S0-AEK-714

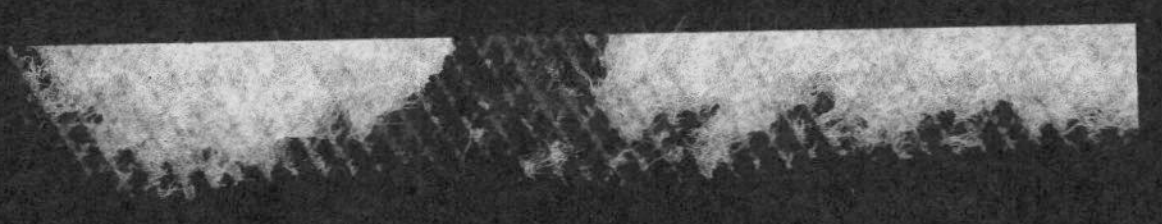

# MASKS OF DIONYSUS

A volume in the series

MYTH AND POETICS

*edited by* Gregory Nagy

A full list of titles in the series appears at the end of the book.

# MASKS OF DIONYSUS

Edited by

THOMAS H. CARPENTER and
CHRISTOPHER A. FARAONE

CORNELL UNIVERSITY PRESS

ITHACA AND LONDON

First published 1993 by Cornell University Press.

Library of Congress Cataloging-in-Publication Data
Masks of Dionysus / edited by Thomas H. Carpenter and Christopher A. Faraone.
p. cm. — (Myth and poetics)
Includes bibliographical references (p. ) and index.
ISBN 0-8014-2779-7 — ISBN 0-8014-8062-0 (pbk.)
1. Greek literature—History and criticism. 2. Dionysus (Greek deity) in literature. 3. Dionysus (Greek deity)—Cult. 4. Euripides. Bacchae. 5. Bacchantes. 6. Dionysia. I. Carpenter, Thomas H. II. Faraone, Christopher A. III. Series.
PA3015.R5D55 1993
880.9'001—dc20 92-54965

Printed in the United States of America

♾ The paper in this book meets the minimum requirements of the American National Standard for Information Sciences—Permanence of Paper for Printed Library Materials, ANSI Z39.48-1984.

# Contents


Foreword
Gregory Nagy vii

Transliteration and Abbreviation ix

Contributors xiii

Acknowledgments xvii

Introduction
Christopher A. Faraone 1

INTERPRETATION

1 "He Has a God in Him": Human and Divine in the Modern Perception of Dionysus
Albert Henrichs 13

2 The Asexuality of Dionysus
Michael Jameson 44

3 Dionysus Poured Out: Ancient and Modern Theories of Sacrifice and Cultural Formation
Dirk Obbink 65

TRAGEDY

4 Mixtures of Masks: Maenads as Tragic Models
Renate Schlesier 89

5 Dionysus as Destroyer of the Household: Homer, Tragedy, and the Polis
RICHARD SEAFORD 115

6 Staging Dionysus between Thebes and Athens
FROMA I. ZEITLIN 147

IMAGE

7 On the Beardless Dionysus
THOMAS H. CARPENTER 185

8 On the Wildness of Satyrs
FRANÇOIS LISSARRAGUE 207

9 Fufluns Pacha: The Etruscan Dionysus
LARISSA BONFANTE 221

MYSTERY CULT

10 Dionysian and Orphic Eschatology: New Texts and Old Questions
FRITZ GRAF 239

11 Bacchic *Teletai* in the Hellenistic Age
WALTER BURKERT 259

12 Voices from beyond the Grave: Dionysus and the Dead
SUSAN GUETTEL COLE 276

Glossary 297

Bibliography 303

Index of Passages Cited 331

Index of Greek, Latin, and Etruscan Words 335

General Index 339

# Foreword

My goal as editor of the Myth and Poetics series is to encourage work that helps to integrate the critical study of literature with the approaches of anthropology and pays special attention to problems concerning the nexus of ritual and myth. Early volumes in the series set the groundwork for a broadened understanding of the very concepts of myth and ritual as reflected in the specific cultural context of ancient Greek poetics. The emphasis of the present volume, *Masks of Dionysus,* is not so much on the specifically poetic testimony about this all-important god in the history of Greek civilization. Rather, it is on the sum total of available empirical evidence about Dionysiac *Religionsgeschichte,* which in turn helps to broaden our perspectives on Dionysiac poetics.

The contributors to this volume have paid special attention to the diversity of the Dionysus figure in the history of Greek religion. The more we understand the rich varieties of Dionysiac myth and ritual, as they show, the more we can appreciate the complexity of Dionysiac poetics, with Euripides' *Bacchae* in the forefront. Thanks to *Masks of Dionysus,* the literary dimension of the Dionysus figure becomes even more interesting than it would be if only the literary evidence were examined, as is the case in most other works on this elusive but compelling god.

GREGORY NAGY

# Transliteration and Abbreviation

In transliterating ancient Greek, we have thought it reasonable, if not entirely consistent, to use a Latinized spelling for words or proper names for which this has become "normal" English usage and in other cases to use a direct transliteration from the Greek. In some instances, such as the nomenclature of clothing or types of Greek vases, the system is unavoidably inconsistent, as it depends more or less on the frequency with which these words have been used in English (e.g., chiton and *krokōtos;* cantharus and *khous*). A similar inconsistency occurs in our rendition of the epithets and alternate names of the god Dionysus himself. Some of his more familiar names, well known to us from the Roman poets, appear in their familiar Latin form (e.g., Bromius or Bacchus), while rarer, epichoric forms (e.g., Meilikhios, Bakkheus, or Omestes) have been directly transliterated from the Greek.

In hope of making the citation of ancient sources clearer to the non-specialist, we have devised the following two-tiered method of reference: (1) the titles of better-known authors are cited either in full by their English titles (e.g., Aeschylus *Seven against Thebes,* Sophocles *Oedipus at Colonus*) or by easily decipherable abbreviations (e.g., Aesch. *Seven* or Soph. *Oed. Col.*); (2) the works of more obscure authors are always cited in full and usually by their Latin titles (e.g., Philostratus *Imagines*). Most references to modern secondary literature consist of author's name and the date of publication; full references can be found to these works in the bibliography at the end of the volume. We have limited our use of abbreviations to the following collections, dictionaries, and frequently used journals (please note that series or collections that are listed below without the name of an editor are the work of many hands).

## Collections of Artifacts or Images

| | |
|---|---|
| *ABL* | C. H. E. Haspels. *Attic Black-Figure Lekythoi*. Paris, 1936. |
| *ABV* | J. D. Beazley. *Attic Black-Figure Vase-Painters*. Oxford, 1956. |
| *ANRW* | *Aufstieg und Niedergang der römischen Welt*. Berlin, 1972–. |
| *ARV*[2] | J. D. Beazley. *Attic Red-Figure Vase-Painters*. 2d ed. Oxford, 1963. |
| *CSE* | *Corpus speculorum Etruscorum*. |
| *CVA* | *Corpus vasorum antiquorum*. |
| *ES* | B. Gerhard, A. Klugmann, and G. Korte. *Etruskische Spiegel*. Berlin, 1840–97. |
| *Gens antiq* | *Gens antiquissima Italiae: Antichità dall 'Umbria a Leningrado*. Perugia. |
| *Para* | J. D. Beazley. *Paralipomena*. Oxford, 1971. |

## Collections of Inscriptions

| | |
|---|---|
| *CIE* | *Corpus inscriptionum Etruscarum*. Leipzig and Rome, 1893–present. |
| *CIG* | *Corpus inscriptionum Graecarum*. Berlin, 1828–77. |
| *CIL* | *Corpus inscriptionum Latinarum*. Berlin, 1863–present. |
| *CIRB* | *Corpus inscriptionum Regni-Bosporani*. Leningrad, 1965. |
| *GV* | W. Peek, ed. *Griechische Vers-Inschriften*. Berlin, 1955. |
| *IG* | *Inscriptiones Graecae*. Berlin, 1873–present. |
| *IGBR* | G. Mihailov, ed. *Inscriptiones Graecae in Bulgaria repertae*. Sofia, 1956–66. |
| *IGSK* | *Inschriften griechischer Städte aus Kleinasien*. Bonn, 1972–present. |
| *IGUR* | L. Moretti, ed. *Inscriptiones Graecae urbis Romae*. Rome, 1968–present. |
| *IKlaudiu Polis* | F. Becker-Bertau, ed. *Die Inschriften von Klaudiu Polis*. IGSK 31. Bonn, 1986. |
| *IKyzikos* | E. Schwertheim, ed. *Die Inschriften von Kyzikos und Umgebung*. IGSK 18 and 26. Bonn, 1980–83. |
| *IMagnesia* | O. Kern, ed. *Die Inschriften von Magnesia am Maeander*. Berlin, 1900. |

| | |
|---|---|
| *INikaia* | S. Sahin, ed. *Katalog der antiken Inschriften des Museums von Iznik (Nikaia)*. Bonn, 1979–82. |
| *IPergamon* | M. Fraenkel, ed. *Die Inschriften von Pergamon*. Altertümer von Pergamon 8. Berlin, 1890–95. |
| *ISmyrna* | G. Petzl, ed. *Die Inschriften von Smyrna*. IGSK 23, 24.1, and 24.2. Bonn, 1982–90. |
| *LSAM* | F. Sokolowski, ed. *Lois sacrées de l'Asie Mineure*. Paris, 1955. |
| *LSCG* | ———, ed. *Lois sacrées des cités grecques*. Paris, 1969. |
| *LSS* | ———, ed. *Lois sacrées des cités grecques: Supplément*. Paris, 1962. |
| *OGI* | W. Dittenberger, ed. *Orientis Graeci inscriptiones selectae*. Leipzig, 1903–5. |
| *SEG* | *Supplementum epigraphicum Graecum*. Leiden, 1923–present. |
| *SIG*³ | W. Dittenberger, ed. *Sylloge inscriptionum Graecarum*. 3d ed. Leipzig, 1921–24. |
| *TAM* | *Tituli Asiae Minoris*. Vienna, 1901–present. |

## Collections of Literary Fragments

| | |
|---|---|
| *EGF* | M. Davies, ed. *Epicorum Graecorum fragmenta*. Göttingen, 1988. |
| *FGrH* | F. Jacoby, ed. *Die Fragmente der griechischen Historiker*. Berlin and Leiden, 1923–58. |
| *FHG* | C. Müller and T. Müller, eds. *Fragmenta historicorum Graecorum*. Paris, 1841. |
| *FVS* | H. Diels and W. Kranz, eds. *Die Fragmente der Vorsokratiker*. Berlin, 1952. |
| *Nauck*² | A. Nauck. *Tragicorum Graecorum fragmenta*. 2d ed. Leipzig, 1889. |
| *OF* | O. Kern, ed. *Orphicorum fragmenta*. Berlin, 1912. |
| *PCG* | R. Kassel and C. Austin, eds. *Poetae comici Graeci*. Berlin, 1983–present. |
| *PLG* | T. Bergk, ed. *Poetae lyrici Graeci*. Leipzig, 1882. |
| *PMG* | D. L. Page, ed. *Poetae melici Graeci*. Oxford, 1962. |
| *SVF* | H. von Arnim, ed. *Stoicorum veterum fragmenta*. Leipzig, 1903–21. |
| *TrGF* | B. Snell and S. Radt, eds. *Tragicorum Graecorum fragmenta*. Göttingen, 1971–present. |

## Collections of Papyri

| | |
|---|---|
| *PAntinoöpolis* | C. H. Roberts, J. W. B. Barns, and H. Zilliacus, eds. *The Antinoöpolis Papyri*. London, 1950–66. |
| *PGurob* | J. G. Smyly, ed. *Greek Papyri from Gurob*. Dublin, 1921. |

| | |
|---|---|
| *PHerc* | M. Gigante, ed. *Catalogo dei papiri ercolanesi*. Naples, 1979. |
| *POxy* | *The Oxyrhynchus Papyri*. London, 1898–present. |

## Dictionaries and Lexica

| | |
|---|---|
| *DA* | C. Daremberg and E. Saglio, eds. *Dictionnaire des antiquités grecques et romaines*. Paris, 1877–1919. |
| *LIMC* | *Lexicon iconographicum mythologiae classicae*. Zurich, 1981–present. |
| LSJ | H. G. Liddell, R. Scott, and H. S. Jones, eds. *Greek-English Lexicon with a Supplement*. 9th ed. Oxford, 1968. |
| *RE* | Pauly-Wissowa. *Real-Encyclopädie der classischen Altertumswissenschaft*. Stuttgart, 1894–1980. |

## Journals

| | |
|---|---|
| *AA* | *Archäologischer Anzeiger*. |
| *AE* | *L'anneé épigraphique*. |
| *AJA* | *American Journal of Archaeology*. |
| *AM* | *Mitteilungen des Deutschen Archäologischen Instituts, Athenische Abteilung*. |
| *AntK* | *Antike Kunst*. |
| *AR* | *Archaeological Reports*. |
| *BCH* | *Bulletin de correspondance hellénique*. |
| *Meded* | *Mededeelingen van het Nederlands Historisch Institut te Rome*. |
| *RA* | *Revue archéologique*. |
| *SBBerlin* | *Sitzungsberichte der Deutschen Akademie der Wissenschaften zu Berlin, Klasse für Sprachen, Literatur und Kunst*. |
| *ZPE* | *Zeitschrift für Papyrologie und Epigraphik*. |

# Contributors

LARISSA BONFANTE is Professor of Classics at New York University. She is author and coauthor of several books and numerous articles on aspects of Etruscan culture and language, including, most recently, *The Etruscan Language* (Manchester, 1983) and *Etruscan Life and Afterlife* (Detroit, 1986).

WALTER BURKERT is Professor of Classics at the University of Zurich. He has published widely on Greek religion. Among his recent books are *Homo Necans: The Anthropology of Ancient Greek Sacrificial Ritual and Myth* (Berkeley, 1983), *Greek Religion* (Cambridge, Mass., 1985), and *Ancient Mystery Cults* (Cambridge, Mass., 1987).

THOMAS H. CARPENTER is Associate Professor at Virginia Polytechnic Institute and State University with a joint appointment in the Center for Programs in the Humanities and the Department of Art and Art History. Among his publications are *Dionysian Imagery in Archaic Greek Art* (Oxford, 1986), *Beazley Addenda,* second edition (Oxford, 1989), and *Art and Myth in Ancient Greece* (London, 1991).

SUSAN GUETTEL COLE is Associate Professor of Classics at the State University of New York at Buffalo. She is the author of *THEOI MEGALOI: Cult of the Great Gods of Samothrace* (Leiden, 1984) and numerous articles on the history of Greek religion, with special emphasis on the mysteries and the cult of Dionysus.

Christopher A. Faraone is Assistant Professor of Classics at the University of Chicago. He is coeditor of *Magika Hiera: Ancient Greek Magic and Religion* (Oxford, 1991) and author of *Talismans and Trojan Horses: Guardian Statues in Ancient Greek Myth and Ritual* (Oxford, 1992) and several articles on ancient Greek magic.

Fritz Graf is Professor of Classics at the University of Basel. Among his numerous books, articles, and reviews on Greek religion are *Eleusis und die orphische Dichtung Athens vorhellenistischer Zeit* (Berlin and New York, 1974) and *Nordionische Kulte* (Rome, 1985).

Albert Henrichs is Eliot Professor of Greek Literature at Harvard University. He is the author of *Die Phoinikika des Lollianos: Fragmente eines neuen griechischen Romans* (Bonn, 1972), *Die Götter Griechenlands: Ihr Bild im Wandel der Religionswissenschaft* (Bamberg, 1987), and numerous articles on Greek religion, especially concerning the cults and myths of Dionysus.

Michael Jameson is Crossett Professor Emeritus of Humanistic Studies in the Department of Classics at Stanford University. He has published extensively on Greek religion, history, inscriptions, and archaeology. He delivered the Martin Lectures at Oberlin College on Greek sacrifice and, recently, the Martin Nilsson Lectures at the Swedish Institute at Athens on Greek religion.

François Lissarrague is Chargé de Recherches at the Centre National de la Recherche Scientifique in Paris. He is a contributor to *A City of Images: Iconography and Society in Ancient Greece* (Princeton, 1989) and is author of *The Aesthetics of the Greek Banquet* (Princeton, 1990) and numerous articles on Greek iconography.

Dirk Obbink is Assistant Professor of Classics at Barnard College. He is coeditor of *Magika Hiera: Ancient Greek Magic and Religion* (Oxford, 1991) and author of the commentary *Philodemus: De pietate* (Oxford, 1993) and a number of articles on Greek religion and philosophy.

Renate Schlesier is Assistant Professor of Religious Studies at the Free University of Berlin. She is editor of the collection *Faszination des Mythos: Studien zu antiken und modernen Interpretationen* (Basel and Frankfurt, 1985) and has published articles and reviews on Greek religion and literature and on the history of classical scholarship.

Richard Seaford is Reader in Greek Literature at the University of Exeter. He is author of *Euripides: Cyclops, with Introduction and Commentary* (Oxford, 1984) and numerous articles and reviews concerning Greek literature and religion.

Froma I. Zeitlin is Charles Ewing Professor of Greek Language and Literature and Professor of Comparative Literature at Princeton University. She is author of *Under the Sign of the Shield: Semiotics and Aeschylus' "Seven against Thebes"* (Rome, 1981) and numerous articles on Greek myth and literature. She coedited *Before Sexuality: The Construction of Erotic Experience in the Ancient World* (Princeton, 1990) and *Nothing to Do with Dionysos? Athenian Drama in Its Social Context* (Princeton, 1990) and edited *Mortals and Immortals* (Princeton, 1991), a collection of essays by Jean-Pierre Vernant.

# Acknowledgments

All the papers published here were originally presented at a conference entitled "Masks of Dionysus" held at Virginia Polytechnic Institute and State University on 11–14 October 1990. This volume is not, however, a conference "Proceedings" and has in fact been organized in an entirely different fashion, one that cannot adequately reflect (nor should it even try) the dynamics of a conference that from the very start was designed to maximize cross-disciplinary dialogue. For the conference eight thematic sections (e.g., "Dionysus and Sexuality," "The Companions of Dionysus," "Dionysus and Sacrifice") were assembled, and whenever possible the dais was shared by individuals of widely varied scholarly interests and training, including archaeologists, literary critics, political and religious historians, epigraphists, and philosophers. The result was a cross-disciplinary discourse of great vivacity and variety—a discourse that informed and transformed all the essays collected here. Because the published collection of essays by its very nature reflects so little of the dynamics of the conference, the reader can have little insight into the extraordinary performances of the conference's "unsung" heroes, Mary Whitlock Blundell, Helene P. Foley, David Halperin, Sarah Iles Johnston, Jon Mikalson, John Oakley, James Redfield, and Charles Segal, who were given the most difficult task of commenting on papers that by design were outside or (at best) at the periphery of their own expertise. In each case the commentaries were insightful and extremely helpful in creating a broader context for the discussion that followed. We also owe special thanks to three of our contributors: to Susan Guettel Cole and Dirk Obbink for their expert advice in the early planning stages of the conference; and to Froma Zeitlin for her wonderful translation of François Lissarague's essay. Our colleague Nicholas Smith also gave much practical advice on planning the conference and this publication.

The success of the conference was guaranteed by a unique amalgam of federal, state, and local resources. Derek Meyers, Chairman of the Art Department, and Robert Landen, Director of the Center for Programs in the Humanities at Virginia Polytechnic Institute and State University, provided the all-important seed money for the conference. Robert Bates, Associate Dean of Arts and Sciences, was an early and staunch supporter of the project, and when looming budget cuts threatened to overwhelm it, both he and Dean Herman Doswald stood by us and provided additional funds at a crucial juncture. We owe thanks to the Virginia Council for the Humanities and Public Policy for several fellowships that allowed broad participation by educators and future educators from all over the Commonwealth of Virginia. Our greatest thanks, however, goes to the National Endowment for the Humanities, which underwrote most of the expense of the conference, and to Christine Kalke of its Research Division, who offered much advice and help throughout the planning process.

T.H.C. and C.A.F.

# MASKS OF DIONYSUS

# Introduction

Christopher A. Faraone

Dionysus has exerted a powerful attraction for scholars, artists, philosophers, and poets for over two thousand years. Part of this attraction can, I think, be attributed to the fact that he was for the ancient Greeks and he remains for us "all things to all people." He is undoubtedly the most complex and multifaceted of all the Greek gods, appearing alternately as the urbane inventor of wine and the symposium, the master of uncontrollable madness and intoxication, the civic patron of Athenian music and drama, the wild hunter who rends his victims with his bare hands and eats them raw, a fertility god represented by the erect phallus, and the mysterious god who comforts the dying and frees them from the fear of death. To the modern observer he is a bundle of contradictions, appearing in one myth as a maniacal and destructive figure and in another as an innocent child who is himself cruelly slain and dismembered. The poets speak of him as a foreign god dressed in Eastern or Thracian garb, a late addition, it would seem to the Hellenic pantheon; yet this image is directly contradicted by the appearance of his name among the divinities listed on Linear B tablets from Pylos, which date to around 1250 B.C. and are among our first written records from the Greek mainland. His worship is strangely conditioned by the gender of the worshiper—men exalted him by drinking wine in symposia, while women danced apart on the mountain. In art and literature he is sometimes depicted as an effeminate youth, but more often as a bearded man distinguishable from Zeus and Poseidon only by his cantharus or an ivy wreath.[1]

On the face of it, it might appear that we have here a number of different gods who, perhaps after a long process of assimilation or syncretization, came to share the name Dionysus. Recent work on the god Apollo suggests a parallel for the assimilation of two or more originally discrete deities into a single multifaceted Panhellenic god.[2] The case of Dionysus, however, is far more complicated, for he frequently appears in myth as a shape shifter or a master of disguise; in Euripides' *Bacchae* he purposely hides his divine form and takes on a deceptive human one designed to further his purposes; to arrogant disbelievers like Pentheus or the Tyrrhenian pirates, he appears in animal form as a bull or a lion. To put it simply: Dionysus is a god who by his very nature is disposed to wear different masks and who was known to reveal himself in different ways at different times to his worshipers. Significantly, these various masks or guises appear not infrequently in a ritual antithesis. At Sicyon on the coast of Attica two images of the god were carried together in a single nocturnal procession, one of Dionysus Bakkheios ("the one who brings madness") and the other of Dionysus Lusios ("the one who frees [one from madness]").[3] A similar polarity seems to underlie the worship of Dionysus at Naxos, where the islanders venerated a mask (*prosōpon*) of Dionysus Bakkheus made from vine wood, as well as a mask of Dionysus Meilikhios ("the mild") made from the wood of a fig tree; here the antithesis seems to lie in Bakkheus as a harsh god and Meilikhios as a gentle one.[4]

For us the central enigma remains: Is Dionysus a unity, a single deity who purposely reveals himself to mortals in a dizzying array of

[1] For a general introduction to Dionysus and his worship, see Otto 1965, 47–119; Henrichs 1979; Simon 1983, 89–105; and Burkert 1985, 161–67. For recent work on his iconography in Greek art, see Carpenter 1986.

[2] Burkert 1985, 143–49, provides an excellent overview of recent work, especially Burkert 1975a and 1975b, Graf 1979, and Jameson 1980.

[3] Versnel 1990a, 139, discusses the main ancient source (Pausanias 2.2.6 and 2.7.6) and gives the most up-to-date bibliography. He does not see any polarity here, preferring to understand Lusios as another facet of the god of wine, i.e., one who "loosens" the cares and sorrows of daily life. On the polarity of Bakkheios/Lusios, see Burkert's essay in this volume, p. 273.

[4] Athenaeus 3.78c. See Burkert 1985, 166–67, for a good discussion of the polarity.

contradictory roles and images? Or is he simply a modern academic and artistic construct—a false unity created from a half-dozen different Dionysi with entirely different cults and myths anchored to specific times and places in the ancient world? Or finally, and less pessimistically, is there a middle ground between the two positions, where we can allow the impossibility of discovering any simple unity or Dionysiac essence in the evidence, admitting at the same time the possibility of developing a coherent conceptual framework upon which we can hang the different masks of the god and appreciate their interrelationships with one another? It is in such a hope that Thomas Carpenter and I have entitled this collection of essays *Masks of Dionysus*.

The book is divided into four sections, each containing three essays. In the first, entitled "Interpretation," three of our contributors explore and critique Dionysiac studies in the nineteenth and twentieth centuries and examine anew three different problems that confront modern interpretations of Dionysus: the emphasis in modern criticism on his humanity, his allegedly ambivalent sexuality, and his central role in the academic conceptualization of all Greek sacramentalism. In the first essay of the section, "He Has a God in Him": Human and Divine in the Modern Perception of Dionysus," Albert Henrichs explores the problematic stress in recent literature on Dionysus as a figure of the human imagination or a projection of the human psyche, arguing that such modern formulations repeatedly obscure the fact that for the Greeks he was first and foremost a supernatural being whose existential status was not only superior to that of humankind but also completely independent of it. Tracing this modern "internalization of Dionysus" back to Nietzsche and (to a lesser degree) the advent of Freudian psychology, Henrichs argues that by taking for granted or neglecting the obvious fact of Dionysus' divinity nearly all twentieth-century scholarship, from the Cambridge Ritualists and their "suffering god" to the most recent work of Jean-Pierre Vernant and Marcel Detienne, tacitly shares a fundamental misperception that frames our modern understanding of the god in a manner that would have been incomprehensible to those who worshiped Dionysus in the ancient world.

Michael Jameson's essay, "The Asexuality of Dionysus," questions recent assertions that the Greeks perceived Dionysus as "asexual" or "sexually ambivalent," and raises two primary objections: the importance of phallic images and processions to the worship of Dionysus, and the central and overtly sexual role the god plays as husband in his annual ritual marriage to the wife of the *basileus* during the Athenian celebration of the Anthesteria. Marshaling three related bodies of evidence (iconography, myth, and cult practices), Jameson suggests that in an effort to understand, for example, the popular depiction of a soft, gentle, unaroused Dionysus presiding over a swirl of often violent sexuality (particularly the activity of his satyr companions), we must see him not as a figure who lacks a clearly defined sexuality, but rather as one who mediates between male and female, a necessarily calming and nonthreatening role because his cult repeatedly releases forces that threaten to destroy social order in the Greek polis.

Dirk Obbink closes the first section of the book with an essay entitled "Dionysus Poured Out: Ancient and Modern Theories of Sacrifice and Cultural Formation" in which he argues that although much of James Frazer's anthropology has been discredited (for example, the notorious "Corn Spirit" and the "Year Daimon"), his concept of the "savage logic" that underlies all sacrificial ritual—if you want to become like god, you must eat god—persists unchallenged in many modern theories of the origin and development of ancient sacrifice. His essay divides neatly into two parts. In the first he surveys a variety of distinctly Dionysiac forms of sacrifice (inter alia, maenadic omophagy and sacramental wine drinking), showing how specific aspects of idiosyncratic Dionysiac rites have been inappropriately used as a general model for all Greek forms of sacrifice. In the second, he goes on to contrast modern theories of Greek sacramentalism with ancient Greek theories in order to reveal that Dionysiac ritual is, in fact, important for understanding the general phenomena of Greek sacrifice, but in a way very different from that envisioned by Jane Harrison or E. R. Dodds.

The second section, "Tragedy," provides new approaches to some old questions about the relationship of Dionysus to tragedy and tragic plot and his relative absence in the Homeric poems. It is, I think, significant that none of our contributors chose to discuss Euripides' *Bacchae* in any detail. Looking instead at Dionysus as the patron of tragedy at Athens and drawing on recent work that stresses the religious setting of tragic performances at the festival of Dionysus,[5] all

[5] E.g., Winkler and Zeitlin 1990; Bierl 1989 and 1991.

three approach the question (once summarily dismissed by an old Greek proverb) of the "Dionysian" or "Dionysiac" as an inherent generic element of central importance to the composition and appreciation of Greek tragedies.

Appearing first in this triad, Renate Schlesier provides a smooth transition from the previous section by opening her essay, "Mixtures of Masks: Maenads as Tragic Models," with a brief survey of the recent surge of scholarly interest in this area, pointing out that the origins of this approach also lie in the work of the Cambridge Ritualists, who despite their obsession with speculations about the origins of tragedy in Dionysiac ritual nevertheless had a great appreciation for the central role of Dionysus in the theater and the civic ideology of fifth-century Athens. Schlesier then goes on to show how references to maenads and maenadic behavior in the extant tragedians, rather than being dismissed as mere metaphors, should be appreciated as important models whereby the intervention of gods other than Dionysus (e.g., Ares, Hera, Aphrodite) or even of the supernatural spirits of the dead (e.g., the Erinyes and the ghost of Polydorus) is presented and understood according to the model of Dionysus' intervention into the human sphere. In this way Dionysus is "subtly included as a vigorous agent and an object of reference even in those plots where the decisive divinity is not Dionysus himself," and tragedy itself is revealed as a genre intrinsically Dionysiac.

Richard Seaford's essay, "Dionysus as Destroyer of the Household: Homer, Tragedy, and the Polis," also examines references to maenadic behavior in tragedy, but he takes a quite different tack by identifying what he calls the "Dionysiac metaphor," a device whereby a female character is labeled or described as a maenad. Beginning with its only appearances in Homer (the description of Andromache in *Iliad* 6 and 22) and then moving on to a variety of scenes from tragedy, he reveals that this Dionysiac metaphor appears repeatedly in combination with a negation of wedding ritual. Seaford argues this is not coincidental, because maenadism at its heart is subversive of the process of marriage, and he suggests that a recurrent Dionysiac pattern in tragedy requires that the salvation of the polis be accomplished only by the destruction of the royal household—a destruction repeatedly evoked in maenadic terms or metaphors as a rejection of endogamy.

Approaching the question of generic Dionysiac factors in tragedy from yet another angle, Froma Zeitlin's contribution, "Staging Dionysus between Thebes and Athens," compares and contrasts the different outcomes of Dionysiac confrontations in those two cities and develops her previous examination of Thebes (as it is portrayed in Attic drama) as a negative configuration of Athens—an "anti-city" that has no viable future because it is closed upon itself by incestuous unions and civil wars. Surveying a number of tragedies, Zeitlin argues that in plays set in Thebes Dionysus is regularly invoked or described in a way that draws him into the circle of destructive deities such as Ares or Aphrodite, and that these plays invariably end in catastrophe. In plays set in Athens, however, or (like Euripides' *Ion*) directly concerned with Attic myth, Dionysus is stabilized by the presence of protective and nurturing goddesses such as Athena or Demeter, and the drama moves from sorrow to joyous finale in which the future greatness of the city is assured.

The third section of the volume, "Image," treats the enormous body of artistic representations of Dionysus and his followers in Greek and Etruscan art. These artifacts, because they can often be dated more precisely than literary texts, provide excellent materials for tracing chronological developments in the ancient perception of the god. All three contributions take their inspiration in part from the growing interest in the last two decades in the iconography of ancient art, a trend that reverses the traditional focus on artistic technique and the development of individual styles. This emphasis on the content instead of the form has reinvigorated and transformed the study of Greek society and religion by breaking down the traditional academic barriers between the previously separate disciplines of archaeology, literature, drama, art history, and history of religions.[6]

Thus Thomas Carpenter in his contribution, "On the Beardless Dionysus," raises the problem of the advent of the young, beardless Dionysus, who begins to appear on Greek vase paintings in the last quarter of the fifth century B.C. and quickly replaces the archaic, bearded figures of the god. In trying to understand this change, Carpenter examines a pair of apparently idiosyncratic images painted some forty years earlier, arguing that the beardless face and the foreign garb of these figures point to a theatrical production of the story of

[6] E.g., Bérard, Bron, and Pomari 1987; Bérard et al. 1984; Carpenter 1986; and Arafat 1990.

Lycurgus in which Dionysus appears to the king in the guise of an effeminate young man. Carpenter closes his essay by pointing out that despite the often pervasive influence of tragic productions on Attic vase paintings, these innovative images of the beardless Dionysus failed to gain popularity, a fact that suggests that some profound changes in the Athenian perception of the god took place in the forty years that separated this first unsuccessful experiment and its spectacularly successful repeat in the Dionysus sculpted for the east pediment of the Parthenon some four decades later.

François Lissarrague begins his essay, "On the Wildness of Satyrs," by pointing out that although the god's more stately and dignified female votaries have been repeatedly discussed over the years, the lowly satyr, that peculiar hybrid of animal and human, has been for the most part ignored. Examining a number of archaic and classical vase paintings, Lissarrague argues that satyrs display their wildness or alterity in a variety of ways, albeit mostly comic, and that in stark contrast to centaurs (those other hybrid "wild men" who in myth live on the margin of the Greek world), satyrs are regularly depicted as subordinates living in the human sphere, either as slaves and servants to Dionysus or engaged in banausic human tasks such as cooking or metallurgy. Lissarrague also illustrates two antithetical ways in which vase painters play upon the animality of the satyrs, either by stressing their close kinship with animals or by masquerading them in the most refined clothing and postures of high Athenian society, with the result that satyrs appear "to invent or deform rules of culture" in a manner that (aside from being comic and entertaining) helps Athenian society to define an image of "normal" human behavior.

The third section closes with an essay by Larissa Bonfante entitled "Fufluns Pacha: The Etruscan Dionysus," in which she surveys one aspect of the fascinating interrelation of Greek and Etruscan culture in the classical and early Hellenistic periods. After a quick survey of the inscriptional evidence for the Etruscan vegetation god Fufluns Pacha, Bonfante shows how he was quickly assimilated to the Greek Dionysus, a process that results in a peculiarly Etruscan modification of traditional Greek iconography. Of crucial importance is the popular Etruscan depiction of the beardless Dionysus as one-half of a divine couple, a configuration rare in Greek art before the late fifth century B.C., but (as Bonfante argues) very predictable in the Etruscan world, where the heterosexual couple and not the individual seems to have been the basic unit of society. Bonfante then uses the images of Dionysus and his mother, Semele, as a focus for her second major point of comparison: the important role of Fufluns as a god of the dead. Bonfante closes her essay by arguing that the popular tradition of pairing images of Fufluns/Dionysus with Ariadne and with Semele seems to be generated by Fufluns' special role as an agent of rebirth.

The conclusion of Bonfante's essay, with its discussion of death and rebirth, provides the perfect bridge to our last triad of essays, all concerned with the Dionysiac mysteries. The most obvious way in which our view of the ancient world changes is by the discovery of new texts, and in recognition of the importance of the newly published gold leaves from Pelinna,[7] we have devoted the entire final section, "Mystery Cult," to the vexed question of the so-called Dionysiac eschatology and the special relationship that the god had with the dying and the dead. Fritz Graf, in an essay entitled "Dionysian and Orphic Eschatology: New Texts and Old Questions," begins by documenting how discoveries in the past two decades have completely altered our understanding of the eschatological beliefs of those individuals buried with inscribed gold tablets that proclaim their special status and provide instructions for obtaining a better lot in the underworld. Graf documents the way in which long-held scholarly distinctions between Pythagorean, Orphic, and Dionysiac eschatological doctrines have collapsed in the face of these new texts and argues that the Dionysiac mysteries, once thought to be a peculiar invention or development of the late classical and early Hellenistic world, were in fact already widespread in the classical period. After a close reading of the new gold tablets from Pelinna, Graf argues that they provide further evidence for the assimilation or blending of Orphic and Dionysiac doctrines. He closes with the important observation that the Pelinna tablets, found in the tomb of a wealthy female devotee of Dionysus, confirm the suspicion raised by earlier archaeological finds that affluent women were as active in these earlier Bacchic groups as they were in the better documented groups of the Roman period.

If, as now seems the case, this new evidence proves that Dionysiac mysteries were spread widely over Magna Graecia, Crete, and parts of

[7] Tsantsanoglou and Parássoglou 1987.

mainland Greece in the classical period, one is forced to see the Hellenistic period as one not of invention of these mysteries, but rather of transformation. Walter Burkert takes just this view in his essay, "Bacchic *Teletai* in the Hellenistic Age," where he focuses in particular on the conditions under which the Dionysiac mysteries were patronized by the political leadership and transformed from an essentially private form of cult into rather elaborate religious and political organizations. He identifies two new features of these transformed mysteries: the role of the theater and the "theatrical artists" (*tekhnitai*), and the appropriation of the patronage of Dionysiac worship and mysteries by the new kings of Egypt and Pergamon. Burkert goes on to argue that as these rituals passed from private ceremony to public spectacle, the older practices of the wandering charismatics were suppressed or closely controlled by the government. He closes his essay with a discussion of an inscription and a sculpted altar, both from the island of Cos, which seem to be the last attestations of the older form of *teletai*.

In the last essay of the "Mystery Cult" section, Susan Guettel Cole questions whether we should generalize the eschatological beliefs of the initiates of Dionysiac mysteries and attribute such doctrines more widely to all devotees of the god. In "Voices from beyond the Grave: Dionysus and the Dead," she presents a wide-ranging survey of funerary inscriptions of individuals who call attention to themselves as special worshipers of Dionysus. Drawing a distinction between private documents (the gold tablets buried in the grave) and public documents (the epitaphs erected in full view over the grave), Cole points out that only rarely do we find any hint in the public documents that the dead or their relations believed that special devotion to Dionysus would result in special treatment in the afterlife. While conceding that much of the iconographical evidence for Dionysiac beliefs in the Roman period (especially the images depicted on sarcophagi) can be interpreted as a continuation of the eschatological doctrines espoused in the gold tablets, she questions how representative these doctrines are for the worshipers of Dionysus in general. She argues, in fact, that the tame conventionality of the epitaphs of Dionysiac worshipers and the very rare expressions of hope for a better afterlife suggest either that the Dionysiac mysteries, despite their wide geographical distribution, undergo some profound change in the later periods with regard to their content or goal or that the eschatological doctrine becomes so secret that it leaves hardly any trace at all in the funerary inscriptions.

The immediate contribution of this collection of essays will, we hope, be a broader and much more diverse discourse about the god, not only as he is rooted in the specific historical and social contexts of the Greek world, but also as he has been taken up by succeeding generations of scholars. This, a work of many voices, is by no means intended to produce consensus or a final, authoritative statement on the god Dionysus or the "correct" critical approach to understanding him. Even to the casual observer there are obvious and fundamental disagreements among the contributors. It is, however, our sincere hope that this volume will appear as a beginning of a more productive, if occasionally discordant, understanding of perhaps the most mysterious and interesting of all the Greek gods.

# INTERPRETATION

CHAPTER I

# "He Has a God in Him": Human and Divine in the Modern Perception of Dionysus

Albert Henrichs

Greek gods aren't easy to get along with, as their myths show. Time and again they destroy the lives of mortals for reasons that are hard to comprehend, and even harder to accept. If judged by their actions and their behavior, these gods don't make much sense, certainly not to our modern minds, which are attuned to the monotheistic theologies and ethics of Judaism and Christianity. The Judeo-Christian god embodies justice, compassion, and a moral code. Perceived as a spiritual rather than corporeal entity, he is invisible and yet intelligible. The gods of Greek myth are the exact opposite. They are anthropomorphic, vindictive, and, in human terms, flagrantly immoral; and while they are highly visible, they are anything but transparent or rationally comprehensible.

Of all the Greek gods, Dionysus is the most visible as well as the most elusive. Present in myth, art, and literature, he conceals his divine identity behind an abundance of physical manifestations that has challenged ancient and modern sensitivities. In the pages of this volume, Dionysus reveals many unexpected traits—he always does—which make him a more interesting and, ultimately, a more familiar figure. But when all is said and done, we are still baffled by the enigma that is Dionysus and by the polymorphous nature with which the Greeks so amply endowed him.

Who is Dionysus? He is first and foremost the god of wine. He is also the god of the mask, who presided over dramatic performances in Athens and Attica and whose name and rituals were closely associated with the origins of tragedy and comedy. In addition, he was believed to inspire the female votaries known as maenads and to lead them to the mountain for their biennial rites of dancing and sacrifice. And finally, he recruited his followers not only among the living but also among the dead. It was in these four provinces—the wine, the theater, maenadism, and the underworld—that Dionysus exercised his power over the Greeks and their imagination.

The Greeks made no attempt to integrate Dionysus' different roles and to reduce them to a common denominator. Modern students of the god, however, have been reluctant to acquiesce in a Dionysus who amounts to nothing more than the sum of his multiple components. In their quest for a more cohesive and integral definition of Dionysus, they have been quick to identify shared elements that connect and consolidate the god's multiple identities. The wine and the theater in particular represent two powerful sources of illusion, escape from the realities of normal life, and a temporary expansion of individual horizons. The maenads and the dead, on the other hand, share several distinctive features, provided we perceive the dead not as corpses but as the spirits of the deceased who return periodically to the world of the living. In Greek tragedy, for instance, ghosts as well as maenads are described as "night stalkers" (*nuktipoloi*) because they come to life only at night.[1] In actual cult, both groups were assigned habitats that lay outside the secure confines of the polis, and while the rituals associated with the practice of maenadism and with the cult of the dead were not identical, they were both strikingly different from ordinary forms of worship. What is more, in the Greek imagination maenads and ghosts inhabited an existential twilight zone where vital energies ebbed and flowed in reciprocal rhythms and where the boundaries of life and death converged.

Dionysus and his followers can be seen as abandoning, shifting, or transcending the limits of everyday experience through their association with exalted or anomalous conditions such as intoxication, mas-

[1] Aeschylus. *Psychagogoi* frag. 273a9 (*TrGF* 3); Euripides *Ion* 717 versus 1048–49; cf. *Helen* 570 and *Cretans* frag. 79.11 (Austin 1968); Henrichs 1991, 190–92. Also relevant here is the similar representation of maenads and Erinyes in art and their affinity in tragedy, first noted by Harrison 1899, 220 (with Schlesier 1991, 208 n. 78); cf. Whallon 1964, 320–22; Napier 1986, 43; Bierl 1991, 90 n. 146, 120, and 122 n. 30.

querade, illusion, trance, or madness. They are thus linked with an expansion of physical and mental faculties—one that leads either to states of heightened self-awareness or to destructive disruptions of the personality and even to the annihilation of life. It is hardly surprising, therefore, that the god whose myths and rituals call into question the normal identities of his worshipers should himself adopt a fluid and changeable identity based on disguise, on transformation, and on the simultaneous presence of opposite characteristics. The question remains, Are we dealing with one coherent divinity? Who is this Dionysus?

## Seeing Is Believing: The Paradox of Dionysus' Self-Revelation

If Dionysus is best defined through his complex image in ancient art and literature, his special place in Greek myth, and his various functions in Greek or Roman society, the present volume covers much of this territory. It opens new perspectives on the cults and rituals associated with Dionysus, on his worshipers and his mythical entourage, on the importance of gender roles and social status, and on his representation in art and in tragedy, not to mention his assimilation by non-Greek cultures. There is one fundamental aspect of Dionysus, however, that as scholars we generally ignore: namely, his divinity. That is the aspect I wish to explore. For the vast majority of the Greeks from Homer to Longus, Dionysus was neither a figure of the imagination nor a projection of the human psyche. He was instead a supernatural being whose existential status was not only superior to that of mortals but also independent of it—he was a god.

Poets ancient and modern have always been more prepared than historians of Greek religion to acknowledge the god in Dionysus and to celebrate his divinity—to experience him rather than analyze his different realms and functions. Ezra Pound can serve as a modern English voice articulating Dionysus' godhood. In the second of his pre-Pisan cantos, first published in 1922, Pound reworks the story of Dionysus and the sailors turned into dolphins as told by Ovid in the third book of his *Metamorphoses*.[2] As the mysterious young boy, ef-

[2] Ovid *Metamorphoses* 3.572–691.

feminate and slightly drunk, staggers into their midst, Acoetes exclaims: "He has a god in him, though I do not know which god" (3.611–12 *quod numen in isto / corpore sit, dubito; sed corpore numen in isto est!*). The fully anthropomorphic appearance of Dionysus, which conceals his divinity, thus becomes the touchstone that polarizes mortals and separates believers like Acoetes from nonbelievers. Here is Pound's vivid recreation of the scene:

> The back-swell now smooth in the rudder-chains,
> Black snout of a porpoise
>         where Lycabs had been,
> Fish-scales on the oarsmen.
>         And I worship.
> I have seen what I have seen.
>         When they brought the boy I said:
> "He has a god in him,
>         though I do not know which god."
> And they kicked me into the fore-stays.
> I have seen what I have seen:
>         Medon's face like the face of a dory,
> Arms shrunk into fins. And you, Pentheus,
> Had as well listen to Tiresias, and to Cadmus,
>         or your luck will go out of you.[3]

Pound here captures the presence of Dionysus as a paradox—a powerful but elusive paradox that Ovid's sailors, like the Pentheus of Euripides' *Bacchae,* failed to understand until it was too late. Pentheus refused to recognize Dionysus as a god because he was deceived by the anthropomorphic guise and did not see the divine in Dionysus. By contrast, the Acoetes of Ovid and Pound feels intuitively that he is in

[3] Canto 2 (Pound 1983, 9). Much has been written on Pound's Dionysus by interpreters tempted to compress Pound's complex and changing perception of the god into ready-made formulae that reflect general trends in the modern discussion of Dionysus—"Pluto or chthonic Dionysus" (Surette 1979, 44), "a symbol of the sacred energies of the cosmos" (Woodward 1980, 88), or "the god of sex and wine" (Terrell 1984, 426). Especially in his later cantos Pound favored a distinctly Frazerian concept of Dionysus, with emphasis on vegetation and agrarian rituals, the Eleusinian mysteries, the Zagreus myth, and sacramental union. A similar emphasis can be found in Dodds 1960, xi–xiii, a passage "vigorously and approvingly initiated [read: initialed]" by Pound during his Venice years (Littlefield 1972, 131). In its Ovidian focus on theophany, the second canto is a remarkable exception to Pound's general treatment of Dionysus (Surette 1979, 53–54).

the presence of a divinity, even though the god is concealed in a human form—*sed corpore numen in isto est;* and when Dionysus finally demonstrates his divine power in the miracle of transformation, Acoetes sees his intuition suddenly confirmed: "I have seen what I have seen."[4] The encounter is acknowledged and its force felt.

Seeing is believing, not only for Acoetes but also for Horace. In the most revelatory of his Dionysiac poems, Horace poses as a true believer who has seen Dionysus and felt the force of this encounter so strongly that he expects his audience to share his belief in the divine revelation: "I have seen Bacchus among the far-off mountain cliffs—believe me, men of future generations—as he was teaching his songs to the attentive nymphs and to the sharp ears of the goat-footed satyrs" (*Odes* 2.19.1–4 *Bacchum in remotis carmina rupibus / vidi docentem—credite posteri—/ nymphasque discentis et auris / capripedum satyrorum acutas*). Horace's vision (*vidi*), poetically projected into the imaginary space of a distant Dionysiac retreat populated by nymphs and satyrs, thus presents itself to the world at large as the poet's personal validation of a universal Dionysiac creed (*credite*). As the unique eyewitness of that vision, the poetic voice recalls the mythical as well as cultic experience of divine revelation.[5] The poet's emphatic avowal *Bacchum vidi* confirms the Greek and Roman perception of Dionysus as an epiphanic god; in particular, it helps to explain why visual representations of the god and his entourage constitute such a prominent aspect of the religion of Dionysus—the god's power manifests itself in his presence, which is revealed and commemorated in his images.[6]

[4] Ovid's Acoetes infers the divinity of Dionysus in human disguise from the god's physical appearance, his dress, face, and gait (*Metamorphoses* 3.609–10 *specto cultum faciemque gradumque: / nil ibi, quod credi posset mortale, videbam*), and he reaches his conclusion long before the series of miracles takes place (658ff.). In Ovid's model, the Homeric *Hymn to Dionysus,* the pious helmsman recognizes Dionysus by his miracles (13–24). By conflating the two traditions, Pound strengthens the visual quality of the recognition.

[5] Some interpreters consider Horace's visionary testimony contrived, if not cynical. But there was more on Horace's mind than mere poetic craftsmanship or religious make-believe. By juxtaposing the dramatic account of the vision with a hymnic catalogue of the god's mythical accomplishments, he merged the traditional form of the literary hymn with the cultic convention of written records, known as "aretalogies," that bear personal testimony to direct divine intervention. The poet's vision thus reproduces the experience of cultic epiphanies and succeeds in capturing its spirit. Cf. Henrichs 1978b.

[6] Dionysus' distinctive epiphanic quality has been explored by Otto (below, n. 42); Oranje 1984, 114–42; Vernant 1986a, 247–55 (= 1988, 390–98); Detienne (below, n. 45); and Versnel 1990a, 137–46, 165–67. One of the most emphatic images of Dionysus' epiphany

The Greeks perceived the divinity of Dionysus as they perceived the divinity of any of their gods, as a cohesive conglomerate of three qualities: immortality, superhuman power, and the capacity for self-revelation, which is an inherent correlate of the anthropomorphic appearance of the Greek gods. While the shared human form minimizes the physical separation of gods and mortals, the existential distance between them is maximized by the gods' immortality and power. In the case of Dionysus, however, each of these divine prerogatives takes on a special significance because it defines the divinity of Dionysus, exceptionally and paradoxically, in terms of his apparent humanity. What distinguishes Dionysus' epiphanies is not only "their physical immediacy" (Walter F. Otto), but also their deceptive human quality, which exceeds the normal expectations of Greek anthropomorphism.[7]

For each of the three categories, I want to draw attention to the unmediated tension between human and divine that abounds in the Dionysiac record: "the contradictory identity of the god who is mortal."[8] First, Dionysus' immortality. Although this is indisputably part of the myth, it is also shot through and even defined by suggestions of mortality. Dionysus has a mortal mother and endures a double birth. He is rarely depicted in the company of other gods—instead, he is accompanied by a constant entourage of satyrs, nymphs, and maenads, who are mortal rather than divine. Finally, the god's death as well as rebirth is emphasized in the myth of Dionysus Zagreus.[9]

Second, his power. Dionysus is powerful because he is a god; but in myth, at least, the god conceals his divinity in order to impress his presence all the more forcefully upon mortals. In his mythical epiphanies, he exercises his destructive power from a position of apparent

---

appears on the Exekias cup, which shares the epiphany theme with the Homeric *Hymn to Dionysus* (above, n. 4) without representing the same myth (Lissarrague 1987b, 116–18 [= 1990c, 120–22]; Henrichs 1987a, 109–11; Siedentopf 1990). Images of Dionysus and his circle: Simon 1985, 269–94; *LIMC* s.v. "Dionysos"; Carpenter 1986; Lissarrague 1987b (= 1990c); Vierneisel and Kaeser 1990. For different ways of interpreting the religious significance of Dionysiac iconography see most recently Bérard et al. 1984 (= 1989); Merkelbach 1988; Schlesier 1987a (review of Carpenter 1986); Henrichs 1982 and 1987a.

[7] Otto 1933, 80 (= 1965, 85). On Otto's Dionysus see below in the section titled "Polarities."

[8] Daraki 1985, 28.

[9] See below in the section titled "The Suffering God."

weakness and inferiority, as in the Lycurgus episode of *Iliad* 6, the Homeric *Hymn to Dionysus,* and the *Bacchae.* When provoked by mortals, he confronts them directly and stares them down—the frontal face and the irritating smile are visual hallmarks of Dionysus' self-revelation in art and literature.[10] But the punishment he inflicts is often indirect, deceptive, and designed to hide his presence and downplay his power; unlike Apollo or Artemis, he does not kill his victims through direct divine intervention but relies on those self-destructive drives within their human nature that cause madness, self-mutilation, or transformation. Similarly, when Dionysus bestows his two ambiguous gifts, the wine and ritual ecstasy, he brings about changes in the personality of the human recipient. The "blessings of madness" in particular, whether they take the form of maenadic *bakkheia* or of mixed *orgia* of men and women, create a powerful emotional bond between Dionysus and his human worshipers, which blurs the boundaries between human and divine.[11]

Third, Dionysus' self-revelation. As perceived by the Greeks, the transformative power of Dionysus is inseparable from his epiphanies. It is his physical presence as an anthropomorphic god that empowers him to interact with mortals. Dionysus, *deus praesentissimus,* "the god of the most immediate presence,"[12] reveals himself more often, more ostentatiously, and with greater emphasis on his anthropomorphic properties than any other Greek god—witness the frequency of epiphany scenes in Dionysiac myth and art, and the close ritual resemblance between the god and his worshipers in cult. More specifically, Dionysus appears as a child surrounded by his nurses in *Iliad* 6, as an ephebic youth in the Homeric *Hymn,* as an effeminate intruder in

[10]On Eur. *Bacchae* 439, 1021 (smile), see Dodds 1960, 131; Segal 1982, 249; and Foley 1980, 127 (= with revision 1985, 247). On the frontal face/mask of Dionysus, "the only Olympian god to be represented facing front" (Frontisi-Ducroux and Vernant 1988, 191 [= 1986, 28]), see Korshak 1987; and *LIMC* s.v. "Dionysos" nos. 6–48; Frontisi-Ducroux 1991, 177–230, 253–63 (catalogue); below, nn. 62 and 64–65.

[11]On wine, maenadism, and ritual gender roles see Henrichs 1978a, 1982, and 1984a; Lissarrague 1987b (= 1990c); and Versnel 1990a, 123–55. Some of the anthropological, psychiatric, and neurophysiological aspects of Dionysiac *mania* and *enthousiasmos* (understood as "possession," "group hysteria," or "trance") have been explored by Dodds 1951, 64–101 ("The Blessings of Madness"); Jeanmaire 1951, 105–56; Simon 1978, 251–57; and Bremmer 1984.

[12]Otto 1965, 90 (= 1933, 85).

Aeschylus' Lycurgus trilogy, and as the youthful and effeminate Lydian stranger in the *Bacchae.* On scores of Attic vases he appears in human form and in the midst of his followers as the divine role model for his thiasos: he leads the Bacchic dance, performs *sparagmos,* both gives and receives his own gift, the wine, adopts the posture of a symposiast, and pours libations.[13] In actual cult, the ritual affinity between Dionysus and the members of his thiasos is so close that the god bears the same name as his worshipers: they are *bakkhai* or *bakkhoi,* while he is the *bakkhos* par excellence, both an ideal participant in and the divine recipient of the Bacchic ritual.[14] As their ritual identities converge and merge, the god and his human entourage act and look alike, but their similarity, though close, merely reflects the performance and mood of the ritual occasion; it does not amount to a "fusion" of god and mortal, let alone to an "identification" with the divine through some kind of sacramental union or even communion.[15] Nor must we conclude, as Jane Harrison did in her quest for ritual origins, that the divinity of Dionysus is nothing but a ritual construct, a "projection from the group," the thiasos.[16] For the Greeks,

[13] Above, n. 6.

[14] On *bakkhos* and its derivatives in the context of ritual identities and identification through ritual see Graf 1985, 285–91.

[15] Rohde (1898b, 14–15 [= 1925, 258 and 272 n. 32]) and Dodds (1951, 278 n. 1, and 1960 on Eur. *Bacch.* 115, 135, 136, 144–50) represent extreme attempts to assimilate the worshiper to the god and to blur the distinction of human and divine; for a critique see Jeanmaire 1951, 58, 372–90, 406; Henrichs 1982, 143–47, 159–60, 218–19, 234–36; Henrichs 1984a, 85–91; and Graf 1985, 287. Gernet (1932, 126), Burkert (1977a, 252 [= 1985, 162]), and Vernant (1981, 2: 81–82 [= 1983, 325], and 1985a, 30 [= 1991, 112]) reject the sacramental theory but retain the misleading notion of an existential (?) "fusion" of god and worshiper. Focusing on metatheater rather than ritual, Segal (1982, 13–14) treats the identification of the actor with his role and that of the audience with the stage characters as integral aspects of a Dionysiac "fusion" and "crossing of boundaries." But the identification was never complete; as Calame (1986 and 1989) reminds us, the dramatic mask was also a means of creating distance between the fictional characters and the civic identities of the actors and the audience, a distance illustrated by the separation of the satyr masks from the actors who carry them on the vase of the Pronomos Painter in Naples; see Simon, Hirmer, and Hirmer 1981, figs. 228–29; Bérard et al. 1984, fig. 195 (= 1989, fig. 195); and Calame 1987.

[16] Harrison 1927, 46–48; cf. Schlesier 1991, 202 n. 62 and 205 n. 70. Harrison was on the right track when she recognized the ritual reciprocity between Dionysus and his thiasos; but like Rohde, she rationalistically suppressed the god in Dionysus—the Bacchus of the *Bacchae* "is one and both, human and divine" because "divinity at its very source is human." A. W. Verrall, a close friend of Harrison, went even farther and argued that the Dionysus of the *Bacchae* was indeed a human impostor, a mere "Man-God," intended as such by Euripides (1910, 1–160, esp. 2–3, 41–42). Below, n. 21.

Dionysus was present whenever his followers gathered at the symposium or on the mountain, but he also existed independently from them, as a god.

According to Ovid's Acoetes, "no god is more near than he" (*nec enim praesentior illo / est deus*).[17] Yet Dionysus' presence is never unproblematic; as Acoetes suggests, the god is most distant from mortals when he is physically present. In Greek myth Dionysus is portrayed as a god who tends to reveal his divinity by concealing it behind a deceptively human mask, thus creating the illusion of a false familiarity and closeness, as his mortal opponents learn at a terrible cost. Euripides' Pentheus, like the sailors in Ovid and Pound, fails to recognize the god in Dionysus even as he rubs shoulders with him. He finally attempts under the god's very eyes, and with his apparent approval, to intrude upon the Dionysiac realm by posing as a member of Dionysus' thiasos. As he surrenders his identity and dresses like a maenad, his alienation both from his polis and from Dionysus is complete, and his doom irrevocable.[18]

In the *Bacchae,* epiphany becomes theater, and the stage becomes the *locus sacer* for divine revelation, miracles, and visions. As the theater god reveals himself as a stage god in disguise, he is seen as a man or imagined as an animal without being recognized as a god, and confusion reigns.[19] The dramatic blurring of ritual identities is such that Dionysus' own followers, the Asian maenads who form the chorus, mistake the "stranger god" for the human leader of their ritual thiasos.[20] Some of Euripides' modern interpreters have added to the confusion and turned the Dionysus of the *Bacchae* into a "Man-

[17] Ovid *Metamorphoses* 3.658–59, a recollection of Eur. *Bacch.* 500–502.

[18] On the ritual irony of the third and fatal encounter between Pentheus and Dionysus, the "robing scene," see Segal 1982, 223–32; Foley 1980, 122–24 (= with revision 1985, 241–42); Goldhill 1988; Zeitlin 1990a, 63–66; Bierl 1991, 203–9.

[19] The convergence of festival and theater, of ritual and dramatic performance, in the *Bacchae* is a major focus in Segal 1982, Foley 1980 (= with revision 1985, 205–58), and, drawing on both, Bierl 1991, 186–218. On the stage epiphanies of Dionysus before Euripides and on the *Bacchae* as a continuous dramatized theophany see most recently Oranje 1984, 121–42; and Bierl 1991, 181–86 (I believe Euripides was much more innovative in his treatment of Dionysus as a stage god than Bierl and Oranje allow).

[20] Cf. Segal 1982, 234–40; Henrichs 1984a, 86; Oranje 1984, 132–33; and Bierl 1991, 194 (who suggests that Euripides is intentionally vague). The playwright pushed the concept of Dionysus' dual nature to its dramatic extreme; in other resistance myths only nonbelievers fail to recognize the god in Dionysus.

God"—"a man masquerading as a god masquerading as a man."[21] But the true status of Dionysus is never in doubt, and it is confirmed by an abundance of vase paintings—it is "the god in him" who joins the thiasos and impersonates the ritual identity of his worshipers. Each time Dionysus acts as the chief *bakkhos,* the god sets an aetiological example, validates the ritual performance, and perpetuates his divinity.

## The God within Us: The Internalization of Dionysus since Nietzsche

A god in human disguise, "he has a god in him"—this paradox of unresolved tension between the human and the divine deceived Pentheus and captured the poetic imagination of Euripides, Ovid, and Pound; it also has led the vast majority of modern interpreters of Dionysus to ignore the existential disparity between god and mortal, to lose sight of the shock of their encounter, and to treat Dionysus as if he were anything but a god. This is what concerns me about the modern perception of Dionysus: we tend to reduce the essential tension between the divine and human in Dionysus by scholarly allegorizing, by interpreting the god as a mere personification of powers located within the individual psyche or in the social environment. To this day, Dionysus is widely perceived as a divine impersonation of human drives, appetites, and behavioral patterns, and the god who was worshiped in antiquity "under the open sky" has almost been effaced by the dark and impersonal Dionysus within us.[22]

It has become fashionable, indeed imperative, to define Dionysus with recourse to psychological and social categories as the divine paragon of illusion and enchantment, of the transcending of boundaries, of ambivalence and polarities, of nonconformity and subversion, or in short, as "the Other" par excellence. This approach has

[21] Dodds 1960, xlix. This is not Dodds's own view but his summary of "the ingenious fancies" of the young Gilbert Norwood, whose rationalistic interpretation of the *Bacchae* was further developed by Verrall (above, n. 16). But Dodds himself was one of the worst offenders; he believed that the Bromius of *Bacch.* 115 was not the god Dionysus but "a male celebrant identified with the god" (Dodds 1960, 82–83; cf. Henrichs 1984a).

[22] On Detienne's "Dionysos à ciel ouvert" see below, n. 74.

given us a Dionysus who is versatile, unpredictable, and intellectually exciting; it has also made it easier to articulate the Dionysiac realm as we encounter it in texts and images. But there is a price to be paid for such schematizing. By locating Dionysus so exclusively either in the external structures of Greek society or in the internal dimensions of the human psyche, we are in danger of growing oblivious to that aspect of him that was foremost in the minds of the Greeks—his divine capacity to appear among mortals when least expected and to make his presence felt by affecting their personalities and changing their lives. As experienced by the Greeks, Dionysus is no abstraction, no intellectualized Other. He is met within the bliss as well as within the chaos his presence produces; the most predictable sign of his appearance among mortals is the recognition of divinity that Dionysus creates.

Published in 1872, Nietzsche's *Birth of Tragedy* was the pivotal study that laid the ground for the modern understanding of Dionysus as a cluster of psychological and social abstractions. The modern concept of Dionysus is markedly different from the pedestrian vegetation and fertility god constructed in the course of the nineteenth century, whose lamentable fate it was to be born again as yet another plant, crop, or tree every time he died. The seemingly unending cycle of death and rebirth, of the making and unmaking of the god's agrarian image, was first broken by Nietzsche, who destroyed Dionysus as a god even as he preserved him as a concept. He did this by transplanting him from the natural world onto the tragic stage and from there into the human psyche.

It is characteristic of Nietzsche's frame of mind that the term "Dionysian" can be found much more often in *The Birth of Tragedy* than the name of Dionysus. I will illustrate some of the stages of the simultaneous internalization as well as dedivinization of the god by discussing major Nietzschean categories and their post-Nietzschean transformations—one could think of them as the modern "masks" of Dionysus or more specifically as human faces that have been superimposed upon the god's divine image by his modern interpreters. These masks come in several different forms: the category of the Dionysian, the suffering god and his human surrogates, Dionysus as the embodiment of polarity, and finally, the mask itself as a sign of the Other. Not all of these masks, however, conceal the god in Dionysus beyond recognition. The masks I find most fascinating are partially transparent and reveal something of the tension between the human and the divine that is the true hallmark of Dionysus.

## The Dionysian versus Dionysus

Already in the opening paragraph of *The Birth of Tragedy,* Nietzsche compartmentalizes both Dionysus and Apollo as "the two art deities of the Greeks." Throughout the essay, he is exclusively concerned with their cultural roles as Greek personifications of two opposite states of mind, the Apollinian and the Dionysian; he is not interested in their divinity. He defines the Dionysian as a transformative emotional experience characterized by the breaking down of boundaries, loss of self, identification with the Dionysiac group, and "the affirmation of life in spite of suffering."[23] In *The Birth of Tragedy,* Dionysus is neither encountered nor recognized as a god. Rather, he is abstracted intellectually and conceptualized as a sign, or symbol, for the tangle of human impulses that Nietzsche called "the psychology of the Dionysian state."[24] Instead of recognizing Dionysus as a divine force outside the human sphere, as the Greeks did, Nietzsche discovered the disruptive presence of the Dionysus within us.

Nietzsche's discovery, reinforced by the advent of Freudian psychology, drastically changed the terms of the modern discussion of Dionysus as its focus shifted from the god himself to the experience of his human followers. In recent decades, interpreters have been preoccupied with the impact of Dionysiac states and activities on social groups as well as the individual, especially as articulated in myth and ritual. The debate has focused on symptoms of mental or civic disorder, on sex-role or status reversals during periods of ritual license, and on the breakdown of natural, social, or conceptual boundaries.[25]

[23] Kaufmann 1967, 20 n. 5.

[24] Nietzsche, *Twilight of the Idols,* X 4–5.

[25] Mental disorder: Dodds 1951, chap. 3 ("The Blessings of Madness"); Simon 1978. Periods of license (such as carnival, "year-festival," and "verkehrte Welt"): Graf 1985, 81–96; Hoffman 1989; Auffarth 1991, 15–34, 249–65 (Anthesteria); cf. Daraki 1985, 10–11 (Dionysus associated with "le carnaval," "la transgression officialisée," and "le paradis sauvage"). Reversals: Segal 1982; Kraemer 1979, 67–68 (role reversals in maenadism). Dissolution of boundaries: esp. Segal 1982; and Segal 1986, 282–93. The classical formulation is that of Nietzsche in *The Birth of Tragedy,* secs. 1 and 7 (pp. 37 and 59 in Kaufmann's translation):

Current definitions of Dionysus reflect these psychological and anthropological categories and trace the specific force of his divinity to its repercussions in the human psyche and in the structures of Greek society. According to Eric R. Dodds, "to resist Dionysus is to repress the elemental in one's own nature."[26] In the same vein, R. P. Winnington-Ingram proposes an even more drastic internalization of Dionysus and claims that the god "symbolizes the power of blind, instinctive emotion." The *Bacchae,* we are told, is concerned with "emotionalism as a factor in human life," and when Pentheus tries to bind the imaginary bull that Dionysus has conjured up before his eyes, he "is performing the futile task of constraining the animal Dionysus within himself."[27] Walter Burkert connects Dionysus not only with the "blurring of the contours of a well-formed personality," but also with the "inversion" of the "normal order of the polis."[28] The concept of social subversion is also emphasized by Froma Zeitlin, who assigns to Dionysus the "paradoxical role as disrupter of the normal social categories."[29] For Charles Segal, Dionysus is "the principle that destroys differences," a definition that is ultimately inspired by Walter F. Otto's fundamental notion of Dionysus as the god who is made up of polarities.[30] Finally, Simon Goldhill defines the Dionysus of the theater as "the divinity of illusion and change, paradox and ambiguity,

"Now [i.e. "under the charm of the Dionysian"] the slave is a free man; now all the rigid, hostile barriers that necessity, caprice or 'impudent convention' have fixed between man and man are broken." "The rapture of the Dionysian state with its annihilation of the ordinary bounds and limits of existence contains, while it lasts, a *lethargic* element in which all personal experiences of the past become immersed." Nietzsche's rhetoric of liberation, which takes its cue from Euripides' *Bacchae* (206–9, 421–23, 498, 613, 649, and 772) and ancient interpretations of Dionysus as Lusios and Eleuthereus (Versnel 1990a, 139 and 167; Seaford in this volume, n. 132), continues to strike a dominant note in the ongoing debate on Dionysus; it is echoed, for instance, by Gernet 1932, 113; Dodds 1951, 76–77; Dodds 1960, xx; Vernant 1981, 2: 81 (= 1983, 324–25); Vernant 1986a, 246; and Bierl 1991, 5.

[26] Dodds 1960, xvi.

[27] Winnington-Ingram 1948, 84 (similar psychologizing can be found on pp. 9, 82, 153–55, 161, and 178–79), which is echoed by Segal 1982, 19.

[28] Burkert 1985, 162 and 165 (= 1977a, 252 and 256). Graf 1985, 74–80 and 294–95, interprets the emphasis on *oreibasia,* omophagy, and human sacrifice in the Dionysiac tradition as a mythical and ritual reflection of the "collapse of everyday normalcy" associated with Dionysus.

[29] Zeitlin 1990a, 66.

[30] Segal 1982, 234; cf. Segal 1986, 292 ("Dionysus as a principle that dissolves boundaries").

release and transgression," whose dramatic festivals enact "the interplay between norm and transgression."[31]

These are some of the prevailing conceptions of Dionysus, which are almost exclusively derived from the mythical record, especially the representation of Dionysus in Greek tragedy; the Dionysus of non-tragic literature and of actual cult, who is much less violent or disruptive, is largely ignored.[32] Within this conceptual framework, each interpreter offers a different definition of Dionysus, but the general tendency is the same: the fact that Dionysus was, in the eyes of the Greeks, a divinity endowed with individual characteristics and capable of self-revelation and interaction with mortals is either taken for granted or neglected, and consequently the god tends to disappear behind the modern conceptual masks that reveal an all-too-human face—the disrupter of civil order, the animal within us, the suffering hero.

## The Suffering God and His Human Surrogates

The abstract and academic quality of modern definitions of Dionysus contrasts sharply with the concrete representation of the god in the Greek imagination. In a myth of unknown origin, contested antiquity, and uncertain meaning, Dionysus is killed by the Titans, who dismember his body and eat from his flesh. The god is eventually restored to a new life.[33] The myth of the dismemberment and rebirth of Dionysus Zagreus carries the anthropomorphic conception of the Greek gods to its very limits. Dionysus as a god is reduced to extremely human dimensions, which include suffering and even death; but in the end, his immortality is confirmed. Beginning with Nietzsche, however, modern interpreters have emphasized some aspects of the story and have ignored others. They have carried the human suffering far beyond the actual myth and turned Dionysus into a permanent sacrificial victim by focusing more on his ritual death than on his rebirth. By the same token, they have transformed the god qua

[31] Goldhill 1986, 78; Goldhill 1990, 127.

[32] Henrichs 1990; Bierl 1991, 17–19.

[33] On the myth of Dionysus Zagreus see Jeanmaire 1951, 372–90; Henrichs 1972, 56–73; Detienne 1977 (below, n. 39); West 1983a, 140–75.

sacrificial victim not only into an animal but, more significantly, into a paradigm of human suffering and mortality. What they have largely lost, however, is the striking conceptual correlation of murder victim and immortal god that defines Dionysus as an immortal mortal, a god who has experienced human mortality but whose ultimate immortality confirms his divine status.

According to Nietzsche, the suffering Dionysus manifested himself on the tragic stage in the guise of the true tragic hero, especially the Aeschylean Prometheus and the Oedipus of Sophocles. The tragic hero qua sufferer thus came to represent the suffering god.[34] By defining tragedy as a reenactment of the suffering of Dionysus, Nietzsche equated divine suffering with human suffering, an equation that obliterates the existential difference between mortals and immortals that forms the basis of the Greek worldview. He thus interpreted the suffering of Dionysus allegorically as the mythical model for the *human* condition as reflected in the suffering hero of Greek tragedy. But as Nietzsche's emphasis shifted irrevocably from the god to his human surrogate, the process I have described in the abstract actually occurred: Dionysus was stripped of his godhood and turned into a convenient symbol of an emotional state more human than divine.

All subsequent attempts to identify Dionysus with his human counterparts are variations of Nietzsche's more complex construct. Erwin Rohde, a close friend of the author of *The Birth of Tragedy,* collapsed the boundary between the human and the divine in the opposite direction from Nietzsche. While recognizing Dionysus as a god and recipient of cult, he deprived him at the same time of his exclusive

[34] Henrichs 1984b, 219–23; Henrichs 1986, 393–95. The theory that the tragic hero is an incarnation of the suffering Dionysus goes ultimately back to Karl Otfried Müller, who died in 1840 (Henrichs 1986, 394). In the wake of Nietzsche, the theory was further explored and reformulated by the Cambridge Ritualists, especially Jane Harrison and Gilbert Murray, who invented and popularized the notorious "eniautos daimon" (rejected by Pickard-Cambridge 1927, 185–208; Jeanmaire 1951, 314–15 and 321–31; Else 1965, 9–31; and Payne 1978; cf. Silk and Stern 1981, 142–50; Henrichs 1984a, 222 n. 35; Versnel 1990b; Bierl 1991, 4–8; Schlesier 1991, 208–9 and 218–22). In the current discussion of the tragic Dionysus, however, the emphasis has shifted from the distant ritual origins of Greek tragedy and their sacrificial repercussions (Burkert 1966) to the polyvalent representation of Dionysus throughout the entire tragic corpus (Bierl 1991; Seaford in his essay in this volume), to the god's role within the polytheism of particular plays (Bierl 1989; Zeitlin 1989 and 1991; and Zeitlin's essay in this volume), and to the poetic construction of complex Dionysiac identities that serve as imaginary "masks" for major tragic characters (below, n. 69).

divinity. According to Rohde, the worshipers of Dionysus became one with their god at the height of their ritual ecstasy; by achieving unity with him, every human follower of Dionysus was temporarily transformed into a god and became not merely godlike, but divine.[35] Dionysus thus had to share his exclusive status as an immortal god with mortals who were hoping to achieve immortality in this life rather than the next.

James Frazer and the Cambridge Ritualists diluted the divinity of Dionysus still further.[36] They believed that Dionysus was rent apart in animal as well as human form and eaten by his worshipers. In Frazer's construct, the god suffers a diminution of his divinity while his worshipers simultaneously rise above their human state by partaking of the divine. It has long been recognized that the pagan rite of communion postulated by Frazer is a modern fiction modeled on the Christian Eucharist.[37] Frazer's Dionysus is hardly more than a mortal link in a food chain that minimizes the difference between god, human, and animal.

The modern fusion of Dionysiac myth and Christian sacramentalism culminated in Jan Kott's eucharistic interpretation of the *Bacchae:* "Eating of the gods—the Dionysian ritual and the Easter rite—is the victory of life over death, a triumphant feast of rebirth, fertility and abundance."[38] Less than a decade later, Marcel Detienne reexamined

[35] Above, n. 15.

[36] On the Dionysus of Frazer and Harrison see McGinty 1978, 71–103; Henrichs 1982, 159–60 and 234–36; Henrichs 1984b, 229–31; Schlesier 1991, esp. 222–26.

[37] Cf. Henrichs 1982, 159–60 and 234–36; Jones 1984; Jones 1991, 111–17; and Obbink's contribution to this volume. Like the dying god, Frazer's Dionysiac sacramentalism (see following note) resurfaces periodically, most recently in an extreme form: "Omophagy, ritual eating of raw flesh, is the assimilation and internalization of godhead. Ancient mystery religion was posited on the worshipper's imitation of the god. Cannibalism was impersonation, a primitive theater. You are what you eat" (Paglia 1990, 95).

[38] Kott 1974, 186–230; the quotation is from p. 222. Dionysus continues to be regarded as a forerunner of Christ, both in terms of sacramentalism and anthropomorphism: "To drink wine in the rites of Dionysus is to commune with the god and take his power and physical presence into one's body. . . . Euripides' popular depiction of the god anticipated the Christian concept of Christ as God incarnate in human form, a man-god [above, n. 16], conceived by a mortal woman from the impregnating action of the Holy Spirit, just as it foreshadowed the image of the miracle-worker who turns water into wine and who is physically present in wine-sacraments conducted in his honor" (Evans 1988, 148, in a chapter entitled "Dionysos and Christ," followed by another called "Dionysos and Us"; Evans' book has added a new dimension to the modern Dionysus by claiming him as a symbol for "the gay liberation movement").

the Zagreus myth without Christian prejudice, but with strict attention to the ritual process of blood sacrifice and to sacrificial as well as structural connections between killing and eating.[39] According to the majority of ancient sources, the Titans boiled the limbs of Dionysus before they consumed them; in a different version reported by Clement of Alexandria, the flesh of the god was first boiled and then roasted.[40] Detienne argues, too ingeniously to my mind, that the sequence of boiling and roasting represents an inversion of the normal sacrificial ritual, and that the Zagreus myth must be seen as an Orphic protest against animal sacrifice, especially in its Dionysiac form of the ritual rending of animals and the eating of raw meat. In the final count Detienne's emphasis on the esoteric Zagreus myth and on the so-called cuisine of sacrifice treats Dionysus not as a god but as food for human consumption.

## Polarities

The Dionysus of Nietzsche, Rohde, Frazer, and Detienne is a god whose divine identity is interchangeable with the human identity of his worshipers—the ultimate goal is oneness with the deity, whether the supposed union is understood as psychological or sacramental. Can a Dionysus who is barely distinguishable from his human followers still be considered a god in the full Greek sense of the term?

An emphatically negative answer to this question was given in 1933 by Walter F. Otto, who construed a radically different Dionysus. Otto was a spiritual disciple of Nietzsche, who inspired Otto's dithyrambic style and emphasis on Dionysian emotionalism.[41] In a striking departure from Nietzsche, however, Otto took Dionysus seriously and

[39] Detienne 1977, 163–217 (= 1979, 68–94, 109–17). Detienne is more respectful of Dionysus' divinity than Frazer, but his alimentary reading of the Zagreus myth makes too much of variable narrative details and ignores the fundamental distinction between myth and ritual. In his most recent book on Dionysus, however, Detienne examines a much more representative spectrum of the Dionysiac record and does so with a fresh emphasis on regional cult and on Dionysus as an epiphanic god (below, n. 45).

[40] Clement of Alexandria *Protrepticus* 2.18.1 = *OF* 35. Cf. Henrichs 1972, 67–68; West 1983a, 160–61.

[41] On Otto's Dionysus see McGinty 1978, 141–80 and 233–43; Cancik 1986; Henrichs 1987b, 26–28 and 44–45 (= Flashar 1990, 139–41 and 157–58).

redirected attention to him as a god whose divinity is absolute, unconditional, and not transferable to human substitutes.

Otto championed a dynamic Dionysus who is revealed in frequent epiphanies and defined by polarities. He is the god who comes, as well as the god who disappears: it is his dual nature that compels him to conceal and to transform his divinity by wearing a human mask.[42] In a dramatic passage, Otto characterizes the two sides of his Dionysus as follows:

> His duality has manifested itself to us in the antitheses of ecstasy and horror, infinite vitality and savage destruction; in the pandemonium in which deathly silence is inherent; in the immediate presence which is at the same time absolute remoteness. All of his gifts and attendant phenomena give evidence of the sheer madness of his dual essence: prophecy, music, and finally wine, the flamelike herald of the god, which has in it both bliss and brutality. At the height of ecstasy all of these paradoxes suddenly unmask themselves and reveal their names to be Life and Death.[43]

Otto's concept of the polar Dionysus is indebted to Euripides and Plutarch, and also to Nietzsche. In *The Birth of Tragedy* Nietzsche had paid but scarce attention to the dual nature of Dionysus and to the mixed emotions of his followers, because he was too preoccupied with the larger polarity of Apollo versus Dionysus to develop the idea of a polar Dionysus and to exhaust its potential. Otto saw the opportunity and seized it.[44]

[42] Otto devoted two chapters of his book to Dionysus as "the god who comes" and who displays his mobility and power in his epiphanies (Otto 1933, 71–81 [= 1965, 74–85]). The nineteenth-century reception of the epiphanic Dionysus from Georg Friedrich Creuzer to Friedrich Hölderlin, who characterized Dionysus as "der kommende Gott," has been studied at length by Frank 1982.

[43] Otto 1965, 121 (= 1933, 113).

[44] Significant Greek examples of a polar articulation of Dionysus include the fifth-century bone tablets from Olbia (unknown to Otto; see the discussions by Graf and Burkert in this volume), the *Bacchae* of Euripides, and various remarks in Plutarch (Henrichs 1984b, 235 n. 85, 236f. n. 88). On Dionysiac polarities in Nietzsche see Henrichs 1984b, 234–36; Henrichs 1986, 395–96. Current rearticulations of Otto's polar Dionysus can be found in Segal 1982; Henrichs 1982, 158–59; Vernant 1986a, 255–57 (= 1988, 398–400); Vernant 1987, 113–14 (= 1990a, 99–100; quoted below at n. 51); Goldhill 1990, 126–27; Bierl 1989, 52–54; Bierl 1991, esp. 13–20, 128–29, and 227 (with emphasis on *both* sides of Dionysus' polarity); Hoffman 1989, 103–7; and Versnel 1990a, 131–37 (Dionysus as "the god of ambiguity").

Dionysus as the embodiment of opposites—Otto's construct—remains to this day the most successful attempt to deal with the multiple identities of Dionysus. The divinity of Dionysus is recognized in his superhuman ability to embody opposite qualities simultaneously. By the same token, the polar qualities that constitute the god also destroy his human followers, who cannot sustain the full force of both of the god's sides at once.

## Dionysus as the Other

The French translation of Otto's book on Dionysus appeared in 1969, and his influence can be seen in the Parisian Dionysus of Jean-Pierre Vernant and, more recently, of Detienne, who has developed one of Otto's most fruitful categories, that of the god's epiphanic presence, his *parousia.*[45] In coming to terms with the Dionysus of Nietzsche and Otto, Vernant in particular has left his own subtle imprint on the modern Dionysus and given new meaning to an old concept—Dionysus as the "strangest" of gods or, more pointedly, as "l'étrange étranger."[46]

In what sense can we speak of the "strangeness" of Dionysus? According to Greek myth, the god came from Lydia, Phrygia, or Thrace; in Euripides' *Bacchae,* the Dionysus in human disguise who returns to Thebes is repeatedly characterized as "the stranger" (*ho xenos*). Rohde took these arrival myths as historical fact and argued that the cult of

[45] Detienne 1986 (= 1989a; summarized in 1987, 360–61). Detienne prefers the term *parousia* to epiphany (cf. Diodorus Siculus 4.3.3: "to praise the presence of Dionysus," *tēn parousian hymnein tou Dionysou*). Of the various epiphanic verbs used by Dionysus in the prologue to Euripides' *Bacchae, hēkō* comes emphatically at the beginning of line 1 and *pareimi* at the beginning of line 5 (cf. Vernant 1986a, 247–50 [= 1988, 390–94]). Unlike Otto, Detienne emphasizes the dual nature and regional characteristics of Dionysus' epiphanies; he associates the god's beneficial presence with Athens and his destructive visitations with the Argolid, Boeotia, and Thrace. I believe this particular polarity has more to do with the different articulations of Dionysus in myth and cult than with regional differentiation.

[46] Detienne 1986, 21 (= 1989a, 10); Vernant 1990a, 96. Renate Schlesier suggested to me in conversation that "l'étrange étranger" as well as Vernant's "déconcertante étrangeté" (below, n. 58) recalls "L'inquiétante étrangeté," the standard French version of Freud's "Das Unheimliche" (1919). For different attempts to articulate Dionysus as the "dieu étranger" in political, historical, or structuralist terms see also Gernet 1953, 392 (= 1968, 85, and 1981b, 66–67); Daraki 1985, 12–14; Detienne 1986, 21–25 (= 1989a, 10–13).

Dionysus had invaded Greece literally "from abroad and as something foreign."[47] He drew attention to the "strange" behavior of the god's "Thracian" followers—their ecstatic dances, overt sexuality, hallucinatory intoxication, ritual dress, and bloodthirsty violence. Inspired by his reading of the second volume of Rohde's *Psyche* (1898), Thomas Mann in *Death in Venice* (1912) transformed the Thracian Dionysus into the mysterious Venetian "stranger" and into the "stranger god" ("der fremde Gott"), whom he understood as a dimension of the human psyche—the dangerous Dionysiac "stranger" within us, a symbol of "freedom, release, forgetfulness."[48] With the intuition of the novelist, Mann had opened a new chapter in the modern study of Dionysus. Yet the scholarly world did not take notice until several decades later. In 1933 Otto pointed out that the mythical image of Dionysus as the "stranger" does not refer to the god's arrival from abroad in the distant historical past but to his disturbing epiphanic presence in the here and now.[49] Otto realized even more acutely than Mann that the strangeness of Dionysus was as much a reflection of the mental state of his worshipers as it was a description of Dionysus' special status as a god.

In retrospect, however, Mann and Otto were mere precursors of a more far-reaching revaluation of Nietzsche's "psychology of the Dionysian state" that continues to be undertaken in Paris. Forty years ago Louis Gernet, the great French social historian, identified Dionysus tentatively, almost casually, as "the Other" ("l'Autre"), a divine power perceived neither as sameness nor as polarity but as alterity or otherness.[50] Of all the conceptual categories marshaled in the modern

[47] Rohde 1925, 283 (= 1898b, 41): "aus der Fremde und als ein Fremdes". The particular arrival myth of the *Bacchae* does have a historical context, but it is very different from the one imagined by Rohde. As Versnel (1990a, 102–31 and 158–63) has made abundantly clear, Euripides modeled his dramatization of the mythical arrival of the stranger god Dionysus in Thebes on the actual introduction of foreign cults and "new gods" into Athens in the late fifth century.

[48] Mann 1963, 4–8 and 67. On Mann's refictionalization of Rohde's fictional construct of the Thracian worship of Dionysus see Henrichs 1984b, 208 n. 8.

[49] Otto 1933, 70–73 (= 1965, 74–76), where he virtually defines Dionysus as the Other without fully exploring the concept (1965, 74): "He entered the world differently ("anders") from the way in which we are told the other gods did, and he encounters man, too, in a very special way. In both instances his appearance is startling, disquieting, violent."

[50] Gernet 1981b, 67 (= 1953, 393, and 1968, 86): "Dionysus brings to mind the *Other*. He would at least be its symbol, since he is, in terms of his function and nature, a god who is beyond our reach." Gernet does not elaborate; it is Vernant who provides the exegesis.

interpretation of Dionysus, that of the Other, with its inherent suggestiveness and polyvalence, promises to become the most popular. It does convey more directly than most other categories something of the shock of the contact between divine and human; but it too suffers from abstraction and schematization. Unlike the polar Dionysus, who is overcharged and overdetermined, Dionysus understood as the Other is defined in terms of what he is not—he is not what the mortal self who faces him expects him to be. Following Gernet, Vernant has articulated most forcefully the concept of the Other:

> Even in the world of the Olympian gods, to which he had been admitted, Dionysos personified, as expressed so well by Louis Gernet, the presence of the Other. He did not confirm and reinforce the human and social order by making it sacred. Dionysos called this order into question; indeed, he shattered it. In so doing he revealed another side of the sacred, one that was no longer regular, stable, and defined but strange, elusive, and disconcerting. As the only Greek god endowed with the power of *māyā* ("magic"), Dionysos transcends all forms and evades all definitions; he assumes all aspects without confining himself to any one. Like a conjurer, he plays with appearances and blurs the boundaries between the fantastic and the real. Ubiquitous, he is never to be found where he is but always here, there, and nowhere at the same time. As soon as he appears, the distinct categories and clear oppositions that give the world its coherence and rationality fade, merge, and pass from one to the other. He is at once both male and female. By suddenly appearing among men, he introduces the supernatural in the midst of the natural and unites heaven and earth. Young and old, wild and civilized, near and far, beyond and here-below are joined in him and by him. Even more, he abolishes the distance that separates the gods from men and men from animals.[51]

In this eloquent statement, Gernet's Other coexists, however precariously, with Otto's polar Dionysus.[52] Elsewhere Vernant defines

[51] Vernant 1987, 113–14 (= 1990a, 99–100). Earlier definitions of Dionysus as "la figure de l'Autre" include Vernant 1981, 2: 82 (= 1983, 325); Frontisi-Ducroux and Vernant 1986, 42–43 (= 1988, 205–6); Vernant 1986a, esp. 246 (= 1988, esp. 389–90); and Vernant 1986b, 291 and 300.

[52] Otto's Dionysus is composed of opposite characteristics; the two sides of each pair are treated as equivalent. By contrast, alterity is a more discriminating category; it establishes a hierarchical relationship between opposites by treating one as normal and the other as abnormal. Vernant and Detienne tend to overemphasize the negative side of the polarity

the Other more appropriately in contradistinction to the concrete manifestations of the self—if the self is perceived as male, Dionysus as the Other is female; if Greek, he is barbarian, if rational, irrational.[53] The particular strength of the concept of the Other, especially in Vernant's articulation, lies in its emphasis on the human psyche and its emotional response to the extraordinary, the deviant, the unknown. To the extent that the Other is a source of apprehension as well as fear, it constitutes a psychological category.[54] For Vernant, every Greek god inspires awe and is by definition the Other. What makes Dionysus the Other par excellence is his tendency to change into whatever one least knows, least expects, or least sees the necessity of fearing. In particular, his deceptive humanity conceals the latent force of his divinity while intensifying its actual impact.[55]

Vernant's Dionysus appeals to our imagination, takes us by surprise, and reminds us that awe, fear, and even terror are inseparable from the Greek notion of divinity. In his concern for the human reaction to Dionysus, however, Vernant also sometimes defines the god in all-too-human terms. While emphasizing the alterity of Dionysus as a divinity, he finds the concrete manifestations of the god's otherness in the "strange" behavior not only of his followers, but also of ourselves: "With Dionysos, the music changes. At the heart itself of life on this earth, alterity is a sudden intrusion of that which alienates us from daily existence, from the normal course of things, from ourselves: disguise, masquerade, drunkenness, play, theater, and finally, trance and ecstatic delirium. Dionysos teaches or compels us to be-

---

because it reflects their notion of the Other as a subversive and disruptive force (cf. Bierl 1991, 14–16, esp. nn. 34, 37, and 40). The two models, though deceptively similar, are difficult to reconcile.

[53] Vernant 1985a, 11–13 and 25–30 (= 1991, 111–12, 195–96, and 204–6); and Vernant 1989, ii (= 1991, 20).

[54] Like Gernet, Vernant derives his notion of the Other rather casually from the Platonic categories of *tāutón* and *to heteron* (1985a, 83 n. 2 [= 1991, 195 n. 2]). In current usage, however, including Vernant's own, the Other is a decidedly post-Freudian, psychological category rather than a Platonic one. Vernant's Other invites comparison with Freud's definition of "das Unheimliche" (above, n. 46) as something that evokes ambivalent feelings because it is at the same time alienating and uncannily familiar, and with Rudolf Otto's concept of the sacred as "the entirely Other" ("das ganz andere"), which inspires a special kind of fear (cf. Schlesier 1987b); it is less comparable to the self/other distinctions found in Lacan and Bakhtin.

[55] Vernant 1986a (= 1988).

come other than what we ordinarily are, to experience in this life here below the sensation of escape toward a disconcerting strangeness."[56] The Dionysus in us, first championed by Nietzsche, has come full circle. Both Nietzsche and Vernant understand Dionysus as the externalized exponent of an inner experience that amounts to a surrender of one's individuality. While Nietzsche saw Dionysus as an innate drive that unites human beings with nature and with their true selves, Vernant now sees him as an intrusive force that alienates us from ourselves as well as from the world in which we normally live. If the Other manifests itself in the mask, cross-dressing, the symposium, and role-playing, we are no longer in the presence of a divine figure, but of the kind of behavior that fits a familiar anthropological pattern—the period of license, rites of reversal, anomie.[57] That the Greeks associated this pattern occasionally with Dionysus tells us something about their self-definition and about the social functions of the god, but it barely touches upon the Greek perception of his divinity.

In its most consistent form, Vernant's concept of the Other thus separates us from Dionysus as a personally conceived god. Vernant's Dionysus quickly ceases to be the divine embodiment of the Other and becomes a mere mediator between the self and "the multiple configurations of the Other," a conductor of psychic energies who "opens for us the path of escape toward a disorienting strangeness."[58] On this reading, Dionysus comes close indeed to being a divine magician "endowed with the power of *māyā*."[59] Magic, illusion, and "strange-

[56] Vernant 1991, 196 (= 1985a, 12–13).

[57] Above, n. 25.

[58] Vernant 1986b, 300: "[Dionysus] joue à faire surgir, dès cette vie et ici-bas, autour de nous et en nous, les multiples figures de l'Autre. Il nous ouvre, sur cette terre et dans le cadre même de la cité, la voie d'une évasion vers une déconcertante étrangeté." See above, n. 46.

[59] Vernant's evocation of the Sanskrit word *māyā* in the first of the two texts quoted above recalls both Gernet's description of Dionysus as "un dieu de *māyā*" (1953, 393 [=1968, 86, and 1981b, 67]; cf. Vernant 1986b, 291: "dieu de magie, de *māyā*") and Nietzsche's *Birth of Tragedy* (secs. 1 and 18), where *māyā* is used in the sense of "illusion" or "mere phenomena," that is, as an Apollinian rather than Dionysian term. Both Nietzsche and Pentheus consider Dionysus a magician, but they attach different values to the word. According to Nietzsche, Dionysus' magic ("Zauber") transforms the world (below, n. 75); in the eyes of Pentheus, Dionysus is not only a "stranger" (Eur. *Bacch.* 233 *xenos*), but also "a magician and charlatan" (*Bacch.* 234 *goēs epōidos;* cf. Versnel 1990a, 116–18). When the god in disguise tricks Pentheus in the so-called palace miracles, he does pose as "the whimsical magician, the master of fantasies" (Dodds 1960, 151).

ness" are important aspects of Dionysus' mythical identity, but they become much less relevant if we look beyond myth and ask how the god was perceived in the context of cult.

With increasing frequency, the concept of the Other is applied to various aspects of the Dionysiac experience—to the wine and the mask, to nonconformity and violence—rather than to the god himself.[60] This tendency reflects a widening of horizons and an ability to mediate between the various realms of Dionysus. At the same time it further contributes to the erosion of the god in Dionysus. Instead of sharpening our eye for the concrete signs of his divinity, the category of the Other, like the related categories of the liminal and the marginal, ultimately invites an indifference that blurs all distinctions by subsuming them under a single denominator, that of alterity.[61]

## The Mask as a Sign of the Other

Associated with cult and drama, art and literature, impersonation and transformation, the mask is of particular interest as a locus in which many Dionysiac ambiguities come simultaneously into play.[62]

[60] Detienne describes the wooden mask of Dionysus retrieved from the sea by the Methymnians as "other in the sense that it is both strange and foreign, reflecting the double meaning of the Greek word *xenos*" (1989a, 9 [= 1986, 19]); also, "the appearance of Dionysos requires the revelation of otherness through its exacting violence" (Detienne 1987, 360). For Lissarrague, "l'expérience du vin, on l'a vu, est aussi expérimentation de l'altérité," translated as "the experience of wine is also the experience of the Other" (1987b, 57 [= 1990c, 10–13, 58]). According to Zeitlin, Thebes, the native city of Dionysus, "functions in the theater as an anti-Athens, an other place" (1990b, 144; cf. her contribution in this volume); along similar lines, Bierl understands Antigone as a Dionysiac figure who represents the Other ("vertritt die Umkehrung des Gewöhnlichen": Bierl 1989, 49 n. 33; cf. Bierl 1991, 1, 15–16, 66).

[61] For Hoffman 1989, Dionysus is by definition the liminal god (esp. p. 114: "Although all deities have liminal characteristics, none is more liminal than Dionysus himself"). A critical assessment of the value and limitations of such general anthropological categories as marginality and liminality for the study of Greek myths and rituals can be found in Versnel 1990b, 50–55, who reminds us that apart from Dionysus gods as different as Apollo, Artemis, Athena, Hermes, Pan, and Poseidon have all at one time or another been labeled "marginal."

[62] The principal studies of the Dionysiac mask as a symbol of ambiguity and mirror of meaning are Otto 1933, 81–86 and 194–95 (= 1965, 86–91 and 209–10); Foley 1980, 126–32 (= with revision 1985, 246–54); Segal 1982, 223–24 and 238–40; Frontisi-Ducroux and Vernant 1986, 38–42 (= 1988, 201–5); Vernant 1986a (= 1988); and Frontisi-Ducroux 1984

According to Otto, whose brief chapter on the mask has inspired much of the recent interest in the subject, Dionysus, "the god of the mask" ("der Maskengott," "le dieu-masque"), is both present and absent in his mask, which thus becomes the symbol of the "duality and paradox" inherent in his epiphany. For Vernant, the enigmatic mask of Dionysus functions as the visible sign of that "otherness" or "strangeness" that disorients and alienates the mortals who encounter him.

The image of the mask conceals more than it reveals; it challenges our imagination and raises questions—"the mask is pure confrontation."[63] A late archaic neck amphora in Tarquinia offers an example of this confrontation and invites us to confront the issue of representation and identity that attaches to every mask. From both sides of the vase, the same frontal image of a bearded, ivy-wreathed head stares at us with big saucer eyes, which seem to epitomize the enigma of the mask. Are we dealing with the image of a face or with the representation of a mask, the image of an image? And who is represented on the vase—Dionysus or one of his satyrs?[64]

Whether used in drama or in cult, masks create the impression of otherness and impose "strange" identities on the wearer as well as the observer. The so-called Lenaia vases depict cultic masks of Dionysus that are suspended from poles or pillars.[65] These masks simulate the

(= 1989) and esp. 1991. Cf. Vernant 1985a, 28–82 (= 1991, 111–38), for a discussion of Gorgo; and Napier 1986 for some cross-cultural comparisons.

[63] Otto 1965, 91 (= 1933, 85: "die Maske ist ganz Begegnung"); Calame 1986.

[64] Tarquinia, National Museum inv. no. RC 1804, ca. 520/510 B.C. (formerly assigned to the Antimenes Painter); *ABV* 275.5; *CVA* Tarquinia 2, pl. 32.4; Simon, Hirmer, and Hirmer 1981, 90 with pl. XXVIII (identified as the "mask of Dionysus"); Bérard et al. 1984, fig. 214 (= 1989, fig. 214); Simon 1985, pl. 268; Carpenter 1986, 97; Frontisi-Ducroux 1991, 183; cf. *LIMC* "Dionysos" nos. 6–48 (Dionysus as "Maskengott"); and Korshak 1987 (frontal images of Dionysus, satyrs). The massive snub nose is the hallmark of satyrs, but the human ears and the ivy wreath around the head link the face iconographically to Dionysus.

[65] Frontisi-Ducroux 1991, 8–9, differentiates between (1) the "cultic masks" of Dionysus represented on the "Lenaia vases," which were objects of worship and which were unparalleled outside of the Attic cult of Dionysus; (2) the "ritual masks" worn by human celebrants on ritual occasions; and (3) the "dramatic masks," especially of tragedy. For an exhaustive dossier of the Dionysus masks see Frontisi-Ducroux 1991, preceded by Durand and Frontisi-Ducroux 1982, Frontisi-Ducroux 1986 and 1987a, and Pickard-Cambridge 1988, 32–34. The history of the ongoing debate over the festive occasion for the cultic display of the mask image of Dionysus—Lenaia or Anthesteria?—has been fully traced by Frontisi-Ducroux 1991, 17–63, who argues that the ritual scenes on the vases evoke the cultic presence of Dionysus as "le dieu-masque" without referring to a specific festival. As for her second category ("ritual masks"), Burkert 1977a, 171 and 288 (= 1985, 104 and 186)

epiphany of a god believed to be present in his image, but they were never worn by men impersonating Dionysus. Wearing a mask on the tragic stage, on the other hand, was tantamount to "playing the other"—mythical heroes, women, non-Greeks, or gods such as Dionysus.[66] The Dionysus of the *Bacchae* is different from any other stage god in tragedy: his presence dominates the entire action, and he masks his "true self," his divinity, behind a deceptively human face. He plays both a human and a divine role and wears two opposite "masks"—a doubling of the Other that reflects Dionysus' own polarity.[67]

---

records a single case of a divine mask (*prosōpon;* on the term see Segal 1982, 248–49) worn by a priest in a ritual setting—the mask of Demeter Kidaria at Pheneos, Arcadia (Pausanias 8.15.3). The various masks worn in the earliest stages of the cult of Artemis Orthia do not portray the image of Artemis (Graf 1985, 89; Carter 1987; Vernant 1989, 173–209 [= 1991, 220–43]). On Frontisi-Ducroux's third category ("dramatic masks") see the following note.

[66]Zeitlin 1990a. On the pictorial and textual evidence for tragic and satyric masks in Attic drama see Pickard-Cambridge 1988, 180–96, and Kachler 1991 (with excellent illustrations); for a fascinating analysis of the dramatic effects generated by tragic masks see Melchinger 1990, 201–16 and 290–98; Kachler 1986 offers a spectacular collection of theater masks made for modern Swiss productions of Greek tragedies and comedies. The fascination of the theatrical mask, whether we call it paradox, illusion, ambiguity, or ambivalence, lies in the interplay of multiple identities, both real and imaginary, that are simultaneously revealed or concealed by the mask. I am thinking particularly of the following: the distance as well as the affinity between the dramatic identities of the masked characters and the civic identities of the individual actors and members of the audience (Segal, 1982, 215–16 and 239; Goldhill 1990; see above, n. 15); the convention of repeated role changes, which required each actor to play several parts, marked by a succession of different masks, in the course of a single play (Pickard-Cambridge 1988, 135–49); the representation of female characters by male actors through the mediation of the mask (Melchinger 1990, 208–10); the contrast between the visible face presented by the mask and the verbal image of the same face mirrored in the tragic text (Frontisi-Ducroux 1991, 226–27), and a related aspect, the tension between the fixed immutability of the mask and the physical or mental transformations that affect many tragic characters (Pickard-Cambridge 1988, 173–74; Melchinger 1990, 213–16; Blume 1978, 91–92); and finally, the double role, enhanced by costume and/or mask, played by dramatic characters such as Pentheus, who cross-dresses as a maenad (above, n. 18), and Dionysus, who assumes a false identity in the *Edoni* of Aeschylus, the *Frogs* of Aristophanes, and the *Bacchae* of Euripides (see following note).

[67]Cf. Segal 1982, 27–31; Vernant 1986a (= 1988); Goldhill 1988; and Frontisi-Ducroux 1991, 225–30. The actor who played the character of Dionysus either wore the same smiling mask throughout (Roux 1970, 110; Foley 1980, 126–31 [= with revision 1985, 246–54]; on Dionysus' smile see above, n. 10) or alternated between the god mask of Dionysus (above, n. 65) in the prologue and the closure scenes and the deceptive "human" mask of the smiling, effeminate Stranger in the three encounters with Pentheus (Segal 1982, 240). There is a third possibility, suggested by Dionysus' emphasis on his human disguise in the prologue, namely, that he wore the god mask and divine costume only for his elevated deus-ex-machina appearance in the closing scene (cf. Mastronarde 1990, 273, 284, no. 15).

"All the celebrated figures of the Greek stage—Prometheus, Oedipus, etc.—are mere masks of this original hero, Dionysus."[68] It was Nietzsche who extended the concept of the Dionysiac mask from the image that reveals the face of the tragic hero to the tragic identities of the characters and of the divine role models that some of them represent. The mask as a metaphor thus signals an interiorized, invisible otherness that either confirms or contradicts the visual mask. In Euripides, for instance, Antigone, Cassandra, and Hecuba are characterized through verbal "masks" that associate their abnormal behavior with the realm of Dionysus, thus adding new facets to their traditional identities.[69] More than five centuries later, Longus closed his Dionysiac novel with the arrival of Dionysophanes, the natural father of Daphnis, who reenacts the divine epiphany reflected in his name, which serves as his verbal mask.[70] From Euripides to Longus, Dionysiac masks, whether visual or verbal, invariably reflect the changing identities that take shape and disintegrate under the sign of Dionysus.

## Recognizing the God

The modern Dionysus is intense and fascinating; at the same time, he is a highly secular product of conceptualization and compartmentalization. We have gone through half of the old myth—during the past 120 years, Dionysus has been dissected and divided into detached concepts that have taken on a life of their own and continue to feed our imagination, just as in the myth Dionysus is dismembered by the Titans, who feed on his limbs. Is it possible to collect the scattered pieces and to bring the god in Dionysus back to life? And where do we find the god in him? The history of Western theology suggests that the notion of pure godhood, undiluted by anthropomorphic accretions, is beyond the comprehension of most people. The Greeks themselves

[68] Nietzsche, *Birth of Tragedy,* sec. 10 (= 1967, 73); cf. sec. 9 (= 1967, 72).

[69] Schlesier 1988a, 1988b, and her essay in this volume; Bierl 1991, 228–31.

[70] Longus 4.13–38; cf. Merkelbach 1988, 143 and 185–97. If it is indeed true that sex and the relation of the sexes are not merely portrayed in *Daphnis and Chloe* but subjected to critical scrutiny (Winkler 1990b, 101–26), Dionysophanes as the embodiment of the married state represents a more complex and ambiguous figure than Longus is normally given credit for.

never attempted to detach the divinity of Dionysus from his physical manifestations. They believed with Aby Warburg that "god lies in the particulars" ("der liebe Gott steckt im détail").[71] Taken literally, this maxim provides a preliminary answer to our question. If it is true that Dionysus was perceived in antiquity essentially as an epiphanic god who revealed himself in concrete physical manifestations, as his myths and images suggest, we need to concentrate on recognition, on the encounter of his particulars. Throughout antiquity, to accept Dionysus was tantamount to being in the presence of the god, whether by a stretch of the imagination or by a leap of faith. His divine status is inseparable from the ability of his worshipers to recognize him not only in his human form, but also behind the particulars of his other manifestations—for instance, his sacred plants or animals, his mythical entourage, or his special gift to mortals, the wine.[72]

In an epigram from Thasos, the local physician Timokleides dedicates to Dionysus, the "Lord of the maenads," a temple "under the open sky, surrounding an altar and covered with ivy," as well as a "handsome evergreen cave."[73] Timokleides goes on to describe how he will mix the wine of Dionysus with the water of the nymphs. The epigram, which culminates in a prayer for the doctor's personal welfare, is a good example of how Dionysus is perceived through the

[71] Cf. Sassi 1983, 86–89; Kany 1987, 131–90, esp. 173–74; Gombrich 1970, 13–14 n. 1, 229, and 286. In this maxim (penned in 1925) the art historian Warburg epitomized the interpretive process as he saw it—a painting's most telling details, understood as "cultural symbols," reveal the true spirit of its epoch and exemplify the formative role of historical recollection in general, which informs all culture.

[72] See above in the section titled "Seeing Is Believing."

[73] A French translation of the epigram was published by Pouilloux (in Ecole d'Athènes 1967, 172) and reprinted with tidbits of Greek by Roux (1972, 633–34); a brief discussion of the epigram can be found in Merkelbach 1988, 19, 60. The first two lines of the iambics can be reconstructed from Roux 1972, 244, 633–34: *hupaithrion soi naon amphibōmion | [s]kepaston ampeloisi, mainadōn ana.* The phrase *kalon antron* followed in line 3 (Roux 1972, 287). In 1976 Jean Pouilloux was kind enough to send me a copy of the entire Greek text, then to be published by F. Salviat, with the proviso "publication réservée." He also confirmed that the inscription dates from the late Hellenistic or early imperial period, and not from the third century B.C. (Roux). Timokleides apparently built a "roofless" temple, that is, a temple with a large skylight (the *hupaithrios naos* is defined as a colonnaded structure without a roof, *medium autem sub divo est sine tecto,* by Vitruvius *De architectura* 3.2.8). The Dionysiac *antron,* "toujours vert," was a bower-grotto, "a frequent setting for Dionysiac symposia" (Rice 1983, 60 and 81–82; Merkelbach 1988, 63–66, with additional bibliography; Nilsson 1957a, 61–63, who compares the Dionysiac grottoes with "Laubhütten").

particulars of the local setting and how his divinity is poetically confirmed by the evocation of a complex divine ambience that includes the "open sky";[74] his female worshipers, the maenads; the Dionysiac grotto; the clubhouse (*oikon . . . euastērion*) where the initiates raise their cry of *euhoi;* and finally, the god's gift to mankind, "the nectar that ends pain, the sweetest thing for mortals" (an echo of *Bacchae* 772). What is more, Timokleides' prayer recognizes Dionysus as a god who receives sacrifice and is worshiped by the initiates. Dionysus' divinity, detailed in the particulars and confirmed in cult, is the focus of the poem rather than conceptualization.

As we struggle to confront Dionysus, the god will emerge from his hiding in those elusive interstices that separate the ancient from the modern world to make an epiphany that invites understanding rather than belief. Dionysus once again joins his entourage of maenads and satyrs, mounts his panther, and embarks upon a conquest that reestablishes him in his traditional provinces and confirms his connection with the wine and the theater, with mystery cults and ecstatic ritual, and with the world of the dead. He appears in this volume too under his contradictory and paradoxical guises, at once masculine and effeminate, bearded and youthful, sober and intoxicated, tragic and comic, ephemeral and timeless, an embodiment of life as well as death, thus incorporating the whole spectrum of human experience. But insofar as we speak of Dionysus as a god whose divinity can be grasped only in his actual presence, neither my rather academic sketch of the modern quest for Dionysus nor my unacademic conclusion is likely to do the job and answer the question with which I began: Who is this Dionysus?

I am not suggesting that we become devotees of the god. What I want to emphasize is that the immediacy of the Greek encounter and the particulars of that encounter must remain central to our scholarly endeavors, whether we look for Dionysus in vase painting or in literature, in inscriptions or on monuments. Too often experts in one or another branch of the Dionysiac record who know everything

[74] Pouilloux's translation of *hupaithrion,* "à ciel ouvert," was adopted by Detienne as the programmatic title of his most recent book on Dionysus (cf. Detienne 1986, 72 and 80–81 [= 1989a, 46 and 51–52]). Like Artemis, Dionysus is indeed "der Gott des Draussen" who frequents the outdoors (cf. Graf 1985, 295, and Merkelbach 1988, 60–61, on Dionysus *pro poleōs*).

about the particulars are not interested in Dionysus. Conversely, some of the scholars who think hardest about the nature of Dionysus and conceptualize him for the rest of us are not always sufficiently attentive to all the particulars. Dionysus would be better served if the two sides joined forces, if a more constructive balance could be achieved.

To conclude what must perforce remain a set of questions and to offer a conclusion that does more justice to Dionysus, it is necessary again to listen to the poets, and especially Pound. In a much later poem, one of the eleven cantos of 1945 composed in the detention camp at Pisa, Pound looks back at his life's work and decides to do things differently. Instead of reviving yet another ancient myth by echoing his predecessors, as he had done in the second canto, he now has the courage to speak in his own voice, to be himself. From his prison cell, his cage, once more he invokes the presence of Dionysus, the god who liberates. The lynx is one of Pound's principal poetic surrogates for Dionysus, and it appears suddenly, like a divine epiphany, halfway into the poem, and in the form of a lyrical refrain: "O Lynx, my love, my lovely lynx, / Keep watch over my wine pot." The refrain undergoes several transformations amid an ever-expanding Dionysiac paradise, or in Nietzsche's poignant phrase, amid a "world bewitched"[75] that is laden with fruit, populated by felines, nymphs, and maenads—"maelid and bassarid among lynxes"[76]—and accentuated with polytheistic invocations of Iakchos, Kore, Pomona, and Kythera—"O Lynx, keep watch on my fire"—"O Lynx, guard this orchard, Keep from Demeter's furrow"—"Lynx, beware of these vine-thorns"—"O lynx, keep the edge on my cider." The canto culminates in a full-scale theophany that is exceptionally rich in Dionysiac detail:

> Therein is the dance of the bassarids
>     Therein are centaurs

[75] In "Die dionysische Weltanschauung" (summer 1870; cf. Cancik 1986, 118) and "Die Geburt des tragischen Gedankens" (December 1870), two precursors of *The Birth of Tragedy,* Nietzsche described the topsy-turvy world of Dionysus as "die verzauberte Welt" (adopted by Otto 1933, 89 [= 1965, 95] as the title of a chapter on Dionysiac miracles). In the first paragraph of *The Birth of Tragedy,* Nietzsche imagines that human individuals and nature will be reunited "unter dem Zauber des Dionysischen." See above, n. 59.

[76] The "maelids," properly Meliai (Hesiod *Theogony* 187; Callimachus *Hymn to Zeus* 47, *Hymn to Delos* 79–81), are tree nymphs, in particular, nymphs associated with the ash tree (*melia*), and by extension with other trees as well.

And now Priapus with Faunus
The Graces have brought 'Αφροδίτην
Her cell is drawn by ten leopards
O lynx, guard my vineyard
As the grape swells under vine leaf
Ἥλιος is come to our mountain
there is a red glow in the carpet of pine spikes.[77]

The principal divinity here is Dionysus. He does not appear in person, nor is he named, but the poet, like Acoetes in the earlier poem, recognizes the god because he is visible in the particulars. "Der Gott steckt im détail"—in the dance of the maenads, in the leopards and the lynx ("safe with my lynxes, feeding grapes to my leopards," says Dionysus to Acoetes in canto 2), in the vineyard, the vine leaf, and the mountain, and most comfortingly in the red glow under the pine trees, sacred to Dionysus.[78]

[77] Canto 79 (Pound 1983, 491–92).

[78] Jan Bremmer (Groningen) and Renate Schlesier (Berlin) have given me the benefit of their advice on various matters. I owe special thanks to Florence Verducci of the University of California at Berkeley for drawing my attention to Pound's Dionysiac cantos and, what is more, for reading and explaining them to me. I gratefully dedicate this paper to her, as well as to the enthusiastic thiasos of Berkeley students who explored the modern Dionysus with me in the spring of 1990.

CHAPTER 2

# The Asexuality of Dionysus

Michael Jameson

In this essay I examine a phenomenon which has been remarked on before—it is so conspicuous that it could hardly be overlooked—but which has received less attention than one might expect. In essence it is this: Dionysus was, of all gods, the most closely associated with the phallus, the erect male member, at once the instrument and symbol of male sexuality. His myths and cults also refer to the liberation, if only temporary, of both women and men from social controls, including sexual controls, which in most cultures are among the most rigid. The god himself is represented to a surprising degree as detached and unconcerned with sex. There certainly are a number of exceptions, as is to be expected in a body of evidence that is spread over a millennium and comes from very diverse sources. I do not suggest, however, that these exceptions are insignificant; there is a persistent ambivalence about the god's involvement with sex.

One can refer to the god's detachment as "asexuality," as I have in the title of this essay. But one might also speak of his bisexuality, the coexistence of elements of *both* genders that may, in effect, cancel each other out, or even of his transcendence of sexuality.[1] There are fre-

[1] "Asexuality" is also used by Hoffman 1989, 105, and by Stephen Fineberg in an unpublished paper, "Dionysos in the New Democracy," which he has kindly let me see and which will be incorporated in a longer study, forthcoming. Both scholars were members of a National Endowment for the Humanities Seminar on Greek religion and society that I

quent references to his effeminacy. Aeschylus in his lost play *Edoni* has that Pentheus-like figure Lycurgus ask, "Where does this woman-man come from?" and in his satyr play *Theori* the god himself protests the satyrs' calumny, that he is a cowardly woman-man who is not counted as a male.[2] There is, indeed, "something feminine in his nature."[3] Is this paradox, the effeminate god of the phallus, the phallic god of women, illusory, trivial, or quite central to the conception of the god and the nature of his cults? The subject can be examined under, roughly, three headings—iconography, myth, and cult.

## Iconography

The contrast is between the environment of the god and the depiction of his person. It is largely in vase painting, which as usual is mostly Attic, that he and his company are to be found. These scenes have been studied intensively, and I draw only on the most generally accepted conclusions.[4] Dionysus' company consists of both females and males—nymphs and maenads (the former usually thought to give way to the latter in the course of the sixth century), and satyrs and sileni. When the god is alone with the females the sexuality is not overt

organized at Stanford University in the summer of 1983. I profited from the stimulating experience the seminar provided, not least from the contributions of Fineberg and Hoffman. "Bisexuality" is the term used by Deutsch 1969 and Zeitlin 1982, while Frontisi-Ducroux and Lissarrague 1990, 232 n. 109, speak of the "alternation . . . between hypervirility . . . and the transcendence of sex."

[2] Aeschylus *Edoni* frag. 61 (*TrGF* 3), quoted by Aristophanes *Women of the Thesmophoria* 136, and *Theori* (or *Isthmiastae*) frag. 78a (*TrGF* 3). Devereux 1973 took the word *khlounēs* in another fragment of the *Edoni,* frag. 62 (*TrGF* 3), to be a reference to Dionysus as a eunuch.

[3] Otto 1965, 175. Otto explores this aspect of the god at some length. He stresses Dionysus' love for women and theirs for him. He cites Philostratus *Imagines* 2.17 (p. 367, 1–7 Kayser 1870): the Bacchant, ignoring the drunken Silenus who reaches for her, desires (*erōsa*) the absent Dionysus and sees him before her eyes (Otto's free rendering [p. 177] is considerably more fervent and mystical). The relevance of this mutual eroticism for the Dionysus of earlier centuries is questionable, but it turns out that, in Otto's view, "true womanliness reveals itself in the slighter importance of sexual desire" when compared with men (p. 178). He sees the maternal, nursing role of Dionysus' women as more significant. The relationship of Dionysus and his mother is also important for the very different, psychoanalytic perspectives of Slater 1968 and Deutsch 1969.

[4] Cf. Rapp 1872; Lawler 1927; Edwards 1960; McNally 1978; Carpenter 1986; Schöne 1987. I omit the South Italian repertoire, in which I have the impression the languid, beardless Dionysus of the later Attic vases prevails.

*Fig. 1.* Dionysus, holding a cantharus and vine branch, moves to the right among satyrs and nymphs. Two nymphs play krotala; one carries a bearded snake. Attic red-figure cup from the late sixth century. (London, British Museum E 16, $ARV^2$ 61.75.)

but latent, if we grant that the swirling dances of young and lovely superhuman women have sexual overtones (fig. 1). When the satyrs too are in the scene they show by their arousal and their behavior that they are not indifferent to their companions (fig. 2). By the second quarter of the fifth century they are usually no longer shown with erections and are generally less enthusiastically indecent in their actions (fig. 3). Perhaps it is worth remarking on what we all take for granted—there are only *male* satyrs. Even a detumescent satyr next to a woman or a nymph embodies male sexuality.[5]

[5]At the same time it is worth noting that only satyrs, not men (except in scenes of actual or anticipated intercourse), are shown with erections, a point Lin Foxhall has made to me. Truly human males, we are to understand, show self-control. The sexuality of satyrs, by

*Fig. 2.* A nymph resists the advances of two satyrs. The nymph, with a snake wrapped around her left arm, swings a thyrsus with her right. One satyr also holds a thyrsus, and both carry wineskins. Attic red-figure cup from the first quarter of the fifth century. (Munich, Direktion der Staatlichen Antikensammlungen und Glyptothek, 2644, *ARV*[2] 461.37.)

The god, meanwhile, is never shown in art as involved in the satyrs' sexual shenanigans. He may dance, he may drink, but he is never paired with or shown taking any interest in any of the female companions of his rout. He is not shown with an erection, but then gods almost never are, except for a single goat-headed Pan chasing a shepherd boy and the semi-iconic pillars of Hermes we call herms, which are shown with phalli at the right height in the archaic and early classical periods.[6] What has not been remarked, as far as I know, is that

contrast, does not need the presence of women for arousal (cf. Lissarrague 1990a, a valuable study that, along with Frontisi-Ducroux and Lissarrague 1990, I was able to use only in the revision of this essay).

[6] Keuls's statement (1984, 291) that gods are never shown with an erection is too sweep-

*Fig. 3.* Dionysus, holding a cantharus and an ivy sprig, moves to the right, led by a satyr playing pipes. Three satyrs follow: one, infibulated, pesters a nymph; the last in the procession carries a pointed amphora on his shoulder and a drinking horn in his right hand. Attic red-figure cup from the first quarter of the fifth century. (Munich, Direktion der Staatlichen Antikensammlungen und Glyptothek 2647, *ARV*² 438.132.)

before the change to a preference for a beardless Dionysus, the god's member is rarely shown, even at rest, though examples can be found (fig. 4). In archaic art and for most of the fifth century Dionysus is a full-bearded, full-grown but youthful male, usually wearing an ankle-length chiton that covers his body completely, on top of which a himation or a deerskin or leopard skin may be draped. Even when he

---

ing. The aesthetic preference for the small penis must also have been a factor (cf. Dover 1978, 125–27; Lissarrague 1990a, 56). The large penis and thus the phallus were comic and grotesque, inappropriate for beautiful and powerful gods. Pan: bell krater by the Pan Painter in the Boston Museum of Fine Arts, 10.185; *ARV*² 550.1; Borgeaud 1988, pl. 4.

*Fig. 4.* A drunken Dionysus, naked except for Thracian boots and a cloak over his left shoulder, holds a thyrsus and a cantharus as he moves to the right in a procession of nymphs and satyrs. The nymph Methyse with a lyre (barbiton) leads the procession. The satyr Oinobios helps the god and is followed by the nymph Chryseis playing pipes and the satyr Maleos with a cantharus and wineskin. Attic red-figure bell krater from the mid-fifth century. (New York, Metropolitan Museum of Art, Rogers Fund, 1907, 07.286.85, *ARV*² 632.3.)

wears a shorter chiton his loins remain hidden.[7] The contrast is not only with the satyrs in these scenes but with the representation of other

[7] On his dress, see Stone 1981, 313–16; Veneri 1986, 414–15; Miller 1989, 314–19; Frontisi-Ducroux and Lissarrague 1990, 230–31.

male gods. Nudity is common both on vases and in sculpture, for Zeus, Poseidon, and especially for the beardless Apollo.[8] The display of their bodies is consistent with their ostentatious masculinity. Dionysus, to be sure, fights in the ranks of the Olympians against Titans and Giants according to the mythographers and in some vase painting.[9] But even though Dionysus, like all Greek gods, could be violent and dangerous, one suspects that the more characteristic images for the Greeks were the terrified Dionysus who takes refuge in the bosom of Thetis (Homer *Iliad* 6.135–37) and the cowardly, if comic, figure who "gilds" his elegant Ionic gown when confronted with the Hound of Hell in Aristophanes' *Frogs* (479).

The dress itself is not a feminine garment. With jewelry in hair worn long it is part of the old-fashioned style of aristocratic Athenians of the archaic period. Other sixth-century depictions of male gods show a similar if simpler costume. Dionysus, however, continues to wear it long after it has been abandoned by the others. The saffron-dyed robe (*krokōtos*) he is described as wearing in comedy has unmistakable feminine connotations.[10]

When the rendering of Dionysus changes from a bearded adult to a beardless youth in the later fifth century the god is shown wholly or partly naked, but, as if to compensate for the absence of the symbolism of dress, his whole image is now even less virile—a graceful, languid figure, a *pais kalos* (fig. 5). This too may be suggested in Euripides' depiction of Dionysus as the young stranger in the *Bacchae* (e.g., 451–60).[11]

Dionysus' chiton is also seen on a cultic image in Athenian scenes of ritual. A trunk or pillar is set up, to which is fastened a mask (some-

[8] On the uses of nudity, see Bonfante 1989.

[9] Diodorus Siculus 3.74.6 and Apollodorus 1.6.2; for the scenes on vases see Lissarrague 1987d.

[10] Cf. Aristophanes *Frogs* 46; Cratinus frag. 40 (*PCG* 4); and Dodds 1944, on Euripides *Bacchae* 453–54.

[11] Evans 1988, 33 (and cf. 134), is convinced that Dionysus tries to seduce Pentheus in this scene and is angered by the king's rejection of him. The latter point is surely mistaken. The king's fate is sealed by his opposition to the new cult. The god only toys with him. But Dionysus' attractiveness as a love object is consistent with the later conception of him. The first, early appearance of the beardless Dionysus is not effeminate, as is shown by Carpenter in this volume ("On the Beardless Dionysus," pp. 185–206). That is not the case when he reappears later in the century. (On this and other points I have profited from Carpenter's knowledgeable comments.)

*Fig.* 5. A beardless Dionysus with a lyre and Ariadne (?) move to the right, followed by Eros who strikes a tumpanon as he hovers beside them. Dionysos carries a lyre, Ariadne a tumpanon. Attic red-figure cup from the last quarter of the fifth century. (London, British Museum E 129, *ARV*² 1414.89.)

times a pair, facing in opposite directions), and draped with a chiton, short or long (fig. 6).[12] The image of Dionysus Eleuthereus set up in the theater in Athens during the dithyrambic and dramatic performances may have been such a pillar topped with the god's head.[13] The

[12] Cf. Simon 1969, figs. 264–65, 274–75; Simon 1983, pl. 32, fig. 2; *LIMC* s.v. "Dionysos" nos. 298–300. The most careful analysis of the vases depicting a pillar and the mask of Dionysus is by Richard Hamilton 1992, 134–38, who shows that they do not form a consistent group representing a single cult. Other Dionysiac rites, such as the Lenaia, the Choes, and private rituals, have been proposed.

[13] Cf. Simon 1969, figs. 263, 274.

*Fig. 6.* Women celebrating in front of an image of Dionysus. The image comprises a mask affixed to a column above a chiton and himation. A table with stamnoi and loaves of bread (?) stands in front of the image. Both women hold drinking cups (skyphoi), and one prepares to fill hers with a ladle. Attic red-figure stamnos from the mid-fifth century. (Florence, Museo Archeologico 4005, *ARV*[2] 621.37.)

column or pillar with a head or simply a face is also found in the cults of Hermes and Zeus.[14] But unlike the images of Hermes the trunk of Dionysus on Attic vases never has a phallus, not even the quiescent penis of later herms.

Should these roughly cylindrical objects perhaps be seen in their entirety as phalli, personified by the addition of a face or head? The herm might then have been not only a representation of Hermes with a phallus attached but itself a large phallus. A difficulty is that stone

[14] Cf. Nilsson 1955, 201–7; Burkert 1985, 85.

versions in the cults of other gods are used for a variety of purposes, for not all of which is a phallic representation plausible. For Dionysus there are some suggestions of phallic-shaped images outside of Attica. At Methymna on Lesbos there was a cult of Dionysus Phallen in which a wooden trunk with a face on it was carried in procession.[15] On Rhodes Dionysus Thuonidas may have had this shape, and the Samians had a Dionysus Enorches, "with Balls."[16] This is not enough, however, to show that the original representation of the god was a phallic figure that, in the course of time, came to be represented in more respectable form.

In Athens and on Delos the evidence for large, ceremonial or commemorative phalli is explicit, but the way they are shown as living creatures is by putting eyes on the head (the glans) and wings or animal legs at the base. The creature is not the god himself but may be Dionysus' companion, Phalles.[17] Should we then interpret the masked and draped trunk as an alternative phallic representation of the god? If so, it is a singularly discrete version in a cult that did not hesitate to exaggerate. In Attica at least we see once again a deliberate avoidance of an easy conflation of the two, god and phallus, and the choice of a neutral rendering.

## Myth

Dionysus and Aphrodite seem a natural pair, representing as they do two of the great joys of life, the pleasures in particular of the

[15] Pausanias 10.19.3: fishermen find a *prosōpon* ("face" or "mask") of olive wood in their nets. Delphi tells them to worship Dionysus Phallen. They honor the *xoanon* ("statue") and send a bronze version to Delphi. Fontenrose 1978, 347, no. Q241 (= Parke and Wormell 1956, no. 337): "perhaps genuine." Cf. an inscription of Methymna, *IG* 12.2, no. 503 (*BCH* 7 [1883]: 37–41).

[16] Hesychius, s.vv. "Thuonidas" and "Enorkhes." Cf. also Lycophron 212. Devereux 1973 interprets the epithet Enorkhes as meaning "in the testicles" and compares Zeus's sewing the unborn Dionysus in his thigh, an indirect reference to his genitals. Dionysus Khoiropsalas, "Cunt-plucker" (?), at Sicyon suggests a lusty Dionysus (Polemon Historicus, *FHG* 3.135.42).

[17] Cf. Aristophanes *Acharnians* 263. For illustrations, see Buschor 1928 and Deubner 1932, pl. 22. An Attic lekythos, black-figure on white ground, shows a large, oblique phallus with an eye on the glans around which satyrs dance (*ABV* 505. 1; Metzger 1951, 49, pl. 26, figs. 1–3; *LIMC* s.v. "Dionysos" no. 153. This has been referred to as Dionysus Phallen (so Veneri 1986, 414–15), but the epithet is not Attic.

symposium. Yet their contacts in mythical genealogy are minor. They are made a couple only for the parentage of the phallic god Priapus of Lampsacus and of the Charites at Orchomenus in Boeotia.[18] The most vivid sexually charged conjoining is in Anacreon's appeal to assist him in a homosexual conquest. Dionysus is the "Lord, with whom Eros the subduer, the dark-eyed Nymphs and bright-faced Aphrodite play."[19] For women Aphrodite and Dionysus are contrasted: Pentheus charges the maenads with ranking Aphrodite before Dionysus, that is, it is for sex that they go to the mountains (Euripides *Bacchae* 225, though Dionysus himself has "the charm of Aphrodite in his eyes," 236). Is there a divergence between an Ionic and an Attic tradition, or between an archaic and a classical? Is Dionysus the patron only of male love? Whatever the case, the potentially powerful image of Dionysus as a force corresponding to Aphrodite was little used.

Dionysus' chief amorous attachment is to Ariadne, and while early versions of their relations may have followed the pattern of the god who loves and then is betrayed by a mortal (Homer *Odyssey* 11.324), the later archaic and classical versions have him rescuing her when she has been abandoned by Theseus.[20] In art they are shown as the embodiment of the happy married couple (fig. 5).[21] While this relationship is hardly asexual, its gentle eroticism is a far cry from the violent swirl of the world of maenads and satyrs. This conjugal aspect of the god, which Eva Keuls has clarified most helpfully,[22] has a ritual correlate in the annual marriage of Dionysus with the *basilinna* (or *basilissa*), the wife of the Athenian archon known as the *basileus* (king), in the days of the festival of the Anthesteria. There were both open and secret phases. The *basilinna* was assisted by fourteen honored women (the *gerarai*) appointed by the *basileus*. The queen performed rites "not to be spoken of" and saw what no one else should see, very likely referring to the handling of representations of sexual parts. The open aspect of

[18] Priapus of Lampsacus: Pausanias 9.31.2; Charites at Orchomenus in Boeotia: Servius *Aeneid* 1.720; cf. also [Orpheus] *Hymns* 46.1–3 and 55.7, of the second century A.D.

[19] Anacreon, *PMG* frag. 12 (= *PLG* frag. 2).

[20] Cf. Otto 1965, 185–86.

[21] *LIMC* s.v. "Dionysos" nos. 708–79 and the comments of Veneri 1986, 417–18. A red-figure pelike of the second quarter of the fourth century has a very sensuous scene of Ariadne and the beardless Dionysus on a bed (*LIMC* s.v. "Dionysos" no. 762). The figure of Eros joins in Dionysiac scenes in the later fifth century as Dionysus becomes a youth (Lissarrague 1990a, 66).

[22] Keuls 1982.

the ceremonies was her passage from the god's sanctuary "in the Marshes" to the *basileus*' headquarters, the Boukoleion, where the marriage took place ([Aristotle] *Constitution of the Athenians* 3.5). The questions of what actually happened and what it may have meant have occasioned a good deal of discussion. Did the archon's wife mate with a mortal man, her husband, or with the priest of Dionysus, perhaps masked and robed as Dionysus? Was the mating a symbolic ceremony, performed in the presence of an image of the god? Or was it purely the imagined consequence of public ceremonies such as the wedding procession, which may have used an impersonation of the god? A number of vases have been cited as evidence for the event, but their connection with this wedding is at best indirect.[23] It is easier to reject than to

[23] The relevant vases are conveniently discussed in Deubner 1932, 104–10; Bieber 1949 (though it is not clear that brides were initiated into Dionysiac mysteries); Simon 1963; Simon 1983, 96–98; cf. Keuls 1984, 293–94. Three types of vases have been thought to refer to this wedding. (1) Vases showing a woman, apparently a bride, being led by a satyr or in the company of Dionysus himself; on one the woman is identified as Ariadne, but a connection with Athens has been seen in the presence of an attendant satyr carrying a cantharus and a *khous,* a reference to the Choes rite at the Anthesteria (Simon 1963, pl. 5, 1, fragment of a calyx krater in Tübingen, no. 5439, "Group of Polygnotos"). (2) Vases showing a tipsy Dionysus (bearded, full grown, and nude); on one he is accompanied by a satyr boy carrying a chous while a woman seated on a bed awaits within (Simon 1963, pl. 5, 3; Simon 1983, pl. 31, 1; Keuls 1984, pl. XX, 14; Keuls 1985, 374, fig. 307; calyx krater in the National Museum in Tarquinia, inv. no. RC 4197, "Group of Polygnotos," *ARV*² 1057.96). (3) On an oinochoe in New York (Metropolitan Museum, 25.190) children seem to be preparing for Dionysus' wedding procession: the god is seated on a decorated two-wheeled cart (he is bearded and carries a cantharus), and a male is about to help a female climb up to join him (Deubner 1932, pl. 11, 2–4; Bieber 1949, pl. 5, 1A and 1B; Parke 1977, pl. 44; Keuls 1984, pl. XXI, 24; *LIMC* s.v. "Dionysos" no. 825).

For group 1 it is not evident that the reference is to the *basilinna* rather than to Ariadne, but it is an attractive notion that the presence of a chous in the scene in which Ariadne is named serves to compare the Athenian rite at the Anthesteria with Ariadne's wedding to the god. (But it is questionable whether we are to think of Theseus' having to relinquish Ariadne to Dionysus as comparable to the *basileus* surrendering his wife to the god, as Simon 1983, 97, suggests. In the best-known version of the story Theseus abandons her.) Seaford 1984, 8, deduces from these vases that men masked and dressed as satyrs accompanied the *basilinna.* In group 2 we seem to have a "realistic" rendering of Dionysus coming home to a wife (but must it be a bride?) after carousing. An allusion to the Choes rite may be implied, but I do not see that we learn anything about the *basilinna*'s wedding. Is some theatrical scene the source? Example 3, the preparation for a procession, would seem to be the most obvious rendering of the wedding, with an imagined or mimed Dionysus, but the scene has been excluded by Rumpf and Simon (see Simon 1983, 98). In the actual procession it is probable that no one represented the god. [Aristotle] *Constitution of the Athenians* 3.5 says that "the *summeixis* with Dionysus takes place there [at the Boukoleion] and the marriage." *Summeixis* is "ceremonial meeting" not "mating" (so Wilhelm 1937; cf. Rhodes 1981, 104–5). This may suggest that they did not meet before.

confirm speculations. Thus, although the Anthesteria had elements of an All Souls festival, when the spirits of the dead returned, the cheerful depictions of the marriage or parodies of it do not allow us to suppose that a dark and sinister side to this ceremony prevailed and that it was seen as the marriage of a woman with the god of the dead.[24]

The public part of the ritual imitates the bridal procession to the house of the groom, which marks the important social change whereby the woman moves from her paternal *oikos* to establish a new *oikos* with her husband. In this rite, however, the move is from the temple to the headquarters of the *basileus* and not vice versa. The god is assimilated to the man. On the vases that have been connected with this wedding one sees the conjugal themes of the marriage of Dionysus and Ariadne but nothing overtly or symbolically sexual, even though actual weddings were not lacking in sexual allusions and symbolism (cf., for example, the end of Aristophanes' *Peace*). The secret rites in which the *basilinna* engages as priestess suggest the controlled, covert sexuality of citizen marriage. Much of what we know of this sacred marriage comes from an allegation that a woman who did not meet the requirements of citizenship and purity had served as *basilinna* ([Demosthenes] *Against Neaera* 73–75). It is a far cry from the exuberant phallicism of the Country and City Dionysia or the abandon of the maenads. The conjugal Dionysus' engagement in sex seems carefully edited—mythologically, a placid marriage with Ariadne; ritually, a blessing of the community's marriages through the annual assimilation of the marriage of the city's most ancient officer, the "king," to that of the god, Dionysus.[25]

What of Dionysus' extramarital adventures? The chorus of Sopho-

[24] So, mistakenly, Daraki 1985, 80–81.

[25] From the extensive literature on the subject, note especially Deubner 1932, 100–110; Parke 1977, 110–13; Simon 1983, 96–97. Burkert 1983, 230–38, stresses restitution and fits this whole ritual into a context of the death, dispersion, reassembly, and revival of the god. He believes the god was represented by his mask fastened to a pillar and it was with this that the *basilinna* was thought to copulate. It is not clear that the mask and pillar have to do with this ceremony (most recently Simon 1983, 100–101, follows Frickenhaus 1912, in attributing all scenes with the mask and pillar to the Lenaia; Hamilton 1992 is skeptical of all identifications). I do not know that a woman who could be identified with the *basilinna* is ever shown alone with the mask and pillar. Hoffman 1989, 110, sees the whole ceremony as a social humiliation of the *basileus,* since he is cuckolded and his wife commits adultery. This is not possible. She *marries* the god in a public ceremony. Nothing in the references we have suggests any shame or humiliation.

cles' *Oedipus the King* (1105–9) wonders if the king may be one of the children presented to a surprised Dionysus by some nymph with whom he disports on Helicon. No asexuality there, but I recall no other such allusions in either literature or art, though no doubt they can be found. A favorite theme of both literature and art is the pursuit by a god of an object of his lust; it would not be surprising if Dionysus had been cast in this role. Only one vase painter seems to have tried to do so, on a single pot where the god and a youth chase each other around a neck amphora of ca. 470–460 B.C.[26] The story in Clement of Alexandria (*Protrepticus* 2.30) that the use of phalli as monuments derives from Dionysus' promise to Prosymnos that he would offer himself for sex in return for directions to the entrance to Hades makes use of the "pathic" rather than the lustful conception of the god.

## Cult

In art and in myth we have seen a god who is essentially detached from the erotic and passionate aspects of sex. In his cult, though there is much more than sex, the image of the phallus is central, however we may wish to explain it—as a celebration of the life force, as a charm for fertility, even as a symbol of life after death. (The apotropaic function of the phallus does not seem important in this cult.) Large and small renderings of the part were made especially for the Country Dionysia celebrated throughout Attica and were carried in public and private
] ... City Dionysia the colonies of Athens were ex-
y year and no doubt to march with them in
wn and then to show them to the assembled
ue of the god in the theater of Dionysus.[27]
is sort were at one time quite widespread in
*lia* 527e). Delos certainly went to great ex-
te a polychrome phallus every year, and we

979, pp. 12 and 80, no. 43, pl. 5, 3–4: a neck amphora by the
inv. 3050); *ARV*² 529.13; 470–460 B.C. The god, bearded,
rsus in his right hand and a vine branch and cantharus in his
; on the other a youth walks away from him while looking
d.
, no. 45), line 17.

have mentioned the processional carrying of a phallic image of the god on Lesbos. These were the most blatant and enthusiastic demonstrations of sexuality, however metaphorical or symbolic, to be found in the ancient world. A cigar may sometimes be only a cigar, as Freud warned, but a phallus, I submit, is always a phallus.[28]

These festivals are not said to have been restricted to men; Dikaiopolis in his private celebration of the Country Dionysia has his daughter carry the basket just ahead of the slave who carries the phallus, while his wife watches from the roof of the house (Aristophanes *Acharnians* 247–79). But we do not hear of Dionysiac rites open to public view in which women carried or manipulated phalli. Herodotus, who was convinced the Greeks took their cult of Dionysus, including the phallic procession, from the Egyptians, noted that the Egyptian celebration lacked dancing and the phallus itself, instead of which women carried wooden figures whose large genitals they raised and lowered by means of cords (Herodotus 2.48–49.1). Although he did not point it out, we should add that, to the best of our knowledge, it was not women who carried the Greek counterpart, the phallus, in Dionysus' cult; it may be that he expected his readers to savor not only the bizarre puppets but the fact that women operated them.[29]

In the closed women's cults of Demeter we hear of the use of representations of female and male sexual parts. Not only men recognized the necessity for the continuing vigor of phalli if the society was to continue, and while most Greek texts on procreation offered a male version in which the male is the dominant factor, the communal cults of Demeter and Kore and the private worship of Adonis helped to right the balance and put the phallus in its place, so to speak.[30] The Demeter cults in particular link the symbolism of human sexual vigor

[28] On the *phallephoria,* see Cole, forthcoming (I am grateful to the author for providing me with a copy of the article). On phallicism, see Herter 1938 and 1972; Jameson 1949. Czaja 1974 is a fascinating study of phallic stones in Japan on which are often represented couples who are symbolically copulating.

[29] Women would seem to be brought into close association with the phallus in a Dionysiac context through the ceremonial surrounding a phallus placed in a *liknon,* a basket used for winnowing grain and for carrying an infant; a mask of Dionysus is also shown in the *liknon.* Cf. Kerényi 1976b, 260–61 and passim; and Slater 1968, 214, who sees the disembodied phallus as significant for "the deprived and resentful Greek matron." But Nilsson 1952b argues that the representations of the *liknon* in ritual use are of Roman date, and denies that it was so used in earlier times. More significant may be the fact that what were evidently private rites, not conducted in public view, were not depicted earlier.

[30] Brumfield 1981; Zeitlin 1982; Winkler 1990b, 188–209.

and fertility with that of agriculture. Dionysus, however, is not demonstrably concerned with fertility, agricultural or human, except in Neoplatonic theory (where the phallus appears as symbol of procreative power) and perhaps by virtue of a place in a Demeter cult.[31] His festivals are agricultural only in their celebration of the vine. Aristophanes has Dikaiopolis, in the Dionysia "in the fields" (*kat' agrous*) that marks his joyful return to the countryside, give free rein to his erotic imagination, without a word on the god's help with his land and crops (*Acharnians* 247–79). At the risk of seeming pedantic, it is worth emphasizing that it is the broader symbolism of sexual ebullience and the new life of springtime that the god and his rites evoke. Sexuality here is much more than a sanitized convention or traditional magic for securing good crops.

The evidence of vase painting, while far from transparent, rather supports our contention that in the cults of Dionysus the phallus is left to men. A number of vases show a naked woman holding a gigantic phallus or a phallus bird or examining a container of phalli, all animated by an eye on the glans.[32] These women are no doubt hetairai like other naked women on vases, not citizen women, and the scenes

[31] Iamblichus (*De mysteriis* 1.11) interprets the phallus as symbol of procreative power. For Dionysus' place in the cult of Demeter, see the learned writer excerpted in the scholia to Lucian *Dialogi meretricii* 7 (= pp. 279–81 Rabe), who reports that the use of clay representations of male genitals in the festival of the Haloa was explained as "a token of human generation [literally *spora*, "seeding"] since Dionysus gave us wine as a tonic drug that would promote intercourse" (Winkler 1990b, 194). He then tells the story of the shepherds who killed Icarius under the influence of wine and attacked Dionysus. Afflicted apparently with satyriasis, they recovered only when they made dedications of clay phalli. "This festival is a memorial of their experience." Nonetheless it does not seem that the Haloa was a festival of Dionysus (Deubner 1932, 60–67; Brumfield 1981, 104–31). The story makes better sense as the *aition* of the Country Dionysia, also held in the month Poseidon (but were clay phalloi dedicated then?). Winkler 1990b, 195–96, sees men and women separately "conducting a memorial rite representing some themes of sex and gender." The scholar quoted in the scholion evidently saw a correspondence between male and female ritual use of genitalia. Dionysus had from an early date a place in the cults of Demeter that modern scholars have tended to slight. But this is the only suggestion we have that Dionysiac cult was concerned with the procreative aspects of sex. The Country Dionysia are often assumed to be directed at the fertility of the countryside, a notion that is even harder to pin down.

[32] E.g., (1) amphora by the Flying Angel Painter in Paris (Petit Palais 307), *ARV*[2] 279.2; Keuls 1985, 84, fig. 77; (2) fragment of a cup in Berlin; Deubner 1932, pl. 3, fig. 2; (3) cup in the Villa Giulia, 50404, *ARV*[2] 1565.1; Deubner 1932, pl. 4, fig. 1; Keuls 1985, 85, fig. 78; (4) column krater by the Pan Painter in Berlin; Deubner 1932, pl. 4, fig. 2; (5) pelike in Syracuse (inv. 20065), *ARV*[2] 238.5; Keuls 1985, 84, fig. 76. Lissarrague 1990a, 65–66, rightly concludes, after reviewing these scenes, that a woman associated with a phallus is not Dionysiac, and vice versa.

do not refer to the community's cults, if they have any cult reference at all. There is a unique scene of a clothed woman sprinkling something on to a row of phalloid plants springing from the ground.[33] We are in the dark about all these scenes, as we are for so much of what went on in the world of Greek women, but perhaps with these scenes we are not missing a great deal. Male artists are saying something about women to a largely male audience, probably that women are wonderfully impressed with the phallus, which is what men like to believe (we may compare the confidence of ancient pornographers in the importance of the dildo).[34] In any case, nothing shown in these scenes points to Dionysus. As far as we can see, overt, exuberant phallicism had no part in the Dionysiac cults of women.

Dionysus was also celebrated privately by means of *kōmoi,* "routs" or "wild parties" at night, in the course of which wine flowed, social barriers were breached, and sexual indulgence was at least thought to occur.[35] One thinks of the Menandrian foundlings, the products of behavior otherwise proscribed. Ostensibly, however, these were occasions for men only (with of course whatever noncitizen women were wanted), while the women of the community had their own rites for the god in which men had limited roles or were excluded.

Maenadism, the withdrawal by women from the community to the mountains to engage in nighttime celebrations, known primarily from literary and artistic depictions, has been much debated—how much is

[33] Red-figure pelike in the British Museum (E 819) by the Washing Painter, *ARV*[2] 1137.25; Deubner 1932, 65–66 and pl. 3, figs. 1 and 3; Winkler 1990b, frontispiece. The scene has been associated with the Haloa, a Demeter festival (so Deubner). Winkler 1990b, 206, describes it as "humorous fantasy not necessarily associated directly with the Adonia . . . but, illustrating the same cultural equation," i.e., that women cultivate and bring to growth the fragile and short-lived vigor of men. I think, however, that Winkler was mistaken in supposing that the woman sprinkles water on the plants. The object she carries would not do for water, nor would such sprinkling induce growth. Something more fantastic may be involved—perhaps she scatters seeds, and instantly phalli spring up.

[34] Cf. Keuls 1985, 83.

[35] A number of illustrations (the so-called Anacreontic vases) and some literary evidence point to the wearing of women's clothes and jewelry at drinking parties. Frontisi-Ducroux and Lissarrague's article in 1990 (stressing the ambivalence of the self and the other which encompasses that of male and female) supersedes earlier studies, but cf. also De Vries 1973 and Slater 1978. Price 1990 came to my attention too late for use in this study. In the worship of Dionysus through participation in the *kōmos* the worshipers, like the god, play with sexual boundaries. Other occasions for cross-dressing in Greece are in rites of initiation and marriage when identities are changed and alien identities are briefly tried out.

imaginary, mythical, or symbolic, and how much corresponds to real life?[36] Ancients and moderns have been at pains to assure us that the expeditions of the women were entirely chaste.[37] It would certainly be surprising if Greek men, in view of their tight control of their women, had allowed them to go to the mountains with the expectation of sexual adventures. And yet it is not without significance that women indulging in wine at night and freed, however briefly, of social constraints were imagined as engaged in sex, as Pentheus repeatedly implies in the *Bacchae*. The situation is by its nature sexually charged. We might say that the communal Dionysia on the one hand and the mountain pilgrimage of the women on the other each emphasizes an aspect of human sexuality, the phallic and the female, and the two are brought together in the imagery of the satyrs and maenads seen on Attic vases. The enigma is the central figure of such scenes, the god who is both male and female but isolated from the sexuality that flourishes all around him.

Dionysus, the phallic god par excellence, is also more closely associated with the rites of women than any other male figure. The reasons for this have received considerable attention in recent years.[38] The god has been seen as a liberating figure in whose worship women found a temporary escape from male domination. There were probably also nonmaenadic rites in which women played the only or the leading parts. But by their nature these were, like the women's rites for Demeter and Kore, secret and remain, therefore, obscure to us. We have seen an example in the sacred marriage of the Athenian *basilinna*. There were consequences for the structure of the god's cult. For him alone among male gods were there priestesses and numerous groups of women with various names (e.g., *gerarai* involved in the *basilinna*'s wedding).[39] An example from Attica is seen in the sacrificial calendar of the deme of Erchia in the second quarter of the fourth century B.C.

[36] See especially Henrichs 1978a and Bremmer 1984.

[37] E.g., Eur. *Bacch*. 314–20, but cf. *Ion* 545–55. Devereux 1973 has no doubt that sexual orgasm, lesbian or heterosexual, was characteristic of most Bacchants. Only the most accomplished women achieved a trance state without it. (His warning that we must not be misled by the obtuse messenger verges on the fallacy of Lady MacBeth's children.) Detienne 1989b, 261, on the other hand, denies that the erotic was for the Greeks a means of leaving oneself and becoming one with the god.

[38] Cf. Kraemer 1979; Segal 1982, 159; Zeitlin 1982.

[39] Cf. Otto 1965, 175; Henrichs 1978a.

Dionysus and Semele received a billy goat and a nanny goat, respectively, on the sixteenth of the month Elaphebolion. The flesh of Semele's goat was handed over "to the women," while the skin of both animals belonged to the priestess.[40] In terms of social organization as well as cult participation we see a predominantly female side to Dionysus' worship, matching the predominantly male and phallic.

## Conclusions

Two cautions are in order before we offer some conclusions. Looking for a consistent whole in the figure of a Greek god and worrying about seeming contradictions are, of course, essentially modern, not ancient, concerns. Furthermore we are able to attempt a reconstruction only for archaic and classical Athens, where alone there may have occurred the particular convergence and balance we think we can see. Dionysiac symbolism makes great play with the male member, on the one hand, and with the concept of liberated women, on the other. Sex may be incidental and not central to the meaning of Dionysus' cult, though our review makes that hard to believe, even if we do not go so far as to say with Keuls that "Dionysiac cult [was] centered around male-female confrontation."[41] But, in any case, his cult lends itself to a powerful nexus of signs. Violence and aggression are portrayed for both male and female, and yet at the center of the commotion stands a figure that presents features of softness, gentleness, and quiet. For women, I suggest, this is especially important. Aggression, the use of the phallus as a weapon, waxes and wanes in the scenes on Attic pots, and corresponding changes have been seen in Athenian society.[42] But while a growing appreciation of conjugality and harmony between the sexes is shown in art, the hostile and aggressive side of male sexuality is not likely to have faded away.[43] While Dionysus presides over

[40] *LSS* nos. 18A, 44–51, 18Δ, 33–40; *SEG* 21, no. 541.

[41] Keuls 1984, 288.

[42] Cf. McNally 1978; Fineberg 1983.

[43] Cf. Sutton 1981, 107–8; Keuls 1985, 174–86; Kilmer 1990. Kilmer compares scenes of sexual violence on Attic red-figure vases with an arbitrary selection of sadomasochistic scenes in European and Japanese art of the recent past to conclude that the Attic examples are relatively innocuous. I do not see that any useful conclusions are to be expected from such methods.

phallic cavortings, he remains detached sexually, except for his rescue of and marriage to Ariadne and his sanctification of the marriage of *basileus* and *basilinna.* The beardless youth of later classical art is still less a threatening and aggressive figure than his bearded predecessor.

To use what has become a cliché, Dionysus is a mediating figure between male and female, needed because the forces his cult releases arouse both men and women in ways that threaten order. The reasons for the development and persistent strength of his potentially explosive cult lie, no doubt, deep within the structure of Greek society, which contained both the psychological tensions of the nuclear family and the wider social and institutional stresses of the approved roles of women and men. Any particular instance of Dionysian activity is not likely to exhibit the full repertoire of elements that we attach to his cult, a construct that is in effect of our own making. Nor are release and resolution of the pressures his cult addresses always achieved, according to some neat, functional model. The most I have hoped to do in this essay is to examine some aspects of a varied and constantly changing pattern.[44]

Two images may provide us with an appropriate conclusion: one is that of the embodiment of the epicene style of modern pop culture, the male leader of the pop group, who for all the violence of music, gestures, and words is neither traditionally masculine nor yet effeminate. To the established order he may be a threat but not to the adoring young, especially the young women. There is a fascination but also a certain horror about such a figure, who cannot be placed and straddles

[44] No one has been more sensitive to the contradictions in the conception of the god than Slater 1968, 210–307. He noted "a quality of dissonance about the god" (211) and his "conglomerate and morphologically unstable character" (212). He also brought out that "even the boundaries between the sexes are to be dissolved." "This," he observed, "was perhaps one of the central psychological functions of the Dionysian cult—it provided the ultimate fantasy solution to the torment which sex antagonism occasioned in Greek life by eliminating the exaggerated differentiation imposed by culturally defined sex roles" (283–84). Segal 1982, 213, who cites this last passage, rightly notes that in the *Bacchae* sexual differentiation is reinforced rather than eliminated and that tragedy by its nature is not concerned with such resolution. Indeed, it could be said that cult and myth in other forms as well may provide opportunities for demonstration and exploration rather than resolution. And yet the recurrent theme of the unclassifiable god seems always to be available as a palliative. It should be added that Slater, who emphasizes the obscuring of boundaries between mother and child and the mother's ambivalence toward child and phallus (conceived of as an isolated object and depicted as the member of depersonalized, inhuman satyrs), sees no resolution of "the Greek cultural sickness" by this route.

or crosses boundaries. The other image is that of Dionysus in the *Bacchae,* who draws Pentheus over a boundary as the king is led to make himself into a *bakkhē*. In that play is there not some of this chilling fascination about Dionysus too, whose gender puzzles Pentheus and who moves quietly between the raucous worlds of the male and the female?

CHAPTER 3

# Dionysus Poured Out: Ancient and Modern Theories of Sacrifice and Cultural Formation

Dirk Obbink

Can anybody be so insane as to think that the food he eats is a god?
Cicero *De natura deorum* 3.41

Inventor of wine, as a god Dionysus himself is poured out to the gods.
Euripides *Bacchae* 284

The blood is the life.
Leviticus 17:11

Whoever eats my flesh and drinks my blood will live in me and I in him.
John 6:56

I am poured out, as a sacrifice.
Philippians 2:17

## Savage Logic

According to a very well-known theory, not only maenadic sacrifice, but also ritual wine drinking in honor of Dionysus, was sacramental in character. Under this theory Dionysiac sacrifice is viewed as communion, with humans sharing in the vital force of the consumed animal, or in the case of libation and wine drinking, in the "blood" of the grape. Under the influence of W. Robertson Smith's totemistic theory of Semitic sacrifice and the anthropology of J. G. Frazer, Jane Harrison applied the theory specifically to Dionysus and concluded that maenadic "sacrifice is a sacrament, that the bull or goat torn or eaten is the god himself, of whose life the worshippers partake in sacramental communion."[1] The theory of Dionysiac sacramentalism[2] received added support from E. R. Dodds. According to Dodds, the practice rested on "a very simple piece of savage logic" ("simple savage" and "savage logic" are Frazer's terms,[3] echoed already by Harrison): "The homoepathic effects of a flesh diet are known all over the world. If you want to be lion-hearted, you must eat lion; if you want to be subtle, you must eat snake; those who eat chickens and hares will be cowards, those who eat pork will get little piggy eyes. By parity of reasoning, if you want to be like god you must eat god (or at any rate something which is *theion*). And you must eat him quick and raw, before the blood has oozed from him: only so can you add his life to yours, for 'the blood is the life.' "[4] Stated in this form, the theory was comprehensive and intriguing, almost irresistible, if lacking epistemological rigor. What Dodds theorized (in what has been called "an excessive fit of comparativism")[5] about Dionysiac sacrifice influenced several generations of work on Greek religion and continues to do so today.

Even after it has been stripped of its Christian overtones (which it quite often is not) and divested of its animistic anthropology, the sacramental theory does not go very far toward elucidating the cul-

[1] Smith 1894, chaps. 8 and 9; Frazer 1912, 138–68 ("The Homoepathic Magic of a Flesh Diet"); Harrison 1912, 119; cf. 118–57; and cf. Harrison 1903, 478–88.

[2] Cf. Harrison 1903, 452–53: "the sacramental mystery of life and nutrition" realized in the "breaking of the bread" and the "drinking of wine." Even Wilamowitz, who resisted the sacramental interpretation (as did Otto, Jeanmaire, Festugière, Winnington-Ingram, and in part Rohde), compared the Milesian *ōmophagion* (see below, pp. 70–71 and 73 n. 22) to the Eucharist. On the scholarly record, see Henrichs 1982, 234–35 with nn. 207–17.

[3] Frazer 1912, 138 and 202. Cf. Harrison 1903, 486: "The idea that by eating an animal you absorb its qualities is too obvious a piece of savage logic to need detailed illustration."

[4] Dodds 1940, 165 (= 1951, 277, and 1960 xvii–viii). So often repeated, the formulation became well known, universally accepted, and endlessly echoed. Dodds's quotation comes from Leviticus 17:11 (cf. Genesis 9:4 and Deuteronomy 12:23), apparently in the canonical rendering of the Cambridge school, as it also appears in Harrison 1903; cf. Dodds 1951, 209.

[5] Versnel 1990a, 145, referring to Dodds 1951, 276.

tic dimension of Dionysus.[6] The theory presumes, for example, the equation of the divinity with his sacrificed victim. But we cannot even be sure that the Greeks ever equated Dionysus with any of his sacrificial animals.

Why then did the sacramental theory gain such popularity and widespread acceptance? No one any longer speaks of the sacrificial animal as a "totem." Much of Frazerian anthropology has been discredited, while the animism of the Cambridge school is as studiously avoided as the term "Corn Spirit" or the elusive "Year Daimon." But the "savage" element entailed by the sacramental theory remains very much a part of current work on sacrifice, not of course in monochromatic ethnological descriptions like "*the* savage" or "savage logic," but in the assumption shared by many modern theories that animal sacrifice originally involved an element of dark and violent behavior demanding ritual atonement for guilt.

Nowhere was this more apparent than in the case of Dionysus, a divinity who had long been recognized as a figure paradoxically composed of, and associated with, polarities such as god/mortal, human/beast, mild/wild, cooked/raw, tame/savage, male/female, and so on.[7] Part of the attractiveness of the sacramental theory lay in the fact that it seemed to bridge the gap between conflicting representations of Dionysus and explain how such contrasting qualities, amply illustrated in myths about Dionysus, could be so closely associated with one and the same divinity. It was, after all, quite clear that Dionysus had *something* to do with both violence and its civilized containment, with killing and eating, with ritual victimization and alimentary consumption. A cult inscription was even found that showed "real" maenads handling raw meat.

[6] There is even some question as to its status as a *theory,* in the sense of a unitary explanation, having scope and economy, for diverse phenomena susceptible to multiple interpretations. I persist in the designation here because Dodds repeatedly referred to his views on the matter as a "theory" and believed it had heuristic validity. On the question see below, n. 55.

[7] Henrichs 1990, 258. Otto 1965 (e.g., 176) was perhaps the first modern scholar to popularize this description of Dionysus' characteristics as pairs of contrasting opposites. Henrichs 1982, 158, points out that this type of characterization of the god actually dates from antiquity: "More than any other Greek god, Dionysus lacks a consistent identity. Duality, contrast and reversal are his hallmark. The wide range of experiences embodied by him was described in pairs of opposites" (with the examples that follow, nn. 193–99).

So while today the sacramental theory has very few outspoken adherents, vestiges of its concept and vocabulary continue to inform many discussions of sacrifice.[8] (A good example is the constant assertion by scholars that the reason the *splankhna* are consumed first in sacrificial procedure is that they contain the vital force or spirit of the sacrificed animal.) Dionysiac sacrifice is certainly no exception in this regard. Indeed conceptions of Dionysus have influenced modern understanding of Greek sacrifice considerably. A survey of the field of Greek sacrifice and a consideration of its role in cultural formation (rather than an exhaustive catalog of the evidence) will show the extent of Dionysus' influence. I will focus on five main features, all of which have been held to involve Dionysus distinctively or which in their Dionysiac manifestations have been regarded as in some way paradigmatic for sacrifice in general. These features are (1) maenadic omophagy, (2) human sacrifice and cannibalism, (3) Dionysiac sacrifice in civic cult, (4) sacrifice and initiation, and (5) sacramental wine drinking. Then, with a view toward clarifying how far modern theories of sacrifice have been misled by the sacramental theory, I will contrast modern theories with some representative *ancient* counterparts on the point of sacramentalism. Although I will ultimately want to abandon the term, I will argue that sacramentalism does in fact obtain in Dionysiac ritual in an important way, but in a sense very different from that envisaged by Dodds and Harrison.

## Maenadic Omophagy

Much of the work done on maenadic sacrifice suffers from excessive reliance on a single literary source, namely, Euripides' *Bacchae,* due in part to the prominence achieved by that work already in antiquity and to the influence that it may have had on later ritual practice and language. Cultic elements are by no means lacking in the play—in fact the play contains quite a variety of references to Dionysiac ritual—but they have been so fully incorporated into the dramatic structure of the play, in order to negotiate the psychological or social experience of Dionysus, as to become almost indistinguishable from other dramatic

[8] For examples see Burkert 1966; Guépin 1968; Daraki 1980.

elements and devices.[9] But the picture presented in the play of roving bands of women, female devotees of Dionysus, who tear wild animals limb from limb for the consumption of raw meat (*Bacchae* 1184 *metekhe nun thoinas,* "Now share the meal") cannot have been a common one in the ancient world—not because it occurs nocturnally, in secret, and to the exclusion of men, but because it is fundamentally an event of myth. (And this fact remains even if we include a historical dimension in the definition of that term.) We have no eyewitness account of such happenings among the later maenadic groups of women who did congregate and dance at Delphi and Thebes and to whom Plutarch and Pausanias talked. It has been pointed out that ritual maenadism in any form was unknown in some parts of the Greek world, including Attica. But it may be wise to guard against minimalism here: what may be significant in this case may not be what was *actually done,* but rather what was *believed* to be done, or (I should prefer to say) what was believed to have *once* been done, in the long history of Dionysus' eternal arrivals and their ongoing reenactments in myth and ritual.

In the worship of Dionysus by private groups the eschatological message of Dionysiac ritual (including sacrifice) was the imaginative acquisition of a lasting Dionysiac identity, either as a member of the god's eternal entourage or through identification with one of the god's mythical roles.[10] In this sense the myth itself, with its sacrificial *sparagmos* and consumption of raw flesh (omophagy), can be placed within a ritual dimension, not in the *drōmena* of cult, but rather in the minds and imaginative role-playing of Dionysiac participants.[11]

I will not, however, want to claim that maenadic omophagy is even a mythic or imaginative example of Dionysiac sacramentalism, for the very reason that it is not sacrifice at all. Instead, it constitutes the inversion of normal sacrificial procedure, in which a domesticated (and not a wild) animal is ritually selected (and not merely chanced upon), killed, systematically cut up (and not dismembered by force), and eaten cooked (and not raw). Maenadic *sparagmos* followed by omophagy thus stands in complete contradistinction to ordinary sacri-

[9] Henrichs 1990, 258.

[10] Henrichs 1982, 160.

[11] Whether this kind of mythic representation can be demonstrated to be a matter of ritual per se remains open to dispute.

fice and can thus be viewed as a kind of inverted charter myth, setting forth the way in which sacrifice should *not* take place, much as the account of the dismemberment of the young Dionysus by the Titans inverts the original, paradigmatic division of the sacrificial victim by (another Titan) Prometheus.[12]

In the case of the *sparagmos* of Dionysus by the Titans we have a clear instance of inverse (or perverse) sacramentalism, an event that occurred once in a distinctly mythic era. Here the Orphic concern was clearly not that the initiate or Orphic adherent should *engage* in theophagy, but rather that animal flesh not be consumed at all (or that restrictions concerning the handling of food, such as "not to boil that which has been roasted," be carefully observed). So also in the case of maenadic *sparagmos* and omophagy, the myth depicts an abnormal form of sacrifice as the expression of a marginal or protest group.[13] In any case the eating of the god is expressly *rejected* in cultic reality. The adverse reaction of the Asiatic maenads to the prospect of eating Pentheus' flesh at Euripides' *Bacchae* 1184 may be profitably compared. When Agave offers them Pentheus' head, saying: *metekhe nun thoinas* ("Now share the meal"), the chorus replies with an outraged *ti; metekhō, tlamon;* ("What!? Am I to partake, O shameful one?").[14] The entire affair is paralleled with curious precision by the reaction (an exclamatory *tlamon*) of Dionysus' satyrs to participation in the Cyclops' cannibalistic sacrifice in Euripides' *Cyclops* (369).[15]

This also provides a key for understanding the handling of the sacrificial meat in the Dionysiac cult inscription from Miletus.[16] Here it is stipulated that the female devotees of Dionysus are to *embalein* (literally, "to toss in or on") the *ōmophagion*.[17] The action is itself

[12] Detienne 1979, 68–94 ("The Orphic Dionysus and Roasted Boiled Meat," an underrated and unjustly maligned account); cf. Detienne 1989a, 57–66.

[13] Detienne 1979, 34.

[14] Cf. Dodds 1960, ad loc.: "The invitation to a feast—presumably with Pentheus' remains as the principal dish—is too much for the nerves of the Chorus: their attitude of forced approval breaks down." In the *Bacchae* this reaction presumably prepares the action for the subsequent (ritual?) reassembly of Pentheus' remains in the (badly preserved) final scene of the play. In any case there is no suggestion that Pentheus' remains may be *properly* eaten; for the later tradition's exaggeration of this possibility for dramatic effect, see Dodds's note ad loc.

[15] Seaford 1981, 274 with n. 214.

[16] On the inscription, see especially Henrichs 1978a, 148–52.

[17] On the disputed meaning of the phrase, see Eisler 1929; Dodds 1951, 276; Festugière 1956; and Henrichs 1978a, 150 with n. 92.

highly unusual and is thus couched in the most unusual of terminology. Here also we can see one of the more imaginatively enacted aspects of the myth being accommodated to ordinary civic cult, for the inscription (actually a contract for the sale of a priesthood of Dionysus Bakkhios designed to guarantee the privileges of the purchaser, who was a woman) specifically stipulates that the priestess must *embalein* the *ōmophagion* first "on behalf of the city" before any of the other participants does so. There can thus be discerned in this case a conflation of aspects of Dionysiac myth with realistic cultic details.[18]

Raw meat in these instances is to be associated with highly marginal, unusual, and infrequent situations of ritual exception and dissolution. One may compare the Hephaestia on Lemnos, a time of dissolution and exception, in which all fire is extinguished for nine days until new fire is brought from Delos.[19] During the exceptional period sacrifices continue to be performed without fire; there is thus no normal food (consumption of raw meat actually is not attested). So also in the case of maenadic sacrifice there is an infrequent ("trieteric," i.e., every other year), periodic (though short-lived) ritual and commemorative regression to an aboriginal period in cultural history, with the mythical worshipers of Dionysus "regressively transformed into bestial predators."[20]

Exactly what form this will have taken in "real" cult (to use a kind of functionalist terminology) is by no means certain. According to Diodorus Siculus (4.3.2), the female devotees of Dionysus did offer their own sacrifices (a highly unusual thing to be said of groups of women in antiquity):

> The Boeotians and other Greeks and the Thracians, in memory of [Dionysus'] campaign in India, have established sacrifices every other year to Dionysus and believe that at that time the god reveals himself to

[18] Compare the later iconographical representations of "mythical" maenads equipped with sacrificial knives known from actual cult, on which see Henrichs 1978a, 151 n. 97, and Henrichs 1982, 220–21 n. 68.

[19] Philostratus *Heroicus* 67.7 (de Lannoy 1977): during the exceptional nine-day period "if the ship bringing new fire from Delos arrives before the funerary sacrifices are over, it may not be brought to anchor on Lemnos." Cf. Burkert 1983, 190–96, especially on the Dionysiac elements, with further bibliography: "Sacrifice was clearly a part of the exceptional period at Lemnos, sacrifice without fire; so that one could eat at most only raw pieces of meat, burying the rest or throwing it into the sea" (193).

[20] Burkert 1987b, 172.

> humans. Consequently in many Greek cities every other year Bacchic bands of women gather, and it is lawful for the maidens to carry the thyrsus and to join in the frenzied revelry, crying out "Euai!" and honoring the god; while the matrons, forming in groups, offer sacrifices to the god and celebrate his mysteries and in general extol with hymns the presence of Dionysus, in this manner acting the part of the maenads who, as history records, were the old companions of the god. . . . And since the discovery of wine and the gift of it to humans were the source of such great satisfaction to them, both because of the pleasure that derives from the drinking of it and because of the greater vigor that comes to the bodies of those who partake of it, it is the custom, they say, when unmixed wine is served during a meal to greet it with the words, "To the Good Deity!" but when the cup is passed around after the meal diluted with water, to cry out "To Zeus Savior!" For the drinking of unmixed wine results in a state of madness, but when it is mixed with the rain from Zeus the delight and pleasure continue, but the ill effect of madness and stupor is avoided.

Thus according to Diodorus, historical maenads offered sacrifices as civilized substitutes for the savage sacrifices of maenadic myth, "in this manner acting out the part of the maenads who were the old companions of the god."[21] I suspect that if you asked a Theban or Delphic maenad if they performed *sparagmos* during their *oreibasiai,* the answer would have been, "No, but we used to do so. It's just we don't do that anymore. *Other* people, *those* people," they might have said, "up there [Thracians, perhaps], *still* do it." (The same is often said by one culture of another culture about cannibalism, on which see below.) Again, though, this absolutely precludes neither the possibility that they nonetheless did engage in such practices anyway (in spite of their denial) nor that they experienced them imaginatively through enactment in ritual or ecstatic states of altered consciousness.

## Human Sacrifice and Cannibalism

Under this heading we have of course to deal with Pentheus, insofar as he is described as a sacrificial victim in Euripides' play. He (or his death) is specifically called a sacrifice (*to thuma*) by Cadmus at *Bacchae* 1246–47. Addressing Agave, he says of the murdered Pentheus:

[21] So Henrichs 1978a, 148.

> A fine sacrifice is this which you fell for the gods,
> while to such a meal as this you invite both Thebes and me.[22]

Agave herself is called a "priestess" who "begins the slaughter or murder" (1114 *mētēr ērxen hierea phonou*—a perverse and ambiguous collocation of words, for *hierea phonou* could mean "priestess of death or murder" and is often so mistaken by commentators). Pentheus himself is eager to make a sacrifice of the women (796) or to sever the stranger's head (724) but himself becomes a decapitated sacrificial victim. So also he intends to sacrifice (631 *sphazōn*) the stranger, which results in his own ritual death (858 *katasphageis*).[23] Most of these are instances of actual terms of cult employed for dramatic and ironic effect in the play. Pentheus' death, of course, is part of a pattern familiar from tales of resistance to Dionysus' cult, the result of which is almost always human death at the hands of or to the glorification of the god. It is uncertain, however, that the violence encountered in resistance to Dionysus reflects the violence of the sacrificial act itself. It may form part of the "dark background" to the sacrificial pattern but need not be seen (even in mythic form) as constituting the sacrificial event itself, even where exaggeration for dramatic purposes, as in the *Bacchae,* gives this illusion.[24]

Allusion to cannibalism is also prominent in the case of the rending of Dionysus Zagreus by the Titans. In this case it is not a human, but a god, albeit as an infant, a detail that has a humanizing effect (only as an infant is the god as helpless as a human). The two aspects (killing of a

[22] *kalon to thuma katabalousa daimosin / epi daita Thēbas tasde ka'me; parakaleis.* Cf. similar language at lines 224 (*mainadas thuoskoous*) and 473 (*thuousin*). The relevance of line 1247 for understanding the term *embalein* (*ōmophagion*) in the Milesian inscription (above, pp. 70–71) appears to have been overlooked. I suspect that the inscription *embalein* bears a technical sense known from cult for the offering of unburnt meat. Dodds cites Euripides *Orestes* 1603 (*sphagia pro doros katabalois*), Isocrates 2.20 (*tous hiereia polla kataballontas*), and Hesychius, s.v. "katabolē (*thusia*)"; see Roux 1972 in his comments on Euripides *Bacchae* 1247 ("désigne le coup frappé sur une victime de sacrifice"). Whether *embalein* (*ōmophagion*) in the Milesian inscription reflects the usage of cult or the language of Euripides' play is not clear. Henrichs 1978a, 122 (cf. also his remarks in Rudhardt and Reverdin 1981, 35–39), at any rate argues that *embalein* (*ōmophagion*) in the inscription represents a reflection of the *action* of the play, as acted out in the cult at Miletus; if so, I suggest that the phrase may be a verbal reflection of *to thuma katabalousa* from the play.

[23] See especially Seidensticker 1979, 181–90, and Foley 1985, 208–18.

[24] Sacrifice of a human that is merely threatened, but averted, usually with the substitution of a standard animal victim, is treated below under initiation.

god and cannibalism) combine to make this form of sacrifice not only unusual, nonstandard, and forbidden, but also officially unspeakable. In the Greek tradition there is long-standing resistance to the concept, familiar from other Mediterranean cultures, of a dying god.[25] Its (largely lost) mythography may have formed part of the mysteries,[26] which suggests that it figured in some way in initiation. Pentheus' death and prospective consumption is thus not unspeakable but clearly rejected in favor of a form of *thusia* practiced by the polis, which contains the violence of unrestrained kin killing; thus the reaction of the Asiatic maenads to the prospect of eating Pentheus' flesh (above, p. 70). The whole complex reminds me of nothing so much as the story about the cannibal and the cook: "I hate my mother-in-law," said the cannibal. To which the cook replied: "Well, at least eat your peas."

Here as well falls under consideration what little evidence we have for Dionysus in actual cult contexts, under such epithets as Anthroporrhaistes ("Man Destroyer"),[27] Omadios or Omestes ("Raw Eater," attested as early as Alcaeus), [28] Mainomenos ("Raging One"), and Agrionios ("Wild One"), as well as the evidence for devotees of Dionysus who were (accidently?) killed in the course of ritual procedures.[29] Such instances *may* preserve an original memory of human sacrifice in actual ritual; but the rites in connection with which they were remembered may equally well have been intended to celebrate Dionysus in his especially dangerous capacity as Lusios ("Loosener") or "Destroyer of the Household,"[30] or to mark the transition from a prehistorical period to a historical one, in which animal husbandry was

[25] Obbink and Harrison 1985, 75–81.

[26] So Seaford 1981, 266 with n. 125; Burkert 1983, 225–26.

[27] Aelian *De natura animalium* 12.34; cf. Porphyry *De abstinentia* 2.55 (who quotes Euelpis of Carystus); Burkert 1983, 165, 183; cf. 21 n. 35, 139 n. 13 (Tenedos). At Tenedos the newborn calf sacrificed to Dionysus Anthroporrhaistes had boots (often identified as cothurni) put on its feet "apparently in order to identify it as closely as possible with the god of tragedy" (Burkert 1983, 183). But the boots are more likely to be the Thracian hunting boots so often depicted in Dionysus' iconography. The sacrificial scene: Cook 1914, 659; Cook 1924, 654–73.

[28] Alcaeus frag. 129.9 (Voigt 1971); Graf 1985, 74–80. Dionysus Omestes: Henrichs 1978a, 144 n. 74, 150, and Henrichs 1981, 208–24; Burkert 1983, 173 n. 23, 183.

[29] Plutarch *Quaestiones Graecae* 38 = *Moralia* 299e–f: "Any one of them that the priest catches he may kill, and in my time the priest Zoilus killed one of them"; Burkert 1983, 175 ("Our one securely attested instance of human sacrifice"): "With the fanatacism of a zealot, Zoilus apparently failed to recognize the theatrical, playacting nature of the ritual and thus pursued it *ad absurdum*. In the Dionysian realm, as elsewhere, animal-sacrifice guarantees that the ritual functions sensibly."

[30] Seaford in this volume, passim.; Burkert 1983, 160 n. 118.

viewed as preserving contemporary order and stability and is thus commemorated by (ordinary) animal sacrifice. The case of the Bassaroi, who ultimately killed themselves off as a result of persisting in the aboriginal form of (human) sacrifice, may be compared in this respect. In Euripides' *Bacchae* the chorus describes Dionysus in the parodos (138–39) as a wild hunter who "hunts" (*agreuōn*) for "blood of the murdered goat" (*haima tragoktonon*), which is a "joy of the feast of raw flesh" (*ōmophagon kharin*). Susan Cole has suggested to me that this refers not to human sacrifice or the eating of the god (as is often alleged) or even to the consumption of raw sacrificial meat, but rather to the fact that Dionysus sometimes gets offerings of uncooked meat.[31] Euripides (*Cretans* frag. 472 [Nauck$^2$]) also mentions a meal of raw flesh (*ōmophagoi daites*) as a Cretan initiation rite in connection with "night-wandering Zagreus." Presumably the great hunter Zagreus shared his prey with his Cretan initiates after the hunt. Euripides may have equated Zagreus and Dionysus, another hunter (*Bacchae* 1192), which may have suggested the reference to omophagy.[32]

To return briefly to the case of the calf at Tenedos, which was sacrificed to Dionysus Anthroporrhaistes ("Man Destroyer") after being dressed in cothurni: in this case we would have an instance of the god identified with his sacrificial victim, though this is nowhere made explicit. At Tenedos the calf's mother is treated as a human mother after childbirth (whatever this was). On the whole, the connection with birth (or rebirth) and the substitution of an animal for a humanized victim is more closely reminiscent of the sacrificial pattern associated with initiation (on which see below).

Various other figures of myth (Icarius, Oeneus)[33] also fall as victims or martyrs to Dionysus. But rather than treating them as sacrificial victims in ritual, it is probably easier to see them as part of the dark background and violence resolved by the institution of ordinary ritual procedure.

## Dionysiac Sacrifice in Civic Cult

In the institutionalized cult of the Greek cities, sacrifices to Dionysus took place quite unexceptionally side by side with sacrifices to

[31] Cf. Henrichs 1978a, 148 and 151: "Neither did the Milesian maenads eat a victim raw; they merely sacrificed raw meat to Dionysus."

[32] Henrichs 1978a, 151 n. 96.

[33] Burkert 1983, 223 and 242 (Icarius), 222 and 245 (Oeneus).

other civic divinities and heroes. Certain stereotyped details of such sacrifices are recorded in the sacrificial calendars (*leges sacrae*) of the Greek cities, and as a result we have quite a large body of data concerning sacrifices to Dionysus.[34] According to Henrichs, the entries typically provide the following kinds of information: "the date and occasion of the ritual; the divine recipient; the place of sacrifice; a description of the kind of animal required; an indication of the type of ritual to be followed, sometimes with additional comments on the technical aspects of the ritual process; instructions concerning the distribution of the sacrificial meat, including the perquisites for the priests or other officials; and finally the price of the victim, that is, the expenditure budgeted for each sacrifice." The calendars do not tell us anything about sacramentalism; they do not mention omophagy, theophagy, or cannibalism, nor do they speak of role reversal, cross-dressing, ecstatic dancing, or the substitution of a human for an animal victim—in other words, the more sensational aspects of ritual associated dramatically and mythically with Dionysus. It is here more than anywhere that the rift between myth and ritual has been perceived most clearly. Institutionalized cult may be by nature "designed to circumvent the sinister element highlighted in myth."[35]

To be sure, the picture of sacrifice that emerges from the cult calendars is a tame and domestic one, which depicts domesticated animals in an elaborate process of selection for killing in infinitely particularized conditions and circumstances. (Though even here the calendars do not give us a full picture; they tell us, for instance, nothing about the domestic production of wine or its consumption.) From a study of the Attic instances alone several important details become clear. First, sacrifices to Dionysus tend to be grouped, as one might expect, around ritual periods in the calendar especially associated with him, such as the Country Dionysia, the Anthesteria (when the wine from the previous season was opened), and the City Dionysia. Second, in the demes, as opposed to the city center, where festivities in the city were supplemented by local offerings, there was probably a closer connection between Dionysus and local heroes, heroines, and figures from Dionysus' own mythography (Icarius, for

[34] Henrichs 1990, 260–64.

[35] So Henrichs 1990, 258; cf. Henrichs 1978a, 148: "Ritual tends to mitigate where myth is cruel."

example). The sacrificial calendar of the deme of Erchia from the fourth century B.C. records separate goat sacrifices on the same altar to Semele and Dionysus on the sixteenth of Elaphebolion (the time of the City Dionysia). Such rites, jointly for Dionysus and Semele, are enjoined already at Euripides' *Bacchae* 998–99 *orgia matros te sas / maneisa prapidi.*[36] In this instance, unspecified women receive the animals entire as a perquisite, probably to conduct their own celebrations in honor of Dionysus.

It is probably fair to say that there was more to Dionysiac sacrifice than can be gathered from the cult calendars. The inscriptions give us the *drōmena* (though not all of them, only certain stereotyped details), but they do not tell us the *legomena,* much less what was imagined or experienced; they do not recount the stories that were told on such occasions or record the dances, and naturally they do not recount any information about the mysteries or initiation (with the exception of the phratries). But in functional terms they are the closest evidence we have to the phenomenon of sacrificial ritual. The portrait of sacrifice they present is one not of sacramentalism but of sociability and domestication.

## Sacrifice and Initiation

Work on initiation ritual has become something of a cottage industry in recent years, and it is probably the most difficult ritual form to evaluate in connection with Dionysus.[37] According to many patterns of initiation the initiate undergoes a symbolic wounding or is otherwise threatened with death, dies, and is "reborn" to assume a new identity as an initiated individual. Such patterns quite naturally encourage the imaginative, if not actual, identification of the initiate with the god's sacrifical victim. The most obvious example is perhaps Strepsiades in Aristophanes' *Clouds.* By extension Pentheus in the *Bacchae* and the Cyclops in Euripides' *Cyclops* have been viewed as figurative initiates threatened with the ritual death of Dionysiac initiation. By a paranoic exaggeration of the pattern in drama both figures

[36] See Henrichs 1990, 264 with n. 31.

[37] For a survey of the methodological problem encountered in approaching myth in terms of initiation see Versnel 1990b, 44–59, with bibliography.

actually suffer death or mutilation at the hands of the god or his devotees.

Nothing of the sort appears to have taken place in the Eleusinian mysteries in connection with Dionysus; initiation into Dionysiac mysteries possibly did not take place in Attica, and anything like evidence for the mysteries of Dionysus at Thebes (on which rests much of the argument for Pentheus in the *Bacchae*)[38] is nonexistent.

On the other hand, instances of such procedures (substitution of an animal victim for a threatened initiate) are well known in Greek cult (e.g., Artemis at Brauron). So the theory remains attractive for the very reason that the motif of initiation may be independently preserved in Dionysus' mythography, namely, in the story of Dionysus' double birth (Zeus's thigh wounding and the second birth of Dionysus from Zeus's thigh reflect initiatory patterns). In the Orphic version, Dionysus, reduced to the childlike state typical of the threatened initiate, is threatened with sacrifice. In both cases the god both dies and does not die, as in initiation.

## Sacramental Wine Drinking

In many parts of the Greek world (including Attica) Dionysus was associated first and foremost with the production and consumption of wine. Wine poured in honor of the god was regarded as a type of sacrifice (*thusia*). Drinking of the new wine in the *khoes* at the Anthesteria fulfilled the function of a consecrated sacrificial meal. As a result, the ritual complex of blood sacrifice was transferred to the labors of the wine maker and the pleasures of the wine drinker.[39] Hand in hand with this process went the identification of Dionysus himself with wine, an identification attested as early as the fifth century B.C. Tiresias in the *Bacchae,* in his defense of Dionysus, points out to Pentheus that Dionysus is responsible for the gift of wine to humankind (as Demeter is for the gift of grain) and states that Dionysus is "himself poured out to the gods, and as a result men have good things."[40] (Odysseus' praise of Dionysus as wine at Euripides *Cyclops*

[38] Seaford 1981, 263–74.

[39] Burkert 1983, 224–25.

[40] Eur. *Bacch.* 284–85 *houtos theoisi spendetai theos gegōs, / hōste dia touton tagath' anthrōpous ekhein.*

519–26 and the perplexed Cyclops' questions about gods who choose to live in a bottle also treat Dionysus in this aspect.) Consequently, the drinker of wine would be drinking the god himself.

This was clearly not just a metaphor, but a way in which Dionysus was experienced, playfully theomorphized into the substance he invented and the sacrifice most often offered to him, in a form literally internalized and thus in turn *im*personated. It is only in this sense that we can speak about something like sacramentalism in connection with Dionysus. People consumed Dionysus himself; yet Dionysus was not actually sacrificed. I am suggesting that there was a "consumption" (rather than "sacramental") ritual, distinctive to Dionysus, in which the substance consumed was stylized in ritual as the blood of the god or hero, and yet the consumption did *not* imply that the god or hero was ritually sacrificed. As a result descriptions of the suffering, death, and transformation of the god became superimposed upon myths about the death of the inventor of wine (as in the story of Icarius). Behind the image lay the process of the preparation of the wine, the tearing apart of the "bloody" grape, and an infinitely particularized process of selection and gradation in the parceling out and ritual handling of the year's crop.

The range of Dionysus' influence in this sphere is illustrated by the role played by wine drinking in the Greek symposium, which also suggests an initiatory aspect in the lives of Greek men. In many Greek cities women were not allowed to drink wine. Young men too were not allowed to drink wine but were rather employed as wine pourers. That they had to pour the wine but were not yet allowed to drink it "stressed the difference of status between them and the adult men."[41] In aristocratic symposia the present of a drinking cup meant admission as a qualified member to the world of adult men.

## The Domestication of Dionysus

In connection with ritual wine drinking and its association with sacrifice, it is instructive to compare modern theories of sacrifice where Dionysus is concerned with their ancient counterparts. Though

[41] Bremmer 1980, 286, collects the ancient evidence relevant to the initiatory role of ritual wine drinking.

the views of ancient authorities do occasionally inform modern theories, they have received very little attention as theories. I do not want to suggest that ancient theories on the matter have necessarily any greater chance than modern theories of being right. They are often demonstrably wrong; paradoxically, their very proximity in time and cultural context to the phenomena in question puts them at a distinct heuristic disadvantage. But from an anthropological perspective it would be premature to rule them out of account, insofar as they do constitute a significant contribution as evidence of what ancient players themselves said about their rites and customs.

Like modern theories, ancient theories are very much concerned with origins and with communication. But in contrast to modern theories of Dionysiac sacrifice, which assume a close correlation between ritual and myth and therefore assume for ritual the same violent, guilt-ridden, sinister background found in myth, ancient theories are basically commemorative and mimetic and view Dionysiac ritual primarily as reenacting the *civilizing* and *domesticating* role of Dionysus in cultural history. That is to say, they view ritual basically as a reenactment or commemoration of (pre)historical manifestations of the god's presence and power.

This can be demonstrated and illustrated from a brief look at some representative ancient theories of Dionysiac ritual: those of the historian Diodorus Siculus, the Peripatetic philosopher Theophrastus, the Atthidographers Philochorus and Phanodemus, and finally the Sophist Prodicus. All mention Dionysus specifically and deal with known sacrificial rituals performed in his honor. Diodorus, for example, makes it clear that the female devotees of Dionysus did perform sacrifices but in doing so provided civilized substitutes for the savage sacrifices of maenadic myth (see above, p. 72).

In contrast to modern theories, ancient expositions of Dionysiac ritual overwhelmingly stress not the sacrifice of animals to Dionysus or the deaths of potential worshipers, but rather Dionysus' role in the domestic production and consumption of wine. In his account of the development of sacrifice from earliest times, Aristotle's successor, Theophrastus, theorized that early peoples had at first sacrificed simple vegetable substances recognized as essential to life. Only much later in human history was the killing of animals introduced (and even this was something of an accident, a substitution for cannibalism *in extremis*). In the case of libated sacrifices, water was originally poured as an offering along with simple vegetable substances.[42] The pouring of wine in libation entered human history only in the intervening agricultural stage. Both wine and water were poured as offerings to the gods long before the inception of the practice of sacrificing animals.[43] For Dionysus wine was the aboriginal sacrifice. Theophrastus posited a later, fortuitous event for the first killing of a goat in honor of Dionysus. Theophrastus regarded this step as something of a misfortune or accident, resulting in a devolution in cultural history. The first murder of a goat had nothing to do with Dionysus.

The accounts of early Attic history by the historians Philochorus and Phanodemus similarly stress Dionysus' role in the development of Attic cult by recounting Dionysus' invention of wine, and attribute the practice of drinking wine to ritual commemorations of Dionysus' aboriginal introduction of viticulture and wine making. Phanodemus relates the origin of the *khoes* at the Anthesteria as a reenactment of the mixing and drinking of the first wine:

> At the temple of Dionysus in the Marshes the Athenians mix the must (*to gleukos*) that they bring from their casks in honor of the god, and then drink it themselves; hence Dionysus was called god of the marsh, because the must was mixed and drunk with water on that occasion for the first time.[44]

This was dated to a precise point in cultural history, and Dionysus' visit to Attica was made by Philochorus to coincide with the reign of a historical king, Amphictyon:

> (*a*) Philochorus in the second book of his *Attic History* says: "In those days the custom was established that after the food only so much

[42] On libations of water as distinct from those of wine, see below on the Atthidographers' theories of how water came to be customarily mixed with wine, and further on Prodicus' theories of the divinization of water among early humankind. For ritual distinctions between different liquids poured in libations see Graf 1980 with further bibliography; Henrichs 1983, 88–89 with n. 6; and Cole 1988. On Theophrastus' theory of libations in cultural development and its borrowing by Jane Harrison and the Cambridge school, see Obbink 1988, 277 with n. 10.

[43] Obbink 1988, 272–95.

[44] Phanodemus, *FGrH* 325 F 12 (= Athenaeus 11.465).

> unmixed wine should be taken by all as should be a taste and sample of the good god's power (*tēs dunameōs*), but after that all other wine must be drunk mixed. Hence the nymphs were called nurses of Dionysus."
> (*b*) Philochorus has this: "Amphictyon, king of Athens, learned from Dionysus the art of mixing wine and was the first to mix it. So it was that men came to stand upright, drinking wine mixed, whereas before they were bent double by the use of unmixed wine. Hence he founded an altar of the "upright" Dionysus in the shrine of the Seasons; for these make ripe the fruit of the vine. Near it he also built an altar to the nymphs to remind devotees of the mixing;[45] for the nymphs are said to be the nurses of Dionysus. He also instituted the custom of taking just a sip of unmixed wine after meat, as a proof of the power of the good god, but after that they might drink mixed wine, as much as each one chose. They were also to repeat over this cup the name of Zeus the Savior as a warning and reminder to drinkers that only when they drink in this fashion would they surely be safe."[46]

According to Philochorus the practice of sampling a small amount of unmixed wine and then freely drinking wine mixed with water was a reenactment of the original benefit conferred on the Athenians, not only in the original gift of wine, but in the civilized custom of drinking it mixed with water. In the background of the account lies the story of Icarius, who was killed in reaction to the effects of the original consumption of the god himself (or his *dunamis*). Dionysus thus provided the antidote, in the form of mixed wine, to this potentially disastrous outbreak of violence. Ritual violence, to be sure, lies in the background but even in the story is superseded by the generally benign effect of Dionysus in the Atthidographer's account.[47] Dionysus is thus made to account for the spontaneous outbreak of violence, while the

[45] This explanation of the "upright" Dionysus (as connected with wine drinking and the necessity of drinking mixed wine in order to stay "upright") competes with other ancient understandings of the epithet with reference to the role of the phallus in Dionysiac cult. The two explanations are hardly mutually exclusive. On Dionysus Orthos see Jacoby's comments on *FGrH* 328 F 5, and Burkert 1983, 217 and 224.

[46] Philochorus, *FGrH* 328 F 5a (= Athenaeus 15.693d–e) and 5b (= Athenaeus 2.38c–d).

[47] Cf. Philochorus, *FGrH* 328 F 173 (= Athenaeus 14. 656a): "The Athenians, according to Philochorus, do not roast the meat when they sacrifice to the Seasons [presumably in the sanctuary of Dionysus in the Marshes], but boil it, entreating the goddesses to defend them from excessive heat and drought and to bring to ripeness growing things by moderate warmth and seasonable rains. For, he declares, roasting affords less benefit, whereas boiling not only takes away the rawness, but can soften tough points and ripen the rest."

containment of that violence is located securely in ritual conducted in his honor.

Dionysus also figured in an important way in Prodicus' theory, notorious in antiquity, of the development of belief in the gods—a theory closely related to Tiresias' identification of the god Dionysus with the substance wine in the Euripides' *Bacchae*. According to Prodicus the belief in the gods had arisen out of the deification first of the substances that contributed to life; at a later stage, Prodicus explained, individuals, such as Demeter and Dionysus, who came to be regarded as responsible for the original introduction or invention of such substances, were worshiped:

> Prodicus of Ceos says: "Primitive mankind regarded as gods the sun and moon and rivers and springs and in general all the things that are of benefit for our life, because of the benefit derived from them, just as the Egyptians do the Nile." And he says that it was for this reason that bread was accorded divine stature as Demeter, and wine as Dionysus, and water as Poseidon, and fire as Hephaestus, and so on with each of the things that are good for use.[48]

Here Dionysus appears in a prominent connection with wine and viticulture, second only in the list to Demeter, who is linked with grain and agriculture. The two divinities appear in the same order and are identified with the same substances by Tiresias at Euripides' *Bacchae* 274–85:

> There are two powers that are supreme in human affairs: first, the goddess Demeter; she is the Earth—call her by what name you will; and she supplies humankind with solid food. Second, Dionysus, the son of Semele; the blessing he provides is the counterpart to the blessing of bread; he discovered and bestowed on humankind the service of drink, the juice that streams from the vine clusters; humans have but to take their fill of wine, and the sufferings of an unhappy race are banished, each day's troubles are forgotten in sleep—indeed this is our only cure for the weariness of life. Dionysus, himself a god, is poured out in offering to the gods; so that through him humankind receives benefits.

Tiresias' description of Dionysus as a benefactor who originally introduced wine and viticulture to humankind alludes to the story found in

[48] Prodicus, *FVS* 84 B 5 (= Sextus Empiricus *Adversus mathematicos* 9.18).

the Atthidographers and treated above. But his (very different) claim that in each and every act of libation Dionysus was himself poured out as a offering to the gods reflects both linguistic usage (according to which wine was commonly referred to as "Dionysus"[49] and an equation of the divinity with his sacrifical substance.[50] In an intriguing parallel, Prodicus had theorized that Dionysus *had originally been wine;* only later was this divine stature accorded to the (originally human) benefactor believed to have been responsible for the introduction of wine and viticulture. Recently our testimony for the first stage of Prodicus' theory was significantly augmented by a papyrus from Herculaneum.

> ὑ]πὸ [τ]ῶν
> ἀνθρώπων νομιζο-
> μένους θεοὺς οὔτ' εἶ-
> ναί φησιν οὔτ' εἰδέ-
> ναι, τοὺς δὲ καρποὺς
> καὶ πάνθ' ὅλως τὰ χρή-
> σιμα πρ[ὸς τ]ὸν βίον
> τοὺς ἀρ[χαίο]υς ἀγα-[51]

> [Prodicus] says that the gods believed in by people do not exist nor do they have knowledge,[52] but that primitive humans, [out of admiration, deified] the fruits of the earth and virtually everything that contributed to their subsistence . . .

Here *karpous,* the substances in Prodicus' view originally regarded as divine, suggests above all the grain or bread associated with Demeter and the grapes or wine known as "Dionysus." These are said to have

[49] For the equation wine = Dionysus see Burkert 1983, 224–25.

[50] It is not entirely clear to me whether the equation of Dionysus with wine in cult is an explanation of linguistic usage (ritual etymology) or whether linguistic usage here mirrors ritual practice and belief. The matter clearly requires further study. It is significant that Tiresias at *Bacchae* 286–97 instructs Pentheus in the proper interpretation of Dionysus' *name* and related words (*ho mēros = to meros = ho homeros*) as revealing the true origin of the myth about his birth from Zeus's thigh and the original form of his name (accepting Dalmeyda's correction *dialusin* for *Dionuson* in 294 with no lacuna, as defended by Willink 1966, 40–44; cf. Versnel 1990a, 166 with n. 261).

[51] Philodemus *De pietate* (*PHerc* 1428 frag. 19). See Henrichs 1975, 93–123, for discussion.

[52] For this meaning of *eidenai* (lines 15–16) see Henrichs 1976, 15–21.

been divinized because they were "useful things" (*ta khrēsima*), directly parallel to the "good things" (*ta agatha*) that the pouring out of Dionysus provides to humans at *Bacchae* 285. Dodds suspected that Tiresias' statement that Dionysus is "himself poured out to the gods, and as a result mortals have good things" (*Bacchae* 284–85) owed much to Prodicus' theory.[53] But the more significant point is that Prodicus (and possibly Euripides as well) will have found the basis of his theory, the identification of individual divinities with the essential goods of life, reflected or imbedded and already celebrated in cult.[54] (This is presumably part of Tiresias' point.) As a result, what Prodicus chose to emphasize about Dionysus was not his connection with violence and irrational killing, but rather his benign, beneficial influence on the development of human civilization in the introduction of ritual wine drinking and libation. Dionysus was originally accorded divine stature because, according to Prodicus, he was poured out and consumed.

I am not of course suggesting that we should hastily credit the explanations provided by the ancient theories; there is even some doubt as to their exact heuristic status as theories.[55] They are cultural glosses and as such should be accorded no more or less privilege than those of Nietzsche or René Girard. But they have the decided advantage of being things that contemporaries and participants in the cults themselves actually said about the divinities in question. They form a part of the pattern. In this respect they depict an important dimension of Dionysus and his cult, perhaps prominent in, though not confined to, Attica, focusing on the god's benefactions during life. Dionysus is poured out, expended in ritual, yet returns, and is present to be poured again in each new year's vintage. In Dionysus' sanctuaries, fountains flow with wine, vines bloom and produce overnight. In this very domesticated view Dionysus represents the perpetually full cup, from which, when mixed with water in a civilized fashion, humans can

[53] Dodds 1960, ad loc.

[54] For "Dionysus" consumed as wine in cult see Dodds 1960, xiii; Dodds 1960 on Eur. *Bacch.* 284–85; Kirchner 1910, 87–90; Frazer 1912, 167; Eisler 1925, 198–217; Henrichs 1972, 74–77. A good example is Achilles Tatius 2.2.1–3.3, on which see Smith 1974.

[55] James Redfield in particular expressed grave doubts on this score, especially with regard to their scope of explanation. In traditional cultures myth often functions as a kind of theory. In discussion Walter Burkert noted that the explanations of Prodicus et al. were as much "theories" as his own.

drink as much as they like. The only social conflict here is over the question, Does Dionysus taste great, or is he less filling?

More important, the ancient theories depict Dionysiac ritual as positive, as an expression of order and solidarity and health in a world of sometimes uncontrollable conflict with humans and with nature. It is a picture that contrasts vividly with the representation of Dionysiac ritual in tragedy and in much of Dionysus' iconography, in which ritual tends toward an inversion of its expression of order and prosperity and is instead an instrument of uncontrollable violence and disaster. In the end we should not, I think, exclude these savage and perversely sacramental depictions from the cultic dimension of Dionysus, from the experience of the god himself. As another member of the Cambridge school, Gilbert Murray, observed (also reflecting on the image of Dionysus poured out), the tragedies reflect Dionysiac ritual as "outer shapes dominated by tough and undying tradition, an inner life fiery with sincerity and spiritual freedom; the vessels of very ancient religion overfilled and broken by the new wine of reasoning, and still shedding abroad the old aroma, as of eternal and mysterious things."[56]

[56] Murray 1912, 363.

# TRAGEDY

CHAPTER 4

# Mixtures of Masks: Maenads as Tragic Models

Renate Schlesier

## Tragedy and Dionysus Today

In the early 1980s, an eminent expert in the stagecraft of Greek tragedy argued in a review: "Despite Nietzsche, it should not be taken for granted that there is anything intrinsically or essentially Dionysian about Greek tragedy."[1] In the meantime, although as a rule the Nietzschean term "the Dionysian" has been carefully avoided,[2] an increasing number of adventurous scholars have detected a prolific range of Dionysiac features not only in Euripides' *Bacchae* but throughout the corpus of Attic tragedy.

This trend can be briefly summarized as follows: most of these scholars are not as fascinated by speculations about the origins of Greek tragedy as were their forerunners, especially the Cambridge Ritualists Jane Harrison, Gilbert Murray, and Francis Cornford.[3] They start rather soberly from the historical phenomenon that the ancient Greeks themselves thought of Dionysus as the theater god—patron of comedy, tragedy, and satyr play—and as "the god of the mask"[4] even

[1] Taplin 1983 on Segal 1982; see also Taplin 1978, 162.

[2] An exception is, for instance, Carpenter 1986, a book that has, ironically enough, otherwise nothing to do with Nietzsche's Dionysus. See Schlesier 1987a.

[3] See Harrison 1903 and 1912; Murray 1912; Cornford 1961; see, especially on Harrison, Schlesier 1990a and 1991.

[4] See Wrede 1928; Otto 1933, 80–85; Burkert 1972, 260–62; Vernant and Frontisi-Ducroux 1986; Vernant 1985a; and Frontisi-Ducroux 1991.

outside the civic theatrical sphere, in visual art and in maenadic cultic experience. Yet many modern critics, not unlike Harrison "and her partners,"[5] and to some extent in their footsteps, rely heavily upon anthropological and sociological analyses of the striking status of Dionysus that place the god and his cults between city and country, culture and nature, inner and outer spheres, order and revelry, and fixed norms and their subversion, transgression, or inversion.[6] Corresponding to these insights, several Dionysiac patterns have been discovered in the plots and the characters of the tragic plays, especially reversals of clear-cut polarities, like the fixed differences between participant and spectator, divine and mortal, female and male, human and beast, hunter and hunted, sacrificer and victim, and so on, polarities that in Greek mythology and ritual are much more frequently and spectacularly blurred by Dionysus and his circle than by any other divinity.

Methodologically and systematically, then, Euripides' *Bacchae* and its evident or assumed cultic references are taken as something like a retrospective "model" of previous tragedies whose mythological themes are not concerned with Dionysus at all. Several authors have nevertheless recently tried to demonstrate from different points of view that a character like Aeschylus' Clytemnestra,[7] for instance, or entire plays such as Sophocles' *Antigone*[8] as well as Euripides' *Hecuba*[9] and *Ion* stand "under Dionysos' auspices."[10]

Whether or not these investigations are valid in every detail, it seems clear that a reversal of an old-fashioned *communis opinio* has begun in the study of Greek tragedy, and it should not be surprising that this reversal is announced under the sign of Dionysus himself, as the god of expected and unexpected reversals. For a long time, the traditional approach was summed up in the saying, transmitted from

[5] Ridgeway 1915, 47.

[6] See especially Dodds 1960, xi–xx; Jeanmaire 1951; Gernet 1953; Guépin 1968; Segal 1978a, 1978b, 1982; Seaford 1981; Zeitlin 1982; Henrichs 1982, 1990; Vernant 1985a; Hoffman 1989; Goldhill 1990.

[7] Seaford 1989a.

[8] Bierl 1989.

[9] *Hecuba:* Schlesier 1988b; Zeitlin 1991. On the Dionysiac features in Euripides' *Hippolytus* and *Heracles,* see Schlesier 1985, as well as 1988a, which also discusses Euripides' *Suppliant Women, Trojan Women,* and *Electra.*

[10] Zeitlin 1989, 164.

antiquity, that the tragedies had "nothing to do with Dionysus."[11] The title of a recent book has transformed this sentence into a rhetorical question.[12] Independently, the title of a recent article refers to a similar ancient formulation and transmutes it into an issue to be taken seriously: "What has tragedy to do with Dionysus?"[13] Although these inquiries are certainly not convincing in every respect and for everybody, their promising results encourage the supposition that ancient tragedies do indeed have a lot to do with Dionysus.

The impression of a strong "Dionysiac" trend in the present-day fin-de-siècle studies of Greek tragedy is reinforced when one considers a further goal emerging there, up to now less systematically pursued: the main tenets of Aristotle's theory of tragedy are being reconsidered in order to match them with the nature of Dionysus and his cult, an approach as much inspired by prior anthropological and psychological researches as are the "Dionysiac" readings of the tragic plots themselves. Mimesis and catharsis,[14] for instance, are deciphered as Dionysiac features as well as anagnorisis and peripeteia.[15] There is certainly room for further suggestions. Of course the absence of an explicit reference to Dionysus in Aristotle's *Poetics* itself does not a priori invalidate this kind of analysis.

[11] Already referred to by Chamaeleon, *TrGF* 1, 1 Thespis T 18; see also Plutarch *Quaestiones convivales* 1.1.5 (= *Moralia* 615a).

[12] Winkler and Zeitlin 1990. Unfortunately, the articles compiled there have, on the whole, less to do with Dionysus in tragedy than one would expect.

[13] Bierl 1989; see also Bierl 1991.

[14] The pioneers include Müller 1833, 191, on Dionysiac catharsis (see also below, n. 15); Rohde 1898b, 44, on the Dionysiac quality of the art of the actor, and 50–51, on Dionysiac purification; Thomson 1973, 358–59, on catharsis as a "common function" of "the orgy of the Dionysiac *thiasos,* initiation into the mysteries, and tragedy"; and Jeanmaire 1951, 316–21, on mimesis and catharsis. Cf. now Zeitlin 1989, 156, on Dionysiac mimesis and "the mysteries of identity" in Euripides' *Ion,* and more generally 1990a, 84–96.

[15] Müller 1833, 191, had already emphasized that the pattern of reversal was basic to the Dionysiac cult and to tragedy as an originally Dionysiac genre. A similar attempt in this direction was made by Murray 1912, 342–44, although without mentioning Müller. On Müller's far-reaching influence on Nietzsche, Rohde, and the Cambridge Ritualists, for instance, see Schlesier 1991, 191–93, esp. nn. 26 and 32. Cf. now on Dionysiac *anagnorisis,* Seaford 1981, 271, with reference to Thomson 1973; see also Goldhill 1988, esp. 151, 155; dramatic peripeteia as the central feature of the (Eleusinian) mysteries was also stressed by Dieterich 1908, 183, as Murray himself acknowledged. On the peripeties of Euripides' *Ion* that evoke mystic experience, cf. now Zeitlin 1989, 161. On *mania* in tragedy as a reversal that is paradigmatic for Dionysiac metabole, see Schlesier 1985, esp. 41–45; cf. also Schlesier 1988a and 1988b.

Let us leave now this brief and indeed oversimplified survey. Arguments against this trend in Dionysiac criticism are easy to find. In addition to the complaints mentioned at the beginning of this essay, more general objections have been accumulating for decades against the ritualistic approach of the Cambridge school.[16] One of the main arguments objects to the obvious reductive aspect of a one-sided Dionysiac interpretation, because it tends to neglect the polytheistic nature of Greek religion, and the nonreligious features of Greek tragedy, too. In my view, these (and other) objections are to some extent reasonable, but I nonetheless think that the "Dionysiac" tendency in interpreting Greek tragedy is legitimate and fruitful. My limited aim in this essay, then, is to consider paradigmatically one figure widespread in tragedy, the maenad, as tragic model, in order to confirm the importance of Dionysiac features for the understanding of Greek tragedy. The tragic paradigm of the maenad depends on the particular relationship between madness and the mask in tragedy.

## Madness, Masks, and Truth in Tragedy

Until Nietzsche's *Birth of Tragedy* and to a large extent until today, interpreters of the plays of the three Attic tragedians were quite reluctant to take Dionysus into account.[17] As far as tragedy (as a genre) is concerned, the impact of Aristotle is still heavily felt.[18] Perhaps in the

[16] Fundamental arguments against the ritualistic interpretation of tragedy proffered by the Cambridge school: Pickard-Cambridge 1927, 185–206; his criticism of Murray 1912 was partly revoked by Webster, the editor of the second edition; see Pickard-Cambridge 1962, 128–29. On the controversy, its antecedents, and its aftermath, see Payne 1978; Henrichs 1984b; Versnel 1990b. A highly influential, non-Dionysiac ritualistic interpretation of Greek tragedy was developed by Burkert 1966; see Burkert, pp. 113–14 n. 61, against the concept of "eniautos daimon," basic for the Cambridge Ritualists.

[17] Nietzsche 1872, chap. 10 (= 1972, 67), suggested that all tragic heroes are nothing but "masks of Dionysus" and conceived the god as the "original hero" of the earliest tragedies; but see already Müller 1825, 395. Since Wilamowitz 1872 and 1873, this assumption has been violently rejected by most scholars. Dionysiac interpretations of the works of the three Attic tragedians were—without mentioning Nietzsche or Müller—first offered by Murray 1912 and renewed by Guépin 1968, who, however, does not agree with Harrison's and Murray's "eniautos daimon" concept but accepts the connection to the Eleusinian mysteries. For more recent and modified Dionysiac interpretations of Greek tragedy, see above, n. 15.

[18] Cf. Taplin 1977, 25, who complains that in the footsteps of Aristotle readers of tragedy easily "lose sight of its visual meaning." For Aristotle's lack of interest either in staging or in

*Poetics* he does conceptualize some Dionysiac features, but as a matter of fact Dionysus himself is mentioned there neither as a concept nor as a god.[19] It seems to me significant, then, that Aristotle does not at all relate to tragedy one particular Dionysiac feature that is quite prominent in tragedy, namely, Bacchic madness.[20]

Since the earliest beginnings of Greek literature Dionysus has, however, been defined by madness. Homer refers to him as *mainomenos,*[21] and the subsequent tradition connects Bakkhos, Bakkheios, and related epithets of the god with Dionysiac *mania.*[22] Correspondingly, *bakkhai* is one of the main cultic terms for his ecstatic female followers, the maenads.[23] The three Attic tragedians associate Bacchic madness

---

masks, see also Jones 1962, 43–46. For a comprehensive outline of Aristotle's theory of tragedy and the scholarly debate on it, see Flashar 1984; Halliwell 1986, esp. 168–201.

[19] Dionysus figures only in an example regarding Aristotle's theory of metaphor (*Poetics* 21, 1457b20–22); see Schlesier 1986–87, 75. See also Most 1987, 21–22. For an ancient conceptual interpretation of Dionysus, see Plutarch *De E apud Delphos* 9 (= *Moralia* 388e–389c), claiming that Apollo and, above all, Dionysus, were perceived by some "theologians" as gods of transformation (metabole), and describing *mania* as a form of metabole specifically connected with Dionysus. On metabole as a tragic feature par excellence, see Aristotle *Poetics* 7, 1451a14, among other passages. But note that among Aristotle's examples of tragic metabole there is mention neither of *mania* in general nor of Bacchic madness in particular.

[20] Recent investigators of Dionysiac features in tragedy (apart from Euripides' *Bacchae*) have generally failed to take Bacchic madness into account; but see Schlesier 1985, 1988a, and 1988b; now Seaford, in this volume.

[21] Homer *Iliad* 6.132. Henrichs 1978a, 143, considers this passage the first in ancient literature to reflect "maenadism as practiced."

[22] The earliest unequivocal evidence is Herodotus (4. 79), who presents Dionysus Bakkheios as a god who induces *mania* in men and presides over mysteries. Cf. Jeanmaire 1951, 88–90. On the problems of the etymology and the use of *bakkhos* and related terms, see Chantraine 1968, 159; Burkert 1985, 163, with 412 nn. 12 and 14; West 1978, 374–75. Xenophanes (*FVS* 21 B17) uses *bakkhoi* to mean "branches" (of pine wood). West's suggestion that the term *bakkhos* therefore refers to the branches carried by Dionysus and his followers does not preclude its association with madness; cf. Cole 1980, 229: "Those who carry the branch are named for the branch itself, and the ritual activity, where the madness of the god manifests itself in the dancing and inspired behavior of the worshippers, is described by the verb *bakkheuein.*" See also Burkert 1987a, 112: " 'Madness' is a distinctive feature of *bakkheia* in its full sense." Note that Plato *Phaedrus* 265b presents the *mania* of Dionysus as specifically associated with mysteries. See furthermore Casadio 1982 and 1983.

[23] Cole 1990 emphasizes that the generic ritual term for an ecstatic female worshiper of Dionysus was *bakkhē* (and many synonymous terms, like *lēnē,* etc.), while *mainas* was a literary epithet that was not used as a cult title in the inscriptions before the third century B.C.; cf. Henrichs 1982, 146, 223 nn. 89–93. Dodds 1951, 270–82, insists that the Bacchants were not mere revelers; see also his illuminating definition of the corresponding verb: "*bakkheuein* is not to have a good time, but to share in a particular religious rite and (or) have

with the plots and the tragic characters of the majority of their extant plays.[24]

Bacchic madness in tragedy is a puzzling thing, however. Most of the time it is not presented as the madness of actual Dionysiac maenads but of figures who are compared or identified with *bakkhai* or *mainades,* and sometimes with *bakkhoi*.[25] On the one hand, then, tragic figures are very clearly defined, at least by their masks, as representing one specific character and nothing else, in any case not a Dionysiac character at all. On the other hand, it sometimes happens that such a character is temporarily mixed up with another kind of character, precisely, a figure that is, terminologically at least, connected with Dionysiac myth and cult.[26] One particular figure is therefore doubled,

---

a particular religious experience—the experience of communion with a god which transformed a human being into a *bakkhos* or a *bakkhē*" (278 n. 1).

[24] *Bakkhos* and related terms, especially *bakkheuein*—"to be maddened by Dionysus," or, more generally, "to rave madly"—occur in Aeschylus *Seven against Thebes* (498; cf. 836 *thuias*), *Libation Bearers* (698), and *Eumenides* (25); cf. also *Suppliant Women* (564 *thuias*); in Sophocles *Trachinian Women* (219 et al.), *Antigone* (136 et al.), *Oedipus the King* (211, 1105), and *Oedipus at Colonus* (678); and in twelve Euripidean tragedies: *Hippolytus* (550 et al.), *Hecuba* (121 et al.), *Suppliant Women* (1001), *Heracles* (897 et al.), *Trojan Women* (169 et al.), *Iphigenia at Tauris* (1243), *Ion* (218 et al.), *Helen* (543, 1364), *Phoenician Women* (21 et al.), *Bacchae* (40 et al.), *Iphigenia at Aulis* (1061), and *Orestes* (338 et al.); cf. also *Electra* (1032 *mainas*).

[25] Tragic characters (including the chorus) as Dionysiac Bacchants or participants in a specific (mystical?) Dionysiac celebration (*bakkheia*): Aesch. *Lib. Bearers* (*bakkheia:* Clytemnestra); Soph. *Trach. Wom.* (*bakkheia:* the chorus); Eur. *Ion* (550–53, feast of Dionysus Bakkhios, with maenads: Xouthos), *Phoen. Wom.* (21 *bakkheia* [*bakkheion* codd.]: Iocaste, with Laios; 1752: Antigone as one of the *mainades*), *Bacch.* (the chorus; Agave). Tragic characters (including the chorus) compared or identified with maenads or *bakkhoi* outside an explicitly Dionysiac context are found in Aesch. *Seven* (836 *thuias*), *Eum.* (500 *mainades:* the chorus); Eur. *Hipp.* (954: Hippolytus), *Hec.* (Hecuba; the chorus), *Supp. Wom.* (Evadne), *Heracles* (Lyssa; Heracles), *Tro. Wom.* (Cassandra), *Helen* (543: Helen), *Phoen. Wom.* (1489: Antigone), *Or.* (Orestes). For figures who are not characters within the play but who are compared or identified there with maenads or *bakkhoi,* see Aesch. *Seven* (498: Hippomedon), *Supp. Wom.* (564: Io); Soph. *Ant.* (136: an anonymous warrior, probably Capaneus); Eur. *Hipp.* (Iole), *Hec.* (Cassandra), *El.* (1032: Cassandra), *Or.* (the Erinyes); cf. the dying pigeon in *Ion* 1204. Apart from the actual identification of tragic characters or other mythological figures with maenads or *bakkhoi,* Dionysiac myth or cult (including Bacchic madness) is referred to by the chorus, and sometimes by characters, in several narrative or hymnic passages, in Aesch. *Eum.* (24–26: the Pythia on Pentheus); Soph. *Ant.* (parodos; fourth and fifth stasima), *Oed. King* (parodos; third stasimon), *Oed. Col.* (first stasimon); Eur. *Hipp.* (339: Phaedra on Ariadne; 454: the nurse on Semele; first stasimon), *Her.* (second stasimon), *El.* (497: the *paidagōgos,* bringing wine), *Iphig. Tauris* (third stasimon), *Ion* (parodos), *Helen* (second stasimon), *Phoen. Wom.* (parodos; first stasimon), *Bacch.* (passim), and *Iphig. Aulis* (third stasimon).

[26] The main examples (in extant Greek tragedy) are Euripidean; see n. 25.

one might say, by means of another mask,[27] this time referring to a specific Dionysiac feature, Bacchic madness. But that does not mean that one of these "masks" or roles is less true or less significant than the other. Neither "mask" is a fraud. No truth lies behind them. All the truth lies upon the masks and nowhere else. But like the mask, the truth is a double one; it blurs the principle of identity.[28]

Such a concept of truth and of the simultaneous truthfulness of different meanings and modes of reality is, I think, a specific feature of ancient Greek tragedy that has much to do with Dionysus. Nothing could be more strikingly antagonistic to the goals of ancient philosophy, above all to the goals of Plato's thinking. Hence modern philosophy and criticism in the footsteps of Plato and his pupils are still haunted by dualistic presuppositions of truth and falsehood. One thing seems to be either true or false, and a third possibility is excluded. The mask, therefore, becomes a metaphor for mere appearance, deceit, illusion.[29]

[27] One could also say "by means of another role," as Helene Foley pointed out to me. To avoid misunderstanding, I am talking about a particular way in which the tragedians stimulate the imagination of the audience. I am of course not suggesting that a second mask is actually put over the first one, but that such a second mask is created verbally and thus, I claim, appears before the eyes of the spectators. My hypothesis is that the "visual meaning" of Greek drama sometimes implies the transformation of words heard into a vision. I am arguing that a figure described as *bakkheuōn,* for instance, is seen as performing a Bacchic role and is therefore temporarily seen with a Bacchic mask, a phenomenon that modern psychologists would call a hallucination. But on the semantical closeness of mask and face, aspect, person, stage figure (*prosōpon*) in ancient Greek, see Jones 1962, 44–45; Foley 1980, 128; and especially now Frontisi-Ducroux 1991, 226–28 with n. 59. On the "magical validity of words" in Aeschylus with respect to vision, but not to mask, see also Walsh 1984, 63ff.; I am not convinced by Walsh's conventional claim (p. 132) that there is an unequivocal trend to disenchantment in Euripides that fundamentally changes the former aim of tragedy.

[28] Cf. Nietzsche 1872, chap. 8 (= 1972, 57–60), who considers "enchantment" the "precondition of all dramatic art" and describes "Dionysiac excitement" as the state of mind of the ancient audience that enables it to see not a mere masked man but a figure out of a vision ("Visionsgestalt"). On the quality of twofoldness operative in the mask and on its Dionysiac implications, cf. Otto 1933, 189–90; Kerényi 1966, 342–43: the mask as implement of a "unifying transformation" and "transforming unification"; Vernant 1985c, 325–38; 1979, 105–37; 1986a. Napier 1986 should be used with caution.

[29] I do not agree with Jones's assumption (1962, 270), followed by Foley (1980, 128–33), that Euripides went beyond the ancient masking convention. I am arguing that in Aeschylus and Sophocles "mask-exploiting" effects are to be found no less than in Euripides. I am inclined to think that the "mask-piercing effect" is a typical feature rather of comedy than of tragedy, including Euripides' *Bacchae;* cf. Calame 1989. Foley 1980, 129, says that "by convention a tragic mask represents one character and one meaning." I do not think that a tragic character is defined by one single meaning, in any of the three tragedians.

Tragedy, then, I think, presents both the concept of truth and the mask in a different way. There is not one single truth but two (or even more) truths that are simultaneously operative and equally valid.[30] This double truth is actually represented by two very different kinds of "masks," and by two different modes of looking at them. One kind of mask, the one that is only verbally applied, is indeed not a mask that can actually be touched or that can be grasped by an ordinary kind of looking. It is evoked by means of words, which are able to engender a sight or vision that emerges as a nonmaterial image before the eyes of the spectators. Nevertheless one should not understand this additional imagined "mask" as a projection of the alleged inner self of the character[31] or as a casual private pleasure of the most imaginative among the contemporary audience and in later scholarship. The described evocation of complementary "imaginary" masks is, I believe, a procedure consciously inflicted by the tragedians upon the spectators in order to lead them to a distinctive, and to some extent religious, experience. This experience is no less real and specifically theatrical than the experience of looking at the actual material masks that are present on the stage or of imagining those masks that are temporarily absent from the stage. But in addition to these common modes of watching and imagining practiced by both ancient and modern audiences, this experience had to do, in the ancient Greek theater at least, with mystery cult and with *ekstasis*.[32] The so-called Bacchic metaphor is not a meta-

[30] I am skeptical about the assumption that the term "ambiguity" suffices to specify this quality of tragedy, as Oudemans and Lardinois 1987 suggest, albeit I do feel rather sympathetic to their attempt to establish a sharp distinction between "tragic" and philosophical modes of thought. Stanford 1939, 61–68, tries to distinguish clearly between ambiguity and irony, and he objects on p. 66 to the scholarly habit of designating "all kinds of ambiguous and suggestive phrases in drama" as tragic irony. Vellacott 1975 was not at all aware of these problems, whereas Foley 1985, acknowledging the impact of religious practice even upon Euripidean tragedy, nevertheless keeps the notion of irony.

[31] In my view, when one speaks about a dramatic inner self one tends to use modern psychology to explain tragic characters and runs the risk of anachronistic misunderstandings. I do not consider Hippolytus' famous line "My tongue swore, but my mind remains unsworn" (Eur. *Hipp.* 612) a violation of the dramatic convention. Tragic characters constantly express and represent tensions and contradictions between states of mind and behavior. It seems to me decisive for tragedy, then, that all of these tensions and contradictions are operative and that the existence or the truthfulness of any side of the contradictions is never denied, as it can be in a modern psychology of self.

[32] On the vacillation, in Greek tragedy, "between the imagined scene and the actual mechanism visibly used to present it," see Dale 1969, 121 and 119–29 passim. On visions and

phor in the Aristotelian (or more recent) sense of the word,[33] but the creation of an imaginary mask that has religious reality. It doubles the actual character, who not only behaves like a maenad or like Dionysus but who appears before the eyes of the spectators as actually transformed into a Bacchic figure, at least for a while. If that is true, one should not be surprised that modern readers or spectators of tragedy, who live in a society without the ancient religious background,[34] are usually not even aware of the possibility of such a dizzying experience as a feature that is specifically tragic precisely because it is Dionysiac.

## Death, Love, and the Model of the Maenad

Maenads and *bakkhai,* the maddened female followers of Dionysus,[35] are frequently associated in Greek literature with violent death, especially with the murder of their own male offspring. Best known is the story of Agave, who, together with the other sisters of Dionysus' mother, Semele, kills her son Pentheus.[36] Both here and elsewhere

---

epiphanies, as religious experiences induced by performances during mystery cults, that aimed to produce fear and lamenting, and finally blessed joy, see, for Eleusis, Burkert 1972, 303–21, esp. 317; Burkert 1985, 288; Burkert 1987a, 89–114 and 162–71 (including Bacchic mysteries and their specific ecstasy, in his chapter on "transforming" experience). Seaford 1981, who emphasizes correspondences between "the Dionysiac drama and the Dionysiac mysteries," takes the similar visual effects into account, but his only major example is Euripides' *Bacchae*. I am arguing that these correspondences can also be demonstrated for previous plays and playwrights.

[33] Cf., in general, Nietzsche 1872, chap. 8 (= 1972, 56), who argues that the "genuine poet" does not use the metaphor as a rhetorical figure but as a "vicarious image" that replaces a concept and that actually "hovers" before the eyes of the poet: "Die Metapher ist für den ächten Dichter nicht eine rhetorische Figur, sondern ein stellvertretendes Bild, das ihm wirklich, an Stelle eines Begriffes, vorschwebt." See also below, n. 42.

[34] On the difficulties inherent in the modern scholarly interpretation of ancient mysteries or even of modern anthropological records of rituals, see Burkert 1987a, 90–91: "The gap between pure observation and the experience of those involved in the real proceedings remains unbridgeable." I venture the surmise that this applies to Greek tragedy too and that, correspondingly, the modern reader (or spectator) is virtually unable to imagine the experience of the ancient audience.

[35] On the differences (and some correspondences) between mythical and ritual maenadism, cf. Rapp 1872; Jeanmaire 1951, 157–219 and 491–93; Dodds 1951, 270–82; Henrichs 1978a; Bremmer 1984. For an extensive survey of the material and of the present state of the debate, and the least biased position, see now Versnel 1990a, 131–55.

[36] For a selective bibliography on Euripides' *Bacchae,* see Saïd 1988, 496–98. Versnel 1990a, 156–205 ("Ambiguities in the *Bacchae*"), does not focus on Agave.

(albeit not always) the murderous assaults committed by maenads are explained in myth as the result of the wrath of the god, who punishes the women for their resistance to his cult.[37]

Furthermore then, even outside the Dionysiac sphere, the main tragic characters identified with maenads either are drawn to kill children and even members of their own family or do indeed murder them. The most spectacular example is Euripides' Heracles, who in a Bacchic frenzy inflicted by Hera kills his sons and his wife. Hecuba, another notorious figure belonging to the series of Euripidean protagonists presented as *bakkhai* or maenads, even kills intentionally. She does not, however, slay her own children but the sons of her enemy, the murderer of Hecuba's last surviving son. A similar pattern occurs already in Aeschylus: the Erinyes, who as divine agents of Clytemnestra's revenge threaten to kill her son and murderer, Orestes, call themselves *mainades*.[38]

The fury of the fighting and murdering maenad is even used by the tragedians in some of their narrative passages, independently of tragic characters and of the aggression against children and kin. Bacchic frenzy can also characterize excited figures of warriors, such as two of the Seven against Thebes: Hippomedon, who is possessed by Ares (Aeschylus *Seven against Thebes* 498), and the anonymous warrior in the parodos of Sophocles' *Antigone*.[39] In both instances, as in the comparable case of Euripides' Heracles, the maenad is a female model for a male behavior.[40]

[37] For myths of resistance to Dionysus, especially involving Lycurgus, the daughters of Cadmus, the Proetids, and the Minyads, see Dodds 1960, xxv–xxvii; Massenzio 1970, 49–98; cf. also Massenzio, pp. 13–45, on murder, within the scope of the Dionysiac *xenia,* that does not result from resistance to the god. Cf. furthermore Seaford 1988.

[38] *Eum.* 500: cf. Whallon 1964, 322; Guépin 1968, 27–28; Seaford 1989a, 303. Sommerstein 1989, ad loc., finds only a resemblance here of the Erinyes to Dionysiac maenads, whereas Lloyd-Jones 1979, 41, translates *mainades* as "who send madness." Loraux 1990b, 265, interprets it as a hint to "la présence absente de Dionysus"; see also Loraux, p. 266.

[39] *Ant.* 136 *bakkheuōn;* i.e., Capaneus, in my view, not Polynices, as has sometimes been argued, recently by Bierl 1989, 47, following Segal 1981 and Lonnoy 1985. But it is more likely that Capaneus is meant, for, among the Seven against Thebes, it is his overwhelming frenzy that is traditionally emphasized. Note that this *theomakhos* is going to be hit by the lightning of Zeus (Eur. *Supp. Wom.* 496–99; cf. Aesch. *Seven* 423–36), as was Dionysus' mother, Semele.

[40] I am not concerned here with the association between war and frenzy in general, or between maenadism and war in particular. These associations are of course much too complicated to develop here. The same is true for the notorious blurring of the differences

But only with women can the tragic model of Bacchic frenzy also denote another state of mind and behavior, one that does not automatically lead to murder, although it may include it: the excitement of violent and painful love. The first example in tragedy is Zeus's goaded lover Io, who is described as a "maenad of Hera" by the chorus of Aeschylus' *Suppliant Women*.[41] Among the tragic characters themselves, the most striking case of a loving woman who displays a maenadic state is Aphrodite's victim Phaedra in Euripides' *Hippolytus*, to whom I will return later.

This brief (and by no means complete) sketch—with illustrations taken from three Aeschylean and three Euripidean tragedies as well as one tragedy of Sophocles—can be summed up as follows: maenads as tragic models occur particularly in three contexts: the killing of kin; war; and love.

These contexts, especially the first and the third, are also reflected in the three examples, one chosen from each of the tragedians, that I shall attempt to investigate in the final section of this essay, namely, Aeschylus' *Libation Bearers*, Sophocles' *Trachinian Women*, and Euripides' *Hippolytus*. First, however, some general remarks are in order. The instances of Bacchic madness mentioned above (as well as analogous passages from other plays) are usually considered in modern scholarship to be mere metaphors.[42] The argument underlying such an inter-

---

between male and female activities in connection with maenadism. For my purposes it is important, however, to stress that at least in the case of the warrior in Aesch. *Seven* 498 (*bakkhāi pros alkēn thuias hōs*, "he raves madly, like a maenad, to the fight"), the model of the warrior is clearly a female one, namely, the maenad.

[41] *Supp. Wom.* 562–64 *mainomena . . . thuias Hēras*. Vürtheim's excursus (1928, 220–23) on *thuias Hēras*, although confused, has not yet been improved upon. On the *kentron* designed, in this Aeschylean passage and elsewhere, to induce *mania*, especially of the Bacchic and of the erotic type, see Schlesier 1985, 24–25. On the evidence concerning the *thuiades* in general, see Villanueva Puig 1986.

[42] Seaford, in a most stimulating essay in this volume, now uses the term "Dionysiac metaphor" throughout and wants it to mean "any explicit or implicit comparison of behavior to the frenzy inspired by Dionysus." Although I strongly sympathize with his analysis and with many of his arguments, I wonder whether the term "model" is not preferable to the term "metaphor." Concerning "explicit comparison," on the one hand, I would prefer to call a comparison a comparison and to restrict the term "metaphor" to contexts remote from religious reality—a remoteness that Aristotle's (and his followers') definition of the term refers to and even requires; see Schlesier 1986–87; see also Most 1987, 31 n. 21, on the "crucial difference . . . between metaphor and the really quite disparate phenomenon of simile." On the other hand, I do not agree that the use of the verb *bakkheuein* in tragedy generally implies nothing other than an "implicit comparison of behavior to the

pretation is that Bacchic madness in its proper sense should be confined to Dionysiac contexts, while in other contexts it should be understood as figurative or deviating from the proper sense. But the Bacchic madness in the cases already alluded to is presented by the tragedians as no less real, and generally no less destructive, than the Bacchic madness of, for example, Agave in Euripides' *Bacchae*. The origin of this madness is always a divine one, and the difference lies only in the particular divine agent who is responsible for it. Whereas Agave's maenadic frenzy is caused by Dionysus, a non-Dionysiac Bacchic state can be produced by other divinities or even by the dead as powers of the underworld.

The Bacchic terminology, then, in contexts other than the Dionysiac, has not been transferred from its proper meaning to a metaphorical one, but from an exclusive connection with one divinity, Dionysus, to a connection with a wider range of divine powers. The main divinities who induce Bacchic madness in tragic figures include, besides Ares, Hera (in the case of Aeschylus' Io and Euripides' Heracles)[43] and Aphrodite (in the case of the Euripidean Phaedra)—precisely those divinities who, along with Dionysus, are ranged in the Greek pantheon as the most important producers of madness, even outside of tragedy. Apollo could indeed be added to these gods, for he is the master of the prophetess Cassandra, who is presented as the god's *mainas* (literally, "mad woman") in Euripides' *Trojan Women* (307, 349, 415) and *Electra* (1032).

Beside these five gods, almost equally important as producers of Bacchic madness are the dead: for instance, Clytemnestra, who awakens the fury of the Erinyes in Aeschylus' *Eumenides,* and the young Polydorus, who causes the maenadic violence of his mother in Euripides' *Hecuba.*[44] Likewise Antigone, in Euripides' *Phoenician Women,* becomes "a maenad of the dead" (1489 *bakkha nekuōn*)[45] after the

frenzy inspired by Dionysus," as Seaford puts it. I am arguing that the use of that verb, on the tragic stage, points to the simultaneous, let's say implicit, participation of Dionysus even in a frenzy inspired by other gods.

[43] Hera is said to inflict madness on Dionysus himself in Eur. *Cyclops* 3; see Seaford 1984, ad loc.; on the mythical and ritual accords and oppositions between Hera and Dionysus, see furthermore Seaford 1988.

[44] See Schlesier 1988b.

[45] See Seaford 1990, 89, who relates this passage to the final (confused?) part of the play where Antigone refers to her previous, and this time truly Dionysiac, maenadism.

reciprocal killing of her brothers Eteocles and Polynices in their duel, and the subsequent suicide of her mother, Iocasta.

The use of Bacchic terminology in all these contexts makes clear, I think, that the tragedians were not dealing there with mere metaphors.[46] Violent frenzy of several kinds,[47] even when caused by distinct divine forces, is classified in tragedy under the sign of Dionysus Bacchos and is fundamentally related to him. In this way, Dionysus is subtly included as a vigorous agent and object of reference even in those plots where the decisive divinity is not Dionysus himself. The maenad as a model explicitly occurs in the majority of the extant tragedies and, I dare to assert, implicitly also in the rest of them. The maenadic model has thus to be perceived as a specific device of tragedy that further shows that tragedy is a Dionysiac genre. This model connects tragic plots to the god who institutionally presides over Greek tragedy in its civic and ritual environment. The tragedians, then, attempted to demonstrate that Dionysus, on the tragic stage, exerts his transforming power even on the great many figures and myths from which, outside the theatrical sphere, he is usually excluded. And this power, dynamically woven into the tragic texts, turns out to be cohesive and destructive at the same time. The cohesive force of Dionysus is most obvious and even harmonizing in the satyr plays, in which each and every mythic figure has something to do with Dionysus and his hybrid male followers. In tragedy, however, the passionate and painful significance of the Dionysiac power for human beings is strikingly exemplified by a female model, that of the maenad. The specific function of the maenadic model in tragedy is further confirmed if one considers the antecedents of this feature. In fact, the maenad emerges in Greek literature as an epic model before appearing as a tragic one.

[46] Cf., more generally, Loraux 1989, 179: "Dans le texte tragique, il n'est pas à proprement parler de métaphore. Parce qu'entre le mot et 'l'image' il n'est pas sûr que l'on puisse introduire la distance qui permettrait que s'établisse un rapport sur fond d'écart. Comme si toujours les mots devraient être pris au mot." She argues that in tragedy metaphors in the technical sense do not occur at all, and she does not share the assumption that in tragedy the distance between the word and the "image" should be understood as a digression. She rather believes that the words always keep their literal meaning. Loraux, however, does not, in this context, investigate the religious implications of tragedy, Dionysiac or other.

[47] Although not of all kinds—the most instructive exception is Sophocles' *Ajax;* cf. Schlesier 1985, 21–22.

The two loci classici are found in Homer and in a Homeric *Hymn*. In book 22 of the *Iliad* Andromache, who does not yet know that Hector has been killed by Achilles, but already hears the laments of his mother, Hecuba, begins to rush through the palace "like a maenad, with her heart in palpitations."[48] In the Homeric *Hymn to Demeter,* at the very moment when Kore-Persephone appears before the eyes of her mother, Demeter "rushes upon her like a maenad down the mountain shadowy with its forest."[49]

The "maenads" Andromache and Demeter have many things in common with the maenadic model in tragedy. First of all, they both share the particular rushing motion and the violent emotion excited by sound or sight that are standard characteristics of maenads. Second, and related to that, they have a common connection to death and to love: Andromache suddenly hears cries of distress and is shaken by the grievous presentiment of the death of her husband. Demeter jumps up at the joyful sight of her daughter who has returned from the underworld. Third, and most important, the maenadic quality emerges at the turn of the events, as hope turns into despair for Andromache and deepest grief into highest delight for Demeter. One might recall that such a precipitous change to the opposite state of things was considered by Aristotle the main characteristic of the course of a tragic plot, under the names of metabole and peripeteia.[50]

Still, the maenad as a tragic model differs from these maenadic models in epic in a decisive respect. Unlike their epic predecessors, tragic characters who follow the maenadic model usually become murderers, either of their mates or of their male children.[51] In fact,

[48] *Il.* 22. 460–61 *mainadi isē / pallomenē kradiēn.* According to Wilamowitz 1973, 60, *mainas* does not here refer to a Dionysiac maenad; cf. Richardson 1974, 281: "simply 'a mad woman.' " Against this view, Privitera 1970, 62: "esplicitamente 'simile a una menade.' " See also Detienne 1986, 89, who takes Andromache as an example of "un corps de ménade": "Son coeur de ménade bat la chamade." On Andromache in the *Iliad* and her Dionysiac connotations, see now the exhaustive interpretation of Seaford in this volume.

[49] Homeric *Hymn to Demeter* 386 *ēix' ēute mainas oros kata daskion hulēs.* Cf. Richardson 1974, ad loc., holding that *mainas* "is here a maenad"; see also Henrichs 1978a, 144. Clay 1989, 254, quotes the passage without an attempt at interpretation.

[50] Metabole and peripeteia thus turn out to be maenadic features, even before tragedy; see also above, nn. 15 and 19.

[51] Cf. Seaford 1989b, 95, and his essay in this volume; Seaford does not mention the fact that the children killed by Dionysiac mothers (or fathers) in tragedy are always sons.

tragic mothers in general do not kill their daughters,[52] but they frequently attempt to kill their sons. And if they do so unwittingly, such as Creusa in Euripides' *Ion,* Dionysus is always explicitly involved.[53] Euripides' Medea, however, murders her children deliberately; consequently she is not presented as a maenad at all.[54]

The maenadic model is dramatized in the three examples to which I will now turn: Clytemnestra with Orestes in a somewhat enigmatic passage in Aeschylus' *Libation Bearers;* Deianira, the unwitting murderer of her husband, Heracles, in Sophocles' *Trachinian Women;* and Euripides' Phaedra with her beloved stepson Hippolytus, whose death she provokes.

## Clytemnestra, Deianira, Phaedra: Three Cases of Displaced Maenadism

Aeschylus' Clytemnestra, Sophocles' Deianira, Euripides' Phaedra: each of these three women dies in the course of the play, Deianira and Phaedra by suicide, and Clytemnestra at the hand of her son. Yet in each case, the prospect of a maenadic state appeals to the woman, a prospect that is linked to her desire for union with her beloved one. If this desire had been realized, she would perhaps not have had to commit murder or to die a violent death. In other words, there would have been no tragedy.

What are the specific starting points? Let us begin with the mother of Orestes. If the attribution of *Libation Bearers* 691–99 to her is correct,[55] Clytemnestra says that the return of her son alive should

[52] The loss of daughters by sacrifice belongs to the most dolorous experiences of tragic mothers, but they do not kill their daughters, at least not as maenads. The only mother who agrees with the death of her daughter (by sacrifice) is Praxithea in Euripides' *Erechtheus;* cf. Loraux 1990a, 26–27, 79, with 143 n. 126.

[53] Zeitlin 1989 does not include this point in her subtle analysis of the Dionysiac features in Euripides' *Ion*. These features are completely elided in an otherwise stimulating article by Loraux (1990c), as well as in her interpretation of the murdering mothers of sons in tragedy (1990a).

[54] See now the similar assessment of Seaford, in this volume.

[55] I am convinced neither by Turnebus' attribution of the passage to Electra, recently revived by Seaford 1989a, nor by Portus' conjecture *kakēs* (*kalēs* M) in line 698, essential for this attribution and for the conventional interpretations as well.

have been an occasion for a "beautiful Bacchic celebration." Comparable is the situation of Heracles' wife, Deianira, who is encouraged by the women of the chorus as she desperately waits for the return of her husband to her bed. They believe that the renewed marriage of the couple allows them to begin an exciting Bacchic revelry (*Trachinian Women* 216–20). For her part, Phaedra actually claims to be starting an *oreibasia:* under the influence of Aphrodite's *mania* she hints at her longing for a maenadic companionship with her adored stepson Hippolytus in his hunting activities (*Hippolytus* 215–18). But in the course of the plot of each of these tragedies, such pious wishes are completely frustrated when less harmonious forces (equally at home in the Bacchic pattern) bring about dire catastrophes.

The first two cases belong, so to speak, to the tragic type of a failed Bacchic feast. This pattern has something in common with the type of the tragic wedding,[56] especially the surprising absence of a happy ending. (In the second case the two types are actually linked together.) The hopes of Clytemnestra and Deianira, and also the frustration of them, correspond to a model that is followed elsewhere in tragedy, too. As a matter of fact, the idea that the return of the beloved males to the house provides an occasion for a Bacchic feast is expressed by several tragic figures and choruses. In Sophocles' *Antigone,* for instance, the chorus, at the end of its parodos, expresses the conviction that now, after the victory over the Seven against Thebes, the city should find forgetfulness in nocturnal dances—on the premise that these revelries should be governed by the god Bakkheios himself, who would make the city whirl around (153 *elelikhthōn*).[57] Analogous desires are expressed by the old men in Euripides' *Heracles* after the return of the hero (682–84). But instead of these wishes being fulfilled, in both plays the murdering continues in the precincts of the city and in the royal palace, and a Bacchic topsy-turvy is part of it.[58]

[56] On this topic, see the path-breaking study of Seaford 1987.

[57] Cf. Segal 1981, 452 n. 147, who emphasizes the tension between the Dionysiac mood in the parodos and in the fifth stasimon of Sophocles' *Antigone*. I cannot, however, accept his assumption on p. 200 that, simultaneously with the parodos, the Dionysiac feast in the city has already started.

[58] On the "sinister import" of the chorus's appeal to Dionysus in the parodos of Sophocles' *Antigone,* cf. Winnington-Ingram 1980, 116. All too-positive interpretations of the Dionysiac features in this tragedy miss this point: for instance, Vicaire 1968, 354–65; see also Bierl 1989, 52–53, who unconvincingly argues that an epiphany of Dionysus actually takes

This happens most strikingly in the *Trachinian Women*. Upon hearing that Heracles is about to return to his wife, the chorus of the Trachinian girls and women (who call themselves *parthenoi* but are repeatedly called *gunaikes* by Deianira)[59] strikes up a wedding song that begins by honoring Apollo, Artemis, and the Nymphs. At the end (216–20), the women clearly evoke the Dionysiac sphere, although without explicitly naming the god:

> I am raised up and I will not reject
> the flute, o ruler of my mind.
> Look, he stirs me up,
> euhoi,
> the ivy now
> whirls me round in Bacchic contest (*bakkhian hamillan*).[60]

This is not a mere invocation of Dionysus. The thrill of the god, for the women, is already there. By means of the Bacchic implements, the flute, the maenadic cry *euhoi,* and the ivy, the chorus is actually transformed into a thiasos possessed by Dionysus.[61] Furthermore one should note that apart from Euripides' *Bacchae,* this passage is the only one in extant Greek tragedy in which the maenadism is actually performed on stage and is not simply alluded to.[62]

In fact, the maenadism of the *Trachinian Women* has a powerful

---

place—but the point is precisely that Dionysus does not respond in this tragedy to his invocations, neither in the parodos nor in the fifth stasimon; cf. furthermore Henrichs 1990, 266–69 and 276–77, who likewise denies the fifth stasimon its "ambivalence." Oudemans and Lardinois 1987, 154–59, on the contrary, stress its "tragic ambiguity" and its "ominous undertones" similar to those of the parodos.

[59] 211 *parthenoi;* cf. 1275; 821 *paides;* cf. 871; 202, 225, 385, 663, 673 *gunaikes*. Iole herself is called *parthenos* by Heracles (1219), who has previously raped her. The common translation of *parthenos* by "virgin" is therefore often misleading.

[60] Cf. Lloyd-Jones 1972, 264–65, 270.

[61] Most commentators speak at best of an "ecstatic dance": Easterling 1982, ad loc.; or of a "Bacchic dance": Gardiner 1987, 130.

[62] In other words, the chorus here adopts a maenadic role in which imagination and reality are indissolubly mingled—as is usual in maenadism. There the Dionysiac coloring of the chorus is even more emphasized than in other Sophoclean choruses (cf. above, n. 25); however the thyrsus, the Dionysiac implement par excellence, is not mentioned; but the Greek term *thursos,* before becoming so prominent in the *Bacchae,* appears for the first and only times in extant Greek tragedy at Eur. *Her.* 890 and *Phoen. Wom.* 792 (in a compound form: *thursomanei*). On the passage in the *Trachinian Women,* see also Vicaire 1968, 354, who does not find an actual trance there.

dramatic function.[63] It aims to include Deianira as well as her beloved husband in the Bacchic ecstasy. This frenzied revel, then, is a fight, a race, or, more precisely, a contest (220 *hamillan*) in which the love of the man should be recaptured.[64] But a peripeteia follows straightaway. An unexpected adversary makes a sudden appearance, which seems to show that the contest is already decided, since at that very moment, it is not the eagerly awaited Heracles who arrives, but instead the women he has captured in his own last struggles, and among them the silent figure of Iole. Her winning beauty says enough about the past and the future. It is not Deianira herself but the chorus who immediately realizes the danger and conjures the healing god, Paean (221),[65] just as the chorus in Euripides' *Heracles* (820) does at the appearance of Hera's Furies Iris and Lyssa. The girls, in solidarity with Deianira, therefore do not classify the foreign women as "subjugated," with respect to Heracles, but rather they call them threatening, "face-to-face" enemies (223 *antiprōira*),[66] with regard to his spouse. In my view,

[63] This point is overlooked by many commentators; see, for instance, Beck 1953, 17, who interprets the song of the chorus as nothing but joyful and as "the only moving pause for rest" ("der einzige, ergreifende Ruhepunkt der Tragödie"), followed by Seale 1982, 187 and 212 n. 17. Segal 1981, 91, notices the dramatic function of this passage, but only with respect to the much later turn of events. Seaford 1987, 128, who remarks that "the return of Herakles is envisaged here as the re-enactment or final completion of the marital transition of Deianeira," does not take the simultaneous tragic reversal into account; but cf. his more recent analysis in this volume in the section entitled "Iole."

[64] The meaning of the word *hamilla* in this passage has been intensely disputed; the translations are either "contest," "competition" (see especially Jebb 1892, ad loc.) or, more recently, "race," in the sense of "speedy course," without a competitive meaning: Kamerbeek 1959, ad loc.; Lloyd-Jones 1972, 270; Easterling 1982, ad loc. I would suggest that the aggressive overtones of this passage should be taken seriously. As the song ends, the beginning of an actual competition becomes obvious, with the arrival of Iole among the other captives, and Deianira's part in her competition with Iole will soon reveal itself to be under Bacchic auspices. On the erotic connotations of a bridal *hamilla* ending with the departure—into death—of the potential groom, cf. also Eur. *Hipp.* 1140–41.

[65] This invocation is often interpreted as "joyous refrain"; see for instance Seale 1982, 187; but cf. Schiassi 1953, ad loc.: "dio soccorritore"; see also Kamerbeek 1959, ad loc., who mentions the simultaneity with the arrival of the captives. I have found no commentary that points to the parallelism with the passage in Euripides' *Heracles*.

[66] Kamerbeck 1959, ad loc., translates "face-to-face" and remarks: "The nautical metaphor has faded." But the chorus here is really frightened and points out the captives to Deianira, describing them precisely as "prows" in front of her, i.e., like ships about to attack. In fact, outside this Sophoclean passage, *antiprōira* is used (especially by Herodotus and Thucydides) exclusively in this sense. The *hamilla,* then, actually turns out to be a deadly competition.

there is no reason to interpret this as "irony" or "paradox." Rather the appearance of these women actually starts a reversal that is about to take place in the plot. And the reversal—itself a Dionysiac feature, I would argue—is indeed brought about in this play under Bacchic signs.

The ending of the "Bacchic race" of the chorus upon the sight of the captives does not mean that Bacchic forces are from this point on suspended or that the contest is over. On the contrary. Deianira does not accept her defeat as a final one. In order to overcome the rival, she soon ventures a risky maneuver. Yet the magic potion that she applies to Heracles as a love charm (in the form of an anointed robe) works the other way round. It will kill him and will eventually lead to her own death as well.[67]

This unlucky maneuver does not, however, lack Bacchic connotations, although it differs considerably from the Dionysiac contest that the chorus had celebrated before. Later in the course of the play, we are told that such a contest had already happened in the life of the queen. It was actually the contest that led to her marriage, since Heracles, who was driven to conquer Deianira, "came from Bacchic Thebes with his arrows that possess opposite tensions,"[68] and defeated his rival, the stream god Achelous.

What does Sophocles mean when he speaks of arrows that possess "opposite tensions"? The play gives the following answer: the arrows do defeat the adversaries of Heracles, but in the end they defeat Heracles himself, since the magic potion that Deianira uses is a mixture of the poison smeared on Heracles' arrows and the blood of one of his adversaries, Nessos, a rival suitor of Deianira, whom Heracles killed with the very same arrows.

[67] On the virile form of Deianira's suicide, albeit attacking the left (= female) side of her body, see the acute remarks of Loraux 1985, 90–91. Deianira, however, does not die for her son and for her husband, as Loraux says: "à cause d'Hyllos, pour l'amour d'Hérakles" (51). The specifically tragic reason for her suicide is the fact that she has unwittingly killed her beloved man precisely by trying to regain his love. See also the striking comment of Zeitlin 1990a, 82: "The point is that, innocent as Deianira may be of conscious intent to harm her husband, she still easily proves a better and more successful plotter than he. Masculine guile is repaid in full—even when retaliation does not openly bear the name of revenge."

[68] *Trach. Wom.* 510–12 *Bakkhias apo / ēlthe palintona Thēbas / toxa.* I am not going to deny the generally accepted technical meaning of *palintona toxa,* "back-bent," "resilient bow," but I cannot help noticing here an additional allusion to Heraclitus: *palintropos harmoniē hokōsper toxou kai lurēs* (*FVS* 22 B51).

Yet the fatal force of this mixture is finally recognized by Deianira under Dionysiac auspices. This time, the connotations are taken neither from love nor from war but from viticulture. How did Deianira realize that her maneuver would lead to catastrophe? She finds in her room the remains of the piece of wool that she had used before to anoint Heracles' robe with the mixture of poison and blood. This piece of wool is now in decay and transformed into foam, "like the opulent drink of the blue fruit that pours to earth from the Bacchic vine."[69] How can we explain the occurrence of this comparison here? First, Deianira should indeed be familiar with such a procedure, since she is the daughter of Oeneus, the ominous wine king, as is often stressed in the play from the very beginning. But most of all, this comparison coincides here with a further peripeteia: the anagnorisis, in this tragedy, turns out to be a Bacchic feature, too.

The plot of the *Trachinian Women* is of course ruled by the goddess of love, who decides the outcome of the different struggles, whether it be the contest for Deianira, and later the contest for Iole (both won by Heracles), or the contest for Heracles that was ventured by Deianira, and of which Iole was the only survivor. The Bacchic god, however, and his characteristically antagonistic and cohesive powers play a reversing and the revealing part in the tragic course of the events, since the shifting of desire into intended or involuntary destruction is repeatedly expressed in Bacchic terms.

From this point of view, numerous analogies are to be found in Euripides' *Hippolytus*. Before Phaedra betrays her secret, namely, her illicit love for her stepson Hippolytus, she exhibits her desire in a rather obscure but nevertheless revealing way, possessed as she is by Aphrodite. She proclaims a great many of her desires, and all of them point to the activities of the young man:[70] the fresh air outside the

[69] *Trach. Wom.* 703–4 *glaukēs opōras hōste pionos potou / xuthentos es gēn Bakkhias ap' ampelou*. Reinhardt 1933, 61, feels compelled to blame the author for the "almost overwhelming" significance of this piece of wool, which "als ein Stückchen Wolle fast mit allzugrosser Wucht des Sinnes beladen wird." In the context of the whole range of Dionysiac features in this tragedy, however, the decomposed piece of wool reveals once again the manifold and polymorphous Bacchic texture of the plot. See also Segal 1981, 91, who points to the connection between wine and blood stressed in this passage.

[70] This fact has frequently been analyzed in scholarship; see especially the sensible remarks of Zeitlin 1985a, 110, arguing that Phaedra's longings surpass "any simple or single mimetic identification" and express "impossible ambiguities" that all have to do with mixtures of several kinds; cf. also Luschnig 1988, 5; on Phaedra's yearning "to *be*" Hippolytus, cf. now Goff 1990, 34, 67.

house, the meadow with its clear water, the hunting of deer with the dogs on the woody mountain, and the taming of horses on the sands of the lagoon belonging to Artemis. The most ecstatic parts of her evocative utterances are presented as preparations for an action that is about to start.[71] She gives the order for her hair to be loosed (202); she announces her immediate departure for the hunt in the wood. And at this point (215–18), although no term is used that is inappropriate to the vocabulary of hunting, almost every word has an unmistakable further sense, a Bacchic one:

> Escort me to the mountain (*eis oros*). I am coming toward the forest
> and to the pines, where the killers of wild beasts
> tread, the bitches (*kunes*)
> hot on the heels of the spotted hinds (*baliais elaphois*).[72]

Phaedra commands the women to lead her to the mountain. It is indeed exactly the way the hunter Hippolytus goes every day. But a *pompē* to the mountain can also imply a ritual relegation of illness and of polluted or otherwise dangerous things beyond the boundaries of human civilization.[73] This could be said to apply to Phaedra, but less to Hippolytus. There is, moreover, another striking implication that is further illuminated by the next set of images: a kind of hunting particular to the maenads.[74] The most typical cry announcing the maenadic *oreibasia* is actually *eis oros,*[75] a cry that is not of course used by Hippolytus and his fellow hunters. Whereas it is not specified what these men are hunting, the "spotted hinds"[76] are the *bakkhai*'s favorite

[71] Phaedra's "delirium" does not exclude action, as some commentators seem to presuppose. On the contrary. Cf. Barrett 1964, at 215.

[72] I have not found any previous attempt to investigate the Bacchic overtones of this passage, which are, in my view, essential for the dramatic turn of events in this tragedy. But on some structural parallels between Phaedra and Agave, see Segal 1978a, 199; between Hippolytus and Pentheus, Segal 1982, 167.

[73] See Versnel 1977, 41–42; Schlesier 1990b.

[74] On the maenads (and Dionysus himself) as hunters (and as hunted), cf. Guépin 1968, 26–32; with respect to the reversal of sex roles, see especially Segal 1978a, 196–98 and 201 n. 21, and Segal 1982, 34–36 and 195.

[75] Cf. Henrichs 1969, 230 n. 24, 232 with nn. 30–31; Henrichs 1978a, 149; on the ambiguity of *eis oros,* cf. now Versnel 1990a, 134 n. 159. Note that the *mainas* Demeter quoted above also acts out an *oreibasia.*

[76] A striking parallel to the *baliais elaphois* desired here by Phaedra as her favorite prey is the *balia elaphos* seen by Hecuba in a dream (Eur. *Hec.* 90). In my interpretation, this points to the Bacchic sacrifice of Hecuba's son Polydorus, which may include his castration, see

prey, and from such skins, the garments of full-fledged maenads are made.[77] In contrast to the custom of male hunters, dogs are absent from maenadic hunting, but as huntresses, this time of men, the maenads are themselves called "running bitches," by Agave in Euripides' *Bacchae* (731 *dromades . . . kunes*), as well as in his *Hecuba* (1077).[78] Phaedra, too, emphasizes the female gender of the hounds. But why does she stress the species of the trees? The term that she uses, *peukai,* "pine trees," is actually often employed by the tragedians in a more restricted sense, meaning "torches of pine wood." It specifically denotes the torches that are brandished by the maenads and that belong to their nocturnal revelries.[79] If that is also implied in Phaedra's use of the term, it becomes clear, at last, that nothing could be more spectacularly opposed to the serene hunting of Hippolytus, which requires daylight and rejects wild ecstasy.

Phaedra is indeed alluding in this passage to her desire to join the beloved hunter in his main activities, but at the same time a less idyllic feature emerges in her words. It is maenadism, and therefore, as the other mythical examples show, it is mortally dangerous for a young man, particularly for a son. Indeed Hippolytus himself will in the end be killed, and Phaedra, the polluted "bitch," provokes intentionally the death of the beloved one who has refrained from loving her.[80]

---

Schlesier 1988b, 129 n. 50. Perhaps in both cases the female sex of the animal alludes to mutilation of males in Bacchic contexts. In any case, the dismemberment of the young men is no less emphasized at the end of the *Hippolytus* (1344 *dialumantheis*) than it is in the *Hecuba* (cf. 716 and 1076 *diamoiraō*); see Schlesier 1988b, 123–24 n. 36. Cf. Guépin 1968, 14: "It is certainly possible to discern an allusion to the Dionysiac *sparagmos* in the rending apart of Hippolytus in Euripides' tragedy."

[77] On the fawn skin (*nebris*) along with the leopard skin (*pardalis*) as the distinguishing features of most full-fledged maenads in Attic vase painting, especially the red-figure, see Edwards 1960, 80; and cf. Henrichs 1987a, 100–105 and 117–21 nn. 45ff.

[78] See Schlesier 1988b, 124 n. 36. On the maenads as hounds in the *Bacchae,* cf. Winnington-Ingram 1948, 107 and 122. The interpretations of *Hippolytus* 217–18 generally comment neither on the female gender of the hounds nor on the parallelism with the maenadic bitches in the *Hecuba* and the *Bacchae.* As applied by Phaedra to herself, *kuōn* of course bears here a further meaning, a sexual one, denoting shamelessness and audacity: the prototype is Homer's Helen, *Il.* 6.344, 356; but cf. also the insult of Artemis by Hera, *Il.* 21.481.

[79] For *peukai* designating torches of pine wood in the Bacchic sphere, see, for instance, Soph. *Oed. King* 215, where they are described as efficient weapons of Dionysus and the maenads against Ares; see the commentary of Bollack 1990, 135–36; cf. also Eur. *Ion* 716; Aesch. *Bassarae* frag. 23a2 (*TrGF* 3). This does not of course exclude other uses of the term.

[80] To summarize: the manifold explicit and implicit meanings of *Hippolytus* 215–18, which include hunting, reversal of sex roles, animality, bloodthirstiness, female shameless-

Yet before it comes to that, the nurse, in the precinct of the house, makes an attempt to convince Hippolytus that he should yield to the desires of his stepmother. Simultaneously, the chorus of the women of Troezen sings its first stasimon, a hymn that praises the all-embracing power of Eros and Aphrodite. The second strophic pair elaborates mythical paradigms that, as has often been shown, relate to the fates of Hippolytus and Phaedra.[81] Both examples mentioned there have a strong Dionysiac emphasis, especially the story of Dionysus' mother, Semele, who was loved and killed by Zeus. Yet the first model is again that of Iole. She is described as an unbridled filly, unmarried before, "like a running naiad and a Bacchant,"[82] who was given by Cypris (i.e., Aphrodite) to Heracles with "bloody wedding songs."[83]

It has sometimes been argued that, like the paradigm of Semele, the figure of Iole offers here a warning example for Phaedra.[84] The passage indeed recalls her maenadic inclinations quoted above. But in the particular context of that strophe, Iole actually functions much more as a model for Hippolytus than for Phaedra: Hippolytus, like Iole but unlike Phaedra, is still unmarried. The unbridling of horses is already evoked by his name[85] and returns in the graphic description of his downfall at the end of the play. Furthermore, he was given by Cypris

---

ness, pollution, and purification, are bound together by the maenadic pattern that is simultaneously concealed and revealed.

[81] See Luschnig 1988, 57: "The chorus' examples, like those of the Nurse, tell of loves that ended unhappy not for the lover but for the beloved"; see also Goff 1990, 63.

[82] *Hipp.* 550–51 *dromada naïd' hopōs te Bakkhan.* On Euripides' maenadic Iole, see now Seaford's brilliant analysis in this volume of tragic maenads as destroyers of the household. He does not, however, relate this exemplum to the plot of the *Hippolytus.* On the comparison of maenads to unyoked fillies in *Bacch.* 1056, cf. Segal 1982, 58–60.

[83] I refer to the text of the manuscripts at *Hipp.* 552: *phoniois th' humenaiois.* According to Barrett 1964, ad loc., this "gives bad metre and bad sense"; he says himself that metrical arguments are not here sufficient in themselves to the extent that this would necessitate conjectures, and he goes on to ask: "But more important; what *are* these 'bloody wedding-songs'?" I would suggest that they do not in fact allude to the union of Iole and Heracles but to its aftermath, the death of Heracles and his wife Deianira. One might recall that in Sophocles' *Trachinian Women,* the—Bacchic—wedding song of the chorus is part of the action that leads to the destruction of that couple. In his earlier analysis Seaford 1987, 129, with n. 239, did not take this possibility into account, but he now relates the two passages to each other (see his essay in this volume, in the section entitled "Iole"), still following Barrett's conjecture *phonioisi numpheiois.*

[84] I cannot follow Goff 1990, 63, in assuming that both exempla, Iole and Semele, refer *only* to Phaedra. Goff herself actually relates other passages of the *Hippolytus* to the presentation of the young man as a bride "yoked to catastrophe" (64).

[85] Cf. Burkert 1979, 112–13.

to Phaedra, and he is the reason for her death, as Heracles died because Iole was given to him. The "bloody wedding songs," on the one hand, seem to recall the wedding song in Sophocles' *Trachinian Women,* treated above, with its strong Bacchic emphasis. As has been demonstrated, the wedding song opens the course of bloodshed in that play. But on the other hand, "bloody wedding songs" in the context of Euripides' *Hippolytus* also have a more specific sense. After the death of Phaedra and Hippolytus, Artemis herself institutes, as a premarital ritual for the young brides of Troezen, the singing of a song that rehearses the deadly love of Phaedra for Hippolytus.[86]

The chorus seems to anticipate these prospects and also points to the analogy between Phaedra's fate and that of Heracles, the conqueror of Iole. Yet Phaedra, who will not manage to violate her beloved one, does not completely follow this male model.[87] A similar twisting of the model occurs in the case of Hippolytus. The analogy between him and Iole indeed provides him with a further female model that has to be added to his other female or, more precisely, virginal characteristics, which have often been analyzed.[88] Yet, unlike Iole, who survives her violator, the virgin Hippolytus, sexually untouched, will himself die. With his death, however, inflicted by the woman who loves him, he finally reaches a male status, although smashed and even dismembered.[89] Phaedra, in her longing for the bloody pleasures of a running maenad, had already alluded to such an erotic aggression. Through the form of his death and its maenadic background, Hippolytus reveals the Bacchic pattern of his own fate. But as a murderer of a mother (albeit a stepmother), he is also prefigured by Orestes.

A last brief glance, then, at that other son who refrained from loving a mother and who was much loved by her—though (as I would argue) in a Bacchic way, too.[90] In Aeschylus' *Libation Bearers,* at the

[86] *Hipp.* 1425–30. In anticipatory fashion, a mournful bridal song has already been celebrated by the chorus in its third stasimon, 1131–50, after the departure of Hippolytus into exile, and thus in fact simultaneously with his deadly accident; but here it is exclusively Hippolytus who is glorified—as the object of the bridal aspirations of the girls of Troezen—and not Phaedra and her love for him.

[87] Phaedra's failure to become a violator underlines the "fundamental asymmetry" analyzed by Zeitlin 1986b, 150, with respect to "configurations of rape in Greek myth."

[88] See especially Zeitlin 1985a, 66–67, 195 n. 38. On the "feminization" of Hippolytus, cf. now Goff 1990, 65–67.

[89] Hippolytus finally acknowledges Aphrodite and her power (1401), albeit only in words he speaks as a mutilated, dying man. See Zeitlin 1985a, 105.

[90] This does not of course mean that I am going to deny the opposite conduct of

message of the alleged death of Orestes, Clytemnestra claims that he was, up to this fatal news, "the salutary hope of a good Bacchic celebration in the house."[91] The question is, What can be meant by such maenadism at home[92] in companionship with a son? I would venture the suggestion that a kind of private initiation cult like the one enacted in the famous story of Aeschines and his mother, reported by Demosthenes,[93] is not improbable.

---

Clytemnestra toward her son, which seems to be the most obvious part of her figure, although I find it less prominent in Aeschylus than in Sophocles or Euripides. Still there is no proof, I think, that the character of Clytemnestra lacks ambivalence or, in other words, that she represents nothing but an unequivocal hatred of her children and particularly of her son, as most interpretations seem to presuppose. On Aeschylus' Clytemnestra as the loving mother of Iphigenia, cf. Loraux 1990a, 77, who, on the other hand, ignores Clytemnestra's ambivalence when she assumes that Clytemnestra killed her husband exclusively "pour sa fille, et non à cause de son amant."

[91] *Lib. Bearers* 698–99 *hēper en domoisi bakkheias kalēs* [*kakēs* Portus] / *iatros elpis ēn*. For a different interpretation of this passage and a discussion of previous comments, see Seaford 1989a. I do concede that it seems more plausible to read *iatros* as a masculine noun, not as feminine (but such a use is attested, too), and to make *bakkheias* dependent not on *elpis* but on *iatros* (but *elpis* with a genitive of object is frequently to be found). Although many commentators connect *en domoisi* to *elpis*, "Bacchic celebration in the house" is a possible reading. Above all, I then see no justification for Portus' conjecture, because *bakkheia kalē* is a regular feature of Bacchic mysteries and their bliss, as is clear in particular from inscriptions; see Henrichs 1969, 238–39; Versnel 1990a, 152. Portus, at the beginning of the seventeenth century, obviously did not have some of the evidence available today. On *to kalon* as "charakteristische Vokabel der Dionysosmysten," see also Merkelbach 1988, 124–25 and 104 n. 37. In the context of mystic terminology, *ta kala* in the house is also referred to in Euripides *Antiope* frag. 198 (Nauck²), a tragedy in which a mother and her sons are also presented in connection with Bacchic features. In the Aeschylean passage, if the interpretation I have adopted is correct, there is perhaps another allusion to (previously performed?) Bacchic initiations in the enigmatic verse 697: *exō komizōn olethriou pēlou poda*. Muddy wine or lees could be the specific meaning of *pēlos* here, as in Sophocles frag. 783 (*TrGF* 4) and, especially, in Demosthenes *On the Crown* 259. 4, where it denotes the material of the purification during an initiation ritual of Bacchic coloring; in this passage an allusion to the mystic *kalon* is to be found as well.

[92] Maenadism at home is also referred to in Aesch. *Edoni* frag. 58 (*TrGF* 3)—if not already in Homer, with respect to Andromache. Private and secret rituals (including Bacchic celebrations) in city houses fostered suspicions, in both classical and Hellenistic Greece, as well as in Rome; see Versnel 1990a, esp. 122. Cf. furthermore Eur. *Helen* 1353–68. The participation of Orestes, as a young boy, in a risky Bacchic cult performed at home by his mother, is perhaps alluded to also in Eur. *El.* 573–74, where his sister succeeds in recognizing him by the scar of a wound inflicted upon him by "a fawn in the house" (*en domois nebron*); one might recall that in this play Electra herself is designated by the chorus as a *nebros* (860), in a passage very similar to the third stasimon of the *Bacchae* (862–76).

[93] Demosthenes *On the Crown* testifies to the performance of mysteries of Dionysus Sabazius by about 380 B.C. in Athens, according to Burkert 1987a, 19, 33, and 96–97; on a testimony from sixth-century Olbia of the joint participation of a mother and a son in

Orestes, as is well known, did not return home as such a Bacchic servant of his mother. That does not mean, however, that he completely succeeded in escaping the Bacchic features that surround her; for, after he murders his mother, the Erinyes present themselves as maenads (*Eumenides* 500),[94] and the prey they are hunting is actually Clytemnestra's son. As far as Athena and her city of Athens are concerned, at the end of Aeschylus' *Eumenides,* such a tragic maenadism is stopped once and for all. Yet until Euripides' *Bacchae,* Greek tragedies stubbornly continued to evoke stories of maenads as tragic models. Most of the time, however, they so discreetly and ingeniously mingled the maenadic models with other figures, with the result that this fact remained almost imperceptible in later, very different cultures, especially in those exclusively trained in *claritas* and *distinctio* and obsessed with the principle of identity.[95]

---

Dionysiac mysteries, see Burkert, p. 22; on the myth about Chthonian Dionysus and his dismemberment and rebirth as an initiation scenario, p. 100: "But there is no reason to assume that the myth was reenacted exactly in this form in ritual." In the German revised edition 1990, p. 85, Burkert is less skeptical. He seems to assume that private Bacchic mysteries in city houses, such as those performed by Aeschines and his mother, probably date back to the fifth or sixth century. On the later identification of Sabazius with Dionysus, see also Johnson 1984, 1587–88. On the historical value of Demosthenes' account of Bacchic mysteries, cf. now Versnel 1990a, 114–18, 136 n. 163, 149 nn. 211–12, 162.

[94] See above, n. 58.

[95] I owe particular thanks to Simon Srebrny and Albert Henrichs, who considerably improved my English formulations, as well as to Helene Foley, the commentator of the paper at the Blacksburg conference, for her patient and generous criticism, and to Thomas Carpenter and Christopher Faraone for inviting me to the inspiring event they organized at Virginia Tech. I am also most grateful to my friends and colleagues at Columbia, Cornell, Princeton, the University of Illinois at Chicago, and the University of Illinois at Urbana-Champaign for giving me the opportunity to present an earlier draft of this essay in October 1990 and to profit from the useful comments of the different audiences. For additional suggestions I wish to thank Richard Seaford and Hendrik Versnel, as well as my friends and colleagues at Tel Aviv University and the Hebrew University of Jerusalem, where the paper was discussed in May 1991.

CHAPTER 5

# Dionysus as Destroyer of the Household: Homer, Tragedy, and the Polis

Richard Seaford

I will use the term "Dionysiac metaphor" to mean any explicit or implicit comparison of behavior to the frenzy inspired by Dionysus. My main concern is to show what it is about Dionysiac frenzy, and in particular maenadism, that underlies the rare appearance of the Dionysiac metaphor in Homer and its frequent appearance in Greek tragedy. This will lead to the basis for a new, historical approach to the question of why Dionysus is almost entirely absent from Homer.[1]

## Maenadic Andromache in the *Iliad*

In the only Homeric narration of a Dionysiac myth, Lycurgus is said to have pursued the nurses of frenzied Dionysus (*Iliad* 6.132 *mainomenoio Diōnusoio tithōnas*). About 250 lines later Andromache, anxious about Hector, rushes to the wall "like a frenzied woman" (i.e., a maenad: 389 *mainomenēi eikuia*).[2] Much later in the poem Andro-

[1] My thanks go to Jon Mikalson, Renate Schlesier, John Wilkins, and especially to Helene Foley for their comments. It will be clear from the footnotes that this essay takes one stage farther an argument spread among several of my earlier articles.

[2] Cf. Homer *Iliad* 22. 460 and the Homeric *Hymn to Demeter* 386. On the rarity of non-Dionysiac, nonmilitary *mainesthai* in Homer see the final section of this essay. Cf. Segal 1971, 47 n. 31.

mache, again in fear for Hector, rushes through the house "like a maenad" (22. 460 *mainadi isē*) to the wall, where she sees Hector dead. There is, apart from these passages, no other mention of maenadism in Homer. It seems that the author of the Lycurgus narrative of *Iliad* 6.130–40 continued to be influenced by the Dionysiac narrative in his descriptions, a little later, of Andromache leaving home, and that the result influenced the parallel action of Andromache in book 22.[3]

Why does Andromache attract the Dionysiac metaphor? It is not only because she rushes twice in a frenzy from the house, as maenads do.[4] In book 6 Hector fails to find Andromache at home and asks the maids whether she has gone to see her sisters-in-law or to the temple of Athena, where the other Trojan women are propitiating the goddess. The reply comes that she has gone neither to see her sisters-in-law nor to the temple of Athena, but that she has rushed to the city wall, and it is at this point that the Dionysiac metaphor occurs. The careful and repeated specification of the normal reasons for the wife leaving the household increases the sense of anomaly in Andromache rushing to the city wall. Characteristic of the maenadic exit is to confuse not only the spatial differentiation of male and female but also their activities: Dionysiac frenzy typically causes women to abandon their weaving and go out to become warriors and hunters.[5] Andromache rushes to the very border of the town (393) to plead with Hector and give military advice (433–39). Hector then tells her to return home to her weaving: "War will be the concern of the men" (492). But this firm differentiation of the activities of the sexes prefigures (as does so much else in this scene) book 22, in which An-

[3] So Privitera 1970. He argues (61 n. 18) that the word *tithēnē,* which occurs four times in these passages (Hom. *Il.* 6. 132, 389, and 467; 22. 503) but nowhere else in Homer, was associated with maenadism. Elsewhere in Homer "nurse" is designated by the more common term *trophos*.

[4] If it was this that attracted the image, then the image has itself influenced the narrative to contain further points of correspondence. It is impossible, and for my purposes unimportant, to decide between these two alternatives.

[5] Weaving: Euripides *Bacchae* 117–19, 1236; Aelian *Varia historia* 3.42; Antoninus Liberalis 10; Ovid *Metamorphoses* 4.33–36, 390, 394–98; *Fragmenta adespota* 645.9 (*TrGF* 2) (?); also surely Aeschylus *Xantriae*. Warriors: Eur. *Bacch.* 52, 752, and 761–64; Aesch. *Eumenides* 25; for vase paintings of maenads with swords see March 1989, 36; Pausanias 2.20.4 (cf. 4.27.6; Lonnoy 1985, 65–71). Hunting: e.g., Eur. *Bacch.* 1236–37 *tas par' histois eklipousa kerkidas es meizon' hēkō thēras agreuein cheroin*.

dromache will abandon her weaving to return, again like a maenad, to the wall.[6]

But there is yet more to the Dionysiac metaphor than this. It is associated, in an interesting manner, with the ritual of marriage. In brief, the exit of Andromache seems to reenact so as to negate the ritual of her wedding. The same combination of Dionysiac metaphor and the negation of wedding ritual can be seen in the movement of Antigone in Euripides' *Phoenician Women*. That this combination is not merely coincidental is suggested by the subversive relationship of maenadism to the process of marriage and is confirmed by its presence in various other tragedies. There is in fact, as I will show, a broad historical context for the functioning of the Dionysiac metaphor and for the near absence of Dionysus from Homer.

## Maenadic Andromache and Wedding Ritual

In book 22 of the *Iliad* Andromache rushes through the house like a maenad to the wall, from which she sees her husband dead. She swoons and throws from her head its covering, including the headdress or veil (*krēdemnon*) "that golden Aphrodite gave her on the day when Hector of the flashing helm led her [as bride] from the house of Eetion."[7] The undoing of Andromache's marriage here finds symbolic expression in the reversal of an element in the ritual process. Recovered from her swoon, she begins (477–84):

> Hector, I am wretched. It was, then, for a single
> destiny that we two were born, you in Troy in the
> house of Priam, but I in Thebes under wooded Plakos in
> the house of Eetion, who brought me up when little,
> ill-fated he, and me with a wretched fate. He should
> never have begotten me. But now you go to the house
> of Hades under the earth, and leave me in bitter grief,
> a widow in the house.

[6] Hom. *Il.* 6.440–41 and 448, *tēs d'elelikhthē guia, khamai de hoi ekpese kerkis;* cf. Eur. *Bacch.* 118–19 *aph' histōn para kerkidōn t' / oistrētheis Dionusōi.*

[7] 22. 468–72. The *krēdemnon* is discussed at length by Nagler 1974, 44ff., 64ff.

This picture of the future bride and groom each still in the parental home complements the mention just made of the wedding procession, in which Hector led Andromache from her parental home. A feature of the wedding procession was the praise or *makarismos* of bride and groom. Sappho writes of this very wedding procession (frag. 44. 34 [Voigt 1971]): "They hymned Hector and Andromache as like the gods." And Admetus, returning home from his wife's burial, remembers an earlier processional arrival, with his bride, in which the company, rather than lamenting as now, called them happy (*olbizōn*) as being "of good parentage and yoked together from aristocrats on both sides."[8] The praise of the pair's fitness for each other, as both of high origin,[9] comes appropriately during the processional transfer, in which the bride is publicly united with her husband. Hence the irony here of Andromache's "it was for *one* fate that we were born, both of us" (each in our own house)—*iēi apa gignometh' aisēi amphoteroi*. Despite what was promised by the *makarismos,* the oneness of Hector and Andromache has turned out to be a oneness in disaster, with the journey undertaken now not (as in the wedding) by the bride but by the husband—"to the house of Hades."[10]

Another commonplace of the wedding ceremony was the wish that the marriage produce fine children similar to their parents.[11] This idea may be combined with that wish for prosperity (*olbos*) that is also characteristic of the wedding *makarismos*. In the Theocritean wedding song Zeus is asked to give "undying *olbos* to pass down from the well-born to the well-born" (18. 52–53). And the same combination is implicit in the following Homeric observation (*Odyssey* 4. 207–8): "Easily recognizable is the offspring of a man to whom Zeus destines prosperity (*olbos*) as he marries." During Andromache's first exit Hector asks Zeus and the other gods to make his son Astyanax like him (or

[8] Eur. *Alcestis* 918–22; see also Eur. *Suppliant Women* 990–98 (discussed below in the section entitled "Evadne"), *Trojan Women* 311–12, *Helen* 640, 1433–35.

[9] Cf. Menander Rhetor 2. 402. 26–403. 25; [Dionysius] *On Epideictic Speeches* 2. 265.

[10] The irony was suggested in part no doubt by the conception of the bridal journey as a journey to Hades (Seaford 1987, 106–7).

[11] Menander Rhetor 2. 404.27 *texete paidas humin te homoious kai en aretēi lamprous;* 407.9, 23; [Dionysius] *On Epideictic Speeches* 2. 266; Catullus 61.209–13 (cf. Hom. *Il.* 6.466–74), 214–18; 64.323–81 (hymeneal: cf. Aristophanes *Birds* 1734; Eur. *Iphigenia at Aulis* 1063), with 64.343–60; cf. Hom. *Il.* 6.480–81; Theocritus 18.21; Sidonius Apollinaris *Carmina* 15.191; cf. Hesiod *Works and Days* 235 (with West ad loc.); Seaford 1987, 126 n. 204.

even better), preeminent among the Trojans as a soldier and a ruler over Troy (*Iliad* 6. 476–81). But in her second exit Andromache dwells at length (22. 484–506) on the miserable, dishonored life that Astyanax will now lead if he survives the war with the Greeks (487; cf. 24. 726–35). Here another commonplace of the wedding ceremony has turned into its opposite. Further, not only has the wedding process been symbolically reversed, the whole household has been destroyed.

This account of the Homeric passage is confirmed by the fact that the ironic reversal of elements of wedding ritual, including the *makarismos* and the prayer for fine children like their parents, occurs frequently in tragedy. For example, in Euripides' *Andromache* Andromache herself hints at the failed *makarismos* of her wedding, and her abduction from Troy is presented as a cruel wedding procession in reverse.[12] Another example from Euripides is provided by Antigone in the *Phoenician Women*.

## Maenadic Antigone and Wedding Ritual

In Euripides' *Phoenician Women* Antigone appears with the bodies of her slaughtered mother and brothers and sings a monody that begins (1485–92):

> Not covering (*prokaluptomena*) the delicacy (*habra*) of my grapelike cheek, nor because of my maidenhood feeling shame (*aidomena*) at the crimson (*eruthēma*) under my eyes, the redness of my face, I am carried on, a maenad of the dead, throwing the covering from my hair, relinquishing the saffron luxury of the garment, led,[13] sighing much, by the dead.

Antigone shares much with Andromache. Told earlier to return from the city wall to her house (193–94), she emerges again and laments her nearest and dearest killed outside the wall and the complete destruction of her household (1504, etc.). She is in her grief-struck movement like a maenad and sheds her headdress in violent grief. The word *krēdemnon,* which occurs in both passages, is rare after the sixth cen-

[12] Seaford 1987 (for Andromache, see especially 129–30).

[13] See below, n. 17.

tury B.C.[14] No doubt Euripides was influenced by the Homeric passage.

One difference between the two cases is that Antigone is unmarried. Her place in the maidens' quarters is stressed throughout the play (89, 194, 1275, 1636). This allows what I believe to be an evocation, in Antigone's discarding of the veil, of the ceremony of the *anakaluptēria*, the unveiling of the bride at the wedding,[15] which seems to have occurred just before the bride's processional departure to her new home: hence the conjunction "I am carried on . . . throwing the covering" (*pheromai . . . krademna dikousa*) here.[16]

Furthermore, the movement referred to by *pheromai* is qualified by *hagemoneuma nekroisi polustonon*, "led,[17] sighing much, by the dead." This evokes the widespread association of bridal and funereal procession, of which the most famous example is provided by Antigone herself, in Sophocles.[18] And so the arrival of Antigone with her dead at the house to which she has been confined as a maiden is implicitly compared with three kinds of exit from the house: the exit of the maenad, the exit of the bride (after the *anakaluptēria*) for the procession to her new home, and the exit of the funeral procession for the tomb.[19]

Antigone is a virgin, and so her wedding is not (like Andromache's) *recalled* but symbolically *enacted*. However, as Antigone herself has

[14] There is, for instance, only one other example in tragedy (Eur. *Tro. Wom.* 508).

[15] Standard in the descriptions of the bride, sometimes in the wedding song, are delicacy (*habros*): cf., for example, Sappho frag. 44.7 (Voigt 1971) (of Andromache as bride); Sophocles *Trachinian Women* 523—hymeneal, see Seaford 1986b, 53; red coloring (*eruthēma*): Sappho frag. 105.1 (Voigt 1971); Theocritus 18.31; cf. Eur. *Cyclops* 515 (and Seaford 1984, ad loc.); the association of *aidōs* with the bridal veil: Pausanias 3.20.11; *ARV*² 1017.44—the moment after unveiling, it seems (Oakley 1982, 113–18); other vase paintings: Sutton 1981, 185, 186. The veil shed in the *anakaluptēria* seems to have been saffron in color (Cunningham 1984, 9–12; Seaford 1987, 124–25), like the one shed by Antigone here. And of the three other occurrences of *prokaluptein* / *prokalumma* in tragedy, two are the bridal veil (Eur. *Medea* 1147; Aesch. *Agamemnon* 691; Seaford 1987, 124).

[16] The same conjunction occurs in other ironic evocations in tragedy of the *anakaluptēria:* Aesch. *Ag.* 690–92, 1178–81; cf. 239; Soph. *Trach. Wom.* 56–57; Seaford 1987, 124–25.

[17] The usual translation is "leading." But in fact it seems to me that *hagemoneuma* is passive (like *phorēma,* for instance). Antigone is led (*pheromai*) by her dead kin (to the underworld), just as the bride is led by the groom to her new home (itself sometimes imagined as a journey to Hades: see n. 10 above).

[18] Soph. *Antigone* 804, 810–11, 816, 886, 891, 947, etc. Seaford 1987, 107–8.

[19] It may be that in all three exits the headdress was imagined as shed (maenads in vase painting are not veiled; mourning: Eur. *Andromache* 830; Homeric *Hymn to Demeter* 41; Hom. *Il.* 22.468) and that all three exits may have been independently associated with the dead (maenadic: see Seaford 1989a, 304; bridal: see n. 10 above), but this is very speculative.

stressed and will continue to stress,[20] the death of her kin means that she will not marry. Like Andromache's, her wedding is evoked (by the shedding of the veil) so as to be negated—in her case negated by the power of those funeral connotations that in actual life attached even to the exit of a normal bride and acquired reality in the funeral of an unmarried girl, who would normally be buried with connotations of a wedding (as is Antigone herself in Sophocles). It is as if here too, as in Sophocles, Antigone rejects marriage for a bridal-funereal journey to her dead kin.[21]

## Maenadism and Marriage Ritual

Both Andromache and Antigone are compared to maenads. The comparison is, I believe, in both cases based not only on the frenzied departure from the house but also on the destruction of the household expressed in the negation of wedding ritual. The aptness of the comparison will now emerge from a brief account of the relationship between maenadism and marriage.[22] (I mean here maenadism as *imagined* by the Greeks, in particular in myth.)[23]

Maenadism is antithetical in obvious respects to the *state* of marriage. Less obviously, it is antithetical also to the whole *process* by which girls become wives of citizens. Included in this process, at least in the classical period, was a type of premarital ritual, associated in particular with Artemis, by which the city-state prepared its girls for marriage. The girls leave their homes for a temporary stay in the wild periphery, in which they are imagined as animals to be "tamed" or "yoked" in marriage, and the performance of animal sacrifice is imagined as substituting for sacrifice of the girl. The implied female resistance to the yoke of marriage continues into the wedding ceremony itself.[24] Myths reflecting this process exhibit the tension between

20 *Phoenician Women* 1436–37, 1489–92, 1520, 1659, and 1671–81; cf. Soph. *Ant.* 891–904.

21 Seaford 1990, 76–78.

22 Brief, because I have described it in more detail (concentrating on Attica and Argos) in Seaford 1988.

23 I am not concerned here with the problem of the relationship between imagined and actually practiced maenadism.

24 Seaford 1987, 106–7.

Artemis' fierce demand for virginity and the mortal necessity of sex and marriage; a period, in the wild, of resistance to men ends in marriage (Atalanta, the Proetids) or sexual union (Callisto), which may be punished by death or metamorphosis into an animal.[25]

Maenads too leave home collectively for a rite of passage in the wild periphery, where they resist men, become like animals, and perform sacrifice. Hence the frequent association of Artemis with Dionysus.[26] But the two kinds of cult are also opposites. Maenads go to the mountainside not to reject all sexuality, for they give suck there (to animals), and Dionysus is called by Aeschylus a "yoker of maenads" and has a retinue of lascivious satyrs and so on.[27] They go rather to reject the males of their own household and polis. Accordingly, the Dionysiac thiasos contains married as well as unmarried women,[28] whose departure disrupts the household in different ways. In married women maenadism renews that centrifugal opposition to marriage that had supposedly been permanently overcome in their marital transition,[29] so that, for example, in the *Bacchae* the Theban maenads are compared (in a reversal of the image of yoking the girl in marriage) to fillies that have *left* the yoke.[30] This disruption may in myth take the irreversible form of killing offspring. In unmarried women permanent disruption is of the natal household and results from their sexual union with outsiders (Antiope, Erigone, Karya, the Proetids).[31] Accordingly, men try to confine maenads to the house.[32]

In the collective premarital cult of the polis the as-yet-untamed virgins in the wild are in a male-controlled, unrepeated liminal phase

[25] Even Iphigenia, who presides over the Brauronian preparation of girls for marriage, was in one version married (to Achilles).

[26] Seaford 1988, 125; Kolb 1981, 83 n. 20. The earliest example is Homer *Odyssey* 11. 325.

[27] Aeschylus frag. 382 (*TrGF* 3) *mainadōn zeuktērie;* Eur. *Bacch.* 699–702, with Dodds 1960, ad loc.; and Seaford 1988, 125–26.

[28] Note especially Eur. *Bacch.* 35 and 694; Seaford 1988, 126 n. 70.

[29] This means that the ultimate triumph of the negative tendencies of marriage ritual, which is characteristic of tragedy (Seaford 1987), may be called "Dionysiac" in a sense.

[30] Eur. *Bacch.* 1056; cf. Eur. *Helen* 543.

[31] Seaford 1988. The Proetids myth exhibits the contradiction between Dionysus and Artemis within itself, for in the Dionysiac version their eventual marriage destroys their father's realm, whereas in the version presided over by Hera and Artemis the royal household and city are saved.

[32] Eur. *Bacch.* 515 (to weave), 226–27, 231, and 443; note also Antiope, Ino (Hyginus *Fabulae* 4), Karya, and the Proetids; Seaford 1990.

that precedes and consolidates incorporation into the civilized state of marriage. Antithetically, initiation into the maenadic thiasos converts this transitional phase into a destination, to which unmarried and married women may constantly return. In actually practiced maenadism, although there may have been less male control than in premarital cult, the maenad would of course always return to her household. And precisely because of the threat he poses to the marital process Dionysus may be incorporated into it,[33] so that even such a threatening feature of maenadism as female military autonomy, for example,[34] was at Chios a prelude to peace and marriage.[35] In imagined maenadism, on the other hand, the departure (or return) of the women to the periphery produces a disruption that is permanent. Whereas the premarital sacrifice to Artemis of an animal in place of the girl may be projected in myth as the sacrifice of the girl herself (e.g., Iphigenia), for whom even in the myth an animal victim may be substituted, in maenadic myth this sacrifice is reversed into one in which the youthful victim is human, mistaken for the (young) animal. The youthful[36] Pentheus is sacrificed[37] by his maenadic mother, who mistakes him for a young animal, and is even imagined as a babe in her arms.[38] And similar Dionysiac killing of offspring occurs in other myths, most of them to

[33] See, for instance, Seaford 1988, 127 n. 71.

[34] See n. 5 above.

[35] Seleucus *apud* Harpocration, s.v. "Homeridai": "At the Chian Dionysia the women once went mad and did battle with the men, and they stopped fighting by exchanging bridegrooms and brides as hostages." This was no doubt enacted in some way in the festival.

[36] Eur. *Bacch.* 274, 330, 973–76, 985–86, 1226, 1254, 1308, and 1319.

[37] Eur. *Bacch.* 1114; Seaford 1988, 124; Seidensticker 1979, 181ff.

[38] Eur. *Bacch.* 1185–87, 969; Seaford 1981, 268 (cf. maenads attending to the adult head of Dionysus in its *liknon,* "cradle"). March 1989 has recently suggested that the killing of Pentheus by his mother was an innovation by Euripides. But this is most unlikely, given that (*a*) it is a general practice of Dionysus to inspire resisting women to kill their children; (*b*) Aristophanes' hypothesis to Eur. *Bacch,* says *hē muthopoia keitai par' Aiskhulōi en Penthei* (with this formula one expects Aristophanes to note differences by *plēn,* as in the hypothesis to Eur. *Phoen. Wom.*); (*c*) Eur. *Medea* 1282–84 *mian dē kluō mian tōn paros / gunaik' en philois khera balein teknois: / Inō* . . . does not mean (*pace* March) that Agave killing her son was as yet unknown (the aim of the chorus here is not precision, and apart from Agave they do not mention the well-known cases of Procne and of Aedon [Hom. *Od.* 19.518–23], for example); (*d*) we cannot affirm that in the *Medea* Euripides "innovated child-murder by a mother" (March 1989, 51), because we do not know all the versions of the myth (oral and written) before Euripides (and in fact in an early version that we do know something of—Eumelus'—Medea *did* kill her children, albeit unintentionally); and (*e*) similarly, we hardly know anything of the versions (oral and written) of the Agave myth before Euripides.

be found in what we know of fifth-century tragedy: the myths of the Minyads, the women of Argos, Ino, Procne, and Lycurgus.[39]

Whereas the sacrifice to Artemis allows the girl (in reality, as well as sometimes in myth) to be incorporated as wife into a household, the maenad's sacrifice of her offspring renders the disruption of her household irreversible. It expresses and confirms the permanence of her departure from it. Toward the end of the *Bacchae* Cadmus imagines the possibility of Agave remaining in her maenadic state, and so being spared the pain of realizing what she has done, but then proceeds to bring her out of this state by a series of questions, one of which, at a crucial stage of her emergence, reminds her of her identity by evoking her wedding procession (1273): "To what house did you come with your hymeneals?" And the very next question is about the son of her marriage. But, pathetically, she cannot of course reassume this identity. She must now leave the household. Restored to her senses, she takes her leave of household, of polis, and of her father. She calls herself *phugas ek thalamōn,* "a fugitive from the chambers," a phrase that connotes a reversal of the wedding process, a *departure* from the bridal chamber.[40]

But killing her son excludes her also, once brought to her senses, from the thiasos. She emphasizes, at the very end of the play, that she will leave maenadism to others (1366–70, 1386–87). But she does not know, as she leaves Thebes, where she is to go (1366–67, 1383). Between the conflicting collectivities of thiasos on the one hand and Thebes on the other she is finally isolated.

The daughters of Minyas, after their frenzied sacrifice of their offspring to Dionysus, are turned into birds,[41] like the maenadic infanticide Procne. This tragic metamorphosis assigns them permanently, disqualified as they are from civilization, to the realm of nature, but as lonely creatures of darkness—bat, owl, and the lamenting

[39] Minyads: Antoninus Liberalis 10 (they leave their homes and the polis); "like a fawn": Aelian *Varia historia* 3.42 (cf. Plutarch *Moralia* 299e); perhaps also in Aesch. *Xantriae*. Argos: Apollodorus 2.2.2 (= Hesiod *Catalogue of Women* frag. 131), 3.5.2. Ino: Ovid *Metamorphoses* 4. 523, a detail that may derive from Euripides *Ino* (cf. Hyginus *Fabulae* 4, "Ino Euripidis," and also, among others, Lucian *Dialogi meretricii* 9); scholia to Hom. *Od.* 5.334; Hyginus *Fabulae* 2 (Ino apotheosized by Dionysus). Procne: Ovid *Metamorphoses* 6.587–674; Soph. *Tereus* (especially frag. 586 [*TrGF* 4]; Kiso 1984, 67–68, 79–80). Lycurgus: Sutton 1975, 356–60 (Aesch. *Lycurgia*).

[40] 1370; cf. Eur. *Andr.* 103–9 (and Seaford 1987, 129–30).

[41] See especially Antonius Liberalis 10.

nightingale. Even Agave, in embracing the father from whom she must part, is compared to a swan.[42]

Thus we can see that the resemblances between Andromache and Antigone are shared also by the maenads with whom they are compared. All are confined by men in the house, from which they depart in a frenzy. Important in the case of each is the destruction of the household,[43] and each laments the death of her nearest and dearest. And because a household is constituted by marriage, in each case its destruction, and the consequent isolation of the female, is associated with the evocation and negation of the transition from maiden to wife. This conclusion must now be tested on further cases of the Dionysiac metaphor.

## Evadne

In Euripides' *Suppliant Women* Evadne reacts to her husband's death in battle by rushing from the house, in which she has been confined (even guarded),[44] in a "maenadic" frenzy: *pros d' eban dromas ex emōn oikōn ekbakkheusamena.*[45] Her wedding, like Andromache's, is recalled (990–94), but it is also, like Antigone's, enacted (or rather reenacted)—she is, for example, dressed as a bride and sings a wedding song (1025 *itō phōs gamoi te,* etc.) before triumphantly throwing herself onto the pyre for a union, described in erotic terms, with her dead husband. There is in fact the same subtle combination that we find in the *Phoenician Women* of bridal, funereal, and maenadic exit. But there is also a remarkable parallel to the combination of recalled wedding procession and reversed wedding *makarismos* that we found in the maenadic exit of Andromache. The first half of Evadne's opening strophe, which recalls her wedding procession and wedding *makarismos,* is mirrored by the second, which describes her maenadic depar-

[42] Eur. *Bacch.* 1363–65; Seaford 1988, 127 n. 75.

[43] Antigone: Eur. *Phoen. Wom.* 1496, 1504, etc. (also, Antigone will not now marry and continue the line with children); maenad: e.g., Eur. *Bacch.* 1250, 1304, 1308, 1313, 1374–76, etc.

[44] 1038–42. Though she is married, the house is her *father's*. This oddity allows a greater similarity with the bridal departure, and male (paternal) despair at her escape.

[45] 1000–1001; cf. *Fragmenta adespota* 645.9 (*TrGF* 2). At 1062 weaving is mentioned as a preoccupation to be expected of her.

ture for her husband's tomb to end her "painful life and the sufferings of her *aiōn*" (1004–5). The word *aiōn* means a *whole* life. The phrase makes sense when applied to Evadne only[46] as a negation of the wedding *makarismos*. The *olbos* desiderated by the *makarismos* is permanent: it depends on a successfully completed *aiōn*.[47] But the death of her husband has, as in Andromache's case, revealed the true nature of Evadne's *aiōn:* it can now be seen as one of suffering (*aiōnos ponous*). Despite the element of triumph in this reenactment of her wedding, Evadne was after all not blessed (*olbia*), and the wedding *makarismos* failed. Similarly, the speed of her maenadic exit (1000–1001 *dromas ex emōn oikōn*)[48] reenacts but reverses the speed of her bridal departure (993 *ōkuthoā numphā*). Here again the maenadic departure from home is associated with the evocation and negation of the bridal transition and the destruction of her (marital and natal)[49] households.

## Iole

The triumphant but pathetic speed of Evadne's maenadic progress reenacts and contrasts with the joyful speed of her bridal progress.[50] A similar irony reappears in the Sophoclean description, in a clearly hymeneal context,[51] of Heracles' violent leading of Iole, a swift bride (*thoan numphan*) from Oechalia:[52] the joyful urgency of the wedding procession here becomes the ruthless urgency of the conqueror.[53] This same combination of the wedding with the brutal abduction of Iole

[46] Collard's comment (1975, 2:367: "Ev.'s whole life has not been full of *ponoi,* but only since the recent death of Cap.; her statement is exaggerated to suit the *sententia* 1006–8") misses this point. Cf. Seaford 1987, 121–22.

[47] Cf., for instance, Aesch. *Ag.* 928–29; Herodotus 1.32; Soph. *Trach. Wom.* 1–3.

[48] Cf. 1038–39 *domōn exōpios / bebēke pēdēsasa.*

[49] 1095; cf. 1133. Evadne also offends against the spirit of the classical polis as expressed in the funerary legislation (attributed, in Athens, to Solon).

[50] Other examples of the speed of the bridal procession are Sappho frags. 44.11 and 23(?) (Voigt 1971); Eur. *Helen* 724.

[51] Seaford 1987, 128–29; note especially the agency of Aphrodite, which was important at a normal wedding.

[52] Soph. *Trach. Wom.* 857–61; cf. also 841–43, where we should probably retain *aoknon:* Seaford 1987, 129.

[53] There may have been, for the bride, an element of this ruthless urgency even in the normal wedding procession: Seaford 1987, 106–7.

from the conquered city reappears, in the same hymeneal context,[54] in Euripides' *Hippolytus:*

> Aphrodite yoked the Oechalian filly, the previously unyoked virgin, from her father's house running like a naiad and a maenad (*bakkhān*), and gave her, with blood and with smoke, in a murderous wedding, to Herakles. O excessive (*tlamōn*) in his/her wedding.[55]

The maenadic image here is apt obviously because the girl runs, and so do maenads, but also for two other reasons. First, because it is specifically to avoid the male yoke that she runs, like Helen in Euripides' *Helen* running from the "wild man" (in fact her husband) "like a running filly or a maenad of the god."[56] Second, because her "wedding" is violently destructive. It is significant that the word *bakkhan* ("maenad") introduces the theme of the wedding celebrated with blood and smoke. Maenads cause violent destruction, and the smoke of their torches is well known.[57]

Returning to the Sophoclean passage, we find the irony that Heracles' "wedding" with Iole means the destruction of her new household as well as of her old one.[58] And so it is too, surely, in the strikingly similar passage in the *Hippolytus,*[59] where the word order gives the

[54] Here too (cf. n. 51) the agent of the disastrous transition is Aphrodite.

[55] 545–54 *tan men Oikhaliai / pōlon azuga lektrōn, / anandron to prin kai anumphon oikōn / zeuxas' ap' Eurutiōn* (Buttman; *apeiresian* MSS) */dromada naid' hopōs te bakkhan sun haimati sun kapnōi / phonioisi numpheiois* (Barrett; *phoniois th' humenaiois* MSS) / *Alkmēnas tokōi Kupris exedōken; ō / tlamōn humenaiōn.*

[56] Eur. *Helen* 543–45 *hōs dromaia pōlos ē bakkhē theou.* Cf. Eur. *Bacch.* 1056. Conceivably the Dionysiac metaphor is inspired also by the "tomb" (544); cf. n. 19 above. But this is merely speculative.

[57] E.g., Soph. *Ant.* 1126–27; cf. Eur. *Bacch.* 144–46; *Ion* 550; Aesch. *Xantriae* frag. 171 (*TrGF* 3); and see the section entitled "Cassandra" below. Vase painting: Arias, Hirmer, and Shefton 1962, 372–73.

[58] Soph. *Trach. Wom.* 842–43 and 893–95; Seaford 1987, 128–29. The death of Herakles is described in terms of erotic union: 662, 767–68, and 833; Seaford 1986b, 56.

[59] This ambiguity (missed entirely by Barrett 1964) strengthens the allusion to the destruction of Theseus' household: the same irony of the arrival of the bride bringing catastrophe (also in a triangular situation) occurs in the very next song, with Phaedra herself as bride: 755–56 *eporeusas eman anassan olbiōn ap' oikōn / kakonumphotaton onasin.* And if Renate Schlesier is right to regard 215–22 as maenadic (see pp. 108–10 of her essay in this volume), then Phaedra is another *maenadic* bride destroying the household. Another catastrophic bridal arrival is Helen's: Eur. *Andr.* 103–4.

impression that the resistance of the "maenad" has brought death, that the violence used by Heracles to master his maenadic bride has somehow destroyed *him,* so that he and his bride are each *tlamōn*[60] in the wedding. The yoking of the girl, which is a feature of normal marriage, has disastrously failed. And so the maenadic image is here again associated with the destruction of the household through the reversal or negation of the marital transition (here the taming process in that transition).

## Cassandra

Comparable to Iole is Cassandra in Euripides' *Trojan Women*. In her brief appearance before being taken off to the ships as Agamemnon's "bride" she is constantly compared to a maenad.[61] In maenadic fashion, she appears from within at a frenzied run: *mainas thoazei deuro Kassandra dromōi* (307). But there is, once again, more to the Dionysiac metaphor than that.

First, like a maenad (see n. 57), she carries torches. Whereas the destructive power of the maenadic torch was merely implicit in the *Hippolytus* passage, here it creates alarm.[62] Hecuba, when asked to catch the Bacchic girl (342 *bakkheuousan ou lēpsēi korēn;*), removes her torches from her with a bitter reflection on the distinction between wedding torches and maenadic torches, which Cassandra has in her maenadic enactment of a wedding confused.[63]

Second, not only does the "wedding" of Cassandra occur along with the destruction of her natal family, but it will also, Cassandra three times stresses (359, 364, 461), destroy completely the household (*domous, oikous*) of her husband. In this dual destruction she resembles Iole and (more remotely) Evadne. Similarly, in the *Iliad* Andromache stresses, before losing her husband as well, that all her natal family has been killed.[64]

[60] The adjective *tlamōn* means both "suffering" and "going too far."

[61] 307, 342–43, 349, 367, 408, 415, and 500. Also at Eur. *Hecuba* 121, 676; *Alexandros* frag. 7 (Snell).

[62] 298–99 and 342–43 (cf. 344–51).

[63] 343–49: *ou gar ortha purphoreis mainas thoazousa,* etc.

[64] 6.429–30: "Hector, but you are my father and honored mother and brother, and you are my sturdy husband."

Third, she utters a wedding *makarismos* more bitter even than Andromache's and Evadne's.[65] Like Evadne's it is both pathetic and seriously meant, even triumphant. The pathos is that both bride and groom will be killed. But the triumph is the ghastly joy of revenge on the groom.[66]

Here again, then, the maenadic image is associated with a marital transition that brings not life but death and destruction to the bride, groom, and the whole household.[67] And we also find the same combination of bridal, funereal, and maenadic exit that we found with the Euripidean Antigone and Evadne.[68]

## Three Generalizations

On the basis of these and other examples, which we are about to survey, it is possible to make some general observations about the fluidity in tragedy between the Dionysiac metaphor and actual Dionysiac frenzy, and the range of the metaphor's application in tragedy. Of course exceptions to these generalizations exist, and we will consider those, too, briefly.

First, the metaphor and actual frenzy. The Dionysiac metaphor may easily pass into the frenzy actually inspired by Dionysus.[69] For example, Clytemnestra, who in at least one and probably two places in the *Oresteia* attracts the Dionysiac metaphor (basically because she kills kin),[70] is in vase painting (probably inspired by tragedy) actually dressed as a maenad.[71] The story of Procne killing her own children,

[65] 311–13, 327, and 336.

[66] 340, 353–54, 359–60, 404–5, and 460–61.

[67] It is in fact not only wedding ritual that will be subverted: Cassandra knows well that she will also be denied death ritual, thrown out to be a lonely prey for the wild animals (448–50).

[68] 445 (*en Haidou numphiōi gēmōmetha*), 344, 351–52, 449, and 455–57. The ironic wedding of Cassandra and Agamemnon (in death) is a constant theme of Aeschylus' *Agamemnon:* Seaford 1987, 127–28.

[69] Just as it often combines with frenzy inspired by another deity (Cassandra by Apollo, Heracles by Lyssa, Orestes by the Furies).

[70] Aesch. *Ag.* 1235 (quoted, n. 76 below), reading Weil's emendation: *Haidou mainad';* the phrase *bakkheias kakēs* at Aesch. *Libation Bearers* 698 refers to Clytemnestra; see Seaford 1989a.

[71] Seaford 1989a, 305.

serving them to her husband, and being turned into a nightingale (he into a hoopoe) was the theme of Sophocles' lost play *Tereus*. Procne seems a prime candidate for the Dionysiac metaphor. But it seems that in the play, as in Ovid, she was actually dressed as a maenad for a Dionysiac festival (see the section "Maenadism and Marriage Ritual" above). It seems that in Euripides' lost *Ino* Agave's sister Ino was an actual maenad and also (although perhaps not simultaneously) the killer of her own child (see the same section above).

An interesting case of this fluidity between metaphor and reality is provided by Antigone. At the end of the play the Dionysiac metaphor (discussed above) is followed by a passage in which Oedipus tells Antigone to go where Dionysus and the maenads' precinct are in the mountains (Euripides *Phoenician Women* 1751–53). Antigone rejects this, saying that her previous maenadism in the mountains won no favor from the gods.[72] This sudden mention of maenadism may perplex. But one function of the passage, whether or not it is interpolated (or misplaced), seems to be to assimilate the extreme desolation of Antigone to that of, say, Agave, who at the end of the *Bacchae* (1383–87), faced like Antigone with exile from Thebes after the destruction of her household, emphatically puts maenadism behind her as well. We will see in due course (in the section "Tragedy: A Dionysiac Pattern") that the passage has another function, and that as it seems in Euripides' lost *Antigone* Antigone actually appeared as a maenad. There is a difference, however, between the *Bacchae* and the *Phoenician Women*. In the former the maenadic frenzy of Agave destroyed her household, whereas the (metaphorical) maenadic frenzy of Antigone in the latter was a *response* to the destruction of her household. This distinction brings me to my second general point.

The Euripidean Heracles is said several times, when killing his children, to be in a Bacchic frenzy,[73] and when he comes to his senses he asks whether in his Bacchic frenzy he destroyed the home (*oikos*).[74] But at the onset of his madness he is asked whether his Bacchic frenzy resulted from the killing of his enemies (Lycus et al.): 966–67 *ou ti pou*

[72] Or reading *ge* after *kharin* in 1757 and ending the question with *anekhoreusa,* Antigone says that for her to resume her maenadism would be to give thankless service to the gods.

[73] Eur. *Heracles* 966, 1085, 1119, 1122. Note also 896–97. A model for a *father* inspired by Dionysus to kill his children is the myth of Lycurgus, dramatized by Aeschylus.

[74] 1142: the text is corrupt, but the sense is clear: *ē gar sunērax' oikon ē bakkheus' emon?*

*phonos s'ebakkheusen nekrōn hous arti kaineis?* This means that Bacchic frenzy may be imagined either as a cause or as a result of slaughter. It is as a *result* of killing his mother that Orestes suffers the "Bacchic frenzy" inflicted on him by the Furies;[75] but in one of the three passages in which the metaphor occurs something more is implied: line 411, *hautai se bakkheuousi suggenē phonon,* suggests an intimate, internal connection between kin killing and Dionysiac frenzy. C. W. Willink (1986, 153) comments that "the polluting 'blood' is not simply the *cause* of the punitive 'madness' but also its *essence.*"

And so our metaphor may cover the states of mind that precede, accompany, and follow the killing of kin and destruction of the household. Clytemnestra is "a maenad of Hades, and breathing truceless Ares on her kin. And how, all-daring, she raised the cry of triumph, as if at the turning-point of battle!"[76] It is as "a maenad of Hades" that she kills Agamemnon. And the cry of triumph in battle is typical of a maenad,[77] as is the idea of breathing violence against kin.[78] This latter is one element, along with the illicit sexual relationship (with Aegisthus) and the destruction of the household, in Clytemnestra's *continuing* "wicked Bacchic revel in the house," which is denounced in the *Libation Bearers* (698; see n. 70), a state that involves hostility to her own children, a kind of frenzy that can be "cured"[79] only by the matricide. Here the wicked maenadism threatens to be permanent.

The maenadic exit of Antigone in the *Phoenician Women* is a reaction to the death of kin and the destruction of the household, as is the "Bacchic" song (*nomon bakkheion*) sung by Hecuba over the dead body of her only surviving son, Polydorus (Euripides *Hecuba* 686–87). The flight from reality characteristic of Dionysiac frenzy may also be found in the immediate reaction to bereavement.[80] Polydorus has, his mother complains, been cut up (716 *diamoirasō*)—a rare verb certainly

[75] Eur. *Orestes* 339, 411, and 835. This is one element in the application of the maenadic metaphor to the Furies themselves (Aesch. *Eum.* 500). Pursued by the Furies to Athens, Orestes participates in the Dionysiac Anthesteria (Eur. *Iphigenia at Tauris* 941–60, etc.).

[76] Aesch. *Ag.* 1235–37 *Haidou mainad'* (Weil; *mēter'* MSS) *aspondon t' Arē* (Franz; *aran* MSS)/*philois pneousan. hōs d'epōloluxato/hē pantotolmos, hōsper en makhēs tropēi.* See Seaford 1989a.

[77] See nn. 5 and 85.

[78] Cf. Soph. *Ant.* 136–37; Eur. *Bacch.* 1094, *Phoen. Wom.* 789 and 794 (and n. 87 below).

[79] 699 *iatros.* Maenadism may be "cured": see, for example, Apollodorus 2.2.2.

[80] Note, for instance, Eur. *Hec.* 689: *apist' apista,* etc.; de Martino 1958, 151–56.

associated later in the play (and elsewhere) with Dionysiac ritual dismemberment (*sparagmos*).[81] Hecuba's frenzied lament turns into the fierce desire for revenge on the Thracian Polymestor, who (like Dionysus' Thracian enemy Lycurgus) is blinded, as his children are torn apart by the "maenads of Hades" (1077 *bakkhais Haidou diamoirasai*), the mothers (1157 *tokades*),[82] who at first behave like nurses and then draw swords—a contradiction typical of maenads.[83]

In the *Hecuba,* then, the Dionysiac metaphor applies both to the reaction to the dismemberment of offspring and to the dismemberment of the children in revenge. Similarly, the maenadism of Cassandra is both a frenzied reaction to the destruction of her natal family and a frenzied prophecy of the destruction she will wreak in revenge on her new household as a maenadic bride. Much the same is true of Iole. And the maenadism of Evadne is also both a frenzied reaction to loss and the frenzy that accompanies further destruction—the suicide that leaves her father lamenting the desolation (*erēmia*) of his household (see n. 49).

I have to this point referred, with four exceptions, to every person who in Homer or Greek tragedy attracts the Dionysiac metaphor: Andromache, Antigone, Evadne, Hecuba and her women, Helen, Heracles, Ino, Iole, Cassandra, Clytemnestra, Orestes, and Procne. In every case (except that of Helen) there is destruction of the household,[84] just as there is when the frenzy is actually inspired by Dionysus

[81] Eur. *Hec.* 1077; *OF* 210; I am indebted in the analysis of this passage to Schlesier 1988b, 129. The theme is prefigured a little earlier (656) in the picture of a Spartan mother lamenting for her son and tearing her cheeks (*sparagmos*). *Sparagmos* occurs elsewhere in Euripides (outside the *Bacchae*) only of the frenzied actions of the "maenadic" Antigone (*Phoen. Wom.* 1525) and the "maenadic" Cassandra (*Tro. Wom.* 453).

[82] The term *tokas* usually refers to the mothers of animals and occurs elsewhere of humans only with regard to "the mother of Bacchus" (Eur. *Hippolytus* 560). This suggests the animal nature of the maenads (see the section above entitled "Maenadism and Marriage Ritual"). With the phrase *hosai de tokades ēsan* (1157) compare Eur. *Bacch.* 35–36 *hosai gunaikes ēsan* (of maenads).

[83] E.g., Eur. *Bacch.* 699–701, 733, 752, etc.; Apollodorus 3.5.2; n. 5 above; maenads are imagined as nurses of Dionysus.

[84] This is not to say that, conversely, kin killing and the destruction of the household always attract the Dionysiac metaphor. A notable exception is the Euripidean Medea—although Seneca's repeated comparison of Medea to a maenad (*Medea* 383, 806, and 849) presumably derives from Greek tragedy. Medea is an exception perhaps because she, horrifically, *means* to kill her own children. The metaphor occurs of Demeter *reunited* with her daughter at line 386 of the Homeric *Hymn to Demeter.* As well as "rushing," Demeter is a female without a male, recalcitrant, isolated, and wandering, her veil torn. The metaphor

(Agave, Lycurgus, etc.). And in five instances the destruction of the household is expressed in the evocation and negation of wedding ritual: Andromache, Antigone, Evadne, Iole, Cassandra.

As for the four exceptions, even they confirm that the metaphor is almost always more complex than it seems. First, Aeschylus calls Io a maenad of Hera (*Suppliant Women* 564 *thuias Hēras*). Given the well-known opposition between the goddess of marriage and Dionysus, the actual or potential enemy of marriage (see n. 94 below), the phrase "maenad of Hera" is an oxymoron. Io is maenadic because she wanders, apparently unceasingly, as an animal, in a god-sent frenzy far from home, avoiding contact with the male. She is a "maenad of Hera" because in this case it is paradoxically Hera who, although goddess of marriage, is trying to preserve Io's virginity by sending her off in a frenzy.

Second, in Aeschylus' *Seven against Thebes* a warrior attacking Thebes "raves like a Bacchant" (498 *bakkhai . . . thuias hōs*). Here the point of comparison is not just the frenzy of war (*entheos d' Arei*) but also the snakes (around his shield) and the triumphant war cry—both characteristic of maenadism,[85] as well as the "military" defeat of the selfsame city of Thebes by Dionysus and his maenads.[86] This last point also underlies our third case, from Sophocles' *Antigone:* Capaneus is "in a Bacchic frenzy" (*bakkheuōn*) as he rushes against Thebes with the maenadic attributes of war cry and destructive torch (133–37).[87] Finally, in Aeschylus' *Seven against Thebes* (836) the chorus applies to itself the word *thuias* when lamenting the fratricidal slaughter of the royal Theban brothers. Although it is uncertain here that *thuias* by itself is Dionysiac, this is a passage to which I will return.

## Dionysus, Household, and Polis

The connection between Dionysus as destroyer of the household and Dionysus as a god of the whole polis, I suggest, provides a basis

---

may also subtly qualify the joy of reunion: Persephone will in fact have to leave her mother to return to Hades.

[85] Eur. *Bacch.* 1133; Seaford 1988, 134; Seaford 1989a, 303; cf. my discussion above at the beginning of the section entitled "Three Generalizations."

[86] Aesch. *Eum.* 25–26; Eur. *Bacch.* 52; and the other references given above in n. 5.

[87] Eur. *Phoen. Wom.* 783–800 exploits the similarities and differences between martial and Dionysiac frenzy, again in the attack of the Seven against Thebes.

for understanding historically the place of the Dionysiac metaphor in Homer on the one hand and in Greek tragedy on the other. Whereas in Homer Hector explicitly reserves war for men as he instructs Andomache to return to house and weaving, in tragedy the Thebans are militarily defeated by the maenads, who have left house and weaving. The threat of frenzied female confusion of the gender division basic to the polis must be contained. It must therefore be embodied so as to be propitiated, and the god employed to embody it is Dionysus.[88] Just as Apollo both sends and heals illness,[89] so Dionysus both threatens the gender division of the polis and is consequently propitiated and honored by the whole polis: "He wishes to have collective honors from all."[90]

All festivals of the polis draw the worshipers from their homes, thereby transcending the division into the households of which the polis is composed. But with Dionysus this function is especially prominent. He is to be worshiped by the citizens "in the streets . . . all mixed up together"—*ammiga pantas,* as the Delphic oracle quoted by Demosthenes has it (*Against Meidias* 52). Moreover, the tendency of the house-

[88]Dionysus is older than the polis. What qualifies him for his role in the polis is, at least in part, his earlier association with the thiasos, a body that seems to represent a survival, in a modified form, of an ancient cultic and *social* unit distinct from the household on the one hand and the emergent polis on the other: see, among others, Gernet and Boulanger 1970, 123; Seaford 1981. (This view is, I believe, confirmed by the range of application of the word *thiasos* in the classical period.) As well as being outside household and polis, the ancient thiasos contained features that were later used to express its symbolic function in the polis: initiation into it involved the ritual disorientation and the ritual death needed as rites of separation before entry into the new group, and these came to acquire new significance as the frenzy required to destroy the household by killing offspring. The secret ritual of the thiasos remains at the heart of the democratic festival of Dionysus, a combination that underlies the contrast expressed at Eur. *Bacch.* 860–61: *en telei theos / deinotatos, anthrōpoisi d'ēpiōtatos* (*telos* here means "initiation ritual"; Seaford 1981).

[89]Burkert 1985, 146–47 and 267. The ambiguity of Dionysus is well known (see, for example, Eur. *Bacch.* 860–61, quoted in n. 88). An example not cited is Pausanias 2. 23.7 (having warred against Perseus, Dionysus laid aside his hostility and was greatly honored by the Argives). Henrichs 1990 has recently driven too firm a wedge between the benign and the dangerous Dionysus.

[90]Eur. *Bacch.* 209 *ex hapantōn bouletai timas ekhein koinas.* Cf., for instance, Ovid *Metamorphoses* 3. 529–30 *turba ruit, mixtaeque vires matresque nurusque / vulgusque proceresque ignota ad sacra feruntur.* Dionysus in general creates concord in place of civil strife: Diodorus Siculus 3.66. He is at home in the *agora:* Kolb 1981. He is in various cities variously entitled Polites, Arkhegetes, Demoteles, Demosios, ho pro poleōs, Kathegemon, Saotes, Aisumnetes: Farnell 1909, 135–38; Privitera 1970, 36.

hold to self-sufficiency is opposed by Dionysus not only on the streets but within the household itself. I am thinking here not just of the well-known stories of the god driving from out their homes the women who resist him, but also (for example) of the annual sexual union of Dionysus with the wife of the "king archon" in what was believed to be the ancient royal palace ([Aristotle] *Constitution of the Athenians* 3.5). The invasion of the royal household by a publicly escorted[91] stranger who symbolically destroys its potential autonomy by having sex with the "king archon's" wife is of benefit, it is clear from a source dating to the fourth century B.C.,[92] to the whole polis.

Three weeks before this event the sacred marriage of Zeus and Hera, king and queen, celebrated at the Theogamia, benefited Athens in an antithetical way, by marking (it seems) the season for the marriages of citizens.[93] Dionysus and Hera are of course natural enemies.[94] Plutarch associates the careful separation of their rituals with Hera's roles as goddess of marriage and leader of the bride in the wedding.[95] When we do find Zeus, Hera, and Dionysus together, in Lesbos in the seventh century B.C., it is in a sanctuary (*temenos*) that, Alcaeus tells us, the Lesbians founded as "conspicuous, great, and common (*xunon*)."[96] Dionysus is honored there as Omestes, "raw-eater." The eating of raw food that puts him outside civilization is here combined with the divine embodiment (in Zeus and Hera) of the civilized idea of marriage, so as to create a sanctuary for the whole community. The frequently noted role of Dionysus as "the Other" badly needs a *historical* explanation. By a familiar mechanism,[97] the power of Dionysus to unite the community derives in part from his coming from outside it, as he does for his sacred marriage.

At Patrae this mechanism is unusually explicit. There Dionysus was

[91] See Jameson in this volume, pp. 54–56.

[92] [Demosthenes] *Against Neaera* 73.

[93] Seaford 1988, 128.

[94] Seaford 1988, 126 n. 66.

[95] Plutarch frag. 157 (Sandbach 1969) = frag. 78 (Tresp 1914), *apud* Eusebius *Praeparatio evangelica* 3.1.2.

[96] Alcaeus frag. 129 (Voigt 1971); cf. Sappho frag. 17 (Voigt 1971). The adjective *xunon* presumably means "common to all the people" (cf., for example, *SIG*[3] no. 1044. 29: *to de temenos einai [koi]non*) but could conceivably mean "common to the three gods."

[97] Cf. Burkert 1985, 260: "Once again the community creates its solidarity through the veneration of one who does not belong to it."

honored as Aisumnetes,[98] a term implying impartial power over all. During his festival images of the god are brought to his sanctuary, each image being named after one of the three ancient cities from which Patrae was composed. His attendants are an equal number of men and women elected by and from the whole people (Pausanias 7.20.1 *ek pantōn ho dēmos,* etc.). The aetiological myth of his cult is as follows. Prevented from marrying by their parents, a young couple have sex in the sanctuary of Artemis, with the result that they are sacrificed, as is thereafter the fairest couple every year. This practice of sacrificing the marriageable young was to cease only when an outside (*xenos*) king came bearing an outsider (*xenikos*) deity. This turns out to be King Eurypylus, who had been frenzied by an image of Dionysus Aisumnetes but was to find a new home where the people offered a strange (*xenos*) sacrifice. And so when he arrives at Patrae (by sea, like Dionysus for his sacred marriage) his frenzy and the human sacrifice are ended, and the cult of Dionysus Aisumnetes is installed. The whole polis makes Dionysus, the impartial outsider, its own and thereby may reproduce itself through the civilized institution of marriage without sacrificing the young.[99]

There is a similar relationship between Dionysus coming from outside and the sacrifice of the young at Megara.[100] Here a founder of the city is Alcathous, who after killing a lion builds a temple to Artemis and Apollo and with the help of Apollo builds the city wall. The pattern of killing followed by the incorporation of deity is then repeated, but with the violence this time of an opposite kind, directed not outwards, at a wild animal, but inwards, at Alcathous' own son, whom he kills in anger because the young man was disrupting a sacrifice (i.e., he kills him at the altar). To purify Alcathous of the murder there comes to Megara an outsider, Polyidus, great-grandson of the Dionysiac priest Melampous, who came from outside to purify the Argive Proetids. Polyidus also builds at Megara a temple of Di-

[98] The cult was an ancient one: see Privitera 1970, 32–33. Information on myth and cult is from Pausanias 7.19–21.

[99] The people of Patrae had also introduced an image of Dionysus from Calydon, where the god had imposed frenzy on the Calydonians after his priest had been resisted by a girl he loved, and demanded that the girl be sacrificed to him. The priest sacrificed himself instead, and the girl committed suicide (Pausanias 7.21.1–5). This represents the reverse side of Dionysus' power (frenzy and death replace marriage), safely located in another city.

[100] Pausanias 1.41–43. Cf. Bohringer 1980.

onysus Patroios. The crisis produced by a parent killing a child is here resolved in the introduction from outside of the cult of the god who so often inspires that very act, and who becomes as Patroios a deity of the whole polis. To take another example, in the myth preserved in detail in the *Bacchae* parental killing of offspring in the royal family is, again, followed by the installation of the outsider god to be honored by the whole polis (39–40, 209–10, etc.).

In embodying the communal principle of the polis Dionysus is a potential destroyer of the household, presenting a latent threat to the tendency of the household to autonomy. Whereas in *ritual* the threat is heeded, in the controlled temporary disruption of the royal marriage to the benefit of the whole polis, in *myth* the threat is generally imagined as realized, in the permanent disruption of the household by the horror of intrafamilial killing, a horror that warns that the god must be honored.

This communality of the polis is established at the expense of women, who, without power in the public sphere, were easily imagined as adhering excessively to the household and as resisting their public powerlessness. These two female threats to the polis may seem antithetical to each other, the one a rejection of the public sphere, the other an attempt to control it. But the Homeric Andromache, for example, combines them: it is out of exclusive concern for her household, which contrasts and conflicts with Hector's sense of public duty, that Andromache threatens to confuse, spatially and functionally, the gender division of the polis. And so the threat she presents attracts the Dionysiac metaphor: it is as if inspired by Dionysus.

Normally, in ritual, Dionysus as god of communality draws women out of the household, inspiring them with a temporary, controlled resistance to public gender division. In this way he counters the two antithetical threats to the polis—offsetting excessive adherence to the household by bringing the women out from their homes, and gender confusion by bringing them out for only a temporary, controlled period. Because he is honored by the whole polis, Dionysus both presents a latent threat to the household and, if deprived of that honor, will destroy the gender division on which the polis is based. Indeed, if Dionysus is resisted, both threats are activated. Female adherence to the household is violently reversed by a frenzy in which women leave their homes and even destroy their families. And this frenzy also endangers male control of the public sphere. In the Theban myth these two reversals of female adherence to the household culminate together in the killing of Pentheus, which, because Pentheus is ruler as well as offspring, means both the destruction of the household and the final victory of the maenads over the men.[101]

At the end of the *Bacchae* the royal household has, with help from the god, destroyed itself, with its surviving members to be exiled. But the polis is to benefit (it is now to be endowed with the salutary cult of Dionysus). This pattern, which may be called Dionysiac, reappears in tragedy (again in Thebes) in the three successive disasters of the family of Oedipus, each of which, as we are about to see, involves Dionysus in his role as the enemy of familial introversion, a role he performs through his sexuality, his liberation of women, or his imposition of frenzied self-destruction.

## Tragedy: A Dionysiac Pattern

First, and very briefly, in Sophocles' *Oedipus the King,* as in the *Bacchae,* the salvation of the polis is linked to the self-destruction of the royal household. As so often, in reality and particularly in myth, the tendency of the household or clan to autonomy takes the form of endogamy.[102] Dionysus is accordingly the enemy of endogamy.[103] And so the chorus's fantasy, just before the catastrophe, that (apparently) Oedipus might turn out to be the son of Dionysus is the direct opposite of the truth. Dionysus has the same significance in the same

[101] The Argive myth contains all these elements, but not in the same combination. In the surviving versions of the Minyads myth the maenadic Minyads are opposed by other maenads, but male opposition does occur in the associated ritual (Plutarch *Moralia* 299e–f).

[102] Seaford 1990. A famous example from Greek history is the Corinthian Bacchiads (Herodotus 5.92). Endogamy and its extreme manifestation as incest (and even endocannibalism) are practices both of tragic kings (*turannoi*) and of the *turannos* in political thought: Plato *Republic* 571c and 619b; Diogenes Laertius 1.96 (Periander sleeps with his mother, significantly named Crateia). Incest and endocannibalism: Clymenos and Harpalyke (Hyginus *Fabulae* 206; Euphorion frag. 26 [Powell 1925]); Thyestes and Pelopia (Hyginus *Fabulae* 88); Uranos and Gaea; the sons of Aegyptus (Aesch. *Suppliant Women* 223–26); Plato *Republic* 571c; cf. Tereus and Philomela and others. Cf. Lévi-Strauss 1972, 105. In Eur. *Bacch.* Agave intends to eat what is in fact Pentheus (1184 and 1242), and an incestuous link between the two is suggested by 812 (cf. 223), taken together with 966–70. Cf Zeitlin 1990b.

[103] Seaford 1990 and 1988.

position (in an optimistic choral song just before the catastrophe) in Sophocles' *Antigone,* as we shall soon see.

Then there are Oedipus' children. In Aeschylus' *Seven against Thebes* King Eteocles, with the enemy at the gates, tries to stop the female chorus running around in flight (191). It is as if the Thebans are being destroyed (194 *porthoumetha*) from within by their own women, he says, and he insists on the spatial and functional division between men and women (200–201), unsuccessfully ordering them inside (201). But in the end he will be lamented by the same chorus, "maenadic" in their frenzy over the bodies of "self-slaughtering" brothers.[104] The city, however, has been saved. The contrast between the salvation of the city and the mutual killing of the royal brothers is stressed twice.[105] The family, it is emphasized several times, has been destroyed.[106] Laius would have saved the polis by having no offspring.[107] Accordingly, the polis is now saved only through the destruction of his line,[108] and this ends the trilogy. The myth, in other versions of which the family in fact lives on, has been reshaped to the Dionysiac pattern.[109] Moreover, the crisis of the play, the point at which Eteocles goes out to fight his brother, is marked by a Dionysiac metaphor that, once again, has not been understood.

"The Fury of the black goatskin will go out from the house when

[104] 836 (but cf. the section above entitled "Three Generalizations"); *autoktonos/ōs* (681, 734, 805) refers to the *reflexive* aspect of kin killing.

[105] 811–17, 820–21; perhaps at 804 as well (see below). Hutchinson 1985 deletes 820–21. But his only objections are the inept ones that *polis sesōtai* is "intolerably abrupt and bare" (here stylistic insensitivity combines with the failure to understand the issue of the city's salvation) and that *basileus* is "reserved in fifth-century tragedy for actual monarchs" (this fails to take account of the way in which the brothers are in this part of the play associated with each other—note the dual in 820—almost to the point of identity; consider 681, for example, as well as the importance of the contrast here between the *royal* household and the polis). Lines 820–21 may originally have been between 803 and 805. Certainly, to delete 804 (with Hutchinson 1985) leaves 803 oddly unanswered until 815. Finally, even were the lines interpolated, this would hardly affect my argument, which is not specifically about Aeschylus.

[106] 689–91, 801–2, 813, 828 (*ateknous* should not of course be changed), 877, 880, and 953–60.

[107] 748–49 *thnaskonta genn/as ater sōizein polin.*

[108] Note especially 801–2. This logic (somewhat perverse, it is true) escapes those who see in it a reference to saving Thebes from the Epigoni (see Hutchinson 1985, ad loc.).

[109] Although the old myth may reappear in interpolations: see, for instance, Hutchinson 1985, ad 903. Cf. Antigone claiming to be the last of the royal clan (Soph. *Ant.* 941) and so ignoring Ismene.

the gods receive sacrifice from hands" (699–700 *Melanaigis exeisi domōn Erinus hotan ek kherōn theoi thusian dekhōntai*). These words of the chorus fail to affect Eteocles. In the *Eumenides* (500) Aeschylus bestows the maenadic metaphor on the Furies persecuting Orestes. Similarly, in Euripides' *Orestes* the Furies impose a "Bacchic" frenzy on the matricidal Orestes.[110] The points of correspondence between Furies and maenads are aggressive movement, the frenzy associated with kin killing, and a similarity of appearance and accoutrements such that in vase painting they may be hard to distinguish: they both have snakes, wands, or torches and are often similarly dressed.[111]

Now Melanaigis is, we shall soon see, a Dionysiac term. As with Orestes, the Fury driving Eteocles is associated with the kin-killing frenzy of a maenad, and that gives *exeisi domōn* part of its point: Eteocles, like a maenad, goes out to destroy in a frenzy his household by killing his kin. But here, unlike the case of Orestes, the Fury is actually inspiring the destruction. (The frenzy inspired by the Fury may, like "Dionysiac" frenzy, be either a cause or an effect of kin killing.) And so the Fury is also associated here, by the term Melanaigis, with the god who will (unless honored with sacrifice) inspire kin killing, namely, Dionysus. For Melanaigis, "of the black goatskin," occurs elsewhere only as a title of Dionysus. Dionysus Melanaigis had an important cult in Attica.[112] In the briefly recorded aetiological myth, in which he maddens the daughters of Eleuther, there is a clear implication that he enters the house with his black goatskin and drives them out in a frenzy.[113] They are restored to sanity by the institution of the cult. Analogously, in the *Seven against Thebes,* the Melanaigis Erinus will leave the house if the gods are given sacrifices, and so the kin-killing frenzy so often inspired by Dionysus (and here inspired by this Dionysiac Fury) will be avoided. This gives the phrase *exeisi domōn* the other part of its point.

This double association of the Fury with both maenad and god is

[110] Eur. *Or.* 339, 411, and 835.

[111] Whallon 1964, 321.

[112] Scholia to Aristophanes *Acharnians* 146; Nonnus 27.302.

[113] *Suda,* s.v. "Melan": (1) They see a *phasma* of Dionysus with his black goatskin—no doubt in their house (as in other myths of this type); (2) *exemēnen:* cf. Eur. *Bacch.* 36 *exemēna dōmatōn;* (3) the name Eleutherae seems to derive from the thiasos of females driven "free" from their homes, who in the aetiological myth become the daughters of Eleuther.

facilitated by the degree to which Dionysus and his maenads share each other's qualities and attributes (frenzy, animal skins, etc.). The Furies also do occasionally wear animal skins,[114] albeit far less frequently than maenads do. The designation of the Fury as Melanaigis is facilitated by the Furies' black appearance and black clothes, which Aeschylus refers to several times in the *Oresteia*.[115] I have elaborated this point partly because the latest commentator on the play (Hutchinson 1985) not only fails to notice all this but prefers to take *melanaigis* as a hapax legomenon meaning "like a black storm wind." This implies the odd idea of a black storm wind *leaving* the house.

In Antigone's case the tendency of the household to autonomy is represented not only by her flouting of the public edict by performing death ritual for her dead kin but also (cf. n. 102) by various suggestions that the family of Oedipus remains doomed to catastrophic endogamy: in particular, Antigone's explicit prioritization of natal kin over marriage, and her being left to die in confinement, such confinement being in Greek myth generally a symbol of familial introversion.[116] As in the *Oedipus the King,* just before the catastrophe the chorus sings to Dionysus (1140–45): "As the polis with its whole people is in the grip of a violent disease, come with purifying foot over the Parnassian slope or the sounding channel." As so often, Dionysus is to come from outside to liberate the female,[117] in the interest of the whole city (*pandamos polis*), from a confinement that expresses the introversion of the household.

Euripides' version of the myth reproduces essentially the same complex of ideas. The suggestions of a quasi-erotic relationship between Antigone and her brother are stronger than in Sophocles. The destruction of the household is expressed, as we have seen, in the maenadic metaphor for Antigone. And the ending of the *Phoenician Women,* whether genuine or not, expresses the victory of the tendency of the household to introversion: Antigone fiercely rejects marriage, expressing the desire to "lie next to" her brother and to stay with, and

[114] *LIMC* s.v. "Erinys" nos. 11 and 109.

[115] Aesch. *Ag.* 462, *Lib. Bearers* 1049, and *Eum.* 52, 352, and 370; cf. Eur. *Electra* 1345, *Or.* 321 and 408.

[116] Seaford 1990.

[117] There is also a suggestion here of his role in the polis festival of the Eleusinian mysteries, in which Persephone was liberated from below the earth: Seaford 1990, 88.

die with, her father. It is highly appropriate that along with all this she should reject the invitation to become (once more) a maenad.[118] Accordingly, when in Euripides' lost *Antigone* Antigone does marry and have offspring she also appears as a maenad.[119] In these three versions of the story of Antigone the Dionysiac has, in its various forms (invocation of the god, Dionysiac metaphor, rejection of maenadism, maenadism), the same essential significance.

## Homeric Exclusions

I return finally to my initial question: Why is Dionysus almost entirely absent from Homer? The old answers—that Homer predates the arrival of Dionysus in Greece and that as a god of the common people Dionysus was of little interest to the aristocratic Homeric milieu—have been shown by others to be untenable: Dionysus was neither newly arrived nor a god merely of the common people.[120] In fact the near absence of Dionysus from Homer is, we shall see, part of the near absence from Homer of a whole complex of ideas that is frequent in tragedy.

The case of Andromache, which shares so much with our tragic passages, is in fact unique in Homer. It combines (as we saw at the beginning of this essay) detailed attention to the irreversible destruction of a household with the permanent subversion of ritual, and the maenadic metaphor. The first two of these are in Homer most unusual, and the third unique, whereas in tragedy they are frequent and belong together. The exits of Andromache represent a pattern that is both tragic and Dionysiac and as such unique in Homer.[121] They are

[118] For the detail of this argument see Seaford 1990; cf. my discussion above at the beginning of the section entitled "Three Generalizations."

[119] Seaford 1990, 89.

[120] See especially Privitera 1970. His own explanation is in terms of genre: Dionysus, for the aristocratic tradition, has his own kind of poetry and is unsuitable as a theme for other kinds. This may be true as far as it goes.

[121] It may be no coincidence that they contain another example of pathetically dislocated ritual, so rare in Homer but frequent in tragedy: sent back to the house by her husband, Andromache laments him (with the maids), even though he still lives (*Il.* 6.500 *hai men zōon goon Hektora hōi eni oikōi*). Cf., among other examples, Aesch. *Ag.* 1322–23; Soph. *Ant.* 801–22.

also, let it be mentioned in passing, among those passages argued (on quite different grounds) to be relatively late in the *Iliad*.[122]

This tragic complex of ideas (the destruction of the household, the permanent subversion of ritual, the Dionysiac) includes two further phenomena, which are accordingly also generally excluded from Homer, namely, violence between members of the same household, and frenzy (outside battle). I shall take these two in turn.

First, the central narratives of the *Iliad* and the *Odyssey* are entirely without violence between members of the same kinship group. And stories in which it occurs are on the whole either not mentioned or mentioned in versions in which it is almost or entirely excluded—for example, the punishment of Lycurgus for opposing Dionysus is to be blinded by Zeus, not the frenzied killing of his wife and son that we find imposed on him by Dionysus in classical vase painting, which probably reflects Aeschylus' version of the story.[123]

Second, not only the frenzy of Lycurgus but frenzy in general (outside battle) is largely excluded from Homer. In particular, the noun *lussa* ("frenzy") and the verb *mainesthai* ("to be maddened") and their cognates are, when used of human beings, almost entirely confined to frenzy directed against the alien group, the frenzy of battle. There are six exceptions, and they all prove the rule.

The first exception, and the only hint of the word *lussa* (outside battle), is the verb *alussō,* a form of *aluō* thought to have been influenced by *lussa*.[124] The verb is used by Priam (*Iliad* 22.70) of the dogs who will drink his blood and disfigure his corpse, dogs whom he has raised, he says, at his own table. The same idea is found in the *Bacchae:* the example of Actaeon, "whom the raw-eating dogs he reared tore apart" (338–39), prefigures the tearing apart of Pentheus by the "dogs of frenzy" (977 *lussas kunes*). The frenzy of Priam's dogs accompanies both the violence inflicted on a member of the same household *and* the negation of ritual (death ritual).

The remaining exceptions are as follows. The participle *mainomenos*

[122] Shipp 1972, 256 and 311.

[123] Sutton 1975; Apollodorus 3.5.1. Further examples: Seaford 1989b, 87. See also Carpenter in this volume, pp. 198–99.

[124] Chantraine 1986, s.v. "*aluō.*" Cf. Hom. *Il.* 8.299: *kuna lussētēra* (military). Even the verb *aluō* in Homer is used (of human beings) only of Achilles (*Il.* 24.12); further on Achilles below.

("raving mad") is used of the entirely passive Dionysus in the Lycurgus narrative. And Andromache is twice compared to a maenad. In the fifth exception, Zeus disapproves of Achilles retaining the corpse of Hector "with his heart in a mad rage" (*Iliad* 24. 114 *phresi mainomenēisin*). Here again, frenzy threatens the performance of death ritual, disfigurement of the corpse this time not by dogs but by a human being. But this threat occupies, significantly, a central role in the structure of the *Iliad,* an importance expressed in its unique status in the poem as attracting something like merely moral disapproval from the gods: the narrative closure of the *Iliad* is achieved by the resolution of the anomaly caused precisely by this frenzy of Achilles. Both Achilles' frenzied, isolating, excessive revenge and the consequent negation of death ritual are ended in his surrender of the corpse to Priam for the public funeral that concludes the poem.

There was a comparable kind of closure in the version of the *Odyssey* that ended at 23.296 with the arrival of Odysseus and Penelope at the bed where they celebrated their first nuptials; for it can be shown that the disorderly, prolonged feasting of the suitors represents a subversion of the due ritual process of the wedding, and that ritual normality is restored by the reunion of Odysseus with Penelope, which is described in a series of parallels to wedding ritual that culminates in 23. 296.[125] The culmination of the *subversion* of the marriage process, in the suitors' disorderly feasting, is marked by Telemachus' accusation that they "are raving mad" (*Odyssey* 18. 406 *mainesthe*).[126] This is the sixth and final exception. And so each of the exceptions is associated with one or more of the elements of our tragic complex of ideas: violence within the household, the negation of ritual, and the Dionysiac.

The restoration of ritual normality in the *Odyssey* is also the restoration of the threatened household.[127] The *Iliad* also concludes in ritual restored, but one that is public, performed by the whole community

[125] For this whole argument see my forthcoming book, *Reciprocity and Ritual: A Study of Homer and Tragedy in the Developing City-State* (Oxford), chap. 2.

[126] This occurs just after the suitors' own admission that "worse behavior was prevailing" (*ta khereiona nikai*) at the house. It is significant that one of the (rare) applications of *mainesthai* to nonhumans is to the Centaur's drunken disruption of Pirithous' wedding (*Od.* 21.298).

[127] The inadequacy of the household ritual to restore *public* order to Ithaca required at a certain point the addition to the narrative of that part of the "continuation" in which the inevitable dispute between Odysseus and the kin of the dead suitors is resolved.

of Trojans and recognized in the truce agreed by the Greeks; whereas the wedding ritual of Andromache remains, in contrast to Penelope's, irreversibly negated. Her household is, despite restoration of ritual normality in the public sphere, irreversibly destroyed. And so Andromache's frenzied negation of ritual remains, in contrast to Achilles', in the end uncontained.[128]

This implicit distinction between household and community is prefigured in the scene between Hector and Andromache in book 6, a scene perhaps unique in Homer for its stark presentation of the contradiction between a man's feelings for his family and his feelings for his community.[129] Andromache tries to move Hector by describing what will happen to his family if he continues to take the fight to the Greeks and is killed. But Hector then sends her back home to weave. With the strongest statement that exists in Homer of a man's sense of duty to the community (441–46) he contains the threat that her "maenadic frenzy" poses to the spatial and functional differentiation of male and female in the city (see above, the section entitled "Maenadic Andromache and Wedding Ritual").

Hector's duty to the community threatens to destroy his household. Hence Andromache's maenadic frenzy. And so the contradiction between household and community is here at the heart of our tragic complex of ideas. That is why the contradiction, like the complex, is frequent in tragedy but in Homer unique to the case of Andromache. This suggests, moreover, a historical explanation for the near absence of the complex from Homer. Also nearly absent from Homer is the functioning polis. This is, at least partly, because Homeric epic is the product of an earlier stage in the development of the polis than is tragedy. Whatever the prehistory of Dionysus, there was something in it that qualified him for an important role in the development of the polis.[130] Homeric epic partly predates and partly excludes this role and this development. The near absence of the functioning polis from Homer entails the near absence of the contradiction between polis and

[128] Despite Hector's containment of it in book 6 and despite the (no doubt traditional) expression of her feelings about the destruction of her household in the due process of lamentation in book 24.

[129] See, among others, Arthur 1981.

[130] See n. 88 above. This is to say that Dionysus' new role (e.g., he seems to have taken over ancient cults of Artemis at Patrae—see the section above entitled "Tragedy: A Dionysiac Pattern"—and Argos—the various versions of the Proetids myth) is no doubt an adaptation of his earlier one.

household, of nonmilitary frenzy, of violence within the household, of the permanent subversion of ritual, and of the expression of these anomalies in the Dionysiac.

The statement that the polis barely functions in Homer may, I am aware, be controversial, but it cannot be demonstrated at length here. Let it be said merely that all the main features of the polis (an assembly conducting public business, a judicial authority, state organization in general, an urban center with public buildings, communal ritual, citizenship, a sense of belonging to a polis, and so on) are either entirely absent from the Homeric narrative or, if present, marginal or ineffective. For example, all that can be found in Homer to compare with the religious festival of the polis is contained in three passages, of which by far the most substantial is the account of the offering made to Athena in her temple on behalf of the city by some noble women of Troy led by Hecuba.[131] This exception actually provides another link in our argument, for it is in fact in the sixth book of the *Iliad*. Hecuba is instructed by Hector to perform the offering. And it is shortly thereafter, when Hector returns to his own home and finds Andromache absent, that he asks the question that produces in reply the Dionysiac metaphor: "No, she has gone neither to see her sisters-in-law nor to the temple of Athena with the other Trojan women to propitiate the goddess. She has gone rather to the city wall like a maenad." The women's offering to Athena represents a role for women in the public sphere, a role instigated by the man who is himself uniquely associated with the public sphere, Hector. It is not coincidental that the full significance of this ritual, by far the closest in Homer to a polis cult, emerges in the contrast it provides to the maenadic action of Andromache. In this action, circumscribed in book 6 but reactivated in book 22, we approach the world of tragedy. But tragedy, it is I hope no longer unfashionable to say, actually originates in a polis cult, a cult celebrating the potentially catastrophic triumph of Dionysus Eleuthereus, or Liberator, originally perhaps the liberator of women from their homes.[132]

[131] Hom. *Il*. 6. 297–311 (note line 300, the priestess appointed by "the Trojans"). Cf. *Od*. 3. 567 and 20. 276–78 (cf. 21. 258–59).

[132] The epithet Eleuthereus may mean just "of Eleutherae," but Eleutherae itself may derive from the women running "free" from their homes (cf., for example, the place-names Aphetae and Clazomenae), i.e., liberated by Dionysus: cf. n. 113 above and Thomson 1946, 172. Dionysus as liberator: cf., for instance, n. 117 above; Eur. *Bacch*. 445, 498, 613, 649; and Connor 1989. Plutarch (*Moralia* 716b) takes Dionysus Eleuthereus to be (psychic) "Liberator."

CHAPTER 6

# Staging Dionysus between Thebes and Athens

Froma I. Zeitlin

## Setting the Stage

The genre of tragedy was a civic institution of the Athenian polis and, like all such institutions, highly ideological in nature, construct, and outlook. This definition holds true for the circumstances of performance—a public spectacle on the occasion of a civic festival, which, with its ritual and political preliminaries, celebrated the city with magnificent display both on and off the stage.[1] It also applies to the ensemble of that aesthetic creation we call tragedy, with its highly codified conventions that range from dramatic structures, formal protocols, and patterns of plot to the staging of distinctive religious and political concerns.[2]

As the god who lent his auspices to the dramatic productions, Dionysus retained a highly visible presence in the theater. His advent

[1] See, for example, Goldhill 1990 and Winkler 1990a.

[2] The fact that tragedy can lay claim to universalizing value, praised as such in Aristotle's philosophical analysis of the genre (in which the name of Dionysus is never mentioned) and proven by its eventual status as an exportable product to be performed far and wide in the Greek-speaking world, should not obscure its original fusion with the city of Athens and its self-representation both on stage and in other idealizing forms of performance. Indeed, that same universalizing value should be taken as consonant with fifth-century Athens' idea of itself both in its claims to cultural hegemony and its own liberal political policies, not only amply demonstrated in tragedy but praised in the genre of the *epitaphios,* which in the hands of the fourth-century orators (and eulogists of Athens) betrays the influence of Athenian drama. The standard work on the *epitaphios* and civic ideology is Loraux 1986.

under the title of Eleuthereus was celebrated each year in the first ceremonies of the festival, which reenacted an original journey from Eleutherae that marked the transfer of his cult from Boeotia to Attica and from a frontier position on the boundaries of the two regions into the civic heart of Athens by the theater precinct.[3] The priest of his cult, not unreasonably, occupied the best seat among those reserved for dignitaries in the audience who were spectators of the drama. But what of the dramatic productions themselves? Was the god merely a privileged but impartial spectator at celebrations in his honor? Or, belying the maxim, "nothing to do with Dionysus" (if indeed this enigmatic saying referred to the tragic genre), was not his divinity also made manifest on stage—in direct impersonation or in discernible traces of his powerful influence? If this was the case, let us take one further step. Can some worthwhile distinctions be made among the various Dionysiac elements in the dramatic repertory in order to demonstrate that these too are subject to certain rule-governed conventions that operate under specified conditions and with definite aims in the unfolding of a given tragic scenario?[4] In particular, does Dionysus perform in one way when Athens represents itself on stage, and in another when it comes to dramatizing that other city, Thebes, from whose territory the god was imported into the Athenian theater? If indeed Dionysiac energy is deployed to different effects according to the dramatic setting, as I suggest it is, then we might have much to learn from the pursuit of this question—first, of course, with regard to the practical workings of the tragic genre, but second as to the part Dionysus is asked to play in the ideological uses of the theater to which he gives his name. Thus to evaluate the god's performance on stage in these two dramatic locales we must explore the range and tenor of Dionysiac allusion in the different theatrical representation of Thebes and Athens, as both are stylized in the work of the tragic poets. I stress

[3] For the most recent discussion of the evidence, see the stimulating work of Connor 1989.

[4] In addition to Zeitlin 1985a, 1985b, 1986a, 1989, and 1991, see Schlesier 1985, 1988b, and in this volume, and Bierl 1989, who also argue for the key value of Dionysiac allusions in the theater. While I dissent in some aspects from their modes of interpreting these references, in principle I agree with Bierl's formulation that allusions to Dionysus are not just "mythological asides" or evidence of a "theological superstructure of a general kind. Rather, each naming of Dionysus and related words plays a definite function in the course of the action of that tragedy which stands in a direct relation to the essence of the god" (45).

the notion of stylization, for neither does this "Thebes" (or this "Athens") precisely mirror any historical reality nor are the uses of Dionysus (or of any of the other gods, for that matter) to be extrapolated in any literal sense from cultic reality.[5] Both are, rather, theatrical elements that also serve to shape the dynamic operation of tragic politics and theology across a spectrum of dramatic plots. By so doing, both contribute too to the larger design of Athenian theater as a forum for projecting and testing certain cherished images of the self, the city, and the world.

In an earlier piece I proposed that Thebes in the theater was configured in the negative as the "anti-city" to Athens' manifest image of itself with regard to the proper management of the polis in social, political, and religious affairs.[6] I argued that this "Thebes," unlike "Athens," consistently sets the stage for a drama that can furnish no enduring way of escaping the tragic through the provision of a familial or civic future beyond the world of the play. In Thebes, we cannot look forward to the continuation of lineage or the assurance of legitimate rule, nor do we hear prophecies that forecast alliances with other parties or promote institutional foundations such as the establishment of law courts and the beneficial inauguration of commemorative cult.[7] This general rule seems to prevail, whatever the cast of characters and whatever the different myths deployed that share a common terrain in Thebes—Cadmus and the Sown Men; the house of Laius, including Oedipus and his progeny; even Heracles in his Theban provenance; and, of course, the god Dionysus himself.

On a grander and more abstract level, I proposed that Thebes offered the paradigm of a city closed in upon itself, maintaining powerful psychological, social, and political boundaries that matched the enclosure of defensive walls and circular ramparts that defined its physical space. Site of autochthony in the founding myth of the Spartoi and of incestuous marriage in the house of Laius, the city suffers a fundamental malaise. It has no means of activating a workable system of relations and differences, either within the city or without,

[5] On the relations between Dionysus in drama and Dionysus in cult, see Henrichs 1978a, 1990; Longo 1986; and Detienne 1989a.

[6] Zeitlin 1986a. See also Sabbatucci 1978 and Vidal-Naquet 1988.

[7] See also Sabbatucci 1978, 117–41, whose argument, although cogent and daring in many respects, is everywhere ruled by an a priori opposition between *genos* and polis.

or between the self and any other, including those relations that regulate the respective domains of humans and gods. Unable to bring outsiders successfully into its system and fixed on the priority of blood relations of the *genos,* Thebes seems to move between the extremes of rigid inclusions and exclusions on the one hand and radical confusions of distinctions on the other. Eteocles in Aeschylus' *Seven against Thebes* and Pentheus in Euripides' *Bacchae,* for example, "are intent on not letting the women *inside* come outside but fail in their attempts, and Dionysus and Polynices are both outsiders who press their claim to being insiders, with destructive results."[8] In short, I argued that this Thebes has no opening to the future; it is a place where civil strife drenches the earth with blood; it has no viable way of stabilizing a ruling order that so easily passes into actual or would-be tyranny, or of resolving its complex of family relations. In Thebes, even the secure identity of the self is in jeopardy: Oedipus and the stranger at the crossroads turn out to be one and the same; Eteocles and Polynices merge their separate identities when they destroy one another in mutual fratricide. Pentheus and Dionysus, kin cousins on either side of the mortal divide, are, at first, equally adversaries and doublets of one another, costumed finally as look-alikes at the climactic moment of the drama.

Oedipus, above all, exemplifies this tragic configuration on all fronts. He is either subjected to an enforced seclusion within the house (as in Euripides' *Phoenician Women*) or, more typically, is found in a state of precarious wandering too far from home. The longer life story of Oedipus corresponds, in a sense, to the two states of Theban maenads in the *Bacchae,* who also oscillate (even if only for the duration of the play) between the spatial extremes of inside and outside—either imprisoned by Pentheus within the palace or roving far off on the mountain of Cithaeron—the site, we might add, that is common to both the myth of Oedipus and the cult of Dionysus.

Oedipus is not a maenad, of course (although his act of self-blinding is represented as the result of a sudden madness), nor is he in any strict sense a Dionysiac victim,[9] as is, for example, the figure of Heracles,

[8] Zeitlin 1986a, 121. Bacon 1964, 27–38, has excellent remarks on this topic. See also the discussion in Zeitlin 1981.

[9] Oedipus' self-blinding is represented as the result of a sudden onrush of madness (*mania*) and frenzy (*lussa*) (Aeschylus *Seven against Thebes* 781–83; Sophocles *Oedipus the King* 1255–

who in Euripides' play turns into a "Bacchant of Hades" and, like Agave in the *Bacchae,* is driven to destroy his kin, misrecognizing them for another's (*Heracles* 1119).[10] But Oedipus, Thebes' most famous son, and Dionysus, god of maenads and of the theater, have a common and significant pattern: at Thebes Dionysus, like Oedipus, is the *xenos* ("stranger") who is also native-born (*suggenēs*); like Oedipus, he is the unacknowledged offspring of the ruling dynasty who will divulge his true identity to the city and claim his patrimony, and despite the crucial differences in status and in the resolution of their respective stories, neither at the end remains in Thebes. Dionysus, even as he tells us in the prologue, will, in keeping with his itinerant character, continue his journeying once he is recognized at Thebes (*Bacchae* 48–50), while Oedipus in Sophocles' and Euripides' versions makes his way to that other city—the antitype to Thebes that is Athens. This is the city that is depicted as admitting outsiders: Euripides' Heracles is led away by Theseus to sanctuary in Athens, and both heroes (Heracles and Oedipus) repay their common benefactor with profitable cults for the city in Attic territory. Admission into Athens appears to be the only alternative to the typical finale at home, which ends with the destruction of the ruling family or the unhappy dispersal of its remaining members.

In the operation of this Theban "master plot," whether in the *Bacchae* or elsewhere, we can detect throughout the consistent and pervasive influence of the tragic Dionysus in theatrical, religious, and sociopolitical terms. In the first, the theatrical realm, we see traces of the god at work in those familiar techniques of doublings and reversals that are essential to dramatic moments of anagnorisis and peripeteia, along with fatal confusions of identity and disastrous blurring of all the boundaries that ordinarily maintain a system of defined polarities.[11] In the ritual and religious sphere, we recognize the god's effects, starting

59, 1299–1302) in the Bacchic idiom, but it is Apollo and not Dionysus who is named as the divine agent in question.

[10] Heracles is not strictly a Theban personage because he has many other geographical associations and never remains for long in that city. Nevertheless, the situation in Euripides' *Heracles* is demonstrably appropriate to Thebes in every respect. Even in Sophocles' *Trachinian Women,* which does not take place in Thebes but at Trachis, where Heracles and his family are in exile, the paradigm of Bacchic Thebes still seems relevant and is, in fact, explicitly mentioned (510–11). On maenadism in the play, see now Schlesier in this volume.

[11] Foley 1980 and 1985; Segal 1982; Vernant 1988.

from the uncertain margin between mortals and immortals (that can be referred to the anomalous status of the god whose identity requires recognition) and extending to the shape of tragic and inverted sacrifice that crosses the lines between animal and human categories.[12] We see too the uses of maenadism and madness, and the transformation of life-giving Dionysiac ecstasy and revelry into the madness of passion, vengeance, and bloodshed.[13] Finally, from a sociopolitical viewpoint, we discern the god's role as an agent of change and cultural innovation, when he comes, especially involving categories of both "otherness" and the status of the "other" with respect to the self, the family, and the community as a whole.

Although an acknowledged poliadic god in Thebes, Dionysus remains in many respects the god who comes from the outside. He is a stranger who brings the strange, and he compels acceptance, under tragic pressure, of altered states of perception and modes of cognition that challenge a limited, often male-centered view of the world. Seen from a human perspective, he subverts the ostensibly rational order through his capacity to turn things upside down (*anō katō*) and to bring about tragic metabole (reversal) and even metamorphosis of bodily form. In short, it is Dionysus whose arrival demands expansion of cultural and cognitive horizons to include and incorporate the "other" (including himself) into a wider network of alliances and relations,[14] a

[12] On tragic sacrifice and Dionysus, see Burkert 1966; Guépin 1968; Detienne 1979; Segal 1982.

[13] Guépin 1968; Schlesier 1985; Burkert 1985; Seaford 1981.

[14] Marcello Massenzio's study (1969) of Dionysiac *xenia,* although not expressly pertaining to tragedy (with the exception of Pentheus), is the trailblazer here. To summarize, he notes the position of Dionysus in many of his myths as a *xenos,* either a stranger or a guest, and its important implications for understanding the power of the god (especially pp. 71ff. and 110–13). In brief, he argues that the series of myths that relate the advent of Dionysus among mortals belongs to a single system of acculturation with three major elements: (1) the acceptance of a new god, (2) the acceptance of a new type of agriculture (the vine), whose product, when used correctly, serves as a "cultural instrument of social relations" that requires (3) the acceptance of relations between non-kin and indeed facilitates such relations. Hence, Dionysus the *xenos*—both a stranger and a guest, the one who both gives gifts and must be received in turn—stands at the heart of a complex system of reciprocal exchange. The logical outcome of the refusal of the god and his gifts is a retaliation that takes the form of some autodestructive action within the family. Vernant 1988 places the emphasis on Dionysus' power to introduce "otherness" into the here and now within the workings of the polis; see too Auger 1988; Bourlot 1988; and Seaford 1988, 1990 (the latter expanding upon Massenzio).

move that tends to be negatively resisted in Thebes and creatively carried out in Athens.

To insist on these distinctions between different locales is not, of course, to imply that Dionysiac elements occur only in the contexts of Thebes and Athens. Even beyond the general influence of Dionysus in regulating the dynamics of tragic plots, Bacchic references appear throughout the tragic corpus that, at strategic moments, recall the power of the god, whether in explicit invocation and language or in identifiable theme, action, or metaphor.[15] I select Thebes and Athens, however, as the two endpoints of a theatrical spectrum that respectively define a negative and a positive pole of Dionysiac action in the city. The key factor is the outcome of the scenario and the extent to which a given drama succeeds in "stabilizing" the very figure of instability and in converting its energies into progressive (nontragic) results.

To test this hypothesis in brief, let us approach the problem from three different perspectives. First, we will examine certain Dionysiac references in a selection of relevant dramas (mainly of Sophocles and Euripides). The aim is to establish the power of the god, especially in relation to the different company he keeps (notably, Ares and Aphrodite at Thebes, Athena and Demeter at Athens), and I will read these associations as symbolic codings of the two patterns indicated earlier. Here Thebes holds the center stage, and Athens serves as foil and counterpart. Second, we will turn to some specific Athenian examples and, in particular, to the working of Dionysiac conventions in the instance of a single play, Euripides' *Ion,* that in many of its aspects comes closest to Theban categories and concerns.[16] Finally, we will move into more unfamiliar territory to take up a triad of Euripidean dramas, two of which are extant only in fragments. All contain strong Dionysiac referents, and by reason of their subjects and scenic locations, they address the question of Thebes from the vantage points of both center and periphery, including that of Eleutherae, the traditional

[15] For a list of explicit mentions of Dionysus and the Dionysiac in the extant plays, see Bierl 1989, 44 n. 6. The relevant plays are Aesch. *Seven, Suppliant Women, Libation Bearers, Eumenides;* Soph. *Antigone, Oed. King, Trach. Wom., Oedipus at Colonus;* Eur. *Hippolytus, Hecuba, Suppliant Women, Electra, Her., Iphigenia at Tauris, Trojan Women, Ion, Helen, Phoenician Women, Orestes, Iphigenia at Aulis, Bacchae.* See also Oranje 1984, 114–30, for fuller discussion of Dionysus in the tragic corpus.

[16] See Zeitlin 1989 for full exposition of this thesis.

home of theater itself. These three plays, *Hypsipyle, Phoenician Women,* and *Antiope* (in that order), may well have comprised an actual trilogy, according to how we interpret one important ancient source, but if not, they certainly belong to the same late period in Euripides' career and represent, as I shall argue, a further validation of the distinctive uses to which Dionysus is put in the vicinity of Thebes.

## Dionysus in Thebes

Given the significance of Thebes in the myth and cult of Dionysus, it is hardly surprising that there are numerous direct allusions to the god in Theban plays, whether referring to the city itself or to other places that are sacred to him in both Greek and barbarian locales. He may be summoned among the poliadic divinities of Thebes or named in the context of his cultic associations with joyous celebration or maenadic ecstasy. Evocations of his positive ambience, however, are most often relegated to the idyllic past of the city (Euripides *Phoenician Women* 638–56) or the individual (Sophocles *Oedipus the King* 1105–9) or are displaced to a distant elsewhere (e.g., Euripides *Bacchae* 134–67). As a general rule, appeals to the saving powers of Theban Dionysus in time of crisis are advance indications of an illusory hope (e.g., Sophocles *Oedipus the King* 209–15), ironic pointers warning the audience to expect some reversal of situation that will release the destructive potential of tragedy. The true measure, however, of the import of Dionysiac references in tragic drama depends not just upon any isolated usage, but on the precise nature of each occurrence and the interrelations among them in the context of a given play.

Sophocles' *Antigone* is an exemplary, even schematic, case in point. First, it contains a series of references, strategically placed in the choral odes, that attest to the changing dynamics of Dionysiac power as the drama proceeds. Second, it includes key invocations of those other divinities whose naming is essential for defining and determining the differing modalities of that power. Finally, it organizes Dionysiac influence in spatial terms through an extensive network of geographical allusions to other locales that by assimilation or contrast affect the situation in Thebes.[17]

[17] Bierl 1989 also takes *Antigone* as his example of "how the god of tragedy can be present

Three times Dionysus himself is mentioned, but it is not until the last occurrence in the fifth stasimon (the hyporcheme) that the god emerges into full focus. This is the pivotal moment of the plot, when Creon has departed to bury Polynices and rescue Antigone and everyone's hopes run high that disaster may yet be averted. Twice addressing Dionysus as a god of the city in the course of the ode (1122–23: "O Bacchus, dweller in Thebes, mother city of Bacchants"; 1136–37: "You hold Thebes, of all cities, first in honor"), the chorus calls upon Dionysus to reveal himself at Thebes and invokes his powers of epiphany by following the itinerary of his cults—in Italy, Euboean Nysa, Delphi, and, above all, in the Athenian setting connected with Eleusis and the cult of Demeter, where Dionysus bears the title of Iacchus, the very name that brings the ode to its close (1151).

The jubilant associations of Dionysus with the nocturnal dances and blazing torches of his rites on the mountain peaks of Delphi are a continuing refrain in the choral lyrics of tragedy.[18] However, the explicit reference to Eleusis and the Eleusinian circle of gods in the setting of Dionysiac tragedy bears closer inspection, both because the reference pertains unequivocally to Athens and because it points to a possible and significant dramatic tension between Dionysiac and Eleusinian elements of myth and cult. In this instance, the mention of Demeter toward the opening of the ode (1119–20) and of Iacchus at the end (1151) is directly relevant, as others have observed, to Antigone's earlier reference to Persephone as receiver of the dead (894) and thus also supports the analogy of Antigone to Kore as a bride of Hades (917–20; cf. 1240–41). The cultic allusion to Eleusis in the company of Iacchus suggests, to be sure, a mystic alternative to the finality of death and a potentially positive conclusion to the Kore's scenario.[19] Yet it also introduces an implicit contrast between the beneficial alliance of Dionysus and Demeter in Attic cult and the destructive one here at Thebes that will end at the last in a tragic merger with Hades (cf. 777, 780, 1075, 1144, 1240–41, 1284). What determines this unhappy out-

---

in a tragic play with a different heroic myth," but he treats Dionysus alone and without special consideration of the Theban milieu.

[18] Aesch. *Eum.* 24–25; Eur. *Ion* 714–17, *Bacch.* 306–8, *Phoen. Wom.* 226, *Hypsipyle* frag. 752 (Nauck$^2$); cf. Aristophanes *Clouds* 603.

[19] See the excellent discussion of Segal 1981, 179–83, 200–206, who argues well for the ambivalence of Kore (promise of salvation or a bride of death). Henrichs 1990 opts for the salvational meaning only.

come, however, depends, as we shall see, on the changing relations of Dionysus with Ares and Aphrodite in the preceding choral odes and on a spatial displacement in myth to a still more negative locale—Thrace of the famed wintry winds and savage cults.

This is the second time that Theban Dionysus has been explicitly summoned to the city. In the opening parodos the chorus had sung of the city's recent victory over the attacking Argives and had concluded with an invitation to Dionysus to lead nocturnal dances in celebration of Ares' defeat of Polynices (or Capaneus), "the Bacchant who had come raging against Thebes with the madness of war" (135–37, 150–54).[20] But madness, it turns out, has not departed from Thebes nor have the images of warfare and victory. Quite the contrary. All these elements return in a different guise, transferred now to another site of familial conflict (Creon and Haemon) and another motive (Haemon's erotic passion for Antigone), marked as such in the third stasimon, where the chorus sings of the figures of Eros and Aphrodite. Both deities are called invincible (781 *Erōs anikate makhan;* Aphrodite: 801 *amakhos*), and desire (*himeros*) is said to win the day (795–96 *nikai;* cf. 133, 147); Eros stirs up again the "kindred strife" of men (793–94 *neikos andrōn xunaimon*). The quarrel between the brothers that had seemingly been laid to rest by the military defeat of the man of "much strife"—*Polu-neikes*—shifts to Haemon and Creon (cf. 131). The battle lines form again, this time through the agency of Eros, who "maddens" the one to whom he comes (790).[21]

In the parodos Ares was named first as the personification of war itself (126) and then as the god who dispatched the other attackers, once Zeus had struck down the warrior who came against the city with a violent "Bacchic frenzy" (134–40). In the third stasimon, as we have just seen, Aphrodite and Eros enter the fray. But Ares returns, along with a fully maenadic Dionysus in the fourth stasimon, which intervenes at the moment when Antigone has been led away to her rocky tomb, just before the entrance of Tiresias. The ode consists of three

[20] On the relation between the parodos and the hyporcheme, see especially Rosivach 1979 and Oudemans and Lardinois 1987, 151–59. See also Coleman 1972. Most commentators, including Schlesier in this volume, identify the "Bacchant" as Capaneus (on the basis of Aesch. *Seven* 423 and Eur. *Phoen. Wom.* 1180). Along with Segal 1981, 166, 170, 197, 202, Lonnoy 1985, 68, and Bierl 1989, 47, I prefer Polynices, although the ambiguity of the allusion may well be significant in its own right.

[21] The pun is noted by Segal 1981, 190, and discussed further by Oudemans and Lardinois 1987, 144, with reference to the extended powers of Eros.

mythic exemplars. In the first, the power of Aphrodite is implied perhaps in the story of Danaë.[22] In the second and central panel, Dionysus plays the leading role as the agent of Lycurgus' madness (955–65).[23] But Ares, already previewed in passing as the generic name for war (in connection with Danaë's fate, 952), is explicitly (and oddly) mentioned in the ensuing strophe as witness to an event of family violence (that might well be enrolled in a Dionysiac context).[24] Both the story of Lycurgus and the subsequent one of the Phineidae and their mother, Cleopatra, are set in the wild reaches of Thrace, where Dionysus and Ares are both known to have received special worship.[25] Thrace is the one famous geographical locale *not* included later in Dionysus' recuperative itinerary in the next stasimon, which closes its hopes of cathartic salvation in a pointed reference, as we have seen, to Iacchus at Eleusis (and, implicitly, to Athens). The Lycurgus ode also ends on a specific Athenian note, but it is a negative one, focusing on the unhappy person of Cleopatra, a descendant from the Erechtheid line (981–82) through her mother, Oreithyia (whom the North Wind, Boreas, abducted from Athens). The fate of an Athenian daughter, it seems, may provide a parallel for a daughter of Thebes, but only if she is first displaced to a barbarian milieu.[26]

[22] Winnington-Ingram 1980, 108; Oudemans and Lardinois 1987, 148–49.

[23] The myth of Lycurgus is attested first in Homer (*Iliad* 6.130–41 with scholia) and was later elaborated in Aeschylus' lost Dionysiac trilogy, the *Lycurgia,* as well as in other sources (e.g., Eumelus frag. 1 [*EGF*]; Apollodorus 3.5.1; Hyginus *Fabulae* 132 and 242; Servius *Aeneid* 3.14; Diodorus Siculus 3.65.5–6; Nonnus 21.166).

[24] The questions of how these various myths are interrelated and what precise message they bear as a whole have given rise to many attempts at interpretation. For the mythic values in particular, see Sourvinou-Inwood 1988, and for a specialized view, see Seaford 1990. Those most relevant to my concerns with Dionysus in the company of Ares and Aphrodite are Winnington-Ingram 1980, 98–110, and, following his lead, Oudemans and Lardinois 1987, 145–51. We may note that a mother's blinding of another man's children (Phineus' second wife) recalls the events of Euripides' *Hecuba,* a play also staged in Thrace and one given a highly Dionysiac coloring. See the recent discussions of Schlesier 1988b and Zeitlin 1991. At the same time, the Theban connection is maintained if we can trust the scholiast (ad 981) who states that Sophocles in his *Tympanistae* (which treated the story of Phineus) named the second wife as Eidothea, sister of Cadmus. Seaford 1990, 87, suggests that perhaps there was a Dionysiac chorus of *tumpanon* players.

[25] Strictly speaking, the mention of Ares is intrusive in this ode, and the fact that he is introduced not once but twice, alerts us to the symbolic valence of his invocation in connection with Dionysus. See the sensible remarks of Winnington-Ingram 1980, 108–9. For the cults of Thrace, see Perdrizet 1910, 29–32; Farnell 1909, 400; and Harrison 1922, 375–76.

[26] The fates of both the Phineidae and their mother, Cleopatra, are relevant to the situation of Antigone and her own family as well as to Creon and his, in ways too complex to

In its emphasis on the theme of imprisonment, the fourth stasimon fills the interval between Antigone's departure for her rocky tomb and her subsequent (and literal) marriage of death that will put an end to Eleusinian hopes and the appeals to a curative epiphany of Dionysus expressed in the later ode. But once the *mania* of Eros/Aphrodite has been assimilated to Ares in the third stasimon, and Ares is recalled in the fourth in proximity to the Dionysiac madness of Lycurgus in Thrace,[27] the Theban scenario is set inexorably upon its tragic course[28] to its true destination, which is Hades (1284).[29]

---

explain here. See, in particular, the subtle analysis of Sourvinou-Inwood 1988. I note only that the ambiguity of the word *gonan* (980), which, as Seaford 1990, 87, rightly points out, can mean both "birth" and "offspring," may well be used to encode an allusion to Anti*gone* herself. On the myth itself and its many variants, see Bouvier and Moreau 1983.

[27] The previous mention of Thrace's turbulent winds in the second stasimon (585) foreshadows the savage violence associated with the myths of this locale in the fourth, which ends in fact with reference again to those wintry storms (984). Like Thebes and Athens in the theater, Thrace assumes a distinctive character as a tragic topos, starting with Aeschylus, at least, in his Dionysiac trilogy, the *Lycurgia,* and the pattern continues with Sophocles himself, who is thought to have turned King Tereus from a Megarian into a Thracian in his lost play the *Tereus*. In the *Hecuba,* Euripides deliberately displaces his scene from Troy to Thrace, with telling effects, and probably invented the villainous king of the place, Polymestor, who is brought into association with the local Dionysus at the end of the play (see Schlesier 1988b and Zeitlin 1991). Likewise, his patriotic Athenian play, the *Erechtheus* (to be discussed in another context below), makes the traditional Eleusinian Eumolpus into a savage Thracian king, coming to invade Attica with a barbarian host. For discussions of some of the associations of Thrace in the theater, see Chalkia 1986, 194–200, 49, and Hall 1989, 103–10, 133–36, 151–53, with appropriate bibliography.

[28] The process of displacement from Thebes to a barbarian locale as a paradigm for the conversion of Dionysiac celebration into madness, death, and destruction begins with a reference to another Dionysiac site with Antigone's comparison of herself to Niobe, the *xenē,* in Phrygia (824–31). Niobe herself, wife of Amphion and queen of Thebes, is displaced (or rather "replaced") in her country of origin after the disaster that befalls her children. The Dionysiac cue is small but telling in Antigone's curious and complex image of Niobe's gradual petrifaction, described as growing upon her like the creeping encroachment of ivy (825–26). The transformation of the body into static mineral becomes itself a perversion of the Dionysiac symbol of exuberant vegetation that in the oxymoron of stone and ivy takes over and stifles (*damasen*) living matter.

[29] Despite his chthonic associations, Dionysus (*pace* Bierl 1989) does not take on the role of Hades in this play. The contrast between them is between the god with the power to purify (1144 *katharsiōi podi*) and the one who resists purification (1284 *duskathartos Haidou limēn*). Nor should Eros, Hades, and Dionysus be taken together merely as evidence of the irruption of the irrational into the human world (Segal 1981, 200). In a formal sense, the drama may be said to belong to Hades in his dual roles as a typical divinity (who demands the honors due him and exacts retribution for any deprecation of his godhood) and as a universal fact of life for all mortals: whatever else man may accomplish, says the chorus in the first stasimon, there is no way to escape Hades (361). The entire drama, in fact, can be read from

It is just this positioning of the god between the two antithetical forces of an Ares and an Aphrodite that seems to typify the workings of Dionysus in the tragic theater of Thebes, by which the powers of passion and madness he inspires oscillate between the spheres of war and love. All three divine figures can be invoked as protective gods of the city in the roles they played in its foundation, as indeed Antigone does in her allusion to the *progeneis theoi* just before the Lycurgus ode (938). Cadmus, we may recall, was given Harmonia, the daughter of Ares and Aphrodite, for his wife.[30] Her name logically signifies the result of a union between the two antithetical principles of Ares and Aphrodite, and it represents too the idealized emblem of the marriage act, whose function it is to conjoin the opposite sexes. But in Thebes, Harmonia is finally only an unhappy delusion. How can it be otherwise in a place where both War (Ares) and Love (Aphrodite) stand for illegal impulses in both the city and the family, where their union leads not to domestic or political tranquillity but, as in the house of Laius, to internal strife and incestuous mixtures?[31]

If in the *Antigone* Dionysus is drawn into the destructive orbit of both Aphrodite and Ares,[32] in the *Bacchae* the framing of Dionysus

---

this moment on as dedicated to the validation of this gnomic statement. (Note the numerous other references to Hades: 519, 542, 575, 581, 654, 777, 780, 810, 822, 905, 1075, 1205, 1241, 1284). The means to this end is Eros (Aphrodite), an equally "inescapable force" (this time, "for both mortals and immortals alike," 786), who is also connected, as we have seen, with both Ares (military idiom) and Dionysus (madness), and whose power is celebrated at the exact midpoint of the play. Dionysus is rather the catalyst who mobilizes the passions of the drama, which, once they have emerged in the central scene between Haemon and Creon, will lead to the domino sequence of deaths (Antigone, Haemon, Eurydice) that completes the destruction of the family and wrings from Creon the acknowledgment of the power of Hades cited above (1284).

[30] So Jebb 1892 suggests ad loc.: "She thinks of Ares and Aphrodite, the parents of Harmonia, wife of Cadmus" as well as of "Dionysus, the son of 'Cadmean' Semele," who is named as such in the fifth stasimon (1115). See too Winnington-Ingram 1980, 109, who suggests that one organizing principle of the fourth stasimon may be that it is "built around these three great gods who played a role in the story of the Theban royal house—gods whose nature was not irrelevant to the disastrous action of our play."

[31] See the important discussion of Ramnoux 1968, who, starting from Lévi-Strauss' famous structuralist analysis of the Oedipus myth, revises his terms in the light of both Theban myth and pre-Socratic thought (Empedocles), each organized around the antithetical principles of War and Love, Conjunction and Disjunction. Note the importance of *harmozō* in Soph. *Ant.* 569 with reference to the bond between Antigone and Haemon, and the comments of Winnington-Ingram 1980, 93.

[32] Aphrodite together with Dionysus may well have played an even larger part in Euripides' treatment of Antigone in a lost play of the same name that dramatized the love

between these same two divinities recurs symbolically in a different key, with Ares, as it were, enlisted to fight against Aphrodite. Pentheus' intention, we may recall, is to go forth from the city as a warrior, leading an army against Dionysus and his female followers (e.g., 50–54, 780–85) precisely because he imagines that the Theban women in the mountains are engaged not in the god's mysteries, as he is told, but in unholy unions of Aphrodite (221–25; cf. 459). The benign Aphrodite is indeed located elsewhere, and the chorus of Lydian Bacchants, in their longing for escape from the oppressive confines of Thebes, envisage the goddess of love far away on her sacred island of Cyprus, the romantic site of "heart-melting Erotes and the profusion of river's streams that make the earth fertile" (402–9). Dionysus himself is poised between his role as the seductive stranger ("he has the charms of Aphrodite in his eyes," says Pentheus at 236) and a stated affinity with Ares (302), and, like Pentheus, Dionysus is ready to engage his troop of Lydian maenads in battle against the army of the king (50–52).[33] As it turns out in the *Bacchae,* Dionysus does not choose the way of Ares to demonstrate his power and destroy his earthborn adversary. Instead he arouses the king's voyeuristic desire (813 *eis erōta . . . megan*) to bring him to the mountain. On the other hand, in the case of the sons of Oedipus, it is Ares *mainomenos* who properly fuels the maddened passion for strife in Thebes, starting with Aeschylus' *Seven* (341–44) and reaching its full expression in the metaphorical merging of Dionysus with Ares in an extended choral passage of the *Phoenician Women* (784–800) whose import will be discussed further below.

To return now to the *Antigone,* the invocation of Demeter and Eleusis at the end of the hyporcheme does not bring the longed-for Dionysus, who was summoned to come with "healing foot" (1144

---

affair between Haemon and Antigone and in which Antigone herself appeared as a maenad and Dionysus was the deus ex machina. For recent discussion of this play, see Seaford 1990, 89 n. 93.

[33] Note that Tiresias reduces the link between Dionysus and Aphrodite, which has a powerful hold over the mind of Pentheus ("the god neither compels a woman to be chaste with regard to Cypris nor will he corrupt her," 314–18; cf. 686–88, 940), but he confirms those between Dionysus and Ares ("he shares in a certain portion of Ares' domain," in his capacity to induce panic and madness in the troops, 302–4), even though Dionysus and Ares are never associated in cult. On Ares and Dionysus in Theban dramas, see Longo 1986 and also Lonnoy 1985.

*katharsiōi podi*). It brings on the messenger, bearing the news of a dreadful "marriage of death" that united Haemon and Antigone in the tomb, and prepares the way for Creon's final apostrophe to Hades *duskathartos* (1284). Even more marked is the failure of appeal to another saving goddess, which occurs at the turning point of the play, since the intention is announced but never fulfilled. Creon's wife, Eurydice, was just venturing forth to address prayers to Pallas Athena when news of a household disaster (*oikeiou kakou*) reached her ears (1183–88), and she remains on stage in silence to hear the messenger's full report. Why Pallas Athena in the first place? And why mention a purpose that will not be carried out? There were two shrines of Pallas among those of the other Theban gods, as we learn from the chorus in the parodos of Sophocles' *Oedipus the King* (20). One was dedicated to Athena Onka (cf. Aeschylus *Seven against Thebes* 487, 501), and the identity of the other is uncertain. Athena was not the most important of official divinities in Thebes,[34] but Eurydice's mention of Pallas following her greeting of the chorus as *astoi* ("citizens") suggests her mission was prompted by concern for the city's welfare. Once the disaster is revealed, however, as a family affair, what is the use of asking for *Athena*'s intervention? Thus, just at the moment when the weight of the play shifts decisively from polis to *genos,* it is marked as such by this wife's unspoken prayer to Athena, which is followed by her return in silence whence she came—back to the woman's place inside the *oikos* (1244), never to emerge again.[35]

Athena's civic function can also be detected in the part she played in the events that led up to the city's foundation, as we learn in the *Phoenician Women,* where the chorus relates how Cadmus slew the dragon with a stone as his weapon and, at the goddess's behest, sowed

[34] The scholiast to Soph. *Oed. King* 20 suggests an Athena Cadmeia or Ismenia. Pausanias reports only a statue and altar of Pallas or Athena Onka (9.12.2) and a statue of Athena Zosteria (9.17.3). Vian 1963, 139–41, notes that Athena in Thebes was neither a goddess of the acropolis nor a "protectress of the city" (Poliouchos) but rather a guardian of the gates (Pylaitis): as Athena Onka with a sanctuary outside the walls and as Athena Ismenia or Pronoia at the entry of the Ismenion with the functions of a Promachos, that is, of an advance sentinel who guards the city from external attack. On her mythic role in the foundation of the city, see further below.

[35] The messenger, attempting to put the best interpretation on Eurydice's abrupt return into the house, sets out the rules: it is inside and not in public (*es polin*) that it is appropriate to mourn a private grief (1246–50 *penthos oikeion*).

the earth with its teeth to produce the earthborn Spartoi (667–70, 1062–64).[36] Ever the "gigantomachic" goddess and upholder of the Olympian order, she exercises the same power at Thebes yet again, this time in Euripides' *Heracles,* when during the hero's Dionysiac mad scene she intervenes directly in the dramatic action to fell Heracles with a stone before he can commit the further and inexpiable crime of parricide (906–8, 1002–4)—not so much for the sake of Thebes, but as a necessary precaution if Heracles is ultimately to be conveyed to Athens. Her value as a goddess of public life is still more apparent later on in the *Phoenician Women* when the women of the chorus pray to Athena that they too may be mothers "blessed in their children" (*euteknoi*). The context might seem to be ironic, for the prayer is uttered at the moment of the death of Creon's son. But the young Menoeceus' death is a heroic act of patriotic sacrifice to save the fatherland, an act required of him as the last autochthon to expiate the wrath of Ares for the ancient slaying of his dragon in which Pallas herself was involved (1040–62).

The chorus's earlier mention of the goddess occurred in an ode that celebrated the idyllic beginnings of the city—Cadmus' arrival in a fertile land nourished by the abundant waters of Dirce, by whose streams, shaded with luxuriant ivy, the infant Dionysus was born, "the origin of Bacchic dances for Theban maidens" (639–66). The story includes, as it must, the subsequent combat of the Sown Men, instigated by Athena (the "motherless goddess," 666), but, to counter the negative recall of the earth drenched with their blood, the epode of the choral song concludes with references to nurturant feminine powers and highlights again the figures of Demeter and her daughter.

After mention of Io, ancestress (*promatoros*) of the Phoenician maidens (named in their appeal to her progeny Epaphus), they call upon "the two goddesses named together—Persephone and dear goddess Demeter, mistress of all" (*pantōn anassa*), and, lastly, upon Earth herself (*Ga*), "nurse of all things" (*pantōn trophos*), who is asked to send

[36] For the development of the mythic tradition concerning Athena's role in the city's foundation that even makes her the recipient of Cadmus' original sacrifice (scholia to Eur. *Phoen. Wom.* 1062; scholia to Aesch. *Seven* 164) and a discussion of the relevant figured monuments, see Vian 1963, 26–30, 46–47, 33–34, 109–10. Perhaps this is why Eteocles, just before the duel with his brother, appeals to the martial goddess ("golden-shielded Pallas") to grant victory to his spear (Eur. *Phoen. Wom.* 1372–76).

the "fire-bearing goddesses" to protect this land of Thebes (676–89). Earth is here allied with the beneficence of Demeter, a move that is further reinforced by the Eleusinian epithets of mother and daughter (*diōnumoi,* "twin-named," and *purphorous,* "fire- or torch-bearing"), names and functions not typical in Thebes. Although Demeter Thesmophoros had a well-known cult in Thebes, the mention of Persephone in the passage above is sufficiently strange to elicit the scholiast's resort to an obscure tradition that Zeus gave Thebes to Persephone as a wedding gift. However this may be, the strategy of appeal proves futile. The Eleusinian deities are not to assure the well-being of the land nor is Pallas either, whose significance we have noted above. Rather, in a replay of the myth of the Spartoi, nurture turns to destruction and fertility to blood in the sinister identification of Earth as the continual breeder of monsters. Antigone, in her grief over her slain brothers, turns into "a Bacchant of corpses" (1489). Marriage remains in the sphere of death. Although Antigone will not, in this play, match Persephone as bride of Hades, she will identify herself as a potential Danaid if she is forced to marry Haemon, as Creon demands (1675). As she goes into exile with her father, Oedipus, it is clear that she, above all (and as her name Anti-gone, "anti-generation," suggests),[37] will never be blessed as a mother of glorious children for the city, as the Phoenician maidens, in their entreaty to Pallas, had wished for themselves.

Such is the recurrent situation in the territory of Thebes, where Dionysus, as I have suggested, is drawn into the circle of Ares and Aphrodite, both protectors and destroyers of the family and polis, and where Demeter and Athena have no efficacious role to play in the averting of disaster. But in Athens, it is precisely these two goddesses, Demeter and Athena, who between them can be said to "stabilize" Dionysus and to divert his potentially negative effects or to capture his creative powers for the benefit of the city. Athena is, of course, the poliadic goddess who rules over the city, while Demeter's influence is more complex, and this for two reasons: in the first place, it is shared between her Thesmophoric and Eleusinian functions in the promotion

[37] For this etymology of Antigone's name, see Benardete 1975, 156: "Her name, whose meaning—'generated in place of another'—bears witness to success, proves to mean 'anti-generation.' " See also Benardete's fuller discussion of this point, pp. 156–57.

of Athens, and, second, the fact of Kore's descent into the underworld is itself susceptible of a double and antithetical meaning. Taken in its entirety, the myth follows the trajectory from sorrow and loss to recovery and joy and thus provides the regenerative patterns we may sometimes find in the theater. This is the case especially in Athens, as we shall see in the *Ion,* but never in Thebes, where, for example, in both the *Antigone* and the *Phoenician Women* the emphasis falls instead on the tragedy of a mother's sorrow and on the deathly union of Persephone and Hades.

## Dionysus in Athens

If Sophocles' *Antigone* sets the terms for Dionysiac reference in Thebes through the progress of its choral odes, the same poet also conversely provides the exact Athenian configuration I have just described. The drama in question is appropriately enough the *Oedipus at Colonus* in which the accursed Oedipus chooses Athens over Thebes as his final resting place, where he will be transformed into a source of blessings for the land. The ode to which I refer is none other than the famous "nightingale" chorus in praise of Athens (668–719). Each element is in its proper place in the sequence, according to my hypothesis. Dionysus, we may note, is invoked first in the list: his is the presence in the grove where the nightingale sings, where the bird "haunts the glades, the wine-dark ivy, dense and dark the untrodden, sacred wood of god/rich with laurel and olives never touched by the sun/untouched by storms that blast from every quarter—where the Reveler (Bakkhiōtas) Dionysus strides the earth forever / where the wild nymphs are dancing round him / nymphs who nursed his life."[38] Next come the Great Goddesses (Demeter and Kore), associated also with the undying streams of the river Cephisus as well as with the choruses of the Muses, ending finally with reference to "Aphrodite of the golden rein." Athena follows after, in the ensuing strophe, through the evocation of her miraculous olive tree, self-renewing, "a terror to the spears of enemies," and nurse of children (*paidotrophou phullon elaias*), over which she and Zeus stand guard with their ever-vigilant

[38] Trans. Fagles 1982.

gaze.[39] One could hardly hope for a more idealizing and ideological statement in which the burgeoning abundance of Dionysus sets the tone (and the paradigm) for the proliferating images of fertility, growth, and nurture, invoked here and now in the present tense of the play—not, as in Thebes, where such hopes of Dionysiac blessings serve only as a distant point of reference and where Eleusinian echoes end in the barrenness of a bride of death. Tiresias in the *Bacchae* links Demeter and Dionysus as emblems both of the necessities of life (bread and wine) and of complementary principles (the dry and the wet) in his explication to Pentheus of Dionysus' benefits (274–85), and indeed, ordinarily the two have much in common both in cult and in popular belief (e.g., *Bacchae* 274–83). But in tragic convention, and especially in Thebes, they are finally separated from one another, with Dionysiac mysteries taking the path of bloody destruction and the Eleusinian rites fulfilling their salvational promise elsewhere, as—above all—on the soil of Attica.

The allusions to Eleusis in the *Oedipus at Colonus* are a cue to the spectators to consider the patterns of the mysteries in connection with the mysterious passing of Oedipus.[40] But in three Euripidean plays, Eleusis itself occupies an important position in the economy of the drama. In the *Erechtheus* it is the city in armed conflict with Athens. In the *Suppliant Women* it serves as the location on stage where the grieving Argive mothers appeal to Athens at Demeter's altar to assist them in procuring for their dead sons the burial denied to them by Thebes. In the *Ion,* a play that directly concerns the future of the Erechtheid dynasty in Athens, although set at Delphi, the nocturnal mysteries of Eleusis are celebrated in the most significant choral ode of the play (1048–1105). In all three dramas, Athena makes a personal appearance at the end as the dea ex machina, and in her role as poliadic goddess, she gives different sets of directions to the participants, according to the specific themes of each of the plots: in the *Erechtheus,* she decrees

[39] The antistrophe that closes the ode appeals to Poseidon, both to complete the roster of protectors of Athens and to pay special homage to the horseman god who had a special cult at Eleusis. Poseidon is not always in such a favorable position in Athens, and indeed Euripides' *Erechtheus,* to which I shall shortly refer, pits Athena against her old rival Poseidon in the matter of Eleusis until the goddess effects a reconciliation at the end of the play.

[40] See Winnington-Ingram 1954; Winnington-Ingram 1980, 264–78, 324–26.

cult honors in both Athens and Eleusis;[41] in the *Suppliant Women,* she establishes binding political oaths upon Argos to honor its alliance with Athens (1183–1226); and in the *Ion,* the goddess certifies the legitimacy of Ion and forecasts the genealogies to come that will secure his place in the city and give his progeny credit for eponymous founders on the Greek mainland and in Ionia (1553–1605). Each of these three plays can be said to include some distinctive elements of Bacchic activity, and we may ask How and under what circumstances does the Dionysiac erupt into the Athenian milieu, and how is it resolved?

I cannot treat the first two plays here in any detail. Suffice it to say, in both the *Erechtheus* and the *Suppliant Women,* Dionysiac motifs are displaced to other contexts and turn up only briefly, if tellingly, toward the end of the action.[42] By contrast, the *Ion* is pervaded by the presence

[41] For Athena's cultic pronouncements, clear with regard to the family of Erechtheus but unfortunately fragmentary in the passage relating to the Eleusinian mysteries, see *Erechtheus* frag. 65. 109–14 (Austin) = frag. 18 (Cararra). On the *Erechtheus,* produced probably in 422 or 423 (but this is still contested), see the editions of the fragments, Austin 1967 and 1968; and Cararra 1977; and also Picard 1931; Parker 1987, 202–5; and Zeitlin 1989, 60.

[42] In frag. 65 (Austin) of the *Erechtheus,* the Dionysiac moment directly precedes and indeed motivates the entrance of Athena herself. The women of the chorus have just begun their lament over the dead in the name of Deo (Demeter) as a prelude to the Athenian queen's full expression of grief over her lost daughters and husband, when suddenly the earth shakes and the ground of the city is set to dancing (line 47); the roofs topple; the palace shakes with Bacchic energy (*bakkheuōn*). The god in question is not Dionysus but Poseidon the Earth Shaker, the mighty god worshiped as father at Eleusis (Pausanias 1.38.6) and the previous, still unplacated rival of Athena for control of the city. Yet the sudden irruption of violence in the action itself and the language used to describe it are Dionysiac in nature (cf. Aesch. *Edoni* frag. 58 (*TrGF* 3); Eur. *Bacch.* 585, *Her.* 898, 905). This Bacchic terror, however, lasts for just an instant, since Athena emerges almost immediately to command Poseidon to "turn his trident away from earth and not to destroy the earth and ruin her lovely city." Poseidon had gotten his due in the death of Erechtheus, Athena's favorite, who is now hidden deep within the earth, and even more, the temple she orders to be built in honor of Erechtheus will bear the double name of Erechtheus-Poseidon. Ever the wily political strategist, Athena not only deflects the Bacchic violence of Poseidon but integrates the god into the city and gives him the presence on the Acropolis he had long desired, and she does so precisely through a merger with his former adversary, Erechtheus, so that the two are now welded into a single and powerful unity.

In the *Suppliant Women,* the scene in question strangely intervenes between two sets of mourners (before: the women and Adrastus; after: the Argive boys bearing the bones of their fathers, which is the prelude to Athena's appearance on stage). Evadne, wife of Capaneus, one of the Argive dead, and daughter of Iphis (who had also lost his son in the expedition), rushes forth like a Bacchant (1000) and climbs a rocky crag just above the flames of the funeral pyre, determined to make a daring leap to join her husband in death and to arrive, as she says, in Hades (1004) and the chambers of Persephone (1042). A bride of death going to join her husband in an outburst of Bacchic frenzy, Evadne also means to win a heroic victory,

and power of Dionysus in both literal and figurative ways, and the play demonstrates in fullest fashion how Athena and Demeter may be said to deflect the scenario of a destructive Dionysiac action that more properly belongs in Thebes. Displaced in locale from Athens to Delphi, the play belongs officially not to Dionysus but rather to Apollo; Ion is Apollo's child, born from his violent union with the Erechtheid daughter, Creusa, and it is around the god's sacred shrine-oracle and not on the mountains of Parnassus that the play is spatially organized, with its parade of comings and goings and its developing themes of secrecy and revelation.

Creusa has come to Delphi to inquire about her present childlessness, with secret hopes of discovering the fate of the child she had exposed long ago, who, as it turns out, was mysteriously rescued through Apollo's agency and was brought up as a temple servant in the holy precinct. The oracle, however, gives Ion to Xuthus as his son, and the complications begin when Creusa acts to prevent this bastard scion of her husband from leaving Delphi for Athens and contaminating the pure blood of her autochthonous lineage. Her instrument is the baneful drop of the Gorgon's blood, given by Athena to Creusa's ancestor Erichthonius; her agent, the old servant of the house who defends the rights of the Erechtheids; and the occasion, a festive banquet organized by Ion and Xuthus. Ion would have died of the poison mixed in with his wine were it not for an ill-omened utterance

---

a *kallinikos,* over all women, not in the usual feminine way through the works of Athena, but in the epic valor of *aretē* (1048–71). The flames of the marriage torch merge with the funeral fires and echo too the fate of her husband, who was struck by lightning (860–61, 985).

The Dionysiac tenor of her action here at Eleusis revives the fate of Persephone, but although it is an Argive bride who stages this disruptive scene, the chorus gives her action a Theban context when first it addresses Adrastus: "Bitter the wedding you saw / bitter the word of Phoebus; a Fury, bringing of grief / has abandoned Oedipus' house and come to yours" (832–35). In the ensuing scene, however, in which Adrastus is bidden by Theseus to give a formal funeral eulogy (or *epitaphios*) over the war dead, as is the Athenian custom, he is, in a sense, brought over to the side of Athens. But the spirit of Oedipus himself will not be stilled and returns now not to the one whose daughter married the cursed son of Oedipus (i.e., Adrastus), but to a man who now resembles Oedipus himself—the father Iphis, who having lost both son and daughter, declares himself to be the most miserable man on earth—to which the chorus can only agree: "What suffering is yours! A share of Oedipus' doom / has befallen you, old man, and me, and my poor city" (1077–78). Even though Thebes has now been vanquished by Athens and Argos has succeeded in burying its dead, a tragic Bacchic event and its aftermath can find its true paradigm only in Thebes, assimilated to this pattern in a variant of the father-daughter relation we have met before with Antigone and Oedipus as well as with Agave and Cadmus.

that prompted him to order all the cups to be poured on the ground and for a subsequent influx of birds that swooped down to dip their beaks into the spilled libations. Ion's bird is the only one to die, and die she does in the spasms of a miniature Bacchic seizure (1203–5). The crisis motivates the events of the rest of the play: Ion pursues his unknown mother, who has taken refuge at Apollo's altar; the Pythia reveals the basket with its tokens, which she had kept all these years in the hidden recesses of the shrine; mother and child unite in a joyful reunion; and, finally, Athena appears at the end to resolve Ion's doubts about his paternity, sending him home and arranging all good things for the future of Athens and Ion's line.

I have treated this play elsewhere in extensive detail and will give only the briefest summary here of the pertinent elements.[43] Dionysus appears first on the sculptured facade of the temple, in company with Athena and in a scene from the Gigantomachy, which the chorus of Athenian women describes in the parodos (216–18). In subsequent odes, they invoke the god twice more in his ritual, and especially mystic, aspects, the first pertaining to Thyiadic rites at Delphi on Mount Parnassus (714–17), the other to those at Eleusis where Iacchus-Dionysus leads the preliminary procession of initiates along the Sacred Way from Athens to Eleusis (1074–86). Xuthus is not present at Ion's banquet, because he has gone to make blood sacrifices to Dionysus on Mount Parnassus as a belated thank-offering for Ion's birth (653, 1130), thinking that he must have sired the boy at Delphi during a nocturnal Dionysiac festival, when he was enjoying "the pleasures of Bacchus" (553). And, finally, Ion's banquet itself is a Dionysiac scene at which convivial celebration is almost transformed into a fatal merger of blood and wine and where the bird, in its death throes, imitates sacred madness (1231–35).

Ion's story is made to follow the pattern of the first autochthon child, Erichthonius, as Nicole Loraux has persuasively shown, and once discovered in his true identity, he is represented as an Erechtheus redivivus who has regained his youth: light shines once again in the royal house of Athens (1465–67).[44] But the action of the play suggests that the hidden pattern that governs the construction of Ion's identity conforms far better to the story of Dionysus himself.

[43] Zeitlin 1989, where the relevant documentation can be found.

[44] Loraux 1990a.

Ion, like Dionysus, was born of a union between a god and a mortal and, like Dionysus, can be said to be twice-born. Ion was separated at birth from a mother he presumes may have died, and he, for his part, was transferred to his father's domain (by the same Hermes who brought Dionysus to Nysa) to remain among the living. The circumstances of Dionysus' double birth further strengthen the analogy, for the secret of Ion's birth (the basket and its tokens) was hidden in the inmost shrine of Apollo. This space, as we are reminded several times, contained an omphalos in the form of a sacred stone (6, 223, 933) but was expressly forbidden to all women (222–32) (except the Pythia) and, as such, bears a suspicious resemblance to that "male womb" from which Dionysus issued forth as the son of Zeus. Additionally, when the basket is brought out for the recognition scene, the ensuing reunion evokes Creusa's exultant cry "He died but did not die" (1440–44). Ion's wicker basket itself is also significant. We are told explicitly that the placement of Ion in his basket imitates the family custom that began with Erichthonius (19–21), but Erichthonius too may be said to follow the earlier pattern of the baby Dionysus Liknites, in honor of whom Thyiadic rites were enacted on Mount Parnassus in the very nocturnal mysteries to which the chorus had earlier referred (711–21).[45]

The Dionysiac model holds true for the subsequent phase of Ion's development as well. Ion, like Dionysus, was born of a god and a mortal, destined to return home to claim his rightful place and identity. He too meets with resistance from those, his kin, who resent his intrusion and, as in the *Bacchae,* do not believe his father was a god. In addition, he also embodies the paradox of being both stranger, *xenos,* and native-born.

Despite these doublet relations, Ion and Dionysus are also antitheses of one another. As an immortal's offspring, Dionysus comes to claim his divinity, while Ion leaves his pedigree behind as the child of the god in order to take up mortal status. For the child of Creusa, however, mortal status means autochthony, and as the plot unfolds, he is aligned with that other autochthon who is Dionysus' adversary, so that Ion too risks becoming the doomed Dionysiac child in the near-tragic scenario by which he almost plays Pentheus to his mother's Agave.

[45] For discussion and relevant bibliography, see Zeitlin 1989, 157 n. 48.

Indeed, we might almost be back in Thebes again. No wonder perhaps, since Athens in this play comes closest to "Theban" categories with respect to the problems of autochthony as the basis of membership in the city and the difficulties of incorporating an "other," a stranger, into one's midst. Ion's first hesitation in going to Athens as Xuthus' son is predicated precisely on his knowledge that this Athens—unlike the city we know elsewhere in tragedy, which prides itself on supporting suppliants and rescuing fallen heroes—is one that resists the advent of outsiders and jealously guards the privileges of citizenship for its own (585–657). The cherished Athenian belief that autochthony validates a collective civic identity is countered by the destructive valence of the earthborn with its monstrous and violent associations. The ambiguity is perfectly exemplified in the two drops of the blood of the Gorgon, who in this play alone is said to have been born from the earth (989). It is this two-sided legacy that accounts for the curious but somehow logical fact that one drop will provide good nourishment and the other a deadly poison (1003–5). The images on the facade of the temple already recall the Gigantomachy, and although Athena and Dionysus are depicted as winning their victory over these earthborn rebels, the events of the play suggest the possibility of another, more Theban, outcome in the matter of the earthborn.

What assures the good news in Ion's story is finally the alliance not only between Athena and Dionysus, but also between Dionysus and Demeter. The pattern of the "twice-born" joins up with the other motif of the "lost one safely found," so as to fulfill a soteriological promise of joy and brilliant light after a long period of darkness and sorrow. The Eleusinian ode is placed at the turning point of the play, when the Paidagogos has gone on his lethal Dionysiac errand to Ion's tent, and the entire recognition scene between mother and child, arranged by the hieratic Pythia, who controls the mysteries of Ion's identity in the secrets the basket contains, is constructed as a revelation reserved only for those who are meant to know. Moreover, the mythic patterns of the Eleusinian story can also serve as the model for Creusa, who is *both* the Kore, raped while picking flowers in the meadow, *and* now the grieving Demeter, searching for her lost child. In this sense, Ion, whom Creusa had thought was "dwelling with Persephone beneath the earth" (1440–44), may be said to play the mythic role of Kore to Creusa's Demeter, but in a ritual setting he can equally represent the mystic child of Eleusis, whom some authorities have been identified as Iacchus himself.[46]

In Ion's present situation, however, it is Dionysus' affiliation with the youthful Iacchus of the sacred procession (to which the choral ode refers) that directly links the god to the boy and offers a joyous alternative to a tragic Dionysiac ending. Thus Iacchus-Dionysus is the figure of transition, whose ritual passage to Eleusis will be matched in the political return of the "twice-born" to Athens, where he can receive the status due him in the city to which he belongs.[47] In this sense, Dionysus, flanked by Athena on one side and Demeter on the other, deflects the plot from the kind of tragic closure that in Thebes cancels dynastic continuity, negates the idea of civic harmony, and proves unable to create new institutions, whether ritual, familial, or political, for the salutary future of the polis.[48]

## Another View: *Hypsipyle, Phoenician Women,* and *Antiope*

The last illustration of the different ways in which Dionysiac power can be mobilized in the theatrical settings of Thebes and Athens requires one more itinerary through Euripidean drama. This route will lead us back to Thebes but will also extend in other directions, includ-

[46] On the birth of a mystic child at Eleusis, see, for example, Burkert 1983, 288–89 and Lévêque 1982, 188–90. The identity of the child is disputed (he is called Brimos in mystic terminology) and may refer to Plutus, Iacchus-Dionysus (see scholia to Aristophanes *Frogs* 482), as well as to other candidates. For the best discussion, see Richardson 1974, 316–21.

[47] This ode works through a number of ironic reversals that are discussed in Zeitlin 1989, 161–63. The reference to Iacchus is as follows: the chorus says it would be "ashamed, if in the presence of the much hymned god [Iacchus], the newcomer [Ion] would witness (*theōros . . . opsetai*) the nocturnal torch when all of nature (starry aither, moon, and Nereid maidens) danced to the two goddesses by the springs of the Callichoron" (1074–86). The text is difficult here. Some have thought that the viewer is Iacchus himself (or even Apollo) rather than Ion. The syntactical ambiguity may well be significant, as implying a reciprocal relation between Ion and Iacchus. There are other problems, although the general sense seems clear. I accept Diggle's version, reading *theōros* for *theōron* and *ennukhion* for *ennukhios*. The word *theōros* has a ritual connotation of an observer at a festival and fits well too with the earlier proposal of Xuthus that he first bring Ion to the city as a *theatēs* or spectator (656).

[48] In addition to Athena's prophecy of descendants for Xuthus, Creusa, and then for Ion, the play validates alliances among non-kin as well as the institutions of fosterage and adoption.

ing a return visit to the town on the frontiers of Boeotia and Attica from which theatrical performances were reputedly introduced into Athens. I want to look in particular at the one play we know (albeit in fragments) that takes place at Eleutherae itself—that is, the *Antiope*—and to situate it in relation to the two other plays (*Hypsipyle, Phoenician Women*) that may well have been presented along with it at the City Dionysia in the same year. The evidence is not secure, but there is good support for this hypothesis, especially the presence of important Dionysiac references in all three plays.[49]

The *Phoenician Women* is Euripides' Theban extravaganza, which, in treating the expedition of the Seven and the hostile encounter of the sons of Oedipus, takes a wide-angle view over the entire dramatic history of the city, starting from Cadmus' Phoenician origins and including the foundation of the city as well as the past and present of Oedipus and his kin. The first and third plays, *Hypsipyle* and *Antiope,* extend the perspective over the earlier fortunes of the city in both time and space, each in a different and distinctive way. In following the journey of the expedition of the Seven on its way from Argos to Thebes, the action of the *Hypsipyle* immediately precedes the events of the *Phoenician Women* that take place once the Argives reach their destination at Thebes. The *Antiope,* on the other hand, looks back to a period in the dynastic history of Thebes well before the house of Laius and, in so doing, fits in with the panoramic sweep of the *Phoenician Women.* In both plays, the settings are peripheral to the center that is the city of Thebes, either as a transitional stopping point (*Hypsipyle*) or as a territory on its margins (*Antiope*).[50]

[49] In commenting on Dionysus' report of having lately read Euripides' *Andromeda* (Aristoph. *Frogs* 53), the scholiast queries: "Why not one of the good plays that has recently been produced, *Hypsipyle, Phoenician Women, Antiope?* The *Andromeda* was produced eight years ago." On the other hand, a corrupt passage in the hypothesis to the *Phoenician Women* suggests it was produced with *Oenomaus* and *Chrysippus* and Kambitsis 1972, xxxii–xxxiv, concurs in this opinion (against Webster 1966 and 1967). The merit of this grouping, it is claimed, is that all the plays concern the history of the house of Laius, culminating in the drama of the sons of Oedipus. But the *Phoenician Women,* which ranges so widely over Theban myth, makes no allusion whatsoever to any of the events of these particular plays. Although it is true that the scholiast's information tells us no more than the fact that his list was chosen from among all the plays presented between 412 and 407, there are excellent internal grounds (both thematic and metrical) to suppose he was recalling a single trilogy. For a list of some of these parallels, see Bond 1963, 144 n. 1.

[50] Webster 1967, 215, prefers to change the order to *Hypsipyle, Antiope, Phoenician Women,* contending that the first "gives an ill-omened prelude to the expedition, the *Phoeni-*

In the first instance, the *Hypsipyle,* the play is set at Nemea, where Amphiaraus is on his way with the Argive expedition to Thebes and meets up with Hypsipyle, a figure from the Argonautic saga, and asks her to lead him to fresh flowing water from a spring for sacred libations. Exiled from Lemnos and separated from the two sons she had there by Jason, Hypsipyle is now in service at the house of the local rulers (Lycurgus and Eurydice) as nurse to their child Opheltes, who dies in the course of the play, crushed by the serpent who guards the holy spring. The reason for her exile is that earlier, in defiance of the Lemnian women's determination to slay all the men on the island, she had saved her father, Thoas, the son of Dionysus himself. Now she in turn will be saved from the wrath of Eurydice, first by the intervention of Amphiaraus and then through the timely reunion with her long-lost sons. Dionysus continues to exert a strong influence in the play; the rescue of Thoas at sea had succeeded through the god's "contrivances" (*mēkhanai*). A Dionysiac sign, the *sēmeion* of the golden vine, will serve as the token of the sons' identity in the recognition scene near the end of the play, after they have won victories in the Nemean Games, newly established in honor of the child Opheltes (renamed Archemoros). Dionysus himself entered the scene as the deus ex machina.[51]

The other drama, the *Antiope,* although directly concerned with Thebes and the founding of the city, is an independent episode in Theban history, since it does not link up with the dynastic lineage of Cadmus, the Spartoi, and the house of Laius. It too takes place in a frontier zone—Eleutherae—situated, as we know, between Thebes and Athens, which is set as the Dionysiac milieu for the recognition between Antiope and her sons, Amphion and Zethus. Born of her enforced union with Zeus, exposed at birth, and raised in the rustic

*cian Women* starts with the attack on Thebes," and since "the setting is Thebes," references to Amphion, Dirce, and Dionysus are "natural links back to the *Antiope*." It can be equally argued, however, that the references in the *Phoenician Women* look ahead to the *Antiope,* where they will be fully developed. The exact order, however, is not of crucial significance to my general argument.

[51] This is the barest summary of what we know about this long and unusually complicated play from the extant fragments (including the substantial papyrus fragment, *POxy* 852) and other mythological sources, and it is possible, as Aélion 1983, 1:191, suggests, that it was Euripides' innovation to combine the Lemnian and Argive stories of Hypsipyle with the founding of the Nemean Games. For the basic edition and commentary, see Bond 1963, and for further interpretation, see, in addition to Bond, Webster 1967, 212–15; Aélion 1983, 1:187–95; and Aélion 1986, 82–84, 128–35. I have not seen the edition of Cockle 1987.

setting of Eleutherae, they are destined, as the play will conclude, to go to Thebes as builders and rulers of the city.[52]

Structurally, all three plays share the motif of two brothers antithetically opposed to each other in function, position, or name. But while the *Phoenician Women* demonstrates again and in abundant detail how the fratricidal conflict results in the loss of difference between the two sons of Oedipus, the case of the two other fraternal pairs follows a very different course. Although both sets of brothers are contrasted by role in that one is a poet-musician (Euneus for the *Hypsipyle,* Amphion for the *Antiope*) and the other a man of war (Thoas, Zethus), the potential for hostile dissension is turned into amicable complement. This is especially the case as we know from the debate between Amphion and Zethus in the *Antiope,* celebrated in Plato's *Gorgias* (485e3–486d1), which extended the argument between a poet's and a warrior's vocation to weigh the relative merits of a contemplative versus an active life.[53]

In addition, each of these dramas represents its pair of brothers in a significant relation to their mother. Once again, the outcome of the *Phoenician Women,* the middle term, differs sharply from the two other dramas that frame its action on either side. A mother, Iocasta, tries to save Eteocles and Polynices from the fateful combat, intervening not once, but twice, to prevent their fateful confrontation, but, once arrived on the field of battle to find them already slain, she kills herself in grief over their corpses. While an important fragment of Stesi-

[52] The myth of Amphion and Zethus represents, in some sense, a second and perhaps competing claim regarding the foundation of the city of Thebes. The problems associated with Antiope's myth and lineage are too complex, however, to discuss here. The numerous variations may well be due, as Vian 1963, 70–73, 193–202, suggests, to the political rivalry between Thebes and Boeotia, each claiming Antiope and her sons, with the added complication of Sicyon's interest, based on Antiope's sojourn there and her marriage with Epopeus. See also Aélion 1986, 17–20, 109. On the play and its fragments, see, in addition to Aélion, Snell 1967, 70–98; Webster 1967, 205–11; and, above all, the edition and commentary of Kambitsis 1972. The ancient sources are mainly the scholia to Apollonius Rhodius 1.735 (and note the context: the myth of Amphion and Zethus is depicted as the second image in the ekphrasis of Jason's cloak, which he dons on his way to his first meeting with Hypsipyle in Lemnos); Apollodorus 3.5.5; Hyginus *Fabulae* 7–8; and Pacuvius frag. 12; *Palatine Anthology* 3.7 (on which see further below, n. 55); Propertius 3.15.11–42; and Dio Chrysostomus 15.9 (2.234 Arnim). For recent discussion of the myth of Antiope, with emphasis only on her marital status as a daughter and bride, see Seaford 1988, 129–30; Seaford 1990, 83–84.

[53] The best account of the poetic/philosophical questions involved in the debate is Walsh 1984, 109–16; and see too Snell 1967, 82–97.

chorus shows us a precedent for Iocasta's active, mediating role between the brothers,[54] Euripides' emphasis on the maternal presence of Iocasta and the tragic consequences of her extreme devotion are surely his own elaboration, decisively shifting the mythic and dramatic perspective to spotlight the affective bonds between mother and sons at this, the last stage in the history of the paternal house of Laius.

In the *Hypsipyle* and *Antiope,* this relationship is the very heart of the plot, and the tragic scenario is reversed: a mother is separated from her sons at their birth or in their babyhood; she has fallen on hard times and is in service to a woman, another man's wife, who makes her life wretched (Eurydice, wife of Lycus of Nemea; Dirce, wife of Lycus in Thebes). In each case, the sons arrive unrecognized and eventually rescue their mother from a crisis that threatens her welfare, and a happy reunion takes place at the end, accompanied by a series of beneficent prophecies for the future.

This type of plot, which revolves around a mother and her sons, is a familiar pattern in the theater and a favorite plot of Euripides, in particular, who returned to it again and again, not only in these two plays but in those, for example, concerning Melanippe, Auge, and Ino, as well as those that involve a mother but only one son (e.g., Cresphontes). The ending is invariably joyful; fatal danger is averted, and mother and sons are successfully reunited in a variant of what I earlier termed a Demetrian scenario of the "lost one safely found." But in these cases, the ruling paradigm has nothing strictly to do with Demeter and Kore. Rather, it conforms far better to the rescue of Semele from the underworld by her son Dionysus, in which he brought her back to the upper world and to life, restoring her to a proper position of honor.[55] In the complementary motif of the woman

[54] *PLille* 76A–C; see Davies 1988, 213–18, for most recent text and full bibliography.

[55] The descent of Dionysus in search of Semele is located variously at Troezen (Pausanias 2.31.2) and Argos through the marsh of Lerna (Pausanias 2.37.5; scholia to Lycophron 12; Diodorus Siculus 4.25.4; Apollodorus 3.5.3). The arrangement and themes of the second-century Cyzicene epigrams further support the hypothesis that Dionysus' filial devotion to Semele serves as the paradigm for other non-Dionysiac plots. The nineteen epigrams, preserved in the third book of the *Palatine Anthology,* were inscribed on the supports between the twenty columns of a Hellenistic temple to accompany a series of mostly mythological reliefs. The temple was dedicated by Attalus II (Philadelphus) and Eumenes II to the memory of their mother, Apollonis. This is why virtually all the epigrams (and reliefs) concern sons who deliver their mothers from misfortune or avenge their wrongs, beginning with Dionysus and Semele and ending with Romulus and Remus. It is also worth noting that

who oppresses this maternal figure (e.g., Eurydice, Dirce), we might also read the antagonism of the goddess Hera, which can be combined with the theme we are tracing in these two plays of enslavement, persecution, and subsequent deliverance.[56] Since none of these "Semele and Dionysus" dramas survive in their entirety, it is not surprising that we tend to overlook the significance of this recurrent mythic pattern, when considering the repertory of dramatic plots in the tragic corpus as well as the range of Dionysiac effects in the theater.

As for the actual Dionysiac elements, each play highlights a different facet of the god's power and mode of manifestation. In schematic form these can be rendered as follows: in the *Hypsipyle,* an association with wine as the distinguishing mark of the family of Dionysus' son, exemplified in the token of the golden vine that secures the identity of Hypsipyle's sons;[57] in the *Antiope,* a connection with satyrs and maenads, as befits the extraurban ambience, both in the fact that Zeus disguised himself as a satyr to seduce Antiope (a detail seemingly unknown before Euripides) and, more significantly, in the maenadic connections of Antiope and her antagonist, Dirce. Antiope is imprisoned in the palace of Thebes, but her fetters miraculously loosen of their own accord (Apollodorus 3.5.5), and she flees from the city to make her way to Eleutherae. Dirce, in pursuit, also arrives at Eleutherae as a maenad with her own band of Bacchant women. The typical reversal of roles between oppressor and victim is enacted here as an explicit reversal of a true Dionysiac action by which Dirce, who

Amphion and Zethus, who are represented as tying Dirce to the bull, head the list on the north side (7), while Hypsipyle and her sons (with the golden vine) have the first place on the west (10). The influence of tragedy is evident too in other pairings that describe dramatic moments from the theater: Auge and Telephus (2) (Euripides' *Auge*); Cresphontes and Merope (5) (Euripides' *Cresphontes*); Tyro and her sons, Pelias and Neleus (9) (Sophocles' *Tyro*); Melanippe delivered by her sons Aeolus and Boeotus (16) (Euripides' *Melanippe desmotis*); and another version of the myth of Cleopatra and the Phineidae, in which the sons defend their mother's honor against their Phrygian stepmother (4). On the epigrams themselves, see the summary of Webster 1964, 188–89.

56 Ino, a daughter of Cadmus and securely within the Dionysiac circle, seems to have played both roles—at one time the victim (of Themistio) and at another the oppressor (of Nephele). The story of Ino was treated by Euripides' predecessors in one or the other alternative, but Euripides seems to have dramatized both versions (probably in the *Ino, Phrixos A,* and *Phrixos B*).

57 In *Il.* 7.467–72, Euneus, named as son of Jason and Hypsipyle, sends supplies of wine from Lemnos to the Troad for the use of the Greek host along with a separate allotment as a gift to Agamemnon and Menelaus.

had intended to tear Antiope apart by tying her to a wild bull, meets that same end herself through the agency of Antiope's sons.

As for the *Phoenician Women,* a Dionysiac aura envelops the play, in keeping with the god's part in the history, landscape, and life of the city, and as the mood of the drama dips downward in the atmosphere of impending doom, the god's power is reflected in (and determined by) darkening allusions to Dionysiac cult. The chief signal is given in the second stasimon (784–800), where, at the turning point of the play, the choral lyrics effect the full conversion (and perversion) of Dionysiac celebration and revel into the bloodthirsty Bacchanale of Ares and in this way definitively set the seal on the inevitability of a tragic fulfillment:

> O Ares, bringer of suffering (*polumokhthos*), why in bloodlust
> and death are you possessed (*katekhēi*), out of tune (*paramousos*) with
> the festivals of Bromios?
> Not at the lovely garlanded dance of young girls
> do you sing to the breath of the flute, with hair flowing,
> a strain, in which are the Graces who form the dance;
> but with armed men, having incited (*epipneusas*) the army of Argives
> with bloodlust against Thebes,
> in revelry where no flutes play (*kōmon anaulotaton*) you lead the dance.
> Not at the will of the thyrsus-maddened god, among fawnskins, you
> wheel
> the horse, hooved quadruped, with chariots and bits
> and at Ismenos' streams advancing
> you charge on horseback (*thoazeis*), having incited against (*epipneusas*)
> the
> Argives the race of Sown Men
> in a shield-bearing armed band (*thiason*),
> hostile against the stone walls
> having equipped them with bronze.
> Strife is indeed a deadly goddess; she
> devised these troubles for the rulers of the land,—
> for the deep-suffering (*polumokhthois*) Labdakids.[58]

In this extended rhetoric of inversion, Ares is an anti-Dionysus, a *polumokhthos,* full of trouble, in contrast to the wine god, who is

[58] Translation adapted from Craik 1988.

*polugēthēs,* full of joy (cf. Hesiod *Theogony* 941, *Works and Days* 614). The *kōmos* of happy revelers turns into a dance of death, while the elated band of maenads is transformed into a shield-bearing thiasos. The war god is out of tune (*paramousos*); the music of Dionysus is replaced by strident cacophany, and ecstasy yields to blood lust; Dionysiac possession turns into the brutal madness of war.[59]

Music is the Dionysiac theme that finally seems to organize the three dramas into a triptych or pedimental shape, in which the full force of negation in the Theban scenario, exemplified in the *Phoenician Women,* is contrasted by the two plays on its periphery. They each celebrate the power of Dionysus precisely through the magical and beneficent power of music, which draws its mysterious and creative energy from its associations with the realm of Orpheus, the sweetest singer of all. In both these plays, although, as I have said, one brother is marked as a poet-musician, and the other is trained in the arts of war, their pairing does not lead, as in Thebes, to a fateful collusion between Dionysus and Ares in the madness of battle, but rather to a fruitful coalition that enhances the quieter virtues of a Dionysiac life. Thus, in addition to the major import of the Dionysus-Semele paradigm, the music of Dionysus also has its vital part to play in invoking the redemptive aspects of Dionysiac myth.

In the *Hypsipyle,* we are told that after Jason died, Orpheus took Hypsipyle's two sons to the land of Thrace and there taught one, Euneus, the music of the Asian cithara and trained the other in the weapons of Ares. This we learn from the papyrus fragment of the recognition scene (frag. 64 [Bond 1963]) that takes place at a point close to the end of the play, and it is probably followed soon after by the appearance of Dionysus as the deus ex machina. We do not know for certain what the god decreed. Some evidence suggests that Dionysus bade Euneus to take Hypsipyle back to Lemnos. But what became of the two brothers? Wilamowitz long ago suggested, and G. W. Bond concurs, that Dionysus sent Euneus on from Lemnos to Athens and "enjoined that the Euneidae should always provide sacred music for Athens." We know something from the lexicographers

[59] See Lonnoy 1985 for detailed discussion of the play of oppositions between Dionysus and Ares in this passage. Ares may become a Bacchant, Dionysus a warrior; the vocabulary of madness, possession, and inspiration (*mainomai, entheos, katekhesthai, epipneō*) is common to both.

about this family's official role in the city: under the entry *genos Athēnaisi mousikon,* Photius writes: "From Euneus, son of Jason and Hypsipyle, the *genos* is thus named among the Athenians. They were singers accompanied by lyres (*kitharōidoi*), and provided the liturgy (*khreian*) for the performance of holy rites (*hierourgias*)." The case is further strengthened by an inscription found on an Athenian theater seat (*IG* 2.3[2], no. 5056) that identifies its holder as the priest of Dionysus Melpomenos from the family of the Euneidae (*Hiereōs Melpomenou Dionusou ex Euneidōn*), and it is also worth reporting that the poet Cratinus wrote a comedy called the *Euneidae.*[60] Amphiaraus in the *Hypsipyle* may proceed along the road to Thebes and to the fate that he already knows awaits him there,[61] but the musical powers that dominate this play (Hypsipyle herself is also a singer) are transferred appropriately to Athens.

In the case of Amphion, the musical brother in the *Antiope,* the evidence seems to situate him in an Apollinian milieu. His wife was Niobe, negatively associated later with both Apollo and Artemis, who avenged her insult to their mother, Leto; the seven-gated city recalls Apollo's sacred number; the god was known as a city founder and builder of walls; and under the title of Apollo Ismenios he had an important cult at Thebes.[62] But in this play, it is Hermes, the first inventor of the cithara, as we know from his Homeric *Hymn,* and not Apollo, who gives the instrument to Amphion, and it is the same god who logically takes the part of the deus ex machina, since he comes, as he says, as a messenger from Zeus. Hermes' arrival is perfectly timed to the moment when the twins are about to kill Lycus, the current ruler of Thebes and husband of Dirce, who had come in person to Eleutherae in search of his absent wife. In a long papyrus fragment that is virtually complete (frag. 48), Hermes declares the following: (*a*) Zeus is the true father of Amphion and Zethus, (*b*) Lycus must voluntarily surrender the rule of the city of Cadmus to Antiope's sons, and (*c*) he must give funeral rites to his dead wife. Lycus is then to cast her ashes into the spring of Ares, which henceforth will be called Dirce, and its waters will forever make fruitful the plains of Thebes. Am-

60 For the Euneidae, see the entire discussion in Bond 1963, 20.

61 The shift in the child's name after his death from Opheltes to Archemoros ("beginning of doom") is generally interpreted as a sign of Amphiaraus' impending death at Thebes.

62 See Vian 1963, 81–84.

phion and Zethus are bidden to go to Thebes, once they have been purified: Zethus will have something to do with military prowess (the text here is lacunose). Amphion, however, is instructed to "take the lyre and sing songs to the gods; and the stones and battlements and trees will be charmed by the music and will leave the seat of their mother so as to make an easy task for the hand of the builders."[63] Each brother too will be given a wife, which attests to the presence of a system of marriage exchange, and, continuing the equal distribution of roles, one will take a Theban woman, the other a bride from Phrygia (Niobe; cf. Sophocles *Antigone* 824).

In this divine dispensation (authorized by Zeus himself), all the destructive terms we have come to recognize in the theater as operating in Thebes are reversed. Dionysiac violence, once having spent its maenadic force on Dirce, is subdued at Eleutherae and its energy reused creatively for the spring that will henceforth bear her name and make the land fertile. Family strife is replaced by family reunion, and the twins continue their profitable differences, one by marrying within the city and the other by taking a bride from elsewhere and bringing her home.[64] Political power is not to be won by killing the king and taking his place; the scepter of Cadmus is bestowed voluntarily in goodwill on those who merit it because of their royal descent from Zeus, a dispensation ratified by Lycus himself, who ends the play with the formal words of a binding treaty: *luō de neikē kai ta prin pepragmena.* For the first time, we have a constructive resolution in Thebes, quite literally in Amphion's construction of the walls of the city, and although his progeny, as we know from elsewhere, is not destined to rule the city, this future lies outside the bounds of the play.

What part Athens may have played we do not know, but it seems likely that the chorus consisted of men from Attica and not from Boeotia,[65] which suggests the significance of Eleutherae in the play as a border zone between the two territories. Possibly an important distinction was made between Athens and Thebes at some point during the play.[66]

[63] Eur. *Antiope* frag. 48.92–95. Unless I indicate otherwise, I cite the fragments of the *Antiope* from the 1972 edition of Kambitsis. The connections here with Orpheus are obvious. See further on the topos, Kambitsis pp. 122–23.

[64] There is no reference, of course, to the unhappy sequel of Niobe.

[65] The evidence is not secure. See Kambitsis 1972, xii–xiii.

[66] Oenoe is also mentioned along with Eleutherae, which is at the very edge of Attic territory and is often claimed by the Boeotians (Thucydides 2.18.2; Herodotus 5.74).

It would be worth investigating more fully the special value of music in association with Dionysus in these late Euripidean plays.[67] What can be stressed here in conclusion is the fact that a positive Dionysiac pattern can be shown to operate in a significant relation to Thebes, but only in displacement from its actual territory and the temporal frame of its usual sequence of events. On the other hand, the *Phoenician Women,* the strictly Theban drama with the most pervasive Dionysiac mood, is shaped in such a way as to thwart any such redemptive pattern that might operate in family and civic affairs as well as in cult. Thus, despite all its innovations in plot, the drama gives us, as it turns out, the fullest account of the requisite Theban scenario we know so well, and it fittingly ends with Oedipus' counsel to Antigone to say farewell to Thebes: "Go," he says, "to Bromios' precinct, sacred to the maenads in the mountains." And Antigone can only reply: "Do you mean the Cadmeian fawnskin I once put on when I danced in Semele's sacred thiasos on the mountains? Shall I render to the gods a *kharin akhariton*—a service that is no service, a joy that is no joy?" (1751–57).[68]

I remarked above that we do not know what part Attica or Athens may have played in the plot of the *Antiope*. If the end of the text were still lost, we might be tempted to make an ingenious conjecture. With the orders to build the walls of Thebes, a stage has just been set for performances in this theatrical locale. In suggesting a transfer from prophecy to stage, the conclusion might also have dictated the transfer of the rustic cult of Dionysus from Eleutherae to the god's precinct in Athens, from homely piety in a grotto (frag. 37) to the dramatic festivals of the City Dionysia—a true *aition* of the theater itself.[69] Yet given the reverse outcome of this Theban play, the *Antiope,* in which the salutary path leads now *to* Thebes and not away from it, the identity of the chorus as consisting of Attic and not Boeotian inhabitants (if the hypothesis is correct) may well be significant in another

[67] See the useful discussion of Moutsopoulos 1962.

[68] I accept the authenticity of these lines. See also Craik 1988, ad loc.

[69] Interestingly enough, the text of frag. 224 (Nauck[2]), attributed by Nauck to Euripides' *Antiope* before the discovery of the papyrus, gives an alternate ending (unique in the mythic tradition), which precisely mirrors that of the *Hypsipyle:* some authoritative speaker directs Zethus "to go and dwell on Thebes' sacred soil" and "the very musical Amphion to immigrate to glorious Athens." These iambic lines are part of what seems to be a tragic parody by the comic poet Eubulus, cited in Athenaeus 2.47. If not Euripides, no other candidate is known.

way. Eleutherae, we may recall, was situated on the contested border between these two regions and, as the historical record shows, eventually chose to align itself permanently with Athens. Even without going so far as to suggest that the setting of the play was located in Attic territory, it may well be that the border zone was sufficient in itself to account for Thebes' unusual good fortune. Site of both Dionysiac madness and reconciliation, Eleutherae is a fitting point of departure for a temporary transfer to an "anti-Athens" of those political and familial solutions that the theater of Dionysus normally reserved for the celebration of the god's power at home in the presence of its citizen spectators.[70]

[70] Many thanks to Leslie Kurke and Andrew Ford for helpful comments and to Georgia Nugent for her exacting and indispensable critique of several drafts of this essay. My profound gratitude also to the editors for their patience and encouragement and, above all, to Ariel Zeitlin, whose astute editorial skills were put to lasting use.

# IMAGE

CHAPTER 7

# On the Beardless Dionysus

Thomas H. Carpenter

[Dionysus] was thought to have two forms, men say, because there were two Dionysoi, the ancient one having a long beard, because all men in early times wore long beards, the younger one being youthful and effeminate and young.

Diodorus Siculus 4.5.2

So Diodorus Siculus, writing in the first century B.C., unwittingly described a fifth-century change in the way the god was shown in art. The change is clearest on Attic painted vases, in part because of the large number of surviving examples, but it can also be observed in sculpture and on coins. From his first appearance in art ca. 580 B.C. until the last quarter of the fifth century, the Dionysus of Attic vases is a bearded adult, usually fully clothed.[1] Then, around 425, this form is all but replaced by Dionysus the beardless youth, who is usually naked (or only partially clothed). The change is first seen in sculpture from the Parthenon, but soon thereafter it appears on vases and quickly becomes the dominant form. The bearded god appears infrequently on vases after about 420, while in sculpture the two forms appear side by side on into Roman times.

There are, however, two exceptions to this general rule. On two Attic red-figure vases from about 470, Dionysus appears as a young

[1] See Carpenter 1986, 124–26.

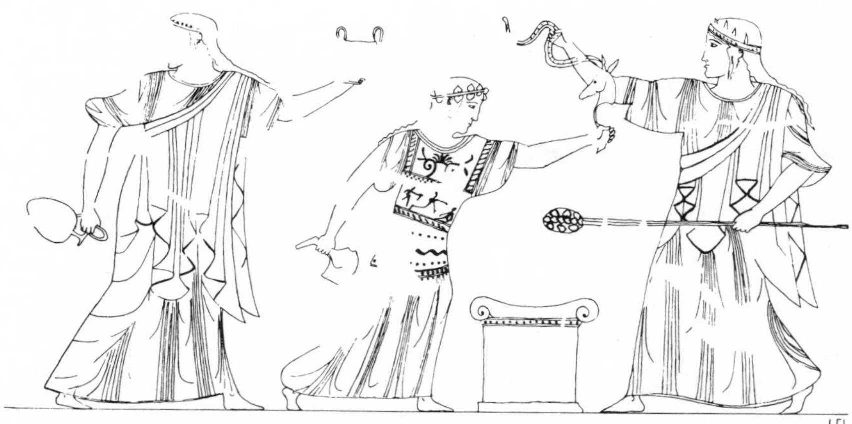

*Fig. 7*. Young Dionysus (*mainomenos*), maddened by Hera, dances between nymphs in front of an altar, with the halves of a torn fawn in his hands. One of the nymphs holds a cantharus and an oinochoe; the other holds a snake and a thyrsus. Attic red-figure hydria by the Niobid Painter from the second quarter of the fifth century. (Private collection, *ARV²* 605.65 *bis*.)

boy.[2] Both vases are from the same workshop, by related painters. One, by the Niobid Painter, is on a fragmentary hydria in a private collection[3] and shows the god with the halves of a fawn in his hands (fig. 7); the other is on a fragment of a krater from Olynthus by the Altamura Painter[4] and is said to show Dionysus fighting a giant (fig. 8). Questions raised by these images about fifth-century perceptions of Dionysus are the focus of this essay. At least four decades separate these depictions from the next appearances of the beardless god on Attic vases.

On the fragmentary hydria by the Niobid Painter, Dionysus and two maenads move about an altar. From the left a maenad, holding up a cantharus in front of her with her left hand, an empty oinochoe in her

[2] Depictions also exist of the infant Dionysus, who is, of course, beardless. See *LIMC* s.v. "Dionysos" nos. 664–707.

[3] Private, *ARV²* 605.65*bis*, unpublished. Drawing by L. C. Lancaster.

[4] Salonica 8.54, *ARV²* 591–28, *LIMC* s.v. "Dionysos" no. 629 (pl. 372).

*Fig. 8.* The young Dionysus holds an ivy branch out in front of him. Fragment of an Attic red-figure krater by the Altamura Painter from the second quarter of the fifth century. (Salonica, Archaeological Museum 8.54, *ARV*[2] 591.28).

lowered right, moves to the right but looks back. In front of her the beardless Dionysus moves toward an altar, holding up the front half of a fawn with his left hand, the hindquarters with his lowered right. From the right another maenad rushes in, brandishing a snake with her right hand and holding a horizontal thyrsus with her left. Dionysus is a head shorter than either of the maenads.

The maenads are dressed alike—a himation over a long chiton. Both wear diadems and have long hair that hangs down over their shoulders. Dionysus' hair is similar to theirs, but he wears an ivy wreath instead of a diadem. He also wears a long chiton, similar to theirs, but over it, instead of a himation, he wears a curious overgarment, which reaches from his neck to mid-thigh. The central panel of this overgarment is decorated with the silhouettes of three figures fighting.

On the Salonica fragment by the Altamura Painter only the head facing right, frontal upper body, and outstretched left arm holding the thick stalk of a grapevine survive. The figure is almost a replica of Dionysus on the hydria; the hair, the ivy wreath, the form of the overgarment, and the short sleeves of the chiton are the same. Even the floral device on the upper panel of the overgarment is a duplicate of the other. The differences are two: on the middle panel of the overgarment there are two dolphins on the Salonica fragment (instead of the three fighting figures on the hydria), and Dionysus holds a grapevine instead of a torn fawn. The similar sleeves suggest that here too he wore a long chiton.

Sir John Beazley, who attributed both of these pieces, called the Altamura Painter, to whom the Salonica fragment is assigned, the "elder brother" of the Niobid Painter, to whom the hydria is assigned. A recent study of the Niobid Painter and his workshop has shown that the two pieces are roughly contemporary and were made about 470.[5] The remarkable similarities, together with the uniqueness of the image, tempt one to see them as part of a set, if not by the same hand.

The first question that arises is, If these are the only depictions of a beardless Dionysus before the last quarter of the century, how do we know that the figure shown is Dionysus and not a maenad?[6] On the hydria, Dionysus' long chiton is the same as those worn by the maenads except that his sleeves are short or pushed up, leaving his arms bare. His facial features and hair are the same as those of the maenads. He differs from them only in his ivy wreath, the halves of the fawn he carries, his smaller size, and the curious overgarment.

Maenads wear similar ivy wreaths (though not the same hairstyle) on other vases by the Niobid Painter;[7] on a vase by the Blenheim Painter,[8] another member of the workshop, a maenad carries the front

[5] Prange 1989, 127.

[6] Of the figure on the hydria Beazley writes: "I take the chief figure to be Dionysus rather than a maenad; for a youthful Dionysus at this period (wearing an *ependutēs*) see the Salonica fragment" (*ARV*[2] 605). His conclusion is clear, but he does not give the basis for it.

[7] E.g., Florence 4007, *ARV*[2] 607.85, *CVA* Florence 2, pls. 66.4, 68.4–5.

[8] Newcastle on Tyne, *ARV*[2] 597.1, Tillyard 1923, pl. 17, no. 115.

half of a fawn, so neither of these elements is unique to the god. On the other hand, the substantially shorter stature of Dionysus on the hydria is clearly intentional and singles him out from the other two figures, who are the same size. Attempts to distinguish actual stages in physical development are rarely attempted on Attic vases before the end of the fifth century; children are usually shown as small adults. On a krater by the Altamura Painter the infant Dionysus, standing on his father's thigh, is shown as a miniature adult.[9] One can probably assume then that the smaller stature of the central figure here simply indicates that he is younger than the others—a boy rather than a youth. It is unlikely that the painter would have singled out a maenad unless he intended to represent a specific figure, and no single female child inflicted with Dionysian madness comes to mind.

Assuming that the two figures represent the same character, the pose of the figure on the Salonica fragment provides further support for his identification as Dionysus. There he holds out in front of him a large branch from a grapevine. The grapevine, of course, belongs to Dionysus, and he is often shown carrying it. On the other hand it is rarely carried by his companions, satyrs or maenads. Furthermore, a bearded Dionysus fighting a giant is shown holding out a vine in just this way on several vases by the Altamura and Blenheim painters,[10] and it is this gesture that has led to an identification of the Salonica fragment as a gigantomachy. For the moment, however, we should reserve judgment on the identification of this scene.

Assuming, then, that the figures on the hydria and on the Salonica fragment are both Dionysus, there are two pictures painted by colleagues at about the same time showing the young, beardless Dionysus in two different scenes. The mature, bearded Dionysus appears in similar scenes on other vases by the same painters as well as on

[9] Ferrara 2738, *ARV*² 593.41, *LIMC* s.v. "Dionysos" no. 705 (pl. 381). Beazley calls the group "Dionysus and Oinopion," but a simple change of the top of the thyrsus from ivy leaves to a scepter makes it Zeus with Dionysus, the more likely subject. See also, for example, depictions of Astyanax on Bologna 268, *ARV*² 598.1, *LIMC* s.v. "Astyanax" no. 23 (pl. 685), by the Niobid Painter, and on Boston 59.178, *ARV*² 590.11, *LIMC* s.v., "Astyanax" no. 24 (pl. 685), by the Altamura Painter, where the young Astyanax is shown as a miniature adult.

[10] E.g., London E 469, *ARV*² 589.1, *LIMC* s.v., "Dionysos" no. 649 (pl. 374); Ancona, *ARV*² 595.66; Leningrad 1149, *ARV*² 598.2, *LIMC* s.v. "Dionysos" no. 621 (pl. 371); Bologna 286, *ARV*² 598.3, *LIMC* s.v. "Dionysos" no. 639 (pl. 373); Boston 00.342, *ARV*² 598.4, *LIMC* "Dionysos" no. 640 (pl. 373).

earlier and later vases. The central questions are, then, Why did the painters choose to break with a very strong tradition and show the god as a beardless youth in these scenes, and what are the implications of this change for an understanding of Dionysus in "postwar" Athens? To answer these we need to consider the meaning of each of the scenes, the thematic connections between them, and their possible sources.

The subject, if not the meaning, of the scene on the Niobid Painter's hydria is clear, and this subject, Dionysus holding a half of an animal in either hand, appears on six other vases, all from between about 480 and 460. The god is bearded on all of the others, and, it should be noted, one is by the Altamura Painter, the Niobid Painter's colleague who painted the Salonica fragment. The vases are[11]

1. London E 439
2. London E 362
3. Amsterdam inv. 372
4. Private collection
5. Gela N 33
6. Louvre G 249
7. Athens A 5349

The earliest of these (1) is probably an unattributed stamnos in London dating to ca. 480, where the god is shown alone, rushing or dancing to the left with the halves of a goat held up in either hand (fig. 9). He wears a leopard skin tied by the paws at his throat over a chiton,[12] Thracian boots, and his traditional ivy wreath on his head. On the other side of the vase a satyr plays pipes. From about the same date is a fragment of a cup found in Athens in 1967 (7), where the god wears a simpler chiton, and the animal he holds up appears to be a fawn rather than a goat.

[11] The literature on these vases is as follows: (1) London E 439, from Vulci: *ARV²* 298, *LIMC* s.v. "Dionysos" no. 151 (pl. 312); (2) London E 362, from Nola: *ARV²* 585.34, *LIMC* s.v. "Dionysos" no. 472 (pl. 355); (3) Amsterdam inv. 372, from Athens: *ARV²* 592.33, *CVA* Scheurleer 1, pl. 3.2; (4) private: *ARV²* 605.65*bis,* unpublished; (5) Gela N33, from Gela: *ARV²* 660.73, *CVA* Gela 3, pls. 34.3–4, 37.1; (6) Louvre G 249, from Italy: *RA* 1982, 206, fig. 7; (7) Athens A 5349, from Athens: *RA* 1982, 203, fig. 5.

[12] Bérard et al. 1989, 147–49, refer to the god's "feminine garments" in this scene and incorrectly, I believe, describe him as "cross-dressing." For a male komast wearing similar dress, see Louvre G 220, *ARV²* 280.11, Boardman 1975, fig. 178. For a discussion see Kurtz and Boardman 1986.

*Fig. 9.* The mad Dionysus dances with the halves of a torn goat (?) in his hands. He wears Thracian boots and a leopard skin over his chiton. Attic red-figure stamnos from the first quarter of the fifth century. (London, British Museum E 439, *ARV*² 298.)

The other five, including the hydria, probably date closer to 470, and on four of them (again including the hydria) the god wears the peculiar overgarment, often called an *ependutēs,* to which we will return. Aside from that on the hydria, the most fully developed scene is on a pelike in London by an early mannerist (2). There the god seems

a

b

*Fig. 10a–d.* The mad Dionysus dances by an altar, with the halves of a torn goat in his hands, amid satyrs and nymphs. Attic red-figure pelike from the second quarter of the fifth century. (London, British Museum E 362, *ARV*[2] 585.34.)

to dance near a flaming altar, with half of a fawn in either hand, while a satyr, wearing a leopard skin, plays pipes, and a maenad dances off to the left (fig. 10). On a fragment of a white-ground vase in the Louvre (6) a fleeing satyr and a dancing maenad flank the god (fig. 11), and on a white-ground lekythos in Gela (5) the god dances alone. Only a fragment survives of the Altamura Painter's depiction of the scene on a krater in Amsterdam (3), and part of a draped arm in the lower right-hand corner shows that the god was accompanied there by a maenad (fig. 12).

The subject of these scenes has been variously interpreted. Jane Harrison describes the figure on the London stamnos (1) as "the Thracian Dionysus drunk with wine, a brutal though still splendid

c

d

savage,"[13] and in a recent study by C. Bérard and C. Bron the same figure is called "the prince of maenads and satyrs in the paroxysm of the ecstatic crisis."[14] Some scholars have discussed the scenes in terms of sacrificial rituals, and for at least one of the scenes the question has been raised whether the dancing figure is perhaps a priest rather than the god.[15] More common, however, is the association of these scenes with ritual *sparagmos*—the tearing to pieces of an animal—and *ōmophagia*—the eating of its raw flesh, with reference to the passage in Euripides' *Bacchae* (137) where it is perhaps the god who is said to eat "the raw flesh of the slaughtered goat."[16]

[13] Harrison 1922, 450.

[14] Bérard et al. 1989, 148.

[15] Cf. Simon 1953, 52ff.; Schmidt 1967, 71.

[16] E.g., *RA* 1892, 231; Maffre 1982, 207. See Henrichs 1984a, 69–91; cf. Dodds 1960, 85–86.

*Fig. 11.* The mad Dionysus with the halves of a torn goat in his hands rushes to the right between a fleeing satyr and a nymph. Fragment from an Attic white-ground vase from the first quarter of the fifth century. (Paris, Musée du Louvre G 249; photo: M. Chuzeville.)

Before settling on an interpretation for these scenes, however, some points about them should be noted. First, all of the depictions of the scene appear within a relatively short period of time around 470. In four of the scenes the god wears a peculiar overgarment that mainly appears in Dionysian scenes and only during the first half of the century. Both of these points would make it more likely that the scenes were inspired by a specific event, such as a production of a play in Athens, than that they were depictions of some element of cult activity or an expression of some realization about the essence of Dionysus.

The torn animals appear to be different species on at least two of the vases. On most, the ears are long and upright, as on the hydria.

*Fig. 12.* Dionysus with the halves of a torn fawn in his hands. Fragment of an Attic red-figure bell krater by the Altamura Painter from the second quarter of the fifth century. (Amsterdam, Allard Pierson Museum 372, *ARV*² 592.33.)

Beazley calls the animal a kid, but it is identical with the animal that often accompanies Apollo and Artemis[17] and is therefore more likely to be a fawn. On two (4, 6), however, the shape of the animal's head is slightly different, and the ears curve back, indicating, perhaps, that these at least are kids. The ambiguity about the nature of the animal would suggest that the painters do not want us to think of the scenes in terms of a specific cult or ritual.

It would obviously be hard to argue that the scenes do not show *sparagmos*—the tearing apart of an animal—but nothing about any of the scenes suggests *ōmophagia*—the eating of raw flesh. Rather, the god seems to be dancing a mad dance as he holds the halves of the rent animal, and in most of the scenes the animal almost seems to be

[17] Cf. Paris, Cabinet des Médailles 443, *ARV*² 606.71, *LIMC* s.v. "Apollon" no. 745a (pl. 246).

toylike, the break between the halves is so remarkably tidy. Contemporary painters do not hesitate to show blood and gore when they depict the death of Pentheus at the hands of the Theban women,[18] so the apparent squeamishness on the part of the painters of the torn animal is puzzling.

A look at the companions of the god in these scenes is also useful. Maenads dance about him, as they are wont to do, and one of them holds up a snake—this is an attribute of maenads and nymphs that goes back nearly a century. None of them actually participate in the mayhem. Furthermore, some of the satyrs who appear in two of the scenes (2, 6) seem positively repulsed by what they see. They bring to mind a passage from the prologue to Euripides' *Cyclops* (3–5) where Silenus tells of the problems he has had trying to keep Dionysus out of trouble. In short, it seems that these scenes have little to do with the bloody goat hunt described by Euripides or with what Dodds calls "the culminating act of the Dionysiac winter dance."[19]

Rather, Dionysus with the torn fawn must bring to mind another image from Euripides' *Bacchae* (737–38): the women of Thebes who, in their madness, imposed on them by Dionysus as a punishment, tear apart animals (and eventually Pentheus). Though that play was written some six decades after these vases were painted, it was by no means the first play on the subject.[20] As the women's behavior was the result of madness inflicted by Dionysus, it is not illogical to wonder if his similar behavior here was also the result of a similarly inflicted madness.

In a passage from the prologue to Euripides' satyr play *Cyclops* (3–5), mentioned above, Silenus tells of a time in the young god's life when Hera drove him mad. Apollodorus (3.5.1) relates that "Dionysus discovered the vine, and, being driven mad by Hera, he roamed about Egypt and Syria," and Nonnus (32.125–50) adds that during his madness Dionysus chased deer and lionesses and that even the satyrs hid from him. I suggest that this madness, inflicted by Hera, is the subject of these scenes and, thus, that they are best understood as narrative scenes depicting an episode from his mythical life.[21]

[18] E.g., Toronto, Borowski, Carpenter 1991, fig. 134.

[19] Dodds 1960, xvi.

[20] Dodds 1960, xxvii.

[21] To the seven scenes already discussed might be added other scenes where the god dances wildly without the rent animal: e.g., London E 75, *ARV*[2] 406.2, *LIMC* s.v. "Di-

Dionysus is one of the most common subjects on sixth- and fifth-century Attic vases, but only a small fraction of the depictions refer to identifiable myths. On the majority he simply stands or walks amid satyrs and maenads. The Altamura and Niobid painters, who are responsible for two of the depictions of the mad Dionysus (3, 4), together with their colleague, the Blenheim Painter, include Dionysus on nearly forty of their surviving vases.[22] And, unusually, narrative scenes that show episodes in the god's life are subjects on nearly half of these. They include

Birth and infancy: *ARV*² 589.3, 593.41
Madness: 592.33, 605.65*bis*
Gigantomachy (and preparation): 589.1, 591.17, 591.28, 595.65, 595.66, 598.2, 598.3, 598.4, 602.24, 602.25
Courting Ariadne: 590.4, 606.83
Return of Hephaestus: 590.4, 591.20, 591.21

With this group of vase painters, then, there is a clear interest in episodes from the mythical life of Dionysus, and the two unusual depictions of the beardless Dionysus by the Altamura and Niobid painters emphasize this interest and become all the more intriguing. If the scene on the hydria refers to the Hera-induced madness with which the young god was inflicted, then, given the remarkable similarities between the depiction of the god on the two pieces, the scene on the Salonica fragment should show another episode from his childhood.

Apollodorus' account of Dionysus' youth (3.5.1), already mentioned, is useful in considering the possible meaning of the scene on the Salonica fragment. After mentioning the madness sent by Hera, Apollodorus explains that Dionysus roamed about Egypt and Syria and eventually arrived in Phrygia:

> And there, after he had been purified by Rhea and learned the rites of initiation, he received from her the costume (*stolē*) and hastened through Thrace. . . . But Lycurgus, son of Dryas, was king of the Edonians, . . . and he was the first who insulted and expelled him. Dionysus took refuge in the sea with Thetis, daughter of Nereus, and the

onysos" no. 470 (pl. 355); and particularly Madrid 11040 and Cyprus C 739 (see below, note 32).

[22] Based on Beazley's lists in *ARV*² 589–608, 1660–61, 1702, and *Para* 393–96.

Bacchanals were taken prisoners together with the multitude of Satyrs that attended him. But afterwards the Bacchanals were suddenly released, and Dionysus drove Lycurgus mad. And in his madness he struck his son Dryas dead with an axe, imagining that he was lopping a branch of a vine, and when he had cut off his son's extremities, he recovered his senses. (Trans. J. Frazer [Loeb])

A very similar passage is assigned to an epic by the Corinthian Eumelus,[23] who by tradition wrote in the eighth century, and E. R. Dodds conjectures that Apollodorus is drawing here on Aeschylus' tetralogy about Lycurgus.[24] M. West sees the passage as a combination of different versions including both epic and dramatic elements.[25] It is not unlikely then that the passage in Apollodorus draws on traditions that go back to before the mid-fifth century. Two points in the account are of particular interest here: the reference to the costume or equipment given to Dionysus by Rhea, to which we will return, and the connection between the god's madness and the subsequent madness of Lycurgus. It should be remembered that Homer, too, seems to link the god's madness with the Lycurgus story, though in the *Iliad* (6.132) Dionysus is still mad (*mainomenos*) when he is chased into the sea.

The madness of the Thracian king Lycurgus is a fairly common subject on South Italian vases during the fourth century,[26] but there is only one certain depiction of it on Attic vases from the fifth century, and that is on a hydria from not long before 450 by a mannerist,[27] who was influenced by the Niobid Painter. Dionysus stands to the right holding out a grapevine with his right hand toward Lycurgus, who, wearing Thracian boots (*embades*) and a Thracian cloak (*zeira*), attacks with an axe a naked youth on an altar while a woman tries to run from him in terror. To the far right a maenad dances, and a satyr seated on a rock plays pipes. The altar is nearly identical with the altar on the Niobid Painter's hydria with the beardless Dionysus, except that here it is marked with blood.

[23] Eumelus *Europia* frag. 1 (*EGF*).

[24] Dodds 1960, xxxii.

[25] West 1983b, 63–71.

[26] For a discussion of Lycurgus in art see Griffith 1983, 217–32; see also Green 1982, 237–48, especially 242–44.

[27] Cracow 1225, *ARV*[2] 1121.17, Trendall and Webster 1971, 49–50, III, 1, 13. See Beazley 1928, 44–46.

Dionysus' gesture with the grapevine in this scene, though reversed, is almost identical with his gesture on the Salonica fragment, and it is the same gesture he uses when he attacks giants on vases by the Altamura and Niobid painters. In the Lycurgus scene the vine is a reminder, on the one hand, that the king thinks he is chopping down a vine when he attacks his son, but, on the other hand, it also carries with it almost magical powers as a destructive weapon, as the gigantomachy scenes suggest, where on occasion it even wraps itself around the victim.[28]

On the bases of this iconographic parallel and the apparent connection between the two depictions of the beardless god by the Altamura and Niobid painters, the Salonica fragment makes more sense if it is seen to belong to a depiction of the madness of Lycurgus rather than to an illustration of a gigantomachy. If this identification is correct, then the distinctive Thracian boots worn by the god on the London stamnos (1), where the god dances alone with the rent fawn in his hands, might be seen as an allusion to the madness of Lycurgus, who wears the same boots on the hydria. In other words, both scenes are part of what might be called the god's Thracian (as opposed to Theban) adventures.

Even if all of this is true, it does little to answer the question asked at the beginning: Why did the painters choose to show the god beardless on the two vases when no one had done it before (and, we might note, no one would do it again for several decades)? Every other depiction of the mad god shows him bearded, and even the Dionysus on the Lycurgus hydria is bearded. Before facing this question head-on, however, we need to consider possible sources for these scenes.

The curious overgarment the god wears in both depictions of him as a youth provides a clue as to the origins of the scene and should be examined more closely. In addition to these two scenes, the god wears a similar garment, as already noted, in three of the six other scenes where he is shown rending an animal (2, 4, 5, 6). The clearest, most fully developed depiction of this garment is on the Niobid Painter's hydria (4).

On each of the four the material seems to have a rigidity to it that it would not have were it a simple linen or woolen pullover. In his description of the Salonica fragment, D. Robinson refers to it as a

[28] E.g., Paris, Cabinet des Médailles 573, *ARV*[2] 417.1. Though in this scene the vine appears to be ivy rather than grape.

"cuirass-like garment."[29] Presumably he has in mind the corselets made of layers of linen that appear on Attic vases after about 500.[30] Dionysus is shown putting on such a garment on a vase roughly contemporary with the vases under discussion, and it is clearly different.[31] Prominent features of those corselets are the two large flaps that come over the shoulders and fasten at the front. In addition, there is usually a short skirt of leather flaps at the bottom.

The distinguishing characteristic of this garment is the rectangular panel at the top, cut to fit around the neck. This must slip over the head or fasten at the back since no fasteners are visible on the shoulders or in the front. The lower part of the garment differs from vase to vase, though on several it seems to end in a fringe, and in all cases it ends above the knee. Dionysus wears a similar garment on at least three other contemporary vases. On two of those he dances, but without the rent animal, and on one he pursues a giant.[32] On another vase from the same period a woman with a sword, whom Beazley describes as a Thracian attacking Orpheus,[33] also wears a similar garment.

Beazley uses the term *ependutēs* for the garment on the London pelike (2) and on the Niobid Painter's hydria. In using this term he probably had in mind the elaborate garment identified by H. Thiersch as having originated in Anatolia and spread to Greece, where it was associated with cult and later, through Dionysus, with the theater.[34] In vases from the second half of the fifth century, Dionysus does, on occasion, wear a different, longer overgarment, more along the lines of the garment described by Thiersch. The Kleophon Painter is one of the first to show him wearing it over his long chiton, ca. 430, in a depiction of the Return of Hephaestus,[35] and his colleague the Dinos Painter uses it a decade or so later in a cult scene where it hangs over a chiton on a column below a mask of the god.[36] It is not clear to me that

[29] Robinson 1933, 95, no. 108.

[30] Snodgrass 1967, 90–91.

[31] Paris, Cabinet des Médailles 391, *ARV*² 286.15, *LIMC* s.v. "Dionysos" no. 609 (pl. 369).

[32] Dancing: Madrid 11040, *ARV*² 568.36, *CVA* 2, pl. 15(72); Cyprus C 739, *ARV*² 683.122, Beazley 1947b, pl. 5. Gigantomachy: London E 303, *ARV*² 636.4, Boardman 1975, fig. 359.

[33] Syracuse 6310, *ARV*² 690.6, Beazley 1947b, 41.

[34] Thiersch 1936.

[35] Munich 2361, *ARV*² 1145.36, *CVA* 2, pls. 74, 75.2, 6–7.

[36] Naples 2419, *ARV*² 1151.2, *LIMC* s.v. "Dionysos" no. 33 (pl. 298).

there is a connection between the earlier and the later overgarments. The later garments are longer and lack the flap at the top, and the gap of four decades between the earlier and the later argues against a connection.[37]

The fact that all of the examples of the earlier form of Dionysus' overgarment appear at about the same time—ca. 470—and then do not appear again is puzzling.[38] There must have been a reason for including it in these specific scenes, and there must have been a model. It is highly unlikely that the garment was invented by vase painters; rather they are more likely to have reproduced a specific garment they knew the god to wear someplace else, but the variations in the form of the garment on the different vases suggest that the model was not sculpture or a monumental painting regularly on view.

If it does represent an actual garment, then the questions arise, Who wore it, and when? As I hinted earlier, there seem to be two likely answers: it could have been either a cult garment or a part of a theatrical costume. But if it was a cult garment, it is difficult to see why its occurrences on vases would be limited to a few years around 470 and why it would be linked so closely to a particular scene. It should also be noted here that the later overgarment has recently been shown not to have cult implications either.[39] If, on the other hand, the garment was worn by an actor or actors in the role of Dionysus in a play or plays performed at the theater of Dionysus around 470, the clustering of depictions might be explained. It is also worth noting here that the Altamura Painter, to whom the Salonica fragment belongs, was one of the early vase painters to include explicit references to the theater in a Dionysian scene by dressing one figure in the satyr shorts with phallus and tail worn by actors portraying satyrs,[40] a point to which we will return.

[37] Simon 1953, 53, argues that the garment worn by the god on the London pelike (2) is not identical with Thiersch's *ependutēs,* because it ends well above the knee. Miller 1989, 315, concurs, noting that "the construction and fabric are different."

[38] For a related garment worn by Dionysus ca. 480, see Munich 8766, *ARV*[2] 198.21*bis*. Cf. one of the Erinyes pursuing Orestes ca. 450, Berlin F 2380, *ARV*[2] 1121.16. See Schauenburg 1977, 250 n. 35.

[39] Miller 1989, 314, has convincingly shown that "the appearance of the garment in [cult and theater] contexts has no greater significance than its appearance in secular contexts. Iconographic evidence portrays fashionably Orientalizing Athenians engaged in a wide variety of public and private activities."

[40] Vienna 985, *ARV*[2] 591.20, *LIMC* s.v. "Dionysos" no. 555 (pl. 362).

The downfall of Lycurgus was the subject of at least two theater productions in Athens during the first half of the fifth century. Polyphrasmon's Lycurgus tetralogy, about which we know nothing but the subject and the date, was produced in 467, and Aeschylus' tetralogy on the subject, about which we know the names of the individual plays but not the date, must have been produced before 456.[41] This is not to argue that scenes or costumes from either of these specific tetralogies influenced our vase paintings, but only to show that such works were produced at the right time. When trying to match scenes on vases to specific theater productions it is always worth remembering that of some one thousand tragedies produced in fifth-century Athens we know the title of fewer than three hundred.[42] That being said, however, it is possible that the Hera-induced madness of Dionysus was shown in a tetralogy about Lycurgus produced in Athens, and, given the Thracian setting for the myth, it is also possible that the actor portraying the god wore a special "foreign" costume in the production or productions.

Apollodorus, in his account of Dionysus' madness, says that "after he had been purified by Rhea and learned the rites of initiation, he received from her the costume (*stolē*) and hastened through Thrace" (3.5.1), and while it is not clear what the costume is, it is worth wondering whether the peculiar overgarment worn by the mad Dionysus on vases could in some way refer to it and whether the vase painters' knowledge of it came from theatrical productions in which it was worn.

An Athenian painter early in the fifth century giving form to a garment received by Dionysus from Rhea in Phrygia would surely give it foreign characteristics, relying on the foreign attire he knew, which for the most part would mean Persian, Thracian, and Scythian.[43] In fact, it is in depictions of foreigners on vases from the first half of the fifth century that we find similarities. On a white-ground lekythos by the Tymbos Painter an oriental archer wears an upper garment with three panels and a fringe that is quite similar to those worn by Dionysus.[44] He also wears oriental trousers, but these, of

[41] For a reconstruction of the plots of Aeschylus' Lycurgus tetralogy, see West 1990, 26–50.

[42] Hall 1989, 1.

[43] See Bovon 1963, 579–602; Raeck 1981; Vos 1963.

[44] Paris, Cabinet des Médailles 496*bis*, *ARV*[2] 758.94, *BCH* 87 (1963): 587, fig. 11.

course, would be inappropriate on Dionysus at this time—he is a Greek god with only touches of the foreign to him. Whether the overgarment worn by the god in these early scenes is Apollodorus' *stolē* or not, it is at the least unlike any costume worn by heroes or other Olympians or contemporary Athenians—in short, it is obviously foreign, and it is my contention that the source of the image is to be found in the theater. If the theater is the source, then it may also be the source for the toylike appearance of the torn fawn. By contrast, the rending of Pentheus was obviously never shown in the theater, only described, and the gruesome depictions of the women with the parts of his body can be only tangentially related to the theater.

There can be no question but that theatrical productions influenced imagery on Attic vases on occasion during the first half of the fifth century. One of the most obvious examples is the Altamura Painter's inclusion of satyr shorts in a depiction of the Return of Hephaestus.[45] These shorts, which hold on an artificial phallus at the front and a tail at the back, were part of the costume worn by members of the chorus in satyr plays, as the famous Pronomos vase in Naples, showing the cast of a satyr play, so clearly illustrates.[46]

The Altamura Painter is one of the early Attic vase painters to experiment with such explicit theater imagery in his depictions of myth, and it is difficult to know just how to interpret his use of it. There is no indication that the satyr wearing the shorts is also wearing a mask, and on a nearly identical depiction of the same subject on a vase now in Naples the satyr has neither shorts nor mask.[47] On both vases, however, the satyr plays a cithara, which is an instrument associated with professional musicians rather than with rural entertainers.

To complicate matters further, the myth is an old one and appears on vases regularly from about 570 on throught the fifth century. Dionysus and Hephaestus look much as they do in other earlier and later depictions of the subject, only here they both walk, while in earlier depictions Hephaestus usually rides a donkey. This change might be inspired by the theater, where, presumably, the donkey could be eliminated for the convenience of staging the story. Whatever

[45] Vienna 985 (see n. 40).

[46] Naples 3240, *ARV*$^2$ 1336.1, Arias, Hirmer, and Shefton 1962, pl. 218.

[47] Naples Stg. 701, *ARV*$^2$ 591.21, Prange 1989, pl. 10, A.30.

the painter is doing, however, he is not giving us an illustration of the theater in the sense of a stop-time moment from a production of the Return. At most he is making an allusion to the theater as he narrates a traditional tale.

This brings us to the important problems associated with the way Dionysus was depicted in theater productions. The few surviving passages from plays from the first half of the fifth century that hint at the physical appearance of Dionysus point to his effeminacy. In a fragment from Aeschylus' *Edoni,*[48] the first play of his Lycurgus tetralogy, someone asks where this "woman-man" (*gunnis*) comes from, what his country is, and what his costume (*stolē*) is. Elsewhere in the play (frag. 59) someone refers to his clothing as a long Lydian chiton and a *bassaras,* a Thracian fox-skin cloak. In a fragment of Aeschylus' *Theori* (78a) it is probably Dionysus who complains about being called womanish, "not to be counted as male" (trans. Lloyd-Jones). This effeminate form is, of course, repeated in Euripides' *Bacchae* and Aristophanes' *Frogs,* yet throughout the first half of the fifth century, the god is invariably depicted (except on our two vases) as a bearded adult—even in those scenes that are almost certainly inspired by plays.[49] He usually wears a long chiton, often with a himation over it. Though women wear similar clothes, there is nothing inherently feminine about this dress. It is also worn by "senior males of myth or contemporary society."[50] The young Triptolemus and the young Apollo wear it as well, neither of whom can be called effeminate.[51] Throughout the sixth and through most of the fifth century, the appropriate form for Dionysus on all occasions was the bearded, fully dressed form. Black-figure painters adopted the bearded form before the middle of the sixth century, and more than one thousand of their depictions of the god have survived. They, in turn, passed the bearded form on to their heirs, the red-figure painters. It was clearly a very strong convention, which makes the two pictures of the beardless god all the more unusual.

When vase painters retold a story about Dionysus that had recently

[48] Aeschylus *Edoni* frag. 61 (*TrGF* 3).

[49] E.g., London E 65, *ARV*² 370.13; see Simon 1982, 123–48.

[50] Kurtz and Boardman 1986, 58.

[51] E.g., London E 140, *ARV*² 459.3, Boardman 1975, fig. 309; Leningrad B 1563, *ARV*² 486.52, *LIMC* s.v. "Apollon" no. 403 (pl. 215).

been shown in a play, they used the conventional, recognizable bearded form of the god, which had its validity by virtue of its antiquity and ubiquity even if the costume for the god in the theater was that of a youth or of an effeminate fop. This was in part justified, no doubt, by the belief that the figure on the stage represented only one of the appearances of the god—one of his masks—not the god himself. Just as in the Homeric *Hymn to Dionysus* (VII) we are told that the god seems to be, rather than is, a beardless youth, so, much later, in the *Bacchae* (4, 53, 54) the god explicitly says several times that he is laying aside the appearance of a god to appear in Thebes as a mortal.[52] The beardless form is, in a way, a disguise.

This brings us back to the two early depictions of the beardless Dionysus, and I suggest that the explanation for his appearance comes from the theater—specifically from a production of a play or plays about Lycurgus. This explains the clustering of the scenes around 470 and the appearance of the foreign overgarment on several of the vases and perhaps of the toylike animal, and the link between the two exceedingly unusual depictions of the god. The two depictions are best understood then as representing something other than the god himself. In other words, they show a disguise—a costume. As any Athenian would have known, the beardless figure on the vases is a mortal disguised as a god disguised as an adolescent. These, then, are further experiments with theatrical imagery from the Niobid Painter's workshop—explicit depictions of a figure from the theater, rather than a figure from myth—and one can only wonder at the motivation.

As mentioned earlier, the remarkable similarities between the beardless figures on the two vases tempt one to see them as parts of a set, and for just a moment I will yield to that temptation. We have a hydria and part of a krater, both symposium vessels, and one wonders if there might have been more—perhaps an amphora, perhaps cups—to make a set commissioned for a particular occasion, perhaps as T. B. L. Webster suggested with reference to another group of vases for a party in celebration of the production of a play.[53] But this is wild surmise. At the least they are companion pieces.

To conclude, these two anomalous depictions of the beardless god

[52] See Dodds 1960, 62; Oranje 1984, 126 n. 313.

[53] Webster 1972, 47, 90–93.

highlight an important contrast in the way the anthropomorphic Dionysus was perceived in Athens during the first half of the fifth century. A rigid convention in sculpture and coins as well as in vase painting insured that the god was always shown as a bearded adult, yet in the theater, at the same time, the god appeared as beardless, effeminate, and even foreign. The two vase paintings are rare exceptions where the two perceptions are joined, and it is surely significant that the experiment was not repeated.

These two depictions seem to refer to the theater. The beardlessness of the god, along with his short stature, is explicitly used to indicate his young age—a particular stage in his life when certain events took place—yet other depictions of the bearded god rending a fawn surely represent the same subject, and it is a bearded god on the mannerist vase who inspires Lycurgus with madness. The convention of depicting Dionysus as a bearded adult, often in somewhat archaic (not effeminate) clothes, held firm until the 430s when Phidias had the god carved as a beardless young man of athletic build on the east pediment of the Parthenon—and vase painters were soon to follow suit. But, as they say, that is another story for another time.

CHAPTER 8

# On the Wildness of Satyrs

François Lissarrague

In Greek tradition, Dionysus is the god who comes from elsewhere. He is the stranger, "the Other." His followers consist of barbarian women, Lydians, or when they are in a wild state, maenads. Their imagery has been examined in detail, both in vase painting and now in the tragic poets.[1] When it comes to masculine attendants, however, it is not men but satyrs who accompany the god. In the marginal world that constitutes the "city of Bromius,"[2] man, as such, has no place; he gives way to the satyr, a hybrid being, a mixture of animal and human traits.

Taking my cue from the iconographical material, I would like to present some observations on the nature of these satyrs in an effort to characterize their form of wildness. These remarks, necessarily limited, will be based essentially on Attic imagery of the end of the sixth and the beginning of the fifth century B.C., at a moment when the figurative repertory is especially rich in this theme and when a certain number of new iconographical series are developed. Rather than providing a history of the origin and development of these motifs, which must, of course, be taken into consideration,[3] I will focus on the

[1] Edwards 1960; McNally 1978; Frontisi-Ducroux 1986. See in this volume Seaford and Schlesier.

[2] Euripides *Cyclops* 99.

[3] On the transformations in the repertory, see Carpenter 1986; Schöne 1987; as well as McNally 1978.

anthropological import of these series: What kind of wildness or alterity is defined by the image of the satyrs? What is the function of this theme in Greek culture?

The satyrs constitute a race of their own, which, from the very first literary reference in a fragment of the Hesiodic *Catalogue of Women,* is judged in clearly negative moral terms: "the race of lazy good-for-nothing Satyrs" (*genos outidanōn Saturōn amēkhanoergōn*).[4]

Images cannot be expressed in a negative fashion, nor can they deliver such a moral judgment in a direct manner. But the iconography does show in many ways the alterity of satyrs, first of all by their bodily appearance. Satyrs are truly hybrids; their human form is always augmented by a tail and horse's ears; sometimes they have hooves or a fully hairy body. These last two features are exceptional,[5] but they are not due solely to a stylistic evolution; it happens that we find these variants on one and the same image. Thus, on an amphora from Berlin showing a lineup of three satyr musicians, the middle one has hooves, while the other two have feet (fig. 13). The same goes for a cup from Leningrad on which two satyrs are covered with dots that indicate a furry coat, while the third one has a smooth skin that looks human.[6] These variants, albeit rare, show that the painters' imagination could entertain degrees of greater or lesser animality in depicting the satyrs' anatomy.

This animal nature, marked on the body of the satyr, is extended in the relationship that the satyrs have with animals themselves.[7] Satyrs are not satisfied, like men, to hunt or domesticate animals; they manage to make them partners—whether in play, in dance, or in amorous relations—and go as far even as to exchange roles with them. On a lekythos in the Louvre,[8] three satyrs carry asses on their shoulders; this visual jesting shows some of the ways in which the universe of satyrs functions as a play of inversion, a topsy-turvy world of a carnivalesque

[4] Hesiod frag. 123 (Merkelbach and West 1967).

[5] Satyrs with footwear or horses' legs: the most famous example on the François vase, Florence 4209, *ABV* 76; see also Brommer 1937, 53 n. 12; Carpenter 1986, 77 n. 4. Hairy satyrs: numerous examples in black figure, especially in Lydos and the Amasis Painter; see Tiverios 1976, pls. 51–52, 53–55, and 96; Bothmer 1985, figs. 40a, 67, 71, 90, and cat. nos. 18*bis,* 19.

[6] Leningrad B 1412 (St. 216), Gorbunova 1983, no. 36.

[7] Lissarrague 1987a, 335–51.

[8] Paris, Louvre CA 1730, not attributed; cf. Lissarrague 1987a, 339, fig. 2.

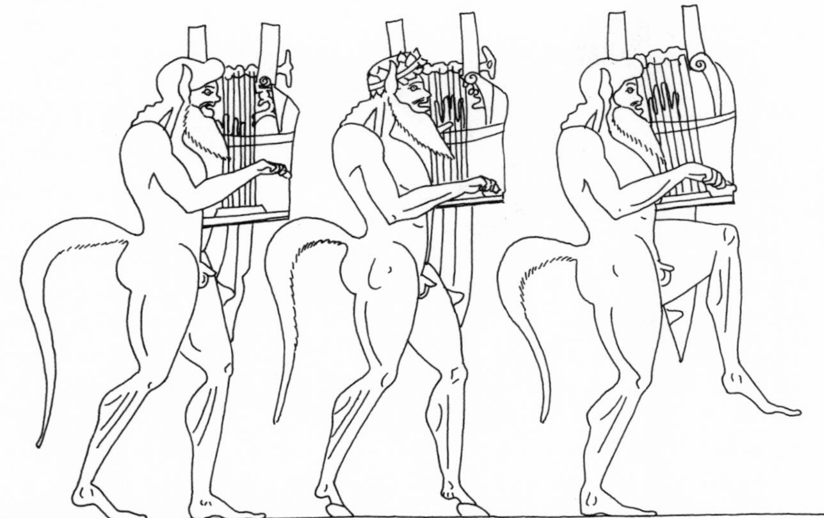

*Fig. 13.* A procession of satyrs playing citharas moves to the right. The middle satyr has hooves rather than human feet. Attic black-figure neck amphora from the last quarter of the sixth century. (Berlin, Antikenmuseum 1966.1, *ABV* 285.1.)

kind. The satyr's ambivalence, his double nature, both human and animal, finally comes to the fore in an explicit way in the images of horse teams where we see satyrs in harness, drawing a chariot like horses and at the same time holding the reins and driving it like a charioteer.[9] Images such as these play on the reversal or juxtaposition of contradictory poses, when compared with human norms. Animals turn human, satyrs turn animal: the boundary between humans and beasts becomes blurred.

Along with anatomical variations that make the satyr a more or less animal being, the painters of images introduce variations of a "cosmetic" or sartorial kind. Satyrs' hair, although usually shaggy and disheveled, is sometimes carefully combed and gathered up into a chignon,[10] and the same goes for their beard.[11] On an amphora in

[9] Cf. Lissarrague 1990d, 174 n. 102.

[10] E.g., on the eponymous amphora of the Berlin Painter, Berlin 2160, *ARV*[2] 196.1 (Oreimakhos).

[11] See Harrow 55, *ARV*[2] 183.11.

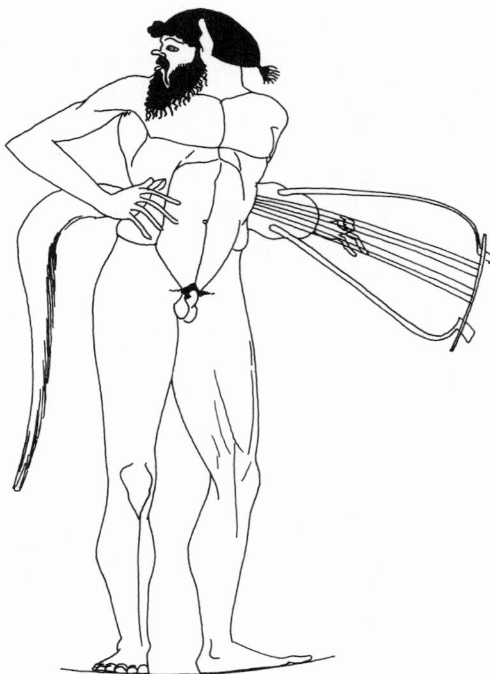

*Fig. 14.* A satyr with an infibulated penis stands holding a lyre. Attic red-figure amphora by the Kleophrades Painter from the first quarter of the fifth century. (Leiden, Rijksmuseum van Oudheden PC 80, *ARV*² 183.7.)

Leiden attributed to the Kleophrades Painter, we notice that, in addition to his well-groomed hair, the penis of the satyr musician is tied up, in the manner of a *kunodesmos,* just like that of an athlete (fig. 14).[12] The body is thus controlled, following the norms of Greek aesthetics.[13] Last, the clothing that certain satyrs wear at times completes the process of making them human, of turning them, one might even say, into middle-class folk. This motif of a satyr in himation seems to exist only on red-figure vases.[14] The first examples come from the Geras Painter around 480–470. On a krater in Geneva (fig. 15),[15] a satyr stands motionless in front of a herm; his clothing, chiton and himation, gives him the dignity of a citizen, but it should be noted that his

[12] Cf. the commentary of M. F. Vos, *CVA* Leiden 3, pl. 120 and p. 21. For the *kunodesmos* used for satyrs, see Lissarrague 1990a, 59–61 and figs. 2.14 to 2.17.

[13] Cf. Aristophanes *Clouds* 1011–14.

[14] Brommer 1959, figs. 36, 56, 63, 64, 67; Bérard et al. 1989, figs. 192–93; Oakley 1990, pls. 14a–b, 35h, 59b.

[15] Attributed by Chamay 1988, 125–27, to the Geras Painter.

*Fig. 15.* A satyr dressed in a chiton and himation with a petasos on his head stands in front of a herm. Attic red-figure column krater from the first quarter of the fifth century. (Geneva, Musée d'Art et d'Histoire HR 85.)

hat—a kind of petasos, characteristic of horsemen—seems displaced in this context. The satyr is all dressed up, but, judged by the sartorial codes of the period, his outfit lacks coherence.[16] Yet in the chronologi-

[16] The same incoherence is apparent on two other vases attributed to the Geras Painter: Oxford 283, *ARV*² 286.11, and Boston 64.2032, *ARV*² 285.2.

cal sequel of this series, there are satyrs in cloaks who are dressed properly, and as the himation conceals their horse tails, they give up their usual antics and gestures. Only their pointed ears still betray them as satyrs, but they have reached their highest degree of humanity.

In certain cases, satyrs are naked, but their feet are not; we find them wearing boots of a Thracian type with broad flaps.[17] This fashion accessory civilizes the satyrs, yet it also marks them as still belonging to the side of the barbarian in a sign that recalls the putative Thracian origin of Dionysus. The same thing happens when they are armed; satyrs are rarely hoplites, but rather peltasts. Marginalized in combat, sometimes they are equipped with a phallus spear: equipped for war, the body reclaims its rights.[18]

Anatomical and sartorial variations are accompanied by variations in gesture. Satyrs are represented in perpetual movement, as though they were incapable of controlling their bodies. (In fact, this is the reason given in Euripides' *Cyclops* for not devouring them as he did the companions of Odysseus.)[19] While they can be observed standing quietly when they are all dressed up, elsewhere we see them leaping, dancing in unruly fashion, crouching, and going on all fours like their animal partners.[20]

In short, in his anatomy, as in his style of dress or in his movements, the satyr oscillates between the animal and the human, the barbarian and the civilized. The hybrid figure who accompanies Dionysus is not just a single strange type whose iconographical model is fixed once and for all: in his quasi-humanness, he demonstrates a variable animality, which may be emphasized to a greater or lesser degree but is nevertheless always present.

Beyond these corporeal and personal aspects, the image of the satyr is characterized above all by his membership in a collective; satyrs band together, often without any perceivable order, and they dance in a group, but rarely as a chorus. In descriptions of this mythic society, satyrs have sometimes been compared to the "wild men" of medieval

[17] E.g., Munich 2645, *ARV*[2] 371.15.
[18] Cf. Lissarrague 1987d, 111–20 esp. 116 n. 62.
[19] Eur. *Cyc.* 220–21.
[20] Cf. the examples illustrated in Hoffmann 1977, pls. VI, 1–4, VII, 4 and 6.

folklore.[21] It happens that Greek tradition itself describes certain wild men (*andras agrious*) like satyrs.[22] Thus in a story quoted by Pausanias from Euphemos the Carian—otherwise unknown[23]—sailors call "Satyrides" those islands of the Atlantic that are inhabited by shaggy, lustful creatures with horses' tails. But this late story seems a unique case (if not entirely fictitious), and it mentions satyrs only as a ground for comparison. Still, the tale is not without interest: in the imagination of sailors—or of Pausanias' interlocutor (it matters little which)—the savage world is indeed the place where one expects to meet satyrs.[24] If these satyr figures can be assimilated to wild men such as M. Mannhardt describes, this view is true, however, only in a very general way; for as soon as we take a closer look, the parallels are not as clear as for another mythic tribe that is not unlike that of satyrs—namely, the centaurs.[25] These are hybrids of the man-horse variety, but with different proportions, in which the human part is less important.

Centaurs, on the other hand, make up a real society of their own, attached to neither a god nor a master, situated outside the human world and civilization. Heracles cannot pass among them without violence. Nessos tries to rape Deianira. The opening of the wine jar entrusted to Pholus by Dionysus drives the centaurs into a frenzy, and the scene of hospitality degenerates into a full-scale battle. We find the same kind of rioting at the wedding of Pirithous, where Theseus has to restrain the centaurs' outburst as they turn into drunken rapists. Inversely, some centaurs, such as Pholus and Chiron, hold secret powers, medical or magical ones. Chiron is also an educator, a famous *paidotrophos*. These hybrid beings are more truly on the borderline between the extremes of wildness and culture, animality and humanity.

In the case of satyrs, the situation is not quite the same. Satyrs

[21] Mannhardt 1877. Cf. Seaford 1976, 213–14; Seaford 1984, 7. On the medieval tradition, see Bernheimer 1952 and more recently the exhibition in New York, Husband 1980–81.

[22] On a black-figure amphora of Cerveteri, one of the satyrs is named Agrios; cf. *Meded* n.s. 6 (1979): 10 n. 20, pls. 4–5. I thank A. Kossatz-Deissmann, who drew my attention to this vase.

[23] Pausanias 1.23.7.

[24] Ptolemy 7.2.30 situates three islands of satyrs in India.

[25] On centaurs, see Schiffler 1976.

do not form an isolated society, far from the civilized world of humans. They accompany Dionysus, who is present among humans with wine, dance, and music, surrounded by maenads. They have a subordinate status, like that of slaves; servants of Dionysus, they also work as artisans at the forge of Hephaestus;[26] sometimes they are sculptors, [27] sometimes cooks.[28] They can be servants of Heracles,[29] who captures them but does not defeat them, unlike the centaurs whom he massacres. By the logic of their servile status, satyrs are depicted as both thieves and gluttons,[30] incorrigible and unrepentant drunkards.

Satyrs can neither keep still nor control their desires. Always thirsty for wine, they are eager to drink, and this is how they get entrapped.[31] But, above all, they are known for their excessive sexual appetite. Vase painters were quite insistent on representing their raunchiness and in their emphasis on the phallus—both in erection and the opposite, in a neatly tied *kunodesmos*. Centaurs may be described as would-be rapists, but they are never seen in erection; satyrs almost always are. Voyeurs and violators, satyrs only rarely achieve their ambitions. More often than not they are reduced to solitary practices. Compared with human behavior, the sexuality of satyrs appears as both excessive and unsatisfied, beyond and below the usual norm.[32] As depicted in images, this quasi-animal character of their sexuality makes the satyrs into homologues of asses and represents a psychological and aesthetic contrast to the eroticism reserved for the figure of Eros, the winged adolescent whom one never sees in erection.[33]

It is clear then that the sexual violence of satyrs is distinct from that of centaurs. There is one exception in this series, a singular and very enigmatic image where several satyrs can be seen torturing a woman tied to a post;[34] the type of punishment inflicted on her has an obvious

[26] Cf. krater fragment from Caltanisetta, *AntK* 12 (1969): 16–21.

[27] Boston 62.613, *ARV*[2] 342.19*bis*.

[28] Berkeley 8.4583, *ARV*[2] 286.10.

[29] Athens 516, *ABV* 508.11, *Para* 248; Prague, private, *Para* 248 (the Oslo lekythos mentioned in *Para* 248 is the same as the Prague vase).

[30] Theft of arms of Heracles: cf. Beazley 1963–64, 3–14; more recently, McPhee 1979, 38–42. Theft from the table: London E 66, *ARV*[2] 808.2.

[31] Lissarrague 1991, 47–61.

[32] See Lissarrague 1990a.

[33] Cf. Greifenhagen 1957.

[34] Athens NM 1129, *ABL* 266.1 and pl. 49. Cf. Halm-Tisserand 1989, 67–82.

sexual connotation, but it is difficult to say more than this. In any case, this violence, far removed from the "classical aesthetic," is utterly unique. In fact, in the Dionysiac thiasos, violence seems rather to belong to the god himself and the maenads who surround him. *Mania* in effect produces a moment of sacrificial violence, which expresses itself in the *diasparagmos,* in radical opposition to the calm of civic sacrifice around the altar. In iconography, it is first of all the dismemberment of Pentheus that is represented from 515 on;[35] here we have a *mania* inflicted by Dionysus as a punishment. Thereafter, around 490, the painters represented an animal *diasparagmos,* practiced by maenads and by Dionysus himself,[36] who, like his companions, can himself enter into a trance (just as, like satyrs, he can get drunk). But it will be observed that satyrs are never depicted in the process of performing a *diasparagmos.*[37] Trance and sacrificial violence are alien to their sphere of activity.

But let us return to the "wild man." What skills are ascribed to satyrs? There are two different levels to his kind of knowledge: that of wisdom and that of invention. There is the wisdom of the educator, in the first place. In a series of images devoted to the birth and infancy of Dionysus—essentially a red-figure series—satyrs are in the minority. It is sometimes Zeus himself or more often Hermes who hands over the divine child to the nymphs of Nysa. Satyrs are rarely present: we meet them only on seven vases, in a series that contains twenty-three examples.[38] Twice they are simply spectators,[39] and five times they are directly involved in the action. On a pelike in New York,[40] it is a satyr and not Hermes who extends the child to a maenad, and the same thing happens on a late lekane;[41] on three other vases, the child is

[35] Boston 10.211, *ARV*[2] 16.14; cf. *Euphronios, Peintre à Athènes, Musée du Louvre exhibition* (Paris, 1990), no. 32.

[36] For a list of these see Schöne 1987, 303–4. Add Gela N 33, *ARV*[2] 660.73 (Dionysus); cf. also Berlin 3223, *ARV*[2] 586.47 (maenad and flute player). Also see Carpenter in this volume.

[37] On a late lekane in Odessa (Metzger 1951, pl. I.3) a satyr and maenad together hold a still-intact deer by the feet.

[38] On this series, see Loeb 1979, 28–59 and 286–300; Brommer 1980, 16–19; Arafat 1990, 39–50 and 188–89. Add to these lists a small red-figure amphora attributed to the Eucharides Painter, on loan to New York, L.1982–27.8.

[39] Paris, Louvre G 478, *ARV*[2] 1156.17; once Vienna, Reuss; see Robert 1919, fig. 262, p. 340.

[40] New York X.313.1, *ARV*[2] 623.69.

[41] Leningrad St. 2007, Metzger 1951, pl. IX, p. 107.

*Fig. 16.* Nymphs bring the infant Dionysus to an elderly satyr (Papposilenus). Attic red-figure bell krater from the third quarter of the fifth century. (Naples, Museo Nazionale SA 283, *ARV*[2] 1080.3.)

entrusted to a satyr, always accompanied by nymphs (fig. 16).[42] In two of these examples, the satyr has white hair. These two vases date from the years 440–430; they represent a remarkable transformation in the series; it is no longer a nymph or a maenad, but a satyr of a new type, an elderly one, who receives the child. This iconographical model appears in the second half of the fifth century and corresponds to an evolution in the imagery: satyrs begin to have an age. No longer just adults, they are also small children, unbearded adolescents, or, as here,

[42] Rome, Villa Giulia 1296, not attributed, Zanker 1965, pl. 6a; Rome, Vatican 16586, *ARV*[2] 1017.54; for the third, see figure 16.

*Fig. 17.* A young satyr (Komos) drinks from a cantharus held by a seated Dionysus. Ariadne stands in front of them, filling the cantharus from an oinochoe, while the nymph Tragodia, with a thyrsus and rabbit, stands behind the chair. Attic red-figure bell krater from the third quarter of the fifth century. (Compiègne, Musée Vivenel 1025, *ARV*² 1055.76.)

old, wise figures. Something like families of satyrs start to appear. The old-man model has its equivalent in the theater in the form of the chorus leader, Papposilenus.[43] In vase imagery, the idea of a wisdom belonging to satyrs is not self-evident and appears only late, when a paternal figure of the satyr is developed that contrasts with the puerile character of the youngest of his fellows. These latter disport themselves like small children,[44] and in a logical reversal, these are the satyrs who are educated by Dionysus: thus on a krater in Compiègne, a very young satyr, Komos, learns to drink from the hand of the god (fig. 17).

A proverbial wisdom belongs to Silenus, from whom King Midas wants to extort secrets. On the vases, it is the moment of Silenus'

[43] A good example is on the Pronomos vase, Naples H 3240, *ARV*² 1336.1. This does not at all imply, as sometimes claimed, that these vases directly illustrate the theater, but the issue is rather a question of parallel evolutions in the theater and in imagery; cf. Lissarrague 1990b, 228–36.

[44] Cf. the examples listed by van Hoorn 1951, figs. 1, 2, 28, 49, 98, 210, 211, 242, 310, 498.

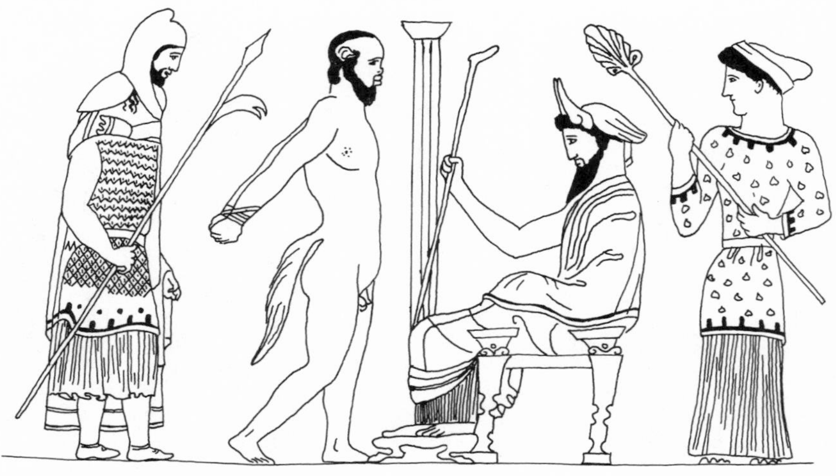

*Fig. 18.* An oriental warrior presents the bound Silenus to the Lydian king Midas. The king has the ears of an ass. Attic red-figure stamnos from the third quarter of the fifth century. (London, British Museum E 447, *ARV*² 1035.3.)

capture that is retained; Silenus, caught by means of a fountain of wine, is a victim of his own inebriation: strange sort of wisdom, indeed. Of his meeting with Midas, however, the images do not say much; but starting from red figure, they show the Lydian monarch with an ass's ears, which makes him something like a royal satyr, as on a famous stamnos in London (fig. 18). The wisdom, it seems, is more like a fool's bargain!

A series of representations—and numerous fragments of satyric dramas—associate satyrs with important inventions in the history of human civilization. Here is a sphere of activity that goes back to the Greek tradition of the "first inventor," *prōtos heuretēs*.[45] In iconography, satyrs are mainly associated with the invention of the *aulos,* "flute." But in this case it is not, properly speaking, a matter of an invention, the product of intelligence and reflection. Rather it is a matter of a discovery. Marsyas picks up the flute invented by Athena.[46] The quality of "cunning intelligence" (*mētis*) belongs to the goddess and not to the satyr. And let us note too that the flute is an

[45] On this theme see Kleingünther 1934.

[46] Cf. Berlin F 2418, not attributed, *CVA* Berlin 2, pl. 147.

invention that devalues its owner, makes him ugly, and disfigures him, and thus is suitable only for satyrs.[47]

In satyric drama, all the scenes of invention we find are in fact of this type: encounters or discoveries, which have an air of the unexpected and are typical of the mode of action of Dionysus himself. Richard Seaford is justified in insisting on this point and in pointing out the close connection in these cases between *heurēmata,* "discoveries," and *terata,* "prodigies."[48] What in fact characterizes satyrs is not their capacity for invention but for astonishment. Thus, when faced with the fire brought by Prometheus, they discover to their cost its chief property: it burns. In the *Omphale* of Achaeus,[49] they discover both the art of reading and the name of Dionysus, but it is really Palamedes who remains the inventor of letters.

Here we discover another essential trait of satyrs: their curiosity. We also note the role of the gaze, in theater as in pictorial images. Satyrs are both eager to see[50] and struck with amazement, susceptible to *thambos,* "astonishment," and also to panic, often indicated on vases by their gestures—a backward movement, hands raised above the head, a fully frontal face. It is important to emphasize the essential role of the specific gesture of *aposkopein,* which signifies bedazzlement,[51] as well as the frequent frontal presentation of satyrs.[52] Everything takes place as if the satyrs were discovering the human world, as if they were being used to explore culture in two ways: through their behavior, which is more or less close to the human model to which they are trying to conform, and through their relationships with the world outside—especially in satyric drama—where they are like naïfs who discover what the spectator knows all too well. As a result, their response suggests a renewal of the world and of culture.

In this sense, their status is close to that of children, whose bodies too are not yet refined or fully formed (but who are, of course, still

[47] Cf. Plutarch *Alcibiades* 2.5.

[48] Seaford 1976, 216.

[49] Achaeus *Omphale* frag. 33 (*TrGF* 1), quoted in Athenaeus 11.466–67.

[50] See Munich 2360, *ARV*[2] 1186.30, where one of the satyrs, leaning toward the pyre of Heracles to observe what remains of him, is called Skopa.

[51] Cf. Jucker 1956.

[52] I refer here to the work in progress of F. Frontisi-Ducroux, who has analyzed the expressive and deictic value of the frontal gaze as a relay between the image and the spectator. Cf. provisionally Frontisi-Ducroux 1984 (= 1989).

asexual) and who are close to animals in their gait and still clumsy in their gestures. This proximity is evident throughout the series of *khoes* of the Anthesteria.[53] These little wine jugs have a double function to perform in this festival of wine and of children; the two iconographical repertories intersect extensively in this series. The world of satyrs, too, has its source in play, understood as a mode of exploration and of experimentation with reality.

It is possible to draw a conclusion based on even this rapid overview of images. The wildness of satyrs is distinct from the wildness of centaurs. The latter, in their positive aspects, are real educators, as Chiron, the master of Achilles, and have real medical knowledge. In their negative aspects, centaurs are a menace to human order; by ignoring the proper customs of mixing and drinking wine, by transgressing the rules of conviviality, they put human society in danger. At Pirithous' wedding, they subvert marriage and laws of hospitality in trying to rape the bride. The violence of centaurs, which Heracles or Theseus confront, characterizes a world outside human culture.

The case of satyrs is very different, for they do not endanger the social order.[54] The wildness of satyrs designates not a prehumanity but rather a subhumanity, which is defined negatively in relation to man. The function of satyrs in images is to invert or deform the rules of culture, a process that not only creates a comic effect but also has an exploratory value; here we find one of the dimensions of the Dionysiac as experimentation with alterity or "otherness."[55]

Comic effects provide here a first level, as a mode of expression; but the essence of this universe is to make the viewer think about humanity. Beyond the man-animal mixture that characterizes the satyrs—through play as an experimentation of the world—one can trace in negative a reassertion of human norms and values.[56]

[53] See n. 44 above.

[54] Collinge 1989, 82–103.

[55] Cf. Frontisi-Ducroux and Lissarrague 1990, 211–56.

[56] I would like to thank once more F. I. Zeitlin, who not only translated this essay but also engaged me in some very helpful discussions concerning it; my warmest thanks also to H. Foley for her stimulating comments during the conference; all errors remain, of course, mine. Thanks also to J. Chamay (Geneva) and R. Cantilena (Naples) for help in their respective museums and permission to publish figures 15 and 16.

CHAPTER 9

# Fufluns Pacha: The Etruscan Dionysus

Larissa Bonfante

A character in Aldous Huxley's *Those Barren Leaves* remarks on the peculiar fascination of Dionysus' Etruscan name for a modern reader:

> "Charming language," he said, "charming! Ever since I learned that the Etruscans used to call the god of wine Fufluns, I've taken the keenest interest in their language. Fufluns—how incomparably more appropriate that is than Bacchus, or Liber, or Dionysus! Fufluns, *Fufluns,*" he repeated with delighted emphasis. "It couldn't be better. They had a real linguistic genius, those creatures. What poets they must have produced! 'When Fufluns *flucuthukhs* the *ziz*' one can imagine the odes in praise of wine which began like that. You couldn't bring together eight such juicy, boozy syllables as that in English, could you?'[1]

It seemed to me useful, in the context of this volume, to examine aspects of the image of the Etruscan Dionysus, Fufluns, and to try to understand how these differ from, or agree with, features of the image of the Greek Dionysus. There is a good bit of evidence for Etruscan religion and life, in spite of the lack of Etruscan literature: some thirteen thousand inscriptions (dating to 600–100 B.C.); some two thousand engraved bronze mirrors, many inscribed; and other repre-

[1] Huxley 1925, 320.

sentations in sculpture, vases, jewelry, and so forth. From this epigraphic and iconographic evidence, there emerges the figure of a local god, Fufluns, who was identified with the Greek divinity, but whose representation in Etruscan art often reflects particularly Etruscan beliefs, attitudes, customs, and rituals. In any case, a barbarian's-eye view of Dionysus is instructive.

Inscriptions show that the god of wine was already at home in central Italy in the seventh century B.C.[2] Italy's cultivation of the olive and the vine, which became important in this period, no doubt favored the introduction of the wine god into Etruscan religion, and his identification with a local god of vegetation, Fufluns. The name seems related to **puple,* or **pople.* The word **pople* itself meant in origin "bud," "sprout," as we see from Umbrian *poplo,* "the [flower of the] youth," "young men at arms"; this is related of course to Latin *populor,* "devastate with the army," and *populus,* "the army," or "people." The Etruscan city of Populonia, called in Etruscan *pupluna,* was apparently the "city of Fufluns," just as Athens was the city of Athena.[3] (A shift from *p* to *f* seems not to have been unusual in Etruscan pronunciation.) Coins of Populonia usually carry the legend *pupluna* or *pufluna.* In one case we have *fufluna,* with the letter *f,* which the Etruscans invented.[4] We see this letter on a red-figure drinking cup of the fifth century B.C., found at Vulci and dedicated to Fufluns Pachies—the Bacchic god. (Etruscan had no sound or letter for *b,* so Greek beta was pronounced and written as *p:* Baccha became Pacha.)[5]

This and two other dedications on vases, "to Fufluns Pacha, at Vulci," show that the local vegetation god, Fufluns, received cult as an important member of the Etruscan pantheon. There is other evidence to prove this, which also gives us some idea as to his nature, or sphere. The name of Pacha appears together with that of Catha, the sun god, in two inscriptions, epitaphs recording the priesthood of Catha and Pacha.[6] On the bronze model of a sheep's liver from

[2] Cristofani 1986, 531.

[3] Pfiffig 1975, 288–89; van der Meer 1987, 53, 55; Cristofani 1983, 126.

[4] Cristofani 1976, 209–14. For the letter *f* see Bonfante and Bonfante 1985, 11.

[5] Cristofani and Martelli 1978, 119–33. Bonfante 1990, 40–41.

[6] Pfiffig 1975, 293; Cristofani 1986, 531; Bonfante 1990, 41; van der Meer 1987, 48–52; Pailler 1988, 468–89.

Piacenza, of the Hellenistic period (designed to serve as a guide for the reading of entrails, a technique in which the Etruscans excelled), Fufluns' name appears twice, along with the names of Etruscan or Italic divinities, native-born or naturalized (in contrast to the Greek mythological figures pictured in the art). Here again Catha's name appears closely related to that of Fufluns (no longer called Pacha here). L. B. van der Meer has pointed to a possible relation with the name of the moon, *tiur,* which appears on the lower surface of the liver, right below Fufluns' name.[7] So both the sun and the moon would appear to be related to Fufluns in his character as a god of vegetation and nature.

Further proof that Fufluns was actually worshiped in Etruria is given by the figure of a middle-aged woman on a stone sarcophagus of the mid-third century B.C. in the British Museum: she is accompanied by all the god's attributes—the cup, the fawn, the thyrsus, and the fawn skin—identifying her as a priestess of Fufluns/Dionysus in Etruria. According to Livy's account (39.8–18) the cult was suppressed by a decree of the Roman Senate in 186 B.C., after a trial in which it was claimed, among other arguments, that the "infection" came from Etruria. But as A. Pfiffig notes, the whole account of the trial is so politicized that it is not possible at this point to draw from it any conclusions concerning the cult of Fufluns/Dionysus in Etruria.[8]

The Greek iconography of Dionysus was well known in Etruria by way of the thousands of Greek vases imported by rich Etruscan families. Many of the scenes were taken over, with little or no change, as in a fourth-century Faliscan vase. Yet rich Etruscans also commissioned works of art—jewelry, vases, bronze mirrors—with scenes that were markedly different from those depicted by the Greeks, or with changes of focus reflecting concerns that distinguished the Etruscans from their Greek contemporaries. In particular, we note (1) the importance of images of goddesses, (2) the importance of couples, married couples especially, and (3) the importance of the ghost (*hinthial*) of the deceased.

The iconography of Fufluns represents various phases of his life and myth that are clearly drawn from Greek accounts and representations

[7] Van der Meer 1987, 53, 56, 133–34.

[8] Pfiffig 1975, 28–29, fig. 1; Macnamara 1973, 52, fig. 64.

*Fig. 19.* Tinia or Zeus, bearded, identified by his crown and thunderbolts, embraces a female figure, perhaps Semele, who lifts her skirt up to her waist. Both wear shoes. The scene may represent the conception of Fufluns/Dionysus. Etruscan bronze mirror with engraved decoration from the end of the fourth century. (Lost, *ES* 81.1.)

of Dionysus. Illustrated are his babyhood, the pirates, his thiasos, his wife Ariadne. He brings Hephaestus back to Olympus (*ES* 1.90) and his mother back from Hades, as we shall see.[9]

A curious scene is related to the god's birth. Two engraved bronze mirrors (figs. 19 and 20) and an Etruscan vase seem to show the solemn moment preceding the conception of Fufluns/Dionysus: On one mirror (fig. 19) Tinia or Zeus, with his crown and thunderbolts (these thunderbolts are prominent in Etruscan religion, as well as in the Greek story of Semele), stands by a female figure, who lifts her skirt. The red-figure vase, a kylix made at Chiusi (or Volterra), is by a fourth-century artist of the Tondo Group who specialized in erotic and Dionysiac subjects. There are no labels; so we cannot be absolutely certain of the identification. But the presence of a satyr on one of the mirrors (fig. 20) makes it likely that Fufluns/Dionysus is involved.[10]

The birth of Fufluns from the thigh of his fond father, Tinia, assisted

[9] Two Caeretan hydriae (*LIMC* s.v. "Dionysos/Fufluns" no. 81) and one mirror from Chiusi (*ES* 1.90; *LIMC* no. 82) show Fufluns/Dionysus accompanying Hephaestus back to Olympus. For Semele, pirates, and so forth, see text below.

[10] For the kylix, see Cianferoni 1984a, 61, no. 41, color pl. on p. 57; Beazley 1947a, 115; Harari 1980, 33, no. 18, 18 *bis*, pl. XI, fig. 3. Mirrors: *ES* 81 (1–2). I thank L. B. van der Meer for advice.

*Fig. 20.* Tinia or Zeus, bearded, with crown and thunderbolt, stands on the right with his arm clasping the waist of a winged, naked female figure wearing necklaces and a headband. A satyr with pipes seems to indicate the god's imminent arrival. The female figure may be Semele: Etruscan art represents figures with wings more often than Greek art. Etruscan bronze mirror with engraved decoration from the end of the fourth century. (Lost, *ES* 81.2.)

by the two solicitous nurses or midwives, Mean and Thalna, is witnessed by his brother Apollo on another mirror (fig. 21). To the left, a goat signifies the presence of the god.[11] Later, Tinia hands the baby over to Turms (Etruscan Hermes) to be taken to the nymphs of Nysa, his nurses.[12] The birth scene is important in Greek myth. Babies are also particularly popular in Etruscan art, which shows such intriguing family groups as Pasiphae with baby Minotaur, and Leda and the egg of Helen.[13]

Etruscan art also provides illustrations of an episode of Dionysus' youth known from the Homeric *Hymn to Dionysus* (VII) and probably

[11] *ES* 1.82. Pfiffig 1975, 290–91, fig. 123; and *LIMC* s.v. "Dionysos/Fufluns" no. 11. For Mean and Thalna, see Sowder 1982, 117–18, 124, with previous bibliography. Mean appears on nine Etruscan mirrors; does her seminudity (*ES* 2.141 and 4.322) identify her as a nurse? Her appearance together with Leinth, who is connected with the underworld, in a scene showing Heracles' return from the underworld (*ES* 2.141), might also represent the contrast between the upper and the lower world, life and death. For this mirror, see Dumézil 1970, 684; Sowder 1982, 115–18; and *Gens antiq* no. 4.7. For the mirror in Leningrad with a seminude Mean (*ES* 4.322; de Grummond 1982, fig. 98; Pfiffig 1975, fig. 121, is the clearest illustration), see *Gens antiq* no. 8.19.

[12] *ES* 4.298; *LIMC* s.v. "Dionysos/Fufluns" no. 10.

[13] Brendel 1978, 344, 349–50, figs. 268, 272; Bonfante, in Rallo 1989, 85–106.

*Fig. 21.* Birth of Fufluns. The baby god, bedecked with a ribbon full of amulets, is taken from Tinia's right thigh by Thalna, a nymph or muse, in the presence of Apulu and Mean, another nymph or nurse who anoints Tinia with a perfume or unguent dipper from an alabastron in her left hand; behind her, on the ground, is the toilette box from which it was taken. Tinia is garlanded and holds an eagle-topped scepter. The bearded head of a satyr or Silenus with a snake (or vine) in his mouth, and the goat (next to Apulu) refer to the world of Fufluns/Dionysus. Etruscan bronze mirror from the mid-fourth century. (Naples, Museo Nazonale, *ES* 82.)

referred to in the beautiful cup by Exekias in Munich.[14] Dionysus was kidnapped by "Tyrrhenian" pirates, who planned to ransom him or sell him into slavery. The god shows his power by covering the ship with vines and ivy and by transforming the pirates into dolphins as they jump overboard in terror at the miracle. On a vase by an Etruscan artist close to the Micali Painter (fig. 22),[15] of the end of the sixth century, we see the human figures as they turn into dolphins. A fourth-century red-figure Genucilia plate found in the Regia in Rome shows the same scene in a very different style, influenced by coin types of this period with the prow of a ship.[16] Despite the temptation to connect the Tyrrhenian pirates with the Etruscans (who were certainly

14 Cássola 1975, 287–88; Cristofani 1983, 117–18. Exekias cup: *ABV* 146.21.

15 Recently acquired by the Toledo Museum of Art, inv. 82.134. Hydria (height: 46 cm) by the painter of Vatican 238, according to Spivey 1987, 59ff., and Martelli 1987, 38, 311, no. 130, pls. on pp. 176–77.

16 Formerly in Rome, Antiquarium del Foro, R 65.75. Coarelli 1973, no. 559; Del Chiaro 1974, 65–67, 136–37, fig. 5; Cristofani 1986, no. 15, believes it to date to 300 B.C.

*Fig. 22.* Dionysus is represented by the vine to the left, while the pirates who kidnaped the god turn into dolphins even as they jump into the water below. Etruscan black-figure hydria from ca. 510–500 B.C. (Toledo Museum of Art 82.134, gift of Edward Drummond Libbey.)

known as pirates in their own time), it is likely that the Tyrrhenians of the Aegean were being referred to.[17]

Numerous representations show Dionysus, looking quite Greek, and his satyrs and maenads, both as couples and separately. The famous Ficoroni cista of the fourth century (made in Rome, as the inscription informs us) has Dionysus with two satyrs for a handle.[18] Satyrs and maenads are extremely popular on the engraved bronze mirrors: dancing, picking grapes from the border of one mirror, or pairing off in chases.[19] Another pair appears on a Praenestine cista handle.[20] Heads of satyrs (or sileni) appear as architectural terracotta decorations, antefixes that decorated temples in Latium and Etruria in the archaic and classical periods.[21] These dancing figures made frequent appearances in the Etruscans' lively art, in terracotta and bronze. Few satyrs and maenads have been found in the tomb paintings, which deal either with real life—banquets, wine drinking after death, and so on—or with the underworld.[22]

Engraved mirrors, on the other hand, show Fufluns/Dionysus caressing his bride Ariadne or, in the words of Emeline Richardson, "rambling with her and his wild thiasos through the wild world" (fig. 23).[23] This wild world was in fact congenial to Etruscan taste—Etruscan artists had even developed a convention for representing air, as Nancy de Grummond has shown, in contrast to the neutral background of Greek art.[24]

Above all, perhaps, the couple was a favorite subject for Etruscan artists. Inside the tomb, the generations of the aristocratic owner's

[17] Cristofani 1983, 57–60; and Torelli 1975, 417–33. According to Thucydides (4.109), the Tyrrhenians lived on the peninsula of Chalcidice.

[18] Rome, Villa Giulia, 330–300 B.C.; *LIMC* s.v. "Dionysos/Fufluns" no. 30; Dohrn 1972, 24–27, pls. 24–25.

[19] Picking grapes: *ES* 313. Satyrs and maenads: *LIMC* s.v. "Dionysos/Fufluns" nos. 43–52 (with Fufluns/Dionysus); *ES* 315 A, 316, and passim.

[20] Rome, Villa Giulia 51195, Jurgeit 1986, 61, no. K 29, 4–6, pl. 49; see also Amsterdam, Allard Pierson Museum 990, Brijder, Beelen, and van der Meer 1990, 188, fig. 190.

[21] Brendel 1978, 247–48; satyrs and sileni: Roncalli 1986, fig. 583 (from Orvieto); Cristofani 1990a, pls. 6, 20, 28 (from Lanuvium and Rome); maenads (it is not always clear they are in fact maenads, unless they are accompanied by satyrs): Cristofani 1990a, pls. 7, 12–13; couples: Cristofani 1990a, pl. 26; Brendel 1978, 247–48. For the nature of satyrs, see the preceding essay of Lissarrague.

[22] See Steingräber 1986, 302 no. 59, 314 no. 74, 360 no. 141.

[23] *ES* 304; Richardson 1979, 189–95, esp. 190.

[24] De Grummond 1982, 3–14. See Homeric *Hymn to Dionysus* (XXVI); and n. 29 below.

*Fig. 23.* A young, beardless, and nude Dionysus with thyrsus moves to the right with a nude young woman holding a down-turned torch, in the company of two maenads and a satyr, along with a number of animals (dogs, rabbit, panthers?) in a rocky, plant-filled landscape. There are no inscriptions, but the attributes would indicate that the couple is Dionysus and Ariadne. The seated figure may be Semele or another representation of Ariadne. Praenestine engraved bronze mirror from ca. 300 B.C. (Mariemont, R. Lambechts, *CSE* Belgique 1.24.)

ancestors were depicted in this way. The normal unit was the couple, male and female, rather than the single citizen, as in the Roman tradition of the *pater familias*. But elsewhere, too, couples appear with striking insistence.[25]

So, too, in Fufluns' case: on a mirror showing the divine pair seated in majesty Fufluns/Dionysus is bearded, in the early style.[26] Generally, however, we see a youthful Fufluns with Areatha (Ariadne), alone or in the company of a variety of figures, including Semla, his mother.[27] Once he appears not with Ariadne, but with an otherwise mysterious Vesuna, dressed in an animal skin, accompanied by Svutaf

[25] Bonfante 1981, 323–43.

[26] *ES* 281; see also Bonamici 1991. On the bearded Dionysus in Greek art, see Carpenter in this volume.

[27] *LIMC* s.v. "Dionysos/Fufluns" nos. 53–77; *ES* 301–2, 307, 299, and passim.

*Fig. 24.* Semla (Semele) embraces and bends down to kiss her young son Fufluns, who is nude, in the presence of Apulu and a seated satyr playing double pipes. Etruscan bronze mirror with engraved decoration from the fourth century. (Berlin, Antikenmuseum Fr. 36, *ES* 83.)

(Eros? Faunus?), and Hercle. The goddess's name occurs in two or three other contexts and apparently refers to a vegetation divinity.[28] Fufluns is young, delicate, wears a necklace and hair decoration, and is noticeably smaller than the statuesque Vesuna. The youth, effeminacy, or ambiguous quality of Dionysus is, of course, a Greek tradition.[29] But the combination of older woman and younger man is an Etruscan characteristic, illustrated in scenes of Turan and Atunis (Aphrodite and Adonis), for example.[30]

[28] Baltimore, Walters Art Gallery, 54.85, *ES* 5.35. Inscribed *h(e)rcle, fufluns, vesuna, svutaf: CIE* 10873. *LIMC* s.v. "Dionysos/Fufluns" no. 78; Mitten and Doeringer 1968, no. 216; Pfiffig 1975, 289–91, 307, fig. 119; van der Meer 1987, 54–56, 134, fig. 21 ("Vesuna wears a lunar emblem on her head"). On Svutaf (Eros?) see Pfiffig 1975, 273.

[29] Cássola 1975, 5, in his introduction to the fragmentary Homeric *Hymn to Dionysus (I),* suggests the name of Dionysus could be interpreted as *Dios* and *nusos,* "the young child of Zeus." His youth or even babyhood is an essential quality. At Delphi, he is Liknites, the child in the cradle; and in many sources, starting from Homer, he is accompanied by his nurses as he wanders in the wild woods, crowned by ivy and laurel (Homeric *Hymn to Dionysus [XXVI]*).

[30] *ES* 4.322 (see above, n. 11); *ES* 112 = de Grummond 1982, fig. 97; Bonfante and Bonfante 1985, 148, no. 27, fig. 20.

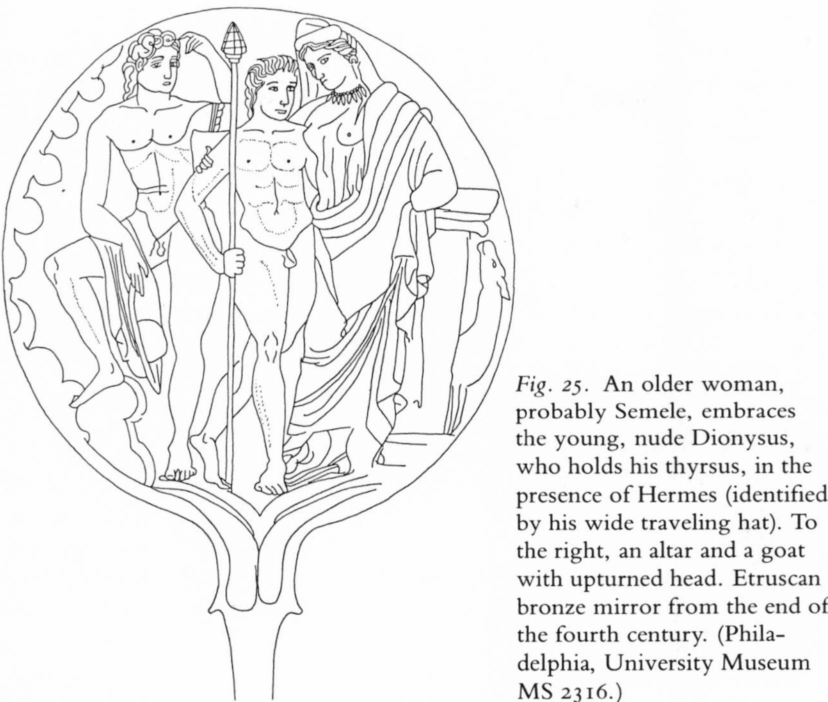

*Fig. 25.* An older woman, probably Semele, embraces the young, nude Dionysus, who holds his thyrsus, in the presence of Hermes (identified by his wide traveling hat). To the right, an altar and a goat with upturned head. Etruscan bronze mirror from the end of the fourth century. (Philadelphia, University Museum MS 2316.)

Fufluns in fact appears on mirrors more than once with his mother, Semla, as a couple, in a somewhat Freudian attitude (figs. 24–25). We have seen that Semla appears also in a scene together with Ariadne.[31] What is Semla doing among the living? The presence of Semla on these mirrors (two are labeled) must illustrate the story of her return to earth from the underworld. Dionysus, when he grew old enough, went to Hades to bring her back. Apollodorus (3.5.3) and Pausanias (2.37.5)

[31] (1) *ES* 83; *CSE:* DDR 1, no. 5; *LIMC* s.v. "Dionysos/Fufluns" no. 76 (inscribed). (2) Unpublished mirror from Vulci in Philadelphia, University Museum, inv. MS 2316; unlabeled, but probably representing the young Fufluns and his majestic mother, Semla: Shelton 1989, no. 18, proposed this interpretation, which is convincing; the mirror is mentioned in Luce 1921, 148 ("Diana and Endymion"); I thank David Romano for the information. (3) Semla and Ariadne: *ES* 4.299 (above, n. 27); an Attic black-figure cup in Naples also shows the return to earth of Dionysus and Semele: *CVA* Italia 20, Naples 1, p. 11, pl. 22, fig. 1 (reference in Richardson 1979, 190); Simon 1973, 34–36, identifies the figures on the back wall of the "Tomb of the Baron" in Tarquinia as Semele introduced to the gods by her son Dionysus (Steingräber 1986, no. 44).

say he went down at Lerna by way of the bottomless Alcyonean lake: "He brought up his mother from Hades, named her Thyone, and ascended with her up to heaven" (Apollodorus 3.5.3). Aristophanes remembered this journey of Dionysus to Hades when he wrote the *Frogs*.[32]

A number of other representations seem to show Fufluns in his role as god of the dead. On a vase in the Villa Giulia Museum in Rome, Hermes wards off a demoness from a dead woman holding a thyrsus. According to Beazley, it is "one of the few monuments that bear witness to the cult of Dionysus as lord of the dead in Etruria, or at least to the belief that his votaries might hope for a privileged position in their passage to the Nether World."[33]

Another scene related to death concerns Ariadne. A fifth-century mirror in Bologna shows an armed Menarva and Fufluns looking toward Artames, who is grasping her bow and the arrows with which she kills young women and is holding in her arms a small figure labeled "Esia" (fig. 26).[34] This has been recognized as an Etruscan version of Ariadne, shown as a dead soul or *hinthial*. According to the *Odyssey* (11.321–25), Artemis killed Ariadne on Dia (Standia, north of Crete) on the testimony or information of Dionysus.

As Richardson points out, "The Etruscan designers of these mirrors understood that to be united with the god and made immortal Ariadne had to die, just as Semele had to be fetched from the land of the dead before she could ascend with Dionysus to heaven (Apollod. 3.5.3). Ovid implies the same thing (*Fast.* 3.510–512) when he makes Liber say to Ariadne: 'We shall seek the heights of heaven together and to thee, when thou art changed, will be given the name Libera.' The 'evidence of Dionysus' in *Odyssey* 11.325, may amount to just this, that 'Ariadne must die because she is destined for immortality with him.' "[35]

[32] Graves 1955, sec. 14 and 27; Pfiffig 1975, 290.

[33] Beazley 1947a, 152. But since then scholars have seen the evidence more and more as pointing to Fufluns as god of the return from the underworld (see below).

[34] *ES* 1.87, 4.52; *CSE:* Italia 1, no. 10; Cristofani 1990b, 264–65, no. 10.5.7; Richardson 1979, 192. Illustrated is the more legible replica in Brussels, Musées Royaux d'Art et d' Histoire: Bonfante 1986, 244, fig. VII.17. See the same motif on a painted plaque from Cerveteri: Roncalli 1965, 19–20, no. 4, pl. IV; Roncalli 1986, fig. 152; and on a painted relief fragment: *Die Welt der Etrusker* (Berlin, 1988), B 6.1.13.

[35] Richardson 1979, 193.

*Fig. 26.* Fufluns, holding a cantharus, and Menarva, wearing her aegis and helmet, look toward Artames, who holds her bow and arrows as she carries off a small, bundled female figure, Esia, an Etruscan version of Ariadne, represented as a dead soul. On the ground, the head of a bearded Silenus looks up menacingly. Etruscan bronze mirror with engraved decoration from ca. 450 B.C. (Brussels, Musées Royaux d'Art et d'Histoire.)

When Dionysus awakened Ariadne from sleep, as we see on the beautiful terracotta pediment from Civitalba, in Etruscan Umbria, we are also seeing a metaphor of death and rebirth.[36] In Etruria Fufluns' satyrs are images of the god's power as well as creatures of the world of the dead. So, too, Fufluns/Dionysus' symbols are often used in the decoration of the painted tombs of the archaic and early classical periods: the ivy, the thyrsus, the panther.[37] (But on mirrors, which

[36] Bologna, Museo Civico, 200–150 B.C.; Sprenger, Bartoloni, and Hirmer 1977, 282–83. Cf. the ash urn from Chiusi in Berlin, which has recently been interpreted as representing Dionysus' discovery of Ariadne: Pairault-Massa 1978, 197–234. The subject is used in other funerary contexts, as Richardson 1979, 194, has noted. Dionysiac subjects appear more frequently in Italy in the later Hellenistic period: Nagy 1988, 46. Particularly popular in the third and second centuries B.C. were bronze relief mirror covers with Dionysos, Eros, and a Muse: Richardson, in *Guide* 1982, 14–21, fig. 18; and Willers 1985, 21–36. Wiman 1990, 106, figs. 11.5–9, points to a group of ivy-garlanded mirrors with Dionysiac subjects.

[37] Pfiffig 1975, 292; and Richardson 1979, 192.

were not *primarily* made for the grave, the ivy border and spiky garland or "Bacchus crown" border are also close to his symbols.)[38]

What then can we conclude about Etruscan Fufluns/Dionysus? The most recent student of the question, Jean-Marie Pailler,[39] sees a complex situation in which we can make out three distinct levels: (1) a properly Etruscan, native divinity; (2) an inherited, long-lived tradition, either native or naturalized early on (for Fufluns Pacha/Bacchus and the closely related god Catha, for example); and (3) a further development in the Hellenistic period,[40] with astral aspects and initiation rites.

The evidence, and the history of Fufluns/Dionysus, is discontinuous in time and space. I have tried to focus here on the characteristics that are most at home in the Etruscan sphere.

The Etruscans used Greek iconography to represent the image and the story of their local vegetation god, Fufluns, identified by the fifth century and probably even earlier, in the seventh century B.C., with the Greek god Dionysus. It was their own vegetation god, Fufluns, who received cult, who had a place on the Piacenza liver next to Catha, the sun god, and over Tiur, the moon. He was portrayed with satyrs and maenads, of course; with his wife Areatha; and with the local vegetation goddess, Vesuna, taller and older. He greets Esia, perhaps Ariadne, as she has died or returns from the dead. And he appears with his mother, Semla, back from the dead, as the Greek myth tells us. Semla/Semele is at one point in Italic religion identified with a local goddess Stimula.[41] And in general, she seems to fit into the Etruscan pattern of the powerful goddess with her young son or lover, like

[38] Wiman 1990, 106, 203, and 209–16. For the plant borders see Edlund 1982, 128–39. De Grummond 1982, 180–86, sees the mirror as an important funerary object for the Etruscans, involving a complex association of the ideas of adornment, love, and fertility with the immortality of the soul. But Wiman 1990, 175, points out that the care taken to ensure its reflecting qualities, even in the late period, would rule out its being used only as tomb furniture. For the apotropaic use of satyr heads as temple antefixes to ward off the evil eye, see references above, no. 21.

[39] Pailler 1988, 489. See Pairault-Massa 1987, 573 ff.

[40] For Etruscan Dionysiac imagery in the Hellenistic period see Nagy 1988, 46; Nielsen 1990, 62–64.

[41] Pfiffig 1975, 294. Other chthonian goddesses, such as Persephone, were also sometimes named as mothers of Dionysus; Semele herself was called Chthonia: Pfiffig 1975, 323; the mother of Zeus's son Dionysus is variously named Demeter, Io, Dione, and Lethe: Graves 1955, 56. She is related to the moon; and Dionysus brought Semele up from the underworld into the temple of Artemis, at Troezen (Pausanias 31.2).

Aphrodite/Turan and Adonis/Atunis. The character and relation of Semla/Semele would be worth studying further.

Fufluns' iconography gives us, as we see, tantalizing glimpses of a transferral and translation of Greek myths concerning Dionysus from Greek art and literature to Etruscan culture; and at the same time it reflects the power and influence of the local god, whose presence was felt on many levels of religion, art, and culture in Etruria, from the archaic through the Hellenistic period.

# MYSTERY CULT

CHAPTER 10

# Dionysian and Orphic Eschatology: New Texts and Old Questions

Fritz Graf

Since about 1970, our knowledge of Dionysian eschatology has been considerably enlarged—not the least by a series of new so-called Orphic texts inscribed on gold leaves. In 1971 Günther Zuntz had thought it possible to present the texts in a clear-cut twofold classification, which he labeled "A group" and "B group."[1] But the implicit assumption in his attempt, that the corpus was more or less closed, quickly proved wrong. New texts were soon to come.

In 1974, Giovanni Pugliese Carratelli published the quite spectacular lamella (*B10) from a tomb in Hipponium (Vibo Valentia), north of Reggio di Calabria. This text belonged to Zuntz's B group but was earlier (late fifth century) and longer, and for the first time it unequivocally proved that at least the B texts formed part of Dionysian eschatology: it ended with a reference to *mustai kai bakkhoi,* in whose bliss the deceased woman would participate. Walter Burkert drew the necessary conclusions in his paper at the 1974 Convegno di Taranto.[2]

Then came a small tablet (*B9) from the J. Paul Getty Museum, said to come from Thessaly and published by J. Breslin in 1977. Its wording was more or less identical with that of six lamellae from Cretan

[1] Zuntz 1971, 277–393; he gives a list on the bottom of p. 286. The appendix to this essay provides a full listing of all extant tablets according to Zuntz's classification of groups A and B.

[2] Foti and Pugliese Carratelli 1974; Burkert 1975c.

Eleutherna (B3–8; all dated to the second century B.C.); these texts present a short dialogue between the dead person and the underworld powers and look like abbreviations from the longer B texts. The Getty tablet seems older (fourth century B.C.), and—more important—it shows that the specific form of the text is not a local development in a marginal Cretan town, since the same text appears nearly two hundred years earlier in Thessaly. The texts must belong to a Panhellenic movement of some duration: most likely Bacchic mysteries.[3]

A year later, A. S. Rusajeva published the still somewhat enigmatic bone tablets from Olbia; Martin West, when republishing them, assigned them their place in Orphism. Though entirely different from anything known up to now, they not only proved that Bacchic mysteries in the later fifth century had a specific eschatology, which promised life after death, they also connected this with the name of Orpheus or a group that called itself Orphikoi.[4]

Finally, in 1987 the two Greek scholars K. Tsantsanoglou and G. M. Parássoglou brought to our knowledge two nearly identical tablets they had found in a grave of Thessalian Petroporos (ancient Pelinna, about ten miles east of Trikka).[5] It is these most recent texts that serve as a starting point for a reconsideration of some more general questions.

## The New Texts

The two new gold lamellae were found in a grave that contained a female body in a marble sarcophagus; they were symmetrically arranged on the chest of the body; coins date the grave toward the end of the fourth century B.C. The two lamellae are cut as two stylized, heart-shaped ivy leaves. Ivy points to a well-defined background, to the world of Dionysus; the texts will confirm this.

The dimensions of the lamellae are, as always, small: the longer text, Pelinna[1] (= P1 in my appendix), measures 40 to 31 mm; the shorter one, Pelinna[2] (= P2), 35 to 30 mm. The two texts are virtually identical, with the exception of scribal mistakes and of two verses missing in Pelinna[2]. At any rate, it is possible to reconstruct a common

[3] See Burkert 1977b; Frel 1977, 19.

[4] Rusajeva 1978; West 1982; see also West 1983a, 15–20.

[5] Tsantsanoglou and Parássoglou 1987.

text from which both were derived; I shall call it text P (P for Pelinna). It reads (without, however, going into the tricky details of the reconstruction of the text here):[6]

($P^1$1 = $P^2$1) *νῦν ἔθανες καὶ νῦν ἐγένου, τρισόλβιε, ἄματι τῶιδε.*
($P^1$2 = $P^2$2) *εἰπεῖν Φερσεφόναι σ' ὅτι Βά⟨κ⟩χιος αὐτὸς ἔλυσε.*
($P^1$3 = $P^2$3) *ταῦρος εἰς γάλα ἔθορες.*
($P^1$4) *αἶψα εἰς γάλα ἔθορες.*
($P^1$5 = $P^2$4) *κριὸς εἰς γάλα ἔπεσε⟨ς⟩.*
($P^1$6 = $P^2$5) *οἶνον ἔχεις εὐδαίμονα τιμήν.*
($P^1$7) *κἀπ̣ιμεν̣εῖ σ' ὑπ̣ὸ γῆν τέλεα ἅσ⟨σ⟩απερ ὄλβιοι ἄλλοι.*

apparatus criticus: $P^1$6 A TIMN, $P^2$5 TIMMN; $P^1$7 ΚΑΠΥΜΕΝΕΙ

Translation:
1 Now you have died and now you have come into being, o thrice happy one,[7] on this same day.
2 Tell Persephone that Bakkhios himself has set you free.
3 Bull, you jumped into milk.
4 Quickly [rather than "Goat"],[8] you jumped into milk.
5 Ram, you fell into milk.
6 You have wine as your fortunate honor.[9]

[6] See, for the problems of text, the *editio princeps* (Tsantsanoglou and Parássoglou 1987) and my contribution to the Geneva symposium on Orpheus and Orphism in the spring of 1988, which has appeared in Borgeaud 1991, 87–102.

[7] The word *trisolbie* (in both texts) is unmetrical; it must have supplanted another word: leaving the content unchanged, *makar* would be the best choice for the original wording; but *nun egenou makar* is both ambiguous ("now you have come into being, o blessed one," or "now you have became blessed") and somewhat flat, so one might have wished to find a clearer and more emphatic wording.

[8] The verse is transmitted only in $P^1$, with the clear wording *aipsa,* "quickly." The adverb sounds somewhat unexpected, though not entirely incongruous, and one thinks of another animal, *aix,* the goat—but a female animal would break the series of male ones.

[9] As it stands, the verse is unmetrical, its end is corrupt in both versions, and the word division in the middle is unclear: obviously, it was copied from an already deficient archetype. $P^2$ reads EUDAIMON without a following A; $P^1$, more carefully written, has EUDAIMONA. With the longer version, it must be either the vocative *eudaimōn,* addressed to the deceased (the A belonging to the final word), or the accusative *eudaimona,* connected with either *oinon* or the final word. The final letters are easily corrected into the accusative *timēn,* which would somewhat more naturally go together with *eudaimona:* this would have to mean, as I translated with some hesitation, "your fortunate portion" or "honor." A vocative *eudaimōn* would be more difficult: it would ask either for deleting the superfluous A in $P^1$ or for reading *atimon* and taking it together with *oinon* to form the expression "wine without price" or "free wine," a thought somewhat alien to our context. I start from the assumption that the verse, though shortened, had some meaning.

7 And below the earth, there are ready for you the same prizes [or "rites"][10] as for the other blessed ones.

## The Interpretation

The text has a marked progression. It begins with a *makarismos:* someone, the bearer of the tablet, is addressed as deceased and resurrected—"now . . . on this same day," that is, at the moment the *makarismos* is spoken: the emphasis on time is noticeable. Death is, at the moment of its occurrence, the beginning of a new existence. Death as the way to real life is a doctrine currently called Orphic. One is reminded, as the original editors were, of Plato's summation of Orphic eschatology (*Meno* 81b): "They say that the soul of man is immortal: sometimes, it ends its existence (what one calls 'death'), sometimes, it comes into being again." Plato, though, speaks about metempsychosis, while the Pelinna text mentions only one cycle of life—death—life. Strictly speaking, we cannot exclude metempsychosis from our text; it might address just this one single moment in the series of cycles—naturally enough, given its use in one specific burial. On the other hand, metempsychosis is not necessarily assumed in the context of Orphism, as one of the bone tablets from Olbia shows: it has just the three words *bios—thanatos—bios:* death (*thanatos*) is a single passage between two phases of life (*bios*). A second inscription on the same tablet connects this with Orpheus.

With verse 2, the situation becomes somewhat clearer: the deceased is instructed what to say in the netherworld, where a confrontation with Persephone will occur. The confrontation will be crucial, and how the deceased replys to Persephone's questions might decide her further destiny. Again, we are in a world where Orphic and Eleusinian details go together: in both Orphism and the Eleusinian mysteries the queen of Hades is the person who decides about the future destiny after death.

There is only one answer possible: the deceased is to refer to the

[10] There is an ambiguity in *telē*. They are either the prizes attained or the rituals to be performed. The performance of rituals in the netherworld is well attested from Aristophanes' *Frogs* onwards. Although it makes sense to assume this significance here, the more general meaning "prize" is not excluded; after all, the performance of the rites is the supreme prize.

*lusis,* the freedom procured by Bakkhios. Lusios is the epiclesis of Dionysus, god of the *bakkhoi,* his ecstatic followers: one becomes *bakkhos* only after personal initiation. The best parallel, once again, is Olbia and its cult of Dionysus Bakkheios, into which the Scythian king Skyles wished to be initiated, after which his countrymen saw him "playing the *bakkhos*" (*bakkheuonta*).[11] Olbian Dionysus Bakkheios is connected with the eschatology of the bone tablet: it is associated not only with Orpheus, but also with Dionysus, whose name appears several times in abridged form. The Pelinna text combines the same features: Dionysus is not only present as Bakkhios but is also symbolized in the shape of the tablets and attested by a small statue of a maenad found outside the sarcophagus. Thus, although the dead woman was initiated into the mysteries of Dionysus Bakkhios and was herself a *bakkhē,* the verses derive from a hexametrical model; the combination suggests that this text should be labeled Orphic.

There is more. The "deliverance" or "freeing" (*lusis*) granted by Dionysus and relevant to Persephone—that is, to her decision about the dead woman's destiny—allows for only one coherent explanation. The term *lusis* cannot just mean death as the freeing of the soul from the body: why should that be the work of Dionysus, and why should that be relevant to Persephone? It has to be more, namely, release from punishment after death that would otherwise be in store for humankind. Although deliverer from underworldly punishment is a rare function of Dionysus, there is one hexametrical fragment of Orpheus, preserved by Olympiodorus, that may provide an answer to our problem. Olympiodorus introduces it by saying that "Dionysus is responsible for deliverance," and then he cites some hexameters of Orpheus that, he says, illustrate why Dionysus is called Luseus, "Deliverer."[12] The verses address Dionysus and assert that he delivers us from the consequences of deeds of our unlawful ancestors (*progonōn athemistōn*) because he has power over them. What these consequences are, is less clear; the "difficult suffering and limitless frenzy" referred to

[11] Herodotus 4.72.

[12] *OF* 232: "That Dionysus is responsible for deliverance and for this very reason the god is [called] 'Deliverer.' And Orpheus says: 'Men send perfect hecatombs in all hours during the whole year, and they perform rites, striving after deliverance from unlawful ancestors. But thou having power over them, you will deliver whomever you wish from difficult suffering and limitless frenzy.' "

in the last line of the fragment could mean illness and madness in life, but also afterlife punishment; perhaps both are implied.

The ancestors mentioned in the fragment are more telling. Generally, punishment can be understood as a result of one's own misdeed, or of that of one's ancestors; Orpheus opts for the second solution, one that (according to Plato *Republic* 2.364c) was also proclaimed by the Orpheotelestai of his own day. But these ancestors are not just ordinary deceased, since Dionysus has power over them: the only ancestors of humans who are closely connected with Dionysus are the Titans, who had killed the god—though it is somewhat unclear what power Dionysus has over them. This at any rate brings us back to Orphic anthropogony and to the famous fragment of a Pindaric dirge (*thrēnos*) where already Herbert J. Rose had seen an allusion to his same myth (frag. 133 [Snell and Maehler 1987]); he suggested we understand the death and dismemberment of the first Dionysus, Persephone's son, to be the reason for her "ancient grief"—an approach that inevitably leads to the Titans as perpetrators of this crime and to humankind as their successor. His suggestion has met with nearly universal approval.[13]

Thus, the combination, in the Pelinna text, of Persephone determining the destiny of a human soul and Dionysus affecting her verdict in a decisive way makes sense when seen in the context of Orphic anthropogony: the Pelinna tablets are the first nonliterary, epigraphical attestation for the doctrine. This alone would be important, given the scarce attestation of it before the Neoplatonists, but there is more to gain: the tablets from Pelinna put it firmly into the context of Bacchic mystery cults and define the function of this mythology in living religion (as opposed to pseudepigraphical and Neoplatonist speculation).

There has always been another text that connected the "Orphic" myth with Bacchic ritual—the gloss in the late lexicon of Harpocration, that those about to be initiated into the "Bacchic rites" (*Bakkhika*) were crowned with a wreath of white poplar, "because the tree is chthonic, and chthonic is also Dionysus, the son of Persephone."[14]

[13] Pindar frag. 133 (Snell and Maehler 1987): "From whom Persephone will accept atonement for ancient grief, their souls she will send forth again into the upper sun in the ninth year." For discussion see Rose 1936, 79–96, who even convinced the skeptic Linforth (1941, 345–50).

[14] Harpocration, s.v. "leukē."

Although the explanation might be late and scholarly and not reflect any real Bacchic ideology, the new text from Pelinna makes one think that, in the end, it may in fact preserve the true lore of the *bakkhoi*.

With this, the hexameters stop, and four unmetrical lines take over, three in the form of closely similar acclamations. They are transformations of an enigmatic formula known from the group of texts Zuntz had labeled the "A group," coming from two tumuli at Thurii in southern Italy. There, two gold leaves had contained the formula *eriphos es gala epeses / epeson,* "A kid, you/I fell into milk." The one addressed to the deceased (A4) had been found in the Timpone Grande, a huge burial mound; the other (A1) in a neighboring mound, the Timpone Piccolo. The formula triggered an immense scholarly literature that now seems quite obsolete—at least all those quite numerous interpretations that had heavily relied on the kid. The kid now seems neither central nor important, as it can be replaced by other domestic animals, a bull or a ram. Some scholars had associated the immersion in milk with a Near Eastern sacrificial ritual of cooking a kid in milk;[15] others had understood the bath in milk as the peak of fortune for a kid[16]—this might be so, but can the same be said about a ram or a bull? Jane Ellen Harrison, finally, even had understood the formula as demonstrating the identity of the deceased with Dionysus: there is a Dionysus Eriphios and a bull-shaped Dionysus, there is even a Dionysus Melanaigis, with a black goat's hide, but there is no ram Dionysus, and there are other explanations for Dionysus Eriphios, Melanaigis, and the bull Dionysus.[17] Nor is it possible to understand kid-ram-bull as different classes of initiates in the Dionysian mysteries, analogous to the somewhat mysterious "horses" (*hippoi*) in the regulations of the Athenian Iobakkhoi:[18] it is impossible to belong to three different degrees at the same time.

There are more constructive remarks. Both in our new text from Pelinna and in the closely related texts of Zuntz's A group, the formula appears in the same context: in all cases, it is preceded by a *makarismos* provoked by the transformation into a new, blessed existence that results from giving the right answers to Persephone. Text A1 begins with a series of statements addressed to the "Lady of the Nether

[15] Bibliography in Burkert 1985, 439 n. 23.

[16] Zuntz 1971, 324–27.

[17] Harrison 1922, 594–95.

[18] Text: *LSCG* no. 51; see Moretti 1986, 247–59, for discussion.

World, Eukles, Eubouleus, and you other gods," then gives their answer, which takes the form of a *makarismos* ("happy and blessed one, you will be god instead of mortal," *olbie kai makariste, theos esēi anti brotoio*), upon which follows the immersion formula ("I fell . . ."). The much shorter text (A4) shows the same basic structure; our text begins with the *makarismos,* adds the right answer to Persephone, then gives a threefold version of the immersion-in-milk formula. Thus the formula is no password: it has no path to open, that had been done by the right answers; rather it is an expression of the bliss following the transformation. If it seems difficult to understand the formula as expressing supreme bliss, one has to understand "to fall into milk" as expressing metaphorically this cardinal transformation. A rare metaphor might help: "to be in milk" (*einai en galaxi*) can mean any new beginning.[19] Bull and ram that "are in the milk" begin a new existence; as for the kid, one has to remember that *eriphos* in Greek does not necessarily mean a very young animal: the Homeric formula *arnes t' eriphoi te* is a collective expression for "sheep and goats" that does not denote only young goats; an *eriphos* thus need not be much younger than a *krios*.

After the immersion-in-milk formulae, the final unmetrical acclamation, "You have wine as your fortunate honor," comes as a surprise, and its exact meaning remains unclear: it should be taken (as by the Greek editors) to point to the well-known *sumposion tōn hosiōn*.[20] For the first editors, who read *oinon atimon,* "free wine," it did so in a rather ironical mood: the deceased finally had come, they thought, to enjoy eternal wine and drunkenness. One knows the eternal drunkenness of the blessed deceased from the heavily sarcastic passage in Plato's *Republic* (363c–d), but sarcasm and irony are entirely out of place in a text like this one: the text is serious, even solemn. Still, we can take the line as reference to the symposium as the final form of existence: the dead continue what was their most intense and enjoyable experience during life.

The text ends with the promise of final bliss: under the earth, the deceased will be among the saints when they are marching in. There are good parallels in two other gold lamellae: in the text of the Hipponium lamella (*B10), after the deceased has avoided all pitfalls when

[19] Aelian *Varia historia* 8.8.

[20] See the material collected in Graf 1974, 98–103.

entering Hades, he is reassured (15–16): "And then, you will go a long way, a holy one, where also the others—the *mustai* and *bakkhoi*—walk in fame"; the Petelia text (B1, now in the British Museum) holds out the final promise (11): "And then, you will be a lord among the other heroes." The structure in these passages is closely similar: an introductory *kai* ("and") connects the verse with the preceding sequence; a verb holds out the promise, either in expressed (B1: *anaxeis;* perhaps *epimeneī* in the new Pelinna text) or implied future (in *B10 the present *erkheai* is preceded by the future *dōsousin,* which expresses the condition under which the deceased will be allowed to start for the final goal); and with *alloi* the group to which the deceased will finally belong (B1: heroes; *B10: *mustai* and *bakkhoi;* new text: the "blessed ones," *olbioi*) is introduced.

## The Ritual Context

There are other formal features to be considered. The first is the combination of hexametrical and nonmetrical lines. Both forms have parallels in the other lamellae, and at least the hexametrical lines must have been transmitted literally, as part of one of these rather elusive Orphic poems. The combination, though, looks rather oral, destined for recitation: Zuntz had argued from the similar combination in the A texts that they were ritual *legomena,* forming part of a "Pythagorean Missa pro defunctis."[21] I very much doubt the Pythagorean provenance, but his insight into the possible oral nature of these texts remains valuable.[22] Another pointer to an oral composition or transmission is the replacement of the metrical *makar* by the unmetrical *trisolbie* in verse 1: the emphasis conferred by the new wording to the detriment of meter is well understandable in a spoken, ritual *makarismos.*[23]

But more important is the emphasis on time in the same verse: anaphoric *nun,* "now," is reinforced and explained by *amati tōide,* "this same day." The other *makarismoi* referring to the life after death, all of

[21] Zuntz 1971, 343–45; he took over an idea of Wieten's (1915).

[22] See also Janko 1984, 98.

[23] Lucian *Nigrinus* 2 calls *trisolbios* an *onoma apo tēs skenēs*—that is, used in a eminently oral situation.

them Eleusinian,[24] are much more vague; they look more general, more literary, than our text: here, the deictic pronoun refers to the moment the verse is spoken and points to a clearly definable ritual situation.

Once this has been established, the text springs to life. It falls into three clearly defined sections: lines 1–2, lines 3–6, line 7. The second hexameter goes closely together with the first; addressed to the deceased and expressed in the form of an order, it gives the reason why she has come into being again. The next section, with its nonmetrical acclamations, is eminently oral but also has ritual associations: it goes from milk to wine. Together with the metaphorical and eschatological content, this looks like a sequence of libations accompanied by the respective acclamations—three times milk, one time wine.

The final hexameter, again, is surprising: the promise that the prizes or rites will wait "below the earth" is clearly spoken from our level of being, addressed to someone going down. The Eleusinian *makarismoi* present the same situation: the Homeric *Hymn* discerns between initiates and uninitiated: the latter will have a different sort "under the dark earth," *hupo zophōi euruoenti;* Pindar and Sophocles address those who will go "under the earth," *hupo khthona,* or to Hades, *eis hadou*. That is, our verse must come from a literary, Orphic text that contained a similar promise for the living (and, maybe, the not-yet initiated); but it could find its place as well in a ritual context.

But what ritual? There are but two possibilities, a funeral or an initiation. The text is uttered the moment death becomes life (*amati tōide*), from the perspective of someone speaking on this earth (*hupo gēn*): this, at first glance, seems to make more sense in the context of a funeral. On closer inspection, the reference to "this same day" is confusing: if taken together with *nun ethanes* ("now you have died"), it is clearly wrong: a funeral—either cremation or burial—usually takes place three days after the occurrence of death. So initiatory ritual would be a plausible alternative: one of the ways initiation conquers death and assures eternal life is by ritually performing death and resurrection.

There is, though, also a possible solution for the awkward designation of time in funeral ritual: one would have to differentiate between

[24] Homeric *Hymn to Demeter* 480–85; Pindar frag. 137 (Snell and Maehler 1987); Sophocles frag. 837 (*TrGF* 4).

physical and ritual death. Though physical death occurred days before the funeral, it is the latter with its destruction or removal of the body and its ritual sequence of separation that makes death final: a person who finds no grave and funeral is not really dead, but a ghost, a revenant with no fixed place down there.

Further, milk and wine find their place in both rituals. Libations of milk and wine form part of the funeral rites in Greece, together with those of oil, water, and honey-milk (*melikraton*); the choice of liquids varies: for example, oil and honey for the pyre of Patroclus; water, milk, wine, and honey on Orestes' grave after his immolation among the Taurians; and three jugs of wine and one jug of oil in a law from fifth-century Ceos.[25] Milk seems rare. As for Bacchic initiations, at least ritual drinking of wine is attested. A relief from the Farnesina depicting the initiation of a boy includes a satyr making ready the wine; another relief on a marble sarcophagus shows the initiation of a woman at which a huge krater is made ready by one of the officials. The initiation, it seems, was concluded by ritual wine drinking, marking the integration of the new member.[26] As for the use of milk in mystery religions, its occurrence is less widespread—but in the mysteries of Attis we hear of a *galaktos trophē hōsper anagennōmenōn,* "feeding with milk, like newborn babies."[27] The symbolism would fit perfectly well into our context.

Both initiation and funeral were important moments in the life of a follower of Bakkhos. Initiatory rituals are depicted in the Roman representations; in earlier times, there were the Orpheotelestai to perform them. The funeral of a *bakkhē* or a *bakkhos,* on the other hand, must also have been a special occasion where the member's special status was once again emphasized: therefore, the Cumaean *bebakkheumenoi* had their separate burial ground, and a Campanian *bakkhē* even had her sarcophagus made in the shape of a maenad.[28] The special status and the future happiness deriving from it would have to be recalled, not the least for the benefit of the survivors: the ritual thus had to have a special form.

As it stands, the sequence of assertion of death and new life, then the

[25] Patroclus: Homer *Iliad* 23.170 (wine is added at line 220); Orestes: Euripides *Iphigenia at Tauris* 633, 159ff.; Ceos: *LSCG* no. 97.

[26] The Farnesina relief: Matz 1963, pl. 9; the sarcophagus: Nilsson 1957a, 90, fig. 19.

[27] Sallustius *On the Gods* 4.

[28] Cumae: *LSS* no. 120; sarcophagus: Horn 1972, 82 and pl. 50.

libations, and finally the *makarismos* over the grave all fit slightly better into the context of a funeral—or does the lack of comparable data from initiations simply mislead us?[29]

## The Other Tablets

In 1971, Zuntz had arranged the lamellae in two clearly distinct groups, A (the Thurii group, and the late and short text from Rome [A5]) and B (the two long texts from Petelia [B1] and Pharsalus [B2], and the short, derivative texts from Eleutherna [B3–8]. His classification was based mainly on two criteria of content: (1) in the A group Persephone is the key figure, while in B it is the sentries (*phulakes*) of the underworld spring; and (2) in the A group the soul referred to its purity as the main argument for admittance, while in B the deceased had to remember the right way in an underworld journey. There were additional features absent in B, such as death through lightning and the immersion-in-milk formula. Despite these distinctions, Zuntz maintained that both groups in the end derived from Pythagorean funeral rites.[30] The Hipponium tablet (*B10) proved this hypothesis wrong, as it clearly points to Bacchic mysteries; but since it was the longest version of the B texts, it served only to widen the gap between B, belonging to Bacchic mysteries, and A, tokens of a local South Italian mystery cult of Persephone.

The new text from Pelinna overrides the boundaries between the two groups. On the one hand, it is undoubtedly Bacchic, as are all the texts of the B group; on the other hand, it shares two characteristics with A: the enigmatic milk formula and, much more important, the role of Persephone as the key figure for admittance to the netherworld. In a way, there were always signals that the classification was not watertight: already Zuntz had pointed out that a further gold tablet from Eleutherna, in a context from which six more or less identical lamellae of the B group came, had the rather laconic inscription

[29] At any rate, I no longer feel as confident as I did two years ago, in my contribution to the Geneva symposium (see n. 6).

[30] Zuntz 1971, 277–393; see his conclusions: "Both A and B derive from verses and acclamations which were recited at Pythagorean funerals. Their combination into one comprehensive 'Guide through the Netherworld' . . . is more likely to have been the end of a gradual development" (385).

*[Plou]toni kai F[ero]ponei chairein,* "Greetings to Pluton and Persephone."[31] Thus Bacchic lamellae and Persephone cannot be kept strictly separated. Similarly, the Hipponium text crosses the borderline: its text, basically belonging to the B group, calls itself *Mnamosunas ērion,* "a leaf of Memory"—a formula that returns in slightly more ordinary Greek and in a metrically equivalent form, in the tablet of Caecilia Secundina (A5), a member of the A group, as *Mnēmosunēs dōron,* "a gift of Memory."[32] Since the latter text dates to the third century A.D., it was dismissed as unreliable; this now seems a misjudgment.

From yet another point of view, the Pelinna tablet stands more on its own. The previous texts presuppose one of two basic narrative situations: either instruction, order, and praise by a virtually omniscient narrator, a guide comparable to Virgil's Sibyl; or address to an underworld power spoken by the deceased himself.[33] This reflects two different dramatic situations: in the second group, the deceased confronts the key figure of the underworld journey, either Persephone (and, maybe, other gods around her, as in texts A1–3 from Thurii) or the sentries that guard the Spring of Memory (in the short texts from Eleutherna [B3–8] and from the Getty [*B9], which derive their wording from the longer texts from Petelia [B1], Pharsalus [B2], and Hipponium [*B10]). In the first group, however, the situation is indeterminate and its occasion unclear; it might even occur before or after death. The one exception is the tablet of Caecilia Secundina (A5), which is spoken by a sort of counselor helping the deceased in her confrontation with Persephone. The Pelinna text is spoken by an omniscient adviser, but for once in a clearly definable situation, at the very moment of death and transfiguration. Thus we arrive at the basic question raised by this text: since it shows that Persephone and Bakkhios go together—a fact best explained with the Orphic myth of Dionysus—could not the Thurii texts from the Timpone Piccolo (A1–3) also belong to Bacchic mysteries?

First point. In three of the tablets from Thurii (A1–3), the speaker claims: "I come from pure ones, being pure myself," *erkhomai ek*

[31] *Inscriptiones Creticae* 2, no. 13.31 *bis;* see Zuntz 1971, 384 (his text B9).

[32] I see no need to change the wording in the first line of the Hipponium tablet, against the many attempts to do so.

[33] In my appendix, column 4, I try to distinguish the different narrative situations.

*katharōn kathara.* The claim to be pure points to specific cathartic rituals that the speaker had performed, while the claim to come from a group of pure ones suggests membership in a closed group who already during their life kept themselves ritually pure. The deliverance (*lusis*) performed by Bakkhios in the Pelinna text must be based on ritual as well.

Evidence of Bacchic initiation ritual is sadly poor—but there is one vital bit of information, Herodotus' famous (and much disputed) statement that *Orphika* and *Bakkhika* were really *Aiguptiaka* and *Puthagorika* (2.81). That is, the things to be explained are the *Orphika* and *Bakkhika,* and Herodotus explains them by referring to Egyptian and Pythagorean creeds and rituals. His remark is stimulated by the Egyptian use of linen and their taboo against the use of wool in temples and in burial, which reminds him of Greek customs: those partaking in these *orgia,* "rituals"—that is, those of Orpheus and Bacchus—could not be buried in woolen garments. There were, then, in Herodotus' time, Bacchic groups with specific cathartic prescriptions, especially those regarding purity in the grave. Herodotus was among the first citizens of Thurii: should not this have been the place where he learned about these things? There is a second coincidence: when opening the grave in the Timpone Grande (source of text A4), the Italian excavator Francesco Saverio Cavallari had come across a "lenzuolo bianco molto fine" that covered the remains of the burnt body.[34] There is no detailed description of this "lenzuolo"; but usually, the word denotes a linen cloth. One would also think that the famous inscription from Cumae that assigns a special burial grounds to the *bebakkheumenoi,* "those who have been *bakkhoi,*" is based on this same quest for purity.[35]

Second point. The three tablets from Thurii (A1–3) with their address to Persephone cannot derive from Pelinna (or from a longer version of it) in a way similar to the relationship between long and short B texts: it is not simply a question of wording being taken over. The Pelinna text advises the deceased to say (*eipein,* imperative) that "Bakkhios himself freed me," and, in the end, holds out the promise of enjoying *telē,* "prizes," or "rites," together with all the rest of the blessed ones; the Thurii texts (A1–3) use a much more complex

[34] Cavallari 1879, 246.
[35] See Turcan 1986, 227–46.

argument: "We belong to your *genos*," say all three. Texts A2 and A3 then continue: "We paid penalty for wrongful deeds," *poinan antepeteis' ergōn henek' outi dikaiōn*, adding that either destiny or Zeus with his lightning had doomed them, and refer to their status as suppliants (*hiketai*) before Persephone; it is for her to decide whether they will be sent to the "seats of the blessed," *hedras eis euhageōn*. Thus the sequence of thought is comparable to that of the Pelinna tablet—by saying the right words, the deceased wins Persephone over and attains his goal; furthermore, with regard to the goal of the soul's migration there is no essential difference between the *telē* in the Pelinna text and the "seats of the blessed" in A2 and A3: the ritual, of course, takes place where the blessed ones stay: in this respect, the traditions at Thurii and Pelinna need not be mutually exclusive.

Thus the central question remains: Is there an essential difference between the two eschatologies—the new text, which relies on deliverance (*lusis*) by Bakkhios, and the tablets from Thurii (A1 and A2), with their references to the penalty (*poina*) for wrongful deeds (*erga adika*), to the common stock of both gods and mortal souls, and to destiny and lightning? Or, to narrow the problem down once more: since the *lusis* mentioned in the Pelinna tablet makes best sense when understood as a reference to the Orphic myth of Dionysus, do the tablets from Thurii presuppose the same myth?

Two answers can be given and have been given in the past. Since their excavation, tablets A2 and A3 had been connected with this myth (after all, that is why they were called Orphic): the reference to the common stock of mortals and gods can be explained with the origin of humans from the combination of Titans and Dionysus, the *erga adika* as the misdeeds of those ancestors who killed Dionysus, and the lightning referring to their death through Zeus's lightning. There is a coherent picture here: the dead man pleads guilty because of his origin and the guilt of his ancestors but appeals for pardon because he had paid the penalty. This reading would bring the two traditions (tablets A2 and A3 and the Pelinna text) closely together and would make them Bacchic.

But there were also those (foremost Zuntz) who thought that although the text referred to a common origin of gods and mortals, this did not imply the one Orphic anthropogony we know; that *poina ergōn adikōn* referred to actual misdeeds in real life; and that the lightning meant actual death by lightning: the Timpone Piccolo became the burial ground of three citizens of Thurii who had died the same unnatural death.

It is impossible to prove or disprove this "realistic" solution; we lack enough data for the actual burial in the Timpone Piccolo, and we have no idea how frequent death by lightning was in that place and time. But from the point of methodology, a solution that gives a coherent picture is more likely to be right, besides being intellectually more satisfactory. Furthermore, the other text from Thurii (A1) can easily be fitted in. It has a different sequence and line of argument: after the reference to the common *genos,* it refers to death through destiny and Zeus's lightning and lists three things performed: "I escaped from the painful cycle, I arrived at the victor's crown with swift feet, I fled into the bosom of the Lady, the Queen of the Nether World"; it ends with a *makarismos* ("You will be god instead of mortal") and the immersion-in-milk formula. Zuntz himself had thought that the differences between the tablets found at Thurii were not casual: the deceased in A1 claimed final liberation from the cycle of reincarnation, whereas in A2 and A3 they had just rounded another cycle from which they would eventually emerge into a new life on earth. Zuntz thus explained the difference with the same doctrine (he labeled it "Pythagorean") that we find, for example, in Pindar fragment 133 (Snell and Maehler 1987), the earliest attestation of the "Orphic" myth of Dionysus. Again, the most economical hypothesis would be to assume the same background for all these texts—the three from Thurii as well as the new finds from Pelinna.

There is a final coincidence. The two Pelinna leaves were arranged symmetrically on the chest of the body, one over each breast. There exist two close parallels. On the one hand, the Hipponium tablet had also been found on the chest of a deceased woman;[36] more interesting, however, is the fact that in the Timpone Grande burial mound at Thurii (the source of text A4), Cavallari found two "small round plates of thick silver" (3.5 cm in diameter), each adorned with a female bust with streaming hair and a necklace, in the same position.[37] As de-

[36] Although Guarducci 1983, 80–81, thinks it probable that it had been in the mouth and had fallen onto the chest only during the decomposition of the body.

[37] Cavallari 1879, 246: "due solidissime pistrelle di argento coll' impronta ognuna di una teste muliebre con capelli radianti ed ornamento al collo."

scribed, the bust is very similar to those found on many Apulian vases where the woman is Persephone: is it a sheer coincidence that in southern Italy her picture had been placed in the same position as the two gold leaves appealing to Persephone for final protection in faraway Thessaly?

## Men and Women, Rich and Poor

The occupant of the Pelinna grave was a woman and a member of a Bacchic group. The same holds true for Hipponium. As for the rest of the texts, it is more difficult to determine the sex of the bearer of the lamella.[38] Claudia Secundina in Rome, of course, was a woman,[39] as was the corpse who carried the tablet found at Mylopetra in Crete (B6): the lamella calls her "a daughter (*thugatēr*) of Earth and Sky." It follows that the five other bearers of the same text (B3–5 and 7–8: all from Crete) were male, as they each call themselves "a son (*huios*) of Earth and Sky." The Hipponium text uses the neutral designation "child" (*pais*). Text A4, from the Timpone Grande in Thurii, perhaps belonged to a man, since he is addressed with a masculine participle (*pathōn*); by the same token, the three people buried in the nearby Timpone Piccolo would have to be women, since they use the feminine adjective *kathara* to describe themselves. Indeed, I should think it likelier that the feminine ending points to the real person and not simply to the soul (in Greek, the feminine word *psukhē*), in view of the fact that in nearly all the other texts, the dead indicate their sexual identity. Unfortunately, it is impossible to use this fact as a further argument for Bacchic mysteries: there are other groups as well—Eleusinian, Pythagorean—that were open to both sexes.

The woman in the Pelinna grave was rather well-off—at least she could afford a marble sarcophagus. There are signs of relative affluence for other bearers of gold lamellae. Both the lamella from Pharsalus (B2) and the Thessalian one in the Getty Museum (*B9) were found in a bronze hydria used as an ash urn. The Pharsalus hydria is a masterpiece of late fourth-century art; the Getty hydria is reported very cursorily. The grave in Pharsalus, furthermore, was quite a compli-

38 See my appendix, column 2.

39 In the text that she carried she is called *tekna,* which the Roman engraver must have taken for a feminine singular: Zuntz 1971, 334.

cated structure, a stone tomb containing a stone *hudriatheke*.[40] The burial mounds at Thurii, of course, could not have belonged to poor or unimportant citizens: the Timpone Grande is singular in size, while the Timpone Piccolo grew together from three single small tumuli that were united by continuous cult.[41] Comparable evidence regarding the wealth or social status of the deceased is entirely lacking for the text found at Petelia (B1),[42] the one owned by Caecilia Secundina (A5: at least she was a Roman citizen), and all of the Eleutherna lamellae (B3–8).[43]

Thus there must have been not a few affluent women among the members of Bacchic groups in the Greek world: one remembers that Olympias, the mother of Alexander, was a follower of the god, as was—much later—the lady Agripinilla in Rome. This calls for modifications in the explanation that Ross Shepard Kraemer tried, following the lead of Ian Lewis.[44] Contrary to the complaints of ancient opponents to the cult of Dionysus, from Euripides' Pentheus to Rome's Livy, the Bacchic mysteries were no lower-class affair: among the marginalized in Greece—women, barbarians, downtrodden males—women, at least, belong to higher social strata, somewhat less unable to formulate their needs, in this life and in the next one.[45] And one of the men we hear of in this context was, after all, a king.[46]

*Addendum*: An Apulian volute crater of the Darius Painter on the Swiss Market (to be published in the Addenda to A. D. Trendall and A. Cambitoglou, *Second Supplement to the Red Figured Vases of Apulia, BICS* Supplement 60, forthcoming) depicts Dionysus at the head of his thiasos, joining hands with Hades who is enthroned in his aedicula opposite a standing Persephone. Even if Dionysus should have come to deliver Semele (not represented), the eschatological meaning—strongly suggested by the deceased in his aedicula on the obverse of the same vase—comes very close to what the new texts presuppose, Dionysus interceding with the powers beyond on behalf of his initiate. (I thank Grazia Berger for her generous help.)

40 Verdelis 1950–51, 80–81 (for the tomb) and 81–98 (for the hydria); Frel 1977, 19.

41 Cavallari 1880, 401—a chance remark by the excavator, the importance of which for the question of chronology has been neglected by all later commentators.

42 See Guarducci 1983, 71–96.

43 See Joubon 1893, 121–24; Verdelis 1953–54, 56–57.

44 Kraemer 1979 and 1980.

45 See Bremmer 1989, 37–47, for the corresponding case of early Christianity.

46 Skyles, king of Scythia; see Herodotus 4.72 and my discussion above.

## Appendix: A Survey of the Gold Lamellae

The following abbreviations have been used: in the column labeled "Burial" the letter *D* refers to manner of death, *B* to manner of burial, and *T* to the position of the tablet with respect to the corpse. The column labeled "Form" refers to the linguistic form of the text: *Ego* refers to first-person singular narratives or boasts; *Mak.* refers to blessings or acclamations (*makarismoi*) in the second-person singular (e.g., "Blessed and holy, you will be a god instead of mortal"); *Milk* refers to the immersion-in-milk formula; *Q* refers to questions asked of the deceased; and *Guide* refers to directions given in the second-person singular to the deceased, indicating the correct movements and pronouncements that are to be made upon arrival in the underworld. In the same column *Hex.*, *Pent.*, and *Pr.* refer respectively to hexameter, pentameter, and prose. Zuntz 1971, 277–393, provides the Greek texts for nos. A1-5 and B1-8. For *B9 see Breslin 1977 and Burkert 1977, and for *B10 see Foti and Pugliese Carratelli 1974.

| *Siglum/Origin* | *Burial* | *Divinities* | *Form* |
|---|---|---|---|
| A Group | | | |
| A1<br>Thurii<br>(Timpone Piccolo)<br>fourth century B.C. | gender?<br>D: lightning<br>B: inhumation<br>T: close to hand | Queen, Eukles, Eubouleus | Ego (1-7), Mak. (8-9); Hex. (1-8), Pr. (9) |
| A2<br>Thurii<br>(Timpone Piccolo)<br>fourth century B.C. | gender?<br>D: lightning<br>B: inhumation<br>T: close to hand | =A1 | Ego (entire); Hex (1-6), Pent. (7?) |
| A3<br>Thurii<br>(Timpone Piccolo)<br>fourth century B.C. | gender?<br>D: lightning<br>B: inhumation<br>T: close to hand | =A2 | =A2 |
| A4<br>Thurii<br>(Timpone Grande)<br>fourth century B.C. | male? v.3 *pathōn*<br>B: cremation in sarcophagus<br>T: in mouth | Phersephoneia | Guide (1-2, 5-6), Mak. (3-5), Milk (4); Hex. (1-3, 6), Pr. (4-5) |
| A5<br>Rome<br>second century A.D. | female | =A1 | Counselor (see above, p. 251)<br>Hex. (entire) |

| | | | |
|---|---|---|---|
| B Group | | | |
| B1<br>Petelia<br>fourth century B.C. | — | *phulakes,*<br>Mnemosyne,<br>Ge | Guide (entire);<br>Hex. (entire) |
| B2<br>Pharsalus<br>fourth century B.C. | female?<br>B: cremation<br>T: in bronze hydria | =A1 | Guide (entire);<br>Hex. (entire) |
| B3<br>Eleutherna<br>second century B.C. | male: "son" (*huios*) | Ge | Ego (1-2, 4), Q (3);<br>Hex. (1-2), Pr. (3-4) |
| B4<br>Eleutherna<br>second century B.C. | =B3 | =B3 | =B3 |
| B5<br>Eleutherna<br>second century B.C. | =B3 | =B3 | =B3 |
| B6<br>Mylopetra, originally<br>second century B.C. | female: "daughter"<br>(*thugatēr*) | =B3 | =B3 |
| B7<br>Stathatos<br>second century B.C. | =B3 | =B3 | =B3 |
| B8<br>Stathatos<br>second century B.C. | =B3 | =B3 | =B3 |
| *B9<br>Thessaly<br>(Getty Museum)<br>fourth century B.C. | gender?<br>B: cremation<br>T: in bronze hydria | =B3 | =B3 |
| *B10<br>Hipponium<br>end of fifth century B.C. | female<br>B: inhumation<br>T: on chest | Mnemosyne,<br>*phulakes*;<br>*bakkhoi* | Guide (entire);<br>Hex. (entire) |
| Between the Groups | | | |
| P1/2<br>Pelinna<br>end of fourth century B.C. | female<br>B: inhumation<br>T: on chest | Persephone,<br>Bakkhios | Milk (3-4), Guide<br>(entire); Hex. (1-2,<br>7), Pr. (3-6) |

CHAPTER 11

# Bacchic *Teletai* in the Hellenistic Age

Walter Burkert

Fritz Graf has shown how much our knowledge of Bacchic mysteries has changed in recent years.[1] First came the gold lamella of Hipponium (ca. 400 B.D.),[2] which established the connection of the gold leaves called "group B" by Günther Zuntz with *mustai kai bakkhoi;* then there were the graffiti on bone tablets of Olbia, which leave no doubt that a group of Orphikoi, with some relation to Dionysus and a markedly dualistic ideology concerning *sōma* and *psukhē,* was in existence by the fifth century B.C., while a mirror from a tomb with the oldest attestation of the Bacchic cry *euai* may even point to "Orphic" myth and ritual in the sixth.[3] Now the new gold lamellae from Pelinna[4] have drawn "group A" of the gold leaves into the realm of Bakkhios too, of Dionysus Lusios and his *telea,* evidently. Thus the whole corpus of these remarkable documents can now finally be attributed to Bacchic mysteries. In this context the well-known but often neglected texts of Heraclitus, of Herodotus, of Aeschines-Demosthenes, and of Plato have received fuller meaning. We find

[1] See Graf's essay in this volume. Cf. Cole 1980; Burkert 1985, 290–93; Burkert 1987a, 5 and 21–23; and the survey entitled "Bacchic Rites in Classical Greece" in Versnel 1990a, 131–55.

[2] Foti and Pugliese Carratelli 1974.

[3] Rusajeva 1978, esp. 96–98; West 1983a, 17–19.

[4] Tsantsanoglou and Parássoglou 1987; Burkert 1990, 27–28.

evidence for Bacchic mysteries from the sixth to the fourth century, with centers at Miletus and the Black Sea, in Thessaly and in Macedonia, Magna Graecia, and Crete; we find special rituals (*teletai*) performed as private initiations by itinerant charismatics to serve as "cures" for various afflictions, good both for this life and for the Beyond, combined with gatherings of private clubs (*thiasoi*) presenting themselves to the city in a public procession (*pompē*). The experience of ecstasy, *mania,* is crucial. Loose forms of tradition are to be assumed, "families" of *telestai* with books and certain theological and anthropological teachings, leaders of thiasoi but normally not founding "sects" in the full sense, as closed societies with permanent organization and ideology, but leaving their "craft" to their successors.

It remains to state that whereas until recently the mere existence of Bacchic mysteries before the Hellenistic age was controversial,[5] by now the most relevant testimonies for these mysteries are seen to belong to the sixth to fourth centuries B.C. It is rather the Hellenistic and imperial evidence that appears barren and unpromising by comparison. At any rate the question about Bacchic mysteries in the Hellenistic age cannot be that of invention but only of transformation.

And transformation indeed must have occurred; apparently it has to do with the interrelation of charismatics and thiasoi. Looking back from the later epoch,[6] it is a striking fact that those wandering charismatics, the practicing "experts in ritual" (*telestai*), who still play their role in the decree of Ptolemy IV Philopator and in the prehistory of the so-called Bacchanalia decree of the Roman Senate in 186 B.C.,[7] have disappeared. On the other hand we find a novel iconography, beginning, as it seems, with the "Villa of the Mysteries" at Pompeii,[8] and some novel terms in the organization of thiasoi, or clubs. The Bacchanalia legislation indeed marks a dramatic crisis in the development of Bacchic mysteries, just at the time when the center of the world was

[5] Still Turcan 1989, 298 (cf. Turcan 1986) would attribute the creation of Dionysian mysteries to the Hellenistic age only, as does Rice 1983, 189–90. See Versnel 1990a, 150–55, who still could not yet use the Pelinna tablets.

[6] Cf. Merkelbach 1988.

[7] Cf. Burkert 1987a, 33–35 (= 1990, 37–39); on the Bacchanalia decree see especially, p. 33 n. 11. Yet some continuity of "telestic" practice is proved by the gold tablet of Caecilia Secundina (A5 Zuntz), about A.D. 260, and the gold tablet from Petelia (B1 Zuntz), worn in Roman times as an amulet (Zuntz 1971, 335).

[8] Matz 1963; cf. in general Merkelbach 1988.

shifting from East to West. Yet the decree of the Roman Senate was not the only force to work changes in the area of Hellenistic mystery cults.

I shall focus my attention here, first, on two indisputably new features of Dionysiac worship that arose with the advent of the Hellenistic age: (1) the role of the theater and the associations of Dionysiac "theatrical artists" (*tekhnitai*), with Euripides' *Bacchae* in the background, and (2) the new kings, the Ptolemies of Egypt and the Attalids of Pergamum, who appropriated the patronage of Dionysiac worship, including Dionysiac *tekhnitai* and Dionysiac mysteries. These developments are to be linked with two new forms of "show" that were gaining control of the "media" in that period: the theater and theatrical life that was spreading everywhere, and the royal parades of the Hellenistic kings. Bacchic cults are found in their wake. Second, I will discuss a little-known document, the reliefs from the altar of Dionysus at Cos, dated to about 150 B.C., the comprehensive publication of which appeared in 1987. While comprising the new elements they still refer to the old practice of *teletai,* as does a Coan inscription of about the same date; this seems to be the last appearance of the older forms of *teletai*.

Royal connections of Dionysus come to the fore already with the Macedonian kings. There is the well-known story in Plutarch about Olympias' addiction to Orphic-Bacchic mysteries: she was seen handling winnowing baskets and snakes, hence the story that she was impregnated by a god in form of a snake, to give birth to Alexander the Great.[9] The celebration of mysteries accounts for the mysterious origin of a great king. The prominence of Bacchic cults in Macedonia and its surroundings at that time is made clear by archaeological evidence, by remarkable "Bacchic" monuments that have come to light in funerary contexts, such as the gilded krater of Derveni, used as an urn, or tombs painted with Dionysiac scenes, such as the one recently discovered at Potidaea.[10] Older and more to the point may be the legend of the royal house of the Argeadae, one form of which was

[9] Plutarch *Alexander* 2–3; and the Nektanebos legend, on which see Merkelbach 1977, 77–83.

[10] Gioure 1978; tomb of Potidaea: *AR* 1984–85, 43, Arch. Museum of Thessaloniki. Four of the gold tablets, including those of Pelinna, come from fourth-century Thessaly.

known already to Herodotus, who reported that it was from the gardens of Midas, where Silenus dwells, that the ancestor of the royal house started to conquer Macedonia; others told how Argaeus, the first king, himself installed the cult of Dionysus with virgin maenads, called Mimallones,[11] hence *Argadistika* and *Bakkhika* constitute the traditional family cult within the dynasty.[12] In consequence the Bacchants in the triumph of Ptolemy II are still referred to as "Macedonians" (*Maketai*) and Thracians.[13] Much more influential was the tradition of how Alexander discovered Dionysus' Nysa in India and came to identify himself with Dionysus, who conversely was turned into the triumphant conquerer of the world. What precisely may be historical fact in these stories is a much-debated problem; there is no question that they molded Dionysiac tradition for the future.[14] The Indian triumph of Dionysus was to become a favorite theme both of poetry and of figurative art, developed even further in the late Bacchic sarcophagi and mosaics;[15] it was the model for any triumph as such.

The diadochs consciously made use of this tradition, beginning at least with Ptolemy II, surnamed Philadelphus. The key document for the glory of Dionysus radiating upon the king of Egypt is the great procession of Ptolemy II in about 280/275 B.C. as described by Callixenus.[16] It is often supposed that the assimilation of king and Dionysus was encouraged by the age-old Egyptian identification of the pharaoh with Horus/Osiris and the later Greek equation of Osiris with Dionysus, but this has been contradicted by the experts.[17] It was simply

[11] Herodotus 8.137–38; Polyaenus 4.1.

[12] Letter of Olympias to Alexander in Athenaeus 15.659–60: Olympias is sending a special cook for Alexander's wedding, one who knows "your family cults, . . . both the *Argadistika* and the *Bakkhika*" (*ta hiera sou ta patrōia . . . kai ta Argadistika* [*Argeadika* Kaibel] *kai ta Bakkhika*). Few will assume that the document is genuine, but it is not part of the fictitious letters that started the *Alexander Romance* (on which see Merkelbach 1977).

[13] Callixenus (see n. 16); Athenaeus 5.198e.

[14] Arrian *Anabasis* 5.1.1; 6.28; 7.10.6; Megasthenes, *FGrH* 715 F 4 (= Diodorus Siculus 2.38); Plutarch *Alexander* 67; see Nock 1928; Jeanmaire 1951, 351–72; Dihle 1981, 22–23; Goukowsky 1981; and Rice 1983, 82–99.

[15] *LIMC* s.v. "Dionysos/Bacchus" nos. 233–36 and 241–47.

[16] Callixenus, *FGrH* 627 F 2 (=Athenaeus 5.196a–203b); Tondriau 1946; Fraser 1972, 1:202–3; for detailed commentary see Rice 1983, who argues for a date 280/275 B.C. against 270, as accepted by the *communis opinio*. Dionysus was just one of the gods in the procession, but his apparently was the most lavish part.

[17] Dunand 1986; see also Nilsson 1957a, 9–10. Cf. in general Tondriau 1946.

Greek propaganda for the Greeks, for all we see. The conquering power bestowing riches and ease of life, this was the main message to be conveyed by the procession of Ptolemy II. There we find Eniautos, the "Year" personified, with a huge cornucopia (Athenaeus 5.198a); the Indian conquest is represented with special luxury (5.200d–201c). There are the *tekhnitai* from the flourishing theater community together with the prominent tragic poet Philiscus as acting priest of Dionysus (5.198b–c), but there are also "many sorts of thiasoi" (5.198e) in the retinue, private associations performing the cult of Dionysus that evidently are anxious to follow suit. These will have included the initiates (*mustai*) of Dionysus. There is also a reference to special rites (*teletai*), unfortunately obscured by corruption,[18] and to various cohorts of sileni and satyrs, who by contrast were without "mystic" intimations and just made a show in the parade notable for their precious outfits.

It was the fourth Ptolemy, Philopator, who took new initiatives as to Dionysiac worship.[19] He not only renamed the demes of Alexandria with Dionysiac names;[20] through his much-discussed "decree,"[21] he tried to get control of private Dionysian mysteries in his kingdom. He even had the ambition to act as a Dionysiac *telestēs* himself, playing the *tumpanon* and collecting gifts in the residence,[22] and he had himself called "New Dionysus"; the poet Euphronius spoke of the "*teletai* of New Dionysus."[23] Philopater had himself branded with the symbol of an ivy leaf, and it is said that he forced the Jews to submit to the same.[24] This would mean that he was trying to use Dionysian mysteries as a form of integration, nay, suppression within his realm. He may have been a psychopath, but characteristic elements of his epoch seem to be reflected in his behavior.

[18] The codex has *perseisteletai;* see Rice 1983, 60–61; cf. 120 ("mystic crown" for the Berenikeion, 202d) and 187–190. See also the Gurob papyrus, *OF* 31, which is dated to the early third century B.C.; cf. Burkert 1990, 59–60.

[19] Fraser 1972, 1:203–4; Dunand 1986. Some sources are apocryphal (3 Maccabees 2:30) but not altogether to be discarded.

[20] Satyrus, *FGrH* 631 F 1; *POxy* 2465; Fraser 1972, 1:44 with n. 48.

[21] Literature in Dunand 1986; Burkert 1990, 110 n. 10.

[22] Plutarch *Cleomenes* 33; *Moralia* 60a.

[23] Powell 1925, 176; Clement of Alexandria *Protrepticus* 48; Fraser 1972, 1:347 n. 117.

[24] *Etymologicum Magnum,* s.v. "Gallos"; 3 Maccabees 2:29; Fraser 1972, 1:348–49 with n. 118; on branding versus tattooing, see Jones 1987, esp. 152.

Royal propaganda and private associations would continue to go hand in hand. Already Philadelphus had become a patron of Dionysiac *tekhnitai* both in Egypt and abroad.[25] The Dionysiac impulse of the Ptolemies was taken up from the outside. *Bakkhistai* from Thera passed a decree, about 150 B.C., by which they made the envoy of the Egyptian king together with his wife and his descendants honorary members of their thiasos.[26]

The last resurgence of Dionysiac ambitions in the realm of the Ptolemies seems to have been the ostentatious display of Antonius and Cleopatra, who were reenacting the triumph of the god once more, organizing a Dionysiac *pompē* at Ephesus and pursuing a life-style of Bacchic relaxation throughout. After their final catastrophe Bacchus abandons Alexandria, or, the story goes, it was the snake crawling from the basket (*kistē*) that killed Cleopatra.[27]

The Pergamene kingdom became an even more important center for Dionysiac activities. The first stages are unclear; much of the subsequent glory of the Attalids seems to have been retrojected on the comparatively humble beginnings. Attalus I Soter had adopted the title of king in about 230 B.C., but Pergamum did not become an important power before the decline of the Seleucids in the wars against Rome, 189/188 B.C. Yet by about 200 B.C. Dionysodorus dedicated the statue of a satyr to Dionysus, son of Thyone, and to King Attalus together, asking for the benevolence of both: Dionysus, with "mystic" allusions, is set in close parallel to the king.[28] A cult of Dionysus Kathegemon, "the Leader," was installed in the city, with a priest appointed directly by the king from his own family,[29] in all probability it was to this Dionysus that the temple at the splendid theater was dedicated; a private chapel in the palace seems to have existed in addition.[30] The old epic tradition of Telephus, king of Mysia-Pergamum,

[25] Callixenus (see above, n. 16); Athenaeus 5. 198b–c, with Rice 1983, 52–58; *OGI* nos. 50 and 51; Fraser 1972, 1:203 and 870 n. 1. See in general Stephanis 1988.

[26] *OGI* no. 735 (= *IG* 12.3, Suppl. no. 1296).

[27] For the Dionysiac displays, see Plutarch *Antonius* 24 and 75; Socrates of Rhodes, *FGrH* 192 F 2; and Fraser 1972, 1:205. Snake: Plutarch *Antonius* 85–86; the *kistē* with the snake appears in the cult of Isis too, but only in later monuments.

[28] Müller 1989; for an emended text, see Kassel 1990.

[29] See especially Prott 1902; Ohlemutz 1940, 90–122; Nilsson 1957a, 9–10. The main document is *IPergamon* no. 248 (= *OGI* no. 331).

[30] Ohlemutz 1940, 94–95; cf. 113, referring to *AM* 35 (1910): no. 43 and *AM* 33 (1908): 423, pl. 24.3.

could be recalled, although his relations to Dionysus Sphaleotas had been ambivalent, to put it mildly. A much more direct link was established by royal propaganda. Oracles, circulating both in the name of the prophetess Phaennis and of Delphi, made the king of Pergamum a descendant of Dionysus himself, referring to the king as "son of the bull fostered by Zeus" or just the "bull-horned."[31]

The most conspicuous document of this affiliation is the official "cistophoric" coinage issued at Pergamum after 166, when, in the aftermath of the fall of Macedonia, Eumenes II was reorganizing his kingdom.[32] The main symbol on these coins is a basket (*kistē*) out of which a snake is crawling. This is the emblem of *mustēria tout court,* concealment with awe lurking from under the lid.[33] *Kistē* and snakes in Dionysiac *teletai* are mentioned already in the fourth century; the snake has especially been related to Sabazius,[34] but it seems that only then was this concentrated into an emblem of mysteries. The snake was probably meant to refer to the divine origin of the dynasty, just as those tales about Olympias handling Bacchic snakes had meant to intimate (see n. 9), though in an allusive way. The "mystery" is half-open and thus allows a glimpse—*sapienti sat.*

Besides the official cult, private clubs were active in the worship of Dionysus, some apparently of "mystic" character; they were under-

[31] Pausanias 10.15.3 (*tauroio diotrepheos philon huion;* cf. 10.12.10 on Phaennis); Diodorus Siculus 34–35.13 (*taurokerōs*) (= *Suda,* s.v. "Attalos" = Parke and Wormell 1956, no. 431 = Fontenrose 1978, no. Q 245). Since this Delphic oracle refers to the end of the dynasty, it is risky to date it before 133 B.C. Cf. Tondriau 1952.

[32] Kleiner and Noe 1977 have established the date; previous studies had assumed earlier beginnings; cf. Seyrig 1963, 22–31.

[33] A relief from Ostia, preserved only in drawings, has the word MYSTERIA written to explain the *kistē;* it is reproduced in Merkelbach 1988, 48, among other places. Cf. Nonnus 9.127–28 for Dionysus' nurse called Mustis and her *kistē.* The *kistē* with snake routinely recurs in two sets of imperial Dionysiac imagery, on funerary altars (Geyer 1977a, 191, no. 327) and sarcophagi. The *kistē* without snakes is found earlier in association with Demeter; Demeter with *kistē* and snake appears on the Lovatelli urn (Burkert 1987a, fig. 4) and the Louvre sarcophagus (Baratte 1974). A *kistē* without snakes is also in a Bacchic tomb painting from Amphipolis, about 250 B.C. (Mus. Kavala), in Theocritus 26.7, and beside Dirke the Bacchant in the statue group known as the "Farnesian bull."

[34] Cf. Kienast 1979, 454, who thinks Eumenes was displaying his piety toward a local cult, without dynastic propaganda. Snake in Sabazius initiation: Burkert 1987a, 106; in the mysteries that Aeschines helped perform: Demosthenes *On the Crown* 260 (read *kistophoros;* cf. Wankel 1976, ad loc.); Plutarch *Alexander* 2 speaks of *likna* and snakes in connection with Olympias. There might be a tradition of Pergamum, claiming "kingship of Asia," behind Cicero *De natura deorum* 3.58 (one Dionysus, "king of Asia," *cui Sabazia sunt instituta*).

standably eager for royal benevolence. "*Bakkhoi*" dedicated an altar to Eumenes, who had become a god after his death: "To King Eumenes, god, savior, benefactor, the *bakkhoi* of the god worshiped with the cry *euhoi* [have dedicated this]" (*Basilei Eumenei Theōi sōtēri kai euergetēi hoi bakkhoi tou euastou theou*).[35] *Bakkhoi* in the old tradition of the term would have been those who had experienced the power of the god through Bacchic frenzy (*bakkheuein*). We are less sure about this at Pergamum. The main inscription about the priest of Dionysus Kathegemon refers to "such great mysteries" (*mustēriōn tēlikoutōn*) performed in the cult of this god—this may simply be a general reference to the whole spectrum of Dionysiac ceremonies.[36]

In the Pergamene cult of Dionysus two further specialities deserve comment:[37] (1) the close interrelation with the theater and the "theatrical artisans" (*tekhnitai*), and (2) the term *boukoloi*. The *tekhnitai* had been present at Teos since the third century. Teos had a cult of Dionysus Setaneios, who was also called "Leader" (Archagetas). We hear of initiates (*mustai*) of Setaneios, or members of religious clubs (*orgeōnes*) devoted to him.[38] The Dionysus temple at Teos was built sometime between 230 and 200 B.C.[39] At that time Teos tried to get international recognition of its right to sanctuary (*asulia*) on account of its cult of Dionysus, claiming that the city and its land were "sacred to Dionysus" (*kathierōsis tas te polios kai tas khōras*). Nevertheless, Teos probably became dependent upon Pergamum at the end of the third century and definitely after 189 B.C. It is probably on account of this fact that among the Tean *tekhnitai* there is a group that explicitly refers to Dionysus Kathegemon, that is, the Pergamene cult.[40]

An interesting though later document for the activities of actors has recently been published. It comes from Amastris, Pontus, and is dated to A.D. 155. A certain Aemilianus has "led the Komos for Dionysus at the trieteric festival (*teletē*) in a mystic way"; at the same time he was a athlete and won victories "with a satyr dance" (*saturōi*) at Cyzicus and Pergamum. Theatrical dance, an official festival of Dionysus,

[35] *AM* 27 (1902): 94, no. 86; cf. Merkelbach 1988, 19, for *oikon euastērion* at Thasos (third century).

[36] *IPergamon* no. 248.38; cf. Ohlemutz 1940, 109–10.

[37] Cf. Geyer 1977b, 180–83.

[38] *RE*, s.v. "Teos," cols. 564–65.

[39] Stambolidis 1987, 198.

[40] Ohlemutz 1940, 98–103.

and "mystic" professionalism go together. It is the dancer/actor who brings the divine alive; does he also hold and transmit the "knowledge" of "mysteries"?[41]

Even more interesting is the designation of *boukoloi* (literally, "cowherds") in the context of the Pergamene cult. In inscriptions from imperial times it appears that *boukoloi* designates the main body of Bacchic initiates (*mustai*). A. Geyer (1977b), reacting against R. Merkelbach, had tried to redate the title *boukoloi* at Pergamum to the imperial period, to the reform of Dionysiac mysteries organized by Aulus Iulius Quadratus at the time of Trajan. This has been disproved recently by a Pergamene inscription published in 1979, an altar dedicated to Dionysus Kathegemon by the "chief *boukolos*" (*arkhiboukolos*) Heroides in the late Hellenistic epoch.[42] The term *boukoloi* at Pergamum thus is positively attested for Hellenistic times, as is the hierarchy within the Bacchic guild (*thiasos*) implied by the prefix *arkhi-*. The *boukoloi* in later Bacchic mysteries may well have Pergamene origins.[43] The term *boukolos* has been connected with the myth of Telephus, who grew up in "bucolic" surroundings; with the sacred marriage of Dionysus at the *boukoleion* of Athens;[44] with the actual cowherds in Euripides' *Bacchae;* and also with representations of Dionysus with bull horns.[45] The tauromorphic imagery is crucial in the oracles referring to the Pergamene king as "son of the bull" or even "the bull" itself. Thus the function of the *boukoloi* appears to be closely related to the identification of king and Dionysus at Pergamum, with

[41] Cf. also Libanius *Epistulae* 1212–13; Burkert 1990, 39.

[42] *AA* 1979, 321–23; *SEG* 29, no. 1264. The altar was found built into the wall of the "Podiensaal," a room for mysteries, as it seems, Bacchic rather than Mithraic: Dahlinger 1979. Further testimony for Dionysian mysteries at Pergamon: *IPergamon* no. 221, statue of a priest (fragmented, no date); of imperial date: *IPergamon* nos. 319, 320 (*Midapedeitōn speira*), 222 (*stibadeion*), 485–88 (*boukoloi, theia mustēria*). See *AM* 24 (1899): 179, no. 31, for inscriptions at the theater terrace (*hoi khoreusantes boukoloi, triet*). For *mustai* of Dionysus Kathegemon in Phrygia, imperial epoch, see *ANRW* 2.18.3 (1990): 1947.

[43] A much earlier testimony has been added from Atrax, Thessaly, a dedication by a *koinon tōn boukolōn* (300–250 B.C.), but the context and even the relation to Dionysus rests in the dark: *SEG* 35, no. 496; cf. *AR* 1987–88, 37. One has referred to *boukoleis Sabazion* (Aristophanes *Wasps* 10)—an unclear allusion. Further evidence on *boukoloi:* Quandt 1912, 251–54.

[44] Aristotle *Constitution of Athens* 3.5.

[45] Sophocles frag. 959 (*TrGF* 4); krater from Thurioi: Kerényi 1976a, fig. 114; Bérard 1976, 61–73. Cf. also the well-known hymn from Elis in Plutarch *Quaestiones Graecae* 36 (= *Moralia* 299b), which invokes Dionysus as *tauros*.

special reference to the king's purported divine origin. Verses preserved in Clement of Alexandria's *Protrepticus* (though probably corrupt) seem to contain the very epitome of this, as they bring together the snake, the bull, the *boukolos,* and the mountain: "Bull, son of the snake, and father of the bull, the snake; in the mountain, the secret goad of the cowherd (?)."[46]

When dealing with the solid but barren evidence for Hellenistic cults provided by coinage and inscriptions we should not forget that the functioning of religion, and of Dionysian cult in particular, rests on the chances for some extraordinary, "divine" experience; in the case of Dionysus, this is especially the "seizure" by the god, transmitted and manipulated by those "ritual performers" (*telestai*) of the old, albeit problematic, tradition; *mania* was to happen and was used for psychosomatic cures. The special possessors of charismatic talents may have been classified as the true *bakkhoi* and thus distinguished from the mere narthex-bearers.[47]

It seems that in Hellenistic society these forms of "charismatic" experience were supplemented and eventually ousted by other forms apt to raise reverential awe (*sebas*) and "enthusiasm." The experience of "epiphany" came to concentrate on the person of the ruler who had acted as a "savior" and inaugurated an age of bliss and abundance—a process that easily assumed a Dionysiac coloring. Royal display in the great parade took the form of a Dionysiac *pompē*. At the same time the theater had made Dionysiac enthusiasm readily available in mimetic play, at least since Euripides' *Bacchae*. The monarch was the victor, the savior, the god, "present" (*epiphanēs*) to a degree gods had hardly ever been. Not only the actors followed in his wake, but "all sorts of thiasoi," including those of *mustai* and *bakkhoi*.

Forms of ruler cult are difficult for moderns to digest; they were ignored by Greek philosophers, but they were real. Poets and orators were less squeamish. We have a few lines in Priapean meter written in honor of Ptolemy IV, the New Dionysus, by the poet Euphronius, who according to ancient tradition was the teacher of Aristophanes of Byzantium and of Aristarchus: "Not uninitiated, O celebrants of the

[46] Clement of Alexandria *Protrepticus* 16.2; Firmicus Maternus *De errore profanorum religionum* 26.1: *Tauros drakontos kai patēr taurou drakōn / en orei to kruphion boukolos to kentron.*

[47] On the Bacchic frenzy (*bakkheia*) of maenads see Bremmer 1984, 275–82; Burkert 1987a, 19 and 33–35.

mysteries of New Dionysus, . . . I too am coming, made to share the rites on account of kindness bestowed, marching to the marsh of Pelusium at dusk."[48] The reference to new forms of Dionysiac mysteries in the retinue of the king could not be clearer. The poet poses as an initiate himself, transformed to celebrate rites (*orgia*) on account of his overwhelming, nay, Bacchantic experience of bliss; with candid simplicity he calls it a "benefit" (*euergesiē*) granted by the king.

In addition there is a papyrus fragment in which M. R. Nilsson discovered "royal mysteries in Egypt." The preserved text is short and fragmentary, but the point seems clear: "Triptolemus. . . , not for you have I now performed initiation; neither Kore abducted did I see nor Demeter in her grief, but kings in their victory."[49] This seems to come from a speech, possibly addressing the king, or from some rhetorical exercise. It is the view of triumphant kings, which surpasses the beatifying "view" proclaimed in traditional mysteries. "God Manifest [and] Victorious" (*Theos Epiphanēs Nikēphoros*) was the title assumed by Antiochus IV,[50] before the Romans reduced his aspirations. Cheering crowds were apt to give resonance to this, at Antioch and at Alexandria. "Royal mysteries" take precedence over private cults practiced in the corner. Once more the procession of Ptolemy Philadelphus seems to provide the model. Even the family of a king's envoy can become members of *Bakkhistai* by decree (see n. 26), without any question of initiation or charismatic talents.

Thus the charisma of power is seen to override other forms of reverential awe (*sebas*); the attraction of royal epiphany seems to be

[48] Euphronius' *Priapeia* in Powell 1925, 176–77: *ou bebēlos, ō teletai tou neou Dionusou . . . ka'gō d' ex euergesiēs ōrgiasmenos hēkō, hodeuōn Pēlousiakon knephaios para telma;* see Powell ad loc. and Fraser 1972, 1: 204 n. 117, 207 with n. 140, and 663 n. 100. That τελέται (probably with this accent; *aliter* LSJ) should mean "initiates" or "mystagogues" was conjectured by Meineke; one compares Demetrius of Phaleron frag. 170 (Wehrti 1949), Cleanthes frag. 538 (*SVF* 1), and a few other texts; see LSJ, s.v.; Fraser 1972, 1:347 and 117. "Marching to the marsh" is reminiscent of the procession to Dionysus "in the marshes" at the end of the Choes day of the Athenian Anthesteria. Choiroboskos says Euphronius addressed the poem "to Priapus," but this may be an overstatement due to the fact that the lines are being used as an example for the Priapean meter. Of course Priapus played his role in Dionysiac contexts.

[49] P. Antinoöpolis no. 18: ὦ Τριπτόλεμε, σ[ . . ο]ὐ σοὶ νῦν μεμύηκ[α?. οὐ γὰρ] τὴν Κόρην εἶδον ἡ[ρπασμ]ένην οὐδὲ τὴν Δή[μητρα λε]λυπημένην, ἀλ[λὰ ν]εικηφόρους βα[σιλέας. Extensive and inconclusive commentary by Delatte 1952; see Nilsson 1957b, still without reference to Euphronius.

[50] Cf. Nock 1928, 41–43 (= 1972, 155–57).

overwhelming. Dionysus was especially suited for this new role, since he is a god of epiphanies, of "being present": *nec enim praesentior illo est deus* (*Ovid Metamorphoses* 3.658–69). "We see you present," the Athenians sang in their notorious hymn in honor of Demetrius Poliorcetes.[51] Monarchic enthusiasm, feigned or real, reaching the level of Bacchic frenzy (*bakkheia*), seems to be at least one factor in the transformation of Dionysiac mysteries from the clientele of individual charismatics into well-organized and officially recognized clubs, even if the "truly religious" element is found to decline. The eclipse of Hellenistic monarchies must have been another shock; but it still left the bourgeois thiasoi we find in the imperial age.

The altar of Dionysus at Cos was built about 150 B.C. at the agora, close to the harbor; it was decorated with a series of Dionysiac reliefs. Some of these had been known for a long time, as they had been built into the walls of a medieval tower; but they had been attributed to Cnidos, from where some comparable reliefs were known, until the Italian excavations, in 1935, brought to light more of these reliefs in situ—there are thirteen now—and the foundations of the altar itself. In 1958 all the plaques were assembled in the local museum. The comprehensive publication and discussion is by N. C. Stambolidis, who has also established the date of the monument.[52]

The reliefs are of moderate quality, and much of the iconography includes standard motifs from the Dionysiac cycle. The cult of Dionysus is well attested at Cos by other, earlier sources as well.[53] It is worthwhile to recall that there are especially close links to the *tekhnitai;* it has been suggested that they chose Cos as their main residence for a while.[54] Among the representations at the altar there are still two that are less common and of special interest in relation to Dionysiac *teletai.*

[51] Athenaeus 6.253d (= Duris, *FGrH* 76 F 13 = Powell 1925, 174). For possible old connections of *thriambos* and royal ritual of a Near Eastern type see Versnel 1970.

[52] Stambolidis 1987, passim; for Cos in general see Sherwin-White 1978, esp. 131–45 (Hellenistic history), 314–17 (Dionysus cult); the altar is mentioned on p. 25. Kabus-Preisshofen 1989 does not deal with reliefs.

[53] New inscriptions mention the recital of honors at the Dionysia festival in the theater (third century B.C.): *ZPE* 25 (1977): 272, no. 3; *ZPE* 27 (1977): 229, no. 1 (= *SEG* 27, nos. 514 and 511).

[54] Sherwin-White 1978, 315–17, with reference to a letter of Sulla, for which see Segre 1938.

One relief (no. 13) has young Dionysus, half-kneeling on a chair, flanked by two Corybants with their characteristically small shields. Dionysus with Corybants is a rare motif, though known from some other monuments.[55] The frieze from the Athenian theater of Dionysus has two Corybants flanking the birth of Dionysus—but this is much later. Stambolidis refers to a comparable scene from the frieze of the Hecate temple of Lagina, which is dated somewhat later than the altar of Cos (100/80 B.C.). The theater of Perge in Pamphylia has a scene that is more similar to ours; little Dionysus is seated on a chair while three Corybants dance around him. With the Corybants an element of Meter cult enters the legend and iconography of Dionysus. It is already in Euripides' *Bacchae* (124–25), and the close association of Dionysus and Meter has been celebrated ever since Pindar (*Dithyramb* 2). The alliance is based on ritual, on corybantic possession. Corybantic dances were practiced as a cure for "madness," a practice largely parallel to Dionysiac *teletai*.[56] Characteristic of Meter and her Corybants was the *tumpanon,* which was hardly less prominent in Dionysiac cult.

As for the scene of young Dionysus amid Corybants, it is tempting to see a reference to the Orphic myth of Dionysus, his enthronement, the Curetes as guardians, and the subsequent attack and assassination by the Titans (*Orphicorum fragmenta* 34–35 and 207–10); this seems a possible interpretation of the relief at Perge, even if the "Orphic" scene is in the midst of "normal" Dionysiac iconography, and definitely in the context of the theater. But at Cos the Corybantic scene is framed by battle scenes that transfer their meaning to the armed dance of the Corybants: Dionysus is the warlike god, the triumphant god. The tradition of Alexander's Indian triumph has made its impact on Dionysus' iconography even at Cos.

More interesting, indeed unique, is the second relief (no. 1). To the

[55] Stambolidis 1987, 69–73, 150–52, pls. 7b and 32d; cf. a sarcophagus fragment in the Vatican depicting the child Dionysus, *kistē* with snake, and Corybants: Stambolidis 1987, pl. 57e = *LIMC* s.v. "Dionysos/Bacchus" no. 140; coins: Stambolidis, pl. 58; Athens: *LIMC* s.v. "Dionysos/Bacchus" no. 253; Lagina: Stambolidis, 151, pl. 57d; Perge: *VIII Kazi Sonuçlari Toplantlsi* (Ankara, 1986), 165, fig. 38; M. J. Mellink, *AJA* 92 (1988): 118; *AR* 1989–90, 120. A later document, clearly Orphic, is the ivory pyxis from Bologna: *LIMC* s.v. "Dionysos/Bacchus" no. 267.

[56] *epi katharmōi tēs manias:* scholia to Aristoph. *Wasps* 119; cf. Burkert 1990, 106 n. 32; Velardi 1989.

left, a *kistē,* out of which a huge snake is crawling; a female with a torch, extending her right hand toward the snake; in the middle, a woman, arms outstretched to either side, evidently dominating the scene; to the right, a bearded man stepping on an altar and somehow reclining on it, within a rocky landscape. The compelling interpretation goes back to O. Benndorf.[57] "Dionysus is purified by Meter in the Cybela mountains and receives his mysteries." Stambolidis concurs; he takes the middle figure to be Meter; the assistant to the left he calls Adrasteia.

Iconographically this scene is without parallel in the extant evidence. But it is attested for Philadelphus' procession: "Dionysus at the altar of Rhea, where he fled, when he was pursued by Hera."[58] There must be some iconographic connection between this tableau and the frieze at Cos. In the background there is the literary tradition to which already Benndorf referred; the main text is in Apollodorus, but virtually the same story is also attributed to the *Europia,*[59] a work of "Eumelus" dated to the eighth century by ancient tradition[60]—whatever that may mean. The passage in Apollodorus seems to be based on an excerpt of "Eumelus" in this case. Earlier and independent is a strange allusion to this mythical incident in Plato's *Laws:* Dionysus was "torn asunder in the wits of his soul" by Hera,[61] hence Dionysus sends his *mania* as a revenge to humans.

The myth as told by "Eumelus" and Apollodorus is evidently a foundation myth for Dionysiac *teletai.* The god himself has suffered what he is inflicting on humans. "Madness" is terrible, a form of sick-

[57] Benndorf and Niemann 1884, 13–14, pl. II; Stambolidis 1987, 29–33, 89–91, pls. 3a, 17d. Rice 1983, 99–101, with n. 201, raises doubts about Benndorf's interpretation, without taking account of the 1935 excavations, which definitely established the Dionysiac context. It is true that the beard of "Dionysus" presents a problem.

[58] Callixenus, *FGrH* 627 F 2 = Athenaeus 5.201c *Dionusos peri ton tēs Rheas bōmon katapepheugōs hote hupo Hēras ediōketo.*

[59] Apollodorus 3.5.1 (quoted in translation and discussed by Carpenter on pp. 197–98 in this volume); Eumelus *Europia* frag. 1 (*EGF*) = scholia A to *Illiad* 6.131 *Dionusos . . . en Kubelois tēs Phrugias hupo tēs Rheas tukhōn katharmōn kai diatheis tas teletas kai labōn pasan para tēs theas tēn diaskeuēn.*

[60] For the possibility that "Eumelus" is the source of *Il.* 6.119ff. see Von der Mühll 1952, 116–17.

[61] Plato *Laws* 672b *diephorēthē tēs psukhēs tēn gnōmēn.* Cf. also Euripides *Cyclops* 3–4; and Carpenter in this volume; a different version of Dionysus' madness appears in [Eratosthenes] *Catasterismi* 24 (pp. 90–91 Robert). For purification as a "science of division" see Parker 1983, esp. 18–31.

ness, but it can be overcome by "purification," and henceforth Dionysus will be the master of *teletai* himself, with all the appropriate paraphernalia,—snakes, *kistē, tumpanon*. Plato's version somehow seems to fuse the tradition preserved by "Eumelus" with the Orphic version of Dionysus' dismemberment; it has the same ambivalence of "madness," the same sequence of falling into *mania* and getting rid of it. The sequence is most clearly expressed by the double nature of Dionysus according to Pausanias: Dionysus Bakkheios, who maddens humans, and Dionysus Lusios, who frees them from madness (2.2.6 and 2.7.6). There are *lusioi teletai* of Bakkhios. The newly discovered gold tablets from Pelinna allude to this most clearly: "Bakkhios himself has set you free" (see n. 4). The god experienced the suffering and salvation that his adherents are going to experience themselves in the course of their "cures." *Mania* is affliction and a means of healing, is revenge or blessing or both; the outcome is purification, "feeling better now," through the acceptance of a rite of initiation (*teletē*).

With this background it is possible to give a more detailed interpretation of the Coan relief. The central, dominating figure, Meter, establishes separation by her imperative gesture, pushing asunder with force and authority the Bacchic female carrying a torch and touching the snake to the left—the epitome of Bacchic frenzy (*bakkheia*)—and the person at the altar seeking catharsis. Purification is in fact an art of "separation." Iconographically the female to the left is similar to a Bacchant in a sarcophagus fragment that figures in the attack of Athamas on Ino.[62] There it is *mania* invading the scene, *mania* in its most terrible, murderous aspect. On the relief from Cos, *bakkheia* is separated from and overcome by *lusis*.

By coincidence we have a written document on Dionysus worship at Cos from about the same time that explicitly refers to the *teletai* and those who perform them. It is cautiously attributed to the "second or first century B.C." by editors.[63] It is a regulation about the sale of the priesthood of Dionysus Thullophoros by the city.[64] A priestess is to be

[62] *LIMC* s.v. "Dionysos/Bacchus" no. 138.

[63] Paton and Hicks 1891, no. 27 (= *SIG*³ no. 1012 = *LSCG* no. 166); Sherwin-White 1978, 314.

[64] There is an earlier law about the sale of the priesthood of Dionysus Thullophoros that dates to the last quarter of the third century; see Sherwin-White 1978, 115 n. 169, quoting Segre 1941, 29–34.

installed for life; she has to pay a certain amount of money, but private activities are to result that will in turn bring revenues for her. The priestess is to be "initiated" (*hopōs de telesthēi*) according to custom, at the cost of the polis. She is allowed to install a "subpriestess" (*huphiereia*) who still must be a citizen of Cos; in the individual districts of Cos (*damoi*), nobody else is allowed to become priestess or perform the *teletai* of Dionysus Thullophoros without being appointed by the priestess, or there will be legal prosecution. It is clear that only women are initiated by the priestess and her deputy. An official festival of Dionysus, a Katagoge, seems to be mentioned too (A 40).

In many respects this inscription is comparable to the well-known decree about the cult of Dionysus Bakkhios at Miletus in 276/275 B.C.[65] There too it is the polis, represented by the "priestess" of the god, that claims precedence in the cult. Private *teletai* are mentioned at Miletus as well; they are allowed "if a woman wishes to perform them" (*ean tis gunē boulētai telein tōi Dionusōi*), but fees are due to the "priestess." At Cos the position of the priestess is more dominant; only those "appointed" by her may perform legal initiations. In this way, a monopoly of the priestess and her deputy with regard to the *teletai* of Dionysus is established. One might compare the form of control the decree of Philopator must have had in view. If the worship of Dionysus seems to be reduced here to a purely bureaucratic arrangement, one may still wonder why the "subpriestess" is provided for. Perhaps, just because the appointment of the priestess is mainly a financial affair, the subpriestess could be chosen on account of "charismatic" qualifications that must still be necessary for the effective performance of *teletai*.[66]

The Dionysus altar at Cos, an official monument of city cult, is found to refer to Corybants and to *teletai,* while the public inscription presupposes a flourishing business of *teletai* but establishes control through the priestess installed by and responsible to the polis. Both

[65] *LSAM* no. 48; cf. Henrichs 1978a, 149–52; cf. epitaph for a priestess of Dionysus from Miletus, third/second century B.C.: *SBBerlin* 1905, 547; Henrichs 1978a, 148–49; regulations between a private club of *bakkhoi* and the polis at Cnidus, about 250 B.C.: *SIG*[3] no. 978 (= *LSAM* no. 55): It is provided that nobody may use the sanctuary (*hieron*) just to stay overnight.

[66] Even Corybantic "cures" were performed by female charismatics; see Plato *Laws* 790d *hai peri' ta tōn korubantōn iamata telousai.*

documents seem to go together. Dionysus at Cos is still the god of madness, of purifications and *teletai,* but also the triumphant god, and the usual imagery of satyrs and maenads is not absent either. Viewed from a historical perspective, the cult at Cos thus seems to combine pre-Hellenistic and the more special Hellenistic features. Private initiations are still routinely performed, but the polis tries to link them to the official cult and to make them dependent on the state-controlled priestess; at the same time, the kings' triumphs have made their undeniable impact.

The situation of Cos at the time of the altar, and possibly of the inscription, was that of a sudden and precarious autonomy. Cos had previously been dominated by Rhodes, which in turn had been humiliated and deprived of its power by the Romans in 166 B.C. At this juncture, pre-Hellenistic times seem to come back, although in reality there is the shadow of a new superpower spreading over the Eastern Mediterranean. The documents of Cos could be called nostalgic, containing as it seems the latest evidence about private Bacchic *teletai* in the function of "cures," while free practitioners are prohibited henceforth by law. This is not yet the form of Dionysian mysteries that was to come to the fore in the imperial age.[67] But the anarchic element dreaded by the Romans in 186, originating from some migrating *sacrificulus et vates,* was out. At a somewhat later point in time *Bakkhiastai* are attested at Cos,[68] probably members of a club of the type that was to last.

[67] It is interesting that a priest of Dionysus Kathegemon at Pergamum, Mithradates, made friends with Caesar in 48 B.C. (*AM* 34 [1909]: 329–30; Ohlemutz 1940, 109)—about the time of the "Villa of the Mysteries." On possible relations of the Villa's iconography to Pergamum see Simon 1961.

[68] Maiuri 1925, no. 492; Sherwin-White 1978, 313, no. 205.

CHAPTER 12

# Voices from beyond the Grave: Dionysus and the Dead

Susan Guettel Cole

The new gold tablets from Pelinna share imagery and vocabulary with two other famous series of gold tablets found in Thessaly, Crete, and Italy.[1] The tablets known before 1985 fall into two groups. One group is concerned with purification and achievement of divine status and mentions Persephone.[2] The other group describes the landscape of the underworld: a spring, a white cypress, cold water from a pool of Memory, and a special road reserved for those who are *mustai* and *bakkhoi*.[3] The Pelinna tablets, because they include variations on themes of both groups, and because they mention the Bacchic god, suggest that all these tablets originated among groups of worshipers who were initiates of Dionysus and had common beliefs about the afterlife. We can therefore now assume that there is a Bacchic context for all these tablets, probably originating either in Thessaly or in southern Italy sometime in the late fifth century B.C. With one exception,[4] all the gold tablets are dated to the fourth and third centuries B.C.

[1] See the essays of Graf and Burkert in this volume.

[2] Zuntz 1971, 299–343; called by Zuntz the "A" group of tablets.

[3] Zuntz 1971, 355–70; the "B" group of tablets. The Hipponium tablet, published originally in 1974, is more complete than the early examples and provides for the first time the lines describing the road in the underworld and the Bacchic context for the whole group; Cole 1980. Janko 1984 gives full bibliography. A new tablet has been found on Lesbos; *AR* 1988–89, 93.

[4] The tablet of Caecilia Secundina, the only tablet to include the name of the deceased, was inscribed in the third century A.D. The tablet, found in Rome, is now in the British

These gold tablets were intended for burial with dead initiates (*mustai*). They seem to have been meant as a reminder of an initiation that promised protection after death to *bakkhoi* who had undergone a special purification and who had been released by the Bacchic one himself. The tablets describing the landscape of the underworld give precise instructions to the dead person, whose soul anticipated obstacles before being accepted among the Bacchic dead by the lords of the underworld. All these tablets were meant to be private, not public, documents, to be read, remembered, and recalled by the dead alone. The texts were not carved in stone for public display but buried with the dead to remind them of ritual responses, perhaps already learned in initiation ceremonies, to be used upon arrival in the underworld. When we compare the content of these tablets to less esoteric and more public evidence for Bacchic beliefs about death and existence after death, most of it dating from the late Hellenistic and Roman imperial periods, we will find that the two groups of evidence, widely separated by time, carry very different messages.

The gold tablets are not the only early epigraphical sources to associate Dionysiac worship with a concern for protection after death. The earliest evidence comes from Olbia, where an inscribed bronze mirror found in a grave seems to record the initiation of two people, Demonassa, the wife (or daughter) of Lenaios, and Lenaios, the son of Demoklos.[5] Also from Olbia are a group of three inscribed bone tablets, one of which carries the following text: "life, death, life, truth . . . Dio⟨nysoi⟩, Orphikoi."[6] The bone tablets, taken within the context of the tradition of Bacchic mysteries in the classical period, show that by the fifth century B.C. rituals associated with Dionysus were concerned with themes of life and death.[7] Even the order of the words "life, death, life" is perhaps significant. Additional evidence for Bacchic groups practicing such rituals is found in the fifth century in

Museum. See Zuntz 1971, 333–35, tablet A5. Zuntz, comparing the tablet to the others in his "A" group, calls it "evidence for the same religion sadly debased."

[5] *Dēmōnassa Lēnaio euai kai Lena⟨i⟩os Dēmokloē e⟨u⟩a⟨i⟩* (sixth century B.C.). Rusajeva 1978, 96–98 and fig. 7; Tinnefeld 1980, 70–71. Burkert 1987a, 22, identifies the female and the male as mother and son, but the male's name is probably to be understood as Lenaios, identical with the name of the woman's *kurios,* and therefore the name of her husband.

[6] *bios thanatos bios aletheia . . . Dio⟨nusoi⟩ Orphikoi*. Rusajeva 1978, 87–89; Tinnefeld 1980, 67–69; West 1983a, 17–20.

[7] For the association of these tablets with the idea of death as transformation, as expressed by Heraclitus, see Seaford 1986a, 14–20.

such authors as Aeschylus[8] and Herodotus.[9] Intensity of commitment may have varied with time and place and from group to group, but there seems to be some consistency in eschatological beliefs. The Hipponium tablet speaks of a special road in the underworld for *mustai* and *bakkhoi*,[10] probably the same road meant by the expression *mustikon oimon epi Rhadamanthun* ("mystic road to Rhadamanthus") in a poem of the third century B.C.[11] A chamber tomb at Cumae in Italy, of the late fifth century B.C., was reserved for those who had participated in Bacchic ceremonies.[12] One imagines that the Bacchic initiates at Cumae reserved their chamber tomb only for those eligible to walk the special road. Just where this road was thought to lead is not made clear, but R. Janko's reconstruction of the prototype of the group of tablets to which the Hipponium tablet belongs suggests that the initiate who takes the special road in the underworld will reach a place where he will rule with the "other heroes."[13] In other words, the initiate, although in the world of the dead, will achieve some sort of divine, heroic status.[14]

The eschatological message so explicit in the early gold tablets does not appear later in the public inscriptions on stone. The detailed description of the underworld and the definite promise of a special status for the Bacchic initiate in the afterlife are missing in the later Dionysiac material dated after the third century B.C. Many claim to find Dionysiac symbolism of life and death in pictorial representations: in vase painting,[15] wall and floor decoration,[16] reliefs carved on

[8] Aeschylus: *Bassarae* frag. 83 (Mette 1959), with West's additions: 1983b, 63–71; 1983a, 12 n. 33. The text is also quoted in *TrGF* 3, p. 138.

[9] Herodotus 2.81, for Bacchic practices; Burkert 1987a, 23. For problems with the text see Linforth 1941, 39–50.

[10] Cole 1980. Euripides *Hippolytus* 952–55 implies the existence of exclusive religious groups with special requirements, but Euripides says nothing about terminology.

[11] Probably by Posidippus of Pella; Lloyd-Jones 1963, 75–99.

[12] *LSS* no. 120; fifth century B.C. For a discussion of the meaning of *bebakkheumenon*, see Turcan 1986, 227–44. Cf. *IG* 14, no. 871, for an even earlier, possibly Bacchic sepulchral inscription at Cumae (ca. 525 B.C.).

[13] Janko 1984, 97–99.

[14] Compare the tablet from Thurii, which addresses the dead person as follows: "Happy and blessed one, you will be a god instead of mortal" (*olbie kai makariste, theos d'esēi anti brotoio*); Zuntz 1971, 301, tablet A 1.8, probably about the middle of the fourth century B.C.

[15] Schauenberg 1953, 38–72; Metzger 1944–45, 296–339; Metzger 1965, 97.

[16] Wall decoration: Nilsson 1957a, 123–27; mosaics: Horn 1972; Dunbabin 1978, 173–85, with reservations about possible religious meaning.

sarcophagoi,[17] and ornamentation on tombs and graves.[18] Dionysiac symbolism, however, takes many forms, and it is not always a simple matter to discern the possible religious meaning of a visual image or the spiritual motivation for a specific iconographic motif. For example, the recently discovered gold tablets from Pelinna, cut in the shape of an ivy leaf, lend new support to R. Merkelbach's suggestion that upright single ivy leaves on two tombstones at Erythrae were meant to imply that the dead were initiates of Dionysus and therefore expected special protection after death.[19] Nevertheless, it is not justifiable to take every decorative ivy leaf, grape cluster, or cantharus on a tomb monument as implying definable beliefs of the person in the grave.[20]

Most of the epigraphical evidence for Dionysiac associations that practiced mysteries and initiations in the Hellenistic and Roman periods is concerned with the rules and regulations of private associations, recognition of special activities, and donations of wealthy members. Public inscriptions do not reveal the secret beliefs of those who practiced Bacchic mysteries. Dionysus was a god whose myths about a double birth, death and rebirth, and a journey to the underworld made him a figure attractive to those who wished to find a way to escape the

17 Lehmann-Hartleben and Olsen 1942; Turcan 1966; Matz 1968–75; Alföldi 1939, 347–59, for bronze objects decorated with Bacchic motifs, which may have ornamented funeral chariots. For skepticism about the symbolic interpretation of Dionysiac scenes, however, see Nock 1946, 148, 150, 166, etc. (= 1972, 616, 618, 637, etc.). Geyer 1977a, 57, points out that Asia Minor, the location of the greatest concentration of inscriptions recording local, private Bacchic groups, produced few sarcophagi with Dionysiac motifs.

18 Andreae 1963; Engemann 1973. For Asia Minor, see Pfuhl and Möbius 1977–79, index, s.v. "Traube." Waelkens 1977 expresses reservations about associating all such symbolism with Dionysus, especially in Phrygia. There is, however, new and unpublished evidence that may prove promising for analysis. Two frescoed tombs, one from Amphipolis (250 B.C., on exhibit in the Archaeological Museum at Kavala) and the other from Potidaea (fourth century B.C., on exhibit in the Archaeological Museum in Thessaloniki), both decorated with distinctive and rich Dionysiac themes, may have been designed for local initiates.

19 Merkelbach 1988, 132–33. The ivy leaf on the tombstone of Antaios Melantou is cast in bronze and attached to the stone. This special treatment implies that this particular leaf had special meaning; see Cumont 1942b, 31, fig. 16.

20 Pfuhl and Möbius 1977–79, no. 2262, a gravestone from Mesembria, third century B.C., illustrates this problem. The stone, decorated with a cantharus in relief, marks the family grave of a man named Botrys (the name means "bunch of grapes") and his wife and son. While the family may have had a special interest in Dionysus, there is nothing about the name or the relief that need necessarily imply that these people were initiates or expected their grave decoration to carry a special meaning.

anxieties of death, but even where Dionysus himself is mentioned, the Dionysiac message is often left vague and cloaked in conventional literary language. An unpublished inscription from Thasos describes him as a god who renews himself and returns each year rejuvenated.[21] The initiate who expected some kind of pleasurable existence after death as a consequence of a Bacchic initiation ceremony could have seen in this description a model for his own future. A similar idea may have prompted Plutarch's remarks to his wife about the meaning of their own Bacchic initiation. After the death of their young daughter he consoled his wife with the thought that their Bacchic initiation had taught them not to fear death. He says that the tokens and responses of the mystery rites for Dionysus (*ta mustika sumbola tōn peri ton Dionuson orgiasmōn*) showed that death is not complete dissolution, as the Epicureans claimed, but release of the soul from the body.[22] Plutarch does not spell out the conditions of that release, nor does he or any other late source refer to the rather specific message of the gold tablets.

In the search for a systematic belief in a Dionysiac afterlife one type of evidence has not yet been fully exploited. This evidence is to be found in inscriptions decorating tombs and graves. When we actually examine sepulchral inscriptions with Dionysiac themes, however, we can see that not all Dionysiac worshipers were as confident as Plutarch about the values of Dionysiac initiation. Some of the texts actually even call into question modern interpretations that see Dionysiac motifs on Roman sarcophagoi and funerary monuments as implicit references to anticipation of a happy afterlife. There are about seventy-five sepulchral inscriptions that refer to Dionysus, Dionysiac activities, Bacchic organizations, or Bacchic mysteries. These inscriptions have been found in all areas of the Mediterranean where Greek was spoken, but the greatest concentration occurs in Asia Minor. Most of these inscriptions were written in Greek, some in prose, others in poetry. Latin occurs in Rome and in Roman colonies like Philippi. Most of the texts date from the imperial period, but comparison of the

[21] Ecole d'Athènes 1967, 172, offers a French translation, republished by Roux 1972, 633–34.

[22] Plutarch *Moralia* 611d–e. Unfortunately the text is badly damaged at just the place where Plutarch seems to be describing the special fate of those who, like his daughter, die young. Plutarch's consolation to his wife is perhaps deliberately vague. Cf. *Moralia* 388a–389a for deliberate obfuscation by riddles of the myths of death and rebirth of Dionysus. On riddles concerning the mysteries in general, see Seaford 1981, 254–55.

earlier with the later texts shows that the tradition of a Bacchic afterlife may not have been the same in all periods, and that the individuals who practiced what we call Bacchic mysteries may not always have shared the same expectations.

The actual tomb inscriptions with Dionysiac themes often differ from their poetic counterparts in the Greek literary anthologies. Funereal texts in the anthologies, often intended for amusement rather than to ornament a real tomb or to remember someone who had actually lived, use Dionysiac themes for humorous effect, while the texts from real graves tend to use Dionysiac themes to palliate the pain of death.[23] In the anthologies wine is a topic of fun. We hear of a man who died of drink[24] and of another who thinks he should blame Dionysus because he died from a fall in the rain while drunk.[25] Wine drinking is also a topic of fun in caricatures of a type well known from Greek comedy, the drunken old woman.[26] When the drinking of wine is mentioned in real tomb inscriptions, however, it is represented as a positive experience and is used to symbolize life's pleasures.[27] When drinking is associated with life's pleasures, Dionysus is paired with Aphrodite,[28] or with the Muses, Graces, and nymphs.[29] In the literary epitaphs only those for Anacreon emphasize these positive aspects of wine.[30] For example, in the literary texts a man who died of drink is described as having committed hubris against the Muses,[31] but in real life death-

[23] The single possible epigraphical exception is a humorous epitaph for a dead pig, killed when struck by the *phallagōgeion,* found at Edessa, third century A.D.; Daux 1970, 609–18.

[24] *Palatine Anthology* 7.104; cf. 105 (where Bacchus drags a drunkard to Hades by his toes); 7.329 (where a drinker of undiluted wine asks for a *pithos* of wine on his grave); and 7.353 (where a wine cup on the gravestone means that the old woman buried there was a hard drinker).

[25] *Palatine Anthology* 7.398; cf. 7.533.

[26] *Palatine Anthology* 7.353, 384, 455, 456, and 457; for the theme in art and literature, see Zanker 1989; Bremmer 1987b, 201–2.

[27] For instance, in *IG* 2$^2$, no. 13151b; *GV* no. 1301, second or third century A.D. I would not include in this group an epigram for a child who appears to have choked on a grape, *ISmyrna* 1, no. 525; see Merkelbach 1984. For choking on a grape as a possible topos, however, cf. the testimonia (nos. 88–90) collected by Radt, *TrGF* 4, p. 67, about the death of Sophocles.

[28] *IGUR* no. 1260, bilingual (Latin and Greek), A.D. 19–37; no. 551, for a singer from Asia who died at Rome; *IG* 14, no. 889, Sinuessa.

[29] *IGBR* 3.2, no. 1579; Augusta Traiana (Thrace), middle of the second century A.D. (where Dionysus is associated with the pleasures of the symposium).

[30] *Palatine Anthology* 7.24, 26–28, 30.

[31] *Palatine Anthology* 7.104.

inducing drunkenness is not seen as a fault. In the single epigraphical example of death while drunk, no blame is attached to drinking. At Amyzon in Caria a young man was brutally stabbed and burned by his slave while in a drink-induced sleep, but his drunken stupor is described as the embrace of the fragrant drafts of Bromius.[32]

Viticulture is also a theme in epitaphs, but it does not always have the same meaning. At Hermopolis Magna in the second century a father found such comfort in the ripening of the grape and the change of seasons that he decided not to weep for his daughter taken by the nymphs in death.[33] However, the family of a young man who tended the vines in Caria did not find the same comfort in the vine. The inscription at his grave describes death as "wretched oblivion" and asks those who pass by to shed a mournful tear and hopes that the gods grant them the blessings of life rather than the emptiness of death.[34] A soldier from Bithynia, buried in Pannonia in the second or early third century, took pleasure in the vine of Dionysus, but the "common fate of life and death" came to him in the end.[35] The same was true for a barkeeper in Egypt who poured "honey-sweet wine for all mortals, the drops that stop pain," but the vine of Bacchus nevertheless mourned for him in death.[36] In these last two texts the joys of the vine are identified with the pleasures of life, not with the compensations in death. Dionysus is considered the source of something that has been lost in death, not something that has been gained.

Other professions associated with Dionysus in tomb inscriptions have to do with the theater. Except for one about a man who fell from a roof and died while watching a play in a theater of Dionysus,[37] the

[32] Robert 1983, 259–66, no. 65; Amyzon (Caria), second century B.C. or earlier. The sweetness of his sleep and the Bacchic pleasure in his inebriation are probably exaggerated to emphasize not only the brutality of his death, but also the pains of the slave's death, who was crucified for his crime and "hung alive for beasts and birds."

[33] Bernand 1969, 350–57, no. 87.

[34] Robert 1957, 15–17; Meander valley, second or third century A.D. For viticulture as a theme in a literary epitaph, see *Palatine Anthology* 7.321 (*GV* no. 1583). For an organization of vine workers that buried a member, see Roesch 1982, 133–34, no. 15; Tanagra, late second or early first century B.C., discussed below.

[35] Jordan, Sasel Kos, and Wallace 1985, 85–89; Poetovio, second or early third century. Bithynia was especially known for its vines. For another soldier buried far from home, cf. the priest of Dionysus Liber from Ankara (Galatia), buried with his family at Istrus (Moesia) in A.D. 157; Bosch 1967, 209–11, no. 160.

[36] Bernand 1969, 107–9, no. 20; Cairo.

[37] *Palatine Anthology* 7.579.

literary epitaphs associated with the theater are about poets and actors and usually correspond closely to examples actually found on stone. In the anthologies we hear of an actor who had died,[38] and of a dead flute player who had dedicated his instruments to Dionysus (Luaios).[39] In another poem the Thyiades are asked to mourn for a flute player who is said to have died at Amphipolis.[40] We also hear of the Sicilian poet Epicharmus, "armed by the Doric Muse," whose grave preserves him for Bacchus and the satyrs.[41] Success in life was recognized after death: even Apollo, the Muses, and Dionysus are said to have mourned one famous actor when he made "his journey on the iron path of Hades."[42] Similar themes appear in the inscriptions. At Athens a famous actor buried among the altars of Dionysus asks those who pass by to acknowledge him with applause.[43] At Rome in the imperial period a teacher and performer of pantomimes and follower of Dionysus is described as overcoming death, not because he was an initiate of Dionysus, but because he lived on in the excellence of his students.[44] A dancer of Bacchic pantomimes in Bithynium-Claudiopolis, who in life won contests in the greatest cities, is represented as having died unhappily because he was unable to embrace his parents before he died at the age of twenty-four years.[45]

The largest category of Dionysiac tomb inscriptions was erected for members, officials, or priests of Bacchic organizations either by the organization or by the dead person's family, and occasionally by both together. There are twenty-five such texts, originating in Asia Minor, Macedonia, Thessaly, Boeotia, the Peloponnesus, Rhodes, and Rome and dating from the third century B.C. through the third century A.D. These texts characteristically emphasize the positive achievements of the dead in their service to the god. Only four were written for women. On Tenos a young woman named Isia was praised for dona-

[38] *Palatine Anthology* 16.289; see Weinreich 1948, 65–68; Ghiron-Bistagne 1976, 114 n.1.

[39] *Palatine Anthology* 16.7; the epithet is known from Mantineia, *IG* 5.2, no. 287 (a dedication of a statue of Dionysus Luaios).

[40] *Palatine Anthology* 7.485.

[41] *Palatine Anthology* 7.82, for Epicharmus, the comic poet.

[42] *Palatine Anthology* 7.412. Cf. 7.410, for Thespis, and 7.414, for Rhintho, who claimed an ivy wreath for his tragic farces.

[43] *IG* $2^2$, no. 12664; first century A.D.; cf. *IG* $2^2$, no. 7857a (*GV* no. 430), an epigram for a poet associated with Bromius.

[44] *IG* 14, no. 2124; Weinreich 1948, no. 7; second or third century A.D.

[45] *IKlaudiu Polis* no. 83, pl. 6; second century A.D.

tions for the roofs of the *megara* in a sanctuary of Demeter and Dionysus,[46] and at Rome a bilingual hexameter text praises a woman who was priestess of Dionysus and attendant of Isis.[47] A difficult Latin inscription from Chekanchevo in Bulgaria describes the services of a priestess of Dionysus who had been initiated at ten years old.[48] At Miletus a Hellenistic text praises the priestess of Alkmeionis for leading the women to the mountain and for taking part in public processions before the whole city.[49] Such inscriptions rarely imply that those who had served Dionysus in an official capacity expected special protection after death, but the last line of the Milesian text describes the priestess of the *bakkhai* as one who "knew her share of the blessings," which might mean that Dionysiac blessings in life corresponded to Dionysiac blessings after death.[50]

The administrative achievements of men recalled at their tombs were more varied. At Attaleia we find two *narthekophoroi;*[51] at Smyrna a *neokoros;*[52] at Julia Gordus a hierophant;[53] priests of Dionysus at Thessalonika,[54] Termessos,[55] and Istros;[56] and at Thessalonika a priest who was also *hudroskopos*.[57] Men are described as initiates with various

[46] *IG* 12.5, no. 972; for a *thussas* of Dionysus, apparently buried by the city. The text is badly damaged.

[47] *IGUR* no. 1150; cf. the Latin inscription from Philippi for a priestess of Sol initiated into the mysteries of Cybele and Dionysus, *CIL* 14, no. 123.

[48] Egger 1950.

[49] Henrichs 1978a, 121 and 148–49; third or second century B.C.: "*Bakkhai* of the city, say 'Farewell, holy priestess,' for this is right for a good woman; she led you to the mountain and carried all the sacred objects and holy equipment, passing before the whole city. And her name, if any stranger asks, was Alkmeionis, daughter of Rhodios; she knew her share of the blessings" (the translation follows Henrichs).

[50] On the meaning of *ta kala,* see Merkelbach 1972.

[51] *TAM* 5.1, no. 817; A.D. 165/166; no. 822; A.D. 198/199: "In the 283rd year, on the sixth day of the month, for their father, Apollonios, his sons Apollonios and Aphianos, his wife, Apphia, his daughter-in-law Hermione, their slaves, the *speira* for their *narthekophoros* and leader, and all of his relatives made this altar for the sake of his memory. Farewell."

[52] *ISmyrna* 1, no. 515; second century B.C.

[53] *TAM* 5.1, no. 744, erected by his wife for a doctor.

[54] *IG* 10 (2.1), no. 503; A.D. 132/133; cf. no. 506; A.D. 209/210, for a priest of the thiasoi of Dionysus.

[55] *TAM* 3.1, no. 841, inscribed rock-cut sarcophagus.

[56] Bosch 1967, 209–11, no. 160.

[57] *IG* 10. (2.1), no. 503; A.D. 16. *Hudroskopia* (divination by water) may be represented at the "Villa of the Mysteries" at Pompeii. In the fifth scene a silenus tips a jar so that a young man can look inside. For bibliography on the fresco and this scene, see Burkert 1987a, 163–64, nn. 24 and 31.

roles. At Cenchreae a Phocian family erected a tomb monument for their *boukolos,*[58] at Miletopolis in Mysia an organization honored a *mustēs* who had led the rites of the *khous,*[59] at Nicaea we find an *arkhimustēs* of Bakkhos Megas,[60] and at Amastris in Pontus a thirty-year-old athlete was known for having "mystically conducted the *kōmos,* the *teletē* for the trieteric god Euios."[61]

Service to Dionysus in life may have been thought worthy of attention after death,[62] but initiation did not necessarily ameliorate the grief of friends and relatives. At Thebes in Thessaly a city council member, initiate of Demeter and "neophyte in the famous mysteries of much-crowned Bacchus," nevertheless left behind "his tiny children and the one who was his beloved wife, wailing pitiably."[63] Simple worshipers of Dionysus are marked in Lydia at Attaleia,[64] in the plain of the Cayster River,[65] and in Bizye (Thrace).[66]

Bacchic organizations, like other corporate and religious associations of the Hellenistic and Roman periods, took responsibility for the burial of members. Bacchic organizations tended the graves of their leaders and officials, but members without rank were also provided with tombstones and rites at the grave. Because all sorts of organizations erected gravestones for their leaders and members, it is probably a mistake to read into these practices any expectations on the part of the membership concerning an afterlife. More likely, the organizations simply intended to provide a decent burial for their members. One organization could even share the expenses with another. At Tanagra the

[58] *IG* 4, no. 207; third century A.D.(?); cf. the inscription for a *boukolos* who died in Phrygia (Ankyra Sidera) at the age of twelve; Henrichs 1982, 226 n. 122.

[59] *IKyzikos* no. 26; first century A.D.(?).

[60] *INikaia* 2.2, no. 1324; third century A.D.

[61] Marek 1985, 137, no. 12; A.D. 155; Jones 1990.

[62] For a young man from Bithynia who danced for Dionysus in the chorus of boys and served wine at symposia while alive and has a statue of Dionysus at his grave to remind him of that service in death, see Cole 1984, 37–48; *SEG* 34, no. 1266.

[63] *GV* no. 694; third century A.D.(?). A fragmentary epitaph from Nicaea, about a Bacchic official who left behind his wife and children, may be similar; *INikaia* 2.2, no. 1325.

[64] *TAM* 5.1, no. 806; fragmentary inscription for a member of a *speira,* second century A.D.

[65] *GV* no. 509; fragment with hexameters marking the grave of a *propolos* of Bromius, first or second century A.D.

[66] *IGBR* 3.2, no. 1864; a husband who is described as performer of initiations buried his wife whom he says he honored as Dionysus honored Semele. The text is in poor condition.

Dionysiastai buried a member in the third century B.C.[67] The same organization, together with the vine workers, provided a similar burial about a century later.[68] We can compare the Iobakkhoi at Athens, whose rules of organization tell us that the group provided a wreath for the funeral of a dead member and wine for the members who attended the funeral.[69] Annual ceremonies for members after death were apparently common in the imperial period. Members left bequests at Philippi,[70] Serrhae,[71] Thessalonika,[72] Magnesia,[73] and Teos. All the texts in the Macedonian group record amounts of money left to pay for libations, sacrifices, or meals at the grave of the deceased, but rites at the grave were common elsewhere in other periods of Greek history and in no way indicate any special concern for the dead on the part of Dionysiac organizations. The list of donations at Magnesia does not specify the purpose of the bequests, which could have been intended to pay for other sorts of festivities for the group. Members of private organizations made bequests because they wanted to be remembered by their friends and associates. At Teos the Dionysiastai honored a priestess for her donations by celebrating the *oinoposia* in her honor as long as she lived and by naming a special day for her after her death, when special rites were to be performed in her honor in thanks for a financial endowment.[74]

Several sepulchral inscriptions describe dedications of a statue or a relief of the dead person dressed as Dionysus. The statue of M. Marius Trophimus, hierophant at Melos, dedicated by the local *mustai*, illus-

[67] Roesch 1982, 132–33, no. 14; Tanagra, late third century B.C. For sepulchral altars erected by the Dionysiastai at Rhodes, cf. Maiuri 1925, no. 46; and possibly *IG* 12.1, no. 155.

[68] Roesch 1982, 133–34, no. 15; Tanagra, late second or early first century B.C.

[69] *LSCG* no. 51, lines 159–63; members who did not attend the funeral were excluded from the drinking of the wine.

[70] *CIL* 2, no. 704 (110 denarii to the thiasos of Liber Pater by a slave); *CIL* 3, no. 703 (300 denarii by a father and son for meals at their grave at the Rosalia for members of the thiasos); and Perdrizet 1900, 305, no. 1 (120 denarii donated by a man for roses to be burned every year at the grave of himself, his wife, and children).

[71] *AE* 1936, Suppl. 17–19 (15 denarii for libations at the grave at the time of the festival of the maenads).

[72] *IG* 10 (2.1), no. 260; third century A.D.; here a priestess of Dionysus left a vineyard with its irrigation ditches to her thiasos so that the income could be used to pay for burned offerings for her at the Rosalia.

[73] *IMagnesia* no. 117; list of bequests to the mystery organization by the priestess, hierophant, *appas*, and *hupotrophos*.

[74] *SEG* 4, no. 398.

trates how these statues may have looked. The hierophant wears a panther skin, holds a thyrsus, and is wreathed with a crown of grape leaves.[75] In Lerna a worshiper named Archelaus seems to have been the object of two such dedications. His friends dedicated to Bacchus (in the sanctuary of Deo) a statue of Archelaus dressed as Bacchus, and his wife dedicated a statue of him as Bacchus for Luaios (Dionysus).[76] In Dascylium the thiasoi of *mustai* dedicated a relief "with the figure of Bromius," showing one of their members as Dionysus, carrying a thyrsus and standing by the side of a tree.[77] Near Acmonia in Phrygia two sons and their mother dedicated an altar to Dionysus with an image of their sons' father, hierophant of a local Dionysiac organization (*speira*), dressed as the god.[78] In Rome a mother and father showed the image of Dionysus on the sarcophagus of their child with the inscription "I am called Saturninus; my mother and father set me up [changed?] from a child to a representation of Dionysus."[79]

These dedications have a literary parallel. Apuleius describes a widow who had a picture of her dead husband represented in the clothes of Dionysus.[80] Identification of the worshiper with Dionysus appears to have been characteristic of Dionysiac cult throughout antiquity, but consecration of a statue of an individual in the form of a god was a custom of the imperial period.[81] Because none of the inscrip-

[75] Wrede 1981, no. 173, pl. 24.1–2; A.D. 160–90, from the Bakcheion at Melos.

[76] *IG* 4, no. 666; the same man recorded his participation in the *taurobolion* for Attis and Rhea at Athens, where he also refers (in line 8) to his Dionysiac initiation, *IG* $2^2$, no. 4841.

[77] Corsten 1988, 72–74, no. 2.

[78] Ramsay 1901, 276–77; A.D. 249–51. Ramsay described the reliefs, severely defaced by deliberate damage, but published no photo. The stone has recently reappeared at Izmir; see Cole 1991. The text reads: "The Aurelii, Epitynchanos and Epinikos with their mother, Tertulla, together with the sacred *speira,* of which he was the hierophant, consecrated their father, Telesphoros, in the 334th year."

[79] *IGUR* no. 1324, first or second century A.D. The sarcophagus has been lost. For a photo of a drawing of the relief, see Wrede 1981, no. 174, pl. 24.5. For a statue from Athens of a child (Hadrianic) dressed as Dionysus, cf. Wrede 1981, no. 172, pl. 23.1. The child wears a panther skin and a crown of grape leaves.

[80] Apuleius *Metamorphoses* 8.7.

[81] The evidence has been collected by Wrede 1981. The list of gods in his catalogue includes at least forty-six figures. Collignon 1911, 322, saw in this custom a promise of immortality in the cortege of the god, but the continuing discovery of more examples since Collignon's day shows that the issue is more complex than he thought. Wrede's list of forty-six divinities does not indicate the possible biases. At Athens alone, for instance, Walters 1988, 30, finds 106 grave *stelai* of the imperial period representing women dressed as the goddess Isis and argues that these were initiates in the cult of Isis. The number for Dionysus

tions describing worshipers in the attire of Dionysus attach any special meaning to the custom, perhaps we should see in these dedications no more than a recollection of the performance of ritual activities, or, at the most, a vague hope of finding consolation in identification with Dionysus.[82] A Latin grave inscription of the imperial period shows that Dionysus was only one of the many possible models for imitation by the dead at the tomb. Young Nepos was told by his mother that he could have himself represented with the Muses or as Pallas, Bacchus, Phoebus, Attis, or any god or hero he chose. Dionysus was just another example in this long list, and Nepos' mother seems to attach no particular significance to his symbols (thyrsus, corymbus, and palmes).[83]

The next largest group of Dionysiac sepulchral texts belongs to the graves of children.[84] All of these seem to have been inscribed in the imperial period. Two themes are prominent, and they strike a dissonant chord. The first is an assumption that initiation into the thiasos of Dionysus before death promises continued participation in that thiasos after death. The second and somewhat contradictory theme is one of the loss and grief of a parent that not even Dionysus can assuage. The more optimistic theme is found at Athens, where a seven-year-old boy, initiated at Eleusis, was also a member of a Dionysiac thiasos.[85] He listed his initiations as if the list itself should offer enough reason for his father to stop wearing out his "sweet heart" with grief. A

---

is far lower, and we can only guess the meaning for the custom. The Hellenistic and imperial custom of calling rulers New Dionysus and representing them as Dionysus has political rather than personal significance. For Mark Antony as Dionysus at Athens in imitation of Demetrius Poliorcetes see Seneca *Suasoriae* 1.6. Antony not only wore the costume of Dionysus but insisted that statues of Dionysus be inscribed with his own name; Plutarch *Antonius* 60. For Caligula in the clothing of Dionysus, cf. Athenaeus 4.148b–c.

[82] The assumption of the name Limnagenes, also known as an epithet of Dionysus (Hesychius, s.v.), by Dionysodoros Pytheou at Cyzicus may imply identification with the god through initiation; Pfuhl and Möbius 1977–79, no. 1187, with pl. 179.

[83] *CIL* 6 (3), no. 21521; Andreae 1963, 152–53.

[84] Children were often initiated by parents; Nilsson 1957a, 115; Burkert 1987a, 52–53. *IG* 10 (2.1), no. 260C.1–3 mentions the "initiates young and old" (*muste mikros megas*). (Sarah Iles Johnston suggests to me that parents may have sought initiation for young children to protect themselves from the spirits of their children in danger of dying too soon and therefore becoming the untimely dead (*aōroi*). However, although the number of Bacchic tomb inscriptions for children may seem high in proportion to the other Dionysiac texts, the number is insignificant when compared with the hundreds of texts collected by Vérilhac 1978 for *aōroi*.)

[85] *IG* $2^2$, no. 11674; second century or later; Vérilhac 1978, vol. 1, no. 190. For a discussion of this text in the context of Dionysiac hopes, see Kaufmann 1897, 66.

similar motivation is behind a text from Iaza in Lydia where a seventeen year old is said to have been chosen by Bromius as a *summustēs,* "fellow initiate," in his dances.[86] The same theme appears in Bithynia, where a young man recalls that he had danced for Dionysus in life and had served wine at the symposium.[87] The idea is especially strong at Philippi, where a Latin speaker imagines that a dead boy is restored or refreshed (*reparatus*) in the Elysian fields, dancing as a satyr with the tattooed *mustai* of Bromius.[88] When relatives mentioned that the dead person was initiated as a child, they must have thought that this merited the attention of the gods at the time of death. The priestess of Dionysus commemorated at Chekanchevo (near Sofia in Bulgaria) had been initiated at ten years old, although she died in middle age, and her initiation is listed as part of her curriculum vitae.[89]

Not all parents were so easily consoled. At Rome a ten-year-old girl who "leads the thiasos in dances" describes the pain of her parents as useless and says that her father in grief gave her as a gift to Dionysus "in honor of whom Dionysus the Bacchic One invited me to dance in his thiasos as leader of my group."[90] At Iconium parents who were themselves attendants of Dionysus set up a statue of their son to alleviate their grief at his death.[91] Other parents felt that an early death deprived a child of life's experiences and life's rituals. A child at Athens who was ready for his first Choes was cheated by death of that Dionysiac experience.[92] A seven year old at Rome mocked his initiation, saying that all the mysteries in the world offered no protection in the face of death.[93] Another seven year old at Rome, named Hero-

[86] *TAM* 5.1, no. 477; A.D. 240/241. The accompanying relief shows a boy holding grapes, a motif that is not itself Dionysiac, but see below.

[87] Cole 1984.

[88] *CIL* 3, no. 686.

[89] Egger 1950; *AE* 1953, 243; Nilsson 1957a, 132.

[90] Merkelbach 1971, 280.

[91] *CIG* no. 4000; Laminger-Pascher 1975, 303–7.

[92] *IG* $2^2$, no. 13139; after the middle of the second century A.D.; see Deubner 1932, pl. 16.1, for relief.

[93] *IGUR* no. 1169, third century A.D.(?): "I lie here, Aurelius Antonius, who was also priest of all the gods, first of Bona Dea, then of the Mother of the Gods and of Dionysus Kathegemon. I always celebrated the mysteries for these gods reverently; now I left the divine sweet holy light of the sun. Well, my *mustai* or friends of each way of life, forget all the sacred mysteries of life, one after the other. For no one is able to dissolve the thread of the Moirae. For I, Antonius the divine, lived seven years and twelve days" (the translation follows Burkert 1987a, 28–29; for suggestions on improving the seventh line of the Greek version, see *Bulletin épigraphique* in *Revue des études grecques* 1988. 101: 305–6, no. 32 [J. Bousquet]).

philus, was even cynical about his short life, concluding that death was so early that he never really came to life.[94]

Grieving parents found little relief in initiation if a child died early. Even the orator Himerius, sometimes cited as evidence for the special care parents took to have young children initiated in the late imperial period,[95] was inconsolable at the loss of his young son Rufinus and blamed Dionysus himself for not watching over the boy more carefully. He says that the lock of hair once grown for Dionysus now lies in the dust, asks the god how he can bear to allow a child dedicated by initiation (*paida ton hieron*) to be snatched from his *temenos,* and ends by asking how he as a father could trust the god who did not watch over and protect his own young initiate.[96] Himerius seems to assume that protection in life was a stronger Dionysiac promise than protection after death.

A balance between the two themes of loss and protection occurs in a poem for a ten year old who died at Caesarea in Mauretania in the first century. Young Proclus, shown in relief holding a bunch of grapes, died early and left behind lamentations and mournful tears for his father, Publius. The boy describes himself as having lost the sweet light of life and any hope of old age and begs the gentle nymph Nysa, nurse of Dionysus, to grant him eternal youth in death.[97] The prayer for protection from Nysa is actually another way of asking to take the place of Dionysus himself, to assume the protection offered to the god as an infant by his own nurse and to regain a chance elsewhere for a life that has been lost.[98] We can compare the text for the priestess who died

[94] *IGUR* no. 1228: "To the gods of the underworld: not yet having tasted of youth, I slipped into the realm of Hades, leaving behind to my parents tears and groans for my short life, nor was I meant to reach the life span of mortals; I lived only seven years and two months, of which I completed three years speaking the rites for Dionysus. And my father and lovely mother called me Herophilus. Passerby, now you know who I was; I was not even brought to life."

[95] Nilsson 1957a, 106, understands the initiation as incomplete. Merkelbach 1988, 88, emphasizes that Himerius expected the boy to be protected in this life as well as in the next.

[96] Himerius *Orationes* 8.7 and 18.

[97] Vatin 1983, 65–74 (*SEG* 33, no. 848); Caesarea (Mauretania), first century A.D. (the text is clumsy and the relief poorly drawn): "Young Proclus, son of Publius, I lie here, having completed twice five years. I did not complete the sweet light of life, but Moira led me to Hades and stopped me, who died early; and I gave to my dear father lamentations and mournful tears. Therefore, since old age is not part of my sacred hope, as I am wretched, gentle nymph Nysa, give boundless youth as my eternal lot."

[98] Nilsson 1957a, 111–15, traces the iconographic tradition of Nysa (Nysai) to the sixth century B.C., arguing that this tradition provided the context later for a parent's hope that a

at Chekanchevo, initiated at ten years old, dead at thirty and still unmarried, but summoned in death to join the followers of Nysian Dionysus. On her tombstone the god himself, seated upon a throne, is waiting to receive her.[99]

Cynicism about death, even in a Dionysiac context, is not confined to epitaphs for children. The plaque recording the epitaph for Herophilus, the cynical child mentioned above, is decorated in the four corners with four small Dionysiac symbols: (clockwise) a bell, a twig switch, a cowherd's crook (*kalaurops*), and a tiny portrait of a child, either Herophilus himself or the god Dionysus as a child.[100] None of these are among the traditional *sumbola* listed by Clement of Alexandria when he describes the mysteries of Dionysus,[101] but all are part of the repertory of Dionysiac imagery of the imperial period. Bells occur as decoration in Dionysiac contexts on reliefs from Asia Minor,[102] a whip is included in one of the scenes of the "Villa of the Mysteries" at Pompeii,[103] and the cowherd's crook is a common image on reliefs and sarcophagi.[104] Such imagery, however, need not always imply optimism about death. The cowherd's crook is not merely a simple pastoral image, but an object with ritual meaning, probably carried by *boukoloi* in Dionysiac organizations. A text on an inscribed sarcophagus in Pisidia gives some clues to its possible extended meaning. The sarcophagus is decorated with a cowherd's crook and a scepter. Morsianos Hermaios, an initiate in the *teletai* of Bacchus, explains both images as symbols of death:

> If you wish to know what the scepter and cowherd's crook have enshrouded here, stop, my friend, and you shall learn this. The scepter (*caduceus*) is what Hermes the Conductor carries, for with this he leads the souls of men under the earth. This cowherd's crook (*kalaurops*)

---

dead child might be identified with the god. See Vatin 1983, 70–73, for a series of grave reliefs found on Rheneia showing a child with a bunch of grapes approaching a seated female figure. Vatin identifies the female figure as Nysa, nurse of Dionysus.

[99] Egger 1950; Nilsson 1957a, 132.

[100] The distinction between Dionysus and the worshiper is often blurred in representations. Cf. the portrait of the child dressed as Dionysus in panther skin and wreath of grape leaves at Athens; Wrede 1981, no. 172, pl. 23.1.

[101] Clement of Alexandria *Protrepticus* 2.22.

[102] For bells in Dionysiac contexts, see Cremer 1986.

[103] See Burkert 1987a, 104 and 168 nn. 90–94, for flogging in Dionysiac contexts.

[104] Matz 1968–75, passim; Geyer 1977a, 164–73, for criticism of the meaning.

> represents the death of mortals. Don't be too proud. Every life rounds its last turn at the farthest turning post. For this reason, this has indeed been written, so that you might know [that you are] mortal.[105]

The epitaph is intended as instruction, to let people who pass by know that they too will have a share in death, and there is nothing in this particular statement to make death at all attractive.

When examined as a group, the grave inscriptions with references to Dionysiac themes are as ambiguous as the visual motifs that often accompany them. To some extent the poetic Dionysiac sepulchral texts are controlled by convention. None of the themes defined here are outside the conventions of the genre. Children who die before their time, parents inconsolable at the death of child, adults who are grim in the face of death—all of these are part of the standard repertory of Greek and Latin epitaphs. What is surprising, however, is that an entirely different set of themes, equally as common, does not appear in clear Dionysiac contexts in the grave inscriptions. By these I mean the sort of epitaph which claims that although the body lies in the earth or dust, the soul is among the blessed, in the heavens, or among the stars.[106] Granted, although the Hipponium tablet mentions the souls of the dead, discussion of the soul does not seem to be part of the Dionysiac tradition. Nevertheless, optimistic themes, like those of the epitaphs about the soul and like the optimistic themes of the gold tablets, are not represented in the sepulchral inscriptions that mention Dionysus. Where such themes do occur, epitaphs that imply happiness or security after death for the initiated do not distinguish between Dionysiac initiates and those of other mysteries. When specific mysteries are mentioned or alluded to, it is normally the Eleusinian mysteries that find attention.[107] There are, to my knowledge, no epitaphs saying that although earth hides the body of the Dionysiac initiate, the

[105] *TAM* 3.1, no. 922; fragment of a sarcophagus from Korkuteli (Pisidia).

[106] Examples are collected by Lattimore 1962, 31–43. The idea of the soul going to the heavens and being received by the air appears for the first time in the epitaph for the Athenians who died at Potidaea, fifth century B.C. Similar images are used of ordinary people in grave inscriptions of the fourth century B.C.—see *GV* nos. 1755 (Piraeus, fourth century B.C.) and 1757 (Athens, fourth century B.C.)—and become common thereafter. The subject is touched on by Kaufmann 1897, 21–22, who attempts, mistakenly, to construct a schematic development of Greek and Roman beliefs about the afterlife.

[107] For instance, *GV* no. 879, found at Eleusis; cf. *AE* 1883, 146, no. 20 (discussed by Kaufmann 1897, 24).

soul has found the special cypress tree, has drunk of the cool water of Memory, or has reached the road of the *bakkhoi*.[108] The dead of the inscriptions reach only the same symbolic level reached by the dead of the sarcophagi. They can dance forever at a great Bacchic party, especially if they die young enough to have the required energy, but there is no promise of a real improvement in status.

When worshipers pray to Dionysus for safety and preservation, their prayers refer to this life, not the next. Two inscriptions from central Thrace promise *sōteria* for the *mustai* of Dionysus,[109] but when the second text says that the altar is for the "initiates whom blessed Dionysus saves" (*mustai hous sōze makar Dionusus*), the use of the term "save" implies protection and preservation rather than salvation.[110] The same meaning occurs in a dedicatory epigram found in the Piraeus where a priest dedicated a *temenos,* temple, and statue to Dionysus, asking the god in return to keep his family and the Dionysiac thiasos safe and sound.[111] An unpublished fragment found built into a private home between Milas and Halicarnassus in Caria describes reliefs on a Bacchic temple as portraying "*bakkhoi* safe and sound" (*sōoi bakkhikoi*).[112] This phrase does not mean that the Bacchic *mustai* are saved from death, but that they are safe and sound in life. We can only

[108] There are epitaphs with images of water or a road to the underworld, but these texts do not refer to Dionysus or include Dionysiac themes. An epigram from Rome (*GV* no. 590, third century A.D.) associates a "divine road" and the soul's achievement of purity in the underworld but makes no explicit reference to Dionysus: "This tomb hides the body of unmarried Kalokairos, but his immortal soul has left the body of the young man. She, his soul, has left far behind the cares of a bitter life and hurries on the divine road so that she might arrive purified."

Another epigram (*GV* no. 1410, second or third century A.D.) prays that the lord of the underworld give to the dead man cold water to drink, but the theme of cold water is also associated with Osiris (cf. *GV* no. 1842, Egypt, first or second century A.D.) and cannot automatically be assumed to refer to Dionysiac beliefs. The epigram for the dead Glykareia at Nymphaeum (Regnum Bospori), *CIRB* no. 913, marks an installation for a spring, but the mention of Bromius together with the water of that spring means only that the speaker mixed his wine with water, and has no obvious implications for the mysteries.

[109] Bizye, two altars to Zeus Dionysus: *IGBR* 3.2, nos. 1864 (*peri sōterias*) and 1865 (*makar* Dionysus saves his *mustai*). Here "save" means "preserve."

[110] For the ambiguities of the Greek terminology of safety and salvation in pagan and Christian contexts, see Kotansky 1991, 120–22. The claims made by Griffiths 1982, 213–15, for punishment and salvation in Dionysiac scenes at Pompeii rely on a subjective interpretation of problematic imagery without support from the literary sources.

[111] *IG* $2^2$, no. 2948; Athens, early second century B.C. Cf. Körte 1900, 414–15, no. 24; Doryleion (Phrygia).

[112] The inscription will be published by W. Blümel and S. G. Cole.

guess that the conventional language of the inscriptions might hide a more esoteric meaning understood by initiates who had participated in the shared secrets of the mysteries, but the public texts give us no clue. It is too bad that we do not have the reliefs that decorated the building near Milas, so that we could see what the Bacchic worshipers were actually doing, but it is likely that they were simply shown as maenads and satyrs, dancing together in the same poses we see so often in imperial art and funereal monuments.

An essay attributed to Plutarch says that the story of the deeds of the Titans and the dismemberment of Dionysus is part of an enigmatic myth about rebirth,[113] but there is no theme of rebirth in the Dionysiac sepulchral texts. One enigmatic epigram from Thessalonika may imply that the sufferings of Dionysus had their ritual counterpart in the experiences of initiation. The inscription describes a sacred initiate who "fled the sacred Bacchic women (*euiades*) on his way to Hades."[114] Pentheus and Orpheus would have had good reason to avoid the *bakkhai* on their way to Hades, and there may have been some reason to associate the myths of their dismemberment with similar stories about Dionysus, but the *bakkhai* (or *euiades*) were not the Titans, and Pentheus and Orpheus were certainly not reborn.

Bacchic organizations, in fact, only rarely mention in inscriptions anything to do with the myth of Dionysus and the Titans. There are only three examples of groups of Dionysiac *mustai* who alluded to myths of Dionysiac rebirth in public inscriptions. At Perinthus a group of *mustai,* with their *arkhimustēs* and their *speirarkhos,* quoted an oracle in iambics, attributed to the Sibyl: "When the Bakkhos crying 'Euai' shall have been struck, then will blood and fire and dust be mixed together."[115] The second example, an inscription from Asia Minor, believed to be from Smyrna, lists the rules of a Bacchic organization and includes in its regulations a prohibition about the Titans.[116] Finally, a Lydian text from Hierocaesarea records a dedication to Dionysus Erikepaios, a figure known from Orphic contexts.[117] Oth-

[113] [Plutarch] *Moralia* 996c.

[114] Sijpesteijn 1983, 287 (*SEG* 31, no. 633), with corrections by Voutiras 1984, 45–50; A.D. 71/72 or A.D. 187/188.

[115] Cyriacus of Ancona, *Codex Vaticanus* 5250; see Bodnar and Mitchell 1976, 31–32, no. 3.

[116] *ISmyrna* 2, no. 728.

[117] Keil and Premerstein 1908, 105–6, no. 112, with fig. 51.

erwise there is no epigraphical evidence that links Bacchic organizations with traditions of Dionysiac *paligenesia,* "rebirth." In the tomb inscriptions of the late Hellenistic and Roman imperial periods, Dionysus is not a savior who promises to his worshipers regeneration, but with the stories of his own rebirth and rejuvenation, he is one who makes this life more sweet and the next one, perhaps, only a little less harsh.

# Glossary

anagnorisis. Recognition, a term used by Aristotle and modern scholars to designate the denouement in a Greek tragedy

*anakaluptēria.* The unveiling, the part of the Greek wedding ceremony when the veil of the bride is lifted up for the first time

Anthesteria. "Festival of the Flowers" at Athens and other Ionian cities, celebrating, among other things, the new vintage and the annual marriage of Dionysus and the *basilinna;* it comprises three days: the Pithoigia ("Opening of the Wine Jars"), the Choes ("Feast of the Cups"), and the Chytroi ("Feast of the Pots")

*aōroi.* The untimely dead, a term usually applied to children who died before their time and were believed to linger about and haunt their survivors

*appas.* Foster father of Dionysus, and subsequently the title of a cult official in Dionysiac cult in Magnesia

*arkhimustēs.* Leader of the initiates at the mysteries

Atthidographers. Hellenistic historians of the city of Athens and of Attica, the territory that encompassed it

Bacchus. "The Frenzied One," an epithet or alternate name for Dionysus in Greece, as well as the wine god in Italy

*bakkhai.* Female worshipers of Dionysus

*bakkheia.* Wild frenzy or revelry that was essential to the maenadic worship of Dionysus

*bakkheion.* A term used in Dionysiac cult inscriptions to refer to a Bacchic organization or to the building used by that organization for its meetings

*bakkhoi.* A generic term for worshipers of Dionysus

*basileus.* King; one of the nine archons (elected public administrators of Athens), who played a central role (allegedly performed by the king in the monarchic era) in important civic festivals

*basilinna.* Queen; the wife of the "king" archon, who played a central role (allegedly performed by the queen in the monarchic era) in important Athenian festivals, especially in the Anthesteria, where she was escorted as a bride and was "married" to Dionysus

*boukolos*. Cowherd, a term for a Bacchic initiate

Bromius. "The Boisterous One," an epithet or alternate name for Dionysus

caduceus. Staff or scepter, especially the one carried by Hermes in his role as the messenger god

cantharus. High-handled drinking cup associated with Dionysus and often seen in the god's right hand in vase paintings

catharsis. Cleansing or purification, a term used by Aristotle and modern scholars to designate the positive effect that the performance of a Greek tragedy has in purging destructive emotions

chiton. Linen gown or tunic worn by both men and women

Choes. "Feast of the Pitchers," the second day of the Anthesteria

chthonian. Epithet of divine powers who belong to the earth or the underworld

cithara. A kind of lyre with seven strings, played by professional musicians

*claritas et distinctio*. Clearness and distinctness, the formulation of the Cartesian test of truth, criticized and developed by Leibniz

corymbus. Cluster of ivy berries, a symbol or token of Dionysus or his devotees

cothurni. Leather buskins of the type worn by actors in performances of Greek tragedies

Dionysia. Various festivals of Dionysus at which the god was celebrated with dramatic performances; the Greater or City Dionysia were held at Athens in the spring in honor of Dionysus Eleuthereus, while the Lesser or Country Dionysia were held in the various demes in the autumn

Dionysiastai. Members of a private religious association devoted to the worship of Dionysus

*drōmena*. Actions (of a ritual), as opposed to words

*ependutēs*. Overgarment, usually a tunic or a robe

epiphany. The self-revelation of a Greek god appearing in human form

*euhoi*. Characteristic ritual cry of *bakkhai* or maenads

*euias* (pl. *euiades*). Rare term for a female follower of Dionysus

Faliscan. Pottery made at Falerii, an Etruscanized city near Rome (Latium)

*genos*. Race, clan, or family

Genucilia plate. A particular type of pottery made at or near Rome

herm. A semi-iconic image, usually of the god Hermes, consisting of a plain shaft surmounted by a head; sometimes a phallus is affixed to the shaft as well

hetaira (pl. hetairai). Courtesan, usually a slave or a noncitizen woman

hierophant. Priest of the mysteries who revealed the sacred tokens

*hieros gamos*. Sacred marriage, a religious celebration enacting the wedding of a divine couple, usually Zeus and Hera

himation. Outer garment or cloak worn over the chiton

hubris. Overweening pride in one's strength or accomplishments, or wanton violence arising from such pride

*hupotrophos*. Nurse of Dionysus, and subsequently the title of a cult official in Dionysiac cult in Magnesia hydria. Large jar, used by women to carry water

hyporcheme. Form of choral lyric found in Greek tragedy, originally performed with dances in honor of Apollo or Artemis

initiation. Ritual procedure marking a transition in the life course or admission into a civic, social, or family group

*Iobakkhoi*. Worshipers of Dionysus connected with the festival of the Iobakkheia

*kalaurops*. Cowherd's crook (see *boukolos*), a symbol or token of Dionysus or his devotees

*kentron*. Goad or sharp point

*khous* (pl. *khoes*). Special pitcher used for drinking wine which gives its name to the second day of the Anthesteria festival at Athens, Choes

*kistē*. Basket or hamper used in Dionysiac processions to carry secret tokens

*kōmos*. Revel, merrymaking, or a band of revelers

krater. Large bowl used to mix wine and water together at the Greek symposium

*krēdemnon*. Woman's headdress or veil that is loosened and lifted during the wedding ceremony

*krokōtos*. Saffron-dyed, Eastern style of dress or robe worn by Dionysus in Aristophanes' play *The Frogs*

lekane. A flat, heavy dish with handles and a lid

lekythos. Small flask, usually used to hold valuable oils and ointments

Lenaia. Festival of Dionysus celebrated with dramatic and other competitions at the Lenaion, a sanctuary to the west of the Athenian acropolis

*lex sacra* (pl. *leges sacrae*). A religious statute (usually inscribed on stone and erected in a public space) that stipulates calendrical sacrifices and other ritual measures for a city, sanctuary, or religious organization

*liknon*. Special basket used for winnowing grain and carrying infants

*lusis*. Deliverance or release, in the context of mystery cults usually indicating a release from trials and tribulations both in this world and in the next

*lussa*. Rage or fury

maenad. Mad woman, a term frequently used to describe a female votary of Dionysus

maenadism. A modern term used to describe the ritual behavior of the ecstatic female followers of Dionysus in myth and in cult

*makarismos* (pl. *makarismoi*). Blessing pronounced at the wedding celebration

*mania*. madness or ecstasy

*māyā*. magic or nature, a Sanskrit term used by Hindus and subsequently by historians of religions to indicate the power by which the phenomenal world is manifested or created

metabole. Transition or transformation, a general term used by Aristotle in his discussion of Greek tragedy to indicate a class of important transitions, the two most important being the anagnorisis and the peripeteia

mimesis. Imitation or representation, a Greek philosophical term used to describe how a work of art imitates or represents reality

*mustēria*. The mysteries, secret cults presupposing initiation

*mustēs* (pl. *mustai*). An initiate into a mystery cult

Nysa. The mountain where the infant Dionysus was raised by nymphs; also the name of the wet nurse and foster mother of Dionysus

*oikos*. Home or household

oinochoe. Small pitcher used for ladling or pouring wine

*olbos*. Prosperity or happiness, in the context of mystery cults usually indicating a much-coveted state of bliss or well-being both in this world and the next

omophagy or *ōmophagia*. The ritual consumption of raw flesh described in mythical accounts of maenadism

omphalos. Navel or center point of the world, said by the Greeks to be located at Apollo's Delphic sanctuary

*oreibasia*. Wandering or dancing on the mountain, part of a biennial maenadic ritual

*orgia*. Secret rites or worship practiced by the initiated in ancient mystery cults

*Orphika*. A body of poems said to have been composed by the legendary singer Orpheus

*Orphikoi*. Followers of Orpheus or his doctrines

palmes. Young shoot of the grapevine, a symbol or token of Dionysus or his devotees

paterfamilias. The head of the ancient Roman family, who had extraordinary absolute power and authority over his own and his sons' families

peripeteia. Sudden change or downfall, a term used by Aristotle and modern scholars to designate an unexpected reversal of fortune experienced by the protagonist of a Greek tragedy

petasos. Broad-brimmed hat worn by travelers and by Hermes, the patron deity of travelers

*phallagōgeion*. Cart used to carry the phallus in processions in honor of Dionysus

poliadic. Tutelary, having to do with the protection of the polis

polis. City-state, the basic political unit in classical Greece

*pompē* (pl. *pompai*). Solemn procession to or from a god's temple during a religious festival

*psukhē*. The spirit or immortal soul of a human being

Pythia. Priestess and prophetess of Pythian Apollo at Delphi

ritualistic. An adjective used to designate a modern theoretical approach that defines myth as a derivation from ritual

Rosalia. Roman festival during which the graves of the dead were decorated with roses

sacramentalism. The mentality or theme of the Christian rite of communion

satyr. Horse-human hybrid, a frequent companion of Dionysus who is prone to cowardice, wine drinking, and sexual license

scapegoat. Sacrificial victim (sometimes human) that is driven out of a community in the belief that it takes along the community's ills with it

silenus. Satyr, usually an old one

*sōma*. Body, as opposed to soul (*psukhē*)

*sōteria*. Deliverance or preservation, in the context of mystery cults usually indicating safety from trials and tribulations both in this world and in the next

*sparagmos*. Ritual dismemberment of animals and humans, described in mythic accounts of maenadic ritual

*speira.* Organization of worshipers, usually (but not always) worshipers of Dionysus

*speirarkhos.* The leader of a *speira*

*splanchna.* Innards (e.g., heart, lungs, liver) of sacrificial animals, which were ritually cooked and tasted by the sacrificers

*stolē.* Sacred or otherwise special vestment or equipment worn or used by those participating in solemn rituals or public performances

*sumbolon* (pl. *sumbola*) Token or sign (usually of deep religious significance), carried and revealed to initiates during the *orgia* of mystery cults

*summustēs.* A fellow initiate in the mysteries

*technitēs* (pl. *technitai*). Skilled artisan, expert; often (in a Dionysiac context) a theatrical artist

*telestēs* (pl. *telestai*). Expert in the rites (*teletai*) of the mysteries

*teletē* (pl. *teletai*). Rite, especially one of initiation into the mysteries

*temenos.* Sacred precinct, usually the land surrounding a temple or sanctuary

*theomachos.* A hubristic person who foolishly fights against a god (e.g., Pentheus)

theophagy. Consumption of a divine being or substance

Thesmophoric. Having to do with the Thesmophoria, a women's festival of Demeter

thiasos. Company or troop of worshipers, usually of maenads but also referring to less exotic religious clubs or institutions

*thuias* (pl. *thuiades*). Raving woman, a generic term for a maenad who worships at Delphi

*thusia.* Burnt offering, a sacrifice of incense or meat that is burnt for the gods on their altars

thyrsus. Wand or staff consisting of a fennel stalk (*narthēx*) with ivy leaves attached at the top; frequently handled by Dionysus and his followers in their processions and dances

Titans. Divine beings of an early generation of gods; in one myth they appear as the enemies of the infant Dionysus, whom they kill and dismember

*tumpanon.* Type of drum or tambourine, often carried by worshipers of Dionysus or of Cybele

*xenia.* The ritual hospitality shown toward a guest and the permanent state of friendly relations that is created as a result

*xenos.* Outsider or stranger, but also a guest, who by virtue of the display of ritual hospitality (*xenia*) becomes a permanent friend

# Bibliography


Aélion, R. 1983. *Euripide: Héritier d'Eschyle*. 2 vols. Paris.

——. 1986. *Quelques grands mythes héroïques dans l'oeuvre d'Euripide*. Paris.

Alföldi, A. 1939. "Chars funéraires bacchiques." *Antiquité classique* 8: 347–59.

Amsler, M., ed. 1987. *Creativity and the Imagination: Case Studies from the Classical Age to the Twentieth Century*. Newark, N.J.

Andreae, B. 1963. *Studien zur römischen Grabkunst*. Heidelberg.

Arafat, K. W. 1990. *Classical Zeus*. Oxford.

Arias, E., M. Hirmer, and B. Shefton. 1962. *A History of Greek Vase Painting*. London.

Arrighetti, G., R. Bodei, and G. Cambiano. 1982. *Aspetti di Hermann Usener filologo della religione*. Biblioteca di studi antichi 39. Pisa.

Arthur, M. 1981. "The Divided World of *Iliad* VI." In Foley 1981, 19–44.

Auffarth, C. 1991. *Der drohende Untergang: "Schöpfung" in Mythos und Ritual im Alten Orient und in Griechenland am Beispiel der Odyssee und des Ezechielbuches*. Religionsgeschichtliche Versuche und Vorarbeiten 39. Berlin and New York.

Auger, D. 1988. "Le jeu de Dionysos: Déguisements et métamorphoses dans *Les Bacchantes* d'Euripide." *Nouvelle revue d' ethnopsychiatrie* 1: 57–80.

Austin, C. 1967. *De nouveaux fragments de l'Erechthée d'Euripide*. Recherches de papyrologie 4. Paris.

——. 1968. *Nova fragmenta Euripidea in papyris reperta*. Berlin.

Bacon, H. 1964. "The Shield of Eteocles." *Arion* 3: 327–38.

Bailey, C., E. A. Barber, C. W. Bowra, J. D. Denniston, and D. L. Page, eds. 1936. *Greek Poetry and Life: Essays Presented to Gilbert Murray*. Oxford.

Baratte, F. 1974. "Le sarcophage de Triptolème au Musée du Louvre." *Revue archéologique*, 271–90.

Barrett, W. S. 1964. *Euripides: Hippolytos*. Oxford.

Bastiaensen, A. A. R., A. Hilhorst, and C. H. Kneepkens, eds. 1989. *Fructus centesimus: mélanges offerts à Gerard J. M. Bartelink à l'occasion de son soixante-cinquième anniversaire*. Dordrecht, Holland.

Beazley, J. 1928. *Greek Vases in Poland*. Oxford.

——. 1947a. *Etruscan Vase Painting*. Oxford.

——. 1947b. *Some Vases in the Cyprus Museum*. London.

——. 1963–64. "Heracles derubato." *Apollo: Bollettino dei Musei Provinciali del Salernitano* 3–4: 3–14.

Beck, A. 1953. "Der Empfang Ioles." *Hermes* 81: 10–21.

Benardete, S. 1975. "A Reading of Sophocles' *Antigone* I." *Interpretations* 4: 148–96.

Benndorf, O., and G. Niemann. 1884. *Reisen im südwestlichen Kleinasien*. Vol. 1, *Reisen in Lykien und Karien*. Vienna.

Bérard, C. 1974. "Silène porte-van." *Bulletin de l'Association Pro Aventico* 22: 5–16.

——. 1976. "Ἄξιε ταῦρε." In *Mélanges d'histoire et d'archéologie offerts à P. Collart*, 61–73. Lausanne.

Bérard, C., C. Bron, J. -L. Durand et al. 1984. *La cité des images: Religion et société en Grèce antique*. Lausanne.

——. 1989. *A City of Images: Iconography and Society in Ancient Greece*. Translation of Bérard, Bron, Durand et al. 1984 by D. Lyons. Princeton.

Bérard, C., C. Bron, and A. Pomari, eds. 1987. *Images et société en Grèce ancienne: L'iconographie comme méthode d'analyse*. Colloque Lausanne 8–11 fév. 1984. Lausanne.

Bernand, E. 1969. *Inscriptions métriques de l'Egypte gréco-romaine*. Paris.

Bernheimer, R. 1952. *Wild Men in the Middle Ages: A Study in Art, Sentiment, and Demonology*. Cambridge, Mass.

Bianchi, U. 1979. *Mysteria Mithrae*. Leiden.

Bianchi, U., and M. J. Vermaseren, eds. 1982. *La soteriologia dei culti orientali nell' impero romano*. Leiden.

Bieber, M. 1949. "Eros and Dionysos in Kerch Vases." In *Commemorative Studies in Honor of T. L. Shear*, 31–38. Hesperia Supplement 8. Princeton.

Bierl, A. F. 1989. "Was hat die Tragödie mit Dionysos zu tun? Rolle und Funktion des Dionysos am Beispiel der 'Antigone' des Sophokles." *Würzburger Jahrbücher für die Altertumswissenschaft* 15: 43–58.

——. 1991. *Dionysos und die griechische Tragödie: Politische und "metatheatralische" Aspekte im Text*. Classica Monacensia 1. Tübingen.

Blok, J., and P. Mason, eds. 1987. *Sexual Asymmetry: Studies in Ancient Society*. Amsterdam.

Blume, H.-D. 1978. *Einführung in das antike Theaterwesen*. Darmstadt.

Boardman, J. 1975. *Athenian Red Figure Vases: The Archaic Period*. London.

——. 1989. *Athenian Red Figure Vases: The Classical Period*. London.

Bodnar, E., and C. Mitchell. 1976. *Cyriacus of Ancona's Journey in the Propontis and the Northern Aegean, 1444–45*. Philadelphia.

Bohringer, F. 1980. "Mégare: Traditions mythiques, espace sacré et naissance de la cité." *Antiquité classique* 49: 5–22.

Bollack, J. 1990. *L'Oedipe Roi de Sophocle: Le texte et ses interprétations*. Vol. 2, *Commentaire, Première partie*. Lille.

Bonamici, M. 1991. "Contributo alla bronzistica etrusca tardo-classica." *Prospettiva: Rivista di storia dell'arte antica e moderna* 62: 2–14.
Bond, G. W. 1963. *Euripides: Hypsipyle*. Oxford.
Bonfante, G., and L. Bonfante. 1983. *The Etruscan Language: An Introduction*. Manchester.
——. 1985. *Lingua e cultura degli Etruschi*. Translation of Bonfante and Bonfante 1983. Rome.
Bonfante, L. 1981. "Etruscan Couples and Their Aristocratic Society." In Foley 1981, 323–43.
——. 1986. *Etruscan Life and Afterlife*. Detroit.
——. 1989. "Nudity as a Costume in Classical Art." *American Journal of Archaeology* 93: 543–70.
———. 1990. *Etruscan*. Reading the Past Series. London.
Borgeaud, P. 1988. *The Cult of Pan in Ancient Greece*. Translated by K. Atlass and J. Redfield. Chicago.
——, ed. 1991. *Orphisme et Orpheé: En l'honneur de Jean Rudhardt*. Recherches et rencontres 3. Geneva.
Bosch, E. 1967. *Quellen zur Geschichte der Stadt Ankara im Altertum*. Ankara.
Bothmer, D. von. 1985. *The Amasis Painter and His World*. New York and Malibu.
Bourlot, M. 1988. "L'orgie sur la montagne." *Nouvelle revue d'ethnopsychiatrie* 1: 7–44.
Bouvier, D., and Ph. Moreau. 1983. "Phinée ou le père aveugle et la marâtre aveuglante." *Revue belge de philologie et d'histoire* 61: 5–19.
Bovon, A. 1963. "La représentation des guerriers perses et la notion de barbare." *Bulletin de correspondance hellénique* 87: 579–602.
Bowersock G., W. Burkert, and M. C. J. Putnam, eds. 1979. *Arktouros: Hellenic Studies Presented to B. M. W. Knox*. Berlin and New York.
Boyancé, P. 1937. *Le culte des Muses chez les philosophes grecs*. Paris.
Bremmer, J. 1980. "An Enigmatic Indo-European Rite: Paederasty." *Arethusa* 13: 279–98.
——. 1984. "Greek Maenadism Reconsidered." *Zeitschrift für Papyrologie und Epigraphik* 55: 267–86.
——, ed. 1987a. *Interpretations of Greek Mythology*. London.
——. 1987b. "The Old Women of Ancient Greece." In Blok and Mason 1987, 191–201.
——. 1989. "Why Did Early Christianity Attract Upper-Class Women." In Bastiaensen, Hilhorst, and Kneepkens 1989, 37–47.
Brendel, O. 1978. *Etruscan Art*. Harmondsworth, U.K.
Breslin, J. 1977. *A Greek Prayer*. Pasadena.
Briggs, W. W., and W. M. Calder III, eds. 1990. *Classical Scholarship: A Biographical Encyclopedia*. New York and London.
Brijder, H., J. Beelen, and L. van der Meer. 1990. *Die Etrusken*. Amsterdam.
Brommer, F. 1937. *Satyroi*. Würzburg.
——. 1959. *Satyrspiele: Bilder griechischer Vasen*. 2d ed. Berlin.

——. 1980. *Göttersagen in Vasenlisten*. Marburg.

Bruhl, A. 1953. *Liber Pater: Origine et expansion du culte dionysiaque à Rome et dans le monde romain*. Paris.

Brumfield, A. C. 1981. *The Attic Festivals of Demeter and Their Relation to the Agricultural Year*. New York.

Burian, P., ed. 1985. *Directions in Euripidean Criticism: A Collection of Essays*. Durham, N. C.

Burkert, W. 1966. "Greek Tragedy and Sacrificial Ritual." *Greek, Roman and Byzantine Studies* 7: 87–121.

——. 1972. *Homo Necans: Interpretationen altgriechischer Opferriten und Mythen*. Religionsgeschichtliche Versuche und Vorarbeiten 32. Berlin and New York.

——. 1975a. "Rešep-Figuren, Apollon von Amyklai und die 'Erfindung' des Opfers auf Cypern." *Grazer Beiträge* 4: 51–66.

——. 1975b. "Apellai und Apollon." *Rheinisches Museum für Philologie* 118:1–21.

——. 1975c. "Le laminette auree: Da Orfeo a Lampone." In *Orfismo in Magna Grecia: Atti del 14° Convegno di studi sulla Magna Grecia, Taranto, 6–10 Ottobre 1974*, 81–104. Naples.

——. 1977a. *Griechische Religion der archaischen und klassischen Epoche*. Die Religionen der Menschheit 15. Stuttgart, Berlin, Cologne, and Mainz.

——. 1977b. "Orphism and Bacchic Mysteries: New Evidence and Old Problems of Interpretation." In *Protocol for the Center for Hermeneutical Studies in Hellenistic and Modern Culture: Colloquy 28, 1977*, 1–10. Berkeley.

——. 1979. *Structure and History in Greek Mythology and Ritual*. Berkeley and Los Angeles.

——. 1982. "Craft versus Sect: The Problem of Orphics and Pythagoreans." In Meyer and Sanders 1982, 1–22.

——. 1983. *Homo Necans: The Anthropology of Ancient Greek Sacrificial Ritual and Myth*. Translation of Burkert 1972 by P. Bing. Berkeley.

——. 1985. *Greek Religion, Archaic and Classical*. Translation of Burkert 1977a by J. Raffan. Oxford and Cambridge, Mass.

——. 1987a. *Ancient Mystery Cults*. Cambridge, Mass.

——. 1987b. "The Problem of Ritual Killing." In Hammerton-Kelley 1987, 149–88.

——. 1990. *Antike Mysterien: Funktionen und Gehalt*. Munich.

Buschor, E. 1928. "Ein choregisches Denkmal." *Mitteilungen des Deutschen Archäologischen Instituts, Athenische Abteilung* 53: 92–108.

Cahn, H. A., and E. Simon, eds. 1980. *Tainia: Festschrift für Roland Hampe*. Stuttgart.

Calame, C. 1986. "Facing Otherness: The Tragic Mask in Ancient Greece." *History of Religions* 26: 125–42

——. 1987. "Quand regarder, c'est énoncer: Le vase de Pronomos et le masque." In Bérard, Bron, and Pomari 1987, 79–88.

——, ed. 1988. *Métamorphoses du mythe en Grèce antique*. Geneva.

——. 1989. "Démasquer par le masque: Effets énonciatifs dans la comédie ancienne." *Revue de l'histoire des religions* 206: 357–76.

Calder, William M., ed. 1991. *The Cambridge Ritualists Reconsidered*. Illinois Classical Studies Supplement 2. Atlanta.
Cancik, H. 1986. "Dionysos 1933: W. F. Otto, ein Religionswissenschaftler und Theologe am Ende der Weimarer Republik." In Faber and Schlesier 1986, 105–23.
Cancik, H., B. Gladigow, and M. Laubscher, eds. 1990. *Handbuch religionswissenschaftlicher Grundbegriffe*. Vol. 2. Stuttgart.
Cararra, P. 1977. *Euripide: Eretteo*. Papyrologica Florentina 3. Florence.
Carpenter, T. 1986. *Dionysian Imagery in Archaic Greek Art: Its Development in Black-Figure Vase Painting*. Oxford.
——. 1991. *Art and Myth in Ancient Greece*. London.
Carter, J. B. 1987. "The Masks of Ortheia." *American Journal of Archaeology* 91: 355–83.
Casadio, G. 1982. "Per un' indagine storico-religiosa sui culti di Dioniso in relazione alla fenomenologia dei misteri I." *Studi e materiali di storia delle religioni* 6: 209–34.
——. 1983. "Per un' indagine storico-religiosa sui culti di Dioniso in relazione alla fenomenologia dei misteri II." *Studi e materiali di storia delle religioni* 7: 123–49.
Càssola, F. 1975. *Inni omerici*. Milan.
Cavallari, F. S. 1879. "XI. Sibari." *Notizie degli scavi di antichità,* 245–53.
——. 1880. "XXVI. Corigliano-Calabro." *Notizie degli scavi di antichità,* 400–410.
Chalkia, I. 1986. *Lieux et espace dans la tragédie d' Euripide: Essai d'analyse socioculturelle*. Thessaloniki.
Chamay, J. 1988. "Quelques inédits à Genève." *Numismatica e antichità classiche* 17: 125–29.
Chantraine, P. 1968. *Dictionnaire étymologique de la langue grecque: Histoire des mots*. Paris.
Cianferoni, G. C. 1984a. *San Martino ai Colli: Un centro rurale etrusco in Val d'Elsa*. Florence.
——. 1984b. "Periodo ellenistico." In Cianferoni 1984a.
Clay, J. S. 1989. *The Politics of Olympus: Form and Meaning in the Major Homeric Hymns*. Princeton.
Coarelli, F., ed. 1973. *Roma Medio Repubblicana*. Rome.
Cockle, W. E. H. 1987. *Euripides: Hypsipyle*. Testi e commenti 7. Rome.
Cole, S. G. 1980. "New Evidence for the Mysteries of Dionysos." *Greek, Roman and Byzantine Studies* 21: 223–38.
——. 1984. "Life and Death: A New Epigram for Dionysos." *Epigraphica Anatolica* 4: 37–48.
——. 1988. "The Uses of Water in Greek Sanctuaries." In Hägg, Marinatos, and Nordquist 1988, 161–65.
——. 1990. "Mail-Order Maenads." Unpublished paper.
——. 1991. "Dionysiac Mysteries in Phrygia in the Imperial Period." *Epigraphica Anatolica* 17: 41–50.
——. Forthcoming. "Procession and Celebration at the Dionysia." In Scodel, forthcoming.

Coleman, R. 1972. "The Role of the Chorus in Sophocles' *Antigone*." *Proceedings of the Cambridge Philological Society* 18: 4–27.
Collard, C. 1975. *Euripides: Supplices*. 2 vols. Groningen.
Collignon, M. 1911. *Les statues funéraires dans l'art grec*. Paris.
Collinge, A. 1989. "The Case of Satyrs." In *Images of Authority: Papers Presented to Joyce Reynolds*. Cambridge.
Connor, W. R. 1989. "City Dionysia and Athenian Democracy." *Classica et mediaevalia* 40: 7–32.
Cook, A. 1914. *Zeus*. Vol. 1. Cambridge.
——. 1924. *Zeus*. Vol. 2. Cambridge.
——. 1940. *Zeus*. Vol. 3. Cambridge.
Cornford, F. M. 1914. *The Origin of Attic Comedy*. Cambridge.
——. 1961. *The Origin of Attic Comedy*. Edited by T. H. Gaster. 2d ed. of Cornford 1914. New York.
Corsten, T. 1988. "Daskyleion am Meer." *Epigraphica Anatolica* 12: 53–78.
Craik, E. M. 1988. *Euripides: Phoenician Women*. Warminster.
——, ed. 1990. *"Owls to Athens": Essays on Classical Subjects Presented to Sir Kenneth Dover*. Oxford.
Cremer, C. 1986. "Der Schellenmann." *Epigraphica Anatolica* 7: 21–34.
Cristofani, M. 1976. "La leggenda di un tipo monetale etrusco." In *L'Italie préromaine et la Rome républicaine: Mélanges offerts à J. Heurgon*. Rome.
——. 1983. *Gli Etruschi del mare*. Milan.
——. 1986. "Dionysos/Fufluns." *Lexicon iconographicum mythologiae classicae* 3: 531–40.
——. ed. 1990a. *La grande Roma dei Tarquini*. Rome.
——. 1990b. "Il culto dei morti." In Cristofani 1990a, 264–65.
Cristofani, M., and M. Martelli. 1978. "Fufluns Pachies: Sugli aspetti del culto di Bacco in Etruria." *Studi Etruschi* 46: 119–33.
Cumont, F. 1942a. *Recherches sur le symbolisme funéraire des Romains*. Paris.
——. 1942b. *La stèle du danseur d' Antibes et son décor végétal*. Paris.
Cunningham, M. L. 1984. "Aeschylus, *Agamemnon* 231–47." *Bulletin of the Institute of Classical Studies* 31: 9–12.
Czaja, M. 1974. *Gods of Myth and Stone: Phallicism in Japanese Folk Religion*. New York and Tokyo.
Dahlinger, S. Chr. 1979. "Der sogenannte Podiensaal in Pergamon: Ein Mithraeum?" In Bianchi 1979, 793–803.
Dale, A. M. 1969. *Collected Papers,* Cambridge.
Daraki, M. 1980. "Aspects du sacrifice dionysiaque." *Revue d'histoire des religions* 197: 131–57.
——. 1985. *Dionysos*. Paris.
Daux, G. 1970. "Epitaphe métrique d'un jeune porc, victime d'un accident." *Bulletin de correspondance hellénique* 94: 609–18.
Davies, M. 1988. *Epicorum Graecorum fragmenta*. Göttingen.
de Grummond, N., ed. 1982. *Guide to Etruscan Mirrors*. Tallahassee.
de Lannoy, L. 1977. *Flavius Philostratus: Heroicus*. Leipzig.

Delatte, A. 1952. "Le papyrus d'Antinoopolis relatif aux mystères." *Bulletin de la classe des lettres de l'Academie Royale de Belgique* 38: 194–208.

Del Chiaro, M. 1974. *Etruscan Red-Figured Vase Painting at Caere*. Berkeley.

de Martino, E. 1958. *Morte e pianto rituale nel mondo antico*. Turin.

Detienne, M. 1977. *Dionysos mis à mort*. Paris.

——. 1979. *Dionysos Slain*. Translation of Detienne 1977 by L. Muellner and M. Muellner. Baltimore.

——. 1986. *Dionysos à ciel ouvert*. Paris.

——. 1987. "Dionysos." *The Encyclopedia of Religion* 4: 358–61.

——. 1989a. *Dionysos at Large*. Translation of Detienne 1986 by A. Goldhammer. Cambridge, Mass., and London.

——. 1989b. "Un phallus pour Dionysos." In Sissa and Detienne 1989, 253–64.

Deubner, L. 1932. *Attische Feste*. Berlin.

Deutsch, H. 1969. *A Psychoanalytic Study of the Myth of Dionysus and Apollo: Two Variants of the Son-Mother Relationship*. New York.

Devereux, G. 1973. "Le fragment d'Eschyle 62 Nauck²: Ce qu'y signifie χλούνης." *Revue des études grecques* 86: 271–84.

Devoto, G. 1932. "Nomi di divinità etrusche: 1. Fufluns." *Studi etruschi* 6: 243–60.

De Vries, K. 1973. "East Meets West at Dinner." *Expedition* 15: 32–39.

Dieterich, A. 1908. "Die Entstehung der Tragödie." *Archiv für Religionswissenschaft* 11: 163–96.

Dihle, A. 1981. *Der Prolog der Bacchen und die antike Überlieferungsphase des Euripides-Textes*. Sitzungsberichte der Heidelberger Akademie der Wissenschaften, No. 2. Heidelberg.

Dodds, E. 1940. "Maenadism in the Bacchae." *Harvard Theological Review* 33: 155–76. Reprinted with slight changes in Dodds 1951, 270–82.

——. 1944. *Euripides: Bacchae*. Oxford.

——. 1951. *The Greeks and the Irrational*. Berkeley and Los Angeles.

——. 1960. *Euripides: Bacchae*. 2d ed. of Dodds 1944. Oxford.

Dohrn, T. 1972. *Die Ficoronische Ciste*. Berlin.

Dover, K. J. 1978. *Greek Homosexuality*. Cambridge, Mass.

Dumézil, G. 1970. *Archaic Roman Religion*. Translated by P. Krapp. Chicago.

Dunand, F. 1986. "Les associations dionysiaques au service du pouvoir lagide (IIIe s. av. J.-C.)." In Ecole de Rome 1986, 85–104.

Dunbabin, K. 1978. *The Mosaics of Roman Africa*. Oxford.

Durand, J.-L. 1986. *Sacrifice et labour en Grèce ancienne: Essai d'anthropologie religieuse*. Paris and Rome.

Durand, J.-L., and F. Frontisi-Ducroux. 1982. "Idoles, figures, images: Autour de Dionysos." *Revue archéologique*, 81–108.

Easterling, P. E. 1982. *Sophocles: Trachiniae*. Cambridge.

Ecole d'Athènes. 1967. *Guide de Thasos*. Paris.

Ecole de Rome. 1986. *L'association dionysiaque dans les sociétés anciennes: Actes de la table ronde organisée par l'Ecole Française de Rome, Rome 24–25 mai 1984*. Collection de l'Ecole Française de Rome 89. Rome.

Edlund, I. 1982. "Floral and Faunal Motifs on Etruscan Mirrors." In de Grummond 1982, 128–39.

Edmunds, L., ed. 1990. *Approaches to Greek Myth*. Baltimore and London.

Edwards, M. W. 1960. "Representation of Maenads on Archaic Red-Figure Vases." *Journal of Hellenic Studies* 80: 78–87.

Egger, R. 1950. *Der Grabstein von Chekanchevo*. Schriften der Balkankommission der Österreichischen Akademie, Antiquarische Abteilung 11.2. Vienna.

Eisler, R. 1925. *Orphisch-dionysische Mysteriengedanken in der christlichen Antike*. Vorträge der Bibliothek Warburg 1922–1923, vol. 2. Leipzig and Berlin.

——. 1929. "Nachleben dionysischer Mysterienriten?" *Archiv für Religionswissenschaft* 27: 171–82.

Else, G. F. 1965. *The Origin and Early Form of Greek Tragedy*. Cambridge, Mass.

Engemann, J. 1973. *Untersuchungen zur Sepulchralsymbolik der späteren römischen Kaiserzeit*. Jahrbuch für Antike und Christentum, Ergänzungsband 2. Münster.

Euben, J. P., ed. 1986. *Greek Tragedy and Political Theory*. Berkeley.

Evans, A. 1988. *The God of Ecstasy: Sex-Roles and the Madness of Dionysos*. New York.

Evjen, H. D., ed. 1984. *Mnemai: Classical Studies in Memory of Karl K. Hulley*. Chico, Calif.

Faber, R., and R. Schlesier, eds. 1986. *Die Restauration der Götter: Antike Religion und Neo-Paganismus*. Würzburg.

Fagles, R. 1982. *Sophocles: The Three Theban Plays*. New York.

Falk, N. A., and R. M. Gross, eds. 1980. *Unspoken Worlds: Women's Religious Lives in Non-Western Cultures*. New York.

Faraone, C. A., and D. Obbink, eds. 1991. *Magika Hiera: Ancient Greek Magic and Religion*. Oxford.

Farnell, L. 1909. *The Cults of the Greek States*. Vol. 5. Oxford.

Festugière, A. 1956. "Omophagion Emballein." *Classica et mediaevalia* 17: 31–34. Reprinted in Festugière 1972, 110–13.

——. 1972. *Etudes de religion grecque et hellénistique*. Paris.

Fineberg, S. 1983. "Dionysos in the New Democracy." Unpublished paper.

Flashar, H. 1984. "Die *Poetik* des Aristoteles und die griechische Tragödie." *Poetica* 16: 1–23.

——, ed. 1990. *Auseinandersetzungen mit der Antike*. Bamberg.

Foley, H. 1980. "The Masque of Dionysus." *Transactions of the American Philological Association* 110: 107–33.

——, ed. 1981. *Reflections of Women in Antiquity*. New York.

——. 1985. *Ritual Irony: Poetry and Sacrifice in Euripides*. Ithaca, N.Y., and London.

Fontenrose, J. 1978. *The Delphic Oracle: Its Responses and Operations*. Berkeley.

Foti, J., and G. Pugliese Carratelli. 1974. "Un sepolcro di Hipponion e un nuovo testo Orfico." *La parola del passato* 29: 91–126.

Foucher, L. 1981. "Le culte de Bacchus sous l'empire romain." *Aufstieg und Niedergang der römischen Welt* 2.17.2: 684–702.

Fournier, D., and S. d' Onofrio, eds. 1991. *Le ferment divin*. Paris.

Frank, M. 1982. *Der kommende Gott: Vorlesungen über die Neue Mythologie*. Frankfurt am Main.

Fraser, P. 1972. *Ptolemaic Alexandria.* 3 vols. Oxford.

Frazer, J. 1912. *The Golden Bough.* Part 5, *The Spirits of the Corn and the Wild.* 3d ed. London.

Frel, J. 1977. "Response [to Burkert 1977b]." In *Protocol of the Center for Hermeneutical Studies in Hellenistic and Modern Culture: Colloquy 28, 1977,* 19–20. Berkeley.

Frickenhaus, A. 1912. *Lenäenvasen.* Winckelmannsprogramm 77. Berlin.

Frontisi-Ducroux, F. 1984. "Au miroir du masque." In Bérard, Bron, Durand et al. 1984, 147–61.

——. 1986. "Images du ménadisme féminin: Les vases des 'Lénéennes.'" In Ecole de Rome 1986, 165–76.

——. 1987a. "Face et profil: Les deux masques." In Bérard, Bron, and Pomari 1987, 89–102.

——. 1987b. "Prosopon: Valeurs grecques du masque et du visage." Diss., Paris.

——. 1989. "In the Mirror of the Mask." Translation of Frontisi-Ducroux 1984 in Bérard, Bron, Durand et al. 1989, 151–65.

——. 1991. *Le dieu-masque: Une figure du Dionysos d'Athènes.* Images à l'appui 4. Paris and Rome.

Frontisi-Ducroux, F., and F. Lissarrague. 1990. "From Ambiguity to Ambivalence: A Dionysiac Excursion through the 'Anakreontic' Vases." In Halperin, Winkler, and Zeitlin 1990, 21–56.

Frontisi-Ducroux, F., and J.-P. Vernant. 1986. "Figures du masque en Grèce ancienne." In Vernant and Vidal-Naquet 1986, 25–43.

——. 1988. "Features of the Mask in Ancient Greece." Translation of Frontisi-Ducroux and Vernant 1986 in Vernant and Vidal-Naquet 1988, 189–206 and 464–66.

Gardiner, C. P. 1987. *The Sophoclean Chorus: A Study of Character and Function.* Iowa City.

Gerhard, E., A. Klugmann, and G. Körte. 1840–97. *Etruskische Spiegel.* 5 vols. Berlin.

Gernet, L. 1932. "Dionysos." In Gernet and Boulanger 1932, 110–50.

——. 1953. "Dionysos et la religion dionysiaque: Eléments hérités et traits originaux." *Revue des études grecques* 66: 377–95. Reprinted in Gernet 1968, 63–89.

——. 1968. *Anthropologie de la Grèce ancienne.* Edited by J.-P. Vernant. Paris.

——. 1981a. *The Anthropology of Ancient Greece.* Translation of Gernet 1968 by J. Hamilton and B. Nagy. Baltimore and London.

——. 1981b. "Dionysus and the Dionysiac Religion: Inherited Elements and Original Traits." Translation of Gernet 1953 in Gernet 1981a, 48–70.

Gernet, L., and A. Boulanger. 1932. *Le génie grec dans la religion.* Paris.

——. 1970. *Le génie grec dans la religion.* 2d ed. of Gernet and Boulanger 1932. Paris.

Geyer, A. 1977a. *Das Problem des Realitätsbezuges in der dionysischen Bildkunst der Kaiserzeit.* Würzburg.

——. 1977b. "Roman und Mysterienritual: Zum Problem eines Bezugs zum dionysischen Mysterienritual im Roman des Longos." *Würzburger Jahrbücher* n.s. 3: 179–96.

Ghiron-Bistagne, P. 1976. *Recherches sur les acteurs dans la Grèce antique.* Paris.

Gioure, E. 1978. *Ο κρατήρας του Δερβενιού*. Athens.

Goff, B. E. 1990. *The Noose of Words: Readings of Desire, Violence, and Language in Euripides' Hippolytos*. Cambridge.

Goldhill, S. 1986. *Reading Greek Tragedy*. Cambridge.

——. 1988. "Doubling and Recognition in the *Bacchae*." *Mètis* 3: 137–56.

——. 1990. "The Great Dionysia and Civic Ideology." In Winkler and Zeitlin 1990, 97–129.

Gombrich, E. H. 1970. *Aby Warburg: An Intellectual Biography*. London.

Gorbunova, K. S. 1983. *Chernofigurnye atticheskie vazy v Ermitazhe*. Leningrad.

Goukowsky, P. 1981. *Essais sur les origines du mythe d' Alexandre*. Vol. 2, *Alexandre et Dionysos*. Nancy.

Graf, F. 1974. *Eleusis und die orphische Dichtung Athens in vorhellenistischer Zeit*. Religionsgeschichtliche Versuche und Vorarbeiten 33. Berlin and New York.

——. 1979. "Apollon Delphinios." *Museum Helveticum* 36: 2–22.

——. 1980. "Milch, Honig und Wein: Zum Verständnis der Libation im griechischen Ritual." In *Perennitas: Studi in onore di A. Brelich*, 209–21. Rome.

——. 1985. *Nordionische Kulte: Religionsgeschichtliche und epigraphische Untersuchungen zu den Kulten von Chios, Erythrai, Klazomenai und Phokaia*. Bibliotheca Helvetica Romana 21. Rome.

Graves, R. 1955. *Greek Myths*. Baltimore.

Green, J. 1982. "Dedications of Masks." *Revue archéologique*, 237–48.

Greifenhagen, A. 1957. *Griechische Eroten*. Berlin.

Griffith, J. 1983. "Myth of Lykourgos, King of the Edonian Thracians in Literature and Art." In Poulter 1983, 217–32.

Griffith, M., and D. J. Mastronarde, eds. 1990. *Cabinet of the Muses: Essays on Classical and Comparative Literature in Honor of Thomas G. Rosenmeyer*. Atlanta.

Griffiths, J. G. 1982. "The Concept of Divine Judgement in the Mystery Religions." In Bianchi and Vermaseren 1982, 192–222.

Grottanelli, C., and N. F. Parise, eds. 1988. *Sacrificio e società nel mondo antico*. Rome.

Gründer, K., ed. 1969. *Der Streit um Nietzsches "Geburt der Tragödie."* Hildesheim.

Guarducci, M. 1983. "Laminette auree orfiche: Alcuni problemi." *Studi scelti sulla religione greca e romana e sul cristianesimo*. Leiden. 71–96.

Guépin, J. 1968. *The Tragic Paradox: Myth and Ritual in Greek Tragedy*. Amsterdam.

Hägg, R., N. Marinatos, and G. C. Nordquist, eds. 1988. *Early Greek Cult Practice*. Skrifter utgivna av Svenska Institutet i Athen 38. Stockholm.

Hall, E. 1989. *Inventing the Barbarian: Greek Self-Definition through Tragedy*. Oxford.

Halliwell, S. 1986. *Aristotle's Poetics*. London.

Halm-Tisserand, M. 1989. "Folklore et superstition en Grèce classique: Lamia torturée?" *Kernos* 2: 67–82.

Halperin, D. M., J. J. Winkler, and F. I. Zeitlin, eds. 1990. *Before Sexuality: The Construction of Erotic Experience in the Ancient Greek World*. Princeton.

Hamilton, R. 1992. *Choes and Anthesteria: Athenian Iconography and Ritual*. Ann Arbor.

Hammerton-Kelley, R., ed. 1987. *Violent Origins: W. Burkert, R. Girard, and J. Z. Smith on Ritual Killing and Cultural Formation*. Stanford.

Harari, M. 1980. *Il "Gruppo Clusium" nella ceramografia etrusca*. Rome.

Harrison, J. 1899. "Delphika." *Journal of Hellenic Studies* 19: 205–51.

——. 1903. *Prolegomena to the Study of Greek Religion*. Cambridge.

——. 1912. *Themis: A Study of the Social Origins of Greek Religion*. Cambridge.

——. 1922. *Prolegomena to the Study of Greek Religion*. 3d ed. of Harrison 1903. Cambridge.

——. 1927. *Themis: A Study of the Social Origins of Greek Religion*. 2d ed. of Harrison 1912. Cambridge.

Heelas, P., and A. Lock, eds. 1981. *Indigenous Psychologies: The Anthropology of the Self*. London.

Henrichs, A. 1969. "Die Maenaden von Milet." *Zeitschrift für Papyrologie und Epigraphik* 4: 223–41.

——. 1972. *Die Phoinikika des Lollianos: Fragmente eines neuen griechischen Romans*. Papyrologische Texte und Abhandlungen 14. Bonn.

——. 1975. "Two Doxographical Notes: Democritus and Prodicus on Religion." *Harvard Studies in Classical Philology* 79: 93–123.

——. 1976. "The Atheism of Prodicus." *Cronache ercolanesi* 5: 15–21.

——. 1978a. "Greek Maenadism from Olympias to Messalina." *Harvard Studies in Classical Philology* 82: 121–60.

——. 1978b. "Horaz als Aretaloge des Dionysos." *Harvard Studies in Classical Philology* 82: 203–11.

——. 1979. "Greek and Roman Glimpses of Dionysus." In Houser 1979, 1–11.

——. 1981. "Human Sacrifice in Greek Religion: Three Case Studies." In Rudhardt and Reverdin 1981, 195–242.

——. 1982. "Changing Dionysiac Identities." In Meyer and Sanders 1982, 137–60 and 213–36.

——. 1983. "The Sobriety of Oedipus: Sophocles *OC* 100. Misunderstood." *Harvard Studies in Classical Philology* 87: 87–100.

——. 1984a. "Male Intruders among the Maenads: The So-Called Male Celebrant." In Evjen 1984, 69–91.

——. 1984b. "Loss of Self, Suffering, Violence: The Modern View of Dionysus from Nietzsche to Girard." *Harvard Studies in Classical Philology* 88: 205–40.

——. 1986. "The Last of the Detractors: Friedrich Nietzsche's Condemnation of Euripides." *Greek, Roman and Byzantine Studies* 27: 369–97.

——. 1987a. "Myth Visualized: Dionysos and His Circle in Sixth-Century Attic Vase-Painting." In *Papers on the Amasis Painter and His World*, 92–124. Malibu.

——. 1987b. *Die Götter Griechenlands: Ihr Bild im Wandel der Religionswissenschaft*. Thyssen-Vorträge "Auseinandersetzungen mit der Antike" 5. Bamberg. Reprinted in Flashar 1990, 116–62.

——. 1990. "Between Country and City: Cultic Dimensions of Dionysos in Athens and Attica." In Griffith and Mastronarde 1990, 257–77.

——. 1991. "Namenlosigkeit und Euphemismus: Zur Ambivalenz der chthonischen Mächte im attischen Drama." In Hofmann and Harder 1991, 161–201.

Herbig, R. 1958. *Neue Beobachtungen am Fries der Mysterien-Villa in Pompeii*. Baden-Baden.

Herter, H. 1938. "Phallos." *Paulys Real-Encyclopädie der classischen Altertumswissenschaft* 19: 1681–1748.

——. 1972. "Phallos." *Der kleine Pauly* 4: 701–6.

Hoffman, R. J. 1989. "Ritual License and the Cult of Dionysus." *Athenaeum* 67: 91–115.

Hoffmann, H. 1977. *Sexual and Asexual Pursuit*. Occasional Papers of the Royal Anthropological Institute 34. London.

Hofmann, H., and A. Harder, eds. 1991. *Fragmenta dramatica: Beiträge zur Interpretation der griechischen Tragikerfragmente und ihrer Wirkungsgeschichte*. Göttingen.

Horn, H. G. 1972. *Mysteriensymbolik auf dem Kölner Dionysosmosaik*. Bonn.

Houser, C., ed. 1979. *Dionysus and His Circle*. Cambridge, Mass.

Husband, T. 1980–81. *The Wild Man: Medieval Myth and Symbolism*. Exhibition at the Museum of Metropolitan Art, New York, Oct. 1980–Jan. 1981. New York.

Hutchinson, G. O. 1985. *Aeschylus: Septem contra Thebas*. Oxford.

Huxley, A. 1925. *Those Barren Leaves*. London.

Jameson, M. 1980. "Apollo Lykeios in Athens." *Archaiognosia* 1: 213–35.

Jameson, R. D. 1949. "Phallism." *The Standard Dictionary of Folklore, Mythology, and Legend* 2: 863–68.

Janko, R. 1984. "Forgetfulness in the Golden Tablets of Memory." *Classical Quarterly* 34: 89–100.

Jeanmaire, H. 1951. *Dionysos: Histoire du culte de Bacchus*. Paris.

Jebb, R. C. 1892. *Sophocles, the Plays and Fragments*. Vol. 5, *The Trachiniae*. Cambridge.

Johnson, S. E. 1984. "The Present State of Sabazios Research." *Aufstieg und Niedergang der römischen Welt* 2.17.3: 1583–1613.

Jones, C. P. 1987. "Stigma: Tattooing and Branding in Graeco-Roman Antiquity." *Journal of Roman Studies* 77: 139–55.

——. 1990. "Lucian and the Bacchants of Pontus." *Echos du monde classique* 24, n.s. 9: 53–63.

Jones, J. 1962. *On Aristotle and Greek Tragedy*. Oxford.

Jones, R. A. 1984. "Robertson Smith and James Frazer on Religion." In Stocking 1984, 31–58.

——. 1991. "La Genèse du Système? The Origins of Durkheim's Sociology of Religion." In Calder 1991, 97–121.

Jordan, D. R., M. Sasel Kos, and M. B. Wallace. 1985. "A Greek Metrical Epitaph from Poetovio for a Soldier from Bithynia." *Zeitschrift für Papyrologie und Epigraphik* 60: 85–89.

Joubon, A. 1893. "Inscription crétoise relative à l'orphisme." *Bulletin de correspondance hellénique* 17: 121–24.

Jucker, I. 1956. *Der Gestus des Aposkopein*. Zurich.

Jurgeit, F. 1980. "Aussetzung des Caeculus-Entrückung der Ariadne." In Cahn and Simon 1980, 269–79.

——. 1986. *Le ciste prenestine*. Vol. 1, *Studi e contributi*. Part 1, *Cistenfüsse: Etruskische und Praenestiner Bronzewerkstätten*. Rome.

Kabus-Preisshofen, R. 1989. *Die hellenistische Plastik der Insel Kos*. Mitteilungen des Deutschen Archäologischen Instituts, Beiheft 14. Berlin.

Kachler, K. G. 1986. *Maskenspiele aus Basler Tradition 1936–1974*. Basel.

——. 1991. *Zur Entstehung und Entwicklung der griechischen Theatermaske während des 6. und 5. Jahrhunderts v. Chr. im Beginn des europäischen Theaters*. Basel.

Kaempf-Dimitriadou, S. 1979. *Die Liebe der Götter in der attischen Kunst des 5. Jhrs. v. C.* Antike Kunst Beiheft 11. Bern.

Kambitsis, J. 1972. *Euripides: Antiope*. Athens.

Kamerbeek, J. C. 1959. *The Plays of Sophocles*. Vol. 2, *The Trachiniae*. Leiden.

Kamper, D., and C. Wulf, eds. 1987. *Das Heilige: Seine Spur in der Moderne*. Frankfurt am Main.

Kany, R. 1987. *Mnemosyne als Programm: Geschichte, Erinnerung und die Andacht zum Unbedeutenden im Werk von Usener, Warburg und Benjamin*. Studien zur Deutschen Literatur 93. Tübingen.

Kassel, R. 1990. "Die Phalaeceen des neuen hellenistischen Weihepigramms aus Pergamon." *Zeitschrift für Papyrologie und Epigraphik* 84: 299–300.

Kaufmann, C. M. 1897. *Die Jenseitshoffnungen der Griechen und Römer nach den Sepulchralinschriften*. Freiburg.

Kaufmann, W. 1967. *Friedrich Nietzsche: The Birth of Tragedy and the Case of Wagner*. Translated with commentary. New York.

Kayser, C. L. 1870. *Flavii Philostrati opera*. Leipzig.

Keil, J., and A. von Premerstein. 1908. *Bericht über eine Reise in Lydien*. Vol. 1. Denkschriften der Akademie der Wissenschaften zu Wien 53. Vienna.

Kerényi, K. 1966. "Mensch und Maske." In *Humanistische Seelenforschung*, 340–56. Munich and Vienna.

——. 1976a. *Dionysos: Urbild des unzerstörbaren Lebens*. Munich.

——. 1976b. *Dionysos: Archetypal Images of Indestructible Life*. London.

Keuls, E. C. 1982. "The Conjugal Side of Dionysiac Ritual and Symbolism in the Fifth Century B.C." *Mededelingen van het Neederlands Historisch Instituut te Rome*. 25–33.

——. 1984. "Male-Female Interaction in Fifth-Century Dionysiac Ritual As Shown in Attic Vase Painting." *Zeitschrift für Papyrologie und Epigraphik* 55: 287–97.

——. 1985. *The Reign of the Phallus: Sexual Politics in Ancient Athens*. New York.

Kienast, D. 1979. Review of Kleiner and Noe 1977. *Gnomon* 51: 452–56.

Kilmer, M. 1990. "Sexual Violence: Archaic Athens and the Recent Past." In Craik 1990, 261–77.

Kirchner, K. 1910. *Die sakrale Bedeutung des Weines im Altertums*. Religionsgeschichtliche Versuche und Vorarbeiten 9.2. Giessen.

Kiso, A. 1984. *The Lost Sophocles*. New York.

Kleiner, F., and S. P. Noe. 1977. *The Early Cistophoric Coinage*. New York.

Kleingünther, A. 1934. *Protos Heuretes*. Philologus Supplementband 26. Leipzig.

Kolb, F. 1981. *Agora und Theater: Volks- und Festversammlung*. Berlin.

Kopcke, G., and M. Moore, eds. 1979. *Studies in Classical Art and Archaeology: A Tribute to Peter von Blanckenhagen*. Locust Valley, N.Y.

Korshak, Y. 1987. *Frontal Faces in Attic Vase Painting of the Archaic Period*. Chicago.

Körte, A. 1900. "Kleinasiatische Studien VI." *Mitteilungen des Deutschen Archäologischen Instituts, Athenische Abteilung* 25: 398–44.

Kotansky, R. 1991. "Incantations and Prayers for Salvation on Inscribed Greek Amulets." In Faraone and Obbink 1991, 107–37.

Kott, J. 1974. *The Eating of the Gods: An Interpretation of Greek Tragedy*. New York.

Kraemer, R. S. 1979. "Ecstasy and Possession: The Attraction of Women to the Cult of Dionysus." *Harvard Theological Review* 72: 55–80.

——. 1980. "Ecstasy and Possession: Women of Ancient Greece and the Cult of Dionysos." In Falk and Gross 1980, 53–69.

Kurtz, D., and J. Boardman. 1986. "Booners." *Greek Vases in the J. Paul Getty Museum,* 3: 35–70. Occasional Papers on Antiquities 2. Malibu.

Kurtz, D., and B. Sparkes, eds. 1982. *The Eye of Greece: Studies in the Art of Greece*. Cambridge.

Laminger-Pascher, G. 1975. "Zu dem Epigramm *CIG* 4000 aus Ikonion." *Zeitschrift für Papyrologie und Epigraphik* 18: 303–7.

Lattimore, R. 1962. *Themes in Greek and Latin Epitaphs*. Urbana, Ill.

Lawler, L. B. 1927. *The Maenads: A Contribution to the Study of Dance in Ancient Greece*. Rome.

Lehmann-Hartleben, K., and E. C. Olsen. 1942. *The Dionysiac Sarcophagi in Baltimore*. Baltimore.

Lévêque, P. 1982. "Structures imaginaires et fonctionnement des mystères grecs." *Studi storico-religiosi* 6: 185–208.

Lévi-Strauss, C. 1972. *The Savage Mind*. London.

Linforth, I. 1941. *The Arts of Orpheus*. Berkeley and Los Angeles.

——. 1946a. "The Corybantic Rites in Plato." *University of California Publications in Classical Philology* 13: 121–62.

——. 1946b. "Telestic Madness in Plato, Phaedrus 244d–e." *University of California Publications in Classical Philology* 13: 163–72.

Lissarrague, F. 1987a. "Les satyres et le monde animal." In *Third Symposion on Ancient Greek and Related Pottery,* 335–51. Copenhagen.

——. 1987b. *Un flot d'images: Une esthétique du banquet grec*. Paris.

——. 1987c. "De la sexualité des satyres." *Mètis* 2: 63–90.

——. 1987d. "Dionysos s'en va-t-en guerre." In Bérard, Bron, and Pomari 1987, 111–20.

——. 1990a. "The Sexual Life of Satyrs." Translation of Lissarrague 1987c in Halperin, Winkler, and Zeitlin 1990, 53–81.

——. 1990b. "Why Satyrs Are Good to Represent." In Winkler and Zeitlin 1990, 228–36.

——. 1990c. *The Aesthetics of the Greek Banquet: Images of Wine and Ritual*. Translation of Lissarrague 1987b by A. Szegedy-Maszak. Princeton.

——. 1990d. *L'autre guerrier: Archers, peltastes, cavaliers dans l'imagerie attique*. Paris and Rome.

——. 1991. "Le vin, piège divin." In Fournier and d' Onofrio 1991, 47–61.

Littlefield, L. 1972. "Letter to the Editor." *Paideuma* 1: 171–72.

Lloyd-Jones, H. 1963. "The Seal of Posidippus." *Journal of Hellenic Studies* 83: 75–99.

——. 1972. "Notes on Sophocles' *Trachiniae*." *Yale Classical Studies* 22: 263–70.

——. 1979. *Aeschylus: Eumenides*. London.

Lobeck, C. 1829. *Aglaophamus sive de theologiae mysticae Graecorum causis*. 2 vols. Königsberg.

Loeb, E. 1979. *Die Geburt der Götter in der griechischen Kunst der klassischen Zeit*. Jerusalem.

Longo, O. 1986. "Dionysos à Thèbes." In *Les grandes figures religieuses: Fonctionnement pratique et symbolique dans l'antiquité*, 93–106. Annales littéraires de l'Université de Besançon 329. Paris.

Lonnoy, M.-G. 1985. "Arès et Dionysos dans la tragédie grecque: Le rapprochement des contraires." *Revue des études grecques* 98: 65–71.

Loraux, N. 1985. *Façons tragiques de tuer une femme*. Paris.

——. 1986. *The Invention of Athens*. Translated by A. Sheridan. Cambridge, Mass.

——. 1989. "Les mots qui voient." In Reichler 1989, 157–82.

——. 1990a. *Les mères en deuil*. Paris.

——. 1990b. "La métaphore sans métaphore: A propos de l' 'Orestie.'" *Revue philosophique* 2: 247–68.

——. 1990c. "Kreousa the Autochthon: A Study of Euripides' *Ion*." In Winkler and Zeitlin 1990, 168–206.

Luce, S. 1921. *The University of Pennsylvania Museum Catalogue of the Mediterranean Section*. Philadelphia.

Luschnig, C. A. E. 1988. *Time Holds the Mirror: A Study of Knowledge in Euripides' Hippolytus*. Leiden.

McGinty, P. 1978. *Interpretation and Dionysos: Method in the Study of a God*. Religion and Reason 16. The Hague, Paris, and New York.

McNally, S. 1978. "The Maenad in Early Greek Art." *Arethusa* 11: 101–36.

Macnamara, E. 1973. *Everyday Life of the Etruscans*. London.

McPhee, I. 1979. "An Apulian Oinochoe and the Robbery of Herakles." *Antike Kunst* 22: 38–42.

Maffre, J. 1982. "Quelques scènes mythologiques sur des fragments de coupes attiques de la fin du style sévère." *Revue archéologique*, 195–222.

Maiuri, A. 1925. *Nuova silloge epigrafica di Rodi e Cos*. Florence.

Malay, H., and G. Petzl. 1985. "Neue Inschriften aus den Museen Manisa, Izmir und Bergama." *Epigraphica Anatolica* 6: 55–69.

Mann, T. 1963. *Death in Venice and Seven Other Stories*. Translated by H. T. Lowe-Porter. New York.

Mannhardt, M. 1877. *Antike Feld- und Waldkulte aus nordeuropäischer Überlieferung*. Berlin.

Mansuelli, G. 1965. "Phuphluns." In *Enciclopedia dell' arte antica* 6: 141–42. Rome.

March, J. R. 1989. "Euripides' *Bakchai*: A Reconsideration in Light of Vase Paintings." *Bulletin of the Institute of Classical Studies* 36: 33–66.

Marek, C. 1985. "Katalog der Inschriften im Museum von Amasra." *Epigraphica Anatolica* 6: 133–56.

Martelli, M. 1987. *La ceramica degli Etruschi: La pittura vascolare*. Novara.

Massenzio, M. 1969. "Cultura e crisi permanente: La 'xenia' dionisiaca." *Studi e materiali di storia delle religioni* 40: 27–113.

——. 1970. *Cultura e crisi permanente: La 'xenia' dionisiaca*. Reprint of Massenzio 1969. Rome.

Mastronarde, D. J. 1990. "Actors on High: The Skene Roof, the Crane, and the Gods in Attic Drama." *Classical Antiquity* 9: 247–94.

Matz, F. 1963. ΔΙΟΝΥΣΙΑΚΗ ΤΕΛΕΤΗ: *Archäologische Untersuchungen zum Dionysoskult in hellenistischer und römischer Zeit*. Abhandlungen der Akademie der Wissenschaften in Mainz 15. Mainz.

——. 1968–75. *Die dionysischen Sarkophage*. 4 vols. Berlin.

Melchinger, S. 1990. *Das Theater der Tragödie: Aischylos, Sophokles, Euripides auf der Bühne ihrer Zeit*. Paperback ed. Munich.

Merkelbach, R. 1971. "Dionysisches Grabepigramm aus Tusculum." *Zeitschrift für Papyrologie und Epigraphik* 7:280.

——. 1972. "Milesische Bakchen." *Zeitschrift für Papyrologie und Epigraphik* 9: 77–83.

——. 1977. *Die Quellen des griechischen Alexanderromans*. 2d ed. Munich.

——. 1984. "Nochmals über den Tod des Knaben Sarapion." *Epigraphica Anatolica* 3: 38.

——. 1988. *Die Hirten des Dionysos: Die Dionysos-Mysterien der römischen Kaiserzeit und der bukolische Roman des Longus*. Stuttgart.

Merkelbach, R., and M. L. West. 1967. *Fragmenta Hesiodea*. Oxford.

Mette, H. J. 1959. *Die Fragmente der Tragödien des Aischylos*. Berlin.

Metzger, B. M. 1984. "A Classified Bibliography of the Graeco-Roman Mystery Religions 1924–73 with a Supplement 1974–77." *Aufstieg und Niedergang der römischen Welt* 2.17.3: 1259–1423.

Metzger, H. 1944–45. "Dionysos chthonien d'après les monuments figurés de la période classique." *Bulletin de correspondance hellénique* 68–69: 296–339.

——. 1951. *Les représentations dans la céramique attique du IVème siècle*. Paris.

——. 1965. *Recherches sur l'imagérie athénienne*. Paris.

Meyer, B. F., and E. P. Sanders, eds. 1982. *Jewish and Christian Self-Definition*. Vol. 3, *Self-Definition in the Graeco-Roman World*. London.

Miller, M. 1989. "The *Ependytes* in Classical Athens." *Hesperia* 58: 313–29.

Mitten, D., and S. Doeringer. 1967. *Master Bronzes from the Classical World*. Cambridge, Mass.

Moretti, L. 1986. "Il regolamento degli Iobacchi ateniensi." In Ecole de Rome 1986, 247–59.

Most, G. W. 1987. "Seeming and Being: Sign and Metaphor in Aristotle." In Amsler 1987, 11–33.

Moutsopoulos, E. 1962. "Euripide et la philosophie de la musique." *Revue des études grecques* 75: 398–447.

Müller, H. 1989. "Ein neues hellenistisches Weihepigramm aus Pergamon." *Chiron* 19: 499–553.
Müller, K. O. 1825. *Prolegomena zu einer wissenschaftlichen Mythologie*. Göttingen.
——. 1833. *Aeschylos Eumeniden: Griechisch und Deutsch, mit erläuternden Abhandlungen über die äussere Darstellung, und über den Inhalt und die Composition dieser Tragödie*. Göttingen.
Murray, G. 1912. "Excursus on the Ritual Forms Preserved in Greek Tragedy." In Harrison 1912, 341–63.
Musti, D. 1986. "Il dionisismo degli Attalidi: Antecedenti, modelli, sviluppi." In Ecole de Rome 1986, 105–28.
Nagler, M. 1974. *Spontaneity and Tradition: A Study in the Oral Art of Homer*. Berkeley and Los Angeles.
Nagy, H. 1988. *Votive Terracottas from "Vignaccia," Cerveteri, in the Lowie Museum of Anthropology*. Rome.
Napier, A. D. 1986. *Masks, Transformation, and Paradox*. Berkeley and Los Angeles.
Nielsen, M. 1990. "Sacerdotesse e associazioni cultuali femminili in Etruria." *Analecta Romana Instituti Danici* 19: 45–67.
Nietzsche, F. 1872. *Die Geburt der Tragödie aus dem Geiste der Musik*. Reprinted in Nietzsche 1972, 17–152.
——. 1967. *The Birth of Tragedy and the Case of Wagner*. Translated, with commentary, by W. Kaufmann. New York.
——. 1972. *Nietzsche Werke: Kritische Gesamtausgabe*. Vol. 3.1. Berlin and New York.
Nilsson, M. R. 1950. "Kleinasiatische Pseudo-Mysterien." *Bulletin de l'Institut Archéologique Bulgare* 16: 17–20.
——. 1952a. *Opuscula selecta*. Vol. 2. Lund.
——. 1952b. "Dionysos Liknites." *Bulletin de la Société Royale des Lettres de Lund*, 1–18.
——. 1955. *Geschichte der griechischen Religion*. Vol 1. 2d ed. Munich.
——. 1957a. *The Dionysiac Mysteries of the Hellenistic and Roman Age*. Skrifter utgivna av Svenska Institutet i Athen 5. Lund.
——. 1957b. "Royal Mysteries in Egypt." *Harvard Theological Review* 50: 65–66. Reprinted in Nilsson 1960, 326–28.
——. 1960. *Opuscula selecta*. Vol. 3. Lund.
——. 1961. *Geschichte der griechischen Religion*. Vol. 2. 2d ed. Munich.
——. 1967. *Geschichte der griechischen Religion*. Vol. 1. 3d ed. Munich.
Nock, A. 1928. "Notes on Ruler-Cult I-IV." *Journal of Hellenic Studies* 48: 21–43. Reprinted in Nock 1972, 1:134–59.
——. 1946. "Sarcophagi and Symbolism." *American Journal of Archaeology* 50: 140–70. Reprinted in Nock 1972, 2: 606–41.
——. 1972. *Essays on Religion and the Ancient World*. 2 vols. Edited by Z. Stewart. Cambridge, Mass.
Oakley, J. H. 1982. "The Anakalypteria." *Archäologischer Anzeiger*, 113–18.

——. 1990. *The Phiale Painter.* Mayence.
Obbink, D. 1988. "The Origin of Greek Sacrifice: Theophrastus on Religion and Cultural History." In Sharples 1988, 272–95.
Obbink, D., and G. Harrison. 1985. "Demeter in the Underworld." *Zeitschrift für Papyrologie und Epigraphik* 62: 75–81.
Ohlemutz, E. 1940. *Die Kulte und Heiligtümer der Götter in Pergamon.* Würzburg.
Oranje, H. 1984. *Euripides' Bacchae: The Play and Its Audience.* Mnemosyne Supplement 78. Leiden.
Otto, W. F. 1933. *Dionysos: Mythos und Kultus.* Frankfurt am Main.
——. 1965. *Dionysus: Myth and Cult.* Translation of Otto 1933 by R. B. Palmer. Bloomington, Ind., and London.
Oudemans, T. C. W., and A. P. M. H. Lardinois. 1987. *Tragic Ambiguity: Anthropology, Philosophy, and Sophocles' Antigone.* Leiden.
Padel, R. 1981. "Madness in Fifth-Century (B.C.) Athenian Tragedy." In Heelas and Lock 1981, 105–31.
Paglia, C. 1990: *Sexual Personae: Art and Decadence from Nefertiti to Emily Dickinson.* London and New Haven.
Pailler, J.-M. 1988. *Bacchanalia: La répression de 186 av. J.-C. à Rome et en Italie.* Bibliothèque des Ecoles Françaises d'Athènes et de Rome 270. Rome.
Pairault-Massa, F. 1978. "Une représentation Dionysiaque méconnue: L'urne de Chiusi (E. 39–40) du Musée Berlin." *Mélanges de l'Ecole Française de Rome, Antiquité* 90: 197–234.
——. 1987. "En quel sens parler de la romanisation du culte de Dionysos en Etrurie?" *MEFRA* 99: 573 ff.
Pallottino, M., and M. Torelli, eds. 1986. *Rasenna: Storia e civiltà degli Etruschi.* Milan.
Parke, H. W. 1977. *Festivals of the Athenians.* London.
Parke, H. W., and D. E. Wormell. 1956. *The Delphic Oracle.* 2 vols. Oxford.
Parker, R. 1983. *Miasma: Pollution and Purification in Early Greek Religion.* Oxford.
——. 1987. "Myths of Early Athens." In Bremmer 1987a, 187–214.
Paton, W. R., and E. L. Hicks. 1891. *The Inscriptions of Cos.* Oxford.
Payne, H. C. 1978. "Modernizing the Ancients: The Reconstruction of Ritual Drama, 1870–1920." *Proceedings of the American Philosophical Society* 122: 182–92.
Perdrizet, P. 1900. "Inscriptions de Philippes." *Bulletin de correspondance hellénique* 24: 209–323.
——. 1910. *Cultes et mythes du Pangée.* Paris and Nancy.
Pfiffig, A. 1975. *Religio etrusca.* Graz.
Pfuhl, E., and H. Möbius. 1977–79. *Die ostgriechischen Grabreliefs.* 2 vols. Mainz.
Picard, C. 1931. "Les luttes primitives d'Athènes et d' Eleusis." *Revue historique* 165: 1–76.
Pickard-Cambridge, A. W. 1927. *Dithyramb, Tragedy, and Comedy.* Oxford.
———. 1962. *Dithyramb, Tragedy, and Comedy.* 2d ed. of Pickard-Cambridge 1927, revised by T. B. L. Webster. Oxford.
——. 1988. *The Dramatic Festivals of Athens.* 2d ed., revised by J. Gould and D. M. Lewis. Oxford.

Poland, F. 1909. *Geschichte des griechischen Vereinswesens*. Leipzig.

Poulter, A., ed. 1983. *Ancient Bulgaria*. Vol. 1. Nottingham.

Pound, E. 1983. *The Cantos of Ezra Pound*. New York.

Powell, J. U. 1925. *Collectanea Alexandrina*. Oxford.

Prange, M. 1989. *Der Niobidenmaler und seine Werkstatt*. Frankfurt am Main.

Price, S. O. 1990. "Anacreontic Vases Reconsidered." *Greek, Roman and Byzantine Studies* 31: 133–75.

Privitera, G. A. 1970. *Dioniso in Omero e nella poesia greca arcaica*. Rome.

Prott, V. v. 1902. "Dionysos Kathegemon." *Mitteilungen des Deutschen Archäologischen Instituts, Athenische Abteilung* 27: 161–88 and 265–66.

Quandt, W. 1912. "De Baccho ab Alexandri aetate in Asia Minore culto." Dissertationes Philologicoe, Halenses 21.2, Halle.

Rabe, H. 1906. *Scholia in Lucianum*. Leipzig.

Radke, G. 1965. *Die Götter Altitaliens*. Münster.

Raeck, W. 1981. *Zum Barbarenbild in der Kunst Athens im 6. und 5. Jahrhundert v. Chr.* Bonn.

Rallo, A., ed. 1989. *Le donne in Etruria*. Rome.

Ramnoux, C. 1968. "Pourquoi les Présocratiques?" *La revue philosophique de Louvain* 66: 397–419.

Ramsey, W. M. 1901. "Deux jours en Phrygie." *Revue des études anciennes* 3: 276–77.

Rapp, A. 1872. "Die Mänade im griechischen Cultus, in der Kunst und Poesie." *Rheinisches Museum für Philologie* 27: 1–22 and 562–611.

Reichler, C., ed. 1989. *L'interprétation des textes*. Paris.

Reinhardt, K. 1933. *Sophokles*. Frankfurt am Main.

Rhodes, P. J. 1981. *A Commentary on the Aristotelian Athenaion Politeia*. Oxford.

Rice, E. E. 1983. *The Grand Procession of Ptolemy Philadelphus*. Oxford Classical and Philosophical Monographs. Oxford.

Richardson, E. 1979. "The Story of Ariadne in Italy." In Kopcke and Moore 1979, 189–95.

Richardson, N. J. 1974. *The Homeric Hymn to Demeter*. Oxford.

Ridgeway, W. 1915. *The Dramas and Dramatic Dances of Non-European Races in Special Reference to the Origin of Greek Tragedy*. Cambridge.

Robert, C. 1919. *Archäologische Hermeneutik*. Berlin.

Robert, L. 1957. "Une épigramme de Carie." *Revue de philologie* 31: 7–22. Reprinted in Robert 1969, 373–88.

——. 1969. *Opera minora selecta*. Vol. 1. Amsterdam.

——. 1983. *Fouilles d'Amyzon en Carie*. Paris.

Robinson, D. 1933. *Olynthus*. Vol. 5. Baltimore.

Roesch, P. 1982. *Etudes béotiennes*. Paris.

Rohde, E. 1898a. *Psyche: Seelencult und Unsterblichkeitsglaube der Griechen*. Vol. 1. 2d ed. Leipzig and Tübingen.

——. 1898b. *Psyche: Seelencult und Unsterblichkeitsglaube der Griechen*. Vol. 2. 2d ed. Leipzig and Tübingen.

——. 1925. *Psyche: The Cult of Souls and Belief in Immortality among the Greeks*. Translation of Rohde 1898a and 1898b by W. B. Hillis. London.

Roncalli, F. 1965. *Le lastre dipinte da Cerveteri*. Florence.

——. 1986. "L'arte." In Pallottino and Torelli 1986, 531–676.

Rose, H. J. 1936. "A Study of Pindar, Fragment 133 Bergk, 127 Bowra." In Bailey et al. 1936, 79–96.

Rosivach, V. 1979. "The Two Worlds of *Antigone*." *Illinois Classical Studies* 4: 16–26.

Roux, J. 1970. *Euripide: Les Bacchantes*. Vol. 1. Paris.

——. 1972. *Euripide: Les Bacchantes*. Vol. 2. Paris.

Rudhardt, J., and O. Reverdin, eds. 1981. *Le sacrifice dans l' antiquité*. Entretiens sur l' antiquité classique 27. Geneva.

Rusajeva, A. S. 1978. "Orfizm i kult Dionisa v Olvii" (Orphism and the Dionysos cult in Olbia). *Vestnik drevnej Istorii* 143: 87–104.

Sabbatucci, D. 1978. *Mito, rito, e storia*. Rome.

Saïd, S. 1988. "Bibliographie tragique 1900–1988: Quelques orientations." *Mètis* 3: 409–512.

Sandbach, F. H. 1969. *Plutarch's Moralia: Fragments*. Cambridge, Mass.

Sassi, M. M. 1983. "Dalla scienza delle religioni di Usener ad Aby Warburg." In Arrighetti, Bodei, and Cambiano 1983, 65–91.

Schauenburg, K. 1953. "Pluton und Dionysos." *Jahrbuch des Deutschen Archäologischen Instituts* 68: 38–72.

——. 1977. "Die nackte Erinys." In von Hoeckmann and Krug 1977, 247–54.

Schiassi, G. 1953. *Sofocle: Le Trachinie*. 2d ed. Florence.

Schiffler, B. 1976. *Die Typologie der Kentauren in der antiken Kunst*. Frankfurt am Main.

Schlesier, R. 1985. "Der Stachel der Götter: Zum Problem des Wahnsinns in der Euripideischen Tragödie." *Poetica* 17: 1–45.

——. 1986–87. "Der bittersüsse Eros: Ein Beitrag zur Geschichte und Kritik des Metapherbegriffs." *Archiv für Begriffsgeschichte* 30: 70–83.

——. 1987a. Review of Carpenter 1986. *Gnomon* 59: 519–24.

——. 1987b. "Das Heilige, das Unheimliche, das Unmenschliche." In Kamper and Wulf 1987, 99–113.

——. 1988a. "Die tragischen Masken des Dionysos: Bakchische Metamorphosen bei Euripides." Habilitationsdiss., Berlin.

——. 1988b. "Die Bakchen des Hades: Dionysische Aspekte von Euripides' *Hekabe*." *Mètis* 3: 111–35.

——. 1990a. "Jane Ellen Harrison." In Briggs and Calder 1990, 127–41.

——. 1990b. "Apopompe" and "Apotropäisch." In Cancik, Gladigow, and Laubscher 1990, 38–45.

——. 1991. "Prolegomena to Jane Harrison's Interpretation of Ancient Greek Religion." In Calder 1991, 185–226.

Schmidt, M. 1967. "Dionysien." *Antike Kunst* 10: 70–81.

Schöne, A. 1987. *Der Thiasos: Eine ikonographische Untersuchung über das Gefolge des Dionysos in der attischen Vasenmalerei des 6. und 5. Jhs. v. Chr.* Göteborg.

Scodel, R., ed. Forthcoming. *Theater and Society in the Classical World*. Ann Arbor.

Seaford, R. 1976. "The Origins of Satyric Drama." *Maia* 28: 209–21.
——. 1981. "Dionysiac Drama and the Dionysiac Mysteries." *Classical Quarterly* 31: 252–75.
——. 1984. *Euripides: Cyclops.* Oxford.
——. 1986a. "Immortality, Salvation, and the Elements." *Harvard Studies in Classical Philology* 90: 1–26.
——. 1986b. "Wedding Ritual and Textual Criticism." *Hermes* 114: 50–59.
——. 1987. "The Tragic Wedding." *Journal of Hellenic Studies* 107: 106–30.
——. 1988. "The Eleventh Ode of Bacchylides: Hera, Artemis, and the Absence of Dionysos." *Journal of Hellenic Studies* 108: 118–36.
——. 1989a. "The Attribution of Aeschylus, *Choephoroi* 691–99." *Classical Quarterly* 39: 302–6.
——. 1989b. "Homeric and Tragic Sacrifice." *Transactions of the American Philological Association* 119: 87–95.
——. 1990. "The Imprisonment of Women in Greek Tragedy." *Journal of Hellenic Studies* 110: 76–90.
Seale, D. 1982. *Vision and Stagecraft in Sophocles.* London and Canberra.
Segal, C. 1971. "Andromache's *Anagnorisis:* Formulaic Artistry in *Iliad* 22. 437–76." *Harvard Studies in Classical Philology* 75: 33–58.
——. 1978a. "The Menace of Dionysus: Sex Roles and Reversals in Euripides' *Bacchae.*" *Arethusa* 11: 185–202.
——. 1978b. "Pentheus and Hippolytus on the Couch and on the Grid: Psychoanalytic and Structuralist Readings of Greek Tragedy." *Classical World* 72: 129–48. Reprinted in Segal 1986, 268–93.
——. 1981. *Tragedy and Civilization: An Interpretation of Sophocles.* Cambridge, Mass.
——. 1982. *Dionysiac Poetics and Euripides' Bacchae.* Princeton.
——. 1986. *Interpreting Greek Tragedy: Myth, Poetry, Text.* Ithaca, N.Y.
Segre, M. 1938. "Due lettere di Silla." *Rivista di filologia e di istruzione classica* 66: 253–63.
——. 1941. "Documenti di storia ellenistica." *Atti Pontificia Accademia di archeologia* 17: 21–38.
Seidensticker, B. 1979. "Sacrificial Ritual in the *Bacchae.*" In Bowersock, Burkert, and Putnam 1979, 181–90.
Seltzer, R. M. 1989. *Religions of Antiquity: Religion, History, and Culture. Selections from the Encyclopedia of Religion.* New York and London.
Seyrig, H. 1963. "Questions cistophoriques." *Revue numismatique* 5: 22–31.
Sharpe, R. B. 1959. *Irony in the Drama: An Essay on Impersonation, Shock, and Catharsis.* Chapel Hill, N.C.
Sharples, R., ed. 1988. *Theophrastean Studies: On Natural Science, Physics, Metaphysics, Ethics, Religion, and Rhetoric.* New Brunswick, N.J.
Shelton, K. 1989. "Etruscan Mirrors in the University Museum." Unpublished paper.
Sherwin-White, S. 1978. *Ancient Cos.* Göttingen.

Shipp, G. P. 1972. *Studies in the Language of Homer*. Cambridge.

Siedentopf, H. B. 1990. "Der Wein und das Meer." In Vierneisel and Kaeser 1990, 319–24.

Sijpesteijn, P. J. 1983. "Remarks on Some Recently Published Inscriptions." *Zeitschrift für Papyrologie und Epigraphik* 52: 288–90.

Silk, M. S., and J. P. Stern. 1981. *Nietzsche on Tragedy*. Cambridge.

Simon, B. 1978. *Mind and Madness in Ancient Greece: The Classical Roots of Modern Psychiatry*. Ithaca, N.Y., and London.

Simon, E. 1953. *Opfernde Götter*. Berlin.

——. 1961. "Zum Fries der Mysterienvilla bei Pompeji." *Jahrbuch des Deutschen Archäologischen Instituts* 76: 111–72.

——. 1963. "Ein Anthesterien-Skyphos des Polygnotos." *Antike Kunst* 6: 6–22.

——. 1969. *Die Götter der Griechen*. Munich.

——. 1973. "Die Tomba dei Tori und der etruskische Apollonkult." *Jahrbuch des Deutschen Archäologischen Instituts* 88: 27–42.

——. 1982. "Satyr-Plays in the Time of Aeschylus." In Kurtz and Sparkes 1982, 123–48.

——. 1983. *Festivals of Attica: An Archaeological Commentary*. Madison, Wis.

——. 1985. *Die Götter der Griechen*. 3d ed. of Simon 1969. Darmstadt.

Simon, E., M. Hirmer, and A. Hirmer. 1981. *Die griechischen Vasen*. 2d ed. Munich.

Sissa, G., and M. Detienne, eds. 1989. *La vie quotidienne des dieux*. Paris.

Slater, P. E. 1968. *The Glory of Hera: Greek Mythology and the Greek Family*. Boston.

Slater, W. J. 1978. "Artemon and Anacreon: No Text without Context." *Phoenix* 32: 185–94.

Smith, M. 1974. "On the Wine God in Palestine." In *Salo Wittmayer Baron: Jubilee Volume on the Occasion of His Eightieth Birthday*, edited by S. Lieberman, 2: 815–29. New York and London.

Smith, W. R. 1894. *Lectures on the Religion of the Semites*. 2d ed. London.

Snell, B. 1967. *Scenes from Greek Drama*. Berkeley.

Snell, B., and H. Maehler. 1987. *Pindari carmina cum fragmentis*. 8th ed. Leipzig.

Snodgrass, A. 1967. *Arms and Armour of the Greeks*. London.

Sommerstein, A. H. 1989. *Aeschylus: Eumenides*. Cambridge.

Sourvinou-Inwood, C. 1988. "Le mythe dans la tragédie, la tragédie à travers le mythe: Sophocle *Antigone* vv. 944–87." In Calame 1988, 167–83.

Sowder, C. 1982. "Etruscan Mythological Figures." In de Grummond 1982, 100–128.

Spivey, N. 1987. *The Micali Painter and His Followers*. Oxford.

Spivey, N., and T. Rasmussen. 1986. "Dioniso e i pirati nel Museum of Art di Toledo." *Prospettiva* 44: 2–8.

Sprenger, M., G. Bartoloni, and M. Hirmer. 1977. *Die Etrusker*. Munich.

Stambolidis, N. C. 1987. Ο ΒΩΜΟΣ ΤΟΥ ΔΙΟΝΥΣΟΥ ΣΤΗΝ ΚΩ. Athens.

Stanford, W. B. 1939. *Ambiguity in Greek Literature*. Oxford.

Steingräber, S., ed. 1986. *Etruscan Painting*. New York.

Stephanis, I. 1988. *Διονυσιακοί Τεχνίται: Συμβολές στην προσωπογραφίαν του θεάτρου και της μουσικής των αρχαίων Ελλήνων*. Athens.
Stocking, G., Jr., ed. 1984. *Functionalism Historicized*. History of Anthropology 2. Madison, Wis.
Stone, L. M. 1981. *Costume in Aristophanic Comedy*. New York.
Surette, L. 1979. *A Light from Eleusis: A Study of Ezra Pound's Cantos*. Oxford.
Sutton, D. F. 1975. "A Series of Vases Illustrating the Madness of Lycurgus." *Rivista di studi classici* 23: 356–60.
Sutton, R. F. 1981. "The Interaction between Men and Women Portrayed on Attic Red-Figure Pottery." Diss., University of North Carolina, Chapel Hill.
Taplin, O. P. 1977. *The Stagecraft of Aeschylus: The Dramatic Use of Exits and Entrances in Greek Tragedy*. Oxford.
——. 1978. *Greek Tragedy in Action*. London.
——. 1983. "Unendingly Hermeneutic." Review of Segal 1982. *Times Literary Supplement*, 11 March 1983, 242.
Terrell, C. F. 1984. *A Companion to the Cantos of Ezra Pound*. Vol. 2. Berkeley and Los Angeles.
Thiersch, H. 1936. *Ependytes und Ephod*. Stuttgart.
Thomson, G. D. 1946. *Aeschylus and Athens: A Study in the Social Origins of Drama*. 2d ed. London.
——. 1973. *Aeschylus and Athens: A Study in the Social Origins of Drama*. 4th ed. London.
Thulin, C. 1919. "Fufluns." *Paulys Real-Encyclopädie der classischen Altertumswissenschaft* 7.1: 210–11.
Tillyard, E. 1923. *The Hope Vases*. Cambridge.
Tinnefeld, F. 1980. "Referat über zwei russische Aufsätze." *Zeitschrift für Papyrologie und Epigraphik* 38: 65–71.
Tiverios, M. 1976. *O Lydos*. Athens.
Tomaselli, S., and R. Porter, eds. 1986. *Rape*. Oxford.
Tondriau, J. 1946. "Les thiases dionysiaques royaux de la cour ptolémaïque." *Chronique d'Egypte* 41: 149–71.
——. 1952. "Dionysos, dieu royal: Du Bacchus tauromorphe primitif aux souverains hellénistiques 'Neo Dionysoi.'" *Annuaire l'Institut de Philologie et d'Histoire Orientales et Slaves* 12: 441–66.
Torelli, M. 1975. "Tyrannoi." *La parola del passato* 30: 417–33.
Trendall, A., and T. Webster. 1971. *Illustrations of Greek Drama*. London.
Tresp, A. 1914. *Die Fragmente der griechischen Kultschriftsteller*. Giessen.
Tsantsanoglou, K., and G. Parássoglou. 1987. "Two Gold Lamellae from Thessaly." *Hellenika* 38: 3–17.
Turcan, R. 1966. *Les sarcophages romains à représentations dionysiaques*. Paris.
——. 1986. "Bacchoi ou bacchants? De la dissidence des vivants à la ségrégation des morts." In Ecole de Rome 1986, 227–46.
——. 1989. *Les cultes orientaux dans le monde romain*. Paris.
van der Meer, L. B. 1987. *The Bronze Liver of Piacenza*. Amsterdam.
van Hoorn, G. 1951. *Choes and Anthesteria*. Leiden.

Vatin, C. 1983. "Une épigramme funéraire grecque de Cherchel." *Antiquités africaines* 19: 65–74.

Velardi, R. 1989. *Enthousiasmòs: Possessione rituale e teoria della comunicazione poetica in Platone*. Rome.

Vellacott, P. 1975. *Ironic Drama: A Study of Euripides' Method and Meaning*. Cambridge.

Veneri, A. 1986. "Dionysos." *Lexicon iconographicum mythologiae classicae* 3.1: 414–19.

Verdelis, N. M. 1950–51. "Χαλκῆ τεφροδόχος κάλπις ἐκ Φαρσάλων." *Archaiologikē ephēmeris*, 80–105.

——. 1953–54. "'Ορφικὰ ἐλάσματα ἐκ Κρήτης." *Archaiologikē ephēmeris*, part 2, 56–60.

Vérilhac, A.-M. 1978. *Paides Aōroi: Poésie funéraire*. 2 vols. Athens.

Vernant, J.-P. 1965a. "Figuration de l'invisible et catégorie psychologique du double: Le colossos." In Vernant 1965b, 251–64. Reprinted in Vernant 1985c, 325–38.

——. 1965b. *Mythe et pensée chez les Grecs: Etudes de psychologie historique*. Paris.

——. 1971. *Mythe et pensée chez les Grecs: Etudes de psychologie historique*. 2 vols. Enlarged two-volume edition of Vernant 1965b. Paris.

——. 1975. "Naissance d'images." *Journal de psychologie normale et pathologique* 72: 133–60. Reprinted in Vernant 1979, 105–37.

——. 1979. *Religions, histoires, raisons*. Paris.

——. 1981. *Mythe et pensée chez les Grecs: Etudes de psychologie historique*. 2 vols. Reprint of Vernant 1971. Paris.

——. 1983. *Myth and Thought among the Greeks*. Anonymous translation of Vernant 1971. London, Boston, and Melbourne.

——. 1985a. *La mort dans les yeux: Figures de l'Autre en Grèce ancienne*. Paris.

——. 1985b. *Mythe et pensée chez les Grecs: Etudes de psychologie historique*. 2 vols. Reprint of Vernant 1971. Paris.

——. 1985c. *Mythe et pensée chez les Grecs: Etudes de psychologie historique*. Paris. New one-volume edition of Vernant 1971.

——. 1986a. "Le Dionysos masqué des *Bacchantes* d'Euripide." In Vernant and Vidal-Naquet 1986, 237–70, and in Vernant 1990b, 215–46.

——. 1986b. "Conclusion." In Ecole de Rome 1986, 291–303.

——. 1987. "Greek Religion." *The Encyclopedia of Religion* 6: 99–118. Reprinted in Seltzer 1989, 163–92. The original French text for this article appeared subsequently in Vernant 1990a, 21–120.

——. 1988. "The Masked Dionysus of Euripides' *Bacchae*." In Vernant and Vidal-Naquet 1988, 381–412 and 501–5. Translation of Vernant 1986a.

——. 1989. *L'individu, la mort, l'amour: Soi-même et l'Autre en Grèce ancienne*. Paris.

——. 1990a. *Mythe et religion en Grèce ancienne*. Paris.

——. 1990b. *Figures, idoles, masques*. Paris.

——. 1991. *Mortals and Immortals: Collected Essays*. Edited by F. I. Zeitlin. Princeton.

Vernant, J.-P., and F. Frontisi-Ducroux. 1986. "Figures du masque en Grèce ancienne." In Vernant and Vidal-Naquet 1986, 25–43.

Vernant, J.-P., and P. Vidal-Naquet. 1971. *Mythe et tragédie en Grèce ancienne*. Vol. 1. Paris.
——. 1986. *Mythe et tragédie en Grèce ancienne*. Vol. 2. Paris.
——. 1988. *Myth and Tragedy in Ancient Greece*. Translation by J. Lloyd of Vernant and Vidal-Naquet 1971 and 1986. New York.
Verrall, A. W. 1910. *The Bacchants of Euripides and Other Essays*. Cambridge.
Versnel, H. S. 1970. *Triumphus*. Leiden.
——. 1977. "Polycrates and His Ring: Two Neglected Aspects." *Studi storico-religiosi* 1: 17–46.
——. 1990a. *Inconsistencies in Greek and Roman Religion*. Vol 1, *Ter Unus: Isis, Dionysos, Hermes: Three Studies in Henotheism*. Studies in Greek and Roman Religion 6. Leiden.
——. 1990b. "What's Sauce for the Goose Is Sauce for the Gander: Myth and Ritual, Old and New." In Edmunds 1990, 25–90.
Vian, F. 1963. *Les origines de Thèbes: Cadmos et les Spartes*. Paris.
Vicaire, P. 1968: "Place et figure de Dionysos dans la tragédie de Sophocle." *Revue des études grecques* 81: 351–73.
Vidal-Naquet, P. 1988. "Oedipus between Two Cities: An Essay on *Oedipus at Colonus*." In Vernant and Vidal-Naquet 1988, 329–59.
Vierneisel, K., and B. Kaeser, eds. 1990. *Kunst der Schale—Kultur des Trinkens*. Munich.
Villanueva Puig, M.-Ch. 1986. "A propos des thyiades de Delphes." In Ecole de Rome 1986, 31–51.
Voigt, E.-M. 1971. *Sappho et Alcaeus: Fragmenta*. Amsterdam.
Von der Mühll, P. 1952. *Kritisches Hypomnema zur Ilias*. Basel.
Von Hoeckmann, U., and A. Krug, eds. 1977. *Festschrift für Frank Brommer*. Mainz.
Vos, M. 1963. *Scythian Archers in Archaic Attic Vase-painting*. Groningen.
Voutiras, M. 1984. "Παρατηρήσεις σε τρία επιγράμματα: 3. Επιτύμβιο για έναν μύστη." *Hellenika* 35: 45–50.
Vürtheim, J. 1928. *Aischylos' Schutzflehende*. Amsterdam.
Waelkens, M. 1977. "Phrygian Votive Tombstones as Sources for the Social and Economic Life in Roman Antiquity." *Ancient Society* 8: 277–315.
Wallach, L., ed. 1966. *The Classical Tradition: Literary and Historical Studies in Honor of Harry Caplin*. Ithaca, N.Y.
Walsh, G. B. 1984. *Varieties of Enchantment: Early Greek Views of the Nature and Function of Poetry*. Chapel Hill, N.C.
Walters, E. 1988. *Attic Grave Reliefs That Represent Women in the Dress of Isis*. Hesperia Supplement 22. Princeton.
Wankel, H. 1976. *Demosthenes: Rede für Ktesiphon über den Kranz*. Heidelberg.
Webster, T. B. L. 1964. *Hellenistic Poetry and Art*. London.
——. 1966. "Three Plays by Euripides." In Wallach 1966, 83–97.
——. 1967. *The Tragedies of Euripides*. London.
——. 1972. *Potter and Patron in Classical Athens*. London.
Wehrli, F. 1949. *Die Schule des Aristoteles*. Vol. 4, *Demetrios von Phaleron*. Basel.
Weinreich, O. 1948. *Epigramm und Pantomimus*. Heidelberg.

West, M. L. 1978. *Hesiod: Works and Days*. Oxford.

——. 1982. "The Orphics of Olbia." *Zeitschrift für Papyrologie und Epigraphik* 45: 17–29.

——. 1983a. *The Orphic Poems*. Oxford.

——. 1983b. "Tragica VI." *Bulletin of the Institute of Classical Studies* 30: 63–71.

——. 1990. *Studies in Aeschylus*. Stuttgart.

Whallon, W. 1964. "Maenadism in the *Oresteia*." *Harvard Studies in Classical Philology* 68: 317–27.

Wieten, J. H. 1915. "De tribus lamineis aureis." Diss., Leiden.

Wilamowitz-Moellendorff, U. von. 1872. "Zukunftsphilologie!" Reprinted in Gründer 1969, 27–55.

——. 1873. "Zukunftsphilologie! Zweites Stück." Reprinted in Gründer 1969, 113–35.

——. 1931. *Der Glaube der Hellenen*. Vol. 1. Berlin.

——. 1932. *Der Glaube der Hellenen*. Vol. 2. Berlin.

——. 1959. *Der Glaube der Hellenen*. 2 vols. 3d ed. of Wilamowitz-Moellendorff 1931 and 1932. Darmstadt.

——. 1973. *Der Glaube der Hellenen*. Vol. 2. Reprint of Wilamowitz-Moellendorff 1959. Darmstadt.

Wilhelm, A. 1937. "ΣΥΜΜΕΙΞΙΣ." *Anzeiger der Österreichischen Akademie der Wissenschaften in Wien* 74: 39–57.

Willers, D. 1985. "Vom Etruskischen zum Römischen: Noch einmal zu einem Spiegelrelief in Malibu." *J. Paul Getty Museum Journal* 14: 21–36.

Willink, C. W. 1966. "Some Problems of Text and Interpretation in the *Bacchae* 1." *Classical Quarterly* 16: 27–50.

——. 1986. *Euripides: Orestes*. Oxford.

Wiman, I. 1990. *Malstria-Malena: Metals and Motifs in Etruscan Mirror Crafts*. Studies in Mediterranean Archaeology 91. Göteborg.

Winkler, J. J. 1990a. "The Ephebes' Song." In Winkler and Zeitlin 1990, 30–62.

——. 1990b. *The Constraints of Desire: The Anthropology of Sex and Gender in Ancient Greece*. New York and London.

Winkler, J. J., and F. I. Zeitlin, eds. 1990. *Nothing to Do with Dionysos? Athenian Drama in Its Social Context*. Princeton.

Winnington-Ingram, R. P. 1948. *Euripides and Dionysus: An Interpretation of the Bacchae*. Cambridge.

——. 1954. "A Religious Function of Greek Tragedy: A Study in the *Oedipus Coloneus* and the *Oresteia*." *Journal of Hellenic Studies* 74: 16–24.

——. 1980. *Sophocles: An Interpretation*. Cambridge.

Woodward, A. 1980. *Ezra Pound and the Pisan Cantos*. London and Boston.

Wrede, H. 1981. *Consecratio in formam deorum*. Mainz.

Wrede, W. 1928. "Der Maskengott." *Mitteilungen des Deutschen Archäologischen Instituts, Athenische Abteilung* 53: 66–95.

Zanker, P. 1965. *Wandel der Hermesgestalt in der attischen Vasenmalerei*. Bonn.

——. 1989. *Die trunkene Alte*. Frankfurt am Main.

Zeitlin, F. I. 1981. *Under the Sign of the Shield: Semiotics and Aeschylus' Seven against Thebes*. Rome.

——. 1982. "Cultic Models of the Female: Rites of Dionysus and Demeter." *Arethusa* 15: 129–57.

——. 1985a. "The Power of Aphrodite: Eros and the Boundaries of the Self in the *Hippolytus*." In Burian 1985, 52–111 and 189–208.

——. 1985b. "Playing the Other: Theater, Theatricality, and the Feminine in Greek Drama." *Representations* 11: 63–94. Reprinted as Zeitlin 1990a, 63–96.

——. 1986a. "Thebes: Theater of Self and Society in Athenian Drama." In Euben 1986, 130–67. Reprinted with revisions as Zeitlin 1990b, 130–67.

——. 1986b. "Configurations of Rape in Greek Myth." In Tomaselli and Porter 1986, 122–51 and 261–64.

——. 1989. "Mysteries of Identity and Designs of the Self in Euripides' *Ion*." *Proceedings of the Cambridge Philological Society* 215: 144–97.

——. 1990a. "Playing the Other: Theater, Theatricality, and the Feminine in Greek Drama." In Winkler and Zeitlin 1990, 63–96.

——. 1990b. "Thebes: Theater of Self and Society in Athenian Drama." In Winkler and Zeitlin 1990, 130–67.

——. 1991. "Euripides' *Hekabe* and the Somatics of Dionysiac Drama." *Ramus* 20: 53–94.

Zuntz, G. 1963a. "Once More the So-Called 'Edict of Philopator on the Dionysiac Mysteries' (*BGU* 1211)." *Hermes* 91: 228–39. Reprinted in Zuntz 1972, 88–101.

——. 1963b. "On the Dionysiac Fresco in the Villa dei Misteri at Pompeii." *Proceedings of the British Academy* 49: 177–202.

——. 1971. *Persephone: Three Essays on Religion and Thought in Magna Graecia.* Oxford.

——. 1972. *Opuscula selecta.* Manchester and Cambridge.

# Index of Passages Cited

For the abbreviations used here, e.g., "*FGrH*" or "Nauck²," see above pages ix–xii; in the case of citations by editor's name and date of publication, e.g., "Demetrius of Phaleron fr. 170 (Wehrli, 1949)," see the Bibliography, pp. 303–29.


Achaeus: *Omphale fr. 33 (TrGF 1)*, 219n
Achilles Tatius: *2.2.1–3.3*, 85n
Aelian: *De Natura Animalium 12.34*, 74n; *Varia Historia 3.42*, 116n, 124n, 246n
Aeschylus: *Agamemnon: 239*, 120n; *462*, 141n; *690–92*, 120nn; *928–29*, 126n; *1178–81*, 120n; *1235*, 129n; *1235–37*, 131n; *1322–23*, 142n; *Bassarae: fr. 23a.2 (TrGF 3)*, 110n; *fr. 83 (Mette, 1959)*, 278n; *Edoni: fr. 58 (TrGF 3)*, 113n, 166n; *fr. 59 (TrGF 3)*, 204; *fr. 61 (TrGF 3)*, 45n, 204n; *fr. 62 (TrGF 3)*, 45n; *Eumenides: 24–25*, 94n, 116n, 155n; *25–26*, 133n; *52, 252, 370*, 141n; *500*, 94n, 98n, 114, 131n, 140; *Libation Bearers: 691–99*, 103; *697*, 113n; *698*, 94n, 103n, 129n, 131; *698–99*, 113n, 131n; *1049*, 142n; *Psychagogoi fr. 273a.9 (TrGF 3)*, 14n; *Seven Against Thebes: 191, 194, 200–201*, 139; *341–44*, 160; *423*, 156n; *423–36*, 98n; *487*, 161; *498*, 94nn, 98, 99n, 133; *501*, 161; *681, 698–91*, 139nn; *699–700*, 139; *734, 748*, 139nn; *781–83*, 150n; *801–2, 804, 811–17, 820–21, 828*, 139nn; *836*, 94nn, 133, 139n; *877, 880, 953–60*, 139n; *Suppliant Women: 223–26*, 138n; *562–64*, 99n; *564*, 94nn, 133; *Theori: fr. 78a (TrGF 3)*, 45n, 204; *Unplaced Fragments: fr. 382 (TrGF 3)*, 122n; *Xantriae: fr. 171 (TrGF 3)*, 127n
Alcaeus: *fr. 129 (Voigt, 1971)*, 74n
Anacreon: *fr. 12 (PMG) = fr. 2 (PLG)*, 54n
*Anthologia Palatina. See Palatine Anthology*
Antoninus Liberalis: *Metamorphoses 10*, 116n, 124nn
Apollodorus: *1.6.2*, 50n; *2.2.2*, 124n, 131n; *3.5.1*, 143n, 157n, 196–98, 202, 272n; *3.5.2*, 132n; *3.5.3*, 175n, 231–32; *3.5.5*, 174n, 176
Apuleius: *Metamorphoses 8.7*, 287n
Aristophanes: *Acharnians: 247–79*, 58–59; *263*, 53n; *Birds: 1734*, 118n; *Clouds: 603*, 155n; *1011–14*, 210n; *Frogs: 46*, 50n; *53*, 172n; *479*, 50; *Wasps: 10*, 267n; *Woman of the Thesmophoria: 136*, 45n
Aristophanes of Byzantium: Hypotheses to Eur. *Bacchae* and *Phoen. Wom.*, 123n
Aristotle: *Constitution of the Athenians: 3.5*, 55, 135, 267n; *Poetics: 7.1451a14, 21.1457b20–22*, 93n
Arrian: *Anabasis: 5.1.1, 6.28, 7.10.6*, 262n
Athenaeus: *2.38c–d*, 82n; *2.47*, 181n; *3.78c*, 2n; *4.148b–c*, 288n; *5.196a–203b*, 262n; *5.198a–c*, 262, 264n; *5.198e*, 262n, 263; *5.200d–201c*, 263, 272n; *6.253d*, 270n; *11.465*, 81n; *11.466–67*, 219n; *14.656a*, 82n; *15.659–60*, 262n; *15.693d–e*, 82n

Biblical passages: *Apocrypha:* 3 Maccabees 2:29, 30, 263nn; *New Testament:* John 5:56, Philippians 2:17, 65; *Old Testament:* Deuteronomy 12:23, Genesis 9:4, 66n; Leviticus 17:11, 65, 66n

Callimachus: *Hymn to Delos 47, Hymn to Zeus 79–81,* 42n
Callixenus: *FGrH 627 F 2,* 262nn
Catullus: *61.209–13, 61.214–18, 61.323–81, 61.342–60,* 118n
Cicero: *De Natura Deorum: 3.41,* 65; *3.58,* 265n
Cleanthes: *fr. 538 (SVF 1),* 269n
Clement of Alexandria: *Protrepticus: 2.18.1,* 29n; *2.22,* 291n; *2.30,* 57; *16.2,* 268n; *48,* 263n
Cratinus: *fr. 40 (PCG 4),* 50n
Cyriacus of Ancona: *Codex Vaticanus 5250,* 294n

Demetrius of Phaleron: *fr. 170 (Wehrli, 1949),* 269n
Demosthenes: *Against Meidias 52,* 134; *Against Neaera 73–75,* 56, 135n; *On the Crown: 259,* 113nn; *260,* 265n
Dio Chrysostomus: *15.9,* 174n
Diodorus Siculus: *2.38,* 262n; *3.65.5–6,* 157n; *3.66,* 134n; *3.74.6,* 50n; *4.3.2,* 71–72; *4.3.3,* 31n; *4.5.2,* 185; *4.25.4,* 175n; *34–35.13,* 265n
Diogenes Laertius: *1.96,* 138n
Dionysius of Halicarnassus: *On Epideictic Speeches: 2.265, 2.266,* 118nn
Duris: *FGrH 76 F 13,* 270n

Eratosthenes: *Catasterismi: 24,* 272n
*Etymologicum Magnum, s.v. "Gallos,"* 263n
Eumelus: *Europia fr. 1 (EGF),* 157n; 198n; 272n
Euphorion: *fr. 26 (Powell, 1925),* 138n
Euphronius: *Priapeia (Powell, 1925),* 269n
Euripides: *Alcestis 918–22,* 118n; *Alex. fr. 7,* 128n; *Andromache: 830,* 120n; *103–4,* 127n; *103–9,* 124n; *Antiope: fr. 16 (Kambitsis, 1972) = fr. 198 (Nauck²),* 113n; *fr. 37 (Kambitsis, 1972) = fr. 203 (Nauck²),* 181; *fr. 48 (Kambitsis, 1972),* 179–80; *fr. 224 (Nauck²),* 181n; *Bacchae: 1,* 31n; *4,* 205; *5,* 31n; *35–36,* 122n, 132n, 140n; *39–40,* 137; *40,* 94n; *48–50,* 151; *50–54,* 160; *52,* 116n, 133n; *53–54,* 205; *115,* 20n; *117–19,* 116n, 117n; *124–25,* 271; *134–67,* 154; *135–36,* 20n; *137,* 193; *140,* 75; *144–50,* 20n, 127n; *206–9,* 25n; *209–10,* 134n, 137; *221–25,* 160; *223,* 138n; *224,* 73n; *225,* 54; *226–27, 231,* 122n; *233–34,* 35n; *236,* 54, 160; *274,* 123n; *274–85,* 83–84, 165; *284,* 65; *284–85,* 84n, 85; *286–97,* 84n; *302,* 160; *302–4,* 160n; *306–8,* 155n; *314–20,* 61n, 160n; *330,* 123n; *338–39,* 143; *402–9,* 160; *421–23,* 25n; *439,* 19n; *443,* 122n; *445,* 146n; *451–60,* 50; *453–54,* 50n; *459,* 160; *473,* 73n; *498,* 25n, 146n; *500–502,* 21n; *515,* 122n; *585,* 166n; *613,* 25n, 146n; *631,* 88; *649,* 25n, 146n; *686–88,* 160n; *694,* 122n; *699–702,* 122n, 132n; *724,* 73; *731,* 110; *733,* 132n; *737–38,* 196; *752,* 116n, 132n; *761–64,* 116n; *772,* 25n, 41; *780–85,* 160; *796,* 73; *812,* 138n; *813,* 160; *856,* 73; *860–61,* 134nn; *862–76,* 113n; *940,* 160n; *966–70,* 138n; *973–76,* 123n; *977,* 143; *985–86,* 123n; *998–99,* 77; *1021,* 19n; *1056,* 111n, 122n, 127n; *1096,* 131n; *1114,* 73, 123n; *1133,* 133n; *1184,* 69, 70, 138n; *1185–87,* 123n; *1192,* 75; *1226,* 123n; *1236–37,* 116n; *1242,* 136n; *1246–47,* 72–73; *1250,* 125n; *1254,* 123n; *1273,* 124; *1304,* 125n; *1308,* 123n, 125n; *1313,* 125n; *1319,* 123n; *1363–65,* 125n; *1366–70,* 124; *1374–76,* 125n; *1383–87,* 124, 130; *Cretans: fr. 79.11 (Austin, 1968) = fr. 472 (Nauck²),* 14n, 75; *Cyclops: 3,* 100n; *3–5,* 196, 272n; *99,* 207n; *220–21,* 212; *369,* 70; *515,* 120n; *519–26,* 78–79; *Electra: 497,* 94n; *573–74, 860,* 113n; *1032,* 94nn, 100; *1345,* 141n; *Erechtheus: fr. 65 (Austin, 1968),* 166nn; *Hecuba: 90,* 109n; *121,* 94n, 128n; *656,* 132n; *676,* 128n; *686–87,* 131; *689,* 131n; *716,* 110n, 131; *1076,* 110n; *1077,* 110, 132; *1157,* 132; *Helen: 50,* 14n; *543,* 94nn, 122n; *543–45,* 127n; *640,* 118n; *724,* 126n; *1353–68,* 113n; *1364,* 94n; *1433–35,* 118n; *Heracles: 682–84,* 104; *820,* 106; *890,* 105n; *896–97,* 130n; *897,* 94n; *898, 905,* 166n; *966–67,* 130–31; *1085,* 130n; *1119,* 130n, 151; *1122, 1142,* 130n; *Hippolytus: 215–18,* 104, 109, 110nn; *215–22,* 127n; *339, 454,* 94n; *545–54,* 127n; *550,* 94n; *550–51, 552,* 111nn; *560,* 132n; *612,* 96n; *755–56,* 127n; *954,* 94n; *1131–50,* 106n; *1140–41,* 110n; *1344, 1401, 1425–30,* 112nn; *Hypsipyle: fr. 64 (Bond, 1963),* 178; *fr. 752 (Nauck²),* 155n; *Ion: 6, 19–21,* 169; *216–18,* 168; *218,* 94n; *222–32,* 169; *545–55,* 61n; *550,* 127n; *550–53,* 94n; *553,* 168; *585–657,* 170; *653,* 168; *656,* 171n; *711–21,* 169; *714–17,* 155n; 168; *716,* 110n; *717,* 14n; *933,* 169; *989, 1003–5,* 170; *1048–49,* 14n; *1048–1105,* 165; *1074–86,* 168, 171n; *1130, 1203–5, 1231–35,* 168; *1240,* 94n; *1440–44,* 169, 170; *1465–67,* 168; *1553–1605,* 166; *Iphigenia at Aulis: 1061,* 94n; *1063,* 118n; *Iphigenia at Tauris: 159, 633,* 249n; *941–60,* 131n; *1243,* 94n; *Medea: 1147,* 120n; *1282–85,* 123n; *383, 806, 849,* 132n; *Orestes: 321,* 141n; *338,* 94n; *339,* 131n, 140n; *408,* 141n; *411,* 131, 140n; *835,* 131n, 140n; *1603,* 73n; *Phoenician Women: 21,* 94nn; *89,* 120; *193–94,* 119–20; *226,* 155n; *453,* 132n; *638–56,* 154; *639–66, 667,* 162; *676–89,* 163; *784–800,* 133n, 160, 177–78; *789,* 131n; *792,* 105n; *794,* 131n; *906–8, 1040–62, 1062–64,* 162; *1180,* 156n; *1275,* 120; *1436–37,* 121n; *1485–92,* 119; *1489,* 94n, 100, 163; *1489–92,* 121n; *1496,* 125n; *1504,* 119, 125n; *1520,* 121n; *1525,* 132n; *1636,* 119; *1659, 1671–81,* 121n; *1675,* 163; *1751–53,* 130; *1751–57,* 181; *1752,* 94n; *1757,* 130n; *Suppliant Women: 496–99,* 98n; *564,* 133; *832–35, 860–61, 985,* 167n; *990–94,* 125–26; *990–98,* 118n; *1000,* 166n; *1000–1001,* 126; *1001,* 94n, 125n; *1004,* 166n; *1004–5,* 126; *1006–7,*

126n; *1025*, 125; *1038–42*, 125n; *1039*, 126n; *1042*, 166n; *1048–71*, 167n; *1062*, 125n; *1077–78*, 167n; *1095*, *1133*, 126n; *1183–1226*, 166; *Trojan Women: 169*, 94n; *298–99*, 128n; *307*, 100, 128; *311–13*, 118n, 129n; *327*, *336*, *340*, 129nn; *342*, 128; *342–43*, 128n, 129n; *343–49*, 128n; *344*, 129n; *344–51*, 128n; *349*, 100, 128n; *351–52*, *353–54*, 129nn; *359*, 128; *359–60*, 129n; *364*, 128; *367*, 128n; *404–5*, 129n; *408*, 128n; *415*, 100, 128n; *429–30*, 128n; *445*, *448–50*, 129nn; *453*, 132n; *455–57*, *460–61*, 129nn; *461*, 128; *500*, 128n

Eusebius: *Praeparatio Evangelica 3.1.2*, 135n

Firmicus Maternus: *De Errore Profanorum Religionum 26.1*, 268n

Harpocration: *s.v. "Homêridai,"* 123n; *s.v. "leukê,"* 244n

Heraclitus: *FVS 22 B 51*, 107n

Herodotus: *1.32*, 126n; *2.48–49*, 58; *2.81*, 278n; *4.72*, 243n, 256n; *5.74*, 180n; *5.92*, 138n; *8.137–38*, 266n

Hesiod: *Catalogue of Women: fr. 123 (Merkelbach and West, 1967)*, 208; *fr. 131 (Merkelbach and West, 1967)*, 124n; *Theogony: 187*, 42n; *941*, 178; *Works and Days: 164*, 178; *235*, 118n

Hesychius: *s.v. "Enorches,"* 53n; *s.v. "katabolê,"* 73n; *s.v. "Limnagenes,"* 288n; *s.v. "Thuonidas,"* 53n

Homer: *Hymn to Demeter: 41*, 120n; *386*, 102n, 115n, 132n; *480–85*, 248n; *Hymn to Dionysus (VII): 13–24*, 17n; *Iliad: 6.119*, 272n; *6.130–40*, 116, 157n; *6.132*, 115, 116n, 198; *6.135–37*, 50; *6.297–311*, 146n; *6.344*, *6.356*, 110n; *6.389*, 115, 116n; *6.393*, *6.433–39*, 116; *6.440–41*, 117n; *6.441–46*, 145; *6.448*, *6.466–74*, 117nn; *6.467*, 116n; *6.476–81*, 119; *6.480–81*, 118n; *6.492*, 116; *6.500*, 142n; *7.467–72*, 176n; *8.299*, 143n; *21.481*, 110n; *22.70*, 143; *22.460–61*, 102n, 115n, 116; *22.468*, 120n; *22.468–72*, 117n; *22.477–84*, 117; *22.484–506*, 119; *22.503*, 116n; *23.170*, 249n; *23.296*, 144; *24.12*, 143n; *24.114*, 144; *24.726–35*, 119; *Odyssey: 3.567*, 146n; *4.207–8*, 118; *11.321–25*, 232; *11.324*, 54; *11.325*, 122n, 232; *18.406*, 144; *19.518–23*, 123n; *20.276–78*, *21.258–59*, 146n; *21.298*, 144n

Homeric *Hymns*. *See* Homer

Horace: *Odes 2.19.1–4*, 17

Hyginus: *Fabulae: 2*, 124n; *4*, 122n, 124n; *7–8*, 174n; *88*, 138n; *132*, 157n; *206*, 138n; *242*, 157n

Iamblichus: *de Mysteriis 1.11*, 59n

Inscriptions: *CIG 4000*, 289n; *CIL: 2.1.686*, 289n; *2.704*, *3.703*, 286n; *6(3).21521*, 288n; *CIRB 913*, 293n; *GV: 430*, 283n; *509*, 285n; *590*, 293n; *694*, 285n; *879*, 292n; *1301*, 281n; *1410*, 293n; *1583*, 282n; *1755*, 292n; *1842*, 293n; *ICreticae 2.13.31*, 251n; *IG 1²: 45*, 57n; *IG* 1³: *46*, 57n; *IG 2²: 2948*, 293n; *4841*, 287n; *5056*, 179; *7857a*, 283n; *11674*, 288n; *12664*, 283n; *13139*, 289n; *13151b*, 281n; *IG 4: 207*, 285n; *666*, 287n; *IG 10: (2.1) 260*, 288n; *(2.1) 503*, *(2.1) 506*, 284nn; *IG 12: 2.503*, 53n; *3 Suppl. 1296*, 264n; *5.972*, 284n; *IG 14: 871*, 278n; *2124*, 283n; *IGBR: 3.2.1579*, 281n; *3.2.1864*, 285n, 293n; *IGUR: 1150*, 284n; *1169*, 289n; *1228*, 290n; *1260*, 281n; *1324*, 287n; *IKlaudiu Polis: 83*, 283n; *IKyzikos: 26*, 285n; *IMagnesia: 117*, 286n; *INikaia 2.2: 1324*, *1325*, 285nn; *IPerg: 221*, 267n; *248*, 264n, 266n; *319*, *320*, 267n; *ISmyrna: 1.515*, 284n; *1.525*, 281n; *2.728*, 294n; *LSAM: 48*, 70–71, 274n; *55*, 274n; *LSCG: 51*, 245n, 286n; *97*, 249n; *166*, 273n; *LSS: 18*, 61–62, 77; *120*, 249n, 278n; *OGI: 50*, *51*, *331*, *735*, 264nn; *SEG: 4.398*, 286n; *21.541*, 62n; *27.511*, *27.514*, 270n; *29.1264*, 267n; *31.633*, 294n; *33.848*, 290n; *34.1266*, 285n; *35.496*, 267n; *SIG: 978*, 274n; *1012*, 273n; *1044*, 135n; *TAM: 3.1.841*, 284n; *3.1.922*, 292n; *5.1.477*, 289n; *5.1.744*, 284n; *5.1.806*, 285n; *5.1.817*, *5.1.822*, 284n

Isocrates: 2.20, 73n

Libanius: *Epistulae 1212–13*, 267n

Livy: *39.8–18*, 223

Lucian: *Dialogi Meretricii 9*, 124n; *Nigrinus 2*, 247n

Lycophron: *212*, 53n

Megasthenes: *FGrH 715 F 4*, 262n

Menander Rhetor: *2.402–3*, *2.404.27*, *2.407.9*, *2.407.23*, 118nn

Nonnus: *21.166*, 157n; *27.302*, 140n; *32.125–50*, 196

Orpheus: *Fragments: fr. 31 (OF)*, 263n; *fr. 34 (OF)*, 271; *fr. 35 (OF)*, 29n, 271; *fr. 207–10 (OF)*, 271; *fr. 210 (OF)*, 132n; *Hymns: 46.1–3*, *55.7*, 54n

Ovid: *Fasti: 3.510–12*, 232; *Metamorphoses: 3.529–30*, 134n; *3.572–691*, 15n; *3.609–10*, 17n; *3.611–12*, 16; *3.658–59*, 17n, 21n, 270; *4.33*, *4.390*, *4.394–98*, 116n; *4.523*, *6.587–674*, 124n

Pacuvius: *fr. 12*, 174n

*Palatine Anthology: 3.2*, *3.4*, *3.5*, *3.7*, *3.9*, *3.10*, *3.16*, 176nn; *7.24*, *7.26–28*, *7.30*, 281n; *7.82*, 283n; *7.104–5*, 281nn; *7.321*, 282n; *7.329*, *7.353*, *7.384*, *7.398*, 281nn; *7.412*, *7.414*, 283n; *7.455*, *7.456*, *7.457*, 281n; *7.485*, 283n; *7.533*, 281n; *7.579*, 282n; *16.7*, *16.289*, 283nn

Papyri: *P. Antinoöpolis 18*, 269n; *P. Gurob 1*, 263n; *P. Herculaneum 1428 fr. 19*, 84n; *P. Lille 76 a–c*, 175n; *P. Oxyrhynchus 852*, 173n; *P. Oxyrhynchus 2465*, 263n
Pausanias: *1.23.7*, 213; *1.38.6*, 166n; *1.41–43*, 136n; *2.2.6, 2.7.6*, 2n, 273; *2.20.4*, 116n; *2.23.7*, 134n; *2.37.5*, 175n, 231; *3.20.11*, 120n; *4.27.6*, 116n; *7.19–21*, 136n; *7.20.1*, 136; *7.21.1–5*, 136n; *8.15.3*, 38n; *9.12.2, 9.17.3*, 161n; *9.31.2*, 54n; *10.12.10, 10.15.3*, 265n; *10.19.3*, 53n
Phanodemus: *FGrH 325 F 12*, 81n
Philochorus: *FGrH 328 F 5, FGrH 328 F 173*, 82nn
Philodemus: *P. Herc. 1428 fr. 19*, 84n
Philostratus: *Heroicus 67.7 (de Lannoy, 1977)*, 71n; *Imagines 2.17 (Kayser, 1870)*, 45n
Pindar: *Dithyramb 2*, 271; *Fragments: fr. 133 (Snell and Maehler, 1987)*, 244; *fr. 137 (Snell and Maehler, 1987)*, 248n
Plato: *Gorgias 485e3–486d1*, 174; *Laws: 672b*, 272n; *790d*, 274n; *Meno 81b*, 242; *Phaedrus 265b*, 93n; *Republic: 363c–d*, 246; *364c*, 244; *571c, 619b*, 132n
Plutarch: *Alcibiades 2.5*, 219n; *Alexander: 2–3*, 261n, 265n; *67*, 262n; *Antonius: 24*, 264n; *60*, 288n; *75, 85–86*, 264n; *Cleomenes 33*, 263n; *de E apud Delphos 9*, 93n; *Fragments: fr. 157 (Sandbach, 1969) = fr. 78 (Tresp, 1914)*, 135n; *Moralia: 60a*, 263n; *299b*, 267n; *299e–f*, 74n, 124n, 138n; *388a–89c*, 93n, 280n; *527e*, 57; *611d–e*, 280n; *615a*, 91n; *716b*, 146n; *996c*, 294n; *Quaest. Conv. 1.1.5*, 91n; *Quaest. Gr.: 36*, 267n; *38*, 74n
Polemon Historicus: *FHG 3.135.42*, 53n
Polyaenus: *4.1*, 262n
Porphyry: *De Abstinentia 2.55*, 74n
Prodicus: *FVS 84 B 5*, 83n
Propertius: *3.15.11–42*, 174n
Ptolemy: *7.2.20*, 213n

Sallustius: *On the Gods*, 249n
Sappho (Voigt, 1971): *fr. 17*, 135n; *fr. 23*, 126n; *fr. 44.7*, 120n; *fr. 44.11*, 126n; *fr. 44.34*, 118; *fr. 105.1*, 120n; *fr. 129*, 135n
Satyrus: *FGrH 631 F 1*, 263n
Scholia: to Aeschylus: *Seven 164*, 162n; *Seven 981*, 157n; to Apoll. Rhod.: *1.735*, 174n; to Aristoph.: *Acharnians 146*, 140n; *Frogs 482*, 171n; to Eur.: *Phoen. Wom. 1062*, 162n; to Homer: *Il. 6.131*, 157n, 272n; *Od. 5.334*, 124n; to Lucian: *Dialogi Meretricii 7*, 59n; to Lycophron: *12*, 175n; to Soph.: *Oed. King 20*, 163n
Seneca: *Suasoriae 1.6*, 288n
Servius: *Aeneid: 1.720*, 54n; *3.14*, 157n
Sextus Empiricus: *Adversus Mathematicos 9.18*, 83n
Sidonius Apollinaris: *Carmina 15.191*, 118n
Socrates of Rhodes: *FGrH 192 F 2*, 264n
Sophocles: *Antigone: 79, 126, 131, 133*, 156; *133–37*, 133; *134–40, 135–37*, 156; *136*, 94nn, 98n; *136–37*, 131n; *147, 150–54*, 156; *153*, 104; *361*, 158n; *569*, 159n; *585*, 158n; *777, 780*, 155; *781*, 156; *786*, 159n; *790, 793–96, 801*, 156; *801–22*, 142n; *804, 810–11, 816*, 120n; *824*, 180; *824–31*, 158n; *886, 891*, 120n; *891–904*, 121n; *894, 917–20*, 155; *938*, 158; *941*, 139n; *947*, 120n; *952, 955–65, 981–82*, 157; *984*, 158n; *1075*, 155; *1115*, 159n; *1119–20, 1122–23*, 155; *1126–27*, 127n; *1136–37*, 155; *1144*, 155, 159n, 160; *1151*, 155; *1183–88*, 161; *1240–41*, 155; *1244*, 161; *1245*, 161n; *1284*, 155, 158–59, 161; *Oedipus at Colonus: 668–719*, 164; *678*, 94n; *Oedipus the King: 20*, 161; *209–15*, 154; *211*, 94n; *215*, 110n; *1105*, 94n; *1105–9*, 57, 154; *1140–45*, 141; *1255–59, 1299–1302*, 150–51n; *Tereus: fr. 586 (TrGF 4)*, 124n; *Trachinian Woman: 1–3*, 126n; *56–57*, 120n; *202, 211*, 105n; *216–20*, 104–5; *219*, 94n; *220–23*, 106; *225, 385*, 105n; *510–11*, 107n, 151n; *523*, 120n; *662*, 127n; *663, 673*, 105n; *703–4*, 107n; *767–68*, 127n; *821*, 105n; *833*, 127n; *841–43*, 126n, 127n; *857–61*, 126n; *871*, 105n; *893–95*, 127n; *1219, 1275*, 105n; *Unplaced Fragments: fr. 783 (TrGF 4)*, 113n; *fr. 837 (TrGF 4)*, 248n; *fr. 959 (TrGF 4)*, 267n
*Suda: s.v. "Attalos,"* 265n; *s.v. "Melan,"* 140n

Theocritus: *18.21*, 118n; *18.31*, 119n; *18.52–53*, 118; *26.7*, 265n
Thucydides: *2.18.2*, 180n; *4.109*, 228n
*Tragic Adespota, fr. 645.9 (TrGF 2)*, 116n, 125n

Vitruvius: *de Architectura 3.2*, 40n

Xenophanes: *FVS 21 B 17*, 93n

# Index of Greek, Latin, and Etruscan Words

*agathos*, 85
*agora*, 134n
*agreuō*, 75
*aidōs*, 120n
*Aiguptiaka*, 252
*aiōn*, 126
*aipsa*, 241n
*aition*, 59n, 181
*aix*, 241n
*aluō*, 143
*alussō*, 143
*amakhos*, 156
*amati tōide*, 247, 248
*ammiga pantas*, 134
*anakaluptēria*, 120
*anaulotatos*, 177
*anō katō*, 152
*antiprōiros*, 106
*antron*, 40n
*aōros*, 288n
*aposkopeō*, 219
*appas*, 286n
*aretē*, 167n
*Argadistika*, 262
*arkhiboukolos*, 267
*arkhimustēs*, 285, 294
*astos*, 161
*asulia*, 266
*ateknos*, 139n
*atimos*, 241n
*aulos*, 218
*autoktonos*, 139n

*Bacchum vidi*, 17
*bakkha nekuōn*, 100
*bakkhē*, 20, 64, 93, 94, 97, 98, 100, 109, 127, 133, 243, 249, 284, 294
*bakkheia*, 19, 93n, 94n, 113n, 268n, 270, 273
*bakkheia kakē*, 129n
*bakkheia kalē*, 113n
*bakkheuō*, 93nn, 94n, 95n, 98n, 99n, 128, 166n, 243, 249, 266, 278n
*bakkhia hamilla*, 105
*Bakkhiastēs*, 275
*Bakkhika*, 244, 262
*Bakkhistēs*, 264, 269
*bakkhos*, 20, 22, 93n, 94, 239, 243, 245, 247, 249, 252, 258, 266, 268, 274n, 276–78, 293
*basileus*, 54–55, 56, 63, 139n
*basilinna*, 54, 55n, 56, 61, 63
*basilissa*, 54
*bassaras*, 204
*bebakkheumenos*, 249, 252, 278n
*bios*, 242
*boukoleion*, 267
*boukolos*, 266–68, 285n, 291

*caduceus*, 291
*claritas*, 114
*credite*, 17

*damazō*, 158n
*deus praesentissimus*, 19
*dialumainomai*, 110n
*diamoiraō*, 110n, 131

*diasparagmos*, 215
*Dionusiastēs*, 286
*diōnumos*, 163
*distinctio*, 114
*domos*, 113nn, 125, 126
*drōmena*, 69, 77
*dunamis*, 82
*duskathartos*, 158n, 161

*eidenai*, 84n
*eis erōta*, 160
*eis hadou*, 248
*eis oros*, 109
*eis polin*, 228n
*ekmainō*, 140n
*ekstasis*, 96
*elaphos*, 109
*elelizomai*, 104
*elpis*, 113n
*embalō*, 70–71, 73n
*embas*, 198
*en domois*, 113nn
*ennukhios*, 171n
*entheos*, 133, 178n
*enthousiasmos*, 19n
*ependutēs*, 188, 191, 200, 201n
*epiphanēs*, 268–69
*epipneō*, 177, 178n
*epitaphios*, 147n, 167n
*eraō*, 45n
*erēmia*, 132
*erga adika*, 253
*eriphos*, 245–46
*eruthēma*, 119, 120n
*euai*, 259
*euastērios*, 41
*eudaimōn*, 241n
*euergesiē*, 269
*euhoi*, 41, 105, 266
*euias*, 294
*euteknos*, 162
*exeisi domōn*, 140

*fufluna*, 222

*genos*, 149n, 150, 161, 179, 253
*gerarai*, 54, 61
*gleukos*, 81
*goēs epōidos*, 35n
*gonē*, 158n
*gunē*, 105
*gunnis*, 204

*habros*, 120n
*hagemoneuma*, 120n
*Haidou mainas*, 129n, 131n
*haima tragoktonon*, 75
*hamilla*, 106
*harmozō*, 159n
*hēkō*, 31n
*heurēma*, 219
*hierea phonou*, 73
*hierougia*, 179
*hiketēs*, 253
*himeros*, 156
*hinthial*, 223
*hippos*, 245
*homēros*, 84n
*hudriathekē*, 256
*hudroskopia*, 284n
*hudroskopos*, 284
*huios*, 253, 258
*hupaithrios*, 40n, 41n
*huphiereia*, 274
*hupo khthona*, 248
*hupotrophos*, 286n
*hupo zophōi euruoenti*, 248

*iatros*, 113n, 131n

*kakos*, 103n
*kalaurops*, 291
*kallinikos*, 167n
*kalos*, 113n, 284n
*karpos*, 84
*kataballō*, 73n
*kat' agrous*, 59
*katasphazō*, 73
*katekhomai*, 177, 178n
*katharos*, 252, 255
*katharsiōi podi*, 158n, 161
*kentron*, 99n
*kharis akharitos*, 181
*khlounēs*, 45n
*khoes* or *khous*, 55n, 78, 81, 220, 285
*khreia*, 179
*khrēsimos*, 85
*kistē*, 264, 265, 271, 272, 273
*kistophoros*, 265n
*kitharōidos*, 179
*kōmos*, 60, 177, 178, 285
*krēdemnon*, 117, 119, 120
*krios*, 246
*krokōtos*, 50
*kunodesmos*, 210, 214
*kuōn*, 109, 110, 143
*kurios*, 277n

*legomena*, 77, 247
*lēnē*, 93n
*liknon*, 58n, 123n, 265n
*locus sacer*, 21
*lusioi teletai*, 273
*lusis*, 243, 252, 253, 273

*lussa*, 143, 150n

*mainadōn zeuktērie*, 122n
*mainas*, 93n, 94, 98, 102n, 109n, 129n, 131n
*mainomai*, 99n, 115n, 143–44, 179n
*mainomenos*, 93, 143–44, 160, 186, 198
*makar*, 241n, 247, 293n
*makarismos*, 118–19, 125–26, 129, 242, 246, 247, 254
*Maketai*, 262
*mania*, 19n, 91n, 93, 99n, 104, 150n, 158, 215, 260, 268, 272–73
*megara*, 284
*mēkhanē*, 173
*melanaigis*, 141
*melia*, 42n
*melikraton*, 249
*meros*, 84n
*metekhō*, 69–70
*mētis*, 218
*Mnamosunas ērion*, 251
*Mnēmosunēs dōron*, 251
*musterion*, 265, 266, 267n
*mustēs*, 239, 247, 259, 263, 266–67, 268, 276–78, 285–89, 293, 294

*naos*, 40n
*narthokophoros*, 284
*nebris*, 110n
*nebros*, 113n
*neikos*, 156
*neokoros*, 284
*nikaō*, 156
*nomos bakkheios*, 131
*nuktipolos*, 14
*numpha*, 126
*nun*, 247

*oikeios kakos*, 161
*oikos*, 41, 56, 131, 161
*oinoposia*, 286
*oinos*, 241n, 247
*olbios*, 126, 247
*olbizō*, 118
*olbos*, 118, 126
*ōmophagia*, 193, 195
*ōmophagion*, 66n, 70–71, 73n
*ōmophagion emballō*, 70–71, 73n
*ōmophagoi daites*, 75
*ōmophagos kharis*, 75
*oreibasia*, 25n, 72, 104, 109
*orgeōn*, 266
*orgia*, 19, 252, 269
*Orphika*, 252

*paidagōgos*, 94n
*paidotrophos*, 164
*pais*, 105n, 255, 290
*pais kalos*, 50
*palingenesia*, 295
*palintona toxa*, 107n
*pandamos polis*, 141
*pantōn anassa*, 162
*pantōn trophos*, 162
*paramousos*, 177, 178
*pardalis*, 110n
*pareimi*, 31n
*parousia*, 31
*parthenos*, 105
*pater familias*, 229
*pēlos*, 113n
*penthos oikeion*, 228n
*peukē*, 110
*phallagōgeion*, 281n
*phallophoria*, 58n
*phasma*, 140n
*pheromai*, 120
*phorēma*, 120n
*phulax*, 250, 258
*poina*, 253
*polis sesōtai*, 139n
*polugēthēs*, 177
*polumokhthos*, 177
*pompē*, 109, 260, 264, 268
*ponos*, 126n
*populor*, 222
*populus*, 222
*portheomai*, 139
*progeneis theoi*, 159
*progonōn athemistōn*, 243
*prokalumma*, 120n
*prokaluptō*, 119, 120n
*promatōr*, 162
*pro poleōs*, 41n
*propolos*, 285n
*prosōpon*, 2, 38n, 53n, 95n
*psukhē*, 255, 259
*pupluna*, 222
*purphoros*, 163
*Puthagorika*, 252

*reparatus*, 289

*sacrificulus et vates*, 275
*saturōi*, 266
*sebas*, 268–69
*sēmeion*, 173
*sōma*, 259
*sōoi bakkhikoi*, 293
*sōteira*, 293
*sparagmos*, 69–70, 72, 110n, 132, 193, 195
*speira*, 284n, 285n, 287
*speirachos*, 294
*sphazō*, 73

*splankhna*, 68
*spora*, 59n
*stolē*, 197, 202–3, 204
*suggenēs*, 150
*sumbolon*, 291
*summeixis*, 55n
*summustēs*, 289
*sumposion tōn hosiōn*, 246

*taurobolion*, 287n
*taurokerōs*, 265n
*tauros*, 267n
*tãutón* (= *to auton*), 34n
*tekhnitēs*, 9, 261, 263, 264, 266, 270
*tekna*, 255n
*telestēs*, 260, 263, 268
*teletē*, 9, 259–61, 263, 265, 266, 269n, 270–74, 285, 291
*telos*, 208n, 242n, 252, 253
*temenos*, 135, 290, 293
*terata*, 219
*thambos*, 219
*thanatos*, 242
*theatēs*, 171n
*theios*, 66
*theomakhos*, 98n
*theōros*, 171n
*thoazō*, 177
*thoina*, 69, 70
*thrambos*, 219
*thrēnos*, 244
*thriambos*, 270n
*thugatēr*, 255, 258
*thuias*, 94nn, 99n, 133
*thuias Hēras*, 99n, 133
*thuma*, 72, 73n
*thuma kataballō*, 73n
*thursomanēs*, 105n
*thursos*, 105n
*thusia*, 74, 78
*thussas*, 284n
*timē*, 241n
*tithēnē*, 116n
*tiur*, 223
*tlamōn*, 127–28
*to heteron*, 34n
*tokas*, 132
*trisolbios*, 241n, 247
*trophos*, 116n, 230
*tumpanon*, 157n, 263, 271, 273
*turannos*, 138n

*xenia*, 98n, 152n
*xenikos*, 136
*xenos*, 31, 35n, 36n, 136, 151, 152n, 158n
*xoanon*, 53n
*xunos*, 135n

*zeira*, 198

# General Index


Achelous, 107
Achilles, 144–45
Acmonia, 287
Acoetes, 16–17, 21, 43
Actaeon, 143
Admetus, 118
Adonis, 58
Adrasteia, 272
Aemilianus, 266
Aeschines, 113
Agave, 70, 72–73, 97, 100, 110, 124–25, 130, 151, 169
Agripinilla, 256
Alcathous, 136
Alexander the Great, 261–62, 271
altar, 186 (fig. 7), 187, 192 (fig. 10), 270–75, 287
alterity, 22–23, 31–38, 135, 152–70, 208, 220
Amastris, 285
Amphiaraus, 173–79
Amphictyon, 81
Amphion, 173–74, 179–80
Amphipolis, 283
Amyzon, 282
Andromache, 102, 114–21, 125–26, 128–29, 132–33, 134, 137, 142–46
Anthesteria, 54–56, 76, 78, 81, 131n, 220, 285, 289
anthropomorphism, 16–21, 26–29, 37–39
Antigone, 119–21, 125, 129–33, 141, 155–59, 161, 181
Antiope, 122, 173, 176–77
Aphrodite, 53–54, 99, 100, 104, 108, 111, 117, 153, 156–60, 163, 164, 281
Apollo, 2, 19, 24, 30, 50, 100, 134, 136, 167, 169, 179, 195, 204, 225; Ismenios, 179
Apollodorus, 197, 198, 202, 231, 272
Areatha, 229, 234
Ares, 98, 100, 131, 153, 156–60, 163, 177–79
Argeadae, royal house of, 261
Argos, 124, 166, 172
Ariadne, 51 (fig. 5), 54–56, 63, 217 (fig. 17), 228
Artames, 232, 233 (fig. 26)
Artemis, 19, 41n, 78, 109, 121–23, 136, 195
Astyanax, 118–19
Athena, 114, 116, 146, 153, 161–63, 164–65, 167–68, 170–71
Athens/Attica, 140, 147–82, 289
Attaleia, 284–85
Attalids of Pergamum, 261, 264–67
Atunis, 230
Aulus Iulius Quadratus, 267
autochthony, 149, 162, 167, 169, 170

Bacchanalia degree, 260–61
Bassaroi, 75
Beazley, J. D., 188, 200, 232
Benndorf, O., 272
Berard, C., 193
Bithynia, 282, 289
Bithynium-Claudiopolis, 283
Bizye, 285
Bond, G. W., 178
boots, Thracian, 49 (fig. 4), 74n, 190, 191 (fig. 9), 198–99, 212
Boukoleion, 55
Brauron, 78

Breslin, J., 239
Bron, C., 193
Burkert, W., 25, 239

Cadmus, 72, 124, 149, 159, 161, 172–73, 179–80
Caecilia Secundina, 251, 255–56
Caesarea, 290
calendars, sacrificial, 75–77
Calydon, 136n
Cambridge school, 27n, 28, 65–68, 81, 86, 89–92
cannibalism, 68, 72–75, 80–81
cantharus, 2, 46 (fig. 1), 48–49 (figs. 3–4), 186 (fig. 7), 187, 217 (fig. 17), 279
Caria, 282, 293
Carratelli, G. P., 239
Cassandra, 100, 128, 132–33
Catha, 222, 234
Cavallari, F. S., 252, 254
Cenchreae, 285
centaurs, 213–14, 220
Ceos, 249
Charites, 54
Chekanchevo, 284, 289, 291
Chios, 123
Christianity, 13, 28, 66–67
Chryseis, 49 (fig. 4)
Cithaeron, 150
Civitalba, 233
Clytemnestra, 90, 98, 100, 103, 104, 113, 131, 132
Cole, S., 75
Cornford, F., 89
Corybants, 271, 275
Cos, altar of Dionysus, 261, 270–75
cothurni, 74n
cowherd, 266–68, 291
Creon, 155, 156, 163
Creusa, 103, 167, 169, 170–71
cult: civic, 68, 71, 74, 75–77; ruler, 268–70
Cumae, 278
Curetes, 271
Cybela, 272, 275

dance, 93n, 104, 105n, 155, 162, 164, 177, 266
Dascylium, 287
death/the dead, 14, 18, 23, 26–30, 32, 41, 242, 277–95
de Grummond, N., 228
Deianira, 103–8
Delos, 57, 71
Delphi, 155, 165, 167–70, 265
Demeter, 58–59, 61, 78, 83, 102, 153–75, 269, 284–85; Thesmophoros, 163
Demetrius Poliorcetes, 270
Derveni krater, 261
Detienne, M., 28–29, 31

Dikaiopolis, 58–59
Dionysia: City, 56, 57, 76, 77, 172, 181; Country, 56, 57, 58, 59n, 76
Dionysiac, ritual, 14, 19–22, 29, 37n, 40–41
Dionysiastai, 286
Dionysophanes, 39
Dionysus
  beardless, 48, 50, 51 (fig. 5), 185–206 (figs. 7–8,) 229–31 (figs. 23–25)
  birth of, 84n, 226 (fig. 21), 169, 271
  bisexuality of, 44
  cult of, 75–76, 82–85, 90–114
  divinity of, 15–24, 26–31, 39–43
  dress of, 50
  effeminacy of, 19, 45, 204–5, 230
  epithets or alternate names: Agrionios, 74; Aisumnetes, 136; Anthroporrhaistes, 74–75; Archegetas, 266; Bakkheios, 2, 71, 243, 273–74; Bakkheus, 2; Bakkhios, 241, 243, 251–52; Bromius, 181, 282, 289; Eleuthereus, 25n, 51, 146, 148; Enchores, 53; Erikepaios, 294; Eriphios, 245; Fufluns, 221–35; Iacchus, 168, 171; Kathegemon, 264, 266, 267; Liber, 232; Liknites, 169; Luaios, 283, 287; Lusios, 2, 25n, 74, 243, 259, 273; Mainomenos, 74; Meilikhios, 2; Melanaigis, 140, 245; Melpomenos, 179; Omadios, 74; Omestes, 74, 135; Patroios, 137; Phallens, 53; Setaneios, 266; Sphaleotas, 265; Thullophoros, 273–74; Thuonidas, 53; Zagreus, 16n, 18, 26–29, 39, 73, 75
  iconography of, 17n, 19–20, 22, 37, 41–42, 185–206, 270–75
  Indian triumph of, 262
  infant, 189, 215, 216 (fig. 16)
  lord of the dead, 232
  madness of, 196–98, 202, 272–73
  marriage to *basilinna,* 54–56, 61, 135, 267
  modern reception of, 15–43, 65–86, 89–97
  nudity of, 50
  his rescue of Ariadne, 232–33
  his rescue of Semele, 175, 231
  "Thracian adventures," 199
Dirce, 175–76, 179–80
Dodds, E. R., 25, 66, 68, 196, 198
dragon (of Ares), 161, 162

Earth, 162–63
Egypt, 261–64, 268, 282
Elaphebolion, 62, 77
Eleusis, 155, 160, 165–66, 168, 171
Eleutherae, 148, 153, 172–74, 176, 179–82
Eleutherna, 240, 250, 256
Elysian fields, 289
endogamy, 138, 141
Eniautos, 263
epiphany, 15–41, 97n, 104n, 268–70

Erchia, 61, 77
Erechtheus, 168
Erichthonius, 167–69
Erinyes, 98, 100, 114, 131
Eros, 51 (fig. 5), 111, 156–58, 214
Erythrae, 279
eschatology, 69, 239–56, 276–95
Eteocles, 101, 139–40, 150, 174
Etruscan culture, 221–35
Eubouleus, 246
Eucharist, 66n
Euios, 285
Eukles, 246
Euneus, 174, 178–79
Euphemos the Carian, 213
Euphronius, 263, 268
Eurydice, 161
Eurypylus, 136
Evadne, 125–26, 129, 132–33

Faliscan vases, 223
fawn, 110n, 113n, 186–90, 192, 195 (fig. 12), 199, 223
felines, 41–43
fertility, 58–59
Ficoroni cista, 228
Frazer, J., 28, 29, 66
frenzy, 98–106, 115–46
Fufluns Pacha, 221–35
funeral, 120–21, 125, 129, 143–44, 248–49, 281
funerary inscriptions, 276–95
Furies. *See* Erinyes

gender roles, 15, 19, 22n, 24, 33–35, 38n, 41
Genucilia plate, 226
Gernet, L., 32–33
Getty Museum, 240, 255
Geyer, A., 267
Gigantomachy, 50, 162, 168, 170, 186, 189, 199
Girard, R., 85
goat/kid, 62, 77, 81, 190, 191 (fig. 9), 193, 194 (fig. 11), 225, 245
Goldhill, S., 25
Graf, F., 259

Hades, 57, 133n, 151, 155, 158, 161, 164, 231–32, 242, 247, 294
Haemon, 156, 161, 163
Haloa, 59n
Harmonia, 159
Harrison, J., 20, 27n, 66, 68, 81n, 89–90, 192
Hector, 102, 115–18, 134, 137, 144, 146
Hecuba, 98, 102, 128, 131–32, 146
Helen, 132, 225
Hephaestia on Lemnos, 71n
Hephaestus, 200, 203–4
Hera, 98–100, 133, 135, 196–97, 272
Heracles, 98, 100, 103–8, 112, 132, 149–51, 162, 214, 220
Hercle, 230
Hermes, 52, 179, 215
Hermopolis Magna, 282
herms, 47, 52, 211 (fig. 15)
hetairai, 59
Hierocaesarea, 294
hierophant, 286–87
Hippolytus, 104, 108–12
Hippomedon, 98
Hipponium, 239, 246, 250–51, 254–55, 259, 278, 292
household, 115–46
hunting, 75, 90, 104, 109, 110, 114, 116
Huxley, A., 221
Hypsipyle, 173, 178–79

Iacchus, 155, 157, 171
Iaza, 289
Icarius, 75, 76, 82
Iconium, 289
immortality, 18, 26–29
infibulation, 48 (fig. 3), 210 (fig. 14)
initiation, 68, 74, 75, 77–79, 113, 239–95
Ino, 124, 130, 132, 175, 273
Io, 99, 100, 133, 162
Iobakkhoi, 245, 286
Iocasta, 101, 174–75
Iole, 106, 108, 111–12, 126, 132–33
Ion, 166–71
Iris, 106
Isis, 284
Istros, 284
ivy, 2, 37, 40, 105, 188, 240, 279

Janko, R., 278
Jason, 173, 178
Judaism of Jews, 13, 263
Julia Gordus, 284

Keuls, E., 54, 62
Komos, 217 (fig. 17)
Kore. *See* Persephone
Kott, J., 28
Kraemer, R. S., 256
krotala, 46 (fig. 1)

Laius, 139, 149, 159, 172–75
Leda, 225
Lemnos, 71n, 173, 178
"Lenaia vases," 37, 52 (fig. 6)
leopard- or panther-skin, 190, 192, 287
Lerna, 287
Lesbos, 57, 135
Lewis, I., 256
libations, 65–68, 81–86

Linear B tablets, 1
Loraux, N., 168
Lycurgus, 115, 116, 124, 132, 143, 157–58, 197–99, 202
Lycus, 179–80
lyre, 49 (fig. 4), 51 (fig. 5), 178–80, 203, 210 (fig. 14)
Lyssa, 106

madness, 15–34, 89–114, 158–60, 178, 182, 272–73
maenads/maenadism, 14–43, 45–49 (figs. 1–4), 54, 60–61, 65–69, 90–114, 115–38, 150–78, 187–89, 192, 196–97, 214, 216, 243, 249
Magnesia, 286
Maleos, 49 (fig. 4)
Mann, Thomas, 32
Mannhardt, M., 213
marriage, 54–56, 104–12, 121–25, 133, 135–36, 158–63
mask, 14, 20n, 21–23, 27n, 30, 35–39, 50, 89–97
Megara, 136
Melampous, 136
Melos, 286
Memory, 276
Menarva, 232, 233 (fig. 26)
Merkelbach, R., 267, 279
Mesembria, 279
metempsychosis, 242
Meter, 271–73
Methymna, 36n, 53
Methyse, 49 (fig. 4)
Midas, 217–18 (fig. 18), 262
Milas, 293–94
Miletopolis, 285
Miletus, 70, 274, 284
milk, 241, 245–46, 248–50
Mimallones, 262
Minyads, 124
mirrors, Etruscan, 223–35 (figs. 19–21, 23–26)
Murray, Gilbert, 27n, 86, 89
Muses, 281, 283, 288
music, 174, 178, 179, 180, 181n
Mylopetra, 255
mysteries, 74, 77–78, 96, 97nn, 239–95; Dionysiac/Bacchic, 165, 240–56, 259–75, 280–81, 285, 288; Eleusinian, 16n, 78, 91n, 92n, 97n, 141n, 155–71, 242, 248, 285, 288, 292
myths of arrival, 31–32

Naxos, 2
Nemea, 173
Neoplatonic theory, 59, 244
Nessos, 107
Nicea, 285
Nietzsche, F., 23–31, 35, 39, 42, 85, 89, 92
Nilsson, M. P., 269
nurses, 115, 132, 162, 164, 225
nymphs, 45–46, 54, 57, 281–82
Nysa, 262, 290

Odysseus, 78, 144
Oedipus, 27, 39, 130, 138, 141, 149–51, 163, 164, 172, 181
Oeneus, 75, 108
Oinobios, 49 (fig. 4)
Olbia, 240, 242–43, 259, 277
Olympias, 256, 261, 265
Olympiodorus, 243
Olynthus, 186
omophagy, 25n, 28n, 68–72, 76
Orestes, 103, 112–14, 131, 132, 140, 249
Orpheotelestai, 244, 249
Orpheus, 178, 200, 242–44, 252, 294
Orphic bone plates, 240, 242–43, 259
"Orphic" gold tablets, 239–58, 259, 278, 292
Orphikoi, 240, 242–43, 259, 277
Orphism, 29, 70, 78, 239–58, 271
Osiris, 262
"Otherness." *See* alterity
Otto, W. F., 18, 25, 29–33, 37

Paean, 106
Pailler, J.-M., 234
Pan, 47
Pannonia, 282
Papposilenus, 217
Parassoglou, G. M., 240
Parnassus, 167, 168, 169
Parthenon, sculpture, 185, 206
Pasiphae, 225
Patrae, 135–36
Pelinna, 240–57, 259
Penelope, 144
Pentheus, 16, 21, 22, 25, 54, 61, 64, 70, 72–74, 77, 97, 123, 138, 143, 150–69, 196, 203, 215, 256, 294
Pergamum, 261, 264–67
Perge, theater, 271
Perinthus, 294
Persephone, 61, 102, 133n, 155, 162–64, 170, 175, 241–55, 269, 276
Petelia, 247
Pfiffig, A., 223
Phaedra, 99, 100, 103, 104, 108–12
Phaennis, 265
Phalles, 53
phallus, 44–47, 52–54, 57–60, 82n, 201, 203, 214
Pharsalus text, 250, 255–56
Philippi, 280, 286, 289
Philiscusi, 263

Phrygia, 197, 202
Piacenza liver, 222–23, 234
pipes, 48 (fig. 3), 105, 190, 218
Piraeus, 293
pirates, 2, 226, 227 (fig. 22)
Plutarch, 30, 135, 280, 294
polarities, 15–16, 21n, 23–25, 29–31, 33–34, 38, 41, 67, 90
polis, 134–39, 141, 145–46
Polydorus, 100, 131
Polyidus, 136
Polynices, 101, 150, 156, 174
Pompeii, 260, 291
Populonia, 222
Potidaea, 261
Pound, E.: Canto 2, 15–17, 21, 22, 42; Canto 79, 42–43
Priapus, 54
priesthood, 71, 73, 74n, 76
Procne, 124, 129–30, 132
Proetids, 122, 136
Prometheus, 27, 39, 70
Ptolemies of Egypt, 261–64, 268, 269, 272
Pythagorean texts, 247, 250, 252, 255

Rhea, 198, 202, 272
Richardson, E., 228, 232
ritual, 65–86
Robinson, D., 199
Rohde, E., 27–32
Roman Senate, 223, 260–61
Rome, 283, 284, 287–91
Rose, H. J., 244
Rusajeva, A. S., 240

Sabazius, 265
sacramentalism, 16n, 20, 28–29, 65–86
sacrifice, 14, 27, 29, 41, 65–86, 90, 121–24, 136, 193
satyrs, 17–18, 27, 41, 45–49 (figs. 1–4), 54, 101, 122, 176, 189, 190, 192–94 (figs. 10–11), 198, 201, 207–20 (figs. 13–17), 224, 234, 249, 263, 283, 289
Seaford, R., 219
Segal, C., 25
Semele, 62, 77, 97, 111, 175
Semla, 229, 231, 234–35
Serrhae, 286
sexuality, 44–64
Sicyon, 2
Silenus, 196, 217–18 (fig. 18), 233 (fig. 26), 262
Smith, W. R., 66
Smyrna, 284, 294
snake, 46 (fig. 1), 47 (fig. 2), 140, 173, 186 (fig. 7), 187, 196, 261, 264–65, 272–73
Spartoi, 149, 162–63, 173
Stambolidis, N. C., 270–72
Strepsiades, 77
symposium, 1, 21, 35, 54, 79, 205, 289

Tanagra, 285
Telephus, 264, 267
Tenedos, 75
Teos, 266, 286
Termessos, 284
Thasos, 280
theater, 14–41, 201–3, 282–83
"theatrical artists," 261, 266–68, 270; costumes, 201–3
Thebes, 78, 107, 124, 130, 133, 138, 147–82, 285
Theogamia, 135
theophagy, 26–29, 70, 78–79
theophany, 16n, 21n, 42
Theophrastus, 80–81
Theseus, 54, 151, 220
Thessalonika, 284, 286, 294
Thessaly, 239–58
thiasos, 20–22, 105, 122–25, 178, 181, 228, 287–88
Thiersch, H., 200
Thoas, 173, 174
Thrace, 156–58, 178, 197–99, 202, 293
Thurii, 245, 250, 253; Timpone Grande, 252, 254, 255–56; Timpone Piccolo, 251, 254, 255–56
Thyiades, 283
Thyone, 232
thyrsus, 47 (fig. 2), 49 (fig. 4), 105n, 186 (fig. 7), 187, 193 (fig. 10), 217 (fig. 17), 223, 287
Timokleides of Thasos, 40–41
Tina/Zeus, 224–26 (figs. 19–21)
Tiresias, 78, 83, 85, 156, 165
Titans, 26, 29, 39, 50, 70, 73, 244, 253, 271, 294
torches, 127–28, 133, 140, 155, 167n, 171n
Tragodia, 217 (fig. 17)
Troy, 119
Tsantsanoglou, K., 240
Turan, 230, 235
Turms, 225

van der Meer, L. B., 223
vase painters: Altamura Painter, 186, 187 (fig. 8), 188–90, 192, 197, 199, 203; Blenheim Painter, 188, 189, 197; Dinos Painter, 200; Exekias, 226; Geras Painter, 210; Kleophon Painter, 200; Kleophrades Painter, 210; Micali Painter, 226; Niobid Painter, 186 (fig. 7), 190, 197–200, 205; Pronomos Painter, 203; Tymbos Painter, 202
vase painting, 17n, 22, 37, 39, 45–53, 110n, 120n, 129, 185–206, 207–20, 223
Vernant, J.-P., 31, 33–35, 37

Vesuna, 229–30, 234
victimization, 65–86
Villa of the Mysteries, 260, 291
vine, 188–89, 196, 199
viticulture, 78–86, 282

war, 116, 123, 131, 133–34
Warburg, Aby, 40
Webster, T. B. L., 205
wedding. *See* marriage
wedding ritual, 117–29, 144–45
West, M., 198, 240
wine, 1, 13–43, 65, 66, 68, 78–86, 94, 108, 113, 167–68, 176–78, 214, 220, 222, 241, 246, 281
wineskin, 47 (fig. 2), 49 (fig. 4)
Winnington-Ingram, R., 25

Xuthus, 167–70

Zeitlin, F., 25
Zethus, 156, 163, 173, 174, 179–80
Zeus, 50, 118, 135, 143, 144, 215, 253–54
Zuntz, G., 239, 245, 247, 250, 254, 259

MYTH AND POETICS

A series edited by

GREGORY NAGY

*Masks of Dionysus*
edited by Thomas W. Carpenter and Christopher A. Faraone

*The Ravenous Hyenas and the Wounded Sun: Myth and Ritual in Ancient India*
by Stephanie W. Jamison

*Poetry and Prophecy: The Beginnings of a Literary Tradition*
edited by James Kugel

*The Traffic in Praise: Pindar and the Poetics of Social Economy*
by Leslie Kurke

*Epic Singers and Oral Tradition*
by Albert Bates Lord

*The Language of Heroes: Speech and Performance in the* Iliad
by Richard P. Martin

*Heroic Sagas and Ballads*
by Stephen A. Mitchell

*Greek Mythology and Poetics*
by Gregory Nagy

*Myth and the Polis*
edited by Dora C. Pozzi and John M. Wickersham

*Knowing Words: Wisdom and Cunning in the Classical Traditions of China and Greece*
by Lisa Raphals

*Homer and the Sacred City*
by Stephen Scully
*The Mute Immortals Speak: Pre-Islamic Poetry and the Poetics of Ritual*
by Suzanne Pinckney Stetkevych
*Phrasikleia: An Anthropology of Reading in Ancient Greece*
by Jesper Svenbro
translated by Janet Lloyd

## Praise for *Future Primal*

"Who can doubt that we need a new paradigm for planetary civilization? Our economic models are projections and arrows when they should be circles. To define perpetual growth on a finite planet as the sole measure of economic well-being is to engage in a form of slow collective suicide. To deny or exclude from the calculus of governance and political economy the costs of violating the biological support systems of life is the logic of delusion. In *Future Primal*, Louis Herman offers a way out, a vision of a new kind of politics for a new era of humanity. Drawing on his time among the Kalahari Bushmen, the lessons of his service as a soldier in the Israeli army, and his experiences as a Jewish lad living through the darkest years of apartheid in South Africa, he has written a seminal book that bears witness to the folly of all those who say we cannot change, as we know we must, the fundamental manner in which we inhabit this planet."

— Wade Davis, National Geographic Society Explorer-in-Residence and author of *Into the Silence* and *The Serpent and the Rainbow*

"*Future Primal* is a masterpiece. It braids together admiration for early societies, respect for science, and profound faith in our ability to create better collective lives on this endangered planet. Louis Herman merges the very old and the very new, the empirical and the mystical; he brings forward artists, shamans, dancers, hunters, and tricksters to beckon us toward a politics more respectful of humanity, of difference, and of the earth. Lively and learned, this book is written with the engaged hand of a practiced teacher. It will be a hit with students who long for Herman's combination of practical examples and sweeping vision."

— Kathy E. Ferguson, professor of political science and women's studies at the University of Hawai'i and author of *Emma Goldman: Political Thinking in the Streets*

"*Future Primal* is an urgent, adventurous, and glistening work. Louis Herman makes a powerful case that in our historical advancement we have lost something deep and fundamental in how we relate to one another, the world around us, and life as a whole. With a rich narrative that mixes the personal, the philosophical, the anthropological, and the spiritual, Herman points to a politics of the future that will be informed by the beauty and power of shamanic and tribal insights that our abstract world has left behind — at our peril."

— Wayne Cristaudo, chair of the politics department at Charles Darwin University, Australia, and author of *Power, Love and Evil: Contribution to a Philosophy of the Damaged*

"Louis Herman's *Future Primal* demonstrates that political science has not completely degenerated into the meaningless accumulation and analysis of empirical data. His book reconnects us with visions of the good life that have been foundational to human existence since the Paleolithic beginnings of humanity in southern Africa. Herman refuses to accept the doctrinal answers of religious orthodoxy and the sterile responses of neo-Marxism, postmodernism, and neoliberalism. His book is a groundbreaking work of creative scholarship and philosophical vision that transcends all civilizational, religious, and political boundaries. It provides a compelling narrative that weaves our new understanding of the origins of human life and the larger community of being into an original vision of the good life that has the philosophical truth quest at its core."

— Manfred Henningsen, political philosopher at the University of Hawai'i

"The author's powerful story of his search for truth over decades in South Africa, England, Israel, and Hawai'i is integral to the fascinating and bold tale he is telling, at once ancient and contemporary, of a cosmos of faith, and of love, and of hope that draws from the best that historical and natural sciences have to offer. A thought-provoking challenge to any philosophy of politics and history."

— Paul Caringella, visiting research fellow at the Hoover Institution at Stanford University and trustee of the Voegelin Literary Trust

"Louis Herman has brought together a rich life journey on several continents with penetrating perspectives from political philosophy and contemporary cosmology. This work is a unique contribution to rethinking our collective story, from a common past out of Africa toward a shared future on our endangered planet. To sink into this perspective is to see with fresh insight how we truly belong here — such a gift!"

— Mary Evelyn Tucker, cofounder and codirector of the Forum on Religion and Ecology at Yale University

# FUTURE PRIMAL

## HOW OUR WILDERNESS ORIGINS SHOW US THE WAY FORWARD

LOUIS G. HERMAN

FOREWORD BY BRIAN THOMAS SWIMME

New World Library
Novato, California

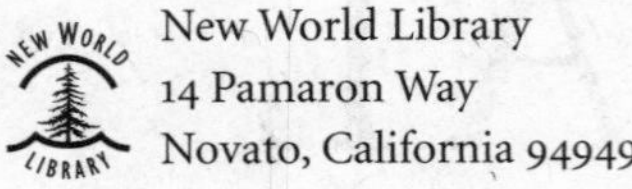

New World Library
14 Pamaron Way
Novato, California 94949



Grateful acknowledgment is given to Christopher Henshilwood at the Institute for Archaeology, History, Culture and Religion in Bergen, Norway, for the use of the Blombos ochre image on page 160; to David Lewis-Williams, senior mentor at the Rock Art Institute of the University of Witwatersrand in South Africa, for the sketches of cave art on pages 251, 254, 255, and 256; and to Craig Foster for the photographs on pages 172 and 281 and the cover.

Text design by Tona Pearce Myers

Library of Congress Cataloging-in-Publication Data is available.

First printing, March 2013
ISBN 978-1-60868-115-0
Printed in the USA on 100% postconsumer-waste recycled paper

New World Library is proud to be a Gold Certified Environmentally Responsible Publisher. Publisher certification awarded by Green Press Initiative.
www.greenpressinitiative.org

10 9 8 7 6 5 4 3 2 1

*To my daughter, Danielle, and her generation,*
*who face unprecedented challenges but also extraordinary opportunities*
*to create a flourishing planetary civilization in balance with nature*

# CONTENTS

FOREWORD BY BRIAN THOMAS SWIMME viii
INTRODUCTION x

## Part I — Where Are We?

CHAPTER 1: *The Truth Quest* 2
CHAPTER 2: *Abandonment of the Quest — A Path with No Heart* 24
CHAPTER 3: *Recovery of the Quest, Part I — Anamnesis: Searching with My Life* 64
CHAPTER 4: *Recovery of the Quest, Part II — Politics of Mystery* 102

## Part II — Where Do We Come From?

CHAPTER 5: *Out of Wilderness* 136
CHAPTER 6: *Lost Worlds* 170
CHAPTER 7: *Primal Politics* 196
CHAPTER 8: *"If You Don't Dance, You Die"* 220

CHAPTER 9: *Boundary Crossing* 260
CHAPTER 10: *The Outer Reaches of Inner Wilderness* 282
CHAPTER 11: *The Primal Polis: Socrates as Shaman* 308

## Part III — Where Should We Be Going?

CHAPTER 12: *Our Primal Future* 336
EPILOGUE: *A Tao of Politics* 376

APPENDIX: *Future Primal Toolkit* 384
ACKNOWLEDGMENTS 393
ENDNOTES 398
INDEX 437
ABOUT THE AUTHOR 465

# FOREWORD

Since the mid-1980s, a number of leading theorists across academic disciplines have been involved in the common endeavor of articulating the outlines of what might be called a planetary civilization. These physicists, economists, poets, cosmologists, sociologists, biologists, political scientists, engineers, city planners, farmers, religious scholars, philosophers, and ecologists all share the assumption that our human societies are undergoing what might prove to be the largest shift of structure since we first settled into villages at the start of the Neolithic era. The primary motivation for this revisioning is the realization that the ecological and social devastation taking place around the planet will only continue until some powerful new ideas take hold in human consciousness. The significance of Louis Herman's *Future Primal* can best be appreciated in terms of this ongoing creative project.

My sense is that, in a number of fields, remarkable progress has been achieved. Some of the landmarks include: in economics, Herman Daly and his articulation of the theoretical foundations for economic sustainability; in technology, Janine Benyus and her recasting of industrial infrastructure as biological mimicry; in agriculture, Wes Jackson and his new paradigm of a perennial polyculture; in physics, Fritjof Capra and his deconstruction of scientism; in human-earth relations, Susan Griffin and her work leading beyond the oppressions of dualism; in religion, Thomas Berry and his vision of the ultimate sacred community as neither humanity nor a subgroup of humanity but the entire earth community itself.

I would place the work of Louis Herman in this company of geniuses. Regularly, at conferences, however satisfied we participants were with what had been accomplished in revising physics or biology or economics, the glaring omission was politics. For years, we have keenly felt this absence of a political philosophy that would support a planetary civilization.

No longer. In *Future Primal* we have a work that deeply resonates with the ideas from the other architects of this new earth era. Drawing from a very wide range of ideas and sources, including contemporary political scientists, the Kalahari Bushmen, and the Axial Greek philosophers, Louis Herman has created a vision of the human being as a microcosm of the entire evolving 13.7-billion-year-old universe itself. Perhaps the best way to describe this creative synthesis is to call it a work of *political cosmology*. For with this new vision of politics we can begin to imagine ourselves not just as consumers, and not just as political units of a nation-state, but as cosmological beings — cosmological beings whose foundations are that same creativity that brought forth a time-developmental universe, and whose struggles are those same ongoing struggles of life itself to give birth to new forms of beauty.

I am convinced that Louis Herman's *Future Primal* provides a cornerstone for this emerging planetary civilization.

— Brian Thomas Swimme, professor of evolutionary cosmology at the California Institute of Integral Studies (CIIS) and coauthor with Thomas Berry of *The Universe Story*

# INTRODUCTION

The universe, at its most basic level, is not only matter, energy, and information. The universe is a story. Each creature is a story. Each human enters this world and awakens to a simple truth: "I must find my own story within this great epic of being."

— **Brian Thomas Swimme**, *The Resurgence of Cosmic Storytellers*

My fellow-men are those who can listen to the stories
That come to them from far-off, floating through the air.
Even now they hear them come from places far away,
These stories like the wind, floating like the winds.

— **//Kabbo**, one of the last of the now-extinct /Xam Bushmen, *Return of the Moon*

We are clearly involved in a dramatic race for time that has no precedent in the entire history of humanity. What is at stake is nothing less than the future of humanity and of life on this planet...humanity [is] at a critical crossroad facing either collective annihilation or an evolutionary jump in consciousness of unprecedented nature and dimension.

— **Stanislav Grof**, 2012 and Human Destiny

## In the Beginning…

Some fourteen billion years ago the entire cosmos, what would become the great wheeling galaxies with their trillions of blazing suns, burst into being from a single point, in an unimaginably violent, unfathomably immense explosion of light and energy. Since that "Great Flaring Forth" the universe has been expanding, cooling, and growing in complexity…and consciousness.*

This is the most astounding discovery of the last four hundred years of modern science and the foundation of our deepest understanding of reality. It is also the limiting case of credulity. If you can believe this, you can believe just about anything. Yet our best science tells us it is so: that the infinitely ordered complexities of the earth — the delicate beauty of birds, flowers, forests, and oceans; the glories and tragedies of self-conscious humanity — *all of this* grows out of that single, infinitely mysterious, explosive beginning. The cosmos is not so much a place as it is a continually unfolding event.

Scientific laws and theories generally deal with universal, repeatable, predictable regularities. In contrast, stories capture the meaning of unique events — novelties — transforming over time. Every individual human life is a unique story told in the living. We could say the evolving universe itself is a story "telling us into existence." Narrative captures something fundamental about the nature of reality. The story becomes a primordial unit of meaning, connecting the present to the past and all things to one another as they emerge from an original unity. All past cultures and civilizations have had some intuitive sense that humans lived within a larger process — a story whose ultimate origin was the most profound and sacred mystery. Each had a cosmology, a story of origins that formed the foundation of its way of life and guided its economics and politics. The viability of a society depended

* Thanks to Brian Thomas Swimme and Thomas Berry for their inspirational framing of "The Universe Story" and for this more fitting alternative term to "the Big Bang."

attunement between inner and outer seemed capable of generating spiritual experiences we commonly call ecstatic or mystical, which have the effect of inspiring and ordering our lives.

When we approach politics from such a perspective, magnificent possibilities open up: of ways of life profoundly "better, truer, and more beautiful" than our sad and frenetic destructiveness. *Future Primal* offers one such vision by weaving together the various narrative layers of my search, from my personal history to the history of civilization, our species, and indeed the universe itself. The vision draws from other models of politics but differs from them in one fundamental respect: at its center is awareness of the ultimate mystery of our origins, and with it the necessity for an ongoing process of creative searching.

## Bringing Soul Back into Politics — the Truth Quest

Our modern use of the word *politics* has become as thoroughly debased and misunderstood as the practice it is commonly used to describe — seeking and wielding power over others for personal gain. On the scale of public opinion, politicians rank somewhere between prostitutes and used-car salesmen. The whole business of politics is considered as far from its Socratic roots in philosophy and "cultivating virtue" as one can get. To move out of this dead end, we need to retrace our steps to find a new way forward. If we go back two and a half thousand years to classical Greece, we can find the origin of the word *politics* in the Greek *polis* — the self-governing, autonomous, democratic city-state — where "politics" simply referred to the affairs of the polis, and as the concern of all, it was regarded as the most ennobling and meaningful of all human activities.

I use the word *politics* in this original, inclusive sense, to mean *the universal human struggle, individually and collectively, to seek and to live the best possible life*. Political philosophy can then be reconnected to its original Socratic intention as the search for the ideal of "the good life." This has two primary aspects: On the one hand, there is what Socrates called "the improvement of one's soul," or what we loosely understand as personal growth, since the Greek word for "soul" is *psyche*, from which we get our *psychology*. On the other hand, there is the improvement of one's society. Traditionally, this sort of Socratic knowledge was called wisdom. By contrast, in today's universities "political philosophy" refers to an obscure subspecialty within the discipline of political science that focuses on the texts of the great philosophers of the past. It has lost its living connection to the primordial questions: "How should I live?" and "How should we all live together?" Part of my purpose is to recover this original search for meaning, what I call "the primal truth quest." Everything we do — the failure and success of all our politics — depends on our grasp of this quest and the reliability of the understanding it produces.

The dangers we face today are compounded by the fact that we have never been more confused or more cynical about what constitutes the good, the true, and the beautiful. We are daily inundated with vast quantities of information but lack the most basic shared understanding of how we should live together. Not only do we lack a shared vision but we are profoundly confused about the way we should search. Science provides only neutral tools. Religion, when based on strict obedience to the Holy Scriptures, remains blind and closed to the search. If we don't know how to look, how will we recognize the truth of a vision of a better way?

Here is our central failing: We have created a political culture that has eliminated *in principle* the need for the individual to consider and take responsibility for the good of the whole. We have abandoned the truth quest in public life. Our system is set up so that economic and political decisions are made according to the conviction that if individuals, organizations, and nations follow self-interest, the "invisible hand of the market" will automatically convert selfishness into the best possible outcome for the largest number. This is reinforced by a prevailing intellectual culture of skepticism and scientific materialism, which assumes that "good" and "evil," and "right" and "wrong" are entirely subjective matters for individual judgment. This sort of relativism has led to a global economic system that rewards a few individuals with grotesque quantities of wealth, rivaling the GDP of small nations, while a billion people go hungry. Never before has so much power over so many been concentrated in the hands of so few in the service of unashamed self-interest. All the while the collective frantic energy of globalized humanity continues to pollute and plunder the planet.

Our situation embodies a stark paradox. We stand on the edge of great danger and great opportunity, both closer to and yet farther than ever from fulfilling some of the most crucial conditions for an enlightened and liberated humanity. No period in history has had the benefit of the staggering vistas of modern cosmology — of how life evolved out of a planet that

4.5 billion years ago was a ball of molten rock. No previous generation has had such reliable detailed knowledge of the diversity of past human societies. This ongoing, exponentially expanding understanding of the human condition is now directly available to masses of ordinary human beings through the miracles of industrialization and electronic communication. The radical democratization of wisdom is a practical possibility for perhaps the first time since hunter-gatherers sat around the campfire every night sharing stories.

Yet emotionally we live in a smaller cosmological space than any previous society. Our daily routine keeps us urbanized and indoors as we go from home to car to office, from health club to shopping mall and back home. Asphalt and concrete bury wilderness, and our city lights blind us to the stars and galaxies. The "liberation technologies" of electronic communication can enlighten and mobilize masses of people, but they are shamelessly captured by commercial culture. The mass media of television, film, and radio are largely controlled by a few corporations who are as disinterested in the truth quest as they are interested is maximizing their profits through entertainment and advertising.

So we endlessly pursue self-interest and wind up feeling alone, meaningless cogs in the machinery of mass society, while congratulating ourselves on being the freest people in history. Globally, contradictions sharpen as we see a rise in murderous fundamentalism and the slow destruction of every traditional culture by consumerism. We are exhausting the resources of our planet and exhausting ourselves in the process. The philosopher Richard Tarnas summed up the paradox well: "The unprecedented outward expansiveness of modernity, its heroic confidence, contrasts starkly with an unprecedented inner impoverishment, uncertainty, alienation and confusion."[4]

To find a way forward we need to know where we are and how we got here; we need to ask in the words of the political philosopher Eric Voegelin how the "spectaculum of modernity" became a "global madhouse bursting with stupendous vitality."[5]

## "Big History" and the Fourth Revolution

Answering the big questions today requires the perspective of "big history" — the vastly expanded story of human emergence from an evolving earth. From this vantage point, we see that civilization's 5,500-year written history is little more than a millionth of the history of the earth, and that the life of the earth is but a small fraction of the life of the universe.[6]

Twenty years ago, physicist and philosopher Peter Russell graphically demonstrated the power of big history's capacity to illuminate our crisis. In his book *White Hole in Time*, Russell used what has since become an unintentionally ominous image to wake us up to the significance of our present moment in human evolution.[7] He took for his scale what was then the iconic achievement of civilization — the world's tallest building — the quarter-mile-high, 108-story World Trade Center. Against this, he imaginatively projected the 4.5 billion years of earth's history. Street level, then, represents the formation of our planet, and the first living cells don't appear until one-quarter the way up, on the 25th floor (about 3.5 billion years ago); plant life starts halfway up, around the 50th floor. Dinosaurs appear on the 104th floor, and mammals and the great apes arrive on the topmost, 108th floor, of the building. *Homo erectus* becomes fully upright only a few inches from the ceiling of the top floor. Already, 99.99 percent of the story of evolution has been told, and civilization has not yet begun. One-quarter inch from the ceiling, *Homo sapiens* replaces Neanderthals, and the first Paleolithic rock paintings appear. Modernity begins at less than the thickness of the coat of paint on the ceiling of the top floor of the quarter-mile-high structure.

Russell's point is as simple as it is obvious and ignored: this exponential rate of evolutionary change in "informational complexity" is approaching a singularity — a leap into a radically different order of being.[8] Wherever this takeoff point is, and whatever lies on the other side, we are getting there fast. Something dramatically different is about to happen. The apocalyptic possibilities of our moment are reinforced by the fact that we can no longer use Russell's metaphor without seeing the twin towers of the World Trade Center collapsing into rubble.

The convergence of these two perspectives — a vastly expanded historical narrative on the one hand, and global destruction on the other — puts extraordinary pressure on our moment. It impels us to consider the possibility that we are poised on the edge of a planetary transformation: of either global catastrophe or some "leap in being" that averts disaster and ushers in something radically novel.

Looking back over the past two hundred thousand years of human existence, we can identify three increasingly sudden leaps in human self-understanding — three revolutionary discontinuities in our way of being

— that are critical in understanding and responding to the uniqueness of our moment. The first was the original primal revolution — the relatively sudden appearance of self-reflective human consciousness in a lineage of upright primates foraging in an African wilderness, which occurred sometime between two hundred thousand and one hundred thousand years ago. The second was the agricultural revolution beginning around ten thousand years ago. The third was the industrial revolution, which had its roots in the sixteenth century and in the gradual convergence of three revolutions — scientific, commercial, and religious. (See chart on page xx.)

The initial "primal revolution" was associated with fire making and the appearance of language and symbolic culture. With this leap into the realm of imagination and self-awareness came an expanded arena of real freedom, creativity, and choice; with choice comes the reality of good and bad choices. Humanity was confronted for the first time by the realm of morality and the question of "the best way to live." In compact bands of nomadic hunter-gatherers, this question was continually addressed and answered in the everyday flow of face-to-face discussion and storytelling. All participated in the life of the self-sufficient, more or less egalitarian community, where the political economy was based on simple reciprocity, cooperation, caring, and sharing. All had some direct experience of the social and cosmological whole.

Around ten thousand years ago, agricultural civilization started walling out wilderness. Ground was held, ploughed, seeded, irrigated, harvested, and defended. The initial domestication of wild plants and cereals was most probably the achievement of the woman-as-gatherer and her plant wisdom. The first Neolithic civilizations in Old Europe were, as far as we know, correspondingly peaceful, egalitarian, nature- and goddess-worshipping societies.[9] Over time, agricultural society made possible growth in population, which was accompanied by an increasing division of labor, specialization in knowledge, and more sharply defined hierarchies of wealth and power. Hunters became soldiers, shamans became priests, and captives became the slaves who built the fortifications and monumental architecture that defined cities. Warrior societies became more patriarchal, and the power and influence of women declined. Religious and political wisdom passed into the hands of scribes, bureaucrats, and professionals who taught what they had been taught, enforced obedience, and eclipsed the authority of the individual's direct experience of the cosmological whole.

The most recent leap in human self-awareness has been accomplished through industrial capitalism, inspired and guided by the political philosophy of Liberalism, which advocated freeing the rational self-interested individual from the constraints of religion, tradition, and arbitrary government. Liberalism helped liberate the individual from a calcified and corrupt feudalism. It produced the astonishing understandings of modern science and its near-miraculous technology. But this revolution has also deformed crucial dimensions of what it means to be human — in particular, the organic connection to other humans and to the larger world of nature from which our humanity emerged. Over the past few centuries the astounding leap in our technological prowess has been supported by an increasingly complex division of labor, held together by hierarchies of wealth and organized violence.

In the past century, while we have applied our scientific intelligence to brilliantly illuminating aspects of the human condition, we have also applied it, with equal passion, to the bureaucratically administered extermination of millions. We have endured two world wars and witnessed how a highly developed industrial nation, Nazi Germany, focused advanced engineering in a production line of mass murder. The transports, gas chambers, and crematoria of one of the death camps, Auschwitz, operated for two years, killing and cremating up to twenty thousand people a day. Altogether somewhere between eleven and seventeen million perished in the Nazi extermination program. After declaring "never again!" we have already witnessed several smaller genocides in Cambodia, Rwanda, Bosnia, and now Darfur. Since World War II we have not had a single day without warfare. The toll of government-directed murder for the twentieth century exceeds 260 million human beings.[10] We face a situation in which humanity has become almost godlike in its technological prowess but demonic in how it directs that power.

Peter Russell's curve of accelerating change suggests that we are on the cusp of a "fourth revolution" in human self-consciousness. Thanks to science and critical scholarship, we have a depth of understanding of all three revolutions that no previous generation could have hoped for. We are in a position to recognize the enduring but partial truths of each and to integrate their wisdom in a higher, more-inclusive synthesis. Such an understanding would join together what has been fragmented; it would integrate the earth-based wisdom of primal societies, which sustained humanity for nine-tenths of the time that we have been human, with the achievements of the classical civilizations and the past four hundred years of science and

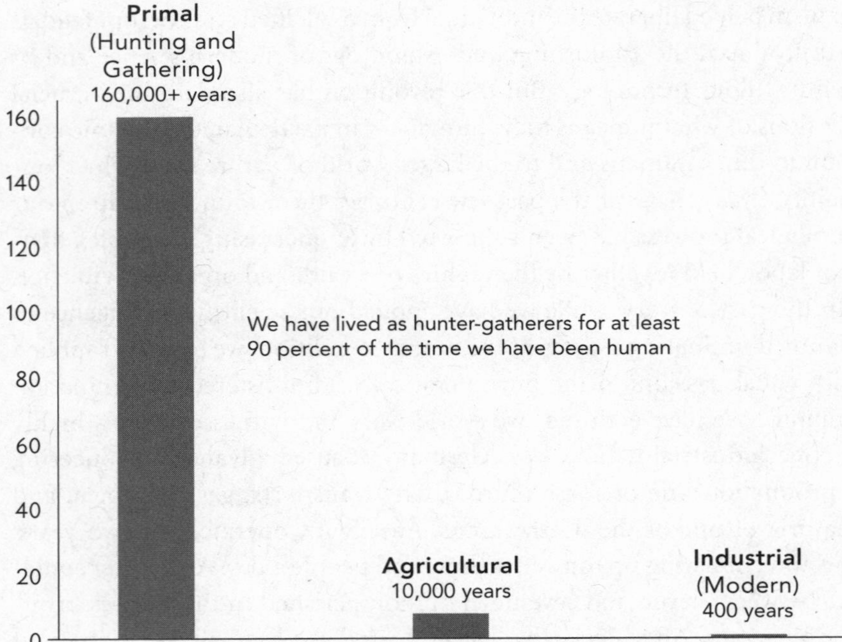


industrial capitalism. It would bring us into a fuller and more creative partnership with the evolving earth community. Such a *future primal* synthesis ultimately requires rethinking almost everything we do and, in the process, living differently.

There are three parts to this enormous undertaking:

- Understanding how the crisis of civilization has emerged within the evolutionary story "telling us into being."
- Grasping the critical role of the psyche of the individual and the significance of choice, constituting the realms of "good" and "evil" in this drama.
- Growing into a fuller humanity by pursuing our capacity for understanding and creativity and by fashioning a wisdom-based way of life — a new politics — guided by a larger, truer vision of the good of the evolving whole.

## The Four-Part Nature of the Quest as a "Tao of Politics"

Today, there are clear signs of something dramatically novel emerging: a vision of an evolving, creative humanity developing out of an evolving and stupendously creative universe. Many all over the world seem to be responding intuitively to the truth of this vision and to the existential reality of our global crisis. They are doing what they can, with what they have, where they are — creatively and courageously struggling to live more conscious, more meaningful, and more satisfying lives in ways that enhance the living diversity of the biosphere. A number of great thinkers, scholars, and artists have already contributed to clarifying and developing this emerging cosmology. What is urgently needed is a corresponding political vision — a political philosophy — that will help us better relate the life of the individual to that of the community, and the life of the whole human community to that of the natural world.

*Future Primal* is my contribution to this enormous work. It presents a model of the truth quest as an archetypal dynamic of the human search for order. I discuss this model on several levels: as I have experienced it in my own life, as it apparently unfolded from the emergence of consciousness in the earliest human society, as it has been variously repressed and cultivated by different societies, and then as it is emerging in our own times.

The model itself identifies four fundamentally interconnected elements — each is both a process and a value, together constituting minimal conditions for the truth quest. As mentioned, the four elements are

1. The self-understanding of the searching, growing *individual*;
2. Honest and ongoing *face-to-face discussion*;
3. Participation in a *democratic community* of fellow seekers;
4. The collective effort to construct an open-ended *big picture* of our single shared reality.

Together, these constitute a four-part structure that can be represented graphically as a circle divided by a cross into four quadrants — a *mandala*. The mandala is also, appropriately enough, the oldest and most universal symbol of order, representing the relationship of the searching individual to the cosmos (see the diagram in chapter 4, page 118).

We see the model most clearly exemplified in one of the last remaining indigenous hunting-gathering societies, the San Bushmen* of the Kalahari Desert. The San have been shown to be one of our closest relatives to that original human population we are all descended from.** If the success of a society is to be judged by longevity and resilience, San hunter-gatherers were probably the most successful society on earth. Despite the assumptions of early modern philosophers, life as a hunter-gatherer in a state of nature was not a "war of all against all." Nor was it a desperate struggle for survival. Under reasonable conditions, ancient and modern hunter-gatherers seem to have enjoyed more leisure than any other form of society. They directed their energies to cultivating a rich social and spiritual life, attuning their existence to "the story telling us." In the pages that follow, I show how the San exemplify this four-part dynamic as both the core of the truth quest and the coordinates of a humanizing politics.

Surprisingly, we can also find the primal structure emerging as the central values of the classical Greek polis — the creative font of Western civilization, the source of our scientific rationality, humanism, and politics. It was as if in the relative freedom and affluence of a mountainous part of the eastern Mediterranean, the Greeks reached back to the primal wisdom of the hunter-gatherer band and integrated it into their own experience in a blaze of creative brilliance. Since the model seems to express an archetypal structure of the search for order that is rooted in the primal human condition — the autonomous creative individual, in face-to-face community, embedded in nature — we find it reappearing at those creative moments of transition in history where one order is collapsing, a new one is emerging, and the big questions resurface. This is the situation we find ourselves in today.

Throughout I show how the mandala structure of the quest can function as a conceptual map — an intellectual, moral, and political compass — helping orient our movement into the future by keeping us organically rooted in our deepest nature. It can help us diagnose our crisis and clarify connections among a growing number of widely separate, liberating political and

---

* There is no single satisfactory name for the indigenous click-language-speaking hunter-gatherers of southern Africa. Each tribe names itself in a different but closely related language. Outsiders have called them variously "Bushmen," "San," "Khoisan," and "Baswara," but there is no Bushman term for all the tribes taken collectively. While scholars favor the composite "Khoisan," surviving groups in Namibia and Botswana tend to use the term "Bushmen," in the way that "black" has been appropriated with pride in the United States. In this book, I use "San" and "Bushmen" interchangeably.

** For the genetic, linguistic, geographic, and archaeological evidence for this, see chapters 5 and 6.

cultural initiatives — ranging from the "Arab Spring" to the Israeli kibbutz, from corporate reform and economic decentralization to eco-villages, Green politics, and what appears to be a mass spiritual revival. In so doing it can hopefully inspire, guide, and accelerate the urgent transformation our situation demands.

We stand at a breathtaking moment in human existence, an evolutionary turning point, where the integrity of the biosphere depends as never before on human understanding and choice. As I write, destruction to the living fabric of the earth accelerates and human suffering intensifies. What we lack are not technologies and tactics as much as political will. And this can only come from a compelling shared vision of our situation and the possibilities inherent in the paradox of the human condition: that the earth that gave birth to the free-thinking human is the very same earth we are choosing to devastate.

*Future Primal* is not a conventional academic work in history, philosophy, psychology, or anthropology, but rather a work of creative synthesis. It draws from a wide range of disciplines, cultures, and historical periods to answer the big questions of personal and political life. Given the broad range of this project, it is inevitable that my treatment will be, in places, oversimplified and superficial. But what I hope to offer is an integrated vision of a better way of life grounded, as any such work must be, in my personal search. In drawing together images of the past, present, and possible future of such a politics, I show how at its center is a model of a way of searching, which is also the core of the good life we seek. This means the vision of *Future Primal* differs from past paradigms of politics in recognizing that the ongoing search itself — the primal truth quest — needs to be at the center of a new politics.

By telling something of how this vision grew out of my search and my story, I invite readers to reflect on how their own worldviews have been shaped by their lives. When we pursue such understandings, and share them openly in face-to-face communication, we start to re-create a living shared cosmology while embodying the politics of questing in our lives. We find, in fact, that our searching becomes the goal; the path becomes the destination in a Tao of politics. Such a practice, if generalized into a political culture, could help constitute that dramatic leap in collective self-consciousness our species so desperately needs.

## Organization of the Book

This book is organized in three parts. Part I, "Where Are We?" takes the measure of our current moment and how we got here. In the spirit of the truth quest, this weaves together both my personal story and society's story. In a sense, chapter 1, "The Truth Quest," begins at the end, describing how I came to recognize the structure of the mandala of primal politics in my life, the life of the San Bushmen, and society at large. Chapter 2, "Abandonment of the Quest," tells the history of our ruling paradigm of the good life — the political philosophy of classical Liberalism and how it has come to constitute an increasingly global political culture that eliminated the quest from public life. Chapter 3, "Recovery of the Quest, Part I," tells the "small story" of my life and my struggle for meaning, out of which this vision of primal politics emerged. Chapter 4, "Recovery of the Quest, Part II," is the philosophical heart of the book, presenting the future primal political model I propose and explaining the dynamic of the four-part mandala structure of the truth quest at its center.

Part II, "Where Do We Come From?" elaborates on the "big story" of humanity and the traditional life of the San Bushmen; it focuses on identifying our original, ancestral primal politics; how that is rooted in the evolution of our species; and how it is exemplified in the lifestyle of San hunter-gatherers. Chapter 5, "Out of Wilderness," tells the story of how both consciousness and the coordinates of the quest evoloved out of an African wilderness. Chapter 6, "Lost Worlds," re-creates what we know of traditional San Bushman hunter-gatherers when the fully nomadic hunting-gathering way of life was still viable; it also examines the intentions, achievements, and limits of the researchers and scholars who did the research. Chapter 7, "Primal Politics," looks at more recent scholarship on San society and presents a fuller picture of how its traditional life exemplifies the four elements of primal politics. Chapter 8, "If You Don't Dance, You Die," describes the spiritual life of the San as expressed through their rock art, mythology, and healing dance, and it shows how shamanic practices are integral to their politics. I explore shamanic practice and its role in the truth quest further and more generally in chapter 9, "Boundary Crossing," and chapter 10, "The Outer Reaches of

Inner Wilderness." Chapter 11, "The Primal Polis: Socrates as Shaman," steps back in time to explore the political parallels in the ancient Greek polis and the role of shamanism in Socratic teaching and the birth of Western politics.

Part III, "Where Should We Be Going?" focuses on our present moment. Chapter 12, "Our Primal Future," highlights instances where we can already see elements of primal politics emerging around the world. In particular, it examines the Israeli kibbutz and the politics of Nelson Mandela for lessons on how we might apply these principles in radically different contexts. The epilogue, "A Tao of Politics," tackles the limitations of all political paradigms and shows how the future primal model differs from past paradigms in recognizing that the process of searching is at the heart of the good life we seek. Finally, the appendix, "Future Primal Toolkit," suggests a range of strategies for bringing our primal future into our lives here and now.

seemed intuitively obvious: to go back to "what was," to imaginatively reconstruct the simplest, earliest form of human society, in order to rethink "what could and should be." Later I came to think of this movement back to go forward as a fundamental aspect of creative renewal — an "eternal primal return."

Personal reasons also drove me back. Until that point I had approached the consciousness of early human societies through texts, libraries, and universities. I felt an urgent need to fix this contradiction, to balance some of the thousands of hours spent indoors with my face turned away from the world, sitting at a desk, staring at books and computer screens. I was hungry for strong, simple experiences of what it meant to be a fully embodied human being in a southern African wilderness. Finally, I was close to burnout and just plain homesick.

The Port Elizabeth airport had barely changed since I was a child. Its single, small terminal building sat in the bush near a rocky wild coastline. As soon as I stepped out of the plane, I took in a deep breath, thick with the smells of salt spray and coastal vegetation, and savored the thrill of being home again. The coastal terrace of southern Africa gets rain throughout the year and is covered with tough, small-leafed, flowering bush — the aromatic *fynbos* or "fine bush" of the Southern Cape. This small area is so ancient and so unique that it constitutes one of the earth's six plant kingdoms, with one of the largest concentrations of biodiversity anywhere.[1] Forest- and bush-covered mountain ranges follow much of the coastline, providing a noble backdrop to enormous curving bays of surf-pounded white sand beaches. Clear rivers and streams, stained amber by forest vegetation, run through valleys and steep gorges to empty into rocky coves and open sandy bays.

When Europeans first arrived, the area was filled with the magnificent big game of Africa — elephant, rhinoceros, lion, leopard, buffalo, and a great variety of buck. Hippopotami waded out of river mouths into the ocean surf to greet the startled Dutch sailors, who named the creatures *zeekoe*, "sea cows." The natural bounty of a region filled with flowers and birds is reflected in the Khoisan name for one of the mountain ranges, Outeniqua, meaning "laden with honey." The coast is dotted with gaping rock shelters, which hold some of the richest evidence for that last leap into modern human consciousness that took place roughly two hundred thousand years ago. Few places on earth could be more evocative of an African Eden than this most southern point of the ancient continent of Africa.

As a child I regularly explored one shelter on the Robberg Peninsula, the Mountain of Seals, which juts off the coast halfway between Port Elizabeth and Cape Town. The eastern edge of the peninsula offers a spectacular view of the former whaling station of Plettenberg Bay. The western coast overlooks a small sandy beach cove fringed by rocks and tide pools. I began my pilgrimage home by returning to the Robberg for the first time after many years. I arrived at the end of the day to find the place deserted. I stepped out of the car, followed the path down the cliff to the cove, and was immediately immersed in the sights, smells, and feel of the coast: the sharp, feral mix of the *fynbos*, seaweed, and salt; the surf crashing on the ocean-scrubbed, bone-white shell-and-stone beach; and the shock of the cold water as I dove in. I scrambled out quickly, spooked by the shadows of large fish next to me in the raised swell. I climbed up and sat inside the mouth of the largest shelter, wide enough for a band of perhaps a dozen people. The floor was made up of fresh and fossilizing shell and bone; in nearby caves, these floors can extend down more than a dozen feet. The whole coastline is rich with archaeological finds from the period when self-conscious *Homo sapiens* emerged over the past two hundred thousand years. Nothing had changed since my childhood except for the addition of a small knee-high fence through which Stone Age relics spilled down the slope. As I sat warming in the golden last light of the day, I could see almost no sign of the intervening thousands of years of civilization. I felt as if I was stepping through a personal dreamscape into our deep past to when some of the first humans lived in that same place.*

We now know in persuasive detail that the earth was once nothing but wilderness: everything, everywhere untouched by human hand, unseen by human eye; nothing tamed, domesticated, or civilized. We know that out of an African savanna, incubated in it, nurtured by it, a primate lineage gradually evolved into hominids. Then hominids slowly developed the self-reflective, creative consciousness capable of language, art, religion, and politics. The very nature of our freedom and creativity emerged gradually, conditioned by the daily rhythms of sunrise and sunset, the seasonal movements of game,

---

* Humanity's oldest symbolic artifact, a piece of carved ochre seventy-seven thousand years old, was found a little farther down the coast in a rock shelter called Blombos near the small town of Stilbaai. More recently, a pair of hundred-thousand-year-old "painting kits" in abalone shells were found in the same shelter. See chapter 5 for more on this.

and the smells and colors of fruit, flower, and veldt. This is the first fact of life — one of the most startling discoveries of modern times: human beings were made by wilderness. Yet all our contemporary political institutions were created by men ignorant of this most basic reality.

Around sixty thousand years ago a population of hunter-gatherers walked out of southern Africa and rapidly spread over the rest of the planet. Most human beings alive today are direct descendants of that small group. Parts of that founder population never left their African Eden; they continued to develop and thrive as nomadic hunter-gatherers into modern times, protected by the harshness of the Kalahari Desert. Today their children barely survive, forced off their ancestral hunting grounds, often living in squalor, at the mercy of government agencies. Recent genetic and linguistic mapping studies support what long seemed clear to many of us who grew up in South Africa: Bushmen populations are the closest living relatives to our shared "African Adam and Eve."* Their traditional cosmology is most likely among the oldest on earth, seeming to recede back into the Paleolithic origins of human consciousness. Traditional nomadic Bushmen led an existence that in some ways seems enchanted, moving in small egalitarian bands held together by an ethos of caring for and sharing with one another, while being sensitively attuned to the natural world.

By contrast, the dominant political and economic institutions of our modern world were created from radically different assumptions about our origins. Political philosophers like John Locke accepted the Genesis account of earth's creation: that the planet was young, that all the plant and animal species appeared as a result of separate acts of divine creation, which culminated on the sixth day in the miraculous appearance of human beings. They believed the natural world existed as raw material for the central human project of productive labor — converting wilderness into wealth. In 1688, when Locke published his *Two Treatises on Government*, the iconic text of modern politics, the global human population was less than half a billion and vast tracts of forest and prairie still covered North America. Southern Africa was an Eden filled with great herds of grazing and browsing animals. To Locke and his contemporaries, all of this existed to feed human appetite and ambition. It was simply "waste" until transformed by human labor:

---

* Chapter 6, "Lost Worlds," discusses the evidence for this.

sinking sun. I found a flat rock, and as we sat together and watched the sun disappear, something deep inside me shifted and settled. For a long moment I had an exquisite feeling of complete identity with the baboons echoing back through the millennia to some old, ancestral primate sitting on a warm rock watching an African sunset. It was an exquisite *feeling* of connection to this place and a bone-deep certainty of the truth of Darwin's insight — "who understands the baboon would do more toward metaphysics than Locke."

This simple revelation was a turning point in my journey and a powerful affirmation of my quest. It had touched some emotional bedrock that gave me the confidence to continue my efforts to reconstruct a deeper, truer way of being human, of living together on this miraculous, evolving, and now-threatened earth.

## The Navel of the World

My subsequent journeys back to South Africa also helped me find meaning in my comfortable Hawaiian exile through an illuminating opposition. Hawai'i is one of the most isolated, ecologically fragile pieces of land on the planet. Surrounded by thousands of miles of Pacific Ocean in every direction, it is the exact antipode of South Africa, both geographically and culturally as far away from my African roots as it is possible to get. As I sit on my lanai writing this, I can look up and see the emerald green Ko'olau mountain range at the back of the valley. Directly beneath the Ko'olaus, on the other side of the planet, are the eroded granite cliffs of Cape Town's Table Mountain. Like the Ko'olaus, Table Mountain rises dramatically from beaches and rocky coves. In photographs the two locations appear strikingly similar. On the ground they couldn't be more different. The Ko'olaus are geologically young, pushed up through a volcano on the ocean floor barely three million years ago. Their valleys and cliffs often seem lonely — no screeching monkeys, no snakes, no leopards, no sunset bark of baboon.

On the other hand, the Cape Fold Mountains are hundreds of millions of years old, scarred, cracked, and weathered by baking sun, storms, cold ocean fog, and the numberless generations of African wildlife living, growing, and dying on its surface. Hiking around the Cape today one still meets baboons foraging in an environment similar to the one that helped shape our shared primate ancestry. Southern Africa is where the great human adventure of globalization began; Hawai'i is where, in a sense, it ended — one of the last places to be colonized by our African ancestors. Kilauea, on the Big Island, is the longest continually erupting volcano in the world — like a *piko*, or "navel," of the earth — still actively giving life to new land. From the oldest to the newest, from the first to the last, this symmetry of opposites made the islands a privileged place for philosophical distance. Distance from my birthplace also helped by putting the sharp edge of homesickness to my reflections on humanity's alienation from our African Eden.

My journey to Hawai'i was circuitous. My family left South Africa for England when I was a boy. After a Cambridge education in science, I emigrated to Israel, lived on a kibbutz, served as a paratrooper in the Israeli army, and survived a Middle Eastern war. Throughout, I made trips to South Africa every few years to visit my parents, who had returned from England in 1970. Most of the trips were confined to the southern coast, where I revived old friendships and started to recover some of those extraordinary states of consciousness I had experienced in wilderness with a child's fresh eyes. By the time of my first university sabbatical in 1998, I had been in Hawai'i twenty years, and I had come to realize that South Africa stood in unique relationship, not only to Hawai'i, but to the rest of the world. The natural and human history of my birthplace seemed to offer a crucial perspective on my times and my species.

I felt ignorant and excited about exploring my neglected homeland more thoroughly. I wanted to experience directly the people and the places that would allow me to imaginatively reconstruct something of the life of the first people of southern Africa — the ancestors of all humans. My goals were modest. I wanted to be able to sit and think in front of some of those ancient Bushman rock paintings that cover the walls of rock shelters throughout southern Africa. There are an estimated fifteen thousand such painted sites — an immense wilderness art gallery filled with tantalizing images from the spirit world of the first people of South Africa. I wanted to find some of the best-preserved examples in the wildest settings, so I could experience them closer to the way the long-dead artists had, surrounded by the multitudes of African wildlife. Finally, I wanted to meet face-to-face, if only briefly, the modern descendants of the human beings who had never left southern

Africa, those who still lived in the desert of the Kalahari and still knew something of the "old ways."

After getting acclimatized in Port Elizabeth revisiting my childhood haunts, many virtually unchanged over the years, I traveled to the urban nightmare of Johannesburg. I was told not to stop at traffic lights when driving at night because hijackers had been shooting the drivers and stealing their cars. But Johannesburg was also home to the world-famous Rock Art Research Institute at the University of the Witwatersrand, where I met David Lewis-Williams, its founder and director, and one of the pioneers of the shamanic interpretation of Bushman rock art. He generously gave me introductions to the wardens who would be able to direct me — sometimes accompanied by armed rangers — to some of the more impressive paintings in the Drakensberg Mountains. Much of the game in the Drakensberg has been hunted out, but large empty areas are protected and being repopulated by herds of eland.

To get a little closer to imagining what life in wilderness must have been like, I spent a few days in a primitive wilderness camp in the *lowveld* of Kruger National Park — a wilderness area the size of the entire country of Israel. Every morning at dawn our small group walked out into the bush led by two armed rangers in search of encounters with the "big five" — elephant, rhino, buffalo, lion, and leopard — supposedly the five most dangerous animals to hunt on foot. The Kruger is one of the first, the largest, and the least-transformed game reserves in southern Africa. It is also one of the few places where it is still possible to find a few Bushman paintings in an indigenous, intact ecosystem with the full variety of animals the painters lived with. Today we often think of a walk in the woods as placid, where nature is a pretty backdrop for what really interests us — the human drama. But an intact African ecosystem is enormously complex and continually fascinating.

One morning we were following the spoor of a lone bull buffalo — regarded by many big-game hunters as the most dangerous of the big five because of its habit of turning off the trail and doubling back to ambush the hunter. We stopped for a break, and I walked out of sight of the group to some bushes at the base of a small outcrop of rock. As I approached the bushes and peered inside, an enormous mass of black muscle exploded out of the vegetation, almost knocking me over with fright, and galloped off in a panic. A lone wildebeest bull had, for some reason, separated from the herd and hidden himself in the shade of the bush. The whole event had taken place out of sight of the rangers, who on hearing my story laughed in disbelief. Wildebeest are herd animals and seldom found alone in a bush. Life in an intact savanna wilderness is full of surprises.

The Bushman paintings in the Kruger were worn, but their mere presence was evocative, reminding me that the theater of Bushman life included a cast of thousands — from the majestic elephant and rhino to the mantis, the little green flying insect, one incarnation of the trickster deity of Bushman mythology.

After a gentle initiation in the Kruger, we proceeded to a more extreme wilderness immersion experience: five days backpacking in the riverine bush of the Hluhluwe-Umfolozi Game Reserve in what used to be called Zululand, and is now Kwazulu, Natal. We carried all our food and slept under the stars. This was the hunting preserve of Shaka and the Zulu kings, and is still home to the full complement of indigenous, savanna megafauna, including the largest rhino population in the world.* Surrounded by large and potentially dangerous animals, guided and protected by two seasoned rangers, I experienced some of the most beautiful and peaceful moments of my life.

The climax of the trip involved flying to Windhoek, the capital of Namibia, renting a Land Rover, and driving into the veldt of Nyae Nyae, East Bushmanland, to visit surviving Ju/twasi** (Ju/hoansi) San communities. After Namibian independence in 1981, the filmmaker and ethnographer John Marshall, who had grown up with the Ju/twasi, helped set up the Nyae Nyae

---

* Much credit goes to Dr. Ian Player for leading the efforts to create this wilderness reserve and initiating the "Save the Rhino" project. Rhinos are again critically endangered by poaching for the Asian market in rhino horn. In South Africa in 2011, over three hundred rhino were slaughtered by poachers.

** There is confusing variation in the spelling of Ju/twasi, ranging from Ju/wasi and Zhun/twasi to the scholarly Ju/hoansi, which follows phonetic convention. Elizabeth Marshall points out that Ju/hoansi reads to the average person like "Jew hone si" and has little resemblance to the actual pronunciation. The "/" is a dental palatal click made by withdrawing the tongue sharply from the back of the front teeth in a sucking sound, as in "tsk." The spelling that comes closest to the actual pronunciation to my ear is the slightly unconventional Ju/twasi (singular: "Jul/twa"). For more on this name, see also chapter 6.

Development Foundation of Namibia with the purpose of helping the people get access to their traditional land — Bushmanland — and gradually transition from hunting and gathering to farming and raising livestock.* As development priorities shifted, the government started working with international aid and conservation agencies — the US Agency for International Development and the World Wildlife Foundation — to establish the Nyae Nyae Conservancy in 1996. This was in part inspired by the idea that Bushmen were best suited for a hunting-gathering way of life, and they should be encouraged to pursue it as much as possible, together with benefiting from trophy hunting and ecotourism. Large numbers of elephants and lions had migrated to the area, attracted by the water of the newly dug bore holes. The tourist and trophy-hunting markets, however, were fickle, lions and elephants did not mix well with farming, and the land base was too small to support a traditional nomadic hunting-and-gathering lifestyle. The result was that the people remained impoverished in what John Marshall called "death by myth" — the myth of the Bushman forever consigned to hunt and gather — the title of the final volume of his five-part film documenting the saga of his family's time with the San.[3]

Amazingly, in 1998, some of the old ways still remained. One of the anthropologists who spent many years working with the community introduced me to a young Bushman guide, /Twi (/Ui) Toma, who helped me connect with some of the old healers and shamans. We camped outside a tiny village consisting of a few simple huts, went hunting with the men, gathered *veldkos* (bushfood) with the women, distributed pouches of the harsh Botswana tobacco that visitors are expected to provide, and shared rounds of tea and biscuits around the campfire. Finally, we found singers and healers in a neighboring village who organized a healing trance dance for the group. The Kalahari Bushmen still practiced the same trance dance that seems to have been universal among diverse Bushman groups throughout southern Africa. The healer-shamans stamped and danced in a tight circle around the singers, who sat shoulder to shoulder around the fire singing and clapping the eerie, complex contrapuntal songs. The healers were bent over, propping themselves up with their dancing sticks, and carried the fly whisk made from

* In 1986 this become the Nyae Nyae Farmers Co-operative, a grassroots advocacy organization for the Ju/twasi.

*Author and /Twi (/Ui) Toma, Bushman guide and interpreter.*
*(Photo: Vicki Nielsen)*

wildebeest hair — the signature of the dancer. Once caught up in the trance-inducing energies of the singing and dancing, some of the healers started entering the spirit world, shaking, sweating, shrieking, talking in tongues, circling the group diagnosing and healing sickness and disorder. That night, under the stars, on the sands of the Kalahari, I witnessed an activity that I had seen depicted in rock paintings over a thousand miles away in South Africa, where the now-extinct southern San — the /Xam — performed the same dances and then painted their experiences on the rock walls of their shelters.

I had no illusions of playing anthropologist or of contributing to the empirical fieldwork on the San, one of the most thoroughly studied groups of hunter-gatherers in the world. One scholar estimated that there are over a thousand published pages for every living San. I simply approached them with the big questions of political philosophy in mind. What can we learn about human nature from one of the last and oldest of such cultures that can guide us now? How did the changing context and circumstances of San life shape their society and politics? How can speculations about our distant past illuminate how we all should live together on this single, increasingly crowded, and fragile planet?

After 1998, I continued making regular trips to South Africa. In 2007 I went to Andriesvale on the edge of the Kalahari to visit one of the last groups of Bushmen to survive within South Africa — the Khomani San. They had inhabited what is now the Kgalagadi Transfrontier Park (which includes the old Gemsbok National Park) on the border between South Africa and Botswana. During apartheid, they had been removed from the park and had scattered, losing their language — perhaps the oldest of all the San languages — and much of their culture. Then in 1999 the new South African government returned to the Khomani some forty thousand hectares, half of which were inside the game reserve. Since then some fourteen surviving language speakers have been found, and there are vigorous attempts to revive the culture and establish a viable local economy.

But the Khomani I saw were still living in shacks in the sand, plagued by poverty, sickness, alcoholism, and boredom. I traveled with one of the leaders — now an Afrikaans speaker with an Afrikaans name, Jan van der Westhuizen, or simply "Oom Jan" — into the central Kalahari of Botswana to D'Kar, where dozens of other Bushman groups had gathered from all over southern Africa for the annual Bushman dance and healing festival. There, filmmakers Craig and Damon Foster were filming /Urugab "Toppies" Kruiper, a young Khomani man who with his family was on a mission to reconnect with the "old ways" and become a fully initiated hunter.* Toppies was all muscle and sinew, his front teeth knocked out and his chest marked with long, jagged white scars from several near-fatal knife fights. He was soft-spoken and laughed as he told me, pointing to his scars, that it was a miracle he was still alive. I spent several days with Oom Jan in the red dunes of the Bushman section of Kgalagadi Park, listening to his stories about how as a young man he had been raised in the park and taught how to hunt with a spear, running down antelope. During the day we followed animal tracks, and

* The film, a full-length high-definition feature, *My Hunter's Heart*, has since been shown throughout South Africa.

at night I did a lot of thinking, sitting in front of the campfire, and then lying on my back, looking up — or was it down?! — dizzyingly into those millions of distant suns glittering in the unpolluted blackness of the desert sky.

## Primal Political Philosophy

The insight I got from repeated and sometimes difficult returns to Hawai'i made me realize that I was no longer primarily interested in being a detached academic, applying critical methodologies to solve scholarly problems. Like it or not, I came to understand that my whole life was a struggle with something like the daunting project of classical political philosophy. This traditionally required nothing less than bringing together the totality of one's lived experience to confront the defining question of the truth quest: "How should we live?" Socrates and Plato, Hobbes, Locke, Rousseau, and Marx, all giants among many others, attempted to articulate an integrated vision in response to this question. Entire societies and ways of life were organized around these visions. In each case the philosopher had responded to a personally felt sense of crisis in the life of the larger society. In each case the creative response required a return to beginnings, to asking and attempting to answer the foundational questions around which every worldview and way of life are constructed: What is the human condition? What connects humans to the rest of creation — the community of being? How can this guide our thinking about good governance, a just and healthy economy, and a satisfying and meaningful life for the individual?

From the perspective of scholarly research, the scope of such a project was clearly huge, and I hesitated to admit my ambition and face the accusation of grandiosity. Then the primal perspective gave me courage, reminding me that in a very basic sense no one escapes the challenge facing the political philosopher. Everyone has to take a stand in the face of the totality of life — even if it is the bad-faith choice of simply going with the flow or living in denial and choosing not to think. We are part of an epic story whose beginning and end are the deepest mystery. We all grow from infancy into adult consciousness asking periodically, "Who am I? What is real? Where am I going? What role shall I play?" All of us answer these questions more or less self-consciously, more or less hurriedly. Ultimately we answer them in the pattern of the daily decisions and actions that make up our lives.

I was also encouraged in this task by the groundbreaking work of Thomas Kuhn in *The Structure of Scientific Revolutions*, first published in 1962, which exposed the inherent limitation of all paradigms — all models of reality in science, and by extension every other area of human knowledge. Kuhn demonstrated convincingly that all scientific theories are inevitably shaped by the context and intention of the scientists and scholars who formulated them. There is no absolutely objective knowledge independent of the perspective and situation of the researcher. Discoveries in modern physics and evolutionary cosmology have confirmed that even at the most fundamental level of elementary particles the observer can never be fully separated from what is observed. So in the late 1990s, it seemed to me that politics was in something of a "postparadigm phase," where we could no longer defer to the great minds of political science and wait for another John Locke to figure it all out for us. Somehow we now all have to be implicated in the business of thinking about how we should live together. We all have to wrestle with the big questions that were reserved for the geniuses of the past.*

I was further heartened by the fact that, as I went back to beginnings and confronted these questions, I could feel myself becoming whole and healthy. The deeper I went into wilderness, the faster the regeneration, and the more I could see the glories and flaws of civilization in sharp relief. I discovered I was also following a path that could be called *shamanic* and that was much more ancient than our written philosophical and religious traditions.

Shamanic practices seem to constitute the earliest form of religion and are central to the lives of hunter-gatherers the world over. Today, related practices can still be found in many religious and spiritual paths across cultures. Shamanic experiences seem to have a common structure in which the ego is overcome, opening awareness to a larger, transpersonal field of information in the service of healing and visioning. The variety of shamanic "psychotechnologies" is truly extraordinary, ranging from chanting, fasting, and self-mutilation to wilderness immersion, incessant dancing, and the ingesting of hallucinogenic plants and mushrooms. The loss of ego can be terrifying but is more typically ecstatic, providing an experience of reality that is often described as larger, deeper, and exquisitely beautiful. Scholar of

---

* I return to Thomas Kuhn in the epilogue, where I consider the model of primal politics as a "metaparadigm."

comparative religion Mircea Eliade described shamanism simply as "archaic techniques of ecstasy."[4] The old shamans seemed to realize that in order to understand society and live more fully attuned to reality, we need periodically to go wild, to travel out of our normal minds to the invisible world of spirit, which underlies the visible. The uninitiated often dismiss such experiences as vague, misty, and emotional. The reality is that the visions are often so incredibly detailed and vivid that one is convinced of having looked through the veil of everyday life into an underlying, normally hidden order of immense complexity and beauty. But shamanic visions are also like mystical experiences in having a powerful, subtle salutary effect of great value in guiding and tuning our lives.*

So while I was developing my theories about politics, I would also regularly pry my rationality-indoctrinated, logic-trained ego from its civilized existence and open myself to the subtle prelinguistic knowledge from the body and the earth. Hawai'i offered me a simple discipline for balancing the poles of civilization and wilderness. I could bookend a workday spent inside — reading, writing, arguing, and teaching — with an hour or two early and late in the day immersed in *mauka* and *makai*, mountain and ocean, the old Hawaiian daily prescription for healthy living. Neither beach nor mountain was more than fifteen minutes from my campus office. By late afternoon I could be alone running on empty mountain trails or swimming half a mile beyond the reef in open ocean. I loved the way I could almost magically exit one world and enter its opposite. Each world — hyperintellectual and urban on the one hand; physical, unfocused, and wild on the other — seemed an essential complement to the other.

After work, I would start running with my head filled with the arguments, encounters, and anxieties of the day. After twenty minutes of deep breathing and sweated exertion, my eyes saturated with greens and blues, my ears full of birdsong, the talk in my head would exhaust itself and slowly be replaced by a blissful sense of peace and boundlessness. I would only realize the absence of the voice in my head when it returned periodically. At certain points I would stop and look back down at Honolulu, shrunk into something I could cover with my outstretched hand, and remind myself that all of it — the stacked white and gray blocks of concrete high-rises fringing the

---

* Chapter 9, "Boundary Crossing," discusses shamanism in more detail.

ocean — only existed because of this richly forested, much-ignored upland, holding the rain clouds, filling the underground aquifers, replenishing oxygen, photosynthesizing carbon dioxide into our food. I bushwhacked up and down the steep slopes and streambeds and learned where the feral pigs lived and where the wild food grew. I learned the patterns of wind, sun, and rain and got to know the trails well enough to run in moonlight — just as I got to know the ocean well enough to swim beyond the reef at sunset, my senses sharpened knowing that tiger sharks swam the same waters and occasionally mistook humans for prey.

After a while I realized that my daily wilderness immersion was not simply a pleasant escape but a kind of meditation, one that literally brought my intellectual life down to earth and helped align mind, spirit, and body. Afterward I would feel more elevated, cleansed, and inspired than I ever did coming out of a synagogue or temple. The intellectual fog would lift, and the reason for my frustrations with academia would become absurdly obvious. Texts, interpretations of interpretations, and language games had been eclipsing all of "what was not text," not-language. What I needed, what any politics needs, is direct experience of how the human being is ultimately connected to the natural world of creation as a whole. I started to think of running trails as part of my philosophical practice, helping restore the balance between opposites: experience and language, body and mind, wilderness and civilization. A huge truth had been so close it was invisible.

Then I discovered Eric Voegelin, the only major political philosopher to recognize the importance of understanding this in-between nature of the human condition for politics. During a lifetime immersed in the scholarship of world civilizations and the history of philosophy, he developed a philosophy of consciousness that was surprisingly congruent with an understanding of an evolving earth and shamanic states of consciousness. Voegelin stressed that we have to keep reminding ourselves that we are born into a drama not of our making. We wake up within the story of our civilization, which in turn emerges from the story of the earth, as the earth itself emerges from the unfolding universe. We have some freedom to write our own script, but like it or not, we are also playing a part in a script written by another hand. Politics involves tuning ourselves and our stories to the "story telling us."*

---

* I return to my expanded use of Voegelin's "in-between" in chapter 4, "Recovery of the Quest, Part II."

This means we are always "looking out" from within our own field of awareness. This is the reason that I make a point to tell something of my own life story, in order to be self-conscious and explicit about my own lived perspective. For the same reason I also make a point of considering the lives and contexts of the scientists, researchers, and thinkers who developed the stories and theories on which modernity has been constructed. For instance, Thomas Hobbes, René Descartes, John Locke, and Adam Smith are primary architects of our current paradigm of the "good life," but it is beyond naive to expect their seventeenth- and eighteenth-century answers to continue to work for us today. Understanding the context for their thinking helps us distinguish what remains vital and illuminating and what does not.

As this unusual mix of political philosophy, shamanism, self-knowledge, and science converged into what I came to identify as the archetypal truth quest, I saw with increasing clarity the failure of our current paradigm in education. I saw that political science was not primarily interested in the big questions of value and meaning; in fact, the very terms *truth* and *wisdom*, *good* and *evil*, were being purged from the curriculum. Even *meaning* had been eclipsed by almighty *critique*. This was strange and disappointing, since it was precisely questions of value and meaning that had led me to political philosophy and had defined it for its founders, Socrates and his pupil, Plato. On the face of it, the situation seemed bizarre. The university, the preeminent institution of higher learning, was ignoring the question of questions, the answer to which was required to justify its own existence. No more an ivory tower, the university has long been an integral part of the larger society. Its focus on specialization without generalization, critique without reconstruction, and its increasingly refined division of labor ultimately served the values and institutions of the ruling political philosophy of classical Liberalism: rationalism, competitive individualism, and efficient production in a global marketplace.

I saw that the primary function of higher education was to equip the individual to contribute to the common good by pursuing self-interest. Across disciplines, there was little consideration of what the "good of the whole" might mean, other than being the unintended outcome of competing self-interest in an ever-expanding free market. Instead of education for responsible participation in the life of a democracy, the focus was on mathematics, science, and literacy in the interests of job training and workforce development. The logic of the factory and the marketplace determined university disciplinary divisions as much as it did most research budgets and methodologies. The sciences thrived, and philosophy, history, and the humanities fragmented and declined, with only cosmetic attempts to address the search for the good through vague references to character, integrity, and ethics.

Reflecting on my dissatisfaction with the current state of the knowledge industry, I considered what distinguished wisdom from mere knowledge or information. First of all, wisdom has a moral concern; it brings all of human experience and knowledge to deal with questions of how we should live — questions of right and wrong, good and bad. I could imagine how, throughout most of human existence, when we lived as hunter-gatherers this sort of teaching was freely shared, as young and old sat around the same campfire every night, under the stars, surrounded by wilderness, talking, arguing, and telling the stories relating one life to another, the living to the dead, and the human community to the great, wide world of nature. Traditionally, wisdom was the special purview of elders, those who had experienced some of the great, archetypal transitions from infancy through adolescence to maturity, adulthood, and then old age; they were those who had tasted the great passions of life — love and hate, beauty and ugliness, the sweetness of victory and the bitterness of loss. Most importantly, elders were closer to the mystery of death, a fate as certain as the fact of our birth and just as crucial for grasping what "life" might mean.

Wisdom is built on self-knowledge — a recognition that our most valuable understanding is energized and shaped by our strongest emotions and deepest experiences. Ultimately, everything we learn and teach is framed and given meaning by the unique stories of individual lives. But the wise individual also knows how to live in society, something learned over years of face-to-face engagement with others — direct, honest, caring communication within a community of similarly seeking individuals sensitive to the great natural community of being. The search for wisdom needs to be the core of the "good life" that the classical political philosophers sought to understand and promote.

I became aware gradually that the threads of the truth quest were spun out of the basic ordering processes in the life of the hunting-gathering band. There was something in the push-pull of life in small, decentralized, democratic, and self-sufficient communities, living in a shamanic resonance with the natural world, that sustained and promoted the quest. My personal search in its own faltering and incomplete fashion had been following an archetypal dynamic embodied in a primal politics.

CHAPTER 2

# ABANDONMENT OF THE QUEST — A PATH WITH NO HEART

With the seventeenth century begins the incredible spectaculum of modernity — both fascinating and nauseating, grandiose and vulgar, exhilarating and depressing, tragic and grotesque — with its apocalyptic enthusiasm for building new worlds that will be old tomorrow, at the expense of old worlds that were new yesterday; with its destructive wars and revolutions spaced by temporary stabilizations on ever lower levels of spiritual and intellectual order through natural law, enlightened self-interest, a balance of powers, a balance of profits, the survival of the fittest, and the fear of atomic annihilation in a fit of fitness; with its ideological dogmas piled on top of the ecclesiastic and sectarian ones and its resistant skepticism that throws them all equally on the garbage heap of opinion; with its great systems built upon untenable premises and its shrewd suspicions that the premises are indeed untenable and therefore must never be rationally discussed; with the result, in our time, of having unified mankind into a global madhouse bursting with stupendous vitality.

— Eric Voegelin, *Published Essays, 1966–1985*

It has no doubt been worth the metaphysical barbarism of a few centuries to possess modern science.

— E. A. Burtt, *The Metaphysical Foundations of Modern Science*

## The Western Revolutions

All the defining institutions of modernity emerged out of western Europe beginning in the sixteenth century as a thousand years of feudalism collapsed and three revolutionary movements converged. Traditionally, historians deal separately with the Protestant Reformation, the scientific revolution, and the commercial revolution.[1] But taking them together we can see how each changed the common cultural and intellectual context in ways that reinforced the most revolutionary ideas of the other two to produce a civilizational shift. During the seventeenth and eighteenth centuries, these ideas solidified into the "metaphysics of modernity," the philosophical underpinnings for global industrial capitalism. It provided the framework for approaching the search for the best way to live, which eventually produced the political philosophy of classical Liberalism. This was most clearly expressed by the writings of the defining Liberal thinkers — Thomas Hobbes, John Locke, and Adam Smith — who together offered a compelling vision of the good life and the just society that remains the default ideology of modernity. Liberalism remains the primary philosophical justification for our dominant institutions and values: free-market capitalism, minimal representational government, the rights and freedoms of the individual, industrial mass production, and a culture of unlimited material consumption.[*]

The Liberal vision inspired a wave of democratic revolutions, including, most notably, the American Revolution, which culminated in the drafting of the Constitution of the United States. The founding fathers of the American

---

* In this sense both modern-day conservatives and liberals with a small *l* are classical Liberals with a capital *L*. Both are committed to the institutional package of individual rights, minimal government, and free-market capitalism. Modern conservatives tend to be ideological purists who resist reforming the established institutions of classical Liberalism (in particular ideas of minimal government in conjunction with free-market forces) and tend to favor cultural norms associated with the eighteenth-century founders. Modern "liberals" are more open to reforming ruling institutions in the light of new knowledge, but in the service of the core mission of the Liberal revolution: the liberation of the individual from internal and external oppression and the promotion of a fuller flowering of what it means to be human. Typically, neither seriously questions the founding assumptions of Liberalism by expanding the metanarrative to include "big history."

republic represented the creative elite of the new revolutionary philosophy. The delegates from the colonies who met in Philadelphia in 1787 to draft the Constitution were exemplars of a triumphant middle class: predominantly successful businessmen, lawyers, and farmers; Protestant, property owning, and imbued with the promise of the new mechanistic science. The country was vast and blessed with great natural wealth. Victory in the War of Independence eliminated the British colonial presence and, with it, the need for the victorious revolutionaries to accommodate an old guard. In this sense, the American Revolution was less a revolution than a war of national liberation against a foreign occupation. Since American Liberals, unlike those in Europe, never had to compromise with the residues of feudal opposition, their vision remained unalloyed. This produced a country so politically homogenous that its revolutionary ideology became almost invisible.[1] The result was that America emerged into the twentieth century as a unified economic and military giant, showing in stark relief all the greatness and the flaws of this quintessentially modern, Western paradigm of the good life.

In *Civilization*, his lively and penetrating comparative history of the rise of Western civilization, the conservative historian Niall Ferguson identifies what he calls six "killer apps" (using unintentionally sinister cyber-slang) for the institutions that most distinguished the West from "the Rest" and that are most responsible for its dramatic rise to global dominance.[2] All the apps were products of the three revolutions of modernity. They are: competition based on a degree of decentralization of political and economic life; science; property rights; medicine, as an application of science; the consumer society; and the work ethic. They were applied aggressively and inventively in the four hundred years between 1500 and 1900 to transform the position of the West from relative insignificance to comprehensive domination of the global population and economy.[3] Western dominance is now in question, says Ferguson, because this quintessentially Western package has become global. "The Chinese have got capitalism. The Iranians have got science. The Russians have got democracy. The Africans are (slowly) getting modern medicine. And the Turks have got the consumer society."[4]

Ferguson keeps the faith that the Western formula still offers human societies the best available set of institutions: "the ones most likely to unleash the individual human creativity capable of solving the problems the twenty-first century faces."[5] His concluding recommendations for the West to retain its edge are surprisingly timid: educational reform, perhaps reinstituting "formal knowledge" and "rote-learning" and reading the classics. He lists his "great books" — the King James Bible, Newton's *Principia*, Locke's *Two Treatises on Government*, Adam Smith's *Moral Sentiments* and *Wealth of Nations*, the complete works of William Shakespeare, and so on.

But Ferguson's *Civilization* operates like most conventional historical analyses, within the time frame of the past 5,500 years of written history. To grasp the larger significance of the crisis of Liberalism, we need to invoke the perspective of big history, within which civilization itself is a very recent event on an evolving earth. From this perspective, the world of industrial capitalism, ushered in by Liberalism, can be seen as dramatically intensifying some of the most conspicuous, defining aspects of civilization: division of labor, hierarchies of wealth and power, specialization in knowledge, and application of instrumental rationality to the mastery of nature and its conversion into wealth. This civilizational trajectory has reached a dead end. The Liberal narrative is exhausted and its institutional forms in their present state are undermining the very conditions necessary for civilization to flourish. The time for a radically more life-affirming vision arrived.

The "big history" perspective helps us see how some of the killer apps are becoming truly deadly. The metaphysics of modernity had a contradictory effect on the truth quest. Liberalism originally supported the truth quest in a number of crucial respects: it liberated the individual from ossified feudal structures and clarified and systematized the scientific method. It also made possible an explosive increase in the human population and our immense achievements in science, art, and the material quality of life. On the other hand, Liberalism's emphasis on an instrumental, mathematical rationality, minimal government, and the invisible hand of the free market effectively eliminated the need for the individual to consider the good of the whole. So here we have a stark irony: Liberalism emerged from the pursuit of the truth quest but its consequences undermined the very quest responsible for its truth. The result is an increasingly corrupt political culture based on self-interest and avarice, while our policies and institutions are leading us to civilizational collapse.

The challenge for our age, in essence, is to advance, deepen, and in a sense complete the Liberal revolution by bringing to bear the larger perspective. This will involve recovering some of the oldest traditional wisdom that Liberalism rejected and then integrating it with some of the newest.

## The Medieval Roots of Our Modern Crisis

One could sum up by saying that the missions of science, the Reformation, and the capitalist revolution converged in a single imperative: to exclude religious, spiritual, and philosophical concerns from political and economic affairs in the interest of transforming nature into ever-larger quantities of wealth. This formula succeeded beyond any of its founders' wildest dreams. But its greatest achievements are now becoming some of its most destructive flaws. We can understand this more clearly when we see Liberalism as an inversion of the feudal worldview, its one-sidedness an extreme reaction to the traumatic collapse of the medieval order and to three centuries of repeated crop failures, famines, plagues, and almost incessant warfare.

The fourteenth century opened with price inflation; ruined harvests in northern Europe then caused a serious famine between 1315 and 1317. This was followed by a massive typhoid epidemic. In 1318 cattle and sheep were decimated by disease. This was followed by another bad harvest and famine in 1321. In Languedoc, poor harvests occurred twenty times between 1302 and 1348, by which time the weakened population was only too vulnerable to the first of a series of bubonic plague epidemics. The Black Death broke out in England in 1361, then again in 1368, 1369, 1371, and 1375. Altogether it killed approximately one-third to one-half of the population. Collective suffering was intensified by "the Hundred Years' War" — actually a series of wars between England and France from 1337 to 1453 — which shattered faith in divine benevolence and the harmonious Great Chain of Being. The result was a profound sense of pessimism and failure.[6]

In the sixteenth and seventeenth centuries, Europe was still scourged by disease, famines, riots, popular uprisings, and war. It should not be surprising to find that the ideology that emerged out of this collective sustained trauma was radically oversimplified and overstated. The result was the replacement of a corrupt religious order and an aristocracy of birth with an increasingly corrupt aristocracy of wealth.

Our focus sharpens as we go further back. Feudalism emerged after the collapse of the Roman Empire as a decentralized, agrarian society based on relatively self-sufficient manorial estates, called *fiefs* or *feudums*, which were loosely held together by local custom, remnants of Roman law, and Christian-Aristotelian cosmology. Peasants swore an oath of loyalty to a warrior aristocracy of knights and lords, who in turn provided defense and administered justice. The whole static order was seen as part of the divine Chain of Being, under the custodianship of the Catholic Church. Trade and craft production were limited and carefully regulated through guilds, which were as concerned with spiritual life as they were with material production. The guilds would set the prices an artisan could charge for a product, with a "just price" being the amount calculated to cover the costs of production and maintain the artisan at his customary place in society. Moneylending for interest — the lifeblood of a capitalist economy — was despised as *usury* and declared a mortal sin, since it took advantage of the needy to enrich the wealthy. The simple act of buying wholesale and selling retail, known as *regrating*, was seen as intrinsically exploitative and became a punishable offense. The ethos of feudal economics was precisely the opposite of a modern market society and could be summed up by the medieval aphorism *homo mercator vix aut nunquam deo placere potest* — "the merchant will never be pleasing to God." Making a profit was inherently sinful.

A story from the tenth century of one pious lord, St. Gerald of Aurrilac, illustrates the stark opposition between medieval and modern attitudes regarding profit. Upon returning from a pilgrimage, St. Gerald showed some Italian merchants a magnificent *pallium* (a religious garment) he had bought in Rome. When they heard what he paid for it, they congratulated him on his bargain. But instead of being delighted, St. Gerald was deeply disturbed and quickly sent the merchant additional money lest he be found guilty in the eyes of God of the sin of avarice.[7] In principle the entire orientation of the social and economic order focused on inner, spiritual life and questions of meaning and value.

By the end of the fifteenth century, however, the corruption of the Catholic Church was undermining its spiritual authority, while a rapidly increasing population and growing need for new sources of raw materials made an expanding mercantile economy essential. The pressure to expand ocean trade intensified after 1453 with the fall of Constantinople to the Ottoman Empire and the closing of Europe's land route to the East. Eastern spices were essential for preserving meat during Europe's long winter, when fields froze and farm animals were slaughtered. At the same time innovations in naval and military technology opened the world's oceans to European shipping. The compass, the brass cannon, and the three-masted, full-rigged ship, which could tack against the wind, opened the stormy Atlantic for transoceanic navigation. This made it possible for Columbus to reach the Americas in 1492, for Vasco da Gama to round the Cape of South Africa a few years later, and for Cortez to arrive in Mexico in 1519. The expansion of long-distance trade and the opening of foreign markets stimulated the shift from guild production to a new class of merchant-manufacturer-entrepreneurs that was able to invest in such risky but lucrative ventures. Overseas trade then provided the capital needed for further technological and scientific innovation, which in turn helped inform, arm, equip, and motivate further expansion. In the fifteenth and sixteenth centuries, a growing cash economy put pressure on the landed aristocracy to enclose and farm previously uncultivated common land. Peasants whose survival had depended for centuries on grazing their animals on the commons were forced off the land. They joined the ranks of the destitute in the growing towns and cities, helping to provide a workforce for an emerging class of property owners. These were neither serfs nor lords, neither peasants nor aristocrats, but a new "middle" class that would provide the base of support for the Liberal revolutions.

In the context of an expanding market society, Protestant notions of "doing God's work" became connected over time to worldly success through thrift and hard work — what Max Weber famously identified as the "Protestant work ethic."[8] When this was combined with notions of religious freedom and the separation of church and state, it reinforced a political culture of growing individualism and materialism. Protestant nations soon led the commercial revolution; first the Netherlands, then England, followed by the United States. The scientific revolution reinforced both tendencies by appealing to the authority of the senses guided by the laws of logic and reason. At the heart of science was a single revolutionary insight — mathematics was the secret language of the world. Whatever could be quantified could be dealt with by mathematics; it could be known with precision and manipulated for our own ends. In practice this meant science focused exclusively on the outer measurable aspects of material reality. Since the method could be replicated by anyone with the right equipment anywhere in the world, results could be verified independently. The objectivity and universality of science undermined arbitrary ecclesiastical and political authority and helped remove traditional fetters on commerce. It also resulted in the rapid development of near-miraculous machinery, which was applied with accelerating effectiveness to the scientific investigation of nature, to the market production of goods, to exploration and navigation, and of course to warfare.

In 1543, King Henry VIII of England broke away from the authority of the Pope and the Catholic Church and established the Church of England with himself as its head. The religious and political conflict that followed ultimately ended in the turmoil of the English Civil War (1642–49) and a tenuously renegotiated relationship between the king and Parliament. The Liberal philosophers Thomas Hobbes and John Locke wrote against the memory of the dark ages of feudalism and its chaotic breakdown into civil war. Generalizing and extrapolating from their experience, they asserted that human nature was fundamentally aggressive, competitive, and selfish. Hobbes put this pungently in the most often quoted lines in modern political philosophy, from his masterwork *Leviathan*, published in 1651. He saw human beings in "a state of nature" without strong central government as naturally free but also selfish and aggressive, caught up in an endless struggle for advantage, in "a war of all against all." In a condition devoid of justice and order, they were condemned to live a life that was "nasty, brutish and short." He concluded that individuals needed to give up some freedom to establish a strong central authority — a "Leviathan" —in order to ensure the common good.

A few decades later, John Locke in his *Second Treatise on Government* softened this bleak understanding by recognizing that human beings also had a natural urge to be productive: to work rationally with hands and tools, crafting wilderness — which he considered simply wasteland — into useful, and thus valuable, products. Value accrued through labor. "Thus the Grass my Horse has bit; the Turfs my Servant has cut; and the Ore I have digge'd in any place where I have right to them in common with others, becomes my Property, without the assignation or consent of anybody."[9] Inspired by the physics of Isaac Newton and Enlightenment ideas of rationality, Locke provided the philosophical foundation for government based primarily on protecting individual rights and freedoms, most especially the right to hold and dispose of property and to enjoy the fruits of one's labor in security. Individual rights increasingly meant property rights, and as we shall see, property rights became the organizing value for the writers of the Constitution of the United States.

From this baseline the Liberal philosophers constructed a theory of society, economics, and government providing for maximum individual liberty. Rebelling against the oppressiveness of aristocratic privilege and the divine right of kings, they sought a political order in which the individual would be neither beholden to nor responsible for others. Government was simplified into a social contract among such rationally calculating, independent, self-interested individuals, who came together to create society by giving up some of their freedom. In so doing, they gained the security necessary to hold and enjoy their wealth. This system made no appeal to altruism or generosity; it had little faith that self-interested individuals would take responsibility for the good of the whole. An impersonal mechanism — the invisible hand of the free market — was assumed to operate according to a semiscientific law of supply and demand, converting individual selfishness into growth in collective wealth. Since corporations barely existed, the threats to individual liberty were seen to come from social chaos on the one hand and big government on the other. It was a minimal vision of government giving maximum rein to self-interest.

During the seventeenth and eighteenth centuries, the North American continent offered Liberal revolutionaries a clean slate — a "state of nature" that from the European perspective was also a political vacuum. Settlers arrived in what appeared to be a vast game-filled wilderness, blessed with an incredible wealth of natural resources and peopled by "savages" who could be easily defeated or "civilized."[10] Under these idealized conditions, without a counterrevolutionary feudal aristocracy, the American Revolution produced the paradigmatic Liberal polity.

A potential counterrevolutionary force existed in the form of spiritually developed, but technologically undeveloped, Native American societies. Within a few centuries this living contradiction to the founding assumptions of Liberalism was crushed by mass immigration and industrial technology. When European settlers first arrived, North America contained about five hundred different indigenous tribes with a total population of perhaps five million. Vast herds of buffalo — some thirty million — covered the continent from east to west, from the current Canadian border to Mexico. As the United States transformed and expanded into an industrialized society, it saw both the native populations and the buffalo as obstacles to progress. By the 1860s, as the final Indian wars approached, the great herds had been destroyed and the survivors were confined to the Great Plains, where they provided subsistence for about three hundred thousand free Native Americans who still resisted the Europeans surrounding them.

Resistance ended with the final slaughter of the herds. Between 1872 and 1874, 3.5 million buffalo were killed. Of these only 150,000 were taken by Indians for subsistence.[11] The rest were shot by Europeans for meat, hide, tongues, and sport and as a matter of military tactics. General Sheridan exhorted the US Congress to pass a bill to exterminate the herds, saying that "every buffalo killed is an Indian less." By the 1880s, the buffalo were virtually extinct. Only a handful of pure specimens remained in the United States. Native Americans saw this blindness to the sacredness of the natural world as a kind of psycho-spiritual disease. The words of Lakota visionary Black Elk capture the gulf between a primal and industrial ethic:

> That fall [1883]...the last of the bison herds was slaughtered by the *Wasichus* [Europeans]. I can remember when the bison were so many that they could not be counted, but more and more *Wasichus* came to kill them until there were only heaps of bones scattered where they used to be. The *Wasichus* did not kill them to eat; they killed them for the metal that makes them crazy, and they took only the hides to sell. Sometimes they did not even take the hides, only the tongues and I have heard that fire-boats come down the Missouri River loaded with dried bison tongues. You can see that the men who did this were crazy. Sometimes they did not even take the tongues; they just killed and killed because they liked to do that. When we hunted bison, we killed only what we needed. And when there was nothing left but heaps of bones, the *Wasichus* came and gathered up even the bones and sold them.[12]

From the primal point of view, wilderness is the closest face of the mystery of creation. From the Liberal point of view, the primary value of wilderness is in its potential for the private production of wealth — ultimately, marketable commodities. Part of the immediate universal appeal of Liberalism comes from its simplicity and the directness of its appeal to the most basic of human impulses: freedom, power, comfort, and wealth. Another part of its appeal is the fact that it presented itself as rational — the application of an empirical, scientific approach to government. A year after Isaac Newton published his monumental *Principia Mathematica*, the grand synthesis of mechanistic science, Locke modestly presented his own work as the contribution of a mere "under-labourer" to the "incomparable Mr. Newton."[13]

But science offered a profoundly materialistic definition of truth, based on measurement and control of the natural world in the service of the production of material wealth. Such a science could not, by definition elucidate the good life. This separation of value and fact, paralleling the separation of church and state, or spirituality and politics, is at the heart of Liberalism's abandonment of the quest. To understand how the use of science is implicated in our crisis and how it might serve in its transcendence, we need to look more closely at the conditions under which it emerged.

## Deformation of the Soul: The Scientific Revolution

The revolutionary founders of the modern Liberal state understood science as the fruit of God-given rationality and the key to human liberation. They were also for the most part devout Christians who still believed in the literal truth of the Bible as God's word. But the practical importance of science as a method of "certain knowledge" grew, and as science increasingly contradicted literal biblical descriptions of the natural world, the political relevance of the entire religious, ethical, and philosophical sphere declined. Religion and philosophy became private matters, as did all questions of value and meaning, other than the self-evident value of Liberal institutions as impersonal, legal mechanisms for checking and balancing individual self-interest. Science became equated with publicly reliable knowledge. The Liberal principles of minimal government and the invisible hand of the market further undermined the role of religion and philosophy.

In 1543 Copernicus initiated what was to become the scientific revolution by publishing an obscure mathematical text, *De Revolutionibus de Oribum Celestium*, in which he argued that the movement of the heavenly bodies could be more elegantly explained, using a simpler geometry, if one assumed that the earth and the planets rotated about the sun rather than the other way around. Copernicus had been inspired to consider this radical hypothesis by the rediscovery of classical Greek texts and the mystical Pythagorean notion that the world was constructed according to mathematical laws. Since medieval Christian cosmology regarded the heavens as the realm of divine perfection, and since mathematical laws were perfectly true, it seemed obvious to Copernicus that God would construct the heavens mathematically. At bottom Copernicus was as much persuaded by the *mathematical elegance* of this new model as he was by its practical capacity to explain and predict the movement of the heavenly bodies. This equation of mathematical elegance, precision, and truth became a cornerstone of the scientific method.

Medieval cosmology, however, was based on the notion of a Great Chain of Being, with the stable immovable earth below and the perfect heavenly bodies spinning above. The fact that the mathematics of Copernican astronomy literally turned medieval cosmology upside down had profound repercussions for epistemology, philosophy, and politics, which are still playing out in our present moment. The elegant certainties of mathematical proofs, and the capacity of mathematical formulations to explain, predict, and then control so much of the natural world, displaced religion and philosophy in intellectual life. Even more unsettling was the fact that science could contradict direct experience. Few things are more obviously true to human senses than the fact that the earth is solid and unmoving and that the blazing sun moves across the sky. Mathematics persuaded us of the opposite. In the ominous words of Galileo, the greatness of Copernicus's intelligence was in allowing mathematics to "rape" his senses.[14] Much of modern philosophy has still not recovered its center after being displaced by science.

The Italian mathematician, physicist, and philosopher Galileo Galilei took Copernicus's insight about the explanatory power of mathematics and helped turn it into a fundamental epistemological and ontological principle. He argued that the deeper significance of Copernicus's achievement was to show us that the universe is constructed mathematically, and so mathematics needs to be understood as the language of a true philosophy and a useful science: "Philosophy is written in that great book...of the universe." And it is written in the language of mathematics, whose "symbols are triangles, circles and other geometrical figures without whose help it is impossible to comprehend a single word of it; without which one wanders in vain through a dark labyrinth."[15] By working closely with practical men — the gunners and artisans in the arsenals of Venice — on the eminently practical matters of ballistics, he developed the experimental method in which the mathematics that explained the heavens so brilliantly was applied to moving objects on earth. In so doing, he directly connected the act of cognition to manipulation, and technology became the embodiment of mathematical reason.

The French philosopher and mathematician René Descartes, inspired by the power of mathematics, then developed a coherent metaphysical system that enthroned this mechanical, mathematical method as the exclusive path to that certain knowledge that would make us "masters and possessors of nature." Since this powerful method of mathematics could only deal with numbers, Descartes's bold philosophical move was to assert an absolute distinction between those experiences that could be quantified (and dealt with by mathematics) and those that could not. Certain knowledge was henceforth confined to the world that could be measured, the world of tangible external things, which Descartes called *res extensa*. These were the unambiguous qualities of shape, weight, and movement — or in the language of physics, mass, extension, and motion — what Galileo called primary qualities. Almost everything else was unknowable, existing only in the realm of *res cogitans*, "things of the mind," what Galileo called secondary qualities. It is hard to overestimate the world-changing significance of this intellectual gambit. Suddenly, in one move, Descartes rendered all the qualities of taste, smell, and color, the full range of human emotions — including all the grand passions of love and hate, grief and joy, despair and hope — unknowable and, by implication, irrelevant to what really mattered!

> When they [*res cogitans*] are judged to be certain things subsisting beyond our minds, we are wholly unable to form any conception of them. Indeed, when anyone tells us that he sees colour in a body or feels pain in one of his limbs, this is exactly the same as if he said that he there saw or felt something of the nature of which he was entirely ignorant, or that he did not know what he saw or felt.[16]

Common sense tells us the opposite is true. The world of emotions and feelings is not only real but where we spend much of our time. When we feel nothing, we value nothing and life loses its meaning. To consign the fullness of our emotional life to the irrational and thus unknowable was an extraordinary act of metaphysical mutilation. By accepting Descartes's proposal, and excluding most of what constitutes our experience from systematic disciplined exploration, society made possible our unfolding modern catastrophe.

Why was this patent absurdity so persuasive to Descartes and, following him, the intellectual elite of early modern Europe? First, Descartes, like many of his contemporaries, was enormously impressed with the sudden profusion in the seventeenth century of clockwork robots, "automata," and machines. Since their workings were a predictable outcome of precisely measurable pieces of matter in motion, machines represented the most fully realized expression of "useful knowledge" based on *res extensa*. The explanatory power of mechanical knowledge was amplified by the fact that a number of the new inventions were instruments for measuring. By the time Descartes published his *Discourse on the Method* in 1637, the microscope, thermometer, pendulum clock, and telescope had all been invented and were radically extending the realm of what could be measured and mathematized.[17]

The application of machinery in the service of commerce added the incentive of profit — also calculated numerically — to manufacturing methods based on mass production of goods in factories. Finally, the superior truth of Cartesian science was demonstrated most emphatically by violence, as the machinery of killing annihilated the traditional societies that stood in the way of European expansion.

In applying the mechanical model to the earth and animals, Descartes was particularly impressed with vivisection — in which living cats and dogs were nailed by their paws onto boards in order to have their chests cut open to expose their still-beating hearts and breathing lungs. In the thrall of his mechanical revelation, Descartes fixated on the obvious similarity between a mechanical pump and the heart, and then he made a bold leap of logic, which was to become a monstrous leap in moral thinking. He postulated that a cat, for example, is nothing more than a kind of clockwork whose parts are so arranged that, when you nail it to a board, screams come out of its mouth.

> [Animals]...are not rational, and that nature makes them behave as they do according to the disposition of their organs; just as a clock, composed only of wheels and weights and springs, can count the hours and measure the time more accurately than we can with all our intelligence.[18]

Cruelty to animals became an unofficial test of being a Cartesian. If you felt compassion for an animal, you simply failed to grasp the absolute separation between things of the mind and things of matter, between sentient humans and mechanical animals. Only humans had reason; therefore, only humans had feelings and could be moral agents. Descartes specifically attacked the notion that animals might have an inner life — a soul — as the most common source of error in the pursuit of reliable knowledge. Things of the mind might be ultimately unknowable, but the mind could recognize itself as absolutely separated from the body and nature. This doctrine, known as Cartesian dualism, eliminated in principle the moral constraints on doing with animals and nature what we would. Despite its obvious absurdity, this notion is almost universally embraced by industrial cultures. We see it on a mass scale in the cruelty of routine testing of pharmaceutical products on laboratory animals and in the heartlessness of our factory farms, in which animals are reared for slaughter as so much protein-per-unit-space-occupied, per-unit-input-of-feed.

Ultimately, we can say that Descartes's ideas took their form to serve short-term human self-interest — the need for certainty under conditions of extreme existential anxiety. When we take a closer, un-Cartesian look at Descartes's psychology, we can see the stages involved in how one man gradually turned away from the truth quest to develop a method that extinguished, in principle, the importance of the quest in public life. By carrying out this exercise, we reverse Descartes's process and find ourselves beginning to recover the quest.

## Descartes's Dream

According to Descartes, *res cogitans*, things of the mind, were unknowable except for a few important exceptions — clear, evident intuitions. One was the reality of the doubting, thinking mind itself, hence his much-celebrated revelation *cogito ergo sum*, "I think, therefore I exist." Also real and knowable were a few propositions of logic, the laws of mathematics, and a few supposedly self-evident propositions of theology. If we reflect for a moment in a wholistic fashion on the contents of consciousness at any particular moment, the fullness of experience becomes apparent. On the face of it the reality of the rational, thinking mind is no more or less self-evident than any other particular content of consciousness revealed through reflection, such as: "I sit contentedly on a warm rock watching a sunset with baboons — therefore I exist." Why, then, was Descartes so convinced that the act of thinking, questioning, and doubting was more real than that of feeling and empathy?

From a psychological perspective, Descartes was like anyone else, an emotionally driven human being on a particular quest conditioned by time and place. Surprisingly, Descartes himself provides us with exactly such an un-Cartesian account of himself in the *Discourse* and more extensively in his journal *Olympica*.[19] What is immediately striking is that he tells a story of an emotional revelation, a drama unfolding over time, taking place as unique events in the supposedly unknowable realm of things of the mind. These writings offer the strange spectacle of Descartes exemplifying elements of the truth quest, then coming to the conclusion that he should prohibit it for others.

He starts by describing how, despite having attended some of the best schools in Europe, he emerged disgusted with the state of philosophy, which seemed "built on mud and sand." He notes that it had been studied by the most outstanding minds for centuries, yet it had failed to produce "anything that was not in dispute and consequently doubtful and uncertain." In conclusion he describes his mental state as wracked by anxiety over the turmoil of the times, and he talks of his despair that he might never find the certain knowledge needed to improve the human condition.[20] Descartes was desperate for certainty. *Libido dominandi* — the lust for power — comes to the fore.

Descartes had spent the summer directly involved in one of the military campaigns of the Thirty Years' War, and this no doubt intensified his general sense of crisis. In late fall, he retired to winter quarters near Ulm. His search climaxed in a waking vision, reinforced by a series of dreams the following night of November 10, 1619. The dreams were highly symbolic but their meaning was clear to Descartes. He saw them as pointing to a new science based on mathematics as the key to that certain and useful knowledge he was seeking. The dreams were so profound, and so directly relevant to his quest, that he was convinced he had been graced with divine revelation. In gratitude he vowed to make an offering of a pilgrimage, on foot, from Venice to the shrine of Our Lady of Lorette, a vow he fulfilled five years later.

Descartes's own account makes it clear that this entire, extraordinary process of discovery takes place within the realm of secondary qualities, the supposedly unknowable things of the mind. He experiences distress at the chaos and confusion of his time, anxiety over the failure of traditional wisdom, and fierce determination in searching for answers. He obviously values the spontaneous dreams and visions and then reflectively interprets them in the context of his life. He reacts, feels, considers, and creates meaning all within the subjective realm of his own mind. In addition, he communicates the meaning and value of his great discovery not through numbers but in the form of a narrative — the *Discourse* — a story describing a series of unique events. Oddly, his own certainty and relief is such that he neglects the decisive flaw in his conclusions: He is so enraptured by the results that he discards the process that led to them.

This is an extraordinary moment in the history of the West, where a drama unfolding in the psychology of one man catalyzes, then becomes emblematic of, a related process of transformation in the entire culture. This moment captures the contradiction that currently splits the modern mind, in which self-reflection attempts to annihilate itself in the spectacle of the genius telling his followers: "Do what I tell you, not what I do!"

By the same token, this account contains the kernel of a process of recovery and transformation for us today. Don't *only* do what Descartes tells you to do. Do *also* what he does: question persistently; be open to the fullness of experience, including ecstatic revelation (like that of Descartes himself); reflect on the full amplitude of human experience in both its measurable and unmeasurable aspects; and then keep making connections between the part and the whole, between the drama taking place in the life of the individual and the story and state of the larger community. Of course, in formulating his ideas, Descartes was not alone. He was heavily indebted to the achievements of Copernicus, Kepler, and Galileo, and his framework was in turn developed, qualified, and articulated by others who followed, culminating in the grand synthesis of Sir Isaac Newton.

The scientific method emerged together with a rapidly growing, global, industrial capitalist economy to produce a remarkably uniform, characteristically Western way of experiencing and thinking about the world. These habits go so deep that even highly intelligent critiques of modernity, like those of many self-proclaimed postmodernists, as we shall see, reveal quintessentially Cartesian, and thoroughly modern, reflexes.

## Deus Ex Machina

Today, we can see one particularly vivid reductio ad absurdum of mechanistic Cartesian science in the hypertechnological fantasies of cryogenicists, roboticists, and nanotechnologists who fantasize about transcending the messy biology of the human condition through robots and androids. Futurists Gregory Paul and Earl Cox point out that humans evolved as better hunter-gatherers, but we are only "marginally adapted for high level physics and novel writing, like the archaeopteryx for flight." Marvin Minksy, MIT professor and researcher on artificial intelligence, laments that we have not become conspicuously smarter since Shakespeare or Euripedes. He notes that humans can only learn and remember about two bits of information per second. Even if we did nothing but learn twelve hours a day for a hundred years, the total sum of information would only be about three billion bits — less than we could store on a memory disk from 1998.[21]

If we start from our self-evident, fully embodied human consciousness, the fallacy is obvious: the mechanists unconsciously assume what they are trying to prove. They implicitly define intelligence mechanically, then triumphantly declare that machines do it better. The roboticist Rodney Brooks's cheerful posthuman futurist fantasy celebrates genetic engineering as indicating "the very deep extent to which we are biological machines... molecules interacting with each other according to well defined laws, combining in predictable ways, and producing, in our case, a body that acts according to a set of specifiable rules. We are machines, as are our spouses, our children, and our dogs. And we are now building machines that will match and surpass us. Resistance is futile."[22] Dr. Robert Haynes, who was the president of the sixteenth International Congress of Genetics, concluded that "it is no longer possible to live by the idea that there is something special, unique or even sacred about living organisms."[23]

These facile pronouncements about the human condition are generated by a method of inference — mechanistic science — that, as we have seen, begins from an already mutilated understanding of human consciousness. The method reproduces the Cartesian error of *forgetting that we have chosen* to focus exclusively on the primary qualities of *res extensa* that can be measured. We forget the freedom of the in-between. We forget we made a choice to treat the world as a machine, not because it is a machine, but because, *if we treated it as if it were a machine*, then we could get a certain type of knowledge useful for practical ends.

Descartes made the archetypal Faustian bargain. His deal with the devil required that we give up the science of soul for the science of wealth and power. Having turned away from considering the soul, we compounded our sin by repressing reflection, and with it the memory of having made the deal in the first place.

Technocrats entirely miss the point when they argue that machines can perform mechanistic functions more efficiently — compute data faster, shoot straighter, dig deeper, lift heavier, travel faster. Efficiency is hardly the point of being human. Cultural historian William I. Thompson says it best: "For the mechanists, the flesh is slow, sloppy, and wet, and, therefore, primitive.... [But] slow and wet is the ontology of birth and the act of making love.... Fast is fine for the programmed crystalline world of no surprises and no discoveries, but slow is better for the creative world of erotic and intellectual play."[24] It is exactly our *inefficiency* that gets to the heart of the human condition. Being embedded in our biological messiness explains our mortality; the sting of death, loss, and grief; and the joy and struggle of loving, of bringing up a child, writing a song, dancing, and philosophizing. Embracing this keeps us close to the irreducible mystery of the way nature works itself into the body, the body into consciousness, and consciousness back into nature.

The philosopher of science E. A. Burtt, in his 1925 masterpiece *The Metaphysical Foundations of Modern Science*, talked of "metaphysical barbarism" as the price we paid for the power of modern science, which he, along with many others since, thought worthwhile. Today, in an age marked by genocide, weapons of mass destruction, and ecocide, it seems long past due to renegotiate the terms of our culture's Faustian bargain.

## The Contradictory Logic of the Heart — Dialectics

One of the great ironies of modernity is that we have now exposed the philosophical absurdity of the Cartesian world-machine at exactly the same time that machinery has become nearly ubiquitous, defining almost every aspect of our direct experience of reality. Virtually every object in the room where I write — books, chairs, tables, computer, phone, and lamp — has been machine made. The components of the house itself — the sheetrock walls, the windows and blinds, the doors and floors — were all fashioned by machines. We live our lives moving from one manufactured interior to another. The primary reality of our wilderness origins has been eclipsed from direct experience, literally buried under our ever expanding cities. Faith in the Cartesian abstraction has led us to create a secondary reality that embodies that abstraction. We experience the world-as-machine because we live in a machine-made world.

The logic that got us here goes back to an original act of splitting: between agriculture and wilderness, or the fence that separated the civilized farm from undomesticated nature. From this has flowed a whole series of related, supporting splits: the outer objective world of matter from inner, subjective life, the rational from the irrational, idea from emotion, the human from the animal. One can trace a philosophical thread from Descartes back to humankind's original alienation from wilderness. In each case of the above pairs, the first term is privileged over the second in a hierarchical dualism that is tearing our world apart. This brings up a fundamental issue about types of logic that we need to be clear about in recovering the quest.

Splitting reality into pairs of absolute opposites requires the deductive *logic of noncontradiction*, also called syllogistic logic. This stipulates that one thing, or A, cannot be something else, such as B, and still be A (A cannot be not-A). This seems self-evident and very useful, since it allows us to define pieces of reality unambiguously, as if they existed like parts of a machine. Each thing is understood as wholly distinct in itself and distinguishable from everything else. Defining each individual thing as isolated requires a related process of abstraction from the field of experience, taking things apart and then analyzing how they fit together. Our primary methodological habits have become *abstraction, analysis,* and *critique*. But the process of dismantling and separating cannot, in principle, make meaning. Meaning requires putting things together, making connections; it requires *narrative description*, *integration*, *reconstruction*, and *synthesis*, all of which run on a different logic.

For example, what of Descartes's poor cat? In strict Cartesian fashion we can describe the beating heart of a living animal in abstract, measurable terms, even accounting for its changing dimensions over time — the volume of its chambers, the force of contraction, and the speed and pressure of the blood flow. But the truth is, when disconnected from the body, the heart no longer works, and neither does its owner. A living heart can only be understood in context. The separated pieces need to be reconnected and related through a process of *creative integration and synthesis*. This recognizes that the beating heart requires breathing lungs and healthy kidneys, oxygenating and detoxifying the blood flowing in the coronary arteries, feeding the heart muscle. We deepen our understanding of the healthy heart by recognizing the role of diet, exercise, environment, and general lifestyle. Further, as we consider these issues, in order to evaluate any particular heart, we ultimately must account for the mental and emotional state of the whole living creature in relationship with its total living environment. The bigger the picture, the more relations established, the deeper and more meaningful the understanding. We refer to this simply as wholistic thinking.

The search for meaning and value — the quest — requires integration and synthesis, which rests on the nonsyllogistic, *contradictory logic* of seeing how opposites give each other meaning. There is no up without connection to down, no hot without cold, no black without white, no A without not-A. Not surprisingly, we see this as a foundational principle in non-Western philosophies like Zen Buddhism or Taoism, where the meaning of yin is in relationship to its opposite, yang: female requires male, outer requires inner, matter requires mind, and so on. Such logic is common in primal and shamanic cosmologies, where knowledge based on direct experience and the closeness of wilderness immediately confronts one with the paradoxical structure of consciousness. We can call this *dialectical* as opposed to *dualistic* logic. This is the logic that is expressed in the *dialektike* of Socratic discussion, which recognizes that meaning begins and ends with unique, fully embodied human beings who inevitably experience the world differently. Understanding comes through face-to-face discussion, where the partial truth of thesis is challenged by the partial truth of *antithesis*, so that both can be integrated and transcended in a more-inclusive *synthesis*. This then becomes a new thesis, and so on. Western thinkers typically stumble over dialectical thinking and get stuck on one side or the other of paradoxical dualisms — mind-body, civilization-wilderness, human-animal.

In practice, we engage in dialectical synthesis all the time; it is necessary and unavoidable. Yet we have also failed to honor it and to cultivate it as a habit. This is striking in higher education, where one hears endless calls for teaching analytical and critical thinking skills but almost nothing about synthesis and constructive and creative skills. Without these complementary opposites we remain stuck. Wholistic, big-picture thinking is either neglected or produces frozen structures of meaning, blocking an understanding of integrated, organic, growing wholes — the whole person, the whole society, the entire species, the planet.

## "There Is No Such Thing as Society"

Descartes helped eliminate the *method* for making meaning from the inner, emotional, qualitative data of the wisdom quest. Classical Liberalism eliminated the *motive* for even pursuing it. The clearest argument for this comes through the lineage of the classical Liberal philosophers, starting with Thomas Hobbes and proceeding through John Locke, Adam Smith, and America's founding fathers, who embodied these ideas in the Constitution of the United States. American democracy offers the clearest example of a society created de novo according to the principles of Lockean Liberalism. This model is now in the final stages of globalizing under the guidance of the United States as the world's preeminent superpower. In this sense the United States is the paradigmatic modern polity, demonstrating with great clarity both its most life-affirming and destructive aspects. While the following discussion focuses on America, in principle it is increasingly applicable globally.

As I've said, the creation of the political vision of Liberalism emerged from the truth quest — from a reflective, passionate concern with the good of the whole. But the Liberal values of personal freedom, private property, and competitive individualism were presented in Cartesian fashion as absolutes, abstracted from the whole without a living connection to their opposites: altruism, generosity, service to and responsibility for others, and love of community. As a result, the less-tangible, hard-to-measure, supreme values — love, beauty, and truth — were increasingly ignored. As Plato and Socrates made clear, any value pursued in isolation as a supreme good inevitably becomes a supreme evil.[25] Any political order that forgets this and assumes certainty becomes deformed and ultimately deadly.

In 1787, after the success of the American Revolution, representatives from the various states gathered in Philadelphia to draft a constitution for a revolutionary theory of government. They were realists and pragmatists, familiar with the struggles among self-interested individuals in the marketplace. They were also aware of the latest advances in science, steeped in the writings of Hobbes and Locke, and imbued with a sense of their historical mission. Following Locke, the writers of the Constitution recognized that in a condition of freedom, where people are born into different social situations, with different abilities and dispositions, some will inevitably acquire more property and others less. Inequality was an inevitable consequence of competition. Thus, government was needed to stop the have-nots from robbing the haves. As Locke put it: "The great and *chief end* therefore of Mens uniting into Commonwealths, and putting themselves under Government, *is the Preservation of their Property*" (emphasis in the original).[26] He assumed reasonable men, recognizing this, would come together to form a social contract and agree to give up some of their natural freedom for the security of a common authority. Such an authority needed to be strong enough to provide protection and order, but not so strong as to quash individual freedom and initiative. Adam Smith put it even more bluntly: "Civil government, so far as it is instituted for the security of property, is in reality instituted for the defense of the rich against the poor, or those who have some property against those who have none at all."[27]

The members of the Constitutional Convention saw themselves as exactly such reasonable men, coming together to draft a social contract for a government that would not attempt to improve human nature but would simply work as a kind of institutional clockwork. A complicated set of checks and balances would ensure a government strong enough to protect private property and to foster trade and commerce, but not so strong as to unnecessarily cramp freedom, enterprise, and initiative.[28] The case for ratification of the draft constitution was laid out in a series of some eighty-five anonymous essays published in New York newspapers, collectively referred to as *The Federalist Papers*. Its authors, now known to be John Jay, Alexander Hamilton, and James Madison, document a remarkable example of applied political philosophy — how institutions of government can be crafted from a philosophical paradigm of the good life.

Much of the focus of the Constitution is on the right to acquire and hold material property as the primary expression of individual freedom. In Federalist No. 10, James Madison argued that the most important function of the Constitution would be to prevent social chaos by guarding us against the violence of the competing interest groups he called factions. Following Locke and Smith, he noted, "The most common and durable source of factions has been the various and unequal distribution of property. Those who own property and those without property — i.e. the rich and the poor — are the most significant of the potentially violent factions."[29] We could say in this sense that class conflict was a founding assumption of the Constitution. Madison rejected the idea of direct democracy, criticizing the small, self-governing "pure" democracies of the ancient Greek polis for their instability and failure to protect inequalities in wealth: "Such societies... have ever been found incompatible with personal security or the rights of property and have in general been as short in their lives as they have been violent in their deaths."[30] Instead, the Constitution established a *republic* that offered the advantages of "a scheme of representation," where the popular will would be refined and enlarged through a process of selection — "a chosen body of citizens, whose wisdom may best discern the true interests of their country, and whose patriotism and love of justice will be least likely to sacrifice it to temporary or partial considerations."[31] The Federalists assumed that the electoral process itself would somehow select the wisest. But would it? And what was wisdom, anyway?

Madison quickly passed over the challenging question of wisdom and moved on to the practical problem of mechanics. He identifies the structural advantage of a republic over a (direct) democracy in protecting private property. Because republics were large they included a greater diversity of interests, particularly the diversity of those factions based on different kinds of property — land owning, slave owning, mercantile, banking, and simply landless. With greater diversity, there is less chance that any particular interest will form a majority and violently impose its will on a minority. Like many of those attending the convention, Madison was deeply disturbed by the nation's postrevolutionary financial crisis and no doubt had in mind Shay's Rebellion, an uprising of impoverished war veterans and poor debtor farmers who took up arms and called for the abolition of debts.

The solution was, as Madison put it, that "ambition must be made to counteract ambition," so that it would be virtually impossible for a single passion to overtake all branches of government. He comments ruefully, "It may be a reflection on human nature, that such devices should be necessary to control the abuses of government." Then he repeats Hobbes's argument for the necessity of strong government: "If men were angels, no government would be necessary. If angels were to govern men, neither external nor internal controls on government would be necessary."[32] In the absence of the wisdom of angels, the Constitution set up intricate rules for establishing the main branches of government — the executive, the legislature, and the judiciary. Then it clearly defined and limited the powers of each, so the net effect would be a pleasingly mechanical, apparently scientific system of checks and balances, which would automatically convert competing selfish interests into the best possible outcome. The machinery of government would make wisdom redundant.

In the eighteenth century, in the aftermath of an order based on a landed aristocracy and a landless peasantry, it must have seemed easier to accept as truth the Lockean assumption that private property was fundamental to human freedom and that wealth would constitute a minimal measure of wisdom and worthiness to govern. In fact, in 1787 most states had property qualifications for voting and holding office, and this probably excluded at least a third of the white male population. Women, Native Americans, and slaves were of course also excluded.[33] Those who attended the convention — white, Protestant, property-owning men — could reasonably assume a larger moral consensus than we can today. In fairness, many of the founding fathers were also imbued with a high-minded sense of service, and none would have been fully satisfied with wealth as a measure of wisdom. But today, when the top 10 percent of the American population owns over 70 percent of the nation's wealth, and where elections are determined by increasingly unregulated and undisclosed financial contributions to media campaigns, we can see the Madisonian formula for what it always was — wishful thinking. It succeeded in replacing an aristocracy of birth with an aristocracy of avarice — the rule of the wealthy.

Instead of seeking a politics that nurtures love of wisdom, the Federalists produced a government that would mitigate the effects of selfishness. The Constitution offered a mechanical arrangement of competing powers and interests intended to produce the best possible collective outcome for all. It provided a moral justification for shifting attention away from the community to the self-interested individual. The reductio ad absurdum of this approach is the notion — attributed to the conservative former British prime minister Margaret Thatcher — that "there is no such thing as society; there are [only] individual men and women and... families." The political culture focused on rights and freedoms and said almost nothing about the individual's responsibilities and duties toward the community — to the good of the social whole. The pursuit of wisdom was made irrelevant to government.

## The Free-Market Machine: Short-Sighted, Narrow-Minded, and Selfish

If modern government was to have only the most minimal role in restricting the freedoms of individuals and providing for the common good, what would regulate the vast arena of economic activity, ensuring the optimum distribution of goods and services? The answer came from Adam Smith, the brilliant Scottish economist and philosopher.

Smith's central work, *The Wealth of Nations*, published in 1776, has been celebrated as having more of an impact in transforming the world than the

Bible. Although Madison never mentions Smith in *The Federalist*, his formula for government assumes the truth of Smith's simple reasoning. Smith claimed to identify a natural law of the market that would automatically convert self-interest into public benefit. He reasoned that in a situation of complete freedom, where all relevant knowledge was available, competition between self-interested individuals, seeking only their own profit, would produce an outcome benefiting all. If every transaction between buyer and seller was voluntary, then, ipso facto, no exchange would take place unless both parties agreed and presumably benefited. It was as if there was an *invisible hand*, the hand of God, that operated in a free market guiding individuals who intended only their own gain to promote an end — the public good — that was no part of their intention. No governmental coercion, no violation of freedom, and no concern for the good of the whole would be required to produce the cooperation necessary for all to benefit. As Smith put it: "It is not through the benevolence of the baker that we get our bread." He added that he had "never known much good to come from those who affected to trade for the public good."

The irony of Smith's genius is that he provided a philosophical and moral justification for the free market that inadvertently resulted in the elimination of philosophical and moral reasoning from economic life. Its impact on economics was equivalent to the effect of Cartesian dualism on metaphysics: "Don't do what I do. Do what I tell you to!"

Smith pointed out that the market mechanism ensured that, not only would both parties to a transaction benefit, but society as a whole would be served by an overall increase in the "wealth of the nation." He gave the famous example of the pin factory to show how the profit motive would impel a division of labor producing dramatic efficiencies in boosting production. Where one man working alone, without machinery, could barely make one pin a day, division of labor enabled ten men with machinery, each doing one piece of the job, to make a total of around forty-eight thousand pins a day, at forty-eight hundred each. "One man draws out the wire, another straights it, a third cuts it, a fourth points it, a fifth grinds it at the top for receiving the head; to make the head requires two or three distinct operations; to put it on is a peculiar business; to whiten the pins is another; it is even a trade by itself to put them into the paper."[34]

The logic was compelling and the practice conclusive. The quickest way to boost profits was to grow the size of the business so as to take advantage of economies of scale: invest in machinery, institute a division of labor, buy raw material more cheaply in bulk, and save on bulk distribution. Labor would be kept cheap so long as the population kept growing, which it would as a consequence of the steady improvement in material existence. Increased profits would feed back into a spiral of continually growing productivity.

Smith's insight brought together the mechanics of Cartesian-Newtonian science, the profit motive, and minimal government in the explosive growth of the mechanized production line. The factory soon became one of the defining institutions of modernity, bringing together raw materials, machinery, and the masses of workers displaced from the countryside. The results were rapid urbanization together with near-miraculous quantities of cheap commodities.[35] City life and shopping reinforced in the most conspicuous way the power, truth, and goodness of the mechanical, materialistic metaphysics of modernity.

Certainly, the rise of America's cities, especially by the late nineteenth century, provided opportunities for cultural creativity, but it also brought overcrowding, exploitation, pollution, and a life chained to the clockwork routine of the production line. The heaviest price was paid in the invisible currency of *res cogitans* — psychology. The production line subjected the working populations to a life-world defined by the division of labor, fragmentation, and hyperspecialization implicit in Descartes's method. Under the feudal system, the individual artisan — fashioning, say, a bow, barrel, or sword — would gather raw materials and control much of the pace and nature of the work. Generally, the work involved learning a craft and some creative expression, and to this degree it reflected the individual who made it and who could take pride in the product. The sale or exchange of the product was also made more meaningful by face-to-face relationships within a localized community.

Now urbanized masses work according to the time clock and assist machinery; they focus endlessly on a few simple, repetitive tasks and produce identical products for distant markets. Depersonalization only increases as state, corporate, and educational bureaucracies apply the mechanical logic of the factory to society as a whole. The resulting irony has been that even though industrial capitalism has globalized, the experience of the urban individual has only become more fractured and narrowly focused. Today, economies are global and interdependent, but people continue to experience themselves as isolated, atomized individuals, no different from any other cog in the machinery of corporate and national bureaucracies. Meaning comes from doing your job and taking care of yourself.

Loss of autonomy and this fragmented experience of both the world and oneself can cause a person's sense of being an integrated whole person and a moral agent with some responsibility for others to collapse entirely. At its most extreme, the modern paradigm for the morally vacuous individual is the Nazi war criminal Adolf Eichmann. Eichmann was the obedient bureaucrat directly responsible for the transport of millions of Jews to the production lines of the Nazi concentration camps. Hannah Arendt's account of his trial, *Eichmann in Jerusalem: A Report on the Banality of Evil*, presents Eichmann as the personification of the modern form of evil: the soulless product of a materialistic, mass society; an individual who has lost the capacity to be the moral authority of his own life.[36]

According to Arendt's account, Eichmann was no anti-Semite. In fact, during the trial, Eichmann took pains to point out that he had good reasons for being sympathetic to Jews. He was indebted to a distant uncle who offered him a job during the Depression and who was married to a Jewish woman. Eichmann had returned the favor by allowing the uncle and his wife to escape while the "final solution" was still under way. At one point during the war, Eichmann had committed the crime of *Rassenschande*, or "racial defilement," by taking a Jewish mistress. Further, his psychological examination revealed him to be "thoroughly normal" with some very "positive attitudes" to family and society.[37]

Eichmann pleaded "not guilty in the sense of the indictment," meaning he never directly killed a Jew with his own hands, and he certainly did not feel he was an *innerer Schweinehund*, a foul and corrupt person. He made it clear, as many of the Nuremburg war criminals did, that he "was doing his job and obeying orders" and that he would only have had a bad conscience had he not done what he was told. Though a nonreligious person, he said he felt "guilty before God" but added more revealingly that he thought "repentance is for little children."[38] For Eichmann, morality had shrunk to obeying orders. Repentance and, by implication, conscience, that inner tension we feel when there is a conflict between satisfying external authority and personal feelings of empathy for others, were childish. Eliminating conscience helps eliminate the tension of emotional conflict. Inner life is simplified. Just obey orders.

The psychologist Stanley Milgram was so disturbed by the implications of Arendt's analysis that he devised an ingenious, and now infamous, experiment to test empirically the degree to which average Americans would follow the orders of an authority figure to inflict physical pain on someone else.[39] In the name of a bogus memory experiment, a scientist urged the subject to give "dangerous" electric shocks to a second subject for failing to memorize word pairs. The second subject was restrained and hidden from view in an adjacent room but could still be heard. Though no shock was actually administered, the second subject would scream as if in intense agony. The results revealed that over half the subjects continued to give 350-volt electric shocks to a restrained, screaming victim pleading to be released and then falling ominously silent. Such obedience was induced by nothing more coercive than a scientist in a white coat intoning, "The experiment must go on.... You have no other choice than to proceed." Milgram's experiment records in painfully precise detail how quickly the anxiety of moral conflict in the increasingly isolated individual gives way before the simple habit of obedience to socially sanctioned authority.[40]

The psychological damage of Liberalism's institutions is real and ubiquitous, and in Milgram's experiment, this becomes measurable in terms of choices made and voltage delivered. Yet we are only shaping ourselves in the ways society asks of us, whether our job is to please the boss or to please the client. For example, one of the largest marketing agencies, Initiative Media, conducted market research to help develop an advertising strategy targeting children; the idea was to give children cues to help them nag their parents more effectively to purchase the product. The research revealed that ads could manipulate children into a type of reasoned nagging that would be more effective than repetitious whining. When the director of strategy was asked whether she thought it unethical to make money by manipulating children, she reflected for a moment: "Yeah. Is it ethical? I don't know." Then she quickly recovered, smiling enthusiastically, "Our role at Initiative is to move products. If we move products... we've done our job."[41] In a culture where the overriding ethical imperative has been narrowed to doing one's job, earning a living, and maximizing profits, there is no sense of responsibility for one's larger impact on society and nature. Ethics dwindles to an afterthought.

## Calculating the Cost of Ethics

Adam Smith was a moralistic thinker who was deeply concerned with society as a whole and well aware that there was more to the good life than material wealth. In making the case for the invisible hand of the free market, he also made a number of critical assumptions and qualifications that we would do well to consider. For example, the nation was still small and relatively homogenous, so he could assume something of a shared moral universe. Since markets were smaller, even when national, the parties to any economic transaction would likely live closer to the consequences of their actions, and they would naturally feel a greater responsibility for the impact on their shared community. Smith was opposed to monopolies, and he assumed that individual businesses would not become large enough to distort the competitiveness of the free market. Most revealing for the present, Smith wanted to outlaw the corporation as fundamentally flawed, since it separated ownership from decision making. The ubiquitous idea of limited liability meant shareholders were only liable for the money they invested, reaping the benefits but taking no moral or legal responsibility for the behavior of the corporation.

In the United States, the problem of "corporate mischief" was compounded after the Civil War as an unintended consequence of the Fourteenth Amendment. Passed in 1868, this amendment to the Constitution was designed to protect the civil liberties of freed slaves, its "due process" clause stipulating that no state should deprive "any person of life, liberty or property without due process of law." This was immediately seized on by clever corporate lawyers to argue that a corporation was in fact a "legal person," and so corporations should enjoy the freedoms and rights of a person. Between 1890 and 1910, corporate lawyers invoked the Fourteenth Amendment 288 times to serve business interests, while African Americans claimed its protection on 19 occasions.[42]

Perhaps most importantly, we tend to forget Smith's model also assumed wide distribution of knowledge of the whole, since voluntary transactions could only be mutually beneficial if all parties had full access to "relevant information." Here, right at the inception of free-market capitalism, is an implicit requirement that something akin to wisdom needs to balance short-term self-interest. I will return to this remarkable caveat later on.

Today few of Smith's assumptions hold. We face a global and growing economic machine that penetrates almost all aspects of modern life, with an overwhelming variety of moving parts and players. We have moved from Smith's world of nations to one increasingly dominated by competing multinational corporations, with incomes that can dwarf the GDP of national economies. Of the 150 largest economic entities on the planet, fewer than half are nation-states. The rest are unelected, undemocratic, multinational corporations, which are free to come and go, manage themselves, shape markets and mass culture, manipulate global finance and government policy — all to serve the bottom line of private profit.[43] Not only is relevant information often hidden, but global markets that make honest attempts to grasp the whole seem almost beyond reach. Obviously, total knowledge is an impossible standard, but as we will see later, dedication to the truth quest provides criteria and methods for developing a "truth of degree" that balances hubris with humility, greed with generosity, and love of wealth and comfort with love of beauty and learning.

Over the past century, as global economic reality has become overwhelmingly complex, centralized, and susceptible to self-interested manipulation by banks and financial institutions, the popular understanding of the economy has become even more simple-minded and ideological. One of the most influential expressions of this comes from Nobel laureate Milton Friedman, whose free-market fundamentalism helped inspire the progressive deregulation of much of the current American economy. Beginning in the 1960s, Friedman advocated a stripped-down, simplified version of Adam Smith's invisible hand, asserting that the *only social responsibility* of business is to maximize its profits. A business will do more good for society, Friedman insisted, by pursuing its own profits than by consciously attempting to work for the collective good.[44] This imperative of "profits first and last" obliges corporations wherever possible to pass on to the public the costs of risk taking.

One result of this is the common corporate practice of balancing the cost of compliance with regulations against the cost of deliberately breaking the law and paying the fine. This is a direct outgrowth of the limited-liability corporate status that Adam Smith argued against: that corporations would have the rights and freedoms of an individual, but no shareholder would be personally liable for its malfeasance. The corporation might be an individual in law, but as Baron Thurlow, an eighteenth-century politician, reportedly said, "It has no soul to save and body to incarcerate." For example, between 1990 and 2001, General Motors, one of the world's largest manufacturers, was caught breaking the law, prosecuted, and convicted on over forty occasions. One of the most revealing cases involved the 1979 Chevy Nova, whose gas tank had been dangerously repositioned to cut costs, making it susceptible to fuel-fed fires. Court documents from a lawsuit filed in 1993 revealed that even after GM realized the car was vulnerable to gas-fueled fires, it chose not to fix the car's design. Initially, upon realizing there was a gas-tank issue, GM management asked the Advance Design Department to provide a comparative cost analysis. They calculated that the cost of paying out anticipated damages came to $2.40 per automobile, whereas the cost of repositioning the fuel tank more safely came to $8.59 per automobile. GM decided its primary responsibility was to shareholder profits and declined to reposition the fuel tanks.[45] Would GM management have decided differently if the executives knew they themselves would have been held personally liable for any deaths or injuries that resulted?

As Joel Bakan, a professor of corporate law, points out, if the corporation were an actual person (as its legal status contends), then the standard practices of many of the largest corporations fit the Personality Diagnostic Checklist of a psychopath: "callous unconcern for the feelings of others; incapacity to maintain enduring relationships; reckless disregard for the safety of others; deceitfulness: repeated lying and conning others for profit; an incapacity to experience guilt and failure to conform to social norms with respect to lawful behavior."[46] No doubt GM's executives didn't regard themselves as psychopaths, yet they justified abdicating responsibility for the harm they knew their choices would cause because Liberal culture and their corporate charter required them to put profits first.

One of the most damaging large-scale expressions of this "ethic of no ethics" is in the work of full-time corporate lawyers and lobbyists who attempt to shape government regulations in the interests of their clients' profit. This is reinforced by corporate-financed media campaigns that, in the name of freedom, whip up an ideological rage against the tyranny of "big government." Self-regulation in the name of private profit regularly leads to environmental damage and public costs that can occasionally be catastrophic. One of the most dramatic examples in recent years was the 2010 blowout of the British Petroleum Macondo Deepwater Horizon drilling rig, which dumped five million barrels of crude oil into the Gulf of Mexico. Over the course of several years leading up to this, BP had cut costs by releasing thousands of older, more experienced, and thus expensive specialists, while at the same time it lobbied to weaken regulation and enforcement.[47] These were all considered reasonable cost-cutting ways to improve the bottom line of boosting profits. The resulting disaster was less an accident than the likely outcome of a system that allowed short-term private gains to be reaped by transferring long-term risks and costs to some third party — the public.

Friedman's simple-minded elimination of ethical thinking in business has helped create a political climate where many leaders in finance and politics no longer seem capable of distinguishing between greed, reasonable self-interest, and the common good. While examples of this are many, some of the most shocking recent events involve the US finance industry and the global financial collapse of 2008, which destroyed the assets of millions of American families and sparked the Great Recession. This occurred after years of corporate-sponsored deregulation of the financial markets made it possible for banks and financial institutions to make enormous profits through a variety of predatory credit and investment schemes. When the whole unsustainable system collapsed, most of the participating firms could reasonably claim they hadn't done anything wrong.

This wasn't, strictly speaking, true, but the pervasive culture of valuing private profit over public good made it difficult for executives to feel responsible. In an interview after the collapse, Lloyd Blankfein, then the chief executive officer of Goldman Sachs — one of the firms implicated in the mortgage crisis, and one of the world's largest, most profitable, and most politically influential investment banking firms — defended the $54 million bonus he received in 2007 by explaining that he was simply "doing God's work."[48]

Such hubris can be seen as a predictable psychological inflation resulting from the politics of self-interest. In 1886, Black Elk, the great Sioux visionary, left his reservation to join Buffalo Bill's *Wild West Show* in the desperate hope of traveling the country and finding a way of helping his defeated, starving people. After a few enervating months in New York City, he saw the noble pretensions of American democracy degenerating into a morally impoverished plutocracy:

> After a while I got used to being there, but I was like a man who had never had a vision. I felt dead and my people seemed lost and I thought

> I might never find them again. I did not see anything to help my people. I could see that the *Wasichus* [whites] did not care for each other the way our people did before the nation's hoop was broken. They would take everything from each other if they could, and so there were some who had more of everything than they could use, while crowds of people had nothing at all and maybe were starving. They had forgotten that the earth was their mother. This could not be better than the old ways of my people.[49]

From such a perspective, the notion that the invisible hand of the market entitles us to whatever we can get away with is a kind of mental and spiritual illness. In practice it means that the rich inevitably grow richer and feel self-righteous doing so. In the United States, in 1965 the average CEO earned 24 times what the average worker earned; by 2007, this had risen to 275 times the average worker's wages,[50] creating what the economists Paul Krugman and Robin Wells dubbed the "creed of greedism."[51] Small-government conservatives, blinded by the dogma of free-market ideology, have great difficulty recognizing that in the absence of wise regulation (imposed from both within and without), such a culture inevitably leads to the "tyranny of the biggest," as the larger, more powerful entities use the competitive advantage of size to further undermine free competition in the service of their own wealth. Unlimited freedom without the guidance of wisdom leads to new forms of tyranny.

## The Eclipse of Wisdom

Classical Liberalism as it has come to be embodied in the United States relies on three impersonal mechanistic understandings that converge in at least one major way: eliminating the need for the individual to consider the good of others and of the whole. The first is the mechanical materialism of Cartesian-based science, which values only the measurable certain knowledge of the tangible world and dismisses as unknowable and unimportant most of the things of the mind. The second is a minimal form of collective decision making and conflict resolution based on a mechanical system of elected representatives, separation of powers, and checks and balances. The third is the law of supply and demand embodied in the invisible hand of the market that supposedly converts self-interest into the collective good. Combined, these ideas and mechanisms release the citizen in principle from the struggle of soul searching and considering the big picture. They make selfishness and a lack of introspection into virtues. The casualty is not only the good but the *truth of the whole*. Greed eclipses a humble opening to the mystery of the human condition. Without openness and humility, deep learning and moral growth are impossible. Truth becomes whatever makes you rich and powerful. Ipso facto, the rich have the truth and should rule.

In the wake of the corrupt and decrepit feudal institutions of the medieval era, the American Constitution was a revolutionary and liberating advance. It was as close as one could imagine to a mechanical form of government congruent with the clockwork universe of Descartes and Newton, in which the various branches of government would act like the cogs and levers of a machine, converting the chaos of selfish humanity into the harmonious order necessary for commerce and agriculture to flourish. Today we rightfully celebrate its achievements: the rights and freedoms of the individual; the efficiencies of industrial production; the cornucopia of wealth; the endless succession of technological miracles; and the massively expanded perspective of science and the reliability of its inferences.

However, America's founders could have had no inkling of how their ideas might translate in a twenty-first-century world. They wrote almost a century before Darwin and Marx and without the revolutionary insights of Freud and Einstein. We now know that neither human beings nor the universe operates like clockwork, and we are also painfully aware of the failings of eighteenth-century clockwork thinking as a basis for politics and society: most particularly, we've witnessed the depersonalization of mass bureaucratic societies and the failures of electoral and market mechanisms to ensure the good of the whole. We see that when individuals are encouraged to give up the search for wisdom, the blind outcome of collective selfishness damages and degrades the natural world while exploiting the weakest and most vulnerable. Without a truth-loving culture, no electoral mechanism can protect us from demagogues who manipulate fear and ignorance in their pursuit of power. The miracle of an ever more productive consumer economy — Adam Smith's promised "wealth of nations" — now confronts us with a double bind: we face an immediate political crisis whenever the economy *fails to keep growing*, and we face the ultimate environmental catastrophe if the economy *continues to keep growing*. All the while, wealth is inexorably concentrated in the hands of the few, who then use part of it to perpetuate the status quo by propagating an ideology of self-interest.

Here we have to face squarely the most damaging and least understood consequence of the Liberal paradigm: the definitive elimination of a culture based on the love of wisdom — the truth quest. In the absence of the quest, which is both an individual and a collective effort, the culture fragments and society lurches between a cynical, pragmatic materialism and a closed-minded fundamentalism. People lose faith in each other and cling tightly to their own beliefs. Today, the majority of Americans regard politicians as morally equivalent to prostitutes, while many hold rigid ideological and religious beliefs in which bizarre individual interpretations are taken as divine certainties.[52]

It is demoralizing and ironic that one result of the Cartesian-based revolution of Liberalism in the United States is the persistence of scientific illiteracy. Today, a significant portion of the electorate defiantly embraces a simple-minded medievalism: one in five Americans believes the sun revolves around the earth, and almost one in two dispute biological evolution, believing instead that God created human beings in their present form within the past ten thousand years.[53] In March 2009, an elected representative, Congressman John Shimkus from Illinois, a Lutheran who believes in the literal truth of the Bible, testified before a House Energy Subcommittee on Energy and Environment by quoting the book of Genesis (chapter 8, verse 22) to reassure the committee that humanity need not worry about global warming because of God's promise to Noah after the flood. He added, "I believe that [the Bible] is the infallible word of God, and that's the way it is going to be for his creation.... The earth will end only when God declares it's time to be over."[54] Soon after this pronouncement, Shimkus made a credible bid to become chair of the House Energy Subcommittee dealing with global warming.

Even at the highest levels of government, dogma eclipses wisdom. Reality becomes what it is convenient to believe. Our political culture is losing its grip on the most elementary criteria for knowledge of what is real. Since industrial capitalism is more immense than ever — global, interlocked, and increasingly impersonal — the idea of radical change seems hopelessly quixotic. What to do?

## We Are Each Responsible for the Good of the Whole

This brings us to another wonderful irony. At the inception of free-market capitalism, Adam Smith assumed that all participants in a transaction would need "relevant knowledge," which suggests the more radical path not taken: invert the understanding that currently rules. Take Smith's condition seriously. Recognize that ultimately markets will only serve justice and the common good to the degree that those involved pursue justice and the common good in their thinking and in their daily decisions. Instead of wishfully assuming, against all the evidence, that selfishness will be automatically converted by the market into the good of the whole, we need to address the heart of the matter — the values, awareness, and motivation of the human individual. Each of us needs to balance selfishness with an openness to others and a concern for the good of the whole, and we need to do this in our various roles and through the various institutions we participate in.

This pursuit of wisdom cannot be simply legislated and bureaucratically enforced. Government — like every other human-created, human-led institution — has a role and an influence in proportion to its power, but ultimately no external regulation will provide the good society we seek. Instead, at the center of such a revolution in political culture and consciousness must be the moral, intellectual, and spiritual regeneration of the individual — what Plato called a *periagoge* — a turning around of the soul toward a love of truth, beauty, and the good.

The rest of this book will examine what this "turning around" looks like and how it could be accomplished, in theory and practice, but it's worth noting here that we can already see it taking place in a variety of arenas in civil society, the economy, and government. The formula is simple: start with where you are and with what you have. For example, one brief, paradigmatic story illuminates in general terms what is at the heart of our problem and the way forward. In 1996, Ray Anderson, the CEO of Interface, one of the largest office carpet manufacturing corporations in the world, became *Forbes* magazine's Entrepreneur of the Year. Anderson's recognition came after a revolutionary two-year process of transformation in his soul, and the ethos of his company, that produced a model of ethical behavior and business more aligned with the truth quest.

The story starts with Interface setting up an environmental task force in response to consumer pressure. The task force approached Anderson as the CEO to give an inspirational kick-off speech presenting an "environmental vision" for the company. With a shock, Anderson realized he had no environmental vision. He had never given a thought to what the company was taking from or doing to the earth in the making of its products. Desperate for inspiration, he read a book that had propitiously landed on his desk, Paul Hawken's *The Ecology of Commerce.* In an interview, he described the moment when he came to a particular phrase that suddenly confronted him with the enormity of the industrial devastation of the earth: "the death of birth," E.O. Wilson's term for species extinction. Anderson said, "It was a point of a spear into my chest... and as I read on the spear went deeper, and it became an epiphanal experience, a total change of mind-set for myself and a change of paradigm... for the company."

As he investigated his company's processes, Anderson was shocked to discover that, for every ton of finished product, his company was responsible for thirty tons of waste. It was, he realized, the "way of the plunderer... plundering something that is not mine, something that belongs to every creature on earth." He then faced squarely the political dimension of the issue and realized that "the day must come when this is illegal, when plundering is not allowed... [and] people like me will end up in jail." Anderson translated his *periagoge* into action and institutional change. He decided that if Interface couldn't produce carpets more sustainably, then maybe it shouldn't be producing them at all. He instituted "Mission Zero" for the company — a model program for recycling and eliminating negative impacts on the environment. In 2007, he was named as one of *Time* magazine's Heroes of the Environment. By 2009, Interface was about halfway to its goal.[55] Implicit in what Anderson called his "mid-course correction" was the moral revolution of giving priority to the truth quest, inverting the market principle and making a concern for the good of the whole a condition of pursuing profit.

This sort of turning around of the soul can be seen in a variety of citizen groups now pushing for greater corporate responsibility. There is a related consumer movement advocating "socially responsible investing" and "triple bottom line" accounting, where the bottom line of *profit* is balanced with concern for *people* and *planet*. Since 2005, the United Nations has developed and supported Principles for Responsible Investing (PRI) dealing with sustainable environmental, social, and corporate governance. What is most encouraging is that as consumers become more aware of the bigger picture and push for moral reform, such measures increasingly make good business sense.[56] There is even a new grassroots campaign in the United States to amend the Fourteenth Amendment to the US Constitution, which, as noted, has been the basis for corporations claiming the rights and freedoms of "personhood." Called Move to Amend, the movement has passed resolutions in over thirty counties and cities across the United States to reaffirm that "constitutional rights and freedoms apply only to persons and not corporations, partnerships, and organizational entities."[57] Such initiatives taken together signal the beginning of a shift in business and corporate culture — one that is driven by the growing number of morally reawakened individuals working, shopping, and living differently.[58]

This turning around of the soul toward the quest inverts the current Liberal assumption that self-interest — and private profit — should be the main driver of every economic calculation and replaces it with a consideration of the whole. When individuals try to balance self-interest with a consideration of the bigger picture, they discover, as Socrates did, that deep self-interest actually includes concern for of the good of the whole.

As we slowly come to terms with the larger narrative of our runaway global economy, we are realizing that our two-hundred-year-old moral holiday in the interests of economic growth is an indulgence we can no longer afford. It was difficult to create a form of consciousness that would set about destroying the living biosphere that created us. We strain against our deepest nature to maintain this destructive one-sidedness, while we secretly crave wholeness and good health. Yet we can be encouraged by the fact that some of the more thoughtful of our founding fathers recognized that love of truth would inevitably require us periodically to rethink the foundations of government. Here are the words of Thomas Jefferson on this subject:

> But I know also, that laws and institutions must go hand in hand with the progress of the human mind. As that becomes more developed, more enlightened, as new discoveries are made, new truths disclosed, and manners and opinion change with change of circumstance, institutions must advance also, and keep pace with the times. We might as well require a man to wear still the coat which fitted him when a boy,

as civilized society to remain ever under the regime of their barbarous ancestors.[59]

We need to remember that Jefferson owned slaves and that the Constitution implicitly endorsed slavery as part of its political vision. Today we have a radically expanded understanding of the human condition. Jefferson himself recognized that as our understanding changed, so our institutions needed to follow. This is our political challenge today, to clarify a reliable method for understanding the human condition and its possibilities for improvement, so we can rethink government and economics.

This recovery of the truth quest proceeds as it has always done, on two levels, following the simple ancient wisdom of the alchemists: "as above so below; as within so without." To know the world, one must know oneself; to know oneself, one must know the world. We are reminded that the search for the grail of the good life begins and ends with self-exploration — reflecting on *anamnesis* and discovering and telling one's story.

The next chapter tells something of my individual story of opening to the wisdom quest. Then chapter 4 overviews the "big" story of self-reflective humanity's emergence from nature and of how the core structure of the quest emerges from the paradoxical nature of consciousness. In the process of weaving together our personal and our collective stories, guided by a concern with the common good, we make a surprising discovery: *we find ourselves already on a path with a heart, engaged in the practice of a new ethics and a new politics.*

CHAPTER 3

# RECOVERY OF THE QUEST, PART I — ANAMNESIS: SEARCHING WITH MY LIFE

I have no Ideology. My life is my Message. — Mohandas Gandhi

A philosopher, it appeared, had to engage in an *anamnetic* exploration of his own consciousness in order to discover its constitution by his own experience of reality, if he wanted to be critically aware of what he was doing. This exploration, further, could not stop short at the more recent events in political and personal life, but had to go as far back as his or her remembrance of things past would allow in order to reach the strata of reality-consciousness that were least overlaid by later accretions. The *anamnesis* had to recapture the childhood experiences that let themselves be recaptured because they were living forces in the present constitution of his consciousness.

— Eric Voegelin, *Anamnesis*

In myths the hero is the one who conquers the dragon not the one who is devoured by it. And yet both have to deal with the same dragon. Also, he is no hero who never met the dragon, or who, if he once saw it, declared afterwards that he saw nothing. Equally, only one who has risked the fight with the dragon and is not overcome by it wins the hoard, the "treasure hard to attain." He alone has a genuine claim to self-confidence, for he has faced the dark ground of his self and thereby has gained himself.... He has arrived at an inner certainty which makes him capable of self-reliance, and attained what the alchemists called the *unio mentalis*. As a rule this state is represented pictorially by a *mandala*.

— C. G. Jung, *Mysterium Conjunctionis* #756

## Home

I have a mother in Africa who used to send me packages of kudu *biltong*. *Biltong* is Afrikaans for the strips of sun-dried venison the Boer trekkers took on their ox-wagon journeys into the wilderness interior of southern Africa. The kudu is one of the most regal of the African antelopes; the male, with its long spiraling horns, is well chosen as the emblem of the South African National Parks. *Biltong* is enjoyed as a delicacy by most native-born South Africans, perhaps most of all by the Bushmen. It is all lean muscle and sometimes so dry it can be snapped like a twig or peeled off in long thin strips. It tastes like no other food and has little resemblance to the fatty, marbled steaks of our corn- and antibiotic-fed cattle. Kudu *biltong* smells wild, gamey, infused with the herbs and shrubs of the antelope's diet — the flavor of the veldt. At times of "meat-hunger," a Bushman hunter has been known to run most of the day in the summer heat of the Kalahari Desert chasing down an adult kudu. I share some Bushman tastes. I loved long-distance running, and kudu *biltong* is my soul food — the taste of home. Savoring the tough strips of flesh fills me with a nostalgia so strong it's a kind of communion. For a moment I feel like I am an African back in Africa.

At other times I also feel myself to be a Jew, an Englishman, an Israeli, and a *kama'aina*, a dweller in the land of Hawai'i. My quest began as a search to find myself in a world where identity could be a matter of life and death. Today, identity can still be a matter of life and death, and since the pieces identifying me do not make a familiar category, I risk being badly misunderstood by all.

My Jewish identity preoccupied me for much of the first three decades of my life. The time I spent working on a kibbutz and soldiering in the Israeli army empowered and healed me. But more surprisingly, Jewish nationalism opened me to the wisdom of indigenous peoples. I found myself participating in activities that gave me insight into some of those archetypal experiences that define what it means to be human, and this, paradoxically, helped liberate me from a purely "tribal" identity.

Biblical Israel was the site for the original monotheistic revelation and marked the beginning of written history as a drama of divine revelation in human affairs — what Eric Voegelin called the "leap in being."* Modern Israel may well prove to be the catalyst in history's next unfolding — another leap in being — or its catastrophic unraveling. Today the Middle East can be seen as the epicenter of the global crisis. Israel is armed with nuclear weapons, led by a hard-line government, and caught in a regressive cycle of fear, anger, and brutality. The surrounding Arab governments are rushing to become equivalent powers. At the same time, their people are starting to assert a form of direct democracy in an "Arab spring," whose course currently oscillates between Islamic fundamentalism and Western consumerism but is still pregnant with the promise of something truly creative.

Beneath the furiously battling, bleeding tribal religions is the contested territory — an expanding, drying desert containing some of the largest remaining oil reserves on the planet. Climate change, drought, limited fresh water, and a rapidly degrading ecosystem threaten the protagonists as well as everyone else. For simple practical reasons all of our problems are now increasingly interlocked. A sustainable resolution to the Middle East conflict cannot be separated from global concerns about living on a habitable earth. Clearly, a bigger story of meaning and identity is required — something that goes to the shared "indigeneity" of both Israeli and Palestinian. Ultimately, this needs to express a shared love for the single indivisible homeland that is planet earth — a primal-planetary culture.

It took my own self-imposed Hawaiian "exile" to distance me sufficiently from my various homelands to recognize a deeper dynamic working in my life. Life in these warm, welcoming islands helped me envision a politics within which the unique stories of individuals, tribes, and nations could express the truth of their particularity and still flourish in a single planetary community.

So, I offer my story as a personal example of the dynamic of the future primal politics I advocate. Telling my story is simultaneously an invitation to the reader to recognize the role of his or her own story in the collective, cooperative creation of meaning that is at the living center of a future primal politics.

---

* In the next chapter I discuss Voegelin's philosophy of consciousness and how the biblical revelation has helped both define and deform the truth quest.

## Exile in Eden

Just beyond the suburbs and pavements of my hometown, Port Elizabeth, are miles of spectacular beach and bush. The city is situated in a region where two very different climates meet and mix, creating one of the most unique and ancient ecosystems in southern Africa. To the west along the southern coast is the winter-rainfall Mediterranean climate. The beaches are fringed with *fynbos*, rich with the remains of the first human seafood culture. In the background, following the ocean and watering the coastal plain are serried ranks of mountains. To the east and north is the summer-rainfall region of the tropics. Where they meet east of Port Elizabeth is a transitional zone of extreme contrasts and diversity — the distinctive tangled *bushveld* of the Eastern Cape.

The Fish River marks the end of this intermediate region and the beginning of the undeveloped Wild Coast of the Transkei north to Zululand. About two thousand years ago, cattle-owning Bantu-speaking people migrated down the east coast, where there was rich pasture for their herds and a suitable climate for their summer-rainfall crops. As they moved south they displaced the original first people, the San Bushman hunter-gatherers, and their close relatives the pastoralist Khoikhoi. At the beginning of the nineteenth century, Dutch and English settlers moved from the southern coastline to the east and north. They met the Xhosas just east of Port Elizabeth, where they clashed in the Xhosa wars, which were more numerous and bitterly fought than the better-known Zulu wars. This was the true frontier separating climate, people, and culture. It was settled by the British, who developed a relatively enlightened attitude to the native population and started a number of mission schools and universities. This British-educated area was the home of some of the great leaders of the struggle against apartheid — Nelson Mandela, Govan Mbeki, Walter Sisulu, and Steve Biko.

The frontier land itself is full of contradictions. Some seasons are wet and rainy, others stone dry. This gives the Eastern Cape bush an utterly unique quality symbolized by the bitter-juice aloes and their bristle-topped, red-hot-poker "flowers of thirst." Gray beard lichen hangs from the tangle of thorn bushes, giving the impression of a primeval forest. Noel Mostert, the historian of the Xhosa wars, describes in his book *Frontiers* the intense impression this landscape makes on the traveler:

> [Here] nature flowers and fruits in a willful and undependable manner, in a fantasy of colour of feverish combinations, the soft and the

> delicate with the violently brilliant, blooms that poison and bulbs that feed the starving, all of it expressing the alternating bounty and generosity and malevolent caprice of the land itself.... One moment it is a land that seems to be all English meadows, parkland. Roses and carnations bloom, orchards hang with soft fruit.... Then, at no distance at all... mere yards it sometimes can seem, one confronts the other side of it all: drought, dust, despair. It is here that the aloes burn, among vast cracked granite boulders that radiate heat like furnaces, and serve as altars for coiled and venomous serpents, which add a new aberration to their threat by spitting their venom unerringly into the eyes. And all about, mile after mile, stretches thick mimosa bush, a hardy greenery, wielding massed thorns the size of small daggers, which stab and strike at whatever passes.... Sometimes in this country there is a breezy freshness blowing in from the distant, hazily seen ocean: vinegar for the crucified.[1]

In the heart of this wilderness around Sunday's River is an area called Addo, named from the Bushman (Khoisan) *Kadouw*, meaning "river crossing." It is one of the few relatively intact fragments of the ancient ecosystems that once covered the paleo-continent of Gondwanaland two hundred million years ago. In the early nineteenth century, miles of impenetrable mimosa thorn bush were alive with the full complement of big game. The only way to move through the bush was to follow paths made by elephants and the aggressive black rhino. One professional big-game hunter called it "a hunter's hell," meaning it was also "animal heaven." This allowed a unique subspecies of the African elephant to flourish. Addo elephants were slightly reddish in color to match the earth, and many females were tuskless, probably an adaptation to intense hunting pressure. The original San Bushman hunters were driven into the mountains, but the tall, thick bush, full of *spekboom* — a dark green succulent also called "elephant's food" — made it possible for the elephants to survive repeated attempts at extermination.

Today the elephants prosper in Addo, which is now the only game reserve in southern Africa extending down to the ocean and hosting the "big seven" — with whales and great white sharks in addition to lion, rhinoceros, elephant, buffalo, and leopard. As a child, I was moved deeply by our family weekend outings to Addo. Driving out of the city on dirt roads into the bush in the hope of encountering elephants was like traveling back to some incredibly wild and wise old Africa. I felt deeply connected to the place and the animals, but I had no story to make meaning of my experiences, no way of connecting them to the rest of my city life.

I grew up as an Orthodox Jew in racist South Africa during the fifties, when the Nazi death camps were still fresh in Jewish memory. The president of the country during the time I discovered politics was Hendrik Verwoerd, the architect of apartheid, who had developed his vision of strict racial segregation while a student in prewar Germany. It was not much of a leap from apartheid to anti-Semitism. South African Jews were legally white, but definitely not Dutch-white. My deeply tanned father was once mistaken for Coloured* and turned off a whites-only bus. Like many middle-class children, I was well loved by my parents but spent much of my time in the close company of Africans — warmly cared for by housemaids, cooks, "garden boys," and nannies; playing with them, eating their food, listening to their music, fascinated by their click-inflected Xhosa language.

In a society that was obsessed by race and tribe, I experienced my Jewishness as a problem — a peculiar tribalism in a world of tribal warfare. Both my parents were Ashkenazi Jews whose parents came from eastern Europe. My father grew up in a small anti-Semitic Afrikaans village; he was the last of five brothers in the solitary Jewish family, which true to stereotype owned the only shop in the village. His first language was Yiddish, which he spoke at home to his parents and brothers, then Afrikaans, used in school. Only later did he become fluent in English. Yiddish was the language of the Ashkenazi ghettos — a mixture of Hebrew, German, and Slavic languages written in the Hebrew alphabet. By their neighbors and themselves, the Ashkenazi were considered a people apart, distinguished by ethnicity, language, dress, and religious practice.

During the Middle Ages, when the majority of the European population was illiterate, Jews had achieved almost universal literacy in Hebrew. Literacy was a condition of religious practice, which involved reading and ritually reenacting an epic story of identity — of tribal, desert nomads, bonded by shared revelation and then shaped by over a thousand years of history amid

* "Coloured" or "Cape-Coloured" is an apartheid category for the mixed-race offspring of Europeans and Bushmen (San and Khoikhoi). For more on this term, see the footnote on page 177.

the arid crossroads between Africa, Asia, and Europe. Since religious practice was tied to a story of identity, Judaism had little interest in converting outsiders.[2] Eventually, Ashkenazi Jews became one of the most genetically isolated and culturally distinct ethnic groups in all of Europe.[3] By the nineteenth century this group constituted the heart of world Jewry, with some five million concentrated on the western boundary of Russia, in a gigantic reservation known as the Pale of Settlement. Here they lived in largely self-governing communities, practicing an exclusive religion, dressing and eating differently, speaking Yiddish, and praying and studying in Hebrew. It was a peculiarly contradictory tribe, insular and fiercely protective of its culture and religion, yet simultaneously landless, rootless, and cosmopolitan.

According to a czarist survey at the end of the nineteenth century, the largest group of Jews in the world constituted the most impoverished and destitute of all the oppressed ethnic minorities in Russia.[4] They were also the most politicized, disproportionately represented in the leadership of progressive, revolutionary, and utopian movements of the time. This was the crucible of modern political Zionism, a movement that created the modern State of Israel, widely admired in its early years, much reviled today. But Zionism also produced a unique utopian community — the agrarian, democratic kibbutz — which in the words of the Jewish philosopher and mystic Martin Buber was the "experiment that did not fail."

After the anti-Jewish massacres at the end of the nineteenth century, some Jews moved to Palestine, inspired by the Zionist dream of building a new country in the ancient homeland. There they joined the small, impoverished Sephardic (Spanish) communities that had returned to the Holy Land in the fifteenth century when the Inquisition expelled the Jews of Spain. But the bulk of the Ashkenazi emigrants left for the rapidly growing capitalist economies of the West. The Jewish community of South Africa came almost exclusively from the Lithuanian part of the Pale. Of those who remained in Lithuania, 90 percent were exterminated during the Holocaust.

South African Jews enjoyed the benefits of honorary white status, doing well in business and professional life, and suffering only indirectly from cultural anti-Semitism. But their political sensitivity inspired a disproportionate number to join, and sometimes lead, the struggle against apartheid. For example, in 1955, when police arrested 156 antiapartheid activists for treason, more than half of the 23 whites arrested were Jewish. In 1963, the South Africa security service raided the headquarters of the underground antiapartheid

African National Congress (ANC). As a result, Nelson Mandela and nine of his comrades were charged with sabotage. Of the nine, four were black, five were white, and all five whites were Jews. All but one received life sentences. The first white elected as a member of the ANC national executive was a Jew, Joe Slovo, who remarkably went on to become chief of staff of its military wing, *Umkhonto we Sizwe*, "Spear of the Nation."[5] My sense of being part of a minority in opposition to brutal, powerful rulers was a source of some pride, but also anxiety. We still lived with the ancient tension of a tolerated, sometimes privileged outsider, aware of past and impending persecution.

My father's hero was the pacifist Mahatma Gandhi, who had spent his early years fighting apartheid in South Africa. In my ignorance and insecurity, I rejected this as the traditional Jewish path of passivity, perhaps cowardice. Like most of my peers, I was drawn to a more assertive Jewish nationalism. I joined the South African branch of a global kibbutz-Zionist youth movement, *Habonim* — "The Builders," based on a mix of the utopian socialism of the Israeli kibbutz, the back-to-nature movement of the German *Wandervogel*, and the heroic vision of returning the Jews to their biblical homeland after two thousand years of exile and persecution. Habonim made sense of the weirdness of being a Jew in Africa and started framing my political worldview.

Zionism attempted to grasp the entirety of Jewish existence in a single passionate narrative: millennia of struggle, culminating in the present moment as an opening for creative politics — redemption through a return to the land of origins. The narrative began with Jewish identity forming around the monotheistic revelation, and the creation of the biblical Kingdom of Israel, followed by a succession of wars, foreign occupation, exile, and return. This ended with the final conquest by Rome in the first century and the global dispersal of the Jews into the Diaspora — the *Galut*. For centuries Jewish history in the Diaspora was a cycle of oppressive decrees, anti-Semitic riots, massacres, and expulsions, only to be followed by acceptance into a new country and accommodation, until the inevitable cycle of persecution and expulsion returned.

Toward the end of the nineteenth century and during the first part of the twentieth century, small groups of young Jews from eastern Europe organized themselves through the international Zionist youth movements and moved back to the biblical homeland to form communal agricultural settlements. Land was purchased by the Jewish National Fund through the Keren Hayesod and held collectively for the nation; it was given to these young groups of idealists. Technically they were colonists, but of a radically different sort from the European colonists who came to America, Canada, Australia, and South Africa. First of all, they were without a motherland and without state backing. They were not part of commercial ventures by chartered companies in search of profit. Nor were they looking for gold or silver or opportunity in a fertile land or for good jobs in a growing economy. They were idealists who were united in a near-mystical notion of transformation, a dream of remaking self and society through hard physical labor on the ancestral homeland. Out of this grew the agrarian, communal settlement — the kibbutz — that became one of the founding institutions of the State of Israel. Like most nationalist movements of liberation, Zionism was almost wholly self-absorbed; it never creatively engaged the indigenous Palestinian population. Early Zionists conveniently saw "a land without a people" for a persecuted "people without a land." Palestinians saw outsiders and colonists arriving, buying up land, and asserting an alien identity. Only a handful of visionaries saw the larger, more complex reality and struggled, vainly, for creative coexistence.

Conflicting needs and mutual incomprehension resulted in violence. Escalation of violence eroded the vestiges of mutual empathy and set in place the vicious cycle that today is the tragedy of the Israeli-Palestinian conflict. In my youth I was oblivious to Palestinians. Zionism healed me by explaining my alienation as an outcome of a collective condition — life in exile. I felt empowered, wholly absorbed in the drama of Jewish redemption, which would be simultaneously *or la'goyim*, a moral example to the world. I felt part of the Kabbalist ideal of *tikkun ha'Olam* — healing and repairing the world through practical action.

South Africa might have been the original Garden of Eden, but most of my childhood was spent in an indoor hell. I attended what was regarded as the best boys' school in town — an authoritarian, whites-only, Christian establishment. Every morning when the rest of the school would gather in the assembly hall to sing hymns of praise to Jesus, a small knot of Jewish boys would be excused to stand outside in the playground, self-consciously with yarmulkes on our heads, to chant and sing our Hebrew prayers. Classes were hours of soul-sucking boredom, punctuated by sudden violent dramas.

Some of the teachers had long ago given up on love of learning as motivation, and they would get our attention by periodically whipping us — getting "cuts," we called it — one at a time in front of the rest of the class for a variety of obscure transgressions. One bored biology teacher once started class with a surprise quiz; twenty questions, and for each wrong answer we got one cut of the cane. We spent the rest of the period getting whipped. Teachers intimidated us in class, and the bigger boys persecuted the smaller in the playground. It disheartened and enraged me. I developed a loathing for bullies and hated school.

Alienation from South African society deepened with my early discovery of the Nazi Holocaust. One day exploring my uncle's medical library, I opened a book on Nazi medical experiments and found myself looking at photographs of mutilated children. I was horrified to discover the Nazis had slaughtered two-thirds of the Jews who had stayed behind in Europe. The shock reverberated in the small daily cruelties of apartheid I witnessed around me. Injustice was brought close to home when I first confronted starving children dressed in rags, coming to the kitchen door begging for "bread and sugar water." I remember my confusion at being stopped from acting on my childish generosity and sharing the contents of the fridge. This sudden encounter with evil cracked my world apart forever. I began the quest without knowing it as a way of healing this fracture.

I would live for weekends and holidays, when the miles of bush and the clean, empty beaches offered an escape from human-inflicted misery and a spectacular playground for my imagination. Vervet monkeys thrived in the bush, and the tidal rock pools were rich underwater gardens, crusted with black and brown mussels and volcano barnacles that cut bare feet; there were also limpets tending their little lawns of algae and bright red and orange plum anemones, spiny sea urchins, and the camouflaged, quick-darting *klipvis* — the rock fish, which we caught and released. With so much food in plain sight, it was easy to imagine the "beach-Bushmen" — whom the Dutch settlers called *strandloopers* — living a life of plenty in the wild, protected from the elements by cozy campfires in the spacious rock shelters that dot the coast.

My early wordless love for Africa and Africans remained unbroken, since our family emigrated before I had to renounce the black friends and loving caretakers of my childhood. There were many obvious privileges associated with being a white African, and many were guilty, but perhaps the most noble and the least celebrated lay in being able to regularly escape civilization into moments of "wilderness rapture." Having direct access to wilderness as a child gave me an early introduction to crossing boundaries and being comfortable with living in the *in-between*. It allowed a part of me to resist being socialized and, in staying wild and African, paradoxically remain more human.

## The Cave

Plato's allegory of the cave is philosophy's most famous metaphor for consciousness entrapped, enlightened, and entrapped again. It appears at the climax of the most celebrated text in the history of political philosophy, Plato's *Republic*, as part of the discussion of the education of the philosopher-king, the ruler who must love wisdom more than power. Socrates asks his pupil Glaucon to imagine the unenlightened — by implication all of us to some extent — as prisoners in a cave, chained by the leg and neck since birth. The prisoners sit facing the back wall, on which are projected shadows of a fire-illuminated puppet show taking place behind the prisoners' backs — a primitive movie theater. All the prisoners know of life is their experience of the shadows projected on the wall and their shared interpretations of what they see. The allegory suggests that to some degree we are prisoners in the cave of our past experience. Any worldview becomes a cave the moment it is taken for reality.

One of the prisoners is somehow liberated. Stepping out of the cave into the larger sunlit world, the liberated prisoner is blinded by the light and disoriented. As he takes stock and explores the larger world, he remembers his journey out of the cave and is led to construct a larger universe of meaning, within which he can recognize the limits of life in the cave as a small part of a larger whole. "Anything is better than to go back and live as they do," Plato tells us. But despite the joy of escaping, the prisoner returns to the cave. Why? We are told it is his duty to liberate his fellows. Why do we feel compelled to help, to enlighten others? Why is it good for the philosopher to be concerned with the well-being of his fellows?

On returning to the cave the philosopher finds his eyes are unaccustomed to the dark, and he has lost his easy familiarity with the world of shadows. When he tries to enlighten his companions, they ridicule his awkwardness and think he has lost his mind. Plato, in the voice of Socrates, gives us a warning. If the philosopher persists too stridently in his mission, the prisoners will turn on him and kill him. The warning is well taken, since we know the *Republic* was written after the polis executed the unrepentant Socrates for questioning authority. In contrast to the comforts of contemporary academia, Socratic philosophy is not an obscurantist escape from public life — but an urgent, practical, life-and-death matter. Why take the risk?

To answer this we need to reflect on what we know about the Socratic practice. Socrates wrote nothing and saw face-to-face discussion, with anyone, about the big questions, as the royal road to truth. To pursue wisdom the philosopher needed to share his knowledge and to keep learning from others. On returning to the cave, the philosopher has to acknowledge that life outside the cave has transformed his ability to live harmoniously as a prisoner. Yet to win the trust of the inmates, he needed to reconnect, to sit and listen to their stories of life in the cave. One cannot "enlighten" without listening and learning something from the "ignorant." Having demonstrated the sincerity of his concern for their mutual well-being, the philosopher can point to the obvious asymmetry of the relationship between "those who stayed and the one who returned." The return embodied the fact that the philosopher had undergone a conversion experience. He had opened himself to experiencing something larger and truer that illuminates the nature of the quest. Socrates and Plato called this process a "turning around of the soul," a *periagoge*, an opening to the mystery of self-awareness and the possibility of living in the light of greater consciousness. This has democratic implications. To put it simply, however fixated on the shadows the prisoners might be, they are still capable of the most minimal act of reflection, which at the very least reveals that one cannot evaluate "life in the cave" without comparing it to something larger — "life out of the cave." Everyone can benefit from the philosophical quest.

Here the metaphor needs to be expanded to serve the Socratic intention of clarifying the quest. We are all in caves of our own limited experience of life. We all need to teach and learn from each other in order to pursue the good life *together*. We all get the greatest benefit by opening to the experience of those who differ the most from us. We teach most effectively when we learn from those we are trying to teach, and we learn most effectively by being allowed to teach those who are trying to enlighten us. The process of face-to-face Socratic enlightenment is reciprocal and endless.

The Athenian jury gave Socrates three choices: give up the practice of philosophy, leave Athens, or die. Socrates chose death. His last act becomes his most unambiguous and eloquent teaching: "The unexamined life is not worth living." And this examination needs to take place within a community of like-minded seekers. As Aristotle famously noted, human beings are indeed "political creatures." Once one has grasped the liberating capacity of reflection in the face-to-face situation, there is no going back. The prisoner is initiated into philosophy — the truth quest — as a minimal condition of the good life.[6]

## Out of the Cave

At the age of twelve, a few months before my bar mitzvah, I escaped from the cave of South Africa, together with my parents and sister. We exchanged the brutalities of apartheid for the mild liberal climate of England. The small, long-established Jewish community of Plymouth welcomed us as part of the tribe and then witnessed my initiation into Jewish manhood as I sang my assigned portion of the Bible.

But coming from a South African school, I scored poorly on the standardized "thirteen plus" — a placement test taken at age thirteen — and was consigned to a nonacademic "secondary modern" school to learn a trade. After a year we moved to the small picturesque university town of Cambridge, where, thanks to private tutoring, I was accepted into the academic Cambridge Grammar School for Boys. It was an enlightened institution that had abolished corporal punishment and had been chosen to pioneer the integrative Nuffield approach to science education. My teachers were young, well qualified, some with PhDs, and fired up about the rapidly growing fields of evolutionary biology, cosmology, quantum physics, and biochemistry. They enjoyed teaching, and I started loving school.

However, I had escaped the cave of apartheid only to find myself in another — an exclusively human-shaped environment devoid of wilderness. The town had the pretty River Cam running through it, and like Port Elizabeth, it was comfortably human scale. But it was surrounded by a relentless patchwork of field, hedgerow, pasture, and village; everywhere worked by human hand. There would be no weekend escape into the miles of deserted beach and mountain, no encounters with the animals of the veldt. At times I felt as if I was suffocating, and I pitied my English school friends who had never known the ecstatic expansion of the soul when alone in truly wild places.

My efforts to assimilate put me in the position of Plato's returning prisoner. During my infrequent visits to South Africa, it became obvious that I could no longer step into my old life. In some important ways I had seen a larger, "truer" reality, and I had a critical perspective on both England and South Africa unavailable to those who had never left either cave. Every new experience was changing me. South Africa was also changing. Like it or not, I was out of the cave and on the journey. There was no going home.

While one part of me was successfully being educated in science and becoming English, the Jewish exile in me was becoming a passionate nationalist. I helped found a Cambridge branch of Habonim, which was already well represented in the larger European cities. My life out of school was taken up by the movement's program of self-education, seminars, campouts, and campfires. At the end of the day we would gather for hours of wild Israeli folk dancing, shouting out Hebrew songs, spinning in circles of horas. We felt part of a creative vanguard of history, drawing energy and enthusiasm from the counterculture of the sixties, but amplified and focused by a three-thousand-year-old Jewish narrative climaxing in liberation here, now. Unlike much of the youth revolt, we had a utopian model under construction — the democratic, self-organizing, idealistic kibbutz. Increasingly I identified with the new State of Israel — a place I had never actually visited.

Meanwhile, science was capturing an unrelated track of my imagination. In my senior year of high school I started realizing that the compelling perspective of quantum physics, biochemistry, and evolutionary biology were interlocking pieces telling a story of a single evolving reality. I have a glowing memory of an epiphany walking home from school on one of those rare sunny English afternoons thinking about what we were learning and, in a flash, realizing that the wilderness I thought I had left behind in Africa was present right there, in every glistening rain-washed piece of vegetation. Inside every green cell were the same chlorophyll-containing chloroplasts — invented by evolution two billion years ago. They were still silently at work, absorbing photons of light traveling from the nuclear furnace of the sun, ninety-three million miles away, energizing the conversion of water and carbon dioxide into sugars. I could visualize the molecular structure of the simple sugars being joined together into the more complex starches and celluloses that make up the green living matter of all the plants on which the rest of life feasts. All of it, every sunlit, fluttering leaf on the poplar trees in the backyard, every green blade of grass on the lawn, every clod of earth, indeed every animal and every human being that had ever lived — including my own idiosyncratic self — was part of our one and only, still-evolving biosphere. This single reality had been steadily growing and unfolding for millions, indeed billions, of years before there were human eyes to gaze at it, human hands to work it, and human consciousness to be amazed at it all.

It was a vision beyond words — utterly astounding — a true revelation. It was made all the more astonishing by the fact that no one, Christian, atheist, or Jew, seemed to notice. Even the teachers who had convinced me of its scientific truth were primarily concerned about the usefulness of the information. No one cared about the big picture. I vaguely sensed that if people really took the time to see and feel this larger reality, everything would have to suddenly stop and change. Business as usual depended on keeping our eyes averted and our thoughts to ourselves. How and why this should be was beyond me. But more importantly, the vision seemed to have nothing to do with the other track of my imagination — the Zionist narrative that was giving my life meaning. The evolutionary revelation was left hanging.

By the time I graduated, the carpet had been rolled out, my choices made by my success in the sciences. I followed the urging of parents and teachers and accepted a scholarship to study medicine at Cambridge University. Barely three weeks into the term, it hit me that I had made a terrible mistake. After my recent initiation into the beauties of cosmology, medicine seemed mundane, like a kind of biological mechanics. I came from a family of doctors — including almost all my uncles and one of my aunts — in a world that seemed to have no shortage of doctors. I felt no passion to heal sick bodies. I did, however, feel a compulsion to understand and respond to human-inflicted misery, particularly that playing out in the drama of Jewish persecution and its recent heroic redemption in the creation of the State of Israel.

The packed medical curriculum with its labs, lectures, and tutorials left me little time to think. I went into depression and then panic. Finally I rebelled. I considered a variety of options, from philosophy to archaeology and even Arabic (which seemed an obvious choice, since I planned to live in the Middle East), but I realized I had no gift for languages, and finally I shocked family and friends by getting accepted into the history department.

At that point, my anatomy professor and director of studies, Bernard Towers, intervened. He had been educated in the best tradition of the public school "good-all-rounder" and had come to medicine after a degree in the classics — Greek, Latin, and philosophy. He offered a compromise. Instead of burning my bridges with medicine, and risking my relationship with both my parents and common sense, he reminded me I could gain a respectable, practical medical degree after two years. I could then use my third year of the Cambridge Tripos system to specialize in the history and philosophy of science, deal with some big questions, and still graduate with honors.

In one of those coincidences whose meaning would only become clear many years later, Towers also happened to be president of the British Teilhard Association. He encouraged my compromise with medicine by giving me a copy of a slim biography of Teilhard de Chardin he had recently authored. Teilhard had the distinction of being both a Jesuit priest and a paleontologist. He was also one of the most original theologians of the past century and one of the first thinkers to recognize that the scientific *discovery* of the evolutionary narrative could itself constitute an evolutionary leap in self-reflective consciousness, with enormous implications for human affairs. Here at last was a Cambridge-sanctioned intellect who could put words to my wordless high school revelation.

Teilhard's genius was to be able to take in the detailed big picture as a whole and recognize in the entirety of the evolution of the universe a single direction. That is, over time there is a gradual unfolding from simplicity to complexity, and with complexity of structure there is an increase in that mysterious interior aspect of reality we recognize in ourselves as consciousness. For example, we can understand the evolution of life on earth as the successive appearance of concentric spheres, each compounding the complexity of what previously existed. Four and a half billion years ago the earth started as a molten ball, of which the core — the *barysphere* — still persists today at the center of the planet, periodically erupting as volcanic lava. Over the eons the planet cooled and crusted over, creating the *lithosphere*. As the cooling continued, millions of years of rain created the layer of oceans covering the earth — the *hydrosphere*. Within the water layers, molecules aggregated into more complex megamolecules, which in turn self-organized in the primeval soup into the first simple cells and then organisms, all of which constituted another layer of complexity — the *biosphere*. Each new layer was an emergent property of the preceding layers that compounded the number of possible relationships with those preceding layers, stimulating further emergence of novelty and complexity. Finally, organisms developed a central nervous system and self-reflective consciousness, creating the most complex layer interacting with all the others — the *noosphere* — the layer of creative, culture-producing, freely choosing humanity.

Teilhard recognized this tendency to grow in complexity and consciousness as a fundamental feature of the evolving universe, which he stated as the *law of complexity-consciousness.* This meant simply that over time increasing complexity of structure was associated with increasing consciousness. Consciousness was not a foreign implant, seeded on our planet by some extragalactic alien, but a fundamental, emergent property of matter. Consciousness could be simply regarded as the *interior* aspect of matter gradually manifesting through the eons of the evolutionary drama, expanding its interiority, as material complexity increases over time. This continued until it reached its most self-conscious form to date — the knowledge-seeking, ethically awake human being. Teilhard summed up his revelation with the statement that the "atomic physicist is the atom's way of looking at itself." We could rephrase that as "the philosopher is the planet's way of knowing itself," *and then choosing its future.* Descartes was wrong. Inner and outer are not absolutely separated; they are two faces of a single reality. Consciousness is a facet of matter.

The Teilhardian vision didn't end there. The superclusters of galaxies are still racing apart with the energy from the initial Big Bang; the universe is still cooling and complexifying. There is no reason why this trajectory, which has been unfolding for billions of years, should suddenly stop dead once the noosphere has produced a civilization that has discovered consumerism. As humanity stumbles to grasp itself through the symbolic narrative of science, history, and philosophy, the cosmic process seems to be reaching some sort of threshold. The obvious question is: What is impending? What would a further leap in complexity-consciousness look like? Given our current reality, what would a more fully self-conscious realization of human agency and creativity look like?

Teilhard made the crucial connection between the evolutionary vision and the political project of seeking the best way to live. But he expressed his anticipated leap in the language of Christianity — as the emergence of a Christ consciousness — the "Christosphere." This left me cold. Christianity was still, for me, contaminated by centuries of anti-Semitism. Nothing in the Christosphere resonated with the Zionism that by now had become the guiding passion in my life. What sort of personal and collective politics could the Teihardian vision support? At some level I must have known I would eventually have to reconcile my politics with scientific cosmology. But more urgent existential issues intervened. I would have to commit fully to the Israeli drama before I returned to philosophy years later, when I could think more freely in the peace and beauty of a tropical island in the middle of the Pacific Ocean.

## Redemption Land

By the time I graduated, I had a degree in medical science and the history and philosophy of science, but intellectual life had lost its enchantment. Graduate work seemed like another layer of verbiage added to an infinite regress of words and reflections on other people's experiences of life. I felt unbalanced, unsure of my grounding in the world. My indoor bookish life seemed a continuation of two thousand years of alienated Jewish existence in exile — escapist intellectualism, study, prayer. The overheated brilliance of Cambridge accentuated what was missing: the world of nature and the body, and direct experiences of the primary realities of existence.

I started reading Micah Berdichevsky, the Nietzschean Zionist writing at the turn of the twentieth century, and all my doubts disappeared. I suddenly saw my path clearly. Berdichevsky was born in the Russian Pale, the son of a long line of rabbis and scholars, and was himself a brilliant scholar of the Talmud and Kabbalah. His father disowned him when he discovered him reading forbidden enlightenment literature. Berdichevsky responded:

> I recall from the teaching of the sages: Whoever walks by the way and interrupts his study to remark, How fine is that tree, how fine is that field, forfeits his life!
>
> Is it any wonder there arose among us generation after generation despising nature, who thought of all God's marvels as superfluous trivialities?
>
> Is it surprising that we became a non-people, a non-nation — non-[human], indeed?
>
> But I assert that then alone will Judah and Israel be saved, when another teaching is given unto us, namely: Whoever walks by the way

> and sees a fine tree and fine field and fine sky and leaves them to think on other thoughts — that man is like one who forfeits his life!
>
> Give us back our fine trees and fine fields! Give us back the Universe![7]

I wanted to experience trees and fields — the natural universe that I felt I had shut out for years. I needed to get out. I needed action.

In three more years I could have been a fully qualified doctor. Instead, as soon as I graduated, I turned down my place at a teaching hospital, left the *golah*, the Jewish exile, and made *aliyah* — the ascent to Israel. I moved to a kibbutz, where I worked as a laborer in the banana plantations while improving my Hebrew.

Kibbutz Zionism seemed to offer a respectable, even noble, respite from academia. While at Cambridge I had considered some of the other radical political philosophies of the sixties. But none of the visions to emerge from the amorphous counterculture came close to the richly realized utopia of the modern Israeli kibbutz.[8] Kibbutz Zionism in its most complete form offered more than agrarian communal living. It included a passionate narrative of meaning in which the Jewish return to the land was offered as a kind of psycho-spiritual healing. Scholar and mystic Aaron David Gordon preached a "religion of labor" in which physical work on the biblical homeland would unite body and soul in a liberated life. Without access to a life on the land, Jews would always be at the mercy of others, lacking the basis for true self-sufficiency. This was a matter not simply of economics and politics but of a psycho-spiritual disease that could only be healed by contact with the living earth. As Gordon put it:

> The Jewish people have been completely cut off from nature and imprisoned within city walls these two thousand years. We have become accustomed to every form of life, except to a life of labor — of labor done at our behest and for its own sake.[9]

Gordon was, like many of the other *chalutzim* — the early pioneers — the son of a family of scholars. He came to Israel at the age of forty-seven, a frail, slight, white-bearded figure, revered as *Hazken* — "the Old Man." He spent the rest of his life working the land, living an ascetic existence, and preaching his philosophy based as much on Kabbalist mysticism as Zionist agrarianism. During the day he sweated in the fields extolling "labor not to make a living, not work as a deed of charity, but for life itself...one of the limbs of life, one of its deepest roots."[10] At night after an exhausting day of work, he would join the spinning circles of hora dancers, caught up in the joy of bonding with his beloved community of farmers.

For Gordon this reconnection with the primal realities of human existence was the movement's moral and spiritual center, the source of its vitality and creativity. Another thinker, Ber Borochov, used a graphic image to support this insight: for centuries in exile the Jewish pyramid of labor had been upside down, balancing on its point with the base up in the air. The majority of Jews, the base, were intellectuals, scholars, rabbis, and professionals — *luftmenschen* — literally "air people." Only a tiny minority, the point of the pyramid, worked on the land in the primary productive process without which no society can survive. The labor Zionist vision in its essence was simple: set the pyramid back on its base; replace the vulnerable, neurotic intellectual with muscular, earthy farmers and soldiers. Or as fellow Zionist Jeffrey Goldberg summed it up sharply: "Only donkey work could straighten the crooked back of Jews in exile."[11]

But the kibbutz was meant to be more than tribal therapy. It saw itself as a specifically Jewish contribution to the utopian vision of creating a democratic egalitarian community. The average kibbutz had a few hundred members and functioned, like the Athenian polis, as a self-governing direct democracy. Unlike Athens, the kibbutz insisted on complete gender equality, with all adult members, men and women, involved directly in government, gathering face-to-face in the general assembly (*assifah klali*) to discuss and decide issues of collective concern. The economy was based on the noble principle of caring and sharing similar to that of hunter-gatherers: from each according to his or her ability; to each according to his or her need. All four polarities of the primal politics of simple hunting-gathering bands were present, at least in principle, if not always in practice: the small-scale, egalitarian, democratic community; the self-actualized whole person in the image of the farmer-soldier-philosopher; a way of life guided by a vision, a big picture, a shared narrative of meaning; and finally a creative and spiritualized relationship to the living earth.

It was as if under the extreme pressures of persecution and revolution in Europe at the turn of the century, Ashkenazi Jews had reached back through the depths of their own history and psychology to retrieve the archetypal practices and norms of primal politics. But the vision of Kibbutz Zionism was incompletely developed in theory, and it was ultimately overwhelmed in practice by a strange mix of warfare and consumerism. Like almost all political movements of the twentieth century, the four elements were never fully grasped as converging in the value of all values — the creative and spiritual life of the primal truth quest.

Without a clear vision of the quest at its center, the kibbutz remained vulnerable to corruption by the universal temptations of wealth and power — ego battles, selfishness, parochialism. The vision of political community had no meaningful place for Palestinian Arabs, nor was there place for the larger community of beings, our animal relatives from our wilderness birth. The kibbutz emerged out of a universal commitment to liberation, but its ideals never extended to our shared planetary predicament. There was little to inspire the community to think beyond tribe, nation, and civilization.

However, in its early days, the kibbutz was still infused with the charisma of its creative founders and had an enormous influence in building up the country. Kibbutzim were responsible for producing the food and growing the export crops. They shaped the new institutions, provided the political leadership, and generated an Israeli national culture of *chalutziut*. This is most often translated as "pioneering," but as Amos Elon points out in *The Israelis*, the English fails to capture the sense of selfless service to an ideal of the Hebrew with all its biblical resonance, ranging from "liberation" and "exaltation" to "expedition" and "rescue." Each kibbutz, depending on its ideological taste, was affiliated with one of the three main national kibbutz movements, which in turn were affiliated with one of the major political parties.[12] A coalition of kibbutz- and labor-based political parties ran the country until 1977, when religious and political conservatives came to power, initiating deep changes in Israeli society. Within a few years the army's response to the Palestinian intifada had shifted the global image of Israel from noble David to Goliath. Until that time few nations had been shaped for so long by such an ethos of utopian idealism. Nevertheless, it was an idealism that tragically neglected the "other." Both Jews and Palestinians remained prisoners in their caves, largely ignorant of, and unconcerned with, the aspirations and the suffering of each other.

In the summer of 1970 I enrolled for an *ulpan* — a kibbutz-based Hebrew language study-work program — and I was assigned to Kibbutz Hanita on the northern Lebanese border. My sense of heroic mission was deflated when I found the *ulpan* full of American Jewish volunteers. They were mostly refugees from the burnout of the counterculture who knew little about Zionism and Israel and seemed to care even less. Many were attracted by stories of the kibbutz as a utopia realized; some came for the free board and lodging in return for work in the fields. They were playful and irreverent, pacifists and spiritual seekers. Despite my initial disdain, they intrigued me and planted the seed of a vision of America as "the land of the free." Years later this helped me make a move to another new world.

## The Jewish Primal

After five months I was sick of peace-loving hippies and impatient for something more intense. I followed the example of my cousins and volunteered for an Israeli army combat unit. I knew robust army service was the quickest, most effective initiation into Israeli society. But I was also hungry for what seemed then to be that quintessentially masculine initiation in a world of wars fought by men. I felt compelled to test my courage, to face death and even, if necessary, kill in defense of myself and my community.

I volunteered through the framework of Nachal — the acronym for Noar Chalutzi Lochem, or "fighting pioneering youth" — which was organized to integrate military service with establishing new kibbutzim on the borders. After basic training I volunteered for Sayeret Habika, a ranger unit based outside Jericho near the Dead Sea. We spent a summer completing advanced training, running and shooting in one of the hottest places on earth. During the day, gunmetal would be too hot to touch, and at nights our shirts would dry white and stiff with sweated salt. Training was followed by four months of active duty. We spent alternate weeks sitting night ambushes on the banks of the Jordan River and doing dawn patrols in the mountains above the Dead Sea during the most peaceful time in the country's history. Our patrols were like picnics, bouncing in command cars along mountainous dirt roads, scaring off ibex, below us the "Sea of Salt," the lowest point on the surface of the earth. At the end of the patrol we would stop to brew coffee with our Bedouin tracker while watching the sun appear above the hills of Jordan.

Wanting to test myself more strenuously I requested transfer to the paratrooper battalion of Nachal. Unlike the armed forces of the United States, the

Israeli Defense Force (IDF, or TZAHAL in Hebrew, for Tzva Haganah Le Yisra'el) is very much a people's army. Israel is one of the few modern countries to conscript all men and all women at age eighteen, with men serving for three years and women for two. Men are then obliged to do a month's reserve duty every year until age forty-five. The IDF is also exceptional in having the flattest hierarchy of any modern military, being intentionally understaffed at the highest levels in order to drill responsibility, improvisation, and flexibility at lower levels. This makes the fierce Israeli martial spirit quite unique in being connected to an assertive individualism. One of the most common army terms of abuse for a soldier who is too ready to obey orders is *sabon*, or "soap," a brutal reference to the Jews of Europe who were seen as obediently marching into the Nazi gas chambers and letting their bodies to be boiled into soap.*

During reserve duty a university professor can find himself under the command of a kibbutznik or a bus driver, and a twenty-five-year-old can be training his uncle. The closeness of combat means there is little attention given to parade-ground drills, saluting, or any of the other rituals of military discipline, and a private has been known to tell a general if he thinks he is doing something wrong. Such informality reinforces a sense of shared purpose and responsibility. Since units tend to be kept together through training and subsequent active service, lifelong friendships are made and then sustained during annual reserve duty. An infantry soldier will travel all over the country, much of the time on foot, and mix with people from all walks of life. The "nation" is not an idealistic abstraction but a matter of direct experience. This makes the army crucial in creating a sense of national solidarity and the single most powerful and respected institution in the country.[13]

In 1971 Israel was a very different country compared to the Israel of world news today. It was still something of a second-world democracy — poor, egalitarian, well educated, doing noble development work in Africa, and even admired in the West for its moral example. There were no beggars, no homeless, and no hungry. America had only recently started supplying the air force with fighter planes; all our infantry equipment came from France and Europe and was generally inferior to that of the surrounding

---

* There seems to be no documented evidence of large-scale manufacture of soap from the bodies of Jewish victims of the death camps, although there is evidence of several experimental programs that attempted this. See Michael Shermer, Alex Grobman, and Arthur Hertzberg, *Denying History: Who Says the Holocaust Never Happened and Why Do They Say It?* (Berkeley: University of California Press, 2000).

Arab armies. Our assault rifles were the long, ungainly Belgian FNs, which jammed easily in the desert sand and weighed twice the compact, more reliable AK-47s supplied to the Arabs by the Russians.[14] Our combat webbing was World War II vintage, canvas and brass, which rubbed the skin off our hips and was impossible to run with until home customized with strips of foam padding. In the field we slept in two-man tents made by pairing up and buttoning together two rain ponchos, which were only waterproof when covered with plastic sheeting (which we had to buy ourselves). We slept on an army blanket spread on the ground, and the food was simple but healthy: plenty of raw vegetables to make our own salads — Israel is the only country where it is not unusual to eat salad with all three meals — supplemented with eggs, cheese, yogurt, hummus, black bread, and tea.* We ate chicken and turkey, but red meat was a rarity and coffee a treat for special occasions. It all seemed frugal and improvised. High morale was our secret weapon.

At the time, the IDF defended borders and fought wars. There was no intifada and no policing of civilian populations. We naively thought of our occupation of the West Bank, barely four years old, as enlightened compared with the surrounding Arab police states. There was still talk of *tohar haneshek* — "purity of arms," or minimal violence in the defense of the community. We gave no thought to the fact that when the British handed their Palestine Mandate to the United Nations in 1948, and the United Nations voted to partition the land into a Palestinian-and-Israeli state, Palestinian Arabs still constituted the majority of the population.[15] We saw the situation in simple ethnocentric terms: This was the ancient homeland of the Jews heroically resurrected as a modern state. Its existence was a condition for Jewish survival. If Israel lost one war, it would cease to exist. The country at its narrowest is twenty kilometers wide; the largest airport, Ben Gurion International, is within easy rocket range of the Palestinian West Bank. Our job was to defend the borders. The enemy was within view and furiously dedicated to "driving the Jews into the sea." Knowing this, we competed strenuously to be chosen for the most difficult and dangerous work. But for all its nobility of purpose, the IDF remained an army, grimly committed to the business of killing, and necessarily brutalizing.

I welcomed the brutality as an inversion of my Cambridge existence and a way of bringing me back to my body and my senses. I went from a world of

---

* Israel has one of the highest rates of consumption per capita of fresh fruits and vegetables.

words, books, and ideas to a world of action and feeling. Most of the training involved running and shooting. We ran everywhere, all the time. We ran to our meals, to the training ground, during training, and then back to camp. Since the IDF specializes in night fighting, after dark we would repeat, at a run, everything we had learning during the day. We were punished with running, called *kader*, the acronym for *kidum derech raglayim* — "progress through the legs." If you survived the training, you got to love running. We ran carrying our battle packs and our kitbags. We ran carrying one another on our backs and in stretchers, and always carrying our guns. From the day I enlisted until the day I was released, I had a weapon next to me. On our rare weekends off, we would take our rifles home and sleep with them under the mattress.

The Israeli army was one of the first modern armies to abandon water discipline,* after some terrible deaths through dehydration, but it still practiced sleep deprivation. During one particularly excruciating month in the field, we slept an average of three and a half hours a night for a week at a time. Thursday night, the night before the Sabbath, was sleepless, spent on a forced march, jogging most of the night with full battle gear, which if you carried the platoon machine gun, as I did, meant a backbreaking forty pounds of equipment. We called it *kniat Shabbat*, "buying the Sabbath." Our officers pushed us till we dropped and then made those still upright carry the fallen. If we complained, officers would curtly inform us, "There is no such thing as 'I cannot'; there is only 'I don't want to,' " and that meant the ultimate humiliation of being kicked out of the unit. Our one day of rest would be spent sleeping off muscle fever. After one such week I was traveling on a full bus back to the kibbutz, standing up, one hand holding the handrail, the other my rifle, and fast asleep. A middle-aged woman woke me up and offered her seat. I sat down gratefully and fell asleep. The very extremity of my experiences fascinated me and took the sting out of the pain. I was pushing my limits and getting to know myself in a hard, sure way. At the same time I was being welcomed into the country and treated as a hero.

As our experiences overwhelmed language, conversations contracted. I stopped reading. Like soldiers in all armies, we resorted to obscenities to express the inexpressible, so we swore constantly, but we had to use Arabic, since spoken Hebrew had only recently been revived from the Bible. One day

* "Water discipline" was based on the erroneous notion that soldiers could be trained to go without water.

I suddenly realized with startling clarity the philosophical gulf between concept and experience. I also saw its visceral connection. The cultural currency at Cambridge was eloquence, wit, and literacy. Now we prized the simple virtues of friendship and loyalty, courage and generosity. We defined these concepts not by words but by actions: by how many kilometers you would carry your friend; how much of a food parcel from home someone would share; how much danger another would risk for you. It was an elemental tribal existence — intensely physical, outdoors, exposed to the elements, and exposed to one another. Language lost its omnipotence.

At first I found my fellow soldiers rude and crude and the lack of privacy claustrophobic. But we were trained to recognize that survival depended on helping one another, and I quickly got over myself. One day I woke up to the fact that I was enjoying the simple bluntness that comes with close living under harsh conditions. The rough life cut through persona and culture and exposed the best and worst in us. At one time or another we all looked ridiculous and learned to laugh at ourselves. We made brutal jokes about what scared us most — killing and being killed. Since our relationships were face-to-face, and everything was on public display, we lived with a high degree of honesty, in the truth of direct experience. Trust and understanding that might have taken years in civilian life could be made and broken in seconds. At the same time, witnessing someone else's shadow helped each of us become a little more conscious of our own. No situation could have been better constructed to turn a group of strangers into a tightly bonded band of brothers. We started growing up quickly.

One of the glories of Israeli infantry life is that one is constantly outdoors in some of the wildest, most beautiful parts of that ancient, eroded landscape. I rediscovered the power of wilderness healing. We moved through great untouched areas of sun-blasted, stony desert and mountain, some of it covered with burnt thorny vegetation, now without the desert lions of the Bible, but still roamed by jackals, ibex, and the occasional hyena. Native forests of stunted oak survive in the Galilee, where vineyards cover stony terraced hillsides; groves of olive and almond, fig and pomegranate dot the valleys. Scattered throughout the country are ruins and relics from the Israelite kingdoms of David and Solomon and the civilizations that followed — Roman, Muslim, Crusader, Turk, and British. Israeli army initiation rites are pilgrimages to two-thousand-year-old ruins — the last standing wall of the

Second Temple and the desert fortress of Masada, where, as the story goes, the Jewish garrison committed suicide rather than surrender to the Romans. Our dawn patrols passed the Qumran Caves on the barren cliffs above the Dead Sea, where the Dead Sea Scrolls were found, written in the same language we took our orders in. We assumed an astounding continuity: that we were living in the crucible of the primary revelation that helped shape Jewish identity, an identity preserved through those ancient Hebrew texts, which after centuries of persecution in exile helped inspire a return to this battered, violently contested homeland. I saw firsthand how ideas and stories could be immense political forces shaping reality.

Months passed running, falling, and crawling over the stones and thorns, with dust and sand in nose and mouth, salty with sweat, soaked with the icy winter rain of the Judean hills, at times feverishly tired, and at others wildly exuberant. I started to understand what it meant to "live in one's body." I became more continually aware of sensations on my skin and in my muscles, bones, breath, and beating heart. Our animal nature represents one pole of our *in-between* situation; ego consciousness is the other pole. The animal is the source of the passions, instincts, and impulses — related to what Freud called Eros — the life force that ego consciousness channels, sublimates, and represses according to the norms of our culture and our quest. This is the biological and emotional foundation of our existence. For this reason the animal is also at the core of the shadow, what we have to repress and forget in order to be acceptable to ourselves and civilized society. As the animal came alive, I lost my neuroses. I was at home in my body, here, now, with my people — welcomed, accepted, connected — whole and happy.

Sometimes on our all-night "fast marches," we were allowed to sing as we ran. We would chant as we jogged, stamping the rhythm of songs of defiance and survival in a kind of ecstasy:

Am Yisrael, Am Yisreal,
Am Yisrael, CHAI!
(The people of Israel LIVE!)

Od Avinu, Od Avinu,
Od Avinu CHAI!
(Our father still LIVES!)

Singing the old songs on that ancient landscape, under the stars of the desert night, in the charged atmosphere of warfare, became a kind of shamanic channeling. As we sang about the spirit of Kind David still walking the land, we felt it coming alive in us. But more than alive and connected, we felt powerful and dangerous.

Such emotions frighten secular liberal intellectuals, and with good reason. When they are mobilized by simple stories of absolute right and wrong, they can generate seismic social forces that drive bold actions with heroic and horrendous consequences. The Nazis mobilized exactly such experience through narratives of blood and soil, oppression and liberation. But it is equally true that such passion is an expression of life energy — Eros — lust for life. Simply squelching such emotional resonance with the past is ultimately deadly. But as the Nazis showed us, Eros can also be deformed and harnessed for destruction — Thanatos — the death impulse.

We all need big-picture narratives to inspire and guide our actions, to take us beyond short-term self-interest and help us find meaning, to help us be of service to our immediate and expanded community of life. The big picture, a worldview, is an essential component of knowledge of the Good. But the great danger of visionary narratives is that they become *disconnected from the truth quest*. When this happens, they easily get hijacked by *libido dominandi* — the lust for power.

Clearly, most narratives of tribal and national identity are truncated, without an authentic species dimension and thus lacking a grounding in the truth quest. The possibility of our present moment is to go beyond such limitations. A science-guided, truth-loving narrative can now, perhaps for the first time, take us back before the origin of all tribes and all civilizations to the roots of a shared humanity born in an African wilderness. In doing so it can give us a passionate basis for taking all nations and all tribes forward into a truly global humanity.

None of this was clear to me then. I was too caught up in the imminence of war and in the exhilaration of my own healing to pay attention to what should have been obvious: the parallel narrative of meaning connecting Palestinians, Arabs, and Muslims to that same ancient landscape. I was integrating some opposites at the expense of neglecting others.

Standing guard alone one night, under the glittering winter stars, breaking discipline by smoking one of the cheap Nadiv cigarettes the kibbutz sent us, I thought back on my life in South Africa and England. I realized at that moment that I was better at soldiering than anything else I had ever done, except perhaps passing exams. I had moved around the medicine wheel 180 degrees from my starting point. Whether my service was ultimately compromised or noble, I knew I was growing and becoming more of a whole human being, and that seemed enough to justify the hardship and the danger.

Much later in Hawai'i, when reading Native American literature, I immediately appreciated the esprit of the Dog Soldier Society of the Cheyenne as that of a closely bonded brotherhood of young men, living a life of the body, outdoors, defending tribal boundaries. Kibbutz and the army had given me a taste of a more indigenous, primal way of being Jewish. I felt wide awake as if for the first time in my life.

## Philosophy in a War Zone

In October 1973, the Yom Kippur War blasted apart my healing revelations. On the holiest day of the Jewish year, Egyptian and Syrian forces attacked simultaneously and overran Israeli defenses. I had been discharged before the war started and was in South Africa visiting my parents. Since I was not an Israeli citizen — having volunteered as a Jew of the Diaspora — I had not been assigned a reserve unit and was not called up for one of the emergency flights to Israel. By the time I found my way back, the war was half over, and it was clear Israel would prevail. I returned not so much to help save the country as to be with my closest friends, who were going through that ultimate test — what we had spent those hard months preparing for. Most of them were serving as corporals dispersed among new platoons. Some had been guarding the frontline positions overrun on the Syrian border on the first day of the war. I went to my old base, which was empty except for a skeleton staff who told me the brigade had regrouped. It had joined the paratrooper counteroffensive across the Suez Canal and was now fighting "somewhere in Egypt." No one knew exactly where. Had I checked in with central command, I knew, in the confusion of war I would have been ordered to some menial job away from the fighting, away from my friends. I decided to go and find them on my own.

I had no rifle or helmet, but I still had my olive fatigues, boots, and the dog tags, prisoner-of-war card, and plastic-wrapped field dressing soldiers carry with them at all times. I put on my uniform, stood at the roadside, and in minutes had caught a ride south to the fighting in Egypt. I got out of my first ride near the edge of the Sinai desert and an empty truck immediately stopped. It was driven by a jittery young infantry lieutenant who had lost his platoon on the Golan Heights on the Syrian border. He had made his way to the fighting in Egypt, where he was given the job of driving out of the battle zone every other day, carrying the bodies of dead Israelis home.

By late afternoon we could see the pontoon bridge across the Suez Canal a few kilometers ahead. We stopped behind an enormous traffic jam of military vehicles snaking across the single-lane bridge, trying to get back into Egypt before dark. My driver warned me that, at dusk every day for the past week, several Egyptian Katyusha missile trucks would race up close to Israeli lines and fire dozens of rockets zeroed in on the traffic jam at the bridge, and then escape under cover of dark. He indicated the fresh bandage on his hand from a shrapnel wound the night before. He warned me we would have maybe a second or two to take cover once we saw the rockets streaking toward us, like "little red birds." We sat and waited and watched the view ahead. It is hard to overstate how utterly gripping the spectacle of war can be. Israeli jets were swooping low over the canal triggering Egyptian missiles and then climbing rapidly, blowing up the missiles behind them. By the time we crossed the canal, the sun had set and I was feverish with excitement.

As soon as we drove off the pontoon bridge onto Egyptian soil, I saw the "little red birds" flaming toward us. Then in one long second, with panicked screaming around me, I found myself somehow out of the truck, my face buried in the sand in the middle of a firestorm of rockets, ground-shaking explosions blasting shrapnel over me from all sides. I felt a sharp impact on my back. I thought, "You fool — now your adventure is over." I felt behind to check the damage, but it was only a piece of packing crate sent flying by the blasts. Then for the strangest second, I saw in my mind's eye the Egyptian soldier firing the battery — a full-grown man, scared, sweating, heroically trying to kill me. The vision couldn't have been more unexpected or less welcome. I felt for the first time with crushing force that I was on someone else's land, and he wanted me dead. At that moment I started to feel a personal responsibility for the whole murderous entanglement. I had chosen to be there.

For two days I hitched rides trying to find my battalion while watching a war going on around me in a fog of horror. A passing officer gave me an Egyptian helmet and a captured Russian Kalashnikov AK-47, which I cleaned, oiled, and loaded. I found a resupply unit preparing a truck of ammunition for my battalion and rode with them. Scorched, bloated bodies and burnt jeeps and trucks casually littered the roadside. Israeli tanks inexplicably charged across our path, chasing something through the sand dunes and firing just out of sight. Occasionally fighter jets screamed low overhead, making us leap out of the truck into the sand with rifles cocked. But by then the jets were all Israeli. I had grown up on my share of war comics, action movies, and stories of heroic combat. But this had no connection to any of my fantasies about war. I couldn't get past the obscenity of the butchery — the simple fact that humans were blasting one another into pieces of burnt, bloody meat and splintered bone, left to lie and rot in the sun. Where was the glory?

The next morning my unit found us, and my friends gave me a warm welcome. That night they had charged an Egyptian position overlooking the canal and killed the garrison. Some were in shock, most simply thrilled to be alive. None of our boys had even been seriously injured. I sat with them in the newly occupied trenches listening to the crazed stories of those fresh from killing. Below us were bunkers and bodies; the air was still thick with that strange sweetish, sickening smell of fresh blood drying on the warming sand. We looked over the Suez Canal into the Sinai Peninsula where the Egyptian Third Army was now trapped, surrounded by Israelis on all sides. We could see the streams of tracer rounds from small arms as they fired in fear.

As I sat in the trench looking over the bunkers, without warning, an Egyptian soldier jumped up perhaps twenty yards below me. I saw him clearly, middle-aged, heavyset, unarmed, with sweat stains under his arms, sprinting across the sand. Someone yelled, "Egyptian! Shoot!" Before anyone else reacted, in a single automatic movement, I had my rifle to my shoulder, dropped the safety catch, pulled the bolt back, and fired a single shot. But I deliberately aimed a meter behind his running heels as he dove into another bunker. At that range, had I wished to, I could have shot hit him square in the chest. But suddenly it seemed pointless. Strangely, there was no follow-up, and we let a potentially dangerous combatant escape. Everyone was sick of killing. But the moment I pulled the trigger, I knew I had crossed a line. There was no doubt, had I felt even slightly threatened, I would have shot to kill. I realized with grim satisfaction that I had transformed myself from a sensitive scholar into a soldier who would do his murderous duty mechanically, without feeling very much at all. It was an encounter with some dark part of myself I had previously doubted existed. It was a bottoming out, both sobering and empowering. I started to realize all possibilities are within us. Saint or sinner, killer or hero, it all depends on circumstance and choice. And choice depends on awareness.

When I met up with my company, they had been moving south toward the city of Suez, fighting down the Egyptian side of the canal. As they advanced, their commander, my old lieutenant, ordered that all wounded Egyptians were to be taken along and cared for. A close friend told me how he had watched an Egyptian soldier die slowly of terrible wounds we had inflicted, dying with a bloodstained photograph of loved ones in his hand. We were sharing intimacies with strangers we were trying to kill. It was a sad and wretched business. At one time I had imagined signing on for officers' school. Now the adventure of a lifetime had dead-ended in another cave — a mausoleum.

Two months later, the peace accord with Egypt was under way, and we hitched home. For days and weeks afterward, when I would see a bundle by the roadside as I drove along, I would think I was looking at a corpse. Yet I was very fortunate. The war was a glancing blow, not enough to damage or disable me, but enough to get my full attention. I returned to civilian life with no interest in pursuing family and professional life. Instead of leaving me cynical, the war reinforced my conviction that the quest was critical. The question "What's it all about?" took on a life-and-death urgency. A life of action pushed me back into the university and back into philosophy.

## A Path with a Heart

In January 1974, at Hebrew University, I began graduate work in political science, the one discipline that seemed the most inclusive of all the others, and the one explicitly concerned with the role of human choice in shaping social reality. Israel and kibbutz life had fallen short of my noble but naive utopianism. However, there was no question about my gratitude for the way the country helped heal me. Two months after the war, I was living with my Israeli girlfriend, who later became my wife. She was an eleventh-generation native-born Israeli. Her mother's family was Sephardi, dark-skinned Jews who were expelled from Spain during the Inquisition and had been living in the Holy Land for the past five centuries. Her father was a German Jew who escaped before Hitler came to power. They adopted me as a son; I started feeling Israeli, and I enjoyed being treated as such. With solid ground underfoot, I could resume my search with greater confidence.

But Israeli society was clearly becoming cynical and increasingly brutalized by the struggle for existence. I still believed the kibbutz vision had come close to providing a blueprint for a democratic society of free-thinking, creative individualists. But the new generation of native-born Sabras — named after the prickly pear, tough and thorny on the outside, sweet inside — tended, however, to be abrasively pragmatic and seemed disinterested in spiritual and intellectual life. They were understandably eager to travel outside the country and enjoy more of consumer culture — the good life, American-style. Kibbutzim were becoming insular and self-absorbed. Gone was the vision of labor as worship. Farming was rapidly industrializing and Arabs were being hired to do the hardest, dirtiest work. The noble vision of *chalutziut* and of a religion of labor was sinking in a sea of materialism.

Plus, the long-neglected and most painful and confusing question of all remained: What about the Palestinians? I had enjoyed their food and their music, and I had spent enough time living, walking, and running around the ancient stone villages, thorny hills, and olive groves to recognize Arab Palestinian culture as indigenous. It was connected to the land in ways some of the original Zionists aspired to re-create for an exiled, alienated Jewry. My South African experience had sensitized me to the arrogance of dismissing the indigenous. How could I not try to see things from an Arab point of view? I noticed similarities between some Israeli attitudes to Arabs and that of Afrikaners to blacks. There were also equally striking differences. The Dutch who colonized the southern tip of Africa never claimed to be returning home from two thousand years of exile to the land that shaped their language, their culture, and their religion. European colonialism was part of a movement of imperial conquest motivated by shameless commercial gain and the manifest destiny of bringing civilization to the natives. Zionism was a movement of cultural, spiritual, and national redemption for a people in extremis. It healed me by giving me an experience of a tribal, earth-based identity. But it also confronted me with the limits of tribe and nation.[16]

Zionism had no creative response to an increasingly angry, militant, and desperate Palestinian nationalism. In the irony of ironies, the Jewish return had created a yearning among displaced Palestinians to return home — a kind of "Palestinian Zionism." There no longer seemed a simple hard line between right and wrong. All were implicated to varying degrees in both good and evil. Certainly the degrees mattered, but it was a tangle I did not yet have the intellectual or emotional resources to sort out.

The inspiring example of South Africa's reconciliation between the races was still decades off. In 1973, apartheid was still tightening its grip and Nelson Mandela was hidden from view in prison on Robben Island. None of us had any inkling that years later he would emerge as the statesman who by the power of his moral example would avert a race war and heal the nation. Mandela had the psychological strength to get close to his enemy. He came to understand and empathize with the racist Afrikaners so well that they felt truly understood; and in being understood, they opened themselves to understanding and trusting him. At the same time, by taking Afrikaner psychology into his own, Mandela transformed himself, growing into a wiser, more loving, and more complete human being. More than any other political figure in the twentieth century, Mandela embodied what was missing in the Middle East — the paradoxical dynamic of a primal politics of transformation through engaging opposites in the service of the greater good.

Even after a few years in university I still struggled with academic Hebrew, so I took whatever courses were offered in English. One was taught by Henry Kariel, a visiting professor from the University of Hawai'i. When he arrived in 1976, he had just completed the manuscript of *Beyond Liberalism*, which thirty years later is still one of the most creative responses to the philosophical collapse of Liberalism.[17] Kariel's approach was bold and playful. He simply claimed the authority to do what the classical political philosophers themselves did. Instead of interpreting the great works of the past — which he did with impressive erudition — he followed their example in practicing political philosophy as the "Royal Art," the art of seeing how all the other arts of life fit together to improve the human condition. By definition, everything that really mattered to living the best life possible was relevant. Kariel opened the whole field of human experience for me. This was the path with a heart I had been looking for.

In the absence of a coherent alternative worldview, Kariel adopted the role of philosopher as trickster-shaman. The great unexplored new frontier was consciousness. Everything depended on the reliability of our grasp of reality; this, in turn, depended on how mind and matter, imagination and reality, were mysteriously interwoven. I started reading widely: history, philosophy, the rise of the West, anthropology, psychology, shamanism, psychoanalysis, Eastern philosophy, American history, and Native American literature — anything that could shed light on the human condition and the mystery of consciousness. I realized why I had been so disappointed with conventional political philosophy: Hobbes, Locke, Madison, Smith, Descartes, Mill, and Hume were dealing with forms of consciousness shaped by the European self-understanding of the seventeenth and eighteenth centuries. They were living in a tiny, mechanical, box universe. I had been confronted with the ecstatic, mind-dissolving vistas of an evolving cosmos.

Doors opened. Kariel offered to sponsor my move to the USA and guide my PhD at the University of Hawai'i. I would be able to rethink everything free from the constraints of family, tradition, and periodic warfare. Meanwhile, I was weaving myself more tightly into the fabric of Israeli life. I married my Israeli girlfriend, and in 1977 we moved to Hawai'i together, fully intending to return to Israel after my studies.

## Paradise, Family, and Philosophy

When the British explorer Captain Cook arrived in Hawai'i in 1778, he was stunned by the beauty and high level of development of Hawaiian civilization. He thought the Polynesians to be among the strongest, healthiest, happiest people he had encountered. He found them with a population close to that of modern Hawai'i — just over one million — living in total self-sufficiency with Stone Age tools and an economy based on aquaculture, ocean fishing, and taro horticulture.[18] Today, Native Hawaiians are the poorest and most disadvantaged of the ethnic groups in the state. Hawai'i now imports more than 80 percent of its food and 90 percent of its energy, degrading ocean, land, and water in the process and achieving the dubious distinction of having the most endangered species of any US state. Honolulu is a premier shopping destination for Asian tourists, while the state hosts the largest concentration of military bases outside the mainland United States.

Hawai'i is also where East meets West. It is one of the most multicultural states in the union, where Caucasians are a minority, where almost half of all marriages are interracial, and where the indigenous culture is still palpable. Since the 1970s, a Native Hawaiian renaissance has been under way with the revival of the Hawaiian language and the tradition of aloha — a warmth and generosity rooted in a reverence for all living things. It is fitting tribute to Hawai'i's exceptionalism that this is where Barack Obama was born and raised — the son of an African man and a white woman, the first black president of the United States and the first president to be nearly universally acclaimed as a global statesman.

Hawai'i's natural beauty and its distance from South Africa offered me a perfect vantage for taking the most global and inclusive perspective on my Jewish past. My everyday life was transformed: the compact geography of a metropolis like Honolulu on a small tropical island made the extremes of ocean, city, and mountain easy to grasp in a single view and to experience in a single day. I could begin and end a workday of teaching and writing with a morning ocean swim and an afternoon run along rough mountain trails.

The political science department was equally exceptional. Although it was ranked as one of the top twenty national research departments in terms of quoted publications, many faculty seemed more concerned with establishing a supportive and creative community of thinkers. Isolated in the middle of the Pacific, thousands of miles from any center of political power, it attracted some free spirits who created a unique intellectual culture: open, curious, supportive of experimentation, and infused with a touch of "Hawaiian style" — the more relaxed, contemplative approach to life. It suited me perfectly.

For the first time I had an opportunity to explore and experiment. I discovered Hawai'i is a gardener's paradise, with rich volcanic soil, plenty of sun and rain, and growing seasons year-round. Gardening helped keep one pole of my thinking literally grounded, close to the living earth, while the other explored the farthest reaches of inner and outer space.

Up to this point, I had no interest in the conventional paths of profession, marriage, and family; this was a result of both inner confusion and my gloomy perception of the chaotic state of civilization. It seemed irresponsible to settle into comfortable domesticity and bring children into a dangerous and damaged world. Yet my wife wanted a family and missed Israel. Ultimately, Hawai'i was changing me, and I knew there was no turning back. We went through a friendly divorce, and she returned home. Soon after, I fell in love again and promptly had my heart broken. Then my next love unexpectedly initiated me into fatherhood. My self-directed life of exploration and adventure seemed to be over. I grieved briefly for my lost freedom, but as soon as I held my newborn daughter in my hands I fell in love again.

Until that moment I feared the responsibility of fatherhood. Now the question of the meaning in my life was self-evident — attending to the immediate needs of a baby girl. I was surprised at how much it settled and satisfied my restlessness. As I softened and became more sensitive to my daughter, I felt myself becoming whole. Male mothering helped balance the angry young warrior. As my daughter grew up, so did I, returning to my scholarly quest with a heightened sense of urgency. My concern with the fate of the earth became less of a pious abstraction and more a simple extension of the love and concern I felt for her. This was her planet, we were her species. I came to see her birth as the most revolutionary event in my life.

After six years of graduate study, I had traveled over wildly varied intellectual landscapes and been blessed by a succession of amazing insights, but I had no PhD. I was still working as a casual lecturer, and in the eyes of the world of professionals that meant failure. I felt that every attempt at putting my learning into a narrowly focused dissertation topic seemed like giving up, as it forced me to abandon what I felt was most critically needed — the illumination of the big picture. How does one make an argument for the big picture seem practical, without actually trying to say everything? My advisers kept recommending focusing on a single, narrow topic.

One night during this protracted crisis, I went to sleep and had a long vivid dream with a simple narrative thread. I saw the path my peers had taken — scientific professionals in white coats, working in hospitals and laboratories — serious men and women being taken seriously. It was all shades of gray; no joy, no beauty, no meaning. Then I saw myself lying on the floor, happily playing like a child, painting a picture in brightly colored oils. I was with friends in a glass-walled apartment at dusk overlooking the hills above a small town — perhaps Port Elizabeth or Jerusalem. When I looked at the picture, it looked childlike and unfinished. One of my friends came over, picked up a brush, and showed me how to make a few small changes. Suddenly the elements gelled into a perfectly formed image. It was more powerful than anything I could ever have imagined painting. It was a miniature version of the view through the window, but somehow luminous and intensified — rounded hills in soft shades of gold, red, and purple, with the lights of a village sparkling in the distance. As I held the painting up so others could see, it merged with the view through the window. Then the painting magically came to life. A human figure appeared in the picture holding a roman candle of exploding fireworks, which sent a cascading rainbow of light over the landscape. I woke up the next morning feeling excited and energized. The dream seemed to bring the most critical elements of my journey into a creative work. It affirmed my rejection of medicine for philosophy. It celebrated the happily playing child and the importance of creativity. It showed the decisive intervention of friends, and the importance of cooperation and community in the creative political work. Finally, it seemed to connect the beauty of nature to human creativity, which, mediated by shamanic magic, brought the outer and the inner world into resonance. I was back on the path with a heart.

The image of a mandala came to me soon after, as the obvious organizing structure for a big picture. Each quadrant represented a distinct thread of my search as well as the core elements of the politics of compact egalitarian societies — those of hunter-gatherers, the San Bushmen, the classical polis, even the utopian kibbutz. The center, where the four quadrants met, unified all the processes within the truth quest. The mandala was quite unlike all the traditional models of political order in at least one critical respect. Instead of pretending to offer a final answer or an absolute truth, the mandala at its deepest also represented the structure of the ongoing quest itself. I finished the dissertation quickly, and "primal politics" became the core of the vision of *Future Primal.*

CHAPTER 4

# RECOVERY OF THE QUEST, PART II — POLITICS OF MYSTERY

Mystery is the most beautiful thing we can experience. It is the source of all true art and science.

— Albert Einstein

The old Lakota were wise.... They could despise no creature for all were of one blood, made by the same hand and filled with the essence of the Great Mystery. They knew that man's heart, away from nature, becomes hard; they knew that lack of respect for growing, living things soon led to lack of respect for humans too. So they kept their youth close to its softening influence.

— Chief Luther Standing Bear

## The Big Story

The very science that has helped precipitate a crisis of scarcely imaginable proportions also tells a story of humanity's place in the cosmos that is so detailed, so compelling, and yet so utterly astounding that it makes all previous creation myths seem cartoonish and one-dimensional. This new understanding directly undermines the philosophical foundations of our global industrial civilization. It calls us to shift from a way of thinking and living shaped by a crude mechanical materialism to one that recognizes the human as an organic outgrowth of an evolving earth. The great challenge is not simply to understand this astonishing new reality intellectually but to start *to feel* this new relationship, and then, feeling it, to live accordingly. As we do this we find ourselves reconnecting with some of the most profound and most ancient human experiences. By reflecting on this convergence of the very old with the very new, we can start to reconstruct a more authentic basis for both the truth quest and politics.

For most of history, human beings could see no more than a few thousand stars in the night sky. They assumed what was obvious to the senses: that the stars — like the sun, moon, and planets — moved across the sky around the massive immovable earth. Thanks to the mathematics of Copernicus and the following centuries of modern science, we now know that it is the earth and the planets that circle around our enormous sun, and that the thousands of stars we can see with the naked eye are all distant suns that constitute but a tiny handful of the two hundred billion in our Milky Way galaxy. We also now know that the Milky Way is only one galaxy in a universe composed of billions of galaxies. Science helps us *know* these things as facts, but its method often blocks us from experiencing their *meaning*.

For example, even though we know as a basic fact of life that the earth rotates around its axis and orbits the sun, most of us, most of the time, still experience the earth as massive and stationary and the sun as a small, blazing body traveling across the sky and *setting* below the horizon. We can start to feel what it is like to live in our new cosmology by practicing the poetic yet scientifically informed sunset meditation of cosmologist Brian Thomas Swimme.[1] At the end of a clear day, we can focus attention on where the sun will disappear, and then as the sun sets during its last few visible seconds, we remind ourselves that it is in fact the earth which is continuously rotating as it orbits the sun. If we hold this thought as we hold our gaze, we can, if we concentrate, experience the novelty of a second of vertigo as the great earth beneath us rolls "backward" on its axis and the horizon comes up in front of us to cover the sun. In Swimme's words, it is as if, for an instant, "in a single surprising shudder," we feel ourselves "standing on the back of something like a cosmic whale that is slowly rotating its great bulk on the surface of an unseen ocean." In this way we can actually feel the thrill of being part of a spinning planet orbiting a star.[2]

We know that when Descartes watched a sunset, he had little idea of what was taking place inside the solar furnace. Today, his scientific method has led to an understanding of matter so detailed and so precise that we can, if we wish, ignite our own small suns on earth. When we set off the first hydrogen bomb on Bikini Atoll, we watched an immense thermonuclear reaction, explosively compressing atoms of hydrogen under sun-like temperatures and pressures until they fused into heavier helium atoms. In the process some of the hydrogen matter is transformed into heat and light energy in a staggeringly powerful explosion — the most destructive force human beings had ever unleashed. Something similar takes place continuously in the heart of the sun on a vastly multiplied scale. Every second, 600 million tons of hydrogen under immense pressures and temperatures are fused into 595 million tons of helium. The 5 million tons of hydrogen that "disappear" are converted into heat and light energy equivalent to a billion one-megaton hydrogen bombs going off every second.[3]

This solar conflagration is so enormous that it could swallow a million earths, so bright it can blind us ninety-three million miles away. Yet at this perfect distance its violence is nurturing — warming and lighting the earth, feeding plants and animals, and giving us our daily and seasonal cycles. The sun has been steadily exploding for the past 4.6 billion years. It will continue for another 5 billion years until it consumes all the hydrogen fuel and the heavier helium ash causes it to collapse in on itself under such pressure that the helium, in turn, ignites in an even more spectacular explosion and fuses into heavier carbon atoms. This explosion will be so immense as to engulf the inner planets and appear from a distant point in the Milky Way as a "red giant." Even suns are subject to the great mystery of existence in which everything that comes into being grows, matures, and dies. Yet the violent death of suns is creative, producing the heavier, more complex elements from which, ultimately, life on earth evolved. All the known, naturally occurring elements are born in such hydrogen fusion explosions in the hearts of exploding stars, some many times larger than our sun.

Our experience of the mystery of existence is compounded when we try to grasp the *scale* of the universe. Such reflection provides an opportunity for an even more profound reorientation to the nature of consciousness and the human condition. The most distant object humans can see with the naked eye is Andromeda. Early hunter-gatherers could make this out as a faint cloud of light in the night sky. Our telescopes now reveal Andromeda to be an entire galaxy, larger than the Milky Way, containing around one trillion suns. It is so far away that the photons of light that strike the retina of our eye today left Andromeda 2.5 million years ago, shooting through space at 186,000 miles a second. When we look at Andromeda, we are literally looking back in time, seeing Andromeda as it was when our hominid ancestors first started chipping stone tools in Africa. Andromeda is only one galaxy in our "local cluster" of galaxies in a visible universe with at least two hundred *billion* galaxies.[4]

Sometimes on a warm clear Hawaiian night, I lie outside on the lawn looking up at the night sky and try to picture myself from the perspective of someone in South Africa — the other side of the planet. Suddenly, for a second, I can feel myself pinned by gravity, with my back pressed against the earth, looking down into the blackness of intergalactic space below me — and I instinctively want to grab something to stop myself falling. The science writer Dava Sobel describes well how imagination short-circuits trying to grasp these immensities:

> When I try to imagine the depths of space,... when pushed to visualize those extremes, my brain just stalls. Silence clogs my ears, as though my thoughts were starved for air in the vast emptiness they are struggling to encompass. At the same time I feel I am falling, as often happens while falling asleep, when the drift into unconsciousness is interrupted by an image — part dream, part memory — that pitches me off a swing or down a staircase and my whole body lurches to save itself.[5]

As if the mere scale of the known universe is not enough to induce this sort of dizzying, paralyzing, "radical amazement" — as the Jewish mystic

Abraham Joshua Heschel put it — science is now compelling us to consider that *all of it* exploded out of a single point, at a single moment in time. The notion that the universe is expanding was implied by Albert Einstein's general theory of relativity, but he rejected this as too fantastic and modified his field equations to fit an unchanging universe. He was subsequently compelled to reverse himself when he looked through Edward Hubble's telescope and confirmed empirically the "red shift," indicating that the clusters of galaxies were all racing away from one another. By extrapolating back in time, we have been forced to conclude that everything exploded into existence in an unimaginably immense primordial "flaring forth" some 13.7 billion years ago. Einstein subsequently regarded his altering of the field equations as the greatest scientific blunder of his career.

We could say that this understanding of how the universe came into existence is one of the greatest achievements of our search for knowledge; it is the culmination of thousands of years of civilization and the past four hundred years of modern science. It means simply that everything — all of existence — is an interconnected whole in a continual process of transforming. The universe is not a place within which events happen as much as an event in itself, and humanity is part of that event, which continues to unfold as human awareness of it expands. We are only just beginning to grasp what it means to emerge from a growing universe. Full realization requires rethinking everything.

But for the most part we continue to revere institutions constructed on eighteenth-century assumptions of a clockwork "box" universe — an empty place within which things happen according to universal mechanical laws. Our political culture confidently marches forward, treating mystery as a problem to be solved or simply dismissed as woolly-mindedness, a distraction from the serious practical business of business. But philosophers, mystics, and shamans from all times tell us the experience of mystery is of immense practical importance. They encourage us to open to the experience and let its passion grip us. They suggest that, rather than being the antithesis of knowledge, such fascination with the miracle of existence is integral to its pursuit and helps keep us on track. Einstein knew this and put it clearly: "Mystery is the most beautiful thing we can experience. It is the source of all true art and science."

Healthy children are natural mystics. They generally start life immersed in this experience of sheer amazement at the beauty of the world. The simplest things — a stone, a butterfly, a sunlit leaf — are magical and endlessly fascinating. As we grow up, society trains us to ignore the distractions of the beauty of existence and to focus on what is practical and useful. But the memories of childhood remain to be awakened at quiet and unexpected moments, surprising us with a fresh experience of the world. At these times, we are reminded that our consciousness, our very capacity to know the world, is a product of some larger, ultimately unknowable order. Mystery remains as the ever-receding horizon of our knowing.

The heart of the problem of our contemporary civilization is that we have forgotten this primal experience of the natural world of creation as a sacred miracle. We don't recognize its truth, nor do we appreciate its importance for ordering human life, and so we fail to create our institutions accordingly. We can extend Einstein's insight by saying, "Mystery should also be the source of all true politics."

## The Politics of Mystery

At one time most human beings experienced this miracle of existence directly as a primary fact of life. Indigenous and hunting-gathering cultures living in wilderness seemed to know intuitively that they were part of an exquisite sacred creation whose source was unfathomable. Chief Luther Standing Bear was one of the last of the Lakota raised on the Great Plains of North America as a nomadic hunter-gatherer and one of the few to author his own book in English. He describes with simple eloquence how "mountains, lakes, rivers, springs, valleys, and woods" were all experienced by the Lakota as "finished beauty," pervaded by the mystery of existence.[6] The infinite connections between all forms of life and the beauty of the whole was part of a single creative force named, simply and precisely, Wakan Tanka, "the Great Mystery." Wakan Tanka was not a supernatural person or thing, or an abstraction, but something visceral, the experienced presence of a "unifying life force flowing in and through all things — the flowers of the plains, blowing wind, rocks, trees, birds, animals." The kinship humans felt for one another extended to the teeming animal communities the Lakota lived among.[7]

While human beings are part of nature, they are also *apart* from it. The gift of self-reflective consciousness gives us freedom and choice, makes us "determiners," and so distances us from the rest of creation. We get distracted by our cleverness, by the endless novelty of our creations. We confuse our god-like creativity with being God and forget our *createdness* — our emergence from and connectedness to a larger creative reality. Our egos inflate and we are tempted to confuse our best understanding with certainty. We forget humility, that freedom is meaningless without the possibility of making mistakes, without the reality of good and evil and the necessity of love and forgiveness.

Many traditional Lakota teachings, like those of other indigenous cultures, functioned as religion in the original sense of the word's Latin root, *religare* — to "bind again" or reconnect. Religion seems to have emerged in part as a corrective to growing ego-driven action, reminding the individual to come down to earth, to return to the source, to remember that "all things are kindred and brought together by the same Great Mystery." This awareness humbles us but also fills us with a love of life that permeates all relationships. Standing Bear elaborates:

> This concept of life and its relations was humanizing and gave to the Lakota an abiding love. It filled his being with the joy and mystery of living; it gave him reverence for all life; it made a place for all things in the scheme of existence with equal importance to all. The Lakota could despise no creature for all were of one blood, made by the same hand and filled with the essence of the Great Mystery.[8]

Science helps us embellish this primal insight, showing with great quantitative precision how the biochemical processes keeping us alive are woven into the living fabric of the entire biosphere, how all the atoms that constitute the molecules of our chemistry emerged from the mystery of that great primordial fireball. Ironically, as the precision of our knowledge increases, so the objectifying attitude of science represses our subjective, *felt* connection to reality. Because science understands by objectifying and demeans the logic of emotion, we have an absurd situation in which emotionally neutral objectivity is good and subjectivity is bad. This purging of emotion and subjectivity makes us strangers to our own inner lives, thus cutting the roots of morally ordered action. Having literally lost our souls, we stand autistic in the face of nature.

Our spiritual disorder was transparent to reflective Native Americans, who responded to the arrival of Europeans first with confusion, then with frustration and anger, and finally with despair:

> Nothing the Great Mystery placed in the land of the Indian pleased the white man, and nothing escaped his transforming hand. Wherever forests have not been mowed down; wherever the animal is recessed in their quiet protection; wherever the earth is not bereft of four-footed life — that to him is an unbroken wilderness. But since for the Lakota there was no wilderness; since nature was not dangerous but hospitable; not forbidding but friendly, Lakota philosophy was healthy — free from fear and dogmatism. Here I find the great distinction between the faith of the Indian and the white man. Indian faith sought harmony of man with his surroundings; the other sought the dominance of surroundings. In sharing in loving all and everything, one people naturally found a measure of the thing they sought, while in fearing, the other found need of conquest. For one man the world was full of beauty; for the other it was a place of sin and ugliness to be endured until he went to another world there to become a creature of wings, half-man and half-bird.[9]

When taken back to its primordial source — the creative cosmos — the connection between the mystical experience and human politics is simple and direct. As the quote by Standing Bear at the beginning of this chapter expresses, one of the foundations of the good life is maintaining this living connection to nature. When we can be amazed at the natural world — the mountains and prairies, the wind and weather, the life-world of coyote, bear, bison, and prairie dog — we pay attention to it. And in paying attention we learn how to live in partnership with the life of the earth. This love of life tends to merge into a related appreciation for the variety of human and cultural forms.

In 1493 Christopher Columbus was struck by the warmth and generosity of the natives of Hispaniola (now the Island of Haiti and the Dominican Republic), a typical reaction recorded in many subsequent accounts of first contact. "Of anything they have, if you ask them for it, they never say no; rather they invited the person to share it, and show as much love as if they were giving their hearts." Columbus's response was to kidnap a few of the natives and then inform his royal patrons that, with the handful of men left behind, he could easily destroy the entire society without danger.[10] It was a pattern to be repeated over and over as imperial Europe encountered native populations.

Disrupting the primary relationship between the human and the nonhuman living world disrupts the organic solidarity among humans. Healing the primary relationship with nature helps heal human relationships. Experiencing all of existence as a single, interconnected sacred creation is at the heart of that turning around of the mind and soul, the Socratic *periagoge*, which is ultimately what is at stake in the sort of radical transformation our situation requires.

Of course, Native Americans like the Lakota did not live in perfect harmony with one another or with the natural world. Modern romantics and environmentalists sometimes exaggerate the ecologically "noble savage" as living in static balance with pristine wilderness. We now know early human hunters were at least partly responsible for killing off the large Pleistocene megafauna, as humans spread out of Africa through Eurasia and then into the Americas. Early European explorers also documented cases of Native American tribes overharvesting and overhunting. Some had eccentric beliefs, like the Rock Cree notion that the spirits of animals killed by humans would be replenished in greater numbers, causing them to sometimes wantonly kill nesting birds and destroy the eggs.[11]

Nor were these societies peaceful, loving utopias. Most practiced some degree of warfare, which at times could be marked by great cruelty. The Lakota were consummate mounted hunters and warriors and familiar with killing at close quarters. However, unlike the genocidal violence of our past century, warfare had a limited function and was tempered by codes of chivalry and pan-tribal principles of the sacredness of life. For instance, for Lakota warriors during the eighteenth century, annihilation of an enemy was sometimes less important than "counting coup," using a long, curved coup stick to deliver a blow or hook one's opponent off his horse, a maneuver that simultaneously demonstrated military prowess, courage, and moral restraint.

Like all human beings, indigenous peoples suffered injury, illness, aging, and death, and they were vulnerable to the ego-hardening passions of fear, greed, envy, and lust for power. However, they also understood that human beings were determiners, and their religious and political institutions directly addressed these universal challenges. Many Lakota institutions and rituals served to sensitize the people to the glories of the natural world and heighten the experience of the Great Mystery at its source. At the core of this religious orientation was the love of life as the source of all values, and with it the companion teachings of generosity, courage, and compassion. Lakota elders actively cultivated this experience as the living heart of their politics and as the primary drive for human action and decision making.

The same organizing ethic can also be found in many indigenous societies that lived in intimate balance with wilderness. It is perhaps most directly expressed in an explanation of the human relationship to God offered by the Bushmen of southern Africa: When one acknowledges the presence of a small bird, a tiny thread is formed. After many encounters with that bird, the thread becomes thicker until it becomes a rope. When there are many ropes to many animals and many people, then the rope to God is formed. These ropes are made of the material of love.

## Searching the "In-Between"

Many Western thinkers have written on the universal importance of the mystical experience in human affairs. Rudolf Otto in his famous comparison of Eastern and Western mysticism concluded that there "are indeed strong primal impulses working in the human soul" that are "completely unaffected by differences of climate, of geographical position, or of race" and that show a "similarity and inner relationship of types of human experience and spiritual life which are truly astonishing."[12] William James, in his famous compendium *The Varieties of Religious Experience*, provided a comparable inventory of mystical experiences and concluded that mysticism is at the root of all religious experience.

In characteristic pragmatic-empirical fashion, James offers a list of defining characteristics, noting, first of all, that mystical experiences are typically "ineffable" — so profound and intense as to defy verbal description. They can be cultivated through rigorous disciplines and rituals, but they are often *spontaneous* and *transient*,[13] occurring as acts of grace to quite ordinary people under ordinary circumstances. Then he notes the central paradox of mysticism: that despite this resistance to language, these experiences have an unmistakable "*noetic* quality," giving a sense of reliable insight concerning deeper aspects of reality with great *practical* importance for how to live one's life.

James quotes as a typical example of a spontaneous mystical experience the account of a middle-aged man who on a beautiful sunny day decided to skip going to church with his family and instead take his dog for a walk through the hills. Suddenly on the way back, without warning, he was overtaken by an ecstatic revelation:

> I felt I was in Heaven — an inward state of peace and joy and assurance indescribably intense, accompanied with a sense of being bathed

> in a warm glow of light...a feeling of having passed beyond the body, though the scene around me stood out more clearly and as if nearer to me than before....Today [years later] it stands out as the most real experience of my life.[14]

Such experiences give one the courage and the enthusiasm to take in the big picture of life — to love truth and to be open to the quest. Experiencing reality as an exquisite, awesome, and sacred mystery can then become an emotional, intellectual, and moral anchor for all other values — a self-evident good, a value of values, a *summum bonum* — guiding action and helping shape culture and society.

In the past century, only one Western political philosopher, Eric Voegelin, has systematically explored the tension between the mystical experience, the truth quest, and political order.[15] Voegelin devoted a lifetime to reflecting on the nature of politics through the study of the primary texts of Mesopotamia, Egypt, China, ancient Israel, Greece, Rome, Medieval Christian Europe, and of course ecumenic modernity. His contribution to our quest for a new politics is twofold: first, he clarifies a philosophy of consciousness as a basis for the truth quest, and second, he provides a sweeping, penetrating empirical study of the search for order in the history of world civilizations.[16]

But Voegelin's extraordinary erudition brings its own difficulties. Such a high level of literacy is required to follow his arguments that he has largely been ignored not only by the layperson but by much of mainstream political science. This neglect reinforced his tendency to elitism, which made his work even less appealing to the creative thinkers who might have made the most radical use of it. Despite these difficulties, the enormous body of Voegelin's work is now starting to gain global recognition.[17]

The inaccessibility of Voegelin's scholarship is particularly unfortunate because his crowning insight into the paradoxical nature of consciousness is something that can be simply and directly experienced by the layperson, and this has critical implications for our search for the good life. We can grasp Voegelin's insight with a little focused reflection on one of the first facts of consciousness — that is the awareness we all have of growing from "unconscious" infancy into an adult self-consciousness. We slowly wake up to the fact that we have been born at a particular time and place, within a particular body, and shaped by our family, society, and culture. None of this is of our choosing. Nor can we ever hope to grasp all of it. We are required to play a part in an unfolding reality, never fully knowing where it all comes from nor where it is all going. We know our actions and choices have consequences; we know we can make mistakes and spoil things, sometimes catastrophically, but we cannot simply abstain from the drama of existence. As Voegelin puts it: "Our role in existence must be played in uncertainty of its meaning... as an adventure of decision on the edge of freedom and necessity."[18] We are born into a story not of our making within which we have to find our own way, to live our own lives and tell our own stories.

Voegelin's terms can sharpen this understanding. He calls the "story telling us into being" the "It-reality," which is ultimately the mystery out of which we emerge. We experience it as congruent with what Native Americans call the "Great Spirit" and the experience of what monotheistic religions call God.[*] Then there is also the world we know as an object, the world of things, including those objects, institutions, and relationships made and shaped by humans. Voegelin calls this the "thing-reality." Humans live in a paradoxical situation, in-between these two realities, participating simultaneously in both, unable to step outside of one to grasp the other with certainty.

Since contemporary philosophy has no vocabulary to describe this situation, Voegelin took the Greek term *metaxy*, from Plato's *Symposium*. *Metaxy* simply means "in-between." It refers to the human condition of existing in-between that great mysterious reality from which we came — the It-reality — and the human-created, conceptualized world of objects, institutions, and things — the thing-reality. In evolutionary and primal terms one could say that the It-reality is the principle of creativity emerging with the Big Bang, permeating the natural world and manifesting in a continually evolving universe.[19][**]

We can approach this in even simpler terms by saying we are always dealing with a single split paradoxical reality that has two inseparable

* Monotheistic religions have so thoroughly anthropomorphized "God" that the name is misleading here. It cannot be emphasized enough that Voegelin's It-reality is an ineffable, indescribable, *truly* mysterious creative force that manifests in the infinite variety of the faces of creation.

** Throughout the book I expand Voegelin's idea of the in-between to clarify the relationship between various pairs of opposites.

aspects — an outer and an inner. The inner is known to us through reflecting on our inner life, which of course is only meaningful insofar as we are aware that it is also simultaneously part of an outer reality. The outer is known through science and history and direct experience, which of course is only meaningful insofar as it also relates to our inner reality. This situation is particularly confusing for us moderns, since in our desire for certainty, we tend to focus on the outer, on the "mastery and possession of nature." Grasping both inner and outer aspects of consciousness together — a paradox — means we can never fully know either; we have to accept that all our knowledge is in principle always incomplete.* Making mistakes — and ultimately the reality of good and evil — is built into what it means to be human. Naturally this situation generates a primordial anxiety, and it is this anxiety that helps drive our search for knowledge of better ways to live.

But anxiety isn't the only response. Grasping the bigger picture of the in-between in evolutionary and primal terms can also generate the classical ecstatic, mystical experience. We are conscious of the earth as an independent entity, and at the same time we can recognize that it gives birth to the human and the very same self-consciousness that allows us to grasp the earth as an object! How utterly extraordinary! As the Jewish Kabbalist and mystic Joshua Heschel pointed out, when we allow ourselves to sink into this sort of "radical amazement," we can recognize its sacred dimension. Like Wakan Tanka for the Lakota, the experience of the miracle of conscious existence gives us a reverence for life and a zest for living; it takes us beyond fear and gives us the courage to stay open, to explore our condition, and to live in the light of our ongoing quest. Maintaining this fascination with the mystery of existence becomes an essential condition for the truth quest and thus for politics — a truly human way of life. Dogmatism of either religion or ideology is an implicit denial of our in-between status and blocks openness to the quest. This inability to live in the tension of the in-between is often connected to *libido dominandi* — the lust for power and control. Every time we think we have certainty about life — whether that certainty comes from mathematics, logic, religion, or ideology — we have lost the primary

* This split structure of consciousness is as fundamentally paradoxical as the confounding world of subatomic physics.

experience. We have deformed our essential humanity and closed down the search. Disaster looms. Much of Voegelin's history of world civilizations documents these deformations and their murderous consequences. By the same token, his work emphasizes the importance of embracing the uncertainty of mystery as inspiration for continuing the quest.

Looking back on the history of our species, we can see that self-consciousness gradually unfolds, over hundreds of millennia, until we have an astounding "aha!" experience — a soul-shaking revelation as we look back over our shoulders and recognize consciousness emerging from something that seems utterly other — the It-reality. Voegelin identified the first such recorded, collective recognition as the monotheistic revelation that became the organizing experience for the Jewish people and the Kingdom of Israel. When Moses asks for God's name, the response is "Ehiyeh Asher Ehiyeh," "I am that I am," represented by the four letters yod, heh, vav, heh, or YHWH. The Greeks called this the tetragrammaton, and non-Jews pronounce it as "Yahweh." But when observant Jews encounter the tetragrammaton, they will simply acknowledge it as *adoni* (my lord) and refrain from trying to pronounce the name of the ineffable, unnameable God. YHWH cannot be grasped as a namable thing. As with the Lakota Wakan Tanka, we are dealing with a Great Mystery that permeates all of creation.

While many such revelations have occurred across the world, what was distinctive about the Israelite revelation was the fact that it was the first such event recorded in writing. As Voegelin points out, the appearance of the written Bible itself is a unique event underscoring the singular event of the revelation, creating a "before" and an "after." This initiates written history as a record of a linear process of particular people at a particular time and place attempting to live in the light of a revelation concerning the human condition. Today, we are still involved in that same process, trying to make sense of "the story telling us" and then choosing our own course accordingly. Since this revelation radically changed humanity's self-understanding and way of being in the world, Voegelin called it a "leap in being" — a radical leap forward in human self-awareness, a marker in the history of civilization. The notion of the big story becomes clarified as the fundamental unit of meaning in the life of the individual and society. Modern scientific cosmology now embeds the story of our species in the story of the earth, and indeed the universe itself.

While the written stories of scholars, scribes, rabbis, and priests preserve the founding experience of the mystery of the in-between and record its unfolding, they also tend to freeze interpretation. Institutionalized religion crystallizes around obedience to the literal word of the holy scriptures — the Torah, the Gospels, or the Koran. The sacred scripture replaces the experience of the sacred. Dogma, bureaucratically enforced rituals, rules, and regulations, tends to block the followers from the primary mystical experience of the in-between. As C. G. Jung noted, religion then becomes a defense against authentic religious experience. The quest shuts down and we fall for the deluded certainties of ideology and theology with all their murderous consequences. Convinced it understands the written word of God, humanity acts diabolically.

When the truth quest is shut down, parts of the psyche calcify and become obsessive; other parts dissociate. We lose our grip on the paradoxical structure of consciousness, or what Voegelin called the "tensional complex" of consciousness-reality-language.[20] Delusions of grandeur and persecution proliferate. Voegelin followed Plato in calling this sickness of the soul *anoia* — a forgetting of our in-between status, our partnership in the community of being. When Jung was interviewed toward the end of his life, he warned that this ignorance of the nature of the psyche was ultimately the greatest danger civilization faced.

> The world hangs on a thin thread and that is the psyche of man. Nowadays we are not threatened by elementary catastrophes. The... H-bomb ... is all man's doing. *We are the great danger. The psyche is the great danger!* What if something goes wrong with the psyche? How important is the psyche of man — to know something about it? But we know nothing about it [emphasis in the original].[21]

The upsurge of fundamentalism in our age — whether that of the free market and scientific materialism or of Islam, Christianity, and Judaism — measures our distance from the awareness of living in-between and our closeness to chaos.

The primal perspective reveals that the monotheistic leap in being can be seen as a partial clarification and differentiation through written history of aspects of an earlier, more fundamental leap in being that took place between two hundred thousand and one hundred thousand years ago: the emergence of modern self-reflective consciousness — the primal revolution. This more inclusive view draws our attention back to the preliterate, pre-agrarian politics of hunter-gatherers, where the elements constituting the questing individual in society were still closely related and in primordial balance. So now we have two starting points for rethinking politics — the reflective-philosophical path through Voegelin and the empirical path through science and history.[22]

## The Mandala Structure of the Primal Quest

Reflecting on the questing human individual as he or she emerges within the primal community, we can identify four primary values and processes that constitute the necessary, minimal coordinates of the quest. My suggestion is that this structure functions like a Jungian archetype, a deeply rooted way of thinking and behaving, that becomes luminous — illuminating itself — as it unfolds over time.

This primordial four-part dynamic structure can be represented, appropriately enough, by one of the oldest and most universal symbols of the whole — a mandala (Sanskrit for "circle"), which is typically represented as a circle cut into four quarters (see diagram, page 118). The term was popularized by C.G. Jung, who noticed the appearance of mandalas in religious and healing traditions across time and cultures, from Paleolithic petroglyphs and Navajo sand paintings to medieval alchemy and objects of meditation in early Christianity and Tibetan Buddhism. In all contexts the mandala seems to represent the connection between the whole and the part; the tension between the unity of existence and the infinite ways in which the whole can be fragmented.

Primal traditions can help bring down to earth the rather abstract discussion of the epistemology of the quest. Hyemeyohsts Storm, a contemporary Cheyenne medicine man, gives us several overlapping examples of how to use the structure of the mandala — what the Cheyenne call a medicine wheel — as a guide to the quest.[23] At its simplest the medicine wheel can be represented by a circle of stones on the prairie cut by a cross into four quarters. The circle represents any single integrated whole: for example, the life of the individual from birth to death, or the earth and all its creatures,

## Mandala of Primal Politics

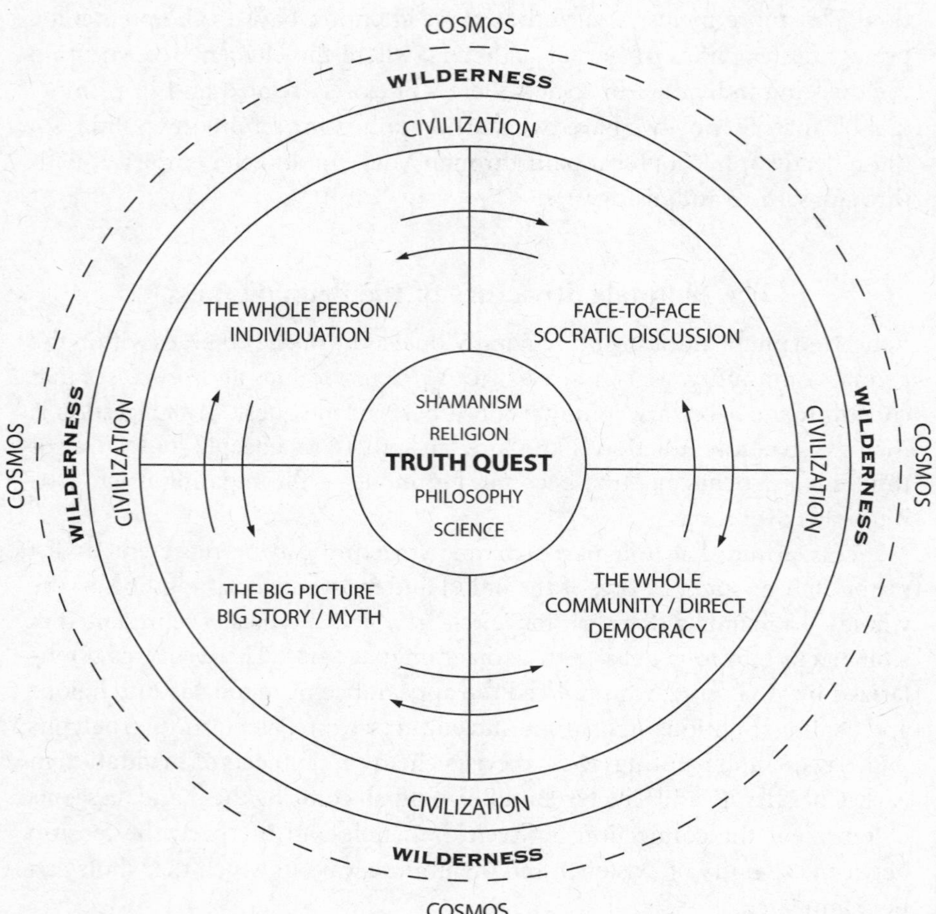


*A model of both a self-transforming politics and a never-ending search for truth. All four quadrants and all the concentric circles are in continual back-and-forth, balancing relationship with one another, partially represented by the arrows connecting the quadrants.* (Diagram: Cyril Ruthenberg)

or ultimately and most importantly the cosmos — all of existence. All creatures, all seasons, all human societies, and all individuals can be represented by stones on the circle showing their unique place in the single whole. As Storm puts it, all creatures and all things have their place in the circle of life, except human beings. Only humans have such an expanded realm of freedom; only humans are "determiners" and only humans have a serious problem in finding their place in the whole. In the language of Genesis, humans have tasted the fruit of the tree of knowledge of good and evil. Attaining self-consciousness means expulsion from the Garden of Eden. The only truly human way forward is through more knowledge; there is no going back.

The four quarters of the mandala represent the distinctiveness of each of these elements. The surrounding circle represents their interconnectedness in continual dynamic interaction, converging in the unity of the single center point — the quest itself. It is helpful to imagine each value of the four quarters as an independent good, an end in itself while simultaneously a necessary means for the realization of the others, in which all collectively constitute the truth quest. Each can be expressed as both a noun and a verb; each describes a goal and a process; each is an end and a means to an end. We need to recognize that all are in constant dynamic interaction — counteracting, complementing, and balancing one another. The rest of this chapter describes the four-part nature of the truth quest. The rest of this book describes how this dynamic operates in the life of small nomadic hunting-gathering societies, and then how it reappears at certain labile, transitional moments throughout history in a variety of contexts, from the Greek polis to the present. As we self-consciously cultivate the mandala dynamic we can start to see its potential for catalyzing a rapid dramatic shift in personal and collective awareness.

### *The Whole Person, or Individuation*

Ultimately, since all our knowing is inevitably refracted by our unique trajectory through life, all we have to teach is contained within our story. As we struggle to grasp a shared reality, we are forced to reflect on our uniqueness and to recognize that of others, and so we find ourselves returning to the wisdom of the Delphic oracle: "Know thyself." Anamnesis becomes an essential component of the quest.

But more than self-reflection is needed. One grows as a human being to the degree that one participates in as many of the archetypal human experiences as possible. We cannot fully know ourselves without knowing life. Our wisdom becomes persuasive to the degree that we live as deeply as possible, that we taste both directly and vicariously as much of the full range of what it means to be human as possible.

Certain social structures enhance this process; others repress it. The small size and self-sufficiency of the primal hunting-gathering group impelled every adult to participate in all the definitively human activities: hunter, gatherer, artist, musician, healer, learner, and teacher. Everyone was a "chief" to the degree that all participated directly in collective decision making, though the degree varied from society to society. The emotionally charged events of the human life cycle — birth, growth, maturity, death, the fights, the loves, the losses, the victories — all took place in the public theater of the camp. The perplexing fullness of life was on display for all to share.

Conversely, the social hierarchy and division of labor of classical and industrial civilizations restrict the degree to which the individual can play multiple parts in the life of the community. Under such conditions the notion of the whole person becomes elevated as an ideal to be struggled for. In the world of hunter-gatherers, the reality of the whole person is taken for granted, and there is little need for its theoretical development. We see one of its first sharp formulations as an ideal of human excellence during the formative period of classical Greece, when the poleis were engaged in a life-and-death struggle with the Persian Empire. The small democratic polis exalted the free creative individual, in contrast to the vast Persian Empire where the citizen was a slave whose life was subject to the whim of the emperor. The Greek ideal of *arete*, or excellence, was the cultivation of the whole person, the consummate amateur who could participate creatively in all areas of life and thus grasp the fullest range of what it meant to be human. The classicist H. D. F. Kitto gives a vivid description of the *arete* of the Homeric hero as

> a great fighter, a wily schemer, a ready speaker, a man of stout heart and broad wisdom who knows that he must endure without too much complaining what the gods send; and he can both build and sail a boat,

> drive a furrow as straight as anyone, beat a young braggart at throwing the discus, challenge the Phaecian youth at boxing, wrestling or running; flay, skin, cut up and cook an ox, and be moved to tears by a song. He is in fact an excellent all rounder; he has surpassing *arete*.[24]

Implicit in this ideal is the deeper principle of balancing opposites — the ideal of the disciplined warrior who the night before battle can also shed tears over a poem. In practice this noble vision of human excellence was truncated by the reality of classical Greece as a patriarchal, slave-owning society that repressed the feminine. Nevertheless, what was unique about the polis was that it grasped the pursuit of wholeness as an end in itself and simultaneously the condition for realizing the democratic and just community. The person with broad vision and wide-ranging experience was better equipped to understand the connection between what was good for the individual and good for the community, and thus more likely to be publicly spirited. Selfless participation in public service was not some abstract duty but an arena for the highest personal fulfillment — the consummate display of *arete*.

In Athens, the most brilliant of all the poleis, the good of the individual and the good of the community converged in the face-to-face discussion of the general assembly — direct democracy. This meant the polis could not be too large or too stratified, so it pursued individual self-sufficiency as a necessary condition for the participation of all citizens in the affairs of the community. It opposed, in principle, division of labor and hierarchy in the service of material profit. In doing so it exemplified precisely the opposite ethos of imperial and industrial societies, which praise the rule-bound bureaucrat and reward the specialist.

An even fuller expression of the whole person is found in the more differentiated, but still egalitarian, shamanic traditions of the Plains Indians of North America. In the Cheyenne teaching offered by Storm, the mandala of the medicine wheel could also represent an individual's entire journey through life, from birth through infancy to youth, maturity, and old age and death. The medicine wheel could also represent the full range of possibilities for human temperament; rather like Jung's basic personality types, Storm's "four directions" of the wheel are roughly equivalent to Jung's "introverted" and "extroverted," "thinking" and "feeling" categories. Everyone starts the quest at a particular point on the wheel with particular gifts, ranging from inherited faculties to culture, geography, and historical period. But every gift is also a limitation that needs to be transcended by relating to its opposite. Growth in wisdom results from moving around the wheel and becoming "what one is not." As Storm puts it:

> But any person who perceives from only one of these Four Great Directions will remain just a partial man [*sic*]. For example, a man who possesses only the Gift of the North will be wise. But he will be a cold man, a man without feeling. And the man who lives only in the East will have the clear far sighted vision of the Eagle, but he will never be close to things. This man will feel separated, high above life, and will never understand or believe that he can be touched by anything. *But none of these people would yet be Whole. After each of us has learned of our Beginning Gift, our First Place on the Medicine Wheel, we must Grow by Seeking Understanding in each of the Four Great Ways. Only in this way can we become Full, capable of Balance and Decision in what we do* [emphasis added].[25]

There is an attraction between psychological and cultural opposites that serves wholeness. As a scholar and intellectual, I found myself drawn to a life of action and the body. As a white in South Africa, I was attracted to black culture; as an Israeli, I fought Arab soldiers but found Palestinian culture fascinating. By following this impulse, we can balance our dominant way of looking at the world; when we seek out and integrate opposites, we get a bigger, truer picture of the human condition. As we participate in the life of a larger humanity, we can grow psychologically, intellectually, and spiritually. Of course, such growth is always a matter of degree. As long as there is more life to be lived, further growth in wisdom and wholeness is always possible.

One of the most vivid examples of a life lived according to this teaching comes, appropriately enough, from another celebrated contemporary Native American medicine man, Lame Deer, who described himself as follows: "It was almost as if I were several different people — a preacher, a spud-picker, a cowhand, a clown, a sign painter, a healer, a bootlegger, a president of the Indian YMCA."[26] Lame Deer ascribed his healing wisdom to having lived through a great range of opposing experiences, becoming both saint and sinner, lawman and outlaw, Christian and heathen. The underlying purpose of this journey was to get a sense of the full range of what it meant to be human, beyond labels and judgments. The wisdom and power of the shaman comes from attunement to the opposites of life rooted in the in-between; he or she resides between God and the world.

The depth psychologist C. G. Jung gives a comparable recommendation to the modern psychiatrist:

> Anyone who wants to know the human psyche would be better advised to bid farewell to his study and wander with human heart through the world. There, in the horrors of prisons, lunatic asylums and hospitals, in drab suburban pubs, in brothels and gambling-hells, in the salons of the elegant, the stock exchanges, socialist meetings, churches, revivalist gatherings and ecstatic sects, through love and hate, through the experience of passion in every form in his own body, he would reap richer stores of knowledge than textbooks a foot thick could give him, and he will know how to doctor the sick with real knowledge of the human soul.[27]

Jung called this process of healing through growth in wholeness *individuation*. The individual grows up, matures psychologically and spiritually, by becoming conscious of his or her personal relations to the entire archetypal constellation of human experience. In the process the person becomes psychologically *individuated* — a morally autonomous, integrated unity, capable of thinking, judging, and acting independently of the prevailing social prejudices. As Jung's thought developed, the notion of individuation increasingly integrated psychological, intellectual, and spiritual growth to form what we might call wisdom.

The process of socialization, which trains us to take our place in the existing social structure, often distorts individuation by forcing compliance through punishment. This has the effect of creating a brittle sense of self that tries to repress from self-awareness everything the ego has been punished into rejecting, disparaging, and fearing as "not-I." Generally, this is whatever the culture identifies as primitive, wild, subversive, disreputable, and dangerous. Jung called this rejected content the "shadow" aspect of the psyche, and he saw it as an inevitable consequence of ego development. Ego implies shadow. Cultivating a conscious relationship with one's shadow instills a humbling relationship to the larger It-reality that creates us — a process that is the core of intellectual and spiritual growth.

The more punishing and rigid the society, the more the ego refuses to recognize its connection to its opposite. This deforms our ability to grasp and accept that we live in-between the great opposites of reality. We then become more and more estranged from the truth quest and from wisdom. The indoctrinated modern individual hates and fears the primitive, just as the white racist hates and fears the black, the Nazi hates the Jew, and so on. The wisdom that comes from psychological maturity affirms that all opposites — the primitive, the modern, the Jew, the Nazi — exist as potentials within us all. By accepting the inevitability of our shadow, we recognize that we are also "what we are not." This humbling recognition restrains us from the madness of trying to eliminate those we hate and fear in the world. Self-mastery, maturity, and wisdom are defined by our ability to hold the tension between opposites.

Nelson Mandela, who struggled against the racist apartheid regime, embodies the individuated, morally mature statesman. His capacity to discover and affirm within his own soul the Afrikaner oppressor transformed both himself and his jailors. His example made it possible for a majority of South Africans, poised on the edge of a racial civil war, to envision a multiracial polity and a nonviolent reconciliation after apartheid. The good life requires this paradoxical individuality, one grounded in a loving relationship to the entire community of beings.

### *Face-to-Face Socratic Discussion*

Self-knowledge is not a process that takes place only inside our heads. It requires relationships with others. "Humans are political animals," Aristotle famously said, generalizing from the teaching implicit in Socrates' heroic death. When faced with death or exile from his beloved Athenian community, Socrates chose death, expressed in the immortal words, "The unexamined life is not worth living." For Socrates, exile was as unacceptable as silence because he believed the examined life must take place in community, with peers. Face-to-face discussion confronts our personal truths with that of others, with those embodied human beings who share our particular moment in space and time. The face-to-face situation can be the site of the richest, deepest interaction between humans, since it is an encounter between undeniably irreducible subjectivities. This is the friction point of politics, the "rub" where conflicts arise but also where decisions can be made in the most inclusive way.

Hyemeyohsts Storm offers a clear example of what this means in his teaching of the medicine wheel. He asks us to imagine a circle of people, symbolizing the primal political community, sitting on the prairie facing one another. A drum with different images painted on its sides is placed in the center. Each person sees and understands something different about the drum depending on their position in the circle. In order for everyone in the group to get the most complete understanding of the drum, each person must offer a personal description, based on his or her particular position. Not only is everyone's perspective necessarily incomplete, but some might have other limitations: some might have weak vision, while others might be color-blind or hard of hearing or have no experience of drums. When the object in the center is a course of action, an idea, or a political system, the challenge of creating a shared understanding and agreement is compounded. Further, each individual's past experience shapes his or her understanding of our shared reality. One person on a mountaintop at night might be filled with fear and anxiety, while another person experiences peace and beauty.

The example of the primal circle confronts our in-between situation in the most direct and inescapable way. We face diverse individuals, each on his or her own trajectory through life. The circle makes it obvious that no one can sit in the exact position of another at the same time. No one can live another's life, and thus no one can share another's exact point of view. This also helps make us more aware of our shadows, which are by definition unseen by us but are often comically obvious to those on the other side of the circle — as when we project our reality, lose our tempers, or become too full of ourselves. Mental health ultimately requires the honest loving feedback of others, who help us create and relate to the bigger picture. The circle makes it equally obvious that we cannot deny that we share an overarching reality — the single community, humanity, the earth and its creatures, the universe itself. Knowledge of the whole is essential, but always a matter of degree, and it is enhanced by the inclusion of all.

For instance, consider Nelson Mandela and his negotiations with his jailors. Mandela met Jimmy Kruger, the racist Afrikaner minister of justice, while incarcerated in Kruger's prison on Robben Island. As they sat face-to-face, speaking in Afrikaans, the language of the oppressor, Mandela talked of the Afrikaner heroes who fought British rule in South Africa and were imprisoned for treason. Mandela surprised Kruger with his sympathetic grasp of the Afrikaner experience. Mandela then showed how the black struggle mirrored the heroic Afrikaner precedent in a way that implicitly affirmed their shared humanity — the African notion of *Ubuntu* — connecting Afrikaner and African. Over years, as such face-to-face meetings were repeated between many Afrikaners and Africans throughout the country, a larger understanding emerged that became a shared vision of the good that helped dissolve apartheid and avert a race war.

Face-to-face communication offers a direct way for grasping the dialectical logic of truth through contradiction, since it confronts us in the most inescapable way possible with our in-between situation. We each see the same reality but from ultimately different positions. I cannot see myself but I can see you, as you cannot see yourself and vice versa. We are both forced to acknowledge a blind spot at the center of all our knowing. Together, with trust and cooperation, using the dialectic of back-and-forth discussion, we can help each other grasp more of our shared reality. In the process we build relationships and community. Face-to-face discussion allows the partial to become more complete by offering each participant immediate access to the perspective of the other.

One classic example comes from the Socratic discussion of courage in Plato's *Laches*. A thesis is presented: "courage means not running away in battle."[28] Thinking about this, those present consider what has been left out and propose an antithesis: for example, refusing to run when the army is in strategic retreat would be idiotic. The group ponders the partial truths contained in thesis and antithesis and is driven to construct a more inclusive synthesis, such as, "courage means refusing to succumb to fear in serving the community." This constitutes a new thesis, which can be further expanded and qualified by a new and more inclusive antithesis. In this fashion, discussion can move toward an ever-larger, deeper synthesis, a bigger picture of the human condition.

The process is never ending. Truth is a matter of degree: the bigger the picture, the deeper the meaning and value given to the part. Scale is not the only measure of truth. Evaluations are compelling to the degree that they include the diversity of perspectives of the relevant community. Both integration and individuation are present in the dynamic of face-to-face discussion, the Socratic *dialektike*, the royal road to truth.

To emphasize the point, Socrates wrote nothing and disparaged lectures and books as incapable of responding to questions. Ironically, it was Plato, his student, who preserved this teaching, only to distance us from its practice by producing the paradigmatic philosophical text and founding the first "academy" in the Grove of Academus. The more we share the life of a community of wisdom-loving individuals, who are committed to opening themselves to the experience of others, the greater the possibility of a compelling, shared, bigger picture. It is significant that the Greek polis that gave us philosophy and direct democracy grounded both in face-to-face discussion. For this reason Plato thought the ideal polis should have around five thousand citizens. Any larger, and it couldn't be self-governing through face-to-face discussion. Any smaller, and it couldn't be self-sufficient and autonomous.

Not surprisingly, we find the most expanded arena for discussion in the small, egalitarian bands of preliterate hunter-gatherers like the San Bushmen, who called themselves "lovers of argument."[29] Bushman politics swam in an ocean of discussion and storytelling. In such a situation the individual was stimulated and challenged to keep thinking and moving around the medicine wheel of life — to keep growing as an individual. At the same time, the face-to-face situation gave everyone some direct experience of the emerging, growing consensus. This shared consensus fostered effective decision making and a more just and egalitarian society. Knowledge of the good of the whole grows as it is shared with others in trusting face-to-face relationship. Today, when multinational media conglomerates can routinely inundate millions with a single message, we find ourselves at the precise antipode of the primal situation.

### *The Whole Community and Direct Democracy*

*Direct democracy* expresses the value of communication free from the distortions of concentrated wealth and power. It also expresses a society's commitment to providing the education and resources necessary to maximize the individual's participation in face-to-face decision making. The more democratic and egalitarian the community, the more discussion can approach a version of Jürgen Habermas's "ideal speech community," with the added qualification that the free expression of the individual can spin into solipsism without a balancing concern for the good of the community.[30] Democracy and egalitarianism promote individuation and provide conditions for such individuals to share their truth without fear. The wider and deeper the pool of shared truths, the greater the likelihood that democratic decision making will produce just and compelling outcomes. This body of shared truths constitutes political culture, and it needs to include the realization of the primacy of the truth quest itself. This commitment to the quest is the ingredient most often missing in dysfunctional democracies.

Nelson Mandela gives us a vivid description of direct democracy from his youth, when he lived with the regent at Mqhekezweni, the seat of the tribal chiefdom of his Thembu people. When problems arose, the regent would call a meeting. Surrounded by his council of wise elders, he would listen to every individual speak his mind fully and without inhibition, although, as Mandela notes with regret, women were not included.

> Everyone who wanted to speak did so. It was a democracy in its purest form. There may have been a hierarchy of importance among the speakers, but everyone was heard, chief and subject, warrior and medicine man, shopkeeper and farmer, landowner and laborer. People spoke without interruption and the meetings lasted for many hours.... At first I was astonished by the vehemence — and candor — with which people criticized the regent. He was not above criticism — in fact he was often the principal target of it. But no matter how flagrant the charge, the regent simply listened.[31]

Here we see a deep respect for the free and forceful expression of individuality. But in the small, self-contained, organic community of the tribe, the self-interest of the individual remains in dynamic balance with the good of the community:

> The meetings would continue until some kind of consensus was reached. They ended in unanimity or not at all. Unanimity might be an agreement to disagree, to wait for a more propitious time to propose a solution.... Majority rule was a foreign notion. A minority was not to be crushed by a majority.[32]

The individual counts, but so does the community. The face-to-face situation mediates the back-and-forth dynamic organically.

We can see an imperfect attempt at this in the town hall meeting of the early days of the United States, although a truly democratic culture of concern for the common good was often overwhelmed by narrow vision and self-interest. We also see something approximating direct democracy in the early days of the Israeli kibbutz, where all adult members of the community gathered in the general assembly to make collective decisions for the community through face-to-face discussion. We have the opposite of direct democracy in contemporary military dictatorships with their presidents-for-life. Where there is only one voice, pounding one story into the minds of a terrorized population, we find monstrous and ultimately doomed regimes constructed around the grotesquely inflated personalities of men like Adolf Hitler, Kim Jong-il, Robert Mugabe, and Muammar Gaddafi. Surrounded by sycophants and mercenaries, such leaders deny themselves the sanity of the truth-speaking community.

The Athenian general assembly of classical Greece provides the West with its first template for connecting the whole person to direct democracy through face-to-face discussion. What is extraordinary is that the polis, so often taken as emblematic of high civilization, seemed to understand that this nexus required *reversing* the trajectory of definitive aspects of civilization. At its wisest the polis recognized that this required a small scale and economic self-sufficiency — *autarkia* — which minimized division of labor and the need for centralization of authority. This also meant material demands needed to be modest. A compact community was essential if each citizen was to participate in all aspects of community life and make decisions face-to-face. The Athenian polis failed when the expansion of trade and the temptations of empire required specialization, division of labor, and a professional navy and army. The experience of the polis teaches us that direct democracy and the *arete* of the whole person are promoted by small-scale, relatively autonomous communities. The good of the whole tends to suffer when these conditions are not met.

By comparison with that of the polis, the direct democracy of the primal band of hunter-gatherers rested on an even stronger foundation — the radical autonomy of the community-loving individual. For example, virtually every adult Bushman could, if necessary, live directly off the land and feed, clothe, and shelter him- or herself. Although the sociable San would have found such isolation unbearably lonely, individual self-sufficiency removed some of the stark necessity that compels obedience in our more stratified societies. The San had no powerful chiefs, or as one hunter responded in answer to an anthropologist's question about their famed egalitarianism: "Of course we have chiefs. Each one of us is a chief over himself!"[33]

In the primal band, we typically find two opposite tendencies held in balance through endless discussion: on the one side is a talkative, argumentative individuality; on the other side, a love for the community. Since there is no political hierarchy, decision making and conflict resolution converge in a single dynamic — the continual flowing ocean of conversation, argument, and storytelling that proceeds until a consensus is reached. Means and ends combine in this dynamic: trust, mutual concern, individuation, and a love of truth are all preconditions and outcomes of the quest.

It is important to note that this notion of direct democracy is not to be reduced to Rousseau's "general will" of civil society. As with all the other values, it is realized only when cultivated together with its counterbalancing opposites. Unlike mob rule, democracy requires the guidance of the big picture and the wisdom of the citizen committed to individuation — spiritual growth.

### *The Big Picture, the Big Story — Mythos*

Big pictures are symbolic representations of the whole. They are visions, paradigms, worldviews, and epic narratives that serve to connect the lives and passions of the individual to larger, more encompassing realities — family, tribe, nation, civilization, species, and ultimately the living earth and the evolving cosmos. Without such nested pictures of wholes within wholes, or stories within stories, we drift, unprepared, easily surprised and distracted. Our energies become dissipated, and we lapse into selfishness and cynicism.

A cosmology offers the largest frame of meaning — the biggest picture — telling the story of how the universe came into being, where it might be going, and what our place in it might be. Cosmologies provide guidance to the individual in living for something more than an ego-based life of self-indulgence, comfort, and pleasure. In this sense big pictures can be symbolic aids to the experience of transcendence.

Cosmologies are immense works of individual and collective creativity that tend to emerge over generations and shape how we organize our lives in society. For example, the synthesis of early Christianity and Aristotelian philosophy ordered feudal Europe for a thousand years. No society and no identifiable way of life can persist without drawing from and expressing such big pictures. But all such creations precipitate in the imagination of individuals as visions, epiphanies, and revelations. They only become politically significant and morally compelling to the degree that they are processed through the mill of the other mandala components — self-reflective individuals, similarly motivated, in free discussion within the community. Again, we get the clearest exemplification of this process in the primal hunting-gathering band, where most members have direct experience of many if not all areas of life. In such a situation each individual is better equipped to have an original relationship with the universe, and thus to be "author and agent of his or her own world view."[34]

The result is not a collection of self-absorbed, solipsistic, asocial individuals. Rather, each individual vision floats in a pool of conversation that gradually dissolves the individual creation into a fluid shared worldview, joining all into a caring community. From the flow of discussion, new individual visions then crystallize to illuminate the way forward.

Today we are in crisis because we are between cosmologies. Liberalism was a radically truncated cosmology that undermined big picture thinking and attempted to turn material self-interest into a transcendent principle of order. The bankruptcy of its eighteenth-century assumptions about nature and human nature are becoming obvious, and a new cosmology is slowly emerging. This effort involves an extraordinary synthesis of the wealth of accumulated civilizational wisdom woven together within the great arc of the evolutionary story, what Teilhard de Chardin called the "light illuminating all facts," the "curve that all lines must follow."[35] Everything — all of human knowledge — is now finding a place within an enormous narrative of a single evolving humanity within a single evolving cosmos. As this picture is extended back in time to our deepest origins, and extrapolated forward into the future, it confronts us with unfathomable mystery, an experience that is at once radically humbling and thrilling.

The outlines of this new cosmology are already clearly visible, but institutions have a life of their own. We created our institutions out of a constricted and distorted worldview. We can re-create them in light of our larger, truer understanding, and in doing so we will start healing ourselves, our society, and the planet.

## The Mandala of Primal Politics as an Ideal

Since the components of the quest emerge out of the deepest energies of what defines us as human, the mandala can function as an archetypal dynamic for meaning. It can operate in any situation, providing us with a template or ideal for diagnosing political disorder and redirecting our actions toward a more satisfying and life-loving politics.

As we have seen, the mandala dynamic emerged in small-scale, self-sufficient, self-organizing communities still living close to nature — the original human condition. However, we can see it reappear throughout history in times of social upheaval and transformation. We see it in the creative ferment of the Renaissance, with an explosion of interest in the natural world and the celebration of the whole person as "the Renaissance man." We see it again emerging out of the chaos of the English Civil War in the seventeenth century before the institutions of Liberalism had hardened, when peasants, driven off manorial estates, seized public land and organized themselves into a variety of democratic and spiritually based communes like the Levellers and the Diggers.[36]

We find elements of the primal now reappearing during our contemporary crisis. We have seen it in the early Israeli kibbutz, and more recently in a steadily growing eco-village movement that builds from the kibbutz-model ideal, integrating the principles of self-sufficiency and sustainability with a spiritual relationship to the larger community of being. These same principles are also evident at a variety of levels in the political mainstream: from informal environmental organizations to the more organized international Green movement, along with the election of Green representatives to public office in most European countries. We can see primal principles emerging in the small Buddhist nation of Bhutan, and we see them exemplified by spiritually attuned leaders of liberation movements, like Mahatma Gandhi, Martin Luther King, and Nelson Mandela.

The lesson of the primal polis is that all moves to decentralize power need to proceed in parallel with strategies for universalizing commitment to the truth quest. Democratizing wisdom requires cultivating the ability to move between opposites: local and global, the individual and the collective, humanity and wilderness. Decentralization backfires if it focuses exclusively on electoral mechanics, which can simply privilege the lowest common denominator of prejudice — for example, racists voting to reinstate segregation and expel foreigners, or fundamentalists voting to whip women without veils. Every step toward devolving power requires a corresponding effort to augment the truth quest — to grasp the bigger picture and to see the connections between part and whole, self and other, enemy and friend.

Since the mandala of primal politics is rooted in the deep structure of what it means to be human, it can function effectively as an ideal and offer criteria for development, without having to be fully embodied in small-scale, self-sufficient communities. Its values can guide us in whatever institutional or historic setting we find ourselves. The more completely we understand the big story telling us into being, the better able we are to respond creatively to the challenges of our moment by applying the discipline of the mandala.

# PART II

# WHERE DO WE COME FROM?

## CHAPTER 5

# OUT OF WILDERNESS

He who understands the baboon would do more towards metaphysics than Locke.

— **Charles Darwin**

Baboons speak Bushman, speak sounding like Bushmen.

When we hear them talking there, we are apt to think that other people are to be found there…

…then we see that they were baboons talking like people.

…My parents used to say to me, that the baboons were once people at the time when we who are people were not here.

— **Dia!kwain**, /Xam Bushman, *Customs and Beliefs of the !Xam Bushmen*

## The Journey Out and In

Rethinking our politics in light of the scientific story of our evolutionary origins requires us to connect the hard evidence of archaeology and paleontology to the "soft evidence" of our inner experience of what is good, true, and beautiful. This journey out and in recognizes that the outer wilderness world of primates is related to the inner wilderness of our psyche, that there remains an ancient consciousness that still breathes and pulses inside every one of us. In this sense our relationships with nonhuman primates can trigger connection to the primate within and so be a doorway to self-knowledge. Conversely, self-knowledge can open us to the mystery of our wilderness origins. This is the story of the evolution of the paradoxical structure of human consciousness; it is also the story of the emergence of the original, primordial political community and with it the truth quest.

The overwhelming consensus of the scientific community is that early prehuman hominids, the first humans, and then modern *Homo sapiens* all emerged in southern Africa, south and east of the Great Rift Valley. This geological feature appeared about seven million years ago, when climatic and tectonic shifts, part of the earth's slow evolution, pushed up a series of mountains, which cut deep gorges, lakes, and rivers that run all the way from Ethiopia down the east coast of Africa and curve into the tip of South Africa. This dramatic escarpment created a border between the lush canopy rain forests to the west and the totally novel environment to the east — the drier, more open, grass-covered, game-filled plains of the savanna, the *bushveld*, or the "real Africa" of popular imagination. It was this habitat that incubated the first ground-living simians and then, over millions of years, modern humanity.[1]

The great gift of southern Africa to paleoanthropology is its relative isolation. Significant sections of savanna remain populated by some of the last of the Pleistocene megafauna: remnant herds of grazing and browsing animals — elephant, rhino, buffalo, zebra, wildebeest, and a wide variety of antelope — along with the predators that follow the herds — lion, hyena, wild dog, and cheetah. Until modern times, many archaeological sites remained mostly undisturbed in relatively wild environments. Even more extraordinary was the persistence of San Bushmen, who continued to hunt and gather in that ancestral species birthplace. The proximity of wild creatures similar to the ones that kept the first humans company makes it easier to throw our imagination back into the deep past and coax meaning from the stones and bones we can still find on the open veldt and in the rock shelters along the coast.[2]

## Baboon Metaphysics

The epiphany I experienced sharing a sunset with wild baboons on that perfect, sunny, winter afternoon in the empty foothills of the Drakensberg gave me a taste of what was possible in retuning our inner life to the larger truths of the outer universe. When I searched out others who had been similarly moved, I found the writings of a fellow South African, Eugène Marais, a turn-of-the-twentieth-century author and naturalist. His experiences living with wild baboons inspired him to write one of the founding classics in modern primate ethology, *The Soul of the Ape*. Marais was something of a melancholic, tragic figure who lost his young wife during the birth of their first child. He witnessed the suffering of his people during the Second Boer War, when over twenty thousand Afrikaner women and children died in the first modern concentration camps, established by the British during their scorched-earth policy. This was followed by World War I, when the mechanized armies of the European nations massacred one another at the rate of six thousand people a day for fifteen hundred days.

Heartbroken, disgusted with civilization, Marais retreated to the remote Waterberg Mountains of the Western Transvaal to heal. This is still quite a wild area close to the famous limestone cave of Makapansgat, where archaeologists later found the remains of our three-million-year-old ancestor *Australopithecus africanus*. Marais spent three years living within a few score yards of a troop of wild baboons who became habituated to his presence. He was particularly struck by the change in mood that overcame the troop every evening at sunset:

> Silence fell upon them gradually. The "talking" ceased. The little ones crept cuddlingly into the protecting arms of their mother. The romping

> young folk joined different groups, generally on the higher flat rock from which a view could be had of the western horizon. The older ones assumed attitudes of profound dejection, and for long intervals the silence would be unbroken except for the soft whimpering complaints of the little ones and the consoling gurgling of the mothers. And then from all sides would come the sound of mourning, a sound never uttered otherwise than on occasions of great sorrow — of death or parting. I do not think there is any possibility of mistaking the state of mind which determines this behavior — even by one not well acquainted with the character and ways of the animal. One need only compare them with a native village under the same conditions to realize beyond any shadow of doubt that you have here a representation of the same inherent pain of consciousness at the height of its diurnal rhythm.[3]

Marais observed a similar emotional transformation he called "Hesperian depression" in rural villages. As the sun sinks below the western horizon it signals the death of the day, an intimation of our mortality and the mystery of the cycles of life. He recognized in the baboon that unmistakable spark of reflective awareness that in us becomes the full flame of self-consciousness.

Prone to depression, Marais perhaps overemphasized the melancholic aspect of this experience. But this sort of fascination with baboons can also contain a moment of transcendence as one experiences oneself as part of the bigger evolutionary story binding baboon to human. Such experiences of identification with obviously wild and conscious animals heighten our awareness of our in-between nature. This is simultaneously humbling and exhilarating, both disturbing our civilized ego and comforting us as we feel once more connected to the cosmic community of life.

As we might expect, traditional San Bushmen, who inherited a culture that developed in proximity to baboons, recognized them as incipiently "in-between," sometimes calling them "the people who sit on their heels." According to San cosmology, there is a first order of being — "the early times" or the "first times," when present-day animals had human attributes, and present-day humans were still like animals. Or as Dia!kwain, a nineteenth-century

/Xam* Bushman, explained, "Baboons were once people at the time when we who are people were not here."[4] Because of the ontological ambiguity of certain animals, Bushmen still feel some ambivalence about eating their flesh, despite the passion with which men hunt and the people enjoy meat. Some animals, like the elephant and the baboon, are still "too much like humans" and are generally not hunted.[5] According to the now-extinct southern /Xam Bushmen, baboons take wives like humans, have speech and songs, understand human language, and call Bushmen by their names. They have diseases like humans and medicines, like *sso/a*, that also cure humans.[6]

Then at some point in the distant past, the early times transformed into the present order of being. This primal revolution seems to be a universal element in the mythology of widely dispersed, linguistically distinct Bushman tribes. One old story from the nineteenth-century Bleek and Lloyd collection of Bushman folklore describes an "adventure with a family of baboons" that seems to be an iconic fragment of collective memory from this transitional time.

In the story, /Khui-/a is out hunting when he encounters a baboon family. In a reckless moment — perhaps he was hungry — he shoots a mother baboon holding a baby. The mortally wounded mother hides the baby in a cleft in the rock. The male baboon comes up and sees the dead female:

> The male baboon sat weeping; he wiped the tears from his eyes.
>
> /Khui-/a...put in his arm...to drag out the baby baboon....And the little baboon screamed, and the male baboon rose up...and said "O /Khui-/a, leave me the child, for you have killed its mother."... /Khui-/a left the little baboon alone....The male baboon went up to the little baboon and put it under his arm. He went up to the baboon mother. He examined her, while /Khui-/a, quite frightened, went away.[7]

---

* As noted, San languages are enormously complex with many more phonemes than English. They include the characteristic "clicks" so difficult for outsiders to pronounce. All the clicks are made by drawing the tongue sharply away from various points on the roof and side of the mouth, and they are signified in the text as follows: The first is the dental click "/"; this sounds like "tsk, tsk!" and is made by putting the tongue just behind the front teeth and drawing it sharply back. The second is the alveolar click " ≠"; this sounds like a soft "pop" and is made by putting the tongue just behind the ridge of the palate at the back of the front teeth and pulling sharply away. The third is the alveolar-palatal "!"; this makes a sharp "pop" by drawing the tongue down quickly from the roof of the mouth. The fourth click is the lateral "//"; this is made by pulling the tongue away from the side of the mouth, as when urging on a horse.

The story tells how /Khui-/a gets caught up in the tragedy he has caused for the baboon family, how he is shocked into his culpability. Such stories would help keep fresh archaic memories of the early times, when humans were still like animals and animals were like humans. In this sense, the early times are like the dreamtime of Australian Aborigines, a primal order that generated the present order and yet is still a living layer — the interface between inner and outer nature — the in-between. As we shall see later, telling the old stories and myths, like performing the rituals and applying the "psychotechnologies" of shamanism, helps bring the energy and insight of the dreamtime into consciousness and daily life.

Marais's example of the sunset melancholy of baboons helps connect evolutionary science to the poetry and politics of Bushman life. Marais's approach shows how we can explore the world of things, objects, and animals from both inside and outside. The dialectical movement of consciousness back and forth can be understood as a corrective to Cartesian dualism, which gets stuck on the outside. A philosophically reflective science requires looking out and looking within; exploring, analyzing, dissecting, measuring the material outer world and then periodically stepping inside and reflecting on how we are experiencing that outer reality. This is the core of the primordial discipline of "boundary crossing," which defines the shaman as one who can travel out of body, who transgresses ego boundaries, going back and forth between the human and the animal, civilization and wilderness, the present and the past. Boundary crossing helps generate a larger picture of the human condition, while staying aware of the in-between and the impossibility of certainty. This allows us to remember our partnership in the community of being and thus heal and grow.

## Jung in Africa, Africa in Jung

The Swiss psychoanalyst C. G. Jung was the first psychologist to explore this inner-outer dialectic systematically and to develop a psychology of healing and spiritual growth congruent with shamanism. Jung describes his own experience of dropping down into the early times of our African ancestry while traveling in Africa. He woke up early one morning on a train from Mombasa to Nairobi and looked out the window at the first rays of sunlight as the train curved around a steep cliff. There on a jagged rock above the track he saw a slim brownish-black figure standing motionless, leaning on a long spear and looking down at the train.

> It was as if I were this moment returning to the land of my youth, and as if I knew that dark-skinned man who had been waiting for me for five thousand years. . . . I could not guess what string within myself was plucked at the sight of that solitary dark hunter. I knew only that his world had been mine for countless millennia.[8]

Powerful experiences of connection and identification out of space and time — as well as across species, as with baboons — have a numinous quality that gives them the force of a revelation. One feels as if the veil has been lifted and a crucial fact of human existence has been revealed with the conviction of a mathematical theorem. The whole experience is suffused with a beauty that compels reflection and exploration. Such experiences can change one's life.

Jung was Freud's most brilliant disciple, who was once referred to by the master as "the crown prince of the psychoanalytic movement." But Jung had a much broader philosophical foundation than Freud. He had an early interest in archaeology and read widely in the history of religion and of science. He was also fascinated by the discoveries of atomic physics and evolutionary cosmology, and he immediately recognized in them implications for understanding the paradoxical nature of human consciousness. His correspondence with the physicist Wolfgang Pauli encouraged his exploration of the strange phenomenon of synchronicities. These are extraordinary coincidences in which events in the outer world seem to be meaningfully connected for us, yet they cannot be explained by normal causality; for example, the instantaneous connections between people and events separated by great distances. Such experiences contradict the Newtonian-Cartesian box universe, but they are widely recognized by shamanic cultures the world over.

Jung was well aware of the limits of Cartesian science and the mechanical model of the universe for understanding the invisible realm of the psyche. This liberated him from Freud's struggle to make psychology a hard, mechanical science with the predictive reliability of the natural sciences. His own experiences among the Swiss peasantry, and subsequent meetings with African "witch doctors" and Native American shamans, opened him to the in-between and the full range of parapsychological, occult, and shamanic phenomena, which are present throughout the history of culture and religion.[9] In this sense Jung was a more daring empiricist than Freud and could develop a more philosophically radical and universal psychology.

He discovered a striking repetition of symbols, narratives, and themes across cultures and times. These ranged from those we share with primates — giving birth, mothering and fathering, gathering and hunting wild foods — to those associated with the human stages of growth from infancy to adulthood. They included death and rebirth symbolized by the *uroboros*, the serpent eating its tail; creation myths; symbols of the Great Mother; the separation of the World Parents; the birth of the hero; the slaying of the father; and the virgin birth of messianic saviors.[10] Jung was amazed to discover that such themes not only recurred throughout history but periodically reappeared in the dreams and imagination of some of his naive patients at significant moments in their lives.

At first, these mythic symbols seemed to be an expression of inherited, inborn aspects of the psyche as it emerged from the animal matrix of instincts, expressing the most fundamental categories of human experience. Jung called them patterns or archetypes of a collective unconscious — which he initially expressed crudely as a sort of "self-portrait of the instincts." In this sense, archetypal themes in art and mythology constituted a kind of history and archaeology of the psyche. Yet archetypes are not historical detritus but exist as living, formative creative forces in the present, helping organize experience and emotion into meaning.[11]

These earlier formulations tended to see archetypes as fixed, inherited Platonic forms, but as Jung's thought matured, he came to consider archetypes as part of an ongoing evolutionary dynamic that changes over time. Furthermore, an aspect of consciousness seemed to exist beyond normal ego-brain-defined space and time (consonant with Voegelin's notions of consciousness). Individuals and generations not only seemed to express and draw from this matrix but in some mysterious way also contributed to this collective unconscious. Jung offered no explanatory mechanism but simply noted and cataloged the evidence from experience.

Thus, even without defining the mechanism, Jung's work allows us to understand mythology as the inner history of the archetypes mediated through the creative imagination of individuals and cultures and canonized in religion, art, and cosmology. The retelling of mythology helps access the creative energy of the ancient past within the present. In this understanding, past, present, and future become separate faces of a single reality — in the words of Jean Gebser, an "ever-present origin."[12]

Events in the outside world can trigger archetypal responses. Thus, for instance, we can understand the revelatory quality of my baboon meditation as the activation of the archaic psyche resonating with events in the present. Laurens van der Post, an author and popularizer of the Bushmen, was another white African who grew up in the veldt near the boundary of the Kalahari Desert, sensitized to the power of wilderness immersion as a spiritual ordering experience. He helped inspire Dr. Ian Player's Wilderness Leadership School, which takes people on foot into a savanna wilderness as a form of education and healing. In the introduction to a collection of testimonies from those who walked the trails, van der Post observed:

> Those who have taken people into such wild areas and lived with them there, have witnessed a change in them.... Somehow they emerge transformed as if they were coming from a highly sacred atmosphere.... [Wilderness is an instrument for]...enabling us to recover our lost capacity for religious experience,...presenting us with a blueprint as it were, of what creation was about in the beginning, when all the plants and trees and animals were magnetic, fresh from the hands of whatever created them. This blueprint is still there, and those of us who see it find an incredible nostalgia rising in us, an impulse to return and discover it again.[13]

As we might expect, immersion in an outer African wilderness is a powerful cue for reordering and activating that inner African wilderness — the conduit to Voegelin's It-reality.

First-time visitors to southern Africa often experience a powerful déjà vu — a feeling of knowing this landscape and being deeply at home in it. Wilderness guides love to remind you that "it's not that Africa gets into your blood. It has been there all the time." Or as Thomas Brown, the nineteenth-century poet and scholar, put it, "We carry with us the wonders we seek without us: there is all Africa and her prodigies in us."[14] In this sense southern African wilderness immersion can offer a powerful pilgrimage experience beyond creed and religion.

## Face-to-Face: The Baboon in Community

Our materialistic culture can accept the African primate in our blood and body but resists the penetration of the primate into our psychic and spiritual life. Staying close to the rub between the two — the primate-human nexus — helps tune us more deeply to the in-between. The evolution of primate intelligence reveals the depth of the tension between the individuating individual and the tightly bonded community. This gives us a more profound foundation for rethinking the modern polarities of the atomized individual and the crush of mass society.

Chimpanzees share with humans between 87 and 98 percent of DNA sites, and consequently they are more closely related, both genetically and behaviorally, to modern humans than baboons are.[15] However, baboons are particularly helpful in reconstructing a political story precisely because they are so conspicuously wild, yet at times so surprisingly, and sometimes embarrassingly, human. They force us to acknowledge the weaving of the wild into the human and the human into the wild. Baboons are unlike chimps and other higher apes and more like us in that they share the open-ground savanna habitat where human and baboon coevolved over hundreds of thousands of years. And when we look more closely at baboon social life, we can already see the emergence of the rudimentary polarities of the paradox of consciousness and the four-part structure of primal politics based on individuality in tension with a rich face-to-face social life.

Baboons exemplify the "surplus intelligence" that is the striking feature of primates. In most mammals, the neocortex, the center of higher mental functions, is a little over 30 percent of the brain volume; in baboons it is 60 percent, in chimpanzees and other apes 70 percent, and humans 80 percent. Why the surplus? Until recently anthropologists focused on tool use as the evolutionary catalyst, an obvious extrapolation of our own obsession with technological materialism. In the sixties, popularizers of paleontology and sociobiology like Robert Ardrey expanded on this backward projection of modernity, suggesting a human nature rooted in the violence and territoriality of primates. Ardrey's image of the "first man" was that of an "armed killer, whose evolutionary survival from his mutant instant depended on the use, the development and the contest of weapons."[16] Ardrey, a disillusioned socialist, offered a concept of human nature that confirmed Hobbes's pessimism and underwrote the inequalities and ruthless competitiveness of a market-driven society: "The carnivorous predatory australopithecines [are] the unquestionable antecedents of man and...the probable authors of man's constant companion, the lethal weapon."[17] The narrow research Ardrey drew on has now been discredited, and the bigger picture of early human societies contradicts this dismal picture.[18]

In fact, primate tool use is rare and comparatively insignificant. Rather, intelligence and self-consciousness seem to be a product of a complex social life based on the novelty of face-to-face communication. This in turn is a part of what Paul Shepard, the poet laureate of primate evolution, calls "the primate patrimony of the flowers." Face-to-face communication emerges together with attunement to the colors and distances of life in the forest canopy — between earth and sky, surrounded by "leaf, bud, flower, fruit, seed, tender culm and shoot."[19] This flowering, fruited forest canopy was itself an evolutionary novelty emerging out of the ecological devastation and mass extinction of the Cretaceous sixty-five million years ago. This most likely occurred because of extreme volcanic activity coinciding with a gigantic asteroid that collided with the earth. The impact ignited immense fires and threw up clouds of dust that blocked sunlight for years and destroyed much of the terrestrial forests of conifer and fern. Out of the ashes came a new ecological space, rapidly colonized by flowering and fruiting plants and the insects that fed off and pollinated them. This was the evolutionary crucible for the proliferation of the world of mammals.

Primates branched off soon after this ecological shift, separating from ancestral tree shrews, by taking fuller advantage of the colors and contrasts of the new environment. Shepard points out that shrew eyes do not see what whiskers and paws touch. As primates evolved, the snout shortened, the numbers of teeth were reduced, and claws became nails to support sensitive fingertips. The thumb became more flexible, and the texture of the skin, with fingerprints and sweat glands, made hands supple and improved their grip, enabling climbing, "picking and peeling fruit, handling, gripping and grooming."[20]

Binocular vision is important in judging distances, near and far. With binocular vision, the face flattens and becomes more mobile. Shepard notes that with the face in a plane, the lips and tongue are free for "sobs, screams, chuckles and chatter." Shepard also notes that often modern humans, civilized and protected by their personas, are no longer as attuned to facial expressions as primates. "Pet monkeys confronted with poker-faced men who no longer attend as well to faces as they do to print, quickly discover that they must exaggerate in order to be understood, like someone shouting into deaf ears."[21] Looking, holding, leaping, grabbing, and face-to-face socializing set up a series of feedback loops in which the appearance of one evolutionary novelty reinforces the development of related novelties, and this in turn feeds the original novelty in a process known as autocatalysis. Monkey life is intensely social — characterized by alertness, close observation of troop members, and sensitivity to complex signals when assessing rank, role, and gender and developing strategies of cooperation and competition. Bullying by dominant males is a relatively small part of a social life that is "full of long attachments, companionships, grooming, play groups, kinship allegiance, sex-group loyalties and play with infants."[22]

Shepard identifies the sudden appearance of a distinctive primate mode of intelligence that is simultaneously arboreal, social, and face-to-face. To "see" is also to understand, to grasp and apprehend. To "attend" means to watch and care for. Barbara Smuts, a fieldworker who spent years living with baboons in Kenya, describes a courtship "worthy of a scene in a singles bar," involving a male, Alex, who had recently joined the troop and was looking for a female. He chose Thalia:

> Alex stared at Thalia until she turned and almost caught him looking at her. He glanced away immediately, and then she stared at him until his head began to turn towards her. She suddenly became engrossed in grooming her toes. But as soon as Alex looked away, her gaze returned to him. They went on like this for more than fifteen minutes, always with split second timing. Finally Alex managed to catch Thalia looking at him. He made the friendly eyes-narrowed, ears back face, and smacked his lips together rhythmically. Thalia froze, and for a second she looked into his eyes. Alex approached, and Thalia still nervous, groomed him. Soon she calmed down, and I found them together on the cliffs the next morning. Six years later they were still friends.[23]

We can all recognize the familiar push-pull of staring at someone we are attracted to. We glance, look away, glance again — wanting and not wanting to reveal our desire, hoping it might be returned but fearful that it won't be.

And then, all at once, everything is communicated through a moment of eye contact. The Harvard research psychologist Gregg Jacobs talks of the shock of intimacy when two mammalian brains recognize each other through the optic nerve, the major sensory channel to the outside world, and resonate in mutually self-conscious recognition. Laboratory experiments suggest we respond to images emotionally and unconsciously within milliseconds. When images of happy, angry, and sad faces are flashed too fast to be consciously recognized, subjects still respond emotionally. Some researchers suggest that up to 90 percent of face-to-face communication during conversation might be nonverbal. The power of the face-to-face situation in amplifying communication is not of our choosing. We are physiologically wired this way. To ignore this is foolish; to repress it, dangerous.[24]

We can also see the rudimentary capacity to distance oneself, to make choices, and to make deals emerging with primates. Primatologists recognize that baboons show a high degree of agency and even a capacity for deception. The individual can mentally distinguish him- or herself from the community and then make choices based on enough of an inner life to remember past experience and project self and other in some future relationship. Richard Leakey retells Barbara Smuts's story of the baboon Cyclops, who had scavenged some meat, a piece of antelope. Then Triton, the prime adult male of the group, spotted the prize and challenged Cyclops for it. "Cyclops grew tense and seemed about to abandon the prey.... Then Cyclops's friend Phoebe appeared with her infant Phyllis. Phyllis wandered over to Cyclops. He immediately grabbed her close and threatened Triton away from the meat." Had Triton advanced, he would have been threatening Phyllis as well, and he would have risked being mobbed by Phoebe and her relatives and friends. Triton backed down.[25]

Here we can see the beginnings of what becomes in the human intersubjectivity — the capacity to experience the world from the perspective of another. The baboons were involved in politics. Both Cyclops and Triton were aware of the interplay of group dynamics, and they were evaluating and manipulating them with regard to their own desires. So already in baboons we can see the defined polarities of consciousness emerging — self-interest on the one hand and connectedness, mutuality, and reciprocity on the other.

These are the rudimentary coordinates making possible the Cartesian deal. We can choose between domination and empathic connection.

When Socrates insisted that the truth quest be based in the *dialektike* — discussion — he turned the practice of philosophy into a mode of cognition that draws on thirteen million years of primate imprinting. The face-to-face situation not only adds the powerful emotional cues of body language and facial expressions but also confronts us in the most direct way with the in-between situation in which the other person is simultaneously an object and a subject. The face-to-face encounter makes us realize that the meaning of any assertion, any piece of knowledge, begins and ends with unique human beings in all their contradictory complexity. The power of the face-to-face interaction is that it encourages us to integrate different perspectives in a single reality — the indisputable fact of sharing the same place at the same time. Shared understanding is not only possible but essential. Certainty, however, is impossible. Hubris is the pathology of the unhinged, isolated intellect.

For primates, the relative security of social life in the canopy lowers infant mortality, reduces litter size, and extends childhood learning. Mother-and-child bonding generally lasts a lifetime, while a baby monkey without a mother quickly becomes a psychotic wreck. We can see intimations of "mother worship" in the deference, special attention, and interest other adult primates show new mothers and their infants; no one gets more grooming than a new mother. In monkeys we also start to see year-round sexual activity with the reproductive cycle becoming disconnected from the seasons. The close and continued presence of a male next to mother and child, which is so characteristic in humans, begins with monkeys, particularly forest-dwelling chimpanzees, our closest genetic relatives.

However, in terms of group dynamics, or societal politics, what's intriguing is how similar humans are to ground-living simians like baboons. There seems to be some correlation between living on open ground, like the savanna, and simian social complexity. Baboons spend more time on two legs and have much more tightly organized societies with stricter hierarchies and ranks than the free-flowing troop of arboreal monkeys. Ground living seems to promote an increase in individual size, group size, and general toughness, even a disposition to hunt. Baboons are highly adaptable, inhabit a variety of environments, and eat a wide range of food, from seeds to marine jellyfish and small antelope.

Among primates, the evolutionary transition from quadrupedal running to swinging and hanging from branches produces a more upright posture and requires the sort of mobile shoulder, elbow, and wrist joints that makes throwing and handling weapons possible. An upright gait confers an enormous advantage in scanning open ground (for both prey and predator), running, endurance, and general biomechanical versatility. But it limits the width of the hips, the narrow-hipped male physique being better adapted for running than the slightly larger-hipped female's. Since female mobility is also critical, upright gait sets an upper limit to the size of the birth canal in the mother. This in turn sets an upper limit to the size of the newborn infant brain, and this puts selective pressure on having more infant brain development take place after birth. This, then, requires an extended childhood, giving the infant brain sufficient time to enlarge to adult size. By adulthood, the chimpanzee infant brain has doubled in size, and in humans this increase is three to four times. The longer period of infant helplessness requires the cooperative care of mother and father and the support of the community at large. The human infant is born helpless and matures slowly, increasing the need for social cooperation, communication, and education of young. Here we can see the feedback accelerating, as the benefits of the larger brain can only be supported by a more cooperative and complex society, while social complexity is compounded by more independent and self-conscious individuals.

Ground-living primate adults seem to enjoy petting and playing with their young more than their forest-living relatives. Once posture has become upright, the hands are available for grasping, throwing, and handling tools. This starts to free the jaw from its role in grasping and makes possible the restructuring of the face, jaw, tongue, neck, and throat for resonance of the pharynx, glottal noises, and the use of the tongue and lips for vocalizations. These primate sounds come surprisingly close to those of humans; the Drakensberg baboons certainly fooled me. Then, in humans, these vocalizations become language, which also feeds back, augmenting the realm of learning and culture and intensifying individuation. The individual becomes simultaneously more independent of its environment — more able to remember, to anticipate, and to control outcome through choice. By the same token, the individual becomes more of a unique integrated subject and a center of action and meaning independent of external stimuli. As the more sharply defined individual increases the variety of relationships, so communication is further refined. This autocatalytic process begins in primates and intensifies with the appearance of language and fire, catapulting us into the primal revolution and politics.

## Love and Cruelty: Looking at Ourselves Looking at Primates

Scientists and those who live with primates and presume to identify "human-like" traits are often accused of anthropomorphizing animals. At this point, it's instructive to remember that the truth quest requires the journey out and in, and this also means looking at ourselves in the act of looking at primates. In fact, anthropomorphization is implicit in the initial Cartesian mutilation of the human condition. Science's attitude of objectification obstructs our grasp of the in-between nature of human existence. Descartes excluded a priori what was self-evident to primal people and what is now confirmed through evolution: that humans are constituted by nature, as primates within nature. The primate is already within the human — lost, lonely, and ignored, perhaps, but there to surface in unguarded moments when the controlling ego loses control. By taking a more inclusive, more reflective point of view and observing ourselves observing, we can come to recognize our inner primate, which enables us to make meaning of the baboons on the edge of the cliff, who sit and watch the sunset together with us.

Scientists take two fundamentally different approaches to researching primate reality. On the one hand there is the quantitative rigor of hard science, notoriously exemplified by Harry Harlow's behaviorist studies on love in infant monkeys. Harlow developed experiments on caged animals in laboratories in which relevant variables could be controlled and precisely correlated into statistical regularities. On the other hand there is the soft, sensitive approach of the participant-observer like Eugène Marais, Barbara Smuts, and the better-known primatologists Dian Fossey and Jane Goodall, all of whom approached primates as fellow creatures. Their investigations involved an empirical approach of a different sort, that of reflective attention to their own feelings in the process of studying other living beings.

Let's look at the soft approach first: Between 1977 and 1983, Smuts made several trips and spent many months living near the Eburru Cliffs' troop of olive savanna baboons, about one hundred kilometers north of Nairobi, near a settlement called Gilgil in the Great Rift Valley. Her primary method was a type of free-floating observation that grew from her fascination with the daily drama of baboon life, which she compared to "watching soap operas." There is not much action in her stories, but the "thick" descriptions of baboon families make clear the irreducible importance of storytelling in understanding the emergence of self-reflective consciousness in the individual in community. In one meticulously detailed story that gives us a sense of the range of baboon expressiveness and the complexity of their social life, Smuts describes a family group settling down for the night. There is Virgil, the adult male; Pandora, the adult female; and two of Pandora's offspring — Plutarch, an infant male, and Pyrrha, an infant female.

> There was no hint of shyness in Virgil's face when he spotted Pandora, shuffling along behind him, apparently intent on finding a tasty bug or two under the small rocks she was turning over, one by one. He hunched his shoulders, pulled his chin in still further, flattened his ears against his skull, and made the skin around his eyes taut, showing the bright white patches of skin above each eyelid. At the same time, he alternately smacked his lips together rhythmically and grunted deeply with the slight wheeze that distinguished Virgil's voice from those of the other adult males. Pandora...looked up and made a similar face back at Virgil and then, abandoning her rocks, headed toward him with the ungainly trot of a baboon anxious to get somewhere fast, but too lazy to run. As she approached, Virgil lip-smacked and grunted with increasing intensity, as if encouraging her to make haste. When she arrived, she plopped herself down on her back next to him and, dangling one foot in the air, presented her flank in an invitation for grooming. Virgil responded promptly, gently parting the sparse hairs on her

> belly with his hands, every now and then lightly touching her skin with his lips to remove a bit of dead skin or dirt from her fur.

Here we can see the importance of the structure of narrative — the story — in expressing the meaning of unique individuals in particular relationship with other individuals.

> After a few moments, they were joined by two of Pandora's offspring, Plutarch, a juvenile male, and Pyrrha, an infant female. Pyrrha was in a rambunctious mood, and she used Virgil's stomach as a trampoline, bouncing up and down with the voiceless chuckles of delight that accompany baboon play. Every now and then Virgil opened his half-shut eyes, peered at Pyrrha, and gently touching her with his index finger he grunted, as if to reassure her that he did not mind the rhythmic impact of her slight body against his full stomach.

We watch the contented father absentmindedly playing with the daughter and fondly recognize ourselves. Then we are momentarily disturbed by the image of Virgil using his lips to remove a bit of dirt from Pandora's fur. Such back-and-forth helps us become more aware of the tension between the human and the animal in ourselves.

> After a while, Pandora stopped grooming, and Virgil moved away, slowly clambering up the cliff face where the troop would spend the night. He glanced back every few steps at Pandora and her family, who followed right behind. Finding a good spot halfway up the cliff, Virgil made himself comfortable. Sitting upright, he leaned backward against the rock face, and grasping his toes in his hands, let his head sink to his chest — a typical baboon sleeping posture. Pandora sat next to him, leaning her body into his, one hand on his knee, her head against his shoulder. Her offspring squeezed in between Pandora and Virgil, and in the dimming light, I could not tell where the body of one baboon began and the other left off. This is how they would remain for the rest of the night.[26]

Smuts's approach involves something touchingly archaic — "sitting, thinking, telling stories." We feel the presence of the sensitive, empathetic researcher, all senses alert, mind wide open, taking in the full context of a family group of unique individuals. Smuts's literary description of face and body language reminds us how much is communicated in "languages older than words," to use Derrick Jensen's phrase. Here we have the beginning of a truly dialectical science; that is, a science that integrates the empiricism of measurable facts about the outer world (primary qualities, or *res extensa*) with an empiricism attuned to the qualitative facts of psychic life — descriptions of feelings and meanings (secondary qualities, or *res cogitans*).

Harry Harlow's work at the Primate Research Center in Madison, Wisconsin, provides a brutal contrast, reminding us how far "exemplary research" has strayed from "a path with a heart." Although today Harlow's work would be regarded as unethical, it still provides a dramatic example of the double bind that current Cartesian-based science inevitably produces. That is, Harlow's work presupposed close connection between the monkey and the human, yet its methodology precluded experiencing this kinship in a way that would lead to action consistent with empathy.

Like Smuts, Harlow was also interested in primate family life, particularly the importance of the most tender of all bonds — that between mother and child. There the similarity ended. Instead of studying intact wholes — the individual within the family, the family within the troop, the troop within the ecology — he followed the Cartesian model of analysis by experimentally isolating measurable variables, controlling one, and measuring changes in the others. He began by raising baby monkeys in bare wire cages, using wire-and-cloth surrogate mothers with various features mimicking variables of mothering.

Harlow's initial, stunningly unremarkable conclusion was that physical contact was critically important. More specifically, infant monkeys showed a strong preference for the cloth-covered rather than the bare-wire surrogate mothers. They also preferred the lactating to the nonlactating, the rocking to the nonrocking, and the warm to the cold surrogates. Harlow further concluded that nursing strengthened the mother-child bond. Then, in a rare admission of the self-induced obtuseness of a science that equates meaning and value exclusively with control and precision, he added: "Thus by this ingenious research we learned what had been totally obvious to everyone else, except psychologists, for centuries."[27]

Harlow then attempted to create psychopathology in the infants with a series of "monster mothers" on the rather obvious assumption that maternal rejection might be a critical variable:

> Four different forms of evil artificial mothers emerged, and although all were designed to repel clinging infants, each had its own unique means by which to achieve this end. One surrogate blasted its babies with compressed air, another tried to shake the infant off its chest, a third possessed an embedded catapult which periodically sent the infant flying, while the fourth carried concealed brass spikes beneath her ventral surface which would emerge upon schedule or demand.[28]

The results were disappointing. "These surrogates produced temporary emotional disturbance in the infants, but little else. When displaced from their artificial mothers, the infants would cry, but they would return to the mother as soon as she returned to normal." Commenting on the obvious, Harlow notes: "To what else can a frightened, contact-seeking infant cling?"

His team then raised newly born monkeys for periods of up to a year in total isolation in a stainless-steel chamber. During this time, each monkey had no contact with any animal or human. Harlow found that the effects of such isolation produced profound behavior abnormalities: catatonic symptoms, self-rocking, indifference, apathy, lack of sexual activity, and finally an emotional state in which the primary response was fear. Such monkeys kept alive for years never demonstrated any vestige of social ability. Not satisfied with these pathetic creatures, Harlow tried to impregnate the females. Since they showed no interest in copulation, they had to be impregnated with what Harlow refers to as a "rape rack" that, in "consideration for the reader," he leaves to the imagination.

Finally, in these motherless mothers, Harlow created the monster he had been seeking. Most of the mothers ignored their infants, but others abused their babies by crushing the infant's face to the floor, chewing off the infant's feet and fingers, and in the case of one mother, "putting the infant's head in her mouth and crushing it like an eggshell." He noted that monkey mothers who had never experienced love of any kind were devoid of love for their infants. Then, in a twilight moment of unwitting self-incrimination, he added, "a lack of feeling unfortunately shared by all too many human counterparts."

Here we can see a momentary flash of empathy as Harlow connects the interior life of humans and monkeys. But Harlow was operating in a research culture that had no epistemological framework for exploring this sort of resonance. The experimental setup itself reproduced the cultural schizophrenia that made it possible for Harlow to abuse monkeys as research objects precisely because he assumed they had humanlike subjectivity and could express the most tender of emotions — the mother-child bond.

A 1977 special edition of *Scientific American*, showcasing "current trends in psychology," described Harlow's work as "some of the best research in psychology in the last ten years." Since Descartes, this capacity for distancing, manipulation, and domination has been considered integral to understanding the world. The method allowed Harlow to demonstrate precisely and conclusively that isolated, unloved, brutalized primates tend to be abusive and murderous parents. The irony, of course, is that Harlow never saw a possible connection between this method of objectification and manipulation, for which he was lauded, and society's prevailing empathy-impoverished culture in which others are regularly objectified and hundreds of thousands of children are abused every year by their parents and caretakers. According to the executive summary of the Child Maltreatment Report, over three million reported cases of abuse or neglect involving six million children occurred in the United States in 2009.[29]

Exploring such connections requires practicing science self-reflectively within the context of the truth quest, guided by awareness of our in-between situation and our connectedness to all living creatures. *Scientific American*'s acclaim for Harlow's conclusive demonstration of the obvious suggests a more important conclusion: a connection between our culture's celebration of brutal objectivity in the interests of "knowledge" and its inability to diagnose and prevent epidemic levels of violence, abuse, and neglect of its children. Perhaps the most redeeming lessons we can learn from captive primates come from being confronted by research objects we have turned into embodiments of our own psychopathology.[30]

## The Evolving Primate: Upright, Walking, and Thinking

Hominids gradually diverged from their primate ancestors through a series of evolutionary novelties that seemed to reinforce one another in conferring selective survival advantage. What most distinguishes humans from apes and monkeys is our upright gait, our capacity to run long distances on two legs, language, our degree of social complexity, and our high level of self-reflective consciousness, giving us the capacity for creativity and choice. As early hominids like *Australopithecus africanus* moved out of the forest canopy to colonize the newly open savanna, the upright posture conferred a distinct survival advantage. It offered a larger field of vision, and it made running more efficient by minimizing heat stress, since less of the body surface area was exposed to direct sunlight. This feature became increasingly critical as the brain, a heat-sensitive organ, enlarged. Running long distances also made it possible to chase down game, supporting the omnivorous diet necessary for the rapid development of the brain in a growing child.

Upright gait also frees the hands. By 2.5 million years ago, as we entered the lower Paleolithic, or the early Stone Age, we find evidence for the appearance of a smallish (seventy-pound), upright, large-brained, still apelike creature, together with a large number of the first crude stone tools. *Homo habilis*, or "handy man," had arrived. In general, as hunting and fishing efficiency slowly increases, so does the availability of high-quality protein. Primates showed almost a gram-for-gram trade-off in the expansion of the brain with the reduction of gut length, as the nutritional value of the diet improved from the predominantly vegetarian australopithecines to the more omnivorous *Homo*.[31]

Further, as we have noted, the biodynamics of walking and running limits the size of the hips, and this shapes another series of complementary evolutionary changes: narrower female hips mean infants are born smaller and mature more slowly; thus child rearing necessarily involves more social cooperation and communication; and this selects for greater intelligence, making possible greater individuation. This process is also aided by vocalization, which becomes possible as the face and neck are aligned by the upright posture. Upright posture also seems associated with the evolution of human sexual dimorphism — the anatomical and physiological differences between the sexes — and sexual behavior. Humans developed enlarged breasts and protruding penises as part of sexual display, which in turn stimulated year-round sexual activity, further compounding social complexity.[32]

A society composed of more highly individuated individuals shows a greater range and complexity of relationships. Negotiating this complexity feeds back, putting selective pressure on intelligence, in an autocatalytic process that accelerated until around 1.7 million years ago, when *Homo erectus* appeared for the first time (separated from an earlier putative *Homo ergaster*), fully upright, capable of walking and running long distances, and probably fortified with rudimentary language and simple hunting tools. Globalization began with *erectus* setting out from Africa, exploring, colonizing, and thriving in Europe and Asia, where it might have remained in some places until a hundred thousand years ago.[33]

Earlier humans were "habitat specialists" who lacked the ability to exploit a wide variety of environments during seasonal fluctuations. Modern humans are extravagantly adaptable, capable of colonizing environments from arctic tundra and rain forest to polluted, overcrowded cities and sterile space stations. Suddenly, around sixty thousand years ago, these fully developed humans seemed to burst out of Africa and almost instantaneously appeared throughout the Eurasian continent, moving down Southeast Asia to populate New Guinea and Australia. Until about forty-five thousand years ago, Neanderthals had western Europe to themselves. By twenty-seven thousand years ago, they had completely disappeared.[34]

Most of the earlier archaeological work on the emergence of modern human behavior was originally conducted by European scholars on the European *Homo sapiens sapiens*, which scholars named Cro-Magnon. The radical discontinuity between Neanderthal and Cro-Magnon sites and the absence of comparable evidence for modernity outside of Europe suggested a European "creative explosion," both flattering to Europeans and convenient for their archaeologists. This long-reigning theory is now challenged by a wealth of new evidence uncovered in the rock shelters and middens — the piles of shell and bone debris made by early humans — along the South African coast over the past few decades. This provides powerful evidence for a much earlier, more gradual emergence of *Homo sapiens sapiens*, which now seems to have started along the southern African coastline roughly two hundred thousand years ago.

Literally thousands of Paleolithic shell middens dot the beaches of this coastline. Thirty-five hundred have been documented between the shore's high-water mark and five kilometers inland, and this is estimated to be about 10 percent of the total. In other words, there are perhaps thirty thousand middle and late Stone Age middens along this coast, not including those that were covered as ocean levels rose to their present state about twelve thousand years ago.[35] In addition to the middens, the rock coastline is full of widely gaping rock shelters with remains going back to the middle Paleolithic, some thirty of which have been extensively excavated. Evidence from these middle Stone Age sites indicates that group size and within-group kin relations were the same as those in the later stone age and among present-day hunter-gatherers.[36]

Curtis Marean, who has guided much of the recent research, points out that between one hundred ninety-five thousand and one hundred twenty-five thousand years ago the world was in a glacial ice age, with much of the African continent dry and desertified. His analysis of the paleo-environmental data of ocean currents, weather patterns, and geological formations indicates there were few sites in sub-Saharan Africa that could have supported a human population. One was at Pinnacle Point near the town of Mossel Bay on the South African coast. When his international team of archaeologists excavated the site, it discovered the oldest evidence of a human seafood diet, together with small stone blades, finely worked points, and, most importantly, traces of worked ochre, generally used for symbolic purposes, going back some one hundred sixty thousand years.[37]

Farther east along the same coastline is Blombos Cave, where Chris Henshilwood found one of the oldest pieces of clearly symbolic representation, a seventy-seven-thousand-year-old chunk of ochre with a complex cross-hatched design (see photograph, page 160). Additional pieces of more crudely engraved ochre have since been found at the same site going back one hundred thousand years, with traces of ochre at the one-hundred-sixty-thousand-year level.[38]

Then in 2011 Henshilwood made another dramatic discovery of two ochre "painting kits" at the one-hundred-thousand-year level of the cave. The kits consisted of abalone shell containers with remains of a complex pigment mix, including fat from a heat-treated seal bone, charcoal, and ground ochre, found together with simple grinding tools. The nearest source of ochre is thirty to forty kilometers away. The kits were found close together without any surrounding detritus, as if brought there for a short period and forgotten. The painting kits reveal the first known use of a container and the first instance of deliberate planning, production, and curing of a compound. While the production of a complex pigment is suggestive of symbolic activity, the seventy-seven-thousand-year-old carved ochre discovery constitutes hard evidence for symbolically mediated human behavior at least forty thousand years prior to the cave paintings of Europe.[39]

*Piece of carved ochre, seventy-seven thousand years old, found by Chris Henshilwood at Blombos Cave on the South African coastline. This is currently the oldest piece of symbolic representation in the world.* (Photo: Christopher Henshilwood)

Henshilwood and Marean have marshaled this new evidence to reveal a subtle circularity and Eurocentric bias in the older theory of the European creative explosion. They suggest shifting the definition of modern human behavior from the standard laundry list of necessary traits — the behavioral "b's": blades, beads, bone tools, barter, and beauty — to the more fundamental criterion of the use of symbols in mediating behavior.[40] Accordingly, they define modern human behavior as "behavior that is mediated by socially constructed patterns of symbolic thinking, actions and communication that allow for material and information exchange and cultural continuity between and across generations and contemporaneous communities."[41] Symbols allow us to store information outside of the brain, and more importantly, they allow us to communicate the information to others and to deepen and complexify our relationship to the past and the future. Symbols sharpen the poles of our in-between situation as "created" and "creators," marking the beginning of the quest in storytelling, politics, religion, and ethics.

This more sophisticated theory and the wealth of new evidence support the recently proposed "southern dispersal" theory of human migration out of Africa. This argues that as the remnant coastal population thrived on the wealth of seafood, it expanded and started walking rapidly east and north, up the coast of South Africa into Arabia, Southeast Asia, and eventually New Guinea and Australia.

## The Quest by Running

We can see the mandala of primal politics gradually emerge as a single tensional complex in the transition from *Homo erectus* to *Homo sapiens*. At one pole is the self-reflective independent individual who becomes increasingly individuated in the process of relating in ever more complex ways to the opposite pole — the tightly bonded, cooperative, caring community. Conversely, the community becomes increasingly cooperative and bonded with the growth in the self-reflective capacity of the individual. With the appearance of language and symbolic painting, the two polarities of face-to-face discussion and storytelling start to synergize, and the four coordinates of the mandala of primal politics shift firmly into place.

All the while, this individual-group dynamic is conditioned by an increasingly complex and intimate relationship to the wilderness within which everyone lives, the larger community of animals and plants. We cannot, obviously, talk to ancient peoples and have them describe this relationship in their own terms. We can, however, make imaginative reconstructions based on a number of extrapolations. We know we are part of a single continuous biological lineage going back to a common ancestor, and so we can reflect on our own range of experiences in wilderness. We can study historical and contemporary hunters and gatherers who have lived continuously within wilderness and examine their cultures. This is largely the focus of chapter 8, in which I look at the relationship between rock art and trance states in San Bushman culture, and of chapter 9, where I explore its wider context.

For now, a brief example helps indicate how we can imaginatively extrapolate from the present concerning what our ancestral relationship to wilderness might have been like. A recent remarkable documentary film, *The Great*

*Dance*, tells the story of one of the last groups of San Bushman hunters who were raised in a traditional nomadic culture. It highlights how the activity of tracking and then running down an antelope — the endurance hunt — can induce profound alterations in consciousness, where the hunter goes into shamanic trance and accesses paranormal powers.[42] The film follows three hunters from the /Gwi and !Xo bands of Bushmen of the Central Kalahari Desert as they track and chase an adult kudu — a large desert-adapted antelope. The hunt takes place during the midday heat with temperatures reaching 110 degrees. Once the kudu is spotted, they chase, running barefoot for four hours without pausing, until the animal, exhausted, gives itself up to the hunters. Afterward, one of the hunters talks about how he entered an altered state of consciousness, where barriers between inner and outer, hunter and kudu, human and God seemed to break down. He describes "entering kudu mind" and "controlling her." He compares tracking to the shamanic, ritual dancing, the primary religious activity in traditional Bushman life, in which "you are talking with God." Here we see hunting converge with peak religious experience, so that even an act of killing becomes a direct experience of communion with nature as sacred.

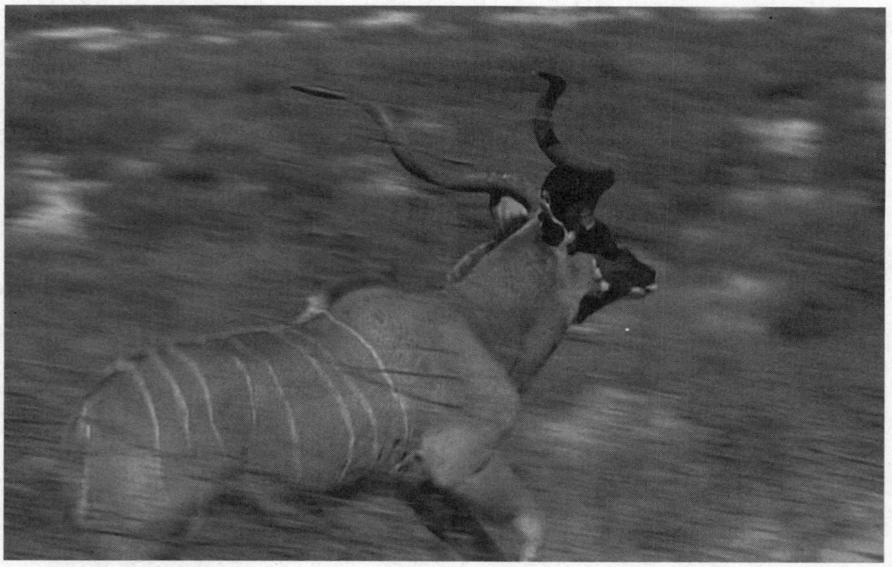

*Adult male kudu in flight.* (*Photo: Craig and Damon Foster*)

*Hunter in pursuit: the endurance hunt as recorded in the film* The Great Dance. *(Photo: Craig and Damon Foster)*

As indoor, sedentary humans in a thoroughly mechanized, symbol-saturated society, plagued by inactivity, obesity, and stress, we can easily forget just how well prepared our species is for tracking and running down game over a sun-baked savanna. Not only do we forget our toughness and versatility — the fact that the human is the only animal that can run a marathon, then swim a river and climb a tree — but as we sit inside at our desks in front of our computers, we tend to forget how embedded our consciousness is in our body. In our spiritually autistic culture, the "runner's high" is reduced to endorphin chemistry — a feel-good recreation allowing us to return to work refreshed. But running across open veldt and along mountain trails can give us a profound inner experience of an outer reality to which our culture is oblivious: how our self-conscious humanity emerged from, and remains connected to, the primate body in vigorous action across a wilderness landscape. The Bushman hunter makes the simple equation between tracking, dancing, and "talking with God." Such disciplines (and there are many) keep our thinking anchored in the experience of the in-between. Ultimately, it is this inner experience of connection to the mystery of our wilderness origins that can function as the experiential center of the moral gyroscope of primal politics.

## A Childlike Species

If we step back and look at humanity's leap into self-awareness against the broad outlines of the past six million years of primate evolution, we notice adult humans have more in common with the juvenile chimpanzee than we have with the adult. As with the adult human, the young chimp's head is bigger in proportion to the rest of the body, the face is flatter, the bones are thinner, and there is a dramatic rising of the forehead. The skulls of infant apes are rounded like those of a human, and their body proportions are closer to those of humans. Similarly, the adult human seems closer in appearance to the children of Neanderthals than to the adults. This suggests the operation of an evolutionary mechanism called *pedomorphism*, which is the retention, by adults in a species, of traits previously seen primarily in juveniles.

Even more dramatic is the way human pedomorphism manifests those aspects of primate childishness most associated with creativity — play and imagination. All higher mammals have periods of childhood openness where the behavior and awareness of the young are disconnected from any fixed action-pattern response, and the young need to be cared for and taught, well or badly, by the adults. With *sapiens* this period of openness is so extended and enlarged that it becomes one of the defining marks of the species. The range in which human consciousness can stray from fixed action-pattern response seems almost limitless. We could say we are genetically coded for transgenetic or epigenetic coding; we are wired to go beyond wiring into freedom, culture, and creativity.

When something enters into animal consciousness, the animal responds with an automatic action pattern. Two lions approach a group of grazing zebras. The zebras notice, stiffen, and watch carefully. When the lions reach a certain distance, the zebras gallop off. Once the lions have made their kill and are busy eating, the zebras will graze peacefully nearby. Most of this is automatic. On the other hand, when something new enters human consciousness, we don't automatically respond. We have the capacity to stop, notice, and let ourselves simply be amused and amazed. We love to play.

Brian Thomas Swimme points out that all other species are magnificently and intricately specialized to know instinctively what to do. "Birds have colonized the air, dolphins and whales are fully integrated into an ocean existence. But with specialization comes limitation. Fins cannot craft tools, fondle a baby, perform surgery or operate a computer. We lose the highly refined senses of smell and hearing; we lose the great muscular strength of the apes."[43] Humans are consummate generalists, amateurs, childishly open, flexible, playful, creative, insatiably curious, and easily distracted. Our specialization is our lack of specialization.

Swimme gives the example of how play could have operated in humanity's acquisition of fire. Imagine a scene a couple of hundred thousand years ago on the highveld during a tremendous summer electrical storm. Lightning strikes. Humans watch as a tree bursts into flames. Monkeys, birds, antelope all flee from fire. They immediately and automatically know what to do as the event enters their consciousness. Not so humans. We can imagine an early ancestor watching, fascinated, approaching the fire, picking up a burning branch, waving it, playing with it, no doubt getting burned — all the while not really knowing what he or she is getting into.[44]

We need to recognize how enormous a novelty the appearance of human creativity and self-consciousness is — an evolutionary leap perhaps comparable to the movement of vertebrates onto land about 370 million years ago. Creativity emerges within a natural world from which it can imaginatively separate itself. Rather than being dominated by the anxious radical doubt of Descartes, it likely emerged closer to the radical amazement of philosophers like Heschel. Like Socrates, Heschel recognized that wonder fuels our fascination with the world and energizes us to engage life as a whole, through all the senses and faculties available to us.[45] It drives our thinking toward the bigger picture, the ever larger story. This stimulates personal growth in wholeness and an enthusiasm for tasting the full amplitude of human experience. Wonder at the miracle of existence balances anxiety and fear.

We need to remember that our coming to consciousness takes place on a planet of stunning natural beauty and relative plenty. Anxiety is balanced by ecstasy. Today we are so jaded by our immersion in artificial and polluted environments, so desensitized to natural beauty, so anxious and fearful that we automatically sneer at the nostalgia of romantics who would attribute to primal peoples an enhanced appreciation for the beauty and numinosity of wilderness. The bigger picture helps us keep our balance between amazement and fear. It encourages us to go more deeply into our childlike creativity, so we can grow and mature without losing our capacity for wonder. The big story helps remind us of the fact that words and concepts

— language itself — emerge from the natural world. It helps correct hubris by honoring the larger creativity out of which we emerge, cautioning us against worshipping the secondary realities of our own creations.

## Fire for the Quest

Fire making, language, and art seem to constitute a powerful complex of evolutionary novelties that reinforce one another, catapulting human beings into full self-reflective consciousness. This full flowering of consciousness can be regarded as the original or primal leap in being making possible that last migration of *Homo sapiens* out of Africa to colonize the planet.

Fire making — the ability to produce fire at will — was certainly in place by a hundred thousand years ago and possibly as far back as five hundred thousand years.[46] Fire is power, warmth, protection, cooked food. More importantly, it is the primordial technology of consciousness. The campfire burns at the literal center of both the community and the truth quest. Anyone who has spent time in wild places knows the importance of the campfire as the center of camp life. Night is free from the focused struggles of the daily round of hunting and gathering, yet darkness typically means sleep. With the campfire, humans created the ideal playground for imagination, language, and culture.

Melvin Konner, a Harvard biologist who lived with the San for two years in a remote part of the Kalahari, speculates on the importance of fire as a catalyst for language.

> When we slept in a grass hut in one of their villages, there were many nights when its flimsy walls leaked charged exchanges from the circle around the fire, frank expressions of feeling and contention beginning when the dusk fires were lit and running on until the dawn. Surely a potent selection pressure for the evolution of language must have been the respect gained by a person whose voice commanded attention around such fires.
>
> ...I came to think of the Pleistocene epoch of human history (the three million years during which we evolved) as one interminable marathon encounter group.[47]

The circle of people, young and old, men and women, sitting around the campfire, talking, telling stories, joking, and singing is the original embodiment of the mandala of primal politics. The people sit and confront one

*Painted figures on the wall of a rock shelter in the Drakensberg. The dancing stick and distortion suggest trance experience.* (Photo: Author)

another face-to-face, as unique individuals yet also self-evidently a part of the unity of the circle, which, like the circle of humanity, is surrounded by the circle of wilderness. The primordial cosmological elements are matters of direct experience and accessible to all. Above, the sun moves by day, and the moon and stars by night; below, all beings walk, sit, and sleep on the sandy earth. Even around the campfire the worlds interpenetrate. The surrounding bush comes alive with noise, the bark of antelope, anonymous grunts, squeals, rustling, crashing. Lions can be heard roaring miles away, or sometimes, mysteriously, they will visit the human camp, seldom causing harm so long as they are not harmed.

The realms interpenetrate. In traditional San Bushman culture, the stories tell of the creatures of the early times, which one can also encounter in trance through the shamanic healing dance and which are painted on the walls of the shelter, imbuing the walls with magical potency. During the shamanic dance, the group of singers sits around the fire clapping and singing. Around them a circle of dancers stamps in time to the rhythm for hours, until the exertion, dehydration, and magical songs propel them into shamanic states of consciousness, where they have the experience of traveling outside their bodies and can access the entities and forces of the spirit world, the early times, for healing and guidance.

The most dramatic hard evidence for the first expression of complex symbolic activity is the exquisite cave paintings going back over thirty thousand years found in underground caverns in southwestern Europe. Because the European paintings were well preserved deep underground, and because they were near European universities, they have received a disproportionate amount of scholarly attention. Only relatively recently did scholars discover that a comparable but far richer rock painting tradition exists in southern Africa. The southern African paintings are far more numerous and not only extend back into prehistory but carry forward into the nineteenth century. Even more illuminating is the fact that they can be connected to a Bushman cosmology and shamanic-religious practice centering on the trance dance.

Chapter 8, "If You Don't Dance, You Die," discusses this southern African rock art in detail. While it remains difficult to verify exactly what the images mean, what's unmistakable is that the paintings were of supreme importance to the people who painted them. Like ritual religious dancing, the art was part of the larger storytelling that occurred around those same campfires. Bushman mythology today seems to be a kind of living, breathing archaeology of consciousness, bringing the deep past into the present. It preserves in metaphoric form some of the first glimmerings of conscious self-awareness. Still today, the old stories, the *hua*, are told and retold around the fire, the teller often giving a personal inflection. The two most popular and widely distributed myths across all the Bushman groups deal with the acquisition of fire and the awareness of death — both defining aspects of the in-between.[48] Fire is a catalyst for consciousness, and with greater self-consciousness comes a sharpened sense of mortality, the coming into being and passing of all things.

In one Bushman retelling of the fire myth, it is mantis, the trickster deity and the intermediary between human and animal, who steals fire from the animals. He discovers the ostrich roasting its food and then hiding the fire under its wing in its armpit.[49] Mantis tricks ostrich by offering to lead her to a delicious fruit. He then persuades her to reach for the highest, tastiest fruit. As she opens her wings to balance, the mantis snatches some of the fire. Much of the metaphoric resonance of such a story would be lost on an audience that never sat looking into the face of a mantis or successfully tricked an ostrich and stole its eggs. Such stories emerged out of the early days of consciousness and, like half-remembered dream fragments, convey a compact meaning in metaphors of the bush that defy simple translation into the language of city dwellers. What does translate is that fire is stolen, which is a universal theme in world mythology. The stealing suggests a capacity for deception and the possibility of human society falling into disorder inherent in the leap into greater awareness. Animals losing fire revert to an unambiguous animality. Humans gaining fire become fully human and usher in the present order.

Bushman storytelling can be understood as a primary way of healing the split, of mediating the anxiety of the in-between, and thus tuning human politics to the great mysterious community of being. Today instead of family and community gathering around the campfire, we sit in front of the television set. Instead of being connected to an embodied community through face-to-face discussion and storytelling, we follow the lives of celebrities in the news and familiar characters in soap operas; our communication is through cell phone and Internet. Our city lights hide the stars and planets; wilderness is paved over and walled out. Brian Thomas Swimme points to the tragic irony of modernity: our discoveries of the immensity of the cosmos remain academic abstractions, while emotionally we live in an imaginative world still constricted by artifacts, things, cities, offices, and homes of our own making.

As we lose the direct visceral contact with the larger community of being, so the telling and retelling of the big story of origin becomes increasingly critical to remind us that "all the wonders of Africa are within us." Today walled off in the urban prisons of our own making, we cannot fully free ourselves without science and history, technology and philosophy. The knife that cuts also heals. We need the technologies associated with our alienation from nature to help us relearn the amazing reality of our condition: that we all wake up within a single story telling us into being. We are all fundamentally connected, dependent on a larger order not of our making; yet we are free and creative.

CHAPTER 6

# LOST WORLDS

What the world lacks today is not so much knowledge of these first things as experience of them. We know so much intellectually, indeed, that we are in danger of becoming the prisoners of our knowledge. We suffer from a hubris of the mind. We have abolished superstition of the heart only to install a superstition of the intellect.

— Laurens van der Post, *Heart of the Hunter*

"Bushmen" and "San" are invented categories…ethnographic reification[s]…. Nostalgia for an innocent past before we Europeans were cast out into the sorrows of self-awareness spawned the current form of "Bushmen"; it is a negative form of metaphor predicated on an urge to retain a mythic image of the childhood of humanity.

— Edwin Wilmsen, *Decolonizing the Mind: Steps toward Cleansing the Bushman Stain from Southern African History*

In the olden days the times were very good, they were very, very good. Today we have gone back, back, back, backwards, we have been put down, why, why? That time long ago when we were alone, when there were no whites, no army, no politics, when it was just us Bushman people, we fixed everything ourselves, then the white people came and brought politics here.

— Kxao, to Paul Weinberg, *Once We Were Hunters*

## Those Who Never Left

Some sixty thousand years ago, when modern humans moved out of Africa and eventually colonized every habitable continent on the planet, some humans remained in southern Africa. Their direct descendants are the San Bushmen, who until recently lived a traditional hunting-gathering way of life in the great Kalahari Desert covering eastern Namibia, northern South Africa and much of Botswana. After decades of intense debate among scholars as to the origin and identity of Bushmen, the click-language-speaking hunter-gatherers of the Kalahari are now being accepted as most likely the closest living relatives to that aboriginal African population from which all modern humans are descended.*

Hunting-gathering ancestors of San Bushmen occupied most of South Africa relatively undisturbed until about two thousand years ago, when the closely related but distinct Khoi-speaking herder people started moving down the east coast. Genetic and linguistic evidence suggests the Khoi — also Khoikhoi, sometimes spelled "Khoe" and "Khoekhoe" and derogatorily known as "Hottentot" — were earlier northern Bushmen who had acquired domesticated sheep and cattle from their Bantu neighbors. As the Khoi moved south down the east coast of South Africa, they were closely followed by Bantu-speaking farmers migrating down from central Africa's Great Lakes region. Although all three groups influenced one another (all the clicks in Xhosa and Zulu are thought to come from contact with Bushman languages), the nomadic hunters and gatherers retained some autonomy by progressively retreating from the fertile well-watered coastal plain into the more arid and mountainous interior.

---

* To reiterate an important and often misunderstood point: "shortest distance" to common ancestor doesn't mean Bushmen haven't developed or evolved since that period, as all other humans have. But "closeness" does imply that many more features (genetic, linguistic, and presumably cultural) of the original population have been retained when compared to populations that evolved outside Africa.

At the time of European settlement in the eighteenth-century, there were an estimated one dozen separate Bushman language groups confined to specific geographic regions of southern Africa. The now-extinct /Xam-speaking Bushmen, the largest and most widely dispersed group, provided the source for the extensive ethnography compiled by the nineteenth-century German philologist Wilhelm Bleek and his sister-in-law, Lucy Lloyd.[1]

*/Akunta, one of Bleek's collaborators.*
*(Photo: Craig Foster/archive)*

Some of the most significant new evidence for identifying the ancestors of the San as the founder population comes from an enormous global genetic mapping project based on analysis of mitochondrial and Y-chromosome DNA. Mitochondrial DNA is inherited without mixing entirely from the mother; and Y-chromosome DNA, possessed only by men, is similarly inherited without mixing from the father. As mutations occur, they are passed on to progeny unchanged. The identification and mapping of these markers across different distinct populations has made it possible to construct a rough genetic tree for all of modern humanity and then to measure the distance of any geographically and genetically isolated population from a common ancestry.

The basic principle is that genetic diversity, measured by the inheritance of specific mutations — markers — on Y and mitochondrial DNA, decreases with distance from ancestry. This might at first seem counterintuitive, but the reason is simply that not all members of the earlier population moved on to populate the new area; therefore, only a fraction of the full range of genetic diversity in the original pool was carried forth out of Africa. Thus we find that the hunting-gathering populations of San Bushmen of Namibia and Botswana have the *highest level of genetic diversity* of all human groups studied, indicating that they are the closest living relatives to that ancestral population from which all other humans branched.[2]

Another line of research supporting the close connection between Bushmen and the founder population comes from linguistics. Bushman languages are famously distinguished by their complexity, their unpronounceable clicks, and their diversity. As with genetics, the antiquity of a language can be inferred from its complexity as measured by the number of phonemes it contains. Phonemes are the basic units of sounds that make up words, and the general principle is that the greater the number of phonemes, the more complex and ancient the language. Thus, Hawaiian, one of the youngest languages, is at one extreme with 13 phonemes; English has around 45 phonemes; Bushman languages have the largest number — !Xo, for example, has 126 identifiable phonemes — strongly suggesting their status as a founder language.[3]

The genetic, linguistic, and geographic evidence has recently been reinforced by dramatic archaeological findings at an exceptionally well-preserved site — Border Cave — in the foothills of the Lebombo Mountains in northern South Africa. The site contains a wealth of artifacts dating back forty-four thousand years that are strikingly similar to those used by contemporary San Bushmen. The list includes digging sticks with perforated weighted stones, the distinctive ostrich eggshell beads that even today adorn San jewelry, fine bone points for awls and arrowheads, traces of resin and beeswax used to attach arrow- and tool heads; and, most extraordinary of all, a wooden poison applicator with traces of poison mixed with beeswax.[4] Use of small poisoned arrows is one of the most complex and characteristic of traditional San hunting methods and suggests a high level of cognitive and cultural development.

This recent accumulation of hard evidence supports extensive ethnographic studies showing common ritual and mythological elements shared by widely dispersed, distinct Bushman groups across southern Africa. The most striking of these is the characteristic healing trance dance practiced by most traditional San, which has now been connected to the extensive and ancient pictorial record of the rock paintings going back almost thirty thousand years.

The picture emerging is that of the original hunter-gatherer continuing to develop in wilderness close to the sites of our last leap into modern human culture and consciousness. While conditions have changed many times over the past hundred thousand years, and the San themselves continue to change and develop, nevertheless they hold a privileged position among all living societies in helping us imaginatively reconstruct the "lost world" of that original population from which we all descended.

This chapter continues the story of who we are by piecing together the accounts of the first explorers and then of the amateur adventurers and professional anthropologists who encountered Bushmen still living a hunting-gathering lifestyle. As noted before, any story is inevitably shaped to some degree by the life-world and purpose of the storyteller, and most of the first-hand accounts of the traditional life of the Bushmen have been shaped by the methods, motives, and perspective of professional academia, a world that couldn't be further from that of the subjects themselves. In that sense, from a Bushman perspective, we could say that scholars live in another lost world, cut off from that shared hunting-and-gathering, wilderness-immersed way of life that originally defined what it meant to be human. Bringing these two radically different life-worlds together takes us further along in our quest for a healing vision of a primal-postmodern synthesis — a *future primal* politics.

## Contact

The Portuguese nobleman-explorer Bartholomew Diaz was the first European to round the southern tip of Africa, in 1488, opening up the vital sea route to the Indies. But Portuguese navigators avoided stopping at the Cape unless forced, partly because of the dangers of the rocky, stormy coastline and partly because of possible conflict with the native inhabitants. By this time most Bushmen along the southern coast had been displaced by Khoikhoi and their large herds of sheep and oxen. In 1510, Admiral Don Francisco de Almeida, first Portuguese viceroy of India, was compelled to land at Table Bay, the site of present-day Cape Town, to replenish his supplies of water and food. His experience with the groups of Khoikhoi he found onshore followed a pattern that was to be repeated throughout the New World as Western imperialists encountered indigenous peoples still living on intimate terms with wilderness.

According to the Portuguese accounts, the encounter went well enough until the Khoi started helping themselves to more trade goods than were offered. A fight broke out, and the trading party was beaten back to the ship, bruised, bleeding, and humiliated. The Portuguese then rashly attempted to punish the Khoi by stealing their cattle and kidnapping a few of their children. The Khoi were unconcerned about the animals, who were trained to come when called, but the capture of their children infuriated them. They charged after the Europeans, whistling and calling to their herds, who, unknown to the Portuguese, were also trained as war oxen. The cattle stampeded through the Portuguese forces causing considerable injury and death. The remaining Portuguese were driven back to their ships, chased by furious Khoi racing nimbly across the sand wielding their fire-hardened sticks and pelting the invaders with well-aimed stones from their slingshots. Half the Portuguese forces were killed in the encounter. The Khoikhoi were left in peace and remained masters of the Southern Cape for the next century and a half, until the Dutch arrived in force.[5]

In general, Europeans saw the leather-clad Khoikhoi, in the words of Reverend Terry in 1616, as "beasts in the skins of men, rather than men in the skins of beasts."[6] A typical seventeenth-century Dutch traveler described Khoikhoi pastoralists as "having everything in common with dumb cattle, barring their human nature, from which, occasionally some co-ordination of the senses may bring forth a spark of intelligence.... They are thus very dissolute and in every way like animals, for they are wild rough and unclean in their habits.... There are no signs of Beliefs or Religion to be found among them and it is for this reason they are called *Cafres* (*Kaffirs*)."[7] Few Europeans actually had the opportunity or desire to live among Khoikhoi or Bushmen. Among those who did were two Dutch sailors who spent two years at the Cape after their ship, the *Haerlem*, was wrecked in 1648. Less concerned with racist ideology than their own experience, they denied that Hottentots were "brutish and cannibals" and noted that, where conflict did occur with settlers, it had more to do with the "uncivilized and ungrateful conduct of our folks."[8] There are repeated accounts by English seafarers of the friendly, courteous, and generous behavior of the natives.[9] However, self-serving prejudice prevailed, as indicated by an entry from the 1889 *Oxford English Dictionary*, which defined *Hottentot* figuratively as a "person of inferior intellect or culture." In the nineteenth century, some of the more imaginative and adventurous traveler-scholars discovered elements of religion, mythology, and ritual, but for the most part (with a few exceptions) scholars were incapable of moving beyond condescension or at best simple confusion.

As the Dutch settlement in southern Africa grew, independent settlers moved east along the coast, displacing Khoikhoi and eventually coming into conflict with the Bantu-speaking Nguni (including Zulus and Xhosas), who had moved down the east coast to the Fish River area. Surviving nomadic hunting-and-gathering Bushmen were increasingly pushed into remote mountain and desert wilderness, where they survived into the nineteenth century. By the twentieth century, there was no longer a coherent Bushman cultural entity in South Africa. Tribes were fragmented, and survivors worked under serflike conditions on isolated farms. However, hunter-gatherers survived farther north in the great sand-and-scrub desert of the Kalahari.

## "The Lost World of the Kalahari"

The Kalahari, one of the largest sand deserts in the world, is approximately one hundred thousand square miles in area and has no surface water for about three hundred days of the year. But unlike the Sahara, it is covered with grasses, tough bushes, and acacia thorn trees, which survive by sending roots deep into supplies of underground water. In the 1950s, when the first serious Bushman studies started, some ten thousand Bushmen still lived a hunting-and-gathering way of life for at least parts of the year, in a sustainable population density of one person to every ten square miles.

The accounts of amateurs, adventurers, and anthropologists of the lives of these people over the next few decades have given us a wealth of first-hand information about the Bushmen's more or less self-sufficient hunting-gathering lifestyle. Given the distance between the life-world of modern academia and life in the bush, it is not surprising that some of the more evocative accounts of Bushman existence come from amateurs. Less constrained by the rigors of professional and methodological paradigms, they relied more on common sense and creative imagination to express the truth of direct experience and served a different rigor — that of the search for meaning.

Perhaps the best known and most controversial of the amateur poet-anthropologists was the Afrikaner writer, soldier, and explorer Laurens van der Post, whose romanticized first-person account of finding wild Bushmen living in the Kalahari Desert captured the imagination of readers all over the world. At roughly the same time, the Marshall family — father, mother, son, and daughter — went to live with an isolated nomadic band of Bushmen in Nyae Nyae. The Marshalls returned for a total of eight expeditions covering several decades. The experience changed them profoundly and made it possible for them to lay the foundations for subsequent scholarly work on the Bushmen.

Van der Post's story, as he told it, was an allegorical quest of a white African in search of soul.[10] He was born in 1906 into an Afrikaans-speaking family, descended from the earliest Dutch-Huguenot pioneer farmer Voortrekkers. He was raised on his grandfather's farm, Bushmansprings, in the Southern Free State near the banks of the Orange River — wilderness frontier territory that until the nineteenth century had been Bushman country. Van der Post's grandfather helped organize one of the Boer commandos that exterminated the last nomadic Bushmen from the southern edge of the Kalahari. During one raid, two young boys were captured and taken back to the farm as servants. They became van der Post's mentors and closest companions, along with Klara, his Coloured* nursemaid. Van der Post's mother reinforced this indigenous education by reading him "Bushman fairy tales" — the recently published collection from Wilhelm Bleek and Lucy Lloyd's archives of /Xam Bushman mythology. All of this moved van der Post so deeply, as he tells it, that he made a childhood pact with himself, recorded in his journal in High Dutch, to one day go out into the desert, try to find surviving Bushmen, and atone in some way for the genocide inflicted on them.

---

* As mentioned, "Coloured" or "Cape-Coloured" (*Kleuring* in Afrikaans) is an apartheid-era category that refers to the mixed Khoisan (San-Khoikhoi)/European/Malay/African population around the Western Cape. Genetic mapping, following the mitochondrial DNA of the mother's lineage, indicates South African Coloureds have the highest level of mixed ancestry of any population in the world. See Sarah A. Tishkoff et al., "Genetic Structure and History of Africans and African Americans," *Science* 22, no. 324 (May 2009): 1035–44. Coloureds speak Afrikaans as their first language, and for this reason they are sometimes called Bruin Afrikaners ("Brown Afrikaners"). Many to this day still exhibit the delicate Bushman features described by van der Post. There is now a movement among some groups to recover their lost Khoisan identity.

Van der Post was self-conscious about the mythic and heroic dimensions of his own story: he was an Afrikaner farm boy who eventually became adviser to a British prime minister, counselor to the future king of England, godfather to Prince William, authority on the Swiss psychiatrist C. G. Jung, and an internationally acclaimed writer. During World War II, he commanded a British guerrilla force behind Japanese lines in Java until he was captured, and then he spent the rest of the war as a prisoner in a Japanese concentration camp. After the trauma of war, he returned to heal in South Africa. In 1950 he led a British government–sponsored expedition to the Kalahari Desert, at the time one of the least explored wilderness areas in southern Africa, and he returned convinced that there were "wild" Bushmen living in its remotest areas. Five years later he again set out, leading his own expedition, and eventually he encountered nomadic Bushmen still living as self-sufficient hunter-gatherers.

Van der Post's writings were another bridge to my own lost past. While still an undergraduate at Cambridge, I had ignored the recommendation of a fellow South African to read this "amazing Afrikaner." At the time I was in the full flush of newfound intellectualism. My politics were utopian and Zionist. South Africa seemed a backwater of history, still in the grip of Calvinist fundamentalism and serving the doomed fantasy of a racist state. I couldn't imagine I might learn something important from someone raised on an Afrikaans farm. It was only years later, in Hawai'i, my certainties gone, that I opened *The Lost World of the Kalahari*. I recognized with some shame how cold and hard our proud scientific detachment was compared to van der Post's evocation of the Bushman's passionate full-bodied knowing:

> He knew the animal and vegetable life, the rocks and the stones of Africa as they have never been known since. Today we tend to know statistically and in the abstract. We classify, catalogue and subdivide the flame-like variety of animal and plant according to species, sub-species, physical property and use. But in the Bushman's knowing, no matter how practical, there was a dimension that I miss in the life of my own time. *He knew these things in the full context and commitment of his life.* Like them, he was utterly committed to Africa. He and his needs were committed to the nature of Africa and the swing of its wide seasons as a fish to the sea. He and they all participated so deeply of one another's being that the experience could almost be called mystical. For instance

> he seemed to know what it actually felt like to be an elephant, a lion, an antelope, a steenbuck, a lizard, a striped mouse, mantis, baobab tree, yellow-crested cobra or starry eyed amaryllis, to mention only a few of the brilliant multitudes through which he so nimbly moved. Even as a child it seemed to me that his world was one without secrets between one form of being and another. As I tried to form a picture of what he was really like, it came to me that he was back in the moment which our European fairy-tale books described as the time when birds, beasts, plants, trees and men shared a common tongue, and the whole world, night and day, resounded like the surf of a coral sea with universal conversation.[11]

I was overwhelmed with longing for something I never knew I had lost. Van der Post's Africa seemed so familiar, yet none of it had been part of my conscious identity. I had never been to the Kalahari, knew very little of its history, and had never knowingly met a Bushman. Only after years of absence, on my return pilgrimage in 1998, did I start to recover my earliest African memories. I remembered flashes from the first two years of my life in Greyton, a small farming village in the Western Cape situated on the slopes of the Riviersonderend Mountains. My father was the only doctor for the district. The village was so remote that I still had to approach it by dirt road. In the early days before the apartheid Group Areas Act, the town was racially mixed. The Coloured population was then forcibly removed to the neighboring village of Genadendal located in the Baviaanskloof — "the ravine of the baboons." Some of my earliest memory fragments surfaced: a whitewashed sunny courtyard, roosters crowing, and the loving care of my nursemaid. I realized that like van der Post, my earliest caretaker was a young part Khoisan, Cape-Coloured woman named Rosie. This was also no doubt the first and last time I heard the bark of baboons in the nearby ravines — a sound I would not consciously recognize until many years later watching that sunset with baboons in the Drakensberg. Van der Post opened the ground under my Jewish identity. For the first time I felt like a child of Africa.

However limited his anthropology, van der Post seemed to have grasped a profound political insight: that the war between the opposite forces of his childhood represented the sickness of our civilization in microcosm, the split between Afrikaner and African, "civilized" and "wild," modern and primordial. A recent biography has focused on van der Post's personal lapses, exaggerations, omissions, and dishonesties.[12] But it fails to explain the most important fact about him — why his stories resonate so deeply with so many people. He offered his life story as an instrument tuned by the archetypal opposites of life in apartheid South Africa. It was unapologetically mythic in the archaic sense of an emotionally gripping narrative of meaning that bridges the chasm between outer and inner, wilderness and civilization.[13]

## A Kalahari Family

The Marshall family moves us deeper into politics by providing the first systematic, detailed firsthand account of Bushman life — the fruit of years of living and working with the people. They laid the empirical foundations of subsequent scholarship, helping to make the Bushmen the most thoroughly studied hunter-gatherers on the planet. The Marshalls are also an inspiring example of boundary crossers, pursuing the wisdom that comes from engaging opposites.

Unlike van der Post, the Marshalls were Americans and could approach the Bushmen without preconceptions, knowing almost nothing of them. They were well educated, well-off, self-confident, and curious. All were amateurs. Laurence Marshall, the father, had retired from a distinguished career as an engineer and was looking for "an interesting project to do together with his family." He had been president of Raytheon, which had played a key role in the Allied war effort. Lorna, the mother, was a scholar of English literature; Elizabeth, the daughter, was nineteen and had just started college. John, the son, was just out of high school. Lorna became the grande dame of hunter-gatherer anthropology. Elizabeth went on to write fiction and nonfiction, most notably *The Harmless People*, a popular ethnography of the Bushmen that has been in print since 1959. John was perhaps the most profoundly affected. He learned to speak the language fluently, and at the age of twenty he fell in love with and married a young San woman. Although they later separated, he retained his sense of responsibility to the extended family throughout his life. John documented the life of the people on film, developing a style that allowed the people to speak for themselves. He returned throughout his life, continuing to film their lives and champion their causes, eventually producing a unique film archive of nomadic hunters and gatherers.[14]

In 1951 the Marshalls were guided by friends to the Nyae Nyae region of the Western Kalahari between present-day Namibia and Botswana. The Nyae Nyae region had only Bushmen — the Ju/twasi* — as permanent residents. They were divided into nineteen groups of approximately thirty to fifty individuals, with each group based on a land-right area, called *n!ores*, with enough food and water for each season. All the large predators were present — lion, leopard, cheetah, and hyena — indicating the abundance of game and the health and stability of the ecosystem.

In 2006, Elizabeth completed a poetic, deeply felt retrospective of her experiences, *The Old Way: A Story of the First People*. Her book is particularly helpful in reconstructing a more wholistic understanding of primal politics because of her special interest in the ways in which the lives of ancient humans, plants, animals, and earth were interwoven.[15] When modern hunters moved out of southern Africa some sixty thousand years ago, their arrival in every new environment in Europe, Asia, Australia, and the Americas was followed by the mass extinction of the megafauna, from woolly mammoths to saber-toothed tigers. In southern Africa, the picture was different. Only there had the big game and human hunters evolved together for most of the previous two hundred thousand years. Consequently, many animals had time to develop successful evasive and survival strategies, putting pressure on the human population to develop more sophisticated hunting strategies. The animals were just elusive enough to avoid extinction, but not fast enough to outstrip the quick-learning hunters. In this fashion, stable balance was maintained into the present.

Elizabeth noted that just as antelope responded to lions by signaling warnings, so they responded to human presence by staying just out of bowshot, a distance they seemed to know well. Giraffes would always keep a shield of tall bush between themselves and the hunter's arrows. Even the plant ecology seemed to have adapted to the human presence. Bushman veldt fires kept a certain thorn bush from taking over, opening space for a

---

* Ju/twasi is also spelled Ju/wasi (Ju/wa is singular), Zhun/twasi, and, as the linguists prefer, Ju/hoansi. This is the Bushman language group around the Nyae Nyae and Dobe areas of the Western Kalahari. They are also confusingly referred to as !Kung by earlier anthropologists. Elizabeth Marshall translates "Ju/wasi" as "the harmless people," as in the title of her first book. The Ju/twasi name for stranger is *zhu dole*, meaning "dangerous person." Non-Bushman black is *zo si*, meaning "animals without hooves" because, as they say, "non-Bushmen are angry and dangerous like lions and hyenas." The "/" is the click sound made by sharply withdrawing the tip of the tongue from behind the front teeth of the upper palate, rather like the English sound "tsk." See Elizabeth Marshall Thomas, *The Harmless People* (New York: Vintage, 1958/1989), 23.

greater variety of grasses to germinate, which in turn helped sustain a larger variety of animals. Thus the small stable populations of hunters and gatherers actually seem to have increased the biodiversity of the area.[16] Contained within this old way is the germ of a model of how the human and nonhuman worlds might continue to grow more attuned to each other in a more life-enhancing balance.

This stands in contrast to our modern Hobbesian assumption concerning the old way — that it was an endless, desperate struggle for survival, a war of all against all, in which life was "nasty, brutish, and short." Economic anthropologists found that even in the desert under reasonable conditions, Bushmen adults worked only two to three days a week to provide sufficient food for the band.[17] During the dramatic thunderstorms of the short rainy season, water collects in enormous shallow pans. Plants and animals quickly reproduce, turning the desert into a garden with a rich and ready supply of wild food, making it possible for bands to gather in large groups. Elizabeth describes the rainy season from what could well have been the point of view of our ancestors as a time of plenty:

> Roots that had been dormant during the dry season would put out their vines of melons or ground growing nuts, the thornbushes would cover themselves with berries, and the trees would put out nuts, fruits and pods of peas and beans. Animals also took advantage of the rains to multiply, so that our ancestors found edible caterpillars, baby birds, and swarms of large ants that tasted of honey.[18]

Contrary to the image of a society dominated by "man the hunter" popularized by writers like Robert Ardrey and Desmond Morris, the Bushman diet was predominantly vegetarian. This was gathered through the consistent labor of San women and children, who spent the day in the veldt and returned sometimes carrying their own body weight in nuts, roots, and other bush-food. Elizabeth compared their own store-bought vegetables to the variety of the Ju/twasi diet: "We had potatoes, sweet potatoes, onions and carrots, plus dry beans, canned pears, and canned peaches." The Ju/twasi could identify some two hundred species of plants, of which they ate about eighty: "twenty-five kinds of roots, seven or eight kinds of berries, five kinds of nuts, sixteen or seventeen kinds of fruits, three or four kinds of melons, four kinds of leaves of which two resembled spinach, eleven kinds of tree gum, and two kinds of beans from pods. They also ate palm hearts."[19]

The attunement to wilderness was most dramatically displayed in hunting and tracking. In general the men didn't need to hunt to survive, but they hunted all the time — enthusiastically encouraged by the rest of the community. The hunters favored the six big game animals — giraffe, eland, kudu, wildebeest, gemsbok, and hartebeest. Smaller animals — warthog, ostrich, duiker, steenbok, porcupine — were also hunted but not pursued with the same passion. Meat was so highly valued that the Ju/twasi had developed a separate word for "meat hunger," used in times when other food might still be plentiful. Like most South African children, I grew up addicted to the unique taste of wild meat in the form of *biltong* — sun-dried antelope meat, mainly kudu and springbok, which my family would get from friends who hunted on farms farther north. No treats or sweets could tempt me like those hard, blackened, sun-baked strips of meat. In *Women Like Meat*, Megan Biesele's study on Bushman folklore, she links craving for meat to the passions of courtship and suggests the importance of animal protein and hunting in the shift from largely vegetarian hominids to the big-brained, omnivorous modern humans.

The most common method of traditional hunting was bow and poisoned arrow. The bow is small and looks almost toy-like; the poisoned arrow, really a dart, weighs less than an ounce. Yet the poison on the tip is absolutely deadly; once it reaches the bloodstream, there is no known antidote. A single drop is enough to kill a person, and a few drops are sufficient for a big antelope. The poison is made from the grubs of certain beetles, and their equally toxic parasite, found under marula and *Commiphora africana* trees. Later in the book, I explore how early hunters might have discovered such obscure properties of the natural world through shamanic states of awareness.

The poison arrow is made in three parts. Once the arrow strikes the quarry, the impact splits a short connecting stalk, leaving the poisoned tip inside the animal while the shaft falls to the ground. The shaft provides evidence for the hunter to examine for signs of a positive strike. The poison can take a day to work, or several days for larger animals like the giraffe. During this time the hunters track the wounded animal continuously — for days, if necessary, as John Marshall documented dramatically in his classic 1957 film *The Hunters*.

Bushman sensitivity to the ecology is extraordinary. A wounded antelope might be part of a herd that splits, joins together, and then splits again, so the hunter has to be able to distinguish the tracks of the darted animal

*The hunter's quiver of poisoned arrows. The tip is free of poison to prevent lethal accidents. The poison is along the metal shaft, which is attached by a short collar to a torpedo-shaped piece of bone sharpened at both ends, the other end of which plugs into the main shaft. When the arrow strikes an animal with sufficient force, the collar breaks, leaving the poisoned shaft in the animal.* (Photo: Author)

from those of the others in the herd. In the 1990s, the filmmaker Craig Foster spent several years living with and filming master trackers (while making the film *The Great Dance: A Hunter's Story*). He describes one occasion on which a tracker seemed to make impossible inferences:

> He casually glanced some distance away and said, "Look, the tracks of a steenbok mother [small antelope], she was calling her baby." Somewhat skeptical I asked how he knew. He replied patiently, "Can you see her front hooves have dug a little deeper into the ground than the back ones? That's where she lifted her head to call and shifted her weight."[20]

Our incredulity is a measure of how far we are from a life in which success in feeding one's family depends on attention to animals and one's ability to decipher tracks in the sand.

In the 1950s, Elizabeth was amazed that Bushmen and lions seemed to have negotiated a truce, echoing the enchanted world of van der Post rather than the more common vision of terrorized humans as prey. Modern lions and humans evolved together on the savanna as ecological neighbors, both as apex predators hunting the same community of herbivores. Elizabeth pointed out that a typical Bushman group of about twenty or thirty was roughly comparable to the weight of the typical lion group of six or seven (both roughly three thousand pounds). A meal large enough for a band of people was also large enough for a group of lions. Human hunters with traditional weapons, pushed to the limits of their skill, were about as successful in the hunt as a group of lions.[21]

Elizabeth described how the Gautscha water hole near one of their camps was shared with a pride of lions, at least five hyenas, and a pair of leopards. The groups politely avoided one another, and the Bushmen never hunted or harmed the lions. Their flimsy four-foot spears were hardly a defense against a charging lion; their weapons were quite unlike those of the Maasai and Samburu, the East African pastoralists who protected their herds and hunted lions with a shield and a heavy, bladed nine-foot spear. Similarly, the tiny Bushman arrows would only infuriate an attacking lion, the poison taking hours, sometimes days, to work.

The lions seemed to show a reciprocal respect for the Bushmen. On one occasion Elizabeth's brother, John, was out filming four hunters tracking a wounded wildebeest. They found it lying down near a clump of bushes surrounded by an unusually large pride of about thirty lions and lionesses. Fragments of the encounter were captured by John on film.[22] Years later, Elizabeth retold his story:

> The four Juwasi took in the situation then slowly advanced on the lionesses, speaking firmly but respectfully, saying that the meat belonged to people. The lionesses rumbled unpleasantly. Some stood their ground. But others turned tail and retreated to the bushes. And then, although the bushes seemed alive with huge tan forms pacing and rumbling, the Juwa hunters descended on the wildebeest, tossing clumps of earth at the lionesses who were still in the open, and continuing to speak firmly and respectfully. At last the lionesses slowly, unwillingly, backed off. As soon as the lions and lionesses were screened in the bushes, the Juwa hunters seemed to give them little further thought, and turned their attention to the wildebeest; they surrounded it, killed it, skinned it, and cut it into strips to carry home, leaving nothing behind but a green cud of partly chewed grass.[23]

The Ju/twasi seemed to be matter-of-fact about the incident. As one of the Bushmen put it, "The lions around here don't harm people. Where lions kill cattle and men shoot at them, the lions are dangerous. Where lions aren't hunted, they aren't dangerous. As for us, we live in peace with them."[24] Van der Post tells legends of Bushmen using lions as hunting dogs, driving game toward where lions were known to be hiding, letting the lions make the kill and eat a share, and then driving the lions off to claim their portion. In some cases, hunter and lion would get to know each other and develop a relationship, hunting cooperatively.

Particularly fascinating to Elizabeth was that the truce with lions went beyond grudging respect to a mutual curiosity. Bushman shamans in trance tell of encountering or transforming into lion spirits, and lions appear in Bushman mythology and in the trance-related rock paintings that cover South Africa. Lions, for their part, seemed equally interested in humans and would periodically approach the camp for obscure purposes. On their second trip to Gautscha, the Marshalls arrived late in the day, after hard traveling. Too tired to put up tents or even build a fire, they spread out their sleeping bags in the open some fifty feet from the Bushman huts. During the night they heard some loud words from the Bushman camp but paid no attention. In the morning they found lion paw prints around where their sleeping heads rested on the sand. The lions had sniffed each one in turn and passed on.

On another night a large group of lions surrounded the camp and started roaring in unison, first synchronously and then one after the other. Elizabeth pointed out that the roar of a lion is the loudest noise on the veldt; under some conditions it can be heard up to twenty miles away. The earth shook and the tent rattled. The lions kept this up for twenty minutes with no gaps in the roaring. Then silence. Elizabeth went out with a lantern, but the lions were behind the tent where she couldn't see them. They seemed to want something. What? No one knew. Then out of the darkness came one of the Ju/twa men who had been on the far side of the ravine when the roaring began. Armed with only his small spear, he had woven his way through the roaring lions to be with his wife and children. There were other such occasions that Elizabeth could only explain as unsuccessful attempts on the part of lions to communicate — something — to the humans. But what?[25]

In these moments of reciprocal behavior between lion and Ju/twasi, we can recognize that some level of nonverbal communication is taking place. As we open to this we find ourselves somewhat humbled and awed as we participate in the primal epistemology of crossing the boundary between human and animal, getting a more grounded understanding of our own nature in-between the world that made us and the things we make. Animal-speak might be forgotten, but Ju/twa hunters retained a sense of communion with nature that helped tune their existence to the reality of life in the veldt.

We see such communion in the previously mentioned film *The Great Dance: A Hunter's Story*,[26] which documents a persistence or endurance hunt, when in the middle of summer in the midday heat the hunters try to outrun an antelope.

No doubt the endurance hunt is the oldest form of hunting — an activity that shaped some of the most definitive aspects of what it means to be a modern human being: the connection between our upright gait, our complex social life, and our intelligence. Since our cognition seems to be tied so viscerally to our ability to run on two legs, the experience of running after a wild kudu for hours across the veldt can evoke some profound, archaic states of consciousness. The running hunter describes an experience of entering the animal's consciousness, of "putting on kudu mind" and becoming kudu, controlling its mind and controlling its movement. This seems to be not so much a simple projection as an entry into shamanic states of awareness, which transcend space and time in some still-mysterious fashion (I explore this in more detail in chapter 8).[27]

Human-animal relations are not all on the level of sublime enchantment. Bushman hunters can also become detached during the gory business of killing and butchering, which can seem brutal, if not outright cruel, to an outsider. I had a small taste of this "natural brutality" in 1998 when I went on a hunt with a group of Ju/twasi in the Nyae Nyae area. After several hours following spoor that led nowhere, the hunters trapped a spring hare deep in its burrow. They had brought a long flexible pole for just such a situation. It was assembled from sections joined with sinew and glue, altogether about ten to fifteen feet long, with a large hook at the end. They probed the pole down the burrow hole, which went down at a slight angle, pushing and hooking until eventually they speared the hare like a fish with a gaff. Once the animal was held in place, they started digging straight down through the earth at a point some distance from the entrance and above where they estimated they had trapped the hare.

After half an hour and sharing a pipe full of tobacco, the Ju/twasi had dug a hole big enough for the oldest and smallest of the hunters to jump in. Smiling broadly, the diminutive hunter held up the struggling, surprisingly large animal by its hind legs. It had thick orange-and-white fur and looked at us with enormous terrified eyes. After I photographed it, the hunter grabbed hold of the back legs with two hands and then sharply bent them against the joint, snapping both like dry twigs with a sharp crack. The animal let out an almost human scream and shook violently. The hunter held it up from its broken legs, then took a club and smashed both sides of the rib cage. Only then did the hunter give two hard blows behind the head, killing the animal before unceremoniously dumping it in his hunting bag.

Quite shocked at this seemingly gratuitous brutality, I asked Twi, our interpreter, to quiz them for an explanation. The only reply I received was "it is traditional." I'm not sure how typical this method was, nor did I get any further explanation for why it was done. On reflection, it did make a certain practical sense; even if the hare wriggled free, it couldn't run with broken legs and a shattered ribcage. First secure the food, then tend to compassion. The brutality might also have been a psychological defense against the abomination of cannibalism — since for Ju/twa, the animal-human connection is so real. By treating the hare as the next meal, the connection to the human is broken. Traditional San still show an ambivalence about hunting and eating certain animals, like the baboon and the elephant, that they consider too much like humans. As during the kudu hunt, the connection between hunter and prey can be so profound as to approach a mystical identification. This thread of ambivalence, the ability to move between opposite attitudes, seems to permeate Bushman politics. As we shall see, such coexistence of opposites is not simply a "mess," "a complex tied up in knots," but is woven into a paradoxical metaphysics that has its own lived coherence. It helps attune Bushman politics to the paradoxical reality of the human condition as being both like and unlike animals.

In reconstructing the politics of the old way, we need to make and remake the imaginative journey from our urban Hobbesian, science-saturated prejudice about nature to the sands of the Kalahari, and then go further back still to recreate the richly varied ecosystem of southern African, when the wilderness of the Cape coastline most closely represented our African Eden, in which one of the world's richest fisheries met one of the world's most diverse botanical kingdoms. Early Europeans found this land filled with unimaginably

*Bushman hunters check tracks around a water hole, Nyae Nyae Conservancy, Western Kalahari, Namibia. Note the long probe to hook a spring hare in its burrow.* (Photo: Author)

*The spring hare, hooked and dug out, soon to be killed and eaten.* (Photo: Author)

vast herds of Africa's grazing and browsing animals. As late as the nineteenth century, when South Africa was already relatively crowded with both black and white farmers, a mesmerized European traveling in a wagon through the Karoo reported being passed for hours by a single mass of migrating springbok. All were potentially targets for Bushman spear, trap, and poisoned arrow. In addition to rich supplies of venison, the thousands of piles of Stone Age beach middens testify to a large population of "beach Bushmen," *strandlopers*, who regularly feasted on an abundance of seafood. With leisure and comfort in some of the most interesting, complex, and noble environments in the world, ancient people were free to let the imagination run, to play, think, argue, tell stories, sing, dance, paint, and make music.

Today, we in the industrialized West sicken on our wealth and confuse ourselves with incomprehensible mountains of information. Our overstimulated children, raised indoors, suffer epidemic levels of obesity and diabetes, while attention deficit and hyperactivity disorders continue to rise. When scientific studies diagnose the obvious — that we are suffering from a "nature-deficit disorder" — we are delighted to find that when children spend more time being physically active in nature, obesity declines, diabetes is mitigated, depression and anxiety dissipate, and learning improves.[28] Sadly, safe accessible wilderness is vanishing, having been poisoned and paved over by "progress." Humanity's perennial nostalgia for a golden age could well be due to a species imprinting of those periods in our deep past when humans flourished in a southern African Eden. The San, even today — constrained, compromised, and impoverished as they are — should not be seen as lost, exotic, or pathetic but rather should also be honored as custodians of a global cultural treasure — inheritors of a culture consistently fashioned by an unbroken connection to the original human homeland.[29]

## The Lost World of Academia

In the decades after the Marshalls' first expedition in the fifties, San Bushman life was studied with increasing critical rigor by Western academics. A considerable amount of important fieldwork was conducted by the Kalahari (Harvard) Research Group, directed by Irven DeVore but more commonly associated with the writings of Richard Lee and others.[30] The project followed the impulse of van der Post's quest into primal humanity, but since it was disciplined by the methodology of science, this meant a shift in emphasis from meaning to precise measurement of the more easily quantifiable aspects of material and social culture. While the methodology was positivistic, the motivation was also broadly political, no doubt in part influenced by the radical climate on American university campuses in the sixties. This critical approach to the established order received some high intellectual wattage from the Frankfurt School philosophers, who fled Nazi Germany to settle in the United States. Only an intellectual elite could penetrate the complexity of their writing and grasp the subtlety of their arguments, but their conclusions were simple and radical and reinforced the zeitgeist — civilization was in crisis, and the possibilities for reinventing politics were wide open.

By 1978, the Third World Conference on Hunter Gatherers, in Paris, was guided by a heightened political sensitivity and focused on the fundamental political question: "What was human social life like when people lived directly from the fruits of the earth?"[31] The consensus was unequivocal. It flatly contradicted the ruling Hobbesian assumptions on which the institutions of modernity were founded. Hunter-gatherers might be poor in personal material wealth, but in general, under reasonable conditions, they had more leisure than any society since, living in what anthropologist Marshall Sahlins described as a kind of "Zen affluence." Furthermore, theirs was not a dog-eat-dog world where the most brutal and ruthless triumphed, but rather it was composed of self-sustaining communities based on mutual caring and sharing. Some individuals were more influential than others, but decisions were made collectively, and there were no powerful chiefs. Far from being crushed by the collective, individuals were assertive and free to go their own way. Hunter-gatherers like the San seemed as close as one could get to a classless society without extremes of rich and poor, where each worked according to his or her ability and received according to his or her need. The San Bushmen themselves looked like "the harmless people," flower children of the veldt, and primitive exemplars of a democratic egalitarian utopia.

This research in turn helped inspire some of the more utopian projects associated with the counterculture, from hippie communes to visions of a fully liberated decentralized eco-tech society. Anarchist thinkers like John Zerzan saw in Bushman politics a model for order without bureaucratic coercion, where the primary political institution was the whole person — the creative autonomous individual in continuing conversation with a small group of other such individuals.[32] Here was a model of order and social responsibility that came from love of community rather than fear of punishment. However, such idealistic extrapolations paid little attention to the epistemology of the quest: "How does one get reliable knowledge of the best way to live?"

Meanwhile, the situation on the ground was becoming much more complex. Bushman society was in rapid transition as the outer world of farming and commerce made a nomadic hunting-gathering lifestyle increasingly difficult. In 1961 when Botswana was still the protectorate of Bechuanaland, at the urging of anthropologists, the British administration established the Central Kalahari Game Reserve in the heart of the country, giving special hunting privileges to the approximately five thousand San living there. In 1978 this arrangement was underwritten by the newly independent government of Botswana, which a year later, under outside pressure, established a system of "special game licenses" for qualified San to hunt and gather for subsistence purposes. But subsistence hunting and gathering was hardly compatible with the political priorities of a government bureaucracy, and Bushmen were increasingly forced out of wilderness areas and into surrounding farms, villages, and towns.[33]

In the Nyae Nyae region of South West Africa, the situation was complicated by the South African administration's bush war with SWAPO — the guerilla army fighting for Namibian independence. The South Africans attempted to move most of the Ju/twasi into a settlement at Tsumkwe and recruited the young men to special combat units in the South African Defense Forces. When Namibia eventually won its independence, various attempts were made to help San preserve a hunting-gathering way of life while slowly integrating them into a subsistence-farming, wage-labor economy. Their success was limited.

By the 1980s anthropological research was also producing a more complex and confusing picture. Accumulated advances in ethnography, archaeology, and colonial history made it clear that at least for the past thousand years the "lost world of the Kalahari" had never been totally lost. While hunting and gathering seemed to have constituted the primary way of life, evidence had accumulated to show confusing flexibility and variability. Thus at different times different Bushman groups acted as "hotshot traders" in salt, ivory, and skins; as small-scale pastoralists entering into a variety of relationships with surrounding Bantu societies; and even at times as fierce defenders of their own crude but rich copper mines that they worked for export. Such contradictions made it difficult for scholars to come to a clear consensus.

The larger political and philosophical context of academia was also changing. After the burnout of the sixties, something of an academic counterreformation gave rise to a more cynical deconstructionist mood that ridiculed idealistic and visionary projects. Imagination and creativity disappeared from political discourse. Revisionist anthropologists, deeply suspicious of all generalizations, criticized the earlier idealizations of San life and tended to see the San and Bushmen as components of a rural *lumpenproletariat* — a sort of "bag people" of the veldt, part of a global political economy in which the significant actors were either exploiters or victims.[34] A powerful reaction against the naive excesses of the youth rebellion put conservatives into power in the United States, England, Europe, and Israel, and Francis Fukuyama's *End of History* celebrated the global triumph of industrial capitalism.

Continental philosophy — the French postmodern deconstructionists in particular — shifted the intellectual center of gravity from the more emancipatory thrust of the Frankfurt School's dialectical critique to relentless one-sided critique without any redeeming reconstruction of meaning. Terms like *reality*, *truth*, and *meaning* went out of fashion. Scholarship became fascinated with the surfaces of things, appearances, and the multiplication of subtle distinctions, voices, and meanings. Some of this was a valuable corrective to an essentialism that saw the world in terms of simple, absolute opposites — black and white, right and wrong. But scholars at times seemed to rejoice in their impotence — perversely celebrating entrapment in an infinite regress of interpretations and language games. The only posture of political integrity seemed a cool and ironic detachment.[35]

The climate of critique and deconstruction reinforced a vigorous revisionism in anthropology, which challenged the prevailing view expressed by Lee and Leacock that Bushmen were, with qualifications, something like the paradigmatic primal society. In 1989, Edwin Wilmsen launched the broadside, in what came to be known as the Kalahari Debate, with his long-awaited *Land Filled with Flies*. The title itself measured the depth of disenchantment.

He argued that "Bushmen," "San," and "Kalahari foragers" were invented categories — constructed to serve European agendas — and that hunting and gathering was simply one of several subsistence strategies engaged in by all the rural poor of Botswana and Namibia. Wilmsen admitted that modern ethnographers' attempts to discover "authentic," "isolated" Bushmen might have noble motivations for "Europeans... who... had become all too aware of the fragility of existence in a violent environment of their own creation." But he dismissed as nostalgia their hope of finding "a place of primeval simplicity... offering a degree of existential respite from the complex cares of the moment."[36] Wilmsen stressed that anthropology was an intensely idealogical practice and implied that all we could do was deconstruct our own projections.[37]

Robert J. Gordon's archival work was a good example of the retreat of anthropology from the quest for meaning. On the one hand, it was a valuable piece of research, providing historical context and deconstructing some of the more simpleminded myths of Bushman barbarity and nobility. Yet his fear of any generalization being exploited in the name of some murderous political project paralyzed any attempt at meaning. He proclaimed the "major intellectual and moral task of anthropology" as "exposé ethnography... debunking dangerous contemporary myths."[38] Thus reduced in purpose, his work became a valuable collection of details that at times dissolved into a bewildering multiplicity of images and interpretations. For every thesis, there was an antithesis, but nowhere a synthesis in sight. Nowhere was there much mention of anthropology's moral and political responsibility to illuminate the meaning of "Bushman," let alone cast light on the human condition.[39]

Jacqueline Solway and Richard Lee responded by defending the classical position: that the San were traditionally independent hunter-gatherers and their egalitarianism reflected cultural continuity with an ancient way of life. Most of the hunter-gatherer anthropologists joined in to give variously qualified support.[40] The debate continued through the 1990s, in the pages of *Current Anthropology*, and produced a much more detailed and nuanced picture of how San have been impacted by outsiders over the past few centuries.

Today, as we have seen, the recent archaeological, genetic, linguistic, and ethnographic research supports the antiquity and integrity of San identity. As a result, the heat of the scholarly debate has subsided, yet the critical deconstructionist approach still pervades much of academia and continues to hamper attempts to construct the sort of big picture that could spur us to meaningful action. As I have argued, this unbalanced commitment to deconstruction is itself an artifact of modernity, the culmination of an intellectual genealogy going back from Descartes to Galileo to Copernicus. It is based on the notion that we only gain reliable knowledge by taking things apart, by analyzing and deconstructing wholes into self-evident measurable pieces, ideally those that can be quantified and dealt with mathematically.

There are layers of irony in the Kalahari revisionist debate. Where the romanticists and classicists were at least explicit about having an agenda — critiquing the one-sidedness of modernity and searching for a way forward — the revisionists seemed to believe that relentless critique somehow escapes any agenda. Ideologically hostile to the big picture, they were incapable of recognizing that an exclusively critical methodology, and the refusal to look at the whole, was itself a kind of agenda. For it is exactly the big picture that reveals that one-sided, unrelenting critique is perfectly congruent with the central thrust of Liberalism — where the objectivity of the scientific method and the amorality of the market converge in the death of meaning. Precisely because of the vigor of their protestations to the contrary — their compulsive skepticism — deconstructionists end up as the *reductio ad absurdum* of modernity.

In a further and final irony, reflective ethnographic studies of Bushman shamanism have today uncovered exactly the sort of dialectical boundary-crossing logic that is needed to transcend the one-sidedness of deconstructionism.[41] Fortunately, there is also a slowly growing realization that critique without construction, analysis without synthesis, and quantification without qualitative evaluation make it impossible to create alternatives to the status quo and rob us of our agency.

How, then, might this wealth of accumulated knowledge on the Bushmen — a society grounded in the defining experience of what it means to be human living on a wild earth — help guide a more sustainable and life-loving politics?

CHAPTER 7

# PRIMAL POLITICS

When a young man kills much meat he comes to think of himself as a chief or a big man, and he thinks of the rest of us as his servants or inferiors. We can't accept this.

— /GAUGO to Richard Lee, "Christmas in the Kalahari"

Beset with contradiction and ambiguity, Bushman society is in need of constant vigilance by its members so that its key values of communalism — egalitarianism, co-operation, mutual aid, sharing, reciprocity, generosity, sociability — are maintained, while at the same time, the individual's personal autonomy and fulfillment are safe guarded.

— MATHIAS GUENTHER, *Tricksters & Trancers*

When we reflect on the lives of traditional Bushman hunter-gatherers and ask the basic questions of political philosophy, we find they exemplify a political economy that embodies the dynamics of the four values of primal politics in a tight, stable, yet flexible balance. Life in the compact nomadic band shows how each value is realized in the process of contributing to, and drawing from, the realization of the others — constituting the good life, Bushman style.

## A Paradoxical Politics — Untying the Knot

By the late 1990s, after some of the furor of the revisionist debate had abated, anthropologists could reflect back on half a century of fieldwork on the San, together with rapidly accumulating archaeological, genetic, and linguistic evidence, and most important what Bushmen actually said about themselves and their culture. Jiro Tanaka, an anthropologist from the Center for African Area Studies at Kyoto University, marked this shift by reminding us that "good fieldwork is possible only if the fieldworker feels, in his heart, respect for the people he studies." This appeal to respect and heartfelt intention has a refreshing humility. It evokes shamanic and ancient systems of knowing, which tell us that attitude and intention are as much determining factors of the success of the truth quest as the hard facts of bones and stones. Descartes's method notwithstanding, feeling is required to make meaning. If we feel nothing for our subject, how can it have meaning and value for us?

Referencing the scholarly battle, Tanaka concludes by asking, "Who… respects the San more deeply, the group that is content with calling them 'the poor' or the one that has expressed appreciation of their cultural uniqueness? Even if there are some defects in his work, as Wilmsen and Denbow point out, as a fieldworker and an anthropologist I feel more sympathy with Lee."[1]

In 1999, Mathias Guenther, a seasoned fieldworker, brought this more respectful and reflective attitude to the accumulated body of research and produced an illuminating synthesis of Bushman politics, religion, and cosmology: *Tricksters & Trancers: Bushman Religion and Society*. At first gloss, his work seemed filled with contradictory and confusing detail, but Guenther was committed to making meaning. He took in the full ambiguity and variability in Bushman life and discovered a hidden order in the chaos — effectively untying the "knotted complex" that had confounded early explorers. His work surveyed all the major studies on the great variety of Bushman groups, but he focused on the Nharo, a group in the central Kalahari he worked with closely for years, as exemplifying what he calls "the foraging band blueprint."

Guenther first described the Nharo as showing a perplexing variability. During the course of the previous century they lived, on and off, as classic egalitarian, nomadic hunter-gatherers. Then, when the market was good and the game plentiful, some became big-game hunters, hunting on horseback and trading in ivory and skins. When hunting-and-gathering conditions were difficult, they worked on farms as serfs or servants and in villages as small-scale entrepreneurs. This variability applied to other Bushman groups, who at various times in the past even worked their own copper and salt mines and traded the products in regional markets. In the nineteenth century, when they were threatened by expanding cattle farmers, both black and white, the apparently harmless "flower children of the desert" banded together in large groups, built palisades, and organized themselves under war captains. Guenther describes how they developed highly effective hit-and-run tactics based on fast-running warriors armed with deadly poison arrows, augmented by mastery of the terrain and by superior hunting and tracking ability. Among whites and the neighboring Batswana, the Nharo gained a reputation as "black serpents of the desert."

This range of political expression seemed to confirm the revisionists' despair of finding any overarching Bushman identity. But Guenther artfully showed that if one takes the longer historical view and the bigger picture, it became apparent that as soon as conditions are suitable, Bushman communities like the Nharo snap back into the "foraging band blueprint." It's as if a kind of organic elasticity pulled the community back into its most balanced, enduring, and satisfying way of life: nomadic bands of hunters and gatherers, egalitarian, decentralized, tightly bonded, yet fiercely individualistic. Guenther concluded that as recently as the 1960s and 1970s the band remained as the underlying social blueprint of Nharo Bushmen in the Kalahari's Ghanzi area. He quoted Alan Barnard, who in 1988 confirmed that "the ideal of band society is in many parts of the Kalahari very much intact."[2]

The most original element of this thesis is that the extreme outer variability of Bushman society does not represent an absence of inner coherence. On the contrary, it expresses a quintessential Bushman flexibility rooted in a shamanically mediated grasp of the paradox of the human condition — what I've called living in the *in-between.*[*]

Guenther's foraging band blueprint is a more nuanced reformulation of Bushman culture as the paradigmatic compact, egalitarian society with minimal, flexible division of labor, without any externally imposed grid or enforced boundaries among roles. Most participate in all social roles within the limits of age, ability, and sex — hunter, gatherer, healer, home builder, dancer, singer. Everyone has direct access to valued resources — the water holes, the great dry lake beds or pans, the plants and animals of the veldt. Relevant knowledge is openly discussed, easily overheard, and readily shared.[**]

Both hunting and gathering are opportunistic, open-ended activities, guided by individual intuition, dream, and luck. People work together in a relaxed stop-go style, making and repairing tools, clothing, and jewelry and exchanging items as needed while constantly talking, joking, and telling stories. Despite the fluidity of roles, most of the gathering is in fact done by groups of women and children, and most of the hunting is done by men, who hunt alone or in small groups.[3] Women work harder at child care than men, but since children are included in virtually all activities, they continue to participate fully in productive work and in public and social life. Fathers are attentive and loving and spend much of their leisure time playing with and holding children.

---

* I explore the shamanic dimension of the in-between in chapters 8, 9, and 10.

** I mostly use the present tense in the following description despite the fact that, as I have mentioned, the fully nomadic hunting-gathering way of life of the San no longer exists. Nevertheless, various aspects of their social, economic, and political life survive in certain places and at certain times, and present tense communicates that ongoing vitality. I also use the present tense in the spirit of Guenther's insight into the resilience and flexibility of the foraging band blueprint. While much knowledge of the old ways may be gone, a surprising amount remains in the collective memory and oral culture of the people, as well as in the wealth of anthropological and scholarly studies. It is not inconceivable that under special circumstances, with wise government help, some San might find opportunities to snap back into some version of the "foraging band blueprint."

Marriage is informal. Traditionally, the couple will live with or next to the wife's parents, with the husband performing bride service to feed the extended family until his own children are teenagers. Divorce is even more informal; it is generally initiated by the woman, who announces to the group that the marriage is over simply by moving out of the husband's hut. Most Ju/twasi are monogamous, but occasionally a woman will take two husbands or a man two wives. Rape is virtually unknown, and domestic violence is rare. Women desire children and often complain of not having as many as they would like. Childbirth is entirely their domain. Upon giving birth, the mother examines the new baby for signs of defect and decides whether or not to invest the enormous energy required to care for it. Though infrequent, infanticide remains an option if necessary and is solely the mother's decision. Her announcement of a stillbirth is accepted without question.[4]

San communalism is balanced by its opposite — fierce individualism, argumentativeness, and assertiveness. In all spheres of San life, we see a fluid crossing of boundaries back and forth between all the opposites of politics — between individuality and communal bonding; argumentativeness and agreement; assertiveness and egalitarianism; recognizing excellence while putting down boastfulness. No one in the band has formal authority over others; there is no mechanism for the group to enforce its will on members. The San can only persuade one another using eloquence, skill, and wisdom. Tension between individuals and the group is mediated by discussion, which is ongoing and includes everyone. Coherence is maintained by collections of stories, myths, and teachings — a shared but open-ended cosmology.

## Power and Wealth — The Christmas Ox

We can see the tug-of-war between the individual and the community clearly in hunting, since this is often a solitary activity whose outcome varies greatly, depending on luck, age, and skill. Meat is loved with a passion and highly valued, but egalitarianism requires that the successful hunter not lord it over his fellows. To prevent this, Bushmen have developed complex mechanisms of "reverse dominance," the most straightforward being the custom that the skilled hunter is sometimes expected to hold back, giving the others a chance to bring back meat. In the case of a bow hunt, the meat belongs not to the hunter who fired the arrow but to the owner of the arrow. Arrows are traded and given as gifts, so a hunter's quiver can contain many distinctively marked arrows belonging to others — such as a young woman or a man too old to hunt. In this way the chance to "own" and distribute the meat is circulated widely and randomly.[5]

Richard Lee tells of his initiation while doing fieldwork and living with a group of Ju/twasi in the sixties. He arrived with the visitor's usual hoard of tinned and preserved food, which in the interests of anthropological objectivity, he felt obliged to refrain from sharing. However, as was customary and polite, he gave generous handouts of tobacco, being the only source in a thousand square miles. He also shared medicine freely. The San were well aware of his conspicuous wealth and regularly criticized him for his stinginess. With Christmas approaching, Lee decided to make amends by sponsoring a feast and buying the fattest ox he could find from a neighboring Herero herder. The Bushmen had little knowledge of Christmas, but Lee got the idea from the surrounding Tswana Herero farmers, who would customarily slaughter an ox on Christmas Day for their Bushman neighbors as a sign of goodwill. Lee eventually purchased an impressive animal that he arranged to be delivered on the day. Since food consumption calculations were his specialty, Lee was confident that, without bones and viscera, the ox would provide a very generous four pounds of meat for each of the 150 individuals in the area.

Word of his purchase got out ahead of time, and over the next few days members of the band took turns berating him for his stinginess in choosing such a puny animal, "a bag of skin and bones." They complained it was so "sickly, old, and meager" that it was bound to cause fights over the small amount of meat it would provide. Lee was at first confused; then, after several days of relentless complaining, he became so irritated that he was tempted to forget the whole thing and leave for Christmas. But his scientific curiosity got the better of him, so he endured the insults to see for himself how the ox turned out. When the day arrived and the animal was slaughtered, it turned out to be even meatier and fattier than Lee had hoped. He responded indignantly:

> "Hey /Gau," I burst out, "that ox is loaded with fat. What's this about the ox being too thin to bother eating? Are you out of your mind?"

> "Fat?" /Gau shot back. "You call that fat? This wretch is thin, sick, dead!" And he broke out laughing. So did everyone else. They rolled on the ground, paralyzed with laughter. Everybody laughed except me; I was thinking.[6]

Afterward, /Gaugo, one of the men, came over and explained, smiling:

> "It is our way.... Say there is a Bushman who has been hunting. He must not come home and announce like a braggart, 'I have killed a big one in the bush!' He must first sit down in silence until I or someone else comes up to his fire and asks, 'What did you see today?' He replies quietly, 'Ah I'm no good for hunting. I saw nothing at all [pause] just a little tiny one.' Then I smile to myself," /Gaugo continued, "because I know he has killed something big."[7]

Of course, the successful hunter feels proud, and the people are thrilled. Meat is loved and important for the health of the group. But at the same time and equally critical to the Bushmen, every individual must feel respected and valued regardless of age, ability, or hunting success. The hunter's pride, in fact everyone's pride, needs to be tempered by regular reminders of this. Later, when Lee asked another hunter, Tomazo, for clarification, he was told:

> "We refuse one who boasts, for someday his pride will make him kill somebody. So we always speak of his meat as worthless. This way we cool his heart and make him gentle."[8]

While generosity and sharing are encouraged and expected, no special reward, honor, or power accrues to the one who has more to give.

When, historically, chiefs have arisen within Bushman society from time to time, they received no extra wealth, nor did they command much more respect than others. Europeans accustomed to hierarchy would arrive, ask who the chief was, and often find an obliging individual pointing to himself or someone else. But as Lee found out when quizzing one of the men about chiefs, every Bushman is considered "chief" over him- or herself.[9] Writing in the nineteenth century, Dorothea Bleek described a conversation with a Nharo Bushman, /Kurib Hartebeeste, who told her privately in Afrikaans that he was the son of an important chief and a chief himself. But in front of the group, speaking in Nharo, he denied this and chimed in with the rest that there were no chiefs anymore.[10]

The Ju/twasi word for "leader" or "chief" is *//Kaiha* (derived from *//kai*, meaning "wealth"). They apply it to the headmen and chiefs of the surrounding Tswana and Herero peoples, and even to English kings and queens, but only rarely and then often mockingly to one another. Bushman chiefs were most conspicuous in the nineteenth century, when nomadic bands were under the greatest pressure from more powerful stratified neighbors. Then, Bushman bands built stockades, acquired cattle, and organized around charismatic and powerful war chiefs. Once the threat disappeared, the bands resumed their nomadic, egalitarian, hunting-and-gathering lifestyle, exemplifying Guenther's default "foraging blueprint." As Lorna Marshall put it, "Chiefs are as thin as the rest." Even when they are recognized today, their most marked common trait is their freedom from pretension, arrogance, and boasting. Chiefs are as modest and down-to-earth as any other member of the band.[11]

## An Economy of Caring and Sharing

In a land where food is seasonal and the hunter can come back from days of hunting either empty-handed or with an eland bull that can feed the band for a week, an ethos of sharing is a survival necessity. But the value goes deeper. Without the market pressure to compete, relationships and social life can be enjoyed for their own sake, as ends in themselves. Lorna Marshall noted the intense sociability of Bushmen, and how separation and loneliness are the most unendurable of hardships, almost deathlike. People are unselfconscious about demanding signs that they are cared for. Lorna quotes a long monologue from a woman talking in her presence but mostly to herself:

> "I am sick. That is why I don't go out for plant foods. I want my mother [meaning Lorna] to give me some and she does not give me any. I am lying down sick. I am starving. If my mother... [meaning her own birth mother] were here she would give some plant foods. She is not here. So I am starving.... [Lorna and Laurence] do not favor me. They do not give me food. Only mielie-meal (corn meal). That is what I am living on. Why does not [Lorna] give me some fat? My ankle is sore. If she gave me fat, my ankle would be better and I could go out for plant foods.... [Laurence] wants me to go to the mangetti trees. I do not think I shall be able. He wants me to go to the mangetti trees. That place is far. That

is what I say. The place is far. The people who stay there are not people who favor others. Not sympathetic. They do not give food."[12]

Children are socialized from an early age on the importance of giving and generosity. The stingy are "bags without openings." The idea of eating alone and not sharing is shocking. "Only lions do that, not people." Those who have some conspicuous wealth are badgered to give until it hurts. Lorna Marshall noted another case where a woman visitor from another band who felt she had not received a sufficiently generous share of hunted meat went into a sort of trance, "saying over and over for perhaps half an hour... [in the hunter's presence]... that he had not given her as much meat as was her due. It was not said like an accusation. It was said as though he were not there. I had the eerie feeling that I was present in someone else's dream. [The hunter] did not argue or oppose her. He continued doing whatever he was doing and let her go on."[13] Such ways of talking are also important in reducing conflict and tension by getting things out in the open without confrontation, keeping everyone in touch with what others are thinking and feeling, preventing pressure from building until it bursts out in aggression.

The pressure to share, and the begging and pestering, can be particularly irritating to visitors who arrive in their 4x4s bursting with luxuries. Elizabeth Marshall gives a graphic measure of the distance between the two societies by comparing their respective inventories.

> We had tents, cots, sleeping bags, folding chairs and tables, maps, a compass, cameras, film, recording equipment, reference books, notebooks, pens, ink, pencils, disinfectants, antivenin kits for snakebites, brandy, cases of canned foods, boxes of dry foods, dishes, cooking pots, frying pans, knives, forks, spoons, cigarettes, matches, spare tires, auto parts, inner tubes, tire patches, jacks, toolboxes, winches, motor oil, drums of gasoline, drums of water, bars of yellow soap, towels, washcloths, toothpaste, toothbrushes, coats, sweaters, pants, boots, sneakers, shirts, underwear, socks, reading glasses, safety pins, scissors, a sewing kit, binoculars, bullets, a rifle.
>
> The *Ju/wasi* had sticks, skins, eggshells, grass.[14]

Comparing the two, we can feel our sense of self-sufficiency buckling under the weight of our possessions. Part of our self-consciousness about this is no doubt due to the starkness of so much next to so little, but part is no doubt due to our sense of vulnerability should we also be obliged to live naked in the bush with nothing but sticks, skins, eggshells, grass, and our skill. Despite their material poverty, Bushmen show a restraint when eating and sharing food that Lorna found touching.

> On several occasions we gave small gifts of corned beef to be shared with a group. The person who received the food from us would take only a mouthful. Once an old man who received the meat first only licked his fingers. The lump of food would be passed from one to another. Each would take a modest bit. The last person often got the most. I found it moving to see so much restraint about taking food among people who are all thin and often hungry.... We observed no unmannerly behavior and no cheating and no encroachment about food.[15]

Perhaps the most elaborate institution for generating an ethos of caring and sharing is *!hxaro* — a Bushman system of making, giving, and receiving gifts. The gifts are generally any nonfood item of value, most typically something decorative that becomes a conspicuous symbol of mutual concern and willingness to share in times of need. The system also opens the way for visiting and hospitality and thus the enduring wealth of companionship, caring, and sharing.[16]

A child may be introduced to *!hxaro* between the ages of six months and a year. For example, a grandmother would give a bead necklace to the child, then at some point she would cut off the beads, wash them, and put them in the child's hand to give to a relative. She then replaces the necklace and repeats the procedure, whether the child likes it or not, encouraging the child to give the beads to an interested adult, until the child starts to develop a taste for the joy of giving and initiates the *!hxaro*.

Most adults generally have from twelve to twenty-four *!hxaro* partners from both sexes and all ages, including relatives and friends from other groups up to several hundred kilometers away. In one study among the Ju/twasi in the 1980s, more than two-thirds of all the possessions in various bands were obtained in this fashion, while the remaining third were either bought or made by the owner and destined to be given away. The gift is not necessarily sex or status related, nor always valued for its usefulness. Women can give and receive hunting arrows, as men can give and receive a woman's apron. As gifts circulate, they are often repaired, remade, embellished, or marked in some way to personalize the next giving. Store-bought woolen caps might be unraveled and reknitted in different patterns many times as they circulate. Considerable time and effort can be spent on making some of the gifts; elaborate beadwork may take several days of systematic labor. There seems to be little concern over intrinsic value. The nature of the gift is more a function of the resources and ability of the giver and the consideration, time, and effort put into the making.[17]

The making of gifts itself is intensely social. This is not wage labor, nor does it require time away from family and friends. Rather, it is conducted at a leisurely pace in company, with all the usual talking, joking, and storytelling that mark the sociability of Bushman life. Gifts belong to the receiver, but they are generally held by one person for a few months, but no more than two years, before being passed on to some other partner. It is important that the return gift be delayed. If it was reciprocated immediately, this might imply unwillingness to sustain the *!hxaro* bond.

In a competitive market economy, relationships can often become a means to enhance one's own material wealth. *!Hxaro* inverts this by understanding wealth as a resource to develop the symmetrical bonds of friendship.[18] It is for this reason that Marshall Sahlins argues (in the spirit of E.F. Schumacher's "Buddhist economics") that we could regard hunter-gatherers like the San, under reasonable conditions, as "the original affluent society." But theirs is a "Zen affluence" that minimizes material demands and creates a wealth of time and energy to serve a life rich in relationships and mutual care.[19]

The contrast with our own economy of competitive avarice is stark, as is the contrast with our society's pathological material excess. There are tantalizing signs, however, that a primal ethic resembling *!hxaro* is reemerging in the West. There is a rise in grassroots networks based on caring and sharing. These range from more formal co-ops to informal bartering networks, where relationships are given weight as "social capital" and "time dollars," allowing socially useful labor to be exchanged. There are also early signs of a fundamental shift in food production, away from distant oil-intensive factory farms to local small-scale organic gardens. Collectively, such strategies and institutions can help buffer individuals from global market forces, while personalizing economies and helping rebuild face-to-face communities based on trust and reciprocity.*

---

* I consider a range of such examples exemplifying future primal principles in chapter 12.

## Direct Democracy — "Everyone a Chief"

From the point of view of market-based economies, we tend to assume that a culture of caring and sharing would crush individuality. The opposite seems to be true among the San. The individual stands out sharply in band life — each is a "big frog in a very small pond," as Guenther puts it. Lorna Marshall described how people sit closely together, often touching, ankles interlocked, chatting endlessly, but this doesn't stop the same individuals from being assertive, argumentative, and fiercely self-interested. Sharing and reciprocity seem to be the first law of Bushman existence, but Marshall also noticed the paradox of an atmosphere of "jealous watchfulness," especially when a kill is being shared. Accusations of unfairness can lead to arguments suddenly flaring up. She went so far as to note that altruism, kindness, sympathy, and generosity are not conspicuously displayed. As Richard Lee discovered, it's considered bad manners for someone to say, "Look at how generous I am!" Perhaps this is because the values of reciprocity, caring, and sharing are so fundamental and so taken for granted that distribution is fine-tuned by the individual expressing need loudly without embarrassment. Guenther notes, as with so many other aspects of Bushman life, we find ourselves affirming one value only to qualify it by affirming the opposite. How does this work?[20]

Part of the answer lies in different notions of individualism. In the West we have an individualism of competition leading to division of labor, specialization, and hierarchies of wealth and power. Bushmen have an individualism of cooperation leading to an egalitarian democracy that promotes universal access to the full range of humanizing experience — cultivation of the whole person. The Bushman formula is rooted in the economy of hunting and foraging, which provides the most unshakable economic foundation of any society for individual self-sufficiency. Since the division of labor is minimal, virtually all individuals have the basic knowledge, ability, and resources to live directly off the land, gather food, make clothing, and build shelter. Children grow up with a deeply rooted sense of security, surrounded by a caring community and in direct contact with a wilderness environment that supplies everything needed. Because of this independence and security, friendships and marriage, while taken seriously, are free from dire economic sanctions and don't require absolutely binding long-term commitments and dependencies. People feel free and secure enough to speak their minds, often with a directness that is disconcerting to outsiders. Very little energy is spent constructing and maintaining a persona, the carefully cultivated self-image that seems so essential to success in competitive economies.

Childhood is a time of exceptional freedom, spontaneity, and self-indulgence. During the day, groups of children play freely around the huts and roam the surrounding veldt enjoying whatever adventures they please. Since all ages tend to play together, competitiveness is tempered with cooperation. Performance is less a matter of comparison with others than a kind of internal self-evaluation, a process that strengthens self-direction and autonomy. Modern Western parents are reluctant to let young children play alone in public. How would they feel at the thought of their children wandering around a wilderness populated by poisonous snakes, lions, leopards, and other large animals? But as Standing Bear reminds us, it is rather our crowded cities and towns — with their traffic, pollution, toxic waste, and human predators — that pose the greater threat to the health of children. Writing of his Lakota childhood spent following the bison herds of the Great Plains, he points out, "There were not the dangers that seem to surround childhood of today. I can recall days — entire days — when we roamed over the plains, hills, and up and down streams without fear of anything. I do not remember ever hearing of an Indian child being hurt or eaten by a wild animal."[21]

As in other traditional hunting-gathering societies, child rearing tends to be unstructured and permissive. Bushman children are not pressured into doing chores. Boys, for example, will only go hunting when they feel moved to do so. Children are never disciplined by being beaten. Instead, as one woman put it, "we talk to them a lot." A child will be allowed to scowl back when scolded without being punished into blind obedience. Parents regard this venting of emotion as healthy and warn against beating a child; as one parent explained: "If you beat a child too much, they will become stubborn, and you cannot win that child over again," and then, "It is better to give a child a reward when they do something right, than to beat him/her when doing something wrong."[22]

At puberty the situation changes somewhat when girls begin an initiation into womanhood. The initiation of boys tends to come later and is associated with the first big kill, signifying the ability to feed a family and contribute to the community. But apart from a few taboos relating to menstruation rites and hunting, there are no "adults only" areas and no externally imposed structures. Adults and children intermingle freely around all public activities. All are free to join the healing dances and to listen to the discussions and storytelling; children are free to make their own interpretations. Education takes place continuously, merging invisibly with participation in everyday life.

This freedom continues into adulthood. Each person follows intuition, passion, and home-crafted wisdom in charting the course of his or her own life. Should the group become oppressive or unsatisfying, there is always the real option of getting up, wandering off, and joining another band; individual Bushmen can also live for a time on their own, as hermits, though this is almost unknown. Deeply rooted autonomy sharpens the joys of communal life, making ostracism the greatest punishment.

The voluntary nature of Bushman association refutes the ideas of economists, even those of relatively enlightened ones like Robert Heilbronner, who asserts it is only "the pure need for self-preservation... that pushes [primitive] society to the cooperative completion of its daily labors." On the contrary, the hunter-gatherer band knows and honors the value of communal effort, but it cultivates an autonomous self-sufficiency that provides a real freedom of choice. Ironically, it's "the pure need for self-preservation" that compels the rule-bound bureaucrat and the obedient wage earner to conform to the hierarchies of our industrial societies. We are educated to fit into the most extreme division of labor of any civilization, which directly constrains our choices of dress, speech, and behavior. Often, the memberships, affiliations, and personas we create and maintain determine how and whether we prosper in a complex variety of corporate structures, from school and business to church and state. Deviance can jeopardize a livelihood.

Much of the stress of modern life — the insecurity and anxiety — seems to be due to this lack of direct control over the conditions for survival. Few of us could feed our families by hunting, gathering, or growing our own food. Even fewer could build and repair a house, computer, car, or phone. We cannot heal sickness, nor can we expect to have unmet needs fulfilled by loudly complaining to our neighbors. Here, rich and poor alike are free to compete for both necessities and luxuries, with no legal or moral limit to the accumulation of wealth, and no obligation to share with or care for one another. When an entire working lifetime can be spent on the production line of a factory, the individual becomes isolated, anxious, and self-absorbed and collapses into a fragile one-dimensionality — personified in the bureaucrat, citizen, or soldier for whom obedience to authority becomes one of the highest virtues.

Here is the paradox: precisely *because of the material simplicity* of Bushman society, each individual can develop a greater inner wealth, cultivating a whole human life. For the most part, each member of the band participates in all the definitive humanizing activities: producer, provider, teacher, learner, leader, follower, artist, musician, dancer, and healer. Everyone has a direct voice in the ongoing discussions and helps create the consensus that constitutes governance. The archetypal events of a human life cycle — birth, growth, maturity, and death — are ubiquitous and public. The full range of human emotions — love and hate, anger and tenderness, meanness and generosity — are similarly on public display in the full context of the lives of the protagonists. As with the medicine wheel, the very compact structure of the primal band exposes the individual to a complexity that is a stimulus to growth around the wheel of life.

## Face-to-Face Discussion — The Pleasure of Politics

Before the anthropology of the sixties and seventies, Europeans who looked at Bushmen from the perspective of modern complex societies were hard-pressed to find anything that looked like politics. Bushman chiefs, as we have seen, were generally insignificant, and there seemed to be no institutions or procedures for decision making and conflict resolution. Then and now, there is little evidence for the beneficence of the sort of politics defined by Adam Smith, which begins with the acquisition of valuable property and whose prime purpose is defending the rich from the poor.

But if we think of politics in terms of its classical Greek origins, we can see that, stripped to its essentials, politics deals with the tension between the competing goods of the individual, society, and the natural world, and that, as Socrates proposed, the primary mode of exploring and mediating this tension is face-to-face discussion. By this definition, politics is ubiquitous in Bushman society. All four components of primal politics are well developed. Life is lived in a sea of conversation: chatting, arguing, storytelling, teasing, and joking. The Ju/twasi call themselves "owners of argument... people who talk too much."[23] Lorna Marshall called them the most loquacious people she knew.

I had a taste of this during my brief stay in a Ju/twasi village in Nyae

Nyae. On one occasion I drove five hunters to a distant water hole where we hoped to find more game. Our interpreter and my research assistant sat with me in front. We barely spoke a word, while the five hunters, crammed in the back of the Land Rover, immediately started a lively chatter that they kept up without a break for the hour-long journey. Despite differences in age and status (the youngest was the so-called headman, apparently because he was the only one who spoke a little Afrikaans), no single voice dominated the conversation. Comment and response overlapped so quickly that it almost sounded orchestrated. The hunters had spent most of their lives together in this apparently featureless bush and sand. What could they be talking about with such enthusiasm? When I asked Twi for a translation, I discovered that each kilometer of the journey set off chains of memories, stories, and associations. Everyone talks and everyone is listened to. It was as if the little group was still filled with the enthusiasm of the novelty of language, having just discovered its magical capacity to give them an entry into the souls of others.

Below the foaming surface of conversation, anthropologists have identified a range of conversational styles and strategies for investigating problems, understanding opposing points of view, coming to consensus, and acting collectively. Decisions are seldom the outcome of a single formal debate. Men, women, young, and old participate, talking together, for days if necessary, until every point of view has been considered. Lorna Marshall quoted a relaxed conversation to show how the style reinforces reciprocity, point and counterpoint punctuated by agreement and repeating what someone has just said:

> "Yesterday," "eh," "at Deboragu," "eh," "I saw old /Gaishay." "You saw Old /Gaishay," "eh, eh." "He said that he had seen the great python under the bank." "EH!" "The python!" "He wants us," "eh, eh, eh," "to help him catch it."

She points out that the "ehs" overlap and coincide with the other speaker's words, and with everyone often talking at once, one sometimes wonders how anyone knows what is being said.[24]

Elizabeth, Lorna's daughter, remarked how our notions of secret ballots and majority rule would have seemed strange to the Bushmen she met, as disrespectful of the contribution of each person. The San preferred consensus, with everyone knowing the thoughts and feelings of everyone else and everyone agreeing to go along. Consensus is not necessarily unanimity. It is agreement to accept a collective decision after everyone has had access to a common pool of relevant information, time to think, and an opportunity to hold forth.[25]

George Silberbauer, who did fieldwork with the /Gwi San in the Central Kalahari Reserve of Botswana from 1958 to 1960, tells a story of group involvement in a domestic conflict that illustrates how the logic of discussion can move to consensus. The situation involved a husband who was a difficult character, slow to understand and quick to anger, vain, pompous, and moody. Eventually, his wife went off to another band with the husband's recently widowed best friend, "a dwarf, a virtuoso dancer…successful hunter…and rumored to be a bit of a demon as a lover." The abandoned husband was inconsolable at the loss of both his wife and his best friend. As custodian of the *!nore* (the water hole), he could not be expected to move, but he refused to remarry and generally made a pest of himself. The band suffered his misery for more than a year. Every time he threw a tantrum, the band resumed discussion about what to do. Eventually they sent word of his suffering to the ex-wife and friend. In the meantime, the wife had been missing her daughter and mother but refused to leave her new partner. The band resumed its discussions until some bright spark suggested that since both husband and wife wanted to be with the friend, why not a ménage à trois? This was unprecedented in /Gwi history, but after more discussion, the polyandrous marriage was agreed to by all three. The novel arrangement lasted, though not without problems, as an original collectively constructed solution.[26]

Leadership in decision making can be assumed by anyone initiating an issue of shared concern. The course of the discussions and the time taken depend on the issue's urgency. In dealing with something controversial, someone in the band may begin a long, slow campaign of quiet and serious discussion with one person at a time, or the person might test the wind by discussing it with one or two individuals within earshot of the real target and then paying attention to the reaction. This forced eavesdropping avoids direct confrontation with the other person, who would be guilty of bad manners if he or she was to join in the conversation. However, opponents are free to do the same. George Silberbauer describes the band being treated to "the occasionally comic spectacle of two sets of orators making their conflicting arguments, each pointedly ignoring the other, but striving desperately to avoid a breach of either logic or etiquette, trying to answer point with counter-point without being seen to attack directly."[27] When a discussion becomes too angry, some of the more placid participants might defuse the situation by politely withdrawing attention, by fussing with an apparently well-attended cooking fire, or creating some distraction. Without an audience, the overheated rhetoric soon cools, and the discussion can be resumed when everyone is calmer. Since all people affected by a decision generally have access to the relevant information and plenty of opportunity to speak and be heard, there tends to be little competition. The emotionally calm atmosphere helps separate idea from personality, while maximizing the incorporation of the collective experience of the group.[28]

Nevertheless it is important not to idealize the San. They are fully capable of the range of human foibles — including selfishness, envy, anger, and even homicidal violence. Despite the numerous mechanisms reinforcing reciprocity, caring, and sharing, arguments do occasionally become passionate and fights break out. With spears, knives, and poison arrows at hand, the most serious fights sometimes quickly turn lethal.

For instance, historically the San have surprisingly high homicide rates. In 1972, Richard Lee calculated that there were a total of 22 killings in a base population of approximately 1,500 Ju/twasi over the previous 50 years, resulting in a homicide rate of 29.3 deaths per 100,000. This is high by both African and European standards. As a comparison, in 1972 in the United States, there were 18,880 homicide victims, for a rate of 9.2 per 100,000. Only in a few American cities did the rate exceed that of the San (Washington, DC: 32.8; Baltimore: 36.8; Detroit: 40.1; and Cleveland: 40.3). However, Lee argues that the raw data do not provide a good measure of social violence. He points out that the relatively low American homicide rate is due in large part to the nation's excellent hospital emergency room facilities, which treat gunshot and knife wounds that in a wilderness situation would almost certainly be fatal. There is also no doubt underreporting of auto-accident deaths resulting from homicidal road rage and of domestic violence. More tellingly, when the total deaths due to the Vietnam War were factored in, the homicide rate was elevated to 100 deaths per 100,000 people.[29]

Lee noted that fights among Bushmen were unpredictable, even hysterical in nature, and he came to regard the violence among the Ju/twasi as a kind of "temporary insanity" or "running amok" rather than an instrumental or calculated act. Violence was not a means to an end.[30] The Ju/twasi displayed a pervasive fear of violence, and groups were quick to intervene when a fight broke out. There was also a complete absence of any ritualized fighting — no contact sports or mock combat. The bottom line is that Bushmen tend to regard violence as a pathological aberration, and they direct considerable energy and ingenuity toward dealing with conflict creatively.

The most effective method for resolving conflict before disagreement becomes violent is discussion, constantly mediating competing claims and needs. The San exemplify what Socrates proposed: that the power of discussion is not simply a mechanism to resolve conflicting ideas; it's a mode of inquiry that in itself helps individuals recognize a deeper shared unity of need and purpose. This is why Socrates insisted on the *dialektike* of face-to-face discussion as both the heart of philosophy and the primary mechanism of Athenian democracy.

Like the nomadic San, Socrates wrote nothing, and repeatedly drew attention to the superiority of discussion over text and lecture. He pointed out that discussion, unlike text, connects ideas and abstractions to their authors as whole embodied human beings. Each faces the other, sharing the same space and time, fully exposed as an instrument and embodiment of political truth. Unlike the prepared lecture with its one-way flow of information, discussion requires all participants to think on their feet. More information is available. Voice, tone, facial expression, and body language can reveal unscripted meaning: degrees of warmth and hostility, respect, trust, and finally intention. For Socrates, as in shamanic systems of knowing, intention helps determine outcome. Most importantly, the simple fact of sharing language, space, time, and self-consciousness reinforces the need to care for a shared humanity. We need one another to be most fully ourselves.

## The Politics of the Iroquois

At the time of European contact, some six hundred indigenous nations occupied North America, each with its own language or dialect, customs, history, and political order. They were more differientiated than the San but all exemplified in varying combinations and degrees the principles of primal politics. They tended to be egalitarian, to respect the unique individual and to govern by discussion and consensus. For example, the Yakimas of the Columbia River area governed through direct democracy, with all members of the tribe meeting in a daily general council. The Lakota had a more differentiated system based on civil societies of wise elders, *nacas*, meeting as a tribal council.[31] Like the Bushmen, the Lakota council acted only after consensus. While some tribes were sedentary farmers and fishermen, and others were nomadic hunters, all hunted to some degree and all were in daily direct contact with wilderness. All shared some notion of a political order guided by spiritual practices attuning humans to the sacredness of all creation. Religion and politics were woven into everyday life.

One of the better-known and more complex examples of a spiritual politics comes from the Iroquois — the Haudenosaunee, or People of the Longhouse. This was a confederation of five nations, the Mohawk, Oneida, Onondaga, Cayuga, and Seneca that later included the Tuscarora. The moral authority of the chiefs at the center of political order was established in part on an egalitarian ethic of voluntary simplicity. In order to hold office, the elected representatives on the Great Council were obliged to give away surplus wealth, ensuring that they were *poorer* than the people they led. As Cadwallader Colden, an eighteenth-century English colonial governor, reported:

> Their Great Men, both Sachems (civil chiefs) and captains (war chiefs) are generally poorer than the common people, for they affect to give away and distribute all the Presents of Plunder they get in their Treaties or War, so as to leave nothing for themselves. If they should be once suspected of selfishness they would grow mean in the opinion of the Country-men and would consequently lose their authority.[32]

Our difficulty today in imagining a vow of poverty as a requirement for holding office gives a stark measure of the materialist foundations of our politics.

The constitution of the Iroquois confederacy emerged sometime between the twelfth and fifteenth centuries as a result of a vision received by a messianic figure, Deganawidah. His Great Law of Peace (Kaianerekowa) provided the spiritual basis for democratic and peaceful governance unlike anything that existed in Europe. It gave women a key role as custodians of moral authority. Clan mothers would nominate chiefs to serve on the Grand Council and then observe the sessions without participating directly, but retaining the power to impeach any leader who failed to serve the collective good. Since women had a primary role in caring for the very young, they were assumed to be less tempted by power and glory. So they were also put in charge of moral education, as custodians of a political culture based on honesty, generosity, and love of community.

Cadwallader Colden, who spent more than half a century in colonial service in America, finishing his career as lieutenant governor of the colony in 1761, is one of the primary sources from the period. He was adopted by the Mohawks, and in 1747 he published the second extant book on the Iroquois. He was struck by the extraordinarily high-minded quality of their leaders who "never execute their Resolutions by Compulsion or Force Upon any of their People." Rather, "Honour and Esteem are their principal Rewards, as Shame and being Despised are their Punishments."[33]

Like Bushmen, the Iroquois are an example of an attempt to institutionalize something like the Platonic ideal: that kings and chiefs should be lovers of truth and righteousness rather than wealth and power. Implicit in this is the insight that the ultimate foundation for the just and good society resides in the souls of its members. No institutional order can produce justice if those in charge are small minded or corrupt. Not surprisingly, a number of the framers of the US Constitution were deeply impressed by this example of indigenous democracy. Benjamin Franklin, like Colden, was moved to invoke the political wisdom of these so-called "ignorant savages" in exhorting his fellows to construct a union.

> It would be a very strange thing if Six Nations of Ignorant Savages should be capable of a Scheme for such an Union and be able to execute it in such a manner, as that it has subsisted Ages, and appears indissoluble, and yet a like union should be impracticable for ten or a dozen English colonies.

Ultimately, the Constitution of the United States incorporated key structural features of the Iroquois confederacy, in particular the principles of the separation of powers and of checks and balances. However, more radically democratic ideas like female suffrage were ignored. Oren Lyons, a contemporary "faithkeeper" of the Onondaga and a political philosopher, has pointed out that the most important omission was the spiritual law on which all other principles and practices rested: the notion of the sacredness of the natural world and all its creatures... including humans.[34]

Instead, the European founding fathers inserted Adam Smith's pseudo-scientific law of the invisible hand of the free market, a well-intentioned rationalization that encouraged individuals who own property to focus exclusively on immediate self-interest. From an Iroquois point of view, the outcome was easily predictable: rule of the wealthy, by the wealthy, for the wealthy — a plutocracy. Over two centuries ago Colden was honest and astute enough to see how elevating private interest as the primary principle for public conduct was inevitably corrupting.

> Alas! we have reason to be ashamed that these Infidels, by our Conversation and Neighborhood have become worse than they were before they knew us. Instead of Vertues, we have only taught them Vices that they were entirely free of before that time. The narrow Views of private interest have occasioned this.[35]

Colden's image of the contrast between the moral integrity of Iroquois leadership and the corruption of our politicians brings us back to the central issue for politics and philosophy, the psyche, or soul, of the individual and its attunement to the good of the whole — the big picture.

## The Big Picture — Everyone a John Locke

No community, tribe, nation, or society can persist as a coherent entity without a shared narrative of meaning. Such narratives function as mythologies, answering the fundamental questions of mythology: Who are we? Where do we come from? What allegiance do we have to this shared way of life? What should we seek?

Our existence is deformed without emotionally resonant *and true* mythologies. Poststructuralist scoffing at such grand narratives of meaning and the refusal to construct any sort of big picture to guide action results in the reproduction of the status quo — the anthropocentric and materialistic narratives of industrial capitalism. The shared mythic framework of Bushman cosmology is compact but locates the human condition emphatically in the in-between. Shamanically assisted openness to paradox dissolves ego-driven certainty and fosters empathy, generosity, and good feeling, helping keep opposing principles in balance. Mutual understanding and mutual concern are much easier in such a spiritually attuned frame of mind. Discussion flows more smoothly and moves toward the bigger picture.

In the Bushman band, their natural tendency to consider the whole is reinforced by the fact that the social whole is not an abstraction like the nation-state. Rather, it is concrete and easily grasped: a collection of individuals, present and accounted for, each with his or her own idiosyncrasies, frailties, and virtues. Everyone is part of a human-animal complex, walking on the same earth, sleeping under the same moon and the same constellations of stars. The very structure of the primal band, represented by the circle of discussants facing one another around the campfire, requires that people live much of their lives in front of one another. In this situation, mendacity and hypocrisy are more quickly exposed. Facing one another, people find it easier to empathize with opposing positions around the circle and accordingly less risky to expose themselves. We can imagine going around the circle questioning ourselves, questioning others, thinking about the contribution of each. Knowing the stories that shape differing perspectives drives the discussion toward inclusivity. When focused by the truth quest, a multiplicity of viewpoints can be integrated into a shared bigger picture.

With the rise of civilization, the construction of such normative, numinous big pictures of the human condition has been increasingly reserved for the "chiefs," the professionals and experts of political philosophy. In the primal band, everyone participates in discussions concerning the good of the whole; everyone grapples directly with the primordial mysteriousness of the early times; everyone is philosopher-royalty.

Just as each individual draws from and contributes to this shared mythological context, so each Bushman adult has direct access to experiencing the spirit world of the early times through shamanic trance. Each individual has what Emerson demanded: a philosophy based on an original experience of the universe. This situation is both empowering and humbling. We all have something to say about the big issues, but none of us has all the answers. There are no certainties. However, this is not the relativism of every opinion being equally significant. Perspectives are meaningful — truthful — to the degree that they follow the discipline of the primal dynamic. Minimal criteria are embodied in the four elementary practices and values of primal politics, the discipline of the quest.

In summary, the three dimensions of experience most characteristic of traditional Bushman life are also the three most removed from our own way of life. They offer a dramatically expanded and deepened vision of what it means to be human and thus a more reliable foundation for the quest and for a new politics. These three dimensions are as follows:

- Politics and the quest take place in public, through open-ended face-to-face-discussion and storytelling in an egalitarian and democratic situation where children, adults, and the elderly all face one another and express their needs, opinions, and visions directly. This is symbolized as the innermost core of the mandala of primal politics (page 118).
- Politics and the quest are embedded in a living wilderness ecology where animal and human communities regularly cross the boundary separating them, and where this boundary crossing can be experienced as ecstatic and enchanted — having the aura of the sacred. This is symbolized by the area surrounding the outermost circle in the mandala of primal politics.
- Politics and the quest are equally embedded in the inner invisible dimension of the psyche — the "nonmaterial pole" of consciousness. Bushmen called this inner reality the spirit world, which is also a part of the early times, equivalent to the Australian Aborigine dreamtime. We can regard this dimension of reality as the inner depths of outer wilderness as it is experienced by the self-reflective searching individual also represented by the innermost circle, the truth quest.

From the point of view of the classical Greek polis we can regard the Bushman band as the ultra-polis: smaller than the polis, more personal, more egalitarian, totally self-sufficient, and with universal participation in discussion as the primary medium of both the truth quest and governance. This is the political-economic foundation of deep democracy, a discussion-based epistemology that feeds and is fed by the *arete* of the whole person. It supports and is supported by each individual's direct participation in constructing a shared normative big picture. The preliterate bushman, while ignorant of the sad and brilliant history of civilization, and largely unaware of the impending crisis of globalization, is ironically closer to a political philosophy of original insight than we are. In a real sense, each Bushman is the author and creative agent of his or her own political cosmology in a far more robust fashion than the citizen of the bureaucratic nation-state…everyone is a Socrates, everyone is a John Locke.

# CHAPTER 8

# "IF YOU DON'T DANCE, YOU DIE"

The springbok seems to be coming, I can feel the dark hair on the springbok's flanks. Go climb up on the rocks over there so you can look around on all sides! I feel the springbok feeling.... I am used to feeling that way: I have a sensation in my calves as if the blood of the springbok dripped down on them.

— Bushman hunter-shaman[1]

In that place far-off, where //Kabbo once lived,
the sorcerers, dancing, would fall into a trance.
Wanting us to believe they were no longer men,
our sorcerers would turn themselves into birds....

In //Kabbo's place, far off, and still farther...
We lived, then, in a world of men become birds.

— Dia!kwain, a nineteenth-century /Xam Bushman[2]

Tracking is like dancing. You are talking with God when you are doing these things.

— !Nqate, Bushman hunter, *The Great Dance: A Hunter's Story*

## The Veil between the Worlds

In 2010, the idiosyncratic filmmaker Werner Herzog took the general public, for the first time, on a filmic journey into the previously restricted cave of Chauvet-Pont-d'Arc in southern France. In *The Cave of Forgotten Dreams*,[3] he confronts us with vivid, beautifully formed painted images from the early days of human symbolic consciousness. The cave was discovered in 1994 when spelunkers entered the Chauvet vault, which had been sealed by a rockfall for twenty thousand years, and found on its walls some of the oldest painted images in the world, going back some thirty-two thousand years. As Herzog's handheld camera tracks over the torch-lit wall, the images seem to leap off the textured surface. In the Megaloceros Gallery of ancient herbivores, a series of four shaggy-maned horse heads gives the impression of animation. Below, sketched in confident outline, two rhinos face each other, horns locked in what looks like the sort of gripping encounter our hunting ancestors must have periodically witnessed.

One does not have to be an anthropologist to sense the passion and focused intention that went into the execution of the art. These are not doodlings or the casual sketches of a playful child. The original hunting-gathering cultures, like the animals depicted, have disappeared from the landscape of Europe, making it difficult to know anything of the intention of the long-dead artists or the meanings of the paintings. The power and precision of the images, however, make it clear that something profound was stirring in the human imagination many thousands of years before civilization.

Southern Africa has a tradition of rock art related to that found in Europe, but it differs in a number of important respects. The most significant is a connection to a living indigenous, shamanic culture — that of the San Bushmen, whose lineage has continued to hunt the big game of southern Africa since the great global human migration. This connection, established over the past few decades of intensive research, makes it possible to understand the shamanic significance of many of the South African paintings. Since there are a number of connections between the southern African and the

European tradition, it is also now possible to make a reasonable guess at some aspects of the European art. Considering the two traditions together reinforces our understanding of the shamanic religion of hunter-gatherers as ubiquitous and ancient. As we now examine how seamlessly politics and religion were interwoven for the San, we can imagine ideas for healing our own morally and spiritually debased way of life.

The European paintings are contained in some three hundred underground rock art sites, which are generally dark and inaccessible and often dangerous. The southern African art adorns some fifteen thousand open-face rock shelters — often with breathtaking views — where people lived, ate, danced, and sang. Since the paintings are exposed to the elements, they quickly fade, making dating much more difficult. However, pieces of buried painted rock from the Apollo 11 cave in Namibia have been positively dated to between twenty-seven and twenty-five thousand years old — roughly within the time frame of the oldest European paintings.[4] The southern African tradition also includes numerous rock engravings, some of which have been dated as several thousand years old.[5]

In addition, already mentioned discoveries of a seventy-seven-thousand-year-old piece of carved ochre — ochre being one of the primary ingredients in the rock painting — and one-hundred-thousand-year-old ochre painting kits at Blombos Cave on the coast of South Africa suggest this tradition of symbolic rock art might be very much older. This evidence, together with the findings of San material culture at Border Cave, dated to forty-four thousand years ago, indicates a southern African tradition of symbolic and possibly shamanic activity forty thousand years or more prior to the European paintings.

While there are significant differences between the African and European traditions, there are striking similarities. These include naturalistic representations of many animals, including in Europe some now-extinct species like bison, lion, and mammoth. More interestingly, both traditions contain abstract, complex patterns of grids and the distinctive enigmatic *therianthropes* — images combining human and animal features in a variety of combinations of limbs, hooves, fins, wings, and horns. The Drakensberg painting that helped initiate my baboon revelation contains a classic therianthropic figure in the form of an upright human figure with antelope hooves and an antelope face. Both traditions have fantastic creatures that seem utterly mysterious. Many of the paintings in both traditions were executed with the sort of focused intention and effort indicative of their value and meaning to the artist.

What did the paintings mean? Why, in Europe, were they painted in such inaccessible, dark, dangerous, and uncomfortable caverns? Why in southern Africa did they adorn thousands of open-air rock shelters where the people chose to live? Why were figures superimposed on one another? What of the part-human, part-animal therianthropes and the mysterious monster-like pictures? Why did they suddenly appear as if out of nowhere?

The history of the academic study of prehistoric art is a cautionary tale of arrogance and the power of preconceived ideas to determine perception. Because most of the paintings were first discovered in France and Spain, European scholars dominated the field, and in fact, many of the European paintings have been off-limits to the general public since their discovery. Revealingly for the power of wholistic thinking, it was some of the early amateurs — like Marcelino Sanz de Sautuola, who in 1879 found the first prehistoric rock paintings in the cave at Altamira — who immediately intuited their great antiquity. Sautuola's estimation of the great age of the paintings was almost universally ridiculed by an academic community, caught up in Eurocentric conceits of linear progress, refusing to believe that the magnificently painted bison could be the work of our barbarous ancestors. It was only after Sautuola's death, and after twenty-three years of his being vilified and accused of fraud, that scholars examined the paintings carefully, recognized their error, and apologized. The apology was most dramatically delivered in an article "Mea culpa d'un sceptique" (mea culpa of a skeptic) by one of the leading prehistorians and skeptics, Emile Cartailhac.[6] Ironically, years later the apology continued to receive more acclaim than the much maligned Sautuola for his correct interpretation.

European scholars were also hampered by the fact that they worked without any surviving tradition of European hunting-and-gathering cultures, which might have given clues as to the intention of the artists. Once more caves were discovered and the antiquity of the Altamira art was more generally accepted, a variety of fairly arbitrary interpretations were proposed for the images, ranging from art for art's sake and hunting magic to a complicated scheme of animal totemism. Some scholars even postulated intricate patterns linking the position, gender, and presumed meaning of the painted animal to the architecture of the cave, as if the early artists were anticipating academic fashion in a kind of primal structuralism.

By the 1980s, all the theories advocated up to then, including the orthodoxies that had dominated the field, had been thrown out as worthless. The European scholars, chastened by the clumsy dogmas of the past, seemed to retreat into a know-nothing skepticism, very much in the spirit of the revisionist deconstructionists of the Kalahari debate. Meanwhile, exciting advances were being made by South African scholars in interpreting the southern African rock paintings.[7]

Their work now makes it possible to synthesize a number of bodies of recent research into a reasonably coherent hypothesis: that Bushman shamanism is a contemporary expression of one of the oldest forms of religious-spiritual practice, one depicted in much of the southern African rock art. Since there are some fairly obvious connections between the southern African and the European paintings, the South African research suggests a similar shamanic meaning for at least some of the European paintings. Taken together, the two bodies of scholarship deepen our understanding of the role of spiritual experiences in ordering human society. The research fields this involves are as follows:

- The wealth of southern African rock art paintings that extend from prehistory into modern times, giving European scholars access to some of the last firsthand accounts from Bushmen familiar with this type of painting.
- Recent research from archaeology and genetic mapping that suggests that the European Paleolithic artists were most likely the descendants of the southern African hunter-gatherers who moved out of Africa some fifty thousand years ago.
- One of the world's largest collections of nineteenth-century ethnographic sources — the Bleek and Lloyd collection — recording the language and cosmology of the now-extinct South African Bushman cultures associated with the paintings.
- Ethnography on contemporary Bushman shamanism in the Kalahari Desert, where there are no rocks and therefore no existing rock art tradition but where the trappings of shamanic dance and accounts of living shamans can be linked to the ancient paintings farther south.
- The larger context of comparative shamanism, and the psychology and philosophy of altered states of consciousness.

What this research suggests is that the humans who left Africa to populate the planet most likely already had protoshamanic practices linked to ochre paint and quite possibly a shamanic rock-painting tradition. My hypothesis is that this shamanic Ur-religion emerged as a primordial balancing and guiding response to the evolutionary emergence of self-reflective consciousness and the human predicament of living in the in-between. The following three chapters suggest that shamanism in general and Bushman shamanism in particular have lessons that can be applied today in helping us recreate a spiritually based truth quest as a foundation for a new politics.

## Connecting the Dots

The foundation for understanding Bushman cosmology, and using it as a framework for understanding Bushman shamanism and southern African rock art, was laid by a German philologist, Wilhelm Bleek, who came to South Africa as an interpreter and in 1862 became curator of the Grey collection of the South African Library. Bleek was first introduced to Bushman culture in the 1860s when a number of /Xam Bushmen were brought back to Cape Town as prisoners of war from the frontier territory on the edge of the Kalahari Desert. He obtained permission from the governor to have a few of the prisoners live with him, his wife, and his sister-in-law, Lucy Lloyd, for the purpose of learning their language and culture. Fascinated, Bleek started recording their folklore, mythology, and stories, and spent the rest of his short life working with six main /Xam collaborators. At least one of them, a man named //Kabbo (whose name means "dream"), seems to have been a shaman.

Between 1870 and his death in 1881, Bleek, together with Lucy Lloyd, compiled a /Xam dictionary and recorded over twelve thousand pages of folklore and stories in the largest ethnographic collection on any single group of hunter-gatherers.[8] Bleek was also one of the first scholars to come across accounts from San who had direct experience of the rock-painting tradition, and so he became one of the first to recognize the religious significance of much of the art.[9]

One of the key sources for Bushman interpretations of the paintings comes from Joseph Orpen, who in 1873 was appointed British magistrate of an area in the northeast of South Africa near the Drakensberg mountains. Misleadingly called "Nomansland," the area was in fact occupied by San, various Bantu tribes, and Griqua (a nomadic Coloured group descended from the

Khoikhoi Griqua). In 1874, Orpen was ordered to go into the mountains to capture a Bantu (Hlubi) chief named Langalibalele. Realizing he needed an expert guide, he hired what he called a "half-tame" Bushman by the name of Qing.

Today, the Drakensberg still contains one of the greatest concentrations of the most complex and the most explicitly shamanic rock paintings. Orpen already had an interest in the rock paintings, had made copies of some, and had been in communication with George Stow, a self-taught geologist who also made many vivid copies of paintings from all over South Africa. Orpen was an educated and sensitive person who got on well with Qing and encouraged him to talk about his culture. Qing, it turned out, had firsthand knowledge of the methods and intentions of the painters and started interpreting the paintings for Orpen, who, without fully understanding, dutifully copied down what he was told. Confusion about the meanings of the paintings was compounded by the fact that Qing's explanations had to be translated into sePhuti (a Bantu language), which was then translated into English. Plus, as we now know, Qing was talking about trance experiences that were utterly unfamiliar to Victorian England, and he was doing so using highly metaphorical language.

Bleek obtained copies of Orpen's drawings without Orpen's detailed report, which was only published later in *The Cape Monthly Magazine*. Bleek immediately questioned his /Xam collaborators about the meaning of the images, and so established an independent line of interpretation. When Bleek put all this together, he was convinced that the paintings were not "mere daubings" or an "idle pastime" but expressed "ideas that most deeply moved the Bushman mind, and filled it with religious feeling."[10] Today, we can read Orpen's record of Qing's comments with the benefit of subsequent scholarship, and it is quite clear that Qing used terms to describe events that correlated with shamanic practices and experiences. These brief but friendly encounters between Bushman and European constitute the most detailed direct insight we have about the intentions and meaning of the southern African paintings.

At the time, the notion that Bushmen possessed a subtle and complex religious sensibility went against the prevailing racism, which preferred to see Bushmen as little more than animals of the veldt who had no moral claim to the land they occupied — land that the colonists coveted. So this early interpretive approach was sidelined; it was effectively buried in the fifties and sixties under the avalanche of quantitative fieldwork, which focused on counting and measuring the paintings and trying to draw simple statistical correlations between image, frequency, and location. Bleek and Lloyd's work was largely ignored until the 1970s, when an interdisciplinary team rediscovered its significance for connecting the dots between the paintings, contemporary Bushman ethnography, and cross-cultural studies on shamanism. At the heart of this interpretation is the trance experience of the shaman, which stands at the center of the religious and political life of the San Bushmen.

## Stories of the Early Times

Bushman mythology, or *kumkummi* — the Bushman oral tradition of stories, myths, folklore, and history that Bleek and Lloyd recorded — helps provide the big-picture cosmological framework for understanding Bushman politics with the trance experience at its center. Mythic narrative itself can be understood as a kind of living archaeology of consciousness connecting the experiences of the storyteller to the oldest and deepest patterns of meaning through complex metaphors and stories. As consciousness differentiates into self-consciousness, stories surface in the inspiration of individuals as if "coming from far off." In the words of one of the last surviving nineteenth-century /Xam Bushman shamans, //Kabbo:

> My fellow men are those who can listen to the stories
> That come to them from far-off, floating through the air.
> Even now they hear them come from places far away,
> These stories like the wind, floating like the winds.[11]

Stories float across the veldt between isolated groups of Bushmen, but they also float up, unasked, from the deepest, earliest glimmerings of consciousness to be welcomed and put into words in moments of quiet receptivity. Only narrative, the story, grasps the fundamental feature of consciousness emerging, not as a fact, but as an event unfolding over time. We still participate in that continuous process, moving it forward as we live and tell the stories of our individual and collective lives.

The largest narrative frame, the biggest picture, is the story of the creation of the cosmos within which the searching human emerges. The Bushman creation story focuses on a primary disruption — a fall from an earlier undifferentiated state that the Bushmen call the "first times" or the "early times," when "humans were like animals and animals like humans." During the transition from the early times to the present, humans acquired fire and language, discovered their mortality, and started living according to norms. This is the primordial "leap" into human being — the appearance of a self-conscious humanity separating itself from Voegelin's larger It-reality.

Megan Biesele, who spent many years collecting Bushman folklore in the 1970s, points out that storytelling is continually creative, existing only in memory and each new performance. Most of us who encounter folktales in print forget that every printed collection is an artifact of the time and place of the collection. What is remarkable is how the basic structure of the myths persists across time and place, making mythology simultaneously conservative and innovative. The fact that a core cosmology is shared among diverse Bushmen groups, in spite of the fact that everyone is free to tell his or her own version, is testimony to the depth and universality of the meaning.

The story of the hare and the moon is one of the most widespread of the myths dealing with the emergence of the human condition — the anxiety of mortality — the in-between. The fact that Mathias Guenther recorded some seventy versions of this myth reveals both its importance and how variability is taken for granted. The version quoted below is told from the perspective of the moon, which dies every month, only to be reborn. The moon first asks the hare — a trickster figure of the early times — to be its messenger to the village of the people and to tell them that from now on, when they die, they will not die forever but will be reborn like the moon. The hare gets it wrong, and he tells the people that, when they die, they will die forever. The hare's mistake costs humans their immortality, and with fear of death comes the anxiety of living in the in-between and of making mistakes.[12]

The style of the telling carries as much meaning as the content itself. The moon contrasts her own immortality with the mortality of all the creatures who, when they die, die forever. Biesele suggests the form of storytelling is almost a magical act, an invocation of a Noah's ark list of some twenty species conjuring the presence and personality of the animals. "There is a certain way of stressing the syllable that appears in no other context.... The list becomes a singsong. The eyes glaze over. The first syllable goes way down in tone. The second, the pluralization, goes up high and then comes down again, trailing off from near-singing into silence.... The effect it conveys is of a dream landscape dotted with an impossible plenty of 'kudus,... buffaloes,... eland,... giraffes.'"[13]

[The moon speaks]
I die, I live; living, I come again;
I become a new moon.
Man dies; man, indeed, dies; dying he leaves his wife.
When I die, I return, living.
The gemsbok. The gemsbok dies, the gemsbok dies, altogether.
The hartebeest. The hartebeest dies, the hartebeest dies, altogether.
The she-ostrich. It dies, it indeed dies.
The kudu. The kudu indeed dies, and dying, it goes away.
The springbok. The springbok dies and, dying, it goes away forever.
Myself, I die; living again, I come back.
The korhaan [bustard]. The korhaan dies; the korhaan dying,
goes away.
The cat does [die]; it dies. The cat goes away, dying.
The jackal. The jackal dies; dying, the jackal goes away.
The lynx goes away, dying.
The hyena. The hyena dies, it goes away, dying, dying.
The eland. The eland dies and dying, it leaves.
Myself, I die. Living again, I come back.
People see me; people say: "Look, the Moon does indeed lie here;
it is grown, it is a Full Moon."
Things which are flesh must indeed die.[14]

Biesele notes that storytellers approach this listing with a kind of relish. They love to count off the animals at any opportunity. If they think they missed one, they will start over from the beginning. This kind of passionate individualized telling and retelling, while the band sits face-to-face around the fire, represents the primordial political community in its essential elements. Anyone can tell the story his or her own way. Yet the telling is also conservative, symbolically connecting the individual to the human group and the animal community, and then both human and animal to the cosmic story. The creative, ritual telling becomes an act of participation, healing the anxiety of the in-between by symbolically invoking the community of being and making the human at home in the cosmos.

## Trickster Metaphysics

In the story of the moon and the hare, human beings become mortal because the hare is behaving like a bumbling trickster. The Bushman trickster, like trickster figures in mythologies the world over, is an agent of transformation, and transformation is directly connected to the trickster's typical character as a shape-shifter, neither fully one thing nor the other, someone betwixt and between all moral and ontological categories. The trickster is the embodiment of contradiction, creator and destroyer of norms, clown, monster, giver of fire, creator of worlds. Having such a confounding figure at the center of one's worldview helps to keep the mind nimble as it moves between opposites, both creating meaning and tearing it down to make room for new creation.

As Mathias Guenther points out, the trickster forms are prodigious. Usually but not always male, the trickster can take the form of a jackal or a louse or, as with the /Xam Bushmen, a little green flying insect — Kaggen (or trickster) — the mantis. He can also be humanoid, as in a black man "tall as a windmill,"* dressed in a loincloth and riding a giant dog, or a tall white man on a horse with a dark beard and "a chalk white face which shifts back and forth from handsome to hideous." He can be part-human, part-animal, as in the therianthropic antelope-shamans depicted in the rock paintings. He can be incorporeal like the wind or sunshine, or monstrously deformed, as in this description by Guenther:

> His thin body is ruffled and covered all over with spidery fibers. Numerous big toes stick out from his cocoon-like cover, as though to compensate for his having only one, eight-toed, crippled and misshapen leg.... His body was of such huge size that, when in pain of death, he gouged out the dry riverbeds of the central Kalahari with his thrashing, as well as formed rivers and rain clouds from his putrefying flesh and hair.[15]

As the agent of transformation, the trickster is the giver of norms, but as the prankster, he is also the enemy of all boundaries, flagrantly desecrating the order he has created. He plays tricks on others and also becomes the victim when they backfire. He is lustful and greedy, a parody of human excess who flouts the taboos surrounding the most powerful of animal drives, eating and sex. In one story, frantic gluttony drives this repulsive creature to cut off and eat pieces of his own flesh, screaming in pain as his greed overrides his agony. In another story, lust drives the baby trickster deity to kill

---

* Southern African farmers typically get water by digging boreholes on their land and installing simple windmills to pump the groundwater into a dam.

his father and try to rape his mother with comical results.[16] Outrageous self-contradiction seems his only consistent feature. In the ultimate reversal, this contradictory creature is also the creator of the universe. No wonder naive early Europeans dismissed such stories as barbaric — perverse and childish nonsense.

After many years living with the Ju/twasi, Lorna Marshall finally realized such self-contradiction could not just be dismissed as evidence of a failure of rationality. Rather, it seems to be an intentional expression of the irreducible paradox of human consciousness living in the in-between, caught in the tension of good and evil.

> The people obviously imagine the two ≠Gao N!a's as different and speak of them in different manners. They tell tales of the old ≠Gao N!a without restraint, say his name out aloud, howl and roll on the ground with laughter at his exploits and humiliations. When they speak of the great one in the eastern sky, they whisper and avoid speaking his name. They offered no explanation for the radical difference of character and function between the two beings. Yet they think that somehow in the rightness of things these two beings must be one, so one they are said to be.[17]

Today, we have even more reason to be reflective and respectful of Bushman cosmology, for our own cosmic story rests on a similar trickster-like paradox. On the face of it, Western science, based on empirical rationalism, is antithetical to paradox and mystery. And yet our best scientific understanding of our origins tells us with increasing precision that billions of years ago the entire universe burst forth in an unimaginable explosion of energy…out of a point. What could be more contradictory than this first fact of modern cosmology — that the intricate magnificence of the earth, and by extension human consciousness, unfolded out of an event of unimaginable cosmic violence? The trickster reminds us that when talking about ontologically primary realms, we are invariably forced into expressions of *coincidencia oppositorum*, a unity of opposites.

Some of our most creative scientists who uncovered the story of the universe emerged on the other side of objectivity, fired up into mystics. Albert Einstein, the paragon of mathematical rationality, discovered, over and over, that the higher the mountain of knowledge, the larger the shadow of mystery. Knowing exists in a fundamental relationship to not-knowing. All norms exist in tension with the chaos of no norms. The only absolute is that there are no absolutes. And this absolute itself might not be absolute.... The trickster rules!

Imagining the trickster as the creator of the universe encourages us not to take ourselves too seriously, to be more humble in the push-pull between inner and outer, self and other, individual and community, right and wrong. Trickster stories stimulate us to think dialectically about the lesser contradictions of life and to be patient with those who argue with us. They coax us to stay open to the flow of thought from thesis to antithesis to creative resolution in a more expanded synthesis.

This democratizing effect of trickster metaphysics is underlined by the fact that there is no Bushman Bible, no sacred scripture, no priestly bureaucracy, no fatwas or papal edicts. Modern scholars can be easily misled by the fact that the *kumkummi* come to us in published volumes as authoritative primary sources. But the text freezes the process of storytelling and obscures a primary function of myth as public performance, as politics. Primal politics gives individuals the freedom to embellish stories as they feel appropriate, including contemporary references to windmills, horses, dogs, and even the Boer farmer. For example, as a result of missionary work by the Afrikaans Dutch Reformed Church, even Jesso Cristo (Jesus Christ) makes an appearance. But Jesus is no longer the incarnation of sublime reason. Instead he has become a shape-shifting Bushman trickster, turning water into wine, feeding the multitude with a few loaves, and seducing Mary at the well. The metaphors are Christian, the meaning shamanic. All can retell the story in their own way, while still preserving the older, larger, more universal meaning.

## Dancing Makes Our Hearts Happy

The healing or trance dance is a way of directly experiencing the life-enhancing energies of the trickster-mediated early times. Both historically and today, the dance is as democratic as storytelling — the *kumkummi* — in that it is a part of normal socialization and open to all. Everyone joins in, young and old, children, teenagers, and women with babies slung under their arms or tied to their backs. While older children might join the circle, the younger ones often play on the edges imitating the adults, stamping out the steps, clapping, pretending to go into trance, doubling over, collapsing, shaking, screaming, and laughing. Most adults attempt to enter deep trance, but only about half the men and a third of the women succeed in becoming accomplished and recognized healers. Since the dance is communal and open to all, it represents a radical democratization of shamanism. Almost all experience the shamanic world of spirit directly to some degree.

Twele, a contemporary Bushman, describes the dance as the single most important ritual activity in the life of the traditional Bushman band:

> [The dance]...is the favorite thing for all Bushmen to do. We dance when we are happy and we dance when we are sad. When we get ready to hunt we dance because it helps us find the animal, and then after the kill we bring home the meat and dance again. We also dance when we feel sick. It helps us take away the sickness and it keeps us well. The dance is the most important aspect of our lives. It is our prayer, our medicine, our teaching and our way of having fun. Everything we do is related to that dance.[18]

As Twele indicates, dances are initiated for various reasons: before a hunt to control game, after a hunt to resolve any ill feelings caused by an unfair division of meat, to heal the sickness of a particular individual, or, as among the /Xam and Southern Bushmen, to bring rain by catching and killing a mythic rain animal. Whatever the pretext, everyone present is invigorated, everyone receives healing and guidance. The collectively generated ecstasy of the people who love to dance, like the collectively generated wisdom of the people who love to argue, bonds a collection of separate, and at times contentious, individuals into a more loving, sharing band.

The way the dance is described in the literature is very similar to the way I have experienced it on two occasions. One time was as an observer-participant at Nyae Nyae in 1999, and then a number of times over several days in the central Kalahari near D'Kar in 2007. What follows is a composite description based on published accounts and my own firsthand observations.

Typically, like most Bushman activities, the dance begins informally, with a few people collecting a stash of firewood large enough to keep the fire going throughout the night.[19] Women gather around the fire, sitting in a circle, and start to clap and sing the ancient, haunting songs; these are intricate, contrapuntal chants, with clapping weaving together several different rhythms at once. The songs have few words, but the tunes, together with the clapping and dancing, concentrate a kind of spiritual energy present in the dancers and the group, which Bushmen refer to as */num*. This can be understood as roughly equivalent to Henri Bergson's *élan vital*, Chinese *chi*, Sanskrit *prana*, Hawaiian *mana*, or Hebrew *ruach*. The fire is the focal point, generating warmth, light, and its own */num*, which holds and concentrates the group energy. As more people gather, dancers start stamping out a circle surrounding the singers.

There is no fancy choreography, and the dance is not particularly pretty. The point is not display but transformation of consciousness. The dancers move with short staccato jumps, lifting their feet only a few inches and stamping down; the typical sequence of four steps barely moves the dancer forward. Some dancers wear long belts of rattles made from dried caterpillar cocoons, with small pieces of stone and ostrich eggshell carefully inserted into the cocoons. Despite its simplicity, the dance is performed with such intensity that every step produces a rattling rainstorm of sound, shaking the flesh on the dancers' bones and making their heads bob up and down. As the dancing, stamping, singing, and clapping continue for hours, the collective */num* of the group gradually builds like a charge of static electricity, concentrating in the bodies of the individual healers.

According to the Bushmen, */num* normally rests at the base of the spine, but with activation it builds, slowly traveling up the spinal column. When it reaches the head, it boils, producing a highly agitated emotional state called *kia*, which is typically accompanied by jerking spasms, shaking, and shrieking. As Kinachau, one of the old Ju/twasi healers, said, "You dance, dance, dance, dance. Then the */num* lifts you up in your belly and lifts you in your back and you start to shiver. */Num* makes you tremble; it's hot. Your eyes are open, but you don't look around: you hold your eyes still and look straight ahead." Another powerful Ju/twasi healer, Kau Dwa, put it this way: "In your backbone you feel a pointed something and it works its way up. The base of your spine is tingling, tingling, tingling, tingling. Then */num* makes your thoughts nothing in your head."[20]

*Kia* is talked of as the deepest mystery, ultimately unknowable. Bushmen who have an unusual capacity to activate and work with */num* are called */num k"ausi*, "owners of */num*." In the West, they would be called shamans, healers, or medicine men and women. Scholars have noted the similarity between the Bushman experience of *kia* through dance and the Indian yoga activation of kundalini energy through a variety of disciplines. Kundalini energy, like */num*, resides at the base of the spine, sometimes imagined as a coiled snake. As it is activated, it rises, passing through and energizing a hierarchy of emotional-cognitive centers called chakras. When it reaches the crown chakra, kundalini explodes in ecstatic visions and paranormal healing powers. The ancient Jewish mystical tradition of Kabbalah has a similar, even more intricate map of this inner emotional-cognitive landscape. The ten *sphirot* (numbers) seem to be a more finely differentiated version of the yogic chakras, arranged in a complex tree of life configuration, culminating again in the *keter*, or crown chakra.

When the Brazilian psychiatrist and medical hypnotist Dr. David Akstein studied trance in a variety of contemporary Afro-American religions like Umbanda and Candomblé, he realized a new term was needed — "kinesthetic trance" — to describe how repetitive dancing could lead to the expanded states of awareness of shamanic trance. It is precisely the *extra*-ordinariness of the discipline — the endless, repetitive stamping, chanting, and clapping — that gradually overwhelms the rational everyday mind and opens consciousness to the larger extrarational field of information and energy. This is the sense in which I use the term *trance*. While many Western and Eastern traditions access transcendence through meditational disciplines, which quiet the mind and the body, the dance attains similar states by the opposite approach — hyperarousal of the body.[21]

Since the ego is identified with the everyday self we rely on for survival within a particular society, disabling the ego is ipso facto a bit like dying a "little death." The purpose, of course, is to be "reborn" more whole and healed. For this reason *kia*, like the hallucinogenic journey, is both exhilarating and frightening, healing and dangerous. While everyone dances, only a few go through the little death into deep trance and become powerful healers. Katz describes one initiate new to the experience:

> He has a look of tremendous fear as he dances. The singing, clapping and dancing in general are at a high pitch of intensity. *Kia* is threatening to overwhelm him, and he runs away from the dance. But instead of letting him stay away from the dance, two people go and take hold of him, one from the front, the other from behind, and physically bring him back to the dance. The three of them then continue dancing in the circle, remaining in physical contact, as the singing reaches a new level of intensity. They bring the fearful one back to what he most fears, but they are now physically with him. He is able to go through his fear and into *kia*.[22]

Sometimes the healers will fall to the ground shaking, trembling, moaning, and shrieking. Others will come around and massage the fallen healer, helping the */num* to flow. Sometimes the dance is so prolonged and so intense that the shaman will bleed from the nose (most likely due to a combination of exertion and dehydration). This was so common that early European explorers to South Africa also described it as the "dance of blood." The blood itself is then thought to contain */num* and will be wiped in characteristic streaks on the face. Typically, dancers will use dancing sticks to help prop themselves up so they can control the */num* and move their intention between deep trance and attending to the healing of the surrounding community.

With *kia*, the */num k"ausi* acquire extraordinary powers, as can some yogis who activate kundalini energy. In the case of Bushmen, this includes handling fire, "seeing the insides of people," diagnosing illness, traveling great distances, negotiating complex but invisible inner landscapes, climbing the "ropes" or "ladders" of light to "God's home," and then through these exertions bringing balance and healing to human affairs. As the Ju/twasi healer Kau Dwa said, "When you *kia*...you see people properly just as they are.... You're looking around because you see everything, because you see what is troubling everybody."[23] Sometimes sickness is understood as the attempt of the dead to pull one of the living into their realm. The healer might then engage in a struggle with the ancestral spirits on behalf of the sick living relative. Other times healing involves removing "arrows of sickness" and sending in good arrows of healing. Some dancers carry fly whisks made from the tail of wildebeest, eland, or giraffe; these appear only during the dance and are used to flick away arrows of sickness. As we will see, they are sometimes depicted quite clearly on the rock paintings.

There is no strict sequence, but a typical progression to deep trance might start off with a range of perceptual and bodily distortions — flashing lights like the illuminated zigzag patterns and nested arcs associated with the onset of a migraine headache and a common theme in rock paintings. This is also often followed by feelings of legs and arms elongating, and experiences of floating, flying, or swimming, another common theme in rock paintings. In the mythology of shamanic societies animals are often the gatekeepers to the spirit world and shamans commonly report experiences of encountering animal spirits or, more dramatically, "becoming animal" or "connecting to" the animal within — the realm of psychic life normally kept under lock and key by the civilized, focused ego. Reports from some of the old /Xam shamans describe entering trance and feeling the hair on the nape of the neck standing up as one turns into a spirit lion, which can then travel great distances, gather information, and when necessary act against enemies. A common spirit animal connected with the trance experience is the prized food antelope, the eland, which when killed releases its */num* to be channeled by anyone present. This encounter with the animal within — the shape-shifting werewolf of European folklore — metaphorically expressed the encounter with wilderness, both inner and outer, which gives us a perspective outside of ourselves necessary for insight and healing. Once this boundary has been crossed, the shamanic universe opens.

## The White Man Dances

The life of the urban Westerner is so radically different from that of the Kalahari Bushmen that the technique of the dance might strike us as bizarre and the descriptions of the trance experience fanciful. There is one European anthropologist — Bradford Keeney — who has succeeded in penetrating the depths of the Bushman trance experience and bringing back some universal wisdom. Keeney did more than successfully enter trance; he eventually became a powerful healer in his own right, recognized by some of the most revered Bushman shamans as well as by Western scholars.

Keeney was perhaps an unlikely candidate for his role of boundary crosser, as a southern white who was raised a devout Baptist in his grandfather's church in Missouri. Yet he was also primed for shamanism by a passionate Christianity and natural gifts for improvisational jazz, modern science, and spontaneous mystical ecstasy. He went through a rigorous Western academic initiation, gaining a PhD in psychology, training as a psychotherapist, and collaborating briefly with the famous Gregory Bateson before integrating this all in his own form of Bushman shamanism.

The first dramatic stage of his initiation occurred spontaneously while a student at the University of Missouri in 1971, when he was suddenly gripped by a classic kundalini-awakening religious experience. Late one unusually sunny and warm winter afternoon he was casually walking along a campus sidewalk when a general feeling of peace and well-being started to build until it slowly climaxed into a full-blown ecstatic mystical vision. As the experience grew in intensity, Keeney found his way into the empty university chapel, where he sat for the rest of the evening, swept up in the most profound experience of his life.

> The inside of my body began to get heated. The base of my spine felt like an oven that was getting progressively warmer until it burned with red-hot coals. As the inner heat turned into what felt like molten lava, my body began to tremble.... The fireball began to crawl slowly up my spine. It had a purpose of its own and nothing was going to stop it. Like a baby, after the breaking of its mother's water, this birth was determinedly on its way. As the lava like movement crept upward, heat spread throughout every cell in my body. I was on fire. My legs, abdomen, arms and especially my hands felt as though they could melt through metal.
>
> When the fire came to my heart, the spiritual lightning struck. It was like being pierced in some unintelligible way. My heart was opened and, rather than bursting, it grew and grew.... Soon my body had no boundaries — my head had encompassed all of space and time.[24]

The expansion of consciousness climaxed as an ultimate big picture, where the point of consciousness became identified with the entire physical universe. Keeney writes, "There was no 'I' having 'the experience' — there was only unexamined experience." His point of consciousness then plummeted to the emotional depths of meaning and value in human life, a profound love. So far this account could be that of any Bushman shaman experiencing *kia* — the boiling energy of trance. Then Keeney describes the appearance of images that have meaning only in terms of his religious and cultural frame: Jesus Christ, the Virgin Mary, and then a procession of saints. This soon led to the revelation that all religions were unified in the experience of love as healing:

> My vision soon went beyond the Christian tradition, becoming a global revelation of what seem to be the truths of all the world religions. I witnessed images of Gandhi, the Buddha, Mohammed, holy medicine people, shamans, yogis, mystics, and a host of other sacred beings, all residing in immediate luminosity.
>
> In this way I was shown that all religions and spiritual practice come from and return to the same source — a divine light born out of unlimited and unqualified love. This love boils inside the inner spiritual vessel and makes the body quake at the slightest awareness of its presence. As I received what others later told me was "direct transmission," "*sartori*," "cosmic consciousness," and "spiritual rapture," my body dripped with sweat and was baptized with tears that would not stop flowing. I

> knew, without any doubt, that I was having the most important experience a human being could ever have. And I have never doubted since that time that an experience of that kind is the greatest gift a person can receive.[25]

The revelation was a turning point in Keeney's life and inspired him to devote his life to healing. He eventually developed his own unique therapeutic modality, part psychoanalysis, part improvisational therapy, part body work.

Then in 1990 he saw John Marshall's 1969 film *N/um Tchai*[26] on Bushman trance healing and immediately realized that this ancient culture had at its center the sort of ecstatic "shaking" healing that had come to him spontaneously. Keeney tells a scarcely believable story of vivid dreams, waking visions, and synchronous encounters that eventually guided him to a place in the Kalahari where he would meet Twele, a teacher he had earlier seen in a dream. Twele appeared, greeted Keeney as if he had been waiting for him, and later introduced him to the dance:

> I didn't dance that night. It's more correct to say that I was danced — I exerted absolutely no effort or willful intention. Twele and Mantag gracefully moved over to me and brought me into the line of men who were dancing around the fire. I had entered the dance and was doing it with no choreography, dance lessons, or understanding of what was taking place.[27]

Keeney was convinced that the dance activated something deeply imprinted in human psychology, which both he and the Bushmen immediately recognized: "The dance had caught me. The Bushmen noticed and clapped their hands, shouting with joy. They, too, knew that I had been snared."

We need to remember that Keeney approached the Bushmen as both a scientific observer and an eager participant. By that time Keeney was also an artist, mystic, and improvisational therapist. He was supremely prepared for that night, both in having had comparable prior experience of trance states and in his readiness to drop objectivity and participate in creating a collective experience. The researcher who maintains objectivity must in principle repress subjectivity. This, almost by definition, blocks attention to subtle changes in inner states that would be required for participation in something like an all-night Bushman rave under the stars in the middle of the Kalahari.

While the repressive ego has to discipline the impulses of the body in the interest of the workday world, the collective dance reverses the process. The ego takes the body to the dance, but once there the "African body electric" takes over and, as Keeney puts it, "the ego listens." His experience was one of "being danced," with information and healing coming spontaneously and gratuitously from the larger reality that creates and sustains us:

> As I dance and shake, my material body feels as though it is dissolving. That is my experience. I become a cloud floating in the air. Images shift. Some people look like cloudy x-rays. I see dark spots on others that cry out to be touched. I act without thought or understanding. My hands are dowsing rods. They feel the tug of other bodies that want to be touched and shaken. All of this happens in a mind that is not mine but is all its own. This mind is outside the boundary of my skin. It is the mind of the dance. Everyone inside the circle is minded and mended by the greater pattern of connectivity. . . . I have become a human electrical transformer, a carrier of the life force.[28]

The dance is passionate, both visceral and spiritual. Much of the healing takes place through touch, skin on skin, a technique Keeney calls "skinship." Hands are used as dowsing rods, touching, stroking, fluttering, following their own wisdom. Healers in the depths of *kia* will even lie on top of those receiving healing, rubbing themselves to wipe the */num*-rich sweat onto the other. Boundaries dissolve. It is not sexual but sensual; it is a collective ecstasy, a release of tension and stress, together with a mobilization of loving energy that produces collective healing.

Since then, Keeney's authenticity as a shaman healer has been recognized by both Bushman healers and leading scholars on Bushman spirituality. A few years later, Megan Biesele, a leading Bushman ethnographer, spoke to two healers named /Kunta and ≠Ouma who danced with Keeney, and she concluded:

> There was no question in their minds but that [Brad's] strength and purposes were coterminous with theirs. I know this not only from [Keeney's] books, [but] from talking myself, a year or two later, with */Kunta*, *≠Ouma*, and others who had danced with Brad. They affirmed his power as a healer and their enjoyment of dancing with him. His work honors them by taking the details of their healing tradition in an effective way to a wider public, as they requested him to do.[29]

As in all other activities, the community recognizes that each person brings different life experiences, attitudes, and attributes to the dance. This means that everyone can have a slightly different experience of what may still be a single multifaceted spiritual reality.[30] Keeney is emphatic about the universal nature of the source and effect of */num*: "It is love, the 'big medicine.'" He continues, writing that

> *n/om* is variously talked about as a kind of spirit, an energy-like electricity, and a divine power. Its source is love, arising from the deepest kind of passionate relationship human beings are capable of experiencing — the same overpowering love that touches a couple when their child has just been born.[31]

We can approach love quite pragmatically, without slipping into either mawkishness or metaphysics, by looking at its effects. When we love something, or someone, we enjoy it for its own sake. We lavish energy and attention on it simply for what or who it is, without regard to its practical benefit. When in the presence of the beloved, we experience it as a source of joy, we experience it as beautiful in itself, independent of its utilitarian value. At the same time we feel drawn to it, connected, related, and, in being related, at home and healed. As Keeney writes:

> The Bushman's spiritual gift pierces the sheltering armor of your psyche, deflates its ego-centered self-importance, and then paradoxically fills you with a spiritual essence that cannot be confined. This "filling" arises from an unspeakable mystery, compassionate love so strong you feel gentle empathy for everyone, including your enemies.[32]

Here, then, we have a reliable, authentic Western translation of the Bushman trance dance that clarifies its role in Bushman society. Since, as we've seen, Bushman culture maintains a remarkable connection to ancient times, this translation helps us unravel a number of mysteries: the ethical egalitarianism of Bushman society, its fostering of the moral autonomy of the whole person, its storytelling and mythology, and even the evolutionary significance of shamnism.

## Paradoxical Ethics

Shamanism is an essential aspect of this book's model of primal politics, since it exemplifies a life dedicated to crossing boundaries and balancing opposites, resulting in intense experiences of connection to the entire community of being. The mother of all boundaries is that between the human being and the rest of the natural universe. In rapture and other heightened states of consciousness, we cross from everyday consciousness into that great mysterious, creative life force coursing through each and every one of us from the day of our conception to the day of our death. This manifests as an inner aspect of the outer universe and is no less diverse and mysterious. It also impels us to follow our deepest passion, to be creative, to individuate, to cross the less rigid boundaries of everyday political life: the tensions between self and other, enemy and friend, wife and husband, parent and child. In this way shamanic ecstasy provides the spiritual energy that connects people to one another and to the community of all being while giving them the courage and vitality to be fully themselves.

Bushmen recognized this process of boundary crossing and cultivated it as *thuru*,[33] the process whereby things become "what they are not" and, in so doing, paradoxically, *become more themselves. Thuru* also describes the process by which someone goes into rapture — *kia* — which the */num k"ausi* describe as "going beyond their normal selves." Yet at the same time, they will say, "I want to have a dance soon so that I can really become myself again." We also see *thuru* at work in the seasonal changes and the human life cycle of birth, growth, aging, and death. This is something similar to the dynamic interplay of yin and yang in Chinese philosophy or the unification of opposites in the flow of the Tao. Western philosophy has a related concept in the dialectical exploration of the in-between — the flow of awareness from thesis to antithesis into the larger truth of synthesis, which in turn provokes a new antithesis. And so the beat of *thuru* goes on, embodied in the shapeshifting trickster of mythology.

Following this boundary-crossing logic, the Ju/twa make little distinction between levels of healing — physical, spiritual, social, and cosmic. On the contrary, healing is precisely a matter of reconnecting what has been separated. It is self-evident to the small community living on the veldt that a healthy mind requires a healthy body, which together depend on a healthy society in harmonious relation to heaven and earth.

The crossing of boundaries also deepens the four primal values — each within itself as well as the back-and-forth dynamic among them. *Kia* expands the soul beyond the socially constrained persona, actualizing hidden potential. The dance begins by crossing the mind-body boundary as the stamping, singing, and clapping come together in a single shared intention. "Dancing makes your body happy," one shaman has said. Deeper levels of trance give the experience of encountering the animal within, the gatekeeper of the spirit world. Since "animal" is one of the complementary opposites of "human," moving into animal consciousness helps expand one's sense of self to include a richer spectrum of opposites — beyond what is conventionally good and bad. Keeney learned this earlier in his quest from a Cheyenne medicine man, William Tall Bull. Keeney writes that Tall Bull asked him: "How can you help others unless you know what it feels like to be drunk, financially broke, and filled with guilt?"

Tall Bull tells Keeney he knows too much about being good; he says, "Go out and make a fool of yourself. Then you can come back and I might teach you something else." So Keeney practiced being a bad boy, flunking out of class, cursing, drinking, and generally going over the top.

> I learned to recognize and appreciate the integrity of scoundrels, gangsters, tricksters and outsiders. Different truths are revealed when you change where you stand in life. From the muddy swamps, the successful city slicker looks rather moronic in the manicured suits and sterilized fingernails. As all good and low-down radicals know, from the outlook of Deep Truth the whole culture appears as a greed machine devoted to making profit off of ignorance and addictions. I went way down and got some views that changed me forever. That was part of my becoming a shaman.[34]

This is also the teaching of the whole person C.G. Jung recommended to the would-be psychoanalyst: "to bid farewell to his study and wander with human heart through the world" in order to "know how to doctor the sick with real knowledge of the human soul."[35] We can also understand this teaching as a therapeutic version of the Greek ideal of the whole person — that is, pursuing *arete*, human excellence, by exploring strong and extreme experiences, by integrating opposites into the health and beauty of the whole human being.

As I discussed earlier, for Jung a central part of this process involved integrating the shadow aspects of our psyche into consciousness. Everything ugly, primitive, abnormal, antisocial, and evil fills this cauldron of forgotten traumas, transgressions, impulses, and potentialities. Erich Neumann was one of the first of the Jungian thinkers to develop an ethic and a politics out of this Jungian concept. In *Depth Psychology and a New Ethic*, he points out that the processes of individuation, or psychological maturity and spiritual growth, all converge in the cultivation of a "living relationship with the shadow." Such a relation brings home to the ego its solidarity with the whole human species and its history, "since it discovers within itself a host of prehistoric psychic structures in the form of drives, instincts, primeval images, symbols, archetypes, ideas and primitive behavior patterns."[36] All of this humbles the ego's certitude and reminds us that it occupies only a very small and very recent part of psychic life. Rigid beliefs and ideologies reinforce the isolation of the brittle ego and its childish repression of everything naughty and bad.

Such maturity expands the compassion of the judge who can see himself sitting in the dock of the accused, or the adult who empathizes with the cowering child, or the person who feels pain when seeing a dog beaten. As we saw earlier, this resonates with the original meaning of *religion*, from the Latin *religare*, "to reconnect." Contained within the experience of reconnection is a sense of lost kinship recovered. There is an implied reciprocity in kinship, a sense of being recognized and feeling more at home and at peace in the universe, and in the process becoming more compassionate and loving.

A similar sense of *thuru* exists in the interplay between opposites in the Kabbalist teachings of Jewish mysticism, which, like shamanism and unlike some monastic and ascetic orders, is concerned with practical spirituality — *tikkun ha'olam* — healing and repairing the world.[37] Like shamanism, Kabbalah recognizes the authority of direct experience empowering the individual and dissolving bureaucratic authoritarianism. The same action can be transformed from good to bad depending on its place in the larger drama of life. The Kabbalist recognizes all judgments are inevitably made with imperfect knowledge of the whole situation. A background of mystery always remains. Taking this to heart humbles certitude. Adin Steinsaltz, one of the great contemporary Kabbalists, writes in *The Thirteen Petalled Rose*:

> As a general rule, there are no attributes of the soul that are good or bad. . . . In certain societies and cultures, love, pity, compassion may be considered good; and yet there may also be occasions, outside these cultures and even within them, when these qualities could be considered bad, leading one astray into sadness or sin. Similarly, pride, selfishness, and even hate are not always bad attributes. As the sages have said, there is no attribute that lacks it injurious aspect, its negation and failure, just as there is no attribute — even if connected with doubt and heresy — that has not, under some circumstances, its holy aspect.[38]

Steinsaltz points out that in Hebrew good attributes are called good *measures*, which suggests that the value of an attribute or action is a matter of *proportion*. There is an implicit reference to the whole, that of the life of the individual, the community, and the cosmos. The same act can be good in one context and evil in another. Good and evil ultimately take their meaning from the bigger picture — whether the action augments or diminishes life in its most expansive and conscious aspects (what Teilhard de Chardin called "complexity-consciousness"). This is where ideologues, fundamentalists, and simpleminded bigots get shipwrecked. If all value judgments are situational, then good and bad are matters of degree. There are no simple moral slide rules, no books of exhortations and prohibitions that can be unthinkingly applied to give the one true, good answer. Each human individual has to assume the burden of conscience and struggle for himself or herself to apply the discipline of the primal complex — self-knowledge, open free discussion, facing opposite experiences with openness, and then relating the part to the whole, the particular action to the bigger picture, in order to determine the more righteous action.

The primal ethic shifts the weight of responsibility from an authoritarian church or ideological bureaucracy to the conscience and wisdom of the individuals most directly involved, guided by the loving community. An impatient and insecure mind, with no capacity for the tension of the in-between, wants a world of black and white, where some external authority dictates quick and clear choices. When all one has to do is obey some external authority, decisions can be quick and clear even if the consequences are horrendous for others. As Bushmen demonstrate, decision making without an imposed authority is rarely quick and efficient since it includes the loud opinions of everyone affected as the group calculates the consequences. But face-to-face democracy serves a high "efficiency" in creating a more honest and caring community.

## Democracy and Spirituality

One of the most striking features of Bushman religion is its radical egalitarianism. Unlike the esoteric Kabbalah and other hidden teachings, the dance is performed regularly in public, and its healing energy is available to all. The technique of ecstasy itself requires the cooperative community. The circle of singers and dancers around the fire, the intensity of the singing, the presence of the surrounding animals of the veldt, with the moon and Milky Way above — all these contribute to the ecstasy of *kia*. The power and insight of those in *kia* is then integrated back into the community.

All over southern Africa, non-Bushman healers — variously called *sangomas*, *inyangas*, and witch doctors — tend to recognize Bushmen as children of the veldt who have the special power that comes from crossing the boundary into wilderness. But within traditional Bushman society, no special reward or power accrues to the shaman once the dance is over. There is no priestly class, no exclusive circle of initiates, and little to encourage the accumulation of psychic powers for selfish ends. Like hunting and beadwork, healing is something some do better than others and it is shared freely for the good of all. The ever-present community helps guard against the perennial danger in ecstatic spiritual work of ego inflation or spiritual materialism. The community helps remind us that contact with the divine is not the same as becoming God.[39]

Shamanic insight still remains subject to ongoing discussion, critique, and reconstruction. The community confronts the individual with others who inevitably represent shadow aspects of the person. We can learn our sharpest lessons precisely from those who differ most from us, those who irritate us most, our opposites. What we detest in others is also what we most repress in ourselves — our shadows. Gaining an inner sense of our shadow allows us to take responsibility for it and avoid the pathology of projecting our evil onto others. The great danger for a psychologically immature culture occurs when primal archetypal energies are linked to ego certitudes; this was the case in the catastrophic possession of the German psyche during the Nazi regime. *Thuru* functions as the principle of the dialectic, which forces us to confront consciously in face-to-face discussion what we wish to exterminate in ourselves and others. The *thuru* of discussion inoculates us against dogmatism, protecting us from overripe beliefs and concepts that become too fixed or real. Nelson Mandela's approach to embracing the enemy Afrikaner is a magnificent example of *thuru* working in politics.*

In our society, competitive individualism and short-term profit calculations reinforce ego boundaries and create isolation, anxiety, and loneliness. My gain is often someone else's loss. This has generated colossal wealth together with a poverty of loving-kindness and extreme inequality. The emotional economy of the dance amplifies enthusiasm for life as such, which spills over into loving-kindness toward others. Love, unlike wealth, is not part of a zero-sum transaction. The more one gives, the more the beloved loves life and returns the loving. What we learn from the San is not the simple platitude "all we need is love" but rather the importance of creating cultural and institutional frameworks for balancing materialism and competitive individualism with wealth in loving relationships with the community of beings.

## "Talking with God" — The Rosetta Stone of Rock Art

If we can connect the beloved trance dance of the San to the rock paintings, then we can consider the sudden appearance of rock art as a possible marker in the evolution of consciousness and in the development of shamanism as fundamental to human psychological and political health. In the conclusion to his film *Cave of Forgotten Dreams*, Werner Herzog talks of dreams and speculates on the meaning of the images and on the future of humanity. He also interviews Jean Clottes, director of prehistory for the Midi-Pyrenees, who has the distinction of being one of the first European scholars to recognize the possible relevance of southern African shamanism to the European Paleolithic art.[40] Herzog, however, misses a wonderful opportunity and makes little mention of shamanism in the film.

Herzog was partly inspired to make his film by an engaging article written by Judith Thurman in the *New Yorker* in 2008. Thurman's article gives a vivid account of Chauvet and a brief introduction to the current state

---

* See chapter 12, "Our Primal Future," for an extended discussion of Mandela's politics.

of scholarship. Yet she opens with a skepticism that seems to echo deconstructionists who make a virtue of giving up any attempt to make meaning: "What those first artists invented was a language of signs for which there will never be a Rosetta stone."[41]

But is that really the case? Can we know nothing at all? The original Rosetta stone was an Egyptian tablet inscribed with a decree from King Ptolemy V, in the second century BCE, in three languages. One script was the mysterious ancient Egyptian hieroglyphics, and the other two were Greek and Demotics, which were both known. The known languages describe the same decree, so it could be reasonably assumed that the hieroglyphics would do the same. They could then be decoded using the two known languages. The analogy of the Rosetta stone can be loosely used in a number of ways to make a good guess at the meaning of certain aspects of the European rock art.

Deep in the Drakensberg Mountains of South Africa there is one painting that has been called the Rosetta stone of Southern African rock art. It links the shamanism of the Kalahari San, who, as mentioned, have no rock painting tradition, to the paintings of South Africa, where there is no longer a living shamanic culture. This is the same painting I had been staring at

*Detail of "Rosetta Stone" of Southern African rock art, Game Pass, Drakenberg Mountains.* (Photo: Author)

before my sunset communion with baboons. (See photographs and sketch below and on pages 250 and 251.)[42] The painting depicts a large solitary eland positioned as it would be in its death throes, with an upright human-like figure touching the eland's tail. The figure has an antelope head and similarly crossed legs. Instead of human feet, it has carefully painted quite unmistakable hooves. It also holds what seems to be clearly identifiable as a stick. There is a second figure in the typical bent-over pose of a dancing shaman. A third upright figure has an antelope head and hooves.

When an eland has been shot with a poison arrow and is dying it lowers its head, bleeds, sweats, trembles, stumbles, and falls. Likewise, a dancing shaman who enters the trance also bleeds from the nose, sweats, trembles, stumbles, and falls. We also know that the eland, as the largest and most prized of the antelopes, is believed to be endowed with exceptional life-force potency, or */num*. It is, par excellence, the animal that signifies the spirit

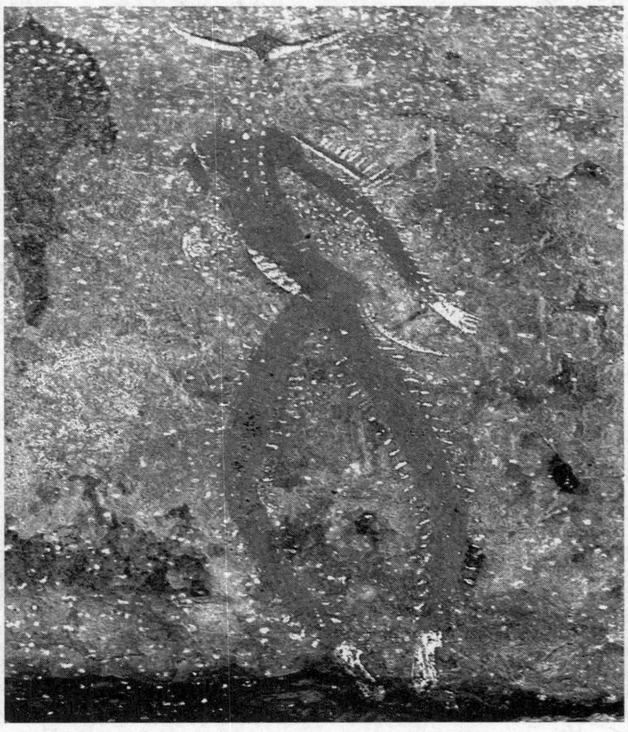

*Detail of therianthropic figure showing antelope head and hooves.* (Photo: Author)

world. Bushmen believe that when the animal dies, the */num* is released and can be absorbed by those around the animal; for this reason, the trance dance is sometimes performed around the dead eland.

So if the painting is the unknown language, we can partially decode it using several known "languages": the stories, myths, and cultural practices described both in nineteenth-century Bushman ethnography associated with the painters and in the recent discoveries from archaeology, linguistics,

*Detail of therianthropic shaman with antelope hooves.* (Photo: Author)

*Sketch showing detail of "Rosetta Stone." Note the crossed legs of the dying eland and the therianthrope form of the "dying" shaman touching the tail of the eland. The lines on the eland and the therianthropic figure on the extreme right represent hair or perhaps* /num, *magical potency, being transferred from eland to shaman. Note also that the shaman holding a dancing stick has antelope hooves and that the adjacent figure is in the characteristic trance posture — bent over with arms outstretched behind.*

*(Sketch: Courtesy of David Lewis-Williams)*

*Adult eland bull, primary spirit animal of the San, in the Southern Kalahari.*
*(Photo: Markus Faigle)*

and genetic mapping connecting the culture of the painters to contemporary San who still practice a shamanic culture in the Kalahari.

Contemporary Kalahari San ethnography tells us that the trance dance is the single most important religious and collective ritual, involving some visually striking markers: dancing sticks, fly whisks, the bent-over posture of the shaman, and nasal bleeding. Further, graphic descriptions connect the little death of the trance to the death of the antelope and the transformation of the shaman into the spirit of the antelope, a verbal equivalent of the therianthropic figure.

The connections between the shamanic experience and the Drakensberg Rosetta Stone are clarified and taken deeper by the already-mentioned documentary film *The Great Dance: A Hunter's Story*.[43] The film-makers record three hunters from the modern-day /Gwi and !Xo bands of Bushmen of the Central Kalahari Desert as they track and hunt an adult kudu by running it to death. We watch the hunters finding the tracks and starting to act out the behavior of the kudu — what they call "putting on kudu mind," trying to feel and think like the animal they are tracking. This is already a boundary-crossing discipline, stimulating more of the animal within to surface. At midday the hunters spot the antelope and give chase. They run barefoot without stopping in what becomes a race against heat exhaustion between hunter and kudu. After several hours, only the master hunter still pursues the exhausted animal. The filmmakers follow at some distance in a jeep until the vehicle gets stuck in the sand, at which point a member of the team — an Olympic athlete — jumps out with a minicamera and runs after the hunter. Finally, the kudu suddenly stops and seems to give itself up to the hunter's spear.

Afterward, the hunter explains his experience of the hunt. He describes how during the course of the hunt the barriers between inner and outer, hunter and kudu, break down. He talks about "entering kudu mind...becoming kudu...feeling her blood boil...controlling her." As her strength diminishes, his energy increases. Finally he makes a decisive connection between tracking and trance when he concludes, "Tracking is like dancing.... It makes your body happy.... You are talking with God when you are doing these things."

The focused discipline of hunting, tracking, and running, like the hyperarousal of the dance, dissolves normal ego boundaries. This makes possible an expansion of consciousness and an experienced connection to the animal within. There is also a paradoxical outward expansion of awareness — the classical out-of-body experience described by shamans the world over — to connect with the hunted kudu. In such a state, opposites — the hunter and the hunted— are brought into close relationship. The shaman becomes more himself by leaving himself. His body is "happy" and he is "talking with God." In Voegelin's terms, we could say he experiences his partnership in the community of being as ecstatic communion.

Since we know that the trance dance was also sometimes performed around a big kill, it would make perfect sense for an ancient San shaman to choose to paint such an intense experience — one that integrates a healing epiphany with feeding the community. The Drakenberg painting helps connect the hunt and the meat to the realm of the sacred; it fuses religion, economics, and politics; it expresses a life-giving event that encourages generosity and sharing and that heals and bonds the community.

How could we achieve an economics where full-bodied participation in feeding ourselves becomes talking with God? Such a political economy would cure our *anoia*, the disease of the soul that results when we forget our partnership in the sacred community of being — the spiritual disease that is currently driving our catastrophe. As !Nqate, one the hunter's in *The Great Dance*, sums it up, "If you don't dance, you die."

When we survey the profusion of southern African paintings, we find many other markers of the trance experience. The most explicit are depictions of circles of people sitting and clapping, generating the */num* for the dancers. There are numerous images of figures, some in the bent-over arms-outstretched posture and some holding dancing sticks and fly whisks — both items used primarily for the trance dance. There are depictions of figures, human and animal, showing nasal bleeding, a once-common aspect of the trance dance. We also find many instances of zigzags, cross-hatching, and nested arcs that seem to correspond to "entoptic" visions — the flashing patterns — characteristic of the early stages of trance. Most telling of all, the

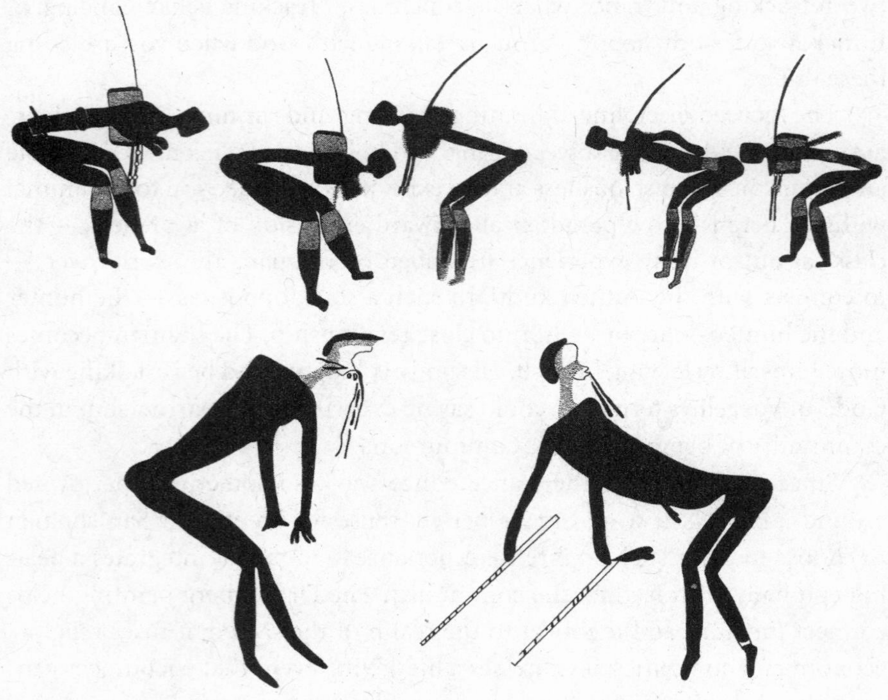

*Dancers in bent-over posture holding dancing sticks. The bottom two figures show bleeding from the nose.* (*Sketch: Courtesy of David Lewis-Williams*)

*Singers and dancers.* (*Sketch: Courtesy of David Lewis-Williams*)

*Trance dance. Note dancing sticks and bent posture of the dancers.* (*Photo: Author*)

profusion of images of part-human, part-animal therianthropes seems to represent one of the most common themes in the shamanic experience of hunter-gatherers.

One particularly complex panel — the Linton Panel — is preserved in the South African Museum. It contains a number of striking icons of the dance, including a prone therianthropic figure with characteristic antelope hooves and blood-streaked lines on his cheek, surrounded by fish and eel-like creatures, suggesting an experience of being underwater (see sketch on page 256). The dotted lines — thought to represent the transmission of spiritual energy, or */num* — enter the back of the shaman's neck, emerge from the base of the spine, and wrap around the legs of an eland. Next to the

*Section of the Linton Panel, preserved in the South African Museum, Cape Town.*
*(Sketch: Courtesy of David Lewis-Williams)*

bent right leg of the supine figure is a small antelope bleeding from the nose. The right hand holds a typical, simple representation of a fly whisk.[44]

The southern African paintings seem to relate to one another in complex ways; they appear not simply to be representations of past spiritually charged experiences but to actually contain */num*. For example, many of the beautifully detailed animals were intentionally superimposed one on another and entangled, despite the fact that there was no shortage of clean surfaces for painting. We know the dances were often performed in the painted shelters, and there is evidence that shamans would intensify their trance experiences by staring at the paintings and sometimes touching particular images.[45] Some of the images were painted so as to give the unmistakable impression of emerging from, and entering, cracks and fissures in the rock surface, suggesting that the rock wall itself represented a veil between the everyday world and the shamanic universe.[46]

At this point, we can regard the entire southern African corpus of knowledge about the connection between rock art and shamanism as something of a Rosetta stone — a cryptographic key — for understanding some of the ancient rock art of Europe. The first language is the scientific narrative from archaeology and genetic mapping, which indicates that the European hunters and gatherers were descendants of the same southern African founder population as modern Bushmen. The second known language is the larger ethnographic record concerning the ubiquity and antiquity of shamanism among hunting-gathering societies (which is discussed further in the next chapter). We can infer that European rock art has a related meaning because of its apparent importance to the painters and because of common visual themes. These include a profusion of geometric patterns, beautifully painted animals, and, most tellingly, the composite animals and the part-human, part-animal therianthropes. As we will see in the next two chapters, the part-human, part-animal figure is the most common theme in the liturgy of the shamanism of hunter-gatherers and an iconic representation of the definitive boundary-crossing shamanic experience.

The most famous European example of a therianthropic figure is the Dancing Sorcerer of Trois Frères, in Ariège, France (see page 258). This arresting Upper Paleolithic painting, about 13,000 years old, combines elements of what appear to be the staring eyes of an owl, the horns of a stag, the nose and ears of a wolf, the tail of a horse, the claws of a lion, and the feet, legs, body, and penis of a human.[47]

Bringing the "known languages" together suggests a story in which at least some of the European paintings developed from a common southern African spiritual-cultural root and most likely had a comparable shamanic significance for the artists.[48]

The Bushman connection to the cosmos was direct and available to all. Today our spiritual impoverishment is such that many can only connect to the sacred through the revelations of long-dead saints and prophets preserved in the holy scriptures. But it seems that humans have an innate need to expand consciousness and to experience direct contact with the divine. When this

*The Dancing Sorcerer, an Upper Paleolithic painting of a therianthropic shaman with elements of several animals combined. It is thought to be approximately 13,000 years old. The sketch was made by Abbé Breuil in the cave at Trois Frères, Ariège, France.*

impulse is frustrated, it emerges in the pathologies of depression and cynicism, addiction and fundamentalism.

In the West there is now an explosion of popular interest in what were once oppressed and ridiculed spiritual practices — from yoga to Kabbalah, from Buddhism and Tai Chi to techno-shamanism — which suggests we could be on the cusp of a revolution in human spirituality. Since the reality of the soul has been so thoroughly expunged from our materialistic culture, much of its recovery is still ad hoc — uninformed and unsupported by institutions of higher learning. It is easily trivialized and corrupted. However, as the next chapter explores, these shamanically grounded spiritual disciplines are ancient, pervasive, and potent, and they are still available to all who feel called — constituting a wealth of resources for personal and political transformation.

CHAPTER 9

# BOUNDARY CROSSING

We know ourselves to be made from this earth,
We know this earth is made from our bodies.
For we see ourselves,
And we are nature.
We are nature seeing nature.
We are nature with a concept of nature.
Nature weeping.
Nature speaking of nature to nature.

— SUSAN GRIFFIN, *Woman and Nature*

Werewolves are persons who are able to *dissolve* "within themselves" the boundary between civilization and wilderness, who can step across the fence separating their "civilization side" from their "wilderness side," their "wolf's nature." These are people who can look their "animal nature" in the eye, something usually kept under lock and key in their culture, and in this way can develop a consciousness of their "cultural nature."

— HANS PETER DUERR,
*Dreamtime: Concerning the Boundary between Wilderness and Civilization*

We need wilderness because we are wild animals. Every man needs a place where he can go crazy in peace once in a while.

— EDWARD ABBEY, *The Journey Home*

## Boundaries

In order to understand the political importance of the boundary-crossing dialectic of shamanism, we need to review how the mandala model of primal politics works (see diagram, page 118). In hunting-gathering cultures like that of the San Bushmen, the truth quest takes place in daily direct contact with the living earth below, the starry sky at night, and the creatures and plants of the surrounding bush. The outermost field encircling the mandala represents this wilderness community of being framing the psychology of the searching human. At the very center of the quest are the healing and visioning practices of shamanic religion. These two practices — the shamanic visionary journey and wilderness immersion, symbolized by the innermost and outermost circles of the mandala — set up a resonance, which we can imagine as the force fields between two poles of a magnet. This holds the four quadrants of the truth quest in a synergistic balance — a primal politics.

This resonance can also be understood metaphorically as a back-and-forth movement of awareness across the boundaries separating all pairs of opposites: the primary boundary separating the inner circle of civilization from surrounding wilderness, and the lesser boundaries separating the four components of the mandala — the individual and the group, the big picture and discussion. This back-and-forth, dialectical movement of awareness can be represented graphically as parallel but opposing arrows cutting all the solid lines that separate the components of the mandala. This helps remind us that each element of politics, each one of the four quadrants and each concentric circle, can only be understood in dynamic relationship with what it is not — its opposite. Thus, the impulse to individuate needs to be understood in relation to, and practiced in balance with, the need to connect to the community, and community life needs to promote individuation. Similarly, the construction of the big picture needs to be balanced with its deconstruction through argument among questioning, free-thinking members of the community, and so on.

This boundary-crossing logic of course applies to our understanding of all dimensions of reality. For example, to grasp a deeper understanding of traditional Bushman life, one must cross a series of related boundaries: between modern and ancient, between life in the academy and life in the bush, and between shamanism as an object of research and as a personal practice. The philosophical truth quest not only includes the study of shamanism but is a kind of transformative shamanic practice itself, dissolving certainties and questioning blind obedience to social authority in the service of love of life. In this sense, the serious searcher puts his or her own life on the line.

Shamanism seems to be practiced by virtually all wilderness-based cultures. The trouble is, the pathways to attaining shamanic ecstasy are so varied, so culture bound, and so far from the prevailing Western models of healing and searching that today the whole field of study has become an undergrowth of ethnographic exotica and scholarly jargon. The situation becomes even more confusing when one considers the role of sacred hallucinogenic plants and mushrooms, which have long been used by many indigenous cultures as one of a variety of methods for inducing these expanded states of consciousness and accessing the spirit world. Western society, already deeply suspicious of transcendence, reacts in a near-hysterical fashion when drugs are involved. The use of shamanic hallucinogens as religious sacraments has been widely ridiculed, responsible research has been crippled, and possession and use have been criminalized. Thankfully, this sad situation may now be changing.

This chapter starts off by considering "softer" techniques of shamanism by focusing on the boundary-crossing relationship of the human to the animal and of civilization to wilderness. The next chapter considers the "harder" techniques, in particular the shamanic use of hallucinogens as the quickest, most reliable, but sometimes the most frightening way of accessing shamanic states of consciousness. In all cases the purpose is to assist the search for health and wisdom.

## Shamanism as Ur-Religion

I use the term *shamanism* very broadly to refer to the earliest forms of religious practice and truth seeking associated with the emergence of the in-between structure of self-reflective consciousness. At its center are the extraordinary states of awareness variously labeled "altered," "nonordinary," "expanded," or "extraordinary," and also more vaguely identified as "trance." These are bland and pallid terms for experiences that range from visions of such beauty that one sheds tears of joy to realities so awesome and terrifying that one is forever changed.

Mircea Eliade's classic work *Shamanism: Archaic Techniques of Ecstasy*[1] defines *shamanism* simply and succinctly in its title. The word *ecstasy* comes from the Greek *ex stasis* — meaning to stand outside of one's ego-defined body. As mentioned, San Bushmen describe the trance experience as a fantastic journey to an invisible but nevertheless vitally real and important encounter with the spirit world, variously called the "first times," the "early times," or simply "God's home." The relationship of the shamanic realm to the everyday world of ego concerns is fundamentally paradoxical, being both "other than" and yet somehow essential. Joseph Campbell called this dimension "the inner reaches of outer space." In evolutionary terms, it might be thought of as the inner aspect of the outer universe, a realm as strange, vast, and at times exquisitely ordered as the external universe.

Shamanic states of consciousness can be attained by an astonishing variety of "psycho-technologies," many of which have been incorporated into the practices of the world's religions. These include dancing, chanting, drumming, fasting, thirsting, self-mutilation, immersion in freezing pools, wilderness isolation, and ingesting hallucinogenic plants and mushrooms. In Europe, Asia, and North America, the most widespread traditional techniques are rhythmic drumming, chanting, and dancing. In the Southern Hemisphere, especially South America, the most common method involves the ingestion of hallucinogenic plants, generally in combination with drumming, music, chanting, and singing. In Central Africa, the Bwiti of Gabon, who practice the *iboga* cult, use the hallucinogen-containing root of the *Tabernathe iboga* tree to "break open the head." The San Bushmen, as we have seen, more typically enter trance without hallucinogens, solely through persistent dancing, clapping, and chanting. In all cases the techniques of ecstasy seem to constitute ways of temporarily breaking down, dissolving, or overwhelming the ego structures of consciousness that keep us focused on socially defined patterns of behavior and experience.

In this understanding, shamanic ecstasy is one of the most dramatic ways in which an individual can experience emerging from imprisonment in Plato's cave. As the prisoner breaks the chains of conditioning and emerges into the light of day, the initial view is overwhelming, confusing, and terrifying, but also magnificently expansive — ecstatic. The released prisoner cannot doubt he or she is experiencing a larger, more compelling reality. The cave is still there — a hole in the hillside — but now within a vastly expanded, brilliantly illuminated, yet ultimately mysterious reality. With this leap, the quest is under way.

Eliade noted that shamanic ecstasy often has the hallmarks of the classical mystical experience, in which the connection to the larger reality is experienced as life enhancing, beautiful, sacred — a *numinosum*. In the process the individual is reinvigorated, feels healed, and can find more joy and meaning in life. The difference between the shamanic and the classical mystical experience — which William James, Rudolf Otto, and others have recognized as the living font of religious life — is probably a matter of emphasis. Whereas mystical rapture is generally associated with a more diffuse, undifferentiated sense of joyful unity with all of existence, shamanic trance tends to lead to more dramatic encounters with specific entities, spirits, and creatures communicating detailed, often-complex information. Both mystical and shamanic experiences overlap and can cover a wide range of nonordinary, numinous, life-enhancing experiences.

In the relatively compact, egalitarian, and democratic culture of nomadic hunter-gatherers, shamanic journeying is generally open to all who feel called. Since the walls between civilization and wilderness are easily crossed, most have some direct sense of the mystery of the *in-between-ness* of the human condition. No religious bureaucracy codifies and enforces dogmatic routes to salvation; religious authority is based on direct experience — that of the journeying shaman and the community of witnesses.

Some have speculated on the likelihood that midwives played a key role in early shamanic religion because of their expertise in birth as one of the most dramatic boundary-crossing experiences. One of the earliest figurative carvings, which is some thirty-five to forty thousand years old, is that of a female figure — the Venus of Holen Fels — with exaggerated breasts and genitalia. The figure is small with a protuberance at the head, suggesting it might have been worn as a pendant. Clearly, early human communities would have valued the herbal knowledge and skill of mothers and midwives who were adept in dealing with the crisis of labor and mystery of birth. Venus figurines found in early Neolithic sites further suggest the importance of the feminine principle in nature-worshipping goddess religions of early Europe. Much of what remained as a sort of folk shamanism in Europe was the preserve of the herbalist-healer-midwives, many thousands of whom were tortured and burned at the stake during the mania of the witch hunts.

## The Werewolf, the Witch, and Wilderness

The German cultural historian Hans Peter Duerr, in his remarkable work *Dreamtime: Concerning the Boundary between Wilderness and Civilization*, reinforced this evolutionary understanding of shamanism with a simple formula. He surveyed the astounding diversity of shamanic traditions and then showed quite compellingly that they all shared the primal discipline of "boundary crossing," which he described variously as dissolving, removing, shattering, straddling, or sitting astride the walls between civilization and wilderness. For example, Duerr pointed out that the word *hagazuzza* as late as the Middle Ages referred to the witch, the *hag*, who sat on the fence (also called a *hag*) separating the gardens and villages from the surrounding wilderness: "She was a being who participated in both worlds. As we might say today, she was semi-demonic." We could also say she was semidivine. "In time, however she lost her double feature and evolved more and more into a representation of what was being expelled from culture, only to return, distorted, in the night."[2]

Witches, shamans, and the tricksters of mythology are all involved in rituals of reversal. Their contradictory character allows them to mediate between opposites — in particular between the ordered chaos of wilderness and the chaotic order of civilization. Seen within the larger evolutionary narrative, two intimately interrelated barriers are being crossed. One movement involves crossing over the literal hedge or fence that was built to wall out wilderness (literally, "the place of the wild deer"). The other boundary is internal, within the individual's identity, when crossing from the culturally constructed, "civilized" ego into the psychic "wilderness" of the instincts, impulses, intuitions, dreams, and visions bubbling up from the unconscious.

Duerr's point is simple, obvious, and profound: for archaic societies the boundary between wilderness and civilization was not insurmountable, and at certain times the fence was torn down to serve a vital political purpose — self-knowledge:

> Those who wanted to live consciously within the fence had to leave the enclosure at least once in their lives. They had to roam the forests as wolves and savages. To put it in more modern terms they had to experience the wilderness, their animal nature, within themselves.[3]

Every social order provides its members a cultural framework for structuring everyday experience and functioning in the everyday world. Out of this crystallize the ego and the personality of each individual. Of course, one cannot fully understand or evaluate the adequacy of this order, this description of reality, unless one can stand outside it. This is precisely the purpose of shamanic disciplines, which offer an encounter with the transpersonal and transcultural dimensions — the inner wilderness — of the psyche. Such boundary-crossing experiences remind us that we live in the in-between and help keep the quest open.

Another way to think of the deep roots of the boundary-crossing impulse is that it functions as an evolutionary balancing process that developed as consciousness and then civilization literally separated itself from immersion in wilderness through the efforts of the ego. Shamanism can then be regarded as mind-body techniques for retracing the steps back to our evolutionary origins. But this is not simply a regression. The traveler always returns from the spirit world to everyday consciousness with more information — a bigger picture. Shamanism can thus be considered a way of regularly tuning the inner and outer aspects of our wilderness nature in a life-affirming resonance. It can show us the way forward.

One of the most common ways this shamanic journey into wilderness expresses itself is through animal identification. Indigenous shamans commonly talk of special relations with specific animals as familiars, guides, and protectors. As we saw in the last chapter, the half-human, half-animal therianthropes in southern African rock paintings give pictorial expression to the accounts of shamanic transformation into animal spirits, giving access to special power and special information. The shamanic encounter with the animal seems to be a way of intensifying the experience of the in-between, since human consciousness emerges from our animal brains and bodies.

Duerr reminds us that in medieval Europe, before the full frenzy of the witch hunts, people were much more in touch with their animal aspect. They still lived surrounded by vast tracts of wild forest inhabited by elk, wolves, and bears. From the residues of shamanic tradition emerged the idea of the werewolf as a demonic form of the animal within. But Duerr asserts that moderns are naive to think of werewolves as fantastic humans who suddenly start growing fangs and sprouting fur. Rather, werewolves were those who could *dissolve* the inner boundaries between their civilized selves and their "wolf nature" and in so doing access special power.

Not surprisingly, this is an archetypal theme in great literature. Popular culture treats the werewolf as a monster to be avoided, despised, and killed, but the more shamanic attitude is expressed by Hermann Hesse in his perennially popular novel *Steppenwolf*, which is a testimony to the healing power of confronting the wild animal within. In the story, repressed scholar Harry Haller gradually realizes that underneath his polite, respectable bourgeois exterior is the seething, wild, and untamed animal part of his nature — the ravenous wolf of the steppes. Homeless, isolated, and appalled by the barbarism of his society, no less than by that lurking in his chest, Harry decides to commit suicide. On his way home that fateful night, he stops at a bar and meets Hermine, a beautiful, wise young woman, radiating the mystery of life, who playfully invites him into the magic theater of the soul — "for madmen only... the price of admission... your mind." Harry eventually accepts this invitation and encounters the inner universe of the psyche. In the magic theater of the mind he lives out the emotions of his wolf nature, tearing a living rabbit apart in his jaws, with his human side sickened by the taste of warm blood and fur in his mouth. In the process of fully encountering his wolf nature, Harry is shocked back into life. Having discovered the range of possibilities of human experience, Harry grows, heals, discovers the laughter of the Gods, and joins the immortals.[4]

For moderns, our society's physical separation from outer wilderness makes contact with our inner wilderness elusive, and boundary crossing requires exceptional exertions. For hunter-gatherers, the physical boundary between wilderness and civilization was no more than the perimeter of the village huts on the veldt or the tepees on the plains. Although the boundary between inner and outer was real, it was also easily crossed. As the Lakota chief Standing Bear put it, "wilderness was tame," and the Lakota felt surrounded by the "blessings of the Great Mystery." Nevertheless, traditional hunter-gatherers seemed well aware of the significance of the human leap into self-consciousness and with it the uniquely human problem of living in the in-between — the problem of freedom of choice and the attendant reality of good and evil.

Bushmen were quite clear that humans both *are* and *are not* animals and that culture *is* and *is not* nature. David Lewis-Williams gives an example of this by examining an old /Xam Bushman myth preserved in the Bleek and Lloyd archives entitled "A Visit to the Lion's House." He points out that the mythology implicitly assumed two bisecting axes of reality, one horizontal, the other vertical (see diagram, below). The horizontal axis extends between the camp and wilderness. The camp is civilization — the realm of human culture, a place of security, norms, ritual, meat sharing, healing, caring, and conversation. Outside the camp is the hunting ground — wilderness — a realm of uncertainty, difficulty, struggle, and possibly danger, but also the source of all life. Between the two is a transitional zone — the water hole — a mile or so from the camp, where both humans and animals share water. In Bushman mythology, the water hole is a point of entry into the shamanic world — both for the upper spirit world and for the underworld. Thus, the vertical axis connects the poles of the invisible spirit world — the sky above and the underworld below — with earth in between.

During ordinary times, people lived on the horizontal axis, but at special times, as in trance, they could travel the vertical axis to an upperworld of spirits and to an underworld of the departed.[5]

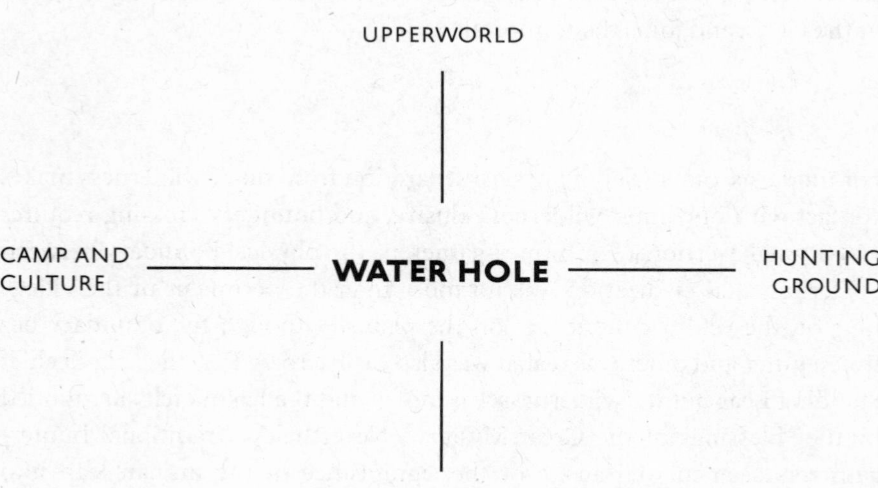

An individual who had regular direct experience of the cosmological whole — camp, water hole, veldt, sun, moon, planets, and stars — had an ego that was less rigid, more flexible, and more conditioned by the experience of boundary crossing in all its dimensions than an ego exclusively conditioned by the concrete, steel, and crowds of city life. The inner world of primal societies — the world of intuition, dreams, visions, and spirits — could be as close to the surface of everyday consciousness as the lions, hyenas, baboons, and buck of the veldt. This made it easier for individuals to go in and out of the spirit world spontaneously.

Traveling the vertical axis deepened and developed what was also the first fact of life for a hunting-gathering society — that wilderness contained and sustained all living creatures, including the whole conflicted human species. But the gift of self-consciousness and freedom confused human beings. With choice and freedom came the necessity of uncertainty and the inescapable drama of the search for right action and the possibility of wrong action. As humans embraced their split-off but connected state, *the whole* became an indispensable ordering ethical principle. Humans needed to be reminded, over and over, that from Wakan Tanka — the Great Mystery — came a great unifying life force that flowed in and through all things: the flowers of the plains, blowing wind, rocks, trees, birds, and animals. The medicine wheel symbolizes that perfect wholeness enclosing the imperfect human.[6]

The living mysterious whole was thus experienced as the source of truth as well as beauty, and this sensitivity pervaded Lakota culture. We find it, movingly, even in battle-hardened warriors like Tatanka Yotanka (Sitting Bull). During one set of negotiations with the United States government, witnesses described him concluding an eloquent speech and sitting down to the cheers of his people. He then dramatically stood up again to emphasize the essential point:

> I wish all to know that I do not propose to sell any part of my country, nor will I have the whites cutting our timber along the rivers, more especially the oak. I am particularly fond of the little groves of oak trees. I love to look at them, because they endure the wintry storm and the summer's heat, and — not unlike ourselves — seem to flourish by them.[7]

The higher value of the little groves of oak was not in utility, as timber for housing, but in beauty, as guidance and inspiration for human behavior. For the traditional Lakota, nature was the outer face of the Great Mystery, which guided and healed and thus needed to be the normative foundation for a wise and compassionate politics. The translation into human politics was simple: if animals, birds, fish, insects, and plants were all worthy of gratitude and kindness, then human beings should be so much more deserving of respect and kindness. As we have seen, wilderness becomes something like a supreme good in itself, an ultimate temple for healing and guiding lost souls.

Today, scientific cosmology allows us to understand the larger whole in immense detail, as the single interconnected evolving cosmos, within which humans are struggling to find their place and their role.

## The Shaman as a Whole Person

The Sioux were originally East Coast woodland horticulturists. But with the arrival of Europeans in North America, they were moved into the Great Plains, and along with the Cheyenne, the Arapaho, the Blackfoot, the Crow, and other Plains Indians, they acquired the horse and developed a magnificent hunting-and-gathering culture following the great herds of bison. The return to a nomadic hunting-gathering way of life after a more sedentary existence seemed to sharpen and deepen the Plains Indians' expression of shamanic religion. As we saw earlier the teaching of the medicine wheel is a Native American version of the mandala, where the four cardinal points represent four personality types (similar to Jung's psychology of types). The teaching is that individuation and growth are achieved through moving around the medicine wheel and so balancing the dominant function with its shadow opposite.

The life of the Sioux medicine man Lame Deer is a dramatic embodiment of the paradoxical ethic of the shaman. Lame Deer grew up in the early twentieth century between the Pine Ridge and Rosebud Sioux reservations, raised by grandparents who were among the last of the nomads of the Plains. He described his initiation as a healer in terms of an archetypal journey around the medicine wheel of life.

> When I was a young man I roamed the country on foot like a hippie, sleeping in haystacks or under the stars on the open prairie. I joined five or six churches, worked at many jobs. It was almost as if I were several different people.... I managed to be both... a fugitive and a pursuer, a lawman and an outlaw. I was uneducated but soaked up knowledge like

> a sponge. All that knowledge as yet undigested made a big racket in my brain...but I also spent many quiet months as a budding healer and medicine man.[8]

In this process, Lame Deer exposes the deeper wisdom underlying the surface anarchy of "anything goes." Wholeness is the path to health, as suggested by the old Anglo-Saxon root of the word *health* in *hal* — "to make whole." Moving around the wheel to the opposite point is the route to expanding one's soul and attaining the larger vision. One of the original forms of shamanic initiation seems to have been self-initiation through recovery from deathly illness. The shaman would then have the insight of "the healed healer"; having made him- or herself whole by experiencing the opposites of sickness and health, he or she is then able to bring them together to serve the health of the community. What applies to physical imbalance applies even more to spiritual and intellectual imbalance. As we saw in previous chapters, the medicine man, the shaman, is capable of drawing wisdom from the tension between opposites in the service of healing:

> A medicine man shouldn't be a saint. He should experience and feel all the ups and downs, the despair and joy, the magic and the reality, the courage and the fear, of his people. He should be able to sink as low as a bug, or soar as high as an eagle. Unless he can experience both, he is no good as a medicine man. Sickness, jail, poverty, getting drunk — I had to experience all that myself. Sinning makes the world go round. You can't be so stuck up, so inhuman that you want to be pure, your soul wrapped up in a plastic bag, all the time. You have to be God and the devil, both of them.[9]

In the traditional tribal life of the Lakota and other Plains Indians, this wisdom of healing through the integration of opposites is ritualized and acted out for the community in the bizarre antics of the *heyoka*, a contrary or clown. A *heyoka* was an individual who, in a vision, received a calling to do everything backward. On a freezing winter's day, he would walk around camp with his shirt off complaining of the heat. In summer, he would shiver wrapped in buffalo robes. The jester in the medieval royal courts performed a similar function, symbolically reversing the existing order by shaking a stick at the king. As the jester admired himself in a mirror held backward, he reflected the court to itself and thereby restored some measure of balance to royal pomposity.

This metaphysics of balancing opposites seemed to make traditional Native American cultures much more accepting of a spectrum of identities, particularly concerning gender. In many societies, the transsexual, the feminized man, and more occasionally the masculinized woman played an important role in the life of the community. The Cheyenne call the transsexual a *hemaneh*; the Lakota, the *winkte*; the Navajo, the *nadle*; and Hawaiians, the *mahu*. Among anthropologists, this figure is known as the berdache. Ridiculed and persecuted in Western culture, the berdache was often someone of considerable intelligence, artistic ability, and shamanic power. Since transsexuals had the ability to experience the world from both male and female perspectives, they were understood to have the special power and wisdom associated with bringing opposites into a harmonious unity and in some tribes they were responsible for rituals that brought together young men and women for courting. Among the Navajos, where women are people of consequence, the *nadle* was virtually deified.[10] Clearly, both the clown and the berdache have something of the creative, healing role of the mythological Bushman trickster.

This understanding of the healer as a whole person is congruent with the depth psychology of C.G. Jung, in which the individual is, in some mysterious sense, a microcosm of the macrocosm. We contain within us the whole universe of archetypal human possibilities. We are animals, but we are also, paradoxically, human. All the opposites — good-evil, human-animal, masculine-feminine, introvert-extrovert — are potentials within us.

When this shamanic understanding of self is missing, society punishes transgressions of identity, which produces anxious, one-dimensional individuals with pathologically constricted, brittle egos terrified of taking responsibility for their shadows. Whatever represents evil or corruption is projected outward, onto something or someone else, and must be destroyed in order to protect or preserve whatever is "absolutely good." Societal and historical examples of this are rife: the demonization of Jews and others by the Nazis, the institutional racism of America in the Jim Crow era and the homophobia of gay bashing. For the individual, this often leads to crisis; as happened with Harry Haller in *Steppenwolf*, any sign of the unacceptable nature within jeopardizes one's entire sense of self and social standing. By contrast, the shamanic approach to self is flexible. It accepts ambiguity and otherness; it encourages a politics of transformation, growth, and inclusiveness. Through shamanic practice, individuals learn to balance first one side, then the other, in ways that are meant to serve the larger good and the health of the community. As we saw in Bushman society, under such conditions there are no ethical absolutes. Decision making is a matter of context and degree. Actions and policies are ultimately judged according to how they serve the circle of life.

## Nature Healing — "Soft" Shamanism

Since shamanism heals and guides through boundary crossing, and since the boundary between wilderness and civilization is an outer equivalent of that between body and mind, we should expect external contact with wilderness to heal and balance both body and mind. This was my revelation in Hawai'i when immersion in ocean and mountain helped expand and balance my indoor understanding of civilization. However, unlike the hallucinogen-induced "hard" shamanism, the healing effect of nature is often subtle and easy to miss.

E.O. Wilson and other sociobiologists have attempted to research this in a more controlled fashion. Their *biophilia hypothesis* proposes simply that since modern human beings have lived for most of their existence in a wilderness environment, we have an innate emotional "affiliation for nature." It follows that an exposure to natural and wilderness settings will be associated with increased measures of well-being, meaning, and happiness.[11] For example, modern medicine recognizes that optimum human health requires not only good food, water, and exercise but also an optimum daily cycle of night and day. Seasonal affective disorder (SAD) is a recognized clinical syndrome associated with restricted daylight as summer moves into winter. The World Health Organization has identified a "sick building syndrome" suffered by people who work indoors for extended periods and who are exposed to a high level of synthetics. Most of us, when given a choice, prefer to live and work with views of natural settings rather than walls, alleys, and traffic. All of this seems like a fairly obvious, self-evident expression of who we are as a species.[12]

Researchers have now demonstrated that this psychological effect is so deeply rooted in our physiology that it can have a measurable effect in promoting healing in patients recovering from surgery. A Pennsylvania hospital studied comparative recovery rates of patients who underwent the same surgery. Pairs of patients were matched for significant factors. One from each pair was randomly assigned to one of two groups of identical rooms with windows, except one group of windows looked out onto a clump of deciduous trees, while the other looked out onto a blank brick wall. Patients who could watch the growing, living trees had a shorter postoperative stay, needed significantly less pain medication, received fewer negative notes in nurses' comments, and had fewer minor postsurgical complications.[13] Surprisingly, even *pictures* of natural settings seem to produce a similar healing effect. An experiment at Uppsala University Hospital in Sweden investigated the postoperative recovery of 166 patients who underwent similar open-heart surgery. They were also randomly assigned rooms with four different wall-size pictures: an open nature view with a water feature, a moderately enclosed forest scene, an abstract painting dominated by curves or rectangles, and a blank wall (as a control). Those assigned the picture of open parkland had the smoothest, least complicated recovery, perhaps indicating the extent to which our perception is responsive to the sort of open savanna humans evolved in. Those recovering under the influence of the busy abstract painting actually experienced more recovery complications than the control group![14]

If, as this study suggests, images evoking wilderness can assist healing, what about the real thing? What about full-body immersion in an intact wilderness savanna?

## Wilderness Rapture — The "Big Medicine"

Dr. Ian Player, a South African game ranger who has spent much of his life in the bush, created the Wilderness Leadership School based on his observation of how the experience of immersion in wilderness seemed to heal and empower leaders who could in turn heal a sick civilization. Player is something of a legend in the world of wilderness conservation as the founder of the World Wilderness Congress. He became famous in the late sixties for his Operation Rhino, which helped save the white rhino population of southern Africa from extinction through the establishment of the Umfolozi Game Reserve in Zululand. This is a well-watered area of wilderness savanna north of the east coast city of Durban, which used to be the private hunting ground for Chaka and the Zulu kings. Player converted the Umfolozi into the largest rhino reserve in the world. He then broke with game reserve protocol by taking small groups of novices on foot for a few days of zero-impact backpacking through thick bush populated by the full complement of African big game.[15]

I joined one of Dr. Player's five-day trails as part of my African pilgrimage in 1998. My purpose was to anchor my thinking about hunter-gatherers like the San by spending a few days on foot, camping and walking through an intact southern African wilderness ecosystem. I began the trek in turmoil. Three months before the trip I went through a series of domestic disasters that set in motion a cycle of depression, anxiety, and illness. Then as I arrived in South Africa at the beginning of a stormy winter, my father died suddenly. Stressed and depressed, I caught the flu and couldn't recover. I approached the date of the trail barely able to walk half an hour without losing my breath. One of the requirements was that participants carry all their food and equipment for five days in the bush — a load weighing some forty-five pounds. It seemed hopeless. But I knew this might be the opportunity of a lifetime, and so, along with the other four participants, I signed the waiver of responsibility, which warned that once on the trail there would be

> no protection in the form of fences, buildings and vehicles in which to take cover and that one or more of the following ... [might cause injury] ... a lion, hyena, buffalo, rhinoceros, leopard, hippo, buck, warthog, bushpig, wildebeest as well as poisonous snakes, insects and plants ... and that once in the wilderness there will be no means of electronic communication with the outside world.

Our safety would depend on the bushcraft of our two rangers.

Our first ranger was Gqakaza, an elderly Zulu who walked with a limp and was blind in one eye. He had been patrolling the trails since he was a teenager in a *beshu*, a loincloth, armed with nothing but an *assegai*, the short Zulu stabbing spear. He had survived being gored by a rhino and had seen friends taken by crocodile. A lifetime in the bush had given him an uncanny ability to detect the presence of animals long before we became aware of any signs. Our second ranger, Rupert, was a white South African, a college graduate who knew the bush both through science and through having led many groups of novices along the trails. Both were armed with large-bore hunting rifles.

We drove to the end of the track, parked, and locked our truck. As we shouldered our unfamiliar packs and followed our guides into the hot, dusty bush, my mind inventoried my anxieties. After half an hour, sweating and breathing heavily under our loads, we stopped at a rhino path for the rangers to explain bush protocol: we were to walk in silence behind them watching them for signals and listening for warning sounds, particularly the call of the oxpecker, a bird that perches on the backs of rhinos and other large grazing animals to feed on ticks. We learned the important difference between white and black rhinos. White rhinos are grazers, generally found in the open, and so are less easily surprised and more placid and predictable. Black rhinos are browsers, more likely to be surprised in thick bush, and thus more unpredictable and aggressive. Confusingly, both black and white are the same color and they can be distinguished only by slight differences in head, face, and shoulder. (Early explorers distinguished them by the color of mud in their different habitats.) We were told the story of how one of the school's rangers had been gored in the thigh when he stepped between his group and a charging rhino. He was fortunate to survive. While an attack was unlikely, the danger was real. If charged, we were to pull the quick release on the pack and climb the nearest tree. I glanced around and noticed that most of the bushes were covered in needle-sharp thorns.

As he talked, Rupert took his water bottle and started washing a mud-covered tree stump shaped like a giant finger. What emerged was a smoothly rounded, glistening, golden sculpture of fragrant hardwood *umthomboti*. Generations of rhinos had used it as a rubbing post, scratching the mud-encrusted ticks off their backs while polishing the stump into a gleaming piece of original rhino art. It was the first of many small and large revelations.

The first night we camped near a pool of stagnant green water surrounded by the spoor of animals. Boiled and disinfected, the water made an unappetizing salty tea, which we nevertheless drank gratefully. The campfire was kept burning throughout the night as we took turns staying awake keeping guard. I sat alone for an hour and a half while everyone else slept, watching the flames, listening, fascinated by the noisy nightlife of the veldt — barks, snorts, yelps, and sudden crashes. Then, once, far in the distance, I heard a male lion roaring.

After another day of walking we found a campsite under an enormous wild fig tree on the banks of the Umfolozi River. Looking out for crocodiles, we washed and drank fresh water. That afternoon we hung our packs in the tree, away from wild dogs and jackals, and followed the rangers to do some exploring. At sunset we were making our way back to camp, winding between high bush, tired, relaxed, and happy after a full day and looking forward to tea and supper around the fire. Gqakaza suddenly stopped, held up his hand, and unslung his rifle. No more than thirty feet in front of us stood the great bulk of a black rhino looking startled. It had just emerged from the bush and was staring straight at us, black eyes glinting, ears swiveling, enormous horn hooking the air as it tried to catch our downwind scent. I smelled its sourness and held my breath, conscious of my pounding heart and grateful I was free of the pack. I noticed how the rhino seemed all compact muscle and armor, unlike the lumbering elephant or the blubbery hippo. With its quick, anxious movements, it looked capable of charging into us with the speed of a boxer's punch. We stood immobilized for maybe half a minute, staring at each other, rhino and human. Then slowly, very slowly, we backed out. It was frightening and thrilling all at once — an initiation. This was no walk in a park.

After the encounter, it was as if a dam had broken within our group. Pretenses fell away. We relaxed and warmth flowed as we saw each other in our shared human vulnerability. I thought of Loren Eisley's observation that "one doesn't meet oneself until one catches the reflection in an eye other than human."

From then on we walked wide awake. Hiking in the bush, following a rhino trail, bears no resemblance to a distracted stroll along a city sidewalk. The veldt is anything but monotonous. Something new and surprising was always going on. Birds would explode out of the bushes — impossible metallic-blue starlings in noisy flocks, an assortment of iridescent hummingbirds — and then when we stopped for a drink, a Bateleur eagle suddenly swooped down, loudly flapped onto the top branch of a nearby tree, and sat staring at us. As we walked we also looked at the ground to notice the animal spoor, each telling a different story. I looked more closely and saw that an ant-lion, a predatory insect, had dug a thimble-sized, cone-shaped pit of sand to trap an ant; I bent down to watch the tiny drama as a passing ant fell into the trap and was dragged under by the ant-lion. I felt as if I was seeing color for the first time — unnameable shades of greens, yellows, browns, and blues. Buck and baboon would appear and disappear. We walked through high bush onto an open grassy plain and found ourselves facing a herd of buffalo. Every single head turned to us in a frozen stare — every head armed with a pair of horns built to chase off lions. We held their gaze until Gqakaza shouted at them in Zulu and waved them off like a herd of cattle.

On the fourth day I realized I was quite well — as clear and refreshed as if I had just woken up after being asleep for years. It occurred to me that I had been healed by beauty. I had been outside on the earth under the open sky every day, every moment of which had been filled with natural beauty, even when sharpened by danger. Wherever I looked from sunrise to sunset, from the campfire at night to a sky blazing with stars — everywhere was beauty. Even the dark-gray clouds that gusted over for a brief storm seemed to punctuate the beauty of the perfectly still, sunny winter days. That night, camped on a rocky plateau above a bend in the river, watching the sunset, I found myself saying, "Thank God — home at last!"

Then I had to ask myself, "Why do I feel so much at home here?" Why here, in this wild bit of Africa, and not paradisiacal Hawai'i, where I was raising a daughter and had been living for the past few decades? With a shock I recognized that the last time I had come close to feeling so good, so deeply at peace with myself, and so connected to everything and everyone around me, was over twenty-five years earlier while in the Israeli army, learning to be a hunter and killer of men, defending the tribal borders. I suddenly understood why I loved my time in the army. Both experiences replicated elements of the primal condition — living simply and strenuously, in close quarters with others while sharing extreme experiences, all the while immersed in the beauty of wild country. It was like a slow, gentle, sustained version of a shamanic-mystical ecstasy, culminating in a deep feeling of integration, of connection to the primordial coordinates of what it means to be human.

After five days, with our food running out, we came to the end of the trail. We all became silent and withdrawn, thinking ahead, preparing to pick up the threads of our old lives. Once out of the reserve, we stopped at a roadside café for toasted sandwiches. It all looked a bit sad and tawdry. We drove through the industrial outskirts of the big city of Durban feeling deflated. I stared out the window at the passing cars, at the gray blocks of buildings and tangles of power lines. It suddenly occurred to me that much of what I would be looking at from now on — that is, until my next wilderness immersion, whenever that might be — would be less beautiful. Most of it would be human-made and more or less ugly, expressing the busy, short-term, utilitarian, profit-minded priorities of its human creators.

Then it all seemed to fit into place. Beauty is not simply subjective or

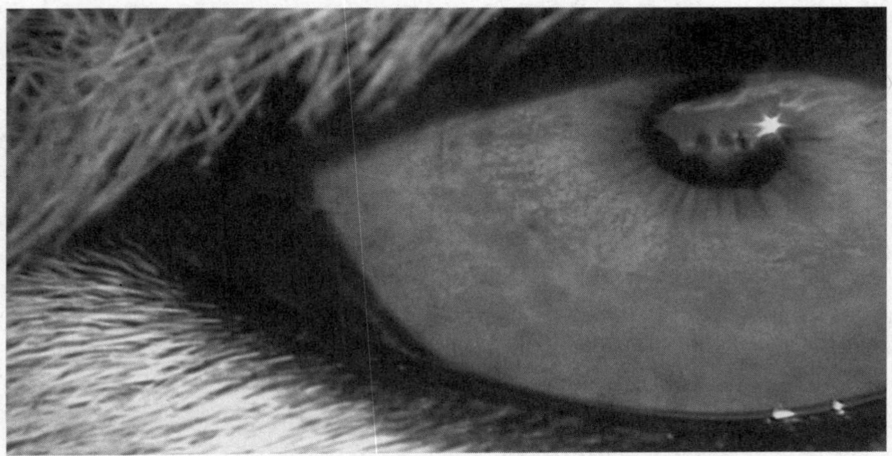

*Cheetah eye. "One doesn't meet oneself until one catches the reflection in an eye other than human." — Loren Eisley* (Photo: Craig Foster)

arbitrary; it's not just in the eye of the beholder. Something is beautiful when we experience joy in contemplating it simply for what it is, without consideration for any material or utilitarian benefit. Like the other defining human orientations to the world, human sensitivity to beauty evolved within a wilderness environment. We could say the experience of pleasure in contemplating the beauty of nature is a kind of resonance between us and the wilderness that crafted our capacity for contemplation. It is a template for aesthetic experience. Some traditional Native Americans became sharply aware of this when they traveled to European cities. Tatanga Mani, Walking Buffalo, one of the leaders of the Stoney Indians, visited England as an old man and tried to explain the quality of the primal convergence of the good, the true, and the beautiful in wilderness:

> Hills are always more beautiful than stone buildings, you know. Living in a city is an artificial existence. Lots of people hardly even feel real soil under their feet, see plants grow except in flower pots, or get far enough beyond the street light to catch the enchantment of a night sky sudden with stars. When people live away from scenes of the Great Spirit's making, it's easy for them to forget his laws.[16]

David Cumes, a physician working in the United States and, like me, another homesick South African, has attempted to systematize this wilderness effect. He came to the realization that much of his medical intervention merely treated symptoms rather than the whole complex of body-mind-spirit. Following the models of van der Post, Ian Player, and his own exposure to Bushman culture, Cumes developed a similar but more structured program leading small groups into wilderness areas but with designated periods for yoga, meditation, and ritual.

The results of his program seemed to confirm this convergence of shamanism with wilderness immersion. The most dramatic and consistent effect was what he called "wilderness rapture" — an intense sense of connection with nature and comfort with one's surroundings. This approached Abraham Maslow's "peak experience" — the classic mystical, ecstatic experience of identification with the larger cosmic unity. Cumes found such experiences to have a powerful healing effect, particularly in inducing positive life changes, ranging from a release from addictions and unhealthy habits to significant reevaluation of the meaning of one's life and being able to make appropriate changes.

Cumes was also struck by a paradoxical "reentry depression" as the group returned to civilization. This seemed more pronounced the more intense the wilderness experience, and it occurred even when there were demonstrably positive lifestyle changes. It is as if wilderness puts one in touch with what is deepest and truest — the primary reality of the human condition, thus opening new possibilities. But by the same token, it sharpens one's sensitivity to what is deficient in our civilized world.

Since African savanna is the wilderness ecology that shaped us most directly, it can provide the most direct route back to an experience of our wilderness Eden. As van der Post puts it:

> How is it that the individual finds a sense of himself, a sense of home in wilderness? Why is it we have lost our sense of belonging in this other, rational world of ours? It seems as if we need to be conscious of the relationship between that within us that gives us our values, and that which makes us instinctively turn to and save wilderness.[17]

An essential creative challenge for politics is to reintroduce initiation into the beauty of wilderness as criterion for both leadership and citizenship. We need to reconnect our self-understanding, through anamnesis, through the various levels of identity — personal, tribal, national, and civilizational

— to our shared African and wilderness origins. Then we need to bring living wilderness back into the direct experience of our urbanized masses, not simply as decoration or recreation, but as a vital intellectual, psycho-spiritual, and political resource — what Cumes calls the "Big Medicine."

*"Dendro-thrope," the face of //Kabbo, dream shaman and one of Bleek's Bushman teachers, on a kokerboom tree in the Northern Cape — //Kabbo's country.*

*(Photo: Craig Foster)*

CHAPTER 10

# THE OUTER REACHES OF INNER WILDERNESS

There is a world beyond ours, a world that is far away, nearby, and invisible. And there it is where God lives, where the dead live, the spirits and the saints, a world where everything has already happened and everything is known. That world talks. It has a language of its own. I report what it says. The sacred mushroom takes me by the hand and brings me to the world where everything is known. It is they, the sacred mushrooms, that speak in a way I can understand. I ask them and they answer me. When I return from the trip that I have taken with them, I tell what they have told me and what they have shown me.

— Maria Sabina, Mazatec shaman, quoted in Joan Halifax, *Shamanic Voices*

Whatever specific symbolic form the shamanic journey takes, the common denominator is always the destruction of the old sense of identity and an experience of ecstatic connection with nature, with the cosmic order, and with the creative energy of the universe. In this process of death and rebirth, shamans experience their own divinity and attain profound insights into the nature of reality. They typically gain an understanding of the origin of many disorders and learn how to diagnose and heal them.

— Stan and Christina Grof, *The Stormy Search for the Self*

## Entheogenic Shamanism

If wilderness immersion can be considered "soft" shamanism, one that gently dissolves boundaries, then as I have suggested hallucinogens constitute "hard" shamanism: shattering the ego, cracking apart our paradigms of reality — or as the Iboga-using Fang of Gabon say "breaking open the head." The purpose is to connect with the wilderness within, to access the archaic coordinates of a good, true, and beautiful primal politics.

Hallucinogens* have an enormous advantage over most other shamanic technologies, in that they produce very dramatic effects on cue, every time. Although cultural context and intentions make an enormous difference, even the naive and unprepared subject may have a life-changing experience upon ingesting hallucinogens. The easy accessibility of hallucinogens has also opened up the whole shamanic realm to systematic laboratory research by Western scientists, making possible an extraordinary mapping of the psyche and exploration of the paradox of "consciousness-reality-language." However, this approach hasn't been without problems. During the 1960s, the reintroduction of these powerful, sacred substances into the popular culture resulted in their often irresponsible misuse as recreational drugs, and this helped feed a culture-wide fear of all drugs. This fear has failed to make critical distinctions in type, context of use, and intent. Increasingly,

---

* *Hallucinogen* is the medical term for a class of compounds, both natural and synthetic, that have a dramatic effect on consciousness (including thought, perception, and mood). The classical hallucinogens — lysergic acid diethylamide (LSD), psilocybin, mescaline, and dimethyl tryptamine — typically produce these effects without stupor or narcosis. Memory impairment is minimal, and these substances are nonaddictive. The term *hallucinogen* is problematic, though, partly because in common usage *hallucination* refers to mental phenomena that appear realistic but have no basis in reality. In fact, subjects under the influence of these classical hallucinogens are aware of the passing and personal nature of their experiences. While a widely used alternative term is *psychedelic*, meaning "mind manifesting," both *psychedelic* and *hallucinogen* are misleading because of their association with the irresponsible use of recreational drugs. This obscures the ancient and widespread use of hallucinogens in shamanic religions. Scholars sensitive to these issues have proposed the term *entheogen*, meaning "manifesting the divine," since one of the most generic features is that of encountering a sacred, deeper, more meaningful reality — the realm of the creative source or the divine.

to distinguish the use of hallucinogens in a sacramental religious context, scholars are using the term *entheogen*, meaning "manifesting the divine." I follow this convention, generally using the term *entheogen* when referring to hallucinogens used by shamans, and using *psychedelic* and *hallucinogen* interchangeably in other contexts.

Given the extent of this distorted understanding, it will help to make three major points clear at the outset:

- Shamanic experiences, like related mystical experiences, seem to be universal, ancient, and accessible by a wide variety of nondrug techniques.
- Shamanic hallucinogens, or entheogens, are heuristically important, since they can offer outsiders a relatively quick method for accessing shamanic states of consciousness. Such states are otherwise capricious or require arduous training.
- Since entheogens can sometimes be identified in the historical and archaeological record, they are also useful in helping determine the antiquity and ubiquity of shamanic practices. In this way, they help establish shamanism as a kind of primordial Ur-religion.

To some degree, the prejudicial attitude among scholars against hallucinogens began with Mircea Eliade, whose research published in the early sixties occurred prior to the outpouring of studies on cross-cultural shamanism and the medical research on shamanic entheogens over the past fifty years. Eliade focused on highly ritualized, specialized Siberian shamanism,* which he took to be paradigmatic. His encounters with the shamanic use of alcohol and tobacco led him to disparage entheogens as "narcotics," a choice of term that was botanically and pharmacologically inaccurate. Narcotics dull the senses, relieve pain, induce deep sleep, and are highly addictive. For example, alcohol is also a highly addictive neurotoxin that suppresses central nervous system function. While such toxins can transform consciousness, their psychopharmacological mechanism is quite different from that of hallucinogens and has effects that are more often pathological than healing and mind opening. By contrast, most of the common hallucinogens are nonaddictive alkaloid

---

* The word *shaman* comes from the Turkic and Tungusic *saman*.

analogues of serotonin and other neurotransmitters. For instance, LSD, the most powerful known hallucinogen, has almost no consistent measurable physiological effect. Not only are hallucinogens nonaddictive, but there is growing evidence that they might actually be *antiaddictive*, and, as we'll see, they have been shown to produce dramatic results in curing alcoholism and drug addiction.

Psychiatric researchers in the fifties and early sixties at first understood hallucinogens as *psychotomimetic* — mimicking psychosis — and valuable for offering doctors an unparalleled opportunity to actually experience the psychic landscape of their mentally ill patients. Very quickly it became clear that the compounds also produced the opposite effect — an expansion of awareness that led to dramatic insights into oneself, often with therapeutic benefits. The healing and illuminating effects of hallucinogens seemed to be associated with their *psycholytic* capacity to loosen or temporarily dissolve the structure of ego armor and personality. Long-repressed biographical material was released for inspection, greatly facilitating the psychoanalytic process; in many cases, this method offered a quite sudden release from intractable neurotic, obsessive, and addictive patterns of behavior. This release was most dramatic when subjects reported the classical mystical epiphany — a powerful encounter with the ground of being, the creative force of the universe.

There were, of course, dangers. In a very few susceptible and unprepared individuals, the dissolution of the ego became permanent. In those cases, the journey was one-way, leaving the poor explorer stranded — a psychotic. But in the vast majority of cases, under proper supervision, it seemed that entheogens could help individuals attain the extraordinary states of consciousness with their attendant benefits, described by shamans and mystics throughout the ages. Since their effects could be produced on demand in the lab, entheogens became powerful research tools for throwing light on the role of shamanic practices in primal societies.[1]

It seems quite likely that as early humans moved out of Africa, they took some sort of rudimentary shamanic practice with them, and this might have included the hallucinogenic potential of plants. Terence McKenna has argued that early humans must have noticed and ingested the entheogenic mushrooms — *Strophari cubensis* — growing on the dung of the herds they followed. In Tassili n'Ajjer, in what is now the Sahara Desert, remains of a Neolithic civilization going back twelve thousand years include engravings associated with what is called the Round Head Culture. Some of these included shamanic-like figures embellished with clearly depicted mushrooms, strongly suggesting a mushroom religion.[2]

There is now evidence that, Eliade to the contrary, hallucinogenic mushrooms played an important role in Siberian shamanism — specifically the red-tipped, white-dotted mushroom *Amanita muscaria*. No doubt the early herders were struck by the fact that reindeer had a penchant for the brightly colored mushrooms, consuming them to the point of inebriation.[3] Gordon Wasson, the famous mycologist who identified the mushroom religion of the Aztec, made a strong case for *Amanita muscaria* being the ingredient in the mysterious sacred brew *soma* described in the ancient Vedic hymns, the *Rig Veda*, of the early Aryans.[4] McKenna has pointed out that *Amanita muscaria*, which contains the hallucinogen muscimol, seems to be unreliably psychoactive and suggested instead that *soma* could well have been *Stropharia cubensis*, which contains the more powerful hallucinogen psilocybin and was widely distributed throughout Africa and the Old World.[5]

As we will see in the next chapter, there is considerable evidence that one of the most important and enduring of the Greek mystery religions, the Eleusinian Mysteries, involved a sacred entheogenic drink, the *kykeon*. Consumed at the climax of elaborate rituals, the drink produced ecstatic visions, bringing joy and meaning to one's life and giving participants a conviction in the existence of an afterlife. Socrates, Plato, and Aristotle are all known to have participated in the Mysteries.

When early hunter-gatherers moved from the Siberian mainland across the Bering Strait during the last ice age, they seem to have brought with them an early form of the Siberian shamanism Eliade encountered. Once isolated in the New World, shamanism continued to develop and incorporate the entheogenic potential of its new environment. More toxic hallucinogens, like the red mescal bean, are known to have been part of the diet of early Paleo-Indians during the late Pleistocene, ten to eleven thousand years ago, and the red bean remained part of the ecstatic visionary shamanic societies of the southern Plains Indians until it was replaced by the more benign peyote cactus in the nineteenth century.[6] Today, this tradition continues in the syncretistic Native American Church, where practitioners from the Rio Grande to the Canadian Plains are now legally allowed to practice their peyote religion.

According to Peter Furst, Native Americans knew and used some eighty to one hundred hallucinogenic plants and mushrooms; this contrasts starkly with the mere eight to ten used by the Old World cultures of Europe.[7] The explanation appears to be less a matter of botany or geography than one of culture. The rise of bureaucratized, patriarchal Christianity meant the vigorous repression of the earlier egalitarian shamanic religions, which offered the individual direct contact with the divine. This repressive attitude didn't arrive in the New World until the late fifteenth century, and as we have seen it has continued into the present.

## "Going Native"

Perhaps the best-known but most controversial example of a Western scholar crossing over and looking at our industrial world from the perspective of indigenous shamanism is Carlos Castaneda. While an anthropology graduate student at UCLA, he claimed to have apprenticed himself to Don Juan Matus, a Yaqui *brujo* — a "man of knowledge," a sorcerer, witch, or shaman — and then he published a series of books purporting to be based on field notes of his experiences. The first three books were taken seriously enough to form the basis for an MA and then a PhD from UCLA. Subsequently, the works became bestsellers and generated something of a cult following.

Castaneda's books describe a terrifying initiation into "separate realities" through ingestion of powerful hallucinogenic, sometimes poisonous plants and mushrooms. Castaneda quickly gave up the idea of comprehending Yaqui shamanism according to the categories of structuralism, and he allowed himself, as he put it, to be swallowed up into the "stupendous, awesome, mysterious and unfathomable" world of primordial shamanism. His work is now widely regarded as a brilliant hoax. Castaneda blended a combination of genuine ethnography, paraphrased chunks of other anthropologists' research, and pure fiction, and he did it so well he succeeded in bewitching the reader into feeling the shattering, exhilarating otherness of shamanic states of consciousness.[8] The phenomenal popularity of his work — translated into seventeen languages with eight million copies sold and generating a cult following — is a testimony to both its literary power and the reading public's hunger for something other than the claustrophobic ubiquity of rationalist materialism. But in the end Castaneda disappoints, leading us into a labyrinth of other realities with little relationship to the one we keep waking up in.

The anthropologist Michael Harner was a less flamboyant but more trustworthy guide whose personal transformation exemplified the healing power of shamanism. Part of Harner's fieldwork involved years of living with the Jivaro and then the Conibo Indians of South America. In 1961, well before the publication of Castaneda's first book, Harner's Conibo informants persuaded him that, if he really wanted to understand them, he needed to undergo shamanic initiation by drinking the powerful hallucinogenic brew *ayahuasca* (also called *yage*, the "vine of souls," "vision vine," or "vine of the dead"). As happened to Castaneda, Harner's ontological categories were blown apart as he experienced fantastic dimensions of other realities.

At the onset of his first experience Harner describes being paralyzed with terror, convinced he was dying and privy to truths reserved only for the dead. Once he recovered, Harner talked of being shocked to his core by the overwhelming conviction that the visions and insights belonged to a depth dimension of reality not normally available to everyday consciousness. Yet in some mysterious way, this strange level of reality seemed more fundamental, more real, and more instructive than the world of normal waking consciousness.

> I found myself, although awake, in a world literally beyond my wildest dreams. I met bird-headed people, as well as dragon like creatures who explained that they were the true gods of this world. I enlisted the services of other spirit helpers in attempting to fly through the far reaches of the Galaxy.[9]

The dragon-like creatures, the "true gods," said they were contained deep within all living matter, and they showed Harner — with a vividness he found impossible to describe — how they guided the course of the whole evolution of life.

After Harner recovered, he struggled to make sense of what he had experienced. He consulted an old blind *ayahuasquero* shaman and was stunned to find that the shaman already knew details of his "dragon" vision before he described them. When he shared some of his experiences with a Christian missionary couple, they pulled out a copy of the Bible and pointed to striking similarities to some of the visions in the book of Revelations. Much later Harner was even more amazed when he realized that the "dragons" inside all of life corresponded strikingly with the role and structure of DNA, which had yet to be elucidated by Crick and Watson.*

Harner felt forced to confront what he called Western *cognicentricism* — the assumption that the only way to reliable knowledge was through rationalist materialism, or the reductive, mechanistic Cartesian worldview. Utterly shaken by the revelation he experienced, Harner decided to devote the rest of his life to studying shamanism. He eventually developed "softer," nondrug techniques — specifically, drumming and visualization — for helping Westerners enter shamanic states of consciousness. Harner became one of the modern pioneers of that immense work of psychic cartography that is now under way, providing some initial maps, metaphors, and models to help navigate an inner geography as vast and extraordinary as that of the outer cosmos.

With the wide availability of plant, mushroom, and pharmaceutical psychedelics in the 1960s, a whole generation got a taste of what Harner and other scholars were experiencing. The extraordinary, controversial history of LSD constitutes a scientific story that provides astounding insights into this realm while at the same time exposing the limits of a mechanical science of mind.

Lysergic acid diethylamide, or LSD-25, was first synthesized in 1938 by Arthur Stoll and Albert Hofmann at the Sandoz pharmaceutical laboratories in Switzerland. It was made from the same ergot fungus that was subsequently identified as the most likely ingredient of the entheogenic *kykeon* of the Eleusinian Mysteries. The substance Hofmann synthesized was initially discarded when animal testing for its use in obstetrics, gynecology, and the treatment of migraines produced no interesting results.

Five years later, Hofmann was disturbed by a series of strange dreams and intimations, which eventually led him to do something he had never done before: he reviewed the results of a previously discarded compound, in this case the twenty-fifth in the series he had synthesized from ergot. In

* Interestingly, Crick himself admitted he had regularly used the powerful psychedelic LSD-25, when it was still legal, as a "thinking tool," and that the idea for the double helical structure had come to him during one of these extraordinary states of consciousness. See Graham Hancock, *Supernatural: Meetings with the Ancient Teachers of Mankind* (New York: Disinformation Co., 2006).

the process of producing a new batch of the diethylamide of lysergic acid, he inadvertently ingested a small quantity, probably through skin contact, and so began a strange and terrifying journey into a kind of madness, which soon turned out to be the most fascinating experience of his life. In the process, science embarked on an equally strange and revolutionary journey of discovery.

The professional psychiatric community initially focused on the most striking aspect of the LSD experience is the dissolution of everyday ego functioning, opening consciousness to a barrage of internal and external information, a kind of temporary psychosis. As normal volunteers experimented with the substance, it quickly became apparent that the drug experience often producing a storm of profound and therapeutic insights, ranging from liberating leaps in self-knowledge to an intuitive understanding of complex issues in aesthetics, religion, and metaphysics. Sandoz started marketing it as a psychiatric drug under the name Delysid, stimulating a flurry of fairly indiscriminate research, but also some dramatic therapeutic breakthroughs. For example, Humphry Osmond found administering LSD to alcoholics in a therapeutic context could produce astounding and consistent cure rates of around 50 percent.[10]

By 1967, few drugs had been more thoroughly tested, with over a thousand papers published. The problem was that the results were so widely variable that each new piece of research seemed to contradict the previous one. Jay Stevens summed up the situation well in his cultural history *Storming Heaven: LSD and the American Dream*:

> There were hunches and hypotheses and horror stories and glowing reports and experiments that worked for some and not for others. But there was no consensus. Every type of madness, every type of parapsychological phenomenon, every type of mystical ecstatic illumination, Jungian archetypes, past lives, precognition, psychosis, sartori-samadhi-atman, union with God — it was all there, in the scientific record.[11]

LSD blew apart the simple behaviorist ego psychology already under assault by the youth rebellion. It shook the ontological foundations on which the scientific method itself rested by confronting scientists with the mystery of an inner dimension to reality that seemed to transcend space and time. The scientific and political establishment reacted by looking the other way: it ignored the anomalies, ostracized those working with hallucinogens, and finally helped criminalize the entire field of psychedelic exploration. By 1968 lysergic acid had been labeled a Schedule I drug and declared to have no therapeutic or research value.

## The Telescope of the Psyche

By this time it was becoming clear to the few who continued to study hallucinogens seriously that part of the variability of response was due to the capacity of these substances to dissolve the conditioning that held personality together and then to amplify a whole range of normally unconscious psychic processes. This variability was compounded by the fact that the preparation, mind-set, and situation of the participant at the time of the session — the "set" and "setting" — seemed to be critical in determining the general course and outcome of the experience.

The most systematic and extensive empirical fieldwork on LSD to date came out of Czechoslovakia in the fifties and sixties. It was interpreted and developed into a revolutionary understanding of the psyche by Stanislav Grof, who was one of the first to grasp just how powerful a tool LSD could be for exploring the inner universe of the psyche. Eventually, Grof came to recognize that LSD could revolutionize psychology in much the same way that the telescope had revolutionized astronomy, and the microscope, biology.[12]

Grof began working with LSD as a conventional medically trained psychiatrist at the Psychiatric Research Institute in Prague. The research started as part of a large study on maladjustive interpersonal patterns in neurotic patients. As the astonishing results accumulated, the project developed into a more ambitious and open-ended exploration of the effects of LSD on the human psyche. Grof personally observed some twenty-five hundred sessions and had access to the records of another fifteen hundred sessions collected by colleagues. By any standard of conventional empirical science, this constituted a massive pool of data.

Grof was initially astounded by the enormous variability in responses, not only among individuals, but within the same individual using the same dose at different times. Gradually, he realized that rather than causing a toxic psychosis, LSD seemed to be a nonspecific amplifier of mental processes, a "powerful catalyst... activating unconscious material from various deep levels of the personality." There tended to be a rough progression during each journey. First, a typical session started with perceptual distortions and pseudo-hallucinations, like seeing sounds, hearing images, and sensations of the limbs elongating, as well as floating or flying, rather like the accounts of Bushman shamans. Material from the personal unconscious would then surface, starting with recent buried memories, then older unresolved conflicts and forgotten traumas. This progression tended to mirror a standard Freudian psychodynamic model, with repeated sessions exposing deeper and deeper layers of the unconscious. Patients described the experience of returning again and again to similar clusters of visions and emotions, each time penetrating deeper until the visions converged into a core traumatic experience. Once the core trauma was fully understood and reexperienced from an adult, therapeutic perspective, the patient would generally gain dramatic relief from pathological symptoms. The drug seemed to accelerate dramatically the process of conventional psychotherapy. Results requiring months or even years of conversational psychoanalysis could be accomplished within a few sessions.

Beyond the psychodynamic level, LSD seemed to have the capacity to open awareness to the most extraordinary range of experiences beyond space and time. Over and over, subjects reported the ability to directly experience distant geographical areas and past historical periods. There were descriptions of identifying with and becoming animals that rivaled in emotional intensity the accounts of Bushman shamans in deep trance and exceeded in graphic detail the rock paintings of therianthropes. They reported extraordinarily vivid insights into biological and natural processes they had no previous knowledge of. These were often corroborated so convincingly that Grof was forced to consider that in some mysterious way an individual's awareness in these expanded states could connect to, and experience directly, inner aspects of the whole human and evolutionary drama. As Daniel Pinchbeck points out so incisively, one of the most shocking features about such hyperreal hallucinations is their "organized precision"; they are "as fully realized as the data seen in the eyes-opened world" and cannot be accounted for by the "pallid scientific thesis" — that they were simply self-generated by-products of an overstimulation of the neocortex.[13]

Despite the astounding range of their experiences, subjects reported a general healing effect. After many thousands of hours of LSD therapy with patients and years of reflection, Grof came to the conclusion that LSD very often brought about what he called "holotropic" states of consciousness that were "oriented toward wholeness," connecting the individual to the world and to the deepest levels of existence in a new way. As Grof puts it:

> Holotropic experiences are the common denominator in many procedures that have throughout the centuries shaped the ritual, spiritual and cultural life of many human groups. They have been the main source of cosmologies, mythologies, philosophies and religious systems describing the spiritual nature of the cosmos and existence. They are the key for understanding the spiritual life of humanity from shamanism and sacred ceremonies of aboriginal tribes to the great religions of the world. But most important they provide invaluable practical guidelines for a rich and satisfying life strategy that makes it possible to realize to the fullest our potential.[14]

After being predictably ignored by the mainstream medical and academic establishment, Grof's work is now slowly being recognized as a major contribution to an emerging science and philosophy of mind. Not only does his work incorporate and refine the achievements of the existing medical and Freudian paradigms, but it also constitutes the most extensive empirical confirmation of Jung's ideas about archetypes of the collective unconscious. In addition, it brings the teachings of the wisdom traditions of mystics and shamans throughout the ages into a constructive dialogue with medical science and psychoanalysis. Finally, it provides a model of psychic life fully congruent with the paradoxical relations between consciousness and matter suggested by Eric Voegelin's philosophy and by quantum physics and modern cosmology. One measure of Grof's slowly growing recognition comes from the philosopher Richard Tarnas, who concludes his monumental, celebrated history of Western civilization, *The Passion of the Western Mind*, by showcasing Grof's work. He describes it as constituting one of "the most epistemologically significant developments in the recent history of depth psychology, and indeed the most important achievement in the field as a whole since Freud and Jung themselves."[15] Such a psychology of course undercuts the Lockean Liberal assumptions about mind and nature, on which our institutions rest, and inspires us to reimagine a neo-shamanic politics.

Today, a number of trends are converging to produce a more mature approach to the shamanic and therapeutic use of hallucinogens. First of all, we are slowly facing up to the hypocrisy of our society waging a vicious war on mind-expanding entheogens while facilitating the addiction of millions to alcohol and nicotine, tranquilizers and antidepressants.[16] Second, we are slowly becoming aware of the long and rich history of the human use of entheogens as aids to healing and visioning. Finally, the astounding breakthroughs in physics and cosmology are dissolving long-held certainties about the nature of reality and creating possibilities for radical transformation of culture and politics.

In 2006, one of the most rigorous studies ever conducted on the subjective and observable effects of hallucinogens was completed on psilocybin. As mentioned earlier, psilocybin is the primary hallucinogen in *Stropharia cubensis*, the divine mushroom of Mesoamerica. The project was directed by Professor Roland Griffiths at one of the most prestigious institutes of medical research in the United States — the Johns Hopkins Department of Neuroscience, Psychiatry, and Behavioral Medicine.[17] The experiment involved thirty individuals in two eight-hour sessions at two-month intervals.

Each subject went through two sessions, one with the psychedelic, the other with methylphenidate (Ritalin) as the active placebo. Griffiths set up a third red herring group that was given the placebo and told it was the hallucinogen, in an attempt to account for distortion due to expectation. Subjects were briefed before and after and given multiple, detailed surveys to complete. More than two-thirds of the participants who took psilocybin rated the experience as being among their five most meaningful and spiritually significant ever. *One-third declared their session to have been the single most meaningful experience of their lives.* Almost 80 percent reported "increased well being and life satisfaction," an estimation supported by follow-up interviews with family and friends. As expected there was no such response from those taking the Ritalin or those in red herring groups.[18] The results, hailed as "landmark" by Charles Schuster, the former director of the National Institute on Drug Abuse (NIDA), confirmed what had been self-evident to shamanic cultures for millennia — that psilocybin regularly produces primary mystical experiences associated with dramatic, positive life changes, and these seem to be sustained over time.

On the face of it, this should be astounding news for a society that champions individual meaning and fulfillment as a supreme political value. Two-thirds of the people in the group that ingested a nonaddictive, nontoxic chemical afterward claimed to have had a life-changing mystical experience comparable to the accounts in religious literature from the saintly and enlightened.

As more evidence like this emerges, the medical profession is finally taking some responsibility for reversing the fear-driven repression of hallucinogens. A recent interdisciplinary investigation published in the venerable, conservative British medical journal *The Lancet* criticized the prevailing system of drug scheduling as "medically unsupported...and completely unjustified." It proposed instead a more consistent evidence-based, nine-point scale of "harm assessment," and then it went on to demonstrate that when applied by a wide range of health professionals, there was a compelling consistency. The results repeatedly ranked the hallucinogens LSD, mescalin, and psilocybin *lower than alcohol and tobacco* in terms of overall social and physical harm and risk of abuse.[19] Clearly, the current drug scheduling has less to do with medical evidence and more to do with the repressive politics of consciousness.

Not only are entheogens nonaddictive but as mentioned some of the early studies using LSD in the treatment of alcoholics demonstrated that hallucinogens might actually be *antiaddictive*. The initial studies, performed in Saskatchewan during the 1950s and 1960s by Humphry Osmond, Abram Hoffer, Colin Smith, and Sven Jensen, produced an astounding, consistent 50 percent cure rate over periods of around six months.[20] Alcohol, in contrast to hallucinogens, produces an ersatz transcendence by releasing the ego from anxiety, but at the expense of obliterating the superego, wittily described as "that part of the psyche soluble in alcohol." Current research using other entheogens, like Ibogaine, are also producing dramatic results.[21]

Grof, among others, has proposed that addictive behavior is in part a consequence of a frustrated yearning for authentic religious experience. Such experiences, as we have seen, give us a passionate connection to the larger community of being, and in so doing bring meaning to our lives and help release us from compulsion and addiction. Bill Wilson, the cofounder of Alcoholics Anonymous, was consulted during these early alcoholism studies and was tremendously impressed with the capacity of LSD to produce a "spiritual experience," which seemed critical to sustained healing. He went on to incorporate the recognition of some mysterious "higher power" — a transcendent dimension into his 12-step program.[22]

The ecstatic peak experience — whether entheogen induced or not — seems to put one in touch with a deeper dimension of the everyday world that is primary, eternal, creative, and in that sense, divine. The enthusiasm and love of life engendered by this encourages one to deepen one's immersion in life, often expressed in a desire for meaningful work, for engaging the lives of others, for being of service, and for making a positive creative contribution. Finally we need to note that such acts of service can, in and of themselves, generate something akin to ecstasy, a feeling of deep connection to the preciousness of existence.

## The Shamanic Journey

We move toward a postmechanistic politics of consciousness as we triangulate research on comparative shamanism, psychopharmacology, and evolutionary psychology. Since this emerging big picture needs to be pursued in tandem with self-exploration, it is unfortunate that many scholars who argue so vehemently about the meaning of shamanism have little, if any, direct experience of shamanic ecstasy. Some show a related tendency to dismiss the rapidly growing number of testimonials of initiated Westerners in favor of obscure accounts from exotic indigenous cultures. This scholarly distance from experience has at times led to a profusion of categories and specious distinctions. Some scholars would deny the label "shamanic" to states of consciousness induced by hallucinogens. They endeavor to confine authentic shamanism to the more structured Siberian and Asian models and make hard distinctions between "mystical," "religious," and "shamanic" states. Graham Hancock observed that sometimes the scholarly hairsplitting sounds like virgins arguing which of the sexual positions described in the *Kama Sutra* are the most pleasurable. When it comes to meaning, experience matters.[23]

A more helpful approach is to follow William James's pragmatism and remain open to a spectrum of consciousness — an inner universe — as it presents itself to us, and then proceed with mapping through multiple modes of exploration. The *ayahuasca* brew that Michael Harner experienced in the 1960s is particularly helpful in connecting shamanic ecstasy to our wilderness origins in the recovery of a quest-based politics. First, *ayahuasca* seems to have played a central role in the politics of indigenous and hunting-gathering societies throughout the Amazon basin for millennia. The fact that at the time of first contact its use was already widespread and integrated in the self-understanding of the native cultures suggests its great antiquity.

Second, *ayahuasca* is undergoing something of a revival as its use has spread into syncretistic churches, which combine Christianity with indigenous shamanic practices. Its use is also spreading through nonindigenous societies via ad hoc groups that mix shamanic and other spiritual traditions.[24] Although one of *ayahuasca*'s primary hallucinogenic ingredients, DMT, is a Schedule 1 drug in pure form, and its use is regulated by international convention, the plant itself and the brew are legal in Brazil for sacramental purposes. Its use is also legal in the United States and France for members of União do Vegetal (union of the plant) church.

Third, *ayahuasca* is hardly a recreational drug; taking it is not something one does lightly. Typically, before a ceremony using *ayahuasca*, a strict diet is followed for several days. Alcohol is avoided, as are other drugs, fish, meat, fermented foods like cheese and soy, and other specific proteins. The brew contains a compound inhibiting the enzyme in the human body that normally breaks down the potentially toxic monoamines in the diet. Participants fast on the day of the ceremony, since even if they've followed the diet, the brew often causes extreme nausea and vomiting. Unpleasant feelings tend to pass after the early stages and can then be followed by ecstatic visions of unearthly beauty. But the visions often confront participants with uncomfortable realities in their personal life. Although this can help initiate positive lifestyle changes, an *ayahuasca* session is far from a "feel-good trip."

Finally, *ayahuasca* is particularly interesting because of its botanical complexity, the difficulty of making it, and what its discovery implies about the early human relation to nature. The brew requires the synergistic combination of two plants, each on its own being fairly unremarkable. The leaves of one plant, *Psychotria viridis*, contain the potent hallucinogen N,N-dimethyltryptamine (DMT), but when the leaves are eaten alone, DMT is immediately broken down because of the presence of monoamine oxidase (MAO) enzymes in the human body, and so it has little psychedelic effect. For that to occur, the body must also have an MAO inhibitor to prevent DMT breakdown. This crucial component is provided by the woody liana, *Banisteriopsis caapi*, which also contributes some hallucinogenic alkaloids.

When the two are boiled together in a lengthy process of rendering, a brown, muddy, nauseating concoction is produced containing the DMT in the presence of the MAO inhibitor and other psychedelic harmalines — creating a profoundly hallucinogenic mixture.[25]

One of the great mysteries of ethnobotany is how this combination was discovered, since it strains credulity to think of Amazonian hunter-gatherers systematically going through the vast number of plants in their environment and then boiling various combinations for hours until hitting upon exactly the right mixture to produce DMT in the presence of MAO inhibitors. When questioned about this, some shamans attribute the discovery to an extraordinary, supernatural event. Significantly, this event is often linked to the identity of the tribe, or the origin of the human species and the establishment of the primary relationships among humanity, culture, and the natural world. Such origin stories suggest the centrality of the ecstatic experience to the life of the community. Shamans repeatedly insist that the plants themselves are in some way sentient and can speak to human beings when they are in the special states of consciousness and receptivity associated with dreams, visions, and trance. Taken seriously, this has profound metaphysical implications for the truth quest.[26]

The cognitive psychologist and linguist Benny Shanon undertook an encyclopedic study of *ayahuasca* shamanism in his 2002 book, *The Antipodes of the Mind: Charting the Phenomenology of the Ayahuasca Experience.* Shanon is a highly respected, well-published scholar at my alma mater, the conservative Hebrew University in Jerusalem. He is also something of a methodological boundary crosser, since he brings together both rigorous scholarship and firsthand experience of shamanic rapture. He stumbled on the religious use of *ayahuasca* while visiting South America in 1991 in total ignorance of its history and literature. He drank the brew out of curiosity and was so fascinated by his experience that he made it the center of his research. Over the years he has actively participated in some 130 sessions, in settings ranging from those guided by indigenous healers to prayer meetings of syncretistic churches and small private gatherings. He then conducted interviews with another 178 individuals from a variety of backgrounds and from this research produced an impressive empirical pool of testimonies covering some 2,500 individual *ayahuasca* sessions.[27] Like Harner, Shanon was eventually forced to reconsider deeply held assumptions about the nature of consciousness-reality.

What most perplexed Shanon was the fact that the content of the experiences seemed to contradict the simple, apparently self-evident fact that mind is confined to brain or body. The *ayahuasca* visions were too wide-ranging and too extraordinarily detailed: they included historical scenes, exotic geographical settings, and fantastical places and creatures, as well as revelations about repressed aspects of one's personal life. Many of the visions were so precise, so completely formed, and so self-consistent that they defied any notion of somehow being stored in the brain or simply produced by the brain. There were striking examples of individuals accessing historical information they had no direct knowledge of — as if the information was stored in some fifth dimension outside the brain-body. Then, in the highly sensitized state of the *ayahuasca* trance, the brain acted like a radio receiver tuned to invisible frequencies of energy that transmitted through space and time. *Ayahuasca*, like other entheogens, also seemed to have its own distinct signature; for example, there were recurring themes of jungle animals like jaguars, anacondas, and boas, and then complex fractal structures all in hyperreal, vivid detail.[28] Even more perplexing was the fact that sometimes the visions were shared within the group at the same time and could even be manipulated by the shaman.

When considering shamanic experiences generally, but particularly entheogenic-assisted shamanism, we encounter another paradox. Taking *ayahuasca*, like other entheogens, sometimes involves going through a hellish kind of ego death. One can be confronted with shocking and painful revelations about long-repressed details concerning one's intimate life or long-held assumptions about the nature of reality. Almost by definition, this is profoundly unsettling and at times terrifying. So why would people do it? Why would they repeat the experience, and why would they create ongoing, passionate, disciplined shamanic rituals that center around it? When asked, practitioners across cultures and times are emphatic: "to find our life," as the Huichol say of their peyote hunt, or as Cicero said of the Eleusinian Mysteries, "to live more joyously...and to die with greater hope."[29] The Bushmen simply say, "If you don't dance, you die." One near-universal constant of such experiences is that they break ossified structures of thought and behavior. They make possible psychological and spiritual growth; they confer profound insight, and they infuse life with more meaning and greater, lasting joy.

Let me give two first-person examples, one historic and one contemporary. The first is the story of Manuel Cordova-Rios. At the end of the nineteenth century, at the age of fifteen, Cordova-Rios went off seeking fortune and adventure with four seasoned *caucheros* — Peruvian rubber cutters.[30] They followed one of the upper tributaries of the Amazon River into a region where few Europeans had ventured. One day the camp was ambushed by a group of Amahuaca Indians, Rios's companions were killed, and he was captured. His hands were tied, and for nine exhausting days he was forced to accompany the band, jogging through the jungle until they reached a remote village. There he lived for several years, captive but well cared for while he was slowly taught the language and the way of life of the tribe.

Eventually, he realized he was being recruited into the tribe for some mysterious purpose. Part of his early initiation involved an extended process of learning through drinking *ayahuasca* — which the Amahuaca called *nixi honi xum*a — the "vision vine." In session after session, the shaman chief, Xumu, would conjure and manipulate shared visions of animals with a vividness and detail that exceeded anything Rios had seen in waking life. In the process, the shaman communicated to the amazed boy detailed, practical information about the creatures of the forest. Years later Rios described his first experience of a shared vision:

> The chief said, "Let us start with the birds. You know the medium sized tinamou, the partridge that gives the plaintive call at sunset because he does not like to sleep alone on the ground. Visualize one for me."
>
> There he was! I saw him in infinite detail with his rounded tailless rump, plumage olive gray, washed and barred with shades of cinnamon, chestnut and dusky brown. Never had I perceived visual images in such detail before.... The chief then brought a female and the male went through his mating dance. I heard all of the song, calls and other sounds. Their variety was beyond anything I had known. Finally a simple saucer-shaped nest appeared on the ground between the birds, with

> two pale-blue eggs in it. The male sat on the nest, to my surprise. "Yes, he raises the children," said the chief.
>
> We went from the various tinamous to the trumpeter, the curassows and the other important game birds, all seen in the same infinite and minute detail.[31]

Cordova-Rios was stunned that empirical information about the external world could be directly communicated in trance. The revelation changed his life and impelled him eventually to become a shaman and a healer in his own right.

The second example of a journey to the wilderness within comes from my own modest experience of *ayahuasca* in a less rustic setting. As part of my own search I participated in several *ayahuasca* ceremonies conducted by a *curandera* — a female shaman — with small groups of similarly motivated individuals. My first experience took place under an open-sided shelter in a remote wild valley. After everyone had consumed a small cup of the vile-tasting, thick, dark-brown concoction, the shaman went around the circle smudging the participants with fragrant incense, blowing smoke on our heads, and reciting a series of blessings. After waiting for the brew to start working, the *curandera* began singing in an ancient Quechua dialect. The song was so exquisitely beautiful that it seemed quite otherworldly. As she sang I noticed a feeling creeping up my body as if my insides were melting, leaving me absolutely paralyzed. I felt so terribly weak and nauseous that I feared I had not dieted properly and had been lethally poisoned. The haunting, yearning quality of the song intensified my feelings of being utterly lost in a strange universe. The song also had a pleading quality that made me want to weep with sadness. None of my extensive reading about the brew had prepared me for the intensity of my emotions. Then I realized her singing was actually bringing the spirit of the vine into the gathering and moving it through my body. I suddenly, desperately wanted her to stop; I wanted it to be over. At the same moment I realized it was too late. We had taken off. It was as if the canoe had left the shore, the shaman was in charge, and the song was our solitary paddle. Avoiding the rapids depended on the beauty of the song and the sincerity of the shaman, begging the spirit of the vine to guide and heal us.

Then something I believed absolutely impossible happened: in a flash, a cartoonish elfin figure with a pointed hat appeared and cartwheeled around the circle, from head to head. The fact that it was so completely unexpected, so unrelated to anything else going on, made it simultaneously terrifying and funny. As it spun from person to person, it tickled, and we each let out a little peal of silvery laughter. It was clearly not a three-dimensional entity — yet it seemed too perfectly formed and too utterly random to be generated by my own overstimulated brain. It was also "real" in the sense of entering shared space and time, as others in the circle who saw it later confirmed. "Oh," I said to myself, "the spirits, whatever they might be and wherever they might come from, are now in charge and playful." If this was no mental projection, what was it? Where did it come from? I started shivering and then vomited violently into my purging bowl, as if heaving out the last of my dogmatic assumptions about reality. The relief was immediate.

I remember very little of the rest of the night. I had a vague sense of being shown visions of astounding beauty. The next day my companions informed me that I couldn't stop proclaiming loudly, over and over: "Thank you, God! Thank you, God!" This went on until my noisy rapture prompted one of the assistants to lead me out of the circle to walk under the stars until I had quieted down.

The next morning, having slept no more than a couple of hours, I felt humbled, weak, and wordless. I was convinced I had somehow looked under the lid of reality and survived visions not meant for mortals. I was still in shock and couldn't imagine ever wanting to repeat the experience. The following night I went to bed early and woke up the next morning feeling very different. It was one of the most peaceful, beautiful days of my life. I couldn't stop looking at the sunlit, gleaming garden, the shades of green on the trees, and the bright-blue sky. It looked like the first day of creation. I felt healed — like a child again — clean, fresh, innocent. I was filled with gratitude at being alive in such a miraculous world.

My old routine — coffee in the morning, beer in the evening — now seemed crude and desensitizing. The feeling of purity and clarity remained for weeks, though it gradually faded as my old world reasserted itself. The otherworldly elf seemed to be completely irrelevant to the mystical rapture of the morning after. Only later, when I discovered that trickster stories are central themes in the mythology of indigenous shamanic cultures, did the vision start to make a bit of paradoxical sense. The details meant little; what mattered was waking up to the beauty of the mystery of the world. My *ayahuasca* journey had taken me on a roller-coaster ride, leaving me, two days later, clear and functional, in a state of gently sustained mystical awe.

The supernatural education of Cordova-Rios, a young man in a pristine rain forest, living with the Amahuaca, proceeded in a more orderly, focused, and practical fashion. After several months this resulted in something like a fine-tuning of his waking state, which he found enormously helpful in improving his relations with members of the tribe.

> During my training I became aware of subtle changes in my mental process and modes of thought. I noticed a mental acceleration, and a certain clairvoyance in anticipating events and the reactions of the tribe. By focusing my attention on a single individual I could divine his reactions and purpose and anticipate what he would do or what he planned to do. This was all important to the way Xumu governed the tribe, and I began to see what lay under the surface of his management of their community life. The old man said my power to anticipate and know future events would improve and grow, also that I would be able to locate and identify objects from a great distance. All this, he told me, would help protect and control the tribe.[32]

In contemporary South American settings, the *ayahuasca* ceremony is also called *la dieta* or *la purge* — "the diet" or "the purge" — and healing sessions can go on day after day for a week or more. In some groups on the morning after a ceremony, participants will eat a simple breakfast together and share experiences of the night before. In one of my own sessions, I remember, a young woman was caught up in a fit of heaving sobs that went on much of the night as she relived and then released herself from an abusive relationship with her mother. Witnessing others choosing to face excruciating truths and then going on to enjoy a garden of heavenly delights was a deeply moving experience. I felt full of love and compassion for their courage and commitment to health and truth. I saw how sharing such life-changing experiences powerfully bonds a group of near strangers.

One of the most consistent features of the *ayahuasca* experience is a sense of being both humbled and energized in the face of a natural world revealed to be infinitely sacred in its beauty and awesome in its ego-shattering mystery. Such revelations accelerate individuation while paradoxically bonding individuals in more mutually supportive relationships. Many report gradual release from compulsive, defensive, and addictive behavior. There seems to be a progression in self-knowledge and healing as individuals pursue the *dieta* as a spiritual discipline. Some of the syncretistic religions function like any other church, offering worship ceremonies on a regular basis. After studying accounts of participants in such groups, I could see the truth of Grof's insight that at the heart of much addictive behavior is a frustrated hunger for ecstasy. It is as if our modern condition of alienation and anxiety has sharpened a craving for the primal condition marked by those extended periods of gentle intoxication in the beauty of a life in wilderness, all the while supported by a loving community of similarly inspired companions. Shamanic ecstasy, religious epiphany, and wilderness rapture all share at their deepest a love for the beauty of life. This love of life is in turn the living inspiration for the truth quest — the lodestone for a future-primal politics.

## A Neo-shamanic Metaphysics

Benny Shanon's repeated, consistent experiences with *ayahuasca* provoked him to consider the possibility of a realm of consciousness-reality that is primary and exists in some sense independently of the individual brain. He struggled with this issue in ways that indigenous cultures like the Bushmen do not. The intellectual division of labor he was trained for, and that is emblematic of Western society, stood in the way of acceptance. In his writings, he repeatedly declares such questions metaphysical and beyond the boundaries of cognitive psychology. Yet Shanon is philosophically sophisticated and seems well aware of how consciousness is mysteriously woven into the external reality in ways that contradict Cartesian dualism and that are consonant with the entheogenic experience. In one of his more speculative papers he considers circumstantial evidence that some of the miracles, visions, and revelations described in the Bible might have been the result of ingesting an *ayahuasca*-like mixture of common desert plants. He points out that equivalent results are produced by a mixture of extracts from acacia trees, which are widespread in the Middle East, and that the hallucinogenic *Peganum harmala* is also a fairly common bush. In one suggestive anecdote Shanon describes following the advice of a pharmacologist and expert on medicinal plants in Israel and finding a patch of *Peganum* growing outside the entrance to the Qumran caves. This is where the mystical sect of the Essenes lived from the second century BCE to the second century CE and where the famous Dead Sea Scrolls were found.[33]

Until fairly recently, there was simply no way of conceptualizing a mechanism for the extraordinary transpersonal experiences encountered during shamanic trance. Western science found it easier to dismiss them as fantasy, fraud, or schizophrenia, since they so glaringly contradicted the ruling mechanistic paradigm of behaviorist psychology and the Newtonian-Cartesian "box" model of the universe, where everything happens within three-dimensional space in linear time. This is no longer the case. This mechanistic model of reality has now been demolished by the consolidation of the revolutions in physics, biology, and cosmology. Creative thinkers in biology and physics are now suggesting different mechanisms to explain how mind is enmeshed with matter. These revolutions in our scientific understanding of reality are strangely concordant with the astounding experiences of archaic shamanism in an evolving universe.

Since consciousness is an emergent property of evolving wilderness — the inner face of the external cosmos — we cannot set preestablished limits to experience. As W. I. Thompson put it so elegantly:

> Since the mind is part of nature, we make a mistake when we imagine that the act of perception is through a window in which we are on one side and nature on the other. We are in nature, so there is no reason that subjectivity and objectivity should be so dissonantly arranged; it is more than likely that the key in which the nerves and the stars are strung is the same.[34]

We need to open ourselves, like the shamans of old, to an interwoven, incredibly complex ecology of consciousness.

As Thompson's statement implies, the shamanic notion that humans might receive specialized learning directly from the plants, animals, and even places of the natural world is implicit in the emerging evolutionary understanding of consciousness as an intrinsic facet of matter. We can understand consciousness as an invisible but inwardly self-evident dimension of reality. As the universe evolves from the primordial simplicity of the fireball, cooling into complexity, so this self-organization produces increasingly autonomous, complex beings, from plants to insects, animals, and eventually humans. As complexity and individuation increase, we find a related dimension of what Teilhard de Chardin called "interiority," where information is collected, stored, and processed to redirect the behavior of the creature. With the human, this inner dimension becomes conscious of itself and capable of augmenting its own autonomy through reflection, imagination, the creative use of technology, and so on, setting in play the whole human drama of the in-between with all its dangers and distractions. Shamanic practice can be understood as a balancing, or self-correcting, mechanism, augmenting creative self-awareness in a variety of ways while reconnecting that expanded awareness to its organic roots in a primordial reality. In this way complexity consciousness* can be fostered without the human becoming unhinged from the animal and without civilization destroying wilderness.

We saw how we became unhinged through the one-sided development of mechanical, mathematical science in the service of power and profit — the primordial sins of hubris and idolatry. In the process, modernity viciously repressed the shamanic journey of ecstatic remembering and reconnecting. This doesn't mean, of course, that science is dispensable. Galileo was partly correct when he asserted that the universe is written in the language of numbers and the laws of mathematics. This is self-evidently true in the reliability of our cars, submarines, and rockets. But the bigger evolutionary story supports the shamans of old, who assert that the universe is also written in the language of words and stories, music and dance. Shamanism and science are both essential to making sense of our primary experience of the world. Discovering and living by truth require practicing each in dynamic balance with the other.

For example, in regard to the mystery of the discovery of the *ayahuasca* mixture, it is not impossible that there is some sort of communication between the plant and human worlds more subtle than the trial and error of blind science. There is every reason to think human consciousness is open to the sort of prelinguistic, prescientific, intuitive knowing that animals regularly demonstrate. Although we might not yet know the mechanism, we can imagine this sort of communication as a sixth sense that makes it possible for buck and baboon to know which of the bland or brightly colored fruits, flowers, and herbs of the veldt are poisonous and which are nourishing and healing. It would be absurd to think that emerging humanity suddenly lost this animal inheritance with the advent of self-consciousness and language. The evolutionary story suggests that the break was slow and progressive,

* For a fuller explanation of Teilhard de Chardin's notion of "complexity consciousness," see chapter 3.

increasing sharply with the constriction of consciousness associated with the hierarchical warrior civilizations, and culminating in the construction of the absolute boundaries of Cartesian metaphysics. Shamanism can then be understood quite simply as a collection of techniques for expanding consciousness and so healing the rift between civilization and wilderness. In doing so it reconnects humanity to the great natural community of being and so becomes part of the foundation for a wilderness-loving planetary politics.

CHAPTER 11

# THE PRIMAL POLIS: SOCRATES AS SHAMAN

"How should I proceed to ask the question properly, don Juan?"

"Just ask it."

"I mean, is there a proper method, so I would not lie to myself and believe the answer is yes when it really is no?"

"Why would you lie?"

"Perhaps because at the moment the path is pleasant and enjoyable."

"That is nonsense. A path without a heart is never enjoyable. You have to work hard even to take it. On the other hand, a path with a heart is easy; it does not make you work at liking it."

— Carlos Castaneda, *The Teachings of Don Juan*

You, my friend — a citizen of Athens — are you not ashamed of devoting yourself to acquiring the greatest amount of money and honor and reputation, and caring so little about wisdom and truth and the greatest improvement of the soul, which you never regard or heed at all?...

...For know that this is the command of God; and I believe that no greater good has ever happened in the state than my service to God. For I do nothing but go about persuading you all, old and young alike, not to take thought for your persons or your properties, but first and chiefly to care about the greatest improvement of the soul. I tell you that virtue is not given by money, but that from virtue comes money and every other good of man, public as well as private.

— Socrates, *The Apology*

The conventional understanding sees the Greek polis of the classical period as a primary creative source for Western civilization, and it naturally emphasizes those aspects of Hellenistic culture that are contiguous with the present: the spirit of critical rationalism, individualism, creativity in the arts and architecture, and the development of mathematics as a key to certain knowledge. The polis is also closer to industrial society than it is to the primal band in being more hierarchical and differentiated, more deformed by warfare and imperial ambition. Yet the defining values of the polis — and, as I will argue, the source of its creative brilliance — are precisely those characterizing the values of primal politics with the shamanically informed truth quest at its center.

Given the more complex, stratified, and conflicted nature of Greek society, these values had to be clarified in theory and fought for in practice. In this way the polis offers a clearer picture of how the complex of primal politics can, when consciously cultivated, function as an ideal, generating a flowering of creativity and wisdom or, when neglected, fragment into violent conflict. In this way the polis helps clarify the challenges of actualizing the mandala ideal under current conditions of social complexity and hierarchy.

We can see a similar process of differentiation and clarification in the life and teachings of Socrates, the emblematic genius of the polis and a founding inspiration for Western rationalism. But Socrates was a complex, contradictory character, and in many ways he was closer to the primal shamanic truth quest than the mathematical rationalism that characterizes modernity. For example, his practice of philosophy was the embodiment of primal democracy, since it consisted of little more than discussing in public, with anyone interested, the big questions of life. His method was similarly primal, privileging truth seeking through face-to-face discussion — the *dialektike* — as compared to the frozen texts of the elitist Platonic academy. Socrates also took for granted the syncretistic religious context of Athens, in which shamanic practices were commonplace, and he experienced directly the entheogen-induced ecstasy of the Eleusinian Mysteries. His story is appropriately paradoxical. Although he was a patriotic citizen, held office at least once, and fought bravely in a number of battles, he was contemptuous of the democracy of the general assembly, which he saw as corrupted by sophistry and demagoguery. The general assembly, in turn, became equally disillusioned with Socrates, putting him on trial at the age of seventy and eventually executing him. As we look back over the past few thousand years of civilization and seek to integrate primal wisdom into our postmodern politics, we can get crucial guidance from both the achievements and the failures of Socrates and the polis.

## The Birth of the Ideal of the Whole Person

The ideal of the classical Greek polis was that of a small, self-sufficient, self-governing, relatively egalitarian, and highly cultured community that valued and supported individual creativity. All of this went against the larger trajectory of civilization toward increasing centralization, division of labor, and hierarchy. By the sixth century BCE, Greek political culture had coalesced around one thousand independent poleis, of which we have written constitutions for about two hundred. Each was a self-governing "city-state" — typically a fortified town on a hill, like the appropriately named Acropolis of Athens — surrounded by fields and villages, making it to varying degrees self-sufficient. This unique system was partly a matter of choice and partly imposed on the Greeks by the geography of the country. With its rocky indented coastline and rugged interior, Greece was very different from the open plains and the great river deltas around which the imperial civilizations of Egypt, Mesopotamia, India, and China arose. The mountains provided security and encouraged decentralized self-sufficiency, while Greece's position on the eastern Mediterranean made possible some degree of trade and provided stimulating contact with other cultures and competing models of order.

The Greeks considered the relatively small scale and the independence of the polis as necessary conditions for the flourishing of the whole human individual as an end in itself. This quintessentially Greek ideal stood in sharp contrast with its opposite — imperialism, where the individual was simply a means to the end of imperial glory. One of the defining episodes in Greek self-understanding occurred when the Athenian polis confronted the might of the Persian Empire at the Bay of Marathon in 490 BCE. The Persian king,

Darius, had conquered one Greek city after another and was preparing to take Athens. At the decisive moment, the Athenians found themselves alone. The runner Pheidippides was sent on his legendary run to enlist the help of the Spartans. He sprinted 240 kilometers in two days but to no avail. Isolated and massively outnumbered, the Athenian citizen army faced the Persian hordes on the plains of Marathon. The Athenian general Miltiades put his strength in the flanks. When fighting began, the weakened Athenian front broke and ran. The Persian mercenaries pursued them, flogged into battle by their officers. The Athenians then swiftly counterattacked on the flanks, sprinting into the face of the enemy and slaughtering the Persians. It was an astounding victory for Athens. According to the historian Herodotus, the Athenians lost only 192 men, while the Persians lost 6,400. Whatever the actual figures, the moral for the Greeks was clear: strength in numbers was no match for the passion and determination of free men fighting for their freedom.

We could say the Greeks rediscovered the beauty and wisdom of the creative individual of the primal band and made it a central organizing political ideal. They recognized that through freedom we become more fully individuated, more fully human, and thus more fully alive. To experience this was to know it as a self-evident good. But in contrast to the hyperindividualism of today's consumer capitalism, the Greeks balanced this ideal with its opposite — the good of the community. Freedom could not be unbounded. Like all other virtues, it was seen as a vice when pursued in isolation, without regard for its opposite. Without a healthy and just community, without constraint and limits, there could be no free individual. Without the free individual, there could be no healthy or just community. The simple secret for mediating these opposing polarities was the primal alchemy of face-to-face discussion. As we have seen from the beginning, first with primates and then flowering fully in the Bushman band, face-to-face discussion brings together diverse individuals in seeking to create a shared reality as a basis for decision making concerning the good of the whole.

Scale is also critical for balancing the good of the individual with that of the community through personal relationships. For Plato and Aristotle, the ideal size for a polis was five thousand, large enough to be self-sufficient but not so large that citizens could no longer know one another and meet face-to-face. *Autarkia*, self-sufficiency, was almost the first law of existence for the polis.[1] This in turn required a degree of egalitarianism, a certain modesty in material demands and minimal division of labor. The ideal was that everyone, as much as was possible, should participate in all areas of communal life, for both the good of the individual and the good of the community. The small scale and self-sufficiency of the community required and facilitated cultivation of the whole person through political participation.

Direct democracy was inextricably linked to the ideal of the whole person.

The reforms of the aristocratic Greek rulers Solon, Pisistratus, and Cleisthenes offer noble examples of the philosopher-kings — wise aristocrats giving up power in order to liberate the ordinary citizen in the name of the greater good of all. When Solon came to power in 594 BCE, he eliminated enslavement for debt, put a limit on the size of estates, and restored land that had been confiscated for nonpayment of debt. He recognized that Athenian soil was thin for corn but excellent for olives and grapes, so he encouraged some degree of specialization and trade. But he promoted collective and individual self-sufficiency by requiring parents to teach their children a trade. Pisistratus, who followed Solon and administered Athens from 546 to 527 BCE, extended these economic reforms and democratized high culture by directing tax revenues into theater, epic poetry, and the celebrations of the festivals. Unlike the anti-intellectual vulgarians of modern tyrannies, the aristocratic founders of Greek democracy recognized that expanding the wealth of the privileged few, at the expense of the poverty and ignorance of the masses, ultimately impoverished all. What we see emerging in these early reforms is a revival of the primal insight that the good of the individual is in principle inseparable from the good of the community.

Cleisthenes completed the democratic revolution in 507 with a radical constitution creating artificial tribes (*demes*) as fighting, voting, and cultural units. Each tribe included a cross section of the whole polis — artisans, farmers, and fishermen — so self-interest would be informed and balanced by contact with a wide range of life-worlds. This helped promote both the well-rounded individual and a more-informed consideration of the good of the whole. The general assembly was the sole legislative and executive body and included all adult male citizens. It was the right *and duty* of the ordinary citizen to speak frankly and sincerely to the entire political community. The agenda was set by the executive committee, the *boule*, consisting of five hundred citizens *chosen by lot* every year. Since it was forbidden to serve more than twice, most citizens could expect to serve at least once during a lifetime — all would get a chance to be a leader.

Over time the polis increasingly connected the individual's direct participation in a wide range of activities to an ideal of excellence rooted in the Homeric ideal of the hero as a "good-all-rounder," a whole person. Nevertheless, "all" did not mean everyone; it meant adult, male Greek citizens. Unlike in the Bushman band, the idea of wholeness was truncated. The polis remained a patriarchal, slave society excluding women, slaves, and foreigners from politics.

What is remarkable is that the entire structure of the polis was designed to *limit professionalization* and to maximize participation in all areas of life. Inefficient though this might have been in terms of modern decision making, it served a higher efficiency of two converging values — the cultivation of the *arete* of the whole person and the search for the more compelling truth of the bigger picture motivated by concern for the good of all.

## Deep Democracy

Athenian democracy at its deepest provided a framework for self-actualization in the service of the good of the whole community. Linking these was face-to-face discussion and decision making driven by a love of wisdom. But the two poles — on the one side personal wisdom and the truth of one's own experience; on the other side the truth of the collective — also represented opposites in tension that were never fully clarified and resolved in theory. Socrates criticized his fellow Athenians precisely because crass self-interest was usurping love of wisdom. And the polis executed Socrates in misguided defense of the common good — for corrupting the youth and failing to respect the customs and deities of the city.

At first sight, face-to-face discussion might appear to undermine any attempt to construct a shared big picture or worldview, since it critiques, dissects, and deconstructs meaning. Closer reflection reveals an equal and opposite movement of thought. When the people in a group debate a proposition, each person refines the idea from his or her own perspective; ideally, this leads to a final result that includes the partial truth in each position in a larger synthesis. Thesis provokes antithesis, which compels a synthesis. In this fashion, heartfelt discussion drives toward an ever larger and deeper picture of the current situation and, by extension, increasingly illuminates the human condition. In Plato's allegory of the cave, the bigger picture reveals to the prisoners that the cave is simply one feature in a staggeringly immense and ultimately mysterious cosmos.

By the same token, the meaning and value of any given proposition, policy, or action depend on their relation to the larger context, the bigger picture. Whatever the intention of the author, the highest good in one context can become the basest evil in another. This applies to the various roles and institutions of society as a whole, as Max Horkheimer points out in his discussion of Plato's *Gorgias*:

> The trades of the baker, the cook, and the tailor are in themselves very useful. But they may lead to injury unless hygienic considerations determine their place in the lives of the individual and of mankind. Harbours, shipyards, fortifications, and taxes are good in the same sense. But if the happiness of the community is forgotten, these factors of security and prosperity become instruments of destruction.[2]

Horkheimer sums up the original aim of philosophy for Plato as being the attempt to negate one-sidedness in thought through a more comprehensive system inclusive of a larger reality:

> to bring and maintain the various energies and branches of knowledge into a unity, which would transform these partially destructive elements into productive ones in the fullest sense. This is the meaning of his demand that the philosopher should rule.[3]

The truth quest for the individual requires considering the whole, and a just collective decision making requires considering the multitude of diverse individuals pursuing the quest. We seem to have a convergence of Socratic philosophy and Athenian democracy in face-to-face discussion. How, then, do we explain the paradox of the Socratic critique of Athenian democracy and the ultimate hostility of the polis to Socratic philosophy?

Socrates taught at a time when the role of moral intention in education was under threat. The lure of power and wealth was corrupting love of wisdom. Philosophy for the Greeks meant a literal "love (*philia*) of wisdom (*sophia*)." For Socrates it was an even more passionate affair than *philia*, which was a kind of friendship or brotherly love. Socratic philosophy was driven by the passion of Eros, something closer to hot shamanic ecstasy than the cool curiosity of the text-bound scholar. The focus was on the expansion of awareness as the highest expression of life energy. But by the middle of the fourth century BCE, education was becoming utilitarian and professionalized. Teachers — confusingly called *sophists* — were traveling the country giving lessons to anyone who could pay, teaching them the skills necessary for success in public life or, as Socrates put it: "the art of making the weaker argument seem the better." The notion of wisdom tied to moral intention was eroding.

What sophistry threatened in particular was a type of morally driven, philosophically inspired oratory essential to democracy, which the Greeks called *parrhesia*. This type of face-to-face speech was characterized by utter frankness: one said everything on one's mind, speaking from the heart, without holding back, without fear of consequences on all matters relevant to the issue.[4] It included a readiness to express unpopular thoughts, criticize the holders of power, demand change, and risk immediate self-interest, all in the service of a higher public good. Polished oratory was suspect, since it obscured intention and made possible the flattery and manipulation of an audience to serve the speaker's self-interest. Ridiculing one's opposition and winning a debate were not to be confused with wisdom. The display of sincere passion for the public good was the highest value in political discussion, as opposed to eloquence or flawless logic for its own sake. Talking with *parrhesia* meant revealing something of who one was, what one cared about, and how one chose to live; the assumption was that the wisdom of one's talk is connected to the life one lived.[5]

Since putting one's life on display entails real risk, *parrhesia* demanded an equivalent moral earnestness from the listeners, whose convictions were also hanging in the balance. This sounds laughably quaint today. For those who bother, participation in American democracy means voting, and not necessarily fostering the creative and original expression of each unique citizen. Today, we count only insofar as we can be counted, on the average, statistically. It is small wonder that almost half the American electorate do not even bother voting in national elections and have utter contempt for most politicians.

Recently, two American scholars, Bruce Akerman of Yale and James Fishkin of Stanford, suggested taking small steps to institutionalize some thoughtful reflection and discussion in the democratic process by establishing a "deliberation day." This would take place sometime before elections, and citizens would be paid for a day's work to gather in groups of about five hundred to discuss and prioritize election issues. Merely adopting such a measure would be a teachable moment by focusing attention and energy on the eroding core of democracy — the process of teaching and learning about the good of the whole through face-to-face encounters. The Internet and other forms of electronic communication have an obvious important role to play in mass societies. But they can never replace the ultimate locus of human politics — the fully embodied face-to-face relationships, in a particular community, at a particular time and place, in which we fully actualize our humanity.[6]

In the compact band, where people live out much of their lives in front of one another, all can, to stretch the allegory, "move in and out of their own and each other's caves." In such a situation, words can be more easily checked against actions and intention. Boundaries are more easily crossed and recrossed. Everyone gets regular reality checks — that is, honest feedback on how others experience the world and each other. Anyone who has done community work or team building knows how communication can be dramatically clarified and consensus more readily achieved when people share strong experiences. We see how quickly an extraordinary understanding and trust can develop among soldiers in combat. Simple action in extremis can bond people more effectively than days and years of conversation. We also see this in the extraordinary bonds of community among strangers that develop during natural disasters. In mass societies so much of our experience of public life is mediated electronically, at a distance, and this is often distorted by the intention to entertain and profit. Without face-to-face encounters our understanding of public affairs swings from cynicism to wishful thinking and seeing only what we want to see. We can easily remain stuck in our caves.

The lesson from the "primal polis" is that deep democracy rests on more than the superficial mechanics of electoral politics. What justifies democracy as a more advanced, more human, wiser form of government is the realization that the free, creative, unique individual is more deeply and more fully human than the obedient member of the herd, the replaceable unit of a corporation, church, or nation. Our creative freedom is the hallmark of our humanity. This is the great revelation at the heart of Greek philosophy, drama, and politics. The great irony is that Western civilization is founded on a society that attempted to engineer what came naturally to the hunting-gathering band: a polity compact enough to allow the community to meet face-to-face and share in one another's lives while guided by a love of learning.

While the ideal of the whole person became clarified through the Greek polis, its realization was compromised by the civilizational context of chronic warfare, slavery, and patriarchy. All of this constrained what it meant to be a whole human being. Athens, the most brilliant of all the poleis, was one of the largest. With a citizen population of around thirty thousand, it was heavily dependent on trade and thus required a more rigid division of labor, including the professionalization of the navy and army. All this contradicted the ideal of the freely searching, whole individual at the center of the polis. It was also contrary to the teaching and life of Socrates, who, when forced to choose between the quest, exile, and death, chose death, leaving us with the famous epitaph: "the unexamined life is not worth living."

## The Essence of the Good: Face-to-Face with Socrates

Socrates was Plato's teacher, the central figure in the Platonic dialogues, and the man Plato regarded as "the wisest and most righteous in all of Athens." If, as Alexander North Whitehead remarked, the whole history of Western philosophy is nothing but footnotes to Plato, then the place of Socrates should be even more exalted. He is the primal figure for Western philosophy.

In order to understand the deep wisdom of the Socratic teaching and how it can help us apply the mandala model to the present, we need to widen the lens and put both the polis and Socratic philosophy in the context of shamanism. Modern scholars tend to read Socrates through the lens of their own skeptical rationalism; they gloss over his cryptic references to transcendence and mysticism and downplay its role in the life of the polis. The primal perspective can help sensitize us to the role of shamanic practices in helping generate and sustain the creativity and humanity of the polis.

We can get to the depth dimension — the metaphysics of Socratic philosophy — by searching the record for passages where Socrates asks and answers the question of questions: What is the essence of the Good? And how does that help us to live "the good life"?

We find one of his most unambiguous definitions of the quest in *The Apology*, when he is under threat of death, defending his practice of philosophy from the charge of "following false gods and corrupting the youth of Athens." The most direct answer to what constitutes the good life is contained in the opening epigraph to this chapter, and it is worth examining more closely. Socrates anchors his life — and by extension his notion of the good life — in the practice of philosophy, which he defines in very simple terms: "[to] do nothing but go about persuading you all, old and young alike, not to take thought for your persons or your properties, but first and chiefly to care about the greatest improvement of the soul." The term *soul* is a direct translation from the Greek *psyche*, which we can take to refer very broadly to one's inner life — one's *psych*ology, the realm of Descartes's *res cogitans*. Socrates continues his manifesto, contrasting virtue with the lure of wealth: "I tell you that virtue is not given by money, but that from virtue comes money and every other good of man, public as well as private." *Virtue* is a translation from *arete* and refers in this context to our essential or deepest humanity and suggests the excellence of the whole person committed to the quest. Thus, Socrates champions the spiritual project of improvement of the soul — spiritual growth — from which flows the political project of seeking the good of the community.

The rather platitudinous exhortation becomes more concrete and radical when we focus on what Socrates did: he questioned everything — himself, others, the status quo, accepted values and perceptions. Again, the questioning is reflective and guided by the central moral intention: How does this or that piece of knowledge, which we can agree on, help us to live the best possible life, together, in a society of other freely questing individuals? The second component of Socratic philosophy is the already-mentioned dialectic — undertaking this quest in public, through continuing face-to-face discussion with anyone interested. Then, finally, imaginatively integrating what has been uncovered in an ever-growing and -changing big picture.

At first gloss such a practice seems to be perfectly congruent with the highest values and the central practices of the democratic polis. Yet by the time of Socrates' trial, Athenian culture had changed to the point that the Socratic practice of questioning authority came to be seen as a deadly threat. This conflict between Socrates and the polis represents a fundamental tension between the life-loving search for wisdom and the fear-driven quest for power. It offers a cautionary tale, and some guidance, as we try to integrate the truth quest into our lives and our politics.

We get additional insight into the shamanic depths of Socratic philosophy from Socrates' answer to the question "What is the essence of the Good?" This appears in the most important chapter in the most important text in the history of political philosophy — Plato's *Republic*. The chapter (23) is titled "The Good as the Highest Object of Knowledge," and it deals with the education of the philosopher-king — what the holders of power must know to ensure a just and good society. Alan Bloom, the much-acclaimed modern translator, points out that if *The Republic* is an ascent, this chapter (together with the adjacent "Allegory of the Cave") is the summit.[7] The chapter is a dialogue between Socrates and Glaucon, Plato's older brother. The philosopher-king is the embodiment of the wise ruler. He understands that only when those who hold power love wisdom more than power will human beings see an end to unnecessary suffering.

Socrates begins by pointing out that the most important knowledge the king must possess is knowledge of the Good, since it is of no use to possess anything or know anything without understanding it.[8] And how can we know this without first knowing what we mean by "the Good"? It is reasonable to expect Socrates to know the answer, since he is emphatic that his practice (of philosophy) is "good" for the citizens of Athens. What, then, is the essence of the Good?

Instead of a straight answer, we get what seems on first reading to be a rambling argument full of unexpected twists, turns, and perplexing disclaimers. First, Socrates observes that "most people identify the Good with pleasure, whereas the more enlightened think that it is knowledge." This sounds reasonable enough, especially to the professional intellectual. Glaucon readily agrees. Then Socrates continues: "And further that these latter cannot tell us what knowledge they mean, but are reduced at last to saying, 'knowledge of the good.'" Glaucon rejects this as a tautology — "That is absurd." To the reader's surprise, Socrates agrees and emphatically dismisses what might have been a suggestive paradox:

> It is [absurd]; first they reproach us with not knowing the Good, and then tell us that it is knowledge of the Good, as if we did after all understand the meaning of that word "Good" when they pronounce it.[9]

Socrates continues, digresses, then discusses briefly, and dismisses, the notion of pleasure as the highest Good, since there are many "bad" pleasures. He tantalizes Glaucon by restating the importance of getting an answer to the question about "the essence of the Good": "Every nerve must be strained ...to achieve...precision and clarity with regards to this question." Glaucon is now getting exasperated and presses Socrates to answer this, "the question ...you cannot hope to escape." Finally, pushed into a corner, Socrates stuns us with a complete about-face, telling Glaucon that the real meaning of the Good, on which the meaning and value of everything else depends, is something he can't explain!

> But I am afraid it is beyond my powers; with the best will in the world I should only disgrace myself and be laughed at. No for the moment let us leave the question of the real meaning of the good.[10]

How can Socrates not know, after telling us that without this knowledge nothing else matters? As consolation, he offers to describe the "offspring or child" of the Good. He briefly recapitulates the theory of forms, or Ideas, and then, finally, he gives this metaphoric answer: It is the sun that stands there "in the same relation to vision and visible things as that which the Good itself bears in the intelligible world to intelligence and to intelligible objects." Without skipping a beat Socrates elaborates by doing precisely what he has just told us is beyond his powers: he gives an explicit definition of the essential nature of goodness.

> This then, which gives to the objects of knowledge their truth and to him who knows them his power of knowing, is the Form or essential nature of Goodness.[11]

Amazing! We are back where we started. This elusive answer, produced through contradictions, disclaimers, and analogies, seems almost identical to the initial paradox he rejected earlier without hesitation — "the essential nature of the Good is knowledge…of the Good." Something crucial, however, has been added: "the conditions and processes which make possible knowing a knowable world." Here we need to stop and consider what these conditions and processes might be. The obvious place to start is with what Socrates actually did as a philosopher. When we do, we come up with the same simple elements: questioning self, others, and society; seeking the best way to live through face-to-face discussion with a community of fellow seekers — the essence of the Good is the truth quest at the center of primal politics.

Since this perplexing section has something of the flavor of a Zen riddle, a cross-cultural comparison helps reinforce the point and bring out its primal dimension. The Zen scholar Daisetz Suzuki's book *What Is Zen?* introduces Zen Buddhism as a search for enlightenment, which we can take as similarly concerned with the Socratic question of questions: "What is the essential nature of the Good?" In the introduction, Suzuki offers a riddle, a *koan*, in which the student asks the master, "What is Zen?"

> You ask, "What is Zen?"
>
> I answer, "Zen is that which makes you ask the question," because the answer is where the question arises. The answerer is no other than the questioner himself.[12]

The answer refers the questioner back to him- or herself, *to the way the question is being asked*. Suzuki continues the story:

> Student: "Do you then mean that I am Zen itself?"
>
> Master: "Exactly. When you ask what Zen is, you are asking who you are, what your self is. It is for this reason that the Zen masters often tell you not to ask where the donkey is when you are right on it, or not to seek for another head when yours has been on your shoulders ever since you were born. It is the height of stupidity to ask what your self is when it is this self that makes you ask the question."[13]

The point of the riddle is to shock the questioner awake, to provoke deep reflection on why and for what the student is searching. The response that "the answer is you" is trite unless one has already experienced something of life and is asking the question with all one's heart and soul. The answer is clearer the deeper and broader one's experience of life, the more impelled one is to make sense of it all. In other words the answer is in the asking to the degree that "one searches with the whole of one's life."

So, Socrates' evasions, repetitions, and infuriating contradictions are rather like Zen riddles. They function to provoke Glaucon and the reader into an "aha!" moment. We are meant to reflectively leap back, look within, look around, and recognize that the quest we are already engaged in is the answer we seek. At that point, we don't pat ourselves on the back and quit, but we continue, more committed than ever, with greater enthusiasm and joy.

Glaucon doesn't really get it. He pays lip service to the virtue of thinking for oneself: "Well Socrates, it does not seem fair that you should be ready to repeat *other* people's opinions but not state *your own*, when you have given so much thought to this subject." (Emphasis added.) But he is still mesmerized by Socrates and makes the neophyte's mistake, thinking all answers, including "self-knowledge," come from the expert, the charismatic guru. Of course, what Socrates and others say and think certainly matters. The quest takes place in community and is concerned with how to live with others, and Socrates is a particularly thoughtful member of the community. But the deeper answer requires grasping one's own life — and one's own search — as the primary instrument of philosophy as well as part of its goal.

Socrates' response is teasing: "There you are!...I could see all along that you were not going to be content with what other people think." Yet Glaucon remains focused on what Socrates thinks. He stares at the finger Socrates is pointing at the moon, rather than the moon, which in this case is Glaucon himself and everything that brings Glaucon to that moment of asking the question. The "essence of the Good" is every aspect of human questing — thinking, arguing, expressing, exploring and experiencing life, and putting it all together — as well as everything that makes it possible — the miracle of a knowable world within which there are searching minds striving for greater awareness:

> It is the cause of knowledge and truth; and so, while you may think of it as an object of knowledge, you will do well to regard it as something beyond truth and knowledge and, precious as these both are, of still higher worth.[14]

Understanding this intellectually is very different from feeling it emotionally, and when one does feel it, the experience can hit one as an epiphany. My own epiphany occurred, appropriately enough, while I was a neophyte teacher trying to teach this chapter of the *Republic* to a small class of undergraduates. I had recently arrived as a graduate student at the University of Hawai'i, and I found myself in charge of the sort of introductory class I had never myself taken, teaching students who at times knew conspicuously more than I did about local politics. From the outset I had to abandon the posture of an all knowing professor. I began the semester by telling my story as a way of introducing why I teach, what I had to offer, and why I felt a democratic discussion-based pedagogy was essential. We then went around the class and the students told their stories. Since the course was offered within the College of Continuing Education, the students represented a wide range of ages and life situations, as well as the usual Hawaiian rainbow of ethnicities — Asian, Polynesian, Filipino, *hapa* (mixed race), and *haole* (white). As the discussions progressed throughout the semester, a pool of shared study, thought, and life experiences accumulated.

By the time we came to this crucial passage in the *Republic*, the course had already covered a wide sweep, beginning with the various aspects of the global crisis — environmental, geopolitical, spiritual — and then looking at the history of political societies from the hunting-gathering bands of the San to the Liberal nation-states in a corporate-dominated world order still plagued by genocide and warfare. Class discussions were now flowing more naturally and personal testimonies had become more honest. At times the frankness and passion of the participants was quite touching. The more I really listened to and learned from my students, the more I was humbled by their range of experience and sincerity of purpose. I also found, to my surprise, on those occasions when I was forced reluctantly to reveal myself as listening and learning, I did my most effective teaching. Growing trust between student and teacher made role reversal possible. Teaching and learning were becoming two aspects of a single process. As we approached the "essence of the Good," a sense grew that the passionate discussion of the previous weeks was approaching a climax. Something important was at stake for all of us.

I divided the class into small discussion groups and charged them with trying to understand the way Socrates was answering the question of questions: "What is the essential nature of the Good?" After about half an hour, with the class buzzing with discussion, I reassembled the groups and took stock. Together we traced Socrates' contradictory back-and-forth with Glaucon. Suddenly, I felt caught up in something larger than my own intellectual process: there seemed to be a resonance between my understanding of the text and the experience I was sharing with the class. Over the previous weeks, we had been bringing our personal lived experiences to the issues raised in class. A number of students told me they continued thinking about the discussions after class; they shared them with friends and family members and looked forward to the next class. I felt similarly involved. As I slowly put all this into words and spoke it out loud, the whole class suddenly grew still and quiet, as if everyone was holding their breath. The air in the room took on a crystalline quality, and the walls separating our inner experiences from one another seemed to become transparent. Something special was happening. The face of one student lit up, and she raised her hand and spoke out: "Aren't we doing it?! Isn't this the sort of thing Socrates is talking about when he says the good is what makes knowing a knowable world possible? Honest arguing where we all really care about what we are saying and we all try to come to some deeper understanding of what it's all about?"[15] Other students smiled in a kind of happy amazement and agreement. It was a shared realization that, not only were we "getting it" as individuals, but our individual knowing depended on our cooperative arguing, and the truth of what we each knew was reinforced by our "getting it" together. It was as if for a moment we all stepped outside of ourselves into a collectively generated experience of illumination — a kind of gentle ecstatic knowing.

I had experienced similar moments in intimate personal relations, but never in a public setting or in a classroom. It was an intense experience of the joy of Eros — the passion of the quest in the company of a community of similarly motivated others. It also made me realize how important the classroom could be as an arena for transformation; how it could give us a hint of what it might be like to live in a wisdom-loving community. Such ecstatic illuminations are rare in academia, where "the Socratic method" usually refers to critical rationalism, forensic interrogation, and winning arguments.

It is true that Socrates developed a powerful critical method, but the whole Socratic enterprise was energized by a passion for wisdom — Eros — a passion powerful enough to override the competing temptations of wealth, status, and power. We get the strongest evidence for this from Socrates himself during his trial, when he defends his philosophy in mystical language, declaring to the assembled citizens in Plato's *Apology*: "I am given to you by God.... Know that this [my practice] is the command of God; and I believe that no greater good has ever happened in the state than [this] service to God." He repeatedly made references to his "inner voice," or *daimon*, as something akin to a shamanic spirit helper:

> You have heard me speak at many times and places of a divine sign from God which comes to me, and which, I suppose, is the divinity that Meletus attacked and ridiculed in the indictment. This sign, which is a kind of voice, first began to come to me when I was a child; it always forbids but never commands me to do anything which I am going to do.[16]

To give up listening to this inner voice, the soul of the lover of wisdom, would be a fate worse than death.

## Socrates and the Eleusinian Mysteries

The hallmarks of the more egalitarian shamanic religions are all present in Socrates: the personal relationship to a higher power, the truth of direct experience, the method of endless discussion with anyone concerned on all matters of importance, the passion for wisdom, and the fearlessness in talking truth to power. We now also know that Socrates participated in the Eleusinian Mysteries, drank the mysterious *kykeon*, and likely experienced the extraordinary dimensions of reality opened up by entheogens. We tend to forget that Greek philosophy operated in a shamanistic world in which dreams, divination, necromancy, and mystical revelation were still compelling realities.[17] As Carl Ruck points out, the connection between philosophy and shamanism was quite taken for granted at the time.

> The common suspicion about people like Socrates was that they were apt to have derived their ideas about other realities and about the relativity of everything to be found in this present world from drug-induced visions.... To [Socrates' contemporaries] he seemed to speak of experiences that resembled those of a shaman, and his unconventional manner of life and his novel deities made it likely that he acted as a mystagogue for the young men devoted to him. He was, in fact, not unlike other early philosophers whose lives and ideas have been recognized as shamanistic.[18]

The Eleusinian Mysteries were by far the most important single religious event in the Hellenic world. They were put on every year virtually without fail for almost two thousand years. The practice of the Mysteries began around 1500 BCE and ended when Alaric, king of the Visigoths, conquered Rome in 396 CE and helped establish a repressive, bureaucratized Christianity. The Mysteries offered anyone who could afford the months of preparation an expectation of the culminating mystical experience of a lifetime. Up to several thousand people a year were initiated, including Socrates, Plato, and Aristotle, as well as other notables like Pindar, Aristophanes, and later Cicero and Plutarch.

Greek shamanism differed from the egalitarian shamanism of the San and other primal societies in that it was shrouded in mystery. As its name suggests, the Eleusinian Mysteries were a closely guarded secret, with a penalty of death for anyone revealing the rites. Consequently, most of the surviving accounts are cryptic, and the secret remained hidden until 1978, when three scholars triangulated their expertise to argue that the climactic life-changing visionary moment involved drinking a hallucinogenic brew, *kykeon*. The classicist Carl A.P. Ruck, the pharmacologist Albert Hofmann, famous for having synthesized LSD, and R. Gordon Wasson, one of the founders of the field of ethnomycology, collaborated to produce a groundbreaking work of synthesis, *The Road to Eleusis: Unveiling the Secret of the Mysteries*. Their account was made even more compelling because they all shared expertise in the primary text of personal experience; they had all experimented with entheogens and all experienced the shamanic realm revealed as the socialized ego structures of perception dissolve. Together they provided a fascinating and compelling case that the mysterious sacred brew — the *kykeon* — almost certainly contained hallucinogenic lysergic acid alkaloids, most likely derived from ergot-infected barley, one of the main ingredients of the drink.[19]

Hofmann synthesized LSD beginning with the purple rust-colored fungus ergot (generally *Claviceps paspali* or *purpurea*), which is parasitic on barley, rye, and other grains. Ergot contains a variety of alkaloids, some of which are toxic; however, some of the nontoxic hallucinogenic amides are water soluble and can be separated out with a simple water solution, a treatment well within the capability of Greek herbalists.[20]

Ruck suggests the Mysteries were a Hellenized version of Indo-European shamanism, which had been practiced in Afghanistan and the Indus valley from at least the second millennium BCE. This practice involved the sacred drink *soma* described in the *Rig Veda*, which seems to have relied on another hallucinogenic fungus that Gordon Wasson argued was the fly agaric mushroom, *Amanita muscaria*.[21] The Mysteries involved a ritualized reenactment of the myth of Demeter that combined archaic themes we find in Minoan and other preclassical agrarian cultures — female procreation, the acquisition of agriculture, and the cycles of death and rebirth. Above all the Mysteries ritually mediated the primary duality at the core of the human condition — wilderness and civilization split apart by the domestication of grain but brought back into divine balance by the poisonous ergot, safely transformed by the wisdom of the herbalist into the sacred *kykeon*.[22]

As in Bushman mythology, the myth appears in a number of versions, each thick with metaphoric resonance regarding the seasonal cycles of death and rebirth, the origins of agriculture, and questions of human nature, destiny, and the afterlife. One version is the anonymous Homeric Hymn to

Demeter composed in the seventh century BCE, some seven centuries after the Mysteries were first practiced. According to this version, Persephone, the daughter of the goddess Demeter, is gathering wild flowers at Nysa when she is kidnapped by her uncle Hades, god of death and the underworld. In her grief Demeter brings a drought, causing the world above ground to wither and die. Since the gods also require regular sacrifices from the fruits of human agriculture, a balance is required. Hades relents and agrees to release Persephone, providing she has eaten nothing during her stay. He tricks Persephone into betraying her godly Olympian status by tempting her to eat six pomegranate seeds. Hades releases her anyway, but on the condition that she return to the underworld every year for the number of months equal to the number of seeds she has eaten (the number varies according to the version of the myth and the length of the seasonal cycle). Every year when Persephone returns to Hades, the earth above dies in autumn. Each spring she returns to the upperworld, and with her return come the life-giving rains that allow the earthbound seeds to sprout. While underground, Persephone produces a child, thus sanctifying marriage and birth as a way of healing the tension of life and death in the mystery of female procreation. Meanwhile, Demeter, as part of her struggle to find Persephone, makes the gift of cultivated barley to the mysterious Triptolemus, a royal prince in the citadel of Eleusis. Triptolemus then becomes the apostle of the new civilized order, traveling throughout the world on a serpent chariot spreading the knowledge of agriculture.[23]

As with Bushman mythology, the elements of the myth also work through emotional associations that would be lost on the modern reader. However, certain archetypal themes are made clearer by aspects of its ritual reenactment. The Mysteries were divided into two parts. The Lesser Mystery took place in nearby Athens and involved several months of preparation and ritual purification as priming for the climactic Greater Mysteries. The Greater Mysteries began with initiates leaving the gates of the city on foot and crossing a bridge, which was intentionally constructed too narrowly for wagons to pass, symbolic of crossing the boundary between worlds. The initiates walked the fourteen or so miles on the sacred road to the village of Eleusis near the Rarian Plain, supposedly the site where barley was first cultivated. Along the way elements from the story were vigorously reenacted. After all-night dancing in honor of Dionysius, the god of ecstasy, the initiates would be taken into the great Telestrion, the initiation hall in the sanctuary, where they drank the *kykeon*.

The little we know of the *kykeon* experience tells us that typically it started with fear and trembling, then nausea and vertigo, but soon passed to revelations so intense as to make "all past seeing like blindness." It completely transformed the initiate's attitude about the meaning of human existence. In the words of the poet Pindar:

> Blessed is he who, having seen these rites,
> Undertakes the way beneath the Earth.
> He knows the end of life,
> As well as its divinely granted beginning.[24]

These experiences were incommunicable, not only because of the prohibition on revealing the secrets, but simply because words could not describe an experience that gave one "the reason to live more joyously" and also to "die with greater hope." It is beyond credulity to think that any mere ritual theatrical production could have produced something so overwhelming for up to three thousand people at a time for over a millennium.[25]

We know that the *kykeon* was made with barley from the nearby Rarian fields, which was mixed with water and *blechon*, or mint. We also know the mint symbolized other aspects of the mythic abduction and was not the psychoactive agent. The Rarian fields would almost certainly have been infected from time to time with the hallucinogenic ergot. The purple of Persephones' robes, associated with the ritual performance of the Mysteries, probably suggested the purple of the ergot fungus. Ergot often selectively infects a more primitive form of wild barley, *aira* or darnel, which farmers regard as a pernicious weed. Consuming a drink made from *aira* — the threat to domesticated grain — would add another layer of symbolic meaning to the boundary-crossing ritual.

It is also quite possible that the *kykeon* contained other psychoactive compounds. Greek herbalists were well aware of natural psychoactives and certainly had the botanical sophistication to separate the soluble, non-toxic hallucinogens from the toxic, insoluble ergotamine and ergotoxin.[26] Greek wine, for example, like that of other ancient cultures, relied primarily not on alcohol as its intoxicant but rather on a mixture of psychoactive plants, herbs, and mushrooms.[27] There is some evidence that the Greeks had acquired knowledge of hallucinogenic mushroom cultivation from the Egyptians. In any event, it seems almost certain that a number of Greek herbalists would have discovered the psychoactive properties of ergot, and no doubt they had some role in the famous scandal in 415 BCE, when prominent Athenians were accused of serving the sacred *kykeon* at their private drinking parties.

The Mysteries present us with the missing dialectical opposite of Western rationalism: a form of visionary shamanism involving fungal hallucinogens as a central, ordering practice at the beginning of philosophy and politics. But like Greek politics, the Mysteries had already diverged from the more compact, integrated, and egalitarian shamanism of the primal band. Where Bushman shamanism was open to all and relevant knowledge was shared willingly, the Mysteries were a violently guarded secret, controlled by a religious bureaucracy — the two hierophantic or priestly families. The experience itself was rigidly structured around the mythic reenactment of the shift from a nomadic existence in wilderness to agriculture and settled communities. Yet democratic dimensions remained, especially when compared to the bureaucratic Christianity that arose in its place. The Mysteries still offered everyone, from aristocrat to slave, a transformative, direct experience of the sacred aspects of the in-between nature of human consciousness.

The work of Ruck, Hofmann, and Wasson makes it easier to understand the deeper Socratic teaching in primal terms. The overwhelming quality of the entheogenic experience — the "breaking open of the head" — exemplifies in the most dramatic way exiting the cave of illusions and turning the soul around to understand the constructed dimension of all socially reproduced knowledge. It also underscores the necessity for regular boundary crossing in approaching the truth quest and its politics.

We can then understand the Eros of philosophy as a spectrum extending from the ecstatic shamanic journey to the more gradual boundary-crossing bonding experience of face-to-face discussion. Both disciplines open one to the sacred mystery of creation and help inspire, humble, and guide thought and action. Within this context Socrates appears closer to a mystic and shaman like Pythagoras than his own pupil Plato, the author and founder of the Academy.[28]

But we also we need to recognize that the focus of the Socratic teaching represents a redirection of the quest away from wilderness and toward the city. In the opening of *Phaedrus*, Phaedrus and Socrates are walking outside the city and talking. Phaedrus teases Socrates about his reluctance to set foot outside the walls of the town. Socrates replies, "You must forgive me, dear friend; I'm a lover of learning, and trees and open country won't teach me anything, whereas men in the town do."[29] We need to understand this in the context of the ubiquity of nature in the life of the Greeks. In the fifth and fourth century BCE, Greek towns were small, most of the population lived by farming, and much of the country was still wild. Herodotus describes lions roaming northern Greece in the first millennium BCE, and in 480 BCE the Persian army under Xerxes encountered a few lions in Macedonia. Wilderness was still a conspicuous dimension of everyday reality.

In such a world, it is easy to understand the appeal of city life — the "town" — as a nexus for face-to-face encounters and for amplifying the variety and depth of human experience. The town concentrates human diversity, multiplying relationships, increasing opportunities for creativity in the arts, the sciences, and of course philosophy. The intensity of town life made it possible for Socrates and Plato to clarify and differentiate elements of the quest. But the deeper Socratic teaching of the dialectic brings us back to boundary crossing, to regularly returning to "trees and open country" to keep civilization in balance with widerness. In the same dialogue we already get a sense of this balancing dimension in Socrates' sensibility. Just before the passage in *Phaedrus* quoted above, Socrates describes their resting place in the rapturous terms of a nature lover:

> Upon my word, a delightful resting-place with this tall spreading plane, and a lovely shade from the high branches of the agnus: now that it's in full flower, it will make the place ever so fragrant. And what a lovely stream under the plane-tree, and how cool to the feet! Judging by the statuettes and images I should say it's consecrated to Achelous and some of the Nymphs. And then too, isn't the freshness of the air most welcome and pleasant: and the shrill summery music of the cicada-choir! And as crowning delight the grass, thick enough on a gentle slope to rest your head on most comfortably.[30]

No doubt rites like the Eleusinian Mysteries, which gave the participants access to the inner wilderness of the spirit, also helped sensitize them to the miracle of the outer world of wilderness. And this profound boundary-crossing experience must have helped maintain the ideal of the compact primal order as the centripetal forces of civilization and empire were tearing the polis apart.

## The Death of Socrates and the Quest in Athenian

As I've noted, the primal ideal was never fully realized in th because it was incompletely developed in theory and because historical conditions undermined it in practice. The polis achieved its highest levels of self-reflection during the classical period, when it also asserted itself as a warrior-based, patriarchal community in a world of warfare, slavery, and empire.* The trial and execution of Socrates in 399 BCE is the emblematic tragedy of the moral and spiritual collapse of the polis, a process that we can date as beginning with the Peloponnesian War in 431 BCE.

Athens managed to be both the epitome and the antithesis of the polis. At the outbreak of the war, Athens was at the apex of her glory, head of an empire, wealthy and rightfully proud of her democracy and her culture. By 404, five years before the trial and execution of Socrates, she had lost it all.

Because of the contingencies of geography, Athens had specialized in the cultivation of olives and vineyards and become increasingly dependent on trade for survival. This impelled Athenians to develop a powerful professional navy — eventually the strongest in Greece, making it possible for them to assume control of the Delian League. Wealth provided the conditions for the flowering of creativity and the arts, but division of labor and specialization undermined the political economy of the amateur — the *arete* of the good-all-rounder — and with it the conditions for a direct democracy guided by concern with the good of the whole.

Growth in population — which by 431 had reached over 250,000 residents, of whom perhaps 40,000 were citizens — was also making a deliberative democracy of face-to-face discussion impossible. Politics was becoming increasingly vulnerable to demagoguery. Education, as mentioned, was also becoming professionalized. Until then education had consisted of training in music and gymnastics, with the rest left up to family and participation in the rich public life of the polis. The sophists created a culture of critical questioning, but they inadvertently undermined inquiry into the good of the

---

* The classical period is usually dated beginning with the war against the Persian Empire in 500 BCE. The famous battle of Marathon in 490 BCE signaled the beginning of the successful assertion of Greek independence and the glorious period of independent poleis. This is generally taken to have ended with the defeat in the battle of Chaeronea in 338, when Philip II of Macedon became supreme ruler and incorporated the poleis into his expansionist Hellenic Empire (soon to be expanded by his prodigiously aggressive son, Alexander the Great).

whole. Here was an ancient anticipation of deconstructionist postmodernists — ethical relativists who provided strategies for demolishing meaning without offering anything in its place. All of this contributed to the erosion of a culture of *parrhesia*.

The dramatic decline of Athens started soon after the war, with plagues in 430 and 426 killing about one-third of the Athenian population. In 415 a large, reckless invasion of Sicily ended with the destruction of the entire fleet and the death of half the force. This catastrophe was foreshadowed shortly before the expedition, when the citizens of Athens woke up one morning to find that the *hermae* — the sacred statues of naked figures protecting the streets and entrances to the city — had been castrated. At the same time, reports were circulating that the Eleusinian Mysteries were being profaned by a dining club of young aristocrats, the *kakodaimonistai* (literally, "devil worshippers"), who used the sacred *kykeon* as a recreational drug to invoke the spirits of the dead for entertainment.[31] By 404 Athens was defeated, and the Peloponnesian War over. A Spartan garrison occupied the city and enforced the brutal rule of the Thirty Tyrants, who soon set about murdering some fifteen hundred leading democrats and exiling another fifteen hundred. There was a pervasive sense that the old order had broken down and the gods had forsaken the city.

All of this is important for understanding the likely mind-set of the jurors at the trial of Socrates. In 399, Meletus and two others, Lycon and Anytus (whom we know as a patriotic and responsible political leader), brought Socrates to trial on charges of impiety and subverting the old ways. The affidavit accused Socrates of "not believing in the gods in which the city believes, and of introducing new divinities." It also accused him of "corrupting the young."[32] The penalty proposed was death. Socrates was tried in front of a jury of 501 of his peers chosen by lot. After accuser and accused had presented their cases, the jury voted immediately, with 281 declaring Socrates guilty and 220 not guilty. This initial verdict was clearly no landslide condemnation of Socrates. Then the penalty had to be discussed and voted on. When Meletus argued for death, Socrates defended his life in the famous passage recorded by Plato in *The Apology*, and he suggested that instead of death he be given the highest honor and supported for life at state expense. This apparent frivolity must have infuriated many on the jury, since 80 changed their vote to guilty. The final count was 361 to 140 for executing Socrates.

Why did the polis kill Socrates? As the classicist M. I. Finley points out, introducing false or strange deities was hardly a serious offense, since Athens at this time supported a complex syncretistic religious culture, with new gods and practices being introduced fairly regularly. There is also evidence that Socrates was indeed pious and respectfully performed the customary religious rituals and rites. The more serious charge was that of corrupting the youth. His habit of inducing his young followers, including a number of young aristocrats, to question everything could easily have been misunderstood as sophistry. The great playwright Aristophanes, who was no friend of Socrates, must take some of the blame, since his famous play *The Clouds*, performed in 423, parodied Socrates mercilessly as a bumbling sophist.

Perhaps far more significant, although never directly addressed in the indictment, was the fact that two well-known associates of Socrates, Critias and Charmedies, were part of the brutal rule of the Thirty Tyrants. There was also Socrates' close association with Alcibiades, who had suggested the disastrous expedition to Sicily and who had been appointed one of its generals. But just before the expedition departed, he was accused of being involved in the desecration of the *hermae* and the profanation of the Mysteries. He requested a trial before departure but was refused. Outraged at this refusal, he later changed sides during the war.

The Thirty Tyrants were removed in 403 BCE, and traditional democracy was restored and remained in place for another century. Immediately after the removal of the tyrants, a general amnesty was declared for all those involved. Nevertheless, the charge of corrupting the youth must have certainly brought to the minds of the jurors the horrors of the previous thirty years. It seems reasonable to assume that in a time of extreme demoralization, such associations were too much for them. Socrates was a danger to the polis.

Socrates' critique of Athens was conspicuous, but his definition of the Good was subtle and required exactly what, he claimed the polis lacked — a love of truth that was greater than fear, greed, and ambition.

## The Socratic Quest Today

The convergence of the Socratic quest and the democracy of the polis holds unrealized potential for addressing the moral and existential crisis of our politics. The West has now ameliorated some of the structural deformities of the Greek polis, most notably the abolition of legal slavery and the incorporation of female participation in politics. In addition, we now have the wealth and technology to make available to vast masses of human beings the wisdom of all past civilizations, greatly enhanced by the epic visions of modern science. But in other ways, we have amplified the perennial problems of the Athenian polis. Our civilization has the most extreme divisions of labor of any society ever. Sophistry runs rampant in academia, and shameless commercialism and cynical appeals to narrow self-interest in public life undermine attempts to educate for the good of the whole. There is also a dimension to our crisis that would have been inconceivable to the Greeks: the fact that we have nearly amputated our connection to the living earth on which the well-being of all depends. The corruption that Socrates criticized in the polis, part of the larger deformation in the differentiation of civilization, seems to be reaching its terminus in our times. Having forgotten our partnership in the community of being, we confront a crisis that is in essence a crisis of meaning and values — a spiritual crisis.

Looking back over the ensuing centuries, and informed by our larger vision of the human condition, we can recognize in the experience of the classical polis an attempt to retain the most deeply humanizing aspects of the primal human group — the balance among the polarities of politics, represented by the components of the mandala. At its greatest, the polis groped for a framework in which philosophy and democracy would guide and inform each other as two faces of a single process: a vision of politics based on the uninhibited exploration of the fullness of human experience, fueled by a passion for living and knowing life so strong that it could eclipse the temptations of wealth and power.

For a brief while the Greek polis managed to hold the balance by integrating primal structures and shamanic practices together with the discovery of the philosophical truth quest. This sort of dialectical reversal through the past into the future seems to be a fundamental aspect of truly creative advances. A similar principle seems to apply to cultural transformation. The energy and brilliance of the Renaissance were in part sparked by a rediscovery of the culture and philosophy of classical Greece. This process of a creative movement forward by periodic visits to the past can also be seen as the heart of the discipline of shamanic religion, which heals and guides by going back and reconnecting with "the ground of being" in an eternal primal return. This is what our present moment is calling for.

# PART III

# WHERE SHOULD WE BE GOING?

CHAPTER 12

# OUR PRIMAL FUTURE

Suddenly the human species as a whole has a common cosmic story. Islamic people, Dineh people, Christian people, Marxist people, Hindu people can all agree in a basic sense on the birth of the Sun, on the development of the Earth, on the complex history of human cultures. For the first time in human existence, we have a cosmic story that is not tied to a cultural tradition, or to a political ideology, but that gathers every human group into its meanings.... Every statement of the cosmic story will be placed in its own cultural context.... But even so, we have broken through to a story that is pan-human, a story that is already taught and developed on every continent and within every major cultural setting.

— BRIAN THOMAS SWIMME, *The Resurgence of Cosmic Storytellers*

*!k e: /Xarra //Ke.* ("People who are different join together.")

— /Xam Bushman motto on South Africa's new coat of arms[1]

Human history suggests that without a social vessel to hold the wine of revelation, it tends to dribble away.... The next research question, it seems to me is: What conditions of community and practice best help people to hold on to what comes to them in those moments of revelation, converting it into abiding light in their own lives?

— HUSTON SMITH[2]

## The Primal Resurgence

Obviously we can no longer follow the truth quest by hunting and gathering in wilderness. Even if we wanted to, we have lost the vast expanse of unspoiled, game-filled country needed to keep more than a handful of humans alive. But we can recognize the complex of primal politics as ubiquitous, within us all. Our wilderness origins fashioned our creative self-consciousness, which is both expanded and balanced by following the primal dynamic: face-to-face communication within a caring community of individuals, passionate for living and learning in a mutually enhancing resonance with the natural world. This is the truth quest, and it is our primal inheritance. We can ignore and repress it, or we can cultivate it in all our endeavors and bring it into a creative engagement with the reality we find ourselves caught up in: a civilization rushing to self-destruction while displaying tantalizing possibilities of a more beautiful, joyful way of life.

Today, hunting and gathering has been replaced by agriculture as our most fundamental and intimate relationship to the natural world. Agriculture is the area in which humanity touches the earth most directly; agriculture shapes and is shaped by the most fundamental values of society.

In his book, *Collapse*, the polymath Jared Diamond provides a fascinating, magisterial survey of a range of agricultural societies, from Easter Island and the Anasazi to Norse Greenland and Rwanda, identifying, as his subtitle puts it, "how societies choose to fail or succeed." As we might expect, ecological devastation — "ecocide" — is a major factor in societal collapse. Diamond then breaks this down into eight categories: "deforestation and habitat destruction, soil problems (erosion, salinization, and soil and fertility losses), water management problems, overhunting, overfishing, effects of introduced species on native species, human population growth, and increased per capita impact of people." All of these are conspicuous aspects of our current crisis. In addition, Diamond identifies four new problems facing us: "human-caused climate change, buildup of toxic chemicals in the environment, energy shortages, and full human utilization of the Earth's photosynthetic capacity."[3] He goes on to clarify contributing factors, the most decisive being society's ability to grasp its environmental problems and then respond creatively.

From the point of view of the primal quest, success in understanding any specific historical reality is in turn dependent on how well a society comprehends the paradox of the human condition — of being free and creative, yet ultimately constrained by the mysterious evolutionary story "telling us into being." Diamond's comparative inquiry sets the stage for identifying a future primal politics that includes institutions that promote the quest while simultaneously embodying its truth, ensuring a sustainable and flourishing way of life.

One of the hard realities the big picture of the quest confronts us with — and perhaps the one that is most likely to cause our collapse — is the failure of the current model of farming. We are enmeshed in an oil-intensive, corporate-dominated, mechanized, wasteful, polluting industry that is eroding the soil, destroying wilderness, and accelerating climate change. Forty percent of the terrestrial surface of the earth has been transformed by farming, which now uses 70 percent of all fresh water consumed. Agriculture is the largest single contributor to global warming — more than transport or industry — now producing some 30 percent of all carbon dioxide emissions. Most countries are losing topsoil at an unsustainable rate, and we are already failing to feed the seven billion human beings on the planet. One person in seven doesn't know where his or her next meal will come from, and projections indicate we will have to double food production to feed nine billion people by 2050.[4] Since we cannot expand agricultural land without dramatically adding to climate change and destroying biodiversity, we have two immense practical challenges: we have to control our global population; and we have to farm both more intensively and more sustainably. To do this we need to come to a compelling shared understanding of our reality, and for this we need to make the truth quest the center of our politics.

When Huston Smith, in an opening quote to this chapter, speaks of a social vessel — "conditions of community and practice" — that can best help people hold on to the "wine of revelation," he raises the question of politics, of finding social and economic practices concordant with the primary revelation of our time — the story of humanity's place in an evolving universe. This story includes the understanding that our consciousness, with its capacity for freedom and creativity, grows from the womb of wilderness. We are a product of the evolving earth, and this both empowers and constrains us. As we have seen, primal societies, still close to this experience, generally organized their politics in the ways described by the mandala structure, with the shamanic quest at their center.

Today immense cultural and economic forces seem to undermine all efforts to live according to this primal dynamic. Locked into the self-interest and materialism of industrial capitalism, facing environmental devastation and social collapse, we find it too easy to despair and indulge in escapism or fatalism, as if it were already too late to do anything but go shopping and wait for the arrival of the apocalypse. But such a response is based on a distorted perception of the larger reality. The bigger, deeper picture reveals that our capacity to respond creatively to our predicament is amplified by the breadth and depth of our vision, and that as we grasp the bigger picture the way forward is illuminated and we become empowered and transformed.

This chapter surveys the modern, global political landscape from this expanded perspective and identifies a growing number of creative responses embodying aspects of the mandala dynamic. The examples come from all scales of human social organization; they come from individuals like Nelson Mandela to eco-villages like Findhorn, EVI at Ithaca, and Gaviotas in Colombia. There is also the idealistic agrarian kibbutz movement, which became the backbone of the young country of Israel; there are "Green cities" and models of democratization and decentralization, such as Porto Alegre and Belo Horizonte, that help make urban centers more sustainable and educate their populations. At the national level, Bhutan shows the success of a commitment to the spiritually based ideal of the "gross national happiness" of its people; and at the international level we have organizations like the United Nations and the European Union and then mass movements of resistance to tyranny.

But by definition there can be no single institutional fix, no one size fits all, in a quest-based politics. Only when taken together, connected, and deepened by the vision of primal politics can these examples be seen as seeds of a coherent, self-transforming political culture — the sort of leap in consciousness we so desperately need.

This perspective reveals how on one level the universe story is the ultimate container for our politics, since we are all born into the evolving wilderness of the cosmos. But on another level the universe story itself is only one quadrant — the big picture — of the mandala dynamic. This means that while the story is panhuman and planetary, it also needs to be told, understood, and lived through the local embodied realities — the land, languages, and cultures — of the individuals and communities telling the story.

## The *Periagoge*: A Revolution in the Soul

There is an invisible dimension to the social and political examples in this chapter. They are all external manifestations of an inner transformation in the souls of the individuals and societies involved. They are all rooted in a change of mind and heart away from short-term material self-interest to a concern for the good of the whole as ultimately inseparable from the highest good for the individual.

The primal perspective makes us aware that one of the primary political "institutions" is the individual. Ultimately, any political change begins, ends, and is carried forward in the life of each person. For this reason, a *periagoge* — the waking up of the soul and its reorientation to the truth quest — is at the center of primal politics.

Concern with the well-being of others, which extends to the entire non-human community of being, is inherent in our nature and expresses an intrinsic connectedness and a need to be of service to others. Primal societies exemplify and reinforce this attitude. Science's recent discovery of "mirror neurons" provides some hard evidence that this cognitive connectedness to others is literally wired within us. Experiments have demonstrated that when one subject views another suffering an injury or performing a task, "mirror" neurons fire along similar pathways in the empathic observer. Indeed, this makes perfect sense given the crucial role of face-to-face relationships and the caring community in the evolution of primate intelligence. Altruism, generosity, and heroic sacrifice in the protection of the community seem to be as much a part of the human condition as our more often celebrated selfishness and greed.[5] Societies like the San make us aware that we choose to cultivate sharing or selfishness, aggression or cooperation.

Since Liberalism sanctifies a self-centered, materialistic, and competitive worldview, waking up to the convergence of the good of the individual with that of the whole is often experienced as an epiphany, a dramatic expansion of awareness — as when the prisoner in Plato's cave walks outside into the larger reality. Once out of the cave and liberated, the prisoner becomes a philosopher and returns in solidarity with those left behind. A life alone is hard to bear. Just as importantly, the imperative of the *periagoge* means we serve our higher selves by serving others, by tending to the good of the whole. Consider Ray Anderson, the CEO of Interface. After his ecological epiphany, Anderson pledged that his company — the largest carpet-manufacturing corporation in the world — would not produce carpets unless it could do so sustainably and serve a triple bottom line of profit, people, and planet. Implicit in this action is a revolutionary understanding — a turning away from a culture of greed, which systematically valorizes and rewards selfish behavior as "being realistic," toward one that honors a generous concern for the welfare of others.

Another way to put this is that all of the stories of positive change presented in this chapter will be enduring only to the degree to which they create a culture that nurtures honest, open, compassionate individuals and a commitment to the quest. No institutional solution will ultimately succeed if it's administered by those who are driven by greed, fear, or self-interest. We can't fix society if we don't also fix ourselves; any social or cultural revolution can only be as successful as the inner revolution that cultivates individuation and a concern for the good of the whole. Ultimately, this inner revolution is part of a cultural revolution that cannot be legislated or enforced; it can only be exemplified, encouraged, and cultivated. Public policy and educational institutions can promote the quest or repress it, but it is the individual and society who must experience the truth of the larger reality that we are all in this together.

## Nelson Mandela's *Periagoge* and the Negotiated Revolution

One of the most striking and inspiring stories in recent times of an individual opening to truth, becoming transformed, and then catalyzing a comparable process in an entire nation is that of Nelson Mandela — the first black president of postapartheid South Africa, whose leadership helped avert a race war in the final days of apartheid. His story is well known, but its connection to primal politics is not, and it's instructive to revisit it in that light. Mandela's actions and attitudes at that critical historical moment exemplified the defining elements of the quest, and the primal political dynamic he embodied helped transform an entire political culture.

Beginning in 1948, apartheid was the South African government's policy of strictly enforced racial segregation that confined the vast majority of the nation's black population to a life of rural poverty and urban disenfranchisement. The country was divided up along racial lines, with the vast majority of the best land given to the minority white population. For example, about fifty thousand Afrikaans-speaking white farmers owned twelve times more arable land than the fourteen million rural blacks. Racial separation was strictly enforced at all levels of society, and blacks could not travel or work in white areas without a permit, or a "pass."

The early antiapartheid coalition, the African National Congress (ANC), had been strongly influenced by Mahatma Gandhi's brief stay in South Africa and his nonviolent struggle for the civil rights of its small Indian population. It was then that Gandhi coined the term *satyagraha* — literally "insistence on truth" or "soul force" — to express the idea that acting peacefully in accordance with the truth of the good of the whole is a force more powerful than violence in overcoming oppression. At first, the ANC followed a strict policy of nonviolent resistance to apartheid. This changed in 1960 after the Sharpeville incident when police opened fire on a peaceful crowd protesting the law that would require women to carry at all times a legal document — a pass — in order to reside near their husbands working in white areas. Sixty-nine people were killed; most of the dead were women.

Under Mandela's leadership the ANC took up arms, went underground, and began sabotaging government installations. Mandela was soon hunted down, arrested, and, in 1963, sentenced to life imprisonment for treason. He was sent to Robben Island, South Africa's Alcatraz, off the coast of Cape Town, a prison designed to crush the spirit of the political opposition. Separated from wife and family, condemned to a life of hard labor, Mandela might have been consumed with hatred for Afrikaners. Instead the opposite happened; he discovered the humanity of the oppressor and in the process he expanded his own humanity. This personal transformation made it possible for him to catalyze a comparable transformation in the psychology of the nation, culminating in the "miracle" of the negotiated revolution.[6]

Mandela had the good fortune to be "raised by a village," enjoying the benefits of an extended family and a warm caring community surrounded by the beautiful rolling hills of the Transkei in the Eastern Cape. He grew up herding cattle, gardening, roaming the veldt, living in the mud-and-thatch huts of a Xhosa village. In his autobiography, he describes witnessing the tribal form of direct democracy* and being enormously impressed by the importance of consensus as a way of balancing the interests of the individual

* Described in chapter 4.

and the collective. This early grounding in the human and national community later made it easier for him to recognize a common humanity with his Afrikaner enemy.

Mandela's point of entry into the world of his adversary was fluency in the Dutch-based Afrikaans language, universally hated by black South Africans as the language of oppression. In 1976 when the government passed a law requiring that all black students be taught not in English but in the despised Afrikaans, the black shantytowns around South African cities erupted in mass demonstrations. The police responded by opening fire on the unarmed students. So when Mandela exhorted his fellow prisoners on Robben Island to speak Afrikaans as a way of engaging their wardens, his comrades were outraged. They only agreed after he presented it as the first law of warfare: know your enemy. But something more significant started working below the surface — the primal principle of growing through engaging opposites to generate a bigger, truer picture of a shared reality.

Mandela carefully studied the psychology of his oppressor. He read widely in Afrikaans history, poetry, and literature and took every opportunity to engage his white wardens, always politely, always in Afrikaans, always as an equal demanding respect. He was surprised to find that many were poor country boys with little education, who must have reminded him of his own simple beginnings. Some had never had a face-to-face relationship with a black man, and much of their fear was rooted in simple ignorance. Mandela saw clearly that their fear was real; they felt that everything they loved — their language, history, and culture, their entire way of life — meant nothing to blacks and would be quickly swept aside once a black majority was in power. From the Afrikaner perspective, agreeing to "one person, one vote" meant national suicide. Apartheid was first a strategy for survival, which then became a strategy for exploitation.

Mandela demonstrated the power of the whole person armed with the bigger vision in his face-to-face meeting in 1976 with his jailer in chief, Minister of Justice Jimmy Kruger. Mandela surprised Kruger by addressing him fluently in Afrikaans and then treating him to a brief history of modern South Africa. He then made his case for the release of ANC political prisoners by citing the Afrikaner heroes General Christiaan de Wet and Robey Leibbrandt, both of whom were political prisoners under the British. In 1914, during World War I, de Wet led twelve thousand troops in a bloody revolt opposing South Africa's support of the Allies. During World War II,

Leibbrandt, a Nazi sympathizer, had set up an underground organization, again to resist South Africa's alliance with the Allies. Both de Wet and Leibbrandt were released. The ANC prisoners were not, but Mandela had gained Kruger's respect.[7] More importantly, Mandela developed a strategy for subsequent negotiations with Kruger's more sophisticated successor, Kobie Coetsee, which would eventually persuade the Afrikaner leadership to accept the fact that giving up apartheid did not mean the end of the Afrikaner.

Mandela's strategy was primal and Socratic. He descended into the cave of the tyrant imprisoned by fear and ignorance. By addressing the Afrikaner in his own language, by using examples from the Afrikaner's world of experience, and by embodying in his own speech and bearing a more inclusive humanity, Mandela gained a measure of credibility and respect. Once this became trust, Mandela could then help the Afrikaner find his way out of the cave of racism into a larger reality — a shared love of a multiracial, multicultural South Africa.

Years after his release, when a television interviewer asked him who his political hero was, Mandela shocked political correctness by answering "Kobie Coetsee," his jailer. He explained that when Coetsee first visited him in jail, he was still the minister of justice and a hardliner at a time when negotiating with a terrorist was considered political suicide. Mandela recognized that it took a heroic exertion of imagination and moral courage for Coetsee to open himself to Mandela's world. Coetsee exemplified a value higher than the principle of multiracial democracy, and that was commitment to continued growth in awareness — the truth quest.

In 1994 when Mandela was inaugurated as president of South Africa, he invited three of his former prison wardens to be guests of honor. He subsequently appointed Coetsee president of the senate. In emphasizing the commonality between the two peoples, Mandela underlined his faith in the universal value of what Africans call *ubuntu* — the notion that under the deformations of ideology, creed, and dogma, one finds a deeper common humanity.

Mandela's strategy followed the boundary-crossing wisdom of Lame Deer, which was also the *thuru* of the Bushman shaman and the dialectic of Socrates: one gains a bigger picture and grows by engaging opposites. As we saw in primal societies, such a discipline requires a degree of psychological wholeness — the inner security that comes from the process of individuation.

Conversely, it is also through this process that one individuates and gains a measure of integrity and grows in wholeness. Looking back on Mandela's life, one can infer that his exceptional capacity for this sort of openness to the truth of the enemy, and his trust that he would find a common humanity, was a product of his early years. Healthy village life, the company and caring of the extended family, the experience of consensus decision-making, and the contact with the beauty of wilderness — all gave him a deep love of life and trust in humanity.

This expansion of consciousness peaked and for a moment united a whole country in 1995, when the Rugby World Cup was held in South Africa after years of international boycott. Mandela had barely been in office one year. The country was still poised on the edge of the abyss. The Afrikaner extreme right — the Volksfront — was supported by many who had served in the military, including the conservative general Constand Viljoen, who had commanded South Africa's combined armed forces. Mandela had evidence that Viljoen might consider leading some hundred thousand armed, trained members of the Volksfront in a secessionist revolution to establish an independent Afrikaner nation. But for the first time since the rugby boycott began ten years earlier, the national team was being allowed to participate in the Rugby World Cup.

Rugby was South Africa's national sport, but to the Afrikaner it was much more than a sport. It was in fact probably the most important public event in the life of the nation apart from attending church. It was a white man's game dominated by the Boers — the tough, big-boned Afrikaner farmers — and to blacks it had come to symbolize apartheid. The national rugby team, the Springboks, or simply Boks (or Bokke), had exactly one nonwhite player, Chester Williams, and he was an Afrikaans-speaking, mixed-race Coloured. Blacks in South Africa played soccer, and during apartheid they would only attend international rugby games to cheer madly for any opposing team. At the height of apartheid, in 1985, massive, angry demonstrations in New Zealand had prevented the visiting Springboks from playing. From then on, South African rugby teams were shunned. For a small nation that had once dominated world rugby and had little else to be proud of, the boycott stung more than the rest of the world's sanctions combined.

During his time in prison, Mandela had studied rugby and used his knowledge of the players and the teams to engage his prison wardens. He understood the depths of the Afrikaner passion for the game. He also knew how much joy could defuse anger and dissipate fear. Now he was faced with an opportunity to do on a national scale what he had learned in prison. He understood that if the nation could celebrate a Bok victory over the New Zealand team — known, disconcertingly, as the All Blacks — it would be a glorious vindication of Afrikaner vitality. But far more importantly, if black South Africans could for the first time celebrate the victory of an Afrikaans team playing the white man's game, it would symbolize a cultural and moral revolution — the triumph of forgiveness and a new pride in a truly multiracial South Africa.

It began with the name. At a critical point the ANC leadership wanted to replace "Springbok" as the team's name and get rid of the little leaping springbuck as the emblem. The old flag had been replaced and the national anthem changed. The springbok was deeply associated with Afrikaner pride. Aware that a right-wing Afrikaner group was plotting a coup, and knowing the gift of rugby pride to Afrikaners might defuse the situation, Mandela intervened decisively, scolded the executive for its failure of vision, and insisted on keeping the old springbok emblem.[8]

As for the competition itself, winning was a long shot, since the South African team made it to the final round in part by virtue of being the host country. The New Zealand All Blacks were universally rated as the stronger team. Mandela put his faith in morale and intention — the power of consciousness focused by the bigger picture of what was at stake. He went on an intensive publicity campaign for the team with the slogan "one team, one country." Mandela had a private meeting with the captain and met all the team members. The black masses were dubious. On the day of the final, the nation held its breath. As the players took the field for the national anthem, Mandela walked out to greet the team and stunned everyone by wearing a rugby jersey with the number of the Afrikaner captain François Pienaar. The crowd went wild, chanting "Nel-Son! Nel-Son! Nel-Son!" The team members stood at attention for the multiple national anthems and then sang, for the first time in their lives, what for years had been the outlawed rallying hymn of the underground ANC, "Nkosi Sikekele I'Africa" — "God Bless Africa." Afterward, the Afrikaner captain Pienaar talked of being so choked up he had to bite his lip to stop from shedding tears, tears of pride at his new South Africa.[9]

It was a desperate, messy game with few opportunities for scoring. After halftime the score was even. If South Africa lost, the event would be remembered as a noble effort that failed in an embarrassing anticlimax. At the end of the second half the score was still even, and the game went into extra time. After the first ten minutes the score was again even. The exhausted players went into the second half of extra time. With seven minutes to go, the South African Joel Stransky got the ball and drop-kicked the winning goal from the twenty-five-yard line. The nation went hysterical with joy. As Mandela presented François Pienaar with the world cup he smiled widely, put a hand on Pienaar's shoulder, and said, "François thank you for what you have done for our country." Pienaar met his gaze and replied, "No, Mr. President. Thank you for what you have done for our country." The next day newspapers were filled with pictures of blacks and whites hugging one another and dancing in the street. Mandela's generous spirit and bold vision orchestrated an act of improvisational political theater that swept the nation in an orgy of forgiveness and reconciliation.

Mandela's leadership exemplifies a revolutionary shift from a political culture of "doing God's work by getting rich at the expense of others" to the primal ethic of "doing God's work by serving others generously." This is the ancient moral nexus connecting love of life, expansion of the soul, and breadth of vision to justice and democracy. All of this is a deeply rooted archetypal potential, expressed in the mandala, that helps define what it means to be human. Such a future primal politics becomes a reality as these connections are seen, understood, and cultivated in our hearts, actions, and institutions.

For Nelson Mandela and South Africa, the miracle of the negotiated revolution was a moment of transcendence within a wider culture of materialism and power politics. It is not really surprising that his example was insufficient on its own to lead to rethinking the foundations of the nation-state or industrial capitalism. The result was an ANC government that was multiracial and based on constitutional democracy, but it was also in some respects more dysfunctional and corrupt than the apartheid regime it replaced.[10]

At its deepest, the sort of political nobility Mandela displayed and for a while evoked in others is sustained by the courage and enthusiasm we get from loving life and loving truth. It contains the recognition that we are all in this together; that despite its horror and suffering, life is ultimately a miraculous gift. Our time on earth is too short to experience even a small fraction of its wonders, so it behooves us to be humble, grateful, and generous.

## Future Primal Agriculture

Nelson Mandela's love of life also expressed itself in a lifelong love of gardening, which he talks of in his autobiography as a profound philosophical and psychological discipline. As soon as he was imprisoned on Robben Island, he asked permission to start a garden. For years this request was rejected. Eventually, permission was granted and the garden prospered, to the point that Mandela was able to share some of his prize tomatoes and onions with the wardens.

Successful gardening requires that we pay attention to natural living processes. It teaches us gentleness and humility in nurturing new life. It connects us to the miracle of a growing universe. Communal agriculture not only feeds our bodies but brings our hearts and minds closer to the primal roots of the truth quest in an evolving earth. Such a gardening ethic needs to guide our industrial approach to farming to create a sustainable society aligned with the quest. This sort of relationship to the local conditions of the earth on which one lives and from which one feeds becomes a geographic "container" for politics and the quest. Kirkpatrick Sale identifies this basic unit for human community as a "bioregion." What he describes as a bioregional sensibility then becomes the cultural basis for a healthy human community and sustainable politics. This is built on an understanding of

> place, the immediate specific place where we live. The kinds of soils and rocks under our feet; the source of the waters we drink; the meaning of the different kinds of winds; the common insects, birds, mammals, plants, and trees; the particular cycles of the seasons;... the carrying capacities of its lands and waters; the places where it must not be stressed; the places where its bounties can best be developed; the treasures it holds and the treasures it withholds — these are the things that must be understood. And the cultures of the people, of the populations native to the land and of those who have grown up with it, the human social and economic arrangements shaped by and adapted to the geomorphic

ones, in both urban and rural settings — these are the things that must be appreciated. That, in essence, is bioregionalism.[11]

Sale's point is that, as we come to understand how bioregions function as integrated unities of land, water, climate, and plant and animal populations, we need to redraw our economic and political boundaries accordingly in order to sustain the health of such local ecosystems. This sort of sensitivity to the regional ecosystem is not only the key to our physical sustenance but a key to self-knowledge, self-actualization, wholeness, and health. We cannot know ourselves without understanding the details of our earthly constitution.

As we have seen, hunter-gatherers give us the most intimate and complete expression of a bioregional sensibility, where the relationship to place is so finely tuned and so ancient that it gradually shapes the language, the collective memory, the culture, the sensibility, and even the physical appearance of the people. Thus we have the often-quoted examples of Inuktitut ("Eskimo" hunter-gatherer) words for snow,[12] and the wealth of terms for rain and horticulture in Hawaiian. It is precisely this unique transaction between people and place that makes a culture indigenous. Tribal, ethnic, and national identities form around these unique, subtle, and passionate experiences of connection and attachment to place, guiding the lives of their members.

Traditional Native Hawaiian society gives us a beautifully realized model for a sustainable fishing and farming bioregional political economy, one that maintained its large population at an exceptional level of health and apparent happiness. In ancient Hawai'i, political chiefdoms divided each island into a number of wedge-shaped, self-sufficient bioregions called *ahupua'a*. Typically, an *ahupua'a* consisted of the valley between two ridges extending from the central mountain spine down to the beach and fringing reef fisheries. Each *ahupua'a* was a more or less integrated geographic and ecological unit capable of providing most of the resources the community needed. The forested uplands supplied timber and other wild resources while catching the heavy regular rains to feed the fast-flowing streams and to water the flooded taro patches. Taro, or *kalo*, was the staple food, producing leafy greens and a nourishing root. The fringing reef and cleverly constructed ocean fishponds provided a rich diet of fish. While each *ahupua'a* was obliged to pay tribute to an aristocratic warrior class of *ali'i*, in practice the Hawaiian commoners — the *maka'ainana*, the farmers and fishermen — shared their produce and enjoyed considerable autonomy.[13] Every individual could grasp directly the self-sustaining ecology of the *ahupua'a*, and the entire island community naturally thought in terms of the health and integrity of the whole. It would have been unthinkable to overfish the reef or block or pollute the fresh stream waters from which people drank, which fed the taro patches and carried nutrients to the fisheries on the reef.

Ancient Hawaiian stories, chants, dance, and mythology expressed and enhanced this sort of loving attention to the natural world — the clouds, the ocean swells, the tides, the movement of the stars, the wind, the textures and fertility of the earth. All of this tuned and guided the daily life and political economy of the society.

This spiritualized agriculture was expressed by a creation mythology in which *kalo* — taro — was the first child of Wakea, the Sky Father, and Papa, the Earth Mother, making it the elder sibling of the Hawaiian people. The plant itself is strikingly beautiful; the leaves glow luminous green in the brilliant Hawaiian sunlight, accented by the wet, black mud of the *loi* — the flooded paddies. Working in the *loi* would "tune the soul" of the farmer, becoming a kind of worship that inspired a rich liturgy of love poetry to *kalo*, farming, and the land. The Native Hawaiian historian Samuel Kamakou describes the farmer's sensibility:

> The stems were exposed to the sunshine that shone down on the farmer, causing his lungs to flutter with joy. He rejoiced in his labors, as he saw the banana stalks bent over with the weight of their fruit, the tall bunches of sugar cane with their ripened stalks tied together lest they become uprooted by the wind, and the *wauke* plants [used for *tapa* bark cloth] luxuriant as the candlenut tree. Moved with delight, he leaped with joy; and at night as he rested he thought of them with happiness and desire, as a lover of his beloved one. His hands were eager to grasp his *o'o* [digging stick]. As he slept through the night, his hands throbbed to till the soil. When the morning star arose, the farmer's *o'o* was heard thumping amid the rocky soil, as he made mounds and dug holes for planting.[14]

Precontact Hawaiian economy combined the healing and guiding effect of wilderness immersion with efficient production of food through a sustainable and sacralized agriculture. Few things would do more to rapidly turn around our way of living on the earth than a shift to such a spiritually guided bioregionally based agriculture. This doesn't have to be all or nothing. It can be applied at every level of scale, from city roof garden to farming.

Intentional agricultural communities are well positioned to take such models to a higher level by mobilizing the quest: building on local indigenous earth-wisdom; refining their practices with scientific precision, aided by appropriate technologies, and guided by the bigger picture. One such modern initiative, founded in 1998, is MA'O Organic Farms on the Hawaiian island of Oahu. Taking its inspiration from traditional Hawaiian agroecology, this is not quite an eco-village but rather a transitional framework — a "social nonprofit enterprise" located in one of the largest concentrations of Native Hawaiians, the Wai'anae community on Oahu's southwest coast.[15]

This community has been plagued for decades by unemployment, drug addiction, domestic violence, and poor health. MA'O offers its at-risk youth internships in running a fully certified organic farm together with a monthly stipend, a tuition waiver to the local community college, and a collection of support services. The farm supplies organic produce to both the community and local high-end restaurants. It mixes a business model with that of a self-organizing, educational-training venture, in which the interns help manage the program. The wider mission aspires to revive the traditional Hawaiian values of caring for the earth, its food systems, and one another. Such a project could in time, with the right change in political culture, transform into a more integrated, cooperative eco-village rooted in the *ahupua'a* bioregion of Wai'anae and organized more explicitly on the primal dynamic of the quest.

## Eco-villages and Intentional Communities

One of the practical lessons of the primal band and the polis is that certain minimal structures of political economy facilitate keeping the mandala components of the quest in balance. These small-scale societies fostered a personal face-to-face politics, direct democracy, and a cooperative culture that prized generosity and a concern for the whole. Their relative self-sufficiency encouraged each person to individuate at the fundamental level of full-bodied participation in the humanizing roles of food producer, house builder, artisan, healer, politician, musician, and priest. Each person had the opportunity to directly participate in governance and to relate directly to the wilderness earth community.

Today, the intentional agrarian community of the eco-village is the social vessel that comes closest to replicating the scale of the primary political community. We can see a number of quite striking examples of people voluntarily and intuitively joining together to create such self-contained, self-supporting, cooperative communities along primal lines within existing local, national, and global economies. Something like a global eco-village movement is now emerging, with the potential to take the agrarian kibbutz model (which I discuss below) to a higher level. Eco-villages are small-scale, intentional communities with varying degrees of democratic cooperative integration; they are created explicitly to serve an earth-based way of life that is sustainable into the indefinite future and that ensures the well-being of all life-forms. At their most self-conscious, they seek to ground themselves in the sort of spiritualized bioregionalism of the Hawaiian *ahupua'a*, but expanded and deepened to include the living planet.

The founding model for the modern spiritually based eco-village is Findhorn in the north of Scotland. Findhorn grew out of the personal quest of three people, Peter and Eileen Caddy and Dorothy Maclean, who found themselves homeless and living together in a small caravan, supported by welfare and trying to supplement their meager income with an organic vegetable garden. Their spiritual discipline slowly led to a mystical-shamanic communion with the spirits of the plants, the soil, and the place. This guided their gardening until they found themselves producing near-miraculous harvests. Their story became a succession of synchronicities, leading to the establishment of the Findhorn eco-village and its related educational foundation, all based on a spiritually guided form of organic gardening.

Today Findhorn has some 450 resident members and is the largest intentional community in the United Kingdom. It has been measured as having the lightest ecological footprint of any community in the country (with half the average use of resources and half the environmental impact), and it has been given a Best Practices award by the United Nations Center for Human Settlement.[16] Although it has no formal ideology, it is committed to demonstrating the synergy between social, ecological, educational, and spiritual practices. It displays the defining elements of the primal complex by nurturing individuation in a relatively egalitarian, cooperative community where decision making is guided by an open-ended big picture.

Gaviotas in eastern Colombia provides another good example of a model eco-village and intentional community. Gaviotas was founded in 1971 by Paolo Lugari, who gathered a group of scientists, artisans, peasants, street children, and Guahibo Indians to set up a sustainable agrarian community in a relatively inhospitable environment. He chose the Llanos, an arid, infertile plain in eastern Colombia, which in pre-Columbian times had been covered with Amazonian rain forest. Since the soil was found to have near-toxic levels of aluminum, agronomists tested hundreds of crops before recommending a native tropical pine. The trees flourished, and by 1995, some six million pines covered the area in one of the largest reforestation projects in Colombia. The trees held groundwater, provided shade, and generated a moist understory, which was soon colonized by indigenous forest species. With the return of the shaded understory came animal populations of deer, anteater, and capybaras. At one count, biologists found some 240 species that had not been seen on the open Llanos for millennia. Meanwhile, in a strange twist, the pines were found to be sterile, whereupon the community decided to allow them to be taken over by regrowth of native vegetation. The pines also produced an exceptionally thick resin, which Colombia had been regularly importing for multiple uses, from turpentine to cosmetics, paints, and varnishes. Suddenly, Gaviotas found itself with a market for its resin, and a steady income while practicing a kind of agro-forestry that actually increased the biodiversity of the region.[17]

The village now consists of around 200 individuals, all receiving the same modest salary, free housing, health care, food, and education. Since basic needs are taken care of, there is no crime, no police, and no jail. Music and the arts are vigorously cultivated in a life that seems remarkably peaceful, relatively sustainable, and satisfying. The community of scientists and artisans has developed inexpensive, ingenious technologies for sustainable energy, including cheap solar panels and windmills. In order to bring the deep artesian groundwater to the surface, they designed a simple, effective pump and then attached it to children's seesaws. The "seesaw pump" has become a symbol of the imaginative and playful pragmatism that made Gaviotas the United Nations "model village for a sustainable world."

There are related initiatives in developing countries, like Sarvodaya Shramadana, a nonprofit education foundation working with existing traditional villages in rural Sri Lanka. The organization runs on minimal capital, preferring to mobilize the volunteer help of retired elders who have the time, skill, and need to be of service to the new generation. The volunteers go out among some fifteen thousand villages offering technical assistance and advice in shifting from a market-dominated model of production to a "no poverty, no affluence" form of sustainable agriculture. Sarvodaya's visionary statement of rights includes not only water, food, and shelter but, in the spirit of the quest, the right to a beautiful environment and a meaningful life.[18]

The eco-village is not an all-or-nothing framework. It is by definition intentional, voluntary, and creative, allowing for a wide mix and degree of primal attributes. For example, in New York State, the EcoVillage at Ithaca, or EVI, mixes cooperative living with private ownership and considerable individual independence. It was founded in 1991 by Liz Walker, a community organizer, who set up a nonprofit organization to purchase land to create "an attractive viable alternative lifestyle to American life," based on Green buildings, renewable energy systems, cohousing communities, an independent organic farm, open-space preservation, and social entrepreneurship.[19]

By 2007, EVI had 160 members living on 175 acres. The nonprofit is run by a board of directors together with the residents. The homes are privately owned by residents, who pay monthly fees for common buildings and shared facilities. They eat several meals a week together, prepared by volunteer cooks, and share a rich social life. Much of the produce consumed comes from the independent organic farm. The village has established connections with surrounding communities and organizations, including Cornell University and the local community college. Education is built into the vision of EVI through a nonprofit educational organization called Center for Sustainability Education (CSE), committed to meeting human needs in ways that "are aligned with the long-term viability of Earth and its inhabitants." In this hands-on learning program, the primary teaching tool is the eco-village itself — a "laboratory for the future." The whole EVI-CSE project is part of an umbrella organization — The Center for Transformative Action — which offers a model of nonviolent social action "that moves us beyond complaint, competition, and 'us versus them' thinking." Its three basic components are all implicit in the structure of the primal truth quest: "breaking the silence that surrounds injustice; building an inclusive movement where adversaries become allies; and articulating an inspiring, proactive vision."[20]

In 1995, Findhorn assumed a leadership role in the eco-village movement by organizing a conference called "Eco-villages and Sustainable Communities," drawing community leaders from all over the world. This led to the formation of the Global Eco-village Network, which now links some four hundred similar projects around the world that previously had little awareness of one another. There are now self-identified aspiring eco-villages in some seventy countries on six continents. Most draw on principles of ecological design, eco-architecture, permaculture, organic gardening, Green production, and use of alternative and renewable energy sources. Also common to most is some recognition of the humanizing magic of small face-to-face social structures in which people have an opportunity to express their individual uniqueness and creativity *by serving and being served by the community*. The movement seeks to shift from a single homogenous consumer economy to a collection of more sustainable, self-sufficient bioregional economies, focusing on the nonmaterial values of human relationships, creativity, beauty, and meaningful work. At their most ambitious, eco-villages try to integrate the best and lightest of industrial technology with science and agriculture guided by a shamanic sensibility.

## Kibbutz — The Experiment That Both Succeeded and Failed

In 2007 I returned to Israel for the first time after many decades. I had been warned repeatedly that the country had changed and in many ways for the worse. I heard the kibbutz was in decline, and the people more cynical, more urbanized, less idealistic, and much more materialistic. I was told Israel now had more start-up companies per capita than any other country in the world, it had more companies listed on NASDAQ than any country outside North America, that 85 percent of households had solar water heaters and that 80 percent of wastewater was recycled. Much was true. As I drove through the country, I was overcome with emotion: the energy and informality of the people, the dry desert air, the smell of the pine forests in the Jerusalem hills, the olives and salad with every meal — all were wonderfully familiar. I reconnected with old friends, family, and loved ones as if I had never left. I thought I had lost my Hebrew, but on my second day back, I got into an argument with a clerk at city hall, negotiating a water bill for my English-speaking friend. Suddenly, in the familiar heat and frustration, my army-learned Hebrew poured out. I was stunned. It was as if the language was there, waiting for me to come back and open my mouth so it could slip onto my tongue. People treated me as an Israeli. If South Africa gave me my species identity, being in Israel felt like coming home to my tribe.

Despite the changes in the country, much of the legacy of the old days remained. I realized how indebted I was to the kibbutz for giving me such a fully realized example of primal politics. I also realized more starkly than ever where the kibbutz vision was deficient, and what a way forward could look like — for the country, the kibbutz, and the planet. For these reasons, it's worth looking at the kibbutz more closely from our expanded perspective.

The Israeli kibbutz was an intentional agrarian community midway in size between the hunting-gathering band and the polis. Like the eco-village, it was in part a utopian social experiment that expressed the four components of primal politics: it had a passionate narrative of meaning and was driven by a powerful democratically organized international movement. But it primarily served the relatively narrow mission of nation building. The Jewish scholar and Kabbalist Martin Buber called it the "experiment that did not fail," and it succeeded conspicuously in shaping the political culture of the early State of Israel. But unlike the eco-village, the kibbutz was founded in the days before the environmental movement, and it lacked an ecological perspective. It also failed to sustain the truth quest at the center of the primal dynamic that made it so powerful in the first place. Therefore, it was unable to provide Israel with an alternative to the rapidly globalizing model of industrial capitalism. The kibbutz movement also failed conspicuously, as did Zionism itself, in engaging the local Palestinian population. In both its successes and failures, the kibbutz demonstrated the critical importance of an explicit commitment to the quest.

Kibbutz philosophy at its best expressed the Kabbalist imperative of *tikkun ha'olam*, to "repair or heal the world." This is the idea that the role of the human being in the cosmic drama of existence is to mitigate suffering, minimize destruction, and foster the beauty and profusion of conscious life on earth. The kibbutz movement offered to satisfy that deep need we have for a purpose in life beyond simple self-gratification. This was connected to, and over time increasingly in conflict with, its other primary mission: a pragmatic response to the needs of early Zionism. The kibbutz was based on a passionate vision of meaning and redemption through a return to Zion, the biblical promised land, the formative homeland of the

Jewish people. This inspired large numbers of young, idealistic, impoverished ghetto Jews with no capital and no farming experience to move to Israel and settle on land in a hostile environment and create an enlightened farming community amid swamp and desert. The movement's pragmatism was driven by the crisis in Jewish existence at the end of the nineteenth century, a crisis that in the middle of the twentieth century became the catastrophe of the Holocaust.

In 1948, when the United Nations voted to partition Palestine into two states — one Jewish, the other Arab — the surrounding Arab nations invaded the new country. During the subsequent struggle for survival, Israeli pragmatism became increasingly ruthless.[21] The more recent rise of suicidal Islamic fundamentalism has further intensified a cycle of violent polarization between Israeli and Palestinian, Jew and Arab. If the most glaring failure of the Zionist vision was its inability to grasp and respond creatively to an indigenous Arab presence,[22] then the legacy of this failure has been continuous bloody conflict and the corruption of the political cultures of both Israelis and Palestinians, each in different ways.[23]

### *The Beloved Community*

The average kibbutz was a small agricultural community consisting of no more than a few hundred individuals. It was based on the key primal principles of voluntary cooperation, democratic decision making, and conflict resolution through direct face-to-face discussion. Its ethos was that of each individual taking responsibility for the whole, while the community concerned itself with the unique needs of individuals. Communalism was balanced by a culture of discussion in which, in theory, individuality was cultivated and respected. In practice the communalist ethic at times crushed individuality. This was due in part to an overreaction to the prevailing culture of competitive individualism. But there was also a failure in theory. The kibbutz ideology lacked a philosophy of consciousness and an adequate notion of individuation — the fundamental human need to grow and explore as much of the full range of human experience as possible, and then to express one's uniqueness creatively. It lacked a spiritual aesthetic.

But the kibbutz had no class structure and did establish complete gender equality. Resources were owned communally and apportioned collectively according to the ethos "from each according to his or her ability, to each according to need." Management positions were rotated and decisions were made by the members in face-to-face discussion of the general assembly.

In the first few decades after its founding, the kibbutz movement succeeded admirably. Two members of Kibbutz Kfar Blum describe this in terms reminiscent of the balance between the opposites of the primal polis. It was a society based on

> co-operation without coercion, equality without reducing cultural or intellectual standards to the lowest common denominator; freedom without disorder; work with neither boredom nor need of economic incentives; self expression without license; specialization without stratification; guidance of public opinion without repression; moral concern without dogmatism; industrialization without urbanization; rural life without idiocy.[24]

At its height, about 300 kibbutzim were responsible for the bulk of the agricultural produce in the country. In 2010, there were still 273 kibbutzim, with a total population of 126,000, including children.[25] In addition to the kibbutz, Israel has the more numerous, more loosely organized communal villages called *moshavim*, where houses and farms are privately owned but produce is marketed collectively and many services are shared. Although kibbutz members never constituted more than about 6 percent of the population, they had an enormous influence in building up the country, shaping its institutions, providing leadership, and generating an Israeli national culture of *chalutziut*, or "pioneering idealism."

Most of the kibbutzim belonged to one of three main kibbutz movements, which in turn were affiliated with the ruling labor parties, which were often led by kibbutz members. The first prime minister of Israel, David Ben-Gurion was a member of Kibbutz Sde Boker and lived in the same material modesty as his fellow farmers, returning periodically to help with the harvest and work in the kitchens. *Chalutzim* — the agricultural pioneers of the country — comprised half the elected members of Israel's first parliament in 1948, and fully one-third of the cabinet were kibbutzniks. Kibbutz members dominated the officer corps of the elite fighting units in the army and air force. One-quarter of all casualties in the Six-Day War were kibbutz members. Most importantly, the impact of the kibbutz was felt in the first half of the century in creating an Israeli culture based on equality, informality in dress and manners, service to the community, and a shared agrarian, communitarian vision.[26]

### *The Kibbutz Abandons the Quest*

In many ways the material success of the kibbutz accelerated its failure. The kibbutz became a powerful reality because it was driven by revolutionaries whose lives were caught up in the passion of a high art — that of creating the beautiful and beloved community. Like the modest San, their psychological and moral center of gravity was spiritual and creative. Once the creative work had been done and the community provided with security and a decent material standard of living, children were expected to fit into the existing structure. To paraphrase Karl Mannheim, "the utopia of the parents became the ideology of the children."

Many of the children grew up to find kibbutz life parochial and boring. After military service, they would follow the pattern of other young Israelis and take off for a year or two of travel abroad. Some never returned. City life and the wider world offered new experiences, adventure, and the sort of creative challenge that had motivated their revolutionary parents. How does one institutionalize revolutionary creativity?* In the absence of a creative and spiritual political life, pragmatism and materialism took over.[27]

The kibbutz general assembly became an instrument for the solution of practical problems of administration and efficient farming and production. It lost its connection to the process that had energized the revolutionaries — the long nights of passionate discussions and the search into the big questions of meaning necessary to create a new way of life. Euphoric folk dancing and singing were increasingly replaced by commercial pop and rock music at the kibbutz disco. The urgent struggle for military and economic survival produced a generation of strong, hardworking, pragmatic farmers and fighters, officers in the elite units, but not so many philosophers, artists, and mystics.

The original asceticism of some of the earlier pioneers gave way to the outside pressure of a growing global market society and to internal pressure for more individual freedom. Agrarianism gave way to light industry as factories were built on fields. Labor as worship quickly became oil driven and industrialized following the factory model of mechanization, division of labor, and specialization, and all this was done in the service of maximizing the bottom line of profit — albeit the profit of the community. When it

* I return to this question in the epilogue, where I discuss a revolutionary approach to revolutions.

became profitable, cheap Arab labor was hired, then foreign workers were imported. In 2007 immigrant workers from Thailand — Tailandim — with no connection to the land, the produce, or the community, provided the new agricultural labor force. Lost was any vision of organic, sustainable agriculture for local consumption. Lost was any notion of the aesthetic, psychological, and spiritual value of working on the land with growing, living things.

Many kibbutzim now pay their members wages. Growing numbers work in adjacent towns and cities, and some have started functioning as landlords, renting houses to outsiders who appreciate what remains of rural community life. Without the creative passion of the idealistic revolutionaries, the community has become increasingly defenseless against the surrounding pressures of corporate-driven consumer capitalism.

Changes in kibbutz proceeded in parallel with larger changes in the political culture of the country. By the 1980s the ruling kibbutz-and-labor coalition of parties had been replaced by the neoclassical economists of the right, and government support of kibbutzim had dwindled. Since then the political center of gravity has continued to shift toward free-market capitalism and the religious right. This shift is also visible in army leadership. In the past the elite combat units were typically led by sons of the kibbutz; today they are more often commanded by the young Jews who wear the knitted skullcap of the Orthodox religious community. The inspiring big picture expressing the passionate connection to the land and mobilizing readiness to sacrifice for the community has now been taken over by the religious right. Utopian agrarianism has been replaced by biblical messianism.

Perhaps the heart of the problem was that Gordon's and Buber's ideas about a spiritual relationship to the land through creative labor failed to take root in the arid soil of the scientific materialism that supported kibbutz ideology. Like most political movements of both the left and the right in the nineteenth and twentieth centuries, kibbutz lacked a philosophy of consciousness adequate to the quest, and it periodically lapsed into ideological rigidity. There was little understanding of the sacred, of aesthetics and their relation to the quest for the good of the individual and the community. Despite its roots in the messianic narrative of Jewish exile, and the mystique of labor on the land, these elements were never explicitly integrated into a social and philosophical self-understanding. They were never institutionalized.

This brings us back to the perennial dilemma of creative political transformation: How can a community sustain the Eros of creative political transformation and still remain a coherent functioning community?[28] The scientific-materialistic ideologies of the past century have no answer.

Ironically, we can find part of the answer by looking closely at what the founders actually did. They were caught up in the primal quest — questioning their lives and their society, crossing boundaries, radically expanding their vision of the possible into a grand narrative of meaning, and, finally, collectively creating a real society from their imagination that would preserve the most obvious elements of their quest. Together these elements gave a quality of transcendence — "spirituality" — to their pragmatic action that humbled and guided individual egos and generated a passion for life that deepened individuation and made possible heroic achievement in the service of the community.

While to some degree the kibbutz consciously pursued each of the primal values represented by the four quadrants of the maṇdala, it failed to clarify both the truth quest and the shamanic-spiritual relationship to the all-encompassing wilderness context — the *fons et origo* of human existence.

Without a practice of the quest at the center of its politics, the kibbutz movement, like Zionism in general, had little hope of generating a picture inclusive enough — a cosmology capacious enough — to inspire a symbiosis of the two nationalist movements, Israeli and Palestinian.[29] Institutions matter, but ultimately no institutional reform — a single binational state or two-state solution — will flourish in the Middle East without transformation in the minds and souls of the individuals involved.[30]

Without commitment to a shared vision based on the quest there can be no deep healing between the two competing narratives of meaning and identity connected to the same piece of land. Ironically, both Israeli and Palestinian identities are rooted in the same monotheistic revelation; both revere Abraham and Moses. But typically, the narratives of the protagonists stop short. They don't extend beyond culture, nation, or religion. The radical way forward is to attempt to resolve the conflict by integrating the two national and religious narratives within a larger, ultimately more compelling story of our common humanity — our shared African origins, our rootedness in a single story of earthly evolution.

### *Healing through Engaging Opposites*

Much of the achievement of the kibbutz remains. There is still an ethos respecting hard work, sharing, and communal living. The fact that the kibbutz survives as a recognized entity is testimony to the flexibility of its democracy. There are still prospects for a recovery of creativity based on a more expanded and spiritual vision. The kibbutz can now draw from models of eco-villages like Findhorn and Gaviotas, and the more spiritualized agriculture of the ancient Hawaiians.[31] For instance, Kibbutz Harduf in the northern Galileo organizes itself within the spiritual individualism of Rudolf Steiner's anthroposophical philosophy. The economy is based on organic farming and running a Waldorf school. The school welcomes surrounding Arab teachers and students, and the curriculum includes Arabic and Islamic studies. When I visited in 2007, the kibbutz also supported a peace camp, Sha'ar le-Adam — Gateway to Humanity — located in the nearby woods. Founded and run by a young kibbutz war veteran and the son of the mukhtar (head) of the nearby Bedouin village, the camp brought young Jews and Arabs together for programs in the arts held outdoors and exposed to the healing power of the land both peoples love so much. The purpose was open-ended: to create a more expanded social container within which the stories and experiences of both peoples can be expressed and integrated.[32]

Nelson Mandela and the kibbutz offer two complementary approaches to changing political culture. Mandela demonstrated the power of a vision-inspired individual, a boundary-crossing strategy. In a complementary fashion, the early success of the kibbutz demonstrates the importance of an inspiring narrative of meaning and the power of organization — the international kibbutz movement — in large-scale political change. The spiritual eco-village and kibbutzim like Harduf suggest the possibility of combining the two examples in an indigenous Israeli-Palestinian bioregional agriculture supported by social institutions aligned with the quest.

## Future Primal Cities and Nations

The eco-village and kibbutz movements showed how primal elements in village life could shape the culture of cities and nations. But we don't have to go back to the village to bring the primal back to the surface. Since the primal complex exists within us, we can activate it wherever we are, working with what we have. And where we are is increasingly in cities. By 2005 more than half the population of the planet lived in cities. Jaime Lerner, the mayor of the model city of Curitiba in Brazil and leader of the Green City Movement, has argued that cities can actually be the most effective units of social change. Like the Greek polis, many cities are small enough to mobilize the population yet big enough to impact the larger arena of national politics and be engines for cultural change. Their concentrations of population and resources also allow them to support culture and the arts, and for this reason they have traditionally been centers of political and social creativity.[33]

Cities exist within living ecologies, and their ultimate viability depends on understanding and nurturing those natural systems. One approach to enhancing a bioregional sensibility is suggested by the American eco-architect and urban planner Richard Register, who advocates allowing streams and rivers to run free through the hearts of our cities. Canals and drains could be brought back to the surface, creating arteries of green that would allow for some wildlife to move from the country through cities. This would help preserve the integrity of the surrounding ecosystem and watershed while also calming, sensitizing, and healing our frenzied populations.[34]

We can nurture fragments of nature in multiple small but often profound ways. Converting empty city lots into community gardens helps feed people and provides a focus for community building. Rooftop gardens cool cities in the summer and absorb storm runoff in the winter while providing food and shelter for insects and birds and bringing the healing effect of nature — a taste of the "big medicine" — into urban landscapes.

By reducing light pollution — the glare from streetlights — with specially designed and more economical street lamps, we can turn backyards, parks, and waste lots into sites for amateur observatories, giving everyone direct access to that ultimate wilderness landscape — the night sky and its billions of exploding suns and spiraling galaxies. In 2001, Flagstaff, Arizona, reduced its light pollution so dramatically that it was awarded the title of the world's first international "dark sky city." Flagstaff now offers visitors and residents a cosmic wilderness-immersion experience without leaving city limits.

The easiest way to connect with nature is to simply jump the fence and explore the wilder country that remains outside our cities and suburbs. The positive health benefits of being outside in nature are well documented, and these are amplified when focused by the boundary-crossing discipline of the quest. Experienced in this way, mountains are not simply picturesque backdrops for cities, and wilderness is not simply empty space for our recreational machinery. Instead, we can we experience wilderness as the primary source of spiritual, moral, and physical regeneration we so badly need.

One of the major problems in greening and humanizing our cities is centralization of power. In this regard, a number of Brazilian cities have made bold moves to reverse this trend and move toward more participatory forms of governance. For example, in 1989 the ruling political party of the city of Porto Alegre in Brazil decided to decentralize and democratize city government in the interest of the good of the community. Fifty thousand citizens were given the opportunity to participate directly in deciding how the budget of two hundred million dollars would be spent. The process started with dozens of assemblies across the city maximizing grassroots participation. First, citizen assemblies met to receive instruction on the issues and the budgeting process, and then they discussed priorities and forwarded them on through elected representatives to the city council. The city then made recommendations and reconciled competing priorities, but it had no authority to change the priorities.

The face-to-face situation brought the most critical, real shared needs to the surface — food, health, education. The results were dramatic. In twelve years the number of public schools increased from twenty-nine to eighty-six and literacy reached 98 percent. Water, sewage, and public transport improved. Political, cultural, and neighborhood civic groups doubled, producing a noticeable elevation in civic responsibility and a significant drop in crime and corruption. Implicit in these outward manifestations of improved quality of life was an inner process of individuals taking responsibility, coming together to understand their shared reality, and cooperatively create a better way of life for all — the truth quest. Since Porto Alegre's initiative, one hundred Brazilian cities have tried to implement similar strategies.[35]

The Brazilian city of Belo Horizonte gives us another example of participatory budgeting in the service of the good of the whole. By 1993, the city population was 2.5 million people, of which 11 percent lived in absolute poverty and almost 20 percent of children went hungry. Like Porto Alegre, the city had already instituted participatory budgeting, and then in 1993 it went further and declared food a right of citizenship. With this, participation in the budgeting process suddenly doubled to more than thirty-one thousand. City agencies brought together the interests of producers and consumers by offering farmers choice spots in the city to sell their produce directly to urban consumers. This curbed retail markups, which often reached 100 percent, but actually made farming more profitable and more attractive. As farming thrived, the population had access to fresher, healthier, cheaper food, and the city moved closer to food sovereignty.

The city also set up Restaurante Popular — People's Restaurants — which served subsidized meals of locally grown food to some twelve thousand people a day for about fifty cents a meal. Today, some 40 percent of the population benefits from these initiatives. In less than a decade Belo Horizonte cut the infant death rate by more than half. Future primal cities like Belo Horizonte and Porto Alegre demonstrate primal principles in interaction with existing structures. They show how a more enlightened political culture, based on a more expanded understanding of "the good life," can inspire centralized power structures like city governments to devolve power and resources to the people for the greater good of all.

### *Bhutan's Gross National Happiness*

The small Himalayan country of Bhutan, located between India and China, provides a unique example of these primal principles elevated to a national level. Bhutan has several natural advantages. The country is largely unspoiled, with magnificent, richly forested mountain wilderness and carefully cultivated valleys. Its population has never been conquered or occupied and is bonded by a deeply rooted tradition of Mahayana Buddhism, related to a kind of nature mysticism. With a population of some eight hundred thousand, covering an area twice the size of the State of Israel (40,000 sq km), it is not exactly polis-sized, yet it is small enough and homogenous enough to be relatively self-sufficient and sustain a high level of participatory governance.

Until recently it was an absolute monarchy. In 1972, King Jigme Singye Wangchuck returned to his country after studying abroad, armed with a British education and a clear understanding of the failures of development based on consumerism. He immediately set about redirecting the process of modernization in accordance with the central values of Buddhism — the sacredness of all of life, compassion for all sentient beings, and living in harmony with the natural world. In a bold move, he threw out GDP — gross domestic product — as the primary measure of well-being and replaced it with a Buddhist-based notion of "gross national happiness," or GNH. The great challenge for Bhutan was to globalize humanely, to incorporate the benefits of science and technology while avoiding the seduction of materialism. As the minister for home and cultural affairs, Lyonpo Jigmi Thinley, explained simply, "What good is the material national wealth of the nation if it doesn't bring happiness?"[36]

GNH is based on "four pillars": economic self-sufficiency, preservation and enhancement of the natural environment, preservation and promotion of the traditional culture, and good governance. The king realized that a government that gave all the decision-making power to one individual was inherently unstable, and that good governance was the key condition for pursuing the other pillars. He set up a council to draft a constitution for a representative democracy with radically decentralized power. The council surveyed some fifty other democratic constitutions and in 2001 came up with a draft that was circulated among the villages and voted on. It consolidated a representative national government based on the unit of the self-governing village. Each village elected a leader by secret ballot, then sent representatives to subdistrict committees of ten villages or more, and so on to the national council. The national body fashioned policies that promoted the four pillars of GNH while enhancing the autonomy, self-sufficiency, health, and education of the lower subsidiary units. Universal free health care and universal free education became additional necessary conditions for effective grassroots participatory government. In other words, central government committed to providing all citizens with the information, education, and access needed for constructing a big picture of the good of the whole.

The ambitious program of teacher training, clinic building, and democratization was financed in large part by Bhutan's major export — hydroelectric power to India — which in 2005 accounted for some 40 percent of all government revenues. Instead of large storage dams, more modest run-of-the-river technologies were constructed in narrow gorges, which diverted part of the flow to the turbines of power plants constructed deep underground. This approach together with cleverly constructed "fish ladders" ensured minimal impact on the surrounding ecosystem. Such run-of-the-river technologies meant periodic power outages during the dry season, but this was seen as a relatively minor problem and a small price to pay for avoiding damage to the ecosystem. Logging was another source of revenue, but raw material was managed in a sustainable fashion by a law requiring at least 60 percent of the land remain forested at all times. There is now more land under forest cover than before the development program began.

Following the principle that it could not ignore the benefits of science and industrialization, in 1999 Bhutan became the last country on earth to introduce television. Within six months the country had gone from one cable channel to forty-five broadcasting twenty-four hours a day. A year later the Internet followed. This sudden exposure to a relentlessly commercial culture exploiting sex and violence in the interests of consumerism had predictably negative results. There was a sudden dramatic increase in drug and alcohol abuse, violence, burglary, and murder.

Television confronted the Bhutanese model with its central challenge, which, in essence, is the same as that facing the rest of humanity: how to engage modernity creatively without being swamped by its destructiveness. Government officials and media experts responded unequivocally by saying "education," but this of course begged the question, "What sort of education?" The deep answer to this requires the quest, and one example of a mass educational program has been encouraging. Faced with the threat of AIDS, many traditional villages resisted protective contraception as disrespectful of life. The government responded by recruiting teams of highly respected priests to teach the people the difference between taking life and preventing unwanted pregnancy. Here, we see Bhutan following the spirit of the quest by approaching the sacred pragmatically and approaching practical matters by invoking the bigger picture of the sacred. The goal is a synthesis of the best of modernity with the most life-enhancing values of primal wisdom, which in Bhutan's case comes through Buddhism.

The Bhutanese model is now attracting global attention as many NGOs and international organizations realize that economic growth and increasing material productivity cannot be the supreme measures of political, societal, and economic health. There is a growing global interest in developing comparable measures to GNH that track genuine progress serving the collective good.[37]

## Movements and Revolutionary Transformations

On the one hand, there is great power when individuals choose to come together to assert their freedom in some mass action in a public space; on the other hand, there is also the perennial danger that the crowd will become a mob — inflamed by a sense of injustice and communal power, swept along by charismatic demagogues, it easily loses the respect for individual life that inspired the revolution, and succumbs to violence. A dictator can be violently deposed, but then what? The power vacuum is too often filled by new power-hungry elites who provoke further violence and betray the values of the original revolution.

Future primal politics clarifies how the truth quest can mediate the tension between individual creativity and conformity to the collective to ensure that action serves the good of the whole. There have been several dramatic examples of this over the past century. Mahatma Gandhi's *satyagraha* — soul force — mobilized masses of ordinary Indians in nonviolent civil disobedience that helped make India ungovernable and impelled the colonial British government to leave. Martin Luther King Jr. used this same approach to great effect in the civil rights movement in the American South, as did Nelson Mandela in South Africa. In all cases the depth of commitment of the leadership to "soul force" helped evoke a comparable level of self-awareness and courage in many of their followers while shaming the oppressors. In such mass actions, the outcome depends directly on the level of consciousness of the leaders and of the individuals composing the movement.

Today, worldwide access to the Internet enables the very rapid lateral diffusion of information, making it easier to put a human face on oppression and to coordinate strategies of resistance. This also means in principle that there can be multiple fluid centers of leadership. Any one individual in private can instantaneously address the collective and be a catalyst for action. This was most dramatically demonstrated during the Arab Spring of 2010–11, in which popular protests against dictatorships were catalyzed by a young Tunisian vegetable seller who set himself on fire in protest against police abuse and oppressive government. This story and others like it were rapidly retold and circulated through a variety of social media by a key revolutionary demographic — urban, fairly well-educated youth. The media then made it possible for masses of citizens to organize themselves into a series of rolling protests and strikes, which in some cases escalated into pitched battles.[38] Long-entrenched, stupefying dictatorships in Tunisia, Egypt, and

Libya fell in quick succession. Clearly, many more repressive regimes are ripe for overthrow, and this transformation is no doubt in its early stages. What will emerge in their place depends directly on the collective level of awareness of a critical mass of citizens.

In the 1960s, the United States was shaken by a cultural revolution of the nation's youth — the counterculture. The post–World War II situation produced an unprecedented, large generation of affluent middle-class, well-educated, leisured students — the baby-boom generation — which became radicalized as it confronted a series of crises: vicious racism in the American South, a controversial war in Vietnam, movements of national liberation throwing out their colonial overlords, indigenous peoples demanding to be recognized, and the first unmistakable signs of the environmental devastation of the planet. The generation started questioning the most basic values and assumptions of its society, and it experimented, sometimes recklessly, with a new universe of political and cultural options. This period saw the emergence of the nonviolent civil rights movement as well as the Black Power movement, the antiwar movement, the environmental movement, back-to-the-land communes, the women's movement, the American Indian Movement, the terroristic Weather Underground, widespread experimentation with entheogens, considerable interest in Eastern religions, enormous creativity in music and the arts, and a host of other more exotic cultural and political expressions. While these movements changed American culture in significant ways, they never really cohered into something larger. There was no integrating philosophical vision nor were there any viable political containers. Instead, seeds of transformation were sown in many areas of culture, society, and politics. Those seeds now seem to be sprouting.[39]

Today in the West we see a new assertion of individual autonomy and resistance to political corruption, as grassroots movements of the right and the left, also mobilized by social media, are taking to the streets to demand a more direct voice in governance. On the conservative right, the Tea Party movement, critical of big government, asserts a right to directly participate in decision making. But the Tea Party, like many conservative movements, is hampered by Eurocentric principles of eighteenth-century Liberalism. On the left, the more open and informed Occupy Wall Street movement is inclusive and democratic enough to grasp the reality of a corporate oligarchy. Yet its worldview is still far from demonstrating a coherent political philosophy that could guide creative transformation of the powers that be. Both pale in comparison to the mass demonstrations and cultural upheaval of the sixties.[40]

The impulse of such grassroots movements is primal and democratic — a simple assertion of the individual's right to self-rule, a desire to participate in the decisions affecting how we live. What has changed are the means — global electronic communication — and this, as Marshall McLuhan noted decades ago, contains its own message. The nature of modern communication contains a global awareness even as it gives expression to the unique individual voice, tweet, or film clip. Politics is moving from the family, tribe, and nation to the planet and then back to the individual person. The basis for political order lies in the order of the soul of the individual.

Internet-based civic organizations like MoveOn.org and Avaaz.org are becoming significant change agents through educational campaigns, petitions, and civic action campaigns on human rights, climate change, corruption in business and government, poverty, and conflict resolution. These include sit-ins, phone-ins, email-your-leader campaigns, demonstrations, and media-friendly stunts. The director of Avaaz, Ricken Patel, insists it has no ideology but it does have a mission "to close the gap between the world we have and the world most people everywhere want. Idealists of the world unite!" Avaaz appears in fifteen languages in 193 countries and has over sixteen million members, and since 2009 it has not taken donations from foundations or corporations, nor has it accepted payments of more than five thousand dollars. In 2008, Avaaz organized a petition to the Chinese president, Hu Jintao, calling for the opening of meaningful dialogue with the Dalai Lama. In seven days the petition had garnered more than one million signatures, making it the largest and fastest-growing online petition in history.

Although Avaaz claims to have no explicit ideology, the great range of issues it has supported reveals an implicit, open-ended vision of "the world we want": one that is ecologically sustainable, fosters expanding individual awareness, is politically empowering, and satisfies the basic human rights including the need for food, shelter, and education — in short, a more life-loving, biocentric vision congruent with the primal vision.

We also see something of a future primal transformation taking place in electoral politics in the proliferation of Green political parties competing for office in regional, national, and supranational governing bodies. The principles of the rather amorphous Green movement were formalized in the German Green Party platform of the late 1970s as ecological wisdom, sustainability, social justice, participatory democracy, nonviolence, localized economies, and respect for cultural integrity and diversity. The degree of commitment to these principles varies widely from country to country depending on local and political conditions, but most Green parties tend to share these aspirational values.

In 1995 the Finnish Green Party was the first European Green party to be part of a national cabinet. Greens have participated in national governments in Belgium, France, Ireland, and the Netherlands. Green parties now exist in most countries with democratic systems of government, including South Africa, Mexico, Mongolia, and Peru. Greens have formed a party in the European Parliament, where in 2009 they held over forty seats.

Perhaps the most elusive but portentous expression of the primal resurgence is in what Paul Hawken has identified as a global democratic mass movement of independent, nongovernmental nonprofits. They are "research institutes, community development agencies, faith-based groups, trusts and foundations, organizations working to safeguard nature, ensure greater equality and justice and create a more life-loving world."[41] Hawken calculates that there are at least one million (and quite possibly two million) such organizations mobilizing tens of millions of idealists in what might be the largest mass movement in history. This movement coalesced from three converging root issues: environmentalism, social justice, and the struggle of indigenous peoples for cultural survival in the global consumer economy.

Hawken notes that the movement has been ignored because it is intrinsically decentralized, and commercial mass media are notoriously incapable of connecting the dots — synthesizing and evaluating information. "When we hear about a chemical spill in a river, it is never mentioned that more than four thousand organizations in North America have adopted a river, creek, or stream. We read that organic agriculture is the fastest growing sector of farming in America, Japan, Mexico and Europe, but no connection is made to the more than three thousand organizations that educate farmers, customers, and legislators about sustainable agriculture."[42]

The most crucial and elusive point of the movement is a quintessentially primal, boundary-crossing dialectic expressed by the movement's ability to hold the tension between opposites: the individual and the community, the global and the local, the practical and the spiritual. According to Hawken, in this "invisible revolution" there is no single unifying ideology, no dogma, no doctrine; rather, there is a grassroots independence, and a respect for diversity and location, which exists alongside a fierce commitment to create a just global community conducive to a flourishing earth. The big questions for all mass political and protest movements remain: How adequate is the diagnosis? What comes after the dictator is overthrown? What structures can deal with our most critical global and local crises? Everything depends on the level of consciousness of the participants, on their grasp of our shared reality, and thus on the clarity of their commitment to the ongoing quest. We can no longer escape the challenge of creating a politics with the truth quest at its center, capable of generating an inspiring vision of a way forward.

## A Vision of Future Primal Planetary Politics

Obviously, none of the examples in this chapter could, in principle, provide a single blueprint for a planetary politics. But when we step back and connect the dots, we can see how they all — from African presidents and American eco-villages to Sri Lankan peasants — embody various dimensions and varying degrees of a quest-based primal politics. We can imagine that as people begin to realize their commonality in the dynamic of the quest emerging from the universe story, they deepen and extend their efforts; connecting and co-operating with one another and creating an evolving, increasingly integrated, decentralized, self-transforming, future-primal, planetary politics.

We can imagine people applying the primal values to realize that leaders like Gandhi, King, and Mandela are great not so much because they are "special" and unlike us but precisely because they exemplify in concentrated form what is most human about us. Such fully individuated human beings can act like seed crystals dropped into a supersaturated solution — in our case a highly charged political situation — causing the entire solution to suddenly crystallize into a more highly ordered, harmonious state. They have discovered that you can achieve the highest sort of personal self-actualization through serving the growth of the community. As Bishop Desmond Tutu explained, when you serve others, you experience satisfaction that approaches a kind of quiet ecstasy, and this can be contagious.

We can imagine eco-villages like Gaviotas in Colombia, EVI at Ithaca, and Findhorn in Scotland incorporating primal principles more explicitly into their educational programs. We can see them deepening their vision to include the quest and the great cosmic story out of which the questing individual emerges. We can imagine this vision inspiring whole communities to live more politically engaged lives, to travel beyond the boundaries of their villages, acting as leaders and examples — "seed crystals" — for organizing social and cultural movements.

We can imagine that the *ahupua'a* system of old Hawai'i and the spiritual community of Findhorn could inspire both kibbutzniks and Palestinians to become natural collaborators in re-creating a kind of cooperative, sustainable agriculture that enriches the soil, enhances biodiversity, and deepens their spiritual relationship to the living land both love.

We can imagine cities committing more sincerely to the "urban Green revolution" of Jaime Lerner and Richard Register. We can see them instituting the participatory forms of government of Porto Alegre and Belo Horizonte. We can imagine citizens and leaders in these ecologically aware cities collaborating with surrounding organic farmers, eco-villages, and conventional farms to integrate their economies in a more bioregionally sensitive way. We can see city councils fostering urban agriculture by expanding community gardens, encouraging edible landscapes and rooftop gardens, bringing rivers and streams to the surface, and making nature immersion part of everyone's education.

We can imagine populations becoming more aware of the range of possibilities for change and pushing their leaders to follow the model of King Jigme Wangchuck of Bhutan, so that "the good life" is measured not by GDP but by gross national happiness, replacing standards of wealth with sustainable standards of happiness guided by the quest.

We can imagine an organization like the United Nations representing nations inspired by the quest, who recognize the need for coordinated global action while understanding that the quest also requires strengthening the integrity, self-sufficiency, and sustainability of the subsidiary social units — from nation and bioregion down to city, village, and ultimately the ordinary individual.

Finally, we can imagine the great cosmic story of the unfolding universe being taught all over the world, in schools and places of worship, in universities and public festivals as the epic narrative gathering together all our personal, tribal, national, and religious stories. We can imagine this vision emerging from the quest as a kind of numinous revelation, giving us courage and enthusiasm to embrace this unprecedented opportunity for human choice and creativity — for consciously guiding the future of life on earth. For this vision reveals that the dark night of the industrialized soul of humanity can also be the prelude to the early dawning of a new consciousness, a way of being more fully human in harmony with a flourishing earth.

## Our African Adam and Eve

One of the great redeeming contributions of Western science to the creation of a life-loving planetary politics is its discovery of the great story of the unfolding universe. The cosmic story inspires each of us to find and tell our own stories and then take that creative leap back to our common southern African ancestry — the story of our shared Bushman Adam and Eve. It is within this universe story that the first storytelling humans emerge, hunting and gathering in the veldt of southern Africa. As we listen to this story we can recognize the Bushmen as the custodians of our species' birthplace. They remind us that however deeply buried in our urban landscapes we might be, or however far into space we might travel, we remain, in our deepest essence, made by the southern African veldt. We don't all have to dance under the Kalahari stars, but we can give primacy of place in our cosmology to the story of the Bushmen and our shared African ancestors.

Their story is also our story, a singular species treasure, connecting us most directly to that wilderness reality that is the closest face of the miracle of creation from which humanity emerges. When deeply experienced, this story can heal and balance the deformities of religions and ideologies by revealing wilderness as the great natural temple of our primary revelation, the site and inspiration of our first religious practice.

Humanity might well be lost if we lose the troops of wild baboons, the monkey and the meerkat, the prides of free-roaming lions and the great herds of zebra and wildebeest. Every encounter with a wild animal can help remind us of the miracle that we are part of and that makes us human. For the cosmic story tells us that we come to moral consciousness within a body crafted by a natural wild world, on a single ball spinning around in space, orbiting one star — our sun — in a galaxy of two hundred billion stars in a universe of hundreds of billions of galaxies…

This new story is taking us into a metareligious awareness by providing a framework of meaning for all religions and all political ideologies. The more we tell it and understand it, the more extraordinary it becomes, until we find ourselves again and again confronted by radical amazement, and we come to recognize in this experience the core of the sacred — the beauty and truth at the heart of the good life we seek.

EPILOGUE

# A TAO OF POLITICS

The Way that can be named is not the unchanging Way,
The names that can be named are not the unchanging names,
It was from the nameless that the Heavens and the Earth sprang. . . .

In harmony with the Tao,
the sky is clear and spacious,
the earth is solid and full,
all creatures flourish together,
content with the way they are,
endlessly repeating themselves,
endlessly renewed.

When man interferes with the Tao,
the sky becomes filthy,
the earth becomes depleted,
the equilibrium crumbles,
creatures become extinct.

— *Tao Te Ching*

Beauty is truth, truth beauty, that is all
Ye know on earth, and all ye need to know."

— KEATS, *Ode on a Grecian Urn*

## Paradigm Phobia

Today, skepticism is becoming a new fundamentalism. Many academics dogmatically reject the very attempt to grasp the human condition as a whole, and they ridicule even the possibility of developing new paradigms for a more balanced, better way of life. Part of this rejection is driven by fear of the appalling violence associated with ideologically driven social experiments in the past. But another part of this skepticism is unwittingly also ideological, rooted in one-dimensional Cartesian thinking, with its absolute dualisms, rationalist materialism, and the triumph of critique over creativity in intellectual life. This deep-seated skepticism has gained additional support from the groundbreaking work of Thomas Kuhn, which exposed the way in which even the "hardest" of the sciences required constructed frameworks of meaning, or paradigms.

Kuhn used the word *paradigm* broadly in many contexts, rather like I use "big picture" or "meaning narratives" to indicate integrated symbolic structures of meaning that ultimately give us what we want in our engagement with reality.[1] One of Kuhn's great achievements was to show how sociocultural context and intention shape paradigms even in supposedly objective sciences like physics and astronomy. Since such constructions depend in part on the standpoint of the scientist, they can never in principle grasp "reality in itself" — a point dramatically exemplified at the subatomic level by Heisenberg's uncertainty principle and at the cosmological level by the simple fact that we find ourselves in an evolving universe emerging from the deepest mystery. Ultimately, we can never be certain of the lasting truth of a particular paradigm because we lack a *metaparadigm* that somehow stands outside our constructions and tells us what makes a paradigm more or less true. Thus in his own way Kuhn confronted the in-between, recognizing that since reality is constituted between us and the world, research is inherently surprising, confronting the scientist with novelty at each new question.

So if science itself cannot offer certainty about reality, how can we know the human condition with the assurance we need to undertake the ambitious and risky project of its improvement? Many scholars take Kuhn's work as authority for avoiding the attempt to reconstruct political paradigms and for promoting a skepticism so vigorous it becomes a kind of dogmatic relativism. Ironically, despite inadvertently reinforcing this radical relativism, Kuhn also provided an analysis of paradigms that helps us focus on the revolutionary process and think more constructively about a metaparadigm for the evolving truth quest.

Kuhn's concept of paradigms allows us to distinguish between two fundamentally different, but related, modes of cognition in scientific research — normal and revolutionary. Normal science fits the popular image of the laboratory scientist conducting systematic manipulations of relevant variables, accumulating data, and coming up with new insights. This is closer to rule-guided puzzle-solving than those creative breakthroughs associated with the revolutionary achievements of science, like the sun-centered astronomy of Copernicus, the atomic theory of Dalton, the evolutionary biology of Darwin, and the quantum physics of Einstein, Heisenberg, and Bohr. Such revolutionary science establishes new paradigms that provide the framework — the rules and models — that make normal science possible. The process of revolutionary science is more chaotic and creative, since by definition it challenges the established rules and procedures of the dominant paradigm. Once established, the revolutionary paradigm sets up its own rules and regulations for a new tradition of puzzle-solving normal science.

Since no paradigm can ever fit reality perfectly, normal science eventually starts producing unanticipated results that cannot be explained by the ruling paradigm. As these anomalies accumulate, the dominant paradigm loses authority, normal science breaks down, and the discipline enters a crisis. For example, by the sixteenth century, the geocentric Aristotelian Christian cosmology was becoming impossibly unwieldy as it attempted to deal with new observations in the night sky — like the apparently erratic movements of the planets — and to make useful predictions in terms of an earth-centered cosmos. Similarly, at the beginning of the twentieth century, explorations of the structure of the atom produced results that could not be explained by the ruling Newtonian mechanical paradigm. As the existing paradigm is challenged by inexplicable and anomalous observations, the scientific community tends to split. One the one hand is an old guard defending the status quo and discussing the anomalies; and on the other hand are the creative boundary crossers, who propose alternative frameworks of meaning that compete for the allegiance of the community. Eventually, one framework gains ascendancy by providing a more inclusive explanation of the old data and the accumulating anomalies as well as by offering a more productive practice of normal science. The Copernican heliocentric cosmology achieved this for astronomy, as did the new quantum physics of Einstein for the subatomic world, and as did Darwin's evolutionary paradigm for the biological world.

Kuhn remained somewhat baffled by the process of revolutionary science, but he nevertheless made a number of suggestive observations. For example, he noted that the great discoveries often came from mavericks or those located at or beyond the margins of the discipline. Darwin was an amateur naturalist, and Einstein worked as a clerk in a patent office when he began his groundbreaking research. Such individuals tend to be less invested in the established norms of professional practice and less bound to the rules of normal science. Often the outsiders have the benefit of a larger world of experience and are more adept at crossing intellectual boundaries. Revolutionary science also seems more like art or philosophy, since it appears to rely on the freely roaming imagination and inspiration of the searching individual. The process by which new paradigms become established is almost like an emotional conversion experience — rather like Descartes's revelation. This creative process does not follow rules of logical inference from new observations. One suddenly grasps the new vision as a whole gestalt — an "aha!" moment — in which one sees a larger field offering a more inclusive, useful, and ultimately life-enhancing understanding.

As mentioned, Kuhn's insights were used to reinforce the blanket skepticism in political philosophy concerning grand narratives of meaning — or paradigms of political order. The recent history of ideological certainties being used to justify murderous concentrations of power has turned skepticism into a kind of "paradigm phobia," a visceral rejection of large-scale explanations of the world as tools for radical transformation. We saw milder versions of this in the postmodern revisionist attack on the meaning of "Bushmen" and implicitly on the meaning of meaning.

As I have argued throughout, to reject all paradigms in principle is a self-defeating denial of the ubiquity of paradigms that simply makes one vulnerable to the tyranny of the ruling paradigm by default. As Kuhn and others have subsequently shown, as long as there is a semblance of consensus and consistency regarding order in reality, there is a paradigm at work. The less it is recognized and subject to critical scrutiny *and reconstruction*, the greater the possibility that "self-evident truth" will be used to support all sorts of abuse in the service of the good. What is needed is a paradigm for politics that recognizes the necessity of paradigms of the good but somehow also incorporates the discipline by which paradigms are critiqued, reformed, and replaced by newer, truer paradigms — that is, a metaparadigm.

## A Revolutionary Approach to Revolutions

We can now apply Kuhn's analysis to our current political crisis. First of all, we can understand political philosophies as "paradigms of the good life" that give rise to political societies that function according to the rules and regulations established by the ruling paradigm. Liberalism, as discussed in chapter 2, can be seen as precisely such a paradigm, constituting our ruling model of the good life. As Liberalism has globalized, it has become almost invisible and increasingly synonymous with the reality we have to accept. In 1992, Francis Fukuyama celebrated this view from "inside the cave" in his *The End of History and the Last Man*, in which he proclaimed the end of both history and ideology as the world settled on the Liberal formula of free-market economics and constitutional democracy.[2] But the bigger, more reflective picture reveals that an endlessly growing human economy within a declining earth economy is an absurdity.

Liberalism was a human creation to serve specific needs at a particular time and place. As we saw, thinkers like Thomas Hobbes, John Locke, and Adam Smith collectively constructed a more inclusive explanation of the failures of feudalism and the possibilities of transformation. Their work in turn provided the philosophical framework for new institutions for governance and economics, which would give us what we thought we wanted: domination over nature, unlimited wealth, and freedom from tyranny. As I have argued, this paradigm succeeded beyond our wildest dreams in achieving the first two goals, but it has replaced the personalized tyranny of monarchs and dictators with the impersonal tyranny of limited-liability corporations and corrupted market mechanisms. Human intelligence — wisdom, knowledge of the good of the whole — has been sidelined, with catastrophic consequences not simply for our way of life, but for life on earth as such. The anomalies of global industrial society are pushing our paradigm into a state of terminal crisis.

In politics, revolutions are resisted for the same reasons they are in science. Retooling is expensive, and the community sustained by the existing paradigm has a vested interest in preserving the status quo. In the case of a political society, the stakes are ultimate, since we are dealing with a framework for a total way of life, protected by wealthy elites, armed with the power of law, the police force, propaganda, and the army. Revolutionary change in politics is often associated with terrifying violence.

Academic political science tends to be of little help in this situation. It functions like a kind of "normal political science" operating within the market-driven, bureaucratically administered system of rewards and patronage of the university, which is of course shaped by the institutions of Liberalism. Under such conditions, political philosophy (often called "theory") has become a vestigial activity, a specialization *within* academic political science, primarily concerned with interpreting, deconstructing, and critiquing the classical works of the past according to prevailing intellectual fashions. None of this can be really transformative, since without the creation of alternative structures of meaning — the task of an authentically revolutionary political science — critique leaves existing power structures unchallenged by an alternative. The status quo rules by default.

## A Metaparadigm for Politics and a More Balanced State of Existence

This is where the larger evolutionary perspective of big history offers the possibility of a breakthrough in understanding both revolutions and the unique possibilities for our moment. When we look at what the great revolutionary paradigm builders of Western civilization *actually did*, as opposed to what they told us we should do, we can see some patterns roughly equivalent to the practices constituting the truth quest described by the primal complex. Socrates and Plato, Machiavelli, Hobbes, Locke, Rousseau, and Marx were all passionately involved in the troubles of their times. They all responded out of heightened awareness of the human predicament of living in the in-between. They experienced the limitations of the prevailing big picture as a personally felt crisis of order, requiring diagnosis and therapy according to a vision of political health. Their visions tended to be worldviews, big pictures, creative works of synthesis touching on the foundational issues of politics: human nature, the individual, the community, the natural world, government, economics, and epistemology. These symbolic constructions were shaped by the life story and situation of the philosopher, and to some degree by the logic of the dialectic — reflective self-examination and discussion carried out in a spirit of egalitarianism among a virtual, if not an actual, democratic community of similarly motivated philosophers. Finally, they were all concerned, directly or indirectly, with action and saving or transforming their worlds. Here we can see their method reflects the four defining elements of the primal dynamic — individuation, democratic discussion, and integration of knowledge into big pictures that guide action.

This enlarged perspective clarifies the depth dimension of the primal truth quest. It is a method of revolutionary political science that is also the core of a new politics; or to put it the other way around, it is a model of political order that is also a way of searching for order. The primal political complex inserts into the heart of practical democratic politics the revolutionary discipline previously reserved for the creative geniuses of classical political philosophy. Using the language of paradigms, we can understand the primal mandala as a paradigm for a radically democratic politics that has at its center the practice of political paradigm deconstruction and reconstruction. In this sense, it could also be regarded as that elusive metaparadigm for politics that constitutes a revolution in our understanding of revolutions.[3]

The reference to such a metaparadigm would help lift competing ideologies to the level of discourse of the primal quest, where the four quadrants of the mandala — self-knowledge, face-to-face discussion, democratic relationships, and the ongoing construction of the big picture — would all be mobilized in decision making. It would constitute a reflective leap that would be both a radical novelty and the recovery of the core of something very ancient. It would establish as the mainspring of political action an ongoing process of psychological, intellectual, and spiritual growth in the soul of the questing individual in community. This would help create a culture in which the community regularly pursues the big questions in personal and political life and is thus more capable of responding to change without waiting for the system to crash. Such a model embodies the ancient Socratic wisdom that the never-ending search for the best way to live is *itself* the *summum bonum*, the core practice of the good life we seek.

Like a spinning gyroscope, the primal dynamic keeps our thinking and our actions moving around the essentials of what it means to be a conscious, questing human at this extraordinarily decisive moment on our marvelous evolving planet. There can be no end to history, or the quest, as long as there is more life to be lived, thought about, and understood. The mandala offers a model for political transformation without violence, since it works continually to challenge the lure of power and privilege with love for the beauty of the path with a heart — the pursuit of the truth quest — a *tao of politics.*

APPENDIX

# FUTURE PRIMAL TOOLKIT

This toolkit offers a few practical applications of the mandala dynamics of *Future Primal* to everyday life. Since the vision of *Future Primal* goes to the roots of the human condition, practical applications can be multiplied endlessly as you reflect on the implications for your own life.

## Cross and Re-cross the Boundary between Wilderness and Civilization

The first fact of primal wisdom is that in order to evaluate our human existence we have to look at it, periodically, from the other side, from our animal or wild nature. We have to cross and re-cross the boundary between wilderness and civilization. This is the eternal primal return, the foundation of the search for political order — the search for the good life. At the same time, boundary crossing *helps constitute this order* by connecting us to others, to nature, and to the cosmos. It deepens each quadrant of the mandala by connecting it to both wilderness and civilization. The logic of balancing opposites also promotes the push-pull relationship among the primal values. Cultivating boundary crossing as part of the quest helps keep the balance between opposites — for example, embracing a growing planetary consciousness while promoting localized, sustainable, self-sufficient, democratic political economies. Very generally, we could say the overarching political imperative is to do some of what we are doing now, *but in balance with its opposite*: balance globalization with localization; centralization with decentralization; creation of the new with conservation of the ancient; a democracy of numbers with an aristocracy of wisdom (determined, paradoxically, by dedication to the *democratic* discipline of the mandala), and so on. Our current growing big picture concerning the best way to live guides us in weighting the balance. Here are six boundary-crossing practices that can help you encounter, integrate, and balance opposites in your daily life:

1. **Live in the primate body.** Walking and running outdoors; swimming in oceans, rivers, and lakes; practicing yoga, lifting weights, and all types of bodywork: these are all opportunities to tune our minds and actions to the fact that the template for the human body — the breath, the ever-pumping heart and blood vessels, our mood-altering hormones — was honed hunting and gathering on an African savanna. Benefits can be immediate. For example, researchers have found that thirty minutes of brisk walking three times per week is as effective at alleviating depression after four months as the antidepressant Zoloft, and it is *considerably more effective* than Zoloft after six months. Exercise changes the brain chemistry by increasing dopamine and serotonin activity. This happens no matter where we exercise, but adding the sensory cues of nature dramatically enhances the effect. Even five minutes of such "green therapy" has been shown to have a measurable impact on mood elevation.
2. **Practice sunrise and sunset meditations.** As Brian Thomas Swimme points out, the rising and setting sun offers potent opportunities for experiencing one's place in a wilderness cosmos. At day's end, watch the western horizon and focus attention on the feeling of the earth rolling back on its axis as it comes up to cover the setting sun. Conversely, face east at sunrise and feel the earth rolling forward as the horizon drops to expose the morning sun. As you watch the sun appear or disappear, imagine the blazing immensity of the nuclear fusion reaction that is the solar furnace. Turn attention to the rotating

earth beneath your feet, fixed firmly by gravity. Picture the earth spinning slowly on a tilted axis in relation to the sun, which it orbits once a year, producing the cycle of the seasons.

3. **Develop summer and winter solstice rituals.** The shortest and longest days of the year, midsummer and midwinter, are opportunities for remembering that the seasons are determined by the tilt of the earth in conjunction with its orbit around the sun. During the winter solstice, try to feel the tilt of the earth leaning away from the sun; during the longest, laziest summer afternoon of the year, imagine the earth leaning toward the sun. Imagine the warming rays — photons traveling at the speed of light, which take almost ten minutes to reach your skin — activating photosynthesis in all green living things, fusing water and carbon dioxide into simple sugars. The sugars then recombine into starches and cellulose — the substance of our fields and forests — the food on which the rest of life flourishes.

   Remember the power of circular motion — the fact that the spring sprouting and the fall harvests are triggered by the patterns of the heavenly bodies spinning circles within circles. Engage in simple celebrations when eating the first of the local seasonal fruits and vegetables, as in the Jewish festival of Succoth; these can remind us of our cosmic connections. On the day of the solstice, mark the point at which the sun rises and sets on the horizon, noting that the direction will be reversed the next day. Remember that the seasons form pairs of opposites — summer-winter, autumn-spring — which unite in the earth's annual circle around the sun — another whole symbolized by the four quadrants of the mandala. Ritual connection with cosmic realities helps mitigate ego isolation and fear, ennobling human action by connecting us to the whole evolutionary miracle.

4. **Practice a night-sky meditation.** On a clear warm night, lie on the ground away from suburb or city lights. Use GPS-guided star maps (available on smartphones) to distinguish stars and planets and their relative distances from us. Stare up at the sky and remember the gentle twinkling pinpricks are blazing nuclear furnaces, each more or less comparable to our sun, each more or less equivalent to hundreds of millions of continuously exploding hydrogen bombs. Realize that from the perspective of a point opposite us on earth, we are not only looking up but also *looking down into an unfathomable*

*void below us*, our backs literally pinned by gravity to the earth beneath us. We can use our taste for science fiction to imagine gravity letting go as we hurtle facedown into the inky blackness, rushing toward those unimaginably distant suns and galaxies.

5. **Eat local and organic; grow your own; grow cooperatively.** On the individual level, few things attune you more to the earth, its seasons, and your own body than growing and eating your own food. Growing food in backyards, community gardens, roof gardens, city waste lots, and window boxes can foster the most basic form of political and economic autonomy. On the global level, few things would shift the political economy of industrial society more quickly and more profoundly than a mass movement to eat locally grown organic food. This could happen relatively quickly. During World War II, Eleanor Roosevelt's backyard "victory gardens" eventually mobilized some twenty million Americans to produce 40 percent of the vegetables consumed nationally.

   Organic local food systems use dramatically less energy and oil for transport and eliminate entirely the need for synthetic pesticides and fertilizers. Soil erosion and watershed and waterway contamination would be ameliorated. Food would be less contaminated, fresher, and healthier. More people would be occupied doing interesting and creative physical work, out-of-doors in the natural world. The growth of local farms, community gardens, roof gardens, and "edible landscapes" of fruit trees and vegetables would mitigate urban sprawl, help beautify cities, and calm their populations. The greening of cities would reduce the cost of air-conditioning and damage from rainwater runoff. Localizing food production would increase the food sovereignty of communities and bioregions and reduce dependence on centralized corporate and government bureaucracies. Food sovereignty is the ultimate foundation for political autonomy. Follow the shamanic context of the mandala and the example of indigenous societies in resacralizing food production as a mode of experiencing directly the Great Mystery of Creation.

6. **Pursue related political action.** Seek out and defend wild places, especially those near cities, as natural temples and places of healing. For instance, campaign and educate for dark sky cities and suburbs. Encourage city planners to follow the example of Flagstaff, Arizona,

which became the first dark sky city. What are the ecological and environmental issues where you live?

## Treat Each Quadrant of the Mandala as a Practice

Each quadrant of the mandala describes both a value or ideal and a practice. Each practice helps constitute the quest and contribute to a balanced way of life. Try to cultivate all four in a dynamic balance. Each practice can be cultivated in a myriad of ways:

1. **The whole person — individuation.** Learn and express your story. Deepen self-awareness by seeking opposite experiences. The scholar should seek the physical and earthly; the farm worker, the ashram and library. Think of your life as a journey around the medicine wheel from birth to death. What can you learn? What do you have to share, to teach? What can you leave for the next generation? Deepen reflection with inner practices — meditation, prayer, and the shamanic technologies for expanding consciousness.

   Practice dreamwork: Pay attention to nightly dreams, when the conscious ego lets go and the larger psyche pushes up into the dreamworld images, stories, and metaphors, teasing the waking ego into greater awareness of what has yet to be integrated in the interests of growth and wholeness. Dreams are a manifestation of the psyche's natural impulse to heal through growth toward wholeness. Just as when we cut our finger, the skin automatically starts a process of self-healing and making whole, so the larger psyche pushes into consciousness what is struggling to be recognized and integrated in the interests of growth and health. We can invite vivid dreams by consciously programming our unconscious mind as we go to bed. Very simply, ask for dreams as you prepare to shift from the work and worry of daily wakefulness to sleep. Keep a dream journal. Immediately on waking, write down the dream images and stories. Free-associate as you write, looking for emotional resonance (not necessarily linear, logical connection) with troubling aspects of your waking life. Work with a dream analyst, trusted friend, or dream group to help tease out what our watchful, wakeful ego resists.

2. **Face-to-face discussion.** This is relevant to any relationship or small group situation — classroom, neighborhood board, NGO, or any social situation where difficult decisions have to be made, conflicts resolved, or a shared understanding arrived at. Use stories to frame the issues and introduce each point of view. Begin with personal introductions — where you come from; what brings you to the issue, topic, or problem; what you hope to get out of the transaction. This starts the process of transforming a group of strangers into a community of cooperative, caring individuals. Make intentions explicit. Stories within stories remind all participants that no one has the whole truth; we all benefit by integrating multiple perspectives. Use the face-to-face talking circle to emphasize that everyone makes a different contribution to a shared reality. When faced with disagreement and conflict, move back and forth between imaginative empathy, expressing one's own truth, and cooperatively constructing a shared story. Acknowledge power differentials — such as between teacher and student, facilitator and group, employer and employee — and then work toward sharing responsibility for and the benefits of a successful outcome.
3. **Direct democracy and cooperative community life.** Set up and support cooperative, community-based organizations of caring and sharing. Set up bartering and time-trading relations with friends and neighbors. Avoid money transactions whenever possible. Learn useful skills that enhance autonomy and can be traded for services — car and computer repair, gardening, web design, editing, and so on. Promote cooperative networks in the workplace, classroom, neighborhood, and all other venues of civil society. Use global communication and information networks to inform and empower local action.
4. **The big picture.** Construct and keep reconstructing the bigger picture, the larger story. Keep relearning and retelling the big story. Human and earth communities are held together by stories of origin, identity, and destiny. Remember that "without a vision the people perish." Start with your own story. Follow the imperative of

the truth quest to grow, engage opposites, listen, empathize, express and expound, and keep integrating new knowledge into a growing picture of an evolving humanity within an evolving cosmos. Enjoy the journey — the quest — as the view keeps getting bigger, more complex, more detailed.

## Pursue the Truth Quest

The following practices constitute the truth quest at the center of the mandala. They emerge from the Socratic search and come to constitute the core of primal politics. We can regard them as a sort of *neoprimal Socratic method* — the core of a pedagogy and an epistemology in which participants both teach and learn from others in the back-and-forth dialectic of face-to-face discussion.* The face-to-face group situation constitutes the nexus of the truth quest, where the process of the search transforms the participating individuals into a primal political community. The value of all values, the ultimate goal, is the ongoing quest itself — the *search* for knowledge by which to live — the good life.

1. **Reflect on your intention.** Intention determines outcome. Follow your heart. Intention includes the Socratic-Platonic truth quest; the search for meaning and value; emerging from Plato's cave and then returning; seeking a bigger picture; gaining self-knowledge or, in Socratic terms, perfection of the soul; making ethical and moral choices; and pursuing Plato's "royal art" of weaving all the other arts and departments of knowledge into an *open-ended* picture of a good and just society.
2. **Question.** Question power. Question accepted authority and the dominant big picture. Question your own assumptions and beliefs to test their truth. This is the beginning of *critical* and *analytical* thinking. It is also the foundation of a democratic culture. Admitting

* For applying the truth quest in the university classroom, see my "Personal Empowerment" in Theodore L. Becker and Richard Cauto, *Teaching Democracy by Being Democratic* (Westport, CT: Praeger, 1996).

ignorance is a precondition for authentic discussion and wisdom. Intellectual and spiritual growth require changing one's mind. Refuse to let fear restrict your questioning.

3. **Experience.** Expand experience. *Direct experience* is full-bodied knowledge with an emotional content. It is distinguished by degree from *vicarious*, secondhand, or culturally mediated experience. Libraries, the Internet, film, and the arts in general can all be powerful ways of expanding and interpreting direct experience of life. Think about your passions — strong positive and negative emotions; what you fear, hate, love, and so on. Ultimately, knowledge only matters if it has some emotional resonance for us. Our lives are our primary texts in the search for the good life. Crossing boundaries, exploring opposites, and reversing roles can accelerate expanding experience. Refuse to let fear automatically restrict experience; face fear thoughtfully, guided by the big picture, especially with high-risk experiences such as joining an army, skydiving, drug taking, and so on. Experience should feed and expand life, not injure or end it.
4. **Think.** Look within. Balance fact gathering with imagination. Reflect, contemplate, meditate, fantasize. Let questioning and critique be guided by the playful working of the imagination, which can reorganize remembered experiences and make new connections, revealing new possibilities, enhancing creativity, and expanding choice. Remember Einstein's dictum: "Imagination is more important than knowledge." Refuse to let fear crush imagination.
5. **Express.** Speak out. Philosophy includes the art of putting words to experience. The arts — writing, painting, dance, music, even public speaking — preserve individual and collective experience for the public work of understanding and creating a better way of life. Giving others the benefit of your best understanding of the moment is a condition of your learning from them, and vice versa. One way to really know a subject is to try to teach it. Talk truth to power with love and art. Don't let fear shut you up.
6. **Argue, discuss.** Discussion is the heart of the Socratic arts of philosophy and politics. Argument can stimulate all aspects of the Socratic method: reflecting on intention, questioning, expanding experience, thinking, expressing, and integrating. Discussion expands experience through *active listening* — repeating what you have understood

to the satisfaction of the one who disagrees with you. Discussion confronts your own unique and best understanding of the moment with that of others who experience the world differently. Use both imagination and compassion in trying to put yourself in the situation of those who disagree with you. Deep discussion is the process of collectively and cooperatively creating an ongoing vision of the good life. Socratic discussion at its highest can become the "royal art," fusing the eros of truth seeking with the joy of creating a trusting, caring community. Don't let fear stop you from changing your mind.

7. **Integrate knowledge into an ongoing big picture.** Make connections. Synthesize. The logic of argument — the *dialectic* — drives thinking to connect the truth of *thesis* and *antithesis* into the larger truth of *synthesis*. This constructive and creative activity is a necessary complement to the *deconstructive*, *analytical*, and *critical* activity initiated by questioning. It is a never-ending process connecting isolated pieces of experience, thoughts, and propositions to a growing and more consistent *big picture* or story — ultimately, a cosmic creation story. Be explicit about your current big picture in evaluating the meaning and worth of individual statements, actions, policies, and so on. Keep revising your big picture in light of new thought, new experience, and more living.
8. **Question the current big picture.** Go back to item 1 and start over. Reexamine intention; question; experience; think; express...and so on, repeating endlessly. Keep learning, teaching, and growing. Most importantly, enjoy the journey!

# ACKNOWLEDGMENTS

It took a tribe to write this book. The vision grew out of an extended process of "searching with my life," and so virtually all the people who constitute my community contributed something uniquely valuable to the work. In a surprising and gratifying way, the process of writing came to embody the primal political dynamic I was describing. Adequately thanking each person would take another chapter.

The support of Alan Doran has been critical. Alan shared my early idealism and joined me as brother on the quest many years ago. Decades later, he reappeared, spent several days on my lanai in Hawai'i reading the manuscript, saw its potential, and revived my enthusiasm. His unfailingly honest and caring feedback guided and inspired the development of the project. I am also enormously grateful to the Doran Foundation for providing essential financial support, without which there might well have been no book.

Gene Awakuni, the chancellor of the University of Hawai'i–West O'ahu played a vital role by appreciating the value of the book and enthusiastically supporting my work. No scholar could have wished for more visionary, creative, and inspiring leadership. It is hard to imagine how the book could have been written without his steadfast support.

The present form and scope of the book owe much to Brian Thomas Swimme. Early in the writing process, when I first heard him tell the great cosmic story with his unique mix of poetry, passion, and scientific precision, I realized I had found the voice and the vision to give larger meaning to my work. Several years ago he read drafts of the manuscript and immediately grasped the deepest dimensions of what I was struggling to express. His example and his enthusiasm for the project gave me the confidence I needed to say what I had to say directly and honestly. I feel truly blessed by our meeting.

Manfred Henningsen is one of the most erudite people I know and one of the rare Socratic scholars in academia. After I became disillusioned with graduate study, he guided me back into political philosophy by encouraging me to write from the truth of my experience. Subsequently he has read and critiqued almost everything I have written. His dinner parties were modern-day Socratic symposia, providing the core of an intellectual life that nourished my writing.

No one has spent more time working on the manuscript than my good friend and fellow philosopher Andy Hoffman. More than twenty years ago he read the first formulation of these ideas in my PhD dissertation and encouraged me to turn it into a book. He has since provided a crucial quadrant of the truth quest — the truly honest friend who holds nothing back in the interest of growth. Our frank and passionate discussions about every aspect of this work — almost every sentence — were consummate examples of the Socratic dialectic. They turned what could have been an excruciatingly lonely process into joyful collaboration.

My thanks to Twi (/Ui) Toma, my guide and translator in Nyae Nyae, Bushmanland, who understood my sincerity and took me to some of the traditional hunters and healers and encouraged them to share their knowledge with me. Oom Jan van der Westhuizen was my Khomani Bushman guide and a living example of a wise leader in touch with the old ways. His help was invaluable. My thanks also go to the anthropologists and archaeologists who helped guide me in new territory: Bion Griffin, Polly Weissner, David Lewis-Williams, and, more recently, Sven Ouzman.

Craig and Damon Foster are living examples of the future primal synthesis I advocate. They have pioneered a shamanic style of filmmaking that helps open souls and change minds. I am enormously indebted to them for sharing with me the profound knowledge they gleaned in some of the wildest regions of Africa and through their years of working with the last surviving Bushman hunter-gatherers. Special thanks go to them for generously allowing me to use their pictures in this book and for providing the cover image.

My thinking was also inspired and guided by the work on the land and in the Hawaiian community of Eric Enos, Poka Laenui, Puanani Burgess, Mahealani and Glen Davis, the brothers Charlie and Paul Reppun, and Gary and Kukui Maunakea-Forth. Jeff Dunn introduced me to Hawaiian wilderness as a spiritual resource and showed me another way forward as a nature-mystic-artist and modern-day hunter-gatherer.

Neil Abercrombie and Nancie Caraway, part of my *hanai* (adopted) family in Hawai'i, have been a source of unfailing encouragement in this work. My special thanks go to Neil for his loyalty, his belief in me, and his bold and generous support for this project. Nancie has been like a sister to me over the years. She also has my heartfelt gratitude for her stimulating intellectual engagement and her gift of attracting good-hearted people and turning them into a loving community of friends — part of the tribe.

My guide and mentor in the world of the soul, Dr. Ramon Lopez-Reyes, read pieces of the manuscript and counseled me during troubled times. His capacity to understand and integrate an astonishing variety of human experiences into loving wisdom has helped me find and live my own truth.

Kathy Ferguson gave me a rare and inspiring example of creative, productive scholarship that helped keep me constructively engaged with the political science profession. Many pieces of writing benefited from her astute editorial eye. Much gratitude goes to Gilli Ashkenazi, my Israeli brother in Hawai'i, who has always been there watching my back, arguing incessantly about everything, and helping keep me honest. I thank both of them for making their home open to me at all times.

Markus Faigle and Jeannette Koijane have also provided a haven for regular debriefing, advice, and encouragement over home-cooked meals. My special thanks to Markus for joining me at the last minute on the second journey into the Kalahari. I have been very fortunate to have his generous assistance with innumerable aspects of the project, from strategy and logistics to photography and graphics.

Lavinia Currier helped decisively by offering warm friendship, editing, and advice. In boldly pursuing her vision, so closely related to my own, she inspired me to follow mine; in living so much of what I advocate with such artistry, she gives me hope for the possibilities of transformation.

Karen Bouris provided a vital link in a chain of synchronicities leading to publication. When I had no clue how to find a publisher, she very kindly read the manuscript, saw its worth, and passed it on to her colleague John Loudon, who then became my literary agent. A big thank-you to John for finding me the right publisher — New World Library, a press that manages to flourish in the marketplace while being guided by a vision of the good of all.

I am extremely grateful to my editor, Jason Gardner, for his sensitivity to the creative process, his enormous patience, and his hard work. Jason deftly guided me through the many stages of editing to make this an incomparably better book. I owe another debt of gratitude to my copy editor, Jeff Campbell. He performed heroically, quickly reading through the whole manuscript, grasping the many threads of narrative, and skillfully reweaving them into a more coherent whole. Thanks to the staff at New World Library — particularly Jonathan Wichmann, Kristen Cashman, Tracy Cunningham, Tona Pearce Myers, and Monique Muhlenkamp — for their dedication and thoroughness.

Cheryl Genet of the Orion Institute provided a welcoming venue for expressing some of the key ideas in the book through the Evolutionary Epic Conference and the Collins Foundation Press. My thanks go to Paul Caringella and Wayne Cristaudo, who made it possible for me to present my ideas to a gathering of scholars at the University of Hong Kong. The faculty at the California Institute of Integral Studies — Rick Tarnas, Sean Kelly, David Ulansey, and Eric Weiss — provided stimulating constructive feedback on an early draft. Thomas Swimme's perceptive comments on my writing cheered me enormously.

Over the years many have contributed ideas, critical feedback, inspiring examples, heartfelt encouragement, and help with editing. These include Chris Aikin, Ted Becker, Richard Castillo, Stuart Coleman, Clarence Dingliwize, Sue Doran, Nanette Flemming, John Goss, Pat Johnston, Kapiolani Kealohalaulii, Lizelle Kleinhans, Christine and Michael Le, Sue Martin, Laureen McCoy, Joe Mobley, Paula Rayman, Jen Rodwell, Catherine Sanja, Cindy Silbert, Christa Slayton, Mike Sukhov, and Amber Volpe. Bob Cahill gave me an unparalleled example of intellectual integrity and taught me the power of teaching through listening. My friend Chris Conybeare introduced me to the world of documentary film production and helped me write for a larger audience. Rob Kay provided valued companionship on mountain walks and good counsel during the final stages of writing.

Cyril Ruthenberg did last-minute, skillful graphic work on the mandala. Bryan Sanders helped with artistry and images and with his magical ability to connect me with key people and resources at critical times. Shanah Trevenna's energy and leadership in creating a sustainable Hawai'i already gives me nostalgia for the future. Patrice Nagley provided me with the perfect writing environment framed by noble views of *mauka* and *makai*.

In Israel, my friends, my kibbutz family Collins, and my extended families Rabinowitz, Fisher, and Herman gave me the vital, healing experience of belonging. My Israeli "sister" Tutla Freund read and commented on sections of the manuscript and helped me clarify my deep feelings for the country. Thanks to my comrades-in-arms who provided the companionship I needed to learn from the extreme experiences we shared. Particular thanks go to Adrian Barnes, who became like a brother and taught me much about friendship and courage. Also my gratitude goes to Nord (Pikie) Lange, another brother-in-arms who volunteered with me from South Africa. Many thanks to my Arab colleague Ibrahim Aoude, who made it possible for me to really hear the voice of the Palestinians.

I am forever grateful to my family and friends in South Africa; Odette and Richard Mendelsohn provided me with a loving home away from home and generously shared their invaluable, expert insights into the country. Ian and Hilary Meyer and Chuck and Stephanie Volpe all welcomed me as family and inspired me with their examples of how to flourish in the new South Africa. Lez Volpe played a special role as another brother on the quest and helped me reconnect to Africa more deeply. Lez took the lead in starting to make another dream come true — turning this book into a film. His life ended suddenly, too soon. I miss him greatly.

Vicki Nielsen was a loving friend who helped organize the first journey around South Africa, took some of the photographs, and shared some of my most beautiful experiences of wilderness.

The Earhart Foundation, the Sacharuna Foundation, the University of Hawai'i Foundation, and the Hawai'i Council for the Humanities all provided essential financial support to make this work possible. Ian Player sponsored my participation in the Wilderness Leadership School and gave me the inspiring example of his leadership in wilderness conservation.

I am grateful to my dedicated and hardworking colleagues at the University of Hawai'i–West O'ahu, who have continued to support and encourage me in a project that took time and energy away from other tasks. My thanks also go to my students, who never fail to inspire me with their determination to apply their learning to making the world a better place.

Last but not least, I have a huge debt of gratitude to my own family. The birth of my daughter, Danielle, was the most significant event in my life. In presenting me with the challenge of becoming a loving father, she taught me some profound primal truths. My late father, Ron; my mother, Ruth; my sister, Charmaine; my nephew, Neil; and my niece, Nina; all gave me essential unconditional love and support. This book is also for them.

# ENDNOTES

## Introduction

1 Anthony D. Barnosky et al., "Approaching a State Shift in Earth's Biosphere," *Nature* 486 (June 7, 2012): 52–58, doi:10.1038/nature11018. For the term *Anthropocene*, see W. Steffen et al., "The Anthropocene: From Global Change to Planetary Stewardship," *AMBIO* 40, Royal Swedish Academy of Sciences (2011): 739–61.

2 Evolutionary biologist E. O. Wilson estimates that we are eliminating twenty-four thousand species of living organisms from the face of the earth every year — over seventy species a day. Edward O. Wilson, *The Diversity of Life* (New York: Norton, 1992), 280. See also E. O. Wilson, *The Creation: An Appeal to Save Life on Earth* (New York: Norton, 2006), 5. A recent report in the *Sunday Guardian* supports Wilson's gloomy estimates: Juliette Jowit, "Humans Driving Extinction Faster Than Species Can Evolve," *Sunday Guardian*, March 7, 2010, http://www.guardian.co.uk/environment/2010/mar/07/extinction-species-evolve.

3 William van Dusen Wishard, "Sleepwalking through the Apocalypse: The 9/11 Memorial Address," sponsored by the C. G. Jung Institute, Santa Fe, New Mexico, September 11, 2003.

4 Richard Tarnas, *The Passion of the Western Mind: Understanding the Ideas That Have Shaped Our World View* (New York: Ballantine, 1991), 421.

5 Eric Voegelin, "Immortality: Experience and Symbol," in *The Collected Works of Eric Voegelin*, vol. 12, *Published Essays 1966–1985* (Baton Rouge: Louisiana State University Press, 1990), 55.

6 The term *big history* was first used by David Christian in 1989, somewhat jestingly, to describe a history course beginning with the Big Bang. Since then the discipline has spread slowly, due to the rather obvious difficulties of finding it a home in the modern university. A number of United States colleges teach interdisciplinary courses in big history, and now Fred Spier has been appointed to the first university chair in big

history, at the University of Amsterdam. See Cynthia Stokes Brown, "Why Aren't More People Teaching Big History?," in *The Evolutionary Epic: Science's Story and Humanity's Response*, eds. Cheryl Genet et al. (Santa Margarita, CA: Collins Foundation Press, 2009). See also Cynthia Stokes Brown, *Big History: From the Big Bang to the Present* (New York: New Press, 2007); David Christian, *Maps of Time: An Introduction to Big History* (Berkeley: University of California Press, 2004); and Fred Spier, *The Structure of Big History: From the Big Bang until Today* (Amsterdam: Amsterdam University Press, 1994).

7 Peter Russell, *White Hole in Time* (San Francisco: Harper & Row, 1992), 7–10.

8 This acceleration in the rate of transformation is due to the fact that each evolutionary novelty is not simply adding to the sum of past novelties but "complexifies" the relations between preexisting elements of the system and thus amplifies changes to the overall complexity of the system. This tends to provoke the emergence of further novelty, setting up a positive feedback loop. As complexity reaches the level of human self-awareness, as in industrial civilization, and electronic communication weaves a web around the planet of ever "complexifying" layers of information, so the feedback loop accelerates exponentially. Russell points out that if we try to plot the rate of change (related to increasing information and complexity) over time, the graph is a curve that gets steeper and steeper until it approaches the vertical.

9 These are speculative reconstructions based on the archaeological evidence and comparative mythology. The two archaeologists who have done the most work in this area are Marija Gimbutas and James Mellart. Mellart did extensive excavations at Catal Hayuk, and Gimbutas worked on central European Neolithic sites. Some of the evidence for their goddess thesis has been challenged as fraudulent, yet evidence continues to accumulate that supports their theories. Their work was popularized by Riane Eisler in *The Chalice and the Blade: Our History, Our Future* (New York: Harper Collins, 1988). See also Karen Vogel, "Female Shamanism, Goddess Cultures and Psychedelics," *Revision* 25, no. 3 (1998). The preponderance of the evidence supports the notion that early Neolithic civilizations were more egalitarian and more peaceful than the pastoralist warrior nomads and subsequent classical civilizations. This is also congruent with cultural studies in comparative mythology. See, for example, Erich Neumann, *The Great Mother: An Analysis of an Archetype*, Bollingen Series (Princeton, NJ: Princeton University Press, 1974).

10 See R. J. Rummel, *Death by Government* (New Brunswick, NJ: Transaction Publishers, 1994). For updated figures, see Rummel's website, http://www.hawaii.edu/powerkills/20TH.HTM.

## Chapter 1. The Truth Quest

1 The Cape Floral Kingdom, four-fifths of which is *fynbos*, hosts 8,600 plant species, 5,800 of which are endemic, with new species being continually discovered. By comparison, the British Isles are three and a half times larger and have only 1,500 plant species, fewer than 20 of which are endemic. Richard Cowling and David Richardson, *Fynbos: South Africa's Unique Floral Kingdom* (Vlaeburg, South Africa: Fernwood Press, 1998), 7. This biome now seems to be threatened by global warming–induced drought.

2 John Locke, *Two Treatises on Government*, ed. Peter Laslett (New York: Mentor, 1698/1963), 330; Second Treatise, section 42, line 20.

3 John Marshall, *A Kalahari Family, Part 5, Death by Myth* (Watertown, MA: Documentary Education Resources, 2002). I return to the remarkable story of the Marshall family in chapter 6, "Lost Worlds."

4 Mircea Eliade, *Shamanism: Archaic Techniques of Ecstasy* (Princeton, NJ: Princeton University Press, 1964).

## Chapter 2. Abandonment of the Quest — A Path with No Heart

1 Europeans tend to be more ideologically self-conscious than Americans, since Liberalism developed in direct reaction to European feudal institutions and norms. For example, the feudal notion of noblesse oblige expressed the moral obligation of the aristocracy to the commoner; more generally, it expressed the principle that those with wealth and power had a responsibility to those less well-off. This made European society more open to socialist attempts to give government a larger role in redistributing wealth and privilege. Consequently, almost all western European nations have a viable social democratic tradition and all tend to have stronger civil societies. The landmark work on the foundations of American political philosophy is Louis Hartz, *The Liberal Tradition in America: An Interpretation of American Political Thought since the Revolution* (New York: Harcourt, Brace, and Jovanovich, 1955).

2 Niall Ferguson, *Civilization: The Six Killer Apps of Western Power* (London: Penguin Books, 2011), 12, 13.

3 Ibid., 5.

4 Ibid., 323.

5 Ibid., 324.

6 See David Stannard's illuminating comparison of late medieval Europe and precontact Hawai'i, *Before the Horror: The Population of Hawai'i on the Eve of Western Contact* (Honolulu: University of Hawai'i Press, 1989), 41–42.

7 Henri Pirenne, *Economic and Social History of Medieval Europe* (New York: Harcourt, Brace, and Jovanovich, 1937), 27.

8 There are two classic studies on the connection between the Protestant Reformation and the rise of capitalism: Max Weber, *The Protestant Ethic and the Spirit of Capitalism: The Relationships between Religion and the Economic and Social Life in Modern Culture* (New York: Charles Scribner's Sons, 1958), and R. H. Tawney, *Religion and the Rise of Capitalism: A Historical Study* (New York: New American Library, 1922).

9 John Locke, *Two Treatises on Government*, ed. Peter Laslett (New York: Mentor, 1698/1963), 330; Second Treatise, section 28, line 24.

10 Even in the 1970s the liberal (with a small *l*) historians Henry Steel Commager and Alan Nevins could write without a trace of self-consciousness, "Here was a great shaggy continent... filled with wild beasts and peopled by a warlike, cruel, and treacherous people still in the Stone Age of culture.... They were ordinarily no match for well-accoutered and vigilant bodies of whites. For that matter, they had shown little capacity to subdue nature, and, as they lived mainly by hunting and fishing, their resources were precarious." Alan Nevins and Henry Steel Commager, *A Pocket History of the United States* (New York: Washington Square Press Publication, 1981), 2, 4.

11 Dee Brown, *Bury My Heart at Wounded Knee: An Indian History of the American West* (New York: Henry Holt, 1970).

12 John Niehardt, *Black Elk Speaks: Being the Life Story of a Holy Man of the Oglala* (New York: Simon & Schuster, 1975), 181.

13 John Locke, *An Essay Concerning Human Understanding*, ed. A. D. Woozely (New York: New American Library, 1690/1964), 58. Locke balanced Descartes's focus on mathematics as the model for knowledge with an emphasis on observation and experiment.

14 In his *Two Great Systems*, Galileo declared his "boundless admiration" for men like Aristarchus and Copernicus, who could allow "reason," that is, mathematics, "to… commit such a rape on their senses" by letting geometry persuade them that the massive, solid, immovable earth actually spins through space orbiting the sun. Galileo Galilei, *Two Great Systems*, quoted in E. A. Burtt, *The Metaphysical Foundation of Modern Science* (New York: Doubleday, 1954), 79.

15 Here is the full quote by Galileo: "Philosophy is written in that great book which ever lies before our eyes — I mean the universe — but we cannot understand it if we do not first learn the language and grasp the symbols in which it is written. This book is written in the mathematical language, and the symbols are triangles, circles and other geometrical figures without whose help it is impossible to comprehend a single word of it; without which one wanders in vain through a dark labyrinth." From *Opere complete di Galileo Galilei*, 1842, quoted in Burtt, *The Metaphysical Foundation*, 75.

16 Descartes, *Principle Part I*, quoted in Burtt, *The Metaphysical Foundation*, 120.

17 The microscope was developed in 1590, the thermometer in 1592, the pendulum clock in 1592, and the telescope in 1609.

18 René Descartes, *Discourse on the Method of Rightly Conducting One's Reason and Seeking Truth in the Sciences*, trans. Laurence J. Lafleur (New York: Bobbs-Merrill, 1960), 4:43.

19 The original has been lost, but fragments were copied by Liebnitz. I have relied on quotes from Jacques Maritain, *The Dream of Descartes: Together with Some Other Essays*, trans. Mabelle L. Andison (New York: Philosophical Library, 1944). Descartes also refers to the vision in his *Discourse on the Method*.

20 Descartes, *Discourse on the Method*, 7–8.

21 Examples quoted from Bill McKibben, *Enough: Staying Human in an Engineered Age* (New York: Henry Holt, 2003).

22 Ibid., 203.

23 Ibid., 203, 204.

24 William Irwin Thompson, *Self and Society: Studies in the Evolution of Culture* (Charlottesville, VA: Imprint Academic, 2004), 54.

25 For an illuminating discussion on this principle in Socrates and Plato, see Max Horkheimer, "The Social Function of Philosophy," in *Critical Theory: Selected Essays* (New York: Seabury Press, 1972), 253–72.

26 John Locke, *Two Treatises of Government*, ed. Peter Laslett (New York: New American Library, 1688/1965), 395. Some interpreters of Locke, like William Ebenstein, stress the inclusive nature of the definition of *property* in the quote below. However, in the context of a rapidly growing global market economy, the most tangible and consequential expression of property became material wealth:

> If Man in the State of Nature be so free, as has been said; If he be absolute Lord of his own Person and Possessions, equal to the greatest, and subject to no Body, why will he part with his Freedom?… To which 'tis obvious to Answer, that though in the state of Nature he hath such a right yet the Enjoyment of it is very uncertain, and constantly exposed to the Invasion of others. For all being Kings as much as he, every Man his Equal, and the greater part no strict Observers of Equity and Justice, the enjoyment of the property he

has in this state is very unsafe, very insecure. This makes him willing to quit a Condition, which however free, is full of fears and continual dangers: And 'tis not without reason, that he seeks out, and is willing to joyn in Society with others who are already united, or have a mind to unite for the mutual *Preservation* of their Lives, Liberties and Estates, which I call by the general Name, *Property*.

27 Adam Smith, *An Inquiry into the Nature and Causes of the Wealth of Nations*, ed. William Benton (Chicago: Encyclopaedia Britannica, 1952), 311. Before this statement, Smith repeats the Lockean argument for government (p. 309): "The acquisition of valuable and extensive property therefore necessarily requires the establishment of civil government. Where there is no property…civil government is not so necessary."

28 The great American historian Charles Beard argued in his classical work *The Economic Interpretation of the Constitution* (New York: Simon & Schuster, 1918/1986) that the founding fathers drafted a document that simply served their class interest and the interests of the rich. This once widely accepted position has been increasingly refuted as too one-sided. As Richard Hofstadter in *The American Political Tradition and the Men Who Made It* (New York: Random House, 1973) helps clarify, the philosophy of Liberalism provides an intellectual framework in which the founders could with perfect sincerity be patriotic idealists while still erecting a polity based on protecting the interests of property against excesses of democracy. This is a fundamental tension in Liberal theory that only a more expanded understanding of the human condition can resolve at a higher level.

29 James Madison, Federalist No. 10, in *The Federalist by Alexander Hamilton, James Madison and John Jay*, ed. Benjamin Fletcher Wright (Cambridge, MA: The Belknap Press of Harvard University, 1966), 131.

30 Ibid., 133.

31 Ibid., 134.

32 James Madison, Federalist No. 51, in *The Federalist*, ed. Benjamin Fletcher Wright, 356.

33 These are Charles Beard's estimations. See Charles Beard, *An Economic Interpretation of the Constitution of the United States* (New York: Macmillan, 1936), 67–68. After some discussion, the property qualification for voting was eventually removed from the Constitution.

34 Adam Smith, *An Inquiry into the Nature and Causes of the Wealth of Nations* (Charleston, SC: Forgotten Books, 1776/2008), 5, http://www.forgottenbooks.org.

35 In the United States, between 1860 and 1914, the population of New York grew from 850,000 to 4 million; that of Chicago from 110,000 to 2 million; and Philadelphia from 650,000 to 1.5 million. By 1900, nine-tenths of all manufacturing took place in cities. For a general discussion, see Alan Trachtenberg, *The Incorporation of America: Culture and Society in the Gilded Age* (New York: Hill and Wang, 1982), especially 101–39. For the statistics on urbanization, see Howard Zinn, *A People's History of the United States* (New York: Harper Colophon, 1980), 248.

36 Hannah Arendt, *Eichmann in Jerusalem: A Report on the Banality of Evil* (New York: Penguin, 1977).

37 New evidence has been published contradicting Eichmann's claims regarding his anti-Semitism; see Bettina Stangneth, *Eichmann vor Jerusalem. Das unbehelligte Leben eines Massemoerders* (Hamburg: Arche Literatur Verlag, 2001). Stangneth uses, among other sources, interviews the Dutch journalist Willem Sassen conducted with Eichmann in the late 1950s in Argentina. Sassen was a Dutch Nazi fellow traveler and deeply sympathetic to Eichmann. For a discussion about Arendt's own problems with anti-Semitism

and a critique of her "banality of evil" thesis, see Bernard Wasserstein's "Blame the Victim — Hannah Arendt among the Nazis: the Historian and Her Sources," *Times Literary Supplement*, October 9, 2012. Despite these major qualifications, Arendt seems to have identified something important concerning the nature of evil in mass societies through the simple habit of obedience to authority.

38 Ibid., 24, 25.

39 Stanley Milgram, *Obedience to Authority: An Experimental View* (New York: Harper & Row, 1974), 5.

40 Ibid., 9. See also the film record of one of Milgram's experiments, *Obedience* (University Park, PA: Penn State Media Sales, 1969).

41 The interview was recorded in the documentary film *The Corporation* and transcribed in the companion text: Joel Bakan, *The Corporation: The Pathological Pursuit of Profit and Power* (New York: Free Press, Simon & Schuster, 2004), 120.

42 Bakan, *The Corporation*, 16, 172.

43 Of the world's largest 150 economic entities, 95 (or 63 percent) were corporations in 2005. The figures come from the World Development Indicators database of the World Bank, as reported in *Fortune*, July 2005, 6.

44 Milton Friedman, "The Social Responsibility of Business Is to Increase Its Profits," *New York Times Magazine*, September 13, 1970. Friedman repeated this in an interview in the documentary film *The Corporation*; see also the companion text, Bakan, *The Corporation*, 34, 42. See also Milton and Rose Friedman, *Free to Choose: A Personal Statement* (New York: Harcourt, 1980), 2.

45 Bakan, *The Corporation*, 61–65.

46 Joel Bakan cites the Personality Diagnostic Checklist of the World Health Organization, ICD-10 Manual of Mental Disorders DSM-IV. Ibid., 56–57.

47 Joel Bourne Jr., "Is Another Deepwater Disaster Inevitable? Special Report: The Spill," *National Geographic* 218, no. 4 (October 2010): 47.

48 Johan Arlidge, "I'm Doing God's Work: Meet Mr. Goldman Sachs," *Sunday Times*, November 8, 2009, http://www.timesonline.co.uk/tol/news/world/us_and_americas/article6907681.ece.

49 Johan Niehardt with Black Elk, *Black Elk Speaks: Being the Life Story of a Holy Man of the Oglala* (New York: Simon & Schuster, 1975), 184.

50 David Own, "The Pay Problem: What's to Be Done about CEO Compensation," *The New Yorker*, October 12, 2009.

51 See Paul Krugman and Robin Wells, review of *The Age of Greed: The Triumph of Finance and the Decline of America, 1970 to the Present*, by Jeff Madrick, *The New York Review of Books*, July 14, 2011, 28.

52 James Patterson and Peter Kim, *The Day America Told the Truth: What People Really Believe about Everything That Matters* (New York: Prentice Hall, 1991). In the largest survey of public opinion to date, the professional integrity of members of Congress was ranked below that of used-car salesmen and just above that of prostitutes and drug pushers.

53 These details are from 2004 Gallup opinion poll results, as discussed by B. A. Robinson, Ontario Consultants on Religious Tolerance, February 20, 2009, http://www.religioustolerance.org/ev_publi.htm.

54 "'The Planet Won't Be Destroyed by Global Warming Because God Promised Noah,' Says Politician Bidding to Chair U.S. Energy Commission," *Daily Mail*, November 10, 2010, http://www.dailymail.co.uk/news/article-1328366/John-Shimkus-Global-warming-wont-destroy-planet-God-promised-Noah.html.

55 Ray Anderson interviewed in Joel Bakan's documentary film and companion text; see Bakan, *The Corporation*. See also Ray C. Anderson, *Mid-Course Correction: Toward a Sustainable Enterprise: The Interface Model* (New York: Pereginzilla, 1999).

56 The Principles for Responsible Investing (PRI) emerged from an original meeting called by the secretary-general of the United Nations in 2005 inviting representatives of the world's largest institutional investors from twelve countries. They eventually came up with six principles of environmental, social, and corporate (ESG) governance they agreed to be bound by; http://www.unpri.org/about/.

57 See the Move to Amend website for its draft resolution, https://movetoamend.org/democracy-amendments.

58 For clarifying the distinction between Wall Street and Main Street and its importance in understanding the recent economic recession, see David Korten, *Agenda for a New Economy: From Phantom Wealth to Real Wealth* (San Francisco: Berrett-Koehler, 2009).

59 Richard Hofstadter, *The American Political Tradition & the Men Who Made It* (New York: Random House, 1974), 53.

## Chapter 3. Recovery of the Quest, Part I — Anamnesis: Searching with My Life

1 Noel Mostert, *Frontiers: The Epic of South Africa's Creation and the Tragedy of the Xhosa People* (New York: Alfred A. Knopf, 1992), xiii.

2 The story is central to Jewish self-understanding, religious practice, and ethnic identity. The rite of passage into adulthood for a young Jew — a bar-mitzvah for a boy, bat-mitzvah for a girl — involves a test of literacy in which the assigned weekly portion of the Bible is sung in Hebrew in front of the assembled congregation. Religious ritual follows public recitation of the five books of Moses, divided into weekly portions, read every Sabbath until the year's end, when the process is repeated from the beginning. The events and seasons of biblical Israel are retold and ritually celebrated in a succession of annual festivals. Every aspect of daily life is intricately structured by performing the 613 mitzvot, or "blessed duties," symbolically connected to the story of origins. Beneath the surface of scholarship and ritual lies the mystical practice of Kabbalah. It was originally carried in more ancient strata of oral tradition until codified in the *Zohar*, "The Book of Splendor," and integrated into practice by the Chassidic movement. It is a kind of shamanism of text and word. Layers of interpretations of interpretations of the narrative are followed as if descending a staircase to the basement of the Jewish soul, and then deeper still into the psychic bedrock of the prelinguistic collective unconscious, a Jewish version of the San "early times" or the Australian Aborigine "dreamtime."

3 The term *Ashkenazi* came from Ashkenaz, the region along the German Rhineland where this Jewish community concentrated in the Middle Ages, later to spread throughout Europe. The recent breakthroughs in genetic mapping have confirmed what has long been part of Ashkenazi self-understanding — they are an ethnic group unto themselves. High-resolution genetic mapping using the Y chromosome for patrilineal descent and mitochondrial DNA for matrilineal descent shows that widely dispersed Ashkenazi Jewish communities have more in common genetically with one another than they do with their neighbors. For example, when I recently sent a sample of my DNA to the National Geographic Genographic project — the largest genetic mapping project ever undertaken — the results showed I belonged to Y haplogroup J1

(M267). The M267 haplogroup arose in the southern Fertile Crescent, perhaps in what is now Iraq, about ten thousand years ago and carries a strong cultural connection: "Many of its members with European ancestry are Jewish. More than half of all J1 samples in the Genographic database are Ashkenazi Jews, revealing a genetic connection to the Middle Eastern homeland of Judaism." Today, modern members of this haplogroup live in the highest concentrations near its ancestral birthplace in the Middle East, as well as in Arabia, North Africa, and Ethiopia. A significant percentage of Sephardic (Spanish and North African) Jews also share this marker. For research on Ashkenazim, see M. F. Hammer et al., "Jewish and Middle Eastern Non-Jewish Populations Share a Common Pool of Y-Chromosome Biallelic Haplotypes," *Proceedings of the National Academy of Sciences* 97, no. 12 (May 9, 2000): 6769, doi:10.1073/pnas.100115997. See also Almut Nebel et al., "Y Chromosome Evidence for a Founder Effect in Ashkenazi Jews," *European Journal of Human Genetics* (2005): 13, 388–91, doi:10.1038/sj.ejhg.5201319 (published online November 3, 2004).

4 In 1887, a Russian government commission of inquiry found that "90% of the Jews are a proletariat of such poverty and destitution as is otherwise impossible to see in Russia." Quoted in Amos Elon, *The Israelis: Founders and Sons* (New York: Holt, Rinehart, and Winston, 1971), 52.

5 Milton Shain, Adrienne Folb, Albie Sachs, Jon Berndt, Jon Weinberg, Barry Feinberg, and Andre Odendaal, comps., *Looking Back: Jews in the Struggle for Democracy and Human Rights in South Africa* (Cape Town, South Africa: Jewish Publications — South Africa, Isaac and Jessie Kaplan Center for Jewish Studies and Research, University of Cape Town, 2001), 122, 138. See also the more recent definitive work by Richard Mendelsohn and Milton Shain, *The Jews in South Africa: An Illustrated History* (Johannesburg: Jonathan Ball Publishers, 2008), 148. Mohandas Gandhi talked of being "surrounded by Jews" during his years in South Africa. The editor of *Indian Opinion*, the mouthpiece of the Indian struggle in South Africa from 1906 to 1916, was an English Jew, Henry Polak. Gandhi and Polak were imprisoned together for participating in the *satyagraha* nonviolent resistance. For many years the only member of the South African parliament opposing apartheid was Helen Suzmann, the Jewish leader of the progressive party.

6 For a penetrating discussion of the connection between the *periagoge*, the essence of the good (the *Agathon*), and political education, see Eric Voegelin, *Order and History*, vol. 3, *Plato and Aristotle* (Baton Rouge: Louisiana State University Press, 1975), 112–17. I return to the Socratic discussion of the good in chapter 11.

7 Arthur Hertzberg, ed., *The Zionist Idea: A Historical Analysis and Reader* (New York: Temple Antheneum, 1982), 297.

8 The various Marxist, neo-Marxist, Leninist, and Maoist visions, like those of Marx himself, seemed completely captured by the mechanical, scientific materialism that afflicted industrial capitalism. None of this was very inspiring. The Frankfurt School philosopher Herbert Marcuse offered a deeper analysis of consciousness. His critique of consumer culture and monolithic industrial capitalism resonated with my kibbutz ethos. He also gave my rebelliousness some intellectual authority. But the counterculture itself seemed increasingly dissipated and self-indulgent and lacked a comprehensive political philosophy.

9 Hertzberg, *The Zionist Idea*, 372.

10 Elon, *The Israelis*, 114.

11 Jeffrey Goldberg, *Prisoners: A Muslim and a Jew across the Middle East Divide* (New York: Alfred A. Knopf, 2006). This is a powerful account of Goldberg's Zionist "ascent"

to Israel, his time on a left-wing Hashomer Hatzair kibbutz, and his service in the military police of the Israeli army. It is an illuminating story of attempted reconciliation and disillusioned idealism, which leaves the question of transformation open.

12 Elon, *The Israelis*, 112.

13 In the words of a young Israeli air force pilot: "If most air forces are designed like a Formula One race car, the Israeli Air Force is a beat-up jeep with a lot of tools in it.... A US Air Force strike package often consists of four waves of specialized aircraft: a combat air patrol to clear a corridor of enemy aircraft; a second wave to suppress enemy antiaircraft systems; a third wave of electronic warfare aircraft and refueling tankers and radar aircraft; and finally, the strikers themselves — planes with bombs. In the Israeli system, almost every aircraft is a jack of all trades.... The IDF approach is in the short term less efficient but a lot more flexible and durable. It also makes being a pilot a more challenging and creative experience." This feature of the IDF is thought to be one of the reasons for Israel producing per capita the highest number of technology start-ups in the world. Quote from unsigned review of *Start Up Nation: The Story of Israel's Economic Miracle* by Dan Senor and Saul Singer, *Newsweek*, November 23, 2009, 45.

14 Our officers and some elite forces used captured Kalashnikovs.

15 For a sobering and well-researched account of the Palestinian experience, see Rashid Khalidi, *The Iron Cage: The Story of the Palestinian Struggle for Statehood* (Boston: Beacon Press, 2006).

16 This was during the time Israel was still governed by a Kibbutz-Labor left wing coalition. A few years after I left Israel in 1980, the right-wing pro-capitalist Herut party led by Menachem Begin overturned the Labor party, which had controlled Israeli politics since the early days of settlement. This led to the rise of other right-wing leaders, like Yitzhak Shamir, Ariel Sharon, and Benjamin Netanyahu. For a harsh look at Israeli treatment of Palestinians from the point of view of a liberal South African Jew, see Susan Nathan, *The Other Side of Israel: My Journey across the Israeli Arab Divide* (New York: Doubleday/Random House, 2006).

17 Henry S. Kariel, *Beyond Liberalism: Where Relations Grow* (San Francisco: Chandler and Sharp, 1977).

18 For precontact Native Hawaiian population estimates, see the revisions by David Stannard, *Before the Horror: The Population of Hawai'i on the Eve of Western Contact* (Honolulu: University of Hawai'i Press, 1989).

## Chapter 4. Recovery of the Quest, Part II — Politics of Mystery

1 Brian Swimme, a mathematic cosmologist, evolutionary philosopher, and visionary storyteller, guides us through this cosmic meditation in *The Hidden Heart of the Cosmos: Humanity and the New Story* (Maryknoll, NY: Orbis Books, 1996/2004), 27–28. His most recent work, the feature-length film *Journey of the Universe* (PBS, 2011), gives his vision a more appropriately epic format. See http://www.journeyoftheuniverse.org/.

2 See also the video documentary *The Hidden Heart of the Cosmos* (Mill Valley, CA: Center for the Story of the Universe, 1996) for another version of this meditation.

3 Neil deGrasse Tyson, interviewed in *The Universe*, season 1, episode 1, History Channel, A&E Television Network (Flight 33 Productions, 2007). Tyson is the director of the Hayden Planetarium and research associate of the American Museum.

4 This 200-billion-galaxy estimate comes from the Cornell University Astronomy Department website's question and answer section, http://curious.astro.cornell.edu/aboutus.php. According to NASA, the 1999 Hubble Space Telescope found 129 billion galaxies, but more recent NASA estimates put the number at around 500 billion and growing. See the NASA website, http://imagine.gsfc.nasa.gov/docs/ask_astro/answers/021127a.html.

5 Giles Sparrow and Dava Sobel, *Cosmos: A Field Guide* (London: Quercus Publishing, 2007), 6.

6 Chief Luther Standing Bear, *Land of the Spotted Eagle* (Lincoln: University of Nebraska Press, 1933/1978), 196.

7 Ibid., 193.

8 Ibid.

9 Ibid., 197.

10 Christopher Columbus, "Letter on His First Voyage" (also called "Columbus's Letter to Santangel"), original in New York Public Library; reproduced by Samuel Eliot Morison, *Christopher Columbus, Mariner* (New York: New American Library, 1955), 149–53.

11 Martin Lewis, *Green Delusions: An Environmentalist Critique of Radical Environmentalism* (Durham: Duke University Press, 1992), 63. This is an important nuanced corrective to overgeneralizing the primal and oversimplifying a neoprimal radical environmentalist politics.

12 Rudolf Otto, *Mysticism East and West: A Comparative Analysis of the Nature of Mysticism* (New York: Macmillan, Collier Books, 1962), 14.

13 William James, *The Varieties of Religious Experience: A Study in Human Nature* (New York: Collier Books, 1961), 299, 300.

14 Ibid., 313.

15 Voegelin, a non-Jew, acknowledged the Jewish mystics like Gershom Scholem, Martin Buber, and to a lesser extent Walter Benjamin as sharing his general approach. Dan Avnon's work on Martin Buber's "hidden dialogues" and his exposition of Buber's "between" illuminate their similarity to Voegelin's philosophy of consciousness. See Dan Avnon, *Martin Buber: The Hidden Dialogues* (Lanham, MD: Rowman Littlefield, 1998). But Voegelin is distinguished by the encyclopedic extent of his exploration of the importance of this experience across the great world civilizations.

16 Eric Voegelin, *Order and History*, 5 vols. (Baton Rouge: Louisiana State University Press, 1958/1987).

17 Surprisingly, Eric Voegelin panels now constitute the largest single section at the annual meetings of the American Political Science Association, the largest professional gathering of political scientists in the United States. The section seems to attract as many theologians, philosophers, and historians as political scientists. With the recent publication of the final and thirty-fourth volume of Voegelin's collected works, and translations appearing in Chinese, French, Italian, Portuguese, and Spanish, his importance is being more widely recognized.

18 Eric Voegelin, *Order and History*, vol. 1, *Israel and Revelation* (Baton Rouge: Louisiana State University Press, 1986), 1.

19 Voegelin traces the a historical formulation of this mystery of consciousness at the beginning and end of his five-volume series *Order and History*. His most precise formulation is in volume 5. Unfortunately, since this is the most condensed and abstract of his works, it is often neglected. Voegelin puts it like this: "Consciousness has a structural

dimension by which it belongs, not to man in his bodily existence, but to the reality in which man, the other partners to the community of being, and the participatory relations among them occur. If the spatial metaphor be still permitted, the luminosity of consciousness is located somewhere 'between' human consciousness in bodily existence and reality intended in its mode of 'thingness.'" Eric Voegelin, *Order and History*, vol. 5, *In Search of Order* (Baton Rouge: Louisiana State University Press, 1986), 16.

20 Since we live *within* this in-between situation, we cannot grasp either reality or consciousness as fully separate things. We are always dealing with both together, and do so primarily through language. So we need to remember that our search always takes place *within* three interrelated dimensions: *consciousness*, *reality*, and *language*. The three really constitute a single "tensional complex," as Voegelin called it: *consciousness-reality-language*. The attempt to separate one from the others — for instance, to see language as separate from the reality it describes, or reality separate from the consciousness that perceives it — deforms the primary in-between structure of human existence, and we fall for the destructive certainties of ideology and dogma. See Eric Voegelin, *Order and History*, vol. 5, *In Search of Order*, 14–18.

21 Carl Jung, interview by John Freeman, *Face to Face*, BBC documentary, October 22, 1959. Also excerpted in the documentary film *Matter of Heart*.

22 Voegelin confined his analysis to the appearance of the great settled civilizations beginning ten thousand years ago. He never explicitly located the story of civilization within the drama of evolutionary cosmology. Nor did he deal with prehistory and archaic and shamanistic systems of wisdom. However, there is evidence in his correspondence toward the end of his life that he was becoming increasingly interested in prehistory. See in particular Voegelin's letters to Marie Koenig in Thomas Hollweck, ed., *The Collected Works of Eric Voegelin*, vol. 30, *Selected Correspondence 1950–1984*, trans. Sandy Adler, Thomas A. Hollweck, and William Petropolus (Baton Rouge: Louisiana State University Press, 2007).

23 Hyemeyohsts Storm, *Seven Arrows* (New York: Harper & Row, 1972).

24 H. D. F. Kitto, *The Greeks* (London: Penguin Books, 1951/1987), 172.

25 Storm, *Seven Arrows*, 6.

26 Lame Deer and Richard Erdoes, *Lame Deer, Seeker of Vision: The Life of a Sioux Medicine Man* (New York: Simon & Schuster, Touchstone, 1972), 79.

27 C. G. Jung, *Collected Works*, vol. 7, 409, quoted in *C. G. Jung: Word and Image*, ed. Aniela Jaffe (New York: Bollingen, 1978), 123.

28 This example is presented by Max Horkheimer to clarify the movement of thought in discussion toward greater inclusiveness. See Max Horkheimer, "The Social Function of Philosophy," in *Critical Theory: Selected Essays* (New York: Seabury Press, 1972), 265.

29 Lorna Marshall, *The Kung of Nyae Nyae* (Cambridge, MA: Harvard University Press, 1976). See especially chapter 9, "Sharing, Talking and Giving: Relief of Social Tensions," 287–312.

30 Jürgen Habermas, *Theory of Communicative Action*, vol. 1, *Reason and the Rationalization of Society*, trans. Thomas McCarthy (Boston: Beacon Press, 1981). But Habermas's minimal conditions for free speech constitute a thin theory for democratic communication. Shared positive intention — living the good life in community — is another critical requirement for truth-loving community.

31 Nelson Mandela, *Long Walk to Freedom: The Autobiography of Nelson Mandela* (New York: Little, Brown, 1994), 21.

32 Ibid., 22.

33 Richard Borshay Lee, *The !Kung San: Men, Women, and Work in a Foraging Society* (Cambridge: Cambridge University Press, 1979), 457.

34 This notion is illustrated in great detail in Mathias Guenther, *Tricksters & Trancers: Bushman Religion and Society* (Bloomington: Indiana University Press, 1999). See especially p. 56.

35 Pierre Teilhard de Chardin, *The Phenomenon of Man* (New York: Harper Collins, 1965), 219.

36 These small sparks were snuffed out as Cromwell abandoned his open vision in favor of a defensive centralism. See, for example, Christopher Hill, *The World Turned Upside Down: Radical Ideas during the English Revolution* (New York: Penguin, 1985).

## Chapter 5. Out of Wilderness

1 Until 1925 all the major hominid fossils were found in Eurasia, confirming and reinforcing the Eurocentric conceit that our definitive humanity could not have emerged from the "backward dark continent of Africa." When the South African anatomist Raymond Dart identified a skull found at the limestone quarry Taung as from a hominid several million years old, few took him seriously. Decades passed before the monumental achievements of the Leakey family and a new generation of paleontologists discovered and identified in the southern African Great Rift Valley the most continuous and complete record of fossils marking the significant evolutionary leaps between ape and *Homo sapiens*. Only here do we find the evidence linking the first dispersion out of Africa between 2 and 1.5 million years ago, from *Homo erectus*, to the final dispersion of modern *Homo sapiens* around fifty thousand years ago. The oldest stone artifacts, dated to 2.5 million years ago, are from the Gona and Awash regions of the Rift Valley, Ethiopia. But the richest evidence for modern human behavior comes from rock shelters — as at the Robberg, Blombos, Klasiers River, and Pinnacle Point — along the coastline of South Africa.

2 The Leakey family's remarkable contribution to constructing the scientifically persuasive story of our emergence from wilderness was a model of interdisciplinary synthesis, weaving among such diverse subjects as taphonomy (the weathering of old bones), primatology, geology, and studies on contemporary hunter-gatherers.

3 Eugène Marais, *The Soul of the Ape* (Harmondsworth, Middlesex: Penguin Books, 1973), 105–6.

4 W.H.I. Bleek and L.C. Lloyd, "Customs and Beliefs of the !Xam Bushmen. Part I: Baboons," *Journal of Bantu Studies* 5 (1931): 167.

5 Mathias Guenther, *Tricksters & Trancers: Bushman Religion and Society* (Bloomington: Indiana University Press, 1999), 74–75.

6 Bleek and Lloyd, "Customs and Beliefs," 167.

7 J.D. Lewis-Williams, ed., *Stories That Float from Afar: Ancestral Folklore of the San of Southern Africa* (College Station: Texas A & M University Press, 2000), 93. This selection comes from the Wilhelm Bleek and Lucy Lloyd archives of nineteenth-century San Bushmen ethnography.

8 C.G. Jung, *Memories, Dreams, Reflections*, ed. Aniela Jaffe (New York: Vintage Books, Random House, 1965), 254–55.

9 For Freud the id contained the basic drives and instinctual responses — hunger, thirst, sleep, self-preservation, sexual arousal, territoriality — which we know to be controlled by structures like the reticular formation at the brainstem, sitting at the top of the

spinal column. For Freud the unconscious is thus the seething repository of inherited drives and instincts as well as the forgotten acts of repression and punishment of expression of instinctual urges — particularly sexuality — which conflict with the disciplines and values of civilization. It is a sort of psychic rubbish heap of forgotten trauma. Jung rebelled against Freud's authoritarian and dogmatic insistence that he make this sexual theory an "unbreachable bulwark against the tide of occultism." C.G. Jung, *Memories, Dreams, and Reflections*, 150. Jung's incorporation of religious experience and transcendence in healing helps connect depth psychology to ancient shamanism.

10 See, for example, Erich Neumann, *The Origins and History of Consciousness* (Princeton, NJ: Princeton University Press, Bollingen Foundation, 1970).

11 "The unconscious, as the totality of all archetypes, is the deposit of all human experience right back to its remotest beginnings. Not, indeed, a dead deposit, a sort of abandoned rubbish-heap, but a living system of reactions and aptitudes that determine the individual's life in invisible ways — all the more effectively because invisible. . . . From the living fountain of instinct flows everything that is creative; hence the unconscious is not merely conditioned by history, but is the very source of the creative impulse. It is like Nature herself — prodigiously conservative, and yet transcending her own historical conditions in her acts of creation." From C.G. Jung, *The Structure and Dynamics of the Psyche, Collected Works, Vol. 8*, in *The Portable Jung*, ed. Joseph Campbell (New York: Viking Press, 1971), 44.

12 Jean Gebser developed a clarification of consciousness which can be related to that of Eric Voegelin. His idea of "integral consciousness" allows us to grasp the past as a living force in the present moving into the future. See Jean Paul Gebser, *The Ever-Present Origin*, trans. Noel Barstad with Algis Mickunas (Athens: Ohio University Press, 1985).

13 Laurens van der Post in Elizabeth Darby Junkin, ed., *South African Passage: Diaries from the Wilderness Leadership School* (Golden, CO: Fulcrum, 1987), x, ix.

14 Thomas Brown quoted in Vance Marin and Mary Inglis, eds., *Wilderness: The Way Ahead* (Findhorn, Scotland: The FindHorn Press, 1984), 170.

15 See, for example, Jeff Hecht, "Chimps Are Human, Gene Study Implies," *New Scientist*, May 19, 2003, http://www.newscientist.com/article/dn3744.

16 Robert Ardrey, *African Genesis: A Personal Investigation into the Animal Origins and Nature of Man* (New York: Dell, 1970), 14. Ardrey focused on the now-rejected interpretation of the remains of *Australopithecus africanus* found at Taung by the South African Raymond Dart as a meat eater, killer ape, possibly cannibalistic, who was our direct ancestor.

17 Ibid., 14.

18 See, for example, Richard Leakey, *Origins Reconsidered: In Search of What Makes Us Human* (New York: Bantam Doubleday, 1993).

19 Paul Shepard, *The Tender Carnivore and the Sacred Game* (Athens: University of Georgia Press, 1998), 42–43. Paul Shepard is one of our more philosophically sensitive guides through the past sixty million years of primate evolution.

20 Ibid., 43.

21 Ibid., 52.

22 Ibid., 58.

23 This quote is actually Richard Leakey summarizing and quoting Barbara Smuts in Leakey, *Origins Reconsidered*, 288. For the original, see Barbara B. Smuts, *Sex and Friendship in Baboons* (New York: Aldine, 1985), 4–5.

24 Experiments with subliminal processing of images of facial expressions show responses (such as sweating palms) can be produced via the autonomic nervous system without passing through conscious awareness. Sensory information passes through the thalamus — the traffic cop of the brain regulating emotional response — and then follows the high road of the hominid brain to the cortex and the low road of the mammalian brain to the amygdala. Research has demonstrated that information reaches the amygdala, stimulating involuntary action (we jump, our skin prickles), before it reaches the cortex. See Gregg Jacobs, *The Ancestral Mind* (New York: Penguin, 2004). For subliminal emotional responses to natural landscapes and urban scenes, see Roger S. Ulrich, "Biophilia, Biophobia, and Natural Landscapes," in Stephen R. Kellert and E. O. Wilson, *The Biophilia Hypothesis* (Washington, DC: Island Press, 1993).

25 Leakey, *Origins Reconsidered*, 288. This is Richard Leakey's pithy summary of an incident recounted in Barbara Smuts, *Sex and Friendship*. Leakey recounts another example of deception among baboons (ibid., 299): "Paul, a young baboon, approached and watched a female, Mel, who was digging in the hard dry earth for a rhizome to eat. Paul looked around: in the undulating grassland habitat no baboons were in sight, although they could not be far off. Then he screamed loudly, which baboons do not usually do unless threatened. Within seconds Paul's mother, who was dominant to Mel, rushed to the scene and chased her, both going right out of sight. Paul walked forward and began to eat the rhizome."

26 Smuts, *Sex and Friendship*, 3–5.

27 Harry Harlow, "Love in Infant Monkeys," *Scientific American* 68 (June 1959): 70–74.

28 Ibid., 96.

29 Child abuse or neglect is defined by the US Department of Health and Human Services as "any recent act or failure to act on the part of a parent or caretaker which results in death, serious physical or emotional harm, sexual abuse or exploitation; or an act or failure to act which presents an imminent risk of serious harm." From Department of Health and Human Services: Administration for Children and Families, *Child Maltreatment 2009* (2010), vii, http://www.acf.hhs.gov/programs/cb/pubs/cm09/cm09.pdf.

30 Shepard points out that captive apes are more like modern humans than like their wild relatives. "They get tuberculosis, spinal lordosis, and other human diseases and afflictions associated with life in a cell. They walk more on their hind legs, develop an exaggerated fear of heights, spend more time building nests or other structures, are more fascinated by their own excrement, more interested in killing birds, mice or other accidental intruders, and more interested in eating meat. At maturity they become sullen and vicious, more introverted, and develop swaying movements symptomatic of neurosis. They may become hypersexual deviants or refuse to mate." Shepard continues, "There is evidence that [captive apes] improve at problem solving and at those kinds of learning directed toward objects instead of other apes. These are also symptomatic of human prisoners, and to some extent of urban [humans] in general.... Movies and animal acts with baby chimpanzees who are not yet broken in spirit perpetuate the fiction of the chimpanzee as a happy and clever rascal delighted to be in captivity." He concludes: "The tragic figures of adult apes in captivity are exactly what they seem: hopelessly despairing of life, psychopathic and deformed. Only by denying what we see can we fail to realize the sickness of the zoo, circus, pet, medical and experimental primate." See Shepard, *The Tender Carnivore*, 82.

31 J. Allman, *Evolving Brains* (New York: Scientific American Library, 2000).

32 H. J. Deacon and Janette Deacon, *Human Beginnings in South Africa: Uncovering the Secrets of the Stone Age* (Walnut Creek, CA: Sage Publications, 1999), 51.

33 Richard Leakey, who found the most complete skeleton of *erectus*, the approximately 1.5-million-year-old "Turkana Boy," talks of holding the *erectus* cranium in his hands and feeling for the first time "in the presence of something distinctly human." The 5 to 6 million years of hominid evolution before *erectus* had taken place exclusively within Africa.

34 For a succinct summary of this event, see David Lewis-Williams, *The Mind in the Cave: Consciousness and the Origins of Art* (New York: Thames and Hudson, 2002), 97. Lewis-Williams notes that the perceived modern "explosion" in human consciousness is sharpened by the fact that modern archaeology began in Europe and centered around the early discovery of Neanderthals, a Eurasian variant of archaic *Homo sapiens*. By 130,000 years ago Neanderthals had been in Eurasia long enough to have diverged from the lighter, more agile African stock into larger, thicker-boned, muscular *Homo neanderthalensis*, which was better adapted to big-game hunting in the cold climate of northern Europe. Neanderthals have larger brains, their skull is much thicker than and shaped differently from that of modern humans, and the angle of the skull on the vertebral column suggests that the larynx was not open enough for the sort of finely turned vocalization that makes possible the complexities of language. Superior communication and a culture of learning and teaching would have given modern *Homo sapiens* a dramatic competitive advantage and been a major factor in the disappearance of Neanderthals. There are four to five times as many Cro-Magnon as Neanderthal sites. The genetic, population, and archaeological evidence suggests that Neanderthals were largely replaced by Cro-Magnons, although there is evidence that Eurasian human beings carry up to 4 percent Neanderthal genes.

35 Deacon and Deacon, *Human Beginnings*, 150.

36 Ibid., 98.

37 Curtis W. Marean et al., "Early Human Use of Marine Resources and Pigment in South Africa during the Middle Pleistocene," *Nature* 449 (October 2007): 905–8. For a more recent update, see Curtis W. Marean, "Pinnacle Point Cave 13B (Western Cape Province, South Africa) in Context: The Cape Floral Kingdom, Shellfish, and Modern Human Origins," *Journal of Human Evolution* (2010): 59, 425–43.

38 Blombos Cave has deposits going as far back as 140,000 years ago. The cave was sealed by shifting sand dunes around 70,000 years ago. There are also more recent deposits above the dune layer. Christopher S. Henshilwood, Francesco d'Errico, and Ian Watts, "Engraved Ochers from the Middle Stone Age Levels at Blombos Cave, South Africa," *Journal of Human Evolution* 57 (2009): 27–47, doi:10.1016/j.jhevol.2009.01.005.

39 Christopher S. Henshilwood et al., "A 100,000-Year-Old Ochre-Processing Workshop at Blombos Cave, South Africa," *Science* 334 (October 14, 2011): 219–22, doi: 10.1126/science.1211535. See also *Science* podcast interview with Chris Henshilwood, October 14, 2011.

40 Henshilwood and Marean offer a more inclusive, more theoretically robust argument based on causal mechanisms derived from behavioral ecological theory and well-known patterns of behavior of contemporary hunter-gatherers in changing climates. For example, complexity of tools and food storage technology increase as groups move from tropical to arctic environments and are not necessary requirements for behavioral modernity. Chris S. Henshilwood and C.W. Marean, "Remodelling the Origins of Modern Human Behaviour," in *The Human Genome and Africa, Part One: History*

*and Archaeology*, ed. H. Soodyall (Cape Town, South Africa: Human Sciences Research Council Press, 2006), 9.

41 Ibid., 9.

42 Christopher McDougall has written a bestseller based on the notion that humanity evolved to be capable of running down game in what is known as the "persistence hunt." See Christopher McDougall, *Born to Run: A Hidden Tribe, Superathletes and the Greatest Race the World Has Never Seen* (New York: Alfred A. Knopf, 2009), 229–39. McDougall quotes the scholar Louis Liebenberg's description of this event but not the remarkable film by the Foster brothers, who participated in the hunt and made history by documenting it in their film *The Great Dance: A Hunter's Story*.

43 Brian Swimme, "The Nature of the Human," *Canticle to the Cosmos*, episode 8, directed by Catherine Busch (San Francisco: Center for the Story of the Universe, 1994).

44 Brian Swimme, *The Earth's Imagination* (San Francisco: Center for the Story of the Universe, 2000). We have evidence for fire tending going back at least five hundred thousand years — like that from Swartkrans — but only evidence for fire making at will, presumably with fire sticks, from a hundred thousand years ago (Deacon and Deacon, *Human Beginnings*, 69).

45 Abraham Joshua Heschel, *Man Is Not Alone: A Philosophy of Religion* (New York: Noonday Press, Farrar, Straus & Giroux, 1976), 11.

46 Deacon and Deacon, *Human Beginnings*, 69.

47 Melvin Konner, *The Tangled Wing: Biological Constraints on the Human Spirit* (New York: Holt, Rinehart, and Winston, 1982), 5.

48 Sigrid Schmidt counted some fifty-seven varieties of mythic story concerning the origin of death and twenty-eight stories about the acquisition of fire. Sigrid Schmidt, "The Relevance of Bleek/Lloyd Folktales to the General Khoisan Tradition," in *Voices from the Past: /Xam Bushmen and the Bleek and Lloyd Collection*, eds. Janette Deacon and Thomas Dowson (Johannesburg: Witwatersrand University Press, 1996). Mathias Guenther counts seventy story versions of the origin of death; see Guenther, *Tricksters & Trancers*, 102, 160.

49 /Gwi story retold by Laurens van der Post. The preying mantis, or /Kaggen, is for the Southern /Xam Bushmen the embodiment of the in-between state of the early race, with magical abilities to change form between human and animal. Laurens van der Post, *Heart of the Hunter* (Harmondsworth, Middlesex: Penguin Books), 168.

## Chapter 6. Lost Worlds

1 Alan Barnard, *Hunters and Herders of Southern Africa: A Comparative Ethnography of the Khoisan Peoples* (Cambridge: Cambridge University Press, 1992). Sven Ouzman, "Silencing and Sharing Southern African Indigenous and Embedded Knowledge," in *Indigenous Archaeologies: Decolonizing Theory and Practice*, eds. Claire Smithe and H. Martin Wobst (London: Routledge, 2005), 4, 208–25.

2 The landmark project on global genetic mapping, the largest ever undertaken, was led by the Oxford geneticist Spencer Wells as scientist in residence at National Geographic. See Spencer Wells, *Deep Ancestry: Inside the Genographic Project. The Landmark DNA Quest to Decipher Our Distant Past* (Washington, DC: National Geographic, 2006). See also his earlier work and the BBC documentary by the same name, *The Journey of Man: A Genetic Odyssey* (Princeton, NJ: Princeton University Press, 2002). For a

popular synthesis of the recent genetic and archaeological research on human origins, see Nicholas Wade, *Before the Dawn: Recovering the Lost History of Our Ancestors* (New York: Penguin, 2006).

In 2011, more extensive research was showcased in a special feature article from the National Academy of Sciences "dealing with events of exceptional significance." A targeted analysis of hunter-gatherer genomes in Africa, including data for the Tanzanian Hadza, the Sandawe, and the South African ≠Khomani and Namibian Bushmen, concluded, "Analyses of… [the data]…suggest that HG's, especially the click-speaking ≠Khomani and Namibian Bushmen, are among the most diverse of all human populations." See Brenna Henn et al., "Hunter-Gatherer Genomic Diversity Suggests a Southern African Origin for Modern Humans," *Proceedings of the National Academy of Sciences* (February 3, 2011): 7, http://www.pnas.org/cgi/doi/10.1073/pnas.1017511108.

In related research, the journal *Nature* reported in February 2010 on the complete sequencing of the genome of five southern African men, four of whom represented four different tribes of the San Bushmen. Each tribe speaks a different language, but all are part of the Khoisan click-language group. The findings support the understanding of Bushmen as having the greatest genetic diversity of all human populations. The study also identified genes conferring possible survival advantage in a desert-adapted hunting-gathering way of life. See Stephen C. Shuster et al., "Complete Khoisan and Bantu Genome from Southern Africa," *Nature* 463 (February 18, 2010): 857, 943–47.

3 Quentin D. Atkinson, "Phonemic Diversity Supports a Serial Founder Effect Model of Language Expansion from Africa," *Science* 332, no. 6027 (April 15, 2011): 346–49. The *Encyclopaedia Britannica* entry on Khoisan languages by Anthony Traill and Oswin R. Kholer (http://www.britannica.com/) points out the complexity of the mixing that took place over millennia between Khoikhoi herders and San hunters. Thus some hunter-gatherers speak a Khoi language, while some San speakers live as herders. In general the non-Khoi San languages have a much greater number of phonemes than those of their Khoi neighbors. For example, the Khoi language of Nama has 32, while the San Ju system has 105, and the !Xoo system has 126. In an interesting variation on this story, the Bayaka "pygmies" (also called Aka) of Central Africa, who also have a very high level of genetic diversity, have apparently lost their original language and now speak versions of Bantu and Nilotic languages. The long history of relative isolation but symbiotic association with surrounding Bantu societies has produced a situation in which one group, the Babenzele Bayaka, actually speak a Bantu language that is no longer spoken by any Bantu. Louis Sarno, *Bayaka: The Extraordinary Music of the Babenzele Pygmies* (New York: Ellipsis Art, 1995), 8.

4 Francesco d'Errico et al., "Early Evidence of San Material Culture Represented by Organic Artifacts from Border Cave, South Africa," *Proceedings of the National Academy of Sciences* 109, no. 33 (August 14, 2012): 13214–19; date of electronic publication: July 30, 2012. See also Paola Villa et al., "Border Cave and the Beginning of the Later Stone Age in South Africa," *Proceedings of the National Academy of Sciences* (July 30, 2012), doi: 10.1073/pnas.1202629109.

5 Noel Mostert, *Frontiers: The Epic of South Africa's Creation and the Tragedy of the Xhosa People* (New York: Alfred A. Knopf, 1992), 85.

6 Ibid., 108.

7 Leonard Thompson, *The Political Mythology of Apartheid* (New Haven, CT: Yale University Press, 1985), 72.

8 Ibid., 74.

9 Mostert, *Frontiers*, 105, 106.

10 Van der Post, largely discredited by anthropologists, has become even more controversial as a result of a recent biography by J. D. F. Jones, *Teller of Many Tales: The Lives of Laurens van der Post* (New York: Carol and Graf, 2002). This is in part the inevitable hatchet job that larger-than-life characters like van der Post attract, and van der Post is particularly vulnerable, since he is an unashamed romantic in the business of mythologizing. Jones's book is remarkable both for its meticulous research into every inconsistency, exaggeration, and lie and for its failure to explain why Laurens's stories had such enormous appeal for so many.

11 Laurens van der Post, *The Lost World of the Kalahari* (New York: Harvest Books, Harcourt, Brace, and Jovanovich, 1958), 15.

12 Jones, *Teller of Many Tales*.

13 Interestingly, the respected anthropologist Alan Barnard gives van der Post credit for dramatically exemplifying an important model for anthropology based on the "dual journey": an outer journey into the world in tandem with an exploration of the changes taking place in the inner world of one's soul. He notes it is similar to the work of self-reflective participatory anthropology, which is also based on an intertwining of these elements. Van der Post's writings "give us a more extreme version of the literary task with which enthnographers, indeed especially Bushman ethnographers, have to cope." Alan Barnard, "Laurens van der Post and the Kalahari Debate," in *Miscast: Negotiating the Presence of the Bushmen*, ed. Pippa Skotnes (Rondebosch, Cape Town: University of Cape Town Press, 1996), 243.

14 John Marshall's first major work, *The Hunters*, is one of the great classics of ethnographic filmmaking. He continued filming the ongoing story of the people and his family relationship with the band until the 1980s, producing some twenty-six finished films. His final work, *A Kalahari Family*, is a five-part filmic document of the story of his family. See John Marshall, *A Kalahari Family* (Watertown, MA: Documentary Education Resources, 2002). Lorna Marshall published most of the systematic ethnography. See Lorna Marshall, *The !Kung of Nyae Nyae* (Cambridge, MA: Harvard University Press, 1976), and the more recent companion volume, Lorna Marshall, *Nyae Nyae !Kung: Beliefs and Rites* (Cambridge, MA: Harvard University Press, 1999). The first is "about the !Kung as they were before profound change began," and both are indispensable texts.

15 Elizabeth Marshall Thomas, *The Old Way: A Story of the First People* (New York: Farrar, Straus & Giroux, 2006). The sections dealing with lions were first published in a more expanded form in Elizabeth Marshall Thomas, "Reflections: The Old Way," *New Yorker*, October 15, 1990.

16 As noted in chapter 4, modern evolutionary biology has made it clear that hunter-gatherers have always had a complex interaction with their wilderness environment. The mass extinction of the Pleistocene due to the spread of modern human hunters is probably the most dramatic example. For a more detailed deconstruction, see Martin Lewis, *Green Delusions: An Environmentalist Critique of Radical Environmentalism* (Durham, NC: Duke University Press, 1995). See also Jared Diamond, *Guns, Germs, and Steel* (New York: W. W. Norton, 1997). Diamond asks the question: "Given that modern humans evolved in southern Africa, why, with this head start, had all the innovations of plant and animal domestication, technological and 'civilizational complexity' developed elsewhere?" His reasons are biological, evolutionary, and geographic, and

he accounts for the dispersal, or lack of dispersal, of innovation meticulously. For instance, by a quirk of natural history, Africa had few animal species that fulfilled the minimal criteria for domestication: fast breeding, instinctively herding, and suitability for milk, meat, and/or work and transport. Thus, zebras might look like horses but are far too aggressive to tame; rhinos are too slow breeding; antelope too high-strung. None of Africa's wild grains are suitable for domestication for various reasons. The question Diamond then doesn't ask is: "Why so few suitable species?" At least with regard to animals of the savanna, one answer might be the same reason southern Africa never suffered the mass extinctions of megafauna in the Pleistocene. Since humans and animals coevolved in southern Africa, the animals had time to develop strategies for evading the ever more intelligent and resourceful hunters and gatherers. Consequently, the human and animal communities remained in a higher state of dynamic balance and therefore had more stability than elsewhere.

17 Among the Ju/twasi (Ju/hoansi) of the Kalahari in the 1960s, this was on average 2.7 days for men and 2.1 for women, according to Richard Lee, "Politics, Sexual and Non-Sexual in Egalitarian Society," in *Politics and History in Band Societies*, eds. Eleanor Leacock and Richard Lee (New York: Cambridge University Press, 1982), 40.

18 Thomas, *The Old Way*, 25.

19 Ibid., 106. Richard Lee identified 105 species of edible plants constituting the bulk of the subsistence diet. Richard Lee, *The !Kung San* (Cambridge: Cambridge University Press, 1979), 438. Women were further empowered as providers and feeders of the family by the innovation of fire making and cooking, which significantly increase the nutritional value of gathered food.

20 Craig Foster and Damon Foster, *The Great Dance: A Hunter's Story*, documentary film press kit (June 2001), 10.

21 Thomas, "Reflections: The Old Way," 81.

22 John Marshall, *A Kalahari Family: Part One, A Far Country* (Waterton, MA: Documentary Educational Resources, 2002).

23 Thomas, "Reflections: The Old Way," 80.

24 Ibid., 81–83. In the early 1980s Claire Ritchie and John Marshall did a study on the causes of death; they spoke to some three thousand Ju/twasi individuals who recalled fifteen hundred deaths going back one hundred years. Those caused by animals most commonly involved snakes and leopards. During Elizabeth's stay in the Kalahari, she heard of several people who had been killed by leopards. Leopards were also known to scavenge temporarily unburied dead, a habit they seemed to develop during the smallpox epidemics of the past. Since leopards (also genus *Panthera*) did kill people, the Bushmen showed them no respect and feared them. The only healthy Bushman ever injured by a lion in the collective generational memory of the people was a man who had been mauled while helping a group of Herero ranchers to hunt a cattle killer during the 1966 lion wars in Botswana. A young paraplegic Juwa girl was also killed by a lion. In this regard, Elizabeth notes that her daughter is a paraplegic and was a source of intense interest to captive lions and tigers. She proposed that the girl's slow, uneven movement close to the ground caused lions to regard her differently than they regarded able-bodied people.

25 Ibid., 90. Elizabeth recounts other perplexing encounters. One night Elizabeth was alone in her tent, with her family and most of the Bushmen gone. A lioness suddenly appeared between the two camps and began a deafening roaring near her tent. Terrified, trembling, unable to think clearly, Elizabeth went outside with a lantern and found an edgy, nervous, impatient lioness pacing back and forth, her tail sweeping

angrily from side to side looking at the Juwa camp. The lioness occasionally leapt back out of range of the lantern's beam. This time everyone kept quiet. No one knew what she wanted. She kept this up for thirty-five minutes (Elizabeth timed her) and then left. No one ever figured out what she wanted.

26 Craig Foster and Damon Foster, *The Great Dance: A Hunter's Story* (Amsterdam, Cape Town: Earthrise and Liquid Pictures, Off the Fence Productions, 2000).

27 Foster and Foster, *The Great Dance.*

28 Francis Kuo, "A Potential Natural Treatment for Attention-Deficit/Hyperactivity Disorder: Evidence from a National Study," *American Journal of Public Health* 94, no. 9 (September 2004): 1580–86. See also the advocacy work of "No Child Left Inside," Chesapeake Bay Foundation, 2008.

29 See Jared Diamond, "The Worst Mistake in the History of the Human Race," *Discover*, May 1987, 64–66. In this opinion piece, Diamond comments on the evidence from paleo-anthropology to argue that the Paleolithic diet and lifestyle of our hunter-gatherer ancestors were far superior to those of the agricultural civilizations that followed, which sacrificed variety and high protein for larger quantities of carbohydrates. Modern nutritionists seem to be returning to the "Paleolithic Prescription," a diet based on a great variety of vegetables, some fruit, high protein, and low carbohydrates. When we factor in a low-stress lifestyle, flexible hours, physical activity in fresh air, closeness to family and friends, and often environments of stunning natural beauty, it is hard not to agree with Sahlins that this represents a "Zen affluence"; Marshall Sahlins, *Stone Age Economics* (Chicago: Aldine Atherton, 1972), 1.

30 Richard B. Lee and Irven DeVore, eds., *Kalahari Hunter-Gatherers: Studies of the !Kung San and Their Neighbors* (Cambridge, MA: Harvard University Press, 1998), 10.

31 Richard Lee and Eleanor Leacock, eds., *Politics and History in Band Societies* (New York: Cambridge University, 1982), 1, 7, 8.

32 John Zerzan, *Future Primitive and Other Essays* (New York: Autonomedia, 1994).

33 The controversial game license program continued until 1990. By 1999 the population in the reserve was around 450. In 2006, as a result of a successful lawsuit against the Botswana government, about 189 of the survivors who filed the lawsuit were allowed to return with their families. But the nomadic way of life of the original hunter-gatherers is over. See Kristin Broyhill, Robert Hitchcock, and Megan Biesele, "Current Situations Facing the San Peoples of Southern Africa," *Kalahari People's Fund* (2007), http://www.kalaharipeoples.org/index_htm_files/Current%20Situations%20of%20the%20San.pdf. For an overview of the San in the context of contemporary African hunter-gatherers, see Richard B. Lee, "African Hunter-Gatherers: Survival, History and the Politics of Identity," *African Study Monograph*, Suppl. 26 (March 2001): 257–80.

34 Edwin N. Wilmsen and James Denbow, "Paradigmatic History of San-speaking Peoples and Currrent Attempts at Revision," *Current Anthropology* 31, no. 5 (December 1990): 490.

35 For a more explicit epistemological engagement of some the French postmodernists, see my paper "Beyond Postmodernism: Restoring the Primal Quest for Meaning to Political Inquiry." *Human Studies* 20: 1997 (Kluwer Academic Publishers: The Netherlands, 1997), 75–94. The most penetrating and best written single piece I know on the double bind of postmodernism is the chapter entitled "The Postmodern Mind" by Richard Tarnas in his magisterial *Passion of the Western Mind* (New York: Ballantine/Random House, 1991), 395–410.

36 Edwin Wilmsen, *Land Filled with Flies: A Political Economy of the Kalahari* (Chicago: University of Chicago Press, 1989), xii. Wilmsen took this a step further to impugn the entire ethnographic enterprise as "construct[ing] alien cultures" (p. xv), specifically

notions of "Bushmen" and "hunter-gatherers" in order to "provide empirical support for Euroamerican moral philosophy by creating a primitive 'other,' in order...to authenticate its own form of [civilized] existence."

37 Edwin Wilmsen, "Decolonizing the Mind: Steps toward Cleansing the Bushman Stain from Southern African History," in *Miscast: Negotiating the Presence of the Bushman*, ed. Pippa Skotnes (Cape Town, South Africa: University of Cape Town Press, 1996), 187. Wilmsen mocks the motivation: "Nostalgia for an innocent past before we Europeans were cast out into the sorrows of self awareness spawned the current form of 'Bushman';...it arises from the European conception of the 'naturalness' of small-scale societies as opposed to the 'artificiality' of industrial society, often expressed in the fear that wherever 'civilization' materializes the 'primitive' in people is attenuated."

38 Robert J. Gordon, *The Bushman Myth: The Making of a Namibian Underclass* (San Francisco: West View Press, 1992), 9. In reviewing the variety of images of Bushmen from brutal to noble savage, Gordon observes (p. 219): "The changing image appears to be more the product of the increased alienation/urbanization of the writer *than a portrayal of the actual situation* [emphasis added]." Hidden in his critique is the notion that deconstruction is somehow more true, or closer to knowing the actual situation. Yet, as I argue, the relentlessly critical posture is itself another agenda. Ultimately, any description of the actual situation will only be true, real, and meaningful to the degree to which it is a synthesis of multiple and opposing perspectives, taking into account the fullest context of each perspective, guided by the best current big picture available.

39 Long after the revisionist debate began, we can still see how the deconstructionist spirit ties researchers on this subject in methodological knots. A good example is Robert Kelly's survey of hunting-gathering societies, *The Foraging Spectrum: Diversity in Hunter-Gatherer Lifeways* (Washington, DC: Smithsonian Press, 1995). As the title suggests, this is a well-researched and generally illuminating survey of the range of variation. Full of nuance and detail, it is striking in avoiding coming to any coherent conclusion about hunter-gatherers. Kelly begins with a clear revisionist manifesto, rejecting the central meaning project of anthropology: "I hope this book helps [the reader]...avoid falling prey to the temptation to use a modern hunter gatherer people, or some amalgam of foraging societies, as an analogy for reconstructing the past" (p. xiii). But in the concluding chapter Kelly seems to have second thoughts, realizing the danger of the discipline degenerating into a dazzling, but ultimately meaningless, display of surfaces. He acknowledges that an anthropology that fails to illuminate the human condition is worthless, and he refers to the search for human nature as a "worthy enterprise...the heart of anthropology" (p. 337). Chastened by decades of relentless deconstructionism, Kelly pays lip service to this "worthy enterprise" but refuses to take up the challenge himself: "Whether or not there is such a thing as human nature is not a question I am prepared to debate here." However, being left with an encyclopedia of detail is transparently unsatisfying and clearly fails the mission of anthropology Kelly affirmed a little earlier, so one is only slightly amazed to find Kelly reversing himself yet again:

> I am of course sympathetic to the use of ethnographic data in reconstructing the past. I am sympathetic to it because if people hunt and gather and if interaction with the environment exerts any kind of influence over their life-ways, *then how living people make decisions should bear some resemblance to how people in the past made decisions as well. This does not mean that living people are identical to those of the past, but it does assume that living foragers operate under the same general evolutionary principles as did prehistoric*

*hunter-gatherers, albeit under some new conditions and constraints and different historical circumstances and cultural particulars* [p. 341, emphasis added].

Implicit in this is the well-established fact that we inherit a human nature forged under conditions of hunting and gathering in wilderness. So Kelly ends up agreeing with the classicists like Lee and Leacock for whom, as Lee put it, "it seems implausible that the behavior of ancient foragers would fall entirely outside the range of behaviors of the modern ones" (Lee, *The !Kung San*, 433, 434).

40 Jacqueline S. Solway and Richard Lee, "Foragers, Genuine or Spurious?" *Current Anthropology* 31, no. 2 (April 1990): 109–46.

41 After diagnosing this particular form of the "eclipse of reason," the Frankfurt School started to reconstruct an emancipatory epistemology rooted in Socratic and Platonic notions of dialectical thinking. See especially Max Horkheimer, *Eclipse of Reason* (New York: Seabury Press, 1974), and Herbert Marcuse, *Reason and Revolution: Hegel and the Rise of Social Theory* (Boston: Beacon Press, 1960).

## Chapter 7. Primal Politics

1 Jiro Tanaka, "Paradigmatic History of San-Speaking Peoples and Currrent Attempts at Revision," *Current Anthropology* 31, no. 5 (December 1990): 515–16.

2 Mathias Guenther, *Tricksters & Trancers: Bushman Religion and Society* (Bloomington: Indiana University Press, 1999), 22.

3 Guenther points out that among the Khutse Bushmen, snare hunting is mostly done by women, who also occasionally hunt larger game (Guenther, *Tricksters & Trancers*, 27). There are hunting-gathering societies in which women hunt, such as the Agta of the Philippine rain forest, where women regularly hunt with bow and spear. See Bion Griffin, "*Agta* Forager Women in the Philippines," *Cultural Survival Quarterly* 8, no. 2: 21–23.

4 Richard Lee, "Politics, Sexual and Non-sexual in an Egalitarian Society," in *Politics and History in Band Societies*, eds. Eleanor Leacock and Richard Lee (New York: Cambridge University, 1982), 44. According to Elizabeth Marshall Thomas most couples had between one and four children. Nine live births was the highest number on record for any Bushman woman — much lower than in any other human population that does not use contraception. The average age for a first pregnancy was 19.5 years for Ju/twasi women. The strenuous work and absence of body fat prevented hunter-gatherer women from menstruating at an early age. Extended breast-feeding and lactation, often for the first four to five years after birth, continued to inhibit menstruation and thus served as a natural form of birth control. See Elizabeth Marshall Thomas, *The Old Way: A Story of the First People* (New York: Farrar, Straus & Giroux, 2006), 192.

5 Craig Foster and Damon Foster, directors of *The Great Dance: A Hunter's Story* (Earthrise and Liquid Pictures, Off the Shelf Production, 2000).

6 Richard Lee, "Christmas in the Kalahari," *Natural History*, December 1969, 14–22.

7 Ibid., 3.

8 Ibid., 4.

9 Lee, "Politics, Sexual and Non-sexual," 45.

10 Quoted in Guenther, *Tricksters & Trancers*, 44.

11 Lee, "Politics, Sexual and Non-sexual," 47.

12 Lorna Marshall, *The !Kung of Nyae Nyae* (Cambridge, MA: Harvard University Press, 1976), 293.

13 Ibid., 293–95.

14 Thomas, *The Old Way*, 62.
15 Marshall, *The !Kung*, 294.
16 Polly Weissner defines *!hxaro* as "reciprocal delayed gift making, giving and receiving of any non-food item of value." In the framework of *!hxaro*, personal property is defined as a resource "to develop symmetrical bonds of friendship between a variety of individuals." Polly Weissner, "Risk Reciprocity and Social Influences on !Kung San Economics," in *Politics and History in Band Societies*, eds. Eleanor Leacock and Richard Lee (New York: Cambridge University, 1982).
17 Ibid. See also Polly Weissner, "Historical Dimensions of !Kung (Ju/hoan) *Hxaro*" in R. Vossen and E. Wilmsen, *Khoisan Studies: Interdisciplinary Perspectives* (Hamburg: Helmut Buske, 2001).
18 While the archaeological evidence for the antiquity of an *!hxaro* economy is skimpy, it is not unreasonable to assume that this emerged early on, enhancing the survival advantage for those *Homo sapiens* who developed a capacity for high levels of communication, cooperation, and bonding. See Alan Barnard and James Woodburn, "Property, Power and Ideology in Hunter-Gatherer Societies: An Introduction," in *Hunters and Gatherers 2: Property, Power and Ideology*, eds. Tim Ingold, David Riches, and James Woodburn (New York: Berg, 1988), 22.
19 Marshall Sahlins, *Stone Age Economics* (Chicago: Aldine Atherton, 1972), 1. For the landmark work on "Buddhist economics," see E. F. Schumacher, *Small Is Beautiful: Economics as If People Mattered: 25 Years Later… With Commentaries* (Dublin, Ireland: Hartley & Marks Publishers, 1999).
20 Guenther, *Tricksters & Trancers*, 48.
21 Chief Luther Standing Bear, *Land of the Spotted Eagle* (Lincoln: University of Nebraska Press, 1933/1978), 37.
22 Willimien Le Roux, "The Challenges of Change: A Survey of the Effects of Preschool on Basawara Primary School Children in the Ghanzi Distrinct of Botswana," Ghanzi Kuru Development Trust (1995), as quoted by Guenther, *Tricksters & Trancers*, 51.
23 Ibid., 34.
24 Marshall, *The !Kung*, 290.
25 Thomas, *The Old Way*, 210. Richard Lee estimated that men tend to do about two-thirds of the talking in discussions involving both sexes, and they act as group spokespersons more frequently than women, but on some issues, the older women do most of the talking and are listened to with respect. For an analysis of power and gender among the !Kung San (Ju/twasi), see Lee, "Politics, Sexual and Non-sexual," 37–59.
26 See George Silberbauer, "Political Process in G/wi Bands," in *Politics and History in Band Societies*, eds. Eleanor Leacock and Richard Lee (New York: Cambridge University, 1982), 27–28.
27 Ibid., 27.
28 Other mechanisms of reverse dominance reinforcing egalitarianism (common to many hunting-gathering societies) include a rich variety of mocking put-downs, teasing, and joking as well as ritualization of conflict, like the song duels of Eskimos. Some antagonists become so engrossed in the artistry of singing they forget the cause of the grudge (Guenther, *Trickers & Trancers*, 36). When an argument is turning ugly and in danger of breaking out into violence, the camp gathers around the furious combatants, shouting, laughing, and jeering — a response that at first might provoke further intensification of anger but quickly produces confusion at the inappropriateness of the group's response and generally ends in collective mirth. Laughter is also used often to dispel tension even in a threatening situation, as when someone is bitten by a poisonous

snake and is in pain and mortal danger. For a comparative discussion, see Richard Borshay Lee, *The !Kung San: Men, Women, and Work in a Foraging Society* (New York: Cambridge University Press, 1979).

29 Ibid., 398.

30 Ibid., 397.

31 Sharon O'Brian, *American Indian Tribal Governments* (Norman: University of Oklahoma Press, 1989), 24. This was written by O'Brian at the request of the National Congress of American Indians, who were looking for a text on tribal government that could be used in Native American schools.

32 Cadwallader Colden is quoted in Bruce Johansen, *Forgotten Founders: How the American Indian Helped Shape Democracy* (Harvard, MA: Harvard Common Press, 1982), 39.

33 Ibid., 38.

34 Oren Lyons, interview with Bill Moyers, *The World of Ideas*, PBS, July 3, 1991.

35 Johansen, *Forgotten Founders*, 37. For the relevance of the Haudenosaunee experience to contemporary politics, see Taiaiake Alfred, *Peace, Power, and Righteousness: An Indigenous Manifesto* (Ontario, Canada: Oxford University Press, 1999).

36 C. G. Jung, in interview on "Face to Face: Professor Jung," BBC, 1959. Distributed under license from BBC Worldwide Americas, by Kino International Corporation, as additional original footage in *Matter of Heart: The Extraordinary Journey of C. G. Jung into the Soul of Man*, directed by Mark Whitney (New York: Kino Video, 2001).

## Chapter 8. "If You Don't Dance, You Die"

1 As quoted in H. P. Duerr, *Dreamtime: Concerning the Boundary between Civilization and Wilderness* (Oxford: Basil Blackwell, 1985), 110.

2 As in Stephen Watson's poetic rendering of the Bleek and Lloyd translations in *Return of the Moon: Versions from the /Xam* (Cape Town, South Africa: Carrefoure Press, 1991), 21.

3 *Cave of Forgotten Dreams*, directed by Werner Herzog (2010), DVD; http://www.ifcfilms.com/films/cave-of-forgotten-dreams.

4 W. E. Wendt, " 'Art Mobilier' from the Apollo 11 Cave, South West Africa: Africa's Oldest Dated Works of Art," *The South African Archaeological Bulletin* 31, no. 121/122 (June 1976): 5–11, http://www.jstor.org/stable/3888265. One image is a feline therianthrope that Wendt estimates with "near certainty" was created between twenty-seven thousand and twenty-five thousand years before the present.

5 For example, the site at Driekopseiland in the Northern Cape contains some 3,500 engravings of geometrical figures and animals, some of which date from before 2,500 years ago. See David Morris, *Driekopseiland and the Rain's Magic Power: History and Landscape in a New Interpretation of Northern Cape Rock Engraving Site* (master's thesis, University of the Western Cape, 2003).

6 Jean Clottes and David Lewis-Williams, *The Shamans of Prehistory: Trance and Magic in the Painted Caves* (New York: Harry Abrams, 1996), 38.

7 David Lewis-Williams, one of the leaders in the field, gives one of the most thoughtful accounts of its history in *The Mind in the Cave: Consciousness and the Origins of Art* (New York: Thames and Hudson, 2002) and in his introduction to Thomas A. Dowson and David Lewis-Williams, eds., *Contested Images: Diversity in Southern African Rock Art Research* (Johannesburg: Witwatersrand University Press, 1994). See also the illuminating account from Graham Hancock, one of the few people who has both studied the literature exhaustively and has direct firsthand experience of shamanic states of

consciousness, *Supernatural: Meetings with the Ancient Teachers of Mankind* (New York: Consortium Books, 2006). He provides a funny, scathing indictment of the narrow-minded arrogance of the early scholars.

8 For an important collection of papers providing an assessment of this invaluable collection, see Janette Deacon and Thomas A. Dowson, eds., *Voices from the Past: /Xam Bushmen and the Bleek and Lloyd Collection* (Johannesburg: Witwatersrand University Press, 1996). Most of the Bleek and Lloyd collections were housed in four different institutions and have now been brought together and digitized. This archival wealth (from the South African National Library, Iziko South African Museum, the University of South Africa, and the University of Cape Town) is indexed, cataloged, and made available free online at http://lloydbleekcollection.cs.uct.ac.za/.

9 One of the first Europeans to try to understand the southern African art was Sir John Barrow, who explored the Cape in 1797 and 1798. He marveled that such sensitive paintings could have been composed by the same people colonists regarded as little more than animals. In a rare moment of critical self-reflection, he suggested that perhaps Bushmen had been made more barbaric by their contact with Europeans. In 1835 Sir James Alexander developed Barrow's ideas, going beyond a purely aesthetic appreciation to seeing the paintings as narratives of San life. Barrow and Alexander were intrigued by the conspicuous obscurity of some of the images; at least they knew that they did not know. Anticipating future enlightenment, George William Stow in the 1860s started making detailed painted copies of rock paintings, collecting an archive for those modern researchers who would eventually find in ethnography and neuropsychology crucial interpretive keys. David Lewis-Williams, *Discovering Southern African Rock Art* (Cape Town, South Africa: David Phillip, 1996), 35.

10 David Lewis-Williams, *Images of Mystery: Rock Art of the Drakensberg* (Cape Town, South Africa: Double Storey, 2003), 25.

11 Stephen Watson, *Return of the Moon: Versions from the /Xam* (Cape Town, South Africa: Carrefour Press, 1991), 71.

12 This version is one of the seventy Mathias Guenther recorded. See Mathias Guenther, *Tricksters & Trancers: Bushman Religion and Society* (Bloomington: Indiana University Press, 1999), 77.

13 Megan Biesele, *Women Like Meat: The Folklore and Foraging Ideology of the Kalahari Ju/'hoan* (Bloomington: Indiana University Press, 1993), 61.

14 Guenther, *Tricksters & Trancers*, 77.

15 Ibid., 98.

16 Ibid., 107.

17 Lorna Marshall, *The Nyae Naye !Kung: Beliefs and Rites,* Peabody Museum monographs (Cambridge, MA: Harvard University, 1999), 9.

18 Bradford Keeney, *Bushman Shaman: Awakening the Spirit through Ecstatic Dance* (Rochester, VT: Destiny Books, 2005), 49.

19 Richard Katz was the first to do an in-depth study of trance healing with the Ju/twasi San, as part of the Harvard Kalahari Research Group in the late sixties. As a community psychologist, Katz recognized the futility of false objectivity and included his reactions in his observations. At the same time he wanted to avoid distorting the uniqueness of a Bushman experience by reducing it to categories familiar to other religious and healing traditions. See his *Boiling Energy: Community Healing among the Kalahari !Kung* (Cambridge, MA: Harvard University Press, 1982) as the standard systematic study. It has been updated with Megan Biesele and Verna St. Denis, in *Healing Makes Our Hearts*

*Happy: Spirituality and Cultural Transformation among the Kalahari Ju/hoansi* (Rochester, VT: Inner Traditions, 1997).

20 Katz, *Boiling Energy*, 42.

21 Keeney, *Bushman Shaman*, 74–75.

22 Katz, *Boiling Energy*, 48.

23 Ibid., 42.

24 Keeney, *Bushman Shaman*, 17–18.

25 Ibid.

26 John Marshall, *N/um Tchai* (Watertown, MA: Documentary Educational Resources, 1969).

27 Keeney, *Bushman Shaman*, 51. Keeney elaborates: "At first I stood outside the dance circle watching.... It took only a few minutes for me to feel the now familiar tingling in my legs. My calves and thighs felt like sharp needles were being stuck into them. They twitched and jerked as the pricking gave way to the flow of an inner current.... Then, without expectation, I felt my hip muscles start to move. It was as if there were strings attached to my hips held by some puppeteer in the sky who was lifting them up and down."

28 Ibid., 139.

29 Biesele's comments are quoted in Keeney, *Bushman Shaman*, 183. David Lewis-William similarly endorsed Keeney: "Eventually, after many astounding experiences, the people accepted him [Keeney] as a "doctor," a *n/om k"au*, one who is believed to possess and control a supernatural essence or power that can be harnessed to heal people with physical and social ills. Other anthropologists, so the Bushmen told him, had attempted to become *n/om k"ausi*, but they had not succeeded in pushing through to the deeply altered state of consciousness that is key to Bushman spirituality. At once, hitherto closed doors began to open.... The healers had not jealously kept secret from others certain aspects of what they told him. Rather, they simply believed that they would not be understood by earlier researchers. The openness of Bushmen about their belief has always been there. Over and above that, the mutual high regard and esteem between Keeney and his teachers is patent. The Bushmen want the world to know as fully and accurately as possible, what they truly believe." See Bradford Keeney, *Ropes to God: Experiencing the Bushman Spiritual Universe* (Philadelphia: Ringing Rocks Press, 2003), 161.

30 In this way Keeney avoids the misplaced concreteness we sometimes find in some scholars who have not shared the experience and compensate by slavishly transcribing translated stories and turning metaphors into things. We see a bit of this in Mircea Eliade's rather rigid notions of "pure" and "degenerate" shamanism, and his tendency to treat accounts of the upperworld, the underworld, and the world tree as definitive. In the supernatural, as in the natural world, the meaning of the experience is ultimately refracted through the life, language, and situation of the searcher.

31 Keeney, *Bushman Shaman*, 130.

32 Ibid.

33 Ibid., 42.

34 Ibid., 84–85.

35 C. G. Jung, *Collected Works*, vol. 7, 409, quoted in *C. G. Jung: Word and Image*, ed. Aniela Jaffe (New York: Bollingen, 1978), 123.

36 Erich Neumann, *Depth Psychology and a New Ethic* (New York: Putnam Press, 1969), 96.

37 Both Kabbalah and yoga texts similarly warn of the dangers involved in activating these enormous psychic energies without the psychological maturity and cultural framework

to handle them. C. G. Jung also warned of the delusions of grandeur associated with "psychic inflation." The history of Kabbalah contains stories of wild messianic attempts to mobilize divine energies to alleviate the sufferings of the persecuted Jewish masses. Many such attempts ended in death, madness, or apostasy, as in the infamous case of the false messiah Sabbatai Tzvi, who, after mobilizing masses of ordinary Jews, then converted to Islam. For this reason, the esoteric practice of Judaism was restricted, generally only permitted to those over forty years of age. In the eighteenth century there was a revival of a more democratic practice of Kabbalah in the Chassidic movement among the impoverished masses of eastern European Jews. It was repressed by the more critical rationalistic western European communities — the *mitnagdim*, or skeptics and deniers. Most Jewish religious communities still focus on a ritualistic and rule-guided approach to Judaism and tend to invoke the traditional prohibition on Kabbalistic study and practice.

38 Adin Steinsaltz, *The Thirteen Petalled Rose*, trans. Yehuda Hanegbi (New York: Basic Books, 1980), 103

39 These comments apply to healing in the traditional context of the nomadic hunting-and-gathering San. With sedentarization and the need to engage in wage labor, gifted healers are now charging outsiders for their services. In 1998 the Ju/twasi of Nyae Nyae were charging a standard fee to outsiders to perform a more or less authentic healing dance. Since the dance requires a community, the income is shared. There is some evidence that this practice of payment or barter goes back to earliest contact between San and Bantu along the east coast of South Africa. Bantu would hire Bushman healers to help with rain making, treating illness, and various forms of divination.

40 Clottes and Lewis-Williams, *The Shamans of Prehistory*. While poststructuralists criticized this as "importing meaning from other traditions," the work is an excellent example of collaboration and how synthesis — the bigger picture — can illuminate meaning.

41 Judith Thurman, "Letter from Southern France: First Impression. What Does the World's Oldest Art Say about Us?," *New Yorker*, June 23, 2008.

42 The black-and-white sketch comes from a South African Museum reprint of a lecture by David Lewis-Williams, *The World of Man and the World of Spirit: An Interpretation of the Linton Rock Painting*, Margaret Shaw Lecture 2 (Cape Town: South African Museum, 1988). For a beautiful photographic collection, see Lewis-Williams, *Images of Mystery*.

43 *The Great Dance: A Hunter's Story*, directed by Craig Foster and Damon Foster (Earthrise and Liquid Pictures, Off the Shelf Production, 2000). This work is a landmark in both ethnographic filmmaking and as a work of film art. It is unique in dealing with shamanic states of consciousness through a type of shamanically inspired filmmaking, which expresses eloquently the experience of the persistence hunt as a transcendent experience.

44 Lewis-Williams, *The World of Man*. The Linton Panel was found in a rock shelter in the Cape Province and was so impressive, and thought to be so vulnerable to vandalism, that it was cut out of the solid rock wall in a single slab two meters long and almost one meter tall. It is now housed in the South Africa Museum in Cape Town.

45 David Lewis-Williams, "Southern African Shamanistic Rock Art in Its Social and Cognitive Contexts," in *The Archaeology of Shamanism*, ed. Neil Prince (New York: Routledge, 2001), 33–34.

46 David Lewis-Williams and Thomas A. Dowson, "Through the Veil: San Rock Paintings and the Rock Face," *South African Archaeological Bulletin* 45 (1990): 5–16. See also

Lewis-William's detailed commentary on some particularly striking images and photographs in his *Images of Mystery: Rock Art of the Drakensberg* (Cape Town, South Africa: Double Storey Books, 2003).

47 For a lively, illuminating discussion on therianthropy, and this picture in particular, see Hancock, *Supernatural*, 80–81.

48 For a general discussion of paleolithic rock painting and the connection between the European and South African paintings, see Lewis-Williams, *The Mind in the Cave*, and Clottes and Lewis-Williams, *The Shamans of Prehistory*. See also Lewis-Williams's many papers on this subject, especially his closely argued, heavily footnoted "Harnessing the Brain: Vision and Shamanism in Upper Paleolithic Western Europe," in *Beyond Art: Pleistocene Image and Symbol*, eds. M. Conkey et al. (Memoirs of the California Academy of Sciences, no. 23, 1997); and "Agency, Art and Altered Consciousness: A Motif in French (Quercy) Upper Palaeolithic Parietal Art," *Antiquity* 71, no. 274 (December 1997).

## Chapter 9. Boundary Crossing

1 Mircea Eliade, *Shamanism: Archaic Techniques of Ecstasy* (Princeton, NJ: Princeton University Press, 1964).

2 Hans Peter Duerr, *Dreamtime: Concerning the Boundary between Wilderness and Civilization* (Oxford: Basil Blackwell, 1985), 46.

3 Ibid., 64.

4 Hermann Hesse, *Steppenwolf* (New York: Holt, Reinhardt, and Winston, 1990).

5 David Lewis-Williams, "A Visit to the Lion's House: The Structure, Metaphor and Sociopolitical Significance of a Nineteenth Century Bushman Myth," in *Voices from the Past: /Xam Bushmen and the Bleek and Lloyd Collection*, eds. Janette Deacon and Thomas A. Dowson (Johannesburg: Witwatersrand University Press, 1996), 122–41.

6 Chief Luther Standing Bear, *Land of the Spotted Eagle* (Lincoln: University of Nebraska Press, 1933/1978), 192.

7 Stanley Vestal, *Sitting Bull: Champion of the Sioux* (Norman: University of Oklahoma Press, 1989), 107.

8 Lame Deer and Richard Erdoes, *Lame Deer, Seeker of Vision: The Life of a Sioux Medicine Man* (New York: Simon and Schuster, Touchstone, 1972), 79.

9 Ibid., 79, 80.

10 Walter Williams, *The Spirit and the Flesh: Sexual Diversity in American Indian Culture* (Boston: Beacon Press, 1992).

11 Stephen R. Keller and Edward O. Wilson, *The Biophilia Hypothesis* (Washington, DC: Island Press, 1993), 21.

12 Roger S. Ulrich has demonstrated that people looking at images of nature scenes have more relaxed encephalograms (measuring brain-wave activity) than those watching urban displays. See Roger S. Ulrich, "Biophilia, Biophobia, and Natural Landscapes" in Keller and Wilson, *The Biophilia Hypothesis*, 73–137.

13 Ibid., 106. All patients were recovering from gall-bladder surgery. The pairs were matched according to age, sex, weight, tobacco use, and previous hospitalization. These restorative effects seem to be most dramatic when people are under high stress and experience anxiety for long periods, especially in places of confinement, such as hospitals, prisons, and certain work environments.

14 Ibid., 107. Postoperative recovery response was measured in a number of ways, including blood pressure, need for painkillers, and length of postoperative hospitalization. Useful though it might be to have precise quantitative confirmation of the physiological depth in the human response to nature, I can't help thinking of the words of the notorious Harry Harlow: "by these means we were able to demonstrate conclusively what had always been obvious to everyone for years except psychologists." At least the primates in these studies were not tortured to induce experimental stress.

15 In contrast to Ian Player's more spiritually oriented wilderness immersion, programs like Outward Bound and National Outdoor Leadership (NOLS) tend to focus on "hard skills" — navigating, rock climbing, rappelling, finding bush food and water, making shelter, kayaking, and so on. These require left brain–disciplined attention to the outer world. The left-right brain distinction refers to the approximate division of labor in the human brain, whereby the more focused instrumental means-ends tasks are controlled by the left hemisphere, while the more creative and integrative activities are controlled by the right hemisphere. While left-brain skills are a necessary prerequisite for surviving in the bush long enough to have other experiences, such focused attention tends to block the more relaxed, less directed states of minds associated with the right hemisphere, which facilitate reflection and more integrative spiritual experiences.

16 Tracy McCluhan, ed., *Touch the Earth: A Self Portrait of Indian Existence* (New York: Promontory Press, 1971), 23.

17 The van de Post quote is in Elizabeth Darby Junkin, ed., *South African Passage: Diaries of the Wilderness Leadership School* (Golden, CO: Fulcrum, 1987), viii.

## Chapter 10. The Outer Reaches of Inner Wilderness

1 For interviews with some of the key researchers in this area, see the documentary film *Entheogenesis: Awakening the Divine Within* (San Francisco: CMP Group in association with Critical Mass Productions, 2007), http://www.entheogen.tv/.

2 Terence McKenna makes an intriguing case for this early Neolithic use of hallucinogenic mushrooms in *Food of the Gods: The Search for the Original Tree of Knowledge: A Radical History of Plants, Drugs, and Human Evolution* (New York: Bantam, 1992); see especially 69–74.

3 Peter Furst, *Hallucinogens and Culture* (New York: Chandler and Sharp, 1972), 5.

4 R. Gordon Wasson, *Soma: Divine Mushroom of Immortality* (New York: Harcourt, Brace, and Jovanovich, 1968). Valentina and Gordon Wasson were among the first to document in magnificent detail the traditional use of psychedelic psilocybin mushrooms in Mesoamerican shamanism.

5 McKenna, *Food of the Gods*, 97–120.

6 Furst, *Hallucinogens and Culture*, 7–8.

7 Ibid., 2.

8 See the incisive detective work of Richard de Mille, *Castaneda's Journey: The Power and the Allegory* (Santa Barbara, CA: Capra Press, 1978), and *The Don Juan Papers: Further Castaneda Controversies* (Santa Barbara, CA: Ross Erikson Publishers, 1980).

9 Michael Harner, *The Way of the Shaman: A Guide to Power and Healing* (San Francisco: Harper & Row, 1980), 16.

10 Erika Dyck, "'Hitting Highs at Rock Bottom': LSD Treatment for Alcoholism, 1950–1970," *Social History of Medicine* 19, no. 2 (2006): 313–29. See also Abram

Hoffer and Humphry Osmond, *New Hope for Alcoholics* (New Hyde Park, NY: University Books, 1968).

11 Jay Stevens, *Storming Heaven: LSD and the American Dream* (New York: Grove Press, 1987), xiv.

12 Stanislav Grof's first major empirical and theoretical work was *Realms of the Human Unconscious: Observations from LSD Research* (New York: E. P. Dutton, 1976). It is still perhaps his most gripping and comprehensive introduction to his research.

13 Daniel Pinchbeck, *Breaking Open the Head: A Psychedelic Journey into the Heart of Contemporary Shamanism* (New York: Broadway Books, 2002), 191.

14 Stanislav Grof, *The Cosmic Game: Explorations of the Frontiers of Human Consciousness* (New York: State University of New York Press, 1998), 9.

15 Richard Tarnas, *The Passion of the Western Mind* (New York: Ballantine/Random House, 1991), 425.

16 One in ten Americans now take antidepressants. There was a 400 percent increase between the two periods, 1988–1994 and 2005–2008. Peter Wehrwein, "Astounding Increase in Anti-depressant Use by Americans," *Harvard Health Blog*, Harvard Medical School, October 20, 2011, http://www.health.harvard.edu/blog/astounding-increase-in-antidepressant-use-by-americans-201110203624.

17 R. R. Griffiths et al., "Psilocybin Can Occasion Mystical-Type Experiences Having Substantial Sustained Personal Meaning and Spiritual Significance," *Psychopharmacology*, January 2006, http://www.hopkinsmedicine.org/sebin/s/m/GriffithsPsilocybin.pdf, doi:10.1007/s00213-006-0457-5. See also Roxanne Khamsi, "Magic Mushrooms Really Cause 'Spiritual' Experiences," *New Scientist*, July 11, 2006, http://www.newscientist.com/article/dn9522-magic-mushrooms-really-cause-spiritual-experiences.html.

18 To prevent adverse side effects, each subject met several times with a medical professional monitor who stayed with the subject during the session. The session took place in a room designed like "a comfortable upscale living room." Lighting was indirect (no laboratory fluorescent strips or spotlights) and soft music was played. There were nine questionnaires and a follow-up survey. To eliminate expectation influencing results, a "red herring" group was given an additional session where they were told wrongly that they were receiving psilocybin. See Griffiths, "Psilocybin Can Occasion." For commentary, see Harriet de Wit et al., "Commentaries and Editorial on Article by Griffiths et al.," *Psychopharmacology*, July 2006, http://www.hopkinsmedicine.org/Press_releases/2006/GriffithsCommentaries.pdf.

19 David Nutt et al., "Development of a Rational Scale to Assess the Harm of Drugs of Potential Misuse," *The Lancet* 369, no. 9566 (March 24, 2007): 1047–53, http://www.thelancet.com/journals/lancet/article/PIIS0140673607604644/fulltext?_eventId=login 8/11/09.

20 Dyck, "'Hitting Highs at Rock Bottom,'" 313–29. See also Hoffer and Osmond, *New Hope for Alcoholics*.

21 Other psychedelics, like *ayahuasca* and psilocybin, seem to be capable of having similar effects for the same reason. Ibogaine is another. This is an enormously powerful hallucinogen capable of producing sometimes hellish journeys lasting up to thirty-six hours. It has been used traditionally by the Fang of Gabon "to break open the head" and find one's life. Dr. Deborah Mash, a neuropharmacologist, is conducting the first FDA-approved clinical trials using Ibogaine to treat alcoholics and narcotics addicts. For more about Ibogaine, visit http://www.ibogaine.org/.

22 Dyck, "'Hitting Highs at Rock Bottom,'" 313–29.

23 Daniel Pinchbeck gives a passionate, brilliant firsthand account of contemporary entheogenic shamanism in *Breaking Open the Head*.

24 The two major syncretistic Christian churches that use *ayahuasca* are the Church of Santo Daime (*Daime* being a colloquial Portuguese term for *ayahuasca*) and União do Vegetal (union of the plant). There is a third, smaller sect, Barquinha, which is syncretistic between the Afro-Brazilian religions of Umbanda and the Daime.

25 Tryptamine chemistry plays an important role in the regulation of consciousness. The best-known tryptamine is the ubiquitous serotonin 5-hydroxytryptamine, which is of course nonpsychedelic. Psilocybin, found in magic mushrooms, is a powerful psychedelic tryptamine. Ibogaine, the African hallucinogen, is made from the bark of a tree and has a tryptamine core. The most famous hallucinogen, LSD (lysergic acid diethylamide), also has a tryptamine core. DMT is actually found in the human brain, but only in very small quantities and for very short periods, since it is quickly broken down by MAO enzymes. Dennis McKenna, "Ayahuasca: An Ethnopharmacological History," in *Ayahuasca: The Sacred Vine of Spirits*, ed. Ralph Metzner (Rochester, VT: Park Street Press, 2006), 40–41.

26 Benny Shanon, *The Antipodes of the Mind: Charting the Phenomenology of the Ayahuasca Experience* (New York: Oxford University Press, 2002), 17.

27 Ibid., 41–44.

28 Each hallucinogenic plant and chemical, like each of the other varieties of shamanic technologies, seems to tune consciousness with its own typical menu of experiences. The broad characteristics overlap to some degree. For example, the *ayahuasca* experience tends to evoke more organic visions, like snakes, panthers, and plant deities. Telepathic phenomena are also more common with some mixtures of *ayahuasca*. The original name of one of the harmalines in the brew was "telepathine." Dimethyltryptamine (DMT), smoked on its own, will often conjure clownish mechanical elves and reveal exquisite geometrical fractal structures. Psilocybin mushrooms favor qualitatively different visions. Maria Sabina, the Mazatec shaman who introduced Gordon and Valentia Wasson to the mushroom religion of Mexico, saw her sacred mushrooms as "children with violins, children with trumpets, clown children who sing and dance around me" and emphasized the healing power of laughter and tears associated with the all-night *velada*. For Maria Sabina's poetry, see Jerome Rottenberg, ed., *Maria Sabina: Selections* (Berkeley: University of California Press, 2003), 155.

29 Albert Hofmann, "The Message of the Eleusinian Mysteries for Today's World," in *Entheogens and the Future of Religion*, ed. Robert Forte (San Francisco: The Council on Spiritual Practices, 2000), 33.

30 The story was told to F. Bruce Lamb, who translated and published it in Bruce Lamb, *Wizard of the Upper Amazon: The Story of Manuel Cordova-Rios* (Boston: Houghton Mifflin, 1974).

31 Ibid., 92.

32 Ibid., 97.

33 See Benny Shanon, "Biblical Entheogens: A Speculative Hypothesis," *Time and Mind: The Journal of Archaeology of Consciousness and Culture* 1, no. 1 (March 2008): 51–74. He points out that the desert shrub *Peganum harmala* (*harmal* in Arabic) contains the MAO inhibitors harmine and harmaline found in the vision vine, *Banisteriopsis caapi*, from which *ayahuasca* is prepared. This is also the bush some scholars suggest was the ingredient in the *soma* of the Hindu Vedas and the sacred drink of the ancient

Zoroastrian religion. While there are no biblical references to *Peganum* (a number of biblical plant names remain unidentified), there are numerous biblical references to acacia trees (*etzei shittim*), which were especially valued and which do contain the same DMT found in *ayahuasca*. In fact, the mixture of the two plants — the *Peganum* with the monoamine oxidase inhibitor and the acacia with the DMT — is used in South America to produce results similar to those of *ayahuasca*. The two plants are also used by traditional Bedouin and Arab healers.

34 William Irwin Thompson, *At the Edge of History* (San Francisco: Harper & Row, 1971), 109–10.

## Chapter 11. The Primal Polis: Socrates as Shaman

1 For Athenian democracy see H. D. F. Kitto, *The Greeks* (New York: Pelican, 1962); M. I. Finley, *The Ancient Greeks* (New York: Penguin, 1985); M. I. Finley, *Economy and Society in Ancient Greece* (New York: Penguin Books, 1983); Mogens Herman Hansen, *The Athenian Democracy in the Age of Demosthenes* (Oxford: Blackwell Publishers, 1992); and J. Peter Euben, J. R. Wallach, and J. Ober, eds., *Athenian Political Thought and the Reconstruction of American Democracy* (Ithaca, NY: Cornell University Press, 1994).

2 Max Horkheimer, "The Social Function of Philosophy," in *Critical Theory: Selected Essays* (New York: Continuum, 1975), 266.

3 Ibid., 265.

4 Susan Monoson, "Frank Speech, Democracy, and Philosophy: Plato's Debt to a Democratic Strategy of Civic Discourse," in Euban, Wallach, and Ober, *Athenian Political Thought*, 172–97.

5 Ibid.

6 Bruce A. Akerman and James Fishkin, *Deliberation Day* (New Haven, CT: Yale University Press, 2005). See also Jim Holt, "Export This?," *New York Times Sunday Magazine*, April 23, 2006.

7 Alan Bloom, *The Republic of Plato* (New York: Basic Books, 1968), 401. In dealing with the text of *The Republic*, I prefer to follow the earlier, more popular translation by the renowned Cambridge classicist Francis M. Cornford, *Republic of Plato* (New York: Oxford University Press, 1969), rather than the newer, celebrated translation by Alan Bloom. Cornford was raised in the British public school system at the turn of the century, during a neoclassical revival, when education was synonymous with literacy in Latin and Greek. Cornford's translation is more of a passionate, imaginative re-creation that is closer in spirit to the Socratic polis than the fastidious but sometimes clunky and obscurantist literalism of Bloom's translation. This is especially the case regarding the crucial chapter on the Good. For Bloom's defense of his "literal translation" against Cornford's imaginative sympathy, see Bloom, *The Republic of Plato*, vii–xx.

8 Cornford, *Republic of Plato*.

9 Ibid., 215.

10 Ibid., 217.

11 Ibid., 220.

12 Daisetz Suzuki, *What Is Zen?* (New York: Harper & Row, 1972), 1.

13 Ibid.

14 Cornford, *Republic of Plato*, 220.

15 Christopher Bache gives a wonderful account of such transpersonal moments in the

classroom in his book *Dark Night, Early Dawn: Steps to a Deep Ecology of Mind* (New York: State University of New York Press, 2000); see the chapter "Teaching in the Sacred Mind," pp. 183–212. Christopher Bache is a professor of theology at Youngstown State University.

16 Richard Livingstone, ed., *Plato, Portrait of Socrates: The Apology, Crito, and Phaedo* (London: Clarendon Press, 1966), 29.

17 See the classic work E. R. Dodds, *The Greeks and the Irrational* (Berkeley: University of California Press, 1951/2004).

18 Carl A. P. Ruck, "Mushrooms and Philosophers," *Journal of Ethnopharmacology* 4, no. 179 (1981): 205.

19 R. Gordon Wasson, Albert Hofmann, and Carl A. P. Ruck, *The Road to Eleusis: Unveiling the Secret of the Mysteries* (Berkeley, CA: North Atlantic Books, 2008). Their work was first published in 1978 in a limited edition, which quickly went out of print and was virtually unobtainable for many years. Library copies would disappear off the shelves. It has recently been republished as a commemorative edition on the thirtieth anniversary of the first publication. The work was largely ignored by scholars, demonstrating the truth of the notion that when ideas are controversial they are discussed, but when they are revolutionary they are ignored. For example, in 1994 Ed Beach's otherwise useful article on the Mysteries focuses on an old hermeneutic dispute between George Mylonas (*Eleusis and the Eleusinian Mysteries* [Princeton, NJ: Princeton University Press, 1961]) and Karoly Kerenyi, "Kore" in *Essay on a Science of Mythology: The Myth of the Divine Child and Mysteries of Eleusis*, eds. C. G. Jung and C. Kernyi (Princeton, NJ: Princeton University Press, 1963). The argument proceeds through layers of esoteric hermeneutic clarification and textual analysis in support of theoretical positions regarding the nature of ancient religion. Nowhere is the possibility mentioned of giving philosophy some experiential legs to stand on, that is, that there might be more or less universal categories of human religious experience at stake here, versions of which might even be directly accessible to scholars today. See Edward A. Beach, *The Eleusinian Mysteries* (1995), http://users.erols.com/nbeach/eleusis.html.

20 Ergot alkaloids play a rich and complex role in human history. They are found in morning glory seeds, from which the Aztecs made the sacred mixture *ololiqui*, consumed for shamanistic purposes as a gateway to the gods. In Europe, bread made from grain infected with ergot is thought to have been responsible for outbreaks of a mysterious disease — a gangrenous-like condition called the Holy Fire or St. Anthony's Fire — in the Middle Ages. The disease was named in honor of the saint to whose shrine those infected could journey to find relief. The relief is thought to be due to the fact that the traveling pilgrims would have moved through regions free from the infected bread.

21 See Ruck, "Mushrooms and Philosophers," 205. For general background, see Gordon Wasson's masterwork, *Soma: The Divine Mushroom of Antiquity* (New York: Harcourt, Brace, and Jovanovich, 1968).

22 For a characterization of this, see Wasson, Hofmann, and Ruck, *The Road to Eleusis*, 14: "It was something from the midwife's pharmacopoeia that had opened the passageway for the initiate's experience, a deadly poison that posed a final recidivist threat to both the cereal foods and the humans who depended on them for sustenance; but something from which, by knowledgeable intervention, like the old lore of the witch Hekate's herbalism, a birthing potion could be extracted. The drink of the ceremony was emblematic of the polarity of primitivism and culture, as was appropriate, since

birthing brought every woman close to the gates of death, which were also the source of life."

23 Danny Staples, trans., "The Homeric Hymn to Demeter," in Wasson, Hofmann, and Ruck, *The Road to Eleusis*, 69–83.

24 Albert Hofmann, "The Message of the Eleusinian Mysteries for Today's World," in *Entheogens and the Future of Religion*, ed. Robert Forte (San Francisco: Council on Spiritual Practices, 2000), 33.

25 Wasson, Hofmann, and Ruck, *The Road to Eleusis*, 33. Ruck (p. 47) also points out that there are no records for any expenditure on actors, stage, or dramatic paraphernalia. The structure of the *telestrion* and the forest of columns would have obscured the vision of much of the crowd. The life-changing experience could not have been simply theatrical; theater was a regular part of Greek life. "What was seen was a *phasmata*, a ghostly vision of the reality of another dimension and this revelation changed in a profound way one's relationship to this world."

26 Ibid., 43, 44. Hofmann points out that it is also highly probable that the Greeks would have also discovered another related source of ergot on the grass *Papsalum distichum* (unrelated to the grain rye), which is widespread in the Mediterranean basin. Since this tends to be nontoxic, it could be used in simpler powder form. It is also quite possible *kykeon* contained additional psychoactive plants or mushrooms.

27 The Greeks were ignorant of the nature of alcohol and the arts of distillation, which means the alcohol concentration of their wine could not have been more than 14 percent, at which levels it kills the fungus and stops the fermentation process. Yet Greek wines are regularly described as exceedingly strong, needing dilution to avoid causing illness, insanity, or death. They were generally diluted with three to eight parts water. Additional intoxicants were added in the form of psychoactive herbs, perfumes, and spices depending on the occasion. For example, the composition of wine drunk at symposia would be determined by the leader, the *symposiarchos*, who manipulated the ingredients depending on the desired effect. Wines consumed on sacred occasions were even stronger, according to one source, and sometimes produced madness. There are also accounts of suicides assisted by appropriately doctored wine. See Wasson, Hofmann, and Ruck, *The Road to Eleusis*, 100, 101.

28 Gorman's description of the shamanic Pythagoras could apply to Socrates: "Like the Buddha he converted his followers by producing an inward change in them, yet he held them spellbound, not by threats or admonitions, but by his sheer psychic and intellectual power. He was not essentially a moralist or an ascetic, but a thaumaturge and *intellectual who had triumphed over the boredom of pedantry and transformed learning into something mystical* [emphasis added]." See Peter Gorman, *Pythagoras: A Life* (New York: Routledge & Keegan Paul, 1979), fn42. For shamanic themes in *Plato's Socrates*, see Barry Cooper, "A Lump Bred Up in Darknesse: Two Tellurian Themes of the Republic," in *Politics, Philosophy, Writing: Plato's Art of Caring for Souls*, ed. Zdravko Planinc (Chicago: University of Missouri Press, 2001).

29 R. Hackforth, trans., *Plato's Phaedrus* (London: Cambridge University Press, 1972), 25.

30 Ibid., 24–25.

31 For an excellent analysis of the trial of Socrates and the profanation of the Mysteries, see M. I. Finley, *Aspects of Antiquity: Discoveries and Controversies* (New York: Pelican Books, 1977), 69–71.

32 Ibid., 69.

## Chapter 12. Our Primal Future

1 For a translation, see Benjamin Smith, J. D. Lewis-Williams, Geoffrey Blundell, and Christopher Chippindale, "Archaeology and Symbolism in the New South African Coat of Arms," *Antiquity* 74 (2000): 467–68.

2 The Huston Smith quote is from an interview with Roland Griffiths, published in a press release by the Johns Hopkins Medicine News and Information Services, http://www.hopkinsmedicine.org/Press_releases/2006/GriffithspsilocybinQ.

3 Jared Diamond, *Collapse: How Societies Choose to Fail or Succeed* (New York: Penguin, 2006), 6–7.

4 Geoff Dabelko, "Jon Foley: How to Feed Nine Billion and Keep the Planet Too," *New Security Beat*, October 12, 2011, http://www.newsecuritybeat.org/2011/10/jon-foley-how-to-feed-nine-billion-and-keep-the-planet-too/; see also TED lecture by John Foley, "The Other Inconvenient Truth," http://www.youtube.comwatch?v=uJhgGbRA6Hk.

5 For an excellent discussion of research on mirror neurons and its implications for our self-understanding, see Jeremy Rifkin, *The Empathic Civilization: The Race to Global Consciousness in a World in Crisis* (New York: Tarcher/Penguin, 2009), 82–90. Rifkin retells the history of civilization, making a powerful case that evolving human nature is at least as naturally empathetic as it is aggressive, competitive, and selfish. He then goes on to discuss the paradoxical relationship among increasing empathy, expanding human awareness, and energy use (entropy) as a way of framing the challenge of the epic shift in global human society already under way.

6 Patti Waldmeir, *The Anatomy of a Miracle: The End of Apartheid and the Birth of a New South Africa* (New York: Penguin, 1998), 91.

7 Nelson Mandela, *Long Walk to Freedom: The Autobiography of Nelson Mandela* (New York: Little Brown & Company, 1995), 482.

8 John Carlin has written a thrilling account of this remarkable piece of true-life political theater in *Playing the Enemy: Nelson Mandela and the Game That Made a Nation* (New York: Penguin Press, 2008), 169–70.

9 See the interview with François Pienaar in the documentary film *The 16th Man*, directed by Clifford Bestall, written by John Carlin (ESPN Films, 2010). See also the book by John Carlin, *Playing the Enemy*. Clint Eastwood directed a Hollywood feature film version, *Invictus*, starring Matt Damon and Morgan Freeman.

10 See, for example, "Sad South Africa: Cry, the Beloved Country. South Africa Is Sliding Downhill While Much of the Rest of the Continent Is Clawing Its Way Up," *The Economist*, October 20, 2012, http://www.economist.com/news/leaders/21564846-south-africa-sliding-downhill-while-much-rest-continent-clawing-its-way-up.

11 Kirkpatrick Sale, *Dwellers in the Land: The Bioregional Vision* (San Francisco: Sierra Club, 1985), 42.

12 Inuktitut terms for different forms and conditions of snow include: "snow that is falling, fine snow in good weather, freshly fallen snow, snow cover, soft snow that makes walking difficult, soft snow bank, hard and crystalline snow, snow that has thawed and refrozen, snow that has been rained on, powdery snow, windblown snow, fine snow with which the wind had covered an object, hard snow that yields to the weight of footsteps, snow that is being melted to make drinking water, a mix of snow and water for glazing sled runners, wet snow that is falling, snow that is drifting, and snow that is right for snow house building." Hugh Brody, *The Other Side of Eden: Hunters, Farmers and the Shaping of the World* (New York: Farrar, Straus & Giroux, 2000), 47.

13 E. S. Craighill Handy and Elizabeth Handy with Mary Kawena Pukui, *Native Planters in*

*Old Hawaii: Their Life, Lore and Environment*, Bishop Museum Bulletin 233 (Honolulu: Bishop Museum Press, 1991), 311, 323.

14 Quoted in ibid., 313.

15 See the MA'O farm website, http://maoorganicfarms.org/.

16 See the Findhorn eco-village website, http://www.findhorn.org.

17 Alan Weisman, *Gaviotas: A Village to Reinvent the World* (White River Junction, VT: Chelsea Green Publishing Company, 1995).

18 See the Sarvodaya website, http://www.sarvodaya.org.

19 Bryan Walsh, "Green Acres," *Time*, September 17, 2007, 55. See also Liz Walker, *Ecovillage at Ithaca: Pioneering a Sustainable Culture* (Canada: New Society Publishers, 2005). See the EVI-CSE website, http://ecovillageithaca.org/evi/.

20 See the Center for Transformative Action website, http://www.centerfortransformativeaction.org.

21 For evidence of the forced expulsion of civilian Arab populations, see the book by the notorious anti-Zionist Israeli historian Illan Pappe, *The Ethnic Cleansing of Palestine* (Oxford: Oneworld Publications, 2008). This is one of the more recent examples of a school of revisionist Israeli histories that began in the 1980s with books like Tom Segev, *1949: The First Israelis* (New York: Free Press, 1986) and Benny Morris, *The Birth of the Palestinian Refugee Problem* (Cambridge: Cambridge University Press, 1987). Such works contribute to a vital revisioning of official history. But as others have noted, there is a long lineage of self-hating zeal among Jewish scholars, what Yoram Hazony has described as the ideal of the Jew as "suffering servant." Benny Morris still affirms his Zionism in spite of his critique of its moral blindness.

22 Some early more utopian socialist Zionists naively imagined Palestinian Arabs welcoming Jews as liberators from feudalism and benefiting from the new society. Others, like Max Nordau and Ben Yehuda, the author of the first Hebrew dictionary, were shocked to find a country filled with Arabs, and they were deeply disturbed that Zionism might displace or cause injury to another oppressed group. But the exigencies of Jewish survival quickly trumped such qualms. At the turn of the century, Palestinian nationalism was still in its infancy, and the Jewish struggle focused on the imperial powers. The country had been a Turkish province for generations. It was then taken by the British in World War I and administered under a mandate from the League of Nations. The British, more attuned to rising Arab nationalism, had mixed feelings about a Jewish homeland, and they eventually closed the borders to Jewish immigration as Hitler came to power. This led to violent confrontation with the Jewish self-defense militia, the Haganah, and the underground right-wing Irgun. See the excellent chapter on this in Amos Elon, *The Israelis: Fathers and Sons* (New York: Holt, Rinehart, and Winston, 1971), 148.

23 Martin Buber had been concerned about Zionism becoming corrupted by the inevitable power struggle in building a nation-state. He promoted Zionism as a movement of cultural and spiritual Jewish revival and tended to favor a single binational state. In retrospect, he was right about corruption but naive about binationalism — at least then. The two national movements were already too self-absorbed and too violently polarized. The intellectual, spiritual, and material resources for a creative symbiosis were not yet in place. Today, the situation is very different, and resources — material and philosophical — are available for considering creative alternatives to warfare between two people who love the same land. For a penetrating account of the contemporary crisis in Zionist thinking and its connection to the conflict between Buber and the

statist Zionists, see Yoram Hazony's *The Jewish State: The Struggle for Israel's Soul* (New York: Basic Books, 2000).

24 Yosef Criden and Saadia Gelb, *The Kibbutz Experience: Dialogue in Kfar Blum* (New York: Shocken Books, 1976), 20.

25 Details from http://www.kibbutz.org.il/eng/081101_kibbutz-eng.htm.

26 Elon, *The Israelis*, 145–46.

27 Paula Rayman gives a neat analysis of this quandary in *The Kibbutz Community and Nation Building* (Princeton, NJ: Princeton University Press, 1981), 140–41.

28 Melford Spiro, *Kibbutz: Adventure in Utopia* (Cambridge, MA: Harvard University Press, 1970), 251.

29 Rashid Khalidi has made an important contribution to clarifying a shared narrative with *The Iron Cage: The Story of the Palestinian Struggle for Statehood* (Boston: Beacon Press, 2007). There were early but short-lived attempts at an Israeli-Palestinian collaboration. For example, Prince Faisal of Arabia signed a treaty of collaboration with the Zionist statesman Chaim Weizmann in 1918 acknowledging the "racial kinship... and ancient bonds between the two people." A generation later, his younger brother, King Abdullah of Jordan, expressed willingness to negotiate a peace treaty with Israel, but he was immediately assassinated. Some of the early Zionists even saw the Palestinian *fellah* (peasant farmer) as a direct descendant of the ancient Hebrews and thought they could eventually be won over to the new state. In 1939, Martin Buber expressed a more thoughtful approach to Palestinian nationalism in an open letter to Mahatma Gandhi. He recognized the competing Palestinian and Jewish claims to the same land and the need to reconcile and honor both. He also emphasized the moral quality of the Jewish effort to return to the land and make it fertile for all, not just themselves (quoted in Arthur Hertzberg, ed., *The Zionist Idea: A Historical Analysis and Reader* [New York: Temple Antheneum, 1982], 465):

> I believe in the great marriage between man (*adam*) and earth (*adamah*). This land recognizes us for it is fruitful through us; and precisely because it bears fruit for us it recognizes us. Out settlers do not come here as do the colonists from the Occident to have natives do their work for them; they themselves set their shoulders to the plough and they spend their strength and their blood to make the land fruitful. The Jewish farmers have begun to teach their brothers, the Arab farmers, to cultivate the land more intensively...; together with them we want to cultivate the land — to serve it, as the Hebrew has it. The more fertile this soil becomes, the more space there will be for us and for them. We have no desire to dispossess them: we want to live with them.

Here we can see Buber's famous I-Thou philosophy applied to politics. This is the notion that we become fully human and find meaning not in the I-It relationship, where I experience the other as an object, an "It," but rather in reciprocal I-Thou relationship. Justice and the good life require relating to others as equivalent, morally autonomous human beings, part of a single humanity on a single planet. What is conspicuously missing in Buber, in the days before ecology had become a science, was an understanding of the critical importance both practically and spiritually of basing human community in a mutually enhancing relationship with its natural environment.

30 Rabbi Michael Lerner, editor of the journal *Tikkun* and founder of Network of Spiritual Progressives, is exemplary in this regard. Over several decades he has developed

a coherent political philosophy, which in the spirit of Nelson Mandela affirms both Israeli and Palestinian nationalism within a context of a global spirituality. See *Tikkun* magazine online, http://www.tikkun.org/nextgen/. See Rabbi Michael Lerner's *Embracing Israel/Palestine: A Strategy to Heal and Transform the Middle East* (Berkeley, CA: North Atlantic Books, 2012).

31 There are now some urban kibbutz initiatives that integrate wage labor with cooperative living. They tend to operate within the rather confining framework of the socialist youth movement Hanor Ha'Oved ve'halomed. Nevertheless, they suggest possibilities for all sorts of hybrid communities in many different situations. There are about one hundred of these small communities, with about two thousand members living communally in cities, pooling their resources, and generally working in education with disadvantaged city youth. The vision is still limited by secular socialist ideology. There is little reflection on what the truth quest is, little spiritual life, and no necessary connection to nature, wilderness, and the earth crisis that unites us all.

32 Goel Pinto, "Pioneers of an Organic Lifestyle," *Ha'aretz*, May 22, 2007, http://www.haaretz.com/weekend/week-s-end/pioneers-of-an-organic-lifestyle-1.221221. See also Kibbutz Harduf website, http://www.kamah.org.il/eng/Kibbutz_Harduf.html. The Israeli/Palestinian group of war veterans Lochamim Le'Shalom (Combatants for Peace) provides another courageous example of a boundary-crossing politics. Two related organizations of IDF veterans who refuse specific types of duties, such as policing the civilian population in the Occupied Territories, are Yesh Gvul ("There's a Limit" [lit. "border"]) and Ometz Le'Sarev (Courage to Refuse).

33 Leif Utne, "The Urban Green Revolution," *Utne Reader,* September-October 2005, 61–63.

34 Richard Register, *Ecocities: Building Cities in Balance with Nature* (San Francisco: Berkeley Hills Books, 2001).

35 Gianpaolo Baiocchi, "Participation, Activism, and Politics: The Porto Alegre Experiment and Deliberative Democratic Theory," *Politics and Society* 29, no. 1 (March 2001): 43–72. For a summary, see David Lewit, "Porto Alegre's Budget, of, by and for the People." *Yes! A Journal of Positive Futures*, Winter 2003, 21–22.

36 Interview in the documentary film *Bhutan: Gross National Happiness in Bhutan*, directed by Karma Wangchuck (Foundation FAVACH, Switzerland, and Bhutan Broadcasting Service, 2005). See also *Bhutan: Taking the Middle Path to Happiness*, directed by John Werheim (Maui, HI: Vendetti Productions, 2007).

37 Obviously, GNH doesn't represent a strictly objective measurement that can be copied wholesale into other contexts; by definition, "happiness" is a nonquantifiable, qualitative, subjective concept. Yet many aspects of well-being are fairly obvious and can be quantified, such as the ratio among average income and consumer price index, personal debt, income distribution, and crime. Environmental health can be measured according to resource depletion, pollution, crowding, and traffic. Med Jones, "The American Pursuit of Unhappiness — Gross National Happiness (GNH) — A New Socioeconomic Policy," executive white paper of the International Institute of Management, working draft (January 15, 2006), http://www.iim-edu.org/grossnationalhappiness/. For a global "happiness" ranking, see Nic Marks's Happy Planet Index at the New Economic Foundation, http://www.happyplanetindex.org/.

38 Philip N. Howard et al., "Opening Closed Regimes: What Was the Role of Social Media in the Arab Spring?" Project on Information, Technology and Political Islam, working

paper (2011), http://dl.dropbox.com/u/12947477/publications/2011_Howard-Duffy-Freelon-Hussain-Mari-Mazaid_pITPI.pdf.

39 For a solid history and perceptive analysis of the counterculture, see Todd Gitlin, *The Sixties: Years of Hope Days of Rage* (New York: Bantam, 1993).

40 For a thoughtful overview of the Occupy movement, see Todd Gitlin, *Occupy Nation: The Roots, the Spirit, and the Promise of Occupy Wall Street* (New York: Harper Collins, 2012).

41 Paul Hawken, "A Global Democratic Movement Is about to Pop," *Orion*, May 2007. This article is excerpted from the book, Paul Hawken, *Blessed Unrest: How the Largest Social Movement in History Is Restoring Grace, Justice, and Beauty to the World* (New York: Penguin, 2007).

42 Ibid., 3.

## Epilogue: A Tao of Politics

1 The widespread use of the word *paradigm* is largely because of Thomas Kuhn's groundbreaking book *The Structure of Scientific Revolutions* (Chicago: University of Chicago Press, 1970). This was, strictly speaking, a work in the historiography of science, focusing on the way the history of science was written. But it revealed something fundamental about the human quest to know reality, and it quickly became one of the most widely quoted and influential books across all academic disciplines in the past half century.

2 Francis Fukuyama, *The End of History and the Last Man* (New York: Simon and Schuster, Free Press, 1992).

3 Soon after Kuhn's publication, Sheldon Wolin was inspired to analyze political philosophers in this fashion and move toward a theory of a revolutionary political philosophy. See Sheldon S. Wolin, "Paradigms and Political Theories," in *Politics and Experience: Essays Presented to Professor Michael Oakeshott on the Occasion of His Retirement*, eds. Preston King and B. C. Parekh (Cambridge: Cambridge University Press, 1968). Thomas Spragens did this a little more systematically in *Understanding Political Theory* (New York: St. Martins Press, 1978). Neither Wolin nor Spragens saw the possibility of the *practice of political philosophy* itself becoming the basis for a way of life — the core of a new politics.

# INDEX


Abbey, Edward, 260
Abdullah (King of Jordan), 434n29
acacia trees, 304
addiction, 258, 284–85, 295–96, 427n21
Addo (South Africa), 68–69
advertising, 52
Africa, southern
archaeological artifacts in, 173, 222, 409n1
ecology of, 188–90
European exploration, 174–76
human origins in, 4, 6–7, 6n, 11, 158–61, 160 *fig.*, 171–74, 415n16
isolation of, 137–38
megafauna in, 137–38
migration from, 171
rock paintings in, 168 (*see also* rock art, San Bushman)
African National Congress (ANC), 70–71, 342, 344, 346
Afrikaans Dutch Reformed Church, 232
Afrikaans language, 343, 344
agrarianism, 359, 360
agricultural revolution, xviii, xx *fig.*
agriculture, xii
future primal, 348–51, 372–73
hunting/gathering replaced by, 337
industrialization of, 96
intentional communities/eco-villages, 351–55, 362, 372–73 (*see also* kibbutzim)
localization of, 387
societal collapse and, 337–38
sustainable, 338, 353–54, 371, 387
urban, 363, 373, 387
agro-ecology, 350
Agta people, 419n3
*ahupua'a*, 349–51, 352, 373
AIDS, 367
Akerman, Bruce, 315–16
Akstein, David, 235
/Akunta, 172 *fig.*
Alaric, 325
alcohol, 284, 295, 431n27
Alcoholics Anonymous, 295
alcoholism, 285, 290, 295–96, 427n21
Almeida, Francisco de, 174–75
Altamira Cave (Spain), 223

altruism, 45, 340
Amahuaca Indians, 300, 303
*Amanita muscaria*, 286, 326
American Indian Movement, 369
American Political Science Association, 407n17
*American Political Tradition and the Men Who Made It, The* (Hofstader), 402n28
American Revolution, 25–26, 32, 45
anamnesis, 63, 120, 281
anarchism, 191
Anderson, Ray, 60–61, 341
androids, 40–41
Andromeda galaxy, 105
Anglican Church, 31
animal cruelty, 37–38, 154–56
animal domestication, 416n16
animal identification, 266
animal nature, 90
animal research, 151–56, 411n30
*anoia*, 253–54
Anthropocene epoch, xii
anthropology
  academic San Bushman studies, 190–95, 197–99
  amateur San Bushman studies, 176–90, 415n10, 415n13
  revisionist debate in, 192–95, 197, 417–19nn36–39
anthropomorphization, 151
antidepressants, 294, 427n16
*Antipodes of the Mind, The* (Shanon), 298
anti-Semitism, 402–403n37
antiwar movement, 369
Anytus, 332
apartheid, 97
  Afrikaner justifications for, 343
  anti-apartheid leadership, 67, 124, 342
  author's witnessing of, 73
  Mandela and, 124, 125–26, 342
  racial categories under, 69, 69n, 177n
  racial mixing preceding, 179
  racial segregation during, 341–42
  San Bushmen displaced because of, 16
  South African Jews under, 70–71
  Verwoerd as architect of, 69
Apollo 11 cave (Namibia), 222, 421n4
*Apology, The* (Plato), 317, 324, 332
Arab-Israeli conflict, 66, 357, 358, 361, 373, 433–34nn21–23, 434n29
Arab nationalism, 433n22
Arab Spring (2010–2011), 66, 368–69
Arapaho Indians, 270
archaeology, 137, 192, 412n34, 414n2
archetypes, 143–44, 210, 327, 410n11
Ardrey, Robert, 145–46, 182, 410n16
Arendt, Hannah, 51–52, 403n37
*arete*, 120–21, 219, 243, 312, 318, 331
Aristarchus, 401n14
Aristophanes, 325, 333
Aristotelian philosophy, 130
Aristotle, 76, 124, 286
arrows, poisoned, 183–84, 184 *fig.*, 249–50
Ashkenazi Jews, 69–70, 83–84, 404–5n3
Athens, 121, 129
  decline of, 331–33
  democracy in, 312, 313–17, 332–33
  in Greco-Persian Wars, 310–11
  political culture of, 318, 331
  Socrates tried and executed in, 75–76
Auschwitz concentration camp, xix
Australian Aborigines, 141, 219, 404n2
*Australopithecus africanus*, 138, 146, 410n16
*autarkia*, 311
authority, obedience to, 51–52, 245
Avaaz.org, 370
avarice, 48, 57, 206, 341

Avnon, Dan, 407n15
*ayahuasca*, 306
 author's experience, 301–3
 ceremony accompanying, 301, 303
 effects of, 297, 299–300, 303–4, 427n21, 428n28
 ingredients for, 297–98, 428–29n33
 use of, in syncretistic churches, 297, 428n24
 Western crossover experiences, 288–89, 298, 300–301, 303
Aztecs, 430n20

baboons, 374
 author's experience, 9–10, 138, 179
 human similarity to, 149–50, 411n25
 Marais's research, 138–39
 San Bushman view of, as in-between, 139–41
 scientific research on, 152–54
 societal politics of, 149–50, 152–54
 sunset melancholy of, 138–39
 surplus intelligence of, 145
Bache, Christopher, 429–30n15
Bakan, Joel, 55
*Banisteriopsis caapi*, 297, 428n33
Bantu speakers, 67, 171, 176, 225–26, 414n3
bar-/bat-mitzvahs, 404n2
Barnard, Alan, 199, 415n13
Barquinha, 428n24
Barrow, John, 422n9
bartering, 389
Beach, Edward A., 430n19
Beard, Charles, 402n28
beauty, healing through, 278, 279
Bechuanaland, 192
Begin, Menachem, 406n17
Belo Horizonte (Brazil), 339, 364–65, 373
Ben-Gurion, David, 358
Benjamin, Walter, 407n15
Benyus, Janine, viii
berdache, 272
Berdichevsky, Micah, 81–82
Bergson, Henri, 234
Berry, Thomas, viii
"Beyond Postmodernism" (Herman), 417n35
Bhutan, 132, 339, 365–67, 373, 435n37
Biesele, Megan, 183, 228–29, 240, 422–23n19
Big Bang theory, xi, xin, 80, 106, 398n6
"big history," xvi–xx, 25n, 27, 398–99n6
big-picture construct, xxi
 cosmology and, 130–31
 face-to-face discussion and, 313–14
 in kibbutzim, 83
 mandala dynamic and, 101, 339
 as mandala quadrant, 118 *fig.*, 261, 382
 practical applications, 389–90, 392
 questioning, 392
 in San Bushman culture, 217–19
 in Socratic philosophy, 318
 Teilhard de Chardin and, 79–80
 visionary narratives and, 91
Biko, Steve, 67
*biltong*, 65
binationalism, 433–34n23
biochemistry, 77–78
biodiversity, 5, 338, 373, 399n1
biophilia hypothesis, 273, 425–26nn12–14
bioregionalism, 348–51, 352, 362, 363, 373, 432n12
biosphere, 78, 79–80
*Birth of the Palestinian Refugee Problem, The* (Morris), 433n21
Black Death, 28
Black Elk, 33, 56–57
Blackfoot Indians, 270
Black Power movement, 369
Blankfein, Lloyd, 56
Bleek, Dorothea, 202

Bleek, Wilhelm, 140, 172, 177, 224, 225, 226, 268
Blombos rock shelter (South Africa), 6n, 159–60, 160 *fig*., 222, 409n1, 412n38
Bloom, Alan, 429n7
body language, 149, 154
Bohr, Neils, 378
Border Cave (South Africa), 173, 222
Borochov, Ber, 83
Bosnia, xix
Botswana, 192, 194, 417n33
*boule*, 312–13
boundary crossing
  author's experience, 73–74
  dialectics and, 141
  human-animal connections, 186–87, 219, 265–67
  by Mandela, 344–45
  mind-body, 243, 266
  NGO movement and, 371–72
  political significance of, 261
  practical applications, 384–88
  primal ethic and, 241–46
  revolutionary science and, 378–79
  in San Bushman culture, 200
  shamanism and, 141, 241–42, 261–62
  during trance dance (*kia*), 252–53
  transitional zones, 268–69
  into wilderness, 242, 265–70, 330
  wilderness immersion, 274–81
  *See also* shamanism
Brazil, urban-level participatory democracy in, 364–65, 373
British Petroleum, 55–56
British Teilhard Association, 79
Brooks, Rodney, 41
Brown, Thomas, 144
Buber, Martin, 70, 356, 360, 407n15, 433–34n23, 434n29
bubonic plague, 28
Buddhism, 365–66, 367
Burtt, E. A., 24, 42
Bushmanland, 13–14
Bushmen. *See* San Bushmen
Bwiti religion, 263

Caddy, Peter and Eileen, 352
Cambodia, xix
Cambridge Grammar School for Boys, 76–77
Cambridge University, 78–79, 87, 89, 178
cannibalism, 188
"Cape-Coloured," 69n, 177n
Cape Floral Kingdom, 399n1
Cape Fold Mountains, 10–11
*Cape Monthly Magazine, The*, 226
Cape Town (South Africa), 10
capitalism, industrial
  depersonalization as result of, 50–51
  environmental impact of, 4, 339
  ethics overlooked in, 53–56
  global triumph of, 50–51, 193, 356
  growth of, 402n35
  industrial revolution spurred by, xviii–xx
  in Israel, 360
  Liberalism and, 27
  mission of, 28
  moneylending for interest and, 29
  primal dynamic undermined by, 339
  *See also* free market economies
Capra, Fritjof, viii
Carlin, John, 432n8
Cartailhac, Emile, 223
Castaneda, Carlos, 2, 287–88, 308
Catal Hayuk, 399n9
Catholic Church, 29, 31
*Cave of Forgotten Dreams, The* (film; 2010), 221, 247
Center for Sustainable Education (CSE), 354
Center for Transformative Action, 354
centralism, 385, 409n36

Central Kalahari Game Reserve, 192, 417n33
*Chalice and the Blade, The* (Eisler), 399n9
*chalutzim*, 82, 358, 359
*chalutziut*, 84, 358
chanting, 263
Chassidic movement, 404n2, 424n37
Chauvet-Pont-d'Arc cave (France), 221, 247–48
Chevy Nova, design flaws in, 55
Cheyenne Indians, 92, 117–19, 121–22, 243, 270, 272
chiefs, role of, 202–3
child abuse, 156, 411n29
Child Maltreatment Report, 156
children
  advertising directed at, 52
  as mystics, 106–7
  in San Bushman culture, 207–9, 419n4
  socialization process, 204
chimpanzees, 145, 149, 150, 164
Christian, David, 398n6
Christianity
  Aristotelian philosophy merged with, 130
  bureaucratic, shamanism repressed by, 287
  Jesus as trickster deity, 232
  medieval cosmology, 34–35, 130, 378
  San Bushman shamanism and, 232
  syncretistic churches, 297, 428n24
  Teilhard de Chardin and, 80–81
"Christosphere," 80
Church of England, 31
Church of Santo Daime, 428n24
Cicero, 299, 325
citizenship, criteria for, 280
*Civilization* (Ferguson), 26–27
civil rights movement, 368, 369
civil society, 130
class conflict, 46
Cleisthenes, 312
climate change, xii, 337–38
Clottes, Jean, 247
*Clouds, The* (Aristophanes), 333
Coetsee, Kobie, 344
cognicentrism, 289
Colden, Cadwallader, 215, 216, 217
*Collapse* (Diamond), 337–38
Colombia, eco-villages in, 339, 353, 362, 372
colonialism, 96
"Coloured," 69, 69n, 177n
Columbus, Christopher, 29, 109
Combatants for Peace (Lochamim Le'Shalom), 435n32
Commager, Henry Steel, 400–401n10
commercialism, 334, 367
commercial revolution, xviii, 25, 30
communalism, 357
communes, 369
community
  earth, and mandala dynamic, 339
  good of the, 311, 313
  intentional communities/eco-villages, 351–55, 362, 372–73 (*see also* kibbutzim)
  in kibbutzim, 83
  love of, and Liberalism, 45
  as mandala quadrant, 118 *fig.*
  Mandela's background in, 342–43
  primal ethic and, 245–46
  requirements for, 408n30
  San Bushman trance dance and, 424n39
  truth quest in, 321–22
community gardens, 363
compassion, 110
competition, 26, 45, 146, 206, 207
complexity-consciousness, 80, 245
conflict resolution, 214
Conibo Indians, 288
consciousness
  complexity-consciousness, 80
  dialectical movement of, 141

consciousness (*continued*)
expansion of, during trance dance, 238
integral, 410n12
luminosity of, 407–8n19
revolutions in, xvii–xx, xx *fig.*, 25–27
self-reflective, 107–8, 166–69
shadow aspects of, 244
split structure of, 114, 114n
consciousness-reality-language, 116, 283, 295, 408n20
consensus, 211–12, 214, 342–43
conservatism, modern-day, 25n, 57, 369
Constantinople, fall of (1453), 29
Constitutional Convention, 46, 48
consumer society, 26, 50, 365, 367, 371
Cook, James, 98
Copernicus, Nikolaus, 34–35, 40, 103, 195, 378, 379, 401n14
Cordova-Rios, Manuel, 300–301, 303
Cornell University, 354
Cornford, Francis M., 429n7
corporate personhood, 53, 54–55, 62
corporations, 4, 53–56, 60–62, 380, 403n43, 404n56
corruption, 29, 84, 334, 364
cosmology
as big pictures, 130–31
contemporary, as exhausted, xii, xv–xvi
contemporary foundations, xi
defined, 130
of early societies, xiii–xiv
evolutionary, 408n22
medieval Christian, 34–35, 378
modern, 231, 293
new, 103–4, 131
scientific, xiii, 115–16
social viability through, xi–xii
traditional Bushman, 7, 139
counterculture, 290–91, 369
courage, 110
Courage to Refuse (Ometz Le'Sarev), 435n32
Cox, Earl, 40
creativity, emergence of, 165–66
Crick, Francis, 289, 289n
Cro-Magnon Man, 158, 412n34
Cromwell, Oliver, 409n36
Crow Indians, 270
cryogenicists, 40–41
Cumes, David, 280
*Current Anthropology*, 194
cynicism, xv, 258

*daimon*, 324
Dalai Lama, 370
Dalton, John, 378
Daly, Herman, viii
dancing, 263
*See also* trance dance, San Bushman
Dancing Sorcerer of Trois Frères (France), 257, 258 *fig.*
Darfur, xix
Darius (King of Persia), 310–11
*Dark Night, Early Dawn* (Bache), 429–30n15
Dart, Raymond, 409n1, 410n16
Darwin, Charles, 10, 58, 136, 378, 379
Dead Sea Scrolls, 90, 305
decentralization, 26, 339, 364–65, 366, 385
decision making, 212–13, 245
deconstructionism, postmodern, 193, 194–95, 224, 248, 331–32, 417–19nn36–39
Delian League, 331
demagoguery, 58, 331, 368
Demeter, myth of, 326–27
democracy
American, 56–57
Athenian, 309–10
constitutional, 380
deep, 219, 313–17
participatory, 364–65

democracy, direct
    Athenian, 312
    community and, 127–30
    as mandala quadrant, 118 *fig.*, 382
    Mandela and, 342–43
    in Native American cultures, 215
    practical applications, 389
    republic vs., 46
    in San Bushman culture, 207–10
    in small-scale societies, 351–52
democratic community, xxi, 127–30
democratization, 339
Denbow, James, 197
depersonalization, 50–51, 58
depression, 258, 385
*Depth Psychology and a New Ethic* (Neumann), 244
*De Revolutionibus de Oribum Celestium* (Copernicus), 34
Descartes, René, 80, 165, 305
    anthropological deconstructionism and, 195
    dream of, 39–40, 379
    human-primate nexus and, 151
    mechanistic science of, 36–38, 40–42, 401n13
    scientific method of, 35–36, 40, 104
    truth quest of, 38–39
    *See also* dualism, Cartesian; science, Cartesian
DeVore, Irven, 190
De Wet, Christiaan, 343–44
Dia!kwain, 136, 139–40, 220
dialectics, 42–44, 313–14, 318, 344, 392, 419n41
    inner-outer, 141–44
*dialektike*, 149, 214, 309
    *See also* face-to-face discussion
Diamond, Jared, 337–38, 415–16n16, 417n29
Diaz, Bartholomew, 174
dictatorships, 129
diet, omnivorous, 157, 182–83
Diggers, 132
*Discourse on the Method* (Descartes), 37, 38, 39
discussion, deep, 391–92
DMT, 297–98
DNA, 172–73, 289, 404–5n3
dogma, 59, 114, 116, 247
Dog Soldier Society, 92
Drakensberg Mountains, 8–10, 138, 150, 222–23, 225–26, 248–52
dreamtime, 404n2
*Dreamtime* (Duerr), 265
dreamwork, 388–89
Driekopseiland (South Africa), 421n5
drumming, 263, 289
dualism, Cartesian, 37–38, 49, 141, 304, 377
Duerr, Hans Peter, 260, 265–67
Dutch exploration, 67, 175–76

Ebenstein, William, 401n26
ecocide, 42, 337
ecological sensitivity, 183–87, 366–67
*Ecology of Commerce, The* (Hawken), 61
economic growth, 58–59
*Economic Interpretation of the Constitution, The* (Beard), 402n28
economics
    cosmology behind as exhausted, xii
    inequality promoted in, xv
    *See also* capitalism, industrial; free market economies
economies of scale, 49–50
EcoVillage at Ithaca (EVI), 339, 354, 372
eco-villages, 339, 351–55, 362, 372–73
education, 314–15, 331, 334, 354, 364, 366
educational reform, 27
egalitarianism, xviii, 127
    in Greek polis, 311–12
    in Native American cultures, 214–15
    in Neolithic civilizations, 399n9
    in San Bushman culture, 200–203, 241, 419n3, 420–21n28

ego, 123–24, 240, 244, 246, 253, 285
ego death, 235, 299
Egypt, 92, 368–69
Eichmann, Adolf, 51, 402–3n37
*Eichmann in Jerusalem* (Arendt), 51–52
Einstein, Albert, 58, 102, 106, 107, 231–32, 378, 379
Eisler, Riane, 399n9
Eisley, Loren, 277
eland, 249–50, 252 *fig.*
electoral politics, 316
elephants, 68
Eleusinian Mysteries, 286, 289, 299, 309, 325–30, 333, 430n19, 430–31n22, 431n25
Eliade, Mircea, 263, 284, 286, 423n30
Eliot, T.S., 2
Elon, Amos, 84
*Embracing Israel/Palestine* (Lerner), 434–35n30
Emerson, Ralph Waldo, 218
*Encyclopedia Britannica*, 414n3
*End of History and the Last Man, The* (Fukuyama), 193, 380
endurance hunt, 161–63, 162 *fig.*, 163 *fig.*, 187, 413n42
energy shortages, 337–38
England
  author's experience in, 76–82
  plague epidemics in, 28
English Civil War, 132, 409n36
English exploration, 67, 176
Enlightenment, 31
entheogenic shamanism
  *ayahuasca* ceremony, 296–304
  early roots of, 285–87, 309
  ergot and, 430n20
  neo-shamanistic metaphysics from, 304–7
  as paradoxical experience, 299–300, 303–4
  research studies of, 298–99
  Western crossover experiences, 287–89, 298
entheogens, 283n, 284, 369
  *See also* hallucinogens
environment, corporate responsibility for, 60–62
environmental degradation, 55–56, 58–59, 337–38, 339
environmentalism, 110, 369, 371
epiphanies, 322–24, 340–44
  *See also periagoge*
ergot, 326, 328, 430n20, 430–31n22, 431n26
Eros, 90, 91, 314, 324, 329, 361
escapism, 339
Essenes sect, 304–5
ethics
  corporate abuses, 53–56
  corporate responsibility, 60–62
  new, 63
  obedience to authority and, 51–52
  paradoxical, and shamanism, 242–46
*Ethnic Cleansing of Palestine, The* (Pappe), 433n21
ethnography, 192, 252, 257, 415n14, 417–18n36
Eurasia, 409n1
Eurocentrism, 160, 369, 409n1
Europe
  human-animal connections in, 266–67
  rock art in, 221–24, 257, 258 *fig.*
  shamanic religions in, 264–65
  social democratic tradition in, 400n2 (ch. 2)
European colonialism, 96
European Union, 339
evolutionary biology, 77–78
experience, direct, 391

face-to-face discussion, xxi
  big-picture construct and, 313–14
  emergence of, 161
  in Greek polis, 311, 313–14, 351–52

human-primate nexus and, 146–48
in kibbutzim, 358
as mandala quadrant, 118 *fig.*, 382
practical applications, 389, 391–92
in San Bushman culture, 127, 210–14, 420n25
in small-scale societies, 351–52
Socratic, 75, 124–27, 318
facial expression, 149, 411n24
factory farming, 38
Faisal, 434n29
Fang people, 283
farmer-soldier-philosopher, 83
fatalism, 339
fear, 341
*Federalist, The*, 46, 49
female suffrage, 334
feminine principle, 264–65
Ferguson, Niall, 26–27
feudalism, 25, 26, 28–29, 50, 130, 380, 400n2 (ch. 2)
financial collapse (2008), 56
Findhorn (Scotland), 339, 352, 355, 362, 372–73
Finley, M.I., 333
Finnish Green Party, 371
fire, 234
fire making/acquisition, 165, 166–69, 413n44, 413n48
fire myth, 168–69
Fishkin, James, 315–16
Flagstaff (AZ), light pollution reduced in, 363, 387–88
food, subsidized, 365
*Food of the Gods* (McKenna), 426n2
"foraging band blueprint," 198–99, 199n, 203
*Foraging Spectrum, The* (Kelly), 418–19n39
*Forbes* magazine, 60
Fossey, Dian, 152
Foster, Craig, 16, 184, 413n42
Foster, Damon, 16, 411n42
Frankfurt School, 191, 193, 403n8, 417n41
Franklin, Benjamin, 216
freedom, personal, 45, 47–48
free market economies
as amoral, 195
competitiveness of, 145–46
ethics overlooked in, 53–56
global triumph of, 380
inequality as result of, 145–46, 217
"invisible hand of," xv, 27, 32, 34, 49, 53, 54, 57–58, 216–17
kibbutzim and, 360
truth quest abandoned through, xv, 48–51, 57–59
*See also* capitalism, industrial
Freud, Sigmund, 58, 90, 142, 143, 409–10n9
Friedman, Milton, 54, 56
*Frontiers* (Mostert), 67–68
Fukuyama, Francis, 193, 380
fundamentalism, 116, 258, 357, 377
Furst, Peter, 286
future primal politics, 174
agriculture, 348–51
author's history as example of, 66
in cities/nations, 362–67, 435n31
cosmic story and, 373–75
identifying, 338
intentional communities/eco-villages, 351–55, 362, 372–73
Israel and, 66
mandala and, 118, 383
metaparadigm for, 380–82
movements and revolutionary transformations, 368–72
practical applications, 384–92
requirements for, xx
vision of, 372–74
*fynbos*, 5, 67, 399n1

Gaddafi, Muammar, 129
Galileo Galilei, 35, 40, 195, 306, 401nn14–15
Gama, Vasco da, 29–30

Gandhi, Mohandas, 64, 71, 132, 342, 368, 372, 405n5, 434n29
gardening, 348, 363, 387
/Gaugo, 196, 202
Gaviotas (Colombia), 339, 353, 362, 372
Gebser, Jean Paul, 144, 410n12
Genadendal (South Africa), 179
General Motors, 54–55
generosity, 45, 110, 340, 351–52
genetic diversity, 172–73, 414nn2–3
genocide, xix, 42, 177
Gerald of Aurrilac, Saint, 29
German Green Party, 370–71
Gimbutas, Marija, 399n9
Glaucon, 74, 319–20, 321–22
Global Eco-village Network, 355
globalization, 4, 45, 50–51, 53–54, 158, 356, 385
global warming, xii, 338
God, 49, 113, 113n
goddess worship, xviii, 399n9
Goldberg, Jeffrey, 83, 405–6n11
Goldman Sachs, 56
Gondwanaland, 68
Good, the, 91, 317–24, 333
Goodall, Jane, 152
Gordon, Aaron David, 82–83, 360
Gordon, Robert J., 194, 418n38
*Gorgias* (Plato), 314
Gorman, Peter, 431n28
government
  "big," 55
  minimal representational, 25, 32, 46–47, 57, 402n27
  participatory, 364–65, 366, 373
Gqakaza, 275, 277
Great Chain of Being, 28–29, 35
*Great Dance, The* (film; 2000), 161–63, 184, 187, 252–53, 254, 413n42, 424n43
Great Mystery, 267
Great Recession, 56
Great Rift Valley, 137, 152, 409n1
Greco-Persian Wars, 310–11, 331n
Greece, ancient, xxiin
  classical period, 331, 331n
  conflicted nature of society in, 309
  direct democracy in, 129
  entheogenic shamanism in, 286, 289
  philosophy in, 314
  political culture of, 310
  Renaissance rediscovery of, 334
  shamanism in, 325–26
  whole person as viewed in, 120–21, 243, 310–13, 316–17
  wines in, 431n27
  *See also* Athens; polis
Green City Movement, 339, 363
Green movement, 132, 370–71
Greyton (South Africa), 179
Griffin, Susan, 260
Griffiths, Roland, 294
Grof, Christina, 282
Grof, Stanislav, x, 282, 291–93, 295, 304, 427n12
gross national happiness, 339, 366–67, 373, 435n37
Group Areas Act (South Africa), 179
Guenther, Mathias, 196, 197–99, 199n, 207, 228, 230, 413n48, 419n3
Gulf of Mexico, oil rig disaster in (2010), 55–56
*Guns, Germs, and Steel* (Diamond), 415–16n16
/Gwi Bushmen, 162–63, 212–13, 252

Habermas, Jürgen, 127, 408n30
Habonim, 71, 77
*Haerlem*, 175
Halifax, Joan, 282
hallucinogens, 263
  awareness heightened by, 291–92
  diseases caused by, 430n20
  empirical fieldwork on, 291–93, 294–95

as "hard" shamanism, 273, 283 (*see also* entheogenic shamanism)
healing power of, 292–93, 295–96, 427n21
LSD, 289–94, 428n25
menu of experiences, 428n28
nonaddictive qualities of, 284–85, 295
psilocybin, 286, 294–95, 426n4, 427n18, 427n21, 428n25
use of term, 283n, 284
Western culture-wide fear of, 262, 283–84, 290–91, 294
Hamilton, Alexander, 46
Hancock, Graham, 296, 421–22n7
Hanita Kibbutz, 84–85
Hanor Ha'Oved, 435n31
happiness, gross national, 339, 366–67, 373, 435n37
Harduf Kibbutz, 362
hare-and-the-moon myth, 228–29
Harlow, Harry, 151, 154–56, 426n14
Harner, Michael, 288–89, 296
Hashomer Hatzair Kibbutz, 405–6n11
Hawai'i, 10, 11, 272
ancient bioregionalism in, 349–51, 352, 362, 373
author's "exile" in, 66, 98–101
multiculturalism of, 98–99
Hawken, Paul, 61, 371–72
Haynes, Robert, 41
Hazony, Yoram, 433n21
healing
human-animal connections and, 267
levels of, 242
nature, 273–74
trance healing, 422–23n19
*Healing Makes Our Hearts Happy* (Katz, Biesele, and St. Denis), 422–23n19
Hebrew University (Jerusalem), 95, 97–98, 298
Heilbronner, Robert, 209
Heisenberg, Werner Karl, 378
Hellenistic culture, 309
Henry VIII, 31
Henshilwood, Chris, 159–60, 412–13n40
Herero people, 201, 203
*hermae*, desecration of, 332, 333
Herman, Louis G., 15 *fig.*
academic career of, 4, 11, 99, 101, 322–24
bar mitzvah of, 76
"Beyond Postmodernism," 417n35
birthplace of, 3, 67
education of, 11, 72–74, 76–79, 81, 95, 97–98, 178–79
family background, 69
as father, 99–100
IDF experience of, 87, 88–89
Jewish identity of, 65–66, 69–72, 92
marriage of, 95–96, 99
return to South Africa, 4–5, 179
South African identity of, 65, 73–74
wilderness immersion experience of, 274–79
*See also* truth quest, author's
Herodotus, 311, 330
Herut Party (Israel), 406n17
Herzog, Werner, 221, 247
Heschel, Abraham Joshua, 114, 165
Hesse, Hermann, 267, 272
*heyoka*, 271
Hinduism, 428–29n33
historical revisions, 433n21
Hitler, Adolf, 129
Hluhluwe-Umfolozi Game Reserve, 13, 274–278
Hobbes, Thomas, 25, 31–32, 44, 47, 145–46, 182, 380, 381–82
Hofmann, Albert, 289–90, 326, 430n19, 430–31n22, 431nn25–26
Hofstader, Richard, 402n28
Holocaust, 70, 73, 86, 86n
holotropic experiences, 293
Holy Fire, 430n20

Homeric Hymn to Demeter, 326–27
hominids
evolution from primates, 156–61, 412nn33–34
fossil evidence, 409n1, 412n33
*Homo erectus*, xvii, 158, 161, 412n33
*Homo ergaster*, 158
*Homo habilis*, 157
homophobia, 272
*Homo sapiens*, xvii, 6, 137, 161, 164, 412n34
*Homo sapiens sapiens*, 158
Horkheimer, Max, 408n28
Hottentots, 176
*See also* Khoikhoi people
Hubble telescope, 106
Huichol people, 299
Hu Jintao, 370
human-animal relationships, 184–88, 265–67
human-primate nexus
childishness, 164–66
language development, 150–51
self-knowledge as result of, 137
societal politics, 149–50, 411nn24–25
Hundred Years' War, 28
hunter-gatherers
academic studies of, 191
Andromeda as viewed by, 105
bioregional sensibilities of, 349
diet of, 182–83, 417n29
direct democracy among, 129–30, 209–14
disappearance of, 337
egalitarianism among, 200–206, 420–21n28
San Bushman ancestors as, 171
social hierarchy/labor divisions among, 120
whole person as viewed by, 120
wilderness and, 415–16n16
*Hunters, The* (film; 1957), 183, 415n14
hunting, 183–84, 184 *fig.*, 189 *figs.*, 249–50
endurance hunt, 161–63, 162 *fig.*, 163 *fig.*, 187, 413n42
snare hunting, 419n3
*!hxaro*, 205–6, 420n16, 420n19

Ibogaine, 295, 427n21, 428n25
imagination, 105–6, 391–92
immigration, 32
"in-between, the," 90, 111–17, 114n, 139–44, 145, 186–87, 199, 242, 267–68, 408n20
Indian wars (North America), 32–33
indigenous peoples, cultural survival of, 371
individualism, 4, 25, 30, 45, 200, 207–8, 247, 311
individuation
during *ayahuasca* experiences, 303, 306
boundary crossing and, 242, 270
community and, 261, 351–52
democracy and, 130
in depth psychology, 123–24, 244
face-to-face discussion and, 126–27
Greek polis and, 311, 312
in human evolution, 150–51, 161
interiority and, 305–6
kibbutzim and, 357
as mandala quadrant, 118 *fig.*, 119–24, 339
Mandela and, 344–45
practical applications, 388–89
societal complexity and, 157–58
*See also* whole person, the
industrial agriculture, 38
industrial civilizations, 32, 120
industrial revolution, xviii–xix, xx *fig.*
inequality, 27, 45, 46, 57, 58–59, 207
informational complexity, xvii, 399n8
Initiative Media, 52
intention, 390
interconnectedness, 110, 119
Interface, 60–61, 341

Internet, 367, 368, 370
intuition, 38, 306
Inuktitut language, 349, 432n12
investing, responsible, 61, 404n56
Iroquois Confederacy, 214–18
Islam, 357
Israel, Kingdom of, 65–66, 71, 115
Israel, State of
- author's identity in, 356
- author's immigration to, 11, 95
- author's return to, 355–56
- communal villages (*moshavim*) in, 358, 406n12
- creation of, 70, 87, 433n22
- diet in, 87, 87n
- future primal politics and, 66
- national culture (*chalutziut*) of, 84, 358
- political culture of, 84, 360, 406n17
- revisionist histories in, 433n21
- as second-world democracy, 86–87
- Six-Day War (1967), 358
- technological start-ups in, 406n14
- Yom Kippur War (1973), 92–95
- *See also* kibbutzim

Israeli Air Force, 406n14
Israeli Defense Force (IDF), 278
- author's experience in, 85, 88–95
- creativity in, 406n14
- mission of, 87
- as people's army, 86
- training conditions in, 88, 88n, 89–91
- wilderness immersion in, 89–90
- during Yom Kippur War (1973), 92–95

*Israelis, The* (Elon), 84
Israel-Palestine conflict, 72, 84, 357, 361, 373, 433–34nn21–23
I-Thou philosophy, 434n29
"It-reality," 113–14, 113n, 115, 124, 144, 228
Jackson, Wes, viii
James, William, 111–12, 264, 296
Jay, John, 46
Jefferson, Thomas, 62–63
Jensen, Derrick, 154
Jensen, Sven, 295
jesters, 271, 272
Jewish Diaspora, 71
Jewish National Fund, 71–72
Jigme Singye Wangchuck, 365–66, 373
Jivaro Indians, 288
Johannesburg (South Africa), 8, 12
Johns Hopkins University, 294
Jones, J. D. F., 415n10
Judaism, 70, 404n2, 423–24n37
Jung, C. G.
- in Africa, 141–43
- archetypes, 117, 143–44, 410n11
- Freud and, 409–10n9
- individuation as viewed by, 123–24, 243–44
- on mandalas, 64
- personality types, 121
- on psychic inflation, 423–24n37
- on religion vs. religious experience, 116
- shamanism and, 142–43
- van der Post as authority on, 178

Ju/twasi San people, 13–14, 13n, 181–83, 181n, 185–88, 200, 204–6, 210–11, 213–14, 242, 416n17, 424n39

Kabbalah, 72, 235, 244–45, 356, 404n2, 423–24n37
//Kabbo, x, 220, 225, 227, 281 *fig.*
Kalahari Bushmen, 14–15, 248–52
Kalahari Debate, 192–95, 197, 224
Kalahari Desert, 7, 171, 176
*Kalahari Family, A* (film), 415n14
Kalahari Research Group (Harvard University), 190–91
Kamakou, Samuel, 350
Kariel, Henry, 97–98, 417n35

Katz, Richard, 235, 422–23n19
Kau Dwa, 234, 236
Keats, John, 376
Keeney, Bradford, 237–41, 243, 423n27, 423n29, 423n30
Kelly, Robert, 418–19n39
Kepler, Johannes, 40
Keren Hayesod, 71–72
Kerenyi, Karol, 430n19
Kfar Blum Kibbutz, 358
Kgalagadi Transfrontier Park (South Africa), 16–17
Khoikhoi people, 67, 171, 174, 414n3
Khalidi, Rashid, *The Iron Cage*, 434n29
Khoi language, 414n3
Khoisan, 177n, 179, 414nn2–3
Kholer, Oswin R., 414n3
Khomani San people, 16
*kia*, 234–36, 238, 242, 243, 246
kibbutzim
- agrarian model, 339, 352
- author's experience, 82, 84–85, 95
- current promise of, 362
- direct democracy in, 128–29
- founding of, 71–72
- founding philosophy of, 70, 71, 82–83, 356–58
- numbers of, 406n12
- primal politics in, 83, 132
- success of, 358, 359
- truth quest abandoned in, 84, 96, 359–61
- urban initiatives, 435n31
- Zionism and, 70, 71

Kibbutz Zionism, 82, 84
Kilauea (Hawai'i), 11
Kim Jong-il, 129
King, Martin Luther, Jr., 132, 368, 372
Kitto, H. D. F., 120–21
Klasiers River, 409n1
knowledge and mystery, 103–7
Konner, Melvin, 166
Ko'olau Mountain Range (Hawai'i), 10
Kruger, Jimmy, 125–26, 343–44
Kruger National Park (South Africa), 12
Krugman, Paul, 57
Kruiper, Toppies, 16
kudu, 65
"kudu mind, putting on," 252–53
Kuhn, Thomas, 377–80, 436n1
kundalini energy, 234–35
/Kunta, 240
/Kurib Hartebeest, 202
Kxao, 170
*kykeon*, 286, 289, 325, 326, 327–29, 430–31n22, 431n26
- *See also* Eleusinian Mysteries

Kyoto University, 197

labor
- division of, 27, 49, 207, 312, 334, 359–60
- kibbutz philosophy of, 82–83, 96, 359, 360–61
- wage, 424n39

laboratory animals, drug testing on, 38
Labor Party (Israel), 406n17
*Laches* (Plato), 126
Lakota Indians, 107–10, 114, 115, 215, 267, 269–70, 272
Lame Deer, 122–23, 270–71, 344
*Lancet, The* (journal), 295
*Land Filled with Flies* (Wilmsen), 193–94
language, development of, 150–51, 157, 161, 166
Leacock, Eleanor, 193, 419n39
Leakey, Richard, 148, 409n2, 411n25, 412n33
leap in being, 115–17
Lee, Richard, 190, 193, 194, 196, 201–2, 207, 213, 419n39, 420n25
Leibbrandt, Robey, 343–44
Leninism, 405n8
leopards, 416n24
Lerner, Jaime, 363, 373

Lerner, Michael, Rabbi, 434–35n30
Levellers, 132
Lewis-Williams, David, 12, 268, 412n34, 421n17, 424–25n46
Liberalism, classical
  as cosmology, 131
  death of meaning and, 44–45, 195
  emergence of, 28, 400n2 (ch. 2)
  Eurocentrism of, 369
  globalization of, 380
  ideology of, 28
  industrial revolution spurred by, xviii–xix
  modern-day liberalism vs., 25n
  Native Americans as obstacle to, 32–33
  as paradigm, 380
  as philosophical justification for modern institutions, 25–27
  political philosophy of, 31–32, 402n28
  psychological damage from, 52
  revolutions in, 25–27, 30
  truth quest and, 27, 45, 57–59
  in United States, 57–59
  values of, as absolutes, 45
  wilderness as viewed in, 33
liberalism, modern-day, 25n
liberation movements, 132
*libido dominandi*, 39, 91, 114
Libya, 369
Liebenberg, Louis, 413n42
light pollution, 363, 387–88
Linton Panel, 255–56, 424n44
lions, 184–87, 330, 374, 416–17nn24–25
lion spirits, 186, 237
Lithuania, 70
Lloyd, Lucy, 140, 172, 177, 224, 225, 268
Lochamim Le'Shalom (Combatants for Peace), 435n32
Locke, John, 7, 25, 276 33, 381–82
  Liberal philosophy of, 31–32, 380, 401n13
  nature as viewed by, 7–8
  on property and material wealth, 401–2n26
  truth quest abandonment and, 44–46
*Lost World of the Kalahari, The* (van der Post), 178–79
Lycon, 332
Lyonpo Jigme Thinley, 366
Lyons, Oren, 216
lysergic acid diethylmide (LSD), 285, 289–94, 289n, 326, 428n25

Machiavelli, Niccolò, 381–82
Maclean, Dorothy, 352
Macondo Deepwater Horizon oil rig disaster (2010), 55–56
Madison, James, 46–47, 49
Makapansgat cave (Western Transvaal), 138
man, first, 145–46
mandala
  future primal politics and, 347–48
  as political ideal, 131–33
  popularization of, 117
  of primal politics, 83, 101, 118 *fig.*, 131–33, 161, 166–67, 197, 210, 214, 219, 243, 309, 317, 337, 339–40, 351–52, 381–82
  as truth quest structure, xxi, xxii–xxiii, 117–31, 118 *fig.*
Mandela, Nelson
  birthplace of, 67
  on direct democracy, 128, 342–43
  face-to-face discussion as employed by, 125–26, 343–44
  as gardener, 348
  imprisonment of, 71, 97, 348
  as individuated human being, 97, 124, 372
  *periagoge* of, during imprisonment, 341–44

Mandela, Nelson (*continued*)
 primal principles exemplified by, 132, 339, 368
 Rugby World Cup (1995) and, 345–47, 432n8
Mannheim, Karl, 359
mantis, 168–69, 230, 413n49
Maoism, 405n8
MA'O Organic Farms (Hawai'i), 351
Marais, Eugène, 138–39, 141, 151
Marathon, Battle of (490 BCE), 310–11, 331n
Marcuse, Herbert, 405n8
Marean, Curtis, 159, 412–13n40
Maria Sabina, 282, 428n28
Marshall, Elizabeth, 13n, 177, 180–82, 181n, 184–86, 204, 211–12, 416–17nn24–25
Marshall, John, 13–14, 177, 180–81, 183, 185, 186, 239, 415n14, 416n24
Marshall, Laurence, 177, 180–81
Marshall, Lorna, 177, 180–81, 203–4, 205, 207, 210, 211, 231, 415n14
Marx, Karl, 58, 191, 381–82, 405n8
Marxism, 405n8
Mash, Deborah, 427n21
Maslow, Abraham, 280
mass production, 25, 50
materialism, 25, 30, 33–34, 103, 145, 206, 259, 339, 377
mathematics, 34–36, 306, 401nn13–15
Mbeki, Govan, 67
McDougall, Christopher, 413n42
McKenna, Terence, 285, 286, 426n2
McLuhan, Marshall, 370
"meat hunger," 65, 183, 202
mechanization, 4, 36–38, 40–42, 50, 57–58, 103, 142, 305, 359–60, 401n17
medicine wheel, 117, 121–22, 125, 269
 *See also* mandala
meditation, 103–4, 385–87, 388
megafauna, 137–38, 181, 416n16
Meletus, 332
Mellart, James, 399n9
mescal bean, 286
mescalin, 295–96
Mesoamerica, 294, 426n4
metaparadigm, 377, 380
*Metaphysical Foundations of Modern Science, The* (Burtt), 42
metaxy, 113
middens, 158–59, 190
midwives, 264–65
Milgram, Stanley, 52
Milky Way, 103
Miltiades, 311
*Mind in the Cave, The* (Lewis-Williams), 421n7
Minsky, Marvin, 40–41
modernity
 cosmology of, 231
 irony of, 169
 political/economic institutions of, 4, 25
 revolutions in, 25–27
 stress as result of, 209–10
monotheism
 "God" anthropomorphized in, 113, 113n
 leap in being in, 116–17
morality, 314–15, 318
Morris, Benny, 433n21
Morris, Desmond, 182
*moshavim*, 358, 406n12
Mostert, Noel, 4, 67–68
MoveOn.org, 370
Move to Amend, 62
Mugabe, Robert, 129
multiculturalism, 98–99
mushrooms, entheogenic, 285–86, 294, 326, 328, 426n2, 426n4, 428n28
*My Hunter's Heart* (film), 16n
Mylonas, George, 430n19
mystery
 boundary crossing and, 267–68
 the "in-between," 111–17

knowledge and, 103–7
politics of, 107–11
scientific method vs., 103–5
during trance dance (*kia*), 234–36
mystical experience, 264
mysticism
children and, 106–7
Jewish, 407n15
nature, 365
religion vs., 116
spontaneous experiences, 111–12
mythology
archetypes and, 143–44
Greek, 326–27
Hawaiian, 350
meaning narratives as, 217
San Bushman, 227–32, 241, 268–69, 413n49
*See also* storytelling

Nachal, 85–86
Namibia, 13–14, 192, 194, 222
nanotechnology, 40–41
narcotics, 284
National Congress of American Indians, 421n31
National Geographic Genographic project, 405n3
National Institute on Drug Abuse (NIDA), 294
National Outdoor Leadership (NOLS), 426n15
nation-state, 4
Native American Church, 286
Native Americans
beauty as viewed by, 279
boundary crossing by, 243
entheogenic shamanism among, 286–87
Euro-American campaigns against, 32–33
European spiritual disorder as viewed by, 108–9
face-to-face discussion among, 125
"Great Spirit" of, 113
Liberal view of, 400–401n10
mystery as viewed by, 107–10, 269–70
nature as viewed by, 109, 110, 269–70
whole person as viewed by, 121–23, 270–73
nature
healing through contact with, 273–74, 425–26nn12–14
human exploitation of, 7–8, 27
Liberal assumptions regarding, 27, 131
mysticism, 365
Native American view of, 109, 110, 269–70
primary relationship with, 109–10, 363–64
shamanic relationship with, 83, 339
"state of," North America as, 32, 400–401n10
*See also* wilderness
*Nature* (journal), 414n2
Navajo Indians, 272
Nazism, xix, 51, 73, 86, 86n, 91, 246–47, 272, 344
Neanderthals, 158, 412n34
neighborhood civic groups, 364
Neolithic Era, xviii, 285–86, 399n9, 426n2
Netanyahu, Benjamin, 406n17
Neumann, Erich, 244
Nevins, Alan, 400–401n10
Newton, Isaac, 31, 33, 40, 305
*New Yorker*, 247–48
New Zealand All Blacks, 346–47
NGOs, independent, 371–72
Nguni people, 176
Nharo Bushmen, 198–99
night-sky meditation, 386–87
*1949: The First Israelis* (Segev), 433n21

Noar Chalutzi Lochem (Nachal), 85–86
noblesse oblige, 400n2 (ch. 2)
Nordau, Max, 433n22
North America
  Indian wars in, 32–33
  Liberal view of, 32, 400–401n10
  *See also* United States
!Nqate, 220, 254
*/num*, 233–37, 240, 249–50, 254, 255–56
*/num k"ausi*, 234, 236, 242
*N/um Tchai* (film; 1969), 239
Nyae Nyae Conservancy, 14, 177, 180–81, 189 *figs*., 210–11, 233
Nyae Nyae Development Foundation (Namibia), 13–14
Nyae Nyae Farmers Co-operative, 14n

Obama, Barack, 98–99
obedience, 51–52
O'Brian, Sharon, 421n31
Occupy Wall Street movement, 369–70
ocean trade, 29–30
*Old Way, The* (E. Marshall), 181–82
*ololiqui*, 430n20
*Olympica* (Descartes), 38
Ometz Le'Sarev (Courage to Refuse), 435n32
Operation Rhino, 274
opposites, balancing, 241–42, 244–45, 265, 270–73, 384
  *See also* boundary crossing
oratory, 315
*Order and History* (Voegelin), 407–8n19
Orpen, Joseph, 225–26
Osmond, Humphrey, 290, 295
ostracism, 209
Otto, Rudolf, 111, 264
≠Ouma, 240
out-of-body experiences, 253
Outward Bound, 426n15
*Oxford English Dictionary* (1889), 176

paleoanthropology, 137–38
Pale of Settlement, 70, 81
Paleo-Indians, 286
Paleolithic era, 157, 158–61, 190, 417n29
paleontology, 137
Palestine
  Jewish emigration to, 70
  partitioning of (1948), 87, 357
  West Bank occupation, 87
  *See also* Israel-Palestine conflict
Palestine Mandate, 87
Palestinian nationalism, 96–97, 433n22, 434n29
Papa, 350
Pappe, Illan, 433n21
*Papsalum distichum*, 431n26
paradigm
  fear of, 379
  normal vs. revolutionary, 378–79
  ubiquity of, 379–80
  use of term, 377, 436n1
*parrhesia*, 315
*Passion of the Western Mind, The* (Tarnas), 293
Patel, Ricken, 370
Paul, Gregory, 40
Pauli, Wolfgang, 142
pedomorphism, 164
*Peganum harmala*, 304–5, 428–29n33
Peloponnesian War (431–404 BCE), 331, 332
*periagoge*, 60, 61, 75, 340–44
Persian Empire, 120, 310–11, 331n
peyote, 286, 299
*Phaedrus* (Plato), 329–30
Pheidippides, 311
Philippines, 419n3
philosopher-kings, 319
philosophy, 34, 76, 97–98, 100–101, 314–15, 317–18, 325, 391
Pienaar, François, 346–47
Pinchbeck, Daniel, 428n23
Pindar, 325, 328
Pinnacle Point (South Africa), 409n1
Pisistratus, 312

Plains Indians, 270–71, 286
Plato
  author's experience teaching, 322–24
  cave allegory of, 74–75, 77, 263–64, 314
  on courage, 126
  as Eleusinian Mysteries participant, 286, 325
  elitist academy of, 309
  on the Good, 317–20
  on ideal polis size, 127, 311
  influence of, 116
  metataxy as defined by, 113
  *periagoge* as defined by, 60
  Socrates's teachings preserved by, 127
  truth quest of, 381–82
  on values in isolation, 45
Plato, works
  *The Apology*, 308, 317, 324, 332
  *Gorgias*, 314
  *Laches*, 126
  *Phaedrus*, 329–30
  *Republic*, 74–75, 318–20, 321–24, 429n7
  *Symposium*, 113
play, 164–66
Player, Ian, 13n, 144, 274–75, 280, 426n15
Pleistocene epoch, 166, 286, 415–16n16
Plutarch, 325
plutocracy, 48, 56–57, 217
Polak, Henry, 405n5
polis, xxiin, 121, 127, 129
  civilization and, 330
  corruption of, 334
  defining values of, 309
  face-to-face discussion in, 311
  height of, 331
  individual vs. community in, 311–12
  modern moral/political crisis and, 333–34
  primal, 132, 351–52
  whole person in, 310–13
political action, 387–88
political philosophy
  Liberal, 31–32
  as paradigm, 380
  revolutionary, 436n3
  use of term, xiv–xv
politics
  Bushman, 127
  cosmology behind, as exhausted, xii
  electoral, 316
  of mystery, 107–11
  new, 63
  reconnection with wilderness and, 280–81
  revolutions and, 380
  truth quest abandoned in, xv
  use of term, xiv–xv
  *See also* primal politics
population growth, 331, 338, 402n35
Port Elizabeth (South Africa)
  as author's birthplace, 3, 67
  author's return to, 4–5
  geography of, 3–4, 5, 67–68
  human origins near, 67
Porto Alegre (Brazil), 339, 363–65, 373
Portuguese exploration, 174–75
postmodernism, 193, 194–95, 217, 379
  *See also* deconstructionism, postmodern
power hierarchies, 27, 207
prayer, 388
primal ethic, 241–46
primal politics
  of the Iroquois, 214–18
  in kibbutzim, 83
  mandala of, 83, 101, 131–33, 161, 166–67, 197, 210, 214, 219, 243, 309, 317, 337, 339–40, 351–52, 381–82
  modern undermining of, 337–39
  *periagoge* as central to, 340
  resurgence of, 339–40

primal politics (*continued*)
shamanism as central to, 241–42, 306–7
wilderness origins and, 163
*See also* San Bushmen, primal politics of
"primal revolution," xviii, xx *fig*., 117, 140, 151
primate, inner, 137, 151
primate body, living in, 385
Primate Research Center (Madison, WI), 154–56
primates
anthropomorphizing of, 151
in captivity, 411n30
face-to-face communication among, 146–48
ground-living vs. arboreal, 149–51
human evolution from, 156–61
intersubjectivity among, 148–49
scientific research on, 151–56, 411n30
surplus intelligence of, 145
upright gait in, 150
*See also* baboons; chimpanzees; human-primate nexus
*Principia Mathematica* (Newton), 33
Principles for Responsible Investing (PRI), 61, 404n56
professionalization, 313, 315, 317, 331
profit, 37, 49–50, 52, 54, 359–60
property qualifications, 47–48
property rights, 26, 45–46, 47–48, 399–402n26
Protestant Reformation, 25, 28
psilocybin, 286, 294–95, 426n4, 427n18, 427n21, 428n25, 428n28
Psychiatric Research Institute (Prague), 291
psychic energy, activation of, 423–24n37
psychology, depth, 409–10n9
psychopathology, 55
psycho-technologies, 263
*See also* entheogens; hallucinogens
psychotherapy, 292
*Psychotria viridis*, 297
Pythagoras, 431n28

Qing, 226
quantum physics, 77–78, 293
questions, 320–21, 390–91, 392
Qumran caves (Israel), 90, 304–5

rationality, 27, 31, 34, 377
*Realms of the Human Unconscious* (Grof), 427n12
Register, Richard, 363, 373
relativism, xv, 378
religion, xiii–xiv, xv, 34
addiction and, 295–96
etymology of, 244
institutionalized, vs. mystical, 116
syncretistic, 309, 428n24
Ur-religion, shamanism as, 262–65
religious revolution, xviii
religious right, 360
Renaissance, 334
*Republic* (Plato), 74–75, 318–20, 321–24, 429n7
republic vs. democracy, 46–47
*res cogitans*, 36, 38, 50, 154, 318
*res extensa*, 36–37, 41, 154
Restaurante Popular (People's Restaurant; Brazil), 365
"reverse dominance," 200–201, 420–21n28
revolutions
negotiated, 347
politics and, 380
rhinoceros, 13n, 68, 274, 276
Rifkin, Jeremy, 432n5
*Rig Veda*, 286, 326
Ritchie, Claire, 416n24
*Road to Eleusis, The* (Ruck, Hofmann, and Wasson), 326, 430n19, 430–31n22, 431n25
Robben Island (South Africa),

Mandela's imprisonment at, 97, 342, 348
Robberg Peninsula (South Africa), 6, 8, 409n1
robots, 40–41
rock art, European, 221–24, 248, 257
rock art, San Bushman, 167 *fig.*
- academic studies of, 224–27, 421–22n7, 422n9, 424–25n46
- age of, 421nn4–5
- author's experience, 8–9
- European rock art compared to, 168, 221–25, 257
- intention/meanings of, 226–27
- in Kruger National Park, 12, 13
- Linton Panel, 255–56, 424n44
- number of sites, 11
- Rosetta Stone of, 248–51 *figs.*, 248–52
- shamanic significance of, 221, 224–25, 248–52, 257, 266
- trance dance and, 174, 236, 253–56, 254–56 *figs.*

Rock Cree Indians, 110
rock shelters, 158
Rome, Visigoth conquest of (396 CE), 325
Roosevelt, Eleanor, 387
Rosetta Stone, 248, 257
Rosie, 179
Round Head Culture, 286
Rousseau, Jean-Jacques, 130, 381–82
Ruck, Carl A. P., 325, 326, 430n19, 430–31n22, 431n25
Rugby World Cup (1995), 345–47, 432n8
running, human development of, 157–58
Rupert, 275
Russell, Peter, xvii, xix, 399n8
Rwanda, xix

sacrifice, 340
Sahlins, Marshall, 191, 206, 417n29
Sale, Kirkpatrick, 348–49
San Bushmen
- academic studies of, 190–95, 197, 199n
- amateur anthropological studies of, 176–90, 415n10, 415n13
- author's meeting with, 11–17, 210–11
- baboons as viewed by, 139–41
- boundary crossing by, 242, 344
- child-rearing among, 207–9, 419n4
- cosmology of, 7, 139, 217, 225, 231, 257
- cultural identity of, 176
- death causes among, 416n24
- diet of, 65, 182–83, 202, 416n19
- "early times" of, 404n2
- ecological sensitivity of, 183–87
- endurance hunt of, 161–63, 162 *fig.*, 163 *fig.*, 187, 413n42
- European contact with, 67, 174–76
- as related to founder population, 171–74, 171n, 374
- four-part quest model exemplified in, xxi–xxii
- genetic diversity among, 172–73, 414nn2–3
- as hunter-gatherers, 138, 183–84, 184 *fig.*, 189 *figs.*, 198, 199, 416n17, 417n33
- *!hxaro* gifting tradition of, 205–6
- individualism as viewed by, 207–8
- languages of, 140n, 172, 173
- marital relations, 200, 212
- mythology of, 168–69, 227–32, 268–69, 413n49
- persistence of, in southern Africa, 138
- religious sensibility of, 226–27
- "reverse dominance," 200–201, 420–21n28
- sociability of, 203, 209
- societal transition of, 192, 199n, 417n33, 424n39

San Bushmen (*continued*)
storytelling of, 167–69
use of term, xxiin
violence among, 213–14
wilderness as viewed by, 111, 182–83
*See also* rock art, San Bushman; trance dance, San Bushman
San Bushmen, primal politics of, 191–92
academic studies of, 197–99
big-picture construct, 217–19
caring/sharing ethos, 203–6, 420n16, 420n19
chief role, 202–3
conflict resolution, 214
direct democracy, 129, 207–10
egalitarianism, 200–203, 241, 419n3
face-to-face discussion, 127, 210–14, 420n25
Iroquois politics compared to, 214–18
modern Western politics contrasted with, 218–19
as paradoxical, 198–200
trance dance and, 241
violence, 213–14
Sandoz, 290
Sarvodaya Shramadana (Sri Lanka), 353–54
Sassen, Willem, 403n37
*satyagraha*, 368
Sautuola, Marcelino Sanz de, 223
savanna, 137–38, 152, 184–86, 280
Save the Rhino project, 13n
Sayeret Habika, 85
Schmidt, Sigrid, 413n48
Scholem, Gershom, 407n15
Schuster, Charles, 294
science
author's education in, 77–78
Cartesian, 36–38, 40–42, 50, 57, 142, 154, 156, 377, 411n30
future primal synthesis and, xix–xx
historiography of, 436n1
illiteracy in, in US, 59
mystery and, 103–5, 108
normal vs. revolutionary cognition in, 378–79
shamanism and, 306
value/fact separation in, 34
Western dominance and, 26
*Scientific American*, 156
scientific method, 34, 35–36, 40, 103–5, 195, 290–91
scientific revolution, xviii, 25, 30, 34–38
Scotland, eco-villages in, 339, 352, 355, 362, 372–73
Sde Boker Kibbutz, 358
seasonal affective disorder (SAD), 273
sea trade, 29–30
*Second Treatise on Government* (Locke), 31
Segev, Tom, 433n21
self, shamanistic understanding of, 272–73
self-consciousness, 112–17, 165, 267–68, 306–7
self-expression, 391
self-interest, xv, 32, 53–56, 57–58, 62, 216–17, 313, 334, 341
selfishness, 58
self-knowledge, 265–66, 382
self-sufficiency, 311
self-understanding, individual, xxi, 281
Sephardic Jews, 70
sePhuti language, 226
*Sex and Friendship* (Smuts), 411n25
sexual dimorphism, 157
Sha'ar le-Adam peace camp (Israel), 362
shadow, 123–24, 244
shamanic dance, 167–68
shamanic ecstasy, 262–65, 284, 296–97
shamanic technologies, 388
shamanism, xiii–xiv, 14–15, 141
academic studies of, 423n30
boundary crossing and, 141, 241–42, 261–62

as central to primal politics, 241–42, 306–7
Christian repression of, 287
democratization of, 233, 246–47
depth psychology and, 409–10n9
ecstasy in, as Ur-religion, 262–65, 284
endurance hunt and, 162–63
etymology of, 284n
evolutionary significance of, 241
goals of, 244, 266
Greek, 325–26
"hard" (hallucinogen-assisted), 273, 283
healing power of, 261, 288
in Judaism, 404n2
Mesoamerican, 294, 426n4
paradoxical ethic of, 270–73
philosophy and, 325
rock art and, 221–22, 224–25, 248–52, 257
Socratic philosophy and, 318–20
"soft" (nature healing), 273–74, 283
use of term, 262–63
visionary practices of, 261
wilderness and, 262, 296–97, 306–7, 339
*See also* boundary crossing; trance dance, San Bushman
*Shamanism: Archaic Techniques of Ecstasy* (Eliade), 263
shamans
therianthropic, 250 *fig.*, 255
as whole persons, 270–73
Shamir, Yitzhak, 406n17
Shanon, Benny, 298–99, 304
Sharon, Ariel, 406n17
shell middens, 158–59, 190
Shepard, Paul, 146–47, 410n19, 411n30
Sheridan, General Philip, 33
Shimkus, John, 59
Siberian shamanism, 286
Sicily, Greek invasion of (415 BCE), 332
"sick building syndrome," 273
Silberbauer, George, 212–13
Sioux Indians, 56–57, 270–71
Sisulu, Walter, 67
Sitting Bull, Chief, 269
Six-Day War (1967), 358
skepticism, 377–78, 379
slavery, 334
Slovo, Joe, 71
Smith, Adam, 25, 44–45, 48–50, 53, 54, 58, 210, 380, 402n27
Smith, Colin, 295
Smith, Huston, 336, 338
Smuts, Barbara, 147, 148, 151–54, 411n25
Sobel, Dava, 105
social contract, 32, 45–46
socialism, 400n2 (ch. 2)
socialization process, 123–24
social justice, 371
societal collapse, 337–38, 339
Socrates, 165
cave allegory of, 74–75
dialectics of, 149, 344
as Eleusinian Mysteries participant, 286, 325–30
exile and, 124
face-to-face discussion and, 210, 214
on the Good, 308, 317–24, 333
paradoxical history of, 309–10
as shaman, 318–20, 329, 431n28
teachings of, recorded by Plato, 127
trial/execution of, 75–76, 124, 313, 317, 318, 331–33
truth quest of, 149, 317–18, 333–34, 381–82
on urban life, 329–30
on values in isolation, 45
Socratic discussion. *See* face-to-face discussion
Socratic philosophy, 314–15, 318–20, 390
Solon, 312
solstice rituals, 386

Solway, Jacqueline, 194
*soma*, 286, 326, 428–29n33
sophistry, 315, 331–32, 333, 334
*Soul of the Ape, The* (Marais), 138
South Africa
author's education in, 72–74
author's identity in, 73–74, 77, 356
biodiversity in, 5, 399n1
history of, 67
Jewish population of, 69, 70–71
Mandela as president of, 341
*See also* apartheid
South African Defense Forces, 192
South African Museum, 255–56, 424n44
Sparta, 332
specialization, 207, 359–60
species extinction, 4, 61, 181, 398n2, 415–16n16
Spier, Fred, 398n6
spirituality, modern Western interest in, 258–59
Spragens, Thomas, 436n3
Springboks, 345–47
Sri Lanka, sustainable agriculture in, 353–54
Standing Bear, Luther, Chief, 102, 107, 108, 208, 267
Stangneth, Bettina, 402–3n37
St. Anthony's Fire, 430n20
St. Denis, Verna, 422–23n19
Steinsaltz, Adin, 244–45
*Steppenwolf* (Hesse), 267, 272
Stevens, Jay, 290
Stoll, Arthur, 289
Stoney Indians, 279
Storm, Hyemeyohsts, 117–19, 121–22
*Storming Heaven* (Stevens), 290
storytelling
cosmic story, 336, 339–40, 373–75
emergence of, 161
one's own, 389–90
practical applications, 389–90
by primates, 152–54
as public performance, 232
San Bushman, 166–69, 228–29, 241
"telling us into being," 113
*See also* mythology
Stow, George William, 226, 422n9
Stransky, Joel, 347
*Stropharia cubensis*, 285–86, 294–95
*Structure of Scientific Revolutions, The* (Kuhn), 436n1
sun, the, 104–5
sunrise meditation, 385–86
sunset meditation, 103–4, 385–86
sustainability, 338, 349–51, 353–54, 371
Suzmann, Helen, 405n5
Suzuki, Daisetz, 320–21
SWAPO, 192
Swimme, Brian Thomas, x, 104, 164–65, 169, 336, 385, 406–7n1
symbolic representation, early development of, 159–60, 160 *fig.*, 161, 167 *fig.*, 168
*See also* rock art, San Bushman
*Symposium* (Plato), 113
synchronicities, 142
syncretistic religion, 309
Syria, 92

Table Mountain (South Africa), 10
Tall Bull, William, 243
Tanaka, Jiro, 197
Taoism, 242
*Tao Te Ching*, 376
Tarnas, Richard, xvi, 293
Tassili n' Ajjer, 285–86
Tatanga Mani, Chief, 279
Tatanka Yotanka, Chief, 269
Taung limestone quarry (South Africa), 409n1, 410n16
Tea Party movement, 369–70
technology, 32
Teilhard de Chardin, Pierre, 79–81, 131, 245, 305–6
television, 367

*Teller of Many Tales* (Jones), 415n10
"tensional complex," 116
Terry, Rev., 175
Thanatos, 91
Thatcher, Margaret, 48
There's a Limit (Yesh Gvul) 435n32
therianthrope, 250–51 *figs.*, 255, 257, 258 *fig.*, 266
"thing-reality," 113–14
Thirty Tyrants, 332, 333
Thirty Years' War, 39
Thompson, William I., 41–42, 305
thought, 391
Thurlow, Edward, Baron, 54
Thurman, Judith, 247–48
*thuru*, 242, 244–45, 246–47, 344
*tikkun ha'olam*, 72, 356
*Tikkun* magazine, 434n30
*Time* magazine, 61
time trading, 389
Toma, /Twi, 14, 15 *fig.*
Towers, Bernard, 79
trade, 29–30
Traill, Anthony, 414n3
trance dance, San Bushman, 9, 14–15, 174
  author's experience, 233
  boundary crossing during, 252–53
  community required for, 424n39
  described, 233–37, 252
  egalitarianism of, 246–47
  initiation of, 233
  performance of, for money, 424n39
  rock art and, 236, 253–56, 254–56 *figs.*
  shamanic ecstasy attained through, 263, 423–24n37
  socialization through, 232–33
  storytelling and, 232
  Western experience/translation of, 237–41, 423n27, 423nn29–30
trance healing, 422–23n19
transsexuals, 272
trickster deities, 97–98, 168–69, 228, 229–32, 265, 272, 413n49
*Tricksters & Trancers* (Guenther), 198
Trois Frères cave (France), 257, 258 *fig.*
truth quest
  anthropology and, 194
  author's, xiii, 4–5, 8–11
  communal agriculture and, 348
  community and, 321–22
  components of, 118 *fig.*, 131–32
  defined, 337
  in early societies, xiii–xiv
  four-part model for, xxi–xxiii
  individual creativity/collective good mediated in, 368
  Liberalism and, 27, 45
  mandala structure of, xxi, xxii–xxiii, 117–31, 118 *fig.*
  *periagoge* and reorientation to, 340
  Platonic cave allegory and, 76
  practical applications, 390–92
  primal, xv, 118 *fig.*, 161–63
  recovery of, 62–63
  science-informed, xiii
  Socratic, 317–18, 333–34
truth quest, author's
  in England, 76–82
  future primal politics and, 66
  in Hawai'i, 98–101
  in IDF, 85, 88–95
  in Israeli kibbutzim, 82–85
  Jewish identity and, 65–66, 69–72
  mandala dynamic and, 101
  original purpose of, 65
  path with a heart, 97–98
  Platonic cave allegory and, 74–76
  in South Africa, 67–74
truth quest, modern abandonment of, 48–49
  "big history" and, xvii, 27
  in free-market economics, 48–51, 53–56
  in government, 45–48

truth quest, modern abandonment of (*continued*)
  institutions behind, 4–5
  in kibbutzim, 84, 96, 359–61
  Liberalism and, 32–34, 57–59
  medieval roots of, 28–32
  as paradox, xv–xvi
  Socratic quest and, 333–34
  spiritual disease driving, 253–54
  in United States, 57–59
  value/fact separation as central to, 34
  visionary narratives and, 91
  Western revolutions and, 25–27, 34–38
tryptamine, 428n25, 428n28
Tswana people, 201, 203
Tunisia, 368–69
"Turkana Boy," 412n33
Tutu, Desmond, 372
Twele, 239
*Two Treatises on Government* (Locke), 7, 27, 401n26
Tyson, Neil deGrasse, 406n3

*Ubuntu*, 126
Ulrich, Roger S., 425–26nn12–14
Umfolozi Game Reserve (Zululand), 274–79
Umfolozi River, 276–77
Umkhonto we Sizwe, 71
unconscious, the, 143, 410n9, 410n11
União do Vegetal church, 297, 428n24
United Nations, 61, 87, 339, 352, 353, 357, 373, 404n56
United States
  antidepressant use in, 427n16
  child abuse in, 156, 411n29
  civil rights movement in, 368, 369
  counterculture in, 290–91, 369
  direct democracy in, 128, 315–16
  eco-villages in, 339, 354, 372
  finance industry and economic collapse in (2008), 56
  founding fathers of, as classical Liberals, 45–47
  identity transgressions punished in, 272
  Liberalism as embodied in, 57–59
  as plutocracy, 56–57
  scientific illiteracy in, 59
  urbanization in, 50, 402n35
United States Agency for International Development (USAID), 14
United States Congress, 403n52
United States Constitution
  Fourteenth Amendment, 53, 62
  Iroquois Confederacy influence on, 216
  as Liberal vision, 25–26, 58
  property rights enshrined in, 45–46, 402n28
  truth quest abandoned in, 45–47, 58
universe
  18th-century view of, 106
  scale of, 105–6
University of Amsterdam, 398n6
University of Hawai'i, 4, 99, 322–24
University of Missouri, 237–38
University of the Witwatersrand, 12
Uppsala University Hospital (Sweden), 274
urbanization, xii, 50, 402n35
urban kibbutzim, 435n31
urban life, 329–30, 359, 362–64, 373
usury, 29

van der Post, Laurens, 144, 170, 177–80, 186, 191, 280, 415n10, 415n13
*Varieties of Religious Experience, The* (James), 111–12
Vedas, 428–29n33
veldt, 4, 4n, 277
Venus figurines, 264–65
Verwoerd, Hendrik, 69
victory gardens, 387

Vietnam War, 369
Viljoen, Constand, 345
violence, 213–14, 377
virtue, 318
Visigoths, 325
visions, shared, 300–301
"Visit to the Lion's House, A," 268
visualization, 289
vivisection, 37
Voegelin, Eric, 20, 24, 253
  on anamnesis, 64
  civilizamtions covered by, 408n22
  consciousness, split structure of, 113, 113n, 143, 293
  consciousness-reality-language, 116, 408n20
  influence of, 410n12
  It-reality as part of the in-between, 113–15, 144
  Jewish mysticism and, 407n15
  Jung and, 143
  leap in being, 66, 115–16
  modernity as viewed by, xvi, 24
  publications of, 407–8n19
  reflective-philosophical path of, as truth quest starting point, 117
  reputation of, 112, 407n17
  scholarship of, 112–13
  on truth quest, 2
Volksfront (South Africa), 345

Wai'anae community (Hawai'i), 350
Wakan Tanka, 107–9, 114, 115, 267, 269–70
Wakea, 350
Walker, Liz, 354
walking, human development of, 157–58
Walking Buffalo, Chief, 279
Wasson, R. Gordon, 286, 326, 426n4, 428n28, 430n19, 430–31n22, 431n25
Wasson, Valentina, 426n4, 428n28
Waterberg Mountains, 138–39
water discipline, 88, 88n
Watson, James D., 289
*Wealth of Nations, The* (Smith), 48–49
Weather Underground, 369
Weber, Max, 30
Weinberg, Paul, 170
Weissner, Polly, 420n16
Weizmann, Chaim, 434n29
Wells, Robin, 57
Wells, Spencer, 413n2
Wendt, W. E., 421n4
werewolves, 237, 260, 266–67
West, the
  as cognicentric, 289
  hallucinogens feared/disrespected in, 262, 283–84, 290–91, 294
  individualism as viewed in, 207
  "killer apps" responsible for dominance of, 26
  moral/political crisis in, 333–34
  shamanism disrespected in, 262
  sharing ethos reemerging in, 206
  spiritual revival in, 258–59
West Bank (Palestine), 87
Westhuizen, Jan van der ("Oom Jan"), 16–17
*What Is Zen?* (Suzuki), 320–21
Whitehead, Alfred North, 317
*White Hole in Time* (Russell), xvii
whole, good of the, 62, 311, 351–52, 368
whole person, the, 119–20
  autonomy loss and feelings of, 51
  Greek ideal of, 120–21, 243, 310–13, 316–17
  holotropic experiences and, 293
  in Jungian psychology, 123–24, 243–44
  in kibbutzim, 83
  as mandala quadrant, 118 *fig.*
  Mandela and, 344–45
  moral autonomy of, 241
  in Native American cultures, 121–23
  practical applications, 388–89
  in San Bushman culture, 241
  shaman as, 270–73
  *See also* individuation

wilderness
- ancestral relationship with, 161–63, 415–16n16
- beauty of, 278, 279, 280
- boundary crossing into, 242, 265–70, 330
- civilization vs., 329–30
- degradation of, 4, 337
- healing through contact with, 273–74, 425–26nn12–14
- human origins in, 6–7, 296–97, 337
- indigenous views of, 110–11, 269–70
- inner, 144, 330
- politics and, 280–81
- primal vs. Liberal views of, 33
- shamanism and, 262, 296–97, 306–7, 339
- *See also* nature

wilderness ecology, 219
wilderness immersion, 89–90, 261, 274–81, 350, 426n15
Wilderness Leadership School, 144, 274
wilderness rapture, 280
Williams, Chester, 345
Wilmsen, Edwin, 170, 193–94, 197, 417–18nn36–37
Wilson, Bill, 295–96
Wilson, E. O., 61, 273, 398n2
Windhoek (Namibia), 13–14
Wishard, William van Dusen, xii
witches, 265
Wolin, Sheldon, 436n3
*Women Like Meat* (Biesele), 183
women's movement, 369
work ethic, 26, 30
World Bank, 403n43
World Conference on Hunter Gatherers (1978), 191
World Health Organization, 273
World War I, 433n22
World War II, 343–44
World Wildlife Federation, 14

/Xam people, 8, 15, 136, 172, 177, 225, 233, 236–37, 268, 336, 413n49
Xhosa language, 171
Xhosa people, 67, 342–43
!Xo Bushmen, 162–63, 252
Xumu, 300

Yakima Indians, 214–15
Yaqui shamanism, 287–88
Yehuda, Ben, 433n22
Yesh Gvul (There's a Limit), 435n32
YHWH, 115
yin/yang dynamic, 242
yoga, 423–24n37
Yom Kippur War (1973), 92–95
youth rebellion (1960s), 290–91, 369

Zen Buddhism, 320–21
Zerzan, John, 191–92
Zionism, 70, 71–72, 81, 82, 84, 96–97, 356–57, 406n11, 433–34nn21–23, 434n29
*Zohar*, 404n2
Zoroastrianism, 428–29n33
Zulu language, 171

# ABOUT THE AUTHOR

Louis G. Herman is a professor of political science at the University of Hawai'i–West O'ahu (UHWO). He was born in an orthodox Jewish community in apartheid South Africa, and his earliest memories were of "wilderness rapture"— intoxication with the rugged beauty of the South African *bushveld* and coastline. At age twelve his family moved to England, where he received a science education that culminated in degrees in medical sciences and the history and philosophy of science at Cambridge University. Disillusioned with academia, he gave up a medical career, sought out his "tribal" roots, moved to an Israeli kibbutz, and volunteered for military service in a combat infantry unit. His wartime experience confronted him with two hard realities. One was the long-ignored, obvious fact that Arabs were also indigenous to the land; the other was the absurdity of war as a long-term solution to political conflict. He felt compelled to start over, to return to the Socratic question "How should we live?"

After studying political philosophy at the Hebrew University and completing his PhD at the University of Hawai'i, he found that the two tracks of his search, the personal and the political, led him back to southern Africa, the birthplace of modern humanity. His search increasingly converged on the wisdom of the oldest culture on earth, the San Bushmen. *Future Primal* represents the culmination of this search.

For the past twenty years, Herman has been at UHWO developing a political science curriculum and pedagogy based on the principles of the primal truth quest. Also, he is co–executive producer and principal investigator for a feature-length documentary on the issues raised in *Future Primal.* The film is a joint UHWO/Earthrise production with Craig and Damon Foster, inspired by *The Great Dance*, their award-winning documentary on the last of the nomadic San Bushman hunter-gatherers.

NEW WORLD LIBRARY is dedicated to publishing books and other media that inspire and challenge us to improve the quality of our lives and the world.

We are a socially and environmentally aware company, and we strive to embody the ideals presented in our publications. We recognize that we have an ethical responsibility to our customers, our staff members, and our planet.

We serve our customers by creating the finest publications possible on personal growth, creativity, spirituality, wellness, and other areas of emerging importance. We serve New World Library employees with generous benefits, significant profit sharing, and constant encouragement to pursue their most expansive dreams.

As a member of the Green Press Initiative, we print an increasing number of books with soy-based ink on 100 percent postconsumer-waste recycled paper. Also, we power our offices with solar energy and contribute to nonprofit organizations working to make the world a better place for us all.

Our products are available
in bookstores everywhere.
For our catalog, please contact:

New World Library
14 Pamaron Way
Novato, California 94949

Phone: 415-884-2100 or 800-972-6657
Catalog requests: Ext. 50
Orders: Ext. 52
Fax: 415-884-2199
Email: escort@newworldlibrary.com

To subscribe to our electronic newsletter, visit
www.newworldlibrary.com

Environmental impact estimates were made using the Environmental Defense Fund Paper Calculator @ www.papercalculator.org.

P9-CMF-751

# PREFACE.

By an act approved June 23, 1874, Congress made an appropriation "to enable the Secretary of War to begin the publication of the Official Records of the War of the Rebellion, both of the Union and Confederate Armies," and directed him "to have copied for the Public Printer all reports, letters, telegrams, and general orders not heretofore copied or printed, and properly arranged in chronological order."

Appropriations for continuing such preparation have been made from time to time, and the act approved June 16, 1880, has provided "for the printing and binding, under direction of the Secretary of War, of 10,000 copies of a compilation of the Official Records (Union and Confederate) of the War of the Rebellion, so far as the same may be ready for publication, during the fiscal year"; and that "of said number, 7,000 copies shall be for the use of the House of Representatives, 2,000 copies for the use of the Senate, and 1,000 copies for the use of the Executive Departments."*

This compilation will be the first general publication of the military records of the war, and will embrace all official documents that can be obtained by the compiler, and that appear to be of any historical value.

---

*Volume I to V distributed under act approved June 16, 1880. The act approved August 7, 1882, provides that—

"The volumes of the official records of the war of the rebellion shall be distributed as follows: One thousand copies to the executive departments, as now provided by law. One thousand copies for distribution by the Secretary of War among officers of the Army and contributors to the work. Eight thousand three hundred copies shall be sent by the Secretary of War to such libraries, organizations, and individuals as may be designated by the Senators, Representatives, and Delegates of the Forty-seventh Congress. Each Senator shall designate not exceeding twenty-six, and each Representative and Delegate not exceeding twenty-one of such addresses, and the volumes shall be sent thereto from time to time as they are published, until the publication is completed. Senators, Representatives, and Delegates shall inform the Secretary of War in each case how many volumes of those heretofore published they have forwarded to such addresses. The remaining copies of the eleven thousand to be published, and all sets that may not be ordered to be distributed as provided herein, shall be sold by the Secretary of War for cost of publication with ten per cent. added thereto, and the proceeds of such sale shall be covered into the Treasury. If two or more sets of said volumes are ordered to the same address the Secretary of War shall inform the Senators, Representatives or Delegates, who have designated the same, who thereupon may designate other libraries, organizations, or individuals. The Secretary of War shall report to the first session of the Forty-eighth Congress what volumes of the series heretofore published have not been furnished to such libraries, organizations, and individuals. He shall also inform distributees at whose instance the volumes are sent."

The publication will present the records in the following order of arrangement:

The **1st Series** will embrace the formal reports, both Union and Confederate, of the first seizures of United States property in the Southern States, and of all military operations in the field, with the correspondence, orders, and returns relating specially thereto, and, as proposed, is to be accompanied by an Atlas.

In this series the reports will be arranged according to the campaigns and several theaters of operations (in the chronological order of the events), and the Union reports of any event will, as a rule, be immediately followed by the Confederate accounts. The correspondence, &c., not embraced in the "reports" proper will follow (first Union and next Confederate) in chronological order.

The **2d Series** will contain the correspondence, orders, reports, and returns, Union and Confederate, relating to prisoners of war, and (so far as the military authorities were concerned) to State or political prisoners.

The **3d Series** will contain the correspondence, orders, reports, and returns of the Union authorities (embracing their correspondence with the Confederate officials) not relating specially to the subjects of the *first* and *second* series. It will set forth the annual and special reports of the Secretary of War, of the General-in Chief, and of the chiefs of the several staff corps and departments; the calls for troops, and the correspondence between the National and the several State authorities.

The **4th Series** will exhibit the correspondence, orders, reports, and returns of the Confederate authorities, similar to that indicated for the Union officials, as of the *third* series, but excluding the correspondence between the Union and confederate authorities given in that series.

ROBERT N. SCOTT,
*Major, Third Art., and Bvt. Lieut. Col.*

WAR DEPARTMENT, *August* 23, 1880.

**Approved:**

ALEX. RAMSEY,
*Secretary of War.*

# CONTENTS.

CHAPTER XXIV.

Page.
**Operations in Northern Virginia, West Virginia, and Maryland** .......... 1-818

# CONTENTS OF PRECEDING VOLUMES.

## VOLUME I.


CHAPTER I. Page.

Operations in Charleston Harbor, South Carolina. December 20, 1860–April 14, 1861 ........ 1–317

CHAPTER II.

The secession of Georgia. January 3–26, 1861 ........ 318–325

CHAPTER III.

The secession of Alabama and Mississippi. January 4–20, 1861 ........ 326–330

CHAPTER IV.

Operations in Florida. January 6–August 31, 1861 ........ 331–473

CHAPTER V. Page.

The secession of North Carolina. January 9–May 20, 1861 ........ 474–488

CHAPTER VI.

The secession of Louisiana. January 10–February 19, 1861 ........ 489–501

CHAPTER VII.

Operations in Texas and New Mexico. February 1–June 11, 1861 ........ 502–636

CHAPTER VIII.

Operations in Arkansas, the Indian Territory, and Missouri. February 7–May 9, 1861 ........ 637–691


## VOLUME II.


CHAPTER IX. Page.

Operations in Maryland, Pennsylvania, Virginia, and West Virginia. April 16–July 31, 1861. 1–1012


## VOLUME III.


CHAPTER X. Page.

Operations in Missouri, Arkansas, Kansas, and Indian Territory. May 10–November 19, 1861. 1–749


## VOLUME IV.


CHAPTER XI. Page.

Operations in Texas, New Mexico, and Arizona. June 11, 1861–February 1, 1862. 1–174

CHAPTER XII.

Operations in Kentucky and Tennessee. July 1–November 19, 1861 ........ 175–565

CHAPTER XIII. Page.

Operations in North Carolina and Southeastern Virginia. August 1, 1861–January 11, 1862 ........ 566–721


## VOLUME V.


CHAPTER XIV. Page.

Operations in Maryland, Northern Virginia, and West Virginia. August 1, 1861–March 17, 1862. 1–1106


## VOLUME VI.


CHAPTER XV. Page.

Operations on the coasts of South Carolina, Georgia, and Middle and East Florida. August 21, 1861–April 11, 1862 ........ 1–435

CHAPTER XVI. Page.

Operations in West Florida, Southern Alabama, Southern Mississippi, and Louisiana. September 1, 1861–May 12, 1862. 436–894


## VOLUME VII.


CHAPTER XVII. Page.

Operations in Kentucky, Tennessee, N. Alabama, and S. W. Virginia. Nov. 19, 1861–Mar. 4, 1862. 1–946


## VOLUME VIII.


CHAPTER XVIII. Page.

Operations in Missouri, Arkansas, Kansas, and Indian Territory. Nov. 19, 1861–April 10, 1862. 1–834

## VOLUME IX.


CHAPTER XIX. Page.

Operations in Southeastern Virginia. January 11–March 17, 1862 ..... 1–71

CHAPTER XX.

Operations in North Carolina. January 11–August 20, 1862 ..... 72–480

CHAPTER XXI. Page.

Operations in Texas, New Mexico, and Arizona. February 1–September 20, 1862 ..... 481–736


## VOLUME X—IN TWO PARTS.


CHAPTER XXII.

Operations in Kentucky, Tennessee, North Mississippi, North Alabama, and Southwest Virginia. March 4–June 10, 1862.

| | Page. |
|---|---|
| **Part I**—Reports ..... | 1–927 |
| **Part II**—Correspondence ..... | 1–642 |


## VOLUME XI—IN THREE PARTS.


CHAPTER XXIII.

The Peninsular Campaign, Virginia. March 17–September 2, 1862.

| | Page. |
|---|---|
| **Part I**—Reports, March 17–June 24 ..... | 1–1077 |
| **Part II**—Reports, June 25–September 2 ..... | 1–994 |
| **Part III**—Correspondence ..... | 1–692 |

## CHAPTER XXIV.

# OPERATIONS IN NORTHERN VIRGINIA, WEST VIRGINIA, AND MARYLAND.

**March 17–September 2, 1862.**

## PART I.

**REPORTS—March 17–June 25.**

### SUMMARY OF THE PRINCIPAL EVENTS.*

March 18, 1862.—Skirmish at Middletown, Va.

19, 1862.—Skirmish at Elk Mountain, W. Va.
Skirmish at Strasburg, Va.

20, 1862.—Maj. Gen. Nathaniel P. Banks, U. S. Army, assumes command of the Fifth Army Corps.
Skirmish at Philippi, W. Va.
Reconnaissance to Gainesville, Va.

20–21, 1862.—Reconnaissance to Dumfries, Va.

22, 1862.—Skirmish at Kernstown, Va.
Middle Military Department constituted, under command of Maj. Gen. John A. Dix, U. S. Army.

23, 1862.—Battle of Kernstown, Va.

25, 1862.—Skirmish at Mount Jackson, Va.

27–31, 1862.—Operations in the vicinity of Middleburg and White Plains, Va.

28–31, 1862.—Operations on the Orange and Alexandria Railroad, Va., including affairs at Bealeton and Rappahannock Stations.

29, 1862.—Maj. Gen. John C. Frémont supersedes Brig. Gen. William S. Rosecrans in command of the Mountain Department.

April 1, 1862.—Skirmish at Salem, Va.

1– 2, 1862.—Advance of Union forces from Strasburg to Woodstock and Edenburg, Va.

2, 1862.—Skirmish at Stony Creek, near Edenburg, Va.
Reconnaissance to the Rappahannock River, Va.

3, 1862.—Skirmish at Moorefield, W. Va.

4, 1862.—Departments of the Rappahannock (under Maj. Gen. Irvin McDowell) and of the Shenandoah (under Maj. Gen. N. P. Banks) constituted.

---

* Of some of the minor conflicts noted in this "Summary" no circumstantial reports are on file.

April 7, 1862.—Reconnaissance to the Rappahannock River, Va.
Skirmish at Columbia Furnace, Va.
12, 1862.—Major-General Banks, U. S. Army, assumes command of the Department of the Shenandoah.
Raid from Fairmont to Valley River and Boothsville, Marion County, W. Va.
Skirmish at Monterey, Va.
15, 1862.—Reconnaissance to the Rappahannock, Va.
16, 1862.—Reconnaissance to the Rappahannock, Va.
Reconnaissance to Liberty Church, Va.
Skirmish at Columbia Furnace, Va.
17, 1862.—Occupation of Mount Jackson, skirmish at Rude's Hill, and occupation of New Market, Va.
Skirmish at Piedmont, Va.
17-19, 1862.—Skirmishes near Falmouth and occupation (18th) of Fredericksburg, Va., by the Union forces.
17-21, 1862.—Expedition from Summerville (Nicholas Court-House) to Addison, W. Va.
18, 1862.—Reconnaissance to the Rappahannock, Va.
Skirmish at Chapmanville, W. Va.
19, 1862.—Skirmish on South Fork of Shenandoah, near Luray, Va.
Occupation of Sparta, Va.
21, 1862.—Skirmish at Monterey, Va.
22, 1862.—Harrisonburg, Va., occupied by Union forces.
Occupation of and skirmish near Luray, Va.
23, 1862.—Skirmish at Grass Lick, W. Va.
24, 1862.—Skirmish nine miles from Harrisonburg, Va.
26, 1862.—Skirmish at the Gordonsville and Keezletown Cross-Roads, Va
27, 1862.—Skirmish at McGaheysville, Va.

May 1, 1862.—Skirmish at Clark's Hollow, W. Va.
Skirmish on Camp Creek, in the Stone River Valley, W. Va.
Skirmish at Rapidan Station, Va.
2, 1862.—Skirmishes at Trevilian's Depot and Louisa Court-House, Va.
4- 5, 1862.—Reconnaissance to Culpeper Court-House, Va.
5, 1862.—Skirmish at Princeton, W. Va.
Skirmish at Columbia Bridge, Va.
Skirmish at Franklin, W. Va.
6, 1862.—Skirmish at Camp McDonald and Arnoldsburg, W. Va.
Skirmish near Harrisonburg, Va.
7, 1862.—Skirmish at and near Wardensville, W. Va.
Action at Somerville Heights, Va.
8, 1862.—Engagement near McDowell (Bull Pasture Mountain), Va.
9, 1862.—Skirmish near McDowell, Va.
10, 1862.—Action at Giles Court-House, W. Va.
10-12, 1862.—Skirmishes near Franklin, W. Va.
11, 1862.—Skirmish at Princeton, W. Va.
Skirmish on the Bowling Green Road, near Fredericksburg, Va.
12, 1862.—Skirmish at Lewisburg, W. Va.
Skirmish at Monterey, Va.
13, 1862.—Affair on Rappahannock River, Va.
14, 1862.—Skirmish at Gaines' Cross-Roads, Va.
15, 1862.—Skirmish at Linden, Va.
Skirmish at Ravenswood, W. Va.
Skirmish at Gaines' Cross-Roads, Rappahannock County, Va.
Action at Wolf Creek, W. Va.

May 15-17, 1862.—Actions at and in the vicinity of Princeton, W. Va.
15-June 17, 1862.—Operations in the Shenandoah Valley.
17, 1862.—McDowell ordered to form junction with Army of the Potomac.
20, 1862.—Raid on Virginia Central Railroad at Jackson's River Depot, Va.
23, 1862.—Action at Lewisburg, W. Va.
25, 1862.—Call made for all Volunteers and Militia in Illinois, Indiana, Iowa, Maine, Massachusetts, Michigan, New Hampshire, New York, Ohio, Pennsylvania, Rhode Island, Vermont, and Wisconsin.*
26, 1862.—Skirmish near Franklin, W. Va.
29, 1862.—Skirmish near Wardensville, W. Va.
30, 1862.—Skirmish at Lewisburg, W. Va.
Raid to Shaver's River, W. Va.

June 4, 1862.—Skirmish at Big Bend, W. Va.
7, 1862.—Skirmish at Big Bend, W. Va.
8, 1862.—Skirmish at Muddy Creek, W. Va.
9, 1862.—Maj. Gen. John E. Wool, U. S. Army, assumes command of the Middle Military Department.
10, 1862.—Skirmish at mouth of West Fork, W. Va.
17, 1862.—Jackson's forces move from Weyer's Cave for the Peninsula.
18, 1862.—Reserve Army Corps constituted, under command of Brig. Gen. Samuel D. Sturgis, U. S. Army.
18-19, 1862.—Skirmishes near Winchester, Va.
22-30, 1862.—Scout from Strasburg to Moorefield and New Creek, W. Va., and Winchester, Va.
24, 1862.—Skirmish at Milford, Va.
25, 1862.—Skirmish at Mungo Flats, W. Va.
26, 1862.—The Mountain Department and the Departments of the Rappahannock and of the Shenandoah merged into the Army of Virginia, under Maj. Gen. John Pope, U. S. Army. First, Second, and Third Army Corps, Army of Virginia, constituted.

## GENERAL REPORTS.

No. 1.—Maj. Gen. John C. Frémont, U. S. Army, of operations March 29-June 27.
No. 2.—Record of the McDowell Court of Inquiry.

## No. 1.

*Report of Maj. Gen. John C. Frémont, U. S. Army, of operations March 29-June 27, 1862.*

NEW YORK, *December* 30, 1865.

SIR: I have had the honor to receive your communication of the 4th ultimo requesting a report of operations in the Mountain Department during the period of my command in 1862. Unavoidable engagements have interfered to prevent an earlier compliance with your request, and having been specially ordered shortly after I was relieved to turn over to my successor all books, records, and documents pertaining to the department, I am also without the data necessary to complete and full statements.

Under the order of the President, bearing date March 11,† I proceeded to the designated headquarters of my department, Wheeling,

* This requisition and resulting correspondence to appear in Series III, Vol. II.
† Creating the Mountain Department. See Series I, Vol. V, p. 54.

Va., relieving Brigadier-General Rosecrans, and assuming command March 29, 1862. The disposition and numbers of troops upon my arrival within the department were reported to me as follows:

Within the District of the Cumberland, comprising all east of the Alleghanies and west of the Department of the Potomac, three regiments of infantry and one company of cavalry; the district commanded by Brig. Gen. R. C. Schenck.

Within the Cheat Mountain District, comprising all west of the Alleghanies, south of the railroad lines, north of the valley of the Gauley, and east of the Weston and Summerville road, six regiments and five companies of infantry, four companies of cavalry, and two batteries of artillery; district under command of Brig. Gen. R. H. Milroy.

Within the Railroad District, comprising all north and west of the railroad lines, thirty-four companies of infantry of different regiments, eight companies of cavalry, and three batteries of artillery; Brig. Gen. B. F. Kelley commanding.

Within the District of Kanawha, comprising all the valleys of the Kanawha and Guyandotte Rivers and mouth of the Big Sandy, twelve regiments and three companies of infantry, fifteen companies of cavalry, and two batteries of artillery; district commanded by Brig. Gen. J. D. Cox.

Within the Districts of Big Sandy Valley and the Gap, commanded respectively by Colonels Garfield and Carter, were troops estimated in the total at a fraction over 9,000 men.

The total of troops within the department, as ascertained or estimated—that is to say, of infantry thirty-five and two-tenths regiments; of cavalry thirty-six companies, and of artillery nine batteries—stood in figures at 34,271 men.

Shortly after assuming command I was informed by the Secretary of War that the troops in Eastern Kentucky and Southwestern Virginia, although included within the limits of my department, would not be subject to my command or control. This deducted, agreeably to the estimates turned over to me, 9,195 men. Adding to these the percentage allowed in estimates as sick, &c., and not available for duty, a further decrease took place of 6,269 men; leaving balance of 18,807 effective force—say, in round numbers, 19,000 men.

With these troops it was necessary to guard a frontier of 350 miles, approached by roads more or less at rectangles with lines in occupation, and having few interior cross-communications. They were also employed to guard the depots, bridges, and tunnels on 300 miles of railroad and over 200 miles of water communication. Several partially formed regiments and companies were found waiting at different localities on my arrival at Wheeling, and asked only to be mustered in and furnished with arms to do good and loyal service. Recent orders, however, of the War Department concerning enlistments and the increase of regiments forbade my acceptance of more than a limited proportion of these troops, and this proportion only as a remainder upon previous quotas of the State. By special permission two howitzer batteries were afterward organized, but at a date so late as to compel a detail from troops already in service to make up the rank and file, thus failing to increase the total of enlisted men within the department.

The enemy, beginning already to gain strength by re-enforcements opposite the whole extent of my lines, was not hesitative in his demonstrations. Early in April General Milroy, within the Cheat Mountain District, was attacked near Monterey by a force of over 1,000 rebels with cavalry and artillery. After a short engagement the enemy were put to rout, and driven with heavy loss beyond the Shenandoah Mountains. At this point pursuit was restrained, partly owing to absence of supports, but mainly because of the want of horses to get forward artillery. Guerrillas also began to be active, and later in the month a small body of infantry sent out by General Schenck from Romney was attacked on Grass Lick near Lost River. The skirmish was severe, our men losing several killed and wounded. A re-enforcement of cavalry coming up, however, under Lieutenant-Colonel Downey, of the Potomac Home Brigade, the rebels were driven and pursued, with the loss of their leader and others killed, besides a number wounded and 20 captured. Still later in April an expedition of infantry and cavalry was sent out from Weston by Colonel Harris, of the Tenth Virginia, against guerrillas infesting Webster County. The cavalry, under Lieutenant Lawson, being attacked near Addison, after killing 5 of the enemy fell back upon the infantry under Captain Darnall. A running fight then ensued, in which the guerrillas were assailed in their own style. The skirmish continued for several hours, at the end of which time the bushwhackers were routed, with a further loss of 12 killed, several wounded, and 4 or 5 captured.

The village of Addison being deserted by its original inhabitants, and found to be a rendezvous for the enemy, was burned. Some cattle and horses were also captured. The loss of Captain Darnall's command was but 3 wounded in all. The lesson inflicted upon the guerrillas in this instance was severe, and induced their leader to send in a letter offering terms of compromise.

Other affairs and skirmishes took place between detached parties of our troops and the guerrillas up to and within the month of June. It was ascertained that, under expectation of entire immunity by virtue of commissions issued at this time broadcast by Governor Letcher, these irregular bands were drawing together in considerable strength, and waited only for the coming of the leaves to harass with robbery and murder our lines from right to left. As a preventive measure certain of their class were, after full and fair trial by military commission, promptly executed by hanging. The effect was to correct a mistaken belief in immunity for their crimes, and to render more secure interior points and roads, as well as loyal inhabitants of the military districts. In connection with the irregular but often prolonged and severe contests with guerrillas, it is just to name Colonels Harris and Rathbone, of Virginia troops; Lieutenant-Colonel Downey, of the Potomac Home Brigade; Captain Latham, of Ohio Infantry, and Captain Fish, of Connecticut Cavalry, as specially active and successful.

The troops of my command, however, though equal to the maintenance, for the time being, of lines established, were, owing to their necessarily scattered condition, unavailable in any large proportion to form active or movable columns or for operations of a general character against the enemy. In view of this fact, as also of a plan submitted for movements in the direction of Knoxville and the Virginia and Tennessee Railroad, the President had, prior to my leaving Washington in March, promised me ample re-enforcements. The number of these re-enforcements, as determined and urged by the Secretary of War, was 17,000. They were to consist of infantry, cavalry, and artillery, and to have attached a pontoon train complete. On the 1st of April a dispatch from the Secretary of War informed me that the division of Brigadier-General Blenker had been detached from the Army of the Potomac and put *en route* for my department. The order as originally issued to this division directed it to proceed by way of Harper's

Ferry, and from that point report. As, however, up to the 12th of April it had failed to reach Harper's Ferry, I telegraphed a request that it be ordered to move by the most direct and shortest road to Moorefield, this arrangement suiting best my plans as up to the time developed. Brigadier-General Rosecrans, who in the mean time had been placed in temporary command to conduct the division, was accordingly instructed to the above effect.

Next to the want of troops within my department in numbers sufficient or available for extended operations had been, as it continued to be, the absolute and pressing need of transportation. As early as the beginning of April no less than five batteries in the field were found to be without horses, and the case represented to the War Department. From lack of horses also to get forward guns at least one opportunity had been lost in the Cheat Mountain District to pursue and capture a retreating rebel force. The Sixth Ohio Cavalry, an excellent regiment, eager for service, was kept unmounted, and by consequence inactive, for the sole reason that animals could not be obtained to supply it. Requisitions reported made by my predecessor in command as early as February for cavalry and artillery horses, mules, wagons, &c., had not been met. Requisitions made direct by myself, under special permission, lingered in unknown channels, and that which was asked for was but partially obtained. My earnest and repeated requests for authority to order the purchase of animals needed without delay and in the open market were not acceded to. It was replied that the mode of supply, through requisitions in the ordinary form, was "sufficient for all purposes, and the only mode consistent with a proper regard for public expenditure." Delays suffered were certainly remarkable, inasmuch as the Secretary of War constantly and kindly assured me that transportation had been or would be speedily ordered through the proper department. The frequent and earnest dispatches of General Rosecrans also showed that the troops ordered to re enforce my department were even worse off than my own, and difficulties in the way of rapid and efficient operations, at a distance from main points of supply, were increased instead of being diminished. Over forty horses were demanded by General Rosecrans to get the batteries of the Blenker division out of Martinsburg. Thirty-six ambulances and teams were also called for. Forage was scarce, and animals already on hand were reported "starving." In addition, it appeared, as late as April 19, that so illy provided in other respects were the coming re-enforcements that thirty-eight days had been passed by them without tents or other shelter, and this during the inclemencies of a spring seldom paralleled for severity in the history of the Virginia Valley. To obviate a delay in payments and an issue of clothing expected to be made I directed the troops as fast as cared for to be sent forward by regiments or other sufficient bodies to Moorefield.

After much correspondence I had begun to think the difficulties of the Blenker division at length removed, and was looking for their immediate appearance in the department, when finally I was informed that the men were too badly in want of shoes to march. With things at this ebb, a dispatch from the Secretary of War, bearing date of April 21, stated the desire of the President to know at what time I purposed moving against Knoxville and by what route.* In reply I had the honor to submit for consideration, through my chief of staff, dispatched to Washington for the purpose, the two separate plans which are set out in the following letter:

---

* See "Correspondence, etc.," Part III, p. 96.

HEADQUARTERS MOUNTAIN DEPARTMENT,
*Wheeling, Va., April 21, 1862.*

To His Excellency ABRAHAM LINCOLN,
*President of the United States:*

SIR: In answer to a telegram from the Secretary of War, desiring me to submit to the President my proposed plan of operations for the occupation of Knoxville, I beg leave to state that my first intention was, after guarding the Baltimore and Ohio Railroad and the loyal inhabitants of the department with a force of about 10,000, to transport 25,000 men by railroad and the Ohio to Maysville, Covington, and Louisville, Ky.; thence, partly by rail and partly by turnpike, to Nicholasville, and from that point march directly upon Knoxville, turning the enemy's position at Cumberland Gap. The difficulties, however, in the way of obtaining the requisite number of troops have led to a change of my plan, which is as follows:

The first base of operations being the Baltimore and Ohio Railroad, the division of General Blenker, which, from the best information I can obtain, numbers about 9,000 men, will take position at Moorefield. At this point or at Franklin it will unite with the troops now under command of General Schenck, numbering about 3,000. With these, acting in conjunction with General Banks, I propose to move up the valley of Virginia by a course which you will see on the accompanying map, over roads which are as dry and as good at all seasons of the year as any in Virginia, and through a country where forage is easily obtained. At Monterey I shall be joined by the troops under General Milroy, numbering 3,500 effective men, and can then strike the railroad at or near Salem, while General Cox with his 7,000 men takes possession of Newbern, or can first effect a junction with General Cox, and seize the railroad with a force thus increased to about 22,000.

The base of operations will then be changed to Gauley. To this place, by the Ohio and Kanawha Rivers, abundant supplies for the army can be transported with the means now on hand and being prepared. Having thus destroyed the connection between Knoxville and the army in Eastern Virginia, and perhaps seized some rolling stock, we can advance rapidly along the railroad toward Knoxville, turning the position at Cumberland Gap. The forces now under General Kelley and the Virginia troops will be left as we proceed to guard the Baltimore and Ohio Railroad and to protect the loyal inhabitants of the State from guerrillas. The latter is to be effected by the establishment of a few posts strongly held, from which sudden and frequent attacks can be made upon any organizations existing or forming in the department. Knoxville taken, a third base of operations can be made upon Nicholasville, from which place supplies can be easily obtained and transported over level and good roads. The army will thus be in a position to co-operate in any way in the general plan of operations for the prosecution of the war.

The original plan above mentioned possesses the advantages of rapidity in execution, the throwing us forward immediately into the heart of the enemy's country, the striking of the enemy's railroad in the first instance at the most important point, and a base of operations in a friendly country, through which provisions can be drawn with comparative safety. The second has been suggested only because it enables us to collect the troops now scattered throughout the department, and thus increase the small force sent.

Respectfully,

J. C. FRÉMONT,
*Major-General, Commanding.*

The proposed plan of operations up the valley of Virginia was approved by the President and Secretary of War, but, as subsequently indicated in telegrams from the War Department, it was adopted in view of the ultimate closing in of my columns toward Richmond, rather than Knoxville.*

On the 3d of May I moved with my staff to New Creek, on the Baltimore and Ohio Railroad, my proposed depot of main supply for operations in the field. On the 4th of May I was apprised by the Secretary of War of the evacuation of Yorktown by the rebel forces. Foreseeing by this event and the release of so large a body in the east that the enemy would be enabled to augment westwardly his force along my front, I judged it desirable to get forward and concentrate at an early moment my strongest available supports. Leaving New

* Copy of Frémont's letter and of the instructions given him were furnished to McDowell by the Secretary of War, under date of April 25, 1862.

Creek on the 5th, and taking with me upon the route the Sixtieth Ohio, a portion of the Eighth Virginia, a company of Indiana cavalry, and a body of men sent forward with baggage from Blenker's division, I proceeded toward Petersburg, arriving on the evening of the 7th.

General Schenck, who had been ordered early in April to advance from Romney and Moorefield, to operate on the road leading by Elkhorn to Franklin, in connection with movements with General Banks up the Shenandoah Valley, was already well in advance. Overcoming many obstacles in the form of swollen streams and difficult roads, he had by the 6th of May reached Franklin.

Farther to the front, and occupying McDowell, a small village about 12 miles east from Monterey, was General Milroy. General Cox, in the district of the Kanawha also, under orders previously given, was moving in force in the direction of Lewisburg and Peterstown.

The command of General Kelley, posted to guard the Baltimore and Ohio Railroad, as well as to watch and punish guerrillas, was necessarily left in rear. A small portion of his force, however, from the Potomac Home Brigade subsequently reported to me at Petersburg, under Lieutenant-Colonel Downey.

The Blenker division, though ordered on the 1st of April, had not so much as entered within the limits of my department until the 4th or 5th of May. Taking into view their ill-provided condition, as reported and set forth in the foregoing, their delay upon the route was less a matter of surprise with myself than had been expressed to me in dispatches from the War Department.

Upon the 7th the brigade of General Stahel being reported at Romney and still in need of shoes, a supply was ordered from New Creek. The issue was made while the men were upon the road, companies halting for the moment to receive what could be spared them.

On the 9th of May the advance of General Blenker's division joined me at my camp near Petersburg, and by the 11th his whole command had arrived. The division was composed of three brigades, commanded respectively by Generals Stahel and Bohlen and Colonel Steinwehr. Assuming the data as then sent in, General Blenker stated his effective force at over 8,000. Subsequent investigation placed the number of men and officers actually present and fit for duty at considerably below 7,000.

The condition of the men, as exhibited upon review, was not such as could have been desired. They were worn and exhausted by hardships scarcely credible, and in spite of efforts by myself and others to supply their wants, a large proportion were without articles of first necessity for service in the field. Of shoes, blankets, and overcoats there was especially great need. Wagon and artillery teams, brought forward by the several batteries and regiments, were found on inspection to be very much jaded and weak from the long march and want of forage. The horses of a portion of the cavalry were so nearly starved and broken down as to be well-nigh useless. The number of wagons was much below the standard for supply on any lengthened route. By report of my medical director, afterward sent in, but about one-fifth of the necessary ambulances had been brought along. One regiment had none.

In the important matter of arms there was great deficiency, Belgian or Austrian muskets of old and indifferent patterns being carried by many of the regiments. Having fortunately at hand a superior lot of Enfield rifles, I was enabled to rearm the corps most needing them. Ammunition was also supplied as far as resources would then permit.

A pontoon train having been previously ordered from Pittsburgh upon my personal responsibility, though the Government afterward sanctioned the contract, and being already well upon its way to Petersburg, it was of less moment that none was found attached to my re-enforcing column. Restrictions upon my chief quartermaster at Wheeling having been at this time in a technical form removed, it was reported in encouragement that team and cavalry horses were coming freely in. These, together with wagons, harness, and other equipage, would be promptly forwarded. The Sixth Ohio Cavalry, having now the opportunity, procured their mount, joining by companies according as they were furnished and equipped. A battery of mountain howitzers for one of the companies heretofore alluded to as specially authorized had also arrived at New Creek. Being brought forward as packed, with carriages, implements, harness, &c., they were, on the last night of my stay at Petersburg, mounted and made ready for the field.

With a view to future service a brigade of light troops was made up at Petersburg, consisting of the Sixtieth Ohio, Colonel Trimble, and the Eighth Virginia, under Major Oley. Colonel Cluseret, of my staff, a French officer of experience, and especially so in the tactics of skirmishers, was assigned to the command.

In the mean time General Banks had been withdrawn from his advanced position near Staunton, and my left became dangerously exposed. Seeing his advantage, the enemy was not slow to profit by it. Turning promptly to the west, and uniting with his own the forces of Johnson and Ewell, the rebel leader Jackson, upon the 7th of May, attacked the outposts of General Milroy. The simultaneousness of his onset indeed, with the retirement of Banks, argues strongly that, by whatever means obtained, the rebel general had early information of the projected movement. On the 8th of May, with an aggregate of upward of 14,000 men and thirty pieces of artillery, Jackson advanced upon the main body of General Milroy's force at McDowell. Pushing forward in a march of 34 miles in twenty-four hours General Schenck arrived from Franklin in time to unite with and support General Milroy. An obstinate engagement took place. Official reports of the action were at the time sent in by me to the War Department. Under the leadership of their gallant commander the men of Milroy's brigade repeatedly attacked and charged a greatly superior force, exhibiting a courage and tenacity worthy the highest praise. The Ohio troops behaved with equal gallantry and suffered severely. After several hours of fighting, however, our troops, outnumbered at every point, reluctantly yielded portions of the field to the odds flowing in against them. The enemy's loss was over 40 killed and between 200 and 300 wounded. Our loss was 31 killed and missing and 217 wounded.

Finding his position at McDowell untenable, and looking to the chances of a night attack, General Schenck, now in command, decided to withdraw toward Franklin. The retrograde was executed with skill and address, and bringing safely off his trains, artillery, and wounded, General Schenck re-entered the above-named town on the 10th of May. Here, disposing his troops to guard against farther advance of the enemy, he awaited the approach of re-enforcements from Petersburg.

Less than twenty-four hours' rest had been given to portions of the command arriving with General Blenker, but deeming the situation of increased importance I determined to move at once to the relief of General Schenck. I was unable to carry forward with me necessary supplies, owing to the still entirely inadequate transportation, but was obliged to rely upon renewed efforts at the rear to get forward in time whatever should be most needed to sustain my troops.

At 4 o'clock on the morning of the 12th my advance had forded the Shenandoah at Petersburg, and on the forenoon of the 14th, after a camp of one night upon the route, I reached Franklin. Preferring to avoid any immediate encounter with my force as concentrated, Jackson, leaving temporarily a thin curtain of his people to disguise the movement, began an early retreat. By sundown of the 15th he had disappeared in a southeasterly direction from my front, taking the road toward the Shenandoah Mountain. Although hitherto crippled for want of transportation, and needing more than ever supplies of every description, I had reason to expect that with economy in the camp as well as just effort on the part of agencies elsewhere deficiencies would yet be made good. Accordingly for the ten days next following upon my arrival at Franklin I addressed myself to the task of getting into order and condition my troops, as well as to details of the movements projected against Knoxville and the Virginia and Tennessee Railroad. While thus occupied I received from the Secretary of War the following urgent dispatch, which made me still more deeply regret the embarrassments of my situation:

WASHINGTON, *May* 16, 1862.

Major-General FRÉMONT, *Franklin:*

The President desires to know whether you design to move on to the Virginia and Tennessee Railroad, and break it between Newbern and Salem, according to the plan you proposed and he approved; and also whether, having reached and broken that road, you cannot move forward rapidly upon Richmond by that route, and by what time you can reach the railroad, and how long it will take you from there to reach Richmond. Please answer immediately.*

EDWIN M. STANTON,
*Secretary of War.*

In the mean time the campaign was being well carried forward. In execution of the plan upon my right the operations of General Cox were resulting in brilliant success. Moving forward as directed, with a view to reach and sever the railroad, his forces were attacked at Lewisburg, May 23, by a body of the enemy over 3,000 strong, under the rebel leader Heth. After an engagement of several hours the enemy were routed and fled in disorder from the field. Four pieces of artillery were captured by General Cox's troops, 200 stand of small-arms, and over 100 prisoners. Our loss was 10 killed and about 40 wounded. In this brilliant affair the conduct of Colonel Crook's brigade, bearing the brunt of the attack, cannot be too highly praised. The rebel loss in killed and wounded in the action was also severe.

But events were now taking place in another direction which had the effect to terminate suddenly my proposed campaign and divert my column intended for Knoxville upon a line of march entirely new. The rebel General Jackson, quitting my front and turning abruptly to the north into the Shenandoah Valley, had, with his customary impetuosity, attacked General Banks at Front Royal, pressing him backward toward Strasburg and Winchester, and threatening the whole valley of the Potomac.

With the intelligence of these events dispatched to me under date of May 24 came also an order from the President directing me to break camp and march against Jackson at Harrisonburg. As stated in the order, the objects of the movements were, first to relieve General Banks, secondly to cut off and capture Jackson and his force in the valley of the Shenandoah. It was the seventh or eighth day of a

* See Frémont to Stanton, same date, in "Correspondence, etc.," Part III, p. 197.

storm. Urging forward by forced marches troops already worn with fatigue, I had reached Franklin in advance of supplies to relieve Schenck and Milroy. The streams at my rear were swollen by the incessant rains and the roads had become almost impassable. With a complement of wagons much exceeding that upon the route the supply would have been but meager even in fair weather. With the limited number available, together with the hinderances encountered, the supply was far below the need. Not so much as one-quarter forage was got forward, and except an incomplete ration of bread no rations had been got up for the men. For days together fresh beef, with a little salt, was the only provision on hand for issue. Coffee, so essential and desirable in the field, was becoming a luxury almost unknown. Subsistence arriving under invoice to a particular brigade was taken by order and so far as it would go distributed among all. Sick lists were largely on the increase, and such was the demoralization induced by privations endured that demonstrations among the men, amounting almost to open mutiny, had in instances to be put down with the strong hand. Of forage in the country about scarcely a single pound could be gleaned. It had already been too well stripped by rebels. Our animals, then, were starving, dying in fact, and by scores, as even prior to my reaching Franklin they had from the same causes begun to do out of the command of General Schenck.

With the order directing my march authority was now given me to order the purchase of horses, or otherwise, in the language of the dispatch, "to take them wherever or however I could get them." But it came too late to aid me. Naturally upon the absence of forage and the causes which led to it animals also had disappeared. As to waiting for the arrival of horses or mules from Wheeling, that was impossible under the terms of the order. I was to move at once.

Of the different roads leading from Franklin to Harrisonburg all but one had been obstructed by Jackson in his retreat. Bridges and culverts had been destroyed, rocks rolled down, and in one instance trees felled across the way for the distance of nearly a mile. The road still left open ran southwardly, reaching Harrisonburg by a long detour. Granting, however, that loss of time by removal of obstacles, or by taking the longer route, were no consideration, tending to lengthen my line of supplies, was a little better than a physical impossibility. The condition of my troops forbade it. Strategically speaking, also, a movement toward Harrisonburg would not have endangered simply—it would have been fatal to my lines of supply. Jackson retreating from his raid could strike westwardly from Strasburg or Winchester by way of Romney or Moorefield, or both. Indeed, as the sequel will develop, it was afterward regarded probable by higher authorities that he had taken these very directions.

Reaching New Creek, then, and Petersburg, the rebel leader would have destroyed my depots at these points and captured every train upon the route. Again, while as a practical relief to General Banks the movement by way of Harrisonburg would have been of no greater importance than a movement striking the valley farther north or lower down, it would at the same time have permitted the enemy to avoid all chance of collision with my force. My own and the rebel columns would have been constantly moving in opposite directions upon opposite sides of a species of parallelogram, having for its four corners Franklin, Harrisonburg, Strasburg, and Petersburg—or otherwise, Winchester, Romney, &c. Our relative positions only would have been changed, with the difference that the gain would have been all upon the side of the rebels, the loss upon mine. Defying contact, Jackson would have escaped intact with his prisoners and plunder. This was a contingency not desired by the President nor contemplated in his dispatch.

Accepting, then, the spirit rather than the letter of the order, or if the letter, the added expression to "operate against the enemy in such way as to relieve Banks," I judged it within my discretion to select another than the route specifically set down—this even though ample means had existed with a fresh and active column to move southward upon my original destination or toward the immediate east. Instead, then, of the attempts through a barren district by any of the above-named routes, I determined to move rearward as far as Petersburg, thence striking easterly by way of Moorefield and Wardensville to Strasburg. Retracing thus for a short distance my supply line I could feed my hungry troops, gather stores, and possibly by vigorous effort reach the Shenandoah Valley in time to intercept Jackson going south. Happily, before leaving camp the next morning (May 25), a later order was received from the Secretary of War confirming previous conclusions, and leaving me free to choose my line of march. I was to "direct my attention to falling upon the enemy wherever I could find him with all speed." With the Secretary's dispatch came also the information that General Banks had abandoned Strasburg, been driven from Winchester, and was in full retreat upon Harper's Ferry. That the enemy would of his own will relinquish pursuit was not consistent with his manifest objects in entering the valley. I was therefore fully apprised of the situation. General McDowell, it was further stated to me in reference to the movement about to be made, would operate toward the same object as myself with his troops.

Looking to the chances of a possession of the telegraph wires at any moment by the rebels I did not at this time communicate my plan of march to the President. It was not desirable that the enemy should by any process be informed. Upon the road out from Franklin were met at various points my stalled and scattered trains, laden with provisions and forage for the command. From the stores contained I was enabled to supply present necessities, and by liberal issues to men and animals afford the necessary strength for coming fatigue and travel.

At Petersburg was found an accumulation of imperfect rations for five days. Causing three days' rations to be cooked and placed in haversacks, I ordered trains made up to carry forward the remainder, together with supplies of ammunition and forage. Tents, with the exception of a very few for indispensable staff and hospital purposes, were at this point required to be abandoned and placed in store. In like manner all surplus personal baggage was directed to be cast off, it being my object to put the column in the lightest possible marching order.

My movement northward leaving the department much exposed, and particularly to the west and south, General Cox was enjoined to double vigilance against the enemy, and ordered to do the best he was able in his position. General Kelley, within the Railroad District, was directed to concentrate, as far as practicable, his force, with a view to the safety of New Creek and other important points.

My column had reached Petersburg on the afternoon of May 26. On the 27th, at daybreak, the march was resumed. The troops, fording the Shenandoah and camping at night near Moorefield, arrived on the 28th at Fabius, about 10 miles easterly from Moorefield, upon Branch Mountain. At this latter point, upon the written protest of my medical director against further marching of the command without one day's rest, a halt was called for the 29th. Hundreds of stragglers and broken-down men from the Blenker division had been left along the road in the ascent of the mountain, and it was plain their condition demanded consideration. They were weak and reduced not only from recent fatigue and want of food, but from previous hardship and privation on the route from the Potomac. I could not venture to proceed with them in disorder and with safety undertake the work in prospect.

During the day's delay an inspection was had and roll calls ordered in presence of officers specially designated for the purpose. The result disclosed material inaccuracies in returns thus far accepted from General Blenker's command, and exhibited a falling off in the aggregate of effective force at this time most unwelcome. In Blenker's division the number reported present and fit for duty was below 6,000. As an accession, a remaining company of the Sixth Ohio Cavalry, having just obtained horses, joined at this camp.

While halting here at Fabius a party of Maryland cavalry, scouting well to the front, came upon a reconnoitering party of the enemy near Wardensville, and attacked them briskly. The enemy were driven with a loss of 2 killed and several wounded; Colonel Downey, in command of our force, having his horse shot under him.

Later, upon the 29th, a dispatch sent forward from telegraph station brought an order from the President directing me, under date of the 29th, to halt my command at Moorefield, or otherwise, "if I heard of the enemy in the general direction of Romney," to march upon him. This order was based upon the conclusion that Jackson had by this time pressed General Banks as far backward as Williamsport along the northern end of the parallelogram I have indicated. It having been subsequently ascertained, however, that the rebels were still occupied with their work in the valley of Winchester and Martinsburg the order was withdrawn, and I was again directed to move upon the enemy "by the best route I could."

On the 30th I moved forward with my command from Fabius. A renewed storm had made the roads heavy, and the march was most fatiguing. On the 31st my column passed the summit of the mountain between Lost River and Cedar Creek, marching most of the night, and closing up in a drenching rain and amid intense darkness at Cedar Creek. I had now reached the point indicated in the following telegrams:

WASHINGTON, *May* 29, 1862—[12 m.]

Major-General FRÉMONT:

General McDowell's advance, if not checked by the enemy, should, or [and] probably will, be at Front Royal by 12 noon to-morrow. His force when up will be about 20,000.

Please have your force at Strasburg, or, if the route you are moving on does not lead to that point, as near Strasburg as the enemy may be by that time.

Your dispatch No. 30 received and satisfactory.

A. LINCOLN.

WASHINGTON, *May* 30, 1862—4 p. m. [2.30 p. m.]

Major-General FRÉMONT:

Yours saying you will reach Strasburg or vicinity at 5 p. m. Saturday has been received and sent to General McDowell, and he directed to act in view of it.

You must be up to time of your promise, if possible.

A. LINCOLN.

At Cedar Creek the road forks, one branch leading to Strasburg and the other in a northeasterly direction to Winchester. Expecting to learn something of General McDowell's movements, early in the day I had sent forward Major Haskell, of my staff, with a party of scouts. He fell in with a party of the enemy's cavalry and two of my scouts were captured at Strasburg, but no information was obtained.

With the arrival of the rear the leading corps of my command again stretched forward, taking the road to Strasburg. At 7 in the morning of this day, June 1, my advance, under Lieutenant-Colonel Cluseret, first touched Jackson's main body, driving in the advanced pickets of General Ewell's brigade. Pressing forward and encountering and driving stronger bodies of skirmishers the column within a short distance came upon cavalry and a battery in position, which immediately opened fire. The enemy's artillery was engaged by detachments from the Eighth Virginia and Sixtieth Ohio, under Major Oley, supported afterward by a section of artillery under Lieutenant-Colonel Pilsen. The fire of the enemy's musketry now brought into action indicated the presence of two or three regiments. I was entirely ignorant of what had taken place in the valley beyond, and it was now evident that Jackson in superior force was at or near Strasburg. In anticipation, therefore, of possible demonstrations on his part before some needed rest could be taken, my command as they came up were ordered to position.

About noon the enemy's batteries ceased fire, and my troops were ordered to encamp. Our cavalry, being pushed forward, found the enemy withdrawing and a strong column of infantry just defiling past our front. A reconnaissance by Colonel Cluseret with the Eighth Virginia, pushed to within 2 miles of Strasburg showed the enemy withdrawn, and at night-fall this officer, with his brigade, accompanied by a battalion of cavalry and a section of artillery, was ordered to move forward upon Strasburg and determine the position of the enemy.

The day closed with one of the most violent rain-storms I have ever seen, with really terrific lightning and thunder, and the night being very dark, and Colonel Cluseret being without guides or knowledge of the country, his troops passed the town of Strasburg, and marching to the light of the enemy's fires, about 11 o'clock came into contact with Ashby's cavalry, which occupied the road forming the rear of Jackson's position, about 2 miles beyond Strasburg, on the road to Woodstock. Disobeying the order to charge, after a scattering fire our cavalry broke in a shameful panic to the rear, passing over and carrying with them the artillery.

To the honor of the Sixtieth Ohio, which at this moment formed the head of the reconnoitering column, not a man of them followed the disgraceful example, but delivered their fire steadily, and checked any movement on the part of the enemy. The officers and men, without exception, of the Sixtieth Ohio and Eighth Virginia, which composed this brigade, deserve special mention for the steadiness and bravery which distinguished them during the affairs of this day, when both regiments were for the first time under fire. Having ascertained the position of the enemy, Colonel Cluseret withdrew his men and returned to camp. The reconnaissance showed the enemy in retreat.

With daylight of June 2 my command moved in pursuit. Passing Strasburg I was joined by General Bayard, who had been sent forward by General McDowell with a cavalry force of about 800 men and four pieces of artillery, with a battalion of the Pennsylvania Bucktails, under Colonel Kane. Farther along the locality of Colonel Cluseret's engagement of the night before was marked by one of our caissons, which had been disabled and left for the night on the ground and by several of the enemy's killed and wounded, some 10 of whom had already been cared for by Colonel Kane. The route now followed lay along the turnpike, stretching southerly from Strasburg toward Staunton. Its more even and compact surface was a welcome exchange for the mire and sloughs of the mountain regions passed.

Closely pressed by my advance, the enemy at about 10 a. m. turned to make a stand. He was vigorously shelled by Buell's and Schirmer's batteries, under direction of Colonel Pilsen, aide-de-camp and chief of artillery, supported by General Bayard's command of cavalry, augmented by about 600 men from my own column, under Colonel Zagonyi, aide-de-camp and chief of cavalry. After determined resistance for an hour the enemy were driven from position and again pursued. Repeatedly during the day they faced about and were as often compelled to relinquish the fight. The pursuit was rapid, not less than 18 miles being made in the space of five hours. In one instance scarcely a hundred yards separated my advance from the enemy, the latter, however, gaining a small bridge and unlimbering rapidly upon a rocky rise beyond. Colonel Pilsen lost at this time his horse, shot from under him, and was himself slightly wounded by a volley from the rebels. But notwithstanding the excellent marching made by our infantry it was impossible to get forward in time for effective operations.

By sunset the enemy had reached for the night the higher points beyond Woodstock. The retreat was reckless. Over 500 prisoners fell into our hands, and a number of our own men captured from General Banks were recovered. Several hundred stand of small-arms cast away or left in stacks by the rebels were also gathered. Of gray-coated stragglers at least a thousand were in the woods along the road and country adjoining. Broken ambulances, clothing, blankets, and articles of equipment lined the route. Our loss was small, but one or two killed, and a proportionate number wounded. At the last stand made by the enemy he lost 7 killed, with a number of horses. His total loss during the day must have been considerable. At about 5 in the afternoon General Stahel's brigade occupied Woodstock.

Although much fatigued by the forced march of the day previous, my command at an early hour of the morning of June 3 were upon the road to resume pursuit. Again the rear guard of the enemy turned to cover his main body, or to gain time for placing obstacles, tearing up the road, or destroying culverts and bridges. The fire of the opposing batteries was mutually brisk, with at intervals an accompaniment of the dropping shots of small-arms. Strenuous effort was made by the rebels to destroy the bridge over Stony Creek, at Edenburg, about 5 miles out of Woodstock. A portion of the planks were torn up and the timbers so far cut that the structure sank, partially broken, about midway of the current. So prompt, however, were my advance troops that the party left by the enemy was compelled to retreat in haste without further execution of its design. A ford was found at a short distance up the stream, and with some difficulty cavalry and artillery were gotten across. Ultimately my baggage and supply trains passed safely. After some hasty repairs infantry was enabled to cross the bridge. On account of depth of water at the ford ammunition was removed from caissons and wagons and carried over by hands of men. For further and more permanent repairs of the bridge Colonel Raynolds, of my staff, engineer, was left with a small detail.

By noon my command were mainly upon the farther bank and again in rapid motion. The bridge over Cedar [Mill] Creek at Mount Jackson, was saved nearly intact by the celerity with which the enemy was overtaken. The rebel General Ashby barely escaped capture at this point by Captain Conger's company of Third Virginia Cavalry. This company, pressing forward under their persevering leader, were in season to come upon a body of the enemy about to fire the larger and more important bridge beyond Mount Jackson, crossing the North Fork of the Shenandoah. A gallant charge was made, but volleys of grape and musketry drove back the small command. General Bayard in the mean time arrived with the main body of the cavalry upon an elevation overlooking the bridge, but it is to be regretted that artillery could not possibly be gotten up in time to warrant his demonstration in heavier force. The bridge was successfully fired, burning rapidly, with thick volumes of flame and smoke. By the time my main column entered Mount Jackson village it had fallen to the stream below.

A body of the enemy incautiously attempting to go into camp within range across the river were speedily shelled by batteries run up upon the bluffs, and after some excellent practice on the part of our artillerists driven out. Our total loss during the day was 1 killed and a few wounded.

The pontoons procured by me at Pittsburgh, having been kept well up with the column, were now ordered to the front, and preparations immediately made to gain passage by rebridging the Shenandoah. The stream was at this point wide and rapid, and had been swollen by recent rains. Major Haskell, of active California experience, plunged with his horse into the current, and by swimming to the opposite bank was enabled to fix fast the preparatory ropes. A corps of employés, acting as pontoniers, under Lieutenant Robinson, of Ohio troops, together with liberal details from infantry regiments, were also put promptly at work. A heavy rain set in, but operations were continued throughout the night. By 6 in the morning the bridge was made available for crossing and a force of infantry and cavalry gotten over. Suddenly, however, the river began to rise to a yet greater height. In the space of four hours, flooded by the storm and its mountain tributaries, it had gained fully 12 feet, with a current correspondingly turbulent and swift. The drift borne down was working great mischief, and several of the boats were swamped. To save the bridge from utter destruction the ropes were cut and the pontoon swung round to the northern shore. Much of the planking and timber was lost.

The troops already across being well posted and amply covered by our batteries upon the bluffs, little apprehension was felt as regarded their immediate safety. Toward night the stream, as suddenly as it had risen, began to subside, and parties at work renewed their efforts. Their task was arduous, and it was not until 10 a. m. of the next day that the bridge was again in condition for crossing.

It will be remembered that at the date of my march from Franklin information was conveyed to me that General McDowell would operate toward the same objects as myself, in capturing or driving out Jackson. Very earnest assurances to this effect were subsequently given me while upon the route both by the President and Secretary of War. Whether in General McDowell's case, as in my own, departmental lines or technicalties of previous orders were temporarily to be lost sight of, was not explained. Arriving, however, within the Shenandoah Valley, I deemed it not extravagant to expect of that officer that he should so far co-operate as, if not himself in advance, to send me troops to secure and hold fast prisoners, as well as to keep intact points of my line in rear. Accordingly, during the delay at Mount Jackson, I dispatched to General McDowell Captain Howard, of my staff, with orders substantially to the above effect. A copy of his reply, declining to recognize authority on my part, here follows:

HEADQUARTERS DEPARTMENT OF THE RAPPAHANNOCK,
*Front Royal, June 6, 1862.*

Maj. Gen. J. C. FRÉMONT,
*Commanding Mountain Department, Mount Jackson, Va.*

GENERAL: I received to-day a letter from your acting assistant adjutant-general ordering me in your name to send some of my troops to Strasburg. Before the receipt of this paper I had written to Major-General Banks, commanding Department of the Shenandoah, at Winchester, calling his attention to this point, for such action in the case as he might see fit to take. I did this after failing, on account of the bridges being carried away and all communication cut off, to get the prisoners transferred to this place to send them to Washington.

I beg you to call the attention of your staff officer to the terms he has employed in his communication to me, making it in the nature of a positive, peremptory order, as if to me under your command. Being like yourself the commander of a separate, independent military geographical department, with certain troops assigned to me by the Secretary of War, and being here in a neighboring department for a special temporary purpose, under the direct orders and instructions of the President, I cannot receive orders from any officer save in the accidental temporary case provided for in the Sixty-second article of war—a case which arose when you came in contact with my cavalry brigade at Strasburg.

In reference to this brigade I have the honor to refer to General Orders, No. 29, of March 22, 1862, and say that I wish you would direct this brigade to march at the first opportunity to join Major-General Shields at Luray Court-House, it being necessary there to further the instructions under which I am acting.

I have the honor to be, very respectfully, your most obedient servant,

IRVIN McDOWELL,
*Major-General, Commanding Department Rappahannock.*

Of the operations of General McDowell through the column of General Shields up the valley of Luray the value will hereafter be seen.

From General Banks, to whom I had in like manner sent a messenger, a reply, though exhibiting the utmost cordiality, informed me that he was "without supplies or transportation and unable to move." He would, however, endeavor to send me some cavalry.

General Sigel, subsequently addressed, although he would "try his best," found his troops in a condition such as would render them "an incumbrance and not a help to me."

It was not until after I had left Mount Jackson that any of the dispatches embodying the above were received; but the fact stood that at the date of my departure from this town (June 5) the contest with Jackson, so far as concerned Shenandoah Valley proper, remained upon my hands. Although I had crossed the mountains on an errand of aid to others, I found myself without conjunction or combination either with the forces relieved or with a force sent toward the same object as my own from an opposite direction. I present the point with the object only that it may be both understood and realized, and with no other. On the 5th of June, then, crossing safely the bridge of pontoons, my column, with scarcely more than half the numbers of the enemy in advance, retook the trail and pushed steadily forward. A lapse of more than thirty hours since the burning of the main bridge over the Shenandoah had given the enemy an advantage he proved not slow to use. He was not overtaken upon the 5th, and having made 18 miles and passing on the way the enemy's fires still burning, my command was bivouacked beyond New Market, the enemy's camp being but a few miles ahead.

On the 6th I was enabled by an early and rapid march to restore the lost contact. Our progress was a little retarded by the burned and blazing culverts which had been fired by the enemy along the road, but sharp artillery and cavalry skirmishing was renewed during the forenoon, and at about 2 o'clock my advance drove his rear guard through Harrisonburg. The direction taken by the main force of the enemy being uncertain, my troops were ordered into camp around the town.

Later in the afternoon the First New Jersey Cavalry, with a battalion of the Fourth New York Cavalry, came suddenly upon the enemy's camp in the woods several miles to the southeast, and was driven out with serious loss, leaving Colonel Wyndham and Captains Shelmire, Clark, and Haines in the hands of the enemy.

A little before sundown General Bayard entered the woods with four companies of Kane's Rifles (Bucktails) and the First Pennsylvania Cavalry. Almost immediately after getting into the timber the Rifles encountered a regiment of cavalry with artillery and a regiment of infantry, from which they received a very damaging fire. A very severe engagement of half an hour followed, during which the Rifles lost upward of 40 in killed, wounded, and missing. Colonel Kane was wounded and taken prisoner, Captain Taylor a prisoner, Captain Blanchard shot through both legs, and Lieutenant Swayne wounded. This noble body of Riflemen is entitled to the expression of my warm admiration for excellent conduct and efficiency during the march and for distinguished bravery on this occasion.

General Bayard, in this as in all other instances of the kind during the pursuit, evinced the qualities of the true soldier.

Colonel Cluseret coming up with his brigade to the support of the Riflemen, the enemy retreated in disorder, leaving him in possession of their camp. On their part, the enemy in this sharp affair suffered still more severely, losing among the killed General Ashby, who up to this time had covered their retreat with admirable audacity and skill. Leaving their dead and wounded on the ground, with the growing darkness the enemy continued their retreat, precipitated by the several assaults of our troops.

On the 7th a reconnaissance in force was sent under General Milroy in the direction of Port Republic, and reconnaissances pushed toward Keezletown and McGaheysville and on the Staunton turnpike to the Middle River, where the bridges were found destroyed. These reconnaissances showed that Jackson, abandoning the turnpike, had struck by a difficult and troublesome road toward Port Republic, and that he was about to turn in force to dispute our farther advance. Accordingly a movement in the new direction taken by him was determined on for the 8th, and early upon the morning of this day the march was resumed, the command taking the road leading directly through the woods from Harrisonburg to Cross Keys.

My column, as constituted and now upon the road, was as follows:

The advance, Colonel Cluseret's brigade, consisting of the Sixtieth Ohio and Eighth Virginia Infantry, re-enforced by the Thirty-ninth New York (Garibaldi Guard); the main column comprising:

1st. Dickel's Fourth New York Cavalry.

2d. General Stahel's brigade, consisting of the Eighth, Forty-first, and Forty-fifth New York and Twenty-seventh Pennsylvania Infantry, Dilger's, Buell's, and Schirmer's batteries.

3d. General Bohlen's brigade, composed of the Fifty-fourth and Fifty-eighth New York and Seventy-fourth and Seventy-fifth Pennsylvania Infantry, and Wiedrich's battery.

4th. General Milroy's brigade, composed of the Twenty-fifth Ohio, the Second, Third, and Fifth Virginia Infantry, and Hyman's, Johnson's, and Ewing's batteries.

5th. General Schenck's brigade, composed of the Thirty-second, Seventy-third, Seventy-fifth, and Eighty-second Ohio Infantry, De Beck's and Rigby's batteries, and a small detachment of cavalry. Rear guard following upon ambulances and ammunition trains. General Steinwehr's brigade, under command of Colonel Koltes, consisting of the Twenty-ninth and Sixty-eighth New York and the Seventy-third Pennsylvania Infantry, and Dieckmann's battery.

Special investigation and roll call at Fabius May 29 had given as present effective strength of all arms something over 11,000. Deducting from this number garrisons, guards, working parties, &c., left in rear, together with disabled, sick, and stragglers upon the route, and 10,500 men is a liberal estimate of force in hand and for duty with above column June 8. Our lowest estimate of Jackson's force gave him 18,000. Many of the horses of General Bayard's cavalry having been reported unserviceable for want of shoes, his command was left temporarily at Harrisonburg, in charge of baggage trains.

My chief quartermaster having fortunately provided for contingencies of the kind, such animals as proved in need were duly attended to, and General Bayard at a later hour came forward. Part of his force was retained as escort to baggage and the remainder disposed to cover the line of communication against parties which might threaten it from the many by-roads or cross-roads striking the main route.

At about 8.30 a. m. my advance, under Colonel Cluseret, came up with the enemy at a point near Union Church and immediately engaged him. The rebels fell stubbornly back through the timber and open ground, Colonel Cluseret vigorously pursuing for the distance of about a mile. At the locality now reached he came upon Jackson's main force in order of battle. In the mean time my own main body coming promptly up, the several brigades were successively directed upon lines selected with a view to general attack.

The formation was substantially upon Colonel Cluseret's brigade, which had pushed the forces opposed to it fully back upon their supports, and now held firmly a good position well to the front.

General Stahel's brigade, advancing along the main road till past Pirkey's farm, took position in the open ground, forming the left of the first line.

General Milroy's brigade, leaving the main road and turning sharply to the right, formed in with a lessened interval upon Cluseret's right, becoming then the right of the first line.

General Bohlen's brigade was conducted in nearly the same direction as Stahel's, taking position opposite to the interval between Stahel and Cluseret, and, pending the arrival of Steinwehr's brigade, acting as reserve to both.

General Schenck's brigade, following in the direction taken by Milroy's, was placed in position, bringing his line in echelon to the right and rear, securing thus our right against any flank demonstrations by the enemy.

My directions for the general disposition were promptly and skillfully carried out by my chief of staff, Colonel Albert. Through a like skill and energy on the part of my chief of artillery, Colonel Pilsen, as also of his assistant on the occasion, Captain Dilger, eight and a half of my ten batteries were within the brief space of thirty minutes got into positions favorable to the work required of them.

Our line of battle then stood thus: Right wing, Milroy, with Schenck in reserve; left wing, Stahel; center, Cluseret; reserve to Stahel and Cluseret, Bohlen. Colonel Dickel's Fourth New York Cavalry occupied position upon the extreme left, guarding approaches in our direction. Watching our right and rear were the cavalry of Schenck's brigade. Captain Conger's company were held in position near headquarters.

The enemy occupied a position of uncommon strength, commanding the junction of the roads to Port Republic. He had chosen his ground with great skill and with a previous full knowledge of the localities. His main line was advantageously posted upon a ridge, protected in front by a steep declivity, and almost entirely masked by thick woods and covered by fences. Near his center, and on the summit of an abrupt ascent, bordered at the base by the high perpendicular bank of a marshy creek, he had massed, in addition to his guns elsewhere, three of his best batteries. From superiority of numbers his flanks both at the right and left considerably overlapped my own. It was almost impossible to force this position by a regular attack in front, which would have exposed us to cross-fires and flank attacks, and to have attacked him irregularly and at random on either of his flanks would have carried us off the roads into wooded and broken ground of which I was entirely ignorant, and would very certainly have resulted in disaster.

To give this effort any chance of success it would have been necessary to lose valuable time in reconnoitering the ground, during which he could have withdrawn his troops, crossed and destroyed the bridge at Port Republic, and possibly, too, the command of General Shields.

I was without reliable maps or guides, but from what could be seen of the roads, and from the understood position of the bridge at Port Republic, I judged that the enemy's right was his strategic flank. I decided, therefore, to press him from this side, with the object to seize, if possible, his line of retreat, and accordingly gave all the strength practicable to my left.

Continuous firing had been kept up during the time occupied in getting my forces into position, and with the full establishment of my lines the battle became general. Urging vigorously forward his brigade, General Stahel encountered in the first belt of woods a strong line of skirmishers, which with hard fighting was driven out of the timber and pushed by the Eighth and Forty-fifth New York over the open ground beyond to the edge of the woods, where these regiments suddenly came upon the right of the enemy's main line, held by the troops of General Trimble, and composed in part of the Sixteenth Mississippi, the Fifteenth and Sixteenth Alabama, the Twenty-first North Carolina, and Twenty-first Georgia. Two of General Stahel's best regiments, the Twenty-seventh Pennsylvania and Forty-first New York, had been diverted to the right in the timber, and the shock of the entire force here was sustained by the Eighth and Forty-fifth New York, and principally by the Eighth, which was attacked in front and flank by four regiments. This regiment behaved with great gallantry, charging with impetuosity into the enemy's ranks, and for a time holding its own, but yielding at length to the great superiority of numbers was driven, together with the Forty-fifth, back over the open ground and through the woods upon Bohlen's brigade, which had in the mean time advanced to Stahel's support and joined in the action, supported by our batteries.

Steinwehr's brigade coming up was deployed in rear of the batteries, and General Blenker arriving, took command of his division.

The enemy now brought up additional artillery into the open ground on my extreme left, and General Taylor's reserve brigade entering the woods, the fighting continued with great severity continuously along the timber in front of our position. A Mississippi regiment, charging with yells upon Buell's battery, was gallantly met with a bayonet charge by the Twenty-seventh Pennsylvania, under cover of which the battery was withdrawn. A Louisiana regiment of Taylor's brigade, undertaking a charge upon Dilger's battery, was received with a fire of canister and grape, delivered with such precision and rapidity as nearly destroyed it.

Every attempt of the enemy to emerge from the cover of the woods was repulsed by artillery and counter-attacks of infantry, and his loss at this portion of the field, inflicted especially by artillery, was very great. On our part the loss was heavy the Eighth New York alone losing 46 killed and 134 wounded.* One of my aides-de-camp, Capt. Nicolai Dunka, a capable and brave officer, was killed by a musket-ball while carrying an order to this part of the field. Colonel Gilsa, of the Forty-first New York, Captain Miser, and Lieutenant Brandenstein, of General Blenker's staff, were severely wounded.

The enemy's movement in the bringing up of artillery and fresh troops threatening entirely to envelop my left, a new position was taken at the edge of the timber on the line B, and the enemy reoccupied the belt of woods lost by them at the beginning. Up to this point the musketry and artillery fire had been incessant and the fighting throughout the field generally severe. Farther to the right our artillery, under the immediate direction of Colonel Pilsen, had been hotly engaged with the batteries of the enemy's center. Milroy and Cluseret were opposed to Generals Elzey and Early, commanding the enemy's right and center. Our own center, under Cluseret, after an ineffectual attempt upon the enemy's batteries, had held obstinately every foot of its advanced ground, repelling with steadiness and gallantry repeated assaults of the enemy. General Milroy had been warmly engaged driving in a strong line of the enemy's skirmishers, attacking their main body at close quarters, and suffering severely in an attempt to plant a battery upon the heights. Upon the extreme right General Schenck, in support of Milroy, had advanced his line, extending it into contact with the enemy, occupying them with skirmishers, shelling the woods, and checking their advance in flank.

Notwithstanding the fair promise held out to an effort on the right, I judged it best at this point to re-establish my whole line in conformity to the change on the left preparatory to a renewal of the battle. Accordingly the brigades of the right were withdrawn for a space, and, except from a portion of Cluseret's strong position at the center and occasional exchanges of artillery shots, the firing subsided, the enemy meantime remaining in his position and our pickets occupying securely the points temporarily relinquished by the main line.

Pending these preparations I received from the hands of one of my scouts the following letter from General Shields:

LURAY, *June* 8—9.30 a. m.

Major-General FRÉMONT,
*Commanding Pursuing Forces:*

I write by your scout. I think by this time there will be twelve pieces of artillery opposite Jackson's train at Port Republic, if he has taken that route. Some cavalry and artillery have pushed on to Waynesborough to burn the bridge. I hope to have two brigades at Port Republic to-day. I follow myself with two other brigades to-

*But see revised statement, pp. 664, 665.

day from this place. If the enemy changes direction you will please keep me advised. If he attempts to force a passage, as my force is not large there yet, I hope you will thunder down on his rear. Please send back information from time to time. I think Jackson is caught this time.

Yours, sincerely,

JAS. SHIELDS,
*Major-General, Commanding Division.*

This was most welcome intelligence. Hitherto I had received no direct information from General Shields, and beyond the fact that he was somewhere near Luray I had no positive knowledge of his whereabouts or intentions. As the moment approached when it became of critical importance that we should act together I had the day before pushed my scouts into the Luray Valley. Several of them were taken by the enemy, but one succeeded in reaching me with this letter. With the certainty now that General Shields was already holding the bridge in force I at once decided to defer until morning a renewal of the battle. My men had been marching and fighting since early in the morning. They were fatigued and hungry and needed rest, and I knew they required every advantage I could give. I therefore directed the command to bivouac and operations for the day to be brought to a close. My force was established for the night upon the line B B, Colonel Cluseret's brigade being withdrawn into the woods near Union Church, and our pickets remaining, as stated, in occupation of other points of the battle ground.

The night was busily spent in preparations to have the command in readiness for a general advance, planned to take place in the morning, and in gathering and caring for the wounded and burying the dead. My loss during the day in killed, wounded, and missing had been upward of 600.* At dawn the enemy was found to have retired from his lines in our immediate front. At about 7.30 a. m. the line was extended, and at a given signal, expecting very soon to come upon the enemy in position, the command moved forward, maintaining admirable steadiness and exactness. The enemy's dead in great numbers lay upon the field, and some 20 horses lying together upon the height occupied by his center batteries showed the effect of our artillery.

Emerging into the more open ground beyond Dunker Church, a black column of smoke, rising about 5 miles in advance, showed the Port Republic bridge on fire, and soon afterward the sound of cannon and white wreaths from rapidly exploding shells along the line of the river showed an engagement in progress in the vicinity of the bridge. Closing in, the several corps of my command took the direction of the burning bridge, and pushing forward reached as quickly as practicable the crest of a ridge overlooking the Shenandoah and beyond it Port Republic village.

The battle which had taken place upon the farther bank of the river was wholly at an end. A single brigade sent forward by General Shields had been simply cut to pieces. Colonel Carroll, in command, had for his own reasons failed to burn the bridge, though occupying it in time with his guards. Jackson, hastening across, had fallen upon the inferior force, and the result was before us. Of the bridge nothing remained but the charred and smoking timbers. Beyond, at the edge of the woods, a body of the enemy's troops was in position and a baggage train was disappearing in a pass among the hills. Parties gathering the dead and wounded, together with a line of prisoners, awaiting the movements of the rebel force near by, was all in respect to troops

*See revised statement, pp. 664, 665.

of either side now to be seen. A parting salvo of carefully aimed rifled guns, duly charged with shell, hastened the departure of the rebels, with their unlucky though most gallant convoy, and the whole were speedily out of sight.

My pontoon bridge having of necessity been left behind at Mount Jackson to keep whole my line of communication and supply, measures were at once taken to construct a bridge out of such material as might be found at hand. Meantime Major Haskell, of my staff, was sent with a strong party of cavalry with orders to cross the river and find out what had become of General Shields.

Proceeding rapidly down the river, and discovering on his way down bodies of the enemy—cavalry, infantry, and artillery—returning from the pursuit of Shields' troops, Major Haskell left his force concealed at a ford about 7 miles below and crossed the river in rebel disguise with a single attendant.

After imminent risks in getting by parties or partisans of the enemy he came up late at night with the remnant of Colonel Carroll's command, moving rapidly in the direction of Luray. From Colonel Carroll he learned that General Shields' corps was on its way to Richmond. Pushing forward, Major Haskell succeeded in finding General Shields' assistant adjutant-general, by whom he was informed that General Shields, with his whole force, was under immediate and imperative orders for Richmond by way of Fredericksburg. Having executed his mission with his usual boldness and celerity, Major Haskell reached me toward morning with this report.

The subjoined letters, all received within a few days following from General Shields, more fully explain the circumstances of Jackson's escape:

HEADQUARTERS SHIELDS' DIVISION,
*Columbia Bridge, June 8, 1862—6.30 p. m.*

Maj. Gen. JOHN C. FRÉMONT:

I pushed forward Colonel Carroll with one brigade and four pieces of artillery to move on Port Republic to burn the bridge and check the advance of the enemy. He went forward, I fear, imprudently, crossed the bridge, which is still standing, and drove the small force there defending it before him. While pursuing this force he was attacked by the enemy in force, lost two pieces of artillery, and is now in retreat to Conrad's store. Part of the enemy, it seems, is on this side and part on the other side of the river. There is one brigade *en route* for Conrad's store from this direction and another brigade at this point which I am moving forward to re-enforce them in front. I will also order a fourth brigade, with the exception of one regiment, which I will leave at Luray to check Longstreet, who is supposed to be in the mountains.

I will earnestly urge that you attack the enemy in their rear at once with all your force, and will get my command up as quickly as possible to operate in front

JAS. SHIELDS,
*Major-General.*

HEADQUARTERS SHIELDS' DIVISION,
*Columbia Bridge, June 8—8.15 p. m.*

Major-General FRÉMONT,
*Commanding U. S. Forces, Harrisonburg, Va.:*

The enemy, as you are aware, is on the Port Republic road, with perhaps four or five of his brigades on this side of the river. If not attacked in force to-night and hurled upon the river by your command, I apprehend that he may pass the bridge during the night and then burn it, so that you could render me no assistance. If such be the case, having but two brigades in front, I might find it difficult to resist him. Your only resource then would be to come around by way of New Market and cross the ferry at Columbia Bridge. If you are unable to employ your whole force sufficiently in his rear, I would respectfully suggest that a portion of it join me in this way anyhow.

JAS. SHIELDS,
*Major-General.*

HEADQUARTERS SHIELDS' DIVISION,
*Luray, June 12, 1862.*

Maj. Gen. JOHN C. FRÉMONT:

My advance guard was driven back on the 9th after a sanguinary engagement of four hours. I re-enforced it, and determined, in connection with you, to renew the attack next morning. After handing the dispatch to your messenger a peremptory order reached me from Washington directing me to get my command together and return at once to this point, preparatory to marching to Fredericksburg. I never obeyed an order with such reluctance, but no option was left me. The mismanagement of one of my generals left the route open to Jackson. He failed to burn the bridge at Port Republic, according to orders, and the result has been the defeat of his small command and the escape of Jackson. Here I found orders to remain till Banks is in position at Front Royal. The moment he is there I am to march to Catlett's Station to report to Fredericksburg, thence to Richmond. The cavalry attached to you, designated as Bayard's cavalry, are to report to me. They must come to Front Royal. If I march before they reach me they must join me at Catlett's, by way of Chester Gap and Warrenton.

I have the honor to be, your friend and obedient servant,

JAS. SHIELDS,
*Major-General, Commanding Division.*

With the receipt of the intelligence brought by Major Haskell I regarded the movement against Jackson as closed. Whatever of the original objects of my mission I had been enabled to accomplish was now fairly fulfilled. That the retreat of the rebel leader had been conducted with skill and ability is what no just enemy can deny him; but had he been less favored by circumstances of weather and by the absence of combinations beyond my control, though easy enough to have been made during Jackson's earlier pursuit, it is for consideration whether he would have been able even to reach the Shenandoah, and still less to cross that river, with or without a bridge to invite his transit. To what degree he had thus far been affected by contact with my column is manifest by his destruction of the valuable bridge he unmolestedly passed, as well as by his rapid disappearance after the rout of the operating force sent by General McDowell.

The withdrawal of Shields had left my command an isolated body far in advance of all other troops, and all expectation of aid or concert of action with others was now cut off. My troops had been long without proper food or shelter; their march had been exhausting, and I had expended their last effort in reaching Port Republic. I determined, therefore, to fall back at once upon my supplies, and accordingly during a day of stormy rain I marched my command back to Harrisonburg.

Here in the evening of the 10th I received the following telegram from the President, two days after the battle of Cross Keys:

WASHINGTON, *June* 9, 1862.

Major-General FRÉMONT:

Halt at Harrisonburg, pursuing Jackson no farther. Get your force well in hand and stand on the defensive, guarding against a movement of the enemy back toward Strasburg or Franklin, and wait further orders, which will soon be sent you.

A. LINCOLN.

Harrisonburg, however strong in a strategical point of view for an army of larger proportions, was to my small command dangerous in the extreme. Distant 22 miles from the enemy's main railroad line at Staunton, and approached by nine different roads, it left constantly exposed my lines of supply and communication. For these reasons my troops were upon the 11th and 12th withdrawn to Mount Jackson, a position strongly defensible, lying behind the Shenandoah, and being a key to the surrounding country.

In this movement the President acquiesced, in the following postscript to a telegram dated:

WASHINGTON, *June* 12.

Major-General FRÉMONT:

Yours, preferring Mount Jackson to Harrisonburg, is just received. On this point use your discretion, remembering that our object is to give such protection as you can to Western Virginia. Many thanks to yourself, officers, and men for the gallant battle of last Sunday.

A. LINCOLN.

On the 13th General Whiting's division, including Hampton's and Hood's brigades, arrived at Staunton. At Mount Jackson a rest was had for several days.

After what has been already stated relative to the condition in which a large portion of my command was turned over to me from the Potomac, as well as concerning hardship and exposure endured by all it is almost superfluous to pursue the subject further. From the continued want of transportation but a very limited amount of supplies had been got forward since leaving Petersburg. Some corn meal and flour, which the rebels in their haste proved unable to carry away from Mount Jackson, had been seized and issued to the troops. Mills also, in which the above were found and which the enemy had not time to fire, were set at work, and eked out a scanty supply. Further than this, added to fresh beef obtained or driven along upon the hoof, it is difficult at this moment to say what constituted the subsistence of my command after the five days' partial rations found at Petersburg became exhausted. It was reported almost in remonstrance by General Bayard, in regard to both men and animals, that the cavalry should never have been sent forward as they were at Harrisonburg—"the horses staggering in the ranks from exhaustion, and the men having been without rations, other than fresh beef, for two or three days."

On the evening of the 7th, preceding the battle of Cross Keys, it was ascertained that less than one full ration in any form remained for issue, and it was only upon the certainty of a fight the next day that the council assembled decided for my plan to move forward. These circumstances cannot but go forcibly to illustrate the physical condition of my men four days after Cross Keys, on their return to Mount Jackson. It was, indeed, less a matter of surprise that their fatigues and privations had begun unmistakably to tell upon the most robust than that the mass had been got forward at all. More than 200 had up to this time, after careful examination by a board of surgeons, been discharged for disabilities incident to their hard service, while the remaining sick and wounded, brought along mainly in army wagons, owing to want of ambulances, upward of 1,000 were now at Mount Jackson. The hospitals were full, and I was deficient in the necessary medicines, as well as the requisite number of surgeons to give attendance. The heroism, the uncomplaining patience, with which the soldiers of my command endured the starvation and other bodily sufferings of their extended marches, added to their never-failing alacrity for duty against the enemy, entitle them to my gratitude and respect. For their good conduct on the march and on the field I take this opportunity to thank them, as well as their officers, regretting that within the limits of this report I cannot dwell upon the many signal cases of individual merit that came under my notice.

The conduct of such of my staff officers as were permitted by their duties to be present during the numerous affairs and skirmishes taking place in the pursuit up the Shenandoah Valley, and especially their energy and promptness on the occasion of the battle at Cross Keys, merit without exception my warmest commendation. To the officers generally of my staff I take pleasure in making my thanks. They are entitled to the most honorable mention I can make for the gallantry, loyalty, and capacity that especially qualified them for the responsible duties, which they discharged with courage and fidelity. And particularly, although it is almost unjust to make any distinction, I desire to present to the notice of the Government, for meritorious service during the campaign, Capts. J. R. Howard, R. W. Raymond, and G. W. Nichols, among the younger, and Cols. Albert Tracy, Anselm Albert, Charles Zagonyi, and Lieut. Col. John Pilsen, among the older officers. To the four last mentioned I feel especially bound to record personally also my acknowledgments. Their uncommon professional ability, joined to previous long experience in the field, rendered their services of the greatest value to me throughout a very laborious and hazardous campaign. All but two of the staff officers present with the command during the engagements are now out of the army, having either resigned or been mustered out. Doubtless, however, some just form of recognition of past services would be grateful to them even at this day. My chief quartermaster in the field, Captain Goulding, as also my chief of subsistence, Captain Mallory, performed each his duties with energy and ability. My medical director in the field, Surg. George Suckley, never failing in zeal and activity in the mass of labors crowding upon him, stands entitled to my earnest commendation and thanks. I would also mention as most worthy and efficient in his duties Brigade Surg. and Medical Inspector A. C. Hamlin.

Major Clary, chief quartermaster at department headquarters at Wheeling, and Major Darr, provost-marshal-general, rendered at all times zealous and efficient services during the period of my command in the Mountain Department.

Significant demonstrations of the enemy, who had been reported largely re-enforced, taken in connection with the still isolated position at Mount Jackson, induced my farther withdrawal down the valley to Strasburg, and subsequently to Middletown, where I arrived with my command June 24, effecting a junction with the forces of Generals Banks and Sigel.

The tents and baggage left at Petersburg on the 27th May having been brought forward to Middletown, and camps and hospitals established at healthful points, having due regard to positions of defense, the troops of my command were made comparatively comfortable, and the sick began to improve. For the first time since they had started on the campaign the men here received full rations. While thus occupied in preparing my corps for active service, which telegrams from the War Department were preparing me immediately to expect, I received from the Secretary of War the President's order of June 26, which placed my own and the corps then with me under the command of Major-General Pope.

Having the conviction that consistently with a just regard for the safety of my troops and what was rightfully due to my personal honor I could not suffer myself to pass under the command of General Pope, I asked to be relieved from the duty to which I had been assigned under him. On the 27th of June, having been relieved of my command by direction of the President, I proceeded to New York to await further orders.

**Respectfully, your obedient servant,**

J. C. FRÉMONT,
*Late Major-General, U. S. Army.*

NEW YORK, N. Y., *December* 31, 1865.

In connection with others specially alluded to, the following telegrams, extracts, reports, &c., gleaned from private memoranda of myself or members of my staff, and numbered 1 to 30, are appended to the foregoing report of operations in the Mountain Department. It is not unlikely that dispatches received from the President may be also on file at the War Office. I will ask, however, to have his own included with the rest, as they serve to make clearer points presented. I would here add that for the topographical map of Cross Keys forwarded with report,* I am indebted to my late chief of artillery, Lieutenant-Colonel Pilsen.

J. C. FRÉMONT,
*Late Major-General, Commanding Mountain Department.*

[No. 1.]

HARPER'S FERRY, *April* 12, 1862.

Major-General FRÉMONT:

Secretary sends me after Blenker. No news of him here. Will dispatch you when I learn his whereabouts. Anything to me will reach at Winchester.

W. S. ROSECRANS,
*Brigadier-General, U. S. Army.*

[No. 2.]

WHEELING, *April* 12, 1862.

Brigadier-General ROSECRANS,
*Winchester:*

Secretary telegraphs me Blenker's division at Salem. I recall an officer I had sent after it. When you find the division let me know its force, and bring it directly across to Moorefield.

J. C. FRÉMONT,
*Major-General, Commanding.*

[No. 3.]

WINCHESTER, *April* 12, 1862.

Major-General FRÉMONT:

Will bring Blenker's division to Moorefield.

W. S. ROSECRANS,
*Brigadier-General.*

[No. 4.]

WOODSTOCK, *April* 15, 1862.

Major-General FRÉMONT:

Rosecrans left this morning for Blenker's division, now at Berry's Ferry. One brigade goes at once to Moorefield. Rain all day and night.

N. P. BANKS,
*Major-General, Commanding.*

---

*To appear in Atlas.

[No. 5.]

WINCHESTER, *April* 17, 1862.

Major-General FRÉMONT:

Blenker has 138 four-horse teams for twelve regiments and three batteries. Will require thirty-six ambulances and some fresh horses.

W. S. ROSECRANS,
*Brigadier-General.*

[No. 6.]

HARPER'S FERRY, *April* 19, 1862.

Major-General FRÉMONT:

Must have 42 horses sent to Martinsburg to move the batteries. Cannot get them from Washington.

W. S. ROSECRANS,
*Brigadier-General.*

[No. 7.]

HARPER'S FERRY, *April* 19, 1862.

Major-General FRÉMONT:

We are bivouacked 5 miles out of Winchester, after thirty-eight days without tents or shelter. Troops wanting shoes too badly to move. Wait for shoes, provisions, and forage. Horses much jaded and nearly starved.

W. S. ROSECRANS,
*Brigadier-General.*

[No. 8.]

MCDOWELL, *May* 8, 1862.
(Received May 9, 7.30 a. m.)

Col. ALBERT TRACY,
*Assistant Adjutant-General:*

There is not a particle of forage here. The last has given out, and all the horses of cavalry, artillery, and others have been without food to-day. The place is otherwise untenable and unfit for military defense. The rebels have appeared on the hills overlooking us to-day and we have shelled them and had skirmishing, with no particular result. I have permitted General Milroy to go up to the mountain with four regiments to prevent the planting of a battery which might shell us out and perhaps a night attack. I hope this may prove a diversion in our favor, but we cannot hold such a place without a very large force against superior numbers, and at all in the present destitution of forage. If our horses starve a day longer they will not be able to draw away the train or carry us off. I greatly regret the necessity of this conclusion, but I believe every officer here concurs in my views.

R. C. SCHENCK,
*Brigadier-General, Commanding.*

[No. 9.]

MCDOWELL, *May* 8, 1862.
(Received Petersburg, May 9, 7.30 a. m.)

Col. ALBERT TRACY,
*Assistant Adjutant-General:*

It is now 11.30 p. m. The reconnaissance of Milroy this afternoon became a sharp engagement, in which we lost several killed and perhaps 75 or 80 wounded. The rebel loss is at least as large or larger, but not known. Johnson was found to have been largely re-enforced by Jackson during the afternoon. His whole force has come up from Buffalo Gap. There is a large army in the hills about us. This place is indefensible altogether, by the unanimous agreement of officers, in our present condition and with our relative forces. I find at least two of the regiments without ammunition, and not a particle of forage. The horses are starving. We must retreat to-night. I am sending off trains and all the property for which there is any transportation. At 2 a. m. I will get the troops in motion. This is a sad experience for the first day of arrival, but nothing else seems to be thought of. We shall probably be followed by the enemy. The general commanding we expect to re-enforce us with any force he has.*

R. C. SCHENCK,
*Brigadier-General, Commanding.*

[No. 10.]

PETERSBURG, *May* 9, 1862.

COMMANDING OFFICER,
*German Division, Romney:*

GENERAL: Push forward the whole of your division by a forced march, so that it may reach here to-morrow.

By order of General Frémont:

ALBERT TRACY,
*Colonel and Acting Assistant Adjutant-General.*

[No. 11.]

PETERSBURG, *May* 11, 1862—8 p. m.

Brigadier-General SCHENCK, *Franklin:*

The condition of the troops on arriving here was such that we cannot leave before 3 in the morning. If, therefore, you cannot fall back with safety, defend and hold the place. You will be supported. We shall make every exertion to arrive in time. Answer, and let us know during the night how you get on. We shall have an operator with us along the road, and shall be in constant communication. At what do you estimate the enemy's force? †

J. C. FRÉMONT,
*Major-General, Commanding.*

[No. 12.]

PETERSBURG, *May* 10, 1862.

Captain LOOMIS,
*Assistant Quartermaster, New Creek:*

If you have not sent me any forage, for God's sake forward at once.

G. I. STEALY,
*Captain and Assistant Quartermaster.*

---

*Other dispatches of this date from Schenck to Frémont appear in "Correspondence, etc.," Part III.

†Other dispatches to and from Schenck of this date in "Correspondence, etc.," Part III.

[No. 13.]

FRANKLIN, *May* 13, 1862.

Maj. R. H. CLARY,
*Chief Quartermaster, Wheeling, Va.:*

Not a pound of forage here. Horses suffering for want of some. Will you hurry up Loomis?

By order of Major-General Frémont:

C. N. GOULDING,
*Captain and Assistant Quartermaster.*

[No. 14.]

MOUNTAIN DEPARTMENT, OFFICE OF MEDICAL DIRECTOR,
*Headquarters Army in the Field, Franklin, May* 22, 1862.

Col. ALBERT TRACY,
*Acting Assistant Adjutant-General:*

COLONEL: In the name of humanity I respectfully call the earnest attention of the commanding general to the sanitary condition of the division under the command of Brigadier-General Blenker. In addition to the facts given in the report of Brigade Surg. Augustus C. Hamlin, inspector, ordered by Special Orders, No. 12, May 18, 1862, I would state that nearly 200 men of Blenker's division are left behind in hospitals or straggling in our rear. There are about 200 more sick in this encampment. The division left Hunter's Chapel near Alexandria on the 7th of March. Its condition now, according to the data furnished by Surgeon Hamlin, is as follows:

There are but few ambulances—in one regiment none. In fact, there is not in the whole division more than one-fifth the necessary ambulance transportation. Even for the few wretched vehicles possessed there is a deficiency of animals, and of those they have and call "horses" several are little better than living skeletons. There are seven medicine panniers, yet not a horse or mule for their transportation. In the whole division there is but one hospital tent. Most of the medical stores are left behind. The question naturally arises whether the necessary measures were taken to have them forwarded. As a military officer I well know the exigencies of the service in an active campaign necessarily cause much human suffering, but I can think of no excuse for a lack of proper endeavor to mitigate these evils. By bringing this subject before Major-General Frémont, so as to secure his early attention, you will be doing officially a charitable action.

I have the honor to be, colonel, very faithfully, your obedient servant,

GEORGE SUCKLEY,
*Brigade Surgeon and Medical Director Forces in the Field.*

[No. 15.]

PETERSBURG, *May* 26, 1862.

Mr. J. B. FORD,
*Supt. Baltimore and Ohio Railroad, Wheeling, Va.:*

Baggage being behind, your telegram not translated till now. What you are doing is of the greatest possible service (sending forward animals, wagons, and commissary stores). No cause for alarm in this department. Am at this place to afford aid. Had transportation been furnished our aid would have been anticipatory.

J. C. FRÉMONT,
*Major-General, Commanding.*

[No. 16.]

PETERSBURG, *May* 27, 1862.

T. B. A. DAVID, *Green Spring:*

Communicate in cipher, or by sure hand, the following dispatch to Major-General Banks:

Our force is on the march to Moorefield, intending to meet the enemy wherever he may be found I send this for your information. You can communicate anything you may have for me to Mr. T. B. A. David, our telegraph superintendent, now at Cumberland. It will give me pleasure to join you.

J. C. FRÉMONT,
*Major-General, Commanding.*

[No. 17.]

WASHINGTON, *May* 28, 1862.

Major-General FRÉMONT:

The following dispatch has been received from General Rufus King:

I sent out cavalry, both on the Bowling Green and Telegraph roads, to Richmond this morning to collect information. They proceeded from 12 to 15 miles; saw nothing of the enemy, but learned from contrabands, who left Hagner's Station yesterday, that the whole force reconnoitering in our front left the junction to re-enforce Jackson Monday morning, the 26th. They were about 15,000 strong—fourteen regiments of infantry, six batteries of artillery, and four companies of cavalry. They were well informed as to our force and movements, but had no intention of abandoning their position in our front till last Saturday, when sudden orders were received from Richmond to march at once, with four days' rations. They moved off the same night. Such is the substance of Colonel Kilpatrick's report, who directed the reconnaissance. I shall push the cavalry still farther out to-morrow, in hopes of obtaining further information.

EDWIN M. STANTON.
*Secretary of War.*

[No. 18.]

MOUNTAIN DEPARTMENT, OFFICE MEDICAL DIRECTOR,
*Headquarters Army in the Field, Fabius, May* 29, 1862.

Col. ALBERT TRACY,
*Assistant Adjutant-General:*

COLONEL: Last evening, while in the camp of Blenker's division, I noticed the weary and haggard appearance of most of the men. Stragglers were coming in until after dark, most of them weary and foot-sore, and many sick. I was informed that, for various reasons, some of the regiments have had but little beef. They were weak in consequence, and forced marches are wearing them down. I would respectfully recommend that a rest of twenty-four hours be allowed.

Very respectfully, your obedient servant,

GEORGE SUCKLEY,
*Brigade Surgeon and Medical Director.*

HEADQUARTERS,
*Winchester, June* 6, 1862.

Major-General FRÉMONT, *in the Field:*

DEAR SIR: The freshet has destroyed for the moment our communications. At Williamsport the river, higher than for ten years, has divided my command, and separated me from all my supplies and transportation. I am here without supplies or transportation, unable to move. The river is falling, however, and I hope our trains have crossed to-day. They will cross to-morrow at any rate, and, the Baltimore and Ohio road in operation, by to-morrow night we shall be afloat again. Harper's Ferry bridge is swept away, but a steam-tug will temporarily supply its place. The Winchester road will be in operation in two or three days. We shall therefore be able to supply your wants soon.

I have sent to-day a strong detachment of cavalry, with instructions to reach you if possible, and to look to your prisoners at Strasburg, gather up arms or supplies on the way, and arrest suspicious persons in the guise of citizens. Colonel De Forest, commanding, is an excellent officer. We will protect your communications, telegraph lines, &c. There is no news of importance here. Nothing from Richmond.

Very truly, yours, &c.,

N. P. BANKS,
*Major-General, Commanding.*

[No. 23.]

WINCHESTER, *June* 8, 1862—11 p. m.

Maj. Gen. JOHN C. FRÉMONT:

GENERAL: Your letter dated Harrisonburg, June 7, is received. I am exceedingly sorry that I could not proceed at once to the scene of action to assist you, but the troops under my command brought from Harper's Ferry could scarcely reach Winchester, and were in such a condition that it is necessary to prepare them for field service before they leave this place, otherwise they would be an incumbrance and not a help to you. I will nevertheless try my best and see whether I can add some of my most serviceable forces to the division of General Banks, and send them on without delay. Captain C——— gave me some valuable information relative to your position and that of the enemy, as well as that of Shields. I immediately had a consultation with the adjutant-general of General Banks, and hope that some of our troops will be sent to-morrow night.

I am, general, your obedient servant,

F. SIGEL,
*Major-General.*

[No. 24.]

HEADQUARTERS FIRST DIVISION, FIRST ARMY CORPS,
*Luray, June* 13, 1862.

Maj. Gen. JOHN C. FRÉMONT, *Comdg. Mountain Dept., Mt. Jackson:*

GENERAL: I have the honor to acknowledge the receipt of your polite note, and avail myself of the return of General Bayard's aide-de-camp to drop you another line. I have sent a communication to the War Department, in which I bear testimony to the energy, activity, and ability with which you conducted the pursuit. The general who

*Nos. 19, 20, and 21, here omitted, are duplicates of Lincoln to Frémont, May 29 and 30, and McDowell to Frémont, June 6, which are quoted at length in Frémont's report. See pp. 13, 17.

led my advance (2,500) committed two grave errors: One in not burning the bridge at Port Republic; the other in taking up an indefensible position and waiting until he was attacked in force by Jackson. But the gallantry with which my poor fellows fought is beyond all praise. But the odds were too great. General Tyler stripped the left and left two batteries without support, and their sharpshooters rushed from the woods and shot down the men. Forty horses were killed of our batteries. They were then compelled to fall back, which they did in good order. I joined them with the main body, and then Jackson fell back in haste. I hurried to attack him next day. You by throwing a pontoon-bridge across and I attacking him at the same time would have cut him up. This was my proposition to your messenger, which he started to take to you when peremptory orders arrived to set out for Fredericksburg. This was one of the mistakes of the war. We ought to have ended Jackson first. He should not have been left behind in this valley. Had we fallen upon him next morning he would never have come back to this valley, and we could have destroyed the railroad at Waynesborough and Gordonsville. General McDowell knew nothing of our situation. He acted upon some preconceived plan, without reference to the condition of things in this valley. We must still destroy the railroad at Gordonsville before we march on Richmond. Any other course would be madness. Pray represent this at the War Department. I want to do that from Fredericksburg.

With my best wishes for your private and public success, I remain, general, yours, sincerely,

JAS. SHIELDS,
*Major-General, Commanding.*

[No. 25.]

HDQRS. FIRST DIVISION, FIRST ARMY CORPS,
*Front Royal, Va., June* 18, 1862—8.30 p. m.

Major-General FRÉMONT:

In pursuance of the following extract of a telegram from General McDowell, dated Manassas, June 18, 1862, to wit:

Let Major-General Frémont be informed by General Shields of the withdrawal of his division from Luray to Front Royal, to the end that if the enemy return down the valley on Front Royal General Frémont may fall on his rear.

I take this occasion to communicate to Major-General Frémont that I arrived in Front Royal on the evening of the 16th. Scouts came in from Sperryville and Luray the evening of the 17th, and report no indications of the enemy, but that 40,000 were approaching. My pioneers are sent out to try and establish some means of crossing the Shenandoah. If the pontoon train which you have could be spared a short time it would make our communication between Front Royal and General Banks' command practicable. I would ask as a favor that this be done, and also to know your position and intelligence.

Yours, respectfully,

JAS. SHIELDS,
*Major-General, Commanding Division.*

[No. 26.]

HDQRS. FIRST BRIG., WILLIAMS' DIV., DEPT. SHENANDOAH,
*Near Front Royal, Va., June* 23, 1862.

Col. ALBERT TRACY, *A. A. G., Mountain Department:*

COLONEL: The general commanding the brigade desires me to express to General Frémont his thanks for the pontoon train, which arrived promptly, and, under the energetic charge of Lieutenant Robinson, was speedily put together for immediate use.

I am, sir, very respectfully, your obedient servant,

EDWARD F. BLAKE,
*Major and Actg. Asst. Adjt. Gen., First Brigade.*

[No. 27.]

WINCHESTER, *June* 13—4 p. m.

General FRÉMONT:

MY DEAR SIR: Yours of the 12th I have just received. I know nothing of the plan of defense adopted by the Government except by telegrams from the President that one was being considered, pending which I was to place my command on the Shenandoah at or opposite Front Royal. We know nothing of Shields' movements toward Richmond, but hear, via Front Royal, he is at Luray. I concur with you entirely in the suggestion of the impolicy of divided commands, and hope that system will be abandoned at once. General Sigel's orders are like mine at present. Mount Jackson is not a position to meet the enemy, unless he moves directly down the pike. The strong position, we think, is near Middletown, which commands all the valleys that open upon the North Branch of the Shenandoah. I will see General Sigel this evening. Your movements have had a splendid success.

Very truly,

N. P. BANKS.

[No. 28.]

WINCHESTER, *June* 17, 1862.

Major-General FRÉMONT:

General Shields and 8,000 men are at Front Royal. Jackson in large force at Luray. Rumors from significant sources say the enemy is working into your rear. Dispatch from General Banks says it will be impossible to get re-enforcements.

R. MORRIS COPELAND,
*Assistant Adjutant-General and Major.*

[No. 29.]

WASHINGTON, *June* 12, 1862.

Major-General FRÉMONT:

Accounts, which we do not credit, represent that Jackson is largely re-enforced and turning upon you. Get your forces well in hand and keep us well and frequently advised, and if you find yourself really pressed by a superior force of the enemy fall back cautiously toward or to Winchester, and we will have in due time Banks in position to sustain you. Do not fall back of Harrisonburg unless upon tolerably clear necessity. We understand Jackson is on the other side of the Shenandoah from you, and hence cannot in any event press you into any necessity of a precipitate withdrawal.

A. LINCOLN.

P. S.—Yours, preferring Mount Jackson to Harrisonburg, is just received. On this point use your discretion, remembering that our object is to give such protection as you can to Western Virginia. Many thanks to yourself, officers, and men for the gallant battle of last Sunday.

[No. 30.]

MOUNTAIN DEPARTMENT, ADJUTANT-GENERAL'S OFFICE,
*Hdqrs. Army in the Field, Middletown, Va., June 25, 1862.*

Maj. Gen. JOHN C. FRÉMONT,
*Commanding Department:*

GENERAL: In compliance with your verbal order of this date to furnish a statement of the number of additional aides-de-camp credited to your staff in orders from the War Department, and also the number generally employed at headquarters or elsewhere, under your immediate orders, I have the honor to submit the following:

The whole number of additional aides-de-camp announced in orders of the War Department as pertaining to your staff is ninety-two. Of this number fifty-six, appointed as a convenience to the service merely, and as I understand without your agency or recommendation, have reported neither in person nor by letter. They performed duty, if at all, in the suites of other commanders. A small number, appointed as above, and directed to report at your headquarters, have done so. It is to be regretted that one or two of these have since proved of a character so unworthy as to induce your request for their dismissal from the service.

Of the remaining number asked for by yourself a proportion have, on application, been assigned to different general officers of the command, leaving an average of about twenty-five on duty at your headquarters or elsewhere under your immediate orders. The withdrawal of several officers of the general staff, on your assuming command of department has necessitated the assignment of a number of your personal staff as substitutes on general duties.

Officers of headquarters staff are employed as follows: Col. Anselm Albert, chief of staff; Col. Albert Tracy (captain, Tenth Regulars), acting assistant adjutant-general; Col. John T. Fiala, chief of topographical engineers, department headquarters; Col. W. F. Raynolds (captain, U. S. Regular Service), chief of topographical engineers in the field; Col. Charles Zagonyi, chief of cavalry; Lieut. Col. John Pilsen, chief of artillery; Maj. R. M. Corwine, judge advocate (absent on detached service during campaign); Col. R. N. Hudson, provost-marshal-general in the field (on leave from May 23); Capt. John C. Hopper, chief of scouts and spies; Capts. R. W. Raymond and T. J. Weed, mustering officers; Capt. G. Ward Nichols, in charge of postal service; Capt. Cyrus Hamlin, acting commissary of subsistence; Lieut. Col. James W. Savage, Majrs. Adolf C. Warberg and Burr Porter, and Captains Nordendorf and Dunka, assistants to chief of staff; Lieut. Col. Philip Figyelmesy and Maj. Leonidas Haskell, assistants of chief of cavalry; Capt. John R. Howard, in charge of telegraphic correspondence. Col. Gustave P. Cluseret, aide-de-camp, though present, is not included as a staff officer at headquarters, he being in command of light brigade.

Respectfully submitted.

ALBERT TRACY,
*Additional Aide-de-Camp and Actg. Asst. Adjt. Gen.*

## No. 2.

### *Record of the McDowell Court of Inquiry.*

Proceedings of a Court of Inquiry convened in the city of Washington, D. C., on the 21st day of November, 1862, by virtue of the following order:

SPECIAL ORDERS, No. 350. } HEADQUARTERS OF THE ARMY, ADJUTANT-GENERAL'S OFFICE, *Washington, November* 17, 1862.

* * * * * * *

III. The Court of Inquiry ordered to assemble the 27th ultimo by Special Orders, 313, Headquarters of the Army, October 25, 1862, is hereby dissolved, and at the request of Major-General McDowell, U. S. Volunteers, a Court of Inquiry will assemble in this city at 11 o'clock a. m. on the 21st instant to inquire into certain charges against him.

*Detail for the court.*—Maj. Gen. George Cadwalader, U. S. Volunteers; Brig. Gen. John H. Martindale, U. S. Volunteers; Brig. Gen. James H. Van Alen, U. S. Volunteers; Lieut. Col. Louis H. Pelouze, assistant adjutant-general, recorder of the court.

* * * * * * *

By command of Major-General Halleck:

E. D. TOWNSEND,
*Assistant Adjutant-General.*

---

*FIRST DAY.*

JUDGE-ADVOCATE-GENERAL'S OFFICE,
*Washington, D. C., November* 21, 1862.

The court met pursuant to the foregoing order.

Present, Maj. Gen. George Cadwalader, U. S. Volunteers; Brig. Gen. John H. Martindale, U. S. Volunteers; Brig. Gen. James H. Van Alen, U. S. Volunteers.

The presiding officer informed the court that Lieut. Col. Louis H. Pelouze, the recorder of the court, would not arrive in the city until to-morrow, the 22d instant, he having received a dispatch to that effect. Also, that he had communicated to Major General McDowell that his presence in court to-day would not be required, by reason of the absence of the recorder of the court.

The court adjourned to meet to-morrow, the 22d November, 1862, at 11 o'clock a. m.

GEO. CADWALADER,
*Major-General, President of the Court.*

---

*SECOND DAY.*

COURT-ROOM, 467 SOUTH FOURTEENTH STREET,
*Washington, D. C., November* 22, 1862—11 a. m.

The court met pursuant [to] adjournment.

Present, Maj. Gen. George Cadwalader, U. S. Volunteers; Brig. Gen. John H. Martindale, U. S. Volunteers; Brig. Gen. James H. Van Alen,

U. S. Volunteers; Lieut. Col. Louis H. Pelouze, assistant adjutant-general, recorder of the court, and Major-General McDowell, U. S. Volunteers.

The order convening the court was read by the recorder.

Major-General McDowell was informed that if there were no objections entertained to any member of the court the oath would be administered according to law.

No objections were made.

The court was then duly sworn by the recorder, and the recorder was duly sworn by the presiding officer of the court in the presence of Major-General McDowell.

The charges referred to in the order convening the court not having been received, the recorder was instructed to address a communication to the Assistant Adjutant-General, Headquarters of the Army, stating that the court of inquiry instituted in Special Orders, No. 350, dated Headquarters of the Army, November 17, 1862, have organized, and to request that a copy of the charges referred to in said order be furnished the court.

The court adjourned to meet Monday, 24th November, 1862, at 11 o'clock a. m.

L. H. PELOUZE,*
*Lieutenant-Colonel and Assistant Adjutant-General, Recorder.*

---

*THIRD DAY.*

COURT-ROOM,
*Washington, D. C., November* 24, 1862—11 a. m.

Thee court mt pursuant to adjournment.

Present, Maj. Gen. George Cadwalader, U. S. Volunteers; Brig. Gen. John H. Martindale, U. S. Volunteers; Brig. Gen. James H. Van Alen, U. S. Volunteers; Lieut. Col. Louis H. Pelouze, assistant adjutant-general, recorder of the court, and Major-General McDowell, U. S. Volunteers.

The proceedings of the preceding days were read by the recorder and approved by the court.†

The recorder here stated that, in compliance with the instructions of the court, given at its last sitting, he addressed a communication to the Headquarters of the Army in words as follows:

COURT-ROOM,
*Washington, D. C., November* 22, 1862—1.30 p. m.

ASSISTANT ADJUTANT-GENERAL,
*Headquarters of the Army, Washington, D. C.:*

I am instructed to communicate that the court of inquiry ordered to assemble in Special Orders, No. 350, dated Headquarters of the Army, Washington, November 17, 1862, have organized, and, further, to request that the court may be furnished with a copy of the charges referred to in said order.

Very respectfully, your obedient servant,

L. H. PELOUZE,
*Lieutenant-Colonel and Recorder Court of Inquiry.*

---

* The daily record henceforward is attested by the signature of Lieutenant-Colonel Pelouze.

† So much of the daily journal as sets forth the meeting of the court, the names of members and others present, and the reading and approval of the previous record will be omitted. Exceptional entries on these subjects will be noted.

And that said communication was returned with the following indorsement thereon:

HEADQUARTERS ARMY,
*November* 23, 1862.

The General-in-Chief is not aware that the Government has any charges against Major-General McDowell.

The court was ordered at the request of General McDowell to investigate his conduct and any charges which should be produced.

None have been filed at the Headquarters of the Army.

Respectfully,

J. C. KELTON,
*Assistant Adjutant-General.*

The communication, of which the foregoing is a copy, with the indorsement, is appended to the proceedings and marked A.*

The court was cleared for discussion.

The court was opened.

Major-General McDowell here presented to the court a communication of which the following is a copy, the original being appended to the proceedings and marked B.*

WASHINGTON, *November* 24, 1862.

Maj. Gen. GEORGE CADWALADER,
*President of the Court of Inquiry instituted in Special Orders, No.* 350:

GENERAL: It appearing from the indorsement on the recorder's letter of the Assistant Adjutant-General at the Headquarters of the Army that there are no charges against me in the possession of the Government, and that therefore the literal reading of the order convening the court, directing it to investigate "certain charges" against me, does not apply, I beg the court to obtain a copy of my letter to the President of September 6, 1862, asking for a court, and on which this court has been instituted; and, further, that the investigation in my case may be as therein requested.

I have the honor to be, general, very respectfully, your obedient servant,

IRVIN McDOWELL,
*Major-General.*

The court is of the opinion that it is not the proper medium through which this communication should reach Headquarters, particularly as an application from the court for a copy of the charges referred to in the order convening the court has been returned indorsed "The General-in-Chief is not aware that the Government has any charges against Major-General McDowell."

Further, as the General-in-Chief has communicated that "the court was ordered at the request of General McDowell to investigate his conduct," the court decide that time be allowed Major-General McDowell to apply for an enlargement of the scope of investigation by the court so as to embrace the subject referred to in this communication.

The court instructed the recorder to inform General McDowell of the action of the court on his communication, by furnishing an extract of the proceedings so far as related thereto.

The court adjourned to meet to-morrow, 25th November, 1862, at 11 o'clock a. m.

---

*FOURTH DAY.*

COURT-ROOM,
*Washington, D. C., November* 25, 1862—11 a. m.

* * * * * * *

Major-General McDowell read to the court a communication of which the following is a copy, and which is appended to the proceedings and marked C.*

---

* Not reprinted in appendix.

WASHINGTON, *November* 24, 1862.

The ASSISTANT ADJUTANT-GENERAL,
*Headquarters of the Army:*

SIR: I inclose a copy of correspondence of this date with the court of inquiry instituted in Special Orders, No. 350, current series, agreeably to the action taken by the court. I have the honor to request it may be furnished, with a copy of my letter of September 6, 1862, to His Excellency the President, asking for a court of inquiry; and that, instead of being directed to investigate "certain charges" against me, as the order now reads, the court be directed to make the investigation asked for in my letter above referred to, and be directed to report the facts and their opinion in the case.

I have the honor to be, very respectfully, your most obedient servant,

IRVIN McDOWELL,
*Major-General.*

The recorder stated to the court that during last evening he received a communication from the Headquarters of the Army in words as follows:

HEADQUARTERS OF THE ARMY,
*Washington, D. C., November* 24, 1862.

Lieut. Col. LOUIS H. PELOUZE,
*Recorder of the Court of Inquiry:*

The General-in-Chief having been informed that the court of inquiry convened to investigate charges against Major-General McDowell has adjourned owing to a statement from these Headquarters that there were no charges against that officer, directs me to call your attention to General McDowell's letter asking for a court of inquiry, and to say that matter for investigation may be found therein.

Very respectfully, your obedient servant,

J. C. KELTON,
*Assistant Adjutant-General.*

P. S.—Since writing the foregoing your communication has been received, and the order by which the action of the court will be governed has been changed as suggested.

A copy of the order will be furnished to the court from the Adjutant-General's Office.

Respectfully,

J. C. KELTON,
*Assistant Adjutant-General.*

The recorder stated that he had made no application to the Headquarters of the Army to which the P. S. to the foregoing letter refers, and that the P. S. evidently applies to the letter just read by General McDowell.

The court expressed such to be its understanding. The letter with its P. S., of which the foregoing is a copy, is appended to the proceedings and marked D.*

The recorder here read an official copy of General McDowell's letter to the President, which copy was inclosed in the communication from the Headquarters of the Army received by the recorder last evening:

WASHINGTON, *September* 6, 1862.

His Excellency the PRESIDENT:

I have been informed by a Senator that he had seen a note, in pencil, written by a colonel of cavalry mortally wounded in the recent battle, stating, among other causes, that he was dying a victim "to McDowell's treachery," and that his last request was that this note might be shown to you.

That the colonel believed this charge, and felt his last act on earth was a great public service, there can be, I think, no question.

This solemn accusation from the grave of a gallant officer, who died for his country, is entitled to great consideration; and I feel called on to endeavor to meet it as well as so general a charge, from one now no longer able to support it, can be met.

---

* Not reprinted in appendix.

I therefore beg you to please cause a court to be instituted for its investigation; and, in the absence of any knowledge whatever as to the particular act or acts, time or place, or general conduct the deceased may have had in view, I have to ask that the inquiry be without limitation, and be upon any points and every subject which may in [any] way be supposed to have led to his belief.

That it may be directed to my whole conduct as a general officer, either under another or whilst in a separate command, whether in matters of administration or command; to my correspondence with any of the enemy's commanders or with any one within the enemy's lines; to my conduct and the policy pursued by me toward the inhabitants of the country occupied by our troops with reference to themselves or their property; and, further, to any imputations of indirect treachery or disloyalty toward the nation or any individual having like myself an important trust.

Whether I have or have not been faithful as a subordinate to those placed over me, giving them heartily and to the extent of my capacity all the support in my power.

Whether I have or have not failed, through unworthy personal motives, to go to the aid of, or send re-enforcements to, my brother commanders.

That this subject of my alleged treachery or disloyalty may be fully inquired into I beg that all officers, soldiers, or civilians who know, or who think they know, of any act of mine liable to the charge in question be allowed and invited to make it known to the court.

I also beg that the proceedings of the court may be open and free to the press from day to day.

I have the honor to be, very respectfully, your most obedient servant,

IRVIN McDOWELL,
*Major-General, Commanding Third Army Corps, Army of Virginia.*

HEADQUARTERS ARMY,
*Washington, November 24, 1862.*

Official copy.

J. C. KELTON,
*Assistant Adjutant-General.*

The official copy of the foregoing letter of General McDowell to the President is appended to the proceedings, marked E.*

The recorder then read to the court Special Orders, No. 362, current series, from the Headquarters of the Army, as follows:

SPECIAL ORDERS, No. 362. HDQRS. OF THE ARMY, ADJUTANT GENERAL'S OFFICE,
*Washington, November 25, 1862.*

I. The Court of Inquiry instituted in Special Orders, No. 350, of November 17, 1862, from the Headquarters of the Army, will make the investigation asked for by Major-General McDowell, U. S. Volunteers, in his letter to the President, dated September 6, 1862, and will report the facts and an opinion in the case.

* * * * * * *

By command of Major-General Halleck:

E. D. TOWNSEND,
*Assistant Adjutant-General.*

The court was cleared for discussion.

The court was opened and the following decision respecting a proposition for deciding a course of investigation was announced:

1. That General McDowell be informed that the court invite and will receive any plan of investigation which he is prepared to submit in writing to be considered by the court.

2. That the members of the court individually digest for consideration their several plans of investigation.

General McDowell informed the court that by to-morrow he would prepare the plan of investigation, as invited.

The court adjourned to meet to-morrow, November 26, 1862, at 11 o'clock, a. m.

---

* Not reprinted in appendix.

*FIFTH DAY.*

COURT-ROOM,
*Washington, D. C., November* 26, 1862—11 a. m.

* * * * * * *

Major-General McDowell then read to the court the following, being a plan of investigation for the consideration of the court which he was invited by the court to prepare at its last sitting:

The original is appended to the proceedings and marked F.*

WASHINGTON, *November* 26, 1862.

With reference to the intimation that I should submit in writing for the consideration of the court "a plan of investigation," I beg to state as follows:

I was appointed a brigadier-general in the Army on the 14th of May, 1861, and a major-general of volunteers on the 14th of March, 1862.

Under the former commission I was placed in command of the troops on the right bank of the Potomac in the then Department of Northeastern Virginia, and retained that command, under Lieutenant-General Scott, until superseded by Major-General McClellan.

Soon after, the military departments of Washington and Northeastern Virginia being suppressed, I was given the command of a division in the Army of the Potomac, which I retained till promoted to that of the First Army Corps, Army of the Potomac.

My next command was that of the Department of the Rappahannock, which was created on the 4th of April, 1862, and had for its limits Virginia between the Potomac and the Aquia, Fredericksburg and Richmond Railroad on the east and the Blue Ridge on the west, and so much of Maryland as is between the Patuxent and the Potomac, including the District of Columbia and the city of Washington. This command was exercised under the orders of the War Department and the President. It was retained till suppressed, together with the Mountain Department, commanded by Major-General Frémont, and the Department of the Shenandoah, commanded by Major-General Banks, and all the troops in each consolidated into the Army of Virginia, under Major-General Pope.

In this army I commanded the Third Army Corps up to the 6th of last September, when I was relieved to undergo this investigation.

The details of the disaster of the battle of Bull Run of July 21, 1861, where I commanded, having become fully known to the country, having been investigated by a joint committee of Congress, and I having since been appointed by the President and confirmed by the Senate a major-general, I have not thought it necessary to ask the court to take up that campaign, and for the further reason that it would tax heavily their time and extend their investigation into questions for which at this distance of time it would be difficult to bring together the necessary witnesses. If, however, the court wish, or should think it proper, I am ready to go also into that part of my military history. But, without seeking to limit the court or wishing to limit myself, if hereafter it should seem advisable to extend the investigation, I do not propose now to go further back than shall be necessary to bring before the court so much of my conduct as a general officer as has been under my commission as major-general. This to take in such events as had commenced before and were passing when that commission was conferred.

The question which stands forth prominently in this case, and which may be assumed as the charge to which all the other points can be regarded as specifications, is that of treason.

Knowing of no specific act, none having been charged, I have the difficult task of proving a negative. By direct proof this is of course impossible, and the only way I know of doing so is by such evidence as shall cause innocence to be inferred.

It was with this in view I wrote to the President the letter now before the court, and asked an investigation on such points as would, if the result of the investigation should prove favorable, leave no doubts to my prejudice.

In addition, therefore, to the question of my general conduct as an executive and administrative officer, I have asked inquiry to be made on those points I supposed may have had in the minds of others a direct bearing on the main question, as follows:

1st. *An investigation of my correspondence with the enemy's commanders or with any one within the enemy's lines.*

If the present limitation I have indicated be adopted, the only correspondence I am aware of was with the secession commander opposite Fredericksburg, which my chief of staff, Colonel Schriver, can produce.

If it is wished or should be wished to go back to my command of the Department

---

* Not reprinted in appendix.

of Northeastern Virginia, there will be found some correspondence with the secession commander at Manassas, and which was forwarded at the time to the Headquarters of the Army.

I know of no correspondence with any one within the enemy's lines, unless it be with Mrs. Robert E. Lee and Mrs. Fitzhugh, who wrote from Ravenswood on some personal matters in June and July, 1861, and whose letters, with my replies, were forwarded at the time to the Headquarters of the Army, and are, I suppose, now in the War Department.

2d. *An investigation of my conduct and the policy pursued by me toward the inhabitants of the country occupied by our troops with reference to themselves or their property.*

This matter has been severely commented upon throughout the country and in both Houses of Congress, and may possibly have had much to do with the charge of treason.

As to my conduct toward the inhabitants with reference to themselves, I wish to offer my general orders concerning rape, robbery, and pillage, and those concerning the interference with the railroads and telegraph, and the testimony of those officers mentioned in the margin.

Brigadier-General Haupt, Colonel Schriver, Maj. J. C. Willard.

As to my conduct toward the inhabitants with reference to their property, I wish to offer my general orders and instructions concerning contributions and the taking of supplies—the form of certificate to be given for supplies taken; and as to the particular cases of a Mr. Hoffman, whose fences were ordered to be guarded, and that of the fences around the wheat fields of Chatham, or the Lacy house, which had been destroyed and were ordered to be replaced, I wish the testimony of those mentioned in the margin.

Brigadier-General Haupt, Colonel Schriver, Lieut. Col. F. Myers, assistant quartermaster; Major Sanderson, commissary of subsistence; Maj. S. Breck, assistant adjutant-general; Maj. S. Barstow, Major Willard, Captain Hodge.

3d. *As to whether or not I have been faithful to those placed over me, &c.*

For so much of my service as was under him, and particularly with reference to the events which immediately preceded the embarkation of the bulk of his army for the Peninsula, and the plans, so far as they may be necessary for the investigation, &c., which led to that campaign, I wish the testimony of Major-General McClellan, Governor Dennison, of Ohio; Brigadier-General Wadsworth, and Colonel Key, aide-de-camp.

For so much of my service as was under him, I wish the testimony of Major-General Pope, and of Brigadier-General Roberts, General Welch, commissary general New York; Colonel Morgan, aide-de-camp; Lieutenant-Colonel Smith, First Ohio Cavalry; Colonel Ruggles, assistant adjutant-general; Colonel Schriver, &c., and, if the court see fit to go back that far, that of Lieutenant-General Scott (by deposition, for I should dislike to trouble him with a disagreeable journey) for so much of my service as was under him.

4th. *As to whether I have failed through any unworthy personal motives to go to the aid of, or send re-enforcements to, my brother commanders.*

I wish inquiry made as to whether, whilst in command of the Department of the Rappahannock, I did or not, so far as my means and instructions permitted, operate so as to aid, or endeavor to aid, Major-General McClellan in his campaign on the Peninsula; whether or not I was active, zealous, and efficient in the discharge of the duties of my command in preparing it for this object.

Whether or not I refused, neglected, or failed to go to him before Richmond when I had my forces at Fredericksburg; and, if so, why?

Whether or not at the last moment I left Fredericksburg for the valley of the Shenandoah to avoid coming under Major-General McClellan's command.

Whether or not, when the compaign in the Shenandoah Valley was considered as ended, I endeavored to take active measures to go to his aid before Richmond.

Brigadier-General Wadsworth, Major Tillson, Maine artillery; Colonel Lyle, Ninetieth Pennsylvania Volunteers; Colonel Biddle, Ninety-fifth New York.

On the foregoing I have mostly to offer the official correspondence between myself and His Excellency the President, the honorable Secretary of War, Major-General McClellan, and others, and the testimony of those mentioned in the margin.

I wish inquiry made as to whether, when ordered to co-operate with Major-General Frémont for the relief of Major-General Banks, I took active measures to do so.

Brigadier-Generals Ricketts and Hartsuff and Haupt, Colonel Schriver.

On this I have to submit my official correspondence, and wish the evidence of those mentioned in the margin.

I wish inquiry made as to whether, in the late Army of Virginia, I at any time neglected or failed to go to the aid of, or send re-enforcements to, either Major-General Banks or Major-General Sigel, commanding the Second and First Army Corps, when it was my duty to do so, and particularly with reference to General Banks at the battle of Cedar Mountain and General Sigel at the battle of Groveton, or Manassas.

Major-Generals Pope and Sigel, Brigadier-General Ricketts, Colonel Buchanan, Major Tillson, Captains Cutting, Krebs, and Jewett, Brigadier-General Roberts.

On this I have to submit official papers, and wish the evidence of those mentioned in the margin.

5th. ***Finally, I ask an investigation into the charge very generally made against me, and which affects seriously my character, to wit, that of drunkenness.***

On this I wish the evidence of the following persons (those absent by deposition): Lieutenant-General Scott, Major-Generals Hunter, Pope, Wool, Sumner, Heintzelman, Keyes, Franklin, Hooker, Schuyler Hamilton; Brig. Gens. Lorenzo Thomas, Andrew Porter, King, Ricketts, Wadsworth, Martindale, Barry, Butterfield, Hancock, French, Brannan, Wood, (T. J.,) Augur, Patrick, Hartsuff, Gibbon, Morris (William); Colonel Delafield, Engineers; Colonel Taylor, commissary-general; Professors Mahan, Bartlett, and Church, Military Academy; Colonel Townsend, assistant adjutant-general; Lieutenant-Colonel Clitz, commanding cadets; Colonel Schriver, Majors Shiras and J. C. Willard, Messrs. Goold, Hoyt, and Herman Leroy and T. d'Orimieulx, New York City; Mr. Henry Burden, Troy, N. Y.; Mr. Gouverneur Kemble, Cold Spring, N. Y.; W. B. Cozzens, West Point; Mr. J. W. Andrews and Judge Joseph Swan, Columbus, Ohio; Michael Sullivant, Illinois.

As far as possible I beg leave to suggest that it may be well to take up the subjects in chronological order.

If in the foregoing it shall appear I have omitted anything, I trust to the indulgence of the court to permit me to add whatever may be wanting.

Very respectfully,

IRVIN McDOWELL,
*Major-General.*

The court was cleared.

The court was opened, when it was decided to adjourn until to-morrow, the 27th November, 1862, at 11 o'clock a. m.

---

### *SIXTH DAY.*

COURT-ROOM,
*November* 27, 1862—11 a. m.

* * * * * * *

The court was cleared.

The court was opened, and its decision respecting a plan of investigation announced.

The court, having carefully considered the foregoing proposition of Major-General McDowell, decide to proceed to the investigation in accordance with the following, making hereafter such modifications or amplifications as may be suggested by the course of the proceedings and be deemed necessary:

To examine and inquire into any and all accusations or imputations of treachery or disloyalty on the part of General McDowell, and to examine and inquire into his whole conduct as a general officer since August 24, 1861, being the date on which General McClellan assumed command of the Army of the Potomac.

For the convenience of the investigation the aforementioned time will be divided as follows, being the periods of time when General McDowell commanded:

1st. A division in the Army of the Potomac, under Major-General McClellan, from August 24, 1861, to March 13, 1862.

2d. The First Army Corps, Army of the Potomac, under Major-General McClellan, from March 13, 1862, to April 4, 1862.

3d. The Department of the Rappahannock, under the orders of the President and the War Department, from April 4, 1862, to June 26, 1862.

4th. The Third Army Corps, Army of Virginia, under Major-General Pope, from June 26 to September 6, 1862.

With a view to a statement of facts and an expression of opinion the court will—

1st. Examine the correspondence of General McDowell with the enemy's commanders or with any one within the enemy's lines.

2d. Examine and inquire into the conduct pursued by General McDowell toward the inhabitants of the country occupied by United States forces with reference to themselves or their property.

3d. Inquire whether General McDowell has fulfilled his duty as a commander to those placed under him and as a subordinate officer to those placed over him, giving heartily, and to the extent of his capacity, all the support in his power.

4th. Inquire whether General McDowell has or has not failed to go to the aid of, or send re-enforcements to, a brother commander; and, if he has so failed, for what reasons.

The attention of the court was called to an article in a newspaper of which the following is a copy, and the recorder was directed to summon the writer as a witness to appear before the court:

68 SAINT MARK'S PLACE,
*New York, September* 24, 1862.

General IRVIN MCDOWELL:

SIR: I have recently noticed in the New York Herald your modest request, by letter, that the President would cause a court to be instituted to investigate charges brought against you by a "dying officer," &c.

In your letter you also send forth the following challenge:

"That this subject of my alleged treachery or disloyalty may be fully inquired into, I beg that all officers, soldiers, or civilians who know, or think they know, of any act of mine liable to the charge in question be allowed and invited to make it known to the court."

Now, sir, I don't know what frame of mind you was in when you wrote such a defiant letter. I cannot say you were then under the influence of liquor, as I have seen you at other times, both in the field and out, but that you are one of those brazen-faced Christians who bid defiance to truth I have not the least doubt.

And as I have no greater hope than yourself that any such court will be called, I will take this opportunity of making a few brief statements of facts, which you may also deny.

On the 3d of July, 1861, I was in Ellsworth's camp; I there visited and heard the sad stories of many sick soldiers—sick, purged, and vomited from living on musty crackers, salt fat junk, and bad water. This was all the food allowed them. They offered to pay for vegetables, but the rebels of Alexandria would not sell them. One man was complained of for plucking an ear of corn. You, as a general, instead of seeing to the wants of your army, issued an order to the rebels, authorizing them to shoot any man who would trespass upon their property; but you did not make any provision for the health of your troops. These same men were constantly being shot at while on picket duty, but your peremptory orders were not to return fire upon the rebels.

A negro servant, owned by Richard Windsor, went to Ellsworth's camp, and informed against his master as being a colonel in the rebel army and then about to go to his regiment. The captain in command went with a squad of his men and overtook Colonel Windsor on the road. He had his carpet-bag, containing his uniform, a brace of pistols, dirk, &c., with him. He offered the captain all his money ($500) if he would let him off, but the captain was one of those who would not be bought. The temper of the rebel then gave way, and he declared that he was a secessionist, and would never be anything else; also that he would soon be out of the scrape. He forthwith wrote a letter to you, general, when you promptly sent orders for your friend's release, at the same time ordering the brave captain into confinement because he had done what he thought was his duty, but whom you never brought to trial.

These, with others, were the causes of mutiny in the regiment, as some may remember. The men declared they would not stand up to be shot whilst they were not allowed to defend themselves.

Is this what you call loyalty? If this alone be true (and I do believe my many authors, both officers and men), I wonder you have escaped hanging.

If a drunken man is incapable of holding office I am satisfied you are, for I have seen the proofs at Fairfax Court-House and in Washington, and I am sorry to say there are more of the same sort in command of our army, whose time would be short if we had not such a good-natured man for President.

We have the bravest soldiers the world ever saw, and I wish I could say the same of their leaders; "but it is a long lane that has no turning."

Your obedient servant,

Colonel R. D. GOODWIN.

The court informed Major-General McDowell that it would receive the depositions of the witnesses named by him on the charge of drunkenness.

The court instructed the recorder to address a communication to the assistant adjutant-general, Headquarters of the Army, requesting that the following-named witnesses be summoned to appear and give evidence before this court, viz: Major-Generals McClellan, Pope, and Sigel; Brigadier-Generals Ricketts, Roberts, Hartsuff, Haupt, Wadsworth: Cols. E. Schriver, Key, aide-de-camp, Morgan, aide-de-camp, Lyle, Ninetieth Pennsylvania Volunteers, Biddle, Ninety-fifth New York Volunteers, Ruggles, assistant adjutant-general, Buchanan, U. S. Army; Lieutenant-Colonels Myers, assistant quartermaster, Smith, First Ohio Cavalry; Majrs. J. C. Willard, Sanderson, commissary of subsistence, S. Breck, assistant adjutant-general, S. F. Barstow, assistant adjutant-general, Tillson, Maine Artillery; Captains Krebbs, Jewett, Cutting, and Hodge.

The court adjourned to meet to-morrow, the 28th instant, at 11 o'clock a. m.

---

*SEVENTH DAY.*

COURT-ROOM, 467 SOUTH FOURTEENTH STREET,
*Washington, D. C., November* 28, 1862—11 a. m.

* * * * * * *

The recorder stated that, in compliance with instructions of the court at its last sitting, he addressed the following communication to the Headquarters of the Army.

COURT-ROOM, 467 SOUTH FOURTEENTH STREET,
*Washington, D. C., November* 27, 1862.

ASSISTANT ADJUTANT-GENERAL,
*Headquarters of the Army, Washington, D. C.:*

COLONEL: I am instructed by the court of inquiry convened pursuant to Special Orders, No. 350, current series, from the Headquarters of the Army, to request that the following-named witnesses may be summoned to give evidence before the court, viz: Major-Generals McClellan, Pope, and Sigel; Brigadier-Generals Ricketts, Roberts, Hartsuff, Haupt, Wadsworth, Augur (if he can be spared), and Welch, commissary-general, of New York; Cols. E. Schriver, aide-de-camp, Key, aide-de-camp, Morgan, aide-de-camp, Ruggles, assistant adjutant-general, Lyle, Ninetieth Pennsylvania Volunteers, and Biddle, Ninety-fifth New York Volunteers; Lieutenant-Colonels Myers, assistant quartermaster, and Smith, First Ohio Cavalry; Majrs. J. C. Willard, Sanderson, commissary of subsistence, S. Breck, assistant adjutant-general, S. F. Barstow, assistant adjutant-general, and Tillson, Maine Artillery; Captains Krebbs, Jewett, Cutting, and Hodge.

I am, very respectfully, your obedient servant,

L. H. PELOUZE,
*Lieutenant-Colonel and Recorder.*

To the foregoing an answer was received as follows:

HEADQUARTERS OF THE ARMY,
*Washington, D. C., November* 28, 1862.

Lieut. Col. LOUIS H. PELOUZE,
*Recorder Court Inquiry:*

COLONEL: In reply to your communication of the 27th I am directed by the General-in-Chief to authorize you to summon (paragraph 890, Army Regulations) the following-named officers, viz: Major-Generals McClellan, Pope, and Sigel; Brigadier-Generals Ricketts, Roberts, Hartsuff, Haupt, and Wadsworth, and Commissary-General Welch, of New York; Colonels Schriver, Key, Morgan, Ruggles; Lieutenant-Colonel Smith, and Major Breck.

The other officers called for by the court are in the field, or are supposed to be in charge of duties from which they cannot be spared.

Very respectfully, your obedient servant,

J. C. KELTON,
*Assistant Adjutant-General.*

The recorder stated that, in pursuance of the instructions of the court of yesterday, he summoned Col. R. D. Goodwin to appear as a witness before this court, as follows:

COURT-ROOM, 467 SOUTH FOURTEENTH STREET,
*Washington, D. C., November* 27, 1862.

Col. R. D. GOODWIN,
*No.* 68 *Saint Mark's Place, New York City:*

I am instructed to summon you as a witness, to appear before the court of inquiry in the case of Major-General McDowell, U. S. Volunteers, now in session in this city, and convened pursuant to Special Orders, No. 350, from the Headquarters of the Army, dated Adjutant-General's Office, Washington, D. C., November 17, 1862.

I am, very respectfully, your obedient servant,

L. H. PELOUZE,
*Lieutenant-Colonel and Recorder.*

The court was cleared.

The court was opened.

The recorder was directed to address a communication to the Headquarters of the Army, requesting that the following official records be furnished the court for examination:

1st. Those pertaining to the division of the Army of the Potomac, commanded by General McDowell, from August 24, 1861, till March 13, 1862.

2d. Those pertaining to the First Army Corps, Army of the Potomac, commanded by General McDowell, from March 13, 1862, till April 4, 1862.

3d. Those pertaining to the Department of the Rappahannock, commanded by General McDowell, from April 4, 1862, till June 26, 1862.

4th. Those pertaining to the Third Army Corps, Army of Virginia, commanded by General McDowell, from June 26, 1862, till September 6, 1862.

General McDowell was informed that the court would receive for examination the official papers referred to in his communication to the court, dated November 26, 1862, and the recorder was instructed to call for the same.

General McDowell stated he would be pleased if the court would add a fifth clause under the general heading, which embodies the subject-matter for investigation—a clause that will embrace the subject of drunkenness.

The question was discussed in open court, and General McDowell informed that the plan of investigation as proposed by the court would not exclude evidence on the charge of drunkenness, and that if in the course of the investigation such additional clause should be deemed necessary the court would have it adopted.

General McDowell here requested that Colonel Schriver be first called, to give evidence on the matter of correspondence with the enemy's commanders.

Colonel SCHRIVER, aide-de-camp, a witness, was duly sworn.

Question by General MCDOWELL. State your rank and position on General McDowell's staff and how long you have been with him.

Answer. I am colonel and chief of his staff. I have been with him about eight months, and in the capacity of chief of staff.

Question by General McDOWELL. Lay before the court all the correspondence had between Major-General McDowell and any of the enemy's commanders.

The witness handed the recorder a paper, which the witness stated was a letter from Brig. Gen. J. R. Anderson to General McDowell, dated May 18, 1862, which letter was read by the recorder as follows, and which is appended to these proceedings and marked G:*

HEADQUARTERS ARMY OF THE RAPPAHANNOCK,
*May* 18, 1862.

Maj. Gen. IRVIN McDOWELL,
*Commanding U. S. Forces:*

GENERAL: You are perhaps informed of the circumstances connected with the death of the Hon. Robert E. Scott, of Fauquier County, one of the most respected and renowned citizens of this Commonwealth. His widow and her family of small children are left in a painful situation. I send one of my aides, Captain Worthington, under a flag of truce, to inquire whether you will permit her brother, Dr. Lyons, to pass your lines to her residence near Warrenton, and to bring her, with her family, within my lines. If so, will you allow me to send an escort of five mounted men, armed, with Dr. Lyons, or would you prefer to send an escort, all of course under a safe-conduct from you to go and return.

Awaiting your reply, I have the honor to subscribe myself, general, your obedient servant,

J. R. ANDERSON,
*Brigadier-General, Commanding.*

One private accompanies Captain Worthington.

J. R. A.

Colonel Schriver, the witness, here presented to the court a book, as containing General McDowell's answer to the foregoing letter, which answer is dated Headquarters Department of the Rappahannock, opposite Fredericksburg, Va., May 18, 1862, and reads as follows:

HEADQUARTERS DEPARTMENT OF THE RAPPAHANNOCK,
*Opposite Fredericksburg, Va., May* 18, 1862.

Brig. Gen. JOSEPH R. ANDERSON,
*Commanding near Massaponax:*

GENERAL: I have just received your communication of this date. It was only today I heard of the death to which you refer. It gave me great pain, and I assure you it is with real distress I cannot find it consistent with my duty to grant your request for Dr. Lyons to return after passing through my lines. He may come within them and go to Mrs. Scott's and bring her and her family to Fredericksburg, if that will in any way be agreeable to them and him, and I will see he has safe conduct in doing so; but more than this I am unable to grant. I regret to have detained your aide-de-camp so long and to have put him to some unnecessary inconvenience. It grew out of the negligence or ignorance of my troops.

I have the honor to be, general, very respectfully, your most obedient servant,

IRVIN McDOWELL,
*Major-General, Commanding.*

The witness stated that reply was sent at the time of its date, and is recorded in the book of letters kept at the headquarters. (The book submitted.)

The witness here submitted a second letter, dated May 19, 1862, from the same commander to Major-General McDowell, which was read by the recorder as follows, and is appended to the proceedings and marked H:*

* Not reprinted in appendix.

HEADQUARTERS ARMY OF THE RAPPAHANNOCK,
*May* 19, 1862.

Maj. Gen. IRVIN MCDOWELL,
*Commanding U. S. Forces:*

GENERAL: Your communication of 18th current was duly received.

I beg you will excuse me for troubling you further upon this subject. In my brief note of yesterday I omitted some delicate details of the case, supposing that the usages of civilization would guarantee to the widow of a fallen citizen a passport to the home of her kindred. It is, however, proper before you make a final disposition of the application that I should make you acquainted with facts which I think invite to it the sympathies of our humanity.

The lamented Scott was not connected with the military service of his country, but was, as I am informed, quietly residing on his farm, when he was called to unite with his neighbors of like status to defend their domiciles from the depredations of an unauthorized marauding party from your army. In a conflict with these assassins he fell in defense of all that was dearest to him. I say this party was unauthorized, because I am sure such a warfare on non-combatants would never receive your sanction, and am satisfied you will cause an investigation to be made and the guilty parties to be punished if the facts have been correctly reported to me.

But to my immediate subject. By the death of her husband I learn that Mrs. Scott is left alone with her children, the family of her husband having fled from that section. She expects soon to give birth to a child, who will never be privileged to behold the manly form of its gifted, murdered father.

It is natural, general, that this gentle, refined, deeply bereaved lady would anxiously desire to return to her native city, to receive the consolation and friendly offices of her family in the day of her deep tribulation.

I respectfully leave the case in your hands, adding an extract from a letter just received from her father:

"I received yesterday a few lines from my poor child, begging imploringly for relief."

I have not yet been able to communicate the arrangement proposed in your letter of yesterday to the family, but think I would be safe in saying it would be impracticable: First, because the important point with the afflicted lady is to be restored to her family, whilst in Fredericksburg she would be among strangers. Secondly, it would seem that her brother would not be allowed to return to his home through your lines, though I don't think you design that construction to be placed upon your letter.

This letter will be carried by one of my aides-de-camp, Captain Worthington.

I have the honor to be, general, your humble and obedient servant,

J. R. ANDERSON,
*Brigadier-General, Commanding.*

The witness stated that the reply to the communication just read is recorded in the same letter-book, and dated May 21, 1862, which reply the recorder read as follows:

HEADQUARTERS DEPARTMENT OF THE RAPPAHANNOCK,
*Opposite Fredericksburg, Va., May* 21, 1862.

Brig. Gen. JOSEPH R. ANDERSON,
*Commanding near Massaponax:*

GENERAL: I have the honor to acknowledge the receipt of your letter of the 19th instant. I am fully disposed to do whatever is in my power for the relief of the lady to whom you refer. If, as I understand, she is now near Warrenton, I will, if it should be agreeable to her and her family, have the general commanding near that place see that suitable transportation for her and her children—a separate car, if possible—is provided by railroad to Alexandria, and thence by steamboat and railroad to this place, and will see that she is sent in a proper way hence to your headquarters. To insure this being done in a manner as little trying to the lady as possible, and to guard as far as may be against inconvenience to her, I will send an officer of my personal staff to see that this is carried out, and to accompany her from Warrenton to your lines.

You cannot be more anxious than I am that this war should be conducted with the least amount of suffering to the innocent and the non-combatants. I know of few, if any, who labor as incessantly and untiringly to this end as I have done and am doing. I take some pleasure in the fact that the bitterest of the inhabitants of Fredericksburg are in candor constrained to admit the good conduct and discipline of the troops now with them.

The letters you sent me for parties in Fredericksburg have been sent to the mayor for distribution.

I have the honor to be, general, very respectfully, your most obedient servant,

IRVIN McDOWELL,
*Major-General, Commanding.*

The witness here presented a communication from Brig. Gen. Joseph R. Anderson to Major-General McDowell, dated headquarters, May 22, 1862, which the recorder read as follows, and which is appended to the proceedings and marked I:*

HEADQUARTERS, *May* 22, 1862.

Maj. Gen. IRVIN MCDOWELL, *Commanding:*

GENERAL: I avail myself of the flag of truce this morning to acknowledge receipt of your courteous letter of yesterday's date.

The plan you propose for bringing Mrs. Scott and her family to this neighborhood I will at once communicate to her relatives at Richmond.

I have the honor to remain, general, your very obedient servant,

J. R. ANDERSON,
*Brigadier-General, Commanding.*

Question by General McDOWELL. Were or not the letters for persons in Fredericksburg, alluded to in my letter to General Anderson of May 21, 1862, received from him opened, and were they examined at my headquarters before being sent to the mayor for distribution?

Answer. They were. This same commander, General Anderson, wrote a letter concerning Generals Buckner and Tilghman, dated 22d May, 1862. General McDowell replied, and his letter is recorded on page 208 in the letter-book submitted to the court.

The recorder then read the letter:

HEADQUARTERS DEPARTMENT OF THE RAPPAHANNOCK,
*Opposite Fredericksburg, Va., May* 22, 1862.

Brig. Gen. JOSEPH R. ANDERSON, *Commanding near Massaponax:*

GENERAL: I have the honor to acknowledge the receipt of your letter of yesterday's date, inclosing a letter concerning Generals Buckner and Tilghman.

I have no knowledge whatever of the treatment shown these gentlemen, and am unable to state anything concerning them.

The letter you have inclosed will be immediately transmitted to Washington, whence only authentic information on the point in question can come. As soon as I receive any it will be immediately communicated to you.

I have the honor to be, general, very respectfully, your most obedient servant,

IRVIN McDOWELL,
*Major-General, Commanding.*

The witness continued:

On the 24th May General McDowell addressed to General J. R. Anderson a letter on the same subject, which is recorded at page 212 in the letter-book.

The recorder read the letter as follows:

HEADQUARTERS DEPARTMENT OF THE RAPPAHANNOCK,
*Opposite Fredericksburg, Va., May* 24, 1862.

Brig. Gen. JOSEPH R. ANDERSON, *Commanding near Massaponax:*

GENERAL: I have just received the following from the Secretary of War:

"You may answer that Generals Buckner and Tilghman are not confined in dungeons. I have directed a specific report to be made as to how they are confined, which when received will be transmitted to you."

I have only to add that when that report shall be received I will lose no time in communicating with you again on the subject.

I have the honor to be, very respectfully, your obedient servant,

IRVIN McDOWELL,
*Major-General, Commanding.*

---

* Not reprinted in appendix.

The witness continued:

That is all the correspondence I am aware of that took place between General McDowell and the Confederate commanders.

Question by the COURT. Do you know, or have you reason to suspect, that any correspondence of any kind was held by General McDowell with the enemy while you were on his staff not included in that which has just been produced by you?

Answer. I know of none and have no reason to suspect that any existed.

1. Question by the COURT. Can you state when you entered on the duties of chief of staff of General McDowell?

Answer. General McDowell issued an order on the 28th March, 1862, announcing me as chief of staff—I think between the 10th and 28th March, 1862.

2. Question by the COURT. When was the record of the letters in the letter-book of General McDowell made with reference to their date?

Answer. Sometimes letters are recorded at their date, sometimes days after. I cannot answer about those particular letters, whether they were recorded immediately or not.

3. Question by the COURT. In respect to the receipt of open letters from the enemy's lines and distributed through the mayor of Fredericksburg, state whether such practice was according to the usages of war.

Answer. I do not know the usages of war on that subject, but I have heard that commanders in our Army in this contest have sent open letters to their address.

4. Question by the COURT. By whom were the letters received from or forwarded to parties within the enemy's lines examined?

Answer. By General McDowell or some of his staff.

5. Question by the COURT. Was any record made of such letters; and, if so, what?

Answer. I am not aware of any.

Col. JOSEPH TAYLOR, commissary-general of subsistence, was duly sworn.

Question by General McDOWELL. Were you acquainted with the late Robert E. Scott, of Fauquier County, Virginia? If so, state what character he bore, whether a Union man or secessionist, where he lived, how he died, and in what place he left his family.

Answer. I knew Mr. Robert Scott intimately for years. I regarded him as a Union man, and have talked with him frequently on that subject. He was residing about 5 miles from Warrenton, Fauquier County, Virginia. I do not know when or where he was killed. I have seen letters from his family dated at the homestead since his death.

The court had no questions to ask this witness. Colonel Schriver, the first witness before the court, stated that since giving his testimony certain other matters had been recalled to memory which should form part of the testimony required from him. Colonel Schriver was requested to have the same put in form for reception by the court to-morrow.

The court adjourned to meet to-morrow, 29th November, 1862.

*EIGHTH DAY.*

COURT-ROOM
*Washington, D. C., November 29, 1862.*

* * * * * * *

The recorder stated that, in compliance with the instructions of the court, he addressed a communication to the Headquarters of the Army, as follows:

COURT-ROOM, 467 SOUTH FOURTEENTH STREET,
*Washington, D. C., November 28, 1862.*

ASSISTANT ADJUTANT-GENERAL,
*Headquarters of the Army, Washington, D. C.:*

COLONEL: I am instructed by the court of inquiry convened pursuant to Special Orders, No. 350, current series, from the Headquarters of the Army, to request that the following official records be furnished for examination by the court:

1st. Those pertaining to the division of the Army of the Potomac, commanded by General McDowell, from 24th August, 1861, to the 13th March, 1862.

2d. Those pertaining to the First Army Corps, Army of the Potomac, commanded by General McDowell, from 13th March, 1862, till the 4th of April, 1862.

3d. Those pertaining to the Department of the Rappahannock, commanded by General Dowell, from 4th April, 1862, till 26th June, 1862.

4th. Those pertaining to the Third Army Corps, Army of Virginia, commanded by General McDowell, from 26th June, 1862, to the 6th September, 1862.

I have the honor to be, very respectfully, your obedient servant,

L. H. PELOUZE,
*Lieutenant-Colonel and Recorder.*

Mr. WILLIAM D. WALLACH, a witness, was duly sworn.

Question by General MCDOWELL. Did you know Robert E. Scott, of Fauquier County, Virginia? If so, state what was his character, Union man or secessionist, the manner of his death, and the place (exposed or otherwise) in which his widow was left at his death.

Answer. I did know Robert E. Scott for between thirty and forty years before he was killed. He was universally regarded, not only as a gentleman of high personal character and great public utility, but as the Union leader in the State of Virginia. He was understood to have been perhaps the last man in the Virginia Convention that adopted the ordinance of secession to submit to its enactment or adoption, declining, if I am rightly informed, even to sign the ordinance as a member of that body. After its adoption he returned to his estate in Fauquier, and I lost sight of him personally, though it was well understood in his county and in mine, adjoining each other, that while submitting to the rule of secession in arms, he did not change his sentiments with reference to the entire impropriety of the act. It is notorious in the counties of Fauquier and Culpeper that from the time of his return to Richmond until his murder he was continually under the surveillance of the authorities, according to the common understanding in the county in which he resided and those surrounding him. He was killed under the following circumstances:

A small party of deserters from the Union forces then in Fauquier County were roaming that region with arms in their hands, entering the houses, marauding and ravishing in the neighborhood. They had ravished two respectable females residing within a few miles from Mr. Scott's home. He hearing of it sent a message to the nearest Union command, urging the apprehension of these desperadoes, and at the same time started, accompanied by his overseer and a half-dozen neighbors, and in attempting to apprehend these men they shot him and killed him. His death caused infinite consternation in the community, as the marauders escaped, and did more to destroy the remaining Union feeling existing in that section of Virginia than any other event of the war that had occurred up to that time.

The court had no questions to ask this witness.

Col. EDMUND SCHRIVER, aide-de-camp, a witness, was recalled.

Question by the COURT. Have you examined the book of letters; and, if so, on what pages are those to be found to which the attention of the

**court was called by you yesterday, after your testimony was concluded?**

Answer. They are respectively numbered—140, page 173; number 153, page 177; number 230, page 213, in the official letter-book of Headquarters Department of the Rappahannock.

The court was closed with a view of examining said letters ere they were received.

The court was opened and the following decision announced:

That the evidence contained in said papers is immaterial to the matter for investigation before the court and would not be received.

Question by General McDOWELL. Lay before the court General Orders, Nos. 12 and 19, Headquarters Department of the Rappahannock.

The recorder read General Orders, Nos. 12 and 19, from Headquarters Department of the Rappahannock, dated—the former dated opposite Fredericksburg, Va., May 16, 1862, the latter Front Royal, Va., June 5, 1862, as follows:

GENERAL ORDERS, No. 12. HEADQUARTERS DEPARTMENT OF THE RAPPAHANNOCK, *Opposite Fredericksburg, Va., May 16, 1862.*

It has come to the knowledge of the major-general commanding that some of the few men among us who are evilly disposed have attempted the commission of a crime which will justly draw upon the troops universal condemnation. It is due to the good men of the army, to the service, to the country, to the sisters, daughters, mothers, and wives of all that the stain be effaced by the infliction of the only fit punishment due such acts. That we are here with arms in our hands, and that the people have no practical redress from our wrong-doings but heightens our obligation to protect the helpless. That this may be done promptly and effectively military commissions will be instituted in each division for the punishment of all crimes committed by any one in the military service or by any one "following the army," and which may not be cognizable by courts-martial.

For ordinary offenses or crimes such commissions will be detailed from the roster in the same way as a court-martial; but whenever it shall be deemed necessary by the division commander, or orders to that effect shall be received by him from the headquarters, a special military commission, to consist in each division of the brigade commanders, the chiefs of the division artillery and cavalry, and two of the regimental commanders, or as many, not less than a majority, as can be immediately convened, will be assembled to try such cases, as, from the persons implicated or the crime committed, the interests of the service shall require to be disposed of in a summary manner.

The form of the proceedings in the case of an ordinary commission shall be the same as that of court-martial. The form of proceedings in the case of a special commission will be such as the division commander may determine; but will not be such as will interfere with summary justice. The punishment for rape will be death; and any violence offered a female, white or colored, with the evident intent or purpose to commit a rape, will be considered as one, and punished accordingly.

In cases of conviction and sentence for rape, as above defined, the division commander, if he approve the findings and sentence, will order immediate execution by hanging, or by shooting if the former should not be convenient. That the order may have full effect, all good men in the army, whether officers, non-commissioned officers, musicians, or privates, and all who may be in any way connected with or following the army are especially charged and entreated to do whatever in them lies to bring this crime to its merited punishment.

By command of Major-General McDowell:

SAML. BRECK, *Assistant Adjutant-General.*

GENERAL ORDERS, No. 19. HEADQUARTERS DEPARTMENT OF THE RAPPAHANNOCK, *Front Royal, Va., June 5, 1862.*

Any person detected in placing obstructions on the track of any of the railroads used by the United States for military purposes, or of injuring the bridges, or doing anything with the object of interrupting military trains, will be shot on the spot. Residents in the vicinity of accidents occurring from hostile act will be held responsible in their persons and property, and will not be suffered to remain passive, but must use vigilance and personal influence to prevent injury.

The same will apply to injury to the military telegraph lines.

By command of Major-General McDowell:

SAML. BRECK, *Assistant Adjutant-General.*

Question by General McDOWELL. Lay before the court Special Orders, No. 65, and paragraph 2, General Orders, No. 10, Headquarters Department of the Rappahannock.

Answer. The order is recorded in the general-order book, page 116, and special-order book, page 135, submitted to the court.

The recorder read the order, as follows:

SPECIAL ORDERS, No. 65. } HEADQUARTERS DEPARTMENT OF THE RAPPAHANNOCK, *Opposite Fredericksburg, Va., May* 13, 1862.

In visiting this afternoon the graves of those who fell in the advance on this place the major-general commanding was pained at seeing that in paying a tribute of respect to their companions some of the men of his command had despoiled a neighboring tomb—that of a woman. Such conduct is undoubtedly to be ascribed to nothing worse than thoughtlessness; yet how thoughtless to pay respect to the dead of to-day by a desecration of the dead of yesterday. Can the graves of these brave men be respected hereafter when it is seen that their friends have not respected that of her who sleeps beside them?

Brigadier-General Augur will detail a party of bricklayers and others, and will obtain the necessary materials for fully restoring the tombs which have been injured, and will at the same time have suitable head-pieces placed over the graves of our men, giving full names, residence, company, and regiment, and inclose the little cemetery neatly and substantially.

By command of Major-General McDowell:

SAML. BRECK,
*Assistant Adjutant-General.*

GENERAL ORDERS, No. 10. } HEADQUARTERS DEPARTMENT OF THE RAPPAHANNOCK, *Opposite Fredericksburg, May* 10, 1862.

* * * * * * *

II. The colored fugitives who have sought the protection of the army will be taken up for the public service, and will be enrolled and registered as heretofore prescribed. This is made necessary to relieve, as far as possible, the troops from labor at depots and on railroads.

These fugitives will wear a uniform badge, to be furnished by the quartermaster's department, made to designate them in gangs of tens and hundreds.

By command of Major-General McDowell;

SAML. BRECK,
*Assistant Adjutant-General.*

Question by General McDOWELL. Lay before the court General Orders, No. 8 and No. 18, and form of certificate ordered to be given for property taken for the public service.

Answer. General Orders, No. 8, is found on page 115, general-order book, and General Order, No. 18, on page 121, general-order book, and the form of certificate may be found on the same page.

These orders and form read, as follows:

GENERAL ORDERS, No. 8. } HEADQUARTERS DEPARTMENT OF THE RAPPAHANNOCK, *Opposite Fredericksbury, May* 7, 1862.

The following is announced as the only recognized method of taking supplies of al descriptions, such as forage, provisions, animals, tools, &c., from citizens. The authority of the division commander, or brigade commander of troops not belonging to division, must first be obtained; nothing will be taken without this authority. Receipts for the property taken must be made out in duplicate, according to prescribed form, and signed; one copy to be given to the person from whom the articles are taken, and one to be forwarded at the end of the month, with an abstract of all receipts given during the month, to the chief of the staff department for which the supplies are taken, at these headquarters. The only persons authorized to sign the above receipts are the division and brigade quartermasters and commissaries and persons specially authorized to do so from these headquarters. Blank forms will be furnished on application to the chief quartermaster of this department.

By command of Major-General McDowell:

SAML. BRECK,
*Assistant Adjutant-General.*

[Inclosure.]

GENERAL ORDERS, No. 18. } HEADQUARTERS DEPARTMENT OF THE RAPPAHANNOCK, *Front Royal, Va., June* 3, 1862.

There has been recently so much irregularity on the subject of levying contributions, and so much misconception on the part of many commanders and other officers as to their powers and duties in this respect, that it has become necessary to call the attention of all concerned to the subject, to the end that the gross abuses which have been committed may cease.

*Paragraph* 491, *Army Regulations.*—"When the wants of the Army absolutely require it, and in other cases under special instructions from the War Department, the general commanding the Army may levy contributions in money or kind in the enemy's country occupied by troops. No other commander can levy such contributions without written authority from the general commander-in-chief."

This paragraph applies to domestic as well as to foreign enemies. No other commander than the general-in-chief of an army can levy contributions without the written authority from said general-in-chief. Yet not only do other commanders, but corporals and privates even undertake to assume the power without authority from any one. Such conduct is simple pillage, theft, or robbery. When in the judgment of the major-general commanding the wants of the army under his command require it, he will exercise—as he has already most freely done—this extraordinary power, and will prescribe fully by whom, when, in what way, to what extent, and in what nature these contributions shall be levied. The allowance of the Government to the Army, issued through the quartermaster's and subsistence departments, are to be obtained by commanders, by requisitions on the proper officers of these departments; and if they have not the supplies to meet these requisitions they will apply to their superiors in the department, and the articles will be furnished, if on hand, if the requisition be approved, or means will be taken to procure them. No one has the right to take private property for public uses than those whom the major-general commanding may authorize. Those who take for private uses will be tried by a military commission for stealing. Commanders are especially enjoined to protect growing crops, and not suffer them to be trodden down save in cases of manifest necessity. No one has a right to enter private houses, and thus disturb non-combatants, women, and children. The above, without in any way wishing to seem even to interfere or suggest to others the course to be pursued in respect to the subject here in question, will apply to the troops of the Department of the Rappahannock, whether within or beyond the department limit.

By command of Major-General McDowell:

SAML. BRECK,
*Assistant Adjutant-General.*

DEPARTMENT OF THE RAPPAHANNOCK,
——— —, 1862.

This certifies that there has been received from the farm of ——— ——— the following military supplies: ———. Such supplies will be accounted for on the property returns of ——— ———, quartermaster, U. S. Army, for the quarter of ———. The owner of said property will be entitled to be paid for the same after the suppression of the rebellion, upon proof that he has, from this date, conducted himself as a loyal citizen of the United States, and has not given aid or comfort to the rebels.

Done under authority of ——— ———.

——— ———,
*Quartermaster.*

The recorder here stated to the court that he believed he had as much matter as he would have time to record.

The court authorized the recorder to employ a citizen as clerk at a daily compensation to be fixed at a future period.

The recorder was directed to summon Professor Tefft, now or late chaplain of a Massachusetts regiment, whose name has been communicated to the court as having knowledge of facts inculpating General McDowell.

The court adjourned to meet on Monday, December 1, 1862, at 11 o'clock a. m.

*NINTH DAY.*

COURT-ROOM,
*Washington, D. C., December* 1, 1862.

* * * * * * *

Col. EDMUND SCHRIVER, a witness, was recalled.

Question by General MCDOWELL. Lay before the court your letter of June 4, 1862, to Brigadier-General Shields.

Answer. The letter is numbered 270, and is found on page 233 official letter-book, dated "Headquarters Department of the Rappahannock, Front Royal, Va., June 4, 1862," which the witness read, as follows:

HEADQUARTERS DEPARTMENT OF THE RAPPAHANNOCK,
*Front Royal, Va., June* 4, 1862.

Maj. Gen. JAMES SHIELDS,
*Commanding Division:*

GENERAL: In transmitting the inclosed general order* I am directed by the major-general commanding to convey to you authority, while your division is acting at a distance from these headquarters, to take such supplies as the troops may need; but in doing so the regular receipts issued for the government of the supplying departments are to be strictly observed.

It is impossible to supply your command with forage, and you must rely upon grazing for the support of the animals.

The same freshet which is delaying your march has taken away both bridges in the Shenandoah, and those in rear of us are reported as going also. This may endanger our supplies. Subsistence for your army has been supplied here to your quartermaster for transportation.

Very respectfully, your obedient servant,

ED. SCHRIVER,
*Colonel and Chief of Staff.*

P. S.—There is no communication with Generals Frémont or Banks.

Question by General MCDOWELL. Where was General Shields at the time this letter was written?

Answer. Near Luray and up the valley of the Shenandoah.

Question by General MCDOWELL. Do you, or not, know if supplies for the army were not frequently and largely ordered to be taken from the inhabitants of the country in which we were operating?

Answer. I do.

Question by General MCDOWELL. What knowledge have you that supplies have been ordered to be taken in large quantities from the inhabitants for the use of the army?

Answer. I have heard General McDowell give such orders repeatedly and I have given them myself in his name.

Question by the COURT. Was there any account kept at your headquarters of supplies drawn from the inhabitants of the country for the support of General McDowell's command? If you answer yes, where is that account?

Answer. I know that orders were given to chiefs of the supplying departments to keep such accounts, but I do not know that it was done regularly or that the accounts would show all the property that was seized under their direction. There were some accounts kept, but I do not know that they were kept regularly, for want of returns from the subordinates or from those who made the seizures.

Question by the COURT. What attention, if any, was given by General McDowell or any member of his staff under him to compel the re-

*No. 18, of June 3, p. 54.

turns or to ascertain what certificates had been given by his commissaries or quartermasters pursuant to his General Orders, Nos. 8 and 18?

Answer. I have repeatedly myself called attention of the chief quartermasters and chief commissaries to the importance of a compliance with the requirements of those orders, and they as frequently replied by stating the difficulties of getting reports and returns of the articles seized. This was done by General McDowell's direction.

Question by the COURT. Have those orders in respect to returns of property seized ever been complied with?

Answer. Yes, in both of the supplying departments.

Question by the COURT. Do you know whether General McDowell gave attention to the sanitary condition and comfort of the troops under his command, by personal inspection, by orders, or in any other manner? And, if yes, state what he has done on the subjects of which you have knowledge.

Answer. I know that General McDowell was solicitous on that subject, and by orders and communications to the commanders and the staff he enjoined upon them attention to the subject, and by his own inspection or through his own staff officers he ascertained the condition of the command in that respect.

Question by the COURT. State what was the condition of the troops under General McDowell in this respect while you were chief of staff.

Answer. It varied; sometimes perfectly satisfactory in my opinion; at other times, after forced or rapid marches, men suffered, and of course were more or less sick.

Question by the COURT. When these circumstances of unusual sickness occurred did General McDowell give any special attention to the subject; and, if so, what?

Answer. Whenever it was necessary, directions were given to the medical department as to the disposition to be made of the sick and of providing necessaries for their comfort.

Question by the COURT. Did General McDowell make the instruction and discipline of his troops the subject of his personal attention? And, if yes, state in what manner, by what means, and to what extent.

General McDowell here stated that he had endeavored to bring the evidence before the court in the order adopted by the court as its plan of investigation.

The question has bearing on the fourth clause of said plan, and as yet the testimony on the second clause has not been exhausted.

General McDowell stated to the court, however, that he did not make these remarks as an objection to the mode of proceeding, but that the witnesses present were intended to give evidence on matter pertaining to the second clause.

The court was cleared.

The court was opened, and the following decision announced by the recorder:

The court are desirous to pursue, as far as they can properly do so, the general course indicated by them for the examination. Embarrassment has arisen in the case in the absence of charges, specifications, witnesses, and judge advocate. When, therefore, a witness is on the stand the court will make such pertinent examination on the whole subject as will assist them in finding and procuring material for further investigation, and will call forth answers to matters arising in the case which are suggested by the witnesses' testimony and the subjects introduced.

Answer. He did, by the issuing of verbal and written orders to the commanders under him, and by inspections, with a view to the enforcement of those orders and instructions, by the correction of abuses on the spot when they came to his knowledge, entering into minutiæ not unfrequently himself, when other means—the usual means—did not effect the object desired.

Question by the COURT. How did the troops under General McDowell's command compare with the troops of the other corps which you have seen in respect to their instruction and discipline?

Answer. I have had no opportunity of making comparisons, except when a division, for instance, joined his corps from abroad and became part of his command. These I found invariably inferior in every respect, as far as I could judge, to his command. I mean by that his command before they joined.

Question by the COURT. Have you any knowledge that his treatment of his officers or men was the occasion of any complaint against him by them or any of them?

Answer. I cannot call to mind any cases at present.

Question by the COURT. Have you been present with him at engagements with the enemy; and, if so, state when and where? State fully.

Answer. I have, at the battle of Cedar Mountain, on the 9th of August, I think; battle of Bull Run, on the 29th and 30th, I think they were, and three days' engagement, more or less, at the Rappahannock Station some time in August.

Question by the COURT. Have you knowledge of any complaints made by his officers or men as to his conduct in battle; and without now stating what the complaints, if any, were, name the persons making them?

Answer. Not of my own knowledge.

Question by the COURT. Have you knowledge of any complaints made by his officers or men as to his arrangement of troops in battle; and without now stating what the complaints, if any, were, name the persons making them?

Answer. No, sir.

Question by the COURT. Have you seen anything in his conduct or management of his troops at such times showing indecision, indiscretion, or want of proper qualities for the command of a division, corps, or department? If so, state fully and particularly what you have seen.

Answer. I have not.

Question by the COURT. Have you known of any occasion of engagement with the enemy by the troops of any other commander or portions of his command when he could have co-operated with them or rendered assistance and failed to do so? If you answer yes, state the occasion and the reasons for such omission?

Answer. I answer no.

Question by the COURT. How long since you entered the military service of the country and during how many years have you served?

Answer. I entered the Military Academy in 1829 and remained in the service till 1846, and resigned. I re-entered the service at the beginning of this war; was reappointed in the service in May, 1861, and have been in the Army since that time.

The court took a recess of 10 minutes.

Question by the COURT. State what orders were given, if any, discriminating between loyal and rebel property-holders in respect to the seizure of supplies for the army, and in respect to the detail of guards and other measures for the protection of persons and property.

Answer. Not being able to call to mind at present any particular cases of discrimination, I will answer that the aim of General McDowell was to protect Union men, and to take the property of rebels for the use of the army without paying for the same. I know two or three cases of Union men's property being taken, which was paid for on it being proven that they were really Union men. I remember also of one safeguard having been given to a Union man. Guards were given, when it was thought proper, to Union and rebel people.

Question by the COURT. State what divisions, brigades, regiments, and batteries composed the different commands of General McDowell, dating from the time of his assignment to a division in the Army of the Potomac, and the names of the officers commanding said divisions, brigades, and regiments.

Answer. I am not prepared to answer it now, but will endeavor to submit it at an early moment.

Question by the COURT. Do you know any other matter or thing relating to the conduct of General McDowell as a general officer, and tending to show that he had at any time been treacherous, inefficient, incapable, or unfaithful? And, if you do, state it fully, as though you were thereto particularly interrogated.

Answer. I do not.

Question by General MCDOWELL. What was General McDowell's command whilst you were with him? Was it ever less than a corps?

Answer. No.

Question by General MCDOWELL. What was done by General McDowell to promote the efficiency of his troops—their mobility and their discipline?

Answer. By making timely calls upon the sub-commanders for reports, or returns, as to the state or condition of supplies of all kinds in possession of their respective commands, with a view to the procurement of any deficiencies in the same, and by ordering the chiefs of the supplying departments to take immediate measures to supply what was needed; by causing commanders of divisions to divest themselves or their troops of all unnecessary articles that would require more transportation than was deemed fit and proper, and by impressing upon them frequently the importance of reducing their trains before going into the field or on marches to the smallest possible limit. With respect to discipline, the issuing of orders and their enforcement, as far as possible, had his particular attention.

Question by General MCDOWELL. Examine the records, and lay before the court the orders and instructions given by General McDowell for promoting the mobility of his army or any part of it.

Answer. I am unable to do it at present, but will submit it.

Question by General MCDOWELL. What was done by General McDowell at Rectortown for the care and comfort of the men left from sickness when he arrived there on his march to Front Royal?

Answer. Finding a detachment of men left there, made up I suppose of different regiments or corps, uncared-for sick men, the general took especial pains personally to have their wants supplied and to rebuke the surgeon in charge for neglecting this important duty toward the men of his command.

Question by General MCDOWELL. What was done by General McDowell in the case of several sick men ordered to Washington from Fredericksburg and who were not cared for by the surgeon in charge?

Answer. On ascertaining the fact he caused the subject to be inquired particularly into, and ordered the arrest and trial of the delinquent officer.

The court adjourned to meet December 2, 1862, at 11 o'clock a. m.

*TENTH DAY.*

COURT-ROOM,
*Washington, D. C., December* 2, 1862.

* * * * * * *

Col. R. D. GOODWIN, a witness, was duly sworn.

Question by the COURT. The witness will examine the letter now handed to him, dated 68 Saint Mark's Place, New York, September 24, 1862, addressed to General Irvin McDowell, signed R. D. Goodwin, and say if he was the author of that letter. The witness examined the letter and said:

Answer. I presume it is. The letter is dated September 24, and is contained in the Sunday Mercury of September 28, 1862, and the letter was written on the 6th September. The editor of the paper changed it to the 24th.

The witness handed to the court a copy of the paper referred to, which letter is same as recorded in proceedings of sixth day.

The witness said:

I beg the court to take into consideration the fact that I have not had sleep for some time, and wish to take this letter and consider it. I do not feel in condition to testify. I feel somewhat nervous this morning, having been detained on the road on my way hither to attend this court. I feel willing, however, if the court insist upon it, to go on. In order, however, to do justice to all parties, and myself in particular, I ask until to-morrow to explain. I do not feel bright enough to go into a lengthy investigation. I will feel better to-morrow.

The court informed the witness that under the circumstances of the case his testimony would not be taken till to-morrow at 11 o'clock a. m.

General McDowell read to the court an extract from the proceedings of Congress of June 25, contained on page 2930 Congressional Globe, of June 27, as follows: (See appendix to this day's proceedings.)

Maj. DAVIS TILLSON, Maine Artillery, was duly sworn:

Question by General MCDOWELL. What was your rank and where were you stationed in May, 1862?

Answer. I was captain of artillery, and stationed at least a portion of the month at Belle Plain, Va. I am not sure of exact dates; I may have been part of my time there and part of the time at Falmouth.

Question by General MCDOWELL. What knowledge have you of a Mr. Hoffman, of Belle Plain, Stafford County, Virginia, and of his property, taken for the public service?

Answer. I recollect distinctly having seen a person of that name at Belle Plain, Va., who stated that he was the owner of the property in that vicinity, including two buildings containing corn. I recollect that he asked me repeatedly how he was to obtain payment for the corn, as it was being taken from these buildings by the quartermaster for the use of public animals; and that, further, I witnessed the removal of the corn from time to time until it all had been taken from the two buildings to which I refer.

Question by General MCDOWELL. How far from the landing at Belle Plain was Mr. Hoffman's house?

Answer. I am unable to say. I do not recollect having been to his house or of having had it pointed out to me.

Question by General MCDOWELL. What do you know of a clover field belonging to Mr. Hoffman used for Government cattle?

Answer. I recollect that some quarter of a mile beyond the encampment of my battery there was a fine field of clover and it was well fenced, and that soon after my arrival at Belle Plain this field was used to graze public animals until the field was completely exhausted. I think the field was afterward used for purposes of drilling. I think I so used it myself.

Question by General MCDOWELL. Have you ever formed an estimate, or can you now form an estimate, of the number of bushels of corn contained in the two houses you refer to?

Answer. I did not make the estimate and have never made it.

Question by General MCDOWELL. How long were you stationed at Belle Plain?

Answer. About a fortnight.

Question by the COURT. Had you knowledge of Special Orders, No. 68, a copy of which has been read to you this morning?

Answer. I had, so far as that portion of it referring to destruction of fences.

Question by the COURT. At what time had the corn in the barns been all taken away?

Answer. Some five or six days, I should say, before my battery was ordered to Falmouth—some time in May.

Question by the COURT. Do you know to what corn this special order of the 26th May is intended to apply? [The order was here shown the witness.]

Answer. I do not know to what particular quantity of corn the order referred.

Question by the COURT. How large was the estate occupied by Mr. Hoffman?

Answer. I have somewhat indistinct recollections of his telling me that it contained some three or four thousand acres. I know that he told me the number of acres, but I do not remember distinctly how many.

Question by the COURT. State, as far as you can from observation, how extensively it was fenced.

Answer. I only saw a comparatively small portion of the estate; that portion, however, was quite well fenced, being divided into several tracts, one of which was a large corn field. Perhaps some two hundred acres may have come under my observation.

Question by the COURT. Was Mr. Hoffman reported to be a Union man or a rebel?

Answer. He avowed himself to be entirely neutral. I can only say, to please the court, that among the soldiers—the only persons present—he had the reputation of being a rebel.

General McDowell here explained, at the suggestion of the court, what he proposed to prove on the subject of this order in connection with the testimony of the witness.

Question by the COURT. Have you knowledge that there were members of Mr. Hoffman's family on his estate, and servants; and, if so, how many persons were there in all?

Answer. I have no knowledge whatever as to the number of persons in his family.

Maj. CLARENCE BROWN, aide-de-camp, a witness, was duly sworn.

Question by General MCDOWELL. What is your rank and position in the military service?

Answer. I am major in the District of Columbia Militia and aide-de-camp to Major General McDowell.

Question by General MCDOWELL. State what you recollect of a Mr. Hoffman, of Belle Plain, coming to see General McDowell in May last, near Brooke's Station, in Stafford County, Virginia, concerning payment for property taken by the army and protection for his home and growing crop. State who were present on the occasion and what was said.

Answer. A Mr. Hoffman, of Belle Plain, asked General McDowell, at Brooke's Station, for a guard to protect his houses and barns. He also asked that the cattle might be kept out of a field of growing grain, and that the Government cattle were tramping down the grain. He stated he had already received an order to have his field protected, and had applied to the officer commanding at Belle Plain to no purpose. General McDowell told me to write to the officer commanding at Belle Plain to furnish guards to protect Mr. Hoffman's property, to rebuild the portion of the fence burned and around the growing grain, and to report compliance with the order to these headquarters. General McDowell said that he could not pay for the property that had been taken—the grain; told Mr. Hoffman to get receipts from the quartermasters who took it.

There were present at Brooke's Station at the time Mr. Hoffman was there the Secretary of War, the Secretary of the Treasury, and the Secretary of State, and some gentlemen accompanying them. There were two gentlemen within hearing, and whom, I think, approved the order written—the Secretary of the Treasury, and I do not remember the name of the other. There was another gentleman there.

Question by General MCDOWELL. Does the witness recollect hearing General McDowell say why he would not pay the claimant?

Answer. I do not recollect.

Question by General MCDOWELL. Have you a copy of the note that you wrote on that occasion?

Answer. I gave it in at the adjutant-general's office headquarters.

Question by General MCDOWELL. Was the guard detailed to protect Mr. Hoffman's house and growing crop in the vicinity of it or his whole plantation?

Answer. The guard was merely to protect what was necessary to the sustenance of Mr. Hoffman's family and the buildings they lived in.

Question by General MCDOWELL. Does the witness know the whereabouts of Mr. Hoffman's house?

Answer. I do not, and never was there.

Question by General MCDOWELL. Was the strength of the guard specified or was it left to the discretion of the commanding officer?

Answer. The strength of the guard was not specified.

Question by the COURT. State whether you have knowledge that any other orders, similar in stringency, were given by General McDowell for the protection of the property of loyal citizens.

Answer. I know that in all cases when it was possible General McDowell protected growing grain and gave orders to that effect.

Question by the COURT. In giving such orders did he discriminate between rebels and Union men; that is, in his orders respecting growing grain?

Answer. I do not remember the orders sufficiently well to answer.

General McDowell here admitted to the court that he protected all growing grain.

Maj. SAMUEL BRECK, assistant adjutant-general, U. S. Army, a witness, was duly sworn.

Question by General MCDOWELL. What position did you occupy in May last on the staff of General McDowell?

Answer. That of assistant adjutant-general.

Question by General McDOWELL. Under what circumstances was Special Orders, No. 68, of May 26, issued?

The witness here referred to the special-order-book before the court.

Answer. General McDowell directed me to order Colonel Meredith to have the house and corn of Mr. Hoffman protected, and he told me at the same time that a similar order had already been given, and directed me to make this order strong and peremptory. With these directions I wrote the order. General McDowell did not see the order I drew up to my knowledge. Those directions that I speak of was all he had to do with it, so far as I know.

Question by General McDOWELL. Did the witness understand the instruction to make the order peremptory to refer to the failure of the commanding officer to comply with previous orders?

Answer. I understood that the cause of the previous directions given me to make the order peremptory was because the first order had not been obeyed, the property having been injured since; and, further, to enforce military discipline.

Question by the COURT. Did General McDowell, in giving you instructions to prepare this order, indicate to you where the corn was, whether in the house or in the barns?

Answer. I do not recollect. I will say further that the impression left on my mind was that Colonel Meredith had violated an express written order, and he was to be given to understand that he had one more opportunity, and only one, to comply with it.

Question by the COURT. Did he indicate to you that corn had been taken from the property of Hoffman for public use or anything on that subject?

Answer. I have no recollection of anything about corn or grain for public use.

Question by the COURT. Have you knowledge whether any measures were taken under the direction of General McDowell to ascertain how much corn would be protected by that order or how many persons would be fed upon it?

Answer. I can only give my general impression. All that I know in regard to this matter, except the directions of General McDowell himself in regard to the order, was derived from conversation with other persons. My impression was that General McDowell had been at Belle Plain, and was familiar with all the circumstances of the case. What other ends he may have had in view, besides those expressed in his directions to me, I did not know.

Question by the COURT. Was there any general rule established by General McDowell defining the quantity of corn or other food to be reserved for persons belonging to the family of the owner?

Answer. None that I know of.

Question by the COURT. Were there any means or sources of information through which the officers and men under the command of General McDowell were instructed as to the special reasons why this order was issued?

Answer. That question I cannot answer. I don't know that there were any, of my own knowledge.

Question by General McDOWELL. Were not the subjects of obtaining supplies and taking property from the inhabitants more especially the duties of the administrative branches of the staff?

Answer. Certainly.

Question by General McDOWELL. Please lay before the court letter of May 16, 1862, to Inspector-General Van Rensselaer, particularly so much as indicates a rule for taking supplies.

Answer. This letter is found on page 189, letter-book, Headquarters Department of the Rappahannock, dated "Opposite Fredericksburg, Va., May 16, 1862," which the witness read, as follows:

HEADQUARTERS DEPARTMENT OF THE RAPPAHANNOCK,
*Opposite Fredericksburg, Va., May 16, 1862.*

Brigadier-General VAN RENSSELAER,
*Inspector-General, &c.:*

GENERAL: It is the direction of the major-general commanding that you proceed with a suitable escort to the cavalry camps of Bayard and Wyndham and thoroughly inspect the same.

You are desired to give special attention to the subject of supplies for the men and horses of their commands, with a view to ascertain what, if any of these, have been improperly acquired from the inhabitants living in the vicinity; such as taking the same without giving the specified receipt to the owner, omitting to take up the same on the quartermaster's and subsistence returns, and issuing them regularly as other supplies.

*You will also inquire whether in any case persons have been left without a reasonable quantity sufficient for the uses of their households.*

An examination of copies of requisitions for the various rations for the last twenty days or more will show whether these regiments have relied chiefly on the regular sources of supply or have resorted to seizures. If the latter, then the necessary receipts, &c., will have to be produced.

Mrs. Seddon, Mrs. Gray, and Mrs. Morson (the latter's letter of complaint is inclosed) have preferred complaints to the general.

He desires you to visit these persons, and, by inquiring of others as well as from them, to learn the justice of their allegations, which are serious.

The general does not wish you to confine your visits to the houses of the persons above named, but expects you to go to others in the neighborhood of the camps, with a view to learning what you can to enable you to make a full report on the subject of these repeated depredations, as alleged.

I am, general, very respectfully, your obedient servant,

ED. SCHRIVER,
*Chief of Staff.*

**The court adjourned to meet at 11 a. m. December 3.**

---

APPENDIX.

**I have here an order from General McDowell that I ask to have read, just to show the principle upon which this accursed war is prosecuted.**

**The secretary read as follows:**

SPECIAL ORDERS, No. 68. } HEADQUARTERS DEPARTMENT OF THE RAPPAHANNOCK,
*Opposite Fredericksburg, Va., May 26, 1862.*

Colonel Meredith, commanding the Fifty-sixth Pennsylvania Volunteers, will furnish from his regiment a guard for the house and property of Mr. L. J. Hoffman, who lives near Belle Plain. Colonel Meredith will see that no more corn is taken from Mr. Hoffman and that no more fencing is disturbed. The guard will be so placed as to make this sure, even if it should be necessary to place a sentinel over every panel of fence.

By command of Major-General McDowell:

SAML. BRECK,
*Assistant Adjutant-General.*

**Mr. WADE. I am told that that Hoffman, whose every panel of fence is to be guarded by a soldier paid for out of our pockets, is as arrant a traitor as there is on the face of God's earth. Now, sir, what say you? Can we reach that property? Can we forage on the enemy? The Senator says no. Restrained by the Constitution, are we? We cannot even take it in the field.**

True copy.

L. H. PELOUZE,
*Lieutenant-Colonel and Recorder Court of Inquiry.*

*ELEVENTH DAY.*

COURT-ROOM,
*Washington, D. C., December* 3, 1862.

* * * * * * *

The recorder stated to the court that the letter contained in the Sunday Mercury of September 28, 1862, presented the court by Col. R. D. Goodwin as a true copy of a letter from himself, is correctly copied in the body of the record of the proceedings of the court on pages 31–35.

Col. R. D. GOODWIN, a witness, was recalled.

Question by the COURT. In your letter you state concerning General McDowell that you have seen him under the influence of liquor both in the field and out. 1st. Have you so seen him? 2d. If so, state fully and particularly when and where.

Answer. I believe I have so seen him. I have seen the general several times in various places. The times I have reference to—first, the first time I thought I noticed him under the influence of liquor was on Pennsylvania avenue, between Fourteenth and Thirteenth streets. We were walking in the same direction—toward Thirteenth street—and my attention was drawn toward him when he reached that portion of the Avenue where there is a kind of inclosure. The general had on an overcoat, which he usually wore in them days, his hand resting upon the hilt of the sword, and walking, not on the sidewalk, but partially toward the middle of the street. He was on foot. I made up my mind at the time of observation that he was certainly under the influence of liquor from the manner in which he was walking and his general appearance. This period I have reference to was previous to General McClellan's going with the army to Fairfax Court-House. It might have been a week; it may have been more; I did not charge my mind with the matter at the time.

Question by the COURT. In this connection state what were the manner and the appearance of General McDowell which gave you the impression that he was under the influence of liquor.

Answer. As I have stated before, I have seen the general at various times. I knew his appearance to be that of a gentleman of full habits, ruddy complexion, &c., but I have never seen him in such a blooming appearance before. His manner of walking seemed to be that of a zigzag manner, apparently very much heated. I am in the habit of seeing parties in that condition, and as it was fashionable here in those days I did not take as much notice of it as I might have otherwise.

Question by the COURT. How near were you to General McDowell on the occasion referred to? State if you had any conversation with him at the time. State more fully the time and place.

Answer. The general passed on the right of me and got a little ahead of me before I noticed his presence; it might have probably been 8 or 10 feet before me, to the front and to the right of me. I did not have any conversation with the general. As regards the hour of the day I could not be positive. I think—I know it was in the afternoon, but what period of the afternoon I cannot readily state. My memory as to time and dates is rather treacherous. The next occasion was at Fairfax Court-House. I was there when General McClellan had a portion of his army there. I think, if my memory serves me, the day I have reference to might have been on the 12th, 13th, or 14th March. It was either the day before or the same day upon which General McClellan ordered a counter-march to Alexandria from that station. From that place I went up to see General McClellan, to have a conversation with him if I could. In front of his headquarters I met General McDowell. I advanced to speak with the general, when I again thought I discovered that he was under the influence of liquor, so much so that I myself felt bad at the time, and I recollect asking myself the question, What we could expect of our Army if they were to be led by such generals? I turned from him sorry and with a considerable degree of disgust. I did not speak with him. I went into the headquarters and did my business there—my errand. I came out. The general was still in front of the building. I did not choose to speak with him. I went on about my business. That is about the sum and substance of what I've got to say on those two points.

Question by the COURT. On this last occasion were there any other persons with you or with General McDowell?

Answer. There were no persons with me. I went alone. There were no officers present on the occasion that I could designate. I did not know a soul present except the general. There were other officers present. There might have been four or five persons. They were to the right of me—to the right-hand side of the building as I was going up. Some four or five persons were there. The general was near enough to me to touch clothes.

Question by the COURT. Describe the manner and appearance of General McDowell which attracted your attention.

Answer. I do not know that I have the powers to describe—that I have to judge when I see a man under the influence of liquor—but I will describe as near as I can. He had a loose, unsteady appearance; his eyes dull. I caught his eye when I looked at him He did not look as he generally looks. In all he bore that appearance that is customary to a man under the influence of liquor. There seemed to be a laxity of the nervous system—rather a careless appearance. There seemed an unsteady gait as he sauntered around. I seen him pause and look vacant. I stood upon the steps of the buildings. I turned around and stood upon the step of the building for the purpose of observing. I here wish to state, Mr. President and gentlemen, I am a friend to humanity, and it grieves me to have to say what I have said; but when I read the general's letter in the Herald I got up from the dinner table——

The witness was here interrupted by the court, which informed him that explanations of the kind were unnecessary, and would only tend to confuse and increase the length of the record.

Question by the COURT. Were you in Ellsworth's camp on the 3d of July, 1861?

Answer. I have in my possession a pass from Colonel Heintzelman dated on that day, and on that day I visited that camp.

Question by the COURT. How long did you remain at that camp?

Answer. I cannot positively say, sir, how long—in the neighborhood of two hours.

Question by the COURT. Was that the occasion to which you refer in your letter, when you visited sick soldiers and heard their stories?

Answer. It was.

Question by the COURT. Had you any opportunity at that time to learn, of your own knowledge, what was the food allowed to the soldiers?

Answer. I think I had; I saw some of their food.

Question by the COURT. What did you see?

Answer. I saw some very hard-looking fat meat, that I would be very hungry to eat it. I was shown a piece of cracker; I've pretty good teeth, but it would be a hard job for me to masticate; I think I tried it. I tasted of the water; it wasn't palatable to me. That is all the food that I understood they had.

Question by the COURT. Where did you see this food?

Answer. In the camp.

Question by the COURT. Did you know the person who exhibited it to you?

Answer. They were all strangers to me.

Question by the COURT. While you were there were you present at any delivery of rations to the men?

Answer. I was not.

Question by the COURT. Was the information—the knowledge rather—of the food furnished to the men, which you acquired at that time, wholly derived from complaints or statements made to you?

Answer. Yes, sir.

Question by the COURT. Did you see any attempt by the soldiers to purchase vegetables?

Answer. I did not, sir.

Question by the COURT. Was the information which you got on that subject derived from the same persons who showed to you the crackers and meat of which you have spoken?

Answer. No, sir.

Question by the COURT. From whom then did you get this information?

Answer. Several soldiers verified the fact.

Question by the COURT. Have you any personal knowledge that any soldier was complained of for plucking an ear of corn?

Answer. Nothing but from the statements made by those parties.

Question by the COURT. Have you any personal knowledge that General McDowell published an order to the rebels authorizing the shooting of any man who trespassed on the property of rebels?

Answer. I have not seen such an order; nothing but the same statement I got in the camp on that occasion. I've heard it talked of by others since.

The Court took a recess of five minutes.

Question by the COURT. Have you any personal knowledge that these same men referred to in your letter were shot at while on picket duty?

Answer. I have not seen them shot at.

Question by the COURT. Have you any personal knowledge of any orders by General McDowell not to return fire upon the rebels?

Answer. I have seen no such orders, except what might appear in newspaper statements.

Question by the COURT. Did you inspect to see what provision was made for the health of General McDowell's troops?

Answer. On that occasion I did, as far as a man without authority could do. I have reference to the occasion when I passed two hours at Alexandria.

Question by the COURT. Are you able to communicate to the court the names of officers or men who can testify as to their knowledge of those facts referred to in your letter and about which you have now been interrogated?

Answer. I am able to give you the name of the leading party who conversed with me on that occasion—John A. Smith. I hold in my hand a memorandum-book which I had with me on that occasion. I don't know where he resides, sir. He was one of Ellsworth's Zouaves—if I recollect aright, a sergeant. There were quite a crowd of them rallied around me in front of the main entrance of the camp. This was after I visited the tents and seen the sick soldiers lying there. They were in a very excited condition; stated they would not serve; seemed to be in a state of mutiny. I begged of them for God's sake to remember their duty to their country. They brought me forward and showed me the place they had been shot at—at [a] little distance from the camp, on the skirt of a ravine, near woods that were there. I have here the name of John Johnson.

Question by the COURT. Did you seek on that occasion an interview with any of the officers belonging to the regiment and did you procure it?

Answer. I did, sir. I asked only after the colonel. I found the colonel was absent from the camp. I did not see any other officer by request.

Question by the COURT. Did you talk with any officers belonging to the camp on that occasion?

Answer. I did.

Question by the COURT. Who were they?

Answer. I don't know the name of any person except the person whose name I have given.

Question by the COURT. Can you state the rank of the officer or officers with whom you conversed?

Answer. I think they were both lieutenants.

Question by the COURT. Did you ask for their names?

Answer. I did not, sir; but I received the name of the captain who was arrested, or said to be arrested.

The presiding officer of the court read to the witness that part of his letter contained between the words "A negro servant" and "never brought to trial," inclusive, found on page 44 of this record.

Question by the COURT. Have you any personal knowledge of any of the facts contained in the paragraph just read to you?

Answer. The only knowledge I have of such facts are that they are *verbatim* as told me by this Smith and verified by those surrounding us.

Question by the COURT. Was this part of the information which you obtained on the occasion of your visit to Alexandria, July 3, 1861?

Answer. Yes, sir.

Question by the COURT. Have you any personal knowledge of a mutiny in that camp?

Answer. I have heard it. As I understand mutiny, I would think insubordination was mutiny. Those parties told me that they were discouraged, and one or more emphatically damned if they would obey any more orders. They would not stand up to be shot at when they had not the opportunity of returning fire; stated that they believed General McDowell to be a rebel sympathizer. I begged them to keep cool and so on.

Question by the COURT. Is this your personal knowledge of a mutiny?

Answer. That is about all, sir. I was only in the camp about two hours.

Question by the COURT. These parties to whom you refer in your answer next preceding the last, were they the same from whom you received the complaints regarding food?

Answer. I don't know as any of them were present who complained of the food; they were those mostly confined in their tents sick whom I seen in reference to the food.

Question by the COURT. Will you give us a statement of persons who can testify from personal knowledge as to the facts set forth in the paragraph of your letter just read to you?

Answer. As I stated before, I was a stranger in that camp. The only name I put to paper was John A. Smith, as an informant. I should think you could get the captain's name—certainly the colonel's—the captain who was arrested.

The court here stated to the witness that if, pending the examination of this case, he can obtain any knowledge of the names of any witnesses whose testimony may be material on any of the points contained in his letter they would wish him to communicate them to the court.

Question by General McDOWELL. What is the position of the witness in the military service of the United States or of his own State?

Answer. I belong to the outside department just now. It is a question to me of doubt, sir. I have my authority from the President and Secretary of War as a colonel, which has never been revoked, but I have not the command.

Question by General MCDOWELL. What does the witness mean by his statement that he has the authority of the President and Secretary of War as a colonel; a colonel of what?

Answer. A colonel of volunteers, from the State of New York.

Question by General MCDOWELL. Of what regiment and what arm of volunteers of the State of New York?

Answer. That known as the President's Life Guards. Infantry, sir. Gotten up by myself.

Question by General MCDOWELL. Did such a regiment as the President's Life Guards, a regiment of volunteers of the State of New York, as the witness refers to, actually exist at the time the witness states he had the authority in question?

Answer. At one time I had under my control 1,200 men. At one time part of the regiment was mustered into service. I base my claim as a colonel on the decision of the Attorney-General of the United States in the case of William Weir, and which I am determined to force upon the Government. I don't wish to mislead the court. I wish to answer questions honorably and truthfully. I have got my letter of withdrawal from the second regiment I was appointed to. I will answer that the regiment did exist under authority of the United States, not under the authority of Governor Morgan, whose authority I ignored, rather as a politician than a patriot. I got my letter of withdrawal from my second regiment at my own request before I got authority to raise the President's Life Guard. I got my letters of acceptance from the President and Secretary of War.

Question by General MCDOWELL. Was the authority given the witness an authority for him to be received as a colonel in a certain contingency, or did it confer upon him the grade of colonel at and from the time it was given him?

Answer. I consider that it conferred upon me the grade of colonel from the time it was given me. I can produce the letter.

Question by General MCDOWELL. Have you ever issued circulars, &c., stating that you were authorized to raise a brigade? If so, state who gave you the authority.

Answer. I have issued those circulars, and the authority was given me by the President of the United States on the 29th day of August, 1861, three or four days, I believe, prior to Governor Morgan's following me here to get his orders.

Question by General MCDOWELL. Have you ever issued circulars signing yourself "General," and by what authority?

Answer. I have, and by the same authority.

Question by General MCDOWELL. Were you ever in the United States service as a general officer?

Answer. I have never been.

Question by General MCDOWELL. Have you ever been in the State service as a general officer? If not, by what authority did you sign yourself a general officer?

Answer. I have never been in the State service as a general officer, and the only authority I have for so doing I have already stated. My authority as colonel is in writing. My authority as general is oral, from the President, who solemnly assured me my men should be accepted. He reiterated that pledge.

Question by General MCDOWELL. Was the regiment of volunteers which the witness states he was authorized to raise ever raised and organized? If so, why was it not mustered into service?

Answer. I have stated that it was in part mustered into the service of the United

States during my stay in New York. There was one full company and fragments of others, as they came in. I had sworn in myself about 800 men. As far as I could organize it, it was. The way I understand it, sir, I would not think the regiment organized until it was entirely full. They were regularly mustered into the service by an order which reads as follows:

The witness read:

WAR DEPARTMENT, *July* 22, 1861.

Col. R. D. GOODWIN,
*Commanding President's Life Guard, Present:*

SIR: Your regiment is accepted, and will be mustered in at once.
Respectfully, your obedient servant,
By order of Secretary of War:

JAMES LESLEY, JR.,
*Chief Clerk.*

And that I might go on toward completion I requested the President to assure me that my men should be accepted if I laid out any money.

The court authorized the payment of $3 per diem to clerk employed by the court.

The court adjourned to meet at 11 a. m. December 4, 1862.

---

## *TWELFTH DAY.*

COURT-ROOM, NO. 467 SOUTH FOURTEENTH STREET,
*Washington, D. C., December* 4, 1862.

* * * * * * *

Question by General MCDOWELL. What organization had the regiment to which you have referred; how many companies? What field officers, if any, besides yourself? Was any enrollment made? If so, was this enrollment by companies?

Answer. May it please this much respected court, previous to going into the cross-examination, believing I notice a disposition on the part of the gentleman—General McDowell—to try and impeach my veracity and lessen me in my own estimation, if not that of the nation——

The court objected to the course which the reply of the witness was taking as containing matter wholly irrelevant.

The witness continued: I simply ask the opportunity of asking a few questions—one or two—and offer a few remarks, that may expedite the proceedings of the court. I owe this to myself and do it in my own defense. I do not propose an address. I came here as an unwilling witness, and am fully aware of the grave charges I have made against the officer.

The court here informed the witness that he had the right to state his objection to any question, against answering which he is entitled to protection. The witness continued: I would ask the general if he means to impeach my veracity.

The court informed the witness that it did not see that the questions thus far propounded gave rise to the construction placed upon them by the witness.

The recorder again repeated the question.

Answer. On yesterday I stated there was one full company enrolled and mustered in by the regular United States officer, fully armed and equipped and uniformed, and provided for by the United States under me, and, by my authority as colonel, I appointed, I forget the first name—the surname—I think it was George W. Fisher; however, it was Fisher, as my lieutenant-colonel; also ——— Whitney as my major. George W. Fisher had been an officer in the service and Major Whitney had served as a colonel in the New Hampshire Militia. The post of adjutant remained vacant, as I wished to fill it by a very competent person.

At the instance of a member the court was cleared.

The court was opened and the following decision was announced.

On cross-examination of a witness General McDowell has the right to elicit facts tending to impair the credibility of the testimony against him.

Within reasonable limits he may inquire into the previous history of the witness, but the answers must be directly responsive.

If this line of examination shall appear to the court to be unduly extended the court will arrest it.

The court directs that so much of the answers of the witness as describe the qualifications of his officers and his reasons for omitting to appoint an adjutant be erased from the record.

The court directed the recorder to read again the question.

By the WITNESS. Previous to the reading of the question, will the court permit me to state that I have some important facts——

The court interrupted the witness, informing him that a question for his answer is now before the court.

The recorder read the question.

Answer. I find on my regimental rolls Charles J. Whitney as my major.

The witness continued: Pardon my simplicity. I wish to answer the questions properly. I do not understand a field officer——

The court interrupted the witness, and requested that the answer of the witness might be responsive to the question.

The witness continued:

I had my lieutenant-colonel and my major as field officers. If you want my line officers, I will say I had my captains and lieutenants. They were enrolled by myself. There was an enrollment made by companies and sanctioned by the Government of the United States. There was a legal enrollment made. There was but one full company.

Question by General MCDOWELL. In your last answer you state there was but one full company. How many incomplete companies had you?

Answer. I suppose the court is aware how those regiments were organizing—incomplete companies. If I take my own view of the matter all the companies were incomplete except one; that is full. I had nine incomplete companies.

Question by General MCDOWELL. Does the witness remember where his complete company was mustered into the service of the United States, and by what United States officer it was so mustered in?

Answer. On Staten Island, in Camp Washington, by Captain Hemans [Hayman?]—I think it was—Seventh Regiment U. S. Regulars.

Question by General MCDOWELL. Did the witness mail to General McDowell's address or otherwise send to him the letter which was published in the New York Sunday Mercury?

Answer. I did not know [the] general's address. I did not know where he was—did not know his address at the time, and did not care.

Question by General MCDOWELL. Witness states he wrote the letter which is dated September 24, 1862, on September 6, 1862. Is the witness positive as to the date on which he actually wrote the letter in question?

Answer. I could only say it was on the same day that the letter was published in the New York Herald. I think it was on the 6th.

Question by General MCDOWELL. At the time you state you saw General McDowell on Pennsylvania avenue under the influence of liquor, state if the general continued to walk in the roadway of the Avenue itself as long as he remained within your sight.

Answer. You walked in the roadway, sir, as long as I saw you at that time.

Question by General McDOWELL. How far from the sidewalk?

Answer. It might have been—if you recollect at that point there is a street diverging; from that there is a flagging which crosses the converging point. It might have been 6, 8, or 10 feet south of the north side of the Pennsylvania avenue, or where pedestrians walk.

Question by General McDOWELL. How near was he to Fourteenth street when you first saw him?

Answer. I can't exactly say how far.

Question by General McDOWELL. Where were you at the time you first saw General McDowell on that occasion?

Answer. I was walking on the avenue.

Question by General McDOWELL. What particular part of the Avenue?

Answer. Just at the converging point there of the Avenue. I think it was E street. I took the course toward E street.

Question by General McDOWELL. How far up the Avenue toward E street did you walk, having, as you have stated, General McDowell to the front and right of you?

Answer. I walked toward the junction of these two streets. I took E street and he went on the Avenue.

Question by General McDOWELL. How long did you have General McDowell in sight when you went up E street and he went up the avenue?

Answer. Not but a very short time. I did not turn my attention toward him after we separated.

Question by General McDOWELL. Did you speak to him?

Answer. I never spoke to the general in my life until in the court.

Question by General McDOWELL. Did he speak to you or to any one at the time you saw him?

Answer. No, sir; not that I see.

Question by General McDOWELL. What object did the general seem to have in view at the time he was walking up the Avenue? Were there any persons in the Avenue near him either on foot or on horseback.

Answer. I am sure I could not tell you what his object was; there was people around as usual—nothing remarkable—nothing that I remarked, except himself.

Question by the COURT. To what letter do you refer as having read it in the Herald and as being defiant, and which you think was on the 6th of September?

Answer. The letter purporting to come from General McDowell, addressed to the President of the United States.

Question by the COURT. When you first observed General McDowell, and thought him under the influence of liquor, do you mean to be understood that he was near the crossing over E street?

Answer. Well, he took the Avenue direct. I took the Avenue direct to the crossing over E street. It was near to the crossing.

Question by the COURT. Can you state the month in which this occurred?

Answer. Yes; it must have either been the commencement of March or the latter part of February.

Question by the COURT. Do you remember whether the roads were dry or muddy at the time?

Answer. Well, I cannot very well. I don't think that they were very dry. I do not recollect.

(The witness was shown a diagram.)

Question by the COURT. Point out on the diagram as near as you can where General McDowell was when you saw him.

The witness pointed out upon the diagram the relative position occupied by General McDowell and self on the diagram, which is appended to this day's proceedings.*

Question by the COURT. On which side of E street did you continue your walk?

(The witness referred to the diagram.)

Answer. I crossed over E street, and passed along the north side.

The court informed the witness that they would receive from him a written list of any witnesses who could give important testimony in the case, and that the question or statement which he stated he desired to make will be considered if in writing.

The evidence of the witness was read by the recorder.

The witness here desired that the following corrections be made:

I think you called my lieutenant-colonel "Whitely" when you mentioned him the second time; his name is Whitney.

You are again in error in saying Charles J.; it should be Charles K.

Col. GEORGE D. RUGGLES, aide-de-camp, and assistant adjutant-general, a witness, was duly sworn.

Question by General MCDOWELL. What was your military rank and position in the summer of 1861?

Answer. On the 1st day of July, 1861, I was assistant adjutant-general in the Regular Army, with the rank of captain. I held that position during the remainder of the summer. In the month of June I was lieutenant and adjutant Second Regiment of infantry.

Question by General MCDOWELL. By your official position in the Adjutant-General's Office was it your special province to keep the records, &c., of all the volunteer forces?

Answer. It was, from the time I entered the office on duty on the 2d day of July, 1861, till I left it on the 28th June, 1862.

Question by General MCDOWELL. Do you know of a R. D. Goodwin having been a colonel of volunteers in the United States service in the summer of 1861; and also whether he was in the United States military service as an officer of any other rank in 1861?

Answer He never was in the United States service. I know such a man.

Question by General MCDOWELL. Are you acquainted with R. D. Goodwin and had you any official intercourse with him? If so, please state it.

Answer. I am acquainted with him. I had official intercourse with him during the year I was in the Adjutant-General's Office. I first saw him 22d July, 1861. He came to the War Department, offering to the Secretary of War a regiment of volunteers. He stated that he "had then 500 men on the Battery in New York, and could raise many more." This regiment was accepted on that day.

The court desire to know of General McDowell what he desires to prove by the question propounded the witness before the court.

---

*Omitted as unimportant.

General McDowell replied "the character and credibility of the witness."

The court was cleared.

The court was opened, and the following decision announced:

General McDowell having avowed that the object of his question was to impeach the character and credibility of the witness, the court rule that the question is incompetent for that purpose, so far as it calls for facts contradicting the testimony of the witness in relation to the organization, &c., of his regiment or brigade.

The cross-examination on that subject was by General McDowell on collateral points, in respect to which he cannot make new issues and introduce rebutting witnesses for the purpose of impeachment; but the court will receive competent testimony to contradict the witness in his evidence on material points or impeach his general character for truth and veracity.

The court adjourned to meet to-morrow, the 5th December, 1862, at 11 o'clock a. m.

---

*THIRTEENTH DAY.*

COURT-ROOM, No. 467 SOUTH FOURTEENTH STREET,
*Washington, D. C., December* 5, 1862.

The court met pursuant to adjournment. Present, * * * .

Col. GEORGE D. RUGGLES, aide-de-camp and assistant adjutant-general, the witness under examination.

* * * * * * *

The recorder informed the court that he has received a communication from R. D. Goodwin, dated Washington, December 5, 1862, which was read, as follows:

LOUIS H. PELOUZE,
*Lieutenant-Colonel and Recorder, Court of Inquiry:*

By request of the court I do hereby inform you that P. Clark, esq., late of Fredericksburg, Va., now stopping at Willard's Hotel, in this city, has informed me of very grave charges which he can make against Major-General McDowell as to his disloyalty, &c. He may leave the city soon if not summoned. I expect more facts this evening from another person; if so, I will inform you.

Respectfully, your obedient servant,

R. D. GOODWIN.

WASHINGTON, D. C., *December* 5, 1862.

The court instructed the recorder to send for Mr. Clark, with a view to ascertaining what is the character of his testimony as pertaining to the matter under investigation.

Question by General McDOWELL. What do you know of the general character of R. D. Goodwin for veracity and what is his character in that respect?

The court was cleared at the instance of a member.

The court was opened, and the following decision announced:

The question is incompetent. The witness cannot be examined as to particular facts, but ought first to be asked substantially whether he has the means of knowing the general character of the witness for truth and veracity. If the witness answers that he has such knowledge, then the question will be competent, inquiring as to the character in that respect.

General McDowell here presented to the court a paper, which was read by the recorder, and which is appended to this day's proceedings.

General McDowell stated that he had no more questions to ask this witness at present.

The court had no questions to ask the witness.

Maj. Gen. S. P. HEINTZELMAN, U. S. Volunteer Army, witness, was duly sworn.

Question by General McDOWELL. What command had you on the 3d of July, 1861? About how long prior to the 3d of July, 1861, did you exercise that command?

Answer. I commanded the troops stationed in and around Alexandria. I think I went to Alexandria about the last day of May from here.

Question by General McDOWELL. Was the regiment of volunteers known as Ellsworth's a part of your command at the time mentioned? If so, in whose brigade was it and where was it stationed?

Answer. It was part of my command. It was stationed near Fort Ellsworth. I am not certain, but think it was in Willcox's brigade.

Question by General McDOWELL. Examine the letter of R. D. Goodwin of September 24, 1862, and state what you know concerning the statements therein made.

The letter referred to was handed to the witness.

Answer. Some of these statements I know nothing about; but those that I am familiar with are not true. In relation to drunkenness, I have known the general a long time, and have never seen him drink. I have sat at the table for weeks at a time with him and have met him at various times and places. He was at my headquarters on the 3d July. (I recollect the date from a conversation we had about some military matters relating to the Army.) Ellsworth's regiment was remarkably healthy at that time. I don't recollect any complaints about musty crackers, bad provisions, or bad water. When the men first came out to the field they wouldn't drink out of a clear running stream, but would crowd around a pump or a spring. As to whether the rebels would sell them vegetables or not I know nothing about it. I never saw any order authorizing rebels to shoot people for trespassing. There were great efforts to stop this picket firing.

About the case of Richard Windsor I know nothing at all; never heard of it before that I recollect. Such cases usually came to me. There was a man by the name of Windsor, who lives a few miles below Alexandria. I believe he is a secessionist. He was outside our lines for a long time. I don't recollect that there was any mutinous conduct in the regiment of Zouaves or not; they were very troublesome and hard to manage. There were constant complaints of their depredations by the inhabitants. The volunteers disliked the hard bread very much, and there were constant complaints on that subject. The hard bread was good. There was no difficulty in getting provisions. If there was any deficiency, it was owing to the neglect of their own officers. There were no greater difficulties there than there always are when new troops come into the field.

Question by General McDOWELL. What do you understand to be the practice at present sought to be maintained in the army as to picket firing, so called?

Answer. We made every effort on the Peninsula to discourage it.

Question by the COURT. During how many years have you been intimately acquainted with General McDowell?

Answer. I do not recollect. 'Tis so long that I've forgotten the number of years.

Question by the COURT. During the time you have known him have his habits, in respect to the use of intoxicating liquors, been the subject of any particular observation and remark?

Answer. Yes. I have heard it frequently spoken of. He was considered remarkably abstemious. I believe he don't drink tea or coffee, no wines or liquors; totally abstemious.

Question by the COURT. Would an order from General McDowell, at the time you were under his command, from May to July, 1861, authorizing soldiers to be shot when trespassing on property, have passed through your office?

Answer. Orders of that kind would pass through my office.

Question by the COURT. If there had been any official complaint as to the provisions, would they have been known to you and have passed through you to General McDowell?

Answer. That is the usual course; but persons have often gone to the President and Secretary of War, and we have got complaints from that quarter. I frequently got complaints of depredations by the Zouaves from General Scott and the Secretary of War generally through General McDowell, who was commander of the troops on the other side of the river. I might add, there were no well-founded complaints about provisions that could not have been remedied by the officers of the regiments themselves. The Government made ample provision for the feeding of the troops.

Question by the COURT. Did you hear of the arrest of Colonel Windsor by a captain and squad of men belonging to the Ellsworth regiment, referred to in the letter of Colonel Goodwin?

Answer. I've no recollection of anything of the kind. Those men did so many outrageous things, I don't know what they didn't do. Such matters usually came to me, and I decided them.

Question by the COURT. Was there any order for the arrest of a captain of the Ellsworth regiment, transmitted by General McDowell, having any relation to Mr. Windsor?

Answer. I don't recollect anything of the kind, and I don't think there was.

Question by the COURT. Did the orders at that time prohibit firing by our pickets when such pickets were fired at by the rebels?

Answer. I don't recollect that there were any specific orders on the subject, but I think not. We tried to prevent it in every way we could.

The testimony of the witness was read by the recorder.

Major-General Heintzelman stated that the words "I think not," in his answer to the last question, are intended as a reply to the question as it reads. The witness added: I do not mean to say that there were no orders on the subject of picket firing.

Maj. CLARENCE BROWN, aide-de-camp, a witness, was recalled.

Question by General McDOWELL. Did you ever make any inspection by order of General McDowell, to see that the property taken from the inhabitants of the country for the use of the troops was regularly taken up and accounted for?

Answer. I did, opposite Fredericksburg, at Falmouth; the Second New York Volunteer Cavalry.

The court had no questions to ask the witness.

The court adjourned to meet to-morrow, December 6, 1862, at 11 o'clock a. m.

---

## APPENDIX.

I am and have been loth to consume the trial and tax the patience of the court in the matter of the character of R. D. Goodwin. I have thought in this case, which the court has already ruled was an exceptional one, I could show what I am assured and believe is the fact, that the witness has attempted to pass forged papers on the Government, and has been an inmate of one of the New York penitentiaries. I am not acquainted with the practice of civil courts, and have felt in this case such acts must be sufficient to discredit the witness among military men.

IRVIN McDOWELL,
*Major-General.*

DECEMBER 5, 1862.

---

*FOURTEENTH DAY.*

COURT-ROOM, No. 467 SOUTH FOURTEENTH STREET,
*Washington, D. C., December* 6, 1862.

* * * * * * *

Brig. Gen. HERMAN HAUPT, U. S. Volunteers, a witness, was duly sworn.

Question by General McDOWELL. What official connection had you with the late Department of the Rappahannock?

Answer. I held the position of chief of construction and transportation on the military railroads.

Question by General McDOWELL. What was the principal work you performed in connection with the construction and management of the railroads in the late Department of the Rappahannock?

Answer. The reconstruction of the wharf and buildings at Aquia Creek; the reconstruction of about 3 miles of railroad which had been torn up and the iron removed by the enemy, and the bridges across Accokeek and Rappahannock Rivers and Potomac Creek. In addition to this, the reconstruction of seven bridges on the Manassas Gap road, the relaying of a portion of the track on that road, and the forwarding of supplies to the army by both roads.

Question by General McDOWELL. What is your present position with respect to the railroads in Virginia? Have you again had to rebuild some of the Aquia Creek Railroad?

Answer. I have at present the general charge of the construction and transportation of the railroads in Virginia and Maryland, with other duties prescribed in Special Orders, 248, Adjutant-General's Office, and I have again rebuilt a portion of the Fredericksburg and Potomac Railroad.

Question by General McDOWELL. Look at the statement herewith in the New York Tribune, comparing the time required to rebuild the Aquia and Fredericksburg Railroad under General McDowell's administration and the time taken under the present commander in Virginia, and state if the contrast is a just one; if not, wherein is it not so.

The statement, as embraced between the words "a ride" and "inspiration," is as follows:

A ride upon the cars to Aquia Creek to-day gave me a view of what General Haupt has accomplished within the past ten days in repairing the road from the Potomac to Falmouth. What it took nearly ten months last spring to reconstruct has been accomplished in about one-sixth of that time. Nearly all the labor then was performed by soldiers, this time by contrabands; or, to call them by a better name, loyal blacks have performed nearly all the hard labor. I saw hundreds of them at work to-day all along the line of the road, at the depots, upon the wharves, on the boats, or wherever there was anything to be lifted, carried, driven, or raised. They were working, too, with a will, not with one arm slowly following the other up and down, or one leg moving after the other as if they were on their way to the gallows, but with a rapid swing and a quick step, giving one to see in every blow and every movement that fifty cents a day, food and rations, and individual freedom are the sources of inspiration.

Answer. The statements in the Tribune are correct in several particulars. The work was not commenced on the Aquia Creek and Fredericksburg road before the 1st day of May, 1862, and before the 1st day of June we were operating on the Manassas Gap road; consequently the time required to reconstruct that road was less than one month, instead of requiring ten days, as has been stated. The difficulties at that time in performing the work were much greater than at present. The weather was rainy, the roads excessively muddy, the nights very dark, and rails were laid at night by the use of lanterns; whereas in the recent reconstruction the night work was done by the light of the moon; the amount to be reconstructed was not so large as at first, and the destruction of the wharf was not as complete as in the first place, and no portion of the track had been torn up. This would be sufficient to account for the difference in time, the exertions in both cases being equal. When first reconstructed General McDowell was daily upon the work, giving it his personal attention and urging it forward with all possible celerity. There was less bridge work during the last reconstruction than on the former occasion, part of the bridges being found standing.

**Question by General McDowell. Were colored fugitives employed by General McDowell's orders in the construction and management of the railroads in the departments under his command? If so, to what extent?**

Answer. They were employed, and to the extent of all that could possibly be procured. I will remark, informally, that at that time it was very difficult to keep men on the road. They were all bound for Washington, as they said, to see "Massa Lincoln."

**Question by General McDowell. Under what regulations as to food pay, &c., were they so employed?**

Answer. The amount of pay was prescribed in a printed order, I believe, issued by General McDowell, giving them, I believe, one ration and a certain price per day. The amount now I do not recollect. I think it was 40 cents, but I am not positively certain.

**Question by General McDowell. Was the amount of pay graduated according to industry or capacity?**

Answer. I don't remember any special orders on that subject; but those who would not work were promptly discharged.

**Question by General McDowell. What rule did General McDowell establish as to the property of the inhabitants of the country required for the use of the troops under his command?**

Answer. That it should be taken whenever necessary for the use of the army, but always by proper requisition. General McDowell claimed the privilege, as he frequently said, of being the only plunderer in the Army of the Rappahannock. He would take what he needed for the use of the army, but would not permit his men to plunder on private account. When property was taken, receipts were given as evidence of the fact. Orders were given to leave subsistence sufficient to keep families from starvation.

**Question by General McDowell. To what extent was the property of the inhabitants taken for the reconstruction of the railroad and the bridges over the Rappahannock, Potomac Creek, &c., and for the management of the road in Fredericksburg?**

Answer. Lumber was taken wherever it could be found. Nearly all the timber suitable for bridging was exhausted in the vicinity of Potomac Creek, and all of the timber of suitable dimensions that could be found in Fredericksburg was used in reconstructing the bridge across the Rappahannock. A large machine shop and foundery, with all the machinery and tools pertaining thereto and the materials on hand, were appropriated for the use of the road in Fredericksburg.

**Question by General McDowell. What attention did General McDowell give to the preparation of his command and the improvement of the means of communication with his forces and preparations for their advance beyond Fredericksburg?**

Answer. The attention given by General McDowell to the details of the work frequently excited my surprise. He was almost constantly upon the road, and sometimes anticipated wants before I had thought of them myself. This was particularly illustrated in ordering a large number of oxen to haul timber at Potomac Creek before any workmen were upon the ground. He was daily engaged in discussing with me plans to secure the earlier completion of the communications, and was very impatient to advance beyond Fredericksburg, with a view to co-operate with General McClellan in his movements against Richmond.

Question by General McDOWELL. What arrangements were made by General McDowell for the reconstruction of the bridge over the Massaponax, south of Fredericksburg, at the time it was in the possession of the enemy?

Answer. That the enemy had prepared combustibles and placed them in position for the purpose of burning the bridge across the Massaponax, 6 miles south of Fredericksburg; that the reconstruction of this bridge would give him 25 continuous miles of railroad over which supplies could be thrown. He asked me if it were not possible to have a bridge ready, and what time would be required to reconstruct it. I replied that I could have a bridge framed and loaded on cars and put it up in half a day. The arrangement then was to move forward on the following Monday, leaving me to reconstruct the communications and forward the supplies, until which time he would rely upon his wagons. It was on Monday, 26th of May, that the forward movement was to take place, this time having been arranged a day or two previous—I do not recollect how long, but it was on the occasion of a visit from the President. I recollect that General McDowell was anxious to march on Sunday. General McDowell used expressions to this effect to the President in my presence: "I will not be quite ready to move on Saturday, as Shields' command is badly off for supplies, which will be received on that day, but by Sunday morning I will be ready." The President remarked, "Take a good ready, and move on Monday morning," or words to that effect.

Question by General McDOWELL. What means of communication had General McDowell established over the Rappahannock at Fredericksburg for the passage of his army?

Answer. A very substantial bridge of barges and a pontoon bridge, previous to the construction of the railroad bridge. By his direction the railroad bridge was also planked to admit of the transportation of artillery, infantry, and wagons; subsequently a wire-suspension bridge was constructed; also a trestle bridge; in all, four bridges.

Question by General McDOWELL. Had you an opportunity of seeing General McDowell's forces at Fredericksburg? If so, state what was their state as to discipline and efficiency, and how supplied and equipped at the time they were about to leave for Richmond.

Answer. I merely saw a portion of the forces in passing to and from headquarters. I know that they were well supplied, but can give no information in regard to other particulars.

Question by General McDOWELL. What was the effect of the murder of Robert E. Scott on the inhabitants of the country? Did you mention this to General McDowell?

Answer. The effect was to excite a very strong feeling of indignation throughout the community, and the fact was used against us with great effect. Robert E. Scott was represented as a very influential man, opposed to secession, and so strongly in favor of the Union as to gain the ill-will of many of his friends and neighbors. He was shot down, as I understood, by our men when in the performance of some friendly mission. The case was frequently referred to by residents along the line of the road as an evidence of the character of the Union forces. I believe that I did repeat to General McDowell the representation that had been made to me on this subject.

Question by General McDowell. What acts of violence on the women of the country came to your knowledge near Fredericksburg? Did you report anything of this to General McDowell?

Answer. I reported one case, which occurred within 3 miles of Potomac Bridge. A rape was committed upon the daughter of a farmer who had rendered me material assistance in searching for timber through the woods. I inquired of the parents in regard to the facts, and found that the act had been perpetrated by one of the numerous stragglers who were continually passing through the country in every direction, and from whose ravages not a single farm-house in the vicinity of the road was exempt, except when guarded, and not always even then. While searching for timber I met these stragglers in every direction, often miles from the road. I reported these facts to General McDowell previous to the issue of his order on the subject of rape.

Question by General MCDOWELL. What discrimination did General McDowell make in paying for property taken by his order; whom did he pay and whom not?

Answer. I am not familiar with that subject. I only recollect in general that he directed receipts to be given, payable on the termination of the war, on proof of loyalty. I am not even certain that this is the precise condition on which receipts were given, but it was something to that effect.

Question by General MCDOWELL. What do you know of General McDowell's conduct at Rectortown, when he first arrived there on his way to Front Royal last May, with respect to the men left sick at that place by the advance divisions?

Answer. All I recollect about it is the use of some very strong expressions of indignation against some surgeon who had not properly attended to the sick under his charge.

Question by the COURT. Do you know any matter or thing tending to show that General McDowell has been treacherous, incompetent, or inefficient as a general officer, or that he has failed in the employment of his forces to co-operate with other commanders as far as he had any discretionary power?

Answer. No facts have ever come to my knowledge tending to show that such was the case. All that I have seen or heard from reliable sources would tend to convey the contrary impression.

Question by the COURT. Have you personal knowledge that his treatment of his officers or men was the occasion of any complaint against him by them or any of them?

Answer. I have some knowledge of that subject. I have heard complaints by members of his staff that he worked them to death; and on one occasion, at which I was personally present, three officers of his staff were sent to Piedmont through a drenching rain, and required to remain all night, to superintend personally the unloading of cars. This was a subject of some complaint at the time. No facts have come to my knowledge in regard to the treatment of the men.

Question by the COURT. Have you knowledge of any complaint made by his officers or men as to his conduct in battle or of his arrangement of troops in battle?

Answer. I have no knowledge of any complaints. I have heard members of his staff speak highly of his conduct in battle and of the personal courage he had exhibited on several occasions. I have heard no criticism on the subject of his arrangements of troops from either his officers or men.

Question by the COURT. Have you seen anything in his conduct or management of troops showing indecision, indiscretion, or want of proper qualities for the command of a division, corps, or department? If so, state fully and particularly what you have seen?

Answer. My answer is, I have not.

Question by the COURT. When did you first enter the military service and how long have you been in it?

Answer. I entered as a cadet at West Point in 1831; resigned from the Army in the fall of 1835, and was not again engaged in the military service until last spring, when telegraphed by the Secretary of War to come to Washington.

Question by General MCDOWELL. What were the circumstances or exigencies of the service at the time you refer, of complaints on the part of certain officers of their being required to superintend the unloading of cars in the rain?

Answer. A necessity existed for a prompt unloading of the cars in order to return them for additional supplies I don't recollect any other exigency at this time.

Question by General McDOWELL. Had you not great difficulty in getting cars unloaded at this time, and were we not on a forced march to reach Front Royal by a given time for an important purpose?

Answer. Such is the fact.

Question by General McDOWELL. Was not General McDowell himself actively engaged during that same night, directing the operations for opening the road, unloading the cars at Rectortown?

Answer. I can't tell whether it was the same night or the preceding night he was so engaged. It was one or the other; and either the same night or the next night he rode to Front Royal on horseback.

Maj. DAVIS TILLSON, Maine Artillery, a witness, was recalled.

Question by General McDOWELL. You have testified in your previous examination that you were in command of a battery at Belle Plain, Va., in May, 1862. State, as far as you know, the position of Belle Plain as respects the military operations then going on at Fredericksburg.

Answer. Belle Plain is 8 miles, I think, below Aquia Creek. Upon my arrival there there were no wharves, bridges, or preparations of any kind for landing troops or supplies. It was immediately made a depot by the erection of the necessary works. Lieutenant Ross was placed in command, and large amounts of stores of different kinds were landed, from whence they were taken to Fredericksburg.

Question by General McDOWELL. What personal attention, if any, did Major-General McDowell give to this station, the works progressing, and the troops stationed there?

Answer. General McDowell went from Aquia Creek with the troops under the command of Lieutenant-Colonel Leech, Ninetieth Pennsylvania Volunteers, the first, I think, that was sent there. My own battery arrived soon after. Before the troops were landed General McDowell went up to the place selected for landing, and personally superintended the construction of a small bridge from the bank to one or more canal-boats that were fastened conveniently for that purpose. Soon after, on the same day or the next, the men of my own battery were landed, and under the immediate supervision of General McDowell cut down the lumber and built a new bridge, over which horses, mules, and a battery of artillery, and a heavily loaded train of pontoon wagons were disembarked. I recollect this bridge occupied in its construction between three and four hours. I afterward had the curiosity to measure it, and found it to be a little over 70 feet in length. I saw General McDowell repeatedly after this at this station, and received from him orders to do everything possible to forward supplies with the greatest rapidity. I know that he gave similar orders to a Lieutenant Ross and other officers.

Question by General McDOWELL. What supplies, if any, for your command did you take from the neighborhood, under what orders, and through what forms?

Answer. I took, I think, just 41 bushels of corn for the use of my battery horses. I did this in compliance with orders from Lieutenant-Colonel Myers, General McDowell's chief quartermaster. The form was in substance this: It stated the place and person to whom the property belonged, the amount taken, and that it would be paid by the United States at the expiration of the war should the owner thereof be able to prove satisfactorily that he had been a true and loyal man from the date of the certificate. My own certificate given in this instance may have varied somewhat from this.

Question by General McDOWELL. What orders, if any, did you receive, as chief of artillery, as to the employment of colored men as drivers of battery wagons, &c.? On what basis was the rate of pay established, if you know?

Answer. While at Falmouth, and having already employed several negroes as drivers of army transportation wagons, I received an order from the division headquarters to which I was attached—an order stating, in substance, that contrabands would no longer be employed as drivers, they having shown themselves unfit to have the care of public animals. As the batteries could not well dispense with the services of these negroes, or contrabands, I went to the department headquarters and inquired of Major Myers, General McDowell's chief quartermaster, as to what should be done in the case. He directed me to continue employing them as drivers, and gave them an order setting forth the rates of pay which they were to receive. I am quite sure that the lowest price was one ration and 25 cents per day, and the highest one ration and 40 cents. Some time I think in July—I'm not sure as to the date—I made formal application to be allowed to employ negroes as drivers of battery wagons and forges of the batteries. The application went up to General McDowell through the usual channels, and an order was received from him giving permission to so employ negroes. I recollect also that all the negroes coming to Belle Plain were employed by Quartermaster Ross in various ways—in unloading subsistence and moving stores.

Question by General McDOWELL. What was the condition of General McDowell's command as to discipline and efficiency? How did it compare with other commands that have come under your observation?

Answer. Its discipline and efficiency compared very favorably with any troops I have seen, surpassing in almost every respect the troops that joined his command while at Fredericksburg. I mean General Shields' division. I remember that when General Shields' troops encamped beside my own encampment they immediately began to destroy and burn up the fences, cut down shade trees, and in other ways utterly disregarding the orders relative to the preservation of property, and I know that previous to their arrival such acts were not committed by the troops encamped in the vicinity of my own battery.

A letter was submitted to the court signed R. D. Goodwin, of this date, requesting that General McDowell be permitted to prove all or any charges against the writer, giving him the right to defend himself, which letter was read, as follows:

WASHINGTON, D. C., *December* 6, 1862.

*May it please this honorable court:*

Inasmuch as a letter of impeachment (by way of protest) was read to the court yesterday from General McDowell, I beg that the general be permitted to prove all of any charges against me, giving me the right to defend myself.

I here emphatically deny that I ever was in prison for any crime or that I ever tried to defraud the Government; but I cannot deny that the Government has defrauded me. I believe as far as I stated in my New York letter of General McDowell I have sustained my position before this court. But drunkenness in our nation may be considered no crime. This nation has been on a drunken frolic for years, during which she has been eating up niggers, body and soul, and drinking the heart's blood of the poor white man, whilst she hunted down and manured her soil with the flesh and blood of the red man. But now the "doctor" has given her an emetic, from which she is suffering. Her brain is maddened and her blood is at fever heat. She has *delirium tremens*, and is now tearing the flesh off her own bones, premeditating self-destruction. The head is deranged. I mean the Cabinet is not a unit; the Congress is divided, and the heads of our Army are distracted, not knowing what to do or how to do it. But our Great Father will bring her to know herself. He will give her a cathartic and will purge her of all her dross and filth, after which she will become cool and collected, when she will again return to her senses, and be found clothed and sitting in her right mind once more.

I am the friend of God and humanity, and shall condemn wickedness wherever I see it.

Yours, for truth,

R. D. GOODWIN.

The court decided that in the examination before them such an inquiry would be irrelevant and could not be permitted.

The court adjourned to meet on Monday, December 8, 1862, at 11 o'clock a. m.

---

### *FIFTEENTH DAY.*

COURT-ROOM, 467 SOUTH FOURTEENTH STREET,
*Washington, D. C., December* 8, 1862.

The court met pursuant to adjournment. Present, * * *

Maj. DAVIS TILLSON, Maine Artillery, the witness under examination.

* * * * * * *

Question by General McDOWELL. What, if anything, was done by General McDowell as respects the mobility of his troops?

Answer. I received orders while at Falmouth to make a return of my camp and garrison equipage and means of transportation. It came to my knowledge that other troops encamped near had received similar orders. Immediately thereupon an order was received setting forth the amount of equipage and transportation that would be allowed the troops, and greatly reducing the amount then in our possession.

Question by General McDOWELL. Was this reduction of baggage in the division to which you were then attached the cause of complaint or dissatisfaction or grumbling?

Answer. It was.

The court had no questions to ask this witness.
The court was cleared.
The court was opened.

Mr. PELEG CLARKE, jr., late of Fredericksburg, Va., was duly sworn.

Question by the COURT. Where did you reside in the month of April last; and if at Fredericksburg, Va., when and under what circumstances did you leave there?

Answer. I resided in Fredericksburg, Va., and left to escape arrest by the rebels about the 23d, 24th, or 25th of April. I can't give the exact date; about a week after the Federal Army arrived. They arrived there about the 18th.

Question by the COURT. On leaving, to what place did you go; and if to the Federal Army, where was that army at that time?

Answer. I crossed the river into Stafford County at General King's headquarters, which was at the Phillips house, where his army or division, or whatever he commanded, was there, or a portion of them was there. General Augur's division at that time was at Falmouth.

Question by the COURT. At that time did you know a man by the name of William A. Little; and, if so, what knowledge did you then have that he was in the rebel service?

Answer. I did know a man by the name of William A. Little. He did reside in Fredericksburg at that time. I knew—that is, by the papers at Richmond and our Fredericksburg papers, by reading the fact in the papers—that William A. Little, of Fredericksburg, had an adjutant's appointment. This was four or five months previous to the arrival of the Federal Army. I saw him during this time, after having seen the notice in the papers, repeatedly on the streets of Fredericksburg in rebel uniform whilst the rebel army was quartered there, and mounted, on the streets of Fredericksburg, acting in the capacity of adjutant. I have seen where he had signed his name several times during the winter in that capacity. Saw him on the streets, I think, in that capacity the same day the Federal Army arrived at Falmouth; that is, the day the rebel army evacuated Fredericksburg.

Question by the COURT. After you left Fredericksburg and reached the United States forces did you see this William A. Little; and, if so, where, when, and under what circumstances?

Answer. I did. Saw him at General King's headquarters or directly in front of the house of his headquarters. I saw him at various places within the lines of the Federal Army at various times. The first time I saw him I think I had been across the iver—the second day I was there—and I saw him after that nearly every day that I remained across the river. It was nearly eleven days in all.

Question by the COURT. Did you have any conversation with said adjutant during the eleven days?

Answer. Nothing, except speaking as we passed each other.

Question by the COURT. Did you communicate to General King who this Little was and did he refer you to General McDowell? Did you

**inform General McDowell what you had said to General King and what he had said to you? And, if you answer that you did, then narrate what took place between you and General King and you and General McDowell.**

Answer. At the time I mentioned of seeing Mr. Little, in the first place my attention was called to him and two other gentlemen by a Mr. De Johns, whose tent I sat in reading a newspaper. He came in and asked me to get up and look out of the tent to see if I knew who they were. I done so, and told him that I knew them, and gave him the names of each, and told him that this Mr. Little was an adjutant in the rebel army. I afterward saw General King; told him who the man was and his position. He referred me to General McDowell. I think the same evening or the next day saw General McDowell, and told him that this man Little was in his lines and beyond doubt a spy for the rebels. I don't think I told General McDowell of the conversation I had with General King or that I was referred by General King. I don't think I did. General McDowell replied that he had no doubt that there would be spies within his lines and were there every day. It was always the case with large armies that they had spies in each other's lines; that he had sometimes spies in their lines. I don't think I told General McDowell at this interview that Little was an officer in the rebel service, but told him that fact on the second interview. This second interview was, I think, the next day after. Seeing Little in the lines, and having learned that morning, from parties from Fredericksburg who I knew to be Union men, that Little was met on returning back to Fredericksburg in the afternoon by Mayor Slaughter, Thomas Barton, Marye, and others, citizens of Fredericksburg; that on his arrival they escorted him to the mayor's office one day and another day to Barton's office, and after being in with closed doors some fifteen minutes or a half hour they came out with packages of letters, and dispatched, by a man in each case, a package of letters out of Fredericksburg toward General Field's headquarters, which was about 6 miles in rear of Fredericksburg, as near as I learned. On that day I called on General McDowell and told him the above facts. I then told General McDowell, after informing him of the above facts, "this man Little was an adjutant in the rebel army." General McDowell turned so as to face me, and, in a stern voice, said, "Mr. Clarke, can you swear that that man Little ever held a commission in the rebel army?" I replied that I, never having seen his commission, would not, but that I had seen notice of his appointment in the Richmond papers, and seen him riding the streets, as I have stated before, in the character of adjutant. General McDowell replied that we could hardly convict him of being a spy under such proof. The night of this day, about sunset, there were some six or eight other men, that were in the Federal lines under the same circumstances as myself, came to see me in regard to this man Little, to know if I had mentioned the fact of his being in the lines to any of the commanding officers. I told them I had, but the trouble was to prove that he ever held a commission in the rebel army. Mr. George Morrison and two Armstrongs said that everybody knew that; that he was adjutant of the regiment that they belonged to. Mr. George Morrison then handed me a paper from his pocket, which was given him by this Mr. Little, where he signed his name as adjutant of the Fourteenth Virginia Regiment. It was a written paper, and which I knew to be in the handwriting of Mr. William A. Little. I took that paper the next day—saw Mr. Little again in the lines—called to General McDowell's headquarters; was told by the clerk, a young man in his office, that he had rode up to General King's headquarters. General McDowell arrived. I handed him this paper that Morrison handed me, telling him at the same time the question he put to me the day before, which I was unable to reply to, was there solved, and that I would swear that was Little's handwriting, and that Little was that day in the lines again. General McDowell took the paper and read it; handed it back to me, and remarked if Little told nothing but the truth it would do him no harm, and that if he lied it would do the rebels no good.

**Question by the COURT. How was Little dressed when you saw him on these various occasions within the Federal lines? What did he do; where did he go?**

Answer. He was dressed in citizen's dress and was always on horseback; he went in almost all directions, as a new division or any move seemed to be taking place or any change. He seemed to be posted up and went through. If a new division came in, when he came up he would turn to the right or left and go to it or go through it.

**Question by the COURT. Had he any other business in the Federal lines, except as you have stated, that you have any knowledge of?**

Answer. This man Little was one of the committee who were appointed by the town council of Fredericksburg to meet General Augur in regard to the surrender of the town to the Federal forces of Fredericksburg. I might say, further, that Mr. Little is interested as part owner of a farm about 3 or 3½ miles north of the Rappahannock River, in Stafford County.

Question by the COURT. What was the contents of the paper which you handed to General McDowell and signed by Little?

Answer. As near as I remember—

This is to show that the bearer, Mr. George Morrison, is employed at Scott & Slaughter's iron furnace, in Spottsylvania County, Virginia, they having a contract to furnish the Confederate Government with a large amount of iron. So long as said Morrison is thus employed he is exempt from all military duty or militia duty [military duty I think it was].

WILLIAM A. LITTLE,
*Adjutant Fourteenth Virginia Regiment.*

The date of the paper I have forgotten, but it was about eighteen days old when it was handed to me.

Question by the COURT. You say that Mr. Little was the adjutant of the same regiment to which the two loyal citizens of Fredericksburg whom you have named belonged? State whether he was the adjutant of a regiment which then was, or had been, in the rebel service.

Answer. Yes, sir; the regiment had been in the rebel service, and one of the men I speak of had done service in the regiment. I have seen him in the regiment on duty. These men were conscripts, and one of them had deserted the regiment—Mr. Armstrong—and come into the Federal lines, and the Mr. Morrison had got exempt from the fact that he was employed on work for the rebel government, as the paper stated.

Question by the COURT. Have you personal knowledge of any other matter or thing tending to show treasonable or unfaithful conduct of General McDowell as a general officer?

Answer. Not of my own knowledge, sir.

The court informed the witness that if he had knowledge of any other witnesses who could communicate facts to the court material to its investigation he was invited to send to the court the names of such in writing.

Question by the COURT. State whether you know if Mr. Little was subsequently in active service—that is, in the rebel army, and where he now is, and what position he now holds.

Answer. I know nothing about the position he now holds; he was in the service of the rebel army last winter. Subsequently to the period named I have no knowledge of him or where he is now.

Question by General MCDOWELL. You state you first saw Mr. Little at General King's headquarters; please state when it was you saw him.

Answer. I can't give the date. It was the second day after I went into the Federal lines across the river. It might have been a week after the advance of the Federal Army arrived; it might have been more. I recollect of seeing General McDowell's wagons at the Lacy house—just north of the Lacy house, in the yard—on the covering marked "General McDowell's Headquarters."

Question by General MCDOWELL. Where was General McDowell when you first saw Mr. Little; near General King's headquarters?

Answer. I do not know, sir; I do not think I had ever seen General McDowell. The first time I saw General McDowell was the day I went to him the first time. Don't think I ever saw him before.

Question by General MCDOWELL. What time was it you told General King of Little's presence within the lines of the Union Army? What time with reference to your leaving Fredericksburg?

Answer. I think it was the second day I was in the Federal lines; it might have been the third day; it was not the first, I know.

Question by General McDOWELL. How did you cross the river when you first came within the Federal lines?

Answer. I crossed at Falmouth in a small skiff.

Question by General McDOWELL. On which side of the river was Little living at the time you first saw him near General King's quarters?

Answer. Living in Fredericksburg, on the south side of the river.

Question by General McDOWELL. How long after you first came across the river was it before you returned to Fredericksburg?

Answer. I returned the next night after dark, and then returned back the next morning, or during the night, and remained on this side of the river eight or ten days, until the Federal Army crossed the river, as near as I can recollect.

Question by General McDOWELL. You say you saw Mr. Little within the lines of the army some eleven days in all; do you mean eleven days from the day you first saw him?

Answer. I don't think I said I saw him eleven days in all; don't think I made such a statement.

Question by General McDOWELL. What transactions did you have with the rebel Government prior to the arrival of the Union Army opposite Fredericksburg?

Answer. I never had any. I will state that I have sold the rebel army lumber and had made in my establishment hospital bedsteads for the rebel army—that is, for the surgeons in the hospitals in charge of the sick.

Question by General McDOWELL. Did you not seize rebel property and endeavor to have General McDowell pay you United States money for the same in order thus to get your pay from the rebels?

Answer. No, sir; I never seized any rebel property and never applied to General McDowell to pay me for any.

The court was cleared at the instance of a member.

The court was opened.

The court directed the recorder to dispatch a telegram to Major-General McClellan, stating that "The court is awaiting your arrival."

The court adjourned to meet on Tuesday, December 9, 1862, at 11 o'clock a. m.

---

## *SIXTEENTH DAY.*

COURT-ROOM, NO. 467 SOUTH FOURTEENTH STREET,
*Washington, D. C., December* 9, 1862.

The court met pursuant to adjournment. Present, * * *

Mr. PELEG CLARKE, jr., the witness under examination.

* * * * * * *

Question by General McDOWELL. Why, in your first interview with General McDowell, did you not tell him Little was in the rebel service?

Answer. My interview was very short; General McDowell seemed to be engaged and in a hurry to attend to other business. It was with considerable difficulty, after waiting some time, that I saw him at all.

Question by General McDOWELL. At what place had you this interview with General McDowell?

Answer. I think it was at the Lacy house; I'm sure it was at the Lacy house. He came out of his office on his way out of the house, and I met him in the hall on his way.

Question by General McDOWELL. Who was present on the occasion?

Answer. I could not tell, sir. It was the first time I had been there; nearly all of his officers and men were strangers. I had never seen any of them before.

Question by General McDOWELL. Were there other officers besides General McDowell?

Answer. I think there were other officers sitting on their horses at the door. I could not say that there were any in the hall at that time or that there were not. The hall was as wide as this room nearly.

Question by General McDOWELL. Where was General McDowell on the second interview you had with him?

Answer. I think it was at the Lacy house—on the west portico of the house.

The witness here stated—

I stated yesterday that I had three interviews with General McDowell; it may have been four.

Question by General McDOWELL. Who was present on that occasion—of your second interview?

Answer. I don't know, sir, that any one was directly present. I do not remember. General McDowell's men were all busy and passing by.

Question by General McDOWELL. Where was General McDowell the third interview you had with him?

Answer. I stated in my direct examination yesterday on the east steps of the Lacy house; that was the interview—the last one—when I handed him the paper.

Question by General McDOWELL. Who was present on that occasion?

Answer. There was at the foot of the steps, I suppose, some twenty or thirty men on horseback.

Question by General McDOWELL. You state you had a fourth interview with General McDowell. State where that interview occurred and who were present.

Answer. I believe I didn't state I had a fourth interview. It may have been four. I had communication with General McDowell the day the English officers were there and had a review in front of General King's headquarters. I then handed him a paper, which was, I think, in regard to some other matters.

Question by General McDOWELL. What was the paper you handed him?

Answer. It was in regard to some rebel deserters who had come into his lines and were then there present; some four of them, I think.

Question by General McDOWELL. What was the purport of that paper?

Answer. It was in regard, I think, to those four rebel deserters. I was asked by some officer to look at those prisoners and report to General McDowell, I think, whether they were spies or rebel deserters.

Question by General McDOWELL. Had you permission to pass and repass the river at Fredericksburg?

Answer. I had after the Federal Army crossed into Fredericksburg. I don't think I had any pass until about the time the Federal Army crossed the river.

Question by General McDOWELL. Did you ever mention Little's case to General Patrick, the governor of Fredericksburg?

Answer. I don't know that I ever did. I had a great many interviews with General Patrick after his headquarters was in Fredericksburg. Never knew or spoke to General Patrick before.

Question by General McDOWELL. Where were General McDowell's headquarters during the eleven days in all you state you saw Little?

Answer. I never knew of General McDowell's headquarters being in any other place than the Lacy house.

Question by General McDOWELL. Did you frequently see General McDowell during those eleven days besides the times you state you had interviews with him?

Answer. I don't know that I did, sir. I might have seen him as he was riding through the fields.

Question by General McDOWELL. How do you know that Little went up to and through the divisions as they came up, as you have stated?

Answer. I don't know that he went through all of them as they came up, but saw him in several cases soon after divisions came up riding in the lines and through them.

Question by General McDOWELL. What else did you manufacture for the rebel army besides bedsteads.

Answer. Hospital accouterments, tables, and I think I made some tent poles.

Question by General McDOWELL. How old a person was Little and what was his general appearance?

Answer. I suppose Little must be thirty-five years old; small man; a man, I suppose, weighing 120 or 130 pounds; well dressed, and smart looking man, and is a smart man; lawyer by profession.

Question by General McDOWELL. Did you speak to General King more than once about Little?

Answer. I don't think I did. After he referred me to General McDowell I had no occasion to.

Question by General McDOWELL. Was there complaint of Union men being taken from Fredericksburg and property being carried off after the Union Army reached Falmouth and before it crossed to Fredericksburg?

Answer. Yes, sir; there was. A large portion of the machinery of a woolen mill was carried out of Fredericksburg after the arrival of the Federal Army; also rice, corn, bacon, and other stores.

Question by General McDOWELL. Who was said to be to blame for this?

Answer. Well, it was charged on the Federal officers in command there.

Question by General McDOWELL. What Federal officers?

Answer. I don't know any names of any particular persons. The charge was general.

Question by General McDOWELL. Was General McDowell ever blamed for this?

Answer. I don't think that he was, sir; I don't know that General McDowell's headquarters were on the Rappahannock at the time this was done.

Question by General McDOWELL. Have you ever seen General McDowell under the influence of intoxicating liquors?

Answer. I never have, sir.

Question by General McDOWELL. Do you know from others in the vicinity of Fredericksburg that he has been so seen?

Answer. No, sir; I never heard such a charge made against General McDowell till after I went North, about the 1st of June. The question was asked me frequently, almost daily, with reference to his being drunk while I was traveling through the North. General McDowell, I will say, was very much sunburned—his complexion—and looked as if he had been out in the weather a good deal. I was surprised when such a question was put to me. I found it common report there.

Question by General McDOWELL. Who asked you such questions when you went North and in what places (towns) were they asked?

Answer. I was asked in the city of Washington, and in every place I went through, large and small; heard it in hospitals and every place almost I went to.

Question by the COURT. State whether to your knowledge the enemy received salt, coffee, sugar, boots, shoes, small-arms, or supplies of any kind from us while General McDowell was in command opposite Fredericksburg.

Answer. No, sir; not from the army, but they passed through the lines.

Question by the COURT. State whether any regular mails or communication of any kind were passed through General McDowell's lines with the apparent knowledge of General McDowell or of any of his subordinate officers.

Answer. I think—yes, sir; I don't know that there were any regular mails every day or every second day. I think they were as often as every second day and sometimes every day, but not to my knowledge or to General McDowell's knowledge.

Question by the COURT. State whether notorious rebels were to your knowledge passed from or into our lines.

Answer. They were. William S. Scott, Dr. Herndon, George Guest, John F. Scott, William F. Brodhurst, Montgomery Slaughter, Henry A. Jones, and a man by the name of Smith, who lived out in the country; James L. Vagine, James Kendall, John L. Marye, jr., and some others—Charles Scott. I can name quite a number of others—William H. Morton, Adam Cox.

Question by the COURT. Do you know the name or names of any officer or officers by whom these persons were passed into or without our lines; those persons or any other rebels?

Answer. I do. Captain Mansfield, who acted provost-marshal, passed the most of them. General Patrick passed some of them. Those parties claimed to be British subjects; and after I found General Patrick was passing them back and forth, he (General Patrick) told me Mr. George Guest, one particular instance I have reference to, had papers claiming to be a British subject. I told General Patrick that he had been voting there for the last four years to my certain knowledge and had been one of the leaders of the rebellion. General Patrick replied that his lines that day were extended beyond Mr. Guest's house and he should not go beyond them. People came in through the lines with the pretense that they had business in town—in Fredericksburg; two of them I knew to be in the rebel service at the time. General Patrick took immediate steps to stop their passing back and forth as soon as he was informed of the facts.

Question by the COURT. State whether you know that guards were placed over houses belonging to or inhabited by rebels, and whether any orders were issued by General McDowell prohibiting his own men from obtaining water or seeking temporary shelter from the rain under the front porch, or portico.

Answer. I do; that answers the first part. I do not; that answers the latter part. I know that parties whose property was so guarded prohibited the soldiers who were on guard from coming onto their porch when it rained or from getting water from the well. By whose orders the guard was so stationed of course I know not, but under Captain Mansfield's instruction, as I was told.

Question by the COURT. At the time you furnished lumber, bedsteads, and hospital accouterments and tent poles to the rebel army, what was your regular business?

Answer. Manufacturing lumber, steam-planing mill, wood-working machinery of nearly all kinds, and keeping a lumber-yard. I'll state when the rebellion broke out I stopped all operations entirely, and before I commenced this was carried by special orders to Quartermaster Cone, and then notified that I was either to go to work with my establishment or go to Richmond jail, and they would take possession of my property.

Question by the COURT. Were the rebel forces then in possession of Fredericksburg and were you residing there with your family?

Answer. Yes, sir.

Question by General McDOWELL. Do you know if these cases of persons refusing to allow sentinels to enter their porches or obtain water were ever reported to the governor of the town or his superiors? Whose was the house where this occurred?

Answer. I understood they reported to Captain Mansfield. I know that they were reported to Captain Mansfield. Mrs. Owens is one, and house where Mr. Temple lived was another.

Question by General McDOWELL. When did these occurrences take place; between what dates?

Answer. Those that came under my observation were in July. I can't give the exact date; about the 6th, 8th, or 10th.

Question by General McDOWELL. Where were General McDowell's headquarters at that time; were they at or near Fredericksburg?

Answer. I don't know. I don't think they were, sir.

Question by General McDOWELL. Between what dates or periods were these supplies you have referred to, such as shoes, salt, &c., allowed to pass through the lines at Fredericksburg?

Answer. About the same time I speak of—just prior to that.

Question by General McDOWELL. Who was military governor of Fredericksburg at those times?

Answer. I think that General King had his headquarters on this side of the river. There was considerable changing about. I am not sure. Captain Mansfield seemed to have the matter in hand.

Question by General McDOWELL. In what way were these supplies allowed to pass?

Answer. By teams coming in from the country beyond our lines, and getting small parcels, perhaps a sack or two of salt, depositing them beyond the lines until they obtained enough to load a two-horse wagon, and then put out to Richmond, as parties have since told me.

Question by General McDOWELL. Were these practices ever reported to the military governor of Fredericksburg or General King, whom you state had his headquarters on this side of the river?

Answer. I have been told by parties who said they notified both Mansfield and General King.

Question by General McDOWELL. Do you know if any practice such as you have stated occurred prior to July last?

Answer. I left there about the 27th May, I think it was, and returned the forepart of July; that is, early in July, and knew of no such thing until after my return.

Question by General McDOWELL. Do you know if General McDowell was ever informed by yourself or others of these occurrences; that is, of irregular mails, supplies, &c., having passed to the enemy?

Answer. I do not, sir.

Col. EDMUND SCHRIVER, aide-de-camp, a witness, was recalled.

Question by General McDOWELL. State to the court the rules established by General McDowell for the government of the town of Fredericksburg and for granting passes to and fro.

Answer. The subject was with General King, who had full power in the case. King also had the government of the town.

Question by General McDOWELL. Did General McDowell, save in some exceptional cases, interfere and in person take charge of the subject—the government of the town or intercourse with its inhabitants?

Answer. No.

Question by General McDOWELL. When were General McDowell's headquarters established near Fredericksburg? When did they leave there?

Answer. Early in May they were established—the 4th or 5th of May, I think, and they were removed then on the evening of the 26th of May to various places. Front Royal was the destination of the general when he left Fredericksburg.

Question by General McDOWELL. During his command of the left of the Rappahannock were his headquarters ever again established at Fredericksburg after he left there?

Answer. No.

Question by General McDOWELL. Were any cases ever reported to General McDowell of persons passing supplies of salt, shoes, sugar, &c., or passing noted rebels through the lines of Fredericksburg either before or after his headquarters were removed from that place?

Answer. None to my knowledge.

Question by General McDOWELL. What were General McDowell's personal habits with respect to intercourse with the inhabitants of Fredericksburg?

Answer. I never knew him to go there or to associate in any way with the inhabitants of Fredericksburg, or to see them, except on business.

Question by General McDOWELL. What were the rules established by General McDowell with respect to the constant attendance of an aide-de-camp? Who were the aides required for service with him personally?

Answer. Daily one of four aides was detailed to be in attendance on the general from early in the morning until in the evening. The four were Major Brown, Captain Wadsworth, Captain Drouillard, and Captain Cutting. I want it to be understood the aides served twenty-four hours, day and night, if their service was required.

Question by the COURT. Had you information, while you were on the Rappahannock, that any officer or officers in the rebel service were suffered to pass through your camps, with opportunity to collect information, and then return to the rebel lines without arrest or hinderance?

Answer. Never heard of any.

Question by the COURT. Had such a circumstance come to your knowledge would you have deemed it your duty to report the fact and take immediate measures for the arrest of such officer or officers?

Answer. Yes.

Question by General McDOWELL. What rules as to trade between Fredericksburg and the loyal States were enforced whilst General McDowell was at Fredericksburg? State as far as you can of any instance where the subject came before General McDowell.

Answer. General [McDowell] refused license to trade or to establish shops in Fredericksburg, because the rules of the blockade would be violated thereby.

The court took a recess of five minutes.

Maj. Gen. GEORGE B. MCCLELLAN, U. S. Army, as witness, was duly sworn.

Question by General MCDOWELL. I desire General McClellan to inform the court as fully and as distinctly as he can on the following heads:

First. As to General McDowell's conduct whilst in command of a division in the Army of the Potomac.

Second. As to General McDowell's conduct whilst in command of the First Army Corps, Army of the Potomac.

Third. As to General McDowell's conduct so far as it bore on his plans and operations whilst he was in command of the Department of the Rappahannock.

Answer. In regard to the first question, the conduct of General McDowell, so far as he was a division commander, was entirely satisfactory. His division was in an excellent condition and all that I could wish. While the general was in command of the First Army Corps, prior to the movements on the Peninsula, I received the fullest co-operation at his hands in preparing the plans and arranging for the movement generally. In fact he frequently, at my request, went beyond his strict duties as a corps commander to facilitate preparations. I don't know that I can make it more full, but I wish to impress the idea that I received from General McDowell's hands the fullest co-operation in the preparations for the Peninsula Campaign. I know nothing personally of General McDowell's conduct while in the Department of the Rappahannock, except that I received two telegrams from him, about the 20th of May, I think; the first informing me that by a certain date he would move to my assistance; the other that some unlooked-for circumstance had caused a delay of a few days in his preparation. I do not know officially, but have every reason to be morally certain that the cause of his failure to advance to my assistance was due to circumstances beyond his control.

Question by General MCDOWELL. Do you remember if the regiments assigned to constitute General McDowell's division were especially designated or were they taken indiscriminately and with reference to their stations at the time?

Answer. My recollection is that they were selected with reference to their stations, being in the vicinity of Arlington, with some few changes subsequently made for particular reasons.

Question by General MCDOWELL. How did this division compare in discipline, drill, and efficiency with your other divisions?

Answer. Very favorably. I might add to that, so much so that upon one occasion a general order was issued complimentary to the division.

Question by General MCDOWELL. Was there a second occasion when the hard labor done by this division on the outworks on the Virginia side attracted your especial attention?

Answer. In the construction of the works in the vicinity of Upton's Hill my attention was drawn to the remarkable rapidity with which troops of this division completed the works.

Question by General MCDOWELL. Do you know personally or by report whether General McDowell took unusual pains in the drill of his division as a division (*i. e.*, the entire body drilled together in the same field) when it was under your command?

Answer. I think he did. I think he paid more attention to the division drill than some other commanders. I think there were no division commanders who paid more attention to it.

Question by General MCDOWELL. Whilst he was under your command was General McDowell ever intrusted by you with the handling on the same field of all the divisions on the Virginia side of the Potomac? If so, state the occasion and state the manner in which the duty was discharged.

Answer. On the occasion of a review of all the troops on the Virginia side, in the month of November, I think, he was intrusted with the selection of the ground and the entire control of the review, and discharged the duty in the most satisfactory manner.

The court adjourned to meet to-morrow, the 10th December, 1862, at 11 o'clock a. m.

---

*SEVENTEENTH DAY.*

COURT-ROOM, NO. 467 SOUTH FOURTEENTH STREET,
*Washington, D. C., Wednesday, December* 10, 1862.

Court met pursuant to adjournment. Present: * * *.

Maj. Gen. GEORGE B. McCLELLAN, U. S. Army, the witness under examination.

* * * * * * *.

Question by General McDOWELL. What communication from the President, by General Franklin or otherwise, did you receive as to the separation of General McDowell's corps from your army? Please state fully what you know concerning that separation, so far as relates to General McDowell, and what communication, if any, you have made to the President concerning him in that connection?

Answer. The substance of the communication by General Franklin from the President was that the President assumed the responsibility of the change of destination of General McDowell's corps, regarding that corps as necessary for the defense of Washington, although the troops actually left in Washington and in front of it, disposable for its defense, were rather more than double the garrison fixed by the engineer and artillery officers, and considerably more than the largest number recommended by any of the corps commanders to be left in the vicinity of Washington. I do not at present recall any communication made to the President in regard to the separation of General McDowell's corps. It would be necessary for me to consult my papers ere I could answer the question.

Question by General McDOWELL. Do you recollect having received any telegram from General Franklin, prior to his joining you in the Peninsula, concerning General McDowell, in connection with the separation of the latter corps from your army?

Answer. Yes. I remember merely the general tenor of the dispatch, which was, in General Franklin's opinion, from his knowledge of the case, General McDowell had nothing to do with the separation of his corps from the Army of the Potomac.

Question by General McDOWELL. What was General Franklin's official position with respect to General McDowell at the time he wrote that dispatch?

Answer. He commanded a division, and was in the corps of General McDowell.

[Here paper was handed to witness.]

Question by General McDOWELL. Please examine this copy of the New York Herald, of October 31, containing the speech of the Hon. J. B. Haskin, at Tarrytown, N. Y., and state if the following remarks therein attributed to you, to wit—

I have been unfortunate in not taking Richmond in consequence of my (your) plan not having been carried out, because McDowell did not re-enforce me, as he should have done and as it was agreed would be done,

are either true, in either letter or spirit, so far as relates to General McDowell. If not true in either, wherein are they not so?

Answer. The incident related in the speech is entirely new to me. I never received any dispatches informing me that General Halleck was made Commander-in-Chief, and am very sure I never made the remark attributed to me in the connection as stated. I have no doubt said, for it has ever been my opinion, that the Army of the Potomac would have taken Richmond had not the corps of General McDowell been separated from it. It is also my opinion that, had the command of General McDowell joined the Army of the Potomac in the month of May by way of Hanover Court House from Fredericksburg, we would have had Richmond within a week after the junction. I do not hold General McDowell responsible in my own mind for the failure to join me on either occasion.

Question by General McDOWELL. Did or not General Franklin, on his joining you on the Peninsula, give you a verbal message from General McDowell that he would endeavor to make a demonstration or diversion in your favor by going to Fredericksburg?

Answer. I think he did.

Question by General McDOWELL. After the change of base to Fort Monroe and Yorktown, on the Peninsula, was it any part of your plan that any of your forces should go to Fredericksburg?

Answer. If you mean the original plan, no; it was not. All the active troops were to move in the general direction of the Peninsula.

General McDowell stated that he wished at this stage of the proceedings to introduce to the court certain correspondence heretofore referred to by him, if the court would suspend for a short time the examination of the witness.

Colonel Schriver, aide-de-camp and chief of staff to General McDowell, here presented to the court a number of papers, stating they have been authenticated by Colonel Stager, superintendent of military telegraphs, by himself, as chief of staff, and by Captain Cutting, one of the general's aides, and Colonel Schriver read the same. These papers are as follows, and are appended to the proceedings of this day.*

1. Dated War Department, April 11, 1862, from Edwin M. Stanton, Secretary of War, to Major-General McDowell.
2. Dated War Department, Washington City, D. C., April 24, 1862, from Secretary of War to Major-General McDowell.
3. Headquarters Department of the Rappahannock, Aquia, April 22, 1862, from Major-General McDowell to Secretary of War.
4. Dated Headquarters Department of the Rappahannock, Aquia Creek, April 26, 1862, from General McDowell to Secretary of War.
5. Headquarters Department of the Rappahannock, near Aquia Creek Landing, April 29, 1862, from General McDowell to Secretary of War.
6. Dated Washington, April 30, 1862, from Inspector-General Van Rensselaer to Major-General McDowell.
7. Dated War Department, Washington City, D. C., May 17, 1862, from Secretary of War to Major-General McDowell.
8. War Department, Washington City, D. C., May 17, 1862, from Secretary of War to Maj. Gen. George B. McClellan.
9. Dated Headquarters Department of the Rappahannock, May 20, 1862, from General McDowell to Secretary of War.
10. Dated Headquarters Department of the Rappahannock, May 21, 1862, from General McDowell to Secretary of War.
11. Dated Headquarters Department of the Rappahannock, May 22, 1862, from General McDowell to Secretary of War.
12. Dated Headquarters Department of the Rappahannock, May 22, 1862, from General McDowell to General McClellan.
13. Dated War Department, May 24, 1862, from Secretary of War to Major-General McDowell.
14. Dated Headquarters Department of the Rappahannock, May 24, 1862, from General McDowell to Secretary of War.

*Omitted, except Nos. 7 and 8, from appendix. They will be printed in chronological order in the "Correspondence, etc.," Part III.

15. Dated War Department, May 24, 1862, from Abraham Lincoln to General McDowell.
16. (Same), May 24, 1862, from General McDowell to the President.
17. War Department, May 24, 1862, from Abraham Lincoln to General McDowell.
18. Dated Headquarters Department of the Rappahannock, May 24, 1862, from General McDowell to His Excellency the President.

The examination of Major-General McClellan was resumed.

A book was here handed the witness containing telegrams, and the telegrams referred to in the following questions are appended to the proceedings of this day and marked Alpha and Beta.

Question by General McDOWELL. Examine the telegrams, pages 252 and 266 and dated June 10 and June 12, and state if you received them.

Answer. I received them.

Question by General McDOWELL. Did you also receive the telegram of May 22, 1862, which has been read to the court?

Answer. Yes.

Question by General McDOWELL. Did you frequently and daily see General McDowell when he was at Fairfax Court-House in March last past, and did you see him on the day the troops were ordered back to Alexandria? If so, state what was his condition at that time or at any time he was at Fairfax Court-House when the army was there in March last, as to his being or not under the influence of intoxicating liquor. How long have you known General McDowell; and have the habits of General McDowell, as to the use of, or abstinence from, every species of distilled vinous or fermented liquors been a subject of remark among those who know him? If so, what has been his habit or is the general character borne by him in this regard?

Answer. I saw General McDowell several times every day in March last at Fairfax Court-House and also on the day the troops were ordered back to Alexandria. He was in his usual condition, entirely free from any effect of intoxicating liquors. I have known General McDowell for nearly twenty years, and have known him as one who abstained entirely from the use of any wine or spirituous liquors, and I think even from tea and coffee. I know that has been his reputation among all who have known him, and I can imagine nothing more absurd than the charge of his being in any way under the influence of intoxicating liquor.

Question by the COURT. State whether General McDowell was under your command at the time of your movement from the Potomac to the Peninsula.

Answer. He was.

Question by the COURT. What orders were given by you to General McDowell having reference to the movement to the Peninsula and how did those orders affect the general plan of movements for the Army of the Potomac?

Answer. The orders were for General McDowell to embark his corps upon the return of the transports then engaged in carrying troops, and having his whole command embarked to report to me for further orders at Fort Monroe or wherever else I might happen to be, the intention being to move that corps as a unit by the York or Severn River, according to circumstances; that movement being an essential part of the plan of the campaign.

Question by the COURT. Were these orders ever changed by you or by others higher in authority; and, if so, how?

Answer. They were not changed by me, but by the President of the United States. When in front of Yorktown, with a considerable portion of the army under fire, I received the first intimation of any intention to change the destination of General McDowell's corps. That intimation was a telegraphic dispatch from the War Department, informing me that General McDowell's corps had been withdrawn from the Army of the Potomac.

Question by the COURT. Did you, after the investment of Yorktown, send any orders to General McDowell or did you request any orders to be sent to General McDowell? If so, what were the tenor and object of such orders and what reply was received from General McDowell or from those to whom the request was made?

Answer. I sent no orders to General McDowell after the investment of Yorktown, for the reason that I received the information that he was detached from my command on the very day we arrived in front of Yorktown.

Question by the COURT. When you caused the occupation of Hanover Court-House did you expect the co-operation of General McDowell's corps? On what were such expectations based, for what purpose was the co-operation desired, and what would have been the probable result of a junction of McDowell and Porter at that time or shortly afterward?

Answer. I hoped for the co-operation of General McDowell's army, although that expectation was not the only reason for occupying Hanover Court-House. The hope of co-operation was based on information I received at various times from Washington. The purpose for which co-operation was desired was to increase our available strength sufficiently to insure the capture of Richmond, and, in my opinion, the junction of McDowell and Porter would have enabled us to have accomplished the object of the campaign; that is, the capture of Richmond.

Question by the COURT. Was such co-operation practicable and by what routes, and was it consistent, in your opinion, with the safety of the capital?

Answer. The co-operation was practicable either by the direct land route from Fredericksburg to Hanover Court-House or by the water route, and was consistent, in my opinion, with the safety of the capital.

Question by a MEMBER. What forces at that time could the enemy have disposed of for the threatening of Washington, and by what routes and in what time could they have been moved?

Answer. The witness here desired permission to ask whether or not the questions propounded were relevant to the matter under investigation.

The court was cleared.

The court was opened and the following decision announced: "That the question be withdrawn."

Question by the COURT. What was the distance at any one time between the pickets of Generals McDowell and Porter?

Answer. I do not know what the position of General McDowell's pickets were. I understood some time after the occupation of Hanover Court-House by General Porter that when General Porter was at Hanover Court-House General McDowell's cavalry force (which I understood to be a reconnaissance) were 12 miles from them, but I do not know the position of General McDowell's pickets.

Question by the COURT. You state that you received the fullest co-operation from General McDowell in preparing the plans for the Peninsular Campaign as corps commander; had he knowledge of those plans and was he consulted in respect to them?

Answer. Yes.

Question by the COURT. Were those plans for the Peninsula Campaign which embraced the employment of the corps of General McDowell known to the War Department or the President?

Answer. Yes.

Question by the COURT. You have stated that troops were retained for the defenses of Washington. Did those plans provide for a force to be retained from the troops then under your command; and, if so how large was the force to be detained and what troops were to compose it?

Answer. The witness stated that he had no objection to answer the question if within the latitude of the court, but was under the impression that it was outside of the inquiry.

The court informed the witness that the series of questions now being propounded have been considered with a view of avoiding the clearing of the court.

The witness here asked that, as a new branch of inquiry was being opened, he might have time to consider the question. The answer to this question was postponed.

Question by the COURT. Have you knowledge of the circumstances which led to the detention of General McDowell and the formation of the Department of the Rappahannock at the time that department was formed?

Answer. I had none at the time.

Question by the COURT. Did the formation of that department and the detention of General McDowell reduce the means which had been arranged before you left Washington to prosecute the campaign?

Answer. Yes.

Question by the COURT. Do you know whether General McDowell had any complicity in promoting or inducing the formation of the Department of the Rappahannock or reducing your force?

Answer. I do not.

Question by the COURT. Was there any reply by you to the telegrams of General McDowell or other notice to him showing that you desired his co-operation?

Answer. I think no reply to General McDowell, but the War Department was informed that I wanted troops.

Question by General MCDOWELL. Do you recollect of the order to General McDowell informing him his corps would be the last to embark, *i. e.*, after Sumner's was sent to him from the steamer Commodore after you had left for the Peninsula?

Answer. I think it was. I wrote a great many papers on the Commodore, and I think such an order was sent from that steamer.

The court now adjourned to meet to-morrow, December 11, 1862, at 11 o'clock a. m.

—

## APPENDIX.

### Alpha.

WAR DEPARTMENT,
*Washington, D. C., June* 10,* 1862.

Major-General MCCLELLAN,
*Commanding Department of Virginia, before Richmond:*

For the third time I am ordered to join you, and this time I hope to get through.

In view of the remarks made with reference to my leaving you and my not joining you before by your friends, and of something I have

*Another copy of this dispatch is dated June 8.

heard as coming from you on that subject, I wish to say that I go with the greatest satisfaction, and hope to arrive with my main body in time to be of service. McCall goes in advance by water. I will be with you in ten days with the remainder by land from Fredericksburg.

IRVIN McDOWELL,
*Major-General, Commanding Department Rappahannock.*

Beta.

HDQRS. DEPARTMENT OF THE RAPPAHANNOCK,
*Manassas, June* 12, 1862.

Maj. Gen. GEORGE B. McCLELLAN,
*Commanding Department of Virginia, before Richmond:*

The delay of Major-General Banks to relieve the division of my command in the valley beyond the time I had calculated on will prevent my joining you with remainder of the troops I am to take below at as early a day as I named. My Third Division, McCall's, is now on the way. Please do me the favor to so place it that it may be in a position to join the others as they come down from Fredericksburg.

IRVIN McDOWELL,
*Major-General, Comdg. Department of the Rappahannock.*

No. 7.

WAR DEPARTMENT,
*Washington, May* 17, 1862.

General McDOWELL,
*Commanding Department of the Rappahannock:*

GENERAL: Upon being joined by General Shields' division you will move upon Richmond by the general route of the Richmond and Fredericksburg Railroad, co-operating with the forces under General McClellan now threatening Richmond from the line of the Pamunkey and York Rivers.

While seeking to establish as soon as possible a communication between your left wing and the right wing of General McClellan you will hold yourself always in such position as to cover the capital of the nation against a sudden dash of any large body of the rebel forces.

General McClellan will be furnished with a copy of these instructions, and will be directed to hold himself in readiness to establish communication with your left wing, and to prevent the main body of the enemy's army from leaving Richmond and throwing itself upon your column before a junction of the two armies is effected.

A copy of his instructions in regard to the employment of your force is annexed.

By order of the President:*

EDWIN M. STANTON,
*Secretary of War.*

No. 8.

WASHINGTON, *May* 17, 1862.

Maj. Gen. GEORGE B. McCLELLAN,
*Commanding Army of the Potomac, before Richmond:*

GENERAL: Your dispatch to the President asking re-enforcements has been received and carefully considered.

* See also memorandum of same date in Series I, Vol. XI, Part III, p. 176.

The President is not willing to uncover the capital entirely, and it is believed that even if this were prudent it would require more time to effect a junction between your army and that of the Rappahannock by the way of the Potomac and York Rivers than by a land march. In order, therefore, to increase the strength of the attack upon Richmond at the earliest moment General McDowell has been ordered to march upon that city by the shortest route. He is ordered—keeping himself always in position to save the capital from all possible attack—so to operate as to put his left wing in communication with your right wing, and you are instructed to co-operate, so as to establish this communication as soon as possible, by extending your right wing to the north of Richmond. It is believed that this communication can be safely established either north or south of the Pamunkey River. In any event you will be able to prevent the main body of the enemy's forces from leaving Richmond and falling in overwhelming force upon General McDowell. He will move with between 35,000 and 40,000 men.

A copy of the instructions to General McDowell are with this. The specific task assigned to his command has been to provide against any danger to the capital of the nation.

At your earnest call for re-enforcements he is sent forward to co-operate in the reduction of Richmond, but charged, in attempting this, not to uncover the city of Washington, and you will give no order, either before or after your junction, which can put him out of position to cover this city. You and he will communicate with each other by telegraph or otherwise as frequently as may be necessary for sufficient co-operation. When General McDowell is in position on your right his supplies must be drawn from West Point, and you will instruct your staff officers to be prepared to supply him by that route.

The President desires that General McDowell retain the command of the Department of the Rappahannock and of the forces with which he moves forward.

By order of the President:

EDWIN M. STANTON,
*Secretary of War.*

---

*EIGHTEENTH DAY.*

COURT-ROOM, No. 467 SOUTH FOURTEENTH STREET,
*Washington, D. C., Thursday, December* 11, 1862.

The court met pursuant to adjournment. Present, * * *.

Maj. Gen. GEORGE B. MCCLELLAN, U. S. Army, the witness under examination.

* * * * * * *

The recorder then read the question proposed yesterday and held by the witness for consideration.

Question by the COURT. You have stated that troops were retained for the defense of Washington. Did these plans provide for a force to be retained from the troops then under your command; and, if so, how large was the force to be retained and what troops were to compose it?

Answer. The troops to be retained for the defense of Washington were almost entirely from those under my immediate command. I cannot give from memory alone an accurate statement of their composition and strength. On the 1st April, I think it was, I wrote a letter to the Secretary of War, giving full information in regard to these points. I have not a copy of that letter with me, but will submit it to the court as soon as I can reach my papers. The force left disposable for the defense of Washington and its dependencies was about 70,000 men, independent of the troops of General McDowell.

Question by the COURT. Will the letter to which you refer disclose what portion of the troops, 70,000 in number, were present and fit for duty; and, if it does not, state your knowledge on the subject.

Answer. No; the letter does not. My recollection is that the number stated in the letter were present with their regiments. I cannot answer the questions without referring to the returns, which I will do.

Question by the COURT. Explain what you refer to as the dependencies of Washington.

Answer. I referred then to the approaches to Washington, both in the direction of the Orange and Alexandria Railroad and by the Shenandoah Valley. The instructions given in regard to the position of these troops contemplated posting the mass of them in the vicinity of Manassas, and on the line of the Manassas Gap Railroad near Front Royal, so that the whole force would be available on either approach to the city. On the 12th April, the date of the letter referred to, I wrote a letter of instruction to General Banks, for his guidance in posting troops in front of Washington, which letter would be a more full answer to the question than the general one I have given, which I will also submit to the court, if they desire it.

Question by the COURT. General McDowell having made known to the court that in his opinion it was safe and proper for him to proceed to co-operate with you against Richmond and having yielded his purpose so to do only in obedience to higher orders, you will state your judgment as to the soundness of that opinion and the military propriety of that purpose on the part of General McDowell, and to that end you will inform the court what, in your judgment, was the object of Jackson's movement against Banks on or about the 24th of May; what were the probabilities of the success of that movement if left unaided by the forces of the enemy at Richmond and if Richmond were at the time additionally threatened by McDowell's proposed cooperation with you; what forces had the enemy to spare at that time to aid Jackson or otherwise to threaten Washington; what were the probabilities of forces so disposed of reaching Washington and at what time and in what manner?

Answer. I think that General McDowell was correct in his opinion that it was safe and proper for him to unite with the Army of Potomac. I think that immediately after the occupation of Hanover Court-House by a portion of the Army of the Potomac there was no rebel force of any consequence between Hanover Court-House and General McDowell. I think that the main object of Jackson's movement against General Banks was to prevent re-enforcements being sent to the Army of the Potomac, and expressed that opinion in a telegram to the President within a day or two from the time I received information of Jackson's movements. I think that if General McDowell had moved directly upon Hanover Court-House instead of in the direction of Front Royal Jackson would have rapidly retraced his steps to rejoin the main rebel army at Richmond. With a strong army of our own in the vicinity of Richmond and threatening it I do not think the rebels would ever detach a sufficient force to seriously endanger the safety of Washington.

Question by the COURT. Had General McDowell knowledge of your letter to the Secretary of War and what it contained, communicating information as to the strength and composition of the troops left to cover Washington?

Answer. I don't know that he had. I sent him no copy.

Question by the COURT. Had General McDowell knowledge of the facts disclosed in that communication, either derived from consultations with you or otherwise, especially in respect to the number of troops left to cover Washington?

Answer. I think he had a general knowledge of the facts resulting from the conversations we had, but probably not a full knowledge as to the number of troops left.

Question by the COURT. State as nearly as you can what knowledge he had on that point.

Answer. I cannot recollect. Busy with the details of an expedition so large as that, I would not pretend to recollect what knowledge General McDowell had. We talked, however, very fully over the details.

Question by the COURT. Did you, in your consultations to which General McDowell was a party, talk over the number of troops which would be left when you should move with the bulk of the army for the Peninsula?

Answer. Yes.

Question by the COURT. What was the largest number of troops suggested by any corps commander to be left to cover Washington and its dependencies? And in this connection state, if you can, the number proposed by General McDowell.

Answer. My recollection is that the suggestions as to the forces to be left varied from 40,000 to 50,000. I think General McDowell proposed the latter number. Of one thing I am confident, that with the facts fresh in my mind I thought that I left more than suggested by any corps commander.

Question by General MCDOWELL. After Jackson marched to attack General Banks did not forces leave Richmond to re-enforce him before he joined the enemy's main army, or had you not reliable information that such was the case, and did you not so report to the Government?

Answer. Yes.

Question by General MCDOWELL. Does the witness recollect if it was not at one time, prior to his own embarkation at Alexandria, arranged or understood that General Sumner's corps should remain in front of Washington till we should learn the enemy's force at Gordonsville had fallen back and should be opposed by the corps first sent off?

Answer. Yes.

Question by General MCDOWELL. Do you recollect if this was not the understanding up to the time you changed the order of embarkation and directed Sumner's corps to precede that of McDowell's?

Answer. I think it was.

Question by General MCDOWELL. Were the other corps commanders besides General McDowell advised or informed in any way by you as to the composition or number of the forces to be left for the defense of Washington?

Answer. They were not informed in writing and only in a general way in conversation. My recollection is that I talked over the matter with them individually and collectively.

Question by General MCDOWELL. Will the witness please state if the force to be left in the Shenandoah Valley was counted in the number for the defense of Washington?

Answer. Yes.

Question by General MCDOWELL. Can the witness state from memory about the strength of the command to be left in the Shenandoah Valley?

Answer. I cannot recall it, but the letter of instructions to General Banks, to which I have referred, will give full information on the whole subject.

Question by the COURT. Do you mean to be understood that one corps designed tc be employed in your movement by the route of the Peninsula was to be left to cover Washington until the first corps sent off to the Peninsula should be opposed by the enemy's force falling back from Gordonsville; and, if so, was General McDowell's corps left behind for that duty?

Answer. The means of water transportation we had rendered it necessary to embark the army in successive portions, andt he idea was to leave a corps or more, which would be the last to embark, in position to cover Washington so long as there was danger of its being attacked by the enemy. Before I left Washington I was satisfied that it was not then in danger, and I directed Sumner's corps to be embarked before General McDowell for the reason that I wished to employ General McDowell's corps as a unit. I did not leave General McDowell's corps behind for the purpose of covering Washington. I expected it to follow me the moment transportation for it was ready.

Question by the COURT. Had General McDowell orders to that effect?

Answer. Yes; that is, to follow me when transportation was ready.

General McDowell presented to the court a communication marked A, which was read by the recorder and is appended to the proceedings of this day.

Maj. Gen. ERASMUS D. KEYES, U. S. Volunteers, a witness, was duly sworn.

Question by General McDOWELL. Please state to the court your present rank and command, and if you have served under General McDowell when he commanded a division in the Army of the Potomac and with him as commanding army corps in that army?

Answer. My present rank is major-general of volunteers. I command the Fourth Army Corps. I served under Major-General McDowell when he commanded a division, as brigadier in the Army of the Potomac. I also served with him as a corps commander, that is, he commanded the First and I the Fourth Army Corps, but not for a great length of time.

Question by General McDOWELL. State to the court as fully as you can concerning General McDowell's conduct as division commander whilst you served under him.

Answer. I served under General McDowell as a division commander from about the 1st of August till about the middle of November following as a brigadier. The conduct of General McDowell during that time was in my opinion that of an attentive officer, who understood the duties of his command perfectly well. It was my impression and knowledge that he examined the details of his command daily. He would pass through the camp very frequently; make frequent and very careful inspections of the men; saw his command frequently under arms and exercised them all. That is my answer to his military conduct.

Question by General McDOWELL. State to the court as fully as you can concerning General McDowell's conduct as army corps commander whilst you and he served in that capacity in the Army of the Potomac.

Answer. While I served with him as corps commander, which was not far from the 12th of March until the end of the month, when I left for the Peninsula, I saw him frequently. During that time I did not see him actually on the field more than two or three times; that I had frequent conversation and discussions with him in reference to the plan of campaign and the conduct of the war. General McDowell appeared to be very active, and it struck me he had studied the subject of the campaign thoroughly, and that he understood and performed the duties of his command with a great deal of alacrity and intelligence. I thought his conduct indicated that his heart was zealous in the cause. It was my impression that his ability and his intelligence were fully equal to his command. I should add, at the time I refer to, about the 10th March, the discussions of corps commanders were very important of course, as the subject of the campaign was under frequent discussion, and I saw more of General McDowell and heard his views more in detail than I did those of any other corps commander.

Question by General McDOWELL. Were you ever present at any consultation with General McDowell when General McClellan informed you, him, or any other corps commander of the amount and composition of the force which he intended to leave for the capital? If so, state the amount and composition of the force he intended so to leave.

Answer. I was present at a consultation of General McDowell, when General McClellan spoke to me, General McDowell, and other corps commanders of the force to be left behind for the defense of Washington, but I do not remember whether General McClellan proposed any definite amount or composition of the forces to be left.

Question by General MCDOWELL. Were you present at any other consultation with the corps commanders after the one you refer to at Fairfax Court-House, when General McClellan informed you or General McDowell of the amount and composition of the forces to be left behind?

Answer. I was present, I think, on a subsequent occasion, when General McClellan spoke of the force to be left behind; but I don't remember whether it was a consultation of all the corps commanders or not. The subject having been settled by the corps commanders, I allowed the matter to pass from my mind in subsequent discussion. General McDowell, it is my impression, was present on a subsequent occasion when that subject was mooted.

Question by General MCDOWELL. Can the witness recollect when this occurred?

Answer. I don't remember at this moment.

Question by General MCDOWELL. Does the witness remember what troops General McClellan designated at that time as those he intended should form the defense of Washington?

Answer. The witness desired time to refresh his memory ere he answered the question.

The court instructed the recorder to make a preliminary examination of such persons as may be represented to the court as knowing matter pertaining to the subjects under investigation by this court.

The court adjourned to meet to-morrow, December 12, 1862, at 11 a. m.

---

## APPENDIX.

### A.

In laying before the court such official communications as have seemed to me to bear more especially on the matter in hand, I may have omitted some which if they were known to the court it might consider important. I therefore beg to say that I have here, for the inspection of the court, my order books, letter book, and books of telegrams received and sent; and if at any time the court should think any particular event or subject might or should be more fully given than I should present it, I beg the recorder may have leave to examine the books with reference to the same.

IRVIN MCDOWELL,
*Major-General.*

---

## *NINETEENTH DAY.*

COURT-ROOM, 467 SOUTH FOURTEENTH STREET,
*Washington, D. C., December* 12, 1862.

The court met pursuant to adjournment. Present * * * .

Maj. Gen. ERASMUS D. KEYES, U. S. Volunteers, the witness under examination.

* * * * * * *

The recorder repeated the following question, propounded yesterday and held by the witness under consideration:

Question by General McDOWELL. Does the witness remember what troops General McClellan designated at that time as those he intended should form the defense of Washington?

Answer. To the best of my remembrance he spoke of some troops then in the Shenandoah Valley as one portion, and another portion were unattached regiments in the neighborhood of Washington; that is, regiments that had not been attached to any corps, and I think he referred to other troops expected to arrive in Washington, but not in definite terms.

Question by General McDOWELL. What was the resolution adopted by the corps commanders at Fairfax Court-House as to the force to be left for the defense of Washington?

Answer. It was resolved by the corps commanders, at a meeting at Fairfax Court-House, held about the 12th of March, that all the forts on the Virginia side of the Potomac, right bank, must be fully garrisoned and all the forts on the Washington side occupied, and that there should be in addition a covering force or movable force of 25,000 troops on the Virginia side. This was the opinion of three of the corps commanders; that is, McDowell, Heintzelman, and myself. General Sumner's opinion was that the whole number of troops to be left for the defense of Washington, including the forts, should be 40,000.

Question by General McDOWELL. What were the duties imposed on the corps commanders by the President with reference to the movement of the Army of the Potomac and the force to be left for the defense of Washington?

Answer. The President imposed upon the corps commanders the duty of making definite arrangements for the defense of the capital, and he required that they should specify the force to be left behind—not the definite regiments, but the amount of force. I understood he required this arrangement to be made before he would permit the army to change its base.

Question by General McDOWELL. After the occasion you refer to at Fairfax Court-House, were the corps commanders ever assembled as a body for consultation, advice, or other purpose?

Answer. They were not—before moving to the Peninsula.

Question by General McDOWELL. Were the corps commanders ever as a body informed as to action taken or to be taken by General McClellan with a view to a fulfillment of the orders of the President concerning the amount of force to be left behind for the defense of Washington?

Answer. They were not.

Question by General McDOWELL. How long have you known General McDowell intimately? What are his habits as to the use of intoxicating liquors?

Answer. I've known him intimately since the month of June, 1844. His habits, so far as I have ever seen or known or heard, until recently, were those of total abstinence from the use of intoxicating liquors. Recently I have seen in the papers and have heard it said that he drank too much; but this change, if there be such a change, is entirely unknown to me.

Question by General McDOWELL. What was the feeling expressed in the Peninsula concerning General McDowell for his not coming from Fredericksburg to join the Army of the Potomac before Richmond?

This question was objected to by a member, as tending to elicit matter not essential to the defense of General McDowell.

General McDowell stated, at the instance of a member of the court, that he had been maligned and abused in the Army of the Peninsula; that there existed a strong feeling against him, and that for months the press seemed filled with every species of abuse, attributing to him bad motives for not joining the Army of the Potomac.

A member stated it was not the province of the court to inquire into imputations on the part of the public by false accusations; but rather whether General McDowell's conduct has been such as to justify accusation.

General McDowell stated that the fact, if admitted by the court, would be all that he deemed necessary in the case.

General McDowell was informed that a statement, in writing, of his wishes on the subject would be received by the court.

Question by the COURT. At the consultation of corps commanders referred to by you did the force of 40,000 named by General Sumner or the garrisons of the forts and movable force of 25,000 agreed to in the resolution passed by the majority of the commanders in any way include the force in the Shenandoah Valley?

Answer. It did not.

Question by the COURT. Did you or do you consider the force that was then or afterward in the Shenandoah Valley as properly applicable to the defense of Washington and to be properly included in the number which were to be left for said defense in obedience to the inquiry of the President?

Answer. I did not consider that force as properly applicable to the defense of Washington at that discussion myself.

A paper (or slip) was read by the recorder and handed the witness, which is appended to proceedings of this day, and marked A.

Question by General McDOWELL. Will the witness examine this slip and see if it is the rough of the resolution adopted by the corps commanders at Fairfax Court-House at the time in question?

Answer. It is.

Question by the COURT. Was General McClellan present at the consultation where this resolution was adopted?

Answer. He was present in the same house, and in and out of the room several times while the discussion was going on, and it was announced and made known to him at the time at his headquarters, Fairfax Court-House.

General McDowell having been summoned to attend the court-martial in the case of General Fitz John Porter as a witness, the court adjourned until to-morrow, December 13, 1862, at 11 o'clock a. m.

---

## APPENDIX.

### A.

That with the forts on the right bank of the Potomac fully garrisoned and those on the left bank occupied a covering force in front of the Virginia line of 25,000 men would suffice.

KEYES.
HEINTZELMAN.
McDOWELL.

A total of 40,000 men for the defense of the city would suffice.

SUMNER.

*TWENTY-FIRST DAY.**

COURT-ROOM, NO. 467 SOUTH FOURTEENTH STREET,
*Washington, D. C., December* 15, 1862.

* * * * * * *

Col. EDMUND SCHRIVER, aide-de-camp and chief of staff to Major-General McDowell, a witness, was recalled.

Question by General MCDOWELL. State what orders were given by General McDowell concerning the fences around some wheat fields near the Lacy house in April or May last.

Answer. Finding them in a condition that endangered the growing crops of wheat, the general ordered them to be restored. I think it was by Colonel Wyndham, commanding cavalry regiment. There was another case in that vicinity where the fences were ordered to be restored by some of General King's division that was encamped near the place. I remember another order that was given to General McCall to restore the fences of a colored man, I think, in the neighborhood of his camp. None others occur to me now.

Question by General MCDOWELL. Was there any wood near at hand to these wheat fields or to the cabin of the colored man which could have been used for fuel by the troops?

Answer. An abundance.

Question by General MCDOWELL. Were any orders given to General Shields' division, or any part of it, requiring them to rebuild fences, or to return to near the Lacy house, when they had marched away from it, for this purpose?

Answer. I have no knowledge of any such order having been given.

The court took a recess for thirty minutes.

General McDowell here requested that the following official papers be laid before the court; which papers were read by Colonel Schriver, the witness under examination, and are appended to the proceedings of this day and in the following order: †

1. From Major-General McDowell to P. H. Watson, Assistant Secretary of War, dated Headquarters Department of the Rappahannock, opposite Fredericksburg, May 11, 1862.
2. From Major-General Shields to E. M. Stanton, Secretary of War, dated Headquarters Shields' division, Fredericksburg, May 24, 1862.
3. From E. M. Stanton, Secretary of War, to Major-General McDowell, at Fredericksburg, dated War Department, Washington City, D. C., May 25, 1862.
4. From Major-General McDowell to E. M. Stanton, Secretary of War, dated same, May 25, 1862.
5. From E. M. Stanton, Secretary of War, to Major-General McDowell, dated War Department, Washington City, D. C., May 25, 1862.
6. From E. M. Stanton, Secretary of War, to Major-General McDowell, at Falmouth, dated War Department, Washington, May 25, 1862.
7. From Major-General McDowell to Secretary of War, dated Headquarters Department of the Rappahannock, May 25, 1862.
8. From Major-General McDowell to Secretary of War, dated Headquarters Department of the Rappahannock, May 25, 1862.
9. From E. M. Stanton, Secretary of War, to Major-General McDowell, dated United States Military Telegraph, War Department, Washington City, D. C., May 25, 1862.
10. From E. M. Stanton, Secretary of War, to Major-General McDowell, at Fredericksburg, dated War Department, Washington City, D. C., May 25, 1862.
11. From E. M. Stanton, Secretary of War, to Major-General McDowell, at Falmouth, dated Washington, May 25, 1862.
12. From Major-General McDowell to Secretary of War, dated Headquarters Department of the Rappahannock, May 25, 1862.
13. From Major-General McDowell to Secretary of War, dated Headquarters Department of the Rappahannock, May 25, 1862.

---

* On the twentieth day, December 13, the court met and immediately adjourned, Major-General McDowell being detained as a witness in the Fitz John Porter trial.

† Omitted from appendix. They will appear in chronological order in "Correspondence, etc.," Part III.

14. From Major-General McDowell to Secretary of War, dated Headquarters Department of the Rappahannock, May 25, 1862.
15. From Major-General McDowell to Secretary of War, dated Headquarters Department of the Rappahannock, May 25, 1862.
16. From Major-General McDowell to Secretary of War, dated Headquarters Department of the Rappahannock, May 25.
17. From Major-General McDowell to Secretary of War, dated Headquarters Department of the Rappahannock, May 26, 1862.
18. From Major-General McDowell to Brigadier-General Ricketts, dated May 26, 1862.
19. From A. Lincoln to Major-General McDowell, dated Washington, May 26, 1862.
20. From Major-General McDowell to His Excellency the President, dated Fredericksburg, May 26, 1862.
21. From General J. W. Geary (signed E. M. Stanton) to Major-General McDowell, dated Washington, May 26, 1862.
22. From General J. W. Geary (signed E. M. Stanton) to Major-General McDowell, dated Washington, May 26, 1862.
23. From Maj. Gen. E. O. C. Ord to Major-General McDowell, dated Aquia Creek, May 26, 1862.
24. From Maj. Gen. E. O. C. Ord to Major-General McDowell, dated Aquia Creek, May 26, 1862.
25. From Maj. Gen. E. O. C. Ord to Major-General McDowell, dated Aquia Creek, May 26, 1862.
26. From E. M. Stanton, Secretary of War, to Major-General McDowell, dated Washington, May 27, 1862.
27. From Major-General McDowell to General Shields, at Catlett's, dated Washington, May 27, 1862.
28. From Major-General McDowell to Secretary of War, dated Headquarters Manassas, May 27, 1862.
29. From Major-General McDowell to Secretary of War, dated Manassas, May 27, 1862.

Maj. Gen. GEORGE L. HARTSUFF, U. S. Volunteers, a witness, was duly sworn.

Question by General McDOWELL. What command have you held under General McDowell? When did you come under his command? In what condition was the brigade when you first joined it?

Answer. I commanded a brigade under General McDowell. I came under his command on the 1st of last May. The general condition of the brigade was good.

Question by General McDOWELL. How was it as to means of transportation, and camp equipage when you joined it?

Answer. The means of transportation and the amount of camp equipage were very abundant; unusually so.

Question by General McDOWELL. What reduction was made in the means of transportation and in the camp equipage on your coming under General McDowell's immediate command at Fredericksburg?

Answer. The number of wagons to each regiment was reduced to seven or eight, I think. The Sibley tents, with which the command were furnished, were changed to shelter-tents; officers' baggage was necessarily considerably reduced, and the baggage of company messes, and baggage generally of officers and men.

Question by General McDOWELL. Do you know if the reduction of means of transportation and camp equipage was the cause of any feeling or the subject of any remark in the brigade?

Answer. It was the cause of considerable feeling and of many remarks of ill-feeling or ill-will toward General McDowell by officers and men. I did not hear the remarks of the men, but am satisfied remarks of the kind were made.

Question by General McDOWELL. State if you know of another cause of ill-feeling toward General McDowell or dissatisfaction with him in that brigade connected with their having been under another department commander, where these restrictions had not been made.

Answer. Three of the four regiments composing my brigade had been under the command of General Banks. The brigade was, as they believed, temporarily attached to General McDowell's command. They were very desirous of getting back under General Banks' command, believing the amount of transportation they brought to General McDowell's command would be restored to them, and with it their baggage and comforts.

Question by General MCDOWELL. Was anything done at Front Royal or at Warrenton to lead these regiments to continue in this belief that they would not continue under General McDowell?

Answer. At Front Royal some officers of Massachusetts regiments visited General Banks, who was then, I believe, at Middletown, and brought from him the assurance that the brigade would soon be again under his command. At Warrenton, in July last, General Banks visited the command one evening and spoke to the regiments separately, I believe, telling them, as I heard, that they would soon be again under his command; that he was making efforts to get them back. I did not hear him myself.

Question by General MCDOWELL. What was the nature of the forced march, as to severity, of the brigade from Alexandria to Front Royal?

Answer. The weather at that time was very hot, and the march, considering the weather, was made as quickly as troops could perform it and be at all efficient at the end of the march.

Question by General MCDOWELL. Was that march the cause of complaint, so far as you know, in the brigade?

Answer. It was the cause of complaint, and I saw afterward letters written by officers of the brigade and published in Boston newspapers containing severe strictures on General McDowell as the author of suffering on the marches. The letter was filled with falsehoods.

Question by General MCDOWELL. Was there any complaint that the men were forced over the Blue Ridge in the rain and without tents or shelter?

Answer. There was such complaint.

Question by General MCDOWELL. Where did the brigade stop and how were they occupied the night before they reached Front Royal?

Answer. They stopped between 2 and 3 miles of the town of Front Royal, and bivouacked in some pine bushes by the road-side.

Question by General MCDOWELL. What kind of weather was it that night?

Answer. There was a severe rain-storm during nearly the whole of the night.

The court adjourned to meet to-morrow, December 16, 1862, at 12 o'clock m.

---

*TWENTY-SECOND DAY.*

COURT-ROOM, 467 SOUTH FOURTEENTH STREET,
*Washington, D. C., December* 16, 1862.

* * * * * * *

Maj. Gen. GEORGE L. HARTSUFF, U. S. Volunteers, the witness under examination.

* * * * * * *

Question by the COURT. Do you know any matter or thing tending to show that General McDowell was treacherous, incompetent, unfaithful, or otherwise disqualified for the command of a division, corps, or department; and if you do, state what you know as fully as though you were specifically interrogated in respect thereto?

Answer. I do not know any such cause.

The court requested that General McDowell would state the names of necessary witnesses whom he proposes to introduce and the points to which their evidence will relate.

Major-General McDowell presented to the court the following papers, which were read by the recorder, and will be appended to the proceedings of this day.*

1. From General Shields to Major-General McDowell, dated Manassas, May 27, 1862.
2. From Secretary of War to Major-General McDowell, dated Washington, May 27, 1862.
3. From Major-General McDowell to General Wadsworth, dated Manassas, May 28, 1862.
4. From General Wadsworth to Major-General McDowell, dated Washington, May 28, 1862.
5. From Major-General McDowell to Secretary of War, dated Headquarters Department of the Rappahannock, Manassas, May 28, 1862.
6. From General Saxton to Major-General McDowell, dated Washington, 7 p. m., May 28.
7. From General Shields to General McDowell, dated Catlett's, May 27, 1862.
8. From General Shields to General McDowell, dated Catlett's, May 27, 1862.
9. From General Shields to General McDowell, dated May 27, 1862.
10. From General Shields to General McDowell, dated Catlett's, May 27, 1862.
11. From General Shields to General McDowell, dated Catlett's, May 27, 1862.
12. From General Shields to General McDowell, dated Catlett's, May 27, 1862.
13. From General Shields to General McDowell, dated Catlett's, May 27, 1862.
14. From General McDowell to Secretary of War, dated Manassas, May 27, 1862.
15. From Colonel Schriver to General Shields, dated Headquarters, Alexandria, May 27, 1862.
16. From General McDowell to General Shields, dated Washington, May 27, 1862.
17. From General Saxton to Major-General McDowell, dated Washington, May 28, 1862.
18. From Secretary of War to General McDowell, dated Washington, May 28, 1862.
19. From Secretary of War to General McDowell, dated Washington, May 28, 1862.
20. From A. Lincoln to General McDowell, dated Washington, May 28, 1862.
21. From General Shields to Colonel Schriver, dated Rectortown, May 28, 1862.
22. From Secretary of War to General McDowell, dated Washington, May 28, 1862.
23. From A. Lincoln to General McDowell, dated Washington, May 28, 1862.
24. From same to same, same date.
25. From Secretary of War to General McDowell, dated Fredericksburg, May 28, 1862.
26. From same to same, dated Washington, May 29, 1862.
27. From General McDowell to Secretary of War, dated Headquarters, Manassas, May 28, 1862.
28. From same to same, same date.
29. From same to same, same date.
30. From same to General Shields, dated Headquarters Department, May, 1862.
31. From same to Secretary of War, dated Headquarters Department of the Rappahannock, May 28, 1862.
32. From same to same, dated headquarters, May 28, 1862.
33. From same to His Excellency the President, dated Headquarters Department of the Rappahannock, May 28, 1862.
34. From same to same, same date.
35. From same to Secretary of War, dated Headquarters Department of the Rappahannock, May 28, 1862.
36. From same to same, same date.
37. From General McCall to General McDowell, dated Falmouth, May 28.
38. From A. Lincoln to same, dated Washington, May 28.
39. From General Shields to same, dated Rectortown, May —.
40. From same to same, dated Rectortown, May 29, 1862.
41. From same to Colonel Schriver, dated Rectortown, May 29, 1862.
42. From Secretary of War to General McDowell, dated Washington City, D. C., May 29, 1862—4.30 p. m.
43. From General Frémont to the President, dated Moorefield, May 29, 1862.
44. From the President to General McDowell, dated War Department, Washington, D. C., May 29, 1862—12 m.
45. From General Shields to General McDowell, dated Rectortown, May 29, 1862.

* Omitted from appendix They may be found in chronological order in "Correspondence, etc.," Part III.

46. From same to same, same date.
47. From same to same, same date.
48. From same to same, same date.
49. From same to same, same date.
50. From same to same, same date.
51. From General McDowell to Secretary of War, dated Headquarters Department of the Rappahannock, Manassas, May 29, 1862.
52. From same to same, dated Headquarters, Manassas, May 29, 1862.
53. From same to General Shields, dated Headquarters Department, Manassas, May 29, 1862.
54. From same to same, same date.
55. From same to same, same date.
56. From same to same, same date.
57. From same to same, same date.
58. From same to same, same date.
59. From same to same, same date.
60. From A. Lincoln to General McDowell, dated War Department, Washington City, May 30, 1862—9.30 p. m.
61. From General Saxton to Secretary of War, dated Harper's Ferry, May 30, 1862.
62. From General Wadsworth to General McDowell, dated War Department, May 30, 1862.
63. From Secretary of War to General McDowell, dated War Department, May 30, 1862.
64. From A. Lincoln to same, dated War Department, Washington, May 30, 1862—10 a. m.
65. From Secretary of War to same, same date.
66. From same to same, same date.
67. From A. Lincoln to same, same date.
68. From same to same, same date.
69. From Secretary of War to same, same date.
70. From General King to General McDowell, dated Catlett's Station, May 30.
71. From General Shields to same, dated Front Royal, May 30, 1862.
72. From same to same, same date.
73. From General McDowell to Secretary of War, dated Rectortown, May 30, 1862.
74. From same to same, same date.
75. From same to General Shields, no date.
76. From same to same, dated Manassas, May 30, 1862.
77. From same to President, same date.
78. From P. H. Watson (Assistant Secretary of War) to General McDowell, dated Washington, May 30, 1862.
79. From Secretary of War to same, same date.
80. From General Saxton to same, same date.
81. From Secretary of War to same, same date.
82. From General Banks to same, same date.
83. From General Saxton to same, same date.
84. From General McDowell to Secretary of War, dated Rectortown, May 31, 1862.
85. From same to same, same date.
86. From same to same, same date.
87. From Secretary of War to General McDowell, dated Washington, June 1, 1862.
88. From same to same, same date.
89. From General McDowell to Secretary of War, dated Front Royal, June 1.
90. From same to same, same date.
91. From General Shields to Colonel Schriver, dated Monday morning, 5 a. m.
92. From Secretary of War to Generals McDowell and Frémont, dated Washington, June 2, 1862.
93. From A. Lincoln to General McDowell, dated Washington, June 3, 1862.
94. From General McDowell to Secretary of War, dated Front Royal, June 3, 1862.
95. From same to same, dated Headquarters Department of the Rappahannock, Front Royal, June 3, 1862.
96. From same to same, dated Headquarters Department of the Rappahannock, June 3, 1862.
97. From same to same, dated Headquarters Department of the Rappahannock, Front Royal, June 4, 1862.
98. From same to same, same date.
99. From same to same, same date.
100. From same to same, same date.

The court adjourned to meet in the room southwest corner of Pennsylvania avenue and Fourteenth street to-morrow, December 17, 1862, at 11 a. m.

*TWENTY-THIRD DAY.*

COURT-ROOM, SW. COR. PA. AVE. AND FOURTEENTH ST.,
*Washington, D. C., December* 17, 1862.

* * * * * * *

Brig. Gen. RUFUS KING, U. S. Volunteers, a witness, was duly sworn.

Question by General MCDOWELL. How long have you served under General McDowell and what commands have you held under him?

Answer. I have served about a year under General McDowell; first as commander of a brigade, afterward as commander of a division.

Question by General MCDOWELL. At the time your division was opposite Fredericksburg, in April and May last, how was it posted? Who was governor of Fredericksburg, and what were the duties which were devolved on you, as commander of the division, with reference to passes to and from the town?

Answer. One brigade of my division was posted in Fredericksburg. Three on this side of the river, opposite the town. General Patrick was the acting military governor. I don't recollect that I had special instructions on the subject of passes to and from the town, though there was an order on the subject, the terms of which I do not now recollect.

Question by General MCDOWELL. What knowledge have you of a man named Little, said to be a rebel adjutant?

Answer. I recollect a man by that name, whom I supposed then, and still suppose, to be a private citizen of Fredericksburg. He was frequently at my headquarters, and I understood, either from him or some friend of his, that he had been in the militia of Virginia some months previous, but was not so any longer. I think he told me so himself.

Question by General MCDOWELL. Do you recollect if any report was made to you by Peleg Clarke of Little's being a spy and asking you to have him arrested or of his being a rebel adjutant then in the service?

Answer. No, sir; except that he told me that Little was or had been a rebel adjutant.

Question by General MCDOWELL. Was any report made to you from General Patrick concerning this Little of his being a spy or rebel officer?

Answer. No, sir.

Question by General MCDOWELL. State what was done with the growing grain (wheat) which was in the fields near Chatham house, and which had been protected by General McDowell whilst his headquarters were opposite Fredericksburg.

Answer. The instructions, I recollect, were to protect the growing crops in our neighborhood, and the reason assigned was that we should need the wheat if the rebels didn't.

Question by General MCDOWELL. Was the wheat in those fields harvested for the Government?

Answer. I think it was, but am not sure.

Question by General MCDOWELL. State the effect on the discipline of the troops of General McDowell's orders and the policy pursued by him with reference to marauding or taking property without authority.

Answer. The effect upon the troops was excellent, and the policy, in my judgment, the best that could have been pursued.

Question by General MCDOWELL. Was a supposed change in that policy the source of any falling off in the discipline?

Answer. Yes, sir; very great and serious.

Question by General McDOWELL. Was that falling off in discipline the cause of any representation to the then commanding general? If so, what was the effect of that representation?

Answer. I don't distinctly recollect what the representation made was. My impression is that it led to such orders as made a change for the better, but am not certain.

Question by General McDOWELL. Do you know if the arrival near your division of troops more abundantly provided than they were with wagons, tents, &c., was the cause of any remark or feeling with reference to the allowances made to your division:

Answer. It was.

Question by General McDOWELL. What do you know of Peleg Clarke, at Fredericksburg, in connection with the presence of our army at that place, and in reference to rebel mails and illicit trade said to be authorized or permitted at that place, and with reference to his own connection with the property of the rebel army left by it in Fredericksburg?

Answer. I knew Mr. Peleg Clarke, and when I first went to Fredericksburg he was represented to me as one of the three or four Union men in that town. I don't recollect that he had any connection with the rebel mails or illicit trade. I do remember on the day we entered Fredericksburg that my quartermaster was directed to proceed to the railroad station and seize some grain said to be there and belonging to the rebel Government. He reported to me that he found 20,000 bushels of corn in sacks, marked "C. S. A.," which I directed him to take and use for forage for our army. This Mr. Clarke soon afterward claimed 2,000 bushels of that corn. I referred the question to my quartermaster, Captain Robinson, and directed him to investigate the claim, which he did, and reported to me.

The witness was here interrupted by a member, who stated, in substance, that the statement of the quartermaster on this point is not competent testimony.

The court was cleared, and the objection of the member sustained.

The witness continued.

I was about stating my knowledge of the last clause of the question when I was interrupted, my knowledge of the facts being derived from that report, which I believe is an official paper, in writing, and may be found.

Question by General McDOWELL. Will the witness please explain more fully his answer to the question as to what was done with the growing wheat near Chatham house?

Answer. I stated, I think, that we were directed to protect it; that if the rebels did not need it we would. I meant by that to say, and so understood it at the time, that we were to protect it for our own use.

Question by the COURT. Do you remember whether or not Peleg Clarke made any communication to you in regard to Little?

Answer. I think he did. I think he told me that Little was or had been an adjutant in the rebel service.

Question by the COURT. Are you able to say whether or not, after an interview between you and Peleg Clarke, you did not refer him to General McDowell?

Answer. My recollection is not distinct about that, though I think it is quite likely that I did refer him to General McDowell, as my commanding officer.

Question by General McDOWELL. State what orders, if any, were given by General McDowell for the guidance of his officers in respect to the admission of disloyal citizens into and out of his lines.

Answer. I can't remember precisely the orders given. I can only state my general impression from the instructions we had; these were that no disloyal citizens should be permitted to come within our lines.

Question by the COURT. Do you know any matter or thing tending to show that General McDowell, as a general officer, has been treacherous or inattentive to his duties, or wanting in reasonable discretion or personal bravery, or delinquent in the proper disposition of his troops for battle, or in using earnest efforts to co-operate with his brother commanders? If you answer in the affirmative in respect to either of these particulars, then state what you know on the subject fully, as though you were specifically interrogated.

Answer. All I know of General McDowell, all that I've seen of him during the year's service under his command, has satisfied me entirely of his zeal, fidelity to the Government, and devotion to duty. I have seen him under fire, and have no doubt as to his personal courage, his skill in the disposition of his troops, and his readiness to co-operate with any and every officer associated with him in the armies of the Republic. I know no matter or thing tending to show the contrary.

Question by the COURT. Have you information of any matter or thing (not within your personal knowledge) tending to inculpate General McDowell in either of the particulars specified in the foregoing interrogatory, and which, in your judgment, is entitled to the consideration of the court? If you have, please communicate that information in writing to the recorder for the consideration of the court.

Answer. None whatever, sir.

Question by the COURT. Does the court understand you to state that you have no knowledge that any disloyal citizen was ever permitted to pass into or from our lines while General McDowell was in command at or near Fredericksburg?

Answer. I don't recollect. I don't think I can give a positive answer to the question.

Brig. Gen. JAMES S. WADSWORTH, U. S. Volunteers, a witness, was duly sworn.

Question by General MCDOWELL. What is your rank in the United States service?

Answer. Brigadier-general of volunteers.

Question by General MCDOWELL. What official relations have you had with General McDowell since you have been in the United States service?

Answer. I served on his staff as a volunteer aide from 29th June till 9th August, 1861, and from 9th August to 15th March I commanded a brigade in his division.

Question by General MCDOWELL. What was General McDowell's conduct as division commander? Did he pay unusual attention to the instruction of his division? How was he as to its discipline and police? How as to the administrative duties of the division?

Answer. It was my impression at the time, from what I saw of other divisions near us, that General McDowell's division drilled quite as much as any and much more than some, and the general himself gave a great deal of attention to the drills, the police, and the discipline of his division.

Question by General MCDOWELL. What was General McDowell's conduct toward the inhabitants of the country whilst he was division commander, either as respects themselves or their property?

Answer. As respects their persons, he protected non-combatants from disturbance or molestation by the soldiers as far as possible. As respects their property, he took a large amount of forage for the public service at the time when it was needed—much needed—paying loyal citizens in money, and giving to those of questionable loyalty verbal or written assurances that they would be paid after the war if they were loyal from that time on. He did not allow marauding by soldiers.

Question by General McDOWELL. Was the same policy or conduct continued by him whilst he commanded the Department of the Rappahannock?

Answer. As far as I know.

Question by General McDOWELL. What position and command have you had in the service since you were relieved from General McDowell's division?

Answer. From the 15th March up to about the 20th or 25th of November I have been military governor of the District of Columbia, and for the first three or four months of that time in command of the troops assigned for the defense of the capital.

Question by General McDOWELL. Were you not under General McDowell's command whilst the Department of the Rappahannock existed?

Answer. I was.

Question by General McDOWELL. What was General McDowell's conduct whilst in command of the Department of the Rappahannock with reference to the efficiency and mobility of his army and his conduct in preparing his command for active service?

Answer. It appeared to me that he exhibited great activity in preparing for the field. I cannot answer the other questions. My command was not intended for the field.

Question by General McDOWELL. State if your official position and connection with the Government and your personal relations with General McDowell were such at the time as to enable you to know or to give you good grounds for judging as to General McDowell's having or not, in April last, sought, induced, or procured the separation of his army corps from the Army of the Potomac with a view to having a separate command for himself; and, if so, whether or not the retention of the corps was, to the best of your knowledge and belief, sought, induced, or procured by him or was made by the Government for public reasons, based on the representations of others?

Answer. I can only say that, from General McDowell's declarations to me, his separation from the Army of the Potomac was a matter of serious regret to him, and from what I saw when he received intelligence of the organization of the Department of Rappahannock from the Secretary of War it was a surprise to him.

Question by General McDOWELL. What was the force, what was its composition and character, which was left under your command for the defenses of the city of Washington by General McClellan at the time he embarked, in April, 1862, for the Peninsula, and what drafts were ordered from that force by him at that time?

Answer. About the 2d of April, the time of his embarkation, my report shows that I had between 19,200 and 19,400 effective men under my command. This embraced six companies of cavalry mounted, and no light artillery fit for service. I can give other details from my reports, which I can lay before the court if they desire it. I had received orders at that time to dispatch four of the best regiments from that force to the Army of the Potomac. I received orders likewise to send 4,000 men to Manassas to relieve General Sumner. I considered this force, however, as part of the force for the defense of the capital, and was part of the aforementioned 19,000 and odd men. The troops under a command for this purpose were the newest and least effective from the Army of the Potomac.

Question by General McDOWELL. State if your personal relations to General McDowell have been such as to enable you to know as to his habits with respect to the use of intoxicating liquors, and whether you know of the reputation he bears as to the use of intoxicating liquors with those who are intimate with him. If so, state what his habits are or what they are reputed to be in this particular.

Answer. I never knew him to drink anything but water. I believe it is notorious in the Army that he does not drink anything but water.

Question by General MCDOWELL. Do you recollect if General McDowell did not write or telegraph you to discourage the coming of traders to Fredericksburg at the time his headquarters were opposite that place?

Answer. I recollect of receiving a communication of that sort from him.

Question by the COURT. Can you state the reasons and causes for the detention of General McDowell from the Army of the Potomac, together with his corps, and the consolidation of that corps with the troops left for the defense of Washington under his command?

Answer. I can give my impression. Because the troops left for the defense of Washington were not deemed adequate.

Question by the COURT. Can you state at what points the 19,400 men named by you were located when General McClellan embarked for the Peninsula; especially was this force or not wholly in the fortifications or did it include any movable force?

Answer. The force employed in provost-guard duty was about 3,500 men. I think there was about as many more that were movable; not located in the forts, but ready for duty wherever they might be required. Some of these troops which I reported as movable were two regiments of cavalry, without horses or arms except sabers.

Question by the COURT. Where was the movable force to cover the city of Washington located?

Answer. I have stated all that was under my command and of which I have any direct knowledge. I understood that General Abercrombie was at Warrenton or Catlett's with a brigade of infantry and some cavalry. Two regiments from that brigade shortly after came in here to be paid off, their term of service having expired. General Banks was at Winchester, the other side of the Blue Ridge, and about 80 miles from here; but I cannot think his force was intended to cover Washington. I know of no other troops in any way connected with the defenses of Washington or available for its defense.

Question by the COURT. When you were left in command of the defenses of the city were you furnished with statements showing the location of the troops confided to your command? To what means did you resort to ascertain the number and location of the troops?

Answer. I was not furnished with an accurate list. I took the command just as the troops were leaving for the Peninsula. I published an order for the commanders of all troops within my command to report to me.

Question by the COURT. State whether you consider the troops at Centreville, Manassas, in the valley of the Shenandoah, at Baltimore, or elsewhere in the department then commanded by Major-General Dix as being part of the forces designed for or properly applicable to the defense of Washington?

Answer. I should consider troops at Centreville and Manassas as covering Washington, but not troops the other side of Bull Run Mountains or at Baltimore or elsewhere in the department of General Dix. I understood that there were very few troops at Baltimore, not more than was required for the police duty and safety of the place. I ought to add, perhaps, that I had a communication from General McClellan indicating that my right would rest on General Banks' left at Manassas. I, however, received the subsequent order to send 4,000 troops to Manassas.

Question by the COURT. How many troops did General Abercrombie have in the brigade to which you referred and how much was it reduced by the discharge of the two regiments whose time had expired? How many troops had General Banks under his command?

Answer. I cannot answer as to General Abercrombie any nearer than I have. I supposed that he had a brigade, but do not know its strength. From subsequent developments I should say that General Banks had about 17,000 men in Winchester and the valley of the Shenandoah.

Question by the COURT. Do you know of any communication addressed by General McClellan to the Government giving the number of troops left for the defense of Washington and their location? If so, state whether the forces in the valley of the Shenandoah and in Maryland were not included in said list, and whether such enumeration and assignment were not virtually adopted by the Government, and these troops relied upon for the defense of the capital?

Answer. I know nothing of it.

The court adjourned to meet to-morrow, December 18, 1862, at 12 o'clock m.

---

## *TWENTY-FOURTH DAY.*

COURT-ROOM, COR. PA. AVE. AND FOURTEENTH ST.,
*Washington, D. C., December* 18, 1862.

* * * * * * *

Lieut. Col. FREDERICK MYERS, aide-de-camp and assistant quartermaster, U. S. Army, a witness, was duly sworn.

Question by General MCDOWELL. What was your position on General McDowell's staff whilst he was in command in Virginia, during the present year, 1862?

Answer. I was his chief quartermaster.

Question by General MCDOWELL. Lay before the court such of your reports or returns as you may have at hand of property taken from the inhabitants of the country occupied by our troops when you were under General McDowell's command. State the amount and kind of stores taken, the amount paid for, if any, and the amount and kind for which claim was made on you for payment; and, if any payment was refused state the grounds for so refusing, and whether you paid any disloyal person or refused to pay any person; and, if so, state fully why you so refused.

The witness referred to a book, showing means of transportation, quartermaster's stores taken up, and colored fugitives from service employed.

Answer. I have no other returns than those contained in the book, for the reason that the others were captured by the enemy at Catlett's Station. I have no recollection of any stores being paid for except in one case, which was paid on my order by Captain Loomis, at Warrenton. It was to a loyal citizen, who voted against secession, as the records of the county clerk's office in Warrenton will show. He was one of the four who voted against secession in that county. His name I have forgotten. In taking stores, a certificate of that form was made out and issued to all the quartermasters.

(A form was handed the recorder and was read by the witness, and is appended to the proceedings of this day, and is marked A.)

The witness continued:

Here is a copy of an order to General Abercrombie.

(Which letter the witness read, and is appended to this day's proceedings and marked B.)

The witness read a letter to Captain Willard, acting quartermaster, which is appended to this day's proceedings and marked C.

The witness continued:

Here is a letter directed to a quartermaster to get corn from certain farms.

(Which letter is appended to this day's proceedings and marked D.)

The witness continued:

Similar letters were written to other quartermasters; also a letter to General Patrick, directing the examination of certain reported pressed hay.

(Which letter is appended to the proceedings of this day and marked E.)

The witness continued:

The letters I hold, written by myself, I will read as part of my answer to the question propounded.

(The letters were read by the witness, and are appended to this day's proceedings and marked F, G, H, and I.)

The witness continued:

As far as I have returns for there were taken 682,895 pounds of corn, 12,416 pounds of oats, 19,574 pounds of hay, 13,850 pounds of fodder, and 5 mules.

There was of this corn taken 147,702 pounds marked "Confederate States," taken from the store-house of Peleg Clarke, and certificate given by Capt. J. Springstead, assistant quartermaster, and 99,272 pounds corn marked "Confederate States," taken from store-house of Peleg Clarke, and certificate given by same person, Captain Springstead. I think claim was made on me for nearly all these stores. None were paid for, however, as far as my knowledge goes. Payment was refused on the ground of their being rebels, antagonistic to the Government. Payment was always refused to disloyal persons, on the ground that they were disloyal. Mr. Clarke never made any claim on me for payment. He was known to me by sight, but never spoke to me.

Question by General McDowell. You say you refused payment to Mr. Clarke for his claim on account of property taken from his store-house marked "Confederate States;" on what ground did you so refuse?

Answer. I did not so state. Mr. Clarke never called upon me for payment.

Question by General McDowell. Did Mr. Clarke, as far as you know, ever call on any of your subordinates for payment for the Confederate corn found in his store-house?

The court was cleared at the instance of a member.

The court was opened and the following decision announced:

The question is immaterial and is excluded. The court has already decided that evidence will not be received to contradict the testimony of Mr. Clarke on matters wholly collateral, nor to impeach him except by proof of general character, and not of particular parts of his conduct. It is desired that this decision will not be overlooked in propounding questions to the witness.

The court had no questions to ask this witness.

General McDowell here submitted to the court a book containing official letters emanating from the Headquarters Department of the Rappahannock, from which book the recorder read the letters dated and marked as follows, copies of which are to be appended to the proceedings of this day.*

1. From General McDowell to General James Shields, dated Headquarters Department of the Rappahannock, opposite Fredericksburg, May 25, 1862.

2. From Lieutenant-Colonel Schriver, chief of staff, to Maj. Gen. E. O. C. Ord,

*Omitted from appendix, to appear in chronological order in "Correspondence, etc.," Part III.

dated Headquarters Department of the Rappahannock, Rectortown, Va., May 31, 1862.

3. From Lieut. Col. Ed. Schriver, chief of staff, to General Shields, dated Headquarters Department of the Rappahannock, Rectortown, Va., May 31, 1862.

4. From Lieutenant-Colonel Schriver, chief of staff, to Brig. Gen. J. W. Geary, dated Headquarters Department of the Rappahannock, Piedmont, Va., May 31, 1862.

5. From Lieutenant-Colonel Schriver to Brig. Gen. J. B. Ricketts, dated Headquarters Department of the Rappahannock, Front Royal, Va., June 1—11 a. m.

6. From Lieut. Col. E. Schriver, a memorandum for General Ricketts, dated Headquarters Department of the Rappahannock, Front Royal, June 1, 1862.

7. From Lieutenant-Colonel Schriver, chief of staff, to Brigadier-General Bayard, dated Headquarters Department of the Rappahannock, Front Royal, June 1, 1862.

8. From Lieutenant Colonel Schriver to commanding officer First Maine Cavalry, dated Headquarters Department of the Rappahannock, Front Royal, Va., June 2, 1862.

8½. From General McDowell to Maj. Gen. John C. Frémont, dated Headquarters Department of the Rappahannock, Strasburg, June 2, 1862.

9. From Lieut. Col. E. Schriver to Lieutenant-Colonel Thompson, chief quartermaster Shields' division, dated Headquarters Department of the Rappahannock, Front Royal, Va., June 3, 1862.

10. From Colonel Schriver to Brig. Gen. J. W. Geary, dated Headquarters Department of the Rappahannock, Front Royal, June 3, 1862.

11. From Colonel Schriver to Maj. Gen. E. O. C. Ord, dated Headquarters Department of the Rappahannock, Front Royal, Va., June 3, 1862.

12. From Major-General McDowell to Maj. Gen. J. C. Frémont, dated Headquarters Department of the Rappahannock, Front Royal, June 3, 1862.

13. From Col. E. Schriver to commanding officer United States troops at Strasburg, dated Headquarters Department of the Rappahannock, Front Royal, Va., June 3, 1862.

14. From Colonel Schriver to Maj. Gen. E. O. C. Ord, dated Headquarters Department of the Rappahannock, Front Royal, Va., June 3, 1862.

15. From Colonel Schriver to Maj. Gen. E. O. C. Ord, dated Headquarters Department of the Rappahannock, Front Royal, Va., June 3, 1862.

16. From Col. E. Schriver to Maj. Gen. E. O. C. Ord, dated Headquarters Department of the Rappahannock, Front Royal, Va., June 3, 1862.

17. From Colonel Schriver to Maj. Gen. E. O. C. Ord, dated Headquarters Department of the Rappahannock, Front Royal, Va., June 3, 1862.

17½. From Col. E. Schriver to Major-General Shields, dated Headquarters Department of the Rappahannock, Front Royal, June 3, 1862.

17¾. From Col. Ed. Schriver to Maj. Gen. E. O. C. Ord, dated Headquarters Department of the Rappahannock, Front Royal, Va., June 4, 1862.

18. From Samuel Breck, assistant adjutant-general, to Major-General Shields, dated Headquarters Department of the Rappahannock, Front Royal, June 6, 1862.

19. Samuel Breck, assistant adjutant-general, to Maj. Gen. E. O. C. Ord, commanding division, dated Headquarters Department of the Rappahannock, Front Royal, June 6, 1862.

20. From General McDowell to Maj. Gen. N. P. Banks, dated Headquarters Department of the Rappahannock, Front Royal, Va., June 5, 1862.

21. From General McDowell to Major-General Frémont, dated Headquarters Department of the Rappahannock, Front Royal, Va., June 6, 1862.

The court adjourned to meet to-morrow, December 19, 1862, at 11 o'clock a. m.

—

## APPENDIX.

### A.

*Form of certificate.*

DEPARTMENT OF THE RAPPAHANNOCK,
———— —, 1862.

This certifies that there has been received from the farm of ———— ———— the following military supplies ————:

Such supplies will be accounted for on the property returns of ———— ————, quartermaster, U. S. Army, for the ———— quarter of 186–.

The owner of said property will be entitled to be paid for the same after the suppression of the rebellion upon proof that he has from this date conducted himself as a loyal citizen of the United States and has not given aid or comfort to the rebels.

Done under authority of ——— ———.

——— ———,
*Quartermaster.*

*Instructions.*

CHIEF QUARTERMASTER'S OFFICE,
*April* 24, 1862.

For all quartermaster's supplies so received a receipt will be given, as in the preceding form, to the person of whom such supplies were received.

A report in abstract form will be made at the end of each month to this office, giving the date, the name of the person from whom, the place where, and the quantity, received.

FRED. MYERS,
*Captain, Assistant Quartermaster and Chief Quartermaster.*

B.

HDQRS. DEPARTMENT OF THE RAPPAHANNOCK,
CHIEF QUARTERMASTER'S OFFICE,
*Catlett's Station, April* 18, 1862.

General ABERCROMBIE,
*Commanding, &c., Warrenton Junction:*

I have the honor to request that your quartermaster be directed to obtain all the information he can in reference to forage in advance of your division, and advise me as early as possible in the premises.

Very respectfully, &c.,

FRED. MYERS,
*Captain, Assistant Quartermaster and Chief Quartermaster.*

C.

HDQRS. DEPARTMENT OF THE RAPPAHANNOCK,
CHIEF QUARTERMASTER'S OFFICE,
*Opposite Fredericksburg, Va., April* 23, 1862.

Capt. J. C. WILLARD,
*Acting Assistant Quartermaster, Headquarters:*

I understand that you can obtain corn at the farm of Mr. ——— ———, about 2 miles from here. You will send your teams to haul sufficient from there to this place for this day's supply for animals at these headquarters.

Very respectfully, &c.,

FRED. MYERS,
*Captain, Assistant Quartermaster and Chief Quartermaster.*

D.

HDQRS. DEPARTMENT OF THE RAPPAHANNOCK,
CHIEF QUARTERMASTER'S OFFICE,
*Opposite Fredericksburg, April* 24, 1862.

Capt. J. HODGE,
*Assistant Quartermaster, General Augur's Brigade:*

You will report at these headquarters on this day, the 24th instant, at 8 o'clock a. m., with a sufficient number of teams, to collect and transport forage for two days for the animals in General Augur's brigade, including cavalry and artillery.

Very respectfully, &c.,

FRED. MYERS,
*Captain, Assistant Quartermaster and Chief Quartermaster.*

E.

HDQRS. DEPARTMENT OF THE RAPPAHANNOCK,
CHIEF QUARTERMASTER'S OFFICE,
*Opposite Fredericksburg, May* 6, 1862.

Brig. Gen. M. R. PATRICK, U. S. A.,
*Fredericksburg, Va.:*

Major-General McDowell informs me that there is reported a lot of pressed hay near the basin. He (general commanding) wishes it to be examined and reported to this office, as early as possible, whether such is the fact, or whether it is only baled straw or wheat.

Very respectfully, &c.,

FRED. MYERS,
*Captain, Assistant Quartermaster and Chief Quartermaster.*

F.

HDQRS. DEPARTMENT OF THE RAPPAHANNOCK,
CHIEF QUARTERMASTER'S OFFICE,
*Opposite Fredericksburg, May* 9, 1862.

Lieut. E. ROSS,
*Acting Assistant Quartermaster, Aquia Creek Depot:*

The major-general commanding directs that all property useful to the Government brought into your depot by "colored fugitives from service" be taken in charge by you for the benefit of the United States.

You will take up such property on your returns, as required by paragraphs 786 and 1013 Revised Army Regulations.

Very respectfully, &c.,

FRED. MYERS,
*Captain and Chief Quartermaster.*

(Copy sent to Capt. H. A. Lacy, assistant quartermaster at Falmouth.)

G.

HDQRS. DEPARTMENT OF THE RAPPAHANNOCK,
CHIEF QUARTERMASTER'S OFFICE,
*Opposite Fredericksburg, May* 12, 1862.

Capt. C. HALL,
*Assistant Quartermaster, General McCall's Division:*

The major-general commanding directs me to call your immediate attention to General Orders, No. 8.

You will make a return without delay to these headquarters of all quartermaster's stores taken up by you from citizens in the month of April, 1862. You will direct each of the brigade quartermasters who have not already done so to forward at the earliest moment possible to these headquarters a report of all quartermaster's stores that have been taken up by their respective brigades in the month of April.

Your attention is called to my letter of the 7th instant, inclosing General Orders, No. 4, to which your response has not been received.

Very respectfully, &c.,

FRED. MYERS,
*Captain and Chief Quartermaster.*

H.

HDQRS. DEPARTMENT OF THE RAPPAHANNOCK,
CHIEF QUARTERMASTER'S OFFICE,
*Opposite Fredericksburg, May* 15, 1862.

Capt. JUSTIN HODGE,
*Assistant Quartermaster, General Augur's Brigade:*

In answer to your letter of the 13th instant I would state that Mr. J. H. Hoffman should make his affidavit of the facts in reference to the corn taken by the troops at Belle Plain, for which no receipts were taken, to accompany your statement and explanation in reference thereto. For the corn taken up by you your receipt in duplicate should be given, blank copies of which I herewith inclose.

You will also find inclosed General Orders, No. 8, in reference to all supplies taken up from citizens.

Very respectfully, &c.,

FRED. MYERS,
*Captain and Chief Quartermaster.*

I.

HDQRS. DEPARTMENT OF THE RAPPAHANNOCK,
CHIEF QUARTERMASTER'S OFFICE,
*Opposite Fredericksburg, May* 24, 1862.

Capt. H. A. LACY,
*Assistant Quartermaster, at Depot:*

You will without delay take possession, for the use of the United States of a lot of lumber at the saw-mill near the headquarters of General McCall, for the purpose of constructing temporary warehouses, sheds, stables, &c.

You will call upon Brigadier-General Doubleday, commanding at this place, for what assistance you may require in erecting such buildings.

By order of Major-General McDowell:

FRED. MYERS,
*Major and Chief Quartermaster.*

---

*TWENTY-FIFTH DAY.*

COURT-ROOM, COR. FOURTEENTH ST. AND PA. AVE.,
*Washington, D. C., December* 19, 1862.

* * * * * * *

The recorder then read from the official books of telegrams received at and sent from the Headquarters of Department of the Rappahannock the following telegrams, which are appended to the proceedings of this day,* as follows:

---

*Omitted from appendix, to appear in chronological order in "Correspondence, etc.," Part III.

1. From Secretary of War to Major-General McDowell, dated Washington, June 4, 1862.

2. From Colonel Haupt, aide-de-camp, to Major-General McDowell, dated Rectortown, June 4, 1862.

3. From General McDowell to Hon. E. M. Stanton, dated Headquarters Department of the Rappahannock, Front Royal, June 5, 1862.

4. From General McDowell to Hon. E. M. Stanton, dated Headquarters Department of the Rappahannock, Front Royal, June 5, 1862.

5. From E. M. Stanton, Secretary of War, to General McDowell, dated Washington, June 6, 1862.

6. From L. Thomas, Adjutant-General, to Major-General McDowell, dated Washington, June 6, 1862.

The court took a recess of thirty minutes.

7. From General McDowell to Hon. E. M. Stanton, dated Headquarters, Front Royal, Va., June 6, 1862.

8. From General McDowell to Edmund Schriver, chief of staff, dated Washington, June 7, 1862.

9. From same to same, dated Washington, June 8, 1862.

9½. From same to same, same date.

10. From same to same, same date.

11. From J. DeW. Cutting, captain and aide-de-camp to Colonel Schriver, dated Washington, June 8, 1862.

12. From General McDowell to Colonel Schriver, chief of staff, dated Washington, June 8, 1862.

13. From same to same, same date.

14. From same to same, same date.

15. From same to same, same date.

16. From same to same, same date.

General McDowell here handed the recorder a copy of a letter (extract) from L. Thomas, Adjutant-General, to Major-General McDowell, dated War Department, Adjutant-General's Office, Washington, June 8, 1862; which was read by the recorder, and is appended to the proceedings of this day, and marked A.*

The recorder continued the reading of the dispatches sent from and received at Headquarters Department of the Rappahannock, and which are appended, as follows:

17. From Col. E. Schriver, chief of staff, to General Shields, Luray, dated Front Royal, June 8, 1862.

18. From E. Schriver to Major-General McDowell, dated Front Royal, June 8, 1862.

19. From E. Schriver to Major-General Shields, dated Front Royal, June 8, 1862.

20. From General McDowell to Colonel Schriver, dated Washington, June 9, 1862.

21. From same to same, same date.

22. From same to same, same date.

23. From Brig. Gen. George A. McCall to Major-General McDowell, dated Seven miles below Fredericksburg, June 9, 1862.

24. From Ed. Schriver, chief of staff, to Major-General Shields, dated Front Royal, June 9, 1862.

25. From same to same, same date.

26. From same to same, same date.

27. From General McDowell to Col. Ed. Schriver, dated Washington, June 10, 1862.

28. From Gen. Rufus King to General McDowell, dated Catlett's, June 10, 1862.

29. From General McDowell to Col. E. Schriver, dated Washington, June 10, 1862.

30. From same to same, same date.

31. From L. Thomas, Adjutant-General, to Major-General Frémont, dated Adjutant-General's Office, Washington, June 10, 1862.

32. From General McDowell to Major-General Shields, dated Washington, June 10, 1862.

33. From R. Morris Copeland, major and assistant adjutant-general, to Col. Ed. Schriver, dated Headquarters Department of the Shenandoah, Winchester, June 11, 1862.

34. From General Shields to General McDowell, dated Luray, June 12, 1862.

35. From Maj. Gen. N. P. Banks to Hon. E. M. Stanton, dated Headquarters Department of the Shenandoah, Winchester, June 12, 1862.

*To appear in "Correspondence, etc.," Part III.

36. From E. M. Stanton to Major-General McDowell, dated Washington, June 12, 1862.
37. From Major-General Shields to Colonel ——, dated June 12, 1862—Columbia Bridge 9 a. m.
38. From Ed. Schriver, colonel and chief of staff, to Hon. E. M. Stanton, dated Headquarters Department, Manassas, June 12, 1862.
39. From Ed. Schriver, colonel and chief of staff, to Major-General Shields, dated Manassas, June 12, 1862.
40. From Ed. Schriver, colonel and chief of staff, to General Ricketts, dated Manassas, June 12, 1862—4 p. m.
41. From same to same, dated Headquarters Department, Manassas, June 12, 1862.
42. From same to same, dated Headquarters Department of the Rappahannock, Manassas, June 12—3.30 p. m.

The telegrams referred to in the foregoing are numbered 37 and 38, this series.

43. From Col. Ed. Schriver, chief of staff, to General Ricketts, dated Headquarters Department of the Rappahannock, June 12, 1862.
44. From General McDowell to Hon. E. M. Stanton, dated Headquarters Department, Manassas, June 12, 1862.
45. From same to same, dated Headquarters Department of the Rappahannock, Manassas, June 12, 1862.
46. From Brigadier-General Bayard to Col. E. Schriver, dated New Market, June 12, 1862.
47. From Brig. Gen. R. King to Colonel Schriver, chief of staff, dated Catlett's, June 12, 1862.
48. From General McDowell to Hon. E. M. Stanton, dated Headquarters Department of the Rappahannock, Manassas, June —, 1862.
49. From General McDowell to Major-General Banks, dated Headquarters Department of the Rappahannock, Manassas, June 13, 1862.
50. From General McDowell to Hon. E. M. Stanton, dated Headquarters Department of the Rappahannock, Manassas, June 13, 1862.
51. From General McDowell to Hon. E. M. Stanton, dated Headquarters Department of the Rappahannock, Manassas, June —, 1862.
52. From Colonel Schriver, chief of staff, to Brigadier-General Ricketts, dated Headquarters Department of the Rappahannock, Manassas, June 13, 1862.
53. From Colonel Schriver, chief of staff, to Major-General Shields, dated Headquarters Department, Manassas, June 13, 1862.
54. From Brigadier-General King to Major-General McDowell, dated Catlett's, June 13, 1862.
55. From Brigadier-General Ricketts to Colonel Schriver, dated Front Royal, June 13, 1862.
56. From E. M. Stanton to General McDowell, dated Washington, June 13, 1862.
57. From General N. P. Banks to General McDowell, dated Winchester, June 13, 1862.
58. From E. M. Stanton to Major-General McDowell, dated Washington, June 14, 1862.
59. From General N. P. Banks to General McDowell, dated Winchester, June 14, 1862.

The court adjourned to meet to-morrow, December 20, 1862, at 11 o'clock a. m.

---

### *TWENTY-SIXTH DAY.*

COURT-ROOM, COR. FOURTEENTH ST. AND PA. AVE.,
*Washington, D. C., December* 20, 1862.

* * * * * * *

Maj. MALCOLM McDOWELL, additional paymaster, U. S. Volunteers, a witness, was duly sworn.

Question by General McDOWELL. What relation are you to Major-General McDowell? What relation or connection, by blood or marriage, is there or has there been between General McDowell and the Hon. S. P. Chase, Secretary of the Treasury, or the Hon. E. M. Stanton, Secretary of War?

Answer. I am his own full brother. To the latter question I answer there is no relation whatever.

Question by General McDOWELL. Is there or has there been any relationship or connection, by marriage or blood, between General McDowell and any of the enemy's generals?

Answer. None that I know of.

The court had no questions to ask this witness.

Maj. Gen. FRANZ SIGEL, U. S. Volunteers, a witness, was duly sworn.

Question by the COURT. What is your rank in the service of the United States?

Answer. I am major-general of volunteers.

Question by the COURT. Have you held command in any corps or department where you have operated in connection with General McDowell or in a department contiguous to one in which General McDowell had command; and, if so, when and where? Describe fully and particularly.

Answer. At the time when General Banks was in the Shenandoah Valley and General Frémont I marched from Harper's Ferry to Winchester, where I learned that the forces of General McDowell were at Front Royal. Afterward, during the campaign of General Pope, I knew that the forces of General McDowell were at Warrenton and the vicinity, whilst my corps was at Sperryville and Luray.

During the operations on the Rappahannock I was under the direct orders of General Pope, co-operating with General McDowell. After the engagements at Freeman's Ford, Sulphur Springs, and Waterloo Bridge I received an order from General Pope that my corps was attached to the command of General McDowell. I regarded myself under his orders from this time until after the battle of Bull Run. I cannot give exact dates without reference to my papers. I cannot give the date when I left Harper's Ferry for Winchester. It was, however, about the 4th of June we arrived at Harper's Ferry, and I left the same day for Winchester with the troops I found at Harper's Ferry.

We marched to Sperryville from Winchester and Middletown about the last of June or first of July. I arrived at Culpeper on the 9th of August, during the battle of General Banks at Cedar Mountain. After the battle of Cedar Mountain my corps marched to Robertson River and Crooked Creek. We left this position in the middle of August and marched by Aestham River to Sulphur Springs, and from Sulphur Springs to Rappahannock Station, where we joined General McDowell's corps. On the 24th August we were at Waterloo Bridge, and on the 27th in Warrenton. On the 28th we marched from Gainesville toward Manassas, General McDowell following the First Corps—my corps—at that time the First Corps, Army of Virginia. I do not know how far General McDowell followed my movements on that day. I had orders to march to Manassas, and took the shortest road I could find. During this march from Gainesville to Manassas I heard firing to my left, marched toward that point, and formed in line of battle, when I received orders from General McDowell to march to Manassas. When my advanced guard arrived at Manassas it was reported that there was no enemy there, and that he had retreated toward Centreville. I therefore sent my aide-de-camp to General Pope to get permit to march to New Market. He there directed me to march to Centreville.

On this march, and arriving near New Market, I met a detachment of the enemy, which I attacked immediately and advanced toward Groveton. During this engagement we heard firing on our left, which we supposed was coming from part of General McDowell's corps. It had become dark, and we encamped that night on the heights near Mrs. Henry's farm, near Groveton. On the morning of 29th I received direct orders from General Pope to attack the enemy, which I did about 6 o'clock in the morning. I did not know where General McDowell's corps was at that time or where any other troops were except those of the enemy. During the 29th, and toward noon, when all the troops of my corps were engaged with the enemy, I received a dispatch from General Pope, saying that General McDowell and General Porter would attack the enemy's right flank and would come in on my left, and that we had probably to go back to Centreville that night to get provisions.

This is what I remember: I can probably find the original dispatch of General Pope in regard to this matter. I do not know whether any attack was made by General

McDowell or when his troops arrived on my left, because I was too much occupied on the right, where the battle was fought principally. I did not see General McDowell during that day until 6.30 minutes p. m., when I saw him and his staff arriving.

On the next day, the 30th August, I did not know where General McDowell's corps was, and I did not see General McDowell during the whole day, as much as I can remember, but I knew that General Reynolds' division was on the left of our line, or near the left of our line, on the 29th and 30th. During the 30th August, same day when General Porter made his attack on the center and was forced to retreat, I received a dispatch, which I believe was transmitted to me by an officer of General McDowell's staff, but the dispatch was written by General Porter, as much as I can remember. In this dispatch it was said that probably the conflict would end fatally, and that General McDowell should push my corps forward. I did not receive an order, but made all preparations to assist General Porter or to take his troops up, who were at that time coming out by squads—out of the woods by squads. I did not receive any order from General McDowell during the day.

I have also to add in regard to the connection between this corps and that of General McDowell, that when at Sulphur Springs General Pope wrote to me that General McDowell would support me at Waterloo Bridge, but I did not see any troops of General McDowell's there for some miles from that point; and at Waterloo Bridge on that same day I received an order, through General McDowell of which one page was missing, so that I do not know what my orders were. I immediately sent to General McDowell for instructions, but he answered that he could not give me any. I am not sure when I received my order from General Pope, which showed exactly when my corps was attached to General McDowell's, but I can find it out. The officer whom I had sent to General McDowell then proceeded to Warrenton Junction to find General Pope. He returned when it was nearly dark with an order of General Pope's for my corps to march to Warrenton that night, which I did. When the corps was at Warrenton with the main force, and I came in with the rear guard about 2.30 a. m. On the next day I met an officer of General McDowell's at the entrance of the town, who delivered me a dispatch, in which it was said that I should force with my corps the passage of the bridge at Waterloo on that same morning, which was an impossibility. This is to show that I received an order from General McDowell on that day at that hour. When my corps had arrived at Gainesville I received an order from General McDowell at about 3 o'clock in the morning, saying that I should march to Manassas. I asked the orderly when he had left General McDowell, and he said that he had left him two hours ago, although the headquarters of General McDowell were not more than 200 paces from my own.

These are the principal facts I can give you.

Question by the COURT. Have you knowledge of any matter or thing occurring during the period of the operations detailed by you in the answer to the last interrogatory tending to show that General McDowell was either treacherous, inattentive to his duties as a general officer, neglectful or otherwise in co-operating with his associate commanders, or going to their aid or the aid of his subordinate commanders, or wanting in personal courage or discretion in battle, or in the disposition of his troops, or otherwise unfaithful or inefficient as a general officer, and if you do, detail your knowledge specifically as though particularly interrogated in respect thereto?

Answer. I must say, gentlemen, that these are extensive questions, and you will allow me to take them up in detail. The first question, "tending to show whether General McDowell has been treacherous," &c. Now treacherous might relate to his connection with me or the enemy. Now you want me, I suppose, to say with regard to the enemy. In regard to treachery, I have no proof or no knowledge of such actions of General McDowell which deserves the name of treachery, as far as relates to connection with the enemy or communication with the enemy or other such acts. In regard to the second point, "inattention to his duties as a general officer," as relates to myself and my judgment, he was not attentive enough, and to qualify my judgment I will give you a few points. In the first place I do not believe that General McDowell did what he could under the circumstances to hinder General Longstreet to join General Jackson. I am not certain, but I believe that he left not a sufficient force at Thoroughfare Gap, or in the neighborhood, to prevent the enemy's troops to pass by this defile, which is very easy to defend. I further believe that there was not the necessary co-operation between the two corps of the [two] corps on their way to Manassas—my corps and that of General McDowell's—by which want of co-operation we lost the opportunity to attack the enemy on his left flank while he was retreating from Manassas.

On the 29th August, at the first battle of Bull Run, it would have been necessary that General McDowell had made a disposition by which our two corps could act with more unity. I believe that he could be on the battle-field with the greater part of his troops at an earlier hour of the day. I also believe that he did not give his troops the right direction on the 29th, because instead of attacking the enemy on his right flank, by coming in on our left, his troops, as much as I could see, came in from the rear; that is to say, instead of coming in the direction of New Market he came in the direction of Centreville—I do not know for what reason. I cannot understand for what reasons General McDowell left the position which he held on the 28th, in the evening, which would have been, according to my opinion, the right place for attacking the enemy in his right flank on the 29th.

There is on the next point, "neglectful or otherwise in co-operating with his associate commanders." I think that General McDowell neglected to get a personal knowledge of the affairs of my corps on the 29th of August, and that it was therefore impossible for him to make his arrangements as they had to be made or as they were intended. I also must mention a remark of General McDowell, which he made to one of my staff officers during our march from Gainesville to Manassas.

General McDowell asked, at this point in the examination, if this is proper evidence to be received by the court; that it was his impression that the court declined to receive like evidence coming from a witness a day or two since.

The court was cleared.

The court was opened.

The court asked the witness the name of the staff officer to whom he referred; where he is, and if his presence before the court could be produced.

Answer. It is Captain Dahlgren, one of my staff; he is here now present before the court.

The following decision of the court was announced:

If it were in proof that General McDowell had made an improper remark, relating to the operations in question, to a staff officer of General Sigel, it would be competent to prove that the remark was duly reported to General Sigel equally as though it were a written message sent to him. It is desirable to observe this order in obtaining the proof in this case if it were practicable, but General Sigel is now called from the field, and it appears to be necessary to receive the testimony. If not supported by direct proof that General McDowell made the remark to such staff officer, it will not operate to General McDowell's prejudice.

The court informed General McDowell that if he considers that it might prejudice his case to continue the examination of General Sigel upon this point, they would suspend the further examination of the witness for the present, with a view to introducing the testimony immediately of Captain Dahlgren.

General McDowell stated that it would please him to have the present witness continue, but would ask that Captain Dahlgren might withdraw from the court while testimony is being given on the matter upon which Captain Dahlgren is to be questioned.

The court requested Captain Dahlgren to withdraw, and to hold himself in readiness to appear as a witness before this court.

The witness continued:

When our troops were on their march to Manassas, the head of the column about 1 mile distant from Manassas, I was of the opinion that a battle would be fought near the point where the troops of General McDowell were at that time. I ordered all the troops back and formed them in line of battle, advancing about a mile toward Groveton, so as to come on the right of General McDowell's corps. I sent first one of my engineers back to see where General McDowell was and to bring me instructions, but as his answer was not satisfactory to me, as he did not speak English very well, I sent Captain Dahlgren, who came back and told me that General McDowell directed me to march to Manassas immediately, and that after having questioned General McDowell in regard to the position I should take the general made a remark, "General Sigel shall fight his own corps." I said nothing and marched to Manassas, but I thought that this was a great mistake. This is what I have to say about that point. I must, although unwillingly, add that after the battle of Bull Run, induced by this remark of General McDowell, I refused to have any private conversation with General McDowell, but to receive only his official communications.

In regard to this point—going to their aid—I have no special point which I could mention.

In regard to personal courage or discretion in battle or in regard to the disposition of his troops, I had no opportunity to gain knowledge of General McDowell as to his personal courage or discretion. I was not in his own immediate neighborhood during the battle.

In regard to the disposition of his troops for attack or defense I had not opportunity enough to form a judgment.

What relates to this point, "otherwise unfaithful or inefficient as a general officer," my relations with General McDowell were only of a short duration. I only saw that he was an officer of great learning and military knowledge. I have given the facts independent from the general coherence of military operations, which may naturally modify my own judgment. I think I have now answered the question.

I would like to make an explanation with regard to my movement after having formed in line of battle between Gainesville and Manassas. By saying that it was a mistake, I meant to say that the troops lost time in marching and counter-marching to come to the same point, nearly, on the evening, which they left at noon, in compliance with the orders of General McDowell.

The testimony of the witness was read by the recorder, when he stated as follows:

The division of General Reynolds was on the 29th near our left wing, commanded by General Schenck, but I do not know whether they had taken any action on that day and whether they had been ordered to attack the enemy. The troops of General McDowell, who came from the Centreville road when it was nearly dark, were, as much as I could distinguish, those of General King, which troops had fought on the evening before at or near Groveton.

The court adjourned to meet on Monday, December 22, 1862, at 11 o'clock a. m.

---

## *TWENTY-SEVENTH DAY.*

COURT-ROOM, COR. FOURTEENTH AND PA. AVENUE,
*Washington, D. C., December* 22, 1862.

The court met pursuant to adjournment. Present, * * * and Maj. Gen. FRANZ SIGEL, U. S. Volunteers, the witness under examination.

The proceedings of the preceding day were read by the recorder and approved by the court, when General Sigel asked permission to make additional remarks respecting his testimony of preceding day, which was granted by the court.

I take liberty to say that I felt exceedingly of the attack made on General King's division on that evening by the enemy, on the 28th, under such circumstances, because this division had to fight alone, whilst it could have been supported by my corps at the right time. I thought that these troops of General King became unnecessarily exposed. I further forgot to say in my record what was reported to have been said by General Milroy regarding his asking assistance from General McDowell, as is contained in the official report of General Milroy.

Question by the COURT. Was General Milroy in your command?

Answer. Yes.

Question by the COURT. Did General Milroy communicate to you the matter referred to in his report; and, if so, when and where?

Answer. General Milroy did not report to me this fact himself except in his official report after the battle.

The witness was asked by the court if he had any further remarks to make on the record of his testimony of the preceding day, to which he replied:

Answer. I have nothing to say at present.

Question by the COURT. Where were you when you received an order from General Pope placing you and your corps under command of General McDowell and where was General McDowell?

Answer. I believe I received that order after my arrival at Warrenton, where I found General McDowell, and reported to him in his tent. I remember that he wished me to state the strength of my troops.

Question by the COURT. Did you report to General McDowell when you found him in his tent in pursuance of such order, and did he give orders to you, as your immediate commander, agreeably to the order of General Pope?

Answer. Whether the order attaching my corps to the corps of General McDowell came directly from General Pope to me or from General McDowell I don't remember very well, but I found the order in my book, so that I know it was given me. I reported to him, as much as I remember, because he directed me to do so. I remember that when we were together (General McDowell and myself) conversing about our situation and that the enemy had marched to Manassas, he questioned me whether it was not good to march to Salem with our troops; whereupon I proposed to march to Gainesville with the whole army, so as to come between Jackson and Longstreet. General McDowell approved, and said that he would report to General Pope in regard to this movement. During the day I read a telegraphic dispatch from General Pope, wherein he said that General McDowell should execute the movement proposed by him (General McDowell). I afterward received the order by General McDowell to march to Buckland Mills, on the road to Gainesville. Whether it was a written or verbal order I cannot remember.

Question by the COURT. On what day did you send to General Pope to get orders to march to Centerville? Where were you at that time?

Answer. It was on the 28th of August, at noon, when my advance guard, under General Milroy, had arrived at Manassas Junction, and the main force was near Bethlehem Church. I sent my adjutant to Manassas Junction to gain knowledge about matters there and to report to General Pope, to tell him where we were. The adjutant came back with a verbal order of General Pope's. (I must add that I proposed to General Pope to march to New Market instead of Manassas, for the enemy had left Manassas.)

Question by the COURT. If you were then under the command of General McDowell, why did you not send to him.

Answer. I knew about the position of the corps of General McDowell, and I sent my adjutant forward because I did not know anything that was going on at Manassas.

The recorder was instructed to repeat the question.

Answer. It was not my intention to send for orders but for my adjutant to see what was going on in front, and to report to General Pope where we were. I supposed General McDowell knew that we were on our way to Manassas, and I thought it was unnecessary to send to him.

Question by the COURT. Did you furnish General McDowell with a statement, orally or in writing, in answer to his application to you for information as to the strength of your corps?

Answer. As much as I know, I did immediately, in writing.

Question by the COURT. When did General Longstreet join General Jackson, and where, by what route? What did General McDowell omit to do, which he could and ought to have done, to prevent such junction?

Answer. When we arrived at Gainesville with the corps, after a skirmish at Buckland Mills, between Warrenton and Gainesville, we made about 300 prisoners, and upon examination of many of them we found that no one of them belonged to the corps of General Longstreet. These troops which were made prisoners came through Thoroughfare Gap on their way to Gainesville. The day before this happened, on the 27th, I received news by my scouting parties that General Longstreet was on his way, by Salem and White Plains, to Manassas (that leads by Thoroughfare Gap to Hopeville) [Hopewell], and that Jackson had already passed Thoroughfare Gap to Manassas. During the battle of the 29th General Longstreet was reported to me, at about 1 o'clock, on his march from Gainesville to the battle-field, which I reported to General Kearny. I thought that General Longstreet must have passed Thoroughfare Gap and Gainesville on the night of the 28th or morning of the 29th. I believe that on the 28th, in the morning, one division should have been posted so as to hinder General Longstreet to pass either Thoroughfare Gap or Hay Market, if it was too late to occupy the Gap.

Question by the COURT. What knowledge have you that General McDowell was aware of the approach of Longstreet? Did you communicate to him the facts which you had learned from your scouts on the 27th?

Answer. I communicated this fact to General McDowell the night of the 27th, at Gainesville, when he proposed to march to Salem. I said to him that Longstreet must be between Salem and Gainesville, and if we were marching to Salem, Longstreet and Jackson would unite and separate General Pope and our troops. Besides this, I received an order from General McDowell, at Warrenton, to send my whole cavalry force with General Bayard to Salem on an expedition. I gave the order to this effect to Colonel Beardsley, the commander of my cavalry, who was at Salem, and when he returned to me on the 29th, during the battle, he said that Longstreet's forces were near Salem. I supposed, as it was natural, that General McDowell had received the report from the commander of the cavalry to which my cavalry was attached. On the same night of the 27th the question arose between General McDowell and myself what troops should stay against General Longstreet, and I left it with General McDowell to make his dispositions, which shows that General McDowell was aware of the approach of General Longstreet.

Question by the COURT. How far would it have been necessary to march a division to reach Thoroughfare Gap? By what route was it practicable to do so? What was the number of Longstreet's force?

Answer. Thoroughfare Gap is about 5 miles from Gainesville and 3½ miles from Hay Market. The best road leads from Gainesville by Hay Market to the Gap; another road from Buckland Mills by Carter's Switch, leaving Hay Market to the right. I believe that General Longstreet had about 35,000 men—infantry, cavalry, and artillery.

Question by the COURT. Where were the divisions, and what ones, which could have been sent to Thoroughfare Gap?

Answer. My whole corps could have been sent there, and General McDowell's corps was behind me at Buckland Mills. It is 3 miles from Buckland Mills to Gainesville and 5 miles by Hay Market. The direct route from Buckland Mills by Carter's Switch to Thoroughfare Gap must be shorter. The road from Gainesville to Thoroughfare Gap is excellent.

Question by the COURT. At that time what was the numerical strength of your corps and of the part of the army of General McDowell then with him? Where was Jackson at that time and what was the numerical strength of his command?

Answer. My corps was about 11,000 men strong, with one brigade of cavalry and nine batteries of artillery included. I did not know at that time what troops belonged to General McDowell's corps and do not know it exactly now.

I saw, when I returned from Gainesville that night, the Pennsylvania Reserves at Buckland Mills. I also learned that General King's division was there. I think that General McDowell's corps, then with him, was at least 15,000 men. It was night, and I could not see very well what troops were there. Jackson must have been at that time near Manassas Junction and beyond, toward Kettle Run; so at least I thought at that time. From his stragglers and other sources I learned that he had with him his own division, that of Ewell, and that of General A. P. Hill, amounting to about 40,000 men.

Question by the COURT. What number of troops would have sufficed to defend Thoroughfare Gap against the 35,000 men under Longstreet?

Answer. I would have sent about 10,000 men, with the intention to retard the movements of General Longstreet. I do not believe that these troops are sufficient to fight them all day, but I think they were sufficient to retard his movements.

Question by the COURT. Did General McDowell make any, and, if so, what, efforts to hold Thoroughfare Gap against the approach of Longstreet?

Answer. I cannot answer the question. It was my impression that it must have been easy for General Longstreet to march through the Gap and to march to the battle-field. I did not hear of any engagement near Hay Market and the Gap. This induces me to say I do not believe the necessary arrangements were made to hinder Longstreet from joining the army.

Question by the COURT. What advantages would have resulted from preventing or delaying the passage of Thoroughfare Gap by Longstreet on the night of the 28th and morning of the 29th of August?

Answer. The troops of General Longstreet had made a long march, and if they had to form in line of battle near Thoroughfare Gap or Hay Market they would not have arrived, probably, in the afternoon of the 29th at Groveton, and would not have been able to support General Jackson on the evening of the 29th, and to make the great attack against our left wing on the next day, which attack resulted in the defeat of our army.

Question by the COURT. State particularly the points in which there was want of co-operation between your corps and that of General McDowell on the 29th of August on the march to Manassas. What did General McDowell omit to do which he ought to have done, and through which omission opportunity was lost to attack the left flank of the enemy; and in this connection state what forces of the enemy could have been so attacked, at what place, and with what results. State particularly.

Answer. When General McDowell's troops and my own were on the march to Manassas Jackson changed his position, and was on his march between Manassas and Gainesville. He therefore was not in order of battle, and presented us his left flank. If my corps and a division of General McDowell's would have attacked him he would not have been able to come so early to the point which he intended to reach—a point between Groveton, Centreville, and New Market; and, secondly, if my corps had not been ordered to march to Manassas, we would have been able to assist General King, or those troops which were attacked, on the evening of the 28th. By sending away my corps either of these opportunities were lost—first to attack the enemy, and second to assist the division under General King. I do not think it probable that they would have defeated the enemy, but we would have retarded his movements, brought him to a stand, where he, perhaps, would not have liked to fight, and given an opportunity to the commander-in-chief to see clearly where was the enemy's position and to what points he should direct his troops.

Question by the COURT. On the 29th what particular disposition of the troops of your corps and General McDowell's did he omit, and which he could have made, so that the two corps would have acted in unity at Bull Run? What advantage would have resulted from such disposition?

Answer. From the letter of General Pope I supposed that the whole corps of General McDowell would attack the enemy on the right, and I would stay in front with my corps to check the enemy in his advance or to follow up advantages. Under this supposition I covered the whole front and extended my lines more than I would have done under other circumstances, to make the enemy believe we were very strong in front. The enemy directed his principal attack against our center and right wing, which was about 7,000 men strong. My left I had to cover by one division, as I did not know in the morning and up to 12 or 1 o'clock that General Reynolds was on my left. I could not make any disposition of the division of General Schenck to assist my right wing and the center, because he had to cover my left wing. I also did not receive a report when I sent different officers that General McDowell had really arrived on my left. Now, if this corps of General McDowell's had advanced toward Groveton and continued the movement they must have come into the rear and on the right flank of the enemy. I do not know what orders the division of General Reynolds had and what they did. My opinion is that they did not understand their task—to attack the enemy in his right flank or in his rear. I also am of the opinion that if the division of General King had been united with that of General Reynolds on that same day at noon or in the afternoon, that is, if 15,000 men had marched forward against the right flank of the enemy, he must have been routed.

Question by the COURT. At what hour did General McDowell arrive with his troops on the battle-field on the 29th? Where had he passed the preceding night, and at what distance from the battle-field?

Answer. I speak, in answering, about the division of General King. I supposed that this division, after the fight, had remained on the field at the place where the fight was on the night of the 28th. I supposed that these troops were, on the morning of the 29th, about 5 or 6 miles from the battle-field of the 29th and not more, and as I did not know, and do not now, which road they had taken, and supposed that they should have taken the shortest road to the battle-field, which was about 5 or 6 miles, I did not and cannot understand why they arrived on the battle-field at sunset on the 29th. I supposed that the division of General King had remained where they were on the night of the 28th, and I did not know where the division of General Reynolds was.

Question by the COURT. If General McDowell's troops had come from New Market, on your left, on the 29th, what would have been the result? What did General McDowell omit to do, which he ought to have done and could have done, to obtain a personal knowledge of the affairs of your corps on the 29th?

Answer. In regard to the first part of this question, I think that Jackson could hardly resist an attack in front, especially when General Heintzelman's troops, under Generals Hooker and Kearny, had arrived. I believe that Jackson wanted all his men to protect himself in front and on his left, and that therefore he cannot have had many troops or a sufficient number of troops to oppose an attack of General McDowell, and therefore he could have been routed or forced at least to give up his position. In regard to the second part of the question, I think that it was the duty of General McDowell to gain a personal knowledge of the position of my troops and of the extension of the battle-field, so as to be able to give his own corps the necessary directions. I would have gone to him personally, but could not leave the battle-field, and, as much as I remember, sent an officer to General McDowell, who could not find him. I do not know whether it was possible for General McDowell to have come personally to the battle-field, but I think it would have been of advantage to our operations. I do not remember that General McDowell sent a staff officer to me to obtain the information he might have desired to have. On the 28th, in the morning, I sent an officer to see where General McDowell was, and I received news that General McDowell would be at Centreville, in some house, of which the name I do not remember. I do not remember that he sent to me on the 29th and 30th, except what I have stated in regard to those dispatches in regard to General Porter. There is something which reminds me of my connection with General McDowell's troops on the 29th. On the 29th or 30th I I sent Lieutenant-Colonel Deans [Deems] to the left to see what troops were there and how matters were going on; besides this, I sent an officer of General Milroy's [to] the left, but the latter was made a prisoner, and the other was also nearly made a prisoner, and lost one or two of his orderlies.

Question by the COURT. Where were Heintzelman's troops, under Kearny and Hooker, at the time that you were in line of battle on the 29th, and when General McDowell came from the direction of Centreville, in your rear, instead of New Market, on your left?

Answer. I do not know and did not know where they were.*

Question by the COURT. What force was opposed to Jackson at the time when McDowell approached from Centreville, in your rear, so that Jackson would have been unable to oppose him had McDowell approached on your left from New Market?

Answer. Between 5 and 6 o'clock in the evening, when General King's division, which I suppose it was, came from the rear, our line was formed of the following troops,

---

* See p. 131.

as much as I can remember: On the right was General Kearny; in the center was my corps and that of General Hooker's troops, which had partially relieved my corps, but the troops so relieved were again in good order and ready to advance; on the left of this line was General Reno, in support of General Schenck. General Stevens commanded one brigade of Reno's, and it was posted with two regiments and one battery in the line of General Schenck. The whole number of these forces must have been about 30,000 men, which is a low number, not including Reynolds' division or any of General McDowell's. The enemy had lost ground during the whole day and in the afternoon.

The court adjourned to meet to-morrow, December 23, at 11 o'clock a. m.

---

### *TWENTY-EIGHTH DAY.*

COURT-ROOM, COR. PA. AVE. AND FOURTEENTH ST.,
*Washington, D. C., December* 23, 1862.

The court met pursuant to adjournment. Present * * * , and Maj. Gen. FRANZ SIGEL, U. S. Volunteers, the witness under examination.

* * * * * * *

The witness desired to correct the first answer, recorded on page 314 of the record [p. 130], which is in words as follows: "I do not know and did not know where they were." From some oversight in reading the question I said I did not know where Generals Kearny's and Hooker's troops were, which is incorrect, as will be seen from the answer to the subsequent question. I probably had in mind the troops of General Sumner or General Porter, of which I did know nothing.

Question by General McDOWELL. You say that after the battle of Bull Run you were induced by a remark of General McDowell, made to your aide-de-camp, that you should fight your own corps, to refuse to have any private conversation with General McDowell, &c. Was this remark the single and only cause of your so refusing?

Answer. It was not; but it was the principal cause.

Question by General McDOWELL. Please state the other cause.

Answer. Although I did regard this matter as a private matter, which I will now bring before the court, and which I did avoid to mention, as I thought that some understanding could hereafter take place between General McDowell and myself in a private way, I will mention it. When on the march from Gainesville to Manassas I sent Captain Asmussen, one of my staff officers, back to General McDowell to report to him some matters in regard to our march and to see whether he could not find out something relative to the firing on our left. Captain Asmussen came back and reported to me that General McDowell seemed very irritated, and used, in presence of his staff officers, expressions which seemed to him (Captain Asmussen) improper. This report regarding the behavior of General McDowell Captain Asmussen made to me in private. This is the cause.

Question by General McDOWELL. Will the witness please state if this cause just stated is the only additional cause. If not, will the witness please give the other causes?

Answer. I have nothing to say about this matter, as I do not believe that they are of importance in regard to our operations. I must say, further, that these two causes, one mentioned before and the latter mentioned to-day, did influence my mind, and brought me to the remark I made to General McDowell.

The recorder was instructed to repeat the question.

Answer. This is the only additional cause which induced me to my private remark to General McDowell.

Question by General McDOWELL. The witness refers in his last answer to unimportant matters, not in his judgment bearing on the subject of our operations, but which he refers to in connection with the question as to the cause of his refusing private conversation with General McDowell; were these matters such as to irritate and influence the witness in his personal feelings toward General McDowell? If so, will the witness please state them?

Answer. There was no point in my whole communication with General McDowell which I can say irritated me, but I regarded expressions used by General McDowell toward two of my staff officers as a personal insult to me, and therefore I thought that it was due to my honor to make him understand that I felt this insult or impropriety of conduct toward a general officer. All matters of a military character which may have influenced my judgment in regard to General McDowell as a commanding officer I do not believe bearing to this personal affair. I think that is the substance of the question answered.

The court was cleared at the instance of a member.

The court was opened, when the following was read by the recorder:

The court desires the witness to state whether there were or were not any other incidents which irritated or influenced his feelings against General McDowell than those already named by him. The witness can answer "Yes" or "No."

Answer. Well then I answer "Yes."

Question by General McDOWELL. What are the causes of bias in your mind?

Answer. I stated two reasons which I regarded as personal. I will now state some reasons which induce me to believe that General McDowell did not like to co-operate with me. These reasons formed my judgment in regard to the political and military character of General McDowell at that time, when we were operating together, but I have given to this judgment a proper expression when I said that I did not think General McDowell a traitor, as there are many things in military operations which cannot be explained fully unless we know all the circumstances connected with them. I will now give the different instances which were occupying my mind before and after the operations with General McDowell.

I hope the court will allow me to state all these instances in chronological order and as short as possible.

1st. When I was at Winchester and General Frémont at Mount Jackson and Port Republic I could not perceive why the corps of General McDowell did not assist better the troops under General Frémont, and that Jackson was allowed to overcome General Shields and to go to Richmond to fight against General McClellan.

2d. When our troops had arrived at Culpeper, on the day of the battle at Cedar Mountain, after a march of one day and one night, and were unable to march 7 miles farther to assist General Banks, I was of the opinion that General McDowell's troops were at Culpeper before, and I did not understand why they did not assist General Banks on that day, and why he had to fight alone with 9,000 men against 25,000, the battle resulting almost in the destruction of General Banks' corps. I thought also that General Pope and General McDowell must have been informed of the strength of General Jackson, as I had sent a letter to General Pope from Madison Court-House or Sperryville stating that Jackson was advancing against Culpeper with 25,000 men.

3d. When at Waterloo Bridge I was under the supposition that General McDowell would support my corps, at least protect my right wing, according to a letter received from General Pope. As this was not done, and as General Roberts, chief of staff of General Pope, had expressly told me that the cavalry of General McDowell would be on my right, and as I, under the supposition, sent away nearly my whole cavalry to Sulphur Springs, exposing thereby my own position, and as I afterward found out this cavalry was 4 or 5 miles behind me and not on my right, I thought that something must be wrong in this matter, either by neglect or otherwise.

4th. I have already stated in my evidence matters in regard to the movements of General McDowell's troops which I also could not well explain to myself. These circumstances, in connection with the old remembrance of Fredericksburg and the first battle of Bull Run, did not contribute to give me full and undivided confidence in Major-General McDowell, but I must also declare that this is only an individual opinion, which I never and under no circumstances have proclaimed and defended publicly, for the simple reason that I had not the true knowledge of all these matters in their connection with higher authorities, and as I have not to this day read an official report which could give me satisfaction. I was never irritated against General McDowell, and maintained in private conversation with my friends that I was not, and I would not like to belong to that class of men who take the misfortune of a man as treason or intentional malignity, and that the people [are] ordinarily more led by sudden impressions in regard to military operations than by clear understanding of the case. I have to add, as a proof to this, that under no circumstances I neglected to hold communication with General McDowell and to execute all orders given me.

Question by General MCDOWELL. Will the witness please explain what he means by "Fredericksburg," which he refers to as a cause of bias, and by what the words "*political character*," as connected with General McDowell?

Answer. In regard to "Fredericksburg" I mean that General McDowell was at one time at Fredericksburg, according to my knowledge, when General McClellan was near Richmond. It was said that General McDowell could have assisted General McClellan in his movement against Richmond, and I did never hear for what reason that it was not done. Under "*political character*," I meant that if I thought all his military acts as intentional he could be called a traitor to his country, but as I had no proof of such an intention I did not regard nim as a traitor. This is why I spoke about his political character.

Question by General MCDOWELL. You have stated that an order from General Pope attached your corps to the corps of General McDowell after the engagements at Freeman's Ford, Sulphur Springs, and Waterloo, and that you regarded yourself under his orders from this time until after the battle of Bull Run. Have you not stated in your official report of September 16, 1862, of the operations of your corps in the late campaign in Virginia, that you were under General McDowell's command from the time of your arrival at Waterloo?

Answer. I must say that in giving my evidence on this point that I was not very much certain when I got the order from General Pope, and in writing my official report I did not think it of much importance. It may be that I have received the order at Waterloo Bridge, but I am not certain. What I said in my official report I thought was true.

Question by General MCDOWELL. You have stated in regard to the connection between your corps and that of General McDowell that General Pope wrote to you that General McDowell would support you at Waterloo Bridge, but that you did not see any troops of General McDowell there for some miles from that point. What day was this, and how far were these troops of General McDowell from Waterloo at the time to which you refer?

Answer. I believe I received a dispatch from General Pope on the 24th at Sulphur Springs, or on the 25th of August at Waterloo Bridge. On these two days I supposed that the troops of General McDowell were at Warrenton, about 10 miles I think, and on the 25th a brigade of cavalry was between Warrenton and Waterloo Bridge; such at least is my recollection.

Question by General MCDOWELL. With reference to the connection of the First and Third Corps at Waterloo, as related by you, have you not stated in your official report, which has appeared in the public papers, that when you retreated under cover of the night of the 25th of August from Waterloo to Warrenton there were no troops within 8 or 10 miles of you at the time, except the cavalry of General Buford?

Answer. Certainly, that I have stated; but whether it was the cavalry of General Buford or that of General Bayard I cannot say.

Question by General MCDOWELL. Did you not know, or were you not informed, that there was a division of General McDowell's corps between you and Warrenton, and did not General Roberts report to you that General Ricketts' division would support you? This on your retreat from Waterloo Bridge or preceding that retreat?

Answer. I am not aware of that, because I had sent three or four times during the day officers and mounted orderlies from Waterloo Bridge to Warrenton to see if any troops were on the roads, and they did not find any; so at least they reported to me. I must, however, state that I personally did not take the direct road from Waterloo Bridge to Warrenton that night of the 25th. This road was taken by the division of General Schurz and the brigade of General Milroy. I marched with General Schenck's division across the fields to strike the Warrenton turnpike; arrived at the joining point or crossing point of the roads, I let pass all my troops toward Warrenton and waited for the rear guard of General Milroy. As soon as they had arrived I rode to Warrenton. I did see no troops of General McDowell's on my way except a large wagon train, which was said to belong to the cavalry. General Roberts told me that I would be supported, but I do not know whether he spoke about General Ricketts' division. I told him that I hoped that at least the cavalry would come on my right.

Question by General MCDOWELL. You state that at Waterloo Bridge, on that same day you arrived there, you received an order through General McDowell one page of which was missing, so that you did not know what your orders were. Did you not state in your official report that you received this order or dispatch from General McDowell? State also where this order or dispatch was written or by whom signed, and to what did it seem to relate, and in what way or to what extent General McDowell was concerned in it or connected with it, otherwise than to furnish the means of its being transmitted to you.

Answer. As much as I remember I received the order through General McDowell, and I really do not know whether it was signed by General McDowell or General Pope or one of their officers, or whether it was signed at all. My impression is that it was signed, and I believe by a staff officer of General Pope. I do not know whether the order was written at Warrenton or Warrenton Junction. As I was greatly surprised and embarrassed I showed the order immediately to General Schenck, as I did not like to take alone the responsibility, and with the intention to show him in what form I received the papers. These papers consisted of two sheets of yellow paper; one of the papers was addressed to General Banks and was finished. In this paper General Banks was asked why he did not send any information, or that he should send information. The other sheet contained only a few lines, with no address, and no commencing lines or introduction. Something was said about my pontoon train, so that General Schenck and myself were of the opinion that this was an end of an order; that one sheet was missing, which must have contained the principal points. I sent this order as it was to General Banks, to hear what was his opinion about my movements, whilst I also sent to General Pope and to General McDowell to Warrenton to receive an explanation. The officer who was sent there came back in the evening, and said to me that he could not get any instructions from General McDowell and that he could not find General Pope, and had to go to Warrenton Junction. The officer's name was, as I remember, Major Fish, on the staff of General Schenck. Whether he brought me the final order from General Pope to march to Warrenton I cannot say with certainty.

A piece of yellow tissue paper was here laid before the witness which is appended to the proceedings of this day, marked L. H. P.

Question by General MCDOWELL. What kind of yellow paper was it on which the order was given; like this now before you or was it a thick yellow paper?

Answer. I think it was a thin paper like this. I did not make a thorough investigation of the paper, but think it was a thin paper. I am almost sure it was a thin paper.

Question by General MCDOWELL. You state you received at the entrance of the town of Warrenton a dispatch from an officer of General McDowell, in which it was said that you should force with your corps the passage of the bridge at Waterloo that same morning. State, as far as you know, what connection General McDowell had with that dispatch other than that the officer who carried it to you was on his staff.

Answer. I do not know any other connection General McDowell had with this order.

Question by General MCDOWELL. Do you know he had any connection with it?

Answer. No, except that his officer brought the order to me. I did not ask him.

Question by General McDOWELL. Is the witness to be understood, as he has stated, that he received an order from General Pope for his corps to march from Waterloo Bridge to Warrenton in the night, and that this order was received by the witness at Waterloo before his corps had commenced to march, and that it was in obedience to this order of General Pope's that witness marched his corps in the night from Waterloo to Warrenton, as is stated in his official report? If so, will the witness please state if the order was written or verbal?

Answer. The order sent to me was written; it directed me to march to Warrenton. When I received the order I made my preparation to evacuate my position and to march to Fayetteville, because I thought from the reference in the paper that I would find my pontoon train at Fayetteville. I thought that the original programme was taken up, and that my first order, of which a part was missing, was an order directing me to march to Fayetteville. During these preparations, and when my corps had not left yet its position, I received the order from General Pope. It was not dark yet when I received this order, and it was perfectly dark when my first troops marched off from the field. Whether it was said that I should march at night or not I cannot well remember. I thought only that it was necessary under the circumstances to march as soon as possible, because I thought we would have a battle near Warrenton, and as I thought this my position was really exposed, the enemy having already flanked it.

The court adjourned to meet to-morrow, December 24, 1862, at 11 o'clock a. m.

---

*TWENTY-NINTH DAY.*

COURT-ROOM, COR. FOURTEENTH AND PA. AVENUE.,
*Washington, D. C., December* 24, 1862.

The court met pursuant to adjournment. Present, * * * , and Maj. Gen. FRANZ SIGEL, U. S. Volunteers, the witness under examination.

* * * * * * *

Question by General McDOWELL. Did the order you refer to in your last answer of yesterday require you to march to Warrenton?

Answer. As much as I remember, it was said in the order either that I should march to Warrenton or the neighborhood of Warrenton, which I understood was Warrenton, or a place in the neighborhood of Warrenton, where troops can be camped.

Question by General McDOWELL. With reference to the connection between the First and Third Corps and the support you say General McDowell was to give you at Waterloo Bridge, have you not stated in your official report that, in accordance with an order of General Pope, General Milroy should have been relieved in the morning by a brigade of General McDowell? If so, state what order of General Pope's was it that required General McDowell to send a brigade to Waterloo and one to Sulphur Springs?

Answer. There were different orders given to me in regard to the movement of our army or of my corps at that time. One order directed me to march to Waterloo Bridge. The next order was an order from General Pope. I do not know exactly at what time I had received this order, but it was a general order, giving instructions to all the different commanders of corps. According to this order my corps should have marched to Fayetteville, and General McDowell, as much as I can remember, should occupy Warrenton, and send a brigade to Waterloo Bridge and one to Sulphur Springs. During the day I was waiting for his brigade because I did not like to evacuate a position in the face of a strong enemy without having other troops there, and I really thought that one brigade would not be enough. Whilst I was waiting for the brigade of General McDowell General Roberts brought me the verbal order that I should not march to Fayetteville, but stay at Waterloo Bridge. Whilst I was waiting for the troops of General McDowell, and had received that fragmentary paper of which I have spoken, I expected that General McDowell would tell my officer whom I had sent to him what were his instructions and how I should move, so as I should direct myself according to his movement; and when this movement was past, and I had received orders by General Roberts to stay at Waterloo Bridge, he promised me assistance from General McDowell, at least by his cavalry, which I did not receive, although I had no cavalry with me, because I had sent mine to Sulphur Springs, to prevent the enemy to come into my rear and on my flank. When I say I had no cavalry, I mean no cavalry except the small force mentioned in my official report. There are therefore two points which have a tendency to this question. First, that I was not relieved, and could therefore not march to Fayetteville, as I could have done. Second, that what General Roberts promised to me was not fulfilled. There is another dispatch of General Pope, which I, as much as I remember, received at Sulphur Springs, wherein General Pope said that in marching against Waterloo Bridge General McDowell would support me.

Question by General McDOWELL. You say you were not relieved at Waterloo Bridge. Did you or did you not receive an order from General Pope telling you that you were not to wait at Waterloo Bridge for General McDowell?

Answer. I did not, as much as I remember; and if I did, this order must have been in conflict with other orders or circumstances of which I have no knowledge now. I would like to add that if I had received that order at the moment when I saw the enemy's army across the river I would have sent immediately to General Pope to apprise him of the fact and to get further instructions.

Question by General McDOWELL. What forces of our army were in your rear at the time you sent your cavalry to Sulphur Springs, when you were, as you state, at Waterloo Bridge?

Answer. There were no forces in my rear within 4 or 5 miles. I hint to that cavalry which was 4 or 5 miles behind us, but I did not know at the time when I sent my cavalry that there was any force between my corps and Warrenton, and I had no control over these forces which might have been behind me.

Question by General McDOWELL. Were not the commands of General Banks and General Reno in your rear, or on your rear and left, at the time you refer to, or on the 25th of August?

Answer. I supposed at that time that they were there, but when I sent my officer with that fragmentary dispatch of General Banks he said that General Reno and General Banks had marched to Fayetteville. They were at least not within my reach, and must have been at that time about 8 miles from me. I would not pretend to say when they had to march.

Question by General McDOWELL. How far is it from Sulphur Springs to Waterloo Bridge?

Answer. I think it is about 5 miles to march with troops.

Question by General McDOWELL. Where was General Banks or General Reno at the time your cavalry were at Sulphur Springs?

Answer. I cannot say where they were. I only knew that they had marched off, because General Banks told me by the officer that he had orders to move away, and that he would advise me to march.

Question by General McDOWELL. At the time you refer to, of a visit to General McDowell's tent at Warrenton, you have stated he wanted to march on Salem. Are you to be understood as saying it was his purpose or plan to march the whole force to Salem or a reconnoitering party only?

Answer. I was under the impression that he meant that we should march; that is, his corps and mine, to Salem, and there was no question about a reconnoitering party, but about an operation of our army.

Question by General McDOWELL. You state you did not know what troops belonged to General McDowell's corps. Did you not receive a note from General McDowell informing you of the divisions which were following you on your march to Buckland Mills?

Answer. I did not state that I did not know what troops belonged to General McDowell's corps. I said that I had seen the Pennsylvania Reserves at Buckland Mills.

Question by General MCDOWELL. Referring to your interview with General McDowell on the morning of the 27th of August, state where this interview took place, and what were the dispositions General McDowell made that evening for the next day.

Answer. The interview took place in my own headquarters, near Buckland Mills. We were speaking about what troops should be left at Thoroughfare Gap. During the conversation, and when General McDowell had not given me yet definite instructions, I told him that I was very much tired, and, as much as I remember, laid down on the sofa, but told General McDowell that as soon as he had come to an understanding with himself he should please notify me. I think it was between 11 and 12 o'clock at night, and this is what I remember.

Question by General MCDOWELL. When you were on the sofa was not General McDowell writing at the piano in the same room?

Answer. I do not know whether he was writing or not. He was at the piano, and had his map, and was thinking about our operations. I do not know that he was writing.

Question by General MCDOWELL. Did you go to sleep on the sofa whilst General McDowell was writing or examining maps on the piano?

Answer. I think so, because I had not slept for three days, I believe, and was marching day and night.

Question by General MCDOWELL. Does the witness remember what General McDowell said to him would be the disposition for the succeeding day? Does he remember whether it was the witness' corps, or the witness' corps with a division of General McDowell's added to it, that General McDowell decided to leave for the defense of Thoroughfare Gap?

Answer. I do not know anything about that; at least it must have been so indefinitely said to me that I did not mind it.

Question by General MCDOWELL. What did General McDowell propose to witness at his headquarters concerning the defense of Thoroughfare Gap and holding the enemy in check at that point?

Answer. He did not make any definite proposition.

Question by General MCDOWELL. Did not the witness understand he was to have a division of General McDowell's corps added to his own, and did he not send word to General McDowell after he had left his (General Sigel's) headquarters to ask what division it would be, and to ask that the division might be directed to report to him?

Answer. I have no knowledge about such an understanding, because I would have been very glad to have it; at least our discussion was not in the form of an instruction or order, but only an exchange of opinions or expressions of opinion of General McDowell. I am certain that I did never know anything about a division added to my corps from General McDowell's corps, and I do not remember that I did send to General McDowell in regard to the division to be attached to me.

Question by General MCDOWELL. What were those opinions or expressions of General McDowell on that occasion with reference to the subject of holding the enemy in check at Thoroughfare Gap or this side of it?

Answer. Many different opinions were expressed by General McDowell. He was not sure whether a corps should be sent there or a division, or what corps or what division, and I therefore, as I did not like to impress upon him my own judgment, left it with him to decide and to order and to give me instructions.

Question by General McDOWELL. When you left Buckland Mills, on the morning of the 28th, did you or did you not know General McDowell had made any provision for meeting Longstreet at or this side of Thoroughfare Gap?

Answer. I did not know anything at all.

(A paper was laid before the witness, which is appended to the proceedings of this day and marked A.)

Question by General McDOWELL. Will the witness see if this is acknowledgment of the order for his march from Buckland Mills to Manassas Junction, and dated at 2.45?

Answer. This is.

A paper purporting to be a copy of General Orders, No. 10, dated "Headquarters Third Corps, Reynolds' Camp, August 28, 1862," was handed the witness, and which paper is appended to the proceedings of this day and marked B.

Question by General McDOWELL. Will the witness state if this is not a copy of the order of march of which he acknowledged the receipt?

Answer. I confess that I have never read this order, at least I do not remember to have read it, because it is in contradiction with my acts and my understanding of our situation at that time, and if I had read it it would be in my memory I think.

The General Orders, No. 10, just referred to, was read by the recorder.

The witness desired to make a correction of his last answer.

From a reperusal of the order I would like to have the words "because it is in contradiction with my acts and my understanding of our situation at that time" considered no part of my answer. I add, in regard to this, that the order I received was written on thin paper, and I believe in pencil.

Question by General McDOWELL. What order did you receive from General McDowell of which you acknowledged the receipt, and in compliance with which you marched from Buckland Mills?

Answer. I received the order to march to Manassas Junction, and it may be that it is the same order as this here, but I do not remember that it was such a general order.

General McDowell here asked a suspension of the examination of the witness with a view of proving the delivery of this order on that day.

The court informed General McDowell that a delay or a suspension in the examination of this witness for the reason stated was unnecessary.

The witness continued:

Very often, when a general order is received by a corps commander, he only takes in his mind that part of the order which affects his own corps, and that therefore I may not remember very well now, after the elapse of many weeks, that I received this general order.

Question by General McDOWELL. Does the witness mean to be understood that the whole of that general order did not affect him, and does not the name or designation even of general order indicate this?

Answer. Certainly, I admit that the whole order, if I had read it, did refer to me, but especially what is referred to in the first point, which point I fully admit I understood and acted upon it—I mean the order directing me to march to Manassas Junction.

Question by General McDOWELL. Was it not your duty to have made yourself acquainted with every part of a general order sent you, especially one involving co-operation of your forces with those of another?

Answer. Certainly it was my duty, but if this was the order sent to me I must have regarded it as pretty indefinite, all things taken into consideration.

Question by General McDOWELL. You state that when you left

Buckland Mills, on the morning of the 28th, you did not know anything at all of any provision being made by General McDowell for meeting Longstreet at or this side of Thoroughfare Gap. Does or does not the General Order, No. 10, for the march make provisions for this?

Answer. The order mentioned makes a provision.

The court adjourned to meet on Friday, December 26, 1862, at 11 o'clock a. m.

---

APPENDIX.

A.

Received the order at 2.45.

F. SIGEL,
*Major-General.*

B.

GENERAL ORDERS, No. 10.

HEADQUARTERS THIRD CORPS,
*Reynolds' Camp, August* 28, 1862.

I. Major-General Sigel will immediately march with his whole corps on Manassas Junction, his right resting on the Manassas Railroad.

II. Brigadier-General Reynolds will march on the turnpike immediately in the rear of General Sigel, and form his division on the left of General Sigel, and march upon Manassas Junction.

III. Brigadier-General King will follow immediately after General Reynolds, and form his division on General Reynolds' left, and direct his march upon Manassas Junction.

IV. Brigadier-General Ricketts will follow Brigadier-General King and march to Gainesville; and if, on arriving there, no indication shall appear of the approach of the enemy from Thoroughfare Gap, he will continue his march along the turnpike, form on the left of General King, and march on Manassas Junction. He will be constantly on the lookout for an attack from the direction of Thoroughfare Gap, and, in case one is threatened, he will form his division to the left and march to resist it.

The headquarters of the corps will be at King's division.

By command of Major-General McDowell:

ED. SCHRIVER,
*Colonel, Chief of Staff.*

---

*THIRTIETH DAY.*

COURT-ROOM, COR. FOURTEENTH AND PA. AVENUE,
*Washington, D. C., December* 26, 1862.

The court met pursuant to adjournment. Present * * *, and Maj. Gen. FRANZ SIGEL, U. S. Volunteers, the witness under examination.

* * * * * * *

The witness desired to know if he had permission to make some remarks regarding his testimony of yesterday, he having received certain papers since.

General McDowell objected to the reception of any remarks from the witness at this time, stating that the witness was undergoing a cross-examination; that yesterday's record had been read twice to the witness, and that, at this stage of the examination, he thought it improper for the reception of any remarks.

The court was cleared.

The court was opened and the following decision announced:

If the witness now remembers, after examining his papers, that his statements, or any of them, have been inaccurate, he may correct those inaccuracies; but all other explanations must be delayed until the close of the cross-examination.

The witness replied: I do not remember any inaccuracies in my evidence given.

Question by General McDOWELL. You have stated the general order for the march made provision for meeting Longstreet. Did you or did you not then, or do you or do you not now, know what was the strength of Ricketts' division, indicated in the order for this duty? Did you or not know, or do you or not now know, it consisted of four brigades or sixteen regiments of infantry and four batteries of artillery of twenty-four pieces?

Answer. It is impossible for me——

General McDowell here stated that this interrogatory was one that admitted of an answer affirmatively or negatively.

The witness continued:

It is impossible for me now to know what I knew four months ago on this point, and now I do not know at all what was the strength of Ricketts' division. I hardly remember anything about Ricketts' division.

Question by General McDOWELL. Did you or not know that the Rhode Island Cavalry had been sent up from New Baltimore on the west side of Bull Run Ridge to be on the enemy's flank as he should be marching through or to Thoroughfare Gap?

Answer. I did not and do not know anything about that. I would say I do not know anything about that.

Question by General McDOWELL. *Did* you or not know, or do you or not *now* know, that, in addition to Ricketts' division, two brigades of cavalry, under Generals Bayard and Buford, were also sent to aid Ricketts' division to meet Longstreet?

Answer. I do not know.

Question by General McDOWELL. Would you have considered, "under the circumstances," that four brigades or sixteen regiments of infantry, twenty-four pieces of artillery, and two brigades of cavalry, in the aggregate between 11,000 and 12,000 men, a sufficient provision to hold Longstreet in check?

Answer. I would have regarded it as a sufficient provision if these troops were placed at the right point at the right time.

Question by General McDOWELL. Do you know that Longstreet *did* not come through Hopewell Gap, about 5 miles to the north of Thoroughfare Gap? And do you know he actually did come through Thoroughfare Gap?

Answer. I do not know exactly whether he came by Thoroughfare Gap or by Hopewell Gap. I, however, think he came by Thoroughfare Gap. I think that Thoroughfare Gap is 3 miles from Hopewell Gap.

Question by General McDOWELL. You say you did not know that anything had been done to hinder Longstreet. Do you not know now there was an engagement between Ricketts and Longstreet at the Gap or between it and Hay Market, and that Longstreet was actually held in check?

Answer. I know now, from a report of General Longstreet himself, which was published in the papers, as much as I remember, that a skirmish had taken place at or near Thoroughfare Gap. From the description it was my impression that the skirmish was of an insignificant character in regard to the resistance made. This is all the knowledge I have upon that subject.

Question by General McDOWELL. You have stated that you believed that General McDowell did not do what he could under the circumstances to hinder General Longstreet to join General Jackson. You afterward say you cannot answer the question as to what General McDowell did to prevent Longstreet coming through Thoroughfare Gap? How, then, do you know he did not do all that you say he should have done?

Answer. Because, first, I have an exact knowledge of what was done in general; and, secondly, my remarks were made in regard to the result, as I knew that General Longstreet was coming up on the 29th or has come up on the 29th, and I also knew that he has co-operated with General Jackson on the next day, on the 30th of August.

Question by General McDOWELL. You have stated you believe General McDowell did not have a sufficient force at Thoroughfare Gap or in the neighborhood to prevent the enemy's troops from passing by this defile, which is very easy to defend, and you have afterward stated you did not know what General McDowell did to prevent Longstreet coming through that Gap. How, then, do you know he did not leave a sufficient force?

Answer. I said that General McDowell did not leave a sufficient force, because it is my impression that a serious fight would have taken place, of which I would have gained knowledge, and, as I did not, I supposed that there was not a sufficient force there.

Question by General McDOWELL. You have stated you saw General McDowell at your headquarters, in a house near Buckland Mills, on the night of the 27th August. Did you again see General McDowell before you marched from Buckland Mills?

Answer. I think I saw him, and I think it was in his tent. I believe that I went to him that night, and was led there by an officer.

Question by General McDOWELL. What occurred at this second meeting?

Answer. I do not know.

Question by General McDOWELL. Was there any conversation between you and General McDowell?

Answer. I do not know.

Question by General McDOWELL. Did you make any report to General McDowell?

Answer. I do not know.

Question by General McDOWELL. You have stated you received the order for the march upon Manassas Junction at 2.45 o'clock in the morning and that the head of your corps was at Gainesville. What time was it when your corps had all passed Gainesville?

Answer. This I cannot state exactly, because I was at the head of the column, finding out the road to Manassas Junction.

Question by General McDOWELL. When did you leave Gainesville yourself; with what part of your corps did you march?

Answer. I left Gainesville, according to my knowledge, before daybreak—when it was dark yet—because I tried myself to bring my troops in order of march as soon as possible. I marched first with the brigade of General Milroy from Gainesville. Afterward I was with Generals Schurz' and Steinwehr's divisions and the reserve artillery, forming them in line of battle; then I went to the division of General Schenck.

Question by General McDOWELL. Does the witness recollect what hour it was he left Gainesville?

Answer. No.

Question by General McDOWELL. Does the witness recollect any impediment in the road in getting his own troops forward?

Answer. There may have been, but I do not recollect any.

Question by General McDOWELL. Did you or did you not receive orders from General McDowell, at Buckland Mills, on the morning of August 28, 1862, to march your corps immediately to Manassas Junction, with your right on the Manassas Railroad?

Answer. I did.

Question by General McDOWELL. Was or was not this order again given you after you had left Gainesville?

Answer. Soon after leaving Gainesville. I do not believe that this order was repeated to me; but after having formed in line of battle on my march to Manassas I received it again.

Question by General McDOWELL. Was or was not any other order of march than to march on Manassas Junction with your right on the Manassas Railroad given you by General McDowell on the occasion of your march from Gainesville?

Answer. I do not remember such order.

Question by General McDOWELL. You have stated that your troops had to march 5 or 6 miles farther to come again at the evening near the place where they started from and that the men were tired, and you were made to lose time in marching by marching and countermarching, and that this was in compliance with General McDowell's orders. How could your men have been counter-marching in compliance with General McDowell's orders when those orders required of you to march in one direction only, that is, to Manassas Junction, and how could those orders bring you back to near where you started from?

Answer. In making this remark about marching and counter-marching I did not mean Gainesville as the point, but the place between Gainesville and Manassas Junction, where I formed my corps, or a part of my corps, against the enemy; and, as far as I remember my statement, I did not state that I lost time by the orders of General McDowell, but my movements were in compliance with the orders of General McDowell.

Question by General McDOWELL. You have stated that your troops lost time in marching and counter-marching to come to the same points nearly in the evening which they left at noon in compliance with the orders of General McDowell. Is or is not the witness to be understood as saying it was by General McDowell's orders he was made to counter-march to come to the same point nearly which he had left?

Answer. I understand that it was by General McDowell's orders that my corps left the point where it was formed in order of battle at noon, and that this was a mistake, because when I had arrived near Manassas Junction I was ordered by General Pope to march by.

(General McDowell here objected to the reception of such testimony. The question makes reference to an order from him (General McDowell) and not from General Pope.

General McDowell also made the following objection: It is objected to by General McDowell that the witness be now allowed to explain the movements made, qualify the evidence given in chief, or make remarks concerning the evidence so given, at least till after he shall have directly and specifically answered the cross-interrogation propounded to him.)

The court was cleared.

The court was opened, and the following, its decisions on the objections, announced:

"The first objection is not well taken. The question may involve a reference to an order of General Pope."

"The second objection is not applicable to the point before the court."

By direction of the court the recorder read the following:

The witness is directed to answer whether the counter-march made by going to and returning from Manassas was by General McDowell's orders alone; and, if not, he will state directly by whose orders, in connection with General McDowell's, it was made.

Answer. It was not by General McDowell's orders alone. I marched by orders of General McDowell toward Manassas, and by orders of General Pope from near Manassas to New Market.

The court adjourned to meet at 11 o'clock a. m. to-morrow, December 27, 1862.

---

*THIRTY-FIRST DAY.*

COURT-ROOM, COR. PA. AVE. AND FOURTEENTH ST.,
*Washington, D. C., December* 27, 1862.

The court met pursuant to adjournment. Present, * * * , and Maj. Gen. FRANZ SIGEL, U. S. Volunteers, the witness under examination.

* * * * * * *

Question by General MCDOWELL. You have stated (twenty-seventh day's proceedings) that you proposed to General Pope to march your corps to New Market instead of Manassas, as ordered by General McDowell. State whether, therefore, it was not the order he issued for you to march to Centreville via New Market on your own proposal to march to New Market that your troops were counter-marched, if they were counter-marched.

Answer. It was the order of General Pope which directed me to march to Centreville, and it was my proposal to General Pope that I should be permitted to march by New Market, as I was near the road leading by New Market to Centreville. It was by this order of General Pope that I marched to New Market and came back near to the point from which I had started. I have to add that at this time General Milroy was at Manassas, or very near to Manassas, and that he joined me at New Market, whilst I asked General Pope to be allowed to march to New Market to avoid the circuitous road by Manassas.

Question by General MCDOWELL. Was or was it not then on your proposal that troops were made to come back to near where they started from?

Answer. Certainly, and especially because I thought that the enemy was not at Centreville, but somewhere between Centreville and Groveton and New Market, and as I thought that it was our object or my object to march against the enemy on the shortest line.

Question by General McDOWELL. Does the witness wish to be understood as implying it was not the object of the other commanders to march against the enemy?

Answer. I did not say anything about that, because I do not know it. I suppose it was so.

Question by General McDOWELL. You state with reference to your being under the command of General McDowell that you "did not apply to General Pope for orders when you sent your adjutant to see him at Manassas, but that General Pope gave you orders on your proposal." Did you or did you not report to General McDowell the change in your march which those orders you received from General Pope made?

Answer. I object to this question, because it is said here that you "did not apply to General Pope for orders when you sent your adjutant to see him at Manassas, but that General Pope gave you orders on your own proposal." He did not give me orders on my proposal; he only permitted me to march by New Market in compliance with his order.

Question by the COURT. Does the witness mean to object to the question as one which does not recite the evidence given by him?

Answer. It does not.

The recorder was directed to refer to the record and read extracts from pages 302 and 303.

Question by the COURT. Is the ground of objection by the witness understood?

Answer. I object to this, that General Pope gave me orders on my proposal, because I received the orders from him to march to Centreville, which proposition I did not make. I believe I sent to General McDowell whilst we were on the march, and as soon as we had arrived near New Market and became engaged with the enemy. I know that the conversation took place between an officer of General King's division and one of my staff officers, but I do not know whether this is the same officer whom I had sent to communicate with General McDowell. In regard to the first part of the question, I believe I first received the order from General Pope to march to Centreville, and that I sent my officer back to him asking permit to march by New Market instead of by Manassas. I refer to my official report, which I think will give the circumstance as it was, and I do not make it a point whether I proposed to General Pope first and received then the order or that I had received first the order then marched to New Market.

Question by General McDOWELL. Was your report, proposition, or application to General Pope, which you sent your adjutant to make, a verbal one to be made by himself, or was he the bearer of a written dispatch, in which you yourself made direct to General Pope the proposition you have referred to? Was General Pope's order verbal or written?

Answer. I am almost certain that the order of General Pope was a verbal order; but whether my communication to General Pope was written or verbal I cannot say. Captain Meysenberg, my adjutant-general, was the officer whom I had sent to General Pope and who had brought me the reply.

Question by General McDOWELL. Does or does not the witness remember that General McDowell informed him at Buckland Mills that the cavalry he had sent out under Buford had caused Longstreet to deploy his army between Salem and White Plains, thus delaying his march?

Answer. I do not remember that.

Question by General McDOWELL. Did not General McDowell inform you in writing of the troops he was marching to Buckland Mills?

Answer. It may be so. I am not certain of it.

Question by General McDOWELL. After you left Gainesville, on the

28th, did you continue with the troops or did you return to Gainesville that day?

Answer. I did not return to Gainesville. I remained with the troops, partly at the head and partly in the center.

Question by General McDOWELL. With reference to the co-operation of your corps and that of General McDowell, have you not stated in your official reports you were ordered to take position on your march to Manassas with your right resting on the railroad leading from Warrenton Junction to Manassas Junction? If so, who gave you this order?

Answer. I ask to be allowed to see my official report, in order to see if this question is in accordance with my official report.

The report in question was handed the witness.

The witness continued:

I find that this question is not in accordanc with my official report, because I did not say that I should take position on my march to Manassas with my right resting on the railroad.

Question by General McDOWELL. Please examine your official report at the part marked in the margin, and state who gave you the order to take position with your right resting on the railroad leading from Warrenton Junction to Manassas Junction.

The recorder read from the report the following, referred to in the foregoing question:

During the night General McDowell's corps arrived at Buckland Mills, and I received orders at 3 o'clock in the morning to march to Manassas, and to take a position with my right resting on the railroad leading from Warrenton Junction to Manassas Junction; so at least I understood the order.

Answer. I received this order from General McDowell, but I must say that I understood under Manassas Railroad that point of the railroad which is between Manassas Station and the junction of Manassas Gap Railroad and the Orange and the Alexandria Railroad. Therefore I said in my report my right resting on railroad leading from Warrenton Junction to Manassas Junction.

Question by General McDOWELL. Was this order to you in writing?

Answer. I think it was.

Question by General McDOWELL. When and where did you receive it?

Answer. I think it was the order I received at 2.45 a. m. on the 28th.

Question by General McDOWELL. Will the witness please produce the order?

Answer. I will see whether I can find it. I have not received the papers for which I have sent. I suppose that it was a part of Order No. 10, and this may be taken as granted.

Question by General McDOWELL. Witness will please examine this note, dated Gainesville, Va., August 28, 7.30 a. m., and state if it is not from him, and then say if, instead of its being before daybreak and dark when he left Gainesville, as he yesterday stated, it was not two hours after sunrise at least when he so left.

The note referred to in the foregoing question was read by the recorder, and is appended to the proceedings of this day, marked A.

Answer. This is my note; it is from me. In the first place I rode forward on the Centreville turnpike, in advance of my troops, to see what was on that road, and after having made this personal reconnaissance I ordered this note to be written. I further state in my record of yesterday——

General McDowell here stated that he did not want the record of yesterday interfered with. The record had been read and approved.

The witness continued:

I spoke about Gainesville when I really meant Buckland Mills——

General McDowell stated that he would like to have the record of yesterday read over.

The witness continued:

And therefore, as I was not allowed yesterday to make remarks about the record, I wrote this correction down here.

Question by the COURT. Has the witness anything more to say on the point as to whether it was two hours after sunrise when he so left?

Answer. I cannot answer this question directly, because I do not know how long it took me to reconnoiter the country before me, but I admit that it was 7.30 o'clock when I was at Gainesville and sent this dispatch.

Question by General McDOWELL. How long did you remain at Gainesville after you sent the dispatch?

Answer. I do not know exactly how long.

Question by General McDOWELL. Was it an hour or two hours, or half an hour; cannot the witness give some idea of the time?

Answer. I cannot really say whether it was half an hour or two hours. I believe it was rather half an hour than two hours. I only waited for General Milroy to bring in all his pickets and come into marching order. This was the reason why I personally remained at Gainesville, if I did so.

Question by General McDOWELL. Did General Milroy's brigade constitute your advance?

Answer. Yes.

Question by General McDOWELL. How long were you away from Gainesville in your personal reconnaissance on the Centreville road? How far did you go? Who did you see?

Answer. I went forward on all the roads leading to Manassas Junction and Centreville; and, as much as I remember, it was my escort that met the enemy's pickets and reported to me the fact. I do not exactly know how far I went and I myself did not see the enemy, but received the report on the road by my cavalrymen.

Question by General McDOWELL. What report did your escort make to you?

Answer. They reported to me that they saw some of the enemy's cavalry pickets on the road to Centreville.

Question by General McDOWELL. Is that all the report you received on that occasion?

Answer. I received another report a little afterward from a part of my cavalry which I had sent to the right into the woods that they had met the enemy's cavalry in that direction.

Question by General McDOWELL. Were these two reports all that witness received?

Answer. This is what I remember now in regard to this particular moment.

Question by General McDOWELL. As these reports of his cavalry scouts were all he received, how did the witness acquire the knowledge he reported of the enemy's train being between Fairfax and Manassas Junction? How as to Anderson's having apparently taken the northern road from Thoroughfare Gap? How that the main force seemed to be still at Manassas Junction?

Answer. I remember now that I had with me several of my scouts, and I remember one by the name of Switzer, who accompanied me upon the march. I do not exactly know from what sources I received all this information or by what means. It must have been my best knowledge that the enemy was in the neighborhood of Manassas Junction, that means in the direction of Manassas Junction, and with one part of his troops, whilst his main force was in the direction of New Market and Centreville.

General McDowell here stated that this had nothing to do with the question.

Question by the COURT. Do you know how you knew that the enemy's train was between Fairfax and Manassas Junction?

Answer. It is a question about a moment when I was near Gainesville. On the march I inquired where the train was and received it from my officers.

General McDowell here stated that this was not what he asked. The witness continued:

This was at that particular time, and I believe I had that knowledge. I do not remember how I got it, except what I have said before in regard to the prisoners taken, and probably some of this information came from the prisoners.

Question by General MCDOWELL. Does the witness mean to be understood that his officers at any time saw the enemy's train in the place in which he reports it in his letter from Gainesville?

Answer. Yes; I have the proof in writing that one of my officers saw the train. He was sent out by me with cavalry, but I do not know whether he informed me that the train was exactly on the place indicated in my dispatch to General McDowell.

Question by General MCDOWELL. The question is: Whether his officers saw the enemy's train between Fairfax and Manassas?

Answer. I do not know whether the officer reported to me exactly that the train was between Fairfax and Manassas Junction.

Question by General MCDOWELL. When it left Gainesville did your head of column go to the right or south side or the left or north side of the Manassas Railroad?

Answer. We marched beyond Gainesville some distance—I believe three-quarters of a mile, then we took the road which leads nearly parallel and north of the Manassas Gap Railroad. We then crossed the railroad to the south side, and marched south of the railroad until we recrossed it in marching to New Market.

Question by General MCDOWELL. Did you pass Bethlehem Church or Chapel before you crossed the Manassas Railroad to go to New Market?

Answer. I believe we did, but I am not sure.

The witness was handed two papers, purporting to be duplicate orders from Major-General Pope to Major-General McDowell, dated Bristoe Station, August 27, 1862, 9 p. m., which papers are appended to this day's proceedings and marked B.

Question by General MCDOWELL. Does the witness not remember he was shown the following order from General Pope prior to his leaving Buckland Mills?

Answer. I do not remember that this order was shown to me, but it may have been shown to me.

Question by General MCDOWELL. Why did you fail to obey General McDowell's order, which required you to march on Manassas Junction, with your right resting on the Manassas Railroad?

Answer. I believe that I did not disobey the order of General McDowell, because I understood that I should march to Manassas Junction, and having arrived there, form my corps so that the right rested on the Manassas Railroad.

2d. If I would have undertaken to march to Manassas Junction with my right always on the railroad it would have been impossible to do so, according to my best knowledge; and

3d. There seemed to me a contradiction in the order in saying that I should march to Manassas Junction and in the same time to rest with my right on the railroad. I understand that this word "resting" can only relate to the formation of troops, and not to their march.

Question by General McDOWELL. In accordance with orders received at 2.45 a. m. of the 28th of August, you were required to start immediately to Manassas, and why was your advance at 7.30 a. m. still at Gainesville, the place where they remained during the night?

Answer. In the first place my troops were stationed as follows: The advance brigade of General Milroy at Gainesville; the division of General Schurz at North Fork Creek; the division of General Schenck between North Fork Creek and Buckland Mills, and my reserve division at Buckland Mills. This position they held because I encamped them where I could find water, and where they could defend their position against an attack from Hay Market or Thoroughfare Gap. I tried to bring up these divisions to Gainesville and then to march on with my whole corps, instead of marching with separate brigades and divisions. They needed a certain amount of time to form and to come to Gainesville. 2d. I could not march with the brigade of General Milroy from Gainesville or draw in his pickets, which were out for a great distance. I ordered him to draw in his pickets only when I saw that the other troops were near his position. These are the facts. I myself went along the road from Buckland Mills to Gainesville to hasten up the troops and to bring them forward to Gainesville. I must also remark that the whole of my reserve artillery and ammunition train was with my reserve division, behind the bridge at Buckland Mills, which they had to pass. I also remark that these troops marched before daylight, and that they had the greatest part of the night no rest at all after their arrival in their different positions.

The court adjourned to meet on Monday, December 29, 1862, at 11 o'clock a. m.

—

## APPENDIX.

### A.

HEADQUARTERS FIRST CORPS, ARMY OF VIRGINIA,
*Gainesville, Va., August* 28, 1862—7.30 a. m.

Major-General McDOWELL, *Commanding Third Corps:*

As yet I have only met some pickets on the Centreville turnpike, which, it seems to me, makes it necessary to send a force to Centreville to cover our left flank. It might also be well to send an entire division to Centreville, as the enemy's train is between Fairfax and Manassas Junction, which force would at the same time separate the enemy's forces; Anderson apparently having taken the northern road from Thoroughfare Gap, and which would also threaten the enemy's rear.

The main force of the enemy seems to be still at Manassas Junction.

Respectfully, your obedient servant,

F. SIGEL,
*Major-General.*

P. S.—In regard to Anderson or Longstreet coming through Thoroughfare Gap, it may be that they take or have taken the more northern road to Centreville.

### B.

HEADQUARTERS ARMY OF VIRGINIA,
*Bristoe Station, August* 27, 1862—9 p. m.

Major-General McDOWELL:

At daylight to-morrow morning march rapidly on Manassas Junction with your whole force, resting your right on the Manassas Gap Railroad, throwing your left well to east. Jackson, Ewell, and A. P. Hill are between Gainesville and Manassas Junction. We had a severe fight with them to-day, driving them back several miles along the railroad. If you will march promptly and rapidly at the earliest dawn of day upon Manassas Junction we shall bag the whole crowd. I have directed Reno to march from Greenwich at the same hour upon Manassas Junction, and Kearny, who is in his rear, to march on Bristoe at daybreak. Be expeditious, and the day is our own.

JNO. POPE,
*Major-General, Commanding.*

Received dispatch for Major-General McDowell August 28, 1.15 a m.

J. C. BRISCOE,
*Lieutenant and Engineer, Kearny's Division.*

---

*THIRTY-SECOND DAY.*

COURT-ROOM, COR. FOURTEENTH AND PA. AVENUE,
*Washington, D. C., December* 29, 1862.

The court met pursuant to adjournment. Present, * * * , and Maj. Gen. FRANZ SIGEL, U. S. Volunteers, the witness under examination.

* * * * * * *

Question by General MCDOWELL. I desire the witness to take General McDowell's General Orders, No. 10, of August 28, 1862, and show from what therein he is warranted in saying he was to take a position with his right resting on the railroad leading from Warrenton Junction to Manassas Junction. Is or is not that railroad mentioned or referred to in that order? If so, where?

The order in question, appended to the proceedings of the twenty-ninth day, was placed before the witness.

Answer. When I wrote my report I had not the order of General McDowell before me.

General McDowell stated that this is hardly an answer to the question.

The witness asked whether the question referred to what is contained in his report or in his evidence.

The court was then cleared.

The court was opened and the following decision announced:

The question has already been fully answered by the witness during the proceedings of the thirty-first day and is overruled.

Question by General MCDOWELL. Will the witness please point out on the map, as far as the map goes, the Orange and Alexandria Railroad and the Manassas Railroad?

The witness referred to the map from the Bureau of the Topographical Engineers, dated August 1, 1862, of "Northeastern Virginia and vicinity of Washington," which map is appended to the proceedings in the case.*

The witness pointed out the railroads as marked on the map, stating that a small portion of the road (about a half mile), to the west of Manassas Station, was common to the two roads.

---

*To appear in Atlas.

Question by General McDOWELL. Were the divisions of Generals Schurz and Schenck bivouacked on the turnpike between Buckland Mills and Gainesville on the evening of the 27th or the morning of the 28th?

Answer. Yes; they were.

Question by General McDOWELL. How far were they respectively from Gainesville?

Answer. The division of General Schurz was about a mile from Gainesville, probably nearer to Gainesville than a mile. The division of General Schenck was first about 2½ miles from Gainesville, and then received orders to form behind the left wing of General Schurz during the night.

Question by General McDOWELL. Why did you delay the march of the whole force on account of the pickets of General Milroy?

Answer. I did not delay the march. I only did not advance General Milroy's brigade without having the whole corps assembled where he was. There may have been a delay for the reason that I wished to have General Milroy's brigade at the head of my column, and that perhaps his preparations were not all made when the others came up. I have stated why his preparations were made at the last moment before our movement. In relation to General Milroy's brigade, I think it my duty to say that they were under arms the whole night and expected an attack from the enemy. They had nearly no rest—like the other troops of my corps.

Question by General McDOWELL. Was the position of your reserve artillery any cause for delay? If so, what?

Answer. I do not know any more, because my headquarters were on this side of Buckland Mills. I started when it was dark, went to General Schenck, then to General Milroy, to be at the head of my troops. There must have been a delay in crossing the bridge, but I would not say *delay*, because in all such movements we want time.

Question by General McDOWELL. What time did you require to march your reserve division from Buckland Mills to Gainesville, a distance of 3 miles?

Answer. I was not with them, and therefore cannot say how much time they wanted, and I also see by the map that it is not 3 but almost 4 miles to Gainesville from Buckland Mills.

Question by General McDOWELL. What is the usual rate of march per hour in your corps over good turnpike roads, which are unobstructed by anything but the troops themselves?

Answer. I refuse to answer that question, if not ordered by the court.

The court decided the question a proper one.

The witness continued:

In answering the question I remarked that I refused to do so because this question is too general and does not apply to the case. According to circumstances we can march very quick on a good road, but ordinarily troops march 15 miles a day on good roads. This would, if we march 10 hours, be 1½ miles an hour. On the 28th August my corps marched 13 miles and the brigade of General Milroy 16, and this was in the presence of the enemy, where we could march only slowly and had to look out well.

Question by General McDOWELL. Do you know of any cause of delay in your march on the morning of the 28th from your baggage wagons obstructing the road—the turnpike from between Buckland Mills and Gainesville—or from your men stopping in the turnpike to build fires to cook?

Answer. I did not see myself that the baggage train was in the road; I at least do not remember it; but I remember that I rode up to the soldiers of General Schenck, who were trying to cook coffee before daylight, and forced them to fall in and to march.

Question by General McDOWELL. How far had your men marched

on the 27th, and had they not had the whole day and night of the 26th to rest themselves at Warrenton, and what time did they finish their march on the 27th?

Answer. On the 27th, that morning we marched from Warrenton toward Buckland Mills, but found the enemy this side of Buckland Mills. I was therefore compelled to halt and to get information. We then had a skirmish at Buckland Mills with the enemy. He retired and burned the bridge. I took possession of the shores of the creek, and had to restore the bridge by my pioneers, which took about two or three hours. During this time the greatest part of the troops formed on the right and left in line of battle, and were all under arms, and standing, because it was reported to me that 10,000 men were on our front and that 60,000 had marched toward Manassas, which report I sent to General McDowell. The march was finished and the troops had all crossed the bridge before sunset. I do not exactly know when we marched from Warrenton. After having crossed the bridge with all my troops I countermarched my reserve division, because the troops of General McDowell had not arrived yet, and I feared an attack from Hay Market. We then marched slowly on toward Gainesville to gain that point. General Milroy arrived at Gainesville at night—8 or 9 o'clock. The divisions of General Schurz and General Schenck were first kept back near Buckland Mills and then successively advanced, so that they changed their position during the night. One regiment was sent toward Hay Market and one toward Greenwich, over a mile distant from the road. One-third of our troops, I think, were under arms and on picket, and General Milroy's brigade especially. On the 26th and on the night of the 26th and 27th we were at Warrenton, and all my troops were resting.

Question by General McDOWELL. How long before sunset was it when you reached Buckland Mills? How far is it from Warrenton to Buckland Mills?

Answer. I do not exactly know how long. It is from Warrenton to Buckland Mills about 9 or 10 miles.

Question by General McDOWELL. Can the witness give no idea how long before sunset it was when he reached Buckland Mills; was it half and hour, an hour, or two hours? State about how long.

Answer. I cannot say how long.

By General McDOWELL. I beg to ask if the court considers this question responded to—before sunset? The term used will take in the whole day, and therefore fixes no time at all after sunrise.

Question by the COURT. Can you state about how near to sunset it was?

Answer. It was in the afternoon and before sunset. I remember now that I sent from Buckland Mills an officer to Warrenton to General McDowell, which must have taken two hours, making it about 4 o'clock. The officer wrote to me when he arrived there about 6 o'clock p. m. It must have been therefore 4 or 5 o'clock, according to this connection of things. The officer was Captain Este, of General Schenck's staff.

A paper dated Headquarters First Corps, Army of Virginia, Buckland Bridge, Va., August 27, 1862, 11.40, was placed before the witness, which paper is appended to the proceedings of this day, marked A.

Question by General McDOWELL. State if this is not the note you sent at that time, dated at Buckland Mills, at 11.40 a. m.

Answer. This is the note which my adjutant has written. I had gone in advance probably to direct the movement of General Milroy, and I remember that as he could not cross the bridge with his artillery, his cavalry, and afterward his infantry, or a part of it, crossed near the bridge. I also remember that the brigade of General Milroy was a great distance ahead of my principal column, as he was ordered to do so.

Question by General McDOWELL. Look at this order, dated Warrenton, August 27, 1862, and state if it is the order under which you marched to Buckland Mills.

A book was placed before the witness, from which a letter, of which the following is a copy, was read by the recorder:

HEADQUARTERS THIRD CORPS, ARMY OF VIRGINIA,
*Warrenton, August* 27, 1862—7.30 a. m.

Major-General SIGEL:

Push immediately a strong advance along the turnpike from Warrenton to Gainesville, for the purpose of taking possession of the position of Buckland Mills, on Broad Run, and get your corps in hand as soon as possible to follow this advance. No wagons but for ammunition will accompany your corps on this road. Your baggage trains will immediately proceed to Catlett's. Detach three batteries from your troops to report to Major-General Kearny, commanding division, who will be moving by the way of Greenwich to your support.

Further instructions will be given as to the route by which these batteries are to join General Kearny; until they do, they will be kept with your command.

By command of Major-General McDowell:

ED. SCHRIVER,
*Colonel, Chief of Staff.*

Answer. Yes; that is the letter.

Question by General McDOWELL. State if these letters were not sent by you from Buckland Mills on the 27th, and if you know of any other reports made by you to General McDowell that day except the one just presented.

Three papers were read by the recorder, then placed before the witness. These papers are dated as follows: "Headquarters, Buckland Bridge, August 27—12.30 p. m." "Headquarters First Corps, Army of Virginia, Buckland Bridge, Va., August 27, 1862—1.50 p. m." "Headquarters First Corps, Army of Virginia, Buckland Bridge, Va., August 27, 1862—8 p. m.," and are appended to the proceedings of this day, and marked B, C, D.

Answer. These letters have been sent by me to General McDowell. I do not remember any other letter. I only remember that I sent that officer of which I have spoken, but I must remark that I do not believe that my troops held exactly the position which I indicated at 8 p. m. in my letter. This is the only remark I have to make about this matter.

Question by General McDOWELL. State if you received the letters dated August 27, recorded on page 327, of this letter-book.

The official letter-book pertaining to the Headquarters Third Army Corps was placed before the witness, from which the recorder read the following:

HEADQUARTERS THIRD ARMY CORPS, ARMY OF VIRGINIA,
*August* 27, 1862.

Maj. Gen. FRANZ SIGEL,
*Commanding First Corps:*

GENERAL: The major-general commanding directs me to inform you [that] three regiments of cavalry, under General Bayard, have been ordered to join you until yours can be returned to you.

Very respectfully, your obedient servant,

ED. SCHRIVER,
*Colonel and Chief of Staff.*

HEADQUARTERS THIRD ARMY CORPS, ARMY OF VIRGINIA,
*August* 27, 1862.

Maj. Gen. FRANZ SIGEL,
*Commanding First Corps:*

GENERAL: I have just received your note of 12.30 p. m. In default of your cavalry, which is not yet returned, I send you this morning General Bayard, with three regiments. When yours return please send him back to me. I will send word to Catlett's about your regimental provision wagons. Brigadier-General Reynolds' division is immediately behind you. King and Ricketts follow.

Very respectfully, your obedient servant,

IRVIN McDOWELL,
*Major-General.*

Answer. I do not remember very well whether these letters were sent to me, but I admit that they were sent. In regard to the cavalry, I know that they arrived at Buckland Mills—I think after dark.

Question by General McDOWELL. Did you see General McDowell at Warrenton on the 27th, before you marched for Buckland Mills?

Answer. I do not know.

Question by General McDOWELL. Without asking as to the nature or quality of the combination or co-operation, I wish the witness to state if the general order he received at 2.45 a. m. at Buckland Mills, August 28, did or did not imply or provide for a combined movement or co-operation of his own and General McDowell's corps.

Answer. I do not know exactly, but I admit it, because I think it very natural.

Question by General McDOWELL. Did or did not the order, in the opinion of the witness, imply that movement of his own corps and that of General McDowell should all be to the left of, or on the north side of, the Manassas Railroad, that road being taken as the directing line of the movement?

Answer. I did not hear anything about a directing line. I probably had on that night no definite idea what would be the best line of attack.

Question by General McDOWELL. Did you or did you not understand that your corps was to march on the left of, or north side of, the Manassas Railroad?

Answer. I could not understand that fully. I probably thought that on my way I should keep as near as possible on the line of the railroad, and, if I should find the enemy between Gainesville and Manassas, that I should form my corps in line of battle, my right resting as near as possible to the railroad, my left extending to near Groveton or New Market, wherever I was.

Question by General McDOWELL. Did not an aide-de-camp of General McDowell come to the witness when he was at or just beyond Gainesville to tell him from General McDowell he was to march with his *right* on the Manassas Railroad, and did not the witness, when he was marching south of the road, receive through other officers of General McDowell's staff similar instructions?

Answer. I do not remember that an aide-de-camp of General McDowell came to me, but it may have been so; and, in regard to the other officers, I also do not know of having seen any one.

Question by General McDOWELL. The witness gives as a second reason (yesterday's proceedings) that he did not disobey General McDowell's order, that if he, the witness, would have undertaken to march to Manassas Junction with his right always on the railroad it would have been impossible to do so, according to his best knowledge. Does the witness desire to be understood that when he receives an order for an important movement on which the whole army depends, and finds while executing it some part impracticable, that this absolves him from carrying out that part which is practicable, and that where a literal compliance is impossible the spirit of the order is not to be followed?

The court considered this question objectionable and overruled it.

The court decided that $5 per diem be paid the clerk of this court, as a fair compensation for his services, from and to include the 21st December, 1862.

The court adjourned to meet to-morrow, December 30, 1862, at 11 o'clock a. m.

## APPENDIX.

A.

HEADQUARTERS FIRST CORPS, ARMY OF VIRGINIA,
*Buckland Bridge, Va., August* 27, 1862—11.40.

Major-General MCDOWELL,
*Commanding Third Corps:*

I have driven the enemy's cavalry, which was one mile this side of the bridge, from the bridge. The bridge had been set on fire, which was extinguished, and I am now in possession of the same. Two pieces of artillery have been posted this side of the bridge. The brigade of General Milroy is now crossing. The enemy had some cavalry and one piece of artillery shown on the opposite side of the creek. The bridge will be repaired at once by my pioneers.

Respectfully, yours,

F. SIGEL,
*Major-General.*

B.

HEADQUARTERS,
*Buckland Bridge, August* 27—12.30 p. m.

Major-General MCDOWELL:

GENERAL: I am not farther yet than at and over the bridge. Some troops of General Milroy have passed it. The firing of yesterday and to-day is said to have been at Manassas. This is said by all whom I have met and examined. It is also in accordance with all other information.

If we concentrate quickly at Gainesville, or near Gainesville, put all our disposable forces, with the exception of a few at the Rappahannock, we have the only and best chance to defeat the enemy's plans and his army. We have several means and ways to operate from here. Jackson may be at Manassas or elsewhere. We should all be here to-night and press forward to-morrow at daybreak.

Yours, respectfully,

F. SIGEL,
*Major-General, Commanding First Corps.*

P. S.—Please send me to-night without fail my cavalry (Fourth New York, Sixth Ohio, and Ninth New York), and my regimental provision wagons, which I have ordered to Catlett's Station.

C.

HEADQUARTERS FIRST CORPS, ARMY OF VIRGINIA,
*Buckland Bridge, August* 27, 1862—1.50 p. m.

Major-General MCDOWELL,
*Commanding Third Corps:*

The brigade of General Milroy has advanced and is now 2 miles beyond the bridge, after the enemy had made an attempt to burn the bridge. He is directed to push his cavalry on to Gainesville and then take position on the fork to Thoroughfare Gap. General Milroy observed a train, which leaves no doubt that this is the enemy's rear guard which I have before me, and believe that the enemy is at Manassas by this time, and has beaten our forces there, and to proceed from there to Alexandria to destroy our depots.

It seems to me necessary that our forces concentrate at Gainesville in pursuit of the enemy.

Being almost without cavalry, I beg leave to request you to send me one regiment from Warrenton, as cavalry is the only arm which may be of some avail under these circumstances. I cannot be without cavalry. I have only 150 men. Please send the first regiment you can find.

Let the troops advance at once, because the enemy may throw himself on my advance and we could lose the bridge.

Respectfully, yours,

F. SIGEL,
*Major-General.*

P. S.—Please take care of my train, which is now at Catlett's Station.

D.

HEADQUARTERS FIRST CORPS, ARMY OF VIRGINIA,
*Buckland Bridge, Va., August* 27, 1862—8 p. m.

Major-General McDOWELL, *Commanding Third Corps:*

The First Corps is in bivouac between Gainesville and Broad Run, with the cavalry beyond Gainesville.

General Milroy captured about 100 prisoners, stragglers of the rebel army. One brigade formed the rear guard, which was driven back by my advance. It seems to me essential that we attack to-morrow, when it would be necessary to know the relations existing between the different commands here, and to know who will be in command in case of a battle if General Pope or yourself should not be here.

Inasmuch as it is said that another force is said to advance from Salem, under command of General Longstreet, and that Jackson's troops are very tired and have used a great amount of ammunition, I think they should be attacked at once at Manassas Junction.

Please inform me where General Cox's command is, and whether there is any hope of his joining me soon.

I am, general, very respectfully, your obedient servant,

F. SIGEL,
*Major-General, Commanding First Corps.*

---

*THIRTY-THIRD DAY.*

COURT-ROOM, COR. FOURTEENTH ST. AND PA. AVE.,
*Washington, D. C., December* 30, 1862.

The court met pursuant to adjournment. Present, * * *, and Maj. Gen. FRANZ SIGEL, U. S. Volunteers, the witness under examination.

* * * * * * *

Question by General McDOWELL. You state you believe that General McDowell did not give his troops the right direction on the 29th, because instead of attacking the enemy on his right flank, by coming in on our left, his troops, as much as you could see, came in from the rear; that is to say, instead of coming in in the direction of New Market he came in in the direction of Centreville. You do not know for what reason? Do you know that General McDowell's troops did not come by the New Market road?

Answer. I do not know.

Question by General McDOWELL. You have stated you are of the opinion that had General King's division been united to that of General Reynolds on that same day at noon or in the afternoon—that is, if 15,000 men had been marched forward against the right flank of the enemy, he must have been routed. Do you know that General McDowell was not moving forward to so unite them in the afternoon?

Answer. I do not know, but if he did it was too late in the afternoon.

Question by General McDOWELL. In answering the question as to when General McDowell's troops appeared on the field, you speak of their arriving on the battle-field at sunset on the 29th. You have also stated they came on the field from the direction of Centreville. Is that the first knowledge you had of King's division of General McDowell's troops being on the field on that day; that is, when they came up along the Warrenton turnpike?

Answer. That is the first knowledge I had, as much as I can remember.

Question by General McDOWELL. Do you know what orders General McDowell had or under what instructions he acted concerning the bringing his troops into action on the afternoon of the 29th. If you say you do, please state them. If you say you do not, then please state how you know that the direction given General McDowell's troops was given to them by General McDowell.

Answer. I have my knowledge about the movements of General McDowell's troops from a paper which I received from General Pope on the morning of the 29th of August, and which I lay before the court. This is the only knowledge.

The paper referred to by the witness was read by the recorder, and is appended to the proceedings of this day and marked A.

Question by the COURT. Where was General Pope's headquarters at this time?

Answer. I think they were at Centreville.

Question by General McDOWELL. What time of the day was it you received this order which you have produced?

Answer. It must have been at about 10 or 11 o'clock in the morning; but I am not sure of this.

Question by General McDOWELL. You said you did not know on the morning of the 29th and up to 12 or 1 o'clock that General Reynolds was on your left, and that you could not make any disposition of General Schenck to assist your right wing and center because he had to cover your left wing, and that you do not know what orders the division of General Reynolds had and what they did, &c. Did you not send to General Reynolds' division before you commenced the action and request its co-operation?

Answer. I believe I did not, because I wrote a note to General Pope on that morning, asking him who was on my left, whether it was Reno?

Question by General McDOWELL. Did not one of General Reynolds' brigade commanders see you before you went into action on the 29th with reference to the co-operation of Reynolds' division?

Answer. I remember now that two officers were in my quarters, speaking with me very hastily. I supposed they were officers belonging to General McDowell's corps; but whether there was any agreement between us I cannot say. I did never suppose by this conversation that I had to give them any direction or had any command over them. I think they spoke about their troops, but I do not remember the particulars. It may have been about Reynolds' division.

Question by General McDOWELL. You have stated, among the points to qualify your testimony, that General McDowell was not attentive enough as relates to yourself; that you cannot understand for what reason he has left his position on the 28th, in the evening, &c. Have you or have you not any official or personal knowledge of the orders given to General McDowell, or of those given by him to his corps, prior to the 29th, after you received orders from him to march to Manassas?

Answer. I have no knowledge about the orders given to General McDowell on the night of the 28th, or the evening of the 28th, after I had received this order to march to Manassas, and I also did not receive any knowledge of orders given to General McDowell during the day of the 28th. I do not know what orders he has given to his corps.

Question by General MCDOWELL. Do you know anything of the movements of King's division on the night of the 28th, after the engagement; where it went or by whose orders it moved?

Answer. I know that I sent an officer to the place where King's division was during or shortly after the engagement, and that he could not find it there any more. I do not know by what orders they moved or had moved and where they went.

Question by General MCDOWELL. Who was the officer you sent to see General McDowell on the 28th and who reported to you that General McDowell would be in a certain house in Centreville? What time of the day was this?

Answer. The officer whom I sent toward Groveton to King's division was, I believe, Captain Dahlgren. This must have been at night, and the officer who spoke about the headquarters of General Pope and General McDowell was, I believe, Captain Kœnig.

Question by General MCDOWELL. Did Captain Dahlgren report having seen General McDowell on this occasion?

Answer. I think he reported that he did not see him and that he could not find him.

Question by General MCDOWELL. You have stated you considered yourself under General McDowell's orders during the battle at Bull Run and that you saw General McDowell come on the field in the evening of the 29th. State if you, on that occasion, reported to him or gave him any information.

Answer. I did not report to him because I saw General McDowell at a distance going to General Pope's headquarters, while I was going to the left of our position, and my presence was needed very much there. I thought that General McDowell would get all the information necessary from General Pope, with whom I was in direct communication during the battle of the 29th.

Question by General MCDOWELL. When did you consider yourself as no longer under General McDowell's command?

Answer. I regarded myself bound to obey all his orders sent to me until I was separated from his corps at Fairfax Court-House and marched to Vienna. This was on the last of August or the 1st of September.

Question by General MCDOWELL. Did you report to him or send an officer to him to report for orders on the night of the 29th, on the morning of the 30th, or the night of the 30th? Did you do so at Centreville?

Answer. I do not believe that I reported personally to General McDowell, and I do not know whether I have sent an officer to him on the night of the 29th or on the 30th. I was under the impression that General Pope and General McDowell's headquarters were at Centreville, and that General McDowell was in close connection with General Pope, and could receive information of all communications sent by me to General Pope, of whom I had a better knowledge where he was, and besides this I thought that if General McDowell had to give me any orders he would send them to me.

Question by General MCDOWELL. Did General McDowell send you any orders on the 29th or the 30th or after the 30th?

Answer. This I cannot remember very well.

Question by General McDOWELL. You state you received a dispatch which you believe was transmitted to you by one of General McDowell's staff, which dispatch was written by General Porter. On what was that belief founded—that this dispatch was given you by one of General McDowell's staff?

Answer. I thought so because it was an officer of General McDowell's staff, as much as I remember.

Question by General McDOWELL. Do you know who it was?

Answer. No.

Question by General McDOWELL. Did you know by sight all of General McDowell's staff?

Answer. I think I did not know every one of General McDowell's staff.

Question by General McDOWELL. Did you know all of General Pope's staff?

Answer. I think not.

Question by General McDOWELL. When did you report to General Pope the force of the enemy that was marching on Cedar Run Mountain?

Answer. On the day before the 9th of August, when the battle took place, I received a letter from Colonel Cluseret, at Madison Court-House, wherein he stated that he received information that Jackson would advance with 20,000 or 25,000 men. It is my impression that I sent this letter to General Pope. I also reported to General Pope, previous to this letter, what forces composed the army of General Jackson.

Question by General McDOWELL. Was this the occasion you reported Jackson marching on Cedar Run Mountain?

Answer. I did not say that I reported Jackson marching on Cedar Mountain. I said that my letter related to his marching on Culpeper.

Question by General McDOWELL. When were you at Madison Court-House?

Answer. I was in Madison Court-House, or in the neighborhood of Madison Court-House, where Cluseret had his camp, one time or more than once. I do not remember exactly the day.

Question by General McDOWELL. How far from Madison Court House was Colonel Cluseret's camp?

Answer. It was for some time in Madison Court-House and beyond, in a southern direction, and at the time I speak of I believe his camp was between Madison Court-House and the Robertson River. The nearest place to his camp was Madison Court-House. I would not say exactly how far it was, for I do not remember very well.

Question by General McDOWELL. Did you not report to General Pope on the 8th of August that heavy forces of the enemy were advancing through Madison Court-House?

Answer. That may be. I do not know if I did.

Question by General McDOWELL. Do you know that General Buford was stationed in Madison Court-House and reported direct to General Pope; that near about the 8th of August heavy forces of the enemy moved upon Madison Court-House in the direction of Sperryville?

Answer. I know that a brigade of General Buford's was at one time stationed beyond Madison Court-House, and that this brigade had to be supported, if necessary, by Colonel Cluseret. Whether they were on the 8th at Madison Court-House I do not know. I suppose General Buford reported directly to General Pope on the 8th of August, but I do not know. I do not remember that General Buford reported that heavy forces of the enemy moved upon Madison Court-House in the direction of Sperryville.

General McDowell stated he had no more questions to ask on the cross-examination.

By the COURT. Have you information of any matter or thing not within your personal knowledge, and not testified to by you, tending to show misbehavior or want of proper qualifications in General McDowell as a general officer, and which information, in your judgment, deserves the consideration of the court? If you have such information will you communicate it in writing to the recorder for the consideration of the court and the names of witnesses by whom the facts may be established.

Answer. I would like time to consider this question. If there is anything I will communicate it in writing to the court.

The witness here asked the court if he had authority to lay before the court such papers as related to the evidence given by him and whether he could correct such portions of his evidence as his papers suggest to him.

The court propounded the following question to the witness: Is there any portion of your cross-examination in respect to which you desire to make any explanation? If so, you can now make it.

Answer. I would like to read over my evidence to-day and will make these explanations to-morrow. My explanations will be very short.

Capt. ULRIC DAHLGREN, additional aide-de-camp, U. S. Army, a witness, was duly sworn.

Question by the COURT. Were you a staff officer on the staff of General Sigel during the month of August last?

Answer. Yes, sir.

Question by the COURT. Were you present with General Sigel on the march of his corps from Gainesville toward Manassas on the 28th day of August last?

Answer. Yes, sir.

Question by the COURT. Were you sent by General Sigel with any oral or written message to General McDowell on that march; and, if so, what was that message?

Answer. I was. General Sigel sent me to General McDowell for more definite instructions, having previously received orders to halt where he was and form line, with his right resting on the railroad. We were then about a mile on the Manassas Railroad from Gainesville. I went back, and found General McDowell about a mile or a mile and a half to the rear of where we then were. He was then sitting under a tree, with a large map before him. I stated to him that an aide had just come to General Sigel with an order to halt where he was and form line, with his right resting on the railroad, and that General Sigel wished more definite instructions. General McDowell replied that he had not sent any order to halt nor any order since the one directing him to proceed to Manassas. I then asked, for my own information, so that I could explain it better, at what point at Manassas we should form. General McDowell replied, "Let General Sigel fight his own corps," emphasizing the word fight. As I was about leaving General McDowell added that General Sigel should be particular to take the nearest road to Manassas, showing me on the map a road which went to the right and near the railroad, distinguished from the road which, I believe, passed by Milford, to the right and south of Milford, and by Bethlehem Church also.

Question by the COURT. What was the manner of General McDowell when he said General Sigel should fight his own corps?

Answer. I would hardly call it angry; it was somewhat irritated or somewhat indifferent as to what might happen to the corps.

Question by the COURT. Did you encounter the enemy on that day and where?

Answer. We did. Our cavalry were skirmishing and taking prisoners from the time we left Buckland Mills, but the first regular engagement was near Mrs. Henry's farm, as marked on the map. What transpired while I was with General McDowell I do not know.

Question by the COURT. In the course of your march toward Manassas did you ascertain where the enemy was in force?

Answer. We did or thought we did. I think our scouts reported they had left Manassas, which report was soon confirmed by General Milroy's advance.

Question by the COURT. Where were you at that time on your route?

Answer. Very near where the road which we were on intersects the road which passes through New Market.

Question by the COURT. At what time of day was this?

Answer. I am unable to say the exact time of day. It was in the afternoon, about 2 or 3 o'clock; I am not certain.

Question by the COURT. Which way did you learn that the enemy had moved?

Answer. We learned that there was a force near Groveton, and we supposed it was the same which had left Manassas, but I do not know on which road they went, as there were many stragglers in every direction.

Question by the COURT. Do you know whether any communication of this movement of the enemy from Manassas toward Groveton was made to General McDowell?

Answer. I do not know. I think it was reported to General Pope.

Question by General McDOWELL. Is witness to be understood General Sigel formed his line of battle in pursuance of an order which he supposed General McDowell had sent him?

Answer. I do not know. I had just come up to General Sigel at the same time that the supposed order was brought from General McDowell.

Question by General McDOWELL. Does witness remember what time of day it was when he left General Sigel to go to General McDowell?

Answer. No, sir.

Question by General McDOWELL. Does witness remember what officers were near General McDowell when he reported to him and saw him examining a map?

Answer. I do not know or remember the officers. I remember the place very well.

The recorder was directed to request the Secretary of War to transmit any reports or papers on file showing the forces left for the defense of Washington when General McClellan moved to the Peninsula last spring, and tending to explain the reasons and influences which led to the detention of the corps of General McDowell at that time.

The court adjourned to meet to-morrow, December 31, 1862, at 11 o'clock a. m.

---

## APPENDIX.

### A.

HEADQUARTERS ARMY OF VIRGINIA,
*August* 29, 1862.

To Generals HEINTZELMAN, RENO, and SIGEL:

If you find yourselves heavily pressed by superior numbers of the enemy you will not push matters further.

Fitz John Porter and King's division, of McDowell's corps, are moving on Gainesville from Manassas Junction, and will come in on your left. They have about 20,000 men. The command must return to this place to-night or by morning on account of subsistence and forage.

JNO. POPE,
*Major-General, Commanding.*

---

*THIRTY-FOURTH DAY.*

COURT-ROOM, COR. FOURTEENTH AND PA. AVENUE,
*Washington, D. C., December* 31, 1862.

* * * * * * *

A communication from Major-General Sigel, dated Washington, D. C., December 31, 1862, was read by the recorder, and is appended to the proceedings of this day and marked A.

The recorder communicated to the court that he had received a communication from Major-General McClellan, dated New York City, December 21, 1862, with inclosures referred to in his testimony, which inclosures were read by the recorder, and are appended to the record of the proceedings of this day, marked B, C, and D, and subject to further verification.

The recorder here stated to the court that he had as yet been unable to procure copies of the one hundred letters read by him in evidence on the twenty-second day and of many letters read since; and that, in order to avoid a greater confusion of the record, he would ask that the reading of further correspondence be delayed until copies of said letters be furnished.

The court directed the recorder to employ additional assistance in order to complete the correspondence belonging to the back record.

Maj. JOSEPH C. WILLARD, additional aide-de-camp, U. S. Volunteers, a witness, was duly sworn.

Question by General MCDOWELL. Were you with General McDowell on the evening of the 27th of August last at Buckland Mills, on the occasion of his going to see General Sigel?

Answer. I was.

Question by General MCDOWELL. What position did you have on General McDowell's staff on that occasion?

Answer. I was aide-de-camp, with rank of major.

Question by General MCDOWELL. Please state, as nearly as you can recollect, what passed, or the substance of what passed, between General McDowell and General Sigel on that occasion, and particularly as to the dispositions of the forces for the next day.

Answer. I went with General McDowell to the house that was the headquarters of General Sigel, and I heard General McDowell request General Sigel to go with his troops to Manassas, I think, and that he (General McDowell) would give him (General Sigel) one of his divisions. I copied an order which mentioned plainly the place to which General Sigel was to go when General McDowell proposed to give him the division which was to accompany him.

Question by General MCDOWELL. What was said about the defense of Thoroughfare Gap?

Answer. I think, as near as I can remember, that General McDowell requested General Sigel to go with his corps to Thoroughfare Gap.

Question by General McDOWELL. Do you recollect if General McDowell offered for this purpose to give General Sigel a division?

Answer. I do, sir.

Question by General McDOWELL. State if you prepared copies of General McDowell's General Orders, No. 10, of August 28, 1862, providing for the march of General Sigel and General McDowell's corps from Buckland Mills to Manassas Junction.

Answer. I did.

Question by General McDOWELL. Was the copy prepared for General Sigel a full copy of that order and was it sent to General Sigel?

Answer. It was, sir.

Question by the COURT. Did General McDowell state that he considered it expedient to send Sigel's corps, with a division of his own corps, to the defense of Thoroughfare Gap; and, if so, for what reason?

Answer. He considered it expedient, I think, because he considered the enemy as coming through that way.

Question by the COURT. Do you know why he did not send the force which he considered it expedient to send?

Answer. I do not.

Question by the COURT. Do you remember what General Sigel said in reply to the proposal of General McDowell; if so, state it as nearly as you remember?

Answer. No; I do not remember.

The court adjourned to meet on Monday, January 5, 1863, at 11 o'clock a. m.

---

## APPENDIX.

### A.

WASHINGTON, D. C.,
*December* 31, 1862.

Lieutenant-Colonel PELOUZE,
*Recorder Court of Inquiry:*

COLONEL: It has been impossible for me to examine all my papers and arrange them for the purpose of laying them before the court or to prepare the statement in answer to the questions submitted to me by the court.

I will endeavor to have everything ready before 11 o'clock of Friday morning, if this will suit the convenience of the court.

Very respectfully, yours, &c.,

F. SIGEL,
*Major-General.*

### B.

HEADQUARTERS ARMY OF THE POTOMAC,
*March* 16, 1862.

Brig. Gen. JAMES S. WADSWORTH,
*Military Governor of the District of Columbia:*

SIR: The command to which you have been assigned by instructions from the President as military governor of the District of Columbia embraces the geographical limits of the District, and will also include the city of Alexandria, the defensive works south of the Potomac from the Occoquan to Difficult Creek, and the post of Fort Washington.

I inclose a list of the troops and of the defenses embraced in these limits.

General Banks will command at Manassas Junction, with the divisions of Williams and Shields, composing the Fifth Corps; but you should nevertheless exercise vigilance in your front, carefully guard the approaches in that quarter, and maintain the duties of advanced guards. You will use the same precautions on either flank.

All troops not actually needed for the police of Washington and Georgetown, for the garrisons north of the Potomac, and for other indicated special duties should be moved to the south side of the river. In the center of your front you should post the main body of your troops and proper proportions at suitable distances toward your right and left flanks.

Careful patrols will be made, in order thoroughly to scour the country in front from right to left.

It is specially enjoined upon you to maintain the forts and their armaments in the best possible order, to look carefully to the instruction and discipline of their garrisons, as well as all other troops under your command, and by frequent and rigid inspections to insure the attainment of these ends.

The care of the railways, canals, depots, bridges, and ferries within the above-named limits will devolve upon you, and you are to insure their security and provide for their protection by every means in your power.

You will also thoroughly protect the depots of the public stores and the transit of stores to the troops in active service.

By means of patrols you will thoroughly scour the neighboring country south of the Eastern Branch, and also on your right, and you will use every possible precaution to intercept mails, goods, and persons passing unauthorized to the enemy's lines.

The necessity of maintaining good order within your limits, and especially in the capital of the nation, cannot be too strongly enforced.

You will forward and facilitate the movement of all troops destined for the active part of the Army of the Potomac, and especially the transit of detachments to their proper regiments and corps.

The charge of all new troops arriving in Washington and of all troops temporarily there will devolve upon you. You will form them into provisional brigades, promote their instruction and discipline, and facilitate their equipment. Report all arrivals of troops, their strength, composition, and equipment by every opportunity.

Besides the regular reports and returns which you will be required to render to the Adjutant-General of the Army, you will make to these headquarters a consolidated morning report of your command every Sunday morning and a monthly return on the first day of each month.

The foregoing instructions are communicated by command of Major-General McClellan.

Very respectfully, your obedient servant,

S. WILLIAMS,
*Assistant Adjutant-General.*

C.

HEADQUARTERS ARMY OF THE POTOMAC,
*March* 16, 1862.

Maj. Gen. N. P. BANKS,
*Commanding Fifth Corps, Army of the Potomac:*

SIR: You will post your command in the vicinity of Manassas, intrench yourself strongly, and throw cavalry pickets well out to the front.

Your first care will be the rebuilding of the railway from Washington to Manassas and to Strasburg, in order to open your communications with the valley of the Shenandoah. As soon as the Manassas Gap Railway is in running order, intrench a brigade of infantry, say four regiments, with two batteries, at or near the point where that railway crosses the Shenandoah. Something like two regiments of cavalry should be left in that vicinity to occupy Winchester and thoroughly scour the country south of the railway and up the Shenandoah Valley, as well as through Chester Gap, which might perhaps be advantageously occupied by a detachment of infantry, well intrenched.

Block-houses should be built at all the railway bridges.

Occupy by grand guards Warrenton Junction or Warrenton itself, and also some still more advanced point on the Orange and Alexandria Railway as soon as the railway bridges are repaired.

Great activity should be observed by the cavalry. Besides the two regiments at Manassas, another regiment of cavalry will be at your disposal to scout toward the Occoquan, and probably a fourth toward Leesburg.

To recapitulate: The most important points which should engage your attention are as follows:

1st. A strong force well intrenched in the vicinity of Manassas, perhaps even Centreville, and another force (a brigade), also well intrenched, near Strasburg.

2d. Block-houses at the railway bridges.

3d. Constant employment of cavalry well to the front.

4th. Grand guards at Warrenton, and in advance as far as the Rappahannock, if possible.

5th. Great care to be exercised to obtain full and early information as to the enemy.

6th. The general object is to cover the line of the Potomac and Washington.

The foregoing is communicated by command of Major-General McClellan.

Very respectfully, your obedient servant,

S. WILLIAMS,
*Assistant Adjutant-General.*

D.

HEADQUARTERS ARMY OF THE POTOMAC,
*Steamer Commodore, April* 1, 1862.

Brig. Gen. LORENZO THOMAS,
*Adjutant-General U. S. Army:*

GENERAL: I have to request that you will lay the following communication before the honorable Secretary of War:

The approximate numbers and positions of the troops left near and in rear of the Potomac are about as follows:

General Dix has, after guarding the railroads under his charge, sufficient troops to give him 5,000 for the defense of Baltimore, and 1,988 available for the Eastern Shore, Annapolis, &c. Fort Delaware is very well garrisoned by about 400 men.

The garrisons of the forts around Washington amount to 10,600 men; other disposable troops now with General Wadsworth being about 11,400 men. The troops employed in guarding the various railways in Maryland amount to some 3,359 men. These it is designed to relieve, being old regiments, by dismounted cavalry, and to send forward to Manassas.

General Abercrombie occupies Warrenton with a force which, including Colonel Geary, at White Plains, and the cavalry to be at his disposal, will amount to some 7,780 men, with twelve pieces of artillery.

I have the honor to request that all the troops organized for service in Pennsylvania and New York and in any of the Eastern States may be ordered to Washington. I learn from Governor Curtin that there are some 3,500 men now ready in Pennsylvania. This force I should be glad to have sent at once to Manassas. Four thousand men from General Wadsworth I desire to be ordered to Manassas. These troops, with the railroad guards above alluded to, will make up a force under the command of General Abercrombie to something like 18,639 men. It is my design to push General Blenker's division from Warrenton upon Strasburg. He should remain at Strasburg long enough to allow matters to assume a definite form in that region before proceeding to his ultimate destination.

The troops in the valley of the Shenandoah will thus—including Blenker's division, 10,028 strong, with twenty-four pieces of artillery; Banks' Fifth Corps, which embraces the command of General Shields, 19,687 strong, with forty-one guns; some 3,652 disposable cavalry and the railroad guard, about 2,100 men—amount to about 35,467 men.

It is designed to relieve General Hooker by one regiment, say 850 men, being, with some 500 cavalry, 1,350 men on the Lower Potomac.

To recapitulate:

| | |
|---|---|
| At Warrenton there is to be | 7,780 |
| At Manassas, say | 10,859 |
| In the valley of the Shenandoah | 35,467 |
| On the Lower Potomac | 1,350 |
| In all | 55,456 |

There would thus be left for the garrisons and the front of Washington, under General Wadsworth, some 18,000 men, exclusive of the batteries under instructions.

The troops organizing or ready for service in New York I learn will probably number more than 4,000. These should be assembled at Washington, subject to disposition where their services may be most needed.

I am, very respectfully, your obedient servant,

GEO. B. McCLELLAN,
*Major-General, Commanding.*

---

*THIRTY-FIFTH DAY.*

COURT-ROOM, COR. FOURTEENTH AND PA. AVENUE,
*Washington, D. C., January* 5, 1863.

* * * * * * *

The recorder read from the record books pertaining to the Headquar ters Department of the Rappahannock the following official correspondence, copies of which are appended to the record of this day's proceedings, in the following order: *

1. Maj. Gen. Irvin McDowell to Major-General Banks, dated Headquarters Department, June 14, 1862, Manassas.

2. Ed. Schriver, colonel and chief of staff, to Major-General Shields, dated Headquarters Department of the Rappahannock, Manassas, June 14, 1862.

3. Maj. Gen. Irvin McDowell to Hon. E. M. Stanton, Secretary of War, dated Headquarters Department of the Rappahannock, Manassas, June 14, 1862.

4. Major-General McDowell to Hon. E. M. Stanton, dated Manassas, June 14, 1862.

5. Ed. Schriver, colonel and chief of staff, to Major-General Shields, dated Headquarters Department of the Rappahannock, Manassas, June 14, 1862.

6. Ed. Schriver, colonel and chief of staff, to Brigadier-General Ricketts, dated Headquarters Department of the Rappahannock, Manassas, June 14, 1862.

7. Major-General McDowell to Major-General Banks, dated Headquarters Department of the Rappahannock, Manassas, June 14, 1862.

8. Major-General McDowell to Hon. E. M. Stanton, dated Washington, D. C., Manassas, June 14, 1862.

9. Irvin McDowell to Major-General Banks, dated Headquarters Department of the Rappahannock, Manassas, June 14, 1862.

10. E. M. Stanton, Secretary of War, to Major-General McDowell, dated Washington, June 14, 1862.

11. N. P. Banks, major-general, to Major-General McDowell, dated Winchester, June 14, 1862.

12. General Ricketts, dated Front Royal, June, 1862, communicating a dispatch from Major-General Banks.

13. Col. Ed. Schriver, chief of staff, to Brigadier-General Ricketts, dated Headquarters Department of the Rappahannock, Manassas, June 15, 1862.

14. Col. Ed. Schriver, chief of staff, to Major-General Shields, dated Headquarters Department of the Rappahannock, Manassas, June 15—5.15 p. m.

15. Col. Ed. Schriver, chief of staff, to Brigadier-General Ricketts, dated Headquarters Department of the Rappahannock, Manassas, June 15, 1862.

16. Col. Ed. Schriver, chief of staff, to Brigadier-General King, dated Headquarters Department of the Rappahannock, Manassas, June 15, 1862.

17. Colonel Schriver, chief of staff, to Brigadier-General Ricketts, dated Headquarters Department of the Rappahannock, Manassas, June 15—10.30 p. m.

18. Major-General McDowell to His Excellency the President, dated Headquarters Department of the Rappahannock, Manassas, June 15, 1862.

19. Major-General McDowell to Hon. E. M. Stanton, dated Headquarters Department of the Rappahannock, Manassas, June 15, 1862—12.35 p. m.

20. Col. Ed. Schriver, chief of staff, to Brigadier-General Ricketts, dated Headquarters Department of the Rappahannock, Manassas, June 15, 1862—6 p. m.

21. Major-General McDowell to Hon. E. M. Stanton, dated Headquarters Department of the Rappahannock, Manassas, June 16—8 a. m.

22. Major-General McDowell to Hon. E. M. Stanton, Secretary of War, dated Manassas, June 16, 1862—8.15 p. m.

23. Col. Ed. Schriver, chief of staff, to Brigadier-General Ricketts, dated Headquarters Department of the Rappahannock, Manassas, June 16—12.30 p. m.

24. Major-General Shields to Colonel Schriver, chief of staff, dated Headquarters First Division, Luray, June 15, 1862.

25. James Shields, commanding division, to Colonel Schriver, chief of staff, dated Milford, 12 miles from Front Royal, June 16, 1862.

26. Brig. Gen. Rufus King to Major-General McDowell, dated Falmouth, June 2, 1862.

27. Brig. Gen. James B. Ricketts to Col. Ed. Schriver, chief of staff, dated Front Royal, June 16, 1862.

28. Major-General McDowell to Major-General Banks, dated Manassas, Va., June 17, 1862—10.45 p. m.

29. Col. Ed. Schriver, chief of staff, to Major-General Shields, dated Headquarters Department of the Rappahannock, Manassas, June 17, 1862.

30. Col. Ed. Schriver, chief of staff, to Colonel Sanford, superintendent of the telegraph, dated Manassas, June 18, 1862.

31. Major-General McDowell to Major-General Banks, dated Headquarters Department of the Rappahannock, Manassas, June 18, 1862.

32. Col. Ed. Schriver, chief of staff, to Major-General Shields, dated Headquarters Department of the Rappahannock, June 18—10.45 p. m.

---

* Omitted from appendix, to appear in chronological order in "Correspondence, etc.," Part III.

33. Colonel Schriver, chief of staff, to Brigadier-General Ricketts, dated Headquarters Department of the Rappahannock, Manassas, June 18, 1862.
34. Major-General McDowell to Hon. E. M. Stanton, dated Headquarters Department of the Rappahannock, Manassas, June 18, 1862.
35. Maj. Gen. James Shields to Col. Ed. Schriver, dated Front Royal, June 18, 1862.
36. E. M. Stanton, Secretary of War, to Major-General McDowell, dated Washington, June 18, 1862.
37. James Shields, commanding division, to Colonel Schriver, dated Front Royal, June 18, 1862.
38. Major-General Shields to Colonel Schriver, chief of staff, dated Front Royal, June 18, 1862.
39. Assistant Secretary of War to Major-General McDowell (containing dispatch from General Banks), dated Washington, June 19, 1862.
40. Major-General Shields to Col. Ed. Schriver, chief of staff, dated Front Royal, June 19, 1862.
41. Col. Ed. Schriver, chief of staff, to Major-General Shields, dated Headquarters Department of the Rappahannock, Manassas, June 19—12.45 p. m.
42. Col. Ed. Schriver, chief of staff, to Hon. E. M. Stanton, dated Manassas, June 19—8.45 a. m.
43. Colonel Schriver, chief of staff, to Brigadier-General Shields, dated Headquarters Department of the Rappahannock, Manassas, June 19—5.30 p. m.
44. Col. E. Schriver, chief of staff, to Brigadier-General Geary, dated Headquarters Department of the Rappahannock, Manassas, June 19—6 p. m.
45. Colonel Schriver, chief of staff, to Lieutenant-Colonel Thompson, quartermaster, dated Manassas, June 20—4.45 p. m.
46. Col. E. Schriver, chief of staff, to General Shields, dated Headquarters Department of the Rappahannock, Manassas, June 20—4.45 p. m.
47. Col. Ed. Schriver, chief of staff, to Major-General Shields, dated Manassas, June 20—12.30 p. m.
48. Col. E. Schriver, chief of staff, to Hon. E. M. Stanton, dated Manassas, June 20—12.30 p. m.
49. Col. E. Schriver, chief of staff, to General Patrick, Catlett's, dated Headquarters Department of the Rappahannock, Manassas, June 20, 1862—8.45 a. m.
50. E. M. Stanton, Secretary of War, to Colonel Schriver, dated Washington, June 20, 1862.
51. E. M. Stanton, Secretary of War (containing dispatch from General Sigel), dated Washington, June 20, 1862.
52. Major-General Shields to Colonel Schriver, dated Front Royal, June 20, 1862.
53. E. M. Stanton, Secretary of War, to Major-General McDowell, dated Washington, June 21, 1862.
54. E. Schriver, chief of staff, to Colonel Haupt, aide-de-camp, dated Manassas, June 21—8 a. m.
55. Col. E. Schriver, chief of staff, to Major-General Shields, dated Manassas, June 21, 1862.
56. Major-General McDowell to Hon. E. M. Stanton, dated Headquarters Department of the Rappahannock, Manasses, June 21—2 p. m.
57. Col. Ed. Schriver, chief of staff, to commanding officer Catlett's, dated Manassas, June 22.
58. Col. Ed. Schriver, chief of staff, to Major-General Banks, dated Manassas, June 22, 1862.
59. Major-General McDowell to Hon. E. M. Stanton, Secretary of War, dated Headquarters Department of the Rappahannock, Manassas, June 22, 1862.
60. Major-General McDowell to Hon. E. M. Stanton, dated Manassas, June 23—5.30 p. m.
61. Col. E. Schriver, chief of staff, to Brigadier-General Patrick, dated Manassas, June 23, 1862—3 p. m.
62. E. M. Stanton, Secretary of War, to Major-General McDowell, dated Washington, June 22, 1862—12.20 p. m.
63. Major-General Banks to Major-General McDowell, dated Middletown, June —, 1.45 p. m.
64. Brigadier-General Geary to Colonel Schriver, dated Rectortown, June 22, 1862.
65. Major-General Shields to Colonel Schriver, dated Salem, June 22, 1862.
66. Brig. Gen. Rufus King to Colonel Schriver, chief of staff, dated Falmouth, June 24, 1862.
67. Brig. Gen. Rufus King to Colonel Schriver, chief of staff, dated Falmouth, June 24, 1862.

Major-General McDowell here presented to the court a copy of the President's order, dated Executive Mansion, Washington, D. C., June

26, 1862, organizing the Army of Virginia, which copy is appended to the proceedings of this day, marked A.

Capt. WLADISLAS LESKI, additional aide-de-camp, U. S. Army, a witness, was duly sworn.

Question by General McDOWELL. State what was your position on General McDowell's staff in August last. State what instructions General McDowell gave you the night of the 27th and 28th of August. State if you saw General McDowell on the morning of the 28th of August, and what instructions he gave you concerning the movements of troops to hold Longstreet in check at or this side of Thoroughfare Gap. What road did the troops from Buckland Mills take? What regiment was first sent? What did it do? What troops succeeded this regiment? What reports did you make? What instructions did you give?

Answer. In August last I was aide-de-camp, with rank of captain, on General McDowell's staff. On the night of the 27th and 28th of August, about midnight, I think, General McDowell called me to his tent, where he was with General Reynolds, and explained to me his desire to send troops to Thoroughfare Gap immediately off the road from Warrenton to Buckland Mills; that is, this side of the creek, where General McDowell's troops were; the other side from here. He instructed me to go and find whether it would be practicable to send artillery and infantry in that direction. Accordingly I went outside our lines a distance of about 2 miles. I found the road passable so far, but beyond this, where was the mill, I couldn't find any road by which artillery could be sent. I returned then and reported the facts to the general.

I saw General McDowell early on the morning of the 28th and before daylight, when General McDowell sent me to General Sigel for General Bayard's cavalry brigade, which was at the time attached to General Sigel. General Sigel stated that he could not spare the cavalry at that time; that it would be impossible for him to advance if he had no cavalry, but that he would send them as soon as possible. He stated at the same time that one regiment of cavalry (the First New Jersey) was somewhat beyond Buckland Mills, and which regiment General McDowell could use. I reported this to the general, and when we advanced in sight of the cavalry—Colonel Wyndham's regiment—General McDowell instructed Colonel Wyndham, in my presence, to move immediately to Thoroughfare Gap to get news from the enemy, and at the same time that he, Colonel Wyndham, would be re-enforced by other regiments as soon as practicable.

Shortly after that General McDowell sent me also to Thoroughfare Gap with instructions to bring as early news as possible about the enemy. I went to Thoroughfare Gap, and found part of the regiment of Colonel Wyndham inside of the Gap. I advised the colonel to obstruct the Gap, and he ordered a detachment of men to fell the trees in the Gap, which was done. We rode (the colonel and myself) then to see the picket line, and send some scouts forward to see whether the enemy was advancing. Several prisoners were taken during the time in the Gap, from whom I ascertained Longstreet had been during the night at Salem, and was expected to pass the Gap during the day.

About 9.30 a. m. the scouts came back, stating the advance of the enemy was coming near to the Gap; and on the receipt of it I immediately sent the news to General McDowell. Soon afterward I returned to the general. When on the road I met General Bayard, coming with other regiments of cavalry, informing him of the condition of things and that the enemy was showing himself also on our right; that is, north of Hay Market.

On my return to General McDowell I informed him of the topography of the country, for which information I was sent; and the general instructed me to go back to General Ricketts, who got orders to defend the Gap. I met General Ricketts' troops crossing through the country from the Buckland Mills road to Hay Market. The troops advanced rather slowly, being an excessively hot day. I met General Ricketts near Hay Market, who concluded to go to the Gap, sending first a regiment of cavalry in advance, no enemy having shown himself yet this side of the Gap. The Harris Light Cavalry engaged first with the enemy in the Gap, who seemed to be removing the obstructions made for them. Soon after the infantry and artillery of General Ricketts engaged the enemy; and, as much as I remember, the Eleventh Pennsylvania Regiment was mostly in the fight.

While the engagement was going on I returned to General Bayard, at Hay Market, with the desire that he should push his cavalry to the right. The enemy then advanced with rather a strong force of cavalry upon Hay Market from the north. The skirmishing was going on for some time, and as there was danger of our being cut off from the remaining portion of General McDowell's troops, or losing communication with them, General Bayard sent a detachment of cavalry to picket the Gainesville road beyond Gainesville. This was about 3 or 4 o'clock in the afternoon.

The cavalry of the enemy being still re-enforced on the north, General Bayard desired me to find General Buford, who was on the south of us, on our left, to send him a regiment of cavalry to support him at Hay Market, and on my return I was again sent to General Ricketts for a couple [of] light pieces for a battery to take position on the heights at Hay Market. I remained with General Ricketts some time; it was getting toward dark, when General Ricketts stated that he would retire with his infantry and artillery to the high position between Hay Market and Gainesville, as he found it, so he said, too dangerous to remain near the Gap, whilst he received reports from the Harris Light Cavalry that the enemy was crossing Hopewell, and also on the left. General Ricketts desired that the cavalry should cover the retreat of his infantry from the Gap to Hay Market. The retreat was finished, I should think, about 9 o'clock p. m.; that is about the time the rear of the infantry reached Hay Market. The division took position for the night between Hay Market and Gainesville.

The court adjourned to meet to-morrow, January 6, 1863, at 11 o'clock a. m.

---

## APPENDIX.

### A.

EXECUTIVE MANSION,
*Washington, D. C., June* 26, 1862.

Ordered:

I. The forces under Major-Generals Frémont, Banks, and McDowell, including the troops now under Brigadier-General Sturgis at Washington, shall be consolidated and form one army, to be called the Army of Virginia.

II. The command of the Army of Virginia is specially assigned to Maj. Gen. John Pope as commanding general. The troops of the Mountain Department, heretofore under the command of Major-General Frémont, shall constitute the First Army Corps, under command of Major-General Frémont; the troops of the Shenandoah Department, now under General Banks, shall constitute the Second Army Corps, and be commanded by him; the troops under the command of General McDowell, except those within the city of Washington, shall form the Third Army Corps, and be under his command.

A. LINCOLN.

LORENZO THOMAS,
*Adjutant-General.*

---

## *THIRTY-SIXTH DAY.*

COURT-ROOM, COR. FOURTEENTH ST. AND PA. AVENUE,
*Washington, D. C., January* 6, 1863.

The court met pursuant to adjournment. Present, * * * , and Capt. WLADISLAS LESKI, additional aide-de-camp, U. S. Army, the witness under examination.

* * * * * * *

Question by the COURT. What is the distance through Thoroughfare Gap?

Answer. It is said to be about 4 miles from the foot of the east to the foot of the west of the mountain.

Question by the COURT. Describe the passage, its width, and character of natural obstructions in it.

Answer. There are properly two gaps—one near the eastern portion of the mountain and the other toward the western portion. Between the two is a more open space, although with heavy embankments on the side. The eastern part of the Gap is rather narrow, with very steep embankments. The land on both sides is wooded. From the eastern gap it opens toward the east sufficiently to post batteries so as to defend the *débouché* of the Gap. This is about half a mile in the mountain from the base of the mountain. So much as I recollect, the land on both sides of the Gap is too steep or too accidental for troops to cross.

Question by the COURT. What was the whole strength of the force under General Ricketts at the Gap and how far did he penetrate it with his force?

Answer. I could not state positively the numerical strength of General Ricketts' force. He had four brigades of infantry, which amounted to at least 8,000; besides he had about six batteries. Some of the batteries were broken; that is, had lost a piece or so. I could not judge well how far they penetrated inside the Gap, but I know they were fighting in the defile. I was not with the advance.

Question by the COURT. Was General Ricketts driven back before he concluded to retreat to Hay Market?

Answer. No, sir.

Question by the COURT. What was the description of rebel troops which approached Hay Market from the direction of Hopewell Gap?

Answer. I saw only cavalry, but the reports which were received from the Harris Light Cavalry were that large masses of troops were debouching through the Gap.

Question by the COURT. Was any communication made to General McDowell of the approach of these masses through the Hopewell Gap?

Answer. A report was sent to General McDowell stating that General Ricketts concluded to retire to Hay Market on account of his believing himself surrounded by the enemy. I believe that General Ricketts sent a similar report to General McDowell. These are the only communications sent to General McDowell of which I have knowledge.

Question by the COURT. What measures, if any, were taken by General McDowell to prevent the approach of the enemy through Hopewell Gap except sending General Ricketts to operate as you have already described?

Answer. I do not know of any other measures taken by General McDowell, except the sending of Ricketts' division and the two brigades of cavalry to defend the line. These regiments had not only to defend the Gap itself, but also small passes through which cavalry might pass.

Question by General MCDOWELL. About what hour were these reports sent to which you refer—of troops coming through Hopewell Gap?

Answer. About 6 o'clock p. m.; maybe a little later.

Question by General MCDOWELL. From the nature of the defile of Thoroughfare Gap, which would have been the better disposition of the force—to have placed them in the defile where the front could have been no wider than the enemy's front or to have placed them so as to prevent the enemy from debouching from the defile by concentrating the fire of a wide front on the opening?

Answer. From the hasty survey that I made of the ground I should judge that having sufficient artillery, as in this case, it was far better to prevent the debouching of troops from the Gap than to post the artillery in a narrow defile.

The court was cleared.

The court was opened.

The court adjourned to meet to-morrow, January 7, 1863, at 11 o'clock a. m.

*THIRTY-SEVENTH DAY.*

COURT-ROOM, COR. FOURTEENTH ST. AND PA. AVE.,
*Washington, D. C., January* 7, 1863.

*    *    *    *    *    *    *

The court was cleared.

The court was opened and the following announced:

The court has received the communication of General Sigel in response to their request for information, wherein he states that he has nothing additional to the evidence already given that he thinks essential to lay before the court.

Although the communication cannot be used as evidence, the court desires the recorder to retain it until the conclusion of this investigation for reference, if it shall become important for that purpose.

Maj. Gen. FRANZ SIGEL, U. S. Volunteers, a witness, was recalled.

Question by the COURT. Look at the papers now shown to you, marked, respectively, No. 1, No. 8, No. 15, No. 16, No. 17, No. 18, No. 19, No. 20, No. 21. Are these papers the original orders or communications, or true copies of them, referred to in your testimony?

Answer. They are.

The papers were then read as follows:

1. From Cluseret, commanding expedition, to Major-General Sigel, dated Criglersville, August 7, 1862.
2. From Maj. R. O. Selfridge, being general orders, dated Headquarters Army of Virginia, Warrenton, August 25, 1862.
3. From Maj. Gen. Irvin McDowell to Major-General Sigel, dated Headquarters Third Corps, Army of Virginia, near Warrenton, August 26, 1862.
4. From Major-General McDowell to Major-General Sigel, dated Headquarters Third Corps, Army of Virginia, Warrenton, August 26, 1862.
5. From Col. Ed. Schriver, chief of staff, to Major-General Sigel, dated Headquarters Third Corps, Army of Virginia, Warrenton, August 27, 1862—7.30 a. m.
6. From S. F. Barstow, assistant adjutant-general, dated 11.30 p. m., Headquarters Third Army Corps, Buckland Mills, August 27, 1862.
7. From Major-General Sigel to Brigadier-General Schenck, dated Headquarters First Corps, Army of Virginia, August 28, 1862—2.30 p. m.
8. From C. Heintz, officer of the general staff, to Major-General Sigel, dated August 28, 1862.
9. From Captain Heintz, aide-de-camp, to Major-General Sigel, dated August 28, 1862.

The witness stated that the two communications from Captain Heintz were originally in German and that the copies read are true translations.

The foregoing papers are appended to the proceedings of this day in the order in which they were read.

Question by the COURT. Look at the four maps now shown to you. State whether those maps indicate the localities and position of the troops referred to in your testimony of operations from the 27th to the 30th of August.

Answer. The maps marked 3 and 4 can only be approximately correct. In the map marked 2 General Schenck's division should be somewhat to the left, and the distance between the divisions of Schurz and Schenck is a little too near; but in general the map marked 2 is correct. The map marked 1 represents the position of the different corps as intended by the order of General Pope on the 25th of August.

The maps referred to in the foregoing are appended to the proceedings of this day, and marked 1, 2, 3, and 4.

Question by General McDOWELL. From what survey or what map was map No. 1 taken?

Answer. It is not a copy of a map; it is made from Lloyd's map and General McDowell's map, by my directions, and executed by Lieutenant-Colonel Meysenberg. I think he also used a photographic map which was lying on the table, but am not sure.

Question by General McDOWELL. State wherein map No. 3 is correct and wherein only approximately so.

Answer. This plan relates to the supposed position of the enemy, as indicated in the order of General Pope, and the troops drawn up north of the railroad have, therefore, not been in this position. In regard to the troops between Buckland Mills and Gainesville, my corps and that of General McDowell are represented correctly in regard to the order they followed each other. According to order No. 10, Generals Reno's and Heintzelman's troops are supposed to be on march from Greenwich and Bristoe to Manassas Junction.

Question by General McDOWELL. On what authority do you place the enemy in the position marked as being where you say General Pope's order supposed him to be?

Answer. In the order of General Pope it was said, according to my remembrance, that the enemy must be somewhere between Manassas Junction and Gainesville.

Question by General McDOWELL. Would then any other place between Manassas Junction and Gainesville be as correct as the one you have assumed?

Answer. No, I think not. I think that the enemy could have probably been on the road from Manassas Junction to Gainesville—on his march to Gainesville.

Question by General McDOWELL. What conditions as to the time of marching—time of starting—of the enemy's troops and our own have you assumed that would place the forces in the supposed position?

Answer. The drawing relates to the order of General Pope, and not to what I have proposed or supposed, and therefore the question cannot relate to me. It relates to General Pope.

Question by General McDOWELL. What knowledge had you or have you as to General Pope's supposition of the enemy's position, and on which he (General Pope) based his order?

Answer. The troops of General Heintzelman, under General Hooker, had a skirmish with the enemy or a fight on the 27th, and probably he thought that the enemy would try to retreat to Gainesville to unite with General Longstreet. I had no knowledge of what General Pope might have surely known of the enemy—under what supposition he has acted—except what is written in his words.

The court took a recess of five minutes.

Question by General McDOWELL. Do I understand the witness that he has deduced this supposed position of the enemy and his own and General McDowell's corps from the orders he received from General McDowell and the one he may have seen to General McDowell from General Pope for his march from Buckland Mills?

Answer. I deduced this supposed position from the order of General Pope, which I may have seen, and which I saw during the investigation.

Question by General McDOWELL. From what map or survey are your maps Nos. 1, 2, 3, and 4 compiled?

Answer. I really do not know what maps Lieutenant-Colonel Meysenberg has used, and I was not particular in regard to the details of these maps.

Question by General McDOWELL. Wherein is map No. 4 correct and wherein approximately so, as to positions, routes, &c., of the enemy or of our own troops?

Answer. I have already given an explanation in regard to this map No. 4. In addition to it I may state that the position of my corps as given on the map is pretty much correct. Jackson's position seems to be also correct. Now, in comparing the two maps, I find that it is impossible to make a detailed explanation. To do this I should have to make another map. This map should only represent a general idea and the movements in general and not in detail.

Question by General McDOWELL. When did you learn of the position of Jackson that you have marked on the map?

Answer. I already stated that this question, bearing to the details, I can only answer on reference to a better map. At daybreak on the morning of the 28th one of my scouts reported to me about the enemy's train between Manassas Junction and Fairfax. It was between 6 and 7 on the morning of the 28th when we found the enemy's pickets on the road to Groveton. It was about 10 o'clock when the officer, Captain Heintz, sent me his dispatches, and it was at noon that I received news that the enemy was not at Manassas Junction. I forgot to say that I found myself the wood in my front occupied by pickets for at least half of a mile, which indicated to me that a large force must be behind. This was before noon, when I first formed toward the north. They were infantry. I will also mention the report of Major Kappner, my engineer officer, who saw the enemy's infantry moving, and reported this to me at the same time mentioned.

Question by General McDOWELL. Did you report to General McDowell or Pope that Jackson occupied the position indicated on the map; if so, when?

Answer. I reported to General McDowell on the morning of the 28th that the enemy was before me, and told the officer to explain to General McDowell where he was; it was the same position nearly as given on the map. I also made a report to General Pope on the evening of the 28th, when I was engaged with the enemy, and told General Pope, by Captain Kanish, what was our position. This was after I had arrived with the whole corps at Mrs. Henry's farm and taken possession of the turnpike between the stone bridge and Groveton, at Mr. Robinson's farm. The whole army of Jackson at that time must have been between Robinson's farm and Groveton. I thought General Pope knew where the enemy was when I sent to him at Manassas Junction.

The court adjourned to meet to-morrow, January 8, 1863, at 11 o'clock a. m.

---

## APPENDIX.

### No. 1.

CRIGLERSVILLE, *August* 7, 1862.

Major-General SIGEL:

GENERAL: Captain Kennedy has just returned from an expedition along the Rapidan. He brings the following news:

Mr. Hood, who has had charge of General Banks' farm for thirteen years, a Union man, being near Wolftown, and having just returned from down the Rapidan, informed him that Jackson would leave to-morrow morning with 25,000 men toward Culpeper, his first point. He proposed from that place to make the whole tour, probably by Woodville and Sperryville. This information comes from the inhabitants of Ruggles, a town 8 or 10 miles from Wolftown, on the Rapidan, the inhabitants having told Mr. Hood so.

There are about 300 men at Ruggles. I will send you to-morrow the report of Captain Kennedy, who brings some horses and some 30 head of cattle. He did not take the mail nor meet Captain White's company, as we hoped. He crossed the Rapidan some miles and got within 2 miles of Stanardsville.

I shall send immediately scouts in all directions to ascertain whether there is any evidence of a movement. In case I find it so, I shall take measures to fall upon Jackson's rear guard and cut off his train.

Very respectfully, your obedient servant,

CLUSERET,
*Colonel, Commanding Expedition.*

No. 2.

GENERAL ORDERS, } HEADQUARTERS ARMY OF VIRGINIA,
No. —. } *Warrenton, August* 25, 1862.

I. The corps of Major-General McDowell, to which the division of Brigadier-General Reynolds is attached, will occupy Warrenton, with an advance of at least a brigade thrown out toward Waterloo and Sulphur Springs. The cavalry of the corps will be kept along the line of the river.

II. The First Army Corps, under Major-General Sigel, will occupy Fayetteville, and will there be joined by Brigadier-General Cox, whose advance has reached Warrenton Junction. Major-General Sigel will occupy some strong position in the vicinity of Fayetteville, throwing out an advance of at least a brigade toward the fords in front of his position and keeping his cavalry along the line of the river.

III. The corps of Major-General Banks, to which will be added 10,000 men under Brigadier-General Sturgis, will take post with its right resting on Bealeton Station and its left extended along the north side of Marsh Creek; from this corps at least one division will be pushed forward as near as practicable to the railroad crossing of the Rappahannock. If there be any difficulty about water for this corps wells will be dug immediately.

IV. The detachment of the Ninth Army Corps, under Major-General Reno, will resume its station at Kelly's Ford, putting itself in communication immediately with the forces below it on the river.

V. The troops of Heintzelman's corps will take post with the center at Germantown and extended along the Licking River.

VI. Brigadier-General Cox, with the troops under his command, will move forward as soon as possible to Fayetteville and report to Major-General Sigel. Those under Brigadier-General Sturgis will report to Major-General Banks at Bealeton Station.

VII. The Headquarters of the Army of Virginia will be established at a point near Warrenton Junction to be hereafter designated.

By command of Major-General Pope:

R. O. SELFRIDGE,
*Assistant Adjutant-General.*

No. 3.

HEADQUARTERS THIRD CORPS, ARMY OF VIRGINIA,
*Near Warrenton, August* 26, 1862.

Major-General SIGEL, *&c.:*

GENERAL: I am instructed by Major-General Pope to take command of the right and front, for the purpose of strengthening some movements I am ordered to make. Please let me know the position and strength of your command, and especially of the cavalry.

My headquarters are on the hill southwest of Warrenton, on Sulphur Springs road.

Very respectfully, general, your obedient servant,

IRVIN McDOWELL,
*Maj. Gen., Commanding Third Corps, Army of Virginia.*

No. 4.

HEADQUARTERS THIRD CORPS, ARMY OF VIRGINIA,
*Warrenton, August* 26, 1862.

Major-General SIGEL, *&c.:*

GENERAL: I have the honor to acknowledge the receipt of your communication of this date, and I beg now to inquire whether the strength reported by you is effective and reliable. Please inform me also who commands your cavalry.

Have three days' rations cooked and your men prepared in every way for the march early to-morrow morning.

Very respectfully, general, your obedient servant,

IRVIN McDOWELL,
*Maj. Gen., Commanding Third Corps, Army of Virginia.*

No. 5.

HEADQUARTERS THIRD CORPS, ARMY OF VIRGINIA,
*Warrenton, August* 27, 1862—7.30 a. m.

Major-General SIGEL:

Push immediately a strong advance along the turnpike from Warrenton to Gainesville, for the purpose of taking possession of the position of Buckland Mills, on Broad Run, and get your corps in hand as soon as possible to follow this advance. No wagons but for ammunition will accompany your corps on this road. Your baggage trains will immediately proceed to Catlett's. Detach three batteries from your troops to report to Major-General Kearny, commanding divisions, who will be moving by the way of Greenwich to your support.

Further instructions will be given as to the route by which these batteries are to join General Kearny; until they do they will be kept with your command.

By command of Major-General McDowell:

ED. SCHRIVER,
*Colonel and Chief of Staff.*

No. 6.

HEADQUARTERS THIRD ARMY CORPS,
*Buckland Mills, August* 27, 1862—11.30 p. m.

It being understood that a large division of the enemy under Longstreet left Salem at 4 p. m. for the enemy's position in the direction of Manassas, through Thoroughfare Gap, and is now on the march, the following preliminary movements of the left wing of the army will be immediately made:

Major-General Sigel's corps will without delay be concentrated at or near Hay Market and Gainesville.

A division of the Third Corps will be left at Buckland Mills to operate against the flank of the enemy's column or march to Hay Market, as shall be found most expedient. King's and Ricketts' divisions will march to Gainesville, and start at 2 o'clock in the morning to attack the enemy's position in the direction of Manassas. This attack will be supported under the provision of the general orders from Headquarters of the Army of Virginia, by the command of Major-General Heintzelman, now at Gainesville,* and which will be on the right of the attack.

By command of Major-General McDowell:

S. F. BARSTOW,
*Assistant Adjutant-General.*

No. 7.

HEADQUARTERS FIRST CORPS, ARMY OF VIRGINIA,
*August* 28, 1862—2.30 a. m.

[Brigadier-General SCHENCK:]

GENERAL: Put your division in motion immediately, and take position behind and near the left wing of Schurz by battalion in mass.

No signals to be given and no noise made.

F. SIGEL,
*Major-General.*

No. 8.

[Dispatch of C. Heintz, aide-de-camp, on the morning of the 28th of August.]

On a hill, at a distance of about 2 miles, alongside of the Centreville road, is a large train which might be captured, perhaps, if attacked by a strong force of cavalry, by taking a by-road through the woods. If the general should wish to convince himself, I think it would prove of importance.

C. HEINTZ,
*Officer of the General Staff.*

No. 9.

AUGUST 28, 1862—a. m.

Major-General SIGEL:

The enemy has placed four pieces in position in front of the woods against McDowell's advancing column; is firing against him, and has sent us five shots already.

McDowell's firing is very slow and has ceased now entirely. Large bodies of troops do not move, the infantry appearing only to support the batteries. The enemy is retreating on the Centreville road. General Steinwehr is here. He is of my opinion, that the enemy does not intend to break through. His train has gone farther into the woods, and is but little to be seen. General Von Steinwehr intends to attack the enemy's flank with the brigade, and is preparing for the advance. I shall follow with the cavalry on his right, and shall post orderlies to facilitate the rapid sending of dispatches.

The commander of McDowell's division has been informed of our movements.

C. HEINTZ,
*Officer of the General Staff.*

---

* In the rough draught of this order, furnished by General McDowell, Greenwich is given and not Gainesville.

No. 1.

[Hopewell]

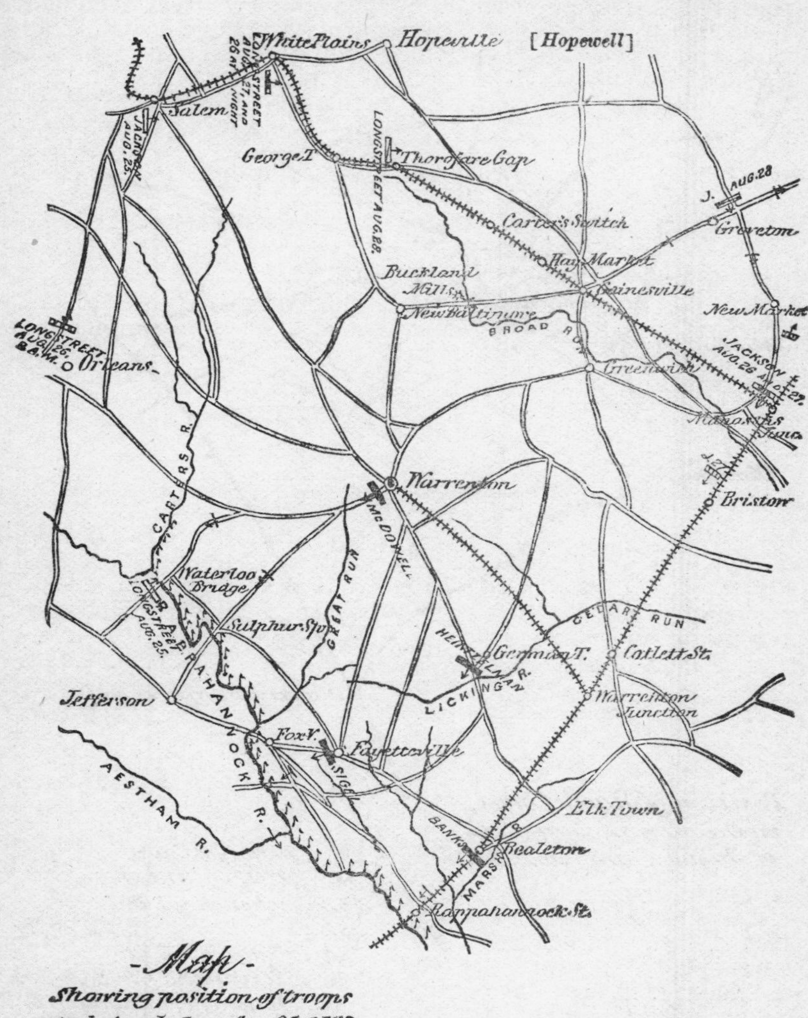


-*Map*-
*Showing position of troops as intended on Aug. 25, 1862, by General Orders of General Pope.*

No. 2.

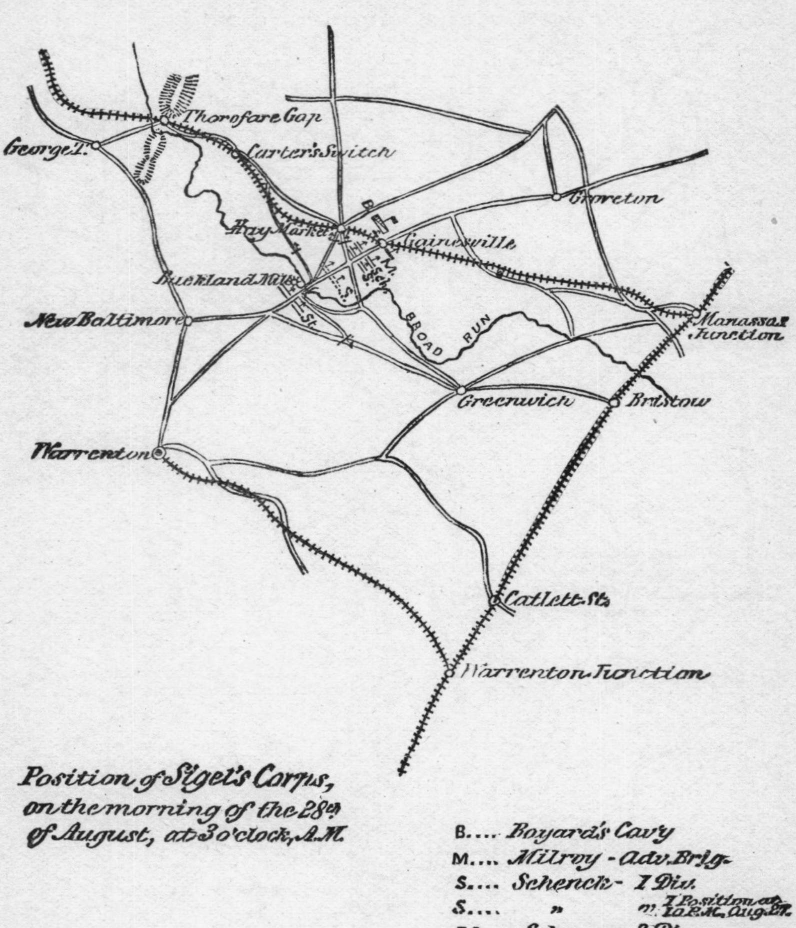


Position of Sigel's Corps, on the morning of the 28th of August, at 3 o'clock, A.M.

B.... Boyard's Cav'y
M.... Milroy - Adv. Brig.
S.... Schenck - 1 Div.
S.... " " 1 Position at 10 P.M., Aug. 27.
Sch.. Schurz - 3 Div.
St.... Steinwehr - 2 Div. (Reserve)
.... Point where dispatch to Gen. McDowell was written.

Nº 3.

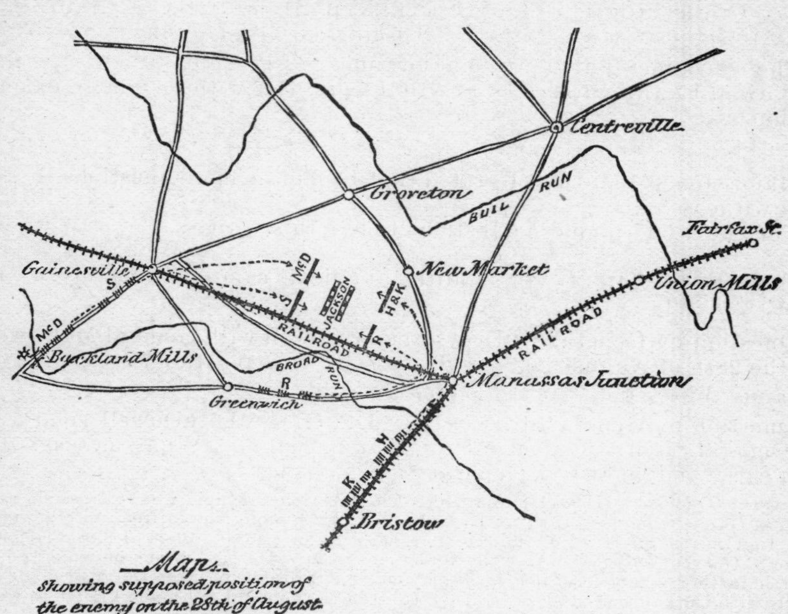
Centreville
Groveton
BULL RUN
Fairfax St.
Union Mills
Gainesville
New Market
McD
S
JACKSON
H&K
R
RAILROAD
RAIL ROAD
Buckland Mills
BROAD RUN
Manassas Junction
Greenwich
H
K
Bristow
Map.
Showing supposed position of the enemy on the 28th of August

Nº. 4.

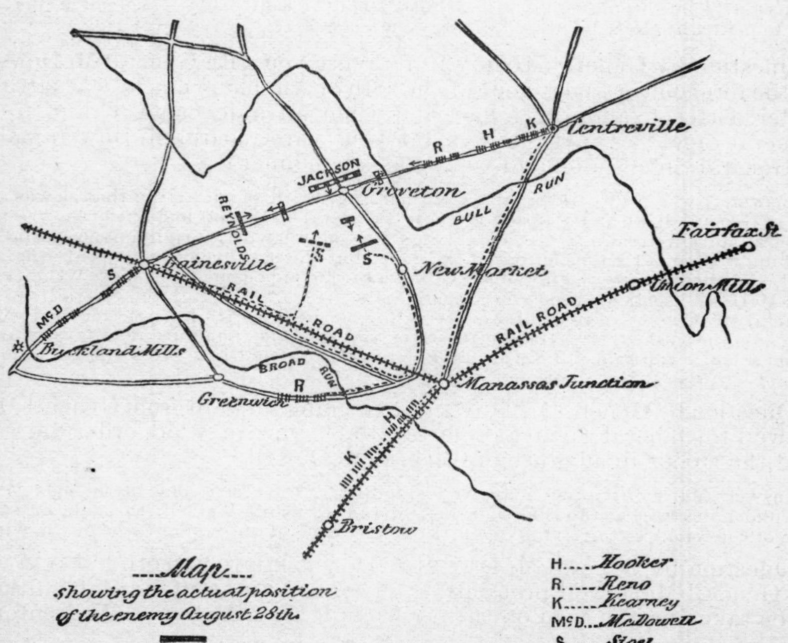
Centreville
R
H
K
JACKSON
Groveton
REYNOLDS
BULL RUN
Fairfax St.
Union Mills
Gainesville
S
New Market
McD
RAIL ROAD
RAIL ROAD
Buckland Mills
BROAD RUN
R
Manassas Junction
Greenwich
H
K
Bristow
Map
showing the actual position of the enemy August 28th.
H.....Hooker
R.....Reno
K.....Kearney
McD...McDowell
S.....Sigel

*THIRTY-EIGHTH DAY.*

COURT-ROOM, COR. FOURTEENTH ST. AND PA. AVENUE,
*Washington, D. C., January* 8, 1863.

The court met pursuant to adjournment. Present, * * *, and Maj. Gen. FRANZ SIGEL, U. S. Volunteers, the witness under examination.

* * * * * * *

Major-General McDowell stated that he had no more questions to ask this witness.

The court had no more questions to ask this witness.

Capt. FRANKLIN HAVEN, additional aide-de-camp, U. S. Army, a witness, was duly sworn.

Question by General MCDOWELL. Were you with General McDowell on the 28th of August last; and, if so, in what position?

Answer. I was; as captain and aide-de-camp.

Question by General MCDOWELL. Did General McDowell send you to General Sigel at Gainesville on that morning? What message did you carry and what was General Sigel's answer?

Answer. General McDowell explained to me that General Sigel was to cross the railroad at Gainesville, then turn to the right and march along the railroad to Manassas, and told me to go forward and see if General Sigel was so doing. I found General Sigel at Gainesville, near where the four roads meet. He said to me he would go on a little farther, a few hundred yards beyond the railroad, because the road made an angle with the railroad, and would then turn off to the right. I made known to General Sigel the message upon which I was sent.

Question by General MCDOWELL. What seemed to be understood by General Sigel as to the route he was to pursue to Manassas with respect to the Manassas Railroad?

Answer. That after crossing the railroad from the south side to the north side he was to march by the side of the railroad to Manassas.

Question by General MCDOWELL. Were you with General McDowell on the forenoon or about noon of the 28th of August, when he was sitting under a tree examining a map and when an aide came to him from General Sigel? What remarks did you hear General McDowell make to General Sigel's aide and what was his manner?

Answer. I was. Two aides came that morning, the first one saying that he was going to General Sigel, and wanting to know if General McDowell had any order to send. General McDowell said, "No; General Sigel is to march with his right on the railroad," nothing further. I knew neither of the aides, but the first one did not speak English well, and shortly after the first one had left a second aide came and asked, "Did General McDowell send an order for General Sigel to go to the right of the railroad?" General McDowell replied emphatically, "No; he is to go with his right on the road." The aide then asked some other questions and one about minute details, at which General McDowell said, "Let General Sigel fight his own corps," in a manner indicative of surprise at the question.

Question by General MCDOWELL. In going forward from General McDowell to General Sigel, as referred to by you, in what order did you find the troops in advance of General McDowell?

Answer. Many of the regiments were standing in the road; some of the men cooking under the trees at the side, and some of the regiments were in the field on each side of the road, resting, lying down, &c. The head of the column was just moving.

Question by General MCDOWELL. Do you know if an order was given by General McDowell prohibiting any wagons, except for ammunition, to be taken on the road on the occasion of the march from Warrenton?

Answer. I did not know that that order had been issued.

Question by General McDOWELL. Do you know if there were any baggage wagons taken on the road which General McDowell caused to be turned off the road to facilitate the advance of the Third Corps?

Answer. There were a great many baggage wagons turned off the road by order of General McDowell as they passed the place where he stood, so that the Third Army Corps might follow right after the troops on the advance.

Question by General McDOWELL. Did you on the night of the 25th or morning of the 26th carry any orders to General Sigel; if so, where did you find General Sigel?

Answer. I did, on the morning of the 26th. I found him about 2 o'clock between 3 and 4 miles from Warrenton, retreating toward Warrenton; that is, about half way between Warrenton and Waterloo Bridge.

The court had no questions to ask this witness.

Col. EDMUND SCHRIVER, aide-de-camp, a witness, was recalled.

Question by General McDOWELL. On the occasion of the march of General McDowell's troops from Buckland Mills what word was sent back to you from General Reynolds as to the cause of the column not moving?

Answer. General Sigel's corps was stopping at Gainesville. He was making no preparation to advance or to organize or form his line, and that his men were stopping, building fires to cook their breakfast, and blocking up the way, so that his division could not get forward.

Question by General McDOWELL. Who was sent forward by General McDowell on this occasion in consequence of this message?

Answer. Major Barstow, assistant adjutant-general.

Question by General McDOWELL. Was the order given to General Sigel, to send no wagons but for ammunition with his corps on the road from Warrenton to Buckland Mills on the 27th of August complied with; if not, to what extent and was there any embarrassment caused to the march of the Third Corps by these wagons?

Answer. No. A large number of baggage wagons, understood to be General Sigel's, were on the road, embarrassing and indeed stopping the march of troops.

The court had no questions to ask this witness at this time.

Maj. S. F. BARSTOW, assistant adjutant-general, U. S. Volunteers, a witness, was duly sworn.

Question by General McDOWELL. Were you sent with an order to General Sigel on the morning of the 28th of August? What was that order? Where did you start from? Where did you find General Sigel? In what state were his troops? What did General Sigel say on its delivery?

Answer. I was sent with an order to General Sigel on the morning of the 28th. We moved out from Buckland Mills on the 28th August before day (General McDowell and staff) and halted by the side of the road; we found a great many wagons of a train which ought not to have been there. The question was asked if they were ammunition wagons, and the answer was "No, they were not." All wagons were ordered to turn out except ammunition wagons.

While we were engaged on that duty General McDowell called me to him and said I must ride on, find General Sigel, and order him to move on and clear the road. I rode on, and found General Sigel about a mile beyond Gainesville at a quarter past 8. I rode up to him and told him that General McDowell's orders were that he should move at once on Manassas Junction. He asked where was General McDowell. I said we were in close column behind him, and when he (General Sigel) halted he halted the column 4 miles back. He then said, "Gentlemen, forward; move," or words to that effect, to the gentlemen around him—to his staff, I presume. The men along the line had pretty generally fallen out; some regiments were in columns. The road was so blocked up that I could not keep the road, but rode in the woods on either side, where I saw the men lying down, halting and resting.

**Question by the COURT. Were you with General McDowell during the 28th, 29th, and 30th of August, and the intermediate nights?**

Answer. I was.

**Question by the COURT. How early in the day of the 28th did the head of General McDowell's corps reach Gainesville?**

Answer. I do not know. When I returned I found General McDowell making a reconnaissance toward Centreville. Shortly after we were being badly shelled. This was about 8.30 o'clock in the morning.

**Question by the COURT. Where did General McDowell go from that position toward Centreville, where you were badly shelled?**

Answer. Moved off to the right toward Manassas Gap Railroad.

**Question by the COURT. From what direction were the shells thrown?**

Answer. From the left of Warrenton pike. We were about a mile on the Centreville road from Gainesville. The pieces of shell were thrown about a mile from the Centreville road.

**Question by the COURT. What was the force of the enemy in the direction from which the shells were thrown?**

Answer. I have no means whatever of judging.

**Question by the COURT. Were any measures taken by General McDowell to ascertain what that force was?**

Answer. He did not communicate with me on the subject. I have no knowledge. I would wish to say at that time I was suffering from fever and ague, and General McDowell would not probably order me on that kind of duty to ascertain what their force was.

**Question by the COURT. After passing toward the Manassas Railroad where did General McDowell go?**

Answer. He remained, as nearly as I can remember, within 2 miles east of Warrenton pike.

**Question by the COURT. Where was his corps at that time and what was he doing?**

Answer. During the short period of time that I was with him he was dismounted, sitting under a tree, receiving and sending dispatches. I do not know where his corps was; I was not with it.

**Question by the COURT. When he left that position where did he go?**

Answer. He moved still farther in the direction of Manassas Station, where we joined General King.

**Question by the COURT. Did you cross the railroad before you joined General King?**

Answer. I do not remember.

**Question by the COURT. Where was General Sigel's corps when you joined General King?**

Answer. I do not know of my own knowledge.

**Question by the COURT. At what time did you join General King and where did General McDowell proceed farther?**

Answer. As nearly as I remember we joined General King early in the afternoon of the 28th, and, I think, about two hours after General McDowell started for Manassas Junction.

Question by the COURT. Where was General King's division when you joined him and where was General Reynolds' division?

Answer. I do not know of my own knowledge where either of them were.

Question by the COURT. Was General King separated from his division?

Answer. I presume his division was with him; I cannot say from my own knowledge. I presume he was moving with his troops to Manassas Junction.

Question by the COURT. At what time did General McDowell reach Manassas Junction?

Answer. I was left behind to see to the disposal of some prisoners. I did not start with General McDowell. I did not see him again that night. I remained that night at the Weir house, near Manassas Station.

Question by the COURT. Did you have any information as to where General McDowell had gone when you arrived at Manassas Station?

Answer. I did not.

Question by the COURT. Did you have any information as to the position of King's and Reynolds' divisions at the time you left the Centreville road, in the forenoon, when you were shelled?

Answer. I did not.

Question by the COURT. What prisoners were they with whom you remained after you were separated from General McDowell?

Answer. The principal prisoner was a captain of infantry. A number of prisoners were brought in just as General McDowell was preparing to leave.

Question by the COURT. Did General McDowell make any inquiry of those prisoners, or any of them, in respect to the direction taken by Jackson?

Answer. He examined the prisoners as to the position of the enemy.

Question by the COURT. What did he learn from them on that subject?

Answer. I do not remember; I don't think I heard the whole examination.

Question by the COURT. Did you encounter any enemy on the march that day except at the point where you were shelled on the Centreville road?

Answer. No, sir.

Question by the COURT. When and where did you next see General McDowell after reaching Manassas?

Answer. At the Weir house, as near as I can remember, which is marked on the map.

Question by the COURT. Where were his troops that morning at the time you met him?

Answer. I don't remember exactly. In regard to King's division, my impression is that it was near Manassas Railroad, about 2 miles from Manassas Station, toward Bristoe. I do not know this, as I was not with the troops, and merely state it as my impression.

Question by the COURT. At what time did General McDowell leave the Weir house, and where did he go?

Answer. He left it about 10 in the morning, as near as I can remember. He went toward Bull Run.

Question by the COURT. Did you go with him during the 27th?

Answer. I was not in his immediate company but a portion of the time.

Question by the COURT. When, so far as you have knowledge, did he first come in presence of his corps on that day?

Answer. I don't remember whether General McDowell was present with some of the staff on the hill opposite the rebel position when the battle was going on or whether he was with General Pope. I don't remember any particular place that I saw him until after the battle of the 29th. I remember one of his staff asking me if I thought the men had better cheer as they charged up the hill. I said I thought they had better. Whether General McDowell was there or not I cannot say; there was so much confusion.

Question by the COURT. When do you remember of first seeing General McDowell after the battle?

Answer. I was lying on the grass beside General Pope when General McDowell came up. It was near the hospital and just after dark—just after having charged the enemy's batteries and carried them. We remained there all night.

Question by the COURT. What troops of General McDowell were engaged in the battle of the 28th, to which you refer?

Answer. I can't state. I have stated before that I was ill, as my reason for not knowing more.

Question by the COURT. Can you give any information or reason why the troops of General McDowell were marched away from the direction of the Centreville road after it was ascertained by the shells thrown at you in the morning that the enemy was in that direction?

Answer. Only that they may have moved to take up a better position.

Question by the COURT. Was General Pope present with General McDowell when the latter, as described by you, was seated under a tree sending and receiving dispatches?

Answer. He was not.

Question by the COURT. Had you any information on the 28th that General Sigel, shortly after commencing his march, had discovered a long line of the enemy's pickets?

Answer. I never heard of it until testified to before the court.

Brig. Gen. BENJAMIN S. ROBERTS, U. S. Volunteers, a witness, was duly sworn.

Question by the COURT. What was your position on General Pope's staff in the late campaign in Virginia?

Answer. In the early part of the campaign I was chief of cavalry of that army; the latter part of it I was inspector-general.

Question by General MCDOWELL. What do you know of the orders of General Pope to General Banks relative to the battle of Cedar Mountain, August 9, 1862?

Answer. Early in the morning of the 9th of August I was sent by General Pope to the front of the army, with directions, when General Banks should reach a position where the night before I had posted General Crawford's brigade, that I should show to General Banks positions for him to take to hold the enemy in check, if it attempted to advance toward Culpeper. Two days previous, the 7th and 8th, I had been to the point, knew the country, and had reported to General Pope my impression that a large force of General Jackson would be at Cedar Mountain, or near there, on the 9th, re-enforcing Ewell's troops, who were already there. General Pope authorized me before going to the front to give any orders in his name to any of the officers that might be in the field senior to me. I understood his object was to hold the enemy in check there that day, and not to attack until the other troops of his command should arrive and join General Banks.

Question by General MCDOWELL. Was the battle of the 9th of August, at Cedar Mountain, brought on by the enemy or by General Banks?

Answer. In the early part of the day the battle was brought on (artillery battle) by the enemy's batteries opening from new positions on General Crawford's artillery. I had been directed by General Pope to send information to him hourly of what was going on; and as I had expressed to General Banks my opinion about 3 o'clock in the afternoon that Jackson had arrived the forces were very large, General Banks expressed a different opinion, saying that he thought he should attack the batteries before night. I stated to General Banks then my reasons for believing that an attack would be dangerous; that I was convinced that the batteries both in Cedar and Slaughter Mountains were supported by heavy forces of infantry massed in the woods. He expressed a different opinion. He told me that he believed he could carry the field. His men were in the best fighting condition, and that he should undertake it. I immediately sent a dispatch to General Pope (I think my dispatch was dated half-past four), telling him that a general battle would be fought before night, and that it was of the utmost importance, in my opinion, that General McDowell's corps, or that portion of it which was between Culpeper and the battle-field, should be at once sent to the field. Ricketts' division of General McDowell's corps was in the immediate vicinity of the crossing of the road leading from Stevensburg with the road leading from Culpeper to the battle-field, or about 2 miles from Culpeper and about 5 from the battle-field.

The court adjourned to meet to-morrow, January 9, 1863, at 11 o'clock a. m.

---

*THIRTY-NINTH DAY.*

COURT-ROOM, COR. FOURTEENTH ST. AND PA. AVE.,
*Washington, D. C., January* 9, 1863.

The court met pursuant to adjournment. Present, * * *, and Brig. Gen. BENJAMIN S. ROBERTS, U. S. Volunteers, the witness under examination.

* * * * * * *

Maj. S. F. Barstow, assistant adjutant-general U. S. Volunteers, a witness examined yesterday, stated that in his testimony of yesterday he fixed the time when the shelling commenced toward Centreville at about 8.30 o'clock, and that it might have been later.

Brig. Gen. Benjamin S. Roberts, the witness under examination, desired to state, with reference to his testimony of the previous day, that such portion of it as reads (page 472)—

General Pope authorized me, before going to the front, to give any orders in his name to any of the officers that might be in the field senior to me.

Needs to be so qualified as to read that—

I was authorized to give any orders, so far as to carry out General Pope's views as had been expressed to me (General Roberts), in relation to holding the enemy there until his forces (General Pope's forces) could come up.

Question by General MCDOWELL. If General Banks had not attacked Jackson in force on the 9th do you think Jackson would have attacked Banks?

Answer. I do not think Jackson would have attacked Banks in a position where he was first posted on coming onto the field. The position was exceedingly strong, and one which a small force, like General Banks', could have held against a larger one of the enemy. General Jackson's troops had made a long march that day, and I do not think they were in a condition to attack General Banks.

Question by General MCDOWELL. Is the witness to be understood that General Banks fought the battle on his own responsibility, and against witness' advice and the known expectation of General Pope?

Answer. When General Banks first came onto the field I met him and went to the front with him, showing him positions where the enemy had batteries already posted and where I had discovered they were posting new batteries, and showed General Banks the positions where his own corps could take position to advantage and hold those positions, as I thought, if attacked. I then told him that General Pope wanted him to hold the enemy in check there until Sigel's forces could be brought up, which were expected that day, and all his other forces united to fight Jackson's forces. I mean to be understood to say that it is my impression that General Banks fought that battle entirely upon his own responsibility and against the expectations of General Pope, and those expectations had been expressed to General Banks, as I have already stated, perhaps more strongly.

Question by General McDOWELL. Do you know why General Banks advanced to make a decisive movement upon the enemy on the 9th of August without the aid of General McDowell's troops? If so, state why.

Answer. I can only state impressions from facts which I can relate. General Banks had seen nothing of the enemy on that day, or not much of the enemy, as the country was such (and well known to them) as to enable them to conceal their movements from General Banks. After he first came onto the field and I had suggested positions to the left of Crawford's brigade, where his main force should take position, he proceeded to put those forces in position in support of Crawford and on his left. I went to the extreme right with one of his brigades (Gordon's) to put it into position, and was gone an hour or more, I should think, as I went some distance to the right, under the belief that a part of the enemy's forces were endeavoring to turn that flank. On returning back to the field I found General Banks had advanced his lines in order of battle considerably toward the enemy, so that very sharp musketry firing had already commenced. I then expressed to General Banks my convictions (and I think this was about 3.30 o'clock) that the enemy was in very large force and massed in the woods on his right. General Banks replied that he did not believe that the enemy was in any considerable force yet, and said that he had resolved to attack their batteries or to attack their main force; it was either the one or the other. From this state of facts I am convinced that General Banks made the attack in the belief that the enemy was not in large force, and that he would succeed in his attack without the aid of other troops. Another reason for this belief is that General Banks supposed that his own force was between 12,000 and 13,000, whereas it was 3,000 less than that number. He was led to this belief by some mistake in returns, which he did not discover until after the battle was fought.

Question by General McDOWELL. Did you know the character of the dispatches General Banks sent to General Pope prior to his engaging the enemy decisively on the 9th of August?

Answer. I did not.

Question by General McDOWELL. What knowledge have you of General Pope's intention to engage Jackson as soon as Sigel's forces should arrive and be in condition to move to the front?

Answer. I know that General Pope intended to attack Jackson the moment he concentrated his forces, and was so confident of attacking him successfully that he conversed with me on the manner of holding Gordonsville, where he supposed he'd drive him. It was his intention to have pushed all his forces on on the 10th with the expectation of fighting that day.

Question by General McDOWELL. What, in your judgment, would have been the result had the battle been delayed till the 10th, and had been fought with all the forces General Pope could have been able to bring up by that time?

Answer. I have no doubt that with the forces General Pope could have brought forward on the 10th he would have defeated and captured the greater part of Jackson's army. With the small force General Banks fought his entire army Jackson was so much damaged that he was unable to renew the battle on the 10th, and I take it that about 26,000 more troops added to those which fought on the 9th would have utterly destroyed Jackson's army. His retreat would have been difficult on account of the Rapidan, which was immediately behind him, where he could have been captured.

Question by General McDOWELL. How long after you sent word back to General Pope of General Banks' intention to engage the enemy decisively was it before you saw General McDowell's troops coming to the field?

Answer. About two hours and a half, as well as I can judge. Perhaps I ought to add that General McDowell was moving with his forces toward the field before my note was received. The orderly had to ride 7 miles to General Pope.

Question by General McDOWELL. What was the position and condition of General Banks' corps when General McDowell's troops arrived on the field?

Answer. At sundown I left General Banks to ride to the rear to bring General McDowell onto the field myself, regarding it as of the utmost importance that General Banks should hold the position on the field and not retreat from it. I met General Pope and General McDowell with Ricketts' division coming onto the field. The division was halted. I was questioned particularly by General Pope and General McDowell of the state of things and the position of General Banks, with a view to pushing General McDowell's troops to support him. I represented the positions of Banks' forces when I left. General McDowell and General Pope were proceeding to make dispositions of their forces on this representation. At this time General Banks came up himself and he was also questioned, and so far as I understood gave to General Pope and General McDowell about the same information that I had already given them. They proceeded to post the troops on this information, in the belief that General Banks' forces still held the field; but it proved that they had fallen back from the field, and General McDowell and General Pope were attacked in the night, and greatly embarrassed by the credit they had given to my representations and the representations of General Banks that his troops were still in front and holding the enemy in check.

Question by General McDOWELL. In what way and to what extent did the nature of the ground assist in this misapprehension as to the position of Banks' corps, as represented by you and him?

Answer. There was a wood of very considerable extent immediately intervening between General Banks' position and the place where General McDowell halted the forces with him, and it was then getting dusk, so that nothing of the position of the field or the troops on it could be seen by General McDowell or General Pope.

Question by the COURT. What troops composed the forces with which General Pope proposed to attack Jackson on the 10th?

Answer. All of McDowell's corps that was present and the corps of Sigel and Banks.

Question by the COURT. Describe the location of these forces on the 9th.

Answer. Banks' forces were on the field; McDowell's as described yesterday, and Sigel about 10 or 12 miles northwest, in the direction of Sperryville.

Question by the COURT. At what time on the 10th did General Pope propose to make the attack?

Answer. He proposed to attack the moment he concentrated his forces—that is, early on the morning of the 10th.

Question by the COURT. In sending General Banks forward to Cedar Mountain, did General Pope give directions to any other corps to operate in supporting distance of Banks?

Answer. Not to my knowledge.

Question by the COURT. Can you give any explanation then why General Banks was placed without troops in supporting distance where he was liable to be attacked by, and did encounter, a largely superior force of the enemy?

Answer. I had no idea General Banks would have been attacked by the enemy on the 9th if he had not made such demonstrations on the forces in front of him as to bring on a battle. I had been in the front three days, and knew where the forces were and what they were, and reported it to General Pope, giving him my opinion that there was no danger of an attack, and that the reports of many of the scouts were greatly exaggerated. It was only the advance of Ewell that reached Cedar Mountain on the 8th; that I considered the brigade of Crawford a sufficient force to hold him in check there that day. I had also information that the most of Jackson's force was behind and crossing the Rapidan late on the 8th and on the morning of the 9th, so that I did not believe that they could have reached the position of Banks and fight him or make the attack on the 9th. I can add I don't think he was liable to be attacked by the enemy. I think he brought the attack on, and that he would not have been attacked but for his own demonstration against the enemy and his belief that there was but a small force of the enemy. I will add that General McDowell's position at the cross-roads (5 miles distant) was within supporting distance, and that it was important he should remain there to protect in the direction of Stevensburg, another way to the Rapidan.

Question by the COURT. What was the force of the enemy at the battle of Cedar Mountain?

Answer. The entire corps of Jackson and Ewell's divisions—about 35,000 men.

Question by the COURT. In the event of any danger to General Banks at Cedar Mountain was it not the duty of General McDowell to go to his aid without further special orders to that effect?

Answer. Had General McDowell known of any danger to General Banks I think it would have been his duty to have gone to him, and I understood that he did go to him; that he started without any orders.

Question by the COURT. You have spoken of batteries being put in position by the enemy, to which you called the attention of General Banks. Did these batteries threaten the position held by General Banks' forces?

Answer. General Banks' forces were under artillery fire all the time they were on the field, and he established his batteries, replying with great effect to the batteries of the enemy, forcing several of them to change position and silencing a number of their guns. The enemy acknowledged that it was the most destructive artillery fire during the war. I have never seen better artillery practice than that under General Banks on that day.

Question by the COURT. State the general direction, by points of the compass, of General Banks' line of battle, the position of his troops before he concluded to advance to an attack of the enemy.

Answer. His general direction was from east to west, his right resting on a farm-house west. The water of Cedar Run was directly behind him; his artillery was formed on the crests of a series of rolling hills.

Question by the COURT. How far were the woods distant from his right, in which woods the enemy was massing the forces referred to in your direct examination, and to which you called General Banks' attention before he made the attack?

Answer. I think those woods were about a thousand yards from the first position General Banks took when I called to his attention that the enemy had massed in the woods; it was after he had advanced his lines so as to bring his right nearer to the woods. Gordon's brigade, however, was behind these woods and to the right of them.

Question by the COURT. To what point, in reference to the right flank of General Banks, did General McDowell's troops advance before they encountered the enemy?

Answer. General McDowell's advance brought him about the center of General Banks' line, considering Gordon's brigade a part of the line.

Question by the COURT. From what direction did the enemy attack General McDowell's forces?

Answer. I was not present when the enemy attacked General McDowell's forces. I was over the ground the next morning, and can state what I know of the position they came in and made the attack.

Question by the COURT. Were the woods which intercepted the view of the enemy when Generals Pope and McDowell arrived at all connected with the woods in which the enemy's troops were massed on the right?

Answer. They were not; they were about 1,500 yards from them toward Culpeper.

Question by the COURT. Was there anything to prevent the enemy which was massed in these woods on the right flank of Banks' force making an attack except the fatigue of the previous march?

Answer. I know nothing else except a want of time and the strength of the position of General Banks, to attack whom the enemy would have had to march 1,000 yards through an open field.

Question by the COURT. How far did General Banks advance his line of battle, to your knowledge?

Answer. I think he had advanced his line from 800 to 1,200 yards.

Question by the COURT. Did you inform General Banks that the attack which he proposed to make would transcend the instructions which you had communicated, that he should hold the enemy in check?

Answer. I informed General Banks that General Pope did not expect him to attack.

Question by the COURT. Are we to understand that General Banks' instructions permitted him to use his artillery against the enemy, but not to advance his troops, if he should judge that to be the best mode of holding the enemy in check?

Answer. I understood that he was to use his artillery, as a matter of course, and that, if he judged it proper to advance his infantry to hold them in check, he could properly do so under the instructions of General Pope.

Question by the COURT. Did he not know that General McDowell's troops were posted on the road 5 miles distant?

Answer. I presume that he did, as he marched by them that morning and reached the battle-field, I should think, between 12 and 1 o'clock.

Question by the COURT. At what time of day did he march by General McDowell's troops?

Answer. I can only judge from the distance; he must have passed about 9 or 10 in the morning to reach the battle-field at the time he did.

Question by General MCDOWELL. Do you know if General Pope's orders on the 9th were that General Sigel should follow General Banks when the latter moved to the front?

Answer. I know that was the order.

Question by General MCDOWELL. From the nature of the position taken up by General Banks was he obliged to leave it for defensive purposes, or was it a better defensive position than any one in front between him and the enemy?

Answer. I think that the first position of General Banks was a much better position for defense than any other in his front, and I am quite sure that he did not advance with any view of securing a better position for defense.

Question by General MCDOWELL. Were the 5 miles you state General McDowell's troops were distant measured from the place where General Banks had taken up his defensive position or from that to which General Banks moved to attack the enemy?

Answer. I referred to General Banks' first position.

Question by General MCDOWELL. Do you know to what corps Crawford's brigade belonged?

Answer. I had supposed, as it had been in Culpeper some time, that it belonged to McDowell's, but I am informed to-day that it belonged to Banks'.

Question by General McDOWELL. Do you know if Crawford's brigade was not in Culpeper when Ricketts' division was between Culpeper and the Rappahannock?

Answer. I understood that it was. I had known that orders were sent to it at Culpeper by General Pope before Ricketts' division had arrived at Culpeper from the Rappahannock.

Question by General McDOWELL. Do you know what cavalry was with Crawford's brigade when it was to the front of Culpeper?

Answer. Bayard's cavalry.

Question by General McDOWELL. Do you know why General Sigel did not follow General Banks to the front on the 9th, as was arranged by General Pope?

Answer. I have no facts of my own knowledge why he did not.

Question by General McDOWELL. Do you know if General Banks sent word back to General McDowell's troops of his intention to make a decisive movement on the enemy or that he would likely need their help?

Answer. I know nothing about it.

Question by General McDOWELL. What orders, if any, did you carry to General Sigel on the 23d and 24th of August, at Sulphur Springs, and on the 25th, at Waterloo Bridge?

Answer. On the 23d I carried an order to General Sigel, who was at Sulphur Springs, that General McDowell's forces on that day would be on his right; that General Banks would support him in his rear and Reno on his left. On the 24th I carried him an order that he should throw immediately his forces across a little creek in front of him (there had been a flood the night before) and push the men to Sulphur Springs and drive any enemy that might be there across the river. General Pope wished that to be done with great dispatch, and I gave him the order that it was to be done forthwith, without waiting for his artillery to be crossed over. I informed him then that we were in possession of Warrenton, and that there was no enemy between his right and Warrenton; that General McDowell's forces had taken possession of that town. On the 25th I bore him an order from General Pope to move all of his forces upon any enemy that might be on the Warrenton side of Waterloo Bridge, and to drive the enemy over the river and to hold the bridge until further orders. I told him that I directed General Banks, who was immediately in his rear and whom I just passed, to co-operate with him in this attack. At the same time I informed him that Buford's cavalry, with a battery, was on the Warrenton road in front of Waterloo Bridge and near it; that the order was imperative and urgent, and that he was to move forward forthwith and execute it at all hazards.

The court adjourned to meet to-morrow, January 10, 1863, at 11 o'clock a. m.

---

## *FORTIETH DAY.*

COURT-ROOM, COR. FOURTEENTH ST. AND PA. AVENUE,
*Washington, D. C., January* 10, 1863.

* * * * * * *

A communication was received to the effect that Brigadier-General Roberts, U. S. Volunteers, the witness under examination, was too unwell to appear before the court this day.

Col. EDMUND SCHRIVER, aide-de-camp, U. S. Army, a witness, was recalled.

Question by General McDOWELL. Where were you on the 28th of August and how engaged that day?

Answer. I was generally in the company of General McDowell, whose headquarters and corps were moving from Buckland Mills in the direction of Manassas Junction.

Question by General McDOWELL. State the incidents of the movement of General McDowell and corps in the direction of Manassas Junction.

Answer. I have already alluded to the delay in the movement by wagons on the road, by troops not going forward who were to lead the advance. After the march was resumed there was some cannonading heard and felt. The march was then continued in the direction of Manassas Junction, and some time in the afternoon there were orders received from General Pope which caused a change in the direction of the corps—the march of the corps. These are the orders:

The witness read the orders, as follows: From Major-General Pope to Major-General McDowell, dated Headquarters Army of Virginia, Manassas Junction, August 28, 1862—1.20 p. m.; from Major-General Pope to Major-General McDowell, dated Headquarters, Manassas Junction, August 28, 1862, which orders are appended to the proceedings of this day and marked A and B.

The witness continued:

These orders were received about 4.15 o'clock in the afternoon. Instructions were then given for the execution of the order last read, and the headquarters were then moved over to Reynolds' division, which we accompanied some time, they getting on the road to Sudley Springs and the headquarters proceeding to General Pope's headquarters at Manassas Junction. The first order I submitted was received a very short time before the second order, and instructions in obedience to it were prepared but not published because of the countermand of the second order from General Pope.

Question by General McDOWELL. What route was given to King's division and what to Reynolds'?

Answer. King was turned right up toward the Warrenton turnpike and directed to advance on that road, and Reynolds was put upon the Sudley Springs road, passing through New Market. I can't define precisely the position occupied by King's and Reynolds' divisions at the time this order was given.

Question by General McDOWELL. Did General McDowell find General Pope at Manassas Junction?

Answer. No.

Question by General McDOWELL. Where did General McDowell go from Manassas Junction and what caused him to take the direction he took?

Answer. He went north, in the direction of the firing, which firing was the reason of his going that way.

Question by General McDOWELL. State where General McDowell staid the night of the 28th, and the time, as near as you recollect, of his reaching that place.

Answer. It was dark when we left Manassas, and thinking to take a short cut we went over fields and got into a wooded swamp, which, with the darkness, caused us to lose our way for some time; and after extricating ourselves took the road by Bethlehem Church and went north, riding till, I suppose, nearly midnight, expecting to find Reynolds' division. Failing entirely in this, the general and his staff laid down in the neighborhood of some of General Sigel's people, who were bivouacked there.

Question by General McDOWELL. Where did General McDowell go on the morning of the 29th?

Answer. Very early, as soon as we could see, he set out, having ascertained where General Reynolds' division was, to join it.

Question by General MCDOWELL. Where did he find General Reynolds' division and what was reported to him by General Reynolds?

Answer. He found it at a place called Conrad's, which is nearer to the pike than marked on the map, and here he learned of the fight which King had the night before.

Question by General MCDOWELL. Did he learn here where King's and Ricketts' divisions had moved to during the night? If so, state the place where they had gone.

Answer. Yes; we heard they had gone to Manassas Junction.

Question by General MCDOWELL. Where did General McDowell go after leaving Reynolds' division and what were the directions he left with Reynolds?

Answer. He went to Weir house, near Manassas Junction, and I think his instructions were to support General Sigel in anything which he might undertake to do in the quarter in which he was.

Question by General MCDOWELL. For what purpose did General McDowell go to Manassas Junction after leaving Reynolds?

Answer. To join the divisions of his corps.

Question by General MCDOWELL. Do you recollect what he said to Reynolds with respect to the disposition he purposed making of these divisions of his corps?

Answer. No; I have no remembrance.

Question by General MCDOWELL. What did General McDowell do after reaching Manassas Junction?

Answer. He directed his divisions on the road to follow General Fitz John Porter's corps, that was marching in the direction of Gainesville, by the Bethlehem Church road, and then proceeded himself with his staff to the front until he reached the headquarters of General Porter.

Question by General MCDOWELL. See if this is an order General McDowell received on the 29th of August last.

The order referred to was from Maj. Gen. John Pope to Major-Generals McDowell and Porter, dated Headquarters Army of Virginia, Centreville, August 29, 1862, which order was read by the witness aloud, and is appended to the proceedings of this day and marked C.

Answer. This is the order.

Question by General MCDOWELL. Where did General McDowell go after leaving General Porter?

Answer. He went over to the right of the headquarters of Porter, and after that I parted with him for a while, and rejoined him at or near Bethlehem Church, where King's division was. It was then pretty well advanced in the day.

Question by General MCDOWELL. What direction did he give King's and Ricketts' divisions?

Answer. To march on the Sudley Springs road.

Question by the COURT. At what time in the morning of the 28th did you hear and feel the cannonading of the enemy?

Answer. I should think it was about noon. I cannot answer positively.

Question by the COURT. Where was the cannonading which you felt?

Answer. It was to our left, but where I do not know.

Question by the COURT. Where were you with reference to the Warrenton pike?

Answer. We were near the Warrenton pike.

Question by the COURT. What means did General McDowell take to ascertain the force present at that cannonading?

Answer. I have no particular recollection of any other means than that of his going out himself and making observations, which he did.

Question by the COURT. Do you not now know that Jackson's force had at that time approached during the preceding night or morning toward or onto the Warrenton pike from the neighborhood of Manassas?

Answer. No.

Question by the COURT. Do you now know where Jackson's forces were at the time of that cannonading?

Answer. No.

Question by the COURT. Did General McDowell give any orders for sending any force against the enemy at the point from which that cannonading proceeded?

Answer. I do not know.

Question by the COURT. What means had General Pope to be informed that the enemy was threatening General McDowell from the course of the Warrenton pike except by information to be obtained or communicated by General McDowell himself?

Answer. I do not know.

Question by the COURT. Was it not the duty of General McDowell to have ascertained what was the force of the enemy then assailing him on the morning of the 28th and to have reported the facts to General Pope?

Answer. I can only give my opinion. It would depend upon circumstances. It would have been proper to ascertain the force making the demonstration and then to report or communicate to General Pope if the magnitude of the force demanded it.

Question by the COURT. Assuming that Jackson's force had approached from Manassas to the neighborhood of the Warrenton pike near Groveton on the morning of the 28th and General McDowell had then proceeded in that direction against him, in your opinion would not Jackson have been defeated?

Answer. I can give no opinion; the result would depend on so many circumstances.

Question by the COURT. On the assumption contained in the last question as to the position of Jackson, and that the fact had been ascertained by General McDowell, ought not General McDowell to have proceeded against him instead of persisting in the march to Manassas?

Answer. I must say again that this must depend upon circumstances—on various things; on the orders received from General Pope; on the reliance he had on his own troops; on comparative numbers, &c.

Question by the COURT. Take for circumstances all the facts in your knowledge except as modified by the assumption as to Jackson's position, and state your opinion.

Answer. I cannot give an opinion that would be satisfactory to myself. I know nothing about Jackson's force or his numbers.

Question by the COURT. Did you not know from the communication of General Pope to General McDowell that Jackson had been driven back on the 27th; also that he was separated from Longstreet; and had you not from the time of encountering Jackson at Cedar Mountain learned this fact?

Answer. I was informed that Jackson and Longstreet were separated, but I did not know the strength of Jackson. I was informed that Jackson had been driven back.

Question by the COURT. At what time were King and Reynolds got in motion toward the Warrenton pike after the receipt of the orders from General Pope on the afternoon of the 28th?

Answer. Orders were given as soon as possible—instantly. The orders were given to King immediately. I was busy at the time on other duties than looking after the time of their departure. We then went to Reynolds' division, and we moved along with it until they took the road toward the north and we took the road to the southeast.

Question by the COURT. How far was it from the point where General McDowell separated from Reynolds to go to Manassas?

Answer. I cannot answer that. I suppose it must have been about 3 miles.

Question by the COURT. You have stated that during the separation of General McDowell from King and Reynolds, King had a fight and fell back to Manassas. What occasion or order had General McDowell to go to Manassas and thus become separated from his corps?

Answer. It was the headquarters of General Pope, and I presume (if I did not hear him say so) he went there to confer with General Pope.

Question by the COURT. Had General McDowell any request or order from General Pope to join him personally, in order to confer with him, at Manassas?

Answer. I am not aware of any at this moment.

Question by the COURT. At what time in the morning of the 29th did General McDowell give instructions to Reynolds to support General Sigel in anything he might undertake to do in the quarter in which he was?

Answer. Of course it must have been prior to his departure from that place. It must have been early, because we left there early.

Question by the COURT. Did General McDowell, to your knowledge, communicate to Sigel the order thus given to Reynolds?

Answer. I have no recollection of it.

Question by the COURT. Had not General McDowell staff officers or other means of bringing back the divisions of King and Ricketts without going to Manassas for them himself?

Answer. Undoubtedly. Messages might have been sent.

Question by the COURT. In your opinion was not the place of General McDowell with Sigel's corps and Reynolds' division, to direct their movements against the enemy, instead of going back for King's and Ricketts' divisions?

Answer. I formed no opinion and can form no opinion on that subject.

Question by General MCDOWELL. After General Pope sent orders to General McDowell at Buckland Mills, on the evening of the 27th, did General McDowell receive any information as to the whereabouts of General Pope up to the time of the receipt of the orders at 4.15 on the evening of the 28th?

Answer. I don't remember any.

Lieut. Col. DAVIS TILLSON, Maine Artillery, U. S. Volunteers, a witness, was recalled.

Question by General McDOWELL. Were you with General McDowell on the 28th of August last?

Answer. I was.

Question by General McDOWELL. State what occurred after General McDowell passed Gainesville.

Answer. Soon after passing Gainesville General McDowell and staff turned to the left and passed by the rear of Sigel's corps, the head of which had turned to the right along the railroad. General McDowell threw out skirmishers to the right and left and in front along the turnpike, and advanced over it, followed at some little distance in the rear by General Reynolds at the head of his division. Arriving at a point a little to the east of where the road from Manassas intersects the turnpike a horseman was noticed, some three-quarters of a mile to the front on the crest of a hill, in the turnpike. Halting his staff and escort, General McDowell sent forward a small body of his escort, under command of Captain Haven, to ascertain what it was. Captain Haven returned and reported that there was a small body of the enemy just beyond the hill before mentioned. About this time the head of General Reynolds' corps arrived at the point where General McDowell had halted, and the enemy opened fire upon the head of his column from a section of a battery placed in the turnpike just beyond the crest of the hill referred to. General Reynolds immediately deployed the head of his column to the left, brought up a rifled battery, and in a few moments silenced the enemy's guns.

Question by General McDOWELL. About what time was it when the shelling took place between the enemy and Reynolds' division?

Answer. I have no means of knowing accurately. I should say it was about noon.

Question by General McDOWELL. State what you know concerning the character and number of the force the enemy had on this occasion and what General McDowell did to ascertain it.

Answer. I have no personal knowledge other than I could obtain from the report of Captain Haven and from the report and amount of the enemy's fire. I am very sure, from the position occupied and the character of the firing, that the enemy did not have more than a section of a battery. Soon after the firing ceased I am very sure I heard General McDowell (who was but a few rods south of the turnpike during the whole of the firing) direct General Reynolds to send out skirmishers, under cover of the woods, each side of the turnpike, and ascertain the strength and character of the enemy, and I know that not long after General Reynolds' division advanced along at or beyond the point the enemy occupied in the morning at the time the shelling took place. It was a very inconsiderable affair. There were only about a dozen shells thrown by the enemy.

Question by General McDOWELL. Did General McDowell receive in your presence any information as to this force of the enemy from any officer—from a cavalry party who were to the south of the pike and to the right and front of Reynolds' position? If so, state the character of the information as to the number and character of the force of the enemy's party?

Answer. I recollect that a mounted officer came up to General McDowell, I think soon after the firing ceased, and stated that his command was to the right and front of the position we occupied at that moment. I got the impression from his description that he was nearly abreast of the position occupied by the enemy. He said that he had been there some time observing the enemy, keeping out of sight as much as possible himself to prevent their shelling him, and I feel quite sure that he stated the enemy's force consisted of a section of a battery and a small support of infantry.

The court adjourned to meet on Monday, January 12, 1863, at 11 o'clock a. m.

## APPENDIX.

A.

HEADQUARTERS ARMY OF VIRGINIA,
*Manassas Junction, August* 28, 1862—1.20 p. m. [4.15 p. m.

Major-General MCDOWELL:

I sent you a dispatch a few minutes ago directing you to move on Gum Spring to intercept Jackson. Since then I have received your note of this morning. I will this evening push forward Reno to Gainesville and follow with Heintzelman, unless there is a large force of the enemy at Centreville, which I do not believe. Ascertain, if you can, about this. I do not wish you to carry out the order to proceed to Gum Spring if you consider it too hazardous, but I will support you in any way you suggest, by pushing forward from Manassas Junction across the turnpike. Jackson has a large train, which should certainly be captured. Give me your views fully; you know the country much better than I do. Come no farther in this direction with your command, but call back what has advanced thus far.

JNO. POPE,
*Major-General.*

B.

HEADQUARTERS,
*Manassas Junction, August* 28, 1862. [4.15 p. m.]

Major-General MCDOWELL:

The enemy is reported in force on the other side of the Bull Run, on the Orange and Alexandria Railroad, as also near Centreville.

I have ordered Sigel to march upon Centreville immediately, as also Kearny and Reno. I will advance Hooker as reserve. Please march immediately with your command directly upon Centreville from where you are.

JNO. POPE,
*Major-General, Commanding.*

C.

HEADQUARTERS ARMY OF VIRGINIA,
*Centreville, August* 29, 1862.

Generals MCDOWELL and PORTER:

You will please move forward with your joint command toward Gainesville. I sent General Porter written orders to that effect an hour and a half ago. Heintzelman, Sigel, and Reno are moving on the Warrenton turnpike, and must now be not far from Gainesville. I desire that as soon as communication is established between this force and your own the whole command shall halt. It may be necessary to fall back behind Bull Run at Centreville to-night. I presume it will be so on account of our supplies. I have sent no orders of any description to Ricketts, and none to interfere in any way with the movements of McDowell's troops except what I sent by his aide-de-camp last night, which were to hold his position on the Warrenton pike until the troops from here should fall on the enemy's flank and rear. I do not even know Ricketts' position, as I have not been able to find out where General McDowell was until a late hour this morning.

General McDowell will take immediate steps to communicate with General Ricketts and instruct him to rejoin the other divisions of his corps as soon as practicable. If any considerable advantages are to be gained by departing from this order it will not be strictly carried out.

One thing must be held in view, that the troops must occupy a position from which they can reach Bull Run to-night or by morning. The indications are that the whole force of the enemy is moving in this direction at a pace that will bring them here by to-morrow night or the next day.

My own headquarters will for the present be with Heintzelman's corps or at this place.

JNO. POPE,
*Major-General, Commanding.*

---

*FORTY-FIRST DAY.*

COURT-ROOM, COR. FOURTEENTH ST. AND PA. AVENUE,
*Washington, D. C., January* 12, 1863.

The court met pursuant to adjournment. Present, * * *, and Lieut. Col. DAVIS TILLSON, Maine Artillery, the witness under examination.

* * * * * * *

The court was cleared.

The court was opened.

The further examination of Lieutenant-Colonel Tillson was suspended in order to receive the evidence of Major-General Meade, U. S. Volunteers.

Maj. Gen. GEORGE G. MEADE, U. S. Volunteers, a witness, was duly sworn.

Question by General MCDOWELL. Did you see General Sigel early on the morning of the 29th of August and before any movements were made by the troops on that day? Where was he at that time?

Answer. I did, sir; and he was at his headquarters on the field at a place usually known as the Robinson house.

Question by General MCDOWELL. Were you at that time the senior officer present on that occasion with Reynolds' division?

Answer. Yes, sir; at least I supposed myself to be.

Question by General MCDOWELL. Did you report your command to General Sigel as the senior officer present, so far as you know and did you inform him of its position with respect to his corps?

Answer. I reported to General Sigel that, in the absence of my superior officer, General Reynolds, who had left the night previous and had not returned and I was ignorant whether his absence was owing to his being captured by the enemy or had lost his way, I had come to report to him the position of my command, to ascertain his position, to know what he was going to do, and to obtain his advice and judgment what I had better do until some officer superior to both of us should arrive to regulate our movements—General McDowell or General Pope.

Question by the COURT. Had Reynolds' division been left the night before without instructions from any officer superior in rank to you, so far as you have knowledge?

Answer. It is not in my power to answer that question. Reynolds was in command of the division. In taking up our position the afternoon previous, whilst moving toward Centreville, under the orders, I understood, to General Reynolds from a superior officer, we turned off the road from Gainesville to Manassas Junction at the Bethlehem Church, and proceeded a short distance in the direction toward the Stone Bridge, when we heard heavy firing on our left and front over in the direction of Groveton. Upon hearing this firing—I was at the head of the column—I received a message from General Reynolds, who was in front, to quicken my movements and to bear off to the left in the direction of that firing. I did so, keeping on the road marked as leading to Sudley Springs. I continued on this road till I reached the vicinity of the Conrad house. It was then quite dark; the firing had entirely ceased, and, so far as I could judge, had receded, leading me to think that our people had fallen back. Hearing nothing from General Reynolds I deemed it prudent to halt the command, and assumed the responsibility of doing so. It seems that General Reynolds reached the scene of action—where the action was—and in returning lost his way, and did not get back till the next morning.

Question by the COURT. Were you at the head of General Reynolds column on the morning of the 28th, when it reached Gainesville, on the march from Buckland Mills?

Answer. Yes, sir; I was.

Question by the COURT. Have you knowledge of any indications of the presence of the enemy in that neighborhood at that time; and, if so, where was the enemy and what was done to ascertain his strength?

Answer. After passing Gainesville and just before reaching Groveton a battery, or section of a battery, was opened by the enemy from the heights immediately adjacent to Groveton, from which they threw some half a dozen (I suppose) of shot and shell at long range at the head of my column, one shell only taking effect, I think, killing 3 and wounding some 4 persons. My brigade was halted and deployed on the open ground on the left of the pike, and a rifled battery placed in position, which opened on the enemy's battery. After a few shots from our battery they withdrew or ceased firing. I saw no exhibition of their force except one or two mounted men in the neighborhood of their guns while they were firing. As to measures taken to ascertain their force, all I know is I made a detail from my brigade of one or two companies of riflemen—probably more—who were directed by General Reynolds, conjointly with a company of cavalry which I understood he obtained from General McDowell's escort, to proceed up a road marked on the map as leading to Sudley Springs and try to ascertain the enemy's force. The result of this expedition I did not hear. A short time afterward my brigade was moved across the country in the direction of Manassas Junction by way of Bethlehem Church.

Question by the COURT. Was the enemy discovered in any other than the direction of Groveton during your march that day to your knowledge?

Answer. No. Not to my knowledge.

Question by the COURT. Had you an impression that any of General McDowell's forces were on the pike from Gainesville toward Groveton at the time you heard the firing in the afternoon toward which you inclined your march?

Answer. I knew that two divisions of General McDowell's corps were in our rear on the same road during that march, viz, Ricketts' and King's, and I presume that it was one of these divisions that was engaged.

Question by the COURT. From your knowledge of what occurred at the first engagement in the morning, and assuming also that Jackson was in the neighborhood of Manassas on the night of the 27th, and that the movement of General McDowell was intended to strike Jackson from the direction of Gainesville, while the other forces of General Pope pressed him from the direction of Manassas, in your judgment was General McDowell's conduct proper in withdrawing all his forces from the Warrenton pike and concentrating them in your rear toward Manassas, if he did do so?

Answer. With the limited knowledge I had at the time of what was known of the position and force of the enemy and of the plans of the commanding generals I am reluctant to advance an opinion which must be deemed a criticism. At the same time I feel bound to say that at the time I thought it was injudicious to pass toward Manassas Junction when he had evidence that the enemy was in the vicinity of Groveton. It is proper I should add that the enemy not taking advantage of our exposing our flank to them led me eventually to conclude he was not in very large force, and that the firing on my column was designed only to check and delay us, which it effected by one or two hours.

Question by the COURT. Did you know that morning that Ricketts division had been sent to Thoroughfare Gap to prevent the approach of Longstreet and his junction with Jackson and was actually there?

Answer. I did not. I knew nothing personally of Ricketts' division, except that he was in our rear.

Question by the COURT. Would the fact that Ricketts was at Thoroughfare Gap to prevent the approach of Longstreet render the march of General McDowell with the rest of his forces to Manassas more or less injudicious, in your opinion, after the demonstration made against him in the morning from the direction of Groveton?

General McDowell offered the following as an objection to the question:

I beg to submit that the opinion of the witness on the construction of orders or on any matter actually before the court should not be asked, for of this the court is to be the judge; that he should only be asked an opinion based on facts which he himself knew, and from which he drew his opinion as a collective judgment, and which basis of opinion is not possessed by the court. The witness says he knows nothing of the movements of Ricketts' division.

The court was cleared, and decided that the question be not put.

The court was opened and its decision announced.

Question by the COURT. Had you any knowledge of the position of King's division, except that it was following Reynolds'?

Answer. I had not.

Question by the COURT. In your opinion, from your knowledge of the country, what would have been the effect on Jackson's forces if General McDowell's forces, including Sigel's corps, had marched against him along the Warrenton pike in the direction of Groveton instead of turning toward Manassas?

General McDowell stated that this question assumed the point at issue, and that there was no evidence to show that Jackson's army was there; that it assumes that the small force, consisting of a section of artillery and its small support, was Jackson's army.

Answer. If Jackson was in the position premised; that is to say, on the heights about Groveton, I presume the effect of advancing would have been to bring on an engagement, the result of which it is not possible to pronounce with certainty.

Question by the COURT. What forces were engaged toward which you inclined your march in the afternoon toward Sudley Springs?

Answer. On our side a portion of King's division. I have no personal knowledge what forces of the enemy were engaged, whether Jackson's or Longstreet's. This was toward sunset, about 6 or 7 o'clock.

Question by the COURT. Have you knowledge, acquired during the ensuing battles, where Jackson's forces were during the 28th; and, if so, where were they?

Answer. I have no knowledge of the position of any of the enemy's forces, so far as being commanded by Jackson. The enemy was on the 28th on the heights to the right or north of Groveton. On the 29th we passed over the ground that General Gibbon had fought on during the 28th.

**The court adjourned to meet to-morrow, January 13, 1863, at 11 o'clock a. m.**

### FORTY-SECOND DAY.

COURT-ROOM, COR. FOURTEENTH ST. AND PA. AVENUE,
*Washington, D. C., January* 13, 1863.

* * * * * * *

Col. EDMUND SCHRIVER, aide-de-camp, U. S. Army, a witness, was recalled.

Question by the COURT. In what formation did General McDowell move his command from Gainesville to Bethlehem Church; in column, by a flank, or in what way?

Answer. As well as I remember it was in a column by a flank—the usual mode of marching *en route*—and by fours.

Question by the COURT. How did the brigades succeed each other; whether over the same ground or in some other and what way?

Answer. I was not with them, so as to answer the question.

Question by the COURT. Can you give us the name of any officer of General McDowell's staff who is present and can give us the information?

Answer. No.

Question by the COURT. Have you any knowledge, or had you any information at the time, that King's division did not follow over the same route behind Reynolds' division?

Answer. No.

Maj. Gen. JOHN POPE, U. S. Volunteers, a witness, was duly sworn.

Question by General McDOWELL. What command did you exercise in the campaign in Virginia last summer?

Answer. I commanded the Army of Virginia.

Question by General McDOWELL. Please state as fully as you can everything concerning the battle of Cedar Run, or Slaughter's Mountain, on the 9th of August, which will show under what circumstances General McDowell's troops were sent forward and brought into action on that day; whether or not General McDowell fully complied with your orders concerning the movement and disposition of his troops, and how it happened that General Banks' corps sustained alone, until driven back, the engagement on the afternoon and evening of that day.

Answer. In order that my statement may be fully understood it will be necessary for me to describe the positions of the army corps and divisions of that army a day or two previous to that battle and the movements that were made up to the time of its occurrence.

On the 6th August the troops were distributed as follows: Sigel's corps at Sperryville; Banks' corps at Little Washington, with Crawford's brigade of that corps occupying Culpeper Court-House; Ricketts' division of McDowell's corps on the march from Waterloo to Culpeper. The disposition of the cavalry to cover the front of the army on that day, and until they were driven in by the advance of Jackson's forces, were as follows: Five regiments of cavalry, under Brigadier-General Buford occupied Madison Court-House, with their advance pickets thrown forward to the line of the Rapidan, and extending westward from Barnett's Ford, on that river, to the base of the Blue Ridge. Bayard, with four regiments of cavalry, was in the neighborhood of Rapidan Station, with his pickets along that river as far east as Raccoon Ford, and connecting with General Buford's pickets, on his right, at Barnett's Ford. From Bayard's left, at Raccoon Ford, to the forks of the Rappahannock, above Falmouth, the river was lined with cavalry pickets. Between Generals Buford and Bayard and on the summit of Thoroughfare Mountain was established a signal station, which overlooked the whole country as far south as Orange Court-House, 8 or 9 miles south of the Rapidan. From these cavalry forces and the signal station on Thoroughfare

Mountain I received frequent and full reports of the movements of the enemy. In rear of General Buford, and at the crossing of Robertson River by the road from Madison Court-House to Sperryville, I had instructed General Sigel to post a brigade of infantry and a battery of artillery as a support to Buford's cavalry in front of him.

Matters stood thus on the 6th August. I instructed General Banks to move forward from Little Washington on the morning of 7th of August and to take post where the turnpike from Sperryville to Culpeper Court-House crosses Hazel River, so that on 7th August the infantry and artillery forces of the Army of Virginia were assembled along the stone turnpike from Sperryville to Culpeper.

On the 7th—that day I reviewed the corps of General Sigel at Sperryville, and remained at that place until 4 o'clock in the afternoon of the 7th. During the whole of this day reports were coming in of movements of the enemy toward the Rapidan from the direction of Gordonsville, portions of his forces having crossed the Rapidan during that day. I reached Culpeper Court-House early on the morning of the 8th of August, where I found Ricketts' division of McDowell's corps and Crawford's brigade of Banks' corps, which latter had been for some days in occupation of that place. By 10 or 11 o'clock on the morning of the 8th it became clear that the enemy had crossed the Rapidan in heavy force and was advancing both upon Culpeper and upon Madison Court-House. My whole force at that time numbered about 30,000 men, it having been considered by the authorities in Washington not judicious to remove King's division of McDowell's corps from Fredericksburg. My instructions required me also to be very careful not to allow the enemy to interpose between myself and Fredericksburg, to which point the forces from the Peninsula were to be brought.

During the 8th August, or at least during the earlier part of that day, it was uncertain whether the main force of the enemy was marching upon Sperryville or upon Culpeper, but in either case I considered it proper to concentrate my forces in the direction of Culpeper, in order constantly to be interposed between the enemy and the lower fords of the Rappahannock.

I accordingly sent orders to Banks to move forward to Culpeper Court-House and to Sigel to move forward to the same place with all speed. Banks arrived at Culpeper in due season, but to my surprise I received a note from General Sigel, dated at Sperryville, about 6.30 in the evening, acknowledging the receipt of my order, and asking me by what road he should come to Culpeper. As there was but one road, and that a broad stone turnpike, that led directly from Sperryville to Culpeper, I was at a loss to know how General Sigel could entertain any doubt upon the subject. This doubt of General Sigel's delayed the arrival of his corps at Culpeper several hours.

When the reports began to come in from General Bayard that the enemy was advancing upon him, and that his cavalry was forced to retire, I advanced Crawford's brigade of Banks' corps to observe the enemy, to support Bayard in holding the enemy in check, and determining his force and movements, as far as possible. Ricketts' division of McDowell's corps was on same day, 8th August, moved to a point 2½ or 3 miles south of Culpeper, and near to the place where the road from Madison Court-House to Culpeper comes into the road from Barnett's Ford to Culpeper.

Early on the morning of the 9th I received information from General Buford, at Madison Court-House, that the enemy was on his right, on his left, and partly in his rear, and that he was retreating toward Sperryville. On the morning of the 9th August I pushed Banks in front, with his corps, to join the brigade of that corps which had gone to the front the day previous. General Banks was instructed by me to move his corps to the position occupied by that brigade; to take up a strong position there to check the advance of the enemy. This instruction was in a personal interview with General Banks at my headquarters at Culpeper. I told General Banks that if the enemy advanced to attack him that he should push his skirmishers well to the front and notify me immediately, it being my wish to gain all the time possible to concentrate our forces at Culpeper Court-House. General Banks' corps at that time, from his consolidated report transmitted to me a few days previous, numbered over 12,000 infantry and artillery, and this I understood to be the strength of his corps when he was pushed to the front. Three miles in rear of the position which I expected him to occupy was Ricketts' division of McDowell's corps.

Desultory artillery firing was kept up all day on the 9th, during which time I received a number of reports from General Banks, in none of which did he consider that the enemy was in any great force in front of him. In one of his notes, dated about 3 o'clock in the day, he mentioned that the enemy was displaying his cavalry ostentatiously; that he had seen no considerable force of infantry, and that he did not believe they intended to attack. The notes received I have, and can submit them to the court if they so desire it. The last note I received from General Banks was dated about 5 o'clock. He spoke then of the skirmishers approaching each other, and did not indicate that he expected any engagement or ask for any assistance. Before I received this note, however, the artillery firing had become so rapid and continuous that I feared a general engagement was going on or might be brought on at any moment. I therefore instructed General McDowell to push forward Ricketts' division as rapidly as possible to the field, and went forward myself with the division leaving behind me in Culpeper the whole corps of Sigel, with orders to push forward as soon as possible to the field. General McDowell was in nowise responsible for anything connected with these movements, but in all respects carried out my instructions faithfully and zealously.

Question by General McDOWELL. Was not General McDowell personally at your headquarters during the 9th prior to his receiving your orders to send Ricketts' division to the front, and was not he there in compliance with your instructions sent to him at his headquarters?

Answer. He was.

Question by General McDOWELL. Was General McDowell's conduct at the battle of Cedar Run Mountain under your immediate notice? If so, state what was his conduct in the management of his troops and otherwise on that occasion.

Answer. He was under my immediate observation near the conclusion of the battle of Cedar Mountain, when he put his troops into the action on Banks' right. His conduct throughout was gallant and efficient.

Question by General McDOWELL. Did you accompany the Third Army Corps on the march from Rappahannock to Warrenton, and were General McDowell's headquarters with yours on the 22d, 23d, 24th, and 25th of August? If so, state if the dispositions made of that corps on those days were made in conformity with your orders.

Answer. I accompanied the Third Army Corps from the Rappahannock to Warrenton on the 23d. On the 22d, 23d, and 24th my headquarters were with those of General McDowell, and part of the day on the 25th. The dispositions of his corps were made by my orders on those days and under my immediate observation.

Question by General McDOWELL. From the time of your leaving Warrenton on the afternoon of the 25th till General McDowell left there can you state if the orders he gave his corps were not immediately reported to you and if these orders were not approved by you?

Answer. Some of the orders that he gave were reported to me and approved by me. I cannot say that he reported to me all the orders given by him, but all that he reported to me were approved.

Question by General McDOWELL. Did or not, so far as you know, General McDowell neglect or fail in any way to carry out any of your orders as to the disposition of his corps at or in the vicinity of Warrenton or Sulphur Springs or Waterloo with reference to any movement you had ordered General Sigel to make?

Answer. He did not. When we commenced the movement toward Sulphur Springs and Warrenton on the 23d August it was on information that large forces of the enemy had crossed the Rappahannock at Sulphur Springs and Waterloo Bridge. The river having risen 6 or 8 feet on the night of 22d, so as to destroy the fords, I purposed to throw my whole force rapidly upon whatever forces of the enemy were on the north side of the river, hoping to be able, on account of the high water, to crush them before they could succeed in recrossing the river. General Sigel commanded the left, and was instructed to push forward to the Waterloo Bridge, following the course of the Rappahannock. I told him I would push forward McDowell's corps from Warrenton to join him, if necessary, near Waterloo Bridge; but on the 24th I sent a strong reconnaissance forward to Waterloo Bridge, under General Buford, from Warrenton, and he reported to me on the afternoon of the 24th that there was no enemy on the north side of the river, and that he had fired the bridge at Waterloo. I immediately informed General Sigel of the whole of these facts; that I was sure there was no enemy between him and Waterloo. I therefore did not consider it necessary to push McDowell's corps any farther in that direction. As soon as the advance of General Sigel's corps reached Waterloo General Buford took post with all his cavalry on his right, and picketed the river for several miles above Waterloo. I make this statement to show why the corps of General McDowell was not advanced toward Waterloo Bridge on the 24th.

Question by General McDOWELL. Were not the communications frequent and full between yourself and General McDowell whilst you were at Warrenton Junction and he was at Warrenton, and did he ever suggest to you that our whole force should be sent to Salem, and was not the movement to Salem a reconnaissance, made in obedience to your orders, to see what had become of the enemy's column which had passed in front of Waterloo Bridge?

Answer. To the first part of that question I would say yes. The communication was full and frequent. No such suggestion was ever made to me by General McDowell. I myself sent him instructions from Wrrrenton Junction to push forward a cavalry reconnaissance toward Salem or White Plains.

Question by General McDOWELL. Did General Sigel report to you from near the crossing of the Sudley Springs road with the road from Manassas to Gainesville between 2 and 3 o'clock p. m. of 28th of August?

Answer. He did, by letter.

Question by General McDOWELL. Were not General Sigel's reports, as commander of the First Army Corps, made to you direct, and were not your orders for him sent to him direct from and after the afternoon of the 28th, when he reported to you from near the crossing of the Sudley Springs road and the Manassas and Gainesville roads and he received your order to march to Centreville?

Answer. I understood General Sigel to be under the command of General McDowell on the afternoon of the 28th, and accordingly informed General McDowell that I had given these instructions to General Sigel on his application; but I did not consider that connection to have continued after the corps became separated during the night of the 28th.

Question by General McDOWELL. Did General Sigel report to you that Jackson's army was at Groveton when he sent you the note before referred to, or in any way give you to believe he thought he was in that direction? Will witness please produce the note of General Sigel?

Answer. He made no report of that kind to me.

The witness produced the note referred to, which was read. It is from Maj. Gen. Franz Sigel to Major-General Pope, dated August 28—2.30 p. m., and is appended to the proceedings of this day and marked A.

Question by General McDOWELL. About what time was it that Jackson left Manassas and what route did he take from that place?

Answer. From information derived at Manassas Junction from prisoners, deserters, paroled prisoners of our own, and our own cavalry reconnaissances I was and am convinced, and in fact sure, as I can be of a thing I have not myself seen, that the larger portion of Jackson's forces left Manassas Junction between 3 o'clock and 9 or 10 o'clock on the morning of the 28th of August and took the road to Centreville. Our cavalry came up to their rear guard at Bull Run Bridge, on that road, on the afternoon of the 28th, and Kearny's division of Heintzelman's corps followed their rear guard into Centreville and beyond. A large part of his force took the road from Centreville around by Sudley Springs, whilst another part followed the turnpike toward Gainesville from Warrenton, destroying the bridges over Bull Run and Cub Run late on the afternoon of the 28th, and in sigh tof the foremost of our cavalry. These facts came to me in so many different ways and through so many different sources that I was so well convinced of their truth that the whole movements of the army as ordered on the night of the 28th were based upon them. Jackson himself in person, with a small escort, left Manassas Junction, after visiting the hospital there, about 11 o'clock on the morning of the 28th and took the road to Centreville. A large part of his cavalry force (I think the larger part from the accounts I received there) left Manassas Junction about the same time and went west of north toward the Warrenton turnpike. A small cavalry force that I had sent out came upon their rear within a mile or two of Manassas Junction.

Question by General McDOWELL. On the 29th of August, after General McDowell's corps came up the Sudley Springs road by New Market, did you send him any orders?

Answer. I did.

Question by General McDOWELL. In the order of the President constituting the Army of Virginia under your command was General Reynolds' division a part of the Third Corps, to be commanded by General McDowell?

Answer. It was not. General Reynolds' division was the advance division of General Porter's corps, coming from the direction of Fredericksburg to re-enforce the Army of Virginia. As it arrived some days before the rest of the corps, and just on the eve of our movement toward Waterloo Bridge, it was temporarily assigned to duty with the corps of General McDowell.

Question by General McDOWELL. Was not the sending of General McDowell's troops up the Warrenton road on the evening of the 29th in conformity to your orders?

Answer. It was.

Question by General McDOWELL. State what was General McDowell's conduct under your command in the late campaign in Virginia.

Answer. Having by the order of the President been placed in command of an army the commanders of the corps of which were my seniors in rank, my position was embarrassing, and likely to lead to unkind feelings between myself and the commanders of the army corps. I am gratified to be able here to bear testimony to the zeal and energy, the ability and the cordial sympathy, of General McDowell from the first to the last day of the campaign in Virginia. In my judgment he has merited and should receive the gratitude of his country and the applause of his countrymen.

The court was cleared.

The court was opened, and the court adjourned to meet to-morrow, January 14, 1863, at 11 o'clock a. m.

---

## APPENDIX.

### A.

AUGUST 28, 1862—2.30 p. m.

Major-General POPE, *Commanding Army of Virginia:*

GENERAL: I am at the road (3 miles from Manassas Junction) which leads to New Market and thence across Bull Run to Centreville.

I have with me all my corps except Milroy's brigade, which has gone in advance toward the Junction. Shall I pursue this road? General Milroy can join us by a direct road from the Junction through New Market. I prefer this, because there is no water here; I can obtain it by going to Bull Run or even this side of New Market, and I understand that Manassas Junction is now crowded with our troops of other corps and divisions.

Respectfully, your obedient servant,

F. SIGEL,
*Major-General, Commanding First Corps.*

---

## *FORTY-THIRD DAY.*

COURT-ROOM, COR. FOURTEENTH ST. AND PA. AVENUE,
*Washington, D. C., January* 14, 1863.

The court met pursuant to adjournment. Present, * * *, and Maj. Gen. JOHN POPE, U. S. Volunteers, the witness under examination.

* * * * * * *

At the instance of a member of the court the recorder read the order from Major-General Pope to Major-General McDowell, dated Headquarters Army of Virginia, Bristoe Station, August 27, 1862—9 o'clock p. m., marked B, and appended to proceedings of thirtieth day.

Question by the COURT. After the order just read to you had Gen. McDowell any discretionary power to send Ricketts' division to Thoroughfare Gap to check the approach of Longstreet?

Answer. At the time that the order in question was written I was satisfied that we had completely interposed between the forces under Jackson and the main body of the enemy yet to the westward of the Bull Run Range. The order directing General McDowell's march would have carried him to the eastward, and in the same direction in which the main body of the enemy was marching to join Jackson. I believed then, and believe now, that we were sufficiently in advance of Longstreet, who was supposed to lead the main body of the enemy, that by using our whole force vigorously we should be able to crush Jackson completely before Longstreet by any possibility could have reached the scene of action. I sent nothing to General McDowell concerning Thoroughfare Gap, and regretted afterward that any portion of his forces had been detached in that direction. General McDowell had the discretion, however, necessarily incident to his position and to his distance from me, to make such a disposition to cover his rear as he might consider necessary. From the order of General McDowell, which he showed me afterward (the order No. 10), I understood that the movement of Ricketts' division was made conditionally and in view of the possibility of an attack upon his rear from the direction of Thoroughfare Gap.

Question by the COURT. Are you familiar with the country near Hay Market, Gainesville, Groveton, and the Warrenton pike to the bridge across Bull Run?

Answer. I am familiar with the country near Groveton and eastward along the Warrenton turnpike to Bull Run. To the west and south of Groveton I have not been, and only know of the country from the accounts of others.

Question by the COURT. Did you or did you not rely on General McDowell for information as to any indications of the presence of the enemy in the neighborhood of the Warrenton pike and Gainesville on the assumption that the forces under Jackson should move in that direction to effect a junction with Longstreet?

Answer. I did not assume that the forces under Jackson would attempt to rejoin the main body by Gainesville, knowing, as Jackson must have known, that he would encounter in attempting to pursue this route a force of our army considerably superior to his own, but from General McDowell, as from every other commander of a corps or a division of that army, I expected to receive all information of the enemy that could be obtained.

Question by the COURT. Did you during the 28th receive information that the enemy had attacked the column of General McDowell with two pieces of artillery from the direction of Groveton as General McDowell was moving from the field toward Manassas?

Answer. I did not.

Question by the COURT. Have you knowledge of any facts or circumstances, either arising from the topography of the country, the orders to General McDowell, or his discretionary power, to authorize a movement of his troops by a flank along the same route across the country to Bethlehem Church from a point on the Warrenton pike about a mile east of Gainesville?

Answer. I had not.

Question by the COURT. What orders or occasion had he to move any of his troops to Bethlehem Church on the 28th?

Answer. The only order that General McDowell had from me till the afternoon of the 28th was the order of the night of the 27th August. I know nothing of circumstances which controlled the details of his movements during the morning of the 28th.

Having received his official report but very lately, and not having yet read it, I am still unacquainted with the details of the movements of the forces under his command during the morning of the 28th. I know of no occasion that would have brought his troops to the point specified in the question.

At the instance of a member the recorder read the two orders marked A and B, and appended to proceedings of the fortieth day, from Major-General Pope to Major-General McDowell, dated respectively Headquarters Army of Virginia, Manassas Junction, August 28, 1862—1.20 p. m., and Headquarters, Manassas Junction, August 28, 1862.

Question by the COURT. What orders or occasion had General McDowell, after your orders to him just read and after putting his divisions in march toward Centreville, to leave them and go in person to Manassas, if he did so?

Answer. I know of no orders to that effect or any occasion.

Question by the COURT. Were you aware that King's division had a fight with the enemy near evening of that day and after the fight fell back to Manassas?

Answer. It was reported to me about 8 or 9 o'clock at night on the 28th that King's division of McDowell's corps had met the enemy retreating from Centreville, and after a severe fight had remained masters of the field, still interposing between Jackson's forces and the main body of the enemy. This report was brought to me by a staff officer, I think, of General King's. Upon receiving this information I stated to several of my staff officers who were present that the game was in our own hands, and that I did not see how it was possible for Jackson to escape without very heavy loss, if at all. Immediately upon receipt of this intelligence I also directed General Kearny, whose division occupied Centreville, to push forward cautiously at 1 o'clock that night in the direction of Gainesville, to drive in the pickets of the enemy, and to keep himself in close contact during the night; to rest his left on the Warrenton turnpike, and to throw his right to the north, toward the Little River, and well to the front. I directed him at the first blush of daylight to attack the enemy with his right advanced, and informed him that Hooker and Reno would be with him immediately after daylight. To my surprise and dissatisfaction I learned toward daylight on the morning of the 29th that King's division had withdrawn in the direction of Manassas Junction, leaving open the road to Thoroughfare Gap. This withdrawal of that division made necessary a great change in the movement and the position of the troops and was a most serious and unlooked-for mistake. I was so impressed with the necessity that that division should hold its ground during the night of the 28th that I sent several orders to General King (one by his own staff officer) during that night to hold his ground at all hazards and to prevent the retreat of the enemy, and informed him that our whole force from the direction of Centreville and Manassas Junction would all upon the enemy at daylight.

Question by the COURT. Do you know any occasion or explanation for the absence of General McDowell from that battle-field and his presence at Manassas, if such was the fact?

Answer. I only know from General McDowell's own explanation to me why he came to Manassas Junction. This explanation was given me some time subsequently; when I cannot state.

Question by the COURT. State, as near as you can, the time when this explanation was made. Was it during the campaign?

Answer. Yes, I think it was, sir. My recollection is not clear, but it occurs to me it was some time after dark on the 29th. Of this, however, I am not certain.

Question by the COURT. State the explanation.

Answer. General McDowell told me that he supposed me to be at Manassas Junction; that he came there to communicate more fully with me than he could do by letter. I had asked him in a note sent him on the afternoon of 28th August—that same day—to give me his views fully, as he knew the country in that vicinity much better than I did. He fully expected to find me at Manassas Junction, and after communicating with me to return immediately to his command. I was, however, not at Manassas Junction, but with the advance near Centreville.

Question by the COURT. Do you mean to be understood that on the morning of the 29th General McDowell was no longer responsible for the movements and command of General Sigel's corps and Reynolds' division; and, if so, produce the orders, if you can, investing him with such command before the 29th, and state any orders which may have been given relieving him.

(The witness produced a certified copy of General Orders, No. —, dated Headquarters Army of Virginia, Warrenton Junction, August 27, 1862; which is appended to the proceedings of this day and marked A.)

Answer. I did not consider General McDowell as having any command over the corps of General Sigel, or as being responsible for the movements of that corps any time during the 29th August. I sent orders to General McDowell on the morning of 29th August, directed to him at Manassas Junction, instructing him to call in Ricketts' division and join it with King's, and in conjunction with Major-General Porter march upon Gainesville by the road from Manassas Junction. On the morning of the 29th August, until the close of the campaign of Virginia, General Sigel's corps, as every other corps of that army, was under my immediate command and received my direct orders. In relation to the division of General Reynolds, I had supposed, until otherwise informed, that it had also fallen back with King's division to Manassas Junction. I sent no orders to General McDowell or to General Sigel changing the relations they had with each other when they marched from Warrenton, for the simple reason that no such orders were needed, the connection between them being dissolved of necessity, either by the separation of the corps or by my own personal presence with them. It is not necessary to state to the court that I had no authority to merge into one two army corps established by the orders of the President; that any temporary connection between them, wherein one corps commander should command both corps, would only last so long as they served at a distance from the general-in-chief of the army to which they belonged.

On the 29th August I received various reports from General Sigel before I reached the field of battle; saw him many times during the day of 29th, and gave him several orders personally and by aides-de-camp. I did not understand, nor did I presume General Sigel to understand, that he was responsible to anybody except myself for any movement of his troops or for any orders he might receive during that day.

Question by the COURT. What did you suppose the force of the enemy immediately under Jackson to have been on the 28th August, 1862?

Answer. The information upon which we deduced an opinion upon that subject was in the nature of things uncertain and to some extent unreliable. I myself supposed Jackson to have, including his own, Ewell's, and Hill's divisions, at the least 25,000 men, or between that and 30,000, though other officers having the same sources of information estimated his forces as high as 35,000 men.

Question by the COURT. Produce the orders to which reference was made in your direct examination of yesterday.

The witness produced an order from Maj. Gen. John Pope to Major-General Sigel, dated Headquarters Army of Virginia, one mile below Warrenton, August 24, 1862—1 p. m.; an order from Major-General Pope to Major-General McDowell, dated Headquarters Army of Virginia, Warrenton Junction, August 26, 1862; which are appended to the proceedings of this day and marked respectively B and C.

The foregoing orders were read by the recorder.

Question by General MCDOWELL. Please state if, under the last order of the afternoon of the 28th, which reported the enemy on the Orange and Alexandria Railroad and which required General McDowell to march his troops to Centreville, he would not be justified in sending his troops by way of Bethlehem Church and New Market, provided that order found one of his divisions nearer that road than any other and that it should be the most direct to Centreville from where the order found it?

Answer. Certainly. The order directed General McDowell to move by the most direct road from where he was to Centreville. Where his troops were I cannot exactly say.

Capt. FRANKLIN HAVEN, additional aide-de-camp, U. S. Army, a witness, was recalled.

Question by General MCDOWELL. Did General McDowell on the afternoon of the 28th send out any parties to scout or reconnoiter to the left or north of the turnpike?

Answer. In accordance with General McDowell's instructions I took a company of cavalry to General Reynolds, which he sent out, with some of the Bucktail regiment, I think, toward Sudley Springs. Other forces, I think, were ordered in that direction, but I do not know of my own knowledge.

Question by General MCDOWELL. Did General McDowell send you to accompany King's division on the afternoon or evening of the 28th, when it was ordered to Centreville?

Answer. He did.

Question by General MCDOWELL. What took place on that march?

Answer. On the march the enemy made an attack on King's division, which was repulsed by Gibbon's brigade and two regiments, I think, in the advance. The enemy's forces were driven off, and General King and General Reynolds (the latter having come up personally) sent me to General McDowell to say that General King would not continue the march to Centreville as ordered, but would remain where he was, and that General Reynolds would bring back his division and join General King at daylight.

Question by General MCDOWELL. Were you not also instructed to say that King would not move from where he was without instructions from General McDowell?

Answer. It was explicitly understood that he would remain where he was until General McDowell should send him fresh orders to the contrary.

Question by General MCDOWELL. When you left General King had not the engagement entirely ceased?

Answer. It had entirely ceased nearly an hour before I left General King.

Question by General MCDOWELL. About how long did it continue?

Answer. About an hour, I thought.

Question by General MCDOWELL. Where did the engagement take place? Was it on the turnpike, or north of it or south of it?

Answer. The troops were marching over the turnpike when they were shelled from the enemy, who was a short distance to the north. General King's forces then left the turnpike and attacked them and drove them off.

Question by General MCDOWELL. Did you bear any order to General King from General McDowell requiring or permitting him to leave the place on the turnpike where he was when you left him?

Answer. No, sir.

Question by the COURT. Did General King strike the turnpike east or west of Groveton, or at Groveton?

Answer. About a mile west of Groveton, I think.

Question by the COURT. How far is Groveton from Gainesville?

Answer. My impression was about 3 miles or 3½ miles.

Question by the COURT. At what time did you leave General King that afternoon or evening to convey a message from him to General McDowell?

Answer. I think it was a little after 9 o'clock.

Question by the COURT. Did you find General McDowell that night?

Answer. I did not.

Question by the COURT. Where was Reynolds' division when the attack was made on King?

Answer. It had advanced over the turnpike, and about that time was about 3 miles in advance of General King from the place of the engagement.

Capt. W. H. W. KREBBS, additional aide-de-camp, U. S. Army, a witness, was duly sworn.

Question by General MCDOWELL. Were you on duty with General McDowell on the 28th of August last?

Answer. I was.

Question by General MCDOWELL. Did General McDowell send you to General Sigel on the occasion of the march from Gainesville toward Manassas Junction on the 28th of August last after the skirmish of Reynolds' division?

Answer. He did.

Question by General MCDOWELL. Where did you find General Sigel's command, on the north or south side of the Manassas Railroad?

Answer. I found General Sigel's command on the south side of the railroad; he and staff. I should think about 4 miles from Gainesville, on the south side of railroad.

Question by General MCDOWELL. Did you represent to General Sigel that he was not on the right road, and that it was General McDowell's order that he should go to the north of it?

Answer. I told him that he was mistaken; that I understood the order that his right should rest on the railroad, his left on our right, which was on the Warrenton turnpike.

Question by General MCDOWELL. Were you sent a second time to General Sigel by General McDowell in the afternoon of the 28th? If so, what did you say to him?

Answer. I was sent to him by General McDowell on the afternoon of the 28th—I should judge it was about 2 o'clock—to find out if the enemy was really at Manassas Junction or not. General Sigel said they were not; he was certain. His cavalry had been there; also Generals Reno and Kearny. I communicated this intelligence to General McDowell as soon as I got back. I found General Sigel the second time three quarters of a mile from the place where I delivered the first message, at a farm-house, about to dine. His artillery horses were unhitched and gone to water, and his men were building fires, preparing to cook their dinners.

Question by the COURT. At what time did you report to General McDowell the answer of General Sigel?

Answer. I should think it was about half an hour after I left General Sigel. I rode as fast as my horse could go, which was my orders from General McDowell.

Question by the COURT. On which side of and how far from the rail road was General McDowell when you found him?

Answer. He was on the north side, near the railroad.

Question by the COURT. How far from the Warrenton pike was he?

Answer. About a half or three quarters of a mile.

Col. EDMUND SCHRIVER, aide-de-camp, U. S. Army, a witness, was recalled.

Question by General MCDOWELL. When General McDowell went to Reynolds' division on the afternoon of the 28th where did he find General Reynolds, and did General McDowell precede his division to Bethlehem Church?

Answer. He found him that afternoon at a farm-house, getting dinner, I think, and we preceded his division to Bethlehem Church.

Question by General McDOWELL. You have stated it was dark when General McDowell left Manassas. Can you, on reflection, state more definitely as to the time he left?

Answer. It was hardly dark, for I remember seeing the remains of the buildings that had been burned the day before, and it was about dark when we were in the swamp and lost our way.

The court instructed the recorder to address a communication to the War Department, calling attention to a communication addressed to the Department on the 30th December, 1862, for certain papers, and also requesting a copy of Major-General Banks' report of the battle of Cedar Mountain, if the same be on file in the War Department.

The court adjourned to meet to-morrow, January 15, 1863, at 11 o'clock a. m.

---

## APPENDIX.

### A.

GENERAL ORDERS, No. —. } HEADQUARTERS ARMY OF VIRGINIA, *Warrenton Junction, August* 27, 1862.

The following movement of troops will be made, viz:

Major-General McDowell, with his own and Sigel's corps and the division of Brigadier-General Reynolds, will pursue the turnpike from Warrenton to Gainesville, so as to reach Gainesville, if possible, to-night.

The army corps of General Heintzelman, with the detachment of the Ninth Corps under Major-General Reno (General Reno leading), will take the road from Catlett's Station to Greenwich, so as to reach there to-night or early in the morning. Major-General Reno will immediately communicate with Major-General McDowell, and his command, as well as that of Major-General Heintzelman, will support Major-General McDowell in any operations against the enemy.

Maj. Gen. Fitz John Porter will remain at Warrenton Junction till he is relieved by Major-General Banks, when he will immediately push forward with his corps in the direction of Greenwich and Gainesville to assist the operations of the right wing.

Major-General Banks, as soon as he arrives at Warrenton Junction, will assume the charge of the trains and cover their movement toward Manassas Junction. The train of his own corps, under escort of two regiments of infantry and battery of artillery, will pursue the road south of the railroad which conducts into the rear of Manassas Junction. As soon as the trains have passed Warrenton Junction he will take post behind Cedar Run, covering the fords and bridges of that stream, and holding that position as long as possible. He will cause all the railroad trains to be loaded with the public and private stores now here, and run back toward Manassas Junction as far as the railroad is practicable. Wherever a bridge is burned so as to impede the farther passage of the railroad trains, he will assemble them all as near together as possible and protect them with his command until the bridges are rebuilt. If the enemy is too strong before him before the bridge can be repaired, he will be careful to destroy entirely the trains, locomotives, and stores before he falls back in the direction of Manassas Junction. He is, however, to understand that he is to defend his position as long as possible, keeping himself in constant communication with Major-General Porter on his right. If any sick, now in hospital at Warrenton Junction, are not provided for and able to be transported, he will have them loaded into the wagon train of his own corps (even if this should necessitate the destruction of much baggage and regimental property) and carried to Manassas Junction. The major-general commanding the Army of Virginia feels assured that he will discharge these duties with intelligence, courage, and fidelity.

The general headquarters will be with the corps of Major-General Heintzelman until further notice.

By command of Major-General Pope:

GEO. D. RUGGLES,
*Colonel and Chief of Staff.*

B.

HEADQUARTERS ARMY OF VIRGINIA,
*One mile below Warrenton, August* 24, 1862—1 p. m.

Major-General SIGEL, *Commanding First Corps:*

General Buford reports his occupation of Waterloo Bridge without finding an enemy. He is ordered to destroy the bridge and await further orders. I think you will find no enemy between Waterloo Bridge and Sulphur Springs on this side of the river.

Ascertain certainly if the enemy has built a bridge at Sulphur Springs, and destroy it if he has done so, and it be possible. As soon as you ascertain that there is no force of the enemy on this side of the river between Waterloo Bridge and Sulphur Springs you will halt, communicate with these headquarters by the direct road from Sulphur Springs to this place, and await further orders.

JNO. POPE,
*Major-General, Commanding.*

C.

WARRENTON JUNCTION,
*August* 26, 1862—[8.10 a. m.]

Major-General MCDOWELL:

I sent instructions last night to make a strong reconnaissance across to Sulphur Springs, intending that Sigel should do the same thing at Waterloo Bridge and Reno at Rappahannock Station. Sigel reports himself unable to do anything until his men are rested. I directed him to halt them somewhere near Warrenton and put them in camp for to-day. Reno, instead of going to Bealeton and thence to Kelly's Ford, has come to this place and is now near here. You must, therefore, under these circumstances, exercise your discretion about the reconnaissance to Sulphur Springs; but it will certainly be well for you to ascertain what there is in the direction of Waterloo Bridge and still farther to your right. Send for General Milroy; he is a courageous man. I think Sigel must be crazy. If you deem it necessary assume command also of Sigel's corps. It is essential that we should watch the movements of the enemy toward our right in some manner. Out of Buford's, Bayard's, and Sigel's cavalry enough can certainly be found to perform this service. Troops are accumulating here, but not very fast. Take charge of the front and use everybody you find there.

JNO. POPE,
*Major-General, Commanding.*

P. S.—I will push Reno to Fayetteville. It will be well to have the men cook three days' rations. Please notify Banks and Sigel.

*FORTY-FOURTH DAY.*

COURT-ROOM, COR. FOURTEENTH AND PA. AVENUE,
*Washington, D. C., January* 15, 1863.

* * * * * * *

Brig. Gen. RUFUS KING, U. S. Volunteers, a witness, was recalled.

Question by the COURT. Where was your division on the morning of the 28th of August, when the head of Reynolds' column was asaulted by a section of the enemy's artillery from the direction of Groveton, on the Warrenton pike?

Answer. As nearly as I can remember my division that morning was near Buckland Mills, on the march between Buckland Mills and Groveton.

Question by the COURT. Do you know where Gainesville is and the railroad from Gainesville to Manassas and Bethlehem Church?

Answer. Yes, sir.

Question by the COURT. Did your division march along the pike from Buckland Mills and change direction toward Manassas on the 28th?

Answer. Yes, sir.

Question by the COURT. At what point of the pike, with reference to Gainesville, did your division change direction toward Manassas?

Answer. I think it was 2 or 3 miles beyond Gainesville toward Centreville.

Question by the COURT. Did you follow in the route of any other division; and, if so, what division?

Answer. My impression is that we did, and that we followed the route of General Reynolds' division.

Question by the COURT. How near were you to the rear of the column in advance of you?

Answer. I do not remember, but I think we were within sight all the while, but am not sure of it.

Question by the COURT. What was your formation of brigades and regiments in your march; that is, did you move by a flank, one regiment following in the same route as the preceding one, or how otherwise?

Answer. My column marched by brigades and regiments in order of seniority; that is, my senior brigade leading the column, and by a flank, all on the same road.

Question by the COURT. When you changed direction from the pike toward Manassas did you march to Bethlehem Church?

Answer. We marched either to the church or to its immediate neighborhood.

Question by the COURT. Did you cross to the south side of the railroad, located between Gainesville and Manassas?

Answer. I don't remember crossing the railroad, but we must have done so if we went as far as Bethlehem Church.

Question by the COURT. By whose orders did you move your division in the manner and by the routes which you have now described?

Answer. The order to march by divisions came from my commanding officer, General McDowell; the manner of the movement was by my own directions.

Question by the COURT. What orders in respect to your movements did you receive from General McDowell? State fully and particularly.

Answer. The only order I recollect of receiving from General McDowell was the general order received that morning to move my division toward Manassas, but the details of the order have escaped my memory. As I remember the order was verbal.

Question by the COURT. On your route that day did you meet General McDowell; and, if so, where?

Answer. I think I saw General McDowell twice at least on that day; on the morning before we marched at or near Buckland Mills, and in the afternoon I think 2 or 3 miles to the right of the Warrenton turnpike, in the direction of Bethlehem Church. My impression is this was about 4 o'clock in the afternoon.

Question by the COURT. Did you receive an order changing the direction of your division that afternoon; and, if so, what was that order?

Answer. I received an order from General McDowell turning my division back to the Warrenton pike, with instructions to march to or toward Centreville, and with the caution to look out for my left flank. This was at the time of the last interview I had with General McDowell.

Question by the COURT. Was this order communicated to you by General McDowell in person, by an aide, or in writing?

Answer. My recollection is that it was a verbal order, communicated through an aide on the general's staff; yet I have the impression that it was the general himself who cautioned me to look out for my left flank.

Question by the COURT. Was or was not the place of this interview, at the point described by you, in the immediate neighborhood of Bethlehem Church?

Answer. No; my recollection is that it was nearer to the Warrenton turnpike than to the Bethlehem Church considerably.

Question by the COURT. Did you turn back to the pike or proceed toward Bethlehem Church?

Answer. We went back to the pike and marched along it.

Question by the COURT. Do you then mean to be understood that you did not go to the immediate neighborhood of Bethlehem Church?

Answer. My first impression was that we went to the Bethlehem Church. Since recalling my last interview with the general I am now under the impression that I went no nearer to the Bethlehem Church than the place of interview.

Question by the COURT. Did you encounter the enemy after returning to the Warrenton pike and where?

Answer. Near Groveton, on the left of the pike. I think the engagement commenced about 6 o'clock.

Question by the COURT. How long did the engagement last?

Answer. I judge about and hour and a half.

Question by the COURT. What was the result of it?

Answer. The attack of the enemy was repulsed and my troops maintained possession of the ground. We collected our dead and wounded. The severity of the action you can judge from the fact that the Second Brigade of my division, under General Gibbon, consisting of four regiments, numbering about 2,300 men, assisted by two regiments from Doubleday's brigade, were engaged in the action. Gibbon's brigade lost in killed, wounded, and missing about 782. The entire loss of Gibbon and Doubleday was about 1,000.

Question by the COURT. How long did you retain possession of the ground, and when you moved where did you go?

Answer. We remained at or near the battle-field till toward 2 o'clock on the morning of the 29th, then we fell back toward the neighborhood of Manassas Junction.

Question by the COURT. What orders or occasion had you to fall back to the neighborhood of Manassas Junction?

Answer. The falling back was in pursuance of a consultation with my general officers, under the opinion that the enemy was in force too strong where we were and that it was our duty to join the main body of our troops.

Question by the COURT. What do you mean by the main body of our troops and where did you suppose them to be?

Answer. I supposed at the time one large body of our troops was at or near Centreville and another at or near Manassas Junction. It was the opinion of my officers that we could not with safety, or without involving the loss of our division, pursue our march to Centreville, and our only alternative, therefore, was to pursue the route to Manassas Junction.

Question by the COURT. What troops did you suppose to be at Manassas Junction?

Answer. I have no distinct impression. I had the general belief that a large body was there; what divisions I did not know.

Question by the COURT. Had you any directions or information from General McDowell as to his headquarters or where to apply to him in any emergency?

Answer. I had with me at the time two or three of General McDowell's staff, one of whom I sent immediately after the action to where I supposed General McDowell to be, which was in the immediate neighborhood of Manassas Junction. I think the officer was Captain Haven.

Question by the COURT. Had you any orders or directions given to you by General McDowell to return that night to Manassas?

Answer. I had no orders on that subject. I acted on my own responsibility.

The court was cleared.

The court was opened.

Question by the COURT. Did General McDowell ever investigate your movements and action in that particular and approve or disapprove them?

Answer. I am not aware that General McDowell investigated the movement, nor do I know whether he expressed approval or disapproval. He did not to me.

Question by the COURT. Had you any information from General McDowell or otherwise as to the position of Sigel's corps and Reynolds' division that night?

Answer. I do not remember to have received any.

Question by General MCDOWELL. After leaving Gainesville to what point did you follow in the route of another division in your march? Did you continue to follow it after you left the turnpike?

Answer. We followed it along the turnpike for some distance and then turned to the right some miles beyond Gainesville. We followed it while on the turnpike, but did not follow it after we left the turnpike.

Question by General MCDOWELL. After the engagement of the evening of the 28th did General Reynolds personally join you before you fell back?

Answer. I have tried repeatedly to recall that circumstance of his joining me and holding a conversation with me, but I cannot recollect the fact.

Question by General MCDOWELL. Did you not quit the command of the division on the forenoon of the 29th?

Answer. I did.

Question by General MCDOWELL. Were you not ill on and after the time of your leaving the division, and have you made any report to General McDowell of the operations of your division in the campaign in Virginia?

Answer. I was ill for some time and unfit for duty, still retaining command of the division, until the 29th of August. After that time I was sick in Washington, and on leave from Adjutant-General's Office. Understanding that General Hatch, my successor, had made the report, I did not consider that one was required from me.

Brig. Gen. JAMES B. RICKETTS, U. S. Volunteers, a witness, was duly sworn.

The court was cleared.
The court was opened.

Question by the COURT. Were you commanding a division in General McDowell's corps on the 28th of August last?

Answer. Yes.

Question by the COURT. At what time did you reach Thoroughfare Gap on the morning of that day with your division?

Answer. I don't know the time of day. I do not know that it was in the morning; I think it was in the afternoon.

Question by the COURT. Had you any orders from General McDowell in respect to your movements that day? If so, how were they communicated, and when, and what were they? State fully and particularly.

Answer. I received an order on that day to send a brigade and a battery of artillery to support Colonel Wyndham at Thoroughfare Gap and to push on to the same place with the rest of my division. I do not know what hour of the day the order was received, but should judge some time in the forenoon. I was at the time with my division on the road from Buckland Mills to Gainesville and marched directly across the country by Hay Market. This order was brought to me by Captain Wadsworth, of General McDowell's staff, and was in writing. Somewhere between Hay Market and Thoroughfare Gap I saw Captain Leski, of General McDowell's staff, who gave directions to go to Thoroughfare Gap; he gave pretty much the same order, to go there and support Colonel Wyndham at the Gap. That is all I recollect.

Question by the COURT. Can you produce the written order referred to?

The witness produced the order, which is in pencil, dated August 28, and signed by Edmund Schriver, colonel and chief of staff. The recorder read the order, which is appended to the proceedings of this day and marked A.

Question by the COURT. On the 28th of August had you any communication with General McDowell designating his headquarters or where to communicate with him if any emergency should require it; and, if so, what was such communication?

Answer. I have a copy of an order sent to me, in which it is stated that General McDowell's headquarters would be at King's division.

The witness produced a copy of General Orders, No. 10, dated Headquarters Third Corps, Reynolds' camp, Army of Virginia, which order is the same as found in appendix B to the proceedings of the twenty-ninth day.

Question by the COURT. At what time did you receive the copy of Orders, No. 10, and was it before or after the order to go to Thoroughfare Gap, already produced by you?

Answer. I don't recollect the time. It must have been received before.

Question by the COURT. Did you have any engagement with the enemy at the Gap; and, if so, at what time?

Answer. I had an engagement in the afternoon of the 28th, which continued until dark.

Question by the COURT. At what time did you retire from the Gap and where did you go?

Answer. I retired from the Gap just after dark on the evening of the 28th, and rested my division that night between Hay Market and Gainesville. I was myself at Gainesville.

Question by the COURT. Did you not receive notice from General McDowell during the afternoon of the 28th, or while you were at Gainesville, that Reynolds' and King's divisions had been directed toward Centreville?

Answer. I don't recollect of receiving that.

Question by the COURT. Where did you move when you left Hay Market and Gainesville and at what time did you start?

Answer. I moved toward Manassas, and started very early in the morning of the 29th—after break of day.

Question by the COURT. Before or after sunrise?

Answer. It is impossible for me to say; it was somewhere about sunrise; whether before or after I cannot say.

Question by the COURT. How near to Manassas did you go?

Answer. I went past Manassas Junction.

Question by the COURT. How far past Manassas Junction did you go and where?

Answer. I was conducted by a guide on the Sudley Springs road, and remained near the road, not far from the Henry house, where the headquarters of my division remained for the night.

Question by the COURT. After leaving Gainesville on the morning of the 29th did you receive any orders from General McDowell; and, if so, where were you when you first received them?

Answer. I received some orders somewhere between Gainesville and Manassas from General McDowell. I think somewhere nearer Manassas than Gainesville. I do not remember the precise point. If not mistaken, the order was brought me by Captain Wadsworth.

Question by the COURT. What orders or occasion had you to go from Thoroughfare Gap to the place last referred to by you, between Gainesville and Manassas?

Answer. I left Thoroughfare Gap because the enemy was turning the right and left flank. I left Gainesville because General King sent me word that he would retire toward Manassas; that was all.

Question by the COURT. Did any communication other than the one referred to in your last answer pass between you and General King during the 28th August and up to the time that you moved from Gainesville on the morning of the 29th? And, if so, state what they were.

Answer. I had two communications from General King; the first stating that he had an engagement with the enemy and had held his ground; the other representing a large force of the enemy in front of him, and that he would retire toward Manassas. In answer to the last I told him that I would retire from my position. I do not recollect of any others.

Question by the COURT. Why did you not await orders from General McDowell to move from Gainesville on the morning of the 29th August?

Answer. When General King sent me word that he would retire I then knew I would be unsupported.

Question by the COURT. Have you knowledge of any neglect or omission of General McDowell in respect to the management of his troops, or keeping them in communication with him, or co-operation with each other, on the 28th or 29th of August? And, if so, state it fully.

Answer. I know of no such neglect or omission.

The court adjourned to meet to-morrow, January 16, 1863, at 11 o'clock a. m.

---

## APPENDIX.

### A.

10.15 A. M.

The enemy is advancing through the pass.

W. LESKI,
*Captain and Aide-de-Camp.*

Colonel Wyndham will halt them as long as he can, and asks to be re-enforced.

W. L.

AUGUST 28.

Send a brigade and a battery to assist Colonel Wyndham, and follow them up by your whole division.

ED. SCHRIVER,
*Colonel, &c.*

General RICKETTS.

---

## *FORTY-FIFTH DAY.*

COURT-ROOM, COR. FOURTEENTH AND PA. AVENUE,
*Washington, D. C., January* 16, 1863.

* * * * * * *

Brig. Gen. JAMES B. RICKETTS, U. S. Volunteers, the witness under examination, appeared before the court.

Question by General MCDOWELL. What o'clock on the 28th of August were you ordered to march from your bivouac beyond Buckland Mills?

Answer. I was ordered to march at 2 o'clock in the morning.

Question by General MCDOWELL. How far did you march on the Warrenton turnpike before you turned off the road to go by Hay Market under the order given you by Captain Wadsworth?

Answer. I had crossed the bridge at Broad Run, and was but a very short distance from it.

Question by General MCDOWELL. Where did the order brought to you by Captain Wadsworth find you; on which side of the bridge?

Answer. On the side nearest Gainesville.

Question by General MCDOWELL. Do you know any cause of delay in your getting forward from your bivouac to the place where you turned off; were there any obstructions in the road?

Answer. The road was very much encumbered by wagons. I saw a very large number in the vicinity of this stream—Broad Run.

Maj. Gen. E. A. HITCHCOCK, U. S. Volunteers, a witness, was duly sworn.

Question by General MCDOWELL. State if your official position and connection with the Government were such at the time as to enable you to know or to give you good grounds for judging as to General McDowell having or not in April last sought, induced, or procured the separation of his army corps from the Army of the Potomac, with a view to having a separate command for himself; and, if so, whether or not the retention of the corps was, to the best of your knowledge and belief, sought, induced, or procured by him, or was made by the Government for public reasons, based on the representations of others? State fully what you know of this matter.

Answer. I was on duty in the War Office, under the immediate orders of the Secretary of War, from the middle of March until the middle of May last. That period embraces the time referred to in this question. The circumstances which led to the detention of General McDowell's army corps in the early part of April, as a covering army for the city of Washington, were, I believe, very fully known to me, and I am very sure that personally General McDowell had nothing whatever to do in procuring the orders which detained him in front of Washington. I am very sure that his first information on the subject was derived from the order itself, directing his detention here. I saw General McDowell soon after that, and his first expressions to me in reference to the order were those of deep regret. He had hoped, as he said to me, to accompany the army to the Peninsula, where he was anxious to be put in a position to do something in his profession as a military man, by which I inferred very plainly that he hoped to have had an opportunity of distinguishing himself as a soldier. His language and his deportment gave me the belief that he was, as he said, truly disappointed, and for the reason he assigned. The facts in the case would be best seen by a recital of the circumstances under which the orders were given.

The witness, with the permission of the court, referred to certain papers in his possession with a view of refreshing his memory in regard to dates, which papers he would place at the disposal of the court, should it so direct.

The witness continued:

In order to understand the case fully I think it necessary to refer to an order from the President, dated 31st January last.

The order was here produced and read by the recorder. It is President's Special Orders, No. 1, dated Executive Mansion, Washington, January 31, 1862, and is appended to the proceedings of this day and marked A.

The witness continued:

On the delivery of the order just read there must have been some plan from General McClellan proposing some other mode of operation. I have not that plan and am not able to produce it; but I have a paper from the President, dated February 3, which evidently followed it.

This paper was read by the recorder, and is from Abraham Lincoln to Major-General McClellan, dated Executive Mansion, Washington, February 3, 1862, and is appended to the proceedings of this day, marked B.

The witness continued:

The President subsequently appears to have yielded his plan to that of General McClellan, but in doing so issued this order, dated March 8.

The order was read by the recorder, and is President's General War Orders, No. 3, dated Executive Mansion, Washington, March 8, 1862, and is appended to this day's proceedings, marked C.

The witness continued:

That order led to a conference of the general officers commanding army corps, the result of which was reported March 13.

The recorder here read the paper referred to, dated Headquarters Army of the Potomac, Fairfax Court-House, March 13, 1862; which paper is appended to the proceedings of this day and marked D.

The witness continued:

The plan alluded to in that paper drew from Mr. Stanton, the Secretary of War, communicating the orders of the President, the following paper, dated March 13.

The paper was read by the recorder; is from the Secretary of War to Major-General McClellan, dated War Department, March 13, 1862, and is appended to the proceedings of this day, marked E.

The witness continued:

This repetition of those conditions shows the importance attached to them by the President. After General McClellan left the front of Washington it was observed in the War Department that his orders for the movement of the troops did not appear to contemplate having such a force for the protection of Washington as the orders of the President required, and a good deal of concern was expressed and felt by the Secretary of War on this subject. On the 2d of April, 1862, General Wadsworth made a report to the Secretary of War, setting forth the amount of the force left under his command in Washington, together with the condition and the character of the troops. That report is the following, which I lay on the table of the court.

The recorder read the report, which is dated Headquarters Military District of Washington, Washington, D. C., April 2, 1862, and addressed to the Hon. Secretary of War, and is appended to the proceedings of this day and marked F.

The witness continued:

On the 19th of April an order was issued by authority of the Secretary of War, the object of which was to ascertain the condition and strength of the force in the city of Washington by actual inspection. I lay before the court a copy of the order, and the report of Major Jones, the inspecting officer.

The recorder read the papers referred to; one from Major-General Hitchcock, by order of the Secretary of War, dated War Department, Washington, D. C., April 19, 1862; the other dated War Department, Washington City, April 19, 1862, and which papers are appended to this day's proceedings, marked respectively G and H.

The witness continued:

It is proper that I should state in this connection that the troops thus paraded did not embrace those of the fortifications on the south side of the Potomac, but did embrace some of the recently arrived recruits from the North, which may account for their unprepared condition in some degree. About that time I held repeated conversations with General Doubleday, who had the immediate command of the forts south of the Potomac, for the purpose of ascertaining the condition of the troops in the forts. He told me on three several occasions, with intervals of a few days, that he had been unable to procure ammunition on his requisition to supply the fortifications. After talking with him the third time I reported the matter to the Secretary of War, who immediately sent for General Doubleday, and the necessary orders were given by which that deficiency was supplied. I now lay before the court a communication from General McClellan, dated April 1, 1862.

The communication referred to was read by the recorder; is from Major-General McClellan to Brig. Gen. L. Thomas, dated Headquarters Army of the Potomac, steamer Commodore, April 1, 1862, and is appended to this day's proceedings, marked I.

The witness continued:

On the 2d April certain papers were referred to General Thomas and General Hitchcock (myself) by the Secretary of War under an order of which this is a copy.

The recorder read the order, which is dated War Department, Washington City, April 2, 1862, from the Secretary of War, and is appended to the proceedings of this day, marked K.

The witness continued:

In obedience to that order General Thomas and myself examined the papers referred to in it, and made a joint report, of which this is a copy.

The recorder then read a report from Major-General Hitchcock and Brig. Gen. L. Thomas, dated Washington, D. C., April 2, 1862, which is appended to the proceedings of this day, marked L.

The witness continued:

I would state here that a part of the force referred to in General McClellan's report—General Blenker's division—had at that time been either ordered out of his department, or was soon to be, by the President himself, and could not properly be considered a part of the force for the defense of Washington in any sense, and was not to be delayed, even in the Shenandoah Valley. It was to go to what was called the Mountain Department, under General Frémont.

It will be observed presently that the President, in a letter to General McClellan, refers to the removal of Blenker's division as if it had been determined with the sanction of General McClellan, though reluctantly. When I heard of the design to remove that division from the front of Washington I expressed my opinion to the Secretary of War that it ought not to be done. He acquiesced at once in that view, and desired me to go with him to the President and explain it to the President, which I did, but without success. On returning to the War Office the importance of the point seemed to be so great that I made a written statement of my reasons March 30, which I gave to the President the next morning. This is a copy of those reasons.

The copy was read by the recorder; is dated March 30, 1862, and is appended to the proceedings of this day, marked M.

The witness continued:

This effort on my part failed. That division left the Shenandoah Valley. General Banks had been ordered into the valley because of the attack made by Jackson upon Shields. This still further reduced the force in front of Washington. I ought to state that Blenker did not leave that valley for some weeks, and because it was under orders which I could not succeed in having revoked; therefore his force was not to be counted upon for the defense of Washington. I had these particulars before my mind in signing the joint report with General Thomas. I considered, further, that the opinion of the four commanders of the *corps d'armée*, setting forth the force necessary for the security of Washington, as confined to the city and its defenses on the other side of the Potomac, extending as far as Manassas and Warrenton—that front in general, but that it did not include the valley of the Shenandoah; that the troops in that valley could not be withdrawn with safety was my clear and decided opinion. Looking, then, to the number of troops which might be counted upon for the protection of the city I could not make out 25,000 men as a unit of force, including the occupation of the garrisons north and south of the river and the force within the city, after allowing the usual deduction for the sick, &c. When these reports came before the President he was manifestly under great anxiety. It was his declared wish to give to General McClellan all the force he called for and all of the means which could be thrown into his hands to execute his purpose, but finally, after much consideration, he determined to order one of the two remaining corps then in front of Washington to be detained here, leaving the selection with the Secretary of War, who designated the corps commanded by General McDowell. As soon as this was reported to General McClellan he complained of it as an interference with his command, calculated to lead to the most dangerous consequences. He asked for two of the three divisions constituting that corps (Franklin's and McCall's), and if he could not get two he was particularly anxious to have Franklin's division. The President came to the War Office in person and held a discussion of some length with several of the chiefs of bureaus in the War Department in the presence of the Secretary of War. I cannot from memory recite the particulars of that discussion. I was present and heard it. Some opinions were averse to sending any part of that force to the Peninsula. I think that one, and one officer only, was in favor of sending the whole of it. At length the President asked me, individually, whether I thought the city would be safe with the two divisions if Franklin should be sent away. I told him I thought it would be safe, and he then wrote the order for Franklin's division to go to General McClellan. General McDowell was not present at this consultation that I remember.

I now lay before the court a letter from the President, dated April 9. It contains the passage in reference to General Blenker which I referred to in my testimony. I place it before the court more particularly because it alludes to the force left for the defense of Washington.

The President's letter referred to was read by the recorder, and is appended to the proceedings of this day and marked N.

The witness continued:

I believe I have given all of the information on that point showing the reasons why General McDowell was detained in front of Washington. I wish to be understood as stating very positively that every step taken in that matter was induced, as I believe, by great public necessity, and with very great reluctance, on the part of the President, so far as General McClellan was concerned. It was the manifest desire of the President and of the Secretary of War to send to General McClellan all the means in their power to enable him to make a successful campaign.

Question by the COURT. When did the enemy evacuate Centreville and Manassas?

Answer. In answer to that question I will state that I have seen an official report from General McClellan, dated Fairfax Court House, March 11, 8.30 p. m., in which he states that the rebels have left all their positions.

Question by the COURT. State in this connection the effect of the movement proposed by General McClellan by Urbana and the York River, referred to in the letter by the President dated February 3, 1862, before the evacuation of Centreville and Manassas by the enemy, and contrast it with the movement proposed by the President, stated in the same letter?

Answer. I can only give my impression or opinion in regard to this. I have never had any doubt myself that the movement proposed by the way of Urbana or the Peninsula was injudicious. It has always appeared to me that if the enemy could have known of this plan before abandoning his position on the Potomac and at Manassas those positions would not have been abandoned; on the contrary, my opinion has been constantly that the proposed movement of a large part of the force in front of Washington would have induced the enemy to make an effort to seize Washington. I have attached very great importance to the possession of Washington, not so much as a military point, but from its political position. Washington is the capital of the United States. The Government is here. The archives of the nation are all here. It is the depository of the original Declaration of Independence and of the Constitution of the United States. It is the residence of foreign ministers. These and many similar considerations give to this city a peculiar character. Its possession, even for a short time by the enemy, would have injured the cause of the country more than the loss of many battles at a distance from this point. I have always thought that the true mode of advance upon the enemy was something like that proposed by the President—keeping the army within striking distance of Washington in the effort to make an effective blow upon the enemy in his positions. The details of such a movement I have not particularly thought about, having had no occasion to do so.

Question by General McDOWELL. So far as you know, what has been the character of the service rendered by General McDowell—faithful and loyal, or otherwise?

Answer. I have known General McDowell many years. I have seen him on duty in the happiest relations with that honored chief Lieutenant-General Scott. I have kept my eyes upon him since this unhappy war broke out, and not the shade of a suspicion has ever crossed my mind touching his entire loyalty. From my knowledge of General McDowell it would be impossible for me to conceive him disloyal. I regard him as a true and faithful patriot.

Question by the COURT. Viewed in a military light, state the responsibilities of the movement of the Army of the Potomac to the Peninsula without leaving the force decided by the President to guard and cover Washington, if such was the fact, and the reasons which such fact would impose for detaining the corps of General McDowell in April last.

Answer. It was the opinion of the President, undoubtedly, that his order of the 8th of March, with respect to the safety of the capital, had not been complied with by General McClellan. In referring to it in his letter of the 9th of April he uses the delicate language that his instruction had been neglected. I certainly was of the same opinion; in plain terms the order had been disobeyed, and I hold it to be a military principle that whenever an officer departs from the instructions of a superior he takes upon himself the entire responsibility of all the consequences; and in the present case, when the President interposed, and by an order of his own made good his original instructions, he performed an act of high duty, to which General McClellan could properly take no exception; and if in that act he diminished the force of General McClellan, and subjected him to any evil consequences whatever, the responsibility for it was with General McClellan and not with the President.

Question by General McDOWELL. Do you know if the Secretary of War reproached General McDowell for failing to fulfill the duty imposed on him as a corps commander by the President in the matter of the force to be left for the protection of the capital?

Answer. I have no recollection of anything of that kind.

Col. EDMUND SCHRIVER, aide-de-camp, U. S. Army, a witness, was recalled.

Question by General McDOWELL. Lay before the court General Orders, No. 2.

Colonel Schriver presented General Orders, No. 2, dated Headquarters Department of the Rappahannock, Fairfax Court-House, April 10, 1862, which is appended to the proceedings of this day, marked P.

The court instructed the recorder to address a communication to the War Department, requesting the notes of the council of division commanders of the Army of the Potomac, held in Washington at the Headquarters of the Army of the Potomac and at the President's in February or March, 1862.

The court adjourned to meet to-morrow, January 17, 1863, at 11 o'clock a. m.

—

## APPENDIX.

### A.

PRESIDENT'S SPECIAL WAR ORDER, No. 1.

EXECUTIVE MANSION,
*Washington, Jan.* 31, 1862.

Ordered, That all the disposable force of the Army of the Potomac, after providing safely for the defense of Washington, be formed into an expedition for the immediate object of seizing and occupying a point upon the railroad southwestward of what is known as Manassas Junction, all details to be in the discretion of the General-in-Chief, and the expedition to move before or on the 22d day of February next.

A. LINCOLN.

### B.

EXECUTIVE MANSION,
*Washington, February* 3, 1862.

Major-General McCLELLAN:

MY DEAR SIR: You and I have distinct and different plans for a movement of the Army of the Potomac: Yours to be down the Chesapeake, up the Rappahannock to Urbana, and across land to the terminus of the railroad on the York River; mine, to move directly to a point on the railroad southwest of Manassas.

If you will give me satisfactory answers to the following questions I shall gladly yield my plan to yours:

1st Does not your plan involve a greatly larger expenditure of time and money than mine?

2d. Wherein is a victory more certain by your plan than mine?

3d. Wherein is a victory more valuable by your plan than mine?

4th. In fact would it not be less valuable in this, that it would break no great line of the enemy's communication, while mine would?

5th. In case of disaster would not a safe retreat be more difficult by your plan than by mine?

Yours, truly,

A. LINCOLN.

C.

PRESIDENT'S GENERAL WAR ORDER, No. 3.

EXECUTIVE MANSION, *Washington, March* 8, 1862.

Ordered, That no change of the base of operations of the Army of the Potomac shall be made without leaving in and about Washington such a force as in the opinion of the General-in-Chief and the commanders of all the army corps shall leave said city entirely secure.

That no more than two army corps (about 50,000 troops) of said Army of the Potomac shall be moved *en route* for a new base of operations until the navigation of the Potomac from Washington to the Chesapeake Bay shall be freed from enemy's batteries and other obstructions, or until the President shall hereafter give express permission.

That any movements as aforesaid *en route* for a new base of operations which may be ordered by the General-in-Chief, and which may be intended to move upon the Chesapeake Bay, shall begin to move upon the bay as early as the 18th day of March instant, and the General-in-Chief shall be responsible that it so move as early as that day.

Ordered, that the Army and Navy co-operate in an immediate effort to capture the enemy's batteries upon the Potomac between Washington and the Chesapeake Bay.

A. LINCOLN.

D.

HEADQUARTERS ARMY OF THE POTOMAC, *Fairfax Court-House, March* 13, 1862.

A council of the generals commanding army corps at the Headquarters Army of the Potomac were of the opinion—

I. That, the enemy having retreated from Manassas to Gordonsville, behind the Rappahannock and Rapidan, it is the opinion of the generals commanding army corps that the operations to be carried on will be best undertaken from Old Point Comfort, between the York and James River, upon Richmond, provided—

1. That the enemy's vessel Merrimac can be neutralized.
2. That the means of transportation sufficient for an immediate transfer of the force to its new base can be ready at Washington and Alexandria to move down the Potomac; and
3. That a naval auxiliary force can be had to silence or aid in silencing the enemy's batteries in York River.
4. That the force to be left to cover Washington shall be such as to give an entire feeling of security for its safety from menace.

Unanimous.

II. If the foregoing cannot be, the army should then be moved against the enemy behind the Rappahannock at the earliest possible moment, and the means for reconstructing bridges, repairing railroads, and stocking them with material sufficient for the supplying the army should at once be collected for both the Orange and Alexandria and the Aquia and Richmond Railroads.

Unanimous.

NOTE.—That, with the forts on the right bank of the Potomac fully garrisoned, and those on the left bank occupied, a covering force in front of the Virginia line of 25,000 men would suffice.

KEYES.
[HEINTZELMAN.]
McDOWELL.

A total of 40,000 men for the defense of the city would suffice.

SUMNER.

E.

WAR DEPARTMENT,
*March* 13, 1862.

Maj. Gen. GEORGE B. McCLELLAN:

The President, having considered the plan of operations agreed upon by yourself and the commanders of army corps, makes no objection to the same, but gives the following directions as to its execution:

1st. Leave such force at Manassas Junction as shall make it entirely certain that the enemy shall not repossess himself of that position and line of communication.

2d. Leave Washington entirely secure.

3d. Move the remainder of the force down the Potomac, choosing a new base at Fort Monroe or anywhere between here and there, or at all events move such remainder of the army at once in pursuit of the enemy by some route.

Seven o'clock 40 minutes.

EDWIN M. STANTON,
*Secretary of War.*

F.

HEADQUARTERS MILITARY DISTRICT OF WASHINGTON,
*Washington, D. C., April* 2, 1862.

Hon. SECRETARY OF WAR:

SIR: I have the honor to submit the following condensed statements of the forces left under my command for the defense of Washington:

| | |
|---|---|
| Infantry | 15,335 |
| Artillery | 4,294 |
| Cavalry (six companies only mounted) | 848 |
| Total | 20,477 |
| Deduct sick and in arrest and confinement | 1,455 |
| Total present for duty | 19,022 |

I have no mounted light artillery under my command. Several companies of the reserve artillery of the Army of the Potomac are still here, but not under my command or fit for service.

From this force I am ordered by General McClellan to detail two regiments (good ones) to Richardson's division (Sumner's corps) as it passes through Alexandria; one regiment to replace the Thirty-seventh New York Volunteers in Heintzelman's old division; one regiment to relieve a regiment of Hooker's division at Budd's Ferry; total, four regiments. I am also further ordered this morning by telegraph to send 4,000 men to relieve General Sumner at Manassas and Warrenton, that he may embark forthwith.

In regard to the character and efficiency of the troops under my command, I have to state that nearly all the force is new and imperfectly disciplined; that several of the regiments are in a very disorganized condition from various causes, which it is not necessary to state here. Several regiments having been relieved from brigades which have gone into the field in consequence of their unfitness for service, the best regiments remaining have been selected to take their place. Two heavy artillery regiments and one infantry regiment which had been drilled for some months in artillery service have been withdrawn from the forts on the south side of the Potomac, and I have only been able to fill their places with very new infantry regiments, entirely unacquainted with the duties of that arm, and of little or no value in thier present position.

I am not informed of the position which Major-General Banks is directed to take, but at this time he is, as I understand, on the other side of the Bull Run Mountains, leaving my command to cover the front from Manassas Gap (about 20 miles beyond Manassas) to Aquia Creek.

I deem it my duty to state that, looking at the numerical strength and character of the force under my command, it is, in my judgment, entirely inadequate to, and unfit for, the important duty to which it is assigned.

I regard it very improbable that the enemy will assail us at this point, but this belief is based upon the hope that they may be promptly engaged elsewhere and may not learn the number and character of the force left here.

I have the honor to be, your obedient servant,

JAS. S. WADSWORTH,
*Brigadier-General, Commanding.*

---

## APPENDIX.

### G.

WAR DEPARTMENT,
*Washington City, D. C., April* 19, 1862.

The Secretary of War desires General Wadsworth to assume a supposed attack by the enemy on Washington; that General Wadsworth hears of it on the receipt of this memorandum, and gives immediate orders to meet it by calling out his force, to be placed in line of battle; that Assistant Adjutant-General Jones, as inspector-general, be directed to report to the War Department in person the number and condition of the troops three hours after this order shall have been given.

By command of the Secretary of War:

E. A. HITCHCOCK,
*Major-General, on duty in the War Department.*

### H.

WAR DEPARTMENT,
*Washington City, April* 19, 1862.

*Report of Assistant Inspector-General Maj. Roger Jones of the forces assembled at 7 o'clock p. m. at north end of Long Bridge and Aqueduct.*

General Wadsworth received the order of the Secretary at 2.45 p. m. Came to War Office at 3.15 p. m. to get the order revoked, which was refused, and at 3.30 p. m. General Wadsworth left to execute it. At 4 p. m. he issued his orders.

At the Aqueduct the following troops assembled:

| | Armed. | Ammunition. | Men. |
|---|---|---|---|
| A German regiment | Muskets | 10 rounds | 948 |
| 102d New York, Colonel Wadsworth, [?] two companies | do | None } | 536 |
| 102d New York, Colonel Wadsworth, [?] four companies | do | 40 rounds } | |
| 86th New York } City Guard, { four companies | do | Little } | 200 |
| 10th New Jersey, } City Guard, { one company | do | do } | |
| | | | 1,684 |

The last-named men reached ground at 8 p. m.

LONG BRIDGE.

| | Armed. | Ammunition. | Men. |
|---|---|---|---|
| 91st Pennsylvania Regiment arrived 7.30 p. m. | Muskets | Sufficient | 560 |
| 10th New Jersey, four companies, arrived 8 p. m. | do | None | 180 |
| 2d Regiment District Volunteers arrived 8 p. m. | do | 35 rounds | 600 |
| 3d New York Cavalry (Colonel Mix): Good horses; all revolvers and sabers, and ammunition; one company, carbines and ammunition. | | | 575 |
| 4th Pennsylvania, three squadrons of cavalry: Sabers and revolvers; no ammunition. | | | 250 |
| Two batteries Rocket Battalion, two companies; one company reached ground 8.45 p. m.; the other company reached ground 9.30 p. m.; eight guns, with ammunition. | | | 160 |
| Maine Artillery, one battery; only obtained guns yesterday; horses to-day; no ammunition; six rifled guns. | | | 115 |
| Total at Long Bridge | | | 2,440 |
| Total at Aqueduct | | | 1,684 |
| Aggregate | | | 4,124 |

Colonel Mix's cavalry regiment the most efficient regiment by far.

I.

HEADQUARTERS ARMY OF THE POTOMAC,
*Steamer Commodore, April* 1, 1862.

Brig. Gen. LORENZO THOMAS,
*Adjutant-General U. S. Army:*

GENERAL: I have to request that you will lay the following communication before the honorable Secretary of War.

The approximate numbers and positions of the troops left near and in rear of the Potomac are about as follows:

General Dix has, after guarding the railroads under his charge, sufficient troops to give him 5,000 for the defense of Baltimore and 1,988 available for the Eastern Shore, Annapolis, &c. Fort Delaware is very well garrisoned by about 400 men.

The garrisons of the forts around Washington amount to 10,600 men; other disposable troops now with General Wadsworth being about 11,400 men.

The troops employed in guarding the various railways in Maryland amount to some 3,359 men. These it is designed to relieve, being old regiments, by dismounted cavalry, and to send forward to Manassas.

General Abercrombie occupies Warrenton with a force which, in cluding Colonel Geary at White Plains and the cavalry to be at his disposal, will amount to some 7,780 men, with twelve pieces of artillery. I have the honor to request that all the troops organized for service in Pennsylvania and New York and in any of the Eastern States may be ordered to Washington. I learn from Governor Curtin that there are some 3,500 men now ready in Pennsylvania. This force I should be glad to have sent at once to Manassas. Four thousand men from General Wadsworth I desire to be ordered to Manassas. These troops, with the railroad guards above alluded to, will make up a force under the command of General Abercrombie to something like 18,639 men.

It is my design to push General Blenker's division from Warrenton upon Strasburg. He should remain at Strasburg, too, long enough to allow matters to assume a definite form in that region before proceeding to his ultimate destination.

The troops in the valley of the Shenandoah will thus, including Blenker's division, 10,028 strong, with twenty-four pieces of artillery; Banks' Fifth Corps, which embraces the command of General Shields, 19,687 strong, with forty-one guns; some 3,652 disposable cavalry and the railroad guards, about 2,100 men, amount to about 35,467 men.

It is designed to relieve General Hooker by some regiment, say 850 men, leaving, with some 500 cavalry, 1,350 men on the Lower Potomac.

To recapitulate:

| | Men. |
|---|---|
| At Warrenton there is to be | 7,780 |
| At Manassas, say | 10,859 |
| In the valley of the Shenandoah | 35,467 |
| On the Lower Potomac | 1,350 |
| In all | 55,456 |

There would thus be left for the garrisons and the front of Washington under General Wadsworth some 18,000 men, exclusive of the batteries under instruction.

The troops organizing or ready for service in New York, I learn, will probably number more than 4,000. These should be assembled at Washington, subject to disposition where their services may be most needed.

I am, very respectfully, your obedient servant,

GEO. B. McCLELLAN,
*Major-General, Commanding.*

K.

WAR DEPARTMENT,
*Washington City, April* 2, 1862.

Adjutant-General THOMAS and Major-General HITCHCOCK:

GENERALS: I beg leave to refer to you the following papers:

1st. The President's War [Order], No. 3, dated March 8, 1862.

2d. The reports of a council held at Headquarters, Fairfax Court-House, March 13, marked B.

3d. The President's instructions to General McClellan, March 13, marked C.

4th. The reports of Major-General McClellan, dated on board the steamer Commodore, April 1, addressed to the Adjutant-General.

5th. The report of General Wadsworth as to the forces in his command, and upon examination, I desire you to report to me whether the President's order and instructions have been complied with in respect to the forces to be left for the defense of Washington and its security; and at Manassas; and if not, wherein those instructions have been departed from.

Yours, truly,

EDWIN M. STANTON,
*Secretary of War.*

L.

WASHINGTON, D. C., *April* 2, 1862.

In compliance with your instructions we have examined the papers submitted to us and have the honor to make the following report:

1. The President's War Orders, No. 3, dated March 8, requires that on taking up any new base of operations the city of Washington shall be left entirely secure. The other points of the order it is unnecessary to consider, as the enemy since its date have abandoned their positions and batteries on the Potomac and retired behind the Rappahannock.

2. The council of general officers held at Fairfax Court-House March 13 took place after the enemy had retired from Manassas and destroyed the railroad in their rear. The council decided unanimously to take up a new base of operations from Fort Monroe, and three of the generals (a majority) decided that the force necessary to be left should be sufficient to fully garrison the forts on the right bank of the Potomac and to occupy those on the left bank, with a covering force of 25,000. It is, we think, the judgment of officers that some 30,000 men would be necessary thus to man these forts, which, with the number of the covering force, would make a total of 55,000.

3. The President's directions of March 13 to General McClellan direct—

1st. To leave such a force at Manassas Junction as shall make it entirely certain that the enemy may not repossess it.

2d. That Washington shall be left entirely secure.

3d. That the remainder of the army move down the Potomac or move in pursuit of the enemy.

In regard to occupying Manassas Junction, as the enemy have destroyed the railroads leading to it, it may be fair to assume that they have no intention of returning for the re-occupation of their late position, and therefore no very large force would be necessary to hold that position.

4. Major-General McClellan's report to the Adjutant-General of April 1, after giving the several positions of the troops proposed to be left for the defense of Washington, gives a representation as follows:

| | Men. |
|---|---|
| At Warrenton there is to be | 7,780 |
| At Manassas, say | 10,859 |
| In the valley of the Shenandoah | 35,467 |
| On the Lower Potomac | 1,350 |
| In all | 55,456 |

and there would be left for the garrisons and the front of Washington under General Wadsworth some 18,000.

In the above enumeration General Banks' army corps is included, but whether this corps, operating in the Shenandoah Valley, should be regarded as part of the force available for the protection of the immediate front of Washington the undersigned express no opinion.

5. General Wadsworth's report of April 2 gives his force as follows:

| | |
|---|---|
| Infantry | 15,335 |
| Artillery | 4,294 |
| Cavalry (six companies only mounted) | 848 |
| | 20,477 |
| Deduct sick, in arrest, and confinement | 1,455 |
| Total for duty | 19,022 |

From this force General Wadsworth is directed to detach two good regiments from Richardson's division (Sumner's corps), which should be deducted from his command; one regiment to replace the Thirty-seventh New York in Heintzelman's old division, and one regiment to relieve a regiment of Hooker's division at Budd's Ferry; total, four regiments. He is also ordered to send 4,000 men to relieve Sumner at Manassas and Warrenton.

General Wadsworth represents that he has no mounted light artillery under his command; states there are several companies of reserve artillery still here, but not under his command or fit for service.

General Wadsworth further reports that nearly all the force is new and imperfectly disciplined; that several of the regiments are in a very disorganized condition, some of them having been relieved from brigades which have gone into the field in consequence of their unfitness for service, the best regiments remaining having been selected to take their places. Two heavy artillery regiments and one infantry regiment which had been drilled for months in artillery service having been withdrawn from the forts on the south side of the Potomac and their places supplied with new infantry regiments entirely unacquainted with the duties of that arm and of little or no value in their present position.

If there was need of a military force for the safety of the city of Washington within its own limits that referred to in the report of General Wadsworth would seem to be entirely inadequate.

In view of the opinion expressed by the council of the commanders of army corps of the force necessary for the defense of the capital, though not numerically stated, and of the force represented by General McClellan as left for that purpose, we are of opinion that the requirements of the President that this city shall be left "entirely secure," not only in the opinion of the General-in-Chief, but that of the "commanders of the army corps" also, has not been fully complied with.

All of which is respectfully submitted.

L. THOMAS,
*Adjutant-General.*
E. A. HITCHCOCK,
*Major-General Volunteers, U. S. Army.*

M.

*Copy of a paper handed to the President by General Hitchcock.*

MARCH 30, 1862.

The main line of the enemy extends from Richmond through Chattanooga and Corinth to Memphis, and at Corinth there is a connection South.

General Halleck (at Saint Louis) is acting upon the west of this line, with General Buell as his immediate commander, having Corinth in view as one object and some point at or near the Cumberland Gap as another object.

General McClellan (before Yorktown) has Richmond for his object, with Washington under his safe-keeping. The immediate interest of the war is connected with the above indications, and all adjacent operations are incidental.

It is necessary to break the line of communication between Richmond and Corinth. This may be done by Buell, and if he should occupy the Cumberland Gap near the railroad this object will be sufficiently accomplished. If some point east of the Gap be also made an object (as proposed by the President), it will require a large force to reach and maintain it, or that force might be destroyed by the enemy. Instead, therefore, of employing a force necessary for seizing a point east of the Gap, it might be better to employ a less force in the protection of the Baltimore and Ohio Railroad (the duty assigned to General Frémont). From present indications it might be better, instead of sending to the Mountain Department all of the force desired by its commander, to divide that force—one part to go to him for the protection of the Baltimore and Ohio Railroad and the country immediately south of it, and the other part to strengthen McClellan's right, now occupied by Shields, the route from Richmond in that direction being open to the enemy, who, though not likely to take it, might be invited by its weakness to make some desperate attempt similar to one already made by Jackson upon Shields.

A movement from McClellan's left is known to the enemy; hence nothing is more natural than a blow on McClellan's right. Nothing has intervened since that made a few days since to prevent a repetition of it with a larger force.

If McClellan should fail (at Yorktown)—not likely to happen; but if he should fail—what would be the movement of the enemy? It might be a desperate attempt to turn the right of the Army of the Potomac (the Shenandoah Valley). This should be guarded against by a part of the force called for by Frémont, instead of sending that force to cut the Richmond and Knoxville Railroad, the success of which might even aid in forcing the enemy to make some desperate attempt on the right of Washington.

N.

WASHINGTON, *April* 9, 1862.

Major-General MCCLELLAN:

MY DEAR SIR: Your dispatches complaining that you are not properly sustained, while they do not offend me, do pain me very much.

Blenker's division was withdrawn from you before you left here, and you knew the pressure under which I did it, and, as I thought, acquiesced in it—certainly not without reluctance.

After you left I ascertained that less than 20,000 unorganized men, without a single field battery, were all you designed to be left for the defense of Washington and Manassas Junction, and part of this even was to go to General Hooker's old position. General Banks' corps, once designed for Manassas Junction, was divided and tied up on the line of Winchester and Strasburg, and could not leave it without again exposing the Upper Potomac and the Baltimore and Ohio Railroad. This presented (or would present, when McDowell and Sumner should be gone) a great temptation to the enemy to turn back from the Rappahannock and sack Washington. My explicit order that Washington should, by the judgment of all the commanders of corps, be left entirely secure had been neglected. It was precisely this that drove me to detain McDowell.

I do not forget that I was satisfied with your arrangements to leave Banks at Manassas Junction, but when that arrangement was broken up and nothing was substituted for it of course I was not satisfied. I was constrained to substitute something for it myself.

And now allow me to ask, "Do you really think I should permit the line from Richmond via Manassas Junction to this city to be entirely open, except what resistance could be presented by less than 20,000 unorganized troops?" This is a question which the country will not allow me to evade.

There is a curious mystery about the number of the troops now with you. When I telegraphed you on the 6th, saying you had over 100,000 with you, I had just obtained from the Secretary of War a statement, taken as he said from your own returns, making 108,000 then with you and *en route* to you. You now say you will have but 85,000 when all *en route* to you shall have reached you. How can this discrepancy of 35,000 be accounted for?

As to General Wool's command, I understand it is doing for you precisely what a like number of your own would have to do if that command was away. I suppose the whole force which has gone forward to you is with you by this time, and, if so, I think it is the precise time for you to strike a blow. By delay the enemy will relatively gain upon you; that is, he will gain faster by fortifications and re-enforcements than you can by re-enforcements alone.

And once more let me tell you it is indispensable to you that you strike a blow. I am powerless to help this. You will do me the justice to remember I always insisted that going down the bay in search of a field instead of fighting at or near Manassas was only shifting and not surmounting a difficulty; that we would find the same enemy and the same or equal intrenchments at either place. The country will not fail to note—is noting now—that the present hesitation to move upon an intrenched enemy is but the story of Manassas repeated.

I beg to assure you that I have never written you or spoken to you in greater kindness of feeling than now, nor with a fuller purpose to sustain you, so far as in my most anxious judgment I consistently can; but you must act.

Yours, very truly,

A. LINCOLN.

P.

GENERAL ORDERS, No. 2. } HDQRS. DEPARTMENT OF RAPPAHANNOCK, *Fairfax Court-House, April* 10, 1862.

I. The powers which, as military governor and commander of the District of Columbia, Brigadier-General Wadsworth may have received from the Headquarters of the Army of the Potomac have in no way been restricted or modified in the creation of the Department of the Rappahannock.

II. In addition to the limits of his command, as heretofore defined, Brigadier-General Wadsworth will, in the absence of the major-general commanding the department, have charge and do whatever may be needful in that part of the department east of the Potomac, and of so much of the counties of Fairfax, Loudoun, and Prince William, Virginia, as are not now and shall not hereafter be occupied by the divisions of Franklin, McCall, and King.

By command of Major-General McDowell:

SAML. BRECK,
*Assistant Adjutant-General.*

*FORTY-SIXTH DAY.*

COURT-ROOM, COR. FOURTEENTH AND PA. AVENUE,
*Washington, D. C., January* 17, 1863.

* * * * * * *

The presiding officer of the court instructed the recorder to produce and read the letter from Major-General McClellan to Major-General N. P. Banks, dated Headquarters Army of the Potomac, on board the Commodore, April 1, 1862, which letter was received by the court January 9, 1863. The letter was read by the recorder, and is appended to the proceedings of this day, marked A.

Lieut. Col. DAVIS TILLSON, Maine Artillery, a witness, was recalled.

Question by General MCDOWELL. Were you with General King's division on or near the Warrenton turnpike at the time it became engaged with the enemy on the evening of the 28th of August last?

Answer. I was.

Question by General MCDOWELL. State the position of the enemy on that occasion with respect to the Warrenton turnpike.

Answer. The enemy were upon a road leading, as I understand, from Sudley Springs to Hay Market, and approaching in the direction, on this road, from Sudley Springs. The head of their column was nearly opposite that point upon the turnpike from which General Reynolds' division had been shelled in the morning by the enemy. The road from Sudley Springs to Hay Market apparently approached Warrenton turnpike slightly, and is about a mile and a half north from Warrenton turnpike.

Question by General MCDOWELL. What was the condition of the artillery and artillery ammunition in King's division after the engagement.

Answer. It was in its usual condition, with the exception that one of Captain Monroe's caissons had been blown up by his own order in consequence of breaking stock and the inability to move it. I think a very few horses had been killed and only a small amount of ammunition expended.

Question by General MCDOWELL. Did you accompany General McDowell on the morning of the 30th of August in a reconnaissance in front of the right of our line?

Answer. I did.

Question by General MCDOWELL. Did you learn, in the course of this reconnaissance, where the left of the enemy had been on the 29th? If so, state where it was, with reference to Bull Run.

Answer. I did learn from General Heintzelman, who was present with General McDowell, and also, I think, from Colonel Allen, of the Maine cavalry, the position previously occupied by the enemy, which was on the Centreville side of Bull Run.

Question by General MCDOWELL. Was this to the north of the Warrenton pike?

Answer. It was.

Question by General MCDOWELL. Can you state how far?

Answer, I can simply say some miles. I should say in the vicinity of 5 or 6 miles, but in this I may be incorrect.

Question by General MCDOWELL. About what hour was it that King's division commenced to withdraw from its position where it engaged the enemy?

Answer. From 11 to 12 o'clock.

Question by General McDOWELL. By what route did King's division retire from the battle-field?

Answer. Over the road leading to Manassas Junction.

Question by the COURT. How near was that road to the route over which he had marched to the Warrenton pike when turned back on the preceding day?

Answer. I think it was the same road, or nearly so.

Question by the COURT. Had you knowledge during the 28th of the order to turn back to the Warrenton pike?

Answer. I had not.

Question by the COURT. How far had you proceeded toward Manassas Junction on the 28th when you turned back?

Answer. About a mile.

Question by the COURT. Were you in the company of General McDowell at the time when you turned back?

Answer. I was.

Question by the COURT. After turning back, how far did you progress before the action with the enemy?

Answer. About 2 miles.

Question by the COURT. Did you remain with the artillery when it retired that night?

Answer. I think I remained until after it had retired, and came away with General King.

Question by the COURT. Was there any difficulty, owing to the darkness of the night or the nature of the roads or country, in finding your way back near to Manassas Junction, either for yourselves or your artillery? And, if so, state it.

Answer. I know of no difficulty whatever. The roads were very good, and through open fields mostly.

Question by the COURT. What was the character of the night as to obscurity?

Answer. It was quite dark. My impression is that [it] was cloudy.

Question by General McDOWELL. Did King's division, in retiring from the engagement, go back over the turnpike before it turned off for Manassas?

Answer. I think it did.

Question by General McDOWELL. Did the road you then took lead you by Bethlehem Church or south of Bethlehem Church?

Answer. I think by Bethlehem Courch.

Question by General McDOWELL. State if the course you took, as described, would be the same as one a person would take in going from Manassas direct to the battle ground?

Answer. No, it would not, looking at the map.

Question by the COURT. Did you start from the battle intending to go direct to Manassas Junction?

Answer. We started to go to Manassas Junction, but whether by the most direct route I do not know.

Question by the COURT. If you have knowledge, state whether there was any other route to Manassas Junction more direct or favorable than the one over which you marched.

Answer. The route we took was the only one of which I have any personal knowledge.

Capt. ROBERT CHANDLER, assistant adjutant-general, U. S. Volunteers, a witness, was duly sworn.

Question by General MCDOWELL. Were you at Falmouth, opposite Fredericksburg, last spring and part of last summer?

Answer. Yes, sir.

Question by General MCDOWELL. Do you know what became of the wheat harvested from the fields in the vicinity of the Lacy house?

Answer. A field of from 40 to 60 acres of wheat on the east of the Lacy house was harvested by the post quartermaster then at Falmouth; afterward thrashed and ground up into flour and furnished to our troops. This was the same field that was protected by General McDowell while our troops were there.

The court adjourned to meet on Monday, January 19, 1863, at 11 o'clock a. m.

---

## APPENDIX.

### A.

HEADQUARTERS ARMY OF THE POTOMAC,
*On board the Commodore, April* 1, 1862.

Maj. Gen. N. P. BANKS,
*Commanding Fifth Corps:*

GENERAL: The change in affairs in the valley of the Shenandoah has rendered necessary a corresponding departure—temporarily at least—from the plan we some days since agreed upon. In my arrangements I assume that you have with you a force amply sufficient to drive Jackson before you, provided he is not re-enforced largely. I also assume that you may find it impossible to detach anything toward Manassas for some days, probably not until the operations of the main army have drawn all the rebel force toward Richmond.

You are aware that General Sumner has for some days been at Warrenton Junction, with two divisions of infantry, six batteries, and two regiments of cavalry, and that a reconnaissance to the Rappahannock forced the enemy to destroy the railway bridge at Rappahannock Station, on the Orange and Alexandria Railroad. Since that time our cavalry have found nothing on this side of the Rappahannock in that direction, and it seems clear that we have no reason to fear any return of the rebels in that quarter. Their movements near Fredericksburg also indicate a final abandonment of that neighborhood. I doubt whether Johnston will now re-enforce Jackson with a view to offensive operations; the time has probably passed when he could have gained anything by doing so. I have ordered in one of Sumner's divisions (that of Richardson, late Sumner's) to Alexandria for embarkation. Blenker's has been detached from the Army of the Potomac and ordered to report to General Frémont.

Abercrombie is probably at Warrenton Junction to-day; Geary at White Plains.

Two regiments of cavalry have been ordered out and are now on the way to relieve the two regiments of Sumner.

Four thousand infantry and one battery leave Washington at once for Manassas; some 3,000 more will move in one or two days, and soon after some 3,000 additional.

I will order Blenker to march on Strasburg and to report to you for temporary duty, so that, should you find a large force in your front, you can avail yourself of his aid. As soon as possible please direct him on Winchester, thence to report to the Adjutant-General of the Army for orders, but keep him until you are sure what you have in front.

In regard to your own movements, the most important thing at present is to throw Jackson well back and then to assume such a position as to enable you to prevent his return. As soon as the railway communications are re-established it will be probably important and advisable to move on Staunton, but this would require secure communications and a force of from 25,000 to 30,000 for active operations. It should also be nearly coincident with my own move on Richmond; at all events not so long before it as to enable the rebels to concentrate on you and then return on me. I fear that you cannot be ready in time, although it may come in very well, with a force less than that I have mentioned, after the main battle near Richmond. When General Sumner leaves Warrenton Junction General Abercrombie will be placed in immediate command of Manassas and Warrenton Junction under your general orders. Please inform me frequently by telegraph and otherwise as to the state of things in your front.

I am, very truly, yours,

GEO. B. McCLELLAN,
*Major-General, Commanding.*

P. S.—From what I have just learned it would seem that the two regiments of cavalry intended for Warrenton Junction have gone to Harper's Ferry. Of the four additional regiments placed under your orders, two should, as promptly as possible, move by the shortest route on Warrenton Junction.

I am, sir, very respectfully, your obedient servant,

GEO. B. McCLELLAN,
*Major-General, Commanding.*

CITY OF NEW YORK, *January* 3, 1863.

**A true copy.**

S. WILLIAMS,
*Assistant Adjutant-General.*

---

*FORTY-SEVENTH DAY.*

COURT-ROOM, COR. FOURTEENTH AND PA. AVENUE,
*Washington, D. C., January* 19, 1863.

* * * * * * *

Lieut. Col. DAVIS TILLSON, Maine Artillery, a witness, was recalled.

Question by General McDOWELL. Were you with General McDowell on the 29th of August last, on the occasion of his march from near Bethlehem Church, with King's and Ricketts' divisions, up the Sudley Springs road to the battle-field?

Answer I was.

Question by General McDOWELL. On that march were you sent forward by General McDowell to the head of the column with orders to the division commander of King's division?

Answer. I was.

Question by General McDOWELL. What were those orders?

Answer. That King's division should form on the left of General Reynolds' division.

Question by General McDOWELL. Did you see General McDowell himself take measures to cause that division to move forward and form on the left of Reynolds?

Answer. I did.

Question by the COURT. What were the measures taken by General McDowell?

Answer. Going to the head of General King's division, directing the chief of artillery to bring up the batteries and move them forward rapidly, sending orders by his aides to the different commanders of King's division to bring up their troops quickly, and, I think, himself going to the front and directing the disposition of Captain Monroe's battery.

Question by the COURT. State as nearly as you can, the time of day.

Answer. I am very doubtful as to the time, but should say it was between 4 and 5 o'clock that these measures were commenced, but later when completed.

Question by the COURT. What was done on the day of the 29th, prior to the beginning of the movement described by you, viz, at 4 p. m.?

Answer. About noon of the 29th—it may have been earlier—General McDowell and staff left Manassas Junction and went forward to where General King's division halted in the morning, gave the necessary directions as to the order in which the troops should march, went forward with the troops, and was occupied in moving forward, as before stated, until after dark. What General McDowell did preceding noon I have no knowledge.

Question by the COURT. Why did he not move earlier than at noon?

Answer. I am not able to say further than it may have been earlier than noon, as I have before stated.

Question by the COURT. Where was General Reynolds?

Answer. I do not know definitely; I was not with him during that day.

Question by the COURT. Why did General McDowell go by Sudley Springs road instead of back by the way the divisions of King and Ricketts came?

Answer. In order more rapidly to get his troops forward and into action, General Porter being in his (General McDowell's) front.

Question by the COURT. How did it happen that General Porter got in General McDowell's front?

Answer. I have no knowledge whatever.

Question by the COURT. Were the movements that day, which were ordered or superintended by General McDowell, made with the rapidity which, under such circumstances, the exigency of the case would seem to demand?

Answer. General McDowell was himself very active and energetic, making every effort to get the troops forward; whether his orders were as promptly and actively executed as they should have been by all the different commanders I am unable to say, not being in a position where I could see but a portion of the command. The movement from the position where the troops started, near Manassas Junction, until they reached the vicinity of the battle-field, was the ordinary rate of march. I should say the distance was about 5 or 6 miles.

Question by the COURT. At what time during the night of the 28th did King's division start for the point it reached during the night and at what time did it halt?

Answer. I think the moving commenced between 11 and 12 o'clock. We halted some time after daylight in the morning. I am uncertain about the time; it was after sunrise, and may have been 8 o'clock. I think the portion of the column that we were with—about the middle of the column—halted at about 8 o'clock.

Col. ED. SCHRIVER, aide-de-camp, U. S. Army, a witness, was recalled.

Question by General MCDOWELL. Can you state if General McDowell was active on the 29th of August in getting his troops on the road to Gainesville, as ordered by General Pope? About what hour was it when the troops got on the way?

Answer. I answer, yes. I think they moved between 8 and 9 o'clock in the morning.

Question by General MCDOWELL. Did General McDowell, after his troops had gotten on the march and had come to a halt, go forward personally to the head of General Porter's column?

Answer. Yes.

Question by General MCDOWELL. Was he not engaged in consultation with General Porter at the head of the column? Was he not also occupied with General Porter in making a reconnaissance of the front?

Answer. Yes.

Question by General MCDOWELL. When he left General Porter did he go rapidly back to the head of his own column? If so, state how rapidly.

Answer. I became separated from General McDowell a moment, and on inquiring where he went was told by an orderly that he had gone in a certain direction, pointing it out. He went so fast that he was out of my sight, and I therefore was unwilling and unable to follow him in the direction he went, not being acquainted in the direction of the route. I therefore retraced my steps (my mode of coming to Porter's headquarters), and thence by the road went back to the head of our column, where I found General McDowell, and where I learned he had gone across the fields by a short cut.

Question by General MCDOWELL. When he reached the head of his own column do you know if he took immediate measures to turn it off on the Sudley Springs road?

Answer. I think I saw the troops moving on that road when I got there.

Question by the COURT. What time did General McDowell turn his column on the Sudley Springs road?

Answer. It was some time in the afternoon, but I cannot tell when. I made no note of it.

Question by the COURT. How far had his column been moved by his orders during the preceding portion of the day?

Answer. I think it must have been 4 to 5 miles; probably more than that. The distance from Manassas to where he halted was probably 3 miles.

Question by the COURT. At what time did General McDowell part with General Porter?

Answer. I can't tell.

Question by the COURT. Early in the morning of the 29th at what time did General McDowell reach Reynolds' division, and how far was it from the place where he bivouacked near Sigel's corps?

Answer. He reached it very early in the morning. I can't tell the hour nor can I now tell the distance.

Question by the COURT. Where did General McDowell learn that King had retired during the night?

Answer. It was at Reynolds' headquarters, I think, but I can't remember when.

Question by the COURT. How long did he remain with Reynolds' division after arriving there?

Answer. I cannot state the time. We took breakfast there.

Question by the COURT. On arriving at Reynolds' division, did General McDowell dispatch any aide-de-camp or other officer or messenger to halt King's column or to intercept Ricketts' division and halt it?

Answer. Not to my knowledge.

Question by the COURT. By what route did General McDowell return to Manassas?

Answer. I cannot remember. I remember that we went to the Weir house first, but the route I cannot tell. I do not know that we did not return by way of Bethlehem Church.

General McDowell informed the court that Major Willard, aide-de-camp, can give evidence on the matter under present consideration.

Question by the COURT. Do you know how it happened that in returning McDowell's corps followed instead of leading Porter's?

Answer. No, I do not know, unless it was so ordered. I do not know whether it was so ordered or not.

Question by General McDOWELL. Witness states General McDowell remained at Reynolds' quarters to take breakfast. Can witness state if General McDowell had eaten a meal since the 27th?

Answer. No, I can't say, but have reason to believe that he had not.

Question by General McDOWELL. Does the witness recollect if, on coming to Manassas, General McDowell did not meet General Porter before he found his own division, and if Porter's division did not get their orders before General McDowell's division got theirs?

Answer. I can't remember that.

Question by General McDOWELL. Does the witness recollect if General Porter, when General McDowell met him, had not already received an order from General Pope to move his corps on the road to Gainesville?

Answer. I do not.

Question by General McDOWELL. Can the witness state if the country between the Warrenton pike, Bull Run, the Sudley Springs road, and the Manassas Railroad does not contain many of the old hutted camps or winter quarters of the enemy?

Answer. Yes.

Question by General McDOWELL. Does the witness recollect if there are not many cross-roads leading to and from these various camps?

Answer. Yes.

Question by General McDOWELL. Does witness recollect if it was not some time after the troops of Porter and King were on the march before Ricketts' division could be brought into the road?

Answer. I have no recollection of it.

Question by General McDOWELL. Lay before the court the communications which passed between General McDowell and General Pope on the 26th and 27th of August.

The communications referred to in the foregoing question were read by the recorder and are appended to the proceedings of this day.*

The court adjourned to meet to-morrow, January 20, 1863, at 11 o'clock a. m.

---

### *FORTY-EIGHTH DAY.*

COURT-ROOM, COR. FOURTEENTH AND PA. AVENUE,
*Washington, D. C., January* 20, 1863.

* * * * * * *

Brig. Gen. WILLIAM F. BARRY, U. S. Volunteers, a witness, was duly sworn.

Question by the COURT. What is your rank in the Army?

Answer. I am a major of artillery in the Army of the United States and a brigadier-general of volunteers.

Question by the COURT. Were you on duty in March and April last? If so, where and in what capacity?

Answer. I was on duty in March and April of last year as chief of artillery of the Army of the Potomac, commanded by Major-General McClellan.

Question by the COURT. State if you made any report at that time to Major-General McClellan respecting the force of artillery to be left in and about Washington for the defense of the capital.

Answer. I did not at that time. I did previously to that time, in connection with General Barnard, the chief engineer of the Army of the Potomac. We made a joint report of the number of troops. I think this was in February. This report was a long one, and one showing the force necessary to garrison the defenses fully and partially. I have no copy of the report. It was an official report, and I suppose is on file. The report stated in detail the amount and strength of the artillery and the number of infantry necessary to be stationed at the forts.

Question by the COURT. State fully and particularly what was the artillery force left by Major-General McClellan for the defense of Washington.

Answer. With regard to the field batteries I can state that seven were left in a camp about three-quarters of a mile east of the Capitol, in the city of Washington. These batteries number, I think, thirty-two guns. At that time the returns of troops in the forts were made to General Doubleday, who had relieved me, and I therefore cannot answer respecting the garrison of the forts. Of the seven batteries, three were fully equipped and fit for service. Three others were fully equipped, with the exception of horses, of which they had an insufficient number. The remaining battery, the Sixteenth New York Battery, had reported but a few days previous, and had no equipments at all. There was at the time an abundance of material at the Washington Arsenal to have immediately equipped this battery. The three batteries without horses could have immediately been furnished with them. There was no design nor intention to withdraw any of these batteries for the Army of the Potomac, and they were not withdrawn.

Question by the COURT. Were those field batteries fully and efficiently manned? Were the artillerists composed of the new levies? Did any portion of the force consist of the regular artillery?

Answer. The field batteries were as fully and efficiently manned as the majority of batteries in the Army of the Potomac. With the exception of the Sixteenth New York Battery they had all been under instruction for about two months. One of them, the Ninth New York Battery, had been under instruction for about six months. They were all volunteer batteries.

---

*These communications, being duplicated in McDowell's report of campaign from August 16 to September 2, are omitted from appendix.

Question by the COURT. Why were the three batteries with insufficient supply of horses not supplied before the departure of the army, and why was not the Sixteenth New York Battery supplied with equipments?

Answer. Those batteries had once been supplied with horses, but at the last hour a division was made up for General Casey, and I was called upon to furnish it with the requisite field batteries. As there was no time then to instruct new horses, or to select others from the quartermaster's yards, I directed the deficiency of horses in the batteries assigned to Casey's division (that deficiency amounting to about 100 horses) to be made good by the batteries which were to be left in Washington, knowing that in a few hours they could get new horses, and would have an abundance of time and opportunity to instruct them. That answers the first part of the question. I have stated that the Sixteenth New York Battery had only reported a few days before. It had also been directed, in special orders from the War Department, to report to General Wadsworth, and I had no further control over it.

Question by the COURT. In describing the field batteries left by you, do you speak from actual personal inspection of them at or near the time when the army went to the Peninsula; and, if so, when did you make such inspection?

Answer. I speak from an actual inspection made by me about the middle of March, and also from an official return made to me by the commanding officer of the camp where these batteries were—about the 3d of April. This return was sent to me while I was on the Peninsula, the commanding officer thinking he was still under my command, which was not the case.

Question by General McDOWELL. Can the witness state the names of the seven field batteries left for the defense of Washington, giving the names of those fully equipped and the names of those partially equipped?

Answer. Battery C, First New York Artillery, Captain Barnes; Battery K, First New York Artillery, Captain Crounse; Battery L, Second New York Artillery, Captain Robinson; Battery A, Second Battalion New York Artillery, Captain Hogan; Battery B, Second Battalion New York Artillery, Captain McMahon; Ninth New York Battery, Captain Morozowicz; Sixteenth New York Battery, Captain Locke. To the best of my recollection the three that were fully equipped were the batteries of Captains Robinson, Hogan, and McMahon, and those partially equipped Captains Barnes, Crounse, and Morozowicz.

Question by General McDOWELL. You have stated you received a return on the 3d of April from the commander of the field artillery; did you not infer from this that he at that time still considered himself as belonging to the Army of the Potomac?

Answer. Yes, I so inferred; but understood it was a mistake of his, and so notified him.

Question by General McDOWELL. Do you know if General Wadsworth knew of there being no design to withdraw these batteries? Did he know they had been detached from the Army of the Potomac at or immediately after the time of General McClellan's embarkation at Alexandria?

Answer. No, I don't know it; but I have the best reasons for believing he so understood it, for the reason that General Wadsworth had dismounted one of the batteries and sent it down to garrison Fort Washington. I learned this much from the captain of the battery, who complained of it.

Question by General McDOWELL. When was the battery sent to Fort Washington?

Answer. I don't know, but I understood from the captain about eight or ten days after the army left—perhaps two weeks.

Question by General McDOWELL. Will witness state if this is the only reason he has for believing General Wadsworth knew these batteries were to remain behind?

Answer. Yes; the only reason.

Question by General McDowell. Can witness state when the Sixteenth New York Battery was ordered to report to General Wadsworth, with reference to the embarkation of General McClellan at Alexandria?

Answer. I cannot, exactly. I know that the battery had only arrived a very short time previous to the departure of the Army of the Potomac, and I believe the order directing the battery to report to General Wadsworth was dated only a very few days previous to the departure of the Army of the Potomac.

Maj. Gen. Fitz John Porter, U. S. Volunteers, a witness, was duly sworn.

Question by the Court. State your present rank in the Army.

Answer. Major-general of volunteers and colonel Fifteenth U. S. Infantry.

Question by the Court. What command did you hold in the Army of Virginia while the latter was under command of General Pope, in August, 1862?

Answer. I was in command of the present Fifth Corps of the Army of the Potomac, at that time composed of a division of volunteers, a division of regulars, and a small brigade of volunteers, which was at times temporarily detached.

Question by the Court. Did you see General McDowell on the 28th or 29th August, 1862?

Answer. I saw General McDowell twice on the morning of the 29th; once at Manassas Junction, again about 3 miles from Manassas Junction, on the road to Gainesville.

Question by the Court. State at what time on that day you saw General McDowell.

Answer. The first time at Manassas Junction, about 9 o'clock; the second time, I presume, between 11 and 12.

Question by the Court. State where was General McDowell's corps at those times.

Answer. General King's division had been assigned to my command when I was at Manassas Junction by General Pope. Ricketts' division, I was informed by General McDowell, was in the vicinity of Manassas Junction, and I think was near Bristoe. Reynolds' division was in the vicinity of Groveton, on the turnpike. (Reynolds' division had belonged to me at one time, but was then claimed by General McDowell.) The second time I met General McDowell King's division was immediately in rear of my corps, and on the road going from Manassas Junction to Gainesville.

Question by the Court. Had General McDowell any command over you prior to the 29th of August?

Answer. No.

Question by the Court. What order did General McDowell give or what authority did he exercise over you, and in virtue of whose order? State fully and particularly.

Answer. General McDowell exercised authority over me in obedience to an order of General Pope, addressed jointly to General McDowell and me, and which I presume is in possession of the court. I have no copy of it. Our commands being united, he necessarily came into the command under the Articles of War.

The witness here stated, in substance, to the court that the question leads to many things pertaining to the recent court in his case, the decision of which has not yet been announced. The question requires a statement of what transpired, and he felt at this time some delicacy in answering, both so far as General McDowell and himself are concerned. I would have to state the orders under which I was moving in that direction.

The court decided that the question was a proper one.

The witness continued:

That joint order refers to a previous order given to me, of which this is a copy.

The witness produced a copy of an order from Major-General Pope, dated Headquarters Army of Virginia, Centreville, August 29, 1862, which was read by the recorder, and is appended to the proceedings of this day and marked A.

The witness continued:

Under that order King's division constituted part of my command. I was moving toward Gainesville when I received the joint order, and was joined by General McDowell, who had also received a copy of the joint order. I had at that time received notice of the enemy being in front, and had captured 2 prisoners. My command was then forming in line preparatory to moving and advancing toward Gainesville. General McDowell, on arriving, showed me the joint order, a copy of which I acknowledged having in my possession. An expression of opinion then given by him to the effect that that was no place to fight a battle, and that I was too far out, which, taken in connection with the conversation, I considered an order, and stopped further progress toward Gainesville for a short time. General McDowell and I went to the right, which was rather to the north, with the view of seeing the character of the country, and with the idea of connecting, as that joint order required, with the troops on my right. But very few words passed between us, and I suggested, from the character of the country, that he should take King's division with him and form connection on the right of the timber, which was then on the left of Reynolds, or presumed to be Reynolds. He left me suddenly, not replying to a call from me, to the effect, "What should I do," and with no understanding on my part how I should be governed. I immediately returned to my command. On the way back, seeing the enemy gathering in my front, I sent an officer (Lieutenant-Colonel Locke, my chief of staff) to King's division, directing it to remain where it was for the present, and commenced moving my command toward Gainesville and one division to the right or north of the road. I received an answer from General McDowell to remain where I was; he was going to the right, and would take King with him. He did go, taking King's division, as I presumed, to take position on the left of Reynolds. I remained where I was. When General McDowell left me I did not know where he had gone. No troops were in sight, and I knew of the position of Reynolds and Sigel, who were on our right, merely by the sound of Sigel's cannon and from information that day that Reynolds was in the vicinity of Groveton. The head of my corps was on the first stream after leaving Manassas Junction, on the road to Gainesville; one division in line of battle, or the most of it.

Question by the COURT. Did you consider the expression of General McDowell, as stated by you, that you were too far to the front and that this was no place to fight a battle in the light of an order not to advance, but to resume your original position?

Answer. I did, when King's division was taken from me, and as countermanding the first order of General Pope under the authority given him by that joint order.

Question by the COURT. Was such an order a proper one under the circumstances? If not, state why.

Answer. I did not think so, and for that reason, when General McDowell left me, I continued my movement as if I had not seen the joint order. My previous order required me to go to Gainesville, and from information received by the bearer of the first order (General Gibbon) I knew it was to prevent the junction of the advancing enemy and Jackson's force, then near Groveton, and that the object was to strike the turnpike to Gainesville before the advancing column should arrive. The sooner we arrived there the more effective would be our action. That order directed me to move quickly or we would lose much. That order had been seen by General McDowell, and when he altered it, as I conceived he had the authority, I presumed he knew more fully than I did the plans of General Pope. I will add that the joint order contemplated forming a line connecting with the troops on the right, and, as I presumed as General McDowell acted, taking King's division with him, that he intended to form such a line. I thought at the time that the attack should have been made at once upon the troops as they were coming to us, and as soon as possible.

Question by the COURT. State, so far as you know, what followed, so far as the movements of General McDowell's troops and your own were concerned, and what orders you subsequently received from General McDowell.

Answer. General McDowell took King off to the right. I know nothing further of his movements. I remained where I was until 3 o'clock next morning; a portion of the command left at daybreak. I received no orders whatever from General McDowell.

Question by the COURT. But for this order, what movement would you have made, and have you reason to suppose that, if you had not been stopped, the junction of Longstreet and Jackson would have been effected?

Answer. I should have continued moving toward Gainesville, and until we got onto the turnpike or met the enemy. I presume we would have prevented the junction or been whipped.

Question by the COURT. Have you any written orders from General McDowell respecting your movements on the 29th? If so, produce them.

Answer. None whatever.

Question by the COURT. Do you know of any other matter or thing tending to show that General McDowell was treacherous, incompetent, unfaithful, or otherwise disqualified for the command of a division, corps or department? And, if you do, state what you know as fully as though you were specifically interrogated in respect thereto.

Answer. I have no reason to know, and never had any reason to suspect, anything whatever of General McDowell which would tend in any way to disqualify him from holding either of such commands.

Question by General McDOWELL. Had you any other warrant for believing that King's division of McDowell's corps was assigned to your command than what was contained in the first order to you from General Pope on the 29th, which directed you to take King's division with you in your movement to Gainesville?

Answer. None other than verbal information, given by General Gibbon.

Question by General McDOWELL. What was that verbal information or the substance of it?

Answer. General Gibbon brought me the order from General Pope. All that I recollect is the impression given to me that General Pope wished me to move quickly.

Question by General McDOWELL. What passed between you and General McDowell at Manassas with respect to King's division?

Answer. He spoke of King's division being under my command or having been assigned to me, and spoke of it with regret. I have no recollection of anything further in reference to King's division.

Question by General McDOWELL. So far as you recollect, did he learn of King's division being under your command from you?

Answer. I think he learned it from General Gibbon. I do not know. He (General McDowell) told me as quickly as I knew it otherwise. I wish to add, now that it is brought to my recollection, I believe it was Captain Piatt who brought me a verbal message from General Pope, directing me to move on Gainesville, and to take King's division with me. This officer I met on the road to Centreville, while going to execute another verbal order sent by General Pope, and before I received the order through General Gibbon. I say it was Captain Piatt, as Captain Ball, of General McDowell's staff, so informed me.

Question by General McDOWELL. Under what relations as to command did you and General McDowell move from Manassas and continue prior to the receipt of General Pope's joint order?

Answer. I did not know that General McDowell was going from Manassas, and I have no recollection of any relations whatever nor of any understanding.

Question by General MCDOWELL. Was there nothing said about General McDowell being the senior, and of his commanding the whole by virtue of his rank?

Answer. Nothing that I know of.

Question by General MCDOWELL. What time did you take up your line of march from Manassas Junction for Gainesville?

Answer. The hour the head of the column left, I presume, was about 10 o'clock; it may have been earlier. Ammunition had been distributed to the men, or was directed to be distributed, and the command to be put in motion immediately.

Question by General MCDOWELL. When you received the joint order where were you personally, and where was your command?

Answer. I was at the head of my column, and a portion of the command, or the head of the column, was then forming line in front; one regiment, as skirmishers, was in advance, and also a small party of cavalry, which I had as escort. The remainder of the corps was on the road. The head of my column was on the Manassas road to Gainesville, at the first stream, as previously described by me.

Question by General MCDOWELL. Please state the order of your divisions, &c., in the column at that time.

Answer. First Morell's; next Sykes'. The other brigade—Sturgis' or Piatt's—I knew nothing of, having left it, in compliance with orders from General Pope, at Warrenton Junction, with orders to rejoin as soon as possible.

Question by General MCDOWELL. Where was King's division?

Answer. I left King's division getting provisions and ammunition near Manassas Junction. I gave personally direction to General Hatch, in command, to move up as quickly as possible. I did not see General King at all.

Question by General MCDOWELL. The witness says he received an order from General McDowell—or what he considered an order—when General McDowell first joined him, which order he did not obey. Will witness state why he disobeyed what he considered an order?

Answer. The order, I have said, I considered an order, in connection with his conversation and his taking King's division from me. I therefore did obey it.

Question by General MCDOWELL. What did you understand to be the effect of General McDowell's conversation? Was it that you were to go no farther in the direction of Gainesville than you then were?

Answer. The conversation was in connection with moving over to the right, which necessarily would prevent an advance.

Question by General MCDOWELL. You state you did not think General McDowell's order (if it was one) a proper one, and that for that reason you continued your movement as if you had not seen the joint order. Is the witness to be understood that this was in obedience of what he has stated to be General McDowell's order?

Answer. I did not consider that an order at that time, and have tried to convey that impression; but it was an expression of opinion which I might have construed as an order; but when General McDowell left me he gave no reply to my question, and, seeing the enemy in my front, I considered myself free to act according to my own judgment, until I received notice of the withdrawal of King.

The court adjourned to meet to-morrow, January 21, 1863, at 11 o'clock a. m.

## APPENDIX.

### A.

HEADQUARTERS ARMY OF VIRGINIA,
*Centreville, Va., August* 29, 1862.

Maj. Gen. FITZ JOHN PORTER:

Push forward with your corps and King's division, which you will take with you, upon Gainesville. I am following the enemy down the Warrenton turnpike. Be expeditious or we will lose much.

JNO. POPE,
*Major-General, Commanding.*

---

### *FORTY-NINTH DAY.*

COURT-ROOM, COR. FOURTEENTH AND PA. AVENUE,
*Washington, D. C., January* 21, 1863.

The court met pursuant to adjournment. Present, * * * , and Maj. Gen. FITZ JOHN PORTER, U. S. Volunteers, the witness under examination.

* * * * * * *

The witness stated that he answered one question propounded yesterday as considering it confined to General McDowell's ability and his faithfulness, and that the answer is not as general as he now finds the question requires.

The witness proceeded:

My further amendment is with reference to his integrity as a witness before the general court-martial of which I was defendant.

At the instance of a member the court was cleared.

The court was opened, and the following decision announced:

Evidence of General McDowell's integrity as a witness on any other trial cannot be received on this inquiry, nor does the question call for such testimony.

Question by General MCDOWELL. What was the effect on your movements of the message you state was brought to you by Colonel Locke (your chief of staff) from General McDowell, that you were to stay where you were; that he was "going to the right and would take King with him?"

Answer. The effect was to post my command, or a portion of the command, in line where the head of the column then was, prepared to resist the advance of an enemy in that direction, and turn a portion of the command a little back on the road. After doing this I sent messages to General Pope informing him of the fact.

Question by General MCDOWELL. Informing General Pope of what fact?

Answer. Of my present position and what there was in my front. I will say that I sent several messengers, conveying, to the best of my recollection, the general information of my location, and one telling him that King's division had been taken to the right. Some of those messengers never returned to me, and I presume were captured.

Question by General MCDOWELL. Did you receive any further message from General McDowell other than the one you state that Colonel Locke brought you, as before stated, which you considered an order?

Answer. None that I recollect of. I had memoranda which I sent to General Morell, and which conveys the general impression that I had received messages from General

McDowell, but I have no recollection of receiving them, nor were they brought to mind till their appearance before the court. That memoranda says General Mc-McDowell informs me all is going well on the right, or something to that effect.

Question by General McDOWELL. Is witness to be understood he did not, on the 29th, after seeing General McDowell the second time, receive any instructions, or directions, or orders from General McDowell to move his troops from where he states he was directed to remain?

Answer. I have no recollection, and I am confident I received no message or order from him other than those that I have mentioned.

Question by General McDOWELL. On his march to Gainesville does witness recollect crossing the Sudley Springs road? Does he know where Bethlehem Church is?

Answer. I now recollect the road. I did not know it at the time I crossed it. I now know where Bethlehem Church is.

Question by General McDOWELL. When General McDowell saw witness the second time how far had the witness gone on the road to Gainesville beyond the Sudley Springs road?

Answer. To the best of my recollection it was 1½ or 2 miles—perhaps a little over 2 miles.

Question by General McDOWELL. How far was it from the head of witness' column to Gainesville?

Answer. I do not know. I had never been over that portion of the country and have not been since.

Question by General McDOWELL. How far was it, in witness' opinion, from Manassas to Bethlehem Church?

Answer. Of those distances I have very little knowledge—very little recollection—and only know them by reference to the map.

Question by General McDOWELL. How long had the witness' head of column been halted when General McDowell joined him?

Answer. I cannot say, but not long. It had halted before I arrived there.

Question by General McDOWELL. Witness speaks of the effect of General McDowell's message (as brought by Colonel Locke) to have been to cause him to remain in position at the place where General McDowell first saw him. How long did witness' troops continue in this position?

Answer. A portion of the command remained there till daybreak the following morning and some till after daybreak. The most of Morell's division was on or near that ground all day.

Question by General McDOWELL. Did witness conceive himself prohibited from making or attempting to make any movement to the front or to the right or to the front and right?

Answer. By that direction or order, taken in connection with the joint order, I considered myself checked in advancing, especially taken in connection with the removal of King's division. I did not consider that I could move to the right, and I consider that General McDowell took King's division to form a connection on the right or to go to the right and form such a connection as was possible. I add, further, that I considered it impracticable to go to the right.

Question by General McDOWELL. Did witness *attempt* to make any movement in either of the directions above named?

Answer. Not directly to the right; I did to the right and front; and when I received the last message from General McDowell to remain where I was I recalled it.

Question by General McDOWELL. Did you make no attempt to go to the front or the right, or the right and front, after that message?

Answer. I made no attempt with any body of troops. I sent messengers through there to go to General Pope and to get information from the troops on the right.

Question by General McDOWELL. After General McDowell left the witness, did the witness not know he was expected by General McDowell to move to the right or the right and front?

Answer. I did not.

Question by General McDOWELL. Witness speaks of having reported to General Pope. When did witness conceive himself as no longer under General McDowell?

Answer. My messages were addressed to General McDowell, I think, all of them. The messengers were directed to deliver them to General Pope if they saw or met him. I considered myself as limited in my operations under General McDowell's orders until I should receive directions from General Pope.

Question by General McDOWELL. How long was witness and General McDowell together before they moved to the right "with a view of seeing the character of the country?"

Answer. I do not think we were together more than four or five minutes, though I have no distinct recollection.

Question by General McDOWELL. How long were they together after moving to the right?

Answer. It may have been ten or twelve minutes; perhaps longer.

Question by General McDOWELL. Witness refers to some conversation between himself and General McDowell when they first met, which, taken in connection with an expression of opinion by General McDowell, witness considered an order. Can the witness state what that conversation was?

Answer. I only recollect the impression left upon my mind at the time, and merely a reference to the artillery contest going on far to our right.

Question by General McDOWELL. Was not the joint order referred to in that conversation?

Answer. I have no recollection of it. It may have been referred to, because we went to the right, my belief is, to look at the country; but I do not recollect anything at all of the order being referred to.

Question by General McDOWELL. Were not the remarks witness has stated to have been made by General McDowell made with reference to the point in the joint order which required the troops not to go to a point from which they could not get behind Bull Run that night?

Answer. I think I have replied to the question by stating I do not recollect.

Question by General McDOWELL. Does not the witness recollect asking General McDowell if he knew of any roads leading to the right or right and front of the head of witness' column?

Answer. I do not. Early in the day General McDowell loaned me a map, and may have given some explanation with it. This is all the information I recollect of receiving, or having in my possession, of the country.

Question by General McDOWELL. Does not the witness recollect of being made acquainted by General McDowell with information received by him from General Buford as to the force of the enemy which had passed through Gainesville?

Answer. I do.

Question by General McDOWELL. When the witness and General

McDowell moved to the right, "with a view of seeing the character of the country," what were "the few words" which witness states passed between them?

Answer. I have given some of the words already; that was, my suggestion to take King's division to the right. I have no recollection of any conversation or any words being used by me or him, except, when reaching the railroad, remarking that the railroad was an obstacle, we having some little difficulty in getting over it with our horses.

Question by General McDOWELL. Does the witness recollect nothing of what was said by General McDowell on that occasion, and of his telling the witness to take his troops across to the Warrenton road, and of General McDowell's intention to go back to take his troops up the Sudley Springs road?

Answer. To the best of my recollection nothing of the kind was conveyed to my mind.

Question by General McDOWELL. You have stated "when General McDowell left me I did not know where he had gone." Have you not stated before the recent court-martial in your defense as follows: "We" (General McDowell and yourself) "soon parted, General McDowell to proceed toward the Sudley Springs road, I to return to the position at which he first spoke to me after our meeting?"

Answer. I know now where General McDowell went. I did not know then.

Question by General McDOWELL. After General McDowell left you you say you sent an officer to King's division, directing it to remain where it was for the present. What was the necessity for this order? Had the division, so far as you then knew, been ordered elsewhere?

Answer. I sent the message to that division to remain where it was for the present in order not to bring it to the front, where I was forming line, before I was ready for it, and intending to use it as the main support.

Question by General McDOWELL. Why did you continue to regard King's division as attached to your command after the receipt of the joint order?

Answer. I never thought of the point before; but General McDowell had left me, and, as I understood, in nowise changing the relations of King's division to my corps.

Question by General McDOWELL. Did not the joint order itself modify the first order you received from General Pope?

Answer. It placed all under the direction of General McDowell.

Question by General McDOWELL. If it placed all under General McDowell how did you regard the fact of its being addressed jointly to you and him, and not to him only, if he was the sole commander?

Answer. I had reason to believe that order was written on an application made by me to General Pope for orders to be given to me in writing; this in consequence of having received verbal orders from him by persons whom I knew nothing of, and which were contrary to some instructions which I had received in writing. I presume the order was written by General Pope because I had a portion of General McDowell's command with me, and the order was intended for both.

Question by General McDOWELL. Did witness send any written order to King's division?

Answer. No, sir.

Question by General McDOWELL. How long was it after you left General McDowell before you sent Colonel Locke to King's division?

Answer. I sent him as soon as I returned to my command after leaving General McDowell. I returned immediately.

Question by General McDOWELL. Did you not ask General McDowell for some cavalry, stating you had none to send with messages; and did you not ask General McDowell to keep you informed when he should be over to the right with the main body?

Answer. I have an indistinct recollection of asking for some cavalry. I do not recollect of asking General McDowell to keep me so informed.

Question by General McDOWELL. Will witness state if this is a copy of a note he addressed to Generals McDowell and King?

The note referred to was shown the witness.

Answer. To the best of my recollection it is.

The note was read by the recorder, and is from Maj. Gen. F. J. Porter to Generals McDowell and King, and is appended to the proceedings of this day and marked A.

The court took a recess of five minutes.

Question by General McDOWELL. Can you recollect the date of that note and about the hour it was written?

Answer. It was written on the 29th. I do not know the hour or about the hour.

Question by General McDOWELL. Did you not receive an order in the afternoon of the 29th from General Pope, addressed to you alone, directing you to make a certain movement?

Answer. I did.

Question by General McDOWELL. With reference to what took place when General McDowell met you, whilst he was with you, when he was leaving you, and with reference to what he did or said, or did not do or say, when he was near Bethlehem Church, have you not spoken of General McDowell's evidence, as given on your recent trial, as having done you great wrong and great harm? If so, can you state wherein that testimony differs from what you have testified to on those points?

This question was objected to by a member of the court, and it was decided the question be overruled.

The witness stated that he had no objection to answer the question.

The court was cleared.

The court was opened, and the court adjourned to meet to-morrow, January 22, 1863, at 11 o'clock a. m.

---

## APPENDIX.

### A.

Generals McDOWELL and KING:

I found it impossible to communicate by crossing the roads to Groveton. The enemy are in strong force on this road, and as they appear to have driven our forces back, the firing of the enemy having advanced and ours retired, I have determined to withdraw to Manassas. I have attempted to communicate with McDowell and Sigel, but my messengers have run into the enemy. They have gathered artillery and cavalry and infantry, and the advancing masses of dust show the enemy coming in force. I am now going to the head of the column to see what is passing and how affairs are going. Had you not better send your train back?

F. J. PORTER,
*Major-General.*

I will communicate with you.

*FIFTIETH DAY.*

COURT-ROOM, COR. FOURTEENTH AND PA. AVENUE,
*Washington, D. C., January* 22, 1863.

* * * * * * *

The court instructed the recorder to place on record a dispatch received from Major-General Burnside, to the effect that Lieutenant-Colonel Locke, a witness, could not be consistently spared from his post at present. (See appendix to this day's proceedings, marked A.)

Col. EDMUND SCHRIVER, aide-de-camp, U. S. Army, a witness, was recalled.

Question by General MCDOWELL. Lay before the court General Orders, No. 103, War Department, 1862; General Orders, No. 16, Headquarters Department of the Rappahannock, May 24, 1862; Special Orders, No. 72, Headquarters Department of the Rappahannock, May 16, 1862; Special Orders, No. 80, Headquarters Department of the Rappahannock, May 19, 1862; letter to General Ord, Headquarters Department of the Rappahannock, May 31, 1862.

The witness handed the recorder the papers referred to, which were read, and are appended to the proceedings of this day, marked B, C, D, E, and F.*

General McDowell stated that he did not propose examining any witnesses until after the testimony of General Milroy and Lieutenant-Colonel Locke had been received.

The court was cleared.

The court was opened at 3.30 o'clock p. m., and the court adjourned to meet to-morrow, January 23, 1863, at 11 o'clock a. m.

—

APPENDIX.

A.

UNITED STATES MILITARY TELEGRAPH—4.15 p. m.
(Received January 21, 1863, from Headquarters Army of Potomac.)

To LOUIS H. PELOUZE,
*Lieutenant-Colonel and Recorder:*

Lieutenant-Colonel Locke cannot consistently be spared from his post at present.

A. E. BURNSIDE,
*Major-General.*

—

*FIFTY-FIRST DAY.*

COURT-ROOM, COR. FOURTEENTH AND PA. AVENUE,
*Washington, D. C., January* 23, 1863.

* * * * * * *

Lieut. Col. BARTON S. ALEXANDER, U. S. Engineers and aide-de-camp, U. S. Army, a witness, was duly sworn.

Question by the COURT. Have you personal knowledge, derived from any communications made by General McDowell or conversations with

*Transferred to "Correspondence, etc.," Part III.

him, that he intended or desired to prevent the departure of his corps with the Army of the Potomac to the Peninsula last spring, under the command of General McClellan, and to obtain a separate command for himself, with a view of promoting his personal interest or for any other reason? And, if you have, state the facts within your personal knowledge fully and particularly.

Answer. I'll state that I never have received any communication from General McDowell on this subject, nor do I know that he ever endeavored to separate his command from the army of General McClellan from any conversation I ever had with him. I would state to the court that I had a conversation with General McDowell, but it occurred during a social visit, and I doubt if it is a matter which the court should inquire into on this occasion.

Question by the COURT. Does the witness mean to qualify his answer?

Answer. Yes, I so intend it.

The court was cleared.

The court was opened.

Question by the COURT. In any conversation of General McDowell, heard by you at any time, did he admit or state, in substance, that he proposed to take or had taken any measures to separate his corps from the Army of the Potomac at the time referred to in the last question?

Answer. In no conversation that I have had with General McDowell or heard from him did I learn that he had ever taken or ever intended to take any measures to have his command separated from the Army of the Potomac at the time referred to in the last question.

In answer to a question by the court the recorder stated that the assistant adjutant-general at Headquarters of the Army had this morning informed him that a general would be ordered to report to General Schenck, with a view of having General Milroy at once relieved, that he may appear as a witness.

Brig. Gen. JOHN H. MARTINDALE, U. S. Volunteers, a witness, was duly sworn.

Question by General MCDOWELL. About what time did McCall's division get into position on the right of General McClellan's army in front of Richmond in June last?

Answer. I cannot speak with entire accuracy, but, from the memory of the events connected with the arrival of that division, I think it was brought into position abou one week before the army commenced to retire to the James River, which was on the 26th of June, the series of battles having commenced on that day at Mechanicsville, where McCall's division was first engaged.

The court was cleared.

The court was opened, and the court at 3 o'clock p. m. adjourned to meet to-morrow, January 24, 1863, at 11 o'clock a. m.

---

### *FIFTY-SECOND DAY.*

COURT-ROOM, COR. FOURTEENTH AND PA. AVENUE,
*Washington, D. C., January* 24, 1863.

* * * * * * *

The recorder informed the court that he had heard nothing further respecting the matter of attendance before the court of Brigadier-General Milroy and Lieutenant-Colonel Locke, who have been summoned as witnesses.

The court was cleared.

The court was opened at 3 o'clock p. m., and adjourned to meet Monday, January 26, 1863, at 11 o'clock a. m.

---

*FIFTY-THIRD DAY.*

COURT-ROOM, COR. FOURTEENTH AND PA. AVENUE,
*Washington, D. C., January* 26, 1863.

* * * * * * *

The recorder, in answer to a question by the court, stated that he had heard nothing further respecting the matter of attendance before the court of Brigadier-General Milroy and Lieutenant-Colonel Locke, who have been summoned as witnesses.

The court was cleared.

The court was opened at 3 o'clock p. m., and adjourned to meet to-morrow, January 27, 1863, at 11 o'clock a. m.

---

*FIFTY-FOURTH DAY.*

COURT-ROOM, COR. FOURTEENTH AND PA. AVENUE,
*Washington, D. C., January* 27, 1863.

* * * * * * *

Lieut. Col. F. T. LOCKE, assistant adjutant-general, U. S. Volunteers, a witness, was duly sworn.

Question by the COURT. What knowledge have you of any order or orders given by General McDowell on the 29th day of August last, and of the whereabouts of General McDowell on that day? State fully and particularly, specifying time and circumstances, as nearly as you remember.

Answer. I was the bearer of a message from General McDowell to General Porter on the afternoon of the 29th August somewhere between 2 and 3 o'clock. At the time of receiving this message of General McDowell he was standing on the right-hand side of the road going to Manassas and near Bethlehem Church. The message was in these words or in words to this effect: "Give General Porter my compliments, and say to him that I am going to the right, and will take General King with me; that I think he had better remain where he is for the present, and if it is necessary for him to fall back, to do so upon my left." This message I carried directly to General Porter. This is the only order I bore General Porter from General McDowell. I heard General McDowell, in the morning or somewhere about noon, make a remark to General Porter which was to this effect: "Porter, you are too far out already; this is no place to have a fight." The first time I saw General McDowell on the 29th was at a brick house at Manassas Junction about 10 o'clock in the morning. I was then in company with General Porter. I subsequently saw him in the place where we were in position, near Gainesville, and about noon. The last time I saw him was on the occasion I have mentioned, near Bethlehem Church. At the time I bore the communication to General Porter the head of General Porter's column was about 2 miles from Bethlehem Church and in the direction of Gainesville. General Porter's column, at about noon, was on an elevated position between the Gainesville road and Manassas Gap Railroad, and about 2 miles from Bethlehem Church in the direction of Gainesville. I am not positive as to the distance, but have always thought it about 2 miles.

Question by the COURT. Do you know of any matter or thing tending to show that General McDowell was treacherous to the country, incompetent, unfaithful, or otherwise disqualified for the command of a division, corps, or department? And, if you do, state what you know as fully as though you were specifically interrogated in respect thereto.

Answer. I do not know of any such thing or believe any such thing.

Question by General McDOWELL. Will witness state under what circumstances he chanced to see General McDowell near Bethlehem Church on the 29th? For what purpose did he come there?

Answer. I was the bearer of a message from General Porter to General King. As I rode down the Gainesville road to Bethlehem Church I saw General McDowell, with another officer, standing by the side of the road. This officer I took to be General King, to whom I delivered my message, first asking this officer if he was General King, to which he assented affirmatively. It was upon the delivery of my message to General King that General McDowell gave me the message to give to General Porter.

Question by General McDOWELL. What was the message you bore from General Porter to General King?

Answer. "To remain where you are till further orders."

Question by General McDOWELL. How long after General McDowell quitted General Porter was it that the latter sent you to General King?

Answer. I don't remember exactly; it may have been an hour.

Question by General McDOWELL. Did you accompany General Porter when he rode from the head of his column with General McDowell to see the country to the right?

Answer. Yes; I rode just in the rear.

Question by General McDOWELL. Did you return with General Porter after General McDowell and he parted?

Answer. I did.

Question by General McDOWELL. How long after he returned to the head of the column was it before he sent you to General King?

Answer. I have no very distinct recollection as to the length of time that elapsed. My impressions are that he stopped behind after we crossed the railroad to give some directions to General Morell. It was very shortly after General Porter returned to the head of the column that I was sent to General King.

Question by General McDOWELL. Did you pass any of General McDowell's troops on your way down the road to see General King up to the point where you state you met him with General McDowell?

Answer. To the best of my recollection they (the troops) were halted just about that place.

Question by General McDOWELL. What was General King's position personally when you saw him—on horseback or on foot, standing or sitting?

Answer. He was standing on the left of General McDowell and leaning against the fence.

Question by General McDOWELL. How long did you remain with Generals King or McDowell?

Answer. But a few moments. It may have been ten minutes, but I hardly think so long.

Question by General McDOWELL. You speak of hearing some remarks made by General McDowell to General Porter on the occasion of his joining General Porter at the head of his column. Did you hear the entire conversation between them?

Answer. No, sir; I did not.

Question by General McDOWELL. Do you know if General Porter was given a part of General McDowell's cavalry on the morning of the 29th?

Answer. I do not know what cavalry General McDowell had. I do not know the fact. I wish to correct my answer. I thought the question referred to a force of cavalry, but there was a small detachment, numbering 12 or 15 men, left with General Porter as messengers.

Question by General McDOWELL. Did you leave with General Porter's message to General King before or after that part of my cavalry escort was given to General Porter?

Answer. I don't recollect.

Question by General McDOWELL. Do you recollect General McDowell's having in his conversation with General Porter referred to the joint order they each had received from General Pope?

Answer. I don't think I heard the conversation to which that refers.

Question by General McDOWELL. Did you hear in what connection the remark of General McDowell to General Porter about being too far out, &c., was made?

Answer. I don't think it was made in connection with any conversation. It appeared to me to be induced by the appearance of the place.

Question by General McDOWELL. Did you hear General McDowell acquaint General Porter with the report of General Buford of the number of the enemy's force that had passed through Gainesville?

Answer. I did not.

Question by General McDOWELL. Do you recollect at the time you left Generals King and McDowell whether they had their horses near them?

Answer. No, I do not remember. My attention was not called to that.

Question by General McDOWELL. Did you leave General McDowell immediately after you received the message you state to carry it to General Porter?

Answer. I did.

The court was cleared.
The court was opened.

Brig. Gen. RUFUS KING, U. S. Volunteers, a witness, was recalled.

Question by General McDOWELL. Did you or not, on the 29th of August, receive a message from General Fitz John Porter, by the hands of Lieutenant-Colonel Locke, at or near Bethlehem Church, in the presence of General McDowell?

Answer. No, sir.

Question by General McDOWELL. Were you and General McDowell together at all on the 29th of August at or near Bethlehem Church and after you and he parted near Manassas?

Answer. No, sir.

Question by the COURT. Did you receive any order from Lieutenant-Colonel Locke?

Answer. I did not.

Capt. DANIEL W. HUGHES, aide-de-camp, U. S. Army, a witness, was duly sworn.

Question by General McDOWELL. Were you with General King on the morning of the 29th of August last, on the occasion of the march of his division from Manassas on the road to Gainesville?

Answer. I was.

Question by General McDOWELL. Were he and General McDowell together at all at or near Bethlehem Church on the 29th and after they parted near Manassas?

Answer. Not at all during the day.

Question by General McDOWELL. What is your rank in the United States service?

Answer. I am captain and additional aide-de-camp.

Question by the COURT. What time did Generals King and Mc Dowell part at Manassas on that day?

Answer. I should judge between 8 and 9 o'clock in the morning. General King was sick, and had been for days previously, and did not exercise any command after 9 o'clock that morning.

Question by the COURT. Do you know that the sickness of General King was known to General McDowell?

Answer. He knew it that morning. General McDowell knew that he had been sick for some days, or at least I think he did.

Question by the COURT. How do you know that?

Answer. I've heard them talking together of his sickness at Warrenton and other places previous to this day. General King complained to General McDowell of feeling very sick several times on the road from Warrenton. General King looked as if he was fatigued out and very weak and sickly.

Capt. DUNCAN A. PELL, additional aide-de-camp, U. S. Army, a witness, was duly sworn.

Question by the COURT. What is your rank in the United States service?

Answer. I am a captain and aide-de-camp on the staff of Major-General McClellan, and assigned to duty with General Burnside.

Question by the COURT. Where were you on the 28th of August last?

Answer. In the morning of the 28th, at about 10 o'clock, I was with the Confederates—the column of General Ewell's division—on Cub Run, somewhere near the crossing of the road from Manassas Junction, and to the northward of it, to some point they had been at the night before. I do not know the place, but think it was Centreville. I made an error in saying the Manassas Junction road; it was the crossing over Cub Run of a road to the north of Centreville and Gainesville road. The troops that I was with halted there for some hours, and then proceeded to a place called Groveton Heights by way of Sudley Springs. They arrived at Groveton Heights about 8 o'clock in the evening. There had been a battle there, in which Doubleday's division was, I think, engaged. I personally reached Groveton Heights at this time. There were troops and wagons in front and in rear of me. I think the greater part of Ewell's division was behind me, and know we passed a great many troops on the road during the day. I left Manassas Junction about 9 o'clock on the evening of the 27th. The rebel troops commenced their march previous to that time. I did not leave with the first of them.

Question by the COURT. Were there any portion of the rebel troops moved from Manassas Junction toward Warrenton on the southwest side of Bull Run?

Answer. I do not know. I had not the means of knowing.

Question by the COURT. Do you know whether any portion of the rebel force proceeded from Cub Run along the Warrenton pike toward Groveton?

Answer. I do not know.

Question by the COURT. Were you present at the engagement at Groveton Heights on the 28th?

Answer. I did not arrive until about half an hour after it was over.

Question by the COURT. Were you present at the battle which took place on the 29th?

Answer. Yes, sir.

Question by the COURT. What opportunities had you for observing what had transpired?

Answer. I at the first part of the day, while they were fighting almost immediately upon the field of the night previous, had very good opportunities for observation, but afterward, when the United States troops occupied that ground, I was sent to the rear of the Confederate Army by A. P. Hill, and had no further opportunity to see the action that day. The rebel force there, from the information I could collect from observation and otherwise, was about 21,000, being the whole of Jackson's corps, three divisions.

Question by the COURT. Did you see or do you know of any movement of our troops which was an improper one, and which, in consequence of its impropriety, inured to the benefit of the enemy? If so, state fully and particularly.

Answer. On Friday, the 29th, which was the only day on which I could well observe the movements of the army, the enemy were decidedly worsted. I did not see our troops except early in the morning.

The court was cleared.

The court was opened at 3 o'clock p. m., and adjourned to meet to-morrow, January 28, 1863, at 11 o'clock a. m.

---

## *FIFTY-FIFTH DAY.*

COURT-ROOM, COR. FOURTEENTH AND PA. AVENUE,
*Washington, D. C., January* 28, 1863.

* * * * * * *

The recorder of the court stated that he had nothing further respecting the attendance of Brigadier-General Milroy as a witness before the court.

The court was cleared.

The court was opened at 3 o'clock p. m., and adjourned to meet to-morrow, January 29, 1863, at 11 o'clock a m.

---

## *FIFTY-SIXTH DAY.*

COURT-ROOM, COR. FOURTEENTH AND PA. AVENUE,
*Washington, D. C., January* 29, 1863.

* * * * * * *

Maj. FRANZ KAPPNER, additional aide-de-camp, U. S. Army, a witness, was duly sworn.

The evidence of Maj. Franz Kappner was interpreted by Charles D. Arnaud (a citizen of Saint Louis), who was duly sworn.

Question by the COURT. State your rank and position in the military service of the United States.

Answer. I am a major and aide-de-camp on Major-General Frémont's staff, and I am assigned voluntarily to General Sigel's staff, on which I rank as chief engineer.

Question by the COURT. Where and with whom were you serving on the 28th day of August last?

Answer. With the First Corps, Army of Virginia, under Major-General Sigel, at Buckland Mills.

Question by the COURT. Narrate the movements made by General Sigel's corps on that day, and in connection therewith state what was known of the position and strength of the enemy on that day.

Answer. General Sigel's corps (at night) by day-time at 3 o'clock was got up—they ordered to fulfill—to march to Manassas. Six o'clock the same morning the advance guard arrived at Gainesville. The same advance guard had met the enemy's pickets while they were advancing, and the enemy's pickets retired beyond Gainesville—that the route from Gainesville to Manassas. They could not pursue the enemy's route, but take the right to Manassas. About 3 miles from Gainesville, toward Manassas, was the center of the army corps, and took their rest. It was about 10 o'clock in the morning. The same time General Sigel's escort came in and told him that the enemy advanced from the right corner of the left flank. In the proper time I have asked General Sigel for to give me 24 cavalrymen for to go out and see if the information of the scouts was correct and for a reconnoitering expedition.

Question by the COURT. Have you made a map of the locality to which you refer? If so, produce it.

Answer. I have.

The witness produced a map, which is appended to the proceedings of this day, marked A.

Question by the COURT. Did you make the map just referred to from your own personal knowledge of the locality it purports to represent?

Answer. From my own personal knowledge and from my observation when I march in these localities.

By the COURT. Continue your narrative of the movements of General Sigel's corps on the 28th August last.

The witness continued:

With the 24 cavalrymen I have made for the same direction where the scouts had informed us—the same position or the same direction; had no road, but one open field. When I made 1½ miles I came to a height near a farm-house. From the same place I had a very far view. I have seen on the turnpike which goes from Centreville and Gainesville a white line on the route. Then I took my glass, then I have seen about 50 of the enemy's wagons, which went toward Gainesville, as I give on my plan. After I have seen this I took my position about 250 yards nearer on the left side, and have seen about 5 vedettes to the front, toward General Sigel's march line, and about a quarter [of a] mile distant from that vedettes. There was about 50 cavalry of the same vedettes, and the route toward Groveton from New Market I saw an infantry column, about three regiments. All this has happened. I immediately let General Sigel, in writing, know. I reported to General Sigel that the army (General Sigel's), with wagons and artillery, could pass along the route without interruptions, as well as the movement of the enemy was reported to General Sigel. I remained at the same point about a half an hour. I saw General Sigel with a part of his army coming before the same position. This was about a quarter to twelve in the morning. General Sigel telled me that before he break his camp he sent a report to General McDowell. When I came to General Sigel, where he was below the hill, and wanted to stretch his column to engage the enemy, then came an ordnance officer from General McDowell—the orderly came with an order to General Sigel to immediately march on Manassas. General Sigel at the same moment took the same route as he came to march toward Manassas, to comply with the order of General McDowell. The same evening we did march so far as the advance guard was—a half a mile before Manassas. I wish to remark that General Sigel did not find any enemy toward Manassas; then he advanced toward New Market. I wish to state a few remarks on the importance of the position where I was at the time on the hill near the farm-house. At the time I was on the hill I observed the enemy marching, and, according with strategic rules, my own impression is that when an enemy is on the march and not yet in position the enemy could be flanked, and it also is my impression that it was only one army corps of the enemy at the time. If at that time we had engaged the enemy, with the aid of General McDowell on the left, I am of the opinion we could have carried the day before re-enforcements could have come to the enemy. For that day this is all I know. By withdrawing General Sigel from that position I believe it gave advantage to the enemy.

At the instance of Major-General McDowell Captain Wladislas Leski was sworn to assist as interpreter during the examination of the witness.

The witness continued:

In consequence of our retreat from that position the enemy had ample time to put himself in position and await re-enforcements. This is all I have to say for the twenty-eighth day.

Question by the COURT. Who was the officer who took the message from General Sigel to General McDowell, referred to?

Answer. Assistant Engineer Burchard, formerly assistant engineer; at present first lieutenant and aide-de-camp on General Cluseret's staff.

Question by the COURT. Did you see Lieutenant Burchard start to go to General McDowell?

Answer. No, not while I was on the hill; but Lieutenant Burchard came back again and informed me while I was there.

Question by the COURT. From that hill could you see Manassas Junction?

Answer. No; it was too far to the left.

Question by the COURT. Could you see Centreville from that hill-top?

Answer. Yes.

Question by the COURT. Did you see any other portions of the enemy than what you have described?

Answer. None but what I have stated. It was not everywhere that I could see, on account of little woods.

Question by the COURT. Could you see General McDowell's corps?

Answer. Not on the 28th; there were woods in the rear of me. It was everywhere woods, but in that particular place open fields.

Question by General MCDOWELL. Was there an apple orchard on that hill-top?

Answer. Not in a position toward the enemy, but toward the left there was.

Question by General MCDOWELL. Was there a road near the hill?

Answer. There was no regular road, but there was a farm road.

Question by General MCDOWELL. Could you see Bull Run stream?

Answer. Part of it.

Question by General MCDOWELL. What part of it; above or below the turnpike?

Answer. On the south side.

Question by General MCDOWELL. Could you see the water?

Answer. No; I could not see the water.

Question by General MCDOWELL. Could you see New Market or Groveton?

Answer. No.

Question by General MCDOWELL. How did you know the column of infantry was on the road from New Market to Groveton?

Answer. I knew it from General McDowell's map. I have seen the enemy moving, and from the map I have learned the enemy's moving. I saw them marching, and took up the map and knew they could be marching over no other route but that one.

Question by General McDOWELL. Could they not have been going on the road from New Market toward Sudley Springs.

Answer. They could not have been going on the other road, for then they would have been going farther to the right. I saw them going right straight toward me.

Question by General McDOWELL. How far was the enemy from you on the hill?

Answer. My impression is about a strong half a mile.

Question by General McDOWELL. How long was the enemy's column?

Answer. One hundred and twenty yards; it might have been more, for they were already turning upon the turnpike, and I could not see all.

Question by General McDOWELL. How long were they in sight?

Answer. About five minutes; then I lost sight of them, as they were turning the road. Whether there was one regiment or three regiments I cannot tell. They might have been going forward a long time, and this may have been their rear.

Question by General McDOWELL. Did you hear any artillery firing on the morning of the 28th?

Answer. I can remember a few shots I heard toward the left in the position of General McDowell, but I do not know from whence they came.

Question by General McDOWELL. What time did you hear this firing?

Answer. I can't remember. It might have been nine or before. I never regarded much about it.

Question by the COURT. The witness has said there might have been but one regiment. Why did he previously say there were three regiments?

Answer. When I have seen the troops march (so I have observed for one hundred and twenty yards), whether they have marched by fours or sixes I could not judge. I have stated they were about three regiments, but there may have been but one.

The court was cleared.

The court was opened at 3 o'clock p. m., and adjourned to meet tomorrow, January 30, 1863, at 11 o'clock a. m.

A.

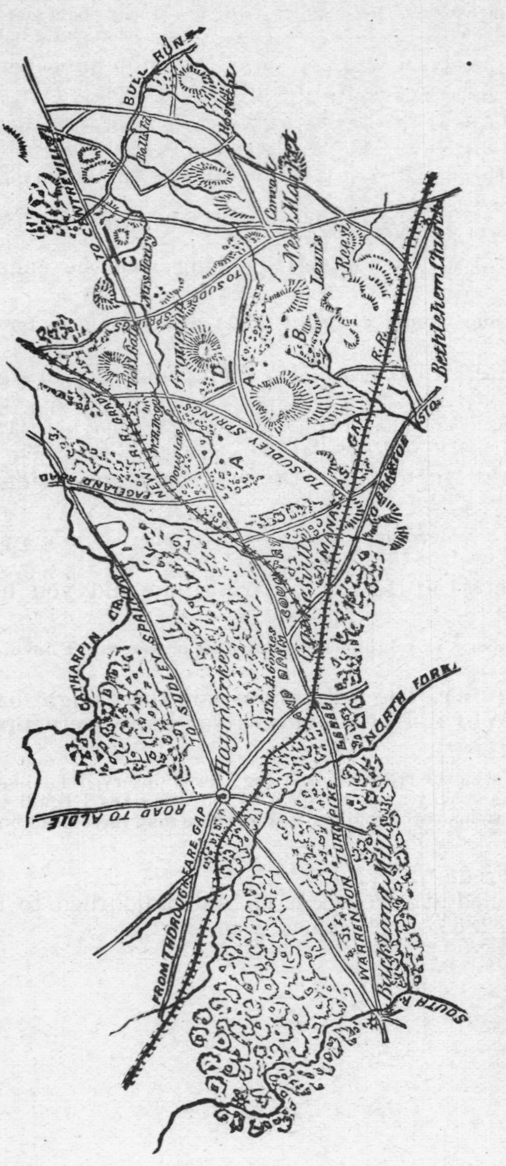


A. Enemy's Pickets
B. Enemy's Vedettes
C. Enemy's train of about 50 wagons
D. Enemy's marching column of infantry, consisting of about 3 regiments.

---

*FIFTY-SEVENTH DAY.*

COURT-ROOM, COR. FOURTEENTH AND PA. AVENUE,
*Washington, D. C., January* 30, 1863.

* * * * * * *

First Lieut. WILLIAM BURCHARD, First Virginia Artillery, a witness, was duly sworn.

Question by the COURT. What was your rank and position in the military service of the United States on the 28th of August last?

Answer. I was engineer, with General Sigel, in the Army of Virginia. I had no military rank—no commission—at that time.

Question by the COURT. Did you take any information from General Sigel to General McDowell on the 28th August last?

Answer. No information from General Sigel to General McDowell.

Question by the COURT. Did you make any communication from anybody to General McDowell relatingto the position of the enemy?

Answer. I gave information to General McDowell relating to the position of the enemy from myself. I received no order from any one.

Question by the COURT. State that information.

Answer. I was sent out by order of General Sigel to our left, after we heard some firing, with 20 men—cavalry. I crossed the field to Fairfax Court-House pike and came near Groveton, where I found the enemy in position. As I came back near Gainesville, and about 1½ miles from Gainesville, I saw General McDowell, and I thought it my business to report to General McDowell what I saw and where I had been sent. General McDowell asked me how far from this place on the Manassas Junction road was General Sigel, and I told him about 4 miles. General McDowell said, "All right; go to General Sigel and tell him he should take position—the right on the railroad, the left on the pike." That is the only communication I took charge of.

Question by the COURT. When you went toward Groveton and before seeing General McDowell did you discover any portion of the enemy; and, if so, state what you saw?

Answer. Yes, sir; I saw some artillery and some cavalry pickets. I think I saw a battery, but I cannot say, only I am sure there was some artillery. I saw of cavalry pickets some 10 or 12 men across the fields, and of cavalry, in all, something about 50 men. I saw no infantry.

Question by the COURT. State whether you informed General McDowell what you had seen.

Answer. I told him that as I was out in that direction about 1½ miles I had seen some of the enemy and a battery in position. I don't recollect whether I said anything about the cavalry and pickets. This is all the information I gave to General McDowell.

Question by the COURT. Have you personal knowledge that any communication was sent to General McDowell on that day informing him of the presence of an infantry force to your left and front or of the movement of a train of wagons on the pike toward Gainesville?

Answer. No, sir.

Lieut. Col. HENRY E. DAVIES, Second Regiment New York Cavalry, a witness, was duly sworn.

Question by General MCDOWELL. Were you for a short time on duty with Major-General Sigel on the 28th of August, 1862?

Answer. I was.

Question by General MCDOWELL. Who placed you with General Sigel, and for what purpose were you so placed?

Answer. Major-General McDowell, for the purpose of showing to Major-General Sigel the country between Gainesville and Thoroughfare Gap and in that vicinity, at General Sigel's request.

Question by General MCDOWELL. At what place and what time was this done?

Answer. In the evening of the 27th August, at or about 10 o'clock, at General Sigel's headquarters, at Buckland Mills.

Question by General McDOWELL. Did you or do you know for what purpose General Sigel wished to know from you the next day concerning the country between Thoroughfare Gap and Buckland Mills.

Answer. I understood that General Sigel had been assigned to the duty of occupying Thoroughfare Gap.

Question by General McDOWELL. Did you on the 28th bring any message from General Sigel to General McDowell which would show that the former knew that General McDowell had taken, or was to take, measures for meeting the enemy coming through or from the direction of Thoroughfare Gap?

Answer. I did. In marching from Buckland Mills toward Gainesville I showed to General Sigel a cross-road leading over to Hay Market. He asked me some questions about the road, and then sent me back to General McDowell, instructing me to say to General McDowell that the division which was to hold Thoroughfare Gap had better go by that road.

The court was cleared.

The court was opened at 3 o'clock p. m., and adjourned to meet to-morrow, January 31, 1863, at 11 o'clock a. m.

---

*FIFTY-EIGHTH DAY.*

COURT-ROOM, COR. FOURTEENTH AND PA. AVENUE,
*Washington, D. C., January* 31, 1863.

* * * * * * *

The recorder informed the court that Brigadier-General Milroy, summoned as a witness before the court, had not yet made his appearance.

The recorder was instructed to make an application for an official copy of Brigadier-General Milroy's report of the operations of his command in the Army of Virginia, and communicate therein the fact that a copy of said report would facilitate the business before the court.

The court was cleared.

The court was opened at 3 o'clock p. m., and adjourned to meet Monday, February 2, 1863, at 11 o'clock a. m.

---

*FIFTY-NINTH DAY.*

COURT-ROOM, COR. FOURTEENTH AND PA. AVENUE,
*Washington, D. C., February* 2, 1863.

* * * * * * *

The recorder informed the court that Brigadier-General Milroy, summoned as a witness before it, had not yet made his appearance.

The recorder stated, in answer to a question by the court, that an application had been made for the report of Brigadier-General Milroy of his operations in the Army of Virginia.

The court decided that the interests of the service would not justify a longer delay to procure the attendance of General Milroy, and in the event of his non-arrival by to-morrow morning his personal examination would be omitted; but his report would be read and counter-testimony, if any, to be produced by General McDowell, would then be received, and the testimony in the case be closed.

Brig. Gen. JOHN BUFORD, U. S. Volunteers, a witness, was duly sworn.

Question by General McDOWELL. Were you present with General

McDowell at his tent near Warrenton on the 26th of August last on the occasion of General Sigel being there?

Answer. Yes, sir.

Question by General McDOWELL. What was the object of the expedition that was then in question in the direction of Salem?

Answer. There was an expedition about being sent out under my command from Warrenton toward Chester Gap. General Sigel was to give me a section of artillery and a portion of his cavalry. The expedition started on the morning of the 27th and got to near Salem, where it came across stragglers from the rear of Jackson's army. I found out that Longstreet's command was close behind and following up. The object of the expedition was to ascertain the position of the rebels, I suppose.

Question by General McDOWELL. Did you make any report to General McDowell of the march of Longstreet?

Answer. I think I did. I sent two dispatches back.

Col. EDMUND SCHRIVER, aide-de-camp, U. S. Army, a witness, was recalled.

Question by General McDOWELL. Lay before the court General Buford's note to General Ricketts concerning the forces passing through Gainesville, and General Orders, No. 160, War Department, of 1862?

Answer. These are the papers. Buford's communication was received on the 29th.

The papers were read by the recorder, and are attached to the proceedings of this day, marked A and B.

Question by General McDOWELL. Did General King, on the afternoon of the 28th of August, report himself as unable to do duty, and was he, to outward appearances, at that time able to do duty?

Answer. He did not report himself sick, to my knowledge, and he seemed to me able to perform duty.

The court was cleared.

The court was opened at 3 o'clock p. m., and adjourned to meet tomorrow, February 3, 1863, at 11 o'clock a. m.

---

## APPENDIX.

### A.

HEADQUARTERS CAVALRY BRIGADE—9.30 a. m.

General RICKETTS:

Seventeen regiments and battery and 500 cavalry passed through Gainesville three-quarters of an hour ago on the Centreville road. I think this division should join our forces now engaged at once.

JNO. BUFORD,
*Brigadier-General.*

Please forward this.

### B.

GENERAL ORDERS, No. 160. } WAR DEPT., ADJT. GEN.'S OFFICE, *Washington, October* 18, 1862.

The following regulations are established for army trains and baggage:

I. There will be allowed for headquarters' train of an army corps four wagons; of a division or brigade, three; of a full infantry regiment, six, and of a light artillery battery or squadron of cavalry, three.

In no case will this allowance be exceeded, but always proportionably reduced according to the number of officers and men actually present. All surplus wagons will be turned over to the chief quartermaster, to be organized, under direction of the commanding general, into supply trains, or sent to the nearest depot. The requisite supply trains, their size depending upon the state of the roads and character of the campaign, will be organized by the chief quartermaster, with the approval of the commanding generals, subject to the control of the War Department.

II. The wagons allowed to a regiment, battery, or squadron must carry nothing but forage for the teams, cooking utensils and rations for the troops, hospital stores, and officers' baggage. One wagon to each regiment will transport exclusively hospital supplies, under the direction of the regimental surgeon; the one for regimental headquarters will carry the grain for the officers' horses, and the three allowed for each battery or squadron will be at least half loaded with grain for their own teams. Stores in bulk and ammunition will be carried in the regular or special supply trains.

III. In active campaign troops must be prepared to bivouac on the march, the allowance of tents being limited as follows:

For the headquarters of an army corps, division, or brigade, one wall-tent to the commanding general and one to every two officers of his staff.

For the colonel, field, and staff of a full regiment three wall-tents, and for every other commissioned officer one shelter-tent each.

For every two non-commissioned officers, soldiers, officers' servants, and authorized camp followers one shelter-tent.

One hospital tent will be allowed for office purposes at corps headquarters, and one wall-tent at those of a division or a brigade. All tents beyond this allowance will be left in depot.

IV. Officers' baggage will be limited to blankets, one small valise or carpet-bag, and a moderate mess-kit. The men will carry their own blankets and shelter-tents, and reduce the contents of their knapsacks as much as possible.

The depot quartermaster will provide storage for a reasonable amount of officers' surplus baggage and the extra clothing and knapsacks of the men.

V. Hospital tents are for the sick and wounded, and, except those allowed for army corps headquarters, must not be diverted from their proper use.

VI. Commanding officers will be held responsible for the strict enforcement of these regulations, especially the reduction of officers' baggage, within their respective commands.

VII. On all marches quartermasters, under the orders of their commanding officers, will accompany and conduct their trains in a way not to obstruct the movement of troops.

VIII. All quartermasters and commissaries will personally attend to the reception and issue of supplies for their commands, and will keep themselves informed of the condition of the depots, roads, and other communications.

IX. All quartermasters and commissaries will report, by letter, on the first of every month to the chiefs of their respective departments at Washington, D. C., their station, and generally the duty on which they have been engaged during the preceding month.

By command of Major-General Halleck:

L. THOMAS,
*Adjutant-General.*

*SIXTIETH DAY.*

COURT-ROOM, COR. FOURTEENTH AND PA. AVENUE,
*Washington, D. C., February* 3, 1863.

* * * * * * *

Lieut. Col. DAVIS TILLSON, Maine Artillery, a witness, was recalled.

Question by General McDOWELL. Were you with General McDowell on the occasion of his return from the head of General Porter's column to the head of his own column, near Bethlehem Church, on the 29th of August last?

Answer. I was.

Question by General McDOWELL. What did General McDowell proceed to do immediately on his return to the head of his own troops?

Answer. To turn the head of his column to the right along the Sudley Springs road.

Question by General McDOWELL. After putting the troops in motion, what position did General McDowell take up and what did he then do personally?

Answer. He went to the north of the road to Manassas and took a position near the railroad, about 150 or 200 yards from the Manassas road and from 50 to 100 yards west of the Sudley Springs road, dismounted, and he remained apparently watching troops as they passed along the road.

Question by General McDOWELL. Did you at any time that day, after General McDowell returned from the head of General Porter's column, see General King with General McDowell?

Answer. I did not.

Question by General McDOWELL. Did you hear of his having been with General McDowell?

Answer. I did not.

Question by the COURT. After the separation of General McDowell from General Porter, did you see Colonel Locke, assistant adjutant-general, or any other staff officer of General Porter, in conversation with General McDowell?

Answer. I did not.

Question by the COURT. Did you hear any communication by General McDowell to any officer whatever, to be delivered to General Porter, to the effect that General Porter had better remain where he was?

Answer. I did not.

Question by the COURT. Were you in the company of General McDowell after his separation from General Porter and until he moved toward Sudley Springs, so that you would have heard such a communication if it had been publicly made?

Answer. I was with General McDowell until a short time before he left the position I have already described near the railroad. I am not sure that I should have known anything about such a communication if it had been delivered. I think, however, that I should have recollected the occurrence had it transpired.

Capt. FRANKLIN HAVEN, aide-de-camp, U. S. Army, a witness, was recalled.

Question by General McDOWELL. Were you with General McDowell on the 29th of August last, on the occasion of his return from the head of General Porter's column to the head of his own column, near Bethlehem Church?

Answer. I was.

Question by General McDOWELL. Did you at any time on the 29th, after leaving the head of General Porter's column, see General King in company with General McDowell?

Answer. No.

Question by General McDOWELL. Did you that day hear of General King's having been in company with General McDowell after the latter had returned from the head of General Porter's column?

Answer. I did not, and I did not see anything of General King until August 30.

Question by the COURT. Where were you after the return of General McDowell from the head of General Porter's column, with reference to General McDowell, until he went with his corps to Sudley Springs?

Answer. I was with the general.

Question by the COURT. During that time did General McDowell send any message, to your knowledge, to General Porter?

Answer. Not to my knowledge.

Question by the COURT. During that time was there any message delivered to him or to any officer in company with him purporting to come from General Porter?

Answer. Not to my knowledge.

Question by the COURT. Were you in a position to have observed such a circumstance if it had occurred?

Answer. I think I was.

Question by the COURT. Do you know Colonel Locke, assistant adjutant-general to General Porter?

Answer. I do not.

Col. EDMUND SCHRIVER, aide-de-camp, U. S. Army, a witness, was recalled.

Question by General McDOWELL. After your return to the head of General McDowell's troops from the head of General Porter's column did you see General King in company with General McDowell? Where did you find General McDowell on your rejoining him?

Answer. No. I found him some distance on the left-hand side of the road to Manassas, under a tree, dismounted.

Question by General McDOWELL. Did you hear of General King having been with General McDowell, on the 29th, after the latter had returned from the head of General Porter's column?

Answer. No.

Question by General McDOWELL. Did you hear or learn of any message having been received by General McDowell from General Porter by any staff officer of the latter?

Answer. No.

Question by General McDOWELL. Did you hear General McDowell send, or hear of his sending, any message to General Porter by any staff officer to the effect that the latter should remain where he was?

Answer. No.

Question by General McDOWELL. Submit to the court General Orders, No. 107, War Department, August 15, 1862.

Answer. That is it.

The order referred to was submitted to the court, was read by the recorder, and is appended to the proceedings of this day, marked A.

Capt. WLADISLAS LESKI, aide-de-camp, U. S. Army, a witness, was recalled.

Question by General McDOWELL. Were you with General McDowell on the 29th of August last, on the occasion of his returning from the head of General Porter's column to the head of his own troops, near Bethlehem Church?

Answer. I was.

Question by General McDOWELL. What did General McDowell do immediately on his return to his own troops?

Answer. On his return to his own troops he ordered General Patrick's brigade to counter-march so as to come back on the Sudley Springs route. This brigade had already passed on the Gainesville road. Then afterward the general went to a place not far from the crossing of the dirt road leading on the south side of the railroad and the Sudley Springs road, and there, in a clump of trees, he dismounted during the passage of General King's and General Ricketts' divisions.

Question by General McDOWELL. Was the place where he dismounted north or south of the road, and about how far was it from that road?

Answer. It was north of the road. I could not exactly say how far; it may have been about 100 yards. It was nearer the Sudley Springs road.

Question by General McDOWELL. Were there any fences near where he dismounted, north of the road to Manassas?

Answer. It was just an open place with a clump of trees; nothing else.

Question by General McDOWELL. Did you see General King with General McDowell on that occasion?

Answer. I did not.

Question by General McDOWELL. Did you hear of General King having been with General McDowell on that occasion?

Answer. I was the whole time with the general, and I did not hear of it.

Question by General McDOWELL. Were you so placed with respect to General McDowell, and was the nature of the ground and the situation of General McDowell such, that you would have been likely to see General King had he been present?

Answer. I was sitting with General Bayard just behind General McDowell the whole time, and of course was obliged to see and hear anybody that was coming.

Question by General McDOWELL. Did you hear or learn of any message having been received by General McDowell from General Porter by any staff officer of the latter?

Answer. I did not.

Question by General McDOWELL. Did you hear General McDowell send, or hear of his sending, any message to General Porter by any officer to the effect that the latter should remain where he was?

Answer. I did not.

Question by the COURT. Was any communication received from General Porter during the time to which you refer by any officer in company with or near to General McDowell, to your knowledge?

Answer. Not to my knowledge.

Question by the COURT. Was there any such communication from General Porter received by General McDowell, or any other officer near him, after you left the head of General Porter's column and before General McDowell proceeded with his corps toward Sudley Springs?

Answer. We left General Porter on full gallop, and on arriving the order was immediately given to General Patrick, of King's division, to counter-march. I was the whole time quite near the general, and did not see any messenger from General Porter. Soon after giving this order General McDowell dismounted in the place previously referred to, and remained there until nearly the whole of Ricketts' division passed. He then mounted again and I went to the head of the column, and did not see any messenger during that time.

Question by the COURT. During the time you have described, did you hear of any message, verbal or written, sent to General Porter that he had better remain for the present where he was or to that effect?

Answer. I did not.

The recorder reported to the court that Brigadier-General Milroy, a witness, had not yet reported his presence. An extract from the report of Brigadier-General Milroy, which report is dated Headquarters Independent Brigade, near Fort Ethan Allen, Va., September 12, 1862, was read by the recorder, and is appended to the proceedings of this day, marked B.

First Lieut. WASHINGTON ROEBLING, Sixth New York Independent Battery, a witness, was duly sworn.

Question by General MCDOWELL. What was your rank and position in the United States service on the 30th day of August last and on what duty were you at that time?

Answer. Second lieutenant. I was assigned to the corps of General McDowell by the Quartermaster-General for the purpose of building military suspension bridges.

Question by General MCDOWELL. Were you present near General McDowell on the 30th of August last, on the occasion of General Milroy's coming to him and asking for re-enforcements?

Answer. I was.

Question by General MCDOWELL. How near did General Milroy ride to General McDowell before he commenced speaking to him?

Answer. He approached to within 50 to 75 feet of him.

Question by General MCDOWELL. How were you placed with respect to General McDowell and General Milroy; to which were you the nearer?

Answer. I was nearest to General McDowell. I was on General McDowell's left and a few feet to his rear, facing General Milroy.

Question by General MCDOWELL. What was General Milroy's manner and state of mind, apparently, when he spoke to General McDowell?

Answer. He was in a very excited state of mind. He spoke at the top of his voice. He was waving his sword and his hat was off.

Question by General MCDOWELL. What was the substance of what he said?

Answer. My impression of what he said is as follows: "For God's sake, general, send a few regiments into these woods; my poor men are being cut to pieces. If you send me some re-enforcements we will be able to drive the enemy back again." In addition to that, General Milroy made use of very many expressions which had apparently no connection with each other and which I don't precisely remember.

Question by General McDOWELL. What did General McDowel say or do to General Milroy?

Answer. He did not make any reply to General Milroy which could have been heard by General Milroy. General McDowell appeared perfectly willing to re-enforce General Milroy, and hesitated for about ten minutes. At that an officer came with a note for General McDowell. General McDowell having read this note, he at once gave orders to a brigade of General Porter's to advance into the woods and took active measures himself to see that was done.

Question by General McDOWELL. Did he say to General Milroy he would not help General Sigel or anything to that effect?

Answer. Not to my knowledge.

Question by General McDOWELL. Did you hear General Milroy say anything about re-enforcements for General Sigel?

Answer. I did not.

Question by General McDOWELL. Did you learn why General McDowell hesitated to send re-enforcements to General Milroy and then immediately sent them on the application of another?

Answer. The impression that I received from what I heard at the time was that he (General McDowell) did not want to take the responsibility of ordering in General Porter's troops when the commander-in-chief was on the field and in the immediate neighborhood.

Question by the COURT. You have stated that General McDowell did not make any reply to General Milroy which he (General Milroy) could have heard. State what General McDowell said at that time which you heard.

Answer. General McDowell was talking to General Porter during the ten minutes I was there, and I do not know positively the language used by General McDowell on that occasion. General McDowell appeared desirous of supporting General Milroy, and he was talking to General Porter about the arrangement of his troops in order to effect that. After having read that note General McDowell said, "Now I have authority; now all is right; let us go in." That was spoken with a great deal of animation.

Question by the COURT. You have stated that you thought General McDowell did not wish to order any of General Porter's command to support General Milroy. Had not General McDowell any portion of his own troops there with which he could have re-enforced General Milroy?

Answer. No, sir, not at that spot; General Reynolds' troops were in the woods and were coming out, and were mostly without ammunition.

Capt. J. De W. CUTTING, aide-de-camp, U. S. Army, a witness, was duly sworn.

Question by General McDOWELL. What is your rank and what duty were you upon on the 30th August last?

Answer. I was captain and additional aide-de-camp, and assigned to duty with General McDowell.

Question by General McDOWELL. Were you near General McDowell on the 30th of August last, on the occasion of General Milroy's coming to him for re-enforcements?

Answer. I was.

Question by General McDOWELL. How far was General Milroy from General McDowell when he asked him for re-enforcements. What was his manner and his state of mind, as far as you can judge?

Answer. When I first saw General Milroy he was about 15 or 20 yards from General McDowell. He was very much excited and gesticulated, having his sword drawn.

His manner was so confusing and his language so indefinite that it was difficult to understand where he needed the assistance which he called for.

Question by General McDOWELL. Were you near to General McDowell? If so, how near?

Answer. I was within 4 or 5 yards of him.

Question by General McDOWELL. State what you know of what was said by General Milroy to General McDowell, and the replies, if any, of the latter.

Answer. I can't remember the words of General Milroy, but they were to the effect that our troops in front were being badly cut up, and that re-enforcements must be sent or else the day would be lost. I do not think that General McDowell made any reply, and am quite sure he said nothing about General Sigel.

Question by General McDOWELL. Was there any question at all raised about re-enforcing General Sigel?

Answer. I do not recollect having heard either General McDowell or General Milroy mention General Sigel's name.

Question by General McDOWELL. Did General Milroy speak in a loud voice?

Answer. He did.

Question by General McDOWELL. Did General McDowell, soon after General Milroy came up, send forward re-enforcements on the application of another officer?

Answer. He did.

Question by General McDOWELL. Did you know why General McDowell hesitated to grant General Milroy's application and then sent off re-enforcements on the application of another?

Answer. I think I did. General Porter's corps, or a part of it, was acting as a reserve, and I supposed that General McDowell scarcely felt authorized to send them forward, unless very urgently required, without an order to that effect from General Pope. General McDowell sent these troops to support General Meade, who a few moments after General Milroy came up had sent a messenger to General McDowell, who said that General Meade was pressed hardly by the enemy and could not hold his position without re-enforcements. General McDowell then spoke a few words to General Porter, and a part of General Sykes' division immediately went forward to re-enforce General Meade.

Question by the COURT. Who was with General Milroy when he approached General McDowell? Was General Milroy alone or was he accompanied by any staff officer or orderly?

Answer. I think he was alone.

Question by the COURT. How do you know that General Porter's corps was acting as a reserve? Was it by the orders of General Pope or of General McDowell?

Answer. I did not know by whose order it was; I saw them drawn up in line of battle quite far to the rear of where the other troops were engaged. I judged they were the reserve from their position.

The court took a recess of five minutes.

General McDowell made the following statement:

I consider the evidence of General Buchanan essential in connection with General Milroy's report, and I request that the court will wait till to-morrow morning to receive it, as I have every reason to believe that he will be here. It is now near the hour of adjournment.

The court adjourned to meet to-morrow morning, February 4, 1863, at 11 o'clock.

## APPENDIX.

### A.

GENERAL ORDERS, No. 107.

WAR DEPT., ADJT. GEN.'S OFFICE, *Washington, August* 15, 1862.

I. Officers of the Regular Army will, as a general rule, receive leaves of absence to accept the rank of colonel in volunteer regiments, but not lower grades. Non-commissioned officers and privates will be discharged on receiving commissions in volunteer regiments.

II. The oath of allegiance will not be administered to any person against his own will; it must in all cases be a voluntary act on his part, nor will any compulsory parole of honor be received. But oaths taken and paroles given to avoid arrest, detention, imprisonment, or expulsion are voluntary or free acts, and cannot be regarded as compulsory. All persons guilty of violating such oaths or paroles will be punished according to the laws and usages of war.

III. The laws of the United States and the general laws of war authorize in certain cases the seizure and conversion of private property for the subsistence, transportation, and other uses of the Army, but this must be distinguished from pillage; and the taking of property for public purposes is very different from its conversion to private uses. All property lawfully taken from the enemy, or from the inhabitants of an enemy's country, instantly becomes public property, and must be used and accounted for as such. The fifty-second article of war authorizes the penalty of death for pillage or plundering, and other articles authorize severe punishments for any officer or soldier who shall sell, embezzle, misapply, or waste military stores, or who shall permit the waste or misapplication of any such public property. The penalty is the same whether the offense be committed in our own or in an enemy's territory.

IV. All property, public or private, taken from alleged enemies must be inventoried and duly accounted for. If the property taken be claimed as private, receipts must be given to such claimants or their agents. Officers will be held strictly accountable for all property taken by them or by their authority, and it must be returned for the same as any other public property.

V. Where foraging parties are sent out for provisions or other stores the commanding officer of such party will be held accountable for the conduct of his command and will make a true report of all property taken.

VI. No officer or soldier will, without authority, leave his colors or ranks to take private property or to enter a private house for that purpose. All such acts are punishable with death, and an officer who permits them is equally as guilty as the actual pillager.

VII. Commanding officers of armies and corps will be held responsible for the execution of these orders in their respective commands.

By command of Major-General Halleck, General-in-Chief of the Army:

E. D. TOWNSEND,
*Assistant Adjutant-General.*

### B.

HEADQUARTERS INDEPENDENT BRIGADE,
*Near Fort Ethan Allen, Va., September* 12, 1862.

Maj. T. A. MEYSENBERG, *Assistant Adjutant-General:*

* * * * * * *

The next morning, 30th, I brought my brigade into the position assigned them, and remained in reserve until about 4 p. m., when I threw it across the road to stop the retreating masses which had been driven back from the front.

I soon received an order to move my brigade off to the left on double-quick, the enemy having massed their troops during the day in order to turn our left flank. I formed line of battle along the road, my left resting near the edge of the woods in which the battle was raging. Soon our troops came rushing panic-stricken out of the woods, leaving my brigade to face the enemy, who followed the retreating masses to the edge of the woods. The road in which my brigade was formed was worn and washed from 3 to 5 feet deep, affording a splendid cover for my men. My boys opened fire on them at short range, driving the rebels back to a respectful distance. But the enemy, being constantly re-enforced from the masses in their rear, came on again and again, pouring in advance a perfect hurricane of balls, which had but little effect on my men, who were so well protected in their road intrenchment. But the steady fire of my brigade, together with that of a splendid brass battery on higher ground in my rear, which I ordered to fire rapidly with canister over the heads of my men, had a most withering effect upon the rebels, whose columns melted away and fast recoiled from repeated efforts to advance upon my road breastwork from the woods. But the fire of the enmy, which had affected my men so little, told with destructive results on the exposed battery in their rear, and it required a watchful effort to hold them to their effective work. My horse was shot in the head by a musket-ball while in the midst of the battery cheering on the men. I got another, and soon after observing the troops on my left giving way in confusion before the rebel fire I hastened to assist in rallying them, and while engaged in this the battery took advantage of my absence and withdrew. I had sent one of my aides shortly before to the rear for fresh troops to support this part of our line where the persistent efforts of the rebels showed they had determined to break through. A fine regiment of regulars was sent, which was formed in rear of my brigade, near the position the battery had occupied. The rebels came around the forest in columns to our right and front, but the splendid firing of the regulars, with that of my brigade, thinned their ranks so rapidly that they were thrown back in confusion upon every attempt made.

About this time, when the battle raged thickest, Lieutenant Esté and Lieutenant Niles, of General Schenck's staff, reported to me for duty, informing me that General Schenck had been seriously wounded and his command thrown back from the field. Most thankfully was their valuable assistance accepted, and most gallantly and efficiently did they assist me on that most sanguine field, until 8 o'clock at night, in bringing up regiments, brigades, and batteries, cheering them on to action and in rallying them when driven back before the furious fire of the enemy.

Shortly after sunset my own brigade had entirely exhausted their ammunition, and it being considered unsafe to bring forward the ammunition wagons where the enemy's shells were constantly flying and exploding, and the enemy having entirely ceased their efforts to break through this part of the line and had thrown the weight of their attack still farther to my left, I ordered my brigade back some one half of a mile to replenish their ammunition boxes and there await further orders. I remained on the field with Lieutenants Esté and Niles, my own [aides] having been sent to see to my regiments.

The enemy continued their attacks upon our left until long after dark, which it required the most determined and energetic efforts to repel. At one time, not receiving assistance from the rear, as I had a right to expect after having sent for it, and our struggling battalions being nearly overcome by the weight and persistence of the enemy's attack, I flew back about one-half mile to where I understood General McDowell was with a large portion of his corps. I found him, and appealed to him in the most urgent manner to send a brigade forward at once to save the day or all would be lost. He answered coldly, in substance, that it was not his business to help everybody, and he was not going to help General Sigel. I told him I was not fighting with General Sigel's corps; that my brigade had got out of ammunition some time before and gone to the rear, and that I had been fighting with a half dozen different brigades, and that I had not inquired where or to what particular corps they belonged. He inquired of one of his aides if General ——— was fighting over there on the left? He answered he thought he was. McDowell replied that he would send him help, for he was a good fellow. He then gave the order for a brigade to start, which was all I desired. I dashed in front of them, waved my sword, and cheered them forward. They raised the cheer, and came on at double-quick. I soon led them to where they were most needed, and the gallant manner in which they entered the fight and the rapidity of their fire soon turned the tide of battle. But this gallant brigade, like the many others which had preceded it, found the enemy too strong as they advanced into the forest, and was forced back by the tremendous fire that met them. But one of General Burnside's veteran brigades, coming up soon after dark with a battery, again dashed back the tide of armed treason, and sent such a tempest of shot, shell, and leaden death into the dark forest after the rebels that they did not again renew the attack.

* * * * * * *

I have the honor to be, very respectfully, your obedient servant,

R. H. MILROY,

*Brig. Gen., Comdg. Indep't Brig., 1st Corps, Army of Va.*

---

*SIXTY-FIRST DAY.*

COURT-ROOM, COR. FOURTEENTH AND PA. AVENUE.
*Washington, D. C., February* 4, 1863.

* * * * * * *

Brig. Gen. R. C. BUCHANAN, U. S. Volunteers, a witness, was duly sworn.

Question by General MCDOWELL. Lay before the court your letter to General McDowell of October 20, 1862, and say if the statements therein made are true.

Answer. That is the letter, and the substance of those statements is true to the best of my recollection and belief.

The letter referred to was handed to the recorder by the witness, was read by the recorder, and is appended to the proceedings of this day, marked A.

The court had no questions to ask this witness.

General McDowell stated that he had no more witnesses to produce.

There being no more witnesses to be called by the court, it was announced "that the evidence in the case is closed."

General McDowell stated that he would submit a statement on Monday, February 9, 1863, at 12 o'clock.

The court adjourned to meet on Monday, February 9, 1863, at 12 o'clock m.

## APPENDIX.

### A.

WASHINGTON, *October* 20, 1862.

Maj. Gen. I. McDOWELL,
*U. S. Volunteers, Washington, D. C.:*

GENERAL: Your note inclosing a printed copy of General Milroy's report is before me, and I will answer your questions *seriatim*.

1. "As to the state of mind General Milroy seemed to be in, his manner, and the impression it produced at the time" to which you refer; that is, when he rode up and asked for re-enforcements.

Answer. General Milroy's manner was very excited; so much so as to attract the special attention of those present, and induced many to inquire who that was that was rushing about so wildly, and what he wanted.

2. "As to whether or not it was a question of my (your) sending re-enforcements to General Sigel, and if I (you) refused to do so."

Answer. General Sigel's name or corps was not referred to in any way in my hearing, as far as I recollect.

3. "As to the part taken by General Milroy with your (my) brigade, which he claims to have led to where they were most needed, but from which they were forced back," &c.

Answer. When re-enforcements were called for to go to the assistance of General Meade I was ordered by General Sykes to take three of my battalions and move up to the front and left to the point most threatened, which I did at once. I left General Milroy haranguing and gesticulating most emphatically in the same place where his conversation with you commenced. He was calling for re-enforcements, and saying if they were sent at once the day would be ours, and that the enemy were ready to run. After I placed my three battalions in position I moved to the right of my line, where, to my surprise, I saw, about 100 yards to my right, the remainder of my brigade, which had been sent to the front after I left, and General Milroy was giving it some orders. I at once rode up to him and told him that those battalions belonged to my brigade of regulars, and that I could not consent to any interference with my command. He said that he did not know they were my men; did not wish to interfere with me, and only wanted to place them in the best position. I told him that I was responsible for the position of my command, and did not want any assistance either in posting or fighting it, when he left me. His own brigade was not near there, and he seemed to be rushing about the field without any special aim or object, unless it was to assist in the performance of other officers' duties wherever he could find one to listen to him. I did not lose one inch of ground after I got my brigade together, which I did immediately, by moving this latter portion to the left, but held the enemy at bay for an hour, and, instead of being "forced back," I maintained my position until ordered to fall back to the position from whence we started. Had the enemy "forced" me back, in the sense of General Milroy's report, he would have obtained possession not only of the turnpike, but of the stone bridge; and what would have then been the result you are well aware. Our defeat would have been disastrous.

I am, sir, respectfully, your obedient servant,

ROBT. C. BUCHANAN,
*Lieut. Col. Fourth Infantry, Comdg. First Brig. Reg. Infantry.*

---

*SIXTY-SECOND DAY.*

COURT-ROOM, COR. FOURTEENTH AND PA. AVENUE,
*Washington, D. C., February* 9, 1863.

* * * * * * *

The whole proceedings of the court having been read by the recorder, Major-General McDowell read the statement referred to by him in the proceedings of the 4th instant (sixty-first day), which statement is appended to the proceedings of this day, marked A.

The court adjourned to meet to-morrow, February 10, 1863, at 11 o'clock a. m.

---

## APPENDIX.

A.

*Statement of Maj. Gen. Irvin McDowell.*

WASHINGTON, *February* 9, 1863.

The unusual position I have occupied, seeking an investigation of so general a character as the one just concluded, whilst there were no charges against me, seems to require a few words of explanation, lest I shall be thought either to have unwarrantably taxed the public service with the time and cost of this court or to have sought an inquiry into my conduct and character in a spirit of vain self-confidence and conceit. It may not therefore be out of place in me to state that at the end of the campaign in September last the outcry against me was so great, that my usefulness as a public officer was thought to be so impaired as to cause it to be intimated to me from high authority that my friends could continue to support and defend me better if I were to have this investigation than they otherwise would be able to do. So I applied for it, though neither the War Department, the General-in-Chief, nor the general commanding the Army of Virginia had said anything to make it necessary or had received charges of any kind against me. The only one I could hear of was from an officer who was then dead, and his general charge of treason had therefore to be made the basis of my application, which, in the absence of any specific allegations, was made in the general terms adopted.

In taking this course I was far from supposing I could submit to such an inquiry as I asked into my whole conduct without something I had done or omitted to do being discovered, which I could not now wish had been otherwise. But if, on the one hand, errors of judgment should appear, on the other, I felt confident errors of intention would not, and that it would be made clear that nothing had occurred to warrant the gross and infamous charges of drunkenness, disloyalty, and treason; and, furthermore, that many intelligent people who did not credit the monstrous things said of me, but who had prejudices and unfavorable opinions, based on the little only that seemed to get abroad, might by a full exposition be disabused and led to believe that I had been unjustly condemned in many matters wherein I was generally if not universally held to be accountable.

So far as I can judge as to the causes of this outcry the first in order of time, as of importance, with reference to the consequences to which it led, was the part I was charged to have taken in the separation of my army corps from General McClellan's army in April last, on the occasion of his going to the Peninsula.

It may be remembered for what a length of time, how deeply, how almost universally, I was censured for having broken up that army. It was, I am told, generally credited throughout that army and the country that not only I sought to have, but succeeded in having, this done for an unworthy personal object—to have an independent command for myself.

## CONCERNING THE FORCE ORDERED TO BE LEFT BY GENERAL MCCLELLAN FOR THE DEFENSE OF WASHINGTON.

As connected with this question and preceding it, it has been thought proper to take up the subject of the number, character, and disposition of the forces left for the defense of the capital by General McClellan or which he intended and ordered to be left on the occasion of his embarking for the Peninsula.

On this point the court has before it the statements of Generals McClellan and Barry, and of Generals Hitchcock, Keyes, and Wadsworth, which fully explain the matter on both sides. I have not been able to see how I am responsible or in any way concerned in this branch of the question. The papers submitted by General Hitchcock show that it was a condition of the President that in changing the scene of active operations General McClellan should leave the capital entirely secure, and that the amount of force to be left by him for this purpose should be not only what he, but his corps commanders, should deem sufficient.

General Keyes states that at Fairfax Court-House, when that matter was acted upon by the corps commanders, I gave the opinion—

> That, with the forts on the right bank of the Potomac fully garrisoned and those on the left occupied, a covering force in front of the Virginia line of 25,000 men would suffice.

After giving this opinion, and its being made known to General McClellan, I had, I submit, no further responsibility in the matter. The whole subject thereafter was between General McClellan and his superior. As General McClellan's subordinate, I could have properly no part, and had none, in seeing that he fulfilled his duty or how he fulfilled it.

It is quite true that up to the time of his embarking for the Peninsula I knew much of General McClellan's plans, and it is equally true there was much I did not know.

I did not know till after he left that my corps was to be the last to embark, for it was understood General Sumner's corps, then in front of Manassas, was to remain until the other corps should reach the Peninsula and we should have become sure the enemy had left Gordonsville and was in their front.

General McClellan's letter of April 1, written on board steamer Commodore, to General Banks, concerning the latter's duties in the Shenandoah Valley, is new to me.*

At the time of General McClellan's embarkation I knew but little, if anything, of the character of the troops that were to be left behind. I did not see the returns nor the reports of these troops, and, as I have before stated, beyond an expression of opinion as to the amount that should be left, I never took any action in the matter nor had any occasion to do so.

## THE SEPARATION OF GENERAL M'DOWELL'S CORPS FROM GENERAL M'CLELLAN'S ARMY.

As to the causes which led the Executive to order my corps to be left in front of Washington, and as to my having procured its being so left, I think there can be no reasonable doubt in any one's mind after the statements of General McClellan himself, General Wadsworth, and General Hitchcock. The latter was at the time on duty in the War Department and in close relations with the Secretary of War and the President; General Wadsworth was military governor of the District, and General McClellan the person said to have been the most injured.

They are, therefore, those whose evidence should have the most influence. They are, moreover, uncontradicted, and agree in freeing me from having had any part in the act.

General McClellan states (in his evidence of December 10):

I do not hold General McDowell responsible in my own mind for the failure to join me.

He further says that he received a telegram from General Franklin, whilst the latter was still with me as one of my division commanders, to the effect that General Franklin, from his knowledge of the case, was of the opinion I had nothing to do with the separation of my corps from the Army of the Potomac, and that General Franklin brought him word from the President as to the causes for the separation of my corps. The President told me he had sent for General Franklin at the time he was under orders to leave me to join General McClellan, and had charged him to acquaint General McClellan with the reasons, which were purely of a public character, that had caused my being kept in front of Washington.

The President, in his letter to General McClellan of April 9 (see proceedings of January 16), states fully his reasons for ordering this separation.

General Hitchcock (see his evidence of January 16) was asked as follows by General McDowell:

State if your official position and connection with the Government were such at the time as to enable you to know or to give you good grounds for judging as to General McDowell's having or not in April last sought, induced, or procured the separation of his army corps from the Army of the Potomac, with a view to having a separate command for himself; and, if so, whether or not the retention of the corps was, to the best of your knowledge and belief, sought, induced, or procured by him, or was made by the Government for public reasons, based on the representations of others? State fully what you know of this matter.

Answer. I was on duty in the War Office, under the immediate orders of the Secretary of War, from the middle of March until the middle of May last. That period embraces the time referred to in this question. The circumstances which led to the detention of General McDowell's army corps in the early part of April, as a covering army for the city of Washington, were, I believe, very fully known to me, and I am very sure that personally General McDowell had nothing whatever to do in procuring the

*See p. 234.

orders which detained him in front of Washington. I am very sure that his first information on the subject was derived from the order itself, directing his detention here, &c.

The general then recites the circumstances under which the order was given, supporting it by official papers; all of which seem to leave no further doubt in the matter, and show the act of the President to have been prompted by considerations of a public character, based on the representations of others than myself.

Lieut. Col. B. S. Alexander, Corps of Engineers, introduced by the court, I suppose, because it had been informed he was acquainted with some facts which might tend to give a different impression from that produced by the other witnesses, on this point was asked:

In any conversation of General McDowell, heard by you at any time, did he admit or state in substance that he proposed to take, or had taken, any measures to separate his corps from the Army of the Potomac at the time referred to in the last question?

Answer. In no conversation that I have had with General McDowell, or heard from him, did I learn that he had ever taken, or ever intended to take, any measures to have his command separated from the Army of the Potomac at the time referred to in the last question.

### GENERAL M'DOWELL'S CONDUCT AT FREDERICKSBURG AND HIS NOT GOING FROM THERE TO JOIN GENERAL M'CLELLAN BEFORE RICHMOND.

Another charge intimately connected with the foregoing is that of my conduct at Fredericksburg, in not going from that place to re-enforce General McClellan before Richmond.

There is hardly a form of reproach that was not used toward me for this. Every possible way my feelings could be hurt seemed to be taken not only by those who opposed the Government under whose very eye I was serving, but the friends and supporters of the Government as well. Those who differed about most matters seemed to agree in this. In addition to the charge of failing, neglecting, or avoiding going to General McClellan's relief, it was also said of me I was idling away the time, doing nothing, on the banks of the Rappahannock; "flitting back and forth between Fredericksburg and Washington for mere personal purposes;" "fearing to cross the river when there was opposed to me not more than the fourth of my force;" "clamoring for re-enforcements to guard against imaginary dangers;" "protecting rebel property for the sake of the rebels instead of using my troops to go against the enemy;" "employing them only to guard the enemy's houses, fences, and fields," and "then, when in hearing of the sound of the cannon of General McClellan at Hanover Court-House, making no sign, but, on the contrary, leaving Fredericksburg to go to the Shenandoah to avoid moving on Richmond and coming under General McClellan.

This and much more was said of me week after week and month after month.

The Army seldom saw my name that it was not coupled with some disparaging remark in connection with the above matters, if indeed not with some denunciation or discreditable charge.

The difficulty of accounting for the Government permitting such neglect, such unprofitable and bad conduct in a general who was within a few hours of the War Department, and with whom instant communication by telegraph was constantly kept up, was sought to be explained by charging that these things were covered up or allowed through the influence of two members of the Cabinet who were General McDowell's brothers-in-law—a statement now proven to be without foundation. In fact, at the time of the inauguration of the present administration I was a stranger to every one of the Cabinet.

Whatever check or disaster the Army of the Potomac incurred on the Peninsula was attributed to my failure to re-enforce that army when I could do so and to my having broken it up as soon as its commander was out of sight of the capital.

I think I have rather underrated this case than otherwise.

I will now give the facts. With the view of combining the protection of the capital with such operations as would aid those of the main army, as soon as my corps was separated from General McClellan I pushed it to the front. At Catlett's I received the order for Franklin's division to leave me and join General McClellan on the Peninsula. and an order from the Department directing me to consider the capital under my especial protection, and—

To make no movement throwing my force out of position for the discharge of this primary duty!

On General Franklin's leaving me, I sent word by him to General McClellan (which the latter acknowledges having received) that I would endeavor to make a demonstration or diversion in his favor by way of Fredericksburg. This General McClellan says was no part of his plan nor was it in obedience to any orders from the Government, though done with the consent of the War Department.

The advance of my forces got to Fredericksburg and drove the enemy from that place, but did not succeed in saving the bridges, which had been prepared for burning and were fired by the enemy as he passed over.

April 22 I telegraphed:

If a steam ferry-boat could be sent there (Fredericksburg) it could be used to great advantage. There are stores in Fredericksburg (more than 1,000 barrels of flour) which I am anxious to save for fear of accident, and am anxious to have free communication with the opposite shore as soon as possible.

I then received the following:

WAR DEPARTMENT,
*Washington, D. C., April* 24, 1862.

Major-General McDOWELL:

The President desires that you should not throw your force across the Rappahannock at present, but that you should get your bridges and transportation all nearly ready and wait further orders.

EDWIN M. STANTON.

On the 26th of April I telegraphed the Department as follows:

Twenty canal-boats and a sterm ferry-boat (which I had asked for) arrived yesterday at Fredericksburg without molestation. It is reported by General King that numerous complaints reach him from Union men in Fredericksburg of outrages received at the hands of secessionists; that small cavalry pickets come into town at night harassing Union men and carrying them off south for no other purpose [reason] than fidelity to the Union. They ask protection. Will it meet with the sanction of the President if I throw not exceeding a battalion of infantry and a small force of cavalry into the town, protected by the artillery on this side, for the purpose of affording protection and saving the supplies?

On the 29th of April I telegraphed the Department as follows:

The enemy's pickets, however, continue to show themselves on the hills in the rear of Fredericksburg, and during the night come into the town to harass the few Union men left there. Five or six have been arrested and carried off toward Richmond. For several nights past the rumbling of wagons leaving town has been heard, and residents say they are loaded with corn and other supplies. Urgent appeals for protection against this oppression by the Confederate authorities reach us through loyal men residing on the other side of the river. By means of our boat bridge, which can be easily made available, in a few hours a sufficient force could be thrown across the river to afford this protection, or it could be withdrawn promptly or re-enforced should circumstances demand it.

Wishing the subject fully laid before the Department, and anxious to get authority, at least for the purposes above indicated, to establish communication with the opposite side, I sent my inspector-general to Washington to see the Secretary on the subject. He communicated the following:

WASHINGTON, *April* 30, 1862.

Major-General McDOWELL,
*Commanding Department of the Rappahannock:*

GENERAL: The Secretary of War has given me authority to inform you that you can occupy Fredericksburg with such force as in your judgment may be necessary to hold it for defensive purposes, but *not* with a view to make a forward movement.

H. VAN RENSSELAER,
*Inspector-General, U. S. Army.*

These communications show fully the position I was in at Fredericksburg and why I did not cross the river before April 30.

The Government was evidently apprehensive that I might, if not put under some restriction, place my force in a position where it could no longer accomplish the purpose for which it was kept from going to the Peninsula. As it was, alarm was expressed about the exposed position I had taken up, and I was urged by one of the most prominent men in the country to strengthen myself by fortifications. I did not do so, because I wished the enemy to believe I was strong and about to march upon him. I did what I could to give the impression I was in large force, and I think I succeeded. In fact I have good reason for believing that the apprehension thus created at Richmond of danger of a large force coming down from Fredericksburg whilst their army was at Yorktown was one of the principal causes for their evacuating their strong works at that place without siege.

Every effort was made by me and my officers and men to get the bridges and transportation nearly ready. I had been assured that as soon as I could do so, and as soon as a sufficient force could be collected, I would receive permission to advance.

A reference to General Haupt's and Major Tillson's evidence, of December 6, will show that I gave my personal attention to this subject, and so far from idling away my time on the Rappahannock, either personally or with my troops, that all were actively engaged in making the preparations necessary to enable me to advance.

When I went to Washington it was because I was summoned there by my superiors. I never went there once for mere personal purposes. Washington and the District were, moreover, part of my command.

The enemy in abandoning the Potomac had as far as possible destroyed the railroad from Aquia; had burned the wharf and the long wooden pier connecting it with the land; had taken up the rails for 3 miles, burnt the cross-ties, and destroyed the large bridges over the Accokeek, Potomac Creek, and the Rappahannock, and was prepared to destroy the one over the Massaponax.

When we reached Fredericksburg the roads between it and the Potomac were still bad, and the damage at Aquia was so great that a temporary depot and landing had to be made at Belle Plain.

Every means within my reach was employed to repair all this. The principal part of the work was done by the troops, aided by such colored fugitives as could be had, and, when possible, the work was pushed night and day.

The large railroad bridge over the Rappahannock, some 600 feet long by 65 high, and the larger part of the one over Potomac Creek, some 400 feet long by 80 feet high, were built from the trees cut down by the troops in the vicinity; and this without those troops losing their discipline or their instruction as soldiers. The work they did excited to a high degree the wonder and admiration of several distinguished foreign officers, who had never imagined such constructions possible by such means and in such a way in the time within which they were done.*

As fast as the means would allow I brought my forces over from Catlett's or down from Alexandria, and, with the verbal consent of the Secretary of War, organized and added to those of McCall and King another division, commanded successively by Generals Ord and Ricketts.

Still, as I did not move forward, what was done, if it was known, did not seem to find favor in the country at large. It was known there was a force within a short distance of Fredericksburg which I did not advance upon, and the world was not in the mood to be charitable to me, and imputed bad motives for my assumed voluntary inaction.

On the 17th of May instructions were issued from the War Department that on being joined by General Shields' division I should move on Richmond. (See appendix, No. 7, December 10.)

This division was ordered to join me, not that I asked for it (as was charged at the time) as a re-enforcement for my command to strengthen it against an attack from the enemy, but that I might carry it with me and strengthen the attack on Richmond, and thus add to the re-enforcement I was to carry below.

General Shields' advance arrived at Falmouth May 22. His division was needing many things—shoes, trousers, ammunition, &c. I had caused supplies to be placed for it at Warrenton and Catlett's, so that it might refit on the march. All the artillery ammunition was condemned by an inspector of ordnance sent from the War Department to inspect it at Catlett's, and new ammunition was ordered from the Arsenal to meet it at Falmouth. This was to have been down so that we could march on Saturday, but the transport grounded near Alexandria and lost a day. Everything, however, was ready to march on Sunday. The wagons—containing five days' bread, coffee, sugar, and salt—were all loaded up, and with beef cattle on the hoof, were distributed to the several brigades. Arrangements were made for General Haupt (see De-

---

* NOTE BY GENERAL MCDOWELL.—The Potomac Run bridge is a most remarkable structure. When it is considered that in the campaign of Napoleon trestle bridges of more than one story, even of moderate height, were impracticable, and that, too, for common military roads, it is not difficult to understand why distinguished Europeans should express surprise at so bold a specimen of American military engineering. It is a structure which ignores all the rules and precedents of military science as laid down in books. It is constructed chiefly of round sticks cut from the woods, and not even divested of bark. The legs of the trestles are braced with round poles. It is in four stories, three of trestles and one of crib work. The total height from the deepest part of the stream to the rail is nearly 80 feet. It carries daily from ten to twenty heavy railway trains in both directions, and has withstood several severe freshets and storms without injury.

This bridge was built in May, 1862, in nine working days, during which time the greater part of the material was cut and hauled. It contains more than 2,000,000 feet of lumber. The original structure which it replaced required as many months as this did days. It was constructed by the common soldiers of the Army of the Rappahannock (command of Major-General McDowell), under the supervision of his aide-de-camp, Col. (now Brig. Gen.) Herman Haupt, chief of railroad construction and transportation in the Department of the Rappahannock.

cember 6) to have a bridge ready to be put across the Massaponax, so that any further supplies which we might require could be sent after us by railroad. I had now ready to march over 40,000 men and over one hundred pieces of artillery. Though I could have started and would have started Sunday, yet it was resolved not to march till Monday; this out of deference to the wishes of the President, who was with me at the time, having come down Friday night, and with the concurrence of the Secretary of War, on account of the day. (See evidence of General Haupt, December 6.)

I had five days' short rations placed in the wagons, intending to have the men take two additional days' in their haversacks. This would have given sufficient for the march to the front of Richmond, which would have taken three days, and left us enough for the train to go to the magazines which General McClellan was to have ordered to be established on the Pamunkey, get another load, and return to the troops. Thus we could have gone independent of the railroad between Fredericksburg and Richmond if the enemy should succeed in destroying it in his retreat.

It was Saturday night that the telegrams announcing the movement of Jackson down the Shenandoah against General Banks began to be received by me at Fredericksburg.

On Sunday, the 24th, I received the order of the President—

> To lay aside for the present the movement on Richmond, and put 20,000 men in motion at once for the Shenandoah.

On the 25th the Secretary of War informed me—

> The movements ordered yesterday should be pressed forward with all speed. The President thinks your field of operations at present is the one he has indicated.

The papers submitted December 10, and appended to that day's proceedings, and those of December 15 will show clearly everything concerning the movements from Fredericksburg to the Shenandoah. I do not purpose to discuss here at all the quality of my judgment in this matter. A certain plan I had much at heart had been adopted and was on the eve of execution when I received orders changing it. I thought whilst obeying the orders, which I immediately proceeded to do, that even if it were not my duty to do so I would be pardoned, both on account of the public service as well as of myself, if, in view of the important trust I held, I should acquaint the President, even unasked, with my own views. This I did in the dispatches to him and the Secretary of War May 24.

These must certainly acquit me of having sought or procured this movement to avoid going to General McClellan.

### MOVEMENT TO THE SHENANDOAH VALLEY.

These dispatches last referred to will also show that I did lay aside "for the present" the movement on Richmond; that "I pressed forward with all speed" the one ordered by the President, accepting it in perfect good faith and acting with all my energy in the field of operations he had indicated, though I certainly left the one I wished to pursue with a heavy heart. But, as I had taken the liberty to say so to the President, I felt it the more incumbent on me to prove that I was doing everything I could to insure the success of the plan he had laid down.

It will be seen that the troops of Ord's division were ordered by the Department to Washington and Alexandria by water. Shields' division, which knew the country better than any other troops I had, having campaigned all through the valley and been selected by me on this account, were sent via Catlett's.

The dispatches give so fully the history of the movements that it is hardly necessary to repeat them here.

It will be seen from those of the President that he wished I should get the advance of my force to Front Royal as early as noon of Friday. It will also be seen what efforts it required to accomplish this. The troops went over the Blue Ridge without other supplies than what they carried on their persons. Ord's division were required to leave their knapsacks behind. This division, having left the Rappahannock to come up to Washington and Alexandria by water, did not take their supply or baggage wagons with them, and had to depend on the railroad till the train I had taken from the depot at Alexandria could arrive, and we found the railroad destroyed by the enemy beyond Rectortown. The evidence of Generals Haupt and Hartsuff and my dispatches to the President and Secretary of War will show that I urged this movement with all the force possible, and that the point was gained an hour before the time appointed, Kimball's brigade and Shields' division driving the enemy out of Front Royal at 11 a. m. on Friday, May 30.

Ord's division got to within a few miles of Front Royal Saturday night, May 31.

That night I reached Front Royal after dark, in the midst of a furious storm. It was arranged, after consulting that same night with General Shields, that on the morning he should take his division, which had all arrived, to Strasburg, and I would, as soon as Ord's could come up next day, send it over to hold the Winchester road, and support the cavalry under Bayard, which I would send in that direction.

Front Royal is on the east bank of the South Fork of the Shenandoah. Strasburg is on the west side of the North Fork of the Shenandoah and several miles beyond.

The next morning, as the troops were moving out, two of General Shields' officers came in from near Strasburg, where the general had sent them to reconnoiter, and reported that the enemy had passed though last night and his rear guard was passing through as they left.

I immediately pushed Bayard's cavalry brigade, eight pieces of artillery, and a battalion of riflemen, who were the most movable of any of the troops at hand, to Strasburg to re-enforce the troops, whom we could then hear cannonading the enemy. General Shields then, on his own proposition—to which I gave great weight, on account of his having been up and down the valley on the Strasburg as well as Luray and Front Royal side, and had positive personal knowledge of a country of which I had a glimpse for the first time that morning—moved up the valley to Luray to intercept Jackson, whilst he should be falling back before General Frémont's advance.

The next day commenced that heavy rain-storm which lasted several days and flooded the country from the Lehigh to Richmond, carrying away millions of property in Pennsylvania and sweeping off all the bridges on the Shenandoah and the Rappahannock. All communication for many days across the Shenandoah was cut off. General Shields found it impossible to cross to General Frémont, or, on account of the roads, to get his artillery and wagons much beyond Luray, and so reported to me June 4.

In sending General Shields up the valley, he was informed that to whatever distance he might, from his better knowledge of the roads and country, feel himself justified in going, he was to have all his force well in hand, with the parts in supporting distance of each other. (See proceedings of December 18.)*

On the 4th of June, seeing that Jackson had been driven through Strasburg by Bayard's brigade of my troops and General Frémont's army, and was now on his retreat up a narrow valley, where a rear guard could hold an army in check, and that it was only a pursuit which could end in nothing decisive for us, I thought the time for resuming my operations from Fredericksburg, which I had been ordered to lay aside for the present, was come. In order to be able to do so I made the communication of June 4 to the Secretary of War, (appendix to proceedings, December 16),† proposing that the limits of General Frémont's department might be extended east to the middle of the Shenandoah Valley; and to compensate General Banks for the part taken from him to extend the limits of his department to the east, taking from my department the much larger country known as the Piedmont District.

I did this that the forces of Generals Frémont and Banks might be united in and hold the valley; in order, as I then stated, to "free the forces of the Department of the Rappahannock to act either in conjunction with those under Major-General McClellan against Richmond, as was arranged, or, if not needed there, to go offensively on the line of the Orange and Alexandria Railroad toward Gordonsville," &c.

On the 6th of June I received from the War Department the order to send McCall's division from Fredericksburg to General McClellan by water down the Rappahannock; to place such additional forces as I might deem necessary at Fredericksburg for the security of that place, and informing me that the President reserved the directions to be given as to the residue of my force. (See dispatches of June 6 from Secretary of War and Adjutant-General, appendix to proceedings of December 19.)†

On conferring personally with the President, he directed instructions to be given me, June 8, to the effect that "after having first provided adequately for the defense of the city of Washington and for holding the position at Fredericksburg, I should operate with the residue of my force as speedily as possible in the direction of Richmond, to co-operate with Major-General McClellan, in accordance with the instructions heretofore given. (See appendix A, proceedings December 19).†

I had, June 7, given orders to move the headquarters to Manassas, and June 8 I gave the orders for General Shields to march, via Warrenton, to Fredericksburg, and two brigades of Ricketts' division to march to Warrenton. The latter order was modified at the instance of the Secretary of War, and only one brigade ordered to move till General Banks should occupy Front Royal.

From this time forth the dispatches brought before the court will show but a constant struggle on my part to get my forces out of the valley to concentrate them upon Fredericksburg. The extended movement of General Shields up the valley and the repulse of two of his brigades, the reports given by Generals Banks and Frémont of the enemy's purpose to come again down the valley, confirmed by a dispatch from General McClellan (see proceedings December 19)‡ that re-enforcements for Jackson had left Richmond, combined to delay the movement ordered on the 8th.

---

* See Schriver to Shields, June 5, 1862, in "Correspondence, etc.," Part III, p. 340.
† See "Correspondence, etc.," Part III.
‡ See Stanton to McDowell, June 12, in "Correspondence, etc.," Part III, p. 373.

It was expected, according to the instructions from the Department,* that Generals Frémont and Banks should hold the valley and I should remain till General Banks should relieve me.*

It will be seen that he was not prepared to cross or was not able to cross the Shenandoah at Front Royal till late in June.

June 11 General Banks, through his chief of staff at Winchester, informed General Ricketts at Front Royal that the orders which he (General Banks) had received from Washington required that he should move his main force to the Shenandoah, at or opposite Front Royal; that General Crawford was near that place; that the remaining (General Williams') division would be there by the last of the week; that General Sigel stated that his command would be in condition to move in six days from that date, his requisitions not having yet been fully answered.†

June 12 General Banks expressed his opinion to the Department, communicated to me by the Secretary:

> That Winchester or Middletown was the place to meet the enemy, and that he had suggested to General Frémont to fall back to that line.‡

I reported as follows to the Secretary of War:

[HEADQUARTERS DEPARTMENT OF THE RAPPAHANNOCK,
*Manassas, June* 12, 1862.]

I have received the telegrams from Major-General McClellan and Major-General Banks you sent me this morning.

The enemy's telegrams from Staunton to Governor Letcher, at Richmond, for re enforcements seem to indicate there was no body of troops between Jackson and Richmond. This is not conclusive, but probable. General McClellan's opinion that some troops left Richmond to join Jackson is strong presumptive evidence that they intended to strengthen their forces in the valley, though hardly by Longstreet's and Smith's divisions. Perhaps it is to make good Jackson's losses. General Frémont intends to occupy Mount Jackson, and his desire that General Banks should join him there, and the latter's wish to occupy Middletown or Winchester, and his opinion adverse to occupying Front Royal, seem to indicate that both these commanders intend or wish to remain on the west side of the Shenandoah. If they can supply themselves by way of Winchester and Strasburg and relinquish the road from Manassas to Front Royal their plan will have the advantage of having their forces move together in better supporting distance and less liable to attack in detail. But in that case it seems to me that as all the forces of both these commanders would be on the same line, they might occupy in force a position farther in advance than Mount Jackson, so as to be able to fall on the rear of any force going on the Luray road or over to Western Virginia, and at the same time be advanced sufficiently as a covering force for Washington to enable the President's plan concerning my command to be carried into effect.

If, under a belief of an advance of a superior force, General Frémont falls back to Mount Jackson, which is within the Massanutten range of mountains, General Shields' division is not safe at Luray, especially since the bridges over the Shenandoah are down and the communication is cut off and he too far distant to be supported from Catlett's. I have sent to him to know if he has a good defensible position at Luray, and have delayed movement of Ricketts' two brigades from Front Royal to Catlett's and ordered him to be ready to move to Luray.

But all this is interfering with the main plan, and if Generals Frémont and Banks think they can operate better both together west of the Shenandoah, I would recommend that no bridge be built on the Shenandoah at Front Royal and the line from Manassas to Front Royal be abandoned, and that I at once bring my forces over to this line.

Again I wrote to the Secretary on the same subject:

Owing to some instructions from Major-General Banks the troops of his department have not crossed the river to relieve General Ricketts at Front Royal. This I understand is under the impression General Banks is under that this is in accordance with his instructions from Washington. It is most desirable that General Banks should at once relieve my troops in the valley or that Front Royal and the line from Winches-

* See letters of June 9–10 to Shields in "Correspondence, etc.," Part III, pp. 364, 367.
† See Copeland to Schriver, June 11, in "Correspondence, etc.," Part III, p. 370.
‡ See May 15–June 17, "Operations, etc.," Report No. 1, p. 522.

ter to that place be abandoned, so that I may be at work getting my forces together. They are too far apart. I want to get a larger force at Catlett's and Fredericksburg at once.

Jackson is either coming against Shields at Luray, King at Catlett's, or Doubleday at Fredericksburg, or is going to Richmond.

None of the places named is in condition to withstand him, and in any case I should get my command together; but I cannot leave the valley and commence to do so till General Banks assumes charge. Cannot he be asked to hasten his troops? General Sigel, who is near Winchester, is waiting for certain supplies. Cannot he move, as we have done, and have his supplies follow him?

Again I telegraphed the War Department:

Has the Department any information as to the position of General Frémont? I ask so as to determine in relation to moving General Shields from Luray and General Ricketts from Front Royal. I am disposed to move both of them as soon as they can march, and without waiting any further on the movements of General Banks.

General Banks is now in force on the Shenandoah opposite Front Royal; and even if Jackson should not have gone to Richmond and should attempt again to go down the valley, General Banks is in the strongest position on the line for resisting him. Such movement on the part of Jackson would only result in abandoning the line from Manassas and Front Royal. General Banks is waiting for a bridge to be built or a ferry larger than the present one to be established.

June 14 I telegraphed the Secretary of War:

The position which I learn from your telegram of last night is now occupied by General Frémont at Mount Jackson leaves General Shields' command exposed at Luray. Either Jackson is falling back to Richmond or is waiting for re-enforcements to renew his offensive operations. If the former, my forces are not needed where they are, but are needed where the President has ordered them. If the latter, then has General Frémont's movements to Mount Jackson, and General Banks' inability to make one, as ordered, up the east bank of the Shenandoah, left the forces of my command too divided to support each other and give that protection to the capital which it is made my duty to afford. I am not in strength either at Luray, on this line, or at Fredericksburg, whilst the valley west of the Shenandoah down to Harper's Ferry is held in superabundant strength. I propose, therefore, to immediately order my troops out of the valley and have General Geary take post at Thoroughfare. General King goes to-day to Fredericksburg with another brigade. If hereafter General Banks shall see fit to cross the Shenandoah at Front Royal and carry out the plan the President ordered he will be able to do so as well as if I were there. If not, no harm will be done, and I will be able to utilize the forces now locked up in his department.

I fear precious time is being lost, so far as I am concerned, by my having to wait for General Banks, and that I am either being exposed to be attacked in detail if Jackson acts offensively or that I am delaying the re-enforcements for Richmond, where they will be needed more than ever, if, as I am led to think may be the case, he is gone to re-enforce Lee.

Please let me know at as early a moment as possible if there is any objection to my acting as I propose.

In answer to my suggestions the Secretary informed me, June 14:

Your telegram has just been received. You have all the knowledge possessed by the Department respecting the position of the forces under command of General Banks and General Frémont, and you also know what orders have been given by the President to those commanders as well as to yourself. I have no further orders.

EDWIN M. STANTON,
*Secretary of War.*

June 14 I telegraphed the Department as follows:

I have ordered General Shields to move as soon as possible to Catlett's. It was from no desire to avoid the full measure of responsibility which belongs to me that I telegraphed the condition in which my troops in the valley are placed. The change of the plan as to General Frémont's position affected me, and I ventured to submit, in the absence of any instructions, what I thought best to be done under the new condition of things.

That day I ordered General Shields to march from Luray to Catlett's at the earliest possible moment.*

---

* See Schriver to Shields, June 14, 1862, in "Correspondence, etc.," Part III, p. 389.

I also telegraphed General Banks as follows:

MANASSAS, June 14, 1862.

Major-General BANKS, *Winchester:*

Permit me to inquire when you will be able to relieve my command at Front Royal, that I may get into position to carry out the orders of the President.

A ferry has been established over the Shenandoah, which was sufficient to bring to this side a regiment of infantry, a section of artillery, and some cavalry, and which therefore I should think would be sufficient to throw over from your command a force to guard the stores and occupy the place till your permanent arrangements can be made. To await for these permanent arrangements would, I fear, delay the movements I am ordered to make beyond the time which would render them effective.

June 15 I telegraphed as follows:

His Excellency the PRESIDENT, *Washington, D. C.:*

So much has been said about my not going to aid General McClellan and his need of re-enforcements that I beg the President will now allow me to take to him every man that can be spared. I make this request in view of what I learn from Front Royal of an intention to have my Second Division broken up and Hartsuff's brigade transferred to General Banks' department.

General Frémont's and General Banks' divisions are now superabundantly strong for all purposes in the valley. Jackson seems to have gone to Charlottesville, and I will have to do with him either on my way to or at Richmond. The rapid marches over the mountains have diminished my force, aside from McCall's division, by at least 4,000 men. At Richmond we will have the heavy work to do, and after providing for the safety of this line and Fredericksburg my force to march upon Richmond will be a much smaller re-enforcement than will be looked for or wanted.

IRVIN McDOWELL,
*Major-General, Commanding.*

The same day I telegraphed the Secretary of War:

[JUNE 15—12.30 p. m.]

Major-General Banks writes to General Ricketts, commanding my Second Division at Front Royal, that General Ricketts must remain with his command until his (General Banks') can be ordered up, which shall not be absolutely beyond the time necessary for its equipment. I learn from another dispatch that he is waiting for blankets, &c., and in one to me that he is waiting for means to cross the river. I have telegraphed him that there is a ferry at Front Royal, on which we have passed a regiment of infantry, a section of artillery, sixty baggage wagons, and a squadron of cavalry, and that with ropes he can build a bridge of scows. I now learn that there is a plan on foot to have Hartsuff's brigade of the Second Division transferred to General Banks, and in anticipation that General Williams has been calling on General Hartsuff for returns of his brigade and that General Banks is now on the way to Washington I am sure it is not expected that I shall wait till bridges are built or troops should get everything in the way of equipments.

My troops also need many things which I shall not wait for. I regret to have to trouble you in this matter, and to beg that I may not be deprived of Hartsuff. They have enough for their defensive purposes, and I shall need more than I have, though I may not ask for them for the work I have to do.

IRVIN McDOWELL,
*Major-General, Commanding.*

General Shields (see his dispatches of June 15, proceedings of January 5), reporting himself unable for want of shoes for his men and horses to march direct from Luray to Catlett's, I had him instructed to move down the valley to Front Royal, where he could be better equipped and could use the railroad from that place over to Manassas; and General Ricketts was instructed, as soon as General Shields' division should reach Front Royal, to commence the march of his division or its transfer in the cars to Manassas.

On the 17th of June (proceedings of January 5) I telegraphed from Manassas to General Banks at Winchester:

I beg to acquaint you that Hartsuff's brigade has moved here to-day; that General Ricketts will follow to-morrow, and that General Shields' division is now at Front

Royal, where I will thank you to support him, in case it should be necessary, until he can be withdrawn. The fords of the Shenandoah are now practicable. All General Bayard's brigade have passed over.

Again, on June 18 (proceedings of January 5), I telegraphed to General Banks:

All of General Ricketts' division will leave Front Royal to-day. General Shields, who is now at Front Royal, will follow General Ricketts to-morrow. There are some commissary stores and beef cattle, more than these troops require, at Front Royal. To avoid bringing them over here, where there is plenty, I beg leave to suggest that you instruct the proper officer in your department to receive them for the use of your command to-day.

On the 20th of June General Shields' division marched from Front Royal to Manassas.

On the 21st (proceedings January 5) the Secretary of War telegraphed me:

General Banks has urgently and repeatedly requested that General Shields' division should remain a short time at Front Royal.

In a note to me this morning the President says: "Tell McDowell what Banks says; tell him we incline to have Shields remain a few days at Front Royal, and ask him to state his strongest objections, if he has any."

You will please answer immediately, and tell us how you are.

To which I replied, June 21—2 p. m. (proceedings January 5):

Your telegram, requesting that Shields' division should be allowed to remain a few days at Front Royal, is just received. In compliance with the orders given after the President was here (Manassas) the advance of Shields' division reached here last night and has moved to Bristoe. The sick, foot weary, and part of the baggage and stores left Front Royal last night; General Shields and the remainder of his division left Front Royal this morning at 5 o'clock.

My reasons for wishing to get General Shields here were, first, that the movements I am ordered to make depend upon it; second, his position at Front Royal, with nothing in advance of him beyond the support of General Frémont and with a river separating him from General Banks, which General Banks' force seems reluctant to cross, was not such as I wanted him, in the condition he is in, to remain in.

General Shields' division is, I learn, in a bad state morally and materially—officers resigning and even men deserting.

I am improving and sitting up, and hope soon to regain my bodily activity.

On the 22d and 23d of June General Shields' command reached Bristoe, near Manassas. On his commencing to arrive, and as fast as it could be safely done, the force held at Catlett's was transferred to Fredericksburg. On the 26th the President's order was issued suppressing the Department of the Rappahannock, and placing me, with the forces I had commanded, under Major-General Pope, to constitute a part of the Army of Virginia.

On the same day Jackson, concerning the renewal of whose attack down the Shenandoah there had been so much speculation in the valley, struck the right of General McClellan's army before Richmond, and commenced that series of battles which resulted in General McClellan taking position on the left bank of the James River.

I had telegraphed General McClellan June 10 that I would be with him in ten days, and could I have disentangled myself from the Shenandoah Valley and commenced to withdraw my forces at the time I ordered—June 8—I would have been with him by the 20th or by the time McCall's reached him by water from Fredericksburg under orders given it June 6.

With the 26th ended my independent command, and with that date I end the account of my conduct in connection with alleged failure to aid or re-enforce General McClellan before Richmond.

## PROTECTING REBEL PROPERTY.

In connection with my command of the Department of the Rappahannock my conduct and the policy pursued by me toward the inhabitants of the country occupied by our troops, particularly with respect to their property, was another subject of much criticism and general condemnation; not only on account of the protection itself, but of the consequent detailing of soldiers to guard their property was especially and bitterly denounced, and was one of the main subjects on which I have supposed, from the language used against me, the charge of treason was founded.

It was not thought the course I pursued was consistent or could possibly have anything to do with a sincere desire to prosecute the war earnestly and zealously, but must have come from a feeling of tenderness or active sympathy with the enemy and a corresponding disregard for the soldiers committed to my charge; that my care for the property of the man in the secession army was greater than the interest I took in the Union volunteer, who was sacrificing his property and business at home to come and fight those whose property I seemed so much to respect.

One of the Senators from my native State, who had been looked upon as being very kindly disposed toward me, was so much moved by the representations made on this subject as to hold me up to the Senate in a disparaging manner as an unprofitable general, misapplying the public force under his command.

My conduct in the matter was made the subject of a resolution in the House of Representatives, founded on a complaint in a newspaper, directing the subject to be inquired into by the Joint Committee on the Conduct of the War, which was done.

Much was said about my making my soldiers rebuild some fences, causing some of General Shields' division to come back some 10 miles for this purpose after they had just come off a long and fatiguing march.

It may be recollected with what joy a supposed change in my policy by my successor was hailed throughout the country: "No more rosewater;" "Now the war will be carried on in earnest;" "No more protection to rebel property;" "No more guards over rebel houses;" "Now the army will live off the enemy," and "The enemy will now be made to feel the war," &c., and much more.

There was perhaps no subject in which more discontent was created than this. I seemed to be universally condemned. As a prominent person told me in reference to this matter, "You are become the most odious man in the nation."

I can truly say I have done things I wish I had done differently, and have omitted much I wish I had done; but I was never less in doubt in my life about anything than I am about my conduct in this respect.

I will try and show why. When I first came into command of the department the policy to be pursued toward the inhabitants of the country occupied by our troops, with respect to their property and the supplies we might find necessary to take for the army, was yet to be determined.

I found the system in force in other commands to be to pay those who took the oath of allegiance and not to pay those who did not.

A serious objection to this, in my opinion, was that a weak or a bad man might take the oath and get the money and be a rebel nevertheless; and then a good man, loyal and true, whose circumstances, family, age, or infirmity might hinder from taking up arms for the Government, and who would willingly take the oath, might, by the changes in the war, be left at the mercy of the rebels when our forces should withdraw from his section of the country. It is well known how much mischief has been done by requiring this prematurely where we did not continue to have the power to protect those whom we called out and thus drive away those who would have been able to give us important aid or information or subjecting them to great hardship and imprisonment. The principle I adopted was to take whatever I needed for the use of my troops, paying only those whom, by investigation, I could satisfy myself were good Union men, and giving all others certificates only, setting forth what was taken from them, and that they would be paid at the end of the war if they could show that they had been loyal citizens and not given aid or comfort to the enemy, thus, to the extent of what was taken, putting them under bonds for good behavior.

That I used freely the resources of the country may be seen from the evidence of Lieutenant-Colonel Myers, my chief quartermaster (see proceedings of December 18), and papers submitted by him, showing the instructions given through him for seizing supplies and accounting for them.

Lieutenant-Colonel Myers says, with reference to the supplies taken:

I think claim was made on me for nearly all these stores. None were paid for, however, as far as my knowledge goes.

Payment was refused on the ground of their being rebels, antagonistic to the Government. Payment was always refused to disloyal persons on the ground that they were disloyal.

General Wadsworth (see proceedings of December 17), in answer to a question as to General McDowell's conduct toward the inhabitants of the country, either as respects themselves or their property, says:

As respects their persons, he protected non-combatants from disturbance or molestation by the soldiers as far as possible.

As respects their property, he took a large amount of forage for public service at the time it was needed, paying loyal citizens in money, and giving to those of questionable loyalty verbal or written assurances that they would be paid after the war if they were loyal from that time on. He did not allow marauding by soldiers.

General Haupt (see proceedings of December 6) being asked, "What rule did General McDowell establish as to the property of the inhabitants of the country required for the use of the troops under his command," says:

That it should be taken whenever necessary for the use of the army, but always by proper requisition. General McDowell claimed the privilege of being, as he frequently said, the only plunderer in the Army of the Rappahannock. He would take what he needed for the use of the army, but could not permit his men to plunder on private account. When property was taken receipts were given as evidence of the fact. Orders were given to leave subsistence sufficient to keep families from starvation.

He further says:

Lumber was taken wherever it could be found. Nearly all the timber suitable for bridging was exhausted in the vicinity of Potomac Creek, and all the timber of suitable dimensions that could be found in Fredericksburg was used in reconstructing the bridge across the Rappahannock. A large machine-shop and foundery, with all the machinery and tools appertaining thereto and the materials on hand, were appropriated for the use of the road in Fredericksburg.

And that as to colored fugitives—

They were employed, and to the extent of all that could possibly be procured.

See Lieutenant-Colonel Tillson's (proceedings, sections 2 and 6) and

Major Brown's evidence (proceedings of December 2) for further details of property taken and colored fugitives employed for the public service.

Colonel Schriver (proceedings of December 1) being asked—

Do you or not know if supplies for the army were not frequently and largely ordered to be taken from the inhabitants of the country in which we were operating?

Answer. I do.

Question. What knowledge have you that supplies have been ordered to be taken in large quantities from the inhabitants for the use of the army?

Answer. I have heard General McDowell give such orders repeatedly, and I have given them myself in his name.

I will here give in full the orders on the subject of taking property from the country and accounting for the same, with the form of certificate prescribed to be given the owner.*

I also give my order respecting the employment of colored fugitives to relieve the troops from the fatigue labor, and thus increase the number for armed service.†

* * * * * * *

It will be seen from Colonel Schriver's testimony (proceedings of December 1) that on the occasion of his march from Front Royal to Luray General Shields was authorized and instructed in Colonel Schriver's letter to him of June 4 to "take such supplies as the troops may require."

From all this it is clear I observed the Regulations of the Army, which are in accordance with all well-regulated warfare.

There are some who think that to live off the enemy's country means to live at free quarters, and for every one to take whatever he needs or desires. This is simply pillage, and no army can exist where it is allowed.

The only safe rule is to lay it down as a law that no one shall interfere with the rights of property save he who represents the Government. That the Government only has the right to take private property for public purposes; that until the Government, through its proper agent, the general commanding-in-chief, seizes private property, it is to be protected, and those taking it without authority are to be considered as much guilty of theft or robbery as if they had done the same thing in their own State; that all supplies seized by proper authority become the property of the Government, and are to be accounted for as regularly as if purchased with Government funds.

This protection to be given not only because these people for the time have no other government than that the general commanding may give them, and are entitled, as long as they are obedient to that government, to be protected by it, but mainly because it is necessary for the army itself—for its discipline, its *morale*, its safety—that it shall be a body of soldiers, not a band of freebooters and *landsknechts*, and for the country that the citizens who have entered the army honest and law-fearing shall not return as thieves and robbers.

The case I have before referred to as having been so condemned by one of the Senators of my own State on the floor of the Senate is that of a Mr. Hoffman, of Belle Plain. This person was a farmer, who had his year's crop of corn in granaries near the temporary landing of Belle Plain—two houses full of corn.

This corn I ordered to be taken (see evidence of Major Tillson, proceedings December 2) for the use of the Government, as well as his

* See, in proceedings of eighth day, General Orders, No. 8, May 7, and No. 18, of June 3.

† See, in proceedings of eighth day, General Orders, No. 10, of May 10.

clover and a field of growing corn. He came to see me; and as I was going from Aquia to Federicksburg, in company with some members of the Cabinet, he met me at the Accokeek, and asked if I would pay him for his grain and if he could have any protection for his growing crop. (See evidence of Major C. Brown, of December 2.)

I questioned him as to his conduct in reference to the war. He claimed to have had nothing to do with it; to have refused to sell anything to the other side, appealing to his full granaries to prove his statement; avowed his sympathies, however, to be with the South. I told him in that case he could not expect I should strengthen his hands by giving him pay for his crops. He then asked if his grain crop near his house, on which his family depended for their sustenance, might be spared; that he was near the high road taken by the trains coming down to the landing, and was molested by the small parties coming with them by their burning his fences and turning his fields out in commons. I promised him his fences should not be further disturbed (there was an abundance of wood near), and that he might go on raising his crop. I was then feeding from the Government stores several hundred women and children who had fled to the army, and as a matter of economical administration of the resources of the country wished as much grain, &c., raised as possible.

None of us then thought we should ever give up a foot of ground north of the Rappahannock, whatever else might come.

The Secretary of the Treasury, whom no one will suspect of not having been and not now being in earnest in the prosecution of this war, was present, and my action in the case struck him as a matter of course.

I had taken all the farmer's grain, giving nothing but a statement of the fact, and promised him protection for the growing crop and the reserve of corn kept at his house for the use of his family. Everything else in this case was but a mere fulfillment of that promise and an enforcement of the orders I gave to carry it out.

I ordered a sentinel to be posted from the command at Belle Plain over Mr. Hoffman's premises. This duty was neglected; he came again; again was the order given; when, finding the order still neglected, I instructed a staff officer to write a peremptory note to the commanding officer, making him accountable that the orders given should not be so disregarded. The terms employed by the officer I did not see, it being a matter of detail into which I did not examine. Major Breck, assistant adjutant-general, the officer in question (see proceedings of December 2), says:

> General McDowell directed me to order Colonel Meredith to have the house and corn of Mr. Hoffman protected, and he told me at the same time that a similar order had already been given, and directed me to make this order strong and peremptory. With these directions I wrote the order. General McDowell did not see the order I drew up, to my knowledge. Those directions that I speak of was all he had to do with it, so far as I know.
>
> Question. Did the witness understand the instruction to make the order peremptory to refer to the failure of the commanding officer to comply with previous orders?
>
> Answer. I understood that the cause of the previous directions given me to make this order peremptory was because the first order had not been obeyed, the property having been injured since, and further to enforce military discipline.

I will now give that part of the debate in the Senate which refers to this case, taken from the Congressional Globe:

> Mr. WADE. I have here an order from General McDowell that I ask to have read, just to show the principle upon which this accursed war is prosecuted.
>
> The Secretary read as follows:

SPECIAL ORDERS, No. 68. } HEADQUARTERS DEPARTMENT OF THE RAPPAHANNOCK, *Opposite Fredericksburg, May 26, 1862.*

Colonel Meredith, commanding the Fifty-sixth Pennsylvania Volunteers, will furnish from his regiment a guard for the home and property of Mr. L. J. Hoffman, who lives near Belle Plain.

Colonel Meredith will see that no more corn is taken from Mr. Hoffman and that no more fencing is disturbed. The guard will be so placed as to make this sure, even if it should be necessary to place a sentinel over every panel of fence.

By command of Major-General McDowell:

SAML. BRECK,
*Assistant Adjutant-General.*

Official:

E. P. HALSTEAD,
*Captain, Assistant Adjutant-General.*

Col. S. A. MEREDITH,
*Commanding Fifty-sixth Pennsylvania Volunteers.*

(Sent by Mr. Hoffman.)

I am told that that Hoffman, whose every panel of fence is to be guarded by a soldier paid for out of our pockets, is as arrant a traitor as there is on the face of God's earth. Now, sir, what say you. Can we reach that property? Can we forage on the enemy? The Senator says no. Restrained by the Constitution, are we? We cannot even take it on the field!

The high place Mr. Wade occupies in my native State and in the Senate, his known ardor in the prosecution of this war, and his devotion to the country, caused, I am told, this unfavorable comment on the little that seems to have reached him respecting my policy, to lower me in the eyes of many good people and to do me much harm with my men.

Another prominent complaint was my protecting certain wheat fields near the Lacy or Chatham house, belonging to an officer in the enemy's service. When we arrived opposite Fredericksburg these fields were green with a promising crop of wheat in drills, then growing most luxuriantly. Contrary to orders, a regiment of cavalry, rather than take the trouble to cut wood, which was near in great abundance, burned several panels of the fence, and thus allowed the animals to enter the fields to tread down the wheat. I caused the regiment to rebuild the fence and the fields to be guarded till the wheat matured. Then it was harvested, thrashed out, taken to a mill near by, ground into flour, and fed to the troops. This matter was simply a question of economy for the Government. (See evidence of Colonel Schriver, proceedings December 15, and Captain Chandler's evidence.)

This is the case on which the charge was built of my harsh conduct to General Shields' division. They were in no way concerned in it.

As to protecting property generally, I did so, and for the reasons stated. There is such a thing as economy in war. There is no need to destroy what you may afterward want yourself. Whether the growing grain was the property of Union men or not I protected it. In either case the army would need it. The same with houses; to burn and destroy simply because the property belongs to the enemy and will irritate him can have no effect on the war, except to strengthen the feeling which causes it to be maintained on the other side.

If the buildings or the crops were likely to fall into the enemy's hands it would be different. In such cases I have caused them to be destroyed.

As to the effect on the discipline of the troops of the policy pursued by me in this respect General King states (evidence of December 17):

The effect upon the troops was excellent, and the policy, in my judgment, the best that could have been pursued.

Question. Was a supposed change in this policy the cause of any falling off in the discipline?

Answer. Yes, sir; very great and serious.

In fact the discipline of the troops at Fredericksburg in the early part of the occupation of that place was a matter of surprise to every one. Nothing was harmed, or when it was every measure was taken to detect and punish the offenders.

It is true I suffered from the representations made in the papers and to Congress, and when a change was supposed to have been made by my successor there was great satisfaction expressed. But soon the great and serious falling off in the discipline became so alarming that, on the representation of it to the commander-in-chief, he issued an order more stringent even than mine had been, and I see by one of the opening paragraphs in his recent report that the subject of his having been supposed to authorize what the papers proclaimed for him was a matter of serious annoyance.

It will be seen by a reference to General Orders, No. ——, that the very system I pursued in my department, and which my successor was supposed to have changed, was adopted by the Government and made general for the whole Army.

## CORRESPONDENCE WITH THE ENEMY'S COMMANDERS.

The subject of my correspondence with any of the enemy's commanders needs but a few words. All the correspondence I ever had is before the court. It was mainly concerning the widow of Robert E. Scott, esq., of Fauquier, whose husband had been murdered by our men, and whose death had made the deepest impression unfavorable to us of anything that had occurred in that part of the country since the beginning of the war. He was the prominent Union man of Virginia. I have been told on good authority that he would have been admitted in the Cabinet on the formation of the present Government.

His death was an event which the enemy sought to turn against us. So on grounds of policy as well as sincere sympathy for a delicate woman, left alone in the country with a young family, I was desirous of doing what I could to carry out her wishes. The correspondence, however, speaks for itself, and it is not necessary to refer to it further.

## REDUCTION OF TRANSPORTATION AND CAMP EQUIPAGE CAUSE OF ILL-FEELING.

On the subject of the mobility of our troops, and the consequent complaints of officers and men, it will be seen from my orders that every effort was early made by me to reduce as far as possible the baggage train of the army, so that the troops might be in condition for active operations. These orders have some time since been made general for the whole Army by orders from the General-in-Chief.

I was, unfortunately, so far as I was personally concerned, ahead of my time in this respect, and the neighboring commanders not having the same rules, when troops from them joined me and came under my more stringent ones, they became dissatisfied, or my own men became so when they served with those who had greater allowance of camp equipage than my orders permitted. On this subject see the following evidence of Major Tillson: (Proceedings of December 8.)

Question. Was this reduction of baggage in the division to which you were attached the cause of complaint or dissatisfaction or grumblings?
Answer. It was.

General King (see proceedings December 17):

Question. Do you know if the arrival near your division of troops more abundantly provided than they were with wagons, tents, &c., was the cause of any remarks or feeling with reference to the allowances made to your division?
Answer. It was.

General Hartsuff (see proceedings December 15):

Question. What reduction was made in the means of transportation and in the camp equipage on your coming under General McDowell's immediate command at Fredericksburg?

Answer. The number of wagons to each regiment was reduced to seven or eight, I think. The Sibley tents with which the command was furnished were changed to shelter-tents. Officers' baggage was necessarily considerably reduced, and the baggage of company messes and baggage generally of officers and men.

Question. Do you know if the reduction of means of transportation and camp equipage was a cause of any feeling or the subject of any remark in the brigade (Hartsuff's)?

Answer. It was the cause of considerable feeling and of many remarks of ill-feeling or ill-will toward General McDowell by officers and men. I did not hear the remarks of the men, but am satisfied remarks of the kind were made.

Question. State if you know of any other cause of ill-feeling toward General McDowell, or dissatisfaction with him in that brigade, connected with their having been under another department commander, where these restrictions had not been made.

Answer. Three of the four regiments composing my brigade had been under the command of General Banks. The brigade was, as they believed, temporarily attached to General McDowell's command. They were very desirous of getting back under General Banks' command, believing the amount of transportation they brought to General McDowell's command would be restored to them, and with it their baggage and comforts.

General Hartsuff (proceedings December 15) being asked if the forced march which I made over the Blue Ridge to Front Royal (to comply with orders given me) was the cause of any complaint, states:

It was the cause of complaint, and I saw afterward letters written by officers of the brigade and published in Boston newspapers, containing severe strictures on General McDowell, as the author of suffering on the marches. The letter was filled with falsehoods.

Question. Was there any complaint that the men were forced over the Blue Ridge in the rain without tents or shelter?
Answer. There was such complaint.

He further says there was a severe rain-storm during nearly the whole of the night.

It will be recollected this was all done to comply with the President's orders, and was nothing more than is incident to military operations; but the troops who made the march were not used to it.

## POLICY PURSUED TOWARD THE INHABITANTS.

As to the policy I pursued toward the inhabitants of the country with respect to themselves I refer to General Orders, Nos. 12 and 19, and Special Orders, No. 65 (proceedings of November 29), which, taken in connection with my orders concerning their property, will show the nature of that policy. It was simply as a matter of justice to them, as one of discipline to my men, to protect their persons from outrage and insult, and so much of their property as was not needed by the army from destruction or damage; in return, to require them, at the peril of their lives, not to harm my communications, either by rail or telegraph, or see them harmed by others.

## PELEG CLARKE'S CASE.

I have now to refer to the testimony of Peleg Clarke, of Fredericksburg (see proceedings of December 8), who alleges that he informed me of the presence of a rebel officer within my lines, and that, being so informed by him on several occasions, I took no steps to arrest him; and, further, that mails, salt, sugar, coffee, boots and shoes, and small-arms were suffered to be taken from Fredericksburg through to the enemy; that sentinels on post in Fredericksburg were prohibited by the inhabitants of the homes they guarded from getting water to drink or taking shelter on their porches when it rained, and that notorious rebels were allowed to enter our lines.

Everything which Peleg Clarke testified to, except the matter of the rebel officer, occurred when I was far away from Fredericksburg and after I had been relieved from the command of the department.

He says as follows to the question:

When did these occurrences—bad treatment of soldiers by citizens and rebels allowed to enter our lines—take place?

Answer. Those that came under my observation were in July. I can't give the several dates—about 6th, 8th, or 10th.

Question. Between what dates or periods were these supplies you have referred to, such as shoes, salt, &c., allowed to pass through the lines at Fredericksburg?

Answer. About the same time I speak of; just prior to that.

Question. Do you know of any practices such as you have stated occurring prior to July last?

Answer. I left there about the 27th of May, I think it was, and returned the forepart of July, that is, early in July, and knew of no such thing until after my return.

Question. Do you know if General McDowell was ever informed by yourself or others of these occurrences; that is, of irregular mails, supplies, &c., having passed to the enemy?

Answer. I do not, sir.

Colonel Schriver, chief of my staff (proceedings of December 9), being asked to state to the court the rules established by General McDowell for the government of the town of Fredericksburg and for granting passes to and fro—

Answer. The subject was with General King, who had full powers in the case. King also had the government of the town.

Question. Did General McDowell, save in some exceptional cases, interfere and in person take charge of the subject—the government of the town or intercourse with its inhabitants?

Answer. No.

In continuation Colonel Schriver states that my headquarters were established near Fredericksburg the 4th or 5th of May and removed from there the 26th of May, Front Royal being the destination when we left, and that they were not again established at or near Fredericksburg, and that he never knew of any cases having been reported to me either before or after my headquarters were at Fredericksburg of persons passing supplies of salt, shoes, sugar, &c., or passing noted rebels through the lines; and, further, that I "refused license to trade or establish shops in Fredericksburg because the rules of the blockade would be violated thereby."

It will be seen that during the time Peleg Clarke states these things to have been done, to wit, in July, I was not near the place. It will be also recollected that I was superseded by General Pope June 26.

On the subject of trade, General Wadsworth (proceedings of December 17) being asked—

Do you recollect if General McDowell did not write or telegraph you to discourage the coming of traders to Fredericksburg at the time his headquarters were opposite that place?

Answer. I recollect receiving a communication of that sort from him.

I utterly refused any one my permission to open trade in Fredericksburg.

There remains now of Peleg Clarke's testimony what he states in relation to Little, whom he says was a rebel adjutant.

He states he spoke to me three times about Little; once in the Lacy house hall as I was passing through to go out of the house, when he says, "General McDowell seemed to be engaged and in a hurry to attend to other business. It was with difficulty, after waiting some time, that I saw him at all."

"The second interview," he says, "was on the west portico of the house; does not remember that any one was directly present; General McDowell's men were all busy and passing by."

"The third interview," he says, "was on the east steps of the Lacy house," and there was at the foot of the steps, I suppose, some 20 or 30 men on horseback.

In the first interview he states he did not mention that Little was in the rebel service. The last time he saw me I was evidently about to mount my horse, as my escort was at the door. In both cases where he states he referred to Little's character no one was with us. He alone can testify what took place, and by the rules the court has adopted I have been unable to establish anything as to the character or the light in which he appeared to me at the time referred to.

The court has restricted me in this case to establishing the general character of the witness for truth and veracity in the community where he resides; a rule inapplicable in his case, as his place (Fredericksburg) is in the hands of the enemy. I did not, however, seek to establish anything as to his general character for truth and veracity.

In a campaign a general in command of an army is approached or has occasion to see and receive statements from men of all kinds, of every degree of intelligence, of every degree of reliability. The weight he may give to the statements he receives will vary with the individual and the circumstances under which he comes before him. The story of of an intelligent negro or a stupid one, a deserter, a prisoner, a rebel officer, a rebel citizen, a Union man, one of his own men, or one of his own officers, or one of his own personal staff, would each, depending on the subject, receive different degrees of credit. In one case a story might be believed when the same story told by another would be utterly discredited. What, therefore, I wish to bring before the court was the light in which, from what had taken place concerning him, Peleg Clarke appeared to me during these moments in which he succeeded in catching me whilst busy in attending to the wants of a large force, concentrating and preparing it for an offensive movement against the enemy. He was living in Fredericksburg when the war broke out; had had transactions—under compulsion, he states—with the rebel army; had sold them supplies; had property marked "Confederate States" in his warehouse; was known in Fredericksburg as a Union man, and came to our troops as soon as they arrived.

He had his private grievances, his claims for compensation, his wrongs, and other personal matters to attend to. I had appointed a governor of the town, and in addition had assigned a general commanding a division to the special duty of attending to all these details, that they might not interfere with the main object of my being there.

Yet Mr. Clarke persisted in coming to me, and therefore saw me with difficulty and in the casual way he describes. My recollection of him is simply of a man annoying me with what seemed far more closely connected with his personal matters and his animosities than with the public service. The cry of traitor, rebel, or secessionist had become so common as to attract but little attention. When a man had anything anybody else wanted he was denounced as a traitor. General King states (proceedings of December 17) concerning Little:

> I recollect a man whom I supposed then, and still suppose, to be a private citizen of Fredericksburg. He was frequently at my headquarters, and I understood either from him or some friend of his that he had been in the militia of Virginia some months previous, but was not so any longer. I think he told me so himself.

The whole matter made but little impression on my mind at the time. In the way it was presented, as far as I can recollect it, it seemed to me to interest Mr. Clarke far more than it concerned the public service.

## GENERAL SIGEL.

I come now to the subject of General Sigel's strictures, &c.

It may be remembered how much was said last August and September of General Sigel's having shot me on the field of battle for being a traitor; how the whole country was filled with the most extraordinary accounts of my treason and his patriotism.

Immediately after the campaign denunciations of me were to be heard, I was told, in every hotel and in every street. The public seemed to have received the impression that though the report that he had killed me was an error, yet that we had had some violent altercations and quarrels, if not actual personal conflicts, on the field itself. I had heard of some of these stories before we left Fairfax Court-House—that of his having shot me on the streets of Warrenton—and it was on this account I sought to speak to him, and that he declined, as he states (December 20), "to hold any private conversation with me." His so declining was the first knowledge or intimation I had of his having any unkind feeling toward me, and up to the time of this investigation I have remained in ignorance of the cause of offense he conceived I gave him. He has now disclosed it. It is inconceivable how such a cause could produce such results. Two staff officers reported to him some expressions of mine they (the staff officers) thought improper. The principal cause of offense, he says (proceedings of December 20), was the remark that I made to his aide-de-camp, Captain Dahlgren, "that General Sigel shall fight his own corps." Captain Dahlgren states (December 30) that this remark was made in answer to a question asked by him for his own information. It was neither a message to General Sigel nor an answer to me from him. Captain Haven (proceedings of January 8) states "the remark was made in a manner indicative of surprise at the question" asked by Captain Dahlgren, which was concerning some minute details.

I have referred thus to the principal cause to avoid speaking of the minor ones.

General Sigel, on being interrogated, stated the following as causes of bias in his mind against General McDowell:

1st. When I was at Winchester and General Frémont at Mount Jackson and Port Republic I could not perceive why the corps of General McDowell did not assist better the troops under General Frémont, and that Jackson was allowed to overcome General Shields and to go to Richmond to fight against General McClellan.

2d. When our troops had arrived at Culpeper on the day of the battle of Cedar Mountain after a march of one day and one night, and were unable to march 7 miles farther to assist General Banks, I was of the opinion that General McDowell's troops were at Culpeper before, and I did not understand why they did not assist General Banks on that day, and why he had to fight alone with 9,000 men against 25,000, the battle resulting almost in the destruction of General Banks' corps.

3d. When at Waterloo Bridge I was under the supposition that General McDowell would support my corps.

The following causes he stated to qualify his judgment that General McDowell was not attentive to his duties as a general officer:

1st. I do not believe that General McDowell did what he could under the circumstances to hinder General Longstreet to join General Jackson. I am not certain, but I believe that he left not a sufficient force at Thoroughfare Gap, or in the neighborhood, to prevent the enemy's troops to pass by this defile, which is very easy to defend.

2d. I further believe that there was not the necessary co-operation between the two corps on their way to Manassas—my corps and that of General McDowell—by which want of co-operation we lost the opportunity to attack the enemy on his left flank while he was retreating from Manassas.

3d. On the 29th of August, at the battle of Bull Run, it would have been necessary that General McDowell had made a disposition by which our two corps could act with more unity.

4th. I believe he could be on the battle-field with the greater part of his troops at an earlier hour of the day. I also believe that he did not give his troops the right direction on the 29th, because, instead of attacking the enemy on his right flank by coming in on our left, his troops, as much as I could see, came in from the rear; that is to say, instead of coming in the direction of New Market, he came in the direction of Centreville.

5th. I cannot understand for what reason General McDowell left the position he had on the 28th in the evening, which would have been, according to my opinion, the right place for attacking the enemy on his right flank on the 29th.

6th. I think that General McDowell neglected to get a personal knowledge of the affairs of my corps on the 29th of August.

As to the first case presented by General Sigel—that of the operations in the valley of the Shenandoah, and that of my not having assisted General McClellan when I was at Fredericksburg, which General Sigel mentions as another cause for his unfavorable opinion of General McDowell—they are so fully given elsewhere in this statement that it will not be necessary to repeat them here.

## GENERAL SIGEL'S CHARGE OF MY FAILING TO SUPPORT GENERAL BANKS AT THE BATTLE OF CEDAR MOUNTAIN.

The next case is that of my not having assisted General Banks at the battle of Cedar Mountain till after he was nearly destroyed.

This is a simple matter, fully explained by the testimony of General Roberts and General Pope (proceedings of January 8 and January 13).

The latter, after stating the movements of the various bodies of troops prior to the 8th and those of the enemy these movements were to meet, says:

> During the 8th of August, or at least during the earlier part of that day, it was uncertain whether the main force of the enemy was marching upon Sperryville or upon Culpeper, but in either case I considered it proper to concentrate my forces in the direction of Culpeper, in order constantly to be interposed between the enemy and the lower fords of the Rappahannock.

I accordingly sent orders to Banks to move forward to the same place with all speed. Banks arrived at Culpeper in due season, but to my surprise I received a note from General Sigel, dated at Sperryville, about 6.30 in the evening, acknowledging the receipt of my order, and asking me by what road he should come to Culpeper. As there was but one road, and that a broad stone turnpike, that led directly from Sperryville to Culpeper, I was at a loss to know how General Sigel could entertain any doubts upon the subject. This doubt of General Sigel's delayed the arrival of his corps at Culpeper several hours.

When the reports began to come in from General Bayard that the enemy was advancing upon him, and that his cavalry was forced to retire, I advanced Crawford's brigade of Banks' corps to observe the enemy, to support Bayard in holding the enemy in check, and in determining his force and movements as far as possible.

Ricketts' division of McDowell's corps was on the same day (8th of August) moved to a point 2½ or 3 miles south of Culpeper, and near to the place where the road from Madison Court-House to Culpeper comes into the road from Barnett's Ford to Culpeper. Early on the morning of the 9th I received information from General Buford, at Madison Court-House, that the enemy was on his right, on his left, and partly in his rear, and that he was retiring toward Sperryville.

On the morning of the 9th of August I pushed Banks in front with his corps to join the brigade of that corps which had gone to the front the day previous. General Banks was instructed by me to move his corps to the position occupied by that brigade; to take up a strong position there to check the advance of the enemy. This instruction was in a personal interview with General Banks at my headquarters at Culpeper.

I told General Banks if the enemy advanced to attack him he should push his skirmishers well to the front and notify me immediately, it being my wish to gain all the time possible to concentrate our forces at Culpeper Court-House. General Banks' corps at that time, from his consolidated report transmitted to me a few days previous, numbered over 12,000 infantry and artillery, and this I understood to be the strength of his corps when he was pressed to the front.

Three miles in rear of the position which I expected him to occupy was Ricketts division of McDowell's corps.

Desultory firing was kept up all day long on the 9th, during which time I received a number of reports from General Banks, in none of which did he consider that the enemy was in any great force in front of him. In one of his notes, dated about 3 o'clock in the day, he mentioned that the enemy was displaying his cavalry ostentatiously; that he had seen no considerable force of infantry, and that he did not believe that they intended to attack. These notes I have, and I can submit them to the court if they so desire it. The last note I received from General Banks was dated about 5 o'clock. He spoke then of the skirmishers approaching each other, and did not indicate that he expected any engagement or ask for any assistance

Before I had received this note, however, the artillery firing had become so rapid and continuous that I feared a general engagement was going on or might be brought on at any moment. I therefore instructed General McDowell to push forward Ricketts' division as rapidly as possible to the field. General McDowell was in nowise responsible for anything connected with these movements, but in all respects carried out my instructions faithfully and zealously.

By referring to General Roberts' evidence in connection with the foregoing it will be seen that General Banks, who was to act on the defensive and hold the enemy in check till the army could be concentrated, believing the enemy not in force, assumed the offensive, and attacked him, contrary to the expectations of the commander-in-chief, and thus was repulsed with heavy loss before the arrangements which the latter had made could be completed.

It will also be seen it was ordered that General Sigel should follow and support General Banks; and from General Pope's testimony, that General Sigel did not do so because of his unnecessary delay in complying with the orders to march to Culpeper, which caused him to arrive too late, it had been arranged by General Pope, as I afterward understood, that Ricketts' division of my corps should constitute the reserve because the other division of the corps (King's) was on the march from Fredericksburg, and he wished to put Ricketts' where King could join him on his arrival, and thus avoid dislocating my command.

The delay in the arrival of General Sigel caused Ricketts to be sent forward in his stead.

It is plain the failure to have troops near to General Banks at the time he moved his corps forward into battle was not due to any neglect of mine, though it will perhaps be noticed from General Pope's evidence that it may have been so from that of my accuser.

### NOT SUPPORTING GENERAL SIGEL AT WATERLOO.

General Sigel was at Waterloo August 24 and 25, leaving there on the night of the 25th.

Major-General Pope, then the commanding officer of General Sigel and myself, marched with my corps from the Rappahannock on the 22d to Warrenton, and remained with its headquarters at Warrenton till the afternoon of the 25th. He testifies that on those days "all the dispositions of my corps were made by his orders and under his immediate observation." (See proceedings of January 12.)

General Pope further states as follows:

Question by General McDOWELL. Did or not, so far as you know, General McDowell neglect or fail in any way to carry out any of your orders, as to the disposition of his corps at or in the vicinity of Warrenton or Sulphur Springs or Waterloo, with reference to any movement you had ordered General Sigel to make?

Answer. He did not. When we commenced the movement toward Sulphur Springs and Warrenton, on the 23d of August, it was on information that large forces of the enemy had crossed the Rappahannock at Sulphur Springs and Waterloo Bridge. The river having risen 6 or 8 feet on the night of the 22d, so as to destroy the fords, I proposed to throw my whole force upon whatever forces of the enemy were upon the north side of the river, hoping to be able, on account of the high water, to crush them before they could succeed in recrossing the river. General Sigel, commanding the left, was instructed to push forward to the Waterloo Bridge, following the course of the Rappahannock. I told him I would push forward McDowell's corps from Warrenton to join him if necessary near Waterloo Bridge, but on the 24th I sent a strong reconnaissance forward to Waterloo Bridge, under General Buford, from Warrenton, and he reported to me on the afternoon of the 24th that there was no enemy on the north side of the river, and that he had fired the bridge at Waterloo. I immediately informed General Sigel of the whole of these facts, that I was sure there was no enemy between him and Waterloo. I therefore did not consider it necessary to push McDowell's corps any farther in that direction. As soon as the advance of General Sigel's corps reached Waterloo General Buford took post with all his cavalry on his right, and picketed the river for several miles above Waterloo. I make this statement to show why the corps of General McDowell was not advanced toward Waterloo Bridge on the 24th.

The dispositions of my corps on the 25th were in strict conformity with General Pope's general order of that day. (Recorded with proceedings of January 7.) From General Sigel's official report it would seem he wished it to appear I was in some way connected with, if indeed not responsible for, his movement from Waterloo Bridge in the night to Warrenton. He says he had been under my command since his arrival at Waterloo; had sent to me for instructions, &c. Yet he has himself presented to the court (proceedings of January 7) a copy of my note, taking command of his corps (for a special purpose, under the instructions of General Pope), which note is dated the 26th. It was in fact issued after his night march from Waterloo, and when he and his whole corps had fallen back behind mine. If he ever sent to me for instructions on the 25th I could have given him none, for he commanded a corps under the orders direct of the general commanding the army. The evidence shows, in fact, that he sought his orders and instructions from the only source that could then give them—General Pope's headquarters, and not mine. He further says, "I was to have relieved General Milroy's brigade at the bridge." In this he mistakes the general order of General Pope of the 25th, which directed the army to be posted with its left on the Rappahannock at Kelly's Ford—to be occupied by Reno—and the right held by my corps at Warrenton. Waterloo was to be held only by cavalry, and Buford was there for the purpose, with a brigade (Tower's) on the Waterloo road to support him, and the other three brigades of Ricketts' division supporting the advance brigade. I know that these troops were so posted, for I visited them in person on the night of the 25th, before General Sigel fell back. The general also refers to having received a mutilated order from me, which confused matters. Whilst in a more correct statement of the case in his testimony he admits "that it was signed, and I believe by a staff officer of General Pope. I do not know," he continues, "whether the order was written at Warrenton or Warrenton Junction."

I refer to these inaccuracies of General Sigel in his report to show the bias of his mind against me, which led him to endeavor to throw the blame on me without cause.

### LONGSTREET AND THOROUGHFARE GAP.

The mountain ridge which runs to the east of north from Warrenton to the Potomac is quite continuous, but with narrow openings every few miles called "Gaps," through which pass the roads from the Potomac to the Blue Ridge.

The first of these openings north of the one taken by the turnpike from Warrenton to Fairfax Court-House, Centreville, and Alexandria is called Thoroughfare Gap. A few miles north of Thoroughfare Gap is Hopewell Gap; next comes Aldie Gap. The railroad from Front Royal to Manassas, and the country road from Salem and White Plains, in the Piedmont District to Manassas, come through Thoroughfare Gap and cross the Warrenton turnpike at Gainesville. There is also an east and west road through Hopewell Gap; and the Little River turnpike to Germantown, Fairfax Court-House, and Alexandria goes through Aldie Gap.

In throwing back the right of the army along the Warrenton turnpike General Sigel, who had fallen behind my corps at Warrenton, was under my command and in front in this retrograde movement, and reached Buckland Mills, with his advance 3 miles beyond, at Gainesville, on the afternoon and evening of the 27th. My corps and Reynolds' division followed and closed up with him that night, one of the divisions having marched from near Sulphur Springs and the other from half way between Warrenton and Waterloo.

It was known to us by telegram from General Pope at Warrenton Junction that Jackson's corps had come through Thoroughfare Gap and was at or near Manassas, and, by a reconnaissance made by General Buford in the direction of Salem, that Longstreet was marching in the same direction after Jackson. It was in reference to what I did or did not do to prevent Longstreet coming through this Gap, or to delay his coming through, that General Sigel finds cause for censure.

General Sigel says (December 20):

> In the first place I do not believe that General McDowell did what he could under the circumstances to hinder General Longstreet to join General Jackson. I am not certain, but I believe that he left not a sufficient force at Thoroughfare Gap, or in the neighborhood, to prevent the enemy's troops to pass by this defile, which is very easy to defend.

He further states:

> I believe that on the 28th, in the morning, one division should have been posted so

as to hinder General Longstreet to pass either Thoroughfare Gap or Hay Market, if it was too late to occupy the Gap.

He continues:

I would have sent about 10,000 men, with the intention to retard the movements of General Longstreet. I do not believe that these troops are sufficient to fight them all day, but I think they were sufficient to retard his movements.

Being asked if he would, under the circumstances,

Have considered that four brigades, sixteen regiments of infantry, twenty-four pieces of artillery, and two brigades of cavalry, in the aggregate between 11,000 and 12,000 men, a sufficient provision to hold Longstreet in check,

Answers:

I would have regarded it as a sufficient provision if these troops were placed at the right point at the right time.

These extracts from his evidence show clearly what General Sigel thought should be, and thinks should have been, done in this case.

He also states:

I did not hear of any engagement near Hay Market and the Gap; this induces me to say I do not believe the necessary arrangements were made to hinder Longstreet from joining the army.

General Sigel acknowledges an interview to have taken place at Buckland Mills, on the night of the 27th, between himself and General McDowell, on the subject of what dispositions should be made for the ensuing day and what troops should be left at Thoroughfare Gap.

As to this interview, being asked by General McDowell (December 24):

Does the witness remember what General McDowell said to him would be the dispositions for the succeeding day? Does he remember whether it was the witness' corps, or the witness' corps, with a division from General McDowell added to it, that General McDowell decided to leave for the defense of Thoroughfare Gap?

Answer. I do not know anything about that; at least it must have been so indefinitely said to me that I did not mind it.

Question. What did General McDowell propose to witness at his headquarters concerning the defense of Thoroughfare Gap and holding the enemy in check at that point?

Answer. He did not make any definite proposition.

Question. What were those opinions or expressions of General McDowell on that occasion with reference to the subject of holding the enemy in check at Thoroughfare Gap or this side it?

Answer. Many different opinions were expressed by General McDowell. He was not sure whether a corps should be sent there or a division, or what corps or what division; and I, therefore, as I did not like to impress upon him my own judgment, left it with him to decide and to order, and to give me instructions.

Question. When you left Buckland Mills on the morning of the 28th did you or did you not know General McDowell had made any provision for meeting Longstreet at or this side of Thoroughfare Gap?

Answer. I did not know anything at all.

Judging from this testimony of General Sigel any one would say he marched from Buckland Mills without knowing anything of General McDowell's arrangements for meeting the enemy the next day in the direction of Thoroughfare Gap.

Yet I shall show he knew that in the first place he himself was assigned to this duty, and that one of my divisions was to remain behind to support him; and, in the second place, that subsequently he knew this duty was assigned to Ricketts' division.

On both these points the court has the best proof, furnished by the testimony of General Sigel himself.

See the following order, introduced by General Sigel, and appended to the proceedings of January 7:

HEADQUARTERS THIRD ARMY CORPS,
*Buckland Mills, August 27, 1862—11.30 p. m.*

It being understood that a large division of the enemy under Longstreet left Salem at 4 o'clock p. m. for the enemy's position in the direction of Manassas, through Thoroughfare Gap, and is now on the march, the following preliminary movements of the left wing of the army will be immediately made, and Major-General Sigel's corps will without delay be concentrated at or near Hay Market and Gainesville. A division of the Third Corps will be left at Buckland Mills to operate against the flanks of the enemy or march to Hay Market, as shall be found most expedient. King's and Ricketts' divisions will march to Gainesville, and start at 2 o'clock a. m., to attack the enemy's position in the direction of Manassas. This attack will be supported under the provision of the general order from headquarters of the Army of Virginia by the command of Major-General Heintzelman, now at Greenwich, and which will be on the right of the attack.

By command of Major-General McDowell:

S. F. BARSTOW,
*Assistant Adjutant-General.*

This order was written by me in General Sigel's room at Buckland Mills after a full conversation with him, and embodied the result of that conversation. General Sigel had gone to sleep while I was writing, and not wishing to disturb him (for we all needed rest when we could get it) I went to my camp and gave the rough of the order to a staff officer to put in form and carry into effect; but before I thought he had done so I received the following order from General Pope:

UNITED STATES MILITARY TELEGRAPH,
(Received at Bristoe Station August 27, 1862, 9 p. m.)

Major-General McDOWELL:

At daylight to-morrow morning march rapidly on Manassas Junction with your whole force, resting your right on the Manassas Gap Railroad, throwing your left well to the east. Jackson, Ewell, and A. P. Hill are between Gainesville and Manassas Junction. We had a severe fight with them to-day, driving them back several miles along the railroad. If you will march promptly and rapidly at the earliest dawn of day upon Manassas Junction we will bag the whole crowd. I have directed Reno to march from Greenwich at the same hour upon Manassas Junction, and Kearny, who is in his rear, to march on Bristoe at daybreak. Be expeditious and the day is our own.

JNO. POPE,
*Major-General.*

This caused a change to be made in the preliminary dispositions I had directed, and the following order was issued:

GENERAL ORDERS, No. 10.

HEADQUARTERS THIRD ARMY CORPS,
*Reynolds' Camp, August 28, 1862.*

1st. Major-General Sigel will immediately march with his whole corps on Manassas Junction, his right resting on the Manassas Railroad.

2d. Brigadier-General Reynolds will march on the turnpike immediately in rear of General Sigel, and form his division on the left of General Sigel, and march upon Manassas Junction.

3d. Brigadier-General King will follow immediately after General Reynolds, and form his division on General Reynolds' left, and direct his march upon Manassas Junction.

4th. Brigadier-General Ricketts will follow Brigadier-General King, and march to Gainesville, and if, on arriving there, no indication shall appear of the approach of the enemy from Thoroughfare Gap, he will continue his march along the turnpike, form on the left of General King, and march on Manassas Junction. He will be constantly on the lookout for an attack from the direction of Thoroughfare Gap, and in case one is threatened, he will form his division to the left and march to resist it.

The headquarters of the corps will be at King's division.

By command of Major-General McDowell:

ED. SCHRIVER,
*Colonel and Chief of Staff.*

This is the order for the march of the troops from Buckland Mills to

Manassas Junction, which General Sigel received at 2.45 o'clock on the morning of the 28th:

Being asked—

Will the witness state if this is not a copy of the order of march of which he acknowledged the receipt?

Answer. I confess that I have never read this order; at least I do not remember to have read it, because it is in contradiction with my acts and my understanding of our situation at that time, and if I had read it it would be in my memory, I think.

(The General Orders, No. 10, just referred to, was read by the recorder.)

The witness desired to make a correction of his last answer. From a reperusal of the order I would like to have the words "because it is in contradiction with my acts and my understanding of our situation at that time" considered no part of my answer. I add in regard to this that the order I received was written on thin paper and I believe in pencil.

Question by General McDOWELL. What order did you receive from General McDowell of which you acknowledged the receipt, and in compliance with which you marched from Buckland Mills?

Answer. I received the order to march to Manassas Junction, and it may be that it is the same order as this here, but I do not remember that it was such a general order.

General McDowell here asked a suspension of the examination of the witness, with a view of proving the delivery of this order on that day.

The court informed General McDowell that a delay or suspension in the examination of this witness for the reason stated was unnecessary.

Major Willard testifies (proceedings of December 31) that he copied a full copy of General Orders, No. 10, of August 28, 1862, for General Sigel, and that it was sent to him.

The witness continued:

Very often when a general order is received by a corps commander he only takes in his mind that part of the order which affects his own corps, and that therefore I may not remember very well now, after the lapse of many weeks, that I received this general order.

Question by General McDOWELL. Does the witness mean to be understood that the whole of that general order did not affect him, and does not the name or designation even of general order indicate this?

Answer. Certainly; I admit that the whole order, if I had received it, did refer to me, but especially what is referred to in the first part, which point I fully admit I understood and acted upon it—I mean the order directing me to march to Manassas Junction.

Question by General McDOWELL. Was it not your duty to have made yourself acquainted with every part of a general order sent you, especially one inviting co-operation of your forces with those of another?

Answer. Certainly it was my duty, but if this was the order sent to me I must have regarded it as pretty indefinite, all things taken into consideration.

Question by General McDOWELL. You state that when you left Buckland Mills on the morning of the 28th you did not know anything at all of any provision being made by General McDowell for meeting Longstreet at or this side of Thoroughfare Gap. Does or does not the General Orders, No. 10, for the march make provision for this?

Answer. The order mentioned makes a provision.

To show further that General Sigel knew of both these orders, and that he did know what arrangements I had made with reference to the enemy's force coming through Thoroughfare Gap, and knew he himself was to have had this service, see evidence of Lieut. Col. Henry E. Davies, Second New York Cavalry, as follows:

Question by General McDOWELL. Were you not for a short time on duty with Major General Sigel on the 28th of August, 1862?

Answer. I was.

Question by General McDOWELL. Who placed you with General Sigel and for what purpose were you so placed?

Answer. Major-General McDowell, for the purpose of showing to Major-General Sigel the country between Gainesville and Thoroughfare Gap and in that vicinity at General Sigel's request.

Question by General McDOWELL. At what place and at what time was this done?

Answer. In the evening of the 27th of August, at or about 10 o'clock, at General Sigel's headquarters at Buckland Mills.

Question by General McDOWELL. Did you or do you know for what purpose General Sigel wished to know from you the next day concerning the country between Thoroughfare Gap and Buckland Mills?

Answer. I understood that General Sigel had been assigned to the duty of occupying Thoroughfare Gap.

Question by General McDOWELL. Did you on the 28th bring any message from General Sigel to General McDowell which could show that the former knew that General McDowell had taken or was to take measures for meeting the enemy coming through or from the direction of Thoroughfare Gap.

Answer. I did; in marching from Buckland Mills toward Gainesville I showed to General Sigel a cross-road leading over to Hay Market. He asked me some questions about the road, and then sent me back to General McDowell, instructing me to say to General McDowell that the division which was to hold Thoroughfare Gap had better go by that road.

Captain Leski, an aide-de-camp on my staff (January 6), states that the force sent under General Ricketts to Thoroughfare Gap consisted of four brigades of infantry, of about 8,000 men, two brigades of cavalry, and six batteries of artillery. He also states (January 5) that by General McDowell's direction he went in the night of the 27th and 28th of August to see if troops could be sent up to the Gap on the west side of the stream running by Buckland Mills, which he found it would be impossible to do; that early in the morning of the 28th, before daylight, General McDowell sent him to General Sigel for Bayard's cavalry (which belonged to my corps and had been sent by me to General Sigel); that General Sigel said it would be impossible for him to advance without cavalry; that he would send them as soon as he could, stating at the same time that the First New Jersey Cavalry was somewhat beyond Buckland Mills and could be used; that as soon as we came in sight of this cavalry it was sent immediately to Thoroughfare Gap to get news of the enemy, and that shortly after General McDowell sent him also to Thoroughfare Gap, with instructions to bring as early news as possible about the enemy.

Captain Leski sent me back the following:

10.15 A. M.

The enemy is advancing through the pass.

W. LESKI,
*Captain and Aide-de-Camp.*

Colonel Wyndham will hold them as long as he can and asks to be re-enforced.

W. L.

This was sent by the hands of my aide, Captain Wadsworth, to General Ricketts, and indorsed as follows:

AUGUST 28.

Send a brigade and battery to Colonel Wyndham and follow them up with your whole division.

ED. SCHRIVER,
*Colonel and Chief of Staff.*

General RICKETTS.

This order General Ricketts received and obeyed.

General Ricketts was asked (January 6) by General McDowell, "What o'clock on the 28th of August were you ordered to march from your bivouac beyond Buckland Mills?"

Answer. I was ordered to march at 2 o'clock in the morning.

Question by General McDOWELL. How far did you march on the Warrenton turnpike before you turned off the road to go by Hay Market under the orders given you by Captain Wadsworth?

Answer. I had crossed the bridge at Buckland Mills and was but a very short distance from it.

Question. Do you know any cause of delay in your getting forward from your bivouac to the place where you turned off; were there any obstructions in the road?

Answer. The road was very much encumbered by wagons; I saw a very large number in the vicinity of this stream—Broad Run.

From all this it is evident—1st, that I took the very measures General Sigel censures me for not having taken; and, 2d, that General Sigel knew I had taken them. It will not fail to be noticed, however, that what General Sigel condemns me for not having done is precisely that which my then commanding general regrets I did. General Pope says (January 14) in reference to his order, dated Bristoe, August 27, 1862—9 o'clock p. m.:

The order directing General McDowell's march would have carried him to the eastward, and in the same direction in which the main body of the enemy was marching to aid Jackson. I believed then and believe now that we were sufficiently in advance of Longstreet, who was supposed to lead the main body of the enemy, that, by using our whole force vigorously, we should be able to crush Jackson completely before Longstreet by any possibility could have reached the scene of action. I sent nothing to General McDowell concerning Thoroughfare Gap, and regretted afterward that any portion of his forces had been detached in that direction. General McDowell had the discretion, however, necessarily incident to his position and to his distance from me, to make such a disposition to cover his rear as he might consider necessary.

From the order of General McDowell, which he showed me afterward (the Orders No. 7), I understood that the movement of Ricketts' division was made conditionally, and in view of the possibility of an attack upon his rear from the direction of Thoroughfare Gap.

It will be seen from General Pope's telegrams to me of the 26th and 27th that after the chances of a battle at or near Warrenton had passed, he expected one might take place near Gainesville; hence his telegraphing me "that we had best move with our whole force to occupy Gainesville, so as to secure our communication with Alexandria." His general order, dated Warrenton Junction, August 27, is to the same end. This order required that my corps, General Sigel's corps, and Reynolds' division should pursue the turnpike as far as Gainesville; that the corps of Heintzelman and Reno, and eventually that of Porter, should concentrate in that direction by way of Greenwich, and that Reno and Heintzelman should support me in any operation against the enemy.

My preliminary order of August 27 was based on this order of General Pope and on the information I had received at Buckland Mills and on my way there, which information was then unknown to General Pope, who was now away from telegraph lines. I directed the holding of the strong position of Buckland Mills and Hay Market, with a support at Gainesville (the three places being nearly equidistant from each other), so as to hold or check any force coming through either gap, whilst two of my divisions, with the corps of Heintzelman and Reno, should go against Jackson in the direction of Manassas. I sent to General Pope soon after I received it the information I had obtained of the near approach of Longstreet and informed him of the dispositions I had made. My communication had hardly gone before I received his order to march my whole force to Manassas. Hence my General Orders, No. 10, changing the arrangements I had made and conforming them to General Pope's orders. It will be seen that whilst I did so I provided for the contingency of an attack from Longstreet from the direction of Thoroughfare Gap, which the information I received left no doubt would be made if we did not get forward most expeditiously and at the earliest moment. To make sure of this I ordered the troops to march at 2 o'clock a. m. General Sigel's rear division had been ordered in my preliminary order of 11.30 p. m. of the 27th to march upon Gainesville immediately, and should have been in motion before the others. The orders I gave General Sigel at Warrenton to march on the turnpike from that place (see January 7) directed him as follows:

No wagons but for ammunition will accompany your corps on this road. Your baggage trains will immediately proceed to Catlett's.

Notwithstanding this order, which was also given to my own command and enforced in it (I had myself nothing but my horse), General Sigel had with his corps nearly 200 wagons, which kept blocking up the road and retarding the movement; and notwithstanding I had seen him on the morning of the 28th, before he left and I had urged on him personally to march immediately and rapidly and had shown him General Pope's orders to me requiring this to be done, yet his advance was so slow that the note written to me by Captain Leski at Thoroughfare Gap at 10.15 a. m. and received by me near Gainesville and then sent to General Ricketts, reached him just this side of Buckland Mills, a distance of about 3 miles from his bivouac of the night before. His division had been on their feet since 2 o'clock a. m.—over 9 hours—and in that time had not gone twice the length of the division front from where they started. For an account of the efforts made to get the troops forward over this fine turnpike road, which General Sigel states had no obstructions on it, see evidence of General Ricketts, Colonel Schriver, Major Barstow, and Captain Haven, from which it will be seen that the provision I had made for Longstreet, and which General Pope says was not in compliance with his orders and could be only justified by the danger I might find myself in from an attack on the rear of my column, was owing entirely to the delays, for which I certainly was not responsible. I knew well the difficulties in moving so large a body of men and artillery over the same road under the most favorable circumstances, and wished therefore it might be unobstructed. The first battle of Bull Run was seriously affected by a small baggage train getting into the column, as in this case, contrary to orders. We had great delay and confusion on account of baggage wagons at Culpeper and on the march to Warrenton. Hence my rigid order that no wagons should go on this road.

I do not feel called upon to go into the question of what was done or what was not done by the force sent to Thoroughfare Gap; that concerns more particularly, so far as personal matters go, the general under whom they were sent. My duty consisted, I submit, in sending—if it was proper I should send at all—an adequate force "to the right place and at the right time." The time was the earliest one possible under the circumstances produced by my accuser, and the place is the one he himself has indicated, and the force a greater one than he has named. So, whatever disapprobation my conduct in this matter may have merited, he of all others should be the last one to censure me. The general (Ricketts) sent to Thoroughfare Gap did hold Longstreet in check during that day.

## WANT OF CO-OPERATION BETWEEN GENERAL M'DOWELL'S AND GENERAL SIGEL'S CORPS ON THE MARCH FROM BUCKLAND MILLS.

In reference to this General Sigel says:

I further believe that there was not the necessary co-operation between the two corps on their way to Manassas—my corps and that of General McDowell—by which want of co-operation we lost the opportunity to attack the enemy on his left flank while he was retreating from Manassas.

And, further:

When our troops were on their march to Manassas I was of opinion that a battle would be fought near the point where the troops of General McDowell were at that time. *I ordered all the troops back* and formed them in line of battle, advancing about a mile toward Groveton.

In reference to having then again received the order from General McDowell to march to Manassas General Sigel continues:

I said nothing and marched to Manassas, but I thought that it was a great mistake. By saying that it was a mistake, I meant to say that the troops lost time in marching and counter-marching to come to the same point nearly on the evening which they left at noon in compliance with orders of General McDowell.

When General McDowell's troops and my own were on the march to Manassas Jackson changed his position and was on his march between Manassas and Gainesville. He therefore was not in order of battle, and presented us his left flank. If my corps and a division of General McDowell's would have attacked him he would not have been able to come so early to the point which he intended to reach—a point between Groveton, Centreville, and New Market; and, secondly, if my corps had not been ordered to march to Manassas we would have been able to assist General King or those troops which were attacked on the evening of the 28th. By sending away my corps either of these opportunities was lost.

I do not think it probable that they would have defeated the enemy, but we would have retarded his movements, brought him to a stand, where he perhaps would not have liked to fight, and given an opportunity to the commander-in-chief to see clearly where was the enemy's position and to what points he should direct his troops.

On the night of the 27th of August the corps of General Sigel was between Gainesville and Buckland Mills; his advance at the former and his reserve at the latter place. General Sigel knew on the 27th that his corps would have to march early the next day. In his note to me from Buckland Mills on the afternoon of the 27th, whilst I was still at Warrenton, he says:

We should all be here to-night and press forward to-morrow at daybreak.

And in another note from the same place he says:

I think they (the enemy) should be attacked at once at Manassas Junction.

General Pope's order of march to Gainesville; my conversation with General Sigel at Buckland Mills; my preliminary order of 11.30 of the 27th; our situation at the time with respect to the enemy, all must have shown him that an early movement was a matter of course.

By the orders of General Pope the whole force was to march rapidly at the earliest dawn of day upon Manassas Junction; the right resting on the Manassas Railroad, the left well thrown to the east.

These orders were sought to be carried out by me in General Orders, No. 10, heretofore referred to in the chapter on Thoroughfare Gap.

In the first place it is to be remarked that General Sigel himself admits that this order does provide for a co-operation between the two corps.

It cannot be said the order was fully carried out. In the first place, though the troops were started early enough in the morning, the march, in spite of every effort on my part, was not a rapid one. It was, on the contrary, a slow one. There is much evidence to show that by noon General Sigel's column was about 2 miles only from Gainesville, where his advance had been the night before. (See General Sigel's, Lieutenant-Colonel Tillson's, Captain Dahlgren's, Major Kappner's evidence.) Under the preliminary order of 11.30 of the 27th he should have had his troops in motion before the others, who started at 2 o'clock.

General Reynolds, who was immediately behind General Sigel's corps, could not get forward, and sent word back that General Sigel was stopping the road. (See Colonel Schriver's evidence.) Major Barstow, who was sent forward, says he found General Sigel halted; Major Kappner, of General Sigel's own staff, speaks of General Sigel "breaking up his camp at about a quarter to 12." (See proceedings January 29.)

The first consequence of this stopping up the communications was the necessity of detaching Ricketts as a rear guard toward Hay Market, to hold Longstreet in check, as has been before described.

The next departure from the orders given General Sigel was in his not going to the north of the railroad, instead of, as he persisted in doing, going to the south of it. He was directed to march with his right resting on the Manassas Railroad. On being asked by General McDowell—

Why did you fail to obey General McDowell's order, which required you to march on Manassas Junction, with your right resting on the Manassas Railroad?

Answer. I believe that I did not disobey the order of General McDowell, because I understood that I should march to Manassas Junction, and having arrived there, form my corps so that the right rested on the Manassas Railroad. 2d. If I could have undertaken to march to Manassas Junction with my right always on the railroad it would have been impossible to do so, according to my best knowledge; and, 3d, there seemed to me a contradiction in the order in saying that I should march to Manassas Junction and in the same time to rest with my right on the railroad. I understand that this word "resting" can only relate to the formation of troops and not to their march.

It is hardly necessary to call attention to the verbal criticism in the foregoing of the use of the word "resting" as applied to a march, which was repeated in General Orders, No. 10, from General Pope's orders, "resting" in this connection being equivalent to "being."

That it was impossible for him to march with his right always on the railroad was proved not to be the case by the march of the other divisions north of the road.

As to his understanding he was to go to Manassas by the most convenient road he could find, and when he arrived to form with his right on the Manassas road, he could not have had this understanding from the orders given him, for the word "formation" and "form" was not used as applied to his corps.

On this same subject he states in his official report:

I received orders at 3 o'clock in the morning to march to Manassas, and to take a position with my right resting on the railroad leading from Warrenton Junction to Manassas Junction; so at least I understood the order.

It will be seen that Warrenton Junction is not mentioned in either General Pope's order or my own.

He seeks to explain this by saying there is a piece of the railroad between Manassas Junction and the station common to both the Orange and Alexandria and the Manassas Gap roads, the station being about a mile east of the Junction. The Junction is, in fact, the only point in common. But admitting what he says as to the piece being in common, it has nothing to do with his statement, for it is the section between the Manassas Junction and the Warrenton Junction on which he says he understood he was to rest his right, and this is all of it west of the Manassas Junction.

Is not the whole manifestly a pretext to excuse his non-fulfillment of the orders he received?

In his evidence General Sigel admits having marched south of the railroad.

Captain Haven, my aide-de-camp, was asked:

Did General McDowell send you to General Sigel at Gainesville on that morning? What message did you carry and what was General Sigel's answer?

Answer. General McDowell explained to me that General Sigel was to cross the railroad at Gainesville, then turn to the right and march along the railroad to Manassas, and told me to go forward and see if General Sigel was so doing. I found General Sigel at Gainesville near where the four roads meet. He said to me he would go a little farther, a few hundred yards beyond the railroad, because the road made an angle with the railroad and would then turn off to the right. I made known to General Sigel the message upon which I was sent.

Question by General McDOWELL. What seemed to be understood by General Sigel as to the route he was to pursue to Manassas with respect to the Manassas Railroad?

Answer. That after crossing the railroad from the south side to the north side he was to march by the side of the railroad to Manassas.

See also Captain Krebbs' evidence (proceedings of January 14).

Question by General McDOWELL. Did General McDowell send you to General Sigel on the occasion of the march from Gainesville toward Manassas Junction on the 28th of August last, after the skirmish of Reynolds' division?

Answer. He did.

Question. Where did you find General Sigel's command, on the north or the south side of the Manassas Railroad?

Answer. I found General Sigel's command on the south side of the railroad—he and staff—I should think about 4 miles from Gainesville, on the south side of the railroad.

Question. Did you represent to General Sigel that he was not on the right road, and that it was General McDowell's order that he should go to the north of it?

Answer. I told him that he was mistaken; that I understood the order that his right should rest on the railroad, his left on our right, which was on the Warrenton turnpike.

First Lieut. William Burchard, on General Sigel's staff, says (proceedings of January 30):

General McDowell asked me how far from this place on the Manassas Junction road was General Sigel, and I told him about 4 miles. General McDowell said, "All right; go to General Sigel and tell him he should take position—the right on the railroad, the left on the pike."

See also evidence of Captain Haven, January 8, as to the interview of one of General Sigel's aides with General McDowell as to the route General Sigel should take. He says:

A second aide (the first did not speak English well) came and asked, "Did General McDowell send an order for General Sigel to go to the right of the railroad?" General McDowell replied emphatically, "No! He is to go with his right on the road."

It will thus be seen it was not for want of reiterated orders, both written and verbal, that General Sigel put himself and persisted in keeping himself south of the railroad, when his orders were that he should go to the north of it. There may have been want of co-operation here, but I feel it is not justly to be ascribed to me. This departure by General Sigel from General Orders, No 10, was the cause of another (Reynolds' division) marching along the turnpike some 2 miles beyond Gainesville and then turning off to go in the direction ordered; and not having General Sigel's corps between it and the railroad, as I had provided for, left so wide a gap that I then brought King's division to the right instead of the left of Reynolds, my object being to have the troops thus marching on Manassas separated by such intervals as would give them the proper space for being brought into line to the front. That this *was* carried out with any great precision or *could* have been so in a broken, partly wooded country, with places impracticable for artillery, is doubtful, but I suppose it might have been sufficiently so for practical purposes. At all events, it was incumbent on us to make every effort to try and do so as nearly as possible to comply with the orders from general headquarters. I did not pretend to superintend the details of the march of either General Sigel's corps or of the divisions, or either of them, or of my own corps. My time and attention were fully otherwise occupied. It has been thought—because later in the day, and when the troops were put in march for Centreville, both Reynolds' division and Sigel's corps passed by Bethlehem Church on the railroad, near which road King had also been—that my whole force, instead of being marched so as to cover a wide front, was marched by a flank along the railroad. General Sigel marched, in spite of my efforts, south of the road; King to the north of the road, with Reynolds to his left. The latter, I am told, tried to move by heads of brigades, but the country was too rough on his left to enable him to continue to do so. When I joined Reynolds' division and gave it orders to go to Centreville it was some distance from Bethlehem Church (see evidence of Colonel Schriver), but went by that place as the nearest way to its destination.

It is to be observed, however, that it is not for any failure in complying with the general order, or in attempting to do so, that General Sigel finds me wanting. It is that for the want of co-operation, as he calls it, between the corps, we lost the opportunity, as he says, to attack the enemy in his left flank while he was retreating from Manassas; that he was of the opinion a battle would be fought near the point where the troops of General McDowell then were, and he ordered all the troops back, and formed them in line of battle, advancing about a mile toward Groveton. To show this to the court, General Sigel has submitted maps, with the position of the enemy placed in a way that supports the view he has taken, and he has sent up the officer of his staff, Maj. Franz Kappner, who saw the enemy at the time he wished to attack them in flank, and when, by my orders to march to Manassas, he was prevented from doing so.

The witness had also a map with the enemy's position all marked down, showing how he might have been defeated, there being, he says, only one army corps of the enemy there at that time, which, being on the march and not in position, was, according to strategic rules, in danger of being flanked and defeated.

In consequence, he adds, of our retreat from that position the enemy had ample time to put himself in position and await re-enforcements. It will be seen with what confidence General Sigel states where the enemy was going and what was his object. He says:

> Jackson changed his position whilst we were on the march to Manassas, and was on his march between Manassas and Gainesville. He therefore was not in order of battle and presented us his left flank, and had he been attacked he would not have been able to come so early to the point he intended to reach between Groveton, Centreville, and New Market.

As it is in Major Kappner's reconnaissance this impression was primarily made on General Sigel, I will refer to it more fully. The major says that at—

> About 10 o'clock in the morning, the center of General Sigel's army corps being about 3 miles from Gainesville and taking their rest, some of General Sigel's escort came in and told him that the enemy advanced from the right corner of the left flank. In the proper time I have asked General Sigel for to give me 24 cavalrymen for to go out and see if the information of the scouts was correct.

Going about 1¼ miles, he came to a cleared hill, from which he had a "very far view," from which he could see Centreville.

> Saw about 5 vedettes to the front toward General Sigel's march line, and about a quarter of a mile distant from that vedettes there was about 50 cavalry of the same vedettes, and [on] the route toward Groveton from New Market I saw an infantry column—about three regiments. All this has happened. I immediately let General Sigel in writing know. I reported to General Sigel that the army (General Sigel's),

with wagons and artillery, could pass along the road without interruption, as well as the movements of the enemy was reported to General Sigel. I remained at the same position about half an hour. I saw General Sigel with a part of his army coming before the same position; this was about quarter to 12 in the morning. General Sigel telled me that before he break his camp he sent a report to General McDowell. When I came to General Sigel, when he was below the hill, and wanted to stretch his column to engage the enemy, there came an orderly officer from General McDowell. The orderly came with an order to General Sigel to immediately march on Manassas. General Sigel at the same moment took the same route as he came to march toward Manassas to comply with the order of General McDowell.

As General Sigel has made it a great point that the line of battle which he had formed to go against the enemy was broken up by me, it may be well to call attention here to what that line amounted to.

According to this officer of his own staff, the chief engineer, it amounted to an intention to form a line and that none was formed, General Sigel going back to the south of the railroad by the route he came.

Question by the COURT. Who was the officer who took the message from General Sigel to General McDowell, referred to?

Answer. Assistant Engineer Burchard, formerly assistant engineer, at present first lieutenant and aide-de-camp on General Cluseret's staff.

Question by the COURT. Did you see Lieutenant Burchard start to go to General McDowell?

Answer. No; not while I was on the hill, but Lieutenant Burchard came back again and informed me while I was there.

Question by the COURT. From that hill could you see Manassas Junction?

Answer. No; it was too far to the left.

Question by the COURT. Could you see Centreville from the hill-top?

Answer. Yes.

Question by the COURT. Did you see any other positions of the enemy than what you have described?

Answer. None but what I have stated. It was not everywhere that I could see, on account of little woods.

Question by the COURT. Could you see General McDowell's corps?

Answer. Not on the 28th; there were woods in the rear of me. It was everywhere woods, but in that particular place open fields.

Question by General McDOWELL. How far was the enemy from you on the hill?

Answer. My impression is about a strong half mile.

Question by General McDOWELL. How long was the enemy's column?

Answer. One hundred and twenty yards. It might have been more, for they were already turning upon the turnpike, and I could not see all.

Question by General McDOWELL. How long were they in sight?

Answer. About five minutes; then I lost sight of them as they were turning the road. Whether there was one regiment or three regiments I cannot tell. They might have been going forward a long time and this may have been their rear.

Question by the COURT. The witness has said there might have been one regiment. Why did he previously say there were three regiments?

Answer. When I have seen the troops march (so I have observed for 120 yards), whether they have marched by fours or sixes I could not judge. I have stated they were about three regiments, but there might have been but one.

The major began with an army corps, which General Sigel adopts as Jackson's army. We have seen it come to a column of three regiments; then it gets to what may be but one regiment of infantry and 55 cavalry.

I will now refer to the testimony of First Lieutenant Burchard, who it is stated was the officer sent to me to acquaint me of this position and force of the enemy.

Question by the COURT. What was your rank and position in the military service of the United States on the 25th of August last?

Answer. I was engineer with General Sigel in the Army of Virginia; had no military rank—no commission at that time.

Question by the COURT. Did you take any information from General Sigel to General McDowell on the 25th of August last?

Answer. No information from General Sigel to General McDowell.

Question by the COURT. Did you make any communication from anybody to General McDowell relating to the position of the enemy?

Answer. I gave information to General McDowell relating to the position of the enemy from myself. I received no orders from any one.

Question by the COURT. State that information.

Answer. I was sent out by order of General Sigel to our left, after we heard some firing, with 20 men—cavalry. I crossed the field to Fairfax Court-House pike and came near Groveton, where I found the enemy in position. As I came back near Gainesville, and about 1½ miles from Gainesville, I saw General McDowell, and I thought it my business to report to General McDowell what I saw and where I had been sent. General McDowell asked me how far from this place on the Manassas Junction road was General Sigel, and I told him about 4 miles. General McDowell said, "All right; go to General Sigel and tell him he should take position—the right on the railroad, the left on the pike;" that is the only communication I took charge of.

Question by the COURT. When you went toward Groveton, and before seeing General McDowell, did you discover any portion of the enemy; and, if so, state what you saw.

Answer. Yes, sir; I saw some artillery, and some cavalry pickets. I think I saw a battery, but I cannot say, only I am sure there was some artillery. I saw of cavalry pickets some 10 or 12 men across the fields, and of cavalry in all something of about 50 men. I saw no infantry.

Question by the COURT. State whether you informed General McDowell what you had seen.

Answer. I told him that as I was out in that direction about 1½ miles I had seen some of the enemy and a battery in position. I don't recollect whether I said anything about the cavalry and pickets. This is all the information I gave to General McDowell.

Question by the COURT. Have you personal knowledge that any communication was sent to General McDowell on that day informing him of the presence of an infantry force to your left and front, or of the movement of a train of wagons on the pike toward Gainesville?

Answer. No, sir.

So it seems that Burchard brought no message to me of General Sigel having formed line of battle, of his having an army corps in front of him, or a brigade, or a regiment, or any infantry at all, or any message from General Sigel or anybody else, but bore one from me to General Sigel that he should get with his right on the railroad, which, however, he did not do.

As to this force which the lieutenant saw, it was the same one which fired into the head of Reynolds' column, and consisted of a section of artillery and some mounted men, evidently a reconnoitering party. (See evidence of General Meade, Lieutenant-Colonel Tillson, and Captain Haven, all fully agreeing on this point.) General Meade thought at first it injudicious in me to leave the road after this evidence of the enemy's being there, but he afterwards thought the party to be a mere demonstration.

There has been an impression that this small force that fired into the head of Reynolds' division, as it was coming up the road from Gainesville, was the same force that that evening became engaged with King's division, and was in fact the head of Jackson's army. General Sigel, it is plain to me, is under this impression. His maps and his theories and assumptions having been made, not at the time of the occurrences of which I am now seeking to explain, but from afterthoughts. It is a pity for the soundness of his theories he had not waited a little longer. He would have found that Jackson, whom he so confidently stated to have been marching by a flank, within striking distance of his head of column, and who was seeking to gain some point between Centreville, Groveton, and New Market was some 8 miles away, and marching in a different direction.

Fortunately, for a true understanding of the matter of Jackson's position, we have the account of Captain Pell, aide-de-camp to General Burnside, who was taken prisoner on the 27th, and was with the enemy's army all of the 28th and 29th.

It is curious, before getting at the exact truth, to recall the different reports or statements made with so much confidence by General Sigel. On the 27th, 1.50 p. m., he informs me—

> The enemy is at Manassas by this time and has beaten our forces there, and to proceed to Alexandria to destroy our depots.

In another he states:

> Jackson may be at Manassas or elsewhere.

Still later:

> Jackson must have been near Manassas Junction and beyond, near Kettle Run.

In the morning of the 28th he reported the enemy's main force still at Manassas Junction.

Still later he says that—

> Jackson was on the march between Manassas and Gainesville to go to a certain point between Centreville, New Market, and Groveton.

And it is on these assumptions he bases his opinions of my neglect of duty; that if I had not broken up his line of battle (which seems now not to have been formed) he would have defeated Jackson and he would have been in position to support King's division in the evening. It will be seen that he says he could not get forward to join King because it was too late in the evening. It may be asked, if he had marched, as he was ordered, rapidly, and thus have been an hour earlier, even if this junction could not have been made.

Captain Pell, fortunately for this case, can give us precise information, free from all speculative error.

He states that he left Manassas Junction about 9 o'clock in the evening of the 27th; the rebel troops commenced their march previous to that time; that he was with Ewell's division of Jackson's army, which consisted, he says, of three divisions, of about 21,000 men; that at about 10 o'clock a. m. of the 28th he was with the column of Ewell's division on Cub Run, somewhere near the crossing of a road to the north of the Centreville and Gainesville road.

He says:

> The troops I was with halted there for some hours, and then proceeded to a place called Groveton Heights, by the way of Sudley Springs. They arrived at Groveton Heights about 8 o'clock in the evening. There had been a battle there, in which Doubleday's division was, I believe, engaged. I personally reached Groveton Heights at this time. There were troops and wagons in front and rear of me. I think the greater part of Ewell's division was behind me, and know we passed a great many troops on the road during the day.

It will be seen from this how little all General Sigel's and his engineer's (Kappner) theories are worth concerning Jackson being at noon on the 28th with his flank within convenient distance of Sigel's column.

We were not only at noon, but since 2 o'clock in the morning, all in error as to the position of the enemy. It was not till the 30th I found out what it had been on the 28th, and it seems General Sigel has yet to find it out, without he has acquired his information since he was before this court.

I have had some difficulty in bringing before the court all the facts connected with these matters of the 28th. It is not always even one's staff—it is so with me at least—know the motives of their chief or know all the facts the chief becomes possessed of. This I find to have been the case about the change of the order of march of King's division and about the means and measurements I took to satisfy myself of the kind, strength, and object of the small force that appeared in the road and fired a half-dozen shots at us from a distant hill. It has been asked if this circumstance was reported to General Pope, and if it should not have been. Of the general principle that the general commanding an army shall be informed of everything that may affect it which comes to the knowledge of his subordinates, there can be no question; yet, on the other hand, nothing is so embarrassing, as I have found it to be in the two armies I have commanded, as to receive crude information of what is called a stampede, which tends more to embarrass than to serve any good end. I did not think of sending information until I found out what the party was, and when I did, it did not impress me sufficiently to make me judge it necessary to send across the country for that purpose only.

It will be seen I had communicated freely with the general commanding throughout the campaign. I would not have made an exception in this case had it seemed to me of importance. The importance it has since received grows out of the error in believing it to have been part of the main army of Jackson, which General Sigel thought was near Groveton at that time.

I do not pretend to be able to stand the test of being judged by "wisdom after the fact." I know nothing short of an omniscient being that could.

It was between 3 and 4 in the afternoon that I got word the enemy were not at Manassas, and soon after I received in quick succession the two notes from General Pope; the first one directing me to go to Gum Springs, some 20 miles off; also directing me to ascertain about certain matters in Centreville, and asking me to give him my views fully, as I knew the country, he said, better than he did; the last informing me that the enemy were in force on the other side of the Bull Run, on the Orange and Alexandria Railroad, and at Centreville, and directing me to march my forces direct for the latter place.

General Sigel had in the mean time reported to General Pope direct, and received orders direct from him to march to Centreville.

King's division, being nearest the Warrenton pike, was, after the receipt of General Pope's orders, directed upon it to go to Centreville; and Reynolds', being farther to the front in the direction we had been marching and nearer the road from Bethlehem Church to New Market and Centreville, was sent by that road. Under the belief the enemy was moving to the south of us to go entirely around and fall on our enormous wagon train under Banks, and was now on the opposite side of Manassas from where I was, and seeing from General Pope's notes that he was making mistakes as to distances and places, I wished, in order to answer his request, to give him fully my views, as I had been doing throughout the campaign—to confer with him personally, and went to Manassas Junction for that purpose.

My knowledge of the country was referred to because the topographical map of Northeastern Virginia had been made at my headquarters and largely under my own directions, and I was therefore supposed to be well acquainted with the whole country. Much of the country was laid down from actual surveys, but much, and particularly that part around Manassas, which had been made when the country was in the hands of the enemy, was entirely conjectural. Still I knew what was correct from what was supposed to be.

I did not find General Pope at Manassas, and just as I reached there I heard the sound of cannonading in the direction of Groveton, and immediately set out for that place. Failing to get there on the straight line we attempted, we had to go around by the Sudley Springs road, and did not reach the vicinity of Warrenton pike till late at night, when we lay down by a camp-fire of General Sigel's men till daybreak.

General King's division had gone along the road till near to Groveton, when, seeing the enemy to the north, they moved across from the turnpike and met them and had a short and severe action, in which only Gibbon's brigade and two regiments of Doubleday's were engaged. They repulsed the enemy and held their ground, remaining masters of the road. (See evidence of General King, Lieutenant-Colonel Tillson, and Captain Haven.) I had sent three of my staff with this division when I left it to go to Reynolds. During the engagement Reynolds' division was moving up the Sudley Springs road to join King, but night-fall stopped its march, and it got no farther than the hill above the Warrenton pike and about a mile from Groveton. General Reynolds had gone personally to King's division, and whilst there it was decided that the division should remain where they were until they had orders to the contrary, and Captain Haven was sent to report this to me. (See evidence of General Meade and Captain Haven.)

I proceeded to join Reynolds' division as soon as it was light enough to move, and found General Reynolds, who also had not been able to rejoin the command during the night, just returned from King's division, which he informed me had, after Captain Haven left, fallen back in the night to Manassas. (For the reasons of this step see evidence of Generals King and Ricketts.)

General King being asked by the court—

*Had you any orders or directions given to you by General McDowell to return that night to Manassas?*

Answer. I had no orders on that subject. I acted on my own responsibility.

The only orders I gave this division were to proceed to Centreville by way of the Warrenton turnpike.

## OPERATIONS OF GENERAL M'DOWELL ON THE 29TH OF AUGUST IN CONNECTION WITH GENERAL SIGEL.

General Sigel charges that I did not make the necessary dispositions on the 29th of August by which his corps and my own should act with more unity. He believes my troops could have been on the battle-field at an earlier hour of the day; that I did not give the right direction to my troops; that instead of attacking the enemy in the left flank I came in from the rear; that is to say, instead of coming in the direction of New Market I came in the direction of Centreville; that I neglected to get a personal knowledge of the affairs of his corps on the 29th of August, which made it impossible for me to make the arrangements as they had to be made, or were intended to be made, and he does not know for what reason I left the position I had on the 28th, in the evening.

The last paragraph refers to King's division, which fell back on General King's own responsibility, without any orders from me, in the night, to Manassas.

The charge of my not having made the necessary dispositions on the 29th for his corps and neglecting to get a personal knowledge of the affairs is based on the assumption he makes that he was under my command from the time we were at Warrenton till we arrived at Fairfax Court-House. To show how much he is in error in this, see his own evidence and that of General Pope.

General Sigel says (December 20):

After the engagements at Freeman's Ford, Sulphur Springs, and Waterloo Bridge I received an order from General Pope that my corps was attached to the command of General McDowell. I regarded myself under his orders from this time until after the battle of Bull Run.

Yet December 30 he says he does not know that he reported to me personally; does not know that he sent an officer to me to report for orders, either on the night of the 29th or on the morning of the 30th or on the night of the 30th, or whether on the 29th or 30th or after the 30th I sent him any orders; nor when he saw me come on the field did he report to me either in person or by his staff. These dates are those of the main battles of last August. If it will be borne in mind how rigid are the rules for reporting to commanding officers in all the German armies, to one of which General Sigel once belonged, it will be seen how little he regarded me as his commanding officer on the occasion.

It is before the court that I took command of General Sigel at Warrenton for a special purpose only, and had command of him on the march, under the orders of General Pope and the provision in such case made and provided by the Articles of War.

General Pope says (January 14):

Question by the COURT. Do you mean to be understood that on the morning of the 29th of August General McDowell was no longer responsible for the movements of General Sigel's corps and Reynolds' division? And, if so, produce the orders, if you can, investing him with such command before the 29th, and state any orders which may be given relieving him.

The witness produced a certified copy of General Orders, No. —, dated Headquarters Army of Virginia, Warrenton Junction, August 27, 1862, which is appended to the proceedings of this day and marked A.

Answer. I did not consider General McDowell as having any command over the corps of General Sigel or as being responsible for the movements of that corps any time during the 29th of August. I sent orders to General McDowell on the morning of the 29th of August, directed to him at Manassas Junction, instructing him to call in Ricketts' division and join it with King's, and, in conjunction with Major-General Porter, march upon Gainesville by the road from Manassas Junction.

On the morning of the 29th of August until the close of the campaign of Virginia General Sigel's troops, as every other corps of that army, was under my immediate command and received my direct orders.

In relation to the division of General Reynolds, I had supposed, until otherwise informed, that it had fallen back with King's to Manassas Junction.

I sent no orders to General McDowell or to General Sigel changing the relations they had with each other when they marched from Warrenton, for the simple reason that no such orders were needed; the connection between them being dissolved of necessity, either by the separation of the corps or by my own personal presence with them. It is not necessary to state to the court that I had no authority to merge into one two army corps established by the orders of the President; that any temporary connection between them, wherein one corps commander should command both corps, would last only so long as they served at a distance from the general-in-chief of the army to which they belonged.

On the 29th of August I received various reports from General Sigel before I reached the field of battle; saw him many times during the day of the 29th, and gave him several orders personally and by aides-de-camp.

I did not understand nor did I presume General Sigel to understand that he was responsible to anybody but myself for any movement of his troops or for any orders he might receive during that day.

Before leaving Reynolds' division to rejoin my corps at Manassas I instructed General Reynolds to support General Sigel. General Meade, of General Reynolds' division, testifies he saw General Sigel early in the morning of the 29th, before the battle, and showed him on the map where the division was. The division was constantly on General Sigel's left, fighting with it all day. Yet General Sigel says as follows in his testimony of December 20:

On the morning of the 29th I received direct orders from General Pope to attack the enemy; which I did about 6 o'clock in the morning. I did not know where General McDowell's corps was at that time or where any other troops were except those of the enemy.

As to the direction I gave my troops on bringing them into battle, which General Sigel says was wrong, I have only to say the direction they took was the one given them by the general commanding the army himself. (See General Pope's evidence.)

I did bring them up in the direction of New Market. They passed through New Market, and then were moving up to the left of Reynolds (see evidence of Lieutenant-Colonel Tillson), when they were recalled and brought over to the Warrenton turnpike by the orders of General Pope.

As to General Sigel's charge that he believed that I could be on the battle-field with the greater part of my troops at an earlier hour of the day, it will be seen that General Sigel says he did not know where my corps was or under what orders it acted. It is therefore more an unfriendly suspicion than a well-founded opinion he here expresses.

When I came up with King's division at Manassas—and I lost no time in joining it by a direct route—I found it getting ammunition and rations, for it had been for some time without food.

General Porter's corps came up from Bristoe and was on the west of it, and on the march to the front, which afterward took place under the orders General Pope had given in the first place to General Porter and then to General Porter and myself, it followed after General Porter's corps. As soon as we got to the front and I saw the condition of things and learned from General Buford the strength of the enemy coming through Gainesville, and that it was much inferior in numbers to General Porter's corps, and bearing in mind the troubles and delays I had experienced in getting ahead with a large force in front on the same road, I turned my troops off to the right, up the Sudley Springs road, to the main field, to come on the left of Reynolds. The testimony of Captain Leski, Lieutenant-Colonel Tillson, and Colonel Schriver will show I came back from the head of General Porter's column where my decision had been made, to the head of my own troops at full speed, and that I immediately set them in motion and took measures to get them into action at the earliest moment. How long this took and at exactly what hour they moved I cannot tell. I know, so far as I was concerned, not a moment was lost.

## GENERAL MILROY.

I have tried to answer all of General Sigel's charges, and there now remains but the one, made by General Milroy, of his corps, which may be looked upon as part of the same subject. General Milroy says as follows in his official report:

> Shortly after sunset my own brigade had entirely exhausted their ammunition, and it being considered unsafe to bring forward the ammunition wagons where the enemy's shells were constantly flying and exploding, and the enemy having entirely ceased their efforts to break through this part of the line and had thrown the weight of their attack still farther to my left, I ordered my brigade back some one-half of a mile to replenish their ammunition boxes and there wait further orders. I remained on the field with Lieutenants Esté and Niles, my own having been sent to see to my regiments. The enemy continued their attacks upon our left until long after dark, which it required the most determined and energetic efforts to repel. At one time, not receiving assistance from the rear, as I had a right to expect after having sent for it, and our struggling battalions being nearly overcome by the weight and persistence of the enemy's attack, I flew back about one-half mile, to where I understood General McDowell was with a large portion of his corps. I found him, and appealed to him in the most urgent manner to send a brigade forward at once to save the day or all would be lost. He answered coldly, in substance, that it was not his business to help every one, and he was not going to help General Sigel. I told him that I was not fighting with General Sigel's corps; that my brigade had got out of ammunition some

time before and gone to the rear, and that I had been fighting with a half dozen different brigades, and that I had not inquired whose or to what particular corps they belonged. He inquired of one of his aides if General ——— was fighting over there on the left. He answered he thought he was. McDowell replied that he would send him help, for he was a good fellow. He then gave the order for the brigade to start, which was all I desired. I dashed in front of them, waved my sword, and cheered them forward. They raised the cheer and came on at double-quick. I soon led them to where they were most needed, and the gallant manner in which they entered the fight and the superiority of their fire soon turned the tide of battle. But this gallant brigade, like the many others that had preceded it, found the enemy too strong as they advanced into the front and was forced back by the tremendous fire that met them. But one of General Burnside's veteran brigades coming up soon after dark with a battery again dashed back the tide of armed treason, and sent such a tempest of shot, shell, and leaden death into the dark forest after the rebels that they did not again resume the attack.

Captain Cutting's and Lieutenant Roebling's evidence shows the state of mind General Milroy was in when he rode up to me, and that Sigel was not referred to. General Milroy's own report, written some time after, when his mind might be supposed to be in its normal state, shows how extravagant and unmeasured he is in the use of language. When he spoke to me he was in a frenzy, not accountable scarcely for what he said, and attracted the attention of every one by his unseemly conduct. He says he had been fighting with six or seven different brigades. How, pray, did he or could he fight with them? What a picture does this present of a general roaming about without any control, interfering with every one. He admits that he was not with his own brigade, which had gone off the field. He used in his conversation with me the most unmeaning generalities, which gave no information whatever.

The troops he asked for were those of General Porter, drawn up as a reserve, and I hesitated to assume the responsibility of using them for fear of deranging the plans of the general commanding the army, whilst General Milroy gave me nothing whatever on which I could be justified in acting; and whilst in doubt for the moment, in view of the circumstances as to the course to be taken, I received a clear and definite message from that intelligent, as well as gallant, officer, General Meade, on which I knew I could rely, and immediately sent the re-enforcements forward.

The following evidence of General Buchanan, who commanded the force sent on that occasion, will show the condition of mind General Milroy was in, and how little his impressions at the time are to be relied on, either as to what he did or what I said. His statement that I refused to send re-enforcements to General Sigel is without foundation in anything I said or thought.

Question by General MCDOWELL. Lay before the court your letter to General McDowell of October 20, 1862, and say if the statements therein made are true.

Answer. That is the letter, and the substance of those statements is true, to the best of my recollection and belief.

"WASHINGTON, *October* 20, 1862.

"GENERAL: Your note inclosing a printed copy of General Milroy's report is before me, and I will answer the question *seriatim*.

"1st. As to the state of mind General Milroy seemed to be in, his manner, and the impression it produced at the time to which you refer; that is, when he rode up and asked for re-enforcements.

"Answer. General Milroy's manner was excited, so much so as to attract the especial attention of those present, and induced many to inquire who that was rushing about so wildly and what he wanted.

"2d. As to whether or not it was a question of my (your) sending re-enforcements to General Sigel and if I (you) refused to do so.

"Answer. General Sigel's name or corps was not referred to in my hearing, as far as I can recollect.

"3d. As to the part taken by General Milroy with your (my) brigade, which he claims to have led to where they were most needed, but from which they were forced back &c

"Answer. When re-enforcements were called for to go to the assistance of General Meade, I was ordered by General Sykes to take three of my battalions and move up to the front and left to the point most threatened, which I did at once. I left General Milroy haranguing and gesticulating most emphatically in the same place where his conversation with you commenced. He was calling for re-enforcements, and urging that if they were sent at once the day was ours, and that the enemy were ready to run. After I placed my three battalions in position I moved to the right of my line, where, to my surprise, I saw almost 100 yards to my right the remainder of my brigade, which had been sent to the front after I left, and General Milroy was giving it some orders. I at once rode up to him and told him that these battalions belonged to my brigade of regulars, and that I could not consent to any interference with my command. He said that he did not know they were my men and did not wish to interfere with me, and only wanted to place them in the best position. I told him that I was responsible for the position of my command, and did not want any assistance either in posting it or fighting it, when he left me. His own brigade was not near there, and he seemed to be rushing about the field without any special aim or object, unless it was to assist in the performance of other officer's duties whenever he could find any one to listen to him. I did not lose one inch of ground after I got my brigade together, which I did immediately by moving this latter portion to the left, but held the enemy at bay for an hour, and, instead of being forced back, I maintained my position until ordered to fall back to the position from whence we started. Had the enemy "forced" me back, in the sense of General Milroy's report, he would have obtained possession not only of the turnpike, but of the stone bridge, and what would have been the result you are well aware—our defeat would have been disastrous.

"I am, sir, respectfully, your obedient servant,

"ROBT. C. BUCHANAN,

"*Lieutenant-Colonel Fourth Infantry, Comdg. First Brigade, Regular Infantry.*"

I have now reviewed what seemed to me to be the principal points in the evidence. There are others I might have noticed had not this statement already grown to a fatiguing length.

It is now more than five months since, on an intimation from the highest authority, I asked for this investigation. It has been held near where all the alleged acts of commission or omission took place. It has been open. All persons have been invited in the most public way to disclose to the court whatever they knew which would tend to show criminality in my conduct as an officer or as a man, and the court have asked witnesses not only what they knew, but what they knew others knew; those who do not wish me well have been asked every question likely to develop anything to my prejudice, and I feel that now, after this tedious and patient investigation which this court has so faithfully made, that as to the past, on all matters concerning my loyalty or sobriety, I may be spared the charges that have been so freely made against me.

Nearly two years ago I was here organizing the small beginnings of the Grand Army of the Potomac. When I commenced we had here in Washington ——— Cooper, now the senior general in the secession army; Lee, commanding at Fredericksburg; Johnston, the commander of the rebel Army of the Mississippi; Magruder, the commander of the enemy's forces in Texas; Pemberton, the commander at Vicksburg; Jones and Field, prominent generals on the other side, besides many others of less rank. Alexandria mostly, if not wholly, secession; Georgetown and Washington very much so. I organized the first hundred, the first thousand, and the first brigade of the loyal citizens of the place, and this in opposition to all the bad influences brought to bear against us. And when the troops from the North came down and the capital had been saved and the opposite shore taken, I organized the army of which the present one is but an extension—a great one, it is true.

I have been in constant active service. No doubt of my loyalty has been entertained by the authorities or my superiors, and no evidence questioning it has been brought before this court. And yet I have had to leave my command and undergo the humiliation of this investigation on a charge in my case as baseless as it is senseless, and this in as intelligent a country as ours claims to be. The charge of treason is a fit pendent to the one of drunkenness and quite as true, seeing that to this day I have never drunk anything but water.

Is it not a bad symptom in the nation when such things can take place? Can its officers sustain themselves under such a system, and render that service which the country needs in its present critical state and must have as a condition of its salvation?

IRVIN McDOWELL,
*Major-General.*

---

*SIXTY-THIRD DAY.*

COURT-ROOM, COR. FOURTEENTH AND PA. AVENUE,
*Washington, D. C., February* 10, 1863.

* * * * * * *

The court was cleared.

The court was opened at 3.30 p. m. and adjourned to meet to-morrow, February 11, 1863, at 11 o'clock a. m.

---

*SIXTY-FOURTH DAY.*

COURT-ROOM, COR. FOURTEENTH AND PA. AVENUE,
*Washington, D. C., February* 11, 1863.

* * * * * * *

Brigadier-General Martindale being absent, and being engaged on certain papers pertaining to the investigation, the court adjourned to meet to-morrow, February 12, 1863, at 11 o'clock a. m.

---

*SIXTY-FIFTH DAY.*

COURT-ROOM, COR. FOURTEENTH AND PA. AVENUE,
*Washington, D. C., February* 12, 1863.

* * * * * * *

The court was cleared.

The court was opened at 3 o'clock p. m. and adjourned to meet to-morrow, February 13, at 11 o'clock a. m.

---

*SIXTY-SIXTH DAY.*

COURT-ROOM, COR. FOURTEENTH AND PA. AVENUE,
*Washington, D. C., February* 13, 1863.

* * * * * * *

The court continued in private session until 4.15 o'clock p. m., when it adjourned to meet to-morrow, February 14, 1863, at 11 o'clock a. m.

*SIXTY-SEVENTH DAY.*

COURT-ROOM, COR. FOURTEENTH AND PA AVENUE,
*Washington, D. C., February 14*, 1863.

The court met pursuant to adjournment.

Present, Maj. Gen. George Cadwalader, U. S. Volunteers; Brig. Gen. John H. Martindale, U. S. Volunteers; Brig. Gen. James H. Van Alen, U. S. Volunteers; Lieut. Col. Louis H. Pelouze, assistant adjutant-general, recorder of the court.

The statement of facts and opinions in the case prepared by the court was read by the recorder, and is appended to the proceedings of this day.

There being no further business before the court, it adjourned *sine die.*

GEO. CADWALADER,
*Major-General and President of the Court.*

LOUIS H. PELOUZE,
*Lieutenant-Colonel and Recorder.*

---

*FACTS AND OPINIONS OF THE COURT OF INQUIRY.*

COURT-ROOM,
*Washington, D. C., February* 14, 1863.

The inquiry directed in this case is of a comprehensive and unusual character. No charges had been preferred against General McDowell and no living accuser had presented himself to make the slightest complaint against him; nevertheless he deemed it important that his whole conduct as a general officer should be made the subject of judicial investigation; and in his letter requesting a court of inquiry he discloses the existence of such extreme dissatisfaction as to induce a dying officer to impute the loss of his life to "McDowell's treachery." No specific act of treason was indicated by that officer.

It must have been foreseen, in view of the high commands intrusted to General McDowell during the present rebellion, and the important part which he has borne in the measures to suppress it, that an investigation into his whole conduct would open a wide field of inquiry. Notwithstanding the presence of civil war, and the difficulty of detailing officers and witnesses to conduct such an investigation, the Government has judged it expedient to direct this court to make it.

In the letter requesting the inquiry General McDowell publishes the following invitation:

> I beg that all officers, soldiers, or civilians, who know or think they know of any acts of mine liable to the charge in question, be allowed and invited to make it known to the court.

In thus inviting a proceeding in which he confronts the whole world the court constituted to conduct it is placed in an attitude to assume that General McDowell was the object of wide-spread discontent in the Army and among civilians.

The investigation would scarcely be complete which did not seek after and find some solution for such general dissatisfaction, at least if it could be found within the appropriate limits of judicial inquiry by pertinent testimony.

To this end much testimony has been received, disclosing the particular conduct of General McDowell since he was assigned to the command of a division in the Army of the Potomac, under General McClellan, on the 24th day of August, 1861.

It is not deemed necessary to furnish an abstract of the testimony in this report except in a few instances, where it appears desirable for an intelligent understanding of the whole subject.

For convenient analysis of the case the court present it in chronological order as nearly as practicable.

GENERAL M'DOWELL AS DIVISION AND CORPS COMMANDER UNDER GENERAL M'CLELLAN.

General McDowell entered on the command of a division in the Army of the Potomac on the 24th day of August, 1861, in which he continued until the 13th day of March, 1862, when he was assigned to the command of the First Corps of the same army, in which he continued until his detention to form part of the force for the defense of Washington, on the 4th day of April, 1862.

During all this period he was under the command of General McClellan, and it appears by the concurrent testimony of every officer who has testified on the subject, and the court report the fact to be, that he was energetic, intelligent, faithful, and without reproach in the performance of the duties of his station.

THE SEPARATION OF GENERAL M'DOWELL'S CORPS FROM THE ARMY OF THE POTOMAC AND FORMATION OF THE DEPARTMENT OF THE RAPPAHANNOCK.

The cause of the detention of General McDowell and the separation of his corps from the Army of the Potomac, when that army proceeded to Fort Monroe to commence the campaign of the Peninsula, has been carefully and thoroughly investigated. The object proposed for that army was the capture of Richmond. The minds of officers and men were deeply imbued with it. It had all the importance and brilliancy of expectation to awaken ambition and a soldier's thirst for glory. The Army of the Potomac contemplated the achievement as one to be accomplished by their united efforts, and for which they had the required numerical strength, discipline, and equipment.

It was to be expected, and it was the fact, that the portion of it which, in the necessary distribution of force, was left behind regarded their separation from their more fortunate comrades with feelings of bitter disappointment.

Public attention had been strongly attracted to the fact that the separation of General McDowell's corps occurred when the Army of the Potomac was taking its position before Yorktown, and a presumption followed, from a want of information as to all the circumstances of the case, that such separation interrupted the plans formed for that army and was the primary cause of the failure of the campaign against Richmond.

It is not difficult to understand how that presumption, when adopted as the real state of the case by officers and men in the Army of the Potomac, would affect their opinions of General McDowell.

That officer immediately succeeded to the command of an independent army and department, known as the Department of the Rappahannock. When the public mind planted itself on the fact that the disruption of the Army of the Potomac, by the detention of General McDowell's corps, was a capricious and unnecessary act; when that officer was beheld invested by it with increased rank and command, it required but another step in this presumptive process of argument to hold him virtually responsible for the disasters of the Peninsular Campaign. To this separation primarily and chiefly associated with the memory of the first battle of Bull Run, the court ascribe the wide-spread discontent with General McDowell throughout the country, his own army, and that of the Potomac.

The court could not perform the duty devolved upon it, in this branch of the case, without a searching investigation into the causes of that separation and the influences through which it was accomplished.

This investigation has revealed, and the court find the fact to be, that the detention of two divisions of General McDowell's corps, amounting in the aggregate to about 20,000 men, and which was the whole force so detained, was not the result of caprice or any unworthy motive whatever, but was in execution of an order of the President, which preceded the departure of the Army of the Potomac to the Peninsula, which order had the substantial concurrence of all the corps commanders, which, under the circumstances at length disclosed before this court, the safety of the capital and common prudence enjoined, and which the President had reason to believe, from a report made to him by three general officers, viz, Generals Hitchcock, Thomas, and Wadsworth, who were on the spot and were specially instructed to investigate the facts, had not been complied with.

In this investigation and report of those generals and the communications which led to it General McDowell had no share whatever. He was not consulted. He expected and desired to proceed to the Peninsula, following the other portions of the Army of the Potomac.

## GENERAL M'DOWELL AS COMMANDER OF THE DEPARTMENT OF THE RAPPAHANNOCK.

Following the natural order of events, and the subjects which have been the occasion of the strongest dissatisfaction manifested toward General McDowell, the court has carefully and thoroughly investigated his operations as commander in the Department of the Rappahannock.

His army was not designed to operate beyond the limits of his own department, while the enemy continued in a position to menace and reoccupy it, including, as it did, the city of Washington.

Still, this attitude of defense was not agreeable to General McDowell; his mind was continually occupied with the idea of participating in the operations of the Army of the Potomac which were then progressing by the route of the Peninsula against Richmond.

With the concurrence of the President, which he yielded only when it appeared that the Army of the Rappahannock could be safely sent forward, it was ready to move from Fredericksburg against Richmond, by the way of Hanover Court-House, on the morning of the 26th of May.

The ambition of General McDowell was deeply interested in this movement. He had for a long time been devoting the most unremitted and energetic efforts to be adequately prepared for it.

So far from manifesting any reluctance to co-operate with the Army of the Potomac the desire to render such co-operation engrossed his mind and heart. Public opinion and censure were never more at fault than in imputing to General McDowell a want of earnest zeal and desire to assist General McClellan from Fredericksburg in the assault on Richmond.

His demonstrations in that direction were timely and useful. They led to a withdrawal of Jackson's forces from Richmond and their renewed menace against the approaches to Washington. The Army of the Peninsula was in this manner relieved of the resistance of a force which it must have expected to encounter, and which numerically was stronger than the portion of General McDowell's corps—20,000—which had been detained to cover Washington.

The movement of Jackson's forces down the Shenandoah Valley, and the jeopardy which menaced the capital, and what was then supposed to be the inflammable and revolutionary sentiments of a part of the population of the State of Maryland, led to an order suspending the march of General McDowell on Richmond and his recall to cover the approaches to Washington on the 24th of May.

It is not possible to determine accurately what would have been the result of persistence in the movement at that time of McDowell's army on Richmond.

Had there been great celerity of movement and co-operation between the armies commanded by Generals McClellan and McDowell, and Richmond had been carried by assault, without a halt and without interruption by the excessive rains which flooded the rivers and streams of Virginia on the following Friday, Saturday, and Sunday, May 30, 31, and June 1—had all this been successfully accomplished before Jackson could have gained any countervailing advantages against the capital and in the State of Maryland, it is quite obvious that General McDowell would have been justified by the results, in his opinion, that it was inexpedient to recall him from his projected movement against Richmond. The court has not found it necessary to decide this hypothetical question. It will remain a fruitful subject of conjecture, perhaps of recrimination, until a time of peace shall reveal all the circumstances calculated to elucidate it.

If it be doubtful whether General McDowell ought to have allowed his mind to be so fully occupied with a campaign beyond the limits of his own department, it is perfectly clear that he yielded a prompt submission to the order of the President, and without reservation or evasion, and with the most commendable alacrity, pushed forward a part of his troops toward Washington and another toward Front Royal, still leaving one division at Fredericksburg.

The whole inquiry into the conduct of General McDowell has disclosed in the most signal manner, however, at Fredericksburg on the occasion in question, that he appreciates the military necessity of submission and obedience to the authority over him. Instead of furnishing any occasion for censure, his whole conduct at Fredericksburg should receive unqualified commendation.

## THE CORRESPONDENCE OF GENERAL M'DOWELL WITH THE ENEMY'S COMMANDERS OR WITH ANY ONE WITHIN THE ENEMY'S LINES.

The only correspondence of General McDowell with the rebel commanders requiring notice relates to the removal of Mrs. Robert E. Scott from near Warrenton, Fauquier County, Virginia, to her friends within the rebel lines after the murder of her husband.

The evidence discloses that her husband was an eminent citizen of Virginia, distinguished for his high character and loyalty to the Government.

In the opinion of the court, both humanity and public policy not only justified but required the course of procedure adopted by General McDowell.

## THE CONDUCT OF GENERAL M'DOWELL TOWARD THE INHABITANTS OF THE COUNTRY OCCUPIED BY UNITED STATES FORCES, WITH REFERENCE TO THEMSELVES OR THEIR PROPERTY.

General McDowell adopted as a principle of administration that the exclusive authority to control and appropriate rebel property was vested in and should be exercised by the commander of the army, and that all interference with it by subordinate officers or soldiers, not sanctioned by that authority, should be denounced and punished as acts which were calculated to demoralize the army and defeat the objects of the war.

In this particular the opinion of the court is that the principle was right, and the measures adopted by General McDowell to enforce it merit commendation.

It is apparent that the censure which was passed upon his conduct during the course of a debate in the Senate on this subject arose from a want of information of all the circumstances relating to it.

From the date of the departure of General McDowell from Fredericksburg to the formation of the Army of Virginia, on the 26th June, 1862, in which the Army of the Rappahannock was merged, his conduct has been the subject of critical investigation by the court. No particular facts were elicited which require special consideration. Throughout this period the court find that his conduct was irreproachable.

It was during this time, and while the enemy's troops under Jackson were operating in the valley of the Shenandoah, that General McDowell sent forward McCall's division of Pennsylvania Reserves, about 10,000 strong, to the Army of the Potomac. This division reached the Chickahominy and got in position on the right of that army at Mechanicsville about the 19th of June, being a week previous to the arrival of the enemy's troops under Jackson and the retirement of the Army of the Potomac to the James River.

## GENERAL M'DOWELL AS A COMMANDER IN THE ARMY OF VIRGINIA, UNDER GENERAL POPE.

When General Pope assumed command of the Army of Virginia, on the 26th of June, 1862, although in order of rank he was below General McDowell, he has testified that he received from that officer the most valuable and cordial co-operation and assistance.

The court dwell with satisfaction on these fine qualities of military subordination, frequently exemplified by General McDowell under circumstances trying to the pride and emulation of a general officer.

The conduct of General McDowell at Cedar Mountain was incidentally called in question by the testimony of General Sigel during his cross-examination as to the unfavorable impressions resting on his mind against General McDowell; but no specific and tangible accusation against him could be predicated on that part of the testimony of General Sigel, nor upon any other part except that which relates to the operations and battles in the neighborhood of Thoroughfare Gap, Gainesville, Groveton, Manassas, and Bull Run, on the 28th, 29th, and 30th days of August last. In respect to the whole conduct of General McDowell preceding those days, and especially the engagement of General Banks with the enemy at Cedar Mountain, the court have found no incident to modify their approval.

The conduct of General McDowell on the 28th and 29th days of August, in the neighborhood of the locality best known as Manassas and Bull Run, has been the subject of specific arraignment in the evidence of General Sigel, and the court have felt bound to examine with critical attention all the testimony relating to the operations of those days. Previous to the 27th day of August the forces of the enemy under Jackson had moved east of Thoroughfare Gap, and came between the army under General Pope and the city of Washington.

This force of Jackson was about 25,000 strong, probably somewhat less. On the 27th General McDowell, with his own corps and that of General Sigel and Reynolds' division, had proceeded eastwardly from Warrenton toward Gainesville across Broad Run at Buckland Mills. He was thus moving along the Warrenton pike, so called, in the direction of Centreville and Alexandria. On the night of the 27th the head of his column, to wit, the command of General Milroy, in Sigel's corps, rested at Gainesville. The rear of his column was at Buckland Mills. At this point of time General Pope was at Bristoe and pressing with Heintzelman's corps and Reno's division on the troops of Jackson, which had been driven to Manassas Junction. The rebel general Longstreet, with the largest portion of the enemy's force, was west of the Bull Run Mountains, and was approaching the passage through Thoroughfare Gap to unite with Jackson.

By looking at the map it will thus be perceived that McDowell, with his whole command, including Sigel's corps and Reynolds' division, was interposed between Longstreet and Jackson, while the latter was being closely pressed by General Pope, within striking distance from the direction of Bristoe and Greenwich.

From Gainesville a highway and the Manassas Railroad lead directly to Thoroughfare Gap, which is 5 miles distant, passing through Hay Market, only 2 miles distant. Another highway leads to Manassas Junction, chiefly on the south side of the same railroad. The Warrenton pike passes from Gainesville through Groveton to Centreville.

On the night of the 27th General McDowell received orders from General Pope to march on Manassas, as follows:

HEADQUARTERS ARMY OF VIRGINIA,
*Bristoe Station, August 27, 1862—9 p. m.*

Major-General McDOWELL:

At daylight to-morrow morning march rapidly on Manassas Junction with your whole force, resting your right on the Manassas Gap Railroad, throwing your left well to the east. Jackson, Ewell, and A. P. Hill are between Gainesville and Manassas Junction. We had a severe fight with them to-day, driving them back several miles along the railroad. If you will march promptly and rapidly, at the earliest dawn of day, upon Manassas Junction we shall bag the whole crowd. I have directed Reno to march from Greenwich at the same hour upon Manassas Junction, and Kearny, who is in his rear, to march on Bristoe at daybreak. Be expeditious, and the day is our own.

JNO. POPE,
*Major-General, Commanding.*

The order was received at about 2 o'clock on the morning of the 28th, and the movement was directed to be made immediately. Without following the succeeding movements in all their details, the court will direct their attention to the single point in the conduct of General McDowell which they cannot pass without disapproval.

In the afternoon of the 28th, at fifteen minutes past 4 o'clock, the several corps and divisions were placed as follows: Ricketts' division of McDowell's corps was in front and on the east side of Thoroughfare Gap, holding in check the advance of Longstreet's forces. Sigel's corps had been turned toward the Warrenton pike and Centreville by the way of New Market. Reynolds' division was on the road leading to Manassas, near Bethlehem Church. King's division of McDowell's corps was between the Manassas Railroad and the Warrenton pike, and about 2 miles southwestwardly from Groveton. A small portion of Jackson's forces were near Groveton, probably less than a brigade; but the main portion was at Centreville and marching toward Sudley Springs, and bearing from that point toward Groveton, on the Warrenton pike, near to which point and on the pike was collected at least fifty transportation wagons of the rebels' train, headed toward Gainesville. General Pope was following the mass of Jackson's forces toward Centreville from Manassas.

At the hour of 1.20 p. m. General Pope transmitted the following order to General McDowell, which was received at about the hour of 4 o'clock p. m.:

HEADQUARTERS ARMY OF VIRGINIA,
*Manassas Junction, August* 28, 1862—1.20 p. m.

Major-General McDOWELL:

I sent you a dispatch a few minutes ago directing you to move on Gum Springs to intercept Jackson; since then I have received your note of this morning. I will this evening push forward Reno to Gainesville and follow with Heintzelman, unless there is a large force of the enemy at Centreville, which I do not believe. Ascertain if you can about this. I do not wish you to carry out the order to proceed to Gum Springs if you consider it too hazardous, but I will support you in any way you suggest, by pushing forward from Manassas Junction across the turnpike.

Jackson has a large train, which should certainly be captured. Give me your views fully. You know the country much better than I do. Come no farther in this direction with your command, but call back what has advanced thus far.

JNO. POPE,
*Major-General, Commanding.*

Shortly after this order had been dispatched another order, as follows, was sent by General Pope to General McDowell, which was received at 4.15 p. m.:

HEADQUARTERS MANASSAS JUNCTION,
*August* 28, 1862.

Major-General McDOWELL:

The enemy is reported in force on the other side of Bull Run, on the Orange and Alexandria Railroad, as also near Centreville. I have ordered Sigel to march upon Centreville immediately, as also Kearny and Reno. I will advance Hooker as reserve. Please march immediately with your command directly upon Centreville from where you are.

JNO. POPE,
*Major-General, Commanding.*

General McDowell immediately turned back King's division onto the Warrenton pike *en route* for Centreville. He then rejoined Reynolds' division, and, passing Bethlehem Church, turned that division northwardly toward the Warrenton pike by the Sudley Springs road. He then proceeded himself with a part of his staff to Manassas Station, being distant about 3 miles eastwardly from the point where he had parted from Reynolds' division. He thus separated himself more than 10 miles from Ricketts' division and certainly not less than 6 miles from King's division, being the two divisions composing his corps, and in a special manner under his command.

Just at dark, while General McDowell was at Manassas Station, King's division, then marching eastwardly along the pike, came in collision with the enemy near Groveton, and a battle ensued. The enemy was driven back. This battle occurred near to a point from which a section of rebel artillery—supposed to form portion of a reconnoitering party—had shelled General McDowell and checked the advance of his troops from one to two hours during the early part of the day, as they were changing direction to the right toward Manassas.

In the course of the night General King, on his own responsibility, as he testifies, and without communicating with General McDowell, retired from the battle-field to a point 2 or 3 miles east of Manassas Station.

At about 9 o'clock in the evening of the 28th General Ricketts had retired with his division from Thoroughfare Gap to Gainesville. Being informed of the intended movement of General King, General Ricketts retired with his division to the neighborhood of Manassas early in the morning of the 29th.

The grave error committed by these movements of McDowell's corps cannot be better explained than by incorporating in this report the following testimony of General Pope:

Question by the COURT. Were you aware that King's division had a fight with the enemy near evening of that day and after the fight fell back to Manassas?

Answer. It was reported to me about 8 or 9 o'clock at night on the 28th that King's division of McDowell's corps had met the enemy retreating from Centreville and after a severe fight had remained masters of the field, still interposing between Jackson's forces and the main body of the enemy. This report was brought to me by a staff officer, I think, of General King's. Upon receiving this information I stated to several of my staff officers who were present that the game was in our own hands, and that I did not see how it was possible for Jackson to escape without very heavy loss, if at all. Immediately upon receipt of this intelligence also I directed General Kearny, whose division occupied Centreville, to push forward cautiously at 1 o'clock that night in the direction of Gainesville, to drive in the pickets of the enemy, and to keep himself in close contact during the night; to rest his left on the Warrenton turnpike, and to throw his right to the north, toward the Little River, and well to the front. I directed him at the first blush of daylight to attack the enemy with his right advanced, and informed him that Hooker and Reno would be with him immediately after daylight. To my surprise and dissatisfaction I learned toward daylight on the morning of the 29th that King's division had been withdrawn in the direction of Manassas Junction, leaving open the road to Thoroughfare Gap. This withdrawal of that division made necessary a great change in the movement and the position of the troops, and was a most serious and unlooked-for mistake. I was so impressed with the necessity that that division should hold its ground during the night of the 28th that I sent several orders to General King—one by his own staff officer—during that night to hold his ground at all hazards and to prevent the retreat of the enemy; and informed him that our whole force from the direction of Centreville and Manassas Junction would fall upon the enemy at daylight.

The court adopt the testimony of General Pope as a faithful statement of the facts.

Had General McDowell been present with his command at the time of these movements of his corps it could not be controverted that he would be justly held responsible for their retreat and the consequent derangement of the plan of battle then formed by General Pope.

What is the explanation of General McDowell's absence?

He went to Manassas to have a personal interview with General Pope, whom he expected to find there.

Granting the good faith of this explanation and General McDowell's honesty of purpose, the court find that he thus separated himself from his command at a critical time, without any order of his superior officer and without any imperative necessity.

It is true that in the first order sent to him and received about 4 o'clock p. m. the following paragraph occurs:

I will this evening push forward Reno to Gainesville and follow with Heintzelman, unless there is a large force of the enemy at Centreville, which I do not believe. Ascertain, if you can, about this.

Again, the following paragraph occurs in the same order:

Give me your views fully. You know the country much better than I do.

But immediately after that order the second one was received, which disclosed that the enemy was near Centreville; that Sigel, Kearny, and Reno had been ordered to march upon Centreville, and directing him, McDowell, to march directly upon Centreville with his command from where he then was.

Clearly this last order contained no implication which can justify the separation of General McDowell from his corps. The moment had arrived for prompt concentration of the whole army against the rebel troops under Jackson. He knew that King's line of march was in the direction of the small force of the enemy by which he had been assailed on the Warrenton pike in the morning. He knew also that Longstreet was approaching by Thoroughfare Gap.

However valuable he might have supposed the expression of his views to General Pope in person, they could be of no avail, while the misconduct of his own corps thwarted a plan the execution of which afforded an opportunity for speedy victory.

He heard the sound of battle while he was yet at Manassas, and made immediate and persistent efforts to rejoin his corps; but he lost his way in the darkness, and, after passing the night with a portion of Sigel's command, found early in the morning that his own corps had retired.

His subsequent efforts on the 29th to repair the consequences of that unfortunate movement of his corps and to press them forward into action were earnest and energetic, and disclose fully that the separation, of which the court has thus stated its disapproval, was inconsiderate and unauthorized, but was not induced by any unworthy motive.

The court also feel bound to report the fact that his commanding officer, General Pope, not only omitted to hold him culpable for this separation, but emphatically commended his whole conduct while under his command, without exception or qualification.

In the course of the investigation General McDowell manifested a just and proper sensibility to the dissemination against him of the charge of drunkenness as well as disloyalty.

The charge of disloyalty was made by an officer of the rank of colonel after being fatally wounded in battle. It was made in general terms, without defining any specific act. The accuser is dead, and the court does not feel at liberty to say more of it than that it is utterly destitute of any foundation in fact; that it is fully disproved by all the evidence bearing on the point, and that the dying officer who made it must have been the subject of deplorable misapprehension, like many others who have formed opinions from calumnious rumors and presumptions.

The court denounces the charge of drunkenness against General McDowell as ridiculous. The fact is that there is no man in the land more free than he from all taint of such vice. Among temperate men he is proved by the testimony to belong to the most temperate and even abstemious.

The court is entirely satisfied that no man ever saw him in the slightest degree under the influence of intoxicating drink.

In taking leave of the many groundless imputations against General McDowell the court call attention to the alacrity of a portion of the public press to disseminate, and a portion of the people to accept, for a time at least, as true such absurd and unjustifiable rumors against general officers, who are thereby disarmed of power and influence essential to the complete performance of their important duties.

It is to be hoped that the public misfortunes entailed by such calumnies will in future lead to greater circumspection and secure for patriotic and meritorious soldiers more considerate treatment from the American press and people.

In the opinion of the court the interests of the public service do not require any further investigation into the conduct of Major-General McDowell.

—

HEADQUARTERS OF THE ARMY,
*February* 21, 1863.

The ADJUTANT-GENERAL:

The facts and opinions of the Court of Inquiry in the case of Major-General McDowell, having been submitted to the General-in-Chief, are herewith returned with his order in the case.

Respectfully,

J. C. KELTON,
*Assistant Adjutant-General.*

—

SPECIAL ORDERS, No. 88. } HDQRS. OF THE ARMY, ADJT. GEN.'S OFFICE,
*Washington, February* 23, 1863.

* * * * * * *

VII. The Court of Inquiry, convened by Special Orders, Nos. 350 and 362, series of 1862, to investigate certain charges and accusations against Major-General McDowell, having completed its investigation, and reported that in its opinion the interests of the public service do not require any further investigation into the conduct of Major-General McDowell, is hereby dissolved.

VIII. Major-General McDowell will report for duty to the Adjutant-General of the Army.

By command of Major-General Halleck:

L. THOMAS,
*Adjutant-General.*

---

## MARCH 20, 1862.—Reconnaissance to Gainesville, Va.

No. 1.—Report of Brig. Gen. Israel B. Richardson, U. S. Army.
No. 2.—Report of Brig. Gen. Oliver O. Howard, U. S. Army.

### No. 1.

*Report of Brig. Gen. Israel B. Richardson, U. S. Army.*

HEADQUARTERS RICHARDSON'S DIVISION,
*March* 21, 1862.

DEAR SIR: General Howard returned last night after dark from his reconnaissance. He reached Gainesville with his infantry, and pushed on his cavalry 3 miles beyond that place. The enemy's scouts have not been there for the last four days. They burned the depot and a considerable quantity of wheat; also the railroad bridge at the Gap. Nothing heard here from General Banks' column.

Yours, truly,

I. B. RICHARDSON,
*Brigadier-General, Commanding Division.*

Captain TAYLOR,
*Assistant Adjutant-General.*

---

## No. 2.

*Report of Brig. Gen. Oliver O. Howard, U. S. Army.*

HEADQUARTERS HOWARD'S BRIGADE,
*Near Manassas, March* 20, 1862.

CAPTAIN: I have the honor to report that I took all the cavalry of the three squadrons present and one of the regiments (Colonel Miller's) of my brigade and made a reconnaissance along the Manassas Gap Railroad. I proceeded carefully to Gainesville, a distance of 9 miles beyond Manassas Junction and 11 miles from this camp. We found that the enemy had burned up tents and other camp equipage at different points. At Gainesville the depot is burned. It contained some 300 or 400 bushels of oats. We had it from pretty good authority that the bridges at Thoroughfare and across the Shenandoah River had been burned. The pickets of the enemy are beyond New Baltimore, on the Warrenton turnpike, and no scouts have been at Gainesville for four days. I sent back Colonel Miller with one squadron to Manassas Junction directly by the railroad, and with the rest of the cavalry proceeded by the Warrenton turnpike to the vicinity of Bull Run, and thence by an easterly course back to this camp.

I feel assured from my scouting yesterday and to-day that there is no sign of the enemy having been north of the Manassas Gap Railroad for the last four days, and that General Jackson did not retreat by this railroad.

General Stuart passed through Gainesville on his retreat. His horses are said to be in bad condition. We found dead horses all along our route. I ought to have said that I know there are no pickets of the enemy within 3 miles of and beyond Gainesville. The roads are very muddy, and yet Colonel Miller, of the Eighty-first Pennsylvania, has made a march of 22 miles with his regiment. The Farnsworth Cavalry always do well. It has been raining moderately the whole day.

Very respectfully,

O. O. HOWARD,
*Brigadier-General, Commanding*

Captain NORVELL,
*Assistant Adjutant-General Division.*

## MARCH 23, 1862.—Battle of Kernstown, Va.

### REPORTS, ETC.

No. 1.—Brig. Gen. James Shields, U. S. Army, commanding division Fifth Army Corps, with congratulations.
No. 2.—Surg. William S. King, U. S. Army, Medical Director Fifth Army Corps.
No. 3.—Return of Casualties in the Union forces.
No. 4.—Maj. R. Morris Copeland, Assistant Adjutant-General, U. S. Army.
No. 5.—Captain R. C. Shriber, U. S. Army, Aide-de-Camp.
No. 6.—Lieut. William W. Rowley, Twenty-eighth New York Infantry, Acting Signal Officer.
No. 7.—Col. Thornton F. Brodhead, First Michigan Cavalry, Chief of Cavalry.
No. 8.—Lieut. Col. Joseph T. Copeland, First Michigan Cavalry.
No. 9.—Capt. John Keys, Pennsylvania Cavalry.
No. 10.—Capt. Andrew J. Greenfield, Pennsylvania Cavalry.
No. 11.—Lieut. Col. Philip Daum, Chief of Artillery.
No. 12.—Col. Nathan Kimball, Fourteenth Indiana Infantry, commanding First Brigade.*
No. 13.—Lieut. Col. William Harrow, Fourteenth Indiana Infantry.
No. 14.—Col. Samuel S. Carroll, Eighth Ohio Infantry.
No. 15.—Lieut. Col. Franklin Sawyer, Eighth Ohio Infantry.
No. 16.—Lieut. Col. Alvin C. Voris, Sixty-seventh Ohio Infantry.
No. 17.—Col. Jeremiah C. Sullivan, Thirteenth Indiana Infantry, commanding Second Brigade.
No. 18.—Lieut. Col. Robert S. Foster, Thirteenth Indiana Infantry.
No. 19.—Lieut. George H. Whitcamp, Acting Adjutant Fifth Ohio Infantry.
No. 20.—Col. Erastus B. Tyler, Seventh Ohio Infantry, commanding Third Brigade.
No. 21.—Col. William D. Lewis, jr., One hundred and tenth Pennsylvania Infantry.
No. 22.—Abstract from "Record of Events" in Williams' division, Fifth Army Corps.
No. 23.—Maj. Gen. Thomas J. Jackson, C. S. Army, commanding the Valley District with resolution of the Confederate Congress.
No. 24.—Return of Casualties in the Confederate forces.
No. 25.—Col. Turner Ashby, Seventh Virginia Cavalry.
No. 26.—Maj. O. R. Funsten, Seventh Virginia Cavalry.
No. 27.—Col. J. W. Allen, Second Virginia Infantry, First Brigade.
No. 28.—Capt. J. Q. A. Nadenbousch, Second Virginia Infantry.
No. 29.—Col. Charles A. Ronald, Fourth Virginia Infantry.
No. 30.—Col. William H. Harman, Fifth Virginia Infantry.
No. 31.—Col. A. J. Grigsby, Twenty-seventh Virginia Infantry.
No. 32.—Col. Arthur C. Cummings, Thirty-third Virginia Infantry.
No. 33.—Capt. William McLaughlin, Rockbridge (Va.) Artillery.
No. 34.—Capt. James H. Waters, West Augusta (Va.) Artillery.
No. 35.—Capt. Joseph Carpenter, Virginia Artillery.
No. 36.—Col. Jesse S. Burks, Forty-second Virginia Infantry, commanding Third Brigade.
No. 37.—Col. John M. Patton, jr., Twenty-first Virginia Infantry.
No. 38.—Lieut. Col. D. A. Langhorne, Forty-second Virginia Infantry.
No. 39.—Capt. D. B. Bridgford, First Virginia Battalion.
No. 40.—Col. Samuel V. Fulkerson, Thirty-seventh Virginia Infantry, commanding Fourth Brigade.
No. 41.—Lieut. Col. Alexander G. Taliaferro, Twenty-third Virginia Infantry.

---

* Colonel Kimball was the senior officer in command in the field—General Shields having been wounded on the previous evening—and consequently reports the general operations.

No. 1.

*Reports of Brig. Gen. James Shields, U. S. Army, commanding division Fifth Army Corps, with congratulations.*

WINCHESTER, VA., *March* 23, 1862.

We have this day achieved a glorious victory over the combined forces of Jackson, Smith, and Longstreet. The battle was fought within 4 miles of this place. It raged from 10.30 o'clock this morning until dark. The enemy's strength was about 15,000; the strength of our division not over 8,000. Our loss, killed and wounded, is not ascertained, but is heavy. The enemy's loss is double that of ours. We have captured a large number of prisoners, some of their guns, and the ground is strewn with the arms they have thrown away in their flight. The cavalry is still in pursuit of the retreating enemy. The particulars cannot be accurately ascertained until daylight.

JAS. SHIELDS,
*Brigadier-General, Commanding.*

S. WILLIAMS, *Brigadier-General.*

---

WINCHESTER, VA., *March* 23, 1862.

The enemy, though severely handled, is still before us. His motions are watched. If he attempts to retreat before morning we will follow up his rear and pursue him to Strasburg. If he keeps his position till morning I expect to annihilate him. General Banks has ordered back one of Williams' brigades, which ought to be here in three hours. I have ordered forward all the force stationed at Martinsburg, Harper's Ferry, Berryville, and Charlestown. I have ordered in all outposts and guards which are on the route in my rear. All are on the march for this place, and will be here by early dawn to re-enforce me. With the whole of this force I will renew the attack as soon as we have sufficient light to point our guns, and feel confident the enemy cannot escape.

JAS. SHIELDS,
*Brigadier-General.*

S. WILLIAMS, *Brigadier-General.*

---

WINCHESTER, VA., *March* 25, 1862.

A dispatch arrived from General Banks, 5 miles below Strasburg, on the road to Mount Jackson. The enemy still on the retreat; our forces in hot pursuit. Their loss must be enormous. They have filled their wagons with the dead and dying they have now abandoned. The houses along the route are found filled with wounded and dead. The houses in the town adjacent to the battle-field are also found filled with wounded. The inhabitants had aided their friends in carrying them off during the day. They are also burying them quickly as soon as they die. Our artillery makes terrible havoc amongst them in their flight. I will keep you advised of everything that takes place. I hope information I am constantly communicating is received.

JAS. SHIELDS,
*Brigadier-General.*

General WILLIAMS,
*Assistant Adjutant-General.*

WINCHESTER, *March* 25, 1862.

Please communicate the following to the general commanding the Army:

I am prostrate from wounds, but hope in a few days to be able to ride in a buggy at the head of my command. General Banks is at Strasburg with my division and part of his own; the rest *en route* to join. He was not able to overtake the enemy. The retreat was a flight. He informs me he means to pursue to Mount Jackson. Rumor makes the re-enforcements now joining Jackson 30,000. He is said to be fortifying at Rude's Hill, between Mount Jackson and New Market, at a point almost unapproachable from this side, and which communicates with the main body under Johnston by a good turnpike through Turet [Luray?], Washington, Springville [Sperryville?], and Culpeper Court-House.

Our prisoners speak with confidence of their strength in front of us and of their immense force on the march to avenge their defeat. I can hardly believe this, but I give it for what it is worth. I am compelled to expend too much of my force in protection to railroad and routes in my rear against guerrilla bands now infesting the country. My cavalry is not efficient in the field, and I mean to employ it principally for this purpose. I sorely need a body of efficient cavalry to feel the enemy in front. I dare not hazard mine in an enterprise of this kind. If the commanding general can give me any information about the exact position of the enemy it would aid us in calculating our movements. Our killed is about 150*; the enemy's 350. Our wounded between 300 and 400*; the enemy's nearly 1,000. I feel distressed at his being able to carry off so many of his guns and baggage. His retreat has been ably conducted. Our men were too much exhausted from fatigue and want of food to convert it into a flight in time. Any information about the enemy will be of great service to us. We are constructing telegraph line to Strasburg, and will keep you constantly advised of movements.

JAS. SHIELDS,
*Brigadier General.*

ASSISTANT ADJUTANT-GENERAL,
*Headquarters Army of the Potomac, Seminary.*

---

WINCHESTER, VA., *March* 25, 1862.

SIR: Knowing your anxiety, I venture to give you a few particulars, without waiting to send it through superior officers. Jackson attacked my division, composed of between 7,000 and 8,000 men, close to Winchester, on the morning of the 23d. The prisoners differ as to the strength of his force; supposed to be absolutely 11,000—the flower of the Southern Army. The battle lasted until night. I was unable, from a wound received the evening before, to leave my bed, where I still lie, and had to direct operations in that condition. The fight between the infantry on both sides was terrible. The enemy disputed every inch of ground, and when they gave way did so in order. Notwithstanding the terrible havoc made in the ranks by the destructive fire of our Western men the slightest evidence of panic never appeared amongst them. No infantry ever behaved better than ours, with the exception of the two Pennsylvania regiments. At night the enemy fell back,

---

* See revised statement, p. 346.

covered by darkness, and established themselves within about 4 miles of our position, which was an advantage of the battle-field. During the night I gave strict orders to watch his movements, with directions to attack him and pursue if he should attempt to retreat. I spent the whole night bringing forward all re-enforcements within my reach, stripping the different posts and routes on my rear of permanent guards. For this purpose I also sent orderlies after General Williams' division, *en route* for Centreville, requesting him to halt, and to send back rear brigade to be in time to re-enforce in morning. General Banks, whom I believed in Washington, was still at Harper's Ferry. He also sent prompt orders to the whole division to fall back to my support. At early dawn on morning of 24th these re-enforcements began to arrive here. General Banks arrived soon after. The attack upon the enemy had already commenced, he retreating in order and our command in vigorous pursuit. As I was utterly unable to leave my bed, General Banks put himself at the head of my division and pushed on in pursuit, forcing the enemy back to the other side of Strasburg last night. I pushed forward re-enforcements as they arrived. At this moment our forces are 5 miles the other side of Strasburg, on turnpike route to Mount Jackson, driving the enemy still before them, and General Banks informs me just now by express that he finds houses along the road filled with the dead and wounded of retreating foe, whom they had been compelled to abandon in their hasty flight. The loss on our side in killed and wounded is naturally great, say 150 killed and 300 wounded.* Most of wounded, I am sorry to say, are not likely to survive, the struggle being so close—most hand-to-hand. The wounds both sides are terribly fatal. The loss of the enemy it is impossible as yet to estimate, he having loaded all his wagons with the dead and dying in order to carry them off and the inhabitants of towns in the vicinity having taken them to their houses to afford shelter and relief to them. Every house is swelling their loss. I can only, therefore, guess at it—say between 400 and 500 killed and about 1,000 wounded. This battle being a close fight of infantry, the wounded bear no proportion to killed.

My cavalry is very ineffective. If I had had one regiment of excellent cavalry, armed with carbines, I could have doubled the enemy's loss.

Our prisoners are not very numerous, not exceeding 200. These were taken on the battle-field, together with two guns and five caissons. Other guns and prisoners are sure to be captured during the retreat. This is mere information, sent for your own private gratification, and not a report, which will be prepared and made soon as full details are ascertained.

I wish I could have Captain Munther, able engineer, now in Washington, sent to me to superintend construction of bridges, &c. I would also beg permission to liberate two rebel prisoners on parole, not to leave our lines or to serve against us until exchanged. Their names are Lieutenant Junkin and Captain Morrison. I make this request for special reasons, which will benefit the service, and which I will communicate hereafter.

JAS. SHIELDS,
*Brigadier-General.*

Hon. E. M. STANTON, *Secretary of War.*

---

* See revised statement, p. 346.

WINCHESTER, VA., *March* 26, 1862.

I hasten to make a correction. Investigation this day has satisfied me that the Pennsylvania regiments behaved as bravely as any on the field. Through the eyes of others I was momentarily misled by misstatements. It affords me infinite gratification to be able to correct them, and to do full justice to a body of brave troops who have suffered dreadfully. You will please expunge that portion of my communication which makes them an exception, as I do in a copy I retain.

JAS. SHIELDS,
*Brigadier-General, Commanding.*

Hon. E. M. STANTON,
*Secretary of War.*

---

WINCHESTER, VA., *March* 26, 1862.

Dispatch this moment from General Banks. He pursued the enemy as far as Woodstock. He thinks they are uniting Jackson's and Longstreet's forces at Luray and Washington, for operations on this side of mountains. Our advance has taken strong position 4 miles beyond Strasburg. Rest of my division occupies strong position near Strasburg. Two brigades (Williams') are 2 miles from Strasburg toward Front Royal. Telegraph line will be completed to Strasburg, to-morrow. Can we get any information of General Rosecrans' position or movements?

JAS. SHIELDS,
*Brigadier-General, Commanding.*

Brigadier-General WILLIAMS, *Seminary.*

---

WINCHESTER, VA., *March* 27, 1862.

Our victory at Winchester has been more fatal to the rebels than at first supposed. It has struck the Shenandoah Valley with terror. Union prisoners escaped from Mount Jackson prison just arrived. Saw eight wagons loaded with dead and wounded enter Mount Jackson on Monday, 10 p. m., 44 miles from the field of battle, in thirty hours. The rebels admitted they had 11,000 in the field; also that they lost between 1,000 and 1,500 in killed and wounded. We are finding their graves some distance from each side of the road. The blow has struck terror to this country.

JAS. SHIELDS,
*Brigadier-General.*

Hon. E. M. STANTON,
*Secretary of War.*

---

HEADQUARTERS SHIELDS' DIVISION,
*Winchester, Va., March* 29, 1862.

SIR: I have the honor to report that during my reconnaissance of the 18th and 19th instant in the direction of Mount Jackson I ascertained that the enemy under Jackson was strongly posted near that place, and in direct communication with a force at Luray and another at Washington. It became important, therefore, to draw him from his position and supporting force, if possible. To endeavor to effect this I fell back to Winchester on the 20th, giving the movement all the appearance of a retreat. The last brigade of the First Division of Banks' *corps d'armée*, General Williams commanding, took its departure for Centreville, by way of Berryville, on the morning of the 22d, leaving only Shields' division and the Michigan cavalry in Winchester.

Ashby's cavalry, observing this movement from a distance, came to the conclusion that Winchester was being evacuated, and signaled Jackson to that effect. We saw their signal-fires and divined their import. On the 22d, about 5 o'clock p. m., they attacked and drove in some of our pickets. By order of General Banks I put my command under arms and pushed forward one brigade and two batteries of artillery to drive back the enemy, but to keep him deceived as to our strength only let him see two regiments of infantry, a small body of cavalry, and part of the artillery. While directing one of our batteries to its position I was struck by the fragment of a shell, which fractured my arm above the elbow, bruised my shoulder, and injured my side. The enemy being driven from his position, we withdrew to Winchester.

The injuries I had received completely prostrated me, but were not such as to prevent me from making the requisite dispositions for the ensuing day. Under cover of the night I pushed forward Kimball's brigade nearly 3 miles on the Strasburg road. Daum's artillery was posted in a strong position to support this brigade if attacked. Sullivan's brigade was posted in the rear of Kimball's, and within supporting distance of it, covering all the approaches to the town by the Cedar Creek, Front Royal, Berryville, and Romney roads. Tyler's brigade and Brodhead's cavalry were held in reserve, so as to support our force in front at any point where it might be attacked. These dispositions being made I rested for the night, knowing that all approaches by which the enemy could penetrate to this place were efficiently guarded.

I deem it necessary in this place to give a brief description of these approaches, as well as of the field, which next day became the scene of one of the bloodiest struggles of the war. Winchester is approached from the south by three principal roads: The Cedar Creek road on the west, the Valley turnpike road, leading to Strasburg, in the center, and the Front Royal road on the east. There is a little village called Kernstown on the Valley road, about 3½ miles from Winchester. On the west side of this road, about half a mile north of Kernstown, is a ridge of high ground, which commands the approach by the turnpike and a part of the surrounding country. This ridge was the key-point of our position. Here Colonel Kimball, the senior officer in command on the field, took his station. Along this ridge Lieutenant-Colonel Daum, chief of artillery, posted three of his batteries, keeping one battery in reserve some distance in the rear. Part of our infantry was first placed in position in rear of and within supporting distance of these batteries, well sheltered in the windings and sinuosities of the ridge. The main body of the enemy was posted in order of battle about half a mile beyond Kernstown, his line extending from the Cedar Creek road to a little ravine near the Front Royal road, a distance of about 2 miles. This ground had been so skillfully selected that, while it afforded facilities for maneuvering, it was completely masked by high and wooded ground in front. These woods he filled with skirmishers, supported by a battery on each flank; and so adroitly had his movement been conducted, and so skillfully had he concealed himself, that at 8 o'clock a. m. on the 23d nothing was visible but the same force under Ashby which had been repulsed the previous evening.

Not being able to reconnoiter the front in person, I dispatched an experienced officer, Col. John S. Mason, of the Fourth Ohio Volunteers, about 9 o'clock a. m., to the front to perform that duty, and to report to me as promptly as possible every circumstance that might indicate the presence of an enemy. About an hour after Colonel Mason returned, reporting that he had carefully reconnoitered the country in front and on both flanks, and found no indications of any hostile force except that of Ashby. I communicated this information to Major-General Banks, who was then with me, and after consulting together we both concluded that Jackson could not be tempted to hazard himself so far away from his main support. Having both come to this conclusion, General Banks took his departure for Washington, being already under orders to that effect. The officers of his staff, however, remained behind, intending to leave for Centreville in the afternoon. These officers afterward participated in the battle, and my whole command, as well as myself, are highly indebted to them for valuable services.

Although I began to conclude that Jackson was nowhere in the vicinity, knowing the crafty enemy we had to deal with I took care not to omit a single precaution. Between 11 and 12 o'clock a. m. a message from Colonel Kimball informed me that another battery on the enemy's right had opened against our position, and that there were some indications of a considerable force of infantry in the woods in that quarter. On receiving this information I pushed forward Sullivan's brigade, which was placed, by order of Colonel Kimball, in a position to oppose the advance of the enemy's right wing. The action opened with a fire of artillery on both sides, but at too great a distance to be very effective. The initiative was taken by the enemy. He pushed forward a few more guns to his right, supported by a considerable force of infantry and cavalry, with the apparent intention of enfilading our position and turning our left flank. An active body of skirmishers, consisting of the Eighth Ohio, Colonel Carroll, and three companies of the Sixty-seventh Ohio, were immediately thrown forward on both sides of the Valley road to resist the enemy's advance. These skirmishers were admirably supported by four pieces of artillery under Captain Jenks and Sullivan's gallant brigade. This united force repulsed the enemy at all points, and gave him such a check that no further demonstration was made upon that flank during the remainder of the day. The attempt against our left flank having thus failed the enemy withdrew the greater part of his force on the right, and formed it into a reserve to support his left flank in a forward movement. He then added his original reserve and two batteries to his main body, and advancing with this combined column under shelter of the ridge upon his left, on which other batteries had been previously posted, seemed evidently determined to turn our right flank or overwhelm it. Our batteries on the opposite ridge, though admirably managed by their experienced chief, Lieutenant-Colonel Daum, were soon found insufficient to check or even retard the advance of such a formidable body.

At this stage of the combat a message arrived from Colonel Kimball informing me of the state of the field and requesting directions as to the employment of the infantry. I saw there was not a moment to lose, and gave positive orders that all the disposable infantry should be immediately thrown forward on our right to carry the enemy's batteries and to assail and turn his left flank and hurl it back on the center. Colonel Kimball carried out these orders with promptitude and ability. He intrusted this movement to Tyler's splendid brigade, which, under its fearless leader, Colonel Tyler, marched forward with alacrity and enthusiastic joy to the performance of the most perilous duty of the day. The enemy's skirmishers were driven before it, and fell back upon the main body, strongly posted behind a high and solid stone wall, situated on an elevated ground. Here the struggle became desperate, and for a short time doubtful; but Tyler's brigade being soon joined on the left by the Fifth Ohio, Thirteenth Indiana, and Sixty-second Ohio, of Sullivan's brigade, and the Fourteenth Indiana, Eighty-fourth Pennsylvania, seven companies of the Sixty-seventh Ohio, and three companies of the Eighth Ohio, of Kimball's brigade, this united force dashed upon the enemy with a cheer and yell that rose high above the roar of battle, and though the rebels fought desperately, as their piles of dead attest, they were forced back through the woods by a fire as destructive as ever fell upon a retreating foe.

Jackson, with his supposed invincible "Stonewall Brigade" and the accompanying brigades, much to their mortifiation and discomfiture, were compelled by this terrific fire to fall back in disorder upon their reserve. Here they took up a new position for a final stand, and made an attempt for a few minutes to retrieve the fortunes of the day. But again rained down upon them the same close and destructive fire. Again cheer upon cheer rang in their ears. A few minutes only did they stand up against it, when they turned dismayed and fled in disorder, leaving us in possession of the field, the killed and wounded, 300 prisoners, two guns, four caissons, and a thousand stand of small-arms. Night alone saved him from total destruction. The enemy retreated about 5 miles, and, judging from his camp-fires, took up a new position for the night. Our troops, wearied and exhausted with the fatigues of the day, threw themselves down to rest on the field.

Though the battle had been won, still I could not believe that Jackson would have hazarded a decisive engagement at such a distance from the main body without expecting re-enforcements. So, to be prepared for such a contingency, I set to work during the night to bring together all the troops within my reach. I sent an express after Williams' division, requesting the rear brigade, about 20 miles distant, to march all night and join me in the morning. I swept the posts and routes in my rear of almost all their guards, hurrying them forward by forced marches to be with me by daylight. I gave positive orders also to the forces in the field to open fire upon the enemy as soon as the light of day would enable them to point their guns, and to pursue him without respite, and compel him to abandon his guns and baggage or cut him to pieces. These orders were implicitly obeyed, as far as possible.

It now appears that I had rightly divined the intentions of our crafty antagonist. On the morning of the 23d a re-enforcement from Luray of 5,000 men reached Front Royal on their way to join Jackson. This re-enforcement was being followed by another body of 10,000 from Sperryville, but recent rains having rendered the Shenandoah River impassable, they found themselves compelled to fall back without being able to effect the proposed junction. At daylight on the morning of the 24th our artillery again opened upon the enemy. He entered upon his retreat in very good order, considering what he had suffered.

General Banks, hearing of our engagement on his way to Washington, halted at Harper's Ferry, and with remarkable promptitude and sagacity ordered back Williams' whole division, so that my express found the rear brigade already *en route* to join us. The general himself returned here forthwith, and, after making me a hasty visit, assumed command of the forces in pursuit of the enemy. The pursuit was kept up with vigor, energy, and activity until they reached Woodstock, where the enemy's retreat became flight, and the pursuit was abandoned because of the utter exhaustion of our troops.

The killed and wounded in this engagement cannot even yet be accurately ascertained. Indeed, my command has been so overworked that it has had but little time to ascertain anything. The killed, as reported, are 103, and amongst them we have to deplore the loss of the brave Colonel Murray, of the Eighty-fourth Pennsylvania Volunteers, who fell at the head of his regiment while gallantly leading it in the face of the enemy. The wounded are 441, many of them slightly, and the missing 24.* The enemy's loss is more difficult to ascertain than our own. Two hundred and seventy were found dead on the battle-field; 40 were buried by the inhabitants of the adjacent village, and, by a calculation made from the number of graves found on both sides of the Valley road between here and Strasburg, their loss in killed must have been about 500 and in wounded 1,000. The proportion between the killed and wounded of the enemy shows the closeness and terrible destructiveness of our fire—nearly half the wounds being fatal. The enemy admit a loss of between 1,000 and 1,500 in killed and wounded.

Our force in infantry, cavalry, and artillery did not exceed 7,000. That of the enemy must have exceeded 11,000. Jackson, who commanded on the field, had, in addition to his own "Stonewall" Brigade, Smith's, Garnett's, and Loring's brigades. Generals Smith and Garnett were here in person. The following regiments are known to have been present, and some from each of them were made prisoners on the field: The Second, Fourth, Fifth, Twenty-first, Twenty-third, Twenty-seventh, Twenty-eighth, Thirty-third, Thirty-seventh, and Forty-second Virginia, First Regiment Provisional Army, and an Irish battalion. None from the reserve were made prisoners. Their force in infantry must have been 9,000. The cavalry of their united brigades amounted to 1,500. Their artillery consisted of thirty-six pieces. We had 6,000 infantry, a cavalry force of 750, and twenty-four pieces of artillery.

I cannot conclude this report without expressing thanks and gratitude to the officers and soldiers of my command for their noble conduct on this trying day. It was worthy of the great country whose national existence they have pledged their lives to preserve. Special thanks are due to Colonel Kimball, commanding First Brigade, and senior officer in the field. His conduct was brave, judicious, and efficient. He executed my orders in every instance with vigor and fidelity, and exhibited judgment and sagacity in the various movements that were necessarily intrusted to his discretion. Colonel Tyler, commanding the Third Brigade, has won my admiration by his fearless intrepidity. His brigade is worthy of such an intrepid leader. This brigade and the regiments accompanying it achieved the decisive movement of the day. They drove the forces of the enemy before them on the left flank, and by hurling this flank back upon the reserve consummated this glorious victory. High praise is due to Colonel Sullivan, commanding the Second Brigade, for the manner in which he contributed to the first repulse of the enemy in the morning. To him, and Colonel Carroll, of the Eighth Ohio Volunteers, who commanded the skirmishers, is the credit due of

---

* But see revised statement, p. 346.

forcing back the right wing of the enemy and of intimidating him, and holding him in check on our left during the rest of the day. The chief of artillery, Lieutenant-Colonel Daum, deserves high commendation for the skillful manner in which he managed his batteries during the engagement. This skillful management prevented the enemy doubtless from using effectually his formidable artillery. The cavalry performed its duty with spirit in this engagement, and under its gallant chief, Colonel Brodhead, and his officers exhibited activity which paralyzed the movements of the enemy.

The commanders of regiments are also entitled to special mention, but sufficient justice cannot be done them in this report. I must therefore refer you on this head to the reports of the brigade commanders. The officers of General Banks' staff were present in the field and participated in the battle. The thanks of myself and command are justly due to them for efficient and gallant services rendered at decisive moments in every part of the field. The officers of my own staff have my thanks and gratitude for the fidelity with which they discharged the trying duties that devolved upon them. They had to penetrate the thickest of the fight to bring me intelligence of the state of the field, and performed their perilous duty throughout the day with fearless alacrity.

It affords me pleasure, as it is my duty, to recommend all the officers whose names I have specially mentioned to the consideration of the Government.

I have the honor to be, your obedient servant,

JAS. SHIELDS,
*Brigadier-General, Commanding.*

Maj. R. MORRIS COPELAND,
*Assistant Adjutant-General, Hdqrs. Fifth Corps d'Armée.*

—

[HEADQUARTERS ARMY OF THE POTOMAC,]
*March* 23, 1862.

Brigadier-General SHIELDS:

The general commanding congratulates you and the brave troops under your command on the splendid achievement communicated in your dispatch, which he has just received. He desires you to follow up rapidly the enemy's troops as far as Strasburg, if possible.

S. WILLIAMS,
*Assistant Adjutant-General.*

—

WINCHESTER, *March* 26, 1862—3 p. m.

Brigadier-General WILLIAMS,
*Assistant Adjutant-General:*

No additional information since my dispatch of yesterday of 4.55 p. m. Rumor says that Jackson fired his train on the other side of Woodstock, and fled to his old position near New Market. General Banks is at Strasburg, making preparations to repair the railroad. The telegraph line will be completed between this and Strasburg to-morrow; men are now repairing; I will know to-night how far they have advanced. I expect a messenger every moment from General Banks. If he brings any additional intelligence I will communicate it. I am arranging a permanent system of posts to protect our rear as far as Strasburg, where I will join the advance again and ascertain the exact position of the enemy.

JAS. SHIELDS,
*Brigadier-General.*

---

HEADQUARTERS ARMY OF THE POTOMAC,
*Seminary, March* 26, 1862.

Brig. Gen. JAMES SHIELDS, *Winchester:*

The commanding general congratulates you and the troops under your command upon the victory gained by your own energy and activity and their bravery on the 23d. He is pained to learn that the wound you received in the skirmish of the day before is more serious than at first supposed.

Sumner, with two divisions of his corps, is 5 miles below Manassas, moving on Warrenton. The telegraph is working to Manassas; will probably be open to Warrenton on Friday. From the best information he can gather the general believes the main force of the enemy has retired beyond the Rappahannock, occupying the line of the Rapidan from Fredericksburg to Gordonsville, and thinks the force you met consisted almost entirely of Jackson's command.

By command of Major-General McClellan:

S. WILLIAMS,
*Assistant Adjutant-General.*

---

WAR DEPARTMENT,
*Washington, March* 26, 1862.

Brigadier-General SHIELDS:

Your two dispatches relating to the brilliant achievement of the forces under your command have been received. While rejoicing at the success of your gallant troops, deep commiseration and sympathy are felt for those who have been victims in the gallant and victorious contest with treason and rebellion. Your wounds as well as your success prove Lander's brave division is still bravely led, and that wherever its standard is displayed rebels will be routed and pursued. To you and to the brave officers and soldiers under your command the Department returns thanks.

EDWIN M. STANTON,
*Secretary of War.*

---

## No. 2.

*Report of Surg. William S. King, U. S. Army, Medical Director Fifth Army Corps.*

MEDICAL DIRECTOR'S OFFICE,
*Strasburg, Va., March* 31, 1862.

SIR: The battle near Winchester, on the 23d instant, was fought by the troops of General Shields' division, the division of General Williams, formerly Banks', having left a few days before in the direction of Centreville. General Shields' division had but recently returned by a forced march from Strasburg. As this division joined us lamentably deficient in medical supplies and with very limited transportation, and has been employed ever since in marching and counter-marching or engaging the enemy, no opportunity has been afforded to supply its wants. When the battle terminated, therefore, we found the supplies inadequate for the occasion, and the medical force not so large as desirable, in consequence of a number of officers being from necessity on duty with their regiments in pursuit of the enemy.

As soon as the action became severe, which was not till 4.30 p. m., the ambulances were ordered to the front, and commenced the work of removing the wounded to a place of shelter. As Winchester was near by, and the night fast approaching, it was thought best to remove the wounded to that place without delay. Camp-fires were made on the field, the wounded collected around, and directed to remain near them until the wagons should pick them up. After making these arrangements, about 8 p. m. I returned to Winchester, and spent most of the night in providing for their accommodation and attending to such cases as required immediate attention. As the medical officers were mostly inexperienced, and some confusion (inseparable to such an occasion) existed, I remained a day in Winchester after the command had advanced until things appeared to be working well, when I left to join headquarters, it being reported that an action was going on near Strasburg.

Complaints of inattention to the wounded having reached me, I again proceeded to Winchester, and found the arrangements not as satisfactory as I could wish, which was owing chiefly to a want of co-operation on the part of the quartermaster's and commissary departments, arising from a want of knowledge, or a want of disposition, to perform their duties. From a consideration of all the circumstances I believe that much of the discomfort of the wounded has been owing to circumstances beyond the control of the medical officers.

I mention these details in explanation of the difficulties known to exist in providing immediately for 400 wounded soldiers suddenly thrown upon us without the means and appliances sufficient to accommodate them, and which cannot be done without some delay.

After writing the above I received a note from Surg. C. C. Keeney to meet him in Winchester, and to him I will refer for further details. I have requested him to send at least 300 bedsteads for the hospitals in Winchester and a supply of stores of all kinds.

I have heard that Dr. Alexander, the medical purveyor of this command, has been ordered away from Baltimore, and I am not aware who has relieved him, and shall be glad to be informed on the subject.

I have to request that a supply for 20,000 men for three months be forwarded to Winchester for this corps, as many of the medical officers are very deficient in medicines and stores of all kinds, and we find that, owing to our frequent change of position, it is impracticable to obtain the supplies called for from the purveyor at Baltimore. A supply of medicines and stores on hand, according to my experience, is as necessary to an army in the field as it is to have a supply of subsistence, so far as availability is concerned. The supplies necessary to establish hospitals we must expect to receive from Washington, as we have no transportation to carry them along with us.

I am, sir, very respectfully, your obedient servant,

W. S. KING,

*Surgeon and Medical Director Fifth Army Corps.*

Surg. Gen. C. A. FINLEY, *Washington City, D. C.*

## No. 3.

### *Return of Casualties in the Union forces.**

[Compiled from nominal lists of casualties, returns, &c.]

| Command. | Killed. | | Wounded. | | Captured or missing. | | Aggregate. | Remarks. |
|---|---|---|---|---|---|---|---|---|
| | Officers. | Enlisted men. | Officers. | Enlisted men. | Officers. | Enlisted men. | | |
| **SHIELDS' DIVISION.** | | | | | | | | |
| Brig. Gen. JAMES SHIELDS (wounded). | | | | | | | | |
| Staff | | | 1 | | | | 1 | |
| *First Brigade.* | | | | | | | | |
| Col. NATHAN KIMBALL.† | | | | | | | | |
| 84th Pennsylvania | 3 | 18 | 2 | 69 | | | 92 | Col. Murray, Capt. Gallagher, and Lieut. Reem killed. |
| 8th Ohio | | 11 | 1 | 40 | | 1 | 53 | |
| 67th Ohio | 1 | 8 | 2 | 36 | | | 47 | Capt. Ford killed. |
| 14th Indiana | | 4 | 5 | 45 | | | 54 | Capt. Kelly died of wounds. |
| Total First Brigade | 4 | 41 | 10 | 190 | | 1 | 246 | |
| *Second Brigade.* | | | | | | | | |
| Col. JEREMIAH C. SULLIVAN. | | | | | | | | |
| 5th Ohio | 1 | 17 | 1 | 31 | | | 50 | Capt. Whitcom killed. |
| 62d Ohio | | | | | | | | No loss reported. |
| 13th Indiana | | 5 | 2 | 35 | | | 42 | |
| 39th Illinois | | | | | | | | No loss reported. |
| Total Second Brigade | 1 | 22 | 3 | 66 | | | 92 | |
| *Third Brigade.* | | | | | | | | |
| Col. ERASTUS B. TYLER. | | | | | | | | |
| 110th Pennsylvania | | 7 | 4 | 39 | | | 50 | Lieut. Kochersperger died of wounds. |
| 1st West Virginia | | 6 | 2 | 21 | | | 29 | |
| 7th Ohio | | 20 | 3 | 59 | | 10 | 92 | |
| 29th Ohio | 1 | 2 | 1 | 9 | | 2 | 15 | Lieut. Williamson killed. |
| 7th Indiana | | 7 | 2 | 31 | | 9 | 49 | |
| Total Third Brigade | 1 | 42 | 12 | 159 | | 21 | 235 | |
| *Cavalry.* | | | | | | | | |
| Col. T. F. BRODHEAD. | | | | | | | | |
| 1st Squadron Pennsylvania Cavalry. Maryland Cavalry, three companies. 1st West Virginia, detachment. 1st Ohio Cavalry, companies A and C. 1st Michigan Cavalry, detachment. | | 3 | 1 | 5 | | | 9 | |
| Total cavalry | | 3 | 1 | 5 | | | 9 | |
| *Artillery.* | | | | | | | | |
| Lieut. Col. PHILIP DAUM. | | | | | | | | |
| West Virginia Light Artillery, Battery A. | | 1 | | | | | 1 | |

*Casualties in skirmish of March 22 included. †Also commanded the division on the field of battle.

*Return of Casualties in the Union forces*—Continued.

| Command. | Killed. | | Wounded. | | Captured or missing. | | Aggregate. | Remarks. |
|---|---|---|---|---|---|---|---|---|
| | Officers. | Enlisted men. | Officers. | Enlisted men. | Officers. | Enlisted men. | | |
| West Virginia Light Artillery, Battery B. | ...... | ...... | ...... | ...... | ...... | ...... | ...... | No loss reported |
| 1st Ohio Light Artillery, Battery H. | ...... | 1 | ...... | ...... | ...... | ...... | 1 | |
| 1st Ohio Light Artillery, Battery L. | | 1 | ...... | 2 | ...... | ...... | 3 | |
| 4th U. S. Artillery, Battery E | ...... | 1 | ...... | ...... | ...... | ...... | 1 | |
| Total artillery | ...... | 4 | ...... | 2 | ...... | ...... | 6 | |
| Signal detachment | ...... | ...... | ...... | 1 | ...... | ...... | 1 | |
| Total Shields' division | 6 | 112 | 27 | 423 | ...... | 22 | 590 | |

## No. 4.

*Reports of Maj. R. Morris Copeland, Assistant Adjutant-General, U. S. Army.*

HDQRS. FIFTH ARMY CORPS, ARMY OF THE POTOMAC,
*Strasburg, March* 26, 1862.

SIR: In reply to your communication of to-day I would say that after receiving your orders on the 23d instant to visit the scene of action and report, I went at once. On my arrival I found we had on our left wing a battery and one or two regiments. The center and right wing were composed of three batteries and about five regiments of infantry, with a considerable force of cavalry. A high and commanding position on our right was occupied by the enemy at about 3 o'clock p. m. and a severe fire opened on our center, which compelled the withdrawal of a portion of our force into a more secure position.

At about 3.30 p. m. Colonel Tyler was ordered to attack the enemy's new position on our right and to take their battery. He moved immediately forward with three or four regiments, a battery, and about 400 cavalry, through a dense woods, which covered the enemy's center and left wing. In about half an hour after Colonel Tyler's movements his skirmishers exchanged shots with the enemy, who were posted behind high stone walls, a rocky hill, and some woods a quarter of a mile in front of his battery. The enemy reserved his fire until our line was very near. They then arose and poured in a very heavy volley. The suddenness and strength of their fire caused our lines to falter, and the extreme left, composed mainly of the One hundred and tenth Pennsylvania Volunteers, broke and ran. The rest of the line soon rallied and maintained a steady fight (falling back on the right and advancing on the left) for at least half an hour, when two regiments came to their assistance up the left flank and through a very severe fire. They advanced steadily, and soon gained a position from which they could flank the enemy, delivering their fire. When they received this new fire the enemy fell back rapidly, but still fighting, to the woods nearest to the hill, from which the battery had been in the mean time withdrawn.

Having in vain attempted to rally the One hundred and tenth Pennsylvania Volunteers (which, with such company officers, as I could see, was in a shameful rout), I joined the advance on the first field which the enemy had held, where there were many dead and wounded. I questioned such as could answer, and learned that Jackson was present with about 6,000 men, having arrived with the largest part of his command at 3 p. m. He had posted about 3,000 in the first field, and had reserved 3,000 more in position behind the offensive battery and in the woods half a mile to the front. Before communicating this to Colonel Tyler I took the liberty of ordering the cavalry to advance by a side road toward the rear of the enemy's reserve, and then communicated to Colonel Tyler, who was advancing, the strength of the enemy before him. Colonel Tyler arranged his force so as to support Colonels Kimball's and Sullivan's forces, which were nearest the enemy, and moved slowly forward.

The enemy now opened on our line with a heavier fire than before. We maintained our position from the first, and soon drove them in utter confusion down the hill, but the near approach of night forbade farther pursuit, and a halt was ordered. Our troops commenced preparations for bivouacking and for removing our dead. I rode over the field and saw that the enemy could not have lost less than 100 killed and 200 wounded, and judged that our loss was about the same. The wounds of the enemy seemed generally more severe than ours. The cavalry came around the hill at a very good time, and captured about 150 prisoners. On the side of the woods in the rear of the enemy's battery there were one cannon and two overturned caissons. There were large numbers of muskets strewed about in the different fields, which I ordered to be stacked for future removal. Also the enemy seemed to have in many cases thrown aside their equipments to expedite their flight.

As there seemed no further reason to expect attack, I returned to the city and reported myself to your headquarters. I afterward learned that the enemy had twenty-eight pieces of artillery in reserve at Kernstown, which were removed as soon as the day seemed to be unfavorable. The report amongst the people along the road is that Jackson carried back 1,000 less than what went to Winchester.

In regard to the enemy at present, I believe he is near Staunton. Ashby and a considerable amount of cavalry, with two pieces of artillery, are about 3 miles from here. The infantry, it is believed, are entirely worn-out and demoralized, but are too far for us to overtake.

I am, general, with much respect, your most obedient servant,

R. MORRIS COPELAND,
*Assistant Adjutant-General and Major Volunteers.*

Brig. Gen. JAMES SHIELDS, *Commanding Division.*

---

HEADQUARTERS FIFTH CORPS D'ARMÉE,
ARMY OF THE POTOMAC,
*Strasburg, Va., March* 26, 1862.

SIR: In reply to your communication I will state what I observed at the first attack by Colonel Ashby on Winchester, March 22. At 2 p. m. a messenger came to General Banks' headquarters, stating that Ashby was advancing on the town. By order of General Banks all the cavalry under his command was immediately sent to the front I rode out, accompanied by 25 men—Company L, First Michigan Cavalry, Captain Brewer. As soon as we emerged from the town two parts of companies joined us, making in all 70 men. We rode out upon the Millwood road about $1\frac{1}{2}$ miles, and were preparing to charge upon a body of the enemy in the edge of some woods, when we received two shots from a battery previously concealed. We immediately moved back to a more secure position, the enemy following with shot and shell and about 200 cavalry. The force was so small that I did not deem it prudent to remain exposed, but put the larger number of men in a hollow, and drew out 12 men on the ridge, to impress the enemy with an idea of a concealed force. An order was at this time received for all the cavalry to return to town. As the order was peremptory, I sent in the two companies, retaining only the 25 men of the escort, still keeping the advance displayed as before. Observing a company of infantry on the left, I ordered them forward as skirmishers, to clear the woods of about 50 men not more than 300 yards in front. The infantry were dismayed by the shell and retreated. Still leaving this small force to check their advance as the infantry retreated the cavalry on the Strasburg road charged down toward the town, but were met by a severe fire of the retreating company, who had formed behind a wall. Soon after this you came out with all your force.

I wish to commend to you the 25 men of Company L, First Michigan Cavalry, Captain Brewer commanding, who during two and a half hours under continuous fire of shot and shell checked the enemy's advance by their resolute bearing, giving the impression that they must have been sustained by a large force; and I firmly believe that had they fallen back the enemy would have charged into the town.

I have the honor to be, general, with much respect, your most obedient servant,

R. MORRIS COPELAND,
*Assistant Adjutant-General and Major Volunteers.*

Brig. Gen. JAMES SHIELDS,
*Commanding Division.*

---

## No. 5.

### *Report of Capt. R. C. Shriber, Aide-de-Camp, U. S. Army.*

WINCHESTER, *March* 26, 1862.

GENERAL: I beg most respectfully to report to you that after having received on Sunday last, the 23d of March, at 9 a. m., an order to report for duty as aide-de camp on your staff, I left headquarters for Kernstown, to assist Colonels Kimball, Tyler, and Sullivan in their efforts, as commanders of brigades, fighting the enemy under General Jackson, and to insure a unity of action of their three respective commands. I reported at 9.30 a. m. to Colonel Kimball, acting brigadier and senior officer on the field, who was stationed upon a hill about half a mile west of Kernstown, which latter place is perpendicularly intersected by the turnpike leading to Strasburg. There I informed myself as to the events which had transpired previous to my arrival on the field, and understood that the enemy, who had been repulsed in endeavoring to drive in our pickets the day before, had opened with his artillery at about 8 a. m. upon our forces again, and that since that time we were engaged in responding to his battery of four guns, which he then had in play, and endeavoring to repel his small but harassing attacks of cavalry upon our chain of sentinels.

Reconnoitering the ground surrounding me, I found that between the hill upon which I stood with Colonel Kimball and the hill opposite us, upon which the enemy's battery was posted, about half a mile distant, a ravine was lying, running from east to west, which is entirely free of wood. When about half a mile to the east a forest connected both hills, through the center of which passes a mud road, and which is bounded on its extreme right by another mud road leading to Cedar Creek. The country to the left (west) of the turnpike is flat, and comparatively little wooded. We placed in position a six-gun battery, commanded by Captain Jenks, First Virginia Artillery, to oppose the enemy's four guns, which latter was soon re-enforced by a whole battery; whereupon Captain Clark's regular battery was put in prolongation of the former named. Both batteries were fought by Colonel Daum, chief of artillery, in person. Our fire from the two batteries became too hot for the enemy, and they brought a third battery in the direction of their right wing in such position upon our two batteries as to enfilade them, but continued their fire.

In the mean time the infantry regiments were moving up to the support of our batteries, and formed into line of battle about 1,000 yards to the rear of our batteries, when at once the enemy's heavier battery moved to the front, and threw in rapid succession a number of well-aimed shells into our batteries and the cavalry and infantry stationed upon the interior slope of the battery hill, and the necessity to storm and take their guns became evident. In conjunction with Colonels Kimball and Tyler the following infantry regiments were drawn up in mass parallel with each other; the right, resting upon the mud road passing through the forest, was held by the Seventh Ohio, the Sixty-seventh and Fifth following, and the Thirteenth Indiana, Eighty-fourth Pennsylvania, and Twenty-ninth Ohio a little to the rear, thus leaving the One hundred and tenth Pennsylvania, Fourteenth Indiana, and three companies of the Eighth Ohio in reserve.

During the time these arrangements were made a messenger was sent to you, general, to have your approval as to this flank movement, and I personally apprised all the commanders in the rear and flanks of our intentions, so as to keep them on the alert. Colonel Daum was enjoined to keep his artillery in lively fire, so as not to divert the attention of the enemy from him, and when the order came to move on everything was ready to respond. General Tyler moved his column by the right flank as far as the Cedar Creek road, rested his right upon the same, and the left upon the before-mentioned mud road, pushing forward upon both roads some cavalry; changed direction to the left right in front, and moved silently but steadily upon the enemy's left, through the woods for about half a mile, when, coming upon a more sparsely wooded ground, he made a half-wheel to the left and came to face of the extreme flank of the enemy, who received him, posted behind a stone wall at about 200 yards' distance with a terrific volley from rifled arms; but still on went the regiments without a return fire, and then threw themselves, with immense cheering and an unearthly yell, upon the enemy, who, receiving at 15 yards our first fire, fell back across the field, thus unmasking two 6-pounder iron guns, which hurled, on being clear in front, death and destruction into our ranks with their canister. But still onward we went, taking one gun and two caissons, and making there a short stand. Again the enemy unmasked two brass pieces, which at last drove us by their vigorous fire back; but I caused the captured gun to be tipped over, so that the enemy, in regaining it, could not drag it away.

The Fifth Ohio and Eighty-fourth Pennsylvania threw themselves once more with fixed bayonets forward, the former losing four times in a few minutes their standard-bearer. Captain Whitcom at last took the colors up again, and cheering on his men, fell also. So Colonel Murray, gallantly leading on his Eighty-fourth. In fact, that ground was strewn with dead and wounded. General Tyler lost there his aide, Lieutenant Williamson, Twenty-ninth Ohio. I hurried back to bring up the One hundred and tenth Pennsylvania and Fourteenth Indiana by a right-oblique movement through the woods, and the enemy, receiving all the combined shock and fire, retired, and left us in possession of our dearly-bought gun and caissons. United we pressed forward again, the enemy's two brass pieces and musketry pouring in their fire into our ranks. Three companies of the Eighth Ohio re-enforcing us, we gained one brass piece and its caissons, and compelled the enemy to fall back. This was at 7 p. m. I moved to the right flank and caused the cavalry to go forward on the now fast-retreating enemy, when I met with 6 of Ashby's cavalry, who shot down my orderly and killed his horse, one of the bullets piercing my cap. I was forced to use my sword to kill one of them. The cavalry captured 230 prisoners and met only with little resistance from the enemy's cavalry.

At 8 p. m. the musketry ceased. A few more of the cannon shots from their extreme left battery were fired, so as to withdraw our attention from the retreating foe, and all was over. Our men remained on the field of battle picking up the wounded, and slept upon their arms, to awake for the pursuit of the enemy on the morning of the 24th, who fell rapidly back beyond Newtown, when at 9 o'clock of the morning of that day Major-General Banks took command, and I reported back to you.

General, I have the honor to be ever ready to serve in this glorious body of soldiers under your able leading.

Most respectfully, your obedient, humble servant,

R. C. SHRIBER,
*Aide-de-Camp and Acting Inspector-General.*

Brig. Gen. JAMES SHIELDS,
*Commanding Second Division, Fifth Corps d'Armée.*

---

## No. 6.

*Reports of Lieut. William W. Rowley, Twenty-eighth New York Infantry, Acting Signal Officer.*

HEADQUARTERS ARMY OF THE POTOMAC,
*Near Yorktown, Va., April* 13, 1862.

SIR: I have the honor to forward the inclosed report relative to the services of signal officers at the battle of Winchester, and the accompanying communication from Lieut. W. W. Rowley, acting signal officer in charge.

The attention of the Secretary of War is respectfully called to the fact that, without recognition or notice of their services, even when rendered on the field of battle and under circumstances of exposure, the best officers now on signal duty become dissatisfied and request their relief from the duty.

I am, sir, very respectfully, your obedient servant,

ALBERT J. MYER,
*Signal Officer, Major, U. S. Army.*

Hon. E. M. STANTON,
*Secretary of War, War Department, Washington, D. C.*

[Inclosure No. 1.]

HEADQUARTERS GENERAL BANKS' DIVISION,
*Strasburg, Va., March* 26, 1862.

MAJOR: I have the honor to report that on Saturday, the 22d instant, the division commanded by General Williams, in the Fifth Army Corps, took up its line of march for Manassas via Berryville and Snicker's Ferry.

On the afternoon of the same day the rebels made their appearance near Winchester; had some little skirmishing, but of no importance. The next day the rebels made their appearance with much force. During the morning there was nothing but the firing of artillery. In the afternoon I took the field with nearly all the signal officers and men. The firing of artillery still continued; the enemy had four guns.

At 3 p. m. the general commanding ordered up one brigade of five regiments to flank the rebels on their right and capture the guns. I had before that established communication with the right, left, and center of our force, and had extended the line back to headquarters in Winchester, making in all six stations. The signals worked beautifully, and were used almost constantly, transmitting messages of an important character, such as ordering up re-enforcements, informing the commander of movements of the enemy, &c. At the movement of our forces to flank the enemy's right I dispatched Lieutenant Taylor, with a flagman, to accompany them. As they approached the place of assault they were greeted by a heavy volley of musketry from the enemy, hid behind a heavy stone fence. The rebels had five regiments to meet ours. At the first volley many of our men fell. Lieutenant Taylor's flagman (Mr. Temple) was wounded in the right forearm; his horse was shot. Lieutenant Taylor remained during the fight, but could not communicate, as his man had returned. He had a button shot off from his overcoat, but was not wounded.

I then sent Lieutenant Byram to a point near the scene of battle, where he opened communication with the center station and kept it finely, although the bullets flew thick around him.

The struggle lasted about two hours, and was, I think, as fierce and closely contested as any of the war.

Several of the officers, with myself, remained upon the field all night, and were employed much of the time in sending and receiving messages. The next day we chased the rebels from Winchester to this point, or near it. At the general's request I located stations on the way, so as to keep up communication with Winchester.

At all times a signal officer was with the foremost of the advance, communicating with the rear.

At General Banks' request I have established three stations around here. The remainder are ready to proceed with our forces toward Manassas. I am certain we were of great service on the field on Sunday, and hope to again have an opportunity of making ourselves very useful.

On Sunday Lieutenants Larned, Spencer, Fralick, Taylor, and Byram were of very great service to me.

I am, truly, your obedient servant,

W. W. ROWLEY,
*Acting Signal Officer.*

ALBERT J. MYER,
*Signal Officer, Major, U. S. Army.*

[Inclosure No. 2.]

HEADQUARTERS GENERAL BANKS' ARMY CORPS,
*Strasburg, March* 29, 1862.

MAJOR: I have the honor to report that the corps under my command are at present around here.

There are but two stations now, but I go to Front Royal to-morrow to establish a station and connect it with this point. It will take at least one intermediate station. As fast as it is safe I push on toward Manassas, desiring to connect the two points, the distance being about 62 miles. I shall establish as far as I can with what I have, and trust to luck for the balance. If it is a fair country, I shall have sufficient to go through the whole distance.

I received yours of the 8th of March to-day, ordering Lieutenant Taylor to Washington. I am very sorry to lose him, he being an excellent officer. You are thinning out my good officers pretty fast. I hardly think it just, after we have labored to work to some degree of proficiency.

I would like to be returned to my regiment, as this service is very expensive and hard. I believe I have labored more than any man in the division, and as yet get no credit. All of us have endeavored to do our duty, but the service is such that no one knows it or seems to appreciate it. As yet I have seen no mention made of us at the battle of Winchester. I know we were of great service. I remained up all night with several others, and was at work transmitting messages a good portion of the time. The general commanding told me we were of great service, and that we should be honorably mentioned. I would like to be returned to my regiment, where I can stand some show for promotion.

I am, yours, respectfully,

W. W. ROWLEY,
*Acting Signal Officer.*

ALBERT J. MYER,
*Signal Officer and Major, U. S. Army.*

---

HEADQUARTERS DEPARTMENT OF THE SHENANDOAH,
*New Market, Va., April* 21, 1862.

SIR: In accordance with your favor of the 15th instant I have the honor to report that on the 22d of March, 1862, in the afternoon, General Jackson made his appearance before Winchester with two pieces of artillery and some cavalry. There was desultory firing, but of not much moment that day. My party was not out all this day, except two or three officers as lookers-on.

On the 23d cannonading was commenced quite early on both sides, and kept up at intervals during the forenoon. About 2 p. m., seeing that the enemy was gathering in some force, I went to the field, accompanied by Lieutenants Wicker, Fralick, Larned, Spencer, Harvey, Byram, Miner, Taylor, Briggs, and Halsted, with their flagmen. I also had two of mine with me. On arriving upon the battle-field we found Colonel Kimball in command. I immediately located a station near Colonel Kimball, placing Lieut. John H. Fralick upon it with his two flagmen. Colonel Sullivan was in command of our left flank, about 1½ miles from Colonel Kimball. I ordered Lieutenant Larned to go to Colonel Sullivan with his flagman and locate a station, which he accordingly did. I afterward sent Lieutenant Briggs to assist him. Then, at Colonel Kimball's request, I established communication between him and General Shields, who was confined to his room with a wound received the day before at Winchester, about 3 miles. I did it at once by sending Lieutenant Miner to General Shields' headquarters, Lieutenants Wicker and Spencer occupying the station next to Lieutenant Miner; Lieutenant Harvey the station next to Wicker's and Spencer's, he communicating with Lieutenant Fralick.

About 3 o'clock p. m. Colonel Tyler was ordered to advance with five regiments to turn the enemy's left and capture a battery which was playing upon our center. I dispatched Lieutenant Taylor, with one flagman to accompany him. After proceeding about 1½ miles he was met with a heavy force, which poured in upon him volley after volley with deadly effect, but our forces under Colonel Tyler answered it with a will. It was here that Lieutenant Taylor's flagman was wounded in the arm. The flagman's horse was shot through the neck, but not killed. Lieutenant Taylor did not succeed in opening communication with Lieutenant Fralick.

I then sent Lieutenant Byram over to our right, so as to get communication with Colonel Tyler, which he did in fine style. The firing lasted until dark, when both sides ceased, the rebels having been routed at all points, we capturing two guns and three caissons.

Lieutenant Taylor joined Lieutenant Byram about dark, and the two worked the station during the night. Lieutenants Larned and Briggs remained upon their station all night upon the left, Byram and Taylor all night upon our right, Lieutenant Spencer and myself upon the station at the center. At dark, with Colonel Kimball's consent, I ordered all the other stations to proceed to the quarters, which they did. The stations at the center and upon the left were almost constantly at work, ordering up re-enforcements, &c. All the stations worked well, no mistake occurring and no reports being called for. Lieutenants Fralick, Taylor, Byram, and myself were in the most exposed part of the field; at times it being very much exposed. Some of the time I acted as aide to Colonel Kimball, carrying messages to different portions of the field. During the night our stations were kept pretty busy sending messages.

The names of the flagmen who worked in the exposed portions of the field are as follows: Lieutenant Larned, Flagman Alonzo H. Hurd, Company H, First Minnesota Volunteers; Lieutenant Fralick, Flagman Edward G. Redner, Thirty-fourth New York Volunteers; Lieutenant Taylor, Flagman Oliver S. Temple, Forty-third New York Volunteers; Lieutenant Byram, Flagman S. W. Shirfey, Sixteenth Indiana Volunteers; Lieutenant Rowley, Flagman Peter Spargo, First Pennsylvania Reserve Volunteers.

All the officers and men did their duty well and faithfully, and I think all are equally deserving. All could not be in the battle, as some were ordered on stations a little removed. They all did their work cheerfully and manfully. I inclose you some of the many messages sent upon the battle-field.* There was not time to preserve a copy of all, the stations were kept so constantly working. I also send copy of messages transmitted by the corps while the army was at Strasburg. They are merely specimens of what we are daily doing. I cannot send but a few; if I should undertake to copy all they would fill a volume.

Yours, respectfully,

W. W. ROWLEY.

Capt. SAMUEL T. CUSHING, *Acting Signal Officer.*

---

## No. 7.

*Report of Col. Thornton F. Brodhead, First Michigan Cavalry, Chief of Cavalry.*

HDQRS. CHIEF OF CAVALRY, FIFTH CORPS D'ARMÉE,
*Strasburg, March* 27, 1862.

MAJOR: In compliance with your circular order of the 25th instant, yesterday received, I have the honor to report that at 2 o'clock p. m., on the 22d instant, Major Paldi, of the First Michigan Cavalry, reported the enemy on the Strasburg road within 2 miles of Winchester. I immediately sent Lieutenant-Colonel Copeland, of that regiment, with the only then available companies, to assume command, and directed Major Chamberlain, of the Virginia Cavalry, to move with his command and report to Lieutenant-Colonel Copeland. These orders given, I joined General Shields and proceeded to the field. Some time before dark General Shields was wounded, and I ordered a portion of the cavalry force to take position some 3 miles on the Strasburg road, where it remained all night, the rest returning to Winchester to await further orders.

On the morning of the 23d we advanced, under the command of Colonel Kimball, at the head of the column, pursuing the enemy until late in the afternoon, when the position of the enemy was stormed by Colonel Tyler, who was efficiently supported by Lieutenant-Colonel Copeland with a cavalry force detailed on the field for that purpose. The attack was successful, and after a severe contest the enemy driven from the field.

On the morning of the 24th I advanced with the cavalry of the corps to Cedar Creek, moving myself with a small party to Strasburg in the evening for the purpose of reconnoitering; after which the force returned, reporting to General Banks, and by his order encamped in front of the position occupied by our troops. My command on the 23d, actively engaged in the battle, consisted of four companies of the First Michigan Cavalry, two companies of the Ohio Cavalry, two companies Maryland, a squadron of the Ringgold and Washington Cavalry (Pennsylvania), commanded by Captain Keys, and six companies of the First Virginia Cavalry, less than 780 men in all. Their position on the march was at all times exposed and at the head of the column, testing well the courage of our gallant men, all of whom, I am proud to say, acquitted themselves nobly. Lieutenant-Colonel Copeland, whose report I have the honor to inclose, gives an accurate statement of the disposition of our forces during the engagement, to which I respect-

---

* Not found.

fully refer. I also inclose the report of Captains Keys and Greenfield, of the Pennsylvania squadron. These excellent officers were assigned to severe duty, but discharged it well. The loss of the cavalry force was 3 killed and 5 wounded, 1 probably mortally.* I sent to Winchester a very large number of prisoners, but reports from the different company commanders have not yet been received to enable me to forward an accurate statement, many being now absent on duty.

I take pleasure in mentioning the prompt and gallant conduct of Lieutenant-Colonel Copeland, of the First Michigan, to whose efficient exertions the whole command are much indebted. He was actively supported by Major Chamberlain, of the Virginia regiment, and by Captain Menken, of the Ohio forces, both of whom during the attack, as a portion of the supporting force, were distinguished for soldierlike bearing. Capt. J. B. Park, who was detached from his company, now under the command of Colonel Geary, was severely wounded while acting as a volunteer in supporting the storming party. This gallant officer deserves high commendation for his gallantry.

I have the honor to be, very respectfully, your obedient servant,

T. F. BRODHEAD,
*Colonel and Chief of Cavalry, Fifth Corps d'Armée.*

Maj. H. G. ARMSTRONG,
*Actg. Asst. Adjt. Gen., Shields' Div., Winchester, Va.*

---

## No. 8.

*Report of Lieut. Col. Joseph T. Copeland, First Michigan Cavalry.*

HEADQUARTERS FIRST MICHIGAN CAVALRY,
*Strasburg, March* 25, 1862.

SIR: I have the honor to report that in obedience to your order of the evening of the 22d instant I proceeded with the companies of this regiment to the Stone Mill, about 1 mile from Winchester, on the pike leading to this place, where Major Paldi, of our regiment, was encamped with one company, and had reported that the enemy were advancing on the town. We held the enemy in check some two hours till re-enforcements could come up. About the time of the arrival of the forces under General Shields Major Chamberlain reported to me with six companies of the Virginia cavalry and Captain Keys with one squadron of Pennsylvania cavalry. After the retreat of the enemy I ordered one squadron of Major Chamberlain's command to patrol the Romney road, Captain Keys with his squadron to patrol the Front Royal road, and two companies the pike in our advance. The balance of the cavalry returned to their quarters, with orders from you to report at your headquarters the next morning at daylight.

On the morning of the 23d I reported with the companies of this regiment not already engaged and away upon detached service at the headquarters of General Shields for orders, as per your direction. I was directed by General Shields to proceed at once and report to Colonel Kimball upon what subsequently became the field of battle. I proceeded thither, and during the morning the following additional bodies of cavalry, by your orders, reported to me for orders, viz: Five companies of Virginia, three of Maryland, two of Ohio, and two of Pennsylvania.

---

* But see revised statement, p. 346.

By order of Colonel Kimball I directed two companies of the Pennsylvania cavalry to patrol the Front Royal road. Two companies were detailed to patrol the Romney road, and one company the cross-road leading from the latter road to the Strasburg pike. Company F of this regiment I directed to support the batteries on the right of our line, and the balance of the Virginia cavalry, under Major Chamberlain, to take position on our right flank.

At about 4 o'clock orders were given to storm the rebel batteries in front of our right, and that the infantry constituting the storming party be supported by all the cavalry that I could collect for the purpose. I concentrated for this purpose three companies of my own regiment, three of Virginia, and two of the Ohio; then I formed in close column of squadron the companies of this regiment in front immediately in rear of the infantry, and proceeded in that order through the woods till we met the enemy. Then we were forced to remain in comparative inactivity till the enemy broke, when I gave the order to charge and pursue them. This order was received with enthusiasm and executed with alacrity, and, notwithstanding the numerous stone walls and fences which retarded our progress, resulted in the capture of between 200 and 300 prisoners—the exact number I have not had an opportunity of ascertaining.

When all did their duty so well, at times under a shower of balls, it would seem invidious to discriminate, and yet I cannot forbear commending Lieutenant Heazlit, the adjutant of our regiment, Lieutenants Gray and Freeman, and Captain Park and Lieutenant Gallagher, of the First Battalion, who, happening to be present, volunteered their services. Captain Park received a severe wound soon after reaching the enemy's position and was obliged to retire from the field.

J. T. COPELAND,
*Lieutenant-Colonel, Commanding.*

Col. T. F. BRODHEAD,
*Chief of Cavalry, Fifth Corps d'Armée.*

---

## No. 9.

### *Report of Capt. John Keys, Pennsylvania Cavalry.*

WINCHESTER, VA., *March* 26, 1862.

Agreeably to your verbal orders and instructions of Saturday, 22d, I took my command, consisting of the Washington and Ringgold Cavalry, numbering 60 men, and proceeded with dispatch and reported at 4 in the evening to Colonel Copeland, who after the enemy began to give back ordered me to take the Front Royal road and proceed cautiously along the same, sending messengers to the rear to report, which was done. We proceeded to a farm-house 3½ miles out, where we captured one of Stuart's (discharged, he says) cavalrymen, with whom we returned to Winchester. Deeming his information valuable, reported him to headquarters General Shields. First picketed the road, and then by your order went into quarters with the balance of the command.

Again on the 23d of March, agreeably to your order, I reported my command to your headquarters, where, by your order, I divided my command, sending Captain Greenfield with the Washington Cavalry on the Front Royal road, with directions to watch the enemy on his right, whilst by your direction I took the Ringgold Cavalry to watch the enemy on his left on the Romney road, and give due notice of his approach by reporting to the rear and headquarters. I proceeded to fulfill this order and followed the Romney road for 7 miles; then sending a scout to the front for 3 miles farther, with instructions as above, I returned 2 miles to where a road intersects the Romney road from Newtown. At this point we had captured two suspicious persons and sent them to headquarters. Here we went off to the southeast and soon heard firing in our front. We next saw some (secesh) rebel cavalry, who upon our approach retired. We advanced until within 800 yards and to the rear of the battle-ground. The fire of musketry was then increasing. The artillery had ceased and the contending forces were approaching each other, but it was dusk, and I was unable, from the smoke of the firing and the dusk of the evening, to distinguish friend from foe, and from my position to the left and rear of the enemy I feared to approach nearer, lest our own forces should open on us. After the firing ceased for the night I, with my company, returned to quarters and reported for further duty.

On the 24th, with my command, numbering 80 men, I reported on the field to you, when again I was referred to Colonel Copeland for orders. Accordingly I went in the advance, sometimes on the right and sometimes on the left, as skirmishers, and sometimes as supporters to the artillery. We pressed the enemy to Newtown, where we were charging the enemy, when we received orders to halt the head of the column. From this point we were sent to the right to cut off a baggage train, but none had passed by that road. We approached the main road again at Cedar Creek and encamped for the night. On the 25th we were again on the march and in the advance, the enemy gradually falling back 4 miles beyond Strasburg. Here, by your order, I reported with my command back to General Williams and Colonel Donnelly.

JOHN KEYS,
*Captain, Commanding Squadron Pennsylvania Cavalry.*

Colonel BRODHEAD, *Chief of Cavalry.*

---

## No. 10.

### *Report of Capt. Andrew J. Greenfield, Pennsylvania Cavalry.*

STRASBURG, *March* 26, 1862.

In pursuance of your order, on the morning of the 23d I proceeded out the Front Royal road about 5 miles with my command of 30 men to watch the enemy's right. I then fell back a short distance, making my position to the left and front of our infantry skirmishers, making it convenient to communicate. I continued to send messengers back to headquarters, reporting position and observation. About 100 rebel cavalry approached about 12 m. within 1 mile of our front and then retired. About 4 o'clock I was over communicating with the commanding officer of the skirmishers, when about 40 rebel cavalry attacked them, but were repulsed before I could bring my command to their assistance. I kept the by-roads well guarded and the front well patrolled. About 12 o'clock, leaving a strong picket, I returned to camp.

Your most obedient servant,

A. J. GREENFIELD,
*Captain, Commanding Washington Cavalry.*

Capt. JOHN KEYS,
*Commanding First Squadron Pennsylvania Cavalry.*

## No. 11.

### *Report of Lieut. Col. Philip Daum, Chief of Artillery.*

HEADQUARTERS ARTILLERY BRIGADE,
*Shields' Division, Strasburg, Va., March* 26, 1862.

On Saturday, March 22, about 4 p. m., the enemy made an attack upon our forces near Winchester and on the turnpike leading to Strasburg. Battery H, First Regiment Ohio Volunteer Artillery, Capt. J. F. Huntington, was promptly placed in position, and opened fire upon the enemy, when they immediately retreated.

Sunday morning, 23d, about 9 o'clock, the enemy opened fire upon our advance guard. I ordered Captain Jenks to advance four rifled guns of his battery, and placed them in position on a hill commanding the enemy's batteries and the village of Kernstown. He opened an effective fire upon them. I immediately ordered Captain Clark's battery to take position on the left of Jenks' battery and upon the same hill. Both batteries kept up an effective fire until the enemy was compelled to change the position of his batteries.

The enemy then attempted to flank our right wing, which they endeavored to do with a column of about 3,000 men, but a very effective salvo from Daum's battery (Captain Jenks) scattered their force, and made them seek cover in the adjoining woods. By this time the enemy had succeeded in placing a battery upon a hill to the right of the one occupied by our batteries, and opened a hot and well-directed fire upon us, which was promptly responded to by Clark's and Jenks' batteries. By this time I had placed Captain Robinson's Ohio battery in a position about 500 yards to the right of Captain Jenks, to cover our right wing from any charge which might be made upon it from the opposite woods, 1,500 yards distant, which was occupied by the enemy. I placed one section of Battery B, First Virginia Artillery, upon our left wing to support Colonel Sullivan. This section did good service. Toward evening, when our forces charged upon the left wing of the enemy, I placed Captain Robinson's battery in such a position as to support the brigade which was to make the charge or cover its retreat if necessary. Our forces having engaged the enemy upon their left wing, I ordered the batteries of Captains Clark, Jenks, and Robinson to cease firing.

The enemy's battery having been taken, I placed Captain Robinson's battery in the position which the enemy had occupied. The batteries commanded by Captains Jenks and Clark having Parrott guns, and being placed in a very commanding position, did excellent execution. The Ohio batteries, commanded by Major Israel, on account of the inferiority of their guns, could not be used to good advantage. Captain Huntington's battery was kept in the rear as a reserve.

The loss sustained by the different batteries is as follows: Captain Clark's battery, E, Fourth Regiment, U. S. Army, Private Bartley Kelley killed and 3 horses disabled; Captain Jenks' battery, A, First Virginia Artillery, Private Charles Schneider killed and 10 horses disabled; Captain Robinson's battery, L, First Ohio Volunteer Artillery, Private Brown killed, Private ——— wounded and missing; on the 22d, Captain Huntington's battery, H, First Ohio Volunteer Artillery, Private Jacob Yeager killed and 2 horses disabled.

Very respectfully, your obedient servant,

P. DAUM,
*Lieutenant-Colonel, Chief of Artillery, Shields' Division.*

Col. NATHAN KIMBALL, *Acting Brigadier-General.*

## No. 12.

*Reports of Col. Nathan Kimball, Fourteenth Indiana Infantry, commanding First Brigade.**

HEADQUARTERS FIRST BRIGADE, SHIELDS' DIVISION,
*Camp near Strasburg, Va., March* 26, 1862

SIR: I have the honor to submit the following report of the battle which was fought near Winchester, Va., on Sunday, the 23d instant, between the forces composing the division which I had the honor to command and the rebel forces under General Jackson:

Early in the morning of the 23d the enemy commenced the attack, advancing from Kernstown and occupying a position with their batteries on the heights to the right of the road and the woods in the plain to the left of the road with cavalry and infantry and one battery. I at once advanced the Eighth Ohio, Colonel Carroll with four companies taking the left and Lieutenant-Colonel Sawyer with three companies the right of the turnpike road. Colonel Carroll advanced steadily, coming up with two companies of the Sixty-seventh Ohio, who had been out as pickets. Uniting them with his command, he drove one of the enemy's batteries which had opened a heavy fire upon him, and after a sharp skirmish routing five companies of the enemy, which were posted behind a stone wall and supported by cavalry, holding his position during the whole day, thus frustrating the attempts of the enemy to turn our left.

The right of the Eighth Ohio remained in front until about 4 o'clock p. m., when they were recalled to support one of our batteries on the heights. The Sixty-seventh Ohio were thrown on a hill to our right to support Jenks' battery, which had been advanced to a position commanding the village of Kernstown and the wood on the right. The Fourteenth Indiana was sent forward to support Clark's battery, which advanced along the road. The Eighty-fourth Pennsylvania was thrown over the hills to the right to prevent a flank movement of the enemy.

The Second Brigade, commanded by Colonel Sullivan, Thirteenth Indiana, composed of the Thirteenth Indiana, Fifth Ohio, Sixty-second Ohio, and Thirty-ninth Illinois, was sent to the left, supporting Carroll's skirmishers, a section of Daum's battery, and Robinson's First Ohio Battery, [L], and to prevent an attempt which was made to turn that flank. We had succeeded in driving the enemy from both flanks and the front until about 4 o'clock p. m., when Jackson, with the whole of his infantry, supported by artillery and cavalry, took possession of the hill on the right, and planted his batteries in commanding position, and opened a heavy and well directed fire upon our batteries and their supports, attracting our attention whilst he attempted to gain our right flank with his infantry.

At this juncture I ordered the Third Brigade, Col. E. B. Tyler, Seventh Ohio, commanding, composed of the Seventh and Twenty-ninth Ohio, First Virginia, Seventh Indiana, and One hundred and tenth Pennsylvania, to move to the right to gain the flank of the enemy, and charge them through the wood to their batteries posted on the hill. They moved forward steadily and gallantly, opening a galling fire on the enemy's infantry. The right wing of the Eighth Ohio, the Fourteenth and Thirteenth Indiana Regiments, Sixty-seventh Ohio, Eighty-fourth Pennsylvania, and Fifth Ohio, were sent forward to support Tyler's brigade,

*See note, p. 334.

each one in its turn moving gallantly forward, sustaining a heavy fire from both the enemy's batteries and musketry. Soon all of the regiments above named were pouring forth a well-directed fire, which was promptly answered by the enemy, and after a hotly contested action of two hours, just as night closed in, the enemy gave way and were soon completely routed, leaving their dead and wounded on the field, together with two pieces of artillery and four caissons. Our forces retained possession of the field and bivouacked for the night.

The batteries, under their chief, Lieutenant-Colonel Daum, were well posted and ably served during the day and the whole action. I respectfully refer you to the several accompanying reports for the details of the engagement.

I regret to report the loss of the gallant Colonel Murray, Eighty-fourth Pennsylvania, who fell while bravely leading forward his gallant men, amidst a perfect storm of shot and shell.

Where all have done so well, both officers and men, and achieved so much, it would be seemingly invidious to particularize any individual officer; yet I can say, without doing injustice to others, that Colonel Tyler deserves the highest commendation for the gallant manner in which he led his brigade during the conflict, and he, with the gallant Carroll, Harrow, Foster, Voris, Patrick, Thoburn, Sawyer, Buckley, Cheek, and Creighton, deserve well of their country. Colonel Sullivan, commanding the Second Brigade, and on the left, though not attacked in force, his batteries and skirmishers engaged the enemy and prevented the turning of that flank. He too merits the highest commendation. I am under many obligations to Colonel Clark, Majors Copeland and Perkins, and Captains Shriber and Scheffler, of Major-General Banks' staff, for valuable assistance rendered, and it is with pleasure I mention their gallantry on the field. To Col. John S. Mason, of the Fourth Ohio, and his adjutant, Lieutenant Green, I am deeply indebted for valuable assistance rendered. To my own staff officers, Actg. Asst. Adjt. Gen. John J. P. Blinn and Aide-de-Camp Lieut. Charles T. Boudinot, I am under many obligations for the gallant and efficient manner in which they discharged their duties on the field.

I herewith submit a plan of the battle, prepared by Captain Mason, of the Sixty-seventh Ohio, to whom I am much indebted for this valuable assistance.

A recapitulation of the killed, wounded, and missing is also appended.*

All of which is respectfully submitted.

NATHAN KIMBALL,
*Colonel Fourteenth Indiana Volunteer Infantry, Commanding.*

Maj. H. G. ARMSTRONG,
*Acting Assistant Adjutant-General.*

---

* Embodied in revised statement, p. 346.

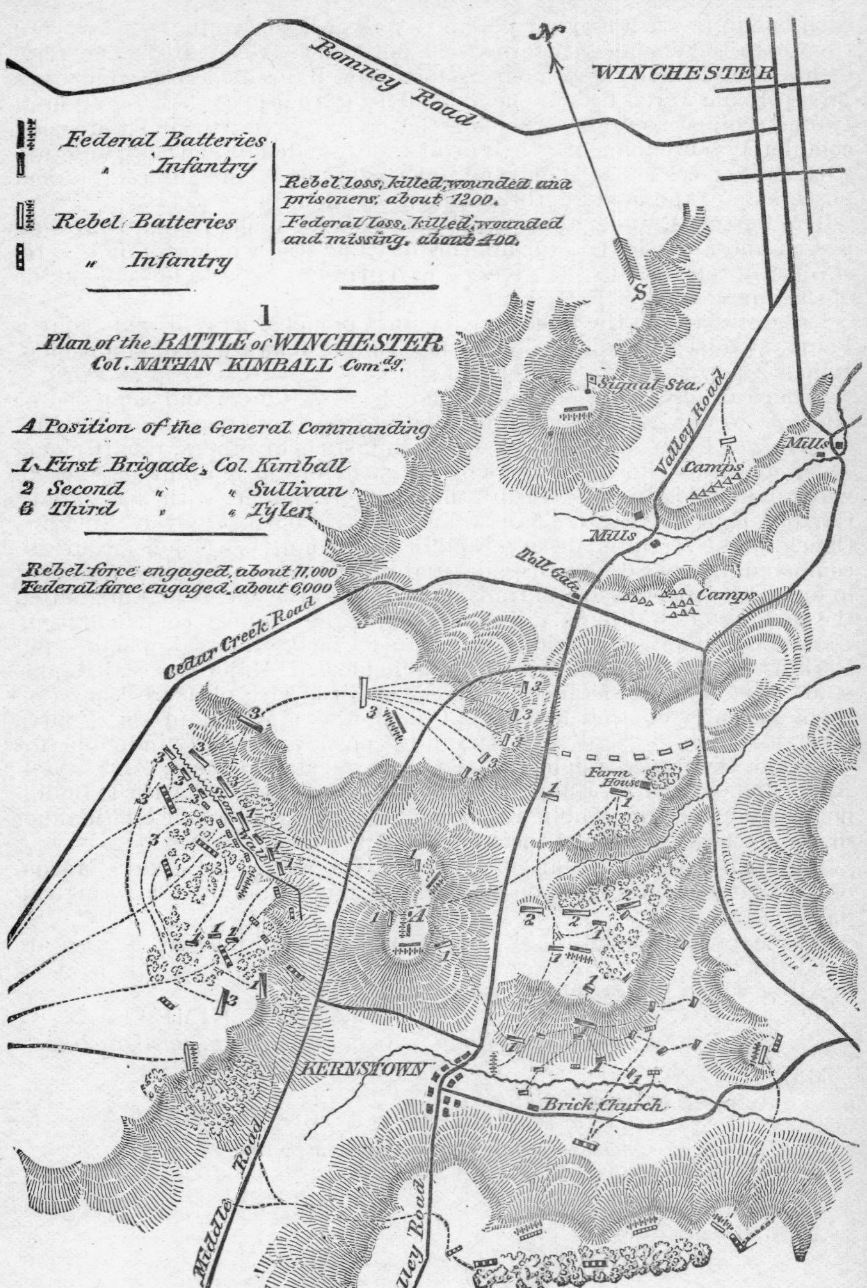
Romney Road
WINCHESTER
N
S
Federal Batteries
" Infantry
Rebel Batteries
" Infantry
Rebel loss, killed, wounded and prisoners, about 1200.
Federal loss, killed, wounded and missing, about 400.
1
Plan of the BATTLE of WINCHESTER
Col. NATHAN KIMBALL Comdg.
A Position of the General Commanding
1 First Brigade, Col. Kimball
2 Second " " Sullivan
3 Third " " Tyler
Rebel force engaged, about 11,000
Federal force engaged, about 6,000
Signal Sta.
Valley Road
Mills
Camps
Mills
Toll Gate
Camps
Cedar Creek Road
Farm House
KERNSTOWN
Brick Church
Middle Road
Valley Road

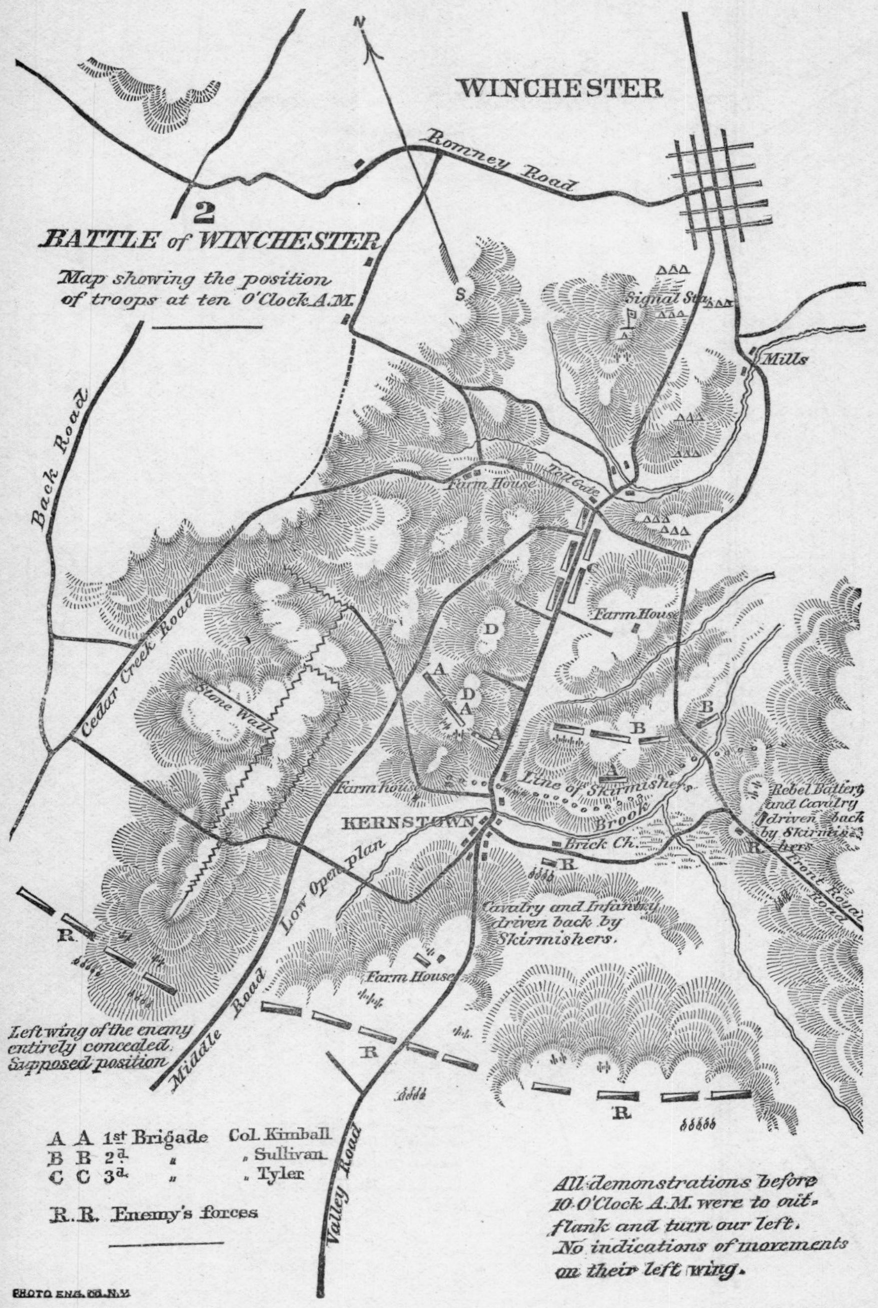
WINCHESTER
Romney Road
2
BATTLE of WINCHESTER
Map showing the position of troops at ten O'Clock A.M.
Back Road
Signal Sta.
Mills
Toll Gate
Farm House
Farm House
Cedar Creek Road
Stone Wall
Farm house
KERNSTOWN
Line of Skirmishers
Brook
Brick Ch.
Rebel Battery and Cavalry driven back by Skirmishers
Front Royal Road
Low Open plan
Cavalry and Infantry driven back by Skirmishers.
Farm House
Left wing of the enemy entirely concealed. Supposed position
Middle Road
Valley Road
A A 1st Brigade Col. Kimball
B B 2d. " " Sullivan
C C 3d. " " Tyler
R.R. Enemy's forces
All demonstrations before 10 O'Clock A.M. were to out-flank and turn our left. No indications of movements on their left wing.

PHOTO ENG. CO. N.Y.

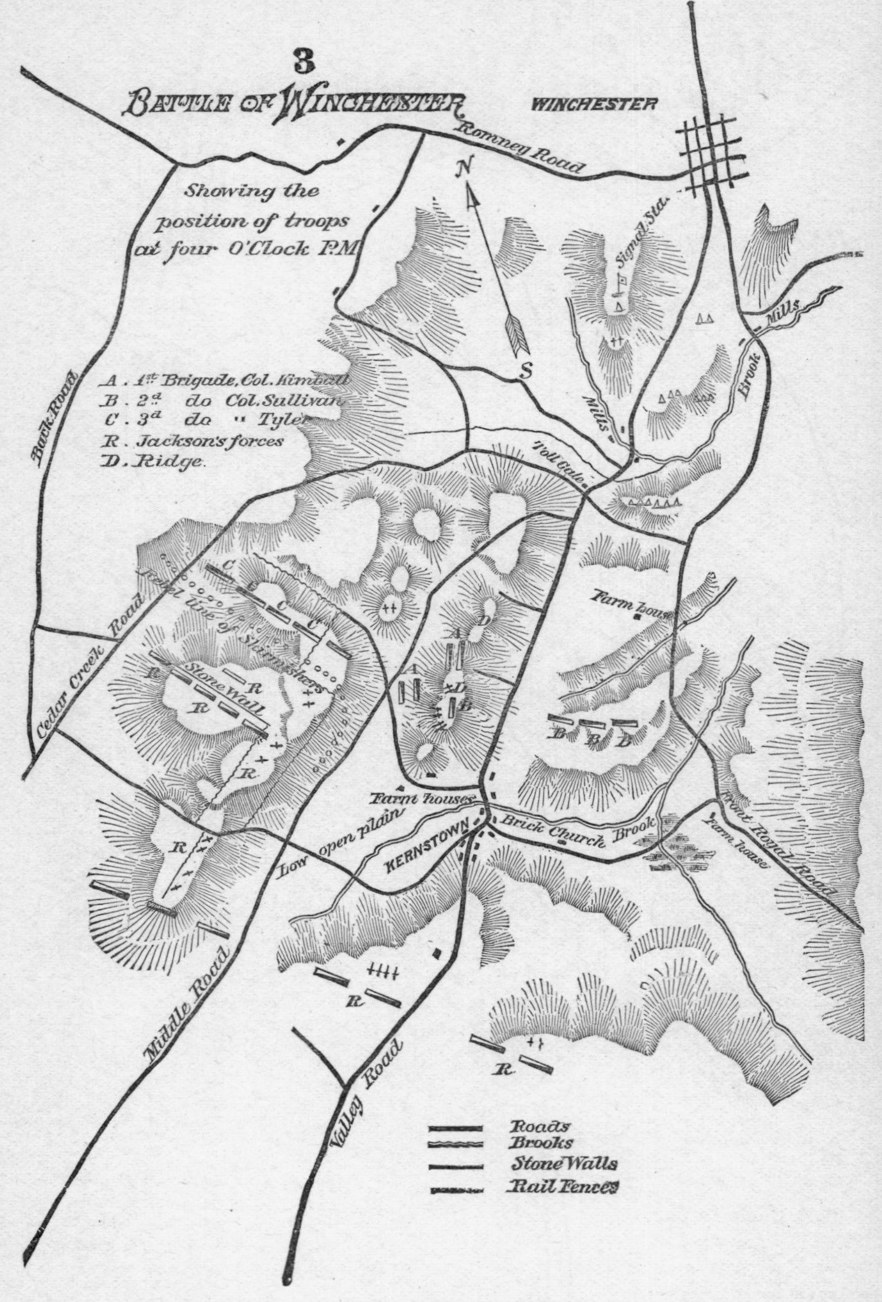
3
BATTLE OF WINCHESTER
WINCHESTER
Showing the position of troops at four O'Clock P.M.
Romney Road
Signal Sta.
Mills
Brook
Mills
Toll Gate
A. 1st Brigade, Col. Kimball
B. 2d do Col. Sullivan
C. 3d do " Tyler
R. Jackson's forces
D. Ridge.
Back Road
Cedar Creek Road
Rebel line of Skirmishers
Stone Wall
Farm house
Farm houses
Low open plain
KERNSTOWN
Brick Church Brook
Farm house
Front Royal Road
Middle Road
Valley Road
Roads
Brooks
Stone Walls
Rail Fences

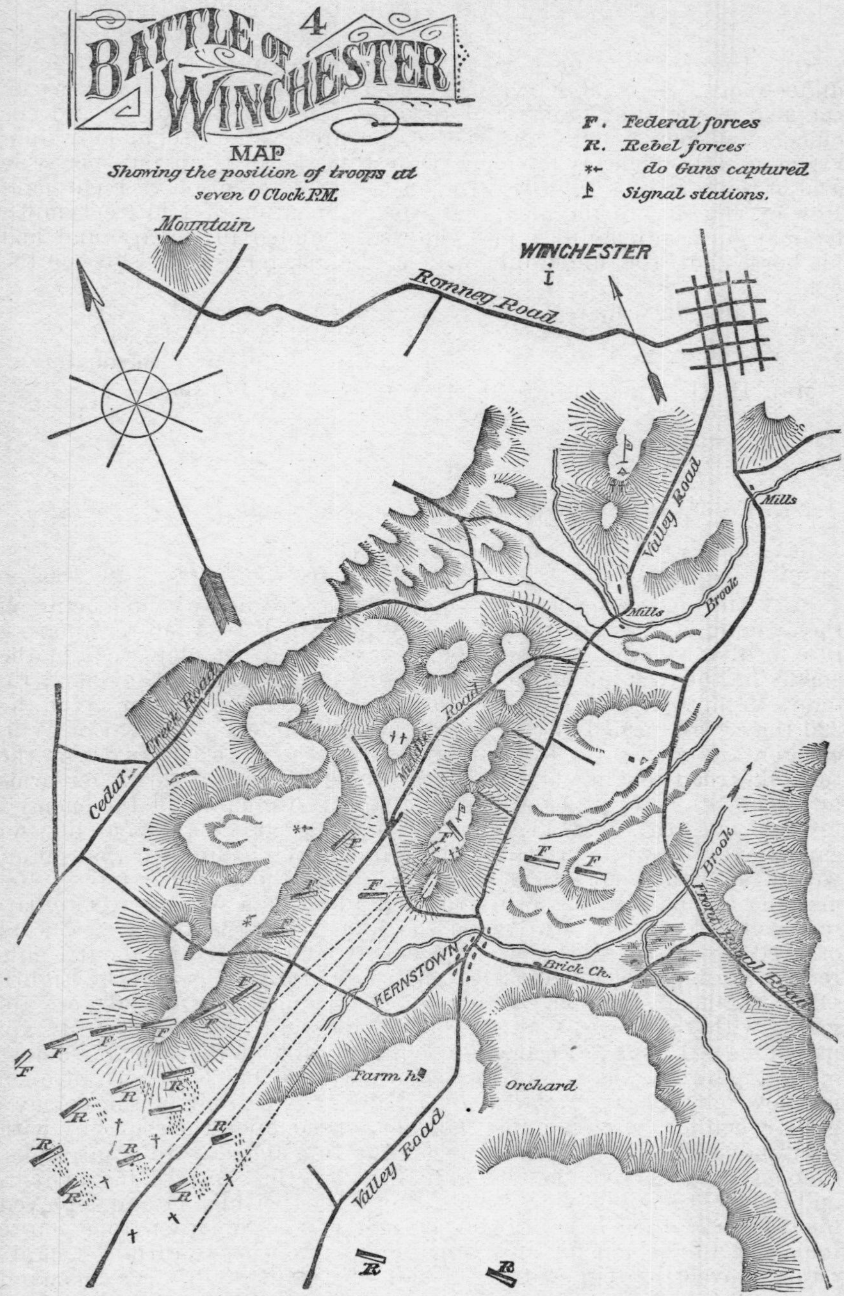

MAP
*Showing the position of troops at seven O Clock P.M.*

F. Federal forces
R. Rebel forces
*← do Guns captured
Signal stations.

Mountain
WINCHESTER
Romney Road
Valley Road
Mills
Mills
Brook
Cedar Creek Road
Middle Road
Brook
Front Royal Road
KERNSTOWN
Brick Ch.
Farm h.
Orchard
Valley Road

HEADQUARTERS FIRST BRIGADE, SHIELDS' DIVISION,
*Strasburg, Va., March* 27, 1862.

SIR: I regret very much that I made no mention of the Signal Corps, under Lieut. W. W. Rowley, who rendered such valuable assistance on the field in signaling orders and reports. Lieutenant Rowley and the officers and men under him deserve the greatest praise, and by their vigilance and efficiency have made the Signal Corps an indispensable arm of the service. I desire to make favorable mention of Lieutenant Rowley, his officers and men, and especial mention of Private Temple, flagman for Lieutenant Taylor, who was wounded in the arm and had his horse shot from under him while in the discharge of his duty on the field.

I am, sir, very respectfully, your obedient servant,

NATHAN KIMBALL,
*Colonel, Commanding.*

Maj. H. G. ARMSTRONG, *A. A. A. G., Shields' Division.*

---

## No. 13.

*Report of Lieut. Col. William Harrow, Fourteenth Indiana Infantry.*

CAMP FOURTEENTH REGIMENT INDIANA FOOT VOLS.,
*Near Winchester, Va., March* 26, 1862.

SIR: During the severe engagement with the enemy commencing on the evening of the 22d instant near Winchester, Va., and terminating in a brilliant victory to the Federal forces and complete rout of the enemy on the evening of the 23d instant, the Fourteenth Regiment Indiana Volunteers bore a conspicuous part. At 5.30 o'clock p. m. on the 22d they were formed at their camp, nearly 2 miles in the rear of Winchester, and moved rapidly forward beyond the town 2 miles out on the turnpike road leading to Strasburg, and there remained under arms upon the left of our batteries during the continuance of the enemy's fire that evening. This regiment lay upon their arms that night, and early next day, while preparing to establish their camp near that point, were again called out by the enemy renewing the attack in force. Remaining at this point near an hour and a half as a support to two batteries of artillery in position on the left of the road, they now were ordered rapidly forward toward the enemy, and proceeding about 1 mile received orders to hasten to position to support, if necessary, the Eighth Ohio Regiment, Colonel Carroll, who had gone forward and were engaged with the enemy's skirmishers, who were reported steadily approaching. Having proceeded to a point favorable for the accomplishment of that purpose, they were formed in line of battle across an open meadow on the left of the road and directly in front of the enemy's guns, when for thirty minutes the enemy fired upon them rapidly with shot and shell, many of their missiles bursting almost within our ranks. Colonel Sullivan's command having by this time formed in our rear, and Colonel Carroll having withdrawn for the time his line and deployed his command upon our extreme left, I received an order from you to look well to the left for any attempt of the enemy to turn that flank. I then moved the regiment to the left of Colonel Sullivan's command and occupied a space between his line and Colonel Carroll. We there remained in position, the enemy continuing to fire shell at our lines until by your order the regiment was moved across the road and was halted near the battery on the hill in your immediate presence.

Remaining in this position one and a half hours, the enemy were discovered moving in force to our right flank. Almost immediately thereafter the collision occurred between the enemy's infantry forces and that portion of our own troops occupying the extreme right. The fire becoming general along our whole right, the Fourteenth Regiment was ordered forward at a double-quick step. Having formed themselves, they eagerly pushed through a slight skirt of timber and crossed an elevation covering the enemy, during the execution of which movement a continuous fire was kept up upon our lines from one of the enemy's batteries. Having crossed a depression in the ground and coming up to the summit we immediately received a terrific fire from the enemy's infantry. At this point several of our men fell wounded and 1 killed.

On our right the Fifth Ohio and Eighty-fourth Pennsylvania Regiments were hotly engaged, when the Fourteenth Indiana rushed forward, cheering at the top of their voices, our right being extended so as to form a connection with the troops in that direction, the left moving directly forward toward a line of stone fencing connecting with a heavy line of timber in our front. At this point of time a portion of our right wing, under the immediate direction of Lieutenant Catterson, acting adjutant, attacked and silenced the enemy's gun, having first received a fire from grape or canister shot at a distance short of 100 yards. This gun the enemy hastily removed under cover, with a loss of 5 or 6 cannoneers killed. The enemy's infantry then rose from their ambush in front and commenced a rapid and murderous fire upon our entire line. This part of their forces, I have since been informed, was the rebel brigade known as General Loring's command. Their fire was promptly, rapidly, and gallantly returned, and for more than an hour the roar of musketry upon each side was terrific, almost beyond conception; during which time Captain Kelly and Second Lieutenant Slocum, of Company K; First Lieutenant Lindsay, of Company I; Captain Martin and First Lieutenant Beem, of Company H, and Sergt. Maj. Thomas C. Bailey fell wounded while bravely sustaining and urging forward their respective commands. During this period also our national and regimental color-bearers each fell wounded, when their places were promptly supplied. The bearer of the regimental colors, who had seized them when the first was wounded, being also wounded, both standards were seized and for a time held up by a private of Company E.

Lieutenant Catterson, being my only mounted officer, became a conspicuous mark by his presence and activity immediately before the enemy. He had his horse killed under him, the animal receiving six balls, two of which barely escaped killing that officer. This escape from instant death is truly wonderful. The smoke from the enemy's guns and our own, together with the lateness of the evening, prohibit any mention of officers or men, if indeed such discrimination was possible when every officer and man engaged performed his duty to himself, his regiment, and country so nobly. Night closing in, the rout of the enemy became general, and another brilliant victory has been chronicled and another hard blow to rebellion has been struck. The entire command lay upon their arms during the night, and for the two days next succeeding pursued the retreating enemy till a point 3 miles beyond this camp was reached, but was unable to overtake them.

All of which is respectfully submitted.

WM. HARROW,

*Lieut. Col. Fourteenth Regiment Indiana Vols., Commanding.*

Col. N. KIMBALL, *14th Ind. Vols., Comdg. 1st Brig., Shields' Div.*

## No. 14.

### *Report of Col. Samuel S. Carroll, Eighth Ohio Infantry.*

HEADQUARTERS EIGHTH OHIO INFANTRY,
*Camp at Strasburg, March* 26, 1862.

SIR: In accordance with instructions from your headquarters I have the honor to make the following report, viz:

On the 23d instant, about 10.30 a. m., I received orders from brigade headquarters to move my regiment forward from camp near Winchester, as skirmishers, on either side of the turnpike toward Newtown and feel the way. Immediately I marched the regiment out, and when about half a mile from camp detached Lieutenant-Colonel Sawyer, with Companies B, H, and E, on the right of the pike; I took Companies F, K, A, and G on the left. Both wings were deployed as skirmishers. Companies C and D were on picket duty on the right of the road, and joined Colonel Sawyer's command soon after it deployed. Company I was on picket near Winchester, and remained there. About the time we deployed, the rebels opened one battery on us. We kept advancing, and the battery fell back to the woods ahead of us and reopened their fire. When about 2 miles from our camp my wing came upon a body of the rebel infantry of five full companies, with a reserve of about 100 cavalry. They were masked behind a stone wall at the edge of a wood, and opened on us about 50 yards distant. My wing replied briskly, and, moving forward, routed them in fifteen or twenty minutes.

We kept on advancing and driving them before us for three-quarters of a mile, when, finding that we were entirely unsupported, I halted my wing. In the mean time Company B had joined us, and Colonel Sawyer's command gotten so far off to the right as to be out of sight.

So soon as I saw support coming I moved forward until the shells from our own batteries fell immediately in front of us, when I halted, not thinking it prudent to expose my men to the fire of our own as well as the rebel batteries. We remained nearly in that position during the remainder of that day and night. In the afternoon, about 3 o'clock, the enemy tried to move a battery on our extreme left flank. I detached one company to deter them, and they were charged upon by about 125 of the rebel cavalry, led by Colonel Ashby. I sent two more companies to their support, and they drove the enemy back and prevented their moving the battery on our flank.

On the morning of the 24th, before daylight, all my regiment joined me except Company I, and Colonel Sullivan ordered me to move forward and support a battery that he wished to get in an advanced position. We did so, and after moving forward three-quarters of a mile the battery finally halted, and I moved forward and continued in the advance until halted by your orders this side of Newtown.

Our loss in the engagement of the morning of the 23d was 2 killed and 9 wounded. The loss of the enemy, killed and wounded, could not have been less than 50, mostly infantry. We had 1 wounded and 2 taken prisoners in the engagement in the afternoon. The enemy left 7 killed and wounded on the field and 5 dead horses, and took away several wounded with them.

Inclosed is Colonel Sawyer's report of the loss in his command.

I would state that my officers and men behaved with great coolness and bravery.

Sir, I have the honor to be, very respectfully, your obedient servant,

S. S. CARROLL, U. S. A.,
*Colonel Eighth Ohio Volunteer Infantry.*

Col. NATHAN KIMBALL,
*Fourteenth Indiana Vols., Comdg. First Brig., Shields' Div.*

---

## No. 15.

*Report of Lieut. Col. Franklin Sawyer, Eighth Ohio Infantry.*

CAMP NEAR STRASBURG, VA.,
*March* 26, 1862.

SIR: In accordance with instructions I have the honor to make the following report:

On Sunday morning, 23d instant, I was detached with three companies to deploy forward as skirmishers on the right of the Strasburg pike, which I at once proceeded to do. We deployed forward about three-fourths of a mile, when I received an order from you, through Surgeon Tappan, to make a careful reconnaissance of the hills to the right, and to recall from picket duty Companies C and D of our regiment and cause them to join my command. This I did. Finding no enemy to the right or immediately in front, we proceeded as far as the village of Kernstown, when I received an order from you, through a mounted orderly, to send you one of my companies, and accordingly sent you Captain Kenny's company. We then deployed forward some distance, resting the center in an open wood near a stone church. At this time a battery came up the road and took position on the left of the road, in advance of our position, and I again moved forward about 40 rods to the front of the battery, halted my men, and rode forward myself to the front of the wood, and came very near a force of the enemy concealed behind a ridge of ground. The battery soon fell back beyond the village, and I ordered the skirmishers back about 60 rods, which position we held until the explosion of our own shells near us admonished me to fall back nearer the battery in our rear.

At this point I received an order from Colonel Kimball through a mounted orderly to call in my skirmishers, fall back to the height where the main batteries were, and support them, which I did. We remained here for some time, when I was ordered to support a battery to our right on a "dirt road" in front of the line of march of Colonel Tyler's brigade, which was then passing in our rear to attack the enemy, who had taken position on the heights on our right and were then shelling us. This position we maintained for a few minutes, when we were ordered to load and fix bayonets for a charge. In a few moments Colonel Daum came with the order to charge, which we obeyed at double-quick, the interval between us and the enemy being about three-fourths of a mile. We charged directly up to a rail fence, from the opposite side of which the enemy in strong force were firing upon us. Our position was at almost a right angle with the position of Colonel Tyler's force. This position we held until the enemy was entirely routed from our front, which was about dusk. We pressed on until the enemy's battery was carried, when I drew off what few of my men were still unhurt, picked up our dead and wounded, and procured ambulances or temporary litters, and bore them from the field.

My whole command consisted of Company C, Captain Butterfield, with Lieutenants Lewis and Hysung and 41 non-commissioned officers and privates; Company D, commanded by Lieutenant Reid, with 45 non-commissioned officers and privates; Company E, commanded by Lieutenant Craig, with 49 non-commissioned officers and privates; Company H, commanded by Lieutenant Wright, with 53 non-commissioned officers and privates.

My officers and men behaved with the greatest coolness and bravery, and I cannot forbear mentioning Captain Butterfield, who was constantly at his post encouraging the men and rendering me every assistance in his power. I might also mention with equal propriety Lieutenants Reid and Craig (who was wounded), Lewis and Wright. They all behaved gallantly, and stood the enemy's fire until he was driven from before us. I joined you the next morning soon after daylight, in pursuance of an order received during the night.

All of which I have the honor to submit.

FRANKLIN SAWYER,
*Lieutenant-Colonel Eighth Ohio Volunteers.*

Col. S. S. CARROLL, U. S. A.,
*Colonel Eighth Ohio Volunteer Infantry.*

---

## No. 16.

*Report of Lieut. Col. Alvin C. Voris, Sixty-seventh Ohio Infantry.*

HDQRS. SIXTY-SEVENTH REGIMENT OHIO VOLUNTEERS,
*March* 26, 1862.

I have the honor to report to you that the Sixty-seventh Ohio Volunteers, on the evening of the 22d, was ordered to report to General Banks for picket duty. In the earliest practicable time the regiment reported to his headquarters and was ordered to report to General Shields on the field, which was done on the Strasburg pike beyond Winchester. We were deployed as skirmishers under the enemy's fire on the left flank, being the first regiment of infantry on the field. We advanced as skirmishers some 2 miles and till after dark. About 10 o'clock were ordered by you to go into camp. Companies A, F, and I were detailed for picket duty, 8 o'clock a. m. of the 23d instant, to the left and front. Companies F and I did not join the regiment till Monday morning. These three companies engaged the enemy as skirmishers on the left early in the day, and gallantly drove the rebel skirmishers under the cover of their artillery. Company A joined my command early in the afternoon. The remaining six companies early in the day were ordered to deploy as skirmishers to the extreme right, which was partially done, when we were ordered to support the battery (Daum's) on the right. Afterward we were relieved by the Fifth Ohio Volunteers, and ordered to hold ourselves as reserve in a wood to the right of the batteries on the right of the pike.

Later in the day we were ordered to support the battery directly in front of the position occupied by the commanding general. After the infantry fight was opened we were ordered to re-enforce our troops. We passed over the open field intervening under a raking fire from the enemy's artillery, and formed line of battle on the right of the first brigade and commenced firing on the enemy's extreme left, and held our first position until the enemy were driven from their position. The Sixty-seventh turned their left flank and terribly punished them from first to last.

I cannot speak in too high praise of my officers (with one or two exceptions) and men. Few of them had ever been under fire before, but they fought with a persistency that never meant to yield. I am proud of my men. Company G was not in the action, having been detailed for guard duty at Winchester on the 18th instant and not yet relieved.

A. C. VORIS,
*Lieut. Col., Comdg. Sixty-seventh Regiment Ohio Vols.*

General KIMBALL,
*Commanding General Shields' Division.*

---

## No. 17.

*Report of Col. Jeremiah C. Sullivan, Thirteenth Indiana Infantry, commanding Second Brigade.*

HEADQUARTERS SECOND BRIGADE, SHIELDS' DIVISION,
*Near Tom's Brook, March* 26, 1862.

I have the honor to make the following report of the part my brigade took in the battle of the 23d, near Winchester:

The Second Brigade, which I commanded, consisted of the Thirteenth Indiana, Fifth Ohio, Thirty-ninth Illinois, and Sixty-second Ohio. My position was on the left wing in a large open field, facing the woods, which were occupied by the rebels. I had no sooner formed my line of battle than the enemy opened on me a heavy and well-directed fire from his artillery, which was sustained for over five hours. The right wing being hard pressed, General Kimball sent to me for re-enforcements. I sent to him one regiment. Again and again were re-enforcements asked for until I was left on the left wing with but one regiment—the Thirty-ninth Illinois—and two pieces of artillery. I, however, advanced and opened fire on the enemy concealed in the woods, and drove back the artillery that was playing on me. The firing on my right had now nearly ceased, but no evidence could be obtained to warrant a belief that the enemy had retired. We rested that night on our arms, expecting every moment an attack. The next morning at daylight I started to attack them, but found that all had retired save a rear guard, which I drove some 3 miles before any re-enforcements reached me.

The loss of the regiments in my brigade is heavy, but owing to our being in advance and yet pursuing the enemy I have no means of ascertaining correctly. Officers and men behaved nobly, and once even gave evidence that their hearts were in this cause. With such soldiers our flag will soon be carried in triumph over the rebellious States.

Inclosed I send copies of the reports of the different commanders on the field. Being in advance and in bivouac, my facilities for obtaining correct information of our loss are small. I am now 25 miles from the field of battle, and surgeons have made no reports.

I remain, respectfully,

JER. C. SULLIVAN,
*Colonel, Commanding Second Brigade.*

H. G. ARMSTRONG,
*Major and Acting Assistant Adjutant-General.*

## No. 18.

### *Report of Lieut. Col. Robert S. Foster, Thirteenth Indiana Infantry.*

HDQRS. THIRTEENTH INDIANA REGIMENT, U. S. ARMY,
*Camp Shields, four miles south of Strasburg, Va.*

SIR: In obedience to your order I herewith submit the following report of the part taken by the Thirteenth Indiana Regiment in the action of the 22d and 23d of March, near Winchester, Va.:

I was ordered by you to withdraw my command (which had been stationed on picket the night of the 21st on the Front Royal and Cedar Creek roads) and to report to you at the toll-gate on the Strasburg pike. Collecting my command I proceeded immediately to join you, and reached the toll-gate at 10 a. m., and moved forward on the right of your brigade and took position in front of and on the enemy's right, which position we held until 5 p. m. under a heavy fire of shell and round shot from his batteries, which were stationed in the edge of a woods. At 5 p. m. you ordered me to move to the enemy's left, to support a part of the First and Third Brigades. We marched over the hills on our right after being exposed to a heavy fire of grape and shell. We took position on the left of the Fourteenth Indiana, whose left had been pressed back by the overwhelming number that had been brought into action by the enemy immediately in front and on the left of the Fourteenth Indiana. Here it was that the Thirteenth Indiana suffered most, being exposed to the galling fire of a whole brigade posted behind a stone fence and in the open woods. Inch by inch the brave and gallant men of my command (Thirteenth Indiana) pressed them back. The Fourteenth Indiana's left rallied to our support, and I gave the command to "Forward! Charge bayonets!" Here it was that the two remnants of the Thirteenth and Fourteenth Indiana went in with a yell and drove from the field a whole brigade, which proved to be Loring's celebrated Irish brigade, of the Provisional Army, and completely routed them, and would have captured their colors had it not been for night coming on, and for fear of firing into our own men I ordered a halt. It was so dark as to prevent us from pursuing the retreating enemy until morning. After gathering up the wounded of our own and the enemy's we slept on our arms until daylight, when I proceeded to join you in the advance toward Strasburg in pursuit of the flying enemy, and have arrived at this camp, after sharing the honors of being in the advance with your brigade and driving the enemy beyond this place.

Before closing this report I must refer to the officers and men of the Thirteenth Indiana. All alike acted nobly and fought bravely, adding new laurels to those already won in Western Virginia. Lest I should be thought preferring one above another I forbear making any personal mention, as they all, both officers and men, fought with a coolness and desperation that proved them not inferior to the brave sons of Indiana who are battling in other localities for our holy cause. Of the medical profession, and more particularly of our own assistant surgeon, requires of me a special mention. Dr. Gall, our principal surgeon, having been detailed during the early part of the engagement to take charge of the wounded who were being sent to Winchester, left Dr. William C. Foster alone on the field, who was in the thickest and hottest of the fight with the band carrying off the killed and wounded as they fell, and but for him our list of dead would be greater than it is.

We captured a number of prisoners, part of them commissioned officers, some of whom are wounded. Among them are a major and an aide to the rebel General Jackson, a number of lieutenants, and some arms, all of which I will report as soon as I can ascertain the exact number of each. Our loss is about 40 killed and wounded, among them Major Dobbs and Captain Sayles, of Company G. It is impossible for me at this time to give you the exact casualties in the Thirteenth, but inclosed you will find a list as correct as it is possible for me to render at this time.*

I am, respectfully,

ROBT. S. FOSTER,
*Lieutenant-Colonel, Comdg. Thirteenth Indiana Volunteers.*

Col. J. C. SULLIVAN,
*Acting Brigadier-General, Commanding Second Brigade.*

---

## No. 19.

*Report of Lieut. George H. Whitcamp, Acting Adjutant Fifth Ohio Infantry.*

MARCH 26, 1862.

The Fifth Ohio was ordered by Acting Brigadier-General Sullivan to turn out under arms on Saturday evening, March 22, at 5 o'clock. There had been some cannonading within hearing of our camp during the day. We marched out the Strasburg road about 3 miles, there halted, and were ordered back to picket the Romney and Cedar Creek roads. On the following morning we had orders to proceed to camp, but were halted on the road to wait for instructions, which we received in about one-half hour, and marched to the right of Kernstown. About 9 o'clock a. m. we were ordered to support Daum's battery. The fire from the enemy was heavy and constant, principally shell and round shot, which continued for about one hour. There was none of our regiment hurt up to that time, although the firing was in line with our battery, but most of the volleys went too far, which was very fortunate for our forces. The battery changed position and moved over to the left of Kernstown, on a level with woods to our left and front. As soon as the artillery was in position and our regiment at their support there came a perfect hurricane of shell from the woods. There must have been a masked battery there, for the fire was tremendous.

We remained under fire about three-quarters of an hour. The battery was forced to retire under a very heavy and destructive fire. We were not aware that the artillery had given way until the piece on the right had gone. They had 1 man killed and we had 2 wounded in our regiment. The lieutenant commanding the battery met our lieutenant-colonel commanding, and said that he could not hold his position any longer than he did; that his battery was not strong enough for theirs, and was forced to abandon his position. We then took up a position in support of the same pieces, with part of Clark's battery, to the right of Kernstown on a hill, where we remained about two hours. The firing continued with the same unabated fury, mostly shell and a few round shot. At this time the enemy marched on a fresh re-enforcement of infantry to flank us on the right.

Our regiment was then ordered by Acting Brigadier-General Kimball to leave the battery and proceed to the right flank. The battery

* See revised statement, p. 346.

by this time was almost if not entirely out of ammunition. After we had got half way to where the infantry were engaged an order came from Acting General Kimball to detach five companies to go back and guard the batteries, which weakened our regiment very materially, and Lieutenant-Colonel Patrick did not know until he was in front of the enemy that he had only a half regiment to fight with. As soon as we got through a little grove of brush and young trees we came in contact with the enemy's fire, which was very rapid and constant as we advanced. The Eighty-fourth Pennsylvania was on our left. We passed them and pressed forward. Lieutenant-Colonel Patrick cautioned our men to "keep cool," "hold their ground," "stand solid," and "every man to do his duty;" "to remember Cincinnati, their homes, and their country," "not to waste their powder." He was still in front of his men when Lieutenant Marshall called out to him to fall behind; that he was unnecessarily exposing himself. Our men advanced steadily, some of them to their last advance. When they reached the brow of the hill the enemy were below and in a front in the trees and small brush. At the first fire from the enemy our two color-bearers fell—B. Isdell, to rise no more, and E. Swaine, wounded in the cheek. He will recover. Five times were our colors shot down, and as quickly did they rise again. The national flag received forty-eight bullet-holes and the regimental flag ten; even the flagstaffs were broken in several places.

It was here that our gallant Captain Whitcom fell. He rushed to the colors after they were shot down for the second time, waved them and drew his pistol, when he received that fatal bullet in his cheek, passing through his head. He fell to the ground and never moved afterward. At that moment it was an almost hand-to-hand fight. The enemy was pressing forward and some of them were within 10 yards of our regiment. The fire was galling, and a perfect whirlwind of balls were flying, as if the air had been suddenly filled with hissing snakes. It appeared to rage with increasing fury. We had no support on our left for some time after we had commenced firing. At last the Eighty-fourth Pennsylvania advanced to support our left flank, but twice they fell back. The third time their brave colonel urged them to follow him and stand fast. It was under that advance that the gallant Colonel Murray lost his life. When the colonel fell his regiment retreated and could not be rallied again. Lieutenant-Colonel Patrick beseeched them not to leave the field, but they had taken the panic, and it became infectious. The regiment on our right flank gave way and fell back. It was a trying moment for the Fifth Ohio. They then received the enemy's whole fire. For a few minutes the tide of success was between the ebb and flow. They stood their ground nobly. Officers and men did their duty.

Our lieutenant-colonel (Patrick) at that moment encouraged the men, telling them not to give way, but stand fast, and there was not a man flinched. The regiment on our right, seeing us remain firm, rallied again. The Fourteenth Indiana, under the command of the adjutant, came on our left and commenced firing behind us, and the first volley they fired Colonel Patrick ran forward to them and ordered them to cease firing; that they were firing on our men. The officer then asked him where the secesh or rebel lines were. He told him that there were no lines here, but to turn his men more to the left and advance and he would see the rebels. The enemy by this time were giving way, and after a few minutes we turned their flank, and they ran and our forces after them, and killing them as they ran.

It was then getting dark and our men were very much fatigued, yet the excitement kept them on their feet. There were a few of them remained behind to take care of the wounded and dying. We kept advancing until we reached their battery and took one piece. In the mean time there was a heavy re-enforcement coming across from the woods to assist the rebels. The Thirteenth Indiana had joined us, and the other five companies of the Fifth, in command of Acting Major Hays, were advancing to our aid. The rebel re-enforcements were seized with the same panic the others had, and they made a very short stand. We kept advancing on them until darkness closed upon us all Had it continued light for one hour longer the whole rebel force would have been captured.

We had hardly completed the task of gathering up our dead and wounded when an order came for our regiment to go out on picket duty. I told Colonel Patrick of the order. He went to see the general about it, and informed him that our regiment had been up two nights and had had very little to eat; that there were other regiments that had not endured so much fatigue. He wanted to know them. The lieutenant-colonel mentioned one. The acting brigadier-general said he did not know where to find it, and we would have to serve, and so we did. The next day we followed the enemy beyond Strasburg.

All of which is respectfully submitted.

GEO. H. WHITCAMP,
*Lieutenant, Acting Adjutant.*

---

## No. 20.

*Reports of Col. Erastus B. Tyler, Seventh Ohio Infantry, commanding Third Brigade.*

HEADQUARTERS THIRD BRIGADE, SHIELDS' DIVISION,
*Camp Kimball, March* 26, 1862.

SIR: I have the honor to submit to you the following report of the action of my command in the battle of Winchester, Sunday, March 23, 1862, together with a report of the killed, wounded, and missing:

On my arrival to the support of General Kimball about 2 p. m. two regiments of my command were brought to the front to support Colonel Daum's artillery—the Seventh Ohio and Seventh Indiana—the other three remaining in the rear. At about 4 o'clock General Kimball ordered me to proceed with my command down a ravine to the rear of a piece of woods on our right, and thence along the woods to the rear of a point on the enemy's left flank, where he had a battery of two pieces planted. Lieutenant-Colonel Daum continued to amuse them in the front while I proceeded to execute the order, and Captain Robinson's battery was sent in the same direction that I moved to a commanding point between the woods and our main point of defense. I succeeded in reaching the enemy's rear unperceived by him, but found him in large force, as I afterward learned from his wounded, consisting of nine infantry regiments, and on the eve of attempting a flank movement similar to ours to capture Robinson's battery. Our front was within musket-range of him when he opened on us, and with such force that I immediately ordered up my reserve. His position was a strong one, and stubbornly maintained for a time, but he was at length forced to fall back before the incessant and well-directed fire of our men. He was protected in front by a stone fence, while our only breastworks were the scattered trees of the woods and a small natural embankment, say, five rods long, and the fact that all his killed and wounded in that locality were struck in the head speaks in stronger terms than I can use of the skill of our men as marksmen.

After my brigade had thus bravely stood their ground for at least an hour, I think I may safely say, the Fourteenth Indiana arrived to my support, followed shortly after by the Eighty-fourth Pennsylvania, Thirteenth Indiana, Sixty-seventh Ohio, and Fifth Ohio, when the complete rout of the enemy was effected, he leaving for me two pieces of artillery—one iron 12-pounder and one brass 6-pounder—with caissons, and all his dead and wounded, amounting, the former to over 300, and the latter unknown, but very large. Considering the enemy's force and position, I consider my loss as noticed below very small. Both the men and officers of my command fought with the most commendable bravery and determination, and are entitled to special mention, but in this brief report I cannot particularize. The colors of the Seventh Ohio were struck by twenty-eight balls, one carrying away the crescent of the spear-head, another breaking the staff; those of the Seventh Indiana by three, and of the Twenty-ninth Ohio by three balls. The darkness of the evening prevented my following the enemy beyond the ground he had occupied, and early on the following morning the pursuit commenced, continuing until last evening. Thus you will perceive that under the present condition of affairs it is extremely difficult to give an accurate report of the loss in killed, wounded, and missing that my command have sustained. I must not neglect to say that to Actg. Asst. Adjt. Gen. E. S. Quay and Aide-de-Camp Henry Z. Eaton, of my staff, I am greatly indebted for the prompt performance of their respective duties. For more definite particulars of the fight I would refer you to my official report to General Kimball.

Respectfully submitted.

I am, sir, your obedient servant,

E. B. TYLER,
*Colonel, Commanding Third Brigade.*

Brigadier-General SHIELDS.

—

HEADQUARTERS THIRD BRIGADE, SHIELDS' DIVISION,
*Camp Kimball, Strasburg, March* 26, 1862.

SIR: I have the honor to submit to you the following report of the part taken by my command in the battle of Winchester, Sunday, March 23:

My command left Camp Shields at 11 o'clock a. m. 23d March, reaching the toll-gate south of Winchester just as our batteries were opened upon the enemy. Remaining in column a short time, I received your order to strike the enemy on his left flank with my brigade, composed of the Seventh Ohio, Lieutenant-Colonel Creighton; Twenty-ninth Ohio, Colonel Buckley; First Virginia, Colonel Thoburn; Seventh Indiana, Lieutenant-Colonel Cheek, and One hundred and tenth Pennsylvania Infantry, Colonel Lewis, jr. The order was executed with the Seventh Ohio on the right, the Twenty-ninth Ohio on the left, First Virginia in the center, Seventh Indiana in the right wing, and One hundred and tenth Pennsylvania in the left wing, advancing in column of divisions. When within easy musket-range the enemy opened fire upon us with their infantry force, consisting of nine regiments. The reception was a warm one, and so heavy was it that I ordered up the reserve at once, when the action became general. The fire of the enemy was poured in upon us from behind a stone wall with terrible effect, yet the column moved forward, driving them from their cover into an open wood, when our men gave them a shower of leaden hail. The timely arrival of the Fourteenth Indiana, Lieutenant-Colonel Harrow, in this unequal contest was of immense service, followed as they were soon after by the Eighty-fourth Pennsylvania, Colonel Murray; Thirteenth Indiana, Lieutenant-Colonel Foster, and still later by the Sixty-seventh, Lieutenant-Colonel Voris, and Fifth Ohio, Lieutenant-Colonel Patrick, routing the enemy just as twilight was fading into night, leaving his dead and wounded on the field. We took from him one 6 and one 12 pounder gun, with their caissons, and about 300 prisoners. The loss of the enemy in killed and wounded could not have been less than 500.

To speak of the heroic acts of those engaged in the battle would require too much space in this brief report. The officers and men behaved as gallantly as ever men did, and are entitled to great credit. The field officers of the different regiments exerted themselves manfully, many of them having their horses shot under them early in the engagement; others were seriously wounded, yet they pressed forward with their men, determined to conquer or die. Where all did so well, and showed so much daring bravery, it would be unjust to mention one without mentioning all. That officers and men discharged their duty the result plainly shows, and to them belongs the victory. To my acting assistant adjutant-general, E. S. Quay, and aide-de-camp, Henry Z. Eaton, of my staff, I am greatly indebted for the prompt performance of their respective duties. Herewith I hand you a report of the dead and wounded of my command.*

All of which is respectfully submitted.

I am, sir, very respectfully, your obedient servant,

E. B. TYLER,
*Colonel, Commanding Third Brigade.*

Acting Brigadier-General KIMBALL,
*Commanding Division.*

---

## No. 21.

*Report of Col. William D. Lewis, jr., One hundred and tenth Pennsylvania Infantry.*

HDQRS. 110TH REGT. PA. VOLS., SHIELDS' DIVISION,
*Winchester, Va., March 27, 1862.*

GENERAL: I have the honor to report that on the afternoon of Sunday, March 23, my command left camp, 3½ miles on the main road east of Winchester, by order of Colonel Tyler, Third Brigade, and proceeded with his command immediately to the scene of action that afternoon. The brigade was ordered to the rear and to the left flank of the enemy, and was marched close column by division into and under cover of a thick wood, when a deadly fire was immediately poured in upon them, which for the moment staggered our troops. They soon recovered, and my command, with the rest of the brigade, advanced to the outskirts of the woods and returned the fire with great spirit. Subsequently, finding that the enemy held a strong position behind a stone fence across a ravine directly opposite our center and were harassing

*Embodied in revised statement, p. 346.

us with their fire, I ordered a charge of my command at "double-quick" upon that point, which was quite successful. The enemy were completely routed on their flank and driven from their position behind the fence. In this charge the command suffered severely from the fire of the enemy. The regiment was rallied after the action in good order, and bivouacked for the night with the brigade on the field adjoining.

I have the honor to be, your obedient servant,

WM. D. LEWIS, JR.,
*Colonel One hundred and tenth Regiment Pennsylvania Vols.*

Brigadier-General SHIELDS.

---

## No. 22.

*Abstract from "Record of Events" in Williams' division, Fifth Army Corps.**

*March* 20.—Division ordered to march with all possible dispatch from Winchester to Centreville. Brigadier-General Williams assumed command.

The First Brigade marched from Winchester for Manassas on March 22. While at Castleman's Ferry, waiting for the Third Brigade to cross the Shenandoah, the brigade, in pursuance of a note from Major Copeland, assistant adjutant-general, counter-marched, and encamped at Berryville, Va. While encamped at Berryville, in pursuance of a note received from General Shields, commanding at Winchester, requesting brigade to support his command, then warmly engaged with the enemy at Kernstown, near Winchester, the brigade marched from Berryville to the field of battle, near Middletown, marching 36 miles in ten consecutive hours, and re-enforcing General Shields' command while engaged with the enemy. Brigade continued the pursuit of the enemy to Strasburg on March 24 and 25, and occupied Strasburg until the close of the month. During the forced march of the brigade from Berryville to Strasburg the shoes of one-half of the men in the brigade were worn-out and rendered worthless. New shoes are urgently needed, but, although repeated requisitions therefor have been made, they have not yet been supplied.

The Second Brigade marched March 21 to Berryville; March 22, to Snickersville; March 23, to Aldie, and thence to Manassas Junction, where it remained detached from the division at the close of the month.

The Third Brigade marched, March 22, from Winchester to Castleman's Ferry; March 23, to Snickersville; March 24, from Snickersville back to Winchester; March 25, from Winchester to Middletown; March 26, from Middletown to Strasburg, where it remained at the close of the month.

The First and Third Brigades picketed the advance of the Fifth Corps, opposite the enemy, in force, from March 25 to 31, being engaged during that time in daily skirmishes with the enemy.

---

* From division and brigade returns First Division for month of March, 1862.

## No. 23.

*Reports of Maj. Gen. Thomas J. Jackson, C. S. Army, commanding the Valley District, with resolution of the Confederate Congress.*

HDQRS. DEPARTMENT OF NORTHERN VIRGINIA,
*Rapidan, Va., March* 25, 1862.

His Excellency the PRESIDENT:

SIR: I have just received the inclosed letter from General Jackson. He evidently attacked the enemy under a misapprehension as to his force. He had previously reported it reduced from about 28,000 to 10,000 men. He now represents the Federal force in the valley as too strong to be driven back by a mere detachment of this army. In such an operation our communications would be completely exposed to McClellan.

It is reported that a bridge over the Shenandoah has been made on the Snickersville road.

Most respectfully, your obedient servant,

J. E. JOHNSTON.

[Inclosure.]

HEADQUARTERS VALLEY DISTRICT,
*Near Newtown, Va., March* 24, 1862.

GENERAL: As the enemy had been sending off troops from the district and from what I could learn were still doing so, and knowing your great desire to prevent it, and having a prospect of success, I engaged him yesterday about 3 p. m. near Winchester and fought until dusk, but his forces were so superior to mine that he repulsed me with the loss of valuable officers and men killed and wounded; but from the obstinacy with which our troops fought and from their advantageous position I am of the opinion that his loss was greater than mine in troops, but I lost one piece of artillery and three caissons.

On Saturday two brigades went down to Berryville with their baggage. The supposition is that they have crossed at Castleman's Ferry. From a prisoner whom we took I learn that more troops had marching orders at Winchester. This fight will probably delay, if not prevent, their leaving, and I hope will retain others. From what I hear there are 15,000 troops at Berryville, Charlestown, and Harper's Ferry. Shields yesterday appears to have had seventeen regiments of infantry. I heard he had much less when I made the attack. To drive him back if he advances I ought to have 5,000 infantry. I have enough artillery. The heavy guns were sent to Gordonsville. I will try and remain on this side of Strasburg. My wagons have gone to the rear and my forces are waiting to see whether the enemy will advance. Ashby is about 5 miles from Winchester.

Respectfully, your obedient servant,

T. J. JACKSON,
*Major-General.*

General JOSEPH E. JOHNSTON, *Comdg. Dist. of Northern Va.*

---

HEADQUARTERS VALLEY DISTRICT,
*Near Mount Jackson, March* 29, 1862.

MY DEAR GENERAL: My information, from a spy who left Winchester on day before yesterday, is that from 8,000 to 10,000 of the enemy came in pursuit of me on Monday, and that nearly the same number has come from Winchester in the direction of Strasburg since then; that they had been leaving in this direction every day since Sunday up to the time of his leaving town, and that there must be about Strasburg between 16,000 and 20,000. From the report of Captain Hess, who has charge of a party of observation, there were about 10,000 who came out on Monday. No passes, not even to negroes, are given to leave Winchester in the direction of Strasburg. On the roads leading northward persons leave town without passes. The enemy continued to return to Winchester from Castleman's from near 10 a.m. till near 4 p.m., and it is believed that all the force that had recently gone to Castleman's, with the exception of about three regiments, returned, and all the force at Winchester, with the exception of two or three regiments, has moved toward Strasburg.

There are no troops left at the encampment near Mrs. Carter's, beyond Winchester. The lowest estimate made in Winchester of the killed and wounded of the enemy is 1,000; the highest 1,500. Mr. Philip Williams, of Winchester, whom you probably know, says that he feels safe in putting the number at 1,200. My impression is that the estimate is too large, though I can only judge from the history of battles and what I saw. Three hundred and forty-one of my command fell into the hands of the enemy, so far as could be ascertained in Winchester; of this number, 81 killed and about 40 so badly wounded that they could not be sent off to the east. A committee of the citizens buried our dead, and the wounded have received that attention which only women can give.

Philip Williams has been told by a gentleman from Baltimore that there is an expedition fitting out against Magruder, and he attaches importance to the statement. It is well to remark that Mr. Williams is a warm friend to our cause, but sustains no other relation to the Army. I make this statement lest this letter might fall into the hands of the enemy.

The Federal troops at Moorefield have taken possession of the keys of the court-house and jail. It appears that one object of their incursion is to unite that section of the State to the Peirpoint government.

Very truly, yours,

T. J. JACKSON.

General JOSEPH E. JOHNSTON.

---

HEADQUARTERS VALLEY DISTRICT,
*Near Mount Jackson, Va., April* 9, 1862.

MAJOR: I have the honor to submit the following report of the battle near Kernstown, Va., on Sunday, March 23:

On the preceding Friday evening a dispatch was received from Col. Turner Ashby, commanding the cavalry, stating that the enemy had evacuated Strasburg. Apprehensive that the Federals would leave this military district, I determined to follow them with all my available force. Ashby, with his cavalry and Chew's battery, was already in front. Col. S. V. Fulkerson's brigade, consisting of the Twenty-third and Thirty-seventh Regiments Virginia Volunteers and Shumaker's battery, was near Woodstock. Brig. Gen. R. B. Garnett's brigade, consisting of the Second, Fourth, Fifth, Twenty-seventh, and Thirty-third Regiments Virginia Volunteers, and McLaughlin's, Carpenter's, and Waters' batteries, was near 2 miles below Mount Jackson. Col. J. S. Burks' brigade, consisting of the Twenty-first, Forty-second, and Forty-eighth Regiments Virginia Volunteers and the First Virginia Battalion, Provisional Army Confederate States, and Marye's battery, was near 2 miles above Mount Jackson.

The three brigades were ordered to march at dawn of the following morning. All the regiments, except the Forty-eighth (Col. John A. Campbell's), which was the rear guard, arrived within a mile or two of Kernstown by 2 p. m. on the 23d, and directions were given for bivouacking.

During the march information had reached me from a reliable source that the Federals were sending off their stores and troops from Winchester, and after arriving near Kernstown I learned from a source which had been remarkable for its reliability that the enemy's infantry force at Winchester did not exceed four regiments. A large Federal force was leaving the valley, and had already reached Castleman's Ferry on the Shenandoah. Though it was very desirable to prevent the enemy from leaving the valley, yet I deemed it best not to attack until morning. But subsequently ascertaining that the Federals had a position from which our forces could be seen, I concluded that it would be dangerous to postpone it until the next day, as re-enforcements might be brought up during the night.

After ascertaining that the troops, part of which had marched over 14 miles since dawn, and Garnett's and Burks' brigades, which had made a forced march of near 25 miles the day previous, were in good spirits at the prospect of meeting the enemy, I determined to advance at once.

Leaving Colonel Ashby, with his command, on the Valley turnpike, with Colonel Burks' brigade as a support to the batteries, and also to act as reserve, I moved with one piece of Carpenter's battery and Colonel Fulkerson's brigade, supported by General Garnett's, to our left, for the purpose of securing a commanding position on the enemy's right, and thus, turning him by that flank, force him back from his strong position in front, which prevented a direct advance.

Soon after, Captain Carpenter brought up his other pieces, also McLaughlin's and Waters' batteries came forward, the eminence was reached, and the three batteries, under their respective captains, commenced playing on the enemy, whose position was now commanded. We continued to advance our artillery, keeping up a continuous fire upon the Federals on our right, while Col. John Echols, with his regiment (the Twenty-seventh), with its skirmishers thrown forward, kept in advance and opened the infantry engagement, in which it was supported by the Twenty-first, under Lieut. Col. J. M. Patton, jr., as no other regiment of General Garnett had yet come up. Well did these two regiments do their duty, driving back the enemy twice in quick succession.

Soon a severe wound compelled the noble leader of the Twenty-seventh to leave the field, and the command devolved upon its lieutenant-colonel, the dauntless Grigsby. Great praise is due to the officers and men of both regiments.

Colonel Fulkerson having advanced his brigade, consisting of the Twenty-third and Thirty-seventh, which were, respectively, commanded by Lieut. Cols. A. G. Taliaferro and R. P. Carson, to the left of Colonel Echols, judiciously posted it behind a stone wall toward which the enemy was rapidly advancing, and opened a destructive fire, which drove back the Northern forces in great disorder after sustaining a heavy loss and leaving the colors of one of their regiments upon the field. This part of the enemy's routed troops having to some extent rallied in another position was also driven from this by Colonel Fulkerson. The officers and men of this brigade merit special mention.

Soon after the Twenty-seventh had become engaged General Garnett, with the Second, Fourth, and Thirty-third Regiments, commanded, respectively, by Col. J. W. Allen, Lieut. Col. C. A. Ronald, and Col. A. C. Cummings, moved forward and joined in the battle, which now became general. The First Virginia Battalion, Provisional Army Confederate States, under Capt. D. B. Bridgford, though it unfortunately became separated in advancing, was in the engagement, and from near 5 to 6.30 p. m. there was almost a continuous roar of musketry. The enemy's repulsed regiments were replaced by fresh ones from his large reserve. As the ammunition of some of our men became exhausted noble instances were seen of their borrowing from comrades, by whose sides they continued to fight, as though resolved to die rather than give way.

Lieutenant-Colonel Ronald, commanding the Fourth, having been injured during the early part of the engagement by being thrown from his horse, the command of the regiment devolved upon Maj. A. G. Pendleton.

Though our troops were fighting under great disadvantages, I regret that General Garnett should have given the order to fall back, as otherwise the enemy's advance would at least have been retarded, and the remaining part of my infantry reserve have had a better opportunity for coming up and taking part in the engagement if the enemy continued to press forward. As General Garnett fell back he was pursued by the enemy, who, thus turning Colonel Fulkerson's right, forced him to fall back.

Soon after this the Fifth Regiment, under Col. W. H. Harman, came up, and I directed it to advance and support our infantry; but before it met the enemy General Garnett ordered it back, and thus the enemy were permitted unresisted to continue the pursuit. So soon as I saw Colonel Harman filing his regiment to the rear I took steps to remedy, as far as practicable, this ill-timed movement by directing him to occupy and hold the woods immediately in his rear; and calling General Garnett's attention to the importance of rallying his troops, he turned and assigned the Fifth a position, which it held until the arrival of Colonel Burks with the Forty-second, under Lieut. Col. D. A. Langhorne. Colonel Burks and the officers and men of the Forty-second proved themselves worthy of the cause they were defending by the spirit with which this regiment took and held its position until its left was turned by the Federals, pressing upon the Fifth as it fell back.

Col. John A. Campbell was rapidly advancing with his regiment to take part in the struggle, but night and an indisposition on the part of the enemy to press farther had terminated the battle, which had commenced near 4 p. m.

Leaving Ashby in front, the remainder of my command fell back to its wagons and bivouacked for the night. Our artillery had played its part well, though we lost two pieces, one belonging to Waters and the other to McLaughlin, the former from having upset when hard pressed by the enemy and the latter from having its horses killed when it was on the eve of leaving the field, which it had so well swept with canister as to have driven back the enemy from a part of it over which he was pressing near the close of the battle.

During the engagement Colonel Ashby, with a portion of his command, including Chew's battery, which rendered valuable service, remained on our right, and not only protected our rear in the vicinity of the Valley turnpike, but also served to threaten the enemy's front and left. Colonel Ashby fully sustained his deservedly high reputation by the able manner in which he discharged the important trust confided to him.

Owing to the most of our infantry having marched between 35 and 40 miles since the morning of the previous day many were left behind. Our number present on the evening of the battle was, of infantry 3,087, of which 2,742 were engaged; twenty-seven pieces of artillery, of which eighteen were engaged. Owing to recent heavy cavalry duty and the extent of country to be picketed only 290 of this arm were present to take part in the engagement.

There is reason to believe that the Federal infantry on the field numbered over 11,000, of which probably over 8,000 were engaged. It may be that our artillery engaged equaled that of the enemy, and that their cavalry exceeded ours in number.

Our loss was, killed, 6 officers, 12 non-commissioned officers, and 62 privates; wounded, 27 officers, 53 non-commissioned officers, and 262 privates, of which number some 70 were left on the field; missing, 13 officers, 21 non-commissioned officers, and 235 privates. Nearly all the missing were captured.

A few days after the battle a Federal officer stated that their loss in killed was 418. Their wounded, upon the supposition that it bears the same relation to their killed as ours, must be such as to make their total loss more than three times that of ours.

Our wounded received that care and attention from the patriotic ladies of Winchester which they know so well how to give, and our killed were buried by the loyal citizens of that town. The hospitality of Baltimoreans relieved the wants of the captured. For these acts of kindness, on both sides of the Potomac, I am under lasting obligations.

The officers and men of the various regiments and batteries deserve great praise.

In consequence of Maj. F. B. Jones, Second Regiment Virginia Volunteers, being familiar with the locality, he was detached from his regiment and acted as a staff officer during the engagement, and from his familiarity with the country, added to his zeal and daring, rendered very valuable service.

Dr. Hunter McGuire, medical director, discharged his duties in a manner which proved him admirably qualified for his position.

Maj. J. A. Harman, chief quartermaster, ably discharged his duties.

Maj. W. J. Hawks, chief commissary, with his usual foresight, had the wants of his department well supplied.

First Lieut. G. G. Junkin, aide-de-camp and acting assistant adjutant-general, faithfully and efficiently devoted himself to his duties until near the close of the engagement, when, I regret to say, he was captured by the enemy.

First Lieut. A. S. Pendleton, aide-de-camp, who is an officer eminently qualified for his duties, discharged them in a highly satisfactory manner.

First Lieut. J. K. Boswell, chief engineer, rendered valuable service.

Though Winchester was not recovered, yet the more important object for the present, that of calling back troops that were leaving the valley, and thus preventing a junction of Banks' command with other forces, was accomplished, in addition to his heavy loss in killed and wounded. Under these circumstances I feel justified in saying that, though the field is in possession of the enemy, yet the most essential fruits of the battle are ours.

Respectfully, your obedient servant,

T. J. JACKSON,
*Major-General.*

Maj. THOMAS G. RHETT, *Assistant Adjutant-General.*

---

GENERAL ORDERS, No. 37. } HDQRS. DEPT. OF NORTHERN VIRGINIA, *Rapidan, April* 8, 1862.

The commanding general has the pleasure to publish to the troops under his command the following resolution of Congress, and at the same time to express his own sense of the admirable conduct of Major-General Jackson and his division, by which they fully earned the high reward bestowed by Congress:

*Resolved by the Congress of the Confederate States of America,* That the thanks of Congress are due, and they are hereby tendered, to Maj. Gen. T. J. Jackson and the officers and men under his command for their gallant and meritorious service in the successful engagement with a greatly superior force of the enemy, near Kernstown, Frederick County, Virginia, on the 23d day of March, 1862.

By command of Major-General Johnston:

THOS. G. RHETT,
*Assistant Adjutant-General.*

---

## No. 24.

### *Return of casualties in the Confederate forces.*

[Compiled from the reports.]

| Command. | Killed. | | | Wounded. | | | Missing. | | | Aggregate. |
|---|---|---|---|---|---|---|---|---|---|---|
| | Officers. | Men. | Total. | Officers. | Men. | Total. | Officers. | Men. | Total. | |
| **Garnett's brigade:** | | | | | | | | | | |
| 2d Virginia | | | 6 | | | 33 | | | 51 | 90 |
| 4th Virginia | | 5 | 5 | | 23 | 23 | 6 | 42 | 48 | 76 |
| 5th Virginia | 1 | 8 | 9 | 2 | 46 | 48 | | 4 | 4 | 61 |
| 27th Virginia | | | 2 | | | 20 | 3 | 32 | 35 | 57 |
| 33d Virginia | | | 18 | | | 27 | | | 14 | 59 |
| McLaughlin's battery | | | | | 10 | 10 | | 1 | 1 | 11 |
| Waters' battery | | | | | 7 | 7 | | | | 7 |
| Total | | | 40 | | | 168 | | | 153 | 361 |
| **Burks' brigade:** | | | | | | | | | | |
| 21st Virginia | | 7 | 7 | 4 | 40 | 44 | | 9 | 9 | 60 |
| 42d Virginia | 2 | 9 | 11 | 5 | 45 | 50 | | 9 | 9 | 70 |
| 1st Virginia Battalion | | | 6 | | | 20 | | | 21 | 47 |
| Total | | | 24 | | | 114 | | | 39 | 167 |
| **Fulkerson's brigade:** | | | | | | | | | | |
| 23d Virginia | | | 3 | 3 | 11 | 14 | 1 | 31 | 32 | 49 |
| 37th Virginia | 1 | 11 | 12 | 7 | 55 | 62 | | 39 | 39 | 113 |
| Total | | | 15 | | | 76 | | | 71 | 162 |
| **Cavalry** | 1 | | 1 | 1 | 16 | 17 | | | | 18 |
| Grand total | | | 80 | | | 375 | | | 263 | 718 |

A summary of casualties, signed by Brigadier-General Garnett, shows 3 officers and 38 men killed 9 officers and 153 men wounded, and 9 officers and 149 men missing; total, 361. But he does not state the loss by regiments.

## No. 25.

### *Report of Col. Turner Ashby, Seventh Virginia Cavalry.*

CAMP NEAR WOODSTOCK, VA., *March* 26, 1862.

DEAR SIR: In reporting the part performed by troops under my command in the engagement of Sunday, the 23d, it is proper to state that four companies of cavalry, under Maj. O. R. Funsten, were, by your order, sent by me to the extreme left of your line, and acted under your orders directly.

Having followed the enemy in his hasty retreat from Strasburg on Saturday evening, I came upon the forces remaining in Winchester within a mile of that place and became satisfied that he had but four regiments, and learned that they had orders to march in the direction of Harper's Ferry.

On Sunday morning I moved my force of cavalry, battery of three guns, and four companies of infantry, under Captain Nadenbousch, to Kernstown, where, after firing a few shots and pressing in the direction of Winchester with cavalry, I learned that the enemy was increasing his force and intended making a stand. He had thrown skirmishers out to threaten my guns, when I ordered Captain Nadenbousch to protect them against him, which he did by driving him from his place in the woods most gallantly; and it was with extreme regret that I found it necessary to order him to fall back, which I did, owing to the enemy's getting in position upon my left with artillery and infantry, to command the position taken by Captain Nadenbousch.

Accompanying this you will find Captain Nadenbousch's report.

Upon falling back, which I did for one-fourth of a mile, I received your order to prepare for an advance, and learned that your force had arrived. My orders being to threaten the front and right, I placed two guns to bear upon the front and one upon his left, where I kept up an incessant fire with some visible effect, gaining ground upon him, when I ordered a charge upon his extreme left, where I drove their advance upon the main line, losing 1 lieutenant (Thaddeus Thrasher) killed and 6 privates wounded. We, however, took 6 or 7 prisoners.

The loss of Lieutenant Thrasher is a great one to his company and regiment, as his boldness and efficiency had made their mark in the regiment.

One man was taken prisoner upon the left of Captain Turner's company, having been thrown from his horse and ordered to the rear.

When the firing ceased at twilight I ordered my guns back to the rear and the cavalry to cover the flank of Colonel Burks' command, coming out in the turnpike, and after they had passed remained at Bartonsville with my companies until 2 o'clock on Monday morning, when the enemy again advanced cautiously.

Respectfully,

TURNER ASHBY,
*Colonel, Commanding Cavalry.*

[Indorsements.]

HDQRS. VALLEY DISTRICT, *April* 7, 1862.

Colonel Ashby will please state the number of men engaged on March 23.

By order of Major-General Jackson:

A. S. PENDLETON,
*Acting Assistant Adjutant-General*

Owing to the arduous duties imposed upon my cavalry companies up to the time that the enemy left Strasburg upon his retreat to Winchester I started in pursuit with one company (Captain Sheetz's), with orders for Captains Bowen and Turner to come on during the night (Friday). After reaching Newtown, or on the way there, I dispatched an order for all of the companies to come up. When I sent Captains Bowen and George W. Myers to Clarke County I left Captains Shands and Harper upon the back road. I proceeded with such of Captains Turner's and Sheetz's companies as were fit for duty toward Winchester, Captains Henderson and Marshall coming up while I was skirmishing with them and Captain Baylor being on the Front Royal road.

These companies having had insufficient forage and rest for one week or more, reduced their number in the fight of the 23d to not more than 150 upon the right with me, and I am informed by Major Funsten that he had but 140 men.

I feel that an explanation is due for my ranks being so small; but when I assure you of the poor condition of my men and horses, and not expecting a fight until next day, will explain the absence of so many.

T. A.

---

## No. 26.

*Report of Maj. O. R. Funsten, Seventh Virginia Cavalry.*

CAMP NEAR HAWKINSTOWN, VA.,
*April* 7, 1862.

COLONEL: I make the following report of the operations of the left wing of the regiment of cavalry commanded by you in the battle near Kernstown, on the 23d ultimo. My delay in making a report has been occasioned by not receiving at an earlier date the reports of Captains Sheetz and Baylor:

On the morning of the 23d nothing of much importance occurred until after the arrival of General Jackson's advance, when I was ordered to send two companies from the left to the right wing.

About 4 o'clock, General Jackson having directed me to hold my command in readiness to make a charge in the event that the enemy were driven back, and my force amounting to only about 70 men, inclusive of pickets, I sent a messenger to request you to send me two companies, if you could spare them from the right. Captains Sheetz's and Turner's companies were sent, and took position on the extreme left soon after the infantry fight commenced.

About 6 o'clock, when the fortune of the day seemed to be turning against us, General Jackson directed me to take a certain position in our rear in the event of our troops falling back, and to charge the enemy as they advanced in that direction, stating at the same time that I would be supported by artillery. I immediately ordered Captain Sheetz's and Turner's companies to report to me, after leaving a strong picket on the extreme left. The position which was occupied by the picket is a high ridge about 800 yards from the battle ground, and commands a view of the Cedar Creek and Opequon turnpike on the west (distant about a mile from the battle ground) and of the intervening valley on the east. In addition to this, I directed Captain Baylor to take 20 men and watch the movements of the enemy between the pickets and our left.

In the course of twenty minutes after these orders were given our troops fell back, and I took the position designated by General Jackson, having been joined by Captains Sheetz's and Turner's companies as we fell back. I remained in this position until all of our troops who retreated in that direction had passed and it became evident that the enemy would not pursue them through the open land in our front, and until the enemy, who advanced through the woods, were a short distance from our right. I then ordered my command to fall back to a ridge about 200 yards to our left and rear. On arriving there I was informed, to my surprise, that the enemy's cavalry were on our left. I believed that I had used every precaution to receive timely information of their advance on our left, having placed more than one-fourth of my command to watch them on that flank.

I have called upon Captains Sheetz and Baylor to report why it was that this information was not communicated to me as soon as the enemy appeared, and herewith inclose their reports.*

I immediately, on hearing of the enemy's cavalry, ordered a charge, and they were driven back. We remained near this position, about three-fourths of a mile in the rear and to the left of the battle ground until about 8 o'clock, covering the retreat of a large number of scattered infantry, and then marched to Newtown, where we arrived about 9 p. m.

The number of cavalry under my command, after the companies of Captains Sheetz and Turner had been added to it, was between 130 and 140, of whom between 30 and 40 were on picket duty on our left.

Respectfully submitted.

O. R. FUNSTEN,
*Major of Ashby's Regiment of Cavalry.*

Col. TURNER ASHBY.

---

## No. 27.

***Report of Col. J. W. Allen, Second Virginia Infantry, First Brigade.***

——, —— —, 1862.

CAPTAIN: In obedience to Special Orders, No. 43, I have the honor to submit the following report of the operations of the Second Regiment Virginia Volunteers, under my command, on Sunday, March 23:

About 6 a. m., with seven companies of my regiment—Companies D, I, and H having been detached under Captain Nadenbousch with Colonel Ashby's regiment of cavalry—we left camp, this side of Cedar Creek, and marched to within 5 miles of Winchester. Being in front of the brigade, I was directed to the left of the turnpike into a piece of woods, where the men were allowed to rest for about half an hour, when they were formed in line, and Company G thrown forward about 300 yards as skirmishers. Soon afterward I was directed to advance and support Colonel Fulkerson, whom I overtook some three-quarters of a mile in front marching in line of battle.

At 2 p. m. I placed my regiment in double column and followed in his rear, Companies D, I, and H having taken their places in line, looking much wearied by their march and subsequent heavy skirmish

---

* Not found.

in the early part of the day with a large force of the enemy's advance guard.

At this point Company B was deployed as skirmishers on our right, and remained in that position until just before crossing the last ridge, when it joined the regiment. Moving the rest of the command in the rear of Colonel Fulkerson's brigade, in the direction of the enemy's battery, to within 300 yards of the edge of the woods, at which point the Fourth Regiment was deployed in front of the Second, I received an order from General Garnett to support it.

While waiting in this position Major [Francis B.] Jones, who had been ordered to report to the major-general commanding, returned with an order for the First Brigade to occupy the wooded height to our left. In getting to this point we were compelled to cross a large field in full view and direct range of the enemy's batteries, which poured in a very heavy fire of shell during the whole passage.

On arriving in the wood I occupied a sheltered position with my command and went across the ridge to report to General R. B. Garnett.

Soon after my return Major Jones again ordered us forward, and after crossing the ridge the firing of musketry began on our left and front. When I reached the last woods I brought my regiment into line by the right flank, and thus advancing came into action in rear of the Thirty-third, on my left, and the Irish Battalion, on my right, about 5 p. m. or soon after. The fire from the enemy was very brisk, but I advanced some paces beyond the line at first occupied. Seeing a wall in front in possession of the enemy, my object was to get possession of it; but owing to the rapid firing of the enemy and thick undergrowth only the right succeeded in reaching it, which they held until the order to retire was given, about 6 p. m. Thus the men were exposed to a severe fire for nearly an hour, during which time they did not lose an inch of ground.

I cannot too highly commend the coolness and bravery of both officers and men, and it would be invidious to draw comparisons. I will, therefore, only confine myself to the field and staff officers and commanders of companies who came especially under my observation.

Lieut. Col. Lawson Botts and Adjutant Hunter, both of whom remained mounted during the day, the first on the left and in front, the latter near me in rear, maintained the position of the line by their coolness and courage.

Major Jones I observed frequently during the day in the most exposed positions in discharge of his duties to the major-general.

I would also highly commend the action of Captains Rowan, Nadenbousch, Hunter, Butler, Colston, and Moore; the latter, though wounded, went back to the fight; also that of Lieutenants Randolph, Burgess, Lewis, and J. B. Davis, who were in command of their respective companies; and especially would I commend the conduct of Lieuts. J. B. Davis, Company K, and R. H. Lee, Company G, each of whom, after Color-Sergeant Crist fell dead at his post, in succession advanced and raised my colors and went forward and cheered on the men until each was shot down, the first struck by a spent ball, the latter badly wounded. I would also mention most honorably the conduct of Lieutenants Hoffman, Company D, and O. S. Colston, Company E, who were both badly wounded in the thickest fight.

My list of killed and wounded is herewith appended, which, under the especial providence of God, who protected us in the thickest of the fight and retreat, is much smaller than could have been expected.*

* List tabulated on p. 384.

Not hearing the order to retire, I did not give it, and only left the field when I found most of the men were drawn off on our left and a heavy force of the enemy were advancing in that direction.

Respectfully submitted.

J. W. ALLEN,
*Colonel Second Virginia Regiment.*

Capt. R. J. WINGATE,
*Assistant Adjutant-General.*

[Indorsements.]

HEADQUARTERS VALLEY DISTRICT,
*April* 7, 1862.

Colonel Allen will please state how many men he had engaged on March 23.

By order of Major-General Jackson:

A. S. PENDLETON,
*Acting Assistant Adjutant-General.*

---

HDQRS. SECOND REGIMENT VIRGINIA VOLUNTEERS,
———, ——— —, 1862.

The number of my regiment engaged on the 23d instant did not exceed 320 rank and file.

By order of Col. J. W. Allen:

R. W. HUNTER,
*Aide-de-Camp.*

---

## No. 28.

*Report of Capt. J. Q. A. Nadenbousch, Second Virginia Infantry.*

CAMP AT BARTONSVILLE, VA.,
*March* 23, 1862.

COLONEL: Companies D, H, and I, of your regiment, and Company H, Twenty-seventh Virginia Volunteers, were ordered forward at dawn on the 23d instant to support Colonel Ashby's command. They moved forward, without breakfast, near Kernstown. After ascertaining the position of the enemy we were ordered forward to protect the battery from a line of skirmishers which were concealed in the woods near by. Company H, under Captain Hunter, and Company I, under Capt. S. J. C. Moore, were at once thrown forward as skirmishers. The line was without delay moved forward into the edge of the woods. Upon arriving at this point the line of the enemy was observed at a distance of about 100 yards. I at once ordered the men to fire on them, which was promptly obeyed. We continued to advance firing, when the enemy retired or fled rapidly, but were soon heavily re-enforced. Seeing this, I at once ordered forward the reserve, Company D, under Lieutenant Hoffman, and Company H, Twenty-seventh Virginia Regiment, under Captain Edmondson. These companies at once moved forward and re-enforced our line, which kept up a brisk fire, doing great execution. Colonel Ashby, seeing heavy columns of the enemy in the rear in the woods, ordered us to fall back, which order was obeyed, and the command fell back to the road.

In this skirmish the following casualties and losses were sustained: Company D, 2 men wounded and brought off the field; Company H, Second Regiment, Lieutenant Link wounded and left on the field, owing to having been thrown, and the horse ran off, and 3 men brought off; Company I, Sergeants Shepherd and N. O. Sowers and Private Roy, and left on the field, 2 of which were wounded in their efforts to carry off their wounded—Corporal Shepherd wounded and brought off the field; Company H, Twenty-seventh Regiment, 1 man wounded and brought off the field.

The conduct of the officers and men in this skirmish was highly commendable. The officers behaved gallantly in encouraging and leading forward their men. The men, with loud shouts, moved forward like heroes, that knew no fear, until the word to fall back was given. Before the men had recovered from their exhaustion from this skirmish we were ordered to join our respective regiments for the general engagement, which order was obeyed, but with rather slim ranks, after which their conduct and operations were under your eye.

With great respect, I remain, your obedient servant,

J. Q. A. NADENBOUSCH,

*Captain, Commanding Detachment under Colonel Ashby.*

Col. J. W. ALLEN,

*Commanding Second Regiment Virginia Volunteers.*

---

## No. 29.

***Report of Lieut. Col. Charles A. Ronald, Fourth Virginia Infantry.***

HDQRS. FOURTH REGIMENT VIRGINIA VOLUNTEERS,

*Camp Buchanan, Va.*, ——— —, 1862.

SIR: The following report of the battle of the valley, near Kernstown, on Sunday, the 23d instant, so far as the Fourth Regiment was connected with it, is respectfully submitted:

On Saturday morning, the 22d, the regiments left camp, near Mount Jackson, and marched to Cedar Creek, below Strasburg, a distance of 26 miles. The roads were very muddy, which made the march more fatiguing than it otherwise would have been.

We rested at Cedar Creek all night, and on Sunday morning, the 23d, took up the line of march toward Winchester. When about 1 mile below Newtown filed to the left, leaving the turnpike. When about half a mile north of the road I was directed to form the regiment in line of battle with the Second. I was soon directed to change this position and form on the left of the Twenty-seventh. In the mean time, advancing gradually toward the right wing of the enemy's line, I was then directed to move the regiment in line of battle across an open field and to cover as much space as possible. This exposed the regiment to the view of the enemy.

I remained in this field about ten minutes, and was ordered to change direction and occupy a position in the woods and more directly toward Kernstown. Here the regiment remained for some twenty-five or thirty minutes, where it was exposed to the shells from the enemy's guns. The firing was so heavy at this point that my horse became ungovernable and ran away with me, hurting me very much.

Here Major Pendleton assumed command and marched the regiment to the extreme left, where the infantry were engaged. Men never behaved better than did the men of the Fourth Regiment. Major Pendleton and Adjutant Langhorne acted well their parts. I could mention others; but all acted (officers and men) so nobly, that I cannot mention one without bringing myself under obligations to number all. I mention Major Pendleton and Adjutant Langhorne merely because they were more conspicuous in command of the regiment.*

I take pleasure in bearing testimony to the promptness and efficiency of Dr. Black, surgeon, who rendered good service during the engagement.

CH. A. RONALD,
*Lieutenant-Colonel, Comdg. Fourth Virginia Regiment.*

Capt. R. J. WINGATE,
*Assistant Adjutant-General, First Brigade.*

[Indorsements.]

HEADQUARTERS VALLEY DISTRICT,
*April* 7, 1862.

Colonel Ronald will please state the number of men engaged on March 23.

By order of Major-General Jackson:

A. S. PENDLETON,
*Acting Assistant Adjutant-General.*

—

The regiment numbered 203, rank and file, when the engagement commenced.

CH. A. R.

---

## No. 30.

### *Report of Col. William H. Harman, Fifth Virginia Infantry.*

HDQRS. FIFTH REGIMENT VIRGINIA VOLUNTEERS,
*March* 27, 1862.

SIR: I have the honor to report, in pursuance of General Orders, No. 43, the operations of my regiment on the day and during the engagement of the 23d instant:

Starting from near Cedar Creek, we marched a distance of 13 miles and to within 5 miles of Winchester, on the Valley turnpike, when we were ordered to the left of the road into Barton's woods, and remained about an hour, a brisk cannonade going on in our front.

My command was then ordered to take position in rear of a stone fence, running in front of an open field, between the woods and road, my right resting on the turnpike, the remainder of the brigade moving off to my left to the battle-field. After remaining in this position for about two hours, during which time there was a continual fire of artillery in my front, and large bodies of the enemy moving around from my right, but not approaching nearer than 1½ or 2 miles, as well as I could judge, I was ordered by Major-General Garnett, through Maj.

* List of casualties here omitted is tabulated on p. 384.

F. B. Jones, Second Virginia Volunteers, to proceed with my regiment to the field of battle, which I did at a quick-march, under his conduct, and proceeded about 2 miles. During the whole time a terrific fire of cannon and musketry was going on in my front. I immediately reported to the major-general commanding (not being aware of the position of General Garnett), who ordered me to support the troops engaged.

I had not, however, proceeded more than a few hundred yards when I received an order, through Major Jones, to file to the left into the woods and occupy a wooded ridge. Almost immediately thereafter, while the regiment was filing to the left, the major-general commanding approached and ordered me to occupy and hold those woods, and while filing into the woods Major-General Garnett approached me and assigned me my position near the top of the wooded ridge. In front of me was an open field and behind it a large and heavily timbered hill. My front was occupied by two regiments of the infantry of the enemy; on my left scattered squads of our men were retiring from the field; on my right a regiment of the enemy was approaching. I immediately ordered my men to open fire on the enemy. In a very short time the regiments of the enemy in my front were broken, one of them retiring and leaving its colors on the field; but they were almost immediately re-enforced by a fresh regiment, upon which they rallied.

At this time a regiment of the enemy opened fire upon my left, thus subjecting me to a heavy cross-fire. Seeing that my right was hard pressed, I rode forward to observe the cause and cheer them on. The regiment which was firing upon them at this moment gave way; but observing that my center and left had given way, I ordered them (the right companies) to cease firing; retired my colors a short distance below my first position; ordered the regiment to form upon them, which was rapidly done; brought the regiment to an about-face, and continued to give the enemy fight.

This position I held for some time, contending with a largely-superior force, the enemy displaying six or seven regimental flags. I was then compelled to fall back to a position near the fence, at the edge of the woods, where I remained some minutes, until I found it was impossible to withstand a force so superior to me in numbers, there being at least six or eight to one engaged against me, and, in addition to that, it being quite dark, and a huge body of the enemy's cavalry threatening me on my left.

The gallant Forty-second Virginia Regiment had taken position on my right and were most efficiently engaged, but none other of our infantry were at that time engaged. After crossing the fence I was joined by General Garnett, with whom I retired from the field, my regiment being in much better order than I could have hoped under the circumstances, and fell back by Bartonsville to the train of wagons, which had retired beyond Newtown.

I believe that, under the providence of God, my regiment had the honor of contributing materially to the protection of the artillery and the preservation of the gallant men of other regiments, who from overpowering force and want of ammunition were compelled to retire from the field.

To the officers and men of my command, without exception, I am greatly indebted for the gallantry, determination, and courage they displayed throughout my participation in this engagement. When the fact is considered that my men had the day before made a march of 26 miles, and before going into the fight had marched 13 miles on a rock pike, I think I may, without fear of criticism, claim for them the highest meed of praise. Where every single company officer displayed the greatest gallantry and intrepidity I cannot distinguish one over the other.

I cannot refrain from expressing the deepest regret at the loss of the following officers, left on the field, viz: Capt. George T. Antrim, Company H, severely wounded; Second Lieut. J. W. Dale, Company C, supposed to have been mortally wounded, and Lieut. John W. Wilson, Company E, killed.

To Maj. Absalom Koiner, the only field officer with me, I am greatly indebted for his zeal and efficiency.

It is due to my personal staff to mention, in the very highest terms, for their gallantry and intrepidity, Adjt. James Bumgardner and Sergt. Maj. John W. Carroll; nor would it be right that I should fail to mention the distinguished conduct of my color-bearer, Sergt. Robert H. Fisher, of Company I.

The casualties of my regiment were, commissioned officers, 1 killed, Lieut. J. W. Wilson, Company E; mortally wounded, Lieut. J. W. Dale, Company C; seriously wounded, Capt. George T. Antrim, Company H. Non-commissioned officers killed, 1; wounded, 6. Privates killed, 7; wounded, 40; missing, 4. Total killed, wounded, and missing, 61; of which I herewith return a list.

Respectfully,

W. H. HARMAN,
*Colonel Fifth Regiment Virginia Volunteers.*

Capt. R. J. WINGATE,
*Assistant Adjutant-General.*

---

## No. 31.

*Report of Lieut. Col. A. J. Grigsby, Twenty-seventh Virginia Infantry.*

HDQRS. TWENTY-SEVENTH REGIMENT VA. VOLS.,
*Camp Stover, Va., March* 27, 1862.

In compliance with General Orders, No. 43, I make the following report of the Twenty-seventh Regiment during the engagement near Kernstown, on Sunday, the 23d instant:

The Twenty-seventh Regiment was ordered by Major-General Jackson to take position in advance of Captain Carpenter's battery and to support the same. This they did, taking position some distance in advance of the battery, with Captain Shriver's company thrown forward as skirmishers. The position where the regiment was first drawn up being untenable, the regiment fell back to the crest of a hill in rear of the first position, the enemy advancing in heavy force.

The enemy was repulsed twice before re-enforcements reached us, which were promptly sent forward as soon as called for.

The position was held until the regiment was ordered to retire, which order was received after the men had fired their last round of cartridges. They retired slowly from a hard-fought field in the face of an overwhelming force.

Colonel Echols fell severely wounded while gallantly leading his regiment in the hottest of the fight.

I cannot speak in terms of too much praise of the officers of the regiment, who acted most gallantly throughout the engagement, constantly exposing themselves to the most galling fire.

The non-commissioned corps and privates bore themselves gallantly throughout the engagement, obeying with alacrity all the orders they received.

The regiment suffered severely, having lost, in killed, wounded, and missing, 57 officers, non-commissioned officers, and privates.*

Among the missing are Captains Holloway and Robertson and Lieutenant Lady.

Respectfully, your obedient servant,

A. J. GRIGSBY,
*Lieut. Col., Commanding Twenty-seventh Virginia Volunteers.*

Capt. R. J. WINGATE,
*Assistant Adjutant-General.*

[Indorsements.]

HEADQUARTERS VALLEY DISTRICT,
*April* 7, 1862.

Colonel Grigsby will please state how many men were in the engagement of March 23.

By order of Major-General Jackson:

A. S. PENDLETON,
*Acting Assistant Adjutant-General.*

---

CAMP NEAR NEW MARKET, VA.,
*April* 7, 1862.

There was in my (Twenty-seventh) regiment when drawn up in Barton's woods 170 guns, all told.

A. J. GRIGSBY,
*Lieut. Col., Comdg. Twenty-seventh Regiment Virginia Vols.*

---

## No. 32.

*Report of Col. Arthur C. Cummings, Thirty-third Virginia Infantry.*

CAMP BUCHANAN, VA.,
*Near Mount Jackson, Va., March* 29, 1862.

SIR: I have the honor to report to the general commanding the First Brigade the part borne by my regiment (the Thirty-third Virginia Volunteers) in the engagement with the enemy, near Kernstown, on the 23d instant.

About 3 p. m. on Sunday we came in sight of the enemy's batteries, having marched a distance of about 40 miles from 8 o'clock the previous morning. After remaining in a strip of woods west of the Winchester turnpike my regiment, by the general's order, was marched by flank about half a mile in a northwesterly direction, when it was formed in line of battle, and advanced in line a short distance through a flat woodland immediately in the direction of the enemy's batteries, planted upon a commanding eminence a little west of the Winchester turnpike and southwest of Kernstown. Here, under a heavy fire from the enemy's

---

* See p. 384.

battery, the regiment was formed, by the order of the general, into column of divisions, and advanced in a northwesterly direction through an open space, when it was formed again in line, and marched by flanks, still in the same general direction, through the open space for about 1,000 yards, all the time within full range of the enemy's guns and exposed to a heavy fire from their batteries. My regiment followed immediately in rear of Colonel Fulkerson's command, deflecting a little to the west, which it was intended to support. After passing through the open space before referred to my regiment crossed a ridge running northeast and southwest, and afterward occupied by our artillery. Colonel Fulkerson's command, which was in advance, formed on the north side of the ridge. My regiment, after passing some 200 or 300 yards along the base of the ridge, remained, somewhat sheltered by the ridge and timber, for about an hour under a most terrific fire of shot and shell from the enemy's batteries (now upon our east), changing position so as to keep within supporting distance of our artillery.

After my regiment had remained in this position it was ordered forward in advance of Colonel Fulkerson's command, which at that time occupied the base of the same ridge immediately in advance. A few minutes after we had reached the first position occupied after crossing the open space and ridge a hot engagement commenced between our infantry, about 300 yards in our advance, and the infantry of the enemy. By your direction I immediately formed my regiment in line of battle perpendicular to the line of the ridge occupied by our artillery. The infantry engagement being immediately in front, I moved forward at once in line of battle to the support of the Twenty-seventh Regiment Virginia Volunteers and what I supposed to be the Twenty-first Regiment Virginia Volunteers, who were occupying the spur of the ridge occupied by our artillery and hotly engaging the enemy in largely superior numbers.

It being but about 300 yards from where my regiment was last formed in line of battle to where our troops were engaging the enemy, my regiment soon arrived upon the ground and immediately opened fire upon the enemy, who occupied the ground in our front and to the right and left of our front. We kept up an incessant fire upon the enemy for about one and a half hours, who were pressing upon us in largely superior numbers and pouring into our ranks a deadly fire. My regiment occupied, with two other regiments, part of the spur upon which our line of battle was formed and immediately on the right of the Twenty-seventh Regiment Virginia Volunteers.

After contending manfully against largely superior numbers for about one and a half hours, many of the men having exhausted their ammunition—the men of two or three different regiments being mingled with mine—it was announced by, I believe, the adjutant of the Second Regiment that it was the order of the general to fall back, when there was a general falling back, after having contended for upward of an hour against large odds, and many being without ammunition and had previously fallen to the rear.

The brave and gallant manner in which the officers, non-commissioned officers, and privates of my regiment did their duty, under the most disadvantageous circumstances, being worn-out by the fatigue of a long march over muddy roads, justly entitles them to the everlasting gratitude of their country. Owing to the fact that there were officers and men of two or three different regiments mingled with my own in the fight, doubtless many instances of daring, bravery, and gallantry were exhibited by officers and men which did not come under my observation, and I therefore refrain from mentioning those that did. I doubt if men are often required to pass through a more severe ordeal than were the officers and men of my regiment on the evening of the 23d. Owing to the severe march, they were not in a physical condition to meet equal numbers, much less immense odds.

I deem it unnecessary to give further particulars, as my regiment was immediately under your eye and orders during the greater part of the time.

Out of 275 men who were in the engagement, a number having given out on the march, there were 18 killed, 27 wounded, and 14 missing, some of whom are doubtless wounded and taken prisoners; others perhaps killed; others will doubtless yet report to their command. A list of the killed and wounded is herewith inclosed.*

All of which is respectfully submitted.

Very respectfully, your obedient servant,

A. C. CUMMINGS,
*Colonel Thirty-third Regiment Virginia Volunteers.*

R. J. WINGATE,
*Assistant Adjutant-General.*

---

## No. 33.

### *Report of Capt. William McLaughlin, Rockbridge (Va.) Artillery.*

CAMP BUCHANAN, VA., *March* 29, 1862.

I have the honor to submit the following report of the operations of the battery under my command in the action of the 23d instant, near Winchester:

We left Cedar Creek about 7 a. m. on the 23d and arrived near the scene of the subsequent action about noon. We were immediately put in position, by order of the major-general commanding, on the hill to the left of the road, so as to protect the approaches from the direction of Winchester.

About 1 o'clock I received an order from General Jackson to move around with four pieces to the left, immediately followed by an order to proceed with the whole battery. I reported to him in person, and was directed to occupy a hill on the left with the least possible delay, as the enemy seemed to be endeavoring to do the same. In proceeding thither we were subjected to a rapid and well-directed fire from a battery of the enemy of six or eight rifled guns, placed in a commanding position on a hill west of Winchester, one of the shots taking effect and completely disabling the seventh (rifled) piece of the battery, rendering it necessary to order it to the rear. When we reached the crest of the hill a well-directed shot from the enemy's battery succeeded in temporarily disabling the third piece of the battery, by killing the wheel-horses and dangerously wounding the driver and one of the cannoneers. The other six pieces promptly took their position and engaged the enemy's battery with marked effect, as his firing became much slower and far less accurate. The horses of the caisson were promptly transferred to the third piece, which also took its position in action.

About 3.30 o'clock a section of the battery, under command of Lieutenant Poague, was ordered to the left, and, with the batteries of Cap-

---

* Embodied in return, p. 384.

tains Carpenter and Waters, played on the enemy's artillery and infantry.

About 4.30 o'clock I joined this section and was immediately ordered to remove it to the position of the rest of the battery. The enemy having engaged our infantry in great force on a line perpendicular to the line of the battery, this section was posted near the straw-stacks, so as to sweep the hill on either side and play on the enemy's re-enforcements, as it did, with effect. The rest of the battery continued to fire upon his artillery and infantry for some time, when it was shifted, so as to sweep the same hill and protect our right flank, should the enemy endeavor to turn it. Our infantry being pressed back, the enemy, with two or three regiments, pressed along the line, evidently for the purpose of turning our right and cutting us off from the turnpike. As they crossed the fence in front of the battery, at a distance of about 250 yards, we opened upon them with a rapid and well-directed fire of canister from four pieces, completely driving them back, and not appearing again in that direction while we remained on the field. Our infantry having fallen back from the woods on our left, which was immediately occupied by the enemy, and the Fifth Virginia Regiment having formed in the edge of the woods near the straw-stacks, about 150 yards in our rear, I ordered these four pieces to limber up and fall back to the rear of the Fifth Regiment, there to be disposed of as occasion might require.

In the mean time, the enemy having emerged from the woods to the left of the position occupied by these four pieces and into the field in which the straw-stacks stood, the section of Lieutenant Poague opened upon them with canister at a distance of about 150 yards, driving them, with the fire of the Fifth Regiment, back into the woods, where they rapidly reformed. As the Fifth Regiment was beginning to fall back this section was limbered to the rear amid a most destructive fire from his infantry, severely wounding 1 of the sergeants and 2 of the cannoneers and killing 2 horses and wounding 3 others, rendering it impossible to bring off one of the pieces. I immediately joined the rest of the battery; but as the infantry were falling back, and it was growing dark and the ground being very unfavorable for moving the carriages, I found it impracticable to reform the battery on the hill in the woods as I had intended, and found it necessary to carry the pieces to the field at the foot of the hill, where I halted and awaited orders.

In a short time I was directed by Lieutenant Junkin, aide of General Jackson, to send the caissons to the rear and to form the battery on a hill in the rear, to protect the retreat. I was proceeding to execute the order when I received an order from the major-general commanding, through Maj. F. B. Jones, Second Virginia Regiment, acting aide, to proceed without delay to the turnpike, which was done in good order.

I desire to express my appreciation of the coolness and gallantry displayed by the officers and men of the battery throughout the entire action, and to the efficiency, skill, and rapidity with which they handled their pieces. Where all did so well it would be improper to discriminate, and I shall content myself with naming the chiefs of sections, Lieutenants Poague, Graham, and Leyburn, and Sergeant Davis, upon whom at different times devolved separate commands, the division of the battery rendering it impracticable for me personally to direct all the movements, and from whom I received invaluable assistance.

The following is a list of the casualties:

| | |
|---|---|
| Wounded, 1 non-commissioned officer and 9 privates | 10 |
| Missing | 1 |
| Total | 11 |

Respectfully,

WILLIAM McLAUGHLIN,
*Captain, Commanding Rockbridge Artillery.*

Capt R. J. WINGATE,
*Assistant Adjutant-General.*

---

## No. 34.

### *Report of Capt. James H. Waters, West Augusta (Va.) Artillery.*

CAMP BUCHANAN, VA., *March* 28, 1862.

I have the honor to submit below a report of the part my company sustained in the engagement with the enemy on Sunday evening, March 23:

Soon after the arrival of our forces upon the field I was ordered to proceed with my battery to a high ridge on the left of the Valley turnpike, and running parallel with the one occupied by the forces of the enemy.

In order to reach this position the battery was compelled to cross a long, low meadow, completely commanded by the enemy's guns, who fired upon us an incessant fire of shell and shot. While crossing this open valley 1 driver and 4 other privates of the piece were struck and knocked down by fragments of shell, which somewhat retarded the rapid movement of one section of the battery. Proceeding forward as rapidly as the wearied condition of the teams and nature of the ground would permit, I brought my battery into position on the ridge above named, and opened fire upon the enemy.

Maintaining this position, a heavy cannonading was kept up for nearly three hours, when the enemy, under cover of the thick woods and a high stone wall which skirted our left, advanced his infantry to within a very short distance of our position unperceived, and commenced a rapid discharge of musketry upon the men working the pieces.

Owing to their position and the nature of the ground, I found it impossible to do them any damage with artillery, and perceiving them pressing us closely, I deemed it prudent to retire from the position then evidently impossible for me to hold. I regret to have to state here that just as one piece of my battery was being limbered up and starting from the field one of the horses attached to the piece was shot by a musket-ball and killed and the piece overturned. Sergt. Charles S. Arnall, who had charge of this piece, after making every exertion to bring it off, was compelled to abandon it, cutting loose the three remaining horses and bringing them away, although the enemy had by this time reached the stone fence on our left, not more than 50 paces distant.

In retiring from the position on the ridge a caisson of one of the pieces, already broken, became so badly damaged as to be immovable and had to be abandoned.

The casualties occurring in my company during the engagement are as follows: Total number wounded, 7; killed, none.

While I greatly regret the loss of the one gun and caisson, I am pleased to be able to report that the non-commissioned officers and privates of my company, while under heavy fire from the enemy's guns, fired these their first shots with a coolness and precision highly gratifying to me, and with evident effect and damage to the enemy.

I was assisted only by one commissioned officer, First Lieut. J. C. Marquis, who performed his duty with judgment and bravery; Second Lieut. T. J. Burke being absent as recruiting officer and Third Lieut. William Blackburn absent on sick furlough.

I have the honor to remain, general, very respectfully, your obedient servant,

JAMES H. WATERS,
*Commanding W. A. Artillery.*

R. J. WINGATE,
*Adjutant-General.*

[Indorsement.]

HEADQUARTERS VALLEY DISTRICT,
*April* 7, 1862.

Please state the number actually engaged and return it.

By order of Major-General Jackson:

A. S. PENDLETON,
*Acting Assistant Adjutant-General.*

---

| | | |
|---|---|---|
| Officers | | 2 |
| Non-commissioned officers | 8 | |
| Privates | 80 | |
| Total | | 88 |
| Whole number engaged | | 90 |

JAMES H. WATERS,
*Commanding W. A. Artillery.*

---

## No. 35.

### *Report of Capt. Joseph Carpenter, Virginia Artillery.*

HEADQUARTERS CARPENTER'S BATTERY,
*March* 27, 1862.

GENERAL: In obedience to General Orders, No. 43, I make the following report of the part taken by my company in the engagement of Sunday, the 23d instant:

I received orders at 1.20 o'clock to take two of my pieces, without caissons, and follow the infantry across a wood west of the Valley turnpike.

After proceeding some half or three-quarters of a mile we observed to our front and right some three regiments of infantry and some cavalry, when we were ordered to open fire upon them; we did so. After firing some ten rounds they retired to the wood in the rear, when I ceased firing.

In a few minutes I received orders to take my battery farther west and on the same ridge upon which the enemy were stationed in strong force. I did so under a very heavy fire of the enemy's battery, which commanded the whole scope of country over which we had to pass; but fortunately we lost not a man. I then proceeded some half a mile under the crest of the ridge to an open field, where I discovered the position of the enemy. I brought my pieces in position and opened fire upon them, which was returned by four pieces of artillery which I had not discovered. I then ordered one of my pieces to fire at the battery. In two or three rounds the enemy's battery was driven from its position. I then directed all my pieces to fire at the infantry and cavalry. They soon retired from view. I then was notified to watch the enemy's movements to our left, and brought my pieces to command the wood to our left, distant some 150 yards, and ordered my pieces to be loaded with canister. Before the order could be executed the enemy made his appearance and opened upon us with small-arms, when I received orders to move my pieces from the field. I did so in good order, losing nothing in our whole operations but one wheel and two horses, which I was compelled to leave.

I am greatly indebted to Lieutenants Carpenter and McKendree for their assistance during the whole engagement, as also to Messrs. Lambie and Fonerden, two of my gunners, for their coolness and the accuracy with which they aimed their respective pieces.

My men generally acted and performed their duty well and like men.

Very respectfully submitted.

JOS. CARPENTER,
*Captain, Commanding Battery.*

[Indorsement.]

HEADQUARTERS VALLEY DISTRICT,
*April* 7, 1862.

Captain Carpenter will please state how many men he had engaged on March 23.

A. S. PENDLETON,
*Acting Assistant Adjutant-General.*

---

We had 48 men engaged.

JOS. CARPENTER,
*Captain, Commanding Battery.*

---

## No. 36.

*Report of Col. Jesse S. Burks, Forty-second Virginia Infantry, commanding Third Brigade.*

HEADQUARTERS THIRD BRIGADE,
*Camp near Woodstock, Va., March* 27, 1862.

SIR: In obedience to an order from Maj. Gen. T. J. Jackson, I beg leave to submit the following report of the part taken by the Third Brigade in the action of March 23, near Winchester, Va.:

My brigade was marching in rear of Major-General Jackson's forces, and on arriving near the field of battle was halted by his order, and I was ordered to take position in a field on our right wing, and was ordered to hold my brigade as a reserve, supporting the batteries stationed there, together with my own battery, which came up with my brigade. I was also ordered to check any advance of the enemy on our right wing. The enemy threatened our right flank, but did not advance.

Soon after the attack was made on the enemy's right wing I was ordered to send forward Captain McLaughlin's battery, supported by a regiment. I obeyed the order, sending the Twenty-first Virginia Regiment, under command of Lieutenant-Colonel Patton. Near the same time I received an order to send Captain Carpenter's battery forward, which I did, supported by the First Virginia Battalion, under command of Captain Bridgford.

Still later in the afternoon I was ordered to bring up the balance of my brigade. I immediately ordered forward my battery, under command of Lieutenant Pleasants, supported by the Forty-second Virginia Regiment, under command of Lieutenant-Colonel Langhorne. At the same time I sent an order to Colonel Campbell, commanding Forty-eighth Virginia Regiment, to bring forward his regiment, which had been left several miles in our rear to protect our baggage (that duty being performed by the different regiments in turn). This regiment (although obeying the order promptly) did not arrive until after the battle was over. The battery and the Forty-second Regiment moved rapidly to the scene of action, and on arriving the regiment was ordered to form on the right of the Fifth Virginia, which they did promptly. The battery was then ordered to retire, by a special order of Major-General Jackson, which they did in good order. The Forty-second Virginia, in conjunction with the Fifth Virginia, opened a terrific fire upon the enemy, causing them to recoil. The Forty-second Regiment's officers and men acted bravely, not one retiring until finding we were flanked. It being nearly dark, I gave the order to retire. They retired some 400 yards, when they were halted and formed by their commandant, Lieutenant-Colonel Langhorne.

It would be invidious to make distinction, as every officer and private, from the lieutenant-colonel down, did his whole duty.

I deem it but justice to state that the Forty-second Regiment was the last to leave the field of battle. The Twenty-first Virginia, under Lieutenant-Colonel Patton, and the First Virginia Battalion, under Captain Bridgford, being detached from the brigade and not coming under my notice, I refer to the reports made by their commandants, and I have been informed that all (officers and men) discharged their duty faithfully.

Below you will find a statement of the casualties of the different regiments engaged.*

Lieut. Robert C. Noonan, of Frederick County, Maryland, was killed while acting as a volunteer lieutenant in Company B, Twenty-first Virginia Regiment.

Capt. R. N. Wilson, my assistant adjutant-general, acted as my aide during the fight, and discharged his duty faithfully. For particulars of names of the parties killed, wounded, and missing I refer to the ac-

---

*See p. 384.

companying reports of the commandants of regiments and the battalion.

Very respectfully,

JESSE S. BURKS,
*Colonel, Commanding Third Brigade.*

Capt. A. S. PENDLETON,
*Acting Assistant Adjutant-General, Valley District.*

P. S.—For the information of the major-general commanding I will state that very few of the wounded men are mortally wounded, and the most of them will be fit for duty in a short time.

---

## No. 37.

***Reports of Lieut. Col. John M. Patton, jr., Twenty-first Virginia Infantry.***

CAMP NEAR MOUNT JACKSON, VA.,
*March* 26, 1862.

SIR: In obedience to orders from headquarters I beg leave to submit the following report of the part borne by the Twenty-first Regiment Virginia Volunteers in the battle near Winchester, on the 23d instant:

On reaching the field of battle we were ordered by you to support the Rockbridge Artillery, commanded by Captain McLaughlin, and, in company with that battery, were shortly afterward ordered into position. In marching to this position the force was exposed for a considerable time in an open field to a severe fire from the enemy's artillery, as also afterward when under cover of a hill in rear of the battery. The enemy's guns were admirably served, their shell bursting in many instances at close quarters, but fortunately with no loss to the regiment, except one man slightly wounded and another stunned for a moment.

McLaughlin's battery was admirably posted on a height equally commanding with that of the enemy's, and my regiment remained immediately in their rear and in supporting distance during the space of two hours or more. While the artillery fight was progressing Colonel Echols' regiment was on the left of our position, and was about this time suddenly attacked by an overwhelming force of the enemy's infantry. As soon as the musketry was heard the major-general commanding, who was near us at the time, ordered me to form line of battle in the direction of the fire and support Colonel Echols in case he was driven back; this occurred very soon.* I threw the regiment forward into line on first company. The movement was well and promptly performed; yet so quick were the movements of the enemy that the regiment received a volley from them before it was quite finished. I immediately ordered the fire to be returned, and from this time forth the rattle of musketry was incessant. Meantime a large portion of Colonel Echols' regiment rallied on our left flank, and this small force for a considerable time held back an overwhelming force of the enemy. The enemy were twice driven back and were substituted by fresh troops.

By this time the ammunition of the regiment was nearly exhausted

---

*See postscript to Patton's second report, p. 404.

and the front was becoming thin by the retirement of those whose cartridges were out and by the loss of killed and wounded. Those who fell back were ordered to rally behind a re-enforcing regiment, which by this time had gotten up and was formed in line about 50 yards in our rear. It was advanced and took the place of our regiment.

At or about this time a regiment of the enemy appeared on our right flank and advanced within about 50 to 70 yards. With the assistance of various officers, among whom Capt. F. D. Irving, Company D, and Sergeant-Major Page were conspicuous, we rallied all of the regiment whom we could find with ammunition and posted them along a fence, by which we flanked in part the flanking enemy. From this point, in co-operation with the skirmishers from the main body, a galling fire was kept up on the enemy. They in their turn were broken and retired. They did not again appear, but were immediately substituted by a fresh regiment, which, in co-operation with those on our front, made a galling cross-fire on our troops. The day was pretty well spent, when an aide of the general commanding ordered me to retire with the regiment.

The regiment went into this battle with 22 commissioned officers, 43 non-commissioned officers, and 205 privates. Out of this number their loss was 60 in killed, wounded, and missing, of whom 9 are missing, and may or may not be wounded.

Paper A,* herewith presented, contains a detailed statement of these losses.

The regiment made a most gallant stand at the close of two days' forced marching. Though foot-sore and weary, their hearts were firm, and they did great execution on the enemy.

The want of commissioned officers was seriously felt. Many lieutenants and eight captains were absent. Almost all the latter and some of the former had been sent home, in obedience to general orders, on recruiting service.

It would be invidious, perhaps, to make mention of individual instances of gallantry which came under my observation. There were many such, both among the commissioned, non-commissioned officers, and privates, and doubtless many occurred which I did not see. I therefore report merely that the officers and men generally behaved well and did their duty.

I cannot close this report, however, without mentioning Lieut. Robert C. Noonan, of Frederick City, Md., lately appointed, as I understand, a lieutenant of artillery in the Confederate Army. While awaiting his appointment he attached himself as a volunteer lieutenant to Company B, of this regiment, and fell while gallantly doing his duty.

Great credit is due to Dr. R. T. Coleman, surgeon of the regiment, for the energy and foresight by which he was enabled to bring from the field almost all of our wounded. We are also indebted both to field officers, cavalrymen, and artillerymen for bringing some of them away on their horses.

Respectfully submitted.

JNO. M. PATTON, JR.,
*Lieutenant-Colonel, Commanding.*

Col. JESSE S. BURKS,
*Commanding Third Brigade.*

---

*Tabulated on p. 384.

HDQRS. TWENTY-FIRST REGIMENT VIRGINIA VOLS.,
*April* 7, 1862.

COLONEL: Since my report of the battle of the 23d ultimo was written I have had a conversation with an officer of Colonel Echols' regiment, and from the facts stated by him I am led to fear that some seeming, though unintentional, injustice to that regiment may be done by a portion of the language I use. To prevent the possibility of such a thing I beg leave to amend it as in the annexed statement, and request that the same may be forwarded and the report altered in these particulars.

Respectfully, your obedient servant,

JNO. M. PATTON, JR.,
*Lieutenant-Colonel, Comdg. Twenty-first Virginia Volunteers.*

Col. JOHN A. CAMPBELL,
*Commanding Second (late Third) Brigade, Army of the Valley.*

On second page of the report, instead of the words, "this occurred very soon," insert "very soon after a considerable body of our men, whom I took to be Colonel Echols' regiment or a portion of it, fell back," and on same page, "Meantime a large portion of Colonel Echols' regiment," insert "Meantime the troops who fell back" rallied, &c.

---

## No. 38.

*Report of Lieut. Col. D. A. Langhorne, Forty-second Virginia Infantry.*

HDQRS. FORTY-SECOND REGIMENT VIRGINIA VOLS.,
———, ——— —, 1862.

SIR: I beg leave to submit the following report of the part borne by the Forty-second Regiment in the engagement of the 23d, near Winchester:

The regiment had been held in reserve until late in the day, when ordered to the scene of action. They marched by flank, right in front, very rapidly, nearly the whole way in double-quick time. While on our way we were exposed to the fire of the enemy's artillery, many of whose shells burst near us, but without effect. We were ordered to form on the right of the Fifth Regiment. The guide led my right up near the right of the Fifth, which immediately commenced to advance. I had, consequently, to bring my regiment into line faced by the rear rank. We formed under the fire of the enemy, who were in line of battle just over the crest of the hill, with skirmishers behind trees on the top.

After commencing our fire we gradually changed our front forward on one of the interior companies without any formal movement, in order to adapt ourselves to the position of the enemy, who otherwise would have gotten around our right flank. Our firing, though a little too hurried at first, was afterward delivered with becoming deliberation, and, I trust, with effect.

The men fought with great bravery and most industriously. The officers all, as far as I observed and have been able to learn, bore themselves gallantly. Among so many it might be deemed invidious to mention any except those whose devoted courage cost them their lives. I refer to Captains Morris and Rector, who fell while gallantly discharging their duties.

Our men stood bravely up to their work until ordered to withdraw by Colonel Burks, whose presence and activity greatly inspired the regiment. The order to retire being imperfectly heard, we fell back very much scattered and in haste, but rallied within 500 yards of the enemy, who advanced only to the edge of the woods. A small portion of the regiment while falling back was separated, and joined us under their officers after reaching the main road; the remainder was placed under charge of Captain Hale, and we entered the main road where we had left it and awaited orders.

Colonel Burks ordered us toward Newtown. So far as I could ascertain we were the last regiment to leave the field.

Respectfully submitted.

D. A. LANGHORNE,
*Lieut. Col., Comdg. Forty-second Regiment Virginia Vols.*

Col. J. S. BURKS,
*Commanding Third Brigade.*

P. S.—Accompanying the above you will find a report of casualties, a summary of which I append below. There were 19 commissioned officers, 52 non-commissioned officers, and 222 privates in the engagement.*

---

## No. 39.

*Report of Capt. D. B. Bridgford, First Virginia Battalion.*

HEADQUARTERS FIRST VIRGINIA BATTALION,
PROVISIONAL ARMY CONFEDERATE STATES,
*Bivouac near Woodstock, Shenandoah Co., Va., March* 26, 1862.

SIR: In obedience to an order received from Col. Jesse S. Burks, commanding the Third Brigade, I have the honor to transmit to you, for his information, a report of the operations of the First Virginia Battalion, Provisional Army Confederate States, under my command, on the 23d instant, after it was separated from the rest of the brigade.

At 3 o'clock in the evening the battalion was ordered to support Captain Carpenter's battery of artillery, and accordingly followed that battery from the position then occupied by the brigade to a point about a quarter of a mile to the left and front. Here the battery halted and opened fire upon a battery of the enemy directly in front of it, which also maintained quite a rapid fire of shot and shell. The firing was kept up on both sides about an hour. Many shell exploded to the rear and on the flanks of the battalion, but none of them did any injury.

At 4.30 o'clock the battalion proceeded, by order of Major Pendleton, about half a mile to the left and front, across an open field, to a hollow in rear of the position occupied by McLaughlin's battery of artillery, for the purpose, as Major Pendleton stated, of reporting to Colonel Burks. Here we found two or more other regiments. The firing of shot and shell continued, and many of the enemy's shell burst near us, but without effect.

About 5 o'clock we heard a discharge of musketry a short distance in front of us. I sent Lieut. Oscar White, acting adjutant of the bat-

---

* Casualties tabulated on p. 384.

talion, to report to Colonel Burks for orders. He was unable to find Colonel Burks, but reported to General Jackson, who sent orders to me to carry the battalion into action. As the battalion was advancing we met General Garnett, who ordered us to move forward into position. We proceeded accordingly over two or three wooded ridges to the point at which the firing of musketry occurred.

Several other corps advanced to the same point along with us. The firing of musketry continued. As we were advancing in line of battle, and had approached very near the crest of a hill occupied by our line, Second Lieutenant Overton, of Company A, informed me that General Garnett had ordered the battalion to be marched to a position nearer the left of our line. But there is some doubt whether the order was given by General Garnett or Colonel Grigsby. I ordered the battalion to march to the left; but before I gave this command the extreme left of the battalion had commenced that movement under the order of a field officer, believed to be either General Garnett or Colonel Grigsby, who addressed the order directly to the men and not through the medium of the officers.

Owing to this fact the left wing of the battalion and a part of the right wing was separated from the remainder of the battalion and some confusion ensued, and a part of the right wing of the battalion, comprising Captain Thom's company (C) and a part of Captain Jones' company (E), not hearing the order, proceeded to the right, while the rest of the battalion marched to the left. After this separation I saw no more of Captains Thom and Jones and the men under their command during the action. The rest of the battalion was assigned a position in an open field just behind the crest of the ridge occupied by our line and next to the regiment on the extreme left of our line, believed to be Colonel Echols'. This position was directly opposite the enemy's line, at a range of not more than 20 yards.

We immediately took part in the action. The firing was general and continuous along both lines. The ground we occupied was soon dotted with dead and wounded men. The fire of the enemy was exceedingly severe.

The colors of the battalion were planted on the crest of the ridge by Color-Sergeant Kenney, under the guidance of Captain Leigh, of Company A. This officer acted with the most conspicuous gallantry during the whole of the action. He took a most exposed position by the side of the colors, and never left it except to bring up his men to the crest of the ridge and point out to them where to aim their fire. He was perfectly cool and collected, and encouraged his men to fight bravely and effectively by example and direction.

Shortly after the firing commenced on our part Second Lieut. John Heth, commanding Company D, fell near the colors, pierced by a ball through the body, while gallantly directing the fire of his men.

First Lieut. John A. Turner, commanding Company B, who insisted upon taking part in the operations of the day, notwithstanding the fact that he was quite ill and feeble, behaved in an exceedingly gallant manner. Second Lieutenant Overton, of Company A, behaved with great gallantry, exerting himself to make the men move forward to the crest of the ridge and deliver their fire effectively. Second Lieutenant Coltram attracted my attention by similar conduct.

Acting Sergeant-Major Duggan fell in advance of the colors with a ghastly wound in his face while in the act of taking aim at the enemy.

The men, especially the non-commissioned officers, acted with great courage.

The action continued with undiminished fury until 6.30 o'clock, when I received orders to fall back, fighting as skirmishers. Before this order was received the whole line to our right, as far as I could perceive, was falling back in great confusion. The retreat became general. After passing over the ridge next behind us an attempt was made by Captains Thom and Leigh and Lieutenants Coltrane and Overton, and perhaps others, to rally the men, and partially succeeded; but the enemy advancing and pouring a heavy fire upon us, and the crowd of fugitives rushing by us, the attempt proved ineffectual and the movement became a general and complete rout. The fugitives were threatened on their right by a detachment of the enemy's cavalry, and many of them would have been captured but for the interposition of a company of our cavalry, commanded, as I have been informed, by Captain Sheetz. Officers and men pursued their course either singly or in squads.

Night soon came on. Many of the officers and men of the battalion gathered together at a bivouac at a point on the Strasburg road 11 miles from Winchester and about 6 miles from the battle ground, where we found our wagons. Here the battalion was reorganized and resumed its place in the brigade.

In respect to that part of the right wing of the battalion which, as I have stated, was separated from the main body, I learn from Captain Thom, of Company C, that at the time of that separation he proceeded with the men under his command to the right, in pursuance of an order to that effect from General Garnett, and took a position in our line; that the firing on both sides was exceedingly hot; that the enemy's line in front of that portion of our line was twice broken; that soon after reaching that position he received a ball against his left breast, which was prevented from penetrating his body by a small copy of the New Testament in a pocket of his shirt, and one through the fleshy part of the palm of his right hand, and fell; that he then gave orders to Lieutenant Randolph to go forward with the company, and that the men under his command did not fall back until the line was entirely broken.

Captain Thom adds that Lieutenant Randolph behaved in a most gallant manner, as did also Second Lieutenant Howard. I learn from Lieutenant Randolph and others that shortly after the firing commenced Captain Jones was seen to get upon a stump and wave his sword, cheering his men forward, and then fall headlong to the earth.

Captain Jones' fate is not yet ascertained. He was left upon the field, and I trust that he still lives; but if he has fallen, he has died a glorious death, sword in hand.

Second Lieutenant Heth was carried off the field and left at a farmhouse in the vicinity. I fear that there is little reason to hope that he will survive his wound.

I cannot close this report without making honorable mention of the active and efficient services rendered during the day by Lieutenant White, acting adjutant of the battalion.

I have the honor to transmit to you along with this report, for the information of Colonel Burks, a detailed statement of our loss. It will be perceived that our battalion went into the action with 11 commissioned officers, 17 non-commissioned officers, and 159 privates. Of these, 6 were killed, 20 wounded, and 21 are missing, making 47 in all.

I have the honor to be, sir, your obedient servant,

D. B. BRIDGFORD,
*Capt., Comdg. First Va. Batt., Prov. Army Conf. States.*

Capt. R. N. WILSON,
*Assistant Adjutant-General, &c.*

## No. 40.

*Report of Col. Samuel V. Fulkerson, Thirty-seventh Virginia Infantry, commanding Fourth Brigade.*

HDQRS. BRIGADE, ARMY OF THE NORTHWEST,
*Camp near Mount Jackson, Va., March* 26, 1862.

SIR: On the night of the 22d instant, while in camp, near Strasburg, I received an order from the major-general commanding to have my baggage packed and move my command, consisting of the Thirty-seventh Virginia Volunteers, commanded by Lieut. Col. R. P. Carson; the Twenty-third Virginia Volunteers, commanded by Lieut. Col. A. G. Taliaferro, and the Danville Artillery, commanded by Lieut. A. C. Lanier, at dawn on the following morning on the road toward Winchester.

Accordingly I marched off and proceeded about 10 miles, when I was filed off from the road to the left about one-half mile and placed in a piece of woods. I was then ordered to take my infantry force and scour a body of woods standing still farther to the left and extending parallel with the road leading to Winchester. I threw forward skirmishers and proceeded through the woods, followed by the Second Virginia Volunteers, Colonel Allen. When I reached the open land, and finding no enemy in the woods, I reported to the major-general commanding, when he rode forward and ordered me to turn a battery of the enemy, which had opened fire upon us from a commanding hill across the fields in my front, and at the same time he informed me that I would be supported by General Garnett.

I threw my command into column by division at full distance, the Thirty-seventh in front, and, after tearing down a portion of a plank fence, entered the fields directly in front of the enemy's position, from which he instantly opened a galling fire upon us. After going in that direction for some distance I turned a little to the left, which brought the right flank of my command next to the enemy's position. The ground at this point being marshy and several fences interposing, the advance was a good deal retarded but steady, the enemy all the while throwing shell and shot into the column with great rapidity.

On the enemy's right and near his position stood a small cluster of trees. I thought that if I could so direct my course as to place that grove between me and the enemy's guns I would be protected from his fire. But so soon as I had reached the desired point a battery placed in the open ground beyond the trees opened a terrible fire upon me. I then turned still farther to the left and took shelter in a piece of woodland, into which the enemy poured a very hot fire of shell and grape for some half an hour.

In the mean time the enemy threw a heavy column of infantry on the brow of the hill below his guns, seemingly for the purpose of resisting a charge upon the position. My advance up to this point, a distance of about half a mile, was under a fire that might well have made veterans quail. But my officers and men pressed steadily forward, instantly closing up when a break was made in the column by the enemy's shot. I then moved across a hill and took position in a hollow, where General Garnett had his brigade sheltered, and reported my position to the major-general commanding. At this point I was much annoyed by the enemy's shell, but only had one man wounded by it.

In a short time the Twenty-seventh Virginia Volunteers (Colonel Echols) moved forward as skirmishers and soon engaged the enemy, when I instantly put my command in line under cover of some timber and moved forward across a field under a most destructive fire of musketry. I reached a stone fence, which extended from the left flank of our forces, already engaged with the enemy, behind which I took position, thus forming the left of our line. On reaching the stone fence I found two regiments of the enemy a short distance in the field beyond, which were evidently trying to get possession of the same fence. My command at once opened a very destructive fire, which in a short time strewed the field with the dead and wounded of the enemy. He withstood the fire but a short time, when he gave way and fled to the woods in his rear and to a stone fence which joined to and ran at a right angle with the fence behind which I was.

I immediately detached a portion of the Thirty-seventh and placed them in position at the junction of the two stone fences for the purpose of dislodging that portion of the enemy which had taken shelter behind one of them. This was soon effected, and the enemy driven entirely from the left flank of our line. He left one stand of colors upon the field.

In a short time the right wing of our line gave way, it being nearly night, and the enemy advancing to the position just left by our right wing, thus placing himself on my right flank, threatening my rear, I ordered my command to fall back to the next piece of woods. Some stone fences and a mill-pond produced some confusion and separated a few of my men from their regiment, and on the opposite side of the pond a few were captured by the enemy's cavalry. I rallied the remainder in the woods, intending to render such assistance as I could to Colonel Burks, who was now engaged with the enemy. But it being dusk and the firing having ceased, and seeing Colonel Burks retiring through an adjoining field, I proceeded to my encampment, near Newtown.

My command had been greatly reduced by furloughs and men on the recruiting service. Many of my officers were also absent on recruiting service or sick. I went into the action with 397 men in the Thirty-seventh and 160 in the Twenty-third, making a total of 557. The artillery was not engaged.

I have to regret the loss of several valuable officers, who were killed or wounded. In the Thirty-seventh Lieut. J. C. Willis was killed. Capt. R. E. Cowan and Lieut. P. S. Hagy were, I fear, mortally wounded, and the latter taken prisoner. Capt. James Vance and Lieuts. George A. Neel and P. S. Hagy were wounded (the latter mortally, I fear) and taken prisoners. Capt. Thomas S. Gibson and Lieut. Charles H. C. Preston wounded. The enemy's cavalry got in the rear and captured some ambulances with some of my wounded.

In the Twenty-third Captain Walton and Lieutenants Crump and Curtis were wounded. Captain Seargeant is missing.

My whole loss is as follows: In the Thirty-seventh, 12 killed, 62 wounded, and 39 missing; total loss in Thirty-seventh, 113. In the Twenty-third, 3 killed, 14 wounded, and 32 missing; total, 49. Aggregate in both, 162.

I cannot speak in suitable terms of the brave conduct of my officers and men, and where all acted so well it would be unjust to discriminate.

To Lieutenant-Colonel Taliaferro, of the Twenty-third, and Lieutenant-Colonel Carson and Major Williams, of the Thirty-seventh, I am especially indebted for their distinguished gallantry throughout the contest.

My adjutant, William S. Rice, exhibited great courage and coolness in executing my orders.

Surgeon Daily and Assistant Surgeon Dennis, of the Twenty-third, deserve great praise for their attention to the wounded under the hottest fire.

Appended I transmit a list of the killed, wounded, and missing.*

Respectfully,

SAM. V. FULKERSON,
*Colonel, Commanding Brigade.*

Lieut. A. S. PENDLETON,
*Acting Assistant Adjutant-General, Valley District.*

---

## No. 41.

*Report of Lieut. Col. A. G. Taliaferro, Twenty-third Virginia Infantry.*

CAMP NEAR MOUNT JACKSON, VA.,
*March* 26, 1862.

COLONEL: As my commanding officer, I beg leave to report the following as to the part taken by my regiment in the late battle fought near Winchester, on the 23d instant, its strength on that day, casualties, &c.:

As you are aware, our operations were upon the extreme left of the army to which your command was ordered.

The morning report of that day gave us only 2 captains, 6 lieutenants, 9 sergeants, and 160 men, rank and file, fit for duty, the regiment being sadly reduced by leaves of absence to re-enlisted men.

Of this number I have to report 3 killed, 14 wounded, and 32 missing.

Where all behaved so well I find it impossible to discriminate; officers and men alike bore themselves bravely and gallantly.

To the members of my medical staff my thanks are especially due for their prompt attention to the wounded, which was fearlessly given, and under showers of shot and shell and small-arms.

All of which is respectfully submitted.

ALEX. G. TALIAFERRO,
*Lieutenant-Colonel, Comdg. Twenty-third Virginia Volunteers.*

Colonel FULKERSON,
*Commanding Fourth Brigade, Virginia Volunteers.*

---

## MARCH 27-31, 1862.—Operations in the vicinity of Middleburg and White Plains, Va.

*Reports of Col. John W. Geary, Twenty-eighth Pennsylvania Infantry.*†

HEADQUARTERS ADVANCE BRIGADE,
*Middleburg, Va., March* 27, 1862—4 p. m.

SIR: Upon reaching here about noon to-day I found there were about 200 cavalry and 200 infantry in and around the town, being advised of

---

* Tabulated on p. 384.

† See also Series I, Vol. V, pp. 511-517, for Geary's report of operations in Loudoun County, Virginia, February 25-May 6, 1862.

their presence by their pickets beyond, who fled upon our approach. The cavalry were of Colonel Stuart's and Captain White's commands. I took possession of the town and pursued the cavalry, who fled precipitately to a woods nearly 2 miles distant, some of my rifles bearing upon them as they started. They at first evinced a design to make a stand just beyond the town, and evidently intended maneuvering to get a pursuing force on the flank with their infantry. We threw a few well-directed shells among them in the woods, when they again fled. No enemy are now in sight. I am occupying a good position here, and will encamp for the night.

I have been informed credibly that General Stuart is at or near The Plains, with a force of about 3,000 men, and it is rumored that about 2,000 are at or near Piedmont. As I now shall probably encounter superior forces, and having horses and men provided, I hope that you will send me the two pieces of cannon belonging to my battery. You will observe the necessity of this to enable me to cope with greater numbers.

Very respectfully, your obedient servant,

JNO. W. GEARY,
*Colonel Twenty-eighth Regiment Pennsylvania Vols., Comdg.*

Lieut. G. B. DRAKE,
*Acting Assistant Adjutant-General, Second Brigade.*

---

HEADQUARTERS ADVANCE BRIGADE,
*White Plains, Va., March* 30, 1862.

GENERAL: In obedience to orders to march to this point on the Manassas Railroad, I reached here yesterday afternoon at 2 o'clock with my whole command, having left Middleburg the same morning at 7 o'clock. The latter place was reconnoitered for some considerable distance in circuit, but no enemy could be found, the rout upon our occupation of the town having effectually driven them toward the mountains. Upon reaching this place I found no troops, and that there had been none for several days, the last having been White's cavalry, who I am informed communicate such of our movements as they can learn to rebel officers below here. I have encamped at the base of a hill, and hold the strongest position in view.

Owing to the great inclemency of the weather, having rained and sleeted from late in the afternoon all night, it continues so this morning, rendering it impossible to reconnoiter with any satisfactory result. As soon as sufficiently clear I will make a tour of examination and report at once thereupon. At present the atmosphere is foggy, the clouds lowering, and the trees and ground covered with ice and snow half an inch thick.

I have received no official documents from headquarters for several days. Major Atwood handed me a memoranda of instructions taken from communications he destroyed to prevent them falling into the hands of the enemy.

I have the honor to be, general, very respectfully, your obedient servant,

JNO. W. GEARY,
*Colonel Twenty-eighth Regiment Pennsylvania Vols., Comdg.*

Brigadier-General ABERCROMBIE,
*Commanding Second Brigade.*

HEADQUARTERS ADVANCE BRIGADE,
*White Plains, Va., March* 31, 1862.

GENERAL: Yesterday afternoon I examined the line of the railroad from this point to Salem, and also to Thoroughfare. The road to Salem is in good running order. The telegraph wire has been pulled down and cut in two or three places and two poles have been cut away. The insulators all remain, and this slight damage can be repaired in a few hours. The road to Thoroughfare is also in good order, the only break being a burnt bridge about 1½ miles this side of the town. It was 40 feet long, in two spans 20 feet each, resting on a stone pier in the center. This pier still stands undisturbed, and the bolts of the bridge are undestroyed. Near it, on the side of the road, are about 50 new rails, and at Thoroughfare between 200 and 300 more. A great stench is noticeable in Thoroughfare, arising from the smoldering remains of a large quantity of meat destroyed by fire by the rebels to prevent it falling into our hands. Since our occupation of this place the rebels have evacuated Warrenton. White's cavalry has retired to Warrenton Springs.

I will continue my investigations to-day and report. All is now quiet, and no enemy in sight.

Very respectfully, your obedient servant,

JNO. W. GEARY,
*Colonel Twenty-eighth Regiment Pennsylvania Vols., Comdg.*

Brigadier-General ABERCROMBIE, *Comdg. Second Brigade.*

---

**MARCH 28-31, 1862.—Operations on the Orange and Alexandria Railroad, Va., including affairs at Bealeton and Rappahannock Stations.**

## REPORTS.

No. 1.—Brig. Gen. Oliver O. Howard, U. S. Army.
No. 2.—Lieut. Marshall H. Rundell, Battery G, First New York Light Artillery.
No. 3. —Brig. Gen. James E. B. Stuart, C. S. Army.

## No. 1.

*Report of Brig. Gen. Oliver O. Howard, U. S. Army.*

HEADQUARTERS CAMP WARRENTON JUNCTION,
*March* 29, 1862.

COLONEL: Having received orders from the headquarters of this Army Corps, dated March 28, 1862, to take command of a reconnoitering force, composed of three regiments of my brigade and one of General Meagher's, and all of the cavalry here present, I have the honor to report that I marched from camp at the appointed time yesterday morning. I organized my force with a large advance guard; thoroughly covered my front and flank by skirmishers. At about 2 miles' distance from this place the scouts of the enemy appeared a mile ahead. As we pressed on they discharged their carbines at my scouts and retired. My scouts and skirmishers returned the fire. Being beyond effective range no harm was done on either side. As soon as the Parrott guns under Lieutenant Rundell reached a fair position I had him open fire on about a company of the enemy just in the edge of some woods. They fled toward our left. This operation was repeated constantly during the march. Sometimes one squadron and sometimes as many as three squadrons appeared and disappeared on our front and flanks. We constantly pressed forward toward the Rappahannock, driving the cavalry before us till within 3 miles of that river. Here a force of infantry was reported advancing at double-quick. I formed in order of battle; ordered the advance guard forward into a good position. I soon ascertained that the remnant of the enemy's infantry on this side of the river was running for a train of cars nearer to me than themselves. As soon as possible Lieutenant Rundell fired in the direction of the train.

As soon as this train had passed the Rappahannock bridge I heard a heavy explosion, much like the blasting of stone. My command was brought forward as fast as possible to a point half a mile this side the river. I then discovered quite a large force on a high ridge. Immediately the Parrott guns were brought into action on a high plat of ground near the railroad. Then the enemy opened upon me with two or three Parrott guns. I moved the battery to a better position and closer range toward my right and front, supporting it by cavalry, and at the same time took possession, by the Fifth New Hampshire Regiment, of a field work which the enemy had left a short time before. I had now ascertained that the entire force opposed was across the river, a battery and apparently infantry on the heights to the left of the railroad, a body of cavalry and a large body of infantry to the right of the railroad. I then ordered up Captain Hazzard's battery to a position near the field works before mentioned. The captain brought it up at a trot, instantly came into action as each piece got upon the ground, and fired in rapid succession upon the cavalry force to our front. He continued firing there till the enemy's cavalry had entirely disappeared in the woods beyond their position. I then sent his battery, supported by the Fifth New Hampshire, to a new position, to shell out some infantry still farther to the right. He fired a few rounds and the enemy disappeared. I kept a strong show of force near the river bank till dark, and then moved back beyond effective cannon-range and bivouacked, picketing strongly at the fords.

At sunrise this morning I put my command in motion for this place, while I made a careful reconnaissance along the river bank with a cavalry guard and sent Major Connor along the railroad to bring me a report of the bridges and depots burned. His guard of infantry fired a few shots into a small body of soldiers apparently endeavoring to remove some hay from the depot opposite him at the burnt bridge. I send a sketch of the works near the burnt bridge, also a map of the railroad, found by a private of the Eighty-first Pennsylvania Regiment. I found quite a large collection of cattle on the abandoned land in that vicinity, and have driven in about 230 head. Some of them may belong to Mr. Bowen, who has taken the oath of allegiance. He claims about 60 head. For these and some forage I receipted to him. The enemy burned what culverts he could and depots and store-houses and the stacks of forage on our route. I found the Rappahannock bridge a burning mass when I reached it. I think the enemy fired about twenty-five rounds from his battery. Lieutenant Rundell fired fifty-one rounds from his section of Parrott guns and Captain Hazzard forty-three rounds. I inclose a report of Lieutenant Rundell. Three prisoners were taken and have been turned over to the provost-marshal. The Fifth New Hampshire Regiment, the Sixty-first New York Regiment, the Eighth Illinois Cavalry, and the artillery were the only portion of my command much exposed to the enemy's fire. One man of Lieutenant Rundell's command was thrown down by a shell striking at his feet, but was unhurt. All without exception behaved well.

Very respectfully, your obedient servant,

O. O. HOWARD,
*Brigadier-General, Commanding.*

Col. J. H. TAYLOR,
*Adjutant-General and Chief of Staff:*

P. S.—The enemy's force a part of two brigades, about 5,000 strong, cavalry included. One man of Hazzard's battery and three of the Sixty-first New York Regiment were wounded by accident, not mortally.

O. O. HOWARD,
*Brigadier-General.*

[Inclosure.]

*Major Connor's memorandum.*

First, Rappahannock bridge burned (four-span bridge). One pier blown up; two stone piers left. It was a Howe truss bridge. Depot buildings of the station near Rappahannock River burned. Six miles this side of the Rappahannock a small three-span bridge burned (22-foot-span). Seven miles this side the Rappahannock a small bridge and about a quarter of a mile of the railroad destroyed. From this point to Rappahannock River railroad in running order, with the above exception. From 8 miles this side the Rappahannock River the railroad track and bridges are all destroyed to Warrenton Junction; track torn up, ties burned, and iron carried off.

---

## No. 2.

*Report of Lieut. Marshall H. Rundell, Battery G, First New York Light Artillery.*

CAMP RICHARDSON'S DIVISION,
*Warrenton Junction, March* 29, 1862.

CAPTAIN: Having been instructed to report to you yesterday morning with a section of 10-pounder Parrott rifled guns, pertaining to Frank's light battery G, First New York Artillery, I accordingly started at 10 o'clock a. m. yesterday, and took my place in the advance guard, composed of the Fifth Regiment New Hampshire Volunteers, Colonel Cross, and one squadron of the Eighth Regiment of Illinois Cavalry, Colonel Farnsworth. After marching about 2 miles I fired one shell at a vedette of the enemy's cavalry. About 1½ miles farther I found a battalion of the enemy's infantry formed in line of battle and fired two shells, which had the effect of immediately dispersing them. Without changing position, threw four shells into some buildings to the left of the infantry, under the impression of dislodging a hidden enemy.

Moving the section upon the ground previously occupied by the enemy's infantry, I directed two shells into the corner of a wood to the right and in a line with the railroad, and likewise three to the left at a small body of cavalry. Next to this I shelled some cavalry nearly 2 miles from the depot and to the right. Having been ordered to the front along the line of the railroad, I shelled another depot and fired into a train. Half a mile farther to the front and right shelled another detachment of cavalry. Moving again to the front, dislodged some of the enemy from a small intrenchment. At this place two pieces of the enemy's artillery opened fire upon us. After moving to the right and front, and sheltering my limbers and caissons behind a building, I opened fire, with the effect of silencing the enemy's artillery.

This closes the proceedings of my section of artillery during the 28th instant; having expended 35 shells, 14 spherical-case, and 2 percussion shells; total, 51 rounds. The fire of my guns, with few exceptions, seemed to be very effective. I returned from this reconnaissance at about 1 o'clock p. m. to-day.

I have the honor to be, very respectfully, your obedient servant,

MARSHALL H. RUNDELL,
*First Lieutenant Company G, First New York Artillery.*

Capt. F. SEWELL,
*Acting Assistant Adjutant-General, Howard's Brigade.*

---

## No. 3.

### *Report of Brig. Gen. James E. B. Stuart, C. S. Army.*

HDQRS. CAVALRY BRIGADE, ARMY OF THE POTOMAC,
*March* 31, 1862.

MAJOR: I have the honor to submit the following report of the operations of the troops under my command for the last few days:

After keeping the enemy under close observation for weeks past by my cavalry pickets, disposed along a front reaching from the Blue Ridge to the close vicinity of the Potomac, frequently penetrating, by the daring boldness of a few scouts, to his rear, it was ascertained that on the 26th [28th] a large column was advancing along the general direction of the railroad 7 miles below. Col. W. E. Jones, First* Virginia Cavalry, was sent with a strong detachment of cavalry to observe the enemy, and his reports from time to time satisfied me that a movement with a force vastly superior to my own was going on. Although having no intention of offering him battle, I determined to keep him observed, threaten him with demonstrations toward his flanks and in front, and by every possible means delay his progress and secure accurate information of his strength and, if possible, his designs. The utmost vigilance was maintained by the cavalry intrusted with this important duty, and is worthy of the highest praise.

Several prisoners were taken that evening, from whom, as well as the observation made by Captain Gaither, whose scouting party first ascertained the movement, I knew that not less than a division composed the force; believed it to be a mere demonstration or reconnaissance, and determined to put on a bold front, and did everything to check its progress compatible with the safety of my command, communicating frequently and fully with the general-in-chief of this army my

---

* There is confusion in the records as to Jones' status. He appears as colonel of the First, Seventh, and Eleventh Regiments Virginia Cavalry.

impressions of the character of the movement as well as every step of its progress.

There was a long and unnecessary delay at Cedar Run, improved by the enemy, confronted by about 50 cavalry, in making a grand display, apparently of his entire force, in battle array on the opposite side of Cedar Run, while an extensive line of skirmishers and a battery of artillery exchanged shots with a few of Captain Blackford's company, First Virginia Cavalry, dismounted, with Sharps carbines.

It was ascertained here that they had a large wagon train, which was very ostentatiously paraded to view. A careful estimate of the force was made from the favorable opportunity this afforded, and Captain Blackford, on duty at the time, set it at 10,000. I believe, therefore, that to be the maximum; but to know whether supporting columns were in rear became of the utmost importance, and I that night, as I wrote to the general, selected Principal Musician David Drake to head a small party of observation to reach the railroad in rear of the enemy's position and report before morning. The officer to whom I specially intrusted starting Drake (Colonel Jones) forgot to deliver my message, consequently the party failed to start until next morning.

The enemy failed to make any move till 11.30 a. m. the next day, at which time their column was observed in motion along the line of the railroad and marched steadily upon Bealeton Station, where my reserves of cavalry and 300 infantry were then located. I made dispositions for defense, determined not to leave till his approach was so near as to make his intention to march to that point unmistakable. From the open ground about Bealeton I commanded a fine view of the column advancing slowly, but steadily, using a caution very characteristic of the enemy, and which greatly facilitated a close observation of his movements, which opportunity I did not fail to improve. When within about a mile of Bealeton they formed line of battle, and having delayed there as much as practicable by a show of resistance, I dispatched the infantry first slowly to the rear and kept part of the cavalry menacing his front, sending Colonel Robertson on the right and Colonel Jones on the left to threaten the enemy's flanks, with orders to carry it as far as compatible with safety, and then retire diagonally toward the railroad bridge. Time was thus given the infantry to retire 4 miles with perfect regularity, even slowness, and to join their respective regiments, under General Ewell, fresh for combat, instead of jaded and panic-stricken. Upon arriving near the bridge, to gain additional time to remove some cars of stores, I ordered Captain Blackford to dismount a few of his men and take post in advance to check the enemy's advance, and I also stationed my own battle-flag so as to show above the crest of the ridge, to represent a regiment. Some half a dozen men thus held the advance of the enemy, with infantry, cavalry, and artillery, at bay till all the stores were removed. My cavalry, having forded the river, were directed by me to extend General Ewell's lines in line, and subsequently I acted under orders of General Ewell.

The scout I sent to the enemy's rear returned next morning while the enemy's skirmishers were reported still in view opposite us, and reported that the wagon train was on its way back the day before beyond Warrenton Junction. Believing the enemy to be already in retreat, I ordered all the cavalry to horse and proceeded immediately to follow in pursuit. Colonel Jones, First Virginia Cavalry, led the way and pressed the pursuit with great vigor and success—capturing about 25 officers and men, mostly cavalry, and wounding several—to the near vicinity of Warrenton Junction, where the enemy was encamped for the night. The other regiments were too slow in their movements to participate in the captures made. I came up with Colonel Jones near Warrenton Junction, near which point three or four of my men of my escort captured four of the enemy.

Colonel Jones' report is herewith inclosed,* including the operations of his regiment since leaving Centreville.

It is proper to remark that the Second, Fourth, and Sixth Virginia Cavalry shared cheerfully the privations detailed in Colonel Jones' report and performed important service in their appropriate spheres of action.

The detachment (four companies) of [the] Second Virginia Cavalry, under Lieutenant-Colonel Munford, has performed distinguished service along the Piedmont region, and I commend to the notice of the general that officer's activity, good judgment, and unceasing vigilance, conspicuously displayed in the signal service he has rendered.

Col. W. E. Jones' excellent service speaks for itself in his accompanying report, while Company L (Washington County Rifles), of his regiment, under the lead of the brave, intelligent, and efficient Capt. W. W. Blackford, distinguished itself no less in the bush than in the saddle, harassing the enemy at every step.

It is not a mere matter of form that impels me to acknowledge the valuable services of my staff throughout the operations of my command since leaving Centreville:

Maj. Dabney Ball, useful in every sphere, displayed on the field of the Rappahannock the dashing boldness of the huzzar, tempered with the cool judgment of the veteran warrior.

I am greatly indebted to Lieut. Chiswell Dabney, aide, and Lieut. J. T. W. Hairston, C. S. Army, acting assistant adjutant-general, who displayed signal ability and efficiency on the field.

Lieuts. Samuel [R.] Johnston and M. W. Henry, C. S. Army; Lieut. Redmond Burke, [and] Captain Towles, volunteer aide, though absent from the action by my authority, in various operations preceding rendered valuable service.

My escort, commanded by Corpl. Henry Hagan, composed of young men of rare intelligence and ability and intrepidity, showed themselves capable of performing in the bivouac or on the field all the various and important duties of the staff officers. Young Farley has been constantly on hand, showing the utmost courage and coolness and doing unmistakable execution.

The casualties to the enemy are not known to [me]. My command, though exposed to artillery fire for half a day, none at all.

A list of prisoners has been already forwarded, consisting of about 50 officers and men, mostly cavalry.

Adjutant Mosby and Principal Musician David Drake, of the First Virginia Cavalry, volunteered to perform the most hazardous service, and accomplished it in the most satisfactory and creditable manner. They are worthy of promotion and should be so rewarded.

Capt. John Pelham, of the Stuart Horse Artillery, while riding alone on his way to join me, came suddenly upon a sturdy veteran, armed with an Enfield gun, took him prisoner, and marched him up to me.

The gallant conduct of Private James Oden has already been the subject of a special report.

[J. E. B. STUART,
*Brigadier-General, Commanding.*]

*Not found.

## APRIL 1-2, 1862.—Advance of Union forces from Strasburg to Woodstock and Edenburg, Va.

### REPORTS.

No. 1.—Maj. Gen. Nathaniel P. Banks, U. S. Army, commanding Fifth Army Corps.
No. 2.—Col. George H. Gordon, Second Massachusetts Infantry, commanding Third Brigade, First Division.
No. 3.—Capt. George W. Cothran, Battery M, First New York Light Artillery.

### No. 1.

*Reports of Maj. Gen. Nathaniel P. Banks, U. S. Army, commanding Fifth Army Corps.*

EDENBURG, VA., *April* 1, 1862—6 p. m.

We have driven the enemy to-day from Strasburg to Woodstock, a distance of 12 miles, and then to Edenburg, 7 miles beyond. He contested the march most of the way, and at a strong position, in which he contemplated making a stand, as at Edenburg, quite a sharp contest occurred. He burned the bridges in his flight except that at Narrow Passage, which we were enabled to reach in time to extinguish the flames. We lost but one man and had but one wounded. The enemy suffered more, but I cannot state the extent. Colonel Ashby received a shot through his cap, which he exhibited with some satisfaction to the people of Woodstock. Others suffered more severely. The men behaved admirably.

N. P. BANKS,
*Major-General, Commanding Fifth Army Corps.*

Hon. E. M. STANTON, *Secretary of War.*

---

EDENBURG, *April* 1, 1862—6 p. m.

GENERAL: At noon to-day we occupied Woodstock and at 4 our troops were in possession of Edenburg, 7 miles beyond. The rebels contested the whole march, and at Narrow Passage, a place of considerable strength, where there had been some preparations for a defense, quite a sharp fight occurred, and also at Edenburg, where we attempted to save the bridges. They burned three bridges, one above Woodstock and two at Edenburg.

The bridge at Narrow Passage we saved by driving them from the position and extinguishing the flames. The others were beyond our reach. Two of the bridges we shall rebuild at once. Few casualties occurred on our side—Private Martin, Twenty-ninth Pennsylvania Volunteers, who was instantly killed by a shell, and a private of the Second Massachusetts, who suffered a flesh wound in his breast, the ball passing through his breastplate, which saved his life. The loss of the enemy I am not able to state. Colonel Ashby received a shot through his cap, which the people of Woodstock said he exhibited with some satisfaction. Others suffered more severely. The utter exhaustion of our supplies will, I fear, prevent pursuit to-morrow. Jackson has retreated to Mount Jackson. The troops behaved admirably and the march was very vigorous.

N. P. BANKS,
*Major-General, Commanding.*

General MCCLELLAN, *Fairfax Seminary*

## No. 2.

*Report of Col. George H. Gordon, Second Massachusetts Infantry, commanding Third Brigade, First Division.*

HDQRS. THIRD BRIG., FIRST DIV., FIFTH ARMY CORPS,
*Edenburg, Va., April* 3, 1862.

SIR: I have the honor to report that the Third Brigade led the advance of the Fifth Army Corps in its march from Strasburg to this town, distant about 15 miles. The following was the order of advance: Five companies of the Second Massachusetts Regiment, deployed as skirmishers, commanded by Lieut. Col. George L. Andrews; all the disposable companies of the [First] Michigan [Cavalry], commanded by Colonel Brodhead, in all about two squadrons; Battery M, First New York Artillery, of 10-pounder Parrott guns, commanded by Captain Cothran; the Twenty-ninth Pennsylvania Regiment, Col. J. K. Murphy; the Third Wisconsin Regiment, Col. Thomas H. Ruger.

Our march was contested during its entire route by the enemy's skirmishers, and at times, when the position was favorable, by a battery of three 10-pounder and one 24-pounder rifled guns, which opened on my advance on three different occasions: First, as I began the descent of the hill into the town of Woodstock; second, as my column was moving through the narrow passage where the turnpike runs between the North Branch of the Shenandoah on one side and high hills on the other; third, from the hills on the south of the town of Edenburg, while my column was moving into that place.

The admirable manner in which the battery was served by Captain Cothran soon silenced the enemy's guns and caused him to retire with precipitation from his strong position. We have evidences of his loss at his second stand; but as all his dead but one was removed I am unable to state the number of his killed and wounded.

Our loss was Private James Martin and Private William D. Richardson, wounded by a shell, both of Company G, Twenty-ninth Pennsylvania Regiment, and Private Edward Bonney, Company I, Second Massachusetts Regiment, slightly wounded by a rifle-shot, his life being providentially saved by his belt-plate.

Many of my command were upon this occasion for the first time under fire. I cannot too highly praise their efficiency and coolness.

I inclose the report of Captain Cothran, with my further comments thereon.

I am, very respectfully, your obedient servant,

GEO. H. GORDON,
*Col. 2d Mass. Regt., Comdg. 3d Brig., 1st Div., 5th Army Corps.*

Capt. WILLIAM D. WILKINS, *A. A. G., First Division.*

---

## No. 3.

*Report of Capt. George W. Cothran, Battery M, First New York Light Artillery.*

HDQRS. BATTERY M, FIRST NEW YORK ARTILLERY,
*Camp Gordon, near Edenburg, Va., April* 2, 1862.

COLONEL: Agreeably to General Orders, No. 7, Headquarters Fifth Army Corps, Army of the Potomac, Battery M, First New York Artillery, preceded by the Second Massachusetts Infantry, proceeded in the direction of Woodstock, Va., on the morning of the 1st instant. On arriving on the heights near Woodstock the enemy opened fire upon the Third Brigade. I ordered the right and center sections to return the fire, which they did. The enemy, after exchanging a few shots without effect, retreated precipitately. I pursued them beyond Woodstock, when several more rounds were exchanged by my battery and the enemy. A short distance farther on the enemy occupied a strong position, and commenced a rapid fire upon our advancing column as we began the descent near Willow Grove. I put the left and center sections in battery and replied to their fire. The contest was spirited, though short, when the enemy again retired. In the position occupied by the enemy at this point our forces to-day picked up 1 dead rebel, who had been killed by our shells, and from observations since made and from the best information that I could gather from residents in the vicinity and others I am confidently of the opinion that the rebel loss was considerable in both killed and wounded. The enemy kept retreating and firing into us from every convenient eminence, but in every instance I succeeded without much difficulty in dislodging them, at times compelling them to temporarily abandon their pieces.

At Edenburg they retreated across the North Branch of the Shenandoah and took position on an eminence under cover of a piece of woods, and commenced shelling our advancing column. I took position on a hill overlooking the town, when the cannonade became general. In less than half an hour the rebel battery was silenced, and my battery occupied the same position during the night. From the accuracy of our firing I have no doubt but what the enemy sustained some loss at this point, but owing to the great distance, and the fact that the enemy was screened by the woods, it was impossible to ascertain to what extent.

Soon after daylight this morning the enemy opened a brisk cannonade from a point near the position last occupied by them yesterday upon my battery, which was promptly responded to. After firing several rounds they ceased firing. One of their shells destroyed a horse-collar and partially destroyed a horse-blanket in my battery. With this exception we sustained no loss or damage from the enemy's fire of yesterday and to-day.

This morning the enemy used an imported percussion shell, but few of which exploded. The cap is of most ingenious and excellent pattern. On removing the cap of several of them I discovered that no percussion cap had been inserted; consequently no explosion could take place. Whether the omission was accidental or intentional, queries. It may be significant and it may not.

The coolness and courage of my men were highly gratifying to me, while the excellence and accuracy of the firing of the left and center sections, commanded by Lieuts. James H. Peabody and John D. Woodbury, were highly commendable.

I have the honor to remain, colonel, your obedient servant,

GEO. W. COTHRAN,
*Captain, Commanding Battery.*

Col. G. H. GORDON,
*Second Mass. Vols., Comdg. Third Brig., Gen. Williams' Div.*

## APRIL 2, 1862.—Reconnaissance to the Rappahannock River, Va.

### *Report of Col. John F. Farnsworth, Eighth Illinois Cavalry.*

HEADQUARTERS EIGHTH ILLINOIS CAVALRY,
*April* 3, 1862.

COLONEL: Yesterday, in compliance with orders from the general commanding this corps, I made another reconnaissance to the Rappahannock River.

Leaving camp at about 9 o'clock a. m., and dividing my regiment into two columns of about equal strength, I detached one company from each column to act as skirmishers. We proceeded in this manner, Lieutenant-Colonel Gamble leading the column which marched upon the right and I that which marched upon the left of the railroad. Our skirmishers, when formed in line, covered a territory of at least 4½ or 5 miles wide, taking the railroad as a center, and the two columns from 3 to 4 miles apart, and striking the river 2 miles above and below the railroad bridge. I found no enemy until within little over 1 mile from the river, when 10 mounted pickets concealed in the skirts of a woods fired upon my skirmishers as they approached through an open field, not, however, hitting either my men or their horses. Instantly upon firing they turned their horses and fled. About an equal number of my men pursued them rapidly down the road to the river, firing upon them as they could get opportunity. The rebels, upon approaching the ford of the stream, turned to the right and left into the woods, no doubt fearing that the water would so check their flight, if they entered it, as to enhance their danger. After following them some distance in the woods I called my men back. At least one of the enemy was badly wounded in the skirmish. Lieutenant-Colonel Gamble saw no enemy until he came around upon the high ground near the railroad bridge, when the rebels commenced firing shells at his column from the other side of the river. They fired twenty-three shots from two guns. They, however, did us no damage. We then returned by routes a little different, taking forage as we came.

I should mention that Lieutenant Hotopp, in command of the company of skirmishers in advance of Colonel Gamble's column, while passing to the extreme right, became entangled in a thicket. When he extricated himself my men were not in sight. In endeavoring to make his way to them he was suddenly set upon by 5 rebels, and had a narrow escape from being captured by them. He shot one or two of their horses, and, being well mounted, escaped from them. Directly afterward the lieutenant met a squad of the Fourth New York Cavalry, told them of his adventure, and desired them to go with him and capture the rebels. Instead of that, however, they took the lieutenant a prisoner and brought him to camp.

My opinion, based upon all the observation and information I have been able to gather, is that there are no rebel soldiers this side the river with the exception of a few scouts and spies, and that there is but a small force still remaining upon the other bank.

Very respectfully, yours, &c.,

J. F. FARNSWORTH,
*Colonel, Commanding Eighth Illinois Cavalry.*

Col. J. H. TAYLOR,
*Chief of Staff and Adjutant-General.*

## APRIL 7, 1862.—Reconnaissance to the Rappahannock River, Va.

*Report of Lieut. Col. Thomas J. Lucas, Sixteenth Indiana Infantry.*

HEADQUARTERS SIXTEENTH INDIANA REGIMENT,
*Warrenton Junction, Va., April* 7, 1862.

SIR: I have the honor to report that in accordance with your order of the 6th instant I made a reconnaissance to the Rappahannock River with five companies of infantry, four of cavalry, and one section of artillery. The route taken was through fields to the right of the railroad line, and much of the road was barely passable for artillery. I arrived at a position within 300 yards of the river, northwest of the burnt bridge, near 11 o'clock a. m., and there halted. I report one small fortification on the north bank of the river abandoned, and one similar opposite, a little to the right on the southwest bank; also a rifle earthwork about 400 yards to the right and rear of the latter on southwest side, both of which were occupied by pickets or small bodies of the enemy.

Having placed the artillery in position under cover of one company of cavalry, and being unmasked, I shelled the fortifications, which were evacuated by the enemy in great haste without returning fire. The earthworks command the ford at the burnt bridge. The river at the ford is about 300 feet wide, and impassable at this time for wagons, though it can be crossed with cavalry. The range of hills on the southwest side of the Rappahannock and northwest of the railroad line approach the river at the point fortified, while on the southeast side of said road there are portions of table-land. Situated on the northeast bank of the river is a large flouring mill, owned by a person in the Confederate Army, and said to contain a considerable amount of grain. The railroad 4 miles northeast of the river is uninjured and in good running order. From the best information I could obtain the enemy are occupying positions on the Rapidan River. I remained in my first position near an hour and a half, and returned by the same route in good order.

The above is respectfully submitted.

T. J. LUCAS,
*Lieut. Col., Sixteenth Indiana Regt., Comdg. Reconnaissance.*

General J. J. ABERCROMBIE,
*Commanding Second Brigade.*

---

## APRIL 12, 1862.—Skirmish at Monterey, Va.

*Report of Maj. Gen. John C. Frémont, U. S. Army.*

WHEELING, *April* 13, 1862.

Dispatch just received from General Milroy at Monterey, under date of yesterday, states as follows: "The rebels, about 1,000 strong, with two cavalry companies and two pieces of artillery, attacked my pickets this morning about 10 o'clock, and drove them in some 2 miles. I sent out re-enforcements, consisting of two companies Seventy-fifth Ohio, two companies Second Virginia, two Twenty-fifth Ohio, and two of Thirty-second Ohio, one gun of Captain Hyman's battery, and one company of cavalry, all under Major Webster. The skirmishing was brisk for a short time, but the rebels were put to flight with considerable loss. The casualties on our side were 3 men of the Seventy-fifth badly wounded. The men behaved nobly."

J. C. FRÉMONT,
*Major-General, Commanding.*

Hon. E. M. STANTON, *Secretary of War.*

---

## APRIL 12, 1862.—Raid from Fairmont to Valley River and Boothsville, Marion County, W. Va.

### REPORTS.

No. 1.—Brig. Gen. Benjamin F. Kelley, U. S. Army.
No. 2.—Capt. John H. Showalter, Sixth West Virginia Infantry.

### No. 1.

*Report of Brig. Gen. Benjamin F. Kelley, U. S. Army.*

HEADQUARTERS RAILROAD DISTRICT,
*Wheeling, Va., April* 12, 1862.

COLONEL: In my order addressed to Captain Showalter I directed him to kill or capture the following-named persons, who were refugees, sent out to raise companies by John Letcher in the western counties of Virginia, viz: John Righter, John Anderson, David Barker, Brice Welsh, John Lewis, John Knight, and Washington Smith.

Respectfully, your obedient servant,

B. F. KELLEY,
*Brigadier-General.*

Col. ALBERT TRACY, *Assistant Adjutant-General.*

---

### No. 2.

*Report of Capt. John H. Showalter, Sixth West Virginia Infantry.*

FAIRMONT, MARION COUNTY, VIRGINIA,
*April* 12, 1862.

SIR: In pursuance with the inclosed order I proceeded with a part of my command in search of the parties named in the order.

Barker was killed by my men on the Valley River, near the railroad. My men were in three squads; they were commanded by one captain, two sergeants, and two corporals. They also killed Ashcraft. Barker made a prisoner of one of my men, who was sick at his home, and took him to Ashcraft's house. They also killed one Kaufman, who belonged to Righter's gang.

These men all belonged to Righter's company. My men were piloted and assisted by the Boothsville Home Guards. The Home Guards killed a man in Boothsville whom I know nothing of.

J. H. SHOWALTER,
*Company A, Sixth Virginia Infantry.*

Brig. Gen. B. F. KELLEY.

## APRIL 15, 1862—Reconnaissance to the Rappahannock River, Va.

### *Report of Capt. Robert F. Dyer, Co. C, First Maine Cavalry.*

CAMP 1ST ME. CAV., *Warrenton Junction, Apr.* 15, 1862.

We left camp at 9.30 a. m. and proceeded on the line of the railroad. Met two contrabands, who informed us that they left camp of General Smith on the opposite side of the river at 9 o'clock last night; also informed us that a portion of the Confederate Army under his command were encamped there, supposed to be from 5,000 to 7,000 troops; that they were constructing a bridge across the river 2 miles above the railroad, with the intention of crossing, and they were also throwing up earthworks. We then proceeded along the line of the railroad, coming to a house occupied by an Irishman, who informed us that the distance to the river was 2 miles, when it could not have been over three-fourths of a mile. We then proceeded about one-half of a mile to an unoccupied house, where we halted. Adjt. B. F. Tucker, accompanied by Musician A. W. Ingersoll, advanced about one-fourth of a mile to an old earthwork to reconnoiter upon the opposite shore, where they discovered plainly with the naked eye a line of rebel earthworks at intervals for 2 miles; could also see the blacks at work upon them, and through a field glass could see everything within the line distinctly; should judge that there were from 150 to 200 horses picketed in the rear of a grove; could also see a large white house, which we supposed was the headquarters, as we could see a rebel flag flying near the house; could not discover any guns within the earthworks, but judge that the encampment contained from 3,000 to 4,000 troops.

Thinking that we had examined sufficiently we were on the point of leaving, when they opened upon us from a masked battery at the southern extremity of their encampment, throwing canister, one shot striking near Lieutenant Tucker and Ingersoll, another striking about 20 feet from the center of my company in the rear. Immediately another battery opened upon us from the center of their line, throwing 10-pound shot, striking about 40 feet in rear beyond the first shot. Then a third battery opened from the extreme north of their encampment, throwing about a 12-pound shell, after which they came thick and fast from the three batteries, making a cross-fire. There were thirteen shots struck within the vicinity of us before we were able to get out of their range. After getting out of range we thought it was not prudent to make the reconnaissance any farther up or down the river, from the fact of their having such a body of horse within their encampment and being able to cross the river by fords and a bridge.

On our return, a short distance from Bealeton Station, two black women having seen us, came about a mile to meet us, and informed us that they had seen 11 mounted men upon this side of the river this morning dressed in gray uniform, some of whom they knew to be rebels; also that they were in the habit of meeting in the vicinity of Liberty Church a blacksmith named Robert Willis, said Willis being in the habit of coming into our camp and gaining information in regard to our pickets and the position of our encampments which he was known to communicate to the enemy, and they were contemplating to cross the river and surround us to-night or to-morrow night. The same information in regard to the blacksmith Robert Willis was given us from various sources. After leaving there we struck off to the left and visited the Randolph plantations, but could discover nothing further in regard to the enemy.

I remain very respectfully, your obedient servant,

ROBT. F. DYER.

## APRIL 16, 1862.—Reconnaissance to the Rappahannock River, Va.

### *Report of Maj. Robert C. Anthony, First Rhode Island Cavalry.*

WARRENTON JUNCTION, *April* 16, 1862.

In pursuance of orders, we started this morning for the Rappahannock River, stopping to take the blacksmith Robert Willis in charge. Arrived at the river about 1 o'clock p. m. I threw out scouts on both sides of the railroad, one of which, in charge of Lieutenant Manchester, had quite a sharp skirmish with the enemy's pickets. Several shots were exchanged. We had one horse badly wounded. There are no bridges on the river, but below the railroad is a ferry-boat large enough to take a horse. Above the bridge is an encampment large enough to hold 2,000 troops. The embankments I should think would extend nearly 2 miles. The river is quite low, and a bridge could be thrown across in a very short time.

Very respectfully,

R. C. ANTHONY,
*Major, Third Battalion First Rhode Island Cavalry.*

General ABERCROMBIE,
*Commanding Brigade.*

---

## APRIL 16, 1862.—Reconnaissance to Liberty Church, Va.

### *Report of Lieut. Col. Willard Sayles, First Rhode Island Cavalry.*

HDQRS. FIRST RHODE ISLAND REGIMENT CAVALRY,
*April* 17, 1862.

SIR: In obedience to Special Orders, No. 36, from Brigadier-General Abercrombie, I took a squadron from First Rhode Island and one from First Maine, and started from camp at 10 p. m. April 16, 1862. We directed our course to Liberty Church, which we reached about 1 o'clock this morning, having learned from a guide, whom we took from a plantation of one Mr. Randolph, that the enemy in small numbers were in the habit of congregating at this place.

Stopping at the house of a Mr. Willis, we were told by one of his servants that a small cavalry detachment of about 10 had visited that place yesterday morning and another of about 14 in the afternoon, the one coming from and the other going in the direction of the Rappahannock. He also told us that a Mr. Olinger was continually giving assistance to the enemy and receiving them at his house, which is situated in the vicinity of the church. We called upon and after a conversation with him, in which he admitted himself a secessionist, and after contradictory statements relative to his connection with the rebel force, we arrested him. Also, upon similar information, we arrested a Dr. Beale.

We learned from all sources that the enemy are in the habit of daily visiting Liberty Church in small numbers. They are mostly cavalry.

Respectfully,

W. SAYLES,
*Lieutenant-Colonel, Commanding Detachment.*

Colonel LAWTON.

**APRIL 16-17, 1862.—Skirmish at Columbia Furnace; occupation of Mount Jackson and New Market, and skirmish at Rude's Hill, Va.**

## REPORTS, ETC.*

No. 1.—Maj. Gen. Nathaniel P. Banks, U. S. Army.

No. 2.—Abstract from "Record of Events" in Cavalry Brigade, Department of the Shenandoah.

### No. 1.

*Reports of Maj. Gen. Nathaniel P. Banks, U. S. Army.*

WOODSTOCK, *April* 16, 1862—7 p. m.

An entire company, more than 60 men and horses, Ashby's cavalry, were captured this morning at Columbia Furnace, about 7 miles from Mount Jackson, by our cavalry and infantry. The capture includes all the officers but the captain. They will be sent to Baltimore to-morrow.

N. P. BANKS,
*Major-General, Commanding.*

Hon. E. M. STANTON, *Secretary of War.*

—

MOUNT JACKSON, *April* 17, 1862.

Our troops occupied Mount Jackson at 7 o'clock this morning, and are now in front of Rude's Hill, where the enemy appears to be in force. The people report that they intend battle there. They resisted our advance in order to gain time for the burning of bridges and railways, cars, engines, &c., that had accumulated at the terminus of the road; but our movement was so sudden, and the retreat of the rebels so precipitate, that we were enabled to save the bridges, two locomotives, and some cars. All these had been prepared with combustible material for instant conflagration. Many prisoners have been taken, and several fine horses captured from the enemy. The troops have acted admirably. They were in motion at 1 o'clock a. m. Colonel Carroll's brigade, of Shields' division, led the advance on the Back road to the rear of Mount Jackson, and General Kimball on the turnpike; General Williams, with his fine division, bringing up the reserve column. We shall occupy New Market to-night. General Shields has so far recovered as to command his division in person.

N. P. BANKS,
*Major-General, Commanding.*

Hon. E. M. STANTON, *Secretary of War.*

—

HEADQUARTERS DEPARTMENT OF THE SHENANDOAH,
*April* 17, 1862.

Our troops occupy New Market to-night. There has been some artillery skirmishing, but no loss on our side. We have many prisoners.

N. P. BANKS,
*Major-General, Commanding.*

Hon. E. M. STANTON, *Secretary of War.*

---

*See also Jackson to Ewell, April 17, in "Correspondence, etc.," Part III, p. 853

WAR DEPARTMENT,
*Washington, April* 17, 1862.

To you and to the forces under your command the Department returns thanks for the brilliant and successful operations of this day.

EDWIN M. STANTON,
*Secretary of War.*

Major-General BANKS, *Mount Jackson.*

---

## No. 2.

*Abstract from "Record of Events" in Cavalry Brigade, Department of the Shenandoah.**

On the 15th instant this squadron [First Squadron Pennsylvania Cavalry], under command of the junior captain, Greenfield, assisted by detachments of infantry from the Fourteenth Indiana, Fifth Connecticut, Twenty-eighth New York, and Forty-sixth Pennsylvania, made a dash upon a company of the enemy's cavalry quartered in a church near Columbia Furnace, and succeeded in capturing the entire force of 3 officers and about 50 men, with all their horses, arms, and baggage.

---

# APRIL 17-19, 1862.—Skirmishes near Falmouth and occupation of Fredericksburg, Va., by the Union forces.

### REPORTS, ETC.

No. 1.—Maj. Gen. Irvin McDowell, U. S. Army, commanding Department of the Rappahannock.
No. 2.—Brig. Gen. Christopher C. Augur, U. S. Army, commanding brigade.
No. 3.—Col. George D. Bayard, First Pennsylvania Cavalry.
No. 4.—Lieut. Col. Judson Kilpatrick, Second New York Cavalry.
No. 5.—Brig. Gen. Charles W. Field, C. S. Army, with instructions from General Lee.
No. 6.—Lieut. Col. W. H. F. Lee, Ninth Virginia Cavalry.

## No. 1.

*Reports of Maj. Gen. Irvin McDowell, U. S. Army, commanding Department of the Rappahannock.*

HDQRS. DEPARTMENT OF THE RAPPAHANNOCK,
*Railroad between Fredericksburg and Aquia, April* 18, 1862.

We occupied the suburbs of the town of Fredericksburg, the left bank of the Rappahannock, this morning at 7 o'clock.

The troops, under the immediate command of Brigadier-General Augur, left Catlett's Station yesterday and made a forced march across the country of 26 miles.

The advance, under Lieutenant-Colonel Kilpatrick, Second Regiment (Harris) Cavalry drove in the enemy's outposts, charged and captured one of his camps. Lieutenant Decker, Second New York Cavalry, was killed by the enemy in the charge. The troops pushed on the next day

* From return for the month of April, 1862.

at 2 o'clock in the morning. The advance, under Lieutenant-Colonel Bayard, First Pennsylvania Cavalry, was attacked by a body of infantry and cavalry and had a hot skirmish, in which we lost 5 men and 15 horses killed and had 16 men wounded. Several of the enemy were killed and wounded in the charge made on them by Colonel Bayard; the number not reported. The colonel, who it seems is always to have some mark of having been in the thickest of every fight in which he is engaged, had his horse shot four times. The command then drove the enemy's forces, which fell back without further resistance, and which consisted of a regiment of infantry, one of cavalry, and a battery of light artillery, across the Rappahannock, but were unable to save the bridges, which were prepared for burning by having tar, shavings, and lightwood in the crib work, and which were fired as soon as the enemy crossed.

As Fredericksburg is a position of manifest importance to us and to the enemy, whatever course the war may take, I have ordered forward the India-rubber bridge train for temporary use, and beg, if the naval force in the Rappahannock can protect their transit, that enough canal-boats to make a substantial bridge, with the necessary lumber for the purpose, be sent up the Rappahannock. I have ordered forward another brigade of King's division and an additional regiment of cavalry (Sir Percy Wyndham's), and, as the railroad cannot be used at present, I need more wagons to supply the force I now have on the Rappahannock, and beg 100 may be sent to me at Aquia.

As the readiest means of having communication with the right bank of the river, I would like one of the steam ferry-boats in the Potomac, with lumber for temporary wharf, may be sent around.

Please order telegraph established between Fredericksburg and Washington.

Very respectfully, your obedient servant,

IRVIN McDOWELL,
*Major-General.*

Hon. E. M. STANTON, *Secretary of War.*

---

HEADQUARTERS DEPARTMENT OF THE RAPPAHANNOCK,
*Aquia, April* 28, 1862.

I sent up by to-day's boat 17 prisoners, taken by our troops in their advance on Fredericksburg. They are mostly of the Ninth Virginia Cavalry. Some are from Mississippi and Alabama.

I have ordered McCall and his Second Brigade over from Catlett's to Fredericksburg.

IRVIN McDOWELL,
*Major-General.*

Hon. E. M. STANTON,
*Secretary of War.*

---

No. 2.

*Report of Brig. Gen. Christopher C. Augur, U. S. Army, commanding brigade.*

CAMP OPPOSITE FREDERICKSBURG, VA.,
*April* 18, 1862—12 m.

CAPTAIN: I have the honor to report the arrival of my command at this point at 7.30 o'clock this morning, but, I am sorry to say, not in time to save either of the bridges. All accounts agree in representing the bridges as being for several days prepared for burning, by having the cribs filled with light-wood and tar and shavings. These were lighted about half an hour before we came in sight of them, and after the enemy's forces on this side the Rappahannock had passed over. We could see a light battery, a regiment of cavalry, and one of infantry going to the rear as we arrived.

Our march has not been without incident. We came upon the first of the enemy's pickets about 18 miles from Catlett's Station, and were only defeated in capturing it by a little girl from a neighboring house discovering our men creeping through the woods and signaling them to the picket. I at the same time learned from some negroes and others that there was a camp of four companies of their cavalry near the Brick Church, about 5 miles from this place, and that a quantity of forage had just been sent there for their use. Although it would make my march a very long one, I determined, as they would learn from their driven-in pickets that we were on the road, to make an attempt to engage them at their camp, and, if practicable, to follow them immediately to Falmouth and try and save the bridges. I organized the light column as was suggested, and leaving Colonel Sullivan in command of the main body, pushed on. On arriving near their camp I directed the Harris Light Cavalry and one battalion of Bayard's Pennsylvania cavalry, under Lieutenant-Colonel Kilpatrick, to move rapidly forward and attack. This was handsomely done, and the camp and its forage and a few horses captured.

I regret to have to report that Lieutenant Decker, of the Harris Light Cavalry, was killed in the charge. The enemy's cavalry fell back about a mile upon a body of infantry. It being now quite dark, and the command very much fatigued by its long march of 26 miles, I determined to halt them some hours.

Some negroes taken in camp reported that an ambuscade had been prepared for us 2 miles in advance. Shortly after a citizen living in the vicinity came into my camp from Falmouth and reported the same thing, and that he had not been permitted to come up the main road, but had reached us by a by-road, on which there were no pickets, and which came into the main road near Falmouth, some 2 miles beyond the point to which they were reported as lying. He said he had left Falmouth just before sunset; that the bridge was prepared, as stated, for burning, and that he would conduct a command by the by-road and enable it to reach and save the bridge, and get in rear of the enemy at same time. I was satisfied from the reports of the negroes and from other evidence that he was a good Union man, and that it was advisable to venture the attempt, as I knew the desire of the general commanding the department to save this bridge.

I intrusted this enterprise to Colonel Bayard, of the First Pennsylvania Cavalry, who had one battalion of his regiment and two battalions of Harris Light Cavalry, under Lieutenant-Colonel Kilpatrick. He left me at 2 a. m. this morning. Unfortunately the enemy in the mean time changed his point of ambuscade to just beyond where the by-road entered the main road, where the command received a volley of about 200 infantry on the watch for them, and were then charged on by cavalry. The road had been barricaded, too, which prevented their farther advance. They wheeled and charged upon the infantry, killing and wounding several (the exact number not known) and capturing 1 man. Colonel Bayard extricated his command with a loss of 5 killed and 16 wounded and a loss of some 15 horses. Thus disappointed in my attempt to secure the bridge by surprise, I advanced at sunrise with my whole command prepared to fight, but with the exception of a few pickets, saw none of the enemy until my arrival at the river.

I am unable at this time to give you any reliable information on the points suggested in my instructions. I send this by the commandant of the squadron ordered to Aquia Creek per my instructions of yesterday. To-morrow I will send the entire train there with a battalion of cavalry.

I have no reason to believe Colonel Bayard was intentionally misled by our guide, for there is abundant evidence of his having suffered greatly in consequence of his Union sentiments.

I regret to add that our valuable scout (Britton) was severely wounded in the leg.

I am, captain, very respectfully, your obedient servant,

C. C. AUGUR,
*Brigadier-General, Commanding.*

Capt. R. CHANDLER,
*A. A. G., Hdqrs. King's Division, Catlett's Station, Va.*

---

## No. 3.

*Report of Col. George D. Bayard, First Pennsylvania Cavalry.*

CAMP OPPOSITE FREDERICKSBURG, VA.,
*April* 19, 1862.

SIR: According to instructions from the general commanding, at 2 a. m. yesterday morning I started from camp for the purpose of getting in rear of the infantry which was reported in our front and of securing the possession of the bridge over the river from Falmouth. I took with me for that purpose seven companies of the Harris Light Cavalry, Lieutenant-Colonel Kilpatrick commanding, and four companies of my own regiment. Pursuant to directions from the general I pushed forward as rapidly as possible and soon reached the vicinity of the enemy. To Lieut. Col. Owen Jones, First Pennsylvania Cavalry, with four companies—F, E, K, and M—of the same regiment, I assigned the duty of seizing the bridge, rushing across it, cutting down the heavy gates which were reported on the opposite side, and throwing out pickets in advance, purposing to cross myself with the Second Battalion of the Harris Light Cavalry, leaving to Lieutenant-Colonel Kilpatrick, with the remaining battalion of his regiment, the duty of holding Falmouth. As soon as I learned that we had come upon the pickets of the enemy I ordered Colonel Jones forward at full gallop. He went up the hill in front rapidly, and when he reached the top was met with a heavy fire of infantry from all sides. The night was dark and the hill on both sides of the road covered with brush, yet the colonel pushed on under this fire until he found barricades across the road. The enemy still kept pouring in their fire until the companies became disorganized and confused and finally broke. Companies K and E—the first commanded by Captain Williams and the latter by Captain French—fled back to camp without having either horse or man injured. Capt. M. L. French, though deserted by his company, still remained on the field, with Sergt. Jesse Fry, of his company, and behaved as became an officer. The greater portion of Companies F and M were rallied in rear by Colonel Jones.

Determined if possible to have the hill, I led forward the Second Battalion of the Harris Light Cavalry, with Captain McIrwin's company in advance. We charged up the hill within 25 yards of the barricades, when they poured upon my column a galling fire, when the companies retreated. I finally rallied them, but as I knew nothing of the enemy's force, except that both infantry and cavalry were in my front, stationed behind the impediments placed in the road, and as from the heaviness of the fire it appeared to be quite a heavy force, I decided to withdraw my command. To Lieutenant-Colonel Kilpatrick, with his battalion, I gave the post of rear guard, with orders to cover my retreat, and to his coolness and good judgment I am much indebted, and he speaks in the highest terms of Major Davies, commanding that battalion, for his good conduct.

I dispatched Lieutenant Thomas, my adjutant, to the general at once to inform him of what had taken place. The enemy made no pursuit, and I withdrew the companies into an open field beyond a pine forest and awaited further orders. When orders came for me to watch the enemy I threw out a squadron of the Harris Light Cavalry for that purpose, who shortly reported the advance of our skirmishers, when I pushed forward as rapidly as possible and soon joined the column.

I inclose the reports of the adjutant of the Harris Light Cavalry and my own surgeon of the casualties among the men; and that our loss has been so small we must attribute to the inaccuracy of their fire. Colonel Jones' loss is 3 killed and 9 wounded, and Colonel Kilpatrick's 4 killed and 7 wounded. My loss in horses has been heavy, the battalion of my own regiment having 11 horses killed and 6 disabled, while the battalion of the Harris Horse which I led in the fire probably lost as many, but I have no report of that. My own horse was badly injured by two or three bullets.

To Lieutenant-Colonels Kilpatrick and Jones I must return my thanks for their coolness and valuable aid throughout the affair.

Capt. A. Davidson, of Company F, First Pennsylvania Cavalry, was taken prisoner by the enemy, but succeeded in capturing his guard and bringing him into camp in turn. He led his company dashingly into the trap which had been laid for us, and I would call the attention of the general to his gallant behavior.

Captain Richards, of Company M, of same regiment, behaved throughout most gallantly.

Both Lieutenants Leaf and Sample, of his company, were hurt, and the latter's horse killed in the *mêlée*.

I regret, sir, my failure to secure the bridge, but there was too strong a force of infantry, artillery, and cavalry, as I have since learned, for me ever to have succeeded with cavalry alone.

I am, sir, very respectfully, your obedient servant,

GEO. D. BAYARD,
*Colonel First Pennsylvania Cavalry, Commanding.*

Captain HALSTED,
*Assistant Adjutant-General, General Augur's Brigade.*

[Indorsement.]

CAMP NEAR FALMOUTH, VA.,
*April* 20, 1862.

Respectfully forwarded.

The object of this expedition was to attempt to surprise the enemy and save the bridge at Falmouth. Col. Bayard, finding the enemy well prepared to prevent this, did right not to advance any farther under the circumstances. His conduct is commended throughout this affair.

C. C. AUGUR,
*Brigadier-General.*

---

## No. 4.

*Report of Lieut. Col. Judson Kilpatrick, Second New York Cavalry.*

HEADQUARTERS HARRIS LIGHT CAVALRY,
*Camp near Falmouth, Va., April* 19, 1862.

GENERAL: I have the honor to report that my advance guard, under Captain E. F. Cooke, Company B, was fired upon and charged by nearly 50 rebel cavalry about 3 miles this side the Spotted Tavern. Captain Cooke charged several times and was completely successful. Maj. H. E. Davies' battalion was then ordered to the front. He skirmished with the enemy for several miles, driving him to within 2 or 3 miles of his camp, when the whole battalion charged, closely followed by the entire regiment. The enemy rapidly fled to his camp, where a stand was made by the whole rebel force, consisting of several companies of cavalry, under Colonel Lee. We reached him with a shout and a blow. The resistance was feeble, and in a moment he was fleeing in all directions. Two we killed or wounded and 4 taken prisoners.

I regret the loss of Lieut. James N. Decker, Company D, who fell at the head of his men, having reached the center of the rebel camp.

The entire regiment—officers and men—hope that, in this their first effort, they have conducted themselves in a manner worthy their honored name and the general under whom they are proud to serve.

Respectfully submitted.

J. KILPATRICK,
*Lieutenant-Colonel, Commanding Harris Light Cavalry.*

Brigadier-General AUGUR.

[Indorsement.]

HEADQUARTERS OF THE BRIGADE,
*Camp near Falmouth, Va., May* 5, 1862.

Respectfully forwarded.

The conduct of the officers and men of this regiment during the day was commendable for enterprise and daring. This report has been delayed in consequence of not receiving a report from Colonel Kilpatrick of the property, horses, and arms captured by him this day. I have called upon him for it frequently, but as he is not under my command I have no means of enforcing the requests.

C. C. AUGUR, *Brigadier-General.*

---

## No. 5.

*Reports of Brig. Gen. Charles W. Field, C. S. Army, with instructions from General Lee.*

BRIGADE HEADQUARTERS,
*Seven miles from Fredericksburg, on Telegraph Road,*
*April* 19, 1862—6 a. m.

GENERAL: I reached this point with my brigade yesterday about noon. A very sharp skirmish occurred about 4 a. m. between the enemy's cavalry and some of my infantry, with complete success on our part. The enemy appearing to be advancing in force, I fell back across the river, burned all the bridges, and retired from the town. As far as accurately ascertained about one brigade is the estimated force, but it is thought that symptoms, such as fires in the interior, indicate more. A prisoner taken (mortally wounded and died in a few hours) made a statement confirming this, though another one gave accounts of much larger force.

My future movements will now depend upon yours. I hope through scouts and other means to get more accurate information in the course of the day. If you carry out the plan of joining General Jackson, the probability is that I shall soon have to fall still farther back. If not, and you propose any other movement, I will co-operate in anything you suggest. Please inform me speedily what your course will be.

I am, general,

CHAS. W. FIELD.

General EWELL.

---

HEADQUARTERS,
*Richmond, Va., April* 19, 1862.

Brig. Gen. C. W. FIELD,
*Commanding, &c., near Fredericksburg, Va.:*

GENERAL: Your letter of the 17th instant is received.* I desire that you shall do everything in your power to prevent the enemy from advancing from Fredericksburg or making that place a base. I shall order to Hanover Junction to support you, in such manner as you may direct, two local regiments of artillery, armed and serving as infantry, a field battery, and a body of horse. I have received information, obtained from a wounded prisoner, that the enemy's force at Fredericksburg consisted of one regiment of cavalry about 500 strong, one regiment of infantry, and two batteries of artillery, and that their entire force on the Lower Potomac is less than 5,000. You will use every exertion to ascertain the strength and movements of the enemy and keep me informed of the same. You will also communicate with General Ewell as to the movements of the enemy, in order that in case of necessity that officer may send you re-enforcements if it be in his power. I desire also that you will render all the assistance you can in obstructing the Rappahannock River below Fredericksburg, to prevent the ascent of the enemy's boats. I am informed by the Secretary of the Navy that some naval officers have been sent to the Rappahannock for that purpose, and also to provide fire-ships to oppose the enemy. You will also watch closely any movements of the enemy from Urbana or Tappahannock in the direction of West Point or the Pamunkey River. Should such an attempt be made you will do everything in your power to prevent it. I call your attention particularly to the importance of exercising the utmost caution in destroying the railroad and bridges. This should not be done except as a measure of extreme necessity, as great injury may result from our advance being retarded or prevented. In connection with the subject of preventing the enemy's boats from ascending the Rappahannock, I am informed to-day that there are six tug-boats off Urbana, two very large, moving up the river.

I am, very respectfully, your obedient servant,

R. E. LEE,
*General.*

---

*Not found.

HEADQUARTERS AQUIA DISTRICT,
*April* 20, 1862.

GENERAL: I have the honor to submit the following report of my recent movements, terminating in the evacuation of Fredericksburg:

My brigade was posted as follows: The Ninth Virginia Cavalry Regiment in two divisions, respectively under command of Colonel Johnson and Lieutenant-Colonel Lee, picketing an arc in my front, its left resting on the river above Fredericksburg, extending by way of Sackett's Mill, Aquia Church, Potomac Creek, &c., to the river below Fredericksburg. Lieutenant-Colonel Lee reporting that the enemy were advancing on the Warrenton road, in the afternoon of the 17th instant I ordered two companies of Colonel Brockenbrough's regiment (Fortieth Virginia) across the bridge to re-enforce the four companies of his regiment, already on that line, to support the cavalry. I ordered Captain Pegram's battery to a position commanding the Falmouth bridge; Colonel Mallory with his regiment (Fifty-fifth Virginia) to a point in Fredericksburg in supporting distance; Lieutenant-Colonel Walker, Fortieth Virginia, commanding the Fifth Alabama Battalion, having charge of the burning of the lower bridges, cotton, &c. All preparations having been made for this object, Captain Lewis, C. S. Navy, was charged with the duty of burning the shipping.

About 3 o'clock on the morning of the 18th instant report was brought of formidable demonstrations of the enemy. The skirmish occurred of which Lieutenant-Colonel Lee's report is herewith transmitted. On hearing the firing Colonel Brockenbrough, previously in position at the Falmouth Bridge, immediately, on his own judgment and afterward sanctioned by me, crossed over with the remainder of his regiment and re-enforced Colonel Johnson, Ninth Cavalry, who was on the Telegraph road.

About 6 a. m. an advance in heavy force was developed, and I proceeded to withdraw all my troops to this side of the river; ordered the bridges to be burned, the shipping, cotton, &c., burned, and every preparation made to retire from the town. All this was done in perfect order and without haste or fear, and with the unanimous concurrence of the senior officers then present and subsequently approved by all.

Up to this hour (6 o'clock) I had hoped his numbers might not be too great for me to resist him successfully on the other side. Whatever the enemy's strength may have been, all share with me the regret that the peculiar situation of the town rendered it impossible to give him such a reception as I think we could have done but for the exposure of the inhabitants and much valuable property, public and private, to certain destruction.

Even supposing but a single brigade opposed to me, with my effective force of not more than 2,200, to have risked an engagement on the other side, with a broad river in my rear, an immense amount of property in the town to be sent back or destroyed, and the country on this side for miles commanded by the opposite heights, I thought very hazardous.

In abandoning the town and destroying the property I knew that interested persons would raise a hue and cry, but I am perfectly willing to bide my time for vindication of the course I thought proper under most trying circumstances to pursue. In carrying out my instructions and the suggestions of humanity, and at the same time making a strong resistance, I barely succeeded in extricating my troops and setting fire to the bridges.

I have the honor to be, very respectfully, your obedient servant,

CHAS. W. FIELD,
*Brigadier-General, Commanding.*

General R. E. LEE,
*Commanding Confederate Forces, Richmond, Va.:*

---

BRIGADE HEADQUARTERS,
*Camp Spottsylvania, April* 20, 1862—12 m.

GENERAL: I have the honor to report that Lieut. Col. W. H. F. Lee has just arrived in my camp, and makes the following statement:

Reconnoitered Fredericksburg on yesterday. Saw what he thought to be the encampment of five regiments; said to be three of infantry and two of cavalry and two batteries. Does not think that the force is less than 5,000. Members of the committee of citizens who visited their headquarters for conference estimate it variously from 5,000 to 13,000. Conversed with members of this committee. General Augur told them he could make no terms with them until the arrival of General McDowell, whom he expected to land to-day (19th) at Aquia Creek with a large force. Afterward heard a report that McDowell was landing. He also told the committee that he expected the trucks up by water and intended building the railroad. Went up in sight of the bridges; no reconstruction of them as yet. All the bridges completely destroyed except one-third of the Falmouth Bridge, saved on the Falmouth side by the enemy.

Reports to-day from several sources six steamers at Aquia Creek; yesterday passed one landing troops; they were passing down.

I will as soon as practicable establish the telegraph operator at Milford.

I have kept up daily communication with General Ewell; he is, however, 40 miles from me, and I only 14 miles from the enemy. I will make a detailed report by to-morrow of the causes and manner of my evacuation of Fredericksburg, as well as of the skirmish with the advance guard.

It is reported from Dr. Stuart, of King George, as obtained from a negro, that the enemy were landing from the Potomac in large numbers. The negro was in their camp. Mr. Taylor, who lives in sight of the obstruction below Fredericksburg, says that five tugs came this morning up to that obstruction and endeavored to pass. These reports, other than Colonel Lee's, are not authenticated, but believed to be entitled to confidence.

I beg leave to add that I believe there is a much larger force of the enemy in my front than the commanding general has any conception of, and that he meditates an advance upon Richmond from this point in force.

I have as yet burned no bridges this side of Fredericksburg, and will not do so until the last moment.

I have the honor to be, very respectfully, your obedient servant,

CHAS. W. FIELD,
*Brigadier-General, Commanding.*

General R. E. LEE.

BRIGADE HEADQUARTERS, SPOTTSYLVANIA CO.,
*Telegraph Road, 14 miles from Fredericksburg, April* 20, 1862.

GENERAL: I have accurate information of the force of the enemy at Fredericksburg—5,000, eight pieces of artillery. Reports of troops landing at Aquia Creek, this not ascertained. By last accounts they had not crossed the river, but supposed to be preparing to do so. I have taken a position here favorable for a stand if I have some re-enforcement. My effective force, all told, is about 2,000. I fell back to this point in order to place the streams subject to high water between me and the enemy. My cavalry are in rear, half the distance perhaps. Give me two or three regiments of infantry and I think we may be able to make formidable resistance here to a force not much exceeding what is represented.

It is reliably ascertained that in our skirmish with them we killed some 25 or 30; their own statement to a spy. Our own loss not known to be more than 3 or 4 killed and wounded, 8 or 10 perhaps captured and scattered; most probably the latter.

Very respectfully,

CHAS. W. FIELD,
*Brigadier-General, Commanding.*

Would it not be well to send the telegraph operator late of Fredericksburg to locate himself at Milford immediately and prepare for operations?

Respectfully,

CHAS. W. FIELD,
*Brigadier-General.*

[Inclosure.]

APRIL 20.

GENERAL: I forward note just handed me by Mr. Gordon from Mr. Barton to yourself. Mr. Gordon also brings a message from Mr. Slaughter (at 5 p. m. yesterday). He had had an interview with Augur, who states that he (Augur) has three brigades (13,000 men) with him, and that McDowell brings twelve more (25,000 men). I have sent the company to Guiney's with full instructions to report to you and me.

Your note to station a picket at Chancellorsville just in. Will do so. Some hours previous to its receipt had sent Captain Crutchfield, who knows the country well, in charge of a scouting party to that point. Will report when he arrives.

Everything quiet on our front so far. Have taken and shall take every possible precaution within my power to guard against surprise.

Respectfully,

J. E. JOHNSON,
*Colonel, Commanding Ninth Virginia Cavalry.*

[Indorsement.]

These papers are just received. I send them for the information of the general commanding.

C. W. FIELD.

[Sub-inclosures.]

FREDERICKSBURG, *April* 19, 1862.

GENERAL: You have been advised of the proceedings of the mayor and council, our resolutions, and an appointment to meet General Augur, commander of brigade, &c.

To-day that committee had an interview with Augur, and we are in the hands of the Philistines. We learn from him that yesterday General McDowell and his division landed at Aquia; that he was expected at his (Augur's) position, just opposite, to-day or to-morrow, and since we left we have seen a large gathering from the position northeast of Augur's brigade. We have reason to suppose this is the arrival of McDowell's brigade, and they say—that is, Augur said—[they had] the means of throwing a bridge over the river in a few moments. He said it might be a day or two before he would cross. I think they are fully informed of your position and numbers. I give you the information, such as it is, that I have. My opinion is that the enemy means to advance; that they have McDowell's division, whatever it is, and that their object is to conceal their purpose by stating that they should require support; should take what is necessary, but would respect private property, &c. I have but a moment to indite this hasty note. The messenger waits.

With much respect, yours,

T. B. BARTON.

APRIL 19, 1862—8 p. m.

DEAR SIR: The Rev. Mr. Lacy conversed with three generals this evening, of whom Augur was not one. They said that General King commanded that division, and it amounted to 13,000; that General McDowell's command landed at Aquia to-day, and the whole amounted to 30,000; that they were on their way to Richmond; that McClellan's army was the finest ever seen in this country; that McDowell's was the flower of that force, &c. That they stated this to Mr. Lacy is certainly so; that a very large accumulation of force is opposite Fredericksburg is also true. I give you the intelligence for what it is worth.

Very respectfully,

T. B. BARTON.

[Indorsement.]

APRIL 20.

This is just received from old Mr. Barton, of Fredericksburg, whom no doubt the general knows well to be reliable. I send it for his information.

Very respectfully,

C. W. FIELD,
*Brigadier-General.*

NEAR PORT ROYAL, CAROLINE COUNTY, VA.,
*Sunday Morning, April* 20.

Colonel JOHNSON:

DEAR SIR: Seven steam tugs anchored at Port Royal yesterday evening and spent the night. They have but few men aboard. I suppose they are carrying provisions up to the army at Fredericksburg. The passing of steamers up and down the river breaks into my arrangements. I must have security of coming back after I cross to the other side. To get over there is easy enough, but coming back is the thing. There are so many negroes to inform against me that I shall have to move with the utmost precaution.

Yours, truly,

W. W. D.

Col. J. E. JOHNSON:

SIR: Mr. Dillard sent me word this morning to stay here and watch. Four of the Yankee gunboats came up about an hour ago. They discovered me and shot at me. They have no troops on board except a few marines. They have landed on the Stafford side of the river. I killed one of the officers, who was about to shoot at me.

J. A. TOOLE,
*At Dickison's Farm, 7 miles below Fredericksburg.*

---

## No. 6.

*Report of Lieut. Col. W. H. F. Lee, Ninth Virginia Cavalry.*

CAVALRY CAMP,
*Spottsylvania, Va., April 20, 1862.*

CAPTAIN: I have the honor to forward a report of the recent engagement between the force under my command and the enemy's cavalry, near Falmouth, on Thursday and Friday, 17th and 18th instant:

At 10 o'clock on Thursday morning my scouts reported the cavalry of the enemy approaching by the Warrenton road. I at once re-enforced my picket in front by ordering Lieutenant Peirce, Lancaster Cavalry, to report with his company to Captain Swan, commanding pickets. I also sent Captain Hatchett, Lunenburg Dragoons, with his company, on the Sackett's Mill road. These companies held the enemy in check, retreating slowly, until 4 p. m. The enemy's force was a full regiment and my force four companies of cavalry. I had but few men in camp, owing to the long line of picket that I was obliged to keep up.

Finding that the enemy was too strong, I determined to fall back toward Falmouth. I took a position at Greeve's [Grove] Chapel, about 1 mile from Falmouth, where I was supported by four companies of infantry of the Fortieth Virginia Volunteers, under Major Taliaferro, and a squadron of cavalry, under Capt. B. B. Douglas. Agreeably to orders I determined not to yield my ground except to superior forces. Major Taliaferro was posted in front with his infantry, and erected a barricade across the road. The cavalry was posted on the right and left and in rear. We remained in position until 1 o'clock Friday morning, when the pickets reported the enemy coming down the Warrenton road at full gallop. We waited in silence until they came within 20 yards of the barricade, when the infantry poured a deadly fire into and repulsed them. Within ten minutes they returned to the charge with a loud yell, and were again repulsed by a destructive volley and driven back. They seemed to be satisfied after the second charge and did not renew the attack.

When it was light enough to make examination 4 dead bodies and several wounded were found; 7 or 8 dead horses in one place. I learn from good authority that the enemy acknowledge in the morning skirmish 3 killed and 7 wounded; among them a lieutenant, whose horse and equipments we have. In the conflict at night they confess to 30 killed.

I testify with pride and gratification to the steady gallantry of my officers and men.

Major Taliaferro merits unqualified commendation for his coolness and gallantry on the occasion. To the unflinching courage and steady, deliberate fire of his men is mainly due the successful repulse of this formidable attack. Our loss was 1 private killed and 6 missing.

I am, captain, your obedient servant,

W. H. F. LEE,
*Lieutenant-Colonel Ninth Virginia Cavalry.*

Capt. G. F. HARRISON,
*Assistant Adjutant-General.*

---

**APRIL 17-21, 1862.—Expedition from Summerville (Nicholas Court-House) to Addison, W. Va.**

*Report of Maj. Ebenezer B. Andrews, Thirty-sixth Ohio Infantry.*

SUMMERVILLE, VA., *April* 22, 1862.

SIR: In obedience to your instructions I left this post for Addison, Webster County, on the morning of April 17, for the purpose of destroying any parties of armed rebels that might be found and of co-operating with certain other Federal troops who were ordered to concentrate at Addison. My command was composed of parts of Company E, Captain Hollister, and Second Lieutenant Patton, with 45 enlisted men; Company G, Captain Palmer, First Lieutenant Stanley, and Second Lieutenant Clarke, with 50 enlisted men; Company I, Captain Nye, and First Lieutenant Clarke, with 51 enlisted men; and Company K, Captain Walden, and First Lieutenant Stearns, with 50 enlisted men; in all, 200 enlisted men.

We started at 7.30 o'clock and reached Andrew Hickman's before noon. In the afternoon we marched to within a mile of Gardner's store and halted for the night, making for the day a march of 22 miles. We captured that evening Jonathan Griffin, a bushwhacker, who confesses to having been in the skirmish at Gardner's store last January.

The next day (Friday) we reached Addison at 2 o'clock p. m. That evening we captured a man named Lynch, who, if not a bushwhacker, has been in sympathy and communion with them, and had just returned from their camp at Holly Creek, a branch of Elk, which empties into the latter stream from the east below Addison. He was well armed when captured.

The next morning (Saturday) Captains Morgan and Murrin, of the Tenth Virginia Volunteers, reached Addison from Upshur County. They had found no armed rebels on their route. About noon Lieutenant Lawson, of the First Virginia Cavalry, from Sutton, and Captain Darnall and Lieutenant Connoly, of the Tenth Virginia Volunteers, with 80 men, from Bulltown, reached Addison. They reported that the cavalry had a skirmish on Thursday with a band of bushwhackers, estimated to be 50 or 60 strong, on Holly Creek, and killed 2 of them. On Friday, re-enforced by Captain Darnall, they met the rebels again and entirely routed them, killing 7. On Saturday morning they killed another of the band. They also reported the capture of a considerable number of horses which had been stolen from Union men, and also some goods recently stolen from a store in Bulltown.

On Sunday morning I started on my return, having sent all the other forces, numbering in all 220 men, to scour thoroughly the infested Holly region. We marched only 13 miles, having halted at the only place where we could obtain shelter from the rain.

The next morning (Monday) we started at 5 o'clock and reached Summerville a little before night, having marched 25 miles. A part of one company, which I sent off the road to capture a rebel, marched 31 miles. It was a rainy day and the marching difficult. All reached camp in good condition; every man in his place in the ranks. No straggling whatever was allowed during the expedition. I attribute the power of endurance shown by the men to the habit of daily drill with their loaded knapsacks.

Although we could find no armed rebels on our own route, nor hear of any, yet the expedition as a whole will, I think, be productive of much good. The people of Webster County have been shown that they are entirely in the power of the Federal Army, and signs of incipient loyalty are seen in many neighborhoods. The bushwhackers have also been taught a lesson by their losses of life and property which they will not soon forget. At Addison I obtained the muster roll of the Webster Dare Devils, a guerrilla company organized at Addison by Duncan McLaughlin, of Addison, now a delegate in the legislature at Richmond. His small salt-works at Addison, which I found in operation and from which the rebels of Webster County have obtained their salt, I ordered to be destroyed.

Respectfully, your obedient servant,

E. B. ANDREWS,

*Major, Thirty-sixth Ohio Vol. Infantry, Comdg. Expedition.*

---

## APRIL 18, 1862.—Reconnaissance to the Rappahannock River, Va.

### REPORTS.

**No. 1.—Brig. Gen. John J. Abercrombie, U. S. Army.**
**No. 2.—Lieut. Col. Timothy M. Bryan, jr., Twelfth Massachusetts Infantry.**

### No. 1.

*Report of Brig. Gen. John J. Abercrombie, U. S. Army.*

HDQRS. SECOND BRIG., FIRST DIV., FIFTH ARMY CORPS,
*Warrenton Junction, Va., April 18, 1862.*

MY DEAR COLONEL: I have just returned from the Rappahannock, where I have been to ascertain, if possible, the true state of affairs there.

I sent Lieutenant-Colonel Bryan, of the Twelfth Massachusetts Regiment, last night, as soon as the moon had risen, with five companies of the Ninth New York, five companies of the Twelfth Indiana, some cavalry, and three sections of artillery, to reconnoiter the position and strength of the enemy. He arrived there about dawn of day, took the most eligible positions he could find for his guns, and commenced firing just as their bands were playing at guard mounting. In a very short time after, however, the rebels opened their batteries and fired rapidly round shot altogether, and from the number visible in the redoubts, and between them infantry and cavalry, I am inclined to think there is quite a large force; but the country is so broken in rear of their batteries it is impossible to make any estimate of it. It is said General Smith is there and some 6,000 or 7,000 men. I do not think their force would exceed 3,000 or 4,000. The cars were running all the time, and some light batteries, drawn by six horses, were seen to approach the earthworks from the direction of the road, which induced the belief they were being re-enforced, probably from Fredericksburg. As soon as Colonel Bryan makes his report I will send you a copy of it. Inclosed I send you a rough sketch* of their works, &c.

Very respectfully, your obedient servant,

J. J. ABERCROMBIE,
*Brigadier-General, Commanding, Warrenton Junction, Va.*

Colonel SCHRIVER,
*Chief of Staff.*

---

## No. 2.

***Report of Lieut. Col. Timothy M. Bryan, jr., Twelfth Massachusetts Infantry.***

HEADQUARTERS TWELFTH MASSACHUSETTS REGIMENT,
*Warrenton Junction, April* 19, 1862.

SIR: In compliance with Special Orders, No. 37, issued from brigade headquarters, I have made a reconnaissance to the North Fork of the Rappahannock River, and have the honor to submit the following as my report:

My command consisted of seven companies Twelfth Massachusetts Volunteers, Major Burbank commanding; five companies Ninth New York State Militia [Eighty-third Infantry], Lieutenant-Colonel Atterbury commanding; five companies Twelfth Indiana Volunteers, Lieutenant-Colonel Humphrey commanding; four companies Rhode Island Cavalry, Captain Gould commanding; two sections Matthews' battery, Lieutenant Godbold commanding; one section Thompson's battery, Lieutenant Brockway commanding; one section Sturmfel's battery, Lieutenant Molitor commanding, making a total of about 1,500 infantry, 160 cavalry, three sections of artillery with the new ordnance gun, and one section artillery with Parrott 10-pounder guns.†

I had issued orders for the command to form in the rear of the camp of the Twelfth Massachusetts Regiment at 10 o'clock, but by some misunderstanding in the change of detail for the cavalry they were not reported present till 12.30 a. m. Another half hour was occupied in detailing the advance and rear guard and flankers and getting the command under way, so that it was 1 o'clock before the rear left. Not having any map of the country or guide, I requested Lieutenant Tucker, of the Maine Cavalry, to accompany me, he having traveled the road once before. I put him at the head of the advance guard, and to his services we are indebted for our early arrival at our destination.

The roads are terrible for artillery, the caissons frequently cutting in hub-deep, so that our march was necessarily impeded much more than we could have wished.

We arrived at a cross-road near our scene of action about 7 a. m., and Lieutenant Tucker thinking they led to fords on our flanks, I dispatched a company of cavalry, about 40 men, down each to reconnoiter and warn me of any attempt to intercept our rear. The road on the left Lieutenant Wyman reports as leading directly to the ford below the bridge, as laid down on the map, about one-eighth of a mile below. Lieutenant Wyman received information from an officer and 2 men

---

* Not found.

† Records show that Lieutenant Brockway commanded a section of Matthews' battery, and that Lieutenant Barry commanded the section of Thompson's battery.

across the river as to the direction of the ford in the river, who also told him it was fordable horseback. When they found the Lieutenant was not inclined to cross they called him to halt and fired upon him, but without effect. The lieutenant on the road to the right, having gone down some 2 miles and not seeing the river ahead, returned nearer the main column to guard the right flank. I then went forward with Lieutenants Godbold and Tucker to select a position for our guns. I found at once that the enemy were strongly fortified. The banks on the opposite shore overlook those on this side some 20 feet at least. Earthworks could be seen in front and on both our flanks on all the prominent hills, and troops could be seen employed building others. These works were laid out with consummate skill, each one in rear commanded and strongly defended by its faces or flanks those in front, and they were so arranged that an enfilading fire could be brought on an enemy opposite in every available position he could occupy. The master-hand of General G. W. Smith was plainly seen in their construction. I soon discovered that there was little choice of position, there being only two hills that were at all tenable should the enemy have many guns. These I occupied, as the inclosed sketch* will show, viz:

The hill on the left by two sections, under Lieutenant Godbold, and one section Parrotts, Lieutenant Barry, their support being the Twelfth Massachusetts Volunteers, Major Burbank.

The hill on the right, distant about three-fourths of a mile, directly north-northeast, was occupied by a section under Lieutenant Brockway, the support being the Twelfth Indiana, Lieutenant-Colonel Humphrey. The section under Lieutenant Molitor and the Ninth New York Militia, Lieutenant-Colonel Atterbury commanding, I left as a reserve. The cavalry I placed on the flanks and in the woods in the rear.

Having thus disposed of my force, I had the pieces run by hand to the crests of the hills, and as the last echo of the rebel band at guard mounting died away I gave them as a chorus the right piece of Lieutenant Godbold. This was a splendid shot. The shell struck nearly the center of the large fort opposite, and bursting, scattered the men on all sides, doubtless killing some. This work was being completed, and the parapet was covered with men at work. The next shot went a little to the right, and the next also. This giving them some encouragement, they returned, and opened fire with two brass 6-pounder smooth-bores, their shot and shell falling short about 30 yards. The fifth shot from Lieutenant Barry's battery blew up the magazine in that work and silenced their guns. When the magazine exploded dark objects were thrown upward, probably men, but I could not say whether they were troops or the logs of which the magazine doubtless was built. This silenced that work.

Lieutenant Barry had thrown a shell through some tents and many in the parapet, tearing it terribly, so that this work was pretty well used up, when suddenly two masked batteries enfiladed us. I made a slight change in our position and replied. These I found were also smooth-bore 6-pounders. We returned their fire briskly for some moments, when I saw two sections of a battery galloping rapidly to our right. I sent word to Lieutenant Brockway, who fired two shells at them, one killing 3 men and a horse. These were seen to fall, the distance being not over 1,500 yards on a level plain. They, however, moved on, getting in the woods, and went I could not ascertain whither, though I sent three good scouts to follow them.

---

*Not found.

Lieutenant Brockway then threw a few shot and shell at a house, said to be headquarters, and near which were some Sibley tents. By the side of one of these tents a trooper dismounted and came forward to reconnoiter. The first shell struck him down and sent his horse flying across the field. The soldier (or officer) struck did not move during the engagement, and laid there when we left, so I presume he was killed. Several shells struck around the earthwork in front and numerous horses ran from the woods in the rear. One round shot went entirely through the house, but not a gun was fired by the enemy from this point.

Two masked batteries, however, opened on Lieutenant Brockway, one a 24 or 32 pounder, which enfiladed the line of skirmishers of the Twelfth Indiana and also the battery. The first ricochetted from the crest of the hill, and making two bounds, passed immediately over Lieutenant-Colonel Humphrey, who, being on foot, fell flat, and I thought him killed. This shot passed down the rear of the whole line of the Twelfth Indiana, between them and their reserves, and several others of the same sort did the same thing, but they never moved an inch till I ordered the battery to take another position and try the earthworks on their extreme left. Hardly had they taken position and opened fire when a masked battery in front, and not over 1,000 yards distant, replied. The brush in front of this being knocked down by their fire, Lieutenant Brockway directed one of his pieces upon it with such effect that at the second fire one of the enemy's guns was knocked over and the horses of the battery seen galloping away over the fields. They fired but one more shot, and were silenced. The heavy gun still kept up its fire on the extreme left of us, and I, having shot and shell brought me from all the batteries, concluded to bring in Lieutenant Brockway and Colonel Humphrey, not knowing where the sections that had passed to our right had gone. I called them in nearer the main body to cover its flank, and started with 3 dragoons to the river's bank to ascertain, if possible, their effective force. I had not proceeded far when a battery within short range opened upon me. I therefore dismounted and crawled to the top of a hill near some low cedars. There I distinctly saw three different regiments under arms in front of their tents back of the woods, two of which had batteries, or sections of batteries, on their right. One of these regiments had tents.

In the woods were tents sufficient for three more regiments, though many of these were wedge-tents, and I might have been deceived. The river was very precipitous on both sides, the less so on that of the enemy, our banks being about 70 feet high. A regiment of cavalry in line was also visible. The river was, I should think, 75 or 80 yards wide. The force of the enemy I estimated at between 5,000 and 7,000 infantry, at least one regiment of cavalry, three full batteries of 6-pounder smooth-bores, and two siege guns, 24-pounders. They used no rifled guns whatever.

Finding no place for my infantry to open an effective fire, even with their rifles, without great exposure from grape and canister, and knowing it was not your wish to risk a general engagement with a force greatly superior to our own and well intrenched, or even a skirmish which might be disastrous to us, I rode back and ordered the entire force back out of range, as I saw them taking a gun, drawn by eight horses, in the masked battery between the woods and their large works which we had silenced.

I had hardly moved my command when they opened there with a 24-pounder shell, but badly out of range and in our rear. They fired four or five times and ceased. I then rode to the right to examine the bridge, and had but just arrived where I proposed to reconnoiter when a masked battery with grape and canister opened so near me I could distinctly see the men working their pieces, the shot flying entirely too close to be pleasant. I changed my position, but only to find a section of light battery drive up, and unlimbering sent a round shot within 10 feet of me, splashing mud over both myself and horse. I therefore saw but little.

The bridge I could not see, as it was hidden by the bluff. Lieutenant Wyman informed me there is but one pier standing, and that somewhat damaged; that the abutments are not entire, and that the place where the second pier should be is vacant, which is between the opposite bank and the first pier. He thinks the building of the bridge would be difficult, and I agree with him, as the river is wide, and just above is a dam, which gives the stream quite a current at present. A large amount of timber was collected near the ford, though in what state of entirety I cannot say. The railroad is entire from the bridge on our side back 4 miles. From this point the rails have either been carried off by the Confederates for their own use or buried in some neighboring fields. The sleepers for about a mile are cut in two, and from there toward Warrenton Junction are removed and burned.

The houses on our road with two exceptions were entirely deserted, one of these, belonging to an officer, Lieutenant Gordon, rebel army, containing a white family, who were taking care of it for him. Hearing they were giving information to the enemy as to our scouts before, I arrested the father and son, a lad of seventeen years, and put a guard over the woman till I returned.

The other is a house of Mrs. Broom. On our approach an Irishman and young Mr. Broom mounted and galloped down toward the river. I sent two cavalry after them across the fields, who soon returned with both. These I kept till I received your orders to release them. The town of Rappahannock, a village of twelve or fifteen houses, is deserted.

The land hereabout is not cultivated, with the exception of two or three fields of thinly-growing wheat. Forage for man or beast is not to be had. I saw but four cows and one two-year-old colt during the trip; not a fowl of any kind at any house. Small streams of very muddy water are numerous, and some of the fields appear to have had clover in them in years gone by. The soil is clayey, and becomes a stiff paste in wet weather. The country is well wooded, generally oak, with some clumps of pines, gently undulating to the river, where it rises abruptly 60 or 70 feet on the bank.

We met no pickets or scouts of the enemy during the entire march, and returned to camp without suffering any loss whatever of men or horses. The position occupied by the enemy I should think difficult to drive them from in front. By making a march so as to throw the men in rifle pits before daylight, and thus cover them from grape and canister on this bank from the other, would force them to cross and attack or drive them back while we did so, as their works are within good rifle range.

This was your expressed wish to me, but unfortunately the cavalry reported too late for me to reach the point designated till 7 a. m. I should have then remained quiet until next day, throwing up works during the night, but I did not know the surrounding country. Besides, I was anxious to engage them, lest they might send re-enforcements toward Fredericksburg, which you desired us to prevent, if possible, and which I think was accomplished.

To attack on the flanks with a considerable force, particularly above on their left flank, having a good guide who knows the fords well, I should think would be successful, as they evidently feared an attack in that quarter, and therefore sent the two sections of a battery referred to in that direction. Their work seemed all open in the rear.

In conclusion, allow me to express to you my heartfelt thanks for your kindness in placing me in command of the picked men of your command, and I believe the Second Brigade (General J. J. Abercrombie commanding) is universally admitted to be the finest body of men in the service, and notwithstanding their fatiguing march, without any sleep at night, they, both officers and men, were ready to undergo any future amount of hardship, and all seemed anxious to acquit themselves as heroes. I would especially mention the fine gunnery of Lieutenants Godbold, Brockway, and Barry. I never saw finer practice by older officers in the U. S. Army. Captain Gould and Lieutenant Wyman, Rhode Island cavalry, rendered much valuable assistance on the march, the former by the precision with which he conducted the advance and rear guards and flankers, and the latter as scout, bringing in much useful information from dangerous points. To Lieutenant Tucker, Maine cavalry, is due our safe-conduct to our point of destination.

The officers and men, without exception, displayed exceeding coolness while under a sharp fire of shot and shell for nearly two hours without firing a gun, which is considered the most trying position in which infantry can be placed.

I am, sir, very respectfully, your obedient servant,

T. M. BRYAN, JR.,
*Lieut. Col., Twelfth Mass. Vols., Comdg. Reconnaissance.*

Brigadier-General ABERCROMBIE,
*Commanding Second Brigade.*

---

**APRIL 19-24, 1862.—Operations in the vicinity of Sparta, New Market, South Fork of the Shenandoah River (near Luray), and Harrisonburg, in the Shenandoah Valley, Va.**

*Reports of Maj. Gen. Nathaniel P. Banks, U. S. Army.*

NEW MARKET, *April* 19, 1862.

Our advance guard occupied this morning the village of Sparta, 8 miles in front of New Market. For the first time in their retreat the rebels burned the small bridges on the road, obstructing by the smallest possible means the pursuit of our troops. Some dozen or more bridges were thus destroyed, but I immediately reconstructed.

N. P. BANKS,
*Major-General, Commanding.*

Hon. E. M. STANTON, *Secretary of War.*

---

NEW MARKET, *April* 19, 1862.

To-day I have been to the bridges on South Fork Shenandoah, Massanutten Valley, with a force of infantry, cavalry, and artillery, to protect the two important bridges that cross the river. We were within sight of Luray. At the south bridge a sharp skirmish occurred with the rebels, in which they lost several men taken prisoners. Their object was the destruction of the bridges. One of the prisoners left the camp on the Rappahannock Tuesday morning. The enemy is at Rappahannock Station, commanded by General Elzey, formerly of U. S. Army; consists of four brigades, five regiments each. No fortifications to that time. Other reports indicate stronger force at Gordonsville and a contest there. The whole resulting in a belief that they are concentrating at Yorktown. I believe Jackson left this valley yesterday. He is reported to have left Harrisonburg yesterday for Gordonsville by the Mountain road. He camped last night at McGaheysville, 11 miles from Harrisonburg. The failure of our supplies made it impossible to continue the pursuit farther.

N. P. BANKS,
*Major-General, Commanding.*

Hon. E. M. STANTON, *Secretary of War.*

---

NEW MARKET, *April* 20, 1862.

The flight of Jackson from the valley, by the way of the mountains, from Harrisonburg toward Stanardsville and Orange Court-House, on Gordonsville is confirmed this morning by our scouts and prisoners.

N. P. BANKS,
*Major-General, Commanding.*

Hon. E. M. STANTON, *Secretary of War.*

---

NEW MARKET, *April* 22, 1862.

Our advance is near Harrisonburg. We have troops across the mountains protecting the bridges on the Shenandoah at Alma and on the Luray road. To-day we pushed a force forward to Luray. The people were greatly alarmed at first on account of the reports circulated by the rebels as to the treatment they would receive from us, but in a few hours they became quite reconciled to the presence of the troops. There is a good road to Warrenton, 25 miles, and a turnpike to Culpeper Court-House, same distance. Some sharp skirmishes with the enemy. We lost 3 men prisoners. Jackson has abandoned the valley of Virginia permanently, *en route* for Gordonsville, by the way of the mountains. The crippled condition of our supplies alone enabled him to escape. When we halted our troops had not a ration left. We are now getting in good condition. Every day brings its prisoners and numerous deserters.

N. P. BANKS,
*Major-General, Commanding.*

Hon. E. M. STANTON, *Secretary of War.*

---

NEW MARKET, *April* 24, 1862.

Our advance guard, Colonel Donnelly commanding, took 3 prisoners to-day at a point 9 miles beyond Harrisonburg. One says he belongs to Company B, Tenth Virginia Regiment Infantry. This regiment has been on the Rappahannock, according to previous information. Prisoner says it joined Jackson at his present location near Stanardsville from Culpeper, ... the retreat of the rebels from that quarter. No ... joined Jackson up to this time.

N. P. BANKS,
*Major-General, Commanding.*

... M. STANTON, *Secretary of War.*

---

## APRIL 23, 1862.—Skirmish at Grass Lick, W. Va.

### *Report of Maj. Gen. John C. Frémont, U. S. Army.*

WHEELING, *April* 23, 1862.

General Kelley sends this evening the following dispatch from Lieutenant-Colonel Downey, in command at Romney:

> Twenty-five of Firey's and Shaw's cavalry encountered Colonel Parsons with some 50 men at Peter Palling's house, on Grass Lick, before day this morning. Two of Firey's men were killed and one of Shaw's. A number of the rebels killed and wounded. I went out with re-enforcements, burned the houses the rebels fired from, and scoured the whole country around.

General Milroy also telegraphs that he made a reconnaissance yesterday with one cavalry and six infantry companies to ascertain the whereabouts of the enemy. He overtook rear guard of cavalry 6 miles this side of the railroad, near Buffalo Gap. They retreated rapidly, pursued by our cavalry. General Milroy was informed that the main body had stopped the night previous 6 miles beyond Buffalo Gap; that they had discovered that they were cut off from Staunton by General Banks, and were bearing off to the right, to go down through Bath and Alleghany Counties to James River.

J. C. FRÉMONT,
*Major-General.*

Hon. E. M. STANTON.

---

WHEELING, VA., *April* 24, 1862.

Information in General Kelley's dispatch of yesterday confirmed and given more in detail by a telegram from General Schenck, which states that a squad of 25 infantry, sent from Romney by Lieutenant-Colonel Downey to look after guerrillas, was attacked yesterday morning on Grass Lick, between Lost River and Cacapon, by the rebels, 40 in number. Our force lost 3 killed, but drove the rebels, who took refuge in the house of one Palling. Colonel Downey went with a re-enforcement of cavalry, but the rebels fled at his approach, carrying off several dead and wounded, among the latter Colonel Parsons, their leader, and Palling, owner of the house. Colonel Downey reports interior of house covered with blood. He burned the house and pursued the flying enemy, taking 5 prisoners. General Schenck sent a re-enforcement of 160 cavalry and one piece of DeBeck's artillery to come on the enemy in rear. These must have reached the place about 4 o'clock. Yesterday afternoon our messengers passing to and fro between Grass

Lick and Romney were fired on 4, 6, and guerrillas. The prisoners will be tried by a if found guilty will be shot.

J.

*Major-Genera*

Hon. E. M. STANTON.

---

## APRIL 27, 1862.—Skirmish at McGaheysville, Va.

*Abstract from "Record of Events" in Cavalry Brigade, Department of the Shenandoah.**

* * * * * * *

On the 26th instant orders were received from the department headquarters to make a reconnaissance toward the enemy's lines at McGaheysville.

At 10 a. m. on the 27th General Hatch, with about 175 men from the Vermont and Michigan regiments and a section of Cothran's battery, moved forward. Orders had been issued for two regiments of infantry from General Williams' division to support the advance, but on arriving at the point designated for a junction they were not upon the ground. General Hatch, therefore, went on, leaving orders for them to follow. When near the town a picket was discovered, when one company of the Vermont regiment (Captain Platt) charged into and through the town and 1 mile beyond, driving two companies of the enemy's cavalry and taking 2 prisoners. The enemy now rallied and opened fire upon the pursuing force. One piece of artillery was now brought forward and a few shells thrown. Lieutenant Ward, of the Vermont regiment, then moved forward and charged upon the enemy, who had before retreated from our advance. They immediately broke, and were followed for some distance to within 2 miles of Swift Run Bridge. Lieutenant Ward then rejoined the main body. General Hatch was then 12 miles from Harrisonburg. The infantry support had not come up, and General Hatch, not deeming it prudent to advance with artillery without any other support than a small force of cavalry, returned to Harrisonburg.

On the 29th and 30th scouts and patrols from the Vermont and Michigan regiments were kept in motion day and night on roads leading into Harrisonburg from the direction of the enemy's lines, but nothing of any great importance occurred.

J. A. JUDSON,

*Captain and Assistant Adjutant-General Cavalry.*

HARRISONBURG, VA., *April* 30, 1862.

---

* From return for the month of April, 1862.

## MAY 1, 1862.—Skirmish on Camp Creek, in the Stone River Valley, W. Va.

REPORTS.

No. 1.—Brig. Gen. Jacob D. Cox, U. S. Army.
No. 2.—Col. E. Parker Scammon, Twenty-third Ohio Infantry.
No. 3.—Col. Walter H. Jenifer, Eighth Virginia Cavalry.

### No. 1.

*Report of Brig. Gen. Jacob D. Cox, U. S. Army.*

CHARLESTON, *May* 2, 1862.

Colonel Scammon's advance guard had a skirmish with about 300 rebels at Camp Creek, a fork of Blue Stone, yesterday morning. Six of the enemy were killed and a considerable number wounded and prisoners. We lost 1 man killed and 20 slightly wounded. The rebels were completely routed and fled. Full particulars will be sent in official report.

Scouting party from Forty-seventh, on Lewisburg road, took 4 prisoners near Sewell Mountain. No additional news of enemy's force or position. Weather clear to-day.

J. D. COX,
*Brigadier-General, Commanding District.*

Col. ALBERT TRACY,
*Assistant Adjutant-General.*

---

### No. 2.

*Report of Col. E. Parker Scammon, Twenty-third Ohio Infantry.*

RALEIGH, *May* 1, 1862.

GENERAL: This morning at daylight the advance guard of Lieutenant-Colonel Hayes, a company of Twenty-third Regiment, under Lieutenant Bottsford, was surrounded and attacked by about 300 rebels at Camp Creek. Lieutenant Bottsford reports 1 man killed and 20 wounded, all but 3 or 4 slightly; 6 or 7 of enemy killed; wounded not yet known. Six prisoners; 3 wounded had been taken and others being brought in when messenger left. The enemy fled, and Lieutenant-Colonel Hayes had reached Camp Creek.

In answering Lieutenant-Colonel Hayes' dispatch, while giving due praise for gallantry, I have not hesitated to speak in rebuke of this matter, because Lieutenant Bottsford was 6 miles in advance, when the whole tenor of my orders has been to keep closed. Happily the men behaved excellently, and defeated and drove the enemy, but this stretching of short lines must cease, or we shall have a break.

It is now raining again; by the time it clears I expect to move forward with the Thirtieth and the artillery. Have ordered five companies of the Thirty-fourth to be here by Saturday, 4 p. m.

E. P. SCAMMON,
*Colonel, Commanding Brigade.*

General COX.

## No. 3.

*Report of Col. Walter H. Jenifer, Eighth Virginia Cavalry.*

HEADQUARTERS DEPARTMENT OF NEW RIVER,
*Wytheville, Va., May 6, 1862.*

GENERAL: I have the honor to submit my report of a skirmish with the enemy near Princeton, Va., on the 1st instant.

On April 30 it was reported to me at Rocky Gap that the enemy was advancing on Princeton from the direction of Raleigh. In consequence of this report I ordered out Lieutenant-Colonel Fitzhugh, with about 120 cavalry (dismounted) and some 70 or 80 militia, to meet the enemy and to detain him, if possible, until I could remove the few remaining stores from Princeton to Rocky Gap. I also ordered up the Forty-fifth Regiment (Colonel Peters) to the support of Colonel Fitzhugh; but before this regiment could reach Princeton the enemy had advanced so rapidly that, fearing Colonel Peters would be cut off, I ordered him back to his camp, and on returning his regiment was ambushed by the enemy and thrown into some confusion. Colonel Peters succeeded, however, in repulsing the enemy, and reached his camp without losing any of his men or property.

In order to enable me to save the stores and property at Princeton it became necessary to engage the enemy's advance column, which Colonel Fitzhugh did, inflicting considerable loss on the enemy. The fight was kept up for thirteen hours, and a distance of 22 miles was well contested by the small force under Colonel Fitzhugh.

During the engagement we lost 1 killed, 4 or 5 seriously wounded, and 8 or 9 slightly wounded. The wounded were all brought off safe from the field; the few who were seriously wounded were taken to houses near the field. The enemy's loss is supposed to be 35 in killed, wounded, and missing.

Colonel Fitzhugh and the officers under him deserve much credit for their gallant conduct during the fight. Colonel Fitzhugh managed his small command with much skill and judgment.

I evacuated Princeton just as the enemy entered it, having first fired the town. All my stores were saved except a few, which the scarcity of transportation prevented me from taking away. No arms or ammunition were destroyed.

After leaving Princeton I fell back in good order to Rocky Gap, at which place I remained some twenty hours. Having only 75 men with me, the remainder of my regiment being on distant duty, I considered it proper to fall back to Walker's Mountain, on the Wytheville road. Having previously ascertained the force of the enemy in Mercer County to be several thousand strong, and knowing that Colonel Peters, whose camp was at the mouth of Wolf Creek, had no artillery to use against the enemy should he make an advance on that line, I ordered him to fall back with his command to Walker's Mountain, a strong position on the Dublin road. The stores at Giles Court-House I had several weeks before ordered to be removed to Dublin. Nearly all of those stores except some flour, which fell into the hands of the enemy, were saved. The reported superior force of the enemy and the very small force under my command rendered it necessary for me to pursue the course I did. I am willing to receive the censure, as I assumed the responsibility, if I have saved any of our gallant soldiers from being captured by a largely superior force of the enemy.

I have the honor to inclose herewith the report of Lieut. Col. Henry Fitzhugh.*

I am, sir, very respectfully, your obedient servant,

W. H. JENIFER,
*Colonel, Commanding Department of New River.*

Brig. Gen. HENRY HETH, *Comdg. Army of New River, Giles C. H., Va.*

---

**MAY 4-5, 1862.—Reconnaissance to Culpeper Court-House, Va.**

REPORTS.

No. 1.—Brig. Gen. George L. Hartsuff, U. S. Army.
No. 2.—Maj. D. Porter Stowell, First Maine Cavalry.

No. 1.

*Report of Brig. Gen. George L. Hartsuff, U. S. Army.*

CATLETT'S, *May* 7, 1862.

Cavalry reconnaissance returned from Culpeper C. H. Drove cavalry pickets 3 miles and into the town. Two companies of cavalry escaped very hurriedly, being notified in time. Captured 7 prisoners and horses trying to escape from the town. No troops between river and Culpeper C. H.; only cavalry outposts there. Two regiments at Rapidan Station and detachments scattered to Gordonsville; number not known—supposed to be large. Generals Ewell, Elzey, and others in command. Town generally occupied, and handkerchiefs waved at our troops. Railroad broken short distance from river; unbroken beyond. River barely fordable at ford below railroad bridge. Occupied town about forty minutes and returned. Send prisoners to Washington to-day. Please send any information about evacuation of Yorktown, present position of enemy's troops which left, and any other news. Get none here.

Respectfully,

GEO. L. HARTSUFF,
*Brigadier-General.*

Hon. E. M. STANTON, *Secretary of War.*

---

No. 2.

*Report of Maj. D. Porter Stowell, First Maine Cavalry.*

HDQRS. 1ST ME. CAV., *Warrenton Junction, May* 5, 1862.

SIR: In accordance with your General Orders, No. —, the available force of this regiment located here took up their line of march Sunday, May 4, 1862, at 5 p. m., for reconnaissance to the Rappahannock River and beyond Culpeper Court-House. After having advanced beyond our line of pickets in that direction I threw out an advance guard and flankers, and proceeded on our route toward the river, without obtaining any important information of the enemy. After proceeding 10 miles the darkness of the night made it necessary for me to obtain a guide, which I did at the house of a Mr. Bowen. We then proceeded to the river 2 miles, and then 2 miles up the river to the only ford which we could cross in this vicinity. We commenced and crossed in file, which took us till about midnight. The water from 4 to 5 feet deep, with a strong current, made it quite difficult for us to go through safely.

*Not found.

I obtained information from our guide that the best and only place for us to stop for a short time to refresh ourselves and horses was the house of Richard Cunningham, the late headquarters of the Confederate Army, on the other side of the river, and about 1½ miles distant from the river. We found the house with some difficulty, as the night was very dark. We were obliged to leave our guide on the opposite side of the river. As he was quite infirm, and with a very small horse, I did not think it safe for him to cross the ford.

After obtaining the consent of the overseer, who resided about half a mile off, and who kindly went and assisted us by opening the house and out-buildings, we fed our horses, and took about three hours' rest ourselves, promiscuously on beds, sofas, lounges, easy chairs, and parlor floors of this well-furnished mansion, and, with very much credit to our officers and men, not a dollar's worth of property was destroyed. I found the overseer of this place to be a very intelligent, well-informed man. His name was Wiltshire. I derived valuable information from him as to the geography of the county of Culpeper, and also much valuable information of the strength of the enemy whilst located there.

Generals Ewell, Taylor, Trimble, and Elzey were in command of the army there. They left there Saturday night, the 19th of April, three days after they were shelled by us from this side of the river. We did them some damage at that time by destroying their magazine, which injured quite a number dangerously by burning, and report said three killed. Their earthworks were 2 miles below their headquarters, and near the railroad bridge, which they destroyed when they retreated from Manassas. Their encampment was 1 mile back from their earthworks, on the high lands in the skirt of a woods. Stuart's Black Horse Cavalry did picket duty for some days after the main body left. They then left for Yorktown, as a Mr. Horace Barber informed Wiltshire. This Barber was a merchant at the railroad bridge, and belonged to that cavalry.

After resting three hours we formed our line and resumed our march, with Wiltshire as our guide. We changed our course, by the advice of our guide, from the main road, which went through a wood and low land, and directed our course south to a range of high lands, 1½ miles distant, where the enemy had recently left. From here we had a very fine view of the river and railroad as well as of the surrounding country on our right and left, thus having a position not to be surprised by the enemy in front or from the right nor to prevent a retreat if obliged to make one, as we had the river and railroad immediately on our left. We then moved forward toward Brandy (a little place with railroad station), 5 miles ahead, and although the country was generally very open, we had thrown out a company of skirmishers and a formidable rear guard, which covered the country for more than 1½ miles.

The attention of the line was called at one time to what was supposed to be a line of army wagons, about 1 mile distant, but proved to be only a herd of white oxen.

The general appearance of the country in this direction is very favorable, gently rolling, open, highly cultivated, and fruitful, rich plantations, with an abundance of forage and subsistence. Vegetation much more forward than in Fauquier County about Warrenton. After crossing the river we found no road leading in the direction of the enemy south and on our left until we arrived at Brandy. Here are the remains of an old plank road of 7 miles' length, connecting with a plank road running from Fredericksburg to Culpeper and so on to Orange Court-House. This branch road is hardly ever used, and of no consequence. On our right, after leaving the Huntington house, is a large brick house, which is owned by a surgeon in the rebel army. The next large plantation on the right abounds with forage and subsistence, which is a fair representation of all the plantations from the river to Brandy.

From all the information I could obtain the strength of the enemy on the Rappahannock fell back to Gordonsville, and there has been no force this side of there of any great amount. The planters on our route, as near as I could judge, are nearly all secesh, and a little bleeding would reduce their fever a little and do them good.

After proceeding beyond Brandy the general appearance of the country is about the same as before described, quite as favorable; the inhabitants likewise, with some noble exceptions. I considered the information I received from the negroes and poor whites very reliable, and they all tell the same story, and are very willing to communicate all the information they are in possession of. After proceeding beyond Brandy about 2 miles we began to obtain information that a line of pickets was established about 3½ miles this side of Culpeper Court-House and about 2 miles ahead of us. We first obtained this information from a very intelligent negro, next from two whites, both overseers out on plantations that owners had left and were in the Army of the Confederate States. I next met an intelligent citizen, who came from the Court-House the night before, and was obliged to procure a pass from the post captain, whose name is Watts. This pass he gave me, and is attached to this report. He informed me the line of pickets was 3½ miles out of the village and about 1 mile ahead, and also that the force in the village was two companies of cavalry, one of 120 and the other 80. I was also informed that all their cavalry had carbines.

After leaving this man opposite the residence of James Barber, who had left and was in the army, we proceeded toward the Court-House. After going about 1 mile Captain Taylor, whose command was acting as skirmishers ahead, sent an orderly back to inform me that the pickets were discovered, and were running in rapidly on the line of railroad, and that Captain Taylor was in pursuit of them. I immediately ordered the column forward as fast as possible, considering the badness of the roads, which in places were very bad, and grew worse as we approached nearer the town. On arriving within a half mile of the town with the right of our column I sent the right squadron forward to cover Captain Taylor. This, however, was after I had sent a non-commissioned officer and 4 men onto a knoll in view of the town to make such discoveries as they could. They reported that they could see horses being driven into a yard. Captain Smith was then sent forward, and in ten minutes I sent forward another squadron. Not having heard from either Captain Taylor or Captain Smith, I did not consider it advisable to move the whole column in at once, not knowing the strength or position of the enemy. The extreme left of our column was out of the village three-quarters of a mile, on an eminence west of the railroad, where we could fall back if necessary and form a line of battle. I here met a young man by the name of Bakham, who resides 6 miles this side of the village. He was a very good Union man, and seemed very much pleased with the idea of Union troops coming forward; said the enemy tried very hard to have his father go with them, but he would not; said our men and horses were much superior to theirs. He was in the village when the news came by one of their pickets that we were approaching the village. He said it produced great excitement. They immediately sent two couriers to the Rapidan, some 8 miles beyond

Culpeper, for two regiments of infantry which were stationed there. I afterward obtained the same information from various other sources, satisfying me of its reliability. He also said that the rebels mounted the horses without regard to ownership, and very many without stopping to saddle them. I also learned from this and other sources that they had two companies of cavalry stationed here, one of 120, the other 80, mounted, with sabers, pistols, and carbines, which made their force, with the addition of carbines, nearly equal to ours.

In view of the fact that the Rapidan was only 8 miles above us, on the line of the Orange and Alexandria Railroad, running parallel with the road we came in on clear back to the river and frequently crossing it, I considered our situation quite critical. Not having heard from Captain Taylor's skirmishers since he first saw the pickets on retreat and the two companies who went to cover him if in town, I had fears that the enemy had taken him, with his command. I immediately left the column and proceeded to the headquarters of the enemy at the Court-House, where the two companies sent forward last had just arrived, but with no tidings of Captain Taylor. Some said they saw him pursuing the rebels up the line of railroad; others saw him in other directions. I then went to their stables, thinking, perhaps, that we might find some spare horses. None were left at the upper stables, and proceeding through the village to some yards where it was said they had some horses, my attention was called by quite a number of our officers to a force of cavalry on the south side of the town. They were trying to observe through their glasses who we were. We were in hopes that it might be Captain Taylor, but all pronounced it not, as this force had light-colored horses and some of it light clothing. To be sure of the fact that it was not Captain Taylor I sent Captain Smith, of Company D, and Lieutenant Stevens, of Company F, to approach as near as possible with safety to ascertain for a certainty. I then proceeded with Lieutenant Virgin, of Company G, to the yards for the rebels, and had not gone far when Captain Smith and Lieutenant Stevens reported that it was not Captain Taylor. Immediately Captain Burbank came and informed me that the enemy's force, as we supposed, were approaching our right. In view of the fact that they had carbines and we had not, and that our only way to meet them was to form a line of battle on the hill from our rear, as we could not possibly form a line in the village, as the streets were very crooked, narrow, and muddy, I ordered the adjutant to go to the rear and change the direction of our column, which was done in good order, and proceeded to go back onto the ridge to form a line of battle. From this position we were near and in sight of the railroad, which if the infantry should come down on we could easily take up the track, and thus save our retreat, not fearing their cavalry, as we could charge them from any direction at this point. Our rear had reached the hill and a part of the column had turned into the field to form a line, when I, on returning to the right, met an orderly from Captain Taylor, stating that Captain Taylor had taken some prisoners, and wished to know what to do with them, thus solving the problem. The supposed enemy was only Captain Taylor. The prisoners' horses, some of them, being light colored, and the men differently dressed, had deceived us all.

Captain Taylor's horses were all dark color. Not having heard from him for more than one hour, and believing that he had no means of knowing that there was a reserved force of infantry at the Rapidan and that sent for, which might possibly cut him off from us, we were all very much rejoiced to see him safely back, more especially as his acts proved that he had discharged his duty so nobly. He brought with him 8 prisoners. We had remained in the village forty-five minutes when I turned the column, which, in view of all the circumstances, was as long a time as was prudent. We searched their headquarters, but found nothing of any great consequence except clothing, which we could not carry off.

Lieutenant Spurling brought away a fine double-barreled gun, and some of the soldiers also brought guns away with them.

After Captain Taylor had arrived with the prisoners we resumed our march back toward the river, feeling safe from any attack of the enemy, as we were near the railroad, and could tear up the track at any time if the cars should approach us with infantry. Went about 4 miles and fed our horses, and then returned to the Rappahannock, thinking it not safe to stop this side for the night, as the enemy could reach us by railroad, but could not cross the ford except with their cavalry, which we did not fear. We arrived at the ford about 6 or half past and commenced to cross, but found the water about 7 inches higher than the night before. We crossed with great difficulty in about two hours' time, and came very near losing two horses and their riders. Also some horses were obliged to swim; others were taken off their legs by the swift current.

Before we crossed the river we thought of camping on the opposite side for the night, but it being stormy and dark, and the men very wet and cold from the rain and fording, we concluded to travel home 12 miles farther, where we arrived about 11 o'clock p. m., thirty-one hours after having left, and having traveled near 60 miles.

Much credit is due to Captain Taylor and Lieutenant Vaughn for the ability shown in the discharge of their duties during the day, and more especially on entering the town. Captain Taylor was appointed to his command from the Regular Army, a fine officer, and knew well his duty. His company acted as skirmishers during the day, and on reaching the town proceeded to flank it. Lieutenant Vaughn, of the same company, who was assigned the left, had reached his point on the left about 50 yards from where the enemy had formed a line of battle, and Captain Taylor, who had much farther to go on the right, would have arrived in five minutes' time and charged them if they had waited; but on discovering Captain Taylor coming from the right they broke their column and dispersed, with Captain Taylor and Lieutenant Vaughn in full pursuit. They succeeded in capturing the prisoners before described. A majority of our officers and all our soldiers deserve much credit for discharging their duty so faithfully.

Our route from Warrenton to the river was on the line of the railroad most of the way, leaving it 2 miles below us on arriving at the river. The rebels destroyed the railroad bridge on their retreat from Manassas. The road is in good running order beyond the river clear to Culpeper Court-House, and also to Rapidan and Orange Court-House, which is 15 miles from Culpeper Court-House, and so on to Gordonsville, which is 10 miles from Orange Court-House, making the whole distance to Gordonsville 49 miles; distance from Culpeper Court-House to Fredericksburg 34 miles. On this side of the Rappahannock River there is a road from the railroad station to Falmouth, 28 miles. Falmouth is on the opposite side of the river and 7 miles from Fredericksburg. I did not consider it necessary to make a sketch of our route, as it was very direct and easily described.

D. PORTER STOWELL,
*Major, Commanding Expedition.*

Brigadier-General HARTSUFF,
*Headquarters Second Brigade, Warrenton Junction.*

## MAY 6, 1862.—Skirmish near Harrisonburg, Va.

*Report of Maj. Gen. Nathaniel P. Banks, U. S. Army, and congratulations from Secretary of War.*

NEW MARKET, *May* 7, 1862.

The Fifth New York Cavalry had a sharp skirmish with Ashby's cavalry yesterday near Harrisonburg. They made a succession of most spirited charges against superior numbers, killing 10, wounding many, and capturing 6 rebels. Their conduct gave the highest satisfaction. Their chief weapon was the saber. The enemy does not show himself except by cavalry. We shall make most vigorous efforts to discover his position. His chief object will doubtless be to prevent a junction of forces on this line with General McDowell.

N. P. BANKS,
*Major-General.*

Hon. E. M. STANTON,
*Secretary of War.*

---

WAR DEPARTMENT, *May* 8, 1862.

Maj. Gen. N. P. BANKS, *New Market, Va.:*

Your account of the repulse of Ashby's cavalry yesterday is received. The New York Fifth Cavalry, by their bravery in the skirmish and the promptness and spirit with which they improved the advantage they gained over the enemy by pursuing and cutting them up, merits praise.

The enemy on the Peninsula have evacuated Williamsburg and continue retiring, but where they intend making the next stand is not yet ascertained.

P. H. WATSON,
*Assistant Secretary of War.*

---

## MAY 7, 1862.—Skirmish at and near Wardensville, W. Va.

### REPORTS.

No. 1.—Maj. Gen. John C. Frémont, U. S. Army.
No. 2.—Lieut. Col. Stephen W. Downey, Third Maryland Potomac Home Brigade Infantry.

### No. 1.

*Report of Maj. Gen. John C. Frémont, U. S. Army.*

HEADQUARTERS IN THE FIELD,
*Franklin, May* 20, 1862.

Lieutenant-Colonel Downey, sent to Wardensville after the party of guerrillas who murdered a party of officers, zouaves, and convalescent soldiers on their way from Winchester to Moorefield, reports that he killed Capt. John Umbaugh, chief of guerrillas, and 3 of his men, wounded 5, and took 12 prisoners, without losing any of his command.

J. C. FRÉMONT,
*Major-General.*

Hon. E. M. STANTON.

No. 2.

*Report of Lieut. Col. Stephen W. Downey, Third Maryland Potomac Home Brigade Infantry.*

DOWNEY'S COMMAND,
*Petersburg, W. Va., May* 20, 1862.

COLONEL: I have the honor to report that on the morning of the 7th instant, at 7 o'clock, I proceeded with Firey's cavalry and 125 infantry from Moorefield in the direction of Wardensville, at which place we arrived at sunset the same day, after a fatiguing march of 30 miles. The town was completely surprised. We took some prisoners and killed 1 man, named Hanson, whom the better portion of the citizens pronounced a very bad man, and one of the participants in the late attack upon Dr. Newhane and his party. From Wardensville we proceeded across the mountain to North River. At the house of one John T. Wilson, situated about 12 miles from Wardensville and 18 from Romney, we surprised and killed Umbaugh and some of his men. Captain Umbaugh, from the best information I could obtain both at Romney and Wardensville, was the prince of the bushwhackers. He held a commission from Governor Letcher authorizing him to recruit men and carry on that guerrilla warfare. When killed he had on clothing taken from the corpse of one of my men killed in the skirmish at Grass Lick a month ago. We surprised several small parties on our route, some of whom we wounded and captured; others escaped. Not a man of my command was killed or wounded. We killed 4, wounded 4, and took 12 prisoners. Some of the latter are probably innocent. I shall examine them as soon as practicable, and release those who prove to be innocent.

The people of Wardensville treated my men with the greatest kindness and respect. No private property was destroyed. The citizens were, however, warned that they would be held strictly accountable for any future demonstrations of guerrilla warfare, and plainly informed that the only way in which they could save their houses from conflagration was for them to defend their territory against incursions of all lawless bands of guerrillas. My men behaved with much gallantry throughout. Their capabilities for hard and long marches were severely tried, and deserve the highest commendation. I was materially aided by Firey's cavalry. Without disparagement of others, I take great pleasure in commending the alacrity and valor of Captain Firey and his company quartermaster-sergeant, John Rivers.

I remain, colonel, very respectfully, your obedient servant,

S. W. DOWNEY,
*Third Regiment Potomac Home Brigade.*

Col. ALBERT TRACY,
*Assistant Adjutant-General, Mountain Department.*

## MAY 7, 1862.—Action at Somerville Heights, Va.

### REPORTS.

No. 1.—Maj. Gen. Nathaniel P. Banks, U. S. Army.
No. 2.—Col. Robert S. Foster, Thirteenth Indiana Infantry.

### No. 1.

*Reports of Maj. Gen. Nathaniel P. Banks, U. S. Army.*

NEW MARKET, *May* 7, 1862—11 p. m.

General Sullivan, guarding Columbia Bridge, made reconnaissance to burned bridge, 5 miles above Columbia Bridge, on Shenandoah, South Fork. Found enemy strongly posted. Sharp skirmish occurred. Enemy suffered severely. Our loss will report to-morrow. Jackson has announced to the people his intention to return to this valley. It is evident the enemy is strongly posted in all directions and in force. Object is doubtless to prevent junction of our forces.

N. P. BANKS,
*Major-General, Commanding.*

Hon. E. M. STANTON.

---

HEADQUARTERS DEPARTMENT OF THE SHENANDOAH,
*New Market, Va., May* 11, 1862.

GENERAL: I have the honor to transmit an official report of the affair which occurred on the 7th inst. on the South Fork of the Shenandoah, near a place called Somerville, between the Thirteenth Regiment Indiana Volunteers, Col. R. S. Foster commanding, with Co. B, First Vermont Cavalry, Captain Conger, and a rebel force of infantry and cavalry, the substance of which was transmitted by telegraph. The report embraces a complete list of 3 killed, 5 wounded, and 21 missing. Measures have been taken to investigate the facts, to some of which a brief allusion is made, of which a full statement will be forwarded.

I have the honor to be, with much respect, your obedient servant,

N. P. BANKS,
*Major-General, Commanding.*

Brig. Gen. LORENZO THOMAS, *Adjutant-General U. S. Army.*

---

### No. 2.

*Report of Col. Robert S. Foster, Thirteenth Indiana Infantry.*

HEADQUARTERS THIRTEENTH INDIANA REGIMENT,
*Columbia Bridge, May* 8, 1862.

SIR: In obedience to your order I beg leave to transmit to you the following account of the affair in which the Thirteenth Indiana Regiment was engaged near Somerville:

The enemy having attacked and driven in our outer pickets you ordered me to take six companies of the Thirteenth Indiana and to hold the other four in reserve under Captain Wilson, and for me to meet and engage the enemy, and if possible to drive him from his position, and if I found him in any considerable force to report the fact to you immediately. I accordingly took Companies A, B, F, G, H, and K, and proceeded beyond Honeyville about 2½ miles, where I found the enemy's advance guard posted on a hill. I immediately deployed Companies A, B, and F on each side of the road, taking Companies G, H, and K and going up the road directly in their front, we found the enemy's force or advance guard to consist of two companies of cavalry and two companies of infantry, with one piece of artillery, which I afterward learned were in command of Major Wheat, of the Louisiana battalion. We drove him from this position and continued to drive him through Somerville and to Dogtown under a heavy fire from our skirmishers, killing 2 of the enemy's cavalry and capturing a carbine and saber.

At Somerville I posted Companies A, F, G, H, and K on the heights on the left of the road, and taking Company B I pushed on to the burned bridge, about 2 miles up the road, and to the right of and distant about 2½ miles from Dogtown. Here I rested my men about half an hour, when Captain Conger, Company B, First Vermont Cavalry, came up and reported himself to me. I told him it was our intention to attack the enemy at daylight, consequently it was not our policy to pursue the enemy any farther at that time, and ordered him not to follow the enemy, but to bring up the rear and follow me back to camp. I withdrew all my skirmishers and started back to camp.

Stopping at Somerville, I called in the companies that were posted on the heights, and proceeded about 1 mile, where I halted to await the cavalry, which I supposed to be directly in my rear. Up to this time not a single casualty had occurred on our side. Here I received your dispatch, per courier, not to pursue the enemy too far—beware of a surprise—and immediately after I received your dispatch I received one from the cavalry: "We are surrounded; come to our assistance." On inquiry of the messenger I learned that the captain of the cavalry, in direct violation of my orders, instead of following in my rear, had gone some 4 miles up the river, and encountered the reserve of the enemy and was surrounded. I caused my command to about-face, and hurried to their assistance. I at the same time ordered Captain Wilson to bring up his reserve. We took position on the heights above the road and to the left of Somerville with Companies A, B, F, E, H, and K, Captain Wilson being immediately on the road with the reserve.

Here we engaged two regiments of infantry and three companies of cavalry at a distance of 100 yards, and drove their skirmishers back 200 or 300 yards on to their main body, which we engaged for half an hour under a most terrific fire from the enemy. Seeing him attempting with another regiment to turn our left flank, I ordered Captain Wilson to move with the reserve at a double-quick to our left, which order he obeyed with promptness. Seeing the enemy were likely to reach there before he did, and seeing their superior numbers, I ordered my men to fall back, which they did in good order, disputing every inch of ground as they went. While we were engaging the enemy the cavalry escaped by swimming the Shenandoah River.

I find our loss in killed, wounded, and missing to be 29, among them Sergeant-Major Vance. The enemy's loss in killed and wounded is greater than ours, and mostly of the Seventh Louisiana Regiment, they being in close column and directly in our front. Most all of our wounded we brought off from the field, and some of our missing I think swam the river, and may yet report themselves.

Too much praise cannot be awarded to the officers and men engaged, they having withstood a most terrific fire from not less than two regiments of infantry, together with cavalry, and bravely stood their ground until I ordered them to fall back, which they did in excellent order, fighting and disputing every inch of ground as they went.

Inclosed you will find a list of the killed, wounded, and missing.*

I am, respectfully, your obedient servant,

R. S. FOSTER,
*Colonel, Commanding Thirteenth Indiana.*

Brig. Gen. J. C. SULLIVAN,
*Commanding Forces at Columbia Bridge, Va.*

Our forces actually engaged, 180. All prisoners taken by us were from the Seventh Louisiana Regiment, all which have been reported to you.

---

## MAY 8, 1862.—Engagement near McDowell (Bull Pasture Mountain), Va.

### REPORTS.

No. 1.—Maj. Gen. John C. Frémont, U. S. Army, commanding the Mountain Department.†
No. 2.—Return of Casualties in the Union forces.
No. 3.—Brig. Gen. Robert C. Schenck, U. S. Army, commanding brigade.
No. 4.—Brig. Gen. Robert H. Milroy, U. S. Army, commanding brigade.
No. 5.—Col. Nathaniel C. McLean, Seventy-fifth Ohio Infantry.
No. 6.—Maj. Gen. Thomas J. Jackson, C. S. Army, commanding the Valley District, including operations since the battle of Kernstown.
No. 7.—Return of killed and wounded in the Confederate forces.
No. 8.—Lieut. Col. R. H. Cunningham, Twenty-first Virginia Infantry, Second Brigade.
No. 9.—Maj. Henry Lane, Forty-second Virginia Infantry.
No. 10.—Lieut. S. Hale, Acting Adjutant, Forty-eighth Virginia Infantry.
No. 11.—Capt. B. W. Leigh, First Virginia Battalion.
No. 12.—Brig. Gen. William B. Taliaferro, C. S. Army, commanding Third Brigade.
No. 13.—Brig. Gen. Edward Johnson, C. S. Army, commanding Army of the Northwest.
No. 14.—Col. W. C. Scott, Forty-fourth Virginia Infantry, commanding Second Brigade.
No. 15.—Col. Michael G. Harman, Fifty-second Virginia Infantry.

### No. 1.

*Reports of Maj. Gen. John C. Frémont, U. S. Army, commanding the Mountain Department.*

HEADQUARTERS MOUNTAIN DEPARTMENT,
*Petersburg, Va., May* 9, 1862.

A dispatch received this morning from General Schenck states as follows:

---

* Nominal list omitted.

† See also Frémont's general report, pp. 9–11.

McDOWELL, *May* 8.

It is 11.30 p. m. The reconnaissance of Milroy this afternoon became a sharp engagement, in which we lost several killed and perhaps 75 or 80 wounded. Rebel loss at least as large or larger, but not known. Johnson found to have been largely re-enforced by Jackson during the afternoon. His whole force has come up from Buffalo Gap. A large army on the hills about us. This place indefensible altogether, by the unanimous agreement of officers, in our present condition and with our relative forces.

SCHENCK.

I have placed on the line of march of Blenker's division shoes and other supplies, and they are being urged forward with all possible dispatch.

J. C. FRÉMONT,
*Major-General.*

Hon. E. M. STANTON,
*Secretary of War.*

---

MOUNTAIN DEPARTMENT, HDQRS. ARMY IN FIELD,
*Franklin, May* 13, 1862.

Arrived here at 10 a. m. with my advance brigade. Find Jackson retreating. Loss on our side, killed and wounded, at fight at McDowell, and in falling back from that place, and also at this point, 200. Enemy's loss reported by prisoners to be 22 killed; wounded not known.

J. C. FRÉMONT,
*Major-General, Commanding.*

Hon. E. M. STANTON.

MOUNTAIN DEPARTMENT, HDQRS. IN THE FIELD,
*Franklin, Va., May* 16, 1862.

SIR: I have the honor to inclose you the official reports of Brigadier-Generals Schenck and Milroy concerning the action of the 8th instant near McDowell.

It will undoubtedly give you pleasure to know, as it affords me great satisfaction to say, that the conduct of the regiments engaged, under the gallant leadership of Brigadier-General Milroy, was distinguished by the admirable courage and tenacity with which they repeatedly attacked and charged a greatly superior force.

More accurate information places the number of the enemy's dead at 42, buried in the neighborhood, and his wounded at 200 or more.

The promptitude with which General Schenck advanced to the relief of the force under General Milroy, and the skill and courage with which he conducted the hazardous retreat, which I found it necessary to order, are worthy of particular notice.

Having anticipated while at New Creek, on the Baltimore and Ohio Railroad, a movement of the enemy in this direction, I advanced as rapidly as possible with my whole available force to this point, where Generals Schenck and Milroy successfully held the enemy at bay until my approach caused him immediately to retire.

The necessity of making this advance before adequate transportation could be collected has caused some suffering among the men, but this has only given me additional reason to commend their conduct. They cheerfully submit to all privations, and are only anxious to have an opportunity of displaying their devotion to their country.

Very respectfully, your obedient servant,

J. C. FRÉMONT,
*Major-General, Commanding.*

Hon. E. M. STANTON,
*Secretary of War.*

---

## No. 2.

### *Return of Casualties in the Union forces.*

[Compiled from nominal lists of casualties.]

| Command. | Killed. | | Wounded. | | Missing. | | Aggregate. | Remarks. |
|---|---|---|---|---|---|---|---|---|
| | Officers. | Enlisted men. | Officers. | Enlisted men. | Officers. | Enlisted men. | | |
| 25th Ohio | ...... | 6 | 1 | 50 | ...... | 1 | 58 | |
| 32d Ohio | ...... | 4 | 3 | 49 | ...... | ...... | 56 | Lieut. C. S. Fugate died of wounds. |
| 75th Ohio | ...... | 6 | 1 | 31 | ...... | 1 | 39 | |
| 82d Ohio | ...... | 6 | 5 | 45 | ...... | 1 | 57 | Lieut. C. W. Deibold died of wounds. |
| 3d West Virginia | ...... | 4 | 1 | 41 | ...... | ...... | 46 | |
| Total | ...... | 26 | 11 | 216 | ...... | 3 | 256 | |

## No. 3.

### *Report of Brig. Gen. Robert C. Schenck, U. S. Army, commanding brigade.*

HDQRS. SCHENCK'S BRIGADE, MOUNTAIN DEPARTMENT,
*Camp Franklin, May* 14, 1862.

I have had the honor in my dispatches, heretofore transmitted through you, to inform the general commanding of my march with my brigade from Franklin to McDowell to the relief of Brigadier-General Milroy, who, with his force, fallen back to and concentrated at the last-named place, was threatened with attack by the combined armies of the rebel Generals Jackson and Johnson. By leaving my baggage train under a guard in my last camp, on the road 14 miles from McDowell, I was able to push forward so as to make the whole distance (34 miles) in twenty-three hours. I added, however, but little numerical strength to the army I was sent to relieve. My brigade, consisting of but three regiments, and with several companies then on detached and other duty, brought into the field an aggregate of only 1,300 infantry, besides De Beck's battery, of the First Ohio Artillery, and about 250 of the First Battalion of Connecticut Cavalry. With this help I reached General Milroy at 10 a. m. on the 8th instant. I was, to use his own expression, "just in time." I found his regiments of infantry partly in line of battle in the plain at McDowell, covering some of the various approaches from the mountain, and partly disposed as skirmishers on the heights in front, and his batteries in position, expecting momentarily that the enemy would attempt to descend into the valley to attack him under cover of artillery that might be brought forward to command the place from different points.

A little observation served to show at once that McDowell, as a defensive position, was entirely untenable, and especially against the largely outnumbering force that was ascertained to be advancing; and if it had been otherwise there was no choice left on account of an entire destitution of forage. I determined, therefore, to obey, with as little delay as possible, your orders to fall back with the force of our two brigades to this place. Such a movement, however, could not with any safety or propriety be commenced before night, nor did it seem advisable to undertake it without first ascertaining or feeling the actual strength of the rebel force before us, and also, perhaps, taking some step that would serve to check or disable him from his full power or disposition to pursue. This was effectually done by our attack of his position on the mountain in the afternoon, and in the night following I was enabled to withdraw our whole little army along the road through the narrow gorge, which afforded the only egress from the valley in which McDowell is situated, in the direction of Franklin. This withdrawal we effected without the loss of a man and without the loss or destruction of any article of public property, except of some stores, for which General Milroy was entirely without the means of transportation.

I submit herewith the reports of Brigadier-General Milroy and of Col. James Cantwell,* commanding the Eighty-second Ohio Volunteer Infantry, of my brigade, giving an account of the affair with the rebel forces that day and of the parts severally taken in the fight by the different regiments engaged.

At 3 o'clock, General Milroy having reported to me that his scouts informed him of re-enforcements continually arriving to the support of the enemy, concealed among the woods on the mountain, and that they were evidently making preparations to get artillery in position for sweeping the valley, I consented to his request to be permitted to make a reconnaissance. The force detailed for this purpose consisted of portions of four regiments of infantry of his brigade—the Seventy-fifth, Twenty-fifth, and Thirty-second Ohio and the Third West Virginia—and the Eighty-second Ohio, of mine, the latter regiment gladly receiving the order to join in the enterprise, although the men were exhausted with the long march from which they had just arrived, with want of food, sleep, and rest. The infantry was supported in a degree also by a 6-pounder of Johnson's battery, which General Milroy had succeeded in conveying to the top of one of the mountain ridges on his left. The movement resulted in a very sharp encounter with the rebels, of which details are given in the accompanying reports. To those details I refer. I will only add, by way of general summing up, that, adding to the 1,768 of Milroy's brigade about 500 of the Eighty-second Ohio, which was the number in the action, the entire force we had engaged was 2,268. That these men were opposed to, I believe, not less than 5,000 of the enemy successively brought into action, besides their reserved force of some 8,000 in the rear; that the casualties on our part amounted in the aggregate to 28 killed, 80 severely wounded, 145 slightly wounded, and 3 missing, making a total of 256.†

---

*Colonel Cantwell's report not found.

†See revised statement, p. 462.

As the evening closed in, and it was ascertained that, from the unexpected severity and protraction of the fight, the ammunition of some of the regiments was almost completely exhausted, I endeavored in person to get a supply of cartridges to the men, and had three wagon loads taken some distance up the Staunton road for that purpose, but the only way it could reach them up the steep mountain side was to be carried by hand or in haversacks. I ordered up the road also the Fifth Regiment West Virginia Infantry, Colonel Zeigler commanding, of my brigade, to the relief of the other troops, if needed, and they most promptly and actively moved to the field, but it was not necessary to bring them into the action. The troops that were engaged, after fighting with a coolness and order and bravery which it is impossible to excel, and after pressing back the enemy over the mountain crest and maintaining unflinchingly and under the most galling and constant fire their ground until darkness set in, were then withdrawn under the immediate order of Colonel McLean, of the Seventy-fifth Ohio, leaving, as I believe, not a prisoner behind, for the 3 men reported missing are supposed to be among the killed.

We took 4 prisoners of the enemy. His loss in killed is thought by all engaged to have much exceeded ours. From prisoners since taken I have ascertained that his killed on the field was admitted to be not less than 30 and his wounded very numerous.

Among the rebels wounded I learn was General Johnson himself and at least one of his field officers. The colonel of a Virginia regiment is known to be among the slain.

Too much praise cannot be awarded to General Milroy himself; to Colonel McLean, of the Seventy-fifth Ohio; Colonel Cantwell, Eighty-second Ohio; Lieutenant-Colonel Richardson, commanding the Twenty-fifth Ohio; Major Reily, Seventy-fifth Ohio; Lieutenant-Colonel Swinney, commanding Thirty-second Ohio; Lieutenant-Colonel Thompson, Third West Virginia Infantry, and the officers and men of their several commands for their steady gallantry and courage manifested throughout the whole affair. No veteran troops, I am sure, ever acquitted themselves with more ardor, and yet with such order and coolness, as they displayed in marching and fighting up that steep mountain side in the face of a hot and incessant fire.

From McDowell I fell back by easy marches on the 9th, 10th, and 11th to this place, the enemy cautiously pursuing.

On a commanding ridge of ground 13 miles from McDowell, at the intersection of the road from that place with the turnpike to Monterey, I stopped from 8 a. m. to 2 p. m. on the 9th, and made my dispositions to receive and repulse the attack of the rebels, who appeared in our rear, but they declined the undertaking.

While awaiting the arrival of the general commanding with re-enforcements at this point on the 11th, 12th, and 13th, the rebel army having advanced to within 2 miles of our position, we were kept constantly engaged in watchful preparation for an expected assault. I had my batteries and the forces so disposed as to feel confident of repelling any attack; but we had no collision, except some skirmishing with my pickets and portions of the infantry advanced on the range of hills to my right as I confronted the enemy's approach, and which resulted only in the loss of 2 men—1 of the Fifth West Virginia Regiment on the 11th, and 1 of the Third Regiment Potomac Home Brigade on the 12th—on our side, and 4 or 5 of the enemy killed by our shells.

The approaches were so guarded as to prevent the enemy from getting his artillery into any commanding position, and in the night of the 13th he withdrew back along the turnpike road to the southward.

I am, respectfully, your obedient servant,

ROBT. C. SCHENCK,
*Brigadier-General.*

Col. ALBERT TRACY,
*Asst. Adjt. Gen., Headquarters Mountain Department.*

---

## No. 4.

*Report of Brig. Gen. Robert H. Milroy, U. S. Army, commanding brigade.*

HEADQUARTERS MILROY'S BRIGADE,
*Camp near Franklin, Va., May* 14, 1862.

GENERAL: I have the honor to report to you the results of the engagement of the 8th instant, near McDowell, on the Bull Pasture Mountain:

As an apology for the delay in transmitting this report I would state that the officers and men of my command have since the occurrence of the engagement been constantly occupied in active field duty, leaving no time for the preparation of the details by the company and regimental commanders, from which alone a correct report could be made.

Upon May 7 I was first advised by my scouts and spies that a junction had been effected between the armies of the rebel Generals Jackson and Johnson, and that they were advancing to attack me at McDowell. Having the day previous sent out a large portion of the Third West Virginia and Thirty-second and Seventy-fifth Ohio Regiments to Shaw's Ridge and upon Shenandoah Mountain for the purpose of protecting my foraging and reconnoitering parties, I immediately ordered my whole command to concentrate at McDowell, and, expecting re-enforcements, prepared for defense there.

In the afternoon of the 7th instant a large force of the rebels was discovered descending the west side of Shenandoah Mountain along the Staunton and Parkersburg turnpike. I ordered a section of the Ninth Ohio Battery (Captain Hyman) on Shaw's Ridge to shell them and endeavor to retard their progress. This they did with such effect as to cause the enemy to retire beyond the Shenandoah Mountain; but observing another heavy force crossing the mountain on our right, some 2 miles distant, I deemed it prudent to fall back and concentrate at McDowell.

Upon the next morning (8th instant) the enemy was seen upon the Bull Pasture Mountain, about $1\frac{3}{4}$ miles distant from McDowell, on my right and front. I commenced shelling them and sent out parties of skirmishers to endeavor to ascertain their numbers. At about 10 a. m. your brigade arrived. Desultory firing of a section of Hyman's battery and occasional skirmishing engaged the attention of the enemy during the morning. Major Long, of the Seventy-third Ohio Volunteer Infantry, with a party of skirmishers, rendered a good service by his efforts in ascertaining the position of the enemy. In the afternoon, at about 3 o'clock, being informed by Capt. George R. Latham, of Second West Virginia Volunteer Infantry, who, with his company, was engaged in skirmishing, that the rebels were endeavoring to plant a battery upon the mountain which would command our whole encampment, with your permission I made a reconnaissance for the purpose of obtaining accurate information of their strength and position. For this purpose the following troops were placed at my disposal: The Twenty-fifth Ohio Volunteer Infantry, Seventy-fifth Ohio Volunteer Infantry, Thirty-second Ohio Volunteer Infantry, Eighty-second Ohio Volunteer Infantry, Third West Virginia Volunteer Infantry. These regiments were by no means full, various companies of each being detailed for special duty. The number of privates, non-commissioned officers, and officers actually engaged are reported to me as follows:

| | |
|---|---|
| 25th Ohio Volunteer Infantry | 469 |
| 75th Ohio Volunteer Infantry | 444 |
| 32d Ohio Volunteer Infantry | 416 |
| 3d West Virginia Volunteer Infantry | 439 |
| Total | 1,768 |

Which is the entire number of field officers, company officers, and privates of this brigade engaged. The exact number of the Eighty-second Ohio Volunteer Infantry engaged is not known to me, but has doubtless been reported to you.

Under my order the Twenty-fifth Ohio and Seventy-fifth Ohio Regiments (the former under the command of Lieut. Col. W. P. Richardson and the latter under the command of Col. N. C. McLean and Maj. Robert Reily) advanced in the most gallant manner up the face of the hill and attacked the enemy in their front. Numbering less than 1,000 men, unprotected by any natural or artificial shelter, they advanced up a precipitous mountain side upon an adversary protected by intrenchments and the natural formation of the mountain, and unsupported drove them (being at least twice their numerical strength) over the crest of the mountain, and for one and a half hours maintained unaided, while exposed to a deadly fire, the position from which they had so bravely driven the foe.

Too much praise cannot be awarded to the officers or men of these regiments. The Twenty-fifth Ohio led the advance, and were rapidly followed and supported by the Seventy-fifth, both acting with the coolness of veterans and the determination of patriot soldiers, willing to sacrifice their lives for the good of the Republic.

At about 4 o'clock in the afternoon, perceiving that the enemy's force was being constantly increased, I ordered the Eighty-second Regiment, of your brigade, the Thirty-second Ohio, and Third West Virginia to turn the right flank of the enemy, and, if possible, attack them in the rear. They obeyed the order with the greatest alacrity, but the enemy, observing the design and having a much superior force, in a handsome manner changed his front to the rear. The regiments named, however, attacked them briskly and kept up a destructive fire, causing the enemy to waver several times; but fresh re-enforcements being brought up by them, and a portion of their re-enforcements coming down the turnpike, the Third West Virginia became exposed to their fire in its front and rear. Unable, however, to withstand the fire of the Third West Virginia, the latter re-enforcements joined the main body of the rebels and the contest became general and bloody. While the Third West Virginia and Thirty-second and Eighty-second Ohio were advancing on the enemy a 6-pounder, of Johnson's battery, under command of Lieutenant Powers, was with the greatest difficulty placed in position on the mountain on the left of the turnpike, and gave efficient support to the attack. During the engagement I also ordered two 12-pounders, of

Johnson's (Twelfth Ohio) battery, to be placed upon the pike, but they could not be placed in position until after twilight.

From 3 p. m. until 8 o'clock our small force engaged with undaunted bravery a force of the enemy which could not have been less than 5,000 men, and maintained the position from which they had driven them, displaying a courage and zeal which has merited the thanks of the country and proved them true representatives of the American citizen soldier. After night-fall the engagement was continued, the firing of our men being guided only by the flashes of the enemy's musketry, until the ammunition of almost all the men engaged was wholly exhausted, when, having achieved the purpose of the attack, our forces were recalled, retiring in good order, bringing with them their dead and wounded.

While I would be glad to bring prominently to the notice of the major-general commanding the names of the officers and men who distinguished themselves in the action, I could not do so without rehearsing the names of all engaged. Neither officer nor man of those engaged faltered in the performance of his whole duty.

The Twenty-fifth and Seventy-fifth Ohio Volunteer Infantry Regiments, in their gallant advance; the Thirty-second Ohio, in a daring bayonet charge, and the Third West Virginia, in their endurance of the most severe fire of the enemy, alike merit his entire approbation.

To Brigadier-General Schenck, for his advice, counsel, and active cooperation, and to the officers and men of the Eighty-second Ohio Volunteer Infantry, who so bravely sustained my brigade, I owe my warmest thanks.

I forward herewith a report of the killed, wounded, and missing of my brigade.

I am, general, very respectfully and truly, your obedient servant,

R. H. MILROY,
*Brigadier-General.*

[Inclosure.]

*Recapitulation of losses.*

| Command. | Number engaged. | Killed. | Wounded severely. | Wounded slightly. | Missing. | Total. |
|---|---|---|---|---|---|---|
| 75th Ohio | 444 | 6 | 13 | 19 | 1 | 39 |
| 25th Ohio | 469 | 6 | 26 | 25 | 1 | 58 |
| 32d Ohio | 416 | 4 | 13 | 39 | ...... | 56 |
| 3d West Virginia | 439 | 4 | 9 | 33 | ...... | 46 |
| Total | 1,768 | 20 | 61 | 116 | 2 | 199 |

## No. 5.

*Report of Col. Nathaniel C. McLean, Seventy-fifth Ohio Infantry.*

HDQRS. SEVENTY-FIFTH REGT. OHIO VOL. INFANTRY,
*Camp Franklin, May 14, 1862.*

GENERAL: I have the honor to submit to you a report of the battle of Bull Pasture Mountain, which occurred on the 8th instant near McDowell. This report would have been sooner made but for the constant duty upon which I have been engaged up to last night. This has rendered it impossible until the present moment for me to devote any time to this report, and is my excuse for the delay.

Under your orders on the afternoon of the 8th instant I marched to attack the Confederate forces, then in position on the top of Bull Pasture Mountain, having under my command seven companies of my own regiment (the Seventy-fifth Ohio) and nine companies of the Twenty-fifth Ohio, commanded by Lieutenant-Colonel Richardson. The remaining three companies and a part of the seven of the Seventy-fifth Ohio were, at the time the order was received, separated from the regiment by your previous orders during the day, and had been engaged in skirmishing with the advance of the enemy, so that I had not the benefit of their strength in the battle. The companies of my own regiment engaged, with the numbers present of each, were as follows: Company A, Captain Friend commanding, 86 men; Company F, Captain Morgan commanding, 51 men; Company I, Captain Fry commanding, 61 men; Company C, Captain Harris commanding, 71 men; Company H, Captain Pilcher commanding, 69 men; Company E, Captain Foster commanding, 46 men; and Company G, Lieutenant Morey commanding, 60 men. Total of Seventy-fifth Ohio engaged, 444 men.

I have not yet ascertained the numbers engaged in the Twenty-fifth Ohio, but have been informed by Lieutenant-Colonel Richardson that his nine companies were incomplete. He will report himself the exact number in the action.

The enemy were in position on the top of the mountain, entirely screened from our view, and the conformation of the ridge permitted them to deliver their fire with only the exposure of a small portion of their bodies, and in reloading they were entirely protected from our fire by the crest of the hill. The side of the mountain up which I was compelled to make the attack was entirely destitute of protection either from trees or rocks, and so steep that the men were at times compelled to march either to one side or the other in order to make the ascent. In making the advance Lieutenant-Colonel Richardson, by my order, deployed two of his companies as skirmishers, in order to more clearly ascertain the position and strength of the enemy. As soon as these companies were deployed properly I ordered Lieutenant-Colonel Richardson to support them with the whole of his regiment formed in line of battle, which order was executed with great promptness, and in a few moments the whole of the Twenty-fifth Ohio was advancing steadily to the front up the mountain, overcoming the difficult ascent with great labor. As soon as the Twenty-fifth Ohio had advanced so as to make room in the open ground for the movement, I formed my own regiment (the Seventy-fifth Ohio) in line of battle and gave the order for the advance, so that the whole force under my command was within easy supporting distance. The enemy did not permit the skirmishers to advance far before a heavy fire was opened upon them from the whole crest of the hill. The mountain was circular in its formation, so that when the whole line was engaged the flanks were in a manner concealed from each other. The enemy received us with so heavy and destructive a fire that I was compelled to bring forward as rapidly as possible the whole of the forces under my command.

I cannot say too much in praise of the conduct of the troops. Under the most heavy and galling fire from a well-sheltered enemy, and without protection themselves, they steadily advanced up the precipitous ascent, firing and loading with great coolness until the enemy was forced to retire from their first position to a second ridge in the rear, which, however, protected them from our fire equally as well as the one which they had abandoned. At this point our troops were halted, and finding that we were attacking a much larger force than I had anticipated, occupying also a most admirable defensive position, I deemed it prudent to make no farther advance, and determined, if possible, to hold on to the ground already acquired. In the position gained my men found partial protection while loading their pieces by taking advantage of the uneven nature of the grounds. This, however, was slight, as the enemy were so placed that many of our men were wounded by their fire some distance below the advanced front. Our position was one of extreme danger and exposure, and the fire of the enemy was heavy, coming sometimes in tremendous volleys, as if they meant by one fire to sweep us from the mountain. Most nobly did our troops sustain themselves.

Both regiments worked together with great coolness, and the men seemed only to be anxious to get steady aim when firing their pieces, without a thought of retiring. We held this position for at least an hour and a half before any troops arrived to re-enforce us, the enemy not daring to make the attempt to drive us back by a charge.

At about this time the Thirty-second Ohio, under command of Lieutenant-Colonel Swinney, and the Eighty-second Ohio, under command of Colonel Cantwell, came to our aid and took position in our midst. The fighting continued around the crest of the hill at this point until I was informed that the Twenty-fifth Ohio were out of ammunition and that some of my own regiment (the Seventy-fifth Ohio) were in the same condition, although every man of my own regiment started in the action with 60 rounds. The evening also was well advanced, so that our men could only see the enemy by the flashes of their guns. The moon was shining, but did not give sufficient light to enable the men to shoot with accuracy. Under these circumstances I determined to withdraw the forces, and so gave the order. I formed the Seventy-fifth Ohio in line of battle under the crest of the hill, sufficiently low down to be out of the worst of the fire, and marched them down the mountain in this order as well as the nature of the ground would permit, so as at any time to be able to face to the rear and fire upon the enemy in case they should attempt to follow us. Upon reaching the road I halted and waited until the Twenty-fifth Ohio, the Eighty-second Ohio, and the Thirty-second Ohio had all returned to the road, when we marched back to McDowell. The action was a most severe one, as is shown by the report of the killed and wounded already in your possession.

My officers and men alike bore themselves most bravely in the action. Lieutenant-Colonel Constable, being sick, was unable to be with us, but Major Reily rendered most important and gallant service during the whole engagement, rallying the men and keeping them to their work, when (as it was the case at times) the enemy seemed by the increase of their fire to have brought new forces into the action.

I had but one officer wounded; and of them all, so far as they came under my observation, I can speak in the warmest terms as regards their gallant conduct during the action.

I have the honor to be, very respectfully, your obedient servant,

N. C. McLEAN,

*Colonel Seventy-fifth Regiment Ohio Volunteer Infantry.*

Brigadier-General MILROY.

## No. 6.

*Reports of Maj. Gen. Thomas J. Jackson, C. S. Army, commanding the Valley District, including operations since the battle of Kernstown.*

VALLEY DISTRICT, VA., *May* 9, 1862.
*Via Staunton, Va., May* 10, 1862.

General S. COOPER,
*Adjutant-General:*

God blessed our arms with victory at McDowell yesterday.

T. J. JACKSON,
*Major-General.*

---

HDQRS. SECOND CORPS, ARMY OF NORTHERN VIRGINIA,
*March* 7, 1863.

GENERAL: I have the honor herewith to submit to you a report of the operations of my command in the battle of McDowell, Highland County, Virginia, on May 8:

After the battle of Kernstown I retreated in the direction of Harrisonburg. My rear guard—comprising Ashby's cavalry, Captain Chew's battery, and from time to time other forces—was placed under the direction of Col. Turner Ashby, an officer whose judgment, coolness, and courage eminently qualified him for the delicate and important trust Although pursued by a greatly superior force, under General Banks, we were enabled to halt for more than a fortnight in the vicinity of Mount Jackson.

After reaching Harrisonburg we turned toward the Blue Ridge, and on April 19 crossed the South Fork of the Shenandoah, and took position between that river and Swift Run Gap, in Elk Run Valley.

General R. S. Ewell, having been directed to join my command, left the vicinity of Gordonsville, and on the 30th arrived with his division west of the Blue Ridge.

The main body of General Banks' pursuing army did not proceed farther south than the vicinity of Harrisonburg; but a considerable force, under the command of General Milroy, was moving toward Staunton from the direction of Monterey, and, as I satisfactorily learned, part of it had already crossed to the east of the Shenandoah Mountain, and was encamped not far from the Harrisonburg and Warm Springs turnpike. The positions of these two Federal armies were now such that if left unmolested they could readily form a junction on the road just named and move with their united forces against Staunton.

At this time Brig. Gen. Edward Johnson, with his troops, was near Buffalo Gap, west of Staunton, so that, if the enemy was allowed to effect a junction, it would probably be followed not only by the seizure of a point so important as Staunton, but must compel General Johnson to abandon his position, and he might succeed in getting between us. To avoid these results I determined, if practicable, after strengthening my own division by a union with Johnson's, first to strike at Milroy and then to concentrate the forces of Ewell and Johnson with my own against Banks.

To carry out my design against Milroy General Ewell was directed to march his division to the position which I then occupied, in the Elk Run Valley, with a view to holding Banks in check, while I pushed on with my division to Staunton. These movements were made.

At Staunton I found, according to previous arrangements, Major-General Smith, of the Virginia Military Institute, with the corps of cadets, ready to co-operate in the defense of that portion of the valley.

On the morning of May 7 General Johnson, whose familiarity with that mountain region and whose high qualities as a soldier admirably fitted him for the advance, moved with his command in the direction of the enemy, followed by the brigades of General Taliaferro, Colonel Campbell, and General Winder, in the order named.

Encountering the enemy's advance near the point where the Staunton and Parkersburg turnpike intersects the Harrisonburg and Warm Springs turnpike, General Johnson pressed forward. The Federals rapidly retreated, abandoning their baggage at Rodgers' and other points east of the Shenandoah Mountain. After the advance had reached the western base of the Shenandoah Mountain the troops bivouacked for the night.

On the following morning the march was resumed, General Johnson's brigade still in front. The head of the column was halted near the top of Bull Pasture Mountain, and General Johnson, accompanied by a party of 30 men and several officers, with a view to a reconnaissance of the enemy's position, ascended Setlington's Hill, an isolated spur of the Bull Pasture Mountain on the left of the turnpike, and commanding a full view of the village of McDowell. From this point the position, and to some extent the strength, of the enemy could be seen. In the valley in which McDowell is located was observed a considerable force of infantry. To the right, on a height, were two regiments, but too distant for an effective fire to that point. Almost a mile in front was a battery supported by infantry.

The enemy, observing a reconnoitering party, sent out a small body of skirmishers, which was promptly met by the men with General Johnson and driven back.

For the purpose of securing the hill, all of General Johnson's regiments were sent to him. The Fifty-second Virginia Regiment, being the first to reach the ground, was posted on the left as skirmishers, and it was not long before they were engaged in a brisk encounter with the enemy's skirmishers, whom they handsomely repulsed. Soon after this three other regiments arrived, and were posted as follows: The Twelfth Georgia on the crest of the hill, and forming the center of our line; the Fifty-eighth Virginia on the left, to support the Fifty-second, and the Forty-fourth Virginia on the right near a ravine.

Milroy having during the day been re-enforced by General Schenck, determined to carry the hill, if possible, by a direct attack. Advancing in force along its western slope, protected in his advance by the character of the ground and the wood interposed in our front and driving our skirmishers before him, he emerged from the woods and poured a galling fire into our right, which was returned, and a brisk and animated contest was kept up for some time, when the two remaining regiments of Johnson's brigade (the Twenty-fifth and Thirty-first) coming up, they were posted to the right. The fire was now rapid and well sustained on both sides and the conflict fierce and sanguinary.

In ascending to the crest of the hill from the turnpike the troops had to pass to the left through the woods by a narrow and rough route. To prevent the possibility of the enemy's advancing along the turnpike and seizing the point where the troops left the road to ascend the hill, the Thirty-first Virginia Regiment was posted between that point and the town, and when ordered to join its brigade in action its place was supplied by the Twenty-first Virginia Regiment. The engagement had now not only become general along the entire line, but so intense, that I ordered General Taliaferro to the support of General Johnson. Accordingly, the Twenty-third and Thirty-seventh Virginia Regiments were advanced to the center of the line, which was then held by the Twelfth Georgia with heroic gallantry, and the Tenth Virginia was ordered to support the Fifty-second Virginia, which had already driven the enemy from the left and had now advanced to make a flank movement on him.

At this time the Federals were pressing forward in strong force on our extreme right, with a view of flanking that position. This movement of the enemy was speedily detected and met by General Taliaferro's brigade and the Twelfth Georgia with great promptitude. Further to check it, portions of the Twenty-fifth and Thirty-first Virginia Regiments were sent to occupy an elevated piece of woodland on our right and rear, so situated as to fully command the position of the enemy. The brigade commanded by Colonel Campbell coming up about this time was, together with the Tenth Virginia, ordered down the ridge into the woods to guard against movements against our right flank, which they, in connection with the other force, effectually prevented.

The battle lasted about four hours—from 4.30 in the afternoon until 8.30. Every attempt by front or flank movement to attain the crest of the hill, where our line was formed, was signally and effectually repulsed. Finally, after dark, their force ceased firing, and the enemy retired.

The enemy's artillery, posted on a hill in our front, was active in throwing shot and shell up to the period when the infantry fight commenced, but in consequence of the great angle of elevation at which they fired, and our sheltered position, they inflicted no loss upon our troops. Our own artillery was not brought up, there being no road to the rear by which our guns could be withdrawn in event of disaster, and the prospect of successfully using them did not compensate for the risk.

General Johnson, to whom I had intrusted the management of the troops engaged, proved himself eminently worthy of the confidence reposed in him by the skill, gallantry, and presence of mind which he displayed on the occasion. Having received a wound near the close of the engagement which compelled him to leave the field, he turned over the command to General Taliaferro.

During the night the Federals made a hurried retreat towards Franklin, in Pendleton County, leaving their dead upon the field. Before doing so, however, they succeeded in destroying most of their ammunition, camp equipage, and commissary stores, which they could not remove.

Official reports show a loss in this action of 71 killed and 390 wounded, making a total loss of 461.

Among the killed was Colonel Gibbons, of the Tenth Virginia Regiment. Colonel Harman, of the Fifty-second, Col. George H. Smith and Maj. John C. Higginbotham, of the Twenty-fifth, and Major Campbell, of the Forty-eighth Virginia, were among the wounded.

To prevent Banks from re-enforcing Milroy, Mr. J. Hotchkiss, who was on topographical duty with the army, proceeded with a party to blockade the roads through North River and Dry River Gaps, while a detachment of cavalry obstructed the road through Brock's Gap.

As the Federals continued to fight until night and retreated before morning, but few of their number were captured. Besides quartermaster and commissary stores, some arms and other ordnance stores fell into our hands.

Dr. Hunter McGuire, my medical director, managed his department admirably.

Lieut. Hugh H. Lee, chief of ordnance, rendered valuable assistance in seeing my instructions respecting the manner in which the troops should go into action faithfully carried out. I regret to say that during the action he was so seriously wounded as to render it necessary for him to leave the field.

First Lieut. A. S. Pendleton, aide-de-camp; First Lieut. J. K. Boswell, chief engineer, and Second Lieut. R. K. Meade, assistant chief of ordnance, were actively engaged in transmitting orders.

Previous to the battle the enemy had such complete control of the pass through which our artillery would have to pass, if it continued to advance on the direct road to McDowell, that I determined to postpone the attack until the morning of the 9th. Owing to the action having been brought on by Milroy's advancing to the attack on the 8th, Maj. R. L. Dabney, assistant adjutant-general, was not with me during the engagement.

Maj. J. A. Harman, chief quartermaster, and Maj. W. J. Hawks, chief commissary, had their departments in good condition.

Leaving Lieut. Col. J. T. L. Preston, with a detachment of cadets and a small body of cavalry, in charge of the prisoners and public property, the main body of the army, preceded by Capt. George Sheetz, with his cavalry, pursued the retreating Federals to the vicinity of Franklin, but succeeded in capturing only a few prisoners and stores along the line of march.

The junction between Banks and Milroy having been prevented, and becoming satisfied of the impracticability of capturing the defeated enemy, owing to the mountainous character of the country being favorable for a retreating army to make its escape, I determined, as the enemy had made another stand at Franklin, with a prospect of being soon re-enforced, that I would not attempt to press farther, but return to the open country of the Shenandoah Valley, hoping, through the blessing of Providence, to defeat Banks before he should receive re-enforcements.

On Thursday, the 15th, the army, after divine service, for the purpose of rendering thanks to God for the victory with which He had blessed us and to implore His continued favor, began to retrace its course.

Great praise is due the officers and men for their conduct in action and on the march.

Though Colonel Crutchfield, chief of artillery, did not have an opportunity of bringing his command into action on the 8th, it was used with effect on several occasions during the expedition.

My special thanks are due Maj. Gen. F. H. Smith for his conduct and patriotic co-operation during the expedition.

Col. T. H. Williamson, of the Engineers, rendered valuable service.

For further information respecting the engagement and those who distinguished themselves I respectfully refer you to the accompanying reports of brigade and other commanders.

I am, general, very respectfully, your obedient servant,

T. J. JACKSON,
*Lieutenant-General.*

Brig. Gen. R. H. CHILTON,
*Assistant Adjutant and Inspector-General,*
*Headquarters Army of Northern Virginia.*

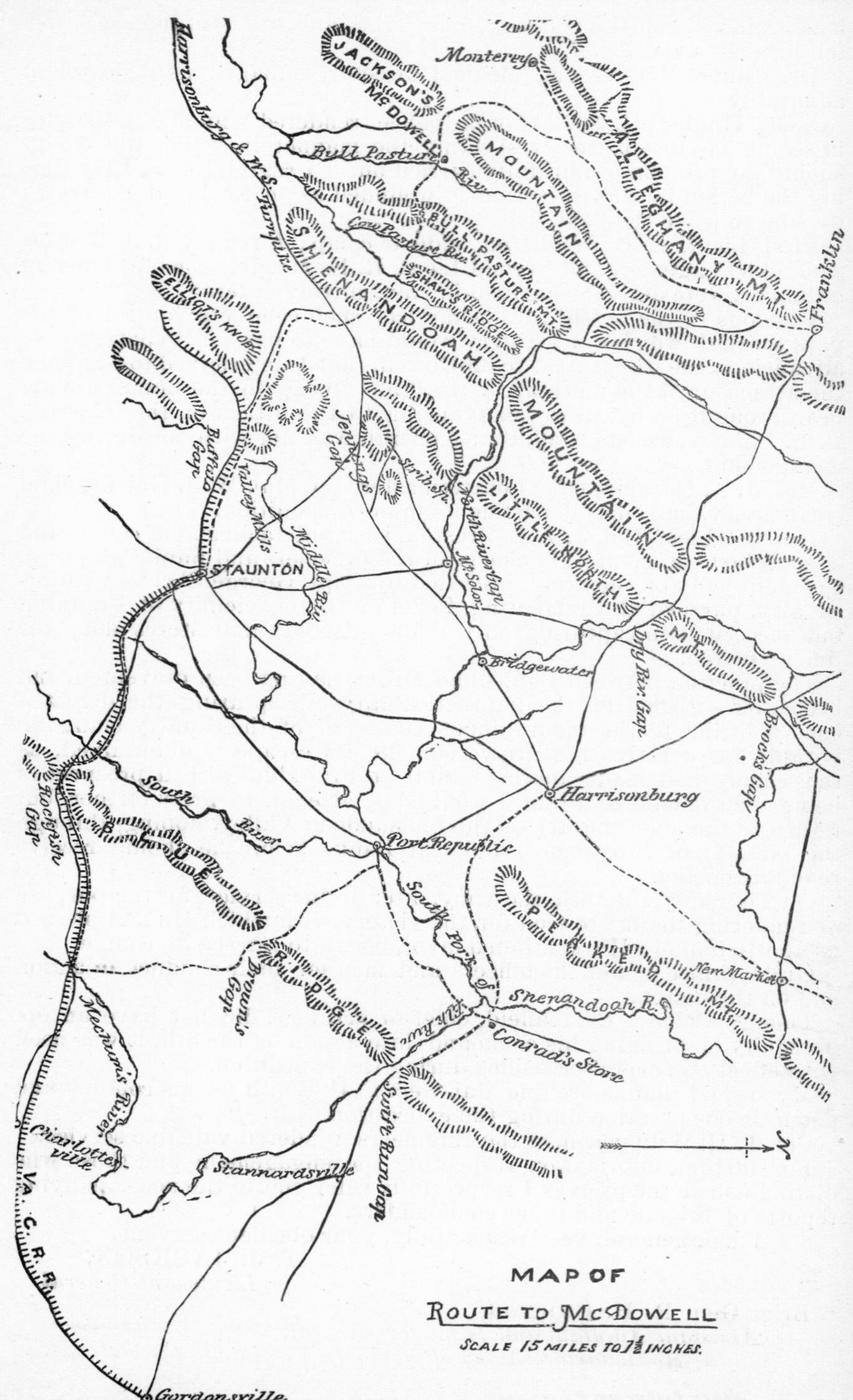


MAP OF

ROUTE TO McDOWELL

SCALE 15 MILES TO 1½ INCHES.

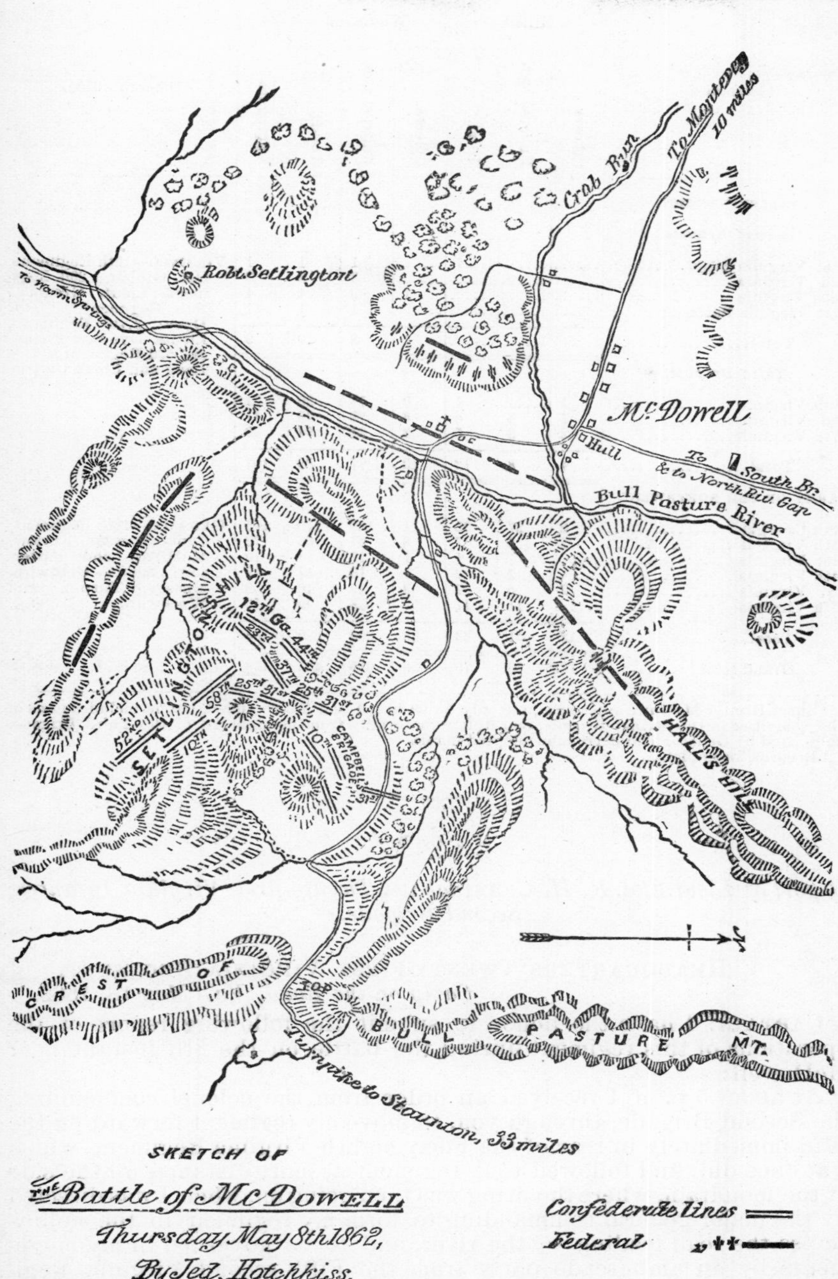


SKETCH OF
THE Battle of McDOWELL
Thursday May 8th 1862,
By Jed. Hotchkiss.
SCALE 1 MILE TO 1⅜ INCHES.

## No. 7.

*Return of killed and wounded in the Confederate forces.*

| Command. | Killed. | | | Wounded. | | | Aggregate. | Officers killed. |
|---|---|---|---|---|---|---|---|---|
| | Officers. | Enlisted men. | Total. | Officers. | Enlisted men. | Total. | | |
| VALLEY DISTRICT. | | | | | | | | |
| *Second Brigade.* | | | | | | | | |
| 21st Virginia | ...... | ...... | ...... | ...... | 1 | 1 | 1 | VIRGINIA.—10th Regiment, Col. Gibbon; 23d Regiment, Lieut. Gregory; 25th Regiment,* Lieut. Dyer; 37th Regiment, Lieuts. Dye and Fletcher; 52d Regiment, Capt. Long and Lieut. Carson. |
| 42d Virginia | ...... | ...... | ...... | ...... | 3 | 3 | 3 | |
| 48th Virginia | ...... | ...... | ...... | 1 | 3 | 4 | 4 | |
| 1st Virginia Battalion | ...... | ...... | ...... | ...... | 1 | 1 | 1 | |
| Total | ...... | ...... | ...... | 1 | 8 | 9 | 9 | |
| *Third Brigade.* | | | | | | | | |
| 10th Virginia | 1 | ...... | 1 | 3 | 17 | 20 | 21 | |
| 23d Virginia | 1 | 5 | 6 | 6 | 29 | 35 | 41 | |
| 37th Virginia | 2 | 3 | 5 | 3 | 31 | 34 | 39 | |
| Total | 4 | 8 | 12 | 12 | 77 | 89 | 101 | |
| ARMY OF THE NORTHWEST. | | | | | | | | |
| 12th Georgia | 8 | 27 | 35 | 11 | 129 | 140 | 175 | GEORGIA.—12th Regiment, Capts. Dawson, Furlow, McMillan, and Patterson; Lieuts. Goldwire, Massey, Turpin, and Woodward. |
| 25th Virginia | 2 | 5 | 7 | 8 | 57 | 65 | 72 | |
| 31st Virginia | ...... | 1 | 1 | 1 | 17 | 18 | 19 | |
| 44th Virginia | ...... | 2 | 2 | 1 | 16 | 17 | 19 | |
| 52d Virginia | 2 | 5 | 7 | 3 | 43 | 46 | 53 | |
| 58th Virginia | ...... | 11 | 11 | 1 | 38 | 39 | 50 | |
| Total | 12 | 51 | 63 | 25 | 300 | 325 | 388 | |
| Grand total† | 16 | 59 | 75 | 38 | 385 | 423 | 498 | |

* Surg. Hunter McGuire's list accounts only for 69 killed and 393 wounded, but it includes none of the casualties in the Second Brigade, and differs materially from nominal list of the Third Brigade, submitted by General Taliaferro, and adopted herein.
† Records incomplete.

## No. 8.

*Report of Lieut. Col. R. H. Cunningham, Twenty-first Virginia Infantry, Second Brigade.*

HEADQUARTERS TWENTY-FIRST VIRGINIA REGIMENT,
*Camp on the Road, Va., May* 18, 1862.

CAPTAIN: I have the honor to submit the following report of the operations of this regiment during the battle on the 8th instant near McDowell:

At about 5 p. m. I received an order from the colonel commanding the Second Brigade, through you, to move my regiment forward on the road immediately in rear of the Forty-eighth Virginia Regiment, which I at once did, and followed that regiment a short distance up the side of the mountain, where the firing was then going on, when I was directed by the major-general commanding to form my regiment in the hollow across the road leading to the river, and to be governed in my movements by an ambuscade party from the Fifty-second Virginia Regiment, which he had sent in front of us. I moved the regiment in line to within 75 yards of the ambuscade party and 150 yards below the ravine where other troops ascended the mountain.

We did not come in contact with the enemy during the evening, but were exposed to a scattering fire while moving to our position, by which one man received a slight contusion from a spent ball.

Very respectfully, your obedient servant,

R. H. CUNNINGHAM,
*Lieut. Col., Commanding Twenty-first Virginia Regiment.*

Capt. R. N. WILSON,
*Assistant Adjutant-General, Second Brigade, Valley District.*

---

## No. 9.

*Report of Maj. Henry Lane, Forty-second Virginia Infantry.*

CAMP OF FORTY-SECOND VIRGINIA REGIMENT,
*May* 17, 1862.

SIR: I herewith report to you the operations of the Forty-second Regiment on the 8th instant in connection with the battle near McDowell:

Late in the afternoon of that day I was ordered to proceed with my regiment along the Monterey road in the direction of heavy firing in front, and after proceeding perhaps half a mile we left the main road and filed to the left up a steep hill. Upon reaching the top of this hill I was ordered to place my regiment in line of battle upon the side of a field to the right of an eminence upon which the main battle was fought, and from which it was separated by a deep ravine, with the view of preventing any attempt on the part of the enemy to turn the right flank of our forces actively engaged with the enemy. I executed this order with as much rapidity as possible, and by the time the regiment was placed in position night had set in and the firing had sensibly slackened, particularly on the part of the enemy.

No demonstration was made in the direction of the ground occupied by my regiment, and, consequently, it was not actively engaged in the fight. We remained in the position assigned us until the firing had entirely ceased, when I was ordered with my command to the top of the hill where the main battle had been fought. Here the regiment remained until a late hour of the night without fires and suffering much from cold.

During the night heavy details were made upon the regiment to assist in carrying from the field the dead and wounded and the arms and accouterments which had been scattered during the engagement; all of which duties were performed with becoming alacrity.

In taking its position the regiment was several times exposed to the fire of the enemy, resulting in the wounding of 3 of my men, but, I am happy to report, only slightly.

Very respectfully, your obedient servant,

HENRY LANE,
*Major, Commanding Forty-second Regiment.*

Capt. R. N. WILSON,
*Assistant Adjutant-General.*

## No. 10.

*Report of Lieut. S. Hale, Acting Adjutant, Forty-eighth Virginia Infantry.*

CAMP OF FORTY-EIGHTH REGIMENT VIRGINIA VOLS.,
*May* 16, 1862.

CAPTAIN: In obedience to the order of Col. John A. Campbell, commanding Second Brigade, Valley District, of this date, I have the honor of making the following report of the part taken by the Forty-eighth Regiment Virginia Volunteers in the battle of the 8th instant, near McDowell:

Late in the evening of the 8th this regiment, under the command of Maj. James C. Campbell, was at its place in the brigade, between the First Battalion Virginia Provisional Army in front and the Twenty-first Regiment Virginia Volunteers in its rear, on the road on the eastern side of Great North Mountain. When the order to march was given Major Campbell led the regiment along the road in rear of the First Battalion until near a log cabin on the right of the road, when, perceiving that the enemy's balls and shells were falling in and near the road, he threw the regiment to the right of the road, causing it to march along a ravine, partially sheltered by the mountains on the right; he, however, continuing to ride along the road near the head of the regiment. Just below the cabin mentioned Major Campbell was wounded and taken from his horse.

Seeing that Major Campbell was wounded I hastened to the front, stated the fact to Senior Captain Vermillion, and notified him that the command fell upon him. He declined, and ordered me to tender the command to Captain Harman, next in rank. He declined, and suggested that I should command. I hastened to the right and reported to Captain Vermillion, and with his consent assumed the command. Just then I met you, and, as you remember, stated the facts, and was directed by you to hold the command of the regiment.

In pursuance of the order to follow the regiment in front the regiment was halted and ordered to load near the creek at the foot of the mountain, and then I followed the battalion up the ravine to the left of the road to the field occupied by our troops during the battle.

After getting into the field the front companies were halted until the rear companies cleared the ravine. I then hastened on to the woods, on the right. Just as I entered the woods the First Battalion was hidden from my view by other regiments, and being informed by a field officer, whose name I do not know, that the enemy had been driven back on the right, and that we were needed on the hill occupied by the Fifty-eighth Virginia and Twelfth Georgia Volunteers, I halted the regiment, ordered the captains to close up their companies, and ran to Col. J. A. Campbell, stated the facts connected with the command of the regiment, and was ordered by him to hasten to the hill mentioned.

During the remainder of the night the regiment was in Colonel Campbell's presence, and I can only state facts that came under his own observation and mention movements made by his direction.

I immediately obeyed his order mentioned, and marched the regiment by the left flank, at double-quick, to a point immediately behind the Fifty-eighth Regiment, halted, closed the regiment, then filed the left companies into line in front of the Fifty-eighth, wheeled the right companies to the left and threw them forward into line, thus forming the whole regiment in front of the Fifty-eighth Regiment, our regiment resting near the left of the Twelfth Georgia Regiment.

After getting into line the regiment fired several rounds at a line of the enemy in front of our left wing, and then ceased firing, in obedience to an order from General Johnson. The regiment was ordered to lie down, and we laid under a heavy fire of the enemy until their line was seen firing on our left again. I then ordered the regiment to fire, and after firing one round again ordered the regiment to cease firing, in obedience to an order from Colonel Campbell. The regiment again laid down, and we were again under heavy fire of the enemy, the bullets whistling just above us and cutting the bushes around until near 8.30 o'clock, when the shout for "Davis and the Confederacy" ran along the line from the right, announcing the retreat of the enemy.

The regiment was immediately called to attention, a picket of 2 men from each company sent to the front, and we remained in our places a few moments, when, by order of Colonel Campbell, I faced the regiment to the right and formed line of battle on the ground occupied by the Twelfth Regiment Georgia Volunteers. Here we remained until near daylight, when I marched the regiment back to its wagons to get the rations for the day, in obedience to the order of Colonel Campbell.

After the firing ceased we made the required details to assist in moving the dead and collecting arms, &c.

One man of the regiment was wounded (slightly) near the log cabin mentioned, and 2 were slightly wounded about the time our line of battle was being formed in front of the Fifty-eighth Virginia Regiment.

The officers and men of the regiment seemed entirely self-possessed while under fire, and the men fired with a great degree of coolness and deliberation.

Very respectfully submitted, by your obedient servant,

S. HALE,

*Actg. Adjt., Comdg. Forty-eighth Regt. Va. Vols. on 8th instant.*

Capt. R. N. WILSON,

*Assistant Adjutant-General, &c.*

---

## No. 11.

### *Report of Capt. B. W. Leigh, First Virginia Battalion.*

HDQRS. FIRST VIRGINIA BATT., PROVISIONAL ARMY,

*Camp near Cross' House, Augusta County, Va., May* 16, 1862.

CAPTAIN: In obedience to an order of Colonel Campbell, commanding the Second Brigade, I have the honor to transmit to you, for his information, a report of the operations of the battalion under my command during the recent engagement near McDowell:

During the latter part of the 8th instant the battalion, along with the rest of the brigade, remained at a halt on the eastern side of the Great North Mountain. The sound of cannon and musketry from time to time in front of us indicated an approaching conflict. About 6.30 o'clock in the evening the brigade was ordered forward to the scene of action. On our way thither the battalion was exposed to a scattering fire from the enemy, which proceeded, as I think, from the summit of a hill which overlooked the valley of a little brook which crossed the road, and one man of Company B was mortally wounded.

On reaching the crest of a hill in the rear of a ridge on which the fight was raging, Colonel Campbell ordered the battalion to proceed to the top of a hill on the right of our position and occupy that point. He accompanied us a part of the way, and cautioned us that we might find the place in the possession of our friends. On reaching the summit of the hill we found it occupied by three companies of the Thirty-first Regiment Virginia Volunteers, and the Forty-second Regiment Virginia Volunteers were drawn up in line of battle immediately on our left.

We remained at this point until a late hour in the night, when we received an order from Colonel Campbell to join the Forty-eighth Regiment Virginia Volunteers on the ridge which had been the principal scene of the conflict. We accordingly proceeded thither, and remained there until the setting of the moon, when the brigade left the battle-field and went back a few miles to get provisions. The battalion kept its ranks well during the whole of this time, notwithstanding the difficulties of the ground, and none of the men left their places. One man of Company A was shot as we were ascending the mountain from the brook I have mentioned; but I am informed and believe that this was accidental. His wound will probably render necessary the amputation of his leg.

While we remained on the summit of the hill which we were ordered to occupy the battle raged with great fury on the principal scene of the conflict until some time after dark. I may be permitted to say that we would have welcomed an order to hasten to succor our comrades.

I have the honor to be, captain, your obedient servant,

B. W. LEIGH,
*Captain, Comdg. First Virginia Battalion, Prov. Army.*

Capt. R. N. WILSON,
*Assistant Adjutant-General, &c.*

---

## No. 12.

*Report of Brig. Gen. William B. Taliaferro, C. S. Army, commanding Third Brigade.*

HEADQUARTERS THIRD BRIGADE,
*Valley District, Va., May* 16, 1862.

MAJOR: I have the honor, in obedience to the instructions of the major-general commanding, to make the following report of the operations of the troops under my command during the engagement with the enemy near McDowell on the 8th instant:

My brigade constituted the advance of the Army of the Valley, and was held in supporting distance of General Johnson's division (Army of the Northwest), which formed the advance of the combined forces under Major-General Jackson.

On the evening of the 8th, learning that the advance was skirmishing with the enemy, I moved my brigade up to the rear of General Johnson's command, and shortly afterward received an order from the major-general commanding to move rapidly to the front to the support of that command, which was by that time hotly engaged with the enemy. My men were under a desultory fire of the enemy from the time they turned the summit of the Bull Pasture Mountain until they reached the field of battle, but pressed forward with enthusiasm and in the best order that the rocky trail through the woods and up a precipitous hill would admit of. On reaching the field I discovered that the enemy were engaging our forces (who occupied an extensive hill, or mountain spur, overlooking the village of McDowell) on the left of our position and in front; that the Twelfth Georgia Regiment was contesting with heroic gallantry the position on the left, well advanced toward the front; that the Twenty-fifth Virginia was holding the front, and I learned that the Thirty-first Virginia was holding a wooded hill across the valley to our right, which was menaced by a large force of the enemy. I at once ordered the Twenty-third Virginia (Colonel Taliaferro) to re-enforce and support the Twenty-fifth, which regiment had expended most of its ammunition, and directed Colonel Fulkerson, with his regiment (the Thirty-seventh Virginia), to move across to the wooded hill on the right, to prevent the enemy from turning our flank and to drive him from his position on the hill. As soon as the Tenth Virginia (Colonel Gibbons), which was the rear regiment, came up I ordered four companies to support the Twelfth Georgia and the remainder to the right of the Twenty-third, which position they maintained with great gallantry until I ordered them under the hill as a reserve to re-enforce any position which might require support. The Twenty-third was immediately thrown forward and opened a heavy fire upon the enemy in front and on a spur of a hill to the right, and maintained the position handsomely under a terrible fire of musketry and artillery, which latter played upon my whole command from a hill beyond the turnpike, out of musket-range.

Colonel Fulkerson moved across, as directed, to the hill on the right with a part of his regiment, which had pressed ahead of the rest in their anxiety to get into the fight; interposed it between our troops and the enemy, who were advancing up the slope of the hill; charged and drove them precipitately before him to the base, and then returned with his command to the main field, when I directed him, with his regiment, to hold the position occupied by the Twenty-third, which I sent to the support of the Georgians.

At this time I moved the Tenth Virginia farther to our right, to prevent any attempt of an advance of the enemy up the valley between the two hills occupied by our troops, which the night (which was rapidly approaching) might render practicable. The troops of my command maintained this position until the close of the fight, which was protracted until after 9 o'clock at night, when the enemy's fire entirely ceased. Knowing that General Johnson, who was near me, had been wounded, I at once, as senior officer in the front, made dispositions for holding the hill during the night and resting our troops. I stationed the several regiments under cover of the declivities and ravines; threw out pickets and skirmishers, and gave orders for the removal of our dead and such of the wounded as had not been carried off the field, and had the arms of our dead and wounded and those that the enemy had left on the field collected.

Soon after this the enemy kindled extensive camp fires beyond the river, and their artillery was heard moving off toward their rear. At 11 o'clock General Jackson ordered me to march my command back to the wagons for rest and refreshments.

I have confined myself in this report to the operations of my own command, and referred to no other except that part of General Johnson's which I supported, viz, the brigade commanded by Colonel Conner.

In conclusion, I desire to bear testimony to the gallantry of the officers and men of my brigade. They fought well under a most severe fire.

To Colonels Fulkerson (Thirty-seventh) and Taliaferro (Twenty-third), who had his horse shot under him, Lieutenant-Colonels Warren (commanding the Tenth) and Curtis (Twenty-third), and Majors Williams (Thirty-seventh) and Walker (Tenth) my thanks are due for the gallantry they displayed and the coolness with which they directed the movements and fire of their men.

I refer to the reports of the colonels for particular notice of the conduct of the officers and men of their respective regiments, and I desire particularly to notice the efficient services rendered me on the field by my adjutant-general (W. B. Pendleton) and my aide-de-camp (First Lieut. Philip A. Taliaferro), both of the Provisional Army.

It pains me to add that some of my best officers were killed and wounded. Colonel Gibbons, of the Tenth, fell early in the action while leading and gloriously cheering his men to the fight. No braver or better soldier or nobler or more Christian gentleman has offered up his life a sacrifice to our holy cause during this struggle for our liberties.

Lieutenants Gregory (Twenty-third) and Dye and Fletcher (Thirty-seventh) paid the last tribute of the loftiest and holiest patriotism by yielding up their lives in the bloom of manhood upon their invaded country's battle-field.

Captain Terry (Thirty-seventh) especially noticed for his gallantry; Captains Saunders and Williams (Twenty-third), Lieutenants Crawford and Myers (Tenth), Southall, Payne, and Garland (Twenty-third), and Wilhelm and Key (Thirty-seventh) were wounded, and deserve especial notice for their good conduct.

I inclose an official list* of the killed and wounded of this brigade, amounting, in the aggregate, to 101 officers and men.

I have the honor to be, very respectfully, your obedient servant,

WM. B. TALIAFERRO,
*Commanding Third Brigade.*

Maj. R. L. DABNEY,
*Assistant Adjutant-General.*

---

## No. 13.

*Report of Brig. Gen. Edward Johnson, C. S. Army, commanding Army of the Northwest.*

STAUNTON, VA., *May* 17, 1862.

MAJOR: I have the honor to submit the following report of the battle of McDowell, which took place between the forces of General Milroy, on the part of the Federals, and a portion of General Jackson's forces, under my immediate command, on the afternoon of May 8:

Early in the day, being in advance with my own brigade, I reached Setlington's Hill, fronting McDowell and to the left of the pike, about 1½ or 2 miles distant. The troops having been halted upon the top of the Bull Pasture Mountain, about 2 miles back, with a party of 30 men and several officers I reconnoitered the enemy's position in the valley of McDowell and also in my immediate vicinity, and found one or two

---

* Embodied in No. 7, p. 476.

regiments posted on the right on a high hill and commanding the position on which I was, but at very long distance. I saw the enemy in McDowell posted in various positions, but such as could be commanded by artillery.

The enemy soon threw out small skirmishing parties, which were engaged by our men and driven in. I then sent back for re-enforcements or some portion of my brigade. The Fifty-second Virginia Regiment first came up, and I posted it on the extreme left of the hill as skirmishers, and it was not long before they entered upon a brisk skirmish with the enemy, repelling them and driving them off handsomely.

Soon after the Forty-fourth and Fifty-eighth Virginia and Twelfth Georgia Regiments came up and were posted as follows, viz: The Twelfth Georgia on the crest of the hill fronting the main body of the enemy, the Fifty-eighth and Fifty-second on the left, and the Forty-fourth on the right, near a ravine. A very heavy fire was opened on the right between 4.30 and 5 p. m., at which time I was making a reconnaissance on the hill on the right of the position of the Forty-fourth. I immediately repaired to the field, and a very sharp fight continued for some time, when the Twenty-fifth and Thirty-first Virginia Regiments coming up I posted them on the right, when the fight became very terrific, my men holding the line upon the crest of the hill and driving back the enemy with great loss.

At this time General Taliaferro's brigade came up. The Twenty-third and Thirty-seventh Virginia Regiments were advanced to support the center of our line, which was occupied by the Twelfth Georgia Regiment, with the most heroic gallantry. The Tenth Virginia Regiment was ordered to support the Fifty-second, which, having driven the enemy from the left, was advanced to make a flank movement upon him.

At this time the enemy advanced a strong column on the extreme right, with a view of flanking our position. General Taliaferro's brigade, with the Twelfth Georgia Regiment, met this movement of the enemy principally. To defeat it, however, I ordered several companies of the Twenty-fifth and Thirty-first Regiments to a position in the elevated woods on the right and rear of our position, but commanding the position of the enemy.

Colonel Campbell's brigade coming up about this time was, together with the Tenth Virginia Regiment, ordered down the ridge in the woods to prevent a flank movement of the enemy, which they effectually did.

The battle raged with terrific violence from about 4.30 to 8.30 p. m., the enemy all the time playing upon us with their artillery.

In all the attempts of the enemy to advance up the hill they were repulsed by the gallantry of our men with very great slaughter.

After dark the fire somewhat ceased. The enemy withdrew from the field with haste, leaving their dead unburied, burned his stores at McDowell, destroyed large quantities of ammunition, camp equipage, &c., and precipitately retreated in the direction of Franklin.

In consequence of a wound received by me in the leg I had no part in the affair after 8 p. m.

Our victory was complete. From information received the loss of the enemy was between 500 and 1,000 killed and wounded. Large numbers of their dead were piled in various places; some in churches and other houses, and some are reported to have been burned up in the house which contained their commissary stores.

Being compelled to leave the field in consequence of my wound, and not having received brigade and regimental reports, I have no certain data of my loss, but I do not believe it to exceed 60 killed and 200 wounded.

The brigade commanders and the regiments generally behaved with remarkable coolness and courage. The following-named officers, commanding brigades and regiments, I would mention as having behaved most gallantly, viz: General Taliaferro, Colonel Conner, Twelfth Georgia Regiment; Colonel Scott, Forty-fourth Virginia Regiment; Colonel Campbell, Forty-eighth Virginia Regiment; Colonel Harman, Fifty-second Virginia Regiment; Lieutenant-Colonel Board, Fifty-eighth Virginia Regiment; Major Hawkins, Twelfth Georgia Regiment; Colonel Smith, Twenty-fifth Virginia Regiment; Lieutenant-Colonel Jackson, Thirty-first Virginia Regiment; Colonel Taliaferro, Twenty-third Virginia Regiment; Colonel Fulkerson, Thirty-seventh Virginia Regiment; Colonel Gibbons, Tenth Virginia Regiment, and Colonel Hoffman, Thirty-first Virginia Regiment, who, though sick, repaired to the field during the engagement and assumed the command of his regiment.

Colonel Gibbons, of the Tenth Virginia Regiment, fell while leading his regiment into the fight. Colonel Harman, of the Fifty-second Virginia Regiment, was wounded early in the engagement, but did not leave the field. Colonel Smith and Major Higginbotham, of the Twenty-fifth Virginia Regiment, were wounded.

To my medical staff I am greatly indebted for the efficiency they displayed, particularly to Surg. R. W. Lunday, medical director of my forces, for his zeal and activity in making preparation for the removal of the wounded from the field and attention to them afterward; and to Assistant Surgeons Opie and Etheridge, whose coolness and efficiency on the field attracted my attention, and the latter of whom was severely wounded.

Lieut. Col. Abner Smead, my assistant adjutant-general, and Col. W. H. Harman, my aide-de-camp, behaved most gallantly throughout the action, affording me great assistance in rallying the men and conveying orders.

Lieut. Ed. Willis, one of my aides, I had placed in charge of my artillery on that day, and he, consequently, was not in the engagement.

Very respectfully, your obedient servant,

E. JOHNSON,
*Brigadier-General.*

Maj. R. L. DABNEY,
*Assistant Adjutant-General.*

---

## No. 14.

*Report of Col. W. C. Scott, Forty-fourth Virginia Infantry, commanding Second Brigade.*

CAMP NEAR GORDONSVILLE, VA.,
*August* 2, 1862.

As I have not heretofore made any report in regard to the battle of McDowell I will now supply the omission:

The Army of the Northwest, commanded by Brig. Gen. Edward Johnson, was divided by him into two brigades, one of which was commanded by me, as senior colonel, and the other commanded by Colonel Conner, of the Twelfth Georgia Regiment. (See appendix.)

I need say nothing of the junction of this little army with General T. J. Jackson's; of the driving in of the enemy's pickets at Mason's shanties; of the stampede of the enemy at Shenandoah Mountain and at Shaw's Fort, and of the final stand made by them on their main body at McDowell.

The turnpike road, as it approaches McDowell from the east, runs through a narrow gorge of the mountains about a mile before it reaches that town.

On May 8 last our army arrived within about 1½ or 2 miles of that town and halted in the turnpike road, General Johnson's two brigades, marching as brigades, in the advance. Generals Jackson and Johnson went forward to reconnoiter. In the afternoon General Johnson's two brigades, and perhaps others, were ordered forward. After proceeding along the turnpike a few hundred yards we were led to the left, through a skirt of woods about half a mile in width, to an open field on a high hill, which overlooked the town of McDowell.

I understood that we were to hold that hill until the next morning, and that in the mean time we would cut a road through the woods, by which we would carry artillery on the hill, with which we were to attack the enemy's camp and defenses. On the top of that hill there was a crest or ridge, running from north to south, except about midway, where the ground was not above the ordinary level of the hill. On this crest General Johnson placed the brigade commanded by me, consisting of the Fifty-eighth, Forty-fourth, and Fifty-second Virginia Regiments, facing it west.

As the enemy were firing shells at us, he placed the men of this brigade in pairs, with intervals between the pairs of about five paces, and caused the men to lie down. In consequence of this disposition my men occupied the whole length, or nearly the whole length, of the crest of the hill in the open field, including the depressed part in the middle. From the right of this crest the ground abruptly descended, and this abrupt descent extended, on a line nearly at right angles to the crest or ridge from its northern termination, back to the woods, some hundred yards to our rear.

The Fifty-eighth Regiment occupied the northern portion of the crest and constituted my right flank; the Forty-fourth occupied the depressed ground and constituted my center, and the Fifty-second occupied the left of the ridge and constituted my left flank.

Shortly after my men were placed in position in pairs, as aforesaid, a regiment of the enemy appeared opposite my left flank, but after remaining there a short time retired to a woods which faced my center and right flank.

After remaining in the woods a short time one or two regiments emerged from them and approached a bluff, which extended from my right flank to the point about —— yards, with the evident intention of shielding themselves behind that bluff. I immediately endeavored to close my regiments to the right. The enemy sent forward a company of skirmishers and I sent forward two to meet them, but on the first fire our skirmishers returned to their regiments. The fire on my right flank, consisting mainly of the Fifty-eighth Regiment, and on a part of my center (the Forty-fourth) then became fast and furious, and was returned by us with equal spirit. I then withdrew the Forty-fourth Regiment from its position on the level or depressed ground in the center and placed it some thirty paces in rear of the Fifty-eighth, and caused its men to lie down where they could not be hurt. My reasons for doing this were the following: 1st, owing to the depressed nature of the ground they occupied the enemy could do them great damage, while they could do the enemy but little, and 2d, because I wanted them as a reserve in case the Fifty-eighth should give way; but after the battle became very animated, and my attention was otherwise directed, a large number of the Forty-fourth quit their position, and rushing forward joined the Fifty-eighth and engaged in the fight, while the balance of the regiment joined some other brigade.

In firing, the front rank of my right flank, after delivering its fire, would retire some three or four paces to the rear and lie down and load, and, as they were shielded from danger while loading, I allowed this system to continue; and I think it was owing to this cause, principally, that my brigade suffered less than Colonel Conner's. But observing that some men retired farther to the rear than necessary, and were lying on their faces and taking no part in the battle, I attempted to rouse them by words, but finding that neither harsh words nor threats were of any avail, I commenced riding over them, which soon made them join the line of battle.

After the battle had continued for some time, and night was approaching, a body of the enemy (the number I do not know) crept up a dark bottom, and their flag was suddenly hoisted within 50 yards of our line of battle. Our men, so soon as they discovered the flag and enemy, received a deadly fire and simultaneously returned it, and then, with the exception of some 15 or 20, broke and ran back. Standing on or near the line of battle, I used all my exertions to rally them, principally by appeals to their State pride, and after they had run back some 20 or 30 yards I succeeded in bringing them to a halt, and after loading they returned to the line of battle with great animation, and poured so deadly a fire into the enemy that they broke and fled. I then proposed three cheers for Old Virginia, which were given with great spirit.

Major Kasey, of the Fifty-eighth, discovering the enemy's flag on the ground a short distance off, went down the hill and brought it up. The flag-staff had been shot in two and the flag-bearer killed.

I suppose that the enemy broke at the same time that our men did, as they were farther off when our men returned to the line of battle than when they left it, which I presume is the reason why every man who remained on the line of battle was not killed.

The enemy, however, soon resumed their attack, and the battle continued with great animation until between 8 and 9 o'clock, when it was terminated by the darkness.

After some time had elapsed from the commencement of the battle the enemy sent some regiments to turn my right flank or to ascend the hill on my right and to my rear, but Colonel Conner's brigade was then placed in position to meet them. His line of battle was then at right angles to mine and his left flank united with my right.

In this battle the officers of the brigade commanded by me (with very few exceptions, and they inferior officers) did their duty nobly.

I derived considerable assistance from Major Ross, of the Fifty-second, who acted with great gallantry.

I must also commend for great gallantry my adjutant, Lieut. Charles Y. Steptoe, and my sergeant-major, William H. Clare. They were with me during the whole action, except when sent off on some errand. They never attempted to shield themselves from danger by lying down or by any other means, and it is singular that neither of them was wounded, though Adjutant Steptoe's clothes were shot through.

Very respectfully, your obedient servant,

W. C. SCOTT,
*Colonel Forty-fourth Virginia Volunteers,*
*Comdg. Second Brig., Army of the Northwest, at McDowell, Va.*

Maj. R. L. DABNEY,
*Asst. Adjt. Gen., Army of the Valley District, Va.*

---

APPENDIX.

The first written order, dividing General Edward Johnson's army (of the Northwest) into two brigades is in the following words and figures, to wit:

ORDERS, }
No. —. }

HEADQUARTERS SECOND BRIGADE,
*Camp at Valley Mills, Va., April 21, 1862.*

I. The troops of this command will be divided into two brigades; the one on the right, Colonel Porterfield commanding, to consist of the Twelfth Georgia and Twenty-fifth and Thirty-first Virginia Regiments, Hansbrough's battalion, and the Star Battery; the one on the left, Colonel Baldwin commanding, to consist of the Forty-fourth, Fifty-second, and Fifty-eighth Virginia Regiments, and Miller's and the Lee battery.

II. All official communications will be sent through the headquarters of the respective brigades. Commandants of brigades will sign all provision returns, requisitions, &c., and will send to this office every morning consolidated reports of their respective brigades.

By order of General Johnson:

A. SMEAD,
*Lieutenant-Colonel and Assistant Adjutant-General.*

[Circular.]

HEADQUARTERS SECOND BRIGADE,
*Camp at Valley Mills, Va., April 22, 1862.*

Commandants of brigades will cause all company officers of the regiments and captains of their commands to quarter with their companies, and field and staff officers with their regiments.

By order of General E. Johnson:

A. SMEAD,
*Lieutenant-Colonel and Assistant Adjutant-General.*

HEADQUARTERS ARMY OF THE NORTHWEST,
*Camp at Valley Mills, Va., May 2, 1862.*

COLONEL: You being the senior officer present with your brigade, you will assume command of it, and will sign all requisitions, provision returns, &c., and will hand in consolidated morning reports of your brigade by 12 m. every day. You will also, as soon as possible, send a consolidated return of the brigade.

Very respectfully, your obedient servant,

A. SMEAD.
*Lieutenant-Colonel and Assistant Adjutant-General.*

This last was directed and sent to me the morning after I regained my regiment after a sick leave of absence. None of the foregoing orders were ever revoked by General Johnson. On the contrary, I have a great number of others recognizing the two brigades. I will only insert one issued just before we commenced our march to McDowell:

[Circular.]

HEADQUARTERS ARMY OF THE NORTHWEST,
*Camp at Valley Mills, Va., May* 5, 1862.

Brigade commanders will cause the different regiments and independent companies of their respective commands to have cooked and put in haversacks the provisions they will draw to-morrow, and be in readiness to march at any moment.

By order of General Johnson:

A. SMEAD,
*Lieutenant-Colonel and Assistant Adjutant-General.*

According to the order of march we marched by brigades, each brigade followed by its wagons.

It is a fact that at the battle of McDowell I commanded the Second Brigade and that Major Cobb commanded the Forty-fourth Regiment.

W. C. SCOTT,
*Colonel Forty-fourth Regiment Virginia Volunteers.*

---

## No. 15.

### *Report of Col. Michael G. Harman, Fifty-second Virginia Infantry.*

———, —— —, 1862.

SIR: I have the honor of submitting to you the following report:

At the battle of McDowell, on May 8, my officers and men behaved with great courage, but it is not necessary to particularize them by name, as they fought under your own eye.

The total loss of my regiment is as follows:

Company B—Officers, Capt. William Long, mortally wounded, since dead. As a brave and faithful officer he is a great loss to my regiment.

Company D—Lieutenant Carson killed.

Companies C and I—Captains Dabney and Humphreys wounded, one in the arm and the other in the mouth, while gallantly leading their companies.

The loss in privates in each company is as follows:

Company B—15 wounded.
Company C—4 wounded; 1 died since the battle.
Company D—2 killed and 3 wounded.
Company E—1 killed and 6 wounded.
Company F—1 killed and 4 wounded.
Company G—5 wounded.
Company I—5 wounded.
Company K—1 killed and 1 wounded.

Early in the action I received a severe and painful wound in my right arm, and with great difficulty remained on the field until the battle was over. To a merciful Providence and your successful leadership and personal bravery we owe our victory on that hotly-contested field.

Respectfully,

M. G. HARMAN,
*Colonel, Commanding Fifty-second Virginia Volunteers.*

General EDWARD JOHNSON,
*Commanding Army of the Northwest.*

## MAY 8-21, 1862.—Scout in Roane and Clay Counties, W. Va.

*Report of Maj. Benjamin M. Skinner, Ninth West Virginia Infantry.*

CHARLESTON, *May* 22, 1862.

COLONEL: I have the honor to submit the following report of my scout into Roane and Clay Counties:

In pursuance to your order we left camp on Elk River on Thursday, the 8th instant, at 11 o'clock, and marched that day to John D. Young's, on Elk River, a distance of 17 miles, when we encamped for the night. The next day we marched up the upper left-hand fork of Sandy, knowing it to be the neighborhood where Comly ranged last season, and encamped at Vineyard, having marched a distance of 28 miles.

That night I threw out scouting parties, who scoured the country around about all night. Hearing there that the rebels had gone to Spencer I marched direct for that place, a distance of 19 miles, where I arrived on Saturday, the 10th instant, at 4 p. m. I rested my men there until Monday morning; found no provisions there except flour and pork. I learned there that the rebels had not been at Spencer, but had changed their course and gone down West Fork to Big Bend, on Little Kanawha.

On Monday morning I left 75 of my men, who were foot-sore, to guard the place, and in their stead I took a company of 40 men, under Lieutenant Bukey, of the Eleventh Virginia Regiment, whom I found stationed at Spencer, and marched with my command to Burning Springs, on Little Kanawha, a distance of 19 miles, arriving there at 6 o'clock Monday evening, 12th instant.

I there found that the rebels had escaped in small squads, finding themselves nearly surrounded. I found General Kelley at Burning Springs, with the Ringgold Cavalry and about 300 infantry; found also Colonel Rathbone, of the Eleventh Regiment Virginia Infantry, they having arrived there a few hours previous. I was ordered by General Kelley to remain with my command at Burning Springs, but upon representing to him the condition of my men, they having no blankets, camp equipage, cooking utensils, &c., and that one detachment of 75 men was at Spencer, I gained his consent to leave one company only at that point, and on Wednesday, 12 m., I left Lieutenant Bukey, with his company, at that place, and with the balance of my command marched up the West Fork of Little Kanawha to within a half mile of the Greathouse settlement (where we intended to encamp), when I heard firing at a distance of about 2 miles in front of us. I then ordered my men on double-quick to the place where the firing was supposed to be, but found nothing, and marched on to the Hiram Chapman place, a distance of 21 miles from Burning Springs, where I expected to find a company of the First Virginia Cavalry encamped, from which I supposed the firing I had heard a few miles back had originated. My advance guard was cautioned to march carefully, as there was danger of encountering their pickets, but the cavalry not having any guards out, my men could have surprised them very easily, taken their horses, and captured the whole company, who were asleep in the house. I then encamped for the night and learned from the cavalry that they had been fired upon by guerrillas at a distance of 600 yards. They returned the fire, but knew nothing of the effect it had on the rebels except to disperse them.

The next morning I broke three squads from the two companies of the

Ninth Virginia Regiment, and sent them, under command of officers, to scour that country, which resulted in the bringing in of 2 prisoners, one of whom was a deserter from Captain West's cavalry; the other was a guerrilla, fully equipped, belonging to Captain Downs' company.

I marched from that place to Spencer, where I arrived at 2 o'clock p. m. Thursday; found there from 600 to 800 infantry and two companies of cavalry. Met General Kelley, who gave me orders to remain there, under the command of Colonel Rathbone.

General Kelley informed me that there was an order for me in possession of Colonel Rathbone from Colonel Lightburn, of the Fourth Virginia, for me to report with my command at Charleston, which order Colonel Rathbone refused to give me.

Friday morning General Kelley left Spencer for Weston, Va. Saturday evening, 17th instant, three guerrillas, named Captain Downs, Perry Hayes, and Silcott, came into Spencer under a flag of truce, stating that they had been requested to do so by a messenger from General Kelley. General Kelley being absent, Colonel Rathbone entered into an agreement that they should cease fighting on both sides for eight days, and that Captain Downs' men should have the privilege of going home to see their families, and that they should not be molested either by the military or civil authority, and at the expiration of eight days they would either give themselves up with their whole command as prisoners of war or take themselves off out of the country to the rebel army, and whatever the rebels decided upon they were to have twenty days after the expiration of the eight days to accomplish. Messengers from each party were to meet at the mouth of Henry's Fork every other day and exchange communications.

On Sunday morning, 19th instant, Colonel Rathbone furnished a company of cavalry to escort the rebel messengers out of the lines to their camp, which company of cavalry returned on Monday morning, bringing with them a lieutenant from the rebels under Captain Downs, who wished a pass, that he might go into Braxton County to see another company of guerrillas, which pass Colonel Rathbone granted. The same day a notorious guerrilla named Dick Greathouse, who had been engaged in fighting at every skirmish had in that country, and had stolen a large number of horses in that section of country, was arrested by the sheriff of the county within a mile of Spencer. The court being in session, he was examined and committed to jail. Colonel Rathbone, hearing of it, ordered his release, and he was escorted out of town under guard.

On Tuesday morning, May 21, I received an order from Colonel Rathbone to report to Colonel Lightburn at Charleston, which order read as follows:

You will report yourself and your command to Colonel Lightburn for duty at Charleston, Kanawha County, Virginia.

By order of Brigadier-General Kelley:

J. C. RATHBONE,
*Colonel, Commanding.*

I notified officers in command of companies to draw three days' rations and prepare to march for Charleston the next day, intending to be three days on the march, but at 9 o'clock on Tuesday I was shown the order from General Kelley, stating that Colonel Lightburn was threatened with an attack from cavalry at Charleston, and ordered to move with haste for that place, which I did, leaving Spencer at 9.30 o'clock Tuesday morning, arriving at Charleston at 5 o'clock on Wednesday p. m. with my command, having taken the nearest route, and marching a distance of 50 miles.

B. M. SKINNER,
*Major Ninth Regiment Virginia Volunteer Infantry, U. S. A*

Col. J. A. J. LIGHTBURN,
*Commanding Fourth Brigade.*

---

## MAY 9, 1862.—Skirmish near McDowell, Va.

*Report of Col. John C. Lee, Fifty-fifth Ohio Infantry.*

HDQRS. FIFTY-FIFTH OHIO VOLUNTEER INFANTRY,
*Franklin, May* 15, 1862.

SIR: On the 9th of May, 1862, while the brigade was at a halt at the intersection of the Monterey and McDowell roads, by your order Lieut. R. F. Patrick, in command of 20 men, was detailed as picket guard, and stationed on the McDowell road. Being attacked by rebel cavalry he was forced to retreat, and met with the following losses: A. D. Stewart, Company B; Milton Cowles, Company C; Henry Fay, Company C; John B. York, Company H; A. Burlingham, Company I, taken prisoners, and James Berry, Company K, wounded and taken prisoner.

I have the honor to be, very respectfully, your obedient servant,

JOHN C. LEE,
*Colonel, Comdg. Fifty-fifth Regiment Ohio Volunteer Infantry.*

Capt. DONN PIATT,
*Assistant Adjutant-General.*

---

## MAY 10, 1862.—Action at Giles Court-House, W. Va.

### REPORTS.

**No. 1.—Brig. Gen. Henry Heth, C. S. Army, commanding Army of New River, Virginia.**
**No. 2.—Col. Walter H. Jenifer, commanding First Brigade.**
**No. 3.—Col. John McCausland, Thirty-sixth Virginia Infantry, commanding Second Brigade.**

### No. 1.

*Report of Brig. Gen. Henry Heth, C. S. Army, commanding Army of New River, Virginia.*

HEADQUARTERS ARMY OF NEW RIVER,
*Giles Court-House, Va., May* 16, 1862.

GENERAL: I have the honor to submit the following report of the battle of Giles Court-House, fought on the 10th instant:

The Forty-fifth Virginia Regiment, Lieutenant-Colonel Peters commanding, stationed at The Narrows of New River, in Giles County, was directed to retire from its position at that point on April 30 by Colonel Jenifer, for reasons which he gives in the inclosed document, marked A.*

---

* Not found.

This regiment fell back as far as the base of Cloyd's Mountain, 10 miles from Dublin Depot, Virginia and Tennessee Railroad. When this occurred I was at the White Sulphur Springs, preparing to withdraw the forces on the James River and Kanawha turnpike to some point at or near the Virginia and Tennessee Railroad, which was rendered necessary in consequence of the abandonment of the Virginia Central Railroad by the withdrawal of all the rolling stock on that road west of Staunton, thus cutting off my source of supplies. At that time I did not know whether my force on the James River and Kanawha turnpike could render better service by re-enforcing General Jackson or strengthening the force defending the approaches to the Virginia and Tennessee Railroad. I wrote and telegraphed General Lee on this subject. On receiving his telegram of the 5th instant I proceeded with all dispatch to strengthen my force covering the approach to the Virginia and Tennessee Railroad at Dublin Depot. As soon as the forces were united I determined to attack the enemy at Giles Court-House and try and retake The Narrows of New River.

On the night of the 9th instant orders were issued to this effect: I divided the command into two brigades and a reserve, the first consisting of the Forty-fifth Virginia Regiment (Lieutenant-Colonel Peters), Otey's battery, and one company of the Eighth Virginia Cavalry, under Colonel Jenifer, and the second composed of the Twenty-second Virginia Regiment (Colonel Patton), Chapman's battery, and one company of the Eighth Virginia Cavalry, under Colonel McCausland, the reserve consisting of fragments of three companies and two mountain howitzers, under Captain Vawter.

We marched at 10 p. m., and discovered the enemy's mounted pickets about 2½ miles from the Court-House. The pickets were driven in and hotly pursued. On reaching a point within 1 mile of Giles Court-House we found the enemy occupying a ridge running from the main road to the mountain (a strong position), sheltered by a fence.

Colonels Jenifer and McCausland, as previously ordered, deployed their commands, the first to the right of the main approach to the Court-House and the second to the left. This was done in handsome style. The battle then commenced by Otey's, Chapman's, and Lowry's artillery opening upon the enemy, the infantry steadily advancing under a line of skirmishers. When within a few hundred yards of the enemy's position, with a determined shout, the force simultaneously charged, driving the enemy before them. The enemy retreated beyond the town of Pearisburg (Giles Court-House), when he made a second stand, but was soon dislodged. He disputed with us a series of hills in rear of Giles Court-House, but was driven from hill to hill until his retreat became a rout. On reaching The Narrows of New River, the great point to be gained, he made his last stand. I ordered two pieces of artillery, under Major King, chief of ordnance, supported by a company of infantry, to cross New River and occupy a commanding position on the right bank. As soon as our artillery opened, which was admirably served (the enemy losing 4 men by the explosion of a single shell from a mountain howitzer), he retreated, leaving in our possession the key to his approach to the Virginia and Tennessee Railroad by way of Giles Court-House.

The force under my command was composed chiefly of the recent levies; they, as all others, acted like veterans. I never witnessed better or more determined fighting. It is with some hesitation, where all did so well, that I mention names. To Colonels Jenifer and McCausland, commanding brigades, my special thanks are due, and they deserve the approbation of the department.

The gallant Colonel Patton fell while leading his regiment and carrying the last and probably most determined stand made by the enemy. I take pleasure in saying his wound is not serious.

Lieutenant-Colonel Peters (commanding Forty-fifth Virginia Regiment) displayed much coolness and gallantry, leading his men in the thickest of the fight. Lieutenant-Colonel Fitzhugh (Eighth Virginia Cavalry) also displayed great coolness and bravery during the engagement. I recommend Colonel Patton (Twenty-second Virginia Regiment) and Lieutenant-Colonels Peters (Forty-fifth Virginia Regiment) and Fitzhugh (Eighth Virginia Cavalry) to your notice.

Captains Otey, Chapman, and Lowry, commanding batteries, all behaved well and did excellent service. The mountain howitzer is found to be exceedingly useful.

To Lieutenant King (elected major of the artillery battalion) I take this occasion of returning my thanks for the energy displayed by him in procuring artillery for my command and for the excellent service performed by him in driving the enemy from The Narrows.

My command was much exhausted when it went into the engagement, a portion of it having lost three nights' sleep. The enemy was pursued 6 or 7 miles, and this at a run.

Our loss was, providentially, small, only 2 killed and 4 wounded. That of the enemy is known to have been comparatively very large, but not accurately ascertained, from the fact that they succeeded in carrying off most of their dead and wounded by the assistance of their cavalry. From the best information I can obtain their loss amounted to about 20 killed and 50 wounded. We captured a considerable amount of quartermaster's and subsistence stores, including a number of horses and a few prisoners.

My special thanks are due to my personal staff—Captain Finney, assistant adjutant-general; Captain Heth, aide-de-camp, and Captain Swann, volunteer aide; also to Mr. Albert Gibboney—for their energy and activity in communicating orders. Captain Selden, aide-de-camp, was absent assisting Lieutenant-Colonel Finney in bringing forward troops and supplies.

I respectfully refer you to the reports of the colonels commanding brigades for additional details.

I am, very respectfully, your obedient servant,

H. HETH,
*Brigadier-General, Commanding.*

General S. COOPER,
*Adjutant and Inspector General.*

---

## No. 2.

*Report of Col. Walter H. Jenifer, commanding First Brigade.*

HEADQUARTERS,
*Camp Success, Va., May* 12, 1862.

GENERAL: I have the honor to submit my report, in reference to my brigade, of the battle of Giles Court-House, which took place on the 10th instant:

Pursuant to orders, I marched from Camp Shannon at 10.30 p. m., in command of the First Brigade of the Army of New River, composed of 650 men of the Forty-fifth Regiment, commanded by Lieut. Col. W. E. Peters; 80 men of the Eighth Virginia Cavalry, under command of Lieut. Col. Henry Fitzhugh, and one 6-pounder rifled gun and one 12-pounder howitzer, with 40 men, under Capt. G. G. Otey.

The march was continued steadily and silently until daybreak, when the enemy's cavalry pickets of 8 men, which were stationed about 2 miles from the Court-House, were driven in by our advance guard. As I approached the town the enemy was seen drawn up in line of battle behind a fence, on a high hill, about 300 yards in advance of the town, with his right wing extending up to the mountain and his left resting on the road leading to the town.

When I had arrived within three-quarters of a mile of the enemy's position I ordered Colonel Peters to march his regiment to the right of the road and deploy two companies as skirmishers. This order was promptly obeyed, and I marched on the enemy in the following order: The Forty-fifth in front, with two companies deployed as skirmishers; the cavalry, under Colonel Fitzhugh, on the right, concealed from the enemy by hills, and the artillery in the rear. This order of advance was continued until we reached within 400 or 500 yards of the enemy's position, when I ordered the artillery to fire, which was replied to by the enemy's howitzer and long-range guns, without injury, however, to our troops. While the artillery kept up a constant fire the infantry and cavalry steadily advanced and obeyed my instructions not to fire until within good rifle-range of the enemy. When within about 150 yards of the enemy the order was given to charge the fence and hill behind which he was posted. This order was beautifully executed, and the regiment was gallantly led by Lieutenant-Colonel Peters.

About the same time the right flank of the enemy was charged and driven back by Colonel McCausland's brigade. My command continued the pursuit through the town and was exposed to a heavy fire during the charge. The cavalry made several charges during the fight.

Lieutenant-Colonel Fitzhugh, Captain Lewis, and Lieutenant Hampton, of the cavalry, behaved with much gallantry during the day.

Lieutenant-Colonel Peters, of the Forty-fifth Regiment, deserves much credit for his coolness and gallantry during the engagement.

Too much praise cannot be given to my staff officers, Lieutenants Kennon and Spotts, for their promptness in carrying orders when exposed to the heaviest fire of the enemy.

Captain Otey and his command were particularly noticed by me, and conducted themselves in a cool and gallant manner, and obeyed with the promptness of old soldiers the orders given them.*

My report is not as complete as I could wish, owing to the duties which require all my attention.

I am, very respectfully, your obedient servant,

W. H. JENIFER,
*Colonel Commanding First Brigade.*

Brig. Gen. HENRY HETH,
*Commanding Army of New River, Giles Court-House, Va.*

P. S.—Inclosed herewith are the reports † of Lieutenant-Colonel Peters and Captain Otey.

---

*Nominal list of casualties 1 killed, 1 mortally wounded, and 3 wounded slightly.
† Not found.

## No. 3.

*Report of Col. John McCausland, Thirty-sixth Virginia Infantry, commanding Second Brigade.*

CAMP SUCCESS, NEAR GILES COURT-HOUSE, VA.,
*May* 13, 1862.

I have the honor to submit the following report of the Second Brigade of the army commanded by Brigadier-General Heth:

In obedience to General Orders, No. 23, I assumed command of the Second Brigade, and at once gave the necessary orders for its movement from the camp at Shannon's toward the enemy, supposed to be at Giles Court-House.

At 10 p. m. on the night of the 9th we took up the line of march, nothing occurring until within a few miles of the town, when the pickets fired, and then the spirit and fire of the men knew no control. They rushed on at a rapid pace. As soon as we arrived at the point indicated in General Orders, No. 23, I at once commenced deploying on the left of the turnpike, keeping the artillery in the road. The infantry was deployed, skirmishers thrown to the front, and an advance ordered.

The enemy were found posted on an eminence protected on the right by a dense forest and on the left by a ravine, the center and main body behind a fence. I at once posted a large 24-pounder gun on an eminence within good range and opened upon the enemy. The first shot passed just above the fence behind which they were posted. The next, a shell, exploded in their midst, scattering them and throwing the rails in every direction. The enemy at once moved toward the forest on the right. I at once threw the left wing of the Twenty-second Regiment up the mountain to meet them. They were soon driven back. Then commenced the pursuit. The enemy again rallied beyond the town. They rallied from time to time, but were soon routed, and in the fight, extending over a space of 7 miles, the officers and men behaved well. My thanks are due to all.

Col. George S. Patton was wounded in the pursuit beyond the town. One private also wounded.

Colonel Patton, Lieutenant-Colonel Barbee, Major Bailey, and Captain Chapman, of the artillery, all behaved well.

To Adjutant Rand and Captains Miller and Ruby, aides-de-camp, my thanks are due.

The result of this victory is important to all in the common defense of the country, and especially of the Virginia and Tennessee Railroad. We have won The Narrows of New River, a point easily defended and a good protection to the country south of it.

The reports of other officers are herewith transmitted.* They will be found to contain more minute information than I could put in this, as I have endeavored to condense as much as possible.

I am, sir, your obedient servant,

JOHN McCAUSLAND,
*Colonel Twenty-sixth Virginia Regt., Comdg. Second Brigade.*

Capt. R. H. FINNEY,
*Assistant Adjutant-General.*

---

* Not found.

## MAY 10-12, 1862.—Skirmishes near Franklin, W. Va.

### *Report of Brig. Gen. Robert C. Schenck, U. S. Army.*

CAMP MILROY, NEAR FRANKLIN,
*May* 10, 1862.

COLONEL: A small scouting party from Franklin was enticed into a house to-day, and, on a signal given by the owner of the house was set upon by bushwhackers. One of my men was taken and his brains beaten out before the door.

I sent out another party when I learned of it, who shot the owner of the house and burnt the house. Another bushwhacker was killed by another of our scouting parties to-day in his attempt to escape after being taken in the very act of firing with his rifle upon one of our cavalrymen.

ROBT. C. SCHENCK,
*Brigadier-General.*

Col. ALBERT TRACY.

---

## MAY 11, 1862.—Skirmish on the Bowling Green Road, near Fredericksburg, Va.

### *Report of Maj. Gen. Irvin McDowell, U. S. Army.*

HDQRS. DEPARTMENT OF THE RAPPAHANNOCK,
*Opposite Fredericksburg, May* 11, 1862.

The enemy advanced upon the Bowling Green road this afternoon, but fell back after losing a lieutenant and 10 men, who were cut off by the gallant Major Duffié, of the Harris Light Cavalry.

IRVIN McDOWELL,
*Major-General, Commanding Department.*

Hon. E. M. STANTON.

---

## MAY 13, 1862.—Affair on Rappahannock River, Va.

### REPORTS.

No. 1.—Brig. Gen. George D. Bayard, U. S. Army, commanding Cavalry Brigade.
No. 2.—Col. Percy Wyndham, First New Jersey Cavalry.
No. 3.—Col. Owen Jones, First Pennsylvania Cavalry.

### No. 1.

### *Report of Brig. Gen. George D. Bayard, U. S. Army, commanding Cavalry Brigade.*

HEADQUARTERS CAVALRY BRIGADE,
*Camp McDowell, Va., May* 14, 1862.

SIR: I have the honor to report that in obedience to orders I started the sloop which was captured a day or two previous up to Falmouth to turn it over to the quartermaster. After it had passed the pickets of the Pennsylvania cavalry the enemy opened fire on the sloop and succeeded in wounding 2 of the Jersey cavalry who were on the boat. In the evening, when we endeavored to take out the wounded, they again opened fire, but the hot fire of the carbineers of the Pennsylvania cavalry drove them from the river banks.

I inclose reports from Colonels Wyndham and Jones.

By the first favorable wind I shall send up the sloop, although it is of no particular value, unless otherwise ordered.

I am, sir, very respectfully, your obedient servant,

GEO. D. BAYARD,
*Brigadier-General, Commanding Cavalry Brigade.*

Capt. SAMUEL BRECK, Jr.,
*Assistant Adjutant-General, McDowell's Corps.*

---

## No. 2.

*Report of Col. Percy Wyndham, First New Jersey Cavalry.*

HEADQUARTERS FIRST NEW JERSEY CAVALRY,
*Camp McDowell, Va., May* 14, 1862.

GENERAL: I have the honor to report that upon receipt of your order yesterday I dispatched an officer with 6 men to proceed with the sloop captured a few days since to Fredericksburg. About half a mile above the pickets of the First Pennsylvania Cavalry the rebels opened a heavy fire upon the vessel. They were in ambush, and some 50 in number, and not more than 3 rods distant. The small party on board returned their fire with great gallantry until re-enforced by a party of the First Pennsylvania. The rebels then retired from the contest.

I regret to state that 2 of my men were badly wounded—Privates James H. Haywood and J. W. Clayhunce. The rebel loss can only be conjectured from their movements. I judge it must have been some 5 or 6 killed and wounded.

I have the honor to be, very respectfully, your obedient servant,

P. WYNDHAM,
*Colonel.*

Brigadier-General BAYARD,
*Commanding Cavalry Brigade.*

---

## No. 3.

*Report of Col. Owen Jones, First Pennsylvania Cavalry.*

HEADQUARTERS FIRST PENNSYLVANIA CAVALRY,
*May* 14, 1862.

SIR: I have the honor to report that on the evening of yesterday (May 13) heavy firing was heard at my camp from the line of my pickets on the Rappahannock. I soon learned that it proceeded from a party of the enemy, and was directed at a vessel in charge of the First New Jersey Cavalry. I at once ordered the carbineers of my command to proceed to the river bank, and found the vessel was fastened to the north bank of the river and in charge of our pickets. I ordered my men to be placed in position to cover the removal of 2 men of the First New Jersey Cavalry that were on board of her and had been badly wounded by the fire of the enemy, giving orders not to fire unless first fired upon. After the first and just as the second wounded man was being removed from the vessel a heavy fire was opened upon her by the enemy. It was instantly replied to by a heavy and well-sustained fire from my men posted along the river bank. As soon as the enemy's fire ceased the order to cease firing was given, and the remaining man was removed to a place of safety.

It gives me great pleasure to state that in the affair none of my men were hurt, and that the officers and men displayed the utmost promptitude, bravery, and coolness.

Very respectfully,

OWEN JONES,
*Colonel First Pennsylvania Cavalry.*

General GEORGE D. BAYARD,
*Commanding Cavalry Brigade.*

---

## MAY 15, 1862.—Skirmish near Gaines' Cross-Roads, Rappahannock Co., Va.

*Report of Col. Thomas T. Munford, Second Virginia Cavalry.*

WASHINGTON, RAPPAHANNOCK COUNTY, VA.,
*May* 15, 1862—7 p. m.

GENERAL: I have the honor to report to you that about 2 o'clock my picket made a dash at a foraging party near Gaines' Cross-Roads with a very small party. My men were driven back. I soon re-enforced them, and dismounted 30 men behind a stone wall. When the enemy came up the dismounted men emptied seven saddles, and I then charged down the road until I met an infantry regiment, who opened upon us in fine style.

The skirmish was the briskest affair I have seen for many a day. The whole army were drawn up to receive us, and by constant firing I kept them in check the whole day. I occupied a commanding hill and could have used a piece of artillery with splendid effect.

The enemy are still between Flint Hill and Gaines' Cross-Roads. They have a heavy train of wagons. I am certain we killed 3 and wounded 4 others. The infantry pressed me too closely to catch the loose horses, though I got one saber and carbine and one six-shooter. I had 2 men slightly wounded, but lost no horses. I have used up all of my small stock of ammunition, but it cost the enemy dearly, and they wasted any quantity of ammunition.

Think of a whole army drawn up in line of battle and kept so six hours by 250 half-armed cavalry.

I send you a letter taken from the Yankee mail. Their wagon trains were hurrying along at a furious rate toward Warrenton and are evidently expecting an attack from you.

Where shall I join you at?

Very respectfully, your obedient servant,

THOMAS T. MUNFORD,
*Colonel, Commanding Second Virginia Cavalry.*

Major-General EWELL, *Commanding.*

## MAY 15, 1862.—Skirmish at Linden, Va.

### REPORTS.

No. 1.—Maj. Gen. Irvin McDowell, U. S. Army.
No. 2.—Brig. Gen. John W. Geary, U. S. Army.
No. 3.—Lieut. Joseph A. Moore, Twenty-eighth Pennsylvania Infantry
No. 4.—Col. Thomas T. Munford, Second Virginia Cavalry.

### No. 1.

*Reports of Maj. Gen. Irvin McDowell, U. S. Army.*

FALMOUTH, *May* 16, 1862.

I have report from Brigadier-General Geary of an attack on the line of the road he is guarding by a party of guerrillas, in which he lost 1 man killed and 14 captured. It looks like a surprise. General Wadsworth, to whom I have given the duty of providing for this road, will inquire into this matter. General Geary writes of being in danger from forces at Luray Court-House. This can hardly be so. If the general places his guards over bridges in log cabins, loop-holed, 14 men can hold out against as large a body of cavalry as can be brought against them. I have told General Wadsworth to so instruct.

IRVIN McDOWELL,
*Major-General, Commanding Department.*

Hon. E. M. STANTON,
*Secretary of War.*

---

FALMOUTH, *May* 16, 1862.

Brigadier-General WADSWORTH:

Brigadier-General Geary reported to me an attack on his line by a party of cavalry, in which he lost 1 man killed and 14 captured. Please call for a report as to this. It appears to me the party was surprised. If General Geary at once causes all his detached parties to build log cabins with loop-holes, and keep them on the alert, 14 men will be able to resist any body of cavalry likely to come against them. This will enable the general to guard bridges with safety with small parties, and give him the mass of his force in hand at such points as may require it. It seems to me that thus arranged he should be able to secure the line with what he has. I would suggest you to send to him some of your dismounted cavalry to aid in this work, but use your own judgment, and I shall be satisfied.

IRVIN McDOWELL,
*Major-General, Commanding.*

---

### No. 2.

*Reports of Brig. Gen. John W. Geary, U. S. Army.*

RECTORTOWN, *May* 15, 1862.

My line was attacked at about 3.30 o'clock this afternoon by a body of rebel cavalry, variously estimated at from 300 to 600, at Linden. One of my men was killed and 14 taken prisoners. My command, consisting of about 1,400 men for duty, is scattered over a distance of 55 miles, and their safety is continually imperiled. I have telegraphed General Wadsworth that I consider it indispensably necessary for the safety of the command that we should be strongly re-enforced without any delay. I am informed that 2,600 cavalry, of Jackson's command, are disbanded to form guerrilla bands for the purpose of attacking this line. General Ewell is also near Luray, with a rebel force of about 8,000 men. I cannot too strongly call your attention to the necessity for re-enforcements.

Very respectfully,

JNO. W. GEARY,
*Brigadier-General, Commanding.*

Hon. E. M. STANTON,
*Secretary of War.*

---

RECTORTOWN, *May* 16, 1862.

SIR: Dispatches have been to-day received from General Wadsworth and orders obeyed. A company of infantry of my command was yesterday ordered to Linden, to remain stationed there. A detachment of 17 men, guarding the company wagon, reached there a short time before the main body of the company, which was on a train. They were attacked by a body of cavalry, variously estimated from 300 to 600, coming upon them from four directions. Our men resisted them, keeping up a sharp firing under shelter of the depot, which was riddled with bullets. My men were overpowered; 1 was killed and 14 taken prisoners, 3 of whom were wounded. When the balance of the company came up the enemy hastily retired under fire, and with some loss.

I have been informed that a portion of General Shields' command had a skirmish with them. Sharp firing was heard from between Chester Gap and Warrenton.

I have reliable authority to-day that the enemy is south of us in threatening attitude. They are represented as being in strong cavalry parties. I will resist any attack to the last extremity. The safety of the roads depends upon an early concentration of forces, as I have from the first stated.

Your orders relative to block-houses, &c., are being executed. I have passed and repassed trains over the road to-day under heavy escort to near Strasburg.

Very respectfully,

JNO. W. GEARY,
*Brigadier-General, Commanding.*

Hon. E. M. STANTON,
*Secretary of War.*

---

## No. 3.

*Report of Lieut. Joseph A. Moore, Twenty-eighth Pennsylvania Infantry.*

LINDEN STATION, MANASSAS GAP RAILROAD, VA.,
*May* 16, 1862.

SIR: After receiving orders from you at Piedmont Station through

Captain Raphael to proceed to this place without delay, and that transportation would be furnished by railroad at the earliest opportunity, I availed myself of the first train yesterday.

At 8 a. m. I sent the company team and wagon* and a two-horse team, in charge of Sergt. Edwin McCabe, 2 corporals, a wagoner, 10 privates, and a colored servant, and took the train at 1 p. m. with the company. When within 1 mile of this place we were met by Sergeant McCabe and Private Joseph Madison, who stated that 500 or 600 rebel cavalry had descended from the mountains suddenly, surprising and capturing the whole party and train except themselves. I ordered the cars to proceed at once to the station.

When arriving at the station we saw the rear guard of the rebel cavalry at a distance of about 500 yards on the road leading south, which, after receiving a volley from my men, fled precipitately into the adjacent wood. I immediately formed my company to take measures to prevent a second surprise.

Having strongly picketed the avenues of approach, I ordered the town to be searched, which was done in a thorough, yet respectful, manner by my men, at the same time arresting every man in the place, and kept them under strict guard.

I found Corpl. George C. Sneath lying in the depot mortally wounded in the abdomen, who died in about an hour. Corpl. Ephraim Baker was slightly wounded in the temple and taken prisoner, with Privates William H. Glazier, John N. Salkeld, Thomas White, George W. Bowersox, Josiah M. Funk, William Cane, George Snyder, Albert Miles, Samuel Rinard, Curtis Maxwell, teamster of Company M, Twenty-eighth Pennsylvania Volunteers, and 3 cavalrymen of the First Michigan Cavalry (Company I), names not known, bearers of mail and dispatches to yourself from Front Royal, and colored servant of Capt. George F. McCabe (Charles Murphy).

I ordered the conductor to return at once with the engine and report. Dr. Logan volunteered to go and report to you particulars. Leaving word at Markham Station, Company G came immediately to our assistance, arriving at this station at 6 p. m. The command was then relinquished to Captain Meyer, who threw out a heavy guard during the night, and at 1.30 a. m. Captain Chapman arrived, relieving Captain Meyer, who returned to Markham.

After a thorough examination of all the persons under arrest (who appeared favorably disposed toward us) I educed the following information: They placed the number of the rebel cavalry at 500 or 600, armed with Minie rifles and carbines—the lowest estimate made was 300—under command of Lieutenant-Colonel Munford, consisting of Captains Dulaney's, Green's, White's, and other companies, of Colonel Stuart's cavalry; they came into the place in three divisions, the right on the main road leading south, the center off the mountain in front of the depot, the left by a mountain road about a quarter of a mile west of the depot and coming to the rear of the depot. So well concerted was the plan, that they supposed them to be thousands.

The inhabitants condemned the rebels very much for the barbarous and treacherous manner they shot and wounded our men after having surrendered their arms. In fact, we were informed by one man, who was very kind to Corporal Sneath, and made him as comfortable as he could under the circumstances, that the rebels were ashamed of it themselves. The company deeply deplore the loss of Corporal Sneath. He

* The rebels left three sets of harness and the company wagon.—J. A. M.

was a brave, generous, and attentive soldier. All is quiet now, and no fears are entertained of a surprise.

Very respectfully, yours,

JOSEPH A. MOORE,
*First Lieutenant, Comdg. Company O, 28th Regt. Pa. Vols.*

Brig. Gen. JOHN W. GEARY.

---

## No. 4.

*Report of Col. Thomas T. Munford, Second Virginia Cavalry.*

WASHINGTON, [*May* 16, 1862]—8.30 a. m.

GENERAL: I cannot conceive why my dispatches to you have not been received. I have sent two dispatches every day since I left you. The enemy, General Shields' command, are now at Flint Hill, on the side of the mountain. Yesterday I went to Linden, hearing that they were moving down the Manassas Gap Railroad. A few troops were passing that way. I captured 15, 2 wagons, and 9 horses. The men were elegantly armed. General Shields has about 6,000 infantry, thirty pieces of artillery, and some little cavalry. They are evidently making for Culpeper Court-House. I presume they will leave Flint Hill this morning. Am on my way to see. They are 5 miles off. I heard that the rest of Banks' command were at Strasburg and fortifying. I sent three dispatches to you, and I now send Major Pearkin's dispatch, on which I predicated my belief that you were on the other side of the mountain, for as soon as they left Luray for Front Royal I sent you a dispatch containing reliable information as to their numbers and their destination, and I crossed the mountain between Chester Gap and Thornton's Gap, and occupied Chester Gap with a picket. Yesterday they marched over.

I sent a dispatch to General Lee, as you directed me, as soon as I found they were at Front Royal and *en route* to join McDowell. I will hang on their rear and watch their movements to-day. If I can do nothing, will join you at once. Will send you another dispatch as soon as I can see them this morning.

Very respectfully,

THOMAS T. MUNFORD,
*Colonel, Commanding Second Virginia Caval y.*

Major-General EWELL,
*Commanding Third Division.*

## MAY 15-17, 1862.—Actions at Wolf Creek and Princeton, W. Va.

### REPORTS.

No. 1.—Maj. Gen. John C. Frémont, U. S. Army, commanding the Mountain Department.
No. 2.—Brig. Gen. Jacob D. Cox, U. S. Army, commanding District of the Kanawha.
No. 3.—Col. E. Parker Scammon, Twenty-third Ohio Infantry, commanding First Provisional Brigade.
No. 4.—Col. Augustus Moor, Twenty-eighth Ohio Infantry, commanding Second Provisional Brigade.
No. 5.—Lieut. Col. Louis von Blessingh, Thirty-seventh Ohio Infantry.
No. 6.—Brig. Gen. Henry Heth, C. S. Army.
No. 7.—Brig. Gen. Humphrey Marshall, C. S. Army.

### No. 1.

*Reports of Maj. Gen. John C. Frémont, U. S. Army, commanding the Mountain Department.*

FARMINGTON [FRANKLIN], *May* 18, 1862.

I am officially informed that General Cox, with the Twenty-eighth and parts of the Thirty-fourth and Thirty-seventh Ohio, attacked the rebels yesterday morning, routed and drove them from Princeton, which they had taken the evening before, capturing from 15 to 20. I am further officially informed that General Heth had fallen back from Lewisburg to Jackson's River Depot, there built boats, and took his stores down to Buchanan, and is now moving them to Bonsack's Station, on the Tennessee Railroad, his forces meanwhile going to Newbern. I still think that any available troops should be sent without delay to Point Pleasant, to sustain General Cox. Please notify me to-day whether these troops will be sent, so that I may know upon what to rely.

J. C. FRÉMONT,
*Major-General.*

Hon. E. M. STANTON,
*Secretary of War:*

—

FRANKLIN, VA., *May* 18, 1862.

Since No. 18 I have report of General Cox. He says:

> We had sharp fight with the enemy at all points yesterday, and inflicted serious damage on him. We lost 3 killed and several wounded. The assault at this post spread the alarm up the line so as to delay our trains and make our supplies short, losing some destroyed in the town.
>
> J. D. COX.

The strength of the enemy is such that if General Cox concentrates to attack them they can fall upon his line of communication from either side. He needs re-enforcements now to enable him to attack. After the enemy is re-enforced by General Heth he would be enabled to hold his position without aid.

J. C. FRÉMONT,
*Major-General.*

Hon. E. M. STANTON,
*Secretary of War.*

## No. 2.

*Reports of Brig. Gen. Jacob D. Cox, U. S. Army, commanding District of the Kanawha.*

No. 2.] PRINCETON, VA., *May* 18 [17], 1862.

I am forced to concentrate my force here instead of advancing, for two reasons:

First. The roads are getting bad again and we are not getting supplies forward to keep us, the new transportation not having arrived in quantities to help us perceptibly.

Second. I find the enemy fully equal to or superior to my force. They hold key position, where if I concentrated to attack them in force they can fall upon my line of communication from either side. Yesterday I was concentrating on the Pearisburg road, when 2,000 men, under Marshall, with three pieces of artillery, pushed in from the Wytheville road and drove the detachment at this post out of it after a severe fight. In the night I marched back Colonel Moor's brigade and drove the enemy out again. He is still hovering in the vicinity, retreating when approached, but taking advantage of the connection of the roads beyond here so as to avoid an action, while he makes it necessary for me to keep so strong a force there as to make that in front entirely inferior to the enemy there. I have to guard in four directions heavily. It is absolutely necessary for me to concentrate here or so split up my command to guard posts that it will be very weak in detail. We had sharp fight with the enemy at all points yesterday and inflicted serious damage on him. We lost 3 killed and several wounded. The assault at this post spread the alarm up the line so as to delay our trains and make our supplies short, losing some destroyed in the town.

I am exceedingly desirous to go ahead, but am satisfied it would be to sacrifice my command.

J. D. COX,
*Brigadier-General.*

Col. ALBERT TRACY,
*Assistant Adjutant-General.*

---

No. 3.] HEADQUARTERS DISTRICT OF KANAWHA,
*Camp near Blue Stone, May* 18, 1862.

After sending No. 2 yesterday (which by error was dated 18th) the enemy in front was largely re-enforced and attacked our position, which, however, we kept without difficulty. Colonel Scammon's brigade joined me in the evening, but he was closely followed up by the enemy in his front. Colonel Scammon brought very reliable evidence that the enemy [had] been largely re-enforced from Eastern Virginia, being commanded by Generals Williams, Marshall, and Heth, and that they numbered not less than 12,000. We also had the most positive evidence that a force, supposed to be about 3,000, were marching from Wytheville road, Wyoming Court-House. One report was that it was Marshall going to Wyoming; another that it was intended to operate upon my line of communication by one of two roads leading from the Wyoming road and coming into the turnpike near my present camp. Our telegraph wires had been cut and our trains and messengers interrupted by small parties. I had no information from the rear for two days, and our last day's rations were issued and the animals suffering for forage. Under these circumstances a council of war strongly urged an immediate return to Flat Top as an absolute necessity for the safety and supply of the army

I accordingly moved at daybreak, and have come 10 miles from Princeton to a point which will prevent the force from the Wyoming road coming on my rear without going to Wyoming Court-House. The movement was made with the most perfect system and order. This may make them abandon their plan and return, unless they are prepared with transportation to follow me up in force. I am trying to get information on which to base my plan for action and to provide measures for the protection of the line. I trust my course will meet the approval of the general commanding. Prudence seemed to demand it and starvation threatened us.

I have no news from Colonel Crook since he reached Lewisburg, and am anxious to hear from him.

The engagement yesterday was warm and continued at intervals through the whole day. During the latter part of the day the enemy did not venture beyond the village. We lost about 30 killed and 70 wounded. Prisoners report the enemy's loss about double or treble that number. Will send you official report as soon as it can be made up. Our officers and men behaved admirably and are in excellent spirits, though outnumbered two to one.

J. D. COX,
*Brigadier-General.*

Col. ALBERT TRACY,
*Assistant Adjutant-General.*

---

HEADQUARTERS DISTRICT OF THE KANAWHA,
*Camp Flat Top, May* 21, 1862.

SIR: I have the honor to submit to the commanding general the following report of the movements of my command on the 16th, 17th, and 18th instant, and the affairs in which they were engaged:

On the evening of the 15th Colonel Scammon's brigade was at Adair's, near the mouth of East River; the main body of Colonel Moor's brigade was at French's, 4 miles above Colonel Scammon's camp, where the road from Princeton to Pearisburg meets the Cumberland Gap road. A detachment of four companies, under command of Lieutenant-Colonel Von Blessingh, Thirty-seventh Ohio Volunteer Infantry, was at the crossing of the Princeton and Wytheville road, with orders to extend their reconnaissance to Rocky Gap and up the Cumberland Gap road as far as possible. A detachment of four companies of infantry and one of cavalry were at Princeton, where I had my headquarters, awaiting the completion of the telegraph to that place, my arrangements being completed for transferring my headquarters to Adair's the next day.

On the afternoon of the 15th Colonel Moor threw a party of two companies of infantry, under Capt. E. Schache, Twenty-eighth Ohio Volunteers, across East River Mountain from French's to reconnoiter the position of the enemy near the mouth of Wolf Creek. They found an outpost of a cavalry company 8 miles from the mouth of the creek, which they attacked and routed, killing 6, wounding 2, and taking 6 prisoners. None of our men were injured. The main force of the enemy was found to be encamped above The Narrows of New River and about the mouth of Wolf Creek, variously reported from 5,000 to 8,000 men.

About noon of the 16th Colonel Moor reported that the detachment on the Wytheville road had a skirmish with 1,500 of the enemy there, killed 3, and retired without loss in the direction of French's; also that

General H. Marshall was reported to be advancing from Tazewell Court-House with 2,500 men. I immediately dispatched an order to Colonel Moor to leave half a regiment at French's and march rapidly with the remainder of his force to the Wytheville Cross-Roads and hold them at all hazards. Meanwhile I kept patrols active on our right and front to ascertain the enemy's movements in those directions. Colonel Scammon reported the enemy still in force in his front, and no apparent change except he was in receipt of reports of considerable re-enforcements reaching them. About 2 o'clock p. m. a cavalry patrol on the Wyoming road 5 miles from Princeton was fired into by a party of the enemy's horsemen. Two companies of infantry and part of the troops at Princeton were immediately sent out, under Major Ankele, Thirty-seventh Ohio Volunteers, to feel the force of the enemy advancing in that direction. It soon became evident that the force which had been met by Colonel Moor's detachment at the Wytheville Cross-Roads was advancing by the Wyoming road, having made a detour to their left to reach it. They advanced cautiously, and were firmly and gallantly met by Maj. F. E. Franklin, Thirty-fourth Ohio Volunteers, and Maj. Charles Ankele, Thirty-seventh Ohio Volunteers, with the detachments of those regiments which garrisoned the post, and Capt. Frank Smith's troop First Ohio Cavalry. Our troops behaved with great steadiness, retiring slowly from point to point as they were outflanked by the superior numbers of the enemy, and maintained the unequal contest for more than three hours.

About 5 p. m., suspecting, from my examination of the advancing force of the enemy, that the principal body of Marshall's command had passed the Wytheville Cross-Roads, I gave orders to Major Franklin to hold the town as long as possible, and if driven from it to retire by the road to French's, sending back to stop trains advancing by the Raleigh road, and then moved my headquarters and baggage upon the Frenchville road, and proceeded immediately to Colonel Moor's headquarters. I there found that, owing to the difficulty of the roads and slowness of communication, he had not yet been able to carry out the order to move his command to the Wytheville Cross-Roads, but had sent to Lieutenant-Colonel von Blessingh six companies of infantry, under Major Bohlender, Twenty-eighth Ohio Volunteers, making the force at the Cross-Roads ten companies of infantry. I immediately ordered the remainder of his command under arms, consisting of three half regiments—the Twenty-eighth, Thirty-fourth, and Thirty-seventh Ohio Volunteers, and a section of Simmonds' battery of artillery—and put them upon the march for Princeton. I ordered Colonel Scammon to move up half a regiment to French's for the night, and to follow at daylight with his whole command, to join me at Princeton. The detachment under Lieutenant-Colonel von Blessingh was notified that, should the enemy appear at Princeton by daylight, he was to move forward from the Cross-Roads in that direction and endeavor to take them in the rear by a simultaneous attack.

I arrived at Princeton at daybreak of the 17th and immediately led forward the whole of Colonel Moor's command upon the place. The enemy made no resistance, but retired before us to the wooded range of hills south and west of the town. We attacked and drove them with considerable loss about the distance of a mile to a strong position commanding both the Wytheville and Wyoming roads, and where they could only be reached by ascending a steep ridge heavily covered with timber, where they had also placed a howitzer battery. On the left of their position they had a rifled 10-pounder and smooth 6-pounder cannon. During the attack in front made by the rest of the command the detachment under Lieutenant-Colonel von Blessingh, marching by the Wytheville road, attacked the enemy's right, but finding the position exceedingly strong and held by greatly superior numbers, they withdrew, and subsequently joined their brigade by a detour to their right.

From prisoners taken during the engagement of the morning we learned that General Williams had joined Marshall, and that the force before us consisted of two brigades—considerably more than double our numbers. This being abundantly corroborated by other information, I did not think it prudent to push the attack farther, but took my position on the outskirts of the town, and awaited the arrival of Colonel Scammon's brigade.

Toward evening Colonel Scammon's brigade arrived. He brought reliable information that the brigades of Generals Williams, Heth, Marshall, and Floyd were united in our front, numbering from 12,000 to 15,000 men; that their movement had been made in the expectation of throwing their principal force in our rear, moving by our right flank on the Wytheville and Wyoming roads, whilst we moved toward our left in the direction of Frenchville and Pearisburg. He also found that the force at The Narrows had promptly followed him up, occupying French's after he left that place, and throwing out outposts quite near those stationed by us on the Pearisburg road. Later in the night the officer of the day brought information that the artillery of the enemy was moving upon the Wyoming road toward our rear by the right, and this information later, taken with that before received, determined me to retire to this position till I could secure my trains, get forward supplies in safety, organize the transportation just arriving in the valley, and fully learn the movements and new force of the enemy. The movement was made at 3 o'clock in the morning of the 18th, and accomplished with the most perfect order and without the least accident.

Upon learning our movement, I am informed that the enemy's left wing abandoned the Wyoming road and turned off toward Tazewell Court-House. For two days prior to their attack on our lines communication had been interrupted and annoyed by small parties cutting the telegraph wires, firing upon messengers and trains. My belief is that the concentration of the enemy's force must be temporary only; that they have drawn in all within reach in the hope of making a successful attack upon this portion of my command, and, having been foiled, that they will separate to guard other points than those immediately in my front. In my present position I feel entirely secure, and am making arrangements to open all communication with Colonel Crook's brigade by way of Pack's Ferry, Palestine, &c., to Lewisburg.

The reports of killed and wounded are forwarded herewith. The conduct of my command has been everything I could desire, and all the movements made with system and precision. The behavior of the detachment at Princeton, under Majors Franklin and Ankele, when the attack began, is peculiarly deserving of praise. They continued the defense of the place, retiring slowly from point to point for a period of six hours, and did not retire from the village until after dark.

I beg leave to call the attention of the commanding general to the fact that the character of this mountain country and the net-work of roads and paths in it is such that no advance movement can be made with entire security to the line of communication without leaving strong detachments at important posts along the line. To do this with my present force would leave an entirely inadequate command at the front. It is quite important that the force in this district should be enlarged enough to enable us to concentrate at least the whole present command in front unweakened by detachments guarding the rear.

As far as we have examined the country it seems to be almost wholly stripped of forage of every sort. This will necessitate an arrangement of transportation in view of this fact. Our movements have been valuable to us as a reconnaissance of the country, and I am very confident a few days will enable us to take the aggressive with increased advantages for success.

Very respectfully, your obedient servant,

J. D. COX,
*Brigadier-General, Commanding.*

Col. ALBERT TRACY, *Hdqrs. Mountain Department.*

The later reports showing that the casualties have been overestimated in first report received, I have ordered them entirely revised, and will forward in another inclosure.

—

***Return of Casualties in Col. Augustus Moor's brigade, District of the Kanawha, in the engagement at Princeton, W. Va., May 16–17, 1862.****

| Command. | Killed. | | Wounded. | | Missing. | | Aggregate. | Remarks. |
|---|---|---|---|---|---|---|---|---|
| | Officers. | Enlisted men. | Officers. | Enlisted men. | Officers. | Enlisted men. | | |
| 28th Ohio | ...... | 5 | ...... | 10 | ...... | 12 | 27 | 9 of the missing prisoners. |
| 34th Ohio | ...... | 5 | 2 | 12 | ...... | 9 | 28 | 5 of the missing prisoners. |
| 37th Ohio | 1 | 12 | 3 | 42 | ...... | ...... | 58 | Lieut. M. W. Blucher mortally wounded, Capt. Lewis Quedenfeld killed. |
| Total | 1 | 22 | 5 | 64 | ...... | 21 | 113 | |

*This is the revised list, dated May 29, 1862, referred to in Cox's report.

## No. 3.

### *Reports of Col. E. Parker Scammon, Twenty-third Ohio Infantry, commanding First Provisional Brigade.*

HEADQUARTERS FIRST PROVISIONAL BRIGADE,
*Camp at East River, Va., May* 16, 1862.

GENERAL: I have very minute directions as to the approach to the enemy by way of French's Mill, but I can get no word from Colonel Moor. There is a rumor that he has gone or sent out to meet Humphrey Marshall, who is said by rumor to be or to have been approaching from Jeffersonville down East River. I have sent to him again this morning, but the messenger has not yet returned. I cannot understand his acting offensively or otherwise without letting me know what he is doing.

All my information goes to show conclusively that former reports as to position of enemy in front are correct; also that the best approach is by French's Mill, for which latter I have pretty minute directions. This road, however, strikes the Wolf Creek road from Tazewell, 7 miles from the mouth of Wolf Creek; thence down the creek the road is a tolerable wagon road.

The place from which the enemy can be seen at mouth of Wolf Creek is about 2 miles up the North River from mouth of Rich Creek and on the heights. There is a report of enemy advancing on Valley road behind us, or rather toward East River Mountain.

Have ordered troops under arms, and sent out to the pickets to verify the report. Will send another messenger immediately.

Very respectfully, your obedient servant,

E. P. SCAMMON,
*Colonel, Commanding First Provisional Brigade.*

General JACOB D. COX.

---

HEADQUARTERS FIRST PROVISIONAL BRIGADE,
*Camp at East River, May* 16, 1862—6.15 p. m.

GENERAL: Your courier just arrived. Have heard from Colonel Moor. He had moved to the front with part of his force or would have communicated sooner. Am glad to hear that Wytheville road is to be held. Will keep up communication with detachment at French's, as directed.

To-morrow morning I had decided to act more offensively toward The Narrows. In view of your plans, as I think I understand them, at least to some extent, I have not wished to make such efforts as would necessitate the pushing up re-enforcements so fast as to disorganize the command. I think The Narrows will be ours, as I have before said, when you give the word.

I will be ready to act when the word comes and as it directs. In saying that I had decided to act more offensively toward The Narrows I did not mean that I will pass them, but drive off the enemy from some field breastworks which they have erected on the opposite side of the river. A few well-directed shots will do it at any time. I think I could pass The Narrows, but apart from orders I doubt if we could keep communication free from annoyance from the other side of the river until it too is cleared of the rebels.

Very respectfully, your obedient servant,

E. P. SCAMMON,
*Colonel, Commanding First Provisional Brigade.*

General JACOB D. COX.

---

## No. 4.

*Report of Col. Augustus Moor, Twenty-eighth Ohio Infantry, commanding Second Provisional Brigade.*

HEADQUARTERS SECOND PROVISIONAL BRIGADE,
*Frenchville, May* 16, 1862.

SIR: I have the honor to report that at 12 o'clock yesterday I received the general's letter, with instructions to send detachments toward Wytheville road. I had already made the details when I received intelligence that a rebel force, stated to be 1,000 to 2,500 strong, had crossed the mountains, coming down Cumberland Gap road. As there was not time to ask for further orders, I detailed for that expedition four companies of the Thirty-seventh, Lieutenant-Colonel Blessingh; four companies of the Twenty-eighth, Major Bohlender; two pieces of Captain Simmonds' battery, and 25 of Captain Emmons' company, Second Virginia Cavalry, all under my command. As it was reported that Humphrey Marshall commanded the rebels, I also detailed Company A, Twenty-eighth, and Company A, Thirty-fourth, Lieut. H. C. Hatfield, under command of Capt. E. Schache, Twenty-eighth Ohio Regiment, to cross East Mountain on bridle-paths and to examine the roads along Wolf Creek. I also detailed Company C, Captain Miller, Thirty-fourth Regiment, to examine a road running east opposite my present position; the whole provided with two days' rations and with written instructions to the commanders. At 1.30 o'clock p. m. the three detachments left camp. I, with the main force, marched 11 miles toward Rocky Gap. As it grew dark I turned over the command to Major Bohlender, Lieutenant-Colonel Blessingh being in the rear, and directed them to bivouac there without fire, rebel pickets being reported to be within a mile at a farm-house. Not feeling justified to stay away overnight from the brigade, I returned with the artillery to Frenchville. At 6 o'clock this morning the detachment under Captain Schache returned with 6 prisoners, 8 Mississippi rifles, 5 Enfield rifles, 1 Harper's Ferry rifle, 3 common rifles, 2 muskets, 5 sabers, and 6 horses. The prisoners and list of names I send to you, under escort of Lieutenant McNally, Second Virginia Cavalry. The arms I stored for the present with Mr. Bogen, at Frenchville.

Please find Captain Schache's report inclosed.* Company C, Thirty-fourth Regiment, returned last night. Captain Miller reported Union people on that road dreading rebel scouts from the mountains south of them. The road comes out on East River again about 2½ miles from here. I have it guarded now.

The detachment to Rocky Gap will return to-day. I shall report the result of that reconnoiter as soon as possible.

I am, sir, very respectfully, your most obedient servant,

A. MOOR,

*Colonel Twenty-eighth Ohio Regt. Infantry, Comdg. Second Brig.*

Capt. G. M. BASCOM,

*Assistant Adjutant-General, District of Kanawha.*

---

## No. 5.

*Report of Lieut. Col. Louis von Blessingh, Thirty-seventh Ohio Infantry.*

CAMP FLAT TOP MOUNTAIN,

*May* 23, 1862.

SIR: On the afternoon of the 15th instant I marched with four companies of the Thirty-seventh Regiment, A, H, C, and F; four companies of the Twenty-eighth Regiment, under command of Major Boehlaender; two pieces of artillery, and one company of cavalry from Frenchville up the East River, following the East River road. Colonel Moor accompanied the column for 7 miles; then returned with the cavalry and artillery, leaving me in command, with instructions to discover the strength of the enemy on the Rocky Gap road and on Cross-Road, and his movements. I marched 1 mile farther and bivouacked, on the road for the night. On the morning of the 16th the command, after marching 6 miles, reached Cross-Roads. Here I heard that the road to Rocky Gap was occupied by 1,500 rebels, and that they intended to intrench themselves near Rocky Gap. At the same time a report was current that General Marshall was on his way from Jeffersonville with 2,500 men.

---

*Not found.

While writing down these reports 26 cavalrymen, the advance guard of Marshall's corps, advanced on the road. I posted our advance guard behind different buildings on the road, and at a distance behind fences three other companies as supports. The cavalrymen came on into the midst of the company and there received a full volley. Seven fell; the balance retreated in haste. While it was the intention to pursue the enemy, the advance guard of the same appeared already in a distance of half a mile in the woods. In order to avoid a collision I retreated 3 miles and concluded there to take an observing position, but seeing, after the fog had parted, at 9 o'clock a. m., that the heights on the other side of East River were strongly occupied by infantry and cavalry, I again retreated about 3 miles to the place where we had camped the night before. One of the dragoons who had been sent back came running into camp saying that he had been shot at. Another mountain path was behind us, and a retreat of 2 miles more brought the same to the front of the column.

Toward evening of the same day (16th) I received the order to keep my present position till the arrival of re-enforcements of two companies—one from the Thirty-fourth and the other from the Twenty-eighth Regiment—and then to march to Cross-Roads and there take position.

During the night, at half past 12, the order came to at once move to Cross-Roads, which was done at 2 o'clock. At 3.45 the aide-de-camp, Lieutenant Ambrosius, came with the order from General Cox to advance from Cross-Roads on the road to Princeton, and to attack the enemy, who had reached there, with every energy.

Three-quarters of a mile east of Cross-Roads I left East River road and reached the road to Princeton without hinderance 3 miles above Cross-Roads, having in this manner flanked Cross-Roads, which, of course, was in possession of the enemy.

Princeton road was occupied by three companies of Virginia troops, who, after a short engagement, took flight, with the loss of 1 killed. This was at 7 o'clock in the morning. With all possible speed I continued the march to Princeton. Rebel cavalry attacked twice, by which a company of the Thirty-fourth, who acted as rear guard and who were most exposed to the attack, killed 2 of the cavalrymen. At 10 o'clock in the morning the heights of Princeton were reached. At the distance of 5 miles the discharge of cannon in Princeton had been heard, which still more drove the men to haste, but when within 3 miles the same ceased. This sudden silence of the cannon left me in uncertainty as to the result of the fight at Princeton and whether our friends had been victorious or not. It did not, though, interrupt our farther advance. Company H was sent out on the right of the road and Company A on the left of the same as skirmishers. Companies C and F, in the center, formed the reserve. These companies were of the Thirty-seventh Regiment.

Hardly had position been taken when the first shots were fired. The skirmishers in a few minutes reached the heights. The reserve, two companies (F and C), Thirty-seventh Regiment, were hid behind fences. The firing on [the] part of the rebels continued to be more lively, while my men could fire with but little success, the enemy being protected by their entrenchments. The five companies of the Twenty-eighth Regiment were drawn up in the rear. Three of them, under command of Major Bohlender, were ordered by me to the left flank to create a demonstration, but without success. The balance of the Twenty-eighth (two companies), who were within reach of the fire, were moved back behind brush-wood on the road. The firing of the enemy became more and more fierce, and it seemed impossible to achieve any result. The position was kept, though, to the last moment. The number of the dead and wounded became larger and larger, and still there was no sign of help reaching us from the brigade in Princeton. Not knowing either what had happened in Princeton, the fighting was broke off in good order and the companies were withdrawn. The retreat was covered by the companies in the rear.

After a motion backward of half a mile I took position on a rather steep hill, and there formed the companies, and believing that we were being pursued I had a part of the wounded brought there, leaving them under the treatment of the assistant surgeon, Dr. J. Schenck, who at once went to work to render them assistance. He remained with them when the column marched away, which was soon after.

It was impossible to return the same road which we had come, and I therefore marched with my command direct into the mountains, trying in some way to reunite with the brigade. To make this possible in Princeton was not very advisable, the enemy occupying a distance of 2 miles from the place. To reach the Princeton, Frenchville road was therefore at first my object. Without a guide we came into a road, and following this brought us into the first camp on East River. It was 3 o'clock in the afternoon. Hoping to find in Frenchville the brigade of Colonel Scammon I sent a spy out, but he returned after an hour with the report that the rebels had just taken possession of the place with a force of 800 men. In consequence of this we at once marched off, taking a farmer, who lived in the neighborhood, with us as guide, and into the mountains, without road or path.

In the evening, at 8 o'clock, a small plateau was reached, where I posted one company of the Thirty-fourth as pickets, taking the balance into a hollow, where I kept them under arms as much as possible until the rising of the moon, at half past 11 o'clock.

At 1 o'clock in the morning (Sunday, the 18th) I passed the road with the command unobserved 4 miles below Princeton, taking the road into the mountains. At 3 o'clock a. m. we took the Logan road and followed the same, thus bringing us around Princeton in a circle of about 4½ miles. Finally, after a tiresome march, we came upon the pickets of the Second Virginia Cavalry Regiment, of whom I learned that the whole division was on the retreat. At 9 a. m. the camp ground of the Twelfth Regiment was reached, on which already a part of the train of the division had arrived.

It is difficult to give the force of the enemy against us in the fight of the 17th. They fired with all sorts and all calibers of balls, even with fire-balls, and hand grenades. The dead of the Thirty-seventh Regiment number 11, so many having been recognized, and 36 severely wounded, have been transported to Princeton, and left there in the hands of the enemy. Seven slightly wounded have been brought back to the regiment, and 18 are still missing from the four companies engaged in this combat. The loss of the Twenty-eighth Regiment is 5 killed and 10 wounded; from the companies of the Thirty-fourth Regiment 2 wounded.*

The march, a most fatiguing one, was made by all companies with great perseverance. Seven slightly wounded men were brought into the camp on Blue Stone River on dragoon horses.

Captain Messner, of the Thirty-seventh, deserves the praise of a

---

*But see revised statement, p. 508.

precautious commander of advance guard; also Captain Reiching, of the Twenty-eighth, on the first day, and Captain West, of the Thirty-fourth, as commanders of the rear guard.

The detachment remained one hour on the ground till the arrival of General Cox, when the different companies joined their regiments.

L. VON BLESSINGH,
*Lieutenant-Colonel, Thirty-seventh Regiment Ohio Volunteers, Commanding Detachment.*

Col. AUGUSTUS MOOR, *Comdg. Second Prov. Brigade.*

---

No. 6.

*Report of Brig. Gen. Henry Heth, C. S. Army.*

HEADQUARTERS NEW RIVER, *May* 19,
*Via Dublin, Va., May* 20, 1862.

By the co-operation of General Marshall, Cox has been driven from this section of the country, losing many prisoners, his entire camp and garrison equipage, baggage, &c. He will be pursued.

H. HETH,
*Brigadier-General, Commanding.*

General R. E. LEE, *Commander-in-Chief.*

---

No. 7.

*Report of Brig. Gen. Humphrey Marshall, C. S. Army.*

CAMP NEAR JEFFERSONVILLE, VA.,
*May* 22, 1862.

GENERAL: In my last letter I advised you that the opportune return of Brigadier-General Heth with his force to Dublin Depot rendered it unnecessary for me to proceed in that direction; but I ventured to suggest to that officer that a lateral movement by me, cutting the line of the enemy's communication at Princeton, might assist him materially in clearing the country of the column which was endeavoring to penetrate to the railroad. General Heth approving the idea, I moved my whole force at once via Saltville toward this place, arriving here on the 12th instant.

I took the responsibility of ordering to the field some skeleton companies just recruited and intended to form part of a new regiment authorized by an order of the Secretary of War of April 9, issued to Major McMahon, formerly General Floyd's aide-de-camp. This corps, composed of seven companies, so called, did not number more than 400 men, and none of them were trained at all. Under my order they elected a lieutenant-colonel for the time only to lead them on this expedition. I also took the responsibility of placing in their hands the old muskets turned in to General Dimmock by Colonel Trigg, which I found at Abingdon.

I left Abingdon with a force composed of the Fifty-fourth Virginia (600 men), the Twenty-ninth Virginia (420 men, four companies, wholly recruits, three raised by me this spring and one by Lieutenant March), the Fifth Kentucky (500 men), Dunn's battalion of recruits (400 men), and Bradley's Mounted Kentucky Rifles (about 275 men), making an aggregate of 2,195 men, to which add Jeffress' battery of six pieces, manned by recruits almost entirely.

General Heth desired a delay of a day or two to reorganize the companies in Floyd's brigade which were under his command. Having dispatched couriers to Colonel Wharton, directing him to meet me in Princeton on the night of the 16th, by advancing from Rocky Gap, and having informed General Heth, who was in position at the mouth of Wolf Creek, that he should attack the enemy at the mouth of East River on the morning of the 17th, I put my column in motion on the 15th and reached Princeton on the night of the 16th.

My advance was unexpected by Brigadier-General Cox, who had his headquarters and body guard at Princeton at the time with a force variously estimated at from 500 to 1,200 men, the former probably nearer the truth than the latter. The pickets of the enemy were encountered by my advance guard about 4 miles from Princeton, and a skirmish continued from that place through the woodlands and brushwood to a point something over 1 mile from the Court-House. This skirmish was conducted by the Fifth Kentucky, from which I lost Capt. Leonidas Elliott, who fell mortally wounded (since dead) at the head of his company while bravely beating the enemy back.

In this skirmish the enemy lost some 16 or 20, who were left on the field. We had only 4 wounded, including Captain Elliott; none killed.

I directed Colonel Trigg to move on the right of the Fifth Kentucky and take the enemy in flank, and so to press on to Princeton. Arriving at the hill (subsequently occupied by me) from which the land drops into the level vale in which Princeton stands, a halt was ordered by Brigadier-General Williams and a line of battle formed, with the view of bringing up the artillery to shell the town from that point. I thought it best to take the place by small-arms, and though the daylight was now nearly gone, I ordered the battalions forward—Trigg leading to the right, May next, Moore's and Bradley's men next—so as to move on the place through the meadows and by the road we had traveled.

In half an hour a sharp, hot fire on the right announced Colonel Trigg in contact with the enemy. Fire from a regiment is seldom more steady than this I refer to. Succeeded by a general shout and then by absolute silence, which lasted at least an hour and a half before I received any message from the troops in front, really I did not know but that we had met a check, and that regimental commanders were arranging for a new assault. As everything had to be left to them, under such circumstances, I waited about half a mile from town, placing my battery in position at once to command the town and our road. I supported the battery with Dunn's battalion.

After a while I was informed that the enemy had fled before us, leaving his tents, clothes, swords, officers' uniforms, and even the lights burning in his tents. It is probable, had we not halted before night-fall, we might have captured many prisoners, possibly the general himself, for I was informed he did not leave town until twilight; but none of us could foresee, and, so far as I know, every one acted for the best; the regiments went in with hearty good will and promptly.

Major Bradley lost one of his men (Weedon, of Holladay's company). Trigg had some 6 wounded, one of whom, Private Carter, of Company I, was mortally wounded.

So the town of Princeton fell into my hands about 10 p. m. on May 16; the line of the enemy's communication with Raleigh was cut, and the headquarters of the Kanawha Division was abruptly stampeded.

A mass of correspondence fell into my hands. Letters and orders, dated from May 10 down to May 16, fully disclosed the intentions of the enemy and his strength. I send you several of these for your perusal.

I learned from the inhabitants of Princeton that on the morning of the 15th two regiments, about 900 men each, had passed through town toward East River, and that two regiments had been expected to arrive at 8 p. m. from Raleigh the very evening I came. I had a knowledge that one or more regiments had passed on to the mouth of East River, by the road from Dunlap's, without coming through Princeton. Combining the information I had, from the letters captured, with the news I received from the people of Princeton, I learned that I was in the neighborhood of at least four regiments, of which General Heth had no knowledge. My own position had suddenly become very critical.

I had only heard from Colonel Wharton that he had not passed East River Mountain on the morning of the 15th. He had not arrived at Princeton on the night of the 16th, as I had directed and desired. I did not know the direction in which General Cox had retired, whether to East River or Raleigh, but whether in the one or the other direction I had no assurance but that the morrow would find me struggling with my force, more than half of whom were undrilled recruits, against largely superior numbers of well-trained troops of every arm.

Casting about us as well as I could at night to catch an idea of the topography, I found that the ruins of Princeton occupy a knoll in the center of some open, level meadows, entirely surrounded by woodlands, with thick undergrowth which fringe the open grounds, and that through the entire circuit about the town the central position at the Court-House can be commanded by the Enfield rifle. Roads lead in through these woods in several directions.

My men had marched 19 miles during the day, had slept none, and were scattering among the houses and tents to discover what had been left by the enemy.

I at once determined to withdraw from the ruins before dawn and to take position within range of the town site, so as to cover the road by which I entered. This I effected; the dawn finding me in the act of completing the operation. My force was masked from the town.

After daylight I received a dispatch from Colonel Wharton, dated the 16th, at the Cross-Roads, 11 miles from Princeton, promising to come to town by 9 a. m. on the 17th. Before he arrived the enemy had re-entered the town, a force I could not estimate, but which was provided with artillery, and displayed more than two full regiments. Colonel Wharton arrived in the neighborhood, by the road leading from the Cross-Roads, a little after 9 a. m.

The enemy was at the time throwing forward his skirmishers to dispute with mine the woods and points overhanging the road which led in from the Cross-Roads to Princeton, which road ran nearly parallel to the one by which I had advanced. I had written to Colonel Wharton to press on and he would have the enemy in flank. The colonel opened with his single piece of artillery a little after 9 o'clock upon my right, and the batteries in town and at my position at once opened upon each other at long range. Colonel Wharton soon came to me to report his position and force. The force was about 800 men. My estimate is I now had some 2,800 men, of whom one-half were raw recruits.

A regiment of the enemy, coming down from the direction of the Cross-Roads to Princeton about this time, appeared in the rear of Colonel

Wharton's command, and were attacked by it furiously. The struggle lasted but a short time. The havoc in the enemy's ranks was terrible. Colonel Wharton reports to me 211 as the dead and wounded of the enemy. I understand that more than 80 bodies were buried on the field.

The enemy appeared with a flag of truce, asking to bury their dead and to remove their wounded. I refused; but hearing, after about an hour, that some officer had allowed it, and that the enemy were then engaged in burying, I directed Brigadier-General Williams to permit the ambulances of the enemy to pass along my right, for the purpose of carrying away their wounded also. There was no further battle.

I waited for news from Brigadier-General Heth, or to learn of his approach to Princeton, as the signal for a general engagement with the enemy. If Brigadier-General Heth had successfully attacked at the mouth of East River in the morning, as requested to do, he might be hourly expected to communicate his approach to Princeton by his couriers or his artillery. If he had not attacked, but was still at the mouth of Wolf Creek, it would be imprudent in me to assail the enemy, for the probability was strong that he would hazard the assault himself against my position, attempting to beat me while he preserved his front against Heth. If General Heth could, by means of my diversion, get through The Narrows of New River our forces should join the night of the 17th, and then, combined, we could fight on the 18th the whole force of the enemy, and, if successful, could pursue his vanquished column to Raleigh, burn his stores, and press our advantage so far as we desired. This was my reasoning. I would not move upon the town in the evening of the 17th because the result would then be problematical, and that problem would likely be solved favorably by the arrival of General Heth's command. A grand result would then be easily obtained. Had I attacked under the circumstances and had I failed nothing could have shielded me from condemnation as a rash officer who imperiled all and lost all when a few more hours would have doubled his force.

I confidently expected at night-fall on the 17th that the enemy, in superior force, would attack me in the morning, or that a junction with General Heth would enable me to attack his whole force, which was apparently concentrating around Princeton. He was in plain view under my glass; his wagons deliberately parked; his regiments exercising, and all the appearances given which indicate the purpose to give battle. My force was masked to him. He could have no idea of its amount. In this fact was my safety until Heth could come up. It seems Brigadier-General Heth did advance to the mouth of East River and found the enemy had abandoned tents and camp equipage both there and at French's, where he had been fortifying. The general passed on until he came within 4 or 5 miles of Princeton, on the evening of the 17th, when, hearing in the country from somebody that I had been repulsed and was retreating, he fell back in the night to the mouth of East River.

His courier arrived at my position, 1 mile from the Court-House, about 9 a. m. on the 18th, conveying to me the information that General Heth's force was now so required in another direction as to forbid farther pursuit of the enemy, with the request to return Colonel Wharton to a post in the district of New River indicated by the general commanding said district.

The enemy had during the night vacated Princeton, taking the Raleigh road, his rear passing Blue Stone River about sunrise. I ordered my battalion of Mounted Rifles to follow him.

I ascertained that on the night of the 18th he encamped about 10 miles from Princeton, in a very strong position, having some seven regiments with him in retreat; in all from 5,000 to 7,000 men.

On the 19th I again sent forward on his line of retreat and ascertained that he had passed the Flat Top Mountains; had burned some of his caissons and gun-carriages, and had abandoned some of his wagons the preceding night. He was now 25 miles from Princeton.

Nothing was now left to me but to return to the district whose interests are under my charge. I left a company of mounted men at Princeton, with orders to remain until General Heth could relieve them, and with the rest of my command I returned to this point. I left 71 of the enemy's wounded in the hospital at Princeton too badly shot to be moved at all. His surgeons were left in attendance and a chaplain was permitted to be with them. I return a list of 29 prisoners. The men themselves have been marched to Abingdon, where 3 others from the same army have been confined, whose names you have already.

My quartermaster has made a return of our captures, among which I may mention about 35 miles of telegraph wire, horses, mules, saddles, pack-saddles, medical instruments, medicines in panniers, tents, a few stores, 18 head of cattle, a number of wagons, and some excellent muskets and rifles. These last have been taken in charge by my ordnance officers, and will be issued to my command unless otherwise ordered.

Reviewing the whole movement, I have only to regret that Brigadier-General Heth did not join me on the 17th and did not communicate to me his whereabouts during the day or night. All was accomplished that I anticipated from the movement except the capture of prisoners. The invasion has been signally repulsed and the enemy has been demoralized and broken; the country he threatened so imminently has been relieved. It is a triumph of strategy merely, without loss on our part.

My list of casualties will only exhibit 2 killed on the field; 2 seriously wounded, who will die, and some 10 or 12 wounded, but not dangerously. The enemy has lost largely, and, indeed, I should not be surprised if in killed and wounded his loss reached 400. One of his regiments scattered in the woods, threw away guns and uniforms, and its members are daily picked up by the country people.

Your obedient servant,

H. MARSHALL,
*Brigadier-General, Commanding.*

General R. E. LEE,
*Commanding, &c., Richmond, Va.*

[Inclosure.]

CAMP AT TIFFANY'S, VA.
*May* 21, 1862.

GENERAL: I have to report the following articles captured from the enemy at Princeton, Va., on the 16th and 17th instant, viz: Twelve bell-tents, 2 wall-tents, and flies, 5 horses, 18 mules, 35 pack-saddles, 4 wagons, a lot of incomplete harness.

Respectfully,

TH. F. FISHER,
*Major and Chief Quartermaster, Army of East Kentucky.*

Brig. Gen. HUMPHREY MARSHALL,
*Commanding, &c.*

## MAY 15-JUNE 17, 1862.—Operations in the Shenandoah Valley.

### SUMMARY OF THE PRINCIPAL EVENTS.

May 15, 1862.—Jackson's command returns from McDowell to Shenandoah Valley.
18, 1862.—Skirmish at Woodstock.
21, 1862.—Reconnaissance from Front Royal to Browntown.
23, 1862.—Action at Front Royal.
Skirmish at Buckton Station.
24, 1862.—Frémont ordered to move from Franklin, W. Va., against Jackson.
McDowell ordered to put 20,000 men in motion for the Shenandoah, &c.
Skirmish at Berryville.
Skirmish at Strasburg.
Action at Middletown.
Action at Newtown.
Skirmish at Linden.
24-26, 1862.—Retreat of Banks' command to Williamsport, Md.
24-30, 1862.—Operations about Harper's Ferry.
25, 1862.—Engagement at Winchester.
26, 1862.—Skirmish near Franklin, W. Va.
27, 1862.—Skirmish at Loudoun Heights.
28, 1862.—Skirmish at Charlestown.
29, 1862.—Skirmish near Wardensville, W. Va.
30, 1862.—Action at Front Royal.
31, 1862.—Skirmish near Front Royal.
Jackson's command retires from Winchester
June 1, 1862.—Skirmish at Mount Carmel, near Strasburg.
2, 1862.—Skirmishes at Strasburg and Woodstock.
3, 1862.—Skirmish at Mount Jackson.
Skirmish at Tom's Brook.
6, 1862.—Action near Harrisonburg.
7, 1862.—Skirmish near Harrisonburg.
8, 1862.—Rearrangement of the Mountain Department and Department of the Shenandoah.
Battle of Cross Keys.
8- 9, 1862.—Engagements at Port Republic.
9, 1862.—Shields' division ordered back to Luray, *en route* for Fredericksburg.
11-12, 1862.—Frémont's command withdrawn to Mount Jackson.
12, 1862.—Jackson's command encamps near Weyer's Cave.
13, 1862.—Skirmish at New Market.
16, 1862.—Skirmish near Mount Jackson.
17, 1862.—Jackson's command moves toward Richmond.

### REPORTS, ETC.

No. 1.—Maj. Gen. Nathaniel P. Banks, U. S. Army, commanding Department of the Shenandoah, of operations May 14-June 16 and including instructions from the President and Secretary of War.

No. 2.—Casualties in the Union forces May 23-25.

No. 3.—Major Hector Tyndale, Twenty-eighth Pennsylvania Infantry, of reconnais, sance from Front Royal to Browntown, May 21.

No. 4.—Col. John R. Kenly, First Maryland Infantry, of action at Front Royal, May 23.

No. 5.—Capt. George Smith *et al.*, First Maryland Infantry, of action at Front Royal, May 23.

No. 6.—Lieut. Col. Charles Parham, Twenty-ninth Pennsylvania Infantry, of action at Front Royal, May 23.

No. 7.—Maj. Philip G. Vought, Fifth New York Cavalry, of action at Front Royal, May 23.

No. 8.—Lieut. Charles A. Atwell, Battery E, Pennsylvania Light Artillery, of action at Front Royal, May 23.

No. 9.—Brig. Gen. John W. Geary, U. S. Army, of skirmish at Linden, May 24.

No. 10.—Lieut. William W. Rowley, Twenty-eighth New York Infantry, Acting Signal Officer, of operations May 24-25.

No. 11.—Capt. James W. Abert, U. S. Topographical Engineers, of operations May 24.

No. 12.—Capt. Samuel B. Holabird, Assistant Quartermaster, U. S. Army, of public animals, wagons, &c., captured, lost, &c., in the retreat from Strasburg to Williamsport.

No. 13.—Capt. Charles H. T. Collis, Pennsylvania Infantry, commanding Body Guard, of operations May 24-26.

No. 14.—Brig. Gen. John P. Hatch, U. S. Army, commanding cavalry, of operations May 24-25.

No. 15.—Lieut. Col. Calvin S. Douty, First Maine Cavalry, of operations May 24.

No. 16.—Lieut. Col. Charles Wetschky, First Maryland Cavalry, of operations May 18-26.

No. 17.—Col. Thornton F. Brodhead, First Michigan Cavalry, of operations May 24-27.

No. 18.—Col. Othneil De Forest, Fifth New York Cavalry, of operations May 24-27.

No. 19.—Lieut. Col. Charles R. Babbitt, Eighth New York Cavalry, of operations May 24-25.

No. 20.—Col. Charles H. Tompkins, First Vermont Cavalry, of operations May 24-25.

No. 21.—Maj. William D. Collins, First Vermont Cavalry, of operations May 24-30.

No. 22.—Brig. Gen. Alpheus S. Williams, U. S. Army, commanding First Division, of operations May 24-25.

No. 23.—Capt. William D. Wilkins, Assistant Adjutant-General, of operations May 25.

No. 24.—Capt. R. B. Hampton, Battery F, Pennsylvania Light Artillery, Chief of Artillery, of operations May 25-28.

No. 25.—Lieut. James H. Peabody, Battery M, First New York Light Artillery, of operations May 23.

No. 26.—Lieut. J. Presley Fleming, Battery F, Pennsylvania Light Artillery, of operations May 24-25.

No. 27.—Lieut. Franklin B. Crosby, Battery F, Fourth U. S. Artillery, of operations May 24-26.

No. 28.—Col. Dudley Donnelly, Twenty-eighth New York Infantry, commanding First Brigade, of operations May 24-26.

No. 29.—Lieut. Col. George D. Chapman, Fifth Connecticut Infantry, of operations May 25.

No. 30.—Col. George L. Beal, Tenth Maine Infantry, of operations May 24-26.

No. 31.—Lieut. Col. Edwin F. Brown, Twenty-eighth New York Infantry, of operations May 24-25.

No. 32.—Col. Joseph F. Knipe, Forty-sixth Pennsylvania Infantry, of operations May 24-26.

No. 33.—Col. George H. Gordon, Second Massachusetts Infantry, commanding Third Brigade, of operations May 24–25.

No. 34.—Col. Silas Colgrove, Twenty-seventh Indiana Infantry, of operations May 25.

No. 35.—Lieut. Col. George L. Andrews, Second Massachusetts Infantry, of operations May 24–25.

No. 36.—Capt. Samuel M. Zulich, Twenty-ninth Pennsylvania Infantry, of operations May 23–26.

No. 37.—Col. Thomas H. Ruger, Third Wisconsin Infantry, of operations May 25.

No. 38.—Brig. Gen. Rufus Saxton, U. S. Army, commanding post, of operations at Harper's Ferry, including instructions and congratulations from the Secretary of War.

No. 39.—Maj. Gen. John C. Frémont, U. S. Army, commanding the Mountain Department, of operations May 24–June 17, and including instructions from the President and Secretary of War.

No. 40.—Casualties in the Union forces at the battle of Cross Keys.

No. 41.—Brig. Gen. Robert C. Schenck, U. S. Army, commanding brigade, of the battle of Cross Keys.

No. 42.—Brig. Gen. Henry Bohlen, U. S. Army, commanding brigade, of the battle of Cross Keys.

No. 43.—Capt. Michael Wiedrich, Battery I, First New York Light Artillery, of the battle of Cross Keys.

No. 44.—Col. Eugene A. Kozlay, Fifty-fourth New York Infantry, of the battle of Cross Keys.

No. 45.—Col. Wladimir Krzyzanowski, Fifty-eighth New York Infantry, of the battle of Cross Keys.

No. 46.—Lieut. Col. John Hamm, Seventy-fourth Pennsylvania Infantry, of the battle of Cross Keys.

No. 47.—Col. Francis Mahler, Seventy-fifth Pennsylvania Infantry, of the battle of Cross Keys.

No. 48.—Capt. Hugh McDonald, Kane Rifle Battalion, of the battle of Cross Keys.

No. 49.—Brig. Gen. George D. Bayard, U. S. Army, commanding cavalry, of operations June 1–13.

No. 50.—Lieut. Col. Joseph Kargé, First New Jersey Cavalry, of operations June 2–13.

No. 51.—Col. Owen Jones, First Pennsylvania Cavalry, of operations June 1–13.

No. 52.—Maj. Gen. James Shields, U. S. Army, commanding First Division, Department of the Rappahannock, of operations May 30–June 9.

No. 53.—Casualties in the Union forces in the engagement at Port Republic.

No. 54.—Col. Philip Daum, Chief of Artillery, of engagement at Port Republic.

No. 55.—Capt. Joseph C. Clark, Battery E, Fourth U. S. Artillery, of engagement at Port Republic.

No. 56.—Brig. Gen. Nathan Kimball, U. S. Army, commanding First Brigade, of action at Front Royal, May 30.

No. 57.—Brig. Gen. Erastus B. Tyler, U. S. Army, commanding Third Brigade, of engagement at Port Republic.

No. 58.—Col. Samuel S. Carroll, Eighth Ohio Infantry, commanding Fourth Brigade, of engagement at Port Republic.

No. 59.—Lieut. Gen. Thomas J. Jackson, C. S. Army, commanding the Valley District, of operations May 14–June 17, with congratulatory orders.

No. 60.—Casualties in the Confederate forces at the battle of Cross Keys and the engagement at Port Republic.

No. 61.—Capt. J. K. Boswell, C. S. Army, Chief Engineer, of operations June 1–9.

No. 62.—Surg. Hunter McGuire, C. S. Army, of medical and hospital stores captured.

No. 63.—Maj. W. J. Hawks, Commissary of Subsistence, C. S. Army, of stores captured.

No. 64.—Maj. John A. Harman, C. S. Army, Chief Quartermaster, of property captured and destroyed.

No. 65.—Col. S. Crutchfield, C. S. Army, Chief of Artillery, of operations May 23–June 9.

No. 66.—Col. T. T. Munford, Second Virginia Cavalry, of operations May and June.

No. 67.—Col. Thomas S. Flournoy, Sixth Virginia Cavalry, of operations May 23–26.

No. 68.—Brig. Gen. Charles S. Winder, C. S. Army, commanding First Brigade, Jackson's division, of operations May 23–June 9.

No. 69.—Col. J. W. Allen, Second Virginia Infantry, of operations May 24–June 9.

No. 70.—Col. Charles A. Ronald, Fourth Virginia Infantry, of operations May 23–June 9.

No. 71.—Col. W. S. H. Baylor, Fifth Virginia Infantry, of engagement at Winchester.

No. 72.—Lieut. Col. J. H. S. Funk, Fifth Virginia Infantry, of the engagement at Port Republic.

No. 73.—Col. A. J. Grigsby, Twenty-seventh Virginia Infantry, of operations May 24–June 9.

No. 74.—Col. John F. Neff, Thirty-third Virginia Infantry, of operations May 23–June 9.

No. 75.—Capt. Joseph Carpenter, Virginia Artillery, of operations May 25–June 9.

No. 76.—Capt. William T. Poague, Virginia (Rockbridge) Artillery, of operations May 23–June 9.

No. 77.—Lieut. Col. R. H. Cunningham, Twenty-first Virginia Infantry, Second Brigade, of operations May 23–25.

No. 78.—Capt. John E. Penn, Forty-second Virginia Infantry, of operations May 23–25.

No. 79.—Lieut. Col. William Martin, Forty-second Virginia Infantry, of operations June 8–9.

No. 80.—Maj. John B. Moseley, Twenty-first Virginia, commanding Forty-eighth Virginia Infantry, of engagement at Winchester.

No. 81.—Lieut. Col. Thomas S. Garnett, Forty-eighth Virginia Infantry, of battle of Cross Keys and engagement at Port Republic.

No. 82.—Capt. B. W. Leigh, First Virginia Battalion, of operations May 25–June 9.

No. 83.—Capt. William H. Caskie, Virginia (Hampden Artillery, of engagement at Winchester.

No. 84.—Col. Samuel V. Fulkerson, Thirty-seventh Virginia Infantry, commanding Third Brigade, of operations May 24–25.

No. 85.—Brig. Gen. William B. Taliaferro, C. S. Army, commanding Third Brigade, of operations June 8–9.

No. 86.—Col. E. T. H. Warren, Tenth Virginia Infantry, of engagement at Winchester.

No. 87.—Col. A. G. Taliaferro, Twenty-third Virginia Infantry, of engagement at Winchester.

No. 88.—Maj. T. V. Williams, Thirty-seventh Virginia Infantry, of operations May 23–25.

No. 89.—Capt. George W. Wooding, Virginia (Danville) Artillery, of operations May 23–25.

No. 90.—Maj. Gen. Richard S. Ewell, C. S. Army, commanding Third Division, of operations May 23–June 9.

No. 91.—Col. W. C. Scott, Forty-fourth Virginia Infantry, commanding Second Brigade, of operations May 23–June 9.

No. 92.—Col. James A. Walker, Thirteenth Virginia Infantry, commanding Fourth Brigade, of operations June 8–9.

No. 93.—Col. Z. T. Conner, Twelfth Georgia Infantry, of action at Front Royal, May 30.

No. 94.—Brig. Gen. Isaac R. Trimble, C. S. Army, commanding Seventh Brigade, of operations May 25–June 9.

No. 95.—Brig. Gen. Richard Taylor, C. S. Army, commanding Eighth Brigade, of operations May 23–June 9.

No. 96.—Col. Bradley T. Johnson, First Maryland Infantry, of operations May 29–June 9.

## No. 1.

*Reports of Maj. Gen. Nathaniel P. Banks, U. S. Army, commanding Department of the Shenandoah, of operations May 14–June 16, and including instructions from the President and Secretary of War.*

STRASBURG, *May* 14, 1862—3.30 p. m.
(Received 5.30 p. m.)

Nothing new has occurred to-day. The enemy has not moved beyond Mount Jackson in this direction except by its cavalry, and then to return again. General Hatch stills occupies Woodstock with cavalry. I have declined to order the bridges burned or the telegraph destroyed as inconsistent with the purposes of the Government, unless absolutely necessary to our safety. Very heavy rain all day.

N. P. BANKS,
*Major-General, Commanding.*

Hon. E. M. STANTON.

—

WAR DEPARTMENT,
*May* 16, 1862—12.30 p. m.

Major-General BANKS:

Please place two of your regiments to guard the railroad from Strasburg to Front Royal, so as to allow Geary to direct his force on other points that are threatened. Answer immediately whether you can do so and how soon they will be in position.

EDWIN M. STANTON,
*Secretary of War.*

—

STRASBURG, *May* 16, 1862—4 p. m.

I will send two regiments to protect the road between this place and Front Royal by to-morrow noon, 17th instant. This will reduce my force greatly, which is already too small to defend Strasburg if attacked.

N. P. BANKS,
*Major-General, Commanding.*

Hon. E. M. STANTON,
*Secretary of War.*

—

STRASBURG, *May* 17, 1862—12 m.
(Received 12.45 p. m.)

Owing to the absence of cars my regiment will not reach Front Royal till toward night. It has to march on the railroad, but will be in season to protect bridges, &c. About 100 of the enemy's cavalry reported at Columbia Furnace, on line with Woodstock. No infantry in that neighborhood. Ewell's force reported by deserters who left him Tuesday to be still at Swift Run Gap.

N. P. BANKS,
*Major-General, Commanding.*

Hon. E. M. STANTON,
*Secretary of War.*

HEADQUARTERS DEPARTMENT OF THE SHENANDOAH,
*May* 18, 1862—10.30 p. m.

No indications of infantry in the valley. Colonel De Forest, with detachment of Fifth New York Cavalry, encountered two companies rebel cavalry this morning and drove them through Woodstock and scoured the country in our front. No signs of enemy in this vicinity with this exception. Three hundred rebel cavalry reported 10 miles from Front Royal, in Chester Gap.

N. P. BANKS,
*Major-General, Commanding.*

Hon. E. M. STANTON.

—

WAR DEPARTMENT,
*May* 21, 1862.

Major-General BANKS, *Strasburg:*

Please report immediately the number and position of the force in your command, and whether any, and what, of Colonel Miles' force has been removed from the Baltimore and Ohio Railroad. Also the position and number of the enemy so far as known to you.

EDWIN M. STANTON,
*Secretary of War.*

—

STRASBURG, VA., *May* 21, 1862—5 p. m.
(Received 8.15 p. m.)

Your dispatch just received. My force at Strasburg is 4,476 infantry, two brigades; 2,600 [1,600] cavalry; ten Parrott guns, and six smoothbore pieces. The larger part of this force is at work on fortifications and constructing lines of defense. I have on the Manassas Gap Railroad, between Strasburg and Manassas, 2,500 infantry; six companies cavalry, and six pieces of artillery. There are five companies cavalry, First Maine, near Strasburg, belonging to Colonel Miles' command. No other troops of his command are here. Of the enemy I received information last night, direct from New Market, that Jackson has returned to within 8 miles of Harrisonburg, west. General Frémont telegraphed me this morning that Jackson had moved from Shenandoah Mountain toward my front, and other information from different sources confirms these reports. I have no doubt that Jackson's force is near Harrisonburg and that Ewell still remains at Swift Run Gap. Their united force is about 16,000. I shall communicate by letter more at length the condition of affairs and the probable plans of the enemy.

N. P. BANKS,
*Major-General.*

Hon. E. M. STANTON,
*Secretary of War.*

—

STRASBURG, *May* 21, 1862—10.30 p. m.
(Received May 22, 9.30 a. m.)

Nothing of importance to-night. Our cavalry encountered Ashby's men near Woodstock this p. m., driving them into town, and killing 4, capturing 6. No loss reported on our side. Prisoners report that Jackson's train was arriving at Harrisonburg yesterday from the west.

N. P. BANKS,
*Major-General, Commanding.*

Hon. E. M. STANTON,
*Secretary of War.*

---

HEADQUARTERS DEPARTMENT OF THE SHENANDOAH,
*Strasburg, Va., May* 22, 1862.

SIR: The return of the rebel forces of General Jackson to the valley, after his forced march against Generals Milroy and Schenck, increases my anxiety for the safety of the position I occupy and that of the troops under my command. That he has returned there can be no doubt. We have information direct from the people of the neighborhood, from prisoners that we have captured from him, from deserters, and also from General Frémont, who telegraphs his march in this direction.

From all the information I can gather—and I do not wish to excite alarm unnecessarily—I am compelled to believe that he meditates attack here. I regard it as certain that he will move north as far as New Market, a position which commands the mountain gap and the roads into the Department of the Rappahannock, and enables him also to co-operate with General Ewell, who is still at Swift Run Gap.

Once at New Market, they are within 25 miles of Strasburg, with a force of not less than 16,000 men. My available force is between 4,000 and 5,000 infantry, 1,800 cavalry, and sixteen pieces of artillery.

We are compelled to defend at two points, both equally accessible to the enemy—the Shenandoah Valley road, opening near the railway bridges, and the turnpike.

We are preparing defenses as rapidly as possible, but with the best aid of this character my force is insufficient to meet the enemy in such strength as he will certainly come, if he attacks us at all, and our situation certainly invites attack in the strongest manner.

We greatly need heavier artillery for the fortification constructing in the town. A battery of 20-pounder Parrott guns will only place us on a level with the guns of the enemy. My infantry should be increased, if possible, both for defense of the town and the protection of the railway and bridges. To guard the railway well it is indispensable that Chester Gap should be occupied, but I have not sufficient force for this. There are two advanced points in front of the railway which should be held by our troops—one at Orleans, in front of Rectortown, General Geary's present position; the other at Chester Gap. These temporarily occupied by a respectable force, say two regiments each, the neighborhood would soon be cleared of guerrillas and scouting parties and the perfect safety of the road secured. At present our danger is imminent at both the line of the road and the position of Strasburg. Our line is greatly extended; the positions and property to be protected of vital importance, and the enemy is in our immediate neighborhood in very great superiority of numbers.

To these important considerations ought to be added the persistent adherence of Jackson to the defense of the valley and his well-known purpose to expel the Government troops from this country if in his power. This may be assumed as certain. There is probably no one more fixed and determined purpose in the whole circle of the enemy's plans. Upon anything like equal ground his purposes will be defeated.

I have forborne until the last moment to make this representation, well knowing how injurious to the public service unfounded alarms become, but in this case the probabilities of danger are so great, that it should be assumed as positive and preparation made to meet it.

Col. John S. Clark, one of my aides-de-camp, knows well the position and purposes of the enemy, and can give you all the information the Department may require.

I have the honor to be, with great respect, your obedient servant,

N. P. BANKS,
*Major-General, Commanding.*

Hon. E. M. STANTON,
*Secretary of War.*

---

STRASBURG, *May* 23, 1862.
(Received 11 p. m.)

Our troops were attacked at Front Royal this afternoon, and, though making a vigorous resistance, were compelled by superiority of numbers to retire toward Middletown. The rebel force is reported at 5,000, and is said to intend advancing on the Middletown road. No definite information has yet been received, the telegraph line having been early destroyed. The force had been gathering in the mountains, it is said, since Wednesday. Re-enforcements should be sent us if possible. Railway communication with Manassas probably broken up. A lieutenant of Captain Best's battery, name not reported, was shot by guerrillas this afternoon. Have requested Colonel Miles to move his available force toward Winchester.

N. P. BANKS,
*Major-General, Commanding.*

Hon. E. M. STANTON,
*Secretary of War.*
(Copies to Frémont and McDowell.)

---

STRASBURG, *May* 23, 1862.
(Received 12 o'clock.)

The following dispatch has just been received:

WINCHESTER, 23*d*.

Colonel Kenly is killed.* Lieutenant-colonel, adjutant, and all the rest of commanding officers First Maryland Regiment taken prisoners. Regiment cut all to pieces and prisoners; First Michigan Cavalry ditto. The enemy's forces are 15,000 or 20,000 strong, and on the march to Strasburg. If you want me to report in person telegraph to Captain Flagg.

SAVILLE,
*Commanding Company B, First Maryland Regiment.*

N. P. BANKS,
*Major-General, Commanding.*

Hon. E. M. STANTON.

---

STRASBURG, *May* 24, 1862.
(Received 2.4 a. m.)

Captain Saville, of the Maryland regiment, whose dispatch I forwarded, has been interrogated by General Crawford in regard to his

---

*A mistake.

dispatch, and reaffirms all its essential details as within his own observation. I deem it much overestimated, but the enemy's force is undoubtedly very large and their possession of Front Royal complete.

N. P. BANKS,
*Major-General, Commanding.*

HON. E. M. STANTON.

---

WAR DEPARTMENT,
*May* 24, 1862—2.6 a. m.

Maj. Gen. N. P. BANKS, *Strasburg:*

Arrangements are making to send you ample re-enforcements. Do not give up the ship before succor can arrive. Your dispatches have been forwarded to General Geary.

P. H. WATSON,
*Assistant Secretary of War.*

---

WAR DEPARTMENT, *May* 24, 1862.

Major-General BANKS:

General Dix has been ordered to forward all the force he can spare to you immediately and other force will be sent from here. Please report the present condition of things.

EDWIN M. STANTON,
*Secretary of War.*

---

STRASBURG, *May* 24, 1862.
(Received 7.5 a. m.)

Colonel Kenly's command of infantry and cavalry has been driven from Front Royal, with considerable loss in killed, wounded, and prisoners. The enemy's force estimated at 5,000 or 6,000. It is reported as fallen back on Front Royal; probably occupies that place this morning.

N. P. BANKS,
*Major-General, Commanding.*

HON. E. M. STANTON.

---

STRASBURG, *May* 24, 1862.
(Received 7.10 a. m.)

Cannot give details this morning of our loss. The force of the enemy was very large; not less than 6,000 to 10,000. It is probably Ewell's force, passing through Shenandoah Valley. Jackson is still in our front. We have sent our stores to the rear, but troops remain here. Thanks for the re-enforcements. Enemy's cavalry reported on the Winchester road this morning by our scouts.

N. P. BANKS,
*Major-General, Commanding.*

HON. E. M. STANTON

---

STRASBURG, VA., *May* 24, 1862—7.15 a. m.
(Received 9.45 a. m.)

Thanks for dispatch. We shall stand firm. Enemy is undoubtedly in strong force. Reported on the road to Winchester this morning, in strength from 6,000 to 10,000.

N. P. BANKS,
*Major-General, Commanding.*

P. H. WATSON,
*Assistant Secretary of War.*

—

WINCHESTER, *May* 24, 1862—8 p. m.
(Received 9.45 p. m.)

I was satisfied by the affair at Front Royal yesterday that I could not hold Strasburg with my force against Jackson's and Ewell's armies, who I believed intended immediate attack. Though I might have saved my command, it would have been impossible to secure the vast stores and extensive trains accumulated there, and, learning from a variety of sources entitled to belief that Ewell intended to put his force between Strasburg and Winchester in order to cut off retreat and prevent re-enforcements, I concluded that the safest course for my command was to anticipate the enemy in the occupation of Winchester. My advance guard entered this town at 5 this evening, with all our trains and stores in safety. A strong attack was made upon our trains at Middletown by rebel cavalry, artillery, and infantry, but it was repulsed by our troops, and the few wagons abandoned by teamsters nearly all recovered. I learn here that the pickets of the enemy were within 5 miles of the town this morning, on the Front Royal road. I shall return to Strasburg with my command immediately. I learn from a prisoner taken to-day, who was at the engagement at Front Royal yesterday, that Colonel Kenly was wounded only and not killed.

N. P. BANKS,
*Major-General, Commanding.*

The PRESIDENT OF THE UNITED STATES.
(Same to General Frémont.)

—

WAR DEPARTMENT,
*May* 24, 1862.

Major-General BANKS, *Winchester:*

In your dispatch of this evening to the President you say that you intend to return with your command to Strasburg. The question is suggested whether you will not by that movement expose your stores and trains at Winchester. The President desires therefore more detailed information than you have yet furnished respecting the force and position of the enemy in your neighborhood before you make a movement that will subject Winchester or Harper's Ferry to danger from sudden attack. You will please report fully before moving.

EDWIN M. STANTON,
*Secretary of War.*

—

WINCHESTER, *May* 24, 1862.
(Received 11.50 p. m.)

I am persuaded that a large force of the enemy occupied positions to-day between Strasburg and Winchester, but had not time to co-operate. The city is full of rumors as to the movements of the enemy, and apprehensions of attack to-morrow are entertained by many. Colonel Miles telegraphs that a rebel party of 60 attacked Colonel Beal's baggage train this afternoon at Berryville, killing 1 and wounding 3.

N. P. BANKS,
*Major-General, Commanding.*

Hon. E. M. STANTON.

—

WAR DEPARTMENT,
*May* 24, 1862.

Major-General BANKS, *Winchester:*

Your movement is regarded by the President as wise and prudent. We have felt deeply concerned for your safety, and have used every exertion to send you re-enforcements. General Frémont has been directed to operate against the enemy in the direction of Harrisonburg. Three regiments have been ordered from Baltimore to Harper's Ferry and Winchester and one regiment left here this evening; another goes to-night for Winchester by way of Harper's Ferry. Geary has fallen back to White Plains. Duryea has sent one regiment to Geary, and will send another immediately. I have ordered General King, formerly of your command, to report to you, if you need him. You may assign him a command or not at your pleasure. Please report particulars of the affair at Front Royal yesterday and what our loss is. Report frequently your condition and operations. If Frémont acts promptly with you the enemy's force ought not to escape.

EDWIN M. STANTON,
*Secretary of War.*

—

HEADQUARTERS,
*Martinsburg, May* 25, 1862—2.40 p. m.

The rebels attacked us this morning at daybreak in great force. Their number was estimated at 15,000, consisting of Ewell's and Jackson's divisions. The fire of pickets began with light; was followed by the artillery, until the lines were fully under fire on both sides. The left wing stood firmly, holding its ground well, and the right did the same for a time, when two regiments broke the line under the fire of the enemy. The right wing fell back. They were ordered to withdraw, and the troops pressed through the town in considerable confusion. They were quickly reformed on the other side, and continued their march in good order to Martinsburg, where they arrived at 2.40 p. m., a distance of 22 miles. Our trains are in advance, and will cross the river in safety. Our entire force engaged was less than 4,000, consisting of Gordon's and Donnelly's brigades, with two regiments of cavalry under General Hatch, and two batteries artillery. Our loss is considerable, as was that of the enemy, but cannot now be stated. We were re-enforced by Tenth Maine, which did good service, and a regiment of cavalry.

N. P. BANKS,
*Major-General, Commanding.*

Hon. E. M. STANTON,
*Secretary of War.*

HEADQUARTERS, BEYOND MARTINSBURG, VA.,
*May* 25, 1862—5.30 p. m.

All communication is cut off. We know not what has occurred at Harper's Ferry, &c. A prisoner captured this p. m. says the rebel force in our rear is to be strengthened; that their purpose is to enter Maryland at two points—Harper's Ferry and Williamsport. He confirms all we have heard in regard to the rebel force here. We all pass the Potomac to-night safe—men, trains, and all, I think—making a march of 35 miles.

N. P. BANKS,
*Major-General, Commanding.*

Hon. E. M. STANTON,
*Secretary of War.*

---

WAR DEPARTMENT, *May* 25, 1862.

General BANKS,
*Williamsport, via Hagerstown:*

Two of your telegrams have been received. They have greatly relieved our anxiety respecting your command. We hope you are by this time entirely safe. Your gallantry and skill and the valiant bravery of your command are deserving of great praise. General Saxton is at Harper's Ferry, with over 3,000 to 5,000 men. We have sent a large force of artillery to that point, which will reach there by daylight. Please report again as soon as possible.

EDWIN M. STANTON,
*Secretary of War.*

---

WILLIAMSPORT, *May* 26, 1862.
(Received 9 a. m.)

We believe that our whole force, trains and all, will cross in safety. The men are in fine spirits and crossing in good order. The labor of last night was fearful. The enemy followed us last night on the march, but has not made his appearance this morning. The news of your movements South has unquestionably caused them to look for their safety. Your dispatch was read to the troops this morning amid the heartiest cheers.

N. P. BANKS,
*Major-General, Commanding.*

Hon. E. M. STANTON,
*Secretary of War.*

---

WAR DEPARTMENT,
*May* 26, 1862.

Major-General BANKS, *Williamsport:*

Your telegram this morning received. We rejoice greatly at your safety. Do you need any ammunition to enable you to dispute the enemy's crossing the river, or anything else?

EDWIN M. STANTON,
*Secretary of War.*

WILLIAMSPORT, *May* 26, 1862.
(Received 2.20 p. m.)

The enemy driving in our pickets across the river. Everything of importance safe—guns, ordnance trains, and nearly all the trains.

N. P. BANKS,
*Major-General, Commanding.*

Hon. E. M. STANTON,
*Secretary of War.*

---

WILLIAMSPORT, *May* 26, 1862—4 p. m.
(Received 10.6 p. m.)

I have the honor to report the safe arrival of command at this place last evening at 10 o'clock and the passage of the Fifth Corps across the river to-day with comparatively but little loss. The loss of men killed, wounded, and missing in the different combats in which my command has participated since the march from Strasburg on the morning of the 24th instant I am unable now to report, but I have great gratification in being able to represent it, although serious, as much less than might have been anticipated, considering the very great disparity of forces engaged and the long-matured plans of the enemy, which aimed at nothing less than entire capture of our force. A detailed statement will be forwarded as soon as possible. My command encountered the enemy in a constant succession of attacks and at well-contested engagements at Strasburg, Middletown, Newtown, at a point also between these places, and at Winchester. The force of the enemy was estimated at from 15,000 to 20,000 men, with very strong artillery and cavalry supports. My own force consisted of two brigades, less than 4,000 strong, all told, 1,500 cavalry, ten Parrott guns, and six smooth-bores. The substantial preservation of the entire supply is a source of gratification. It numbered about 500 wagons, on a forced march of 53 miles, 35 of which were performed in one day, subject to constant attack in front, rear, and flank, according to its position, by enemy in full force. By the panics of teamsters and the mischances of river passage of more than 300 yards, with slender preparations for ford and ferry, it lost not more than 50 wagons. A full statement of this loss will be forwarded forthwith. Very great commendation is due to Capt. S. B. Holabird, assistant quartermaster, and Capt. E. G. Beckwith for the safety of the train. Our troops are in good spirits and occupy both sides of the river.

N. P. BANKS,
*Major-General, Commanding*

The PRESIDENT.

---

MAY 26, 1862—8.20 p. m.
(Received May 27, 2.35 a. m.)

The enemy's pickets have been in our front, and some skirmishing, but not in any force, between this and Martinsburg. I do not think there is any great force there. Shall test it to-morrow. Our troops supposed to have been cut off by enemy are coming in considerable numbers; some by Sharpsburg, others by Hancock. Trains all across river. Everything quiet. Enemy alarmed; has withdrawn, I think.

N. P. BANKS.

Hon. E. M. STANTON

WILLIAMSPORT, *May* 27, 1862—9 p. m.
(Received May 28, 1.15 a. m.)

A detachment of cavalry advanced to-day within a few miles of Martinsburg. Two regiments of the enemy's cavalry and some infantry are in position on the right of the town. A prisoner captured near the town states that a part of Ashby's command left Martinsburg this morning in the direction of Winchester. My reports will be forwarded as soon as the necessary statements can be obtained.

N. P. BANKS,
*Major-General, Commanding.*

Hon. E. M. STANTON.

---

WASHINGTON, *May* 28, 1862—12.45 p. m.

Major-General BANKS,
*Williamsport:*

You will get your force in order for moving speedily as possible, and establish your communication with General Saxton with a view to reoccupying your former lines. Can you not occupy Martinsburg at once? General Shields is moving forward from Manassas to Front Royal, thence to Strasburg. In order to enable General Saxton to move, you will send him a part of your transportation. He has none, and it cannot be sent from here in time.

EDWIN M. STANTON,
*Secretary of War.*

Please acknowledge the receipt of this and the hour it is received.

---

WILLIAMSPORT, *May* 28, 1862—1 p. m.
(Received 3.40 p. m.)

Colonel Pinkney, in command on the other side of the river, reports that they constantly heard the sound of cars running west from Martinsburg during last night. I have no doubt this is a delusion. It constantly occurred last summer on the Potomac. There is something in the night sounds which encourages this idea. I do not credit the report, but think you should be informed of it, as the Department may explain it from other information. I regret to see these reports published with my name, as it presents me to the country as an alarmist, when in truth I am almost incredulous as to them.

N. P. BANKS,
*Major-General, Commanding.*

LORENZO THOMAS,
*Adjutant-General.*

(Copy to McDowell and Frémont.)

---

WILLIAMSPORT, *May* 28, 1862—2.35 p. m.
(Received 4.50 p. m.)

A prisoner captured near Martinsburg this morning by our troops reports that about 2,000 of the enemy were there yesterday. Ashby's force, artillery, and baggage he met upon the road to Winchester yesterday morning. It was understood among the men that Ashby had been ordered to Berryville, on account of forces said to be advancing upon Winchester. The prisoner is intelligent, and seems to be perfectly honest. Our advance is near Martinsburg, and a force also at Falling Waters. My troops are not yet in condition to march.

N. P. BANKS,
*Major-General, Commanding.*

Hon. E. M. STANTON,
*Secretary of War.*

---

WILLIAMSPORT, *May* 28, 1862.
(Received 3.46 p. m.)

Your dispatch received 1.40 p. m. Orders were issued yesterday to put my command in condition to march. My troops are much disabled and scattered, but will be in good condition in a day more. We are near Martinsburg, and will occupy it as soon as possible. Transportation shall be sent to General Saxton immediately.

N. P. BANKS,
*Major-General, Commanding.*

Hon. E. M. STANTON,
*Secretary of War.*

---

WILLIAMSPORT, *May* 28, 1862—4.35 p. m.
(Received 6.20 p. m.)

A skirmish took place this morning between the rebels and Tenth Maine near Falling Waters, 8 miles in front. No one was injured. I have just received information that 4,000 of the enemy are advancing on Falling Waters. It is expected they will make an attack. They have five pieces of artillery.

N. P. BANKS,
*Major-General, Commanding.*

Hon. E. M. STANTON,
*Secretary of War.*

---

WILLIAMSPORT, *May* 28, 1862—8.20 p. m.
(Received 11.35 p. m.)

Have received information to-day which I think should be transmitted, but not published over my name, as I do not credit it altogether. A merchant from Martinsburg, well known, came to inform me that in a confidential conversation with a very prominent secessionist, also merchant of that town, he was informed that the policy of the South was changed; that they would abandon Richmond, Va., everything South, and invade Maryland and Washington; that every Union soldier would be driven out of the valley immediately. This was on Friday evening, the night of attack on Front Royal. Names are given me, and the party talking one who might know the rebel plans. A prisoner was captured near Martinsburg to-day. He told the truth, I am satisfied, so far as he pretended to know. He was in the fight at Front Royal and passed through Winchester two hours after our engagement. Saw the dead carried away. He says the rebel force was very large—not less than 25,000 at Winchester and 6,000 or 7,000 at Front Royal; that the idea was general among the men that they were to invade Maryland. He passed Ashby yesterday, who had twenty-eight companies of cavalry under his command; was returning from Martinsburg, and moving under orders, his men said, to Berryville. There were 2,000 rebels at Martinsburg when he passed that town yesterday. These reports came to me at the same time I received General Saxton's dispatch and the statement from my own officer that 4,000 rebels were near Falling Waters, in my front.

N. P. BANKS,
*Major-General, Commanding.*

Hon. E. M. STANTON.

---

WILLIAMSPORT, *May* 29, 1862.

Everything is quiet this morning. The Signal Corps reports a camp of one company in the vicinity of Back Creek; no evidence of enemy elsewhere in that direction. Sixty to one hundred wagons were sent to General Saxton to-day.

N. P. BANKS,
*Major-General, Commanding.*

Hon. E. M. STANTON,
*Secretary of War.*

---

WASHINGTON, *May* 29, 1862—12 m.

Major-General BANKS,
*Williamsport, Md.:*

General McDowell's advance should and probably will be at or near Front Royal at 12 (noon) to-morrow. General Frémont will be at or near Strasburg as soon. Please watch the enemy closely, and follow and harass and detain him if he attempts to retire. I mean this for General Saxton's force as well as that immediately with you.

A. LINCOLN.

---

WILLIAMSPORT, *May* 29—2.30 p. m.

Hon. E. M. STANTON:

Information from the front 11.30 a. m. is that enemy is drawing in his pickets to Martinsburg.

N. P. BANKS.

(Copy tc McDowell.)

---

WILLIAMSPORT, *May* 29, 1862.

Your dispatch received at headquarters 3.30 p. m. My command is much disabled, but we will do what we can to carry out your views.

N. P. BANKS,
*Major-General, Commanding.*

PRESIDENT.

WILLIAMSPORT, *May* 29, 1862—10 p. m.
(Received midnight.)

No advance has been made by the enemy's pickets to-day. Information direct from Martinsburg to-day assures me that he is withdrawing. I shall put all my available forces on the move in the morning. Regiments all greatly disabled from a great variety of causes.

N. P. BANKS,
*Major-General.*

Hon. E. M. STANTON,
*Secretary of War.*

---

WILLIAMSPORT, *May* 29, 1862—10.15 p. m.

Affairs are more quiet. The rumors of the approach of the enemy at Falling Waters and the extent of his force prove to be unfounded. Every one feels assured of the strength of our positions. Signal officers fail to discover from commanding points any traces of the enemy's camp, and the latest reports from our front indicate his gradual withdrawal.

N. P. BANKS,
*Major-General, Commanding.*

Hon. E. M. STANTON.

---

WAR DEPARTMENT,
*May* 29, 1862—11.30 p. m.

Major-General BANKS:

A dispatch just received (11 p. m.) from Assistant Secretary Watson at Harper's Ferry states that Jackson with his forces was near there at sundown, plainly contemplating an attack.

EDWIN M. STANTON.

---

WILLIAMSPORT, *May* 30, 1862.
(Received 2.35 a. m.)

Information received from General Saxton at Harper's Ferry which renders it necessary for me to move to his assistance rather than in the direction of Martinsburg.

N. P. BANKS,
*Major-General.*

His Excellency the PRESIDENT.

---

WILLIAMSPORT, *May* 29, 1862.
(Received 30th, 3.25.)

Your dispatch received. Have sent force to Sharpsburg upon same information from General Saxton.

N. P. BANKS,
*Major-General, Commanding.*

Hon. E. M. STANTOF.

WASHINGTON, *May* 30, 1862—10.15 a. m.

Major-General BANKS,
*Williamsport, Md., via Harper's Ferry:*

If the enemy in force is in or about Martinsburg, Charlestown, and Winchester, or any or all of them, he may come in collision with Frémont, in which case I am anxious that your force, with you and at Harper's Ferry, should so operate as to assist Frémont if possible; the same if the enemy should engage McDowell. This was the meaning of my dispatch yesterday.

A. LINCOLN.

---

WILLIAMSPORT, *May* 30, 1862.
(Received 4.45 p. m.)

Your communication received. Have sent part of our force to Antietam Ford, near Shepherdstown. Will do all we can to harass the enemy's rear. No indication of enemy this side of Martinsburg, and we believe no considerable force there.

N. P. BANKS,
*Major-General, Commanding.*

The PRESIDENT OF THE UNITED STATES.

---

WILLIAMSPORT, *May* 31, 1862—10.25 a. m.

My advance troops, Fifth New York Cavalry, Colonel De Forest commanding, entered Martinsburg this morning, and passed several miles beyond, where they encountered the enemy's cavalry. They captured several prisoners, a wagon, muskets, ammunition, and an American flag. There does not appear to be a large force in that neighborhood. My command, I regret to say, is not in condition to move with promptitude to any great distance, but everything that can be done will be to press and harass the enemy. Colonel De Forest reports that Colonel Kenly is at Winchester, wounded. My troops are yet much scattered, and want army blankets and cooking utensils, that are required for any movement. We shall move into Martinsburg a larger force to-day.

N. P. BANKS,
*Major-General, Commanding.*

Hon. E. M. STANTON,
*Secretary of War.*

---

WILLIAMSPORT, *May* 31, 1862.
(Received 11.40 p. m.)

We have no report from our forces at Martinsburg to-night. It is quite possible that the demonstration of the rebels against Harper's Ferry is to cover their retreat. They operate between Charlestown and Berryville. Berryville, which they occupied early in our movement, covers Snicker's Ferry. This will take them east of the Blue Ridge. They are probably preparing means of crossing at that point. All their fury and numbers are well spent at Harper's Ferry for that purpose.

N. P. BANKS,
*Major-General, Commanding.*

Hon. E. M. STANTON,
*Secretary of War.*

---

HEADQUARTERS DEPARTMENT OF THE SHENANDOAH,
[*May* 31, 1862.]

SIR: In pursuance of orders from the War Department, Col. John R. Kenly, commanding First Maryland Volunteers, was sent on the 16th day of May from Strasburg to Front Royal, with instructions to relieve the troops under Major Tyndale, attached to General Geary's command, and to protect the town of Front Royal and the railway and bridges between that town and Strasburg. The force under his command consisted of his own regiment (775 available men), two companies from the Twenty-ninth Pennsylvania Volunteers, Lieutenant-Colonel Parham commanding; the Pioneer Corps, Captain Mapes, engaged in reconstructing the bridges; a portion of the Fifth New York Cavalry, and a section of Knap's battery, Lieutenant Atwell commanding. Nearer to the town of Strasburg were three companies of infantry, charged with the same duty. This force was intended as a guard for the protection of the town and railway against local guerrilla parties that infested that locality, and replaced two companies of infantry with cavalry and artillery, which had occupied the town for some weeks, under Major Tyndale, Twenty-eighth Pennsylvania Volunteers, for the same purpose. It had never been contemplated as a defense against the combined forces of the enemy in the valley of Virginia.

Front Royal is in itself an indefensible position. Two mountain valleys debouch suddenly upon the town from the south, commanding it by almost inaccessible hills, and it is at the same time exposed to flank movements by other mountain valleys via Strasburg on the west and Chester Gap on the east.

The only practicable defense of this town would be by a force sufficiently strong to hold these mountain passes some miles in advance. Such forces were not at my disposal, and no such expectations were entertained from the slender command of Colonel Kenly. It was a guerrilla force, and not an organized and well-appointed army that he was prepared to meet.

On the 23d of May it was discovered that the whole force of the enemy was in movement down the valley of the Shenandoah, between the Massanutten Mountain and the Blue Ridge and in close proximity to the town. Their cavalry had captured a considerable number of our pickets before the alarm was given. The little band which was charged with the protection of the railway and bridges found itself instantaneously compelled to choose between an immediate retreat or a contest with the enemy against overwhelming numbers. Colonel Kenly was not the man to avoid a contest at whatever odds. He immediately drew up his troops in the order he had contemplated in case of attack of less importance. The disposition of his forces had been wisely made to resist a force equal to his own, and the best, perhaps, that could have been devised in his more pressing emergency.

About 1 o'clock p. m. the alarm was given that the enemy was advancing on the town in force. The infantry companies were drawn up in line of battle about one-half mile in the rear of the town. Five companies were detailed to support the artillery, which was placed on the crest of a hill commanding a meadow of some extent, over which the enemy must pass to reach the bridges, one company guarding the regimental camp nearer to the river, on the right of the line. The companies, three in number, left to guard the town were soon compelled to fall back upon the main force. There were then four companies on the right of the battery, near the camp, under Lieutenant-Colonel Dushane, and five companies on the left, under Colonel Kenly. The battery, Lieutenant Atwell commanding, opened fire upon the enemy, advancing from the hills on the right and left, well supported by the infantry, doing much damage. A detachment of the Fifth New York Cavalry was ordered to advance upon the road, which was attempted, but did not succeed. They held this position for an hour, when they were compelled to retreat across the river, which was done in good order, their camp and stores having been first destroyed.

On the opposite shore their lines were again formed, and the battery in position opened its fire upon the enemy while fording the river. They were again ordered to move left in front on the Winchester road, and had proceeded about 2 miles when they were overtaken by the enemy's cavalry, and a fearful fight ensued, which ended in the complete destruction of this command.

Colonel Kenly, in the front of his column, was wounded in this action. The train and one gun was captured. One gun was brought within 5 miles of Winchester, and abandoned by Lieutenant Atwell only when his horses were broken down.

The enemy's force is estimated at 8,000. The fighting was mostly done by the cavalry on the side of the rebels, with active support from the infantry and artillery. Our own force did not exceed 900 men. They held their ground manfully, yielding only to the irresistible power of overwhelming numbers.

Prisoners captured since the affair represent that our troops fought with great valor and that the losses of the enemy were large.

It is impossible at this time to give detailed accounts of our losses. Reports from the officers of the regiment represent that but 8 commissioned officers and 120 men have reported. Of these officers 5 were in the engagement, 2 absent on detached service, and 1 on furlough.

All the regimental officers were captured. Colonel Kenly, who was represented to have been killed, is now understood to be a prisoner. He is severely wounded.

Lieutenant Atwell reports that of 38 men attached to his battery but 12 have reported. The cavalry was more fortunate, and suffered comparatively little loss. Undoubtedly large numbers of the command will yet return, but it is impossible to speculate upon the number.

I have the honor to ask attention to the reports of the remaining officers of the First Maryland Regiment, who participated in the engagement, giving their account of the same, and that of Lieutenant Atwell, commanding the battery.

N. P. BANKS,
*Major-General, Commanding, &c*

E. M. STANTON,
*Secretary of War.*

JUNE 1, 1862—8.30 a. m.

Major-General BANKS, *Williamsport:*
Brigadier-General SAXTON, *Harper's Ferry:*

Are you in condition to harass the enemy, who will be hard pressed to-day by McDowell and Frémont?

EDWIN M. STANTON,
*Secretary of War.*

---

WAR DEPARTMENT,
*Washington, June* 1, 1862.

Maj. Gen. N. P. BANKS,
*Williamsport, Md.:*

Jackson reported to be pressing as conscripts, to bear the arms abandoned by your command, all male inhabitants of the valley capable of bearing arms. Direct your quartermaster and ordnance officer to report immediately by telegraph, as nearly as they can, the number of guns, small-arms, accouterments, ammunition, clothing, horse equipments, and other supplies that you lost, that an estimate may be formed of the extent to which Jackson has the means of augmenting his forces, as he can obtain all the men he can arm and equip.

EDWIN M. STANTON,
*Secretary of War.*

---

WILLIAMSPORT, *June* 1.

Not to exceed 1,000 stand of small-arms. Of the arms and equipments at Front Royal we have not been advised. Will send detailed statement soon.

N. P. BANKS.

Hon. E. M. STANTON.

---

WASHINGTON, *June* 1, 1862.

Major-General BANKS, *Williamsport:*

Major-General Sigel has been assigned to command of the troops at Harper's Ferry, numbering about 10,000, and directed to report to you. That force has been added to your command, and it will receive further additions. Immediately on his arrival at Harper's Ferry, for which place he will start this evening, the President desires you to assume actively the offensive against the retreating enemy without the loss of an hour. You will please communicate with General Sigel speedily as possible. You will of course see that Harper's Ferry is left secure.

EDWIN M. STANTON,
*Secretary of War.*

---

WILLIAMSPORT, *June* 1, 1862—1 p. m.
(Received 3.40 p. m.)

Have heard nothing of Frémont. The enemy reported in full retreat from Harper's Ferry.

N. P. BANKS.

Hon. E. M. STANTON.

WILLIAMSPORT, *June* 1, 1862—10.25 p. m.

Our troops are in occupation of Martinsburg, but report no traces of the enemy. We have no news from Frémont. Dispatches from Harper's Ferry state that Jackson retreated in the direction of Winchester. I shall move forward to Martinsburg as soon as possible.

N. P. BANKS,
*Major-General, Commanding.*

Hon. E. M. STANTON.

---

WILLIAMSPORT, *June* 1, 1862—10.30 p. m.

Report from Martinsburg, 6 p. m., just received. Our troops have advanced on Charlestown and Winchester pikes and pickets posted on all roads leading from Martinsburg, but no trace of enemy found. Cavalry has orders to push on and find enemy if possible.

N. P. BANKS,
*Major-General, Commanding.*

Hon. E. M. STANTON.

---

WILLIAMSPORT, *June* 2, 1862—6 a. m.

Your dispatch received 3.30. General Sigel reported his arrival at Harper's Ferry this morning. Have directed him to move troops forward toward Charlestown, and will join him this morning at Harper's Ferry.

N. P. BANKS,
*Major-General, Commanding.*

Hon. E. M. STANTON,
*Secretary of War.*

---

WILLIAMSPORT, *June* 2, 1862—10 p. m.
(Received June 3, 8.45 a. m.)

Our advance troops are near Winchester and several regiments near Martinsburg. It is with great difficulty that they are got ready for marching orders. I hope to-morrow they will all be on the move. Several officers captured at Winchester returned to-night. They represent that the rebels evacuated the town Friday last.

N. P. BANKS.

Hon. E. M. STANTON.

---

MARTINSBURG, *June* 3, 1862.

General Sigel, with 6,000, and Crawford's brigade, Williams' division, 3,000, will be in Winchester to-morrow. There is [no?] positive news of Jackson. Message received from McDowell at Front Royal says he believes Frémont is at Strasburg. The river is very high at Williamsport, and crossing is very slow.

N. P. BANKS,
*Major-General, Commanding.*

Hon. E. M. STANTON,
*Secretary of War.*

MARTINSBURG, *June* 4, 1862—9 a. m.
(Received 10.54 a. m.)

The trains will run over the Baltimore and Ohio Railroad to-morrow night. The telegraph is open east and west to Cumberland. The river is very high, and my last brigade will cross very slowly. Still raining heavily. Damage to bridge is not great.

N. P. BANKS,
*Major-General, Commanding.*

Hon. E. M. STANTON,
*Secretary of War.*

---

MARTINSBURG, *June* 4, 1862—9 a. m.
(Received 11 a. m.)

The best information I can get shows that Jackson left Winchester about 11 a. m. Friday, his train in front. He encountered Frémont's advance near Cedar Creek, which he held in check on Saturday until his troops passed up the valley. His rear guard then took a position upon a hill 2 miles beyond Strasburg, which he held Sunday and Monday. The cannonading there is described as terrific by the people. The last heard of him was that he was at New Market. His entire force is represented as near 40,000 by the people of Winchester.

N. P. BANKS,
*Major-General, Commanding.*

Hon. E. M. STANTON,
*Secretary of War.*

---

WINCHESTER, *June* 5, 1862.
(Received June 6, 10.50 a. m.)

From report of an eye-witness to the retreat of Jackson, being at Strasburg, Jackson reached Strasburg Friday evening late. Frémont arrived within 5 miles of Strasburg some time unknown to Jackson, via Moorefield, Wardensville, and over the mountain by the Hardy grade. A rebel scout in that direction discovered him, showed themselves in two or three places, and then sent a young lad to Frémont's force to say that Jackson was there with his artillery, infantry, &c. This delayed the advance some time. In the mean time Jackson fell back to near Rude's Hill, 5 miles above Strasburg. Fighting began Sunday 1st, a.m., and continued Sunday and Monday all day, with very sharp musketry discharges. Many of our prisoners escaped at Mount Jackson. Frémont's pursuit close and Jackson himself much excited. Tuesday morning Jackson at New Market; last at Harrisonburg. Secessionists say Frémont occupied Rude's Hill and Jackson cut through. This is not true.

N. P. BANKS,
*Major-General, Commanding.*

Hon. E. M. STANTON,
*Secretary of War.*

---

WINCHESTER, *June* 5, 1862—11 a. m.
(Received June 6, 11 a. m.)

The river is yet impassable for men, horses, or wagons; but one brigade of Williams' division is on this side. Supplies are short, but I have ordered the town to be thoroughly searched for stores secreted by Jackson's army. General Sigel's command cannot move for some days. It will be three days before the balance of troops can cross the river and reach this point. Still raining. Have not heard from bridge at Harper's Ferry. Winchester Railroad disabled.

N. P. BANKS,
*Major-General, Commanding.*

Hon. E. M. STANTON,
*Secretary of War.*

---

WINCHESTER, *June* 6, 1862,
*Via Harper's Ferry, June* 7, 1862.

River is falling, and our trains and troops will be over by to-morrow night. The Baltimore and Ohio Railroad will be in operation by Monday; the Winchester road in two or three days at least. We can then send supplies to Frémont. No news from the valley of importance.

N. P. BANKS,
*Major-General, Commanding.*

Hon. E. M. STANTON.

---

ADJUTANT-GENERAL'S OFFICE,
*Washington, June* 8, 1862.

Major-General BANKS,
*Comdg. Dept. of the Shenandoah, Winchester, Va.:*

Send immediately to Front Royal a force to relieve the troops now there under General McDowell.

L. THOMAS,
*Adjutant-General.*

---

WAR DEPARTMENT, ADJT. GEN.'S OFFICE,
*Washington, June* 8, 1862.

GENERAL: I inclose herewith for your information a manuscript copy of General Orders, No. 62.

Instructions have been given to Major-General Frémont to take position with his main force at or near Harrisonburg, to guard against any operations of the enemy down the valley of the Shenandoah.

The Secretary of War directs that you take position in force at or near Front Royal, on the right or left bank of the Shenandoah, with an advance on Luray or other points in supporting distance of General Frémont; also that you occupy with sufficient detachments the former positions of Brigadier-General Geary on the line of the Manassas Gap Railroad as far as the Manassas Junction.

I am, general, very respectfully, your obedient servant,

L. THOMAS,
*Adjutant-General.*

Maj. Gen. N. P. BANKS,
*U. S. Volunteers, Winchester, Va.*

[Inclosure.]

GENERAL ORDERS, } No. 62. }
WAR DEPT., ADJT. GEN.'S OFFICE,
*Washington, June* 8, 1862.

I. The Department of the Mississippi is extended so as to include the whole of the States of Tennessee and Kentucky. All officers on duty in those States will report to Major-General Halleck.

II. The Mountain Department is extended eastward to the road running from Williamsport to Martinsburg, Winchester, Strasburg, Harrisonburg, and Staunton, including that place; thence in the same direction southward until it reaches the Blue Ridge chain of mountains; thence with the line of the Blue Ridge to the southern boundary of the State of Virginia.

III. The Department of the Shenandoah is extended eastward to include the Piedmont district and the Bull Mountain range.

By order of the Secretary of War:

L. THOMAS,
*Adjutant-General.*

---

WINCHESTER, *June* 8, 1862—9 p. m.

Our train is now across the river at Williamsport, another ferry having been constructed. There is an unaccountable delay in forwarding the equipments and clothing needed, but I hope the division will be here by Wednesday. General Sigel's command is not yet ready to move, but will be in a few days. Every possible effort is making to compensate for loss of time occasioned by the rise of the river.

N. P. BANKS,
*Major-General, Commanding.*

Hon. E. M. STANTON,
*Secretary of War.*

---

WASHINGTON, *June* 9, 1862.

Major-General BANKS, *Winchester:*

We are arranging a general plan for the valley of the Shenandoah, and in accordance with this you will move your main force to the Shenandoah at or opposite Front Royal as soon as possible.

A. LINCOLN.

---

WINCHESTER, VA., *June* 9, 1862—10 p. m.

General THOMAS, *Adjutant-General:*

Your dispatches received this morning. I will send a force to Front Royal immediately.

N. P. BANKS,
*Major-General, Commanding.*

---

WINCHESTER, *June* 9, 1862—10.50 p. m.

Two regiments, with a battery and cavalry, moved this morning for Front Royal. The rest of the brigade arrived here to-night and will move on to-morrow. General Williams' Third Brigade has crossed the river and will reach this place Wednesday. General Sigel's command will be able to march in a few days. As soon as possible the President's order shall be carried out. Our supplies, clothing, and equipments have been unaccountably delayed.

N. P. BANKS,
*Major-General, Commanding.*

SECRETARY OF WAR.

WINCHESTER, *June* 10, 1862—11 a. m.
(Received 8.20 p. m.)

A deserter from New Orleans Zouaves, Richmond, ten days since, reports removal of large quantities of stores to Lynchburg. Common rumor among soldiers makes rebel force in and near Richmond 200,000. Came by Lynchburg, Gordonsville, Madison Court-House, and Edenburg. No rebel forces seen or heard of *en route*. At Lynchburg sick and prisoners, but few troops.

N. P. BANKS,
*Major-General.*

Hon. E. M. STANTON,
*Secretary of War.*

---

HDQRS. DEPARTMENT OF THE SHENANDOAH,
*Winchester, Va., June* 12—1.30 a. m. (Received 8.35 a. m.)

General Frémont's chief of staff reports that they have beaten Jackson in two engagements and that Shields has been beaten on the opposite side of the river. Jackson has been re-enforced to the number of 30,000 or 35,000 men, including Smith's and Longstreet's divisions, in consequence of which he is falling back to Harrisonburg, on his way to Mount Jackson, where he desires my command to join him. General Sigel's division is in front of Winchester, at Kernstown—6,000 effective men, with ten pieces of artillery. The First Brigade, Williams' division, is on the Shenandoah, opposite Front Royal, and the Third Brigade will be in Winchester to-morrow; total, with cavalry, 6,000 men and twelve serviceable guns. In my opinion Mount Jackson is no place to meet the enemy. Middletown is a point which commands the opening of the three mountain valleys, and either Middletown or Winchester is the place to meet Jackson if he returns to this valley. My opinion is that Frémont should fall back to this line, and I have so suggested to him, in order to keep the enemy from his rear. If we are compelled to meet the enemy here, more artillery and more troops should be sent, if possible. We expect return of messenger in the morning with further advices, and will communicate.

N. P. BANKS,
*Major-General, Commanding.*

Hon. E. M. STANTON,
*Secretary of War.*

(Copy to McDowell.)

---

WINCHESTER, *June* 12, 1862—10.40 a. m.

Your dispatches by Lieutenant Claassen just received.* The condition of affairs has suddenly changed. Frémont is moving to the rear, and calls upon me to support him at Mount Jackson. This from himself. His chief of staff, in dispatch received at 2 o'clock, confirms this, and states that Jackson has been re-enforced by Smith and Longstreet to the extent of 30,000 to 35,000 men to repeat his invasion of the valley. I believe this to be true. It is confirmed by rumors received from all quarters. I repeat it, that the Department may judge the course to

---

* Probably Thomas to Banks, June 8, inclosing General Orders, No. 62. See p. 541.

be adopted. My troops will be well posted, so as to carry out instructions or to meet an advancing enemy. We need more artillery and re-enforcements if possible. Expect further advices hourly, and will forward information.

N. P. BANKS,
*Major-General, Commanding.*

General LORENZO THOMAS,
*Adjutant-General.*

---

WINCHESTER,
*June* 12, 1862—10.45 a. m.

Dispatch of this morning, 1 o'clock, confirmed by subsequent reports. General Crawford reports two brigades at Front Royal instructed to leave when two of our brigades relieve them. In the changed aspect of affairs I think they should remain until instructed by you, and have so suggested to General Ricketts, in command. If the enemy attacks it will be immediate. Dispatches passed through town from General Frémont, which doubtless inform you fully. I will place my command so as to comply instantly with your instruction received to-day from Adjutant-General, or meet the enemy if he advances.

N. P. BANKS,
*Major-General, Commanding.*

Hon. E. M. STANTON,
*Secretary of War.*

---

WINCHESTER,
*June* 12, 1862—2 p. m.

Our messenger just returned from headquarters. General Frémont confirms all essential statements of my dispatch this morning. General Greene's brigade is here.

N. P. BANKS,
*Major-General, Commanding.*

Hon. E. M. STANTON,
*Secretary of War.*

---

WASHINGTON, *June* 12, 1862—10.40 p. m.

Major-General BANKS, *Winchester:*

Your telegram has just been received. It is not believed to be possible that Jackson has any such re-enforcements as 30,000 or 35,000. McClellan says that two regiments were sent from Richmond to Jackson. What can be the necessity of your falling back before Frémont reaches you? If you abandon Front Royal and your present position, do you not afford a gap for Jackson to pass through as before? The President directs that you hold your positions until further developments.

EDWIN M. STANTON,
*Secretary of War.*

HEADQUARTERS,
*Winchester, June* 12, 1862.

My dispatch has been evidently misunderstood by you. I have never thought of falling back, but am exerting all my power to advance my command night and day to the post assigned me by the President, and have been greatly distressed at the unaccountable delay in getting clothing and equipments, and at the state of the river, which has made crossing impossible. My dispatch related to Frémont's falling back, and expressed the opinion that Mount Jackson is not the best place to meet the enemy in the force represented. I am glad to believe the strength of the enemy exaggerated. We shall not fall back an inch. Telegraph now open to Winchester.

N. P. BANKS,
*Major-General, Commanding.*

Hon. E. M. STANTON,
*Secretary of War.*

---

WINCHESTER, VA., *June* 13—12.45 p. m.

The First Brigade, Williams' division, is on Shenandoah, opposite Front Royal. The Second, General Greene, at Newtown, in supporting distance. General Sigel's division is advanced to Kernstown, to move forward if necessary. They wait only for blankets and equipments to be up to-day and will advance. The river is impassable for troops to Front Royal, but we are making preparations for crossing.

N. P. BANKS,
*Major-General, Commanding.*

Hon. E. M. STANTON,
*Secretary of War.*

(Copy to McDowell.)

---

WINCHESTER, *June* 16, 1862.

Everything is quiet in the valley to-day. The Third Brigade, Williams' division, will move to the Shenandoah to-morrow, making two brigades opposite Front Royal. General Sigel's division will advance in same direction immediately. Unavailing efforts have been made to provide sufficient means of crossing river, but they will be secured immediately. Tuesday morning, if nothing occurs here, I will be in Washington.

N. P. BANKS,
*Major-General.*

Hon. E. M. STANTON.

---

HEADQUARTERS DEPARTMENT OF THE SHENANDOAH,
[*June* —, 1862.]

Information was received at headquarters on the evening of May 23 that the enemy in very large force had descended upon the guard at Front Royal, Colonel Kenly, First Maryland Regiment, commanding, burning the bridges and driving our troops toward Strasburg with great loss.

Owing to what was deemed an extravagant statement of the enemy's strength these reports were received with some distrust, but a regiment of infantry, with a strong detachment of cavalry and a section of artillery, was immediately sent to re-enforce Colonel Kenly. Later in the evening dispatches from fugitives who had escaped to Winchester informed us that Colonel Kenly's force had been destroyed with but few exceptions, and the enemy, 15,000 or 20,000 strong, were advancing by rapid marches on Winchester. Orders were immediately given to halt the re-enforcements sent to Front Royal, which had moved by different routes, and detachments of troops, under experienced officers, were sent in every direction to explore the roads leading from Front Royal to Strasburg, Middletown, Newtown, and Winchester, and ascertain the force, position, and purpose of this sudden movement of the enemy. It was soon found that his pickets were in possession of every road, and rumors from every quarter represented him in movement in the rear of his pickets in the direction of our camp.

The extraordinary force of the enemy could no longer be doubted. It was apparent also that they had a more extended purpose than the capture of the brave little band at Front Royal. This purpose could be nothing less than the defeat of my own command or its possible capture by occupying Winchester, and by this movement intercepting supplies or re-enforcements, and cutting off all possibility of retreat. It was also apparent from the reports of fugitives, prisoners, Union men, and our reconnoitering parties that the three divisions of the enemy's troops known to be in the valley, and embracing at least 25,000 men, were united, and close upon us in some enterprise not yet developed. The suggestion that had their object been a surprise they would not have given notice of their approach by an attack on Front Royal was answered by the fact that on the only remaining point of assault—the Staunton road—our outposts were 5 miles in advance, and daily reconnaissances made for a distance of 12 miles toward Woodstock. Under this interpretation of the enemy's plans our position demanded instant decision and action. Three courses were open to us: First, a retreat across Little North Mountain to the Potomac River on the west; second, an attack upon the enemy's flank on the Front Royal road; third, a rapid movement direct upon Winchester, with a view to anticipate his occupation of the town by seizing it ourselves, thus placing my command in communication with its original base of operations in the line of re-enforcements by Harper's Ferry and Martinsburg, and securing a safe retreat in case of disaster. To remain at Strasburg was to be surrounded; to move over the mountains was to abandon our train at the outset and subject my command to flank attacks without possibility of succor, and to attack the enemy in such overwhelming force could only result in certain destruction. It was determined, therefore, to enter the lists with the enemy in a race or a battle, as he should choose, for the possession of Winchester, the key of the valley, and for us the position of safety.

## THE MARCH.

At 3 o'clock a. m. the 24th instant the re-enforcements (infantry, artillery, and cavalry) sent to Kenly were recalled; the advance guard, (Colonel Donnelly's brigade) was ordered to return to Strasburg; several hundred disabled men left in our charge by Shields' division were put upon the march, and our wagon train ordered forward to Winchester, under escort of cavalry and infantry. General Hatch, with nearly our whole force of cavalry and six pieces of artillery, was charged with the protection of the rear of the column and the destruction of any stores for which transportation was not provided, with instructions to remain in front of the town as long as possible and hold the enemy in check, our expectations of an attack being in that direction. All these orders were executed with incredible celerity, and soon after 9 o'clock the column was on the march, Colonel Donnelly in front, Colonel Gordon in center, and General Hatch in the rear, the whole under direction of Brigadier-General Williams, commanding division.

### A STAMPEDE.

The column had passed Cedar Creek, about 3 miles from Strasburg, with the exception of the rear guard, still in front of Strasburg, when information was received from the front that the enemy had attacked the train and was in full possession of the road at Middletown. This report was confirmed by the return of fugitives, refugees, and wagons, which came tumbling to the rear in fearful confusion.

It being apparent now that our immediate danger was in front, the troops were ordered to the head of the column and the train to the rear, and in view of a possible necessity of our return to Strasburg, Capt. James W. Abert, Topographical Corps, who associated with him the Zouaves d'Afrique, Captain Collis, was ordered to prepare Cedar Creek bridge for the flames, in order to prevent a pursuit in that direction by the enemy. In the execution of this order Captain Abert and the Zouaves were cut off from the column, which they joined again at Williamsport. They had at Strasburg a very sharp conflict with the enemy, in which his cavalry suffered severely. An interesting report of this affair will be found in the reports of Captain Abert and Captain Collis.

### THE FIRST COMBAT.

The head of the reorganized column, Colonel Donnelly commanding, encountered the enemy in force at Middletown, about 13 miles from Winchester. Three hundred troops had been seen in town, but it soon appeared that larger forces were in the rear. The brigade halted, and the Forty-sixth Pennsylvania, Colonel Knipe, was ordered to penetrate the woods on the right and dislodge the enemy's skirmishers. They were supported by a section of Cothran's New York battery. Five companies of the enemy's cavalry were discovered in an open field in rear of the woods, and our artillery, masked at first by the infantry, opened fire upon them. They stood fire for a while, but at length retreated, pursued by our skirmishers. The Twenty-eighth New York, Lieutenant-Colonel Brown, was now brought up, and under a heavy fire of infantry and artillery the enemy were driven back more than 2 miles from the pike. Colonel Donnelly being informed at this point by a citizen in great alarm that 4,000 men were in the woods beyond, the men were anxious to continue the fight, but as this would have defeated our object by the loss of valuable time, with the exception of a small guard they were ordered to resume the march. This affair occurred under my own observation, and I have great pleasure in vouching for the admirable conduct of officers and men. We lost 1 man killed and some wounded. The loss of the enemy could not be ascertained. This episode, with the change of front, occupied nearly an hour, but it saved our column. Had the enemy vigorously attacked our train while at the head of the column it would have been thrown into such dire confusion as to have made the successful continuation of our march impossible. Pending this contest Colonel Brodhead, of the First Michigan Cavalry, was ordered to advance, and, if possible, to cut his way through and occupy Winchester. It was the report of this energetic officer that gave us the first assurance that our course was yet clear, and he was the first of our column to enter the town.

### THE SECOND COMBAT.

When it was first reported that the enemy had pushed between us and Winchester General Hatch was ordered to advance with all available cavalry from Strasburg, leaving Colonel De Forest to cover the rear and destroy stores not provided with transportation.

Major Vought, Fifth New York Cavalry, had been previously ordered to reconnoiter the Front Royal road to ascertain the position of the enemy, whom he encountered in force near Middletown, and was compelled to fall back, immediately followed by the enemy's cavalry, infantry, and artillery. In this affair 5 of our men were killed and some wounded. The loss of the enemy is not known.

After repeated attempts to force a passage through the lines of the enemy, now advanced to the pike, General Hatch, satisfied that this result could not be accomplished without great loss, and supposing our army to have proceeded but a short distance, turned to the left, and moving upon a parallel road, made several ineffectual attempts to effect a junction with the main column. At Newtown, however, he found Colonel Gordon, holding the enemy in check, and joined his brigade. Major Collins, with three companies of cavalry, mistaking the point where the main body of the cavalry left the road, dashed upon the enemy until stopped by a barricade of wagons and a tempestuous fire of infantry and artillery. His loss must have been severe.

Six companies of the Fifth New York, Colonel De Forest, and six companies of the First Vermont, Colonel Tompkins, after repeated and desperate efforts to effect a junction with the main body, the road now being filled with infantry, artillery, and cavalry, fell back to Strasburg, where they found the Zouaves d'Afrique. The Fifth New York, failing to effect a junction at Winchester, and also at Martinsburg, came in at Clear Spring with a train of 32 wagons and many stragglers. The First Vermont, Colonel Tompkins, joined in at Winchester with six pieces of artillery, and participated in the fight of the next morning. Nothing could surpass the celerity and spirit with which the various companies of cavalry executed their movements and their intrepid charges upon the enemy.

General Hatch deserves great credit for the manner in which he discharged his duties as chief of cavalry in this part of our march as well as at the fight at Winchester and in covering the rear of our column to the river, but especially for the spirit infused into his troops during the brief period of his command, which, by confession of friend and foe, had been made equal, if not superior, to the best of the enemy's long-trained mounted troops. From this point the protection of the rear of the column devolved upon the forces under Colonel Gordon.

### THE THIRD COMBAT.

The rear guard having been separated from the column, and the rear of the train attacked by an increased force near the bridge between Newtown and Kernstown, Colonel Gordon was directed by General Williams to send back the Second Massachusetts, Lieutenant-Colonel Andrews commanding; the Twenty-seventh Indiana, Colonel Colgrove, and the Twenty-eighth New York, Lieutenant-Colonel Brown, to rescue the rear of the train and hold the enemy in check. They found him at Newtown with a strong force of infantry, artillery, and cavalry. The Second Massachusetts was deployed in the field, supported by the Twenty-eighth New York and Twenty-seventh Indiana, and ordered to drive the enemy from the town, and the battery was at the same time so placed as to silence the guns of the enemy. Both these objects were quickly accomplished. They found it impossible to reach Middletown, so as to enable the cavalry under General Hatch to join the column or to cover entirely the rear of the train. Large bodies of the enemy's cavalry pressed upon our right and left, and the increased vigor of his movements demonstrated the rapid advance of the main body. A cavalry charge made upon our troops was received in squares on the right and on the road and in line on the left, which repelled his assault and gained time to reform the train, to cover its rear, and to burn the disabled wagons. This affair occupied several hours, the regiments having been moved to the rear about 6 o'clock, and not reaching the town until after 12. A full report by Colonel Gordon, who commanded in person, is inclosed herewith. The principal loss of the Second Massachusetts occurred in this action.

### THE FIGHT AT WINCHESTER.

The strength and purpose of the enemy were to us unknown when we reached Winchester, except upon surmise and vague rumors from Front Royal. These rumors were strengthened by the vigor with which the enemy had pressed our main column and defeated at every point efforts of detached forces to effect a junction with the main body. At Winchester, however, all suspense was relieved on that subject. All classes—secessionists, Union men, refugees, fugitives, and prisoners—agreed that the enemy's force at or near Winchester was overwhelming, ranging from 25,000 to 30,000. Rebel officers who came into our camp with entire unconcern, supposing that their own troops occupied the town as a matter of course and were captured, confirmed these statements, and added that an attack would be made upon us at daybreak. I determined to test the substance and strength of the enemy by actual collision, and measures were promptly taken to prepare our troops to meet them. They had taken up their positions on entering the town after dark without expectations of battle, and were at disadvantage as compared with the enemy. The rattling of musketry was heard during the latter part of the night, and before the break of day a sharp engagement occurred at the outposts.

Soon after 4 o'clock the artillery opened its fire, which was continued without cessation till the close of the engagement. The right of our line was occupied by the Third Brigade, Col. George H. Gordon commanding. The regiments were strongly posted, and near the center covered by stone walls from the fire of the enemy. Their infantry opened on the right, and soon both lines were under heavy fire. The left was occupied by the First Brigade, Colonel Donnelly, Twenty-eighth New York, commanding. The line was weak compared with that of the enemy, but the troops were well posted and patiently waited, as they nobly improved their coming opportunity.

The earliest movements of the enemy were on our left, two regiments being seen to move as with the purpose of occupying a position in flank or rear. General Hatch sent a detachment of cavalry to intercept this movement, when it was apparently abandoned.

The enemy suffered very serious loss from the fire of our infantry on the left. One regiment is represented by persons present during the action and after the field was evacuated as nearly destroyed.

The main body of the enemy was hidden during the early part of the action by the crest of the hill and the woods in the rear. Their force was massed apparently upon our right, and their maneuvers indicated a purpose to turn us upon the Berryville road, where, it appeared subsequently, they had placed a considerable force, with a view of preventing re-enforcements from Harper's Ferry; but the steady fire of our lines held them in check until a small portion of the troops on the right of our line made a movement to the rear. It is but just to add that this was done under the erroneous impression that an order to withdraw had been given. No sooner was this observed by the enemy than its regiments swarmed upon the crest of the hill, advancing from the woods upon our right, which, still continuing its fire, steadily withdrew toward the town. The overwhelming force of the enemy now suddenly showing itself, making further resistance unwise, orders were sent to the left by Captain d'Hauteville to withdraw, which was done reluctantly, but in order, the enemy having greatly suffered on that wing. A portion of the troops passed through the town in some confusion, but the column was soon reformed, and continued its march in order.

This engagement held the enemy in check nearly five hours. The forces engaged were greatly unequal. Indisposed to accept the early rumors concerning the enemy's strength, I reported to the Department that it was about 15,000.

It is now conclusively shown that not less than 25,000 men were in position and could have been brought into action. On the right and left their great superiority of numbers was plainly felt and seen, and the signal officers from elevated positions were enabled to count the regimental standards, indicating a strength equal to that I have stated.

My own command consisted of two brigades, of less than 4,000 men all told, with 900 cavalry, ten Parrott guns, and one battery of 6-pounder smooth-bore cannon. To this should be added the Tenth Maine Regiment of infantry and five companies of Maryland Cavalry, stationed at Winchester, which were engaged in the action. In all, about 5,000 men.

The loss of the enemy was treble that of ours in killed and wounded. In prisoners ours greatly exceeds theirs. Officers whose word I cannot doubt have stated as the result of their own observation that our men were fired upon from private dwellings in passing through Winchester, but I am credibly informed and gladly believe that the atrocities said to have been perpetrated upon our wounded soldiers by the rebels are greatly exaggerated or entirely untrue.

Our march was turned in the direction of Martinsburg, hoping there to meet re-enforcements, the troops moving in three parallel columns, each protected by an efficient rear guard. The pursuit of the enemy was prompt and vigorous, but our movements rapid and without loss. A few miles from Winchester the sound of the steam-whistle heard in the direction of Martinsburg strengthened the hope of re-enforcements and stirred the blood of the men like a trumpet. Soon after two squadrons of cavalry came dashing down the road with wild hurrahs. They were thought to be the advance of the anticipated supports, and were received with deafening cheers. Every man felt like turning back upon the enemy. It proved to be the First Maryland Cavalry, Colonel Wetschky, sent out in the morning as train guard. Hearing the guns, they had returned to participate in the fight. Advantage was taken of this stirring incident to reorganize our column, and the march was continued with renewed spirit and order.

At Martinsburg the column halted two and a half hours, the rear guard remaining until 7 in the evening in rear of the town, and arrived at the river at sundown, forty-eight hours after the first news of the attack on Front Royal. It was a march of 53 miles, 35 of which were performed in one day. The scene at the river when the rear guard arrived was of the most animating and exciting description. A thousand camp-fires were burning on the hill-side, a thousand carriages of every description were crowded upon the banks, and the broad river lay between the exhausted troops and their coveted rest. The ford was too deep for the teams to cross in regular succession. Only the strongest horses, after a few experiments, were allowed to essay the river before morning. The single ferry was occupied by ammunition trains, the ford by the wagons. The cavalry was secure in its own power of crossing. The troops only had no transportation. Fortunately the train we had so sedulously guarded served us in turn. Several boats belonging to the pontoon train, which we had brought from Strasburg, were launched, and devoted exclusively to their service.

It is seldom that a river-crossing of such magnitude is achieved with greater success. There were never more grateful hearts in the same number of men than when at midday of the 26th we stood on the opposite shore. My command had not suffered an attack and rout, but had accomplished a premeditated march of near 60 miles in the face of the enemy, defeating his plans and giving him battle wherever he was found.

Our loss is stated in detail, with the names of the killed, wounded, and missing, in the full report of Brigadier General Williams, commanding division, to which reference is made. The number of killed is 38; wounded, 155; missing, 711. Total loss, 904. It is undoubtedly true that many of the missing will yet return, and the entire loss may be assumed as not exceeding 700.* It is also probable that the number of killed and wounded may be larger than that above stated, but the aggregate loss will not be changed thereby. All our guns were saved.

Our wagon train consisted of nearly 500 wagons. Of this number 55 were lost. They were not, with but very few exceptions, abandoned to the enemy, but were burned upon the road. Nearly all our supplies were thus saved. The stores at Front Royal, of which I had no knowledge until my visit to that post on the 21st instant, and those at Winchester, of which a considerable portion was destroyed by our troops, are not embraced in this statement.

The number of sick men in the hospital at Strasburg belonging to General Williams' division was 189, 125 of whom were left in the hospitals at Winchester, under charge of Surg. Lincoln R. Stone, Second Massachusetts. Sixty-four were left in the hospitals at Strasburg, including attendants, under charge of Surgeon Gillespie, Seventh Indiana, and Assistant-Surgeon Porter, U. S. Army. Eight of the surgeons of this division voluntarily surrendered themselves to the enemy, in the hospitals and on the field, for the care of the sick and wounded placed under their charge. They include, in addition to those above named, Brigade Surgeon Peale, at Winchester; Surgeon Mitchell, First

* But see revised statement, p. 553.

Maryland, at Front Royal; Surgeon Adolphus, Best's battery, U. S. Army; Surgeon Johnson, Sixteenth Indiana, and Surg. Francis Leland, Second Massachusetts, on the field. It is seldom that men are called upon to make a greater sacrifice of comfort, health, and liberty for the benefit of those intrusted to their charge. Services and sacrifices like these ought to entitle them to some more important recognition of their devotion to public duty than the mere historical record of the fact. The report of the medical director, Surg. W. S. King, exhibits the disposition of nearly 1,000 sick and disabled men left at Strasburg by General Shields' division upon its removal to the Rappahannock Valley.

My warmest thanks are due to the officers and men of my command for their unflinching courage and unyielding spirit exhibited on the march and its attendant combats; especially to Brig. Gen. A. S. Williams, commanding the division, General George S. Greene, and General S. W. Crawford, who had reported for duty, but were yet unassigned to separate commands. They all accompanied the column throughout the march and rendered me most valuable assistance. My thanks are also due to the gentlemen of my staff—Maj. D. D. Perkins, chief of staff; Capt. James W. Abert, of the Topographical Corps; Capt. William Scheffler, Captain Munther, and Capt. Frederick d'Hauteville—for their assiduous labors. It gives me pleasure also to commend the conduct of Colonel Donnelly and Colonel Gordon, commanding the two brigades of Williams' division. I would also respectfully ask the attention of the Department to the reports of the several officers commanding detachments separated from the main column, and to the officers named in the report of General Williams, as worthy commendation for meritorious conduct.

The Signal Corps, Lieut. W. W. Rowley commanding, rendered most valuable assistance on the field and on the march. There should be some provision for the prompt promotion of officers and men so brave and useful as those composing this corps.

The safety of the train and supplies is in a great degree due to the discretion, experience, and unfailing energy of Capt. S. B. Holabird and Capt. E. G. Beckwith, U. S. Army.

I have the honor to be, with great respect, your obedient servant,

N. P. BANKS,
*Major-General, Commanding, &c.*

Hon. E. M. STANTON,
*Secretary of War.*

## No. 2.

### *Casualties in the Union forces at Front Royal and Winchester, &c.**

[Compiled from nominal lists of casualties, returns, &c.]

| Command. | Killed. | | Wounded. | | Captured or missing. | | | Remarks. |
|---|---|---|---|---|---|---|---|---|
| | Officers. | Enlisted men. | Officers. | Enlisted men. | Officers. | Enlisted men. | Aggregate. | |
| **FIRST DIVISION.** | | | | | | | | |
| **Brig. Gen. A. S. WILLIAMS.** | | | | | | | | |
| ***First Brigade.*** | | | | | | | | |
| **Col. DUDLEY DONNELLY.** | | | | | | | | |
| 5th Connecticut | ...... | 1 | ...... | 12 | 3 | 68 | 84 | |
| 28th New York | ...... | ...... | ...... | 2 | ...... | 62 | 64 | |
| 46th Pennsylvania | ...... | 2 | ...... | 41 | 2 | 65 | 110 | |
| 1st Maryland | 1 | 13 | 5 | 38 | 21 | 514 | †592 | |
| Total First Brigade | 1 | 16 | 5 | 93 | 26 | 709 | 850 | |
| ***Third Brigade.*** | | | | | | | | |
| **Col. GEORGE H. GORDON.** | | | | | | | | |
| 2d Massachusetts | ...... | 13 | 2 | 45 | 3 | 77 | 140 | |
| 29th Pennsylvania | ...... | 2 | ...... | 5 | 7 | 230 | ‡244 | |
| 27th Indiana | ...... | 3 | 3 | 14 | 3 | 101 | 124 | |
| 3d Wisconsin | ...... | 4 | 2 | 9 | 1 | 85 | 101 | |
| Total Third Brigade | ...... | 22 | 7 | 73 | 14 | 493 | 609 | |
| ***Cavalry.*** | | | | | | | | |
| 1st Michigan (five companies) | ...... | 10 | ...... | 9 | 1 | 34 | 54 | |
| Total cavalry | ...... | 10 | ...... | 9 | 1 | 34 | 54 | |
| ***Artillery.*** | | | | | | | | |
| 1st New York Light Artillery, Battery M. | ...... | 2 | 2 | 2 | ...... | 5 | 11 | |
| Pennsylvania Light Artillery, Battery F. | ...... | ...... | ...... | 7 | ...... | 4 | 11 | |
| 4th U. S. Artillery, Battery F | ...... | ...... | ...... | 3 | 1 | 2 | 6 | |
| Total artillery | ...... | 2 | 2 | 12 | 1 | 11 | 28 | |
| Total First Division | 1 | 50 | 14 | 187 | 42 | 1,247 | 1,541 | |
| ***Cavalry Brigade.*** | | | | | | | | |
| **Brig. Gen. JOHN P. HATCH.** | | | | | | | | |
| 1st Maine, Companies A, B, E, H, and M. | ...... | ...... | 1 | ........ | 3 | 125 | 129 | |
| 1st Vermont | ...... | 1 | 1 | 8 | 2 | 103 | 115 | |
| 5th New York | 1 | 3 | ...... | 15 | 3 | 53 | ‖75 | |
| 1st Maryland (five companies) | ...... | ...... | ...... | ...... | ...... | 5 | 5 | |
| Total Cavalry Brigade | 1 | 4 | 2 | 23 | 8 | 286 | 324 | |

* Includes losses at Front Royal and Buckton Station, May 23; Strasburg, Middletown, and Newtown, May 24, and Winchester, May 25.

† At Front Royal. Capt. Charles W. Wright died of wounds.

‡ Of this number there were 2 men killed and 4 officers and 127 men captured or missing at Front Royal.

‖ Of these 39 occurred at Front Royal. Lieut. Philip Dwyer died of wounds.

*Casualties in the Union forces at Front Royal and Winchester, &c.*—Continued.

| Command. | Killed. | | Wounded. | | Captured or missing. | | Aggregate. | Remarks. |
|---|---|---|---|---|---|---|---|---|
| | Officers. | Enlisted men. | Officers. | Enlisted men. | Officers. | Enlisted men. | | |
| *Unattached.* | | | | | | | | |
| 10th Maine Infantry | ...... | 3 | ...... | 6 | ...... | 54 | 63 | |
| 8th New York Cavalry | ...... | 2 | ...... | 5 | 1 | 23 | 31 | |
| Zouaves d'Afrique | ...... | 1 | ...... | 1 | ...... | 2 | 4 | |
| Pioneer Corps | ...... | ...... | ...... | ...... | ...... | 28 | *28 | |
| Pennsylvania Light Artillery, section Battery E.† | ...... | ...... | ...... | 5 | ...... | 23 | 28 | |
| Total unattached | ...... | 6 | ...... | 17 | 1 | 130 | 154 | |
| Total Department Shenandoah. | 2 | 60 | 16 | 227 | 51 | 1,663 | 2,019 | |

* Not accounted for in their regiments.
† At Front Royal. Detached from General Geary's command.

## No. 3.

*Report of Maj. Hector Tyndale, Twenty-eighth Pennsylvania Infantry, of reconnaissance from Front Royal to Browntown, May* 21.

FRONT ROYAL, VA.,
*May* 22, 1862.

GENERAL: At midnight of the 20th instant I took about 100 men—about 70 of Company I, this regiment, with 30 of Company A, same, the latter temporarily under my command—and marched about 11 miles south of this place on the mountain road, not on any map I have seen. I left orders with Captain Acker, First Michigan Cavalry (Company I), to follow me with 30 men at an interval of two hours; done that the infantry might noiselessly advance at head of column. We found no troops, not even pickets, along the road, although reports had made me believe them there.

We reached Browntown, 10 miles distant, at daylight (3 a. m.) 21st instant and surrounded it, this being the place reported as center of several infantry squads of rebels, but none were found therein. They had, however, occupied one house the night before to the number of 20 men, of the Eighth Louisiana Regiment, Taylor's brigade, Ewell's division, which last heard from was encamped all together in Swift Run Gap, west side. Captain Acker arrived at Browntown about one hour after the infantry, and while going to surround a house 3 miles distant, said to contain a company of infantry—with orders not to engage, but merely to hold them in check if found until his messenger could reach me and the infantry come up—he took prisoner 1 man of the Eighth Regiment Louisiana Volunteers. This man (Cox) was in citizen's dress. He is a Kentuckian, and seems desirous to have quit the rebel service "honorably," and "regrets only" that he was in "citizen's clothes." He was going, he says, back to regimental headquarters to procure a uniform, which to that time they had been unable to give him. I send this man down to you by train. He will tell you of the straits which Ewell's division is reduced to, and this one of the best in the rebel army. He was communicative to me and I credit his story. Captain Acker found no other rebels.

My whole detachment returned safely, after a most wearisome and harassing march, made rapidly, of about 25 miles, yesterday at noon. I heard from several persons more or less reliable of the sound of drums being heard, as coming from the west side of Shenandoah River, westward from a point about 5 miles south of this. Also reports of several parties of cavalry, from 50 to 200, but all on roads other than that I took in returning, which can be defended against fourfold odds. Moreover, the common belief, confirmed by the prisoner, is that infantry forces besides cavalry are expected down in this direction. It was told me by several that we could not get back, if at all, without a fight. The enemy were impressing militia, mostly timid Union men, slaves of all and any ownership, and horses, besides subsistence, using for these objects small detached bodies of foot and horse, and it was to capture or drive these out, as well as to reconnoiter, that I made up my little expedition, which I hope will meet your approval.

I yesterday sent a telegram, after seeing you, to Major-General Banks, who this morning was kind enough to thank me for the energy and enterprise of the little matter.

The officers and men did all possible, and made the most rapid advance I have yet seen, and all came back in order, showing excellent discipline.

With respect, I am, your obedient servant,

HECTOR TYNDALE,
*Major, Twenty-eighth Regiment Pennsylvania Vols., Comdg. U. S. Troops, Detachment at Front Royal.*

General JOHN W. GEARY,
*Commanding Brigade, Rectortown, Va.*

P. S.—I will send down soon the arms, equipments, horse, &c., taken from the prisoner Cox, and arms from the 2 deserters sent you some days ago.

---

## No. 4.

### *Report of Col. John R. Kenly, First Maryland Infantry, of action at Front Royal, May 23.*

WINCHESTER, *May* 31, 1862.

SIR: I have the honor to report that my post at Front Royal was attacked on the 23d instant, between 1 and 2 o'clock p. m., by the Confederate troops under Major-General Jackson.

The entire force under my command consisted of two 10-pounder Parrott guns, with 38 men of Knap's Pennsylvania battery, commanded by Lieutenant Atwell, and nine companies of my regiment, the absent company (E) being on detached service at Linden, on the Manassas Gap Railroad.

At the time of the attack two companies were on picket, one company doing duty as a provost guard, and the remaining six companies were with me in camp, about three-fourths of a mile from town.

It is proper to state that two companies of the Twenty-ninth Pennsylvania Regiment were posted beyond the main branch of the Shenandoah to cover the railroad bridge, and although not under my immediate command, the knowledge of their strength and position had a material influence upon my order of battle and the events of the day.

Not having a single cavalry soldier attached to my command to warn the pickets or the company in town of the approach of an enemy, I had ordered them, in case of an attack by a superior force, to retreat rapidly to camp. This the majority of them were enabled to do, and I had the advantage of their valuable support to my small numbers in resisting the advance of what it very soon became evident was a large army corps.

Two battalions of the enemy's infantry pushed rapidly forward on both sides of the road leading from town toward the camp, and through it to the two bridges in my rear, which crossed the main branch and the North Fork of the Shenandoah, while at the same time a heavy column of infantry and cavalry crossed the railroad, and moved as if to turn my left flank and cross the river below the junction. A battery of artillery was also got into position and opened on us, and heavy clouds of dust indicated the rapid approach of large additional numbers. My situation was critical; but knowing the importance of gaining time, so as to enable our troops at Strasburg to get beyond Middletown before the enemy, I determined to hold on to my position as long as it was possible, and immediately dispatched a courier to Major-General Banks, informing him of the approach and attack of Jackson's army.

I maneuvered my men so as to present the appearance of a much larger force than I had, and whilst Lieutenant Atwell's guns were being well and effectively served, I directed Lieut. Col. Nathan T. Dushane to proceed with two companies to protect my right flank, Maj. John W. Wilson to advance with one company and cover the road leading to the bridges, whilst First Lieutenant Saville marched with his company and the camp guard to prevent the enemy's advance by the railroad toward the bridge.

These orders were promptly and fearlessly executed under a sharp fire from their skirmishers. The fire soon became general along my whole extended front, and the battalion which advanced toward my left was driven back and that on the right held in check under cover of the woods within which it was posted.

In the mean time tents and camp and garrison equipage had been loaded and the train dispatched to the rear, with orders which, if they had been obeyed, would have saved my entire regimental and private property.

About one hour after the battle commenced two small companies of the Fifth New York Cavalry, under Major Vought, came up from Strasburg and reported to me. Their appearance and the cheers with which my men received them had a very beneficial effect, as it induced the enemy to believe that I was being re-enforced, and the movement of their troops gave me additional inducement to gain time by continued resistance, although it was painfully apparent that I was being surrounded.

I kept the cavalry ready for a charge, and moved them about in sight of the infantry, but somewhat sheltered from their artillery, whilst my infantry and artillery kept up a well-directed and continuous fire upon all their troops within range.

At 4.30 p. m. word was brought me that a regiment of cavalry was in my rear beyond the river and rapidly advancing. I went at once to ascertain the correctness of this report and found it too true. In crossing the first bridge I perceived one of the companies of the Twenty-ninth Pennsylvania marching away from its post. I inquired by whose orders they were thus abandoning an important defense. Captain Lane, commanding the company, replied that it was by the order of their lieutenant-colonel. I immediately ordered him back, and the order was promptly and cheerfully obeyed. With loud cheers the company returned to its duty, which to the end was gallantly performed. Returning to the front, I saw that the enemy was massing his troops to force my position, and nothing was now left, if I wished to make a stand on the road to Middletown, but to cross the rivers. This dangerous movement I proceeded to execute, and did withdraw my forces, in the midst of their fire, over the bridges in good order. This was the most trying moment of the day, as I was closely pursued by the enemy, who advanced with shouts and cheers until checked by the fire from the head of the column, which had reached the left or farther bank of the Shenandoah. Posting Lieutenant Atwell, with his two pieces, on an eminence commanding the bridges, and the infantry on the slope of an adjacent height and in full view of the enemy, I waited their advance.

Soon their cavalry came toward us from the direction of the Big Fort Valley Pass, and promptly the guns were at work, and with my infantry checked for nearly an hour their advance and that of their infantry supports. As soon as I crossed the river I ordered Captain Mapes, whom I met with a working party on the road, to burn the bridges, and he proceeded to comply with my orders, but the work was inefficiently done, although the heat from the fire on the nearest bridge must have prevented its being crossed for a considerable length of time. Going in person to superintend their destruction I discovered that the river below the bridges was alive with horsemen, crossing in two different places by fording. Directing Capt. George W. Kugler, commanding Company A, of my regiment, to hold these men in check as long as possible, I ordered off the artillery and infantry, and directed Major Vought to protect my rear with his cavalry.

It was now nearly 6 o'clock, and determining to make a last stand at the cross-road leading to Middletown I hurried on to gain this point. All had so far gone well, and I commenced to indulge a hope that I might yet save my command, when the sudden appearance of cavalry galloping through the fields on my left satisfied me that I was lost. I still pushed on in an orderly military manner, and had actually gained some 4 miles from the river, when Major Vought rode up from the rear and informed me that he was closely pressed. I told him that I would order Lieutenant Atwell to halt with his artillery; that I would march my infantry into the field off the road, and ordered him to charge the enemy, so as to check, if but a few minutes, their advance. He rode back, as if to comply with the order. I dispatched Adjt. Lieut. Frederick C. Tarr to communicate the order to Lieutenant Atwell, and with the assistance of Lieutenant-Colonel Dushane turned the right of the infantry into the field by tearing down a panel of fencing, while Major Wilson did the same with the left wing. In this condition of affairs, seeing that the artillery had not halted, I dashed forward to learn why my orders had not been obeyed, when the discharge of firearms and the rush of cavalry caused me to turn in time to see that the cavalry had not charged the enemy, but were running over my men, who had not yet left the road, and were closely followed by the enemy's horse. The infantry in the field poured in a very close volley, which nearly destroyed the leading company, but did not check the advance of the succeeding squadrons, which charged in the most spirited manner. Large numbers of them, turning into the field, charged upon the men there, who continued fighting desperately until nearly all were captured, some 5 or 6 officers and about 100 men alone escaping.

The cavalry which had been following me upon the left now came in from the front, and assisted those who had charged us in capturing both of the guns and most of the gunners, Lieutenant Atwell, I am happy to say, escaping the general capture of my command. There was no surrender about it.

I beg to report to you the good conduct of Captain White, of the Fifth New York Cavalry, who, with a portion of his command, were taken prisoners, making every effort to assist me, and the gallantry and meritorious services of Lieutenant Atwell and his men.

To Lieut. Col. N. T. Dushane, Maj. John W. Wilson, Surg. Thomas E. Mitchell, and my adjutant, First Lieut. Frederick C. Tarr (the latter severely and the former slightly wounded), I am under the deepest obligations; their distinguished gallantry, coolness, and good conduct merit the highest praise, and to every officer and man of my regiment I return my heartfelt thanks for the bravery, fortitude, and constancy with which they struggled against fearful odds to maintain the cause of our country, and to save from impending destruction our comrades of the First and Third Brigades of the First Division, Fifth Army Corps.

I am also under many obligations to Lieut. J. D. Devin, Ninth Infantry, assistant quartermaster, U. S. Army, and to Mr. A. W. Clarke, a correspondent of the New York Herald, for valuable services rendered me as volunteer aides, and who were both taken prisoners in the discharge of their duties.

I regret that I cannot accurately report my loss, as many are yet missing. Eighteen bodies were buried and I have some 30 wounded. I judge that from 25 to 30 were killed and from 40 to 50 wounded of my command.

The loss of the enemy has been variously estimated at from 180 to 340 killed and wounded.

I desire also to state that since we fell into the hands of the Confederate troops our treatment has been kind and considerate, except that but a scanty allowance of food has been given to us, which I ascribe rather to its scarcity among them than to any disposition on their part to deprive us of it.

I have the honor to be, very respectfully, your obedient servant,

JOHN R. KENLY,
*Colonel First Maryland Regiment.*

Capt. WILLIAM D. WILKINS,
*Asst. Adjt. Gen., First Division, Fifth Army Corps.*

---

## No. 5.

***Report of Capt. George Smith et al., First Maryland Infantry, of action at Front Royal, May 23.***

HEADQUARTERS FIRST REGIMENT MARYLAND VOLS.,
*Hagerstown, Md., May 28, 1862.*

SIR: We beg leave to have the honor to make the following report of facts under our own observation of the engagement at Front Royal, Va., on Friday, May 23:

Our forces at Front Royal consisted of the following troops: First Maryland Regiment Volunteers, nine companies, 775 available men rank and file, one company being absent on picket duty 8 miles below, at a town called Linden; two companies from the Twenty ninth Regiment Pennsylvania Volunteers, about 120 men; also a portion of Pioneer Corps, supposed to be about 40 men; a detachment of Fifth New York Cavalry, about 90 men; two pieces of artillery, with 38 men, making in all 1,063 men.

On the morning of the 23d Companies H, Captain Schley, and I, Lieutenant Coloney, relieved Companies C, Captain Smith, and D, Captain Wright, on picket duty about 1½ miles beyond Front Royal, and Company F, Captain Reynolds, was detailed for provost duty in the town. About 1 o'clock a portion of the outer pickets were captured and the rest driven in. The enemy in considerable force were advancing on the town. The roll was beat, and the six companies in camp were immediately drawn up in line of battle. Five companies were ordered to support the battery a short distance across the field at the edge of a woods, leaving one company to guard the camp. The three companies at and near the town fell back to the camp under a severe fire from the enemy. The then four companies at the camp were placed in position by Lieutenant-Colonel Dushane to prevent us from being flanked on the right.

The battery and the other five companies being on the left, the battery commenced firing on the advancing enemy, doing great execution and throwing them into confusion. Rallying again with greater force, flanking us on right and left, we were ordered to fall back, which we did in good order, having burned our camp and stores.

We continued to fall back until we had crossed both branches of the Shenandoah River, setting fire to the bridge over North Branch. We were again thrown into line, with the battery on the right, and opened fire. The enemy's artillery were stationed on the hills opposite us, across the South Branch, and commenced throwing shells, having a very good range.

The rebel infantry forded the North Branch stream and flanked us on the left. We were again ordered to move, left in front, up the road toward Winchester. We had marched about 2 miles when a wild shout was heard, and rebel cavalry came dashing into our lines, cutting right and left, showing no quarter, displaying a black flag. A portion of their cavalry captured our train, except one wagon and eight horses, which were cut loose by the teamsters to escape on. A severe fight was kept up until our whole force was cut to pieces. We estimate their force to be about 8,000.

As to our number of killed, wounded, and missing we cannot make an estimate.

Since the battle 8 commissioned officers and about 120 men have reported. Of the 8 officers 5 were in the engagement, 2 absent on detached service, and 1 absent on furlough (Captain Johnson).

Respectfully submitted by your obedient servants,

THOS. SAVILLE,
*First Lieutenant, Commanding Company B.*

JOHN McF. LYETH,
*First Lieutenant and R. Q. M., Company H.*

GEO. W. THOMPSON,
*Lieutenant, Company D.*

CHAS. CAMPER,
*Lieutenant, Company K.*

GEO. SMITH,
*Captain Company C.*

Major General BANKS, *Comdg. Fifth Army Corps.*

## No. 6.

*Report of Lieut. Col. Charles Parham, Twenty-ninth Pennsylvania Infantry, of action at Front Royal, May 23.*

HDQRS. TWENTY-NINTH REGT. PENNSYLVANIA VOLS.,
*Williamsport, Md., June* 5, 1862.

SIR: Having just arrived at this point, still an invalid, not yet fully recovered from the bruises, &c., received at Front Royal, therefore I hasten to give a statement of the part my command and self had in that engagement. It is impossible to furnish a full report in detail, owing to the position of my different companies, yet I will try and furnish a correct report or statement of what I witnessed, &c.

Having been detailed by you with five companies to hold the railroad and bridges from Strasburg to Front Royal, I therefore proceeded and posted the several companies as follows: One company of the Second Massachusetts, Captain Russell, on the road beyond the railroad bridge near Strasburg, with guard at the bridge, also cross-road near the railroad station; one company of the Third Wisconsin, Captain Hubbard, about half way between the above station and Buckton Bridge, with guard at the school-house, railroad station, cross-road, &c.; one company of the Twenty-seventh Indiana, Captain Davis, at the Buckton Station, with strong guard at Buckton railroad bridge, cross-roads, &c.; one company of the Twenty-ninth Pennsylvania, Company G., Captain Richardson, on the road between Buckton Station and Pike Bridge, over the North Shenandoah, near Richards' Station; one company of the Twenty-ninth Pennsylvania, Company B, Captain Lane, stationed at the railroad bridge over the South Shenandoah, with guard at the three bridges, giving the commanding officers stringent orders in reference to the importance of their duties, &c.

On Sunday I proceeded to explore and examine the neighborhood and to collect information as to the enemy, &c.

On Monday I, acting according to information, issued the following orders* (No. —) to the several commanding officers. I immediately passed up the road, and gave additional orders as to making a proper and obstinate defense in case of an attack and how and where to fall back to, &c.

On the 22d I addressed the following letter to you (I herein inclose a copy),* deeming still my forces weak, and same day ordered the commanding officers to have erected immediately barriers or breastworks to cover their men in case of an attack, which I now really believed would take place soon, owing to the facts that the bridges and road were now in working order, the importance of the connection, the smallness of the guard, and the reduction of your command in the valley, an excellent turnpike road to Winchester from over the mountain and through Front Royal, with other dirt roads diverging in all directions to your rear.

On Thursday afternoon two of the enlisted men of the Third Wisconsin were captured, which fact I telegraphed to you.

On Friday, about 12.30 o'clock p. m., I collected information that I deemed reliable. I immediately proceeded to write a dispatch to you containing such (copy inclosed),* at the same time preparing my men for a determined and obstinate resistance; also informing Colonel Kenly of a momentary attack. Captain Davis, of the Twenty-seventh Indiana,

*Not found.

and Lieutenant Giddings, of the Third Wisconsin, came down for instructions, &c.; but before I could get the dispatch off to you the attack was commenced in town and railroad broken up and telegraph wire cut off on my side, and also on the other side of the town, and my companies at the Buckton Bridge attacked, which it appears they most bravely defended to the last. There being two locomotives in, they attempted to pass up twice, but were driven back.

Captain Davis and Lieutenant Giddings endeavored to reach their companies, but were prevented; consequently I ordered them to remain with me. They were captured with me, and are still held prisoners.

At the moment of attack I was lying in my bed in great pain, but still I gave orders and collected information, never giving up my command. On hearing the attack I ordered my horse to be saddled, and although I could not stand a moment before nor get on my boots I put on an old pair of shoes, intending if not successful in so doing to mount in stocking feet. I immediately proceeded to place my men in such position as to be most effective and to save them in the attack. I also ordered Captain Mapes' bridge-builders to form and join my command; also the railroad men.

I append a rough plan of my side of the river, position of my men, &c.* On the opposite side of the North Branch at its junction there are hills and bluffs, partly covered with timber. The pike from Winchester passes between two hills and along the base to the bridge over North River. Upon this one hill I ordered Captain Richardson, Captain Mapes' railroad men, &c.; deployed them at intervals, forming the two sides of a square, one side covering the bridge and country opposite, the other side covering the several roads and woods opposite. On the hill on the opposite side of the road stands a brick house, at which I placed 10 men, in command of a lieutenant, to operate in any direction, but principally to cover my men on the hill from attack in the woods opposite, commanding the house, &c.

About this time a squadron of cavalry arrived and reported to me. I ordered them over to the assistance of Colonel Kenly, I taking the opportunity of dispatching two of them (in case one should be captured) to bear the fact of our being attacked by large rebel forces, and with my idea of its being their intention to make Winchester that night.

Immediately at the junction of the rivers there is a rope-ferry and large boat-fording and the railroad bridge, and overlooking these important points is a very high, rugged bluff, covered on its sides with wood. To this point I ordered Captain Lane, he being stationed at the railroad bridge, exposed to the fire of the enemy. My orders were given before the enemy appeared near the bridge for him to fall back, cross over the North River, and occupy the heights, placing his men under cover of the trees, and to command all points; but when the captain was about executing my orders Colonel Kenly ordered him back, at which time the enemy approached in large numbers and shot two of his men. He then fell back, by the orders of Colonel Kenly, Colonel Kenly now retreating safely over the bridges, and I now called in my men and formed in column in road, under the command of Colonel Kenly.

I would also mention that having full knowledge of the enemy crossing both rivers, right and left, to outflank our whole command, and of their presence at the Buckton Station, I posted pickets out both roads leading therefrom, but from my position on the hill I saw by the dust

*Not found.

arising over the woods that an immense cavalry force was rapidly approaching, evidently with the intention of dispersing my remaining companies and cutting off Colonel Kenly's retreat from the town and over the bridge. They drove in my pickets and fired upon them. As they emerged from the woods I opened fire upon them and held them in check, they forming in line in front of us but out of reach of our pieces. There appeared to be at least 2,000 men. Still my men held their position, effectually protecting the bridges until after Colonel Kenly crossed. Colonel Kenly now ordered the two pieces of cannon to take position on the hill just occupied by my men to cover us until we destroyed the North Branch bridge. At this time the enemy brought forward their cannon and opened on us. We now all retired up the road toward Winchester.

I, amidst the confusion, lost my horse, and was compelled to take seat on a caisson, not being able to procure another horse or to walk, still being within commanding distance of my men. As we advanced toward the branching road to Middletown or Newtown Colonel Kenly ordered a halt of some minutes. I advised him to keep moving, as the enemy were fast approaching. He now ordered the column to change direction toward Middletown, but feeling confident that the road and woods were occupied by the enemy, they anticipating that in retreat we would make for Strasburg, and they crossing the fording at Buckton Station, driving my companies over there. It proved true, as we discovered in time that they occupied the road and woods. I called Colonel Kenly's attention to the fact, and advised him to keep the pike for Winchester. From this point we gained 2 or 3 miles. Their cavalry now charged after us from all directions. I am sure there were over 3,000. They closed upon our squadron of cavalry in our rear, which in confusion broke right and left to the front, the rebel cavalry charging after and to our front, bringing us to a halt, shooting every man who moved forward. I, still riding on the caisson, turned my head to notice the cause of the confusion, when the most advanced man raised his saber to cleave my head. At this moment, which was most singular and fortunate for me, the side wheel came off, throwing his horse aside and myself under his horse, and all that charged to the front on the left passed over me before I could drag myself from the road to the fence.

Four of them now came and ordered me up, and to deliver up my pistol, which I proceeded to do good naturedly—not my sword, which I had thrown under the wheel of the caisson, but told them I had lost it. They demanded my scabbard and belt; took off my coat to see what I had underneath, they at the same time threatening to shoot, but I deemed it prudent to be as pleasant as possible, so I laughed them out of the notion, and actually engaged in conversation with them until an opportunity presented for me to escape, which very soon took place in the following manner: One of the rebels dismounted, tying his horse near me, asking for Colonel Kenly. I answered I believed him to be toward the rear. Some person answered that he was wounded and in the ambulance. He then went to it, which was approaching, halted the driver by firing at him, raised the curtain, demanded the occupants to get up and come out. He then fired in the ambulance.

While I lay on the road-side under guard I noticed that that portion of the rebel cavalry that occupied the road in front of us repeatedly turned around, looking up the road. I interpreted it to be a fear of re-enforcements approaching. Instantly I sprang to my feet, shouting, "Here come our re-enforcements, boys; we're good for another fight!"

The ruse took; they in one body put spurs to their horses and filed to left over in field, clearing the road in front. I made for the horse, unhitched him, mounted, and left, shouting for the men to break for the woods, a large number escaping before the rebels discovered the trick. They fired after me, but I had no time to stop.

It was now near dark. The road was strewn with baggage, broken wagons, horses, &c., for the whole distance to Winchester, as I had passed them over the bridge an hour or two before we retreated, so as to get them in safe; but it appeared the teamsters took a panic, and broke horses, wagons, and everything else up by rapid driving. It was some time after dark that I came to a halt from finally giving out and getting on wrong road; so I concluded to get in a house near by, and by considerable coaxing I obtained an entrance.

I was now completely broken down—so much so that the gentleman prepared a liniment for me and actually bound up some of my bruises, while the female portion of his family actually screamed with joy at our defeat, &c. I was helped to bed, and all the attention that Mr. Bitzer could bestow upon me was cheerfully done. I could not sleep for my pains, and consequently could hear the rebel cavalry passing up and down the road. This house is nearly 8 miles from Winchester. Next morning, not being able to walk, Mr. Bitzer brought me to Winchester in his carriage, and during the ride he informed me that he was Captain Bitzer, of the Bitzer cavalry, but was captured, paroled, took oath of allegiance, &c. He is a gentleman in all particulars, but his family the reverse.

I was taken to the Taylor house and engaged a room, to wait for you to come to Winchester, as I was informed you were going to remove your quarters, so that I could report to you my condition; but during my stay there, of some two hours, there was a great panic and all kinds of reports, the enemy being within 2 or 3 miles of the city, &c.

I, finding all things looked decidedly squally, concluded that if I did not get out immediately I would be again captured. By the kindness of the lieutenant-colonel of the Vermont cavalry I was carried to Martinsburg. By being driven over a rough road my bruises pained me the more, and I requiring medical attention and quiet nursing, also a change of linen and clothes, having lost all my clothing, baggage, horse, &c., and being offered by the agent of a baggage train to take me to Baltimore, I concluded to accept of the offer, and from the time I entered the car I took a sleeping bunk, and there remained until I arrived in Baltimore the next afternoon, Sunday.

I now proceeded to Philadelphia, sending immediately for my physician, J. A. Meigs, under whose care I remained until ordered to report back, previous to which I by letter notified yourself and Colonel Gordon of the fact of my being there and my condition.

While in Philadelphia I heard of several of our officers and men being there, all sound and in good health I immediately ordered them back.

The above statement is correctly true and fully corroborated. You have no doubt received a regimental report of those companies ere this.

I am here, unfit for service for some few days. Still, as I believe that the *morale* of the Twenty-ninth is not as it should be, I await your orders, and remain, your obedient servant,

CHAS. PARHAM,
*Lieutenant-Colonel Twenty-ninth Regiment Pennsylvania Vols.*

Major-General BANKS.

## No. 7.

*Report of Maj. Philip G. Vought, Fifth New York Cavalry, of action at Front Royal, May 23.*

On Friday last, the 23d instant, I left Strasburg with my command, Company B and Company D, numbering about 100 men, in accordance with Special Orders, No. 28, to proceed to Front Royal and report for duty to Colonel Kenly, of the First Maryland Infantry. When about 3 miles this side of the town I received a message from the colonel to hurry on with my cavalry; that he had been fighting the enemy since sunrise; that they were in large force, and we much in want of aid. I immediately ordered my baggage to the rear about a mile and put my column under a fast trot, and in less than fifteen minutes we were at the colonel's headquarters.

Finding the colonel with his small command, less than 500 infantry, with only two pieces of artillery, on high ground about 1 mile north of the town, and being in much danger, the enemy having from 5,000 to 6,000 infantry and three pieces of artillery, but at that time not all in sight, I charged with my cavalry down the hill, intending to charge across the plain, being supported by the artillery; but finding such a large force of the enemy behind a stone wall on my left and in a small wood on my right, I withdrew my men under the cover of a hill until I could report to the colonel, who immediately ordered me to bring my men in line in rear of the artillery. We held our position for some two hours, sending out skirmishers and checking the enemy on every side, when we saw a large body of cavalry, from 1,000 to 1,500, deploying out of a wood some 3 miles on the opposite side of the town. We then commenced our retreat, and drew off our force in good order across both branches of the Shenandoah, my cavalry covering the rear and setting fire to the bridges, the enemy following close on us, and wading the river—both cavalry and infantry—with perfect ease.

I held with my cavalry the enemy in check for some 3 miles, making three several charges upon them, and driving them back with considerable loss on their side, until about 6 o'clock p. m., when we made another charge, and in rallying, the enemy having entirely surrounded our entire force, our own infantry fired into my men and very many fell. At this time the fight became general. Colonel Kenly having been wounded and taken prisoner, and most of his officers being killed, and his men being all cut up, I told my men we would take care of ourselves, and we cut our way through the ranks of the enemy, and fled toward Winchester, the enemy following in large force for some 2 miles. When about 3 miles from the battle-field I halted my horse and tried to rally my men, but could not do so with much success. I also urged on the baggage train, and was joined in my efforts by Sergeant-Major Smith, of my own battalion.

Believing that the enemy intended to march on Winchester that night I felt it my duty to ascertain their movements, and, if so, to notify General Banks myself. I therefore secreted myself with my sergeant-major in a thick wood close by the road, and in some fifteen minutes the enemy's cavalry came by, some 200 strong; but having no infantry and so small a force of cavalry I was convinced that they would not venture very far. I remained quietly in my place of concealment until about 11 o'clock, when the enemy returned with three of our baggage wagons; after which I mounted my horse and started for Winchester, which place I reached in safety about 2.30 o'clock on the morning of the 24th.

I am sorry to report the loss of Captain White, of Company D, who fought bravely; Lieutenant Dwyer, of Company B, and Lieut. George H. Griffin, First Battalion adjutant, and First Battalion Quartermaster-Sergeant Haviland; also First Sergeant Watson and Quartermaster-Sergeant Appleby, of Company D, and 21 privates.

Very respectfully,

P. G. VOUGHT,
*Major, Fifth New York Cavalry, Ira Harris Guards.*

Col. O. DE FOREST.

---

## No. 8.

*Report of Lieut. Charles A. Atwell, Battery E, Pennsylvania Light Artillery, of action at Front Royal, May 23.*

WILLIAMSPORT, MD., *May* 27, 1862.

DEAR SIR: On Friday, May 23, at about 2 p. m., the rebel forces, reported to be under command of General Ewell, made a sudden descent upon the town of Front Royal, Va., occupied by the First Regiment Maryland Volunteers, Col. John R. Kenly. Two of the companies were on guard in the town, and barely made their escape. I got my two guns in readiness, and in less than five minutes opened a heavy fire on them to the right of the town, where they were in large numbers, and succeeded in holding them back.

The rebels now moved from here along the top of the hills to the left, and coming down under cover of a hollow crossed under the railroad bridge and kept off to our rear through the woods. I checked them once or twice in this movement, but their numbers were too large to hold them back. The enemy now appeared in large force to the front and right of the town, and we directed both pieces on them, being well supported by our infantry, who were deployed on our right and left.

Two companies of the Fifth New York Cavalry coming up were sent forward along the main road, but had to fall back immediately. Colonel Kenly now ordered me to fall back, cover his infantry, who first fired his camp equipage and stores, and then retired across both branches of the Shenandoah River, burning the bridges.

We took a position on a hill left of the road and the infantry, with two companies of the Twenty-ninth Pennsylvania Volunteers, who were on guard here to the right. We held these positions for nearly an hour, but were compelled to fall back, as the enemy were fording the river above and below us. My section of artillery covered the retreat for about a mile, and I was then ordered by Colonel Kenly to the front, and the cavalry brought up the rear. At this time our loss was very small, but 2 killed and 8 or 10 wounded.

Our last stand was on the main road from Front Royal to Winchester, where the rebels, having advanced on our flanks under cover of the woods, succeeded in surrounding us, and I was unable to use my pieces, as the two forces were mixed up together, and my cannoneers, having no side-arms, were cut to pieces by the rebel cavalry. I had my advanced gun limbered up and ran it through them. The fighting here was terrible, as we were shown no mercy. Our infantry stood up to the work, and were most of them cut to pieces.

As near as I could estimate the enemy's forces they must have numbered between 8,000 and 10,000. The fighting was mostly done by the rebel cavalry. They had three pieces of artillery, but none of the shots fired did any damage to us. Our entire force of infantry, cavalry, and the section of artillery did not reach more than 900. I am not able to say how many of these we lost. Most of the officers were killed or taken prisoners, and I have heard of about 50 of the infantry privates. The cavalry nearly all escaped. I had 38 men in my section of artillery, and have but 12 that I can account for. The gun that I got away I brought within 5 miles of Winchester, and had to leave on the roadside, as the horses gave out.

I reported to Colonel Beal, of the Tenth Maine Volunteers, on my arrival at Winchester, and went out early in the morning with a company of cavalry, but could not get to it, the rebels having thrown their pickets 2 miles nearer the town. The limber I saved and afterward destroyed before leaving Winchester. We had used all our ammunition but about 60 rounds, nearly all of which was canister.

Respectfully, yours,

CHARLES A. ATWELL,
*First Lieutenant, Commanding Section Knap's Battery.*

Maj. Gen. N. P. BANKS,
*Commanding Division.*

---

## No. 9.

*Report of Brig. Gen. John W. Geary, U. S. Army, of skirmish at Linden, May 24.*

HEADQUARTERS,
*Near Rectortown, Va., May* 24, 1862.

Captain Gillingham's company, of the First Maryland, being attacked at Linden by 200 cavalry and two pieces of artillery, fell back into my lines at Markham, and is now at these headquarters; his men all safe.

JNO. W. GEARY,
*Brigadier-General, Commanding.*

Hon. E. M. STANTON.

---

## No. 10.

*Report of Lieut. William W. Rowley, Twenty-eighth New York Infantry, Acting Signal Officer, of operations May 24–25.*

HEADQUARTERS SIGNAL CAMP,
*Williamsport, Md., May* 29, 1862.

SIR: I have the honor to report that, in compliance with your orders, on Saturday, the 24th day of May, I packed all my luggage, camp and garrison equipage, into the wagons, and started them for Winchester early in the morning. I also, under orders, established signal stations along the route from Strasburg toward Winchester, so as to keep communication from the rear to the front. I placed Lieutenant Halsted with 2 men upon the station nearest to Strasburg, with orders to abandon it when General Hatch came forward with his cavalry. Lieutenant Spencer occupied the next station near Middletown, with the same instructions for leaving as I gave Lieutenant Halsted. Lieutenant Wicker occupied the next station, Lieutenant Miner the next, Lieutenant Larned the next, at Newtown.

All had the same orders to remain upon their respective stations until General Hatch came up with the rear guard. I left Strasburg about 10 o'clock a. m., and upon arriving in the vicinity of Middletown I found a general stampede with the teamsters, many turning about, driving pell-mell, causing for a few minutes the greatest consternation. Many wagons were upset, while many were left standing with the teams unhitched and taken away. In a short time quiet and order were restored, and the trains moved on quietly. As near as I could learn, the cause of the stampede was occasioned by the appearance of some rebel cavalry in their front, who fired, or threatened to fire, upon them.

I then went on with the advance guard to Newtown, where I saw a small party of cavalry of the enemy running from the town toward the woods on the right of town. Our advance guard moved on through the town and proceeded about a quarter of a mile, when some rebel cavalry was seen moving toward our rear upon our right. The cavalry halted until the Forty-sixth Pennsylvania, Colonel Knipe commanding, came up to the town, when the Forty-sixth immediately deployed to the right of the town, penetrating into some woods, followed by two pieces of artillery. The rebel cavalry was in fair sight about half a mile distant. The artillery opened upon them, driving them into the woods. After throwing a few shells the guns limbered up, and, with the Forty-sixth, proceeded to the turnpike toward Winchester.

Soon after this, about 2 p. m., Lieutenants Wicker and Harvey were forced from their station by the rebel cavalry. Up to this time the stations had worked finely, transmitting many messages from rear to front and *vice versa.* Lieutenant Miner followed when they joined me. After this time no signals were used during the day. Lieutenant Spencer with his three men started to join me as soon as Lieutenant Wicker left, and upon arriving at Middletown he was forced to fly to the woods upon the right of the town. A company of rebel cavalry being upon the turnpike in front, a regiment of infantry in a field to the right of the road, and another squad of cavalry coming down upon them to the right, Lieutenant Spencer put spurs to his horse, followed by his men, and escaped to the woods, receiving only one volley from the infantry, which did no harm. He arrived at Winchester about 9 p. m. all right. Lieutenant Halsted during this time had been cut entirely off from us, so that he was obliged to take to the mountain road, arriving in camp the 27th instant, crossing the river at Hancock.

The corps encamped at Winchester during the night of the 24th, and on the 25th, as soon as the fog cleared away so that signals could be used to advantage, we proceeded to the field of battle. I was ordered to establish communication between the right and left wings of our forces. Just as I had got the stations established, and before any communication was sent, the retreat commenced, we retreating with the others, Lieutenant Wicker being among the last to leave the field. A portion of our troops retreated in considerable disorder for a short distance from Winchester, but they were soon rallied, and preserved very good order during the rest of the day.

The First Brigade, Colonel Donnelly commanding, proceeded in good order to the right of the road, while the Third Brigade, Colonel Gordon commanding, proceeded to the left, going toward Martinsburg. I dispatched three officers to accompany the First Brigade and three to accompany the Third Brigade, myself remaining upon the road.

We had not much occasion to use our signals during the day until after we passed Bunker Hill, when by some means the officers got detached from the First Brigade and did not come up with it again, thus preventing any communication between the two columns. While at Martinsburg the corps was employed in transmitting signals for a short time. After leaving the latter place no signaling was done until we arrived at this place, when two stations were immediately established, one upon either side of the river, where they were retained until last night, when all the troops were ordered on this side of the river. The corps arrived at this place all safe and well, losing none of our baggage, camp or garrison equipage.

I cannot say too much for the noble conduct displayed by the signal officers and men under my command, ever ready to endure fatigue and exposure upon the slightest call for duty.

I am, respectfully, your obedient servant,

W. W. ROWLEY,

*First Lieut., 28th N. Y. Vols., Chief Signal Officer, in Command.*

R. MORRIS COPELAND,

*Assistant Adjutant-General and Major of Volunteers.*

---

## No. 11.

*Report of Capt. James W. Abert, U. S. Topographical Engineers, of operations May 24.*

HEADQUARTERS OF MAJOR-GENERAL BANKS,

*Williamsport, Md., May 28, 1862.*

GENERAL: I have the honor herewith to report as follows in regard to the operations of Saturday, May 24:

Having been ordered by the general-in-chief to burn the bridge over Cedar Creek as soon as I should receive final instructions, I detained Captain Collis' Zouaves to assist in carrying out your orders, and to hold the enemy in check in case he should rush down upon us and endeavor to save the bridge. In a neighboring barn I procured a tar-barrel, some straw, some commissary pork, and other inflammable materials, lit a fire close by, and waited until 3.30 o'clock. Finding the ford was in much better condition than the bridge, and that its destruction would be of no advantage to us, I concluded to follow on to Winchester.

In approaching Middletown I saw that the enemy had occupied the ridge on the east side of the town and was shelling some of our cavalry, General Hatch's, which turned off to the left (west), and again resumed their route to Winchester.

We were slowly approaching the town, when Captain Collis requested me to post his company. I desired the captain to walk to the top of the ridge to the east and look over it, when he reported the enemy advancing. There was also a regiment of troops advancing along the main street in column by company. I then directed the captain to deploy his company behind a stone wall which ran perpendicularly from the road and across the ridge, whilst I reconnoitered the regiment advancing on the main road. Being in doubt as to their uniforms, and fearing I might fire on friends, we approached quite close, and owing to a number of stragglers and cavalry, who crowded behind him, we received a volley from the leading company. They then marched steadily onward, in perfect ignorance of the locality of the Zouaves, who from a close distance poured in the whole company fire upon them. This staggered them for a few moments, and the Zouaves continued to load and fire until the column to the right threatened to outflank them, when Captain Collis ordered them to retire. This they did, deployed as skirmishers and firing steadily.

By the greatest good fortune we found one of our batteries in position on the hill to the south of the town (Captain Hampton's.) From this place we shelled the enemy, and as he approached near enough gave him some canister, which checked him. We then retired upon Strasburg, where I directed some pieces to be placed in the fort, but the very side of the enemy's approach (to the north) was completely unfinished. I then directed the battery to follow me, and I would try to save it by taking the back road to Winchester, but the officer in command, when I told him that the road ran parallel to the main road, and was only 3 to 4 miles distant from it, said the enemy's flankers would intercept him, and that it would be vain to make the attempt. I therefore left him, and taking that road, pursued it toward Winchester alone. Within 3 miles of that city I found the road occupied by the enemy.

The next morning I started for Martinsburg, and learned I was again cut off. I therefore resolved to strike off for Bath, and if necessary cross the Potomac at Hancock, where I arrived Tuesday evening, and I had the honor to report to the general at Williamsport on Wednesday evening, the 27th of May.

I am, sir, very respectfully, your obedient servant,

JAMES W. ABERT,
*Captain, U. S. Army, Topographical Engineers.*

Major-General BANKS,
*Commanding Fifth Corps d'Armée.*

## No. 12.

***Report of public animals, wagons, harness, and other means of transportation captured, lost, destroyed, and abandoned in the retreat from Strasburg, Va., to Williamsport, Md., May 24–25.***

| In whose possession. | Horses. | Mules. | Spring wagons. | Wagons. | Two-wheel ambulances. | Four-wheel ambulances. | Wheel harness, single sets of. | Lead harness, single sets of. | Wagon saddles. | Saddle blankets. | Riding saddles. | Riding bridles. | Two-horse wagons. | Four-horse wagons. | Remarks. |
|---|---|---|---|---|---|---|---|---|---|---|---|---|---|---|---|
| Capt. S. B. Holabird, assistant quartermaster | 204 | 87 | 1 | 24 | | | | | | | | | 17 | | 160 horses and 20 mules condemned and worthless; 4 mules drowned and 2 stolen; 2 beds washed away. Mr. C. K. Marks, chief wagon-master, rendered the greatest service in managing the train. |
| Capt. G. A. Flagg, assistant quartermaster | | | | | | | | | | | | | | | Not known. Not over two or three wagons. |
| Capt. H. M. Whittelsey, assistant quartermaster | 4 | | | | | 1 | | | | | | | | | Captured. |
| Lieut. R. G. Rutherford, brigade quartermaster, Third Brigade. | 4 | 14 | | 3 | | | | | | | | | | | Captured or burned. Lieutenant Rutherford was very attentive and kept with his train, doing good service. |
| Lieut. C. L. Skeels, brigade quartermaster, First Brigade. | 11 | 25 | | 10 | | | 12 | 17 | 7 | 10 | 2 | 1 | | | Lost or captured by the enemy. Lieutenant Skeels was particularly efficient in every way. |
| Lieut. J. I. David, brigade quartermaster, Cavalry Brigade. | 40 | | | 10 | | | 10 | 10 | 10 | | | | | | Captured by the enemy near Strasburg, Va. Lieutenant David rendered most efficient aid in crossing the river. |
| Lieut. J. M. Jameson, regimental quartermaster, Twenty-seventh Indiana. | 5 | 1 | | | 5 | | 8 | 8 | 4 | | | | | | Captured or burnt at Front Royal. |
| Lieut. G. B. Cadwalader, regimental quartermaster, Forty-sixth Pennsylvania. | 2 | 1 | | 2 | 1 | | | | 1 | 8 | 1 | 1 | | | Captured, lost, broken, and abandoned. Lieutenant Cadwalader was attentive and efficient. |
| Lieut. J. Francis, regimental quartermaster, Second Massachusetts. | | | | | | | | 1 | | | | 1 | | | Lost in crossing the Potomac. |
| Lieut. M. P. Whitney, regimental quartermaster, Fifth Connecticut. | | 2 | | | | | 2 | 2 | | | | | | | Captured by the enemy. |
| Lieut. J. C. Terry, regimental quartermaster, Twenty-eighth New York. | | 5 | | | | 1 | | 1 | 1 | | | 4 | | | Mules died; ambulance broken and abandoned. Harness lost in the Potomac. |
| Lieut. A. S. Dewey, regimental quartermaster, First Vermont Cavalry. | 63 | | | | 2 | | | | | | | | | 19 | Horses were killed or captured by the enemy. The ambulances were abandoned or destroyed. |

| | | | | | | | | | | | | | | | |
|---|---|---|---|---|---|---|---|---|---|---|---|---|---|---|---|
| Lieut. J. G. Knight, regimental quartermaster, Third Wisconsin. | ...... | 6 | .... | 2 | .... | .... | 4 | 4 | 2 | 2 | .... | .... | .... | .... | Lost crossing the river. Lieutenant Knight attended well to his train. |
| Capt. R. B. Hampton, commanding battery | 7 | 4 | .... | 1 | .... | .... | 2 | 2 | .... | .... | .... | .... | .... | .... | Captured by the enemy. |
| Lieut. H. C. Cushing, acting assistant quartermaster, Fourth Artillery. | 1 | ...... | .... | .... | 1 | .... | 2 | .... | .... | .... | .... | .... | .... | .... | Captured or destroyed. |
| Lieut. D. B. Hamilton, acting assistant quartermaster | ...... | ...... | .... | 3 | .... | .... | .... | .... | .... | .... | .... | .... | .... | .... | Broke down and abandoned or burnt. Lieutenant Hamilton rendered good service in managing the 31 wagons saved by way of Hancock, Md. |
| | 341 | 145 | 1 | 55 | 9 | 2 | 40 | 45 | 25 | 20 | 3 | 7 | 17 | 19 | |

**I certify that the above statement is correct, as far as can be known.**

S. B. HOLABIRD,
*Captain, Assistant Quartermaster.*

## No. 13.

*Report of Capt. Charles H. T. Collis, Pennsylvania Infantry, commanding Body Guard, of operations May 24–26.*

WILLIAMSPORT, MD., *May* 28, 1862.

GENERAL: I have the honor to report that on the 24th instant, in obedience to your order, received through Captain Abert, of your staff, I halted my command at Cedar Creek, and made preparation to fire the bridge. Upon consultation with Captain Abert, however, we deemed it inexpedient to fire, inasmuch as the head of the column was then being attacked. So, abandoning the idea, I pushed on after you with all haste.

Arriving at Middletown, I discovered I was effectually cut off from the main body by what I believe to have been the reserve of the enemy—a brigade of four regiments of infantry, a few companies of cavalry, and four pieces of artillery, all formed in or near the town. He observed our approach, and made preparations for an attack upon us. I threw my men quickly as possible behind a stone wall on the east side of the road, running along the south side of the town, and within 150 paces of the enemy's position. Our first reception was a whole volley of musketry from right to left, but, thanks to our little breastwork, I had but one man (Charles Fedalen) injured, and he but slightly. The fire was three times returned by my brave men, whose cool aim, short range, and grand position must have had terrible effect. It at all events held him in check for some ten minutes, when he charged along the whole line at double-quick, intending to outflank me. Perceiving this movement I deemed it advisable to fall back, which was accomplished in wonderfully good order. To the credit of my men be it said that this movement was as orderly as though executed upon the drill ground.

We had fallen back a mile, hotly pursued by cavalry, infantry, and artillery, and losing 3 men killed, when, by an intervention of a generous God, we reached assistance. Captain Hampton, First Pennsylvania Artillery, who I supposed was with you, general, now joined me, and placing his guns in battery afforded my men a half hour's rest.

The enemy now formed his line of battle fully 1½ miles long. Outnumbered and almost surrounded, we fell back to Strasburg, where, taking position on the hill north of Hupp's house, we determined to make a final struggle, in which, thanks to the cool bravery of the men engaged, we were successful, forcing the enemy to retire to their first position at Middletown. Colonel Tompkins, First Vermont Cavalry, with about 500 men, came to our aid at Hupp's house.

Captain Hampton, of the battery, deserves the thanks of all engaged, and of the whole country, for his gallant behavior. His guns were supplied admirably and fired with telling effect.

Still determined to rejoin you, and finding the direct road impracticable, I took the western (dirt) road, which brought me out on the pike within 3 miles of Winchester, Colonel Tompkins and the battery in the mean time, being mounted, taking the direct road. Colonel De Forest, with a detachment of Fifth New York Cavalry, and Lieutenant Hamilton, with his supply train, joined us on this road, but about midnight we found ourselves again cut off by the enemy's pickets. Retracing our steps, we took the Romney pike, and traveling 27 additional miles approached Winchester on Sunday morning in time to see you evacuate the town, while the enemy took possession.

A third time cut off, with nothing but misfortune staring us in the face, though we had spared no human effort to come to your aid, I was at last compelled to provide for our own personal safety; so, placing in the wagons 23 men too fatigued to walk, I left the road with the rest and took to the woods, and providentially having found a pocket-compass and a map, succeeded in reaching Hancock on Monday, the 26th instant, at 2 p. m., and on the following day had the gratification of reporting to you in person.

I have omitted to mention that I brought with me from Strasburg 2 lieutenants and 50 men of various regiments, who had been guarding the commissary stores at that place.

The 23 men who remained with the wagons, I am informed, bravely defended them along the whole route, and rejoined me at Hancock. We lost all our personal baggage, knapsacks, blankets, &c.

I am greatly indebted to Capt. James W. Abert, U. S. Army, Topographical Engineers, for most valuable suggestions during my engagement with the enemy, as also to my brother officers, Lieutenants Barthoulot and Heimach.

Incredible, general, as it may appear, my men marched 141 miles in forty-seven hours, as measured by Captain Abert.

Reassuring you of my desire always to serve you and the cause to the extent of my poor capacity, and congratulating you upon the success of your unparalleled retreat, I have the honor to be, very respectfully, your obedient servant,

CHARLES H. T. COLLIS,
*Captain, Commanding Zouaves d'Afrique, Body Guard.*

Maj. Gen. N. P. BANKS,
*Commanding Department of the Shenandoah.*

---

## No. 14.

*Report of Brig. Gen. John P. Hatch, U. S. Army, commanding cavalry, of operations May 24–25.*

HDQRS. CAVALRY, DEPARTMENT OF THE SHENANDOAH,
*Williamsport, Md., May* 30, 1862.

MAJOR: I have the honor to submit herewith a report of the operations of the cavalry under my command during the 24th and 25th instant:

The composition of the force was as follows: The Fifth New York Cavalry, Colonel De Forest; the First Vermont, Colonel Tompkins, and five companies of the First Maine, Lieutenant-Colonel Douty, afterward joined by five companies of the First Maryland, Lieutenant-Colonel Wetschky, Hampton's battery, and one howitzer of Best's battery attached.

On the morning of the 24th the First Maine and two companies of the First Vermont accompanied the main body of the army on the retreat toward Winchester. Colonel Tompkins with the remainder of his regiment made a reconnaissance into Woodstock by the turnpike, and Captain Krom, of the New York Fifth, with two companies reconnoitered the same distance by the Middle road. Nothing was seen of the enemy on either road.

Orders were then received for the cavalry to follow in the rear of the trains toward Winchester. While the pickets were being withdrawn I advanced with six companies to Strasburg, and on arriving there met an order directing me to hasten to the front with the available cavalry. I pushed forward rapidly with the six companies, sending word to Colonel Tompkins to hasten on with his regiment and the artillery, and directing Colonel De Forest to destroy the Government property at Strasburg, for which there was no transportation, and then to act as a rear guard to the train.

On arriving at Middletown General Banks had directed the Maine cavalry and the two companies of the Vermont, under Major Collins, to make a reconnaissance toward Front Royal. After proceeding about 4½ miles this party had met a large force, consisting of artillery, infantry, and cavalry, and having been driven back by it, were just coming into the town when I arrived there. The enemy almost immediately occupied the road in front of the town with a battery, two regiments of infantry, and a force of cavalry, cutting off my command (all cavalry) from the main body of the army. Supposing our army to be but a short distance off, we turned to the left, and moving parallel to the pike, tried several times without success to make a junction with General Banks, each time finding the enemy upon the road; but on reaching Newtown we found Colonel Gordon's brigade holding the enemy in check, and we there joined it. At dusk we attempted to retire to Winchester, but were attacked by the enemy, and it was not until 10 o'clock p. m. that we entered the town. Major Collins, mistaking in the clouds of dust the point at which the main body of the cavalry left the turnpike at Middletown, charged down the road with one company of the Vermont and two of the Maine cavalry until stopped by a barricade of wagons. The stone wall at the side of the road was there lined with infantry, and I fear the loss in killed and prisoners was great, as but few who were in the charge have returned. The major when last seen was unhorsed, and is either killed or a prisoner.

Colonel Tompkins in advancing toward Middletown was met by returning wagons and stragglers, and received information that the direct road to the front was in the hands of the enemy. He therefore fell back to Strasburg, making a junction with Colonel De Forest and the company of Zouaves d'Afrique. They all moved to the left by a side road, taking with them the wagons and artillery. The column was very long, and in moving over a bad road became divided. Colonel Tompkins, with his regiment, a part of the New York, and the artillery, reached Winchester about 11 p. m. Colonel De Forest with the remainder of the Fifth New York and the infantry attempted at different times to unite with the main body of the army both at Winchester and at Martinsburg without success, each time finding a large body of the enemy in his front. He then bore to the left, striking for the Potomac River, which he crossed successfully at Cherry Run, sending the infantry and baggage to Hancock Ferry. He brought with him 32 baggage wagons, 1 battery wagon, and 1 forge.

The cavalry, arriving in Winchester late on the night of the 24th, and having to disperse throughout the town to obtain forage and shelter for the animals, was with difficulty assembled on the morning of the 25th. By appointing certain streets in which the different regiments were to rendezvous they were finally brought into order, but too late to participate in the action at Winchester. They, however, covered the retreat of the infantry and artillery through the town, and with Cothran's battery formed the rear guard of the army on its march from Winchester to the ferry at Williamsport, which point they reached about 10.30 p. m. The First Maryland Cavalry, which had been doing duty at Winchester, was ordered early in the morning to escort the baggage train to the rear. After proceeding several miles on the road they received an order to return, and marched to the rear of the column, taking up a position in line of battle in fine order, thereby giving confidence to our right wing, which had become somewhat demoralized. The Maine, Vermont, and Michigan cavalry (the latter of Williams' division) are deserving of great praise for their steadiness in ranks in leaving the town of Winchester and upon the march.

I cannot with justice close the report without mentioning with praise Colonel De Forest, of the Fifth New York Cavalry, who by his energy saved a large train; Colonel Tompkins, of the First Vermont Cavalry, who brought Hampton's battery safely to Winchester; Captain Pratt, Fifth New York Cavalry, who, with his company (E), formed the special escort to Cothran's battery on the retreat from Winchester; Majors Davidson and Gardner, of the same regiment, and Lieut. John D. Woodbury, of Cothran's battery, First New York Artillery. This last-named officer, by his coolness and judgment in the management of his guns, gained the well-deserved praise of all employed in covering the retreat of the army.

My personal staff, Capt. John A. Judson, assistant adjutant-general; First Lieuts. James Lyon, Fourth New York Cavalry, and John W. Bennett, First Vermont Cavalry, are deserving of praise for their attention to duty and coolness under fire. Lieutenant Bennett was more particularly exposed, having on the 24th instant carried to the commanding general a message, literally cutting his way through the cavalry of the enemy, and escaping harm as by a miracle.

A report* of killed, wounded, and missing is inclosed with this, together with the detailed reports of the regimental commanders. I also inclose the reports of Lieutenant-Colonel Babbitt, Eighth New York Cavalry (dismounted), and of Major Vought, commanding cavalry, in the affair at Front Royal.

Very respectfully, your obedient servant,

JNO. P. HATCH,
*Brigadier-General, Commanding Cavalry.*

Maj. D. D. PERKINS,
*Acting Assistant Adjutant-General.*

---

## No. 15.

*Report of Lieut. Col. Calvin S. Douty, First Maine Cavalry, of operations May 24.*

HDQRS. FIRST BATTALION FIRST MAINE CAVALRY,
*Williamsport, Md., May* 27, 1862.

GENERAL: On Saturday morning last I proceeded to Middletown, and left my baggage there according to orders. A detachment of cavalry with two pieces of artillery had just returned from a reconnaissance on the road leading across to the Winchester and Front Royal turnpike. They had seen nothing of the enemy. I immediately started across, and struck what I at first took to be their pickets, but afterward proved to be their advance guard. Shots were exchanged,

* Embodied in revised statement, p. 553.

and the enemy fell back. This was about $1\frac{1}{2}$ miles from the Front Royal pike.

I here learned from a person who had just come up from that direction that the enemy was in force upon the road and moving across toward Middletown. I threw out skirmishers to the right and left and awaited their movements, at the same time sending back intelligence of what had happened to the signal officer at Middletown. Seeing no signs of the enemy, after waiting an hour I fell back toward Providence Church, leaving vedettes along the road and small parties at a distance each side to look out for any flank movement of the enemy. My object in so doing was to conceal my force and delay the enemy, in order to save time to the baggage trains, knowing they had a large force of infantry, which would render opposition on my part ineffectual.

At Providence Church I halted my command, expecting to be re-enforced from Middletown. At about 12 o'clock, after waiting an hour or more, the most advanced vedettes came in and reported the enemy's cavalry and infantry advancing. Others coming in and confirming this statement I drew up my command in order of battle, to deceive the enemy and gain time. Their advance guard soon came in sight, and halted at a respectful distance. Their infantry soon came in sight, and also halted. I remained in position, determined to hold them in check as long as possible, at the same time sending intelligence of the condition of affairs to the signal officer, to be forwarded to General Banks.

After a delay of half an hour the enemy opened on us with artillery, throwing shell into my column. I drew off my force, and proceeded slowly to Middletown. I there learned that General Banks had gone on toward Winchester, and that you were coming up with your command. I determined to wait for your arrival. The enemy quickly appeared and commenced shelling the town. I was about giving the order to fall back toward Strasburg when I saw you approaching. I formed my command in column of fours in the main street, and awaited orders. Major Collins, of the First Vermont Cavalry, was attached to my command, and took place with his two companies at the head of the column.

After the end of five or ten minutes I saw the head of the column in motion, as I supposed by your order. My position was then near the rear of the column, looking after Captain Cilley, of Company B, who had been severely wounded by a shell. I rode forward as fast as possible toward the head of the column, which was charging up the pike amid a shower of shell and bullets. The dust was so thick I could neither see nor tell anything in particular, except close by me. I passed over the bodies of men and horses strewn along the road till I had come up to near the center of Company M, the third company from the rear, where I found the bodies of men and horses so piled up that it was impossible to proceed. I saw they were retreating, and heard the order for the same from ahead. I fell back, and reformed the remainder of my command in the street about the middle of the town. At the same time a company of rebel infantry formed across the street at the upper end and opened fire on us. I saw that a second attempt to advance was useless and fell back a few rods, when I made a turn to the left and struck into the fields and proceeded toward Winchester, falling in with your command after marching about 2 miles.

Our loss is as follows: A, 44 men missing; B, Captain Cilley wounded severely and left and 5 men missing; E, Captain Putnam and 42 men missing; H, 1 man missing; M, 33 men missing. It is impossible to tell how many of these were killed and wounded.* Probably some may yet come in who have escaped. Companies A, E, and M lost nearly all their horses also.

I am, sir, very respectfully, your obedient servant,

C. S. DOUTY,
*Lieutenant-Colonel, First Maine Cavalry.*

Brig. Gen. JOHN P. HATCH.

---

## No. 16.

*Report of Lieut. Col. Charles Wetschky, First Maryland Cavalry, of operations May 18–26.*

HEADQUARTERS FIRST MARYLAND CAVALRY,
*Camp near Williamsport, May 29, 1862.*

SIR: Appended please find a report of the duty done by the battalion of cavalry under my command since arriving in this department:

The battalion left Camp Carroll, Md., at about 2 o'clock on Sunday morning, the 18th of May, and arrived at Winchester, Va., on Monday, the 19th, at about midday, and encamped about 1½ miles south of Winchester in an open field. The companies were engaged as pickets on Thursday by order of Colonel Beal, commanding post at Winchester, two companies being posted—one on the road leading to Front Royal and the other on the road from Winchester toward Romney.

On Friday morning the entire battalion was under saddle, and during the day scoured the country from point to point, with a view to ascertaining the whereabouts of the enemy's pickets.

On Saturday morning the battalion (which was still under saddle) was called to the pike leading from Winchester to Strasburg by a report reaching it that the enemy were approaching, and the wagon trains, which had started for Strasburg, rapidly returning.

After proceeding about 6 miles on the pike toward Strasburg we met the enemy's pickets or advance guard, and drove them back some 3 miles, taking from them or recapturing a hospital wagon, a wagon loaded with officers' goods, the enemy, however, cutting the traces and carrying off the horses that were attached. A team was procured from a farmer close by and the wagon sent into camp.

After returning to camp, and before time was had to unsaddle, the enemy's advance attacked a picket, under command of Captain Merritt, and a report reached us that Captain Merritt's company was cut to pieces. The battalion was marched about 2 miles on the Front Royal road and found the rumor incorrect. On returning to camp and before unsaddling the pickets came in and reported that the enemy's main body of cavalry was but a short distance from Winchester and advancing; great consternation among the teamsters, they flying rapidly toward Winchester, numbers of them having upset and deserted the wagons under their charge.

The battalion marched down the Winchester road toward Stras-

* See revised statement, p. 553.

burg, a distance of probably 4 miles, and drew up in line to receive the supposed enemy's attack. After remaining there some time we found that the cavalry that was approaching was the First Michigan. We returned to camp, kept our horses saddled, and at about 10 p. m. a courier came into camp to notify us that a brigade which was at the time passing the camp on the way to Winchester was being followed up by the enemy.

After making some preparation to receive the enemy we concluded that the position of the camp was unfavorable for defense, and we evacuated, marching some 3 miles on the road to Romney, and there bivouacked during the night.

Early on Sunday morning we started with two companies for camp, wishing, if possible, to bring away the tents and other camp equipage, and also the wagon which we had captured; but on arriving in Winchester we were informed that the camp was in the possession of the enemy. By this time the wagon trains were pushing through Winchester toward Martinsburg.

On reporting to Colonel Beal for orders, we were ordered by him to send one company in advance of the trains as an advance guard. Three companies were placed in rear of the baggage and one in rear of the ammunition train. After marching about 7 miles in the aforementioned order we were ordered, in common with all the cavalry, to the rear. The battalion was immediately marched back until it was met by Major-General Banks, who ordered us to again retreat, a great portion of the other cavalry having left before us. We fell into column and joined in the retreat until after passing through Martinsburg, near which place we stopped for nearly two hours, and were then ordered to proceed on with the other retreating forces, and after marching nearly 6 miles from Martinsburg toward Williamsport we returned to the hill west of Martinsburg, intending to act as a rear guard or cover to our retreating infantry.

On arriving near Martinsburg (on our return) we were ordered by General Banks to furnish a rear guard to the brigade commanded by Colonel Donnelly, acting brigadier-general. We proceeded on the route indicated as that on which we would overtake Colonel Donnelly, but found that the main body of his command had started on their march for Dam No. 4, there being some 50 or more of his command still near the bridge. We started in their rear and brought up all the stragglers that we could overtake, reaching Dam No. 4 after night. The adjutant of my battalion then reported to General Donnelly that the cavalry that had been ordered to join him were in the rear. General Donnelly stated that it would be impossible to ford, and that he would march with his command for a ferry some distance up the river. The battalion then accompanied General Donnelly's command to the ferry above mentioned, and one company remained there and assisted in ferrying General Donnelly's command across the river. The remaining companies of the battalion then took up the line of march for Williamsport, accompanied by Captain Curll's independent company, which company we met at the ferry above mentioned. The march from the ferry to Williamsport was executed through by-roads and lanes amid intense darkness, and day had dawned before we reached the Virginia shore opposite Williamsport. We forded the river, and reached Williamsport about 7 o'clock on Monday morning.

When it is remembered that the men and horses had been in active duty from Friday until Monday (the men without rations except such as chanced to fall in their way, and the horses with no forage except the grass which they picked up) it will, I hope, be conceded that the battalion deported itself in a creditable manner.

With great respect, your obedient servant,

CH. WETSCHKY,
*Lieutenant-Colonel, Commanding First Maryland Cavalry.*

Brig. Gen. JOHN P. HATCH,
*Chief of Cavalry.*

---

## No. 17.

*Report of Col. Thornton F. Brodhead, First Michigan Cavalry, of operations May 24–27.*

HEADQUARTERS FIRST MICHIGAN CAVALRY,
*Williamsport, Md., May 28, 1862.*

SIR: Your order of the evening of the 24th instant was received by me while prostrate with lung fever and hemorrhage, which for ten days had confined me to my quarters. The five companies of the regiment present were promptly notified of the intended movement and promptly placed in readiness.

In compliance with your order for detail, Major Paldi, with detachment of three companies of the command, proceeded to Middletown, reported to Colonel Murphy, of the Twenty-ninth Pennsylvania Volunteers, and accompanied him 5 miles on the Front Royal road, where he found the enemy's pickets of infantry and cavalry in large force. They retired to Middletown, where they found the train in disorder from an attack of a party of the enemy's cavalry who had possession of Newtown.

Major Paldi immediately proceeded to the front, without orders, to protect the train and ascertain the enemy's force. On approaching Newtown the enemy retreated to a wood on the right of the road, where they were held in check until the arrival of the artillery and infantry. At this point, with the rest of the command, I moved to the front, leading with my companies the advance of the column.

Under orders from General Banks I now proceeded at once to Winchester, where, on the arrival of our forces, I was ordered to furnish two companies for grand-guard duty on the Front Royal road, which detachment was placed under command of Major Town. The balance of the command bivouacked on the outside of the town. Major Town proceeded on the Front Royal road 2½ miles, where he was joined by two companies of the Tenth Maine Volunteers, and established his grand guard. Several attempts were made during the night by a superior force of the enemy to drive them in, but their position was maintained until 7 o'clock on the morning of Sunday, when they were compelled to retire on the line of the First Brigade. Thereupon the detachment joined the balance of the command.

Finding I had very much overtasked my strength, utterly exhausted by the day's march from Strasburg, I assigned the command to Major Paldi; Lieutenant-Colonel Copeland just recovering from a long illness, and too feeble for duty in the saddle.

About 5 o'clock Sunday morning, when our pickets were being driven in in every direction, a regiment of the enemy's infantry appeared on a hill on the right of the turnpike, driving a small party of our own infantry before them, with the apparent intention of closing immediately on the town. Major Paldi assumed the responsibility of ordering a battery into position to resist their approach, and formed his own command as its support. He remained in this position, under a severe fire of musketry and artillery, until the retreat of both artillery and infantry from the hill. As the last of the infantry were leaving the hill General Williams ordered Major Town, then temporarily in command, to form line of battle on top of the hill, and, if possible, charge the advancing column and hold them in check. Major Town immediately formed his command in the position designated and prepared for action. Directly in his front and within 15 rods of him, advancing at a double-quick, came six full regiments of the enemy's infantry. His appearance before them caused a halt, and they made preparations to receive his charge. This movement delayed the enemy full ten minutes, giving our retreating infantry time to gain the cover of the town. Major Town judged it impracticable to charge on this column with his command of 200 men, and ordered a retrograde movement, which was executed in good order under a heavy fire of musketry. He then proceeded to the opposite side of the town, and was assigned a position on the left by General Hatch, Lieutenant-Colonel Copeland joining and assuming command. When within 5 miles of Martinsburg General Hatch ordered him to join Colonel Donnelly's brigade, on a back road. He proceeded through the woods to this road, and after sending 2½ miles back in search of the brigade, and halting until the enemy's advance was ahead of him, being unable to ascertain anything of Colonel Donnelly's whereabouts, he slowly proceeded to Martinsburg, where he arrived about 4 p. m. The lieutenant-colonel being unable to proceed farther the command devolved upon Major Paldi, who was ordered to proceed on the road to Williamsport in rear of the infantry. The command reached the vicinity of Williamsport during the night, and remained standing in the road until 3 o'clock the next morning, when it was ordered on grand-guard duty on the Martinsburg road, where it remained until 10 o'clock a. m. the 27th instant, observing nothing of moment in the interim. At this time he was relieved and proceeded to Williamsport into camp.

The company commanders not having been able to ascertain the loss in their respective companies precludes the possibility of making an accurate report of the loss in my command. It is known that Second Lieut. William M. Brevoort, of Company G, was wounded on the field, fell from his horse, and was probably captured by the enemy. His conduct was everything that his commanding officer could desire, and his loss will be severely felt in the regiment. A more gallant young officer never trod a battle-field.

It was not until infantry and artillery had begun the retreat, and until ordered to do so, that the regiment—the only cavalry in the field in the action—left it, and then in good order, taking position immediately, and acting throughout the retreat under the eye of the general commanding the division. It was the last regiment that left the field, and reformed immediately in the streets.

Lieutenant-Colonel Copeland, feeble to the extreme from protracted illness, against the remonstrance of the surgeon, for several hours of the march insisted upon taking command of the column, and only left it when utterly unable to keep his saddle.

To the coolness, judgment, and gallant conduct of Major Town, very much of the time in command, every credit is due. His prompt action at critical periods contributed materially to the success of that trying march. His duties were pressing and critical, and always well performed. Second Lieut. and Adjt. William M. Heazlit, and Lieut. D. G. Maynard, adjutant of the Third Battalion, were conspicuous for gallantry and good conduct. First Lieutenants Sprague, Alexander, and Duggan, and Second Lieutenant Snyder, commanding companies—officers all highly distinguished heretofore for good conduct—behaved admirably, and deserve high commendation for gallantry and soldier-like bearing. The notice of the general of division is especially called to the noble conduct of Dr. George K. Johnson, the accomplished surgeon of the regiment. When our train was attacked near Middletown on the march from Strasburg he made a most gallant effort to save it, and commanded in person, assisted by Sergt. A. D. Burdino, a portion of the guard, and a company of the Fifth Connecticut Infantry. The enemy were in force too strong, but it was only after a most determined struggle, in which the hospital steward was killed and several assistants wounded, that the hospital train was abandoned.

Our loss is, 1 officer wounded and prisoner; enlisted men killed, 10; wounded, 9; missing, 34. Total, 54; nearly one-fourth of the force of the command.

I have the honor to be, very respectfully, your obedient servant,

T. F. BRODHEAD,
*Colonel, Commanding.*

Brig. Gen. ALPHEUS S. WILLIAMS,
*Commanding Division.*

---

## No. 18.

*Report of Col. Othneil De Forest, Fifth New York Cavalry, of operations May 24–27.*

HEADQUARTERS FIFTH NEW YORK CAVALRY,
*Camp near Williamsport, Md., May* 29, 1862.

I have the honor to make the following report of my movements from noon of Saturday, the 24th, until evening of Tuesday, the 27th:

Leaving camp at Tom's Brook somewhat after noon on Saturday, the 24th, and moving toward Strasburg, I received orders on the way to order forward Hampton's battery and the First Vermont Cavalry, and to bring up the rear with the six companies (A, C, E, G, K, M) remaining with me, Companies B and D, under command of Major Vought, having gone to Front Royal to join Colonel Kenly on the 23d, and Companies F, H, I, and L having gone forward to Strasburg, under Major Gardner, according to previous instructions.

On the road I received instructions from yourself to destroy the Government stores in Strasburg. Halting my command at the south end of the village, I emptied the church of the ordnance stores and burned them, and then partly emptied the freight depot after loading a supply train of 13 wagons with clothing; but being pressed for time, I finally fired the depot, as well as a large outbuilding to the south, containing tents, and the various piles of tents, poles, &c., lying near together, with some half-dozen vacant wall and A tents that were pitched close by.

Moving now to the summit of the hill north of Strasburg, I found that my own command, as well as a portion of the First Vermont Cavalry, a portion of General Banks' body guard, and Hampton's battery, were cut off from the main body by the rebels. Infantry, cavalry, and wagons were streaming back in wild confusion along the road and the fields on either side as far as the eye could reach. The battery having been at once ordered to the summit of the hill, I supported it with my cavalry, formed in line of battle in the field on either side. A few shell checked the small force of rebels who were pressing on us from Middletown.

After a hasty consultation Colonel Tompkins, Captain Hampton, and myself decided to try and rejoin the main body by a mountain road on the west of the pike, Colonel Tompkins stating that he had a captain who could guide us. Colonel Tompkins, forming the advance with a portion of his regiment, was to move out the cross-road a piece and halt until the column should be formed, the battery and my own command following. I ordered forward Companies A and E to support the battery. I would earnestly call your attention to the fact that I have not since seen Colonel Tompkins and his command, and to the critical situation in which I was placed by his desertion, as he took with him the only guide we had, the Vermont captain. I have subsequently learned that Colonel Tompkins pushed on without the battery, and that Companies A and E, of my regiment, entered Winchester about 1 a. m. on Sunday with the battery. Captain Hampton and his two battery wagons remained with me. I halted a few minutes for Captain Hampton to bring up these two battery wagons from the rear, and then moved rapidly on, but could not overtake the battery.

Before moving I ordered Captain Foster, of Company M, to bring out of the village a loaded supply train of 35 wagons that remained there, which he did in the face of a large body of rebel cavalry who appeared to the south of the village. I also brought up a portion of General Banks' body guard, and some of the First Maine, First Michigan, First Maryland, First Virginia, Tenth Maine, and Fifth Connecticut, some telegraph operators, one of the Signal Corps, &c., who had been cut off near Middletown.

Now, about 5 p. m., I moved forward as rapidly as the battery wagons allowed, and without halting, along rough roads parallel with the pike, making inquiries at every step. Late in the evening we reached a grade running to Winchester and joining the Winchester and Strasburg pike, say 1½ miles south of Winchester.

At one time, just before reaching this grade, we heard the beating of the enemy's drums, and I ascertained that they were not more than three-quarters of a mile from us. About 11 miles from Winchester I came upon a road running westerly again to Pughtown, 14 miles, and easterly 6 miles to Newtown. Learning that the grade I was on entered the Winchester and Strasburg pike, and thinking I might be compelled to take a more westerly road, I halted here, to be sure of a way of retreat, and throwing out pickets on the Newtown road, ordered forward Captain Hammond's company to reconnoiter as far as the pickets of General Banks, if possible, and send me report. While standing here signaling was going on from a height many miles in our rear for a long time, and two rockets, possibly in reply, were sent up from near Winchester.

Standing to horse some hours about daybreak two orderlies returned to me, reporting that Captain Hammond had forced the enemy's pickets and entered Winchester, but that they occupied the pike near the fork of the grade and the Winchester and Strasburg pike, rendering it extremely hazardous for us with our train to attempt to enter Win chester there. I concluded at once to enter the Pughtown road and seek a mountain road that would lead me into the west side of Winchester. I soon discovered a German Unionist, who conducted us through the woods a mile or so to a grade running direct and entering Winchester near Mason's house. Halting on the grade only long enough to bring my train on the rough road well up with the column I lost no time in approaching Winchester, spurred on by the hope of rejoining the main column, so as to assist in the battle I supposed to be raging, as from dawn we heard heavy firing.

At 9 a. m. the head of the column was within a mile of Winchester, moving cautiously lest I might betray our presence to the enemy, whose picket was suspected to be on that road, as we took prisoner a private of Colonel Dudley's Twenty-sixth Kentucky Regiment, who said he had come from Winchester, and that there was a picket on that road, though he refused to tell what it was. Ascertaining through my vedettes that General Banks had nearly evacuated Winchester, closely followed by the enemy, I decided to search for a mountain road to Martinsburg. Counter-marching at once and striking over a bad road for some 3 miles, guided by a Union refugee, we struck the mountain road to Martinsburg, and running parallel with and about 3 miles from the Winchester and Martinsburg pike. Moving rapidly to within about 4 miles of Martinsburg and a mile north of Gerardstown, we halted about two hours to graze our horses, which were much jaded, and meanwhile Pratt, the scout, went forward to within 2 miles of Martinsburg, and returned, reporting that the enemy were shelling the town. Cut off now the third time, I resolved to cross the mountain to the west and strike for McCoy's Ford, on the Potomac, passing through Hedgesville. Counter-marching the column a mile, I passed through Gerardstown and to the west, crossed the mountain by the pass, and took the road to the ford, picking up some guides by the way.

Learning subsequently that a spy had gone to inform the enemy of our intention to cross at McCoy's Ford, I moved the column instead to Cherry Run Ford, arriving within a mile of it about 2 a. m. on Monday, the 26th. I have since learned that McCoy's Ford was occupied Sunday night by a force of the enemy's cavalry and infantry. Finding some hay here, we baited our horses while waiting for dawn, that we might reconnoiter the ford.

At daybreak I became satisfied, by a personal reconnaissance, that fording was impracticable, on account of the rise of the river. I then resolved to move on Hancock, with the view of crossing there, there being some facility for ferrying there. While passing along the river with my command a man reported to me that he had that morning forded the river twice, though it was quite deep, and volunteered to ford it again in my presence. Convinced, on seeing him ford it, of the feasibility of fording, I ordered my cavalry to ford at once, the infantry to cross by the ferry, and the wagon train with Company K, under command of Lieutenant-Colonel Johnstone, to move at once to Hancock and cross. The ford, though rapid and shoulder-deep to the ordinary sized horse, was, I am happy to report, made without a single casualty.

The Maryland bank affording good clover fields, we unsaddled and grazed the horses here for some hours and gave the men some rest, after which we marched 7 miles to Clear Spring, and bivouacked in a grove near the town. The wagon train crossed Monday afternoon on boats, swimming some of the mules, and rested at Hancock Monday night. Tuesday morning it joined my command, and I moved to Williamsport, 11 miles by the pike, and bivouacked.

Except twice that we grazed, once at Gerardstown on Sunday, and again Monday morning, on the Maryland side, after fording the Potomac, our horses had nothing from Saturday at daybreak, and our men nothing until the evening of Monday, except what bread, milk, and pie they picked up hastily on the road.

We marched from Strasburg Saturday at 5 p. m., and moved before halting that night 18 miles. From dawn on Sunday we moved, say, 11 miles, to Winchester, and 37 to Cherry Run Ford, making on Sunday 48 miles. On Monday we marched to Clear Spring, 7 miles; on Tuesday to Williamsport, 11 miles—in all, 84 miles.

The number of men that came in with us was not ascertained, any further than that there were 250 of the First Vermont Cavalry, 65 of General Banks' body guard, and some from the First Maine, First Virginia, First Maryland, First Michigan, and Eighth New York Cavalry, of the Fifth Connecticut and Tenth Maine Infantry, four companies of the Fifth New York Cavalry, some sutlers, telegraph operators, and wagoners, one of the Signal Corps, and some of the First Maryland Artillery.*

Three of the 35 wagons I was obliged to abandon on the road; the remaining 32 I brought in, with an unknown quantity of Government stores.

I have the honor to be, your most obedient servant,

O. DE FOREST,
*Colonel Fifth New York Cavalry.*

General HATCH.

---

## No. 19.

*Report of Lieut. Col. Charles R. Babbitt, Eighth New York Cavalry, of operations May* 24–25.

HEADQUARTERS EIGHTH NEW YORK CAVALRY,
*Williamsport, Md., May* 29, 1862.

CAPTAIN: I have the honor to report that in obedience to orders received from Col. Dixon S. Miles, Second Infantry, U. S. Army, commanding railroad brigade, upon the 24th of May I marched five companies of my command to Winchester, for the purpose of relieving Colonel Beal, Tenth Maine. The command reached Winchester at 6 p. m., and was reported to Colonel Beal by Captain Pope, senior captain. Owing to delay of the train I did not arrive until 9 p. m. Captain Pope's company guarded a wagon train during the night. Early in the morning I inquired for orders, and learned simply that the men were to be ready to fall in at a moment's notice. The command was drawn up in front of Our House upon the main street for about an hour, when I saw our artillery and cavalry passing through the town, apparently upon the retreat. I marched by the left up the main street, receiving fire from the houses as I rose the hill and from the enemy in the rear. The men kept the ranks and marched in good order, column *en route*, until we reached the plain north of the town, when we received the fire of the enemy's skirmishers upon our left, and were thrown into some confusion. The men quickly formed again and proceeded some

* More properly Battery F, Pennsylvania Light Artillery.

distance, when they were again broken up by the sudden breaking of an infantry regiment upon the left, and the crossing of their front by a company of cavalry and section of artillery.

After this the column was not reformed. Part of the men went down the turnpike and the remainder took the railway. Adjutant Ford, of my command, after seeing all efforts to reform the command fruitless, attached himself as volunteer to Major Vought's battalion, Fifth New York Cavalry, and remained with it during the day. I continued along the pike looking up my men, directing them to fall in with the columns of infantry, and reached the Potomac about 9.30 o'clock p. m., and crossed to Williamsport at noon the following day, having, with some that crossed the previous night, 119 men, 2 staff and 8 line officers.

I immediately dispatched an officer to Harper's Ferry for the purpose of learning the situation of the four other companies guarding the railway and the whereabouts of the missing. He reports that as near as could be ascertained 137 of the force at Winchester and the four companies had reached that place safely.

The force at Winchester numbered as follows: Field officer, 1; staff officers, 2; line officers, 10; enlisted men, 279. Accounted for as follows: At this point—field officer, 1; staff, 2; line, 8; enlisted men, 119, of whom 4 are wounded. At Harper's Ferry—line officer, 1; enlisted men, 135; known to have been killed, 2. Missing—line officer, 1; enlisted men, 23.

The line officer missing is Capt. J. W. Dickinson, of Company C. He was last seen from one-half to three-quarters of a mile this side of Winchester, and as he was in ill-health, it is feared that he has fallen into the hands of the enemy.

I beg leave to say that the men were under fire for the first time, conducted themselves creditably, and did not break their column until actuated to do so by force of example.

Respectfully, your obedient servant,

CHARLES R. BABBITT,
*Lieut. Col., Comdg. Eighth New York Cavalry, Dismounted.*

P. S.—The men were armed with Hall's carbines (unserviceable), and but few were brought in. All that had Sharps brought them in.

Captain JOHN A. JUDSON,
*Assistant Adjutant-General.*

---

## No. 20.

*Report of Col. Charles H. Tompkins, First Vermont Cavalry, of operations May 24–25.*

CAVALRY BRIGADE, DEPARTMENT OF SHENANDOAH,
*Williamsport, Md., May* 28, 1862.

SIR: I have the honor to submit the following report of the operations of my regiment on the 24th and 25th days of the present month:

May 24, having received orders through your office, at 12.30 o'clock on the morning of the 24th instant, to send my baggage and regimental and company property to the rear and to hold my regiment in readiness to march at a moment's notice with one day's rations, orders were immediately given to carry out these instructions. Between the hours of 4 and 5 o'clock a. m. my wagons were sent to the rear as far as Cedar Creek, with instructions to await the further orders of the brigade commander.

At 5 o'clock a. m. I was directed by Brigadier-General Hatch, commanding cavalry, to proceed with my regiment to the town of Woodstock, with instructions to reconnoiter the position of the enemy, if there, as well as to hold them in check, to further the advance of the division.

Arriving within half a mile of the town, I directed one squadron (Companies B and D) to precede the regiment as an advance, with instructions to pass through the town and reconnoiter the suburbs beyond.

Upon the return of the squadron, and ascertaining to my entire satisfaction that the enemy had not occupied the town in any considerable force for some time, I counter-marched my regiment, and returned to my camp near Strasburg, arriving there at 9 o'clock a. m.

At 10 o'clock three companies (Companies F, C, and E), under command of Captain Hall, squadron captain, were ordered to report to Major-General Banks for immediate service.

At 12 o'clock m. one squadron, Companies A and G, under command of Senior Major Collins, were ordered to report to Brigadier-General Hatch. At the same time I received instructions to bring up the rear of the army and to destroy all public property after the army had advanced beyond Strasburg.

At 3 o'clock p. m. I mounted my command and left camp to carry out these instructions. Arriving at Strasburg, my instructions were countermanded, and I was to join General Hatch immediately with the remaining five companies of my regiment. Pursuant to this order I proceeded as far as the suburbs of Middletown, where I found the enemy in force. Their line of infantry was very extensive, and was well supported by cavalry and artillery. My regiment was formed in column of squadrons, in readiness to charge. The only troops in the field, independent of my five companies, consisted of a New York battery of 10-pounder Parrott guns and one company of zouaves. These latter were being driven in upon my arrival by the advance skirmishers of the enemy. Perceiving the enemy were advancing in too strong force for a successful opposition to be made, I deemed it advisable to retreat in order, abandon the wagons, and make an attempt to join General Hatch by making a detour to the left of the enemy's right flank, and signifying my intention to Captain Hampton, of the New York battery, immediately commenced the movement, and was so far successful as to join Brigadier-General Hatch at Winchester at 11.30 p. m. of the same day, bringing in with me six pieces of artillery and a portion of the Fifth New York Cavalry. The entire baggage train of the regiment was abandoned and fired, and rendered entirely worthless and useless to the enemy.

My horses were foraged, but the men were without food, and were completely exhausted from the fatigues of the day, but bore their arduous duty with the courage and steadiness of old and well-tried soldiers, and behaved through the day in a manner to surprise and excite the admiration of their commander.

Captains Preston and Conger, and Lieutenants Huntoon, Beman, and Adams, and Private C. P. Stone, of Company F, acting as chief wagoner, are particularly deserving of attention, and I would respectfully recommend them to the attention of the brigadier-general commanding. I must also speak in terms of the highest praise of the efficient and valuable services rendered by Adjt. E. Petkin and Quartermaster A. S. Dewey. To these gentlemen I am particularly indebted, owing to the absence of the lieutenant-colonel, who had availed himself of a sick leave, and of the detachment of my senior major.

In summing up the occurrences of to-day I regret to have to report an accident befalling Major Sawyer, occasioned by the falling of his horse, seriously injuring his ankle joint and rendering him unfit for duty, and thus depriving me of the services of a valuable officer.

The casualties of the day, as soon as correctly ascertained, will be appended to this report.

May 25. My regiment this day being under the immediate eye of the brigadier-general commanding, I deem a lengthened report of its operations unnecessary, and close my report by appending the list of casualties for this and the preceding day.

Very respectfully, your obedient servant,

CHAS. H. TOMPKINS,
*Colonel First Vermont Cavalry.*

Capt. JOHN A. JUDSON,
*Assistant Adjutant-General.*

---

## No. 21.

*Report of Maj. William D. Collins, First Vermont Cavalry, of operations May* 24–30.

WASHINGTON, D. C., *June* 4, 1862.

SIR: I have the honor to report that at early dawn on the morning of the 24th of May, 1862, I received an order from Col. C. H. Tompkins, commanding First Vermont Cavalry, to report with one squadron of my battalion to Maj. D. D. Perkins, chief of your staff, at your headquarters, Strasburg, Va., for special service, forthwith. Pursuant to order I reported with squadron about 6 o'clock a. m., and was instructed to join my command with five companies of the First Maine Cavalry, under Lieutenant-Colonel Douty, and proceed to Middletown, thence in an easterly direction, by the Chapel road, to the Front Royal and Winchester pike; to proceed up toward Front Royal until the force which had been stationed at Front Royal should be found by us; to leave the baggage wagons accompanying the First Maine and part of our cavalry in camp near said force; then to make a reconnaissance with part of our cavalry force to Front Royal, and beyond it, if possible, to gain information, and ascertain the casualties and condition of the force under Colonel Kenly, of the First Maryland Infantry, who it was supposed had been attacked on the afternoon of the 23d by a portion of Jackson's force, with the intention of capturing the stores and transportation located at this point; and, further, if the enemy's forces should be found pressing their way from Front Royal to Winchester, to fall back to that point where the Chapel road intersects the Front Royal and Winchester pike, there make a stand, and keep the enemy in check until orders were received from headquarters. To make frequent communication of facts and incidents occurring on our route which should be deemed of any interest to the nearest signal station, whence it would be transmitted to headquarters.

On arriving at Middletown I found a force consisting of one regiment of infantry, a section of artillery, and about one company of cavalry.

Lieutenant-Colonel Douty halted our column, and after some minutes' delay informed me that this force had been sent out upon the road which we were about to take; that they had reached a point some 3 or 4 miles distant; had then been fired upon by carbineers, whereupon they immediately returned, without having seen anything further of the enemy.

Lieutenant-Colonel Douty asked me what course in my opinion was best to pursue. I replied that I considered our orders imperative; that whenever I had been intrusted with duties of a character similar to the present I always made it a rule to at least see my foe, and, if possible, ascertain their number and purposes before retiring from them. The lieutenant-colonel (Douty) remarked that he agreed with me, and ordered the column forward. We had proceeded to a point within 3 or 4 miles of the Front Royal and Winchester pike when a halt was made. Here Lieutenant-Colonel Douty sent his compliments, requesting me to come to front of column, which I immediately responded to, and found the lieutenant-colonel in front of a house interrogating a lady. He told me that he had learned from her that the enemy was seen (by the lady) some two hours before in considerable force, principally cavalry, and were occupying the road between us and the pike, their cavalry pickets extending to within 1½ miles of her house, at the door of which she was standing, and, further, that a very large force was moving down the pike from Front Royal to Winchester—using her own words, "Wagons and all, reaching some 4 miles long." I turned to the lady, and was making more critical inquiry respecting the enemy and the topography of the road over which we must have passed had we advanced, when our advance guard was fired upon by the enemy's advanced pickets, who instantly retired after discharging their pieces.

It was then proposed by an officer present that he, with the lieutenant-colonel (Douty) and a small escort, should advance. Lieutenant-Colonel Douty again asked me what I thought was best to do. I remarked that I had some delicacy in attempting to dictate to my superiors, but would cheerfully obey any order which he should direct me to execute. Whereupon he remarked that "We are volunteers; have not had very large experience in the field, and would receive with thanks any suggestion or opinion which I should be pleased to give." In reply to which I said that I did not consider it prudent to attempt to press our advance any farther in the direction of the enemy, for the following reasons: First, those deduced from the information obtained from the lady, as above stated; second, the bold attack of Ashby's vedettes upon our advance guard, in my experience with them in the field, was a sure indication to me of the near presence of a superior force. I then proposed that as our flanks were skirted on either side by dense woods, which would enable the enemy by an extended flank movement to surround us unobserved, we should fall back to the vicinity of the chapel, a point where several roads formed a junction with the one which we then occupied, and where there was an extended open area, stationing pickets in our rear as we retired, and there await the issue of events; and, further, I suggested the propriety of sending by courier a dispatch to the signal station notifying you of the information received, the attack of the enemy's pickets, that we were falling back to the vicinity of the chapel, and to ask for further instructions. Lieutenant-Colonel Douty; concurring, immediately ordered the column about, stationing pickets at proper intervals until the main body of our force had reached the point designated, when the column, which had moved at a walk, was halted.

We had been halted some twenty or thirty minutes when shots were heard in the direction of the enemy, and our pickets were seen being rapidly driven in by the enemy's skirmishers, who were issuing from the border of the woods, supported by cavalry in the road. The enemy's skirmishers kept up a brisk fire, while his cavalry formed and threatened to make an immediate dash upon us. Being near Lieutenant-Colonel Douty at the time, he requested me to let him take my field glass to enable him to make a more minute observation of the enemy's movements, and directed me to make such arrangements and disposition of our force as would, in my judgment, best resist the charge with which we were momentarily threatened. Whereupon I ordered the rear guard, which were formed by fours in the road, to be strengthened by the addition of one company, and the remainder of the company, of which the rear guard formed a portion, and their flanks, supported by two companies drawn up in line on their right and left, in the adjoining fields. The residue of our command being formed in column of fours at some distance in our rear, occupied a position commanding the roads diverging from the chapel and its vicinity, with orders to support us if our lines should be broken. This formation had been completed but a few moments when the front of the enemy's cavalry was seen to oblique to the right and left, simultaneous with which the booming of artillery and the screeching of spherical shells, which were falling in rapid succession in our front and on our left rear, gave unmistakable evidence of the strength and manifest intention of our wily foe, being no less (as I then conjectured and afterward learned from them while in duress to be correct) than the immediate possession of Middletown, which would enable Jackson to cut off the baggage trains and more effectually intercept the passage of our retreating column, this movement of Jackson being part of the programme of the day.

Rebel programme: Ewell's force, 12,000 strong, marched from Front Royal at 4 o'clock a. m. of 24th by way of the Front Royal and Winchester pike, with orders to cross over to the Winchester and Strasburg pike between Kernstown and Winchester, to secure the possession of the last-named place with its stores, the occupation of which would secure to them nothing less than the total defeat and capture of your command and cut off all possibility of succor or retreat. Jackson some four hours later, with his Stonewall Brigade, supported by Elzey's division, in all numbering about 13,000, moved upon Middletown, in anticipation of an attack upon his flank in the direction of Front Royal, thence to Strasburg, with the view of surrounding you at that point, and in the event of his being foiled there to pursue your column with such vigor and rapidity as to render the destruction of your gallant little army inevitable. This being done, the accomplishment of which they did not doubt, would leave the route clear for a demonstration on Washington, in which they were to be aided by their rebel sympathizers, whom they claimed had already risen in Baltimore.

From the manner and vigor of the attack, together with the arms employed by the enemy, there was no longer any doubt in my mind respecting the character and purposes of our assailants. I immediately suggested to Lieutenant-Colonel Douty the necessity of moving our main force beyond the range of the enemy's artillery, while the rear guard would cover them as they retired and resist a dash with which we seemed again to be threatened by the enemy's cavalry, and that a dispatch be prepared stating the fact that the enemy had appeared in such force and with such arms as to leave no doubt of their being the advance guard of a very considerable force; that we were falling back on Middletown, and to again ask for instructions; that this be sent by several different couriers until a communication could be gotten to headquarters.

Our column was reformed under the fire of the enemy's battery without receiving any injury, and moved at a trot until it reached a piece of woods through which the road ran leading from the chapel to Middletown. Here the leading squadron of our retiring column, which was now moving left in front, having advanced at a brisker pace than the center and rear, was ordered to halt until the order to advance should be given from the rear, where Lieutenant-Colonel Douty and myself had taken our posts, in rear of the rear guard, between them and the enemy, to watch his maneuvers.

The enemy continued to shell the woods for some time after we had passed it with our main force, with the view, as I afterward learned, of dislodging our troops, whom he conjectured were strongly posted there, supposing us to be the cavalry of your advance guard.

Here I most respectfully beg you will permit me to state that much credit is due to the officers and men of the First Maine Cavalry, whose companies were ordered to the front, for the boldness and celerity with which they prepared to resist this threatened cavalry charge, which feint was made by him for the ostensible purpose of masking the approach of his battery, which opened upon us with such warmth and vigor as to render the abandonment of our position near the chapel an act of necessity. The manifest reluctance with which we retired from before him, and the deliberate coolness exhibited by the rear guard as they hung upon his front, made his advance slow and cautious, he evidently being yet ignorant of the strength and character of the force before him.

From the moment that the enemy's guns opened upon us doubt could no longer be entertained respecting his purposes, but the spirit of our little command was kept buoyed with the hope of finding at Middletown the force of artillery, infantry, and cavalry which were seen by us as we passed through in the morning, as well as instructions in reply to dispatches, looked for with such earnest solicitude by Lieutenant-Colonel Douty and your most humble servant from your headquarters.

We reached Middletown about 11.30 o'clock a. m., and the head of the column, turning to the left, halted in column of fours in the street, at the east side of the village, which runs at a right angle from the Chapel road in a southwesterly direction and parallel to the principal street on the pike. Some disappointment was felt when it was ascertained that the force seen here in the early part of the day was withdrawn, and that nothing had yet been heard in reply to the dispatches sent by courier more than an hour previous to the signal station, in accordance with the instructions given at your headquarters.

The firing, however, from the enemy's battery had ceased. Pickets were again stationed in our rear, supported by a strong rear guard, and the troopers ordered to dismount and rest. The horses having been under the saddle since before daybreak without forage or water, permission was granted to commanders of troops to water by companies. Thus nearly the interval of an hour had elapsed without seeing the enemy, he being hid from view by a belt of woods which intervened in our rear, some half mile or more beyond, in the direction of the Chapel road.

The relative positions of the companies comprising Lieutenant-Colonel Douty's command at this juncture were as follows: Pickets, extending from the rear guard to an approximate distance from the woods in our rear, to watch for the first approach of the enemy; rear guard, posted some 200 yards from the rear of the column in an angle of the Chapel road, each of these being details from the Maine cavalry. The main body of the command, having been halted left in front, gave my squadron a position at the head of the column at the extreme southwest end of the street, alluded to in a preceding paragraph.

I had been scanning the field through my field-glass in the direction of the enemy, when suddenly his artillery was seen to debouch from the woods in our rear, which fact I instantly communicated to Lieutenant-Colonel Douty, who was mounted near me, at the same time handing him my glass. The order to mount was quickly given by him, and the rear guard drawn in. The enemy's guns had in the mean time been brought into action, supported by a strong body of infantry deployed upon the perimeter of the woods, and their right resting on the crest of a gentle slope near the pike, forming a transverse line on our rear. On the left flank of our column was another line of infantry, formed parallel to and in rear of the street occupied by our gallant little band, they being also supported by a light field battery, which I readily recognized as the rebel Ashby's, whose proximity to us would have told with fearful havoc were it not for the buildings behind which our troopers were directed to take cover from the vigorous, though yet to us harmless, fire of his musketry and artillery. At this particular juncture, as I was passing down the column, I met General Hatch, engaged in conversation with Lieutenant-Colonel Douty on the corner of a cross street, who, with his characteristic coolness, deliberately surveyed the enemy for a few moments, when, it being evident that our position was no longer tenable, he gave the order to move down into the principal street on the pike.

A desultory fire had been kept up by his infantry, and Ashby's light battery had taken post near the side of the road, which crossed the street at the point where the head of our column rested. Company G of my squadron, occupying the space at the crossing, and whose gray horses afforded no doubt a splendid mark, had, at the moment the order to move was given, been selected as a special object of attack by him, and so violent were his attempts to shell them from their position that many of the horses, chafing under restraint, had broken their formation, and, in the slight consequent confusion, the order to turn to the right not having been understood, many of them dashed off in the opposite direction. I sent my orderly with an order for them to return, and passed down into the street on the pike, where the column had already halted, right in front, with its head in the direction of Newtown, and found my command re-enforced, Captain Rundlett with his company (E) having joined the column while I was detained in the street above. This change from left to right in front gave our companies the following relative position in column, which was formed by fours: The companies of the First Maine Cavalry occupied the front and center, the First Vermont Cavalry, Companies E, A, and G, the rear, in the order last named.

It was very apparent now that the strength and character of our command was fully known. The enemy closed down upon us, continuing his fire with renewed vigor. Here it was that the mettle and temper of officers and men were severely tried, but nobly did they bear the test, for although we still had the shelter of the houses, yet his artillery was brought to bear upon us from the front, center, and flank, the shells from which were passing and exploding in every direction around us.

Here we were detained for some reason unknown to me for several minutes, during which time I kept constantly moving up and down the column, endeavoring by example to encourage and cheer our men. I was passing toward the rear of the column, and seeing Lieutenant-Colonel Douty on the opposite side of the street, I addressed him with the following interrogatories: "Colonel, what is the order? Do we move?" To which he replied in the affirmative, "Yes," and moved rapidly to the head of the column. I saw that the enemy's infantry had closed down near the fence on our right, and that his cavalry had formed in the road some distance beyond in our front and in the fields on our flanks.

Hearing no other order but that communicated by the lieutenant-colonel as he passed, I ordered my sabers drawn, and took my post at the head of my squadron in the column, the head and center of which had already commenced to advance at a brisk trot. This pace was soon increased to a gallop, and now another enemy presented itself. The dust from the pike began to rise and envelop us in such dense clouds as to shut out all objects from our vision at a distance, and so intense was it at times that our file-leaders were not distinguishable.

We were now moving in column closed *en masse*, and had gained the distance, I should judge, of a mile, under a raking fire from the enemy, when suddenly the column in front of us was brought to a stand, the consequent danger of which instantly occurring to me, I turned and called a halt, directing the saber points to be kept erect, thereby intending to obviate the press which I knew must follow, those in my rear from the impenetrable cloud of dust surrounding us being unable through the organ of vision to guard against it. My horse, as well as others near me, began to sink from the pressure around us, but now the column in front again advanced, and we were relieved.

We again moved forward, but soon came in contact with the rear of the baggage train, which, being deserted by the drivers, was tumbling down the pike in wild confusion, impeding our passage and so seriously checking my advance that when the dust cleared away for a moment I found myself with the command in my rear separated from the main body of the column.

Supposing, from the clouds of dust still visible and not far distant in front, that Lieutenant-Colonel Douty, with the main body of the command, had cut his way through the enemy's cavalry, and conjecturing also, as no special directions or orders had been received or heard by me since that mentioned above in the street, that the object of the movement down the pike and in this direction was to form a junction with the rear guard of your column, which I had good reason to suppose could not be far distant, I pressed my way through the labyrinth surrounding us, and soon gained a clear space in the road.

The enemy, taking advantage of our condition, formed his cavalry again in our front, and concentrating the fire of his artillery and infantry, hurled a shower of lead and shell upon us. At this discharge the fragment of a shell which exploded near me struck my left holster, cutting the brass tip from the end, and striking the end of a Savage pistol, glanced, wounding my left knee, and passed, inflicting a severe wound on the side of my horse. Here I left 2 men who were wounded and their horses shot by fragments of the same shell.

Recovering again from the momentary shock, I saw at a glance that to make a diversion on either flank would be to risk the destruction of my brave companions, and to boldly dash upon the cavalry in front would secure the positive advantage to us as we neared them of causing the tempestuous fire of his infantry and artillery to cease, as the safety of his cavalry as we closed upon them would demand it, and that the chance of cutting our way through and rejoining our column was the most feasible course to adopt. On we dashed amid clouds of dust, and as we neared them, true to their guerrilla tactics, and apparently not daring to meet the shock of the charge that was so closely threatening them, they fell back around a barricade of wagons drawn up in the center of the road, with a passage on each side next to the fence, which they manned, ranging themselves along on the sides of the road near this obstruction, intending no doubt in the collision which seemed imminent to cut us upon our flanks, which would have proved very disastrous. In this they were foiled. Quickly discovering their stratagem, I ordered the head of my command to oblique right and left, and on we rushed to a hand-to-hand encounter. We succeeded in forcing them back at the point of the saber, leaving several of their number weltering in their blood upon the pike, and as far as my knowledge extends without suffering any loss at this point, when I received a saber blow from one of two assailants (the other having fallen) on the side of my head, which deprived me of consciousness. I had fallen from my saddle to the ground, but soon recovered, to find myself surrounded by foes and a prisoner of war.

I find from data in my memorandum of that (May 24) date that it was now over three hours since our advance guard had been fired upon by Ashby's pickets in the advance of Jackson's column. I was now taken into the custody of one of Ashby's lieutenants, who marched me to Front Royal, a distance of some 14 miles, which place we reached a little after 9 o'clock p. m. The next morning (May 25) I found among the prisoners taken only 16 of those engaged with me in the charge upon the enemy's cavalry, 2 of whom were wounded, but not seriously.

On the morning of May 26 all the prisoners taken to Front Royal and vicinity who were able to walk were marched to Winchester. Privates Marcus Hoskins, Company E, John Farley, Company E, and myself, being considered as unable to be removed at this time, were left at Front Royal, where, on the 30th of May, at 10.30 a. m., we were recaptured by the Rhode Island cavalry under Major Nelson, of General Shields' division, having been a prisoner in the hands of the rebels six days.

In justice to our captors I feel it my duty to say that every attention and care were shown to our sick and wounded by their surgeons, and that no act of cruelty was perpetrated by them on any of our prisoners while we remained in durance among them.

I have the honor to be, with high esteem and respect, your most obedient servant,

WM. D. COLLINS,
*Major First Vermont Cavalry.*

General N. P. BANKS,
*Comdg. Fifth Corps d'Armée, Dept. of the Shenandoah, Va.*

---

## No. 22.

*Report of Brig. Gen. Alpheus S. Williams, U. S. Army, commanding First Division, of operations May 24–25.*

HDQRS. FIRST DIVISION, DEPT. OF THE SHENANDOAH,
*Williamsport, Md., May 27, 1862.*

MAJOR: Pursuant to department instructions I have the honor to report the operations of the First and Third Brigades of this division on the 24th and 25th instant. I beg leave to premise that the composition and strength of this division on the morning of the 24th instant, when I received orders to make preparations for an immediate evacuation of Strasburg, Va., were as follows:

First Brigade—Col. D. Donnelly, Twenty-eighth New York Volunteers, commanding: Twenty-eighth Regiment New York Volunteers, Lieut. Col. E. F. Brown; Fifth Regiment Connecticut Volunteers, Lieut. Col. G. D. Chapman; Forty-sixth Regiment Pennsylvania Volunteers, Col. J. F. Knipe.

The First Regiment Maryland Volunteers, attached to this brigade, was on duty at Front Royal. Intelligence then partly received, and since fully confirmed, had reached us on the night preceding the march that this fine regiment was nearly, if not wholly, destroyed on that day by an overwhelming force of the rebels. A company of pioneers, some 50 men, under Captain Mapes, Twenty-eighth New York Volunteers, also on duty near Front Royal, was made up of details from all the regiments. It suffered severely from the same attack, losing in killed, wounded, and missing 28 men.

Third Brigade—Col. George H. Gordon, Second Massachusetts Volunteers, commanding: Second Regiment Massachusetts Volunteers, Lieutenant-Colonel Andrews; Third Regiment Wisconsin Volunteers, Colonel Ruger; Twenty-ninth Regiment Pennsylvania Volunteers, Colonel Murphy; Twenty-seventh Regiment Indiana Volunteers, Colonel Colgrove.

From this brigade five companies were on detached duty along the line of the railroad at or near Front Royal, under Lieutenant-Colonel Parham, Pennsylvania Volunteers. No report has been received from this officer.*

Artillery—1. Best's battery, light Company F, Fourth U. S. Artillery, Lieut. F. B. Crosby, four 6-pounder guns and two 12-pounder howitzers, brass smooth-bores. 2. Cothran's battery, Company M, First New York Artillery, Lieutenant Peabody commanding, six Parrott guns. 3. Hampton's battery Maryland Artillery, Capt. R. B. Hampton commanding, four Parrott guns.

Cavalry—Five companies of First Michigan Cavalry, Col. T. F. Brodhead, numbering for duty less than 250 men.

This small command of not over 3,600 infantry present for duty, ten Parrott and six brass smooth-bore guns, not only comprised my division, but, with the cavalry, under the immediate command of Brigadier-General Hatch, and the major-general's personal escort was the entire force that could be brought to oppose this sudden, although not wholly unlooked-for, combination of the rebel columns under Jackson, Ewell, and Johnson, variously estimated by prisoners, deserters, and fugitives at from 20,000 to 30,000 men, with from fifty to sixty pieces of artillery.

Under these circumstances I hastened the execution of the major-general's order, and before daylight put in movement toward Winchester all the trains of the division, with such escort of cavalry and infantry as the smallness of the command and the uncertainty of the point of attack would warrant. I also ordered Donnelly's brigade, encamped about 6 miles above Strasburg, to join the division, in readiness for a rapid march to the rear. At the same time the Twenty-ninth Pennsylvania Volunteers, Colonel Murphy, of Gordon's brigade, with a section of artillery, was ordered to occupy and reconnoiter the

*But see p. 560.

road from Middletown toward Front Royal, and to oppose the advance of the rebels by that route at all hazards.

The main column was put in march at about 10 a. m. At Middletown I found a part of the train in some confusion from the demonstrations made by the rebel cavalry, but no considerable force presented itself until the head of our force had passed Newtown. At this point Colonel Donnelly encountered and rapidly drove away a large body of the enemy's cavalry by a spirited movement of the Forty-sixth Regiment Pennsylvania Volunteers, with a section of artillery.

Anticipating, from reports received on the route, a stout resistance in front, the leading regiments of the column moved in compact order to within 6 miles of Winchester. At this point five companies of Michigan cavalry were detached as a reconnoitering party, under Colonel Brodhead, who, though suffering from a severe illness, volunteered to mount his horse and lead his command to observe the road leading toward Winchester. At the same time reports were brought that the center and rear of the train had been seriously attacked and were further threatened. The Second Massachusetts, Twenty-seventy Indiana, and Twenty-eighth New York, with several pieces of artillery, were in succession detached for its protection. These regiments, with the artillery, engaged the enemy's infantry, cavalry, and artillery with great spirit and success. The Second Massachusetts Volunteers, Lieutenant-Colonel Andrews, was particularly engaged, and suffered considerable loss in vigorously resisting the advance of the rebels until some time after midnight. Colonel Gordon, commanding Third Brigade, personally joined this rear guard, and surpervised its operations until late in the night.

Having received a report from Colonel Brodhead that the town of Winchester was still in our possession, the head of the column was put in motion, but halted again near Kernstown, to be in position to re-enforce the rear guard should it be seriously menaced. No unfavorable reports coming in, Colonel Donnelly was ordered to occupy, with his brigade in bivouac, the ridges nearest the town, on both sides of the Front Royal road, and Colonel Gordon, with his brigade, the hills near the town, which command the road from Strasburg.

It was after dark before the first regiments were in position, and nearly 1 o'clock in the morning before the last came in. Most of the regiments had marched fully 30 miles, and some more, and all had been under arms since daylight without food, or at most with but one meal. Fortunately, some of the severe labor of outpost and picket duty was assumed by companies of the Tenth Maine Infantry and First Maryland Cavalry, though the opportunities of rest were much disturbed during the night by constant attacks upon our outposts.

Before daybreak on the morning of the 25th I received the verbal order of the major-general commanding—based upon reliable information that the enemy were in overwhelming force before us—to send back the trains of the division toward Martinsburg. At the same time I was notified of his intention to offer such resistance to the rebels as would develop with more certainty their strength and give time for our transportation wagons to move clear of the route of our retreat. The enemy gave us little time to correct our own position or to reconnoiter theirs. They opened with their rifled guns at the earliest dawn, and began the movement of their masses on both flanks for attack immediately afterward.

Before I arrived on the ground the two capable commanders of brigades had made such disposition of their troops as seemed most judicious with reference to our inferior numbers and the extent of ground we were obliged to cover.

On the right Gordon's brigade occupied the interior slopes of the hills nearest town and adjacent to the Strasburg pike. Two sections of Company M, First New York Artillery (Cothran's battery), and one section of Hampton's battery, Maryland artillery, were placed in position on the crest of the central heights.

On the extreme right five companies of Michigan cavalry (attached to the First Division) were held in reserve under cover of the hill. This body of horse were successively under command of Majors Town and Paldi, both Colonel Brodhead and Lieutenant-Colonel Copeland being prevented from assuming command by severe illness, from which they had some time been suffering.

On the left Donnelly's brigade rested its right upon a considerable elevation, which commanded the road toward Front Royal and extended its left in a crescent form, so as to observe and cover the approaches on the southeast direction. The six guns of Light Company F, Fourth U. S. Artillery, Lieutenant Crosby commanding, and one section of Company M, First New York Artillery, Lieutenant Peabody, held commanding positions near the right of this brigade. The narrow valley which intervenes between these two positions and the plain, extending in a fanlike shape beyond, was commanded by a section of Hampton's battery of Maryland Artillery, under Lieutenant Fleming, in position on a central elevation immediately in front of the town, in supporting distance of which General Hatch had ordered the principal position of his cavalry.

The opening of the cannonade was followed within half an hour by an infantry attack in force upon Donnelly's brigade. This was gallantly and successfully repulsed. One of the rebel regiments more audaciously pursuing its attack than the others (said to be the Twenty-seventh North Carolina Volunteers) was almost annihilated, first by the cross-fire of the Fifth Connecticut and Forty-sixth Pennsylvania Regiments, and afterward by one wing of the Twenty-eighth New York Regiment, in its attempt to regain the woods in its rear. This regiment left in front of our lines its dead and wounded thickly strewn over the field so near to our lines that Colonel Donnelly and several of our field officers went forward and conversed with the wounded soldiers.

After this unsuccessful infantry attack the rebels confined their efforts for a long time to artillery firing, opening their batteries from new positions and with increased number of guns. The whole atmosphere for a while was densely and obscurely filled with smoke and fog. Our artillery replied with marked vigor, and, though inferior in number of guns, was decidedly more effective, both in rapidity and precision of fire. At this time Colonel Donnelly reported to me that several rebel regiments of infantry were moving to their right, with the apparent purpose of occupying our line of retreat to the Martinsburg road, and that Lieutenant-Colonel Brown, commanding Twenty-eighth New York, had deployed his skirmishers and moved his regiment in that direction. The colors of nine rebel regiments could be seen at this moment preparing to attack simultaneously this gallant little brigade of not over 1,700 men, who awaited the trying onset with a coolness and composure of both officers and men which was most marked and extraordinary.

With the approval of the commanding general I went in person to observe the progress of events upon the right wing, and, if practicable, to bring up re-enforcements to the support of this seriously threatened part of our line. I had, however, hardly reached the central position between the two wings before a heavy infantry fire commenced on the right, and apparently extending along the whole front of Gordon's brigade, and before I could reach with all possible speed the crest of the hill upon which Gordon's brigade had moved I saw the artillery were limbering up to move to the rear. At the same time stragglers from the Twenty-seventh Indiana Regiment, on its immediate right, were slowly falling back in considerable numbers. With members of my staff I made a strong effort to rally them. The men generally obeyed orders, but before anything valuable could be accomplished the whole regiment apparently was retiring over the hill in much confusion. I observed Colonel Colgrove in their midst striving to restore order and other officers exerting themselves in the same way. The men did not run, but were rapidly retiring in disordered ranks, as if broken by a superior attack. The report of Colonel Colgrove gives, I doubt not, a true statement of this confusion.

Seeing that our right was exposed by this movement I hurried forward to the reserve of Michigan Cavalry, on the extreme right, hoping by a prompt demonstration with this force to hold the enemy in check and protect the remaining regiments of this brigade from a flank attack. Major Town, at the head of the column, spiritedly rode out to meet me, and moving his command to the front with great promptness and gallantry formed in column for charge on the crest of the hill. Meeting with a terrific fire of infantry from a whole brigade, and being menaced on the right by a large column of rebel cavalry, he was obliged to retire, which was done in good order, considering the nature of the ground and the obstacles on the line of his retreat.

Colonel Gordon held the remaining regiments of his brigade unbroken, and checked the advance of the rebels until it became evident that the attacking columns were overwhelming and would soon cut off the avenues of retreat. The regiments were then withdrawn, for the most part in column, after reaching the edge of the town, through which they passed in good order. I immediately dispatched a message to Colonel Donnelly to withdraw his brigade by the east side of the town.

When the right was giving way, I directed Captain Wilkins, my assistant adjutant-general, to endeavor to rally the Twenty-seventh Indiana Volunteers behind a stone wall in the outskirts of the town and cover the rear. This was in a measure successfully done, and the rebels were received with repeated volleys, which greatly checked their advance.

Having retired through the town, my personal efforts and that of my staff were given (for the most part of the time under the immediate supervision of the major-general commanding) to restore order to the fugitives, and to check the growing irregularity of the retreat, which the pressure of an immensely superior force was beginning to create. For this purpose I ordered Lieutenant Fleming to put a section of his artillery in battery on the first elevation near the town, which he promptly and cheerfully did. Other positions were taken by the artillery near the Martinsburg road. The straggling infantry were collected, and the rush of some flying cavalry stopped in the first woods after leaving town. In a short time all disorder was removed, and the retreat was continued with coolness and in order. It is but justice, however, here to acknowledge the important service rendered by Brigadier-General Hatch, with the cavalry under his command, not only on this occasion, but during our whole retreat, by covering the rear of our march, and by offensive demonstrations, which repeatedly deterred threatening attacks from the enemy's pursuing force.

On retiring from town a portion of the Tenth Regiment Maine Volunteers (unattached), Colonel Beal commanding, joined the column, and marching with the other regiments on the left flank, assisted in effectually guarding the road in this direction. Colonel Donnelly's judicious movement of his brigade on the right flank equally protected us in that direction. In consequence our whole march, in face of an immensely overwhelming force, was comparatively unmolested.

After a quiet halt at Martinsburg a sufficient time to give some little rest to the men the whole of the main column reached the Potomac River opposite Williamsport soon after dark, without further molestation. The command and the wagons were transported to the opposite shore during the following day.

Colonel Donnelly, after reporting at the Opequon, within 1½ miles of Martinsburg, continued his march, by order of the major-general commanding, to Dam No. 4, with the Twenty-eighth New York and Fifth Connecticut Regiments (the Forty-sixth Pennsylvania having previously joined the main column), and successfully ferried his men over the river during the night. The division trains and regimental wagons were brought off with little loss. The men of the command, however, by laying aside their knapsacks, under orders to execute rapid movements to repel various attacks which were made during the exhausting retreat, are deprived of their overcoats, blankets, and their entire kit and extra clothing, with which they should be supplied without delay, and I beg to suggest without expense to themselves.

It would give me pleasure to bring to your notice the good conduct of individual officers during these two days of severe hardships and great peril and three nights of sleepless watching; but where all, so far as my observation extended, almost without exception, did their whole duty it would seem invidious to particularize. For more particular mention of those distinguished in their respective commands I would respectfully refer you to brigade, regimental, and detachment reports forwarded herewith. I must, however, commend to the notice of the Government the good judgment, skillful management, and cool conduct of Colonel Gordon, Second Massachusetts Volunteers, and Colonel Donnelly, Twenty-eighth New York Volunteers, commanding brigades.

From the extended and widely separated order of our march in escorting and furnishing protection to several hundred wagons, and from the necessarily isolated conflicts with the enemy at various points on the march, they were necessarily left to their own discretion and judgment in the movements and formations consequent thereon. Whatever was done by them will I doubt not meet with the hearty approval and commendation of the major-general commanding, as it certainly does of mine.

I beg leave also to bring to the favorable notice of the major-general commanding the valuable services rendered by my personal staff, Capt. W. D. Wilkins, assistant adjutant-general; Capt. E. C. Beman, commissary of subsistence, and First Lieut. Samuel E. Pittman, aide-de-camp, who were with me on the field, and were most prompt and efficient not only during the engagement, but during the whole retreat from Strasburg.

Favorable notice is also made of Captain Wilkins in the report of Colonel Donnelly, to which I also refer.

Dr. Thomas Antisell, medical director of the division, charged with duties beyond the immediate command, was active and prompt in the discharge of all.

Capt. H. M. Whittelsey, assistant quartermaster, in charge of the division train, was especially serviceable, attending to its order and rapid movement.

Lieutenant Augustine, Twenty-ninth Pennsylvania Volunteers, division ordnance officer, very faithfully and untiringly discharged his responsible duties, bringing off most of his ordnance wagons under the very guns of the enemy.

Before concluding let me congratulate the major-general commanding on the successful withdrawal of an immense train of supplies and stores, protected by a small but gallant command, over a distance of nearly 70 miles of rebel territory, in the face of an active and overwhelming force of the enemy, prepared for and confident of its destruction, and entirely familiar with the field of operations and with the weakness and absence of supports of the command they were to encounter.

I inclose herewith a complete list* of the killed, wounded, and missing of the troops under my command, except that of the First Maryland Regiment, detached on duty at Front Royal, from which no report has been received. Many of the reported missing will doubtless soon rejoin their colors.

I regret to notice that the veteran Colonel Murphy, of the Twenty-ninth Pennsylvania Regiment, and that gallant young officer Major Dwight, of the Second Massachusetts Regiment, are reported among the missing, and it is thought are in the hands of the rebels.

I cannot close this report without expressing a hope that the rumor relative to the death of that courteous and brave officer Colonel Kenly, of the First Maryland Regiment, will be found incorrect, and that, though a prisoner, he may still be spared for the future service of the Union.

I have the honor to remain, your obedient servant,

A. S. WILLIAMS,
*Brig. Gen. Vols., Comdg. First Div., Dept. of the Shenandoah.*

Maj. D. D. PERKINS,
*Chief of Staff and Acting Assistant Adjutant-General.*

---

## No. 23.

***Report of Capt. William D. Wilkins, Assistant Adjutant-General, of operations May 25.***

HDQRS. FIRST DIV., DEPT. OF THE SHENANDOAH,
*Williamsport, Md., May* 29, 1862.

GENERAL: I have the honor to submit to you a report of such parts of the engagement of the 25th instant, in front of Winchester, as fell under my observation while separated from yourself, while you were engaged in reforming the line of the Third Brigade after their repulse on the hill by a largely superior force of the enemy.

Perceiving a large number of stragglers passing through the head of the main street of the town I succeeded, pursuant to your orders, given just before leaving you, in rallying about three companies of the Twenty-seventh Indiana Volunteers behind a low stone fence traversing the

* Embodied in revised statement, p. 553.

rear of the position just vacated by the artillery on the hill. This had scarcely been done before three regiments of the enemy's infantry came over the brow of the hill and poured in a heavy fire on the small force behind the fence. Our men replied with spirit and accuracy, holding their position for about eight minutes, and enabling the artillery formerly stationed on the hill to get safely to the rear. This accomplished, and seeing the uselessness of a further resistance in presence of such a superior force, I directed the men to rejoin their regiment. I am sorry I cannot designate the companies who rallied, as they are deserving of great praise.

Perceiving that the main body of our little command were retiring through the town, and fearing that the First Brigade, holding our left wing, might be cut off, I rode across the town to their position, and ordered them to retire to the rear. An order to the same effect was given almost simultaneously by Captain Scheffler, of General Banks' staff.

Colonel Donnelly withdrew the three regiments of his brigade through the streets of the city in perfect order and regularity, although menaced by a large force of cavalry on his right, by two regiments of infantry, moving through a street two squares distant on his left, and by two batteries of artillery shelling his rear. His line of retreat lay through open country and light belts of timber, about 2 miles distant from and parallel with the pike. Although continually menaced by an immensely superior force, and moving under a heavy fire from the enemy's batteries, this gallant officer, with his equally gallant command, never broke their step or changed their order of retreat, resorting to the double-quick for but two minutes, when in crossing a ravine the enemy's battery obtained an accurate range upon them.

After marching with Colonel Donnelly about 12 miles I concluded to endeavor to communicate the route of march of his command to you, and after a ride of 2 miles across the woods I succeeded in joining you.

I am, general, very respectfully, your obedient servant,

WM. D. WILKINS,
*Captain and Assistant Adjutant-General.*

Brig. Gen. ALPHEUS S. WILLIAMS,
*Commanding First Divison.*

---

## No. 24.

*Report of Capt. R. B. Hampton, Battery F, Pennsylvania Light Artillery, Chief of Artillery, of operations May* 25–28.

WILLIAMSPORT, MD., *May* 29, 1862.

I have the honor to report that after a short engagement at Strasburg, on the afternoon of the 24th, in which the four guns belonging to my battery and one howitzer belonging to Captain Best participated, and with which we succeeded in holding the enemy in check for some two hours and a half, I was compelled to withdraw the artillery, and started by a circuitous route to Winchester, under command of First Lieut. J. P. Fleming, after which I returned to Strasburg to endeavor to bring forward my battery wagon and forge, and some few men who had remained with them, ordered all wagons, men, &c., to proceed on the Middle road to Winchester, all of which we got in column about dark and proceeded toward Winchester. We halted 7 miles from Winchester, and were sent forward to the front where the roads connect, found we were cut off, and altered our course to another road parallel with the pike, and came within 3 miles of Winchester.

About 9 a. m. Sunday morning I halted the column and train, and went to the rear of Winchester with the adjutant of the Fifth New York Cavalry, and found our forces had retreated toward Martinsburg and the rebels in possession of Winchester, and we again cut off from connecting with our forces. Our column was again ordered to retire and proceed toward Martinsburg by way of the Middle road to within 5 miles of Martinsburg, and sent forward and ascertained that we were again cut off. I then consulted with Colonel De Forest and his officers, and concluded to cross the mountain and go to Hancock, Md., which place we made by marching all night, and arrived at Hancock on Monday at 11.30 a. m.; then employed the boats and crossed the train and men in safety, remaining till dawn on Tuesday, the 28th, losing in our retreat 1 man wounded and 4 missing and my battery wagon abandoned; also 1 wagon loaded with ordnance stores, and 4 mules, harness, and camp equipage.

Your obedient servant,

R. B. HAMPTON,
*Captain, Commanding Artillery.*

Brigadier-General WILLIAMS,
*Commanding First Division, Fifth Corps.*

---

## No. 25.

*Report of Lieut. James H. Peabody, Battery M, First New York Light Artillery, of operations May 23–25.*

CAMP NEAR WILLIAMSPORT.

SIR: In obedience to orders I submit the following report:

On the evening of the 23d one section, under Lieutenant Woodbury, was ordered to report to Colonel Kenly on the road to Front Royal. By some means he missed Colonel Kenly, and narrowly escaped running into the enemy's line. He then retired for the night and encamped beyond Centreville. Having no escort, his position was rather critical. He was rejoined in the morning by Colonel Murphy, with the Twenty-ninth Pennsylvania Regiment; made a reconnaissance up the road about 3 miles and then retreated, as the enemy was in force.

At 11 o'clock on the evening of the 23d the balance of the battery was ordered out and the baggage sent to the rear. One baggage wagon being absent, I was compelled to load the three on hand very heavy.

Sixty spades, twenty-five pickaxes, and ten axes left in my charge were loaded up and brought forward.

About 9 o'clock on the morning of the 24th the column moved forward. Our battery was called into action by sections several times during the day. One skirmish, very creditable to all engaged, occurred near Newtown just at dusk, under Lieutenant Hodgkins. Lieutenant Hodgkins was wounded at this time, narrowly escaping with his life, and from reliable information the enemy had one gun dismounted at this engagement.

About 9 o'clock we went into camp, remaining until daylight, when our pickets came running in, and the enemy's artillery could be distinctly heard taking position on every side. I immediately ordered one section into position on the left and two on the right, Lieutenant Woodbury taking charge of one, Lieutenant Winegar, who was sick and unfit for duty, the other. The enemy first opened on the right, and the left section opened on their infantry, which took a position behind a stone wall.

After pouring eight or ten shots with an enfilading fire on their ranks the enemy replied with artillery. The other guns on the right now opened, but the enemy's fire was directed to the left, as the position was a galling one and exposed their flank constantly. The enemy now opened on the left and the firing became general. We changed position to protect the men and horses a number of times. The brigade on the right finally retired in good order under a heavy fire, as the enemy were completely flanking them in overwhelming numbers. The two sections on the right were ordered to fall back, but first gave them two rounds of canister each. As the enemy on the right were entering the town the order came on the left to retreat, just entering in time to escape the enemy's bullets, which flew in every direction. Women and citizens of the village were actively engaged firing at our forces as they passed through.

The fight became general, and it was with difficulty that we could prevent the infantry from loading our carriages down completely. Our battery was ordered to cover the retreat, and opened on the rebels from every advantageous position. Lieutenant Woodbury took charge of two guns, and under General Hatch ably sustained the reputation of the battery.

In the retreat every officer and man behaved with particular credit. I cannot forget to mention Lieutenants Woodbury, Winegar, and Hodgkins, the former especially, who has conducted himself with unparalleled bravery during the whole movement. Sergeant Weld saved his caisson at the risk of his life, five of his horses being shot down just about the time the enemy charged. Officers and men fought nobly, and I cannot speak too highly of those concerned when all acquitted themselves with so much credit.

The baggage and accouterments (excepting some harness) of the battery were all saved, as far as I can ascertain. Seven horses were killed and 7 wounded.

Most respectfully, yours,

J. H. PEABODY,

*First Lieut., Comdg. Company M, First Regt. N. Y. Arty.*

Colonel GORDON,
*Commanding First Brigade.*

---

No. 26.

*Report of Lieut. J. Presley Fleming, Battery F, Pennsylvania Light Artillery, of operations May 24–25.*

WILLIAMSPORT, MD., *May* 29, 1862.

I have the honor to report that after taking command of the battery we left the Valley turnpike and proceeded to Winchester by the Middle, or Dirt road, and after a forced march reached Winchester at 4 o'clock on the morning of the 25th instant. Shortly after our arrival our pickets were driven in, when I immediately placed the battery in readiness for action and awaited orders.

Owing to our late arrival and the tired and weary state of both men and horses I awaited daylight to report to headquarters. The enemy's operations commencing at such an early hour I immediately proceeded to place my guns in the best position my judgment indicated they were most needed, viz: I ordered one section, under command of Lieutenant Irish, on the right, in support of Colonel Gordon's command; the other section was posted in the center and on the right of the road, and also in support of Colonel Gordon, and continued in these positions during the action, with one exception, when the section under my command was ordered to the support of Colonel Donnelly, but was countermanded before the pieces were in battery. I immediately returned to my original position and resumed firing. The position of the troops of Colonel Gordon's brigade when returning was such that the action of this section was in a great manner retarded, but the section on the right was enabled to do most excellent execution at very short ranges.

During the action of the 25th we had 6 men wounded (by musket-balls), but none of them seriously; also 3 horses. One of the horses was left on the field. Our men are all doing well. We returned to this place, taking position in the rear, and doing such service as was ordered.

I am happy to state that my men are able and in readiness to try their mettle again, under your supervision, in any similar occasion you may see fit to place them.

Very respectfully, your obedient servant,

J. PRESLEY FLEMING,
*First Lieutenant.*

Brigadier-General WILLIAMS,
*Commanding First Division, Fifth Corps.*

---

## No. 27.

***Report of Lieut. Franklin B. Crosby, Battery F, Fourth U. S. Artillery, of operations May 24–26.***

CAMP OF LIGHT COMPANY F, FOURTH ARTILLERY,
*Near Williamsport, Md., May* 27, 1862.

SIR: Pursuant to instructions I would report the operations of this battery during the movement from Strasburg, Va., to this place. Before leaving Strasburg on Saturday morning one 12-pounder howitzer was detached, by orders received from General Hatch, to remain in the rear with the cavalry. This piece returned to the battery at Winchester on Sunday morning before the action commenced, with a loss of 1 private killed, its retreat being effected as the enemy were about to surround it. About 1½ miles this side of Newtown, by order of Colonel Gordon, Lieutenant Cushing, in charge of his section, was sent to report to Colonel Colgrove, Twenty-seventh Indiana Volunteers, in order to protect the rear of the column. He assisted in driving back the advancing rebel cavalry and infantry, which was accomplished without any loss to our men. This section also rejoined the battery early on Sunday morning.

Before the commencement of the action the battery was in position, pursuant to Colonel Donnelly's orders, on Potato Hill, between the roads to Strasburg and Front Royal, and about a quarter of a mile from town.

About 4.30 a. m. the enemy opened fire from a point where the Front Royal road ascends a slight hill, about 1,800 yards from our position. They did not obtain our range, and their firing from this point was not good. About the same time they opened from some guns on our right, and threw shell into us rapidly and with great precision. We replied to these guns, and also threw spherical case and shell at two or three pieces posted on the Front Royal road at about 750 yards' range, and on the infantry advancing on Colonel Donnelly's brigade through the fields on each side of the road. Under the fire of the infantry and artillery the enemy withdrew. A section in charge of Lieutenant Muhlenberg was then sent to strengthen our extreme left and another section placed in reserve. The enemy again advancing, the section under Lieutenant Cushing opened fire on them and on a battery in their support, but with what effect it is difficult to state on account of the fog and smoke which so generally prevailed. Orders were then received to withdraw toward Martinsburg, which was done in good order, all the caissons being placed in advance after leaving the town.

The practice of the opposing batteries was very accurate, and at one time we were exposed to a severe cross-fire. Notwithstanding this, no injury was sustained in men or material while in position on the hill. Upon reaching Martinsburg the battery was placed in position on the west of town, orders to that effect having been received from General Williams, but it was soon moved off by his orders to the Potomac, without an opportunity of firing.

After remaining for some time near the river I received instructions from Major Perkins to move the battery across. In the fording two pieces were left in the river, the horses being so entangled in the harness that it became necessary to cut them out. The pieces were soon after brought over. The depth of the water being so great the ammunition was wet and rendered almost entirely useless.

After crossing the guns were placed to command the south bank of the river, but were soon withdrawn to the present camp, by order of Captain Scheffler, of General Banks' staff.

Our loss is 1 private killed near Strasburg, Va., 2 wounded, both having been run over on the road this side of Winchester, and being now in hospital doing very well, and 2 missing, 1 sent to hospital in Winchester on Sunday morning, he having been sick for some time previous, and the acting hospital steward in charge of the ambulance, which was also lost.

I very much regret to state that Dr. Philip Adolphus, assistant surgeon, U. S. Army, attached to this battery, is missing. When last seen he was in care of the wounded, having refused to leave his duty to secure his personal safety.

One horse was killed by a round shot this side of Winchester and in crossing the Potomac 2 horses were drowned. Two sets of harness, three or four buckets, axes, &c., were also lost. On the route from Strasburg no wagons or mules were lost, nor were any tents, stores, subsistence, or forage left behind or destroyed.

None of the men left the guns during the action, and all crossed the Potomac together on Monday morning, their behavior in every respect being all that could be desired. Lieutenants Muhlenberg and Cushing deserve mention for their coolness and self-possession. The only regret expressed, and I am sure not by myself alone, was that our guns were not of greater range and could not be of more effective service.

I am, sir, very respectfully, your most obedient servant,

FRANKLIN B. CROSBY,
*First Lieut., Fourth Artillery, Comdg. Co. F, Fourth Artillery.*

Capt. WILLIAM D. WILKINS,
*Assistant Adjutant-General.*

---

## No. 28.

*Report of Col. Dudley Donnelly, Twenty-eighth New York Infantry, commanding First Brigade, of operations May 24–26.*

HDQRS. 1ST BRIG., 1ST DIV., DEPT. OF THE SHENANDOAH,
*Williamsport, Md., May* 29, 1862.

GENERAL: In obedience to orders received from you, on the morning of the 24th of May instant, at 1 o'clock, the First Brigade, comprising the Forty-sixth Pennsylvania, Twenty-eighth New York, and Fifth Connecticut Volunteers (the First Maryland being at Front Royal on detached service), and Best's battery of Fourth U. S. Artillery, broke up their encampment at Round Hill and marched to Strasburg, at which place we halted for one hour. I was then directed by Major-General Banks to march to Middletown on the road to Winchester, a large portion of our train having preceded us in that direction.

As the head of the column approached Middletown a portion of the train was met returning in great confusion and disorder, the guards reporting that they were attacked by the rebels in front. The trains were ordered by me to move into a field. The brigade advanced rapidly through the village, when a large body of the enemy's cavalry appeared on the right, half a mile distant, partially covered by woods. The brigade was halted, and two companies of the Forty-sixth Pennsylvania Volunteers were thrown forward as skirmishers, and a section of Battery M, First New York Artillery, supported by the Forty-sixth Regiment Pennsylvania Volunteers, under Col. J. F. Knipe, were advanced in that direction. Five companies of the rebel cavalry appeared in an open field immediately in front of a piece of woods, and our artillery opened upon them. The enemy retired, after receiving a few well-directed shots, to the woods in their rear. The skirmishers advanced and drove the enemy from the woods into and across another open field, where the artillery and the Forty-sixth Pennsylvania Volunteers advanced and occupied the position. The artillery again opened upon them. Our line advanced, the rebels retreating, notwithstanding re-enforcements of cavalry were observed to join them.

At this point, having driven them back 2 miles from the pike, the troops engaged returned to the main road by your order, and our march was continued toward Winchester, the train following in the rear. When within 5 miles of Winchester I detached the Twenty-eighth New York Volunteers and a section of artillery to return to Middletown, by your order, to support General Hatch, an attack having been made in the rear of the train. With the remainder of the force under my command I marched forward, and, by your direction, took a position on the Front Royal road 1 mile from Winchester.

It being dark we could not select our position with care. The Forty-sixth took position on the right of the road, the Fifth Connecticut Volunteers on the left, Best's battery on the hill immediately in the rear. Ascertaining that the hills in front were picketed by two companies of the Tenth Maine and some cavalry the men were allowed to bivouac, but could not rest, being without blankets, overcoats, or knapsacks, and having little or no food.

During the night the enemy kept continually firing on the pickets, but met with such determined resistance that our line remained undisturbed till soon after daylight, when the Twenty-eighth New York Volunteers arrived on the ground. Before the men had prepared their breakfast the enemy drove in the pickets with a large force of infantry and artillery. The regiments rapidly formed in line, the Fifth Connecticut Volunteers deploying from column of companies in the face of a severe fire. The enemy attacked the center, pouring in upon it a storm of shot and shell, and at the same time moved three regiments to the left, menacing our left flank. They were met firmly by the Fifth Connecticut and Forty-sixth Pennsylvania Volunteers at the center, and after a short but decisive conflict fled in disorder, leaving a large number of dead and wounded on the field. As they retired a section of Best's battery, under Lieutenant Cushing, poured in upon them a deadly fire of grape and canister, mowing them down at each discharge. They attempted to rally again as they moved toward the left, but received a volley from the Twenty-eighth New York Volunteers, which completed their entire rout.

Lieutenant-Colonel Brown, with the Twenty-eighth New York, moved rapidly to the left, and by skillfully disposing of his force effectually prevented our flank being turned. The rebel infantry withdrew to their original line on the hill, and made no further attack or demonstration on our position.

A heavy fog having settled over the ground the firing ceased on both sides for almost half an hour. As the mist cleared away the enemy opened upon us from two batteries, which was promptly responded to by our batteries, re-enforced by a section of Battery M, First New York Artillery, under command of Lieutenant Peabody. At the same time we became aware that the right wing of the division was attacked. The rebel batteries continued to shell the left wing, and although their pieces were well served our men stood firm.

I received orders from General Banks through Captain d'Hauteville to retire, as the right of our division was turned. I immediately gave orders to retreat. The brigade retired in good order, taking the right of the pike and a half a mile distant therefrom toward Martinsburg, the head of the column being opposite the rear of the other wing of our division.

We continued to march in this order to Bunker Hill, pursued by the artillery and cavalry of the enemy, near which place the Forty-sixth Pennsylvania fell into the rear of the right wing on the pike.

At this point the sick men and stragglers, who numbered about 50, while resting on the ground, were suddenly surrounded by three companies of cavalry and called upon to surrender, but falling quickly into line they delivered a galling fire into their midst; then, fixing bayonets, they charged and drove them out of the woods. The rebels left 6 dead on the field and we captured 1 prisoner. We were not pursued any farther by the enemy.

On arriving at the Charlestown road opposite Martinsburg I communicated with Major-General Banks, and received orders to move on. We took the road to Dam No. 4, at which place we arrived about 10 o'clock p. m. Finding the river too high to ford we marched 3 miles up the river to Jameson's Ferry, where a boat was found capable of crossing 30 men. After throwing out a strong rear guard, I allowed the men to lie down and sleep, only awaking sufficient numbers to keep the ferry busy.

I am much indebted to Lieutenant-Colonel Chapman, Fifth Connecticut Volunteers, and Captain Bowen, Twenty-eighth New York Volunteers, for their untiring exertions in assisting me in crossing the men with the small means at our command.

At 4 a. m., the entire force having been crossed, the field officers of the regiments, accompanied by the brigade officers, passed the river. The entire crossing was effected without accident or panic after a march of 43 miles without rest or food for twenty-four hours.

The commanders of the regiments, Col. J. F. Knipe, Forty-sixth Pennsylvania Volunteers, who was slightly wounded; Lieut. Col. E. F. Brown, Twenty-eighth New York, and Lieut. Col. George D. Chapman, Fifth Connecticut Volunteers, and the officers and men of their commands, are entitled to great credit for the courage and coolness displayed by them in the face of a superior force.

Owing to the untiring exertions of the officers and coolness and good discipline of the men I was enabled to conduct the retreat in good order and without loss.

I would particularly mention the gallant conduct of Capt. E. A. Bowen, Twenty-eighth New York Volunteers, who commanded the rear guard and effectually protected our retreat. Lieut. E. L. Whitman, of the Forty-sixth Pennsylvania, attached to my staff, alone carried the orders to the different regiments through the thickest of the fight, and is entitled to my warmest approbation. Capt. W. D. Wilkins, assistant adjutant-general First Division, who brought the order to retreat, was unable to rejoin the right wing, and remained with the First Brigade. By his coolness and personal bravery he encouraged the officers and men and rendered valuable assistance, as I had but one staff officer present.

The train of the entire brigade, numbering over 100 heavily loaded wagons, was brought safely through with small loss by the untiring energy and skill of Lieut. C. L. Skeels, acting brigade quartermaster. The whole force of the First Brigade amounted to less than 1,700 men. The reported loss up to this time in killed is 3; wounded, 47; missing, 251. This will be materially lessened, as numerous parties have been heard from who crossed the river at different points above and below this place. The force of the enemy opposed to the left wing was nine regiments of infantry and two batteries of artillery.

I hope the First Brigade has done no discredit to the discipline attained while under your command.

I am, respectfully, your obedient servant,

D. DONNELLY,
*Colonel, Twenty-eighth New York Vols., Commanding.*

Brig. Gen. ALPHEUS S. WILLIAMS,
*Commanding First Division.*

## No. 29.

*Report of Lieut. Col. George D. Chapman, Fifth Connecticut Infantry, of operations May* 25.

HDQRS. FIFTH REGIMENT CONNECTICUT VOLUNTEERS,
FIRST BRIG., FIRST DIV., FIFTH ARMY CORPS,
*Williamsport, Md., May* 28, 1862.

COLONEL: I have the honor to report as follows concerning the late battle at Winchester, in which this regiment was engaged:

About 5 o'clock Sunday morning, as the men were rising from their sleep and heating their coffee in the field which we entered late the night before, a shell suddenly fell amongst them. This was followed by others in rapid succession. The men quickly seized their muskets and fell into line as calmly as if on parade. The inquiry was then sent back whether we should hold the spot or advance. Before receiving a reply I ordered the regiment to a hollow in the field next to the rear, which was done by the right of companies to the rear in good order.

The enemy's infantry soon appeared on the hill in front, charging directly upon us. Companies A and F immediately moved forward beyond the fence and delivered their fire with effect upon the enemy, now within a few rods. The whole battalion then moved up to their line, and, delivering three well-directed volleys, mowed down the enemy in scores, shooting away their flag each time. At the third volley Companies I and B delivered a cross-fire by a half-wheel to the right. The enemy broke and ran in confusion. The order then came from yourself for the regiment to fall back to a line of stone wall in the rear of the field next behind. During this movement Company D deployed as skirmishers, to hold the line we were leaving. A fog then settled down, and for half an hour firing ceased. As it lifted I saw at some distance a large force of the enemy moving by the right flank to turn our left. Our skirmishers fired upon them, but their movement remained unchecked till a few shell from our artillery forced them back. After this their infantry paid but little attention to us, but their artillery poured a heavy fire of shell about us from their right and left batteries as we lay behind the wall.

About 9 o'clock, our regiment being in advance of the other two of the brigade, I ordered it back to their line, and while dressing the ranks received the order to retreat. Company D having been called in, the retreat commenced in closed files at quick-march through the streets on the east side of the city under a heavy fire of artillery in the rear and frequent shots on our flank from citizens and even women in the houses. After leaving the city the regiment fell into the column of the brigade, and by a forced march of 43 miles through by-roads reached the Potomac at 11 o'clock p. m. The last man of the regiment crossed at Dunn's Ferry, 7 miles by land below Williamsport, at 1.20 a. m. Monday afternoon we moved by canal-boat to Williamsport, where we now lie in camp, 537 men, subject to your orders.

During the fight and retreat both officers and men acted calmly and readily. Where all have done exactly as ordered it seems invidious to discriminate; still I desire to especially notice the following officers for gallant conduct: Captain Betts, whom I have since learned to be severely wounded; Captain Lane and Lieutenant Dutton, Acting Regimental Quartermaster Lieutenant Rice, since missing, and Adjutant Blake rendered me efficient service in the field.

I inclose my adjutant's report of killed, wounded, and missing.*

I am, very respectfully, your most obedient servant,

GEO. D. CHAPMAN,
*Lieut. Col., Comdg. Fifth Regiment Connecticut Volunteers.*

Col. D. DONNELLY,
*28th N. Y. V., Comdg. 1st Brig., 1st Div., 5th Army Corps, Williamsport, Md.*

---

## No. 30.

*Report of Col. George L. Beal, Tenth Maine Infantry, of operations May 24–26.*

HEADQUARTERS TENTH MAINE VOLUNTEERS,
*Martinsburg, June 3, 1862.*

GENERAL: In accordance with Special Orders, No. —, Headquarters First Brigade, First Division, Department of Shenandoah, Williamsport, Md., May 31, 1862, I have the honor to submit the following report:

In order to give a connected account of the events of Sunday and Monday, May 25 and 26, I must refer to the movements of my command on the 24th of May. Early in the morning of Saturday I posted Companies C and I as pickets on the Front Royal road, together with a detachment of Maryland Cavalry. The enemy made their appearance on the road about 10 o'clock p. m. 24th of May. Frequent skirmishes occurred during the night.

About 6 o'clock a. m. of Sunday the enemy advanced in force on our pickets and drove them in. The companies then repaired to their quarters. Soon after I gave orders for the regiment to be formed in line near the headquarters, and at 7.30 took up a line of march toward Martinsburg. Soon after leaving Winchester the enemy made their appearance in our rear and commenced throwing shell into our column. The first shell was fired at precisely 8 o'clock. This one exploded far above us and to our right. They soon obtained correct range, and the remainder fired fell into our line. Had they continued their firing they must have injured us severely. Here most of our casualties occurred. One man was mortally wounded and 3 others slightly.

We continued our march without further interruption from the enemy's fire. About 2 o'clock p. m. we reached Martinsburg. A short stop was here made, and then we pushed on to Williamsport, arriving there about 9 o'clock p. m. A portion of our troops crossed over, but most of them, tired and jaded, remained on the Virginia side. Early in the morning we crossed over and occupied the quarters assigned us in Williamsport.

Our casualties are as follows: Six wounded and 77 missing. This number is being reduced daily.

I would here make especial mention of the valuable service rendered by Company I, under command of Captain Furbish, and Company C, commanded by Captain Jordan. The determined manner in which

*Embodied in revised statement, p. 553.

they held the position assigned them no doubt kept the enemy at bay until morning, and prevented them from advancing on our troops until we had an opportunity to retreat. Had they pushed on in force during the night the consequence to our left wing must have been very serious.

A detachment of Maine cavalry, under command of Lieutenant Colonel Douty, covered our retreat in a handsome manner, and no doubt contributed in a great measure to our safety.

Very respectfully, your obedient servant,

GEO. L. BEAL,
*Colonel, Commanding Tenth Maine Volunteers.*

Brig. Gen. S. W. CRAWFORD.

---

## No. 31.

*Reports of Lieut. Col. Edwin F. Brown, Twenty-eighth New York Infantry, of operations May 24–25.*

HDQRS. TWENTY-EIGHTH REGIMENT NEW YORK VOLS.,
*Camp near Williamsport, Md., May* 28, 1862.

SIR: I have the honor to report that on the morning of the 25th instant the regiment under my command took up its position in line of battle on the extreme left of the brigade at about 4 o'clock. A brisk fire from the rebel batteries was soon opened upon us with shot and shell. Our ambulances immediately moved to the rear and the position of our regiment was somewhat altered. Immediately after this a strong column of infantry was seen advancing, and was when discovered within 200 yards of us.

At this time the Twenty-eighth was standing in line of battle directly behind a stone wall, and about 10 rods in rear of the Fifth Connecticut Volunteers, who were standing in column by companies, the men making coffee. A moment later the head of the column of rebels opened fire on the Twenty-eighth New York and the Forty-sixth Pennsylvania, not yet having seen the Fifth Connecticut, who were stationed on low ground. This fire we immediately returned over the heads of the Fifth Connecticut. We continued firing until the Fifth deployed in line of battle, when we immediately moved by our left flank some distance farther to the left, intending to occupy an orchard. We advanced for this purpose, so that the line of battle of the brigade was crescent-shaped, the Fifth Connecticut occupying the center, the Forty-sixth the right.

When the left of the regiment was within about 10 rods of the orchard the enemy were seen moving to their right, and at this short range we poured a volley from the left wing of the regiment with tremendous effect. At this time the fog and smoke were so dense as to make it impossible to see over a few rods. Captain Bush was ordered by Major Cook to advance a platoon as skirmishers on our left to find the enemy. While the skirmishers were advancing Private Bartram, acting as my orderly, being mounted, rode to the top of the hill behind which the rebel column had retreated. Owing to the smoke and fog he was unable to see them until within less than six rods. A volley was fired at him, and strange to say only one ball took effect, wounding the horse slightly. Bartram reported the enemy as no doubt trying to outflank us on the left wing (their right). The position of the regi ment was again changed to counteract this movement. A strong position was taken behind a stone wall, where we waited, expecting the advance of the enemy every moment, but he, taking advantage of the fog and no doubt being satisfied with the morning's work, withdrew to a safe distance. When the fog lifted they were seen in great force about a half or three-fourths of a mile from us, near their batteries, with a line of skirmishers in front, coming on with great caution.

About this time, the right wing of our army having given way, we were ordered to retreat, which order we obeyed in good order under a heavy fire of shot and shell. The aim of the rebel batteries was wonderful, but not more so than the escape of the men, who seemed to bear charmed lives, only 1 man being wounded. We continued our retreat, keeping to the right of the pike. The rebels, being considerably in advance of us on the pike, kept up a brisk fire with their artillery, as opportunity offered, for several miles. When near Bunker Hill their cavalry made a dash at our rear, but were handsomely beaten off and so badly used that they troubled us no more during the day.

We continued our march, reaching the Potomac at Dam No. 4 about dark, a distance of 45 miles from Winchester. Here we hoped to be able to ford the river, but found it impracticable. We again resumed the march, proceeding up the river about 1½ miles, where we found a ferry-boat capable of carrying about 30 men. With this and a small boat by daylight on the morning of the 26th we were all crossed over without panic, confusion, fear, or loss of life.

Owing to the scarcity of commissioned officers Sergeant Casey, of Company A, had command of the rear guard of skirmishers, which duty he performed most admirably and with great credit to himself, as did most of the detail and several volunteers. We were the last regiment on the field, and the pursuit on the pike was pushed with such vigor that we found ourselves considerably in the rear of those on the pike, which made it necessary for us to avoid Martinsburg, which was done under your immediate direction with consummate skill.

Officers and men behaved with admirable coolness during the entire engagement, and during the retreat with wonderful and deliberate energy. Many instances of complete exhaustion occurred, and in several cases the men have shown great skill in eluding the scouts and in many cases made a defense successfully.

I would be delighted to make a special mention of some cases of valor and skill, but my heart is too full of gratitude to all, both officers and men, to disparage one by a more favorable mention of another. The men who were compelled to drop to the rear from exhaustion are coming in singly and in squads.

The reports at the present time show: Killed, none; wounded, 2; missing, 79; and there are strong hopes of reducing this number considerably.* About 60 men have crossed at Harper's Ferry, and all have not yet reported.

We have great reason to be grateful to kind Providence and applaud the skill and energy of our commanding officers for the miraculous escape of our men from utter annihilation.

E. F. BROWN,

*Lieut. Col., Comdg. Twenty-eighth Regiment New York Vols.*

Col. D. DONNELLY,

*28th N. Y. Vols., Comdg. 1st Brig., 1st Div., Dept. Shenandoah.*

---

* See revised statement, p. 553.

HDQRS. TWENTY-EIGHTH REGIMENT NEW YORK VOLS.,
*Williamsport, Md., May* 29, 1862.

SIR: In addition to my former report of the battle at and retreat from Winchester I beg leave to submit this additional report of the skirmish with the rebel artillery and cavalry on the afternoon and evening of Saturday:

About 4 o'clock I received orders to counter-march and return to New town from near Kernstown and report to General Hatch. This we did cheerfully, accompanied by the Second Regiment Massachusetts Volunteers and two sections of artillery, one of Best's and one of Cothran's, and the Twenty-seventh Indiana Regiment. Two companies (B and G), under command of Captain Bush, were deployed on the right as skirmishers, and two on the left (D and C), under command of Captain Bowen. When about 1 mile from Newtown a brisk firing of artillery was commenced by the rebels, which was promptly responded to by ours. They (the rebels) were soon driven from their position, and retired beyond Newtown. We followed them up, and the rebels planted a battery about half a mile beyond the town. One section (Cothran's) took position on the right of the town, supported by Captain Bush and Captain Hardie, and one section on the left, supported by two companies of the Twenty-seventh Indiana. Captain Bowen extended his line of skirmishers nearly a mile on the left and discovered a body of cavalry in the woods, with whom they exchanged several shots. The cavalry concluded it better to keep proper distance, and retired. The main body remained in the town. The artillery practice was vigorously kept up till dusk, when we were ordered to retire toward Winchester. Our skirmishers were deployed as before, and we retired in column by platoon. As we passed the wagons which were disabled and the pontoons left in the highway, I detailed Lieut. George Ellicott, Company F, and 10 men to burn and destroy them. This was successfully done, though frequent shots were exchanged.

We arrived safely at Winchester at 11 p. m., considerably wearied by our day's march, and at 4 o'clock on Sunday morning we took our position in line of battle, as per report previously sent forward.

Very respectfully submitted.

E. F. BROWN,
*Lieut. Col., Comdg. Twenty-eighth Regiment New York Vols.*

Col. D. DONNELLY,
*28th N. Y. Vols., Comdg. 1st Brig., 1st Div., Dept. Shenandoah.*

---

No. 32.

*Report of Col. Joseph F. Knipe, Forty-sixth Pennsylvania Infantry, of operations May* 24–26.

HDQRS FORTY-SIXTH REGIMENT PENNSYLVANIA VOLS.,
*Adjutant's Office, Camp near Williamsport, Md., May* 30, 1862.

DEAR SIR: In accordance with orders received at 3 o'clock a. m. Saturday, May 24, my command was immediately put in readiness to move, and, with the regimental train ahead, reached the turnpike leading to Strasburg at 4.30 o'clock a. m. So prompt were our movements that no time was taken to issue rations, and save a little hard bread, which a few of the men secured, their haversacks were entirely empty.

Pushing on at a rapid rate until we reached Strasburg we were joined by the remainder of General Banks' command, when, with the whole train, numbering some 500 wagons, in front, we again took up the line of march for Winchester. When within a short distance of Middletown an alarm in front caused a stampede of teamsters, sutlers, and civilians, who came rushing back upon us in the wildest confusion.

Receiving orders from Colonel Donnelly to hasten to the front, I ordered my regiment to unsling knapsacks, load at will, and, marching through Middletown at a double-quick, halted about half a mile beyond the town.

Again ordered forward, we reached Newtown, through which we moved at a double-quick, driving the enemy's cavalry before us, and filing to the right at the end of the town I threw Companies A and K forward as skirmishers and drew up in line of battle in a woods, supporting a section of artillery, which shelled the enemy's cavalry and drove them into a woods about a mile beyond.

Again ordered forward, we arrived at Winchester at 9 o'clock p. m., taking position on the Front Royal road about a mile from the town and bivouacked, my men being entirely without blankets, overcoats, or food.

During the night heavy firing from the pickets in front kept us constantly on the alert, and before daybreak I paraded my regiment under arms.

At 4.30 a. m. our pickets were drawn in, and immediately after a battery of rifled pieces on a hill about a mile distant opened a brisk fire upon us. Seeing the exposed condition of my regiment I moved behind a piece of rising ground, and closing column in mass was comparatively sheltered from the enemy's shell, keeping a sharp lookout, ready to deploy should the infantry of the enemy make their appearance. Whilst moving to the rear, however, a large body of infantry, under cover of the rising ground behind which we had taken position, approached to within 100 yards, and from behind a stone wall opened a heavy fire upon us. Deploying my regiment, a severe engagement ensued, when, finding their position gave them great advantage, my regiment being in an open field, I ordered a charge to be made, and drove them back with terrible slaughter. As they fell back in confusion the Fifth Connecticut Volunteers, on our left, poured into them a most galling fire, which did great execution.

At this juncture I received orders to support a section of Best's artillery on an eminence in our rear, and accordingly fell back midst a raking fire of shot and shell to the position assigned me, which we held securely until we received orders to retreat, when we moved through the town in perfect order, the citizens firing upon us from the houses in an inhuman manner.

Seeing large numbers of the enemy within a short distance of our rear I halted the regiment, determined to drive them back, when the number of stragglers (soldiers and citizens) between us caused me to refrain.

After a fatiguing march under fire of the enemy's artillery, who pursued us within 3 miles of Martinsburg, during which the regiment was twice halted and drawn up in line of battle, temporarily checking the vigor of the pursuit, we reached the Potomac opposite Williamsport at 10 o'clock p. m.

To the field officers, Lieutenant-Colonel Selfridge, Major Mathews, and Adjutant Boyd, I am particularly indebted for the prompt and efficient manner in which they supported me, inspiring the men with their own courage and determination. To the company officers and men under their immediate commands too much praise cannot be bestowed for their steadiness under the terrible fire to which they were so long exposed. The gallantry which they exhibited entitled them to a success which the overwhelming numbers arrayed against us rendered hopeless.

For the safety of my regimental train I am indebted to the untiring exertions of Lieut. G. B. Cadwalader, regimental quartermaster, who succeeded in saving the whole train.

Very respectfully, yours, &c.,

JOS. F. KNIPE,

*Colonel, Comdg. Forty-sixth Regiment Pennsylvania Volunteers.*

Capt. BENJAMIN FLAGLER,

*Asst. Adjt. Gen., First Brig., First Div., Dept. Shenandoah.*

---

## No. 33.

*Reports of Col. George H. Gordon, Second Massachusetts Infantry, commanding Third Brigade, of operations May* 24–25.

HEADQUARTERS THIRD BRIGADE,
*Camp near Williamsport, Md., May* 28, 1862.

GENERAL: I take the first moment of leisure from arduous military duties to report in brief the events of an engagement of forces under my command with the enemy on the march of the Fifth Army Corps, under General Banks, from Strasburg to Winchester, on the 24th of May:

Disastrous news from fugitives of the First Maryland Regiment, received the night of the 23d instant, made it apparent that a very large force of the enemy threatened us at Strasburg. The precautionary order to pack and send to the rear my brigade and regimental trains was complied with. They started for Winchester at night, and were thus saved.

The morning of the 24th brought little cheer. The worst reports were confirmed. Frequent reconnaissances during the night and morning of the 24th developed that a very large force of the enemy threatened to surround us at Strasburg. At 10 a. m. my brigade was ordered, in conjunction with the First Brigade of your division, to move toward Newtown *en route* to Winchester, to check an approach of the enemy from that direction. No enemy being found at Middletown or within 4 miles in direction of Front Royal, our march was continued. Our column moved on toward Strasburg in good order, preceded by an immense train of wagons and followed by many that could not be prepared for moving the night before. At 2 p. m. reports from the rear reached us that the train had been attacked by the enemy; that we were entirely cut off from our rear guard; that many wagons had been captured; that the enemy were pursuing us. The sound of his guns we could distinctly hear. With the view of uniting the train, if possible, and with the sanction of General Banks, I proceeded with two regiments of my brigade and two sections of artillery to attack the enemy and do what I might for the rescue of our rear guard and baggage. My force was increased by a third regiment, ordered by General Banks to report to General Hatch, commanding rear guard, if practicable. This regiment, the Twenty-eighth New York, Lieutenant-Colonel Brown, fell also under my command. Upon arriving near Newtown I found some confusion in the trains, and saw perhaps six or seven wagons that had been overset and abandoned.

The Twenty-seventh Indiana, of my brigade (previously ordered with a section of artillery to this point), I found drawn up in line of battle. The rebel battery and force were said to be at the town, distant beyond about half a mile. I made disposition to attack them with artillery and infantry, holding one regiment in reserve for further use. The Second Massachusetts, under Lieutenant-Colonel Andrews, with skirmishers thrown to its front, covered the approaches to the town, supported by its own reserve and the Twenty-eighth New York.

The rebel force was at once driven from the town. A heavy fire of artillery was opened upon my command from a rebel battery, to which we replied with spirit, driving the enemy from his position. After an hour or more of skirmishing, with continued firing of artillery on both sides, I had driven the enemy from Newtown, which I held.

At this time I was joined by General Hatch, who had by a circuitous pathway been able to join the first half of the column. He at once confirmed my fears that the enemy in strong force had taken a portion of the rear half of our train, with such stores as might have been left at Cedar Creek and such forces as had not happily escaped. I became convinced of the impossibility of making headway against the force in my front and I much feared being surrounded, as large bodies of cavalry were seen in the distance toward Winchester, my then rear.

It was now about 8 o'clock; General Hatch was safe; the enemy driven from Newtown; all our train in advance of the center protected from further assault. I determined to withdraw, and, as I could not transport, to burn the 7 or 8 abandoned wagons. This was accordingly done.

The difficult task of keeping the enemy at bay was confided to the Second Massachusetts Regiment, Lieutenant-Colonel Andrews. To aid him I ordered cavalry and one section of artillery to the rear. The column thus proceeded to join the main body at Winchester. Fearful of an attempt on the part of the enemy to seize the road where it enters Winchester (and which they did not an hour after the Second Massachusetts passed), I made rapid progress, reaching the environs of Winchester at about 12 o'clock at night. Frequent reports from Lieutenant-Colonel Andrews advised me of the good progress of the rear, also that they were somewhat annoyed with skirmishing cavalry. I sent him such additional force as I thought might be necessary, but becoming impatient at his non-arrival I went out with an orderly to meet him, and arrived at the head of the regiment at about 1 o'clock. Rather a severe skirmish was then going on between the rear company of the regiment, Captain Underwood, and the enemy. Their temerity punished and their advance checked, we reached our encampment at 2.30 a. m.

The men of my brigade were without shelter, many of them without rations, having imprudently, though intending to offer better service, laid aside their knapsacks. Their capture by the enemy deprived them of food.

The Second Massachusetts Regiment made this day a march of 30 miles, nearly 10 miles of which was a continued running fight. The service performed by this regiment on this occasion reflects the greatest credit upon both officers and men, never shaken by the discharge of artillery and musketry into their ranks. This noble regiment moved in column along the road, undismayed by an enemy they could not see, firing at the flashes of rebel rifles, supporting their wounded and carrying their dead. For more than 8 miles they guarded the rear of the column; then with two and a half hours' slumber upon the earth, uncovered and unprotected, they were aroused by the cannon and musketry that ushered in the battle of Winchester, to do their part in the heroic struggle of that day.

I refer for particulars of this day's duty to the report of Lieut. Col. George L. Andrews, hereto appended.

I cannot too strongly praise the coolness and discretion of this officer upon this trying occasion.

Respectfully,

GEO. H. GORDON,
*Col. Second Massachusetts Regiment, Comdg. Third Brigade.*

General ALPHEUS S. WILLIAMS,
*Commanding First Division, Fifth Army Corps.*

---

HEADQUARTERS THIRD BRIGADE,
*Camp near Williamsport, Md.*

CAPTAIN: Agreeably to instructions received from headquarters of the division, I have the honor to report the movements of my brigade in an engagement with the enemy on the 25th instant in front of and less than a third of a mile from the town of Winchester, Va. At dawn in the morning I received information through the officer commanding the pickets that the enemy in large numbers were driving them in and approaching the town. I immediately formed my brigade in line of battle, the right resting upon the commanding ridge, the left extending into the valley. The ridge surrounds the town, which it holds as in a basin. It is less than one-third of a mile distant, and presents many key-points for positions. I placed my artillery, Battery M, of First New York, composed of six 6-pounder Parrotts, under Lieutenant Peabody, upon the ridge, and thus awaited further developments.

About 5 a. m. skirmishers from the Second Massachusetts, on the right and crest of the hill, became sharply engaged. At about the same time I directed the battery to open upon the columns of the enemy evidently moving into position just to the right and front of my center. This was done with admirable effect. The columns disappeared over the crest. For more than an hour a fire of shell and canister from several rebel batteries was directed upon my position. My brigade, being somewhat protected by a ravine, suffered but little loss. The fire of our skirmishers and the spirited replies of the battery, with heavy musketry and artillery firing on our left in Donnelly's brigade, were the only marked features of the contest until after 6 a. m.

At about 6.30, perhaps nearer 7 a. m. large bodies of infantry could be seen making their way in line of battle toward my right. They moved under cover of the dense wood, thus concealing somewhat their numbers. I directed the Twenty-ninth Pennsylvania Regiment, Colonel Murphy, and the Twenty-seventh Indiana Regiment, Colonel Colgrove, to change position from the left to the right of line, holding the Second Massachusetts, Lieutenant-Colonel Andrews, first on the right, in the center, the Third Wisconsin Regiment, Colonel Ruger, forming the left. This movement I had hardly completed, despite a new battery which opened upon my line, when three large battalions of infantry, moving in order of battle, came out from their cover and approached my brigade. They were received with a destructive fire of musketry, poured in from all parts of my line that could reach them. Confident in their numbers and relying upon larger sustaining bodies (suspicions of which behind the covering timbers in our front were surely confirmed), the enemy's lines moved on, but little shaken by our fire. At the same time, in our front, a long line of infantry showed themselves, rising the crest of the hills just beyond our position. My little brigade, numbering in all just 2,102, in another moment would have been overwhelmed. On its right, left, and center immensely superior columns were pressing. Not another man was available; not a support to be found in the remnant of his army corps left General Banks. To withdraw was now possible; in another moment it would have been too late.

At this moment I should have assumed the responsibility of requesting permission to withdraw, but the right fell back under great pressure, which compelled the line to yield. I fell back slowly, but generally in good order, the Second Massachusetts, in column of companies, moving by flank; the Third Wisconsin, in line of battle, moving to the rear. On every side above the surrounding crest surged the rebel forces. A sharp and withering fire of musketry was opened by the enemy from the crest upon our center, left, and right. The yells of a victorious and merciless foe were above the din of battle, but my command was not dismayed. The Second Massachusetts halted in a street of the town to reform its line, then pushed on with the column, which, with its long train of baggage wagons, division, brigade, and regimental, was making its way in good order toward Martinsburg.

My retreating column suffered serious loss in the streets of Winchester. Males and females vied with each other in increasing the number of their victims, by firing from the houses, throwing hand grenades, hot water, and missiles of every description. The hellish spirit of murder was carried on by the enemy's cavalry, who followed to butcher, and who struck down with saber and pistol the hapless soldier, sinking from fatigue, unheeding his cries for mercy, indifferent to his claims as a prisoner of war.

This record of infamy is preserved for the females of Winchester. But this is not all. Our wounded in hospital, necessarily left to the mercies of our enemies, I am credibly informed, were bayoneted by the rebel infantry. In the same town, in the same apartments where we, when victors on the fields of Winchester, so tenderly nursed the rebel wounded, were we so more than barbarously rewarded. The rebel cavalry, it would appear, give no quarter. It cannot be doubted that they butchered our stragglers; that they fight under a black flag; that they cried as they slew the wearied and jaded, "Give no quarter to the damned Yankees."

The actual number of my brigade engaged was 2,102.

In estimating the force of the enemy I turn for a moment to the movement of the First Division from Strasburg to Winchester on the preceding day, the 24th, and my engagement with the enemy during the march, which assured me of their presence in great force upon our right flank.

The capture and destruction of Colonel Kenly's command (First Brigade) on the 23d at Front Royal while guarding our railroad communication with Washington and the facts set forth in my report of my engagement on the 24th tended to a conviction of the presence of a large force under General Ewell in the valley of the Shenandoah. The union of Jackson with Johnson, composing an army larger by many thousands than the two small brigades, with some cavalry and sixteen pieces of artillery, which comprised the entire army corps of General Banks, furnishes evidence justifying a belief of the intention of the enemy to cut us off first from re-enforcements, second to capture us and our material, beyond peradventure.

From the testimony of our signal officers and from a fair estimate of the number in rebel lines drawn up on the heights, from fugitives and deserters, the number of regiments in the rebel army opposite Winchester was 28, being Ewell's division, Jackson's and Johnson's forces, the whole being commanded by General Jackson. These regiments were full, and could not have numbered much less than 22,000 men, with a corresponding proportion of artillery, among which were included two of the English Blakely guns. Less than 4,000 men in two brigades, with sixteen pieces of artillery, kept this large and unequal force in check for about three hours; then retreating in generally good order, preserved its entire trains and accomplished a march of 36 miles.

Where all the regiments in my brigade behaved so well it is not intended to reflect in the least upon others in mentioning the steadiness and perfect discipline which marked the action of the Second Massachusetts, Lieutenant-Colonel Andrews, and Third Wisconsin, Colonel Ruger. The enemy will long remember the destructive fire which three or four companies of the Third Wisconsin and a like number of the Second Massachusetts poured into them as these sturdy regiments moved slowly in line of battle and in column from the field.

I herewith inclose a list* of the killed, wounded, and missing of the several regiments of my brigade, hoping that the numbers will hereafter be reduced by arrivals of those marked missing. How many were captured it is impossible now to determine.

Colonel Murphy, Twenty-ninth Pennsylvania, is known to be a prisoner. Major Dwight, of the Second Massachusetts, while gallantly bringing up the rear of the regiment, was missed somewhere near or in the outskirts of the town. It is hoped that this promising and brave officer, so cool upon the field, so efficient everywhere, so much beloved by his regiment, and whose gallant services on the night of the 24th instant will never be forgotten by them, may have met no worse fate than to be held a prisoner of war.

To my personal staff, Lieut. C. P. Horton, Second Massachusetts Regiment, my assistant adjutant-general; to Lieut. H. B. Scott, of the same regiment, my aide-de-camp, I am indebted for promptness in transmission of orders, for efficiency and gallant services in action.

I desire to express my thanks to Colonels Murphy, Ruger, Colgrove, and Andrews, and to the officers and men generally of my command, especially to officers and men of Battery M, whose skill and courage tended so much by their destructive fire to disconcert the enemy and hold him in check.

In fine, in the two days of the 24th and 25th of May the larger portion of my brigade marched 61 miles, the Second Massachusetts skirmishing on the 24th for more than six hours with infantry, cavalry, and artillery, the entire command on the 25th fighting a battle.

I herewith inclose such reports of colonels of regiments as have been forwarded.

Respectfully,

GEO. H. GORDON,
*Colonel Second Massachusetts Regt., Comdg. Third Brigade.*

Capt. WILLIAM D. WILKINS, *A. A. G., Fifth Army Corps.*

---

* See revised statement, p. 553.

## No. 34.

*Report of Col. Silas Colgrove, Twenty-seventh Indiana Infantry, of operations May 25.*

HDQRS. TWENTY-SEVENTH REGIMENT INDIANA VOLS.,
*Near Williamsport, Md., May 26, 1862.*

SIR: I have the honor of making the following report of the part taken in the action of the 25th instant at Winchester, Va.:

At an early hour in the morning, about 5.30 a. m., I received orders from Asst. Adjt. Gen. C. P. Horton to form my regiment into line of battle on the extreme left of the brigade, which order was promptly obeyed, the left of my regiment resting on the turnpike. My regiment while occupying this position became the target of the enemy's sharpshooters from the rifle pits on the top of the hill and from the top of a tree standing on the brow of the hill. They kept up a constant fire, with but little effect except wounding a private in Company H in the leg.

This position was held by the Twenty-seventh Regiment until I received an order from you, stating that the enemy was flanking us upon the right, and ordering my regiment to the right of the Second Massachusetts, which order was promptly obeyed. My regiment was marched by the right flank past the Twenty-ninth Pennsylvania, Third Wisconsin, and Second Massachusetts. It had scarcely gained its position to the right of the Second Massachusetts before we received a very heavy fire from the enemy's left, consisting of two full regiments of infantry, posted in a skirt of small scrubby timber about 150 yards in my front. We received the first fire of the enemy while the regiment was still marching by the flank. I immediately halted my regiment, brought it to the front into line of battle, and marched it to the front about 20 paces, to gain the advantage of the ground. These orders were executed by the regiment with promptness and coolness, as if it had been upon parade. I gave the order to fire, which was promptly obeyed, and with telling effect upon the enemy's lines.

About this juncture, the Twenty-ninth Pennsylvania filed past my regiment and took position on my right. My position brought the right wing of my regiment opposite and in front of the right wing of the enemy's left regiment and the left wing of the Second Regiment.

At about this juncture, and before the Twenty-ninth Pennsylvania had fired a gun, the enemy's left regiment from the line of battle formed into column and marched left in front until it had flanked the Twenty-ninth on the right, and then marched by the right flank in column by company, with the evident intention of gaining its rear. From the conformation of the ground I was satisfied that this movement of the enemy, although in plain view of the position occupied by myself, was entirely screened from the observation of Colonel Murphy. I immediately informed him that the enemy had flanked him on the right and was endeavoring to gain his rear. He immediately fell back about 20 paces, gaining a position in view of the enemy and preventing him from gaining his rear.

By a flank movement and filing to the right I brought Companies A and F of my regiment into position, and in connection with the Twenty-ninth Pennsylvania opened fire upon the enemy's left, which checked his flank movement.

At this juncture I discovered that my entire regiment, except Companies A and F, were falling back. As soon as possible I brought them to a halt and about-face and commenced firing. Lieutenant-Colonel Morrison came up to me, and said that he had ordered the regiment to cease firing and fall back. He informed me that he had received the order from you through Aide-de-Camp Lieutenant Scott, and had given the order to the regiment without communicating it to me.

At this time I saw the other regiments falling back, and gave the order to fall back to my regiment. I regret to say that the coolness that had marked every action of the regiment in advancing in the face of the enemy and receiving and returning his fire until the time of the retreat was ordered was by degrees lost, and in spite of every effort of mine ended in disorder to some extent. This fact is attributable to the want of line officers. From various causes I had less than half of my line officers in the action. Company C was without a commissioned officer, and was commanded in the action by Lieut. George Fesler, of Company G.

I wish to state that I am satisfied that the order received by Colonel Morrison did not emanate from your honor, but am satisfied he received the order and acted upon it in good faith, believing it to be from you.

The strength of my regiment in the action was—enlisted men, 431; commissioned officers, 15. Total, 446.

The following is a list of killed, wounded, and missing, so far as I have been able to ascertain. I have no doubt but that the killed and wounded will be materially increased when the full facts shall be ascertained.* Many in the list of the missing are reported to me as having fallen upon the field during the retreat; but I have reported none in the list of killed and wounded except those of whom I have positive information.

Respectfully submitted.

S. COLGROVE,
*Colonel, Commanding.*

Col. GEORGE H. GORDON,
*Commanding Third Brigade, Fifth Army Corps.*

---

## No. 35.

*Reports of Lieut. Col. George L. Andrews, Second Massachusetts Infantry, of operations May 24–25.*

HDQRS. SECOND REGIMENT MASSACHUSETTS VOLS.,
*Camp at Williamsport, Md., May* 26, 1862.

SIR: I have the honor to submit the following report of the operations of the Second Regiment of the Massachusetts Volunteers on the 24th instant:

At about 11 o'clock a. m. the regiment left camp at Strasburg, marching toward Winchester. After a fatiguing march of about 13 miles, when within 5 miles of Winchester I received an order to return toward Strasburg, to assist the rear guard in repelling attacks upon the train. Knapsacks were deposited at the side of the road to relieve the men, already much fatigued with the march over a dry, dusty road. We were followed by the Twenty-eighth New York Regiment, Lieutenant-Colonel Brown, and a section of Best's battery, under Lieutenant Cushing.

---

*Nominal list omitted, but see revised statement, p. 553.

On arriving at Newtown I found the Twenty-seventh Indiana Regiment formed in line on this side of the town with two sections of Cothran's battery, which were firing upon the enemy's cavalry in the edge of the wood on our left. I received an order to advance, take the town, and hold it until further orders. Companies A and C, under Captains Abbott and Cogswell, were deployed as skirmishers, and advanced, followed by the remainder of the regiment and the section of Best's battery, under a well-directed fire of the enemy's artillery, posted in the main street and in full view of their cavalry. The enemy was speedily driven from the town to a position on the heights beyond, from which he continued the fire of artillery, principally directed against the section of Cothran's battery, which had advanced and taken position on our right, but his fire was with little or no effect. The sections of Best's and Cothran's batteries replied by a well-directed fire.

At sunset an order came to withdraw and resume the march to Winchester, the desired object having been attained. This was done, the two companies above mentioned forming the rear guard, and Company B, Captain Williams, thrown out as flankers; the artillery, with three companies of this regiment, leading, followed by the remainder of the regiment in column. We soon overtook the Twenty-seventh Indiana Regiment, which was engaged in the destruction of abandoned property of the train. This caused some delay, but the march was soon resumed. The Twenty-eighth New York was in advance of the Twenty-seventh Indiana. At the place in which the knapsacks were left the regiment was halted, and, the rear guard and flankers remaining in their places, the rest of the regiment were ordered to take their knapsacks. Six companies of the New York cavalry here joined us.

It was now quite dark, and the enemy, who had not before shown himself on our return, made a cavalry charge, which was promptly repelled by a volley from the rear guard, which was delivered at short range with perfect coolness and great effect. The enemy then fired a single shell, which was replied to by another volley from the rear guard, and the enemy ceased for the time his attack. The companies composing the rear guard and flankers were now directed in turn to take their knapsacks; Company I, Captain Underwood, forming the new rear guard, and Company D, Captain Savage, the flankers.

The enemy now sent forward a line of skirmishers, who opened fire on Captain Underwood's company, which, although very severe, was sustained, and replied to with a steadiness most creditable to the officers and men of the company. The firing continuing, I sent forward in support on the right and left platoons of the companies of Captains Cogswell and Williams, and our fire soon produced a marked effect upon the enemy. Everything being now ready, the march was resumed. The enemy followed but a short distance. The march was continued until we reached Kernstown, when a halt was ordered, to rest the men and make arrangements to send forward some of the wounded. From the non-arrival of ambulances some delay occurred, during which the enemy advanced and again opened his fire of skirmishers, which was promptly replied to by the rear guard.

The darkness of the night concealing the enemy deployed, while the column forming a dark mass upon the road was a fair mark, I ordered the march to be resumed, which was done in perfect order. The enemy did not pursue.

At 2 o'clock a. m. the 25th the regiment reached Winchester after a march of 25 miles, having sustained firmly and successfully the reiterated attacks of the enemy, made under cover of the darkness of the night.

The conduct of officers and men was most admirable. Major Dwight, who was in immediate command of the rear guard, displayed much courage and skill.

Our loss in the affair was 3 killed and 17 wounded. I have also to regret the loss of Dr. Leland who was taken prisoner while attending to our wounded men in a house near Kernstown. The loss of the enemy I have no means of estimating.

The regiment bivouacked for the night without fires, with little food, and much exhausted. The company of Captain Cogswell was ordered on outpost duty immediately, but rejoined the regiment in the morning, when the outposts were driven in, having fallen back slowly in good order before the greatly superior forces of the advancing enemy.

Very respectfully, your obedient servant,

GEO. L. ANDREWS,

*Lieut. Col., Second Massachusetts Regiment, Comdg.*

Col. GEORGE H. GORDON,

*Commanding Third Brigade.*

---

HDQRS. SECOND REGIMENT MASSACHUSETTS VOLS.,

*Camp at Williamsport, Md., May* 26, 1862.

SIR: I have the honor to submit the following report of the operations of the Second Regiment Massachusetts Volunteers on the 25th instant:

After less than two hours' rest, following the fatigue of the preceding day, this regiment was called upon to go into action. Our outposts were seen to be driven in at an early hour, and the regiment was ordered to take a position on the heights southwest of the town, forming the extreme right of the line, the Third Wisconsin being the next regiment on the left.

While the regiment was marching to its position a fire of grape was opened upon it from the enemy's battery opposite. Nevertheless it steadily moved on and took its position. The right company, Captain Savage, was deployed as skirmishers on the right of the regiment. It was soon, however, sent forward to a stone wall a few rods in advance, from which its fire seriously annoyed the enemy's battery. A movement being observed on the part of the enemy to drive them away, Captain Carey's company was sent forward in support. Several volleys were also fired by the two right companies, directed at the battery, with evident effect. It was observed that one of the enemy's guns was abandoned by the cannoneers.

The action had continued about an hour and a half when the enemy appeared emerging from behind a wood, which had entirely concealed his movements, and advancing in line of battle directly upon our right flank. This was promptly reported, and the Twenty-ninth Pennsylvania and Twenty-seventh Indiana Regiments were ordered up and formed on the right of the Second Massachusetts Regiment. They opened a fire upon the enemy, but failing to check his rapid advance, which was favored by the ground, they fell back. This exposed the right flank of this regiment to the attack of the enemy's line, and I was obliged to withdraw it, the regiment marching down the hill in good order under a heavy fire from the enemy.

Upon entering one of the cross streets I halted the regiment, which formed in line with perfect steadiness and regularity, with the view of making a stand to check the advance of the enemy. Finding, however, that our forces were all in full retreat, and the regiment becoming exposed to a fire down the street from a large body of the enemy, the retreat was resumed, and we rapidly withdrew from the town, the men preserving their good order admirably. This regiment was the last to leave the town. The retreat was continued without a halt to Martinsburg, a distance of 22 miles; was resumed after a short rest and continued to the Potomac, a distance of 12 miles, making in all a march of 34 miles, almost without food or rest, from 12 o'clock m. on the 24th to 8 o'clock on the evening of the 25th.

The loss of the regiment on the 25th was 7 killed, 28 wounded (including 2 commissioned officers), and 131 missing, besides 2 commissioned officers. Of the missing many are daily coming in, having been compelled to halt from exhaustion, and afterward found their way by different routes. The 2 commissioned officers wounded, both slightly, were Captain Mudge and Second Lieutenant Crowninshield. Major Dwight and Assistant Surgeon Stone are missing.*

Very respectfully, your obedient servant,

GEO. L. ANDREWS,
*Lieut. Col., Second Massachusetts Regiment, Comdg.*

Col. GEORGE H. GORDON, *Commanding Third Brigade.*

---

## No. 36.

*Report of Capt. Samuel M. Zulich, Twenty-ninth Pennsylvania Infantry, of operations May 23–26.*

HDQRS. TWENTY-NINTH PENNSYLVANIA VOLUNTEERS,
*Camp near Williamsport, Md., May* 29, 1862.

SIR: Pursuant to order, on Friday night at 12 o'clock, May 23, the Twenty-ninth Regiment Pennsylvania Volunteers left their encampment on the Woodstock turnpike, near Strasburg, Va., and marched to Middletown. You had ordered Colonel Murphy to take possession of the road at that place leading toward Front Royal, and to hold it at all hazards. We advanced along that road with a section of the First New York Artillery, under Lieutenant Woodbury, a distance of 4 miles. Ascertaining that the enemy were in force in that direction we turned back, and were stationed in the vicinity of Middletown.

At 11 o'clock a. m. of Saturday, 24th, an excitement was created among the teamsters by an advance of the enemy's cavalry from Newtown. This brought the whole force to that point, and we took position on the right of your brigade, retreating toward Winchester. We marched constantly until we arrived in the vicinity of Winchester at 8 o'clock p. m. We lay upon our arms all night upon the right of the turnpike, facing the enemy, within a quarter of a mile of the edge of the town.

At 2 o'clock on Sunday morning Companies E, Capt. S. M. Zulich, and K, Capt. William D. Rickards, were stationed as pickets in advance on the right, extending from the turnpike to the cavalry camp on the hill. Firing continued until daybreak among the pickets, with no loss to us. At 4.30 a. m. the pickets were driven in by an advance of the enemy, who were filing their regiments around us to reach the earthworks on the hill. The regiment was at once drawn in line, and shortly

---

* See revised statement, p. 553.

afterward we received your order to take position on the left of the brigade.

In the mean while the engagement had been opened and was being continued by the artillery of the opposing forces. When the attack was made upon the right wing the Twenty-ninth Pennsylvania Volunteers was by your order moved from the left to the extreme right, and before we had got into position we received a volley of musketry from a large body of the enemy in our front, which was not distinctly visible, on account of a fog arising from the damp ground. This fire we promptly returned, and before we could discern the enemy in front we saw a brigade, consisting of, as near as my observation serves me, four regiments closed *en masse* on our right flank and rapidly approaching our rear. Colonel Murphy promptly changed the front of the regiment perpendicularly to the rear and facing the advancing force. This movement brought us in a gully, with the enemy in front and a ridge of rocks thickly studded with bushes in our rear. We received their fire for some minutes and promptly returned it. For a moment the enemy seemed to stagger, but it was only for a moment; for, feeling confident in their great strength, they charged down the hill upon us, with deafening cheers. Colonel Murphy gave us the order to retire (which order was received through Lieutenant-Colonel Morrison, of the Twenty-seventh Indiana Volunteers, who states that he received it from Lieutenant Scott, your aide-de-camp), which was executed at first in good order, but we found it impossible to preserve our ranks while climbing up these rocks amidst the fire of the enemy.

We were allowed no time to rally and reform our men until we had passed through the town and retreated several miles toward this place. While retreating through the town the citizens poured volley after volley upon our men, who were tired and foot-sore from the fatiguing march of the previous day. We continued in retreat with your brigade until 9 o'clock p. m., when we had reached the Virginia shore of the Potomac River. There we rested for the night, and on Monday morning, the 26th instant, transported our men and trains across the river in safety. We found numerous officers and men missing, but many have since rejoined their regiment, having taken to the woods and crossed the river under many difficulties.

Col. John K. Murphy acted coolly and calmly during the engagement. He had lost his horse upon the field, and being advanced in age, was unable to make a successful retreat. He was captured by the rebel cavalry in the streets of Winchester after bravely attempting a resistance.

Very respectfully,

SAMUEL M. ZULICH,
*Captain Company E, Commanding Twenty-ninth Regiment.*

Col. GEORGE H. GORDON,
*Commanding Third Brigade.*

[Indorsement.]

HEADQUARTERS THIRD BRIGADE,
*Near Williamsport, May* 29, 1862

The statement that Lieutenant-Colonel Morrison received the order to retire from Lieutenant Scott is incorrect, as has been proved to the satisfaction of Lieutenant-Colonel Morrison.

GEO. H. GORDON,
*Colonel Second Massachusetts Regiment, Comdg Third Brigade.*

## No. 37.

### *Report of Col. Thomas H. Ruger, Third Wisconsin Infantry, of operations May 25.*

HDQRS. THIRD REGIMENT WISCONSIN VOLUNTEERS,
*Camp near Williamsport, Md., May 28, 1862.*

SIR: I have the honor to submit the following report in relation to the part taken in the action at Winchester, Va., on Sunday, the 25th of May, 1862, by the Third Regiment of Wisconsin Volunteers:

The enemy having been reported moving to the attack, about daylight I formed the regiment on the ground on which it had encamped the previous night. Soon after I received orders to place the regiment in its place in line of battle next to the left of the Second Massachusetts Volunteers, which was done under fire. The regiment remained in the position assigned to it, two companies from the left of the battalion, under the command of Major Crane, having been thrown forward behind a stone wall some 75 yards in front of their position for about two hours, from 5 to 7 a. m., when I received an order to fall back to the crest of the hill a short distance in rear. Calling in the two companies advanced from the left I faced the battalion about and moved to the rear in good order to the position designated and immediately faced the battalion to the front, almost immediately after which I received orders to fall back and rally behind a stone wall just on the edge of town, which I did with as much regularity and in as good order as the obstructed and broken condition of the ground would admit. After taking position behind the stone wall, which served to cover the right wing only of the regiment, most of the left being exposed, fire was opened on the enemy, who by this time had reached the top of the hill and were preparing to charge down the hill. On receiving the fire that part of the enemy's line at which it was directed halted and commenced firing. About the same time the enemy placed a battery in position on the hill and threw several shells into the inclosure behind the stone wall and against the wall, and also several rounds of canister. Seeing there was no possibility of making a successful stand, as the troops on the right continued to fall back, rendering it certain that my flank would soon be turned, I ordered the regiment to retire, and gave the command for the battalion to face to the left, and passed with the left wing into the street next west of the main street, on which I came out near the Taylor Hotel. The right wing, finding it impossible to follow and perhaps not hearing the command in the noise and confusion, passed through an alley back of the inclosure into the street, and continued on the same street through the town.

The small loss at the stone wall was owing to the sheltered position of the regiment and the inaccuracy of the enemy's fire from the hill, the musketry fire being too high. The retreat from the position behind the wall was effected just as the enemy's cavalry made a dash and succeeded in cutting off a few men from the left. One man was shot while marching through the city from a window on the main street. As soon as the regiment was clear of the town I directed Major Crane to order all men belonging to the regiment and separated from it to join their respective companies.

The men were much worn when the action commenced, but evinced a disposition throughout to do their duty. The officers of the regiment, without exception, as I believe, endeavored to keep the men steady and cool under, to them at least, so unexpected adverse circumstances. The list of killed, wounded, and missing I will transmit as soon as it can be ascertained with anything like accuracy.

Very respectfully, your obedient servant,

THOS. H. RUGER,
*Colonel, Commanding Third Regiment Wisconsin Volunteers.*

C. P. HORTON,
*Acting Assistant Adjutant-General, Third Brigade.*

---

## No. 38.

*Reports of Brig. Gen. Rufus Saxton, U. S. Army, commanding post, of operations at Harper's Ferry, including instructions and congratulations from the Secretary of War.*

WAR DEPARTMENT,
*Washington, May* 24, 1862.

General SAXTON:

You will please proceed with the troops from Washington to Harper's Ferry and operate with them according to your discretion, as circumstances may require, assuming the command of them.

EDWIN M. STANTON,
*Secretary of War.*

---

WAR DEPARTMENT,
*May* 24, 1862—1 p. m.

General SAXTON:

Geary reports Jackson with 20,000 moving from Ashby's Gap by the Little River turnpike, through Aldie, toward Centreville. This, he says, is reliable. He is also informed of large forces south of him. We know a force of some 15,000 broke up Saturday night from in front of Fredericksburg, and went we know not where. Please inform us, if possible, what has become of the force which pursued Banks yesterday; also any other information you have.

A. LINCOLN.

---

WAR DEPARTMENT,
*May* 24, 1862—3.41 p. m.

General SAXTON, *Harper's Ferry:*

A fine battery of artillery will leave Baltimore for you at 4 o'clock. More will leave here this evening. Exercise your own judgment as to your defense. Whatever you do will be cordially approved, be the result what it may.

EDWIN M. STANTON,
*Secretary of War.*

---

HARPER'S FERRY, *May* 25, 1862.
(Received 10.45 a. m.)

I arrived here at 9.15 a. m. The train is 1 mile behind, with the One hundred and ninth Regiment. The other Washington regiment has not arrived One hundred and eleventh Pennsylvania is here, and will go on toward Winchester, taking every precaution against surprise. Five companies of the Maryland Cavalry are getting ready to go out on the turnpike toward Winchester to obtain information. Shall hold the One hundred and ninth Regiment here for the present. The telegraph says this morning that General Banks is retreating from Winchester. I do not think the information altogether reliable. It may be the enemy have got possession of the telegraph.

R. SAXTON,
*Brigadier-General.*

Hon. E. M. STANTON.

---

HARPER'S FERRY, *May* 25, 1862.

Heavy firing was heard near Winchester this morning. To obtain reliable information is difficult; there are so many reports in circulation, started undoubtedly by the enemy. Cavalry for scouting purpose is very much needed. The five companies here are in a shocking condition—horses not shod, and no saddles. The latter have arrived and will be issued at once and the scouts started. I fear it will be to-morrow before they will be ready. One regiment has gone this morning to re-enforce General Banks; the other regiment will go on as soon as I am satisfied it will be prudent to leave the railroad bridge unprotected. If the whole movement of the enemy is not a feint in force to cover a movement on Manassas there is a possibility they may move on this place.

R. SAXTON,
*Brigadier-General.*

Hon. E. M. STANTON,
*Secretary of War.*

---

HARPER'S FERRY, *May* 25, 1862.
(Received 12.20 p. m.)

In case we are attacked two light batteries and two 8-inch howitzers would be of great service to command the river and bridge. There is no artillery here. The facilities for obtaining accurate information are so limited, and so many rumors of danger are in circulation, that I find it difficult to estimate its exact extent. One of the most reliable reports is that General Banks is in full retreat on Martinsburg, the enemy in pursuit as far as Spencer [?] Station. I shall stop the regiment sent forward to Winchester this morning at Charlestown, to fall back on this point if it is necessary. I think it would be of no service to General Banks, as I cannot yet inform myself of the strength or purpose of the enemy. I want all the assistance I can get. I cannot realize yet that we are in any immediate danger here.

R. SAXTON,
*Brigadier-General.*

Hon. E. M. STANTON.

---

WAR DEPARTMENT,
*May* 25, 1862—2.10.

General SAXTON, *Harper's Ferry:*

I have ordered General Dix to send you some artillery from Baltimore. I will send some from here to-night. Put yourself in communication with General Dix, and call upon him as well as upon me for anything you want.

EDWIN M. STANTON.

---

HARPER'S FERRY, VA., *May* 25, 1862.
(Received 2.25.)

All the reports I receive go to show that General Banks is hotly pressed and in full retreat toward Martinsburg. There is a panic, and so few troops here I am satisfied that it is not best to send troops to Winchester, as it is now in the possession of the enemy. The troops have left Charlestown, and are falling back upon this place. This was done before the regiment I sent forward this morning reached there. I do not think, with our present force, it will be wise to reoccupy it. I shall send two regiments to occupy Bolivar Heights, a commanding position near this place, and the force here is too small to follow up the force before which General Banks is retreating, and at the same time defend this place, which I shall do to the last.

R. SAXTON,
*Brigadier-General.*

Hon. E. M. STANTON.

---

HARPER'S FERRY, VA., *May* 25, 1862.
(Received 3.20 p. m.)

Stragglers have come in from Winchester and report that General Banks attacked the rebels this morning in front of Winchester and was driven back into the town. Our troops burned the town. General Banks' army is disorganized and in full retreat on Martinsburg. The enemy is in full pursuit. It may be necessary for us to fight the enemy with the river in our rear or withdraw to the other side and defend the bridge and the crossing. We feel the want of artillery severely.

R. SAXTON,
*Brigadier-General.*

Hon. E. M. STANTON.

---

WAR DEPARTMENT,
*May* 25, 1862—4.15 p. m.

General SAXTON, *Harper's Ferry:*

If Banks reaches Martinsburg is he any the better for it? Will not the enemy cut him off from thence to Harper's Ferry? Have you sent anything to meet him and assist him at Martinsburg? This is an inquiry, not an order.

A. LINCOLN.

---

HARPER'S FERRY, VA., *May* 25, 1862.
(Received 5.30 p. m.)

Stragglers continue to come in in large numbers. General Banks' column too much frightened to give a clear account of affairs. They represent his rout as complete. They report that 15,000 men are moving down upon Harper's Ferry. I believe this is an exaggeration, but I think the rebel force is large—that they have a large amount of artillery. It was this which defeated General Banks. We have no artillery here yet. Have 2,500 men.

R. SAXTON,
*Brigadier-General.*

E. M. STANTON,
*Secretary of War.*

—

HARPER'S FERRY, VA., *May* 25, 1862.
(Received 6 p. m.)

General Banks cannot reach Harper's Ferry from Martinsburg. He had two lines of retreat—one to Harper's Ferry, one to Martinsburg. He took the latter. The most intelligent man I have seen, who was in the battle at Winchester, reports that General Banks' army fought for six hours and then retreated in great confusion—perfectly disorganized. Parts of companies have arrived here who ran away from his column. It is 19 miles from Winchester to Martinsburg, and 23 miles from here to Martinsburg, and 11 or 12 from Williamsport. His only chance is to go there. We could do nothing to assist him, as we could not ascertain line of retreat until it was too late. The whole force here does not amount to over 2,500 men, and 1,000 of these did not get ready to march before 12 o'clock to-day. I am anxiously looking for artillery.

R. SAXTON,
*Brigadier-General.*

His Excellency the PRESIDENT.

—

WAR DEPARTMENT,
*May* 25, 1862—6 p. m.

Brigadier-General SAXTON,
*Harper's Ferry:*

You will have before morning a large force of artillery with officers and artillerymen. Hold firm and keep calm. Mr. Watson is on the road with a train of artillery from here besides that from Baltimore.

EDWIN M. STANTON,
*Secretary of War.*

—

WAR DEPARTMENT,
*May* 25, 1862—6.50 p. m.

General SAXTON, *Harper's Ferry:*

One good six-gun battery, complete in its men and appointments, is now on its way to you from Baltimore. Eleven other guns, of different sorts, are on their way to you from here. Hope they will all reach you before morning. As you have but 2,500 men at Harper's Ferry, where are the rest which were in that vicinity and which we have sent forward? Have any of them been cut off?

A. LINCOLN.

HARPER'S FERRY, VA., *May* 25, 1862.
(Received 9.20 p. m.)

I feel perfectly secure here for the present. The enemy cannot attack before to-morrow noon. If the promised re-enforcement arrives we can then afford to fight them, with the river in our rear. I have every reason to believe they are following General Banks, with a view to capture his army. I hope we shall have force enough to cut them off. Their treatment of prisoners and wounded is barbarous in the extreme. The women in Winchester fired upon our soldiers in the streets. Since I commenced this a dispatch has arrived giving information that General Banks was crossing the Potomac in retreat at Martinsburg [Williamsport].

R. SAXTON,
*Brigadier-General.*

Hon. E. M. STANTON.

---

WAR DEPARTMENT,
*May* 25, 1862—9.46 p. m.

Brigadier-General SAXTON,
*Harper's Ferry:*

Your dispatch received, and your confidence gratifies us. General Hamilton, formerly of Banks' division, was sent forward to join Banks and report to him for orders. He telegraphs that he is on the train with Mr. Watson. If he remains at Harper's Ferry and can render any service I desire him to do so, but not to supersede you in command. By special assignment of the President you are assigned to the command of the forces and operations at Harper's Ferry, without regard to seniority of rank. Please acknowledge the hour at which you receive this and report the state of affairs at that hour.

EDWIN M. STANTON,
*Secretary of War.*

---

HARPER'S FERRY, VA., *May* 25, 1862.
(Received 10.10 p. m.)

All the troops which were in this vicinity—one company and a half of the First Potomac Home Brigade and six companies Eighth New York Cavalry—are here. None of the troops which have arrived since I came here have been cut off, except one sergeant and one private at Winchester this morning, of the First Regiment District Volunteers. This regiment arrived at Winchester just as General Banks commenced retreating. Three companies only got out of the cars. The train returned with the regiment, with the above-mentioned line of retreat, until it was too late. The whole force here does not amount to over 2,500 men, and 1,000 of these did not get ready to march before 12 o'clock to-day. I am anxiously looking for artillery.

R. SAXTON,
*Brigadier-General.*

His Excellency the PRESIDENT.

HARPER'S FERRY, VA., *May* 25, 1862.
(Received 10.24 p. m.)

Everything is now quiet. Pickets out 3 miles on the road toward Winchester and Charlestown. Three companies of cavalry near Charlestown. Six companies of infantry on Bolivar Hill, on outpost service. Three regiments of infantry on a commanding height in front of the village. The remainder of the forces are guarding the bridge and the passage of the river. I have had all the contrabands at work moving the stores across the river, to provide against a possible contingency. I feel sure that I have made the best disposition of the force here. To-morrow, if sufficient re-enforcements arrive, I shall occupy Bolivar Heights in force. Your assignment to the command of operations was received at 10 o'clock. I will do all in my power to merit your confidence.

R. SAXTON,
*Brigadier-General, Commanding.*

Hon. E. M. STANTON,
*Secretary of War.*

---

WAR DEPARTMENT,
*May* 25, 1862.

General SAXTON, *Harper's Ferry:*

I fear you have mistaken me. I did not mean to question the correctness of your conduct; on the contrary, I approve what you have done. As the 2,500 reported by you seemed small to me I feared some had got to Banks and been cut off with him. Please tell me the exact number you now have in hand.

A. LINCOLN.

---

WAR DEPARTMENT,
*May* 25, 1862—12 p. m.

General SAXTON, *Harper's Ferry:*

Banks appears to have reached the vicinity of the Potomac safely and intends to cross at Williamsport to-night. He does not know how you stand at Ferry. Have you opened communications with him? You should send a messenger immediately.

EDWIN M. STANTON,
*Secretary of War.*

---

WAR DEPARTMENT,
*May* 26, 1862.

Brigadier-General SAXTON,
*Harper's Ferry:*

Artillery will be forwarded in the course of an hour from here. Please report the present condition of things.

EDWIN M. STANTON,
*Secretary of War.*

HARPER'S FERRY, VA.,
*May* 26, 1862.

If the artillery arrives in time, so that we can command the bridge, &c., we can hold it with less disaster. The want of artillery is the only thing that would make me think of withdrawing to the other side.

R. SAXTON,
*Brigadier-General.*

Hon. E. M. STANTON,
*Secretary of War.*

---

HARPER'S FERRY, VA.,
*May* 26, 1862.

I have had as careful an estimate made of the force here as is possible at present. It amounts to 6,700 men. Many more are on the way. A portion of the artillery has arrived, including one light battery. No signs of the enemy yet.

R. SAXTON,
*Brigadier-General.*

His Excellency the PRESIDENT.

---

HARPER'S FERRY, VA., *May* 26, 1862.
(Received 1.35 a. m.)

Yes.* I sent scout out 3 miles on Winchester road. No enemy this side of Charlestown. Ashby's cavalry, 1,500 strong, are near Charlestown. Is it better, if we are attacked to-morrow, to risk an engagement on this side of the river, with the river in our rear, or retreat to the other side and guard the bridge?

R. SAXTON,
*Brigadier-General.*

E. M. STANTON.

---

WASHINGTON, *May* 26, 1862.

General SAXTON, *Harper's Ferry:*

You must judge of that yourself, as the emergency arises, and act according to the circumstances in which you are yourself placed. Whatever you do will be approved. You should be on the watch and expect an attack at an early hour in the morning, and be sure to hold your position until artillery arrives. Mr. Watson thinks they will arrive about daylight.

EDWIN M. STANTON.

---

HARPER'S FERRY, VA., *May* 26, 1862.
(Received 2.10 p. m.)

I can get no reliable information to-day of the locality of the enemy. Many reports are circulated that we are to be attacked at this place, and that they mean to force their way into Maryland by way of Har-

---

*Probably answers inquiry in Stanton's dispatch of May 25, 12 p. m., p. 631.

per's Ferry. Everything is quiet here now. I have not been able to communicate with General Banks yet. Have heard nothing of Jackson's movements, except a report that he was marching on this place.

R. SAXTON,
*Brigadier-General.*

Hon. ABRAHAM LINCOLN, *President.*

---

HARPER'S FERRY, VA., *May* 26, 1862.
(Received 6 o'clock.)

Everything is quiet. The Third Delaware arrived this morning. No artillery yet. I shall keep the main body of troops on the Maryland side until the artillery arrives, with the exception of the three regiments in front of the town. Mr. Watson has not yet arrived. There are great delays on the railroad. I have not been able to get any additional news from General Banks.

R. SAXTON,
*Brigadier-General.*

E. M. STANTON,
*Secretary of War.*

---

HARPER'S FERRY, VA., *May* 26, 1862.
(Received 9 p. m.)

Four companies of cavalry, which I have had out in the vicinity of Charlestown, have just come in. They were followed for some distance this side of Charlestown by the rebels, and had 1 horse shot. The commanding officer of the party says that Jackson is in Charlestown, and is moving down here to attack us. I have Reynolds' light battery in position, and expect to hold him in check if he should come. While I am satisfied the rebels are in Charlestown in some force, I believe that Jackson is not there.

R. SAXTON,
*Brigadier-General.*

Hon. E. M. STANTON.

---

HARPER'S FERRY, VA., *May* 27, 1862.
(Received 7.35 a. m.)

Everything is quiet. I shall put the greater portion of the forces here on Bolivar Heights, beyond Harper's Ferry, to-day, and extend my pickets as far as possible. Almost all of the regiments are new and not well instructed. Our movements are consequently slow. If they were old soldiers I would take Winchester in a very short time, and hold it. Cannot a large amount of transportation be sent here? I could use it to very great advantage.

R. SAXTON,
*Brigadier-General, Commanding.*

Hon. E. M. STANTON.

---

HARPER'S FERRY, VA.,
*May* 27, 1862.

The enemy are in some force in the immediate vicinity of this place.

I sent out two companies about dark this evening to scour the woods on Albion Heights, back of the town, where it was reported the enemy had a body of cavalry. After proceeding about 2 miles they were fired upon; 1 of our men killed and 1 wounded.

R. SAXTON,
*Brigadier-General.*

Hon. E. M. STANTON.

---

WASHINGTON, *May* 28, 1862—12.45.

Brigadier-General SAXTON:

Direction has been given General Banks to get his force in order to establish a communication with you for the purpose of reoccupying his former lines. He has also been directed to supply you with transportation. Shields is moving toward Front Royal and Strasburg. It is designed to leave at Harper's Ferry a sufficient force to make that place secure.

EDWIN M. STANTON.

---

HARPER'S FERRY, *May* 28, 1862.
(Received May 28, 1 p. m.)

Information from Martinsburg as late as 1 p. m. yesterday. The rebels had burnt Opequon Bridge and the trestle work at Martinsburg.

R. SAXTON,
*Brigadier-General.*

Hon. E. M. STANTON.

(Copy to McDowell.)

---

HARPER'S FERRY, VA., *May* 28, 1862.
(Received 1.05 p. m.)

I sent out a strong party toward Martinsburg this morning. General Banks sent me a telegram this morning, informing me that two regiments of cavalry and some infantry were there; also that a prisoner says that Ashby was ordered to Winchester yesterday morning, and withdrew with a portion of his cavalry and some artillery. General Banks says he shall occupy Falling Waters to-day. He believes that the enemy is still strong at Winchester. Lieutenants Daniels and Dahlgren have their battery in position on the heights, commanding all the points in this vicinity, and had some splendid practice with the larger Dahlgren, shelling the woods and heights across the Shenandoah, where our scouting party was killed.

R. SAXTON,
*Brigadier-General.*

Hon. E. M. STANTON,
*Secretary of War.*

---

HARPER'S FERRY, VA., *May* 31, 1862.
(Received 8.45 a. m.)

The enemy moved up in force last evening about 7 o'clock, in a shower of rain, to attack. I opened on them from the position which the troops occupy above the town and from the Dahlgren battery on the mountains. The enemy then retired. Their pickets attacked ours twice last night within 300 yards of our works. A volley from General Slough's breastworks drove them back. We lost 1 man killed. Enemy had signal-lights on the mountains in every direction. Their system of night-signals seems to be perfect. They fire on our pickets in every case. My men are overworked. Stood by their guns all night in the rain. What has become of Generals Frémont and McDowell?

R. SAXTON,
*Brigadier-General.*

Hon. E. M. STANTON,
*Secretary of War.*

(Copies to Frémont and McDowell 9 a. m.)

---

HARPER'S FERRY, VA., *May* 31, 1862.
(Received 9.30 a. m.)

Hon. E. M. STANTON:

Telegraph General McDowell to press on with all possible haste. All my pickets driven in last night. Enemy in force in front and I believe on both flanks. My position is strong. Shall try to hold it.

R. SAXTON,
*Brigadier-General, Commanding.*

(Telegraphed to McDowell 9.40 a. m.)

---

WASHINGTON, *May* 31, 1862—9.50 a. m.

General SAXTON,
*Harper's Ferry:*

Shields has already surprised and captured the enemy's rear guard at Front Royal. Shields is close after them. Frémont will be in line to-day. Keep cool and hold your ground.

EDWIN M. STANTON,
*Secretary of War.*

---

WASHINGTON, *May* 31, 1862—10.30 a. m.

General SAXTON, *Harper's Ferry:*

General McDowell telegraphs me to say to you that he is pushing everything ahead; and if you hold on you won't have to do so long, for the enemy will be on the retreat soon and you will be the pursuer.

EDWIN M. STANTON,
*Secretary of War.*

---

WASHINGTON, *May* 31, 1862.

Brigadier-General SAXTON,
*Commanding Harper's Ferry:*

Report immediately by telegraph the particulars of the disgraceful conduct of Maulsby's regiment in abandoning their post night before last.

EDWIN M. STANTON,
*Secretary of War.*

HARPER'S FERRY, VA., *May* 31, 1862.
(Received 3.45 p. m.)

I was absent upon a reconnaissance when your dispatch came. Colonel Maulsby's regiment left their post when in a position to which I had assigned them, and moved down into the town of Harper's Ferry without any authority, and wished to cross the river to the Maryland side, away from the enemy. Colonel Miles, my chief of staff, ordered the colonel to take his regiment back to its position. He informed Colonel Miles and myself that he could not make his men go back; that they were utterly demoralized, and he begged me to allow his regiment to cross the river. Convinced that they would be useless I told them to go, and left their place to a braver regiment. At the time this affair occurred the action of this regiment came near causing a panic while I was changing the position of the entire command by a night march. The entire occupation of my time since the affair occurred has prevented me from sending you a report of it sooner. The regiment has been in a safe position since and has performed its required duty well. There are many brave men in the regiment, but I think the colonel lacks that force and energy of character necessary to the good commander. The regiment did not enlist to serve out of Maryland, which with some might be looked upon as an extenuation of their conduct.

R. SAXTON,
*Brigadier-General.*

Hon. E. M. STANTON, *Secretary of War.*

---

HARPER'S FERRY, 31*st*.
(Received 4.20 p. m.)

The enemy commenced their retreat last night soon after I shelled them from Battery Stanton, and their last company passed through Halltown about 9 o'clock this a. m. I am convinced that they had heard of McDowell's advance, and the attack last night at so unseasonable an hour was a last effort to break through our lines. I have learned that the signals which I mentioned in my last dispatch were made to General R. Taylor's brigade, which was advancing behind Loudoun Heights to cut off our line of communication.

There is no doubt but that the enemy fully expected to cut us off. His force is large and active. It is not best for me to follow him with my present force where he is driven back by Generals Frémont and McDowell. If I move out of my intrenchments he is strong enough to escape me in the open field.

I cannot speak too highly of the services of Lieutenant Daniels, U. S. Volunteers, and his splendid rifled 9-inch Dahlgren. Both he and they did their work well. I have reliable information that fifty cannon passed through Charlestown yesterday with the retreating army. The heaviest portion were with Taylor's brigade, from Loudoun County, which passed behind Loudoun Heights. Taylor impresses everybody, old and young, into service as he goes on. General McDowell has some work before him.

R. SAXTON,
*Brigadier-General.*

Hon. E. M. STANTON, *Secretary of War.*
(Copy sent General McDowell 5.55 p. m.)

HARPER'S FERRY, VA.,
*June* 1, 1862.

I have many reports of heavy firing to-day on the east side of the Blue Ridge. I have reliable information that on Thursday Jackson had ordered his army to storm this place, but the shells from our batteries were so destructive that he drew back out of their range and endeavored to draw us out to attack him.

R. SAXTON,
*Brigadier-General.*

Hon. E. M. STANTON.

---

WASHINGTON, *June* 1, 1862.

Brigadier-General SAXTON,
*Harper's Ferry:*

Your dispatch announcing that the enemy has not reappeared is received. Make a reconnaissance as far as Charlestown to ascertain whether the enemy is there or thereabouts. See that the reconnoitering force maintains strict discipline. Let couriers report the progress and discoveries of the reconnaissance from time to time to your headquarters, and forward the reports here promptly by telegraph.

EDWIN M. STANTON,
*Secretary of War.*

---

HARPER'S FERRY, *June* 1, 1862.
(Received 6.20 p. m.)

My scouts, who have just come in from Charlestown, bring a rumor that Jackson is falling back from Winchester before the advance of our forces. There has been heavy firing there. I shall send out a strong reconnaissance.

R. SAXTON,
*Brigadier-General.*

Hon. E. M. STANTON,
*Secretary of War.*

(Copy to McDowell.)

---

HARPER'S FERRY, VA., *June* 1, 1862.

A reconnaissance commanded by Captain Cole, which was sent to Charlestown, has just returned. Scoured the country on both sides of the road. No signs of the enemy. The inhabitants say the rebel force, 15,000 strong, retreated in great haste yesterday morning. Captain Cole reports heavy firing in the direction of Winchester. Our forces are undoubtedly there.

R. SAXTON,
*Brigadier-General.*

Hon. E. M. STANTON,
*Secretary of War.*

HARPER'S FERRY, VA.,
*June* 1, 1862—8 p. m.

My scouts have returned from Loudoun Mountain. The enemy had been there, but have gone. A shell thrown at night from our batteries passed over the mountain and exploded directly in their camp. All reports are that Jackson is falling back. He may try to get out across General Geary's lines. I can see no other chance.

R. SAXTON,
*Brigadier-General.*

Hon. E. M. STANTON.

---

WASHINGTON, *June* 1, 1862.

Brigadier-General SAXTON:

The forces at Harper's Ferry have been assigned to General Banks' corps, and Major-General Sigel has been placed in command, with directions to report to General Banks and assume active operations against the enemy. You will please report to General Sigel on his arrival, and remain in such command as he may assign to you.

EDWIN M. STANTON,
*Secretary of War.*

---

HARPER'S FERRY, VA.,
*June* 1, 1862.

I have received your dispatch announcing the assignment of General Sigel to the forces here. I beg that you will not forget your promise when I left Washington that my assignment to duty was but temporary and relieve me from further duty with this command on the arrival of General Sigel.

Respectfully,

R. SAXTON,
*Brigadier-General.*

Hon. E. M. STANTON,
*Secretary of War.*

---

WASHINGTON, *June* 1, 1862.

Brigadier-General SAXTON,
*Harper's Ferry:*

I shall not forget my promise, but wish you to remain until General Sigel gets the troops in hand. You can render him very important service in that way until he comes in communication with General Banks and can arrange his command. I will give instructions to relieve you as soon as that takes place. I have reserved to say to you personally what I feel concerning the important service you have rendered the Government and the high sense I have of your skill and ability in the performance of your arduous duties, which have fulfilled my expectations.

EDWIN M. STANTON.

HARPER'S FERRY, VA.,
*June* 2, 1862.

SIR: I have the honor to report that, in obedience to your instructions of May 24, 1862, I assumed command of the forces at Harper's Ferry on the 26th of May. I found Colonel Miles occupying the place with one company of the Maryland Potomac Home Brigade. He had pushed forward that morning a battalion, composed of the First District of Columbia Regiment and One hundred and eleventh Regiment Pennsylvania Volunteers, on the cars to Winchester, to re-enforce General Banks. They were too late, he having retreated, and they returned to Harper's Ferry. The same evening re-enforcements arrived, consisting of the Seventy-eighth New York, One hundred and ninth Pennsylvania, a naval battery of Dahlgren guns, under Lieutenant Daniels, U. S. Navy, and four companies of the Fifth New York Cavalry, from Winchester. On the 27th other troops arrived, with Captain Crounse's and Reynolds' battery of the First New York Artillery. I occupied Bolivar Heights with my troops and Maryland Heights with the naval battery. On the same evening I sent two companies of Colonel Maulsby's First Maryland Regiment, under Major Steiner, to make a reconnaissance of Loudoun Heights, where it was reported the enemy were in position.

They were fired upon whilst ascending, between 9 and 10 o'clock in the morning, by dismounted rebel cavalry concealed in the bushes on both sides of the road. Sergeant Mehrling, of Company I, was killed. The fire was returned, with what effect was not known. Owing to the darkness of the night Major Steiner returned.

On Wednesday I shelled the Heights from Battery Stanton, compelling the enemy to retire, as was proved by a subsequent reconnaissance. In the course of the morning a reconnaissance in force was made toward Charlestown by the One hundred and eleventh Pennsylvania Regiment, Colonel Schlaudecker, and the First Maryland Cavalry, Major Deems, and one section of Reynolds' battery. Our cavalry drove the enemy out of Charlestown, but they were immediately re-enforced, and opening fire from a battery of nine guns, compelled our forces to retire, with a loss of 1 captain and 8 men captured by the enemy. The Seventy-eighth New York and the remaining pieces of Reynolds' battery were at once dispatched to cover their retreat, which was effected in good order without further injury, the enemy's battery following them to a point 2 miles distant from Charlestown. They reported on their return the enemy advancing. Our troops were immediately formed in line of battle, extending along the crest of Bolivar Heights across the peninsula from the Potomac to the Shenandoah.

A body of the enemy's cavalry was seen occasionally emerging from a point of woods about 2 miles distant, a little on the left of the road to Charlestown. Clouds of dust were visible in various directions, as if the enemy were advancing. Our guns shelled the woods in front. The enemy made no response, but seemed, from their movements, desirous of drawing us out from our position. Our men slept on their arms.

On the morning of the 29th the Fifth New York Cavalry was sent out to reconnoiter, and was fired upon by the enemy's infantry and artillery. Our pickets being driven in, our forces were again formed in order of battle, General Cooper's brigade on Bolivar Heights to the right, and General Slough's brigade to the left of the road leading to Charlestown. After two or three hours, the enemy not appearing, a squadron of cavalry was sent out toward Halltown, before reaching which they were suddenly fired upon by a battery occupying a position on the verge of the woods to the left of the road. A body of cavalry and some infantry were seen stationed under cover of the woods in position to support the battery. Having accomplished their object, our cavalry returned. It became evident that the enemy were seeking, as on the preceeding day, to allure us from our strong defensive position to one of their own selection, where their greatly superior force could attack us with certain success.

Learning in the course of the evening from various reliable sources that the enemy, failing in this, contemplated a flank movement—crossing the Potomac with one division above and another occupying Loudoun Heights, so as to command our naval battery and cut off our communication below Harper's Ferry, while the remaining force menaced us in front—it was determined to withdraw our troops from Bolivar Heights and take up a second line of defense on the height known as Camp Hill, immediately above the town of Harper's Ferry. The occupation of this inner line presented a twofold advantage: First, that being much less extended it could be held by a smaller force, the enemy from the nature of the ground being unable to bring into action a larger force than our own; secondly, that it would enable us to bring our naval battery on the Maryland Heights to bear upon the enemy as they advanced down the declivity of Bolivar Heights into the valley which separates it from Camp Hill. They would thus be exposed for a considerable time to a heavy fire from this formidable battery, whose great elevation would enable it to throw shells directly over the heads of our own forces on Camp Hill into the faces of the advancing foe. With the force rendered by this contraction of our front available for other purposes it was deemed prudent to occupy the crest of the hill above the naval battery on the Maryland shore, to frustrate any attempt of the enemy to take this hill in the rear and turn out batteries against us.

The movement having been decided upon, orders were immediately given for its prompt execution. This was about midnight. General Cooper's brigade was at once set in motion, and by daylight had succeeded in crossing the river and occupying the heights on the Maryland side. General Slough's brigade at the same time fell back to the new position on Camp Hill, and when morning dawned our batteries (Companies K and L, of the First New York Artillery), supported by a heavy force of infantry, were in position to command all the approaches in our front and flanks, the remainder of the infantry being posted as reserves along the brow of the hill, under cover of the town and houses. The weak portions of this line were subsequently strengthened by breastworks hastily erected.

On Friday morning Major Gardner, with the Fifth New York Cavalry, was sent to the front to feel the enemy's position and watch his movements. He was later in the day re-enforced by a piece of artillery and 200 sharpshooters. The enemy opened upon him with a scattered fire of musketry along his whole front. The first fire of grape from our piece caused the enemy's skirmishers to fall back in disorder. He then brought six pieces of artillery into action. Major Gardner, having most gallantly accomplished the object of his expedition, retired. The enemy now advanced with his artillery and shelled our former position on Bolivar Heights. Having done this, he withdrew.

General Jackson, the commander of the rebel forces, having given the order to his army to storm our position, they advanced beyond Bolivar Heights in force to attack us. About dark on Friday evening, in the storm, General Slough opened upon them from Camp Hill with Crounse's and part of Reynolds' battery, and Lieutenant Daniels from Battery Stanton, on Maryland Heights. The scene at this time was very impressive. The night was intensely dark; the hills around were alive with the signal-lights of the enemy; the rain descended in torrents; vivid flashes of lightning illumined at intervals the grand and magnificent scenery, while the crash of thunder, echoing among the mountains, drowned into comparative insignificance the roar of our artillery. After an action of about an hour's duration the enemy retired. He made another unsuccessful attack at midnight with regiments of Mississippi and Louisiana Infantry, and after a short engagement disappeared. Signal-lights continued to be seen in every direction.

On Saturday morning, ignorant of the enemy's movements, I sent out a reconnaissance in force to discover his whereabouts, and found that he had retreated. I pushed forward as far as Charlestown and found the enemy's rear guard had left an hour before. Fifty pieces of his cannon passed through Charlestown that morning, the enemy being in strong force, variously estimated at from 18,000 to 25,000, and many reports in circulation that he had repulsed our forces sent to attack him in the rear; and my own forces, of not more than 7,000 effective men, being completely worn-out by fatigue and exposure, I deemed it not prudent to advance, at least until the men rested. On Sunday General Sigel arrived, and on Monday he assumed command. I have not yet received the reports of the subordinate commanders, and cannot particularize individual instances of good conduct. As a general thing the troops bore their fatigue and hardships with cheerfulness.

Great credit is due to Brigadier-Generals Cooper and Slough, commanding the First and Second Brigades respectively, for their untiring exertions during the five days and night siege. Also to Col. D. S. Miles, commanding the Railroad Brigade, and his aides, Lieutenants Binney and Reynolds, as well as my own personal staff, Capt. George Merrill, assistant adjutant-general; Capts. J. C. Anderson and Ulric Dahlgren, additional aides-de-camp; Maj. George W. Brum, volunteer aide, and Mr. Thorndyke, of the Eighth Missouri Regiment, who volunteered his services on this occasion. Lieutenant Daniels, with his naval battery of Dahlgren guns on Maryland Heights, 2,000 feet above the level of the sea, did splendid service throughout the entire siege.

Very respectfully, your obedient servant,

R. SAXTON,
*Brigadier-General, U. S. Volunteers.*

Hon. E. M. STANTON,
*Secretary of War.*

---

WAR DEPARTMENT,
*Washington, June* 17, 1862.

Brig. Gen. R. SAXTON:

GENERAL: The thanks of this Department are cordially tendered to you for your late able and gallant defense of Harper's Ferry against the rebel forces under command of General Jackson. You were placed in command at that point at a moment of extreme danger and under circumstances of extraordinary difficulty.

By your gallantry and skill great service was rendered to the country, which I feel it to be the duty of this Department to acknowledge and place on record, assuring you at the same time of my personal confidence and regard.

Yours, truly,

EDWIN M. STANTON,
*Secretary of War.*

---

## No. 39.

*Reports of Maj. Gen. John C. Frémont, U. S. Army, commanding the Mountain Department, of operations May 24–June 17, and including instructions from the President and Secretary of War.**

WAR DEPARTMENT,
*May* 24, 1862—9.45 a. m.

Major-General FRÉMONT, *Franklin:*

Yesterday the enemy attacked and drove Banks' force from Front Royal, and are threatening Strasburg and Winchester. If you can operate so as to afford him any support do so.

EDWIN M. STANTON,
*Secretary of War.*

---

FRANKLIN, *May* 24, 1862.
(Received 2.30 p. m.)

General Banks informs me this morning† of an attack by enemy. This is probably by Jackson, who marched in that direction some days since. Ewell's force with him. General Banks says he should be re-enforced immediately. May I ask if you will support him? I have no information concerning the real situation of affairs in Eastern Virginia. My own movements are being directed to the object proposed in plan approved, and in connection to the speediest possible support of General Cox, while at the same time protecting country behind our lines from New Creek to Flat Top Mountain, where General Cox now is. Between him and the railroad is a largely superior force. Enemy seems everywhere re-enforced and active. Under the circumstances my force cannot be divided, and if I abandon this line and move eastward to the support of General Banks this whole country to the Ohio would be thrown open, and General Cox also immediately exposed to disaster. If conditions elsewhere will permit General Cox to fall backward and upon my lines, I could in such case cover him without much exposure. Want of supplies has kept this force at Franklin. Beef is now secured, but during the last eight days there has been but one ration of bread, two of coffee and sugar, and nothing else. There is nothing but beef now in camp. This want of food has been nigh to produce disorder, and rendered advance hazardous. Transportation collected at New Creek will begin to tell to-day, and the few days' advance supplies will be accumulated here which are required for active operations. Continued rains have flooded the streams. Raining to-day. Needing much the use of my cavalry. I telegraph to General Meigs asking that he authorize the chief quartermaster and my quartermaster here to purchase

---

* See also general report of operations from March 11 to June 26, pp. 3–35.
† See Banks to Stanton, May 23, p. 525.

immediately, wherever they can be had, 400 horses. Will you approve the requisition?

J. C. FRÉMONT,
*Major-General.*

Hon. E. M. STANTON,
*Secretary of War.*

---

WAR DEPARTMENT,
*May* 24, 1862—4 p. m.

Major-General FRÉMONT, *Franklin:*

You are authorized to purchase the 400 horses or take them wherever or however you can get them.

The exposed condition of General Banks makes his immediate relief a point of paramount importance. You are therefore directed by the President to move against Jackson at Harrisonburg, and operate against the enemy in such way as to relieve Banks. This movement must be made immediately. You will acknowledge the receipt of this order and specify the hour it is received by you.

A. LINCOLN.

---

HEADQUARTERS MOUNTAIN DEPARTMENT,
*Franklin, May* 24, 1862. (Received 6.35 p. m.)

Your telegram received at 5 o'clock this afternoon. Will move as ordered, and operate against the enemy in such way to afford prompt relief to General Banks.

J. C. FRÉMONT,
*Major-General, Commanding.*

His Excellency ABRAHAM LINCOLN.

---

WAR DEPARTMENT,
*May* 24, 1862—7.15 p. m.

Major-General FRÉMONT,
*Franklin, Va.:*

Many thanks for the promptness with which you have answered that you will execute the order. Much—perhaps all—depends upon the celerity with which you can execute it. Put the utmost speed into it. Do not lose a minute.

A. LINCOLN.

---

HEADQUARTERS MOUNTAIN DEPARTMENT,
*On the march, May* 25, 1862.

Dispatch received. Our army will do the best to answer your expectations.

J. C. FRÉMONT,
*Major-General, Commanding.*

President LINCOLN.

WAR DEPARTMENT,
*May* 25, 1862.

General FRÉMONT:

General Banks fell back yesterday from Strasburg to Winchester. To-day he has been driven from Winchester toward Harper's Ferry. You must direct your attention to falling upon the enemy at whatever place you can find him with all speed. McDowell will also operate toward the same object with his force. You must not stop for supplies, but seize what you need and push rapidly forward; the object being to cut off and capture this rebel force in the Shenandoah.

EDWIN M. STANTON.

---

WASHINGTON, *May* 27, 1862.

Major-General FRÉMONT, *Petersburg, Va.:*

General Banks was defeated, and forced to cross the Potomac at Williamsport, which he accomplished with no great loss of troops or stores. Well conducted retreat; brought off all his guns and 500 wagons. The enemy threatened General Geary at Thoroughfare Gap, on the Manassas Gap Railroad, yesterday, but whether in large or small force is not definitely known, nor is the present position of the enemy known. General McDowell has a strong force concentrated at Manassas to pursue the enemy and cut off his retreat, if he can be overtaken. Harper's Ferry strongly occupied by our fresh troops and artillery, and no enemy known to be on the Lower Shenandoah. It is desirable that you move with celerity to prevent the escape of the enemy.

EDWIN M. STANTON,
*Secretary of War.*

---

MAY 27, 1862—9.58 p. m.

Major-General FRÉMONT:

I see that you are at Moorefield. You were expressly ordered to march to Harrisonburg. What does this mean?

A. LINCOLN.

---

HEADQUARTERS IN THE FIELD,
*May* 28, 1862—6 a. m. (Received 10.50 a. m.)

My troops were not in condition to execute your order otherwise than has been done. They have marched day and night to do it. The men had had so little to eat that many were weak for want of food, and were so reported by the chief surgeon. Having for main object, as stated in your telegram, the relief of General Banks, the line of march followed was a necessity. In executing any order received I take it for granted that I am to exercise discretion concerning its literal execution, according to circumstances. If I am to understand that literal obedience to orders is required, please say so. I have no desire to exercise any power which you do not think belongs of necessity to my position in the field.

J. C. FRÉMONT,
*Major-General.*

The PRESIDENT.

MOOREFIELD, *May* 28, 1862.
(Received 11.30 a. m.)

The reasons for my being in Moorefield are, 1st, the point of your order was to relieve General Banks. At the time it was issued it was only known that he had been attacked at Front Royal. When my march commenced I knew he had retreated from Winchester. 2d. Of the different roads to Harrisonburg all but one, and that one leading southward, had been obstructed by the enemy, and if the loss of time by taking the only open road were no consideration, it was still a simple impossibility to march in that direction. My troops were utterly out of provisions. There was nothing whatever to be found in the country except a small quantity of fresh beef, from the effects of which the troops were already suffering, and, in fact, all my men were only saved from starvation by taking the road to Petersburg, where they found five days' rations. With these we are now moving with the utmost celerity possible in whatever direction the enemy may be found.

J. C. FRÉMONT,
*Major-General.*

Hon. ABRAHAM LINCOLN, *President.*

---

WASHINGTON, *May* 28, 1862—1 p. m.

Major-General FRÉMONT, *Moorefield:*

The President directs you to halt at Moorefield and wait orders, unless you hear of the enemy being in the general direction of Romney, in which case you will move upon him. Acknowledge the receipt of this order and the hour it is received.

EDWIN M. STANTON,
*Secretary of War.*

---

CAMP TEN MILES EAST OF MOOREFIELD,
*May* 28, 1862—5 p. m.

Your two dispatches of this date reached me together here at 4.45 p. m. I am camped here, 10 miles east of Moorefield, at fork of roads leading, respectively, to Woodstock, Strasburg, and Winchester. Except Milroy, at Moorefield, my whole force is here. Scouting parties thrown forward to Wardensville. It being late and the men fatigued, I will remain in camp to-night and return to Moorefield in the morning, unless otherwise directed by you. Sent telegraph to Moorefield at 3.30 p. m., directing commanding officer at Romney to make cavalry reconnaissance 15 miles on road to Winchester. My courier will await answer.

J. C. FRÉMONT,
*Major-General.*

Hon. E. M. STANTON, *Secretary of War.*

---

WASHINGTON, *May* 28, 1862—4.50 p. m.

Major-General FRÉMONT, *Moorefield:*

The following dispatch has just been received from General Hamilton, at Harper's Ferry:

HARPER'S FERRY, *May* 28.

Hon. E. M. STANTON, *Secretary of War:*

There is very little doubt that Jackson's force is between Winchester and Charlestown. His troops were too much fatigued to pursue Banks. A large body of rebel cavalry is near Charlestown now. Jackson and Ewell were near Bunker Hill yesterday at noon. Of this last there is no doubt.

C. S. HAMILTON,
*Brigadier-General.*

The above probably indicates the true position of the enemy at this time. President directs you to move upon him by the best route you can.

EDWIN M. STANTON,
*Secretary of War.*

---

HEADQUARTERS NEAR MOOREFIELD, *May* 28, 1862.
(Received 11 p. m.)

Your telegram conveying information from General Hamilton was received at 7 o'clock this evening. The President's order will be obeyed accordingly.

J. C. FRÉMONT,
*Major-General.*

Hon. E. M. STANTON.

---

WASHINGTON, *May* 28, 1862—11 p. m.

Maj. Gen. JOHN C. FRÉMONT, *Moorefield:*

The order to remain at Moorefield was based on the supposition that it would find you there. Upon subsequent information that the enemy were still operating in the vicinity of Winchester and Martinsburg you were directed to move against the enemy. The President now again directs you to move against the enemy without delay. Please acknowledge the receipt of this and the time received.

EDWIN M. STANTON,
*Secretary of War.*

---

WASHINGTON, *May* 29, 1862—2 p. m.

Major-General FRÉMONT, *Moorefield:*

Dispatches from General Saxton, at Harper's Ferry, state as follows:*

HARPER'S FERRY, *May* 28.

Hon. E. M. STANTON:

I have learned from a Union prisoner that my reconnoitering party captured at Charlestown to-day that General Steuart is moving from Winchester to Point of Rocks, intending to cross there, move upon my rear, break up the line of railroad, and burn the bridge. I have sent 100 men to guard it. My troops are posted in strong positions, and unless they disgrace themselves they will hold it, provided the rear is safe.

R. SAXTON,
*Brigadier-General.*

This is all the information we have of the enemy's position. Banks is at Williamsport, having retreated from Winchester. Please acknowledge the receipt of this.

EDWIN M. STANTON.

---

*Copy of Saxton's dispatch sent also to McDowell.

HEADQUARTERS MOUNTAIN DEPARTMENT,
*Army in Field, May* 29, 1862.

Your dispatches of 8 and 10 p. m. were received by me this morning at 2.5 by courier. The President's order will be obeyed as promptly as possible, and I am now engaged in drawing forward my force. My reconnoitering parties out last night 22 miles, to Wardensville, report Jackson's force 4 miles below Winchester; rear guard at Strasburg; headquarters, Winchester. Reconnaissance returned to Romney at 11 last night from 15 miles out. Report Jackson, Johnson, and Ewell at Chester, and rebel cavalry sent from Winchester toward Harper's Ferry and Martinsburg.

J. C. FRÉMONT,
*Major-General.*

Hon. E. M. STANTON, *Secretary of War.*

---

WASHINGTON, *May* 29, 1862—12 m.

Major-General FRÉMONT,
*Moorefield, Va.:*

General McDowell's advance, if not checked by the enemy, should, and probably will, be at Front Royal by 12 (noon) to-morrow. His force, when up, will be about 20,000. Please have your force at Strasburg, or, if the route you are moving on does not lead to that point, as near Strasburg as the enemy may be by the same time. Your dispatch No. 30* received and satisfactory.

A. LINCOLN.

---

HEADQUARTERS MOUNTAIN DEPARTMENT,
*Near Moorefield, May* 29, 1862.

Our advance occupies to-night the bridge at Lost River, 16 miles ahead. The scouting party of Maryland cavalry, sent out last evening under charge of Lieutenant-Colonel Downey, drove the enemy's pickets through Wardensville this morning, killing 2. Colonel Downey's horse was shot under him. My command is not yet in marching order. It has been necessary to halt to-day to bring up parts of regiments and to receive stragglers, hundreds of whom from Blenker's division strewed the roads. You can conceive the condition of the command from the fact that the medical director this morning protested against its farther advance without allowing one day's rest, the regiments being much reduced, and force diminished accordingly. I could not venture to proceed with it in disorder, and cannot with safety undertake to be at the point you mention earlier than by 5 o'clock on Saturday afternoon. At that hour I will be at or near it, according to position of the enemy. Companies in the rear are marching night and day to bring up the entire force. Will be on the road early to-morrow morning, and couriers will be provided to bring on your answer, which please send to-night, and let me know if General McDowell's force can be so controlled as to make this combination.

J. C. FRÉMONT,
*Major-General.*

The PRESIDENT.

(Copy to McDowell May 30.)

---

* Next preceding.

MOOREFIELD, *May* 30, 1862.
(Received 11.30 a. m.)

Scouts and men from Winchester represent Jackson's force variously at 30,000 to 60,000. With him Generals Ewell and Longstreet.

J. C. FRÉMONT,
*Major-General.*

ABRAHAM LINCOLN, *President.*

—

**WASHINGTON, *May* 30, 1862—11.30 a. m.**

Major-General FRÉMONT,
*Moorefield, Va.:*

Yours of this morning from Moorefield just received. There cannot be more than 20,000, probably not more than 15,000, of the enemy at or about Winchester. Where is your force? It ought this minute to be near Strasburg. Answer at once.

A. LINCOLN.

—

WASHINGTON, *May* 30, 1862—2.30 p. m.

Major-General FRÉMONT,
*Moorefield, Va.:*

Yours, saying you will reach Strasburg or vicinity at 5 p. m. Saturday, has been received and sent to General McDowell, and he directed to act in view of it. You must be up to time you promised, if possible. Corinth was evacuated last night and is occupied by our troops to-day; the enemy gone south to Okolona, on the railroad to Mobile.

A. LINCOLN.

—

HEADQUARTERS,
*May* 30, 1862.

Colonel Latham, with a detachment of the Second Virginia, and a company of Connecticut Cavalry, under Captain Fish, who were sent to Saver's River, surprised and routed a gang of guerrillas at that place, killing their captain and 3 men, wounding several others, and capturing and destroying more than thirty guns.

J. C. FRÉMONT,
*Major-General.*

Hon. E. M. STANTON.

—

WASHINGTON, *May* 30, 1862—9.30 p. m.

Major-General FRÉMONT, *Moorefield:*

I send you a dispatch just received from General Saxton, at Harper's Ferry:

HARPER'S FERRY, 30*th*.
(Received 6 p. m.)

Hon. E. M. STANTON, *Secretary of War:*

The rebels are in line of battle in front of our lines. They have nine pieces of artillery in position and cavalry. I shelled the woods in which they were, and they in return threw a large number of shells into the lines and tents from which I moved last night to take up a stronger position. I expect a great deal from the battery on the mountain, having here nine 9-inch Dahlgren's bearing directly on the enemy's approaches. The enemy appeared this morning, and then retired with the intention of driving us out. I shall act on the defensive, as my position is a strong one. In a skirmish which took place this afternoon I lost 1 horse; the enemy 2 men killed and some wounded.

R. SAXTON,
*Brigadier-General.*

It seems the game is before you. Have sent a copy to General McDowell.

A. LINCOLN.

---

WASHINGTON, *May* 31, 1862—1 a. m.

Major-General FRÉMONT, *Moorefield, Va.:*
Major-General MCDOWELL, *Rectortown, Va.:*

I have just returned from Harper's Ferry. The enemy has been before that place and threatening an attack for two days. Deserters report that Jackson is in command, and that in a speech made to his men in Charlestown on Wednesday morning he promised them less marching and better fare in a few days, when they would enter Maryland. It is supposed that the attack on Harper's Ferry has been delayed by an apprehension of the advance of your force to cut off retreat. When do you expect to reach Winchester? Where is Shields?

P. H. WATSON,
*Assistant Secretary of War.*

---

HEADQUARTERS MOUNTAIN DEPARTMENT,
*Wardensville, May* 31, 1862. (Received 8.30 p. m.)

Your telegram of 31st [30th?] received. Main column at this place. Roads heavy and weather terrible. Heavy storm of rain most of yesterday and all last night. Our cavalry and scouts have covered the roads 10 to 15 miles ahead. The enemy's cavalry and ours now in sight of each other on the Strasburg road. Engagement expected to-day. The army is pushing forward, and I intend to carry out operations proposed.

J. C. FRÉMONT,
*Major-General, Commanding.*

To the PRESIDENT.

(Copy to McDowell.)

---

HEADQUARTERS,
*Five miles from Strasburg, June* 1, 1862.

Our advance reached this point last night; became engaged this morning. Main body reached here at 10 a. m. to-day. Advance is under Colonel Cluseret, aide-de-camp. He has eight pieces and two small regiments. Was attacked by enemy in considerable force. Reported by prisoner 15,000, with 8,000 coming up. We hear nothing of McDowell. Our force marched hard all night, and crossed the Shenandoah during an uninterrupted storm. Expect to bring up our entire force by night-fall. Our advance holds its place, and I shall accept battle in our present position, which is an excellent one. Will do more according to opportunity. General engagement will probably take place during the afternoon.

J. C. FRÉMONT,
*Major-General, Commanding.*

To the PRESIDENT.
(Copy to McDowell.)

—

HEADQUARTERS IN THE FIELD,
*Near Strasburg, June* 1, 1862—6 p. m.

Your telegram of this date received at 5 o'clock. The skirmish of this morning was confined to infantry and artillery of our advance and lasted about two hours, at the expiration of which time the enemy retired. Our loss only 7 wounded. State of rebels not known. I am now (6 o'clock) about driving in their pickets, and if that does not bring on a general engagement shall close with him early to-morrow morning.

J. C. FRÉMONT,
*Major-General.*

Hon. E. M. STANTON,
*Secretary of War.*

—

HEADQUARTERS ARMY IN FIELD,
*Strasburg, June* 1, *via Moorefield, June* 2, 1862

A reconnoitering force just in reports the enemy retreating, but in what direction is not yet known. Our cavalry will occupy Strasburg by midnight. Terrible storm of thunder and hail now passing over. Hailstones as large as hens' eggs.

J. C. FRÉMONT,
*Major-General.*

To the PRESIDENT.

—

HEADQUARTERS ARMY IN THE FIELD,
*Strasburg, 2d.*

The engagement of yesterday was renewed and continued until 10 o'clock at night, at which time my advance had driven the rear guard of the rebels into their main camp at a place called Round Hill, some 4 miles from Strasburg. At this point my cavalry attacked and dispersed a body of rebel cavalry, but pursued no farther on account of the storm. The enemy lost many in killed and wounded. We took 11 prisoners. Several wounded on our side, but none killed. My whole force is now (9 o'clock) up and in rapid pursuit of the enemy. I meet here General Bayard, with a regiment of cavalry, one company of infantry, and four guns, forming the advance of General McDowell. The officers who particularly distinguished themselves in the cavalry charge last night are Colonel Figyelmesy, of my staff; Major Finch, temporarily of the Sixth Ohio Cavalry, and Captain Fish, of the Connecticut cavalry.

J. C. FRÉMONT,
*Major-General, Commanding.*

Hon. E. M. STANTON.

P. S.—I have opened and read General Frémont's message and forwarded it, 12.30. General Bayard's brigade, I understand from the messenger, has joined General Frémont, and Hartsuff is on the way. General Shields, who advanced for Luray last night, has his whole division on the march to try and intercept Jackson up the valley.*

IRVIN McDOWELL.

---

WASHINGTON, *June* 2, 1862.

Major-General FRÉMONT, *Strasburg:*
Major-General McDOWELL, *Front Royal:*

Your dispatches received. We are glad to hear you are so close on the enemy. McClellan beat the rebels badly near Richmond yesterday. The President tells me to say to you do not let the enemy escape from you. Major-General Sigel is advancing with two brigades from Harper's Ferry toward Winchester. Let us hear from you often.

EDWIN M. STANTON,
*Secretary of War.*

---

HEADQUARTERS ARMY IN THE FIELD,
*Camp by Woodstock, Va., June* 2, 1862—6 p. m.

The enemy was pressed by our advance this morning until about 10 o'clock, when he made a determined stand of an hour. He was attacked by about 1,000 cavalry, under General Bayard, 600 cavalry of my command, under Colonel Zagonyi, and Schirmer's and Buell's batteries, of General Stahel's brigade, under Lieutenant-Colonel Pilsen, aide-de-camp. He repeatedly faced about, and was as often driven from his position during a running fight of four hours. Our force marched 18 miles in five hours. The pursuit was so rapid that it was impossible to get the infantry up before he reached for the night the heights beyond Woodstock.

His retreat was reckless. About 100 prisoners and 200 stand of arms were taken, and there are at least 1,000 stragglers in the woods along the road and country adjoining. Clothing, blankets, muskets, and sabers are strewn also upon the road.

We have a few killed and wounded. Among the hurt is Colonel Pilsen, though not seriously.

At their last stand the enemy lost 6 or 8 killed, and his loss during the day was undoubtedly considerable. With the infantry at hand we should have taken his guns.

At 4.45 p. m. General Stahel's brigade occupied Woodstock.

J. C. FRÉMONT,
*Major-General, Commanding.*

Hon. E. M. STANTON,
*Secretary of War, Washington, D. C.*

---

HEADQUARTERS IN THE FIELD,
*Mount Jackson, June* 4, 1862.

The pursuit of the enemy was continued to-day, and their rear again engaged. The rebels attempted to destroy all the bridges, and suc-

* Foregoing was telegraphed to Sigel, at Harper's Ferry, by Secretary of War, who added, "I hope no time will be lost in pushing forward to aid General Frémont."

ceeded in burning several, the most important of which was that over the Shenandoah at this place. Our loss to-day is but 1 killed. We have begun to release prisoners taken at Front Royal, about 30 having been recaptured to-day. The late violent rains, which still continue, have raised the rivers so that they are not fordable, but arrangements are being made to-night for crossing, and the pursuit will be continued early in the morning. I hope to-morrow to force the rebels to a stand.

J. C. FRÉMONT,
*Major-General.*

Hon. E. M. STANTON.

---

HEADQUARTERS ARMY IN THE FIELD,
*Mountain Department, June* 4, 1862.
(Received June 6, 1.05 p. m.)

It has rained continuously and hard for twenty-four hours, producing one of the two greatest freshets known for many years. The Shenandoah rose 10 feet in four hours, breaking up the temporary bridge just thrown across. The bridge at Edenburg, partially demolished by the enemy, is also now entirely swept away. A regiment of infantry and two companies of cavalry succeeded in crossing the Shenandoah before the bridge was broken, and are now encamped on the other side of the stream. The effort to cross will be renewed to-morrow morning. The prisoners now number 400. We hear nothing yet of General Shields.

J. C. FRÉMONT,
*Major-General, Commanding.*

Hon. E. M. STANTON, *Secretary of War.*

---

HDQRS. MOUNTAIN DEPT., ARMY IN THE FIELD,
*Harrisonburg, June* 7, 1862. (Received June 9, 9 a. m.)

The army reached this place at 2 o'clock yesterday afternoon, driving out the enemy's rear guard from the town. Severe skirmishing continued from that time until dark, the enemy's rear being closely pressed by our advance. At 4 o'clock the First New Jersey Cavalry, after driving the enemy through the village, fell into an ambuscade in the woods to the southeast of the town, in which Colonel Wyndham, of that regiment, was captured and considerable loss sustained. Colonel Cluseret with his brigade subsequently engaged the enemy in the timber, driving him from his position and taking his camp. At about 8 a battalion of Colonel Kane's (Pennsylvania) regiment entered the woods under the direction of Brigadier-General Bayard, and maintained for half an hour a vigorous attack, in which both sides suffered severely, driving the enemy. The enemy attempted to shell our troops, but a few shots from one of our batteries soon silenced his guns. After dark the enemy continued his retreat. Full particulars will be forwarded by mail. The condition of the force is extremely bad, for want of supplies. We have been obliged to leave our single pontoon train at one of the bridges behind, in order to get our supplies over, and are now without any.

J. C. FRÉMONT,
*Major-General.*

Hon. E. M. STANTON, *Secretary of War.*

HEADQUARTERS ARMY IN THE FIELD,
*Harrisonburg, June* 7, 1862—9 p. m.
(Received June 9, 7.40 a. m.)

The attacks upon the enemy's rear of yesterday precipitated his retreat. Their loss in killed and wounded was very severe, and many of both were left on the field. Their retreat was by an almost impassable road, along which many wagons were left in the woods, and wagon loads of blankets, clothing, and other equipments are piled up in all directions. During the evening many of the rebels were killed by shells from a battery of General Stahel's brigade. General Ashby, who covered the retreat with his whole cavalry force and three regiments of infantry and who exhibited admirable skill and audacity, was among the killed. General Milroy made a reconnaissance to-day about 7 miles on the Port Republic road, and discovered a portion of the enemy's forces encamped in the timber.

J. C. FRÉMONT,
*Major-General, Commanding.*

Hon. E. M. STANTON.

---

WAR DEPARTMENT, ADJT. GEN.'S OFFICE,
*Washington, June* 8, 1862.

Maj. Gen. JOHN C. FRÉMONT, U. S. A.,
*Commanding Mountain Department, Mount Pleasant, Va.:*

GENERAL: I inclose herewith for your information a manuscript copy of General Orders, No. 62.* The Secretary of War directs that you take position with your main force at or near Harrisonburg, with the double object of guarding against any operations of the enemy down the valley of the Shenandoah, and also, in conjunction with your force under General Cox, against any such operations in Western Virginia.

The cavalry force known as Bayard's cavalry brigade, with the artillery and battalion of Bucktail Rifles, heretofore under command of Major-General McDowell, but now operating with you, will be immediately ordered to rejoin General McDowell at Fredericksburg.

Major-General Banks is instructed to take position in force at or near Front Royal, on the right or left bank of the Shenandoah, with an advance at Luray or other points in supporting distance of you, and also to occupy with sufficient detachments the former positions of General Geary on the line of the Manassas Gap Railroad as far as the Manassas Junction.

I am, general, very respectfully, your obedient servant,

L. THOMAS,
*Adjutant-General.*

---

HEADQUARTERS ARMY IN THE FIELD,
*Camp near Port Republic, June* 8, 1862—9 p. m.
(Received June 10, 9.30 a. m.)

The army left Harrisonburg at 6 this morning, and at 8.30 my advance engaged the rebels about 7 miles from that place, near Union Church. The enemy was very advantageously posted in the timber,

---

* See Thomas to Banks, same date, p. 541.

having chosen his own position, forming a smaller circle than our own, and with his troops formed in masses. It consisted undoubtedly of Jackson's entire force. The battle began with heavy firing at 11 o'clock, and lasted with great obstinacy and violence until 4 in the afternoon. Some skirmishing and artillery firing continued from that time until dark. Our troops fought occasionally under the murderous fire of greatly superior numbers, the hottest of the small-arm fire being on the left wing, which was held by Stahel's brigade, consisting of five regiments. The bayonet and canister shot were used freely and with great effect by our men. Loss on both sides very great. Ours very heavy among the officers. A full report of those who distinguished themselves will be made without partiality. I desire to say that both officers and men behaved with splendid gallantry, and that the service of the artillery was especially admirable. We are encamped on the field of battle, which may be renewed at any moment.

J. C. FRÉMONT,
*Major-General.*

Hon. E. M. STANTON,
*Secretary of War.*

---

HEADQUARTERS MOUNTAIN DEPARTMENT,
*Port Republic, June* 9, 1862—noon, *via Martinsburg.*
(Received June 12, 8 a. m.)

There was no collision with the enemy after dark last night. This morning we resumed the march against him, entering the woods in battle order, his cavalry appearing on flanks.

General Blenker had the left, General Milroy the right, and General Schenck the center, with a reserve of General Stahel's brigade and General Bayard's. The enemy was found to be in full retreat on Port Republic, and our advance found his rear guard barely across the river and the bridge in flames. Our advance came in so suddenly that some of his officers remaining on this side escaped with the loss of their horses. A cannonading during the forenoon apprised us of an engagement, and I am informed here that General Jackson attacked General Shields this morning, and after a severe engagement drove him down the river and is now in pursuit. I have sent an officer with a detachment of cavalry to open communication with General Shields, and in mean time preparing to bridge the river, having no pontoon.

This morning detachments were occupied in searching the grounds covered by yesterday's action at Cross Keys for our remaining dead and wounded. I am not fully informed, but think 125 will cover our loss in killed and 500 in wounded. The enemy's loss we cannot clearly ascertain. He was engaged during the night in carrying off his dead and wounded in wagons. This morning upon our march upward of 200 of his dead were counted in one field, the greater part badly mutilated by cannon-shot. Many of his dead were also scattered through the woods, and many had been already buried. A number of prisoners had been taken during the pursuit.

I regret to have lost many good officers. General Stahel's brigade was in the hottest part of the field, which was the left wing from the beginning of the fight. The brigade lost in officers 5 killed and 17 wounded, and one of his regiments alone—the Eighth New York—has buried 65. The Garibaldi Guards, next after, suffered most severely, and following this regiment the Forty-fifth New York, the Bucktail Rifles of General Bayard's, and General Milroy's brigade. One of the Bucktail companies has lost all its officers, commissioned and non-commissioned. The loss in General Schenck's brigade was less, although he inflicted severe loss on the enemy, principally by artillery fire. Of my staff I lost a good officer killed, Capt. Nicolai Dunka. Many horses were killed in our batteries, which the enemy repeatedly attempted to take, but were repulsed by canister fire.

Generally I feel myself permitted to say that all our troops, by their endurance of this severe march and their splendid conduct in the battle, are entitled to the President's commendation. The officers throughout behaved with a gallantry and efficiency which require that I should make particular mention of them, and which I trust will receive the particular notice of the President. As soon as possible I will send a full report, but in this respect I am unable to make any more particular distinction than that pointed out in the description of the battle.

Respectfully,

J. C. FRÉMONT,
*Major-General, Commanding.*

Hon. E. M. STANTON.

---

WASHINGTON, *June* 9, 1862.

Major-General FRÉMONT:

Halt at Harrisonburg, pursuing Jackson no farther. Get your force well in hand and stand on the defensive, guarding against a movement of the enemy either back toward Strasburg or toward Franklin, and await further orders, which will soon be sent you.

A. LINCOLN.

---

ADJUTANT-GENERAL'S OFFICE,
*Washington, June* 10, 1862.

Major-General FRÉMONT, *Harrisonburg:*

The Secretary of War directs that you immediately order the cavalry force known as Bayard's cavalry brigade, with the artillery and battalion of Bucktail Rifles, heretofore under General McDowell, but now operating with you, to rejoin General McDowell's command, and to march to Luray and report to General Shields.

L. THOMAS,
*Adjutant-General.*

---

HEADQUARTERS MOUNTAIN DEPARTMENT,
*Harrisonburg, Va., June* 10, 1862. (Received June 12, 4 p. m.)

In my dispatch of yesterday I omitted to state that Colonel Cluseret's brigade, consisting of the Sixtieth Ohio and Eighth Virginia, afterward supported by the Garibaldi Guard, formed our advance, and commenced the battle of Cross Keys by sharp skirmishing at 9 o'clock in the morning. During the day they obtained possession of the enemy's ground, which was disputed foot by foot, and only withdrew at evening, when ordered to retire to a suitable position for the night. The skill and gallantry displayed by Colonel Cluseret on this and frequent former occasions during the pursuit in which we have been engaged deserve high praise.

Respectfully,

J. C. FRÉMONT,
*Major-General, Commanding.*

Hon. E. M. STANTON,
*Secretary of War.*

---

HEADQUARTERS,
*Port Republic, June* 10, 1862.

The officer sent with a detachment of cavalry to open communication with General Shields returned at 3 o'clock this morning, having found the troops on the march under orders for Richmond. He learns from the adjutant-general of General Shields that the Union forces engaged yesterday were only three brigades, which were almost cut to pieces. Jackson having received re-enforcements, General Shields having been ordered to Richmond with his force, and my own being very much weakened by battle and the hardships and exposures of a severe march, I deem it best to fall back until I can form a junction with the forces of Generals Banks and Sigel and am made acquainted with your wishes.

J. C. FRÉMONT,
*Major-General.*

Hon. E. M. STANTON,
*Secretary of War.*

---

HEADQUARTERS MOUNTAIN DIVISION,
*Harrisonburg, June* 11, 1862. (Received June 12, 10 a. m.)

Your dispatch of yesterday morning finds me here withdrawing upon Mount Jackson, a strong, defensible position behind the Shenandoah, and the key to the surrounding country. General Shields' withdrawal after his action of the 9th, together with the condition of my troops, made this movement imperative. Will you allow me to halt at Mount Jackson instead of Harrisonburg, which is not a line of defense, and exposes me to be cut off from my supplies and communication? My troops are much distressed for want of supplies, which are far in the rear and come up very inadequately. We are greatly in need of surgeons and ambulances.

J. C. FRÉMONT,
*Major-General.*

Hon. ABRAHAM LINCOLN,
*President of the United States.*

---

HEADQUARTERS IN THE FIELD,
*Mount Jackson, June* 12, 1862. (Received June 13, 10 a. m.)

Upon intelligence of General Shields' defeat and withdrawal toward Richmond I retired upon this place, which is a defensible and good position. The regiments composing my command have been rendered very weak by illness, casualties, and deaths. I request that orders be given to recruit them to full strength immediately. Their condition necessitates that they have some days' rest and good and sufficient food. The demand made upon them in the pursuit of Jackson has exhausted them for the present, and they should be supported by fresh troops. At any hour they may be attacked by the enemy, now reported strongly re-enforced, and I ask that General Sigel be telegraphed to report to me with his force without delay. I respectfully suggest to the President that it may prove disastrous to separate the small corps now operating in this region. Consolidated, they could act offensively and efficiently against the enemy. I also suggest that General Shields may be attacked in his march eastward unless supported. My strength should be sufficient to enable me to occupy the Monterey passes and aid General Cox and Colonel Crook, against whom I think the enemy is likely to concentrate a superior force. I have asked for Sigel if possible. Banks also should come. A disaster now would have consequences difficult to remedy.

J. C. FRÉMONT,
*Major-General.*

Hon. ABRAHAM LINCOLN,
*President of the United States.*

---

WASHINGTON, *June* 12, 1862—11 a. m.

Major-General FRÉMONT:

Your dispatch of yesterday to the President has just been received. He directs me to say that Mount Jackson will serve the purpose he had in view as well as Harrisonburg, except that it does not so well guard against the enemy's operations toward Western Virginia. But if, in view of all the circumstances, you prefer the position of Mount Jackson, you will occupy it instead of Harrisonburg.

EDWIN M. STANTON,
*Secretary of War.*

---

HEADQUARTERS ARMY IN THE FIELD,
*Mount Jackson, Va., June* 12, 1862.

I arrived at this place to-day. My officers have been so much engaged with marching duties since the battle of the 8th, at Cross Keys, that full reports of that engagement have not been made to me. Still, wishing to give you a fuller account of that battle than that contained in my telegraphic dispatch, I make the following statement:

The forces under my command left Harrisonburg on the 8th instant, the advance consisting of the Eighth West Virginia and Sixtieth Ohio, being under the command of Colonel Cluseret, aide-de-camp, who was temporarily supported by the Thirty-ninth New York Volunteer Regiment of General Stahel's brigade.

At 9 a. m. the skirmishers of the advance discovered the enemy most advantageously posted in the woods at Cross Keys, on the road to Port Republic. A spirited bayonet charge was immediately made by the Garibaldi Guard, and his right driven back in some confusion. The main body of the army now coming up, General Stahel, commanding the First Brigade, of General Blenker's division, supported by the Third

Brigade, General Bohlen commanding, entered the woods on our left with the Eighth, Forty-first, and Forty-fifth New York Volunteers and the Twenty-seventh Pennsylvania Volunteers. After an obstinate contest of three hours, during which the bayonet was used to extricate one of our batteries from more than three regiments of the enemy, and after some desperate struggles, in which canister-shot was used to repel him from an attempt to take Johnson's and Schirmer's batteries, the brigade (Stahel's) withdrew from the wood in good order, taking up another position under the support of Bohlen's and Steinwehr's brigades.

Meanwhile, on the right, Brigadier-General Milroy, with the Twenty-fifth Ohio, the Second, Third, and Fifth West Virginia, supported by the brigade of General Schenck, drove the enemy steadily forward until the withdrawal of General Stahel's brigade and the near approach of night prevented any farther advance. Colonel Cluseret, commanding the advance, maintained his position throughout the day, steadily resisting the attempts of the enemy to turn his flanks, until, at the approach of night, he was ordered to take position on the right wing. The enemy's force was so largely superior that he was enabled to attempt turning both flanks, and massed overwhelming forces against the brigade of General Stahel, on our left, with the obvious design of interrupting our line of communication. The plan was frustrated by the coolness and courage of our men.

Our troops slept on their arms through the night of the 8th, expecting to renew the contest at an early hour on the following morning. The enemy, however, retreated during the night, leaving behind on the field of battle the most of his dead and many of his wounded. His loss in killed, wounded, and missing cannot be less than 1,200. More than 200 dead were discovered in one field alone and buried by our men.

Our own loss amounts to 106 killed, 386 wounded, and 126 missing.* Of these 43 killed, 134 wounded, and 43 missing are from one regiment, the Eighth New York Volunteers, which fought with the greatest bravery, and yielded ground only when opposed by four rebel regiments at once.

Our artillery, under the command of Lieutenant-Colonel Pilsen, aide-de-camp, was served with the greatest effect and precision, and contributed largely to the final result of the action.

Brigadier-Generals Milroy and Stahel and Colonel Cluseret deserve particular mention for the cool and effective manner in which their troops were handled. For a list of names deserving special commendation I refer to the reports of the brigade and division commanders.

Capt. Nicolai Dunka, one of my aides, and a brave and capable officer, was struck by a rifle-ball and instantly killed while carrying orders to a distant part of the field.

The steadiness and gallantry displayed by the army, after the hardships to which they had been exposed during their forced marches to the scene of action, elicited my warmest admiration, and I hope will give pleasure to the President.

Respectfully,

J. C. FRÉMONT,
*Major-General, Commanding.*

Hon. E. M. STANTON,
*Washington, D. C.*

---

*But see revised statement, p. 664.

HEADQUARTERS MOUNTAIN DEPARTMENT,
*Mount Jackson, June* 13, 1862.

I think General Shields' position at Luray very much exposed. If you will direct him to join me here I will cover his passage over the river. Jackson's force is reported to me by one of General Shields' officers this morning at 38,000.

J. C. FRÉMONT,
*Major-General.*

ABRAHAM LINCOLN,
*President United States.*

---

WASHINGTON, *June* 13, 1862.

Major-General FRÉMONT:

We cannot afford to keep your force and Banks' and McDowell's engaged in keeping Jackson south of Strasburg and Front Royal. You fought Jackson alone and worsted him. He can have no substantial re-enforcements so long as a battle is pending at Richmond. Surely you and Banks in supporting distance are capable of keeping him from returning to Winchester. But if Sigel be sent forward to you and McDowell (as he must be put to other work), Jackson will break through at Front Royal again. He is already on the right side of the Shenandoah to do it and on the wrong side of it to attack you. The orders already sent you and Banks place you and him in the proper positions for the work assigned you. Jackson cannot move his whole force on either of you before the other can learn of it and go to his assistance. He cannot divide his force, sending part against each of you, because he will be too weak for either. Please do as I directed in the order of the 8th and my dispatch of yesterday, the 12th, and neither you nor Banks will be overwhelmed by Jackson. By proper scout lookouts and beacons of smoke by day and fires by night you can always have timely notice of the enemy's approach. I know not as to you, but by some this has been too much neglected.

A. LINCOLN.

---

MOUNT JACKSON, *June* 13, 1862.
(Received June 14, 8.30 a. m.)

Your dispatch of yesterday received. Will you permit me to have put in running order the railroad from Strasburg to this place? For all reasons this is a military necessity and would be a great economy. The repairs mainly would consist in temporary trestle work in place of bridges destroyed.

J. C. FRÉMONT,
*Major-General.*

Hon. E. M. STANTON,
*Secretary of War.*

---

WASHINGTON, *June* 14, 1862—10 a. m.

Major-General FRÉMONT,
*Mount Jackson:*

You are authorized to put the railroad in running order, as requested in your telegram of yesterday, just received, in such manner as you deem proper. The Quartermaster-General will answer requisitions for what you may need.

EDWIN M. STANTON.

---

HEADQUARTERS MOUNTAIN DEPARTMENT,
*Mount Jackson, June* 14, 1862.

I suggest for the consideration of the President that the condition of affairs here imperatively requires that some position be immediately made strong enough to be maintained. As it now stands, a largely superior force can be directed against any one of our small corps in twenty-four hours. It would then be too late to concentrate, and they could not support each other. This position should by all means be maintained. If you design to maintain it, re-enforcements should be sent here without an hour's delay. The enemy's pickets are 10 miles this side of Harrisonburg. Is Sigel under my command? Pray oblige me with an immediate answer.

J. C. FRÉMONT,
*Major-General.*

Hon. E. M. STANTON,
*Secretary of War.*

---

WASHINGTON, *June* 14, 1862.

Maj. Gen. JOHN C. FRÉMONT,
*Mount Jackson:*

General Sigel is under command of Major-General Banks. Major-General Banks will co-operate with you, but he is commander of a separate corps, and does not come under your command.

EDWIN M. STANTON,
*Secretary of War.*

---

HEADQUARTERS MOUNTAIN DEPARTMENT,
*Mount Jackson, June* 15, 1862.

I respectfully remind the President that when assigned to this command I was informed that I should have a corps of 35,000 men. I now ask from the President the fulfillment of this understanding, and ask it only because, under the conditions of the war here, I should be able to render good and immediate service. Such a force would enable me to take Staunton, hold the railroad there, go down through Lexington, seize the railroad between Lynchburg and Newbern, and hold it for General Banks' troops, or destroy it, according to circumstances. Whether from Richmond or elsewhere, forces of the enemy are certainly coming into this region, which the great wheat crop makes a granary for him, and which he will not abandon without a struggle. Casualties have reduced my force to such numbers in many of the regiments as 176, 250, 300, and so on. This makes me very weak, and the small corps scattered about the country, not being within supporting distance of each other, as the topography of the country will show, are exposed to sudden attack by greatly superior force of an enemy, to whom intimate knowledge of country and universal friendship of inhabitants give the advantages of rapidity and secrecy of movements.

I respectfully submit this representation to the President, taking it for granted that it is the duty of his generals to offer for his consideration such impressions as are made by knowledge obtained in operations on the ground.

J. C. FRÉMONT,
*Major-General.*

ABRAHAM LINCOLN, *President United States.*

—

WAR DEPARTMENT,
*Washington City, D. C., June* 15, 1862.

Major-General FRÉMONT:

MY DEAR SIR: Your letter of the 12th, by Colonel Zagonyi, is just received. In answer to the principal part of it I repeat the substance of an order of the 8th and one or two telegraphic dispatches sent you since:

We have no indefinite power of sending re-enforcements; so that we are compelled rather to consider the proper disposal of the forces we have than of those we could wish to have. We may be able to send you some dribs by degrees, but I do not believe we can do more. As you alone beat Jackson last Sunday I argue that you are stronger than he is to-day, unless he has been re-enforced, and that he cannot have been materially re-enforced, because such re-enforcement could only have come from Richmond, and he is much more likely to go to Richmond than Richmond is to come to him. Neither is very likely. I think Jackson's game—his assigned work—now is to magnify the accounts of his numbers and reports of his movements, and thus by constant alarms keep three or four times as many of our troops away from Richmond as his own force amounts to. Thus he helps his friends at Richmond three or four times as much as if he were there. Our game is not to allow this. Accordingly, by the order of the 8th, I directed you to halt at Harrisonburg, rest your force, and get it well in hand, the objects being to guard against Jackson's returning by the same route to the Upper Potomac, over which you have just driven him out, and at the same time give some protection against a raid into West Virginia. Already I have given you discretion to occupy Mount Jackson instead, if, on full consideration, you think best. I do not believe Jackson will attack you, but certainly he cannot attack you by surprise; and if he comes upon you in superior force you have but to notify us, fall back cautiously, and Banks will join you in due time. But while we know not whether Jackson will move at all, or by what route, we cannot safely put you and Banks both on the Strasburg line, and leave no force on the Front Royal line, the very line upon which he prosecuted his late raid. The true policy is to place one of you on one line and the other on the other, in such positions that you can unite on either once you actually find Jackson moving upon it. And this is precisely what we are doing. This protects that part of our frontier, so to speak, and liberates McDowell to go to the assistance of McClellan. I have arranged this, and am very unwilling to have it deranged. While you have only asked for Sigel I have spoken only of Banks, and this because Sigel's force is now the principal part of Banks' force.

About transferring General Schenck's command, the purchase of supplies, and the promotion and appointment of officers mentioned in your letter, I will consult with the Secretary of War to-morrow.

Yours, truly,

A. LINCOLN.

HEADQUARTERS MOUNTAIN DEPARTMENT,
*Mount Jackson, June 16, 1862.*

A portion of the Sixth Ohio Cavalry, under command of Captain Barrett, sent out this afternoon to recover a small foraging party of 15 men and 3 wagons cut off this morning, was charged by the enemy's cavalry, but repulsed them and drove them in upon their pickets, 7 miles from this place. We lost 1 man killed. Enemy left 2 dead on field and 4 prisoners, with a number of horses. Sabers, carbines, and revolvers were taken. Sergeants Austin and Wood distinguished for bravery. Harrisonburg is reported occupied by a large body of enemy's cavalry, and Jackson's main body reported crossing Shenandoah to this side at Port Republic yesterday morning. Lieutenant-Colonel Harris, commanding at Buckhannon, reports that he has captured 3 leading guerrillas—Haymond, Coal, and Goff—killed 3, wounded 5, and taken 11 prisoners and some arms. He reports enemy at Alleghany Summit with one regiment, a squadron of cavalry, and a battery. If you will send the heavy battery by express it may arrive in time to do good service. Pray send a few artillerists with it.

J. C. FRÉMONT,
*Major-General, Commanding.*

Hon. E. M. STANTON,
*Secretary of War.*

---

WASHINGTON, *June* 16, 1862.

Major-General FRÉMONT,
*Mount Jackson, Va.:*

Your dispatch of yesterday, reminding me of a supposed understanding that I would furnish you a corps of 35,000 men, and asking of me the "fulfillment of this understanding," is received. I am ready to come to a fair settlement of accounts with you on the fulfillment of understandings.

Early in March last, when I assigned you to the command of the Mountain Department, I did tell you I would give you all the force I could, and that I hoped to make it reach 35,000. You at the same time told me that within a reasonable time you would seize the railroad at or east of Knoxville, Tenn., if you could. There was then in the department a force supposed to be 25,000, the exact number as well known to you as to me. After looking about two or three days, you called and distinctly told me that if I would add the Blenker division to the force already in the department you would undertake the job. The Blenker division contained 10,000, and at the expense of great dissatisfaction to General McClellan I took it from his army and gave it to you. My promise was literally fulfilled. I have given you all I could, and I have given you very nearly, if not quite, 35,000.

Now for yours: On the 23d of May, largely over two months afterward, you were at Franklin, Va., not within 300 miles of Knoxville nor within 80 miles of any part of the railroad east of it, and not moving forward, but telegraphing here that you could not move for lack of everything. Now, do not misunderstand me. I do not say you have not done all you could. I presume you met unexpected difficulties; and I beg you to believe that as surely as you have done your best, so have I. I have not the power now to fill up your corps to 35,000. I am not demanding of you to do the work of 35,000. I am only asking of you to stand cautiously on the defensive; get your force in order, and give such protection as you can to the valley of the Shenandoah and to Western Virginia.

Have you received the orders and will you act upon them?

A. LINCOLN.

---

MOUNT JACKSON, *June* 16, 1862,
(Received 5.30 p. m.)

Your dispatch of to-day is received. In reply to that part of it which concerns the orders sent to me I have to say that they have been received, and that as a matter of course I will act upon them, as I am now doing.

J. C. FRÉMONT,
*Major-General.*

The PRESIDENT.

---

WASHINGTON, *June* 17, 1862.

Major-General FRÉMONT,
*Mount Jackson:*

It is reported here that you understand the President's order to you as requiring you to remain at Mount Jackson. The President directs me to say that he does wish you to hold your position at Mount Jackson if you can safely do so; but if pressed beyond your strength that you will then fall back toward Strasburg for support from General Banks. General Banks is now here, and will see you immediately upon his return to his command.

EDWIN M. STANTON,
*Secretary of War.*

---

WASHINGTON, *June* 17, 1862.

Ordered, That the military protection and defense of the Baltimore and Ohio Railroad east of Cumberland to the city of Baltimore, and of the railroad between Harper's Ferry and Winchester, is especially assigned to the command of Maj. Gen. John E. Wool. Officers on the line of that road will report to him.

2d. That the Winchester and Potomac Railroad being the line of supply for General Banks, operating the road will remain under his direction.

EDWIN M. STANTON,
*Secretary of War.*

---

HEADQUARTERS,
*Mount Jackson, June* 17, 1862.

Both your telegrams of this date, including the order assigning railroads, received.

J. C. FRÉMONT,
*Major-General, Commanding.*

Hon. E. M. STANTON,
*Secretary of War.*

## No. 40.

### *Return of Casualties in the Union forces at the battle of Cross Keys.*

[Compiled from nominal lists of casualties, returns, &c.]

| Command. | Killed. | | Wounded. | | Captured or missing. | | | Remarks. |
|---|---|---|---|---|---|---|---|---|
| | Officers. | Enlisted men. | Officers. | Enlisted men. | Officers. | Enlisted men. | Aggregate. | |
| General staff | 1 | | | | | | 1 | |
| **BLENKER'S DIVISION.** | | | | | | | | |
| Brig. Gen. LOUIS BLENKER. | | | | | | | | |
| Staff | | | 2 | | | | 2 | |
| *First Brigade.* | | | | | | | | |
| Brig. Gen. JULIUS STAHEL. | | | | | | | | |
| 8th New York Infantry | | 43 | 2 | 132 | 2 | 41 | 220 | |
| 39th New York Infantry | | | | | | | (*) | |
| 41st New York Infantry | | | | | | | (*) | |
| 45th New York Infantry | | | | | | | (*) | |
| 27th Pennsylvania Infantry | 1 | 16 | 3 | 58 | | 14 | 92 | |
| New York Light Artillery, 2d Battery. | | | | | | | | No loss reported |
| West Virginia Light Artillery, Battery C. | | | | 2 | | | 2 | |
| Howitzer battery | | | | | | | | |
| Total First Brigade | 3 | 65 | 12 | 228 | 4 | 86 | 398 | |
| *Second Brigade (Steinwehr's).* | | | | | | | | |
| Col. JOHN A. KOLTES. | | | | | | | | |
| 29th New York Infantry | | | 1 | | | 6 | 7 | |
| 68th New York Infantry | | | | | | 2 | 2 | |
| 73d Pennsylvania Infantry | | | | | | | | No loss reported. |
| New York Light Artillery, 13th Battery. | | | | | | | | No loss reported. |
| Total Second Brigade | | | 1 | | | 8 | 9 | |
| *Third Brigade.* | | | | | | | | |
| Brig. Gen. HENRY BOHLEN. | | | | | | | | |
| 54th New York Infantry | | 1 | | 4 | | | 5 | |
| 58th New York Infantry | | 7 | 1 | 17 | | 4 | 29 | |
| 74th Pennsylvania Infantry | | 3 | 1 | 10 | | 1 | 15 | |
| 75th Pennsylvania Infantry | | 2 | | 16 | | 3 | 21 | |
| 1st New York Light Artillery, Battery I. | | | | 3 | | | 3 | |
| Total Third Brigade | | 13 | 2 | 50 | | 8 | 73 | |
| 4th New York Cavalry | | | | | | | | No loss reported. |
| Total Blenker's division | 3 | 78 | 17 | 278 | 4 | 102 | 482 | |
| *Unattached Cavalry.* | | | | | | | | |
| 3d West Virginia (detachment) | | | | | | | | No loss reported. |
| 6th Ohio | | | | | | | | No loss reported. |
| Total unattached cavalry | | | | | | | | |

* Only partial reports of casualties on file; losses embraced in the brigade total.

*Return of Casualties in the Union forces at the battle of Cross Keys*--Continued.

| Command. | Killed. | | Wounded. | | Captured or missing. | | Aggregate. | Remarks. |
|---|---|---|---|---|---|---|---|---|
| | Officers. | Enlisted men. | Officers. | Enlisted men. | Officers. | Enlisted men. | | |
| ***Advance Brigade.*** | | | | | | | | |
| **Col. G. P. CLUSERET.** | | | | | | | | |
| 8th West Virginia Infantry | ...... | 1 | ...... | 8 | ...... | 3 | 12 | |
| 60th Ohio Infantry | 1 | 2 | ...... | 4 | ...... | ...... | 7 | |
| **Total advance brigade** | 1 | 3 | ...... | 12 | ...... | 3 | 19 | |
| ***Milroy's Brigade.*** | | | | | | | | |
| **Brig. Gen. ROBERT H. MILROY.** | | | | | | | | |
| 2d West Virginia Infantry | ...... | 3 | ...... | 19 | ...... | 2 | 24 | |
| 3d West Virginia Infantry | ...... | 4 | ...... | 23 | ...... | ...... | 27 | |
| 5th West Virginia Infantry | ...... | 9 | 1 | 37 | ...... | ...... | 47 | |
| 25th Ohio Infantry | ...... | 5 | 1 | 39 | 1 | 4 | 50 | |
| 1st West Virginia Cavalry (detachment). | ...... | ...... | ...... | ...... | ...... | 7 | 7 | |
| West Virginia Light Artillery, Battery G. | ...... | ...... | ...... | 1 | ...... | ...... | 1 | |
| 1st Ohio Light Artillery, Battery I. | ...... | 1 | ...... | 1 | ...... | ...... | 2 | |
| Ohio Light Artillery, 12th Battery. | ...... | 1 | ...... | ...... | ...... | ...... | 1 | |
| **Total Milroy's brigade** | ...... | 23 | 2 | 120 | 1 | 13 | 159 | |
| ***Schenck's Brigade.*** | | | | | | | | |
| **Brig. Gen. ROBERT C. SCHENCK.** | | | | | | | | |
| 32d Ohio Infantry | ...... | ...... | ...... | 1 | ...... | ...... | 1 | |
| 55th Ohio Infantry | ...... | ...... | ...... | ...... | ...... | ...... | ...... | No loss reported. |
| 73d Ohio Infantry | ...... | 4 | ...... | 3 | ...... | ...... | 7 | |
| 75th Ohio Infantry | ...... | ...... | ...... | ...... | ...... | ...... | ...... | No loss reported. |
| 82d Ohio Infantry | ...... | ...... | 1 | 1 | ...... | ...... | 2 | |
| 1st Battalion Connecticut Cavalry. | ...... | ...... | ...... | ...... | ...... | 4 | 4 | |
| 1st Ohio Light Artillery, Battery K. | ...... | ...... | ...... | ...... | ...... | ...... | ...... | No loss reported. |
| Indiana Light Artillery, Rigby's battery. | ...... | ...... | ...... | 1 | ...... | ...... | 1 | |
| **Total Schenck's brigade** | ...... | 4 | 1 | 6 | ...... | 4 | 15 | |
| ***Bayard's Brigade*** | ...... | ...... | ...... | ...... | ...... | ...... | ...... | Detached. |
| **Brig. Gen. GEORGE D. BAYARD.** | | | | | | | | |
| 1st New Jersey Cavalry | ...... | ...... | ...... | ...... | ...... | ...... | ...... | No loss reported. |
| 1st Pennsylvania Cavalry | ...... | ...... | ...... | ...... | ...... | ...... | ...... | No loss reported. |
| 13th Pennsylvania Reserves (1st Rifles), battalion. | ...... | 1 | 1 | 6 | ...... | ...... | 8 | |
| Maine Light Artillery, 2d Battery (B). | ...... | ...... | ...... | ...... | ...... | ...... | ...... | No loss reported. |
| **Total Bayard's brigade** | ...... | 1 | 1 | 6 | | | 8 | |
| **Grand total** | 5 | 109 | 21 | 422 | 5 | 122 | 684 | |

NOTE.—Lieuts. Nicolai Dunka, aide-de-camp; James M. Vance, 60th Ohio; Frederick Lueders, 27th Pennsylvania, killed; and Lieuts. Henry Grassau and Bruce B. Rice died of wounds.

## No. 41.

*Report of Brig. Gen. Robert C. Schenck, U. S. Army, commanding brigade, of the battle of Cross Keys.*

HDQRS. SCHENCK'S BRIGADE, MOUNTAIN DEPARTMENT,
*Camp at Mount Jackson, Va., June* 12, 1862.

I have the honor to report the part taken by the Ohio Brigade in the engagement at Cross Keys on the 8th instant.

It was about 1 p. m. when I arrived near the point of the road leading to Port Republic, where the advance guard had already come upon the enemy. A staff officer, after indicating the position where my cavalry was to be left in reserve, informed me that I was to pass into the field and take position on the right, forming my line of battle and placing my batteries so as to support Brigadier-General Milroy, whose brigade preceded mine in the march and was already getting into line. I was entirely without knowledge of the ground, but immediately proceeded to find the best position I could, according to these instructions, in the direction indicated.

I turned my artillery (De Beck's and Rigby's batteries) into and across the fields, supported by infantry, throwing the body of my infantry into line of battle and extending it in the rear of Milroy's brigade. As I advanced, however, upon the open ridge first pointed out as probably the best on which to establish my batteries, about one-fourth of a mile from the main road by which our column arrived, I discovered that I was brought into the rear of a line of woods through which Milroy was passing, also to the right. These woods at the same time concealed the enemy and the character of the ground he was occupying, while they afforded no eligible position for placing my guns so as to reach him. I became satisfied, too, from the character of the ground beyond, as it now opened to us, that the enemy would seek to extend the line of his forces on his left, so as, if possible, to outflank us. I hastened, therefore, to press forward to the right to anticipate any such movement, and to occupy an extended ridge of higher ground half a mile farther to the south, which I found gave me a more commanding range and advanced me farther to the point, while it enabled me also to cover an easy pass leading up from the enemy's position in front between the two ridges and all the open ground sloping away to the valley at the foot of the mountain, by one of which approaches the rebels were to be expected to advance on that side. This position placed my brigade on the extreme right wing, which I occupied for the rest of the day.

To reach this point of advantage I had to cross a road in front of my first position, and passing through the skirt of the wood in which General Milroy had advanced, went over some wheat fields, along the edge of another wood. This I accomplished without loss, though exposed to a pretty severe fire of shell from the enemy, marching my line—composed of the Seventy-third, Fifty-fifth, and Eighty-second Regiments of Ohio Volunteer Infantry—directed by the flank, detaching the Seventy-fifth and Thirty-second Ohio to cover the artillery moving by a more circuitous route. While effecting this I was ordered, by a messenger from the general commanding, to detach Rigby's battery and send it to the relief of General Milroy. This was immediately done.

Reaching the farther position, which I had selected, I found the line of woods extended still to the right and shutting in our front. An examination of these woods by companies of the Seventy-third and Thirty-second, immediately thrown forward as skirmishers, discovered the enemy concealed there in force and still endeavoring to extend himself to the left, with the evident object of turning our right, as I had expected. A few shells thrown into the woods on that side by De Beck's battery checked this movement and drove back the rebel infantry farther to our left. The whole of the Seventy-third, Eighty-second, and Fifty-fifth Regiments, being then deployed in the woods on my left front, formed in line of battle and slowly advanced, feeling the enemy's position and gradually bringing the concealed line of the rebels to close quarters. The firing of small-arms at once became brisk, especially with the Seventy-third, which seems to have been brought nearest the enemy's line, and at this time had several men killed and wounded by the fire. It was at this point of time, too, that Dr. Cantwell, surgeon of the Eighty-second, fell severely wounded by a shot through the thigh, received while he was passing along the line of his regiment carefully instructing the men detailed from each company to attend to conveying the wounded to the ambulances.

I believed that the moment for attacking and pressing the rebels successfully on this wing had now arrived, and I brought forward the Thirty-second to advance also in the woods and form on the Seventy-third, extending thus the line to the right, and intending to order a charge which should sweep around the enemy's left flank and press him back toward our sustaining forces on the left. Never were troops in better temper for such work; but just as the Thirty-second was marching to the front for this purpose, leaving only the Seventy-fifth in the rear to cover the battery, I received the order of the general commanding to withdraw slowly and in good order from my position and go to the relief of the left wing, composed of the brigades of Blenker's division. I felt reluctant to obey, because I was satisfied that the advantageous and promising position and condition of my brigade could not have been known at headquarters. I held my place, therefore, and sent back instantly to ascertain whether the emergency was such as to require me with all haste to retire. The order came back repeated. To prevent my being followed and harassed by the rebels while falling back I then began to withdraw my infantry, moving them carefully by the flank toward the left until I could uncover the enemy's line sufficiently to enable my battery to throw shot and shell into the woods. This done, I returned the Thirty-second to the support of the battery and commenced drawing off the whole of my force to the left along the same lines in which I had advanced them. Here, again, however, I was met by a messenger from the general commanding, informing me that if I thought I could hold my ground I might remain, but stating that Milroy's brigade, my supporting force on the left, had also been directed to retire, I stopped and threw the artillery again into battery at a point a few rods in the rear of the place which it had at first occupied and ordered a number of rounds of quick, sharp firing into the woods occupied by the rebels. The severe effect of this firing was discovered the next day by the number of rebels found lying on that part of the battle-field; but while thus engaged Captain Piatt, my assistant adjutant-general, ascertained for me that General Milroy, under the order he had received, was rapidly withdrawing his brigade, passing toward the left, and sc I had to follow him or be left separated from all the rest of the forces. I returned, however, only to the ridge (half a mile to the left) which I had at first occupied, and there remained, in pursuance of orders, encamped for the night. My other battery (Rigby's) which I understood had been very effectively engaged during the action on the left, was here returned home. It was now perhaps 5.30 or 6 o'clock.

Late in the evening the enemy from the opposite point opened a brisk fire upon our camp and upon Hyman's battery, occupying the point of a hill at our left with what seemed to be a battery of two 6-pounders. This was probably a cover to his retreat, but he was replied to with so quick and hot a return by Hyman, Rigby, and De Beck that his fire was very soon silenced and, as afterward ascertained, both his guns dismounted. Subsequently a company of skirmishers from the Seventy-third had an encounter with skirmishers of the rebels in the woods immediately in front of us, in which we had 1 man killed and another man wounded; but otherwise we rested undisturbed until called to march in pursuit of the enemy again in the morning.

I regret to have to state that in the night a party detailed from the battalion of Connecticut Cavalry—Sergeant Morehouse and 4 men of Company D—being sent to ascertain the position of Colonel Cluseret, commanding the advance brigade, lost their way, and were captured, as is supposed, by the enemy's pickets.

The whole number of effective men of my brigade that I was enabled to take into action was as follows:

| | |
|---|---|
| The 32d Ohio | 500 |
| The 55th Ohio | 525 |
| The 73d Ohio | 295 |
| The 75th Ohio | 444 |
| The 82d Ohio | 374 |
| Total infantry | 2,138 |
| De Beck's battery (six guns) | 94 |
| Rigby's battery (five guns) | 91 |
| Connecticut cavalry | 113 |

The casualties were, altogether, but 4 killed, 7 wounded, and 4 missing. I append in a separate report the names and corps of the killed and wounded.*

I cannot close this report without expressing my satisfaction with the officers and men generally of my command. Although worn down and reduced in numbers by days and weeks of constant fatigue and privation, under long marches with insufficient supplies, which they have necessarily had to undergo, they were actively and cheerfully eager to meet the rebel forces, and only regretted that it could not be their fortune to encounter them for their share in more obstinate and decisive battle.

To the officers commanding my several regiments and detached companies who had any opportunity to be in the engagement my acknowledgments are especially due: Lieutenant-Colonel Swinney, of the Thirty-second; Colonel McLean, of the Seventy-fifth; Colonel Smith, of the Seventy-third; Colonel Lee, of the Fifty-fifth; Colonel Cantwell, of the Eighty-second; Captain De Beck, of the First Ohio Artillery, and Captain Blakeslee, of Company A, Connecticut cavalry, commanding my guard.

To the officers of my staff also—Capt. Donn Piatt, assistant adjutant-general; Captain Margedant, of Engineers; Captain Crane, commissary of subsistence, and my two aides-de-camp, Lieutenants Chesebrough and Esté—I am greatly indebted for their constant energy and activity in conveying orders and attending to other duties during the day.

I am, very respectfully, your obedient servant,

ROBT. C. SCHENCK,
*Brigadier-General.*

Col. ALBERT TRACY, *Asst. Adjt. Gen.*

---

* Embodied in revised statement, p. 665.

## No. 42.

*Report of Brig. Gen. Henry Bohlen, U. S. Army, commanding brigade, of the battle of Cross Keys.*

The brigade received orders to march on the 8th at 6.15 a. m., and marched at that time from their camping ground in the following order: Fifty-fourth Regiment New York Volunteers, commanded by Colonel Kozlay; Battery I, First New York Artillery, commanded by Captain Wiedrich; Seventy-fifth Pennsylvania Volunteers, commanded by Lieutenant-Colonel Mahler; Fifty-eighth New York Volunteers, commanded by Colonel Krzyzanowski; Seventy-fourth Pennsylvania Volunteers, commanded by Major Hamm. Ambulances and ammunition wagons followed in the rear of the brigade. Receiving orders to hurry on the column, I passed the train in front of my brigade and arrived near the place where the engagement should take place, immediately in rear of the First Brigade. Here I received orders to form the battalions in columns, to support the First Brigade, commanded by General Stahel. This order was executed at once, and the brigade at the point A (see diagram)* was put in motion in the following order, the battalions being in double columns, closed in mass: On the right the Fifty-fourth Regiment, followed by the Seventy-fifth; in the center (on the road) the battery of Captain Wiedrich; on the left the Fifty-eighth Regiment New York Volunteers, followed by the Seventy-fourth Regiment Pennsylvania Volunteers.

At the point B a staff officer of General Stahel requested me to order the column forward to support the First Brigade. The Fifty-eighth Regiment, being nearest on hand, was immediately ordered forward, formed in line of battle, and marched to the point C, the direction given by General Stahel. The Seventy-fourth was then ordered forward to the point D, on the left of the Fifty-eighth Regiment, and formed in line of battle. The battery was ordered to form at the point E on elevated ground. Receiving the indication that a force of two regiments with some cavalry was concealed in the wheat field (at point F) and tried to outflank me on the left, I immediately ordered the two regiments in reserve to the left to check the enemy's movements. I regret to say that at that time I received no communications at all as to what was going on on my right, where part of the First Brigade had taken position.

Meanwhile, as is shown in the report of Colonel Krzyzanowski, the Fifty-eighth marched gallantly ahead, supported by a section of Captain Schirmer's battery, which disabled the enemy's pieces placed on a hill on the right of the regiment (point G). The Fifty-eighth met the enemy and drove him back at the point of the bayonet. Being in danger of being cut off by two columns advancing on the right, and also by the enemy's force placed on the left, the regiment had to retire, Captain Schirmer's battery having previously retired. The regiment, being without any support, fell back behind Captain Wiedrich's battery in good order.

Meanwhile the Seventy-fourth Regiment had proceeded in line of battle toward the wheat field (at point D). Here General Blenker ordered to send only two companies of skirmishers ahead, he supposing the New York Eighth Regiment to be in front, the main body of the regiment following slowly. At the outskirts of the woods (at point H)

*Not found.

our skirmishers met the enemy suddenly again, concealed in a wheat field and protected by fences, as appears in the report of Major Hamm, in the strength of two regiments. Major Hamm, being in danger of being outflanked on the left and overpowered by the superior strength of the enemy, was forced to retire, which he did slowly. He then received orders from me to move to the left toward the woods to give the battery of Captain Wiedrich a full sway. This battery soon opened fire and did fearful execution. Before the battery was brought in action the Seventy-fifth Regiment Pennsylvania Volunteers was ordered to advance and relieve the Seventy-fourth Pennsylvania Volunteers. It had already the skirmishers deployed, when the order was given to fall back in a small ravine to give the artillery an opportunity to fire.

The Fifty-fourth Regiment New York Volunteers, Colonel Kozlay, was ordered to the left to deploy in the woods. Captain Schirmer's battery on my right having already retired, he (Captain Schirmer) gave the command to Captain Wiedrich to retire also, against my positive order to remain. The battery then retired.

At this moment a battalion of the enemy deployed in line of battle on the hill opposite our position. The battery then came into action again, pouring grape shot into the line of the enemy, which forced him to retire. After few shots the battery was again ordered by Captain Schirmer to retire, which order was obeyed. Meanwhile the Fifty-fourth Regiment New York Volunteers was ordered to the left into the woods ready to support part of the Seventy-fourth, which was on the extreme left deployed in line of skirmishers. After the battery had retired a retrograde movement of the Seventy-fifth and Fifty-fourth Regiments was visible. They retired slowly about 100 paces when they were ordered to a halt. The Fifty-fourth, being in front, was ordered to deploy at once, which order was executed in the woods (at J). A second regiment of the enemy appearing on the outskirts of the woods, the Fifty-fourth regiment opened fire. After a few shots the enemy retired and did not molest us any longer. General orders being given to fall back, the movement was executed in complete order by my entire command. From the report of Captain Schirmer, whose guns were supported by the Fifty-eighth Regiment, this regiment behaved with great gallantry, under the command of Colonel Krzyzanowski. During the action Capt. P. T. Schopp, assistant adjutant-general, and my two aides-de-camp, Captain Yultman and Captain Chandler, as well as Quartermaster John Weih, were generally under fire and transmitted my orders with great promptitude.

[HENRY BOHLEN,]
*Brigadier-General, Commanding.*

---

## No. 43.

*Report of Capt. Michael Wiedrich, Battery I, First New York Light Artillery, of the battle of Cross Keys.*

MOUNT JACKSON, *June* 12, 1862.

On arriving near the battle-field the Third Brigade, commanded by General Bohlen, formed in order of battle, with the battery in the center, which order was given by General Bohlen. After forming, the brigade advanced about half a mile, when the battery was ordered by General Blenker to break off from the road to the left in an open field. After arriving in said field General Bohlen ordered the battery to take position near and to the left of a road on high ground and shell a piece of wood in front and to the right of the battery. After forming in battery Captain Schirmer arrived, and ordered the battery to the right side of road to assist his battery, and after coming to action front again Captain Schirmer ordered the battery to its former position, but a little farther ahead. After coming to action front again the battery fired a few rounds in the woods in front by order of General Bohlen.

Presently, after firing those few rounds, a regiment made its appearance in front of us in a wheat field, when Captain Schirmer ordered the battery to limber to the rear and take the position first selected by Generals Blenker and Bohlen. The Fifty-fourth Regiment was then ordered by General Bohlen to the left in the woods, to keep the said regiment from outflanking us. Having arrived at our old position we came in battery again and continued our fire, without one man flinching, until Captain Schirmer ordered us to limber to the rear and retire, as Lieutenant Jahn, commanding Schirmer's battery, was obliged to retreat. When the battery was limbering to retire General Bohlen came up and ordered me to stay and keep up the fire, but Captain Schirmer insisted on retiring, and as I had received orders from General Blenker a few days before that all orders from Captain Schirmer should be obeyed the same as before, I withdrew with my battery, against the protest of General Bohlen.

Respectfully, your obedient servant,

M. WIEDRICH,
*Captain, Comdg. Battery I, First Regiment N. Y. Arty.*

---

## No. 44.

*Report of Col. Eugene A. Kozlay, Fifty-fourth New York Infantry, of the battle of Cross Keys.*

FIFTY-FOURTH REGIMENT NEW YORK STATE VOLS.,
*June* 11, 1862.

GENERAL: I have the honor to report that on the 8th of June, about 3 or 4 miles on the other side of Harrisonburg, I was ordered to deploy my regiment into double columns and to proceed on the right of the road leading to Port Republic, parallel with the Fifty-eighth Regiment, who were marching on the other side of the road. Arriving in a small open field I was ordered to cross the road and to proceed with my double columns and take position on a small bare hill on the left of the Seventy-fifth Regiment, which was posted there in double columns. Before I occupied the position assigned to me (and having many difficulties in marching on account of fences and morass which lay before me and which I had to cross), I rode myself on the top of the hill to choose a suitable position for my columns. When on the top of the small hill on my right the Seventy-fifth Regiment already began to move backward, as the fire of the enemy was very severe upon us. Under these circumstances I could not bring my forces on the top of the hill without an unnecessary great loss, and I had ordered them to stay in a little valley, as it is seen in the annexed diagram,* on the side of the same hill, ordering my men to stand for a minute on the side of the hill which

* Not found.

covered them against the fire of the enemy. I hardly stood there two minutes when I received orders to retreat after the Seventy-fifth Regiment, whom I had protected with my double columns against the advancing forces of the enemy.

I hardly marched with my regiment 40 paces when I met General Blenker alone riding through the column, and suggested to him that there is a regiment of the enemy whom we could take prisoners. He at once gave me orders not to retreat, but flank the regiment and proceed into the woods. By a flank movement I at once directed my regiment and marched into the woods, deployed the columns into a line of battle, and opened a severe fire upon the approaching enemy. This fire put the enemy into great confusion, and they gave up not only their object to flank us but began to run before our advance and fled on the other side of the open field. Seeing that the enemy was retreating, I gave directions at once to change direction to the right in order to inflict a more severe chastisement on them, but before I could accomplish this I received orders to withdraw, and I have retreated in good order and without the least confusion.

My officers and men behaved themselves, though exposed to severe fire of the enemy, admirably and bravely. I had in the engagement present 373 men (officers, non-commissioned officers, and privates), and had the misfortune to lose 2 brave soldiers, who were killed, and 3 wounded.* I beg also to state that through the engagement I received a great many conflicting orders, coming from staff officers unknown to me, which I disobeyed. I have also to report that by our fire we have also prevented two regiments of the enemy to advance upon our batteries, who were only stopped by our flank fire, and have suffered by it a considerable loss of lives, while my regiment was protected against the fire of the enemy in the woods, excepting about 100 paces where I had to cross the open field in my retreat. My men were unwilling to retreat, and I was the last who retreated, because I was not supported by other regiments. My men were eager to fight, and if not withdrawn the enemy would have been at this point repulsed. I was not followed by them. My flank fire stopped the enemy's advance.

I am, general, yours, most respectfully,

E. A. KOZLAY,
*Colonel, Commanding Fifty-fourth Regiment New York Vols.*

Brig. Gen. H. BOHLEN, *Commanding Third Brigade.*

---

## No. 45.

### *Report of Col. Wladimir Krzyzanowski, Fifty-eighth New York Infantry, of the battle of Cross Keys.*

HDQRS. FIFTY-EIGHTH REGT. NEW YORK VOLS.,
*Mount Jackson, June* 12, 1862.

I have the honor to submit to you the following report in regard to the engagement of June 8:

After the arrival of my regiment near the field of battle to the left of the battery of the First Brigade, I received your orders to move to the right, when Brigadier-General Stahel asked me to come up to his assistance. I at once formed my regiment into line, being in column by division, and advanced to the place indicated by General Stahel. I was

---

* But see revised statement, p. 664.

at that time in the middle of a large rye field, skirted by woods immediately on the right of the battery and in front of my regiment, into which direction I moved in line up to and just beyond a fence at the outskirts of these woods, looking for the troops I was to assist and for the enemy. On the right of my position was another open field, on the opposite side of which I saw a column move by the flank toward the left of our lines, and upon a hill I perceived a battery opening fire toward our right. In order to find out whether I was on the left I sent one company out as skirmishers to keep up the connection on that side and by throwing them a little forward to give information of the enemy's advance.

Directly after this Captain Schirmer came up, and seeing the battery he told me if I would protect him with my regiment he would bring up a couple of guns and open fire upon the enemy's battery. He did so, and soon silenced the latter, when the enemy engaged my skirmishers, who slowly retired toward the regiment for the purpose of giving my men a chance to fire. Captain Schirmer now withdrew his guns and soon the whole regiment was engaged. Keeping up a constant fire, which told greatly among the enemy's lines, I now gave the command to charge bayonets, and succeeded in driving him back about a hundred yards.

To my greatest dismay I noticed at this instant two regiments coming out of the woods on the right of the enemy's battery, and having no reserve to fall back on I thought it imprudent to remain any longer, and consequently gave the command orders to retire while a heavy musketry fire was poured upon my men. I retired behind the battery of Captain Wiedrich, who now opened a heavy fire upon the enemy.

I remain, general, your obedient servant,

W. KRZYZANOWSKI,
*Colonel, Commanding Fifty-eighth New York Volunteers.*

General H. BOHLEN,
*Commanding Third Brigade.*

---

## No. 46.

*Report of Lieut. Col. John Hamm, Seventy-fourth Pennsylvania Infantry, of the battle of Cross Keys.*

HDQRS. SEVENTY-FOURTH REGT. PENNSYLVANIA VOLS.,
*Camp near Mount Jackson, June* 12, 1862.

On Sunday, at 2.30 o'clock p. m., June 8, 1862, the Seventy-fourth Regiment Pennsylvania Volunteers was formed in line of battle by General H. Bohlen, and remained such for ten minutes, when General L. Blenker in person gave Lieut. Col. J. Hamm the order to detail the right and left companies (Companies A and G) as skirmishers, under command of Maj. F. Blessing, the former company commanded by Capt. A. von Hartung, the latter by Capt. C. Zinn, Lieut. Col. J. Hamm at the same time asking General L. Blenker, with or without reserve, as customary in skirmishing, upon which General L. Blenker ordered the companies to proceed without reserve, remarking at the same time that these skirmishers of the Seventy-fourth Regiment Pennsylvania Volunteers were ordered only to protect the wounded of the Eighth Regiment New York Volunteers; also saying to be very careful and not to fire, as the Eighth Regiment New York Volunteers was ahead of the Seventy-fourth Regiment. This order was rehearsed several times to the adjutant of the regiment, Lieut. F. Klenker, in hearing of the different companies. Maj. F. Blessing received the same order from Lieutenant Brandenstein, by order of General L. Blenker, he (Lieutenant Brandenstein) remaining till the skirmishers ceased firing, after which he (Brandenstein) was shot from his horse, the skirmishers having fired previously by order of Maj. F. Blessing, he (Maj. F. Blessing) recognizing the forces before him were not the Eighth Regiment New York Volunteers, but Second Regiment rebels, in line of battle. The skirmishers, after having gone forward, found themselves about 20 paces from the enemy, and had such volleys of balls discharged at them that Maj. F. Blessing found it necessary to order the skirmishers to fall back toward the left, and ordered Captain Huestmann to send the artillery forward to play upon the enemy.

The regiment being close by, the skirmishers ahead of us received torrents of musket-balls into them, whereupon Lieut. Col. J. Hamm ordered the regiment to fall back to the next fence, 20 paces to the rear, to take a good position, the regiment having returned the fire of the enemy very briskly. General H. Bohlen then ordered the regiment, through Captain Chandler, to fall back toward the left, the enemy's forces being discovered to be entirely too strong for us; also allowing the artillery to have full range at the enemy. Maj. F. Blessing's horse was shot from under him during the engagement. The falling back was conducted in the best possible order, without confusion. Roll call was held upon arriving at camp, and but 6 were missing, not accounted for at the time.

Very respectfully,

J. HAMM,

*Lieut. Col., Comdg. Seventy-fourth Regt. Pennsylvania Vols.*

General H. BOHLEN,
*Commanding Third Brigade.*

---

## No. 47.

### *Report of Col. Francis Mahler, Seventy-fifth Pennsylvania Infantry, of the battle of Cross Keys.*

HDQRS. SEVENTY-FIFTH REGT. PENNSYLVANIA VOLS.,
*Mount Jackson, June* 1 [?], 1862.

Having been informed that serious charges have been made in regard to the conduct of the regiment which I have the honor to command, in the engagement of Sunday last, by General Blenker, it is due to the honor of my regiment that I should report the part that we took in the action. While in the support of the Seventy-fourth Regiment Pennsylvania Volunteers and Fifty-fourth New York Volunteers, on the extreme left of the line, I was met by General Blenker and ordered to the front, advising me at the same time to be very cautious not to fire, as the Thirty-fifth (former number of the Seventy-fourth) was right in our front, and the Eighth New York were removing their wounded from the woods on our right. Arriving on the top of a knoll I perceived that the Seventy-fourth engaged a superior force, and seeing that their line of skirmishers were falling back I halted and immediately ordered my two flank companies to relieve them, which left me only four companies, about 150 men in all, having previously detached two companies by order of General Bohlen for the support of Captain Wiedrich's battery. At the same time, in order to shelter the reserve from the galling fire which was being poured into us, I ordered them to fall back a few paces, to take advantage of the sloping ground until the moment for action should arrive. The enemy at this time making an attack to outflank us, we, in concert with the Fifty-fourth New York, were ordered to the left, to deploy in the woods.

The Fifty-fourth were in advance of us, and had opened their fire just as we arrived on the ground. At this moment our battery was obliged to retire from the attack of a force that deployed from the woods, which General Blenker led me to suppose were occupied by the Eighth New York, and before I was able to open fire I received the order to fall back. I deny totally that my regiment ran away, as charged by General Blenker, and will say for them that they behaved themselves worthy of a better opportunity.

I have the honor to be, respectfully, yours,

F. MAHLER,
*Commanding Seventy-fifth Pennsylvania Volunteers.*

General H. BOHLEN, *Commanding Third Brigade.*

---

## No. 48.

*Report of Capt. Hugh McDonald, Kane Rifle Battalion, of the battle of Cross Keys.*

CAMP NEAR PORT REPUBLIC,
*June* 9, 1862.

DEAR SIR: In obedience to orders I yesterday morning reported with my command to Brigadier-General Stahel, commanding First Brigade, General Blenker's division, and was by him detailed to support Captain Buell's battery of his brigade, and accordingly I accompanied it to the front, where one of our batteries had already engaged the enemy. After waiting for a short time under cover of a wood the rattle of small-arms in advance showed us where our infantry had engaged them, and directly we were ordered to cross the strip of woods on our right and engage the enemy. The movement was executed promptly, and immediately upon our emerging from the wood we attracted the attention of the enemy, who threw a few shot and shell at us, one of which struck Private John McElhaney, of Company C, inflicting a severe wound in the leg; another struck a member of Company A, Twenty-seventh Regiment Pennsylvania Volunteers (which was deployed along a fence in advance of us), blowing him to fragments. Fortunately our course led us down into a ravine under cover, and another hollow at right angles with it enabled the battery to advance across the entire field and take up a position with their caissons well under cover. I placed my command in the first-mentioned hollow, and ordered the men to lie down, which was done in good order, but a few minutes' observation convinced me that I was too far to the right and too nearly in the range of our guns for safety. Accordingly I moved the command more to the left and down the hollow, and again ordered them to lie down. Most of the shells flew over us, but one burst right in our midst, wounding Private Edmond Debeck, of Company G, and tearing the pants of Lieut. T. B. Winslow, of same company.

In the mean time the rattle of musketry steadily advancing toward our position told me that the enemy were gaining ground upon the other side of the wood, and presently orders came to fall back and bring off the battery. The Twenty-seventh formed in column by division and I formed in line of battle upon their left, in which positions we advanced into the wood at a double-quick, and owing to a high fence which we had to clamber over entered it in some confusion, the Twenty-seventh still on my right and the battery coming up on my left We found it already occupied by the enemy, and received a volley, which killed 1 and wounded 5 of Company I, of my command. We immediately opened upon them, driving them out of the wood at the point of the bayonet. The battery also unlimbered two pieces and double-shotted them, but so eager were the men and so rapid the firing that I could not rally the men in time to allow the guns to play without endangering our own men. So soon as possible I rallied my command, and the Twenty-seventh having also retired in rear of the guns, we waited to give them a taste of grape, but the brush was too dense to allow us to see them, and we came on. Upon emerging from the wood we were opened upon by our own batteries, who had retired and taken up a position some distance in the rear. The prompt display of the flag of the Twenty-seventh Regiment soon put a stop to that, with the loss of one or two horses by the battery, and we came in bringing in our wounded.

Where all behaved so well it would be invidious to mention names, and hoping that we may always acquit ourselves as well in future, I have the honor to subscribe myself yours, respectfully,

HUGH McDONALD,
*Captain, Commanding Kane Rifle Battalion.*

Brigadier-General BAYARD, *Commanding Brigade.*

---

## No. 49.

***Reports** of Brig. Gen. George D. Bayard, U. S. Army, commanding Cavalry, of operations June 1–13.*

CAMP AT HARRISONBURG, VA.
*June* 7, 1862.

MAJOR: I write for instructions. Am I to stay here? Am I to regard myself as belonging to General Frémont's army? If not, what am I to do?

Colonel Wyndham was ambuscaded yesterday. He was taken prisoner, the regimental colors lost, and 30 men, including Captains Shelmire, Clark, and Haines.

Colonel Kane had a fight with a regiment of infantry. He was wounded and taken prisoner; also Captains Taylor and Blanchard and Lieutenant Swayne wounded. He lost 25 men. The Bucktails fought splendidly.

We have had the advance ever since we have been here, and have taken about 300 prisoners and released about 40 of Banks' men. We are utterly used up, except Lieutenant Hall's Griffin guns and the Bucktails.

I am, sir, very respectfully, your obedient servant,

GEO. D. BAYARD,
*Brigadier-General, Commanding.*

Maj. SAMUEL BRECK,
*Assistant Adjutant-General.*

CAMP NEAR MANASSAS, VA.,
*June* 20, 1862.

MAJOR: I have the honor to report that, agreeably to General McDowell's order, on June 1 last I proceeded toward Strasburg, with a view of attacking Jackson's train as it passed. Instead of the train being protected by nothing but cavalry, as reported, heavy masses of infantry, artillery, and cavalry were all plainly discernible, drawn up in commanding positions around the town—a force so largely exceeding my own that an attack was utterly out of the question. The enemy threw a couple of shells at us, and just before dark I withdrew my forces from the Strasburg side of the Shenandoah and encamped. Col. T. L. Kane, commanding the Bucktail Battalion, was posted so as to protect the railroad bridge across the river. I was that evening joined by Capt. James A. Hall with four Griffin guns from General Ricketts' brigade.

The next morning early the town was reconnoitered by Lieutenant Colonels Kargé and Kane, and finding it abandoned by the enemy, they moved in and occupied it. I moved through the town, and hearing that General Frémont was advancing I rode out and reported to him. He assigned me the advance, when I immediately pressed on to Colonel Wyndham's support, who was already pressing on toward the enemy. For the particulars of the pursuit I have the honor to refer you to the detailed reports of Colonel Jones and Lieutenant-Colonel Kargé.

The brigade has seen hard service and the men have done well, and it will certainly require at least a week to again get men or horses in the condition they were three weeks ago.

Last Sunday, agreeably to your order, we moved from Mount Jackson to rejoin the forces of General McDowell's department, and arrived here on Thursday, June 19.

I am, sir, very respectfully, your obedient servant,

GEO. D. BAYARD,
*Brigadier-General, Commanding.*

Maj. SAMUEL BRECK,
*Asst. Adjt. Gen., Department of the Rappahannock.*

---

## No. 50.

### *Report of Lieut. Col. Joseph Kargé, First New Jersey Cavalry, of operations June 2–13.*

CAMP NEAR MOUNT JACKSON, VA.,
*June* 13, 1862.

GENERAL: In compliance with your request I have the honor to submit the following report concerning the regiment and its operations, commencing June 2, until date:

June 2, immediately after reveille, I received your verbal orders (being then encamped 1½ miles the other side of Strasburg) to proceed with one battalion of cavalry (about 200 men strong) to reconnoiter the immediate vicinity of Strasburg from an impending hill, quarter of a mile from the above-named place. I followed up your orders, and the result was that, finding no enemy in sight, I sent Lieutenant Sawyer, of Company D, with a platoon, to the town, deploying meantime my skirmishers in all the neighboring woods, reporting facts to you. In consequence of this I received your orders to proceed with my whole command to town, Lieutenant-Colonel Kane, of the Pennsylvania Sharpshooters, following me with his detachment. Just before I reached the interior of the town I was joined by Colonel Wyndham, to whom I immediately reported the state of things, suggesting meantime that by appearances the enemy could not be far off, and it would be advisable to start in immediate and hot pursuit. Colonel Wyndham immediately put himself at the head of the battalion, which had been reduced somewhat from its original number by sending out skirmishers and a platoon to reconnoiter the town, which as yet had not joined the battalion, and started in a lively trot along the Staunton road, myself remaining in town in order to await the arrival of the regiment and dispose of the prisoners, 40 in number, taken by Lieutenant Sawyer.

In less than an hour the regiment made its appearance, and we started, by your orders, in hot pursuit of the enemy. Having trotted pretty briskly along the pike about 6 miles, encountering all the time captured prisoners, and finding the road strewn with arms, blankets, and knapsacks, we closed up with Colonel Wyndham, coming toward us with a detachment of about 25 of his men, having left the remainder of the battalion drawn up in line on the right hand of the road, under command of Major Cumming. The colonel inquired for you. I stated to him that I had seen you only a little while ago at the head of our column, and did not know where you could be found at this very moment. He went to the rear in search of you, ordering me to advance.

I immediately ordered all available carbineers to the front and was approaching a heavy oak wood. Before we got fairly through it the first report of a gun greeted our ears and a sharp buzz of a shell flew over our heads. This very moment the colonel made his appearance at the head of the column, encouraging the men by words and action, who did not show the slightest signs of fear. Immediately after a second report was heard, and the shell fell about 15 feet on the right of the head of our column, scattering its fragments in all directions and grazing the leg of one of the buglers riding close to me. The column was halted, and, in order to get out of the range, drawn up in line about 150 yards on the left side of the road in a heavy grove of timber, waiting meantime for our artillery. Shell and shot came thick and fast through the woods, tearing down limbs and slicing trees, doing no damage to either men or beasts. Finally a battery of six guns came up, and, taking position, commenced forthwith its operation. Emboldened by this, our boys rushed forward with a wild hurrah over fences and fields under a perfect deluge of shell, Major Beaumont taking a part of the First Battalion through a ravine, so as to fall on the enemy's left flank. Myself, with some of the Second and Third Battalions, crossed the field in an oblique direction, aiming directly for the enemy's battery, which had its position on an eminence on the edge of a heavy oak timber. We were not more than 600 yards off—the ground favoring us—when the enemy limbered up and moved off with his pieces, being supported by two divisions of cavalry. In less than a minute I lost sight of him in the dense woods. I proceeded with my men to the pike, which I perceived about 300 yards on my right. I will mention here that while moving toward the enemy's battery we were in imminent danger from our own battery, whose shell fell close to us on all sides.

Leading my men, as I stated above, to the pike, I heard a sharp platoon fire on my right, which lasted about two minutes, and shortly after this I saw Major Beaumont's men rally on a hill on the right of the pike and hastening to a dense wood for protection. I formed my men, consisting of about 60 men, in a gully close to the left on the pike, having in my front a row of buildings, and still farther on a heavy timber. Colonel Wyndham joined me there with the rest of the regiment, and after a few minutes' delay we proceeded onward, following the pike. Colonel Wyndham put himself at the head of about 50 men, mostly belonging to Company D, and proceeded hastily into the woods, ordering me to follow with the remainder. In less than ten minutes I heard a sharp volley of musketry in my front, and shortly afterward straggling bodies of men were falling back on the road. I stopped and rallied them on the left of the road in the woods. In doing so the enemy opened fire upon us with its batteries, and I have to report the loss of a horse, which was shot under me by a shell bursting between the fore-legs, shattering the former and cutting off entirely one of the hind legs; also lacerating his chest. Our own batteries had reached at this moment the ground and opened their fire, which silenced the enemy's.

Our loss amounted to 1 killed and 5 men severely wounded, besides several horses lost.

A drenching rain set in, with a heavy storm, and this ended the action of the day. The regiment encamped for the night on the other side of the woods in sight of the town of Woodstock.

Next morning we marched onward, passing Woodstock and Edenburg. At the latter place we found the bridges burned; had to ford the stream, which was accomplished without accident. Marched all day without encountering the enemy until we reached Mount Jackson. Two miles this side of Mount Jackson the regiment received your orders to advance, the First Pennsylvania Cavalry leading the van, in order to save the bridge over the Shenandoah, which was then on fire. We arrived just in time to behold the smoldering timber of the bridge, and the remains of a private of the First Pennsylvania, killed by a shell. The enemy was secreted, throwing occasionally shell, which did no further damage. The bridge being burned and the stream swollen by wash-out rains, we encamped on the banks, waiting for the construction of a pontoon bridge, which, after a delay of forty-eight hours, was effected, and the army crossed over on Thursday, June 5. We proceeded about 7 miles and halted for encampment 1 mile beyond New Market.

Friday morning the march was resumed, and for the first time we advanced in proper battle array, the artillery and infantry in the center, following the pike, the cavalry on the flanks, toward Harrisonburg.

About 3 p. m. our advanced troops reached the former-mentioned place, and having placed our artillery in position so as to command the surrounding country, you gave orders both to Colonel Wyndham and myself to proceed with our regiment and a part of the Fourth New York Mounted Rifles, consisting of four companies, through the town, and take possession of such a position 1¼ miles beyond the town as would insure us a good reconnoitering point. Furthermore, you stated that if we should encounter cavalry to try to scatter it; but if infantry, to fall back. We succeeded in carrying out your orders without meeting any opposition, drew up our line on an eminence, and were waiting for further orders. Meantime reports came in from scouts that a body of the enemy's cavalry had formed on the other side of the woods right in front of us, and by their representations were urging strongly on Colonel Wyndham to pursue them. The colonel objected, but finally, through some unexplained reasons, he gave the order forward, and our wearied horses and men took up again the march, and onward we went, "waddling" through bottomless roads. We had proceeded about 3¼ miles, partly by platoons, partly by fours, as the nature of the ground would allow it, when a sudden fire was opened on us on our right in an oblique direction. The first division, consisting of Company A, bravely rushed onward, Major Beaumont at the head. Colonel Wyndham, at the head of another division, followed, and myself at the head of the rest of the regiment. The roar of musketry had now opened fairly, and, as far as I can judge in the moment of confusion, I saw fire in our front and on both flanks. The first two platoons suddenly emerged from the woods in a retrograde movement, threatening to throw the rest of the column in confusion which followed. Colonel Wyndham made an oblique movement to the left. I followed, and when in the act of tearing down fences in order to get into a belt of woods which separated us from the enemy, and from behind which he was discharging his deadly missiles, the colonel disappeared from my sight, and I was left alone among a headless mass of men and horses.

All the officers, as far as I could see, behaved bravely in trying to rally their men, but of no avail. They retreated without order and in the greatest confusion—for the most part panic-stricken.

Our loss in killed, wounded, and missing amounts to 32.

The regiment mourns for one of its noblest officers in the person of Captain Haines, who was shot through the body in the moment when he nobly was endeavoring to rally his men.

Colonel Wyndham, Captains Shelmire, of Company A, and Clark, of Company G, were taken prisoners.

The standard of the regiment fell into the enemy's hands after the horse was shot and the standard-bearer himself wounded in the face.

In killed the regiment lost but 4 men. The rest evidently were all taken prisoners.

My own horse was shot by a Minie-rifle ball in the hip, which proves of little consequence.

Our retreat lasted for 1½ miles, when the men again came to their senses and rallied.

Among the officers I especially noticed Captains Boyd and Brodrick, who behaved very coolly and judiciously, being the last in their retreat; also Captain Kester deserves all praise for his personal bravery.

Very respectfully, your obedient servant,

JOSEPH KARGÉ,
*Lieutenant-Colonel, Commanding First New Jersey Cavalry.*

Brigadier-General BAYARD,
*Commanding Cavalry Brigade.*

---

## No. 51.

*Report of Col. Owen Jones, First Pennsylvania Cavalry, of operations June 1–13.*

CAMP NEAR MOUNT JACKSON,
*June* 13, 1862.

GENERAL: In pursuance of your order I have the honor to submit the following report of the operations of this regiment (First Pennsylvania Cavalry) from June 1, when we first came in sight of the rear guard of the enemy to the present date:

On June 1, being with my regiment at Front Royal, I was ordered to proceed to Strasburg to intercept the train of General Jackson, at that time said to be passing through the town. I immediately started, forded the Shenandoah, and came within sight of the town. The train of the enemy was in rear, but was very strongly guarded by a force of cavalry, infantry, and artillery, vastly superior to the force at my disposal. I halted my men and reported the facts to you. In pursuance of your orders then received I recrossed the river and encamped about 1 mile from the ford.

The next day I again advanced on Strasburg; found the town deserted by the enemy and in possession of a portion of your brigade. By your order the pursuit of the enemy was at once commenced, the command being joined by a portion of the army under General Frémont. The enemy retreated southward by the turnpike, and shortly commenced throwing shell from batteries placed in a commanding position. By your command I took charge of the advance on the right, and pressed forward with a portion of my regiment, capturing many prisoners. The enemy retreated from point to point, making stands at all favorable positions to check our advance. The final stand for the day was made at Woodstock. At this point Captain Thomas, of Company M, dismounted his men, and, acting as infantry, attacked the enemy, and drove them from their position by a well-directed fire of carbines. Encamped at a point near Woodstock.

On the morning of the 3d I took the advance and advanced through Woodstock. Found the bridges over the streams at that point destroyed. The ford at this point was in an exceedingly dangerous condition, but was passed after some delay without accident. I immediately formed my men and proceeded in pursuit of the retreating enemy, coming up to the cavalry at a point some miles from the ford, when a sharp skirmish ensued, the enemy being driven under a battery of four guns placed in a position to command the advance. I halted for our artillery to come up; but before it arrived the enemy again retreated, sharply followed by my men. I led the advance with a portion of Companies L and M, under Captains Thomas and Sands, driving the enemy at full speed through the village of Mount Jackson, at which point we had the pleasure of hearing the shouts of quite a number of prisoners taken from General Banks and retaken at this point by our sudden advance. We drove the enemy to the bridge over the Shenandoah at this point, which they fired to check our advance. When my advance appeared on the bluff above the bridge it was met by a violent fire from batteries placed on the other bank of the river, by which, I regret to say, Private Teagarden, of Company F, acting as my orderly, was killed at my side by a shell.

The day following we remained in camp.

On the morning of June 6 we again advanced, my regiment taking the right of the road, and on the evening of the second day arrived, without special incident, at Harrisonburg.

Shortly after we encamped we learned that the First New Jersey Regiment had been ambuscaded a few miles beyond the town and suffered some loss. We saddled up and proceeded with the Bucktails to reconnoiter the position of the enemy. In this advance the gallant Bucktails suffered loss, being attacked by an overwhelming force of the enemy. My men were under fire from a battery, but fortunately suffered no loss.

On the morning of the 8th we left Harrisonburg for Port Republic, but did not participate in the affair of that day.

On the morning of the 10th left Port Republic and returned to this place.

My men and horses are much jaded by the length and severity of the march, but I hope that a rest of a few days will restore them to their former high state of efficiency. The conduct of the officers and men that accompanied me is deserving of all praise.

Very respectfully, your obedient servant,

OWEN JONES,
*Colonel First Pennsylvania Cavalry.*

Brigadier-General BAYARD,
*Commanding Cavalry Brigade.*

---

No. 52.

*Reports of Maj. Gen. James Shields, U. S. Army, commanding First Division, Department of the Rappahannock, of operations May 30–June 9.*

FRONT ROYAL, *May* 30, 1862.

GENERAL: The First Brigade of this division, General Kimball commanding, preceded by four companies of Rhode Island cavalry, under Major Nelson, entered this place at 11 o'clock this morning and drove out the enemy, consisting of the Eighth Louisiana and four companies of the Twelfth Georgia and a body of cavalry. Our loss is 8 killed, 5 wounded, and 1 missing, all of the Rhode Island cavalry. We captured 6 officers and 150 men. Among the officers captured are Capt. Beckwith West, Forty-eighth Virginia; First Lieutenant Grinnell, Eighth Louisiana: Lieuts. J. W. Dixon and Waterman, Twelfth Georgia. We captured 18 of our troops taken by the enemy at this place a week ago; among whom are Maj. William D. Collins, First Vermont Cavalry; George H. Griffin, adjutant Fifth New York Cavalry; Lieutenant Dwyer, Fifth New York Cavalry, and Frederick C. Tarr, adjutant First Maryland Infantry. Captured a large amount of transportation, including 2 engines, 11 railroad cars, 5 wagons with teams, much quartermaster stores, and a quantity of small-arms recently captured from us have been recaptured. The loss of the enemy in killed is not yet known. The names of all prisoners captured and recaptured will be forwarded to-morrow.

Your obedient servant,

JAS. SHIELDS,
*Major-General.*

---

HDQRS. FIRST DIV., ARMY OF THE RAPPAHANNOCK,
*Front Royal, Va., May* 31, 1862—11 p. m.

COLONEL: The Fourth Brigade of this division, General Carroll commanding, was pushed forward in the direction of the Winchester and Strasburg turnpike this afternoon for the purpose of making a reconnaissance. A considerable force of the enemy, consisting of a brigade of infantry, a large force of cavalry, and four pieces of artillery, were found in position in the vicinity of a turnpike about 6 miles from this place. When attempting to form they were briskly attacked by our troops, driven from their position, and pursued back in the direction of Winchester until darkness prevented further pursuit. They covered their retreat with their numerous cavalry, and we, having no cavalry, were unable to make the pursuit effective. We succeeded in capturing 7 prisoners, one 10-pounder rifled gun, 12 wagons, and a number of horses and mules, and recapturing 6 men of the First Maryland Regiment, namely: John Corcoran, William T. Fowler, Edward Lockmond, Henry Roper, Thomas Mitchell, and Sergeant Uhler.

We lost 1 man killed and 2 wounded. The loss of the enemy we are as yet unable to ascertain.

Frémont's forces have not yet made their appearance. We are now running one of the engines saved from the flames yesterday by our troops.

The telegraph station is established 2 miles from this place.

Respectfully, your obedient servant,

JAS. SHIELDS,
*Major-General, Commanding Division.*

Colonel SCHRIVER,
*Chief of Staff, Front Royal, Va.*

---

HDQRS. FIRST DIV., DEPT. OF THE RAPPAHANNOCK,
*Columbia Bridge, June* 8, 1862—7 p. m.
(Received June 9, 4.30 a. m.)

COLONEL: A dispatch has this moment arrived from Colonel Carroll, commanding the advance of this division, stating that he moved forward to-day with some cavalry, infantry, and two pieces of artillery on Port Republic, drove a small force of the enemy from the bridge, and crossed the bridge in pursuit of this force. Three brigades of Jackson's army, covering at least three batteries, assailed them at once on both flanks. The cavalry fled the first fire; his two guns were captured, and he, with the residue of the brigade, is in full retreat on Conrad's Store, where he (Carroll) sent me the dispatch, no time being mentioned. It must have been this morning.

There is another brigade advancing to his support; and a third brigade moving forward at this time from this place to support them. The Fourth Brigade is still at Luray, awaiting the arrival of forces from Front Royal. I have sent information of this to General Frémont, who seems to be lying at Harrisonburg, urging him to attack them with all his force in their rear at once, while I am hurrying forward the others to maintain our position, and try to repulse the enemy. The general commanding will see at once the necessity of immediate action to recover this loss.

Very respectfully, &c.,

JAS. SHIELDS,
*Commanding Division.*

Colonel SCHRIVER, *Chief of Staff.*

---

COLUMBIA BRIDGE,
*June* 12, 1862—9 a. m.

COLONEL: We are now passing this place to Luray. There I must take a few days' rest to refit for the march to Catlett's. At Catlett's I hope to be within reach of ample supplies. I find that about half my command are barefoot and foot-sore. Hard bread and salt are indispensable to take us to Catlett's. Our men fought like devils. The enemy suffered terribly. The odds were overwhelming. The officer (Colonel Carroll) neglected to burn the bridge at Port Republic. This report that the bridge was burned five days ago deceived me. He held it three-quarters of an hour and wanted the good sense to burn it. They took up an indefensible position afterward instead of a defensible one. But notwithstanding all these blunders the men behaved nobly; left the ground in perfect order; brought off everything but the guns, which had to be abandoned, the horses being killed. Eight pieces they report abandoned. I had concerted a combined attack with General Frémont next day, which must have proved successful. The position and peremptory orders compelled me to come on. Please let General McDowell know that my artillery needs refitting, and to let me have the Napoleon guns if possible. I will have a perfect memorandum of our wants forwarded you from Luray as soon as I have time to halt.

JAS. SHIELDS,
*Major-General, Commanding Division.*

Colonel SCHRIVER.

---

HEADQUARTERS SHIELDS' DIVISION,
*Luray, Va., June* 13, 1862—6.30 a. m.

The telegrams from General Banks* and giving extracts from Richmond papers received.

The engagement of Monday, the 9th instant, was between General Jackson's whole force and the advance of this division, under Brigadier-General Tyler, near Port Republic. The unequal contest was maintained successfully for four hours.

On Sunday, at 6.30 a. m., Colonel Carroll, leading a small body in advance, found Jackson's army and train on the opposite side of the river at Port Republic. The river was impassable, and the bridge across it still standing. By some unaccountable misapprehension he neglected to burn it, although he held possession of it three-quarters of an hour. The destruction of the bridge would have insured the destruction of Jackson's army, placing him between General Frémont and us, with an impassable river in his front. This first fundamental error was not redeemed afterward either by Colonel Carroll or General Tyler, who commanded the advance, by falling back at once upon a defensible position. On the contrary, they took up a position utterly indefensible, within 2 miles from Port Republic.

Jackson crossed his whole army over the bridge, thus left, as it were, for his use, on Sunday night and on Monday morning, and attacked our advance, consisting of about 2,500 men, with his whole force. The folly of attempting to hold such a position against such overwhelming odds was redeemed by the fearless and reckless courage of our troops.

They repulsed the enemy at every point for four hours. Our artillery hurled destruction through his ranks. The infantry drove the enemy back from the guns at the point of the bayonet. The artillerists stood to their guns, especially those of Captain Clark's battery (E), Fourth Artillery, until their horses were killed, and then defended themselves in a hand-to-hand fight with the enemy's infantry, and were only compelled to abandon the field at length by a fatal mistake of General Tyler's in stripping the left flank of all infantry support. They then fell back in good order, carrying off all the guns except those whose

---

*See pp. 543, 544.

horses were killed. I reached them in time to cover the retreat with the residue of the command, and took up a strong and defensible position between Conrad's Store and Port Republic, which Jackson feared to attack, falling back at once.

On the evening of the 9th I was concerting a combined attack on Jackson next morning with General Frémont, with whom I kept up constant communication by means of a ferry which we had previously established, when I received a positive and peremptory order to return to Luray. There was no option left me. I never obeyed an order with such reluctance, but I had to return.

Jackson, with that sagacity which characterizes his course, burned the bridge between himself and Frémont after having crossed the river to our side, but General Frémont, whose conduct throughout cannot be too highly praised, had a pontoon bridge to throw across next morning to attack Jackson's flank, while I with my whole command should attack him in front. The result could not have been doubtful. Thus lay a kind of fatality. This man, who dared to insult our capital, whom 2,500 of this division fought for four hours, who fell back in haste before my whole division, not deeming himself safe until he put 5 miles between us, is left to escape. The first fatality was in not burning the bridge on Sunday morning. Colonel Carroll, in whom I placed implicit confidence, was hurried on by an excess of daring to neglect this important duty in his pursuit of the enemy. The second was in attempting to maintain an indefensible position in the face of such tremendous odds. Brigadier-General Tyler, in command of the advance, must have had unbounded confidence to have hazarded this. The third was in recalling my command peremptorily to Luray when General Frémont and myself had the enemy still in our grasp.

The plan for Jackson's destruction was perfect. The execution of it, from inexplicable causes, was not what was to be expected, but the hardihood and indomitable courage of my brave but misguided advance in giving battle to the whole of Jackson's army, in repulsing him for four hours, in destroying numbers of the enemy, which he himself admits was much heavier than in the battle of the previous day with the whole of Frémont's force, and then in carrying everything off the field but the unhorsed guns, is an exhibition of fearless confidence and courage that must extort admiration even from the enemy. This division has not been defeated. The advance, instead of falling back upon the main body as it should have done, gave battle and was repulsed, after killing, as the citizens report, 1,000 of the enemy. Few prisoners were taken on either side.

This is in brief the history of the affair of the 9th, which will be given in detail in the reports now in course of preparation. I beg that this may be forwarded to the War Department, to relieve the President and Secretary from their natural solicitude on our account.

I am, very respectfully, your obedient servant,

JAS. SHIELDS,
*Brigadier-General, Commanding Division.*

Colonel SCHRIVER,
*Chief of Staff, Dept. of the Rappahannock, Manassas Junction.*

—

HDQRS. FIRST DIVISION, DEPT. OF THE RAPPAHANNOCK.

COLONEL: I have the honor to report, now that I have found time to do so, that on the 1st instant it became apparent at Front Royal to the general commanding that the enemy under Jackson had effected his escape through Strasburg the day previous, and that our forces under Frémont were in hot pursuit of him. My division was therefore ordered to take the Luray road, in order to operate against him.

The route which I thus took was parallel to that taken by the enemy, the South Fork of the Shenandoah and a range of mountains interposing between us As the enemy had gained something like a day's march upon us, my first object was to find some mode of crossing the Shenandoah, in order to fall upon his flank while Frémont assailed him in the rear. About 5 o'clock p. m. next day my advance guard reached the Shenandoah at Honeyville, but found the White House Bridge and Columbia Bridge both burned, thus cutting off all hope of attacking his flank at New Market. I then pushed forward the advance as rapidly as possible, in hopes of finding the bridge at Conrad's Store still standing, but that bridge was also found burned. During the whole of this time, which occupied nearly three days, the rain poured down in torrents, so that the Shenandoah overflowed its banks, and the mountain streams became rivers. It became impossible to move forward; the wagons sank in the mud to the axles, and all communication was cut off for a time between the main body and the advance guard. In this condition the first question was to live, to obtain supplies, as none could reach us over such roads.

To meet this necessity we took possession of two mills, purchased wheat, and employed fatigue parties to grind flour, and were soon supplied with an abundance of that necessary article. We were not idle in other respects. It became necessary to open some kind of communication with General Frémont, and to effect this we set to work to construct a ferry across the Shenandoah at the site of the Columbia Bridge. While engaged in these operations our scouting parties discovered General Longstreet's pickets on the Luray side of Thornton Gap, and some deserters brought in gave his force at 10,000, moving from Culpeper to Thornton Gap upon Luray with the view of creating a diversion in favor of Jackson. This compelled me to post two brigades at Luray and remain there in person to make head against Longstreet, so that he might not fall on my rear.

Just at this time Colonel Carroll, commanding Fourth Brigade, then at Conrad's Store, informed me by a dispatch that the bridge at Port Republic had been burned five weeks, and that the enemy's train was on the other side waiting for the river to fall.

Communication having been now opened with General Frémont, I sent a messenger to ascertain his position and that of the enemy. The messenger found General Frémont within 5 miles of Harrisonburg, and brought back intelligence that the enemy had abandoned the turnpike to Staunton, owing to the bridges having been previously burned on that route, and had turned short in the direction of Port Republic. This corroborated the dispatch of Colonel Carroll. The enemy had an impassable river in his front; Frémont's cannon were in his rear. This river could not become fordable in less than three days. It was only necessary to place him between Frémont's artillery and mine, with an impassable river in his front, to insure his destruction, and to prevent him from effecting his escape by any by-road it was only necessary to cut the railroad at Waynesborough, 18 miles distant, to burn the bridge and depot at that place, and he would be compelled to lay down his arms.

The Fourth and Third Brigades were sent forward for this purpose; also fourteen pieces of artillery, under Colonel Daum. Their mission was to guard the river at Port Republic at the place used as a ford in low water, but now impassable, and cut the railroad at Waynesborough—an easy job if the bridge had been burned as reported—while I remained with two brigades (the First and Second), not exceeding 4,000 men, to confront Longstreet, reported to have 10,000, if he should fall on Luray.

These arrangements having been made, and while awaiting the result, at 7 o'clock p. m., 8th instant, I was startled by a dispatch from Colonel Carroll from Port Republic giving me intelligence that he found the bridge at that place still standing; that he dashed upon it, drove the enemy from it, captured it, and pursued him some distance on the other side, when on a sudden he was assailed by three brigades and eighteen pieces of cannon, and compelled to retreat with the loss of three guns, and that he was then in full retreat on Conrad's Store, and should be well satisfied if he could effect it decently.

Conrad's Store is about 15 miles on the Luray side of Port Republic. I acted at once upon this intelligence; sent instant orders to General Tyler, who had command of the advance, as well as to Colonel Daum, chief of artillery, to take up a defensible position at or near Conrad's Store, and that I would join them with the residue of the command as speedily as it could march. I communicated the intelligence to General Frémont at Harrisonburg, with the request that he would fall with his whole force on the enemy's rear, while I would attack him in front in the morning. I sent a dispatch to Front Royal, giving the same intelligence to the general commanding, and earnestly urging that two brigades should be sent to protect Luray against Longstreet during my absence, as I was under the necessity of pushing forward my whole command to support the advance. This being done, I put my two other brigades in motion that night and moved forward as rapidly as the men could march.

About 9 o'clock next morning I reached Conrad's Store, and my surprise and disappointment may be imagined when I learned by a messenger from General Tyler that they were still posted within 2 miles of Port Republic, and urging me to push forward re-enforcements. I cannot describe my feelings when I received this intelligence. I saw our previous efforts and struggles to prevent the escape of the enemy were now worse than thwarted. I needed no further information to assure me that the enemy must secure his only avenue of retreat. He had from Sunday morning till Monday morning to cross his troops without interruption to effect this object, and no enemy could neglect such an opportunity. I sent an order for them to extricate themselves from their false position and fall back as speedily as possible, but they were compelled to fall back before the order reached them.

I pushed forward my command, and placed it in a position upon which the whole force of the enemy would break itself. I proceeded next to post guns and fresh troops on commanding points to cover their retreat, but before I had advanced 10 miles beyond Conrad's Store a crowd of fugitives from the field gave evidence of retreat. It required all my influence to get these fugitives to deploy in the woods as skirmishers. Soon after the main force came in sight, not, however, as fugitives or an army in retreat, but marching as proudly and calmly as if they were on parade, while the Fifth Ohio, a gallant regiment, with two pieces of artillery, under Colonel Carroll, brought up the rear, and by their noble conduct kept the advancing foe in check; but I just arrived in time, as the enemy's cavalry, which is very active, was enveloping the column, and our cavalry, the First Virginia, was nowhere to be seen. Our fresh troops soon drove back the cavalry, and the retreating column reached the other brigades in position without further accident. There I prepared for battle, but the enemy fell back from before it much more rapidly than he had advanced.

At this moment I received a message from Major-General Frémont, giving me an account of his engagement of the previous day. I prepared a dispatch for him in return, giving him the intelligence of the day, and urging him to throw his pontoon bridge across the Shenandoah in the morning (surmising, as it happened, that the enemy would burn the bridge the moment he crossed) and attack Jackson's flank, while I would attack him with my whole force in front.

The messenger with this dispatch had started on his way when an orderly arrived with a dispatch from the general commanding, then in Washington, giving me positive orders to return to Luray immediately. I recalled the messenger and communicated this intelligence to Major-General Frémont, assuring him that I deeply regretted I could be of no further use to him. I report the facts and abstain from all comments, but I cannot omit to notice the courage and confidence which inspired such a small force, whose effective strength did not exceed 2,500 men, to calmly await the attack of an army of from 10,000 to 20,000.

The battle which followed shows that this confidence was not ill-founded; for, although the enemy must have made his dispositions during the previous night to overwhelm them, they contested the field for several hours, repulsing him with great slaughter several times. The artillery generally, in which I took such just pride, was managed splendidly, shattering the enemy's columns with canister, and frequently driving them in dismay from the field. The infantry never failed to repulse the enemy in close conflict. The right wing, as it appears from the reports, not only drove the enemy before it, but took possession of the ground he occupied. Our batteries on the left wing, as it appears, were unfortunately left without adequate infantry support, and it was only when 30 of their horses were killed and the enemy's bayonets at their breasts that Captain Clark and his gallant artillerists withdrew from the field, carrying off all their guns except such as had been wholly unhorsed by the enemy's fire. Nothing could exceed the general courage and daring of the force engaged, but I prefer referring to the reports of the different commanders engaged on the field for the names of those entitled to special praise. The number of guns engaged on our side was eighteen, of which they had to abandon seven, all the horses being killed. Our loss is severe for the number engaged, amounting to 40 killed and 313 wounded.* There were but few prisoners taken on either side. The list of missing is large, but many of them have since joined us. The enemy's loss must have been immense. Their advancing columns were several times broken and repulsed with canister by our batteries, leaving the ground covered with their killed and wounded. The Seventh Louisiana Regiment, 748 strong, left the field, it is said, with only 36 effective men.

Considering the locality, which was not defensible, being liable to be turned on both flanks, and the disparity of forces engaged, it is truly wonderful that our little army was able to effect its escape. This can only be attributed to the splendid manner in which the artillery was handled and the desperate manner in which the infantry fought in its close contests with the enemy. But defeat was unavoidable. It is fortunate they withdrew when they did. My whole division in that position, or rather in that locality, would have protracted the struggle

---

*But see revised statement p. 690.

and made it more bloody, but could not have maintained the field. There is much to be regretted in this affair, but nothing which does not reflect honor upon the courage and conduct of the gallant troops engaged.

Very respectfully, your obedient servant,

JAS. SHIELDS,
*Brigadier-General, Commanding Division.*

Col. E. SCHRIVER,
*Chief of Staff, Department of the Rappahannock.*

[Addenda.]

WASHINGTON, D. C., *October* 3, 1862.

GENERAL: I respectfully inclose a nominal report of the killed and wounded in the engagement had by General Shields' division in the valley of Virginia last June. The report when received was incorrect and had to be returned, and when received back was overlooked.

With reference to the remark made by the general that the order to him to cease following the enemy and return to Luray was received just "as he had planned a combined attack with General Frémont, by which Jackson was to be annihilated," I have to say that the order was given by me from the War Department by direction of the President, who at the same moment wrote a similar order to General Frémont, it being not considered expedient to continue the chase after Jackson up the valley, which could bring on nothing decisive for us, and it being greatly the desire of the President and myself that the forces under my command should as speedily as possible return to Fredericksburg to move on Richmond. Both the condition of General Shields' division and that of the roads and rivers, as represented by him, indicated anything than the success he anticipated.

I have the honor to be, general, very respectfully, your obedient servant,

IRVIN McDOWELL,
*Major-General.*

To the ADJUTANT-GENERAL OF THE ARMY,
*Washington, D. C.*

[Inclosure.]

FRONT ROYAL, *June* 9, 1862.

It being the intention of the President that the troops of this department be employed elsewhere, the major-general commanding directs that you cease all further pursuit and bring back all your division to Luray, and get ready for the march to Fredericksburg.

I send herewith a telegram in cipher to Major-General Frémont,* which I have been directed to inclose to you for transmittal to him.

ED. SCHRIVER,
*Colonel, Chief of Staff.*

Major-General SHIELDS,
*Commanding Division, Luray.*

*See Lincoln to Frémont, p. 655.

FRONT ROYAL, *June* 9, 1862.

I am directed to inform you that it is the order of the President of the United States that Major-General Frémont shall hold the valley in connection with Major-General Banks, and that the forces belonging to the Department of the Rappahannock be immediately marched on Richmond to co-operate with Major-General McClellan.

It has been, and is still, no doubt much desired that Jackson shall be made to pay for his late dash down the valley, and if there is a reasonable expectation of his being caught no doubt the order for the advance on Richmond would be suspended. But it is not clear from your report what is the position of your command at this time, and it is inferred that the force at Port Republic is small, as well as the party expected to be at Waynesborough. If this is so, the general thinks you have forgotten your instructions not to move your force so that the several parts should not be in supporting distance of each other. If, however, you are in hot pursuit and about to fall on the enemy, and can do so with reasonable chance of success without relying on the troops at Front Royal, who are too far in rear to support you in your extended movements, the general is not disposed to recall you; but if you have only detachments thrown out in front your command should not be placed in such positions as to prevent compliance with the President's general plan of operations, and you should at once call in the advance parties and move upon Fredericksburg, there to be refitted for the march to Richmond.

The general desires an immediate reply.

ED. SCHRIVER,
*Colonel, Chief of Staff.*

Major-General SHIELDS, *Commanding Division.*

---

## No. 53.

***Return of Casualties in the Union forces in the engagement at Port Republic.***

[Compiled from nominal lists of casualties, returns, &c.]

| Command. | Killed. | | Wounded. | | Captured or missing. | | Aggregate. | Officers killed. |
|---|---|---|---|---|---|---|---|---|
| | Officers. | Enlisted men. | Officers. | Enlisted men. | Officers. | Enlisted men. | | |
| General staff | | | 1 | | | | 1 | |
| 84th Pennsylvania Infantry | | 1 | | 10 | | 21 | 32 | |
| 110th Pennsylvania Infantry | | 1 | | 10 | | 15 | 26 | |
| 1st West Virginia Cavalry* (detached). | | | | | | | | |
| 1st West Virginia Infantry | 1 | | 3 | 15 | | 48 | 67 | Lieutenant Barnes. |
| 1st Ohio Light Artillery, Battery H. | | 2 | | 4 | | 5 | 11 | |
| 1st Ohio Light Artillery, Battery L. | | 1 | | 4 | 1 | 5 | 11 | |
| 5th Ohio Infantry | 2 | 2 | | 63 | 6 | 191 | 264 | Lieutenants Graham and Smith. |
| 7th Ohio Infantry | | 10 | 3 | 52 | | 10 | 75 | |
| 29th Ohio Infantry | 1 | 16 | 5 | 36 | 10 | 104 | 172 | Captain Luce. |
| 66th Ohio Infantry | | 20 | 5 | 70 | 6 | 104 | 205 | |
| 7th Indiana Infantry | 1 | 8 | 4 | 103 | 1 | 28 | 145 | Captain Waterman. |
| 4th U. S. Artillery, Battery E | | 1 | | 5 | | 3 | 9 | |
| Total | 5 | 62 | 21 | 372 | 24 | 534 | 1,018 | |

* No loss reported.

## No. 54.

*Report of Col. Philip Daum, Chief of Artillery, of engagement at Port Republic.*

HEADQUARTERS OF ARTILLERY,
*Luray, June* 13, 1862.

SIR: I have the honor to submit to you the following report of the actions which took place on the 8th and 9th of June last, near Port Republic, Va.:

I reached Sunday last, June 8, early in the morning, a point 1 mile north of Port Republic, where I found the forces under Colonel Carroll in full retreat from a bridge spanning at that place the Shenandoah. I learned from Colonel Carroll that Captain Robinson, Ohio artillery, with one section, was ordered to take position near that bridge. I immediately started toward the same to recall it, but found bridge as well as guns in possession of the enemy. On my return I found one piece of the same battery abandoned in the field, with only two horses and one driver attached to it, the sergeant being killed and the lieutenant commanding missing. I found Captain Keily, aide-de-camp, making great efforts to rescue the piece. It was impossible to accomplish this, as it was sunk in the swamp. I went to the next infantry regiment, which I found about one-half mile to the rear, and succeeded in procuring the assistance of eight volunteers of the Seventh Indiana Regiment (the names of whom I respectfully attach). With these brave fellows and the help of Captain Keily I was lucky enough to bring the piece to the road, and this under the concentrated fire of eighteen of the enemy's guns. Pursuing the road in retreat with the thus secured gun, I found in the same another piece of the same battery also abandoned, the pole being broken. This piece belonged to the reserve and had not been in action. Officers and men, panic-stricken, had taken off the horses and fled. I mended the pole and had the piece brought to the rear by infantry. Officers, cannoneers, and horses could not be found for four hours afterward.

We now were out of the enemy's range, and took position at a point commanding the road and ground before us, so as to enable the infantry to rally here. I brought two guns from Clark's battery and one howitzer of Robinson's in position. This was at noon. The enemy moved now their baggage train toward the bridge, *en route* to Gordonsville, and a heavy fire was heard to our right and rear across the Shenandoah, which we supposed to be the forces of General Frémont engaged with those of General Jackson. At 2 o'clock General Tyler arrived with the Third Brigade, and I had now the artillery attached to the Third and Fourth Brigades and the reserve, consisting in all of sixteen pieces, under my command. I ordered a 12-pounder howitzer and a 6-pounder smooth-bore to the rear, to guard a ford. I proposed to General Tyler and General Carroll to attempt the destruction of the bridge at all hazards. Jackson's force being then in an engagement with General Frémont, the infantry should move to the woods unobserved by the enemy, the artillery and cavalry to move rapidly along the road after the infantry had started, but the plan was abandoned by order of General Tyler.

Evening now set in, and the troops went into bivouac. By daylight of Monday morning, June 9, everything was apparently quiet, and a heavy fog rested over the ground. At 5.45 the fog had partly disappeared. The enemy opened fire upon us from a battery near the road, within 1,800 yards of my selected position. I promptly replied, and the infantry fell in. I suggested to General Tyler to draw a sufficient infantry force to the left of Clark's battery in the road, because I saw the enemy pour into the same some distance above, fearing a flank movement. The enemy kept up a sharp artillery fire from two batteries. I brought three guns of Huntington's battery into position on the right of Clark's, and the rest of Clark's, under Lieutenant Baker, and two guns of Huntington's battery on our right near the river, to prevent a flank movement, which the enemy attempted. These guns did excellent execution, as they drove the enemy back with canister. The infantry support had not then come up. As soon as the infantry came our troops moved forward and captured one of the enemy's guns.

I now went to the left wing, and found two of Captain Huntington's battery horses had been killed by musket-fire. I earnestly entreated General Tyler to throw infantry into the woods, to clear them of the enemy. He answered me that he had only two regiments to do this, but they were placed in the wrong direction, and were insufficient to check the enemy's advance. The enemy's fire from the wood grew hotter, but Captain Clark succeeded in driving them back with canister, and I now demanded of General Tyler to increase and push forward some more infantry into the woods to the left of the guns, whereupon he rebuked me for asking or suggesting to him.

By General Tyler's order Lieutenant-Colonel Hayward was left in command of artillery on the left wing, and I went to the right wing to follow up our success there. The enemy then was in full retreat, and General Tyler recalled the infantry from the extreme left, stationed in the woods. Shortly afterward the enemy charged from the left flank through a ravine on which Captain Clark's guns could not bear, and they were captured. Seeing this, I ordered the guns of the right wing to fall quickly back, and took position within 200 yards of the captured battery and opened with canister upon them. That and the musketry of some infantry near by was too much for the enemy, and they retreated into the woods, and I again had possession of our lost guns, but for want of horses could not bring off more than one of Captain Clark's guns.

Captain Clark, Lieutenant Baker, and their non-commissioned officers and men stood manfully and bravely to their posts till the last. I could have saved some of Captain Huntington's guns, but his limbers had gone long before this to the rear, nor could I see Captain Huntington himself. The enemy now came in an overwhelming force upon us, and we retreated to the rear in tolerably good order. One of Captain Huntington's guns was carelessly left in the road, half way between the battle-ground and Conrad's Store. The axle-tree had been broken, and although I taught him (the captain) how to mend it, it was left to its fate. The gun was even unspiked, but Lieutenant-Colonel Shriber, acting inspector general, spiked it and destroyed the carriage. In the same dishonorable manner Captain Huntington left his forge upon the field.

I cannot close my report without mentioning the names of a few brave officers and men who deserve to be rewarded for their personal valor: Captain Keily, aide-de-camp, stands at the head; Captain Clark, U. S. Army; Lieutenant Baker, First Sergt. C. F. Merkle, Musician Delmege, and Private John Martin, Company E, light artillery. Further, James M. Lambertson, N. Williams, William Merrill, William Ripkin, N. G. Conley, Company K, Seventh Regiment Indiana Infantry; J. Clark, Company I, Seventh Indiana; William Davis and John Henderson, Company F, Seventh Indiana Regiment; Thomas E. Smith and Corpl. Stephen Slain, Robinson's battery. These men assisted me in rescuing a gun on Saturday, with great perseverance, under the heavy fire of the enemy. Lieutenant-Colonel Shriber rendered valuable service in his endeavors to rally and organize the retreat.

I have the honor to be, sir, your obedient servant,

P. DAUM,
*Colonel and Chief of Artillery.*

Captain PELOUZE, U. S. A.,
*Actg. Asst. Adjt. Gen., Shields' Div., Dept. Rappahannock.*

---

## No. 55.

*Report of Capt. Joseph C. Clark, Battery E, Fourth U. S. Artillery, of engagement at Port Republic.*

CAMP NEAR LURAY, VA.,
*June* 11, 1862.

I have the honor to report the part taken by my battery in the battle near Port Republic on the 9th of June. Three of my Parrott guns, under my command, were placed by your direction on our extreme left in a rather contracted position, which, however, commanded the enemy's guns. The remainder of my battery, under First Lieut. W. L. Baker, was posted on the extreme right of our position. In my rear and on the left flank woods approached within a few yards of my guns. Close to the flank was also a ravine, beyond which the ground rose rapidly, giving a plunging fire upon our guns if occupied by the enemy. Early in the action, while replying to the guns of the enemy, his riflemen appeared in the woods covering this high ground, and opened a sharp fire at short range upon the batteries of the left wing. This was replied to by my guns and one of Battery L, First Ohio, with canister, with such destructive effect as to drive them immediately from the position. Infantry skirmishers in the woods assisted in this repulse.

About an hour later a large force of the enemy suddenly charged through the ravine and down the wooded slope of the hills upon our guns. The thick undergrowth prevented our seeing them until they were quite near us. Our infantry having been principally if not entirely withdrawn from this point, we were unsupported at this critical moment, and it being impossible to bring the guns to bear upon the ravine in time to check the enemy's advance, my men, as well as those of the other guns, were compelled by an overwhelming force to fall back. Nearly all the horses and part of the men were immediately shot down. I afterward succeeded in recovering one of the three guns thus captured, but two were retained by the enemy.

The three guns of my battery under Lieutenant Baker, after engaging the enemy's guns on our right, were charged by the rebel infantry, but gallantly drove them back, assisted by our infantry supports and one gun of Battery H, First Ohio. These guns were shortly afterward ordered to fall back to support the left flank, which had been overpowered. I then took command of two of these guns, and succeeded in recovering one of those captured by the enemy.

I take pleasure in calling your attention to the coolness and fine conduct of First Lieutenant Baker under a galling fire; also to the gallant conduct of First Sergt. C. F. Merkle, Corpl. Francis Dalton, Musician Delmege, and Private John Martin. Where so many deserve to be mentioned it is difficult to discriminate. Two rifled Parrott guns and two caissons were also lost, and 30 horses, most of which were killed by the sharpshooters of the enemy.

I am, respectfully, your obedient servant,

J. C. CLARK,
*Captain Fourth Artillery.*

Col. PHILIP DAUM,
*Chief of Artillery.*

---

## No. 56.

*Report of Brig. Gen. Nathan Kimball, U. S. Army, commanding First Brigade, of action at Front Royal, May 30.*

HDQRS. FIRST BRIG., FIRST DIV., DEPT. RAPPAHANNOCK,
*Front Royal, Va., May* 31, 1862.

SIR: I have the honor to report that in obedience to your orders I moved with my command from Rectortown at 6 p. m. the 29th instant, and after a short rest near Manassas Gap reached Front Royal at 11.30 a. m. the next day, the 30th. I had reason to believe the enemy were in large force in the village, and on approaching the heights commanding the town from the southeast I ordered two guns to be placed in position. This was scarcely done before the enemy was discovered and fire opened upon him. I ordered the Fourth Ohio Volunteers to occupy the hills to the south and southwest, and the Seventh West Virginia and Fourteenth Indiana Volunteers the hills to the northeast and north, reserving the Eighth Ohio Volunteers to support the guns. This disposition of my force was not completed before the enemy commenced a hurried retreat by the road toward Winchester, after setting fire to the railroad depot buildings and the cars near it. A detachment of infantry was hurried forward to extinguish the flames, who by the most strenuous efforts saved several cars loaded with grain, but the buildings were destroyed.

A small body of New Hampshire cavalry, all I had, closely followed by the Fourth and Eighth Ohio Volunteers, were pushed forward in pursuit of the enemy, who was overtaken about 2 miles from the village, and after a sharp skirmish and a decisive charge of the fearfully small body of cavalry he was scattered with loss, and the pursuit abandoned because of the utter exhaustion of my men, they having marched, with but little rest since the evening before, 23 miles. My command rested upon the ground where the pursuit ended.

The enemy's loss in killed and wounded I am unable to ascertain, as he carried them away with him. I succeeded in capturing 155 prisoners and a large quantity of arms, ammunition, clothing, and forage. The prisoners are from the Twelfth Regiment Georgia Infantry; the Sixth, Seventh, Eighth, and Ninth Regiments and Bate's and Wheat's battalions Louisiana infantry; the Second, Fifth, Twenty-fifth, Twenty-seventh, Forty-second, Forty-eighth, Fifty-second, and Fifty-eighth Virginia Infantry, and the Sixth and Seventh Virginia and Ashby's Cavalry; the Twenty-first North Carolina and the Sixteenth Mississippi Infantry. Three commissioned officers and 17 privates were recaptured.

Our loss is 8 killed, 7 wounded, and 1 missing, all of the New Hampshire cavalry. Among the killed is Capt. William P. Ainsworth, of Troop M.

It affords me great pleasure to commend to you Maj. D. B. Nelson, of the New Hampshire cavalry, and the brave few who followed him in the gallant charge upon the enemy in overwhelming numbers.

I cannot speak in too high terms of the officers and men of my command for their fortitude and cheerfulness on a fatiguing march with short rations, and the readiness and determination exhibited by them to drive or capture the enemy without regard to his force.

With this I submit lists* of our killed and wounded, our friends recaptured, and of the enemy captured, and invoice of stores saved from the flames and taken from the enemy.

I am, very respectfully, your obedient servant,

NATHAN KIMBALL,
*Brigadier-General, Commanding.*

Capt. LOUIS H. PELOUZE,
*Assistant Adjutant-General.*

---

## No. 57.

*Report of Brig. Gen. Erastus B. Tyler, U. S. Army, commanding Third Brigade, of engagement at Port Republic.*

HEADQUARTERS THIRD BRIGADE,
*Near Luray, Va., June* 12, 1862.

SIR: In compliance with your order to proceed to Waynesborough I left Columbia Bridge on the 7th instant, reaching Naked Creek the same day, going into camp under orders to march at 4 o'clock a. m. next day, that we might reach Port Republic at the time you indicated to me.

When within about 6 miles of the town I learned Acting Brigadier-General Carroll with the Fourth Brigade had engaged the enemy at or near the town. I immediately halted my train, clearing the road for the troops and artillery, and pressed forward to his support as rapidly as possible, reaching the position occupied by him—some 2 miles north of the town—at 2 o'clock p. m. 8th instant. The position was selected by Colonel Daum, I understood, as the only tenable one in that vicinity. From that officer I learned the enemy had eighteen pieces of artillery planted so as to completely command all the approaches to the town, and from the engagement with General Carroll that morning had obtained the range of the different points.

Immediately on the arrival of my command Colonel Daum urged an attack with the combined forces of infantry and artillery, to which I so far consented as to order the infantry into position under cover of a thick wood which skirted the road, and commenced observing the enemy's position myself, which appeared to me one to defy an army of 50,000 men. I at once sent for Colonel Carroll, Lieutenant-Colonel Shriber, Captains Clark and Robinson, who had been over the ground, they all agreeing in the opinion that an attack would result in the destruction of our little force.

About this time your order to commandant of post at Port Republic

* Nominal list omitted.

was handed me. Upon it and the opinion of these officers I ordered the infantry back to bivouac for the night. A heavy picket was kept well to the front to observe any movement of the enemy, and at 4 a. m. General Carroll and myself went to the outer vedettes, who reported that there had been no movement of the enemy across the bridge during the night. Their pickets only appearing, which we were able to discover ourselves, we returned to camp.

A few moments after your order of June 8, 7.15 p. m., from Columbia Bridge, reached me, and while writing a reply, was informed that the enemy were advancing upon us, or rather into the woods opposite their position, evidently with a view of outflanking us upon the left. Captains Clark and Robinson opened their batteries upon them with effect. Captain Huntington's guns were soon doing the same good work. Two companies of skirmishers and two regiments of infantry were ordered into the woods to counteract this movement of the enemy. The fire of our skirmishers was soon heard, and I ordered two more regiments to their support. A sharp fire was kept up in the woods for a few moments only, when the enemy retired, and was seen coming out of the woods, crossing to join a column moving upon our right.

In the mean time a section of two guns had opened upon our battery on the left and another section was taking position on our right. The Seventh Indiana Infantry, Colonel Gavin, was sent to the extreme right, and was met by two rebel regiments under cover of the river bank. A section of Captain Clark's battery took a position well to the right. The fire of the enemy from their masked position compelled Colonel Gavin to retire a short distance, which he did in admirable order. The Twenty-ninth Ohio was sent to support him, moving forward in splendid style on double-quick. The Seventh Ohio was next sent forward to support Captain Clark's guns; the Fifth Ohio next, to support a section of Captain Huntington's battery. These two last-named regiments moved forward and engaged the enemy in a style that commanded the admiration of every beholder. Regiment after regiment of the enemy moved upon the right, and the engagement became very warm. The First Virginia, Colonel Thoburn, who had been ordered into the woods on the left, was now ordered down to the right, entering the open field with a loud shout.

My entire force was now in position. On our right was the Seventh Indiana, Colonel Gavin; Twenty-ninth Ohio, Colonel Buckley; Seventh Ohio, Lieutenant-Colonel Creighton; Fifth Ohio, Colonel Dunning; First Virginia, Colonel Thoburn, with a section of Captains Clark's and Huntington's batteries. On our left, the key of the position, was a company of the Fifth and one of the Sixty-sixth Ohio Infantry, deployed through the woods as skirmishers; the Eighty-fourth and One hundred and tenth Pennsylvania Regiments also well up into the woods. The Sixty-sixth Ohio, Colonel Candy, was directly in the rear of the battery (composed of three guns of Captain Clark's battery, three guns of Captain Huntington's, and one of Captain Robinson's, under Lieutenant-Colonel Hayward), and upon him and his gallant band depended everything at this critical moment, and the duty was well and gallantly executed. Had they given way the command must have been lost. The left wing of Colonel Candy's regiment was extended into the woods and close in the rear of the battery, which position they held until a retreat was ordered.

Additional re-enforcements of the enemy were coming up on our right, and having abandoned their position on our left, I ordered the

Eighty-fourth and One hundred and tenth down to the right, but before they reached the position assigned them the enemy was in full retreat before our brave men, and I at once ordered them across into the woods again.

Under cover of the engagement on our right the enemy had thrown another force into the woods and pressed them down upon our batteries on the left. So rapid was this movement that they passed the line on which the Eighty-fourth and One hundred and tenth were ordered unobserved, making a dash upon the battery so sudden and unexpected as to compel the cannoneers to abandon their pieces. Colonel Candy met the enemy with his regiment with great coolness, his men fighting with commendable bravery. The Seventh and Fifth Ohio were soon supporting him, driving the enemy from their position and retaking the battery. The artillery officers made a strong effort and used great exertions to remove their guns, but, the horses having been killed or disabled, found it impossible.

The enemy had given way along the whole line, but I saw heavy re-enforcements crossing from the town that would have been impossible for us successfully to resist. After consulting General Carroll I ordered the troops to fall back under his direction, with a view of retreating until we should meet the re-enforcements of Generals Kimball and Ferry. General Carroll took command of the covering of the retreat, which was made in perfect order, and, save the stampede of those who ran before the fight was fairly opened, the retreat was quite as orderly as the advance.

The force engaged under my command could not have exceeded 3,000 men. Of the enemy's force my information comes from the prisoners taken by us; none of them estimated it at less than 8,000 men actually in the engagement.

The loss of our artillery we feel almost as keenly as we should to have lost our colors, yet it was impossible to save them without animals to drag them through the deep mud; the men could not do it. While we deeply feel this loss we have the satisfaction of knowing that we have one of theirs, captured by the Fifth Ohio, and driven off in full view of their whole force, 67 prisoners following it to this post.

It will not be expected that I can mention the many gallant acts of the different officers upon that hard-fought field, yet I cannot do justice to my own feelings without remarking that in my opinion braver, more determined, and willing men never entered a battle-field. General Carroll distinguished himself by his coolness and dashing bravery. Upon him I relied, and I was not disappointed. For heroic gallantry I will place Colonel Gavin, Colonel Buckley, Lieutenant-Colonel Creighton, Colonel Dunning, Colonel Thoburn, Colonel Candy, and Lieutenant-Colonel Hayward beside the bravest men of the U. S. Army. The line officers of the different regiments discharged their duties nobly, and deserve special mention of their colonels. Captains Clark, Robinson, and Huntington served their guns with great credit, and deserve particular notice.

To the members of your staff, Lieutenant-Colonel Shriber, Captain Keily, and Captain Keogh, I am under many, very many, obligations for the prompt, efficient, and officer-like manner in which they discharged the duties assigned them. The two latter were in the field through the hottest of the engagement, exposed to the enemy's fire from first to last. Captain Keily received a severe wound in the face while urging forward the men, and was carried off the field.

For the casualties of the engagement I respectfully refer you to the reports of the several regiments accompanying this paper. The loss of the enemy must have been very heavy; the grape and canister from our batteries and the fire of our musketry mowed them down like grass before a well-served scythe, and the fact of their heavy force retiring before us is an evidence that they suffered severely.

Aide-de-Camp Eaton was the only officer of my own staff present. Captain Quay being too ill to take the field, Chaplain D. C. Wright, of the Seventh Ohio, volunteered to serve me. The duties these gentlemen were called upon to perform were arduous, and led them almost constantly under fire of the enemy, yet they executed their duties with commendable coolness and energy, meriting my warmest thanks.

I have the honor to be, very respectfully, your obedient servant,

E. B. TYLER,
*Brigadier-General, Third Brigade, Shields' Division.*

General JAMES SHIELDS,
*Commanding Division.*

---

## No. 58.

*Report of Col. Samuel S. Carroll, Eighth Ohio Infantry, commanding Fourth Brigade, of engagement at Port Republic.*

HEADQUARTERS FOURTH BRIGADE, SHIELDS' DIVISION,
*Luray, Va., June* 11, 1862.

SIR: I have the honor to make the following report:

In accordance with orders from the general commanding the division I reached the vicinity of Port Republic about 6 a. m. on Sunday, the 8th instant, with about 150 of the First Virginia Cavalry and four pieces of Battery L, First Ohio Artillery. I found the enemy's train parked on the other side of the North Branch of the Shenandoah, with a large quantity of beef cattle herded near by, and the town held by a small force of cavalry only. I chose the most commanding position I could find, about half a mile from the bridge, and planted there two pieces of artillery to command the ends of the same. I then ordered Major Chamberlain, commanding the cavalry, to rush down and take possession of the bridge.

Finding that he had been injured by a fall from his horse, that his command in consequence were in confusion, and hesitated as they came to the South River, and that a body of the enemy's cavalry were assembling at this end of the bridge, giving me fears that they would fire it, I ordered the artillery to open fire upon them, and sent Captain Goodrich to urge the cavalry forward immediately, which he did, and took possession of the bridge, driving part of the enemy's cavalry across it and part of them out of town by the road leading to the left.

I then went into town myself, and took with me two pieces of artillery, one of which I planted at the end of the bridge and the other at the corner of the street commanding the road by which part of the enemy's cavalry had fled. While occupying a position between these, and devising some method by which I could hold the town until my infantry should come up, I suddenly perceived the enemy's infantry emerging from the woods a short distance from the bridge and dashing down upon it at a run in considerable force. As soon as my cavalry, which was now under charge of its own officers, perceived them, they broke and ran in every direction by which they could secure a retreat.

Seeing that I could not hold that position, I ordered the two pieces of artillery to be withdrawn. The enemy's infantry fired so heavily into the limber-horses of the piece at the bridge that they ran away with the limber, and that piece had to be abandoned. The other piece was brought away from its position by Captain Robinson, but instead of taking the road he followed by mistake some of the flying cavalry into the woods, and not being able to extricate it, concealed and abandoned it. In the mean time my infantry had almost reached the position where I had left the two pieces of artillery planted, and they were opened upon by eighteen pieces of the enemy's artillery from the hills upon the opposite side of the river, and partially catching the contagion from the panic-stricken cavalry were retreating amid a heavy shower of shot and shell. The two pieces which I had left upon the hill, superintended by Captain Keily, had been withdrawn from their position, and one of them abandoned in the mud by its cannoneers. The other was also abandoned, with the pole of the limber broken. By the indomitable energy and courage of Colonel Daum and Captain Keily those pieces were saved, and I managed to fall back with my force to a better position without range of the enemy's artillery. At this juncture General Tyler, with his brigade, joined me. After that the enemy made no further attack upon us.

Our loss this day in killed, wounded, and missing was as follows: Seventh Regiment Indiana Volunteers, 8 killed; 2 captains, 1 lieutenant, and 27 men wounded; Battery L, First Ohio Artillery, 1 killed; 1 lieutenant missing. Total loss, 40. Battery L lost two pieces and limbers and fourteen horses.

Too great credit cannot be given to Captain Robinson and Lieutenant Robinson for the noble manner in which they stuck to their pieces after they were deserted by their cavalry support. The latter gallant young officer was either killed or taken prisoner while endeavoring to save his piece.

Early on the morning of the 9th Colonel Daum urged upon General Tyler, under cover of the fog, to move down and destroy the bridge. I rode forward with General Tyler and showed him the impracticability of such a proceeding, and told him that if we could effect a retreat from our present position without disaster we would be doing as well as I could expect. Immediately upon our return the enemy's infantry and cavalry in considerable force were observed passing into the woods opposite our batteries upon the left, and at the same time they opened upon us with a battery near that point.

I then again urged upon General Tyler the necessity of immediately organizing for an orderly retreat, and upon his non-compliance with the same, at my suggestion two regiments from my brigade and two companies from the Third Brigade were sent into the woods upon the left to meet the advancing force above mentioned. At this time Colonel Daum ordered Lieutenant Baker, of Captain Clark's battery, with two pieces, into a wheat field upon our right, whereupon several regiments of the enemy's infantry were observed advancing toward them along the bank of the river. Colonel Gavin, Seventh Indiana Volunteers, was sent to oppose them. At General Tyler's request I took command of the right. Before leaving to do so, however, I impressed upon him the necessity of sustaining the batteries upon our left.

The enemy advanced upon the right in force, and Colonel Gavin was compelled to fall back. I ordered Lieutenant Baker to pour grape and canister into them, which he did with great effect. I sent to General Tyler, requesting assistance upon the right if he could spare it, and he sent me the First Virginia Volunteers, commanded by Colonel Thoburn. I then, with these two regiments and three regiments from the Third Brigade, drove the enemy before me. At this time the enemy's infantry advanced, upon our left and took possession of the batteries planted there. I then told General Tyler that we must organize for a retreat, and at his request I gave orders for the same. The artillery was ordered to be brought to the rear, with the exception of two pieces, which, with the Fifth Regiment Ohio Volunteers, were to cover the retreat. The infantry upon the right was withdrawn, the batteries upon the left retaken, and the retreat was effected as well as could be expected. I myself brought up the rear, General Tyler having gone forward to select a position to make a new stand.

As soon as we commenced the retreat the enemy turned and opened upon us portions of Clark's, Huntington's, and Robinson's batteries, that they had taken from us on the left, which threw the rear of our column in great disorder, causing them to take to the woods, and making it for the earlier part of the retreat apparently a rout. Their cavalry also charged upon our rear, increasing the confusion. I did all I could to organize the rear, but the front was led with such speed that it was impossible to do so under 2 or 2½ miles, when I succeeded in halting the three rear regiments of my brigade and organizing them.

Total loss, 234; loss of day before, 40; aggregate loss, 274. Battery L lost this day one piece and limber, two caissons, and 24 horses. The loss of the enemy was greater than ours, for grape and canister were poured into them with terrible effect, and the ground was strewn with their dead. A Louisiana regiment before our right was almost annihilated. The action lasted about four hours without cessation.

In conclusion I would say that all my command, both officers and men, acted most gallantly, and that, although it may seem invidious to particularize where all did so nobly, I cannot forbear mentioning Captain Keily, of General Shields' staff, who was severely wounded; Captain Goodrich, temporarily assigned to duty with me, and Lieutenants Reid and Lostutter, of my own staff; Colonel Thoburn, First Virginia Volunteers; Colonel Gavin, Seventh Indiana Volunteers; Colonel Lewis, One hundred and tenth Pennsylvania Volunteers; Major Barrett, commanding Eighty-fourth Pennsylvania Volunteers, and Lieutenant Baker, of Captain Clark's battery, who was in my wing during the action.

The enemy contested every inch of ground, but we drove his superior force for nearly half a mile, and continued to drive him until his re-enforcements alone largely exceeded our whole command.

Colonel Gavin, Major Patterson, Seventh Indiana Volunteers, and myself had our horses killed under us in the heat of the action.

Sir, I have the honor to be, very respectfully, your obedient servant,

S. S. CARROLL,
*Commanding Fourth Brigade.*

Capt. LOUIS H. PELOUZE,
*Acting Assistant Adjutant-General.*

## No. 59.

*Reports of Lieut. Gen. Thomas J. Jackson, C. S. Army, commanding the Valley District, of operations May 14–June 17, with congratulatory orders.*

WINCHESTER, *May* 26, 1862.

General S. COOPER:

During the last three days God has blessed our arms with brilliant success. On Friday the Federals at Front Royal were routed, and one section of artillery, in addition to many prisoners, captured. On Saturday Banks' main column, while retreating from Strasburg to Winchester, was pierced, the rear part retreating toward Strasburg. On Sunday the other part was routed at this place. At last accounts Brig. Gen. George H. Steuart was pursuing with cavalry and artillery and capturing the fugitives. A large amount of medical, ordnance, and other stores have fallen into our hands.

T. J. JACKSON,
*Major-General, Commanding.*

---

HDQRS. SECOND CORPS, ARMY OF NORTHERN VIRGINIA,
*April* 10, 1863.

GENERAL: I returned to McDowell on May 14 from the pursuit of Generals Milroy and Schenck toward Franklin.

On the following day I crossed the Shenandoah Mountain, and encamped that night near the Lebanon White Sulphur Springs. Here the troops were halted for a short rest after their fatiguing marches, to enable them to attend divine service and to observe the fast recommended by the proclamation of the President of the Confederate States.

On the 17th the march was resumed toward Harrisonburg. In the mean time, while the pursuit of the Federal troops west of the Shenandoah Mountain was in progress, General Banks had fallen back to Strasburg, which position it was understood he was fortifying. We moved from Harrisonburg down the Valley turnpike to New Market, in the vicinity of which a junction was effected with Ewell's division, which had marched from Elk Run Valley. Leaving the Valley turnpike at New Market we moved via Luray toward Front Royal, with the hope of being able to capture or disperse the garrison at the latter place and get in the rear of Banks or compel him to abandon his fortifications at Strasburg.

To conceal my movements as far as possible from the enemy, Brigadier-General Ashby, who had remained in front of Banks during the march against Milroy, was directed to continue to hold that position until the following day, when he was to join the main body, leaving, however, a covering force sufficient to prevent information of our movements crossing our lines.

My command at this time embraced Ashby's cavalry; the First Brigade, under General Winder; the Second Brigade, Colonel Campbell commanding; the Third Brigade, Colonel Fulkerson commanding; the troops recently under command of Brig. Gen. Edward Johnson; and the division of General Ewell, comprising the brigades of Generals Elzey, Taylor, Trimble; and the Maryland Line, consisting of the First Maryland Regiment and Brockenbrough's battery, under Brig. Gen.

George H. Steuart; and the Second and Sixth Virginia Cavalry, under Colonel Flournoy.

On Thursday, the 22d, my entire command moved down the road leading from Luray to Front Royal, the advance (under General Ewell) bivouacking about 10 miles from the last-named place.

Moving at dawn on Friday, the 23d, and diverging to the right, so as to fall into the Gooney Manor road, we encountered no opposition until we came within 1½ miles of Front Royal, when about 2 p. m. the enemy's pickets were driven in by our advance, which was ordered to follow rapidly. The First Maryland Regiment, supported by Wheat's battalion of Louisiana Volunteers, and the remainder of Taylor's brigade, acting as a reserve, pushed forward in gallant style, charging the Federals, who made a spirited resistance, driving them through the town and taking some prisoners.

The main force of the enemy now retired a short distance beyond Front Royal, and took position on a commanding height, to the right of the turnpike. From this point they opened rifled artillery upon our troops as they advanced beyond the town.

Colonel Crutchfield, chief of artillery, placed some rifled guns in position to dislodge them, and the Sixth Louisiana Regiment was moved to the left, through the woods, to flank their battery; but in the mean time Wheat's battalion, Major Wheat, and the First Maryland Regiment, Col. Bradley T. Johnson, advancing more directly, and driving in their skirmishers, the Federals retreated across both forks of the Shenandoah, attempting in their retreat to burn the bridge over the North Fork; but before they could fully accomplish their purpose our troops were upon them, and extinguished the flames, crossed the river, the enemy in full retreat toward Winchester, and our artillery and infantry in pursuit.

The cavalry, under General Ashby and Col. Thomas S. Flournoy, had crossed the South Fork of the Shenandoah at McCoy's Ford, above the enemy's position, for the purpose of destroying the railroad and telegraphic communication between Front Royal and Strasburg, and also to check the advance of any re-enforcements from Strasburg or the retreat of any portion of the enemy in that direction from Front Royal. Colonel Flournoy kept a short distance west of that river, and, having executed his orders, was now in readiness to join in pursuit of the retreating Federals.

Delayed by difficulties at the bridge over the North Fork, which the Federals had made an effort to burn, Colonel Flournoy pushed on with Companies A, B, E, and K, of the Sixth Virginia Cavalry, and came up with a body of the enemy near Cedarville, about 5 miles from Front Royal. This Federal force consisted of two companies of cavalry, two pieces of artillery, the First (Federal) Regiment Maryland Infantry, and two companies of Pennsylvania infantry, which had been posted there to check our pursuit.

Dashing into the midst of them, Captain Grimsley, of Company B, in the advance, these four companies drove the Federals from their position, who soon, however, reformed in an orchard on the right of the turnpike, when a second gallant and decisive charge being made upon them, the enemy's cavalry was put to flight, the artillery abandoned, and the infantry, now thrown into great confusion, surrendered themselves prisoners of war.

In this successful pursuit our loss was 26 killed and wounded. Among the killed was Captain Baxter, of Company K, while gallantly leading his men in the charge.

While these occurrences were in progress General Ashby, who after crossing at McCoy's Ford had moved with his command farther to the west, so as to skirt the base of the Massanutten Mountain, met with a body of the enemy posted as a guard at Buckton in a strong position, protected by the railroad embankment. Ashby drove back and dispersed the enemy, but with the loss of some of the most valuable of his followers, among them Captains Sheetz and Fletcher. The infantry and artillery pursued but a short distance before darkness rendered it necessary to go into camp.

The results of this first day's operations were the capture of about 700 prisoners, among them about 20 officers, a complete section of rifled artillery (10-pounder Parrotts), and a very large amount of quartermaster and commissary stores. The fruits of this movement were not restricted to the stores and prisoners captured; the enemy's flank was turned and the road opened to Winchester.

In the event of Banks leaving Strasburg he might escape toward the Potomac, or if we moved directly to Winchester he might move via Front Royal toward Washington City. In order to watch both directions, and at the same time advance upon him if he remained at Strasburg, I determined, with the main body of the army, to strike the turnpike near Middletown, a village 5 miles north of Strasburg and 13 south of Winchester.

Accordingly the following morning General Ashby advanced from Cedarville toward Middletown, supported by skirmishers from Taylor's brigade, with Chew's battery and two Parrott guns from the Rockbridge Artillery, and followed by the whole command, except the troops left under command of General Ewell near Cedarville. General Ewell, with Trimble's brigade, the First Maryland Regiment, and the batteries of Brockenbrough and Courtney, had instructions to move toward Winchester. Ashby was directed to keep scouts on his left to prevent Banks from passing unobserved by Front Royal. Brig. Gen. George H. Steuart, who was now temporarily in command of the Second and Sixth Virginia Cavalry, had been previously dispatched to Newtown, a point farther north and 9 miles from Winchester, with instructions to observe the movements of the enemy at that point. He there succeeded in capturing some prisoners and several wagons and ambulances, with arms and medical stores. He also advised me of movements which indicated that Banks was preparing to leave Strasburg.

I accompanied the movement of the main body of the army to Middletown. Upon arriving there we found the Valley turnpike crowded with the retreating Federal cavalry, upon which the batteries of Poague and Chew, with Taylor's infantry, promptly opened, and in a few moments the turnpike, which had just before teemed with life, presented a most appalling spectacle of carnage and destruction. The road was literally obstructed with the mingled and confused mass of struggling and dying horses and riders. The Federal column was pierced, but what proportion of its strength had passed north toward Winchester I had then no means of knowing. Among the surviving cavalry the wildest confusion ensued, and they scattered in disorder in various directions, leaving, however, some 200 prisoners, with their equipments, in our hands. A train of wagons was seen disappearing in the distance toward Winchester, and Ashby, with his cavalry, some artillery, and a supporting infantry force from Taylor's brigade, was sent in pursuit.

But a few moments elapsed before the Federal artillery, which had been cut off with the rear of the column, opened upon us with the evident intention of cutting its way through to Winchester. Our batteries were soon placed in position to return the fire, and General Taylor was ordered with his command to the attack. After a spirited resistance this fragment of the Federal army retreated to Strasburg, and from thence made its escape through the mountains across the Potomac. A large amount of baggage fell into our hands at this point. Entire regiments, apparently in line of battle, had laid down their knapsacks and abandoned them.

Having become satisfied that the main body of Banks' army had already passed this point on its way to Winchester, our troops, which had been halted, moved on in pursuit in that direction. The large number of wagons loaded with stores and abandoned by the enemy between Middletown and Newtown plainly indicated his hurried retreat.

From the attack upon Front Royal up to the present moment every opposition had been borne down, and there was reason to believe, if Banks reached Winchester, it would be without a train, if not without an army; but in the midst of these hopes I was pained to see, as I am now to record the fact, that so many of Ashby's command, both cavalry and infantry, forgetful of their high trust as the advance of a pursuing army, deserted their colors, and abandoned themselves to pillage to such an extent as to make it necessary for that gallant officer to discontinue farther pursuit. The artillery, which had pushed on with energy to the vicinity of Newtown, found itself, from this discreditable conduct, without a proper support from either infantry or cavalry. This relaxation in the pursuit was unfortunate, as the enemy was encouraged by it to bring up, about two hours later, four pieces of artillery, which were planted on the northern skirt of Newtown and opened upon our batteries. Their fire was replied to by Captain Poague's two rifled guns with skill and accuracy.

When I overtook the advance it was thus held in check by the enemy's artillery. We were retarded until near dark, when the Federals retreated and the pursuit was renewed. As we advanced beyond Newtown the same profusion of abandoned Federal wagons loaded with stores met the eye; but we derived no benefit from this property, as the time lost during the disorder and pillage, before referred to, and the consequent delay of our advance at Newtown, enabled the enemy to make arrangements for burning them. Shortly after leaving Newtown the advance was fired upon by a body of the concealed enemy; but they were soon driven off by the Thirty-third Virginia Regiment (Colonel Neff) and the march resumed.

On reaching Bartonsville another ambuscade from the right, left, and front was encountered, and heavy firing kept up for some time. In repelling this, the Twenty-seventh (Colonel Grigsby), Second (Colonel Allen), and Fifth Virginia Regiments (Colonel Baylor) acquitted themselves with credit. Skirmishing continued during the night, the enemy ambuscading from point to point. So important did I deem it to occupy before dawn the heights overlooking Winchester, that the advance continued to move forward until morning, notwithstanding the darkness and other obstacles to its progress. The other troops were permitted to halt for about an hour during the night.

In the mean time Major-General Ewell, with Trimble's brigade, the First Maryland Regiment, and Steuart's cavalry, which had now joined him from Newtown, and Brockenbrough's and Courtney's batteries, was advancing to Winchester by the turnpike from Front Royal to that place, and had occupied a position about 3 miles from the town as early as 10 o'clock in the night, and thrown forward his picket about a mile in advance of his position.

As we approached Winchester soon after dawn the enemy's skirmishers were occupying the hill to the southwest overlooking the town. An order was given to General Winder to seize that height as speedily as possible. The Fifth Virginia Regiment (Colonel Baylor) was accordingly thrown out in advance as skirmishers, and the Second, Fourth, Twenty-seventh, and Thirty-third Virginia Regiments being placed in order of battle the whole line was ordered to advance, which was done in handsome style, and the position on the crest secured, although the enemy made a resolute but unsuccessful effort to dislodge our troops from so commanding a position. Two Parrott guns from the Rockbridge Artillery and the batteries of Carpenter and Cutshaw were promptly posted on the height to dislodge a battery of the enemy which was playing from the front with great animation and effect upon the hill.

At this moment a body of the enemy's sharpshooters was seen crossing the ridge to our left between us and a battery, which soon opened an enfilade fire upon our batteries. Poague's guns were promptly turned to the left, which compelled the infantry to seek shelter behind a stone fence, from which their fire upon our cannoneers and horses was for a while very destructive. By the well-directed guns of Carpenter and Cutshaw the Federal battery in front had now become silenced, but the battery upon the left still kept up a brisk and damaging fire. Withdrawing his battery to the left and rear, so as to avoid the exposure under which he was severely suffering, Poague opened his guns upon the enfilading battery of the enemy. He was also directed by General Winder to throw some solid shot against the stone wall, under the shelter of which their sharpshooters were pouring a fatal fire into our ranks.

During these operations valuable officers and privates suffered; among the number Col. J. A. Campbell, commanding Second Brigade, was wounded.

While the enemy's artillery was playing upon our position his infantry moved to the left, as if designing to get possession of that portion of the hill immediately to the north of us. General Taylor was ordered to advance his brigade to the left and check the movement. Promptly leaving the turnpike, he passed under cover of the hill in rear of Winder, and formed his line of battle in the face of a heavy fire of artillery and musketry from the sharpshooters, the Tenth Virginia Infantry taking position upon the left and the Twenty-third Virginia on the right of his line.

Steadily, and in fine order, mounting the hill, and there fronting the enemy, where he stood in greatest strength, the whole line magnificently swept down the declivity and across the field, driving back the Federal troops and bearing down all opposition before it. In this gallant advance all the troops of General Winder joined except those left as supports to the batteries.

This successful charge being followed by the giving way of the whole Federal army, General Elzey, who had been in reserve on the Valley turnpike, was now ordered to pursue, and eagerly uniting in the general advance soon entered Winchester with the other troops.

On the right the attack, under General Ewell, was executed with skill and spirit. The Twenty-first North Carolina and the Twenty-first Georgia gallantly drove back the advance post of the enemy. The

Twenty-first North Carolina soon became exposed to a destructive fire from a Federal regiment posted behind a stone wall, and after suffering severely, in both officers and men, was forced to fall back. The Twenty-first Georgia, having succeeded in driving that regiment from its shelter, re-enforced its brigade.

With the First Maryland on his left and Trimble's brigade on his right General Ewell now moved toward the eastern outskirts of the town. That advance was made about the time that Taylor's brigade was so gallantly crossing the hill and charging toward the western side of the town. This simultaneous movement on both his flanks, by which his retreat might soon have been cut off, may account for the suddenness with which the entire army gave way and for the slight resistance which it made while passing through the town. The Federal forces were now in full retreat.

As our troops, now in rapid pursuit, passed through the town they were received with the most enthusiastic demonstrations of joy by its loyal people, who for more than two months had been suffering under the hateful surveillance and rigors of military despotism.

Notwithstanding the fatiguing marches and almost sleepless nights to which the mass of our troops had been subjected they continued to press forward with alacrity.

The Federal forces, upon falling back into the town, preserved their organization remarkably well. In passing through its streets they were thrown into confusion, and shortly after, debouching into the plain and turnpike to Martinsburg and after being fired upon by our artillery, they presented the aspect of a mass of disordered fugitives. Never have I seen an opportunity when it was in the power of cavalry to reap a richer harvest of the fruits of victory. Hoping that the cavalry would soon come up, the artillery, followed by infantry, was pressed forward for about two hours, for the purpose of preventing, by artillery fire, a reforming of the enemy, but as nothing was heard of the cavalry, and as but little or nothing could be accomplished without it in the exhausted condition of our infantry, between which and the enemy the distance was continually increasing, I ordered a halt, and issued orders for going into camp and refreshing the men.

I had seen but some 50 of Ashby's cavalry since prior to the pillaging scenes of the previous evening and none since an early hour of the past night. The Second and Sixth Virginia Regiments of Cavalry were under the command of Brig. Gen. George H. Steuart, of Ewell's command. After the pursuit had been continued for some distance beyond the town, and seeing nothing of the cavalry, I dispatched my aide-de-camp, Lieutenant Pendleton, to General Steuart, with an order "to move as rapidly as possible and join me on the Martinsburg turnpike, and carry on the pursuit of the enemy with vigor." His reply was that he was under the command of General Ewell and the order must come through him. Such conduct, and consequent delay, has induced me to require of Lieutenant (now Major) Pendleton a full statement of the case, which is forwarded herewith.

About an hour after the halt of the main body had been ordered Brig. Gen. George H. Steuart, with his cavalry, came up, and renewing the pursuit, pushed forward in a highly creditable manner, and succeeded in capturing a number of prisoners; but the main body of Banks' army was now beyond the reach of successful pursuit and effected its escape across the Potomac.

Before reaching Bunker Hill General Steuart was joined by General Ashby with a small portion of his cavalry. Upon my inquiring of

General Ashby why he was not where I desired him at the close of the engagement, he stated that he had moved to the enemy's left, for the purpose of cutting off a portion of his force. General Steuart pushed on to Martinsburg, where he captured a large amount of army stores.

There is good reason for believing that, had the cavalry played its part in this pursuit as well as the four companies had done under Colonel Flournoy two days before in the pursuit from Front Royal, but a small portion of Banks' army would have made its escape to the Potomac.

On the following day (26th) divine service was held for the purpose of rendering thanks to God for the success with which He had blessed our arms and to implore His continued favor.

In order to make a demonstration toward the Potomac, General Winder, early on the morning of the 28th, left his encampment near Winchester with the Fourth, Fifth, Thirty-second, and Twenty-seventh Virginia Regiments and Carpenter's and Poague's batteries, and took up the line of march for Charlestown by Summit Point. When about 5 miles from Charlestown he received information that the enemy was in possession of that place in heavy force. Upon being advised of this I ordered General Ewell, with re-enforcements, to his support. Notwithstanding the report of the large number of the enemy, and the expectation of re-enforcements in the course of the day, General Winder moved forward cautiously toward Charlestown, and, as he emerged from the woods, less than a mile distant from the town, he discovered the enemy in line of battle about 1,500 strong, and decided to attack them. Upon the appearance of our troops they were fired upon by two pieces of artillery. Carpenter's battery was immediately placed in position, the Thirty-third Virginia Regiment to support it. This battery was so admirably served that in twenty minutes the enemy retired in great disorder, throwing away arms, blankets, haversacks, &c. The pursuit was continued rapidly with artillery and infantry to Halltown.

A short distance beyond that point, observing the enemy in position on Bolivar Heights, General Winder returned to the vicinity of Charlestown.

On the following day the main body of the army took position near Halltown, and the Second Regiment Virginia Infantry was sent to the Loudoun Heights, with the hope of being able to drive the enemy from Harper's Ferry across the Potomac.

In the mean time Shields was moving from Fredericksburg, on my right, and Frémont from the South Branch, on my left, with a view to concentrating a heavy force in my rear and cutting off my retreat up the valley. To avoid such a result orders were issued for all the troops, except Winder's brigade and the cavalry, to return to Winchester on the 30th. Directions were given to General Winder to recall the Second Regiment from Loudoun Heights, and as soon as it should return to its brigade to move with its command, including the cavalry, and rejoin the main body of the army.

Before I reached Winchester the enemy's cavalry had appeared at Front Royal, and Colonel Conner, who held that town with the Twelfth Georgia and a section of Rice's battery, hastily and improvidently abandoned the place, permitting not only Federal prisoners then in our possession but some of his own men to fall into the hands of the enemy. Quartermaster and commissary stores, which we had previously captured at that place, and which Major Harman in his report estimates at the value of $300,000, were, before they could be recaptured by the enemy, through the energy and vigilance of Captain Cole, assistant quartermaster Thirty-seventh Virginia Regiment, fired, with the depot and buildings in which they were stored, and destroyed.

Early on the morning of the 31st the Twenty-first Virginia Regiment (Colonel Cunningham commanding) left Winchester in charge of some 2,300 Federal prisoners and moved up the valley toward Staunton. It was followed by the other troops then near Winchester, which at that time embraced all my command except that part which had been left with Winder. The command encamped that night near Strasburg.

On the following morning General Frémont, who was approaching by way of Wardensville, attacked my outpost in that direction. As it was necessary for me to maintain my position at Strasburg until Winder should arrive with his command, General Ewell was ordered, with his division, to hold Frémont in check. Other troops were subsequently sent to his support, and after a spirited resistance the enemy's advance fell back a short distance.

Toward evening Winder arrived, part of his brigade (the Second Virginia Regiment) having in one day marched 36 miles. The command being again united, the retreat was resumed toward Harrisonburg.

The public property captured in this expedition at Front Royal, Winchester, Martinsburg, and Charlestown was of great value, and so large in quantity that much of it had to be abandoned for want of necessary means of transportation. Major Harman, my chief quartermaster, had but one week within which to remove it, and, although his efforts were characterized by his usual energy, promptitude, and judgment, all the conveyances that within that short period could be hired or impressed were inadequate to the work. The medical stores, which filled one of the largest store-houses in Winchester, were fortunately saved. Most of the instruments and some of the medicines, urgently needed at that time by the command, were issued to the surgeons; the residue was sent to Charlottesville and turned over to a medical purveyor. Two large and well-furnished hospitals, capable of accommodating some 700 patients, were found in the town and left undisturbed, with all their stores, for the use of the sick and wounded of the enemy.

Commissary supplies, consisting of upward of 100 head of cattle, 34,000 pounds of bacon, flour, salt, sugar, coffee, hard bread, and cheese, were turned over to the proper officers, besides large amounts taken by the troops and not accounted for. Sutler's stores valued at $25,000, and for want of transportation abandoned to the troops, were captured. Quartermaster's stores to the value of $125,185 were secured, besides an immense amount destroyed. Many horses were taken by the cavalry. Among the ordnance stores taken and removed in safety were 9,354 small-arms and two pieces of artillery and their caissons.

The official reports of the casualties of my command during this expedition, including the engagements at Front Royal and Winchester, show a list of 68 killed and 329 wounded, with 3 missing, making a total loss of 400.

In addition to the prisoners in Colonel Cunningham's charge there were found in the hospitals at Winchester about 700 sick and wounded of the enemy, and at Strasburg some 50, making the total number who fell into our hands about 3,050. Those left in the hospitals were paroled. Eight Federal surgeons, attending the sick and wounded at

Winchester, were at first held as prisoners of war, though paroled, and the next day unconditionally released.

While I have had to speak of some of our troops in disparaging terms, yet it is my gratifying privilege to say of the main body of the army that its officers and men acted in a manner worthy of the great cause for which they were contending; and to add that, so far as my knowledge extends, the battle at Winchester was on our part a battle without a straggler.

Col. S. Crutchfield, chief of artillery, discharged his duties to my entire satisfaction.

For the prompt transmitting of orders my thanks are due to Maj. R. L. Dabney, assistant adjutant-general; First Lieut. A. S. Pendleton, aide-de-camp; First Lieut. H. K. Douglas, acting assistant adjutant-general, and First Lieut. J. K. Boswell, chief engineer. Dr. H. Black, acting medical director, discharged his duties well.

The commissary and quartermaster's departments were efficiently managed during the expedition by their respective chiefs, Majs. J. A. Harman and W. J. Hawks. My thanks are also due to Second Lieut. R. K. Meade, acting chief of ordnance. Second Lieut. J. M. Garnett, General Winder's ordnance officer, rendered valuable service in removing the captured ordnance from Winchester.

For further particulars respecting the conduct of officers and men and the detail movement of troops I would respectfully call your attention to the accompanying reports of other officers.

Accompanying this report are two maps,* by Mr. J. Hotchkiss—one giving the route pursued by the army from Franklin, Pendleton County, Virginia, to Winchester, and during the pursuit of the enemy; the other is a map of the battle-field.

I am, general, very respectfully, your obedient servant,

T. J. JACKSON,
*Lieutenant-General.*

Brig. Gen. R. H. CHILTON,
*Actg. Adjt. and Insp. Gen., Hdqrs. Dept. of N. Virginia.*

[Inclosure.]

———, ——— —, 1862.

On Sunday, May 25, after the enemy was driven out of Winchester, the pursuit had been carried on with infantry and artillery for some 3 miles toward Martinsburg, when I was directed by General Jackson to find the cavalry, under Brig. Gen. G. H. Steuart, and send them on at once rapidly, in order that the enemy might be pressed with vigor. This was about 10 o'clock in the morning. I rode rapidly to Winchester, and failing to ascertain the whereabouts of the cavalry by inquiry, I determined to go to Major-General Ewell, on the east of Winchester, under whose immediate command General Steuart was acting.

I found the cavalry some 2½ miles from Winchester, on the Berryville road, with the men dismounted and the horses grazing quietly in a clover field. Not seeing General Steuart, I gave the order direct to the colonels of the regiments to mount and go rapidly forward to join General Jackson on the Martinsburg turnpike.

Colonel Flournoy, Sixth Virginia Cavalry, the senior colonel, requested me to ride on and overtake General Steuart and communicate the order to him, as he had directed them to await him there. Going

* Not found.

some half a mile farther, I overtook General Steuart, and directed him, by General Jackson's order, to move as rapidly as possible to join him on the Martinsburg turnpike and carry on the pursuit of the enemy with vigor. He replied that he was under command of General Ewell and the order must come through him. I answered that the order from General Jackson for him to go to join him (General Jackson) was peremptory and immediate, and that I would go forward and inform General Ewell that the cavalry was sent off. I left him, and went on some 2 miles and communicated with General Ewell, who seemed surprised that General Steuart had not gone immediately upon receipt of the order.

Returning about a mile, I found that, instead of taking the cavalry, General Steuart had ridden slowly after me toward General Ewell. I told him I had seen General Ewell and brought the order from him for the cavalry to go to General Jackson. This satisfied him. He rode back to his command, had them mounted and formed, and moved off toward Stephenson's Depot.

Respectfully,

A. S. PENDLETON,
*Major and Assistant Adjutant-General.*

---

GENERAL ORDERS, No. 58. } HDQRS. DEPT. OF NORTHERN VIRGINIA, *Richmond, May* 29, 1862.

The commanding general has the satisfaction to announce to the army another brilliant success won by the skill and courage of our generals and troops in the valley.

The combined divisions of Major-Generals Jackson and Ewell, commanded by the former and constituting a part of this army, after a long, arduous, and rapid march, attacked and routed the Federal forces under Major-General Banks successively at Front Royal, Middleburg, and Winchester, taking several thousands of prisoners and an immense quantity of ammunition and stores of all descriptions. The Federal Army has been dispersed and driven ignominiously from the valley of Shenandoah, and those who have freed the loyal citizens of that district by their patriotic valor have again earned, as they will receive, the thanks of a grateful country.

In making this glorious announcement on the eve of the desperate struggle about to ensue the commanding general does not deem it necessary to invoke the troops of this army to emulate the deeds of their noble comrades in the valley. He feels already assured of their determined purpose to make illustrious in history the part they are soon to act in the impending drama.

By command of General Johnston :

THOS. G. RHETT,
*Assistant Adjutant-General.*

---

BROWN'S GAP, VA., *June* 11, 1862.

MAJOR : On the 8th instant an attack was made on me early in the morning from the east side of the river at Port Republic by troops of Shields' command. This was soon repulsed.

During the same morning, but subsequently, Frémont approached from the west and opened upon Major-General Ewell's division. After several hours' fighting Frémont was also driven back.

Early on Monday morning, the 9th, I attacked the Federals on the east side of the river, and after about four and a half hours' hard fighting the same kind Providence which had so blessed us on Sunday completely routed the enemy. He lost six pieces of artillery. Shields' command also lost two pieces on Sunday, making his artillery loss eight pieces. Many small-arms were also captured.

The Federal troops engaged on Monday appear to have been three brigades of Shields' division, under Brigadier-General Tyler.

Respectfully, your obedient servant,

T. J. JACKSON,
*Major-General.*

Maj. THOMAS G. RHETT,
*Assistant Adjutant-General, Dept. of Northern Virginia.*

---

HDQRS. SECOND CORPS, ARMY OF NORTHERN VIRGINIA,
*April* 14, 1863.

GENERAL: I have the honor herewith to submit to you a report of the battle of Port Republic, fought on June 8 and 9, 1862:

Having through the blessing of an ever-kind Providence passed Strasburg before the Federal armies under Generals Shields and Frémont effected the contemplated junction in my rear, as referred to in the report of the battle of Winchester, I continued to move up the Valley turnpike, leaving Strasburg on the evening of June 1. The cavalry under Brig. Gen. George H. Steuart brought up the rear.

Frémont's advance, which had been near us during the day, soon ascertained that our retreat had been resumed, and, pursuing after dark, succeeded, when challenged by replying "Ashby's cavalry," in approaching so near our rear guard as to attack it. The Sixth Virginia Cavalry, being nearest the enemy, was thrown into confusion and suffered some loss. Disorder was also to some extent communicated to the Second Virginia Cavalry, but its commander, Colonel Munford, soon reformed it, and gallantly drove back the Federals and captured some of their number.

From information received respecting Shields' movements, and from the fact that he had been in possession of Front Royal for over forty-eight hours and had not succeeded in effecting a junction with Frémont, as originally designed, I became apprehensive that he was moving via Luray for the purpose of reaching New Market, on my line of retreat, before my command should arrive there. To avoid such a result I caused White House Bridge, which was upon his assumed line of march, over the South Fork of the Shenandoah River, to New Market, to be burned, and also Columbia Bridge, which was a few miles farther up the river.

On June 2 the enemy's advance came within artillery-range of and commenced shelling our rear guard, which caused most of the cavalry and that part of its artillery nearest the enemy to retreat in disorder. This led General Ashby to one of those acts of personal heroism and prompt resource which strikingly marked his character. Dismounting from his horse, he collected from the road a small body of infantry from those who from fatigue were straggling behind their commands, and posting them in a piece of wood near the turnpike he awaited the advance of the Federal cavalry, now pushing forward to reap the fruits of the panic produced by the shells. As they approached within easy range he poured such an effective fire into their ranks as to empty a number of saddles and check their farther pursuit for that day. Having transferred the Second and Sixth Virginia Cavalry to Ashby, he was placed in command of the rear guard.

On the 3d, after my command had crossed the bridge over the Shenandoah near Mount Jackson, General Ashby was ordered to destroy it, which he barely succeeded in accomplishing before the Federal forces reached the opposite bank of the river. Here his horse was killed by the enemy, and he made a very narrow escape with his life.

We reached Harrisonburg at an early hour on the morning of the 5th, and passing beyond that town turned toward the east in the direction of Port Republic.

On the 6th General Ashby took position on the road between Harrisonburg and Port Republic, and received a spirited charge from a portion of the enemy's cavalry, which resulted in the repulse of the enemy and the capture of Colonel Wyndham and 63 others. Apprehending that the Federals would make a more serious attack, Ashby called for an infantry support. The brigade of Brig. Gen. George H. Steuart was accordingly ordered forward. In a short time the Fifty-eighth Virginia Regiment became engaged with a Pennsylvania regiment called the Bucktails, when Colonel Johnson, of the First Maryland Regiment, coming up in the hottest period of the fire, charged gallantly into its flank and drove the enemy with heavy loss from the field, capturing Lieutenant-Colonel Kane, commanding.

In this skirmish our infantry loss was 17 killed, 50 wounded, and 3 missing. In this affair General Turner Ashby was killed.

An official report is not an appropriate place for more than a passing notice of the distinguished dead, but the close relation which General Ashby bore to my command for most of the previous twelve month, will justify me in saying that as a partisan officer I never knew his superior; his daring was proverbial; his powers of endurance almost incredible; his tone of character heroic, and his sagacity almost intuitive in divining the purposes and movements of the enemy.

The main body of my command had now reached the vicinity of Port Republic. This village is situated in the angle formed by the junction of the North and South Rivers, tributaries of the South Fork of the Shenandoah. Over the larger and deeper of those two streams, the North River, there was a wooden bridge, connecting the town with the road leading to Harrisonburg. Over the South River there was a passable ford. The troops were immediately under my own eye; were encamped on the high ground north of the village, about a mile from the river. General Ewell was some 4 miles distant, near the road leading from Harrisonburg to Port Republic. General Frémont had arrived with his forces in the vicinity of Harrisonburg, and General Shields was moving up the east side of the South Fork of the Shenandoah, and was then at Conrad's Store, some 15 miles below Port Republic, my position being about equal distance from both hostile armies. To prevent a junction of the two Federal armies I had caused the bridge over the South Fork of the Shenandoah at Conrad's Store to be destroyed. Intelligence having been received that General Shields was advancing farther up the river, Captain Sipe with a small cavalry force was sent down during the night of the 7th to verify the report and gain such other information respecting the enemy as he could. Capt. G. W. Myers, of the cavalry, was subsequently directed to move with his company in the same direction, for the purpose of supporting Captain Sipe, if necessary.

The next morning Captain Myers' company came rushing back in disgraceful disorder, announcing that the Federal forces were in close pursuit. Captain Chipley and his company of cavalry, which was in town, also shamefully fled. The brigades of Generals Taliaferro and Winder were soon under arms and ordered to occupy positions immediately north of the bridge. By this time the Federal cavalry, accompanied by artillery, were in sight, and after directing a few shots toward the bridge they crossed South River, and dashing into the village they planted one of their pieces at the southern entrance of the bridge. In the mean time the batteries of Wooding, Poague, and Carpenter were being placed in position, and General Taliaferro's brigade, having reached the vicinity of the bridge, was ordered to charge across, capture the piece, and occupy the town. While one of Poague's pieces was returning the fire of that of the enemy at the far end of the bridge the Fifty-seventh Virginia Regiment, Colonel Fulkerson, after delivering its fire, gallantly charged over the bridge, captured the gun, and, followed by the other regiments of the brigade, entered the town and dispersed and drove back the Federal cavalry. Another piece of artillery with which the Federal cavalry had advanced was abandoned and subsequently fell into our hands.

About this time a considerable body of infantry was seen advancing up the same road. Our batteries opened with marked effect upon the retreating cavalry and advancing infantry. In a short time the infantry followed the cavalry, falling back to Lewis', 3 miles down the river, pursued for a mile by our batteries on the opposite bank, when the enemy disappeared in the wood around a bend in the road. This attack of General Shields had hardly been repulsed before Ewell was seriously engaged with Frémont, moving on the opposite side of the river. The enemy pushed forward, driving in the Fifteenth Alabama, Colonel Cantey, from their post on picket. This regiment made a gallant resistance, which so far checked the Federal advance as to afford to General Ewell time for the choice of his position at leisure. His ground was well selected, on a commanding ridge, a rivulet and large field of open ground in front, wood on both flanks, and his line intersected near its center by the road leading to Port Republic. General Trimble's brigade was posted on the right, somewhat in advance of his center. The batteries of Courtney, Lusk, Brockenbrough, and Raine in the center; General Steuart's brigade on the left, and General Elzey's brigade in rear of the center, and in position to strengthen either wing. Both wings were in the wood.

About 10 o'clock the enemy threw out his skirmishers and shortly after posted his artillery opposite to our batteries. The artillery fire was kept up with great animation and spirit on both sides for several hours. In the mean time a brigade of Federal forces advanced, under cover, upon the right, occupied by General Trimble, who reserved his fire until they reached the crest of the hill, in easy range of his musketry, when he poured a deadly fire from his whole front, under which they fell back. Observing a battery about being posted on the enemy's left, half a mile in front, General Trimble, now supported by the Thirteenth and Twenty-fifth Virginia Regiments, of Elzey's brigade, pushed forward for the purpose of taking it, but found it withdrawn before he reached the spot, having in the mean time some spirited skirmishing with its infantry supports. General Trimble had now advanced more than a mile from his original position, while the Federal advance had fallen back to the ground occupied by them in the morning.

General Taylor, of the Eighth Brigade of Louisiana troops, having arrived from the vicinity of the bridge at Port Republic, toward which he had moved in the morning, reported to General Ewell about 2 p. m. and was placed in rear. Colonel Patton, with the 42d and 48th Virginia Regiments and 1st Battalion of Virginia Regulars, also joined, and with the remainder of General Elzey's brigade was added to the center and left, then supposed to be threatened. General Ewell—having been informed by Lieutenant Hinrichs, of the Engineer Corps, who had been sent out to reconnoiter, that the enemy was moving a large column on his left—did not advance at once, but subsequently ascertaining that no attack was designed by the force referred to, he advanced, drove in the enemy's skirmishers, and when night closed was in position on ground previously held by the enemy. During this fighting Brigadier-Generals Elzey and Steuart were wounded and disabled from command.

This engagement with Frémont has generally been known as the battle of Cross Keys, in which our troops were commanded by General Ewell. I had remained at Port Republic during the principal part of the 8th, expecting a renewal of the attack. As no movement was made by General Shields to renew the action that day, I determined to take the initiative and attack him the following morning. Accordingly General Ewell was directed to move from his position at an early hour on the morning of the 9th toward Port Republic, leaving General Trimble, with his brigade, supported by Colonel Patton, with the Forty-second Virginia Infantry and the First Battalion of Virginia Regulars, to hold Frémont in check, with instructions, if hard pressed, to retire across the North River and burn the bridge in their rear. Soon after 10 o'clock General Trimble, with the last of our forces, had crossed the North River and the bridge was destroyed.

In the mean time, before 5 in the morning, General Winder's brigade was in Port Republic, and having crossed the South Fork by a temporary wagon bridge placed there for the purpose, was moving down the River road to attack the forces of General Shields. Advancing 1½ miles he encountered the Federal pickets and drove them in. The enemy had judiciously selected his position for defense. Upon a rising ground, near the Lewis house, he had planted six guns, which commanded the road from Port Republic and swept the plateau for a considerable distance in front. As General Winder moved forward his brigade a rapid and severe fire of shell was opened upon it. Captain Poague, with two Parrott guns, was promptly placed in position on the left of the road to engage, and if possible dislodge, the Federal battery. Captain Carpenter was sent to the right to select a position for his battery, but finding it impracticable to drag it through the dense undergrowth, it was brought back and part of it placed near Poague. The artillery fire was well sustained by our batteries, but found unequal to that of the enemy.

In the mean time, Winder being now re-enforced by the Seventh Louisiana Regiment, Colonel Hays, seeing no mode of silencing the Federal battery or escaping its destructive missiles but by a rapid charge and the capture of it, advanced with great boldness for some distance, but encountered such a heavy fire of artillery and small-arms as greatly to disorganize his command, which fell back in disorder. The enemy advanced across the field, and by a heavy musketry-fire forced back our infantry supports, in consequence of which our guns had to retire. The enemy's advance was checked by a spirited attack upon their flank by the Fifty-eighth and Fifty-fourth Virginia Regiments, directed by General Ewell and led by Colonel Scott, although his command was afterward driven back to the woods with severe loss. The batteries were all safely withdrawn, except one of Captain Poague's 6-pounder guns, which was carried off by the enemy.

While Winder's command was in this critical condition the gallant and successful attack of General Taylor on the Federal left and rear diverted attention from the front, and led to a concentration of their force upon him. Moving to the right along the mountain acclivity through a rough and tangled forest, and much disordered by the rapidity and obstructions of the march, Taylor emerged with his command from the wood just as the loud cheers of the enemy had proclaimed their success in front, and, although assailed by a superior force in front and flank, with their guns in position, within point-blank range, the charge was gallantly made, and the battery, consisting of six guns, fell into our hands. Three times was this battery lost and won in the desperate and determined efforts to capture and recover it. After holding the battery for a short time a fresh brigade of the enemy, advancing upon his flank, made a vigorous and well-conducted attack upon him, accompanied by a galling fire of canister from a piece suddenly brought into position at a distance of about 350 yards. Under this combined attack Taylor fell back to the skirt of the wood near which the captured battery was stationed, and from that point continued his fire upon the advancing enemy, who succeeded in recapturing one of the guns, which he carried off, leaving both caisson and limber. The enemy, now occupied with Taylor, halted his advance to the front. Winder made a renewed effort to rally his command, and, succeeding, with the Seventh Louisiana, under Major Penn (the colonel and lieutenant-colonel having been carried from the field wounded), and the Fifth Virginia Regiment, Colonel Funk, he placed part of Poague's battery in the position previously occupied by it, and again opened upon the enemy, who were moving against Taylor's left flank, apparently to surround him in the woods.

Chew's battery now reported and was placed in position, and did good service. Soon after guns from the batteries of Brockenbrough, Courtney, and Rains were brought forward and placed in position. While these movements were in progress on the left and front Colonel Scott, having rallied his command, led them, under the orders of General Ewell, to the support of General Taylor, who, pushing forward with the re-enforcements just received, and assisted by the well-directed fire of our artillery, forced the enemy to fall back, which was soon followed by his precipitate retreat, leaving many killed and wounded upon the field.

General Taliaferro, who the previous day had occupied the town, was directed to continue to do so with part of his troops, and with the remainder to hold the elevated position on the north side of the river, for the purpose of co-operating, if necessary, with General Trimble and preventing his being cut off from the main body of the army by the destruction of the bridge in his rear; but, finding the resistance more obstinate than I anticipated, orders were sent to Taliaferro and Trimble to join the main body. Taliaferro came up in time to discharge an effective volley into the ranks of the wavering and retreating enemy. The pursuit was continued some 5 miles beyond the battle-field by Generals Taliaferro and Winder with their brigades and portions of the batteries of Wooding and Caskie. Colonel Munford, with cavalry and some artillery, advanced about 3 miles beyond the other troops.

Our forces captured in the pursuit about 450 prisoners, some wagons, one piece of abandoned artillery, and about 800 muskets. Some 275 wounded were paroled in the hospitals near Port Republic.

While the forces of Shields were in full retreat and our troops in pursuit Frémont appeared on the opposite bank of the South Fork of the Shenandoah with his army, and opened his artillery upon our ambulances and parties engaged in the humane labors of attending to our dead and wounded and the dead and wounded of the enemy.

The next day withdrawing his forces, he retreated down the valley.

On the morning of the 12th, Munford entered Harrisonburg, where, in addition to wagons, medical stores, and camp equipage, he captured some 200 small-arms. At that point there also fell into our hands about 200 of Frémont's men, many of them severely wounded on the 8th, and most of the others had been left behind as sick. The Federal surgeons attending them were released and those under their care paroled.

The official reports of the casualties of the battle show a loss of 16 officers killed, 67 wounded, and 2 missing; 117 non-commissioned officers and privates killed, 862 wounded, and 32 missing, making a total loss of 1,096, including skirmishes on the 6th. Since evacuation of Winchester, 1,167; also one piece of artillery.

If we add to the prisoners captured on the 6th and 9th those who were paroled at Harrisonburg and in the hospitals in the vicinity of Port Republic it will make the number of the enemy who fell into our possession about 975, exclusive of his killed and such of his wounded as he removed. The small-arms taken on the 9th and at Harrisonburg numbered about 1,000. We captured seven pieces of artillery, with their caissons, and all of their limbers except one.

The conduct of officers and men during the action merits high praise. During the battle I received valuable assistance in the transmission of orders from the following members of my staff: Col. Abner Smead, assistant inspector-general; Maj. R. L. Dabney, assistant adjutant-general; First Lieut. A. S. Pendleton, aide-de-camp; First Lieut. H. K. Douglas, assistant inspector-general; First Lieut. J. K. Boswell, chief engineer, and Col. William L. Jackson, volunteer aide-de-camp. The medical director of the army, Dr. Hunter McGuire, gave special attention to the comfort and treatment of the wounded. Maj. W. J. Hawks, chief commissary, and Maj. J. A. Harman, chief quartermaster, had their departments in good condition.

For further information respecting the conduct of officers and men who distinguished themselves, as well as for a more detailed account of the movements of the troops, I would respectfully refer you to the accompanying official reports of other officers.

I forward herewith two maps* by Mr. J. Hotchkiss, one giving the route of the enemy during the retreat from Strasburg to Port Republic and the other of the battle-field.

On the 12th the troops recrossed South River and encamped near Weyer's Cave.

For the purpose of rendering thanks to God for having crowned our arms with success, and to implore his continued favor, divine service was held in the army on the 14th.

The army remained near Weyer's Cave until the 17th, when, in obedience to instructions from the commanding general of the department, it moved toward Richmond.

I am, general, very respectfully, your obedient servant,

T. J. JACKSON,
*Lieutenant-General.*

Brig. Gen. R. H. CHILTON,
*A. A. and I. G., Hdqrs. Dept. of Northern Virginia.*

* To appear in Atlas.

## No. 60.

***Return of Casualties in the Confederate forces at the battle of Cross Keys and engagement at Port Republic.***

[Compiled from the reports.]

| Command. | Killed. | | | Wounded. | | | Missing. | | | Aggregate. | Remarks. |
|---|---|---|---|---|---|---|---|---|---|---|---|
| | Officers. | Enlisted men. | Total. | Officers. | Enlisted men. | Total. | Officers. | Enlisted men. | Total. | | |
| **JACKSON'S DIVISION.** | | | | | | | | | | | |
| ***First Brigade.*** | | | | | | | | | | | |
| 2d Virginia | 1 | | 1 | 1 | 23 | 24 | | | | 25 | |
| 4th Virginia | | | | | 4 | 4 | | | | 4 | |
| 5th Virginia | | 4 | 4 | 3 | 86 | 89 | | 20 | 20 | 113 | |
| 27th Virginia | 1 | 6 | 8 | 2 | 26 | 28 | | 11 | 11 | 46 | |
| 33d Virginia | | | | | | | | | | | No casualties. |
| ***Second Brigade.*** | | | | | | | | | | | |
| 21st Virginia | | | | | | | | | | | No report. |
| 42d Virginia | | 1 | 1 | | 2 | 2 | | | | 3 | |
| 48th Virginia | | 8 | 8 | 2 | 12 | 14 | | | | 17 | |
| 1st Virginia Battalion | | | | | | | | | | | No casualties |
| ***Third Brigade.*** | | | | | | | | | | | |
| 10th Virginia | | | | | | | | | | | No report. |
| 23d Virginia | | | | | | | | | | | No report. |
| 37th Virginia | | | | | | | | | | | No report. |
| ***Artillery (batteries).*** | | | | | | | | | | | |
| Carpenter's | | | | | 4 | 4 | | | | 4 | |
| Caskie's | | | | 1 | | 1 | | | | 1 | |
| Carrington's | | | | | | | | | | | No report. |
| Cutshaw's | | | | | | | | | | | No report. |
| Poague's | | | | 1 | 3 | 4 | | 1 | 1 | 5 | |
| Wooding's | | | | | | | | | | | No report. |
| Total | 2 | 14 | 17 | 10 | 160 | 170 | | 32 | 32 | 218 | |
| **EWELL'S DIVISION.*** | | | | 1 | | 1 | | | | 1 | Division staff. |
| ***Second Brigade*** | | | | 3 | | 3 | | | | 3 | Field and staff. |
| 1st Maryland | | | | 1 | 28 | 29 | | | | 29 | |
| 44th Virginia | 1 | 14 | 15 | 4 | 34 | 38 | | | | 53 | |
| 52d Virginia | 2 | 12 | 14 | 6 | 81 | 87 | | | | 101 | |
| 58th Virginia | 1 | 3 | 4 | 3 | 70 | 73 | | | | 77 | |
| ***Fourth Brigade*** | 1 | | 1 | 1 | | 1 | | | | 2 | Field and staff. |
| 12th Georgia | | 2 | 2 | | 12 | 12 | | | | 14 | |
| 13th Virginia | | 2 | 2 | | 13 | 13 | | 1 | 1 | 16 | |
| 25th Virginia | | | | 4 | 25 | 29 | | | | 29 | |
| 31st Virginia | 2 | 12 | 14 | 3 | 76 | 79 | | 4 | 4 | 97 | |
| ***Seventh Brigade*** | | | | 1 | | 1 | | | | 1 | Field and staff. |
| 15th Alabama | 2 | 7 | 9 | 2 | 35 | 37 | 1 | 4 | 5 | 51 | |
| 21st Georgia | | 4 | 4 | 1 | 22 | 23 | | 1 | 1 | 28 | |
| 16th Mississippi | | 6 | 6 | 2 | 25 | 27 | | | | 33 | |
| 21st North Carolina | | 2 | 2 | 1 | 10 | 11 | | | | 13 | |
| ***Eighth Brigade*** | | | | 2 | | 2 | | | | 2 | Field and staff. |
| 6th Louisiana | 1 | 10 | 11 | 2 | 53 | 55 | | | | 66 | |
| 7th Louisiana | 2 | 8 | 10 | 5 | 117 | 122 | | | | 132 | |
| 8th Louisiana | 1 | 8 | 9 | 3 | 34 | 37 | | | | 46 | |
| 9th Louisiana | 1 | 3 | 4 | | 36 | 36 | | | | 40 | |
| Wheat's battalion | | 2 | 2 | 5 | 14 | 19 | | | | 21 | |

* The losses in this division are stated separately for June 8 and 9 in inclosures to Ewell's reports. No. 90, p. 778.

*Return of Casualties in the Confederate forces at the battle of Cross Keys, &c.*—Continued.

| Command. | Killed. | | | Wounded. | | | Missing. | | | Aggregate. | Remarks. |
|---|---|---|---|---|---|---|---|---|---|---|---|
| | Officers. | Enlisted men. | Total. | Officers. | Enlisted men. | Total. | Officers. | Enlisted men. | Total. | | |
| ***Artillery (batteries).*** | | | | | | | | | | | |
| Brockenbrough's | .... | 2 | 2 | .... | ...... | ...... | .... | .... | .... | 2 | |
| Courtney's | .... | 2 | 2 | .... | 10 | 10 | .... | .... | .... | 12 | |
| Lusk's | .... | 2 | 2 | .... | 3 | 3 | .... | .... | .... | 5 | |
| Raine's | .... | 2 | 2 | .... | 7 | 7 | .... | 8 | 8 | 17 | |
| Rice's | .... | ...... | ...... | .... | ...... | ...... | .... | .... | .... | ........ | No report. |
| Total | 14 | 103 | 117 | 50 | 705 | 755 | 1 | 18 | 19 | 891 | |
| ***Cavalry.*** | | | | | | | | | | | |
| 2d Virginia | .... | ...... | ...... | .... | ...... | ...... | .... | .... | .... | ........ | No report. |
| 6th Virginia | .... | ...... | ...... | .... | ...... | ...... | .... | .... | .... | ........ | |
| Chew's battery | .... | ...... | ...... | .... | ...... | ...... | .... | .... | .... | ........ | |
| Grand total | 16 | 117 | 134 | 60 | 865 | 925 | 1 | 50 | 51 | 1,109 | |

## No. 61.

### *Report of Capt. J. K. Boswell, C. S. Army, Chief Engineer, of operations June 1–9.*

HEADQUARTERS SECOND ARMY CORPS,
*March* 27, 1863.

GENERAL: I have the honor to report that I rejoined you at Strasburg on the evening of May 31, 1862, having just returned from Richmond, whither I had gone on [the] 26th as bearer of dispatches to General J. E. Johnston.

On the morning of June 1 I was directed by you to make a reconnaissance down the Front Royal road to gain information with regard to the movements of the enemy and to find out whether the pickets were properly posted. I took with me a lieutenant and 5 men, and crossed the North River just below the railroad bridge, but had not gone more than a hundred yards before I came in sight of a considerable body of the enemy's cavalry a short distance in front. Seeing that it would be needless to attempt to fight them I recrossed the river as rapidly as possible, and, leaving the cavalry as a picket on the road, returned to headquarters to inform you of the advance of the enemy's cavalry in that direction, and not being able to find you I gave the information to General Ashby, who immediately sent a portion of his command to guard that road. During the retreat from Strasburg to New Market I was engaged, as were Mr. Hotchkiss and Mr. Brown, topographical engineers, in transmitting orders and keeping the wagon train in motion.

On the 4th I took with me Mr. Brown, and went by your order to Mr. Crawford to see if a bridge could be built over the North River. On reaching there I found Captain Mason, acting quartermaster, and Lieut. W. G. Turpin, Engineers. After examining the river we determined that it would be impossible to build a bridge, as the river was higher than it had been for twenty years and extremely rapid. I reported these facts to you by a courier.

Early on the following morning I sent Lieutenant Turpin to Bridgewater to collect lumber for building boats. Captain Mason having built two boats from lumber found at Mr. Crawford's, succeeded in carrying most of the sick across the river.

During the day I built a bridge across Cook's Creek, on the road to Port Republic, and after seeing the ambulances and wagons safely across the bridge I returned to your headquarters, near Harrisonburg.

On the 4th Mr. Hotchkiss, topographical engineer, made for you a map of the region around Port Republic, and on the following morning he took a signal operator to Peaked Mountain, from whence he communicated to you the movements of General Shields, on the opposite side of South River. For the two days following he remained on this duty.

On the morning of June 8, while near Dr. Kemper's, I heard firing in the direction of Port Republic, and saw you, with several members of your staff, riding rapidly in the direction of the bridge. I mounted my horse and followed, crossing the bridge just as the enemy's cavalry entered the town. Lieutenant Willis, who was a short distance behind me, was captured. I found you on the hill a short distance off, and was directed by you to find whether the enemy was in the town. I soon returned with the information that their cavalry were on the bridge, when you ordered up the Thirty-seventh Virginia and rode down to the bank of the river. The enemy brought up a gun and planted it in the south end of the bridge and fired one shot at the Thirty-seventh Virginia as it advanced, but the gun was soon captured by that regiment.

During the engagement at Cross Keys I was engaged in transmitting orders from you to General Ewell.

At 4 a. m. June 9 I was ordered by you to proceed immediately to Mechanic's River Depot, for the purpose of meeting re enforcements which were expected at that point.

Mr. Hotchkiss was unwell during the morning of the 8th and was not on the field. During the evening he conducted Chew's battery, by your order, to Patterson's Ford and placed it in position.

On the 9th he conducted General Taylor's brigade, by your order, through the wood, so as to flank the enemy's battery [near] the Lewis house, which was taken by that brigade.

Very respectfully,

J. K. BOSWELL,
*Captain and Chief Engineer, Second Army Corps.*

Lieut. Gen. THOMAS J. JACKSON.

---

## No. 62.

***Report of Surgeon Hunter McGuire, of medical and hospital stores captured.***

HDQRS. SECOND CORPS, ARMY N. VA., MED. DEPT.,
*March* 5, 1863.

COLONEL: I respectfully submit the following report of medical and hospital stores captured from the enemy at Winchester, Va., on May 25, 1862:

One of the largest store-houses in the town had been appropriated by the United States medical purveyor, and was filled with medicines, instruments, and hospital stores. The supply was very large, and intended, as I was told by the Federal surgeons, for the armies under the command of Generals Shields and Frémont, as well as that of General Banks. Most of the instruments and some medicines (badly needed at that time by our army) were issued to the surgeons and the rest sent to Charlottesville, Va., where they were turned over to a medical purveyor. No invoice was made of them. There were also two large, very well furnished hospitals, accommodating about 700 patients. The stores in these hospitals were left for the use of the sick and wounded Federals, and a few of our own men, who were too ill or badly wounded to be removed.

Respectfully, your obedient servant,

HUNTER McGUIRE,
*Surgeon and Medical Director, Second Corps.*

Lieut. Col. C. J. FAULKNER,
*Assistant Adjutant-General.*

---

## No. 63.

***Reports of Maj. W. J. Hawks, Commissary of Subsistence, C. S. Army, of stores captured.***

SUBSISTENCE DEPARTMENT, SECOND ARMY CORPS,
*Guiney's Station, Va., February* 8, 1863.

GENERAL: The following statement of property captured by your command is as nearly complete as I can make it:

| | | |
|---|---|---|
| **At Front Royal:** | | |
| Flour | barrels.. | 85 |
| **At Winchester and Martinsburg:** | | |
| 103 head of cattle | pounds gross.. | 92,700 |
| Bacon | pounds.. | 14,637 |
| Hard bread | do.... | 6,000 |
| Sugar | do.... | 2,400 |
| Salt | bushels.. | 350 |
| **At Harper's Ferry:** | | |
| Salt pork | pounds.. | 1,315 |
| Salt beef | do.... | 1,545 |
| Bacon | do.... | 19,267 |
| Hard bread | do.... | 155,954 |
| Rice | do.... | 628 |
| Coffee | do.... | 4,930 |
| Sugar | do.... | 209 |
| Candles | do.... | 67 |
| Soap | do.... | 280 |
| Beans | bushels.. | 9 |
| Salt | do.... | 154 |
| Vinegar | gallons.. | 180 |
| Molasses | do.... | 80 |

At McDowell nothing was captured except hard bread, which was issued to troops passing through—an extra ration.

At Winchester, Martinsburg, and Harper's Ferry large amounts of supplies were carried off by division wagons, of which no report was made to me. Full rations were issued to 13,000 of the enemy for two days at Harper's Ferry. The issue was made before an inventory was taken.

Very respectfully,

W. J. HAWKS,
*Major and Com. of Sub., Second Army Corps, Army N. Va.*

Lieutenant-General JACKSON,
*Commanding Second Army Corps.*

*Supplies captured by General Jackson at Winchester and Martinsburg in May, 1862.*

| | |
|---|---|
| 103 head of cattle (gross weight 92,700 pounds), at 7 cents | $6,489 00 |
| 14,637 pounds of bacon, at 35 cents | 5,122 95 |
| 6,000 pounds of hard bread, at 8 cents | 480 00 |
| 2,400 pounds of sugar, at 35 cents | 840 00 |
| 350 bushels of salt, at $5 | 1,750 00 |
| 85 barrels of flour, at $8 | 680 00 |

A large amount of supplies was taken by the troops of General Ewell's and Colonel Ashby's commands from Martinsburg, hauled to their camps, and issued without being receipted for or reported to me. Captain Lock's certificate accompanies this report, showing probable amount received. The contents of four sutlers' stores, filled with a variety of goods, valued at $25,000, for want of transportation, were abandoned to our troops.

W. J. HAWKS,
*Major and Commissary of Subsistence.*

---

*Report of Capt. P. J. Lock.*

Major Snodgrass, quartermaster for General Ewell's command, informed me that they retained for that command fully 20,000 pounds of bacon and 40,000 pounds of hard bread; also salt, sugar, coffee, and cheese. Captain Richardson, commissary for Colonel Ashby, retained for the cavalry supplies for five or six days—about 7,200 rations.

P. J. LOCK,
*Captain and Acting Commissary of Subsistence.*

---

## No. 64.

*Reports of Maj. John A. Harman, C. S. Army, Chief Quartermaster, of property captured and destroyed.*

MOSS NECK, VA., *March* 10, 1863.

GENERAL: In response to your inquiry as to the amount of property captured and destroyed from the United States forces under General Banks at Front Royal, in the latter part of May, 1862, I respectfully submit the following:

It is impossible for me to make an accurate estimate of the property captured, owing to the fact that I was only there a part of one day and night, when I was ordered to Winchester, and left Capt. S. M. Somers, assistant quartermaster, in charge of the public property captured at Front Royal. There was a very large and varied amount of supplies found there, consisting of harness, carpenter's tools, clothing, horse-shoes and nails, blacksmith's tools, forges, axes, sutler's and commissary stores, &c., upon which it is impossible to place a reliable estimate of value.

A very considerable amount of these stores passed at once into our possession, being taken in charge and use by the different quartermasters as they passed through with their trains. Many valuable wagons were thus exchanged, our worn-out and injured ones being left in their stead. The same was done as to harness.

The subsequent capture of Captain Somers prevented any detailed report being made of the property received and turned in to him.

Upon my arrival in Winchester I at once set about making the most ample preparations for removing this property to the rear, and had detailed from each brigade a large number of wagons for that purpose. In addition I ordered up all the available transportation from Staunton, and it had arrived within less than a day's travel of Front Royal when that place was recaptured by a portion of General Shields' army. The trains from the brigades had partially arrived there, and a portion had been loaded and sent off, while a part turned back to Winchester. This train was placed by me in charge of Capt. J. L. Cole, assistant quartermaster, Thirty-seventh Virginia Regiment (since resigned), with instructions to take immediate charge of the shipment to the rear. He proceeded in part to the performance of his duty, but was interrupted by the entry of the enemy into Front Royal. He narrowly escaped capture, having remained behind our troops (on his own motion) for the purpose of firing the depot and an adjoining building, full of stores, both of which were burned to the ground. His estimate of the stores thus consumed is, I am informed, $300,000, in which I concur, from my own recollection of the contents of the buildings. Having accomplished this, Captain Cole followed our retreating forces.

With the preparations made as above, had our forces held possession of Front Royal forty-eight hours longer, all the captured property would have been secured and taken to the rear.

Very respectfully, your obedient servant,

JOHN A. HARMAN,
*Major, Chief Quartermaster, &c.*

General THOMAS J. JACKSON.

---

CHIEF QUARTERMASTER'S OFFICE, SECOND CORPS,
*March* 23, 1863.

COLONEL: In response to your inquiry in regard to the order of quartermaster's stores that came into my hands at Winchester, June 1 last, I beg leave to report that, upon a careful estimate, they amounted to $125,185.

It is proper for me to state that all the quartermaster's stores captured at Winchester did not come into my hands. Horses fell into the hands of the cavalry, and wagons, too, that were never reported to me, and a number of the quartermasters of the army got stores which they reported directly to the Quartermaster-General.

There was an order issued that everything belonging to the quartermaster's department should be turned in to me, but it was not carried out for some reasons not known to me.

Very respectfully, your obedient servant,

JOHN A. HARMAN,

*Maj. and Chief Q. M., Second Corps, Army of N. Virginia.*

Col. C. J. FAULKNER,

*Chief of Staff, Second Corps, Army of Northern Virginia.*

—

*List of articles captured and turned in to the chief quartermaster of the Valley District during the second and third quarters* 1862, *viz:*

| Article | Unit | Quantity |
|---|---|---|
| Saddles | | 12 |
| Wagons | | 19 |
| Artillery saddles | | 27 |
| Artillery valises | | 6 |
| Bridles | | 21 |
| Leg guards | | 2 |
| Artillery harness | pairs | 19 |
| Artillery collars | | 61 |
| Artillery traces | pairs | 100½ |
| Breast straps | | 5 |
| Breeching | | 5 |
| Feed pockets | | 16 |
| Wheel harness | sets | 2 |
| Lead harness | do. | 9 |
| Horses | | 233 |
| Mules | | 21 |
| Envelopes | | 3,425 |
| Cap paper | quires | 64½ |
| Letter paper | do | 94 |
| Note paper | do | 10 |
| Steel pens | | 172 |
| Black ink | bottles | 95 |
| Red ink | do | 1 |
| Mucilage | do | 1 |
| Cards | packs | 12 |
| Wagon bolts | | 25 |
| Wagon harness | | 350 |
| Tar buckets | | 10 |
| Halter chains | | 47 |
| Nails | pounds | 50 |
| Leather | do | 5,300 |
| Wheelbarrows | | 8 |
| Jack-screw | | 1 |
| Iron maul | | 1 |
| Rasps | | 575 |
| Files | | 12 |
| Hats | | 2 |
| Blankets | | 14 |
| Oil-cloth blankets | | 30 |
| Shoes | pairs | 305 |
| Shoes, ladies' | do | 2 |
| Shoes, misses' | do | 2 |
| Shoes, children's | do | 3 |
| Socks | do | 90 |
| Cotton cloth | yards | 545½ |
| Peg-cutter | | 1 |
| Hammers | | 10 |
| Anvils | | 14 |
| Crowbars | | 33 |
| Smith's vises | | 7 |
| Blacksmith's tools | set | 1 |
| Carpenter's tools | sets | 3 |
| Auger | | 1 |

| Article | Unit | Quantity |
|---|---|---|
| Crosscut-saws | | 15 |
| Axes | | 13 |
| Hatchets | | 31 |
| Helves | | 127 |
| Picks | | 272 |
| Shovels | | 212 |
| Spades | | 82 |
| Camp kettles | | 71 |
| Telegraph wire | bundles | 29 |
| Platform scales | | 3 |
| White lead | keg | 1 |
| Horseshoes | pounds | 13,061 |
| Horseshoes | do | 3,816 |
| Horseshoe nails | do | 9,411 |
| Iron | do | 275 |
| Spikes | do | 20 |
| Rope | do | 303½ |
| Tar | barrel | 1 |
| Can of oil | | 1 |
| Artillery grease | kegs | 2 |
| Artillery grease | do | 2 |
| Picket rope | feet | 200 |
| Picket pins | | 28 |
| Chests | | 5 |
| Pulley-block | | 1 |
| Buckles | | 144 |
| Insulators | | 190 |
| Tents | | 134 |
| Camp stools | | 65 |
| Mess pans | | 60 |
| Skillet lid | | 1 |
| Cooking stoves | | 2 |
| Tin plates | | 292 |
| Spoons | | 52 |
| Tin cups | | 20 |
| Table knives | | 80 |
| Table forks | | 31 |
| Neck-ties | dozens | 2¾ |
| Paper collars | boxes | 7 |
| Suspenders | pairs | 7 |
| Handkerchiefs | | 6 |

The above are the articles captured in the quartermaster's department and turned in to me. Besides these, much property was captured and reported direct to the Quartermaster-General by various quartermasters of the command without being reported to me.

Respectfully submitted.

JOHN A. HARMAN,
*Major and Chief Q. M., Second Corps, Army of N. Virginia.*

---

## No. 65.

*Reports of Col. S. Crutchfield, C. S. Army, Chief of Artillery, of operations May 23–June 9.*

HEADQUARTERS VALLEY DISTRICT,
*Near Gordonsville, Va., July 25, 1862.*

SIR: I have to submit the following report of the part taken by the different batteries of this army in the actions of May 23 and 25 at Front Royal and Winchester:

On the morning of Friday, May 23, after our skirmishers advanced upon Front Royal and drove in the enemy's pickets, the main force of the enemy was found to have retired a short distance beyond the town and taken position on a commanding height to the right of the turnpike. Their force consisted apparently of a section of artillery, supported by a regiment or more of infantry. I at once sent back to order up all the batteries of Major-General Ewell's division, which was in front, while I proceeded in person to reconnoiter the ground to the left of the enemy's position, with a view to planting our own guns. The division of Major-General Ewell had only joined us a day or so previous, and I was, therefore, unfamiliar with the composition of his batteries, which I afterward found to contain but three rifled guns in all. Guns of this kind were necessary, on account of the nature of the approaches to the enemy's position, and also because their guns were found to be rifled.

It so happened that the first of our batteries which reported to me consisted of smooth-bore 6-pounder and 12-pounder howitzers, and had therefore to be ordered aside. The next battery which came up, that of Captain Courtney, contained but one rifled gun, which was put in position, under charge of Lieutenant Latimer, and exchanged shots with the enemy, though it was, of course, unequal to the task of silencing their guns.

After a short time Captain Brockenbrough's battery came up, and two of his guns having been planted and opened on the enemy, a brisk cannonade of some ten or fifteen minutes was kept up, with no injury to ourselves and no apparent damage to the enemy. At the end of this time the opposing battery drew off and the enemy began his retreat. Captain Lusk's battery having by this time come up, I took from it two rifled guns and started in pursuit.

About a mile or more from the village the enemy had planted a gun and left a few skirmishers on a ridge commanding the bridge over the river, which they had set on fire. A few shells dispersed them, and the fire being extinguished, the bridge was crossed and the pursuit continued. Owing to the jaded condition of our horses and the rapidity of the enemy's movements our artillery did not overtake them again during the chase, and took no further part in the affair.

Both of the guns of the enemy, with their two caissons, were captured by our cavalry, together with seven battery horses and three sets of artillery harness. The harness was turned over to Captain Cutshaw. One gun and caisson were given to Captain Poague in lieu of a 4-pounder rifled gun belonging to his battery, and the remaining gun and caisson to Captain Brockenbrough, to replace one of his Blakeley 12-pounder guns, which had an assembling-bolt in the cheek broken by the strain on its carriage during the firing. Both the captured pieces were 10-pounder Parrott rifled guns. In this affair our guns were badly served and did no execution.

On the following day (Saturday, May 24) two rifled guns from Captain Poague's battery were detailed to accompany Chew's battery, and the cavalry, under the late Colonel Ashby, from Cedarville toward Middletown. The remaining batteries marched with their brigades. Arriving near the Valley turnpike, on the southern edge of Middletown, the wagon train of the enemy was seen moving down the valley, its right flank covered by a small force, which was quickly dispersed by a few shots, and retired toward Middletown. A few shells quickly fired into the train cut off a large portion of it in the rear, and I was preparing to move our guns down the pike after the rest, when a large body of the enemy's cavalry came dashing down the turnpike from Middletown. As our infantry supports were yet some distance in the rear I threw the guns in battery about 80 yards from the pike, and as the cavalry dashed by a volley of canister scattered them completely. Some hundred or so surrendered; about as many more kept down the road, and the remainder, amounting perhaps to 300, turned off to the left of the pike, and formed in line facing the battery, some 400 yards distant. The dust and smoke hid this movement from my view, and when I first saw them so formed I took them to be our own cavalry, as I observed them with Confederate colors flying. Upon inquiring of Colonel Ashby if they belonged to his command he replied that they did not, and I then opened our pieces on them.

The miserable quality of our ammunition (shells of two-minute fuse, bursting not 50 feet from the muzzle of the guns) prevented any harm being done them, but they rapidly moved off toward the back road and were seen no more.

Our pieces were then limbered up and moved on down the turnpike after the wagon train, shelling it and its escorting cavalry force as occasion offered. The train was repeatedly broken and parts cut off, and no material resistance met with, the enemy only once opposing us with artillery and infantry, both of which were dispersed without difficulty or loss to ourselves.

Arriving on the edge of Newtown, we found ourselves entirely without an infantry support, so I halted the guns and rode back to hurry them forward. I found some hundred or so of the Seventh Louisiana Regiment coming on slowly, much broken down by fatigue and heat. These I hurried on, but going on back I found the remainder of the supporting force busily engaged in plundering the captured wagons. Unable to force or persuade them to abandon this disgraceful employment and return to their duty I returned to Newtown, and after consulting Colonel Ashby we concluded it would be imprudent to push the pursuit farther until other infantry should come up, especially as there were but 50 cavalry, under Major Funsten, remaining with us, the residue being eagerly engaged in plundering the captured train.

This relaxation in the pursuit, though necessary, was unfortunate, as the enemy were encouraged by it to bring up, about two hours later, four pieces of artillery, which, being planted just on the northern edge of Newtown, opened on us. Their fire was returned by Captain Poague's two rifled guns, and the action was kept up until dusk, when the enemy withdrew.

Our only damage was 3 men wounded and 2 horses killed. Enemy's not known.

Captain Poague's guns were well served and their fire remarkably accurate—superior to that of the enemy. Considerable praise is due to this section of his battery and to Captain Chew's battery for the skill and perseverance manifested by them in the pursuit, especially when contrasted with the conduct of the majority of the accompanying infantry force.

None of our guns were engaged during the ensuing night, when the army pressed on toward Winchester.

About one and a half hours before dawn I was sent by the major-general commanding, via Newtown and Nineveh, a distance of 29 miles, with an order for Major-General Ewell, and so had no share in planting the batteries of Captains Poague, Cutshaw, and Carpenter, which were all engaged early next morning (Sunday, May 25), nor any opportunity of a personal observation of their conduct. From the known position they occupied, the results achieved, and the losses they suffered, I feel warranted in saying that their pieces were well served, and both officers and men manifested a praiseworthy courage and steadiness during the action.

On the side I was, where General Ewell's division was acting, I directed the fire of the batteries of Captains Brockenbrough and Courtney. The latter, under charge of Lieutenant Latimer, by an unfortunate mistake, fired repeated rounds at our own troops, on the western side of the town, but without any damage, so far as I could see. That of Captain Brockenbrough engaged and finally silenced an opposing battery of the enemy, and then turned its fire on the retreating infantry with some effect.

The batteries of Captains Caskie and Raine were engaged in the farther pursuit of the enemy, and were handled with uncommon tact, energy, and effect.

In the subsequent advance of our forces toward Harper's Ferry parts of the batteries of Captains Wooding, Caskie, and Raine were lightly engaged.

In the retreat of Col. Z. T. Conner from Front Royal, the Blakely gun belonging to Captain Brockenbrough's battery was by some means lost. On the same occasion a section of Captain Rice's battery (the only artillery present) was charged by the Federal cavalry, which they repulsed, by a close fire at 80 yards distant, unsupported by infantry. Captain Rice had to destroy one of the rear chests of one of his caissons, to relieve himself of its weight in this retreat.

In the retreat of the army from Winchester to Port Republic details were daily made from some one of the batteries of Captains Poague, Raine, Courtney, Cutshaw, and Caskie to act with the rear guard of cavalry, under Colonel Ashby (the best gun of Captain Chew having been disabled during the journey down the valley), and on all occasions in which they were engaged with the enemy their guns were well and efficiently served.

At Strasburg the battery of Captain Lusk was closely engaged with the enemy for a short time, but suffered no loss save from an untoward accident with one of his guns, by which he lost 2 men, and on account of which the gun was condemned and turned over to the ordnance officer.

Respectfully submitted.

S. CRUTCHFIELD,
*Colonel and Chief of Artillery, Valley District.*

Maj. R. L. DABNEY,
*Assistant Adjutant-General, Valley District.*

---

HEADQUARTERS VALLEY DISTRICT,
*Near Gordonsville, Va., July* 28, 1862.

SIR: I have the honor to submit the following report of the part taken by the different batteries of this army in the actions of June 8 and 9 at Cross Keys and Port Republic:

On Sunday morning, 8th instant [ultimo], about 9 a. m., the advance of General Shields' division approached Port Republic on the Swift Run Gap road, and, while a part of their cavalry dashed into the village, they opened fire from a section of artillery on the bridge across North River. Soon these two pieces (a 6-pounder gun and 12-pounder howitzer) were brought across South River and planted in the village. As soon as their firing had disclosed their approach Capt. George W. Wooding brought out his battery on the bluffs across North River and opened on their infantry, which, to the amount of four regiments, was then near the town. The enemy's advance was soon driven out of Port Republic by the Thirty-seventh Virginia Infantry and their 6-pounder gun captured. About this time the batteries of Captains Carpenter and Poague were brought out by Brigadier-General Winder and posted on the heights on the west bank of the South Fork, and their fire directed on the retreating cavalry and still advancing infantry of the enemy. Just then I came up, and encountering the major-general commanding, he directed me to remain there in charge of these batteries, and also for the purpose of forwarding to him—about Cross Keys—any dispatches sent to him by Colonel Munford, commanding Second Virginia Cavalry. The fire of our batteries was capital. The enemy's infantry soon broke and fled down the river, followed up by our guns on the opposite bank for nearly a mile, when they disappeared in the woods around a bend in the road.

I waited till about 2.30 p. m., and there being no signs of any intention on the enemy's part to return, I rode over toward Cross Keys, where the battle had been raging between the forces of Major-General Ewell and Major-General Frémont since about 10 a. m. I found our batteries posted in good positions on a commanding ridge to the left of the road. Their fire had been directed by Brigadier-General Elzey up to the time he was wounded, and I found them holding their ground well, and delivering their fire with accuracy and spirit. Those engaged were the batteries of Captains Courtney, Lusk, Brockenbrough, Rice, and Raine, while those of Cutshaw and Caskie were held in reserve. As I got up I found Captain Courtney's battery withdrawing from the field, as also a part of Captain Brockenbrough's, having exhausted their ammunition. Upon inquiry I found the other batteries getting short of ammunition, and as the ordnance train had taken a different road from the one intended, and was a considerable distance away, I slackened their fire to correspond with that of the enemy.

Some of these batteries suffered a good deal from the enemy's fire of small-arms, but all held their ground. At one time those of Captains Rice and Raine had to be withdrawn to the rear for a short distance for this reason. Captain Raine's battery was particularly well and gallantly managed, he having his horse shot, and serving a gun himself when short of cannoneers. The enemy's fire soon ceased and his guns withdrew from the field. None of our guns or caissons were lost or injured in this affair.

On Monday morning, June 9, about 7 a. m., I rode down from Port Republic on the Swift Run Gap road, and found the pickets of General Shields' advance being driven in by Brig. Gen. C. S. Winder with skirmishers and Carpenter's battery. The enemy had a battery of six guns (five of them rifled) posted on an old coaling at Lewiston, from which they soon opened an accurate fire upon our approaching infantry. Their battery was at once engaged by two rifled guns of Captain Poague's battery, posted in an open field to the left of the road. Just then the major-general commanding sent me back to Port Republic to hurry up the Eighth Brigade of Brig. Gen. R. Taylor. Having done this, I proceeded to order up the rifled guns from our different batteries. Many of them I found short of ammunition from the previous day's engagement and their ignorance of the exact locality of our ordnance train. To supply them consumed some time, and they could only go on into action in succession. Those ordered up were guns from the batteries of Captains Chew, Brockenbrough, Raine, Courtney, and Lusk, the latter of whom did not get his ammunition in time to engage in action. As they came up they were posted near Captains Poague and Carpenter, on the left of the road, and fired, advancing, a part on the battery and part on the infantry of the enemy. Their fire was good, and they were generally well managed, particularly that of Captain Poague, which was subjected to a heavy infantry fire, and only fell back under orders.

At one time the enemy's infantry observing, perhaps, the smallness of our supporting force of infantry, advanced across the field somewhat to our left and front, and by a heavy concentrated musketry fire forced back our infantry supports, in consequence of which our guns had to retire. The enemy's advance was soon checked by an attack on their flank by Major-General Ewell, and our batteries enabled to resume the engagement, but not before the enemy had got one of Captain Poague's 6-pounder guns, which they either carried off or managed to conceal. When the enemy were finally routed the pursuit was continued by parts of the batteries of Captains Wooding and Caskie with great spirit and serious effect, and the enemy forced to abandon the only gun they were seen to carry from the field.

With the exception of the one gun of Captain Poague's battery above referred to, none of our pieces or caissons were lost and none damaged. There were captured from the enemy six guns and a 12-pounder howitzer, with caissons, and all the limbers except one. One or two of their caissons and limbers were slightly damaged, and one gun spiked and the carriage broken and pretty much destroyed. They were all reported to the quartermaster and brought off. The guns were turned over to Brig. Gen. R. Taylor, as also the unhurt caissons, except one gun, which was assigned to Captain Wooding, and a traveling forge given to Captain Brockenbrough.

Most respectfully, your obedient servant,

S. CRUTCHFIELD,
*Colonel and Chief of Artillery, Valley District.*

Capt. A. S. PENDLETON,
*Assistant Adjutant-General, Valley District.*

---

## No. 66.

*Report of Col. Thomas T. Munford, Second Virginia Cavalry, of operations in May and June.*

HEADQUARTERS SECOND VIRGINIA CAVALRY,
*February* 26, 1863.

MAJOR: In obedience to instructions from Lieut. Gen. T. J. Jackson to furnish a report of the operations of the cavalry brigade connected with his brilliant campaign in the valley, I beg leave respectfully to submit the following:

When I joined his army, under Major-General Ewell, the Sixth and Second Virginia Cavalry were attached to his division. Our regiments had just been reorganized, and as the senior cavalry officer I had the outpost. My headquarters were at the Swift Run Gap, and my pickets extended from Culpeper Court-House to the mountains on the east side of the Blue Ridge, and from near Harrisonburg to Wolftown on the west. A heavy scout was kept watching Geary's command on the Manassas Gap Railroad, and General Shields' command, who was marching on Fredericksburg to re-enforce McDowell. After Shields had passed Warrenton my regiment was for the first time assembled. Finding over 100 unarmed recruits added to my regiment, I was sent to Richmond to get arms, and while *en route* for that place General Jackson started after Banks. I joined his command at Winchester and reported for duty. The Sixth and Second Cavalry were then under the command of Brig. Gen. George H. Steuart. My regiment had been employed in tearing up the railroad near Front Royal (Lieutenant-Colonel Watts' report has already been sent in) and guarding the flank of the division and constantly skirmishing with the enemy, and as soon as they had commenced their retreat they were pursued by the Sixth and Second on the turnpike to within 5 miles of Winchester, capturing a number of men, wagons, arms, and stores. My regiment supported the Sixth in their charge upon the First Maryland (Yankee infantry) and were constantly engaged picking up stragglers until the morning of the battle of Winchester; there they supported a battery on the right until after the rout of the enemy, when they pursued them on the road to Martinsburg, capturing many prisoners, wagons, arms, negroes, &c., the enemy making a stand at that place. It was not entered until the next day. Here I joined my regiment. Captains Dickinson, of Company A, and Whitehead, of Company E, were sent to destroy the bridge on Back Creek, on the Baltimore and Ohio Railroad, at North Mountain Depot. They captured many valuable stores, which they sent to Martinsburg, to add to the splendid prize found in that town.

On the 28th of May I took two squadrons of my regiment to within 1 mile of Williamsport, with one piece of artillery from the Baltimore Battery, and had a brisk skirmish with the Yankees, giving them several telling rounds of shell, but was unable to pursue, as they opened their batteries from the other side of the river. I was then recalled by General Steuart, when I sent for the rest of my regiment, and every few hundred yards on the road we found evidences of a complete rout. Wagons and ambulances were burnt, tents and cooking utensils, arms and clothing, were scattered along for miles and miles.

On the 29th we marched to Charlestown; supported the batteries which were engaged in shelling the enemy from Bolivar Heights. That evening I was driven from the heights. My regiment was performing heavy picket duty on all the roads on the Key Ferry road and the Harper's Ferry road, and one squadron was kept bringing Colonel Allen's regiment, Second Virginia Infantry, across the river behind them (they had been occupying Loudoun Heights). We were shelled nearly all night, and had had nothing for men or horses to eat for twenty-four hours.

We marched from Charlestown to Kernstown on the 30th; had no feed for our horses; and on the morning of June 1 we started at early dawn to cover our retreat to Strasburg, at which place we were kept in line of battle nearly the whole day, watching for the approach of both Shields and Frémont. Then we got about a third of a ration of corn for our horses.

That night we were halted in rear of General Taylor's brigade, who were cooking rations about two and one-half hours. The Sixth Regiment (cavalry) was in the rear, and our men were completely worn down and most of them sleeping on their horses. Captain Dulany, now colonel of the Seventh Cavalry, was in command of the rear guard, [and] was approached by the Yankee cavalry. It was dark, and when challenged they replied, "Ashby's cavalry." Having been previously informed that General Ashby had one company out, he allowed them to approach very near, and suddenly they fired a volley and charged him. The Sixth Cavalry were surprised and dashed through the Second, who were sleeping and relying upon the Sixth to guard the rear, as we had alternated each day with that regiment. Colonel Dulany was badly shot in the leg and several of his men were captured. To add to the confusion thus created, a part of the Seventh Louisiana fired into our ranks. This was our first surprise. Many of our men were nearly exhausted from hunger and loss of sleep. We had been in the saddle and had had no regular rations for three days. My command was soon formed and we drove them back, capturing three or four, who in the dark mistook us for their friends.

The next morning, June 2, found us still covering the retreat. Near Woodstock Generals Steuart and Ashby, each with a battery and their cavalry, selected a position. Each seemed determined to do something, as the enemy had become very bold and annoying. My regiment was thrown to the right and rear of Caskie's battery, on the left of the road, coming up the valley, one company acting on my flank. Here the enemy opened a battery and shelled us furiously, and I was ordered by General Steuart to move back out of range, and crossed with my command to the other side of the turnpike, to support a battery there in position, which would check the enemy while Caskie's battery was retiring. In executing this order, after we had gone but a few hundred yards, to my utter surprise I saw the battery and cavalry teeming together down the road pell-mell and the Yankees after them at full speed. The head of my column was under a hill, and as we came out of the woods a part of the Forty-second Virginia Infantry, mistaking us for the Yankees, fired into my advance squadron, causing a stampede, wounding several.

The Yankees pressing on my rear captured 8 men. Such management I never saw before. Had the batteries retired by *échelon*, and the cavalry in the same way, we could have held our position or driven back their cavalry by a counter-charge from ours. But a retreat was ordered and a disgraceful stampede ensued. Mortified and annoyed at such management, Colonel Flournoy, of the Sixth, accompanied me to see General Ewell, who was kind enough to intercede with General Jackson and have us at once transferred to General Ashby's command. Here the gallant Ashby succeeded in rallying about 50 straggling infantry and poured a volley into the Yankee cavalry, emptying many saddles and giving them a check, clearing the road for the rest of the day. Ashby's cavalry, the Sixth, and a portion of the Second, were all equally stampeded. We then marched across the Shenandoah beyond Mount Jackson in a drenching rain all day and night. Encamped for the night, getting rations for both men and horses. The next morning we were ordered to recross the bridge before it was burned, relieving the Sixth, who were bringing up the rear. After burning the bridge heavy picket was thrown out, and we retired to New Market, and had heavy picket skirmishing all day.

On the 5th the enemy got their pontoon bridges over and about one regiment of their cavalry crossed. The army moved up the valley on the 5th and encamped near Harrisonburg.

June 6 we moved on the Port Republic road. About 3 p. m., while the Second and Seventh were grazing their horses in a field on the right of the road, the Sixth bringing up the rear, it was again suddenly charged by the Yankee cavalry; but we succeeded in repulsing them, who in turn were charged by the Second and Seventh and driven back within half a mile of town. In this fight the Yankees lost their colonel

(Sir Percy Wyndham), captured, and 63 officers and men, together with their colors. Major Green, of the Sixth, was severely wounded here, but we sustained no other loss.

Here it was that Ashby determined to ambush them. Leaving me in command of the brigade, he marched with the First Maryland and Fifty-eighth Virginia Infantry under cover of the woods to my right, intending to flank the Yankees, instructing me that as soon as he had dislodged them from the hill to charge them with my whole force. In that enterprise he was baffled and ambushed himself. As soon as our forces became engaged the Yankee cavalry advanced to the support of the Bucktails. I advanced with my command to meet them, and getting within easy range, I opened with two pieces of Chew's battery, which had been masked in rear of the cavalry, and drove them from their position. Finding that a severe engagement had taken place, and that the brave Ashby had fallen, General Ewell ordered me to retire, making a heavy detail from my regiment to bear off our wounded on horseback.

The next morning, June 8, I assumed the command of the brigade. The general commanding having determined to give battle, the cavalry were disposed of as follows: The Second on picket on the McGaheysville road and on General Ewell's right flank; the Sixth and Seventh were thrown across the river, protecting the baggage train. Two companies (Captains Myers' and Chipley's) disgraced themselves by running and leaving the bridge to be burned by the enemy. The night after the battle I was engaged reconnoitering the road between Port Republic and Brown's Gap. Major Breckinridge, with the Second Squadron Second Virginia Cavalry, was thrown on picket on the road to Swift Run Gap, and skirmished with the enemy (Shields' command) until the battle commenced the next morning by the infantry, the Second Regiment bringing up the rear. Lieut. Thomas Waller, Company E, was left on the other side of the bridge watching the enemy, which was burned before he could cross, and in attempting to swim the river was drowned. We were not engaged in the fight until after the enemy had been routed. The cavalry then pursued them about 8 miles, capturing about 150 prisoners, 6 or 7 wagons filled with plunder, and bringing off the field two pieces [of] artillery abandoned by the enemy, and about 800 muskets. Also recaptured one of General Jackson's staff. We encamped about midnight near the top of the mountain, having been without rations for either man or horse for twenty-four hours.

June 10 we were engaged most of the day picking up stragglers and sending off prisoners to Lynchburg by the dismounted men of my command.

June 11 we started again for the valley; crossed the South and Middle Branches of the Shenandoah, camped near Mount Crawford, and captured 2 of the enemy's pickets.

Next morning, June 12, we occupied Harrisonburg; captured about 200 prisoners, many of them severely wounded in the Cross Keys fight. We also captured medicines, wagons, camp equipage, and about 200 Belgian guns. Here we again had evidences of a precipitate retreat by the enemy. I advanced my picket to New Market, and then to Mount Jackson, and held that position until relieved by Brigadier-General Robertson.

On the 13th a Yankee major and surgeon came up with 28 ambulances, under a flag of truce, asking the privilege of carrying off their wounded. For military reasons it was declined by General Jackson, they having enough surgeons within our lines to attend to them.

Having received orders from General Jackson to move back with my regiment to Port Republic and await further orders, I there learned that he was *en route* for Richmond and that I was to follow. His command having had three days' start of me, I did not overtake him until he arrived at Hanover Court-House.

The weather had been extremely hot during our campaign in the valley. The roads macadamized and the cavalry unprovided with horseshoes, and being compelled to subsist them mostly on young grass without salt, I found my command in a most deplorable condition. Our work had been eternal, day and night. We were under fire twenty-six days out of thirty. Having gone in with more than 100 men unarmed, we returned generally well equipped. History bears no record of the same amount of service performed by the same number of cavalry horses in the same time.

I am, general, very respectfully, your obedient servant,

THOMAS T. MUNFORD,

*Colonel Second Virginia Cavalry, Commanding Ashby's Br*

P. S.—I have failed to mention any special marks of gallan hibited by any of my men, supposing that it has been done by under whose orders they were acting. I shall omit in the rest report our Richmond campaign, and begin at Waterloo Bridge, I was ordered again to report to General Jackson, in advance army moving on Manassas.

---

## No. 67.

*Report of Col. Thomas S. Flournoy, Sixth Virgini*
*May 23–26.*

HEADQUA

In obedience to orders from of the Sixth Virginia Cav chester, I make the fo

On the morning under my comm Gap Rai

position, but soon reformed in an orchard on the right of the turnpike, where these companies again charged and put them to complete rout.

The force of the enemy consisted of two companies of cavalry, two pieces of artillery, one regiment of infantry (the First Maryland), and two companies of Pennsylvania Infantry. When the charge was commenced their cavalry took to flight. The two pieces of artillery were abandoned and taken and nearly the entire infantry force taken prisoners.

The enemy lost in killed 15 and 20 wounded. Our loss was, in Company B, 9 killed and 14 wounded; in Company A, 1 killed and 1 wounded; in Company K, Captain Baxter was killed while leading his company most gallantly to the charge; making our loss in killed and wounded 26.

Company D, Captain Richards, and Company I, Captain Row, came [illegible] time to engage in the pursuit of the enemy. The other com[illegible] of the Sixth and the Second Regiments were prevented from [illegible]up in time to take part on account of the difficulty in crossing [illegible]ge, which alone prevented their taking the most active part in [illegible]nt.

[illegible] officers and men engaged acted with the greatest intrepidity and [illegible]ge, executing every order with promptness, and gained a complete [illegible]y over the enemy.

[illegible]he morning of the 24th the Sixth and Second Regiments, under [illegible]f General G. H. Steuart proceeded to Newtown, on the turn[illegible]g from Strasburg to Winchester, to harass the enemy and [illegible]ne wagon train.

[illegible]he day a number of prisoners (some 250) were taken, and [illegible] and ambulances with stores and medicines.

[illegible] command was ordered to move toward Win[illegible]ll's division, to be in readiness to take part in [illegible]hich took place on the morning of May 25, [illegible]y was in full retreat. The cavalry was [illegible]tinued to Martinsburg, and on the [illegible]ver. In this pursuit many strag[illegible]stores taken at Martinsburg.

[illegible]nt servant,

[illegible] FLOURNOY,

*[illegible] Virginia Cavalry.*

ness for the charge and to move forward simultaneously. All were eager for the charge and moved forward rapidly and in good order, sweeping the entire field, the enemy leaving his position some time before we reached it. When he began the retreat and was in some confusion I directed the batteries to be opened on him; but, owing to their disabled and exhausted condition, could get but one piece of Cutshaw's battery, under Lieutenant Carpenter, to bear on his column. This sent a few well-directed shells among them. The enemy retreated, at first in good order, halting near the town to give a parting shot, and then retreating in the greatest disorder. I pressed forward the artillery, having followed up the movements of the infantry, but their exhausted and disabled condition prevented their following rapidly, and two pieces were of necessity left on the field for several hours before they could be brought up to camp. I pressed forward through and beyond the town. Just beyond I reformed the regiments as far as practicable, they having been much scattered in passing through the streets. On getting them partially formed I moved on the Martinsburg road some 4½ miles, when orders were received to encamp. The brigade was encamped in Stephenson's woods.

It affords me sincere pleasure to bear testimony to the bravery, coolness, and handsome conduct of the officers and men under my command.

Colonels Allen, Grigsby, and Baylor conducted their regiments forward in admirable order, driving the enemy from the hill, and with true bravery received a heavy fire of artillery and infantry while inactive, awaiting an opportunity to dash forward, which, when the time came, they did in gallant style.

Colonel Baylor's horse was killed passing through the town and his leg bruised by the ball.

Colonel Neff kept his regiment quietly in position supporting a battery, though exposed to fire.

Colonel Ronald advanced through the town in the place assigned him, though unfortunately was not under fire, the enemy having moved everything to his right.

Of Captains Poague, Carpenter, Cutshaw, and their officers and men I cannot speak too highly. The skill, judgment, and bravery displayed by them at all times, under a heavy fire of artillery and infantry, reflect the greatest credit upon themselves. Opposed by a greater number of guns admirably served, and at times to an enfilading fire, they coolly and manfully stood by their guns, working them with such precision as to silence a greater portion of the enemy's. The loss in these batteries will attest the warm positions they held during the action. The gallant Cutshaw and Barton fell wounded at the same moment, the latter mortally, within sight of his home, containing all most dear to him, for which he was so manfully and courageously fighting, having won the esteem and admiration of all and met a soldier's death in this our glorious cause.

To my personal staff—Capt. John F. O'Brien, assistant adjutant-general, and Lieuts. McH. Howard and J. M. Garnett, aides-de-camp—I tender my sincere thanks for their readiness and promptness in transmitting my orders, frequently under a heavy fire while doing so.

The casualties in the brigade are as follows: Killed, 10, rank and file; wounded, 57 [27], rank and file.

For particulars I have the honor to refer to the reports of the several commanders, herewith transmitted.

The entire strength of the brigade on going into action was 1,529, rank and file.

I am, sir, very respectfully, your obedient servant,

CHAS. S. WINDER,
*Brigadier-General, Commanding.*

Maj. R. L. DABNEY,
*Assistant Adjutant-General, Headquarters Valley District.*

---

HEADQUARTERS FIRST BRIGADE, VALLEY DISTRICT,
*Camp near Weyer's Cave, Va., June* 15, 1862.

SIR: I have the honor to submit the following report of the operations of this brigade on May 28:

In obedience to orders from Headquarters Valley District the Fourth, Fifth, Twenty-seventh, and Thirty-third Regiments Virginia Volunteers, with Carpenter's battery, of four pieces, and Poague's, of six, left their camp, 4½ miles from Winchester, at 5 a. m., taking up the line of march for Charlestown, following the road passing through Summit Point. The march was without incident until within 5 miles of Charlestown, when I learned the enemy had advanced in force, represented from 4,000 to 5,000, and possessed himself of that place.

I at once dispatched Lieut. J. M. Garnett, of my staff, to General Jackson, at Winchester, with such information as I had, asking that re-enforcements might be sent. Being without cavalry, I pressed into service all stragglers of that arm I met on the road, some 15 in number, which the gallant Capt. R. P. Chew, whom I met, volunteered to command and advise me of the enemy's movements in front.

I moved forward cautiously. Captain Chew soon informed me he had met the enemy's pickets (cavalry) and charged them, and they had taken cover in a woods. I ordered two companies of the Fifth Regiment, Lieutenant-Colonel Funk commanding, to be thrown forward, which was rapidly done, under Captain Burke. The enemy's pickets retired after a few shots.

On emerging from the woods, some three-quarters of a mile from Charlestown, I discovered the enemy in line of battle, some 1,500 strong (about the strength of this brigade, the Second Regiment having been left in Winchester as a provost-guard), and decided to attack him. As soon as we were discovered he opened upon us with two pieces of artillery. Carpenter's battery was placed in position, the Thirty-third Regiment being ordered to support it. This battery was admirably worked, and in twenty minutes the enemy retired in great disorder, throwing away arms, blankets, haversacks, &c. The pursuit was continued rapidly with artillery and infantry. Captain Poague was ordered up with a gun and howitzer. These, with Carpenter's guns, were placed in position whenever practicable and used with admirable effect, frequently causing the enemy's cavalry to leave the rear of his column and move parallel to it in fields.

The pursuit was continued to Halltown. On reaching that point I found the enemy in line of battle on Bolivar Heights. I contented myself with the success of the morning, posted my pickets, and encamped a mile from Charlestown. General Ewell arriving about dark, I reported to him.

It affords me the liveliest satisfaction to bear testimony to the gallantry, coolness, and bravery of the officers and men under my command in this little affair—ever enthusiastic and anxious to move forward, freeing this beautiful valley and its citizens, known to be so loyal, from the miserable vandals who then oppressed them. The enemy wantonly burned the market-house, with a hall, &c., over it, giving as an excuse that some 20 bushels of grain would fall into our hands.

We captured 10 horses and equipments, 1 captain, and 8 privates First Maryland Cavalry, with some stores. Our casualties, 1 wounded, in Thirty-third Regiment Virginia Volunteers, by shell.

My thanks are eminently due, and the same are hereby tendered, to Captain Chew for his able assistance and to the great amount of information given me as to the country, thus enabling me to press forward rapidly when totally ignorant of the country myself.

To my staff, Captain O'Brien and Lieutenants Howard and Garnett, I tender my thanks for their services in transmitting my orders rapidly at all times.

The strength of the brigade was 1,337, rank and file.

I am, sir, very respectfully, your obedient servant.

CHAS. S. WINDER,
*Brigadier-General, Commanding.*

Maj. R. L. DABNEY,
*Assistant Adjutant-General, Headquarters Valley District.*

—

HEADQUARTERS FIRST BRIGADE, VALLEY DISTRICT,
*Camp near Weyer's Cave, Va., June* 15, 1862.

SIR: I have the honor herewith to report the part taken by this brigade in the operations of the 8th and 9th instant near Port Republic, Va.:

While quietly in camp on Sunday morning, the 8th instant, between 8 and 9 o'clock, I heard artillery to our right and rear, which I inferred must be that of the enemy. Captain Poague came in at this time and informed me he had ordered his battery to be prepared for action. I approved it, and requested him to transmit to Captain Carpenter, camped just by him, instructions to the same effect. The good judgment of both these officers had anticipated such orders—a most fortunate circumstance indeed, as the enemy were pressing rapidly on our rear. General Jackson rode to my tent at this time and ordered me to send a regiment to the bridge over the Shenandoah at Port Republic in double-quick time. I at once sent orders to Col. J. W. Allen, commanding Second Regiment, to conduct his regiment to that point. Mounting my horse, I rode in the direction of the bridge. Passing Poague's battery, I observed a Parrott gun hitched up and ordered it to follow me. About one-fourth of a mile from camp I discovered the position of a battery of the enemy across the river, it sending shell just across the road, but too high to do any damage. The gun arriving, I turned it to the left, to bear on the aforesaid battery, when General Jackson directed me to send it to him on the right. This I did and awaited the arrival of other guns, which were soon brought up and placed in position on the hill commanding the opposite side of [the] river. The second shot silenced the enemy's battery, causing it to limber up and move off. Carpenter's battery arriving, I ordered it placed on the left of Poague's, and the eight pieces of the two batteries to be directed on the retreating battery and column of infantry advancing up the road. The guns were rapidly and admirably served, pouring a heavy and destructive fire upon the enemy. His column halted, staggered at so warm a reception, wavered, and then retreated down the road, being signally repulsed by the artillery alone. I directed pieces to move to the left, keeping up a constant fire upon him so long as he was within range. Two or more guns were moved a mile beyond the original position. Colonel Allen, Second Regiment, arriving, I directed him to move to the left (General Taliaferro's brigade having gone to the bridge), throwing out skirmishers, guarding against a flank movement by the enemy. The Fourth Regiment, Colonel Ronald, was ordered to support this regiment. The Fifth Regiment, Lieutenant-Colonel Funk, supported Poague's battery. The Twenty-seventh, Colonel Grigsby, supported Carpenter's battery. The Thirty-third Regiment, Colonel Neff, was advanced on the left and held in position to repel a flank movement, and at night picketed near same point.

Some few unimportant changes occurred during the day, but the enemy did not again advance within range of our guns. So heavy and well directed was our artillery fire he was obliged to abandon a howitzer and two limbers, which were found in the woods on the following day, being a portion of the battery used against us in the morning. I had observed him trying to remove it and succeeded beyond my expectations in forcing him to leave it, though I knew he had not taken it off by the road on which it advanced. The brigade moved to camp at dark just above Port Republic. The total strength of brigade was 1,334 rank and file in action.

On the morning of the 9th instant, at 3.45 o'clock, I received orders to have my brigade in Port Republic at 4.45 o'clock. Orders were immediately given, and the head of the brigade reached the point indicated at that hour. I met General Jackson shortly thereafter, who ordered me to move across South River on a temporary foot-bridge being constructed. I sent Lieutenant Garnett to recall Colonel Neff's regiment from picket, and then moved the brigade as indicated. I was ordered to follow the road down the valley. I placed the Second Regiment, Colonel Allen, in front, throwing forward two companies as an advance guard. Having proceeded about a mile, the cavalry in front reported the enemy's pickets. General Jackson being near, I referred the officer to him. I then received orders to drive them in, occupy the woods in front, and attack the enemy. I directed Captain Nadenbousch, commanding advance, to deploy skirmishers on either side of the road and move forward; Captain Carpenter to advance two pieces, take post on left of road, and shell the pickets. These orders were rapidly and well executed; the enemy's pickets disappeared and the skirmishers advanced, the line being supported by Colonel Allen. The enemy here opened a rapid fire of shell with great accuracy on the road and vicinity. I was then ordered to send a regiment through the woods to endeavor to turn their battery, also a battery to get a position above them. I directed Colonel Allen to move with his regiment, he being in advance and near the wood, to accomplish this, and Colonel Ronald, Fourth Regiment, to support him; Captain Carpenter to take his battery in same direction to execute the above order. Captain Poague's two Parrott guns I ordered in position on left of road in a wheat field and opened on enemy's battery, the smoke of which only could be seen, the remaining pieces being under cover. Colonel Grigsby, Twenty-seventh Regiment, I ordered to support this battery. Lieutenant-Colonel Funk, Fifth Regiment, was placed on left and to rear of Twenty-seventh Regiment. The Thirty-third Regiment, Colonel Neff, to take position on right of road, but, being detained in crossing the river, this order never reached him. The enemy's fire was so well directed I found it necessary to separate Poague's two guns, placing one some distance on left, ordering Funk's regiment to follow the movement. Here the fire was resumed. The enemy soon placed a battery of two pieces in front and in a commanding position. I sent Lieutenant Garnett, and afterward Captain Poague, to look for a position nearer and more desirable, but none could be found unless the enemy were driven off. I then learned his skirmishers were advancing, and ordered Funk's regiment forward to support extreme left of line, at same time sending to General Jackson for re-enforcements, being greatly outnumbered. Col. H. T. Hays soon reported to me with the Seventh Louisiana Regiment. I directed him to take position on the right of Funk's, and ordered Grigsby's regiment up, placing it on the right of Hays'.

This line under Hays I ordered to move forward, drive the enemy from his position, and carry his battery at the point of the bayonet. I at the same time directed the remainder of Poague's and a section of Carpenter's battery—the latter having reported it impossible to get through the thick woods or find any position—to be advanced. Colonel Hays moved his command forward in gallant style with a cheer. Seeing his movement I advanced with the artillery, placing the guns in battery just in rear of Hays' line, which I found had been halted behind a fence, the enemy being in such strong force and pouring in such a heavy fire of artillery and rifles. I then sent for re-enforcements, but received none. The men stood it boldly for some time and fought gallantly—many until all their cartridges were gone. Captain Raine reported with two pieces of artillery, one, however, without any cannoneers; this piece I sent from the field, the other being brought into action. I had directed Captain Poague to move with a Parrott gun to the right, and sent Lieutenant Garnett to Carpenter to endeavor to place his section so as to enfilade the enemy. The Thirty-first Regiment Virginia Volunteers (Colonel Hoffman) arrived about this time to relieve Colonel Hays, who was ordered to join his brigade. This change it was impossible to effect, and I held Colonel Hoffman in rear of the batteries for their security, as the infantry line began to waver under the storm of shot, shell, and balls which was being rained upon them. The batteries were moved to rear and I tried to rally the men, placing Hoffman's regiment in line on which to rally; here I partially succeeded, but the enemy so greatly outnumbered us, and, getting within such easy range, thinned our ranks so terribly, that it was impossible to rally them for some time, though I was most ably assisted in my endeavors by my staff, the gallant Hays, Grigsby, Funk, Major Williams (Fifth Regiment), Captains Nadenbousch (Second), and Burke (Fifth Regiment); these came particularly under my observation, though doubtless others did their duty as nobly and bravely. Here one piece of Poague's, I regret to say, fell into the enemy's hands, I having ordered it to halt and fire on his advancing column, where it was disabled, as shown in Poague's report.

I still endeavored to rally the remainder of this force, and succeeded in getting the Seventh Louisiana, under Major Penn, the colonel and lieutenant-colonel both being wounded, and Fifth Regiment, under Funk. I placed two pieces of Poague's battery in the position previously occupied, and again opened fire on the enemy, he having halted in his advance. A sharp fire from the wood on [the] right told General Taylor's and Allen's forces were engaged. I directed the Parrott gun on the enemy's battery, which was now turned on those forces. I was gratified to learn from General Taylor this fire was of service to him.

The enemy now moved to his left flank, apparently to surround this command in the woods. Seeing two regiments lying quietly on their arms to the right under the woods, I dispatched Lieutenant Garnett to order them forward rapidly to press the enemy's rear. I then moved forward the artillery with its supports and obtained a far better position. Captain Chew here reported to me and did good execution with his battery, displaying great skill and accuracy in his fire.

I soon met General Jackson and reported my impressions to him, and was told he had ordered up other troops. Lieutenant-Colonel Garnett (Forty-eighth Regiment) came up, reporting for orders. I directed him to follow the road in double-quick, pressing the enemy hotly in rear and driving him from his position. Major Holliday (Thirty-third Regiment) rode up at this time, and through him I sent orders to Colonel Neff to do the same. The batteries arriving, I continued to advance them as rapidly as possible, pouring in a heavy and well-directed fire on the retreating columns of the enemy, who were now driven from the field, routed at every point. A section of Captain Brockenbrough's battery joined me just as the retreat commenced and was ably handled. The road and woods were shelled and the enemy scattered in every direction. The pursuit was continued some 4 miles, when I met General Jackson, who was in advance, and by his orders halted all the artillery except two pieces of Chew's battery. The enemy being again driven from their ambuscade, I followed with my command to a point some 8 or 9 miles below Port Republic, when I received orders to return and camp with my wagons, which order was executed, my advance reaching camp on the summit of the Blue Ridge at Brown's Gap at midnight and the batteries at daylight.

It again affords me sincere and great gratification to bear testimony to the courage, gallantry, fortitude, and good conduct of the officers and men under my command, and to them I return my heartfelt thanks. They fought gallantly and desperately, as our holy cause urged them to do, and though temporarily repulsed, it was only from overwhelming numbers. Although exposed to such a withering fire, the killed are few in number, a kind Providence having guarded many from the great dangers to which they were exposed. Colonels Allen and Ronald were so far separated from me I must refer to their respective reports for the operations of their regiments. To my staff, Captain O'Brien, Lieutenants Howard and Garnett, I tender my sincere thanks for their assistance in transmitting my orders to different points (though under heavy fire frequently after the fight became general), ever ready and prompt.

The casualties were: Killed—officers, 2; privates, 11. Wounded—officers, 6; privates, 148. Missing—privates, 32. Total, 199. The strength of the brigade was 1,313, rank and file.

For detailed accounts of the affair I respectfully refer to the reports of the several commanders herewith transmitted.

I am, sir, very respectfully,

CHAS. S. WINDER,
*Brigadier-General, Commanding*

Maj. R. L. DABNEY,
*Assistant Adjutant-General, Headquarters Valley District.*

## No. 69.

### *Reports of Col. J. W. Allen, Second Virginia Infantry, of operations May 24–June 9.*

CAMP NEAR NEW MARKET, VA.,
*June* 4, 1862.

CAPTAIN: In obedience to Special Orders, No. —, I have the honor to submit the following report of the part taken by the Second Regiment Virginia Volunteers in the engagement near and at Winchester, Frederick County, Virginia, on Saturday night and Sunday, May 24 and 25:

Arriving near Newtown just before sunset, our advance was delayed by the enemy's fire from the hills beyond until after dusk, when the brigade resumed the line of march, the Thirty-second Regiment in advance, followed by the Twenty-seventh, the Second occupying the center of the brigade, continuing our march in this manner, with light skirmishing in front, until about 1 a. m., when our advance guard of cavalry was driven back by a heavy volley from the enemy, concealed in an orchard near the left of the road. Immediately the advance regiments were ordered to the left and front, and receiving an order from General Winder to that effect, I directed the head of my regiment at right angles to the road, and then by the left flank moved parallel to the turnpike, until arriving at the stream found it impossible to advance by the front, and crossed by the flank on a narrow foot-way; before accomplishing which received, through Lieutenant Garnett, an order to return to the turnpike. The Fifth Regiment had passed before I reached the road.

In this manner we advanced, with four companies as skirmishers (Company F, Second Regiment, being one of them), until after we had passed through Kernstown. Sharp skirmishing occurring at the road at this point, we remained until after dawn, when the order was given to move forward. Arriving at Perkins' Mill, the Twenty-seventh was filed to the left of the road, and I received an order from General Winder to take the direction of the Twenty-seventh, Second, and Fifth Regiments, and occupy the heights to the left of the turnpike, on which there was a breastwork and across which the enemy's line of skirmishers was already extended.

Skirmishers were thrown forward from the Twenty-seventh and Fifth, and the main bodies of the Second and Twenty-seventh, immediately after crossing the run, moved forward promptly and soon occupied the position indicated. Immediately on reaching the crest of the hill a battery about 400 yards in advance opened on my regiment. I drew it back slightly under the crest of the hill, where we remained over an hour, subject to the direct and enfilading fire of the enemy's guns, two shells from which fell and exploded exactly in Companies I and H of my regiment.

The men during this trying time maintained their position with perfect coolness, and when I received an order from General Winder to advance, as the enemy were being driven back by General Taylor's brigade on our left, every man started forward in admirable style. After passing the ridge, behind the crest of which I had taken my first position, I discovered the enemy about to take advantage of a stone wall directly in front of General Taylor's brigade, to make a stand, whereupon I directed my regiment, together with the companies of the Fifth (which had been thrown forward as skirmishers), by the right flank, and passed the end of the wall, thus turning the flank of the force holding it, when a well-directed fire from my men drove them off at a run, closely pursued into the town by the men of the Second and Fifth Regiments. Colonel Baylor and Lieutenant-Colonel Botts dashed down one street. I crossed to Loudoun, or Main, street with the larger part of the Second and some of the Fifth. Finding all the enemy that had been driven from the heights west of town had taken this street, I pressed them closely and drove them entirely through the town, where they united with the column which passed down Railroad street. Having but few men left with me, and these mostly exhausted from the long run and previous march of the day and night before, I halted and gave way to the other troops, which then made their appearance on that side of the town.

I cannot too highly commend the coolness and perseverance of both officers and men during the night march from Newtown to Kernstown, during which there was continual skirmishing with an invisible enemy, and in which some of my men were wounded; and also during the trying time they were exposed to the sharp fire from the battery of the enemy, not more than 400 yards in their front, whose shells were constantly exploding immediately over our position and two of which fell in our midst; also during the pursuit through the town, when, though the ranks were entirely broken and the enemy were constantly turning and firing upon them, still pressed on and captured many prisoners who were overtaken.

List of casualties in the Second Regiment Virginia Volunteers at Winchester, May 25:

| | |
|---|---|
| Killed | 4 |
| Wounded | 14 |
| Total | 18 |

Respectfully submitted.

J. W. ALLEN,
*Colonel Second Regiment.*

Captain O'BRIEN,
*Assistant Adjutant-General.*

P. S.—Strength, rank and file, 392.

—

HDQRS. SECOND REGIMENT VIRGINIA VOLUNTEERS,
*Camp, Brown's Gap Pass, June* 11, 1862.

CAPTAIN: I have the honor to make the following report of the action of my regiment during the engagements of Sunday and Monday, June 8 and 9:

Early on Sunday I received an order to get my regiment under arms as speedily as possible and move down the road in the direction of the bridge at Port Republic, which place had been entered by the enemy's cavalry. Within five minutes after the reception of this order I had my regiment formed and marched out of the woods into the field adjoining the road, where I halted long enough to load, and was proceeding down the road when Captain O'Brien directed me to occupy the woods to the left of the road and guard the left flank. On reaching the woods I deployed Company A as skirmishers and sent it forward to the river bank, and sent Company D, under Captain Nadenbousch, to the left and front, who also went as far as the bank of the river on our extreme left. The remaining five companies (three being on picket at the bridge and in town) I kept in the edge of the wood until ordered to support two pieces of artillery which were left under my charge on the left. I then moved in rear of these guns and remained there until after dark, when I received an order to return to the wagons, which were about a mile beyond Port Republic.

Soon after dawn on the morning of the 9th I received an order to get under arms at once, and moved back through the town and across the river, the Second Regiment being in front of the brigade. After crossing Companies D and I were thrown forward as skirmishers, the former on the left of the road, and Company I, with a portion of Company G, on the right of the road. After advancing some distance down the road the enemy opened on us, and I received an order from General Winder to advance under cover of the woods to the right and take the battery which commanded the road on which we were advancing. I started forward with 177 privates and non-commissioned officers, the Fourth following at some distance as our support. After working our way with much difficulty through the undergrowth and laurel thickets I came within a hundred yards of the battery which I had been ordered to take, but found it supported by three regiments of infantry. I immediately sent to General Winder a report of my position, and at the same time ordered the two left companies (being nearest the guns of the enemy) to take deliberate aim and fire at the gunners. Unfortunately, two chance shots showed our position, and one gun had been brought to bear on us loaded with grape. At my first volley all the gunners were driven off, but the two regiments of infantry opened on us, and returning to their guns they poured in volley after volley of grape on us in such quick succession as to throw my men into confusion, and it was some time before they were reformed.

In the mean time the Fourth, which had come up on my right, was subjected to the fire of the three regiments in reserve. I ordered it back a short distance, and then directed both regiments to retire to a more eligible position, while I reported to General Jackson—General Winder being very hotly pressed by a much superior force to his own on our extreme left—my position and utter inability to carry the battery without assistance. I was told that General Taylor had been sent to my right, and returning I met an officer from General Elzey's brigade, who reported to me for orders. I directed him forward, as the brigade was on my right, and moved back with the Second and Fourth Regiments, but found that General Taylor had passed around my right and carried the battery before we came up. We then followed on in rear until ordered to return to camp.

Accompanying this is a report of my losses.*

Respectfully submitted.

J. W. ALLEN,
*Colonel Second Regiment.*

Captain O'BRIEN,
*Assistant Adjutant-General.*

---

* List omitted shows 1 officer (Lieut. R. M. English) killed, and 1 officer and 23 men wounded, and strength, rank and file, 224.

## No. 70.

***Reports of Col Charles A. Ronald, Fourth Virginia Infantry, of operations May 23–June 9.***

HEADQUARTERS FOURTH VIRGINIA VOLUNTEERS,
*June* 4, 1862.

In the engagement with the enemy on May 23, 24, and 25 I have the honor to submit the following report so far as the Fourth Regiment was concerned:

The regiment did not arrive at Front Royal in time to take part in the engagement of the 23d.

On the morning of the 24th the regiment, with the brigade, took up the line of march at an early hour from Front Royal (the Fourth Regiment in front) for Middletown. Arriving at the forks of the road, the brigade was halted for several hours. The march was then resumed, and marching in quick-time, arrived at Middletown about — p. m. The march was continued a short distance in the direction of Strasburg.

The enemy being in full retreat down the valley, the brigade was ordered to about-face and was counter-marched by regiments, which threw the Fourth in the rear. This being done, the regiment marched in pursuit of the enemy. When about 1 mile west of Newtown I was directed by Lieutenant Howard, aide-de-camp, to file to the left and put the regiment under cover in the woods. While this order was being executed Captain O'Brien directed me back to the road, as the position in the road was out of the range of the enemy's guns.

About sunset the regiment, with the brigade, pushed forward, the Thirty-third being in front. The enemy being in ambush, and the position of the preceding regiments being changed, the Fourth now became the second in the order of march; but no casualty occurred during the night.

On the morning of the 25th the regiment arrived near Winchester. About 5 a. m. Lieutenant Garnett directed me to take up a position on the right of our lines and to support a line of skirmishers that had been thrown out. The point to be occupied was in a wheat field, designated by Lieutenant Garnett as the skirmishers advanced. I advanced the regiment to within about 600 or 800 yards, as I supposed, of the enemy's battery, which battery was on the right of the road. I expected to draw the fire of this battery, but it did not open upon me, although in full view of it.

The regiment did not become engaged during the fight. When the retreat commenced I double-quicked the regiment for the turnpike, taking the nearest route, but before reaching the road I was met by an order to change the direction farther to the right, which I did, and followed the enemy 5 miles below Winchester, on the Martinsburg road.

No casualties. Strength, rank and file, 200.

Respectfully submitted.

CH. A. RONALD,
*Colonel Fourth Virginia Volunteers.*

Captain O'BRIEN,
*Assistant Adjutant-General, First Brigade.*

P. S.—It is proper to state that my reason for reaching the road by the nearest route was with the view of intercepting the enemy's battery, which I believed could be done.

HDQRS. FOURTH REGT. VA. VOLS., *June* 13, 1862.

**SIR:** On Sunday morning, the 8th instant, the enemy, under General Shields, appeared in force on the east bank of South River at Port Republic, whereupon I immediately put my regiment under arms and awaited orders. In a very little while I was directed to move the regiment to a position on the McGaheysville road and to throw out a line of skirmishers. This put me in position on the left, and was the only point from which a flank movement of the enemy was apprehended. I threw out the skirmishers and so deployed them as to prevent surprise.

I remained on the alert in this position until about dark, when I was ordered to withdraw and march the regiment to camp, crossing the Shenandoah at Port Republic, and encamping near the village.

I take no note of the engagement of same day between a portion of the Confederate forces and the enemy under General Frémont. Strength, rank and file, 310.

On Monday, the 9th, at 5.30 a. m., I was ordered to cross the South River at Port Republic. After marching down the river a short distance (I suppose it was discovered that the enemy were preparing to give battle, the Second Regiment, Colonel Allen, was in front of me; his regiment filed to the right through an open field) I was directed to follow and support Colonel Allen, whereupon I filed to the right, following Colonel Allen. In passing through this open field the enemy's battery was brought to bear upon the regiment, but fortunately doing no damage. Arriving at the woods on the right I formed on the right of the Second in line of battle, threw out skirmishers, and advanced through a very dense wood and laurel thicket. Arriving at a point on a hill, that I afterward learned was very near the enemy's battery, two or three of the skirmishers that I had thrown out fired upon the enemy. This drew a considerable volley from the enemy, who were concealed in the brush, and, although at a very close range, no damage was done, the enemy overshooting. At this moment the enemy began to throw grape and canister into the woods, which they continued for a short time with great violence, from the effects of which 4 men were wounded, none mortally. Here Colonel Allen directed me to fall back, which I did. Shortly thereafter he directed me to move forward with his regiment. After advancing a short distance the retreat of the enemy commenced and I followed in pursuit.

Officers and men all acted well, and while not actively engaged with the enemy, yet the conduct of all was such as to justify me in saying that the Fourth Regiment would have been equal to any emergency.

Strength, rank and file, 317.*

CH. A. RONALD,
*Colonel Fourth Virginia Volunteers.*

Captain O'BRIEN, *Assistant Adjutant-General.*

---

No. 71.

***Report of Col. W. S. H. Baylor, Fifth Virginia Infantry, of engagement at Winchester.***

HDQRS. FIFTH REGT. VA. VOLS., *June* 1, 1862.

**CAPTAIN:** I have the honor to report that, in obedience to orders of Brigadier-General Winder, I moved my regiment to the front of the

* Nominal list of casualties shows 4 men wounded.

entire column, near Bartonsville, on the night of the 24th ultimo. I immediately threw forward Companies A and K, under the command, respectively, of Captain Fletcher and Lieutenant Kurtz, as skirmishers, with instructions to advance cautiously and to scour the woods and country on either side of the road, superintending the movement in person, assisted by Lieutenant-Colonel Funk. The remaining eight companies followed some 400 or 500 yards in the rear. Owing to the frequent ambuscades of the enemy, which exposed them to a dangerous fire, the darkness of the night, the roughness of the country, and the exhausted condition of the men, the advance was necessarily slow, but was kept up constantly.

The enemy was driven back, about 20 of his number captured, 3 wounded, and 1 killed.

Finding my men almost broken down, I asked for assistance to relieve them, and one company of the Second Regiment (Captain Burgess) was sent forward for that purpose; but as only three of that company were acquainted with the neighborhood I received but little help from it.

At dawn my skirmishers had advanced as far as Hollingsworth's Mill (taking possession of a camp of the enemy's cavalry, apparently just deserted) and discovered the enemy upon the hill in the suburbs of Winchester, to the left of the road. I ordered Companies E (Captain Newton) and G (Captain Richard D. Simms) to support my skirmishers, and moved the line forward rapidly. The enemy's cavalry made its appearance in the main road, but was soon driven back.

By direction of Brigadier-General Winder I pushed forward Company C, commanded by Lieutenant John F. Litten (Captain Trevey being sick), to drive the enemy from the brow of the above-mentioned hill and advance it in conjunction with the Second and Twenty-seventh Regiments. The remainder of the regiment, under the command of Major Williams, was ordered to follow and support the movement. The enemy retired rapidly, and I placed the skirmishers under the brow of the hill and behind a stone fence, so as to protect them from the enemy's sharpshooters and enable them to drive them back without any loss, which they succeeded in doing.

Perceiving the enemy was shifting his forces to his right (our left), I ordered forward Companies D (Captain Randolph), L (Captain Burke), and I (commanded by Lieutenant Arnold), and placed them on the left of Company C, thus nearly filling up the space between the right of the Second Regiment and the main road. All of the companies thus thrown forward were placed behind the hill and stone fence, and, being armed with long-range guns, did good service, and were in a most excellent position to enfilade, with a raking fire, any force which might attempt to retake the hill, which I thought it was then the intention of the enemy to undertake.

This position had not been occupied long when, perceiving the left of our line moving forward, I ordered my men to charge, which was done with a cheer and in gallant style. Warned by a lady just at the edge of the town that the enemy was still making a stand, I rode in advance, and found that he had formed three sides of a square at the intersection of Loudoun and ——— streets, so as to rake our forces as they advanced in three directions. I directed two companies to attack the enemy on the one side and led two others around the square, so as to attack him on that side also. He did not stand, however, but a short time, and my advance companies, in conjunction with some of the Second Regiment, pursued him down Braddock, Loudoun, and Market streets, capturing many prisoners in their progress. My horse being mortally wounded, and having received a slight hurt myself in the town, I was separated from my regiment for a short time and it became considerably scattered, but continued the pursuit until several of the companies were ordered back to guard the prisoners.

Captain Simms, with some of his company, pursued a regiment of the enemy so closely as to be driven away by our own artillery, which was firing on the regiment.

I cannot speak too highly of Captain Fletcher and Lieutenant Kurtz and the officers and men of their companies for the fearless, untiring, and skillful manner with which they led the advance for 6 miles, under many difficulties, in the darkness of the night and in the face of the enemy.

Captains Randolph, Burke, Newton, and Simms, and Lieutenants Litten and Arnold, and the men and officers of their respective companies, behaved with coolness and gallantry, and were in the thickest of the fight.

Companies F and H, though not actually engaged in the battle (having been held in reserve) kept up the pursuit.

I am much indebted to Lieutenant-Colonel Funk and Major Williams for the ready assistance they gave me by their constant activity and fearless conduct during the night preceding and the day of the battle.

Surgeon Baldwin and Assistant Surgeon Brevard discharged their duties promptly.

It gives me pleasure to mention the gallantry of Lieutenant-Colonel Botts, of the Second Regiment.

I believe that the advance companies of my regiment, with a part of the Second Regiment, are entitled to the honor of having first entered the town. They captured and turned in 373 prisoners, among them many officers.

The list of casualties was providentially small, consisting of 1 killed and 3 wounded.*

I have the honor to be, very respectfully, your obedient servant,

W. S. H. BAYLOR,
*Colonel Fifth Regiment Virginia Volunteers.*

---

## No. 72.

*Report of Lieut. Col. J. H. S. Funk, Fifth Virginia Infantry, of the engagement at Port Republic.*

HDQRS. FIFTH REGIMENT VIRGINIA INFANTRY,
*June* 11, 1862.

SIR: In compliance with an order from headquarters First Brigade I make the following report of my regiment in the engagements of the 8th and 9th instant:

June 8, the drum beat to arms about 9 a. m. Our wagons were unloaded and the men cooking. Hurriedly we loaded the wagons and were ready to move. I received orders to move in the direction of the bridge near Port [Republic], which the enemy were then trying to destroy. Arriving near the bridge, I was ordered to support Poague's battery on the right of the road leading from Harrisonburg to Port

* Nominal list omitted.

Republic. The enemy were in line of battle near a strip of wood beyond the river, on the Swift Run Gap and Port [Republic] road. Our battery fired some well-aimed shots into their lines, causing them to retire in much disorder. I then moved by the left flank some 300 yards across the road, where my command laid behind the battery until 4 p. m., when ordered to Port [Republic]. Immediately after crossing the bridge I received orders to return to the position just left, where I remained until ordered to camp one-half mile beyond Port [Republic], where my command cooked two days' rations.

June 9, early upon this morning I left camp south of Port Republic, passed through the village, crossed the river on a temporary bridge, and marched in direction of Swift Run Gap. Marching some 2 miles we fell upon the enemy, and General Winder ordered me to support Poague's battery, posted in a wheat field on the left of the road. The enemy shelled us furiously. Remaining in this position a half an hour, I received an order to move by the left flank some 400 yards to the left, to support a piece of the afore-mentioned battery. Moved to this point. Company L, Captain Burke, was deployed as skirmishers, who soon came in contact with a company deployed by the enemy from the Fifth Ohio. Driving the enemy's skirmishers back upward of 100 yards, I was ordered to my skirmishers' support. Moving off by the left flank to the river bank I threw my column in line of battle and marched to within 50 yards of my skirmishers. Colonel Hays, of the Seventh Louisiana Volunteers, then came up on my right, and we charged through an orchard and across a wheat field, the enemy prudently retiring 300 or 400 yards. We rushed through a pond of water to the opposite shore, where the enemy opened a terrific fire upon us. We returned it and were exposed to a murderous cross-fire. One regiment of the enemy was in our front in a lane in rear of Mr. Fletcher's house, another regiment laid in a wheat field on our right, and immediately on our left some three or four companies laid behind the river banks. I dispatched one company to try and dislodge the latter. My men stood firmly and poured death into their ranks with all the rapidity and good will that the position would admit. A field officer, mounted on a gray steed, rode in front of my regiment, waving his hat and cheering his men, but he was soon picked off by some of my sharpshooters. Finding that my men's ammunition was nearly exhausted, and that we would soon be compelled to fall back unless relief was sent me, I dispatched Lieutenant McKemy to General Winder, asking for re-enforcements; but before aid reached me many of my men had fired their last cartridge, but remained in ranks for the word charge upon the ranks of the foe.

In the mean time the center of our line gave way, exposing my regiment. The enemy had already attempted to flank my regiment, and I deemed it prudent to fall back. I had nearly reformed my regiment at the edge of the orchard, when the Seventh Louisiana Regiment (which had partly formed) was scattered by a raking fire and rushed through my line scattering my men. General Winder came riding up at a barn some 400 yards from our abandoned position and asked them to go no farther. I succeeded in rallying all that were near me, and sent Major Williams to rally the others, which he did. I was again ordered to support Poague's battery, which had fallen back to their position at the commencement of the engagement. The enemy soon gave way. I followed with my command in pursuit for 4 miles, when ordered back, taking a back road to the furnace. Encamped on top of the mountain, which I reached at midnight. Many of the men fell at the road-side, worn-out and exhausted from the hard labors of the day. In the pursuit we secured the colors of the Fifth Ohio, which was left on the field in their flight.

I deem it proper here to state that the officers and men under my command behaved more gallantly than I ever witnessed them before. The coolness displayed by them on the morning of the 8th was worthy the veterans who have contested with the insolent invaders every step from the Potomac up their beautiful valley, and on the 9th held their position in face of superior numbers under the murderous fire of grape, shell, and musketry, falling back when completely overpowered, and then only to be rallied by the words of their commanders. Maj. H. J. Williams assisted me in the command and acquitted himself honorably, cheering and encouraging the men by example to the work which was so well executed.

Lieut. A. J. Arnold, commanding Company I, fell, mortally wounded, while gallantly leading his company. He was a noble young officer, whose loss will be seriously felt by all who knew him. Lieutenant Wright, Company D, was wounded and is a prisoner. Adjutant Arnold received a wound early in the action and [was] sent to the rear. Robert Fisher, color-sergeant, who bravely bore the colors to the point amid the showers of shell and bullets, was wounded. Corpl. Walter Montero received and supported our banner manfully through the engagement.

The casualties are as follows: Killed, 4; wounded, 89; missing, 20. Total, 113. Strength of regiment, rank and file, 447.

With but one regret, that we were unable to do more in repulsing these vandals who have polluted our fair valley by their presence, I submit, very respectfully,

J. H. S. FUNK,

*Lieut. Col., Comdg. Fifth Regiment Virginia Infantry.*

Captain O'BRIEN,

*Assistant Adjutant-General.*

---

## No. 73.

***Reports of Col. A. J. Grigsby, Twenty-seventh Virginia Infantry, of operations May 24–June 9.***

CAMP NEAR WINCHESTER, VA.,

*May* 27, 1862.

CAPTAIN: I have the honor to submit the following report of the Twenty-seventh Regiment Virginia Volunteers, under my command, in the skirmish at Bartonsville on the night of the 24th instant, and also in the engagement of the 25th at Winchester:

During the night of the 24th, while on the march toward Winchester, the command came in contact with an ambuscade of the enemy at Bartonsville, some 5 miles from the town of Winchester.

The leading regiment having been thrown into confusion by our retiring cavalry breaking through its ranks, my (the Twenty-seventh) regiment was ordered to the front to clear a passage. This it did in a gallant manner, driving the enemy from their position under a heavy fire from an invisible enemy without the loss of a man, 2 being slightly wounded. In the charge Private Charles E. Pemberton, of Company G, captured a stand of colors. The march was continued until about 3 a. m., at which time the command halted for repose.

Shortly after daylight the command was again put in motion, and had marched but a short distance when they came in sight of the enemy on the hills to the left of the Valley turnpike. My command was ordered to move to the left and occupy a piece of woodland near the hill upon which the enemy had already shown themselves.

A short time after taking the position assigned me I was ordered, in connection with the Second Regiment Virginia Volunteers, under Colonel Allen, to drive the enemy from their position and to occupy the same. This we did promptly.

For a space of over two hours we remained under a most galling fire of grape, shell, and long-range guns. The enemy commenced a flank movement to our left. Other troops were brought into position, when a general charge was made and the enemy driven hastily from the field.

In this charge they evinced the most gallant conduct, braving every danger coolly and deliberately. While the charge was not made with as much regularity as I desired, it was owing to the fact that a majority of the men were undrilled, the regiment having been on the march from the day they were attached to the command, with scarce a day of rest, much less time or opportunity for drill.

I cannot speak in terms of too high praise of the conduct of my officers during the battle. Each of them evinced perfect coolness and gallantly led his men to the charge as soon as ordered by me to do so. The order I gave in accordance with instructions received from Brigadier-General Winder. The conduct of my officers was such that to make mention of any one by name would be invidious. The non-commissioned officers behaved well and gallantly.

I must make honorable mention of Sergt. William H. H. Powell, of Company G, for the gallant manner in which he bore himself in the charge. He bore the colors of the Twenty-seventh Regiment through the town of Winchester ahead of all others.

The privates behaved gallantly, cheerfully obeying all orders given them.

The regiment suffered but little, having lost in killed and wounded only 4.*

Respectfully, your obedient servant,

A. J. GRIGSBY,

*Lieut. Col., Comdg. Twenty-seventh Virginia Volunteers.*

Capt. J. F. O'BRIEN,

*Assistant Adjutant-General.*

P. S.—Strength, rank and file, 136.

—

CAMP NEAR PORT REPUBLIC, VA.,

*June* 13, 1862.

CAPTAIN: I have the honor to submit the following report of the Twenty-seventh Regiment Virginia Volunteers, under my command, in the engagements of the 8th and 9th instant, near the town of Port Republic:

The engagement of the 8th was with artillery; the infantry did not participate. The Twenty-seventh Virginia Regiment was ordered to support Captain Carpenter's battery, and remained near it during the day.

At an early hour Monday morning the command crossed the South

* One man killed and 1 officer and 2 men wounded.

River and moved down the road leading to Swift Run Gap. The command had proceeded about $1\frac{1}{2}$ miles when the enemy made their appearance and commenced shelling our advance guard. Captain Poague's battery was ordered up and took position in the field to the left of the road. My (the Twenty-seventh) regiment was ordered to support his battery. I immediately took position a short distance in rear of it, and remained under a heavy fire of shell for over an hour. The battery, by order, changed its position. I made a corresponding change, keeping near it. My regiment was afterwards ordered to move to the left to support a battery placed near a barn. Upon reaching the position the battery was limbered up to move. I was ordered to form in line of battle, move to the front, and take position on the right of the Seventh Louisiana. This I promptly did, when both regiments moved forward across an open field under a heavy fire of grape, by which my ranks were considerably thinned. The Seventh Louisiana took position under cover of a fence; my regiment still advanced some distance farther. Finding myself unsupported, I ordered my command to drop back on a line with the Seventh Louisiana. We remained under a perfect shower of balls for near an hour. In this position my horse was shot twice and so disabled that I was compelled to leave him.

My command, though small, boldly maintained its position until two regiments of the enemy came within 20 paces of their line, when they fell back, by my order, amid a perfect shower of balls, the whole line giving way about the same time. The enemy did not retain his advantage long, as they were compelled to fall back, and were soon driven from the field. A part of my regiment joined our pursuing forces.

In this engagement the Twenty-seventh suffered severely, having lost in killed, wounded, and missing 47 officers, non-commissioned officers, and privates.

Too much praise cannot be given my officers for the gallant manner in which they bore themselves throughout the entire action, braving every danger coolly and deliberately. The non-commissioned officers and men behaved well and gallantly, moving forward in good order under a heavy fire of grape, obeying all orders cheerfully.

To make mention by name of any of my officers would be invidious where all behaved so well. The same of my non-commissioned officers and privates.

Strength, rank and file, 150.*

Respectfully, your obedient servant,

A. J. GRIGSBY,
*Colonel Twenty-seventh Virginia Volunteers.*

Capt. J. F. O'BRIEN, *Assistant Adjutant-General.*

---

## No. 74.

*Reports of Col. John F. Neff, Thirty-third Virginia Infantry, of operations May 23–June 9.*

BIVOUAC NEAR NEW MARKET, VA.,
*June* 4, 1862.

SIR: In relation to the part taken by my regiment in the affairs upon

*List of casualties shows 1 officer (Lieut. James A. Lennon) and 6 men killed, 2 officers and 26 men wounded, and 11 men missing. It appears from records that Lieut. Joseph H. Haynes died from wounds.

the road to Winchester on the 23d and 24th ultimo I have the honor to make the following report:

On the 23d, at dawn, we left camp near Luray, Page County, and marched toward Front Royal. As my command was not engaged at the latter place it is unnecessary to say more than that we bivouacked for the night northeast of Front Royal.

On the morning of the 24th I moved from bivouac at 8 a. m., and marched with the brigade on the Winchester road about 3 miles, where we were halted.

About 12 m. we again moved, taking the Middletown road. Arriving at this place, where the enemy made a brief stand, I was ordered into a woods on the west of the Valley turnpike, immediately in rear of the Twenty-seventh Virginia, and some 400 yards to the left of, I think, Poague's battery.

After remaining quiet for an hour or more I again, pursuant to order, took up the line of march toward Winchester in front of the brigade, except Poague's guns.

About 10 or 11 p. m., when some 2 miles or more beyond Newtown, the enemy was discovered in a woods at Barton's Mill, and I was ordered to send two companies to drive them out. Company A, Capt. P. T. Grace, and Company F, Capt. A. Spengler, were ordered forward. After a moment or two had elapsed the skirmish began, and at the first shots of the enemy, whose fire enfiladed the road, the few cavalry in front rushed to the rear by the battery and through my ranks, riding over and injuring several of my officers and men and creating for the moment a scene of most mortifying confusion. With the assistance of my field officers I soon gathered the men who had broken ranks and took them forward to support my skirmishers; but support was unnecessary, as they had already driven the enemy off and the Twenty-seventh had advanced beyond me.

My loss in the skirmish was: From Company A, 2 wounded, and from Company F, 6 wounded.

I avail myself of this opportunity to express my high appreciation of the gallant manner in which Captains Grace and Spengler, with their men, behaved in this little affair, as they have invariably done in the frequent engagements in which I have observed them.

We continued the march all night, excepting a halt of two hours at Kernstown, and at daylight on Sunday morning, May 25, it was my privilege to aid in the attack upon General Banks at Winchester.

Having already submitted my report for that day, I am, very respectfully, your obedient servant,

JNO. F. NEFF,
*Colonel, Commanding Thirty-third Regiment.*

Capt. J. F. O'BRIEN,
*Assistant Adjutant-General, First Brigade.*

---

HDQRS. THIRTY-THIRD REGIMENT VIRGINIA VOLS.,
*Bivouac near Winchester, Va., May* 27, 1862.

GENERAL: In obedience to an order from Headquarters First Brigade, Army of Virginia, requiring reports from the several regiments and batteries of this command of the part taken in the action of the 25th instant, I have the honor to make the following report:

About 4 a. m. of the 25th the command was aroused from a short repose at Kernstown, where my men had thrown themselves upon the ground for an hour or more; the brigade was started, my regiment being in the rear of the whole, except the artillery. We marched very leisurely for 1½ miles down the turnpike road in the direction of Winchester until arriving at Hollingsworth's Mill. My regiment was again halted in the rear of the Fifth Virginia Infantry, while regiments in front filed to the left and right of the Valley turnpike road, halting for perhaps ten minutes. I again moved on, following the regiment in front of me (the Fifth Virginia), still moving down the road for nearly a quarter of a mile, where, the Fifth filing to the left by a large stone mill, I followed with my command, halting, however, before the regiment had all turned off the turnpike, as I found the Fifth was again halted, and having received no orders from the brigade commander, I conformed with the movements of the regiment immediately in my front.

While halting here the batteries of Captains Poague, Carpenter, and Cutshaw passed my command, going to the left, also the Second Brigade, Colonel Campbell's, going in the same direction. I had halted for nearly an hour in this position, when a lieutenant, whom I recognized as belonging to a company in the Fifth Regiment, came with a verbal order from General Winder to follow on immediately in rear of the infantry, then marching to the left (I think Colonel Campbell's command), and to support Carpenter's battery. I immediately advanced in the direction indicated, and had gone about 200 paces, when, seeing General Winder approaching, I advanced to meet him. I was directed to place my command in a gully a short distance behind the caissons of the pieces I was to support. I caused my men to lie down, that they might be better protected from the shells that were exploding over us.

I had been in this position about half an hour when the battery ceased firing, the pieces being either disabled or out of ammunition, as I supposed. I was ordered still to keep my position, and informed that two pieces of Cutshaw's battery would take the position then occupied by two of Carpenter's battery. While I occupied the position behind the batteries I was partly exposed to a cross-fire from two batteries then playing on two of our own nearly at right angles to each other. My loss here was 1 killed and 1 wounded by the explosion of a shell.

Before the pieces of Cutshaw's battery were well in position General Jackson passed near my command and inquired what my orders were. I replied, "To support that battery," pointing to it. The position of the pieces was slightly altered from what it was when directed where to go by General Winder, and General Jackson directed me to throw my left forward, so as to get my line parallel with the battery, and then move the whole forward, place a few men immediately behind the crest of the hill as skirmishers, and if any battery of the enemy was brought on the neighboring hill immediately in my front, to charge it with the bayonet. I replied, "Very well, general, but my regiment is rather small." His answer was, "Take it."

Although I looked for my orders to the general of the brigade, I felt convinced that I was carrying out his order of supporting the battery by slightly shifting my position, as the battery had done so, and I accordingly carried out a portion of General Jackson's order. It never became necessary to charge with the bayonet. Soon after changing position General Winder approached; the battery was ordered to a new position, and I was ordered (until further orders) to conform to the movements of the battery. Several new positions were taken by the battery, as the enemy was giving way, until their rout commenced, when I faced the regiment by the left flank and followed the battery, at a double-quick most of the way, until we had got a considerable distance north of Winchester.

In going toward the town my command picked up a stand of U. S. cavalry colors, which were turned over to the brigade commander, Lieutenant-Colonel Lee, of the Thirty-third Regiment. I followed, with my command down the Martinsburg road for about 4½ miles, where I was ordered to halt and bivouac with the rest of the brigade.

My casualties on the 25th were but 1 killed and 1 wounded—members of Company F.

I forgot to mention that my loss in the skirmish on the night of the 24th was 4 severely and 2 slightly wounded, exclusive of 2 lieutenants and 4 privates, run over by our cavalry and badly bruised—several, I fear, seriously injured.

During the whole of the engagement of the 25th, both officers and men under my command behaved with great steadiness and coolness under a very warm fire of artillery, and in a great measure regained the confidence I had reposed in them by having witnessed their gallant bearing on many trying occasions in the past campaign, but which confidence was greatly shaken by the mortifying circumstance on the night of the 24th. It must not be forgotten, however, that Companies A (Captain Grace) and F (Captain Spengler) deployed as skirmishers on that night, behaved very well, and that the cavalry, rushing back through my ranks, alone occasioned the confusion and disorder in my reserve.

I omitted to mention that Major Holliday was detailed to act as aide to Major-General Jackson, and acted upon his staff during the entire day.

Respectfully submitted.

JNO. F. NEFF,
*Colonel, Comdg. Thirty-third Regiment Virginia Vols.*

Brig. Gen. CHARLES S. WINDER,
*First Brigade, Valley District.*

P. S.—Strength, rank and file, 150.

---

HDQRS. THIRTY-THIRD REGIMENT VIRGINIA INFANTRY,
*June* 16, 1862.

I have the honor to submit the following report of the killed and wounded of the Thirty-third Regiment Virginia Infantry in the several engagements with the enemy at Winchester and Charlestown:

Battle of Winchester—killed, 1; wounded, 6.

Battle of Charlestown—wounded, 6.

None killed or wounded at the battle near Port Republic.

JNO. F. NEFF,
*Colonel, Commanding Thirty-third Virginia Regiment.*

D. H. WALTON, *Adjutant.*

---

HEADQUARTERS THIRTY-THIRD REGIMENT,
*Brown's Gap, Va., June* 11, 1862.

SIR: In compliance with instructions received I have the honor to make the following report of the operations of my regiment on Sunday and Monday, the 8th and 9th instant:

About 9 a. m. on Sunday last the camp was suddenly startled by several reports of artillery in the direction of Port Republic. I immediately gave orders to pack the wagons and get under arms, anticipating an order to that effect in a few moments from headquarters, in which I was not mistaken; the regiment was soon under arms and in a few moments was put in motion, marching in the direction of Port Republic, my regiment in rear of the brigade. As we moved on the cannonading became quite warm, and on a nearer approach I found two or perhaps portions of three batteries actively engaged, firing from a commanding position on the west side of the river upon the enemy's infantry, several regiments of which were in a flat bottom on the east bank of the river. Halting for a moment near a battery on the left of the road I went forward for instructions, and meeting Captain O'Brien, was ordered to follow the Fourth Regiment, then marching to the left. We marched on for perhaps a mile or more, taking various positions and changing them every few moments until, entering a body of woods, the Fourth formed in line of battle, throwing skirmishers in front and left flank, it moved on down the McGaheysville road. I followed with my regiment in line and about 100 paces in rear. The Fourth Regiment halted after proceeding about a quarter of a mile, and remained in that position during the remainder of the day, my regiment about 100 paces in rear. Here we were idle all day, no enemy making its appearance in that quarter.

At dark we were withdrawn from our position and ordered to encamp on the opposite side of the river. My regiment had just crossed the river when I was ordered back to near the same position for picket duty, and marched back accordingly.

Some time after sunrise on the morning of the 9th I was directed by Lieutenant Garnett to draw in my pickets and join my brigade at once. On inquiring where the brigade was, he replied that he was not sure whether it was on the Brown's Gap road or whether it would go down the river. I had scarcely collected my regiment and started for the bridge when our artillery opened upon the enemy's camp. I pushed on, but before I got to the bridge I found the way blocked by wagons, ambulances, artillery, and infantry; it was with great difficulty and considerable loss of time that I at last got my regiment across the main bridge, and encountered almost every obstacle in crossing the temporary one across the smaller stream. I was without any definite knowledge as to the whereabouts of the brigade, but took it for granted it was somewhere on the battle-field, and I moved on in the direction of regiments which had crossed before me. Marching along the road I was considerably annoyed by the enemy's shells, which were bursting in and over the road almost constantly. I got under shelter of a small skirt of wood near the road and pushed on under this cover for some distance, when I came up to an ambulance which the driver told me belonged to the Second Virginia Infantry, and from him I learned that the Second Regiment had gone up the same road upon which I was then moving. I continued to march in that direction, expecting to meet with General Winder or some of his aides. At all events I was getting nearer the scene of conflict, where I expected to be of some service. I had gone, as I supposed, half a mile farther, when I met several members of the Fourth Virginia, who told me the regiments were falling back, and their regiment was ordered back to support Carpenter's battery. I was now in the woods; there was sharp firing in front of me; I was totally ignorant of our position or that of the enemy, and scarcely knew what to do. I accordingly halted the regiment and rode forward to ascertain, if possible, something of the condition of affairs. I had proceeded but a short distance when I met Elzey's brigade coming back, and was told upon inquiry, that they could get no position ahead and were coming back to a better one; I could get no information from the First Brigade. In this dilemma I concluded to fall in with Elzey's brigade, and sent Major Holliday to report to Colonel Walker until I could hear positively and know what to do. Before reporting to Colonel Walker the major accidentally met with Lieutenant Garnett, and soon after with General Winder and General Jackson. Orders now came in abundance. I do not remember which came first, but one from General Jackson in person—to push to the front at a double-quick—followed by others from other sources, but all tending to urge to the front. I pushed on as fast as I could, passing several regiments, and was in turn passed by others. The enemy were already falling back. The firing was, however, still quite warm, but receded quite rapidly, and I never got up in time to participate in the firing. My regiment followed in the pursuit for 5 or 6 miles until the infantry was halted and ordered back, when I came back, following in the rear of the brigade.

Being but little exposed to danger during the two days that the army was engaged with the enemy, my regiment has sustained no loss at their hands.

My situation on the 9th was a perplexing and unpleasant one. I used my best efforts to reach my brigade in time to be of service and to act with it, but for reasons above stated was unable to do so.

Strength of regiment, rank and file, 260.

Respectfully, your obedient servant,

JNO. F. NEFF,
*Colonel, Commanding Thirty-third Virginia Infantry.*

Capt. J. F. O'BRIEN,
*Assistant Adjutant-General, First Brigade.*

---

## No. 75.

*Reports of Capt. Joseph Carpenter, Virginia Artillery, of engagements at Winchester and Port Republic.*

HEADQUARTERS CARPENTER'S BATTERY,
*Winchester, Va., May* 26, 1862.

SIR: In obedience to your orders of this date I make the following report of the operations of my battery in the battle of Winchester on the 25th instant:

After marching the day previous and nearly all night without sleep, I received orders early on the morning of the 25th to move my battery forward and place it in position to the left and south of Winchester on a height that was pointed out to me by the major-general. I executed this order as speedily as possible.

After placing my pieces in position and opening fire upon the enemy I found that I was exposed to an enfilading fire from a battery of two pieces on my left and a direct fire from a battery of six pieces in my front. However, after firing some 30 or 40 rounds on the battery in front, I was very much rejoiced to see it limber to the rear and move off, as it left me only exposed to the fire of the battery to my left and the enemy's sharpshooters in my rear.

At this time my first lieutenant, John C. Carpenter, was placed in command of Captain Cutshaw's battery, which had lost all the commissioned officers with it, and I was ordered to change my position on an elevated position on the left of the line of battle. I moved as speedily as possible to the left of General Taylor's brigade; but before getting into position I was told by the general that he intended charging the enemy's left flank, and not to fire. His charge completely routed the left flank of the enemy, and I received orders to pursue the enemy as speedily as possible, but in consequence of the worn-out condition of my horses I was unable to get to the front.

The artillery duel was a hot one, as the following list will show: Killed, 1, and wounded, 6. During the engagement I lost 2 horses.

As to the manner in which the company performed its duty, suffice it to say that the brigadier-general must be cognizant, as he was present several times during the engagement.

Very respectfully submitted.

JOS. CARPENTER,
*Commanding Battery.*

General CHARLES S. WINDER,
*Commanding First Brigade.*

P. S.—Strength, rank and file, 52.

---

HEADQUARTERS CARPENTER'S BATTERY,
*June* 11, 1862.

GENERAL: In obedience to your orders I hereby make the following report of the operations of my company in the recent engagements of the 8th and 9th instant near Port Republic:

On the morning of the 8th, while in camp on the heights opposite Port Republic, and, as I supposed, in quarters for one day at least, my horses all turned out to graze, I was very much surprised to hear a brisk cannonading at or near the bridge over the Shenandoah River. Knowing that the enemy was on that side of the river, and believing that he had made his appearance, I immediately ordered my horses to be caught and harnessed and my battery put in readiness for action. At this time I received orders from you to move my battery forward as soon as possible. I did so, and placed it in a position at a point indicated by yourself. Upon looking across the river I saw the enemy's cavalry in full retreat, and upon looking down the river I observed his infantry coming, upon which I turned my pieces and opened fire. He was at first very obstinate and appeared determined to move forward, but a few rounds from our artillery upon the head of his column soon taught him the importance of the about-face and double-quick in his drills. I then kept up a fire upon his retreating column, advancing by half battery so long as it was in sight. After remaining some time at the last position occupied, some half a mile below the bridge, I received orders to move to camp.

Early in the morning on the 9th instant I received orders to move my battery across the South River. After proceeding a short distance down the river, on the road leading to Swift Run, the enemy's pickets were observed. Two of my pieces were unlimbered, and one or two rounds drove them off. I then received orders to limber up and move to the right. About this time the enemy opened fire upon us. I was then ordered to move my pieces forward and through a wood that was just in front of me. After examining the wood I found that it was impossible to move artillery through in consequence of the thick undergrowth. I reported this fact to Captain O'Brien, assistant adjutant-general, when he directed that I should send one section of my battery to the support of the left. I did so, under the command of Lieutenant McKendree, who reported to the general in person, and was ordered to take position on the extreme left. Of the operations of this section the general must be acquainted, as it was under his immediate observation nearly the whole time. With Captain O'Brien's permission I ordered the other section, under command of Lieutenant Carpenter, to take a position on the extreme right, as there was no artillery there, and by so doing to get a cross-fire upon the enemy. He moved forward until within short range of the enemy's guns and opened upon them with shell. Very soon the infantry of the enemy began to advance upon him. Then I ordered a round or two of canister, which staggered them. He continued to pour canister into their ranks and maintained his ground until his ammunition, except a few shell, was exhausted, in consequence of which and the close proximity of the enemy I ordered him to move to the rear and fill his limbers again.

I then went to look after my other section on the left. After getting nearly there I found that it had already been ordered to the rear.

The artillery duel was a sharp one, having been fought principally with canister and short-range shell.

Strength on 8th, rank and file, 70. Strength on 9th, rank and file, 55; 11 not engaged.*

Very respectfully submitted.

JOS. CARPENTER,
*Commanding Battery.*

Capt. JOHN F. O'BRIEN,
*Assistant Adjutant-General.*

---

## No. 76.

*Reports of Capt. William T. Poague, Virginia (Rockbridge) Artillery, of operations May 23–June 9.*

CAMP NEAR WINCHESTER, VA.,
*May* 27, 1862.

CAPTAIN: I have the honor to report that on the 23d ultimo, at about 4 p. m., when distant 5½ miles from Front Royal, I was ordered to report, with my two Parrott pieces, to Major-General Jackson, near Front Royal. I proceeded as rapidly as the jaded condition of my horses would permit, but was unable to get to the scene of action before the retreat of the enemy. I reached the Shenandoah River at dark, and finding the road blocked by artillery and infantry, and not being able to find General Jackson, I went into camp, and awaited the arrival of the brigade.

Following with the brigade the next day, I received orders to report, with my Parrott guns, to Major-General Jackson, who directed me to report to Colonel Ashby, on the road leading to Middletown. I found the colonel about 4 miles from Middletown, driving the enemy's pickets before him. Following along with Captain Chew's battery, supported by a few companies of infantry, we came up with a train of the enemy's

---

* List of casualties shows 4 men wounded.

wagons, escorted by a considerable body of cavalry, making its way toward Winchester. A few rounds drove their cavalry in great confusion down the road. Following on in the pursuit, and firing as often as I could get within range, I finally came up with a regiment of infantry about a mile from Newtown, which seemed disposed to make a stand, but was soon dispersed by a few well-directed shells.

Here I was ordered to halt until an infantry support should arrive. Proceeding with these, and when less than 1 mile from Newtown, three guns of the enemy opened fire upon our infantry and cavalry. This was about 5 p. m. I at once took a position on the left of the road and opened fire upon their battery. The firing was kept up on both sides until about dusk, when the enemy's guns withdrew. In this combat 3 of my men were wounded. Two of my horses were killed by a shell.

I was then ordered by Major-General Jackson to proceed in advance. Afterward a company of infantry was placed on each side of the road, a little in advance of my pieces, and a company of cavalry in front. On arriving at Barton's Mill the enemy fired a volley into the cavalry, which immediately whirled and retreated in great confusion, running over and disabling two of my cannon-drivers. After this two of my pieces marched in rear of the brigade until dawn, when they were again ordered to the front. At this point commences my report of the operations of the battery on the 25th, which has been sent in.

Very respectfully, your obedient servant,

WM. T. POAGUE,
*Captain of Battery.*

Capt. J. F. O'BRIEN,
*A. A. G., First Brigade, Valley District.*

---

CAMP NEAR WINCHESTER, VA.,
*May* 27, 1862.

CAPTAIN: I have the honor to submit the following report of the operations of the battery under my command in the engagement of the 25th near Winchester:

In pursuance of directions from Brigadier-General Winder the two Parrott guns, under charge of Lieutenant Graham, were posted on the top of the ridge about 1 mile south of Winchester. My orders were to fire upon the enemy's artillery, known to be in position across the pike. While unlimbering a regiment of the enemy's infantry was discovered crossing the ridge on my left, about 500 or 600 yards distant, and at the same time a battery wheeled into position about 200 yards beyond the infantry, thus completely enfilading the position first taken. My pieces were instantly turned to the left and several rounds fired at the infantry, compelling them to seek shelter behind a stone fence, from which they commenced firing upon us, wounding several cannoneers and horses.

In the mean time their battery opened a brisk fire, and, not wishing to continue so unequal a contest, I ordered the caissons to a place of security, following soon after with the limber and the piece. During this time Lieutenant Brown, with the remainder of the battery (four guns), had come up, with orders to take a position on the extreme left. Seeing that it would be impracticable to place them in position in that vicinity, I had them brought and posted to the left and in rear of my first position, where the caissons and limbers were well protected and the cannoneers sheltered by the crest of the ridge. From this position fire was opened on the enemy's battery. Shortly afterward I was ordered by the brigadier-general to fire solid shot into the wall from behind which the enemy's infantry were greatly annoying our troops. They were soon driven from their shelter, and but few returned afterwards

By this time my company had suffered considerably, and on reporting its condition to General Winder was ordered to cease firing and draw the pieces under cover. In a short time the enemy commenced retreating, pursued by our troops. I followed as rapidly as possible, but from the exhausted condition of my horses was unable to get to the front.

The following is a list of casualties sustained by the battery during this engagement: Killed, 2; wounded, 15; horses killed, 4; wounded, 5. One wheel of a caisson was injured by a shell.

It gives me pleasure to be able to testify to the good conduct of all the officers, non-commissioned officers, and privates, with a few exceptions among the latter.

Very respectfully, your obedient servant,

WM. T. POAGUE,
*Captain Rockbridge Artillery.*

Captain J. F. O'BRIEN,
*A. A. G., First Brigade, Valley District.*

P. S.—Strength, rank and file, 89.

---

BROWN'S GAP, VA., *June* 11, 1862.

CAPTAIN: I have the honor to submit the following report of the action of the battery under my command on the 8th and 9th instant near Port Republic, Va.:

On the morning of the 8th, in obedience to directions from Brigadier-General Winder, I hastened from camp with one of my Parrott guns, the first hitched up and ready to move, in the direction of the bridge at Port Republic, about three-fourths of a mile distant. Under the direction of Major-General Jackson, in person, this gun was placed in position in the wheat field near the bridge, commanding both it and the country beyond the Shenandoah River. This piece drove the enemy's cavalry from beyond the river, and fired two shots at a 6-pounder stationed by the enemy at the farther extremity of the bridge, when the cannoneers abandoned the gun and retreated across the river, taking the limber with them. After this piece had been placed in position I hurried back, and found my other guns, four in number, taking a position, under the direction of Brigadier-General Winder, on a ridge to the left of the road, and nearly opposite the position occupied by two pieces of the enemy's artillery, which had kept up an irregular fire for some time. After two or three shots from my battery these two guns ceased firing. One of them, I learn, was afterward found in the woods near by. Thereafter my guns, in conjunction with Carpenter's battery, were turned upon the enemy's infantry, several regiments of which were within range. They were soon driven back, retreating in considerable haste, leaving some of their dead along the road. Two of my guns were then moved about a mile down the river, to a position from which to sweep the road if the enemy should again endeavor to advance. This, however, was not attempted, and shortly after dark all of my guns were taken to camp. Strength of company, rank and file, 73.

On the morning of the 9th, having crossed South River, and following the brigade about $1\frac{1}{2}$ miles down the road leading to Swift Run Gap, I received orders to place two Parrott pieces on the left of the road, from which position they opened on the enemy's batteries. The balance of my guns, being of short range, were kept under cover. After firing about two hours, shifting position occasionally to the left, I received an order to take one of my Parrott guns to a point indicated some distance down the road and within short range of the enemy's batteries. From this point, under a hot fire from four of their guns, a rapid fire was kept up, partly on their batteries and partly on their infantry, with canister, until the ammunition was exhausted, when I ordered the piece to retire a short distance up the road. Hastening across to the left, where my other guns had been ordered up, engaging the artillery and infantry of the enemy, I found that they had retired to the position first occupied in the morning. The officer in charge of them, Lieutenant Graham, informs me that after our infantry began to fall back he ordered the guns to be limbered to the rear and retire. Having lost his horse in the engagement, and being some distance behind the guns, he sent three different messengers on to have the guns halted in the orchard. These orders were not received by the lieutenant in charge. After the battery had commenced falling back, the fourth piece, a brass 6-pounder, in charge of Lieutenant Davis, was ordered by Brigadier-General Winder to halt and fire on the advancing infantry of the enemy. While unlimbering, Lieutenant Davis was severely and several cannoneers slightly wounded by the infantry of the enemy; two of the horses also were shot, one of them falling across the pole. But few men being left with the gun, the enemy within 100 yards, and finding it impossible to extricate the wounded horse, it was abandoned. The piece was taken from the field by the enemy, though the limber was afterward secured. A careful search was made for the gun, but nothing heard from it. Three of my pieces were again moved forward and assisted in the final dislodgment and rout of the enemy, joining in the pursuit for about 2 miles, when I received orders to halt.

The conduct of all the men and officers engaged was unexceptionable.

Strength of company, rank and file, 71.*

Very respectfully, &c.,

WM. T. POAGUE,
*Captain of Battery.*

Capt. JOHN F. O'BRIEN,
*A. A. G., First Brigade, Valley District.*

---

## No. 77.

*Report of Lieut. Col. R. H. Cunningham, Twenty-first Virginia Infantry, Second Brigade, of operations May* 23–25.

HEADQUARTERS TWENTY-FIRST VIRGINIA REGIMENT,
*Waynesborough, Va., June* 6, 1862.

CAPTAIN: In obedience to orders I have the honor to submit, for the information of the colonel commanding the Second Brigade, Valley

* List of casualties, all occurring on the 9th, shows 1 officer and 3 men wounded and 1 man missing.

District, the following report of the operations of the Twenty-first Virginia Regiment on the 23d, 24th, and 25th of May, during the engagements with the enemy near Front Royal and Winchester:

The regiment moved, Colonel Patton commanding, in the position assigned it, with the brigade, from camp near Luray, early on the morning of May 23, along the road to Front Royal, keeping well closed with the troops in front of it. We did not become engaged with the enemy, they having been driven from and beyond Front Royal by the troops in our front. We encamped that night, the 23d, about 1 mile west of Front Royal.

Left on the morning of the 24th, at 9 o'clock, taking the Winchester road for about 4 miles, when we were ordered to take the Middletown road; moved on this last road quite rapidly, with skirmishing going on to our front, until we reached Middletown, when we were filed to the left, in the direction of Strasburg. We were at this point for a short time exposed to the fire of the enemy's guns, some few shot falling near us, but doing no harm.

We had marched about half a mile toward Strasburg when we were counter-marched, with the brigade, in the direction of Winchester, on the Valley road, the First Brigade, Valley District, filing immediately in front of us; moved on, with heavy skirmishing in front of us, though not engaged ourselves, during the night of the 24th and morning of the 25th, halting about an hour just before daybreak.

We approached Winchester soon after dawn on the 25th, when it was evident, from the heavy and continued discharges of artillery, that a general engagement was about to ensue or had commenced. We moved on the road to a point opposite a large stone mill on the left, where we were filed to the left, and marched, under cover of the hill, to near the top of the first hill, as you enter the town, immediately on the left of the road, and ordered to support the Rockbridge Artillery, Captain Poague.

We remained in the above position for about an hour, the men lying down, to protect them from a very heavy fire from the enemy's batteries and from the fire of a party of skirmishers posted behind a stone wall 300 yards in front and to our left. While the regiment was in this position I took command of it, Colonel Campbell being wounded and Colonel Patton taking command of the brigade.

The enemy's right having been turned by our troops on the left and the skirmishers driven from the stone wall by the Rockbridge Artillery, they commenced to give way and our troops pursued them, apparently along the whole line. In obedience to orders I moved the regiment immediately in rear of the Rockbridge Artillery until we got on the main road leading into the town from the south, when I was ordered to move forward in pursuit on the Martinsburg road. I moved the regiment rapidly for about 5 miles, immediately in rear of the First Brigade, Valley District, without overtaking the enemy, when we were ordered to go into camp, with other troops.

I am thankful to be able to report that we lost no men, and though we bore no conspicuous part in the various engagements, I have the satisfaction of knowing that we did our duty and went where we were ordered to go.

I wish to take this opportunity to thank most of the officers and men for the promptness and cheerfulness with which they obeyed orders.

It is my painful duty to report that some were not at their posts. Owing to the fact that a large number were broken down by the hard duty we had performed, it is impossible to separate those who were really broken down from those who were so lost to all pride and patriotism as to desert their posts in the hour of danger. One officer, however, about whose case I was satisfied, I have placed under arrest, and shall bring the matter before the proper tribunal at the earliest opportunity.

Respectfully, your obedient servant,

R. H. CUNNINGHAM,
*Lieutenant-Colonel, Comdg. Twenty-first Virginia Regiment.*

Capt. R. N. WILSON,
*A. A. G., Second Brigade, Valley District.*

---

## No. 78.

*Report of Capt. John E. Penn, Forty-second Virginia Infantry, of operations May 23–25.*

HDQRS. FORTY-SECOND VIRGINIA REGIMENT,
*On the Winchester and Martinsburg Road,*
*Four miles from Winchester, Va., May* 10, 1862.

On Friday, May 23, this regiment, constituting a part of the Second Brigade, commanded by Col. John A. Campbell, marched from its camp, on the Luray and Front Royal road, 2 miles from the former place, to Front Royal, arriving there after the engagement of the day had closed. Saturday it continued in pursuit of the enemy on the road to Middletown, thence on the road to Winchester, and rested one hour during the night near the village of Kernstown.

At 5 o'clock on Sunday morning it was ordered to support Captain Cutshaw's battery, occupying the eminence near and to the left of Barton's Mill.

Early in the engagement Maj. Henry Lane, commanding the regiment, was wounded and compelled to leave the field. I, as senior captain, then assumed command. The regiment held the above position during the engagement, protected from the heavy fire of the enemy by the rifle pits, and followed in pursuit of the enemy to this place.*

Respectfully submitted.

JNO. E. PENN,
*Captain, Commanding Forty-second Virginia Regiment.*

Col. JOHN M. PATTON,
*Commanding Second Brigade.*

---

## No. 79.

*Report of Lieut. Col. William Martin, Forty-second Virginia Infantry, of operations June 8–9.*

HDQRS. FORTY-SECOND REGIMENT VIRGINIA VOLS.,
*Camp near Port Republic, Va., June* 15, 1862.

CAPTAIN: I have the honor to transmit to you, for the information of Colonel Patton, commanding Second Brigade, Valley District, the following report of the operations of the Forty-second Regiment Virginia

---

*Nominal list of casualties shows 1 officer and 2 men wounded.

Volunteers during the recent engagements of the 8th and 9th near Port Republic:

Between 8 and 9 o'clock of the morning of the 8th instant the Forty-second Regiment received orders from headquarters to load their wagons, form quickly, and proceed from their encampment, which was about 1½ miles from Port Republic, on the Harrisonburg road. The regiment was promptly conducted to the heights near Port Republic, and stationed on the left of the road in an open field in rear of our batteries, and in view of the retreating enemy on the opposite side of the Shenandoah River. We retained that position until about 1 o'clock, in hearing of heavy cannonading and musketry in our rear, when I was ordered by Colonel Patton to move my regiment quickly in that direction. I accordingly promptly put my regiment in motion, and conducted them back along the Harrisonburg road to a church, a distance of 3 miles, where I was met by Colonel Patton, and received orders to throw my regiment in line of battle to the right of the road and march them in quick-time in the direction of the firing, which I accordingly did, and, after marching them several hundred yards, I received orders to conduct my regiment to the left of the position occupied by our batteries. I accordingly placed myself at the head of the regiment and conducted it through an open field a distance of half a mile in rear of our batteries, under a heavy fire of shells and Minie balls from the enemy.

On reaching the woods I was met by Captain Nelson, of General Ewell's staff, who conducted us a short distance to General Ewell, by whom I was ordered to place my regiment in position on the brow of the hill to the left of our batteries, which position we occupied about a half hour, many shells and Minie balls passing over us. We were then conducted by Colonel Patton about 300 yards farther to the left, and formed on the left of the First Virginia Battalion, when I threw out two companies of skirmishers, commanded by Captain Dobyns. We marched for a short distance, then changed direction to the right, proceeding down quite a steep hill, crossed a small stream, about which place there were traces of repeated and heavy skirmishing on both sides—our skirmishers, as I have been informed by the captain in command, at one time driving back an entire regiment of the enemy, the casualties of which upon our side have been given in a report which I have heretofore had the honor of submitting.

Shortly after crossing the stream the Seventh Louisiana Regiment passed in our rear and formed on our left. We continued our march in the direction of the road, a short time before reaching which a sharp fire from the enemy drove in our skirmishers, and we halted, which was then about dark. We remained in this position until a little before daybreak the next morning, in full view of the enemy's camp-fires and in the hearing of their voices.

About 11 o'clock at night a scouting party, consisting of a sergeant and 4 men of the Fifth Connecticut Cavalry, rode up to a picket posted on the Harrisonburg road and were captured, and were evidently ignorant of the fact that we were in their vicinity.

A little before daybreak on the morning of the 9th instant Colonel Patton returned to my regiment, and conducted us, with the First Virginia Battalion, back to the church where we were thrown in line of battle on the previous day. We were then placed under the command of General Trimble, and brought up the rear of our column, then crossing the bridge at Port Republic, which bridge was burned about 10 a. m., and we marched down the river 2 or 3 miles, and finding the column of General Shields was completely routed, we were ordered across the mountain at Brown's Gap, and camped on the eastern slope of the Blue Ridge.

During the whole of the two days in question, although losing only 1 man killed and 2 wounded, as stated in a former report, we were nevertheless exposed to the fire of the enemy, both artillery and infantry, for several hours on the 8th instant, and I am pleased to say that the officers and men behaved with remarkable coolness and bravery.

I have the honor to be, captain, your obedient servant,

WM. MARTIN,
*Lieut. Col., Comdg. Forty-second Regiment Virginia Vols.*

Capt. R. N. WILSON,
*Assistant Adjutant-General.*

---

## No. 80.

*Report of Maj. John B. Moseley, Twenty-first Virginia, commanding Forty-eighth Virginia Infantry, of engagement at Winchester.*

CAMP NEAR WINCHESTER, VA.,
*May* 28, 1862.

COLONEL: In obedience to Orders, No. —, I beg leave to submit my report of the operations of the Forty-eighth Regiment Virginia Volunteers at the battle of Winchester, on the 25th instant:

On reaching the field of battle I was in my place as major of the Twenty-first Virginia Regiment, which had been ordered to support Poague's battery. While with the regiment in the position assigned it I was ordered by Colonel Patton, who assumed command of the brigade in consequence of the wounding of Colonel Campbell, to take command of the Forty-eighth Regiment, its commander having likewise been wounded. I found the Forty-eighth in its position in a trench in advance of the Twenty-first Regiment. There the regiment remained until the right flank of the enemy was turned by General Taylor's brigade and other troops and the enemy commenced their retreat. We were then ordered to join in the pursuit, which was continued until we were called off and ordered into camp at our present position. While in the trenches the regiment was somewhat exposed to the fire of the enemy, and afterward, while engaged in the pursuit. The men and officers of the regiment behaved well.

The casualties are as follows: Wounded, 7; killed, 2.

Captain Hale was wounded early in the action.

Respectfully, your obedient servant,

J. B. MOSELEY,
*Major, Twenty-first Regt., Comdg., pro tempore, 48th Regt.*

Col. JOHN M. PATTON,
*Commanding Second Brigade.*

## No. 81.

*Reports of Lieut. Col. Thomas S. Garnett, Forty-eighth Virginia Infantry, of battle of Cross Keys and engagement at Port Republic.*

HDQRS. FORTY-EIGHTH REGIMENT VIRGINIA VOLS.,
*Camp near Port Republic, Va., June* 15, 1862.

CAPTAIN: I have the honor to transmit to you, for the information of Colonel Patton, commanding the Second Brigade, a report of the operations of the Forty-eighth Regiment Virginia Volunteers during the recent engagement of the 8th near Port Republic:

At about 8 o'clock on Sunday morning we were marched to the hills overlooking Port Republic, and took up a line of battle, in which we remained during a heavy cannonade of some two or three hours. Orders were then received to march to the rear in the direction of the firing. The Forty-eighth Regiment, followed by the other portion of this brigade, moved rapidly to the scene of action. Colonel Patton then detached the Forty-eighth Regiment and ordered me to move forward to the left of the road to support a battery, strongly threatened with being charged by the enemy. Here General Ewell placed the regiment in position, ordering to the front as skirmishers all the men with long-range guns. We remained at this place until about 8 o'clock at night, when we were ordered back to camp.

Casualties during the day were 3 men killed and 1 officer and 8 men wounded.*

Very respectfully,

THOS. S. GARNETT,
*Lieut. Col., Comdg. Forty-eighth Regiment Virginia Vols.*

Capt. R. N. WILSON,
*Assistant Adjutant-General, Second Brigade.*

---

HDQRS. FORTY-EIGHTH REGIMENT VIRGINIA VOLS.,
*Camp near Port Republic, Va., June* 15, 1862.

CAPTAIN: I have the honor to transmit to you, for the information of Colonel Patton, commanding the Second Brigade, a report of the operations of the Forty-eighth Regiment Virginia Volunteers during the recent engagement of the 9th near Port Republic:

At daylight on the morning of the 9th the Forty-eighth Regiment was ordered to report to Major-General Jackson at Port Republic. On reaching this point I found that the general had left for the field of battle, and I immediately marched the regiment there, when I was ordered to take position with General Winder's brigade, and acted in conjunction with his and the Louisiana brigade until the enemy was routed. The Forty-eighth Regiment then joined in the pursuit, throwing out skirmishers, and succeeded in capturing some 60 prisoners; returning, we reached our camp about 2 o'clock Monday night. Casualties during the day, 1 man killed and 4 wounded.

Very respectfully,

THOS. S. GARNETT,
*Lieutenant-Colonel, Commanding Second Brigade.*

Capt. R. N. WILSON,
*Assistant Adjutant-General, Second Brigade.*

*According to Ewell's report, 3 men killed and 1 officer and 6 men wounded.

## No. 82.

### *Reports of Capt. B. W. Leigh, First Virginia Battalion, of operations May 25–June 9.*

HDQRS. FIRST VIRGINIA BATT., PROVISIONAL ARMY,
*Camp near Mount Jackson, Shenandoah County, Va., June* 3, 1862.

CAPTAIN: I have the honor to transmit to you, for the information of Colonel Patton, commanding the Second Brigade, a report of the operations of the First Virginia Battalion, Provisional Army, during the recent engagement near Winchester:

At about 6 o'clock in the morning of May 25 the battalion, along with the rest of the brigade, left the Valley turnpike at the Milltown Mill, and proceeded a short distance to a point to the left and rear of some fortifications on the top of a hill. Here we were ordered to support, in conjunction with the Twenty-first Regiment Virginia Volunteers, the Rockbridge Battery of Artillery. The battery took a position on the crest of a ridge behind which the Twenty-first Regiment and we were lying, and opened fire upon an enemy's battery and some infantry who occupied the crest of a ridge nearly parallel with that which we occupied. The fire was maintained on both sides for about an hour and a half. Four men of the battalion—all in Company D—were wounded. Col. John A. Campbell, then commanding the brigade, was wounded during this time.

About 7.30 o'clock a number of regiments, consisting, as I have been informed, of the Louisiana Brigade, formed in line of battle in some fields to the left of us and made a charge upon the enemy. At their approach the enemy fled. The Rockbridge Battery immediately engaged in the pursuit of them and the brigade followed the battery. We proceeded rapidly through Winchester, and halted at about 11.30 o'clock at a grove about 4 miles from a town on the Martinsburg road.

I have the honor to be, captain, your obedient servant,

B. W. LEIGH,
*Captain, Commanding First Virginia Battalion, Prov. Army.*

Capt. R. N. WILSON,
*Assistant Adjutant-General, &c.* [*Second Brigade*].

---

HDQRS. FIRST VA. BATT., PROV. ARMY, C. S. A.,
*Camp near Port Republic, Va., June* 15, 1862.

CAPTAIN: I have the honor to transmit to you, for the information of the officer commanding the Second Brigade, a report of the operations of the First Virginia Battalion, Provisional Army, C. S. A., on the 8th and 9th instant:

At about 8.30 o'clock on the morning of the 8th instant the battalion, along with the rest of the brigade, was ordered to load the wagons, form quickly, and proceed from their encampment—which was situated on the road from Harrisonburg to Port Republic, about a mile from the latter place—in the direction of Port Republic. On our reaching the brow of the heights on the left bank of the Shenandoah overlooking Port Republic the battalion was detached from the rest of the brigade and ordered to support a rifled piece belonging to Cutshaw's battery. The piece moved off to the left and assumed a position on the bank of the river near a small mill. We followed it, and laid in a hollow nearly in its rear until about 2.30 o'clock in the evening.

During this time we saw parties of the enemy retreating in confusion, under the fire of our batteries, down the right bank of the Shenandoah. They were pursued by our cavalry until they reached the point where the road enters the woods. At that point the enemy made a stand, and their artillery drove our cavalry back.

About 2.30 o'clock in the evening the battalion was ordered to rejoin the brigade. In order to do so it was necessary for us to march back on the Harrisonburg road to a point near the Three-mile sign-post from Port Republic. At that point we were met by Captain Nelson, of General Ewell's staff, and conducted to a position occupied by Colonel Letcher's regiment [Fifty-eighth] Virginia Volunteers, a short distance to the left of the road, about a mile farther toward Harrisonburg. We took our place in line of battle on the left of that regiment in prolongation of that line. It was then about 4 o'clock in the evening. We remained here about an hour, and during this time a number of shells and Minie balls passed near us. In the mean time Colonel Patton, who commanded our brigade, came up with the Forty-second Regiment Virginia Volunteers, and drew up in line of battle to our left.

About 5.15 in the evening the brigade moved forward in line of battle through the woods. A line of skirmishers preceded us and drove out a few skirmishers of the enemy with some loss on each side. After proceeding a short distance we changed direction to the right, and, proceeding down a considerable declivity and across a small stream, approached the road. Shortly before we reached the road the Seventh Regiment Louisiana Volunteers joined us and formed on our left. As we reached the road a sharp fire from the enemy drove in our skirmishers, and we halted. We remained in this position from about 7.30 o'clock in the evening until a little before daybreak the next morning. From the side of the road, a few yards in front of us, I observed a battery of the enemy about 500 yards to our left at an angle of about 45° with our line. A short distance in front of the battery a line of the enemy's infantry, composed of about two regiments, according to my estimate, were drawn up behind a rail fence. A small wheat field in front of them was occupied by a number of their skirmishers and another body of their troops occupied a large piece of woods in front of us. At dark the latter body moved across the wheat field and joined the troops drawn up behind the fence. They all immediately built fires, and we could see a number of camp-fires behind them. We could distinctly hear the voices of the skirmishers in the wheat field.

In the course of the night a scouting party, consisting of a sergeant and 4 men of the Fifth Connecticut Cavalry, rode up to a picket which we had put out on the road and were captured. They said they were entirely ignorant of the fact that we were in their vicinity.

In the early part of the night I sent back a detail from each company to cook provisions at our previous encampment, whither some of our wagons had been ordered to return for that purpose.

A little before daybreak on the morning of the 9th instant we marched back through the woods to a point near the Three-mile sign-post which I have mentioned. Here the Forty-second Regiment and the battalion were ordered to join General Trimble's brigade. While we were at this point Major Seddon rejoined the battalion and assumed the command of it, but as that officer is now absent I shall continue to give an account of the operations of the battalion during that day.

About 8 o'clock we heard a cannonade to our rear in the direction of Port Republic.

About 8.30 o'clock we commenced our march back toward Port Republic. On the way we halted at our old encampment and furnished the men with provisions, which had been cooked for them, as I have already mentioned.

At 10 o'clock we crossed the bridge at Port Republic.

At 10.15 the bridge was burned. We crossed the South Branch of the Shenandoah on a temporary bridge and proceeded about 2 miles down the right bank of the river.

At about 11.45 o'clock large bodies of the enemy's infantry, cavalry, and artillery commenced to appear on the heights on the left bank of the river, and rapidly deployed in long lines along the heights.

About 12.30 o'clock our troops filed to the right and marched along a cross-road to the road from Port Republic to Brown's Gap. On reaching that road we continued our march across the mountain, and a little before dark halted a short distance from the summit on the eastern side of the mountain.

During the whole of the two days in question not a single man in the battalion was killed or wounded nor did the battalion fire a single shot. We were, nevertheless, exposed to the fire of the enemy, both artillery and infantry, for several hours on the 8th, and regiments not more exposed than ourselves suffered severely.

I have the honor to be, captain, your obedient servant,

B. W. LEIGH,
*Captain, Comdg. First Virginia Battalion, P. A., C. S. A.*

Capt. R. N. WILSON,
*Assistant Adjutant-General, &c.*

---

## No. 83.

***Report of Capt. William H. Caskie, Virginia (Hampden) Artillery, of engagement at Winchester.***

HAMPDEN ARTILLERY,
*Camp, June* 3, 1862.

In obedience to orders I have respectfully to report that early on the morning of May 25 (Sunday) my battery was halted by General Jackson in front of the stone mill, about three-fourths of a mile from Winchester, as there was no desirable position unoccupied by our batteries. Here we remained until the gallant charge of our Louisiana Brigade, which caused the enemy to break and fall back, when I immediately hurried my battery to the front at a rapid gallop, and opened fire first a short distance outside of Winchester. I kept the advance on the Martinsburg turnpike, availing myself of every position to fire upon the retreating column and train of the enemy.

Just before reaching Stevenson's Depot my first lieutenant, James A. Caskie, was wounded in the leg by a piece of the enemy's shell and taken to the rear.

Having no support, General Jackson ordered me to give up the pursuit at Stevenson's Depot, and it was my privilege to receive my orders directly from General Jackson, who superintended my operations.

During the chase Sergeant Etting, of my company, captured 6 of the enemy and duly delivered them to the proper authorities.

As our cavalry was not on the ground, by General Jackson's order the lead horses of my caissons were unhitched, and some of my cannoneers mounted for a charge, but, owing to orders to halt soon thereafter, did not undertake the hazardous duty for which they bravely volunteered.

Most respectfully,

W. H. CASKIE,
*Captain, Commanding Hampden Artillery.*

Capt. R. N. WILSON,
*Assistant Adjutant-General, Second Brigade.*

---

## No. 84.

*Report of Col. Samuel V. Fulkerson, Thirty-seventh Virginia Infantry, commanding Third Brigade, of operations May 24–25.*

HEADQUARTERS THIRD BRIGADE, VALLEY DISTRICT,
*Camp near Winchester, Va., May 28, 1862.*

SIR: In making my report of the part acted by the Third Brigade in the battle near Winchester, on the 25th instant, I have to say that on the morning of the 24th the brigade left its bivouac, 4 miles south of Front Royal, at daylight and marched to Middletown, and thence down the main Valley pike, in the direction of Winchester. Owing to delay, occasioned by the enemy's skirmishers embarrassing the advance of the head of the column, daylight opened upon us near Kernstown, after which we quickly advanced to the mill south of Winchester, at which time a vigorous fire was going on between our own and the enemy's batteries. I was ordered to file my brigade to the left of the pike and take position under shelter of a hill, for the purpose of supporting one of our batteries. I was also ordered to report to General Winder, who was already upon the ground.

I placed the Twenty-third and Thirty-seventh Virginia Volunteers in the position indicated, when General Winder ordered me to occupy a wooded hill to my left, in an adjoining field, with one regiment, which position he informed me the enemy were on the move to occupy. I at once ordered Colonel Warren, with the Tenth Virginia Volunteers, to take position on the hill, which he quickly did.

In a short time General Winder ordered me to place another regiment on the hill with the Tenth, when I ordered Major Williams to march the Thirty-seventh there, which he did with dispatch.

During all of the time of these movements, and in fact from the time when the brigade first entered the field, it was exposed to a severe fire from the enemy's batteries and long-range small-arms.

After these movements had been executed Colonel Taliaferro was ordered to move the Twenty-third forward and charge a battery of the enemy in his front. He pushed forward his regiment in gallant style; but in the mean time General Taylor's Louisiana Brigade had come upon the field, formed, and moved in the direction of the enemy, coming up on the left of Colonel Taliaferro. The Thirty-seventh and Tenth followed immediately after General Taylor's brigade.

On reaching the top of the ridge on which the enemy's batteries had been placed a sharp musketry fire ensued, but soon a general charge was made by our whole line, when the enemy gave way and fled precipitately through Winchester in the wildest confusion. We followed in immediate pursuit on the Martinsburg road for 4 miles, where we were halted.

A list of casualties is herewith furnished,* from which it will be seen that the loss of the brigade is comparatively light.

Colonels Taliaferro (commanding the Twenty-third) and Warren (commanding the Tenth) and Major Williams (commanding the Thirty-seventh) acted in the most gallant and efficient manner.

I refer to the reports of Colonels Taliaferro and Warren and Major Williams for the conduct of the officers and men of their respective regiments.

I with pride bear testimony to the gallant conduct of the whole brigade, both officers and men.

I am indebted to Capt. William B. Pendleton, acting assistant adjutant-general, for his gallant conduct and the prompt and cheerful manner with which he executed my orders.

Captain Wooding's battery was not placed in position during the day.

Respectfully,

SAM. V. FULKERSON,
*Colonel, Commanding Brigade.*

Maj. R. L. DABNEY,
*Assistant Adjutant-General, Valley District.*

---

## No. 85.

*Report of Brig. Gen. William B. Taliaferro, C. S. Army, commanding Third Brigade, of operations June 8–9.*

HEADQUARTERS THIRD BRIGADE, VALLEY DISTRICT,
*Camp near Port Republic, Va., June* 13, 1862.

MAJOR: I have the honor to make a brief report of the operations of my brigade on the 8th and 9th instant:

On the morning of the 8th my camp on the north side of the Shenandoah was disturbed by the sound of artillery close under the hills below us, and apparently in the town of Port Republic. I immediately ordered the brigade to be formed, and as it was about to be formed for inspection the regiments were speedily in line. I received orders to move the regiments as they were formed down to the bridge, which was done. On reaching the crest of the hill overlooking the town and river I perceived that a party of the enemy, consisting of some cavalry and two field pieces, had penetrated the town, and that a piece was planted at the mouth of the bridge, commanding its entrance and the whole distance through it. I found Major-General Jackson on the hill, in person directing the fire of some of our pieces, and he ordered me to charge across the bridge, capture the piece, and occupy the town. We were exposed to considerable fire from the enemy's guns in crossing the hill, and the Thirty-seventh Regiment lost 3 men, but that regiment, Colonel Fulkerson, with the utmost gallantry, after delivering a fire, charged across the bridge, captured the piece, and chased the enemy from the village, killing and capturing several of them. Had I known the topography we could have captured most of the enemy, but we made at first for the lower ford, which I supposed was the only one leading into the town.

---

* Not found.

Lieutenant Duncan, of the Thirty-seventh, perceiving the enemy crossing at an upper ford, promptly detached a part of the regiment and fired upon the retreating enemy at that point, but not in time to cut them off. I threw the Tenth, Colonel Warren, into the town, and occupied with that and the Thirty-seventh the fords near the town, placed a battery (Carrington's) on the hill on the west side, which commanded the upper fords, and sent the Twenty-third Regiment to protect the ford near Weyer's Cave. In the mean time the enemy's infantry, which had advanced toward the town, were driven back by the artillery in great confusion. Captain Wooding's battery, of my brigade, did beautiful service from its position, the precision and accuracy of its fire, and the terrible execution it effected, eliciting the admiration of all who witnessed it.

In obedience to the orders of the commanding general I occupied the town during the night with part of my command, and was ordered at dawn of the 9th to reoccupy the position I had held on the 8th, so as to co-operate with General Trimble's and Colonel Patton's brigades, which were to remain on the north side of the river. The other brigades of the army then passed me to attack Shields' troops down the valley.

After the fight had lasted some time I was ordered to move to the scene of action, which was accomplished by my men with wonderful celerity. I came up with the enemy at Lewis' house, and found them posted in the orchard and under the crest of a hill. General Taylor's Louisiana brigade occupied the hills on the right of the road, from which, with extraordinary gallantry, they had driven the enemy, capturing a full battery.

At this point I could perceive that the enemy were leaving the orchard and slowly retreating down the flat. I hurried up my command as rapidly as possible, fired upon the enemy, who, after delivering two volleys at us from an entire regiment, became demoralized, broke, and precipitately retreated. We pursued them 7 miles with the infantry, and captured between 300 and 400. I do not estimate the number taken by other troops.

Captain Wooding's battery had during this time been rendering most effective service, and the effect of his shot was remarkable. By direction of Major-General Jackson two pieces of his battery were pushed forward and pursued the enemy, with the cavalry, for many miles beyond the infantry, rendering, under the eye of the commanding general, the most effective service.

In conclusion I have to state that my brigade had the opportunity to take but little part in the glorious victory achieved by our troops on this day. They reached the battle-field only just before the enemy retreated, were under fire for a very short time, and only had the satisfaction of securing the fruits of the gallantry of others. Nevertheless I trust I shall be pardoned for referring to the rapidity with which they pressed forward to the fight and the zeal and gallantry manifested by officers and men.

The Thirty-seventh Regiment, Colonel Fulkerson, was in front, and captured most of the prisoners. Captain Wood and Lieutenant Duncan of that regiment rendered remarkable service, and Sergt. Samuel L. Gray, Company D (Thirty-seventh), actually captured at one time a Federal captain and 11 of his men, all armed, and although fired upon by them, seized the captain's sword and made the men throw down their arms.

I am under obligations to the officers of my staff, Captain Pendleton, assistant adjutant-general, Lieutenant Taliaferro, aide-de-camp, and Major Stanard, brigade commissary, for their services and gallant conduct. Colonel Fulkerson, in the advance, managed his command admirably, and Colonel Warren, Tenth Virginia, and Lieutenant-Colonel Curtis, Twenty-third, kept their commands closed up and well in hand for action.

I have the honor to be, very respectfully, your obedient servant,

WM. B. TALIAFERRO,
*Brigadier-General, Comdg. Third Brigade, Valley District.*

Maj. R. L. DABNEY, *Assistant Adjutant-General.*

---

## No. 86.

*Report of Col. E. T. H. Warren, Tenth Virginia Infantry, of engagement at Winchester.*

CAMP NEAR WINCHESTER, VA.,
*May* 27, 1862.

In obedience to orders I have the honor to submit the following report of the part taken by the Tenth Virginia Regiment in the action of the 25th instant:

On arriving at the scene of action I was ordered by Colonel Fulkerson to proceed rapidly to our left and occupy a wooded hill toward which the enemy were advancing. I did so, securing an advantageous position for the regiment, and deployed skirmishers in front, under cover of rocks and trees. These were under the command of Captain Coffman, who behaved most gallantly, and so worried the enemy, posted behind a stone wall, that he succeeded in drawing their fire. At this moment (Colonel Fulkerson having arrived with the Thirty-seventh Virginia Regiment and Brigadier-General Taylor with a portion of his command) a vigorous charge was made (the Tenth forming on General Taylor's left), when the rout of the enemy commenced and the pursuit begun, which was continued by this regiment 4 miles beyond Winchester.

In my operations I was much aided by my field officers, Lieut. Col. S. T. Walker, Maj. J. Stover, and First Lieutenant Kisling, who was acting adjutant, and discharged his duty with great boldness. Men and officers all behaved as well as men ever did, and proved, as they have ever done, that they can be relied on in any emergency.

The loss sustained was 1 killed and 8 wounded, among which was Captain Mauck.

I have the honor to be, very respectfully,

E. T. H. WARREN,
*Colonel Tenth Virginia Volunteers.*

Captain PENDLETON, *Asst. Adjt. Gen., Third Brigade.*

---

## No. 87.

*Report of Col. A. G. Taliaferro, Twenty-third Virginia Infantry, of engagement at Winchester.*

HEADQUARTERS TWENTY-THIRD VIRGINIA VOLUNTEERS,
*Camp near Winchester, Va., May* 28, 1862.

CAPTAIN: In obedience to a Special Order, No. —, I have the honor to submit the following report of the part taken by the Twenty-third Regiment Virginia Volunteers in the late battle of May 25 at Winchester:

Early on the morning of that day orders were received to advance from our position in the road where the night previous we had been halted about 12 o'clock to enable our exhausted troops to acquire a few hours' sleep. The Twenty-third was the front regiment of the Third Brigade at Union Mills, under orders of Colonel Fulkerson, commanding brigade. I filed my command to the left at nearly right angles to the main turnpike, to support a section of Captain Poague's battery, then advancing to take a position in front of the enemy. I subsequently received orders from General Jackson in person, in case the enemy changed his position, to charge the battery. I saw evidences of a change, and ordered my regiment to charge, which it did in gallant style. On passing over the hill we received repeated volleys of grape from the enemy. On emerging from the hill we passed a small valley and passed over the hill, and found one piece and a caisson had been abandoned by the enemy. The object of the move being secured, we formed line of battle and moved forward to the right, pressing the enemy until 4 miles beyond Winchester, when we were ordered to halt. The regiment behaved well during the fight. The following is the number of casualties: Wounded, 7.

All of which is respectfully submitted.

By order of A. G. Taliaferro, colonel, commanding.

G. T. WADDY,
*Sergeant-Major and Acting Adjutant.*

Captain PENDLETON,
[*Assistant Adjutant-General, Third Brigade.*]

---

## No. 88.

*Report of Maj. T. V. Williams, Thirty-seventh Virginia Infantry, of operations May 23–25.*

HEADQUARTERS THIRTY-SEVENTH REGIMENT,
*May* 28, 1862.

CAPTAIN: In making my official report of the part acted by the Thirty-seventh Virginia Regiment, commanded by myself, during the days of the 23d, 24th, and 25th (owing to my position in the column), I am forced to say that I had no opportunity of entering into the skirmishing which took place near Front Royal on the 23d; also the skirmish near Middletown on the 24th.

I marched on the road to Middletown, and my men up to the latter place kept up and marched in very good order, and seemed to endure the fatigue with surprising fortitude. They seemed loath to vacate their position; but loss of sleep and fatigue from the long and continued march forced many of those who would have been proud to have mingled with their companions in the dangers of the battle of the 25th to leave their places, and in consequence of this fact daylight the next morning found me with 300 men ready for action.

At this time I received orders from Col. S. V. Fulkerson, commanding brigade, to load and prepare to march immediately after Colonel Taliaferro's regiment. I followed, as I had been directed, to the field where Colonel Fulkerson had drawn up in line. Colonel Taliaferro's regiment not being where I could receive information at what point Colonel Fulkerson wished me to form, I came to the conclusion that he wished me to form line and move on in supporting distance of the regiment which attracted his attention at that time. I had just drawn my men up in line, when the enemy's battery to our front seemed to get the direction of the right flank of our line, and threw shell with great precision into the ranks of Company A, commanded by Lieutenant Taylor. And here allow me to add that both officers and men remained at their post and gallantly maintained their position, though each shell told with terrible effect in their ranks. As soon as I found that the enemy had my direction I ordered Lieutenant Taylor to take his company to the rear and center, and about the time this was completed I received orders from Colonel Fulkerson to take the regiment to the extreme left flank, as the enemy was making an effort to flank our line in that direction. In marching to that position the regiment was subjected to a heavy fire both from cannon and rifle, and I could not, with justice to officers and men, discriminate which acted most gallantly; suffice it to say that each one performed his duty and acted nobly. After arriving at my position, and having formed line of battle, I threw out skirmishers in front, and remained in that position until Colonel Fulkerson ordered me to advance. And here I would notice the gallantry of Capt. John A. Preston, who was so eager to pursue that I was forced to restrain him while advancing. We continued to advance; but when we arrived on the hill we found a routed enemy in rapid retreat. We pursued along the Martinsburg road 4 miles beyond Winchester. At this point, completely exhausted, we gave up farther pursuit.

Before closing I take great pleasure in noticing the prompt and efficient attention of Surg. Casper C. Henkle and Asst. Surg. M. M. Butler. I am also under obligations to Adjutant Wood for prompt attention.

The following is the number of casualties: Aggregate—Killed, 1; wounded, 19.

T. V. WILLIAMS,
*Major, Thirty-seventh Virginia Regiment.*

Captain PENDLETON.

---

## No. 89.

*Report of Capt. George W. Wooding, Virginia (Danville) Artillery, of operations May 23–25.*

CAMP OF DANVILLE ARTILLERY,
*Near Winchester, Va., May* 27, 1862.

COLONEL: In compliance with instructions received from yourself I hereby transmit you a brief report of the operations of my command (the Danville Artillery) during the engagements of May 23, 24, and 25:

On the evening of the 23d I received an order from Colonel Fulkerson to take my rifled piece to the front. I accordingly left the rear of the brigade with my rifled piece, and moved rapidly on toward Front Royal. On reaching that place, about night-fall, I learned that the enemy had been routed and many of them captured by the advance of our army. Seeing no officer at Front Royal to whom I could report, I moved on some 3 miles beyond the town, when, seeing some pieces of artillery which were in advance of mine returning toward Front Royal,

I halted my men upon the road-side and ordered them to encamp during the night, while I returned to the rest of my command, which I found encamped, with your brigade, near where I left you in the evening.

On the morning of the 24th I received an order from Colonel Crutchfield, chief of artillery, to join my rifled piece with the rest of my battery. I accordingly sent forward to have it halted until we came up to it, and during the whole of this day my wearied men and jaded horses marched immediately in rear of your brigade until 2 or 3 o'clock on the morning of the 25th, when we halted until dawn in the road, our horses standing hitched to the pieces and the men lying down upon the roadside.

At dawn, in the same order of march as on the previous day, we marched toward Winchester. When within a short distance of that place, and in distinct hearing of the enemy's artillery and musketry, which had opened upon our advancing column, I received orders to remain in the road until ordered forward. I had been there but a few minutes when an aide to General Jackson ordered me to move forward. He carried my battery to within a short distance of the enemy's, who kept up an incessant fire from our right toward our forces posted on our left, some of their shells passing over us and bursting very near to us. This aide to General Jackson informed me that an officer had been sent to choose a position for my battery to the right of the road. I remained there some thirty minutes, when I saw the enemy commence a swift retreat toward Winchester, and, believing it useless to remain in that position any longer, I, with my battery, joined in the pursuit, which was followed up to this encampment, when we were ordered to halt.

None of my men or horses were injured by the enemy's fire, and the only injury sustained by my command was the natural consequence of weariness and fatigue resulting from long and incessant marching.

Very respectfully, &c.,

GEO. W. WOODING,
*Captain, Commanding Danville Artillery.*

Col. S. V. FULKERSON, *Commanding Third Brigade.*

---

## No. 90.

*Reports of Maj. Gen. Richard S. Ewell, C. S. Army, commanding Third Division, of operations May 23–June 9.*

HEADQUARTERS THIRD DIVISION,
*New Market, Va., June* 4, 1862.

MAJOR: I have the honor to report the movements of this division from Front Royal to Winchester on May 23, 24, and 25:

The attack and decided results at Front Royal, though this division alone participated, were the fruits of Major-General Jackson's personal superintendence and planning. I will therefore merely state that the attack was made by the First Maryland Regiment (Col. Bradley T. Johnson) and Major Wheat's special battalion (Louisiana Volunteers), supported by the Sixth, Seventh, and Eighth Regiments Louisiana Volunteers, Colonel Kelly, of the Eighth Louisiana, leading his regiment through the river under fire of artillery and musketry. The Federals, having retired their infantry under cover of their artillery, ceased firing after the engagement had continued about three hours.

The pursuit was immediately commenced under the direction of

Brigadier-General Steuart (Maryland Line), and was carried on very successfully by the Sixth (Lieutenant-Colonel Flournoy) and Second Cavalry, under Lieutenant-Colonel Watts. These officers pursued with courage and energy, capturing two pieces of artillery, the field and staff officers, and most of the Maryland (Federal) regiment.

A fine Parrott piece, abandoned within 4 miles of Winchester, was brought off, within sight of the enemy's pickets, by Privates Fontaine and Moore (Company I, Sixth Cavalry), who, using two plow horses from a neighboring field, brought it back to Front Royal—a piece of cool daring hard to match.

At 6 o'clock the next morning my division was again moving toward Winchester. The head of the column had marched about 8 miles, when it was halted by Major-General Jackson. The brigades of Generals Elzey and Taylor were detached from my position on the Front Royal and Winchester turnpike and carried by the major-general commanding with his division of the army to the road leading from Strasburg to Winchester. The service there rendered was not under my observation; but the Federal accounts tell of the havoc in their cavalry by the Louisiana Brigade. Brig. Gen. George H. Steuart, with the Second and Sixth Cavalry, cut the enemy's line at Newtown, between Strasburg and Winchester, capturing some hundreds of prisoners, many wagons, &c.

The Seventh Brigade (General Trimble commanding) remained until 5 p. m. where halted by Major-General Jackson, about 8 miles from Front Royal. Seeing then that the enemy were retreating before General Jackson from Strasburg, I immediately ordered Generals Trimble and Steuart to move forward, and reported to the general commanding what I was doing. I received orders on the march to make this movement. The Twenty-first North Carolina, under Colonel Kirkland, drove in the enemy's pickets that evening and held the position 2 miles from Winchester, occasionally skirmishing during the night. The rest of the command slept on their arms about 3 miles from Winchester.

We moved at dawn, and opened the attack at 5.40 a. m., the Twenty-first North Carolina (Colonel Kirkland) and Twenty-first Georgia (Colonel Mercer) gallantly dashing into the western part of the town and driving back the advanced posts of the enemy. The Twenty-first North Carolina was exposed to a murderous fire from a regiment posted behind a stone wall. Both of its field officers were wounded and a large number of privates killed and wounded. They were forced back, retiring in good order and ready to renew the fight. Colonel Mercer, of the Twenty-first Georgia, drove out this Federal regiment and joined the rest of the brigade in the subsequent movements. The Maryland regiment, under Col. Bradley T. Johnson, had been sent into the suburbs on the left, where it remained. As soon as the balance of my command (the Fifteenth Alabama, under Colonel Cantey, and the Sixteenth Mississippi, under Colonel Posey) came on the field I joined them to the Twenty-first Georgia, and, the mist then admitting a better view, I adopted the suggestion of Brigadier-General Trimble and marched them to the right. This movement was immediately followed by a retrograde one of the enemy, soon converted into a flight, as the attack, conducted by General Jackson in person on the south side of the town, was driving them on. The affair was over between 8 and 9 o'clock.

Captain Courtney having been detached on duty connected with his battery, Lieut. J. W. Latimer was in command of Courtney's battery and was exposed during the whole affair to a heavy cannonade. This young officer was conspicuous for the coolness, judgment, and skill with which he managed his battery, fully supporting the high opinion I had formed of his merits.

Captain Brockenbrough brought his battery into action at a later moment and handled it with energy and effect.

The brilliant service rendered by Taylor's brigade, being immediately under the direction of the commanding general, is not included in my report of the operations.

Except the Maryland regiment and the cavalry, the attack on the east of the town was made by the troops of General Trimble's brigade—the Seventh. I am indebted to that officer on more than one occasion for valuable counsel and suggestion.

The Eighth Brigade, General Taylor leading, had the fortune to be so posted as to make a charge, which closed the action.

My personal staff consisted of Lieut. Col. J. M. Jones and Maj. James Barbour, of the Adjutant-General's Department, and Lieuts. G. Campbell Brown and T. T. Turner, aides. These officers performed all the duties required with coolness and efficiency. Capt. Powhatan Robinson and Lieut. J. Innis Randolph, topographical engineers, and Major Snodgrass, Quartermaster's Department, were also on the field.

Above all I was struck by the uncomplaining endurance of the men, marching and fighting almost incessantly for three days without a murmur, willing to endure to the limit of human power, and only asking to come up to the enemy.

I inclose a report of the killed and wounded, except of the cavalry, which I have not been able to procure. I inclose reports of Brigadier-Generals Trimble and Taylor.

Respectfully,

R. S. EWELL, *Major-General.*

Maj. R. L. DABNEY, *Asst. Adjt. Gen., Department of the Valley.*

[Inclosure.]

*Casualties in the Third Division in the actions of May 23, 24, and 25, 1862.*

| Command. | Officers. | | | Non-commissioned officers and privates. | | | Remarks. |
|---|---|---|---|---|---|---|---|
| | Killed. | Wounded. | Missing. | Killed. | Wounded. | Missing. | |
| *Seventh Brigade.* | | | | | | | |
| General TRIMBLE commanding. | | | | | | | |
| 21st North Carolina Infantry Regiment. | 1 | 4 | ...... | 20 | 55 | ....... | 21st N. C.: Captain Ligon killed. Lieutenant-Colonel Pepper and Captain Hedgcock died of wounds. Colonel Kirkland and Lieutenant Beall wounded. |
| 21st Georgia Infantry Regiment. | ...... | 2 | ...... | 1 | 14 | ....... | |
| Total Seventh Brigade.. | 1 | 6 | ...... | 21 | 69 | ....... | |
| *Eighth Brigade.* | | | | | | | |
| General TAYLOR commanding. | | | | | | | |
| Brigade commissary.......... | 1 | ...... | ...... | ...... | ...... | ....... | Major A. Davis, brigade commissary. |
| 7th Louisiana Infantry Regiment. | ...... | ...... | ...... | 5 | 12 | ....... | |
| Wheat's Battalion.............. | ...... | 1 | ...... | 1 | 5 | ....... | Lieutenant Grinnell wounded. |
| 9th Louisiana Infantry Regiment. | ...... | ...... | ...... | 5 | 37 | ....... | |
| 6th Louisiana Infantry Regiment. | 1 | 3 | ...... | 4 | 39 | 3 | Major McArthur killed, and Captains Hanlon and Offutt and Lieutenant Clarke wounded. |
| Total Eighth Brigade.... | 2 | 4 | ...... | 15 | 93 | 3 | |

SUMMARY.

| | Killed. | Wounded. | Missing. | Total. |
|---|---|---|---|---|
| Officers | 3 | 10 | ..... | 13 |
| Non-commissioned officers and privates | 36 | 162 | 3 | 201 |
| Total | 39 | 172 | 3 | 214 |

R. S. EWELL, *Major-General.*

---

HDQRS. THIRD DIV., VALLEY DIST., *June* 16, 1862.

MAJOR: I have the honor to submit the following report of the action of the 8th instant at Cross Keys between the division commanded by me and the forces under Major-General Frémont:

I was ordered on the 7th by the general commanding to occupy the advance, and my division encamped for that night near Union Church. The enemy made a reconnaissance in the afternoon, and going forward I found General Elzey drawing up his own and General Taylor's brigades in position. I at once determined to meet the enemy on the ground selected by General Elzey.

On the morning of the 8th the enemy advanced, driving in the Fifteenth Alabama, Colonel Cantey, from their post on picket. The regiment made a gallant resistance, enabling me to take position at leisure. The camp-fires left by the regiment—no tents or anything else—were the camps from which the enemy report to have driven us. At this time I had present Elzey's, Trimble's, and Steuart's brigades, short of 5,000 men, Taylor's having been ordered to Port Republic. The general features of the ground were a valley and rivulet in my front, woods on both flanks, and a field of some hundreds of acres where the road crossed the center of my line, my side of the valley being more defined and commanding the other. General Trimble's brigade was posted a little in advance of my center on the right, General Elzey in rear of the center, and General Steuart on the left; the artillery was in the center. Both wings were in woods. The center was weak, having open ground in front, where the enemy was not expected. General Elzey was in position to strengthen either wing.

About 10 o'clock the enemy felt along my front with skirmishers, and shortly after posted his artillery, chiefly opposite mine. He advanced under cover on General Trimble with a force, according to his own statement, of two brigades, which were repulsed with such signal loss that they did not make another determined effort. General Trimble had been re-enforced by the Thirteenth and Twenty-fifth Virginia Regiments, Colonel Walker and Lieutenant-Colonel Duffy, of General Elzey's brigade. These regiments assisted in the repulse of the enemy. General Trimble in turn advanced and drove the enemy more than a mile, and remained on his flank ready to make the final attack.

General Taylor, with the Eighth Brigade, composed of Louisiana troops, reported about 2 p. m., and was placed in rear. Colonel Patton, with the Forty-second and Forty-eighth Regiments and Irish Battalion, Virginia Volunteers, also joined, and with the remainder of General Elzey's brigade was added to the center and left, then threatened. I did not push my successes at once, because I had no cavalry, and it was reported, and reaffirmed by Lieutenant Hinrichs, topographical engineer, sent to reconnoiter, that the enemy was moving a large column 2 miles to my left. As soon as I could determine this not to be an attack I advanced both my wings, drove in the enemy's skirmishers, and when night closed was in position on the ground previously held by the enemy, ready to attack him at dawn.

My troops were recalled to join in the attack at Port Republic. The enemy's attack was decided by 4 p. m., it being principally directed against General Trimble, and, though from their own statement they outnumbered us on that flank two to one, it had signally failed. General Trimble's command, including the two regiments on his right, under Colonel Walker, is entitled to the highest praise for the gallant manner in which it repulsed the enemy's main attack. His brigade captured one of their colors.

As before mentioned, the credit of selecting the position is due to General Elzey. I availed myself frequently during the action of that officer's counsel, profiting largely by his known military skill and judgment. He was much exposed. His horse was wounded early in the action, and at a later period of the day was killed by a rifle-ball, which, at the same time, inflicted upon the rider a wound that forced him to retire from the field. He was more particularly employed in the center, directing the artillery. General George H. Steuart was severely wounded, after rendering valuable aid in command of the left.

I had Courtney's, Brockenbrough's, Raine's, and Lusk's batteries. The enemy testifies to the efficiency of their fire. Captain Courtney opened the fight, and was for hours exposed to a terrible storm of shot and shell. He and Captain Brockenbrough have been under my observation since the campaign opened, and I can testify to their efficiency on this as on former occasions. The loss in all the batteries shows the warmth of the fire. I was well satisfied with them all.

The history of the Maryland regiment, gallantly commanded by Col. Bradley T. Johnson, during the campaign of the valley, would be the history of every action from Front Royal to Cross Keys.

On the 6th instant, near Harrisonburg, the Fifty-eighth Virginia Regiment was engaged with the Pennsylvania Bucktails, the fighting being close and bloody. Colonel Johnson came up with his regiment in the hottest period of the affair, and by a dashing charge in flank drove the enemy off with heavy loss, capturing the lieutenant-colonel (Kane) commanding. In commemoration of their gallant conduct I ordered one of the captured bucktails to be appended as a trophy to their flag.

The gallantry of the regiment on this occasion is worthy of acknowledgment from a higher source, more particularly as they avenged the death of the gallant General Ashby, who fell at the same time. Two color-bearers were shot down in succession, but each time the colors were caught before reaching the ground, and were finally borne by Corporal Shanks to the close of the action.

On the 8th instant, at Cross Keys, they were opposed to three of the enemy's regiments in succession.

My staff at Cross Keys consisted of Lieut. Col. J. M. Jones and Maj. James Barbour, Adjutant-General's Department; Lieuts. G. Campbell Brown and T. T. Turner, aides, and Capt. Hugh M. Nelson, volunteer aide. These officers were much exposed during the day, and were worked hard over an extensive field. Their services were valuable, and were rendered with zeal and ability. Lieutenant Brown was painfully wounded by a fragment of shell toward the close of the fight.

I append a list of casualties, showing 42 killed, and 287 killed, wounded, and missing.* I buried my dead and brought off all the

* List shows 41 killed and 288 total.

wounded except a few, whose mortal agonies would have been uselessly increased by any change of position.

Some of the enemy's wounded were brought off and arrangements made for moving them all, when I was ordered to another field. There are good reasons for estimating their loss at not less than 2,000 in killed, wounded, and prisoners. On one part of the field they buried 101 at one spot, 15 at another, and a house containing some of their dead was said to have been burned by them, and this only a part of what they lost. They were chiefly of Blenker's division, notorious for months on account of their thefts and dastardly insults to women and children in that part of the State under Federal domination.

The order of march of General Frémont was found on a staff officer left in our hands. It shows seven brigades of infantry, besides numerous cavalry. I had three small brigades during the greater part of the action, and no cavalry at any time. They made no bayonet charge, nor did they commit any particular ravages with grape or canister, although they state otherwise. Colonel Mercer and the Twenty-first Georgia tried to close with them three times, partly succeeding in overtaking them once. That officer is represented to have handled his regiment with great skill, and, with the Sixteenth Mississippi, Colonel Posey, was the closest engaged.

Brigadier-General Trimble, Seventh Brigade, had the brunt of the action, and is entitled to most thanks. Col. Bradley T. Johnson (First Maryland), Col. Carnot Posey (Sixteenth Mississippi), Col. J. T. Mercer (Twenty-first Georgia), Captain Courtney (of the Courtney Battery) are officers who were enabled to render highly valuable service.

I regret that I cannot go more into details of those lower in rank, whose gallant services are recompensed by the esteem of their comrades and their own self-approval; after all, the highest and most enduring record.

I inclose a copy of General Frémont's order of march on the day of battle, and detailed reports of the killed and wounded, names and regiments of the officers killed and wounded, and tabular statements of the same according to regiments; also the official report of Col. J. A. Walker, commanding the Fourth Brigade.

Respectfully,

R. S. EWELL,
*Major-General.*

Maj. R. L. DABNEY, *Asst. Adjt. Gen., Valley District.*

[Inclosure No. 1.]

*Casualties in Third Division, action of June 6, near Harrisonburg.*

| Command. | Killed. | | Wounded. | | Missing. | | Aggregate. | Remarks. |
|---|---|---|---|---|---|---|---|---|
| | Officers. | Enlisted men. | Officers. | Enlisted men. | Officers. | Enlisted men. | | |
| *Second Brigade.* | | | | | | | | |
| 1st Maryland | 2 | 4 | ...... | 11 | ...... | ...... | 17 | Capt. Michael S. Robertson and Lieut. Nicholas Snowden killed. |
| 58th Virginia | 1 | 10 | ...... | 39 | ...... | 3 | 53 | Lieut. T. A. Wright killed. |
| Total | 3 | 14 | ...... | 50 | ...... | 3 | 70 | |

[Inclosure No. 2.]

*Casualties in Third Division, action of June 8, near Cross Keys.*

| Command. | Killed. | | Wounded. | | Missing. | | Aggregate. | Remarks. |
|---|---|---|---|---|---|---|---|---|
| | Officers. | Enlisted men. | Officers. | Enlisted men. | Officers. | Enlisted men. | | |
| Division staff | | | 1 | | | | 1 | Capt. G. C. Brown, aide-de-camp, wounded. |
| *Second Brigade.* | | | | | | | | |
| Field and staff | | | 1 | | | | 1 | Brig. Gen. George H. Steuart wounded severely. |
| 1st Maryland | | | 1 | 27 | | | 28 | Lieut. Hezekiah H. Bean wounded. |
| 44th Virginia | | 1 | 1 | 2 | | | 4 | Capt. John T. Martin wounded. |
| 52d Virginia | 1 | 1 | 4 | 20 | | | 26 | Lieut. [C. M.] King killed, and Maj. John D. H. Ross, Lieuts. S. Paul and T. D. Ranson, and Assist. Surg. John Lewis wounded. |
| 58th Virginia | | | | 5 | | | 5 | |
| Brockenbrough's battery | | 2 | | | | | 2 | |
| Lusk's battery | | 2 | | 3 | | | 5 | |
| Total | 1 | 6 | 8 | 57 | | | 72 | |
| *Fourth Brigade.* | | | | | | | | |
| Field and staff | | | 1 | | | | 1 | Brig. Gen. Arnold Elzey wounded. |
| 12th Georgia | | 2 | | 11 | | | 13 | |
| 13th Virginia | | 2 | 1 | 13 | | 1 | 17 | Lieut. R. C Macon wounded. |
| Raine's battery | | 2 | | 7 | | 8 | 17 | |
| Total | | 6 | 2 | 31 | | 9 | 48 | |
| *Seventh Brigade.* | | | | | | | | |
| Brigadier-General TRIMBLE commanding. | | | | | | | | |
| 15th Alabama | 2 | 7 | 2 | 35 | 1 | 4 | 51 | Capt. R. H. Hill and Lieut. W. B. Mills killed, Lieuts. H. C. Brainard and A. A. McIntosh wounded, and Lieut. W. T. Berry missing. |
| 21st Georgia | | 4 | 1 | 22 | | 1 | 28 | Lieut. J. M. Mack wounded. |
| 16th Mississippi | | 6 | 3 | 25 | | | 34 | Col. Carnot Posey and Lieuts. J. B. Coleman and W. R. Brown wounded. |
| 21st North Carolina | | 2 | 1 | 10 | | | 13 | Lieut. L. T. Whitlock wounded. |
| Courtney's battery | | 2 | | 10 | | | 12 | |
| Total | 2 | 21 | 7 | 102 | 1 | 5 | 138 | |
| *Eighth Brigade.* | | | | | | | | |
| Brig. Gen. RICHARD TAYLOR commanding. | | | | | | | | |
| 7th Louisiana | | 1 | 1 | 7 | | | 9 | Capt. —— Green wounded. |
| 8th Louisiana | | 1 | | 7 | | | 8 | |
| Total | | 2 | 1 | 14 | | | 17 | |
| *Patton's Brigade.* | | | | | | | | |
| Col. J. M. PATTON commanding. | | | | | | | | |
| 42d Virginia* | | | | 3 | | | 3 | |
| 48th Virginia* | | 3 | 1 | 6 | | | 10 | |
| Total | | 3 | 1 | 9 | | | 13 | |
| Grand total | 3 | 38 | 19 | 213 | 1 | 14 | 288 | |

* See Second Brigade, Jackson's division, report No. 60, p. 717.

[Inclosure No. 3.]

MOUNTAIN DEPARTMENT, HEADQUARTERS IN THE FIELD,
*Harrisonburg, Va., June* 8, 1862.

*Order of march.*

ADVANCE GUARD.

1. Colonel Cluseret's brigade.
2. The pioneers of all brigades, as also the ax-men of every regiment, to start at 5 a. m.
3. Fourth New York Cavalry.
4. General Stahel's brigade, with Bucktail Rifles as flankers, at 5.30 a. m.

MAIN COLUMN.

5. Cavalry, under command of Colonel Zagonyi, at 5.45 a. m.
6. General Milroy's brigade, at 6 a. m.
7. General Schenck's brigade, at 6.15 a. m.
8. General Steinwehr's brigade, at 6.30 a. m.
9. General brigade train, at 6.45 a. m.

REAR GUARD.

10. General Bayard's brigade.

Each regiment to be accompanied by its ambulances and a sufficient number of wagons to carry their cooking utensils.

The train will move in the order of brigades.

All horses unable to perform service to be left at this place until further orders.

By order of Major-General Frémont:

ALBERT TRACY,
*Colonel and Assistant Adjutant-General.*

---

HDQRS. THIRD DIV., DEPT. OF NORTHERN VIRGINIA,
*July* 8, 1862.

MAJOR: I have the honor to report the movements of my division in the battle near Port Republic on June 9:

When I received the order to march to Port Republic, to join in the attack on the forces under General Shields, my command included, in addition to my own division, the Second Brigade of the Army of the Valley District. This brigade, under the command of Col. J. M. Patton, had been attached to my command during the engagement of the day before.

My command had been engaged with General Frémont throughout the day on June 8, and slept upon their arms. The brigades commanded by General Trimble and Colonel Patton (except one regiment) and the Seventh Louisiana Regiment, Colonel Hays, had before night closed in been advanced within range of the enemy's musketry.

Day was breaking on the morning of June 9 before these troops commenced their march from this position to the other field at Port Republic, 7 miles distant, some of them without food for twenty-four hours.

The commands of General Trimble and Colonel Patton were kept in position to hold the enemy under Frémont in check, and keep him from advancing upon Port Republic or taking any part in the engagement on that day. The difficulty in effecting the crossing of the South Branch of the river at Port Republic occasioned a delay, which separated the forces in my command. When I reached the field the Eighth Louisiana Brigade, commanded by General Taylor, had been sent by Major-General Jackson, under cover of the woods, to attack the enemy in flank and rear. One of the regiments of the Second Brigade of my division was detached to the left, and I placed the Fifty-eighth, Colonel Scott, and the Forty-fourth Virginia, Colonel Letcher, under cover of the woods, with the flank toward the enemy. When, after a severe struggle, from the advantage of position and numbers, the enemy were driving back our forces on the left and the flank of the advancing enemy (at least two brigades) came in front, an advance was ordered. The two regiments, bravely led by Colonel Scott, rushed with a shout upon the enemy, taking him in flank. For the first time that day the enemy was then driven back in disorder for some hundreds of yards. At the same instant, while our artillery was retiring rapidly from the field, one piece was halted and opened fire upon the enemy, showing great quickness and decision in the officer commanding it. These efforts checked the enemy so long that, although Colonel Scott's command was driven back to the woods with severe loss, there was time to rally and lead them to the assistance of the Eighth Brigade, General R. Taylor commanding, which was heard engaging the enemy far to their rear. The remnants of the two regiments reached General Taylor at the moment when, as shown in his report, fresh troops of the enemy had driven him from the battery he had captured. His brigade formed and advanced with these two regiments, and the enemy fled a second time from the battery and the field after exchanging a few shots.

The credit of first checking the enemy and then assisting in his final repulse and of the capture of the battery is due to these two regiments. It would be difficult to find another instance of volunteer troops after a severe check rallying and again attacking the enemy.

To General Taylor and his brigade belongs the honor of deciding two battles—that of Winchester and this one. As soon as his fire was heard in rear and flank the whole force of the enemy turned to meet this new foe.

Colonel Walker, commanding Fourth Brigade, ordered by the major-general commanding to follow the Eighth Brigade, was lost in the mountains, reported to me, and joined in the pursuit.

General Trimble, commanding Seventh Brigade, with part of Colonel Patton's command, was left to hold Frémont in check. The Fifty-second Virginia Regiment was detailed, and fought on the left flank with General Winder.

Colonel Scott reports:

> I particularly commend the gallantry of Lieutenant Walker, Company E, Forty-fourth Virginia. There may have been others equally worthy of commendation, but I could not fail to notice him. When the brigade halted in the field and sat down he alone stood erect, went in front, and attempted to get the brigade to advance still nearer the enemy.

I indorse this report and recommend the officer to executive favor.

Lieut. Col. J. M. Jones, Maj. James Barbour, Lieut. T. T. Turner, and Capt. Hugh M. Nelson, of my staff, rendered invaluable service in rallying the broken troops. Lieut. G. Campbell Brown was absent, owing to the wound received the day previous.

I inclose sub-reports of Colonel Scott and General Taylor; also a detailed list of killed and wounded, amounting to 78 killed and 533 wounded and 4 missing; in all, 615 killed, wounded, and missing.

Respectfully, &c.,

R. S. EWELL,
*Major-General.*

Maj. R. L. DABNEY, *Asst. Adjt. Gen., Valley District.*

[Inclosure.]

*Casualties in Third Division, action of June 9, near Port Republic.*

| Command. | Killed. | | Wounded. | | Missing. | | Aggregate. | Remarks. |
|---|---|---|---|---|---|---|---|---|
| | Officers. | Men. | Officers. | Men. | Officers. | Men. | | |
| *Second Brigade.* | | | | | | | | |
| Col. W. C. SCOTT commanding. | | | | | | | | |
| 1st Maryland | | | | 1 | | | | |
| 44th Virginia | 1 | 13 | 3 | 32 | | | | Lieut. William T. Robertson killed, and Capts. John S. Anderson and T. R. Buckner and Lieut. J. M. Hughes wounded. |
| 52d Virginia | 1 | 11 | 4 | 61 | | | | Capt. Benjamin T. Walton killed, and Lieuts. S. B. Brown, John N. Hanna, L. Harman, and James A. White wounded. |
| 58th Virginia | 1 | 3 | 3 | 65 | | | | Lieut. George W. Teaford killed, and Capt. John P. Moore and Lieuts. E. C. Hurt and W. C. Ridgway wounded. |
| Total | 3 | 27 | 10 | 159 | | | 199 | |
| *Fourth Brigade.* | | | | | | | | |
| Col. J. A. WALKER commanding. | | | | | | | | |
| Field and staff | 1 | | | | | | | Maj. J. H. Chenoweth killed. |
| 12th Georgia | | | | | | | | No loss reported. |
| 13th Virginia | | | | 1 | | | | |
| 25th Virginia | | | 4 | 25 | | | | Capt. William T. Gammon and Lieuts. E. D. Camden, J. J. Dunkle, and John H. Johnson wounded. |
| 31st Virginia | 2 | 12 | 3 | 76 | | 4 | | Capt. Robert H. Bradshaw and Lieut. A. Whitley killed, and Lieuts. Jonathan W. Arnett, J. M. Burns, and W. C. Kincaid wounded. |
| Total | 3 | 12 | 7 | 102 | | 4 | 128 | |
| *Eighth Brigade.* | | | | | | | | |
| Brigadier-General TAYLOR commanding. | | | | | | | | |
| 6th Louisiana | 1 | 10 | 2 | 53 | | | | Capt. Isaac A. Smith killed, and Lieuts. Thomas P. Farrar and James O. Martin wounded. |
| 7th Louisiana | 1 | 7 | 5 | 110 | | | | Lieut. J. H. Dedlake killed, Lieut. Col. C. De Choiseul died of wounds, Col. H. T. Hays and Lieuts. James M. Brooks, W. C. Driver, and L. Pendergast wounded. |
| 8th Louisiana | 1 | 7 | 3 | 27 | | | | Lieut. A. G. Moore killed, and Lieuts. Robert Montgomery, Augustus Randolph, and G. L. P. Wren wounded. |
| 9th Louisiana | 1 | 3 | | 36 | | | | Lieut. W. Meizell killed. |
| Wheat's Battalion | | 2 | 5 | 14 | | | | Lieuts. E. H. Cockcroft, John Coyle, F. P. McCarthy, Bruce Putnam, and Thaddeus A. Ripley wounded. |
| Total | 4 | 29 | 15 | 240 | | | 288 | |
| Grand total | 10 | 68 | 32 | 501 | | 4 | 615 | |

## No. 91.

*Reports of Col. W. C. Scott, Forty-fourth Virginia Infantry, commanding Second Brigade, of operations May 23–June 9.*

———, ——— —, 1862.

### FRONT ROYAL, VA.

When within 2 or 3 miles of Front Royal I received a message from Maj. Gen. T. J. Jackson to send forward as rapidly as possible all the rifled pieces of artillery in my brigade. I did so, by sending forward Captain Lusk with his two rifled pieces, which I understood did excellent execution.

The battle was over before my brigade reached the field of battle, and of course none of our men were killed or wounded.

### WINCHESTER, VA.

My brigade was ordered upon the left of the road to support the attack made on the enemy by General Taylor. Ultimately I was ordered to form line of battle facing to Winchester and to march to the front. I did so, but while the brigade was marching in beautiful order and before it reached the crest of the hill I ascertained that the enemy had taken to flight. Hence I lost no man in this engagement.

W. C. SCOTT,
*Colonel, Commanding Brigade.*

—

——— —, 1862.

The brigade now commanded by me was commanded by General George H. Steuart. It was annexed to the First Maryland, previously under the command of that officer. The whole brigade, having advanced in this direction about 4 miles this side of Harrisonburg, were marched back through the woods toward Harrisonburg, for the purpose of cutting off a regiment of the enemy which we understood was following us. The Fifty-eighth Virginia was leading, the First Maryland next, the Forty-fourth Virginia next, and the Fifty-second Virginia last. We marched by the right flank. The Fifty-eighth was first engaged; the others drawn up in line of battle in the woods. Ultimately General Steuart led the First Maryland and Forty-fourth by the right flank toward the main road, and then, bending around toward the right, approached the place of combat, but halted them in the woods when within 100 or 200 yards of that place.

We had remained halted but a few minutes when General Ewell ordered us to charge bayonets. The First Maryland and Forty-fourth Virginia dashed forward at a rapid rate and with loud cheers, until they came up with the Fifty-eighth, and on delivering their first fire the enemy fled with precipitation. I am not sure they were not fleeing before, as I could not run as fast as the men and did not get up so soon as they did. The Fifty-eighth bore the brunt of the battle and fought gallantly. As re-enforcements were advancing on the part of the enemy we were ordered to retire toward the rear. The Fifty-second did not accompany these movements, but remained in the woods, drawn up in line of battle, where the brigade was first formed, Colonel Skinner, the commander, informing me that he heard no orders to move.

In this action the Fifty-eighth lost 11 killed and 39 wounded and 3 missing. The Forty-fourth and Fifty-second lost none. I do not know the loss of the First Maryland.

Respectfully submitted.

W. C. SCOTT,
*Colonel, Forty-fourth Regiment Virginia Volunteers.*

P. S.—In this action General Ashby was killed.

---

HEADQUARTERS BRIGADE,
*Camp near Mount Meridian, Va., June 14, 1862.*

GENERAL: In regard to the action of the 6th I have only this to remark, that the Fifty-eighth Regiment was the right and leading regiment of the brigade and first came in contact with the enemy, but as the brigade was then under the command of Brigadier-General Steuart I do not know personally what transpired with that regiment. The other regiments—the First Maryland and the Forty-fourth and Fifty-second Virginia—were drawn up in line of battle in the woods in the rear of the Fifty-eighth. After the firing had continued for some time General Steuart led the First Maryland (the leading regiment) toward the turnpike by the right flank, followed by the Forty-fourth, and thence up the fence toward the place from which the firing emanated and halted. The Fifty-second did not follow these movements, as the commander, Colonel Skinner, says he heard no orders, but remained drawn up in the woods. Ultimately you gave the command "charge" to the First Maryland and Forty-fourth, which they did in gallant style until they reached the fence, when, pouring in a volley on the enemy, they fled in great precipitation.

On the 8th the Fifty-second and Fifty-eighth were posted so as to support the batteries on your left wing. The Forty-fourth was divided into two parts, and thrown forward a considerable distance to skirmish the woods on the left and the woods near the main road in front. That part which was ordered to skirmish the woods near the main road in front first came in contact with the enemy, but being too weak to defend itself it fell back, and united with the other portion of that regiment in the woods near your left most advanced battery. At this point the Forty-fourth, numbering not more than 130 men, was attacked by two regiments of the enemy, and after exchanging a few rounds the Forty-fourth charged them gallantly with the bayonet and broke them, chasing them a considerable distance, killing several and taking some prisoners.

On the 9th the Fifty-second was detached and sent forward on our left to support General Winder, I think. When General Winder was driven back the Fifty-second went forward, but was driven back also. The Forty-fourth and Fifty-eighth were placed in a wood on our right wing. You were with them. You know all about the order to charge, the way in which the order was executed, the retirement of these regiments to the wood in consequence of being overpowered, and their being rallied by you, and the ultimate charge under you by a part of the brigade.

The casualties have been sent to General Jackson, from whom you can obtain them. I do not recollect them.

I particularly commend to you the gallantry of Lieutenant Walker, Company E, Forty-fourth Regiment Virginia Volunteers. There may have been others equally worthy of commendation, but I could not fail to notice him. When the brigade halted in the field and sat down he alone stood erect, went in front, and attempted to get the brigade to advance still nearer the enemy.

Very respectfully, your obedient servant,

W. C. SCOTT,
*Commanding Brigade.*

Major-General EWELL.

---

PORT REPUBLIC, VA.,
———, —, 1862.

In this action [near Cross-Keys] in the early part of the day I only commanded the Forty-fourth Regiment. The Fifty-eighth Virginia was placed in rear of our batteries on the left flank to support them. The Fifty-second was farther in the rear. The Forty-fourth was divided into two parts and each part thrown forward as skirmishers. One part, under Major Cobb, skirmished the wood near our most advanced battery on our left; the other part, under Captain Buckner, skirmished the woods near the main road to our front. This latter first came in contact with the enemy, and being overpowered, retired and formed a junction with the first part. They were then attacked by two regiments of the enemy, and after the exchange of a few rounds the Forty-fourth, under Major Cobb, gallantly charged them with the bayonet, drove them back, and charged them, killing several (1 with the bayonet) and taking 5 prisoners. The Forty-fourth numbered in the fight about 120 or 130 men. The Forty-fourth and Fifty-eighth then united, but, the enemy not approaching very near except the sharpshooters, there was no regular fight. I do not know the locality of the Fifty-second in the evening, as I was with the Forty-fourth and Fifty-eighth, and momentarily expected an attack.

In this engagement the Forty-fourth lost 1 killed and 3 wounded. The Fifty-second had 2 killed and 24 wounded, and the Fifty-eighth none killed and 5 wounded. Lusk's battery 2 killed and 3 wounded. Total, 5 killed and 35 wounded.

Respectfully submitted.

W. C. SCOTT,
*Commanding Brigade.*

P. S.—In this action Major Ross, of the Fifty-second, was wounded; so was General Steuart.

---

HDQRS. SECOND BRIGADE, ARMY OF THE NORTHWEST,
*Camp near Mount Meridian, Va., June* 14, 1862.

MAJOR: In obedience to your order I beg leave to submit to you the following report of the operations of my brigade in the battle of the 9th instant near Port Republic:

On arriving on the field of battle the Fifty-second Regiment, under Lieutenant-Colonel Skinner, was ordered to take position on the left flank, in order to support General Winder's brigade, then engaged with the enemy. The Forty-fourth and Fifty-eighth, under my command, were ordered to take position in the woods on the right of the road and on our right flank, in the rear of General Taylor's brigade, which was thrown forward for the purpose of cutting off the most advanced batteries of the enemy. We were ordered to support General Taylor. In a short time after the Fifty-second reached their position on our left flank General Winder's brigade was driven back, and the Fifty-second, advancing to their support, was also overpowered and driven back, and the enemy advanced. Seeing this, General Ewell ordered my brigade, now consisting of the Forty-fourth and Fifty-eighth, to charge the enemy diagonally across the field. This they did with loud cheers, which caused the enemy to fall back, but as General Ewell was with the brigade the remainder of the battle I refer you to his report for an account of its subsequent operations.

In this action Lieutenant Walker, of Company E, in the Forty-fourth Regiment, highly distinguished himself for his gallantry.

The Fifty-eighth had 4 killed and 18 wounded. The Forty-fourth had 15 killed and 35 wounded, nearly one-half of those present at the battle. The Fifty-second had 12 killed and 65 wounded and 7 missing. Among these were Lieut. G. W. Leaford killed, and Capt. John P. Moore and Lieut. W. C. Ridgway wounded, in the Fifty-eighth; Lieut. William T. Robertson killed, and Capts. John T. Martin, Thomas R. Buckner, John S. Anderson, and Lieuts. John W. Omohundro and James M. Hughes wounded, in the Forty-fourth; Capt. B. T. Walton killed, and Lieuts. Lewis Harman, S. B. Brown, John N. Hanna, and James A. White wounded, in the Fifty-second.

Very respectfully, your obedient servant,

W. C. SCOTT,
*Commanding Brigade.*

Maj. R. L. DABNEY,
*Adjutant-General, Valley District.*

---

## No. 92.

***Report of Col. J. A. Walker, Thirteenth Virginia Infantry, commanding Fourth Brigade, of operations June 8–9.***

HEADQUARTERS FOURTH BRIGADE,
*June* 14, 1862.

I have the honor to report the movements of the regiments under my command on the 8th and 9th of the present month:

On the morning of the 8th General Elzey ordered me to take my own (Thirteenth Virginia) and the Twenty-fifth Virginia Regiment, Lieutenant-Colonel Duffy commanding, and proceed to the right of our lines to prevent an attempt to turn that flank. We moved by the right flank until I thought we were on the enemy's extreme left, and then, sending two companies forward, under the command of Lieutenant-Colonel Terrill, as skirmishers, we advanced in line across the cleared ground and through the wood beyond without encountering the enemy.

When the skirmishers reached the skirt of the woods near Ever's house they reported a large body of the enemy close at hand. I halted my command, and going forward to reconnoiter, found a large force of infantry, probably a brigade, and a battery in a wheat field, about 400 yards from our position. Finding myself entirely separated from our troops on the left, and perceiving the enemy were moving a regiment through the woods to our right, I deemed it best to withdraw to the woods and await the coming of other troops. I did so, and encountered General Trimble's brigade advancing on our left. General Trimble informed me that he was going forward to charge the enemy's battery, and directed me to advance on his right. This I did, again sending Colonel Terrill forward with the skirmishers. He soon encountered the enemy's skirmishers that had followed us into the woods. After a brief but active skirmish they were driven back with the loss of several killed and wounded, among the latter an aid of General Blenker.

We again moved forward, under cover of Ever's house and barn, until ordered by General Trimble to move more to the right, so as to leave the house and barn on my left. In moving by the right flank to gain this position we received a heavy volley of musketry from a Yankee force on our left, which wounded several of the Twenty-fifth Regiment, and almost at the same instant the right of the Thirteenth Regiment came into full view of a battery of three pieces, supported by three regiments of infantry, and not more than 400 yards in front. The battery opened a well-directed and heavy fire with grape, which, owing to the unexpected nature of the attack, caused some confusion, but, order having been restored, the troops advanced steadily to the front to a fence 50 yards farther in advance. Finding General Trimble's brigade was detained by a force on our left, I ordered the men to lie down and fire. This they did with such effect as to twice drive the enemy from one of their guns. The fire of the enemy was galling, and seeing no further good could be accomplished by remaining longer in my position, I moved again by the right flank to the cover of a wood and halted. About this time the enemy fell back and I was ordered to remain in my position. About sundown I was directed by General Trimble to join him on the left, which I did, and remained with his brigade until ordered back to camp about 10 o'clock at night. The men and officers of both regiments were exposed to a terrible fire for a few moments, and behaved to my entire satisfaction.

For a report of the operations of the Twelfth Georgia and Thirty-first Virginia Volunteers on the 8th I beg leave to refer to the report of the commanders of the respective regiments, marked A and B.* Lists of the killed and wounded will be found inclosed for each regiment. The report from Raine's battery will be sent as soon as received.

On the 9th I was placed in command of the Fourth Brigade, General Elzey having been wounded on the preceding day. After crossing the river I reported to Major-General Jackson, who ordered me to send one regiment and my battery (Raine's) to support General Winder. I detached the Thirty-first Virginia Regiment, under command of Colonel Hoffman, for this purpose, and saw no more of the regiment or battery during the day. The accompanying report, marked C,* of Colonel Hoffman, will show the operations of his regiment, which I regret to say was badly cut up, being placed in a very exposed position for some time.

With the three remaining regiments, Thirteenth, Twenty-fifth Virginia, and Twelfth Georgia, I was ordered to follow General Taylor's brigade. I attempted to do this, but, having no guide and being totally unacquainted with the nature of the ground, we became entangled in the thick undergrowth and made slow progress, until we arrived at a precipice so matted and grown over with laurel and ivy that we could ad-

* Not found.

vance no farther in that direction. I then marched back and around the end of the bluff, and pushed forward rapidly in the direction of the heavy firing on the right; but just as we came in sight of General Taylor's brigade he had succeeded in taking the enemy's battery, and we were left no part but to follow the retiring foe, which we did until ordered back.

The total casualties in the four infantry regiments were:

| | Killed. | Wounded. | Missing. | Total. |
|---|---|---|---|---|
| On the 8th instant | 5 | 62 | ...... | 67 |
| On the 9th | 15 | 80 | 4 | 99 |
| Total | 20 | 142 | 4 | 166 |

In Raine's battery there were 2 killed and 7 wounded and 18 horses killed or disabled. Lists of the casualties in each regiment are herewith appended.

Respectfully, your obedient servant,

J. A. WALKER,
*Colonel Thirteenth Virginia Vols., Comdg. Fourth Brigade.*

Maj. JAMES BARBOUR,
*Assistant Adjutant-General.*

---

## No. 93.

*Report of Col. Z. T. Conner, Twelfth Georgia Infantry, of action at Front Royal, May* 30.

WINCHESTER, *May* 30, 1862—6.30 p. m.

GENERAL: Just arrived here. Enemy in close pursuit. Shields has been crossing at Berry's Ferry with a large army all day, at least 12,000 men. Unless you can throw re-enforcements here by morning all will be gone.

Your obedient servant,

Z. T. CONNER,
*Colonel Twelfth Georgia Volunteers.*

Major-General EWELL.

[Indorsement.] *

This letter was written by Colonel Conner after abandoning his regiment and flying to Winchester from Front Royal, with the impression that the whole regiment had been captured. Major Hawkins tried to surrender it, but the men refused to give up, and Captain Brown (nearly sixty years of age) took command and brought the regiment safely to Winchester. Colonel Conner was arrested by General Jackson and finally resigned. He was a brave man, but thrown off his balance by responsibility.

---

* Probably of General Ewell.

## No. 94.

*Reports of Brig. Gen. Isaac R. Trimble, C. S. Army, commanding Seventh Brigade, of operations May 25–June 9.*

GENERAL: In compliance with your order I report the losses and principal incidents in the action of yesterday, 25th, at Winchester:

The night previous the Twenty-first North Carolina Regiment, Colonel Kirkland, had been employed in advance as skirmishers, and reached a point about 2½ miles from the town. By daylight they moved forward, driving the enemy's pickets before them, and arrived at a point 1 mile from Winchester by 6 a. m., where it was seen the enemy were drawn up in line of battle in the southwest part of the town.

The Sixteenth Mississippi (Colonel Posey), Twenty-first Georgia, (Colonel Mercer), and Fifteenth Alabama (Colonel Cantey), preceded by Courtney's artillery, of six pieces, followed rapidly on the Winchester road, and all reached the hill, a mile from town, about 7 a. m. Soon after the Twenty-first North Carolina was ordered to advance into town, and was gallantly led forward by Colonel Kirkland until he encountered a destructive fire from ambuscades behind stone walls. He continued to advance, under a galling fire, until supported by the Twenty-first Georgia, Colonel Mercer, who, seeing the position of the enemy, was enabled to drive them by a flank movement quickly from their position into the city, as also a battery of the enemy just posted. The Twenty-first North Carolina and Twenty-first Georgia were then removed, the latter advancing to an eminence on the east of the town, threatening his flank. Courtney's artillery had taken a position on a hill 1 mile from the town, but after a few shots the fog became so dense as to obscure for half an hour both the town and valley.

At about 8 o'clock the fog dispersed, when the Sixteenth Mississippi was moved down the hill within view of the enemy, and took a position on the east of the town, in readiness to make a movement on the enemy's left flank. This movement, with that of the Twenty-first Georgia, no doubt had an immediate influence in deciding the result of the day, as half an hour after a heavy force of the enemy, supposed to be his reserve, was seen to march in good order out of the town and take a northern direction behind woods and was soon lost to our view.

As the fog rose Courtney's artillery opened a rapid fire on the enemy's batteries posted on a hill in the suburbs of the town. For half an hour the fire exchanged between these batteries was incessant and well directed on both sides, displaying a scene of surpassing interest and grandeur on that sunny but far from peaceful Sabbath.

The battle on the west hills of the town, where General Jackson commanded, had raged incessantly, with the single interruption caused by the fog, and about 9 o'clock a hearty cheer from that scene of conflict told the success made on the right flank of the enemy, who were seen fleeing in broken masses toward the Martinsburg turnpike.

At this time I received your order to advance on the enemy's flank and cut them off. Had this movement been permitted half an hour sooner (prevented by causes known to you) the retreat of the enemy's reserves would have been completely cut off. The delay of this half hour enabled them to get so far the start of us that it was impossible to get a further view of them during the next two hours, in which time my brigade was marched 9 miles, until recalled by your order.

I subjoin a list of killed and wounded:

The Twenty-first North Carolina Regiment, as perfect as can now be made out: Killed, 21; wounded, 55—privates, by two discharges.

Among the wounded are Colonel Kirkland, Lieutenant-Colonel Pepper, badly; Captain Hedgcock, badly; Lieutenant Beall and 6 other officers. Captain Ligon, killed.

The Twenty-first Georgia Regiment, Colonel Mercer: Killed, 1; wounded, 16. Among the wounded are 2 officers, Lieutenants Butler and Easley.

The pluck and enthusiasm displayed by my brigade in marching, hungry and partly barefoot, to overtake the retreating foe, and the ready courage and calmness with which they encountered the enemy and met his fire, and the readiness with which my staff officers bore orders cannot be too highly commended.

I have the honor to be, respectfully, yours,

I. R. TRIMBLE,
*Brigadier-General.*

Maj. Gen. R. S. EWELL,
*Commanding Third Division.*

---

HEADQUARTERS SEVENTH BRIGADE,
*Brown's Gap, Va., June* 11, 1862.

In compliance with the orders of Major-General Ewell I send a statement of the operations of my brigade on the 8th and 9th instant in the battle of Cross Keys:

At your request I rode forward with you on the morning of the 8th at about 10 o'clock to examine the ground most desirable for defense. It was decided to post my artillery (Courtney battery) on the hill to the south of the small stream, and immediately on the left of the road from Union Church to Port Republic. You directed my brigade to take the right of our line of defense and occupy the pine hill to the east of the road and the battery, but somewhat retired from the front, *en échelon* position. Previous to assigning my brigade its position in line of battle I rode forward in front and to the right about half a mile, and examined a wooded hill running nearly parallel to our line of battle. Finding this position advantageous, with its left in view and protected by my artillery and its right by a ravine and densely-wooded hill, I at once occupied this position with two regiments (the Sixteenth Mississippi and Twenty-first Georgia) about 10.30 o'clock, leaving the Twenty-first North Carolina with the battery to protect it.

Colonel Cantey, of the Fifteenth Alabama, by General Ewell's orders, had been left on picket at Union Church, one mile in advance. This regiment was the first engaged, resisting the enemy's advance by a destructive fire from the church, the grave-yard, and the woods. Their force was checked, and they did not pursue the regiment, which soon after retired, finding itself outflanked on right and left, and narrowly escaped being cut entirely off from the failure of [the] cavalry picket to do their duty. Colonel Cantey's own pickets, thrown out as a precaution, though told the cavalry was on that duty, alone saved his regiment. In retreating in good order he passed the enemy's flanking forces on the right and left within long gun-shot range, and succeeded in reaching my position with trifling loss. Colonel Cantey was placed on the right of the two regiments before named.

Half an hour later the enemy were seen to advance with General

Blenker's old brigade (among the regiments, as prisoners informed us, the Eighth New York and Bucktail Rifles from Pennsylvania), driving in our pickets before a heavy fire. I ordered the three regiments to rest quietly in the edge of an open wood until the enemy, who were advancing in regular order across the field and hollow, should come within 50 steps of our line. The order was mainly observed, and as the enemy appeared above the crest of the hill a deadly fire was delivered along our whole front, beginning on the right, dropping the deluded victims of Northern fanaticism and misrule by scores. The repulse of the enemy was complete, followed by an advance, ordered by me, in pursuit. As the enemy's rear regiments had halted in the wood on the other side of the valley, I deemed it prudent, after the field in our front had been cleared, to resume our position on the hill and await their further advance.

Remaining in our position some fifteen minutes, and finding the enemy not disposed to renew the contest, and observing from its fire a battery on the enemy's left, half a mile in advance of us, I promptly decided to make a move from our right flank and try to capture the battery, as I reported at the time to General Ewell, who at this stage of the action sent to know our success and to ask if I wanted re-enforcements. To which I replied I had driven back the enemy; wanted no aid; but thought I could take their battery, and was moving for that purpose. I accordingly in person moved the Fifteenth Alabama to the right along a ravine, and, unperceived, got upon the enemy's left flank and in his rear, marching up in fine order as on drill. I had on leaving with this regiment ordered the other two to advance rapidly in front as soon as they heard I was hotly engaged with the enemy. These regiments, before the order was executed, stood calmly under a heavy fire of the enemy's artillery, directed at the woods. The Fifteenth Alabama completely surprised the force in their front (the enemy's left flank), and drove them by a heavy fire, hotly returned, from behind logs and trees along the wood to the westward.

Meantime the Twenty-first Georgia and Sixteenth Mississippi moved across the field and fell in with the remainder of the enemy's brigade, which had reformed in the woods to our left, and delivered a galling fire upon the Sixteenth Mississippi, which omitted to turn up the woods to its left, after the main body of the enemy, thus exposing its men to enfilading fire. Colonel Mercer, of the Twenty-first Georgia, came to their timely rescue, and both soon gallantly drove the enemy out of the woods, killing and wounding large numbers. On marching to the right flank with the Fifteenth Alabama I found parts of the Thirteenth and Twenty-fifth Virginia Regiments, under command of Col. J. A. Walker, of General Elzey's brigade, had been ordered to my support by General Ewell. I ordered Colonel Walker to move on my right through the woods and advance on the enemy in line of battle perpendicularly to his line and in rear of the battery. Unluckily, as the woods tended to his right, he marched directly on, fell in with my regiment (Fifteenth Alabama), and lost time by having to move by the flank to regain his position. In doing this he was exposed to the view of the battery, which turned its fire on him with galling effect, compelling a resort to the woods. At this time the right wing of the Fifteenth Alabama had advanced unperceived, under my direction, to within 300 yards of the battery, then playing rapidly over their heads on the Thirteenth and Twenty-fifth Virginia. Perceiving the Sixteenth Mississippi and Twenty-first Georgia had advanced, I gave orders to charge the battery. Upon reaching the top of the hill I found it had limbered up and rapidly retired, having lost several horses by our fire. Five minutes' gain in time would have captured the guns. This was lost by the Mississippi regiment in misconstruing my orders.

Another brigade of the enemy supporting the battery 200 yards to its left, our right advanced into the open ground, and at the time the [Fifteenth] Alabama and the Thirteenth and Twenty-fifth Virginia reached their position this force was driven back by their united action and retired with the battery. After some minutes' brisk fire by the enemy's sharpshooters their entire left wing retreated to their first position, near Union Church, on the Keezletown road.

At this time General Taylor, with his brigade, joined me. He had previously been ordered to my support, and I had directed him to march up in the open ground between the woods, but he passed too far to the right, and lost time by falling in behind the Thirteenth and Twenty-fifth Virginia Regiments. I called General Taylor to an interview on an eminence in view of the enemy, then a mile distant, where a battery with an infantry force—of what strength we could not discern—was in sight. I proposed to move forward and renew the fight. General Taylor's reply was that we could soon wipe out that force if it would do any good, but proposed to return his brigade to camp, as he had that morning marched rapidly to Port Republic and returned, and his men needed rest and food. I replied that we had better attack the enemy; but as he did not agree with me, and as I at that time understood that he was sent to aid me in the contest, which was then ended, I did not insist on his remaining. He left me about 4 p. m. I then disposed the three regiments in the woods in regular order about one-half mile distant from the enemy, with skirmishers in front and on the flanks, sending word to General Ewell that the enemy had been repulsed on our right, and that I awaited orders.

About half an hour after General Taylor left Major Barbour came to me with orders from General Ewell to "move to the front," and that a force would be sent forward on the enemy's right to make a combined attack before night. It was too late to recall General Taylor. I moved through the woods and halted in line 500 yards from the enemy's front (disposed along the Keezletown road), prepared to attack him as soon as I could hear from their fire that our force on his flank was engaged. I waited half an hour without any intimation of this attack, and sent a courier to General Ewell to say I awaited the movement on our left. Half an hour afterward I sent another courier with the same message, and soon after Lieutenant Lee, of my staff, to say that if the attack was made on their flank, to divert their attention from my movement, I thought I could overpower the enemy in front, but that it would be injudicious to do so alone, as I could plainly see three batteries of the enemy, all able to bear on our force, as we should advance across the open fields, and (what I estimated at) five brigades of infantry. I waited in suspense until after dark, saw the enemy go into camp, light their fires, draw rations, and otherwise dispose themselves for the night, evidently not expecting any further attack. I then sought General Ewell to recommend a night attack, and found he had gone to report to General Jackson. Before leaving I was strongly tempted to make the advance alone at night, and should have done so had I not felt it a duty to secure complete success by waiting for the combined attack before alluded to, and having some scruples in regard to a possible failure, if acting alone, which might have thwarted the plans of the commanding general, whose success the day after would be seriously jeopardized by even a partial reverse after the fortunate results of the day. I regretted that I had not detained General Taylor until Major Barbour reached me, as with his brigade and my own the result would have been reasonably certain without consulting General Ewell.

Finally, convinced that we could make a successful night attack and disperse or capture General Frémont's entire force—certainly all his artillery—I awaited General Ewell's return, and then urged more than ever the attack, and begged him to go with me and "see how easy it was." He said he could not take the responsibility, and if it was to be done I would have to see General Jackson. I accordingly rode 7 miles to see him, obtained his consent to have Colonel Patton's battalion co-operate with me and his directions "to consult General Ewell and be guided by him." On returning to General Ewell with this permission he declined taking the responsibility which he said thus rested on him, and continued, with General Taylor, to oppose it against my urgent entreaties to be permitted to make the attack alone with my brigade. He only replied, "You have done well enough for one day, and even a partial reverse would interfere with General Jackson's plans for the next day." I replied that we should have the army of Frémont pressing us to-morrow if not driven off, and that we had better fight one army at a time. So ended the matter.

My regiments remained under arms all night, and I moved to camp at daybreak with reluctance.

Having received orders to retard the advance of the enemy on the Port Republic road, on the 9th I took up our old position and remained until 9 o'clock, when, being without artillery and finding the enemy had placed a battery to drive us out of the wood where they had sustained so fatal a repulse the day before, I slowly retired toward Port Republic. Receiving from General Jackson two messages in quick succession to hasten to the battle-field where he had engaged General Shields' army, I marched rapidly to obey this order, crossed the bridge, burned it just before the enemy appeared, and reached the field after the contest had been decided in our favor.

To sum up the occurrences of the day, I may state that our handsome success on the right was due to the judicious position selected, as well as to the game spirit and eagerness of the men. The flank movement to the right, totally unexpected by the enemy and handsomely carried out by Colonel Cantey, completed our success, and although we failed to take their battery, it was not attributable to unskillful maneuvering, but to one of those accidents which often decide the result of battles and partial engagements.

To the bearing of all the officers (dismounted by my order except myself and staff) and the men I give most favorable testimony, and cannot withhold my highest admiration of their gallant conduct and fine discipline, and after the contest, as you witnessed, every regiment was in line, as composed as if they had been on drill. The prisoners and wounded say two brigades were opposed to us—General Blenker's old brigade (now Stahel's) and General Train's [?], with reserves—probably not less than 6,000 to 7,000 men (one regiment having brought 800 men on the field), with two batteries of artillery. My three regiments, counting 1,348 men and officers, repulsed the brigade of Blenker three times, and one hour after, with the Thirteenth and Twenty-fifth Virginia Regiments—whose conduct while observed by me was characterized by steadiness and gallantry—the other brigade of the enemy, with their battery, was driven from the field, 1½ miles from the first scene of the contest. On the ground where we first opened fire 290 of the enemy were left dead. I think a moderate estimate would place the killed and wounded of the enemy on their left wing at 1,740. Prisoners said that the famous Eighth New York Regiment and Bucktails, whose gallantry deserved a better fate, were entirely cut to pieces. Their flag was left on the field and secured by the Twenty-first Georgia.

Of the heroic conduct of the officers and men of Courtney's battery, commanded by Captain Courtney, with Lieutenant Latimer as first lieutenant, in holding their position under the incessant fire of four batteries at one time, I cannot speak in terms which would do them full justice. The fact that they stood bravely up to their work for over five hours, exhausted all their shot and shell, and continued their fire with canister to the end of the battle, speaks more in their favor than the most labored panegyric. The most admirable position selected for the battery alone saved it from total destruction, if a special Providence did not guard it from harm.

The Twenty-first North Carolina, left to support this battery, was exposed to the effect of the terrific fire, but under cover of the hill happily escaped with few casualties. When the battery was threatened with an infantry force this regiment was called and readily took its position to repel the enemy's attack, and stood modestly ready to do its duty as gallantly as heretofore.

To Colonel Mercer, for his judicious movements during the day, and to Colonel Cantey, for his skillful retreat from picket and prompt flank maneuver, I think especial praise is due, as well as to my staff, Captain Hall and Lieutenants McKim and Lee, for the promptness and coolness displayed in conveying orders.

I would also call the attention of the major-general to the services performed on this occasion and previously by Captain Brown, of Company A, Sixteenth Mississippi, who, with portions of his company, has within the last few weeks killed 12 of the enemy, captured 64, with their arms, and some 25 horses, with their equipments, and to the conspicuous gallantry of Private Long, of Company B, Twenty-first Georgia, who, while acting as skirmisher on the 8th instant, brought in 10 prisoners—5, with their arms, captured at one time—and shot an officer of General Frémont's staff, obtaining from him the enemy's order of march, herewith inclosed,* from which it appears they had or the field seven brigades of infantry, besides cavalry and artillery.

It is but an act of simple justice to the brave men of my command to say that this battle was fought by their infantry and artillery in fact alone. Colonel Walker's Fifteenth and Twenty-fifth Virginia Regiments aided in the last repulse, General Taylor's brigade not having been engaged or seen by the enemy. The infantry under Brigadier-General Steuart, on the left of the line, encountered at no time of the day more than the enemy's skirmishers, as they made no demonstration on our left. The battery of General Steuart was in the early part of the fight, but was withdrawn after a severe loss of horses, leaving Captain Courtney's battery to contend singly with four batteries of the enemy.

Herewith I hand a list of the killed and wounded.

Very respectfully,

I. R. TRIMBLE,
*Brigadier-General.*

Maj. JAMES BARBOUR,
*Assistant Adjutant-General.*

---

* Printed on p. 785.

*List of killed and wounded:* Twenty-five killed, 25 wounded, and 4 missing, not including Colonel Walker's list, which was small. The names of the officers killed and wounded not now given.

---

## No. 95.

*Reports of Brig. Gen. Richard Taylor, C. S. Army, commanding Eighth Brigade, of operations May 23–June 9.*

HEADQUARTERS EIGHTH BRIGADE,
*May* 26, 1862.

MAJOR: I have the honor to render the following report in regard to the actions of the 23d, 24th, and 25th instant, in which my brigade was engaged:

On the 23d the First Maryland Regiment, Brigadier-General Steuart, being in advance, the brigade reached the heights above Front Royal about 3 p. m., the enemy opening upon us with shell at the same time. Here Major Wheat's battalion, of five companies, was immediately ordered forward into the town, to assist the Maryland regiment in dislodging the enemy, the Sixth Louisiana Regiment following as a reserve.

Major Wheat performed his part in gallant style, charging through the town, and drawing up his command on the bank of the Shenandoah in a position sheltered from the enemy's shells, the three remaining regiments—Seventh, Eighth, and Ninth Louisiana—at the same time advancing in parallel lines through the fields and woods to the south and west of the town.

The details of the engagement having occurred under the eye of the major-general commanding, it is not necessary to mention them further. The whole brigade was under the fire of artillery and behaved well.

On this day the Seventh Louisiana lost 1 (private) killed and 1 badly wounded. Wheat's battalion lost 1 killed and 6 wounded; 1 (an officer, Lieutenant Grinnell) wounded in the hand.

It is with deep regret that I have also to report the loss of Maj. Aaron Davis, my brigade commissary. After crossing the river he became separated from my staff, and, as I afterward learned, led on by a fatal impetuosity, joined in the cavalry charge of Colonel Munford's regiment, and met his death charging at its head. He was killed by a bullet entering his right breast.

On the 24th the skirmishers of my brigade again encountered the enemy's cavalry near Middletown, cutting their column in two and killing and capturing a large number of them; also many horses and wagons, the latter loaded with various stores of value, such as medicines and other hospital stores.

The brigade being constantly in motion, it is impossible to state the exact number of the enemy killed or captured in this skirmish.

I have the honor to hand over to you two flags captured in action on this day by Companies A and B, of the Sixth Louisiana Regiment, under command of Major McArthur. Our loss in the skirmish was 3 killed and 12 wounded.

On the morning of the 25th, being ordered by Major-General Jackson to execute a flank movement upon the enemy's strong position in front of Winchester, the brigade was formed into line of battle in the face of a severe fire of artillery and musketry, the Seventh Regiment acting as a reserve. The advance and subsequent charge were both conducted steadily and in good order, resulting in the dislodgment of the enemy and the capture of the town.

We lost on this occasion, in killed, Major McArthur (Sixth Louisiana Regiment) and 14 privates; wounded, Lieutenant-Colonel Nicholls (Eighth Louisiana) badly, in the elbow, 2 captains, 2 lieutenants, and 85 privates.

Recapitulation for the three days:

| | Killed. | Wounded. |
|---|---|---|
| Officers | 2 | 6 |
| Privates | 19 | 103 |
| Total | 21 | 109 |

Four guidons, captured by the Seventh Louisiana Regiment in the skirmish at Middletown, have just been sent in and are herewith forwarded.

To enumerate all the acts of gallantry and good conduct would extend this report to an improper length.

Colonels Seymour, Hays, Kelly, and Stafford, of the Sixth, Seventh, Eighth, and Ninth Louisiana, led their regiments into action with the most distinguished bravery.

Major Wheat, with a part of his battalion, detached on the left, rendered valuable service in assisting to repel the attempt of the enemy's cavalry to charge our line.

Captain Surget, assistant adjutant-general, and Lieutenant Hamilton, aide-de-camp, carried orders under the hottest fire with coolness and precision, the former having his horse struck several times.

To Private H. B. Richardson, of the Sixth Louisiana Regiment, I am particularly indebted for valuable services in reconnoitering and gaining important information of the enemy's position and movements while acting as a mounted orderly during the engagement of the 25th, and would earnestly recommend him to the Government for an appointment as lieutenant in the Provisional Army.

Very respectfully, your obedient servant,

R. TAYLOR,
*Brigadier-General, Commanding.*

[Indorsement.]

———, ——— —, 1862.

Respectfully forwarded. The recommendation in case of H. B. Richardson is approved, as I am aware of the invaluable services rendered by him on various occasions.

R. S. EWELL,
*Major-General.*

---

HEADQUARTERS EIGHTH BRIGADE,
*June* 11, 1862.

MAJOR: I have the honor to submit the following report of the Eighth Brigade as connected with the actions of the 8th and 9th instant:

On the morning of the 8th I received orders to march the brigade to Port Republic to assist in repelling the attack commenced on the bridge at that point by Shields' forces. When within 1½ miles of the bridge the column was halted, by order of Major-General Jackson, to await further orders. These were shortly received—in effect to return to the front and act as a reserve to the troops there engaged against Frémont. Here the brigade became separated, two regiments, the Seventh and Eighth Louisiana, being ordered to Major-General Ewell to the support of a battery in the center or on the left of our line, while I marched the remaining two regiments and Wheat's battalion to the right to support General Trimble's brigade, then much pressed. The display of force caused the enemy to retire still farther from the position to which he had been driven by the vigorous charge of Trimble's command.

The brigade, though not actually in action on this day, was much exposed to the enemy's shell, and suffered a loss of 1 private killed, 1 officer (Captain Green, Seventh Louisiana) and 7 privates and non-commissioned officers wounded.

On the 9th I marched from camp near Doukard's [Dunkard's?] Church, according to orders, at daylight, and proceeded across Port Republic Bridge to the field where General Winder's troops had already engaged the enemy. Here I received orders from the major-general commanding to leave one regiment near the position then occupied by himself, and with the main body to make a detour to the right for the purpose of checking a formidable battery planted in that locality. The nature of the ground over which we passed necessarily rendered our progress slow.

On reaching the position indicated the charge was made, and the battery, consisting of six guns, fell into our hands after an obstinate resistance on the part of its supporters, our troops being at the same time subjected to a most destructive fire from the enemy's sharpshooters, posted in a wood above the battery. After holding the battery for a short time a fresh brigade of the enemy's troops, moving up from their position on my left flank, and where they had been fronting the troops of Winder's brigade, made a determined and well-conducted advance upon us, accompanied by a galling fire of canister from a piece suddenly brought into position at a distance of about 350 yards. Under this combined attack my command fell back to the skirts of the wood near which the captured battery was stationed, and from this point continued their fire upon the advancing enemy, who succeeded in reclaiming only one gun, which he carried off, leaving both caisson and limber. At this moment our batteries in my rear opened fire, and re-enforcements coming up, led by Major-General Ewell, the battle was decided in our favor, and the enemy precipitately fled.

The Seventh Louisiana Regiment, Colonel Hays, being the regiment left in the front by order of General Jackson, was meanwhile engaged in another portion of the field, and suffered heavy loss. The guns captured by the brigade were five in number, and one other—a brass 12-pounder howitzer—was afterward discovered deserted in the woods near the Brown's Gap road by Lieutenant Dushane, quartermaster of Wheat's Battalion, and by him brought off.

The loss of the brigade on this day was as follows:*

* * * * * * *

*For statement here omitted, see p. 787.

*Recapitulation for the two actions of 8th and 9th instant.*

| | Killed. | Wounded. | Missing. |
|---|---|---|---|
| Officers | 4 | 17 | |
| Non-commissioned officers and privates | 30 | 247 | 9 |
| Total | 34 | 264 | 9 |

The above record is a mere statement of facts, but no language can adequately describe the gallant conduct of the Eighth Brigade in the action of the 9th instant. Disordered by the rapidity of their charge through a dense thicket, making the charge itself just as the loud cheers of the enemy proclaimed his success in another part of the field, assailed by a superior force in front and on the flanks with two batteries in position within point-blank range, nobly did the sons of Louisiana sustain the reputation of their State. Three times was the captured battery lost and won, the enemy fighting with great determination.

Colonel Seymour, of the Sixth Louisiana, and Major Wheat, of the battalion, on the left; Colonel Stafford, of the Ninth, in the center, and Colonel Kelly, of the Eighth, on the right, all acted with the most determined gallantry, and were as gallantly supported by their officers and men. Members of each of the regiments engaged in the charge were found dead under the guns of the captured battery. Captain Surget, assistant adjutant-general, distinguished himself greatly, and rendered the most important service on the left. Lieutenant Hamilton, aide-de-camp, gave me valuable assistance in rallying and reforming the men when driven back to the edge of the wood, as did Lieutenant Killmartin, of the Seventh Louisiana Regiment, temporarily attached to my staff. Circumstances unfortunately retained the Seventh Regiment, under the gallant Colonel Hays, in another part of the field. Its record of 156 killed and wounded—50 per cent. of the number carried into action—shows the service it performed.

Respectfully, your obedient servant,

R. TAYLOR,
*Brigadier-General.*

Major BARBOUR, *Assistant Adjutant-General, Third Division.*

For No. 96 (report of Col. Bradley T. Johnson, First Maryland Infantry), see Appendix, p. 817.

---

## MAY 20, 1862.—Raid on the Virginia Central Railroad, at Jackson's River Depot, Va.

*Report of Maj. Gen. John C. Frémont, U. S. Army.*

HEADQUARTERS, *Franklin, Va., May* 21, 1862.

Colonel Crook, commanding brigade in Greenbrier County, has just returned from a successful dash upon the Central Railroad, 10 miles beyond Covington, at Jackson's River Depot. Dispatches were discovered at the telegraph office in Covington from the provost-marshal of Alleghany County, asking General Jackson, at Staunton, for two or three regiments, and stating that he was endeavoring to raise the militia of Greenbrier and Monroe. Answers were also found promising re-enforcements from Jackson by way of Staunton and from Floyd by way of Sweet Springs. To prevent any immediate advance from Staunton Colonel Crook proceeded from Covington, destroyed the railroad bridge 10 miles in advance of that place, and returned to Callaghan's, and thence to Lewisburg, bringing with him the notorious Captain Sprigg and another guerrilla, captured after firing upon our troops. General Heth is reported to have effected a junction with General Floyd, and to be near Dublin, on the Tennessee Railroad.

J. C. FRÉMONT,
*Major-General.*

Hon. E. M. STANTON, *Secretary of War.*

---

## MAY 23. 1862.—Action at Lewisburg, W. Va.

### REPORTS, ETC.

No. 1.—Brig. Gen. Jacob D. Cox, U. S. Army, with congratulations.
No. 2.—Col. George Crook, Thirty-sixth Ohio Infantry.
No. 3.—Lieut. Col. Melvin Clarke, Thirty-sixth Ohio Infantry.
No. 4.—Col. Samuel A. Gilbert, Forty-fourth Ohio Infantry.
No. 5.—Maj. Gen. William W. Loring, C. S. Army.
No. 6.—Brig. Gen. Henry Heth, C. S. Army.

### No. 1.

*Reports of Brig. Gen. Jacob D. Cox, U. S. Army.*

FLAT TOP, *May* 24, 1862.

My Third Brigade, Colonel Crook commanding, was attacked yesterday morning at Lewisburg by General Heth, with 3,000 men, and after a lively engagement he routed them and they fled in confusion. Four of the enemy's cannon, 200 stand of arms, and 100 prisoners taken. Our loss, 10 killed and about 40 wounded.

J. D. COX,
*Brigadier-General, Commanding District.*

Col. ALBERT TRACY,
*Assistant Adjutant-General.*

---

FLAT TOP, *May* 24, 1862.

COLONEL: The rebels in their retreat burned Greenbrier Bridge. Crook cannot advance far beyond Lewisburg till the new trains are ready to help him with supplies. The same cause operates here. Steady rain for the past twenty-four hours puts our supplies behind, and my hope that we might get some ahead is disappointed for the present. The news from the front is not very consistent or definite. Loring is now reported chief in command, having arrived two days ago. Numbers are reported as before: Heth's 4,000, the rest 9,000 or 10,000. I allow for exaggeration, but no doubt it is a very much larger force than ours. Does the general commanding get any encouragement as to re-enforcements for us?

J. D. COX,
*Brigadier-General, Commanding.*

Col. ALBERT TRACY,
*Assistant Adjutant-General.*

---

FLAT TOP, *May* 24, 1862.

Col. GEORGE CROOK,
*Commanding Third Brigade, Lewisburg:*

Your report of your victory over Heth is received. I congratulate and thank you and your command for your brilliant conduct, and shall immediately transmit the intelligence to department headquarters. I shall urge forward transportation to enable you to move in co-operation with this line. Keep me fully informed of all passing near you. Your retaliation upon the citizens who fired on your wounded will be approved.

J. D. COX,
*Brigadier-General, Commanding.*

---

HDQRS. ARMY IN THE FIELD, MOUNTAIN DEPARTMENT,
*Franklin, May* 24, 1862.

The general commanding congratulates the army on a new victory in the department, won by the skill and bravery of our soldiers against the superior number of the enemy.

The Third Brigade of General Cox's division, commanded by Colonel Crook, was attacked yesterday morning at Lewisburg by General Heth with 3,000 men, and after a lively engagement the enemy were routed and fled in confusion.

Colonel Crook captured four cannon, 200 stand of arms, and 100 prisoners. Our loss was 10 killed and 40 wounded.

The results of this victory will be important. The general commanding is confident that the forces now under his immediate command but lack the opportunity to emulate the gallantry and share the glory of their comrades of the Army of the Kanawha.

This circular will be read at the head of every regiment or separate corps in this command.

By order of Major-General Frémont:

ALBERT TRACY,
*Colonel and Assistant Adjutant-General.*

---

## No. 2.

### *Reports of Col. George Crook, Thirty-sixth Ohio Infantry.*

HEADQUARTERS,
*Lewisburg, May* 23, 1862.

CAPTAIN: I have the honor to inform you that I was attacked this morning about 5 a. m. by General Heth with 3,000 men, some six or eight pieces of artillery, and a small force of cavalry. They came from the direction of Union, crossed the Greenbrier River at the bridge, driving in our pickets. They formed a line of battle on the hill east of town, our camp being on the hill west of town, and shelled the town and our camp. I at once formed my line of battle and marched on them. My men encountered them on the outskirts of the east side of town. We drove them back, they disputing every inch of ground until we gained the top of the hill, when they fled in great confusion, utterly demoralized, throwing away their blankets, hats, coats, accouterments, and some guns. Having only 1,200 or 1,300 men, I was afraid to follow them for fear they had another column to attack us in our rear, which was entirely unprotected, or else I might have followed them and prevented their burning the bridge. We lost some 10 killed, 40 wounded, and 8 missing. The enemy's loss is much greater; have no correct list yet. We captured four cannon, two rifled and two smooth, and some 200 stand of arms, and about 100 prisoners, among them one lieutenant-colonel, one major, and several captains and lieutenants.

I regret to have to report that our wounded men passing to the rear were fired on from the houses and some killed. I have instituted a search, and shall burn all the houses from which was firing from and shall order a commission on those who are charged with firing, and if found guilty will execute them at once in the main street of this town as examples. I will send detailed report by mail.

I am, sir, very respectfully,

GEORGE CROOK,
*Colonel, Commanding Brigade.*

Captain BASCOM,
*Assistant Adjutant-General.*

---

HEADQUARTERS THIRD BRIGADE,
*Lewisburg, May* 24, 1862.

CAPTAIN: Nothing new to-day. Enemy retreated in direction of Union, greatly demoralized; stragglers are still coming in. The rebels left 38 dead on the field, and 66 wounded that we have found, besides carrying a good many of their wounded with them. Besides the four pieces of artillery we have collected some 300 stand of small-arms; have no doubt many are still lying in the brush. We took 100 prisoners. Our loss was 13 killed, 53 wounded, and 7 missing. I send prisoners and some of our wounded and small-arms to Gauley to-day. Various rumors say that Jackson is going to make a descent on us, but we are prepared for him. Greenbrier River is too much swollen to be crossed now. My transportation is so limited that I can scarcely supply myself here, let alone making any advance on the enemy.

GEORGE CROOK,
*Colonel, Commanding Brigade.*

Captain BASCOM,
*Assistant Adjutant-General.*

---

HEADQUARTERS THIRD PROVISIONAL BRIGADE,
*Lewisburg, Va., May* 24, 1862.

CAPTAIN: At 5 o'clock on the morning of the 23d our pickets were driven in by a force under General Heth, and shortly afterward their advance was seen on the crest of a hill beyond Lewisburg. Two companies of infantry from each regiment were ordered forward to ascertain the force of the enemy and to hold them in check until we could form and advance to their relief. The advance companies were met by a very severe fire, and, deploying as skirmishers, fell slowly back, contesting the ground inch by inch. The Forty-fourth Regiment, under Colonel Gilbert, was ordered forward on the right flank; the Thirty-sixth Regiment, under Lieutenant-Colonel Clarke, on the left flank, with instructions to push on rapidly before the enemy had time to form.

General Heth had pushed forward six pieces of artillery, and was throwing round shot and shell into our camp and into the ranks of our troops as they passed through the streets of the town, many of the shells striking the dwellings.

While Lieutenant-Colonel Clarke pushed steadily up the slope of the hill in the face of a severe fire Colonel Gilbert was also advancing on the right flank and by a vigorous movement succeeded in capturing four pieces of artillery, one of which was loaded with canister at the time of the capture. The locality of the battery after the battle showed by the number of the dead and wounded the fierceness of the fight at that point.

Gaining the more open ground on the slope below the enemy a steady, rapid advance was made by our entire line, loading and firing as they advanced, and upon gaining the crest of the hill the enemy fell back in confusion.

Colonel Bolles, of the Second Virginia Cavalry, who had been held in reserve, was ordered forward in pursuit, but their retreat was so rapid and the ground so unfavorable for pursuit, the road passing through narrow and rocky defiles, that they crossed Greenbrier Bridge, burning it behind them, before they could be overtaken, and from the best information in my possession has continued his retreat down the Union road; and as a number of his troops are men who have been pressed into the service under the State conscription, and this is their first engagement, there is every reason to believe that the defeat will be to them very demoralizing. The force actually engaged with us was about 2,500 men, including about 125 cavalry and six pieces of artillery.

We have in our possession as prisoners Lieutenant-Colonel Finney, Major Edgar, and a number of minor officers and 93 privates; also 66 wounded prisoners and 38 dead; four pieces of artillery (two 12-pounder field howitzers and two 6-pounder rifled cannon), and about 300 stand of arms.

We have a loss of 11 killed and 54 wounded, the greater number of whom are not dangerously so. Many of our wounded were fired upon by citizens of the town as they returned on the way to the hospital, and one wounded man shot dead in the street. The houses which can be fully identified as having been fired from will be burned, and if I can capture any of the parties engaged they will be hung in the street as an example to all such assassins.

Our forces engaged were about 1,200 infantry. Had my force been larger, so that I might have left my rear guarded, there being reasonable ground to expect another force in our rear, and had I possessed transportation (which I need very much) the enemy would have been pursued until they were captured or dispersed.

It is unnecessary to eulogize the men whom I have the honor to command. Their steady, firm advance in the face of the fire which met them and the result will speak for itself. I need only say that not an officer or private in my command failed in doing his whole duty as a soldier.

I am, sir, very respectfully, your obedient servant,

GEORGE CROOK,
*Colonel, Commanding Brigade.*

Capt. G. M. BASCOM,
*Assistant Adjutant-General.*

---

## No. 3.

*Report of Lieut. Col. Melvin Clarke, Thirty-sixth Ohio Infantry.*

LEWISBURG, *May* 23, 1862.

SIR: In obedience to your order of this morning, issued on the approach of the enemy under General Heth, I formed the regiment which I had the honor to command on the left of the line of your brigade, my position being to the left of the road leading to Greenbrier Bridge, and at the foot of a steep declivity, having an elevation of some 50 feet, and along the brow of which were several houses surrounded by inclosures, beyond which the larger portion of the enemy's infantry, commanded by General Heth in person, were formed.

Having taken this position I at once marched my battalion to the top of the steep declivity, and passing the houses over numerous fences found myself in front of the enemy, who was posted behind a fence, and immediately opened a brisk fire upon us, which was returned with promptness and alacrity.

For a short time the fight was very sharp. I continued to advance until the line of the battalion was within 40 yards of that of the enemy, when they fled in confusion. The firing ceased only when the enemy had got beyond our range. We pursued the enemy a considerable distance, but as they fled with great speed it was impossible to keep up with them. A large number of their dead and wounded lay behind the fence where they were first posted and scattered through the fields beyond.

Though the first battle in which the regiment was ever engaged, the men behaved nobly. From the time we arrived beyond the houses we had to pass and received the first fire of the enemy the battalion pressed steadily and firmly forward in the face of a galling fire. Not a man flinched. The steadiness, firmness, and determination and vigor with which the line moved on, together with the rapidity and accuracy of our fire, seemed to inspire the enemy—though twice our number or more—with terror. But nine companies of my regiment, having an aggregate of 600 men, were in the engagement.

Of the officers, every one was in his place and did his whole duty, exhibiting a courage and determination worthy of all praise. It would be invidious to specify any as peculiarly worthy of commendation when all so well merit it. The casualties of the engagement in my regiment are—killed, 5; wounded, 41; missing, 4.* The missing were on picket duty on the Greenbrier Bridge road and were probably prisoners.

All which is respectfully submitted.

I have the honor to remain, your obedient servant,

M. CLARKE,
*Lieut. Col., Comdg. Thirty-sixth Regiment Ohio Vol. Infantry.*

Col. GEORGE CROOK, *Commanding Third Brigade.*

---

* Nominal list omitted.

## No. 4.

### *Report of Col. Samuel A. Gilbert, Forty-fourth Ohio Infantry.*

LEWISBURG, VA.,
*May* 12, 1862—12 m.

COLONEL: I have the honor to make the following report of the part taken by my regiment in the affair at this place to-day:

In obedience to your orders I sent forward a company (Company D, L. W. Talley's) to ascertain the nature of the attack that had been made upon our outpost at the Greenbrier Bridge. Near the east end of the town they came upon the enemy in force, who opened a heavy fire of musketry and advanced upon them. The company was deployed to the south of the road, and contested the ground warmly as they fell back.

As soon as the presence of the enemy was known, in accordance with your order I formed the Forty-fourth in line of battle on the south side of the main street of the town and advanced as rapidly as the nature of the ground would admit toward the enemy's position. On emerging from a small grove we came suddenly upon a battery of the enemy, consisting of two rifled 10-pounders and two 12-pounder field howitzers, which was charged with such impetuosity that the gunners had no time to fire. Here some 20 of the enemy were killed, as many more wounded, and many prisoners taken; also about 200 stand of small-arms taken.

Leaving small guards over the artillery and prisoners we pushed on to the top of the hill, where the enemy had first formed into line. Here we reformed our line and relieved our companies that had been deployed as skirmishers; ordered the new line of skirmishers, composed of two companies, to continue the pursuit, feeling their way carefully through the dense woods that cover the greater part of the slope toward Greenbrier River. But the enemy having retired beyond the river and set fire to the bridge any farther pursuit was not attempted.

The casualties in my regiment are as follows: Killed, 6; wounded, 14; of which 3 are very slightly and none very severely; missing, none. Among my wounded are J. C. Langston, captain Company B, ball through calf of leg, and Samuel C. Howell, first lieutenant Company C, ball through the leg above the knee.

In regard to the conduct of my officers and men I am proud to say that without exception they displayed the greatest coolness and energy, and performed the work before them in a soldier-like manner, as the above report will show.

With much respect, I have the honor to be, your obedient servant,

SAMUEL A. GILBERT,
*Colonel Forty-fourth Regiment Ohio Volunteers.*

Col. GEORGE CROOK, *Commanding Third Provisional Brigade.*

---

## No. 5.

### *Report of Maj. Gen. William W. Loring, C. S. Army.*

HDQRS. DEPARTMENT OF SOUTHWEST VIRGINIA,
*Dublin Depot, May* 27, 1862.

MAJOR: I send you the report of General Heth relative to his recent affair.

The general moved for the purpose of cutting off the enemy, who at the time was between Lewisburg and Covington, as we were then informed, and if he found his force sufficient to attack him wherever he could find him. This was commenced before my arrival. Subsequently I received the telegram inclosed, which I sent the general, together with my letter, also inclosed, and his reply. He explains in his communication why it was that he attacked the enemy at Lewisburg, with an account of his withdrawal.

I have no further information with regard to this affair to send you.

I shall leave to-day for General Heth's command, and will repair the damage done as far as I can with the force I have. I regret we cannot get additional strength. I think the enemy, from all I can learn, much larger than Heth estimates him. If possible more troops should be sent. It will take time to raise the rangers. I have been exerting myself to effect the object ever since my arrival.

With respect, I have the honor to be, your obedient servant,

W. W. LORING,
*Major-General, Commanding.*

Maj. W. H. TAYLOR,
*Assistant Adjutant-General.*

[Inclosure No. 1.]

HDQRS. DEPARTMENT OF SOUTHWEST VIRGINIA,
*Giles Court-House, May* 21, 1862.

Brigadier-General HETH,
*Commanding:*

GENERAL: I have the honor to inclose you the within communication and telegram,* just received, and I send them to you for your information.

Unless you can form a junction with the forces mentioned your present direction may bring you rather near the enemy at Lewisburg, which, if true, as has been represented, has been strongly re-enforced.

For the want of information of the country over which you are now passing it is impossible for me to say at what point it would be best for you to move upon in order to communicate, and, if possible, combine, with the forces of Johnson. Unless more definite information can be obtained of the strength of the enemy at Lewisburg and the movements of Johnson's forces would it not be well to strike the road leading to Salem, in order to await further information and protect the railroad at Bonsack's and Salem, and also to enable you to return here in case it is threatened.

I give you this opinion more as a suggestion, because of your better knowledge of the country and means of information.

I shall leave here to-day for Newbern, and shall be pleased to hear from you constantly. I have not up to this time written to the Department at Richmond, but shall to-day write them of the necessity of sending additional troops to guard the lines from Salem to Bonsack's.

Respectfully, your obedient servant,

W. W. LORING,
*Major-General, Commanding.*

---

* Telegram not found.

[Sub-inclosures.]

DUBLIN, *May* 20, 1862—8 p. m.

Major-General LORING,
*Commanding Department:*

GENERAL: Knowing General Heth's movement I hasten to give you the following facts just to hand:

The telegraphic operator, with his papers, at Jackson River was captured by the enemy. Among the undestroyed dispatches was one ordering two of Jackson's regiments and Ashby's cavalry to the rear of the enemy at Covington. As soon as captured the enemy fell back to Lewisburg. At the latter post he has been strongly re-enforced within the last thirty-six hours.

If Heth makes the contemplated move he may easily be seriously threatened and annoyed by a superior force on his left.

The enemy burnt the first railroad bridge between Jackson River Depot.

General Cox's headquarters are at Lewisburg. The operator was making his way off with his instruments, &c., when he was captured. I think this information is entirely reliable.

I am, general, very respectfully, your obedient servant,

W. H. WERTH,
*Lieutenant-Colonel, C. S. Army.*

SALT SULPHUR SPRINGS,
*May* 21, 1862.

Maj. Gen. W. W. LORING:

GENERAL: Yours of 21st instant, with inclosures, to hand. I am at this point with my force, 24 miles from Lewisburg.

I think I have pretty accurately ascertained that the force of the enemy does not exceed three regiments of infantry, 300 or 400 cavalry, with six or eight pieces of artillery.

I am endeavoring to place myself in communication with the forces under General Johnson, supposed to be advancing toward Covington, and if compelled to fall back I will do so in the direction of Bonsack's and Salem, covering those points.

I hope to learn something from General Johnson's force early to-morrow, 22d instant. I will communicate with you by every opportunity daily, if possible.

Very respectfully, your obedient servant,

H. HETH,
*Brigadier-General, Commanding.*

[Inclosure No. 2.]

HEADQUARTERS, ETC.,
*Fincastle, May* 25, 1862.

Brig. Gen. HENRY HETH,
*Commanding Brigade:*

GENERAL: I am just now in receipt of a telegram informing me that you are falling back to The Narrows.

Will not this movement leave the entire country exposed to the enemy? Retiring will give them an impetus which may induce them to move upon the railroad at once, and if you go back to The Narrows there will be no one to stop them. Can you not get supplies so as to enable you to halt at some point to protect the approaches to the railroad in the direction of Bonsack's and Salem, as well as, if necessary, to move upon The Narrows.

Try and effect the protection of the railroad. I have no information of any enemy approaching The Narrows, and until that there is no immediate necessity of going there.

In your note in reply to mine relative to the re-enforcement of the enemy at Lewisburg you informed me that, in case you did not deem it proper upon information to attack the enemy, you would take position so as to afford the protection desired. Cannot this be done now?

I shall be at Dublin Depot to-morrow.

Respectfully, your obedient servant,

W. W. LORING,
*Major-General, Commanding.*

---

## No. 6.

### *Report of Brig. Gen. Henry Heth, C. S. Army.*

UNION, MONROE COUNTY, VA.,
*May* 23, 1862.

GENERAL: I have the honor to state that after the rout of Cox's army by the combined forces of General Johnson and my own I at once concluded to attack the force at Lewisburg, and was the more determined upon this course when I learned that the enemy had divided his force at Lewisburg and sent a portion of it in the direction of Covington.

This plan was communicated to you on assuming the command of the department; in fact, the movement had then already commenced.

I proceeded rapidly in the direction of Lewisburg. I had the most accurate information of the enemy's force in every respect. He numbered about 1,500 men (infantry)—two regiments—two mountain howitzers, and about 150 cavalry. The force I led against him numbered about 2,000 infantry, three batteries, and about 100 cavalry.

My chance of success was good, provided I could surprise the enemy and get into position. This I succeeded in doing far beyond my expectation. Most of his pickets were captured, and I attained without firing a shot that position in front of Lewisburg which I would have selected.

The enemy retired to a range of hills corresponding in height on the west side of the town.

As my regiments and batteries arrived they were deployed as follows:

Finney's battalion on the left, the Forty-fifth Regiment in the center, and the Twenty-second Virginia Regiment on the right; Lieutenant-Colonel Cook's battalion of dismounted men, Eighth Virginia Cavalry, as the reserve.

While deploying and getting my batteries into position the enemy, evidently in order to cover the retreat of his wagons, threw forward his smallest regiment, sending one-half to the right and the other to the left of the main approach to the town.

I advanced to meet him. I directed Lieutenant-Colonel Finney, commanding battalion, to occupy a small body of oak timber. In doing this Colonel Finney had to cross a wheat field. The enemy, numbering only three companies, opened upon his battalion a very severe fire, which possibly compelled his command to fall back. At this time the left of the enemy was in full retreat.

One of those causeless panics for which there is no accounting seized upon my command. Victory was in my grasp, instead of which I have to admit a most disgraceful retreat.

The field officers, among whom none were more conspicuous than the gallant Lieutenant-Colonel Finney, as well as some few captains, threw themselves between the enemy and their retreating men, but threats and persuasions were alike unavailing. The result is, we mourn the loss of many a brave officer.

The only excuse that can be offered for the disgraceful behavior of three regiments and batteries is that they are filled with conscripts and newly officered under the election system.

I cannot as yet ascertain our exact loss, but will furnish you reports at my earliest convenience. By far the greater portion of the casualties was among the officers—a consequence of the panic.

I do not wish to be understood as shifting the responsibility of what has occurred upon the shoulders of my troops, for as a general is the recipient of honors gained, so he should bear his proportion of the result of the disaster. I simply give you a plain statement of facts apparent to all present.

I move to-morrow or next day to my original position at The Narrows, as the tents of my command are there.

I have the honor to be, &c.,

H. HETH,
*Brigadier-General.*

Maj. Gen. W. W. LORING,
*Commanding Department of Southwest Virginia.*

---

## MAY 30, 1862.—Raid to Shaver's River, W. Va.

*Report of Maj. Gen. John C. Frémont, U. S. Army, commanding Mountain Department.*

HEADQUARTERS, *May* 30, 1862.

Hon. E. M. STANTON:

Colonel Latham, with a detachment of the Second Virginia, and a company of Connecticut cavalry under Captain Fish, who were sent to Shaver's River, surprised and routed a gang of guerrillas at that place, killing their captain and 3 men, wounding several others, and capturing and destroying more than thirty guns.

J. C. FRÉMONT,
*Major-General.*

---

## JUNE 3-4, 1862.—Operations in the vicinity of Winchester, Front Royal, Strasburg, and Smithfield, Va.

*Report of Maj. Gen. Franz Sigel, U. S. Army.*

HEADQUARTERS, *Winchester, Va., June* 4, 1862.

The troops under my command arrived in and near Winchester at 12 o'clock to-day. I sent scouting parties to Strasburg and Front

Royal to ascertain the position of our own and of the enemy's troops. One brigade of General Banks is on its march from Martinsburg to this place. General Banks himself will be here to-day. The detachment of cavalry sent out from Smithfield yesterday made about 50 prisoners, and to-day we found here 8 surgeons and 350 sick and wounded, belonging to General Banks' command.

F. SIGEL,
*Major-General.*

Hon. E. M. STANTON, *Secretary of War.*

---

## JUNE 8, 1862.—Skirmish at Muddy Creek, W. Va.

*Report of Maj. John J. Hoffman, Second West Virginia Cavalry.*

CAMP MEADOW BLUFF, W. VA.,
*June* 9, 1862.

COLONEL: In obedience to your order of the 8th I took with me Captains Powell, Dove, and Behan, of the Second Battalion Second Virginia Cavalry, and traveled in the direction of Alderson's Ferry via Blue Sulphur. When within about 2½ miles from the ferry and 1½ miles from the small village of Palestine I found a squad of 14 men, belonging to the Greenbrier and White's cavalry, dismounted and standing picket, under the command of First Lieutenant Hawver, of the Greenbrier cavalry. They retreated to the woods, and I pursued them through the woods and fields about 1½ miles to Muddy Creek. Here 1 man (McClung) surrendered, and in crossing the creek we killed 2, who fell in the stream and floated down.

The creek was deep, the bottom covered with loose stone, and the current swift, and we were delayed some time in crossing.

After crossing we killed Lieutenant Harover, whose body we left in charge of one Baker (citizen), and captured 1 prisoner (Graves, from Lewisburg). We took two double-barreled shot-guns. The picket had left their horses across the river, at the ferry, with a guard. The river was too deep and rapid to ford, and having no boats we were unable to get at them.

There are no boats at this ferry, nor at any of the crossings above or below that I could hear of. I did not go to Haynes' Ferry, about 8 miles below, and a rough road. I learned that near Haynes' Ferry there was a road (very rough) leading on to Lick Creek, and from there across to the Gauley road, near the top of Little Sewell. None of my command were hurt, and both officers and men are entitled to credit for the promptness and zeal with which they executed their orders. Two horses of Captain Powell's company died from fatigue. Four miles beyond Blue Sulphur there is a large quantity of hay, but no grain that I could find. From Blue Sulphur to the ferry the road, with the exception of a few slips, is tolerably good, and on this side the Springs there is a very large slip on the mountain-side.

I could not hear of any Confederate troops this side of the river, and heard that General Heth's forces were still at the Salt Springs, beyond Union.

Respectfully, yours,

J. J. HOFFMAN,
*Major Second Battalion Second Virginia Cavalry.*

Col. GEORGE CROOK, *Commanding Brigade.*

## JUNE 22-30, 1862.—Scout from Strasburg to Moorefield, New Creek, and Winchester, Va.

### *Report of Capt. Charles Farnsworth, First Connecticut Cavalry.*

CAMP NEAR MIDDLETOWN, VA.,
*June* 30, 1862.

SIR: I have the honor to report that in pursuance to a special order I left Strasburg Sunday, June 22, for Moorefield. At Lost River Bridge I found Captain Ten Eyck, of the New York Fourth Mounted Rifles, suffering from wounds. I procured a carriage and took him to Moorefield, from whence he was sent to New Creek. On the 24th, when 5 miles distant from Baker's Tavern, was fired upon from the brush and 1 horse killed and 4 wounded. I learned subsequently that 15 men, said to be Harne's men, slept at a Mr. Inskeep's, 4 miles distant from the place of bushwhacking. I burned all the houses for 4 miles on the road. At the request of Colonel Downey I remained with my command at Moorefield until noon of the 27th, having sent a squad to New Creek for what stragglers were upon the road.

On the 29th I captured a wagon, loaded with United States goods and arms, in the woods near Cacapon Bridge, 3 horses, and 1 man, who said he was one of a party of 18. I found from the inhabitants that the party had plundered citizens and stolen many horses. I delivered the man and property to the provost-marshal at Winchester, from which place I came to ———. I gathered up 15 members of the battalion, whom I have reported to Major Lyon.

Respectfully, yours,

CHARLES FARNSWORTH,
*Captain Company B, First Connecticut Cavalry.*

Captain PIATT,
*Assistant Adjutant-General, Schenck's Division.*

---

## JUNE 24, 1862.—Skirmish at Milford, Va.

### *Report of Maj. Charles H. Town, First Michigan Cavalry.*

CAMP FIRST MICHIGAN CAVALRY,
*Front Royal, Va., June* 24, 1862.

GENERAL: I would respectfully report that, in compliance with your order of this date, I proceeded with detachments of the First Michigan and First Maine Cavalry on the road to Luray, nothing of interest occurring on the route until I reached the vicinity of Milford. Found the enemy in possession of the town, with their pickets stationed some half mile this side of the village. We opened fire upon them and drove them into the village. Upon our skirmishers approaching their line they returned the fire in a rapid manner. Our skirmishers continued to advance and drove their advance from the village. They retired upon their main body in the edge of a wood, extending upon both sides of the road beyond the town. Our skirmishers still continued to advance, and parts of Companies B and M, of the First Michigan Regiment, were thrown over the creek to support them, the detachment of Maine cavalry covering the bridge and acting as a reserve.

As my command neared the wood I found the nature of the ground would not permit a charge; besides, I discovered the wood to be so dense that it would be impossible for cavalry to act efficiently. At this moment I ordered a halt, discovering which the enemy endeavored, with some 40 or 50 dismounted men or infantry, to flank our skirmishers and gain their rear, under cover of the wood on the right of the road. Inasmuch as I had but 20 carbines in the entire command, and as our pistols were altogether too short-range to cope with our adversaries with long rifles, with which all of them were armed, and as they nearly if not quite equaled us in numbers, I deemed it prudent to retire across the bridge, which was admirably executed by the officers and men of both companies in precisely the same order in which they advanced.

Upon reaching my reserve a messenger arrived from the rear guard informing me that the enemy had thrown a body of cavalry to my left and rear, to intercept my return to Bentonville. Upon learning this I ordered a retrograde movement to Bentonville. On reaching that place I learned through a citizen that the enemy's force in and around Milford was estimated to be about 300 mounted men, said to be part of a Louisiana mounted rifle regiment. The enemy were armed with pistol, saber, and rifle. After remaining a few minutes at Bentonville I proceeded on my return to the Manor Line road. Being desirous of discovering whether the enemy had any force at Boyd's Mill, I proceeded on that road to that point. Marshall's company, which had been in that vicinity, and which had been encamped there as recently as Sunday last, was not to be seen, but I was informed by the citizens that they might return at any moment.

The horses of the command being very much jaded I found it necessary to return to camp, having been twelve hours in the saddle. I learned nothing of the enemy's force at Luray. I would respectfully represent that, owing to the topography of the country and the character of the force with which we had to contend, armed as our regiment is with only pistol and saber, barring the few carbines already mentioned, it is next to impossible to encounter our foes successfully, as he is never in position where saber and pistol can be used.

It gives me pleasure to report that the officers and men of both detachments behaved with great coolness and bravery during the encounter.

I have the honor to be, very respectfully, your obedient servant,

CHAS. H. TOWN,
*Major. Commanding Detachment.*

Brig. Gen. S. W. CRAWFORD,
*Commanding First Brigade.*

# APPENDIX.

**MAY 15–JUNE 17, 1862.—Operations in Shenandoah Valley.**

No. 96.

*Report of Col. Bradley T. Johnson, First Maryland Infantry, of operations May 29–June 9.**

HEADQUARTERS MARYLAND LINE,
*Camp on Mountain, June 11, 1862.*

MAJOR: On Thursday, May 29 ultimo, this command, Brigadier-General Steuart, commanding Maryland Line, marched from Martinsburg to beyond Charlestown. On the 30th it was ordered toward Harper's Ferry. The enemy were found on Bolivar Heights, and, after driving in their skirmishers with a few sharpshooters from the First Maryland Regiment, our artillery, Captain Cutshaw's battery, drove them from the hill. I then advanced with Company A, Maryland Cavalry, and my regiment, and took possession of the heights. We captured the camp of the enemy, full of stores and arms. I went to the Potomac. Very soon he opened on me from a battery at Barbour's house, and a gun to our right, when, having no artillery to support me, I was ordered back by Brigadier-General Steuart. I went into camp 2½ miles east of Charlestown, without rations, my wagons having been sent forward. The next day, 31st, I was rear guard of the army, and marched 7 miles beyond Winchester. The next day, June 1, also rear guard; marched beyond Strasburg. On the 6th of June, 2 miles southeast of Harrisonburg, I became engaged with a force of the enemy—one brigade and the First Pennsylvania Rifles (Bucktail Rifles), (Captain [Wilson C.] Nicholas, Company G, captured their colonel, Kane), and, together with the Fifty-eighth Virginia, Colonel [Samuel H.] Letcher, we drove them back. Here I lost Capt. M. S. Robertson, Company I, a gallant officer, who fell at the head of his men, in a charge, shouting, "Go on, my men; don't fall back for me." Here also fell Second Lieut. Nicholas Snowden, a true and brave soldier, who died as became his life, in the arms of victory, with his face to the foe. Near him fell the chivalric Ashby. Here also died Privates [William E.] Harris and [L. R.] Schley, Company H; Murphy, Company G, and [E. W.] Beatty, Company D. Beatty was advanced in years, and has steadily refused promotion at my hand, preferring to carry his rifle in defense of right and honor. Besides these 6 killed outright, I lost 11 men wounded, 4 or 6 mortally, making 17 out of 150 men engaged. My colors fell twice, but were caught before they touched the ground. Color Sergt. Joseph Doyle was severely wounded, and left in a house in the neighborhood; Color-Corporal Taylor was badly shot, and Color-Corporal [Daniel] Shanks carried them the rest of the time. I subjoin a list.†

*Received too late for insertion in proper sequence.

†Not found.

On the 8th of June my regiment was engaged in the center, on the left, and supporting the Baltimore Light Artillery. Soon after getting into position, I was attacked by a regiment slightly to my left. I changed position and drove them back. In a short time another regiment came up, and got behind a fence some 300 yards from me. This place they obstinately held for an hour. I could not charge them, not having 175 men in ranks, and having to cross a branch, a ravine, and a fence. At last, however, I drove them out, leaving some dead and quantities of arms, accouterments, and blankets. Soon after, another regiment was brought up the road, a little to my right, but my men dispersed them rapidly.

No other attack was made on this point during the day. The enemy had a piece of artillery, some 800 yards distant, the whole time, playing on me with grape, but when our rifles sent the last attacking regiment back, it retired. A demonstration was before that made on my left, but the force retired without effecting anything. About 4 to 5 o'clock my ammunition gave out, and the guns became so hot and foul as to be seriously impaired. Major-General Ewell then ordered me back for a new supply, and my regiment did not get into action again. There was no move made on my wing after I left, for I came back myself, and, under General Ewell's orders, pushed Colonel Patton's and Colonel Hays' commands forward on our extreme left.

Our loss was severe. Brig. Gen. George H. Steuart, in command on the left, and of my regiment and the battery, was shot, toward the close of the engagement, in the shoulder, severely, but not dangerously. His acting assistant adjutant-general, Lieutenant [Frank A.] Bond, and his aide, Lieut. Randolph [H.] McKim, each had horses wounded. Second Lieut. H. [H.] Bean, Company I, was wounded, and 24 men. I subjoin a list.* Two men were wounded in the battery.

It is my duty to notice the precision and gallantry with which Captain Brockenbrough served his guns.

I was not under fire on the 9th, but lost 1 man wounded, Private [Joshua] Simpson, Company D, who was fighting with the Fifty-second Virginia.

Your obedient servant,

BRADLEY T. JOHNSON,
*Colonel First Maryland Regt., Comdg. Maryland Line.*

Maj. JAMES BARBOUR,
*Assistant Adjutant-General, Third Division.*

[Inclosure.]

SPECIAL ORDERS, No. 230. } HEADQUARTERS VALLEY DISTRICT, *June* 13, 1862.

* * * * * * *

III. Colonel Johnson, of the First Maryland Regiment, is directed to encamp, with his command, in the vicinity of Staunton, Va., for the purpose of recruiting; and is also ordered to collect all stragglers from the Army of the Valley, and return them to these headquarters under guard.

By order of Major-General Jackson:

R. L. DABNEY,
*Assistant Adjutant-General.*

---

*Not found.

# INDEX.

***Brigades, Divisions, Corps, Armies, and improvised organizations are "Mentioned" under name of commanding officer; State and other organizations under their official designation.***


Page.

**Abbott, Edward G.** Mentioned ... 621

**Abercrombie, John J.**
  Correspondence with Frederick Myers ... 118
  Mentioned ... 114, 115, 165, 226, 227, 234, 235, 425, 445
  Report of reconnaissance to the Rappahannock River, Va., April 18 ... 440

**Abert, James W.**
  Mentioned ... 547, 552, 572, 573
  Report of operations in Shenandoah Valley, May 24 ... 568

**Acker, George S.** Mentioned ... 554, 555

**Adams, Charles A.** Mentioned ... 586

**Addison, W. Va.** Expedition to, April 17–21. Report of Ebenezer B. Andrews. 439
  (See also *report of John C. Frémont*, p. 5.)

**Adjutant-General's Office, U. S. A.**
  Correspondence with
    Army Headquarters ... 332
    Banks, Nathaniel P ... 531, 541–543
    Frémont, John C ... 653, 655
    McClellan, George B. ... 164, 226
    McDowell, Irvin ... 689
  Orders, General, series 1862: **No. 62**, 541; **No. 107**, 271; **No. 160**, 263.

**Adolphus, Philip.** Mentioned ... 552, 604

**Ainsworth, William P.** Mentioned ... 695

**Alabama Troops.** Mentioned.
  Cavalry—*Battalions*: **5th**, 434.
  Infantry—*Regiments*: **15th**, 20, 713, 717, 779, 781, 784, 794–797; **16th**, 20.

**Albert, Anselm.** Mentioned ... 19, 26, 35

**Alexander, Barton S.**
  Mentioned ... 250, 278
  Testimony of, McDowell Court of Inquiry ... 250, 251, 278

**Alexander, George W.** Mentioned ... 581

**Alexander, R. H.** Mentioned ... 345

**Allen, James W.**
  Correspondence with Thomas J. Jackson ... 389
  Mentioned ... 382, 736, 737, 739, 740, 742, 747, 752
  Reports of
    Kernstown, Va. Battle of, March 23 ... 387
    Newtown, Va. Action at, May 24 ... 743
    Port Republic, Va. Engagements at, June 8–9 ... 744
    Winchester, Va. Engagement at, May 25 ... 743

**Allen, Samuel H.** Mentioned ... 232

**Ambrosius, Frederick.** Mentioned ... 511

Page.

**Anderson, John.** Mentioned ... 423
**Anderson, John C.** Mentioned ... 641
**Anderson, John S.** Mentioned ... 787, 791
**Anderson, Joseph R.**
Correspondence with Irvin McDowell ... 47–49
Mentioned ... 47, 49, 146, 148
**Andrews, Ebenezer B.** Report of expedition to Addison, W. Va., April 17–21. 439
**Andrews, George L.**
Mentioned ... 419, 549, 615, 616, 618
Reports of
Newtown, Va. Action at, May 24 ... 620
Winchester, Va. Engagement at, May 25 ... 622
**Andrews, J. W.** Mentioned ... 43
**Ankele, Charles.** Mentioned ... 506, 507
**Anthony, Robert C.** Report of reconnaissance to the **Rappahannock River,** Va., April 16 ... 425
**Antisell, Thomas.** Mentioned ... 598
**Antrim, George T.** Mentioned ... 393
**Appleby, H. John.** Mentioned ... 565
**Armstrong,** Mr. Mentioned ... 83
**Armstrong,** Mr. Mentioned ... 83, 84
**Army Headquarters.**
Correspondence with
Adjutant-General's Office, U. S. A. ... 332
McDowell Court of Inquiry ... 37–39, 45, 51
McDowell, Irvin ... 39
Orders, Special, series 1862: **No. 88,** 322; **No. 350,** 36; **No. 362,** 40.
**Army Trains and Baggage.** Regulations for ... 263
**Arnall, Charles S.** Mentioned ... 398
**Arnaud, Charles D.** Mentioned ... 256
**Arnett, Jonathan W.** Mentioned ... 787
**Arnold,** Adjutant. Mentioned ... 751
**Arnold, A. J.** Mentioned ... 748, 749, 751
**Arnoldsburg, W. Va.** Skirmish at, May 6 ... 2
**Ashby, Turner.**
Correspondence with Thomas J. Jackson ... 385
Mentioned ... 14, 16, 18, 339, 340, 348, 351, 368, 379–387, 389, 407, 411, 415, 418, 426, 456, 470, 523, 531–533, 588, 591, 593, 632, 634, 653, 694, 701–704, 706, 707, 711–713, 718, 721, 725–727, 730–732, 735, 760, 782, 789, 811, 817
Reports of battle of Kernstown, Va., March 23 ... 385, 386
**Ashcraft, ——.** Mentioned ... 423
**Asmussen, Charles W.** Mentioned ... 131
**Atterbury, William.** Mentioned ... 441, 442
**Atwell, Charles A.**
Mentioned ... 536, 537, 555, 557, 558
Report of action at Front Royal, Va., May 23 ... 565
**Atwood, William S.** Mentioned ... 411
**Augur, Christopher C.**
Correspondence with Rufus King ... 431, 432
Mentioned ... 43, 45, 53, 82, 84, 119, 427, 435–437
Reports of operations about, April 17–19, and occupation of, Fredericksburg, Va., April 18 ... 428
**Augustine, William J.** Mentioned ... 599

Page.
**Austin, Eusebius S.** Mentioned ... 662
**Babbitt, Charles R.**
Mentioned ... 575
Report of operations in Shenandoah Valley, May 24–25 ... 584
**Bailey, R. A.** Mentioned ... 495
**Bailey, Thomas C.** Mentioned ... 367
**Baker,** Mr. Mentioned ... 814
**Baker, Ephraim.** Mentioned ... 501
**Baker, W. L.** Mentioned ... 692, 693, 699, 700
**Bakham,** Mr. Mentioned ... 453
**Baldwin,** Dr. Mentioned ... 749
**Baldwin, John B.**
Assignments to command ... 487
Mentioned ... 487
**Ball, Dabney.** Mentioned ... 417
**Ball, Flamen.** Mentioned ... 243
**Baltimore and Ohio Railroad.** Military protection and defense of, assigned to command of John E. Wool ... 663
**Banks, N. P.**
Assignments to command ... 1, 2, 169
Correspondence with
Adjutant-General's Office, U. S. A ... 531, 541–543
Frémont, John C ... 27, 31, 32, 34, 527, 530
Lincoln, Abraham ... 527, 530, 533–535, 542
McClellan, George B ... 164, 234
McDowell, Irvin ... 287, 288, 531, 533, 543
Saville, Thomas ... 525
Saxton, Rufus ... 538
War Department, U. S. ... 285, 427, 456, 522–535, 538–545
Direction and control of Winchester and Potomac Railroad to remain under ... 663
Instructions to. Communications from George B. McClellan ... 164, 234
Mentioned ... 7–13, 15, 17, 24, 26, 31–34, 41, 42, 55, 97, 99, 100, 107, 109, 114, 115, 117, 121–123, 132, 134, 136, 163, 165–167, 169, 174, 184–190, 200–202, 210, 211, 220, 225, 227, 228, 230–232, 277, 282, 284–288, 295, 298–301, 316, 328, 333, 335–341, 343, 344, 348, 351, 352, 355, 370, 383, 419, 447, 470, 472, 473, 502, 543, 555, 556, 564, 574, 576, 578, 579, 582, 583, 586, 605, 606, 613, 614, 617, 618, 626–631, 633, 634, 638, 639, 642–646, 653, 656, 657, 659–661, 663, 676, 681, 684, 690, 701, 703, 704, 706, 707, 710, 720, 721, 730, 734, 754, 814
Reports of
Columbia Furnace, Va. Skirmish at, April 16 ... 426
Edenburg, Va. Advance to, April 1–2 ... 418
Front Royal, Va. Action at, May 23 ... 536
Harrisonburg, Va. Skirmish near, May 6 ... 456
Mount Jackson, Va. Occupation of, April 17 ... 426
New Market, Va. Occupation of, April 17 ... 426
Shenandoah Valley. Operations in
April 19–24 ... 445, 446
May 15–June 17 ... 545
Somerville Heights, Va. Action at, May 7 ... 458
Woodstock, Va. Advance to, April 1–2 ... 418
**Barbee, A. R.** Mentioned ... 495
**Barber, Horace.** Mentioned ... 452
**Barbour, James.** Mentioned ... 780, 782, 786, 797, 798

Page.

**Barker, David.** Mentioned ... 423
**Barnard, John G.** Mentioned ... 239
**Barnes, John.** Mentioned ... 690
**Barrett, Norman A.** Mentioned ... 662
**Barrett, Walter.** Mentioned ... 700
**Barry, John P.** Mentioned ... 441, 442, 445
**Barry, William F.**
Mentioned ... 43, 239, 276
Testimony of, McDowell Court of Inquiry ... 239–241
**Barstow, S. F.**
Mentioned ... 42, 45, 171, 181, 185, 308, 310
Testimony of, McDowell Court of Inquiry ... 181–184
(For correspondence as A. A. G., see *Irvin McDowell.*)
**Bartram, William H.** Mentioned ... 610
**Barthoulot, Severin A.** Mentioned ... 573
**Bartlett, William H. C.** Mentioned ... 43
**Barton, Charles M.** Mentioned ... 736, 737
**Barton, Thomas B.**
Correspondence with Charles W. Field ... 436, 437
Mentioned ... 83, 436, 437
**Baxter, George A.** Mentioned ... 702, 734
**Bayard, George D.**
Mentioned ... 14–16, 18, 19, 24, 25, 63, 117, 122, 128, 133, 140, 152, 168, 169, 190, 200, 201, 211, 267, 283, 284, 288, 300, 306, 428–431, 650–655, 665, 785
Reports of
Fredericksburg, Va. Operations about, April 17–19, and occupation of, April 18 ... 430
Rappahannock River, Va. Affair on, May 13 ... 496
Shenandoah Valley. Operations in, June 1–13 ... 676, 677
**Baylor, Robert W.** Mentioned ... 386, 387
**Baylor, W. S. H.**
Mentioned ... 736, 737, 744
Report of engagement at Winchester, Va., May 25 ... 747
**Beal, George L.**
Mentioned ... 566, 577, 578, 584, 598
Report of operations in Shenandoah Valley, May 24–26 ... 609
**Beale, Dr.** Mentioned ... 425
**Bealeton Station, Va.** Affair at, March 28. (See *Orange and Alexandria R. R.*)
**Beall, James F.** Mentioned ... 780, 795
**Bean, Hezekiah H.** Mentioned ... 784, 818
**Beardsley, John.** Mentioned ... 128
**Beatty, E. W.** Mentioned ... 817
**Beaumont, Myron H.** Mentioned ... 678, 680
**Beckwith, E. G.** Mentioned ... 530, 552
**Beem, David E.** Mentioned ... 367
**Behan, Newton I.** Mentioned ... 814
**Beman, Edgar C.** Mentioned ... 586, 598
**Bennett, John W.** Mentioned ... 575
**Berry, James.** Mentioned ... 491
**Berry, W. T.** Mentioned ... 784
**Berryville, Va.** Skirmish at, May 24 ... 518
**Betts, James A.** Mentioned ... 608
**Biddle, George H.** Mentioned ... 42, 45
**Big Bend, W. Va.** Skirmishes at, June 4–7 ... 3
**Binney, Henry M.** Mentioned ... 641

Page.

**Bitzer, J. H.** Mentioned ... 563
**Black, Harvey.** Mentioned ... 391, 709
**Blackburn, William.** Mentioned ... 399
**Blackford, W. W.** Mentioned ... 416, 417
**Blake, Edward F.** Mentioned ... 609
(For correspondence as A. A. A. G., see *S. W. Crawford.*)
**Blakeslee, Erastus.** Mentioned ... 668
**Blanchard, William T.** Mentioned ... 18, 676
**Blenker, Louis.**
Correspondence with John C. Frémont ... 29
Mentioned ... 5–9, 13, 20, 27, 28, 30, 31, 165, 220, 227, 230, 234, 235, 461, 647, 654, 657, 662, 664, 667, 669, 670–675, 783, 796, 798
**Blessing, F.** Mentioned ... 673, 674
**Blessingh, Louis von.**
Mentioned ... 505–507, 510
Report of actions at Princeton, W. Va., May 16–17 ... 510
**Blinn, John J. P.** Mentioned ... 510
**Blucher, M. W.** Mentioned ... 361
**Board, F. H.** Mentioned ... 508
**Bogen, Mr.** Mentioned ... 484
**Bohlen, Henry.** ... 510
Mentioned ... 8, 18–20, 658, 664, 670, 671, 673–675
Report of battle of Cross Keys, Va., June 8 ... 669
**Bohlender, Alexander.** Mentioned ... 506, 510, 511
**Bolles, William M.** Mentioned ... 807
**Bond, Frank A.** Mentioned ... 818
**Bonney, Edward.** Mentioned ... 419
**Boothsville, W. Va.** Raid to, April 12. Reports of
Kelley, Benjamin F ... 423
Showalter, John H ... 423
**Boswell, J. K.**
Mentioned ... 383, 473, 709, 716
Report of operations in Shenandoah Valley, June 1–9 ... 718
**Botts, Lawson.** Mentioned ... 388, 744, 749
**Bottsford, James L.** Mentioned ... 449
**Boudinot, Charles T.** Mentioned ... 361
**Bowen, Mr.** Mentioned ... 413
**Bowen, E. A.** Mentioned ... 607, 612
**Bowen, Walter.** Mentioned ... 386
**Bowersox, George W.** Mentioned ... 501
**Bowling Green Road, Va.** Skirmish on, May 11. Report of Irvin McDowell. 496
**Boyd, George W.** Mentioned ... 613
**Boyd, Robert N.** Mentioned ... 680
**Bradley, Benjamin F.** Mentioned ... 514
**Bradshaw, Robert H.** Mentioned ... 787
**Brainard, H. C.** Mentioned ... 784
**Brandenstein, E. von.** Mentioned ... 21, 674
**Brannan, John M.** Mentioned ... 43
**Breck, Samuel.**
Mentioned ... 42, 45, 61, 117, 292
Testimony of, McDowell Court of Inquiry ... 61–63, 292
**Breckinridge, Carey.** Mentioned ... 732
**Brevard, E. A.** Mentioned ... 749
**Brevoort, William M.** Mentioned ... 580
**Brewer, Melvin.** Mentioned ... 349

Page.

**Bridgford, D. B.**
Mentioned .... 382, 401
Report of battle of Kernstown, Va., March 23 .... 405
**Briggs, Ephraim A.** Mentioned .... 354
**Britton,** Scout. Mentioned .... 430
**Brockenbrough, J. B.** Mentioned .... 725, 729, 780, 782, 818
**Brockenbrough, J. M.** Mentioned .... 434
**Brockway, Charles B.** Mentioned .... 441–443, 445
**Brodhead, Thornton F.**
Mentioned .... 343, 346, 419, 548, 595, 596
Reports of
Kernstown, Va. Battle of, March 23 .... 355
Shenandoah Valley. Operations in, May 24–27 .... 579
**Brodhurst, William F.** Mentioned .... 88
**Brodrick, Virgil.** Mentioned .... 680
**Brooks, James M.** Mentioned .... 787
**Broom,** Mr. Mentioned .... 444
**Brown,** Mr. Mentioned .... 718
**Brown, Clarence.**
Mentioned .... 60, 75, 90, 291, 292
Testimony of, McDowell Court of Inquiry .... 60, 61, 75
**Brown, Edwin F.**
Mentioned .... 596, 606, 607
Reports of
Newtown, Va. Action at, May 24 .... 612
Winchester, Va. Engagement at, May 25 .... 610
**Brown, G. Campbell.** Mentioned .... 780, 782, 784, 786
**Brown, James.** Mentioned .... 799
**Brown, John H.** Mentioned .... 359
**Brown, Samuel B.** Mentioned .... 787, 791
**Brown, W. F.** Mentioned .... 793
**Brown, William M.** Mentioned .... 761
**Brown, W. R.** Mentioned .... 784
**Browntown, Va.** Reconnaissance to, May 21. Report of Hector Tyndale .... 554
**Brum, George W.** Mentioned .... 641
**Bryan, Timothy M., jr.**
Mentioned .... 440, 441
Report of reconnaissance to the Rappahannock River, Va., April 18 .... 441
**Buchanan, Robert C.**
Correspondence with Irvin McDowell .... 274, 320
Mentioned .... 42, 45, 270, 273, 320
Testimony of, McDowell Court of Inquiry .... 273, 320
**Buckley, Lewis P.** Mentioned .... 361, 697
**Buckner, Simon B.** Mentioned .... 49
**Buckner, Thomas R.** Mentioned .... 787, 790, 791
**Buckton Station, Va.** Skirmish at, May 23.
Casualties. Returns of Union troops .... 553, 554
(See *reports of T. J. Jackson*, p. 703, and *C. Parham*, pp. 560, 561.)
**Buell, Don Carlos.** Mentioned .... 229, 230
**Buford, John.**
Correspondence with James B. Ricketts .... 363
Mentioned .... 133, 140, 144, 158, 169, 190, 200–202, 211, 247, 254, 262, 263, 300–302, 319
Testimony of, McDowell Court of Inquiry .... 262, 263
**Bukey, Van H.** Mentioned .... 489
**Bull Pasture Mountain, Va.** Engagement near, May 8. (See *McDowell, Va.*)

Page.

**Bull Run, Va.** Battle of, August 30.
Communications from Robert C. Buchanan .... 320
Reports of R. H. Milroy .... 271, 319
**Bumgardner, James.** Mentioned .... 393
**Burbank, Augustus J.** Mentioned .... 454
**Burbank, Elisha.** Mentioned .... 441
**Burchard, William.**
Mentioned .... 258, 260, 311, 313, 314
Testimony of, McDowell Court of Inquiry .... 261, 311, 313, 314
**Burden, Henry.** Mentioned .... 43
**Burdino, A. D.** Mentioned .... 581
**Burgess, James B.** Mentioned .... 388
**Burke, Redmond.** Mentioned .... 417
**Burke, Thomas J.** Mentioned .... 399, 738, 741, 749
**Burks, Jesse S.**
Mentioned .... 381, 382, 384, 385, 405–407, 409
Report of battle of Kernstown, Va., March 23 .... 400
**Burlingham, A.** Mentioned .... 49
**Burns, John M.** Mentioned .... 78
**Burnside, A. E.**
Correspondence with McDowell Court of Inquiry .... 256
Mentioned .... 250, 273, 320
**Bush, William W.** Mentioned .... 610, 612
**Butler, G. B.** Mentioned .... 795
**Butler, M. M.** Mentioned .... 777
**Butler, Vincent M.** Mentioned .... 388
**Butterfield, Daniel.** Mentioned .... 43
**Butterfield, Francis W.** Mentioned .... 370
**Byram, S. D.** Mentioned .... 352–354
**Cadwalader, George.** Mentioned .... 36, 37, 323
(For correspondence as President Court of Inquiry, see *McDowell Court of Inquiry.*)
**Cadwalader, George B.** Mentioned .... 570, 614
**Camden, E. D.** Mentioned .... 787
**Campbell, James C.** Mentioned .... 472, 478
**Campbell, John A.** Mentioned .... 382, 401, 471, 472, 476, 478–480, 483, 484, 701, 705, 717, 736, 755, 764, 765, 767, 769
**Camp Creek, W. Va.** Skirmish on, May 1. Reports of
Cox, Jacob D .... 449
Jenifer, Walter H .... 450
Scammon, E. Parker .... 449
**Camper, Charles.** Report of action at Front Royal, Va., May 23 .... 558
**Camp McDonald, W. Va.** Skirmish at, May 6 .... 2
**Candy, Charles.** Mentioned .... 697
**Cane, William.** Mentioned .... 501
**Cantey, James.** Mentioned .... 779, 795, 798, 799
**Cantwell, Jacob Y.** Mentioned .... 667
**Cantwell, James.** Mentioned .... 463, 464, 469, 668
**Carpenter, John C.** Mentioned .... 400, 736, 737, 758, 760
**Carpenter, Joseph.**
Correspondence with Thomas J. Jackson .... 400
Mentioned .... 381, 714, 729, 736, 737, 739–741
Reports of
Kernstown, Va. Battle of, March 23 .... 399
Port Republic, Va. Engagements at, June 8–9 .... 759
Winchester, Va. Engagement at, May 25 .... 758

Page.
**Carroll, John W.** Mentioned ... 393
**Carroll, Samuel S.**
Mentioned ... 22, 23, 342, 360, 361, 366 426, 682–687, 691, 695–697
Reports of
Kernstown, Va. Battle of, March 23 ... 368
Port Republic, Va. Engagements at, June 8–9 ... 698
**Carson, John A.** Mentioned ... 476, 488
**Carson, R. P.** Mentioned ... 381 408, 409
**Carter, Samuel P.** Mentioned ... 4
**Carter, Thomas P.** Mentioned ... 514
**Casey, Michael.** Mentioned ... 611
**Casey, Silas.** Mentioned ... 240
**Caskie, James A.** Mentioned ... 771
**Caskie, William H.** Report of engagement at Winchester, Va., May 25 ... 771
**Catterson, Robert F.** Mentioned ... 367
**Chamberlain, Benjamin F.** Mentioned ... 355–357, 698
**Chandler, Robert.**
Mentioned ... 234, 293, 670, 674
Testimony of, McDowell Court of Inquiry ... 234
**Chapman, G. B.** Mentioned ... 493, 495
**Chapman, George D.**
Mentioned ... 607
Report of engagement at Winchester, Va., May 25 ... 608
**Chapman, Lanceford F.** Mentioned ... 501
**Chapmanville, W. Va.** Skirmish at, April 18 ... 2
**Charlestown, W. Va.** Skirmish at, May 28. (See *reports of Thomas J. Jackson*, p. 707; *John F. Neff*, p. 756; *Charles S. Winder*, p. 738.)
**Chase, S. P.** Mentioned ... 61, 122, 292
**Cheek, John F.** Mentioned ... 361
**Chenoweth, J. H.** Mentioned ... 787
**Chesebrough, William H.** Mentioned ... 668
**Chew, R. P.** Mentioned ... 738, 739, 742
**Chipley, J. J.** Mentioned ... 713
**Church, Albert E.** Mentioned ... 43
**Cilley, Jonathan P.** Mentioned ... 576
**Claassen, Peter J.** Mentioned ... 543
**Clare, William H.** Mentioned ... 486
**Clark, Henry E.** Mentioned ... 18, 676, 680
**Clark, J.** Mentioned ... 692
**Clark, John S.** Mentioned ... 361, 525
**Clark, Joseph C.**
Mentioned ... 359, 688, 692, 695–697
Report of engagements at Port Republic, Va., June 8–9 ... 693
**Clarke, Amos.** Mentioned ... 439
**Clarke, A. W.** Mentioned ... 558
**Clarke, Frank.** Mentioned ... 780
**Clarke, Joshua M.** Mentioned ... 439
**Clarke, Melvin.**
Mentioned ... 807
Report of action at Lewisburg, W. Va., May 23 ... 808
**Clarke, Peleg, jr.**
Mentioned ... 73, 82, 85, 110, 111, 116, 296–298
Testimony of, McDowell Court of Inquiry ... 82–89, 296
**Clark's Hollow, W. Va.** Skirmish at, May 1 ... 2

Page.

**Clary, R. H.**
Correspondence with C. N. Goulding ... 30
Mentioned ... 26
**Clay County, W. Va.** Scout in, May 8-21. Report of Benjamin M. Skinner. 489
**Clayhunce, J. W.** Mentioned ... 497
**Clitz, Henry B.** Mentioned ... 43
**Cluseret, Gustave P.**
Correspondence with Franz Sigel ... 173
Mentioned ... 9, 14, 18-22, 35, 158, 171, 649, 652, 655-658, 665, 668, 785
**Coal, ——.** Mentioned ... 662
**Cobb, Norvell.** Mentioned ... 488, 790
**Cockcroft, Edward H.** Mentioned ... 787
**Coffman, Isaac G.** Mentioned ... 775
**Cogswell, William.** Mentioned ... 621
**Cole, Henry A.** Mentioned ... 637
**Cole, James L.** Mentioned ... 708, 722
**Coleman, John B.** Mentioned ... 784
**Coleman, R. T.** Mentioned ... 403
**Colgrove, Silas.**
Mentioned ... 597, 603, 618
Report of engagement at Winchester, Va., May 25 ... 619
**Collins, William D.**
Mentioned ... 548, 574, 576, 586, 682
Report of operations in Shenandoah Valley, May 24-30 ... 587
**Collis, Charles H. T.**
Mentioned ... 547, 568, 569
Report of operations in Shenandoah Valley, May 24-26 ... 572
**Colston, O. S.** Mentioned ... 388
**Colston, Raleigh T.** Mentioned ... 388
**Coltrane, B. E.** Mentioned ... 406, 407
**Columbia Bridge, Va.** Skirmish at, May 5 ... 2
**Columbia Furnace, Va.** Skirmishes at.
April 7 ... 2
April 16.
Orders, congratulatory. War Department, U. S ... 427
Record of Events, Cavalry Brigade ... 427
Report of Nathaniel P. Banks ... 426
**Comly, ——.** Mentioned ... 489
**Commodore, Steamer.** Mentioned ... 96, 219, 227, 232, 276
**Cone, A. F.** Mentioned ... 88
**Confederate Troops.**
Casualties. Returns of
Cross Keys, Va. Battle of, June 8 ... 717, 718, 784
Front Royal, Va. Action at, May 23 ... 780, 781
Harrisonburg, Va. Action near, June 6 ... 783
Kernstown, Va. Battle of, March 23 ... 384
McDowell, Va. Engagement near, May 8 ... 476
Port Republic, Va. Engagements at, June 8-9 ... 717, 718, 787
Winchester, Va. Engagement at, May 25 ... 780, 781
Mentioned. (See respective States.)
Organization, strength, etc., Army of the Northwest ... 487
**Conger, Everton J.** Mentioned ... 16
**Conger, George P.** Mentioned ... 459, 586
**Congress, C. S.** Resolutions. Battle of Kernstown, Va., March 23 ... 384

Page.

**Conley, N. G.** Mentioned ........ 692

**Connecticut Troops.** Mentioned.

Cavalry—*Battalions:* **1st**, 462, 648, 665, 668, 766, 770, 813, 815.

Infantry—*Regiments:* **5th**, 427, 553, 581, 582, 584, 594, 596, 598, 605, 606, 608-610, 613.

**Conner, Eli T.**

Mentioned ........ 413

Report of operations on the Orange and Alexandria R. R., Va., March 28-31. 414

**Conner, Z. T.**

Mentioned ........ 481, 484-486, 707, 727, 793

Report of action at Front Royal, Va., May 30 ........ 793

**Connoly, James P.** Mentioned ........ 439

**Constable, Robert A.** Mentioned ........ 469

**Cook, Elliott W.** Mentioned ........ 610

**Cooke, E. F.** Mentioned ........ 432

**Cooper, James.** Mentioned ........ 639-641

**Cooper, Samuel.** Mentioned ........ 321

**Copeland, Joseph T.**

Mentioned ........ 355-358, 579, 580, 596

Report of battle of Kernstown, Va., March 23 ........ 356

**Copeland, R. Morris.**

Mentioned ........ 121, 285, 361, 378

Reports of battle of Kernstown, Va., March 23 ........ 347, 348

(For correspondence as A. A. G., see *Nathaniel P. Banks.*)

**Corcoran, John.** Mentioned ........ 683

**Corwine, R. M.** Mentioned ........ 35

**Cothran, George W.**

Mentioned ........ 419

Report of advance to Edenburg and Woodstock, Va., April 1-2 ........ 419

**Council of War.** Army of the Potomac, March 13 ........ 104, 223

**Courtney, A. R.** Mentioned ........ 779, 782, 783, 799

**Cowan, R. E.** Mentioned ........ 409

**Cowles, Milton.** Mentioned ........ 491

**Cox, ——.** Mentioned ........ 554, 555

**Cox, Adam.** Mentioned ........ 88

**Cox, Jacob D.**

Congratulatory orders. Action at Lewisburg, W. Va., May 23 ........ 805

Correspondence with George Crook ........ 805

Mentioned ........ 4, 7, 8, 10, 12, 155, 174, 503, 508, 511, 513-515, 642, 653, 657, 812

Reports of

Camp Creek, W. Va. Skirmish on, May 1 ........ 449

Lewisburg, W. Va. Action at, May 23 ........ 804

Princeton, W. Va. Actions at, May 16-17 ........ 503-505

**Coyle, John.** Mentioned ........ 787

**Cozzens, W. B.** Mentioned ........ 43

**Craig, Alfred T.** Mentioned ........ 370

**Crane, Joseph G.** Mentioned ........ 668

**Crane, Louis H. D.** Mentioned ........ 625

**Crawford, Mr.** Mentioned ........ 718

**Crawford, J. J.** Mentioned ........ 482

**Crawford, S. W.**

Correspondence with John C. Frémont ........ 33

Mentioned ........ 184-186, 188-190, 200, 201, 285, 300, 525, 539, 543-545, 552

**Creighton, William R.** Mentioned ........ 361, 697

Page.

**Crist, Sergeant.** Mentioned ........ 388
**Crook, George.**
  Correspondence with Jacob D. Cox ........ 805
  Mentioned ........ 10, 505, 507, 657, 803–805
  Report of action at Lewisburg, W. Va., May 23 ........ 805, 806
**Crosby, Franklin B.**
  Mentioned ........ 594, 596
  Report of operations in Shenandoah Valley, May 24–26 ........ 603
**Cross Keys, Va.** Battle of, June 8.
  Casualties. Returns of
    Confederate forces ........ 717, 718, 784
    Union forces ........ 664, 665
  Communications from John C. Frémont ........ 653, 655, 785
  Reports of
    Bohlen, Henry ........ 669
    Ewell, R. S ........ 781
    Garnett, Thomas S ........ 768
    Hamm, John ........ 673
    Kozlay, Eugene A ........ 671
    Krzyzanowski, Wladimir ........ 672
    Leigh, B. W ........ 769
    McDonald, Hugh ........ 675
    Mahler, Francis ........ 674
    Martin, William ........ 765
    Schenck, Robert C ........ 666
    Scott, W. C. ........ 789, 790
    Trimble, Isaac R ........ 795
    Walker, J. A. ........ 791
    Wiedrich, Michael ........ 670
  (See also
  *March 29–June 27. Operations in Mountain Department. Report of*
    Frémont, John C.
  *May 15–June 17. Operations in Shenandoah Valley. Reports of*
    Crutchfield, S. Frémont, John C. Johnson, B. T.)
**Crowninshield, Francis W.** Mentioned ........ 623
**Crump, Edward C.** Mentioned ........ 409
**Crutchfield, Corbin.** Mentioned ........ 436
**Crutchfield, S.**
  Mentioned ........ 473, 702, 709, 778
  Reports of operations in Shenandoah Valley, May 23–June 9 ........ 724, 727
**Culpeper Court-House, Va.** Reconnaissance to, May 4–5.
  Reports of
    Hartsuff, George L. ........ 451
    Stowell, D. Porter ........ 451
**Cumming, Alexander M.** Mentioned ........ 678
**Cummings, Arthur C.**
  Mentioned ........ 382
  Report of battle of Kernstown, Va., March 23 ........ 394
**Cunningham, R. H., jr.**
  Mentioned ........ 476, 708
  Reports of
    McDowell, Va. Engagement near, May 8 ........ 476
    Winchester, Va. Engagement at, May 25 ........ 763
**Curtin, Andrew G.** Mentioned ........ 165, 227

Page.
**Curtis, George W.** Mentioned ... 409, 482, 775
**Cushing, H. C.** Mentioned ... 571, 603, 604, 606, 620
**Cutshaw, W. E.** Mentioned ... 725, 736, 737
**Cutting, J. De W.**
Mentioned ... 42, 45, 90, 93, 121, 269, 320
Testimony of, McDowell Court of Inquiry ... 269, 270
**Dabney, Chiswell.** Mentioned ... 417
**Dabney, Ed. M.** Mentioned ... 488
**Dabney, R. L.** Mentioned ... 473, 709, 716
**Dahlgren, Ulric.**
Mentioned ... 125, 157, 159, 298, 309, 634, 641
Testimony of, McDowell Court of Inquiry ... 159, 160
**Daily, R. W.** Mentioned ... 410
**Dale, J. W.** Mentioned ... 393
**Dalton, Francis.** Mentioned ... 694
**Daniels, C. H.** Mentioned ... 634, 636, 639, 641
**Darnall, Morgan A.** Mentioned ... 5, 439
**Darr, Joseph, jr.** Mentioned ... 26
**Daum, Philip.**
Mentioned ... 339, 340, 343, 346, 350, 361, 369, 375, 686, 687, 695, 699
Reports of
Kernstown, Va. Battle of, March 23 ... 359
Port Republic, Va. Engagements at, June 8–9 ... 691
**David, J. I.** Mentioned ... 570
**David, T. B. A.**
Correspondence with John C. Frémont ... 31
Mentioned ... 31
**Davidson, A.** Mentioned ... 431
**Davidson, James.** Mentioned ... 575
**Davies, Henry E.**
Mentioned ... 261, 305, 431, 432
Testimony of, McDowell Court of Inquiry ... 261, 262, 305, 306
**Davis, Aaron.** Mentioned ... 780, 800
**Davis, James C.** Mentioned ... 397, 763
**Davis, Jefferson.**
Correspondence with Joseph E. Johnston ... 379
Mentioned ... 701
**Davis, John B.** Mentioned ... 388
**Davis, William.** Mentioned ... 692
**Davis, William E.** Mentioned ... 560, 561
**Dawson, Samuel** Mentioned ... 476
**Debeck, Edmond.** Mentioned ... 675
**De Beck, William L.** Mentioned ... 668
**De Choiseul, Charles.** Mentioned ... 787
**Decker, James N.** Mentioned ... 427, 429, 432
**Dedlake, J. H.** Mentioned ... 787
**Deems, James M.** Mentioned ... 130
**De Forest, Othneil.**
Mentioned ... 32, 523, 535, 548, 572, 574, 575, 601
Report of operations in Shenandoah Valley, May 24–27 ... 581
**Deibold, Charles W.** Mentioned ... 462
**De Johns, Mr.** Mentioned ... 83
**Delafield, Richard.** Mentioned ... 43
**Delaware.** Military departments embracing ... 1

Page.

**Delaware Troops.** Mentioned.
Infantry—*Regiments:* **3d**, 633.
**Delmege, Patrick.** Mentioned ... 692, 694
**Dennis, J. M.** Mentioned ... 410
**Dennison, William.** Mentioned ... 42
**Devin, J. D.** Mentioned ... 558
**Dewey, A. S.** Mentioned ... 570, 587
**Dickinson, Henry C.** Mentioned ... 730
**Dickinson, J. W.** Mentioned ... 585
**Dilger, Hubert.** Mentioned ... 19
**Dillard, W. W.**
Correspondence with John E. Johnson ... 437
Mentioned ... 438
**Dimmock, Charles.** Mentioned ... 513
**District of Columbia Troops.** Mentioned.
Infantry—*Regiments:* **1st**, 630, 639; **2d**, 226.
**Dix, John A.**
Assignments to command ... 1
Mentioned ... 114, 165, 226, 526, 627, 628
**Dixon, J. W.** Mentioned ... 682
**Dobbs, Cyrus J.** Mentioned ... 373
**Dobyns, Abner.** Mentioned ... 766
**Donnelly, Dudley.**
Mentioned ... 358, 446, 528, 546, 547, 549, 552, 553, 558, 568, 578–580, 594–598, 600, 603, 604, 613, 616
Report of operations in Shenandoah Valley, May 24–26 ... 605
**Doubleday, Abner.** Mentioned ... 120, 213, 219, 239, 255, 286, 315, 317
**Douglas, B. B.** Mentioned ... 438
**Douglas, H. K.** Mentioned ... 709, 716
**Douty, Calvin S.**
Mentioned ... 587–592, 610
Report of action at Middletown, Va., May 24 ... 575
**Dove, David.** Mentioned ... 814
**Downey, Stephen W.**
Correspondence with Benjamin F. Kelley ... 447
Mentioned ... 5, 8, 13, 447, 456, 647, 815
Reports of skirmishes at and near Wardensville, W. Va., May 7 ... 457
**Downs, ——.** Mentioned ... 490
**Doyle, Joseph.** Mentioned ... 817
**Drake, David.** Mentioned ... 416, 417
**Driver, W. C.** Mentioned ... 787
**Drouillard, James P.** Mentioned ... 90
**Duffié, Alfred N.** Mentioned ... 496
**Duffy, Patrick B.** Mentioned ... 791
**Duggan, Andrew W.** Mentioned ... 581
**Duggan, James.** Mentioned ... 406
**Dulany, R. H.** Mentioned ... 730, 731
**Dumfries, Va.** Reconnaissance to, March 20–21 ... 1
**Duncan, C.** Mentioned ... 774
**Dunka, Nicolai.** Mentioned ... 21, 35, 655, 658, 665
**Dunkle, J. J.** Mentioned ... 787
**Dunning, Samuel H.** Mentioned ... 697
**Duryea, Abram.** Mentioned ... 528
**Dushane, Nathan T.** Mentioned ... 537, 556–559
**Dushane, Samuel P.** Mentioned ... 802

Page.

**Dutton, Henry M.** Mentioned ..... 608
**Dwight, Wilder.** Mentioned ..... 599, 618, 622, 623
**Dwyer, Philip.** Mentioned ..... 553, 565, 682
**Dye, Samuel P.** Mentioned ..... 476, 482
**Dyer, Charles E.** Mentioned ..... 476
**Dyer, Robert F.** Report of reconnaissance to the **Rappahannock River, Va.**, April 15 ..... 424
**Early, Jubal A.** Mentioned ..... 21
**Easley, C. B.** Mentioned ..... 795
**Eaton, Henry Z.** Mentioned ..... 376, 377, 698
**Echols, John.** Mentioned ..... 381, 393, 402
**Edenburg, Va.** Advance to, April 1-2. **Reports of**
Banks, N. P ..... 418
Cothran, George W ..... 419
Gordon, George H ..... 419
**Edgar, George M.** Mentioned ..... 807
**Edmondson, James K.** Mentioned ..... 389
**Elk Mountain, W. Va.** Skirmish at, **March 19** ..... 1
**Ellicott, George.** Mentioned ..... 612
**Elliott, Leonidas H.** Mentioned ..... 514
**Elzey, Arnold.** Mentioned ..... 21, 446, 451, 452, 589, 701, 705, 713, 714, 717, 728, 757, 758, 779, 781, 782, 784, 791, 792, 796
**English, R. M.** Mentioned ..... 745
**Este, William M.** Mentioned ..... 151, 272, 319, 668
**Etheridge, James A.** Mentioned ..... 484
**Etting, Samuel M.** Mentioned ..... 771
**Ewell, R. S.**
Correspondence with **Thomas J. Jackson** ..... 801
Mentioned ..... 9, 14, 128, 149, 184, 188, 207, 255, 304, 315, 328, 416, 426, 433, 435, 451, 452, 470, 500, 522–524, 526–528, 555, 565, 589, 594, 617, 618, 642, 646–648, 702–715, 717, 719, 721, 725–729, 731, 732, 734, 738, 766, 768, 788, 791, 793, 795–798, 802, 818
**Reports of**
Cross Keys, Va. Battle of, June 8 ..... 781
Front Royal, Va. Action at, May 23 ..... 778
Port Republic, Va. Engagements at, June 8–9 ..... 785
Winchester, Va. Engagement at, May 25 ..... 778
**Falmouth, Va.** Skirmishes near, April 17–19. (See *Fredericksburg, Va.*)
**Farley, John.** Mentioned ..... 593
**Farley, W. D.** Mentioned ..... 417
**Farnsworth, Charles.** Report of scout to **Moorefield and New Creek, W. Va.**, and Winchester, Va., June 22–30 ..... 815
**Farnsworth, John F.** Report of reconnaissance to the **Rappahannock River**, Va., April 2 ..... 421
**Farrar, Thomas P.** Mentioned ..... 787
**Fay, Henry.** Mentioned ..... 491
**Fedalen, Charles.** Mentioned ..... 572
**Ferry, O. S.** Mentioned ..... 697
**Fesler, George.** Mentioned ..... 620
**Fiala, John T.** Mentioned ..... 35
**Field, Charles W.**
Correspondence with
**Barton, T. B** ..... 436, 437
**Johnson, John E** ..... 436
Lee, Robert E ..... 433, 436, 437

Page

**Field, Charles W.**—Continued.
Mentioned ... 321
Reports of operations about, April 17-19, and occupation of Fredericksburg, Va., April 18 ... 432, 434-436
**Figyelmesy, Philip.** Mentioned ... 35, 650
**Finch, C. M.** Mentioned ... 650
**Finney, R. H.** Mentioned ... 493
**Finney, William W.** Mentioned ... 493, 807, 812, 813
**Firey, William.** Mentioned ... 457
**Fish, William S.** Mentioned ... 5, 134, 648, 650, 813
**Fisher, George W.** Mentioned ... 69
**Fisher, Robert H.** Mentioned ... 393, 751
**Fisher, Th. F.** Report of actions at Princeton, W. Va., May 16-17 ... 517
**Fitzhugh,** Mrs. Mentioned ... 42
**Fitzhugh, Henry.** Mentioned ... 450, 451, 493, 494
**Flagg, George A.** Mentioned ... 525, 570
**Fleming, J. Presley.**
Mentioned ... 596, 597, 600
Report of operations in Shenandoah Valley, May 24-25 ... 602
**Fletcher, C. G.** Mentioned ... 476, 482
**Fletcher, John.** Mentioned ... 703
**Fletcher, L. J.** Mentioned ... 748, 749
**Flournoy, Thomas S.**
Mentioned ... 702, 707, 709, 731, 779
Report of operations in Shenandoah Valley, May 23-26 ... 733
**Floyd, John B.** Mentioned ... 507, 514, 804
**Fonerden, Clarence A.** Mentioned ... 400
**Fontaine,** Private. Mentioned ... 779
**Ford, Albert L.** Mentioned ... 585
**Ford, Hyatt G.** Mentioned ... 346
**Ford, J. B.** Correspondence with John C. Frémont ... 30
**Foster, James D.** Mentioned ... 468
**Foster, Justus P.** Mentioned ... 582
**Foster, Robert S.**
Mentioned ... 361, 458
Reports of
Kernstown, Va. Battle of, March 23 ... 372
Somerville Heights, Va. Action at, May 7 ... 458
**Foster, William C.** Mentioned ... 372
**Fowler, William T.** Mentioned ... 683
**Fralick, John H.** Mentioned ... 353, 354
**Francis, J.** Mentioned ... 570
**Franklin, F. E.** Mentioned ... 506, 507
**Franklin, William B.** Mentioned ... 43, 92, 93, 220, 231, 277, 279
**Franklin, W. Va.** Skirmishes near.
May 5 ... 2
May 10-12. Report of Robert C. Schenck ... 496
May 26 ... 3, 518
**Fredericksburg, Va.** Operations about, April 17-19, and occupation of.*
Communications from
Augur, Christopher C ... 431, 432
Barton, T. B ... 436, 437
Dillard, W. W ... 437

* Includes skirmishes near Falmouth, Va., April 17-19.

Page.

**Fredericksburg, Va.** Operations about, Apr. 17–19, and occupation of—Cont'd.
Communications from
Field, Charles W ..... 436, 437
Johnson, John E ..... 436
Lee, Robert E ..... 433
Toole, J. A ..... 438
Reports of
Augur, Christopher C ..... 428
Bayard, George D ..... 430
Field, Charles W ..... 432, 434–436
Kilpatrick, Judson ..... 432
Lee, W. H. F ..... 438
McDowell, Irvin ..... 427, 428
**Freeman, William H.** Mentioned ..... 357
**Frémont, John C.**
Assignments to command ..... 1, 169
Congratulatory orders. Action at Lewisburg, W. Va., May 23 ..... 805
Co-operation with McDowell ..... 16, 17
Correspondence with
Adjutant-General's Office, U. S. A ..... 653, 655
Banks, Nathaniel P ..... 27, 31, 32, 34, 527, 530
Blenker, Louis ..... 29
Crawford, S. W ..... 33
David, T. B. A ..... 31
Ford, J. B ..... 30
Lincoln, Abraham ..... 7, 13, 24, 25, 34, 643–645, 647–650, 655, 656, 659–663
McDowell, Irvin ..... 17, 647, 649
Rosecrans, W. S ..... 27, 28
Saxton, Rufus ..... 635
Schenck, R. C ..... 28, 29
Shields, James ..... 21, 23, 24, 32, 33
Sigel, Franz ..... 32
Suckley, George ..... 30, 31
Tracy, Albert ..... 35
War Department, U. S. ..... 10, 31, 642, 644–657, 659, 660, 662, 663
**Mentioned** ..... 7, 10, 29, 30, 32–34, 41, 42, 55, 108, 117, 121, 123, 132, 169, 220, 230, 234, 283–288, 298, 460, 523, 524, 528, 533, 535, 538–541, 543–545, 635, 636, 651, 676, 677, 681, 683–691, 707, 708, 710–714, 716, 720, 728, 730, 747, 781, 783, 786, 798, 802
Ordered to move from Franklin, W. Va., against Jackson ..... 10, 642, 643
Proposed operations against Knoxville, Tenn ..... 6–10
Reports of
Grass Lick, W. Va. Skirmish at, April 23 ..... 447
McDowell, Va. Engagement near, May 8 ..... 460, 461
Monterey, Va. Skirmish at, April 12 ..... 422
Mountain Department. Operations in, March 29–June 27 ..... 3
Princeton, W. Va. Actions at, May 16–17 ..... 503
Shaver's River, W. Va. Raid to, May 30 ..... 813
Virginia Central Railroad, Va. Raid on the, May 20 ..... 803
Wardensville, W. Va. Skirmish at and near, May 7 ..... 456
Staff of. Communication from Albert Tracy ..... 35
**French, M. L.** Mentioned ..... 430
**French, William H.** Mentioned ..... 43
**Friend, Charles W.** Mentioned ..... 468

Page.

**Front Royal, Va.**
Actions at.
May 23.
Casualties. Returns of
Confederate troops ... 780, 781
Union Troops ... 553, 554
Communications from
Banks, Nathaniel P ... 525–527
Saville, Thomas ... 525
Reports of
Atwell, Charles A ... 565
Banks, Nathaniel P ... 536
Camper, Charles ... 558
Ewell, R. S ... 778
Kenly, John R ... 555
Lyeth, John McF ... 558
Parham, Charles ... 560
Saville, Thomas ... 558
Scott, W. C ... 788
Smith, George ... 558
Thompson, George W ... 558
Vought, Philip G ... 564
(See also
*May* 15–*June* 17. *Operations in Shenandoah Valley.* *Reports of*
Banks, Nathaniel P. Crutchfield, S. Flournoy, Thomas S. Jackson, Thomas J. Munford, Thomas T. Taylor, Richard.)
May 30.
Communications from R. S. Ewell ... 793
Reports of
Conner, Z. T ... 793
Kimball, Nathan ... 694
Shields, James ... 682
Skirmish near, May 31. Report of James Shields ... 682
**Fry, George.** Mentioned ... 468
**Fry, Jesse.** Mentioned ... 430
**Fugate, Cervantus S.** Mentioned ... 462
**Fulkerson, Samuel V.**
Mentioned ... 380–382, 384, 387, 388, 395, 481, 482, 484, 701, 717, 736, 773, 775–777
Reports of
Kernstown, Va. Battle of, March 23 ... 408
Winchester, Va. Engagement at, May 25 ... 772
**Funk, J. H. S.**
Mentioned ... 738, 740, 741, 748, 749
Report of engagements at Port Republic, Va., June 8–9 ... 749
**Funk, Josiah M.** Mentioned ... 501
**Funsten, Oliver R.**
Mentioned ... 385, 386, 726
Report of battle of Kernstown, Va., March 23 ... 386
**Furbish, Nehemiah T.** Mentioned ... 609
**Furlow, William L.** Mentioned ... 476
**Gaines' Cross-Roads, Rappahannock County, Va.** Skirmishes near.
May 14 ... 2
May 15. Report of Thomas T. Munford ... 498
**Gainesville, Va.** Reconnaissance to, March 20. Reports of
Howard, Oliver O ... 333
Richardson, Israel B ... 332

Page.

**Gaither, George R.** Mentioned ... 415
**Gall, Alvis D.** Mentioned ... 372
**Gallagher, Michael F.** Mentioned ... 357
**Gallagher, Patrick.** Mentioned ... 346
**Gamble, William.** Mentioned ... 421
**Gammon, William T.** Mentioned ... 787
**Gardner, George H.** Mentioned ... 575, 581, 640
**Garfield, James A.** Mentioned ... 4
**Garland, Nelson H.** Mentioned ... 482
**Garnett, J. M.** Mentioned ... 709, 737-743, 746, 757, 758
**Garnett, R. B.** Mentioned ... 342, 380-382, 384, 388, 391, 392, 406-408
**Garnett, Thomas S.**
Mentioned ... 742
Reports of
Cross-Keys, Va. Battle of, June 8 ... 768
Port Republic, Va. Engagements at, June 8-9 ... 768
**Gavin, James.** Mentioned ... 696, 697, 699, 700
**Geary, John W.**
Mentioned ... 106, 117, 165, 167, 227, 234, 286, 356, 410, 499, 522, 524, 526, 528, 536, 541, 554, 626, 638, 644, 653, 729
Reports of
Linden, Va. Skirmishes at
May 15 ... 499, 500
May 24 ... 566
Middleburg, Va. Operations about, March 27-28 ... 410
White Plains, Va. Operations about, March 29-31 ... 411, 412
**Georgia Troops.** Mentioned.
Infantry—*Regiments:* **12th**, 471, 472, 476, 478, 479, 481, 483, 487, 682, 694, 707, 717, 784, 787, 792, 793; **21st**, 20, 705, 706, 717, 779, 780, 783, 784, 794-796, 799.
**Gibbon, John.** Mentioned ... 43, 199, 208, 213, 242, 243, 317
**Gibboney, Albert.** Mentioned ... 493
**Gibbons, S. B.** Mentioned ... 472, 476, 482, 484
**Gibson, Thomas S.** Mentioned ... 409
**Giddings, Ephraim.** Mentioned ... 561
**Gilbert, Samuel A.**
Mentioned ... 807
Report of action at Lewisburg, W. Va., May 23 ... 809
**Giles Court-House, W. Va.** Action at, May 10. Reports of
Heth, Henry ... 491
Jenifer, Walter H. ... 493
McCausland, John ... 495
**Gillespie, William.** Mentioned ... 551
**Gilsa, Leopold von.** Mentioned ... 21
**Glazier, William H.** Mentioned ... 501
**Godbold, Henry L.** Mentioned ... 441, 442, 445
**Goff, ——.** Mentioned ... 662
**Goldwire, John K.** Mentioned ... 476
**Goodrich, Earle S.** Mentioned ... 698, 700
**Goodwin, R. D.**
Correspondence with
McDowell Court of Inquiry ... 46, 73, 81
McDowell, Irvin ... 44
War Department, U. S. ... 69
Mentioned ... 46, 59, 64, 72-75, 81
Testimony of, McDowell Court of Inquiry ... 59, 64-72

Page.
**Goold**, Mr. Mentioned ..... 43
**Gordon**, Mr. Mentioned ..... 436
**Gordon**, Lieutenant. Mentioned ..... 444
**Gordon, George H.**
Correspondence with A. S. Williams ..... 624
Mentioned ..... 186, 188, 528, 547–549, 552, 553, 558, 563, 568, 574, 594–598, 603
Reports of
Edenburg, Va. Advance to, April 1–2 ..... 419
Shenandoah Valley, Va. Operations in, May 24 ..... 2
Winchester, Va. Engagement at, May 25 ..... 616
Woodstock, Va. Advance to, April 1–2 ..... 419
**Gordonsville and Keezletown Cross-Roads, W. Va.** Skirmish at, April 26 ..... 2
**Gould, J. J.** Mentioned ..... 441, 445
**Goulding, C. N.**
Correspondence with R. H. Clary ..... 30
Mentioned ..... 26
**Grace, P. T.** Mentioned ..... 754
**Graham, Archibald.** Mentioned ..... 397, 761, 763
**Graham, Robert.** Mentioned ..... 690
**Grassau, Henry.** Mentioned ..... 665
**Grass Lick, W. Va.** Skirmish at, April 23.
Communications from Stephen W. Downey ..... 447
Report of John C. Frémont ..... 447
(See also *report of John C. Frémont*, p. 5.)
**Graves, David C.** Mentioned ..... 814
**Gray**, Mrs. Mentioned ..... 63
**Gray, Samuel L.** Mentioned ..... 774
**Gray, W. W.** Mentioned ..... 357
**Greathouse, Dick.** Mentioned ..... 490
**Green, Conrad.** Mentioned ..... 784, 802
**Green, John.** Mentioned ..... 361
**Green, J. Shac.** Mentioned ..... 732
**Greene, George S.** Mentioned ..... 542, 544, 545, 552
**Greenfield, Andrew J.**
Mentioned ..... 356, 357, 427
Report of battle of Kernstown, Va., March 23 ..... 358
**Gregory, William H.** Mentioned ..... 476, 482
**Griffin, George H.** Mentioned ..... 565, 682
**Griffin, Jonathan.** Mentioned ..... 439
**Grigsby, A. J.**
Correspondence with Thomas J. Jackson ..... 394
Mentioned ..... 381, 406, 736, 737, 740, 741
Reports of
Kernstown, Va. Battle of, March 23 ..... 393
Newtown, Va. Action at, May 24 ..... 751
Port Republic, Va. Engagement at, June 8–9 ..... 752
Winchester, Va. Engagement at, May 25 ..... 751
**Grimsley, Daniel A.** Mentioned ..... 702
**Grinnell**, Lieutenant. Mentioned ..... 682
**Grinnell, R. M.** Mentioned ..... 780, 800
**Groveton Heights, Va.** Battle of, August 30. (See *Bull Run, Va.*)
**Guest, George.** Mentioned ..... 88
**Hagan, Henry.** Mentioned ..... 417
**Hagy, Pleasant S.** Mentioned ..... 409

Page.

Haines, Thomas R. Mentioned ........ 18, 676, 680
Hairston, J. T. W. Mentioned ........ 417
Hale, Samuel.
Mentioned ........ 767
Report of engagement near McDowell, Va., May 8 ........ 478
Hale, Samuel, jr. Mentioned ........ 405
Hall, Josiah. Mentioned ........ 586
Hall, C. Correspondence with Frederick Myers ........ 119
Hall, James A. Mentioned ........ 677
Hall, W. C. Mentioned ........ 799
Halleck, Henry W. Mentioned ........ 93, 229, 275, 294, 332, 542
Halsted, Edward L. Mentioned ........ 354, 567
Hamilton, C. S.
Correspondence with War Department, U. S ........ 645
Mentioned ........ 630, 645, 646
Hamilton, D. B. Mentioned ........ 571, 572
Hamilton, James. Mentioned ........ 801, 803
Hamilton, Schuyler. Mentioned ........ 43
Hamlin, Augustus C. Mentioned ........ 26, 30
Hamlin, Cyrus. Mentioned ........ 35
Hamm, John.
Mentioned ........ 669, 670, 673
Report of battle of Cross Keys, Va., June 8 ........ 673
Hammond, John. Mentioned ........ 582
Hampton, Joseph J. Mentioned ........ 494
Hampton, R. B.
Mentioned ........ 571, 572, 582, 586, 594
Report of operations in Shenandoah Valley, May 25–28 ........ 600
Hampton, Wade. Mentioned ........ 25
Hancock, W. S. Mentioned ........ 43
Hanlon, Joseph. Mentioned ........ 780
Hanna, John N. Mentioned ........ 787, 791
Hanson, ——. Mentioned ........ 457
Hardie, David. Mentioned ........ 612
Harman, J. A.
Mentioned ........ 383, 473, 707–709, 716
Report of stores captured during operations in Shenandoah Valley, May 15–June 17 ........ 721–723
Harman, Lewis. Mentioned ........ 787, 791
Harman, Michael G.
Mentioned ........ 472, 484
Report of engagement near McDowell, Va., May 8 ........ 488
Harman, William H. (Captain.) Mentioned ........ 478
Harman, William H. (Colonel.)
Mentioned ........ 382, 484
Report of battle of Kernstown, Va., March 23 ........ 391
Harper, Addison. Mentioned ........ 386
Harper's Ferry, W. Va. Operations about, May 24–30.
Communications from
Hamilton, C. S ........ 645
Lincoln, Abraham ........ 626, 628, 629, 631
Saxton, Rufus ........ 626–638, 646, 648
War Department, U. S ........ 626, 627, 629–632, 634, 635, 637, 638, 641
Congratulatory orders. War Department, U. S ........ 641

Page.

**Harper's Ferry, W. Va.** Operations about, May 24-30—Continued.
Reports of
Saxton, Rufus ..... 639
Winder, Charles S., May 28 ..... 738
Saxton, Rufus, assigned to command ..... 626
Sigel, Franz, assigned to command ..... 638
(See also
*May* 15–*June* 17. *Operations in Shenandoah Valley. Reports of*
Jackson, Thomas J. Munford, Thomas T.)
**Harris, A. L.** Mentioned ..... 468
**Harris, Thomas M.** Mentioned ..... 5, 662
**Harris, William E.** Mentioned ..... 817
**Harrisonburg, Va.**
Action near, June 6.
Casualties. Returns of, Confederate forces ..... 783
Communications from John C. Frémont ..... 652, 653, 657
Report of W. C. Scott ..... 788, 789
(See also
*March* 29–*June* 27. *Operations in Mountain Department. Report of*
Frémont, John C.
*May* 15–*June* 17. *Operations in Shenandoah Valley. Reports of*
Bayard, George D. Johnson, Bradley T. Kargé, Joseph.
Jackson, T. J. Jones, Owen. Munford, Thomas T.)
Occupation of, by Union forces, April 22. (See *Shenandoah Valley. Operations in, April* 19–24.)
Skirmishes near.
April 24. (See *Shenandoah Valley. Operations in, April* 19–24.)
May 6.
Communications from War Department, U. S ..... 456
Report of Nathaniel P. Banks ..... 456
June 7 ..... 518
**Harrow, William.**
Mentioned ..... 361
Report of battle of Kernstown, Va., March 23 ..... 366
**Hartsuff, George L.**
Mentioned ..... 42, 43, 45, 106, 107, 283, 287, 295, 651
Report of reconnaissance to Culpeper Court-House, Va., May 4–5 ..... 451
Testimony of, McDowell Court of Inquiry ..... 106, 107, 295
**Hartung, A. von.** Mentioned ..... 673
**Harvey, Isaac J.** Mentioned ..... 354, 567
**Haskell, Leonidas.** Mentioned ..... 14, 16, 23, 24, 35
**Haskin, J. B.** Mentioned ..... 92
**Hatch, John P.**
Mentioned ..... 215, 244, 448, 522, 528, 546–550, 553, 567, 568, 580, 586, 591, 594, 596, 597, 602, 603, 605, 612, 614, 615
Record of Events.
Columbia Furnace, Va. Skirmish at, April 16 ..... 427
McGaheysville, Va. Skirmish at, April 27 ..... 448
Report of operations in Shenandoah Valley, May 24–25 ..... 573
**Hatchett, William H.** Mentioned ..... 438
**Hatfield, H. C.** Mentioned ..... 510
**Haupt, Hermann.**
Mentioned ..... 42, 45, 76, 121, 280–283, 290
Testimony of, McDowell Court of Inquiry ..... 76–80, 290
**Hauteville, Frederic d'.** Mentioned ..... 550, 552, 606

Page

**Haven, Franklin.**

Mentioned .......... 180, 195, 208, 214, 265, 298, 308, 310, 311, 314, 317

Testimony of, McDowell Court of Inquiry .......... 180, 181, 208, 209, 265, 266, 311

**Haviland, William F.** Mentioned .......... 565

**Hawkins, Willis A.** Mentioned .......... 484, 793

**Hawks, W. J.**

Mentioned .......... 383, 473, 709, 716

Reports of supplies captured during operations in Shenandoah Valley, May 15–June 17 .......... 720, 721

**Hawver, G. W.** Mentioned .......... 814

**Hayes, Perry.** Mentioned .......... 490

**Hayes, Rutherford B.** Mentioned .......... 449

**Hayman, Samuel B.** [Hemans.] Mentioned .......... 70

**Haymond, ——.** Mentioned .......... 662

**Haynes, Joseph H.** Mentioned .......... 753

**Hays, Robert M.** Mentioned .......... 375

**Hays, H. T.** Mentioned .......... 741, 750, 787, 801, 803, 818

**Hayward, W. H.** Mentioned .......... 692, 696, 697

**Haywood, James H.** Mentioned .......... 497

**Hazzard, George W.** Mentioned .......... 413

**Heazlit, William M.** Mentioned .......... 357, 581

**Hedgcock, J. C.** Mentioned .......... 780, 795

**Heimach, George.** Mentioned .......... 573

**Heintz, C.**

Correspondence with Franz Sigel .......... 176

Mentioned .......... 171, 173

**Heintzelman, S. P.**

Correspondence with John Pope .......... 160

Mentioned .......... 43, 65, 74, 75, 103, 130, 172, 174, 176, 196, 210, 224, 229, 232, 304, 307, 328–330

Testimony of, McDowell Court of Inquiry .......... 74, 75

**Hemans.** [Hayman, Samuel B.?] Mentioned .......... 70

**Henderson, John.** (7th Indiana.) Mentioned .......... 692

**Henderson, John.** (7th Virginia Cavalry.) Mentioned .......... 386

**Henkle, Casper C.** Mentioned .......... 777

**Henry, W. W.** Mentioned .......... 417

**Herndon,** Dr. Mentioned .......... 88

**Hess, Joseph T.** Mentioned .......... 380

**Heth, Henry.**

Correspondence with W. W. Loring .......... 810, 811

Mentioned .......... 10, 495, 503, 504, 507, 513–517, 804–811, 814

Reports of

Giles Court-House, W. Va. Action at, May 10 .......... 491

Lewisburg, W. Va. Action at, May 23 .......... 812

Princeton, W. Va. Actions at, May 16–17 .......... 513

**Heth, John.** Mentioned .......... 406, 407

**Heth, Stockton.** Mentioned .......... 493

**Higginbotham, John C.** Mentioned .......... 472, 484

**Hill, A. P.** Mentioned .......... 128, 149, 207, 256, 304, 328

**Hill, R. H.** Mentioned .......... 784

**Hinrichs, Oscar.** Mentioned .......... 714, 781

**Hitchcock, E. A.**

Correspondence with

Lincoln, A. .......... 229

War Department, U. S. .......... 227, 228

Page.

**Hitchcock, E. A.**—Continued.
Mentioned ... 218–220, 276, 277, 325
Testimony of, McDowell Court of Inquiry ... 218–222, 277
**Hodge, Justin.**
Correspondence with Frederick Myers ... 118, 120
Mentioned ... 42, 45
**Hodgkins, Thomas.** Mentioned ... 601, 602
**Hoffman, Edmund L.** Mentioned ... 388, 389
**Hoffman, John J.** Report of skirmish at Muddy Creek, W. Va., June 8 ... 814
**Hoffman, John S.** Mentioned ... 484, 741, 792
**Hoffman, L. J. [J. H.]** Mentioned ... 42, 59–61, 63, 120, 291–293
**Holabird, S. B.**
Mentioned ... 530, 552, 570
Report of means of transportation lost, destroyed, and abandoned in the retreat to Williamsport, Md., May 24–25 ... 570
**Holliday, F. W. M.** Mentioned ... 742, 756, 758
**Hollister, Warren.** Mentioned ... 439
**Holloway, Lewis P.** Mentioned ... 394
**Hood,** Mr. Mentioned ... 173
**Hood, John B.** Mentioned ... 25
**Hooker, Joseph.** Mentioned . 43, 130, 131, 165, 172, 196, 206, 224, 227, 229, 230, 329, 330
**Hopper, John C.** Mentioned ... 35
**Horton, C. P.** Mentioned ... 618, 619
**Hoskins, Marcus.** Mentioned ... 593
**Hotchkiss, J.** Mentioned ... 472, 709, 716, 718, 719
**Hotopp, Henry J.** Mentioned ... 421
**Howard, John R.** Mentioned ... 17, 26, 35
**Howard, McHenry.** Mentioned ... 737, 739, 742, 746
**Howard, Oliver O.**
Mentioned ... 332
Reports of
Gainesville, Va. Reconnaissance to, March 20 ... 333
Orange and Alexandria Railroad, Va. Operations on the, March 28–31 . 412
**Howard, W. D.** Mentioned ... 407
**Howell, Samuel C.** Mentioned ... 809
**Hoyt,** Mr. Mentioned ... 43
**Hudson, R. N.** Mentioned ... 35
**Huestmann,** Captain. Mentioned ... 674
**Hughes, Daniel W.**
Mentioned ... 254
Testimony of, McDowell Court of Inquiry ... 254, 255
**Hughes, James M.** Mentioned ... 787, 791
**Humphrey, George.** Mentioned ... 441, 443
**Humphreys, John M.** Mentioned ... 488
**Hunter, David.** Mentioned ... 43
**Hunter, James H. L.** Mentioned ... 388, 389
**Hunter, Robert W.** Mentioned ... 388
(For correspondence as Aide-de-Camp, see *J. W. Allen.*)
**Huntington, James F.** Mentioned ... 692, 697
**Huntoon, Franklin T.** Mentioned ... 586
**Hurd, Alonzo H.** Mentioned ... 354
**Hurt, E. C.** Mentioned ... 787
**Hyman, Henry F.** Mentioned ... 668
**Hysung, Jacob P.** Mentioned ... 370

Page.

**Illinois.** Call of the President for all Volunteers and Militia from ........ 3

**Illinois Troops.** Mentioned.

Cavalry—*Regiments:* **8th**, 333, 414, 421.

Infantry—*Regiments:* **39th**, 346, 360, 371.

**Indiana.** Call of the President for all Volunteers and Militia from ........ 3

**Indiana Troops.** Mentioned.

Artillery—*Batteries:* **Wilder's** (*Rigby*), 19, 665–668.

Cavalry—*Regiments:* **1st**, 8.

Infantry—*Regiments:* **7th**, 346, 360, 375, 376, 690, 691, 696, 699; **12th**, 440–443; **13th**, 341, 346, 350, 360, 371–373, 375–377, 458–460; **14th**, 341, 346, 350, 351, 360, 366, 367, 372, 374, 376, 377, 427, 694; **27th**, 549, 553, 560, 594, 595, 597, 599, 612, 615, 616, 619-622.

**Ingersoll, A. W.** Mentioned ........ 424

**Iowa.** Call of the President for all Volunteers and Militia from ........ 3

**Irish, Nathaniel.** Mentioned ........ 603

**Irving, Francis D.** Mentioned ........ 403

**Isdell, B.** Mentioned ........ 374

**Israel, William P.** Mentioned ........ 359

**Jackson, Alfred H.** Mentioned ........ 484

**Jackson, Thomas J.**

Correspondence with

Allen, J. W ........ 389

Ashby, Turner ........ 385

Carpenter, Joseph ........ 400

Ewell, R. S ........ 801

Grigsby, A. J ........ 394

Pendleton, A. S ........ 709

Ronald, Charles A ........ 391

Waters, James H ........ 399

Mentioned ........ 9–14, 16, 17, 19, 21–24, 29, 31, 33, 34, 99, 100, 124, 127–130, 132, 141, 149, 154, 155, 158, 173, 174, 183–188, 193, 194, 196, 198–200, 203, 205–207, 220, 230, 234, 235, 242, 243, 256, 263, 282–288, 298, 299, 302, 304, 307, 309, 312–316, 326–331, 333, 335, 336, 338–344, 348, 349, 353, 360, 373, 379, 384, 386, 387, 393, 396, 400, 401, 406, 418, 426, 433, 446, 447, 458, 461, 462, 465, 480–482, 485, 492, 500, 523, 524, 526–528, 534, 538–541, 543, 544, 555, 556, 587, 589, 593, 594, 617, 618, 626, 633, 637, 638, 640–643, 645–649, 651, 654–657, 659, 661, 662, 677, 680, 683–686, 688–691, 709, 710, 717, 721, 729–733, 735, 736, 738–742, 745, 755, 756, 758, 760–762, 768, 771–774, 776, 778, 779, 784, 786, 788, 789, 792–794, 798, 800, 802–804, 806, 811

Movement of command of, to the Peninsula ........ 3, 716

Reports of

Kernstown, Va. Battle of, March 23 ........ 379, 380

McDowell, Va. Engagement near, May 8 ........ 470

Shenandoah Valley. Operations in, May 15–June 17 ........ 701, 710, 711

**Jackson, William L.** Mentioned ........ 716

**Jackson's River Depot, Va.** Raid to, May 20. (See *Virginia Central R. R.*)

**Jahn, Herman.** Mentioned ........ 671

**Jameson, J. M.** Mentioned ........ 570

**Jenifer, Walter H.**

Mentioned ........ 491, 492

Reports of

Camp Creek, W. Va. Skirmish on, May 1 ........ 450

Giles Court-House, W. Va. Action at, May 10 ........ 493

**Jenks, John.** Mentioned ........ 350, 359

**Jewett, John E.** Mentioned ........ 42, 45

Page.

**Johnson Bradley T.**
Mentioned ... 712, 779, 782, 783, 818
Report of operations in Shenandoah Valley, May 29–June 9 ... 817
**Johnson, Edward.**
Correspondence with W. C. Scott ... 487
Mentioned ... 9, 29, 461, 462, 464, 465, 470–472, 479–481, 484, 485, 487, 594, 617, 618, 647, 701, 810–812
Report of engagement near McDowell, Va., May 8 ... 482
**Johnson, George K.** Mentioned ... 581
**Johnson, Jarvis J.** Mentioned ... 552
**Johnson, John.** Mentioned ... 66
**Johnson, John E.**
Correspondence with
Dillard, W. W ... 437
Field, Charles W ... 436
Toole, J. A ... 438
Mentioned ... 434
**Johnson, John H.** Mentioned ... 787
**Johnson, Thomas S. J.** Mentioned ... 559
**Johnston, Joseph E.**
Congratulatory orders.
Kernstown, Va. Battle of, March 23 ... 384
Shenandoah Valley. Operations in, May 15–June 17 ... 710
Correspondence with Jefferson Davis ... 379
Mentioned ... 234, 321, 336, 718
**Johnston, Samuel R.** Mentioned ... 417
**Johnstone, Robert.** Mentioned ... 583
**Jones, Francis B.** Mentioned ... 383, 388, 392, 397
**Jones, Henry A.** Mentioned ... 88
**Jones, J. M.** Mentioned ... 780, 782, 786
**Jones, J. Y.** Mentioned ... 406, 407
**Jones, Owen.**
Mentioned ... 430, 431, 497, 677
Reports of
Rappahannock River, Va. Affair on, May 13 ... 497
Shenandoah Valley. Operations in, June 1–13 ... 680
**Jones, Roger.**
Mentioned ... 219, 225
Report of number and condition of troops available April 19, for defense of Washington, D. C. ... 225
**Jones, Samuel.** Mentioned ... 321
**Jones, W. E.** Mentioned ... 415–417
**Jordan, William P.** Mentioned ... 609
**Judson, John A.** Mentioned ... 575
(For correspondence as A. A. G., see *John P. Hatch.*)
**Junkin, George G.** Mentioned ... 337, 383, 397
**Kane, Thomas L.** Mentioned ... 14, 15, 18, 676–678, 712, 782, 817
**Kanish,** Captain. Mentioned ... 173
**Kappner, Franz.**
Mentioned ... 173, 256, 309, 310, 312, 315
Testimony of, McDowell Court of Inquiry ... 256–259, 312, 313
**Kargé, Joseph.**
Mentioned ... 677
Report of operations in Shenandoah Valley, June 2–13 ... 677
**Kasey, John G.** Mentioned ... 486

Page.
**Kaufman,** ———. Mentioned ........ 423
**Kearny, Philip.** Mentioned .. 128, 130, 131, 149, 152, 175, 196, 203, 206, 209, 304, 328–331
**Keeney, C. C.** Mentioned ........ 345
**Keezletown and Gordonsville Cross-Roads, W. Va.** Skirmish at, April 26. 2
**Keily, Daniel J.** Mentioned ........ 691, 692, 697, 699, 700
**Kelley, Bartley.** Mentioned ........ 359
**Kelley, Benjamin F.**
Correspondence with Stephen W. Downey ........ 447
Mentioned ........ 4, 7, 8, 12, 447, 489, 490
Report of raid to Boothsville and Valley River, W. Va., April 12 ........ 423
**Kelly, H. B.** Mentioned ........ 778, 801, 803
**Kelly, James R.** Mentioned ........ 346, 367
**Kelton, J. C.** (For correspondence as A. A. G., see *Army Headquarters.*)
**Kemble, Gouverneur.** Mentioned ........ 43
**Kendall, James.** Mentioned ........ 88
**Kenly, John R.**
Mentioned ........ 525–527, 535–537, 545, 546, 560–562, 564, 565, 581, 587, 599, 601, 617
Report of action at Front Royal, Va., May 23 ........ 555
**Kennedy,** Captain. Mentioned ........ 173
**Kenney, Patrick.** Mentioned ........ 406
**Kennon, P. P.** Mentioned ........ 494
**Kentucky.** Military departments embracing ........ 542
**Kentucky Troops.** Mentioned. (Confederate.)
Cavalry—*Battalions:* **1st** (*Bradley's Mounted Rifles*), 513, 514, 516.
Infantry—*Regiments:* **5th**, 513, 514.
**Kentucky Troops.** Mentioned. (Union.)
Artillery—*Batteries:* **Simmonds'**, 506, 509.
**Keogh, Myles W.** Mentioned ........ 697
**Kernstown, Va.**
Battle of, March 23.*
Casualties. Returns of
Confederate forces ........ 384
Union forces ........ 346, 347
Communications from
Allen, J. W ........ 389
Carpenter, Joseph ........ 400
Grigsby, A. J ........ 394
Jackson, Thomas J ........ 385, 389, 391, 394, 399, 400
Johnston, Joseph E ........ 379
McClellan, George B ........ 343, 344
Myer, Albert J ........ 351
Ronald, Charles A ........ 391
Shields, James ........ 343
War Department, U. S ........ 344
Waters, James H ........ 399
Congress, C. S. Resolution of ........ 384
Congratulatory orders.
Johnston, Joseph E ........ 384
McClellan, George B ........ 344
War Department, U. S ........ 344
Record of Events. Williams' division ........ 378
Reports of
Allen, J. W ........ 387
Ashby, Turner ........ 385, 386

* Also called battle of Winchester, Va.

Page

**Kernstown, Va.—Continued.**
Battle of, March 23.
Reports of
Bridgford, D. B. 405
Brodhead, Thornton F 355
Burks, Jesse S 400
Carpenter, Joseph 399
Carroll, Samuel S 368
Copeland, Joseph T 356
Copeland, R. Morris 347, 348
Cummings, Arthur C 394
Daum, Philip 359
Foster, Robert S 372
Fulkerson, Samuel V 408
Funsten, O. R 386
Greenfield, Andrew J 358
Grigsby, A. J 393
Harman, William H 391
Harrow, William 366
Jackson, Thomas J 379, 380
Keys, John 357
Kimball, Nathan 360, 366
King, William S 344
Langhorne, D. A 404
Lewis, William D., jr 377
McLaughlin, William 396
Nadenbousch, J. Q. A 389
Patton, John M., jr 402, 404
Ronald, Charles A 390
Rowley, William W 352, 353
Sawyer, Franklin 369
Shields, James 335, 336, 338
Shriber, R. C 349
Sullivan, Jeremiah C 371
Taliaferro, Alexander G 410
Tyler, Erastus B 375, 376
Voris, Alvin C 370
Waters, James H 398
Whitcamp, George H 373
Sketches of battle-field 362–365
Skirmish at, March 22 1
**Kester, John W.** Mentioned 680
**Key,** Lieutenant. Mentioned 482
**Key, Thomas M.** Mentioned 42, 45
**Keyes, Erasmus D.**
Mentioned 43, 101, 102, 276
Testimony of, McDowell Court of Inquiry 101–104
**Keys, John.**
Mentioned 355, 356
Report of battle of Kernstown, Va., March 23 357
**Killmartin, John.** Mentioned 803
**Kilpatrick, Judson.**
Mentioned 31, 427, 429–432
Report of operations about, April 17–19, and occupation of, Fredericksburg, Va., April 18 432

Page.

**Kimball, Nathan.**
Mentioned........ 283, 339–342, 346, 348–350, 354–357, 369, 371, 374–376, 426, 682, 697
Reports of
Front Royal, Va. Action at, May 30........ 694
Kernstown, Va. Battle of, March 23........ 360, 366
**Kincaid, W. C.** Mentioned........ 787
**King, C. M.** Mentioned........ 784
**King, J. Floyd.** Mentioned........ 492, 493
**King, Rufus.**
Correspondence with
Augur, Christopher C........ 431, 432
Porter, Fitz John........ 249
War Department, U. S........ 31
Mentioned........ 31, 43, 82–84, 87, 89, 90, 105, 109, 110, 121, 122, 126, 128–130, 139, 152, 156, 157, 161, 166, 167, 175, 182, 183, 191, 192, 194, 198–201, 206–209, 212, 216, 231–233, 235–238, 241–246, 248, 249, 252–255, 263, 265–267, 279, 281, 286, 293, 295, 296, 298, 300, 304, 309, 311, 312, 314–319, 329–331, 428, 437, 528
Testimony of, McDowell Court of Inquiry...... 110–112, 212–215, 254, 295, 298, 317
**King, William S.**
Mentioned........ 552
Reports of battle of Kernstown, Va., March 23........ 344
**Kirkland, W. W.** Mentioned........ 779, 780, 794, 795
**Kisling, W. G.** Mentioned........ 775
**Klenker, F.** Mentioned........ 674
**Knight, J. G.** Mentioned........ 571
**Knight, John.** Mentioned........ 423
**Knipe, Joseph F.**
Mentioned........ 567, 605, 607
Report of operations in Shenandoah Valley, May 24–26........ 612
**Knoxville, Tenn.** Operations against. (Proposed.) Communications from
Frémont, John C........ 7
War Department, U. S........ 10
**Kochersperger, William Henry.** Mentioned........ 346
**Koenig,** Captain. Mentioned........ 157
**Koiner, Absalom.** Mentioned........ 393
**Koltes, John A.** Mentioned........ 19, 664
**Kozlay, Eugene A.**
Mentioned........ 669
Report of battle of Cross Keys, Va., June 8........ 671
**Krebbs, W. H. W.**
Mentioned........ 42, 45, 209, 311
Testimony of, McDowell Court of Inquiry........ 209, 311
**Krom, Abram H.** Mentioned........ 573
**Krzyzanowski, Wladimir.**
Mentioned........ 669, 670
Report of battle of Cross Keys, Va., June 8........ 672
**Kugler, George W.** Mentioned........ 557
**Kurtz, George W.** Mentioned........ 748, 749
**Lacy,** Mr. Mentioned........ 437
**Lacy, H. A.**
Correspondence with Frederick Myers........ 119, 120
Mentioned........ 119
**Lady, John B.** Mentioned........ 394

Page.

**Lambertson, James M.** Mentioned ... 692
**Lambie, William T.** Mentioned ... 400
**Lander, Frederick W.** Mentioned ... 344
**Lane, David F.** Mentioned ... 557, 561, 608
**Lane, Henry.**
Mentioned ... 765
Report of engagement near McDowell, Va., May 8 ... 477
**Langhorne, D. A.**
Mentioned ... 382, 401
Report of battle of Kernstown, Va., March 23 ... 404
**Langhorne, James H.** Mentioned ... 391
**Langston, J. C.** Mentioned ... 809
**Lanier, A. C.** Mentioned ... 408
**Larned, William L.** Mentioned ... 353, 354, 567
**Latham, George R.** Mentioned ... 5, 465, 648, 813
**Latimer, J. W.** Mentioned ... 725, 727, 779, 799
**Lawson, Charles D.** Mentioned ... 5, 439
**Leaf, George D.** Mentioned ... 431
**Lee, Edwin G.** Mentioned ... 756
**Lee, Hugh H.** Mentioned ... 473
**Lee, John C.**
Mentioned ... 668
Report of skirmish near McDowell, Va., May 9 ... 491
**Lee, John E.** Mentioned ... 797, 799
**Lee, Richard H.** Mentioned ... 388
**Lee, Robert E.**
Correspondence with Charles W. Field ... 433, 436, 437
Mentioned ... 286, 321, 492, 502
**Lee, Robert E., Mrs.** Mentioned ... 42
**Lee, W. H. F.**
Mentioned ... 432, 434, 435
Report of operations about, April 17–19, and occupation of, Fredericksburg, Va., April 18 ... 438
**Leech, William A.** Mentioned ... 80
**Leigh, B. W.**
Mentioned ... 406, 407
Reports of
Cross Keys, Va. Battle of, June 8 ... 769
McDowell, Va. Engagement near, May 8 ... 479
Port Republic, Va. Engagements at, June 8–9 ... 769
Winchester, Va. Engagement at, May 25 ... 769
**Leland, Francis.** Mentioned ... 552, 622
**Lennon, James A.** Mentioned ... 753
**Leroy, Herman.** Mentioned ... 43
**Leski, Wladislas.**
Correspondence with Irvin McDowell ... 217, 306
Mentioned ... 168, 169, 215, 258, 267, 306, 308, 319
Testimony of, McDowell Court of Inquiry ... 168–170, 267, 268, 313
**Lesley, James, jr.** (For correspondence, etc., see *War Department, U. S.*)
**Letcher, John.** Mentioned ... 5, 285, 423, 457
**Letcher, Samuel H.** Mentioned ... 817
**Lewis, C. J.** Mentioned ... 494
**Lewis, David.** Mentioned ... 370
**Lewis, H. H.** Mentioned ... 434

Page

**Lewis, John**. Mentioned ... 423
**Lewis, John**. [Asst. Surg]. Mentioned ... 784
**Lewis, William D.,jr.**
Mentioned ... 700
Report of battle of Kernstown, Va., March 23 ... 377
**Lewis, William H. T.** Mentioned ... 388
**Lewisburg, W. Va.**
Action at, May 23.
Communications from
Cox, Jacob D ... 805
Heth, H ... 811
Loring, W. W ... 810, 811
Werth, W. H ... 811
Congratulatory orders.
Cox, Jacob D ... 805
Frémont, John C ... 805
Reports of
Clarke, Melvin ... 808
Cox, Jacob D ... 804
Crook, George ... 805, 806
Gilbert, Samuel A ... 809
Heth, Henry ... 812
Loring, W. W ... 809
(See also *report of John C. Frémont*, p. 10.)
Skirmishes at
May 12 ... 2
May 30 ... 3
**Leyburn, John.** Mentioned ... 397
**Liberty Church, Va.** Reconnaissance to, April 16. Report of Willard Sayles. 425
**Lightburn, J. A. J.** Mentioned ... 490
**Ligon, H. S.** Mentioned ... 780, 795
**Lincoln, Abraham.**
Calls for all Volunteers and Militia, May 25 ... 3
Correspondence with
Banks, Nathaniel P ... 527, 530, 533–535, 542
Frémont, John C ... 7, 13, 24, 25, 34, 643–645, 647–650, 655, 656, 659–663
Hitchcock, E. A ... 229
McClellan, George B ... 222, 230
McDowell, Irvin ... 39, 282, 287
Saxton, Rufus ... 626, 628–632
Mentioned ... 3, 5–7, 10, 12, 13, 16, 17, 24–26, 32, 34, 38–44, 68, 69, 71, 75, 77, 78, 92, 94, 95, 97–99, 103, 104, 106, 108, 109, 162, 166, 167, 204, 207, 218–222, 224, 227–230, 276–279, 282–288, 295, 318, 325, 326, 527, 528, 538, 542, 544, 545, 630, 643, 645–647, 651, 655, 657, 658, 660, 661, 663, 685, 689, 690
Operations in Virginia. Proposed by ... 222
Orders, series 1862, June 26, 169.
Orders, General (*War*), series 1862: **No. 3**, 223.
Orders, Special (*War*), series 1862: **No. 1**, 222.
**Linden, Va.** Skirmishes at
May 15. Reports of
Geary, John W ... 499, 500
McDowell, Irvin ... 499
Moore, Joseph A ... 500
Munford, Thomas T ... 502
May 24. Report of John W. Geary ... 566

Page.

**Lindsay, John.** Mentioned ... 367
**Link, Thomas.** Mentioned ... 390
**Litten, John F.** Mentioned ... 748, 749
**Little, William A.** Mentioned ... 82–87, 110, 111, 297, 298
**Lock, P. J. [J. J.?]** Mentioned ... 721
**Locke, F. T.**
Mentioned ... 242, 245, 246, 248, 250–252, 254, 265, 266
Testimony of, McDowell Court of Inquiry ... 252–254
**Lockmond, Edward.** Mentioned ... 683
**Logan, Samuel.** Mentioned ... 501
**Long, John.** Mentioned ... 799
**Long, Richard.** Mentioned ... 465
**Long, William.** Mentioned ... 476, 488
**Longstreet, James.** Mentioned ... 23, 124, 127–129, 138–141, 144, 148, 155, 168, 172, 175, 194, 199, 205, 243, 263, 285, 299, 302–305, 307, 308, 310, 328, 329, 331, 335, 338, 543, 648, 686, 687
**Loomis, M. D. W.**
Correspondence with G. I. Stealy ... 29
Mentioned ... 30, 115
**Loring, W. W.**
Correspondence with
Heth, H ... 810, 811
Werth, W. H ... 811
Mentioned ... 342, 367, 372
Report of action at Lewisburg, W. Va., May 23 ... 809
**Lostutter, David, jr.** Mentioned ... 700
**Loudoun Heights, Va.** Skirmish at, May 27 ... 518
**Louisa Court-House, Va.** Skirmish at, May 2 ... 2
**Louisiana Troops.** Mentioned.
Infantry—*Battalions:* **Bate's** [?], 694; **Wheat's**, 459, 694, 702, 717, 778, 780, 787, 800–803. *Regiments:* **6th**, 694, 702, 717, 778, 780, 787, 800, 801, 803; **7th**, 459, 460, 688, 694, 714, 715, 717, 726, 731, 741, 750, 753, 766, 770, 778, 780, 784, 785, 787, 800–803; **8th**, 554, 682, 694, 717, 778, 784, 787, 800–803; **9th**, 694, 717, 780, 787, 800, 801, 803.
**Lowry, William M.** Mentioned ... 493
**Lucas, Thomas J.** Report of reconnaissance to the Rappahannock River, Va., April 7 ... 422
**Luce, Horatio.** Mentioned ... 690
**Lueders, Frederick.** Mentioned ... 665
**Lunday, R. W.** Mentioned ... 484
**Luray, Va.** Occupation of, and skirmish near, April 22. (See *Shenandoah Valley. Operations in, April* 19–24.)
**Lusk, John A. M.** Mentioned ... 788
**Lyeth, John McF.** Report of action at Front Royal, Va., May 23 ... 558
**Lyle, Peter.** Mentioned ... 42, 45
**Lynch, ——.** Mentioned ... 439
**Lyon, Judson M.** Mentioned ... 815
**Lyon, James.** Mentioned ... 575
**Lyons, Dr.** Mentioned ... 47
**McArthur, Arthur.** Mentioned ... 780, 800, 801
**McCabe, Edwin.** Mentioned ... 501
**McCabe, George F.** Mentioned ... 501
**McCall, George A.** Mentioned ... 97, 105, 108, 120, 121, 128, 137, 220, 231, 251, 281, 284, 287, 288, 327, 428
**McCarthy, F P.** Mentioned ... 787

Page.

**McCausland, John.**
Mentioned ... 492, 494
Report of action at Giles Court-House, W. Va., May 10 ... 495
**McClellan, George B.**
Co-operation of McDowell with. Communications from
McDowell, Irvin ... 96, 97
War Department, U. S ... 97
Correspondence with
Adjutant-General's Office, U. S. A ... 164, 226
Banks, Nathaniel P ... 164, 234
Lincoln, Abraham ... 222, 230
McDowell, Irvin ... 96, 97
Shields, James ... 343, 344
Wadsworth, James S ... 162
War Department, U. S ... 224
Instructions to Banks ... 164, 234
McDowell ordered to form junction with ... 3
Mentioned ... 41–43, 45, 64, 78, 85, 91–94, 97, 98, 102–104, 113–115, 132, 133, 160, 161, 218–224, 227–230, 232, 239–241, 251, 276–279, 282, 284, 285, 287, 288, 298, 299, 324, 326, 379, 437, 544, 651, 661, 662, 690
Orders, congratulatory. Battle of Kernstown, Va., March 23 ... 344
Testimony of, McDowell Court of Inquiry ... 91–96, 98–101, 277
**McClung, J. S.** Mentioned ... 814
**McDonald, Hugh.** Report of battle of Cross Keys, Va., June 8 ... 675
**McDowell, Va.**
Engagement near, May 8.
Casualties. Returns of
Confederate forces ... 475
Union forces ... 462
Communications from
Johnson, Edward ... 487
Schenck, R. C ... 28
Scott, W. C ... 487
Reports of
Cunningham, R. H., jr ... 476
Frémont, John C ... 460, 461
Hale, S ... 478
Harman, Michael G ... 488
Jackson, Thomas J ... 470
Johnson, Edward ... 482
Lane, Henry ... 477
Leigh, B. W ... 479
McLean, Nathaniel C ... 467
Milroy, Robert H ... 465
Schenck, Robert C ... 461, 462
Scott, W. C ... 484
Taliaferro, William B ... 480
(See also *report of John C. Frémont*, p. 9.)
Sketches ... 474, 475
Skirmish near, May 9. Report of John C. Lee ... 491
**McDowell Court of Inquiry.**
Charges, etc., for investigation. Communications from
Army Headquarters ... 38, 39
Goodwin, R. D ... 44, 81
McDowell, Irvin ... 37–39, 4

Page.

**McDowell Court of Inquiry—Continued.**
Convened ... 36
Correspondence with
Army Headquarters ... 37-39, 45, 51
Burnside, A. E ... 250
Goodwin, R. D ... 46, 73, 81
McDowell, Irvin ... 38, 41
Sigel, Franz ... 162
Course and plan of investigation ... 40-45
Facts and opinions of the ... 323-332
Proceedings of ... 36-332
*Sine die.* Adjournment of ... 323
Statements of McDowell ... 75, 102, 199, 275
Testimony of
Alexander, Barton S ... 250, 251, 278
Barry, William F ... 239-241
Barstow, S. F ... 181-184
Breck, Samuel ... 61-63, 292
Brown, Clarence ... 60, 61, 75
Buchanan, Robert C ... 273, 320
Buford, John ... 262, 263
Burchard, William ... 261, 311, 313, 314
Chandler, Robert ... 234
Clarke, Peleg, jr ... 82-89, 296
Cutting, J. De W ... 269, 270
Dahlgren, Ulric ... 159, 160
Davies, Henry E ... 261, 262, 305, 306
Goodwin, R. D ... 59, 64-72
Hartsuff, George L ... 106, 107, 295
Haupt, Hermann ... 76-80, 290
Haven, Franklin ... 180, 181, 208, 209, 265, 266, 311
Heintzelman, S. P ... 74, 75
Hitchcock, E. A ... 218-222, 277
Hughes, Daniel W ... 254, 255
Kappner, Franz ... 256-259, 312, 313
Keyes, Erasmus D ... 101-104
King, Rufus ... 110-112, 212-215, 254, 295, 298, 317
Krebbs, W. H. W ... 209, 311
Leski, Wladislas ... 168-170, 267, 268, 313
Locke, F. T ... 252-254
McClellan, George B ... 91-96, 98-101, 277
McDowell, Malcolm ... 122, 123
Martindale, John H ... 251
Meade, George G ... 197-199
Myers, Frederick ... 115, 116, 290
Pell, Duncan A ... 255, 256, 315
Pope, John ... 200-207, 299-301, 307, 318, 330
Porter, Fitz John ... 241-249
Ricketts, James B ... 215-217, 306, 307
Roberts, Benjamin S ... 184-190
Roebling, Washington ... 268, 269
Ruggles, George D ... 72-74
Schriver, Edmund ... 46-52, 55-58, 89, 90, 105, 181, 190-194, 200, 209, 210, 222, 237, 238, 250, 263, 266, 267, 291, 296

Page.

**McDowell Court of Inquiry**—Continued.
Testimony of
Sigel, Franz .......... 123-159, 171-173, 180, 302, 303, 305, 308-310, 312, 317, 318
Taylor, Joseph .......... 50
Tillson, Davis .......... 59, 60, 80-82, 195, 197, 232-237, 265, 295
Wadsworth, James S .......... 112-115, 290, 296, 297
Wallach, William D .......... 51
Willard, Joseph C .......... 161, 162, 305
Witnesses, evidence, etc. Communications from
Army Headquarters .......... 45, 332
Burnside, A. E .......... 250
Goodwin, R. D .......... 73
McDowell Court of Inquiry .......... 45, 46, 51, 162

**McDowell, Irvin.**
Assignments to command .......... 1, 169
Co-operation with
Frémont, John C .......... 16, 17
McClellan, George B .......... 96, 97
Correspondence with
Adjutant-General's Office, U. S. A .......... 689
Anderson, Joseph R .......... 47-49
Army Headquarters .......... 39
Banks, Nathaniel P .......... 287, 288, 531, 533, 543
Buchanan, Robert C .......... 274, 320
Frémont, John C .......... 17, 647, 649
Goodwin, R. D .......... 44
Leski, W .......... 217, 306
Lincoln, Abraham .......... 39, 282, 287
McClellan, George B .......... 96, 97
McDowell Court of Inquiry .......... 38, 41
Pope, John .......... 148, 196, 211, 304, 328-331
Porter, Fitz John .......... 249
Ricketts, James B .......... 217, 306
Saxton, Rufus .......... 634-637
Shields, James .......... 33, 55, 689, 690
Sigel, Franz .......... 148, 152, 154, 155, 174, 175, 309, 315
Van Rensselaer, Henry .......... 63, 280
War Department, U. S .......... 97, 279, 282, 285-288, 646, 649-651
Mentioned .......... 7, 12-14, 16, 17, 24, 32, 33, 36-41, 43-47, 49-51, 54-67, 69-96, 98-117, 119, 121-147, 149, 151-153, 155-157, 159-162, 166-174, 176, 180-210, 212-216, 218, 220-222, 230, 232-239, 241-255, 257-259, 261-263, 265-270, 273-275, 277, 278, 281, 284, 288, 290-292, 295-303, 305-314, 317-320, 323-332, 435-437, 456, 502, 533, 535, 538, 539, 541, 635, 636, 644, 646-650, 653, 655, 659, 661, 677, 684, 729
Ordered to form junction with Army of the Potomac, May 17 .......... 3
Ordered to the Shenandoah, etc., May 24 .......... 282
Reports of
Bowling Green road, near Fredericksburg, Va. Skirmish on the, May 11 .......... 496
Fredericksburg, Va. Operations about, April 17-19, and occupation of, April 18 .......... 427, 428
Linden, Va. Skirmish at, May 15 .......... 499
Statements of, McDowell Court of Inquiry .......... 75, 102, 199, 275
Submits plan of investigation desired, and furnishes list of witnesses .......... 41

Page.

**McDowell, Malcolm.**
Mentioned .... 122
Testimony of, McDowell Court of Inquiry .... 122, 123
**McElhaney, John.** Mentioned .... 675
**McGaheysville, Va. Skirmish at, April 27. Extract from Record of Events,** Cavalry Brigade .... 448
**McGuire, Hunter.**
Mentioned .... 383, 473, 476, 716
Report of engagement at Winchester, Va., May 25 .... 719
**McIntosh, A. A.** Mentioned .... 784
**Mack, J. M.** Mentioned .... 784
**McKemy, William C.** Mentioned .... 750
**McKendree, George.** Mentioned .... 400, 760
**McKim, Randolph.** Mentioned .... 818
**McKim, W. D.** Mentioned .... 799
**McLaughlin, Duncan.** Mentioned .... 440
**McLaughlin, William.**
Mentioned .... 381, 402
Report of battle of Kernstown, Va., March 23 .... 396
**McLean, Nathaniel C.**
Mentioned .... 464, 466, 668
Report of engagement near McDowell, Va., May 8 .... 467
**McMahon, J. J.** Mentioned .... 513
**McMillan, John.** Mentioned .... 476
**McNally, John.** Mentioned .... 510
**Macon, R. C.** Mentioned .... 784
**Madison, Joseph.** Mentioned .... 501
**Magruder, John B.** Mentioned .... 321, 380
**Mahan, Dennis H.** Mentioned .... 43
**Mahler, Francis.**
Mentioned .... 669
Report of battle of Cross Keys, Va., June 8 .... 674
**Maine.** Call of the President for all Volunteers and Militia from .... 3
**Maine Troops.** Mentioned.
Artillery—*Batteries:* **2d** (*B*), 665, 676, 677; **6th** (*F*), 226.
Cavalry—*Regiments:* **1st**, 424, 425, 451–455, 523, 553, 573–577, 582, 584, 587, 590, 591, 610, 815, 816.
Infantry—*Regiments:* **10th**, 528, 532, 550, 554, 579, 582, 584, 595, 598, 606, 609, 610.
**Mallory, Francis.** Mentioned .... 434
**Mallory, S. R.** Mentioned .... 433
**Mallory, William L.** Mentioned .... 26
**Manchester, Charles N.** Mentioned .... 425
**Mansfield,** Captain. Mentioned .... 88, 89
**Mapes, William H. H.** Mentioned .... 536, 554, 557, 559, 561, 594
**March, William J.** Mentioned .... 513
**Margedant, William.** Mentioned .... 668
**Marks, C. K.** Mentioned .... 570
**Marquis, J. C.** Mentioned .... 399
**Marshall, Hugh.** Mentioned .... 374
**Marshall, Humphrey.**
Mentioned .... 504, 506–508, 510, 511, 513
Report of actions at Princeton, W. Va., May 16–17 .... 513
**Marshall, James.** Mentioned .... 386

Page

**Martin, James.** Mentioned ... 418, 419
**Martin, James O.** Mentioned ... 787
**Martin, John.** Mentioned ... 692, 694
**Martin, John H.** Mentioned ... 367
**Martin, John T.** Mentioned ... 784, 791
**Martin, William.** Reports of
Cross Keys, Va. Battle of, June 8 ... 765
Port Republic, Va. Engagements at, June 8–9 ... 765
**Martindale, John H.**
Mentioned ... 36, 37, 43, 251, 322, 323
Testimony of, McDowell Court of Inquiry ... 251
**Marye, John L., jr.** Mentioned ... 83, 88
**Maryland.** Military departments embracing ... 1
**Maryland Troops.** Mentioned. (Confederate.)
Artillery—*Batteries:* **Baltimore** (*Brockenbrough*), 701, 703, 704, 713, 715, 718, 725, 727, 728, 730, 742, 780, 782, 784, 799, 818.
Cavalry—*Companies:* **A** (*Brown*), 817.
Infantry—*Regiments:* **1st**, 701–704, 706, 712, 717, 732, 778–780, 782–784, 787–789, 800, 817, 818.
**Maryland Troops.** Mentioned. (Union.)
Cavalry—*Companies:* **Cole's**, 346, 355; **Curll's**, 346, 578; **Firey's**, 5, 13, 447, 457, 647; **Horner's**, 346, 355. *Regiments:* **1st**, 550, 551, 553, 573, 575, 577–579, 582, 584, 595, 609, 627, 639, 739.
Infantry—*Regiments:* **1st**, 525, 526, 536, 553, 555–559, 565, 566, 594, 599, 605, 614, 617, 702, 730, 734, 779; **1st P. H. B.**, 630, 635, 636, 639.
**Mason,** Captain. Mentioned ... 718, 719
**Mason, Eddy D.** Mentioned ... 361
**Mason, John S.** Mentioned ... 340, 361
**Massachusetts.** Call of the President for all Volunteers and Militia from ... 3
**Massachusetts Troops.** Mentioned.
Infantry—*Regiments:* **2d**, 419, 420, 549, 553, 560, 594, 595, 612, 615–623, 625; **12th**, 441, 442.
**Massey, William A.** Mentioned ... 476
**Mathews, Joseph A.** Mentioned ... 613
**Mauck, Robert C.** Mentioned ... 775
**Maxwell, Curtis.** Mentioned ... 501
**Maynard, D. G.** Mentioned ... 581
**Meade, George G.**
Mentioned ... 197, 270, 274, 314, 317, 318, 320, 321
Testimony of, McDowell Court of Inquiry ... 197–199
**Meade, R. K., jr.** Mentioned ... 473, 709
**Meagher, Thomas Francis.** Mentioned ... 412
**Mehrling, Conradt.** Mentioned ... 639
**Meigs, J. A.** Mentioned ... 563
**Meigs, Montgomery C.** Mentioned ... 642, 660
**Meizell, W.** Mentioned ... 787
**Menken, Nathan D.** Mentioned ... 356
**Mercer, John T.** Mentioned ... 779, 783, 796, 799
**Meredith, S. A.** Mentioned ... 62, 63, 292, 293
**Merkle, C. F.** Mentioned ... 692, 694
**Merrill, George.** Mentioned ... 641
**Merrill, William.** Mentioned ... 692
**Merrimac,** U. S. Frigate. (See *Virginia, C. S. S.*)
**Merritt, Joseph B.** Mentioned ... 577

Page.

**Messner, Charles.** Mentioned ............ 512
**Meyer, Conrad U.** Mentioned ............ 501
**Meysenberg, Theodore A.** Mentioned ............ 144, 172
**Michigan.** Call of the President for all Volunteers and Militia from ............ 3
**Michigan Troops.** Mentioned.
Cavalry—*Regiments:* **1st,** 339, 346, 349, 355–357, 419, 525, 553–555, 575, 578–582, 584, 594–597, 815, 816.
**Middleburg, Va.** Operations about, March 27–28. Report of John W. Geary ............ 410
**Middle Military Department.** (Union.)
Constituted ............ 1
Dix, John A., assigned to command ............ 1
Wool, John E., assumes command ............ 3
**Middletown, Va.**
Action at, May 24.
Casualties. Returns of Union troops ............ 553, 554
Reports of
Douty, Calvin S ............ 575
Poague, William T ............ 760
(See also
*May* 15–*June* 17. *Operations in Shenandoah Valley. Reports of*
Banks, Nathaniel P. Donnelly, Dudley. Taylor, Richard.
Collins, William D. Hatch, John P. Tompkins, Charles H.
Collis, Charles H. T. Jackson, T. J. Winder, Charles S.)
Crutchfield, S. Peabody, J. H.
Skirmish at, March 18 ............ 1
**Miles, Albert.** Mentioned ............ 501
**Miles, Dixon S.** Mentioned ............ 523, 525, 528, 584, 636, 639, 641
**Milford, Va.** Skirmish at, June 24. Report of Charles H. Town ............ 815
**Military Commissions.** Instituted in Department of the Rappahannock ............ 52
**Miller, Austin T.** Mentioned ............ 510
**Miller, James.** Mentioned ............ 333
**Miller, Samuel A.** Mentioned ............ 495
**Mills, W. B.** Mentioned ............ 784
**Milroy, R. H.**
Mentioned ............ 4, 7–9, 11, 18, 19, 21, 28, 126, 127, 130, 134, 135, 142, 143, 146, 148, 150, 151, 154, 155, 160, 204, 211, 250–252, 256, 262, 268–270, 274, 275, 301, 319–321, 328, 422, 447, 461–464, 470–473, 482, 524, 645, 653–655, 658 665–667, 701, 785
Reports of
Bull Run, Va. Battle of, August 30 ............ 271, 319
McDowell, Va. Engagement near, May 8 ............ 465
**Miner, B. N.** Mentioned ............ 354, 567
**Miser,** Captain. Mentioned ............ 21
**Mississippi, Department of.** (Union.) Limits extended ............ 541, 542
**Mississippi Troops.** Mentioned.
Infantry—*Regiments:* **16th,** 20, 694, 717, 779, 783, 784, 794–796, 799.
**Mitchell, Thomas.** Mentioned ............ 683
**Mitchell, Thomas E.** Mentioned ............ 551, 558
**Moïtor, Albert.** Mentioned ............ 441, 442
**Monterey, Va.** Skirmishes at.
April 12. Report of John C. Frémont ............ 422
(See also *report of John C. Frémont,* pp. 4, 5.)
April 21 ............ 2
May 12 ............ 2
**Montero, Walter.** Mentioned ............ 751

Page.
**Montgomery, Robert.** Mentioned ... 787
**Moor, Augustus.**
Mentioned ... 504-506, 508-510
Report of actions at Princeton, W. Va., May 16-17 ... 509
**Moore,** Private. Mentioned ... 779
**Moore, A. G.** Mentioned ... 787
**Moore, John P.** Mentioned ... 787, 791
**Moore, Joseph A.** Report of skirmish at Linden, Va., May 15 ... 500
**Moore, Samuel J. C.** Mentioned ... 388, 389
**Moorefield, W. Va.**
Scout to, June 22-30. Report of Charles Farnsworth ... 815
Skirmish at, April 3 ... 1
**Morehouse, John B.** Mentioned ... 668
**Morell, George W.** Mentioned ... 244-246, 253
**Morey, Henry L.** Mentioned ... 468
**Morgan, Benjamin.** Mentioned ... 468
**Morgan, C. A.** Mentioned ... 42, 45
**Morgan, David.** Mentioned ... 439
**Morgan, E. D.** Mentioned ... 68
**Morris, William.** Mentioned ... 43
**Morris, William W.** Mentioned ... 404
**Morrison,** Captain. Mentioned ... 337
**Morrison, Abisha L.** Mentioned ... 620, 624
**Morrison, George.** Mentioned ... 83, 84
**Morson,** Mrs. Mentioned ... 63
**Morton, William H.** Mentioned ... 88
**Mosby, John S.** Mentioned ... 417
**Moseley, John B.** Report of engagement at Winchester, Va., May 25 ... 767
**Mountain Department.** (Union.)
Frémont, John C., assumes command ... 1
Limits extended ... 542
Merged into Army of Virginia ... 3, 169
Operations in, March 29-June 27. Report of John C. Frémont ... 3
Orders, Field, series 1862: **May 24**, 805; **June 8**, 785.
Sanitary condition of Blenker's division. Communications from George Suckley ... 30, 31
**Mount Carmel, Va.** Skirmish at, June 1. Communications from J. C. Frémont. 650
(See also *report of John C. Frémont*, p. 14.)
**Mount Jackson, Va.**
Occupation of, April 17.*
Congratulatory orders. War Department, U. S ... 427
Report of Nathaniel P. Banks ... 426
Skirmish at and near.
March 25 ... 1
June 3. Communications from John C. Frémont ... 651
(See also
*March* 29-*June* 27. *Operations in Mountain Department. Report of*
Frémont, John C.
*May* 15-*June* 17. *Operations in Shenandoah Valley. Reports of*
Jones, Owen. Kargé, Joseph.)
June 16. Communications from John C. Frémont ... 662
**Muddy Creek, W. Va.** Skirmish at. June 8. Report of John J. Hoffman ... 814

* Includes skirmish at Rude's Hill, Va.

Page.

**Mudge, Charles R.** Mentioned ..... 623
**Muhlenberg, Edward D.** Mentioned ..... 604
**Munford, Thomas T.**
  Mentioned ..... 417, 501, 711, 715, 716, 728
  Reports of
    Gaines' Cross-Roads, Rappahannock County, Va. Skirmish near, May 15 ..... 498
    Linden, Va. Skirmish at, May 15 ..... 502
    Shenandoah Valley. Operations in, May 15–June 17 ..... 732
**Mungo Flats, W. Va.** Skirmish at, June 25 ..... 3
**Munitions of War.** Supplies of, etc. Communications from
  Goulding, C. N ..... 30
  McDowell, Irvin ..... 55
  Myers, Frederick ..... 118–120
  Rosecrans, W. S ..... 28
  Schenck, R. C ..... 28
  Stealy, G. I ..... 29
  (See also *report of John C. Frémont*, pp. 6, 8.)
**Munther, Frederick R.** Mentioned ..... 337, 552
**Murphy,** Private. Mentioned ..... 817
**Murphy, Charles.** Mentioned ..... 501
**Murphy, John K.** Mentioned ..... 579, 599, 601, 618, 619, 623, 624
**Murray, William G.** Mentioned ..... 342, 346, 351, 361, 374
**Murrin, Thomas D.** Mentioned ..... 439
**Myer, Albert J.** Correspondence with
  Rowley, William W ..... 353
  War Department, U. S ..... 351
**Myers, A. C.** Mentioned ..... 722, 724
**Myers, Frederick.**
  Correspondence with
    Abercrombie, J. J ..... 118
    Hall, C. ..... 119
    Hodge, Justin ..... 118, 120
    Lacy, H. A ..... 119, 120
    Patrick, M. R ..... 119
    Ross, E ..... 119
    Willard, J. C ..... 118
  Mentioned ..... 42, 45, 80, 81, 115, 290
  Testimony of, McDowell Court of Inquiry ..... 115, 116, 290
**Myers, George W.** Mentioned ..... 386, 712
**Myers, L. C.** Mentioned ..... 482
**Nadenbousch, J. Q. A.**
  Mentioned ..... 385, 387, 388, 740, 741, 744
  Report of battle of Kernstown, Va., March 23 ..... 389
**Neel, George A.** Mentioned ..... 409
**Neff, John F.**
  Mentioned ..... 737, 740, 742
  Reports of
    Charlestown, W. Va. Skirmish at, May 28 ..... 756
    Newtown, Va. Action at, May 24 ..... 753
    Port Republic, Va. Engagements at, June 8–9 ..... 756
    Winchester, Va. Engagement at, May 25 ..... 754, 756
**Nelson, David B.** Mentioned ..... 593, 682, 695
**Nelson, Hugh M.** Mentioned ..... 766, 770, 782, 786
**New Creek, W. Va.** Scout to, June 22–30. Report of Charles Farnsworth ..... 815

Page.

**New Hampshire.** Call of the President for all Volunteers and Militia from. 3

**New Hampshire Troops.** Mentioned.

Infantry—*Regiments:* **5th**, 413, 414.

**Newhane,** Dr. Mentioned ........ 457

**New Jersey.** Military department embracing ........ 1

**New Jersey Troops.** Mentioned.

Cavalry—*Regiments:* **1st**, 18, 168, 306, 428, 497, 498, 652, 665, 677–681.

Infantry—*Regiments:* **10th**, 226.

**New Market, Va.**

Occupation of, April 17.

Congratulatory orders. War Department, U. S ........ 427

Report of Nathaniel P. Banks ........ 426

Operations in the vicinity of, April 19–24.

(See *Shenandoah Valley. Operations in, April* 19–24.)

Skirmish at, June 13 ........ 518

**Newton, James W.** Mentioned ........ 749

**Newtown, Va.** Action at, May 24.

Casualties. Returns of Union troops ........ 553, 554

Reports of

Allen, J. W ........ 743

Andrews, George L. ........ 620

Brown, Edwin F ........ 612

Grigsby, A. J ........ 751

Neff, John F ........ 753

Poague, William T ........ 760

(See also

*May* 15–*June* 17. *Operations in Shenandoah Valley. Reports of*

Banks, Nathaniel P. | Crosby, Franklin B. | Crutchfield, S. | Gordon, George H. | Hatch, John P. | Jackson, T. J. | Knipe, Joseph F. | Peabody, J. H. | Williams, A. S. | Winder, Charles S.)

**New York.** Call of the President for all Volunteers and Militia from ........ 3

**New York Troops.** Mentioned.

Artillery—*Batteries:* **2d**, 15, 18, 651, 658, 664, 669–671, 673; **9th**, 239, 240; **13th**, 19, 441, 442, 664; **16th**, 239–241. *Battalions:* **Rocket** (*Batteries*), **A, B**, 226; **2d** (*Batteries*), **A, B**, 240. *Regiments:* **1st** (*Batteries*), **C**, 240; **G**, 412–415; **I**, 18, 664, 669–671, 673, 675; **K**, 240, 639, 640; **L**, 633, 639–641; **M**, 419, 420, 448, 547, 553, 574, 575, 594, 596, 601, 602, 605, 606, 612, 616, 618, 621, 623; **Hamilton's** (*Batteries*), **L**, 240.

Cavalry—*Regiments:* **2d**, 75, 168–170, 427, 429–432; **3d**, 226; **4th**, 18, 20, 154, 421, 664, 679, 785; **5th**, 456, 523, 535–537, 548, 553, 556–559, 564, 565, 572–575, 581–586, 621, 639, 640; **8th**, 554, 584, 585, 630; **9th**, 154.

Infantry—*Regiments:* **8th**, 18, 20, 21, 654, 658, 664, 669, 673–675, 796, 799; **9th**, 440; **11th**, 74, 75; **28th**, 427, 547, 549, 553, 594–596, 598, 605, 606, 610–612, 615, 620, 621; **29th**, 19, 664; **37th**, 224, 229; **39th**, 18, 654, 655, 657, 664; **41st**, 18, 20, 658, 664; **45th**, 18, 20, 655, 658, 664; **54th**, 18, 664, 669–672, 674, 675; **58th**, 18, 664, 669–673; **61st**, 413; **68th**, 19, 664; **78th**, 626, 639; **83d** (*Ninth State Militia*), 441, 442; **86th**, 226; **102d**, 226; **President's Life Guard**, 68, 69.

**Nicholas, Wilson C.** Mentioned ........ 817

**Nicholls, Francis T.** Mentioned ........ 801

**Nichols, G. Ward.** Mentioned ........ 26, 35

**Niles,** Lieutenant. Mentioned ........ 272, 319

**Noonan, Robert C.** Mentioned ........ 401, 403

**Nordendorf, C. S. de.** Mentioned ........ 35

Page.

**North Carolina Troops.** Menti.ned.
Infantry—*Regiments:* **21st**, 20, 694, 705, 706, 717, 779, 780, 784, 794, 795, 799; **27th**, 596.

**Northern Virginia.** Campaign in, August 16–September 2.
Communications from
Buchanan, R. C ... 274
Buford, John ... 263
Heintz, C ... 176
Leski, W ... 217, 306
McDowell, Irvin ... 139, 152, 174, 175, 217, 304, 306
Pope, John ... 148, 160, 174, 196, 210, 211, 245, 304, 328–331
Porter, Fitz John ... 249
Sigel, Franz ... 148, 154, 155, 176, 204, 309, 315
Sketches. Positions, August 25, 28 ... 177–179, 260

**Northern Virginia, Department of.** (Confederate.)
Orders, General, series 1862: **No. 37**, 384; **No. 58**, 710.

**Northwest, Army of the.** (Confederate.)
Baldwin, John B., assigned to command of Second Brigade ... 487
Orders, Circulars, series 1862: **April 22**, 487; **May 5**, 488.
Orders, General, series 1862: **April 21**, 487.
Organization, strength, etc., April 21 ... 487
Porterfield, G. A., assigned to command of First Brigade ... 487
Scott, W. C., assigned to command of Second Brigade ... 487

**Nye, Reuben L.** Mentioned ... 439
**O'Brien, John F.** Mentioned ... 737, 739, 742, 744, 746, 757, 760
**Oden, James.** Mentioned ... 417
**Offutt, Nat.** Mentioned ... 780
**Ohio.** Call of the President for all Volunteers and Militia from ... 3

**Ohio Troops.** Mentioned.
Artillery—*Batteries:* **12th**, 19, 463, 466, 467, 658, 665. *Regiments:* **1st** (*Batteries*), **H**, 347, 359, 690, 692, 693, 696, 700; **I**, 18, 19, 21, 422, 465, 665, 668; **K**, 19, 447, 462, 665–668; **L**, 347, 359, 360, 375, 690, 691, 693, 696, 698–700.
Cavalry—*Regiments:* **1st**,* 346, 355, 506; **6th**, 6, 9, 13, 154, 662, 664.
Infantry—*Regiments:* **4th**, 694; **5th**, 341, 346, 350, 351, 360, 367, 370, 371, 373–377, 687, 690, 696, 697, 700, 750, 751; **7th**, 346, 350, 360, 375, 376, 690, 696, 697; **8th**, 340, 341, 346, 350, 351, 360, 366, 368–370, 694; **23d**, 449; **25th**, 18, 422, 462–464, 466–469, 658, 665; **28th**, 503, 506, 508–512; **29th**, 346, 350, 360, 376, 690, 696; **30th**, 449; **32d**, 19, 422, 462–467, 469, 665–668; **34th**, 449, 503, 506, 508–512; **36th**, 439, 440, 807, 808; **37th**, 503, 506, 508–512; **44th**, 807, 809; **47th**, 449; **55th**, 491, 665–668; **60th**, 8, 9, 14, 18, 655, 657, 665; **62d**, 341, 346, 360, 371; **66th**, 690, 696, 697; **67th**, 340, 341, 346, 350, 360, 370, 371, 376, 377; **73d**, 19, 665–668; **75th**, 19, 422, 462–469, 665–668; **82d**, 19, 462–464, 466, 467, 469, 665–668.

**Oley, John H.** Mentioned ... 9, 14
**Olinger,** Mr. Mentioned ... 425
**Omohundro, John W.** Mentioned ... 791
**Opie,** Surgeon. Mentioned ... 484

**Orange and Alexandria R. R., Va.** Operations on, March 28–31.† Reports of
Conner, Eli T ... 414
Howard, Oliver O ... 412
Rundell, Marshall H ... 414
Stuart, J. E. B ... 415

*Companies A and C only serving in Virginia.
†Includes affairs at Bealeton and Rappahannock Stations, Va.

Page.

**Ord, E. O. C.** Mentioned ........ 106, 116, 117, 250, 281–283
**Orimieulx, T. d'.** Mentioned ........ 43
**Otey, G. G.** Mentioned ........ 493, 494
**Overton, William.** Mentioned ........ 406, 407
**Owens,** Mrs. Mentioned ........ 89
**Page, Mann.** Mentioned ........ 403
**Paldi, Angelo.** Mentioned ........ 355, 356, 579, 580, 596
**Palling, Peter.** Mentioned ........ 447
**Palmer, Jewett, jr.** Mentioned ........ 439
**Parham, Charles.**
  Mentioned ........ 536, 594
  Report of action at Front Royal, Va., **May 23** ........ 560
**Park, J. B.** Mentioned ........ 356, 357
**Parsons,** Colonel. Mentioned ........ 447
**Patrick, John H.** Mentioned ........ 361, 374, 375
**Patrick, Marsena R.**
  Correspondence with Frederick Myers ........ 119
  Mentioned ........ 43, 86, 88, 110, 116, 167, 267, 268
**Patrick, R. F.** Mentioned ........ 491
**Patterson, Alexander B.** Mentioned ........ 700
**Patterson, James W.** Mentioned ........ 476
**Patton, George S.** Mentioned ........ 493, 495
**Patton, John M., jr.**
  Mentioned ........ 381, 401, 402, 714, 764–770, 774, 781, 784–786, 798, 818
  Reports of battle of Kernstown, Va., March 23 ........ 402, 404
**Patton, Jonathan N.** Mentioned ........ 439
**Paul, Samuel.** Mentioned ........ 784
**Payne, A. W.** Mentioned ........ 482
**Peabody, James H.**
  Mentioned ........ 420, 594, 606, 616
  Report of operations in Shenandoah Valley, May 23–25 ........ 601
**Peale, J. Burd.** Mentioned ........ 551
**Pearkin,** Major. Mentioned ........ 502
**Peirce, Robert T.** Mentioned ........ 438
**Pelham, John.** Mentioned ........ 417
**Pell, Duncan A.**
  Mentioned ........ 255, 314, 315
  Testimony of, McDowell Court of Inquiry ........ 255, 256, 315
**Pelouze, Louis H.** Mentioned ........ 36, 37, 323
  (For correspondence as Recorder, see *McDowell Court of Inquiry.*)
**Pemberton, Charles E.** Mentioned ........ 751
**Pemberton, J. C.** Mentioned ........ 321
**Pendergast, L.** Mentioned ........ 787
**Pendleton, Albert G.** Mentioned ........ 382, 390, 391
**Pendleton, A. S.**
  Correspondence with Thomas J. Jackson ........ 709
  Mentioned ........ 383, 405, 473, 706, 709, 716
  (For correspondence as A. A. G., see *Thomas J. Jackson.*)
**Pendleton, William B.** Mentioned ........ 482, 773, 774
**Peninsular Campaign, Va.** Affairs in, generally. Communications from Abraham Lincoln ........ 230
**Penn, David B.** Mentioned ........ 715, 741
**Penn, John E.** Report of engagement at Winchester, Va., May 25 ........ 765

Page.

**Pennsylvania.**
Call of the President for all Volunteers and Militia from ... 3
Military departments embracing ... 1
**Pennsylvania Troops.** Mentioned.
Artillery—*Batteries:* **C**, 441, 442; **E**, 536, 537, 554–558, 565, 566; **F**, 553, 569, 572–575, 581, 582, 584, 594, 596, 597, 600–603; **1st** (*Batteries*), **F**, 441–443.
Cavalry—*Battalions:* **Ringgold**, 346, 355–358, 427, 489; *Regiments:* **1st**, 18, 429–431, 497, 498, 665, 679–682; **4th**, 226.
Infantry—*Companies:* **Zouaves d'Afrique** (*Charles H. T. Collis*), 547, 548, 554, 568, 569, 572–574, 582, 584. *Regiments:* **11th**, 168; **13th**,* 14, 18, 208, 652, 653, 655, 665, 675–678, 681, 712, 732, 782, 785, 796, 799, 817; **27th**, 18, 20, 21, 658, 664, 675, 676; **28th**, 410–412, 500, 501, 554, 555; **29th**, 419, 536, 553, 555–557, 559–563, 565, 594, 601, 616, 619, 622–624, 702, 734; **46th**, 427, 547, 553, 567, 594–596, 598, 605, 606, 610, 612–614; **56th**, 63, 293; **73d**, 19, 664; **74th**, 18, 664, 669, 670, 673, 674; **75th**, 18, 664, 669–672, 674, 675; **81st**, 333; **84th**, 341, 342, 346, 350, 351, 360, 367, 374, 376, 377, 690, 696, 697; **91st**, 226; **109th**, 626, 627, 639; **110th**, 346–348, 350, 351, 360, 376–378, 690, 696, 697; **111th**, 627, 639.
**Pepper, Rufus K.** Mentioned ... 780, 795
**Perkins, D. D.** Mentioned ... 361, 552, 587, 604
**Peters, William E.** Mentioned ... 450, 491, 493, 494
**Petkin, E.** Mentioned ... 587
**Philippi, W. Va.** Skirmish at, March 20 ... 1
**Piatt, A. S.** Mentioned ... 244
**Piatt, Donn.** Mentioned ... 243, 667, 668
**Piedmont, Va.** Skirmish at, April 17 ... 2
**Pilcher, Thomas M. D.** Mentioned ... 468
**Pilsen, John.** Mentioned ... 14, 15, 19, 21, 26, 27, 35, 651, 658
**Pinkney, Bertine.** Mentioned ... 531
**Pittman, Samuel E.** Mentioned ... 598
**Pleasants, James.** Mentioned ... 401
**Poague, William T.**
Mentioned ... 396, 397, 705, 714, 725, 729, 736–739, 741
Reports of
Middletown, Va. Action at, May 24 ... 760
Newtown, Va. Action at, May 24 ... 760
Port Republic, Va. Engagements at, June 8–9 ... 762
Winchester, Va. Engagement at, May 25 ... 761
**Pope, Edmund M.** Mentioned ... 584
**Pope, John.**
Assigned to command Army of Virginia ... 169
Correspondence with
Heintzelman, S. P ... 160
McDowell, Irvin ... 148, 196, 211, 304, 328–331
Porter, Fitz John ... 196, 245
Reno, Jesse L ... 160
Sigel, Franz ... 160, 204, 211
Mentioned ... 26, 41–43, 45, 123, 124, 127–129, 132–136, 142–144, 147, 155–158, 160, 169, 171–174, 184–187, 189–194, 197, 198, 200, 203–207, 237, 238, 241–245, 247–249, 254, 270, 275, 288, 296, 299–302, 304, 307–310, 316–319, 327–331
Testimony of, McDowell Court of Inquiry ... 200–207, 299–301, 307, 318, 330
**Porter, George L.** Mentioned ... 551
**Porter, Andrew.** Mentioned ... 43
**Porter, Burr.** Mentioned ... 35

* Reserves; also called 1st Rifles.

Page.

**Porter, Fitz John.**
Correspondence with
King, Rufus ........ 249
McDowell, Irvin ........ 249
Pope, John ........ 196, 245
Mentioned ........ 95, 104, 105, 123, 124, 130, 131, 158, 161, 192, 196, 204, 207, 210, 211, 236–238, 241, 245, 249, 252–254, 265–270, 307, 318–320
Testimony of, McDowell Court of Inquiry ........ 241–249

**Porterfield, G. A.**
Assignments to command ........ 487
Mentioned ........ 487

**Port Republic, Va.** Engagements at, June 8–9.
Casualties. Returns of
Confederate forces ........ 717, 718, 787
Union forces ........ 690
Communications from
Frémont, John C ........ 654
Shields, James ........ 23, 24, 32
Reports of
Allen, J. W ........ 744
Carpenter, Joseph ........ 759
Carroll, Samuel S ........ 698
Clark, Joseph C ........ 693
Daum, Philip ........ 691
Ewell, R. S ........ 785
Funk, J. H. S ........ 749
Garnett, Thomas S ........ 768
Grigsby, A. J ........ 752
Leigh, B. W ........ 769
Martin, William ........ 765
Neff, John F ........ 756
Poague, William T ........ 762
Ronald, Charles A ........ 747
Scott, W. C ........ 789, 790
Shields, James ........ 683–685
Taliaferro, William B ........ 773
Trimble, Isaac R ........ 795
Tyler, Erastus B ........ 695
Walker, J. A ........ 791
Winder, Charles S ........ 739
(See also
*May* 15–*June* 17. *Operations in Shenandoah Valley.* *Reports of*
Crutchfield, S. Frémont, John C. Jackson, T. J. Taylor, R.)

**Posey, Carnot.** Mentioned ........ 779, 783, 784

**Potomac, Army of the.** (Union.)
Banks, N. P., assumes command of Fifth Corps ........ 1
Council of war, March 13 ........ 104, 223

**Powell, William H.** Mentioned ........ 814

**Powell, William H. H.** Mentioned ........ 752

**Powers, Albert A.** Mentioned ........ 466

**Pratt,** Scout. Mentioned ........ 583

**Pratt, William P.** Mentioned ........ 575

**Preston, Addison W.** Mentioned ........ 586

**Preston, Charles H. C.** Mentioned ........ 409

Page.

**Preston, John A.** Mentioned ..... 777
**Preston, J. T. L.** Mentioned ..... 473
**Princeton, W. Va.**
Actions at, May 16–17.
Casualties. Returns of ..... 508
Reports of
Blessingh, Louis von ..... 510
Cox, Jacob D ..... 503–505
Fisher, Th. F ..... 517
Frémont, John C ..... 503
Heth, H ..... 513
Marshall, Humphrey ..... 513
Moor, Augustus ..... 509
Scammon, E. Parker ..... 508, 509
Skirmishes at.
May 5 ..... 2
May 11 ..... 2
**Prisoners of War.** Treatment of, exchange, etc ..... 49
**Private Property.** Action touching ..... 53–55, 63, 117–120, 271, 289–294
**Putnam, Black H.** Mentioned ..... 576
**Putnam, Bruce.** Mentiond ..... 787
**Quay, E. S.** Mentioned ..... 376, 377, 698
**Quedenfeld, Lewis.** Mentioned ..... 508
**Railroad or Telegraph lines.** Punishment for obstructing or injuring, in Department of the Rappahannock ..... 52
**Raine, Charles I.** Mentioned ..... 741
**Rand, Noyes.** Mentioned ..... 495
**Randolph, Augustus.** Mentioned ..... 787
**Randolph, George W.** Mentioned ..... 513
**Randolph, J. Innis.** Mentioned ..... 780
**Randolph, Lewis.** Mentioned ..... 407
**Randolph, Robert C.** Mentioned ..... 388
**Randolph, William H.** Mentioned ..... 749
**Ranson, Thomas D.** Mentioned ..... 784
**Raphael, William.** Mentioned ..... 501
**Rapidan Station, Va.** Skirmish at, May 1 ..... 2
**Rappahannock, Department of the.** (Union.)
Constituted ..... 1
McDowell, Irvin, assigned to command of ..... 1
Merged into Army of Virginia ..... 3, 169
Military commissions to be instituted in ..... 52
Orders, General, series 1862: **No. 2**, 231; **No. 8**, **No. 10**, 53; **No. 12**, 52; **No. 18**, 54; **No. 19**, 52.
Orders, Special, series 1862: **No. 65**, 53; **No. 68**, 63, 293.
Railroad or telegraph lines. Punishment for obstructing or injuring in ..... 52
**Rappahannock Line.** Operations on the. Communications from
Cluseret, G. P ..... 173
McDowell, Irvin ..... 63, 279
Van Rensselaer, H ..... 280
War Department U. S ..... 279
**Rappahannock River, Va.**
Affair on, May 13. Reports of
Bayard, George D ..... 496
Jones, Owen ..... 497
Wyndham, Percy ..... 497

Page.

**Rappahannock River, Va.**—Continued.
Reconnaissances to.
April 2. Report of John F. Farnsworth ..... 421
April 7. Report of Thomas J. Lucas ..... 422
April 15. Report of Robert F. Dyer ..... 424
April 16. Report of Robert C. Anthony ..... 425
April 18. Reports of
Abercrombie, John J ..... 440
Bryan, Timothy M., jr ..... 441
**Rappahannock Station, Va.** Affair at, March 29. (See *Orange and Alexandria Railroad, Va.*)
**Rathbone, John C.**
Correspondence with Benjamin M. Skinner ..... 490
Mentioned ..... 5, 489, 490
**Ravenswood, W. Va.** Skirmish at, May 15 ..... 2
**Raymond, R. W.** Mentioned ..... 26, 35
**Raynolds, W. F.** Mentioned ..... 15, 35
**Rector, William B.** Mentioned ..... 404
**Redner, Edward G.** Mentioned ..... 354
**Reem, Charles.** Mentioned ..... 346
**Reiching, Mathias.** Mentioned ..... 513
**Reid, John.** Mentioned ..... 370
**Reid, John G.** Mentioned ..... 700
**Reily, Robert.** Mentioned ..... 464, 466, 469
**Reno, Jesse L.**
Correspondence with John Pope ..... 160
Mentioned ..... 131, 136, 149, 172, 174, 190, 196, 206, 209–211, 302, 304, 307, 328–331
**Reynolds, Hosea C.** Mentioned ..... 641
**Reynolds, John F.** Mentioned ..... 124, 126, 129–131, 139, 152, 156, 168, 174, 181, 183, 191, 192, 194, 195, 197–200, 204, 207–210, 212, 214, 216, 232, 236–238, 241, 242, 269, 302, 304, 307, 309, 311, 312, 314, 316–319, 328, 329
**Rhode Island.** Call of the President for all Volunteers and Militia from ..... 3
**Rhode Island Troops.** Mentioned.
Artillery—***Regiments*****:** **1st** (*Batteries*), **D**, 232–236.
Cavalry—***Regiments*****:** **1st**,* 140, 425, 441, 593, 682, 694, 695.
**Rice, Bruce B.** Mentioned ..... 665
**Rice, Edward J.** Mentioned ..... 609
**Rice, William H.** Mentioned ..... 727
**Rice, William L.** Mentioned ..... 410
**Richards, Thomas S.** Mentioned ..... 431
**Richardson, H. B.** Mentioned ..... 801
**Richardson, Israel B.**
Mentioned ..... 224, 229, 234
Report of reconnaissance to Gainesville, Va., March 20 ..... 332
**Richardson, John D.** Mentioned ..... 721
**Richardson, William D.** (Captain.) Mentioned ..... 561
**Richardson, William D.** (Private.) Mentioned ..... 419
**Richardson, William P.** Mentioned ..... 464, 466, 468
**Ricketts, James B.**
Correspondence with
Buford, John ..... 363
McDowell, Irvin ..... 217, 306

* Sometimes mentioned as New Hampshire Cavalry.

Page.

**Ricketts, James B.**—Continued.
Mentioned ........ 42, 43, 45, 106, 117, 122, 133, 134, 139, 140, 152, 166–170, 175, 185, 187, 190, 192, 194, 196–202, 205, 207, 215, 217, 235, 236, 238, 241, 263, 267, 268, 281, 284–288, 300, 302–304, 306–308, 310, 317, 318, 329, 330, 544, 677
Testimony of, McDowell Court of Inquiry ........ 215–217, 306, 307
**Ridgway, W. C.** Mentioned ........ 787, 791
**Rigby, Silas F.** Mentioned ........ 668
**Righter, John.** Mentioned ........ 423
**Rinard, Samuel.** Mentioned ........ 501
**Ripkin, William.** Mentioned ........ 692
**Ripley, Thaddeus A.** Mentioned ........ 787
**Rivers, John.** Mentioned ........ 457
**Roane County, W. Va.** Scout in, May 8–21. Report of Benjamin M. Skinner. 489
**Roberts, Benjamin S.**
Mentioned ........ 42, 45, 132–136, 184, 185, 190, 299, 300
Testimony of, McDowell Court of Inquiry ........ 184–190
**Robertson, Beverly H.** Mentioned ........ 416, 732
**Robertson, H. H.** Mentioned ........ 394
**Robertson, Michael S.** Mentioned ........ 783, 817
**Robertson, William T.** Mentioned ........ 787, 791
**Robinson, Lieutenant.** Mentioned ........ 16, 34
**Robinson, Charles D.** Mentioned ........ 111
**Robinson, Charles H.** Mentioned ........ 699
**Robinson, Lucius N.** Mentioned ........ 691, 695–697, 699
**Robinson, Powhatan.** Mentioned ........ 780
**Roebling, Washington.**
Mentioned ........ 268, 320
Testimony of, McDowell Court of Inquiry ........ 268, 269
**Ronald, Charles A.**
Correspondence with T. J. Jackson ........ 391
Mentioned ........ 382, 736, 737, 740, 742
Reports of
Kernstown, Va. Battle of, March 23 ........ 390
Port Republic, Va. Engagements at, June 8–9 ........ 747
Shenandoah Valley. Operations in, May 23–25 ........ 746
**Roper, Henry.** Mentioned ........ 683
**Rosecrans, W. S.**
Correspondence with John C. Frémont ........ 27, 28
Mentioned ........ 4, 6, 27, 338
Superseded in command of the Mountain Department ........ 1
**Ross, E.**
Correspondence with Frederick Myers ........ 119
Mentioned ........ 80, 81
**Ross, John D. H.** Mentioned ........ 486, 784, 790
**Rowan, John W.** Mentioned ........ 388
**Rowley, William W.**
Correspondence with Albert J. Myer ........ 353
Mentioned ........ 351, 354, 366, 552
Reports of
Kernstown, Va. Battle of, March 23 ........ 352, 353
Shenandoah Valley, Va. Operations in, May 24–25 ........ 566
**Roy, Richard B.** Mentioned ........ 390
**Ruby, John C.** Mentioned ........ 495
**Rude's Hill, Va.** Skirmish at, April 17. (See *Mount Jackson, Va.*)

Page.

**Ruger, Thomas H.**
Mentioned ... 618
Report of engagement at Winchester, Va., May 25 ... 625
**Ruggles, George D.**
Mentioned ... 42, 45, 72, 73
Testimony of, McDowell Court of Inquiry ... 72–74
**Rundell, Marshall H.**
Mentioned ... 412, 413
Report of operations on the Orange and Alexandria Railroad, March 28-31. 414
**Rundlett, Samuel P.** Mentioned ... 591
**Rutherford, R. G.** Mentioned ... 570
**Salem, Va.** Skirmish at, April 1 ... 1
**Salkeld, John N.** Mentioned ... 501
**Sample, Henderson.** Mentioned ... 431
**Sanderson, James M.** Mentioned ... 42, 45
**Sands, William A.** Mentioned ... 681
**Sanford, E. S.** Mentioned ... 166
**Saunders, H. B.** Mentioned ... 482
**Savage, James W.** Mentioned ... 35
**Saville, Thomas.**
Correspondence with Nathaniel P. Banks ... 525
Mentioned ... 525, 556
Report of action at Front Royal, Va., May 23 ... 558
**Sawyer, Edward B.** Mentioned ... 587
**Sawyer, Franklin.**
Mentioned ... 360, 361, 368
Report of battle of Kernstown, Va., March 23 ... 369
**Sawyer, Henry W.** Mentioned ... 677, 678
**Saxton, Rufus.**
Assignments to command ... 626
Correspondence with
Banks, Nathaniel P ... 538
Frémont, John C ... 635
Lincoln, Abraham ... 626, 628–632
McDowell, Irvin ... 634–637
War Department, U. S ... 626–638, 641, 646, 648
Mentioned ... 108, 109, 529, 531-534, 646, 648
Report of operations about Harper's Ferry, W. Va., May 24–30 ... 639
**Sayles, Stephen D.** Mentioned ... 373
**Sayles, Willard.** Report of reconnaissance to Liberty Church, Va., April 16. 425
**Scammon, E. Parker.**
Mentioned ... 449, 504–507, 512
Reports of
Camp Creek, W. Va. Skirmish on, May 1 ... 449
Princeton, W. Va. Actions at, May 16–17 ... 508, 509
**Schache, E.** Mentioned ... 505, 510
**Scheffler, William.** Mentioned ... 361, 552, 600, 604
**Schenck, J.** Mentioned ... 512
**Schenck, R. C.**
Correspondence with
Frémont, John C ... 28, 29
Sigel, Franz ... 176
Mentioned ... 4, 5, 7–9, 11, 19–21, 29, 126, 129, 131, 134, 142, 148, 150, 151, 156, 171, 251, 272, 447, 460, 461, 467, 471, 524, 654, 655, 658, 661, 665, 701, 785

Page.

**Schenck, R. C.**—Continued.
Reports of
Cross Keys, Va. Battle of, June 8 ... 666
Franklin, W. Va. Skirmishes near, May 10–12 ... 496
McDowell, Va. Engagement near, May 8 ... 461, 462
**Schirmer, Louis.** Mentioned ... 670, 671, 673
**Schley, L. R.** Mentioned ... 817
**Schneider, Charles.** Mentioned ... 359
**Schopp, P. T.** Mentioned ... 670
**Schriver, Edmund.**
Mentioned ... 41–43, 45–47, 50, 51, 55, 89, 93, 105, 108, 109, 116, 117, 121, 122, 166, 167, 171, 181, 190, 200, 209, 215, 222, 237, 250, 263, 266, 284–286, 291, 293, 296, 308, 310, 312, 319
Testimony of, McDowell Court of Inquiry ... 46–52, 55–58, 89, 90, 105, 181, 190–194, 200, 209, 210, 222, 237, 238, 250, 263, 266, 267, 291, 296
(For correspondence as Chief of Staff, see *Irvin McDowell.*)
**Schurz, Carl.** Mentioned ... 134, 142, 148, 150, 151, 171, 176
**Scott, Charles.** Mentioned ... 88
**Scott, H. B.** Mentioned ... 618, 620, 624
**Scott, John F.** Mentioned ... 88
**Scott, Robert E.** Mentioned ... 47, 48, 50, 51, 78
**Scott, Robert E., Mrs.**
Mentioned ... 47–49, 294, 326
Case of. Communications from
Anderson, Joseph R ... 47–49
McDowell, Irvin ... 47, 48
**Scott, W. C.**
Assignments to command ... 487
Correspondence with Edward Johnson ... 487
Mentioned ... 484, 488, 715, 786, 787
Reports of
Cross Keys, Va. Battle of, June 8 ... 789, 790
Front Royal, Va. Action at, May 23 ... 788
Harrisonburg, Va. Action near, June 6 ... 788, 789
McDowell, Va. Engagement near, May 8 ... 484
Port Republic, Va. Engagements at, June 8–9 ... 789, 790
Winchester, Va. Engagement at, May 25 ... 788
**Scott, William S.** Mentioned ... 88
**Scott, Winfield.** Mentioned ... 41–43, 75, 221
**Seargeant, William J.** Mentioned ... 409
**Second Manassas, Va.** Battle of, August 30. (See *Bull Run, Va.*)
**Seddon, Mrs.** Mentioned ... 63
**Seddon, John.** Mentioned ... 770
**Selden, Miles C., jr.** Mentioned ... 493
**Selfridge, James L.** Mentioned ... 613
**Selfridge, R. O.** Mentioned ... 171
**Seward, William H.** Mentioned ... 61
**Seymour, Isaac G.** Mentioned ... 801, 803
**Shands, E. A.** Mentioned ... 386
**Shanks, Daniel.** Mentioned ... 782, 817
**Shaver's River, W. Va.** Raid to, May 30. Report of John C. Frémont ... 813
**Sheetz, George F.** Mentioned ... 386, 387, 407, 473, 703
**Shelmire, John H.** Mentioned ... 18, 676, 680

Page.

**Shenandoah, Department of the.** (Union.)
Banks, Nathaniel P., assigned to and assumes command of ........ 1, 2
Constituted ........ 1
Limits extended ........ 542
Merged into Army of Virginia ........ 3, 169
**Shenandoah River, Va., South Fork of.** Skirmish on, near Luray, Va., April 19. (See *Shenandoah Valley, Va. Operations in, April* 19–24.)
**Shenandoah Valley.** Operations in.
April 19–24. Reports of Nathaniel P. Banks ........ 445, 446
May 15–June 17.
Casualties. Returns of
Confederate troops* ........ 717, 718, 780, 781, 783, 784, 787
Union troops† ........ 553, 554
Communications from
Adjutant-General's office, U. S. A ........ 541, 653, 655
Banks, Nathaniel P ........ 32, 34, 285, 522–524, 526–535, 538–545
Crawford, S. W ........ 33
Ewell, R. S ........ 801
Frémont, John C ........ 31, 642–657, 659, 660, 662, 663
King, Rufus ........ 31
Lincoln, Abraham ........ 13, 24, 25, 34, 282, 533, 535, 542, 643, 644, 647, 648, 655, 659, 661, 662
McDowell, Irvin ........ 17, 33, 55, 285–288, 651, 689, 690
Pendleton, A. S ........ 709
Shields, James ........ 21, 33
Sigel, Franz ........ 32
Suckley, George ........ 31
War Department, U. S ........ 31, 282, 285, 286, 288, 522, 523, 526–529, 531, 534, 538, 544, 642, 644–646, 649, 651, 657, 659, 660, 663
Congratulatory orders. (Joseph E. Johnston) ........ 710
Frémont, John C. Ordered to move from Franklin, W. Va., against Jackson ........ 10, 642, 643
Jackson's command moves toward Richmond ........ 716
McDowell, Irvin. Ordered to put in motion 20,000 men for ........ 282
Reports of
Abert, James W., May 24 ........ 568
Babbitt, Charles R., May 24–25 ........ 584
Banks, Nathaniel P ........ 545
Bayard, George D., June 1–13 ........ 676, 677
Beal, George L., May 24–26 ........ 609
Boswell, J. K., June 1–9 ........ 718
Brodhead, Thornton F., May 24–27 ........ 579
Collins, William D., May 24–30 ........ 587
Collis, Charles H. T., May 24–26 ........ 572
Crosby, Franklin B., May 24–26 ........ 603
Crutchfield, S., May 23–June 9 ........ 724, 727
De Forest, Othneil, May 24–27 ........ 581
Donnelly, Dudley, May 24–26 ........ 605
Fleming, J. Presley, May 24–25 ........ 602
Flournoy, Thomas S., May 23–26 ........ 733

* Losses at Front Royal, May 23; Winchester, May 25; Harrisonburg, June 6; Cross Keys and Port Republic, June 8–9.

† Includes losses at Front Royal and Buckton Station, May 23; Strasburg, Middletown, and Newtown, May 24, and Winchester, May 25.

Page.

**Shenandoah Valley.** Operations in—Continued.
May 15–June 17.
Reports of
Gordon, George H., May 24 ... 614
Hampton, R. B., May 25–28 ... 600
Harman, John A ... 721–723
Hatch, John P., May 24–25 ... 573
Hawks, W. J ... 720, 721
Holabird, S. B., May 24–25 ... 570
Jackson, Thomas J ... 701, 710, 711
Johnson, Bradley T., May 29–June 9 ... 817
Jones, Owen, June 1–13 ... 680
Kargé, Joseph, June 2–13 ... 677
Knipe, Joseph F., May 24–26 ... 612
Munford, Thomas T ... 732
Peabody, James H., May 23–25 ... 601
Ronald, Charles A., May 23–25 ... 746
Rowley, William W., May 24–25 ... 566
Sigel, Franz, June 3-4 ... 813
Taylor, Richard, May 23–June 9 ... 800, 801
Tompkins, Charles H., May 24–25 ... 585
Wetschky, Charles, May 18–26 ... 577
Williams, Alpheus S., May 24–25 ... 593
Winder, Charles S., May 23–25 ... 734
(See also
March 29–June 27. *Mountain Department. Operations in.*
May 18. *Woodstock, Va. Skirmish at.*
21. *Browntown, Va. Reconnaissance from Front Royal to.*
23. *Front Royal, Va. Action at.*
*Buckton Station, Va. Skirmish at.*
24. *Berryville, Va. Skirmish at.*
*Strasburg, Va. Skirmish at.*
*Middletown, Va. Action at.*
*Newtown, Va. Action at.*
*Linden, Va. Skirmish at.*
24–30. *Harper's Ferry, W. Va. Operations about.*
25. *Winchester, Va. Engagement at.*
26. *Franklin, W. Va. Skirmish near.*
27. *Loudoun Heights, Va. Skirmish at.*
28. *Charlestown, W. Va. Skirmish at.*
29. *Wardensville, W. Va. Skirmish near.*
30. *Front Royal, Va. Action at.*
31. *Front Royal, Va. Skirmish near.*
June 1. *Mount Carmel, near Strasburg, Va. Skirmish at.*
2. *Strasburg and Woodstock, Va. Skirmishes at.*
3. *Mount Jackson, Va. Skirmish at.*
*Tom's Brook, Va. Skirmish at.*
6. *Harrisonburg, Va. Action near.*
7. *Harrisonburg, Va. Skirmish near.*
8. *Cross Keys, Va. Battle of.*
8– 9. *Port Republic, Va. Engagements at.*
13. *New Market, Va. Skirmish at.*
16. *Mount Jackson, Va. Skirmish near.*)

**Shepherd, Decatur J.** Mentioned ... 390
**Shepherd, William C.** Mentioned ... 390

Page.

**Shields, James.**
Correspondence with
Frémont, John C ... 21, 23, 24, 32, 33
McClellan, George B ... 343, 344
McDowell, Irvin ... 33, 55, 689, 690
War Department, U. S ... 344
Mentioned ... 17, 20–24, 32–34, 55, 78, 81, 97, 105, 106, 108, 109, 116, 117, 121, 122, 132, 163, 165–167, 220, 227, 230, 281–289, 291, 293, 298, 339, 344, 346, 347, 354–356, 370, 378, 379, 426, 500, 502, 531, 543, 546, 552, 593, 634, 635, 649, 651, 652, 654–657, 659, 689, 707, 710–714, 716, 719, 720, 722, 727–730, 732, 747, 767, 774, 785, 793, 798, 802
Reports of
Front Royal, Va. Action at, May 30, and skirmish near, May 31 ... 682
Kernstown, Va. Battle of, March 23 ... 335, 336, 338
Port Republic, Va. Engagements at, June 8–9 ... 683–685
**Shiras, Alexander E.** Mentioned ... 43
**Shirfey, S. W.** Mentioned ... 354
**Showalter, John H.**
Mentioned ... 423
Report of raid to Boothsville and Valley River, W. Va., April 12 ... 423
**Shriber, R. C.**
Mentioned ... 361, 692, 693, 695, 697
Report of battle of Kernstown, Va., March 23 ... 349
**Sigel, Franz.**
Assignments to command ... 638
Correspondence with
Cluseret, Gustave P ... 173
Frémont, John C ... 32
Heintz, C ... 176
McDowell Court of Inquiry ... 162
McDowell, Irvin ... 148, 152, 154, 155, 174, 175, 309, 315
Pope, John ... 160, 204, 211
Schenck, Robert C ... 176
War Department, U. S ... (Note) 651
Mentioned ... 17, 26, 34, 42, 45, 123, 125, 126, 131, 133, 135, 139, 143, 149, 155, 159–162, 167, 168, 171, 174, 175, 180–182, 184, 186, 187, 189, 190, 192, 194–197, 199–203, 207, 209–211, 214, 237, 242, 249, 257, 258, 261–263, 269, 270, 273, 274, 285, 286, 298–320, 327–329, 331, 538, 539, 541–543, 545, 638, 641, 651, 656, 657, 659–661
Report of operations in Shenandoah Valley, June 3–4 ... 813
Testimony of, McDowell Court of Inquiry ... 123–159, 171–173, 180, 302, 303, 305, 308–310, 312, 317, 318
**Silcott, Captain.** Mentioned ... 490
**Simms, Richard D.** Mentioned ... 749
**Simpson, Joshua.** Mentioned ... 818
**Sipe, Emanuel.** Mentioned ... 712
**Skeels, C. L.** Mentioned ... 570, 607
**Sketches.**
Kernstown, Va. Battle of, March 23 ... 362–365
McDowell, Va. Engagement near, May 8 ... 474, 475
Northern Virginia. Campaign in, August 16–September 2 ... 177–179, 260
**Skinner, Benjamin M.**
Correspondence with J. C. Rathbone ... 490
Report of scout in Clay and Roane Counties, W Va., May 8–21 ... 489

Page.

**Skinner, James H.** Mentioned ..... 788–790
**Slain, Stephen.** Mentioned ..... 693
**Slaughter, Montgomery.** Mentioned ..... 83, 88, 436
**Slaves and Slave Property.** References to ..... 53
**Slocum, Paul E.** Mentioned ..... 367
**Slough, John P.** Mentioned ..... 639–641
**Smead, Abner.** Mentioned ..... 484, 716
(For correspondence as A. A. G., see *Edward Johnson.*)
**Smith, ——.** Mentioned ..... 88
**Smith,** General. [?] Mentioned ..... 342
**Smith, Charles D.** Mentioned ..... 453, 454
**Smith, Charles W.** Mentioned ..... 690
**Smith, F. H.** Mentioned ..... 471, 473
**Smith, George.** Report of action at Front Royal, Va., May 23 ..... 558
**Smith, George H.** Mentioned ..... 472, 484
**Smith, George T.** Mentioned ..... 564
**Smith, Gustavus W.** Mentioned ..... 285, 335, 424, 440, 442, 543
**Smith, Isaac A.** Mentioned ..... 787
**Smith, John A.** Mentioned ..... 66, 67
**Smith, Orlando.** Mentioned ..... 668
**Smith, Thomas C. H.** Mentioned ..... 42, 45
**Smith, Thomas E.** Mentioned ..... 693
**Smith, Washington.** Mentioned ..... 423
**Sneath, George C.** Mentioned ..... 501
**Snodgrass, C. E.** Mentioned ..... 721, 780
**Snowden, Nicholas.** Mentioned ..... 783, 817
**Snyder, Charles J.** Mentioned ..... 581
**Snyder, George.** Mentioned ..... 501
**Somers, S. M.** Mentioned ..... 721, 722
**Somerville Heights, Va.** Action at, May 7. Reports of
Banks, Nathaniel P ..... 458
Foster, Robert S ..... 458
**Southall, V. W.** Mentioned ..... 482
**Sowers, N. O.** Mentioned ..... 390
**Spargo, Peter.** Mentioned ..... 354
**Sparta, Va.** Occupation of, April 19. (See *April 19–24. Operations in Shenandoah Valley.*)
**Spencer, Joseph H.** Mentioned ..... 353, 354, 567
**Spengler, A.** Mentioned ..... 754
**Spotts, G. W.** Mentioned ..... 494
**Sprague, Charles H.** Mentioned ..... 581
**Sprigg,** Captain. Mentioned ..... 804
**Springstead, J.** Mentioned ..... 116
**Spurling, Andrew B.** Mentioned ..... 455
**Stafford, Leroy A.** Mentioned ..... 801, 805
**Stager, Anson.** Mentioned ..... 93
**Stahel, Julius.** Mentioned ..... 8, 15, 18–20, 651, 653, 654, 657, 658, 664, 669, 672, 675, 785, 798
**Stanard, William B.** Mentioned ..... 775
**Stanley, James.** Mentioned ..... 439
**Stanton, E. M.** Mentioned ..... 4–7, 10, 12, 16, 17, 26, 27, 42, 49, 61, 68, 72, 75, 79, 93 98, 99, 105, 106, 108, 109, 113, 121, 122, 160, 164, 166, 167, 218–222, 225, 226, 231, 277, 280–288, 351, 541, 632, 642, 651, 653, 655, 661, 685
(For correspondence, etc., see *War Department, U. S.*)

Page.

**Stealy, G. I.** Correspondence with M. D. W. Loomis .......... 29
**Stearns, Benjamin F.** Mentioned .......... 439
**Steiner, John A.** Mentioned .......... 639
**Steinwehr, Adolph von.** Mentioned .......... 8, 19, 20, 142, 176, 658, 664, 785
**Steptoe, Charles Y** Mentioned .......... 486, 487
**Steuart, George H.** Mentioned .......... 646, 701–704, 706, 707, 709–714, 717, 730, 731, 734, 779, 781–784, 788–790, 799, 817, 818
**Stevens, Isaac I.** Mentioned .......... 131
**Stevens, Jarvis C.** Mentioned .......... 454
**Stewart, A. D.** Mentioned .......... 491
**Stone, C. P.** Mentioned .......... 586
**Stone, Lincoln R.** Mentioned .......... 551, 623
**Stony Creek, near Edenburg, Va.** Skirmish at, April 2 .......... 1
**Stover, Joshua.** Mentioned .......... 775
**Stowell, D. Porter.** Report of reconnaissance to Culpeper Court-House, Va., May 4–5 .......... 451
**Strasburg, Va.** Skirmishes at and near.
March 19 .......... 1
May 24.
Casualties. Returns of Union troops .......... 553, 554
(See *May* 15–*June* 17. *Operations in Shenandoah Valley.* *Reports of*
Banks, Nathaniel P. Collis, Charles H. T. Hatch, John P.)
June 2. Communications from John C. Frémont .......... 651
(See also
*March* 29–*June* 2. *Operations in Mountain Department.* *Report of*
Frémont, John C.
*May* 15–*June* 17. *Operations in Shenandoah Valley.* *Reports of*
Bayard, George D. Jones, Owen. Kargé, Joseph. Munford, T. T.)
**Stuart,** Dr. Mentioned .......... 435
**Stuart, J. E. B.**
Mentioned .......... 333, 411, 452, 501
Report of operations on the Orange and Alexandria Railroad, Va., March 28–31 .......... 415
**Sturgis, Samuel D.**
Assigned to command of **Reserve Army Corps** .......... 3
Mentioned .......... 169, 174, 244
**Suckley, George.**
Correspondence with **John C. Frémont** .......... 30, 31
Mentioned .......... 26
**Sullivan, Jeremiah C.**
Mentioned .......... 339, 340, 342, 346, 348, 349, 354, 359–361, 366, 368, 373, 429, 458
Report of battle of Kernstown, Va., March 23 .......... 371
**Sullivant, Michael.** Mentioned .......... 43
**Sumner, Edwin V.** Mentioned .......... 43, 96, 100, 101, 103, 104, 113, 131, 224, 229, 230, 234, 235, 276, 344
**Surget, E.** Mentioned .......... 801, 803
**Swaine, E.** Mentioned .......... 374
**Swan, Joseph.** Mentioned .......... 43
**Swann,** Captain. Mentioned .......... 493
**Swann, Samuel A.** Mentioned .......... 438
**Swayne, Joel J.** Mentioned .......... 18, 676
**Swinney, Ebenezer H.** Mentioned .......... 464, 469, 668
**Switzer,** Scout. Mentioned .......... 147

Page.

**Sykes, George** Mentioned ... 244, 270, 274, 321

**Taliaferro, Alexander G.**

Mentioned ... 381, 408, 409, 482, 484, 772, 773

Reports of

Kernstown, Va. Battle of, March 23 ... 410

Winchester, Va. Engagement at, May 25 ... 775

**Taliaferro, Philip A.** Mentioned ... 482, 775

**Taliaferro, William B.**

Mentioned ... 471, 472, 476, 483, 484, 713, 715, 740

Reports of

McDowell, Va. Engagement near, May 8 ... 480

Port Republic, Va. Engagements at, June 8-9 ... 773

**Taliaferro, W. T.** Mentioned ... 438

**Tappan, Benjamin.** Mentioned ... 369

**Tarr, Frederick C.** Mentioned ... 557, 558, 682

**Taylor,** Mr. Mentioned ... 435

**Taylor,** Color-Corporal. Mentioned ... 817

**Taylor, Charles F.** Mentioned ... 18, 676

**Taylor, Charles W.** Mentioned ... 777

**Taylor, Constantin.** Mentioned ... 453-455

**Taylor, David A.** Mentioned ... 352-354

**Taylor, Joseph.**

Mentioned ... 43, 50

Testimony of, McDowell Court of Inquiry ... 50

**Taylor, Richard.**

Mentioned ... 21, 452, 636, 701-706, 714, 715, 717, 719, 728-730, 736, 741, 743, 745, 759, 767, 772, 774, 775, 779-781, 784, 786-788, 790-793, 797-799

Report of operations in Shenandoah Vall›y, May 23-June 9 ... 800, 801

**Teaford, George W.** Mentioned ... 787, 791

**Teagarden, George W.** Mentioned ... 681

**Tefft, Benjamin F.** Mentioned ... 54

**Telegraph or Railroad Lines.** Obstruction of, or injury to, in Department of the Rappahannock. Punishment for ... 52

**Temple,** Mr. Mentioned ... 89

**Temple, Oliver S.** Mentioned ... 352, 354, 366

**Ten Eyck, George.** Mentioned ... 815

**Tennessee.** Military departments embracing ... 542

**Terrill, James B.** Mentioned ... 791, 792

**Terry, J. C.** Mentioned ... 570

**Terry, John F.** Mentioned ... 482

**Thoburn, Joseph.** Mentioned ... 361, 696, 697, 700

**Thom, J. P.** Mentioned ... 406, 40-

**Thomas, Hampton S.** Mentioned ... 431, 681

**Thomas, Lorenzo.**

Correspondence with War Department, U. S ... 227, 228

Mentioned ... 43, 121, 163, 219, 220, 227, 228, 235, 284, 325, 332, 543, 544, 653

(For correspondence, etc., see also *Adjutant-General's Office, U. S. A.*)

**Thompson, Ambrose.** Mentioned ... 117, 167

**Thompson, Francis W.** Mentioned ... 464

**Thompson, George W.** Report of action at Front Royal, Va., May 23 ... 558

**Thorndyke,** Mr. Mentioned ... 641

**Thrasher, Thaddeus.** Mentioned ... 385

**Tilghman, Lloyd.** Mentioned ... 49

Page.

**Tillson, Davis.**
Mentioned ........ 42
45, 59, 80, 81, 195, 197, 232, 235, 265, 280, 290, 291, 294, 309, 314, 317, 319
Testimony of, McDowell Court of Inquiry .. 59, 60, 80–82, 195, 197, 232–237, 265, 295
**Tompkins, Charles H.**
Mentioned ........ 572–575, 582, 587
Report of operations in Shenandoah Valley, May 24–25 ........ 585
**Tom's Brook, Va.** Skirmish at, June 3 ........ 518
**Toole, J. A.** Correspondence with John E. Johnson ........ 438
**Tower, Zealous B.** Mentioned ........ 302
**Towles, W. E.** Mentioned ........ 417
**Town, Charles H.**
Mentioned ........ 579, 580, 596, 597
Report of skirmish at Milford, Va., June 24 ........ 815
**Townsend, E. D.** Mentioned ........ 43
**Tracy, Albert.**
Correspondence with John C. Frémont ........ 35
Mentioned ........ 26, 35
Report of number of aides credited to the staff of John C. Frémont ........ 35
(For correspondence as A. A. G., see *John C. Frémont.*)
**Train,** General. Mentioned ........ 798
**Trevey, Jacob M.** Mentioned ........ 748
**Trevilian's Depot, Va.** Skirmish at, May 2 ........ 2
**Trigg, Robert C.** Mentioned ........ 513, 514
**Trimble, Isaac R.**
Mentioned .... 20, 452, 701, 703, 704, 706, 713–715, 717, 766, 770, 774, 779–786, 792, 802
Report of
Cross Keys, Va. Battle of, June 8 ........ 795
Port Republic, Va. Engagements at, June 8–9 ........ 795
Winchester, Va. Engagement at, May 25 ........ 794
**Tucker, Benjamin F.** Mentioned ........ 424, 441, 442, 445
**Turner, John A.** Mentioned ........ 406
**Turner, T. T.** Mentioned ........ 780, 782, 786
**Turner, William.** Mentioned ........ 386
**Turpin, Walter G.** Mentioned ........ 718, 719
**Turpin, William H.** Mentioned ........ 476
**Tyler, Erastus B.**
Mentioned ........ 33, 339, 341, 342,
346–351 354, 355, 360, 361, 369, 377, 684, 685, 687, 691, 692, 699, 700, 711
Reports of
Kernstown, Va. Battle of, March 23 ........ 375, 376
Port Republic, Va. Engagements at, June 8–9 ........ 695
**Tyndale, Hector.**
Mentioned ........ 536
Report of reconnaissance to Browntown, Va., May 21 ........ 554
**Uhler, William H.** Mentioned ........ 683
**Umbaugh, John.** Mentioned ........ 456, 457
**Union Troops.**
Casualties. Returns of
Cross Keys, Va. Battle of, June 8 ........ 664, 665
Kernstown, Va. Battle of, March 23 ........ 346, 347
McDowell, Va. Engagement near, May 8 ........ 462
Port Republic, Va. Engagements at, June 8–9 ........ 690
Princeton, W. Va. Action at, May 16–17 ........ 508

Page.

**Union Troops**—Continued.
Casualties. Returns of
Shenandoah Valley. Operations in, May 15–June 17* ........ 553, 554
Mentioned. (*Regulars.*)
Artillery—*Regiments:* **4th** (*Batteries*), **C**, 413; **E**, 347, 350, 359, 360, 373, 684, 688, 690–694, 696, 699, 700; **F**, 553, 573, 574, 594, 596, 600, 603–606, 612, 613, 620, 621. *Batteries:* **Naval** (*C. H. Daniels*), 634, 639, 641.
(For Volunteers, see respective States.)
Sanitary condition of Blenker's division. Communications from George Suckley ........ 30, 31
Washington, D. C. Strength of, available for defense of, April 19 ........ 226
**Vagine, James L.** Mentioned ........ 88
**Valley District.** Orders, Special, **No. 230**, 818.
**Valley River, W. Va.** Raid to, April 12. Reports of
Kelley, Benjamin F ........ 423
Showalter, John H ........ 423
**Van Alen, James H.** Mentioned ........ 36, 37, 323
**Vance, James.** Mentioned ........ 409
**Vance, James M.** Mentioned ........ 665
**Vance, William.** Mentioned ........ 459
**Van Rensselaer, Henry.**
Correspondence with Irvin McDowell ........ 63, 280
Mentioned ........ 62, 93
**Vaughn, Zenas.** Mentioned ........ 455
**Vawter, Louis A.** Mentioned ........ 492
**Vermillion, John M.** Mentioned ........ 478
**Vermont.** Call of the President for all Volunteers and Militia from ........ 3
**Vermont Troops.** Mentioned.
Cavalry—*Regiments:* **1st**, 448, 458, 459, 548, 553, 572–576, 581, 582, 584–593.
**Virgin, Isaac G.** Mentioned ........ 454
**Virginia**, C. S. S. (U. S. Frigate **Merrimac.**) Mentioned ........ 223
**Virginia.**
Affairs in, generally. Communications from
McClellan, George B ........ 164, 234
McDowell, Irvin ........ 275
Campaign in. Communications from Abraham Lincoln ........ 222
Military departments embracing ........ 1, 542
Operations in. (See
March 18. *Middletown, Va. Skirmish at.*
19. *Strasburg, Va. Skirmish at.*
20. *Gainesville, Va. Reconnaissance to.*
20–21. *Dumfries, Va. Reconnaissance to.*
22. *Kernstown, Va. Skirmish at.*
23. *Kernstown, Va. Battle of.*
25. *Mount Jackson, Va. Skirmish at.*
27–31. *Middleburg and White Plains, Va. Operations in the vicinity of.*
28–31. *Orange and Alexandria Railroad, Va. Operations on the, including affairs at Bealeton and Rappahannock Stations.*
April 1. *Salem, Va. Skirmish at.*
1–2. *Woodstock and Edenburg, Va. Advance of Union forces from Strasburg to.*
2. *Stony Creek, near Edenburg, Va. Skirmish at.*

*Includes losses at Front Royal and Buckton Station, May 23; Strasburg, Middletown, and Newtown, May 24, and Winchester, May 25.

Page

**Virginia**—Continued.

Operations in. (See

April 2. *Rappahannock River, Va. Reconnaissance to the.*
7. *Rappahannock River, Va. Reconnaissance to the.*
*Columbia Furnace, Va. Skirmish at.*
12. *Monterey, Va. Skirmish at.*
15. *Rappahannock, Va. Reconnaissance to the.*
16. *Rappahannock, Va. Reconnaissance to the.*
*Liberty Church, Va. Reconnaissance to.*
*Columbia Furnace, Va. Skirmish at.*
17. *Mount Jackson, Va. Occupation of.*
*Rude's Hill, Va. Skirmish at.*
*New Market, Va. Occupation of.*
*Piedmont, Va. Skirmish at.*
17–19. *Fredericksburg, Va. Operations about, and occupation of.*
18. *Rappahannock, Va. Reconnaissance to the.*
19. *Shenandoah River, South Fork of. Skirmish on, near Luray, Va.*
*Sparta, Va. Occupation of.*
21. *Monterey, Va. Skirmish at.*
22. *Harrisonburg, Va. Occupied by Union forces.*
*Luray, Va. Occupation of, and skirmish near.*
24. *Harrisonburg, Va. Skirmish nine miles from.*
26. *Gordonsville and Keezletown Cross-Roads, Va. Skirmish at the.*
27. *McGaheysville, Va. Skirmish at.*
May 1. *Rapidan Station, Va. Skirmish at.*
2. *Trevilian's Depot and Louisa Court-House, Va. Skirmishes at.*
4–5. *Culpeper Court-House, Va. Reconnaissance to.*
5. *Columbia Bridge, Va. Skirmish at.*
6. *Harrisonburg, Va. Skirmish near.*
7. *Somerville Heights, Va. Action at.*
8. *McDowell (Bull Pasture Mountain), Va. Engagement near.*
9. *McDowell, Va. Skirmish near.*
11. *Bowling Green Road, near Fredericksburg, Va. Skirmish on the.*
12. *Monterey, Va. Skirmish at.*
13. *Rappahannock River, Va. Affair on.*
14. *Gaines' Cross-Roads, Va. Skirmish at.*
15. *Linden, Va. Skirmish at.*
*Gaines' Cross-Roads, Rappahannock County, Va. Skirmish at.*
15–June 17. *Shenandoah Valley. Operations in the.*
20. *Virginia Central Railroad at Jackson's River Depot, Va. Raid on.*
June 18–19. *Winchester, Va. Skirmishes near.*
22–30. *Moorefield and New Creek, W. Va., and Winchester, Va. Scout from Strasburg to.*
24. *Milford, Va. Skirmish at.*)

**Virginia, Army of.** (Union.)

Banks, Nathaniel P., assigned to command of Second Corps ........ 169
Constituted ........ 3, 169
Frémont, John C., assigned to command of First Corps ........ 169
McDowell, Irvin, assigned to command of Third Corps ........ 169
Orders, Field, series 1862: *Corps:* **3d** (*McDowell*), **August 27**, 175, 304.
Orders, General, series 1862: **August 25**, 174; **August 27**, 210. *Corps:* **3d** (*McDowell*), **No. 10**, 139, 304.
Pope, John, assigned to command ........ 169

Page.

**Virginia Central Railroad, Va.** Raid on the, May 20 Report of John C. Frémont ........ 803

**Virginia Troops.** Mentioned.

Artillery—*Batteries:* **Alleghany** (*Carpenter*), 380, 381, 393, 397, 399–401, 405, 705, 707, 713, 714, 717, 726–728, 736–741, 752, 755, 758–760, 762; **Charlottesville** (*Carrington*), 717, 774; **Chew's**, 380, 383, 470, 703, 715, 718, 719, 725–728, 732, 742, 760; **Courtney's**, 703, 704, 713, 715, 718, 725, 727, 728, 779, 782, 784, 794, 795, 799; **Cutshaw's**, 705, 717, 726–728, 736, 737, 755, 758, 765, 769, 817; **Danville** (*Shumaker and Wooding*), 380, 408, 713, 715, 717, 727, 729, 773, 774, 777, 778; **Hampden** (*Caskie*), 381, 715, 717, 727–729, 731, 771, 772; **Lee** (*Raine*), 487, 713, 715, 718, 727, 728, 741, 782, 784, 792, 793; **Lusk's**,* 487, 713, 718, 725, 727, 728, 782, 784, 788, 790; **Lowry's**, 492; **Monroe** (*Chapman*), 492; **Nottoway** (*Jeffress*), 514; **Otey's**, 492, 494; **Purcell** (*Pegram*), 434; **Rice's**,† 487, 707, 718, 727, 728; **Rockbridge** (*McLaughlin and Poague*), 380–382, 384, 396–398, 401, 402, 405, 450, 703–705, 707, 713–715, 717, 725–729, 735–741, 749, 753–755, 760–764, 767, 769, 776; **Vawter's**, 492, 493; **West Augusta** (*Waters*), 381, 382, 384, 397–399.

Cavalry—*Battalions:* **Dunn's**, 513, 514; **White's**, 173, 411, 412. *Companies:* **Chipley's**, 712, 713, 732; **Downs'**, 490; **Greenbrier**, 814; **Marshall's**, 816; **Myers'**, 712, 713, 732; **Righter's**, 423; **Webster Dare Devils**, 440. *Regiments:* **1st**, 415–417; **2d**, 417, 498, 502, 702, 703, 706, 711, 712, 718, 729–734, 779; **4th**, 417; **6th**, 417, 631, 702, 703, 706, 711, 712, 718, 729, 730, 732–734, 779; **7th** (see *Turner Ashby*); **8th**, 450, 492, 494, 812; **9th**, 428, 432, 434, 438; **11th**, 415; **14th**, 814.

Infantry—*Battalions:* **1st**, 342, 381, 382, 384, 388, 401, 405–407, 476, 478–480, 714, 717, 736, 766, 769–771, 781; **Hansbrough's**, 487. *Regiments:* **2d**, 342, 380, 382, 384, 385, 387–390, 408, 674, 694, 704, 705, 707, 708, 717, 730, 735, 736–741, 743–745, 747–749, 752, 757; **4th**, 342, 380, 382, 384, 388, 390, 391, 705, 707, 717, 735–738, 740, 745–747, 757; **5th**, 342, 380, 382, 384, 391–393, 397, 401, 404, 694, 704, 705, 707, 715, 717, 735–738, 740, 741, 743, 744, 747–751, 755; **10th**, 447, 472, 476, 481–483, 705, 717, 772–775; **13th**, 713, 717, 781, 784, 787, 791, 792, 796–798; **15th**, 799; **21st**, 342, 381, 384, 395, 401–403, 471, 476–478, 708, 717, 736, 763–765, 767, 769; **22d**, 492, 495, 812; **23d**, 342, 380, 381, 384, 408–410, 472, 476, 481–483, 705, 717, 772–776; **25th**, 471, 472, 476, 481, 483, 487, 694, 713, 717, 781, 787, 791, 792, 796–799; **27th**, 342, 380–382, 384, 389, 390, 393–395, 402, 404, 406, 408, 694, 704, 705, 707, 717, 735–738, 740, 741, 743, 748, 751–754; **28th**, 342; **29th**, 513, 514; **31st**, 471, 472, 476, 480, 481, 483, 487, 717, 741, 787, 792; **32d**, 707, 743; **33d**, 342, 380, 382, 384, 388, 394–396, 704, 705, 707, 717, 735–738, 740, 746, 753–758; **37th**, 342, 380, 381, 384, 408, 409, 472, 476, 481–483, 717, 719, 728, 772–776; **40th**, 434, 438; **42d**, 342, 381, 382, 384, 392, 401, 404, 405, 476, 477, 480, 694, 714, 717, 731, 765–767, 770, 781, 784; **44th**, 471, 476, 483, 485–487, 717, 784, 786–791; **45th**, 450, 491, 492, 494, 812; **48th**, 381, 382, 401, 476, 478–480, 694, 714, 717, 736, 767, 768, 781, 784; **50th**, 812; **52d**, 471, 472, 476, 483, 485, 487, 488, 694, 717, 784, 786–791; **54th**, 513, 514, 714; **55th**, 434; **57th**, 713; **58th**, 471, 476, 478, 479, 483, 485–487, 694, 712, 714, 717, 732, 770, 782–784, 786, 787–791.

**Voris, Alvin C.**

Mentioned ........ 361

Report of battle of Kernstown, Va., March 23 ........ 370

**Vought, Philip G.**

Mentioned ........ 548, 556, 557, 575, 581

Report of action at Front Royal, Va., May 23 ........ 564

**Waddy, G. T.** (For correspondence, etc., see *A. G. Taliaferro.*)

**Wade, Benjamin F.** Mentioned ........ 63, 292, 293

---

* Originally Miller's. † Also called 8th Star Artillery.

Page.

**Wadsworth, Craig W.** Mentioned ... 90, 215–217, 306

**Wadsworth, James S.**

Correspondence with

McClellan, George B ... 162

War Department, U. S ... 224, 225

Limits of command extended ... 231

Mentioned ... 42, 43, 45, 108, 112, 165, 219, 225–229, 231, 240, 241, 276, 277, 290, 296, 325, 499, 500

Testimony of, McDowell Court of Inquiry ... 112–115, 290, 296, 297

**Walden, William A.** Mentioned ... 439

**Walker, H. H.** Mentioned ... 434

**Walker, J. A.**

Mentioned ... 758, 782, 783, 786, 787, 796, 799, 800

Reports of

Cross Keys, Va. Battle of, June 8 ... 791

Port Republic, Va. Engagements at, June 8–9 ... 791

**Walker, N. D.** Mentioned ... 786, 789, 791

**Walker, S. T.** Mentioned ... 482, 775

**Wallach, William D.**

Mentioned ... 51

Testimony of, McDowell Court of Inquiry ... 51

**Waller, Thomas M.** Mentioned ... 732

**Walton, Benjamin T.** Mentioned ... 787, 791

**Walton, Simeon T.** Mentioned ... 409

**Warberg, Adolf C.** Mentioned ... 35

**War, Council of.** Army of the Potomac, March 13 ... 104, 223

**Ward, John S.** Mentioned ... 448

**Wardensville, W. Va.** Skirmishes at and near.

May 7. Reports of

Downey, Stephen W ... 457

Frémont, John C ... 456

May 29. Communications from John C. Frémont ... 647

(See also *report of John C. Frémont*, p. 13.)

**War Department, U. S.**

Congratulatory orders.

Columbia Furnace, Va. Skirmish at, April 16 ... 427

Harper's Ferry, W. Va. Operations about, May 24–30 ... 641

Kernstown, Va. Battle of, March 23 ... 344

Mount Jackson, Va. Occupation of, April 17 ... 427

New Market, Va. Occupation of, April 17 ... 427

Correspondence with

Banks, Nathaniel P ... 285, 427, 456, 522–535, 538–545

Frémont, John C ... 10, 31, 642, 644–657, 659, 660, 662, 663

Goodwin, R. D ... 69

Hamilton, C. S ... 645

Hitchcock, E. A ... 227, 228

King, Rufus ... 31

McClellan, George B ... 224

McDowell, Irvin ... 97, 279, 282, 285–288, 646, 649–651

Myer, Albert J ... 351

Saxton, Rufus ... 626–638, 641, 646, 648

Shields, James ... 344

Sigel, Franz ... (Note) 651

Thomas, Lorenzo ... 227, 228

Wadsworth, James S ... 224, 225

Page.

**Warren, E. T. H.**
Mentioned ... 482, 772, 773, 775
Report of engagement at Winchester, Va., May 25 ... 775
**Washington, D. C.** Defense of. (Immediate.)
Communications from
Hitchcock, E. A ... 228, 229
Lincoln, Abraham ... 230
McClellan, George B ... 162, 164, 226
Thomas, Lorenzo ... 228
Wadsworth, James S ... 224
War Department, U. S ... 224, 225, 227
Report of Roger Jones, of troops available for, April 19 ... 225
(See also *statement of McDowell*, pp. 276–277.)
**Waterman, E.** Mentioned ... 682
**Waterman, Solomon.** Mentioned ... 690
**Waters, James H.**
Correspondence with Thomas J. Jackson ... 399
Mentioned ... 381
Report of battle of Kernstown, Va., March 23 ... 398
**Watson, P. H.** Mentioned ... 105, 109, 534, 629, 630, 632, 633
(For correspondence as Asst. Secy. of War, see *War Department, U. S.*)
**Watson, William.** Mentioned ... 565
**Watts, Captain.** Mentioned ... 453
**Watts, James W.** Mentioned ... 730, 779
**Webster, George.** Mentioned ... 422
**Weed, T. J.** Mentioned ... 35
**Weedon, Henry T.** Mentioned ... 514
**Weih, John.** Mentioned ... 670
**Weir, William.** Mentioned ... 68
**Welch, Benjamin, jr.** Mentioned ... 42, 45
**Weld, John W.** Mentioned ... 602
**Welsh, Brice.** Mentioned ... 423
**Werth, W. H.** Correspondence with W. W. Loring ... 811
**West, Beckwith.** Mentioned ... 682
**West Fork, W. Va.** Skirmish at mouth of, June 10 ... 3
**West, Samuel R. S.** Mentioned ... 513
**West Virginia.** Operations in. Communications from
Banks, Nathaniel P ... 27
Frémont, John C ... 27, 29, 30
Goulding, C. N ... 30
Rosecrans, W. S ... 27, 28
S[illegible] George I ... 29
Suckley, George ... 30
(See also
March 19. *Elk Mountain, W. Va. Skirmish at.*
20. *Philippi, W. Va. Skirmish at.*
29–June 27. *Mountain Department. Operations in.*
April 3. *Moorefield, W. Va. Skirmish at.*
12. *Valley River and Boothsville, Marion County, W. Va. Raid from Fairmont to.*
17–21. *Addison, W. Va. Expedition from Summerville (Nicholas Court-House) to.*
18. *Chapmanville, W. Va. Skirmish at.*
23. *Grass Lick, W. Va. Skirmish at.*

Page.

**West Virginia.** Operations in—Continued.
(See also
May 1. *Clark's Hollow, W. Va. Skirmish at.*
*Camp Creek, in the Stone River Valley, W. Va.* ***Skirmish on.***
5. *Princeton, W. Va. Skirmish at.*
*Franklin, W. Va. Skirmish at.*
6. *Camp McDonald and Arnoldsburg, W. Va.* ***Skirmish at.***
7. *Wardensville, W. Va. Skirmish at and* ***near.***
10. *Giles Court-House, W. Va. Action at.*
10–12. *Franklin, W. Va. Skirmishes near.*
11. *Princeton, W. Va. Skirmish at.*
12. *Lewisburg, W. Va. Skirmish at.*
15. *Ravenswood, W. Va. Skirmish at.*
*Wolf Creek, W. Va. Action at.*
15–17. *Princeton, W. Va. Actions at and in the* ***vicinity of.***
15–June 17. *Shenandoah Valley.* ***Operations in.***
23. *Lewisburg, W. Va. Action at.*
26. *Franklin, W. Va. Skirmish near.*
29. *Wardensville, W. Va. Skirmish* ***near.***
30. *Lewisburg, W. Va. Skirmish at.*
*Shaver's River, W. Va. Raid to.*
June 4. *Big Bend, W. Va. Skirmish at.*
7. *Big Bend, W. Va. Skirmish at.*
8. *Muddy Creek, W. Va. Skirmish at.*
10. *West Fork, W. Va. Skirmish at mouth of.*
22–30. *Moorefield and New Creek, W. Va., and* ***Winchester, Va. Scout*** *from Strasburg to.*
25. *Mungo Flats, W. Va. Skirmish at.*)

**West Virginia Troops.** Mentioned.
Artillery—*Batteries :* **A**, 340, 346, 350, 359, 360, 370, 373, 375 ; **B**, 347, 359 ; **C**, 15, 18, 21, 651, 664, 675 ; **G**, 19, 665.
Cavalry—*Regiments :* **1st**, 5, 19, 346, 355–357, 439, 582, 584, 665, 687, 690, 698 ; **2d**, 509, 512, 648, 807, 813, 814 ; **3d**, 5, 16, 20, 447, 664.
Infantry—*Regiments :* **1st**, 346, 360, 376, 690, 696, 700 ; **2d**, 19, 422, 465, 658, 665 ; **3d**, 19, 462–467, 658, 665 ; **5th**, 19, 464, 658, 665 ; **6th**, 423; **7th**, 694, **8th**, 8, 9, 14, 18, 655, 657, 665 ; **9th**, 489, 490 ; **10th**, 5, 439; **11th**, 489. *Miscellaneous :* **Boothsville Home Guards**, 423.

**Wetschky, Charles.** Report of operations in Shenandoah Valley, May 18–26 . 577
**Wharton, Gabriel C.** Mentioned ........ 514–516
**Wheat, C. R.** Mentioned ........ 459, 702, 800, 801, 803
**Whitcamp, George H.** Report of battle of Kernstown, Va., March 23 ...... 373
**Whitcom, George B.** Mentioned ........ 346, 351, 374
**White, Amos H.** Mentioned ........ 558, 565
**White, James A.** Mentioned ........ 787, 791
**White, Oscar.** Mentioned ........ 405, 407
**White, Thomas.** Mentioned ........ 501
**Whitehead, Thomas.** Mentioned ........ 730
**White Plains, Va.** Operations about, Mar. 29–31. Reports of J. W. Geary . 411, 412
**Whiting, W. H. C.** Mentioned ........ 25
**Whitley, A.** Mentioned ........ 787
**Whitlock, L. T.** Mentioned ........ 784
**Whitman, E. L.** Mentioned ........ 607
**Whitney, Charles K.** Mentioned ........ 69, 70, 72
**Whitney, M. P.** Mentioned ........ 570

Page.
**Whittelsey, H. M.** Mentioned ... 570, 599
**Wicker, Frank N.** Mentioned ... 354, 567
**Wiedrich, Michael.**
Mentioned ... 669, 670, 673
Report of battle of Cross Keys, Va., June 8 ... 670
**Wilhelm, J. R. S.** Mentioned ... 482
**Wilkins, William D.**
Mentioned ... 597, 598, 607
Report of engagement at Winchester, Va., May 25 ... 599
**Willard, J. C.**
Correspondence with Frederick Myers ... 118
Mentioned ... 42, 43, 45, 116, 161, 238, 305
Testimony of, McDowell Court of Inquiry ... 161, 162, 305
**Willcox, O. B.** Mentioned ... 74
**Williams, Alpheus S.**
Correspondence with George H. Gordon ... 624
Mentioned ... 163, 285, 287, 335, 337–339, 341, 342, 344, 352, 358, 378, 426, 448, 540, 542, 543, 545, 547, 549, 551–553, 575, 580, 604
Record of Events. Abstract from. Battle of Kernstown, Va., March 23 ... 378
Report of operations in Shenandoah Valley, May 24–25 ... 593
**Williams, H. J.** Mentioned ... 741, 748–751
**Williams, John S.** Mentioned ... 504, 507, 514, 516
**Williams, Joseph H.** Mentioned ... 430
**Williams, N.** Mentioned ... 692
**Williams, Philip.** Mentioned ... 380
**Williams, Samuel C.** Mentioned ... 482
**Williams, Seth.** (For correspondence as A. A. G., see *George B. McClellan.*)
**Williams, T. V.**
Mentioned ... 409, 482, 772, 773
Report of engagement at Winchester, Va., May 25 ... 776
**Williamson, T. H.** Mentioned ... 473
**Williamson, William P.** Mentioned ... 346, 351
**Willis,** Lieutenant. Mentioned ... 719
**Willis, Edward.** Mentioned ... 484
**Willis, J. C.** Mentioned ... 409
**Willis, Robert.** Mentioned ... 424, 425
**Wilson, John M.** Mentioned ... 458, 459
**Wilson, John W.** (Lieutenant.) Mentioned ... 393
**Wilson, John W.** (Major.) Mentioned ... 556–558
**Wilson, R. N.** Mentioned ... 401
**Wiltshire,** Mr. Mentioned ... 452
**Winchester, Va.**
Battle of, March 23. (See *Kernstown, Va.*)
Engagement at, May 25.
Casualties. Returns of
Confederate troops ... 780, 781
Union troops ... 553, 554
Communications from
Banks, Nathaniel P ... 528
Gordon, George H ... 624
Reports of
Allen, J. W ... 743
Andrews, George L ... 622
Baylor, W. S. H ... 747

Page.

**Winchester, Va.**—Continued.
Engagement at, May 25.
Reports of
Brown, Edwin F ... 610
Carpenter, Joseph ... 758
Caskie, William H ... 771
Chapman, George D ... 608
Colgrove, Silas ... 619
Cunningham, R. H ... 763
Ewell, R. S ... 778
Fulkerson, Samuel V ... 772
Gordon, George H ... 616
Grigsby, A. J ... 751
Leigh, B. W ... 769
McGuire, Hunter ... 719
Moseley, John B ... 767
Neff, John F ... 754, 756
Penn, John E ... 765
Poague, William T ... 761
Ruger, Thomas H ... 625
Scott, W. C ... 788
Taliaferro, A. G ... 775
Trimble, Isaac R ... 794
Warren, E. T. H ... 775
Wilkins, William D ... 599
Williams, T. V ... 776
Wooding, George W ... 777
Zulich, Samuel M ... 623
(See also
*May* 15–*June* 17. *Operations in Shenandoah Valley.* *Reports of*
Babbitt, Charles R. Banks, Nathaniel P. Beal, George L. Brodhead, Thornton F. Crosby, Franklin B. Crutchfield, S. Donnelly, Dudley. Fleming, J. Presley. Hatch, John P. Jackson, T. J. Knipe, Joseph F. Munford, Thomas T. Peabody, J. H. Taylor, Richard. Williams, Alpheus S. Winder, Charles S.)
Scout to, June 22–30. Report of Charles Farnsworth ... 815
Skirmishes near, June 18–19 ... 3
**Winchester and Potomac Railroad.** Military protection and defense of, to remain under direction of John E. Wool ... 663
**Winder, Charles S.**
Mentioned ... 471, 701, 705, 707, 708, 713–717, 728, 743, 745, 747, 748, 750, 752, 755, 757, 758, 761–763, 768, 772, 786, 789–792, 802
Reports of
Harper's Ferry, W. Va. Operations about, May 28 ... 738
Port Republic, Va. Engagements at, June 8–9 ... 739
Shenandoah Valley. Operations in, May 23–25 ... 734
**Windsor, Richard.** Mentioned ... 44, 74, 75
**Winegar, Charles E.** Mentioned ... 602
**Winslow, T. B.** Mentioned ... 675
**Wisconsin.** Call of the President for all Volunteers and Militia from ... 3
**Wisconsin Troops.** Mentioned.
Infantry—*Regiments:* 3d, 419, 553, 560, 594, 616–619, 622, 625.
**Wolf Creek, W. Va.** Action at, May 15. (See *Princeton, W. Va.* Reports of
Cox, Jacob D. Marshall, Humphrey. Moor, Augustus.)
**Wood,** Sergeant. Mentioned ... 662

Page.

**Wood, Henry C.** Mentioned ... 774
**Wood, James H.** Mentioned ... 777
**Wood, T. J.** Mentioned ... 43
**Woodbury, John D.** Mentioned ... 420, 575, 601, 602, 623
**Wooding, George W.**
Mentioned ... 727, 729
Report of engagement at Winchester, Va., May 25 ... 777
**Woodstock, Va.**
Advance to, April 1-2. Reports of
Banks, Nathaniel P ... 418
Cothran, George W ... 419
Gordon, George H ... 419
Skirmishes at and near.
May 18. Communications from Nathaniel P. Banks ... 523
May 21. Communications from Nathaniel P. Banks ... 523
June 2. Communications from John C. Frémont ... 651
(See also
*March* 29–*June* 27. *Operations in Mountain Department. Report of*
Frémont, John C.
*May* 15–*June* 17. *Operations in Shenandoah Valley. Reports* [illegible]
Bayard, George D. Jones, Owen. Kargé, Joseph. Munford, T. T.)
**Woodward, James T.** Mentioned ... 476
**Wool, John E.**
Assignments to command ... 3
Defense and protection of Baltimore and Ohio and Winchester and Potomac Railroads assigned to command of ... 663
Mentioned ... 43, 231, 663
**Worthington, Captain.** Mentioned ... 47, 48
**Wren, G. L. P.** Mentioned ... 787
**Wright, Charles A.** Mentioned ... 370
**Wright, Charles W.** Mentioned ... 553
**Wright, D. C.** Mentioned ... 698
**Wright, John H** Mentioned ... 751
**Wright, T. A.** Mentioned ... 783
**Wyman, Arnold.** Mentioned ... 441, 442, 444, 445
**Wyndham, Percy.**
Mentioned ... 18, 63, 105, 168, 215, 217, 306, 497, 652, 676–680, 712, 732
Report of affair on Rappahannock River, Va., May 13 ... 497
**Yeager, Jacob.** Mentioned ... 359
**York, John B.** Mentioned ... 491
**Yultman, Captain.** Mentioned ... 670
**Zagonyi, Charles.** Mentioned ... 15, 26, 35, 651, 661, 785
**Zeigler, John L.** Mentioned ... 464
**Zinn, C.** Mentioned ... 673
**Zulich, Samuel M.** Report of engagement at Winchester, Va., May 25 ... 623

O